THE OFFICIAL
NBA BASKETBALL
ENCYCLOPEDIA

SECOND EDITION

THE OFFICIAL
NBA BASKETBALL
ENCYCLOPEDIA

SECOND EDITION

FOREWORD BY JULIUS ERVING

INTRODUCTION BY DAVID J. STERN

EDITED BY ALEX SACHARE

VILLARD BOOKS
NEW YORK 1994

This is a revised edition of *The Official NBA Basketball Encyclopedia* published in 1989 by Villard Books, a division of Random House, Inc.

Library of Congress Cataloging-in-Publication Data

The Official NBA basketball encyclopedia/foreword by Julius Erving; introduction by David J. Stern; edited by Alex Sachare.—2nd ed.
    p.   cm.
    Includes index.
    ISBN 0-679-43293-0
    1. Basketball—United States—History.   2. Basketball—United States—Records.   3. National Basketball Association—History.
I. Sachare, Alex.   II. National Basketball Association.
GV885.7.O44 1994
796.323'64'0973—dc20   94-11858

Design by ROBERT BULL DESIGN

Manufactured in the United States of America

9   8   7   6   5   4   3   2

Second Edition

PHOTO CREDITS

NBA Photo Library: 31 (all), 32 (top), 34, 35, 39, 44 (right), 45 (left), 48, 49 (left), 52, 63 (right), 64, 69 (right), 70, 71, 73, 74 (left), 75, 76, 79, 80 (both), 128 (both), 177 (both), 178, 181, 183, 185, 186, 222, 223, 226; Andrew D. Bernstein/NBA Photos: ii, v, 28 (both), 29, 36, 37, 81, 82, 84 (top), 124, 127, 130, 132 (right), 166, 167 (both), 169 (left), 211, 212, 214, 216, 218, 221, 228, 231 (top), 234, 262, 264, 266 (right), 268, 269, 276 (both), 320, 321, 322; Nathaniel S. Butler/NBA Photos: ix, 85, 88, 129, 131, 132 (left), 133 (left), 164, 165, 169 (right), 170 (both), 213, 217, 224, 227, 229, 230, 231 (bottom), 232, 261; Bill Smith/NBA Photos: 30 (top); Graig Abel/NBA Photos: 30 (bottom); Steve Lipofsky/NBA Photos: 68, 125; Lou Capozzola/NBA Photos: 84 (bottom), 133 (right), 134 (both); Jon Soohoo/NBA Photos: 87; Sam Ferencich/NBA Photos: 168; Jonathan Daniel/NBA Photos: 171; Pete Ceresci/NBA Photos: 235; Rocky Widner/NBA Photos: 266 (left); Bruce Bennett/NBA Photos: 323; UPI/Bettmann: 1, 14, 20, 29 (bottom), 32 (bottom), 33, 45 (right), 46, 47, 50, 51, 62, 63 (left), 72, 86 (bottom), 176, 274; Courtesy Naismith Memorial Basketball Hall of Fame: 2, 3, 4, 12, 18, 19, 44 (left), 61, 74 (right), 77, 78 (left), 174, 175, 265, 310; Sports Photo Source/Dutch Dehnert Collection: 5, 6, 16; Sports Photo Source/Nig Rose Collection: 8; Sports Photo Source/Joe Lapchick Collection: 10; Sports Photo Source/Eric Compton Collection: 26; Malcolm Emmons: 69 (left), 78 (right), 86 (top); AP/Wide World: 43, 49 (right), 89, 275; Rich Clarkson/*Sports Illustrated*: 83, 126; Paul Bereswill: 179; Cliff Barnard: 180; Bert Fox: 182; Bill Randolph: 184; Mitchell B. Reibel: 272; *Sports Illustrated*: 38.

FOREWORD

by Julius Erving

Basketball has, quite literally, opened up an entire world for me. It has taken me from the playgrounds of Long Island to the arenas of the National Basketball Association, allowing me to travel the world and giving me entrée into both corporate business and broadcasting. It has enabled me to realize a global perspective of the world instead of a local one, and that has been very rewarding.

When I was starting out as a professional, I simply loved the fact that I could play basketball and earn a living at it. I knew I'd probably be playing the game somewhere anyway, even if I wasn't getting paid. So to be able to make a living doing what I loved seemed like the best of both worlds, and I'm thankful the sport enabled me to provide for myself and my family.

I've always taken a very artistic approach to the game. The interesting thing to me is that such an approach now seems to be the norm rather than the exception. In the 1960s and 1970s, anything different was viewed as unorthodox; now I see much more creativity among the players, and it's a beautiful sight.

How else has the game changed since my playing days? The biggest change probably has less to do with the sport than with the people who play it. Look at David Robinson of the San Antonio Spurs—he's 7-1 and built like a skyscraper, yet he runs like a deer! The number of seven-footers today who can do so much, who are so coordinated and so agile, is amazing. You also have guards who are bigger, but they still possess all the traditional guard skills. Following in the footsteps of Magic Johnson are Anfernee Hardaway of the Orlando Magic and Steve Smith of the Miami Heat, both at least 6-7, who, despite having the size to play forward, play the point-guard position. Yet Charles Barkley of the Phoenix Suns and Clarence Weatherspoon of the Philadelphia 76ers are two of the game's best rebounders, despite measuring 6-7 or less. I believe it has to do with an increased emphasis on versatility and all-around ability. Today's players have the confidence and skill to assert their individuality on the court, refusing to be cast in traditional roles.

It's so exciting the way the players and the game they play continue to get better. Basketball has never been stronger than it is today. As I travel the world, I find greater and greater interest in the sport wherever I go.

I've always considered myself a student of basketball, always stayed open to learning about the sport both on and off the court. At first I wasn't that familiar with its history, but while I was attending the University of Massachusetts, I frequently visited the Hall of Fame

in Springfield, Mass. I enjoyed the exhibits and quickly learned about the early years, how Dr. Naismith invented the game back in 1891, and about the early stars—the guys who rode the trains and took the buses and barnstormed around the country, playing games wherever they could find an audience. Those were the men who laid the foundation upon which today's sport is built, and to whom today's players owe a debt of gratitude.

At that time, my hope was that I could put in the type of effort required to develop my skills so I might earn a small place in that rich tradition—a tradition that is captured here in the second edition of *The Official NBA Basketball Encyclopedia.*

For Lori and Debbie, who make every day special.

ACKNOWLEDGMENTS

Many people contributed to the creation of this book and are deserving of thanks. They include:

The distinguished writers whose expertise can be found in the special essays in this history: Dave DuPree, Leonard Koppett, Leonard Lewin, Jack McCallum, Terry Pluto and Bob Ryan.

The members of the NBA's Editorial Department, who wrote for the book, did research, fact-checked and otherwise helped make it happen: Clare Martin, Mark Hurlman, Chris Ekstrand, Jamie Rosenberg, Jeanne Tang, Mark Broussard, Kim Brown, Lori Kashouty, Lori Cook and Amy Solomon.

Zander Hollander, coeditor of the first edition of the *Encyclopedia* and editor of many other works on basketball and other sports, and the contributing writers to the first edition: Joe Gergen, Jan Hubbard, Leonard Koppett and Jerry Sullivan.

The statisticians at Elias Sports Bureau, under the guidance of Seymour Siwoff, the Hirdt brothers and Chris Thorn, for their monumental work in compiling both the All-Time Records and the Player Directory.

Bill Himmelman and Robert Tewksbury, whose intensive research and fact-checking plugged many of the holes and made this book as complete as it is. Also Meryl Steinberg of the NBA, whose updates contributed to this effort.

For their leadership and assistance in bringing this project to fruition, NBA Commissioner David J. Stern; Deputy Commissioner Russ Granik; NBA Properties President Rick Welts; and Frank Fochetta and Lee Newell of the NBA's publishing department. Thanks, too, to the members of the PR departments of the NBA and its 27 (soon to be 29) teams for their help along the way.

The people of Villard Books/Random House, who believed in this book and made it a reality, especially Peter Gethers, whose ideas and insight may be found throughout. Also Diane Reverand, Jacqueline Deval, Peter DeGiglio, Richard Aquan, Leta Evanthes, Carolyn Edy, Sue Park, Nicky Weinstock and Andrew Krauss. A special thanks to Chief Copy Editor Amy Edelman and her crew, who did an outstanding job turning a manuscript into a book.

For their varied and valued assistance: Carmin Romanelli, Paul White, Joe Amati and Marc Seigerman of NBA Photos, who helped select the illustrations in this book; Robin Deutsch and Wayne Patterson of the Basketball Hall of Fame, a must visit for anyone interested in hoop history; and the media members and basketball people who have shared their thoughts and insights over the years and who make being a part of this game as much fun as it is.

CONTENTS

INTRODUCTION

by David J. Stern

It's been more than 10 years since I began my term as commissioner of the NBA, and each year seems to bring more excitement and surprises than the one before. Basketball is truly on its way to becoming the most popular sport in the world, and we at the NBA are proud to showcase the finest basketball players in the world.

Millions of fans marvel at the strength of Shaquille O'Neal, the range of skills of Scottie Pippen and David Robinson, the pinpoint shooting ability of Mark Price and the ballhandling wizardry of Kenny Anderson and John Stockton. International fans follow players from their own countries who came to the NBA to play among the best in the world—players like Dikembe Mutombo from Zaire, Detlef Schrempf from Germany, Hakeem Olajuwon from Nigeria, Vlade Divac from Serbia and Toni Kukoc and Dino Radja from Croatia. The NBA is spreading its wings farther than ever now, and basketball is demonstrating its strength globally as well as domestically.

The NBA is developing a rich tradition as well. Michael Jordan and Dominique Wilkins set the standard at which today's high fliers take aim, but before they took to the air, Julius Erving was defying the limits of gravity and imagination—and Elgin Baylor before him. Before there was a Kenny Anderson there was a Magic Johnson, and before him there were Oscar Robertson and Jerry West, and Bob Cousy and Bob Davies before them. Before Shaquille O'Neal and David Robinson there were Kareem Abdul-Jabbar and Moses Malone, and before them there were Bill Russell and Wilt Chamberlain, and George Mikan before them.

Today's NBA involves the best athletes playing the game on an ever-expanding global stage. But it is much more than that. It is the culmination of more than 100 years of basketball tradition that began with peach baskets in a YMCA in Springfield, Mass., and was shaped by teams such as the Buffalo Germans, the Original Celtics, the Rens, the SPHAs and the Harlem Globetrotters.

In text that is accompanied by rare photographs, this second edition of The Official NBA Basketball

Encyclopedia traces the sport's rich history—from the early years of barnstorming teams who played their games in dance halls to the modern era of internationally known superstars who play in luxurious arenas. There is a year-by-year look at the NBA with annual statistical leaders, along with essays by some of the top basketball writers in America on major eras and events in NBA history. This edition also features separate chapters on the All-Star Weekend, coaches, officials, the NBA Draft, the global game and the Hall of Fame, as well as all-time records and the official NBA rules.

A unique feature of *The Official NBA Basketball Encyclopedia* is the All-Time Player Directory, which provides a complete statistical profile of every player who ever appeared in the NBA. With more statistical data than ever before, this edition includes year-by-year ABA and NBA totals for each player, plus career regular-season, playoff and All-Star stats. If you want to "remember" how many rebounds Harry Gallatin had for the New York Knicks in the 1955–56 season, and thereby revive for an instant the image of "Harry the Horse" and his valiant efforts against bigger foes, this is the place to do it.

The Official NBA Basketball Encyclopedia provides the most complete look at the sport of professional basketball ever attempted. It is, I believe, a fitting tribute to the men whose labors receive statistical immortality in its pages. I hope you'll like it and that it will add to your knowledge and enjoyment of the NBA.

THE OFFICIAL
NBA BASKETBALL
ENCYCLOPEDIA

SECOND EDITION

LAYING THE FOUNDATION

ABOVE THE RIM

From the beginning, no team sport aimed higher. In 1891, in a YMCA in Springfield, Mass., a young Canadian-born instructor named James Naismith invented a simple game in which players could raise their sights, extend their reach and stretch their imagination.

Professor Naismith, an instructor at the Springfield Men's Christian Association Training School, established the direction of the sport when he asked a custodian to nail two peach baskets to the gymnasium balcony. Although Naismith could not have foreseen Michael Jordan and Dominique Wilkins, Shawn Kemp and Chris Webber dueling for domination of the air, or envisioned modern sports palaces filled to capacity with cheering fans, he did know enough to look *up* when he set about inventing basketball as an indoor activity for his pupils to play during the long New England winters. He was, after all, a former divinity student!

Naismith reasoned that elevating the baskets would promote finesse and agility over the brute strength associated with football. And while basketball has always been a physical game, its verticality has enabled it to evolve into a showcase for great athletes to perform aerial acrobatics about which Dr. Naismith could only have dreamed.

GAME ONE

The first professional basketball game likely was played in 1896 in Trenton, N.J. This game is better docu-

Dr. James Naismith started it all in 1891 with a peach basket and a ball.

mented than an 1893 event in Herkimer, N.Y., where a group of basketball enthusiasts apparently rented the Fox Opera House, invited a team from Utica and shared the proceeds.

The story of the 1896 game in Trenton highlights something about basketball that is known by any child who ever shoveled snow from a driveway to clear a place to dribble—players have got to play!

In the mid-1890s, amateur teams playing Dr. Naismith's new game were springing up throughout the northeast, and the Trenton team was among the best of them. These teams played their games in YMCAs, competing for time and space against a host of other sports and community activities. The basketball teams often lost out and were turned away from the YMCAs, but the Trenton players were determined to play. Rather than cancel a scheduled game, they rented the local Masonic Hall, charged admission to defray expenses and agreed to split any profits.

Because of the reputation of the Trenton club, the game attracted a sizable crowd and produced a gate that exceeded the night's rent. Each player earned $15, and there was $1 left after the split. This was awarded to

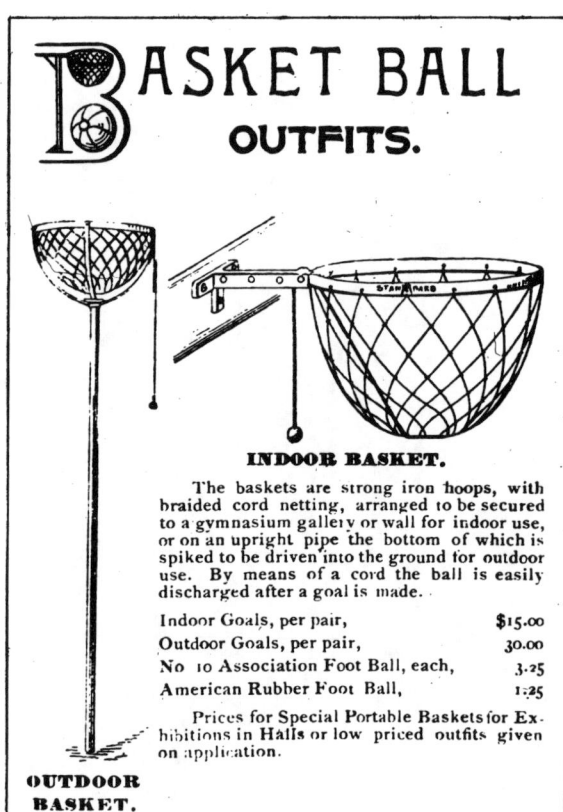

This was the first manufactured basket, made by the Narragensett Machine Company in 1893.

Fred Cooper, the team captain, who thus became pro basketball's first "highest paid player."

THE CAGE

The Trenton team wore uniforms featuring long tights and velvet shorts and played in a wire cage that enclosed the court, protecting the fans from the players and vice versa. It also speeded up the game, since a ball deflecting off a side of the cage remained in play.

Fred Paderatz, the part-time manager of the Trenton team and a full-time carpenter, made the first cage from chicken wire. Not long thereafter, Cooper built a more durable cage of steel mesh. A team in Bristol, Pa., substituted a rope net for the metal cage, and this form of enclosure remained popular throughout Pennsylvania and neighboring states well into the 1920s.

Little wonder that the athletes, who learned to abruptly change direction by bouncing off the siding, preferred netting to metal. "Players would be thrown against the wire," recalled Barney Sedran, one of the great little men of his era, "and most of us would get cut. The court was covered with blood."

Indeed, the safety of participants was not high on the list of the sport's priorities at the turn of the century. Some early games bore a closer resemblance to football scrimmages than to present-day basketball, and players dressed for them with pads covering knees, elbows and even shins. Since no padding had been designed for faces, broken noses were common.

Home-court advantages included raucous fans, who, at many events, took such a personal interest in play that they exchanged insults and/or punches with the competitors. According to Frank Basloe, an early promoter and manager, a Trenton player was knocked cold during a game at Millville, Pa., and the patrons "proceeded to kick him in the face. He ended up with a broken jaw."

Meanwhile, some "fans" amused themselves by jabbing hatpins and lighted cigarettes through the cages at the players' legs. In tough Pennsylvania coal towns, miners favored nails, which they would heat with mining lamps and throw in the direction of the referee or the opposing free-throw shooter. As if that wasn't enough, players frequently had to contend with floors that had been highly waxed—in anticipation of the social dances often held in conjunction with the games.

A team's offense was limited to two basic shots: the layup, which the defense discouraged by placing a "standing guard" in the free-throw lane, and the two-handed set shot, occasionally taken with an underhand motion.

THE GERMANS AND THE TROJANS

Among the foremost teams of the era were the Buffalo Germans, organized in 1895 at the Buffalo "Y," located in a German-American neighborhood on the east side of the city. Starting as 14-year-olds, the Germans dominated amateur tournaments, including the 1901 Pan-American Exposition, where the basketball competition was staged on a grass court.

Led by Al Heerdt and Eddie Miller, they were equally successful campaigning against professionals. As a touring team, they amassed 111 consecutive victories before a 26–21 loss to a team from Herkimer managed by Frank Basloe. Before disbanding in 1929, the Germans claimed a record of 792-86. Among their victims was a Carlisle Indians squad featuring legendary football star Jim Thorpe.

A hotbed of early pro ball, New York also was home to the Troy Trojans, perhaps the most innovative team of the prewar era. The Trojans were organized by Lew Wachter and fashioned around his brother Ed, the foremost center of his day. Ed was 6-6, a factor that contributed to both his success and his fame. Known informally as the Wachter Wonders, the Trojans pio-neered the use of the bounce pass as well as the long pass from one end of the court to the other, setting in motion the first fast break.

National attention was focused on the club in 1915, when they undertook a barnstorming tour through the midwest and won all 38 games. But they had made their reputation in the professional leagues, which attempted to offer some structure and protection to the rapidly developing sport.

THE EARLY LEAGUES

The first of these leagues was formed in 1898. Called the National League by its ambitious organizers, it hardly was national in scope, consisting of six teams in the immediate vicinity of Philadelphia. The Trenton team, coached by Fred Cooper, won the first two National League titles.

After five years the National League folded and many former players found employment in the new Philadelphia League. That, in turn, spawned the Eastern League and Central League. The Troy Trojans dominated the Hudson River League and, when that dis-

The Buffalo Germans were among the great early teams, compiling a 792-86 record from 1895 to 1929.

banded, the New York State League. Unfortunately, the team was too successful for its own good—insufficient competition forced the New York State League out of business, too.

To call the early leagues unstable is an understatement. There were no contracts binding players to one team. Instead, athletes sold their services to the highest bidder on a per-game basis, leading to massive confusion. You could never tell who would be playing for what team. In the 1914–15 season Barney Sedran, the dynamic 5-4 guard who led a superb Carbondale, Pa., team to 35 consecutive victories and the Tri-County League title, managed to play a full schedule for Utica in the New York State League at the same time.

In 1919, Joe Lapchick, a 6-5 center from New York, played for four different teams in four different leagues. Why was he in such demand? At the time there was a jump ball after each basket, so the services of a tall, talented center like Lapchick were at a premium. "My earnings increased by leaps and bounds," recalled

Barney Sedran once scored seventeen baskets in a game—before the introduction of the backboard!

Lapchick, who went on to a long and successful coaching career. "I bargained with the managers for every game. I played one manager against the other and sometimes got as much as $75 a game. The standard rate of pay was $1 a minute, but the rates were gradually increased until I got up to $90 or $100 a game no matter how many minutes I played. When there was a clash of dates, I took the best offer."

Such was the scrambled state of professional basketball at the start of the 1920s—a collection of loosely organized leagues comprised of teams whose outstanding players could shift allegiances on a daily basis, according to the best offer. Ironically, the sport would gain a degree of self-discipline in the 1920s, the most high-spirited and freewheeling decade in American history. It was a time for flappers, bathtub gin—and the Original Celtics.

THE ORIGINAL CELTICS

The Celtics weren't original, not by any means. They were the descendants of the New York Celtics, a team organized in 1914 to represent a settlement house on Manhattan's tough west side. That first group of Celtics, featuring Pete Barry and Johnny Witte, disbanded with America's entrance into World War I.

Jim Furey, a New York promoter, and his brother Tom sought to reorganize the Celtics after the war. Since Frank McCormack, founder of the New York Celtics, refused to relinquish rights to the name, the Fureys called their team the Original Celtics. They added Barry and Witte from the New York Celtics to a group of professionals that included Ernie Reich, Joe Trippe, Eddie White and Mike Smolick.

The following year, with the arrival of Henry "Dutch" Dehnert, Swede Grimstead and Johnny Beckman, the Celtics became the dominant team in the New York region. Through the 1920s Furey continued to add the best players he could find—Horse Haggerty, Nat Holman, Chris Leonard, Lapchick, Davey Banks, Carl Husta, Nat Hickey. Of greater importance, he kept them together. He achieved that stability by renting the 71st Regiment Armory in Manhattan for Sunday night games and signing the Original Celtics to the first individual contracts in the history of basketball. They were paid by the season, not by the game, which meant no more switching teams or leagues at the drop of a $100 bill.

The Original Celtics' impact on basketball was profound. They brought refinements to the game, including the use of the zone defense and a pivot man as an offensive hub. They experimented constantly, fre-

ORIGINAL CELTICS ARE COMING

World's Basketball Champions
vs.

EBER'S
Western New York Champions

2 DAYS
March 9th and 10th
Both Games At
COLUMBUS CIVIC CENTER

Tickets on Sale at
Columbus Civic Center
Central Cigar Store   136 Franklin St·
Raz Cigar Store   351 Central Ave.

2 DAYS
March 9th and 10th
Both Games At
COLUMBUS CIVIC CENTER

Reserved Seats 65c Including Tax
Unreserved 40c
Preliminary 8:15 P. M.

Dutch Dehnert

See The Original Pivot Play Starring The One And Only
'DUTCH' DEHNERT

The Original Celtics, led by Henry "Dutch" Dehnert, popularized pivot play and zone defense.

quently in the course of games against overmatched opponents, staging brilliant passing exhibitions. Throughout the decade, the Celtics averaged more than five victories for every six games, despite a numbing schedule.

They were superb showmen as well as excellent athletes, and few put on a better show than the dapper Holman, one of the game's great passers. He developed the potential of pivot play with his passes to Dehnert, whom he taught to step toward the pass and thus seal off the defender on his back, preventing the pass from being picked off. It's a simple tactic that remains one of the basic keys to success to this day.

What Holman did best on a court, however, was to feint. He had a gift for tying opponents into knots with his clever moves. Whenever the Celtics were involved in a tight game, Holman would handle the ball and invariably draw a foul, frequently as a result of imaginary contact that sent Holman careening and drew a sympathetic whistle from the official. His sleight of hand (and foot) was never displayed to better effect than in a game against the Brooklyn Visitations at Madison Square Garden.

Willie Scrill of the Visitations had a particularly difficult time with Holman, and he grew more incensed by the moment. Finally, he'd had enough. Scrill charged Holman, his fists flailing. They raced the length of the court, Scrill throwing punches with both hands, Holman backpedaling with his arms at his sides. The Celtic bobbed and weaved with such skill that not one of Scrill's several dozen punches landed. Holman never

retaliated; instead, when Scrill finally stopped from exhaustion, Holman calmly stepped to the foul line and sank the free throw awarded to him!

Although the Celtics gained their greatest fame in barnstorming, they occasionally remained in one spot long enough to qualify as a franchise in a professional league. Difficulty in scheduling opponents caused Furey to enter the team in the Eastern League for the second half of the 1921–22 season. Although the Celtics had an unexpectedly difficult time, particularly with the Trenton Bengals, they clinched a first-place finish on the final day of the season and then defeated first-half titlist Trenton in a best-of-3 championship series.

When the Eastern League venture did not produce a financial windfall, the Celtics dipped their toes into the less ambitious Metropolitan League at the outset of the 1922–23 season. There they dominated so thoroughly, piling up a 13-0 record, that they had to withdraw due to lack of competition. So they went back to the Eastern League, this time replacing an Atlantic City team called the Sandpipers.

They continued to win, again too often and too easily for their own good. Attendance in Atlantic City increased, but not enough to cover the $900 weekly guarantee they were receiving. When the owner sought to cut their salaries to $400, Furey pulled the team out of the oceanfront resort and the league, which folded at the end of the season.

So the Original Celtics went back to doing what they had done for years, beating independent teams in New York and touring the country before appreciative

fans. Even the debut of the American Basketball League in 1925 did nothing to diminish their reputation. If anything, their reputation was enhanced because the Celtics dominated members of the new league in 20 financially lucrative exhibition games.

THE ABL (1925–31)

Although the Celtics declined to join the ABL during its initial season, the league had much going for it. Organ-

Nat Holman, one of the stars of the Original Celtics, delighted fans with his ballhandling.

ized by Washington laundry tycoon George Preston Marshall, Chicago Bears owner George Halas and Cleveland department store magnate Max Rosenblum, the ABL represented the first attempt to form a truly national league along the lines of baseball's major leagues. Joe Carr, president of the National Football League and an official in baseball's minor leagues, served as the ABL's first president.

Nine teams, from as far east as Boston and as far west as Chicago, began play under conditions that did much to shape the modern game. Players were signed to exclusive contracts, preventing roster-jumping; backboards were made mandatory; and the cages, still popular in the east, were banned. Rules were standardized to conform with those of the Amateur Athletic Union. This included the elimination of the two-handed dribble, still used by East Coast professionals, thus opening the pro game to college-trained players for the first time, although most ABL teams opted to fill their rosters with veteran pros. Other rules included the disqualification of a player after five personal fouls and the three-second foul-lane violation.

The first ABL season was played in two halves. The Brooklyn Arcadians finished a game ahead of the Washington Palace Five in the first half, and the Cleveland Rosenblums, led by Honey Russell, won the second-half title with a 13-1 record. The two teams met for the championship in what was billed as basketball's World Series, a best-of-5 playoff. Cleveland hosted the first two games in the Public Auditorium and won both before sellout crowds of 10,000. New York, however, did not share the enthusiasm for the event, and only 2,000 spectators showed up at the 71st Regiment Armory to watch the Rosenblums clinch the title with a 23–22 victory.

Despite some moderate success, the ABL didn't prosper in its first year. One team, the Boston Whirlwinds, failed to complete the season, and it became apparent that if the league hoped to achieve major-league status, it would have to deal with the Celtics. Rather than invite the Celtics to join the ABL, Carr and the league's executive committee did something more persuasive—they banned ABL teams from playing exhibition games against the Celtics, thus denying the Celtics the competition they needed to attract large crowds. The strategy worked, and the Original Celtics joined the ABL five games into the 1926–27 season, replacing the Brooklyn Arcadians. In other changes, the second-generation Buffalo Germans folded and the league added two new clubs, the Baltimore Orioles and the Philadelphia Warriors. The Warriors were run by Eddie Gottlieb, whose Philadelphia SPHAs had beaten the

Celtics a year earlier in a nonleague series. Several stars from the SPHAs, an acronym for the South Philadelphia Hebrew Association, wore Warrior uniforms, among them 6-7 Stretch Meehan and Chick Passon.

Because they inherited the Arcadians' 0-5 record, there was no chance for the Celtics to catch the first-half leaders, the Rosenblums, even though they won 13 of 16 games. But the second half was a different story, as the Celtics went 19-2, then swept Cleveland—weakened by the sale of its star, Honey Russell, to George Halas's Chicago Bruins—in the second World Series.

The Celtics dominated the ABL's third year of operation from start to finish and represented New York in the Eastern Division of a league that was divided into geographical regions. With Lapchick, Holman, Dehnert, Barry and Banks as a nucleus, the Celtics won 15 games in a row at one point and finished 40-9, 11 games ahead of Philadelphia. They also convinced Marshall, one of the league's founders and a man who had spent freely and promoted well, that the ABL was not for him. Just after New Year's, with his team's record at 6-14, Marshall sold his players and the franchise to the Brooklyn Visitations, former members of the Metropolitan League. The Detroit franchise, reorganized only that year, folded at almost the same time.

Even Cleveland, once the ABL's showcase team, was in trouble. Vic Hanson, a three-time All-American from Syracuse, announced he was leaving the league because he was unwilling to tolerate the rough play. Shortly thereafter, three important players—Nat Hickey, Carl Husta and Dave Kerr—suffered significant injuries. Following a 15-7 start, the Rosenblums lost 22 of their next 29 games. The Fort Wayne Hoosiers were the prime beneficiaries of Cleveland's problems. Adding Rusty Saunders, the league's high scorer in each of its first two seasons, to a roster that featured the talented Benny Borgmann, Fort Wayne passed the Rosenblums and finished first in the West by five games.

A new playoff format guaranteed the Celtics would have to play more games in order to claim a championship. Under a plan that foretold the sport's emphasis on

postseason competition in later years, the first-place finishers in each division were required to play the second-place teams in a best-of-3 series, followed by a best-of-5 series among the two survivors. The Celtics and Hoosiers won their preliminary series in the minimum two games, then the Celtics claimed a second consecutive championship 3–1.

Officials of the ABL, who earlier had decided they couldn't live without the Celtics, now decided they couldn't live with them. There wasn't enough competition. The cry became "Break up the Celtics," and it became a reality after Jim Furey, the Celtics' dynamic promoter, was convicted of embezzling $187,000 from the Arnold Constable Clothing Company while serving as its head cashier. With Furey in Sing Sing and no businessman to carry on his duties, the Celtics indeed were broken up. Lapchick, Barry and Dehnert were dispatched to Cleveland. Holman and Banks, the league's leading scorer the previous season, formed the nucleus of the New York Hakoahs, an all-Jewish team

In 1919, Joe Lapchick played for four teams in four leagues at the same time.

that was granted a franchise for the 1928–29 season. The Trenton Bengals and the Paterson (N.J.) Crescents, the leading teams in the Metropolitan League, also were accepted for membership in an eight-team ABL, which returned to a split-season format. Carr relinquished his office before the start of the season in order to devote more time and energy to the NFL and was replaced by John O'Brien, who had operated the Metropolitan League.

It wasn't long before people began referring to the Cleveland franchise as the Rosenblum Celtics. At the time of the acquisition of Lapchick, Barry and Dehnert, the Rosenblums already had two former Celtics—Nat Hickey and Carl Husta—on their roster. Trying to avert another potential monopoly, the league forced Cleveland to sell Hickey to Chicago. Undaunted, the Rosenblums bought ex-Celtic star Johnny Beckman from Rochester. While they didn't dominate in the manner of

The Cleveland Rosenblums, bolstered by several former Original Celtics, won the ABL title in 1929.

the Original Celtics, the Rosenblums did edge out Fort Wayne by a single game for the first-half championship. The Hoosiers finished first in the second half, but in the playoffs, now best-of-7, Cleveland swept Fort Wayne in four games for the championship.

Two weeks before the start of the 1929–30 season, which promised the return of the Celtics under their own banner and the leadership of a paroled Jim Furey, the stock market crashed. At the time, ABL officials, along with most of the general population, were only too willing to believe that the economic problems would be resolved and that prosperity was just around the corner. But it was not to be, either for the ABL or the rest of the country.

Furey's revived Celtics, including Holman, Banks, former Eastern League star Stretch Meehan and a 35-year-old Beckman, struggled to a 5-5 start and then disbanded. Syracuse, a first-year franchise that had replaced Trenton, also folded two weeks before the end of the first half. Only the Cleveland Rosenblums appeared oblivious to hard times. Bolstered by the center play of Cookie Cunningham, who had played football for the Chicago Bears, they topped the first-half standings with a 17-7 mark, then defeated the second-half champion Rochester Centrals, who were led by front-courtmen Gordon Chizmadia and Tiny Hearn, in five games in the title series.

By the start of the 1930–31 season, it was clear the Depression was more than a temporary economic setback. Teams were forced to make sharp cuts in their payrolls, as Lapchick learned in a letter from Nig Rose, who operated the Cleveland franchise for Max Rosenblum: "I am enclosing your contract for $1,000 per month, which is less than last year, but will guarantee you four months of play," the letter said in part. "While I am sorry that this cannot be the same as last year, still it is a whole lot more money than what the other clubs can afford, or intend, to pay. Everyone intends to make drastic cuts in salary, as the salaries all along the line were entirely too high for the income that can be attained out of basketball."

Veterans like Holman, Beckman, George Glasco and Tom Barlow weren't even asked back for the ABL's sixth season. Under such conditions, the question was not so much whether the league would expire, but when. For all intents and purposes, the death knell was sounded on December 8, when Max Rosenblum announced that the Cleveland franchise, a cornerstone of the enterprise, was withdrawing from the ABL because he no longer was able to fulfill his guarantee to Lapchick and his other stars. Dumped onto the open market, Lapchick, Dehnert and Barry all signed with the Toledo Redmen, a franchise in its first year. But three weeks later, Paterson also folded, reducing the league to five viable members. And in Chicago, where George Halas had paid Holman $6,000 for half a season the previous year, the Bruins were forced to abandon the high-rent Chicago Stadium for lesser quarters.

For once, there were no Celtics—current or former —in the playoffs. Instead, the Brooklyn Visitations, the first-half champions, defeated a Fort Wayne team led by Branch McCracken, a rookie from Indiana University, 4–2, for the 1931 title. Shortly afterward, the league suspended operations.

Although the ABL would return, it would never again be national in scope. "We had big buildings and players on monthly salaries and we stretched from New York to Chicago," noted Eddie Gottlieb, whose Philadelphia ABL team had a life span of just two years, "but we were just three or four years ahead of our time."

History would show that to be an understatement; a couple of decades or more ahead of their time might have been more accurate. Clearly, however, the timing for such an ambitious project was premature.

The Celtics survived the passing of the ABL because they had something to fall back on. Once again, they became America's best-known road show. Lapchick, Dehnert, Banks, Hickey and Husta went back to barnstorming, although they had to make a few concessions to economic reality. Whereas before the Depression they would never book an appearance for a guarantee of less than $400 (and sometimes they earned as much as $1,000), now they were grateful to receive $250. So much for Pullman cars on the nation's famous trains! Now they were reduced to traveling by automobile. Lapchick not only had to jump center, he also had to drive the team car.

THE RENS

There was one other difference: The road was more crowded than ever. Among the teams battling for a share of the limited entertainment dollar, and the right to call itself the best in the nation, was the New York Renaissance Five, founded by Bob Douglas. The Rens, as they were commonly called, faced far greater hardships than did the Celtics. They were spat upon by some fans, insulted by others. Their postgame meals frequently consisted of cold cuts that had to be eaten on the bus

THE AMERICAN BASKETBALL LEAGUE
UNIFORM PLAYERS' CONTRACT

The Cleveland Rosenblum's herein called the club and... Joe Lapchick of Yonkers, New York herein called the player.

The club is a member of the AMERICAN BASKETBALL LEAGUE and as such, and jointly with the other members of the league, is obligated to insure to the public wholesome and high-class professional basketball by defining the relations between the club and the player and between club and club.

In view of the facts above recited, the parties to this contract agree as follows:

(1) The club shall pay the player a salary for his skilled services during the playing season of 19 30-31 at the rate of $1,000.00 per month. The salary above provided for shall be paid as follows: $500.00 on the 1st and 15th of each month. 90 per cent at the close of each and the remaining 10 per cent at the close of the season, or upon the release of the player by the club.

(2) The player agrees that during the playing season he will faithfully serve the club and pledges himself to the American public to conform to the highest standards of fair play and good sportsmanship.

(3) The player will not play basketball during the season of 19 30-31 other than for the club, except in case the club shall have released the player and such release has been approved by the president of the AMERICAN BASKETBALL LEAGUE.

(4) The player accepts as part of this contract such reasonable regulations as the club may announce from time to time.

(5) This contract may be terminated at any time by the club upon six (6) days notice given in writing to the player.

(6) The player submits himself to the discipline of the AMERICAN BASKETBALL LEAGUE and agrees to accept its decision pursuant to its Constitutions and By-laws.

(7) Any time prior to September 1, 19.31., by written notice to the player, the club may renew this contract for the term of that year, except that the salary rate shall be such as the parties may then agree upon, or in default of agreement, such as the club may fix.

(8) The player may be fined or suspended for violation of this contract, but in all cases, the player shall have the right of appeal to the president of the AMERICAN BASKETBALL LEAGUE, whose decision in the matter shall be final.

(9) In the event of disagreement between the club and the player in regard to the salary rate, the player shall accept the rate set by the club and the player may appeal for readjustment to the president of the AMERICAN BASKETBALL LEAGUE. The decision of the president shall be final and binding on both the club and the player.

(10) The reservation by the club of the valuable right to contract and fix the salary for the succeeding year and the promise of the player not to play during said year other than with the club to whom he is under contract, have been taken under consideration in the fixing of the salary stated herein and the guarantee by the club to pay said salary, is in consideration for playing, the right to reserve the player for the succeeding season and the player's agreement to submit to other agreements as stated above.

(11) In case of any dispute between the player and the club, the same shall be referred to the president of the AMERICAN BASKETBALL LEAGUE and his decision shall be accepted by both parties as final.

(12) In the absence of a regular league contract, agreements in writing which may be executed in an emergency, shall be as binding as a contract, providing a copy is on file with the secretary; however, such agreements must be placed in regular contract form as soon as possible. Verbal contracts and agreements between the club and player will not be considered by the league in the event of a dispute.

Signed this ... 11th day of August A. D. 19.30.

....   CLEVELAND ROSENBLUM'S INC.
                                                                                    Club

....
             Witnesses   Player

This copy to be forwarded to Secretary's office.

Though Joe Lapchick was one of basketball's biggest stars, his contract reflects the Depression.

because many establishments refused to serve them. All this because they were black.

By the time the Rens reached their prime in the early 1930s, the Celtics were in decline. Nevertheless, the two staged some memorable games, drawing as many as 15,000 customers in the midwest and causing promoters to place a premium on ticket prices in New York. They also were the opponents in the first basketball game between black and whites in the south. It was the Celtics who ended the Rens' 88-game winning streak in 1933, but that was their only victory over the Rens in eight meetings that season. The Celtics developed a healthy respect for the Rens, Lapchick calling Charles "Tarzan" Cooper the best center he had ever seen.

As with the Celtics in their peak years, the Rens specialized in teamwork. They had seven outstanding athletes who played together for four years starting in 1932, developing a cohesiveness that was unmatched. The 6-4 Cooper and 6-5 Wee Willie Smith controlled the inside, and 5-7 whiz Clarence "Fat" Jenkins, billed as "the fastest man in basketball," ran a devastating break. Bill Yancey and Eyre "Bruiser" Saitch were the primary outside threats, with John Holt and James "Pappy" Ricks in reserve.

The games invariably were the easiest part of what the Rens had to endure, even when they played two or three contests in a single day. In their barnstorming tours, they were forced to set up command posts in such cities as Chicago and Indianapolis and return from as far as 200 miles away after games because they were denied hotel space. Yet in that four-year period from 1932 to 1936, the Rens compiled a remarkable 473-49 record.

The Rens were well paid by Douglas, who went to great lengths to make sure the team wasn't shortchanged by promoters. Eric Illidge, the club's road secretary, carried a tabulator and personally counted the fans because the team usually was paid a percentage of the gate. He also carried a pistol, although he never had to use it. "Eric would tell the guys not to come out on the court," Smith said, "until he had the money. It was the only way we could survive."

In some instances, the fans presented a bigger threat than the opponents. During a game in Akron, Smith got into a skirmish with a white player and the crowd became so incensed it attacked Smith and his teammates. Gathering in a circle, the Rens fought off the mob until someone hit the light switch, darkening the building and ending the brawl. A similar outburst, provoked by a referee, occurred in Cicero, Ill. Both times, the Rens were provided with a police escort out of town.

On-court incidents were the exception rather than the rule, however. Honey Russell, a respected pro who played frequently against the Rens, said whatever discrimination and abuse they suffered never provoked hostility once the game began. He remembers the Rens as "one of the cleanest teams I ever played against. They just played basketball that was so good they didn't have to resort to any of the rough stuff."

The Rens capped the decade by posting a record of 112-7 in 1939 and winning a tournament of the best professional teams held in Chicago, defeating the Oshkosh All-Stars from the fledgling National Basketball League in the final. It wasn't until after World War II that the team finally disbanded, with an overall record of 2,588 won and 529 lost.

To those who marveled at the Rens' extraordinary success in the face of so many obstacles, Illidge offered a simple explanation. "We would not," he said, "let anyone deny us our right to make a living."

THE HARLEM GLOBETROTTERS

Another team that would not be denied was the Harlem Globetrotters, organized five years after the Rens. It would be decades before the Trotters lived up to their nickname with trips to the far corners of the earth. Their first journey, on January 7, 1927, took them from Chicago to Hinckley, Ill.—all of 48 miles!

Few took notice of the Trotters at the time. "On a crisp January day in 1927, Abe Saperstein, a portly little man with big basketball ideas, took five players, a ramshackle flivver (automobile) and a tattered road map and started one of the most amazing careers of the sports world," wrote Wendell Smith of the *Pittsburgh Courier,* one of the nation's prominent black newspapers, many years later. "This was the unheralded and humble beginnings of the Harlem Globetrotters."

Saperstein was a man of vision. Born in London, he moved with his parents to Chicago when he was four. Without the size or talent to compete successfully in American sports, he invested his energy in youth work and coaching. The Trotters were a product of his love for basketball.

As the team's first manager and coach, he outfitted the Trotters in red-, white- and blue-striped uniforms made in his father's tailor shop and drove the team through the rural midwest, booking games wherever he could. In that first winter of 1927, they won 101 of 117 games before audiences whose exposure to the sport was minimal. Rarely did they leave a town with more than the $75 they received for their first game.

The Rens, or New York Renaissance Five, were a dominant team of the 1930s. From left: Clarence "Fat" Jenkins, Bill Yancey, John Holt, James "Pappy" Ricks, Eyre "Bruiser" Saitch, Charles "Tarzan" Cooper and Wee Willie Smith. Inset: team founder Bob Douglas.

Although Walter "Toots" Wright, Byron "Fats" Long, Willis "Kid" Oliver, Andy Washington and Al "Runt" Pullins did not travel in style, they did develop a game that involved quick cuts and passes while toying with mostly inexperienced pickup teams. For two seasons, they eked out a meager living while extending their reputation through ever-widening circles in the region.

With the addition in 1929 of Inman Jackson, a tall, powerful man with a fine sense of humor who was capable of performing amazing stunts with a basketball, the Globetrotters began experimenting with the clowning that was to become their trademark. It was an idea born of necessity: They realized they weren't going to get return engagements by routing local favorites unless they put on a show.

In order to amuse themselves as well as the paying customers during an exhausting schedule of one-night stands, the Trotters began to spin the ball on their fingers, drop-kick it toward the goal and even bounce it off their heads into the basket. Occasionally, they would line up in a football formation and snap it to Jackson for one of his drop kicks.

The showmanship helped get bookings, but Saperstein and his team still harbored an ambition to become recognized as the best team in the country. To this end, the manager finally lined up a game in 1935 against the Original Celtics. With two minutes left and the score tied at 32, the Celtics called a timeout and walked off the court rather than risk a potential defeat. For the Trotters, it was their ticket to the big time. Their years in the sticks were at an end.

By 1939, not long after they first set foot outside the United States with a foray into Mexico, the Trotters gained entry to the first professional world champion-

ship, held in Chicago. They reached the semifinal round of the tournament, where they were defeated by the Rens. In the following year, they returned to win the tournament with a team comprised of Jackson, Sonny Boswell, Babe Pressley, Hillary Brown, Ted Strong and Bernie Price. Boswell sparked a comeback from a five-point deficit late in the championship game against the Chicago Bruins, and the Trotters triumphed 31–29 in overtime.

That victory gave Saperstein free reign in booking his team into the biggest arenas, against the best competition. Later that year, the Trotters began a long-standing series against a collection of college all-stars. The world was beckoning.

Two of the team's most prominent stars signed on in the 1940s as the Trotters prepared to fulfill their destiny: Reece "Goose" Tatum and Marques Haynes. Tatum was a gifted athlete from Eldorado, Ark., with gigantic hands and an 84-inch wingspan, whom Saperstein lured away from a baseball career and developed into a star attraction. Haynes came to Saperstein's attention while he was leading Langston (Okla.) University to a 74–70 victory over the Trotters. The two would form the backbone of the team that would realize Saperstein's fondest dreams—carrying the message of basketball around the world.

In 1949, they played 14 games in five days during a tour of Alaska. In 1950, Saperstein took the team to Western Europe and North Africa. A year later, they played Central and South America, drawing 50,000 to a game in Rio de Janeiro. But the highlight of those early excursions around the globe was a game in Berlin in the summer of 1951.

At the request of John J. McCloy, the U.S. commissioner for Germany who sought to ease anti-American feelings, they agreed to a game at the Olympic Stadium, where 15 years earlier Adolf Hitler had snubbed America's black Olympians. The Trotters got a rousing reception from the huge crowd of 75,000, who were treated to a special halftime show in which a helicopter flew over the open-air court and then deposited a lone figure in a track suit. As the unannounced figure began to circle the stadium, the fans stood and applauded. It was Jesse Owens, whose four gold medals had made him the star of the 1936 Olympic Games. Both Owens and the Globetrotters officially were recognized as "ambassadors of good will" by the State Department.

The Trotters celebrated their 25th anniversary the following year with an around-the-world tour, traveling more than 50,000 miles. Five Trotters—Babe Pressley, Leon Hilliard, Bill Brown, Clarence Wilson and Josh Crider—performed their famous warm-up routine to the tune of "Sweet Georgia Brown" for Pope Pius XII during an audience at Castel Gandolfo.

In time, the fame of the Trotters would be such that they became the subject of two motion pictures, were invited to appear behind the Iron Curtain and formed the basis of a children's television series. And it all began with an uncomfortable ride in an old jalopy from Chicago to Hinckley.

THE SPHAS

There was one other team that earned a formidable reputation during the Depression, although its fame was confined mostly to the east. Eddie Gottlieb's Philadelphia SPHAs dominated the American Basketball League that John O'Brien reorganized as a regional circuit, but they had been a crack outfit for a long time.

The SPHAs were an outgrowth of a team created in 1918 by Gottlieb, Harry Passon and Hughie Black, all recent graduates of South Philadelphia High School. This team consisted entirely of Jewish youngsters and played under the banner of the Young Men's Hebrew Association, which provided the uniforms. When the YMHA withdrew its sponsorship after three years, they found a new home at the South Philadelphia Hebrew Association, a social club from which the team derived its new identity, and wore uniforms with the acronym SPHAs stenciled across the chest in Hebrew letters. Even after the social club stopped providing uniforms, Gottlieb and his partners continued to call their team by the unusual name.

Eventually, their success earned them an invitation to participate in the Philadelphia League. With the help of Davey Banks, a sharpshooter imported from New York, and Charley Tettemer, a non-Jew from Trenton, the SPHAs won consecutive championships, the last two in the league's history.

After the Philadelphia League disbanded, the SPHAs joined the Eastern League, which went out of business in the same season, forcing the team to book its own games. Fortunately, Gottlieb was more than equal to the task. A shrewd entrepreneur, he used his contacts to set up a series of exhibition games against teams from New York's Metropolitan League and the far-reaching American Basketball League, then in its first year of operation.

When the SPHAs won five of six games, losing only to the ABL's premier team, the Cleveland Rosenblums,

Marques Haynes exemplified the showmanship that made the Harlem Globetrotters popular worldwide.

"Gotty" arranged for best-of-3 series against both the Original Celtics and the Rens. Strengthened by the addition of former Eastern League stars Stretch Meehan and Tom Barlow, the SPHAs defeated the Rens 2–0 and the Celtics 2–1, although the Celtics gained a measure of revenge soon after by signing Davey Banks away from the SPHAs. Thus, within approximately six weeks, Gottlieb's team had won nine of 11 games against some of the most celebrated squads in professional basketball.

For the next two years Gottlieb devoted his energy to the Warriors, Philadelphia's new entry in the ABL that featured former SPHAs stars Chick Passon and Stretch Meehan, but he rebuilt the SPHAs in 1929 with younger talent. By adding former college stars such as Harry Litwack of Temple, Red Wolfe of St. John's, Lou Forman of Dickinson and Moe Goldman of CCNY to holdovers like Passon, Shikey Gotthoffer and Cy Kaselman, Gottlieb re-created the team's success. The

SPHAs joined the third edition of the old Eastern League and promptly won three championships in four years.

That led to an invitation from the American Basketball League, being reorganized by O'Brien in 1933 after a two-year hiatus. This version had no major-league pretensions, with all franchises located within driving distance of each other in the northeast and with games to be played in small arenas, armories and dance halls, a scenario reminiscent of the early 1920s.

The league was considerably better than was indicated by its minimal press coverage. The Brooklyn Visitations had reigned as the last champion of the old ABL, and an outstanding St. John's team, dubbed the Wonder Five after amassing a 70-4 record in three seasons of college competition, moved intact into the new circuit as the New York Jewels. But it was the SPHAs who dominated.

Gottlieb's team won championships in three of the league's first four seasons and claimed seven titles in the 15 years it existed. The team didn't bow out until the end of the 1948–49 season, after its founder and driving force had moved to the Basketball Association of America, forerunner of the National Basketball Association. One of professional basketball's most formidable pioneering teams, the SPHAs passed from the scene after 31 years promoting the sport.

THE NBL (1937–49)

Despite the efforts of the reorganized ABL and the prominence of some barnstorming teams, it was the college game that occupied basketball's center stage during the Depression years. In New York, a young promoter named Ned Irish booked four college teams into Madison Square Garden for a doubleheader and created a sensation. The practice grew into a financial bonanza not only for the Garden but for other major arenas in the east and midwest. Irish started the postseason National Invitation Tournament in 1938, and the NCAA followed suit with its own championship playoffs a year later.

The popularity of the cleaner, faster college game had a profound influence on the people who, in 1937, decided to form the National Basketball League. Their intention was to sign as many college stars as they were able for the venture, which was centered in the midwest. Catalysts in the NBL were the Goodyear and Firestone Rubber companies of Akron and the General Electric Company of Fort Wayne. After fielding successful teams in the Midwest Industrial League, they agreed to match their clubs against 10 previously independent professional teams in the 1937–38 season.

The 13 teams were split into Eastern and Western divisions, but unfortunately the structure of the new league stopped there. Commissioner Hubert Johnson left scheduling to each team's discretion. As a result, teams did not play the same number of games, and some played only a limited number of opponents. Even in the matter of whether the NBL should accept or reject the new NCAA rule that abolished the center jump after each basket, the decision was left to the home team on a game-by-game basis.

Goodyear, Firestone and General Electric all had a decided advantage in stocking their teams, continuing their practice of recruiting talented college seniors by offering them jobs in management—a powerful enticement during those hard times. The independent clubs had to be more resourceful, raiding local leagues and nearby colleges.

Thus did the Whiting All-Americans, one of four teams based in Indiana, sign Johnny Wooden. He was the kind of big-name player the NBL hoped to attract, a three-time All-American at Purdue whose magnificent playing career someday would be eclipsed by his success as a college coach at UCLA. Wooden already was coaching on the high school level and would maintain his vocation while playing pro ball.

A player who had an even greater impact on the NBL was Leroy "Cowboy" Edwards, a 6-4 center who could shoot his hook shot with either hand. Playing for the Oshkosh All-Stars, Edwards averaged 16.2 points per game while leading Oshkosh to a Western Division title in the NBL's first year. The All-Stars, whose founder, Lon Darling, was instrumental in shaping the NBL, were defeated by Eastern leader Goodyear 2–1 in the championship series.

Having learned from its mistakes, the commissioner's office took control of scheduling for 1938–39, with each team playing 26 games. It also dismissed the center jump after each basket and streamlined the league by dropping six franchises, adding the Sheboygan Redskins and approving the transfer of the Whiting All-Americans to Hammond, Ind. Thus, eight teams began the second season, and although the NBL failed to sign two targeted high-profile collegians, Hank Luisetti of Stanford and Meyer Bloom of Temple, it was successful in luring a number of other college stars. The Akron Firestones signed Johnny Moir, the towering Paul Nowak of Notre Dame and Jerry Bush from St. John's. The Warren Penn Oilers recruited playmaker Buddy Jeannette from Washington and Jefferson, and the

Hammond All-Americans added John Townsend from Michigan and Lou Boudreau from Illinois. Boudreau's future, however, lay in baseball, where he became a star shortstop and manager of the 1948 champion Cleveland Indians.

Edwards, at 6-4, had reigned as the tallest player in the NBL's first season, but now he had a few players to look up to. Sheboygan had signed 6-7 Ed Dancker, and the Firestones had two big men in the 6-9 Nowak and 6-11 Slim Shown. Still, Edwards remained the class of the league's centers in the 1938–39 season, leading the All-Stars to another Western Division title and to within one game of the championship. But in the final game of the best-of-5 title series, Edwards was double-teamed in the pivot and limited to nine points as the Firestones captured the championship with a 37–30 victory.

Two new teams joined the league in time for the 1939–40 season, the Detroit Eagles and the Chicago Bruins, one of the ABL originals. Since the Eagles had signed 6-8 Slim Wintermute, one of the stars of Oregon's NCAA champions, and Chicago featured 6-9 Mike Novak from hometown Loyola, Edwards now had the dubious distinction of being the NBL's shortest center.

With the elimination of the center jump after each basket and the adoption of the rule that required a team to advance the ball past a center-court line within 10 seconds, the sport raced ahead. Scores rose dramatically, as evidenced by the championship series, which again pitted Oshkosh against the Firestones and which ended with the Firestones posting a 61–60 victory in the deciding third game.

Although Edwards was displaced as the NBL's leading scorer the following year by Ben Stephens, a second-year player for the Goodyears, the All-Stars again advanced to the championship round, where this time they claimed their first league title with a three-game sweep of the Sheboygan Redskins. That merely whetted their appetite for glory, and they entered the annual world championship professional tournament in Chicago as favorites. NBL representatives had been beaten by the Rens and the Globetrotters in the finals of the previous two tournaments, but this time the NBL's Detroit Eagles eliminated both touring teams to reach the final against Oshkosh. Coached by Dutch Dehnert, one of the great stars of the Original Celtics, Detroit capped a week of upsets in the 16-team tournament by edging the All-Stars 39–37.

The NBL's progress was halted in 1941 by the United States' entry into World War II. Three teams withdrew: the Akron Firestones, one of the founding members; the Detroit Eagles, the defending champion;

The Detroit Eagles, coached by Dutch Dehnert, won the 1941 world pro championship in Chicago.

and the Hammond All-Americans. But replacement franchises were put in place, enabling the league to continue as a seven-team operation. The Indianapolis Kautskys rejoined after a year of independent play. The other new teams were the Toledo Jim White Chevrolets and the Fort Wayne Zollner Pistons, named for Fred Zollner's piston plant.

Of all the organizations that completed the 1941–42 season, the Pistons would have the greatest influence on professional basketball. The first-year team also had an immediate impact on the NBL. Built around fiery guard Bobby McDermott, who had been a high-scoring attraction with the last of the Celtics' great barnstorming teams and later the top scorer in the reorganized ABL, the Pistons reached the championship series against Oshkosh, a five-time finalist. The All-Stars had added 6-5 Bobby Carpenter to the front line, and he and Edwards formed an unusual double-pivot offense.

It was Edwards who rallied Oshkosh to a 68–60 victory in the second game of the best-of-3 series with a spectacular 35-point performance after the Pistons had routed the All-Stars 61–43. Fort Wayne's strategy of denying Edwards the basketball at all costs in the deciding contest was costly, for while Edwards was held to a single point, his teammates led Oshkosh to a second championship.

One of the stars of the NBL's first wartime season was a rookie hook-shot artist from the University of North Carolina, George Glamack. So nearsighted was Glamack that while in college he had acquired a memorable nickname: the "Blind Bomber." Despite his handicap, he was among the leading scorers on the Goodyears.

The Goodyears and the Indianapolis Kautskys dropped out prior to the start of the 1942–43 season, and the NBL was reduced to four teams when the Toledo Jim White Chevrolets, whose two top scorers had entered military service, abruptly canceled the rest of the season after losing their first four games. The situation could have been worse. George Halas had decided to disband his Chicago Bruins, but that franchise was purchased by the United Auto Workers local representing employees of the Studebaker plant in Chicago. As a result, the Chicago Studebakers, a team comprised of two former Bruins, one former Sheboygan Redskin and several former Harlem Globetrotters, were born. While they may have been pioneers in the field of racial integration, their play was weak and they finished in last place, partially because of dissension between black and white players. The Studebakers did not return for a second season.

Sheboygan and Fort Wayne met in the championship series, and the Redskins won the third and deciding game by a single point.

Down to three teams with the disbanding of the Studebakers, the league welcomed the Cleveland Brass into the fold for the 1943–44 season. Neither the Brass nor the Oshkosh All-Stars, however, was a match for the Pistons and the Redskins. The Redskins had four of the tallest players in the league in 6-9 Mike Novak, 6-8 Kleggie Hermsen, 6-7 Ed Dancker and 6-6 Elmer Gainer. The Pistons were smaller, more creative and more explosive, Buddy Jeannette having joined McDermott, the NBL's perennial MVP, in the backcourt while 6-6 strongman Jake Pelkington worked the backboards. It was McDermott—a hard-driving, fast-living man who had a high-arcing two-handed set shot—who set the tempo and the tone for the Pistons. The 5-11 guard, who had dropped out of a New York high school to follow a career with as many bounces as a basketball, was as renowned for his temper as for his scoring feats.

The Pistons finished first in the four-team NBL in 1943–44 and then enjoyed a remarkable postseason. They defeated the Cleveland Brass in two consecutive games to reach the playoff finals, finished off the Redskins in three for the NBL title, then won all three games in the world professional tournament in Chicago for a clean sweep of eight contests and both championships.

This was only a beginning for Fort Wayne, which dominated an enlarged league the following season. With the war winding down and many basketball players returning from military duty, the NBL assisted in the organization of two new franchises, the Chicago Gears and the Pittsburgh Raiders. But the Pistons and the Redskins remained the teams to beat, and they squared off in the 1944–45 playoff finals. Sheboygan's victories in the first two games startled many, but with no margin for error, Fort Wayne won the next three games and claimed its second consecutive NBL title. Then the Pistons again raced through the field in the Chicago world tournament, blasting the independent Dayton Acmes 78–52 in a final game witnessed by a crowd of 15,119.

The Pistons, and especially McDermott, were the talk of basketball. In a vote of league coaches after the 1945 season, McDermott, who had averaged 20.1 points per game, was selected as the greatest player in professional basketball history.

Fort Wayne presaged a new era for pro basketball when it defeated the College All-Stars 63–55 before

23,912 fans at Chicago Stadium prior to the start of the 1945–46 season. The NBL was up to eight teams, with newcomers that included the revived Indianapolis Kautskys and Rochester Royals, a mix of veterans and major college stars.

The Pistons, after finishing the regular season with the league's best record, were upset in the playoffs by the Royals, whose backcourt boasted wily old pro Al Cervi, brilliant playmaker Bob Davies from Seton Hall and steady Red Holzman from CCNY. On the front line, Rochester had "Blind Bomber" Glamack, 6-8 John Mahnken from Georgetown and Fuzzy Levane, captain of the 1943 NIT champion St. John's team. The reserves included some athletes who were to become famous outside basketball: All-American quarterback Otto Graham, major-league baseball catcher Del Rice and a fun-loving two-sport star from Brooklyn named Chuck Connors, who became the star of a popular television series, *The Rifleman.* Coached by Lester Harrison, the

Fiery Bobby McDermott starred in the NBL for the Fort Wayne Zollner Pistons.

Royals upended Fort Wayne in the division playoffs, winning the final game by a decisive 70–54 score, then swept Sheboygan in three games for the NBL championship.

The Royals, however, were upstaged by the professional debut of George Mikan, the most celebrated college player in the history of the game, a 6-10 giant with thick glasses, nasty elbows and a tremendous competitive spirit who had been virtually unstoppable while at DePaul. His signing by the hometown Chicago Gears at the conclusion of the college season created unprecedented public attention for the NBL and the entire league. Although he did not play in the NBL's regular season or the playoffs, he was eligible for the world professional tournament, and with No. 99 in the pivot the Gears advanced to the semifinals, where they were eliminated by Oshkosh and slick center Leroy Edwards.

Any doubts about Mikan's ability to dominate the pro ranks vanished during that Chicago tournament as he scored 100 points in five games and was selected Most Valuable Player. His showing created unprecedented anticipation for the start of the new season, but Mikan sat out the first six weeks in a contract dispute.

Before the 1946–47 season started, the leaders of the NBL decided that the team with the best record in the regular season should be regarded as the league's champion, not the playoff winner. Thus, the Rochester Royals, bolstered by the addition of veteran Dolly King and rookie Arnie Johnson, went into the books as the league's champion, even though they lost to the Gears 3–1 in the playoff finals.

The Gears had been mired in fifth place in the Western Division of a league grown to 12 teams when McDermott, the player-coach of the Pistons, was suspended for punching 6-9 center Milo Komenich in a brawl on a train. As much as Zollner admired McDermott's talent, he had overlooked many fights in the past, but this time he reluctantly agreed to a trade that sent McDermott to the Gears in the same dual capacity of player-coach. Once McDermott joined Mikan, creating an outstanding inside-outside combination, Chicago won 17 of its next 23 games to edge the Anderson Packers for the final playoff spot in the division, then overpowered Indianapolis and Oshkosh to reach the finals against Rochester. Mikan was limited to 14 points in the first game of the best-of-5 series, and the Royals won 71–65 with the help of a 23-point performance by Davies. But the big center broke loose for 27 and 23 points in the next two games, and the Gears won

ROCHESTER ROYALS - NATIONAL LEAGUE CHAMPIONS - 1945-46
FRONT ROW: VOORHEIS, HOLZMAN, GRAHAM, GARFINKEL, CERVI, DAVIES, REAR ROW: LEVANE, RICH, NEGRATTI, MAHNKEN COACH MALANOWICZ, CONNORS, GLAMACK, FITZGERALD,

The 1946 NBL champion Rochester Royals. Front, from left: Bernie Voorhees, Red Holzman, Otto Graham, Dutch Garfinkel, Al Cervi, Bob Davies. Rear, from left: Fuzzy Levane, Tom Rich, Al Negratti, John Mahnken, Coach Eddie Malanowicz, Chuck Connors, George Glamack, Bob Fitzgerald.

three in a row. They appeared to be a dynasty in the making.

What followed was one of the more bizarre developments in the annals of a sport not yet known for stability. Maurice White, president of the American Gear Company, envisioned his own 24-team league in which he would own all the teams and arenas, financing the venture with the fortune he had made selling gears to the navy during World War II. Naturally, the Chicago Gears would be the flagship of the circuit, which he called the Professional Basketball League of America, so he pulled his team out of the NBL, taking with him the biggest star in the game. The grandiose plan collapsed in the first month of the PBLA's operation, and the Gears' players were distributed among other NBL teams. McDermott went to Sheboygan, and Mikan, pro basketball's first "franchise" player, was awarded to a first-year team, the Minneapolis Lakers.

Minneapolis already had forward Jim Pollard, the star of Stanford's 1942 NCAA champions, and playmaker Herm Schaefer. The addition of Mikan enabled

the Lakers to outdistance all competition in the Western Division. They also went unchallenged in the playoffs, dismissing Oshkosh, a Tri-Cities club that featured seven-foot center Don Otten, and, in the finals, the Rochester Royals. The Royals had been weakened by injuries, including a broken jaw that sidelined center Arnie Risen, and only managed to win one game in the best-of-5 title series as Mikan averaged 27.5 points per game. And in the final of what would be the last world professional tournament, Mikan scored 40 points in the Lakers' 75–71 triumph over the Rens.

Once again, it seemed, the NBL had created a potential dynasty. But while some league members spent the summer designing defenses to stop Mikan and his teammates, the Lakers and three other prominent clubs—Rochester, Fort Wayne and Indianapolis—announced they were withdrawing from the league to join the rival Basketball Association of America, which had begun play in 1946. It was a devastating blow to the older league, which was further depleted when the Toledo and Flint franchises folded.

The NBL hastily formed franchises in Denver, Waterloo (Ia.), Hammond (Ind.) and Detroit. Detroit folded after winning only two of 19 games and was replaced by a Dayton team comprised of several former Rens well past their prime. The Anderson Packers won the 1948–49 championship with a three-game sweep of an Oshkosh team whose roster still included Leroy Edwards, now reduced to a reserve role.

Among the bright spots in the NBL's 12th season was the play of two rookies, Alex Hannum of Oshkosh and Dolph Schayes of Syracuse. Schayes, a 6-8 forward with a remarkable outside shot, would become a superstar—but not in the NBL.

In the summer of 1949, after the league had attempted a show of strength by granting a franchise in Indianapolis to graduating members of the University of Kentucky's NCAA championship team, the NBL passed from the scene. Surviving members agreed to join the BAA, and the new merged league was to be called the National Basketball Association.

The world was changing. The building blocks had been formed. Pro basketball was poised to leave the past behind and embrace its future.

George Mikan proudly displays his MVP trophy from the world pro tournament in 1946.

NBA TIMELINE

Following are major dates, from the invention of basketball until the present day.

December 1891—Dr. James Naismith, an instructor at the Springfield Men's Christian Association Training School (now Springfield College) in Springfield, Mass., invents the game of basketball.

1896—The first known professional basketball game is played, in Trenton, N.J.

June 6, 1946—The Basketball Association of America, the forerunner of the National Basketball Association, is founded at the Commodore Hotel in New York. Maurice Podoloff is the league's first president.

November 1, 1946—The Basketball Association of America begins play as the New York Knicks defeat the Toronto Huskies 68–66 in Toronto. Any fan taller than Huskie center George Nostrand (6-8) got in free.

January 11, 1947—The Basketball Association of America outlaws the use of zone defenses.

April 22, 1947—Philadelphia beats Chicago 83–80 to claim the first championship of the BAA, four games to one.

August 3, 1949—Six surviving teams from the midwest-based National Basketball League join the Basketball Association of America. The resulting 17-team league is renamed the National Basketball Association, with Maurice Podoloff as president.

April 23, 1950—The Minneapolis Lakers become the first team to win back-to-back NBA championships by defeating Syracuse in six games.

March 2, 1951—The East defeats the West 111–94 in the first NBA All-Star Game, held at Boston Garden.

1952—The NBA widens the foul lane from six to 12 feet.

April 12, 1954—The Minneapolis Lakers become the first team to win three NBA championships in a row by defeating Syracuse 87–80 in Game 7.

1954–55—The NBA adopts two playing rules that revolutionize the game of basketball: the introduction of the 24-second clock and the awarding of a penalty shot following a team's fifth foul in any one period.

October 30, 1954—The 24-second clock is used in an NBA game for the first time in Rochester, N.Y., the host Royals beating the Boston Celtics 98–95.

April 9, 1959—The Boston Celtics win their first of eight consecutive NBA championships with a 118–113 victory over Minneapolis for a four-game sweep of the NBA Finals.

October 19, 1960—Relocated to the West Coast after 13 years in Minneapolis, the Lakers open their inaugural season as the Los Angeles Lakers with a 140–123 loss at Cincinnati.

1961—The Chicago Packers enter the NBA as an expansion team, the league's ninth franchise, only to move to Baltimore two years later.

March 2, 1962—Wilt Chamberlain scores an NBA record 100 points in a 169–147 Warrior win over the New York Knicks in Hershey, Pa.

September 1, 1963—Walter Kennedy succeeds Maurice Podoloff as the president of the NBA. The job title would be changed to commissioner in 1967.

1964—The NBA widens its foul lane from 12 to 16 feet.

April 28, 1966—The Boston Celtics win their eighth straight NBA title, the longest streak in league history.

1966—The third NBA team to call Chicago home, the Bulls, enters the league as its 10th franchise.

February 1, 1967—The formation of the American Basketball Association (ABA) is announced at a press conference at the Carlyle Hotel in New York. George Mikan is named commissioner of the league, scheduled to begin play in October 1967.

1967—San Diego and Seattle enter the NBA as the league's 11th and 12th franchises.

October 13, 1967—The ABA opens its inaugural season as the Oakland Oaks beat the Anaheim Amigos 134–129.

February 17, 1968—The Naismith Memorial Basketball Hall of Fame opens in Springfield, Mass., on the Springfield College campus, where the game was invented by Dr. James Naismith.

1968—The NBA expands to 14 teams with the addition of Milwaukee and Phoenix.

1970—Expansion franchises begin play in Buffalo, Cleveland and Portland, bringing the number of NBA teams to 17.

January 7, 1972—The Los Angeles Lakers defeat the Atlanta Hawks 134–90 for their 33rd straight win, an NBA record.

March 26, 1972—The Los Angeles Lakers beat Seattle 124–98 to finish the season at 69-13, the best record in NBA history.

1974—ABA/USA officially forms to become the United States' representative in FIBA, the International Basketball Federation.

March 7, 1974—New Orleans becomes the NBA's 18th franchise, bought by a nine-man group for $6.15 million.

August 1974—Moses Malone signs with the Utah Stars of the ABA to become the first professional basketball player of the modern era to go directly from high school to the pros.

April 30, 1975—Larry O'Brien is named the third commissioner of the NBA, succeeding Walter Kennedy.

June 17, 1976—Four former ABA teams—San Antonio, Denver, New York and Indiana—are admitted into the NBA, raising the league to 22 teams.

July 7, 1978—The NBA approves a franchise swap in which Buffalo Braves owners John Y. Brown and Harry Mangurian acquire the Celtics, while Celtics owner Irv Levin acquires the Braves. He soon moved them to San Diego to become the Clippers.

1978–79—The NBA adds a third referee on a one-year experimental basis.

1979–80—The NBA adopts the three-point field goal and votes to eliminate the third referee.

October 12, 1979—Chris Ford of the Boston Celtics scores the first official three-point field goal in the NBA as the Celtics defeat Houston in Boston Garden.

May 1, 1980—Dallas is granted an expansion franchise, bringing the total of NBA teams to 23.

February 1, 1984—David J. Stern succeeds Larry O'Brien and becomes the fourth commissioner of the NBA.

May 12, 1984—The New York Knicks win the first-ever NBA Draft Lottery, enabling them to select Patrick Ewing with the first pick in the NBA Draft.

June 18, 1985—At the annual NBA Draft, the number of rounds is reduced from 10 to seven.

June 30, 1985—The new Naismith Memorial Basketball Hall of Fame in downtown Springfield, Mass., is officially dedicated and opened to the public.

April 13, 1986—The Boston Celtics close out the regular season with a 135–107 win over New Jersey, giving the Celtics a 40-1 record at home. This sets a record for most home-court wins and highest home winning percentage (.976) in a season in NBA history.

April 22, 1987—The NBA grants expansion franchises to Charlotte, Miami, Minnesota and Orlando, raising the number of teams to 27. Charlotte and Miami would join the league in the 1988–89 season, while Minnesota and Orlando would join in 1989–90.

October 23–25, 1987—The first McDonald's Open is played in Milwaukee involving the NBA's Milwaukee Bucks, the Soviet Union's National Team and the Italian League champion, Tracer Milan. This is the first tournament involving NBA teams to be sanctioned by FIBA.

June 28, 1988—At the annual NBA Draft, the number of rounds is reduced from seven to three.

July 25, 1988—The Atlanta Hawks become the first NBA team to play in the Soviet Union as they defeat the Soviet Georgia All-Stars 85–84 in an exhibition game.

1988–89—The NBA votes to return to the three-officials plan that had been abandoned after the 1978–79 season.

April 6, 1989—FIBA votes to drop restrictions on professional basketball players, allowing them to participate in major international competitions beginning with the 1992 Olympics.

June 27, 1989—At the annual NBA Draft, the number of rounds is reduced from three to two.

October 12, 1989—The NBA becomes a member of ABA/USA, the nation's representative in FIBA. ABA/USA changes its name to USA Basketball.

November 2, 1990—The Phoenix Suns defeat the Utah Jazz at the Tokyo Metropolitan Gym in Japan in the first regular-season game played outside North America by any major professional sports league.

December 21, 1991—The game of basketball observes its centennial.

June 24, 1992—The city of Portland becomes the first city besides New York to host the annual NBA Draft.

August 8, 1992—In Barcelona, Spain, the USA Olympic Men's Basketball Team, nicknamed the Dream Team, defeats Croatia 117–85 for the gold medal. This is the first time NBA players are allowed to compete in the Olympics.

June 20, 1993—The Chicago Bulls become the first team in 27 years to win three consecutive championships with a 99–98 Game 6 victory over the Phoenix Suns.

November 4, 1993—The NBA Board of Governors awards an expansion team to Toronto, Canada, bringing the total of teams to 28.

April 27, 1994—The NBA Board of Governors awards an expansion franchise to Vancouver, Canada, raising the number of NBA teams to 29. Both Toronto and Vancouver will begin play in the 1995–96 season.

Team	Span
Cleveland Rebels ('46–'47)	
Detroit Falcons ('46–'47)	
Pittsburgh Ironmen ('46–'47)	
Toronto Huskies ('46–'47)	
Providence Steamrollers ('46–'49)	
Chicago Stags ('46–'50)	
St. Louis Bombers ('46–'50)	
Washington Capitols ('46–'51)	
Philadelphia Warriors ('46–'62)	
San Francisco Warriors ('62–'71)	
Golden State Warriors ('71–Present)	
Boston Celtics ('46–Present)	
New York Knickerbockers ('46–Present)	
Baltimore Bullets ('47–'55)	
Indianapolis Jets ('48–'49)	
Fort Wayne Pistons ('48–'57)	
Detroit Pistons ('57–Present)	
Rochester Royals ('48–'57)	
Cincinnati Royals ('57–'72)	
Kansas City–Omaha Kings ('72–'75)	
Kansas City Kings ('75–'85)	
Sacramento Kings ('85–Present)	
Minneapolis Lakers ('48–'60)	
Los Angeles Lakers ('60–Present)	
Denver Nuggets ('49–'50)	
Anderson Packers ('49–'50)	
Sheboygan Redskins ('49–'50)	
Waterloo Hawks ('49–'50)	
Tri-Cities Blackhawks ('49–'51)	
Milwaukee Hawks ('51–'55)	
St. Louis Hawks ('55–'68)	
Atlanta Hawks ('68–Present)	
Indianapolis Olympians ('49–'53)	
Syracuse Nationals ('49–'63)	
Philadelphia 76ers ('63–Present)	
Chicago Packers ('61–'62)	
Chicago Zephyrs ('62–'63)	
Baltimore Bullets ('63–'73)	
Capital Bullets ('73–'74)	
Washington Bullets ('74–Present)	
Chicago Bulls ('66–Present)	
San Diego Rockets ('67–'71)	
Houston Rockets ('71–Present)	
Seattle SuperSonics ('67–Present)	
Milwaukee Bucks ('68–Present)	
Phoenix Suns ('68–Present)	
Buffalo Braves ('70–'78)	
San Diego Clippers ('78–'84)	
Los Angeles Clippers ('84–Present)	
Cleveland Cavaliers ('70–Present)	
Portland Trail Blazers ('70–Present)	
New Orleans Jazz ('74–'80)	
Utah Jazz ('80–Present)	
New York Nets ('76–'77)	
New Jersey Nets ('77–Present)	
San Antonio Spurs ('76–Present)	
Indiana Pacers ('76–Present)	
Denver Nuggets ('76–Present)	
Dallas Mavericks ('80–Present)	
Charlotte Hornets ('88–Present)	
Miami Heat ('88–Present)	
Minnesota Timberwolves ('89–Present)	
Orlando Magic ('89–Present)	

THE NBA FAMILY TREE

NOTE: Toronto and Vancouver have been granted expansion franchises and will begin competition in the 1995–1996 season.

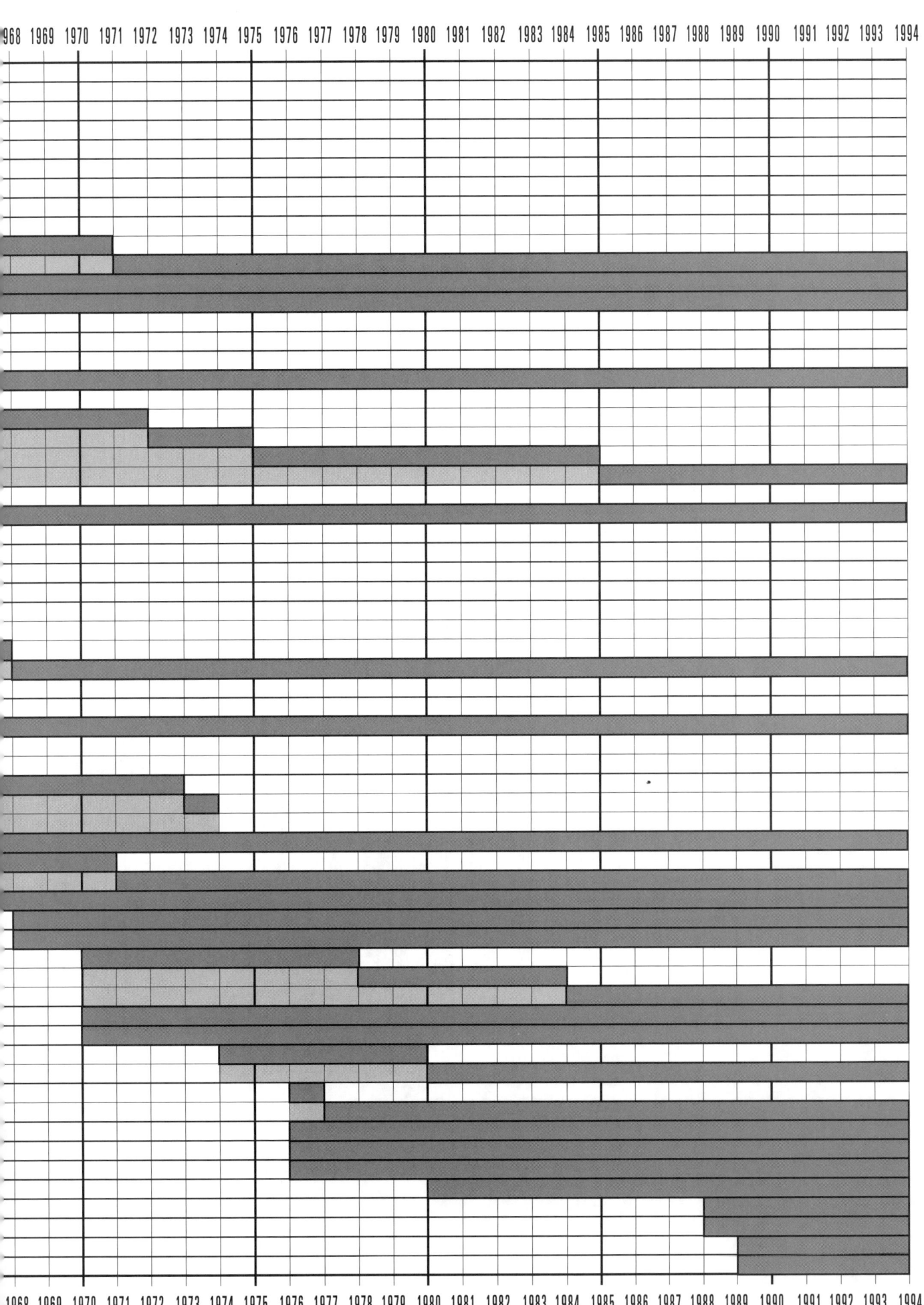

CHAPTER THREE

THE HISTORY OF THE NBA

TIP-OFF: HOW THE NBA BEGAN
by Leonard Koppett

Leonard Koppett, longtime sports writer for the New York Times, Peninsula Times-Tribune *and* Oakland Tribune, *is the author of* Twenty-Four Seconds to Shoot, *a history of the NBA's early years.*

To understand how and why the National Basketball Association started the way it did, one must have some idea of the special characteristics of the world in the spring of 1946. World War II had ended less than 12 months before, but even before it did, all entrepreneurs could see and plan for the immediate aftermath: a tremendous pent-up demand for entertainment. People wanted to spend the money they had accumulated during the war years.

Sports promoters, in particular, were ready to cash in. There were limits, however. College football was

NEW YORK KNICKERBOCKERS
VS.
CHICAGO STAGS
MADISON SQUARE GARDEN   NOVEMBER 11, 1946
24c. N. Y. C. SALES TAX 1c   25c

Cover of the program sold at the New York Knicks' first game at Madison Square Garden, November 11, 1946.

important, but still essentially regional and tied to educational institutions rather than pure profit seekers. Professional football was just coming out of its barn-storming semipro stage; the 10-team National Football League was still looked down upon by the college football public. Golf and tennis were strictly amateur, at least officially. The Olympics had been in limbo since 1936. Hockey meant nothing at all to most of the United States. There were only three big moneymaking sports: baseball, boxing and horse racing.

Baseball was alone as the prototype "big-league professional sport." Its 16 teams, in 10 of the largest cities in the northeast quarter of the United States, had been in place since 1903. Its World Series was the climax of the whole sports year. No one thought of challenging its status; everyone wanted to imitate it to as high a degree as possible.

Boxing was elemental, universally appealing, individual combat. Championships in all weight classes were major events. Local club bouts drew crowds every day of the week in large cities and less frequently in all cities.

Horse racing, of course, was based on the appeal of legalized betting.

So sports promoters looking for an opportunity in 1946 had to make choices. Baseball was a closed corporation, uninterested in expansion. Horse racing was locked into state regulation.

But boxing, back in the 1920s, had created the context for what was already growing. The large-city downtown arenas, with capacities in the 10,000 to 15,000 range, had been built primarily to house major fights. Once built, they had many open dates to fill. The circus, rodeos, dog or horse shows, six-day bike races, political rallies and other special events (but no rock concerts yet) took some. Then hockey was brought to Boston, New York, Detroit, Chicago and a few other places specifically to fill in other dates. And after the 1932 and 1936 Winter Olympics, ice shows became a regular feature.

In the 1930s, college basketball doubleheaders proved to be a big hit. And they were a bigger hit in New York's Madison Square Garden than anywhere else. The most glamorous venue for boxing champions had also become the "Mecca of Basketball."

By now, the arena owners had an umbrella organization, the Arena Managers Association of America, to cooperate on setting ice show and circus dates. (The ice shows were crucial, as they couldn't be put on in theaters or summer tents; the rinks created for hockey gave the arenas a monopoly situation.) But the arenas also owned and operated hockey teams, so their ties were even closer.

Two men were particularly interested in adding pro basketball to their promotional mix: Walter Brown of Boston and Al Sutphin of Cleveland. But a pro basketball league without a New York City entry was inconceivable, and that entry had to be in Madison Square Garden.

Max Kase, sports editor of the *New York Journal-American* and a good friend of Brown's since his own days in Boston, had a New York team lined up. All he had to do was rent the Garden from the man who ran its basketball operations, Ned Irish.

But Irish, who had started as a sportswriter and publicity man, had invented and developed the college doubleheader program. He didn't want or need to fill in any open dates (having none), nor did he need competition for his thriving collegiate program. Also, in line with the general thinking of his day, he didn't really believe in a bright future for pro basketball.

He could not, however, stay out of such a league if there was to be one—nor could he let someone else run a team in his building. Citing a prior agreement among the arena managers that "if one went into pro basketball, all would," Irish joined the movement Brown and Sutphin had been pushing all through 1945. Kase was bought out; the Garden, which owned and operated the National Hockey League's Rangers, would now also own and operate a basketball team.

At an organizational meeting on June 6, 1946, at the Commodore Hotel alongside Grand Central Terminal in New York City, the new league was born and given the name Basketball Association of America, or BAA.

Its heritage was clear: hockey.

• The Boston Celtics belonged to Brown, who ran the NHL Bruins and Boston Garden.
• The Chicago Stags were represented by Arthur Morse, not an arena operator himself but a lawyer with close ties to the Norris family, which ran Chicago Stadium and the NHL Black Hawks (and also were involved in Detroit's Olympia and Madison Square Garden through boxing).
• The Cleveland Rebels were the creation of Sutphin, who also ran the Cleveland Arena and the American

ON TOP OF THE ACTION

With the court so close to the stands and personalities larger than life, the NBA has generated sights and sounds that have become ingrained in the mind's eye of every sports fan. These images tell us something not only about the way we were but the way we are:

Red Auerbach's victory cigar.

Michael Jordan embracing the championship trophy and sobbing, with his father at his side.

Wilt Chamberlain's wristbands.

The gold star in Gus Johnson's front tooth.

Larry Johnson's gold tooth.

Kareem Abdul-Jabbar's goggles.

George Mikan's glasses.

Pat Riley's suits.

Walt Frazier's ''Clyde'' outfits.

The no-look passes of Larry Bird and Magic Johnson.

High fives, low fives, and everything in between.

The special relationship between Jack Twyman and the stricken Maurice Stokes.

The scraps of paper on which Eddie Gottlieb compiled the league schedule.

Feets Broudy operating the clock at Madison Square Garden.

Jack Nicholson sitting courtside at the LA Forum.

Wes Unseld's broad shoulders and his outlet passes.

Tommy Heinsohn's sneer and his running hook shot.

Jerry West's oft-broken nose and his unerring jumper.

The look of eagles in Bill Russell's eyes and the cackle in his voice.

Willis Reed taking the floor in Game 7.

Pete Maravich's floppy socks.

The parquet floor.

The Laker Girls.

Hugo the Hornet and everything teal.

Shaq Attaqs.

Pat Riley's hair, slicked back.

Bill Walton's hair, in a ponytail.

Artis Gilmore's hair, in an eight-inch Afro.

Michael Jordan's hair—where?

Jim Murray's description of Elgin Baylor: ''The only man to look dignified in short pants.''

Dave Zinkoff's ''Gola Goal!'' ''Dipper dunk!'' ''Two for Shue!'' And, of course, ''Julius Errrrrrving!''

Johnny Most's ''Havlicek stole the ball!''

Chick Hearn's ''He put him into the popcorn machine!''

John F. X. Condon welcoming folks to ''the magical world of Madison Square Garden.''

Michael Jordan's tongue in shooting position.

Larry Bird wiping the bottoms of his sneakers.

Magic Johnson's smile.

Goggles don't impede Kareem Abdul-Jabbar's vision as he launches his famed sky-hook.

Jack Nicholson watches his beloved Lakers from his courtside seat at the Forum.

Walter Brown, owner of the Boston Celtics and one of the NBA's founding fathers.

Hockey League Barons. The AHL was the top minor league in hockey's structure.
* The Detroit Falcons were a Norris operation owned by the Olympia, adopting a former name of the NHL Red Wings.

* The New York Knickerbockers, with Irish in command, were the house team of Madison Square Garden, corporate cousins of the NHL Rangers.
* The Philadelphia Warriors were owned by Pete Tyrell, who ran the Philadelphia Arena and the AHL Rockets.
* The Pittsburgh Ironmen were under the control of John Harris, who also had the AHL Hornets and an arena in Pittsburgh.
* The Providence Steamrollers belonged to Lou Pieri, proprietor of the arena there and of the AHL Reds.
* The St. Louis Bombers, under Emory D. Jones, were packaged with the St. Louis Arena and the AHL Flyers.
* The Toronto Huskies were the house team of Maple Leaf Gardens, which also owned the NHL Maple Leafs.
* And the Washington Capitols were owned by Mike Uline, the only one without a hockey connection but owner of Uline Arena, the largest such building in the nation's capital.

Thus began the actualization of a concept totally different from the pro basketball scene that had previously existed:

The BAA absorbed six teams from the NBL and was renamed the National Basketball Association on August 3, 1949. From left: Ike Duffy, NBL president; Leo Ferris, owner, Syracuse Nats; Maurice Podoloff, BAA/NBA president; Ned Irish, owner, New York Knicks; Walter Brown, owner, Boston Celtics.

The BAA was formed in 1946, providing additional events for large downtown arenas like Chicago Stadium (top) and Toronto's Maple Leaf Gardens.

1. Each of the 11 teams was arena-owned, i.e., its own landlord.
2. The emphasis was on college players. Publicity played up the "clean" and "open" game the colleges were making so popular and dissociated the younger players from the "old pros."
3. A hockey-schedule format emphasizing postseason playoff series from the start, not elimination tournaments for postseason championships, was utilized.
4. A conscious effort was made at unified league-entity promotion.

As president, the owners selected someone they knew well: Maurice Podoloff, president of the AHL. A lawyer from New Haven whose family had long run the arena there (the New Haven Ramblers were a farm club of the New York Rangers), he was well suited to deal with exactly the kinds of problems a new league would face: internal diplomacy, helping the have-nots stay alive, keeping the big boys (like Irish) from prematurely imposing "big-league" standards and requirements on smaller operations not ready to handle such burdens,

THE COMMISSIONERS

Four men have headed the NBA: Maurice Podoloff, J. Walter Kennedy, Larry O'Brien and David Stern. Each, in his own way, has left his imprint on the sport and helped make professional basketball the success it is today.

Podoloff was chosen to head the infant Basketball Association of America because he was a man well known to the owners of the league's franchises. His family owned and operated the New Haven Arena in Connecticut, and he was serving as president of the American Hockey League when the basketball organizers requested his services. Born in czarist Russia and a graduate of Yale Law School, Podoloff's strength was his ability to negotiate for the common good.

The BAA lost much money in its first two years, and it was evident that more would follow unless the league could put a better product on the court. While the BAA occupied large arenas in major cities, most of the basketball talent was then in the older National Basketball League, which operated in the midwest. Podoloff's solution was clear.

First he convinced the leaders of the Fort Wayne Zollner Pistons and the Indianapolis Kautskys that their future could be better served by switching from the NBL to the BAA. When word of their move got out, owners Max Winter and Ben Berger of the Minneapolis Lakers decided to go with them—bringing to the BAA 6-10 George Mikan, the sport's first dominant big man and its marquee attraction. The next domino to fall in the direction of the BAA was the Rochester Royals, who were led by Bob Davies, the backcourt whiz who had popularized the behind-the-back dribble and was the sport's No. 2 attraction. On the eve of the 1948–49 season, Podoloff had transformed the BAA into a 12-team league with major stars, and the future of the sport was shaped. One year later, the BAA absorbed the surviving members of the NBL and adopted a new name, the National Basketball Association. Podoloff, who headed the league with the title of president, secured the league's first television contract in 1954 and remained on the job until his retirement in 1963 at the age of 73.

He was succeeded by Kennedy, who had served as the league's first public relations director and then worked in advertising before becoming mayor of Stamford, Conn., a post he resigned to become president (his title would be changed to commissioner in 1967) of the NBA. Kennedy broadened the appeal of the game and oversaw expansion that doubled the size of the league from nine to 18 teams.

Kennedy retired in 1975, yielding to O'Brien, onetime national chairman of the Democratic party, postmaster general and a longtime adviser to former President John F. Kennedy. Coincidentally, O'Brien shared a birthplace with basketball and even played at the "Y" in Springfield, Mass., where Naismith had first devised the sport.

A prominent figure in political circles who was acclaimed for his behind-the-scenes negotiating skills,

Four men have led the NBA in the office of president or commissioner (the title was changed in 1967): Maurice Podoloff (top left), who served from 1946 to 1963; J. Walter Kennedy (top right), 1963 to 1975; Larry O'Brien (lower left), 1975 to 1984; and David J. Stern (lower right), 1984 to present.

O'Brien was an ideal choice to engineer the NBA's absorption of the four surviving members of the American Basketball Association in 1976 and gain congressional approval for the endeavor, which ended a costly nine-year battle between the two leagues and created one national major league of professional basketball.

Stern, an attorney who had worked on several cases involving the NBA, and a lifelong basketball fan, became its first general counsel and was promoted to executive vice president in charge of legal and business affairs under O'Brien, whom he succeeded as commissioner in 1984.

A canny administrator with a keen understanding of marketing and broadcasting and a flair for personal diplomacy, Stern forged a strong relationship with the National Basketball Players Association, which helped the NBA lead all team sports in establishing a progressive free agent system and forming a cohesive and effective policy for dealing with drug abuse. Stern also developed and greatly expanded NBA Properties, the league's marketing arm, as well as NBA Entertainment, and established NBA International to focus on the league's role in the worldwide growth of basketball. He has presided over the NBA at the time of its greatest growth and taken basketball to the forefront of the global sports scene.

When Madison Square Garden was unavailable, the New York Knicks played home games at the 69th Regiment Armory.

scrambling for survival when survival was by no means assured.

What's more, he already had an office, at 515 Madison Avenue. Before long, the BAA would open its own office on the highest level imaginable—the 80th floor of the Empire State Building.

Getting to the top of the basketball world wasn't easy, however. The newly formed BAA had the right

Joe Fulks (10) was the league's first scoring champion, averaging 23.2 ppg in 1947.

idea (college rules, except for having a 48-minute game rather than 40 minutes, with an extra personal foul allowed and zone defense forbidden). It had the right personalities: fresh, attractive names coming out of college. And it had the right cities. But the older leagues, particularly the midwest-based National Basketball League, had the mature professional players. There was a separation of talent and resources that would have to be resolved one way or another.

The major-arena idea failed quickly. For one thing, the Knicks weren't filling Madison Square Garden, so most of their home games were played in the 5,000-seat 69th Regiment Armory. The "Mecca" was doing the BAA no good at all.

After the first season, Toronto, Pittsburgh, Detroit and Cleveland gave up. The remaining seven, in order to keep going, took in Baltimore from the old American League (now called the Eastern League) and cut the schedule from 60 to 48 games.

It had taken only one year to put into focus the good and bad sides of the BAA concept. The arena owners had plenty of business and promotional know-how, qualities in short supply among previous basketball operators. What they didn't know was how to put together, direct and maintain winning basketball teams of pro-level ability. The experienced pros knew one thing the arena operators didn't: *basketball*—the game, the players, the existing audience and the practical lines of development.

Four individuals emerged as key figures in the eventual resolution: George Mikan, Eddie Gottlieb, Maurice Podoloff and Ned Irish.

Mikan, basketball's first truly dominant "big man" (6-10 with good athletic reflexes, not mere size), came out of Chicago's DePaul University in 1946. But he chose to join the National League, with its established pro players, rather than the BAA. When his Chicago Gears left the NBL in an attempt to form a new league and then disbanded, he was awarded to the NBL's Minneapolis Lakers, who were establishing rivalries with the older Rochester Royals and Fort Wayne Pistons.

The concept of cashing in on college stars in general, in 1946 and 1947, was a bit premature because so many top players, back from the war, could continue college careers under the GI Bill. The flood would come, but later; for the moment, Mikan was a unique gate attraction, second only to the independent Harlem Globetrotters, whose exhibition appearances helped BAA revenue.

Gottlieb, brought in by Tyrell to run the Philadelphia Warriors, was the only one of the first set of coaches with deep pro roots. All the other teams sought leaders with college experience or (in the case of Arnold "Red" Auerbach in Washington) no real reputation at all. Gottlieb had run the successful Philadelphia SPHAs in the American League. When his Warriors won the first BAA championship in 1947, his basketball acumen

Eddie Gottlieb (right) coached the Philadelphia Warriors to the first BAA championship in 1947.

got attention. As time went on, his knowledge and experience were leaned upon more and more by Podoloff in particular and by the owners as a group. Among other things, Gottlieb was an expert schedule maker, and proper scheduling was an art essential to solvency.

The first two years were financial disasters. The first year ended with four teams dropping out. The second proved that a 48-game schedule didn't provide enough openings to meet expenses. Podoloff and others saw that the only immediate remedy would be to bring in, somehow, the one obvious moneymaker: Mikan.

Irish was all in favor of that. Mikan had come to stardom as a college player in Madison Square Garden as a visitor and tournament standout; his name on the marquee would certainly work in New York and upgrade the image of the league.

But what Irish didn't want was any compromise with the original "college aura" concept. Mikan, yes; old pros in number and style, no.

The Podoloff camp, of course, recognized that one went with the other. They had to be blended in some way. So Podoloff, using his diplomatic skills to the highest, concentrated on getting Mikan as part of a larger package.

The Lakers themselves, when approached, were content to stay in the National League. Rochester would be glad to switch, but who needed a town that size in the BAA? Fort Wayne and Indianapolis, however, were more eager. If publicity for the businesses of their owners was one rationale for their operation, wouldn't it mean more on a "big-league canvas" to get exposure in the big business centers?

Just before the 1948–49 season was about to start, the move was completed and announced. Fort Wayne and Indianapolis would jump to the BAA.

The Lakers then decided that if the National League was going to have defections, they would jump, too.

And if those three went, what about Rochester? Over the objections of Irish, who also took a dim view of "Fort Wayne" on the uniforms of a visiting team at his "Mecca," the Royals were invited to come along.

Suddenly, the BAA had 12 teams and a full complement of the established pros of the day along with the collegians who would now have no other league of comparable status to contemplate when turning pro.

For all practical purposes, that was the end of the National League and a solid basis for the future of the BAA. But that's hindsight. In 1948, it wasn't at all clear that the transfer would really pay off, that the "college atmosphere" could be maintained or that the forces that had undermined pro leagues in the past wouldn't still have their effect over time.

Nevertheless, the 1948–49 season was a success, with the Lakers winning the championship by beating Auerbach's Washington Caps in the final round. Still very much a second banana to the college game, the BAA had at least stopped the economic hemorrhage that the first two years had produced.

After that season, the remnants of the National League were taken in: Syracuse, Anderson, Tri-Cities, Sheboygan, Denver and Waterloo. In deference to the "merger" and to avoid possible legal complications, the name was changed from "BAA" to the "National Basketball Association." That didn't bother anyone concerned because the name "BAA" had not achieved any particular distinction. But it was definitely the same league with the same governing body, including Podoloff. And with Providence dropping out, it went into the 1949–50 season with 17 teams playing in three divisions.

That was the end of the beginning.

Ned Irish, head of the New York Knicks and Madison Square Garden, favored bringing stars like George Mikan into the NBA.

ROUNDBALL, B-BALL AND HOOPS

NBA players are household names, often on a first-name (or nickname) basis: Shaq and Sir Charles, Larry and Magic, Isiah and Michael, Willis and Wilt, 'Nique and Spud. NBA history is marked by many noteworthy nicknames. Red has been among the most popular, belonging to Arnold Auerbach, William Holzman, Ephraim Rocha, Johnny Kerr and Herman Klotz, among others. Here is a sampling of some of the monikers:

The Big O	Oscar Robertson
Dr. J	Julius Erving
The Skywalker	David Thompson
Jumpin' Joe	Joe Fulks
Pogo Joe	Joe Caldwell
The Kangaroo Kid	Billy Cunningham
Harry the Horse	Harry Gallatin
The Whopper	Billy Paultz
Houdini of the Hardwood	Bob Cousy
The Human Highlight Film	Dominique Wilkins
Tricky Dick	Dick McGuire
Bad News	Jim Barnes
Chet the Jet	Chet Walker
Dollar Bill	Bill Bradley
The Big Dipper, or Wilt the Stilt	Wilt Chamberlain
Bill the Hill	Bill McGill
Easy Ed	Ed Macauley
The Big E	Elvin Hayes
Big Bells	Walter Bellamy
Crash	John Mengelt
Tiny	Nate Archibald
Muggsy	Tyrone Bogues
Cornbread	Cedric Maxwell
Truck	Leonard Robinson
Hondo	John Havlicek
Jungle Jim	Jim Loscutoff
Satch	Tom Sanders
Duck	Don Chaney
Butterbean	Bob Love
Jellybean	Joe Bryant
Bubbles	Robert Hawkins
Tree	Wayne Rollins
Toothpick	Maurice McHartley
Sweetwater	Nat Clifton
World B. Free	World B. Free
Earl the Pearl	Earl Monroe
Clyde	Walt Frazier
Fall Back, Baby	Dick Barnett
Sleepy	Eric Floyd
Happy	Harold Hairston
Doc	Glenn Rivers
Pistol Pete	Pete Maravich

Zeke from Cabin Creek, or Mr. Clutch	Jerry West
The Iceman, or Ice	George Gervin
Sir Charles, or The Round Mound of Rebound	Charles Barkley
The Mailman	Karl Malone
The Human Eraser	Marvin Webster
Mr. Mean	Larry Smith
Slick	Donald Watts
Silk	Jamaal Wilkes
'Nique	Dominique Wilkins
'Zo	Alonzo Mourning
Shaq	Shaquille O'Neal
The Dream	Dean Meminger
The Dream	Hakeem Olajuwon
The Admiral	David Robinson
The Worm	Dennis Rodman
Air	Michael Jordan
Magic	Earvin Johnson

Earl "the Pearl" Monroe

Michael ''Air'' Jordan

"Pistol" Pete Maravich

Julius ''Dr. J'' Erving

"Dollar" Bill Bradley

1946—47

In the first season of the BAA, a new professional star emerged, one who had gained little notoriety in college. Joe Fulks, a 6-5 forward from Kentucky, averaged 23.2 points per game, an astonishing amount considering most games were won by teams scoring in the 70s and 80s, and nearly seven points per game more than any other player in the league. Field-goal percentages were in the 30 percent range, and Ernest Calverley of the Providence Steamrollers led the league with 3.4 assists per game. Other stars in the fledgling league were Washington's Bob Feerick and Bones McKinney, Detroit's Stan Miasek and Chicago's Max Zaslofsky.

The 60-game regular season belonged to the Washington Capitols, coached by Red Auerbach to a 49-11 record, including a 29-1 mark at home. But in the playoffs, Chicago shocked the Capitols behind the play of Zaslofsky and center Chuck Halbert to advance to the Finals. Philadelphia, coached by Eddie Gottlieb, who had the most extensive pro background of anyone in the BAA, defeated St. Louis and New York to advance to the Finals. Fulks, Howie Dallmar and Angelo Musi led Philadelphia past Chicago as the Warriors won the first league title 4–1.

BAA 1946-47

FINAL STANDINGS

Eastern Division

	W.	L.	PCT.
Washington	49	11	.817
Philadelphia	35	25	.583
New York	33	27	.550
Providence	28	32	.467
Toronto	22	38	.367
Boston	22	38	.367

Western Division

	W.	L.	PCT.
Chicago	39	22	.639
St. Louis	38	23	.623
Cleveland	30	30	.500
Detroit	20	40	.333
Pittsburgh	15	45	.250

PLAYOFFS

Quarterfinals

New York 2, Cleveland 1
April 2—Cleveland 77, New York 51
April 5—New York 86, Cleveland 74
April 9—New York 93, Cleveland 71

Philadelphia 2, St. Louis 1
April 2—Philadelphia 73, St. Louis 68
April 5—St. Louis 73, Philadelphia 51
April 6—Philadelphia 75, St. Louis 59

Semifinals

Chicago 4, Washington 2
April 2—Chicago 81, Washington 65
April 3—Chicago 69, Washington 53
April 8—Chicago 67, Washington 55
April 10—Washington 76, Chicago 69
April 12—Washington 67, Chicago 55
April 13—Chicago 66, Washington 61

Philadelphia 2, New York 0
April 12—Philadelphia 82, New York 70
April 14—Philadelphia 72, New York 53

Finals

Philadelphia 4, Chicago 1
April 16—Philadelphia 84, Chicago 71
April 17—Philadelphia 85, Chicago 74
April 19—Philadelphia 75, Chicago 72
April 20—Chicago 74, Philadelphia 73
April 22—Philadelphia 83, Chicago 80

INDIVIDUAL LEADERS

Scoring

	G.	FG	FT	PTS.	AVG.
Fulks, Philadelphia	60	475	439	1389	23.2
Feerick, Washington	55	364	198	926	16.8
Miasek, Detroit	60	331	233	895	14.9
Sadowski, Tor.-Cle.	53	329	219	877	16.5
Zaslofsky, Chicago	61	336	205	877	14.4
Calverley, Providence	59	323	199	845	14.3
Halbert, Chicago	61	280	213	773	12.7
Logan, St. Louis	61	290	190	770	12.6
Mogus, Cle.-Tor.	58	259	235	753	13.0
Gunther, Pittsburgh	52	254	226	734	14.1

Field Goal Pct.
(Minimum 200 FG made)

	FGM	FGA	PCT.
Feerick, Washington	364	908	.401
Sadowski, Tor.-Cle.	329	891	.369
Shannon, Providence	245	722	.339
Gunther, Pittsburgh	254	756	.336
Zaslofsky, Chicago	336	1020	.329

Free Throw Pct.
(Minimum 125 FT made)

	FTM	FTA	PCT.
Scolari, Washington	146	180	.811
Kappen, Pit.-Bos.	128	161	.795
Stutz, New York	133	170	.782
Feerick, Washington	198	260	.762
Logan, St. Louis	190	254	.748

Assists

	G.	NO.	AVG.
Calverley, Providence	59	202	3.4
Sailors, Cleveland	58	134	2.3
Schectman, New York	54	109	2.0
Dallmar, Philadelphia	60	104	1.7
Miasek, Detroit	60	93	1.6
Rottner, Chicago	56	93	1.7

The debut season closed with neither a bang nor a whimper. The new league was acknowledged, with small items on the local teams appearing in newspapers. Television was still in the future, and radio broadcasts were hardly universal.

Still, the franchises did play in major arenas, such as Boston Garden, Madison Square Garden and Chicago Stadium. Most of the teams shared the buildings with hockey teams. The Finals games in Philadelphia were sellouts, and members of the victorious Warriors pocketed about $2,000 per man in prize money—almost half a season's pay for most.

1947—48

When the second season began, several prominent changes had taken place. The league schedule was reduced from 60 to 48 games in an attempt to cut travel expenses. Four teams from the original 11—Detroit, Cleveland, Toronto and Pittsburgh—had folded, leaving the remaining seven with an unbalanced schedule. To correct this problem, the Baltimore Bullets were brought in from a regional circuit called the American Basketball League.

To the surprise of many, Baltimore more than proved it belonged by winning the title in six games over Philadelphia, including a 21-point halftime comeback in Game 2 that stands as the best in NBA playoff history. Baltimore featured 5-11 player-coach Buddy Jeannette, 6-8 center Clarence "Kleggie" Hermsen, guard Chick Reiser, and forwards Paul Hoffman and Connie Simmons. Chicago's Zaslofsky was the only player who broke the 1,000-point barrier; he won the scoring title (determined then by total points, rather than average, as it is now) over Fulks when the Philadelphia star missed five games. The league, which struggled through adversity as the reduction in games also cut into revenues, got a boost when Joe Lapchick, who had played for the Original Celtics and coached at St. John's, brought his experience to the league as coach of the Knicks.

While some teams played in large arenas like Madison Square Garden, Boston Garden or Chicago Stadium, the champion Bullets played in a dingy old coliseum in one of Baltimore's poorer neighborhoods. "It was a real dump," conceded team owner Robert "Jake" Embry. "You could only get 4,000 in if you stood them in all the corners."

"I'll tell you how bad it was," said player-coach Jeannette. "When they quit using it as an arena, they made a garage out of it."

The Coliseum's main function in those days was as a roller-skating rink, and the same floor was used for basketball. "It was raw wood," recalled Hoffman. "They would roller-skate on it the night before we played on it."

Yet the intimacy of the Coliseum gave the Bullets an edge, and they used the home-court advantage to post a 17-7 record there during the regular season, then win all six of their home playoff games. "We were close to our fans," said Hoffman. "We knew practically everybody there!"

BAA 1947-48

FINAL STANDINGS

Eastern Division

	W.	L.	PCT.
Philadelphia	27	21	.563
New York	26	22	.542
Boston	20	28	.417
Providence	6	42	.125

Western Division

	W.	L.	PCT.
St. Louis	29	19	.604
Baltimore *	28	20	.583
Chicago	28	20	.583
Washington	28	20	.583

* Won playoff to break tie

PLAYOFFS

Western Division Tie-breakers

March 23—Chicago 74, Washington 70
March 25—Baltimore 75, Chicago 72

Quarterfinals

Baltimore 2, New York 1
March 27—Baltimore 85, New York 81
March 28—New York 79, Baltimore 69
April 1—Baltimore 84, New York 77

Chicago 2, Boston 1
March 28—Chicago 79, Boston 72
March 31—Boston 81, Chicago 77
April 2—Chicago 81, Boston 74

Semifinals

Philadelphia 4, St. Louis 3
March 23—St. Louis 60, Philadelphia 58
March 25—Philadelphia 65, St. Louis 64
March 27—Philadelphia 84, St. Louis 56
March 30—St. Louis 56, Philadelphia 51
April 1—St. Louis 69, Philadelphia 62
April 3—Philadelphia 84, St. Louis 61
April 6—Philadelphia 85, St. Louis 46

Baltimore 2, Chicago 0
April 7—Baltimore 73, Chicago 67
April 8—Baltimore 89, Chicago 72

Finals

Baltimore 4, Philadelphia 2
April 10—Philadelphia 71, Baltimore 60
April 13—Baltimore 66, Philadelphia 63
April 15—Baltimore 72, Philadelphia 70
April 17—Baltimore 78, Philadelphia 75
April 20—Philadelphia 91, Baltimore 82
April 21—Baltimore 88, Philadelphia 73

INDIVIDUAL LEADERS

Scoring

	G.	FG	FT	PTS.	AVG.
Zaslofsky, Chicago	48	373	261	1007	21.0
Fulks, Philadelphia	43	326	297	949	22.1
Sadowski, Boston	47	308	294	910	19.4
Feerick, Washington	48	293	189	775	16.1
Miasek, Chicago	48	263	190	716	14.9
Braun, New York	47	276	119	671	14.3
Logan, St. Louis	48	221	202	644	13.4
Palmer, New York	48	224	174	622	13.0
Rocha, St. Louis	48	232	147	611	12.7
Scolari, Washington	47	229	131	589	12.5

Field Goal Pct.
(Minimum 200 FG made)

	FGM	FGA	PCT.
Feerick, Washington	293	861	.340
Sadowski, Boston	308	953	.323
Zaslofsky, Chicago	373	1156	.323
Braun, New York	276	854	.323
Reiser, Baltimore	202	628	.322

Free Throw Pct.
(Minimum 125 FT made)

	FTM	FTA	PCT.
Feerick, Washington	189	240	.788
Zaslofsky, Chicago	261	333	.784
Fulks, Philadelphia	297	390	.762
Jeannette, Baltimore	191	252	.758
Dallmar, Philadelphia	157	211	.744

Assists

	G.	NO.	AVG.
Dallmar, Philadelphia	48	120	2.5
Calverley, Providence	47	119	2.5
Seminoff, Chicago	48	89	1.9
Gilmur, Chicago	48	77	1.6
Phillip, Chicago	32	74	2.3
Sadowski, Boston	47	74	1.6

THE MIKAN ERA
by Leonard Lewin

Leonard Lewin is a former sports writer for the New York Post *who covered the NBA since its inception and is now the executive director of the New York Knicks Alumni Association. In 1993 he received the Hall of Fame's Curt Gowdy Award for outstanding contributions to basketball.*

The NBA has seen but two true dynasties in its nearly half century of existence. The most famous, of course, was the Bill Russell–led Boston Celtics' 1957–69 run of 11 championships in 13 seasons, including eight in a row at one point. But the league's first dynasty came much earlier, at a time when it was still struggling to establish its place in American sports. George Mikan, the game's first dominant big man, led the Minneapolis Lakers to five NBA titles in six seasons from 1949 through 1954 and altered forever the way pro basketball is viewed. Players, coaches and rules have changed, but not the fact that Mikan and his teammates established the foundation as well as the future of the NBA.

The original Basketball Association of America was so shaky in its effort to capitalize on the college basketball excitement of the times that it reached out to the older, midwest-based National Basketball League for expansion after only two seasons. Many of the major college basketball names preferred the NBL then because the money and recognition were there.

The 6-10, bespectacled Mikan was the hottest basketball property in the country when the two professional leagues went after him. He had been a devastating college player at DePaul and eventually was voted "Mr.

Basketball of the First Half Century" for his performances as a college and pro player. He chose to ignore the BAA when he moved into pro ball, signing with the Chicago American Gears of the NBL after the Chicago Stags of the BAA failed to entice him. He rejected the Stags and the opportunity to be a charter member of the BAA because of money.

In those days, a few top players would be paid around $5,000. "I turned down the Stags because they wouldn't pay me $12,000," said Mikan. He was promised that amount from the Gears but soon had to go to court to collect it.

In December 1946, early in his first season, he sued over his contract. He was receiving $7,000 a year and cited a series of agreements that added up to another $25,000 over his five-year contract. All of which balanced out to the $12,000 a year he had been seeking.

Both professional leagues were struggling. There was very little risk capital, and the money promised Mikan was high and unusual but reflective of his ability to draw fans and attention. Mikan was a towering figure in all basketball circles, and he knew it—and he was concerned that the Gears seemed not to show any appreciation of his presence and contributions.

Mikan also battled back when he felt the Gears treated other players poorly. For example, during his 1946 lawsuit, he told the court he had complained about the Gears' way of dismissing players without any concern. "It was plainly illustrated two weeks ago," he said. "Four members of our squad were handed dismissal notices when they were in the railroad station boarding a train for a road trip."

Mikan went back to the Gears and finished the season with the lawsuit pending. The following year

Sometimes it took two men to get the angle on 6-10
George Mikan, the NBA's first dominating center.

Jim Pollard, while overshadowed by George Mikan, never failed to average double figures in scoring.

Maurice White, the owner of the Gears, pulled his team out of the NBL in an attempt to form a new league, but that venture lasted for only eight games before it was disbanded. Mikan, without a team, signed with the Minneapolis Lakers of the NBL for the remainder of the 1947–48 season.

When the Gears folded, several teams wanted to sign Mikan, who had led Chicago to the 1947 NBL championship. But Max Winter, the owner of the Minneapolis franchise who later sold out to buy the NFL Vikings, went after Mikan immediately. He had gained the rights in a special NBL meeting. Mikan recalls his negotiations, which took place in a car.

"Rochester and Fort Wayne wanted me, but Minneapolis got my rights," he said. "They brought me into Minneapolis and showed me around. I wasn't too

excited about playing there—too cold for me! I tried to be hospitable, but I wasn't too anxious to sign. They decided to drive me to the airport and continue talking. We went over some roads you couldn't find on a map. They just kept driving me around."

He finally agreed when they guaranteed his $12,000-a-year salary. Then he led the Lakers to the 1948 NBL title.

The Lakers carried a solid roster, built around Mikan and Jim Pollard, into their first BAA season. They also carried a strong rivalry with the Rochester Royals into their new league.

The Lakers and Royals fought it out in the West for all six years of what would become known to NBA

Vern Mikkelsen joined Minneapolis in 1949 and formed a formidable front line with George Mikan and Jim Pollard.

Lester Harrison, owner and coach of the Rochester Royals, couldn't match Minneapolis's George Mikan at center.

The next season, the BAA changed its name to the National Basketball Association. It also expanded to 17 teams and created three divisions after absorbing the surviving teams from the NBL. Rochester and Minneapolis were in the Central Division and wound up the season tied at 51-17. A one-game tiebreaker was played in Rochester because the Royals won the toss for the home court, but the Lakers won 78–76.

Bob Davies of the Rochester Royals was one of the great ballhandling guards of the 1940s and 1950s.

historians as the Mikan era. Mikan, Pollard and Vern Mikkelsen, who joined the team in 1949, comprised a powerful front line that many feel could compete even in today's accelerated game. Mikan was the scorer and rebounder inside, Pollard was the greyhound speedster and driver, and Mikkelsen had a strong body he used to muscle people.

On balance, the Rochester team, owned and coached by Les Harrison, was the Lakers' equal— except at center. Arnie Risen, a 6-9, 200-pounder, carried the load when he came out of Ohio State in 1948–49, but he was no physical match for the stronger Mikan.

The Royals were built around the exceptionally skillful Red Holzman, Bob Davies and Bobby Wanzer. All future members of the Hall of Fame, they helped the Royals pressure the Lakers every year, even though Rochester won only one championship. That was in 1950–51, when Holzman helped beat the Knicks four games to three. (The Knicks did not win their first NBA title until 1970—when Holzman was their coach.) That was the only title Minneapolis didn't win in the Mikan era. Every division battle was tight, though.

The Royals were 45-15 and Minneapolis 44-16 in 1949, but the Lakers beat them 2-0 in the division playoff final before taking the league title 4–2 against Washington.

George Mikan is the center of attention among the Minneapolis Lakers, the 1949 BAA champions.

The top four teams in each division qualified for the playoffs that season. Syracuse, Minneapolis and Anderson, Ind., one of the expansion teams, won their divisional playoffs, and Syracuse received a bye for the semifinals because it had the best regular-season record.

Syracuse was coached by Al Cervi and produced four future NBA coaches in Dolph Schayes, Alex Hannum, Paul Seymour and Fuzzy Levane. The Nats, in the middle of an Eastern Division rivalry with the Knicks, beat them 2–1 to make the NBA Finals. But the Lakers then beat Syracuse, capturing their second straight title, four games to two.

The Lakers had made a few changes in their original lineup. They added Mikkelsen, a big shooting guard in Bob Harrison, a backup forward named Bud Grant (who was to become the Hall of Fame coach of the NFL's Minnesota Vikings), Billy Hassett of Notre Dame (brother of former big-league first baseman Buddy Hassett) and an outstanding backcourtman named Slater Martin. It was Martin, Mikan, Pollard and Mikkelsen who teamed together to win four more championships before the team broke up.

Martin, or "Dugie" as he was called, was a 5-10, 170-pound guard from the University of Texas who added speed to the Lakers. "I was the Muggsy Bogues of

my time," he said some 40 years later, referring to the 5-3 guard who played in the NBA in the 1980s and 1990s. "I'm sure glad the small man has come back into the game." His job was to break down defenses and get the ball to his big men.

He had a strange though successful career with the Lakers. He signed for the munificent sum of $5,000 plus a $1,500 bonus, a lot of money for a small man from Texas coming to a championship team. He considered it good himself, too, until the Lakers swept to their second straight title.

Martin had a solid rookie year, playing in 67 games, but he never did get his bonus. "It so happened that our share from the playoffs that year was $1,500," he explained. "That turned out to be my bonus. That's why I held out every year after that. I wouldn't play unless they gave me a raise. And every year, they kept looking for a big guard to replace me."

The Lakers were clearly the hottest team in the game. "I played as many exhibition games during training camp as I did in college," recalled Martin. "We'd travel around in a Greyhound bus, and we wore out many of them. We played every night, mostly against a team of Minnesota Viking players."

That practice continued through the regular season

Hall of Famer Dolph Schayes was a mainstay of the Syracuse Nationals, appearing in 11 All-Star Games.

as well. Pro basketball was a sport rooted in barnstorming, and whenever the opportunity to pick up $5,000 a game appeared, Lakers management had Mikan & Co. show up. Wherever a hole in the league schedule appeared, it was filled with an exhibition game at the proper price. One game's fee would pay the annual salary for one Laker at the standards that existed then.

Martin remained a star among the Lakers until he was traded to the Knicks in 1956–57. By then, the dynasty was over. Mikan retired after the fifth championship in 1953–54 (he made a 37-game comeback two seasons later before giving it up forever), and Pollard retired after the 1954–55 season.

While the Lakers were slipping, the St. Louis Hawks were making major noises. Owner Ben Kerner had put together a strong team headed by Bob Pettit and Easy Ed Macauley, but he needed a Slater Martin type in the backcourt to add some speed and finesse to the offense.

"The Lakers didn't want to trade me to St. Louis and strengthen a Western rival," explained Martin. "So the Hawks went to Ned Irish and worked out a deal. I'd come to the Knicks, stay there for around three weeks and then go to St. Louis. That's what happened."

Irish and Kerner worked out a deal where the Knicks obtained the services of Willie Naulls, a smooth 6-6 forward out of UCLA who would play for New York for seven seasons. The switch was made after Martin had played 13 games for the Knicks and Naulls six with the Hawks. One season later, Slater was on the St. Louis championship team that beat Bill Russell and the Celtics in the Finals.

Gone are the Minneapolis Lakers, but the memories linger. Mikan, an average-size center by today's standards but a giant in the early '50s, is a legend who left his clear imprint on the game. They changed the foul lane because of him, from six feet across to 12, to try to

Slater Martin's ballhandling and playmaking helped Minneapolis stay on top.

minimize his effectiveness by denying him position near the basket. One time the league even experimented with a 12-foot-high basket to help reduce his advantage over everyone.

Max Winter waged a tough campaign over the league's attempt to legislate against his man. He sent out letters that asked, in essence, why rules should be changed because of Mikan's prowess when baseball never changed the rules for Babe Ruth. It didn't matter to Big George, though. In fact, he welcomed the lane change because it showcased his talent more.

"It gave me the opportunity to be more flexible"

Ben Kerner, owner of the St. Louis Hawks, put together one of the NBA's top teams of the 1950s.

12-foot-high basket than anyone else. The experiment was deemed a failure and abandoned. "It didn't work. It was worthless," said Martin. "I couldn't even hit the bottom of the rim."

No one dunked in those days, although that didn't mean no one was capable of dunking. "They did it in practice but never in a game," explained Martin. "In those days it was considered showboating and embarrassing to the other players, and we didn't want to do that."

Pollard, for one, was capable of taking off at the foul line and flying to the hoop, where he would jam it through. It was a feat performed publicly by a select few through the years, notably Julius Erving and Michael Jordan, but Pollard would do it only in practice for the enjoyment and amazement of his teammates. The championship Lakers didn't need that flair. They had all

George Mikan (99) was too big, too strong and too skillful for rivals of his era.

was his reaction to the rule change doubling the width of the foul lane. "It enabled me to move with more space and show I was a better player than I had been."

Instead of posting up close to the basket, he was now able to use more than his famous elbows to get to the hoop. He also insisted he was now able to make the play and pass the ball because there was more cutting room for the other Lakers, especially Pollard.

The change didn't keep Mikan from dominating the league or winning championships. That dream died faster than the one-game experiment to raise the rims.

The experiment took place in a Minneapolis–Milwaukee Hawks game on March 7, 1954, near the end of the regular season, a game that President Maurice Podoloff authorized to be used because it had no effect on the race for playoff positions.

None of the players was comfortable shooting at the higher baskets, and Mikan still dominated play because he was still bigger and stronger and closer to the

The driving play of Bobby Wanzer helped the Rochester Royals win the NBA title in 1951.

the basic elements they needed to keep winning titles year after year.

The New York Knicks kept coming close to the Lakers but couldn't break through. They just missed a championship in 1951 when they finished third in the East, beat the Celtics and the Nats in the playoffs and faced Rochester in the Finals. They were so confident they would take it all that Ned Irish, the man who "invented" big-time basketball at Madison Square Garden, filled the small chartered plane that took the Knicks to the seventh and final game in Rochester with champagne.

Unfortunately, Holzman, Davies, Wanzer, Risen

and the other Royals won the deciding game by four points, 79–75. That sent the Knicks back to New York, beaten once more. But since the champagne already was on the plane, the team drank it anyway.

It was a small plane with one pilot. Pretty soon a man was seen strolling to the back of the plane, where the champagne was flowing. Joe Lapchick, the coach, turned to someone sitting alongside and asked: "Wasn't that the pilot who just walked by? Who's flying the plane?"

Someone took a look. Sitting at the controls was John "Bud" Palmer, an original 1946–47 Knick out of Princeton. Bud was on the broadcasting team then and

Knicks Coach Joe Lapchick greets Nat "Sweetwater" Clifton, the first black to be signed by an NBA team.

on his way to a career as an ABC network sportscaster. He had also been a navy pilot, so he volunteered to handle the plane while the actual pilot went for some champagne.

The next season, the Knicks were back in the Finals. So were the Lakers, who once more disposed of the Royals along the way. It was Rochester battling Minneapolis in the West every year, with the survivor making it to the championship round. This is the way they finished in their divisional hand-to-hand combat in those years:

    1948−49: Rochester 45-15
                Minneapolis 44-16
    1949−50: Tied at 51-17
    1950−51: Minneapolis 44-24
                Rochester 41-27
    1951−52: Rochester 41-25
                Minneapolis 40-26
    1952−53: Minneapolis 48-22
                Rochester 44-26
    1953−54: Minneapolis 46-26
                Rochester 44-28

In 1952 the Lakers won another championship over the Knicks—benefiting from a basket that went in but never got onto the scoreboard. It came in Game 1 of the Finals. The featured New Yorkers were Max Zaslofsky, Sweetwater Clifton, Harry Gallatin, Ernie Vandeweghe, Vince Boryla and the McGuire brothers, Dick and Al. Al McGuire drove the middle and hit a shot from around the foul line. As the ball dropped through, there was a whistle. A foul had been called, and McGuire was given two shots, starting an uproar that held up the game for about 10 minutes.

"What about the basket?" the Knicks players and Coach Lapchick inquired. "What basket?" asked Sid Borgia and Stan Stutz, the two officials. Borgia had called the foul from underneath. Stutz, working the outside, told Borgia he hadn't seen McGuire's shot go in.

Lapchick pleaded his case with President Maurice Podoloff and Chief of Referees Pat Kennedy, who were sitting on the sidelines. They had seen the ball go through the hoop but advised the Knicks' coach they had no authority to interfere with the officials.

John Kundla coached the Minneapolis Lakers to five NBA titles in six seasons from 1949 to 1954.

Meanwhile, John Kundla, the Lakers' coach, had been all over the refs when the argument started. "How can you give him two shots when the ball went in the basket?" he asked at first. It didn't impress or influence the officials. Their decision stood as made while Kundla, of course, strolled silently back to his bench.

McGuire made one of two free throws, which appeared rather insignificant at that point. However, the game wound up tied at the end of regulation, and the Lakers went on to win 83–79 in overtime. The Knicks figured if they had gotten credit for McGuire's basket (instead of just one made free throw), they would have won the game by a point in regulation. Given that they won the next game in St. Paul and split two at home, they would have had a 3–1 lead instead of a 2–2 deadlock. Since they won the sixth game at home— voilà, the championship.

Of course, the game is not played that way. The teams wound up going back to Minneapolis for the seventh and deciding game, and the Lakers won 82–65.

The Lakers beat the Knicks again in the 1953 Finals,

this time by a 4–1 margin. Mikan considers that one of his favorite championships because the Lakers dropped the first game at home and went on to sweep the next four.

"They were trying to dethrone us, and we won the last four in a row, three of them in New York," he said. "We had a big celebration when it was over. We went to the Copacabana and Joe E. Lewis saluted us. He made us stand up, and we got a big hand from the audience."

Mikan remained durable and dominating as the Lakers continued to reign. There were obstacles, notably some serious injuries to the big center, but he overcame them. Way back in the first championship series against Washington in 1949, Big George was involved in a bad accident. He was driving to the basket on a break when Kleggie Hermsen of the Capitols knocked him into the seats.

"I went flying into the third row and broke an arm," said Mikan. "I played the rest of the series in a cast. I was out there in pain, and I remember Red Auerbach telling the refs: 'Drag him out of here. Let's get the game going.' He was tough even then."

Mikan got some compensation in one respect. Every time the Lakers played in Washington, they had a celebrated rooter. "Senator Hubert Humphrey was at all our games," he said. "He was our cheerleader." The senator (and later vice president) from Minnesota more than made up for Auerbach in the eyes of Mikan and the other Lakers.

In another playoff series, someone ran into Mikan and broke his leg. He actually played three weeks with the injury.

Mikan decided to retire after the Lakers beat Syracuse in seven games for the 1953–54 championship. He reached 30 that June and decided he'd had enough basketball. He had passed the bar exam in 1949 and had a legal career ready for him. "I didn't know who I was," he reflected. "I wanted to be with my children more."

Mikan was at the peak of his athletic career and the decision was difficult, but he finally made it. When he left, the Minneapolis Lakers' championships went with him. So did much of the excitement that he engendered. The NBA hadn't as yet reached maturity and needed attractions like Mikan, though his prominence sometimes led to needling from teammates.

Martin recalled the night the Lakers came to play the Knicks at Madison Square Garden and the marquee read: "Mikan vs. The Knicks." So when the Minneapolis Lakers were standing in the runway, ready to go on the court, they told him: "Go ahead, George. Go out there and play the Knicks."

The Minneapolis Lakers dynasty—five championships in their first six years—ended when Mikan retired. Wilt Chamberlain and Jerry West first, then Kareem Abdul-Jabbar and Magic Johnson won titles once the Lakers franchise moved to Los Angeles. But Mikan and the Minneapolis Lakers own the distinction of being the first dynasty ever seen in the NBA. It established their place in the history of the league.

1948–49

The BAA clearly had the best arenas in the bigger cities, but the National Basketball League, featuring teams in smaller midwestern cities, claimed the best players. This changed, however, prior to the 1948 season, when the NBL's four best teams—Fort Wayne, Rochester, Indianapolis and Minneapolis—jumped to the BAA. Overnight, the best players and the biggest arenas, in the largest media centers, were brought together for the first time.

The Minneapolis team came with the man who would become the sport's star attraction and the first in a long line of great big men, George Mikan. At 6-10 and 245 pounds, Mikan revolutionized the game with his inside scoring, effortlessly throwing in hook shots with either hand on his way to a 28.3 ppg average, earning him the first of three league scoring titles.

The revitalized 12-team league resumed a 60-game schedule, with Washington finishing first in the Eastern Division and Rochester besting Minneapolis by one game in the West. Minneapolis breezed through the Western Division Playoffs and met Washington in the Finals. Mikan scored 42 points in Game 1 and led the Lakers over Washington in six games.

Mikan's arrival signaled many things: the advent of the big man, the demise of the NBL and the rise of the league's first dynasty, in Minneapolis. Washington's Horace "Bones" McKinney, who had the unpleasant task of guarding Mikan, recalled that even a broken hand suffered in Game 4 of the Finals didn't stop Mikan.

"He wore a cast that was hard as a brick," McKinney said. "It fit right in with his elbows. It would kill you. And it didn't bother his shooting a bit."

BAA 1948-49

FINAL STANDINGS

Eastern Division

	W.	L.	PCT.
Washington	38	22	.633
New York	32	28	.533
Baltimore	29	31	.483
Philadelphia	28	32	.467
Boston	25	35	.417
Providence	12	48	.200

Western Division

	W.	L.	PCT.
Rochester	45	15	.750
Minneapolis	44	16	.733
Chicago	38	22	.633
St. Louis	29	31	.483
Fort Wayne	22	38	.367
Indianapolis	18	42	.300

PLAYOFFS

Eastern Division Semifinals

New York 2, Baltimore 1
March 23—Baltimore 82, New York 81
March 24—New York 84, Baltimore 74
March 26—New York 103, Baltimore 99 (OT)

Washington 2, Philadelphia 0
March 23—Washington 92, Philadelphia 70
March 24—Washington 80, Philadelphia 78

Western Division Semifinals

Minneapolis 2, Chicago 0
March 23—Minneapolis 84, Chicago 77
March 24—Minneapolis 101, Chicago 85

Rochester 2, St. Louis 0
March 22—Rochester 93, St. Louis 64
March 23—Rochester 66, St. Louis 64

Eastern Division Finals

Washington 2, New York 1
March 29—Washington 77, New York 71
March 31—New York 86, Washington 84 (OT)
April 2—Washington 84, New York 76

Western Division Finals

Minneapolis 2, Rochester 0
March 27—Minneapolis 80, Rochester 79
March 29—Minneapolis 67, Rochester 55

Finals

Minneapolis 4, Washington 2
April 4—Minneapolis 88, Washington 84
April 6—Minneapolis 76, Washington 62
April 8—Minneapolis 94, Washington 74
April 9—Washington 83, Minneapolis 71
April 11—Washington 74, Minneapolis 65
April 13—Minneapolis 77, Washington 56

INDIVIDUAL LEADERS

Scoring

	G.	FG	FT	PTS.	AVG.
Mikan, Minneapolis	60	583	532	1698	28.3
Fulks, Philadelphia	60	529	502	1560	26.0
Zaslofsky, Chicago	58	425	347	1197	20.6
Risen, Rochester	60	345	305	995	16.6
Sadowski, Philadelphia	60	340	240	920	15.3
Smawley, St. Louis	59	352	210	914	15.5
Davies, Rochester	60	317	270	904	15.1
Sailors, Providence	57	309	281	899	15.8
Braun, New York	57	299	212	810	14.2
Logan, St. Louis	57	282	239	803	14.1

Field Goal Pct.
(Minimum 200 FG made)

	FGM	FGA	PCT.
Risen, Rochester	345	816	.423
Mikan, Minneapolis	583	1403	.416
Sadowski, Philadelphia	340	839	.405
Pollard, Minneapolis	314	792	.396
Rocha, St. Louis	223	574	.389

Free Throw Pct.
(Minimum 150 FT made)

	FTM	FTA	PCT.
Feerick, Washington	256	298	.859
Zaslofsky, Chicago	347	413	.840
Wanzer, Rochester	209	254	.823
Schaefer, Minneapolis	174	213	.817
H. Shannon, Providence	152	189	.804

Assists

	G.	NO.	AVG.
Davies, Rochester	60	321	5.4
Phillip, Chicago	60	319	5.3
Logan, St. Louis	57	276	4.8
Calverley, Providence	59	251	4.3
Senesky, Philadelphia	60	233	3.9

1949–50

The summer of 1949 solidified the professional basketball picture, as the six surviving NBL teams were absorbed into the BAA and the league was renamed the National Basketball Association. The league was split into Eastern, Central and Western divisions. Syracuse, the only NBL team in the East, won that division behind the play of 6-8 Dolph Schayes, who averaged 16.8 ppg. Alex Groza averaged 23.4 for a new Indianapolis team that won the West, while Mikan led the league again with 27.4 ppg and helped the Lakers win the Central Division.

With three divisions, the playoffs were a jumbled mess. Minneapolis had to beat Chicago, Fort Wayne and Anderson to reach the Finals, while Syracuse had to defeat only Philadelphia and New York to qualify for the title round. Syracuse had talented players like Schayes, Al Cervi and Paul Seymour, but couldn't handle the dominance of Mikan, who, surrounded by other stars like Pollard, Martin, Harrison and powerful Vern Mikkelsen, led the Lakers to another title in six games.

The Lakers had talent, and they also had the friendly confines of Minneapolis Auditorium, whose odd dimensions forced the game to be played on a court several feet narrower than the standard court. That made Mikan and his teammates even more dominant defensively.

"They used to say that when Mikan, Mikkelsen and Pollard stretched their arms across that narrow court, nobody could get through," said Cervi. Teammate Seymour added, "Those three big guys made every court look narrow."

NBA 1949-50

FINAL STANDINGS

Eastern Division

	W.	L.	PCT.
Syracuse	51	13	.797
New York	40	28	.588
Washington	32	36	.471
Philadelphia	26	42	.382
Baltimore	25	43	.368
Boston	22	46	.324

Central Division

	W.	L.	PCT.
Minneapolis *	51	17	.750
Rochester	51	17	.750
Fort Wayne *	40	28	.588
Chicago	40	28	.588
St. Louis	26	42	.382

* Won playoff to break ties

Western Division

	W.	L.	PCT.
Indianapolis	39	25	.609
Anderson	37	27	.578
Tri-Cities	29	35	.453
Sheboygan	22	40	.355
Waterloo	19	43	.306
Denver	11	51	.177

PLAYOFFS

Central Division 1st Place Tie-breaker

March 21—Minneapolis 78, Rochester 76

Central Division 3rd Place Tie-breaker

March 20— Fort Wayne 86, Chicago 69

Eastern Division Semifinals

Syracuse 2, Philadelphia 0
March 22—Syracuse 93, Philadelphia 76
March 23—Syracuse 59, Philadelphia 53

New York 2, Washington 0
March 21—New York 90, Washington 87
March 22—New York 103, Washington 83

Central Division Semifinals

Minneapolis 2, Chicago 0
March 22—Minneapolis 85, Chicago 75
March 25—Minneapolis 75, Chicago 67

Fort Wayne 2, Rochester 0
March 23—Fort Wayne 90, Rochester 84
March 24—Fort Wayne 79, Rochester 78 (OT)

Western Division Semifinals

Anderson 2, Tri-Cities 1
March 21—Anderson 89, Tri-Cities 77
March 23—Tri-Cities 76, Anderson 75
March 24—Anderson 94, Tri-Cities 71

Indianapolis 2, Sheboygan 1
March 21—Indianapolis 86, Sheboygan 85
March 23—Sheboygan 95, Indianapolis 85
March 25—Indianapolis 91, Sheboygan 84

Eastern Division Finals

Syracuse 2, New York 1
March 26—Syracuse 91, New York 83 (OT)
March 30—New York 80, Syracuse 76
April 2—Syracuse 91, New York 80

Central Division Finals

Minneapolis 2, Fort Wayne 0
March 27—Minneapolis 93, Fort Wayne 79
March 28—Minneapolis 89, Fort Wayne 82

Western Division Finals

Anderson 2, Indianapolis 1
March 28—Indianapolis 77, Anderson 74
March 30—Anderson 84, Indianapolis 67
April 1—Anderson 67, Indianapolis 65

NBA Semifinals

Minneapolis 2, Anderson 0
April 5—Minneapolis 75, Anderson 50
April 6—Minneapolis 90, Anderson 71

NBA Finals

Minneapolis 4, Syracuse 2
April 8—Minneapolis 68, Syracuse 66
April 9—Syracuse 91, Minneapolis 85
April 14—Minneapolis 91, Syracuse 77
April 16—Minneapolis 77, Syracuse 69
April 20—Syracuse 83, Minneapolis 76
April 23—Minneapolis 110, Syracuse 95

INDIVIDUAL LEADERS

Scoring

	G.	FG	FT	PTS.	AVG.
Mikan, Minneapolis	68	649	567	1865	27.4
Groza, Indianapolis	64	521	454	1496	23.4
Brian, Anderson	64	368	402	1138	17.8
Zaslofsky, Chicago	68	397	321	1115	16.4
Macauley, St. Louis	67	351	379	1081	16.1
Schayes, Syracuse	64	348	376	1072	16.8
Braun, New York	67	373	285	1031	15.4
Sailors, Denver	57	329	329	987	17.3
Pollard, Minneapolis	66	394	185	973	14.7
Schaus, Fort Wayne	68	351	270	972	14.3

Field Goal Pct.
(Minimum 200 FG made)

	FGM	FGA	PCT.
Groza, Indianapolis	521	1090	.478
Mehen, Waterloo	347	826	.420
Wanzer, Rochester	254	614	.414
Boykoff, Waterloo	288	698	.413
Mikan, Minneapolis	649	1595	.407

Free Throw Pct.
(Minimum 170 FT made)

	FTM	FTA	PCT.
Zaslofsky, Chicago	321	381	.843
Reiser, Washington	212	254	.835
Cervi, Syracuse	287	346	.829
Smawley, St. Louis	260	314	.828
Curran, Rochester	199	241	.826

Assists

	G.	NO.	AVG.
McGuire, New York	68	386	5.7
Phillip, Chicago	65	377	5.8
Davies, Rochester	64	294	4.6
Cervi, Syracuse	56	264	4.7
Senesky, Philadelphia	68	264	3.9

1950–51

The NBA went from an unwieldy 17-team league to a more manageable 11 teams in two divisions. Minneapolis, Rochester and Fort Wayne reverted to the Western Division. The Eastern Division began the season with six teams, but Washington, which had lost Coach Red Auerbach to Tri-Cities a year earlier, disbanded after going 10-25.

The season also marked the first appearance of black players in the league. Chuck Cooper became the first black player to be drafted when he was chosen by Boston, Sweetwater Clifton became the first to sign an NBA contract when he signed with New York and Earl Lloyd became the first to play in an NBA regular-season game because the schedule had his Washington team opening one day before the others.

Philadelphia won the East by 2½ games, while Minneapolis bested Rochester by three games in the West. The playoffs were a different story, however. New York blitzed Boston and barely edged Syracuse to reach the Finals, while Rochester, behind 6-9 Arnie Risen and backcourt star Bob Davies, defeated Fort Wayne and finally overcame Minneapolis to meet the Knicks in the Finals. For the first time, the NBA Finals came down to a seventh game and Rochester prevailed 79–75 in a close, exciting finale.

NBA 1950-51

FINAL STANDINGS

Eastern Division

	W.	L.	PCT.
Philadelphia	40	26	.606
Boston	39	30	.565
New York	36	30	.545
Syracuse	32	34	.485
Baltimore	24	42	.364
Washington *	10	25	.286

* Disbanded on Jan. 9, 1951

Western Division

	W.	L.	PCT.
Minneapolis	44	24	.647
Rochester	41	27	.603
Fort Wayne	32	36	.471
Indianapolis	31	37	.456
Tri-Cities	25	43	.368

PLAYOFFS

Eastern Division Semifinals

New York 2, Boston 0
March 20—New York 83, Boston 69
March 22—New York 92, Boston 78

Syracuse 2, Philadelphia 0
March 20—Syracuse 91, Philadelphia 89 (OT)
March 22—Syracuse 90, Philadelphia 78

Western Division Semifinals

Rochester 2, Fort Wayne 1
March 20—Rochester 110, Fort Wayne 81
March 22—Fort Wayne 83, Rochester 78
March 24—Rochester 97, Fort Wayne 78

Minneapolis 2, Indianapolis 1
March 21—Minneapolis 95, Indianapolis 81
March 23—Indianapolis 108, Minneapolis 88
March 25—Minneapolis 85, Indianapolis 80

Eastern Division Finals

New York 3, Syracuse 2
March 28—New York 103, Syracuse 92
March 29—Syracuse 102, New York 80
March 31—New York 77, Syracuse 75 (OT)
April 1—Syracuse 90, New York 83
April 4—New York 83, Syracuse 81

Western Division Finals

Rochester 3, Minneapolis 1
March 29—Minneapolis 76, Rochester 73
March 31—Rochester 70, Minneapolis 66
April 1—Rochester 83, Minneapolis 70
April 3—Rochester 80, Minneapolis 75

NBA Finals

Rochester 4, New York 3
April 7—Rochester 92, New York 65
April 8—Rochester 99, New York 84
April 11—Rochester 78, New York 71
April 13—New York 79, Rochester 73
April 15—New York 92, Rochester 89
April 18—New York 80, Rochester 73
April 21—Rochester 79, New York 75

INDIVIDUAL LEADERS

Scoring

	G.	FG	FT	PTS.	AVG.
Mikan, Minneapolis	68	678	576	1932	28.4
Groza, Indianapolis	66	492	445	1429	21.7
Macauley, Boston	68	459	466	1384	20.4
Fulks, Philadelphia	66	429	378	1236	18.7
Brian, Tri-Cities	68	363	418	1144	16.8
Arizin, Philadelphia	65	352	417	1121	17.2
Schayes, Syracuse	66	332	457	1121	17.0
Beard, Indianapolis	66	409	293	1111	16.8
Cousy, Boston	69	401	276	1078	15.6
Risen, Rochester	66	377	323	1077	16.3

Field Goal Pct.
(Minimum 200 FG made)

	FGM	FGA	PCT.
Groza, Indianapolis	492	1046	.470
Macauley, Boston	459	985	.466
Mikan, Minneapolis	678	1584	.428
Coleman, Rochester	315	749	.421
Gallatin, New York	293	705	.416

Free Throw Pct.
(Minimum 170 FT made)

	FTM	FTA	PCT.
Fulks, Philadelphia	378	442	.855
Smawley, Syr.-Bal.	227	267	.850
Wanzer, Rochester	232	273	.850
Scolari, Was.-Syr.	279	331	.843
Boryla, New York	278	332	.837

Assists

	G.	NO.	AVG.
Phillip, Philadelphia	66	414	6.3
McGuire, New York	64	400	6.3
Senesky, Philadelphia	65	342	5.3
Cousy, Boston	69	341	4.9
Beard, Indianapolis	66	318	4.8

Rebounds

	G.	NO.	AVG.
Schayes, Syracuse	66	1080	16.4
Mikan, Minneapolis	68	958	14.1
Gallatin, New York	66	800	12.1
Risen, Rochester	66	795	12.0
Groza, Indianapolis	66	709	10.7

When Rochester took the first three games of the 1951 Finals, a quick knockout seemed in order. But the Knicks stormed back, winning three games by margins of six, three and seven points to send the series to a seventh and deciding game in Rochester.

The Royals led by as many as 16 points during the first half, but the Knicks battled back to take a two-point lead with two minutes to go. With 40 seconds left and the score tied, Davies was fouled on a drive to the basket and sank two free throws. The Royals hung on for a 79–75 victory and temporarily interrupted the Minneapolis dynasty.

1951–52

The jump shot, first popularized by Joe Fulks, was becoming more prevalent in the game, and its effectiveness was underlined as Philadelphia's Paul Arizin, a young forward from Villanova, wrested the league scoring title from Mikan with 25.4 ppg and led the league in field goal percentage (.448). The lane was widened from six to 12 feet in an attempt to cut down the big man's dominance. But while the jump shot was advancing the game, some of the game's rules were holding it back. Stalling tactics were the norm once a team gained a comfortable lead, and relief, in the form of a shot clock, was still three years away.

Meanwhile, for the first time in several years, all 10 NBA teams played 66 games, and all 10 teams that started the season finished it. The NBA was mining the best college talent. Mikan, Arizin, Ed Macauley and Bob Cousy made the All-NBA First Team, Davies and Schayes sharing the fifth spot. For the second straight season New York overcame a third-place finish to reach the Finals, while Minneapolis reasserted itself by defeating Rochester in the West. Another seven-game NBA Finals resulted, and the Lakers put the home-court advantage to good use, winning Game 7 easily, 82–65.

NBA 1951-52

FINAL STANDINGS

Eastern Division

	W.	L.	PCT.
Syracuse	40	26	.606
Boston	39	27	.591
New York	37	29	.561
Philadelphia	33	33	.500
Baltimore	20	46	.303

Western Division

	W.	L.	PCT.
Rochester	41	25	.621
Minneapolis	40	26	.606
Indianapolis	34	32	.515
Fort Wayne	29	37	.439
Milwaukee	17	49	.258

PLAYOFFS

Eastern Division Semifinals

New York 2, Boston 1
March 19—Boston 105, New York 94
March 23—New York 101, Boston 97
March 26—New York 88, Boston 87 (2OT)

Syracuse 2, Philadelphia 1
March 20—Syracuse 102, Philadelphia 83
March 22—Philadelphia 100, Syracuse 95
March 23—Syracuse 84, Philadelphia 73

Western Division Semifinals

Rochester 2, Fort Wayne 0
March 18—Rochester 95, Fort Wayne 78
March 20—Rochester 92, Fort Wayne 86

Minneapolis 2, Indianapolis 0
March 23—Minneapolis 78, Indianapolis 70
March 25—Minneapolis 94, Indianapolis 87

Eastern Division Finals

New York 3, Syracuse 1
April 2—New York 87, Syracuse 85
April 3—Syracuse 102, New York 92
April 5—New York 99, Syracuse 92
April 8—New York 100, Syracuse 93

Western Division Finals

Minneapolis 3, Rochester 1
March 29—Rochester 88, Minneapolis 78
March 30—Minneapolis 83, Rochester 78 (OT)
April 5—Minneapolis 77, Rochester 67
April 6—Minneapolis 82, Rochester 80

NBA Finals

Minneapolis 4, New York 3
April 12—Minneapolis 83, New York 79 (OT)
April 13—New York 80, Minneapolis 72
April 16—Minneapolis 82, New York 77
April 18—New York 90, Minneapolis 89 (OT)
April 20—Minneapolis 102, New York 89
April 23—New York 76, Minneapolis 68
April 25—Minneapolis 82, New York 65

INDIVIDUAL LEADERS

Scoring

	G.	FG	FT	PTS.	AVG.
Arizin, Philadelphia	66	548	578	1674	25.4
Mikan, Minneapolis	64	545	433	1523	23.8
Cousy, Boston	66	512	409	1433	21.7
Macauley, Boston	66	384	496	1264	19.2
Davies, Rochester	65	379	294	1052	16.2
Brian, Fort Wayne	66	342	367	1051	15.9
Foust, Fort Wayne	66	390	267	1047	15.9
Wanzer, Rochester	66	328	377	1033	15.7
Risen, Rochester	66	365	302	1032	15.6
Mikkelsen, Minneapolis	66	363	283	1009	15.3

Field Goal Pct.
(Minimum 210 FG made)

	FGM	FGA	PCT.
Arizin, Philadelphia	548	1222	.448
Gallatin, New York	233	527	.442
Macauley, Boston	384	888	.432
Wanzer, Rochester	328	772	.425
Mikkelsen, Minneapolis	363	866	.419

Free Throw Pct.
(Minimum 180 FT made)

	FTM	FTA	PCT.
Wanzer, Rochester	377	417	.904
Cervi, Syracuse	219	248	.883
Sharman, Boston	183	213	.859
Brian, Fort Wayne	367	433	.848
Scolari, Baltimore	353	423	.835

Assists

	G.	NO.	AVG.
Phillip, Philadelphia	66	539	8.2
Cousy, Boston	66	441	6.7
Davies, Rochester	65	390	6.0
D. McGuire, New York	64	388	6.1
Scolari, Baltimore	64	303	4.7

Rebounds

	G.	NO.	AVG.
Hutchins, Milwaukee	66	880	13.3
Foust, Fort Wayne	66	880	13.3
Mikan, Minneapolis	64	866	13.5
Risen, Rochester	66	841	12.7
Schayes, Syracuse	63	773	12.3

Point-shaving scandals rocked the basketball world in 1951, but the fledgling NBA was touched only marginally. Although it was revealed that several college players at major programs across the country had taken money to influence the outcome of games, there wasn't a shred of evidence that any pro games had been fixed. Thus, the pro league's reputation was spared during a period that otherwise dealt a black eye to the sport of basketball.

The scandals did, however, cost the league two of its brightest young stars. Alex Groza, one of the NBA's top five scorers in each of his first two pro seasons and one of the league's leading rebounders, along with Ralph Beard, another leading scorer, were implicated for their actions while at the University of Kentucky. Both were summarily banned from the NBA as the league fought to protect its fragile image in the public's eye.

Their team, the Indianapolis Olympians, which had been composed of recent Kentucky stars, lasted just two more years and then disbanded.

1952–53

Excessive fouling was still a big problem, and rule changes relating to the last few minutes of a game failed to bring adequate relief. Coaches liked playing the percentages of hoping for a miss of at least one of two free throws while their own team scored a two-point basket. Fouls rose to 58 per game, and teams set records for free-throw attempts.

Some things didn't change, however, like the dominance of big men. Neil Johnston, a 6-8 hook-shooting center, won the first of his three straight league scoring titles, while last year's champion, Arizin, spent the first of two years in the military. Boston was coming of age, with the exciting backcourt of Bob Cousy and sweet-shooting Bill Sharman, but couldn't get by the Knicks, who had a host of good players such as Carl Braun, Dick McGuire, Harry Gallatin and Sweetwater Clifton who played well together, overcoming their height deficiencies. For the first time, both regular-season division winners, New York and Minneapolis, advanced to the NBA Finals. The Knicks won the first game, but the Lakers then won four straight to send the New Yorkers home empty-handed for the third consecutive year.

NBA 1952-53

FINAL STANDINGS

Eastern Division

	W.	L.	PCT.
New York	47	23	.671
Syracuse	47	24	.662
Boston	46	25	.648
Baltimore	16	54	.229
Philadelphia	12	57	.174

Western Division

	W.	L.	PCT.
Minneapolis	48	22	.686
Rochester	44	26	.629
Fort Wayne	36	33	.522
Indianapolis	28	43	.394
Milwaukee	27	44	.380

PLAYOFFS

Eastern Division Semifinals

New York 2, Baltimore 0
March 17—New York 80, Baltimore 62
March 20—New York 90, Baltimore 81

Boston 2, Syracuse 0
March 19—Boston 87, Syracuse 81
March 21—Boston 111, Syracuse 105 (4OT)

Western Division Semifinals

Fort Wayne 2, Rochester 1
March 20—Fort Wayne 84, Rochester 77
March 22—Rochester 83, Fort Wayne 71
March 24—Fort Wayne 67, Rochester 65

Minneapolis 2, Indianapolis 0
March 22—Minneapolis 85, Indianapolis 69
March 23—Minneapolis 81, Indianapolis 79

Eastern Division Finals

New York 3, Boston 1
March 25—New York 95, Boston 91
March 26—Boston 86, New York 70
March 28—New York 101, Boston 82
March 29—New York 82, Boston 75

Western Division Finals

Minneapolis 3, Fort Wayne 2
March 26—Minneapolis 83, Fort Wayne 73
March 28—Minneapolis 82, Fort Wayne 75
March 30—Fort Wayne 98, Minneapolis 95
April 1—Fort Wayne 85, Minneapolis 82
April 2—Minneapolis 74, Fort Wayne 58

NBA Finals

Minneapolis 4, New York 1
April 4—New York 96, Minneapolis 88
April 5—Minneapolis 73, New York 71
April 7—Minneapolis 90, New York 75
April 8—Minneapolis 71, New York 69
April 10—Minneapolis 91, New York 84

INDIVIDUAL LEADERS

Scoring

	G.	FG	FT	PTS.	AVG.
Johnston, Philadelphia	70	504	556	1564	22.3
Mikan, Minneapolis	70	500	442	1442	20.6
Cousy, Boston	71	464	479	1407	19.8
Macauley, Boston	69	451	500	1402	20.3
Schayes, Syracuse	71	375	512	1262	17.8
Sharman, Boston	71	403	341	1147	16.2
Nichols, Milwaukee	69	425	240	1090	15.8
Mikkelsen, Minneapolis	70	378	291	1047	15.0
Davies, Rochester	66	339	351	1029	15.6
Wanzer, Rochester	70	318	384	1020	14.6

Field Goal Pct.
(Minimum 210 FG made)

	FGM	FGA	PCT.
Johnston, Philadelphia	504	1114	.452
Macauley, Boston	451	997	.452
Gallatin, New York	282	635	.444
Sharman, Boston	403	925	.436
Mikkelsen, Minneapolis	378	868	.435

Free Throw Pct.
(Minimum 180 FT made)

	FTM	FTA	PCT.
Sharman, Boston	341	401	.850
Scolari, Bal.-Ft.W	276	327	.844
Schayes, Syracuse	512	619	.827
Braun, New York	331	401	.825
Schaus, Fort Wayne	243	296	.821

Assists

	G.	NO.	AVG.
Cousy, Boston	71	547	7.7
Phillip, Phi.-Ft.W.	70	397	5.7
King, Syracuse	71	364	5.1
D. McGuire, New York	61	296	4.9
Seymour, Syracuse	67	294	4.4

Rebounds

	G.	NO.	AVG.
Mikan, Minneapolis	70	1007	14.4
Johnston, Philadelphia	70	976	13.9
Schayes, Syracuse	71	920	13.0
Gallatin, New York	70	916	13.1
Hutchins, Milwaukee	71	793	11.2

New York had learned from past experience that it would not be easy to beat Minneapolis without the home-court advantage. But with the 2-3-2 format in place, New York figured it could win if it could somehow take one of the first two games in Minneapolis. The Knicks got their win in Game 1, 96–88, and seemed poised to take control.

But Mikan, who had played in New York many times while in college, and the Lakers had other ideas. The Lakers took all three in New York, two in convincing fashion, to put to rest the home-court advantage—at least for this series.

1953–54

A curious rule was put in place in another attempt to cut down on the excessive number of fouls, which were draining the excitement from the game. Each player was limited to two fouls per quarter; if he committed a third, he would have to be removed for the remainder of that quarter. The number of fouls decreased to 51 per game, but late-game free-throw-shooting contests remained the norm and the two-fouls-per-quarter rule was rescinded.

Indianapolis folded, leaving the Western Division with only four teams, three of which would make the playoffs. Johnston averaged a league-leading 24.4 ppg, and Cousy finished second at 19.2 ppg. He also led the league in assists with 7.2 per game. Mikan, now 30, was playing fewer minutes as the Lakers tried to save him for the playoffs. He still averaged 18.1 points and 14.3 rebounds per game.

The playoffs began with an awkward round robin;

the top three teams in each division played each other to see which two would advance. New York's string of NBA Finals appearances ended as Syracuse came out of the East, while Minneapolis again won the West. In what would prove to be the last championship for the Lakers in Minneapolis, the Lakers took a hard-fought Game 7, 87–80.

John Kundla never received much credit for leading Minneapolis to five NBA titles in six years. Many said that any coach with Mikan, Pollard, Mikkelsen and the rest would win titles without much work. Red Auerbach doesn't buy it.

"I've seen a lot of great teams, at least on paper, that won nothing," Auerbach said. "Sure, Kundla had a great team, but he did great things with them."

NBA 1953-54

FINAL STANDINGS

Eastern Division

	W.	L.	PCT.
New York	44	28	.611
Boston	42	30	.583
Syracuse	42	30	.583
Philadelphia	29	43	.403
Baltimore	16	56	.222

Western Division

	W.	L.	PCT.
Minneapolis	46	26	.639
Rochester	44	28	.611
Fort Wayne	40	32	.556
Milwaukee	21	51	.292

PLAYOFFS

Eastern Division Round Robin

March 16—Boston 93, New York 71
March 17—Syracuse 96, Boston 95 (OT)
March 18—Syracuse 75, New York 68
March 20—Boston 79, New York 78
March 21—Syracuse 103, New York 99
March 22—Syracuse 98, Boston 85

Western Division Round Robin

March 16—Rochester 82, Fort Wayne 75
March 17—Minneapolis 109, Rochester 88
March 18—Minneapolis 90, Fort Wayne 85
March 20—Minneapolis 78, Fort Wayne 73
March 21—Rochester 89, Fort Wayne 71
March 23—Minneapolis at Rochester (cancelled)

Eastern Division Finals

Syracuse 2, Boston 0
March 25—Syracuse 109, Boston 94
March 27—Syracuse 83, Boston 76

Western Division Finals

Minneapolis 2, Rochester 1
March 24—Minneapolis 89, Rochester 76
March 27—Rochester 74, Minneapolis 73
March 28—Minneapolis 82, Rochester 72

NBA Finals

Minneapolis 4, Syracuse 3
March 31—Minneapolis 79, Syracuse 68
April 3—Syracuse 62, Minneapolis 60
April 4—Minneapolis 81, Syracuse 67
April 8—Syracuse 80, Minneapolis 69
April 10—Minneapolis 84, Syracuse 73
April 11—Syracuse 65, Minneapolis 63
April 12—Minneapolis 87, Syracuse 80

INDIVIDUAL LEADERS

Scoring

	G.	FG	FT	PTS.	AVG.
Johnston, Philadelphia	72	591	577	1759	24.4
Cousy, Boston	72	486	411	1383	19.2
Macauley, Boston	71	462	420	1344	18.9
Mikan, Minneapolis	72	441	424	1306	18.1
Felix, Baltimore	72	410	449	1269	17.6
Schayes, Syracuse	72	370	488	1228	17.1
Sharman, Boston	72	412	331	1155	16.0
Foust, Fort Wayne	72	376	338	1090	15.1
Braun, New York	72	354	354	1062	14.8
Wanzer, Rochester	72	322	314	958	13.3

Field Goal Pct.
(Minimum 210 FG made)

	FGM	FGA	PCT.
Macauley, Boston	462	950	.486
Sharman, Boston	412	915	.450
Johnston, Philadelphia	591	1317	.449
Lovellette, Minneapolis	237	560	.423
Felix, Baltimore	410	983	.417

Free Throw Pct.
(Minimum 180 FT made)

	FTM	FTA	PCT.
Sharman, Boston	331	392	.844
Schayes, Syracuse	488	590	.827
Braun, New York	354	429	.825
Seymour, Syracuse	299	368	.813
Zawoluk, Philadelphia	186	230	.809

Assists

	G.	NO.	AVG.
Cousy, Boston	72	518	7.2
Phillip, Fort Wayne	71	449	6.3
Seymour, Syracuse	71	364	5.1
D. McGuire, New York	68	354	5.2
Davies, Rochester	72	323	4.5

Rebounds

	G.	NO.	AVG.
Gallatin, New York	72	1098	15.3
Mikan, Minneapolis	72	1028	14.3
Foust, Fort Wayne	72	967	13.4
Felix, Baltimore	72	958	13.3
Schayes, Syracuse	72	870	12.1

THE SHOT CLOCK THAT SAVED THE NBA
by Alex Sachare

Alex Sachare, former pro basketball editor for the Associated Press, is the NBA's vice president, editorial, and the editor of The Official NBA Basketball Encyclopedia, *as well as a columnist for* Hoop *magazine.*

The National Basketball Association was not yet 10 years old, but, in the eyes of many, it already was dying a slow death—with the emphasis on slow.

The problem in the early 1950s was the pace of the game. All too often it was played at a snail's pace, with one team opening up a bit of a lead and then putting the ball in the deep freeze until time ran out. The other team's only recourse was to foul, since in those days there was no limit on the amount of time a team could hold the ball. Games became foul-shooting contests, and spectators headed to the exits early.

"The game had become a stalling game," recalled the late Danny Biasone, then owner of the NBA's Syracuse Nationals. "A team would get ahead, even in the first half, and it would go into a stall. The other team

Danny Biasone, owner of the Syracuse Nats, was the inventor of the 24-second shot clock.

would keep fouling, and it got to be a constant parade to the foul line. In 1952 we played a game in which neither team took a shot in the last eight minutes. It was a parade between foul lines, and boy, was it dull!"

The problem was widespread. On November 22, 1950, the Fort Wayne Pistons edged the Minneapolis Lakers 19–18 in the lowest-scoring game in NBA annals. Each team had only four baskets, and Fort Wayne outscored Minneapolis by the underwhelming margin of 3–1 in the fourth quarter to win. Three years later, 106 fouls were called and 128 free throws were shot in a playoff game in which Boston's Bob Cousy scored what was then a playoff-record 50 points—30 of them from the foul line! In 1954, Syracuse beat New York 75–69 in another playoff masterpiece in which the teams combined for 75 successful free throws but only 34 baskets. Syracuse attempted only 38 shots in the entire game and won anyway.

"That was the way the game was played—get a lead and put the ball in the icebox," said Cousy, whose skill at killing the clock as well as his adept playmaking made him one of the league's premier players. "Teams literally started sitting on the ball in the third quarter. Coaches are conservative by nature to begin with, and it didn't make much sense to play a wide-open game.

"We'd get a lead, and you'd see good ol' No. 14 doing his tricks out there."

Good ol' No. 14 was joined by other premier ball handlers like Dick McGuire, Slater Martin, Bob Davies, Andy Phillip and more, who would dribble out the clock until they were fouled. Then the parade from one free-throw line to the other would begin.

In 1953 the NBA adopted a rule awarding two shots for a foul that occurred in the backcourt in an attempt to reduce fouling. But it was not enough—the stalling tactics and fouling continued, only now teams waited until the ball was brought over half-court before committing those fouls.

"Coaches will take advantage of anything to win," said Biasone. "If they can win a game 3–2, that's okay with them. And you can't blame them—that's why they're getting paid. But if you're a promoter, that won't do. You've got to have offense because offense excites people."

So Biasone, true to the entrepreneurial spirit that characterized many of the NBA's founding fathers, decided to do something about it.

"We needed a time element in our game," he said. "Pro basketball would not have survived without a clock. There was no way we could stop the stalling and fouling without a time element. Other sports had

Boston's Bob Cousy was among those most adept at killing the clock when his team got the lead.

limits—in baseball you get three outs to score, in football you must make 10 yards in four downs or you lose the ball. But in basketball, if you had the lead and a good ball handler, you could play around all night. The only way for the other team to stop that was to grab him and send him to the foul line. Then you'd foul him back. It was dull.

"After the 1953–54 season, I got 10 players together in Syracuse and tried out my idea with a stopwatch in a little scrimmage game. The Board of Governors agreed to try it out in the exhibition season, and after that they voted it in for the regular season."

The clock prevented stalling, but there was still the matter of excessive fouling. So the Board of Governors also adopted a rule limiting the number of fouls per team per quarter, after which each foul became a shooting foul. The two rules complemented each other perfectly.

The 24-second shot clock made its debut on October 30, 1954, and its effect was immediate. The host Rochester Royals beat the Boston Celtics 98–95 in what would have been the seventh highest-scoring game of the previous season. During the first season with the 24-second clock, NBA teams averaged 93.1 points per game, an increase of 13.6 ppg over the year before—and 10.5 of the extra points came from the field, with only 3.1 from the foul line. In 1955 the Boston Celtics became the first team in NBA history to average over 100 ppg for an entire season; three years later every team in the league bettered that plateau.

Cousy, one of the best at stall ball, immediately recognized the value of the 24-second clock.

"Before the new rule, the last quarter could be deadly," he said. "The team in front would hold the ball indefinitely, and the only way you could get it was by fouling somebody. In the meantime, nobody dared take a shot and the whole game slowed up. With the clock, we have constant action. I think it saved the NBA at that time. It allowed the game to breathe and progress."

"It was the single most important rule change in the last 50 years," said Boston Celtics President Red Auerbach.

"The whole purpose of the 24-second rule—to make the game fast and furious, with plenty of action—was accomplished," said Eddie Gottlieb, who owned and coached the Philadelphia Warriors when the rule was put into effect.

"The adoption of the clock was the most important event in the NBA," said Maurice Podoloff, the NBA's first president.

"Without the clock," said Dolph Schayes, a Hall of Fame forward with the Syracuse Nats who named his son Danny after Biasone, "I think the pro game definitely would have disappeared. That idea saved the game. Somebody else would have done it eventually, like Columbus discovering America, but Danny was the one who did it."

How did Biasone come up with the unusual number of 24 seconds for his time limit? Why not 30 or some other round number?

Dolph Schayes is among many who credit Danny Biasone's shot clock with saving pro basketball.

The shot clock forced teams to go to the basket, as Boston's Bill Sharman does against Detroit's Dick McGuire.

"The number of seconds wasn't that important, as long as we had the time element," said Biasone, who then explained that he and his general manager, Leo Ferris, worked out the formula this way: "By figuring the average number of shots two teams would take during a game, which was about 120, and dividing that into the length of a game, which was 48 minutes, or 2,880 seconds, you come up with 24. But it could have been anything—just so there was some kind of a time limit."

In some sort of poetic justice, Biasone's Nats, with a roster that featured Schayes, Paul Seymour, Red Rocha, Johnny Kerr, Earl Lloyd and George King, won the NBA title in 1954–55, the first year of the shot clock. And they had to rally from a 17-point deficit to beat Fort Wayne 92–91 in the seventh game of the NBA Finals to do so.

"If it wasn't for the shot clock," said Biasone, "it would have been the dullest game in history. Fort Wayne was up by 17, and under the old rules, they would have gone into a stall. Then there'd have been a flurry of fouls.

"Everyone kidded me that I thought of the clock just to win the championship, but that wasn't so. I just wanted to see a whole game."

One of Biasone's early 24-second shot clocks is on display at the Basketball Hall of Fame in Springfield, Mass. Its inventor sold the Nats in 1963, saying, "The price of running a club went up and up and up. I just couldn't afford them anymore." Biasone continued to run his Eastwood Sports Center, a bowling center in Syracuse, until his death in 1992.

It's remarkable that his creation, based on a relatively simple calculation, has remained the same in the NBA for four decades and the league is prospering as never before, thanks in large part to it.

The 1954–55 Syracuse Nationals. Front row, from left: George King, Paul Seymour, Billy Gabor, Billy Kenville, Dick Farley; back row, from left: coach Al Cervi, Wally Osterkorn, Johnny Kerr, Red Rocha, Dolph Schayes, Earl Lloyd.

NBA'S 50-POINT GAMES

Prior to the advent of the 24-second shot clock in 1954–55, there had only been seven instances in which a player scored 50 or more points in a single game, and four of those were by George Mikan.

With the shot clock, there have been 333 50-point performances. Leading the way is Wilt Chamberlain, who scored 50 or more points 122 times in his illustrious career, 46 of them in 1961–62 when he *averaged* 50.4 ppg. Only four other players have had as many as 10 50-point games: Michael Jordan 32, Elgin Baylor 18, Rick Barry 15 and Kareem Abdul-Jabbar 10.

Of the 340 50-point games in NBA history, 318 have come in the regular season and 22 in the playoffs, including five in NBA Finals competition.

1954−55

Two momentous events in NBA history occurred prior to the 1954–55 season. George Mikan, who had been the standard-bearer as the league gained a foothold in the public consciousness, announced his retirement. But if anything could overshadow the departure of the game's greatest player, it was the adoption of the 24-second clock and an accompanying limit on the number of fouls a team could commit in a quarter.

While team scoring soared, individual point totals did not, as the increased points came from the entire team. Johnston, who averaged 22.7 ppg, won another scoring title, while Cousy averaged 21.2 and Arizin, back from military service, 21.0.

With Mikan gone, the opportunity was never better for Syracuse, and the Nationals won what would prove to be their only championship in that city, defeating Fort Wayne in seven games. In Game 7, Syracuse's George King made one of two foul shots with 12 seconds left, then stole the ball to seal a 92–91 victory.

Charley Eckman made one of the more unusual job transitions in 1954. For the previous four seasons an NBA referee whose assignments had included the 1954 NBA Finals, Eckman was hired by Fred Zollner to coach the Fort Wayne Pistons even though he had no prior coaching experience at any level, not even high school.

How'd he get the job? It seems Eckman had refereed a game during the 1953–54 season in which Minneapolis defeated Fort Wayne. Afterward, in a restaurant, Eckman told Lakers star George Mikan, "If I was coaching the Pistons, I'd beat you." Zollner overheard the comment

and filed it away, and when he decided to get a new coach for the Pistons for the 1954–55 season, he tagged Eckman.

All Eckman's Pistons did in his first year as coach was win the Western Division title with a 43–29 record, matching Syracuse for the best record in the league. Those two teams then battled through a seven-game NBA Finals, Syracuse winning the title by one point in Game 7. Eckman is the only man in NBA history to participate in the NBA Finals as both a referee and a coach.

NBA 1954-55

FINAL STANDINGS

Eastern Division

	W.	L.	PCT.
Syracuse	43	29	.597
New York	38	34	.528
Boston	36	36	.500
Philadelphia	33	39	.458
Baltimore *	3	11	.214

* Baltimore disbanded and did not finish the season

Western Division

	W.	L.	PCT.
Fort Wayne	43	29	.597
Minneapolis	40	32	.556
Rochester	29	43	.403
Milwaukee	26	46	.361

PLAYOFFS

Eastern Division Semifinals

Boston 2, New York 1
March 15—Boston 122, New York 101
March 16—New York 102, Boston 95
March 19—Boston 116, New York 109

Western Division Semifinals

Minneapolis 2, Rochester 1
March 16—Minneapolis 82, Rochester 78
March 18—Rochester 94, Minneapolis 92
March 19—Minneapolis 119, Rochester 110

Eastern Division Finals

Syracuse 3, Boston 1
March 22—Syracuse 110, Boston 100
March 24—Syracuse 116, Boston 110
March 26—Boston 100, Syracuse 97 (OT)
March 27—Syracuse 110, Boston 94

Western Division Finals

Fort Wayne 3, Minneapolis 1
March 20—Fort Wayne 96, Minneapolis 79
March 22—Fort Wayne 98, Minneapolis 97 (OT)
March 23—Minneapolis 99, Fort Wayne 91 (OT)
March 27—Fort Wayne 105, Minneapolis 96

NBA Finals

Syracuse 4, Fort Wayne 3
March 31—Syracuse 86, Fort Wayne 82
April 2—Syracuse 87, Fort Wayne 84
April 3—Fort Wayne 96, Syracuse 89
April 5—Fort Wayne 109, Syracuse 102
April 7—Fort Wayne 74, Syracuse 71
April 9—Syracuse 109, Fort Wayne 104
April 10—Syracuse 92, Fort Wayne 91

INDIVIDUAL LEADERS

Scoring

	G.	FG	FT	PTS.	AVG.
Johnston, Philadelphia	72	521	589	1631	22.7
Arizin, Philadelphia	72	529	454	1512	21.0
Cousy, Boston	71	522	460	1504	21.2
Pettit, Milwaukee	72	520	426	1466	20.4
Selvy, Bal.-Mil.	71	452	444	1348	19.0
Schayes, Syracuse	72	422	489	1333	18.5
Mikkelsen, Minneapolis	71	440	447	1327	18.7
Lovellette, Minneapolis	70	519	273	1311	18.7
Sharman, Boston	68	453	347	1253	18.4
Macauley, Boston	71	403	442	1248	17.6

Field Goal Pct.
(Minimum 210 FG made)

	FGM	FGA	PCT.
Foust, Fort Wayne	398	818	.487
Coleman, Rochester	400	866	.462
Marshall, Rochester	223	505	.442
Johnston, Philadelphia	521	1184	.440
Felix, New York	364	832	.438

Free Throw Pct.
(Minimum 180 FT made)

	FTM	FTA	PCT.
Sharman, Boston	347	387	.897
Brian, Fort Wayne	217	255	.851
Schayes, Syracuse	489	587	.833
Schnittker, Minneapolis	298	362	.823
Baechtold, New York	279	339	.823

Assists

	G.	NO.	AVG.
Cousy, Boston	71	557	7.8
McGuire, New York	71	542	7.6
Phillip, Fort Wayne	64	491	7.7
Seymour, Syracuse	72	483	6.7
Martin, Minneapolis	72	427	5.9

Rebounds

	G.	NO.	AVG.
Johnston, Philadelphia	72	1085	15.1
Gallatin, New York	72	995	13.8
Pettit, Milwaukee	72	994	13.8
Schayes, Syracuse	72	887	12.3
Felix, New York	72	818	11.4

1955–56

After a season of adjustment to the new rules, the NBA flourished in its second go-round with the up-tempo game. The league scoring average surged to 99 points per team per game, and quickness and athletic ability were at an all-time premium. Bob Pettit, an exciting rookie with the Milwaukee Hawks in 1954–55, took the league scoring title with 25.7 ppg in his team's first year in St. Louis.

Baltimore had folded the year before, leaving an eight-team league, with the division champions receiving a bye through the first round of the playoffs. Philadelphia, 33-39 the previous year, improved to 45-27 and won the East. Fort Wayne took the West for the second straight year. The Warriors, owned by Eddie Gottlieb and coached by George Senesky, featured a well-balanced lineup of Johnston in the middle, Joe Graboski and Walt Davis at forward and the high-scoring Arizin and prize rookie Tom Gola at guard. They won the championship in five games over Fort Wayne.

NBA 1955-56

FINAL STANDINGS

Eastern Division

	W.	L.	PCT.
Philadelphia	45	27	.625
Boston	39	33	.542
Syracuse *	35	37	.486
New York	35	37	.486

Western Division

	W.	L.	PCT.
Fort Wayne	37	35	.514
Minneapolis *	33	39	.458
St. Louis	33	39	.458
Rochester	31	41	.431

* Won playoff to break ties

PLAYOFFS

Eastern Division 3rd Place Tie-breaker

March 15—Syracuse 82, New York 77

Western Division 2nd Place Tie-breaker

March 16—Minneapolis 103, St. Louis 97

Eastern Division Semifinals

Syracuse 2, Boston 1
March 17—Boston 110, Syracuse 93
March 19—Syracuse 101, Boston 98
March 21—Syracuse 102, Boston 97

Western Division Semifinals

St. Louis 2, Minneapolis 1
March 17—St. Louis 116, Minneapolis 115
March 19—Minneapolis 133, St. Louis 75
March 21—St. Louis 116, Minneapolis 115

Eastern Division Finals

Philadelphia 3, Syracuse 2
March 23—Philadelphia 109, Syracuse 87
March 25—Syracuse 122, Philadelphia 118
March 27—Philadelphia 119, Syracuse 96
March 28—Syracuse 108, Philadelphia 104
March 29—Philadelphia 109, Syracuse 104

Western Division Finals

Fort Wayne 3, St. Louis 2
March 22—St. Louis 86, Fort Wayne 85
March 24—St. Louis 84, Fort Wayne 74
March 25—Fort Wayne 107, St. Louis 84
March 27—Fort Wayne 93, St. Louis 84
March 29—Fort Wayne 102, St. Louis 97

NBA Finals

Philadelphia 4, Fort Wayne 1
March 31—Philadelphia 98, Fort Wayne 94
April 1—Fort Wayne 84, Philadelphia 83
April 3—Philadelphia 100, Fort Wayne 96
April 5—Philadelphia 107, Fort Wayne 105
April 7—Philadelphia 99, Fort Wayne 88

INDIVIDUAL LEADERS

Scoring

	G.	FG	FT	PTS.	AVG.
Pettit, St. Louis	72	646	557	1849	25.7
Arizin, Philadelphia	72	617	507	1741	24.2
Johnston, Philadelphia	70	499	549	1547	22.1
Lovellette, Minneapolis	71	594	338	1526	21.5
Schayes, Syracuse	72	465	542	1472	20.4
Sharman, Boston	72	538	358	1434	19.9
Cousy, Boston	72	440	476	1356	18.8
Macauley, Boston	71	420	400	1240	17.5
Yardley, Fort Wayne	71	434	365	1233	17.4
Foust, Fort Wayne	72	367	432	1166	16.2

Field Goal Pct.
(Minimum 230 FG made)

	FGM	FGA	PCT.
Johnston, Philadelphia	499	1092	.457
Arizin, Philadelphia	617	1378	.448
Foust, Fort Wayne	367	821	.447
Sears, New York	319	728	.438
Sharman, Boston	538	1229	.438

Free Throw Pct.
(Minimum 190 FT made)

	FTM	FTA	PCT.
Sharman, Boston	358	413	.867
Schayes, Syracuse	542	632	.858
Schnittker, Minneapolis	304	355	.856
Cousy, Boston	476	564	.844
Braun, New York	320	382	.838

Assists

	G.	NO.	AVG.
Cousy, Boston	72	642	8.9
George, Philadelphia	72	457	6.3
Martin, Minneapolis	72	445	6.2
Phillip, Fort Wayne	70	410	5.9
King, Syracuse	72	410	5.7

Rebounds

	G.	NO.	AVG.
Pettit, St. Louis	72	1164	16.2
Stokes, Rochester	67	1094	16.3
Lovellette, Minneapolis	71	992	14.0
Schayes, Syracuse	72	891	12.4
Johnston, Philadelphia	70	872	12.5

Paul Arizin had a complete offensive repertoire, everything from long set shots to corner jump shots to driving layups and even hook shots. He had returned from two years in the military and didn't skip a beat, as the new up-tempo style played to his strengths: agility and scoring. In the 10 playoff games in 1956, Arizin scored 289 points, more than anyone but Mikan ever had tallied in postseason.

With the gifted Gola and Jack George in the backcourt to get him the ball and the still formidable Johnston at center, the 6-4 Arizin was a scoring machine that other teams couldn't shut off.

THE BOSTON CELTICS' 16-CHAMPIONSHIP LEGACY
by Bob Ryan

Bob Ryan, sports columnist for the Boston Globe, *is a former Celtics beat reporter and the author or coauthor of several basketball books, including* Drive, *the autobiography of Larry Bird.*

In the beginning there was Red, and the annual postseason theme was "Close, but No Cigar."

That's a metaphorical allusion because yes, there actually was a cigar or two—not quite as many as Auerbach would revel in during that spectacular run when he coached the Boston Celtics to nine championships in 10 years, the last eight in succession, before his surprising departure from the bench at age 48.

A little background: Arnold "Red" Auerbach came to Boston in the first place because Celtics owner Walter Brown needed a coach. His basic basketball knowledge being equivalent to his familiarity with Albanian folksingers (Brown was a born-and-bred hockey man), he came up with a coach by consulting with an informal advisory board. (Just to show how long ago that was, that committee included local sportswriters!) Brown's advisers told him that the Best Man Available was this Auerbach guy, who had been a Basketball Association of America charter coach with the Washington Capitols and then coached the Tri-Cities Blackhawks.

So Brown hired Auerbach for the 1950–51 season and discovered that he now had in his employ a brash, bombastic, opinionated and highly intelligent coach who came armed with a clear basketball philosophy. Auerbach believed that professional basketball should be fast-break basketball. He had been weaned back at George Washington University by Bill Reinhart, a name that has never gotten its proper due in basketball history. Auerbach also believed in aggressive defense and unselfish team play (then again, who doesn't?), and he had a million and one assorted observations about the game, many of which were well ahead of their time. But if there was one thing that characterized his vision of basketball, it was the fast break.

Auerbach put the fast break on display during his first six years in Boston. In Bob Cousy he had the game's preeminent little man to orchestrate it. Cousy, nicknamed "the Houdini of the Hardwood," remains the standard by which all fast-break middlemen are judged. Bill Sharman, his backcourtmate, was the consummate pull-up shooter at the end of the break. Center Ed Macauley was perhaps the most mobile big man in the league. He constantly beat his man down the court to

Championship banners hang majestically above the parquet floor at Boston Garden, saluting sports' greatest dynasty.

become the gleeful and grateful recipient of a Special Delivery from the Cooz.

The early Celtics were, without question, the prettiest team to watch in the NBA. But they weren't the best. Far from it.

In fact, the "B" on their jerseys stood for "Bridesmaids." They peaked with a 46-25 record in 1952–53. Their worst season was a 36-36 campaign in 1954–55. They were an okay team, but they were never really a

serious challenger for the NBA Championship. In each of those first six years they were eliminated from the playoffs by either the New York Knicks or the Syracuse Nationals. Their playoff record during those six seasons was 10-17.

The problem was fairly simple. The Celtics ran better than anyone else when they got the ball. Unfortunately, they didn't get the ball often enough. Macauley was built like a hatrack, and he was the center. The

Celtics put up some nice stats, but when there was a big rebound to grab or a big defensive stand to execute, they couldn't get the job done. They lacked a meaningful presence in the middle.

There was, however, a solution to all Auerbach's problems: a young man playing center for the University of San Francisco in the mid-1950s. He began to attract serious attention as a junior. Left unrecorded is the first time Auerbach actually saw William Felton Russell, but we do know that it was his old college mentor, Bill Reinhart, who made him aware of this interesting prospect as early as Russell's sophomore season. When Auerbach did get the opportunity to size the center up, he saw things in him that were not readily apparent to everyone else.

Russell was a very important college basketball

Although here he hits a running hook shot, Bill Russell was best known for his rebounding and shotblocking.

Bob Cousy (14) and Bill Russell (6) were two cornerstones of the Boston Celtics' dynasty.

player, the center on a two-time national champion, but he also was a different type of center than anyone had seen previously, and this unique flavor bothered some experts. They weren't sure how to project Russell into the professional game, primarily because shooting was the least of his skills.

Cousy recalled that Auerbach took him aside one day to indicate he had a plan and that the plan involved a rare player in the college ranks. There being no *Sports-Center* in those days, Bill Russell might just as well have

been playing in the Aleutian Islands as in San Francisco. East of the Sierra Nevadas, he was largely a rumor.

The Celtics had compiled a 39-33 regular-season record in 1955–56, then sustained their customary First

Nicknames like "Gunner" and "Ack-Ack" attest to Tommy Heinsohn's shooting instinct—and skill.

Round loss to Syracuse in the playoffs. Auerbach had improved the rebounding situation significantly that year by making Oregon's rugged Jim Loscutoff his No. 1 draft pick. Not for nothing was this man nicknamed "Jungle Jim." He stood 6-5 and weighed 225, maybe 230 pounds, and he had the aura of the circus strongman. Moreover, he actually *liked* inflicting punishment. He knew he was never destined to be a great scorer. He set picks and gratefully accepted the few available shots (he actually had a useful one-handed set) that came his way. He worked the boards and in his rookie year established himself as the team's second-leading rebounder with 8.8 rebounds per game.

With Cousy and Sharman at their physical peak, Auerbach clearly had the best backcourt duo in the league. Loscutoff gave him the enforcer-type forward he had always cherished. Auerbach knew the 1956 NBA Draft would be fruitful because he would automatically have the rights to Holy Cross star Tom Heinsohn as a territorial pick. But he would still be one man short if he didn't come up with a plan.

The NBA was a far different enterprise in those days. When draft time came, teams had many factors influencing their decisions. Consider the following scenario.

Auerbach was picking third but would have to give up that pick if he wanted to make Heinsohn a territorial choice. The first two picks in the draft belonged to Rochester and St. Louis, and by this time Russell was no longer a secret. He had led San Francisco to a pair of NCAA championships and seemed certain to lead the United States to an Olympic gold medal in Melbourne. Despite fears that he couldn't score in the pros, it was obvious he should be the first pick in the draft. Ahead of Auerbach were Rochester and St. Louis.

Auerbach started finagling with St. Louis owner Ben Kerner. He offered Macauley and the rights to Kentucky star Cliff Hagan, who was coming out of the army. Macauley, a St. Louis native, was pleased with the idea of returning home to complete his career. Kerner, for whatever reason, didn't think Russell would be that good, and wasn't prepared to meet Russell's expected high salary demands, so he decided to pass on Russell and accept Auerbach's offer.

That left Rochester. The Royals already had one of the game's premier rebounders in Maurice Stokes, the Rookie of the Year in 1956. Some say that because of Stokes's presence, the Royals decided not to select Russell but to open the draft by taking a high-scoring guard named Sihugo Green. Others contend that the machinations had nothing to do with basketball. The

Bill Sharman's scoring ability complemented Bob Cousy's playmaking and gave Boston a great guard tandem.

story goes that Celtics owner Walter Brown steered the Ice Capades into Rochester for two years, and as a quid pro quo the Royals passed on Russell.

The result was that Auerbach managed to maneuver himself into position to acquire one of the greatest American team sport athletes in history. He just didn't get him right away. First there was the customary (for the times) flirtation with the Harlem Globetrotters. Then there was the Olympics, which were being held for the first time in a southern hemisphere country and were thus conducted late in the calendar year.

Auerbach waited patiently, and why not? By the time Russell and teammates brought back the gold, the Celtics were in first place in the Eastern Division with a 16-8 record, in large measure due to the contributions of the high-scoring Heinsohn, who would go on to become Rookie of the Year.

Russell made his NBA debut on December 22, 1956. He helped spark a fourth-quarter comeback against the Hawks in a game ultimately decided by a Sharman jumper at the buzzer. In 21 minutes of play he grabbed 16 rebounds. In the first of countless virtuoso

defensive performances, he blocked three shots by All-NBA star Bob Pettit—in the fourth quarter alone.

The NBA was not quite ready for Bill Russell. "There wasn't much thinking about Bill Russell being a great player," Heinsohn would later say. "When he showed up, nobody quite knew what to make of him."

The NBA of 1956 was very white and, by the athletic standards of late-twentieth-century America, very slow. The benchmark center in the first half century of basketball had been George Mikan, the burly 6-10 hook shooter who liked to plant himself in the low post and dare someone to dislodge him. His game was power, not agility. He was precisely the type of center Russell would render obsolete.

Russell played the game in the air. He also possessed unparalleled quickness. The game of basketball had heretofore been horizontal. In 1956 the two-handed set shot was still a major offensive weapon, as was its first cousin, the one-hand set. Not every guard or forward had a jump shot. Centers relied on hook shots (always considered to be unblockable) or basic inside power moves. Russell came in and from the first moment made the game vertical and diagonal. He disrupted not only the center, but every member of the opposing team. Prior to Russell, blocked shots were rarities; he made them a staple of his game. Unfortunately, it was not until 1973, after Russell had retired, that the NBA made shotblocking an official statistical category.

Latter-day pundits lavish their highest praise on individuals who, they say, "make their teammates better." That concept did not exist until Russell began to tyrannize the NBA. Quite simply, there never before had been a single player who had the capacity to enhance the capabilities of each teammate the way Russell did.

Russell ruined careers. That's a fact. Exhibit A: Neil Johnston. This man had led the NBA in scoring for three consecutive seasons (1953–55) and was still very much a force for the Philadelphia Warriors when Russell showed up. And why not? He was only 26 years old.

Johnston's calling card was a sidearm hook shot. He had never worried about getting it off; he just shot the ball when he felt like doing so. But Russell easily and repeatedly blocked that shot when they met in Russell's rookie year, and that was the beginning of the end for Johnston. He could still play well enough against everyone else, but against Boston he was useless, and within two years he was out of the league. Everyone knew Russell had destroyed him.

Russell did more than annoy sidearm hook shooters. He discouraged men from driving to the basket. He made players hesitate before shooting, especially if Russell wasn't in their line of vision. They never knew where he'd be coming from.

His phenomenal rebounding and even more astonishing outlet passing unleashed the Boston fast break. At last Auerbach's full vision was being fulfilled. Russell would rip the ball down and feed Cousy. The wing men ran their lanes. Cousy now had the complete offensive menu at his disposal. Most of the time he produced a layup for someone, but sometimes he set up Sharman, Heinsohn or Frank Ramsey for a jumper. Occasionally, he fooled everyone and took it to the hoop himself. And on more than a few occasions Cousy flipped the ball

The brilliance of Bob Pettit enabled St. Louis to interrupt Boston's championship run in 1958.

Lakers great Jerry West didn't win a championship until 1972, his path often blocked by the Celtics and rivals like John Havlicek.

back over his shoulder to a trailing Russell, who dunked the ball over a bewildered defender.

The Celtics, invigorated by Russell and Heinsohn, marched into the 1957 NBA Finals. Waiting for them was St. Louis, a 34-38 regular-season team now playing its best basketball under the guidance of player-coach Alex Hannum. Key roles were being played by the men who had been traded for Russell: Macauley and Hagan.

The series went seven rugged games, culminating in a sensational double-overtime epic in Game 7. Cousy and Sharman came up empty, shooting a horrifying 5-for-40 between them. But Russell played a Russell game. Most of all, Tommy Heinsohn established that he was a fearsome clutch performer, notching 37 points and 23 rebounds before fouling out in the overtime portion of this grueling game.

NCAA TO NBA CHAMPIONS

In 1956–57, Bill Russell became the first player in NBA history to play for NCAA and NBA titlists in successive years. In the league's 48 years, only four players have accomplished the feat:

Player	College	NBA
Bill Russell	San Francisco 1956	Boston 1957
Henry Bibby	UCLA 1972	New York 1973
Magic Johnson	Michigan State 1979	LA Lakers 1980
Billy Thompson	Louisville 1986	LA Lakers 1987

The game ended on a bizarre note. With Boston leading by two and one second left, Hannum threw a length-of-the-court inbounds pass off the St. Louis backboard. The ball ricocheted to Pettit, whose putback hung on the rim and fell off. Only then were the Celtics crowned NBA Champions, by a 125–123 score. It was the start of the dynasty that would result in 11 titles in 13 seasons.

St. Louis got revenge the following year. Russell injured his ankle in Game 3 of the Finals and wound up missing two games. He played in the sixth game, but he was not himself. Pettit, a true Hall of Famer, took over the game, dropping in 50 points to give St. Louis the title.

And that was it. Auerbach would never lose a title again. He had Russell, he had Cousy, he had Heinsohn, he had Sharman and he had many others, and he always knew what to do with them.

The Celtics rolled over Minneapolis in 1959, blowing out the overmatched Lakers in four straight. It was nothing more than a glorified Bum of the Month Club from then on. Some teams (St. Louis in '60 and Los

Ballhandling and defense made K. C. Jones an ideal point guard for the Celtics' championship teams.

Angeles in '62 and '66) put up brave battles, but most other Finals were nothing more than affirmations of Celtic superiority.

Sam Jones, who averaged 17.6 ppg in 12 seasons with Boston, was known as a master of the bank shot.

1962: WILT'S REMARKABLE SEASON

Although the Boston Celtics won the NBA Championship in 1962, Wilt Chamberlain of the Philadelphia Warriors enjoyed the most remarkable season any player has ever had in the NBA.

Chamberlain averaged an NBA record 50.4 points per game and became the only player to surpass 4,000 points in one season with 4,029. He also led the league in rebounding with 25.7 per game and was second in field-goal percentage at .506.

Amazingly, Chamberlain averaged 48.5 minutes per game—quite a feat when you consider that an NBA game only lasts 48 minutes. The Warriors played a total of 10 overtime periods in seven games that season, and Chamberlain was on the court for 3,882 of a possible 3,890 minutes. Of the team's 80 games, Chamberlain went the distance in a record 79 of them.

Highlighting Chamberlain's year, of course, was

Wilt Chamberlain's amazing 1962 season remains unmatched in basketball annals.

his 100-point effort against the New York Knicks on March 2, 1962. Following is the box score from that record-setting performance:

WILT CHAMBERLAIN'S 100-POINT GAME

March 2, 1962 at Hershey, Pa.
Philadelphia Warriors (169)

PLAYER	POS.	FGM	FGA	FTM	FTA	PTS.
Paul Arizin	F	7	18	2	2	16
Tom Meschery	F	7	12	2	2	16
Wilt Chamberlain	C	36	63	28	32	100
Guy Rodgers	G	1	4	9	12	11
Al Attles	G	8	8	1	1	17
York Larese		4	5	1	1	9
Ed Conlin		0	4	0	0	0
Joe Ruklick		0	1	0	2	0
Ted Luckenbill		0	0	0	0	0
		—	—	—	—	—
TOTALS		63	115	43	52	169

FG Pct.: .548. FT Pct.: .827. Team Rebounds: 3.

New York Knickerbockers (147)

PLAYER	POS.	FGM	FGA	FTM	FTA	PTS.
Willie Naulls	F	9	22	13	15	31
Johnny Green	F	3	7	0	0	6
Darrall Imhoff	C	3	7	1	1	7
Richie Guerin	G	13	29	13	17	39
Al Butler	G	4	13	0	0	8
Cleveland Buckner		16	26	1	1	33
Dave Budd		6	8	1	1	13
Donnie Butcher		3	6	4	6	10
TOTALS		57	118	33	41	147

FG Pct.: .483. FT Pct.: .805. Team Rebounds: 4.

Score by Periods:	1st	2nd	3rd	4th	Totals
Philadelphia	42	37	46	44	169
New York	26	42	38	41	147

Officials: Willie Smith and Pete D'Ambrosio. Attendance: 4,124.

CHAMBERLAIN'S SCORING BY PERIODS

	MIN.	FGM	FGA	FTM	FTA	REB.	AST.	PTS.
1st	12	7	14	9	9	10	0	23
2nd	12	7	12	4	5	4	1	18
3rd	12	10	16	8	8	6	1	28
4th	12	12	21	7	10	5	0	31
		—	—	—	—	—	—	—
TOTALS	48	36	63	28	32	25	2	100

Known for his defense and rebounding, Tom "Satch" Sanders won eight championship rings with Boston.

The Celtics pummeled people with depth and balance. Celtics did not appear high on the individual scoring lists. Auerbach did more than preach team play; he demanded it. Young talent such as Sam Jones and K. C. Jones waited their turns behind Sharman and Cousy, and by the time Auerbach really needed them to become front-line players they were thoroughly seasoned professionals who knew what it took to win.

Sharman left to go into the fledgling American Basketball League following the 1960–61 season, and that was the beginning of the turnover. It seemed that every year one of the Old Gang was saying farewell. Cousy retired in '63. Ramsey and Loscutoff left in '64. Heinsohn, his knees gone, retired in 1965 at age 30. K. C. Jones left in '67.

Auerbach himself announced to the world prior to the 1965–66 season that everyone could have one more shot at him before he left the bench and became the Celtics' general manager. He managed to go out a

winner, although it took seven games to dismiss the Lakers as Boston claimed its eighth championship in a row. Amid much controversy, he selected Russell as his replacement, reasoning that Russell was the Celtics' best player and would play best for Russell the coach.

By 1968 the Celtics were old and vulnerable. Philadelphia, coached by Alex Hannum, had ended its title streak the year before, and the consensus opinion was that Boston's time had come and gone. In fact, the legend was about to be fortified. The core now consisted of Russell, Sam Jones, Satch Sanders, Don Nelson, Bailey Howell, John Havlicek and Larry Siegfried. Nelson had come off the waiver wire. Howell had come via a brilliant trade in exchange for skinny center Mel Counts. Auerbach now had a reputation of being able to see things in players no one else saw. Of course, it all began with Russell, who was still in the business of making everyone else better.

The Celtics came from 3–1 down in the 1968 Eastern Division Finals against Philadelphia (and Russell's archrival, Wilt Chamberlain) to regain their Eastern Conference title by winning Games 5 and 7 on the road. But that was a mere warm-up for the following season, perhaps the most fondly remembered of all Celtic championships by their die-hard fans.

The 1968–69 Celtics really were ancient. The only important regular under the age of 30 was Havlicek, who began the season at 28. Russell put the word out on opening night that he could still play by hauling in 36 rebounds against Detroit. But he spent most of the season getting ready for the playoffs.

The Celtics finished fourth in their division, which meant they would spend the entire playoffs without the home-court advantage. It hardly mattered, as they dispatched Philadelphia and New York without too much difficulty.

The last hurdle was Los Angeles, where Chamberlain, now wearing a gold uniform, was again the biggest obstacle. It came down to a seventh game in Los Angeles, and when it had to be done, the Celtics did it. Nelson hit a crucial basket, the ball bouncing off the back rim high into the air before falling back in for a 108–106 victory. The tally was up to 11 championships in 13 years.

The only individual constant, the only man who had played on every one of those 11 title teams, had been Bill Russell.

The rest of the NBA was absolutely, positively convinced that Celtic tyranny was over on the eve of the 1969–70 season. Sam Jones had announced his impending retirement during the '68–'69 campaign, so everyone

After being released by the Lakers, Don Nelson enjoyed 11 productive seasons with the Celtics.

knew the Celtics would have one big hole to fill. But the real bombshell was dropped in the summer of 1969 when Russell told the world that 13 years and 11 championships would be enough.

What no one knew was that in four years the Celtics would put together a 68-victory season and that in five they would again be atop the NBA pile.

When Russell retired, the Celtics were reduced to one All-Star. But John Havlicek was not just your garden-variety All-Star. In 1969 he was at his physical peak, a 29-year-old multiskilled swingman who was any coach's answer to the king on a chessboard.

Long acclaimed as the best sixth man in basketball, Havlicek demonstrated once Russell left the squad that he was nothing less than the best all-around player in basketball. He led the '69–'70 Celtics in scoring, rebounding and assists; he was a fabulous defender at both forward and guard; and he never had to leave the game, as he had legendary stamina.

By the '70–'71 season he found himself den mother to a bunch of eager and talented young Scouts. Auerbach had quietly rebuilt the team by securing three interesting young players, first-round draft choices all. The first was Don Chaney, a Houston teammate of

Versatile John Havlicek was effective playing guard or forward, starting or coming off the bench.

from Florida State who had been hidden from full public view because his school had been on NCAA probation and kept off television during his entire career.

When Russell the player had retired, he took Russell the coach with him. The new coach was Heinsohn, who had spent the years following his own retirement selling insurance and dabbling in broadcasting. He was young and smart and eager, but he had never coached anything in his life.

Heinsohn retained Auerbach's fabled seven set plays, while modernizing other aspects of the Celtic attack. Knowing he would not be expected to construct

Though only 6-8, Dave Cowens stepped in at center and led the Celtics to titles in 1974 and 1976.

Elvin Hayes, who entered the league with strong defensive credentials and very limited offense. The second was Kansas All-American Jo Jo White, a very smooth guard who would very likely have been the No. 2 pick in the 1969 draft behind Kareem Abdul-Jabbar had he not had an obligation to Uncle Sam that was subsequently adjusted so he was able to play pro ball right away. Finally, there was Dave Cowens, a 6-8 center/forward

a team overnight, he implemented a long-range plan, his main goal being to implant in the newcomers the concept of 100 percent fast-break basketball. Cowens was the key. At 6-8 he was regarded by many as being too small to be a center in the modern game, but he was a great leaper, which made him 6-8 going on 7-2. He was fast, strong and astonishingly competitive. He also loved the concept of playing center, which is not true of all big men.

Heinsohn fashioned an offense around Cowens, taking full advantage of his mobility. Cowens made mistakes (he committed 350 personal fouls and fouled out of 15 games as a rookie), but he also made plays no other big man could make, thanks to his hustle. He wound up cowinner of the Rookie of the Year Award (with Geoff Petrie) as the Celtics improved their victory total from 34 to 44. That number increased by 12 the following season as the Celtics regained the Eastern Conference's Atlantic Division title from New York. But the Celtics were rudely ousted in the playoffs by the smarter, more physical Knicks, leaving Auerbach, now the president and general manager, to conclude that his team was one player short of true greatness. That player was Paul Silas, and he was playing for the Phoenix Suns.

Two years earlier Auerbach had done an interesting thing during the NBA Draft. He selected players in rounds seven, nine and ten who were already under contract to the rival American Basketball Association. Many people asked, "Why?"

Two years later they found out. One of those players was guard Charlie Scott. After playing for the ABA Virginia Squires, Scott wanted to bolt that club and play instead for the Suns. But guess who held Scott's NBA rights? Come to my den, said the spider to the fly. Auerbach yielded the NBA rights to Scott in exchange for Paul Silas.

Silas was then 29 years of age and coming off an excellent season. He was a superb power forward who could rebound and defend. He was the perfect complement to Cowens and a great locker-room leader. White and Chaney were now the league's best young backcourt. Havlicek was the league's best all-around player. Nelson was a wily veteran forward who could score off the bench or start the game; it made no difference to him.

The team won 68 and lost 14. However, in Game 3 of a 1973 playoff series against the Knicks, Havlicek sustained an injury to his right shoulder when sandwiched between Dave DeBusschere and Bill Bradley. The Celtics wound up losing the series in seven, and the Knicks went on to win the championship.

A consummate power forward, Paul Silas gave the Celtics the defense and rebounding they needed to win.

But it had been a magnificent season for the Celtics. They began to pack the Boston Garden as never before. Cowens was their new hero, and he was rewarded with the MVP trophy. Havlicek made First Team All-NBA.

The first post-Russell championship didn't come until a year later, but it was worth the wait. The 1973–74 Celtics started 29–6, then cruised through the remainder of the regular season. They disposed of Buffalo in six games and the aging Knicks in five. That left only Kareem Abdul-Jabbar and the Milwaukee Bucks in the way of a Boston title.

It was a fascinating series in which the heroes were the coaches. The real subplot in this series was Tom Heinsohn and assistant John Killilea versus Larry Costello and assistant Hubie Brown. The Celtics seized the initiative with a press that disrupted the Bucks and gave them a victory on the road in Game 1, prompting a ceaseless run of coaching punches and counterpunches. It was a series of constant adjustment. It was also a series of road triumphs, with the road team winning Games 1,

Coach Red Holzman's New York Knicks beat the Celtics in the 1973 playoffs en route to the title.

4, 5, 6 and 7. There was an overtime and a historic double overtime.

The marquee game was the sixth. Boston led the series, 3–2, but Milwaukee dominated most of regulation play, leading by six with 2:30 to go. The Celtics rallied, sending the game into overtime. Havlicek took over in the second overtime, scoring nine points, including an arching jumper on the right baseline over Kareem that put Boston ahead 101–100. With ecstatic Boston fans ringing the Boston Garden in anticipation of

another title, Kareem wiped the smiles off those faces and silenced the raucous Garden with an 18-foot hook that gave Milwaukee a 102–101 victory.

That sent everyone to Milwaukee for Game 7. Cowens (a 5-for-19 shooter in Game 6) came out smoking in the first half, and Boston expanded its lead to 17 points before Milwaukee launched its inevitable counterattack, reducing the lead to three. Paul Westphal came up with a huge basket, however, driving the baseline to ignite a Boston run that put the game away.

Five short years after all the Celtic enemies had figured they were done with the Green and White, the Celtics were NBA champions for the 12th time.

There would be no repeat, as the Washington Bullets defeated Boston in six games the following year. By 1976 the Celtics had again been replenished, and by a very interesting person. Does the name "Charlie Scott" ring a bell?

He had arrived in a trade for Westphal. It took a while for him to get adjusted to the Boston scheme of

Jo Jo White stepped into the shooting guard spot for the Celtics and surpassed 18 ppg seven times.

things and to sort out the backcourt duties with Jo Jo White, but by playoff time he was thoroughly comfortable as a Celtic. Boston entered the playoffs with a lot of question marks but managed to scrape by Buffalo and Cleveland in six games each to get out of the East.

The opponent was a curious foe. Phoenix had slogged through a 42-40 regular season, but the Suns suddenly jelled during the playoffs, eliminating defending champion Golden State in a superb seven-game series.

There was one shining moment in the Phoenix-Boston finals. Game 5 is in the discussion whenever the "Greatest Game Ever" argument begins.

Tied at 2–2, the teams put on a memorable show at Boston Garden. The basic story of the game was Phoenix's refusal to give in, no matter how brilliantly the Celtics insisted on playing. Boston led by 22 early. The Suns shrugged. Boston led again and again, and the Suns yawned. The overtimes were electric, gaining in drama as more and more key players fouled out. Havlicek thought he had won the game with a banker at the end of the first overtime, but Phoenix called a timeout it didn't have, giving Boston a technical free throw but also allowing the Suns to inbound the ball at midcourt. With one second to get off a shot, Gar Heard nailed an 18-footer to prolong the game. In the end, Boston's hero was Glenn McDonald, a substitute who had the fresh legs in the third overtime when most others had wobbly underpinnings.

If the instant rebirth of the Celtics following the retirement of Bill Russell had been impressive, what, then, can be said about the lightning revival of the Celtics in the late '70s?

Within two years of the 1976 championship, the Celtics were a bad ball club, the records falling to 32-50 and 29-53. Silas left the team when his salary demands weren't met. Cowens left the team early in '76–'77 for a sabbatical. Havlicek retired amid great pomp and circumstance in 1978. Newcomers Sidney Wicks and Curtis Rowe, talented individuals, never fit into the team concept.

And then along came Larry.

Larry Bird had been drafted by Auerbach as the sixth pick of the 1978 NBA Draft, even though he had one year of college eligibility left. The Indiana State forward opted to finish his college career first, and it turned out to be a wise move. He led Indiana State to 33 straight victories and a berth in the NCAA championship game against Michigan State.

He and agent Bob Woolf had the Celtics in a difficult bargaining position. The Celtics clearly needed

Bill Fitch guided the Celtics to 242 wins in four seasons, including an NBA Championship in 1981.

Bird. Auerbach and owner Harry Mangurian swallowed hard and gave Bird what was then the biggest contract ever bestowed on any rookie in any sport—$650,000 a year. It turned out to be the most colossal bargain in the history of the franchise.

But Bird wasn't the only thing new, different and exciting about the 1979–80 Celtics. There was a new coach, Bill Fitch, who turned out to be the disciplinarian and teacher the Celtics needed. M. L. Carr, a hustling, effervescent forward/guard who was an ideal sixth man, had arrived from Detroit as part of machinations involving the unwanted Bob McAdoo. Another newcomer of note was guard Gerald Henderson. Finally, veteran Tiny Archibald returned as the equivalent of a new man after shedding weight and getting in condition following a washout year in the wake of an Achilles' heel surgery.

Larry Bird drives to the basket against Magic Johnson in one of the great Celtic-Laker Finals.

And if all that wasn't enough, Cowens came back in the best shape of his life, which, in his case, is saying plenty.

So it wasn't just Bird. Then again, it was. For Bird did for the Celtics what he had done for Indiana State with his share-the-wealth philosophy. Bird's passing expertise was contagious. While no one could make all the passes he could, by playing with him a man began to

think in terms of passing. When all five men on the court are committed to that end, wonderful things can happen.

The Celtics were transformed into a crowd-pleasing, devastating team. Bird proved immediately that concerns about his foot speed and jumping ability were groundless. Though not a cheetah up and down the floor, he did have a great first step. Though not in

Larry Bird led little-known Indiana State to 33 victories and the NCAA Finals before signing with the Celtics.

possession of a notable vertical leap, he had the gift of a quick takeoff, enabling him to get to his apex before some higher-jumping opponent could uncoil himself. Bird proved on a nightly basis that running and jumping are only a small part of the athletic whole, that hand-eye coordination, anticipation, timing and knowledge of the game and human nature are equally valuable traits.

The cold, hard facts are that Bird became the team leader the minute he walked onto the court. The Celtics won 61, 62, 63, 56, 62, 63 and 67 games in his first seven years in the league. They won championships in 1981, 1984 and 1986.

After winning those 61 games in 1979–80, the Celtics were dumped, and dumped hard, in the playoffs by their old rivals, the 76ers. Fitch came away from the series believing that as admirable as his team may have been, it was too small to get the ultimate job done. He vowed to change that state of affairs.

He and Auerbach cooked up a deal at draft time, sending their first pick, as well as their 13th, to Golden State for the third spot plus seven-foot center Robert Parish. With the No. 3 selection the Celtics chose

Minnesota center/forward Kevin McHale, a 6-11 kid with arms that effectively made him a 7-6 monster.

Now the Celtics had weapons. Bird, Parish and the rubbery Cedric Maxwell comprised the best starting frontcourt in the league. McHale immediately became the most important sixth man. Archibald was in full flower. Chris Ford was a cagey off-guard. The Celtics demolished Chicago in four straight in preparation for yet another match with Philadelphia, then promptly fell behind, three games to one, against the hated Sixers.

The situation was grim when the Sixers took a six-point lead with 1:40 left in Game 5. The Celtics pulled out that game, however, and came from 10 points behind in the third period to win Game 6 in Philadelphia. Game 7 was more of the same.

Philly led by nine points with just over five minutes to go when the Celtics turned into attack dogs on defense. In their final 10 possessions the Sixers came up with just one point. Bird's banker with just over a minute to go turned out to be the game-winner. "The only place in the world I wanted that ball to be was in my hands," he said with customary bravado.

The outside shooting and passing skills of Larry Bird helped Robert Parish (00) blossom into one of the NBA's top centers after coming to Boston in 1980.

Kevin McHale's long
arms and skillful
touch made him one
of the NBA's best
low-post players.

The 1981 NBA Finals were anticlimactic. The Celtics were simply a better team than the Houston Rockets, and everyone on both teams knew it. Boston had some trouble with the Rockets' deliberate style, but Maxwell took over Game 5 with 28 points and the Celtics nailed down title No. 14 when Bird's three-pointer clinched the sixth game.

It took a little tinkering to return to the Finals, Auerbach's key move being to trade center Rick Robey

to Phoenix for guard Dennis Johnson prior to the 1983–84 season. DJ went on to establish Hall of Fame credentials over the next seven years.

The 1984 Finals were the last of the old-fashioned coast-to-coast odysseys, before the NBA changed the home-road format from 2-2-1-1-1 to 2-3-2. This series had everything, starting with the basic Boston-LA rivalry, back in the limelight after a 15-year absence. Throw in the individual sideshow of a Bird–Magic Johnson

Nate "Tiny" Archibald (10) led the NBA in scoring and assists in 1973, but didn't win a title until he came to Boston.

Larry Bird enjoys a puff from Red Auerbach's trademark victory cigar during a championship celebration.

Magic Johnson and Larry Bird gave basketball fans something to savor with their brilliant rivalry.

professional confrontation, and this had more drama than a trunkful of Shakespearean manuscripts.

The Lakers will always believe that the better team failed to win, and they may be right. LA had more athleticism, but the Celtics had more moxie. They also had more Bird. Larry came through continually, most notably in Game 4 (29 points, 21 rebounds in an overtime triumph in the Forum) and Game 5, the famed "Heat Game."

Boston was hit with unseasonably steamy June weather, and since the Boston Garden lacked air conditioning, the game-time temperature at courtside was a scary 97 degrees. Bird shrugged his shoulders and went to work, shooting 15-for-20 from the floor. He finished with 34 points and 17 rebounds, and the Lakers—most of them, anyway—finished with their faces stuck in oxygen masks.

McHale had turned the series around in Game 4

Has there ever been a better backup center than Bill Walton (5), who helped Boston win in 1986?

when his hard, physical take-down of LA's Kurt Rambis changed the tenor of the series. The Celtics continually helped themselves to extra shots, extra helpings of mashed potatoes and extra anything else they wanted for the remainder of the series.

Maxwell, the 1981 Finals MVP, played his last great game as a Celtic in Game 7, scoring 24 points while giving James Worthy an inside scoring lesson as the Celtics brought home championship No. 15.

Maxwell did have one more valuable service to render. He was the pawn Auerbach used to bring in Bill Walton.

The 1985–86 Celtics may very well have been the greatest of all Boston teams, and Walton was a large part of the reason. The following statements are nonnegotiable: (1) The 1985–86 center tandem of Robert Parish and Bill Walton constitutes the best one-two center punch in NBA history, and (2) Walton in 1985–86 was the greatest so-called backup center ever seen on this planet.

There were further distinctions. This could very well have been the best all-around passing team ever. Surely, Bird, Parish, McHale, Walton and Scott Wedman —all All-Stars at one time or another—represented the greatest frontcourt quintet ever assembled. And few teams have ever possessed this team's defensive capabilities.

The regular season was laughably easy. The Celtics went 40-1 at home. There was one second-half stretch in which they won 13 consecutive games in Boston Garden by an average of 16 points a game.

The playoffs? Not much harder. Michael Jordan's record 63-point game for Chicago did throw a scare into them in the First Round, but after pulling out that 135–131 double-overtime classic the rest was cake and ice cream. Atlanta made the mistake of spoiling a sweep in the second round by winning Game 4, and as punishment the Celtics hit them with a 36–6 third quarter in Game 5. Milwaukee was engulfed in four. Houston put up a fight, but the Celtics blitzed them 114–97 in Game 6 to win the NBA Championship for the 16th and final time.

Bird in Game 6 was transcendent. He totally dominated the game to insure another Finals MVP trophy.

A very serious argument can be made that when the '85–'86 Boston Celtics played their best, that was as good as NBA basketball ever has been.

So there it is, the Boston Celtics' 16-title legacy. Would anyone care to challenge it while keeping a straight face?

The ultimate blue-collar player, Larry Bird squeezes in between three Houston Rockets for a rebound.

BOSTON CELTICS IN THE HALL OF FAME

There are 22 people in the Naismith Memorial Basketball Hall of Fame who spent all or part of their careers with the Boston Celtics. Following are those Hall of Famers, including the category in which they were inducted:

Nate "Tiny" Archibald, player
Arnold "Red" Auerbach, coach
Dave Bing, player
Walter Brown, contributor
Bob Cousy, player
Dave Cowens, player
John Havlicek, player

Tom Heinsohn, player
Bob Houbregs, player
K. C. Jones, player
Sam Jones, player
Alvin "Doggie" Julian, coach
Clyde Lovellette, player
Ed Macauley, player
Pete Maravich, player
Bill Mokray, contributor
Andy Phillip, player
Frank Ramsey, player
Bill Russell, player
John "Honey" Russell, coach
Bill Sharman, player
Bill Walton, player

1956–57

The season marked the beginning of what would become sports' greatest dynasty, the reign of the Boston Celtics that would produce 11 championships in 13 years. The Celtics had employed the group of Cousy, Sharman and Macauley to score points in bunches for some time, but without rebounding and defense they hadn't progressed very far in the playoffs. But Auerbach traded Macauley and Cliff Hagan to St. Louis for the draft rights to center Bill Russell of San Francisco, and Boston used its own pick to grab high-scoring 6-7 forward Tom Heinsohn of Holy Cross.

With Russell and Heinsohn joining Cousy,

Sharman, muscleman Jim Loscutoff and sixth man Frank Ramsey, the Celtics assembled a team that would be the scourge of the league for years to come. Sharman (21.1 ppg) and Cousy (20.6) still piled up the points, but with Russell anchoring a suddenly tough Celtics defense, Boston cruised to a league-best 44-28 record, winning the Eastern Division by a comfortable six games. St. Louis, buoyed by the addition of Macauley (16.5 ppg) and Hagan, advanced to the Finals in the West. A classic seven-game series ensued, with Boston winning a thrilling Game 7 in Boston, 125–123 in double overtime.

NBA 1956-57
FINAL STANDINGS

Eastern Division

	W.	L.	PCT.
Boston	44	28	.611
Syracuse	38	34	.528
Philadelphia	37	35	.514
New York	36	36	.500

Western Division

	W.	L.	PCT.
St. Louis *	34	38	.472
Minneapolis	34	38	.472
Fort Wayne	34	38	.472
Rochester	31	41	.431

* Won playoff to break tie

PLAYOFFS

Western Division Tie-breakers

March 14—St. Louis 115, Fort Wayne 103
March 16—St. Louis 114, Minneapolis 111

Eastern Division Semifinals

Syracuse 2, Philadelphia 0
March 16—Syracuse 103, Philadelphia 96
March 18—Syracuse 91, Philadelphia 80

Western Division Semifinals

Minneapolis 2, Fort Wayne 0
March 17—Minneapolis 131, Fort Wayne 127
March 19—Minneapolis 110, Fort Wayne 108

Eastern Division Finals

Boston 3, Syracuse 0
March 21—Boston 108, Syracuse 90
March 23—Boston 120, Syracuse 105
March 24—Boston 83, Syracuse 80

Western Division Finals

St. Louis 3, Minneapolis 0
March 21—St. Louis 118, Minneapolis 109
March 24—St. Louis 106, Minneapolis 104
March 25—St. Louis 143, Minneapolis 135 (2OT)

NBA Finals

Boston 4, St. Louis 3
March 30—St. Louis 125, Boston 123 (2OT)
March 31—Boston 119, St. Louis 99
April 6—St. Louis 100, Boston 98
April 7—Boston 123, St. Louis 118
April 9—Boston 124, St. Louis 109
April 11—St. Louis 96, Boston 94
April 13—Boston 125, St. Louis 123 (2OT)

INDIVIDUAL LEADERS

Scoring

	G.	FG	FT	PTS.	AVG.
Arizin, Philadelphia	71	613	591	1817	25.6
Pettit, St. Louis	71	613	529	1755	24.7
Schayes, Syracuse	72	496	625	1617	22.5
Johnston, Philadelphia	69	520	535	1575	22.8
Yardley, Fort Wayne	72	522	503	1547	21.5
Lovellette, Minneapolis	69	574	286	1434	20.8
Sharman, Boston	67	516	381	1413	21.1
Cousy, Boston	64	478	363	1319	20.6
Macauley, St. Louis	72	414	359	1187	16.5
Garmaker, Minneapolis	72	406	365	1177	16.3

Field Goal Pct.
(Minimum 230 FG made)

	FGM	FGA	PCT.
Johnston, Philadelphia	520	1163	.447
Share, St. Louis	235	535	.439
Twyman, Rochester	449	1023	.439
Houbregs, Fort Wayne	253	585	.432
Russell, Boston	277	649	.427

Free Throw Pct.
(Minimum 190 FT made)

	FTM	FTA	PCT.
Sharman, Boston	381	421	.905
Schayes, Syracuse	625	691	.904
Garmaker, Minneapolis	365	435	.839
Arizin, Philadelphia	591	713	.829
Johnston, Philadelphia	535	648	.826

Assists

	G.	NO.	AVG.
Cousy, Boston	64	478	7.5
McMahon, St. Louis	72	367	5.1
Stokes, Rochester	72	331	4.6
George, Philadelphia	67	307	4.6
Martin, N.Y.-St.L	66	269	4.1

Rebounds

	G.	NO.	AVG.
Stokes, Rochester	72	1256	17.4
Pettit, St. Louis	71	1037	14.6
Schayes, Syracuse	72	1008	14.0
Russell, Boston	48	943	19.6
Lovellette, Minneapolis	69	932	13.5

Game 7 of the 1957 NBA Finals was the type of game that could advance a sport by its sheer excitement. It was a game that would be talked about for years: how rookies Russell (19 points, 32 rebounds) and Heinsohn (37 points, 23 rebounds) stepped up and provided the win that would set the Celtic dynasty in motion.

"The first one [championship] is always the hardest, and it's also the most satisfying," reflected Red Auerbach. "Everywhere I went that following summer, I could tell myself, 'I'm the coach of the world champions.'"

1957-58

The NBA took giant strides in cementing its big-league image when the Fort Wayne Pistons moved to Detroit and the Rochester Royals moved to Cincinnati. Just three years earlier, half the NBA's teams were based in metropolitan areas with less than a million people; now only Syracuse was in that category. The new fans in Detroit were treated to the league's leading scorer as the Pistons' George Yardley became the first player to score 2,000 points in a season, leading the NBA in scoring at 27.8 ppg.

Boston in the East and St. Louis in the West were clearly the class of the league, with each team winning its division by eight games over a 72-game schedule. Boston took Philadelphia in five games to win what was now a best-of-7 Division Finals, while St. Louis also bested Detroit in five games. When St. Louis and Boston split the first two games in Boston, it seemed another classic series was in the offing. But Russell's sprained ankle in Game 3 turned the series in the Hawks' favor. Boston showed gritty determination by tying the series with a win in Game 4 without Russell, but St. Louis won Game 5 in Boston by two points and Hawks forward Bob Pettit exploded for 50 points in Game 6 to give St. Louis its only league title.

NBA 1957-58

FINAL STANDINGS

Eastern Division

	W.	L.	PCT.
Boston	49	23	.681
Syracuse	41	31	.569
Philadelphia	37	35	.514
New York	35	37	.486

Western Division

	W.	L.	PCT.
St. Louis	41	31	.569
Detroit	33	39	.458
Cincinnati	33	39	.458
Minneapolis	19	53	.264

PLAYOFFS

Eastern Division Semifinals

Philadelphia 2, Syracuse 1
March 15—Syracuse 86, Philadelphia 82
March 16—Philadelphia 95, Syracuse 93
March 18—Philadelphia 101, Syracuse 88

Western Division Semifinals

Detroit 2, Cincinnati 0
March 15—Detroit 100, Cincinnati 83
March 16—Detroit 124, Cincinnati 104

Eastern Division Finals

Boston 4, Philadelphia 1
March 19—Boston 107, Philadelphia 98
March 22—Boston 109, Philadelphia 87
March 23—Boston 106, Philadelphia 92
March 26—Philadelphia 112, Boston 97
March 27—Boston 93, Philadelphia 88

Western Division Finals

St. Louis 4, Detroit 1
March 19—St. Louis 114, Detroit 111
March 22—St. Louis 99, Detroit 96
March 23—Detroit 109, St. Louis 89
March 25—St. Louis 145, Detroit 101
March 27—St. Louis 120, Detroit 96

NBA Finals

St. Louis 4, Boston 2
March 29—St. Louis 104, Boston 102
March 30—Boston 136, St. Louis 112
April 2—St. Louis 111, Boston 108
April 5—Boston 109, St. Louis 98
April 9—St. Louis 102, Boston 100
April 12—St. Louis 110, Boston 109

INDIVIDUAL LEADERS

Scoring

	G.	FG	FT	PTS.	AVG.
Yardley, Detroit	72	673	655	2001	27.8
Schayes, Syracuse	72	581	629	1791	24.9
Pettit, St. Louis	70	581	557	1719	24.6
Lovellette, Cincinnati	71	679	301	1659	23.4
Arizin, Philadelphia	68	483	440	1406	20.7
Sharman, Boston	63	550	302	1402	22.3
Hagan, St. Louis	70	503	385	1391	19.9
Johnston, Philadelphia	71	473	442	1388	19.5
Sears, New York	72	445	452	1342	18.6
Mikkelsen, Minneapolis	72	439	370	1248	17.3

Field Goal Pct.
(Minimum 230 FG made)

	FGM	FGA	PCT.
Twyman, Cincinnati	465	1028	.452
Hagan, St. Louis	503	1135	.443
Felix, New York	304	688	.442
Russell, Boston	456	1032	.442
Lovellette, Cincinnati	679	1540	.441

Free Throw Pct.
(Minimum 190 FT made)

	FTM	FTA	PCT.
Schayes, Syracuse	629	696	.904
Sharman, Boston	302	338	.893
Cousy, Boston	277	326	.850
Braun, New York	321	378	.849
Schnittker, Minneapolis	201	237	.848

Assists

	G.	NO.	AVG.
Cousy, Boston	65	463	7.1
McGuire, Detroit	69	454	6.6
Stokes, Cincinnati	63	403	6.4
Braun, New York	71	393	5.5
King, Cincinnati	63	337	5.3

Rebounds

	G.	NO.	AVG.
Russell, Boston	69	1564	22.7
Pettit, St. Louis	70	1216	17.4
Stokes, Cincinnati	63	1142	18.1
Schayes, Syracuse	72	1022	14.2
Kerr, Syracuse	72	963	13.4

Bob Pettit won only one NBA Championship during his illustrious career, but that says more about the Celtics' dominance during that period than about the desire of the 6-9, 215-pound forward from LSU. Pettit burned with an inner fire that never let him be satisfied with his performance.

"When I fall below what I know I can do, my belly growls and growls," Pettit once said.

Pettit, who led the Hawks to the NBA Finals four times, retired at the end of the 1964–65 season after 11 seasons as the NBA's then all-time leading scorer with 20,880 points.

1958–59

A new superstar burst on the NBA scene with the arrival of Elgin Baylor in Minneapolis. A 6-5 forward from Seattle, Baylor helped a Lakers team that had been 19-53 a year before to a 33-39 record and a playoff berth by averaging 24.9 points and 15.0 rebounds per game, making the All-NBA team as a rookie. But perhaps his most profound impact in his first season came in the playoffs.

Boston had won the East by 12 games, while St. Louis won the West by 16 games. Just about everyone expected a third straight Boston–St. Louis matchup in the NBA Finals. Boston had a tough time with Syracuse, which had acquired Yardley to add to a front line that

already boasted Schayes and Red Kerr. Pushed to the limit, Boston won the seventh game of the Eastern Finals, 130–125. St. Louis, however, did not make it back to the Finals for the expected date with the Celtics. Baylor and the Lakers overcame a 2–1 St. Louis lead to win three straight games and oust the Hawks. Nobody gave the Lakers much chance against the Celtics, and although the Lakers kept three of the four games close, Boston recorded the first 4–0 sweep in NBA Finals history. Nobody knew it at the time, but it was the beginning of the Celtics' run of eight straight championships.

Even in 1959, 6-5 was not considered tall for a forward in the NBA. But Elgin Baylor proved to be more than a handful for taller rivals. As strong as any of his counterparts, Baylor had a smooth scoring style that was ahead of its time, and his ability seemingly to hang in the air would

become the measuring stick for players that followed, like Connie Hawkins, Julius Erving and Michael Jordan.

Baylor's 55-point game in his rookie season was the third highest in NBA history and signaled a new high-scoring era.

NBA 1958-59

FINAL STANDINGS

Eastern Division

	W.	L.	PCT.
Boston	52	20	.722
New York	40	32	.556
Syracuse	35	37	.486
Philadelphia	32	40	.444

Western Division

	W.	L.	PCT.
St. Louis	49	23	.681
Minneapolis	33	39	.458
Detroit	28	44	.389
Cincinnati	19	53	.264

PLAYOFFS

Eastern Division Semifinals

Syracuse 2, New York 0
March 13—Syracuse 129, New York 123
March 15—Syracuse 131, New York 115

Western Division Semifinals

Minneapolis 2, Detroit 1
March 14—Minneapolis 92, Detroit 89
March 15—Detroit 117, Minneapolis 103
March 18—Minneapolis 129, Detroit 102

Eastern Division Finals

Boston 4, Syracuse 3
March 18—Boston 131, Syracuse 109
March 21—Syracuse 120, Boston 118
March 22—Boston 133, Syracuse 111
March 25—Syracuse 119, Boston 107
March 28—Boston 129, Syracuse 108
March 29—Syracuse 133, Boston 121
April 1—Boston 130, Syracuse 125

Western Division Finals

Minneapolis 4, St. Louis 2
March 21—St. Louis 124, Minneapolis 90
March 22—Minneapolis 106, St. Louis 98
March 24—St. Louis 127, Minneapolis 97
March 26—Minneapolis 108, St. Louis 98
March 28—Minneapolis 98, St. Louis 97 (OT)
March 29—Minneapolis 106, St. Louis 104

NBA Finals

Boston 4, Minneapolis 0
April 4—Boston 118, Minneapolis 115
April 5—Boston 128, Minneapolis 108
April 7—Boston 123, Minneapolis 110
April 9—Boston 118, Minneapolis 113

INDIVIDUAL LEADERS

Scoring

	G.	FG	FT	PTS.	AVG.
Pettit, St. Louis	72	719	667	2105	29.2
Twyman, Cincinnati	72	710	437	1857	25.8
Arizin, Philadelphia	70	632	587	1851	26.4
Baylor, Minneapolis	70	605	532	1742	24.9
Hagan, St. Louis	72	646	415	1707	23.7
Schayes, Syracuse	72	504	526	1534	21.3
Sears, New York	71	491	506	1488	21.0
Sharman, Boston	72	562	342	1466	20.4
Cousy, Boston	65	484	329	1297	20.0
Guerin, New York	71	443	405	1291	18.2

Field Goal Pct.
(Minimum 230 FG made)

	FGM	FGA	PCT.
Sears, New York	491	1002	.490
Russell, Boston	456	997	.457
Hagan, St. Louis	646	1417	.456
Lovellette, St. Louis	402	885	.454
Greer, Syracuse	308	679	.454

Free Throw Pct.
(Minimum 190 FT made)

	FTM	FTA	PCT.
Sharman, Boston	342	367	.932
Schayes, Syracuse	526	609	.864
Sears, New York	506	588	.861
Cousy, Boston	329	385	.855
Naulls, New York	258	311	.830

Assists

	G.	NO.	AVG.
Cousy, Boston	65	557	8.6
McGuire, Detroit	71	443	6.2
Costello, Syracuse	70	379	5.4
Guerin, New York	71	364	5.1
Braun, New York	72	349	4.8

Rebounds

	G.	NO.	AVG.
Russell, Boston	70	1612	23.0
Pettit, St. Louis	72	1182	16.4
Baylor, Minneapolis	70	1050	15.0
Kerr, Syracuse	72	1008	14.0
Schayes, Syracuse	72	962	13.4

1959-60

The NBA had seen a big man dominate before, when George Mikan's Minneapolis Lakers won five NBA titles in six years from 1949 through 1954. But in terms of individual dominance, no one had seen anything quite like Wilt Chamberlain. At 7-1 and nearly 275 pounds, Wilt towered over Bill Russell and the other centers of his time. In his rookie season with the Philadelphia Warriors, Chamberlain won both Rookie of the Year and Most Valuable Player, leading the league in scoring (37.6) and rebounding (27.0). Chamberlain scored 50 or more points seven times. A Philadelphia team that had gone 32-40 the previous season improved to 49-26, and Chamberlain's Warriors attracted capacity crowds most nights.

But despite the arrival of Chamberlain, the Celtics were still the league's top team, which was underlined as

Boston won an NBA-record 59 games and the Eastern Division. St. Louis won the West by 16 games in what was now a 75-game season. Boston defeated the Warriors and Chamberlain in six games to advance to the Finals, while St. Louis was pushed to seven games by the Lakers before advancing to once again meet the Celtics. The teams split the first six games, with Boston winning in blowouts and St. Louis just scraping by. The Celtics easily won Game 7 in Boston as Russell starred with 22 points and 35 rebounds.

NBA 1959-60

FINAL STANDINGS

Eastern Division

	W.	L.	PCT.
Boston	59	16	.787
Philadelphia	49	26	.653
Syracuse	45	30	.600
New York	27	48	.360

Western Division

	W.	L.	PCT.
St. Louis	46	29	.613
Detroit	30	45	.400
Minneapolis	25	50	.333
Cincinnati	19	56	.253

PLAYOFFS

Eastern Division Semifinals

Philadelphia 2, Syracuse 1
March 11—Philadelphia 115, Syracuse 92
March 13—Syracuse 125, Philadelphia 119
March 14—Philadelphia 132, Syracuse 112

Western Division Semifinals

Minneapolis 2, Detroit 0
March 12—Minneapolis 113, Detroit 112
March 13—Minneapolis 114, Detroit 99

Eastern Division Finals

Boston 4, Philadelphia 2
March 16—Boston 111, Philadelphia 105
March 18—Philadelphia 115, Boston 110
March 19—Boston 120, Philadelphia 90
March 20—Boston 112, Philadelphia 104
March 22—Philadelphia 128, Boston 107
March 24—Boston 119, Philadelphia 117

Western Division Finals

St. Louis 4, Minneapolis 3
March 16—St. Louis 112, Minneapolis 99
March 17—Minneapolis 120, St. Louis 113
March 19—St. Louis 93, Minneapolis 89
March 20—Minneapolis 103, St. Louis 101
March 22—Minneapolis 117, St. Louis 110 (OT)
March 24—St. Louis 117, Minneapolis 96
March 26—St. Louis 97, Minneapolis 86

NBA Finals

Boston 4, St. Louis 3
March 27—Boston 140, St. Louis 122
March 29—St. Louis 113, Boston 103
April 2—Boston 102, St. Louis 86
April 3—St. Louis 106, Boston 96
April 5—Boston 127, St. Louis 102
April 7—St. Louis 105, Boston 102
April 9—Boston 122, St. Louis 103

INDIVIDUAL LEADERS

Scoring

	G.	FG	FT	PTS.	AVG.
Chamberlain, Philadelphia	72	1065	577	2707	37.6
Twyman, Cincinnati	75	870	598	2338	31.2
Baylor, Minneapolis	70	755	564	2074	29.6
Pettit, St. Louis	72	669	544	1882	26.1
Hagan, St. Louis	75	719	421	1859	24.8
Shue, Detroit	75	620	472	1712	22.8
Schayes, Syracuse	75	578	533	1689	22.5
Heinsohn, Boston	75	673	283	1629	21.7
Guerin, New York	74	579	457	1615	21.8
Arizin, Philadelphia	72	593	420	1606	22.3

Field Goal Pct.
(Minimum 190 FG made)

	FGM	FGA	PCT.
Sears, New York	412	863	.477
Greer, Syracuse	388	815	.476
Lovellette, St. Louis	550	1174	.468
Russell, Boston	555	1189	.467
Hagan, St. Louis	719	1549	.464

Free Throw Pct.
(Minimum 185 FT made)

	FTM	FTA	PCT.
Schayes, Syracuse	533	597	.893
Shue, Detroit	472	541	.872
Sears, New York	363	418	.868
Sharman, Boston	252	291	.866
Costello, Syracuse	249	289	.862

Assists

	G.	NO.	AVG.
Cousy, Boston	75	715	9.5
Rodgers, Philadelphia	68	482	7.1
Guerin, New York	74	468	6.3
Costello, Syracuse	71	449	6.3
Gola, Philadelphia	75	409	5.5

Rebounds

	G.	NO.	AVG.
Chamberlain, Philadelphia	72	1941	27.0
Russell, Boston	74	1778	24.0
Pettit, St. Louis	72	1221	17.0
Baylor, Minneapolis	70	1150	16.4
Schayes, Syracuse	75	959	12.8

The Celtics, with Auerbach at the controls, had built a champion piece by piece, beginning with Cousy in 1950, adding Sharman in 1951, Ramsey in 1954, Loscutoff in 1955, and Heinsohn and Russell in 1956.

But after the first championship in 1957, the Celtics didn't stop adding players who put winning above personal achievements. Sam Jones came aboard in 1957, K. C. Jones and Gene Conley in 1958, and Tom Sanders in 1960. Auerbach's legendary eye for talent and demand for team play had set in motion one of sport's greatest dynasties.

To the untrained eye, Jerry West appeared to be just a skinny kid from West Virginia when he came to the NBA in 1960. But the 6-2 college forward learning to be a pro guard had a desire to be the best and skills that would allow him to get there. As a rookie, West played behind fellow West Virginia legend Hot Rod Hundley, but it was not long before West pleaded for and got more minutes.

"I knew I couldn't learn sitting on the bench," West said. "The only thing I could learn were bad habits. I had to get out there and get rid of those first-year jitters."

1960–61

The NBA was changing rapidly. Baylor and Chamberlain had each brought a special brand of excitement to the league with landmark NBA debuts. In 1960 two guards who would thrill NBA fans for the next 14 seasons—and who would always be inextricably linked —joined the league. Oscar Robertson and Jerry West, both superb collegians, entered together after winning gold medals at the 1960 Olympics. Cincinnati's Robertson had a more immediate impact, averaging 30.5 ppg and leading the league with 9.7 assists per contest. Chamberlain's scoring of 38.4 ppg and Baylor's 34.8 marked the first time in NBA history that three players

scored 30 ppg in the same season. West, on the other hand, came aboard just as the Lakers made a bold move, leaving Minneapolis for the larger market of Los Angeles, and averaged 17.6 ppg as a rookie.

The schedule had been increased to 79 games, and Boston and St. Louis once again outclassed the competition with 57 and 51 victories, respectively. For the second straight season, St. Louis had to fight off the Lakers in a seven-game Western Division Finals to meet the Celtics, who had cruised past Syracuse in five games. Unfortunately for the Hawks, the well-balanced Celtics dismissed them in five games.

NBA 1960-61

FINAL STANDINGS

Eastern Division

	W.	L.	PCT.
Boston	57	22	.722
Philadelphia	46	33	.582
Syracuse	38	41	.481
New York	21	58	.266

Western Division

	W.	L.	PCT.
St. Louis	51	28	.646
Los Angeles	36	43	.456
Detroit	34	45	.430
Cincinnati	33	46	.418

PLAYOFFS

Eastern Division Semifinals

Syracuse 3, Philadelphia 0
March 14—Syracuse 115, Philadelphia 107
March 16—Syracuse 115, Philadelphia 114
March 18—Syracuse 106, Philadelphia 103

Western Division Semifinals

Los Angeles 3, Detroit 2
March 14—Los Angeles 120, Detroit 102
March 15—Los Angeles 127, Detroit 118
March 17—Detroit 124, Los Angeles 113
March 18—Detroit 123, Los Angeles 114
March 19—Los Angeles 137, Detroit 120

Eastern Division Finals

Boston 4, Syracuse 1
March 19—Boston 128, Syracuse 115
March 21—Syracuse 115, Boston 98
March 23—Boston 133, Syracuse 110
March 25—Boston 120, Syracuse 107
March 26—Boston 123, Syracuse 101

Western Division Finals

St. Louis 4, Los Angeles 3
March 21—Los Angeles 122, St. Louis 118
March 22—St. Louis 121, Los Angeles 106
March 24—Los Angeles 118, St. Louis 112
March 25—St. Louis 118, Los Angeles 117
March 27—Los Angeles 121, St. Louis 112
March 29—St. Louis 114, Los Angeles 113 (OT)
April 1—St. Louis 105, Los Angeles 103

NBA Finals

Boston 4, St. Louis 1
April 2—Boston 129, St. Louis 95
April 5—Boston 116, St. Louis 108
April 8—St. Louis 124, Boston 120
April 9—Boston 119, St. Louis 104
April 11—Boston 121, St. Louis 112

INDIVIDUAL LEADERS

Scoring

	G.	FG	FT	PTS.	AVG.
Chamberlain, Philadelphia	79	1251	531	3033	38.4
Baylor, Los Angeles	73	931	676	2538	34.8
Robertson, Cincinnati	71	756	653	2165	30.5
Pettit, St. Louis	76	769	582	2120	27.9
Twyman, Cincinnati	79	796	405	1997	25.3
Schayes, Syracuse	79	594	680	1868	23.6
Naulls, New York	79	737	372	1846	23.4
Arizin, Philadelphia	79	650	532	1832	23.2
Howell, Detroit	77	607	601	1815	23.6
Shue, Detroit	78	650	465	1765	22.6

Field Goal Pct.
(Minimum 200 FG made)

	FGM	FGA	PCT.
Chamberlain, Philadelphia	1251	2457	.509
Twyman, Cincinnati	796	1632	.488
Costello, Syracuse	407	844	.482
Robertson, Cincinnati	756	1600	.473
Howell, Detroit	607	1293	.469

Free Throw Pct.
(Minimum 200 FT made)

	FTM	FTA	PCT.
Sharman, Boston	210	228	.921
Schayes, Syracuse	680	783	.868
Shue, Detroit	465	543	.856
Ramsey, Boston	295	354	.833
Arizin, Philadelphia	532	639	.833

Assists

	G.	NO.	AVG.
Robertson, Cincinnati	71	690	9.7
Rodgers, Philadelphia	78	677	8.7
Cousy, Boston	76	587	7.7
Shue, Detroit	78	530	6.8
Guerin, New York	79	503	6.4

Rebounds

	G.	NO.	AVG.
Chamberlain, Philadelphia	79	2149	27.2
Russell, Boston	78	1868	23.9
Pettit, St. Louis	76	1540	20.3
Baylor, Los Angeles	73	1447	19.8
Howell, Detroit	77	1111	14.4

1961–62

Wilt Chamberlain's rookie performance, coming into the NBA and averaging nearly 38 ppg, was almost beyond belief. But what he did in his third season will likely never be duplicated. Chamberlain, who played all but eight possible minutes of the entire season and averaged 48.5 minutes per game, averaged 50.4 points per game, a full 12 points more than his NBA record set the previous season. On March 2, 1962, Chamberlain scored 100 points against the New York Knicks in Hershey, Pa., in a 169–147 triumph. Although 4,124 were in attendance, tens of thousands more would claim for decades afterward to have been there.

In another outstanding individual performance, Oscar Robertson of the Cincinnati Royals averaged a triple-double of 30.8 points, 12.5 rebounds and 11.4 assists per game.

Chicago had been added to the league as an expansion franchise, and the Packers' center, Walt Bellamy, won Rookie of the Year honors by averaging 31.6 ppg (second in the league behind Chamberlain) and 19.0 rebounds per game and led the league with a .519 shooting percentage.

While Chamberlain was setting records that would hold up for decades, the Celtics were busily continuing their dynasty, winning a record 60 games in an 80-game season. In contrast to Chamberlain's scoring feats, no Boston player appeared among the NBA's Top 10 in scoring. Boston and Philadelphia engaged in one of their legendary battles in the Eastern Division Finals, with Sam Jones hitting a jump shot with two seconds left in Game 7 to give the Celtics the win. St. Louis's run of Finals appearances ended when the Lakers won 54 games and advanced to the Finals against Boston. Boston came back from being down 2–1 and 3–2 in the series to win a fourth straight NBA title in dramatic fashion, 110–107 in overtime in Game 7 at Boston Garden.

Just two years earlier, Boston had blown out St. Louis in the seventh game of the NBA Finals. But in 1962, Frank Selvy of the Lakers had the chance to put Boston away on the parquet. With seconds remaining in Game 7 and the score tied, Selvy, a 29-year-old guard who had played in two All-Star Games, was being guarded by Cousy, who had left him momentarily to double-team West. When Hundley passed him the ball, Selvy had a good look at an eight-foot shot. But it bounced off the rim and the game went into overtime, where Boston prevailed.

"It was a fairly tough shot because I was almost on the baseline," Selvy said. "But I would trade all my points for that last basket."

NBA 1961-62

FINAL STANDINGS

Eastern Division

	W.	L.	PCT.
Boston	60	20	.750
Philadelphia	49	31	.613
Syracuse	41	39	.513
New York	29	51	.363

Western Division

	W.	L.	PCT.
Los Angeles	54	26	.675
Cincinnati	43	37	.538
Detroit	37	43	.463
St. Louis	29	51	.363
Chicago	18	62	.225

PLAYOFFS

Eastern Division Semifinals

Philadelphia 3, Syracuse 2
March 16—Philadelphia 110, Syracuse 103
March 18—Philadelphia 97, Syracuse 82
March 19—Syracuse 101, Philadelphia 100
March 20—Syracuse 106, Philadelphia 99
March 22—Philadelphia 121, Syracuse 104

Western Division Semifinals

Detroit 3, Cincinnati 1
March 16—Detroit 123, Cincinnati 122
March 17—Cincinnati 129, Detroit 107
March 18—Detroit 118, Cincinnati 107
March 20—Detroit 112, Cincinnati 111

Eastern Division Finals

Boston 4, Philadelphia 3
March 24—Boston 117, Philadelphia 89
March 27—Philadelphia 113, Boston 106
March 28—Boston 129, Philadelphia 114
March 31—Philadelphia 110, Boston 106
April 1—Boston 119, Philadelphia 104
April 3—Philadelphia 109, Boston 99
April 5—Boston 109, Philadelphia 107

Western Division Finals

Los Angeles 4, Detroit 2
March 24—Los Angeles 132, Detroit 108
March 25—Los Angeles 127, Detroit 112
March 27—Los Angeles 111, Detroit 106
March 29—Detroit 118, Los Angeles 117
March 31—Detroit 132, Los Angeles 125
April 3—Los Angeles 123, Detroit 117

NBA Finals

Boston 4, Los Angeles 3
April 7—Boston 122, Los Angeles 108
April 8—Los Angeles 129, Boston 122
April 10—Los Angeles 117, Boston 115
April 11—Boston 115, Los Angeles 103
April 14—Los Angeles 126, Boston 121
April 16—Boston 119, Los Angeles 105
April 18—Boston 110, Los Angeles 107 (OT)

INDIVIDUAL LEADERS

Scoring

	G.	FG	FT	PTS.	AVG.
Chamberlain, Philadelphia	80	1597	835	4029	50.4
Bellamy, Chicago	79	973	549	2495	31.6
Robertson, Cincinnati	79	866	700	2432	30.8
Pettit, St. Louis	78	867	695	2429	31.1
West, Los Angeles	75	799	712	2310	30.8
Guerin, New York	78	839	625	2303	29.5
Naulls, New York	75	747	383	1877	25.0
Baylor, Los Angeles	48	680	476	1836	38.3
Twyman, Cincinnati	80	739	353	1831	22.9
Hagan, St. Louis	77	701	362	1764	22.9

Field Goal Pct.
(Minimum 200 FG made)

	FGM	FGA	PCT.
Bellamy, Chicago	973	1875	.519
Chamberlain, Philadelphia	1597	3159	.506
Twyman, Cincinnati	739	1542	.479
Robertson, Cincinnati	866	1810	.478
Attles, Philadelphia	343	724	.474

Free Throw Pct.
(Minimum 200 FT made)

	FTM	FTA	PCT.
Schayes, Syracuse	286	319	.897
Naulls, New York	383	455	.842
Costello, Syracuse	247	295	.837
Ramsey, Boston	334	405	.825
Hagan, St. Louis	362	439	.825

Assists

	G.	NO.	AVG.
Robertson, Cincinnati	79	899	11.4
Rodgers, Philadelphia	80	643	8.0
Cousy, Boston	75	584	7.8
Guerin, New York	78	539	6.9
Shue, Detroit	80	465	5.8

Rebounds

	G.	NO.	AVG.
Chamberlain, Philadelphia	80	2052	25.7
Russell, Boston	76	1790	23.6
Bellamy, Chicago	79	1500	19.0
Pettit, St. Louis	78	1459	18.7
Kerr, Syracuse	80	1176	14.7

1962–63

Significant changes took place prior to the season. The Warriors, who had the league's top gate attraction in Chamberlain, moved to San Francisco and the Western Division. To compensate, Cincinnati, with Robertson, was moved to the East. The Chicago franchise changed its name from Packers to Zephyrs. Bob Cousy, now 34, announced before the season that it would be his final one. Exciting rookies like Zelmo Beaty, John Havlicek and Dave DeBusschere came into the league.

But some things didn't change. The Celtics didn't have a 20 ppg scorer, yet won 58 games and another Eastern title. The Lakers won 53 games and a second straight Western title. Chamberlain won another scoring title with 44.8 ppg and also won the rebounding category with 24.3 rpg. The Division Finals almost upstaged the NBA Finals, each going to a deciding seventh game. Boston belted Cincinnati 142–131 in the East's Game 7, while the Lakers held off a revived St. Louis team 115–100 to advance to the Finals. The Celtics helped Cousy go out on a high note by taking leads of 2–0 and 3–1 in the series before closing out the Lakers in six games, with the clincher coming in Los Angeles.

Red Auerbach was all about winning, and the Celtics did little else during the early 1960s. But Auerbach was never the most popular coach with opposing coaches and players due in part to his sideline manners and victory cigars.

"Anytime you're winning, you get criticism," Auerbach said. "Nothing instigates jealousy like winning."

One opposing player who didn't mind Auerbach's theatrics was Jerry West. "Red was outspoken," West said. "His sideline antics were funny. I happened to like him very much. When you talk to his ex-players, they all have great respect for him. I don't know many players who would tell you that about their former coaches."

NBA 1962-63

FINAL STANDINGS

Eastern Division

	W.	L.	PCT.
Boston	58	22	.725
Syracuse	48	32	.600
Cincinnati	42	38	.525
New York	21	59	.263

Western Division

	W.	L.	PCT.
Los Angeles	53	27	.663
St. Louis	48	32	.600
Detroit	34	46	.425
San Francisco	31	49	.388
Chicago	25	55	.313

PLAYOFFS

Eastern Division Semifinals

Cincinnati 3, Syracuse 2
March 19—Syracuse 123, Cincinnati 120
March 21—Cincinnati 133, Syracuse 115
March 23—Syracuse 121, Cincinnati 117
March 24—Cincinnati 125, Syracuse 118
March 26—Cincinnati 131, Syracuse 127 (OT)

Western Division Semifinals

St. Louis 3, Detroit 1
March 20—St. Louis 118, Detroit 99
March 22—St. Louis 122, Detroit 108
March 24—Detroit 107, St. Louis 103
March 26—St. Louis 104, Detroit 100

Eastern Division Finals

Boston 4, Cincinnati 3
March 28—Cincinnati 135, Boston 132
March 29—Boston 125, Cincinnati 102
March 31—Cincinnati 121, Boston 116
April 3—Boston 128, Cincinnati 110
April 6—Boston 125, Cincinnati 120
April 7—Cincinnati 109, Boston 99
April 10—Boston 142, Cincinnati 131

Western Division Finals

Los Angeles 4, St. Louis 3
March 31—Los Angeles 112, St. Louis 104
April 2—Los Angeles 101, St. Louis 99
April 4—St. Louis 125, Los Angeles 112
April 6—St. Louis 124, Los Angeles 114
April 7—Los Angeles 123, St. Louis 96
April 9—St. Louis 121, Los Angeles 113
April 11—Los Angeles 115, St. Louis 100

NBA Finals

Boston 4, Los Angeles 2
April 14—Boston 117, Los Angeles 114
April 16—Boston 113, Los Angeles 106
April 17—Los Angeles 119, Boston 99
April 19—Boston 108, Los Angeles 105
April 21—Los Angeles 126, Boston 119
April 24—Boston 112, Los Angeles 109

INDIVIDUAL LEADERS

Scoring

	G.	FG	FT	PTS.	AVG.
Chamberlain, San Francisco	80	1463	660	3586	44.8
Baylor, Los Angeles	80	1029	661	2719	34.0
Robertson, Cincinnati	80	825	614	2264	28.3
Pettit, St. Louis	79	778	685	2241	28.4
Bellamy, Chicago	80	840	553	2233	27.9
Howell, Detroit	79	637	519	1793	22.7
Guerin, New York	79	596	509	1701	21.5
Twyman, Cincinnati	80	641	304	1586	19.8
Greer, Syracuse	80	600	362	1562	19.5
Ohl, Detroit	80	636	275	1547	19.3

Field Goal Pct.
(Minimum 210 FG made)

	FGM	FGA	PCT.
Chamberlain, San Francisco	1463	2770	.528
Bellamy, Chicago	840	1595	.527
Robertson, Cincinnati	825	1593	.518
Howell, Detroit	637	1235	.516
Dischinger, Chicago	525	1026	.512

Free Throw Pct.
(Minimum 210 FT made)

	FTM	FTA	PCT.
Costello, Syracuse	288	327	.881
Guerin, New York	509	600	.848
Baylor, Los Angeles	661	790	.837
Heinsohn, Boston	340	407	.835
Greer, Syracuse	362	434	.834

Assists

	G.	NO.	AVG.
Rodgers, San Francisco	79	825	10.4
Robertson, Cincinnati	80	758	9.5
Cousy, Boston	76	515	6.8
Green, Chicago	73	422	5.8
Baylor, Los Angeles	80	386	4.8

Rebounds

	G.	NO.	AVG.
Chamberlain, San Francisco	80	1946	24.3
Russell, Boston	78	1843	23.6
Bellamy, Chicago	80	1309	16.4
Pettit, St. Louis	79	1191	15.1
Baylor, Los Angeles	80	1146	14.3

1963–64

This was an important transition year for the league and its top team. Maurice Podoloff, the only president the league had ever had, retired before the season began and was replaced by J. Walter Kennedy, who had earlier served as publicity director. Meanwhile, in Boston, the Celtics began a season for the first time since 1950 without Bob Cousy. In franchise shifts, the Chicago Zephyrs moved to Baltimore and became the new Baltimore Bullets, while the Syracuse Nats moved to Philadelphia, vacated by the Warriors a season earlier, and became the Philadelphia 76ers.

A pair of impressive rookie big men came into the league, Jerry Lucas (Cincinnati) and Nate Thurmond (San Francisco). Alex Hannum became coach at San Francisco, where he instilled a defensive philosophy in the Chamberlain-led team. The Warriors led the NBA by allowing just 102.6 ppg and won the West by two games over St. Louis. The Warriors fought off a spirited challenge from Pettit's Hawks to win the West Finals in seven games, but were no match for Boston's depth as the Celtics polished them off in five games for a sixth straight title.

NBA 1963-64

FINAL STANDINGS

Eastern Division

	W.	L.	PCT.
Boston	59	21	.738
Cincinnati	55	25	.688
Philadelphia	34	46	.425
New York	22	58	.275

Western Division

	W.	L.	PCT.
San Francisco	48	32	.600
St. Louis	46	34	.575
Los Angeles	42	38	.525
Baltimore	31	49	.388
Detroit	23	57	.288

PLAYOFFS

Eastern Division Semifinals

Cincinnati 3, Philadelphia 2
March 22—Cincinnati 127, Philadelphia 102
March 24—Philadelphia 122, Cincinnati 114
March 25—Cincinnati 101, Philadelphia 89
March 28—Philadelphia 129, Cincinnati 120
March 29—Cincinnati 130, Philadelphia 124

Western Division Semifinals

St. Louis 3, Los Angeles 2
March 21—St. Louis 115, Los Angeles 104
March 22—St. Louis 106, Los Angeles 90
March 25—Los Angeles 107, St. Louis 105
March 28—Los Angeles 97, St. Louis 88
March 30—St. Louis 121, Los Angeles 108

Eastern Division Finals

Boston 4, Cincinnati 1
March 31—Boston 103, Cincinnati 87
April 2—Boston 101, Cincinnati 90
April 5—Boston 102, Cincinnati 92
April 7—Cincinnati 102, Boston 93
April 9—Boston 109, Cincinnati 95

Western Division Finals

San Francisco 4, St. Louis 3
April 1—St. Louis 116, San Francisco 111
April 3—San Francisco 120, St. Louis 85
April 5—St. Louis 113, San Francisco 109
April 8—San Francisco 111, St. Louis 109
April 10—San Francisco 121, St. Louis 97
April 12—St. Louis 123, San Francisco 95
April 16—San Francisco 105, St. Louis 95

NBA Finals

Boston 4, San Francisco 1
April 18—Boston 108, San Francisco 96
April 20—Boston 124, San Francisco 101
April 22—San Francisco 115, Boston 91
April 24—Boston 98, San Francisco 95
April 26—Boston 105, San Francisco 99

INDIVIDUAL LEADERS

Scoring

	G.	FG	FT	PTS.	AVG.
Chamberlain, San Francisco	80	1204	540	2948	36.9
Robertson, Cincinnati	79	840	800	2480	31.4
Pettit, St. Louis	80	791	608	2190	27.4
Bellamy, Baltimore	80	811	537	2159	27.0
West, Los Angeles	72	740	584	2064	28.7
Baylor, Los Angeles	78	756	471	1983	25.4
Greer, Philadelphia	80	715	435	1865	23.3
Howell, Detroit	77	598	470	1666	21.6
Dischinger, Baltimore	80	604	454	1662	20.8
Havlicek, Boston	80	640	315	1595	19.9

Field Goal Pct.
(Minimum 210 FG made)

	FGM	FGA	PCT.
Lucas, Cincinnati	545	1035	.527
Chamberlain, San Francisco	1204	2298	.524
Bellamy, Baltimore	811	1582	.513
Dischinger, Baltimore	604	1217	.496
McGill, Bal.-N.Y.	456	937	.487

Free Throw Pct.
(Minimum 210 FT made)

	FTM	FTA	PCT.
Robertson, Cincinnati	800	938	.853
West, Los Angeles	584	702	.832
Greer, Philadelphia	435	525	.829
Heinsohn, Boston	283	342	.827
Guerin, N.Y.-St.L.	347	424	.818

Assists

	G.	NO.	AVG.
Robertson, Cincinnati	79	868	11.0
Rodgers, San Francisco	79	556	7.0
K. Jones, Boston	80	407	5.1
West, Los Angeles	72	403	5.6
Chamberlain, San Francisco	80	403	5.0

Rebounds

	G.	NO.	AVG.
Russell, Boston	78	1930	24.7
Chamberlain, San Francisco	80	1787	22.3
Lucas, Cincinnati	79	1375	17.4
Bellamy, Baltimore	80	1361	17.0
Pettit, St. Louis	80	1224	15.3

Boston's sixth consecutive championship was one of its easiest, and a question was starting to be asked: Would Boston ever lose again? The title streak drew comparisons to the New York Yankees' five straight from 1949 to 1953, adding prestige to the still young league. Auerbach basked in the titles.

"The thrill never goes from winning," he said. "But maybe the reasons change. First, it was just trying to win a title. Now it is a question of going down as the greatest team of all time. That stimulates you."

1964–65

In an effort to lessen the dominance of big men and keep the game open and moving, the NBA widened the foul lane from 12 to 16 feet. A major trade that took place at the NBA All-Star break would have far-reaching implications for years to come. Chamberlain, in the midst of his greatness at 28 years old, was dealt by the financially strapped San Francisco Warriors to the Philadelphia 76ers for Paul Neumann, Connie Dierking, Lee Shaffer and cash. The immediate results: San Francisco went from 48-32 the season before to 17-63, while Philadelphia improved from 34-46 to 40-40. More important, Chamberlain was back in the Celtics' division and would have to be dealt with even before the Finals.

Meanwhile, Celtics founder Walter Brown died in August 1964, putting more of the team's administrative load on Auerbach. Boston seemed unaffected, however, and broke its own league record with 62 victories despite the retirements of Frank Ramsey and Jim Loscutoff. The Lakers won the West with 49 wins as West (31.0) and Baylor (27.1) finished in the top five in the league in scoring. While the Lakers defeated Baltimore in six games in the West Finals, the East Finals between Boston and Philadelphia were a classic, with the home team winning each of the first six games. Boston won Game 7 by a point, with John Havlicek's deflection producing the famous "Havlicek stole the ball!" radio call from Celtics broadcaster Johnny Most. The Finals were less exciting, as Boston closed out the Lakers, who were without the injured Baylor, in five games.

The seventh game of the Eastern Division Finals in 1965 provided some hope for the rest of the league that the Celtics might be beaten one day soon. If Philadelphia had been able to convert in the last five seconds, the Celtics dynasty would have been halted at six straight NBA championships and Chamberlain and the 76ers might have begun their own dynasty.

But Havlicek deflected the inbounds pass of Hal Greer to Sam Jones, who dribbled out the five seconds and preserved the dynasty for another year. Of such momentous plays are titles won and lost, and for now the Celtics were still on top.

NBA 1964-65

FINAL STANDINGS

Eastern Division

	W.	L.	PCT.
Boston	62	18	.775
Cincinnati	48	32	.600
Philadelphia	40	40	.500
New York	31	49	.388

Western Division

	W.	L.	PCT.
Los Angeles	49	31	.613
St. Louis	45	35	.563
Baltimore	37	43	.463
Detroit	31	49	.388
San Francisco	17	63	.213

PLAYOFFS

Eastern Division Semifinals

Philadelphia 3, Cincinnati 1
March 24—Philadelphia 119, Cincinnati 117
March 26—Cincinnati 121, Philadelphia 120
March 28—Philadelphia 108, Cincinnati 94
March 31—Philadelphia 119, Cincinnati 112

Western Division Semifinals

Baltimore 3, St. Louis 1
March 24—Baltimore 108, St. Louis 105
March 26—St. Louis 129, Baltimore 105
March 27—Baltimore 131, St. Louis 99
March 30—Baltimore 109, St. Louis 103

Eastern Division Finals

Boston 4, Philadelphia 3
April 4—Boston 108, Philadelphia 98
April 6—Philadelphia 109, Boston 103
April 8—Boston 112, Philadelphia 94
April 9—Philadelphia 134, Boston 131 (OT)
April 11—Boston 114, Philadelphia 108
April 13—Philadelphia 112, Boston 106
April 15—Boston 110, Philadelphia 109

Western Division Finals

Los Angeles 4, Baltimore 2
April 3—Los Angeles 121, Baltimore 115
April 5—Los Angeles 118, Baltimore 115
April 7—Baltimore 122, Los Angeles 115
April 9—Baltimore 114, Los Angeles 112
April 11—Los Angeles 120, Baltimore 112
April 13—Los Angeles 117, Baltimore 115

NBA Finals

Boston 4, Los Angeles 1
April 18—Boston 142, Los Angeles 110
April 19—Boston 129, Los Angeles 123
April 21—Los Angeles 126, Boston 105
April 23—Boston 112, Los Angeles 99
April 25—Boston 129, Los Angeles 96

INDIVIDUAL LEADERS

Scoring

	G.	FG	FT	PTS.	AVG.
Chamberlain, S.F.-Phi.	73	1063	408	2534	34.7
West, Los Angeles	74	822	648	2292	31.0
Robertson, Cincinnati	75	807	665	2279	30.4
S. Jones, Boston	80	821	428	2070	25.9
Baylor, Los Angeles	74	763	483	2009	27.1
Bellamy, Baltimore	80	733	515	1981	24.8
Reed, New York	80	629	302	1560	19.5
Howell, Baltimore	80	515	504	1534	19.2
Dischinger, Detroit	80	568	320	1456	18.2
Ohl, Baltimore	77	568	284	1420	18.4

Field Goal Pct.
(Minimum 220 FG made)

	FGM	FGA	PCT.
Chamberlain, S.F.-Phi.	1063	2083	.510
Bellamy, Baltimore	733	1441	.509
Lucas, Cincinnati	558	1121	.498
West, Los Angeles	822	1655	.497
Howell, Baltimore	515	1040	.495

Free Throw Pct.
(Minimum 210 FT made)

	FTM	FTA	PCT.
Costello, Philadelphia	243	277	.877
Robertson, Cincinnati	665	793	.839
Komives, New York	212	254	.835
Smith, Cincinnati	284	342	.830
West, Los Angeles	648	789	.821

Assists

	G.	NO.	AVG.
Robertson, Cincinnati	75	861	11.5
Rodgers, San Francisco	79	565	7.2
K. Jones, Boston	78	437	5.6
Wilkens, St. Louis	78	431	5.5
Russell, Boston	78	410	5.3

Rebounds

	G.	NO.	AVG.
Russell, Boston	78	1878	24.1
Chamberlain, S.F.-Phi.	73	1673	22.9
Thurmond, San Francisco	77	1395	18.1
Lucas, Cincinnati	66	1321	20.0
Reed, New York	80	1175	14.7

1965-66

The Celtics had fought off the challenge of the 76ers in the previous year's Eastern Division Finals, but Philadelphia was ready to cause more problems for Boston this season. A rookie forward from North Carolina named Billy Cunningham made an immediate contribution, averaging 14.3 ppg and joining Chamberlain, Chet Walker and Lucious Jackson up front. Hal Greer and second-year man Wali Jones manned the backcourt.

During the season, the 76ers beat the Celtics six times in 10 meetings and eventually won 55 games, taking the Eastern Division title away from the Celtics for the first time in 10 years. Chamberlain led the league in scoring for what would prove to be the last time, averaging 33.5 ppg and becoming the NBA's all-time leading scorer, passing Bob Pettit.

For the playoffs, though, the Celtics had added

incentive: Auerbach had announced that he would retire from the bench to the front office after the end of the season. Boston recovered from a 2–1 deficit to defeat Cincinnati in five games, then moved on to play Philadelphia, which had been resting for two weeks. The 76ers proved rusty, and the Celtics disposed of them in five games, costing Coach Dolph Schayes his job. Mean-

while, the Lakers sweated out a seven-game Western Finals series over the Hawks to advance to meet Boston. LA took the opener in overtime in Boston, but the Celtics won the next three and, though the Lakers fought back to tie the series, Boston gave Auerbach his desired send-off, his eighth straight NBA title.

NBA 1965-66

FINAL STANDINGS

Eastern Division

	W.	L.	PCT.
Philadelphia	55	25	.688
Boston	54	26	.675
Cincinnati	45	35	.563
New York	30	50	.375

Western Division

	W.	L.	PCT.
Los Angeles	45	35	.563
Baltimore	38	42	.475
St. Louis	36	44	.450
San Francisco	35	45	.438
Detroit	22	58	.275

PLAYOFFS

Eastern Division Semifinals

Boston 3, Cincinnati 2
March 23—Cincinnati 107, Boston 103
March 26—Boston 132, Cincinnati 125
March 27—Cincinnati 113, Boston 107
March 30—Boston 120, Cincinnati 103
April 1—Boston 112, Cincinnati 103

Western Division Semifinals

St. Louis 3, Baltimore 0
March 24—St. Louis 113, Baltimore 111
March 27—St. Louis 105, Baltimore 100
March 30—St. Louis 121, Baltimore 112

Eastern Division Finals

Boston 4, Philadelphia 1
April 3—Boston 115, Philadelphia 96
April 6—Boston 114, Philadelphia 93
April 7—Philadelphia 111, Boston 105
April 10—Boston 114, Philadelphia 108 (OT)
April 12—Boston 120, Philadelphia 112

Western Division Finals

Los Angeles 4, St. Louis 3
April 1—Los Angeles 129, St. Louis 106
April 3—Los Angeles 125, St. Louis 116
April 6—St. Louis 120, Los Angeles 113
April 9—Los Angeles 107, St. Louis 95
April 10—St. Louis 112, Los Angeles 100
April 13—St. Louis 131, Los Angeles 127
April 15—Los Angeles 130, St. Louis 121

NBA Finals

Boston 4, Los Angeles 3
April 17—Los Angeles 133, Boston 129 (OT)
April 19—Boston 129, Los Angeles 109
April 20—Boston 120, Los Angeles 106
April 22—Boston 122, Los Angeles 117
April 24—Los Angeles 121, Boston 117
April 26—Los Angeles 123, Boston 115
April 28—Boston 95, Los Angeles 93

INDIVIDUAL LEADERS

Scoring

	G.	FG	FT	PTS.	AVG.
Chamberlain, Phila.	79	1074	501	2649	33.5
West, Los Angeles	79	818	840	2476	31.3
Robertson, Cincinnati	76	818	742	2378	31.3
Barry, San Francisco	80	745	569	2059	25.7
Bellamy, Bal.-N.Y.	80	695	430	1820	22.8
Greer, Philadelphia	80	703	413	1819	22.7
Barnett, New York	75	631	467	1729	23.1
Lucas, Cincinnati	79	690	317	1697	21.5
Beaty, St. Louis	80	616	424	1656	20.7
S. Jones, Boston	67	626	325	1577	23.5

Field Goal Pct.
(Minimum 210 FG made)

	FGM	FGA	PCT.
Chamberlain, Philadelphia	1074	1990	.540
Green, N.Y.-Bal.	358	668	.536
Bellamy, Bal.-N.Y.	695	1373	.506
Attles, San Francisco	364	724	.503
Hairston, Cincinnati	398	814	.489

Free Throw Pct.
(Minimum 210 FT made)

	FTM	FTA	PCT.
Siegfried, Boston	274	311	.881
Barry, San Francisco	569	660	.862
Komives, New York	241	280	.861
West, Los Angeles	840	977	.860
Smith, Cincinnati	408	480	.850

Assists

	G.	NO.	AVG.
Robertson, Cincinnati	76	847	11.1
Rodgers, San Francisco	79	846	10.7
K. Jones, Boston	80	503	6.3
West, Los Angeles	79	480	6.1
Wilkens, St. Louis	69	429	6.2

Rebounds

	G.	NO.	AVG.
Chamberlain, Philadelphia	79	1943	24.6
Russell, Boston	78	1779	22.8
Lucas, Cincinnati	79	1668	21.1
Thurmond, San Francisco	73	1312	18.0
Bellamy, Bal.-N.Y.	80	1254	15.7

In addition to having some of the best players in the world at the time, Auerbach had beaten opponents for years with mind games, always knowing what buttons to push to frustrate or even infuriate the opposition. When the Lakers took Game 1 of the 1966 Finals, Auerbach pulled out a trump card, announcing that Bill Russell would succeed him as head coach. Russell would become the first black head coach in a major American sports league.

The bombshell announcement had the desired effect: the inspired Celtics went on to capture an eighth straight NBA Championship, the ninth for Boston in 10 seasons.

1966-67

The season would prove to be a watershed year for the NBA. Boston's string of eight championships would come to an end, and another club would set a new standard for victories in one season. Philadelphia, which had hired veteran Alex Hannum as coach, got off to a 46-4 start and never looked back, posting an NBA-best 68-13 record. Walker and Cunningham scored more as Chamberlain concentrated on rebounding and defense. Chamberlain still finished third in scoring (24.1), but he also led the league in rebounding (24.2) and was third in assists (7.8).

The Chicago Bulls were added as an expansion franchise, and the Baltimore Bullets were switched to the Eastern Division. With two five-team divisions, the playoffs were changed so that the division winners no longer received byes and instead played a First Round series against the fourth-place team. Philadelphia polished off Cincinnati in the First Round, then crushed

NBA 1966-67

FINAL STANDINGS

Eastern Division

	W.	L.	PCT.
Philadelphia	68	13	.840
Boston	60	21	.741
Cincinnati	39	42	.481
New York	36	45	.444
Baltimore	20	61	.247

Western Division

	W.	L.	PCT.
San Francisco	44	37	.543
St. Louis	39	42	.481
Los Angeles	36	45	.444
Chicago	33	48	.407
Detroit	30	51	.370

PLAYOFFS

Eastern Division Semifinals

Boston 3, New York 1
March 21—Boston 140, New York 110
March 25—Boston 115, New York 108
March 26—New York 123, Boston 112
March 28—Boston 118, New York 109

Philadelphia 3, Cincinnati 1
March 21—Cincinnati 120, Philadelphia 116
March 22—Philadelphia 123, Cincinnati 102
March 24—Philadelphia 121, Cincinnati 106
March 25—Philadelphia 112, Cincinnati 94

Western Division Semifinals

St. Louis 3, Chicago 0
March 21—St. Louis 114, Chicago 100
March 23—St. Louis 113, Chicago 107
March 25—St. Louis 119, Chicago 106

San Francisco 3, Los Angeles 0
March 21—San Francisco 124, Los Angeles 108
March 23—San Francisco 113, Los Angeles 102
March 26—San Francisco 122, Los Angeles 115

Eastern Division Finals

Philadelphia 4, Boston 1
March 31—Philadelphia 127, Boston 113
April 2—Philadelphia 107, Boston 102
April 5—Philadelphia 115, Boston 104
April 9—Boston 121, Philadelphia 117
April 11—Philadelphia 140, Boston 116

Western Division Finals

San Francisco 4, St. Louis 2
March 30—San Francisco 117, St. Louis 115
April 1—San Francisco 143, St. Louis 136
April 5—St. Louis 115, San Francisco 109
April 8—St. Louis 109, San Francisco 104
April 10—San Francisco 123, St. Louis 102
April 12—San Francisco 112, St. Louis 107

NBA Finals

Philadelphia 4, San Francisco 2
April 14—Philadelphia 141, San Francisco 135 (OT)
April 16—Philadelphia 126, San Francisco 95
April 18—San Francisco 130, Philadelphia 124
April 20—Philadelphia 122, San Francisco 108
April 23—San Francisco 117, Philadelphia 109
April 24—Philadelphia 125, San Francisco 122

INDIVIDUAL LEADERS

Scoring

	G.	FG	FT	PTS.	AVG.
Barry, San Francisco	78	1011	753	2775	35.6
Robertson, Cincinnati	79	838	736	2412	30.5
Chamberlain, Philadelphia	81	785	386	1956	24.1
West, Los Angeles	66	645	602	1892	28.7
Baylor, Los Angeles	70	711	440	1862	26.6
Greer, Philadelphia	80	699	367	1765	22.1
Havlicek, Boston	81	684	365	1733	21.4
Reed, New York	78	635	358	1628	20.9
Howell, Boston	81	636	349	1621	20.0
Bing, Detroit	80	664	273	1601	20.0

Field Goal Pct.
(Minimum 220 FG made)

	FGM	FGA	PCT.
Chamberlain, Philadelphia	785	1150	.683
Bellamy, New York	565	1084	.521
Howell, Boston	636	1242	.512
Robertson, Cincinnati	838	1699	.493
Reed, New York	635	1298	.489

Free Throw Pct.
(Minimum 220 FT made)

	FTM	FTA	PCT.
Smith, Cincinnati	343	380	.903
Barry, San Francisco	753	852	.884
West, Los Angeles	602	686	.878
Robertson, Cincinnati	736	843	.873
S. Jones, Boston	318	371	.857

Assists

	G.	NO.	AVG.
Rodgers, Chicago	81	908	11.2
Robertson, Cincinnati	79	845	10.7
Chamberlain, Philadelphia	81	630	7.8
Russell, Boston	81	472	5.8
West, Los Angeles	66	447	6.8

Rebounds

	G.	NO.	AVG.
Chamberlain, Philadelphia	81	1957	24.2
Russell, Boston	81	1700	21.0
Lucas, Cincinnati	81	1547	19.1
Thurmond, San Francisco	65	1382	21.3
Bridges, St. Louis	79	1190	15.1

the Russell-coached Celtics in five games in the Eastern Division Finals. After the Game 5 win in Philadelphia, 76ers fans rushed the court in jubilation, but Chamberlain and the 76ers knew the big prize was still ahead. The 76ers captured the title in six games over San Francisco, which featured the NBA's new scoring leader, Rick Barry (35.6). Chamberlain had his first championship in the year he relinquished the scoring title.

After so many years of failing to beat the Celtics, the 76ers needed a nearly flawless season finally to topple the champions.

"The whole season was just magical, something where a team played almost perfect basketball," said guard Wali Jones. "We played with a team/family concept."

Even the Celtics had to admit the 76ers were better. "They're playing the same game we've played for the last nine years," said K. C. Jones, who had known nothing but NBA titles in his first eight seasons as a player. "In other words, team ball."

1967–68

The NBA greeted two more expansion franchises, Seattle and San Diego, which were installed in the Western Division while Detroit moved to the East. The NBA was now a 12-team league and played an 82-game schedule for the first time.

The prosperity that the professional basketball league was enjoying was not lost on several outside observers, who figured the time was right for a second, competing professional league. Thus, the ABA was born, with 11 teams playing a 78-game schedule. Major cities that had been unable to attract an NBA franchise like Dallas, Denver, Houston and Oakland now claimed

pro teams in the new league. The league gained credibility with the naming of NBA legend George Mikan as its first commissioner and with NBA star Rick Barry's decision to sign with the new Oakland franchise.

In the NBA, Detroit's Dave Bing became the first guard to lead the NBA in scoring since 1948. But the real story was the return of the Celtics, who came back from a 3–1 deficit to win the Eastern Finals over Philadelphia, then defeated the Lakers to take the NBA Championship back after a one-year hiatus. Russell had proven a success as a coach—thanks largely to the presence of Russell the player out on the court.

NBA 1967-68

FINAL STANDINGS

Eastern Division

	W.	L.	PCT.
Philadelphia	62	20	.756
Boston	54	28	.659
New York	43	39	.524
Detroit	40	42	.488
Cincinnati	39	43	.476
Baltimore	36	46	.439

Western Division

	W.	L.	PCT.
St. Louis	56	26	.683
Los Angeles	52	30	.634
San Francisco	43	39	.524
Chicago	29	53	.354
Seattle	23	59	.280
San Diego	15	67	.183

PLAYOFFS

Eastern Division Semifinals

Boston 4, Detroit 2
March 24—Boston 123, Detroit 116
March 25—Detroit 126, Boston 116
March 27—Detroit 109, Boston 98
March 28—Boston 135, Detroit 110
March 31—Boston 110, Detroit 96
April 1—Boston 111, Detroit 103

Philadelphia 4, New York 2
March 22—Philadelphia 118, New York 110
March 23—New York 128, Philadelphia 117
March 27—Philadelphia 138, New York 132 (2OT)
March 30—New York 107, Philadelphia 98
March 31—Philadelphia 123, New York 105
April 1—Philadelphia 113, New York 97

Western Division Semifinals

San Francisco 4, St. Louis 2
March 22—San Francisco 111, St. Louis 106
March 23—St. Louis 111, San Francisco 103
March 26—San Francisco 124, St. Louis 109
March 29—San Francisco 108, St. Louis 107
March 31—St. Louis 129, San Francisco 103
April 2—San Francisco 111, St. Louis 106

Los Angeles 4, Chicago 1
March 24—Los Angeles 109, Chicago 101
March 25—Los Angeles 111, Chicago 106
March 27—Chicago 104, Los Angeles 98
March 29—Los Angeles 93, Chicago 87
March 31—Los Angeles 122, Chicago 99

Eastern Division Finals

Boston 4, Philadelphia 3
April 5—Boston 127, Philadelphia 118
April 10—Philadelphia 115, Boston 106
April 11—Philadelphia 122, Boston 114
April 14—Philadelphia 110, Boston 105
April 15—Boston 122, Philadelphia 104
April 17—Boston 114, Philadelphia 106
April 19—Boston 100, Philadelphia 96

Western Division Finals

Los Angeles 4, San Francisco 0
April 5—Los Angeles 133, San Francisco 105
April 10—Los Angeles 115, San Francisco 112
April 11—Los Angeles 128, San Francisco 124
April 13—Los Angeles 106, San Francisco 100

NBA Finals

Boston 4, Los Angeles 2
April 21—Boston 107, Los Angeles 101
April 24—Los Angeles 123, Boston 113
April 26—Boston 127, Los Angeles 119
April 28—Los Angeles 118, Boston 105
April 30—Boston 120, Los Angeles 117 (OT)
May 2—Boston 124, Los Angeles 109

INDIVIDUAL LEADERS

Scoring

	G.	FG	FT	PTS.	AVG.
Bing, Detroit	79	835	472	2142	27.1
Baylor, Los Angeles	77	757	488	2002	26.0
Chamberlain, Philadelphia	82	819	354	1992	24.3
Monroe, Baltimore	82	742	507	1991	24.3
Greer, Philadelphia	82	777	422	1976	24.1
Robertson, Cincinnati	65	660	576	1896	29.2
Hazzard, Seattle	79	733	428	1894	24.0
Lucas, Cincinnati	82	707	346	1760	21.5
Beaty, St. Louis	82	639	455	1733	21.1
LaRusso, San Francisco	79	602	522	1726	21.8

Field Goal Pct.
(Minimum 220 FG made)

	FGM	FGA	PCT.
Chamberlain, Philadelphia	819	1377	.595
Bellamy, New York	511	944	.541
Lucas, Cincinnati	707	1361	.519
West, Los Angeles	476	926	.514
Chappell, Cin.-Det.	235	458	.513

Free Throw Pct.
(Minimum 220 FT made)

	FTM	FTA	PCT.
Robertson, Cincinnati	576	660	.873
Siegfried, Boston	236	272	.868
Gambee, San Diego	321	379	.847
Hetzel, San Francisco	395	474	.833
Smith, Cincinnati	320	386	.829

Assists

	G.	NO.	AVG.
Chamberlain, Philadelphia	82	702	8.6
Wilkens, St. Louis	82	679	8.3
Robertson, Cincinnati	65	633	9.7
Bing, Detroit	79	509	6.4
Hazzard, Seattle	79	493	6.2

Rebounds

	G.	NO.	AVG.
Chamberlain, Philadelphia	82	1952	23.8
Lucas, Cincinnati	82	1560	19.0
Russell, Boston	78	1451	18.6
C. Lee, San Francisco	82	1141	13.9
Thurmond, San Francisco	51	1121	22.0

Bailey Howell, a 6-7, 220-pound forward who was a five-time All-Star nearing the end of his career, arrived in Boston just in time to see the Celtics' eight-year reign atop the NBA end. But he was determined to bring a title back to Boston after Philadelphia's triumph the previous year.

"Everywhere we went, especially in Philadelphia, they had a chant: 'Boston's dead. Boston's dead. The dynasty is over,'" Howell said. "Everywhere we went, the fans were real vocal. But it just made you more determined, really. It helped you to play. When you get some help like that from opposing fans, it's really a lift."

1968-69

The Knicks had long been a league doormat, making the playoffs just once from 1956 to 1966. But a couple of interesting developments had occurred in New York during the 1967–68 season that would have an impact down the road. Red Holzman, the former Hawks coach in Milwaukee and St. Louis, replaced Dick McGuire as Knicks coach in midseason and took the 15-22 Knicks to a 28-17 mark the rest of the 1967–68 season. Rhodes Scholar Bill Bradley of Princeton, Walt Frazier of Southern Illinois and Phil Jackson of North Dakota all made their rookie debuts. And in December the Knicks made another important addition, obtaining Dave DeBusschere from Detroit for Walt Bellamy and Howie Komives.

But attention was focused on a much bigger trade, as Wilt Chamberlain went to the Lakers for Jerry Chambers, Archie Clark and Darrall Imhoff prior to the 1968–69 season. Lakers owner Jack Kent Cooke figured the addition of Chamberlain to the tandem of West and Baylor would surely bring him a championship in the 14-team league, which had welcomed Milwaukee and Phoenix as expansion franchises. But it wasn't to be, at least not right away. The Celtics, widely written off due to advancing age, won just 48 games in the regular season, finishing fourth in the East. But they dumped Philadelphia, took the playoff-neophyte Knicks in six games and stunned the basketball world by pulling out one last championship, defeating the Lakers in seven games—the finale a two-point win in Los Angeles, as hundreds of balloons that had been held in netting near the ceiling in anticipation of a Lakers victory celebration never got a chance to be unleashed. It marked the Celtics' 11th championship in 13 seasons.

Two impressive frontcourtmen made their debuts in 1968: Elvin Hayes and Wes Unseld. Hayes, a powerfully built forward for the San Diego Rockets, won the league scoring title as a rookie with 28.4 points and also averaged 17.1 rebounds. Unseld, the second pick (after Hayes) in the 1968 NBA Draft by Baltimore, became only the second player in NBA history to win both the Most Valuable Player and Rookie of the Year awards simultaneously, following in Chamberlain's footsteps. Unseld averaged 13.8 ppg and was second to Chamberlain with 18.2 rpg.

NBA 1968-69

FINAL STANDINGS

Eastern Division

	W.	L.	PCT.
Baltimore	57	25	.695
Philadelphia	55	27	.671
New York	54	28	.659
Boston	48	34	.585
Cincinnati	41	41	.500
Detroit	32	50	.390
Milwaukee	27	55	.329

Western Division

	W.	L.	PCT.
Los Angeles	55	27	.671
Atlanta	48	34	.585
San Francisco	41	41	.500
San Diego	37	45	.451
Chicago	33	49	.402
Seattle	30	52	.366
Phoenix	16	66	.195

INDIVIDUAL LEADERS

Scoring

	G.	FG	FT	PTS.	AVG.
Hayes, San Diego	82	930	467	2327	28.4
Monroe, Baltimore	80	809	447	2065	25.8
Cunningham, Philadelphia	82	739	556	2034	24.8
Rule, Seattle	82	776	413	1965	24.0
Robertson, Cincinnati	79	656	643	1955	24.7
Goodrich, Phoenix	81	718	495	1931	23.8
Greer, Philadelphia	82	732	432	1896	23.1
Baylor, Los Angeles	76	730	421	1881	24.8
Wilkens, Seattle	82	644	547	1835	22.4
Kojis, San Diego	81	687	446	1820	22.5

Field Goal Pct.
(Minimum 230 FG made)

	FGM	FGA	PCT.
Chamberlain, Los Angeles	641	1099	.583
Lucas, Cincinnati	555	1007	.551
Reed, New York	704	1351	.521
Dischinger, Detroit	264	513	.515
Bellamy, NY-Det.	563	1103	.510

Free Throw Pct.
(Minimum 230 FT made)

	FTM	FTA	PCT.
Siegfried, Boston	336	389	.864
Mullins, San Francisco	381	452	.843
McGlocklin, Milwaukee	246	292	.842
Robinson, Chi.-Mil.	412	491	.839
Robertson, Cincinnati	643	767	.838

Assists

	G.	NO.	AVG.
Robertson, Cincinnati	79	772	9.8
Wilkens, Seattle	82	674	8.2
Frazier, New York	80	635	7.9
Rodgers, Milwaukee	81	561	6.9
Bing, Detroit	77	546	7.1

Rebounds

	G.	NO.	AVG.
Chamberlain, Los Angeles	81	1712	21.1
Unseld, Baltimore	82	1491	18.2
Russell, Boston	77	1484	19.3
Hayes, San Diego	82	1406	17.1
Thurmond, San Francisco	71	1402	19.7

PLAYOFFS

Eastern Division Semifinals

Boston 4, Philadelphia 1
March 26—Boston 114, Philadelphia 100
March 28—Boston 134, Philadelphia 103
March 30—Boston 125, Philadelphia 118
April 1—Philadelphia 119, Boston 116
April 4—Boston 93, Philadelphia 90

New York 4, Baltimore 0
March 27—New York 113, Baltimore 101
March 29—New York 107, Baltimore 91
March 30—New York 119, Baltimore 116
April 2—New York 115, Baltimore 108

Western Division Semifinals

Atlanta 4, San Diego 2
March 27—Atlanta 107, San Diego 98
March 29—Atlanta 116, San Diego 114
April 1—San Diego 104, Atlanta 97
April 4—San Diego 114, Atlanta 112
April 6—Atlanta 112, San Diego 101
April 7—Atlanta 108, San Diego 106

Los Angeles 4, San Francisco 2
March 26—San Francisco 99, Los Angeles 94
March 28—San Francisco 107, Los Angeles 101
March 31—Los Angeles 115, San Francisco 98
April 2—Los Angeles 103, San Francisco 88
April 4—Los Angeles 103, San Francisco 98
April 5—Los Angeles 118, San Francisco 78

Eastern Division Finals

Boston 4, New York 2
April 6—Boston 108, New York 100
April 9—Boston 112, New York 97
April 10—New York 101, Boston 91
April 13—Boston 97, New York 96
April 14—New York 112, Boston 104
April 18—Boston 106, New York 105

Western Division Finals

Los Angeles 4, Atlanta 1
April 11—Los Angeles 95, Atlanta 93
April 13—Los Angeles 104, Atlanta 102
April 15—Atlanta 99, Los Angeles 86
April 17—Los Angeles 100, Atlanta 85
April 20—Los Angeles 104, Atlanta 96

NBA Finals

Boston 4, Los Angeles 3
April 23—Los Angeles 120, Boston 118
April 25—Los Angeles 118, Boston 112
April 27—Boston 111, Los Angeles 105
April 29—Boston 89, Los Angeles 88
May 1—Los Angeles 117, Boston 104
May 3—Boston 99, Los Angeles 90
May 5—Boston 108, Los Angeles 106

1969–70

The Celtic dynasty was finally over. Russell retired as player and coach after the 1969 championship, and Sam Jones also retired, K. C. Jones having preceded him two years earlier. The new team to beat in the East was the New York Knicks, who served notice by winning a league-record 18 straight games early in the season. Willis Reed, DeBusschere, Bradley, Frazier, Cazzie Russell and Dick Barnett played as a team on both ends of the floor, no one player dominating the spotlight. The other team to be reckoned with in the East was Milwaukee, which catapulted to 56 wins in just its second season with the addition of 7-2 rookie center Kareem Abdul-Jabbar, then called Lew Alcindor.

New York was extended to seven games in the Eastern Semifinals by Baltimore before advancing, but had a much easier time with Milwaukee, ousting the Bucks in five games. In the West, Jerry West had won the league scoring title (31.2) almost out of necessity as Chamberlain hurt his knee nine games into the season and didn't return until three games remained. As a result Atlanta won the division by two games over the Lakers. But with Chamberlain back for the playoffs, Los Angeles swept the Hawks in four straight to meet the Knicks in the Finals. The first six games were classic battles, with the Knicks winning one, then the Lakers tying the series, until a Game 7 loomed. The Knicks, with an emotional boost from their injured captain, Reed, won to capture New York's first NBA title in 24 years in the league.

NBA 1969-70

FINAL STANDINGS

Eastern Division

	W.	L.	PCT.
New York	60	22	.732
Milwaukee	56	26	.683
Baltimore	50	32	.610
Philadelphia	42	40	.512
Cincinnati	36	46	.439
Boston	34	48	.415
Detroit	31	51	.378

Western Division

	W.	L.	PCT.
Atlanta	48	34	.585
Los Angeles	46	36	.561
Chicago	39	43	.476
Phoenix	39	43	.476
Seattle	36	46	.439
San Francisco	30	52	.366
San Diego	27	55	.329

PLAYOFFS

Eastern Division Semifinals

Milwaukee 4, Philadelphia 1
March 25—Milwaukee 125, Philadelphia 118
March 27—Philadelphia 112, Milwaukee 105
March 30—Milwaukee 156, Philadelphia 120
April 1—Milwaukee 118, Philadelphia 111
April 3—Milwaukee 115, Philadelphia 106

New York 4, Baltimore 3
March 26—New York 120, Baltimore 117 (2OT)
March 27—New York 106, Baltimore 99
March 29—Baltimore 127, New York 113
March 31—Baltimore 102, New York 92
April 2—New York 101, Baltimore 80
April 5—Baltimore 96, New York 87
April 6—New York 127, Baltimore 114

Western Division Semifinals

Atlanta 4, Chicago 1
March 25—Atlanta 129, Chicago 111
March 28—Atlanta 124, Chicago 104
March 31—Atlanta 106, Chicago 101
April 3—Chicago 131, Atlanta 120
April 5—Atlanta 113, Chicago 107

Los Angeles 4, Phoenix 3
March 25—Los Angeles 128, Phoenix 112
March 29—Phoenix 114, Los Angeles 101
April 2—Phoenix 112, Los Angeles 98
April 4—Phoenix 112, Los Angeles 102
April 5—Los Angeles 138, Phoenix 121
April 7—Los Angeles 104, Phoenix 93
April 9—Los Angeles 129, Phoenix 94

Eastern Division Finals

New York 4, Milwaukee 1
April 11—New York 110, Milwaukee 102
April 13—New York 112, Milwaukee 111
April 17—Milwaukee 101, New York 96
April 19—New York 117, Milwaukee 105
April 20—New York 132, Milwaukee 96

Western Division Finals

Los Angeles 4, Atlanta 0
April 12—Los Angeles 119, Atlanta 115
April 14—Los Angeles 105, Atlanta 94
April 16—Los Angeles 115, Atlanta 114 (OT)
April 19—Los Angeles 133, Atlanta 114

NBA Finals

New York 4, Los Angeles 3
April 24—New York 124, Los Angeles 112
April 27—Los Angeles 105, New York 103
April 29—New York 111, Los Angeles 108 (OT)
May 1—Los Angeles 121, New York 115 (OT)
May 4—New York 107, Los Angeles 100
May 6—Los Angeles 135, New York 113
May 8—New York 113, Los Angeles 99

INDIVIDUAL LEADERS

Scoring

	G.	FG	FT	PTS.	AVG.
West, Los Angeles	74	831	647	2309	31.2
Alcindor, Milwaukee	82	938	485	2361	28.8
Hayes, San Diego	82	914	428	2256	27.5
Cunningham, Philadelphia	81	802	510	2114	26.1
Hudson, Atlanta	80	830	371	2031	25.4
Hawkins, Phoenix	81	709	577	1995	24.6
Rule, Seattle	80	789	387	1965	24.6
Havlicek, Boston	81	736	488	1960	24.2
Monroe, Baltimore	82	695	532	1922	23.4
Bing, Detroit	70	575	454	1604	22.9

Field Goal Pct.
(Minimum 700 Attempts in 70 Games)

	FGM	FGA	PCT.
Green, Cincinnati	481	860	.559
Imhoff, Philadelphia	430	796	.540
Hudson, Atlanta	830	1564	.531
McGlocklin, Milwaukee	639	1206	.530
Snyder, Pho.-Sea.	456	863	.528

Free Throw Pct.
(Minimum 300 Attempts in 70 Games)

	FTM	FTA	PCT.
Robinson, Milwaukee	439	489	.898
Walker, Chicago	483	568	.850
Mullins, San Francisco	320	378	.847
Havlicek, Boston	488	578	.844
Love, Chicago	442	525	.842

Assists
(Minimum 70 games)

	G.	NO.	AVG.
Wilkens, Seattle	75	683	9.1
Frazier, New York	77	629	8.2
Haskins, Chicago	82	624	7.6
Goodrich, Phoenix	81	605	7.5
West, Los Angeles	74	554	7.5

Rebounds
(Minimum 70 games)

	G.	NO.	AVG.
Hayes, San Diego	82	1386	16.9
Unseld, Baltimore	82	1370	16.7
Alcindor, Milwaukee	82	1190	14.5
Bridges, Atlanta	82	1181	14.4
Johnson, Baltimore	78	1086	13.9

The events of the 1970 NBA Finals remain indelibly etched in the memories of those who watched, while others latched on to them the way youngsters memorize tales of yore told by family elders. Reed, until he tripped and tore a leg muscle in Game 5, had been having a marvelous Finals, dominating the injury-slowed Chamberlain. The Knicks scrambled with undersized players against Chamberlain and hung on to win that game, but with Reed out of Game 6, Chamberlain poured in 45 points to tie the series.

The Knicks left the locker room before Game 7 in New York not knowing if Reed would be able to play. Just before tip-off, Reed hobbled through the tunnel and onto the floor of Madison Square Garden. The fans erupted, Reed scored New York's first two baskets and the inspired Knicks went on to a 113–99 victory.

"There isn't a day in my life that people don't remind me of that game," Reed said years afterward.

1970–71

The new season brought with it three expansion teams in Buffalo, Cleveland and Portland and a new wrinkle—the advent of four divisions, two in each newly formed conference. In 1965 nine teams had played 360 games in a league with 108 players. Just five years later, the NBA season opened with 17 teams playing 697 games in a 204-player league.

Abdul-Jabbar ruled the NBA with grace uncommon in a seven-footer. His sky-hook had become the most devastating weapon in the game, and he used it to lead the league in scoring (31.7 ppg) and also win the Most Valuable Player Award for the first time. Abdul-Jabbar was surrounded by a group of quality teammates, with Greg Smith and Bob Dandridge at forward and Lucius Allen and Jon McGlocklin assisting Oscar Robertson at guard. During his career, Robertson had led the NBA in scoring and in assists and had won the Rookie of the Year and MVP awards, but he had never won an NBA title, and, at 32, he knew the time was now.

Milwaukee won a league-high 66 games, brushed by San Francisco and Los Angeles in five games each in the Western Conference Playoffs, then prepared for the Finals. Baltimore surprised many by defeating New York in a slugfest seven-game series in the Eastern Conference Finals, but Unseld, Earl Monroe and Gus Johnson all sustained injuries during the series, and the Bucks swept to the championship in four straight, only the second Finals sweep in NBA history.

Larry Costello had retired as a player after the 1968 season and was hired to bring along a young Milwaukee Bucks expansion team. But all that changed when the Bucks signed Kareem Abdul-Jabbar. Sensing that an Abdul-Jabbar-led team could contend, Bucks management went out and traded for veterans Oscar Robertson, Lucius Allen and Bob Boozer. The group clicked almost immediately, due in part to the single-mindedness shared by Costello, Robertson and Abdul-Jabbar.

"Larry, Oscar and I have the same way about us," Abdul-Jabbar said. "We agree that being as efficient as possible cuts down on our chances for errors."

In 1971 Milwaukee avoided most errors, winning 66 games and going 12-2 in the playoffs on its way to the NBA title.

NBA 1970-71

FINAL STANDINGS

Eastern Conference

Atlantic Division

	W.	L.	PCT.
New York	52	30	.634
Philadelphia	47	35	.573
Boston	44	38	.537
Buffalo	22	60	.268

Central Division

	W.	L.	PCT.
Baltimore	42	40	.512
Atlanta	36	46	.439
Cincinnati	33	49	.402
Cleveland	15	67	.183

Western Conference

Midwest Division

	W.	L.	PCT.
Milwaukee	66	16	.805
Chicago	51	31	.622
Phoenix	48	34	.585
Detroit	45	37	.549

Pacific Division

	W.	L.	PCT.
Los Angeles	48	34	.585
San Francisco	41	41	.500
San Diego	40	42	.488
Seattle	38	44	.463
Portland	29	53	.354

PLAYOFFS

Eastern Conference Semifinals

New York 4, Atlanta 1
March 25—New York 112, Atlanta 101
March 27—Atlanta 113, New York 104
March 28—New York 110, Atlanta 95
March 30—New York 113, Atlanta 107
April 1—New York 111, Atlanta 107

Baltimore 4, Philadelphia 3
March 24—Philadelphia 126, Baltimore 112
March 26—Baltimore 119, Philadelphia 107
March 28—Baltimore 111, Philadelphia 103
March 30—Baltimore 120, Philadelphia 105
April 1—Philadelphia 104, Baltimore 103
April 3—Philadelphia 98, Baltimore 94
April 4—Baltimore 128, Philadelphia 120

Western Conference Semifinals

Los Angeles 4, Chicago 3
March 24—Los Angeles 100, Chicago 99
March 26—Los Angeles 105, Chicago 95
March 28—Chicago 106, Los Angeles 98
March 30—Chicago 112, Los Angeles 102
April 1—Los Angeles 115, Chicago 89
April 4—Chicago 113, Los Angeles 99
April 6—Los Angeles 109, Chicago 98

Milwaukee 4, San Francisco 1
March 27—Milwaukee 107, San Francisco 96
March 29—Milwaukee 104, San Francisco 90
March 30—Milwaukee 114, San Francisco 102
April 1—San Francisco 106, Milwaukee 104
April 4—Milwaukee 136, San Francisco 86

Eastern Conference Finals

Baltimore 4, New York 3
April 6—New York 112, Baltimore 111
April 9—New York 107, Baltimore 88
April 11—Baltimore 114, New York 88
April 14—Baltimore 101, New York 80
April 16—New York 89, Baltimore 84
April 18—Baltimore 113, New York 96
April 19—Baltimore 93, New York 91

Western Conference Finals

Milwaukee 4, Los Angeles 1
April 9—Milwaukee 106, Los Angeles 85
April 11—Milwaukee 91, Los Angeles 73
April 14—Los Angeles 118, Milwaukee 107
April 16—Milwaukee 117, Los Angeles 94
April 18—Milwaukee 116, Los Angeles 98

NBA Finals

Milwaukee 4, Baltimore 0
April 21—Milwaukee 98, Baltimore 88
April 25—Milwaukee 102, Baltimore 83
April 28—Milwaukee 107, Baltimore 99
April 30—Milwaukee 118, Baltimore 106

INDIVIDUAL LEADERS

Scoring
(Minimum 70 games played)

	G.	FG	FT	PTS.	AVG.
Alcindor, Milwaukee	82	1063	470	2596	31.7
Havlicek, Boston	81	892	554	2338	28.9
Hayes, San Diego	82	948	454	2350	28.7
Bing, Detroit	82	799	615	2213	27.0
Hudson, Atlanta	76	829	381	2039	26.8
Love, Chicago	81	765	513	2043	25.2
Petrie, Portland	82	784	463	2031	24.8
Maravich, Atlanta	81	738	404	1880	23.2
Cunningham, Philadelphia	81	702	455	1859	23.0
Van Arsdale, Cincinnati	82	749	377	1875	22.9

Field Goal Pct.
(Minimum 700 Attempts)

	FGM	FGA	PCT.
Green, Cincinnati	502	855	.587
Alcindor, Milwaukee	1063	1843	.577
Chamberlain, Los Angeles	668	1226	.545
McGlocklin, Milwaukee	574	1073	.535
Snyder, Seattle	645	1215	.531

Free Throw Pct.
(Minimum 350 Attempts)

	FTM	FTA	PCT.
Walker, Chicago	480	559	.859
Robertson, Milwaukee	385	453	.850
Williams, San Francisco	331	392	.844
Mullins, San Francisco	302	358	.844
Snyder, Seattle	302	361	.837

Assists
(Minimum 70 games)

	G.	NO.	AVG.
Van Lier, Cincinnati	82	832	10.1
Wilkens, Seattle	71	654	9.2
Robertson, Milwaukee	81	668	8.2
Havlicek, Boston	81	607	7.5
Frazier, New York	80	536	6.7

Rebounds
(Minimum 70 games)

	G.	NO.	AVG.
Chamberlain, Los Angeles	82	1493	18.2
Unseld, Baltimore	74	1253	16.9
Hayes, San Diego	82	1362	16.6
Alcindor, Milwaukee	82	1311	16.0
Lucas, San Francisco	80	1265	15.8

1971–72

Through the heyday of Elgin Baylor, the Lakers had never been able to beat the rival Celtics in the NBA Finals. Baylor had been named to the All-NBA First Team 10 times in his career, but nine games into the 1971–72 season, he decided injuries and age (37) had caught up to him and announced his retirement. Bill Sharman, the old Celtic guard, had been brought to LA to instill a winner's attitude as coach. With Chamberlain (35) and West (33) in sight of the end of their careers, Sharman needed to fit the other pieces around his aging stars to win now. Forwards Jim McMillian and Happy Hairston and guard Gail Goodrich were the perfect pieces, as was demonstrated when the Lakers went on a league-record 33-game winning streak that stretched from November 5 to January 7. The Lakers posted a 69-13 record, the best one-season record in NBA history. Chamberlain led the league in field-goal percentage (.649) and rebounding (19.2), while Goodrich (25.9) and West (25.8) handled the bulk of the scoring.

The Lakers swept Chicago in four straight and defeated Milwaukee in six games as Chamberlain outdueled Kareem Abdul-Jabbar. New York defeated Baltimore and Boston in the Eastern Conference Playoffs but, without Willis Reed in the Finals, proved no match for the Lakers, who finally got their championship in five games.

NBA 1971-72

FINAL STANDINGS

Eastern Conference

Atlantic Division

	W.	L.	PCT.
Boston	56	26	.683
New York	48	34	.585
Philadelphia	30	52	.366
Buffalo	22	60	.268

Central Division

	W.	L.	PCT.
Baltimore	38	44	.463
Atlanta	36	46	.439
Cincinnati	30	52	.366
Cleveland	23	59	.280

Western Conference

Midwest Division

	W.	L.	PCT.
Milwaukee	63	19	.768
Chicago	57	25	.695
Phoenix	49	33	.598
Detroit	26	56	.317

Pacific Division

	W.	L.	PCT.
Los Angeles	69	13	.841
Golden State	51	31	.622
Seattle	47	35	.573
Houston	34	48	.415
Portland	18	64	.220

PLAYOFFS

Eastern Conference Semifinals

Boston 4, Atlanta 2
March 29—Boston 126, Atlanta 108
March 31—Atlanta 113, Boston 104
April 2—Boston 136, Atlanta 113
April 4—Atlanta 112, Boston 110
April 7—Boston 124, Atlanta 114
April 9—Boston 127, Atlanta 118

New York 4, Baltimore 2
March 31—Baltimore 108, New York 105 (OT)
April 2—New York 110, Baltimore 88
April 4—Baltimore 104, New York 103
April 6—New York 104, Baltimore 98
April 9—New York 106, Baltimore 82
April 11—New York 107, Baltimore 101

Western Conference Semifinals

Los Angeles 4, Chicago 0
March 28—Los Angeles 95, Chicago 80
March 30—Los Angeles 131, Chicago 124
April 2—Los Angeles 108, Chicago 101
April 4—Los Angeles 108, Chicago 97

Milwaukee 4, Golden State 1
March 28—Golden State 117, Milwaukee 106
March 30—Milwaukee 118, Golden State 93
April 1—Milwaukee 122, Golden State 94
April 4—Milwaukee 106, Golden State 99
April 6—Milwaukee 108, Golden State 100

Eastern Conference Finals

New York 4, Boston 1
April 13—New York 116, Boston 94
April 16—New York 106, Boston 105
April 19—Boston 115, New York 109
April 21—New York 116, Boston 98
April 23—New York 111, Boston 103

Western Conference Finals

Los Angeles 4, Milwaukee 2
April 9—Milwaukee 93, Los Angeles 72
April 12—Los Angeles 135, Milwaukee 134
April 14—Los Angeles 108, Milwaukee 105
April 16—Milwaukee 114, Los Angeles 88
April 18—Los Angeles 115, Milwaukee 90
April 22—Los Angeles 104, Milwaukee 100

NBA Finals

Los Angeles 4, New York 1
April 26—New York 114, Los Angeles 92
April 30—Los Angeles 106, New York 92
May 3—Los Angeles 107, New York 96
May 5—Los Angeles 116, New York 111 (OT)
May 7—Los Angeles 114, New York 100

INDIVIDUAL LEADERS

Scoring
(Minimum 70 games played)

	G.	FG	FT	PTS.	AVG.
Abdul-Jabbar, Milwaukee	81	1159	504	2822	34.8
Archibald, Cincinnati	76	734	677	2145	28.2
Havlicek, Boston	82	897	458	2252	27.5
Haywood, Seattle	73	717	480	1914	26.2
Goodrich, Los Angeles	82	826	475	2127	25.9
Love, Chicago	79	819	399	2037	25.8
West, Los Angeles	77	735	515	1985	25.8
Lanier, Detroit	80	834	388	2056	25.7
Clark, Phi.-Bal.	77	712	514	1938	25.2
Hayes, Houston	82	832	399	2063	25.2

Field Goal Pct.
(Minimum 700 Attempts)

	FGM	FGA	PCT.
Chamberlain, Los Angeles	496	764	.649
Abdul-Jabbar, Milwaukee	1159	2019	.574
Bellamy, Atlanta	593	1089	.545
Snyder, Seattle	496	937	.529
Lucas, New York	543	1060	.512

Free Throw Pct.
(Minimum 350 Attempts)

	FTM	FTA	PCT.
Marin, Baltimore	356	398	.894
Murphy, Houston	349	392	.890
Goodrich, Los Angeles	475	559	.850
Walker, Chicago	481	568	.847
Van Arsdale, Phoenix	529	626	.845

Assists
(Minimum 70 games)

	G.	NO.	AVG.
West, Los Angeles	77	747	9.7
Wilkens, Seattle	80	766	9.6
Archibald, Cincinnati	76	701	9.2
Clark, Phi.-Bal.	77	613	8.0
Havlicek, Boston	82	614	7.5

Rebounds
(Minimum 70 games)

	G.	NO.	AVG.
Chamberlain, Los Angeles	82	1572	19.2
Unseld, Baltimore	76	1336	17.6
Abdul-Jabbar, Milwaukee	81	1346	16.6
Thurmond, Golden State	78	1252	16.1
Cowens, Boston	79	1203	15.2

Like Baylor, West had been brilliant in defeat for many years in the NBA Finals. It almost didn't seem right that he was no longer a dominant player when the Lakers finally won the championship.

"I played terrible basketball in the Finals, and we won," West said. "And that didn't seem to be justice for me personally because I had contributed so much in other years when we lost. Now, when we won, I was just another piece of the machinery. It was particularly frustrating because I was playing so poorly that the team overcame me.

"But maybe that's what a team is all about."

1972–73

Willis Reed returned to the Knicks after injuries had limited him to 11 games the previous season. Earl Monroe and Walt Frazier, longtime adversaries when Monroe was with Baltimore, learned to coexist in the New York backcourt. Jerry Lucas, like Monroe, had been obtained in a trade and shared the center spot with Reed. Bradley and DeBusschere were at their familiar forward spots, and Phil Jackson was again in reserve. But the top team during the regular season was Boston, which had rebuilt around Havlicek with young stars Jo Jo White and Dave Cowens, veteran Paul Silas, and 1969 title team holdovers Don Chaney, Don Nelson and Satch Sanders. Boston won 68 games, just one shy of the league record the Lakers established a season earlier. Meanwhile, the 76ers, who lost Billy Cunningham to the ABA, suffered through an NBA record-worst 9-73 season.

New York breezed past Baltimore in the Eastern Conference Playoffs, then battled tooth and nail with Boston before the younger Celtics succumbed in a surprisingly easy Game 7. The Lakers defeated Chicago in seven games, then moved past a well-balanced Golden State team in five to reach the Finals. With the same Finals matchup for the third time in four years, there were few secrets between the two teams. After the Lakers edged New York in Game 1, the Knicks won four straight closely contested games to bring a second NBA title to New York.

While Boston grabbed the headlines during the regular season with 68 victories and New York won its second championship, a remarkable story was being played out in the unlikely settings of Kansas City, Mo., and Omaha, Neb. The Cincinnati Royals had moved after the 1972 season and were splitting home games between the two cities. Although the team went 36-46 and didn't qualify for the playoffs, the fans witnessed greatness in the form of 6-1 guard Nate "Tiny" Archibald, in his third pro season.

Archibald, a guard with all the New York playground moves, led the NBA in both scoring (34.0) and assists (11.4). More than two decades later, no one has come close to matching Archibald's dual achievement as he belied his slight frame by playing a league-leading 46 minutes per game.

NBA 1972-73

FINAL STANDINGS

Eastern Conference

Atlantic Division

	W.	L.	PCT.
Boston	68	14	.829
New York	57	25	.695
Buffalo	21	61	.256
Philadelphia	9	73	.110

Central Division

	W.	L.	PCT.
Baltimore	52	30	.634
Atlanta	46	36	.561
Houston	33	49	.402
Cleveland	32	50	.390

Western Conference

Midwest Division

	W.	L.	PCT.
Milwaukee	60	22	.732
Chicago	51	31	.622
Detroit	40	42	.488
Kansas City-Omaha	36	46	.439

Pacific Division

	W.	L.	PCT.
Los Angeles	60	22	.732
Golden State	47	35	.573
Phoenix	38	44	.463
Seattle	26	56	.317
Portland	21	61	.256

PLAYOFFS

Eastern Conference Semifinals

Boston 4, Atlanta 2
April 1—Boston 134, Atlanta 109
April 4—Boston 126, Atlanta 113
April 6—Atlanta 118, Boston 105
April 8—Atlanta 97, Boston 94
April 11—Boston 108, Atlanta 101
April 13—Boston 121, Atlanta 103

New York 4, Baltimore 1
March 30—New York 95, Baltimore 83
April 1—New York 123, Baltimore 103
April 4—New York 103, Baltimore 96
April 6—Baltimore 97, New York 89
April 8—New York 109, Baltimore 99

Western Conference Semifinals

Los Angeles 4, Chicago 3
March 30—Los Angeles 107, Chicago 104 (OT)
April 1—Los Angeles 108, Chicago 93
April 6—Chicago 96, Los Angeles 86
April 8—Chicago 98, Los Angeles 94
April 10—Los Angeles 123, Chicago 102
April 13—Chicago 101, Los Angeles 93
April 15—Los Angeles 95, Chicago 92

Golden State 4, Milwaukee 2
March 30—Milwaukee 110, Golden State 90
April 1—Golden State 95, Milwaukee 92
April 5—Milwaukee 113, Golden State 93
April 7—Golden State 102, Milwaukee 97
April 10—Golden State 100, Milwaukee 97
April 13—Golden State 100, Milwaukee 86

Eastern Conference Finals

New York 4, Boston 3
April 15—Boston 134, New York 108
April 18—New York 129, Boston 96
April 20—New York 98, Boston 91
April 22—New York 117, Boston 110 (2OT)
April 25—Boston 98, New York 97
April 27—Boston 110, New York 100
April 29—New York 94, Boston 78

Western Conference Finals

Los Angeles 4, Golden State 1
April 17—Los Angeles 101, Golden State 99
April 19—Los Angeles 104, Golden State 93
April 21—Los Angeles 126, Golden State 70
April 23—Golden State 117, Los Angeles 109
April 25—Los Angeles 128, Golden State 118

NBA Finals

New York 4, Los Angeles 1
May 1—Los Angeles 115, New York 112
May 3—New York 99, Los Angeles 95
May 6—New York 87, Los Angeles 83
May 8—New York 103, Los Angeles 98
May 10—New York 102, Los Angeles 93

INDIVIDUAL LEADERS

Scoring
(Minimum 70 games played)

	G.	FG	FT	PTS.	AVG.
Archibald, K.C.-Omaha	80	1028	663	2719	34.0
Abdul-Jabbar, Milwaukee	76	982	328	2292	30.2
Haywood, Seattle	77	889	473	2251	29.2
Hudson, Atlanta	75	816	397	2029	27.1
Maravich, Atlanta	79	789	485	2063	26.1
Scott, Phoenix	81	806	436	2048	25.3
Petrie, Portland	79	836	298	1970	24.9
Goodrich, Los Angeles	76	750	314	1814	23.9
Wicks, Portland	80	761	384	1906	23.8
Lanier, Detroit	81	810	307	1927	23.8

Field Goal Pct.
(Minimum 560 Attempts)

	FGM	FGA	PCT.
Chamberlain, Los Angeles	426	586	.727
Guokas, Kansas City-Omaha	322	565	.570
Abdul-Jabbar, Milwaukee	982	1772	.554
Rowe, Detroit	547	1053	.519
Fox, Seattle	316	613	.515

Free Throw Pct.
(Minimum 160 Attempts)

	FTM	FTA	PCT.
Barry, Golden State	358	397	.902
Murphy, Houston	239	269	.888
Newlin, Houston	327	369	.886
Walker, Houston	244	276	.884
Bradley, New York	169	194	.871

Assists
(Minimum 70 games)

	G.	NO.	AVG.
Archibald, Kansas City-Omaha	80	910	11.4
Wilkens, Cleveland	75	628	8.4
Bing, Detroit	82	637	7.8
Robertson, Milwaukee	73	551	7.5
Van Lier, Chicago	80	567	7.1

Rebounds
(Minimum 70 games)

	G.	NO.	AVG.
Chamberlain, Los Angeles	82	1526	18.6
Thurmond, Golden State	79	1349	17.1
Cowens, Boston	82	1329	16.2
Abdul-Jabbar, Milwaukee	76	1224	16.1
Unseld, Baltimore	79	1260	15.9

1973–74

The retirement of Wilt Chamberlain from the NBA after more than 31,000 points and 23,000 rebounds signaled a change in the league. The old guard was gone or on its way out. Reed, DeBusschere and Lucas were playing their last seasons for New York, while West in LA and Robertson in Milwaukee were also in their final seasons.

The beneficiary proved to be Boston, which had come of age with a mix of veterans and young stars. Havlicek was still good for 22.6 ppg, and Cowens hauled in 15.7 rebounds per game and baffled opposing centers with his quickness and fiery determination. Tom Heinsohn had nurtured the group as head coach for five years, and Auerbach was still making the key acquisitions to build another contender. The Celtics won 56 games, 12 fewer than the previous year but still the best in the East, and romped past Buffalo and the aging Knicks to reach the Finals for the first time since 1969. In the West, Abdul-Jabbar won his third MVP Award after averaging 27 points and 14.5 rebounds in leading

Milwaukee to a league-high 59 victories. The Bucks toppled the aging Lakers in five games and swept overmatched Chicago to reach the Finals.

The matchup of Cowens and Abdul-Jabbar headlined the series, and each man helped his team to wins as the teams split six games, including a pair of overtime Milwaukee victories. But in Game 7, the Celtics altered their strategy and double- and triple-teamed Abdul-Jabbar. Cowens, thus freed from having to focus on defense, scored 28 points and helped Boston to a 102–87 win.

John Havlicek was 34 by the time the Celtics reached the 1974 NBA Finals, but he seemed to be the same man who had helped Boston win six NBA titles during the 1960s. A link to the Cousy/Russell Celtics, "Hondo" was still the main man for the Celtics a decade later.

"When things are swinging easy, we all get in the flow of it," explained Paul Silas. "And sometimes then it almost looks like we ignore John. But when things don't go well, we look to him all the time to make the tough play. We do this instinctively because he has usually been the guy who's turned bad moments into good ones for us."

NBA 1973-74

FINAL STANDINGS

Eastern Conference

Atlantic Division

	W.	L.	PCT.
Boston	56	26	.683
New York	49	33	.598
Buffalo	42	40	.512
Philadelphia	25	57	.305

Central Division

	W.	L.	PCT.
Capital	47	35	.573
Atlanta	35	47	.427
Houston	32	50	.390
Cleveland	29	53	.354

Western Conference

Midwest Division

	W.	L.	PCT.
Milwaukee	59	23	.720
Chicago	54	28	.659
Detroit	52	30	.634
Kansas City-Omaha	33	49	.402

Pacific Division

	W.	L.	PCT.
Los Angeles	47	35	.573
Golden State	44	38	.537
Seattle	36	46	.439
Phoenix	30	52	.366
Portland	27	55	.329

PLAYOFFS

Eastern Conference Semifinals

Boston 4, Buffalo 2
March 30—Boston 107, Buffalo 97
April 2—Buffalo 115, Boston 105
April 3—Boston 120, Buffalo 107
April 6—Buffalo 104, Boston 102
April 9—Boston 100, Buffalo 97
April 12—Boston 106, Buffalo 104

New York 4, Capital 3
March 29—New York 102, Capital 91
March 31—Capital 99, New York 87
April 2—Capital 88, New York 79
April 5—New York 101, Capital 93 (OT)
April 7—New York 106, Capital 105
April 10—Capital 109, New York 92
April 12—New York 91, Capital 81

Western Conference Semifinals

Chicago 4, Detroit 3
March 30—Detroit 97, Chicago 88
April 1—Chicago 108, Detroit 103
April 5—Chicago 84, Detroit 83
April 7—Detroit 102, Chicago 87
April 9—Chicago 98, Detroit 94
April 11—Detroit 92, Chicago 88
April 13—Chicago 96, Detroit 94

Milwaukee 4, Los Angeles 1
March 29—Milwaukee 99, Los Angeles 95
March 31—Milwaukee 109, Los Angeles 90
April 2—Los Angeles 98, Milwaukee 96
April 4—Milwaukee 112, Los Angeles 90
April 7—Milwaukee 114, Los Angeles 92

Eastern Conference Finals

Boston 4, New York 1
April 14—Boston 113, New York 88
April 16—Boston 111, New York 99
April 19—New York 103, Boston 100
April 21—Boston 98, New York 91
April 24—Boston 105, New York 94

Western Conference Finals

Milwaukee 4, Chicago 0
April 16—Milwaukee 101, Chicago 85
April 18—Milwaukee 113, Chicago 111
April 20—Milwaukee 113, Chicago 90
April 22—Milwaukee 115, Chicago 99

NBA Finals

Boston 4, Milwaukee 3
April 28—Boston 98, Milwaukee 83
April 30—Milwaukee 105, Boston 96 (OT)
May 3—Boston 95, Milwaukee 83
May 5—Milwaukee 97, Boston 89
May 7—Boston 96, Milwaukee 87
May 10—Milwaukee 102, Boston 101 (2OT)
May 12—Boston 102, Milwaukee 87

INDIVIDUAL LEADERS

Scoring
(Minimum 70 games played)

	G.	FG	FT	PTS.	AVG.
McAdoo, Buffalo	74	901	459	2261	30.6
Maravich, Atlanta	76	819	469	2107	27.7
Abdul-Jabbar, Milwaukee	81	948	295	2191	27.0
Goodrich, Los Angeles	82	784	508	2076	25.3
Barry, Golden State	80	796	417	2009	25.1
Tomjanovich, Houston	80	788	385	1961	24.5
Petrie, Portland	73	740	291	1771	24.3
Haywood, Seattle	75	694	373	1761	23.5
Havlicek, Boston	76	685	346	1716	22.6
Lanier, Detroit	81	748	326	1822	22.5

Field Goal Pct.
(Minimum 560 Attempts)

	FGM	FGA	PCT.
McAdoo, Buffalo	901	1647	.547
Abdul-Jabbar, Milwaukee	948	1759	.539
Tomjanovich, Houston	788	1470	.536
Murphy, Houston	671	1285	.522
Beard, Golden State	316	617	.512

Free Throw Pct.
(Minimum 160 Attempts)

	FTM	FTA	PCT.
DiGregorio, Buffalo	174	193	.902
Barry, Golden State	417	464	.899
Mullins, Golden State	168	192	.875
Walker, Chicago	439	502	.875
Bradley, New York	146	167	.874

Assists
(Minimum 70 games)

	G.	NO.	AVG.
DiGregorio, Buffalo	81	663	8.2
Murphy, Houston	81	603	7.4
Wilkens, Cleveland	74	522	7.1
Frazier, New York	80	551	6.9
Bing, Detroit	81	555	6.9

Rebounds
(Minimum 70 games)

	G.	OFF.	DEF.	TOT.	AVG.
Hayes, Capital	81	354	1109	1463	18.1
Cowens, Boston	80	264	993	1257	15.7
McAdoo, Buffalo	74	281	836	1117	15.1
Abdul-Jabbar, Milwaukee	81	287	891	1178	14.5
Hairston, Los Angeles	77	335	705	1040	13.5

Steals
(Minimum 70 games)

	G.	NO.	AVG.
Steele, Portland	81	217	2.68
Mix, Philadelphia	82	212	2.59
Smith, Buffalo	82	203	2.48
Sloan, Chicago	77	183	2.38
Barry, Golden State	80	169	2.11

Blocked Shots
(Minimum 70 games)

	G.	NO.	AVG.
Smith, Los Angeles	81	393	4.85
Abdul-Jabbar, Milwaukee	81	283	3.49
McAdoo, Buffalo	74	246	3.32
Lanier, Detroit	81	247	3.05
Hayes, Capital	81	240	2.96

1974–75

The retirements of West and Robertson left their teams weakened, and the Lakers and Milwaukee each fell to the bottom of their divisions. This spelled opportunity for hungry young teams in the Western Conference, and nobody was hungrier than the Golden State Warriors. Al Attles, a fixture with the Warriors since 1960 as a player and a coach, had developed an 11-deep roster of role players to go with high-scoring forward Rick Barry, still in his prime at 30. Attles had acquired young center Clifford Ray for the aging Nate Thurmond, obtained scrappy guard Butch Beard and drafted forward Jamaal (then Keith) Wilkes from UCLA and guard Charles Johnson from California. This unlikely group won 48 games to top the Western Conference, defeated Coach Bill Russell's Seattle team in six games and used its endless hustle and desire to beat a more talented Chicago Bulls team in seven games to reach the Finals.

The Washington Bullets won 60 games in the East but had a tough time dispatching the Buffalo Braves, led by NBA scoring champ Bob McAdoo (34.5) in seven games in the Eastern Conference Semifinals. The Celtics had also won 60 games and blew past Houston in five games to meet Washington. The Bullets had the inside-outside combination of Elvin Hayes and Phil Chenier working brilliantly and turned back the Celtics in six games. The Bullets were heavily favored to beat the Warriors, but Golden State stunned the basketball world by winning four straight close games to post only the third sweep in the 29-year history of the NBA Finals.

The Bullets had an experienced team in 1975, with powerful Elvin Hayes and Wes Unseld up front joined by feisty forward Mike Riordan, with quick Kevin Porter and sharpshooter Phil Chenier in the backcourt. On paper, the Bullets were far superior to the Warriors. But as the old saying goes, games aren't played on paper. And when the Warriors swept, Rick Barry could afford to celebrate.

"It has to be the greatest upset in the history of the NBA Finals," Barry said. "It was like a fairy-tale season. Everything just fell into place. It's something I'll treasure for the rest of my life."

NBA 1974-75

FINAL STANDINGS

Eastern Conference

Atlantic Division

	W.	L.	PCT.
Boston	60	22	.732
Buffalo	49	33	.598
New York	40	42	.488
Philadelphia	34	48	.415

Central Division

	W.	L.	PCT.
Washington	60	22	.732
Houston	41	41	.500
Cleveland	40	42	.488
Atlanta	31	51	.378
New Orleans	23	59	.280

Western Conference

Midwest Division

	W.	L.	PCT.
Chicago	47	35	.573
Kansas City-Omaha	44	38	.537
Detroit	40	42	.488
Milwaukee	38	44	.463

Pacific Division

	W.	L.	PCT.
Golden State	48	34	.585
Seattle	43	39	.524
Portland	38	44	.463
Phoenix	32	50	.390
Los Angeles	30	52	.366

PLAYOFFS

Eastern Conference First Round

Houston 2, New York 1
April 8—Houston 99, New York 84
April 10—New York 106, Houston 96
April 12—Houston 118, New York 86

Western Conference First Round

Seattle 2, Detroit 1
April 8—Seattle 90, Detroit 77
April 10—Detroit 122, Seattle 106
April 12—Seattle 100, Detroit 93

Eastern Conference Semifinals

Boston 4, Houston 1
April 14—Boston 123, Houston 106
April 16—Boston 112, Houston 100
April 19—Houston 117, Boston 102
April 22—Boston 122, Houston 117
April 24—Boston 128, Houston 115

Washington 4, Buffalo 3
April 10—Buffalo 113, Washington 102
April 12—Washington 120, Buffalo 106
April 16—Washington 111, Buffalo 96
April 18—Buffalo 108, Washington 102
April 20—Washington 97, Buffalo 93
April 23—Buffalo 102, Washington 96
April 25—Washington 115, Buffalo 96

Western Conference Semifinals

Chicago 4, Kansas City-Omaha 2
April 9—Chicago 95, Kansas City-Omaha 89
April 13—Kansas City-Omaha 102, Chicago 95
April 16—Chicago 93, Kansas City-Omaha 90
April 18—Kansas City-Omaha 104, Chicago 100 (OT)
April 20—Chicago 104, Kansas City-Omaha 77
April 23—Chicago 101, Kansas City-Omaha 89

Golden State 4, Seattle 2
April 14—Golden State 123, Seattle 96
April 16—Seattle 100, Golden State 99
April 17—Golden State 105, Seattle 96
April 19—Seattle 111, Golden State 94
April 22—Golden State 124, Seattle 100
April 24—Golden State 105, Seattle 96

Eastern Conference Finals

Washington 4, Boston 2
April 27—Washington 100, Boston 95
April 30—Washington 117, Boston 92
May 3—Boston 101, Washington 90
May 7—Washington 119, Boston 108
May 9—Boston 103, Washington 99
May 11—Washington 98, Boston 92

Western Conference Finals

Golden State 4, Chicago 3
April 27—Golden State 107, Chicago 89
April 30—Chicago 90, Golden State 89
May 4—Chicago 108, Golden State 101
May 6—Golden State 111, Chicago 106
May 8—Chicago 89, Golden State 79
May 11—Golden State 86, Chicago 72
May 14—Golden State 83, Chicago 79

NBA Finals

Golden State 4, Washington 0
May 18—Golden State 101, Washington 95
May 20—Golden State 92, Washington 91
May 23—Golden State 109, Washington 101
May 25—Golden State 96, Washington 95

INDIVIDUAL LEADERS

Scoring
(Minimum 70 games played or 1,400 points)

	G.	FG	FT	PTS.	AVG.
McAdoo, Buffalo	82	1095	641	2831	34.5
Barry, Golden State	80	1028	394	2450	30.6
Abdul-Jabbar, Milwaukee	65	812	325	1949	30.0
Archibald, K.C.-Omaha	82	759	652	2170	26.5
Scott, Phoenix	69	703	274	1680	24.3
Lanier, Detroit	76	731	361	1823	24.0
Hayes, Washington	82	739	409	1887	23.0
Goodrich, Los Angeles	72	656	318	1630	22.6
Haywood, Seattle	68	608	309	1525	22.4
Carter, Philadelphia	77	715	256	1686	21.9

Field Goal Pct.
(Minimum 300 FG made)

	FGM	FGA	PCT.
Nelson, Boston	423	785	.539
Beard, Golden State	408	773	.528
Tomjanovich, Houston	694	1323	.525
Abdul-Jabbar, Milwaukee	812	1584	.513
McAdoo, Buffalo	1095	2138	.512

Free Throw Pct.
(Minimum 125 FT made)

	FTM	FTA	PCT.
Barry, Golden State	394	436	.904
Murphy, Houston	341	386	.883
Bradley, New York	144	165	.873
Archibald, Kansas City-Omaha	652	748	.872
Price, L.A.-Mil.	169	194	.871

Assists
(Minimum 70 games or 400 assists)

	G.	NO.	AVG.
Porter, Washington	81	650	8.0
Bing, Detroit	79	610	7.7
Archibald, Kansas City-Omaha	82	557	6.8
Smith, Buffalo	82	534	6.5
Maravich, New Orleans	79	488	6.2

Rebounds
(Minimum 70 games or 800 rebounds)

	G.	OFF.	DEF.	TOT.	AVG.
Unseld, Washington	73	318	759	1077	14.8
Cowens, Boston	65	229	729	958	14.7
Lacey, Kansas City-Omaha	81	228	921	1149	14.2
McAdoo, Buffalo	82	307	848	1155	14.1
Abdul-Jabbar, Milwaukee	65	194	718	912	14.0

Steals

(Minimum 70 games or 125 steals)

	G.	NO.	AVG.
Barry, Golden State	80	228	2.85
Frazier, New York	78	190	2.44
Steele, Portland	76	183	2.41
Watts, Seattle	82	190	2.32
Brown, Seattle	81	187	2.31

Blocked Shots

(Minimum 70 games or 100 blocks)

	G.	NO.	AVG.
Abdul-Jabbar, Milwaukee	65	212	3.26
Smith, Los Angeles	74	216	2.92
Thurmond, Chicago	80	195	2.44
Hayes, Washington	82	187	2.28
Lanier, Detroit	76	172	2.26

1975–76

Just as the season was about to begin, the ABA's two strongest teams, the New York Nets and Denver Nuggets, applied for admission into the NBA, signaling the beginning of the end for the upstart league. While ABA teams would not enter the NBA for another year, the NBA moved to facilitate the get-together by naming as its third commissioner Larry O'Brien, replacing the retired Walter Kennedy. O'Brien was a prominent political figure whose office as chairman of the Democratic National Committee had been the scene of the famed Watergate burglary. He was renowned for his negotiating skills and political acumen.

On the court, the Warriors team that had been considered a fluke by many refuted that belief by winning a league-high 59 games. Boston, which had acquired shooting guard Charlie Scott from Phoenix

for Paul Westphal, won 54 games to top the Eastern Conference. A bombshell trade took place when Milwaukee traded Abdul-Jabbar to the Lakers for Elmore Smith, Brian Winters, Junior Bridgeman and Dave Meyers. While Abdul-Jabbar was named MVP again after averaging 27.7 points and a league-leading 16.9 rebounds per game, the Lakers went 40-42 and missed the playoffs.

The Celtics defeated Buffalo and Cleveland to reach the Finals in the East. In the West, upstart Phoenix, with Rookie of the Year Alvan Adams, beat Seattle and defeated heavily favored Golden State in seven games to reach the Finals. Boston won its second title in three years and 13th overall in a six-game Finals that is most remembered for a remarkable triple-overtime Game 5 that Boston captured 128–126.

In sport, there are a few games that seem to linger forever in the memory. While not a title-clinching game, Game 5 of the 1976 NBA Finals is one.

At the close of the second overtime, John Havlicek hit a 15-foot jump shot for an apparent 111–110 victory. Jubilant Celtics fans swarmed the court, but the officials ruled one second remained on the clock. After the court was cleared, guard Paul Westphal called a timeout the

Suns didn't have, which produced a technical free throw for Boston but also moved the ball to half-court. After Jo Jo White hit the T, Phoenix inbounded to forward Gar Heard, who launched a 20-footer that swished through, stunning the Celtics and sending the game into a third overtime. However, Boston won 128–126, as reserve forward Glenn McDonald scored six points down the stretch.

NBA 1975-76

FINAL STANDINGS

Eastern Conference

Atlantic Division

	W.	L.	PCT.
Boston	54	28	.659
Buffalo	46	36	.561
Philadelphia	46	36	.561
New York	38	44	.463

Central Division

	W.	L.	PCT.
Cleveland	49	33	.598
Washington	48	34	.585
Houston	40	42	.488
New Orleans	38	44	.463
Atlanta	29	53	.354

Western Conference

Midwest Division

	W.	L.	PCT.
Milwaukee	38	44	.463
Detroit	36	46	.439
Kansas City	31	51	.378
Chicago	24	58	.293

Pacific Division

	W.	L.	PCT.
Golden State	59	23	.720
Seattle	43	39	.524
Phoenix	42	40	.512
Los Angeles	40	42	.488
Portland	37	45	.451

PLAYOFFS

Eastern Conference First Round

Buffalo 2, Philadelphia 1
April 15—Buffalo 95, Philadelphia 89
April 16—Philadelphia 131, Buffalo 106
April 18—Buffalo 124, Philadelphia 123 (OT)

Western Conference First Round

Detroit 2, Milwaukee 1
April 13—Milwaukee 110, Detroit 107
April 15—Detroit 126, Milwaukee 123
April 18—Detroit 107, Milwaukee 104

Eastern Conference Semifinals

Boston 4, Buffalo 2
April 21—Boston 107, Buffalo 98
April 23—Boston 101, Buffalo 96
April 25—Buffalo 98, Boston 93
April 28—Buffalo 124, Boston 122
April 30—Boston 99, Buffalo 88
May 2—Boston 104, Buffalo 100

Cleveland 4, Washington 3
April 13—Washington 100, Cleveland 95
April 15—Cleveland 80, Washington 79
April 17—Cleveland 88, Washington 76
April 21—Washington 109, Cleveland 98
April 22—Cleveland 92, Washington 91
April 26—Washington 102, Cleveland 98 (OT)
April 29—Cleveland 87, Washington 85

Western Conference Semifinals

Golden State 4, Detroit 2
April 20—Golden State 127, Detroit 103
April 22—Detroit 123, Golden State 111
April 24—Golden State 113, Detroit 96
April 26—Detroit 106, Golden State 102
April 28—Golden State 128, Detroit 109
April 30—Golden State 118, Detroit 116 (OT)

Phoenix 4, Seattle 2
April 13—Seattle 102, Phoenix 99
April 15—Phoenix 116, Seattle 111
April 18—Phoenix 103, Seattle 91
April 20—Phoenix 130, Seattle 114
April 25—Seattle 114, Phoenix 108
April 27—Phoenix 123, Seattle 112

Eastern Conference Finals

Boston 4, Cleveland 2
May 6—Boston 111, Cleveland 99
May 9—Boston 94, Cleveland 89
May 11—Cleveland 83, Boston 78
May 14—Cleveland 106, Boston 87
May 16—Boston 99, Cleveland 94
May 18—Boston 94, Cleveland 87

Western Conference Finals

Phoenix 4, Golden State 3
May 2—Golden State 128, Phoenix 103
May 5—Phoenix 108, Golden State 101
May 7—Golden State 99, Phoenix 91
May 9—Phoenix 133, Golden State 129 (2OT)
May 12—Golden State 111, Phoenix 95
May 14—Phoenix 105, Golden State 104
May 16—Phoenix 94, Golden State 86

NBA Finals

Boston 4, Phoenix 2
May 23—Boston 98, Phoenix 87
May 27—Boston 105, Phoenix 90
May 30—Phoenix 105, Boston 98
June 2—Phoenix 109, Boston 107
June 4—Boston 128, Phoenix 126 (3OT)
June 6—Boston 87, Phoenix 80

INDIVIDUAL LEADERS

Scoring

(Minimum 70 games played or 1,400 points)

	G.	FG	FT	PTS.	AVG.
McAdoo, Buffalo	78	934	559	2427	31.1
Abdul-Jabbar, Los Angeles	82	914	447	2275	27.7
Maravich, New Orleans	62	604	396	1604	25.9
Archibald, Kansas City	78	717	501	1935	24.8
Brown, Seattle	76	742	273	1757	23.1
McGinnis, Philadelphia	77	647	475	1769	23.0
Smith, Buffalo	82	702	383	1787	21.8
Drew, Atlanta	77	586	488	1660	21.6
Dandridge, Milwaukee	73	650	271	1571	21.5
Barry, Golden State	81	707	287	1701	21.0
Murphy, Houston	82	675	372	1722	21.0

Field Goal Pct.

(Minimum 300 FG made)

	FGM	FGA	PCT.
Unseld, Washington	318	567	.561
Shumate, Pho.-Buf.	332	592	.561
McMillian, Buffalo	492	918	.536
Lanier, Detroit	541	1017	.532
Abdul-Jabbar, Los Angeles	914	1728	.529

Free Throw Pct.

(Minimum 125 FT made)

	FTM	FTA	PCT.
Barry, Golden State	287	311	.923
Murphy, Houston	372	410	.907
Russell, Los Angeles	132	148	.892
Bradley, New York	130	148	.878
Brown, Seattle	273	314	.869

Assists

(Minimum 70 games or 400 assists)

	G.	NO.	AVG.
Watts, Seattle	82	661	8.1
Archibald, Kansas City	78	615	7.9
Murphy, Houston	82	596	7.3
Van Lier, Chicago	76	500	6.6
Barry, Golden State	81	496	6.1

Rebounds

(Minimum 70 games or 800 rebounds)

	G.	OFF.	DEF.	TOT.	AVG.
Abdul-Jabbar, Los Angeles	82	272	1111	1383	16.9
Cowens, Boston	78	335	911	1246	16.0
Unseld, Washington	78	271	765	1036	13.3
Silas, Boston	81	365	660	1025	12.7
Lacey, Kansas City	81	218	806	1024	12.6

Steals

(Minimum 70 games or 125 steals)

	G.	NO.	AVG.
Watts, Seattle	82	261	3.18
McGinnis, Philadelphia	77	198	2.57
Westphal, Phoenix	82	210	2.56
Barry, Golden State	81	202	2.49
Ford, Detroit	82	178	2.17

Blocked Shots

(Minimum 70 games or 100 blocks)

	G.	NO.	AVG.
Abdul-Jabbar, Los Angeles	82	338	4.12
Smith, Milwaukee	78	238	3.05
Hayes, Washington	80	202	2.53
Catchings, Philadelphia	75	164	2.19
G. Johnson, Golden State	82	174	2.12

1976–77

Prior to the season, four teams from the ABA—the New York Nets, Indiana Pacers, Denver Nuggets and San Antonio Spurs—were admitted as NBA franchises for a fee of $3.2 million per team. The rest of the ABA players, including imposing 7-2 center Artis Gilmore of the Kentucky Colonels, were disseminated throughout the league in a dispersal draft. The NBA now had 22 teams, and the playoffs were restructured so that 12 teams qualified and each of the four division winners received a bye through the First Round.

Portland, which had yet to post a .500 record in its first six seasons in the league, was greatly improved under Jack Ramsay, who had previously coached the 76ers and Buffalo Braves. Bill Walton, the 6-11 center from UCLA who had been hurt most of his first two seasons, now had a scoring and rebounding partner in 6-9 Maurice Lucas, who came in the ABA dispersal draft. The rest of the team was comprised of consummate role players like small forward Bobby Gross, point guard Dave Twardzik and shooting guard Lionel Hollins. Despite not winning their division, the Trail Blazers defeated Chicago, Denver, the Lakers and the 76ers, who now had ABA superstar Julius Erving, to become the improbable NBA Champions.

NBA 1976-77

FINAL STANDINGS

Eastern Conference

Atlantic Division

	W.	L.	PCT.
Philadelphia	50	32	.610
Boston	44	38	.537
New York Knicks	40	42	.488
Buffalo	30	52	.366
New York Nets	22	60	.268

Central Division

	W.	L.	PCT.
Houston	49	33	.598
Washington	48	34	.585
San Antonio	44	38	.537
Cleveland	43	39	.524
New Orleans	35	47	.427
Atlanta	31	51	.378

Western Conference

Midwest Division

	W.	L.	PCT.
Denver	50	32	.610
Detroit	44	38	.537
Chicago	44	38	.537
Kansas City	40	42	.488
Indiana	36	46	.439
Milwaukee	30	52	.366

Pacific Division

	W.	L.	PCT.
Los Angeles	53	29	.646
Portland	49	33	.598
Golden State	46	36	.561
Seattle	40	42	.488
Phoenix	34	48	.415

PLAYOFFS

Eastern Conference First Round

Boston 2, San Antonio 0
April 12—Boston 104, San Antonio 94
April 15—Boston 113, San Antonio 109

Washington 2, Cleveland 1
April 13—Washington 109, Cleveland 100
April 15—Cleveland 91, Washington 83
April 17—Washington 104, Cleveland 98

Western Conference First Round

Portland 2, Chicago 1
April 12—Portland 96, Chicago 83
April 15—Chicago 107, Portland 104
April 17—Portland 106, Chicago 98

Golden State 2, Detroit 1
April 12—Detroit 95, Golden State 90
April 14—Golden State 138, Detroit 108
April 17—Golden State 109, Detroit 101

Eastern Conference Semifinals

Philadelphia 4, Boston 3
April 17—Boston 113, Philadelphia 111
April 20—Philadelphia 113, Boston 101
April 22—Philadelphia 109, Boston 100
April 24—Boston 124, Philadelphia 119
April 27—Philadelphia 110, Boston 91
April 29—Boston 113, Philadelphia 108
May 1—Philadelphia 83, Boston 77

Houston 4, Washington 2
April 19—Washington 111, Houston 101
April 21—Houston 124, Washington 118 (OT)
April 24—Washington 93, Houston 90
April 26—Houston 107, Washington 103
April 29—Houston 123, Washington 115
May 1—Houston 108, Washington 103

Western Conference Semifinals

Portland 4, Denver 2
April 20—Portland 101, Denver 100
April 22—Denver 121, Portland 110
April 24—Portland 110, Denver 106
April 26—Portland 105, Denver 96
May 1—Denver 114, Portland 105 (OT)
May 2—Portland 108, Denver 92

Los Angeles 4, Golden State 3
April 20—Los Angeles 115, Golden State 106
April 22—Los Angeles 95, Golden State 86
April 24—Golden State 109, Los Angeles 105
April 26—Golden State 114, Los Angeles 103
April 29—Los Angeles 112, Golden State 105
May 1—Golden State 115, Los Angeles 106
May 4—Los Angeles 97, Golden State 84

Eastern Conference Finals

Philadelphia 4, Houston 2
May 5—Philadelphia 128, Houston 117
May 8—Philadelphia 106, Houston 97
May 11—Houston 118, Philadelphia 94
May 13—Philadelphia 107, Houston 95
May 15—Houston 118, Philadelphia 115
May 17—Philadelphia 112, Houston 109

Western Conference Finals

Portland 4, Los Angeles 0
May 6—Portland 121, Los Angeles 109
May 8—Portland 99, Los Angeles 97
May 10—Portland 102, Los Angeles 97
May 13—Portland 105, Los Angeles 101

NBA Finals

Portland 4, Philadelphia 2
May 22—Philadelphia 107, Portland 101
May 26—Philadelphia 107, Portland 89
May 29—Portland 129, Philadelphia 107
May 31—Portland 130, Philadelphia 98
June 3—Portland 110, Philadelphia 104
June 5—Portland 109, Philadelphia 107

INDIVIDUAL LEADERS

Scoring
(Minimum 70 games played or 1,400 points)

	G.	FG	FT	PTS.	AVG.
Maravich, New Orleans	73	886	501	2273	31.1
Knight, Indiana	78	831	413	2075	26.6
Abdul-Jabbar, Los Angeles	82	888	376	2152	26.2
Thompson, Denver	82	824	477	2125	25.9
McAdoo, Buf.-NY-K	72	740	381	1861	25.8
Lanier, Detroit	64	678	260	1616	25.3
Drew, Atlanta	74	689	412	1790	24.2
Hayes, Washington	82	760	422	1942	23.7
Gervin, San Antonio	82	726	443	1895	23.1
Issel, Denver	79	660	445	1765	22.3

Field Goal Pct.
(Minimum 300 FG made)

	FGM	FGA	PCT.
Abdul-Jabbar, Los Angeles	888	1533	.579
Kupchak, Washington	341	596	.572
Jones, Denver	501	879	.570
Gervin, San Antonio	726	1335	.544
Lanier, Detroit	678	1269	.534

Free Throw Pct.
(Minimum 125 FT made)

	FTM	FTA	PCT.
DiGregorio, Buffalo	138	146	.945
Barry, Golden State	359	392	.916
Murphy, Houston	272	307	.886
Newlin, Houston	269	304	.885
Brown, Seattle	168	190	.884

Assists
(Minimum 70 games or 400 assists)

	G.	NO.	AVG.
Buse, Indiana	81	685	8.5
Watts, Seattle	79	630	8.0
Van Lier, Chicago	82	636	7.8
K. Porter, Detroit	81	592	7.3
Henderson, Atl.-Was.	87	598	6.9

Rebounds
(Minimum 70 games or 800 rebounds)

	G.	OFF.	DEF.	TOT.	AVG.
Walton, Portland	65	211	723	934	14.4
Abdul-Jabbar, Los Angeles	82	266	824	1090	13.3
Malone, Buf.-Hou.	82	437	635	1072	13.1
Gilmore, Chicago	82	313	757	1070	13.0
McAdoo, Buf.-NY-K	72	199	727	926	12.9

Steals
(Minimum 70 games or 125 steals)

	G.	NO.	AVG.
Buse, Indiana	81	281	3.47
Taylor, Kansas City	72	199	2.76
Watts, Seattle	79	214	2.71
Buckner, Milwaukee	79	192	2.43
Gale, San Antonio	82	191	2.33

Blocked Shots
(Minimum 70 games or 100 blocks)

	G.	NO.	AVG.
Walton, Portland	65	211	3.25
Abdul-Jabbar, Los Angeles	82	261	3.18
Hayes, Washington	82	220	2.68
Gilmore, Chicago	82	203	2.48
Jones, Philadelphia	82	200	2.44

Before 1977 many fans barely acknowledged that Portland had been fielding a team in the NBA. The Trail Blazers didn't command respect, averaging 28 wins in six seasons and failing to earn a playoff berth. But in just one magical season, NBA fans everywhere were introduced to "Blazermania."

The Pacific Northwest embraced the Trail Blazers and their decidedly unconventional red-haired center from California, Bill Walton. Portland played the team game that thrilled basketball purists and that had brought first the Celtics, and later the Knicks, NBA Championship rings.

1977–78

Two violent incidents cast a shadow over the game. Kareem Abdul-Jabbar punched Milwaukee rookie center Kent Benson, breaking his hand and drawing a $5,000 fine from Commissioner O'Brien. Abdul-Jabbar missed 20 games, hurting the Lakers' chances in the playoffs. Benson missed fewer games, but he never fulfilled the promise he'd shown as a collegian at Indiana. An even more serious incident occurred in December. Kermit Washington, a powerfully built forward for the Lakers, got into a fight with Houston center Kevin Kunnert. As Houston's star forward Rudy Tomjanovich ran toward the combatants, Washington turned and swung his fist, inflicting massive injuries to Tomjanovich's jaw, eye and cheek. Washington was fined and suspended for two months, costing him more than $50,000 in salary.

Portland had won a league-high 58 games during

Hard-driving coach Dick Motta and 10-time NBA All-Star Elvin Hayes were vastly different personalities, but in 1978 the two compromised their different basketball philosophies enough to secure the only NBA title in Bullets history. It proved to be the only NBA Championship for Hayes, who played in 1,303 NBA games, and Motta, who coached in 1,719 NBA games (going into his second stint as coach of the Dallas Mavericks in 1994–95).

"We had such diverse talent on that team," Hayes said. "We had Mitch Kupchak, Larry Wright, Charles Johnson and Greg Ballard all coming off the bench. Any one of those guys would have been a great starter on another team. For starters, we had Unseld, Kevin Grevey, Tommy Henderson, Bobby Dandridge and myself. From the bench to the starters, we had great balance."

the season, but saw its playoff chances dwindle with injuries to several players, most notably Walton. Instead, two Cinderella teams, Washington and Seattle, neither of which had won its division, advanced to the Finals.

The Bullets franchise, which had been to the NBA Finals twice before without winning a single game, rebounded from a 3–2 deficit to defeat Seattle in seven games.

NBA 1977-78

FINAL STANDINGS

Eastern Conference

Atlantic Division

	W.	L.	PCT.
Philadelphia	55	27	.671
New York	43	39	.524
Boston	32	50	.390
Buffalo	27	55	.329
New Jersey	24	58	.293

Central Division

	W.	L.	PCT.
San Antonio	52	30	.634
Washington	44	38	.537
Cleveland	43	39	.524
Atlanta	41	41	.500
New Orleans	39	43	.476
Houston	28	54	.341

Western Conference

Midwest Division

	W.	L.	PCT.
Denver	48	34	.585
Milwaukee	44	38	.537
Chicago	40	42	.488
Detroit	38	44	.463
Indiana	31	51	.378
Kansas City	31	51	.378

Pacific Division

	W.	L.	PCT.
Portland	58	24	.707
Phoenix	49	33	.598
Seattle	47	35	.573
Los Angeles	45	37	.549
Golden State	43	39	.524

PLAYOFFS

Eastern Conference First Round

Washington 2, Atlanta 0
April 12—Washington 103, Atlanta 94
April 14—Washington 107, Atlanta 103 (OT)

New York 2, Cleveland 0
April 12—New York 132, Cleveland 114
April 14—New York 109, Cleveland 107

Western Conference First Round

Seattle 2, Los Angeles 1
April 12—Seattle 102, Los Angeles 90
April 14—Los Angeles 105, Seattle 99
April 16—Seattle 111, Los Angeles 102

Milwaukee 2, Phoenix 0
April 11—Milwaukee 111, Phoenix 103
April 14—Milwaukee 94, Phoenix 90

Eastern Conference Semifinals

Philadelphia 4, New York 0
April 16—Philadelphia 130, New York 90
April 18—Philadelphia 119, New York 100
April 20—Philadelphia 137, New York 126
April 23—Philadelphia 112, New York 107

Washington 4, San Antonio 2
April 16—San Antonio 114, Washington 103
April 18—Washington 121, San Antonio 117
April 21—Washington 118, San Antonio 105
April 23—Washington 98, San Antonio 95
April 25—San Antonio 116, Washington 105
April 28—Washington 103, San Antonio 100

Western Conference Semifinals

Denver 4, Milwaukee 3
April 18—Denver 119, Milwaukee 103
April 21—Denver 127, Milwaukee 111
April 23—Milwaukee 143, Denver 112
April 25—Denver 118, Milwaukee 104
April 28—Milwaukee 117, Denver 112
April 30—Milwaukee 119, Denver 91
May 3—Denver 116, Milwaukee 110

Seattle 4, Portland 2
April 18—Seattle 104, Portland 95
April 21—Portland 96, Seattle 93
April 23—Seattle 99, Portland 84
April 26—Seattle 100, Portland 98
April 30—Portland 113, Seattle 89
May 1—Seattle 105, Portland 94

Eastern Conference Finals

Washington 4, Philadelphia 2
April 30—Washington 122, Philadelphia 117 (OT)
May 3—Philadelphia 110, Washington 104
May 5—Washington 123, Philadelphia 108
May 7—Washington 121, Philadelphia 105
May 10—Philadelphia 107, Washington 94
May 12—Washington 101, Philadelphia 99

Western Conference Finals

Seattle 4, Denver 2
May 5—Denver 116, Seattle 107
May 7—Seattle 121, Denver 111
May 10—Seattle 105, Denver 91
May 12—Seattle 100, Denver 94
May 14—Denver 123, Seattle 114
May 17—Seattle 123, Denver 108

NBA Finals

Washington 4, Seattle 3
May 21—Seattle 106, Washington 102
May 25—Washington 106, Seattle 98
May 28—Seattle 93, Washington 92
May 30—Washington 120, Seattle 116 (OT)
June 2—Seattle 98, Washington 94
June 4—Washington 117, Seattle 82
June 7—Washington 105, Seattle 99

INDIVIDUAL LEADERS

Scoring

(Minimum 70 games played or 1,400 points)

	G.	FG	FT	PTS.	AVG.
Gervin, San Antonio	82	864	504	2232	27.2
Thompson, Denver	80	826	520	2172	27.2
McAdoo, New York	79	814	469	2097	26.5
Abdul-Jabbar, Los Angeles	62	663	274	1600	25.8
Murphy, Houston	76	852	245	1949	25.6
Westphal, Phoenix	80	809	396	2014	25.2
Smith, Buffalo	82	789	443	2021	24.6
Lanier, Detroit	63	622	298	1542	24.5
Davis, Phoenix	81	786	387	1959	24.2
King, New Jersey	79	798	313	1909	24.2

Field Goal Pct.

(Minimum 300 FG made)

	FGM	FGA	PCT.
Jones, Denver	440	761	.578
Dawkins, Philadelphia	332	577	.575
Gilmore, Chicago	704	1260	.559
Abdul-Jabbar, Los Angeles	663	1205	.550
English, Milwaukee	343	633	.542

Free Throw Pct.

(Minimum 125 FT made)

	FTM	FTA	PCT.
Barry, Golden State	378	409	.924
Murphy, Houston	245	267	.918
Brown, Seattle	176	196	.898
Newlin, Houston	152	174	.874
Wedman, Kansas City	221	254	.870

Assists

(Minimum 70 games or 400 assists)

	G.	NO.	AVG.
K. Porter, Det.-N.J.	82	837	10.2
Lucas, Houston	82	768	9.4
Sobers, Indiana	79	584	7.4
Nixon, Los Angeles	81	553	6.8
Van Lier, Chicago	78	531	6.8

Rebounds

(Minimum 70 games or 800 rebounds)

	G.	OFF.	DEF.	TOT.	AVG.
Robinson, New Orleans	82	298	990	1288	15.7
Malone, Houston	59	380	506	886	15.0
Cowens, Boston	77	248	830	1078	14.0
Hayes, Washington	81	335	740	1075	13.3
Nater, Buffalo	78	278	751	1029	13.2

Steals

(Minimum 70 games or 125 steals)

	G.	NO.	AVG.
Lee, Phoenix	82	225	2.74
Williams, Seattle	79	185	2.34
Buckner, Milwaukee	82	188	2.29
Gale, San Antonio	70	159	2.27
Buse, Phoenix	82	185	2.26

Blocked Shots

(Minimum 70 games or 100 blocks)

	G.	NO.	AVG.
Johnson, New Jersey	81	274	3.38
Abdul-Jabbar, Los Angeles	62	185	2.98
Rollins, Atlanta	80	218	2.73
Walton, Portland	58	146	2.52
Paultz, San Antonio	80	194	2.43

1978–79

An offseason development would have major ramifications on the entire decade of the 1980s. Larry Bird, a junior eligible from Indiana State, was chosen as the sixth pick of the 1978 NBA Draft by the Boston Celtics. Although Bird elected to remain in school, Red Auerbach, who had for years found players by extraordinary means, had done it again.

Washington won a league-high 54 games and took the Atlantic Division, while San Antonio, behind repeat NBA scoring champion George Gervin (29.6 ppg), won the Central. Kansas City, in its first year under feisty Cotton Fitzsimmons, qualified for the playoffs for only the second time since moving from Cincinnati by winning the Midwest, and Seattle, brimming with confidence after reaching the Finals, took the Pacific.

Only Kansas City, victimized by a high-scoring Phoenix club led by Paul Westphal and Walter Davis, failed to advance to the Conference Finals. Washington fell behind San Antonio 3–1, but won three straight games by a total of 14 points to keep their hopes of two straight titles alive. Seattle won the first two against Phoenix, dropped three straight, then came back to take the last two games by a total of five points to set up a rematch with the Bullets.

Washington took Game 1 by two points when Larry Wright made two free throws with no time remaining. But the SuperSonics, behind NBA Finals MVP Dennis Johnson, won four straight to bring Seattle a title and some overdue respect.

NBA 1978-79

FINAL STANDINGS

Eastern Conference

Atlantic Division

	W.	L.	PCT.
Washington	54	28	.659
Philadelphia	47	35	.573
New Jersey	37	45	.451
New York	31	51	.378
Boston	29	53	.354

Central Division

	W.	L.	PCT.
San Antonio	48	34	.585
Houston	47	35	.573
Atlanta	46	36	.561
Cleveland	30	52	.366
Detroit	30	52	.366
New Orleans	26	56	.317

Western Conference

Midwest Division

	W.	L.	PCT.
Kansas City	48	34	.585
Denver	47	35	.573
Indiana	38	44	.463
Milwaukee	38	44	.463
Chicago	31	51	.378

Pacific Division

	W.	L.	PCT.
Seattle	52	30	.634
Phoenix	50	32	.610
Los Angeles	47	35	.573
Portland	45	37	.549
San Diego	43	39	.524
Golden State	38	44	.463

PLAYOFFS

Eastern Conference First Round

Atlanta 2, Houston 0
April 11—Atlanta 109, Houston 106
April 13—Atlanta 100, Houston 91

Philadelphia 2, New Jersey 0
April 11—Philadelphia 122, New Jersey 114
April 13—Philadelphia 111, New Jersey 101

Western Conference First Round

Los Angeles 2, Denver 1
April 10—Denver 110, Los Angeles 105
April 13—Los Angeles 121, Denver 109
April 15—Los Angeles 112, Denver 111

Phoenix 2, Portland 1
April 10—Phoenix 107, Portland 103
April 13—Portland 96, Phoenix 92
April 15—Phoenix 101, Portland 91

Eastern Conference Semifinals

Washington 4, Atlanta 3
April 15—Washington 103, Atlanta 89
April 17—Atlanta 107, Washington 99
April 20—Washington 89, Atlanta 77
April 22—Washington 120, Atlanta 118 (OT)
April 24—Atlanta 107, Washington 103
April 26—Atlanta 104, Washington 86
April 29—Washington 100, Atlanta 94

San Antonio 4, Philadelphia 3
April 15—San Antonio 119, Philadelphia 106
April 17—San Antonio 121, Philadelphia 120
April 20—Philadelphia 123, San Antonio 115
April 22—San Antonio 115, Philadelphia 112
April 26—Philadelphia 120, San Antonio 97
April 29—Philadelphia 92, San Antonio 90
May 2—San Antonio 111, Philadelphia 108

Western Conference Semifinals

Seattle 4, Los Angeles 1
April 17—Seattle 112, Los Angeles 101
April 18—Seattle 108, Los Angeles 103 (OT)
April 20—Los Angeles 118, Seattle 112 (OT)
April 22—Seattle 117, Los Angeles 115
April 25—Seattle 106, Los Angeles 100

Phoenix 4, Kansas City 1
April 17—Phoenix 102, Kansas City 99
April 20—Kansas City 111, Phoenix 91
April 22—Phoenix 108, Kansas City 93
April 25—Phoenix 108, Kansas City 94
April 27—Phoenix 120, Kansas City 99

Eastern Conference Finals

Washington 4, San Antonio 3
May 4—San Antonio 118, Washington 97
May 6—Washington 115, San Antonio 95
May 9—San Antonio 116, Washington 114
May 11—San Antonio 118, Washington 102
May 13—Washington 107, San Antonio 103
May 16—Washington 108, San Antonio 100
May 18—Washington 107, San Antonio 105

Western Conference Finals

Seattle 4, Phoenix 3
May 1—Seattle 108, Phoenix 93
May 4—Seattle 103, Phoenix 97
May 6—Phoenix 113, Seattle 103
May 8—Phoenix 100, Seattle 91
May 11—Phoenix 99, Seattle 93
May 13—Seattle 106, Phoenix 105
May 17—Seattle 114, Phoenix 110

NBA Finals

Seattle 4, Washington 1
May 20—Washington 99, Seattle 97
May 24—Seattle 92, Washington 82
May 27—Seattle 105, Washington 95
May 29—Seattle 114, Washington 112 (OT)
June 1—Seattle 97, Washington 93

INDIVIDUAL LEADERS

Scoring

(Minimum 70 games played or 1,400 points)

	G.	FG	FT	PTS.	AVG.
Gervin, San Antonio	80	947	471	2365	29.6
Free, San Diego	78	795	654	2244	28.8
M. Johnson, Milwaukee	77	820	332	1972	25.6
McAdoo, N.Y.-Bos.	60	596	295	1487	24.8
Malone, Houston	82	716	599	2031	24.8
Thompson, Denver	76	693	439	1825	24.0
Westphal, Phoenix	81	801	339	1941	24.0
Abdul-Jabbar, Los Angeles	80	777	349	1903	23.8
Gilmore, Chicago	82	753	434	1940	23.7
Davis, Phoenix	79	764	340	1868	23.6

Field Goal Pct.

(Minimum 300 FG made)

	FGM	FGA	PCT.
Maxwell, Boston	472	808	.584
Abdul-Jabbar, Los Angeles	777	1347	.577
Unseld, Washington	346	600	.577
Gilmore, Chicago	753	1310	.575
Nater, San Diego	357	627	.569

Free Throw Pct.

(Minimum 125 FT made)

	FTM	FTA	PCT.
Barry, Houston	160	169	.947
Murphy, Houston	246	265	.928
Brown, Seattle	183	206	.888
Smith, Denver	159	180	.883
Sobers, Indiana	298	338	.882

Assists

(Minimum 70 games or 400 assists)

	G.	NO.	AVG.
Porter, Detroit	82	1099	13.4
Lucas, Golden State	82	762	9.3
Nixon, Los Angeles	82	737	9.0
Ford, Kansas City	79	681	8.6
Westphal, Phoenix	81	529	6.5

Rebounds

(Minimum 70 games or 800 rebounds)

	G.	OFF.	DEF.	TOT.	AVG.
Malone, Houston	82	587	857	1444	17.6
Kelley, New Orleans	80	303	723	1026	12.8
Abdul-Jabbar, Los Angeles	80	207	818	1025	12.8
Gilmore, Chicago	82	293	750	1043	12.7
Sikma, Seattle	82	232	781	1013	12.4

Steals

(Minimum 70 games or 125 steals)

	G.	NO.	AVG.
Carr, Detroit	80	197	2.46
Nixon, Los Angeles	82	201	2.45
Jordan, New Jersey	82	201	2.45
Walker, Cleveland	55	130	2.36
Ford, Kansas City	79	174	2.20

Blocked Shots

(Minimum 70 games or 100 blocks)

	G.	NO.	AVG.
Abdul-Jabbar, Los Angeles	80	316	3.95
Johnson, New Jersey	78	253	3.24
Rollins, Atlanta	81	254	3.14
Parish, Golden State	76	217	2.86
Tyler, Detroit	82	201	2.45

Dennis Johnson won the Most Valuable Player Award in the 1979 NBA Finals, Gus Williams led the SuperSonics in scoring, Jack Sikma in rebounding and "Downtown" Fred Brown in improbable perimeter bombs. But the man Coach Lenny Wilkens pointed to as a key member of the squad was 35-year-old ex-Celtic forward Paul Silas, who averaged just 5.6 points and 7.0 rebounds that season.

"Look anywhere on our team, and you'll see Paul's influence," Wilkens said. Silas was in his 15th season as a player, and he would retire to coaching after one more season. But he had spread a little Celtic magic to the northwest corner of the NBA map.

STAR POWER: MAGIC, LARRY, MICHAEL AND MORE
by Jack McCallum

Jack McCallum is a senior writer for Sports Illustrated *and the author of recent books about Shaquille O'Neal and speed skater Dan Jansen.*

At the time no one was aware of the importance of March 26, 1979, the first meeting of the black kid from

Stars like Magic Johnson and Larry Bird helped spur fan interest in the NBA in the 1980s.

Michigan State with an angel's smile and the white kid from Indiana State with a bad haircut.

Oh, it was a fascinating basketball matchup, all right, still the highest-rated TV final in NCAA history. But beyond Michigan State's expected 75–64 victory and beyond the obvious coronation of Magic Johnson and Larry Bird as professional stars of the future, no one could have known that on that court were the roots of perhaps the most successful turnaround by any league in the history of sport.

The NBA of the late '70s, the one Magic and Bird entered together in 1979, existed as almost a cult phenomenon. It was a major sport in places with a championship tradition, like Boston, but went virtually unnoticed in other parts of the country—for example, that part of the country run by TV executives. David J. Stern, who became NBA commissioner in 1984, had a lot of low moments from the time he became associated with the league as general counsel in 1978, but none lower than May 16, 1980, the night a rookie nicknamed Magic led the Lakers to an incredible Game 6 championship victory over the 76ers—and America saw it on tape delay.

It is simplistic to point to a single reason for that, but clearly this was the major one: The American public just didn't embrace NBA stars. Magic and Bird changed that. Pick your surface reasons: Magic had a great smile, Bird was white, Magic had flash, Bird looked like Everyman. But the bottom line is that, together, they formed a kind of professional partnership, unspoken (certainly by the taciturn Bird) but nonetheless palpable, a model, a way to play the game that the American public could relate to. Years later, speaking of the Magic-Bird phenomenon, Golden State's Chris Mullin had this to say: "What they did, for the player and spectator, was to give the lesson that you played hard on every play, every night, every season. You were unselfish and you were fundamentally sound. And if you did those things, you won."

Ah, there was the key thing—both of them won and won big. Magic and Bird became so identified with each other and with winning that average fans vastly overestimate how many times they actually played against each other in the Finals. They didn't meet in championship competition until 1984 (Bird won), their fifth year in the league, and were matched up only twice after that, in 1985 (Magic won) and in 1987 (Magic won again). But year after year they lifted their teams to prominence, and, moreover, their regular-season meetings had an edge, more like minichampionships than just signposts in an endless season.

The sociological impact of Magic-Larry can't be ignored, either. Had a scriptwriter set out to create two foils for one another, he couldn't have done a better job than the jabbering magician from Michigan and the down-and-dirty farmer from Hoosier Land. Their differences—black and white, West Coast and East Coast, showtime and blue collar, Lakers and Celtics—worked out impossibly well for the NBA, which at last had a matchup it could really sell. Suddenly, America could relate to the NBA. You could be a "Magic guy" or a "Larry guy," and in that choice you were making a statement, saying something about yourself. Golf historians have long talked about the impact Arnold Palmer had on their game, and college football buffs would probably say the same about Red Grange. But pro basketball owes an eternal debt to No. 32 in the purple and gold, and No. 33 in the green and white.

They didn't do it alone, not by any means. Waiting patiently in the wings for the game to get big enough to legitimize him was one Julius Erving. In the pre–Magic and Bird era, the average fan looked at the NBA and saw mostly carnival acts, and Erving, at quick glance, seemed to be one himself, albeit one of the classier variety. But when fans started to appreciate the NBA as an art form, they began to see other things about Erving's game, his odd but effective jump shot, his rebounding, the way he played the passing lanes. There was much flash-and-dash to Erving's game, but there was also substance and passion—witness his famous Boston Garden tussle with Bird during the an exhibition game in 1984.

Erving might never have won a championship, however, if not for the arrival of Moses Malone, who came from Houston before the 1982–83 season, providing the final piece in what was one of the great teams of all time. Erving's 76ers tore through the postseason with only one loss, and the sweep of the Lakers certified the Good Doctor as one of the NBA's all-time greats.

Just as important, the presence of Erving—even in

Magic and Larry: It's hard to think of one without immediately thinking of the other, and their great rivalry.

the twilight of his career—gave the NBA a kind of de facto ambassador. Though millions of youngsters grew up following the example of Michael Jordan, "youngsters" like Michael Jordan grew into basketball players following the example of Julius Erving. While Magic and Bird showed everyone the way to do it on the court, Erving was the paradigm off it as well. Erving's effect on NBA play was profound, for it was he who mainstreamed playground moves and bridged the gap between street ball and the NBA. But his importance off the court was simply incalculable. His message was this: When you're a professional, you conduct yourself as one. You act like a gentleman with your teammates, your coach, your fans and even the media that covers you.

Michael Jordan, of course, was Erving raised to the nth degree. Erving did it first, but Jordan did it better. Jordan was a better shooter, a better defender, a better passer. (We will leave it to the individual to decide who was the better midair acrobat.) And his appeal, both on and off the court, was the final step in the evolutionary

Only 20 years old, Magic Johnson came up with a gem in Game 6 of the 1980 NBA Finals against Philadelphia.

process begun by Dr. J and carried on by Bird and Magic.

There was resistance to Jordan early in his career. He was allegedly frozen out at the All-Star Game in 1985, his rookie year, by Isiah Thomas and others (Thomas always denied it), and many players complained about Jordan's near monopoly on big-money endorsement contracts. But Jordan didn't seem to

notice, or, if he did, he didn't seem to care. Sure, a carefully polished image off the court had something to do with his success and popularity. But image doesn't get you 63 points in a playoff game at Boston Garden, as Jordan did against the Celtics in his second season. Image doesn't get you 37.1 points per game, as Jordan averaged in 1986–87, his third year in the league and the year after his return from a foot injury that cost him

It's hard to believe that they met in only three NBA Finals, Larry Bird's Celtics winning in 1984, Magic Johnson's Lakers winning in 1985 and 1987.

most of the 1985–86 season. What would be Jordan's greatest personal accomplishment was evident from the earliest moments of his career: He was *better* than his hype.

And so the NBA had its ultimate piece in the success puzzle—a great player who obviously loved the game (a clause in Jordan's contract guaranteed that he would be allowed to play pickup ball in the offseason)

and one who was attractive to fans of all ages, all races, all creeds and, to the delight of the global-minded Stern, all countries.

Jordan wasn't the only fascinating personality to come into the league in 1984. Charles Barkley, a brash, trash-talking southern kid with a build more suited to playing linebacker, joined the Philadelphia 76ers. To the NBA, Charles was like the bad-boy brother. You had to

Julius Erving led the influx of ABA stars in 1976 that helped revitalize the NBA.

invite him to the family dinner because he was so much fun, but you couldn't be sure he wouldn't start a food fight.

In many respects Barkley is the most remarkable athlete in the game. Standing around 6-5, with a weight ranging between a never svelte 250 and 260 pounds, Barkley was arguably the league's best rebounder and certainly one of its most creative inside shooters. He could elevate, but the key to his success was his ability to jump quickly and use an unerring built-in radar to guide him toward the ball. "I don't believe in boxing out," Barkley once said. "My idea about rebounding is just to go get the damned ball."

As Barkley's career went on, however, Philadelphia became more and more like prison to him. Gradually, all the veterans from the 1983 championship team— Erving, Malone, Bobby Jones, Andrew Toney, Maurice Cheeks—either retired or were traded away, and owner Harold Katz was unable to replace them with comparable talent. Barkley became the quintessential superstar

in the wrong place, proving the point (once again) that glittering statistics are simply not enough to satisfy true professionals. When Barkley didn't win, he became increasingly disenchanted, criticizing teammates, coaches, fans and media. He was finally traded to Phoenix in 1992 and led the Suns into the 1993 NBA Finals, where they were beaten by Jordan's Bulls.

Another superstar who finally packed his bags after he and his team couldn't find the championship pot of gold was Dominique Wilkins, who played 11½ seasons with the Atlanta Hawks before finally being traded to the Los Angeles Clippers in February 1994. Wilkins, nicknamed the Human Highlight Film for his unbelievable dunks and ability to hang in the air, was a scoring machine (he led the league in 1985–86, the season Jordan was injured, with 30.3 points per game) from the time he came bounding into the NBA in 1982, but basketball purists were slow to accept him. Under Wilkins's offensive leadership, the Hawks began a climb toward the NBA's summit, but for a variety of reasons

Though it's been seven years since his last dunk, Julius Erving remains a global ambassador for basketball.

(yes, Wilkins's early failure to become a complete player was one of them), never made it. Each year there was talk that Dominique would have to be traded, or that the Hawks would never win with Dominique, or that Dominique could never raise his teammates to the next level, and so on.

But Dominique endured. And he became a complete player, improving his rebounding and assist totals as he grew older while remaining every bit as dangerous a scorer. For years the Hawks knew they could never get a player of his caliber in a trade, so they wisely kept him, and, finally, as the decade turned the corner, Wilkins began to get appreciated. He had always been popular with the media because, through bad times as well as good, he never shut anybody out, never was less than forthright. He came back strong from an Achilles ten-

Patrick Ewing's in the way? No problem for Michael Jordan—that's why they call him ''Air.''

Few athletes can match the charisma of Charles Barkley, whether it's on or off the court.

don injury during the 1991–92 season and, at the age of 34, was playing better than ever in 1993 and 1994. But finally, at the 1994 trade deadline, the Hawks sent Wilkins to the Clippers for Danny Manning, a fellow All-Star who was six years younger than Wilkins.

Wilkins's situation in Atlanta was analogous to that of Clyde Drexler in Portland, except Drexler remains a Trail Blazer. The Glide was (still is) a phenomenal athlete, a gifted two guard whom history will remember —well, it's sure to be remembered in Portland, anyway —as the reason Michael Jordan was not drafted by the Trail Blazers. Drexler came into the league the year before Jordan, and, though he averaged only 7.7 ppg playing behind veteran Jim Paxson, he was obviously Portland's shooting guard for the future. So when Jordan came out, Portland said, "We don't need him because we've got Clyde. We'll take the big center from Kentucky, Sam Bowie." Bowie never got untracked because of injuries, and Drexler, great as he was, could never rid himself of the shadow of Jordan.

As with Wilkins, many observers thought that the answer to every Trail Blazer problem was to trade Clyde. But Clyde stayed, and, finally, in 1990, he led Portland into the NBA Finals against Detroit. The Trail Blazers came up short in five games and, in 1992, lost in six to the Bulls. It's unfortunate, but as a consequence of timing, Drexler may go down as a great guard who simply wasn't as great as Michael.

For a stable one-two punch, the league may never do better than the Karl Malone–John Stockton tandem in Utah. Stockton arrived in 1984, Malone one year later, and from the time they breathed their first breath of mountain air, neither wanted to be anywhere else. Throughout the decade of the '80s, one could never think about Malone without also thinking about Stockton and vice versa. "We've got some kind of strange telepathy," Malone once said. "Sometimes I'll make a move that I don't know I'm going to do myself, yet John anticipates it." Again, as with Magic and Bird, they offered a model for how to play the game. Without Stockton, the Mailman would probably have been considered a gunner; without Malone to finish his plays with flair, Stockton might have been rated nothing more than a mechanical playmaker. But together they paved a road (two lanes, of course) into the Hall of Fame.

One of the most intriguing subplots of the late '80s was the sudden reemergence of the center position. The success of the Bulls and the Pistons (more on them later) proved that having a classic, back-to-the-basket pivot-man was no longer an absolute necessity, but there wasn't a team in the NBA that, to varying degrees, wouldn't have liked to have Hakeem Olajuwon, Patrick Ewing or David Robinson, the centers of attention.

The trio offers a fascinating look into the different ways the position can be played. Olajuwon's footwork is nonpareil, the consequence of his having been an outstanding soccer player in his native Nigeria. Yet his utter unpredictability—his moves simply didn't suggest any other center who had ever played the game—led some to doubt his ability.

No one doubted the ability, at the defensive end, anyway, of the Knicks' Patrick Ewing, when, breathing fire, he came out of John Thompson's Georgetown program in 1985. Ewing wound up in New York, instantaneously raising expectations that at long last a winning franchise would return to Madison Square Garden. If there was any example in the decade of the '80s that one player doth not a franchise make, it was Ewing and the Knicks. As Patrick struggled to find consistency as a shooter and particularly as a rebounder, the Knicks went 85-161 in his first three seasons. But

Ewing made himself into a great shooter and, slowly but surely, pulled the Knicks up with him.

Robinson pulled the San Antonio Spurs up right away, taking a team that had won 21 games in 1988–89 to 56 wins and a Midwest Division championship in 1989–90, his rookie year. Like Olajuwon, he was a superb natural athlete—Robinson was a gymnast in high school who could walk on his hands for an entire

city block—and, moreover, he just looked like a classic center, with nice form on his jumper and a feel for the game.

Still, since none of them took his team to a championship right away, critics judged these centers by what they lacked rather than by what they possessed. Olajuwon didn't have the overall floor game, they said. Ewing was too mechanical. Robinson lacked fire and

"The Human Highlight Film," Dominique Wilkins, made the Atlanta Hawks one of the NBA's top teams of the 1980s.

Clyde "the Glide" Drexler led the Portland Trail Blazers to the NBA Finals in 1990 and 1992.

been much poorer without them. They were a wild collection of personalities led by their cocaptains, Isiah Thomas and Laimbeer. Both had a knack for winning and for infuriating the opposition; witness their pitched battles with, first, Bird's Celtics, and then, most memorably, with Jordan's Bulls.

For three straight seasons beginning in the 1988 playoffs, the Bulls were tripped up by the Pistons, whose specialty was hellacious defense, streak shooting (Thomas, Laimbeer, Joe Dumars and supersub Vinnie Johnson were all good enough to win games down the stretch) and taunting, physical play. They even had a way to keep Jordan under control (Coach Chuck Daly called his defense against Chicago the "Jordan Rules") and force his less-than-confident teammates, Scottie Pippen in particular, to try to step up in clutch situations. One of the enduring images of the Pistons' run was Laimbeer, after sinking a free throw in a riotous Chicago Stadium during Game 3 of the 1988 Eastern Semifinals, continuing to hold his arm up in the follow-through

passion. Whether or not those criticisms were true, it is a fact that none of them, even taken collectively, matched the appeal and success of one Michael Jeffrey Jordan.

Yes, as Bird's aching back caused him more and more pain and as the Lakers slowly but surely started to descend, the late '80s became dominated by Jordan. But even as he matured as a player and a person, something stood in his way. Something cocky. Something nasty. Something mean. The Detroit Pistons.

For those fans who thought that the NBA had become a little too touchy-feely in the '80s—there was Erving patiently talking to reporters, there were Magic and the once reticent Bird exchanging compliments, there was Jordan's smile on every billboard from Baltimore to Bangkok—the Motor City Madmen were a breath of fresh air. Or perhaps hot air. Though the NBA had its problems dealing with the Pistons—league executive Rod Thorn used to joke that Detroit center Bill Laimbeer's fines were one of the NBA's best revenue sources—the league in the late '80s would have

Better known for his playmaking, perennial assist king John Stockton crossed up the defense by shooting.

position as he ran back upcourt, simply basking in the torrent of boos that rained down upon him.

"It's who we are," said Thomas of the Pistons' style. "It's not like we can play any other way." And it was effective. After serving a one-year apprenticeship in the Finals, losing to the Lakers in seven games in 1988, Detroit won back-to-back titles in 1989 and 1990, sweeping the Lakers in the former and then taking Portland in five.

Because the media concentrated on Detroit's collective bad-boy attitude, it often missed a crucial point about the Pistons' metamorphosis into a championship team. Only a few years before their first title, the Pistons had been an offensive-minded team comprised of mad gunners, Thomas being one of them. But through sheer determination (and the canny drafting of defensive specialists Dennis Rodman and John Salley), they became a low-scoring team that won with defense. Much of the credit for that must go to the selling job of Daly, perhaps the most delightful sideline personality of the

A burning desire to win helped Isiah Thomas lead the Detroit Pistons to NBA crowns in 1989 and 1990.

David Robinson leaps to block a shot attempt by Patrick Ewing in a matchup of two of the NBA's premier centers.

'80s. The slick-dressing coach, quick with a joke, was a masterful public relations tool for the Pistons, at once defusing much of the criticism directed at his players while at the same time preserving his team's fire. Once, before a crucial playoff game, Daly walked over to a group of reporters at courtside, leaned down, pointed to his tie and said, "You know, the gold in this tie is a perfect match for the subtle pinstripes in my suit."

Daly's uncanny ability to mix an easygoing temperament with a highly competitive demeanor during the game was a major reason he was selected to coach the first U.S. Olympic team to include NBA players. Called the Dream Team, for, truly, there will never be another like it, the Americans stormed through the qualifying competition in Portland and then on to the gold medal in Barcelona in August 1992 with hardly a false step. The unofficial cocaptains were Magic Johnson and Larry Bird, the latter more of an honorary leader since he was in almost constant pain by then and, indeed, did retire a few weeks after the Games. The main forces on

Chuck Daly proved the perfect coach for the Dream Team and led the U.S.A. to Olympic gold in Barcelona.

the court were Jordan and Barkley, who by then had clearly established themselves as the best players in the game. The rest of the team was comprised of many of the major personalities that have been discussed: Karl Malone, Stockton, Robinson, Ewing, Drexler, Pippen and Mullin, the sharpshooting lefty forward from the Golden State Warriors. The final member of the team was the outstanding college player of 1992, Duke's Christian Laettner, who had been drafted by the Minnesota Timberwolves.

After leading the Bulls to back-to-back titles in '91 and '92, Jordan did it again in '93 and, four months later, pronouncing the thrill all but gone, he hung up his Airs in a surprise retirement announcement. It was a truly electrifying moment, the top sports story of 1993. Had a comparable event occurred, say, 14 or 15 years earlier, the NBA would have pushed the panic button. But it didn't. Though Magic (diagnosed with the HIV virus) and Bird were already gone and Barkley was talking about leaving soon due to a nagging back injury, there seemed to be enough young personalities around to carry the torch. They included Orlando Magic Goliath Shaquille O'Neal; the Charlotte Hornets' dynamic duo of Larry Johnson and Alonzo Mourning; Laettner; Miami Heat dazzler Harold Miner, once dubbed "Baby Jordan"; young powerhouse Chris Web-

Bulls owner Jerry Reinsdorf (at microphone) had nothing but praise for Michael Jordan (right), who stunned the world with his 1993 retirement.

ber of Golden State; and rim-rattling dunker Shawn Kemp of Seattle, just to name those at the tip of the iceberg.

That's a lot of talent and a lot of charisma. But remember one thing: The personalities who dominated the game in the decade of the '80s and turned the NBA into a mainstream sport came into a league that was struggling to achieve its identity. Either consciously or subconsciously, they felt a strong urge to help the league, to carry a bayonet in the public relations war;

there was an unspoken bond between the league and the players. The O'Neals and the Miners don't necessarily feel that way. They came in and saw crowded arenas, a worldwide merchandising plan and multimillion-dollar contracts and may not feel the sense of communion that Magic, Bird and Jordan felt. It will be interesting to see whether such a proprietary feeling ever does evolve among the young players.

One thing is for sure: The NBA will never have another decade like the 1980s.

1979–80

Although the season would forever be known as the year Larry Bird and Earvin "Magic" Johnson entered the league, several other important changes also occurred. The three-point field goal, a popular facet of the ABA game, was adopted by the NBA. The New Orleans Jazz moved to Salt Lake City and took the unlikely team name of the Utah Jazz. And the schedule was altered so that teams faced rivals in their own division more often than teams from other divisions.

But the big story of the season was definitely the arrival of two charismatic and talented rookies, Bird and Johnson, materializing on opposite coasts on the rosters of two of the NBA's most successful franchises. The turnaround in Boston was dramatic. Havlicek had retired after the 1978 season, and Boston went 29-53 in 1979. Along with Bird, the Celtics still had Cowens and third-year forward Cedric Maxwell up front, with Archibald and Chris Ford in the backcourt. The team posted a remarkable 61-21 record, a 32-game improvement. But Philadelphia won 59 games and behind Erving's stellar play defeated the Celtics in five games to advance to the Finals.

In Los Angeles, the Lakers experienced a little "Magic," as Johnson's enthusiasm seemed to rejuvenate Abdul-Jabbar, propelling the Lakers to 60 wins and a

berth in the NBA Finals. With Abdul-Jabbar leading the way and Johnson stepping in for the injured center in the clinching game, the Lakers won the first title of the 1980s in six games.

Abdul-Jabbar, who hadn't won an NBA title since 1971 with Milwaukee, dominated the Finals as Johnson fed him the ball in all the right spots in the first five games. But Abdul-Jabbar badly twisted an ankle in Game 5 and couldn't make the trip to Philadelphia for Game 6.

The Lakers, figuring they had nothing to lose, came out and played loose in the Spectrum. Jamaal Wilkes enjoyed one of the finest games of his career and finished with 37 points. But the newspapers the next day heralded the only headline possible—"It's Magic!" Johnson, filling in for Abdul-Jabbar as the starting center and eventually playing every position on the court, scored 42 points, adding 15 rebounds and seven assists as the Lakers wrapped up the title.

"We know you're hurting, big fella," Johnson said for all America, and Abdul-Jabbar, to hear. "But we want you to get up and do a little dancin' tonight."

NBA 1979-80

FINAL STANDINGS

Eastern Conference

Atlantic Division

	W.	L.	PCT.
Boston	61	21	.744
Philadelphia	59	23	.720
Washington	39	43	.476
New York	39	43	.476
New Jersey	34	48	.415

Central Division

	W.	L.	PCT.
Atlanta	50	32	.610
Houston	41	41	.500
San Antonio	41	41	.500
Indiana	37	45	.451
Cleveland	37	45	.451
Detroit	16	66	.195

Western Conference

Midwest Division

	W.	L.	PCT.
Milwaukee	49	33	.598
Kansas City	47	35	.573
Denver	30	52	.366
Chicago	30	52	.366
Utah	24	58	.293

Pacific Division

	W.	L.	PCT.
Los Angeles	60	22	.732
Seattle	56	26	.683
Phoenix	55	27	.671
Portland	38	44	.463
San Diego	35	47	.427
Golden State	24	58	.293

PLAYOFFS

Eastern Conference First Round

Houston 2, San Antonio 1
April 2—Houston 95, San Antonio 85
April 4—San Antonio 106, Houston 101
April 6—Houston 141, San Antonio 120

Philadelphia 2, Washington 0
April 2—Philadelphia 111, Washington 96
April 4—Philadelphia 112, Washington 104

Western Conference First Round

Phoenix 2, Kansas City 1
April 2—Phoenix 96, Kansas City 93
April 4—Kansas City 106, Phoenix 96
April 6—Phoenix 114, Kansas City 99

Seattle 2, Portland 1
April 2—Seattle 120, Portland 110
April 4—Portland 105, Seattle 95 (OT)
April 6—Seattle 103, Portland 86

Eastern Conference Semifinals

Philadelphia 4, Atlanta 1
April 6—Philadelphia 107, Atlanta 104
April 9—Philadelphia 99, Atlanta 92
April 10—Atlanta 105, Philadelphia 93
April 13—Philadelphia 107, Atlanta 83
April 15—Philadelphia 105, Atlanta 100

Boston 4, Houston 0
April 9—Boston 119, Houston 101
April 11—Boston 95, Houston 75
April 13—Boston 100, Houston 81
April 14—Boston 138, Houston 121

Western Conference Semifinals

Los Angeles 4, Phoenix 1
April 8—Los Angeles 119, Phoenix 110
April 9—Los Angeles 131, Phoenix 128 (OT)
April 11—Los Angeles 108, Phoenix 105
April 13—Phoenix 127, Los Angeles 101
April 15—Los Angeles 126, Phoenix 101

Seattle 4, Milwaukee 3
April 8—Seattle 114, Milwaukee 113 (OT)
April 9—Milwaukee 114, Seattle 112 (OT)
April 11—Milwaukee 95, Seattle 91
April 13—Seattle 112, Milwaukee 107
April 15—Milwaukee 108, Seattle 97
April 18—Seattle 86, Milwaukee 85
April 20—Seattle 98, Milwaukee 94

Eastern Conference Finals

Philadelphia 4, Boston 1
April 18—Philadelphia 96, Boston 93
April 20—Boston 96, Philadelphia 90
April 23—Philadelphia 99, Boston 97
April 25—Philadelphia 102, Boston 90
April 27—Philadelphia 105, Boston 94

Western Conference Finals

Los Angeles 4, Seattle 1
April 22—Seattle 108, Los Angeles 107
April 23—Los Angeles 108, Seattle 99
April 25—Los Angeles 104, Seattle 100
April 27—Los Angeles 98, Seattle 93
April 30—Los Angeles 111, Seattle 105

NBA Finals

Los Angeles 4, Philadelphia 2
May 4—Los Angeles 109, Philadelphia 102
May 7—Philadelphia 107, Los Angeles 104
May 10—Los Angeles 111, Philadelphia 101
May 11—Philadelphia 105, Los Angeles 102
May 14—Los Angeles 108, Philadelphia 103
May 16—Los Angeles 123, Philadelphia 107

INDIVIDUAL LEADERS

Scoring
(Minimum 70 games played or 1,400 points)

	G.	FG	FT	PTS.	AVG.
Gervin, San Antonio	78	1024	505	2585	33.1
Free, San Diego	68	737	572	2055	30.2
Dantley, Utah	68	730	443	1903	28.0
Erving, Philadelphia	78	838	420	2100	26.9
Malone, Houston	82	778	563	2119	25.8
Abdul-Jabbar, Los Angeles	82	835	364	2034	24.8
Issel, Denver	82	715	517	1951	23.8
Hayes, Washington	81	761	334	1859	23.0
Birdsong, Kansas City	82	781	286	1858	22.7
Mitchell, Cleveland	82	775	270	1820	22.2

Field Goal Pct.
(Minimum 300 FG made)

	FGM	FGA	PCT.
Maxwell, Boston	457	750	.609
Abdul-Jabbar, Los Angeles	835	1383	.604
Gilmore, Chicago	305	513	.595
Dantley, Utah	730	1267	.576
Boswell, Den.-Utah	346	613	.564

3-Pt. Field Goal Pct.
(Minimum 25 made)

	FGM	FGA	PCT.
Brown, Seattle	39	88	.443
Ford, Boston	70	164	.427
Bird, Boston	58	143	.406
Roche, Denver	49	129	.380
Taylor, San Diego	90	239	.377

Free Throw Pct.
(Minimum 125 FT made)

	FTM	FTA	PCT.
Barry, Houston	143	153	.935
Murphy, Houston	271	302	.897
Boone, L.A.-Utah	175	196	.893
Silas, San Antonio	339	382	.887
Newlin, New Jersey	367	415	.884

Assists
(Minimum 70 games or 400 assists)

	G.	NO.	AVG.
Richardson, New York	82	832	10.1
Archibald, Boston	80	671	8.4
Walker, Cleveland	76	607	8.0
Nixon, Los Angeles	82	642	7.8
Lucas, Golden State	80	602	7.5

Rebounds
(Minimum 70 games or 800 rebounds)

	G.	OFF.	DEF.	TOT.	AVG.
Nater, San Diego	81	352	864	1216	15.0
Malone, Houston	82	573	617	1190	14.5
Unseld, Washington	82	334	760	1094	13.3
C. Jones, Philadelphia	80	219	731	950	11.9
Sikma, Seattle	82	198	710	908	11.1

Steals
(Minimum 70 games or 125 steals)

	G.	NO.	AVG.
Richardson, New York	82	265	3.23
Jordan, New Jersey	82	223	2.72
Bradley, Indiana	82	211	2.57
Williams, Seattle	82	200	2.44
Johnson, Los Angeles	77	187	2.43

Blocked Shots
(Minimum 70 games or 100 blocks)

	G.	NO.	AVG.
Abdul-Jabbar, Los Angeles	82	280	3.41
Johnson, New Jersey	81	258	3.19
Rollins, Atlanta	82	244	2.98
Tyler, Detroit	82	220	2.68
Hayes, Washington	81	189	2.33

1980–81

The biggest news of the season came a full four months before the season started. On June 9, 1980, Auerbach pulled off the type of trade that had earned him a reputation for thievery in his more than three decades in the league. Auerbach dealt the first and 13th picks in the 1980 NBA Draft to Golden State for the third pick in the draft and four-year veteran center Robert Parish. The Warriors selected Purdue center Joe Barry Carroll

with the first pick and tabbed Mississippi State forward Rickey Brown 13th. The Celtics took forward Kevin McHale of Minnesota, and thus added Parish and McHale to a frontcourt that already featured Bird and Maxwell. In one trade, Auerbach had fashioned a frontcourt for the next decade.

Thus, the NBA's 35th season started with the Celtics in a strong position just over a year after a 29-53 finish in 1979. The Lakers, meanwhile, were dealt a big blow when Magic Johnson suffered torn cartilage in his left knee just one month into the season, forcing him out of 45 games. As a result, the Lakers failed to win the Pacific Division and were knocked out of the playoffs in the First Round by Houston, which made it all the way to the Finals despite a 40-42 record in the regular season. Moses Malone, the 25-year-old center already in his seventh professional season, averaged 27.8 ppg and led the NBA in rebounding with 14.8 rpg. The Celtics swept Chicago, defeated Philadelphia in seven games after trailing 3–1 and overmatched Houston in six games to win their first title of the Bird-Parish-McHale Era.

In conjunction with the NBA's 35th anniversary, pro basketball writers selected their "All-Time NBA Team." It was made up of Bill Russell, Kareem Abdul-Jabbar, Elgin Baylor, Wilt Chamberlain, Bob Cousy, Julius Erving, John Havlicek, George Mikan, Bob Pettit, Oscar Robertson and Jerry West, and the coach was Red Auerbach.

NBA 1980-81

FINAL STANDINGS

Eastern Conference

Atlantic Division

	W.	L.	PCT.
Boston	62	20	.756
Philadelphia	62	20	.756
New York	50	32	.610
Washington	39	43	.476
New Jersey	24	58	.293

Central Division

	W.	L.	PCT.
Milwaukee	60	22	.732
Chicago	45	37	.549
Indiana	44	38	.537
Atlanta	31	51	.378
Cleveland	28	54	.341
Detroit	21	61	.256

Western Conference

Midwest Division

	W.	L.	PCT.
San Antonio	52	30	.634
Kansas City	40	42	.488
Houston	40	42	.488
Denver	37	45	.451
Utah	28	54	.341
Dallas	15	67	.183

Pacific Division

	W.	L.	PCT.
Phoenix	57	25	.695
Los Angeles	54	28	.659
Portland	45	37	.549
Golden State	39	43	.476
San Diego	36	46	.439
Seattle	34	48	.415

PLAYOFFS

Eastern Conference First Round

Chicago 2, New York 0
March 31—Chicago 90, New York 80
April 3—Chicago 115, New York 114 (OT)

Philadelphia 2, Indiana 0
March 31—Philadelphia 124, Indiana 108
April 2—Philadelphia 96, Indiana 85

Western Conference First Round

Houston 2, Los Angeles 1
April 1—Houston 111, Los Angeles 107
April 3—Los Angeles 111, Houston 106
April 5—Houston 89, Los Angeles 86

Kansas City 2, Portland 1
April 1—Kansas City 98, Portland 97 (OT)
April 3—Portland 124, Kansas City 119 (OT)
April 5—Kansas City 104, Portland 95

Eastern Conference Semifinals

Boston 4, Chicago 0
April 5—Boston 121, Chicago 109
April 7—Boston 106, Chicago 97
April 10—Boston 113, Chicago 107
April 12—Boston 109, Chicago 103

Philadelphia 4, Milwaukee 3
April 5—Philadelphia 125, Milwaukee 122
April 7—Milwaukee 109, Philadelphia 99
April 10—Philadelphia 108, Milwaukee 103
April 12—Milwaukee 109, Philadelphia 98
April 15—Philadelphia 116, Milwaukee 99
April 17—Milwaukee 109, Philadelphia 86
April 19—Philadelphia 99, Milwaukee 98

Western Conference Semifinals

Houston 4, San Antonio 3
April 7—Houston 107, San Antonio 98
April 8—San Antonio 125, Houston 113
April 10—Houston 112, San Antonio 99
April 12—San Antonio 114, Houston 112
April 14—Houston 123, San Antonio 117
April 15—San Antonio 101, Houston 96
April 17—Houston 105, San Antonio 100

Kansas City 4, Phoenix 3
April 7—Phoenix 102, Kansas City 80
April 8—Kansas City 88, Phoenix 83
April 10—Kansas City 93, Phoenix 92
April 12—Kansas City 102, Phoenix 95
April 15—Phoenix 101, Kansas City 89
April 17—Phoenix 81, Kansas City 76
April 19—Kansas City 95, Phoenix 88

Eastern Conference Finals

Boston 4, Philadelphia 3
April 21—Philadelphia 105, Boston 104
April 22—Boston 118, Philadelphia 99
April 24—Philadelphia 110, Boston 100
April 26—Philadelphia 107, Boston 105
April 29—Boston 111, Philadelphia 109
May 1—Boston 100, Philadelphia 98
May 3—Boston 91, Philadelphia 90

Western Conference Finals

Houston 4, Kansas City 1
April 21—Houston 97, Kansas City 78
April 22—Kansas City 88, Houston 79
April 24—Houston 92, Kansas City 88
April 26—Houston 100, Kansas City 89
April 29—Houston 97, Kansas City 88

NBA Finals

Boston 4, Houston 2
May 5—Boston 98, Houston 95
May 7—Houston 92, Boston 90
May 9—Boston 94, Houston 71
May 10—Houston 91, Boston 86
May 12—Boston 109, Houston 80
May 14—Boston 102, Houston 91

INDIVIDUAL LEADERS

Scoring

(Minimum 70 games played or 1,400 points)

	G.	FG	FT	PTS.	AVG.
Dantley, Utah	80	909	632	2452	30.7
Malone, Houston	80	806	609	2222	27.8
Gervin, San Antonio	82	850	512	2221	27.1
Abdul-Jabbar, Los Angeles	80	836	423	2095	26.2
Thompson, Denver	77	734	489	1967	25.5
Birdsong, Kansas City	71	710	317	1747	24.6
Erving, Philadelphia	82	794	422	2014	24.6
Mitchell, Cleveland	82	853	302	2012	24.5
Free, Golden State	65	516	528	1565	24.1
English, Denver	81	768	390	1929	23.8

Field Goal Pct.

(Minimum 300 FG made)

	FGM	FGA	PCT.
Gilmore, Chicago	547	816	.670
Dawkins, Philadelphia	423	697	.607
Maxwell, Boston	441	750	.588
King, Golden State	731	1244	.588
Abdul-Jabbar, Los Angeles	836	1457	.574

3-Pt. Field Goal Pct.

(Minimum 25 made)

	FGM	FGA	PCT.
Taylor, San Diego	44	115	.383
Williams, San Diego	48	141	.340
Hassett, Dal.-G.S.	53	156	.340
Bratz, Cleveland	57	169	.337
Bibby, San Diego	32	95	.337

Free Throw Pct.

(Minimum 125 FT made)

	FTM	FTA	PCT.
Murphy, Houston	206	215	.958
Sobers, Chicago	231	247	.935
Newlin, New Jersey	414	466	.888
Spanarkel, Dallas	375	423	.887
Bridgeman, Milwaukee	213	241	.884

Assists

(Minimum 70 games or 400 assists)

	G.	NO.	AVG.
Porter, Washington	81	734	9.1
Nixon, Los Angeles	79	696	8.8
Ford, Kansas City	66	580	8.8
Richardson, New York	79	627	7.9
Archibald, Boston	80	618	7.7

Rebounds

(Minimum 70 games or 800 rebounds)

	G.	OFF.	DEF.	TOT.	AVG.
Malone, Houston	80	474	706	1180	14.8
Nater, San Diego	82	295	722	1017	12.4
Smith, Golden State	82	433	561	994	12.1
Bird, Boston	82	191	704	895	10.9
Sikma, Seattle	82	184	668	852	10.4

Steals

(Minimum 70 games or 125 steals)

	G.	NO.	AVG.
Johnson, Los Angeles	37	127	3.43
Richardson, New York	79	232	2.94
Buckner, Milwaukee	82	197	2.40
Cheeks, Philadelphia	81	193	2.38
R. Williams, New York	79	185	2.34

Blocked Shots

(Minimum 70 games or 100 blocks)

	G.	NO.	AVG.
G. Johnson, San Antonio	82	278	3.39
Rollins, Atlanta	40	117	2.93
Abdul-Jabbar, Los Angeles	80	228	2.85
Parish, Boston	82	214	2.61
Gilmore, Chicago	82	198	2.41

A shot by Larry Bird late in the fourth quarter of Game 1 of the NBA Finals remains a staple of highlight videos. Bird launched an 18-footer from the right side, knew instantly that the shot was off, hustled in to rebound his miss, caught the ball as his momentum was carrying him to the baseline, switched the ball to his left hand in midair and swished a 12-footer. The Boston Garden faithful fell about the place.

"It was the one best shot I've ever seen a player make," Auerbach claimed.

1981–82

Frustrated by their playoff failure in 1981, the Lakers started the season determined to make a better showing. But an early-season disagreement between Coach Paul Westhead and Magic Johnson led to Westhead's dismissal just 11 games into the season, despite his having won at least 50 games in each of his two seasons at the Lakers' helm. Johnson, cast as the villain, was actually booed at the Forum, which had previously been unthinkable. But out of the chaos emerged Pat Riley, the former Laker who had been part of the 1972 championship team. Riley had been brought down by Westhead from the broadcast booth to serve as an assistant coach two years earlier and was thrust into the top job when Jerry West, then a personnel consultant to the team, declined.

Riley installed a freewheeling offense and aggressive, trapping defense, and the Lakers responded by winning 57 games. Boston won a league-high 63 games and the Eastern Division, and Philadelphia and Boston advanced to meet in the Eastern Conference Finals for the third straight year. Philadelphia went up 3–1 for the

Bob McAdoo had won three consecutive league scoring titles as a member of the Buffalo Braves. But his teams never got past the Eastern Conference Semifinals. After several injuries and trades, the former All-Star had fallen into the category of many high-scoring players: admired for his point-producing ability but disdained for his teams' lack of playoff success. The night before Christmas 1981, the 30-year-old McAdoo was traded to the Lakers. Although the trade received little notice, McAdoo became a key player for Los Angeles, averaging 16.7 ppg in the playoffs. The championship ring was a fine fit for him.

"This is the happiest moment of my life," he said in the moments after the Lakers' victory. "People have said bad things about me during my career, but this makes up for it."

second straight year, but Boston again won two games to send it to a seventh game in Boston. This time, Philadelphia triumphed 120–106 and moved on to meet the Lakers in the Finals. Los Angeles had swept Phoenix and San Antonio to reach the Finals and had been enduring two-a-day practice sessions in order not to be rusty for the Finals. The Lakers won Game 1 by seven points, the closest game of the Finals, and captured the series in six games.

NBA 1981-82

FINAL STANDINGS

Eastern Conference

Atlantic Division

	W.	L.	PCT.
Boston	63	19	.768
Philadelphia	58	24	.707
New Jersey	44	38	.537
Washington	43	39	.524
New York	33	49	.402

Central Division

	W.	L.	PCT.
Milwaukee	55	27	.671
Atlanta	42	40	.512
Detroit	39	43	.476
Indiana	35	47	.427
Chicago	34	48	.415
Cleveland	15	67	.183

Western Conference

Midwest Division

	W.	L.	PCT.
San Antonio	48	34	.585
Denver	46	36	.561
Houston	46	36	.561
Kansas City	30	52	.366
Dallas	28	54	.341
Utah	25	57	.305

Pacific Division

	W.	L.	PCT.
Los Angeles	57	25	.695
Seattle	52	30	.634
Phoenix	46	36	.561
Golden State	45	37	.549
Portland	42	40	.512
San Diego	17	65	.207

PLAYOFFS

Eastern Conference First Round

Philadelphia 2, Atlanta 0
April 21—Philadelphia 111, Atlanta 76
April 23—Philadelphia 98, Atlanta 95 (OT)

Washington 2, New Jersey 0
April 20—Washington 96, New Jersey 83
April 23—Washington 103, New Jersey 92

Western Conference First Round

Phoenix 2, Denver 1
April 20—Denver 129, Phoenix 113
April 23—Phoenix 126, Denver 110
April 24—Phoenix 124, Denver 119

Seattle 2, Houston 1
April 21—Seattle 102, Houston 87
April 23—Houston 91, Seattle 70
April 25—Seattle 104, Houston 83

Eastern Conference Semifinals

Boston 4, Washington 1
April 25—Boston 109, Washington 91
April 28—Washington 103, Boston 102
May 1—Boston 92, Washington 83
May 2—Boston 103, Washington 99 (OT)
May 5—Boston 131, Washington 126 (2OT)

Philadelphia 4, Milwaukee 2
April 25—Philadelphia 125, Milwaukee 122
April 28—Philadelphia 120, Milwaukee 108
May 1—Milwaukee 92, Philadelphia 91
May 2—Philadelphia 100, Milwaukee 93
May 5—Milwaukee 110, Philadelphia 98
May 7—Philadelphia 102, Milwaukee 90

Western Conference Semifinals

Los Angeles 4, Phoenix 0
April 27—Los Angeles 115, Phoenix 96
April 28—Los Angeles 117, Phoenix 98
April 30—Los Angeles 114, Phoenix 106
May 2—Los Angeles 112, Phoenix 107

San Antonio 4, Seattle 1
April 27—San Antonio 95, Seattle 93
April 28—Seattle 114, San Antonio 99
April 30—San Antonio 99, Seattle 97
May 2—San Antonio 115, Seattle 113
May 5—San Antonio 109, Seattle 103

Eastern Conference Finals

Philadelphia 4, Boston 3
May 9—Boston 121, Philadelphia 81
May 12—Philadelphia 121, Boston 113
May 15—Philadelphia 99, Boston 97
May 16—Philadelphia 119, Boston 94
May 19—Boston 114, Philadelphia 85
May 21—Boston 88, Philadelphia 75
May 23—Philadelphia 120, Boston 106

Western Conference Finals

Los Angeles 4, San Antonio 0
May 9—Los Angeles 128, San Antonio 117
May 11—Los Angeles 110, San Antonio 101
May 14—Los Angeles 118, San Antonio 108
May 15—Los Angeles 128, San Antonio 123

NBA Finals

Los Angeles 4, Philadelphia 2
May 27—Los Angeles 124, Philadelphia 117
May 30—Philadelphia 110, Los Angeles 94
June 1—Los Angeles 129, Philadelphia 108
June 3—Los Angeles 111, Philadelphia 101
June 6—Philadelphia 135, Los Angeles 102
June 8—Los Angeles 114, Philadelphia 104

INDIVIDUAL LEADERS

Scoring
(Minimum 70 games played or 1,400 points)

	G.	FG	FT	PTS.	AVG.
Gervin, San Antonio	79	993	555	2551	32.3
Malone, Houston	81	945	630	2520	31.1
Dantley, Utah	81	904	648	2457	30.3
English, Denver	82	855	372	2082	25.4
Erving, Philadelphia	81	780	411	1974	24.4
Abdul-Jabbar, Los Angeles	76	753	312	1818	23.9
Williams, Seattle	80	773	320	1875	23.4
King, Golden State	79	740	352	1833	23.2
Free, Golden State	78	650	479	1789	22.9
Bird, Boston	77	711	328	1761	22.9

Field Goal Pct.
(Minimum 300 FG made)

	FGM	FGA	PCT.
Gilmore, Chicago	546	837	.652
S. Johnson, Kansas City	395	644	.613
B. Williams, New Jersey	513	881	.582
Abdul-Jabbar, Los Angeles	753	1301	.579
Natt, Portland	515	894	.576

3-Pt. Field Goal Pct.
(Minimum 25 made)

	FGM	FGA	PCT.
Russell, New York	25	57	.439
Toney, Philadelphia	25	59	.424
Macy, Phoenix	39	100	.390
Winters, Milwaukee	36	93	.387
Buse, Indiana	73	189	.386

Free Throw Pct.
(Minimum 125 FT made)

	FTM	FTA	PCT.
Macy, Phoenix	152	169	.899
Criss, Atl.-S.D.	141	159	.887
Long, Detroit	238	275	.865
Gervin, San Antonio	555	642	.864
Bird, Boston	328	380	.863

Assists
(Minimum 70 games or 400 assists)

	G.	NO.	AVG.
Moore, San Antonio	79	762	9.6
M. Johnson, Los Angeles	78	743	9.5
Cheeks, Philadelphia	79	667	8.4
Archibald, Boston	68	541	8.0
Nixon, Los Angeles	82	652	8.0

Rebounds
(Minimum 70 games or 800 rebounds)

	G.	OFF.	DEF.	TOT.	AVG.
Malone, Houston	81	558	630	1188	14.7
Sikma, Seattle	82	223	815	1038	12.7
B. Williams, New Jersey	82	347	658	1005	12.3
Thompson, Portland	79	258	663	921	11.7
Lucas, New York	80	274	629	903	11.3

Steals
(Minimum 70 games or 125 steals)

	G.	NO.	AVG.
M. Johnson, Los Angeles	78	208	2.67
Cheeks, Philadelphia	79	209	2.65
Richardson, New York	82	213	2.60
Buckner, Milwaukee	70	174	2.49
R. Williams, New Jersey	82	199	2.43

Blocked Shots
(Minimum 70 games or 100 blocks)

	G.	NO.	AVG.
G. Johnson, San Antonio	75	234	3.12
Rollins, Atlanta	79	224	2.84
Abdul-Jabbar, Los Angeles	76	207	2.72
Gilmore, Chicago	82	220	2.68
Parish, Boston	80	192	2.40

1982–83

When Julius Erving came to Philadelphia prior to the 1976–77 season, an NBA Championship was predicted for the 76ers. While the 76ers did make three trips to the NBA Finals in Dr. J's first six years with the team, the title continued to elude them. But when Moses Malone, the league's MVP, played out his option and became available as a free agent, Philadelphia swooped in and signed him, giving up Caldwell Jones and a first-round draft pick to Houston as compensation. The trade solidified the 76ers up front, and Philadelphia went on to 65 victories and the Atlantic Division title. When asked how Philadelphia would perform in the playoffs, Malone issued what would become a famous prediction: "Fo', Fo', Fo'," meaning that the 76ers would win each round in a sweep on their way to the championship.

But the Lakers would have something to say about that. Bolstered by the addition of smooth forward James Worthy, the top pick in the 1982 NBA Draft, they won 58 games and another Pacific Division title, their third in four years. But in the last week of the season, Worthy fractured his leg coming down from a tip-in. It would be a bad break for the Lakers. In the playoffs, they easily moved past Portland and San Antonio to advance to the

Julius Erving had won two ABA championships with the New York Nets in 1974 and 1976. Although Erving and the other ABA players proved they were good enough for the NBA from the start, the NBA title forecast for the 76ers with Erving had not come to pass. Then Moses Malone, another ABA star, came to Philadelphia. The 76ers went 12-1 in the playoffs, recording a sweep over the Lakers in the Finals.

"Let's not make believe," said 76ers Coach Billy Cunningham, a member of the 76ers' last title team in 1967. "The difference from last year was Moses. He gave us the consistency inside that the Lakers had always gotten from Abdul-Jabbar. We got that and more from Moses."

Finals. The 76ers swept the Knicks and defeated Milwaukee in five games to meet the Lakers. But Los Angeles, already without Worthy, also lost Norm Nixon and Bob McAdoo for much of the Finals, and Philadelphia swept to its first title since the days of Wilt Chamberlain. Malone's prediction had to be updated to "Fo', Fi', Fo'" for the championship rings.

NBA 1982-83

FINAL STANDINGS

Eastern Conference

Atlantic Division

	W.	L.	PCT.
Philadelphia	65	17	.793
Boston	56	26	.683
New Jersey	49	33	.598
New York	44	38	.537
Washington	42	40	.512

Central Division

	W.	L.	PCT.
Milwaukee	51	31	.622
Atlanta	43	39	.524
Detroit	37	45	.451
Chicago	28	54	.341
Cleveland	23	59	.280
Indiana	20	62	.244

Western Conference

Midwest Division

	W.	L.	PCT.
San Antonio	53	29	.646
Denver	45	37	.549
Kansas City	45	37	.549
Dallas	38	44	.463
Utah	30	52	.366
Houston	14	68	.171

Pacific Division

	W.	L.	PCT.
Los Angeles	58	24	.707
Phoenix	53	29	.646
Seattle	48	34	.585
Portland	46	36	.561
Golden State	30	52	.366
San Diego	25	57	.305

PLAYOFFS

Eastern Conference First Round

Boston 2, Atlanta 1
April 19—Boston 103, Atlanta 95
April 22—Atlanta 95, Boston 93
April 24—Boston 98, Atlanta 79

New York 2, New Jersey 0
April 20—New York 118, New Jersey 107
April 21—New York 105, New Jersey 99

Western Conference First Round

Denver 2, Phoenix 1
April 19—Phoenix 121, Denver 108
April 21—Denver 113, Phoenix 99
April 24—Denver 117, Phoenix 112 (OT)

Portland 2, Seattle 0
April 20—Portland 108, Seattle 97
April 22—Portland 105, Seattle 96

Eastern Conference Semifinals

Milwaukee 4, Boston 0
April 27—Milwaukee 116, Boston 95
April 29—Milwaukee 95, Boston 91
May 1—Milwaukee 107, Boston 99
May 2—Milwaukee 107, Boston 93

Philadelphia 4, New York 0
April 24—Philadelphia 112, New York 102
April 27—Philadelphia 98, New York 91
April 30—Philadelphia 107, New York 105
May 1—Philadelphia 105, New York 102

Western Conference Semifinals

San Antonio 4, Denver 1
April 26—San Antonio 152, Denver 133
April 27—San Antonio 126, Denver 109
April 29—San Antonio 127, Denver 126 (OT)
May 2—Denver 124, San Antonio 114
May 4—San Antonio 145, Denver 105

Los Angeles 4, Portland 1
April 24—Los Angeles 118, Portland 97
April 26—Los Angeles 112, Portland 106
April 29—Los Angeles 115, Portland 109 (OT)
May 1—Portland 108, Los Angeles 95
May 3—Los Angeles 116, Portland 108

Eastern Conference Finals

Philadelphia 4, Milwaukee 1
May 8—Philadelphia 111, Milwaukee 109 (OT)
May 11—Philadelphia 87, Milwaukee 81
May 14—Philadelphia 104, Milwaukee 96
May 15—Milwaukee 100, Philadelphia 94
May 18—Philadelphia 115, Milwaukee 103

Western Conference Finals

Los Angeles 4, San Antonio 2
May 8—Los Angeles 119, San Antonio 107
May 10—San Antonio 122, Los Angeles 113
May 13—Los Angeles 113, San Antonio 100
May 15—Los Angeles 129, San Antonio 121
May 18—Los Angeles 117, San Antonio 112
May 20—Los Angeles 101, San Antonio 100

NBA Finals

Philadelphia 4, Los Angeles 0
May 22—Philadelphia 113, Los Angeles 107
May 26—Philadelphia 103, Los Angeles 93
May 29—Philadelphia 111, Los Angeles 94
May 31—Philadelphia 115, Los Angeles 108

INDIVIDUAL LEADERS

Scoring
(Minimum 70 games played or 1,400 points)

	G.	FG	FT	PTS.	AVG.
English, Denver	82	959	406	2326	28.4
Vandeweghe, Denver	82	841	489	2186	26.7
Tripucka, Detroit	58	565	392	1536	26.5
Gervin, San Antonio	78	757	517	2043	26.2
Malone, Philadelphia	78	654	600	1908	24.5
Aguirre, Dallas	81	767	429	1979	24.4
Carroll, Golden State	79	785	337	1907	24.1
Free, G.S.-Cle.	73	649	430	1743	23.9
Theus, Chicago	82	749	434	1953	23.8
Cummings, San Diego	70	684	292	1660	23.7

Field Goal Pct.
(Minimum 300 FG made)

	FGM	FGA	PCT.
Gilmore, San Antonio	556	888	.626
S. Johnson, Kansas City	371	595	.624
Dawkins, New Jersey	401	669	.599
Abdul-Jabbar, Los Angeles	722	1228	.588
Williams, New Jersey	536	912	.588

3-Pt. Field Goal Pct.
(Minimum 25 made)

	FGM	FGA	PCT.
Dunleavy, San Antonio	67	194	.345
Thomas, Detroit	36	125	.288
Griffith, Utah	38	132	.288
Leavell, Houston	42	175	.240

Free Throw Pct.
(Minimum 125 FT made)

	FTM	FTA	PCT.
Murphy, Houston	138	150	.920
Vandeweghe, Denver	489	559	.875
Macy, Phoenix	129	148	.872
Gervin, San Antonio	517	606	.853
Dantley, Utah	210	248	.847

Assists
(Minimum 70 games or 400 assists)

	G.	NO.	AVG.
M. Johnson, Los Angeles	79	829	10.5
Moore, San Antonio	77	753	9.8
Green, Utah	78	697	8.9
Drew, Kansas City	75	610	8.1
Johnson, Washington	68	549	8.1

Rebounds
(Minimum 70 games or 800 rebounds)

	G.	OFF.	DEF.	TOT.	AVG.
Malone, Philadelphia	78	445	749	1194	15.3
Williams, New Jersey	82	365	662	1027	12.5
Laimbeer, Detroit	82	282	711	993	12.1
Gilmore, San Antonio	82	299	685	984	12.0
Sikma, Seattle	75	213	645	858	11.4

Steals
(Minimum 70 games or 125 steals)

	G.	NO.	AVG.
Richardson, G.S.-N.J.	64	182	2.84
Green, Utah	78	220	2.82
Moore, San Antonio	77	194	2.52
Thomas, Detroit	81	199	2.46
Cook, New Jersey	82	194	2.37

Blocked Shots
(Minimum 70 games or 100 blocks)

	G.	NO.	AVG.
Rollins, Atlanta	80	343	4.29
Walton, San Diego	33	119	3.61
Eaton, Utah	81	275	3.40
Nance, Phoenix	82	217	2.65
McHale, Boston	82	192	2.34
Gilmore, San Antonio	82	192	2.34

1983–84

The season saw a significant change off the court. Larry O'Brien, who had presided over the peaceful merger between the NBA and ABA, retired as commissioner. In O'Brien's place came David Stern, an energetic attorney who had been the NBA's executive vice president. As the league's fourth commissioner, Stern would oversee tremendous expansion in the marketing of the NBA, develop a cohesive and profitable broadcasting strategy and become the driving force behind the NBA's profound increase in global popularity. Stern would move quickly to ensure the stability of NBA franchises by increasing licensing revenues, developing corporate sponsorships and bolstering the league's image with a groundbreaking antidrug policy.

On the court, the playoff system underwent a radical expansion. The format was expanded to include 16 teams instead of 12, which eliminated the First Round, best-of-3 miniseries. Instead, each First Round series would be a best-of-5, and even the division winners would have to play in the First Round. Now the

NBA Champions would have to win four series for the first time in NBA history.

The Celtics emerged as the dominant team during the regular season, winning 62 games and taking the Atlantic Division by 10 games over the defending champion 76ers. Philadelphia won 52 games, but was ousted in the First Round by New Jersey, the high point in that franchise's NBA history. The Celtics eased past Washington, defeated the Bernard King–led New York Knicks in seven games and easily moved past Milwaukee to reach the Finals. The Lakers, who won 54 games, defeated Kansas City, Dallas and Phoenix, losing only three games along the way, to meet Boston. In what would eventually become a trilogy of epic meetings in the NBA Finals over the next four seasons, Boston outlasted the Lakers to win a 15th NBA Championship.

The Lakers' Kareem Abdul-Jabbar became the NBA's career scoring leader on April 5, 1984, when he surpassed Wilt Chamberlain's mark of 31,419 points.

Four seasons had gone by since Magic Johnson and Larry Bird had entered the NBA in 1979. Magic's Lakers had won two titles and Larry's Celtics had captured one. But the two greatest players in the game had yet to meet in the NBA Finals, their on-court meetings limited to two a year during the regular season. But 1984 was going to change all that.

For years afterward, the Lakers would rue the title that got away from them. The Lakers won the first game in Boston and led Game 2 115-113 with 18 seconds left and possession of the ball. With the series shifting back to Los Angeles after Game 2, the thought of a series sweep was on the minds of players on both sides. But James Worthy's crosscourt pass was intercepted by Gerald Henderson, who went in for an uncontested layup to tie the score. Boston won the game in overtime and, after winning again in overtime in Game 4, managed to pull it out in seven games.

"To be honest, they should have swept," Bird said.

NBA 1983-84

FINAL STANDINGS

Eastern Conference

Atlantic Division

	W.	L.	PCT.
Boston	62	20	.756
Philadelphia	52	30	.634
New York	47	35	.573
New Jersey	45	37	.549
Washington	35	47	.427

Central Division

	W.	L.	PCT.
Milwaukee	50	32	.610
Detroit	49	33	.598
Atlanta	40	42	.488
Cleveland	28	54	.341
Chicago	27	55	.329
Indiana	26	56	.317

Western Conference

Midwest Division

	W.	L.	PCT.
Utah	45	37	.549
Dallas	43	39	.524
Denver	38	44	.463
Kansas City	38	44	.463
San Antonio	37	45	.451
Houston	29	53	.354

Pacific Division

	W.	L.	PCT.
Los Angeles	54	28	.659
Portland	48	34	.585
Seattle	42	40	.512
Phoenix	41	41	.500
Golden State	37	45	.451
San Diego	30	52	.366

PLAYOFFS

Eastern Conference First Round

Milwaukee 3, Atlanta 2
April 17—Milwaukee 105, Atlanta 89
April 19—Milwaukee 101, Atlanta 87
April 21—Atlanta 103, Milwaukee 94
April 24—Atlanta 100, Milwaukee 97
April 26—Milwaukee 118, Atlanta 89

Boston 3, Washington 1
April 17—Boston 91, Washington 83
April 19—Boston 88, Washington 85
April 21—Washington 111, Boston 108 (OT)
April 24—Boston 99, Washington 96

New York 3, Detroit 2
April 17—New York 94, Detroit 93
April 19—Detroit 113, New York 105
April 22—New York 120, Detroit 113
April 25—Detroit 119, New York 112
April 27—New York 127, Detroit 123 (OT)

New Jersey 3, Philadelphia 2
April 18—New Jersey 116, Philadelphia 101
April 20—New Jersey 116, Philadelphia 102
April 22—Philadelphia 108, New Jersey 100
April 24—Philadelphia 110, New Jersey 102
April 26—New Jersey 101, Philadelphia 98

Western Conference First Round

Dallas 3, Seattle 2
April 17—Dallas 88, Seattle 86
April 19—Seattle 95, Dallas 92
April 21—Seattle 104, Dallas 94
April 24—Dallas 107, Seattle 96
April 26—Dallas 105, Seattle 104 (OT)

Utah 3, Denver 2
April 17—Utah 123, Denver 121
April 19—Denver 132, Utah 116
April 22—Denver 121, Utah 117
April 24—Utah 129, Denver 124
April 26—Utah 127, Denver 111

Los Angeles 3, Kansas City 0
April 18—Los Angeles 116, Kansas City 105
April 20—Los Angeles 109, Kansas City 102
April 22—Los Angeles 108, Kansas City 102

Phoenix 3, Portland 2
April 18—Phoenix 113, Portland 106
April 20—Portland 122, Phoenix 116
April 22—Phoenix 106, Portland 103
April 24—Portland 113, Phoenix 110
April 26—Phoenix 117, Portland 105

Eastern Conference Semifinals

Boston 4, New York 3
April 29—Boston 110, New York 92
May 2—Boston 116, New York 102
May 4—New York 100, Boston 92
May 6—New York 118, Boston 113
May 9—Boston 121, New York 99
May 11—New York 106, Boston 104
May 13—Boston 121, New York 104

Milwaukee 4, New Jersey 2
April 29—New Jersey 106, Milwaukee 100
May 1—Milwaukee 98, New Jersey 94
May 3—Milwaukee 100, New Jersey 93
May 5—New Jersey 106, Milwaukee 99
May 8—Milwaukee 94, New Jersey 82
May 10—Milwaukee 98, New Jersey 97

Western Conference Semifinals

Los Angeles 4, Dallas 1
April 28—Los Angeles 134, Dallas 91
May 1—Los Angeles 117, Dallas 101
May 4—Dallas 125, Los Angeles 115
May 6—Los Angeles 122, Dallas 115 (OT)
May 8—Los Angeles 115, Dallas 99

Phoenix 4, Utah 2
April 29—Utah 105, Phoenix 95
May 2—Phoenix 102, Utah 97
May 4—Phoenix 106, Utah 94
May 6—Phoenix 111, Utah 110 (OT)
May 8—Utah 118, Phoenix 106
May 10—Phoenix 102, Utah 82

Eastern Conference Finals

Boston 4, Milwaukee 1
May 15—Boston 119, Milwaukee 96
May 17—Boston 125, Milwaukee 110
May 19—Boston 109, Milwaukee 100
May 21—Milwaukee 122, Boston 113
May 23—Boston 115, Milwaukee 108

Western Conference Finals

Los Angeles 4, Phoenix 2
May 12—Los Angeles 110, Phoenix 94
May 15—Los Angeles 118, Phoenix 102
May 18—Phoenix 135, Los Angeles 127 (OT)
May 20—Los Angeles 126, Phoenix 115
May 23—Phoenix 126, Los Angeles 121
May 25—Los Angeles 99, Phoenix 97

NBA Finals

Boston 4, Los Angeles 3
May 27—Los Angeles 115, Boston 109
May 31—Boston 124, Los Angeles 121 (OT)
June 3—Los Angeles 137, Boston 104
June 6—Boston 129, Los Angeles 125 (OT)
June 8—Boston 121, Los Angeles 103
June 10—Los Angeles 119, Boston 108
June 12—Boston 111, Los Angeles 102

INDIVIDUAL LEADERS

Scoring
(Minimum 70 games played or 1,400 points)

	G.	FG	FT	PTS.	AVG.
Dantley, Utah	79	802	813	2418	30.6
Aguirre, Dallas	79	925	465	2330	29.5
Vandeweghe, Denver	78	895	494	2295	29.4
English, Denver	82	907	352	2167	26.4
King, New York	77	795	437	2027	26.3
Gervin, San Antonio	76	765	427	1967	25.9
Bird, Boston	79	758	374	1908	24.2
Mitchell, San Antonio	79	779	275	1839	23.3
Cummings, San Diego	81	737	380	1854	22.9
Short, Golden State	79	714	353	1803	22.8

Field Goal Pct.
(Minimum 300 FG made)

	FGM	FGA	PCT.
Gilmore, San Antonio	351	556	.631
Donaldson, San Diego	360	604	.596
McGee, Los Angeles	347	584	.594
Dawkins, New Jersey	507	855	.593
Natt, Portland	500	857	.583

3-Pt. Field Goal Pct.
(Minimum 25 made)

	FGM	FGA	PCT.
Griffith, Utah	91	252	.361
Evans, Denver	32	89	.360
Moore, San Antonio	28	87	.322
Cooper, Los Angeles	38	121	.314
Williams, New York	25	81	.309

Free Throw Pct.
(Minimum 125 FT made)

	FTM	FTA	PCT.
Bird, Boston	374	421	.888
Long, Detroit	243	275	.884
Laimbeer, Detroit	316	365	.866
Davis, Phoenix	233	270	.863
Pierce, San Diego	149	173	.861

Assists
(Minimum 70 games or 400 assists)

	G.	NO.	AVG.
Johnson, Los Angeles	67	875	13.1
Thomas, Detroit	82	914	11.1
Nixon, San Diego	82	914	11.1
Lucas, San Antonio	63	673	10.7
Moore, San Antonio	59	566	9.6

Rebounds
(Minimum 70 games or 800 rebounds)

	G.	OFF.	DEF.	TOT.	AVG.
Malone, Philadelphia	71	352	598	950	13.4
Williams, New Jersey	81	355	645	1000	12.3
Ruland, Washington	75	265	657	922	12.3
Laimbeer, Detroit	82	329	674	1003	12.2
Sampson, Houston	82	293	620	913	11.1

Steals
(Minimum 70 games or 125 steals)

	G.	NO.	AVG.
Green, Utah	81	215	2.65
Thomas, Detroit	82	204	2.49
Williams, Seattle	80	189	2.36
Cheeks, Philadelphia	75	171	2.28
Johnson, Los Angeles	67	150	2.24

Blocked Shots
(Minimum 70 games or 100 blocks)

	G.	NO.	AVG.
Eaton, Utah	82	351	4.28
Rollins, Atlanta	77	277	3.60
Sampson, Houston	82	197	2.40
Nance, Phoenix	82	174	2.12
Gilmore, San Antonio	64	132	2.06

1984–85

The 1984 NBA Draft was one for the ages, yielding Michael Jordan, Hakeem Olajuwon, Charles Barkley and John Stockton, as well as many other fine players. Olajuwon had been chosen first by Houston, Jordan third by Chicago, Barkley fifth by Philadelphia and Stockton 16th by Utah. Their impact would be felt for years to come. In New York, Bernard King clinched the scoring title (32.9 ppg) despite suffering a serious knee injury with 27 games left in the season.

But the NBA was focused intently on the Celtics-Lakers matchup. During the regular season, Boston was the class of the East with 63 victories, and Bird enjoyed his best season to date, averaging 28.7 points, 10.5 rebounds and 6.6 assists per game. Each member of Boston's starting five—Bird, Parish, McHale, Dennis Johnson and Danny Ainge—played more than 2,500 minutes during the season. The Lakers, meanwhile, had endured a full offseason of questions about how they had let the title slip right through their fingers in 1984. Magic Johnson in particular seemed to use every game as a stepping-stone toward a rematch with the Celtics. The Lakers won 62 games and easily dispatched Phoenix, Portland and Denver to reach the Finals. Boston had beaten Cleveland, Detroit and Philadelphia to make the finals a return engagement. Led by the 38-year-old Abdul-Jabbar and a revitalized Worthy, the Lakers rebounded from a horrible 148–114 defeat in Game 1 to win the series in six games. After eight losses to Boston in the NBA Finals, the Lakers won the clinching Game 6 on the parquet at Boston Garden.

NBA 1984-85

FINAL STANDINGS

Eastern Conference

Atlantic Division

	W.	L.	PCT.
Boston	63	19	.768
Philadelphia	58	24	.707
New Jersey	42	40	.512
Washington	40	42	.488
New York	24	58	.293

Central Division

	W.	L.	PCT.
Milwaukee	59	23	.720
Detroit	46	36	.561
Chicago	38	44	.463
Cleveland	36	46	.439
Atlanta	34	48	.415
Indiana	22	60	.268

Western Conference

Midwest Division

	W.	L.	PCT.
Denver	52	30	.634
Houston	48	34	.585
Dallas	44	38	.537
San Antonio	41	41	.500
Utah	41	41	.500
Kansas City	31	51	.378

Pacific Division

	W.	L.	PCT.
L.A. Lakers	62	20	.756
Portland	42	40	.512
Phoenix	36	46	.439
L.A. Clippers	31	51	.378
Seattle	31	51	.378
Golden State	22	60	.268

PLAYOFFS

Eastern Conference First Round

Boston 3, Cleveland 1
April 18—Boston 126, Cleveland 123
April 20—Boston 108, Cleveland 106
April 23—Cleveland 105, Boston 98
April 25—Boston 117, Cleveland 115

Milwaukee 3, Chicago 1
April 19—Milwaukee 109, Chicago 100
April 21—Milwaukee 122, Chicago 115
April 24—Chicago 109, Milwaukee 107
April 26—Milwaukee 105, Chicago 97

Detroit 3, New Jersey 0
April 18—Detroit 125, New Jersey 105
April 21—Detroit 121, New Jersey 111
April 24—Detroit 116, New Jersey 115

Philadelphia 3, Washington 1
April 17—Philadelphia 104, Washington 97
April 21—Philadelphia 113, Washington 94
April 24—Washington 118, Philadelphia 100
April 26—Philadelphia 106, Washington 98

Western Conference First Round

Portland 3, Dallas 1
April 18—Dallas 139, Portland 131 (2OT)
April 20—Portland 124, Dallas 121 (OT)
April 23—Portland 122, Dallas 109
April 25—Portland 115, Dallas 113

Denver 3, San Antonio 2
April 18—Denver 141, San Antonio 111
April 20—San Antonio 113, Denver 111
April 23—Denver 115, San Antonio 112
April 26—San Antonio 116, Denver 111
April 28—Denver 126, San Antonio 99

Utah 3, Houston 2
April 19—Utah 115, Houston 101
April 21—Houston 122, Utah 96
April 24—Utah 112, Houston 104
April 26—Houston 96, Utah 94
April 28—Utah 104, Houston 97

L.A. Lakers 3, Phoenix 0
April 18—L.A. Lakers 142, Phoenix 114
April 20—L.A. Lakers 147, Phoenix 130
April 23—L.A. Lakers 119, Phoenix 103

Eastern Conference Semifinals

Boston 4, Detroit 2
April 28—Boston 133, Detroit 99
April 30—Boston 121, Detroit 114
May 2—Detroit 125, Boston 117
May 5—Detroit 102, Boston 99
May 8—Boston 130, Detroit 123
May 10—Boston 123, Detroit 113

Philadelphia 4, Milwaukee 0
April 28—Philadelphia 127, Milwaukee 105
April 30—Philadelphia 112, Milwaukee 108
May 3—Philadelphia 109, Milwaukee 104
May 5—Philadelphia 121, Milwaukee 112

Western Conference Semifinals

Denver 4, Utah 1
April 30—Denver 130, Utah 113
May 2—Denver 131, Utah 123 (OT)
May 4—Utah 131, Denver 123
May 5—Denver 125, Utah 118
May 7—Denver 116, Utah 104

L.A. Lakers 4, Portland 1
April 27—L.A. Lakers 125, Portland 101
April 30—L.A. Lakers 134, Portland 118
May 3—L.A. Lakers 130, Portland 126
May 5—Portland 115, L.A. Lakers 107
May 7—L.A. Lakers 139, Portland 120

Eastern Conference Finals

Boston 4, Philadelphia 1
May 12—Boston 108, Philadelphia 93
May 14—Boston 106, Philadelphia 98
May 18—Boston 105, Philadelphia 94
May 19—Philadelphia 115, Boston 104
May 22—Boston 102, Philadelphia 100

Western Conference Finals

L.A. Lakers 4, Denver 1
May 11—L.A. Lakers 139, Denver 122
May 14—Denver 136, L.A. Lakers 114
May 17—L.A. Lakers 136, Denver 118
May 19—L.A. Lakers 120, Denver 116
May 22—L.A. Lakers 153, Denver 109

NBA Finals

L.A. Lakers 4, Boston 2
May 27—Boston 148, L.A. Lakers 114
May 30—L.A. Lakers 109, Boston 102
June 2—L.A. Lakers 136, Boston 111
June 5—Boston 107, L.A. Lakers 105
June 7—L.A. Lakers 120, Boston 111
June 9—L.A. Lakers 111, Boston 100

INDIVIDUAL LEADERS

Scoring
(Minimum 70 games played or 1,400 points)

	G.	FG	FT	PTS.	AVG.
King, New York	55	691	426	1809	32.9
Bird, Boston	80	918	403	2295	28.7
Jordan, Chicago	82	837	630	2313	28.2
Short, Golden State	78	819	501	2186	28.0
English, Denver	81	939	383	2262	27.9
Wilkins, Atlanta	81	853	486	2217	27.4
Dantley, Utah	55	512	438	1462	26.6
Aguirre, Dallas	80	794	440	2055	25.7
Malone, Philadelphia	79	602	737	1941	24.6
Cummings, Milwaukee	79	759	343	1861	23.6

Field Goal Pct.
(Minimum 300 FG made)

	FGM	FGA	PCT.
Donaldson, L.A. Clippers	351	551	.637
Gilmore, San Antonio	532	854	.623
Thorpe, Kansas City	411	685	.600
Abdul-Jabbar, L.A. Lakers	723	1207	.599
Nance, Phoenix	515	877	.587

3-Pt. Field Goal Pct.
(Minimum 25 made)

	FGM	FGA	PCT.
Scott, L.A. Lakers	26	60	.433
Bird, Boston	56	131	.427
Davis, Dallas	47	115	.409
Tucker, New York	29	72	.403
Ellis, Dallas	42	109	.385

Free Throw Pct.
(Minimum 125 FT made)

	FTM	FTA	PCT.
Macy, Phoenix	127	140	.907
Vandeweghe, Portland	369	412	.896
Davis, Dallas	158	178	.888
Tripucka, Detroit	255	288	.885
Adams, Phoenix	250	283	.883

Assists
(Minimum 70 games or 400 assists)

	G.	NO.	AVG.
Thomas, Detroit	81	1123	13.9
Johnson, L.A. Lakers	77	968	12.6
Moore, San Antonio	82	816	10.0
Nixon, L.A. Clippers	81	711	8.8
Bagley, Cleveland	81	697	8.6

Rebounds
(Minimum 70 games or 800 rebounds)

	G.	OFF.	DEF.	TOT.	AVG.
Malone, Philadelphia	79	385	646	1031	13.1
Laimbeer, Detroit	82	295	718	1013	12.4
Williams, New Jersey	82	323	682	1005	12.3
Olajuwon, Houston	82	440	534	974	11.9
Eaton, Utah	82	207	720	927	11.3

Steals
(Minimum 70 games or 125 steals)

	G.	NO.	AVG.
Richardson, New Jersey	82	243	2.96
Moore, San Antonio	82	229	2.79
Lever, Denver	82	202	2.46
Jordan, Chicago	82	196	2.39
Rivers, Atlanta	69	163	2.36

Blocked Shots
(Minimum 70 games or 100 blocks)

	G.	NO.	AVG.
Eaton, Utah	82	456	5.56
Olajuwon, Houston	82	220	2.68
Bowie, Portland	76	203	2.67
Cooper, Denver	80	197	2.46
Rollins, Atlanta	70	167	2.39

Wilt Chamberlain had two NBA Championship rings. Jerry West got his in 1972. A ring was the only honor Elgin Baylor hadn't won in the NBA. But none of the great Lakers had known the sweet bliss of beating the Boston Celtics in an NBA Finals. Only the St. Louis Hawks of Bob Pettit in 1958 had ever beaten the Celtics in the Finals. Boston's response to that had been eight straight titles. Save for the 1958 championship, the other 15 times the Celtics had made it to the Finals, they had gone home wearing rings.

It took a team with two of the NBA's all-time greats, Kareem Abdul-Jabbar and Magic Johnson, to put the leprechauns to sleep. The Lakers won two of the three games in Boston, including the final one, Game 6. The sound of silence in Boston Garden was sweet music, indeed, for generations of frustrated Laker faithful.

"All of our skeletons are out of the closet," said Lakers Coach Pat Riley. "I don't want to hear about history anymore. The history is this: This was our year. And we did it on the parquet floor—maybe that's the ultimate test."

1985–86

Larry Bird had won his second consecutive Most Valuable Player Award the previous year, but the loss to the Lakers in the Finals weighed heavily on his mind. In much the same way that Magic Johnson had been driven all during the previous season by the Lakers' failure in the 1984 Finals, Bird set out to find a way to lead the Celtics back to the top. He did so by finishing in the NBA's Top 10 in five categories: scoring (25.8 ppg), rebounding (9.8 rpg), steals (2.02), free-throw percentage (.896) and three-point field-goal percentage (.423).

The Celtics had also made an important addition with the acquisition of Bill Walton, who came from the Los Angeles Clippers in a trade for Cedric Maxwell. Walton, plagued by injuries for years, shocked NBA observers by playing a career-high 80 games as a valuable backup to Parish and McHale. The contributions of Walton and fellow reserves Scott Wedman and Jerry Sichting alleviated some of the burden from the Celtics' starters and propelled Boston to a franchise-best 67-15 record, including an astounding 40-1 home record. The Celtics swept Chicago, defeated Atlanta in five games and swept Milwaukee to reach the Finals.

The Lakers had won 62 games, but were shocked in the Western Conference Finals in five games by the Houston Rockets, who under former Boston pilot Bill Fitch were employing a Twin Towers look with 7-4 Ralph Sampson and 7-0 Hakeem Olajuwon playing together. Houston had won the Midwest Division and two playoff series, but when the Lakers took Game 1 in the Western Finals, NBA fans got ready for another Boston-LA meeting. But the Rockets surprised everyone by taking the next four games to advance to the Finals. Playing at the top of his game, Bird averaged 24.0 points, 9.7 rebounds and 9.5 assists and led Boston's double-teams of Olajuwon and Sampson as Boston took its 16th title in six games.

With Olajuwon and Sampson, the Rockets had brought a new wrinkle to the NBA. In the days of Mikan, and later, with Chamberlain, Russell, Thurmond and Reed, success in the league had been measured by how good your best big man was. Houston decided to take that formula a step further with their two uncommonly agile big players. But the Celtics, unlike most teams, had the answer with Parish, Walton and McHale, complemented by double-teaming from Bird and Dennis Johnson. Although the Celtics received much praise for their unselfish, crisp-passing offense, it was their defense that brought down Houston.

"I don't remember the last time I was hounded by a team more than I was today," Sampson said after Game 6. "Every time I touched the ball, there were two and three guys around me. And that went for Hakeem, too."

NBA 1985-86

FINAL STANDINGS

Eastern Conference

Atlantic Division

	W.	L.	PCT.
Boston	67	15	.817
Philadelphia	54	28	.659
Washington	39	43	.476
New Jersey	39	43	.476
New York	23	59	.280

Central Division

	W.	L.	PCT.
Milwaukee	57	25	.695
Atlanta	50	32	.610
Detroit	46	36	.561
Chicago	30	52	.366
Cleveland	29	53	.354
Indiana	26	56	.317

Western Conference

Midwest Division

	W.	L.	PCT.
Houston	51	31	.622
Denver	47	35	.573
Dallas	44	38	.537
Utah	42	40	.512
Sacramento	37	45	.451
San Antonio	35	47	.427

Pacific Division

	W.	L.	PCT.
L.A. Lakers	62	20	.756
Portland	40	42	.488
L.A. Clippers	32	50	.390
Phoenix	32	50	.390
Seattle	31	51	.378
Golden State	30	52	.366

PLAYOFFS

Eastern Conference First Round

Atlanta 3, Detroit 1
April 17—Atlanta 140, Detroit 122
April 19—Atlanta 137, Detroit 125
April 22—Detroit 106, Atlanta 97
April 25—Atlanta 114, Detroit 113 (2OT)

Boston 3, Chicago 0
April 17—Boston 123, Chicago 104
April 20—Boston 135, Chicago 131 (2OT)
April 22—Boston 122, Chicago 104

Milwaukee 3, New Jersey 0
April 18—Milwaukee 119, New Jersey 107
April 20—Milwaukee 111, New Jersey 97
April 22—Milwaukee 118, New Jersey 113

Philadelphia 3, Washington 2
April 18—Washington 95, Philadelphia 94
April 20—Philadelphia 102, Washington 97
April 22—Philadelphia 91, Washington 86
April 24—Washington 116, Philadelphia 111
April 27—Philadelphia 134, Washington 109

Western Conference First Round

Dallas 3, Utah 1
April 18—Dallas 101, Utah 93
April 20—Dallas 113, Utah 106
April 23—Utah 100, Dallas 98
April 25—Dallas 117, Utah 113

Denver 3, Portland 1
April 18—Denver 133, Portland 126
April 20—Portland 108, Denver 106
April 22—Denver 115, Portland 104
April 24—Denver 116, Portland 112

Houston 3, Sacramento 0
April 17—Houston 107, Sacramento 87
April 19—Houston 111, Sacramento 103
April 22—Houston 113, Sacramento 98

L.A. Lakers 3, San Antonio 0
April 17—L.A. Lakers 135, San Antonio 88
April 19—L.A. Lakers 122, San Antonio 94
April 23—L.A. Lakers 114, San Antonio 94

Eastern Conference Semifinals

Boston 4, Atlanta 1
April 27—Boston 103, Atlanta 91
April 29—Boston 119, Atlanta 108
May 2—Boston 111, Atlanta 107
May 4—Atlanta 106, Boston 94
May 6—Boston 132, Atlanta 99

Milwaukee 4, Philadelphia 3
April 29—Philadelphia 118, Milwaukee 112
May 1—Milwaukee 119, Philadelphia 107
May 3—Philadelphia 107, Milwaukee 103
May 5—Milwaukee 109, Philadelphia 104
May 7—Milwaukee 113, Philadelphia 108
May 9—Philadelphia 126, Milwaukee 108
May 11—Milwaukee 113, Philadelphia 112

Western Conference Semifinals

L.A. Lakers 4, Dallas 2
April 27—L.A. Lakers 130, Dallas 116
April 30—L.A. Lakers 117, Dallas 113
May 2—Dallas 110, L.A. Lakers 108
May 4—Dallas 120, L.A. Lakers 118
May 6—L.A. Lakers 116, Dallas 113
May 8—L.A. Lakers 120, Dallas 107

Houston 4, Denver 2
April 26—Houston 126, Denver 119
April 29—Houston 119, Denver 101
May 2—Denver 116, Houston 115
May 4—Denver 114, Houston 111 (OT)
May 6—Houston 131, Denver 103
May 8—Houston 126, Denver 122 (2OT)

Eastern Conference Finals

Boston 4, Milwaukee 0
May 13—Boston 128, Milwaukee 96
May 15—Boston 122, Milwaukee 111
May 17—Boston 111, Milwaukee 107
May 18—Boston 111, Milwaukee 98

Western Conference Finals

Houston 4, L.A. Lakers 1
May 10—L.A. Lakers 119, Houston 107
May 13—Houston 112, L.A. Lakers 102
May 16—Houston 117, L.A. Lakers 109
May 18—Houston 105, L.A. Lakers 95
May 21—Houston 114, L.A. Lakers 112

NBA Finals

Boston 4, Houston 2
May 26—Boston 112, Houston 100
May 29—Boston 117, Houston 95
June 1—Houston 106, Boston 104
June 3—Boston 106, Houston 103
June 5—Houston 111, Boston 96
June 8—Boston 114, Houston 97

INDIVIDUAL LEADERS

Scoring
(Minimum 70 games played or 1,400 points)

	G.	FG	FT	PTS.	AVG.
Wilkins, Atlanta	78	888	577	2366	30.3
Dantley, Utah	76	818	630	2267	29.8
English, Denver	81	951	511	2414	29.8
Bird, Boston	82	796	441	2115	25.8
Short, Golden State	64	633	351	1632	25.5
Vandeweghe, Portland	79	719	523	1962	24.8
Malone, Philadelphia	74	571	617	1759	23.8
Olajuwon, Houston	68	625	347	1597	23.5
Mitchell, San Antonio	82	802	317	1921	23.4
Free, Cleveland	75	652	379	1754	23.4

Field Goal Pct.
(Minimum 300 FG made)

	FGM	FGA	PCT.
Johnson, San Antonio	362	573	.632
Gilmore, San Antonio	423	684	.618
Nance, Phoenix	582	1001	.581
Worthy, L.A. Lakers	629	1086	.579
McHale, Boston	561	978	.574

3-Pt. Field Goal Pct.
(Minimum 25 made)

	FGM	FGA	PCT.
Hodges, Milwaukee	73	162	.451
Tucker, New York	41	91	.451
Grunfeld, New York	26	61	.426
Bird, Boston	82	194	.423
Free, Cleveland	71	169	.420

Free Throw Pct.
(Minimum 125 FT made)

	FTM	FTA	PCT.
Bird, Boston	441	492	.896
Mullin, Golden State	189	211	.896
Gminski, New Jersey	351	393	.893
Paxson, Portland	217	244	.889
Gervin, Chicago	283	322	.879

Assists
(Minimum 70 games or 400 assists)

	G.	NO.	AVG.
Johnson, L.A. Lakers	72	907	12.6
Thomas, Detroit	77	830	10.8
Theus, Sacramento	82	788	9.6
Bagley, Cleveland	78	735	9.4
Cheeks, Philadelphia	82	753	9.2

Rebounds
(Minimum 70 games or 800 rebounds)

	G.	OFF.	DEF.	TOT.	AVG.
Laimbeer, Detroit	82	305	770	1075	13.1
Barkley, Philadelphia	80	354	672	1026	12.8
B. Williams, New Jersey	82	329	657	986	12.0
Malone, Philadelphia	74	339	533	872	11.8
Sampson, Houston	79	258	621	879	11.1

Steals
(Minimum 70 games or 125 steals)

	G.	NO.	AVG.
Robertson, San Antonio	82	301	3.67
Richardson, New Jersey	47	125	2.66
Drexler, Portland	75	197	2.63
Cheeks, Philadelphia	82	207	2.52
Lever, Denver	78	178	2.28

Blocked Shots
(Minimum 70 games or 100 blocks)

	G.	NO.	AVG.
Bol, Washington	80	397	4.96
Eaton, Utah	80	369	4.61
Olajuwon, Houston	68	231	3.40
Cooper, Denver	78	227	2.91
Benjamin, L.A. Clippers	79	206	2.61

1986–87

Not since Wilt Chamberlain's exploits in the early 1960s had the NBA seen the individual scoring brilliance it saw in the 1986–87 season. Michael Jordan, who had missed most of the previous season with a broken foot, signaled what was to come when he returned to score 63 points against the Boston Celtics in a playoff game. Now fully healthy, Jordan tore through the league with a vengeance, scoring 3,041 points for a 37.1 ppg average, marking the first time a player had eclipsed the 3,000-point mark since Chamberlain in 1963.

Aside from Jordan, the player who had been asked to do the biggest job for his team was Magic Johnson. As Kareem Abdul-Jabbar approached 40, Lakers Coach Pat Riley asked Magic to take on more of the scoring load in addition to running the team. Johnson responded by averaging a career-best 23.9 ppg while still leading the league in assists with a 12.2 average. The Lakers won 65 games during the regular season and devastated the competition in the West, going 11-1 in the Western Conference Playoffs on the way to a showdown with Boston. The Celtics won 59 games, but what had been a deep bench was decimated by injuries to Walton and Wedman. As a result, Bird, Parish, McHale and Johnson each played more than 37 minutes per game and Ainge played 35. Boston showed a bit of fatigue as it was extended to seven games by both Milwaukee and Detroit before advancing to the Finals

"Showtime," the moniker given to the Lakers' fast-breaking, freewheeling offense, was in high gear as the Lakers took a 2–0 Finals lead on their home court. But Boston won Game 3 behind a 30-point effort from Bird. Game 4 came down to one sequence. With the Lakers trailing 106–104, Abdul-Jabbar was fouled, made the first and missed the second. But the rebound was batted out of bounds and ruled the Lakers' ball. Magic Johnson took an inbounds pass on the left side, drove into the key and was met by McHale, Bird and Parish. Magic lofted a hook shot over Boston's tall trio and when the shot found the net, the Lakers led by one. With two seconds left after a timeout, Bird somehow got open for a jumper, but the shot rimmed out. The Lakers had stolen a game in Boston and would eventually win the series back in Los Angeles.

"You expect to lose on a sky-hook," Bird said later. "You don't expect it to be from Magic."

for the fourth straight year. But the Lakers were rested and ready, jumped out to a 2–0 lead, won a critical Game 4 at Boston Garden and went on to capture their fourth NBA title during the 1980s.

The NBA, a 23-team league since the Dallas Maver-

icks began play in the 1980–81 season, announced in April 1987 that it would add franchises in Charlotte and Miami in 1988 and Orlando and Minnesota in 1989, expanding to 27 teams for the 1989–90 season.

NBA 1986-87

FINAL STANDINGS

Eastern Conference

Atlantic Division

	W.	L.	PCT.
Boston	59	23	.720
Philadelphia	45	37	.549
Washington	42	40	.512
New Jersey	24	58	.293
New York	24	58	.293

Central Division

	W.	L.	PCT.
Atlanta	57	25	.695
Detroit	52	30	.634
Milwaukee	50	32	.610
Indiana	41	41	.500
Chicago	40	42	.488
Cleveland	31	51	.378

Western Conference

Midwest Division

	W.	L.	PCT.
Dallas	55	27	.671
Utah	44	38	.537
Houston	42	40	.512
Denver	37	45	.451
Sacramento	29	53	.354
San Antonio	28	54	.341

Pacific Division

	W.	L.	PCT.
L.A. Lakers	65	17	.793
Portland	49	33	.598
Golden State	42	40	.512
Seattle	39	43	.476
Phoenix	36	46	.439
L.A. Clippers	12	70	.146

PLAYOFFS

Eastern Conference First Round

Atlanta 3, Indiana 1
April 24—Atlanta 110, Indiana 94
April 26—Atlanta 94, Indiana 93
April 29—Indiana 96, Atlanta 87
May 1—Atlanta 101, Indiana 97

Boston 3, Chicago 0
April 23—Boston 108, Chicago 104
April 26—Boston 105, Chicago 96
April 28—Boston 105, Chicago 94

Detroit 3, Washington 0
April 24—Detroit 106, Washington 92
April 26—Detroit 128, Washington 85
April 29—Detroit 97, Washington 96

Milwaukee 3, Philadelphia 2
April 24—Milwaukee 107, Philadelphia 104
April 26—Philadelphia 125, Milwaukee 122 (OT)
April 29—Milwaukee 121, Philadelphia 120
May 1—Philadelphia 124, Milwaukee 118
May 3—Milwaukee 102, Philadelphia 89

Western Conference First Round

Seattle 3, Dallas 1
April 23—Dallas 151, Seattle 129
April 25—Seattle 112, Dallas 110
April 28—Seattle 117, Dallas 107
April 30—Seattle 124, Dallas 98

L.A. Lakers 3, Denver 0
April 23—L.A. Lakers 128, Denver 95
April 25—L.A. Lakers 139, Denver 127
April 29—L.A. Lakers 140, Denver 103

Golden State 3, Utah 2
April 23—Utah 99, Golden State 85
April 25—Utah 103, Golden State 100
April 29—Golden State 110, Utah 95
May 1—Golden State 98, Utah 94
May 3—Golden State 118, Utah 113

Houston 3, Portland 1
April 24—Houston 125, Portland 115
April 26—Portland 111, Houston 98
April 28—Houston 117, Portland 108
April 30—Houston 113, Portland 101

Eastern Conference Semifinals

Detroit 4, Atlanta 1
May 3—Detroit 112, Atlanta 111
May 5—Atlanta 115, Detroit 102
May 8—Detroit 108, Atlanta 99
May 10—Detroit 89, Atlanta 88
May 13—Detroit 104, Atlanta 96

Boston 4, Milwaukee 3
May 5—Boston 111, Milwaukee 98
May 6—Boston 126, Milwaukee 124
May 8—Milwaukee 126, Boston 121 (OT)
May 10—Boston 138, Milwaukee 137 (2OT)
May 13—Milwaukee 129, Boston 124
May 15—Milwaukee 121, Boston 111
May 17—Boston 119, Milwaukee 113

Western Conference Semifinals

L.A. Lakers 4, Golden State 1
May 5—L.A. Lakers 125, Golden State 116
May 7—L.A. Lakers 116, Golden State 101
May 9—L.A. Lakers 133, Golden State 108
May 10—Golden State 129, L.A. Lakers 121
May 12—L.A. Lakers 118, Golden State 106

Seattle 4, Houston 2
May 2—Seattle 111, Houston 106 (OT)
May 5—Seattle 99, Houston 97
May 7—Houston 102, Seattle 84
May 9—Houston 117, Seattle 102
May 12—Houston 112, Seattle 107
May 14—Seattle 128, Houston 125 (2OT)

Eastern Conference Finals

Boston 4, Detroit 3
May 19—Boston 104, Detroit 91
May 21—Boston 110, Detroit 101
May 23—Detroit 122, Boston 104
May 24—Detroit 145, Boston 119
May 26—Boston 108, Detroit 107
May 28—Detroit 113, Boston 105
May 30—Boston 117, Detroit 114

Western Conference Finals

L.A. Lakers 4, Seattle 0
May 16—L.A. Lakers 92, Seattle 87
May 19—L.A. Lakers 112, Seattle 104
May 23—L.A. Lakers 122, Seattle 121
May 25—L.A. Lakers 133, Seattle 102

NBA Finals

L.A. Lakers 4, Boston 2
June 2—L.A. Lakers 126, Boston 113
June 4—L.A. Lakers 141, Boston 122
June 7—Boston 109, L.A. Lakers 103
June 9—L.A. Lakers 107, Boston 106
June 11—Boston 123, L.A. Lakers 108
June 14—L.A. Lakers 106, Boston 93

INDIVIDUAL LEADERS

Scoring

(Minimum 70 games played or 1,400 points)

	G.	FG	FT	PTS.	AVG.
Jordan, Chicago	82	1098	833	3041	37.1
Wilkins, Atlanta	79	828	607	2294	29.0
English, Denver	82	965	411	2345	28.6
Bird, Boston	74	786	414	2076	28.1
Vandeweghe, Portland	79	808	467	2122	26.9
McHale, Boston	77	790	428	2008	26.1
Aguirre, Dallas	80	787	429	2056	25.7
Ellis, Seattle	82	785	385	2041	24.9
M. Malone, Washington	73	595	570	1760	24.1
Johnson, L.A. Lakers	80	683	535	1909	23.9

Field Goal Pct.

(Minimum 300 FG made)

	FGM	FGA	PCT.
McHale, Boston	790	1307	.604
Gilmore, San Antonio	346	580	.597
Barkley, Philadelphia	557	937	.594
Donaldson, Dallas	311	531	.586
Abdul-Jabbar, L.A. Lakers	560	993	.564

3-Pt. Field Goal Pct.

(Minimum 25 made)

	FGM	FGA	PCT.
Vandeweghe, Portland	39	81	.481
Schrempf, Dallas	33	69	.478
Ainge, Boston	85	192	.443
Scott, L.A. Lakers	65	149	.436
Tucker, New York	68	161	.422

Free Throw Pct.

(Minimum 125 FT made)

	FTM	FTA	PCT.
Bird, Boston	414	455	.910
Ainge, Boston	148	165	.897
Laimbeer, Detroit	245	274	.894
Scott, L.A. Lakers	224	251	.892
Hodges, Milwaukee	131	147	.891

Assists

(Minimum 70 games or 400 assists)

	G.	NO.	AVG.
Johnson, L.A. Lakers	80	977	12.2
Floyd, Golden State	82	848	10.3
Thomas, Detroit	81	813	10.0
Rivers, Atlanta	82	823	10.0
Porter, Portland	80	715	8.9

Rebounds

(Minimum 70 games or 800 rebounds)

	G.	OFF.	DEF.	TOT.	AVG.
Barkley, Philadelphia	68	390	604	994	14.6
Oakley, Chicago	82	299	775	1074	13.1
B. Williams, New Jersey	82	322	701	1023	12.5
Donaldson, Dallas	82	295	678	973	11.9
Laimbeer, Detroit	82	243	712	955	11.6

Steals

(Minimum 70 games or 125 steals)

	G.	NO.	AVG.
Robertson, San Antonio	81	260	3.21
Jordan, Chicago	82	236	2.88
Cheeks, Philadelphia	68	180	2.65
Harper, Cleveland	82	209	2.55
Drexler, Portland	82	204	2.49

Blocked Shots

(Minimum 70 games or 100 blocks)

	G.	NO.	AVG.
Eaton, Utah	79	321	4.06
Bol, Washington	82	302	3.68
Olajuwon, Houston	75	254	3.39
Benjamin, L.A. Clippers	72	187	2.60
Lister, Seattle	75	180	2.40

1987–88

No NBA team had won back-to-back championships since the Boston Celtics turned the trick in 1968 and 1969. Many believed that the league's expansion had spread the talent pool so widely that repeating had become nearly impossible. One man who disagreed with that theory was Pat Riley. Not satisfied with the Lakers' position as the "Team of the 1980s" after four titles, Riley decided that back-to-back championships would stamp his team as one of the all-time greats. So he did a peculiar thing. A day after the 1987 Finals, Riley guaranteed the Lakers would repeat. Not maybe—a *guarantee.*

The Lakers fashioned the NBA's best record at 62-20, as Byron Scott (21.7 ppg) and James Worthy (19.7 ppg) assumed a greater share of the scoring load from Abdul-Jabbar and Johnson. The Lakers' bench was at its deepest. Mychal Thompson, a key reserve on the 1987 title team, was now sharing the center spot with Abdul-Jabbar. Third-year forward A. C. Green, who was coming of age, and veterans Michael Cooper and Kurt Rambis made important contributions.

As the Lakers looked to repeat, a new challenger was rising in the East. Boston won an East-high 57 games, but Detroit, which had pushed the Celtics to the limit on their way to the Eastern Finals the previous year, won 54 games and the Central Division. General Manager Jack McCloskey and Coach Chuck Daly had surrounded 6-1 superstar guard Isiah Thomas with rugged rebounders Bill Laimbeer and Rick Mahorn, scorers Adrian Dantley, Joe Dumars and Vinnie Johnson and young, aggressive defensive forwards Dennis Rodman and John Salley.

Each team was battle-tested on its way to the Finals, with Detroit going 11-5 and the Lakers 11-6. The

Isiah Thomas yearned for recognition, not as one of the NBA's top guards, or top little men, but as one of the game's top players. He had entered the league with Detroit after the Pistons had suffered through a 21-61 campaign in 1980–81. By Thomas's third season, the Pistons had a head coach, Chuck Daly, who had figured out how to maximize his superstar's strengths so that a team built around a point guard could contend.

Although Detroit lost the 1988 NBA Finals in seven games, Thomas's effort in Game 6, when he sustained a seriously sprained ankle but still scored 43 points, stamped him as an NBA legend in the making. Thomas scored 25 points in the fourth quarter, which remains an NBA Finals record.

"What Isiah Thomas did in the second half was just incredible," marveled Lakers Coach Pat Riley.

Pistons defeated Boston by winning two of three games at Boston Garden. The Lakers outlasted Dallas in seven hard-fought games with the home team winning each time. In the Finals, Los Angeles needed every bit of its home-court advantage, coming back from a 3–2 deficit to win two close games in the Forum to become the first repeat champions since the 1968–69 Boston Celtics.

NBA 1987-88

FINAL STANDINGS

Eastern Conference

Atlantic Division

	W.	L.	PCT.
Boston	57	25	.695
Washington	38	44	.463
New York	38	44	.463
Philadelphia	36	46	.439
New Jersey	19	63	.232

Central Division

	W.	L.	PCT.
Detroit	54	28	.659
Atlanta	50	32	.610
Chicago	50	32	.610
Cleveland	42	40	.512
Milwaukee	42	40	.512
Indiana	38	44	.463

Western Conference

Midwest Division

	W.	L.	PCT.
Denver	54	28	.659
Dallas	53	29	.646
Utah	47	35	.573
Houston	46	36	.561
San Antonio	31	51	.378
Sacramento	24	58	.293

Pacific Division

	W.	L.	PCT.
L.A. Lakers	62	20	.756
Portland	53	29	.646
Seattle	44	38	.537
Phoenix	28	54	.341
Golden State	20	62	.244
L.A. Clippers	17	65	.207

PLAYOFFS

Eastern Conference First Round

Atlanta 3, Milwaukee 2
April 29—Atlanta 110, Milwaukee 107
May 1—Atlanta 104, Milwaukee 97
May 4—Milwaukee 123, Atlanta 115
May 6—Milwaukee 105, Atlanta 99
May 8—Atlanta 121, Milwaukee 111

Boston 3, New York 1
April 29—Boston 112, New York 92
May 1—Boston 128, New York 102
May 4—New York 109, Boston 100
May 6—Boston 102, New York 94

Chicago 3, Cleveland 2
April 28—Chicago 104, Cleveland 93
May 1—Chicago 106, Cleveland 101
May 3—Cleveland 110, Chicago 102
May 5—Cleveland 97, Chicago 91
May 8—Chicago 107, Cleveland 101

Detroit 3, Washington 2
April 28—Detroit 96, Washington 87
April 30—Detroit 102, Washington 101
May 2—Washington 114, Detroit 106 (OT)
May 4—Washington 106, Detroit 103
May 8—Detroit 99, Washington 78

Western Conference First Round

Dallas 3, Houston 1
April 28—Dallas 120, Houston 110
April 30—Houston 119, Dallas 108
May 3—Dallas 93, Houston 92
May 5—Dallas 107, Houston 97

Denver 3, Seattle 2
April 29—Denver 126, Seattle 123
May 1—Seattle 111, Denver 91
May 3—Denver 125, Seattle 114
May 5—Seattle 127, Denver 117
May 7—Denver 115, Seattle 96

L.A. Lakers 3, San Antonio 0
April 29—L.A. Lakers 122, San Antonio 110
May 1—L.A. Lakers 130, San Antonio 112
May 3—L.A. Lakers 109, San Antonio 107

Utah 3, Portland 1
April 28—Portland 108, Utah 96
April 30—Utah 114, Portland 105
May 4—Utah 113, Portland 108
May 6—Utah 111, Portland 96

Eastern Conference Semifinals

Boston 4, Atlanta 3
May 11—Boston 110, Atlanta 101
May 13—Boston 108, Atlanta 97
May 15—Atlanta 110, Boston 92
May 16—Atlanta 118, Boston 109
May 18—Atlanta 112, Boston 104
May 20—Boston 102, Atlanta 100
May 22—Boston 118, Atlanta 116

Detroit 4, Chicago 1
May 10—Detroit 93, Chicago 82
May 12—Chicago 105, Detroit 95
May 14—Detroit 101, Chicago 79
May 15—Detroit 96, Chicago 77
May 18—Detroit 102, Chicago 95

Western Conference Semifinals

Dallas 4, Denver 2
May 10—Denver 126, Dallas 115
May 12—Dallas 112, Denver 108
May 14—Denver 107, Dallas 105
May 15—Dallas 124, Denver 103
May 17—Dallas 110, Denver 106
May 19—Dallas 108, Denver 95

L.A. Lakers 4, Utah 3
May 8—L.A. Lakers 110, Utah 91
May 10—Utah 101, L.A. Lakers 97
May 13—Utah 96, L.A. Lakers 89
May 15—L.A. Lakers 113, Utah 100
May 17—L.A. Lakers 111, Utah 109
May 19—Utah 108, L.A. Lakers 80
May 21—L.A. Lakers 109, Utah 98

Eastern Conference Finals

Detroit 4, Boston 2
May 25—Detroit 104, Boston 96
May 26—Boston 119, Detroit 115 (2OT)
May 28—Detroit 98, Boston 94
May 30—Boston 79, Detroit 78
June 1—Detroit 102, Boston 96 (OT)
June 3—Detroit 95, Boston 90

Western Conference Finals

L.A. Lakers 4, Dallas 3
May 23—L.A. Lakers 113, Dallas 98
May 25—L.A. Lakers 123, Dallas 101
May 27—Dallas 106, L.A. Lakers 94
May 29—Dallas 118, L.A. Lakers 104
May 31—L.A. Lakers 119, Dallas 102
June 2—Dallas 105, L.A. Lakers 103
June 4—L.A. Lakers 117, Dallas 102

NBA Finals

L.A. Lakers 4, Detroit 3
June 7—Detroit 105, L.A. Lakers 93
June 9—L.A. Lakers 108, Detroit 96
June 12—L.A. Lakers 99, Detroit 86
June 14—Detroit 111, L.A. Lakers 86
June 16—Detroit 104, L.A. Lakers 94
June 19—L.A. Lakers 103, Detroit 102
June 21—L.A. Lakers 108, Detroit 105

INDIVIDUAL LEADERS

Scoring
(Minimum 70 games played or 1,400 points)

	G.	FG	FT	PTS.	AVG.
Jordan, Chicago	82	1069	723	2868	35.0
Wilkins, Atlanta	78	909	541	2397	30.7
Bird, Boston	76	881	415	2275	29.9
Barkley, Philadelphia	80	753	714	2264	28.3
Malone, Utah	82	858	552	2268	27.7
Drexler, Portland	81	849	476	2185	27.0
Ellis, Seattle	75	764	303	1938	25.8
Aguirre, Dallas	77	746	388	1932	25.1
English, Denver	80	843	314	2000	25.0
Olajuwon, Houston	79	712	381	1805	22.8

Field Goal Pct.
(Minimum 300 FG made)

	FGM	FGA	PCT.
McHale, Boston	550	911	.604
Parish, Boston	442	750	.589
Barkley, Philadelphia	753	1283	.587
Stockton, Utah	454	791	.574
Berry, San Antonio	540	960	.563

3-Pt. Field Goal Pct.
(Minimum 25 made)

	FGM	FGA	PCT.
Hodges, Mil.-Pho.	86	175	.491
Price, Cleveland	72	148	.486
Long, Indiana	34	77	.442
G. Henderson, N.Y.-Phi.	69	163	.423
Tripucka, Utah	31	74	.419

Free Throw Pct.
(Minimum 125 FT made)

	FTM	FTA	PCT.
Sikma, Milwaukee	321	348	.922
Bird, Boston	415	453	.916
Long, Indiana	166	183	.907
Gminski, N.J.-Phi.	355	392	.906
Dawkins, San Antonio	198	221	.896

Assists
(Minimum 70 games or 400 assists)

	G.	NO.	AVG.
Stockton, Utah	82	1128	13.8
Johnson, L.A. Lakers	72	858	11.9
Jackson, New York	82	868	10.6
Porter, Portland	82	831	10.1
Rivers, Atlanta	80	747	9.3

Rebounds
(Minimum 70 games or 800 rebounds)

	G.	OFF.	DEF.	TOT.	AVG.
Cage, L.A. Clippers	72	371	567	938	13.0
Oakley, Chicago	82	326	740	1066	13.0
Olajuwon, Houston	79	302	657	959	12.1
Malone, Utah	82	277	709	986	12.0
Williams, New Jersey	70	298	536	834	11.9

Steals
(Minimum 70 games or 125 steals)

	G.	NO.	AVG.
Jordan, Chicago	82	259	3.16
Robertson, San Antonio	82	243	2.96
Stockton, Utah	82	242	2.95
Lever, Denver	82	223	2.72
Drexler, Portland	81	203	2.51

Blocked Shots
(Minimum 70 games or 100 blocks)

	G.	NO.	AVG.
Eaton, Utah	82	304	3.71
Benjamin, L.A. Clippers	66	225	3.41
Ewing, New York	82	245	2.99
Olajuwon, Houston	79	214	2.71
Bol, Washington	77	208	2.70

1988–89

Although two new teams began play in Charlotte and Miami, some things remained the same. Michael Jordan won his third straight NBA scoring crown. Magic Johnson won his second Most Valuable Player Award. And the Detroit Pistons played the best team defense in the NBA. But the team's hierarchy sensed that the elusive team chemistry wasn't quite what it should be, so three days after the All-Star Game, the Pistons traded Adrian Dantley and a No. 1 draft pick for forward Mark Aguirre of the Dallas Mavericks. The trade seemed a gamble, but the Pistons responded to the trade and finished the regular season with a league-best 63-19 record.

The Lakers, meanwhile, were determined to send their captain, Kareem Abdul-Jabbar, into retirement with three straight titles. Abdul-Jabbar had announced that this season, his 20th, would be his last. The 42-year-old center had won the league MVP six times, had become the NBA's all-time scoring leader and had played on six NBA title teams. When the Lakers swept through the first three rounds of the playoffs without a loss in 11 games, it seemed the fairy-tale ending was in place. But Byron Scott pulled his hamstring prior to Game 1 of the Finals, and Magic Johnson also suffered a hamstring injury, during Game 2. The Pistons, who had nearly captured a championship the previous year, outplayed what was left of the Lakers and swept four straight games, including the clincher at the Forum.

NBA 1988-89

FINAL STANDINGS

Eastern Conference

Atlantic Division

	W.	L.	PCT.
New York	52	30	.634
Philadelphia	46	36	.561
Boston	42	40	.512
Washington	40	42	.488
New Jersey	26	56	.317
Charlotte	20	62	.244

Central Division

	W.	L.	PCT.
Detroit	63	19	.768
Cleveland	57	25	.695
Atlanta	52	30	.634
Milwaukee	49	33	.598
Chicago	47	35	.573
Indiana	28	54	.341

Western Conference

Midwest Division

	W.	L.	PCT.
Utah	51	31	.622
Houston	45	37	.549
Denver	44	38	.537
Dallas	38	44	.463
San Antonio	21	61	.256
Miami	15	67	.183

Pacific Division

	W.	L.	PCT.
L.A. Lakers	57	25	.695
Phoenix	55	27	.671
Seattle	47	35	.573
Golden State	43	39	.524
Portland	39	43	.476
Sacramento	27	55	.329
L.A. Clippers	21	61	.256

PLAYOFFS

Eastern Conference First Round

Milwaukee 3, Atlanta 2
April 27—Atlanta 100, Milwaukee 92
April 29—Milwaukee 108, Atlanta 98
May 2—Milwaukee 117, Atlanta 113 (OT)
May 5—Atlanta 113, Milwaukee 106 (OT)
May 7—Milwaukee 96, Atlanta 92

Detroit 3, Boston 0
April 28—Detroit 101, Boston 91
April 30—Detroit 102, Boston 95
May 2—Detroit 100, Boston 85

Chicago 3, Cleveland 2
April 28—Chicago 95, Cleveland 88
April 30—Cleveland 96, Chicago 88
May 3—Chicago 101, Cleveland 94
May 5—Cleveland 108, Chicago 105 (OT)
May 7—Chicago 101, Cleveland 100

New York 3, Philadelphia 0
April 27—New York 102, Philadelphia 96
April 29—New York 107, Philadelphia 106
May 2—New York 116, Philadelphia 115 (OT)

Western Conference First Round

Phoenix 3, Denver 0
April 28—Phoenix 104, Denver 103
April 30—Phoenix 132, Denver 114
May 2—Phoenix 130, Denver 121

Golden State 3, Utah 0
April 27—Golden State 123, Utah 119
April 29—Golden State 99, Utah 91
May 2—Golden State 120, Utah 106

Seattle 3, Houston 1
April 28—Seattle 111, Houston 107
April 30—Seattle 109, Houston 97
May 3—Houston 126, Seattle 107
May 5—Seattle 98, Houston 96

L.A. Lakers 3, Portland 0
April 27—L.A. Lakers 128, Portland 108
April 30—L.A. Lakers 113, Portland 105
May 3—L.A. Lakers 116, Portland 108

Eastern Conference Semifinals

Chicago 4, New York 2
May 9—Chicago 120, New York 109 (OT)
May 11—New York 114, Chicago 97
May 13—Chicago 111, New York 88
May 14—Chicago 106, New York 93
May 16—New York 121, Chicago 114
May 19—Chicago 113, New York 111

Detroit 4, Milwaukee 0
May 10—Detroit 85, Milwaukee 80
May 12—Detroit 112, Milwaukee 92
May 14—Detroit 110, Milwaukee 90
May 15—Detroit 96, Milwaukee 94

Western Conference Semifinals

Phoenix 4, Golden State 1
May 6—Phoenix 130, Golden State 103
May 9—Golden State 127, Phoenix 122
May 11—Phoenix 113, Golden State 104
May 13—Phoenix 135, Golden State 99
May 16—Phoenix 116, Golden State 104

L.A. Lakers 4, Seattle 0
May 7—L.A. Lakers 113, Seattle 102
May 10—L.A. Lakers 130, Seattle 108
May 12—L.A. Lakers 91, Seattle 86
May 14—L.A. Lakers 97, Seattle 95

Eastern Conference Finals

Detroit 4, Chicago 2
May 21—Chicago 94, Detroit 88
May 23—Detroit 100, Chicago 91
May 27—Chicago 99, Detroit 97
May 29—Detroit 86, Chicago 80
May 31—Detroit 94, Chicago 85
June 2—Detroit 103, Chicago 94

Western Conference Finals

L.A. Lakers 4, Phoenix 0
May 20—L.A. Lakers 127, Phoenix 119
May 23—L.A. Lakers 101, Phoenix 95
May 26—L.A. Lakers 110, Phoenix 107
May 28—L.A. Lakers 122, Phoenix 117

NBA Finals

Detroit 4, L.A. Lakers 0
June 6—Detroit 109, L.A. Lakers 97
June 8—Detroit 108, L.A. Lakers 105
June 11—Detroit 114, L.A. Lakers 110
June 13—Detroit 105, L.A. Lakers 97

INDIVIDUAL LEADERS

Scoring
(Minimum 70 games played or 1,400 points)

	G.	FG	FT	PTS.	AVG.
Jordan, Chicago	81	966	674	2633	32.5
Malone, Utah	80	809	703	2326	29.1
Ellis, Seattle	82	857	377	2253	27.5
Drexler, Portland	78	829	438	2123	27.2
Mullin, Golden State	82	830	493	2176	26.5
English, Denver	82	924	325	2175	26.5
Wilkins, Atlanta	80	814	442	2099	26.2
Barkley, Philadelphia	79	700	602	2037	25.8
Chambers, Phoenix	81	774	509	2085	25.7
Olajuwon, Houston	82	790	454	2034	24.8

Field Goal Pct.
(Minimum 300 FG made)

	FGM	FGA	PCT.
Rodman, Detroit	316	531	.595
Barkley, Philadelphia	700	1208	.579
Parish, Boston	596	1045	.570
Ewing, New York	727	1282	.567
Worthy, L.A. Lakers	702	1282	.548

3-Pt. Field Goal Pct.
(Minimum 25 made)

	FGM	FGA	PCT.
Sundvold, Miami	48	92	.522
Ellis, Seattle	162	339	.478
Price, Cleveland	93	211	.441
Hawkins, Philadelphia	71	166	.428
Hodges, Pho.-Chi.	75	180	.417

Free Throw Pct.
(Minimum 125 FT made)

	FTM	FTA	PCT.
Johnson, L.A. Lakers	513	563	.911
Sikma, Milwaukee	266	294	.905
Skiles, Indiana	130	144	.903
Price, Cleveland	263	292	.901
Mullin, Golden State	493	553	.892

Assists
(Minimum 70 games or 400 assists)

	G.	NO.	AVG.
Stockton, Utah	82	1118	13.6
Johnson, L.A. Lakers	77	988	12.8
K. Johnson, Phoenix	81	991	12.2
Porter, Portland	81	770	9.5
McMillan, Seattle	75	696	9.3

Rebounds
(Minimum 70 games or 800 rebounds)

	G.	OFF.	DEF.	TOT.	AVG.
Olajuwon, Houston	82	338	767	1105	13.5
Barkley, Philadelphia	79	403	583	986	12.5
Parish, Boston	80	342	654	996	12.5
Malone, Atlanta	81	386	570	956	11.8
Malone, Utah	80	259	594	853	10.7

Steals
(Minimum 70 games or 125 steals)

	G.	NO.	AVG.
Stockton, Utah	82	263	3.21
Robertson, San Antonio	65	197	3.03
Jordan, Chicago	81	234	2.89
Lever, Denver	71	195	2.75
Drexler, Portland	78	213	2.73

Blocked Shots
(Minimum 70 games or 100 blocks)

	G.	NO.	AVG.
Bol, Golden State	80	345	4.31
Eaton, Utah	82	315	3.84
Ewing, New York	80	281	3.51
Olajuwon, Houston	82	282	3.44
Nance, Cleveland	73	206	2.82

Joe Dumars was the best-kept secret in the NBA prior to the 1988–89 season, which took some doing considering he had made the NBA All-Rookie Team in 1986 and played in the NBA Finals in 1988. The long shadow cast by All-Stars Isiah Thomas and Bill Laimbeer was large enough to obscure Dumars's solid contributions. When Mark Aguirre was acquired, it merely put another All-Star between the spotlight and Dumars. But his fine play on both ends of the court in the NBA Finals once and for all ended his anonymity as he was named NBA Finals MVP. Next to the flashy Thomas and bombastic Laimbeer, Dumars knew he was viewed as a straight arrow.

"I can understand that people want to see the fancy stuff," Dumars said. "But believe me, we've got enough fancy stuff on the Detroit Pistons where I don't have to be fancy."

1989–90

For the first time in 20 seasons, the NBA got things under way without Kareem Abdul-Jabbar. The Lakers relied on Magic Johnson's all-around talents more than ever before, and he responded by scoring more than 22 points per game for the second straight year and also averaging 11.5 assists. Without Kareem, the Lakers used 35-year-old Mychal Thompson and rookie Vlade Divac at center. The new formula, with most of the old ingredients still intact, worked well enough for the Lakers to post a league-best 63-19 record, including a stellar 37-4 home record.

The Pistons looked a bit different as well. The loss of Rick Mahorn in the expansion draft to stock the new teams in Minnesota and Orlando meant more minutes for veteran James Edwards, who was nowhere near the physical presence Mahorn was but gave the Pistons a needed low-post scorer in addition to Aguirre. The Pistons won 59 games and their third straight Central Division title, but they also had to contend with Chicago, which had slowly built a team around Jordan that won 55 games under new coach Phil Jackson, the former Knicks forward from the 1970s.

In the playoffs, Detroit blitzed Indiana and New York, but needed seven games to dismiss the increasingly troublesome Bulls. The Lakers defeated Houston, but were stunned in the Western Conference Semifinals by Phoenix in five games. The Suns were in turn upset by the Portland Trail Blazers, a team that had lost in the First Round of the playoffs four straight years. The Trail Blazers, led by high-scoring Clyde Drexler, had won 59 games, but didn't get much respect until outlasting San Antonio in seven games to reach the Western Conference Finals. When Portland won Game 2 in Detroit by one point in overtime to tie the Finals at 1–1, the young Blazers seemed poised to score a major upset. But the veteran Pistons, behind Thomas's 27.6 ppg, took three straight games in Portland to capture a second straight title. After going 19 years without back-to-back champions, the NBA now had back-to-back repeaters.

The Pistons felt they hadn't received their due for winning the NBA title in 1989, what with the Lakers hobbled by injuries to Scott and Johnson. While the 1989 title may have been for the loyal Detroit fans, the 1990 crown was one the Pistons won more for themselves.

"You rank this one as more of a satisfaction for a job well done," said Bill Laimbeer after it was over. "We wanted to repeat as champions, but not so much to prove it to anybody else. We wanted to do it for ourselves."

"You can say what you want about me," declared Thomas, "but you can't say that I'm not a winner."

NBA 1989-90

FINAL STANDINGS

Eastern Conference

Atlantic Division

	W.	L.	PCT.
Philadelphia	53	29	.646
Boston	52	30	.634
New York	45	37	.549
Washington	31	51	.378
Miami	18	64	.220
New Jersey	17	65	.207

Central Division

	W.	L.	PCT.
Detroit	59	23	.720
Chicago	55	27	.671
Milwaukee	44	38	.537
Cleveland	42	40	.512
Indiana	42	40	.512
Atlanta	41	41	.500
Orlando	18	64	.220

Western Conference

Midwest Division

	W.	L.	PCT.
San Antonio	56	26	.683
Utah	55	27	.671
Dallas	47	35	.573
Denver	43	39	.524
Houston	41	41	.500
Minnesota	22	60	.268
Charlotte	19	63	.232

Pacific Division

	W.	L.	PCT.
L.A. Lakers	63	19	.768
Portland	59	23	.720
Phoenix	54	28	.659
Seattle	41	41	.500
Golden State	37	45	.451
L.A. Clippers	30	52	.366
Sacramento	23	59	.280

PLAYOFFS

Eastern Conference First Round

New York 3, Boston 2
April 26—Boston 116, New York 105
April 28—Boston 157, New York 128
May 2—New York 102, Boston 99
May 4—New York 135, Boston 108
May 6—New York 121, Boston 114

Chicago 3, Milwaukee 1
April 27—Chicago 111, Milwaukee 97
April 29—Chicago 109, Milwaukee 102
May 1—Milwaukee 119, Chicago 112
May 3—Chicago 110, Milwaukee 86

Philadelphia 3, Cleveland 2
April 26—Philadelphia 111, Cleveland 106
April 29—Philadelphia 107, Cleveland 101
May 1—Cleveland 122, Philadelphia 95
May 3—Cleveland 108, Philadelphia 96
May 5—Philadelphia 113, Cleveland 97

Detroit 3, Indiana 0
April 26—Detroit 104, Indiana 92
April 28—Detroit 100, Indiana 87
May 1—Detroit 108, Indiana 96

Western Conference First Round

Portland 3, Dallas 0
April 26—Portland 109, Dallas 102
April 28—Portland 114, Dallas 107
May 1—Portland 106, Dallas 92

San Antonio 3, Denver 0
April 26—San Antonio 119, Denver 103
April 28—San Antonio 129, Denver 120
May 1—San Antonio 131, Denver 120

L.A. Lakers 3, Houston 1
April 27—L.A. Lakers 101, Houston 89
April 29—L.A. Lakers 104, Houston 100
May 1—Houston 114, L.A. Lakers 108
May 3—L.A. Lakers 109, Houston 88

Phoenix 3, Utah 2
April 27—Utah 113, Phoenix 96
April 29—Phoenix 105, Utah 87
May 2—Phoenix 120, Utah 105
May 4—Utah 105, Phoenix 94
May 6—Phoenix 104, Utah 102

Eastern Conference Semifinals

Chicago 4, Philadelphia 1
May 7—Chicago 96, Philadelphia 85
May 9—Chicago 101, Philadelphia 96
May 11—Philadelphia 118, Chicago 112
May 13—Chicago 111, Philadelphia 101
May 16—Chicago 117, Philadelphia 99

Detroit 4, New York 1
May 8—Detroit 112, New York 77
May 10—Detroit 104, New York 97
May 12—New York 111, Detroit 103
May 13—Detroit 102, New York 90
May 15—Detroit 95, New York 84

Western Conference Semifinals

Phoenix 4, L.A. Lakers 1
May 8—Phoenix 104, L.A. Lakers 102
May 10—L.A. Lakers 124, Phoenix 100
May 12—Phoenix 117, L.A. Lakers 103
May 13—Phoenix 114, L.A. Lakers 101
May 15—Phoenix 106, L.A. Lakers 103

Portland 4, San Antonio 3
May 5—Portland 107, San Antonio 94
May 8—Portland 122, San Antonio 112
May 10—San Antonio 121, Portland 98
May 12—San Antonio 115, Portland 105
May 15—Portland 138, San Antonio 132 (2OT)
May 17—San Antonio 112, Portland 97
May 19—Portland 108, San Antonio 105 (OT)

Eastern Conference Finals

Detroit 4, Chicago 3
May 20—Detroit 86, Chicago 77
May 22—Detroit 102, Chicago 93
May 26—Chicago 107, Detroit 102
May 28—Chicago 108, Detroit 101
May 30—Detroit 97, Chicago 83
June 1—Chicago 109, Detroit 91
June 3—Detroit 93, Chicago 74

Western Conference Finals

Portland 4, Phoenix 2
May 21—Portland 100, Phoenix 98
May 23—Portland 108, Phoenix 107
May 25—Phoenix 123, Portland 89
May 27—Phoenix 119, Portland 107
May 29—Portland 120, Phoenix 114
May 31—Portland 112, Phoenix 109

NBA Finals

Detroit 4, Portland 1
June 5—Detroit 105, Portland 99
June 7—Portland 106, Detroit 105 (OT)
June 10—Detroit 121, Portland 106
June 12—Detroit 112, Portland 109
June 14—Detroit 92, Portland 90

INDIVIDUAL LEADERS

Scoring
(Minimum 70 games played or 1,400 points)

	G.	FG	FT	PTS.	AVG.
Jordan, Chicago	82	1034	593	2753	33.6
Malone, Utah	82	914	696	2540	31.0
Ewing, New York	82	922	502	2347	28.6
Chambers, Phoenix	81	810	557	2201	27.2
Wilkins, Atlanta	80	810	459	2138	26.7
Barkley, Philadelphia	79	706	557	1989	25.2
Mullin, Golden State	78	682	505	1956	25.1
Miller, Indiana	82	661	544	2016	24.6
Olajuwon, Houston	82	806	382	1995	24.3
Robinson, San Antonio	82	690	613	1993	24.3

Field Goal Pct.
(Minimum 300 FG made)

	FGM	FGA	PCT.
West, Phoenix	331	530	.625
Barkley, Philadelphia	706	1177	.600
Parish, Boston	505	871	.580
Malone, Utah	914	1627	.562
Woolridge, L.A. Lakers	306	550	.556

3-Pt. Field Goal Pct.
(Minimum 25 made)

	FGM	FGA	PCT.
Kerr, Cleveland	73	144	.507
Hodges, Chicago	87	181	.481
Petrovic, Portland	34	74	.459
Sundvold, Miami	44	100	.440
Scott, L.A. Lakers	93	220	.423

Free Throw Pct.
(Minimum 125 FT made)

	FTM	FTA	PCT.
Bird, Boston	319	343	.930
E. Johnson, Phoenix	188	205	.917
Davis, Denver	207	227	.912
Dumars, Detroit	297	330	.900
McHale, Boston	393	440	.893

Assists
(Minimum 70 games or 400 assists)

	G.	NO.	AVG.
Stockton, Utah	78	1134	14.5
Johnson, L.A. Lakers	79	907	11.5
K. Johnson, Phoenix	74	846	11.4
Bogues, Charlotte	81	867	10.7
Grant, L.A. Clippers	44	442	10.0

Rebounds
(Minimum 70 games or 800 rebounds)

	G.	OFF.	DEF.	TOT.	AVG.
Olajuwon, Houston	82	299	850	1149	14.0
Robinson, San Antonio	82	303	680	983	12.0
Barkley, Philadelphia	79	361	548	909	11.5
Malone, Utah	82	232	679	911	11.1
Ewing, New York	82	235	658	893	10.9

Steals
(Minimum 70 games or 125 steals)

	G.	NO.	AVG.
Jordan, Chicago	82	227	2.77
Stockton, Utah	78	207	2.65
Pippen, Chicago	82	211	2.57
Robertson, Milwaukee	81	207	2.56
Harper, Dallas	82	187	2.28

Blocked Shots
(Minimum 70 games or 100 blocks)

	G.	NO.	AVG.
Olajuwon, Houston	82	376	4.59
Ewing, New York	82	327	3.99
Robinson, San Antonio	82	319	3.89
Bol, Golden State	75	238	3.17
Benjamin, L.A. Clippers	71	187	2.63

1990–91

Michael Jordan had won four straight NBA scoring titles by the time the 1990–91 season began, and his vast array of endorsements had made him a household name. But he was dogged by the Wilt Chamberlain syndrome. Every sports fan with even a passing familiarity with the NBA would quote how no NBA team with the league scoring champion had won the NBA title since Kareem Abdul-Jabbar had led the Milwaukee Bucks to the NBA title way back in 1971.

Jordan had been the NBA's Rookie of the Year in 1985, had been named to the All-NBA First Team four straight years and had even been named to the NBA All-Defensive First Team three straight times. But Jordan's Bulls couldn't seem to get by Detroit, having lost to the Pistons in the Eastern Conference Finals each of the past two years. But the Bulls had made drastic changes since Jordan's rookie year. John Paxson was

signed as a free agent in 1985. Horace Grant and Scottie Pippen were added as a result of the 1987 NBA Draft. Bill Cartwright was acquired for Charles Oakley in 1988. B. J. Armstrong was selected in the 1989 NBA Draft. By 1990 the Bulls were ready to supplant the Pistons.

Chicago won a franchise-record 61 games and blew through New York, Philadelphia and their nemesis, Detroit, on the way to the NBA Finals. The Lakers, now a defensive unit under new coach Mike Dunleavy, moved past Houston, Golden State and Portland to advance to the Finals. The Lakers won Game 1 in Chicago on Sam Perkins's three-point basket, but that was to be their only victory. The Bulls, behind the incomparable Jordan, took four straight to secure Chicago's first NBA title.

The 1991 NBA Finals were billed as a matchup between two larger-than-life superstars, Michael Jordan and Magic Johnson. But as the series played out, it became obvious that it took a team, not one superlative individual, to win an NBA Championship. Jordan was superb, as his series averages of 31.2 points, 11.4 assists and 6.6 rebounds demonstrated, but the Bulls were no one-man team. Their defense held the Lakers to a Finals record-low 458 points for a five-game series. Jordan, who had won his fifth straight scoring title in April, had finally silenced those who said he couldn't lead the Bulls all the way.

"I never thought I'd be this emotional," said Jordan, who cried and repeatedly hugged the NBA's Championship trophy. "I've never been this emotional publicly."

NBA 1990-91

FINAL STANDINGS

Eastern Conference

Atlantic Division

	W.	L.	PCT.
Boston	56	26	.683
Philadelphia	44	38	.537
New York	39	43	.476
Washington	30	52	.366
New Jersey	26	56	.317
Miami	24	58	.293

Central Division

	W.	L.	PCT.
Chicago	61	21	.744
Detroit	50	32	.610
Milwaukee	48	34	.585
Atlanta	43	39	.524
Indiana	41	41	.500
Cleveland	33	49	.402
Charlotte	26	56	.317

Western Conference

Midwest Division

	W.	L.	PCT.
San Antonio	55	27	.671
Utah	54	28	.659
Houston	52	30	.634
Orlando	31	51	.378
Minnesota	29	53	.354
Dallas	28	54	.341
Denver	20	62	.244

Pacific Division

	W.	L.	PCT.
Portland	63	19	.768
L.A. Lakers	58	24	.707
Phoenix	55	27	.671
Golden State	44	38	.537
Seattle	41	41	.500
L.A. Clippers	31	51	.378
Sacramento	25	57	.305

PLAYOFFS

Eastern Conference First Round

Detroit 3, Atlanta 2
April 26—Atlanta 103, Detroit 98
April 28—Detroit 101, Atlanta 88
April 30—Detroit 103, Atlanta 91
May 2—Atlanta 123, Detroit 111
May 5—Detroit 113, Atlanta 81

Boston 3, Indiana 2
April 26—Boston 127, Indiana 120
April 28—Indiana 130, Boston 118
May 1—Boston 112, Indiana 105
May 3—Indiana 116, Boston 113
May 5—Boston 124, Indiana 121

Chicago 3, New York 0
April 25—Chicago 126, New York 85
April 28—Chicago 89, New York 79
April 30—Chicago 103, New York 94

Philadelphia 3, Milwaukee 0
April 25—Philadelphia 99, Milwaukee 90
April 27—Philadelphia 116, Milwaukee 112 (OT)
April 30—Philadelphia 121, Milwaukee 100

Western Conference First Round

Golden State 3, San Antonio 1
April 25—San Antonio 130, Golden State 121
April 27—Golden State 111, San Antonio 98
May 1—Golden State 109, San Antonio 106
May 3—Golden State 110, San Antonio 97

L.A. Lakers 3, Houston 0
April 25—L.A. Lakers 94, Houston 92
April 27—L.A. Lakers 109, Houston 98
April 30—L.A. Lakers 94, Houston 90

Utah 3, Phoenix 1
April 25—Utah 129, Phoenix 90
April 27—Phoenix 102, Utah 92
April 30—Utah 107, Phoenix 98
May 2—Utah 101, Phoenix 93

Portland 3, Seattle 2
April 26—Portland 110, Seattle 102
April 28—Portland 115, Seattle 106
April 30—Seattle 102, Portland 99
May 2—Seattle 101, Portland 89
May 4—Portland 119, Seattle 107

Eastern Conference Semifinals

Detroit 4, Boston 2
May 7—Detroit 86, Boston 75
May 9—Boston 109, Detroit 103
May 11—Boston 115, Detroit 83
May 13—Detroit 104, Boston 97
May 15—Detroit 116, Boston 111
May 17—Detroit 117, Boston 113 (OT)

Chicago 4, Philadelphia 1
May 4—Chicago 105, Philadelphia 92
May 6—Chicago 112, Philadelphia 100
May 10—Philadelphia 99, Chicago 97
May 12—Chicago 101, Philadelphia 85
May 14—Chicago 100, Philadelphia 95

Western Conference Semifinals

L.A. Lakers 4, Golden State 1
May 5—L.A. Lakers 126, Golden State 116
May 8—Golden State 125, L.A. Lakers 124
May 10—L.A. Lakers 115, Golden State 112
May 12—L.A. Lakers 123, Golden State 107
May 14—L.A. Lakers 124, Golden State 119 (OT)

Portland 4, Utah 1
May 7—Portland 117, Utah 97
May 9—Portland 118, Utah 116
May 11—Utah 107, Portland 101
May 12—Portland 104, Utah 101
May 14—Portland 103, Utah 96

Eastern Conference Finals

Chicago 4, Detroit 0
May 19—Chicago 94, Detroit 83
May 21—Chicago 105, Detroit 97
May 25—Chicago 113, Detroit 107
May 27—Chicago 115, Detroit 94

Western Conference Finals

L.A. Lakers 4, Portland 2
May 18—L.A. Lakers 111, Portland 106
May 21—Portland 109, L.A. Lakers 98
May 24—L.A. Lakers 106, Portland 92
May 26—L.A. Lakers 116, Portland 95
May 28—Portland 95, L.A. Lakers 84
May 30—L.A. Lakers 91, Portland 90

NBA Finals

Chicago 4, L.A. Lakers 1
June 2—L.A. Lakers 93, Chicago 91
June 5—Chicago 107, L.A. Lakers 86
June 7—Chicago 104, L.A. Lakers 96 (OT)
June 9—Chicago 97, L.A. Lakers 82
June 12—Chicago 108, L.A. Lakers 101

INDIVIDUAL LEADERS

Scoring

(Minimum 70 games played or 1,400 points)

	G.	FG	FT	PTS.	AVG.
Jordan, Chicago	82	990	571	2580	31.5
K. Malone, Utah	82	847	684	2382	29.0
King, Washington	64	713	383	1817	28.4
Barkley, Philadelphia	67	665	475	1849	27.6
Ewing, New York	81	845	464	2154	26.6
Adams, Denver	66	560	465	1752	26.5
Wilkins, Atlanta	81	770	476	2101	25.9
Mullin, Golden State	82	777	513	2107	25.7
Robinson, San Antonio	82	754	592	2101	25.6
Richmond, Golden State	77	703	394	1840	23.9

Field Goal Pct.

(Minimum 300 FG made)

	FGM	FGA	PCT.
Williams, Portland	358	595	.602
Parish, Boston	485	811	.598
Gamble, Boston	548	933	.587
Barkley, Philadelphia	665	1167	.570
Divac, L.A. Lakers	360	637	.565

3-Pt. Field Goal Pct.

(Minimum 50 made)

	FGM	FGA	PCT.
Les, Sacramento	71	154	.461
Tucker, New York	64	153	.418
Hornacek, Phoenix	61	146	.418
Porter, Portland	130	313	.415
Skiles, Orlando	93	228	.408

Free Throw Pct.

(Minimum 125 FT made)

	FTM	FTA	PCT.
Miller, Indiana	551	600	.918
J. Malone, Utah	231	252	.917
Pierce, Mil.-Sea.	430	471	.913
Tripucka, Charlotte	152	167	.910
Johnson, L.A. Lakers	519	573	.906

Assists

(Minimum 70 games or 400 assists)

	G.	NO.	AVG.
Stockton, Utah	82	1164	14.2
Johnson, L.A. Lakers	79	989	12.5
Adams, Denver	66	693	10.5
K. Johnson, Phoenix	77	781	10.1
Hardaway, Golden State	82	793	9.7

Rebounds

(Minimum 70 games or 800 rebounds)

	G.	OFF.	DEF.	TOT.	AVG.
Robinson, San Antonio	82	335	728	1063	13.0
Rodman, Detroit	82	361	665	1026	12.5
Oakley, New York	76	305	615	920	12.1
K. Malone, Utah	82	236	731	967	11.8
Ewing, New York	81	194	711	905	11.2

Steals

(Minimum 70 games or 125 steals)

	G.	NO.	AVG.
Robertson, Milwaukee	81	246	3.04
Stockton, Utah	82	234	2.85
Jordan, Chicago	82	223	2.72
Hardaway, Golden State	82	214	2.61
Pippen, Chicago	82	193	2.35

Blocked Shots

(Minimum 70 games or 100 blocks)

	G.	NO.	AVG.
Olajuwon, Houston	56	221	3.95
Robinson, San Antonio	82	320	3.90
Ewing, New York	81	258	3.19
Bol, Philadelphia	82	247	3.01
Dudley, New Jersey	61	153	2.51

1991–92

Just a few days into the season, Magic Johnson delivered the shocking news that he had contracted the human immunodeficiency virus (HIV) that causes AIDS. Johnson announced that he would retire immediately from the NBA and devote his time to educating the public about HIV and AIDS. Just like that, a 12-year NBA career that included five NBA titles and three Most Valuable Player Awards was over. The season would also prove to be the last for Larry Bird, who played through enormous back pain to appear in 45 games, averaging 20.2 ppg.

While two of the NBA's all-time greats were leaving the scene, the Chicago Bulls and their superstar Michael Jordan were just getting started. Not satisfied with the club-record 61 wins of a season ago, the Bulls improved to 67-15, tying for the fourth-best season mark in NBA history. The incandescent Jordan won his third MVP Award and sixth straight scoring title, but he averaged only 30.1 ppg, his lowest average in six seasons. More than ever, Jordan worked to capitalize on the burgeoning talents of Pippen (21 ppg) and Grant (14.2 ppg, 10 rpg). Cleveland, with All-Stars Mark Price and Brad Daugherty, won 57 games to tie Portland for the league's second-best record. The Cavaliers played well all season, but had no answer for Jordan and succumbed in six games in the Eastern Conference Finals. Portland, hungry to get back to the Finals after a disappointing playoffs in 1991, defeated the Lakers, Phoenix and tough Utah, which had All-Stars John Stockton and Karl Malone, to gain the Finals for the second time in three seasons. Just as in 1990, the Trail Blazers managed a split on the road in the first two games. But Chicago took two of three in Portland and staged a remarkable comeback at home in Game 6 to repeat as NBA Champions.

Portland had taken it on the chin at home, losing two of three games to return to Chicago down 3–2 in the Finals. Most expected an easy triumph for the Bulls in Game 6, but after three quarters, the Trail Blazers led 79–64 and seemed ready to push the series to a seventh game. But an improbable lineup of Pippen plus reserves Scott Williams, B. J. Armstrong, Bobby Hansen and Stacey King turned the tide, outscoring the Trail Blazers 14–2 to open the fourth quarter and cut the seemingly insurmountable lead to 81–78. Jordan and Pippen took over from there, scoring the Bulls' last 19 points to grab the series from the stunned Trail Blazers.

"We needed a different matchup," Bulls Coach Phil Jackson explained afterward. "That's what we got from those young guys. They had fresh legs. It's either daring or stupid, depending on which way it comes out."

Score one for daring.

NBA 1991-92

FINAL STANDINGS

Eastern Conference

Atlantic Division

	W.	L.	PCT.
Boston	51	31	.622
New York	51	31	.622
New Jersey	40	42	.488
Miami	38	44	.463
Philadelphia	35	47	.427
Washington	25	57	.305
Orlando	21	61	.256

Central Division

	W.	L.	PCT.
Chicago	67	15	.817
Cleveland	57	25	.695
Detroit	48	34	.585
Indiana	40	42	.488
Atlanta	38	44	.463
Charlotte	31	51	.378
Milwaukee	31	51	.378

Western Conference

Midwest Division

	W.	L.	PCT.
Utah	55	27	.671
San Antonio	47	35	.573
Houston	42	40	.512
Denver	24	58	.293
Dallas	22	60	.268
Minnesota	15	67	.183

Pacific Division

	W.	L.	PCT.
Portland	57	25	.695
Golden State	55	27	.671
Phoenix	53	29	.646
Seattle	47	35	.573
L.A. Clippers	45	37	.549
L.A. Lakers	43	39	.524
Sacramento	29	53	.354

PLAYOFFS

Eastern Conference First Round

Boston 3, Indiana 0
April 23—Boston 124, Indiana 113
April 25—Boston 119, Indiana 112 (OT)
April 27—Boston 102, Indiana 98

Chicago 3, Miami 0
April 24—Chicago 113, Miami 94
April 26—Chicago 120, Miami 90
April 29—Chicago 119, Miami 114

Cleveland 3, New Jersey 1
April 23—Cleveland 120, New Jersey 113
April 25—Cleveland 118, New Jersey 96
April 28—New Jersey 109, Cleveland 104
April 30—Cleveland 98, New Jersey 89

New York 3, Detroit 2
April 24—New York 109, Detroit 75
April 26—Detroit 89, New York 88
April 28—New York 90, Detroit 87 (OT)
May 1—Detroit 86, New York 82
May 3—New York 94, Detroit 87

Western Conference First Round

Seattle 3, Golden State 1
April 23—Seattle 117, Golden State 109
April 25—Golden State 115, Seattle 101
April 28—Seattle 129, Golden State 128
April 30—Seattle 119, Golden State 116

Utah 3, L.A. Clippers 2
April 24—Utah 115, L.A. Clippers 97
April 26—Utah 103, L.A. Clippers 92
April 28—L.A. Clippers 98, Utah 88
May 3—L.A. Clippers 115, Utah 107 (game played in Anaheim)
May 4—Utah 98, L.A. Clippers 89

Portland 3, L.A. Lakers 1
April 23—Portland 115, L.A. Lakers 102
April 25—Portland 101, L.A. Lakers 79
April 29—L.A. Lakers 121, Portland 119 (OT)
May 3—Portland 102, L.A. Lakers 76 (game played in Las Vegas)

Phoenix 3, San Antonio 0
April 24—Phoenix 117, San Antonio 111
April 26—Phoenix 119, San Antonio 107
April 29—Phoenix 101, San Antonio 92

Eastern Conference Semifinals

Cleveland 4, Boston 3
May 2—Cleveland 101, Boston 76
May 4—Boston 104, Cleveland 98
May 8—Boston 110, Cleveland 107
May 10—Cleveland 114, Boston 112 (OT)
May 13—Cleveland 114, Boston 98
May 15—Boston 122, Cleveland 91
May 17—Cleveland 122, Boston 104

Chicago 4, New York 3
May 5—New York 94, Chicago 89
May 7—Chicago 86, New York 78
May 9—Chicago 94, New York 86
May 10—New York 93, Chicago 86
May 12—Chicago 96, New York 88
May 14—New York 100, Chicago 86
May 17—Chicago 110, New York 81

Western Conference Semifinals

Portland 4, Phoenix 1
May 5—Portland 113, Phoenix 111
May 7—Portland 126, Phoenix 119
May 9—Phoenix 124, Portland 117
May 11—Portland 153, Phoenix 151 (2OT)
May 14—Portland 118, Phoenix 106

Utah 4, Seattle 1
May 6—Utah 108, Seattle 100
May 8—Utah 103, Seattle 97
May 10—Seattle 104, Utah 98
May 12—Utah 89, Seattle 83
May 14—Utah 111, Seattle 100

Eastern Conference Finals

Chicago 4, Cleveland 2
May 19—Chicago 103, Cleveland 89
May 21—Cleveland 107, Chicago 81
May 23—Chicago 105, Cleveland 96
May 25—Cleveland 99, Chicago 85
May 27—Chicago 112, Cleveland 89
May 29—Chicago 99, Cleveland 94

Western Conference Finals

Portland 4, Utah 2
May 16—Portland 113, Utah 88
May 19—Portland 119, Utah 102
May 22—Utah 97, Portland 89
May 24—Utah 121, Portland 112
May 26—Portland 127, Utah 121 (OT)
May 28—Portland 105, Utah 97

NBA Finals

Chicago 4, Portland 2
June 3—Chicago 122, Portland 89
June 5—Portland 115, Chicago 104 (OT)
June 7—Chicago 94, Portland 84
June 10—Portland 93, Chicago 88
June 12—Chicago 119, Portland 106
June 14—Chicago 97, Portland 93

INDIVIDUAL LEADERS

Scoring

(Minimum 70 games played or 1,400 points)

	G.	FG	FT	PTS.	AVG.
Jordan, Chicago	80	943	491	2404	30.1
K. Malone, Utah	81	798	673	2272	28.0
Mullin, Golden State	81	830	350	2074	25.6
Drexler, Portland	76	694	401	1903	25.0
Ewing, New York	82	796	377	1970	24.0
Hardaway, Golden State	81	734	298	1893	23.4
Robinson, San Antonio	68	592	393	1578	23.2
Barkley, Philadelphia	75	622	454	1730	23.1
Richmond, Sacramento	80	685	330	1803	22.5
Rice, Miami	79	672	266	1765	22.3

Field Goal Pct.

(Minimum 300 FG made)

	FGM	FGA	PCT.
Williams, Portland	340	563	.604
Thorpe, Houston	558	943	.592
Grant, Chicago	457	790	.578
Daugherty, Cleveland	576	1010	.570
Cage, Seattle	307	542	.566

3-Pt. Field Goal Pct.

(Minimum 50 made)

	FGM	FGA	PCT.
Barros, Seattle	83	186	.446
Petrovic, New Jersey	123	277	.444
Hornacek, Phoenix	83	189	.439
Iuzzolino, Dallas	59	136	.434
Ellis, Milwaukee	138	329	.419

Free Throw Pct.

(Minimum 125 FT made)

	FTM	FTA	PCT.
Price, Cleveland	270	285	.947
Bird, Boston	150	162	.926
Pierce, Seattle	417	455	.916
Blackman, Dallas	239	266	.898
J. Malone, Utah	256	285	.898

Assists

(Minimum 70 games or 400 assists)

	G.	NO.	AVG.
Stockton, Utah	82	1126	13.7
Johnson, Phoenix	78	836	10.7
Hardaway, Golden State	81	807	10.0
Bogues, Charlotte	82	743	9.1
Strickland, San Antonio	57	491	8.6

Rebounds

(Minimum 70 games or 800 rebounds)

	G.	OFF.	DEF.	TOT.	AVG.
Rodman, Detroit	82	523	1007	1530	18.7
Willis, Atlanta	81	418	840	1258	15.5
Mutombo, Denver	71	316	554	870	12.3
Robinson, San Antonio	68	261	568	829	12.2
Olajuwon, Houston	70	246	599	845	12.1

Steals

(Minimum 70 games or 125 steals)

	G.	NO.	AVG.
Stockton, Utah	82	244	2.98
M. Williams, Indiana	79	233	2.95
Robertson, Milwaukee	82	210	2.56
Blaylock, New Jersey	72	170	2.36
Robinson, San Antonio	68	158	2.32

Blocked Shots

(Minimum 70 games or 100 blocks)

	G.	NO.	AVG.
Robinson, San Antonio	68	305	4.49
Olajuwon, Houston	70	304	4.34
Nance, Cleveland	81	243	3.00
Ewing, New York	82	245	2.99
Mutombo, Denver	71	210	2.96

1992–93

The Phoenix Suns had won 50 or more games four straight years from 1988–89 to 1991–92 under veteran coach Cotton Fitzsimmons. The Suns made a major leap in 1988, trading for point guard Kevin Johnson and signing free agent Tom Chambers. With the development of young guards Jeff Hornacek and Dan Majerle, the Suns seemed assured of being in the playoff picture for years to come. But just making the playoffs wasn't what the Suns had in mind. Three days after the 1992 Finals ended, Phoenix announced it was trading Hornacek, starting forward Tim Perry and backup center Andrew Lang to Philadelphia for superstar Charles Barkley, who was about to star on the Dream Team that would win the gold medal at the 1992 Olympic Games.

Immediately, the Suns were in a position to challenge for the NBA title. They won a league-best 62 games, survived a First Round scare against the Lakers, then defeated San Antonio to meet Seattle in the Western Conference Finals. The SuperSonics, a 12-deep unit with no top star, pushed the Suns to seven games before losing in Phoenix.

The Bulls, who had set as a goal a third straight NBA Championship, coasted through the regular season with 57 wins, but lost the home-court advantage to New York, which surged to a 60-22 record. After the Bulls and Knicks easily advanced to the Eastern Conference Finals, the two teams split the first four games, the home team winning each time. Chicago won a pivotal Game 5 in New York and closed out the Knicks back in Chicago. Chicago won the first two games in Phoenix, prompting predictions of a sweep, but the Suns won two of three in Chicago before bowing out in Game 6 at home. The series was unusual in that the home team won only one game, Chicago in Game 4, and it also featured a remarkable triple-overtime game, Phoenix taking Game 3 129–121. The Bulls became only the third team in NBA history to win as many as three consecutive championships, joining Boston (1959–66) and Minneapolis (1952–54).

Michael Jordan had heard the warning from Dream Team teammate Magic Johnson before the season even began: "If the Bulls thought winning two in a row was hard, they'll find out that winning three in a row will be the hardest thing they ever do."

When Chicago appeared on the brink of becoming the third team to accomplish that feat, slogan writers worked overtime to dream up a suitable title.

"I think the motto that struck me the most was 'Three the Hard Way,'" said victorious Bulls Coach Phil Jackson when it was all over.

NBA 1992-93

FINAL STANDINGS

Eastern Conference

Atlantic Division

	W.	L.	PCT.
New York	60	22	.732
Boston	48	34	.585
New Jersey	43	39	.524
Orlando	41	41	.500
Miami	36	46	.439
Philadelphia	26	56	.317
Washington	22	60	.268

Central Division

	W.	L.	PCT.
Chicago	57	25	.695
Cleveland	54	28	.659
Charlotte	44	38	.537
Atlanta	43	39	.524
Indiana	41	41	.500
Detroit	40	42	.488
Milwaukee	28	54	.341

Western Conference

Midwest Division

	W.	L.	PCT.
Houston	55	27	.671
San Antonio	49	33	.598
Utah	47	35	.573
Denver	36	46	.439
Minnesota	19	63	.232
Dallas	11	71	.134

Pacific Division

	W.	L.	PCT.
Phoenix	62	20	.756
Seattle	55	27	.671
Portland	51	31	.622
L.A. Clippers	41	41	.500
L.A. Lakers	39	43	.476
Golden State	34	48	.415
Sacramento	25	57	.305

PLAYOFFS

Eastern Conference First Round

Chicago 3, Atlanta 0
April 30—Chicago 114, Atlanta 90
May 2—Chicago 117, Atlanta 102
May 4—Chicago 98, Atlanta 88

Charlotte 3, Boston 1
April 29—Boston 112, Charlotte 101
May 1—Charlotte 99, Boston 98 (2OT)
May 3—Charlotte 119, Boston 89
May 5—Charlotte 104, Boston 103

Cleveland 3, New Jersey 2
April 29—Cleveland 114, New Jersey 98
May 1—New Jersey 101, Cleveland 99
May 5—Cleveland 93, New Jersey 84
May 7—New Jersey 96, Cleveland 79
May 9—Cleveland 99, New Jersey 89

New York 3, Indiana 1
April 30—New York 107, Indiana 104
May 2—New York 101, Indiana 91
May 4—Indiana 116, New York 93
May 6—New York 109, Indiana 100 (OT)

Western Conference First Round

Houston 3, L.A. Clippers 2
April 29—Houston 117, L.A. Clippers 94
May 1—L.A. Clippers 95, Houston 83
May 3—Houston 111, L.A. Clippers 99
May 5—L.A. Clippers 93, Houston 90
May 8—Houston 84, L.A. Clippers 80

Phoenix 3, L.A. Lakers 2
April 30—L.A. Lakers 107, Phoenix 103
May 2—L.A. Lakers 86, Phoenix 81
May 4—Phoenix 107, L.A. Lakers 102
May 6—Phoenix 101, L.A. Lakers 86
May 9—Phoenix 112, L.A. Lakers 104 (OT)

San Antonio 3, Portland 1
April 29—San Antonio 87, Portland 86
May 1—Portland 105, San Antonio 96
May 5—San Antonio 107, Portland 101
May 7—San Antonio 100, Portland 97 (OT)

Seattle 3, Utah 2
April 30—Seattle 99, Utah 85
May 2—Utah 89, Seattle 85
May 4—Utah 90, Seattle 80
May 6—Seattle 93, Utah 80
May 8—Seattle 100, Utah 92

Eastern Conference Semifinals

New York 4, Charlotte 1
May 9—New York 111, Charlotte 95
May 12—New York 105, Charlotte 101 (OT)
May 14—Charlotte 110, New York 106 (2OT)
May 16—New York 94, Charlotte 92
May 18—New York 105, Charlotte 101

Chicago 4, Cleveland 0
May 11—Chicago 91, Cleveland 84
May 13—Chicago 104, Cleveland 85
May 15—Chicago 96, Cleveland 90
May 17—Chicago 103, Cleveland 101

Western Conference Semifinals

Seattle 4, Houston 3
May 10—Seattle 99, Houston 90
May 12—Seattle 111, Houston 100
May 15—Houston 97, Seattle 79
May 16—Houston 103, Seattle 92
May 18—Seattle 120, Houston 95
May 20—Houston 103, Seattle 90
May 22—Seattle 103, Houston 100 (OT)

Phoenix 4, San Antonio 2
May 11—Phoenix 98, San Antonio 89
May 13—Phoenix 109, San Antonio 103
May 15—San Antonio 111, Phoenix 96
May 16—San Antonio 117, Phoenix 103
May 18—Phoenix 109, San Antonio 97
May 20—Phoenix 102, San Antonio 100

Eastern Conference Finals

Chicago 4, New York 2
May 23—New York 98, Chicago 90
May 25—New York 96, Chicago 91
May 29—Chicago 103, New York 83
May 31—Chicago 105, New York 95
June 2—Chicago 97, New York 94
June 4—Chicago 96, New York 88

Western Conference Finals

Phoenix 4, Seattle 3
May 24—Phoenix 105, Seattle 91
May 26—Seattle 103, Phoenix 99
May 28—Phoenix 104, Seattle 97
May 30—Seattle 120, Phoenix 101
June 1—Phoenix 120, Seattle 114
June 3—Seattle 118, Phoenix 102
June 5—Phoenix 123, Seattle 110

NBA Finals

Chicago 4, Phoenix 2
June 9—Chicago 100, Phoenix 92
June 11—Chicago 111, Phoenix 108
June 13—Phoenix 129, Chicago 121 (3OT)
June 16—Chicago 111, Phoenix 105
June 18—Phoenix 108, Chicago 98
June 20—Chicago 99, Phoenix 98

Scoring

(Minimum 70 games played or 1,400 points)

	G.	FG	FT	PTS.	AVG.
Jordan, Chicago	78	992	476	2541	32.6
Wilkins, Atlanta	71	741	519	2121	29.9
K. Malone, Utah	82	797	619	2217	27.0
Olajuwon, Houston	82	848	444	2140	26.1
Barkley, Phoenix	76	716	445	1944	25.6
Ewing, New York	81	779	400	1959	24.2
Dumars, Detroit	77	677	343	1809	23.5
O'Neal, Orlando	81	733	427	1893	23.4
Robinson, San Antonio	82	676	561	1916	23.4
Manning, L.A. Clippers	79	702	388	1800	22.8

Field Goal Pct.

(Minimum 300 FG made)

	FGM	FGA	PCT.
Ceballos, Phoenix	381	662	.576
Daugherty, Cleveland	520	911	.571
Davis, Indiana	304	535	.568
O'Neal, Orlando	733	1304	.562
Thorpe, Houston	385	690	.558

3-Pt. Field Goal Pct.

(Minimum 50 made)

	FGM	FGA	PCT.
Armstrong, Chicago	63	139	.453
Mullin, Golden State	60	133	.451
Petrovic, New Jersey	75	167	.449
Smith, Houston	96	219	.438
Les, Sacramento	66	154	.429

Free Throw Pct.

(Minimum 125 FT made)

	FTM	FTA	PCT.
Price, Cleveland	289	305	.948
Jackson, Denver	217	232	.935
Johnson, Seattle	234	257	.911
Williams, Minnesota	419	462	.907
Skiles, Orlando	289	324	.892

Assists

(Minimum 70 games or 400 assists)

	G.	NO.	AVG.
Stockton, Utah	82	987	12.0
Hardaway, Golden State	66	699	10.6
Skiles, Orlando	78	735	9.4
M. Jackson, L.A. Clippers	82	724	8.8
Bogues, Charlotte	81	711	8.8

Rebounds

(Minimum 70 games or 800 rebounds)

	G.	OFF.	DEF.	TOT.	AVG.
Rodman, Detroit	62	367	765	1132	18.3
O'Neal, Orlando	81	342	780	1122	13.9
Mutombo, Denver	82	344	726	1070	13.0
Olajuwon, Houston	82	283	785	1068	13.0
Willis, Atlanta	80	335	693	1028	12.9

Steals

(Minimum 70 games or 125 steals)

	G.	NO.	AVG.
Jordan, Chicago	78	221	2.83
Blaylock, Atlanta	80	203	2.54
Stockton, Utah	82	199	2.43
McMillan, Seattle	73	173	2.37
Robertson, Mil.-Det.	69	155	2.25

Blocked Shots

(Minimum 70 games or 100 blocks)

	G.	NO.	AVG.
Olajuwon, Houston	82	342	4.17
O'Neal, Orlando	81	286	3.53
Mutombo, Denver	82	287	3.50
Mourning, Charlotte	78	271	3.47
Robinson, San Antonio	82	264	3.22

1993–94

The biggest news of 1993–94 came a full month before the season got under way. On October 6, Michael Jordan, three-time NBA regular-season and NBA Finals Most Valuable Player, announced his retirement from the sport at age 30, saying he had accomplished all he set out to do in basketball. Not since Jim Brown's retirement from the NFL had a star of such magnitude stepped away while he was at the pinnacle, having won NBA championships in his final three seasons and scoring titles in his final seven. But Jordan's departure had an energizing effect on the league, as the championship now seemed within reach of any number of teams.

Seven teams went on to win at least 55 games, led by Seattle, which had come within one game of the NBA Finals a year ago. The SuperSonics won 63 games to lead the West, while Houston, led by NBA Most Valuable Player Hakeem Olajuwon, won 58. In the East, a pair of defensive stalwarts, New York and Atlanta, won 57 games apiece, while the Jordan-less Chicago Bulls did surprisingly well, winning 55. Phoenix, which battled through injuries to Charles Barkley and Kevin Johnson, won 56 games, and San Antonio, with David Robinson enjoying his best season, won 55.

In the postseason, a young Denver squad achieved what was thought impossible, becoming the first No. 8 seed to defeat a No. 1 seed when it came back from a 2–0 deficit and ousted Seattle in the First Round. Houston disposed of Portland easily, came back from a 2–0 deficit to beat Phoenix in seven games, and beat Utah in five games to advance to the NBA Finals for the first time since 1986. New York, which took the hard road all season with its grinding defense, dismissed New Jersey, then survived seven-game series against Chicago and Indiana to reach the Finals for the first time since 1973. But New York came up short in its third consecutive seven-game series as Houston captured its first NBA title by winning Game 7 at home, 90–84, closing out the first Finals since 1955 where neither team reached 100 points in any game.

Hakeem Olajuwon had long been the NBA's most underrated superstar, quietly flourishing in the background while charismatic stars like Larry Bird, Magic Johnson, Michael Jordan, Isiah Thomas and Charles Barkley captured the spotlight. Olajuwon made it to the NBA Finals in his second NBA season in 1986, but didn't make it back to the NBA's premier stage until 1994, when he capped his MVP season by bringing the city of Houston its first major-league championship in any sport.

Olajuwon had a magnificent NBA Finals, winning his private duel with Patrick Ewing and scoring 26.9 ppg in a series where Houston managed just 86.1 ppg. He also averaged 9.1 rebounds, 3.6 assists and 3.86 blocked shots, and it was his block of John Starks's last-ditch three-pointer that preserved Houston's 86–84 win in Game 6. In the company of Jordan at last, Olajuwon added a championship ring and the NBA Finals MVP award to his regular-season MVP trophy.

NBA 1993-94

FINAL STANDINGS

Eastern Conference

Atlantic Division

	W.	L.	PCT.
New York	57	25	.695
Orlando	50	32	.610
New Jersey	45	37	.549
Miami	42	40	.512
Boston	32	50	.390
Philadelphia	25	57	.305
Washington	24	58	.293

Central Division

	W.	L.	PCT.
Atlanta	57	25	.695
Chicago	55	27	.671
Cleveland	47	35	.573
Indiana	47	35	.573
Charlotte	41	41	.500
Detroit	20	62	.244
Milwaukee	20	62	.244

Western Conference

Midwest Division

	W.	L.	PCT.
Houston	58	24	.707
San Antonio	55	27	.671
Utah	53	29	.646
Denver	42	40	.512
Minnesota	20	62	.244
Dallas	13	69	.159

Pacific Division

	W.	L.	PCT.
Seattle	63	19	.768
Phoenix	56	26	.683
Golden State	50	32	.610
Portland	47	35	.573
L.A. Lakers	33	49	.402
Sacramento	28	54	.341
L.A. Clippers	27	55	.329

PLAYOFFS

Eastern Conference First Round

Atlanta 3, Miami 2
April 28—Miami 93, Atlanta 88
April 30—Atlanta 104, Miami 86
May 3—Miami 90, Atlanta 86
May 5—Atlanta 103, Miami 89
May 8—Atlanta 102, Miami 91

Chicago 3, Cleveland 0
April 29—Chicago 104, Cleveland 96
May 1—Chicago 105, Cleveland 96
May 3—Chicago 95, Cleveland 92 (OT)

Indiana 3, Orlando 0
April 28—Indiana 89, Orlando 88
April 30—Indiana 103, Orlando 101
May 2—Indiana 99, Orlando 86

New York 3, New Jersey 1
April 29—New York 91, New Jersey 80
May 1—New York 90, New Jersey 81
May 4—New Jersey 93, New York 92 (OT)
May 6—New York 102, New Jersey 92

Western Conference First Round

Denver 3, Seattle 2
April 28—Seattle 106, Denver 82
April 30—Seattle 97, Denver 87
May 2—Denver 110, Seattle 93
May 5—Denver 94, Seattle 85 (OT)
May 7—Denver 98, Seattle 94 (OT)

Phoenix 3, Golden State 0
April 29—Phoenix 111, Golden State 104
May 1—Phoenix 117, Golden State 111
May 4—Phoenix 140, Golden State 133

Houston 3, Portland 1
April 29—Houston 114, Portland 104
May 1—Houston 115, Portland 104
May 3—Portland 118, Houston 115
May 6—Houston 92, Portland 89

Utah 3, San Antonio 1
April 28—San Antonio 106, Utah 89
April 30—Utah 96, San Antonio 84
May 3—Utah 105, San Antonio 72
May 5—Utah 95, San Antonio 90

Eastern Conference Semifinals

Indiana 4, Atlanta 2
May 10—Indiana 96, Atlanta 85
May 12—Atlanta 92, Indiana 69
May 14—Indiana 101, Atlanta 81
May 15—Indiana 102, Atlanta 86
May 17—Atlanta 88, Indiana 76
May 19—Indiana 97, Atlanta 79

New York 4, Chicago 3
May 8—New York 90, Chicago 86
May 11—New York 96, Chicago 91
May 13—Chicago 104, New York 102
May 15—Chicago 95, New York 83
May 18—New York 87, Chicago 86
May 20—Chicago 93, New York 79
May 22—New York 87, Chicago 77

Western Conference Semifinals

Utah 4, Denver 3
May 10—Utah 100, Denver 91
May 12—Utah 104, Denver 94
May 14—Utah 111, Denver 109 (OT)
May 15—Denver 83, Utah 82
May 17—Denver 109, Utah 101 (2OT)
May 19—Denver 94, Utah 91
May 21—Utah 91, Denver 81

Houston 4, Phoenix 3
May 8—Phoenix 91, Houston 87
May 11—Phoenix 124, Houston 117 (OT)
May 13—Houston 118, Phoenix 102
May 15—Houston 107, Phoenix 96
May 17—Houston 109, Phoenix 86
May 19—Phoenix 103, Houston 89
May 21—Houston 104, Phoenix 94

Eastern Conference Finals

New York 4, Indiana 3
May 24—New York 100, Indiana 89
May 26—New York 89, Indiana 78
May 28—Indiana 88, New York 68
May 30—Indiana 83, New York 77
June 1—Indiana 93, New York 86
June 3—New York 98, Indiana 91
June 5—New York 94, Indiana 90

Western Conference Finals

Houston 4, Utah 1
May 23—Houston 100, Utah 88
May 25—Houston 104, Utah 99
May 27—Utah 95, Houston 86
May 29—Houston 80, Utah 78
May 31—Houston 94, Utah 83

NBA Finals

Houston 4, New York 3
June 8—Houston 85, New York 78
June 10—New York 91, Houston 83
June 12—Houston 93, New York 89
June 15—New York 91, Houston 82
June 17—New York 91, Houston 84
June 19—Houston 86, New York 84
June 22—Houston 90, New York 84

INDIVIDUAL LEADERS

Scoring

(Minimum 70 games played or 1,400 points)

	G.	FG	FT	PTS.	AVG.
Robinson, San Antonio	80	840	693	2383	29.8
O'Neal, Orlando	81	953	471	2377	29.3
Olajuwon, Houston	80	894	388	2184	27.3
Wilkins, Atl.-L.A.-C.	74	698	442	1923	26.0
K. Malone, Utah	82	772	511	2063	25.2
Ewing, New York	79	745	445	1939	24.5
Richmond, Sacramento	78	635	426	1823	23.4
Pippen, Chicago	72	627	270	1587	22.0
Barkley, Phoenix	65	518	318	1402	21.6
Rice, Miami	81	663	250	1708	21.1

Field Goal Pct.

(Minimum 300 FG made)

	FGM	FGA	PCT.
O'Neal, Orlando	953	1591	.599
Mutombo, Denver	365	642	.569
Thorpe, Houston	449	801	.561
Webber, Golden State	572	1037	.552
Kemp, Seattle	533	990	.538

3-Pt. Field Goal Pct.

(Minimum 50 made)

	FGM	FGA	PCT.
Murray, Portland	50	109	.459
Armstrong, Chicago	60	135	.444
Miller, Indiana	123	292	.421
Kerr, Chicago	52	124	.419
Skiles, Orlando	68	165	.412

Free Throw Pct.

(Minimum 125 FT made)

	FTM	FTA	PCT.
Abdul-Rauf, Denver	219	229	.956
Miller, Indiana	403	444	.908
Pierce, Seattle	189	211	.896
Threatt, L.A. Lakers	138	155	.890
Price, Cleveland	238	268	.888

Assists

(Minimum 70 games or 400 assists)

	G.	NO.	AVG.
Stockton, Utah	82	1031	12.6
Bogues, Charlotte	77	780	10.1
Blaylock, Atlanta	81	789	9.7
K. Anderson, New Jersey	82	784	9.6
K. Johnson, Phoenix	67	637	9.5

Rebounds

(Minimum 70 games or 800 rebounds)

	G.	OFF.	DEF.	TOT.	AVG.
Rodman, San Antonio	79	453	914	1367	17.3
O'Neal, Orlando	81	384	688	1072	13.2
Willis, Atlanta	80	335	628	963	12.0
Olajuwon, Houston	80	229	726	955	11.9
Polynice, Det.-Sac.	68	299	510	809	11.9

Steals

(Minimum 70 games or 125 steals)

	G.	NO.	AVG.
McMillan, Seattle	73	216	2.96
Pippen, Chicago	72	211	2.93
Blaylock, Atlanta	81	212	2.62
Stockton, Utah	82	199	2.43
Murdock, Milwaukee	82	197	2.40

Blocked Shots

(Minimum 70 games or 100 blocks)

	G.	NO.	AVG.
Mutombo, Denver	82	336	4.10
Olajuwon, Houston	80	297	3.71
Robinson, San Antonio	80	265	3.31
Mourning, Charlotte	60	188	3.13
Bradley, Philadelphia	49	147	3.00

SHAQ, 'ZO AND BEYOND: A PEEK INTO THE FUTURE
by David DuPree

David DuPree is the senior pro basketball writer for USA Today *and a columnist for* Hoop *magazine. He previously covered the NBA for the* Washington Post.

As great as the past has been, the future of the NBA looks even brighter. State-of-the-art arenas, a new generation of stars and basketball's global explosion all point to an exciting, wide-open bonanza for players and fans.

The league has successfully gone through many eras. The post–Michael Jordan era promises to be one of the most exciting. This is the time when parity has truly taken hold.

The superstars of past generations like George Mikan, Joe Fulks, Bill Russell, Wilt Chamberlain, Bob Pettit, Kareem Abdul-Jabbar, Bob Cousy, Oscar Robertson, Jerry West, Julius Erving, Larry Bird, Earvin "Magic" Johnson, Michael Jordan and others have all given way to present-day stars like Scottie Pippen, Charles Barkley, Karl Malone, Patrick Ewing, Hakeem Olajuwon, David Robinson, John Stockton and more. The future, however, belongs to Shaquille O'Neal, Alonzo Mourning, Chris Webber, Shawn Kemp, Latrell Sprewell, Oliver Miller, Kenny Anderson, Derrick

From the moment he burst on the NBA scene in 1992, Shaquille O'Neal exuded star power.

Coleman, Jamal Mashburn, Anfernee Hardaway and other youngsters still honing their skills and waiting for their chance to compete at basketball's highest level.

O'Neal is compared to Chamberlain as Chamberlain was to Mikan. David Robinson was the new Kareem, and now Mourning is the next Russell. Hardaway continues the legend of Magic Johnson, and Toni Kukoc just may remind the world of what the game was like when Michael Jordan still played it. Barkley is an improved Pettit and Magic passed his torch to Jordan. It goes on and on.

The game has gotten better over the years, and so have the players. When it was hard to imagine any player ever comparing to Chamberlain, along came Abdul-Jabbar. After Magic we had thought we had seen it all, and then in floated Mr. Jordan.

The new stars have brought changes in the game. The players are so much bigger and stronger than in previous decades, and the trend continues, leading to speculation about rules changes in the future. The baskets already have changed over the years to take into account the physical skills and size of the players. A hydraulic system was installed to withstand the onslaught. Then came collapsible rims to avoid the shattering of backboards. Six inches were trimmed from the bottom of the backboard because modern players, taller and able to jump so much higher, were constantly banging into it.

The players with the big advantages today are those who can use their off hands—right-handers with the ability to go to the left and left-handers who can go to the right. This ability will be even more valuable in the future as defenses and scouting reports become ever more sophisticated.

The positions on the floor, once clearly defined, simply aren't anymore. It used to be easy to tell the point guard from the shooting guard and the small forward from the power forward and everybody else from the center. Not anymore. Even the terminology has changed. A point guard is referred to as a 1, the shooting guard a 2, the small forward a 3, the power forward a 4 and the center a 5.

These designations used to define the players. Now they merely define positions on the floor, positions capable of being filled by any number of players in the lineup at a given time. It won't be long before any position will be able to be played by nearly any player. That's all muddled now, as we head for a time when coaches just put players on the floor and let them play. Whoever takes the inbounds pass will become the point guard. What positions often do, anyway, is restrain the

individuality of the players and limit the options of the coach.

Pat Riley was the first to talk about this. When he coached the Los Angeles Lakers from 1981 to 1990, he spoke of a team with five players capable of playing all five positions. Of course, he had Magic Johnson, a human wild card, so it was easy for him to envision five players all standing around 6-9, muscular and quick, playing together without restrictions on who was playing which position. With the offensive game presently designed to get a mismatch somewhere on the floor, this universal lineup would force that philosophy to change. There is no such thing as a mismatch when all the players are interchangeable, and so a whole new set of plays and options must be developed. Riley, for one, relished the challenge.

In the '70s and early- to mid-'80s, teams got the ball to the point guard, who ran everything.

Then came the Chicago Bulls. They won three consecutive NBA titles from 1991 to 1993, without

Strong and skillful, Alonzo Mourning is the center of attention in Charlotte.

Though he never played college ball, exciting Shawn Kemp has grown up to be an All-Star in Seattle.

a traditional point guard. John Paxson and B. J. Armstrong, who played that position, were primarily jump shooters. The ballhandling was done as much by shooting guard Michael Jordan and small forward Scottie Pippen as it was by the so-called point guards. That put a new kind of pressure on the opposition.

The Dream Team, which captured the gold medal at the 1992 Olympics in Barcelona, took that team concept even further under Coach Chuck Daly. Patrick Ewing and John Stockton were the only players who played just one position. Everyone else played two, three or four of them.

Youngsters today recall Magic Johnson and want to play like him, do the things he did on the basketball floor. In the past a youngster who was tall was forced to play an inside position. A 6-7 player at the high school level was made to play center, taught post-up moves and rebounding techniques at the expense of learning to dribble and pass effectively. He was also told that he shouldn't even think about shooting from outside. Today, however, if a 6-7 or even 6-9 player shows great ballhandling skills, he is allowed to play guard and his skills at that position are utilized, creating unique problems for the opposition.

His nickname may be "Penny," but Anfernee Hardaway is worth his weight in gold to the Orlando Magic.

Dream Teammates Magic Johnson (15) and Charles Barkley set standards at which the younger generation can take aim.

Chris Webber of the Golden State Warriors was the NBA's top rookie in 1994.

Where is the game headed? How giddy would a coach be if he could put on the floor a starting lineup of Toni Kukoc (6-11), Detlef Schrempf (6-10), Anfernee Hardaway (6-7), Chris Webber (6-10) and Walt Williams (6-8)? That's a starting team of players all 6-7 or taller, all five capable of playing any of the five positions.

Perhaps that is where the game is headed, although the 1993–94 NBA season saw the reemergence of the traditional centers. Pivotmen like Hakeem Olajuwon, Shaquille O'Neal, Patrick Ewing and David Robinson moved to the forefront following the retirement of Michael Jordan and took their teams with them.

As the game shifts toward rewarding the large and the versatile, there is, however, still a place for the little man. There always will be. But trends have been established that will continue. A traditional starting

lineup may well become a thing of the past in the not-too-distant future. Most coaches of today pick a lineup and stay with it, making changes only grudgingly. In years to come, starting lineups may be looked at differently. Who starts may depend on the opponent. Coaches might be more apt to try different things, and players may be more open to accepting them.

As the players increase in size and versatility, some rules may have to be reexamined to keep up with the game. Raising the basket, though frequently mentioned, is not regarded by most people as a good idea. Taller players would still be closer to the basket even if you raised it, and besides, drives and dunks are among the game's most spectacular plays.

The most likely long-term changes may be in the size of the court. It may become longer and wider, the lane could be widened or changed to the trapezoidal shape used in international play, even the radical idea of four players to a side could be employed. Each of these concepts would serve to open up the game, which has

Germany's Detlef Schrempf was a college star at Washington before becoming an NBA All-Star.

Croatia's Toni Kukoc was the object of several years of recruiting by the Chicago Bulls.

been the driving philosophy behind rules changes since the league was founded. These are extreme changes, however, and not likely to happen in the immediate future. The NBA is booming right now, and, as the saying goes, if it ain't broke, don't fix it.

There could be more subtle changes, too, like a larger ball or a smaller rim. But one trouble with any such change is how it would affect the records. For a sport just beginning to develop a sense of its heritage, this becomes a very real concern. Will every new record require an asterisk after it? It's hard enough to compare players from different eras now; imagine if you changed the size of the basket or did other such tinkering.

The NBA game already has become a global affair, and it will continue to grow in the next decade. Already there are NBA players from Germany (Schrempf), Venezuela (Carl Herrera), Nigeria (Hakeem Olajuwon), Romania (Gheorghe Muresan), Lithuania (Sarunas Marciulionis), Serbia (Vlade Divac), Croatia (Toni Kukoc

Nigerian-born Hakeem Olajuwon shoots over Jamaican-born Patrick Ewing in NBA playoff action.

the look-away pass. It used to be that a behind-the-back dribble or pass was hot-dogging it. Now it's an integral part of the game, designed to give the offensive player an advantage, not to show up the opposition.

Recently, the NBA has concentrated on defense. Coaches have found that good defense keeps their teams in virtually every game, even if the offense isn't working. Shots come and go, but good defense is a constant. As a result of this, scoring has taken a downward trend, and

The driving, slashing style of Lithuania's Sarunas Marciulionis helped him make it in the NBA.

and Dino Radja), Sudan (Manute Bol) and Zaire (Dikembe Mutombo) in the league, just to mention a few. NBA exhibition games have been played in Mexico and England and regular-season games in Japan. NBA players now also play every two years in a major global event, either the Olympics or the World Championship of Basketball.

Though NBA Commissioner David Stern repeatedly has said the league has no plans to expand outside North America, preferring to work with federations and leagues in each country to grow the sport of basketball, the concept of a global league remains a topic of speculation among fans. Divisions could be in Europe, Asia, Africa and South America as well as in North America, leading to some truly global pro championship each year.

The game's style also has gone through many changes. The jump shot was the biggest innovation of its time. Then came the dunk. Today, it's the lob pass and

Born and raised in Zaire, Dikembe Mutombo learned his basketball at Georgetown and is now an NBA All-Star.

in the near future teams may find it even more difficult to score.

Youngsters have found new heroes, too. It used to be that everyone wanted to be like Mike. Now, some youngsters grow up wanting to play like Dennis Rodman, a unique player who doesn't like to shoot and seldom does, virtually never from outside the lane. But Rodman became one of the league's most valuable commodities because he was a relentless rebounder and defender, capable of guarding any player at any position.

And if he doesn't care about scoring, that simply leaves more shots for his teammates, who certainly love him for that!

The future of basketball may have us in a quandary. On one hand, as described above, the game may go to a team of five interchangeable parts. On the other hand, specialists may become more valuable than ever. You can carry a defensive-rebounder specialist like Rodman if you have other players to take up the scoring slack, for instance. And instead of another 6-7 shooter on your

bench, why not a 5-9 spark plug who can wreak havoc with his quickness and change the pace of a game each time he steps onto the floor?

The game is also going the sophisticated route. Coaches are continually stretching the boundaries of the illegal defense guidelines, devising ways to make it more difficult for opponents to score. Complicated traps and presses are a staple in every team's playbook.

NBA basketball has always been a forerunner in terms of fashion. What NBA players do and wear sets the standard for colleges, high schools, junior leagues and playgrounds. Just look at a picture of George Mikan in uniform and compare it with one of Alonzo Mourning of the Charlotte Hornets. Mikan's shoes are canvas, his trunks are short and tight. The numbers on his jersey are small and there's no name on the back of his shirt. Team colors were simpler in those days, with many clubs using basic colors like blue and white, and the uniforms often were designed and even made by a coach's or owner's wife.

Mourning's uniform was created by innovative fashion designer Alexander Julian. The principal color is trendy teal. The numbers are large and distinctive. Thin stripes, widely separated, suggest the look of a fine Italian suit. Mourning's name is on the back of his jersey. His shorts are long and full. He also wears two wristbands on each arm. And then there are the shoes, leather with overlapping Velcro straps for extra support, an air cushion sole and heel—and a new pair worn every game.

The future? The name will still be on the back, but the uniforms may well be full body suits, gleaming and aerodynamic. The shoes may be boots worn over the uniform and fitted to the ankle, making sprains virtually obsolete.

Statistics will evolve as well. Already the NBA has gone to computerized stat systems at courtside, but this could be just the beginning. Perhaps the ball could be programmed to record each player's fingerprints in sequence, so a computer could instantly tally every pass, every rebound, every assist—without having to rely on a statistician's eyes and judgment as the standard.

Last-second shots always will be dramatic, but the new baskets might be designed so that when the clock reaches 00:00.0, a force field won't allow a shot to go through the hoop.

These ideas may seem far-fetched, but remember, there was a time when there was no three-point shot, no dunking, a smaller lane, and it was considered rude to block another player's shot. Today, the blocked shot is one of the most exciting plays in the game.

Who knows what tomorrow will bring?

NBA NUMBER RETIREMENTS

Having his number retired is one of the great honors that can be bestowed upon an athlete. Following is a complete list of the NBA's retired numbers:

				K. C. Jones	(25)
				Kevin McHale	(32)
Atlanta:	Bob Pettit	(9)		Larry Bird	(33)
	Lou Hudson	(23)		Jim Loscutoff	(LOSCY)[2]
Boston:	Walter Brown	(1)[1]		Johnny Most	(microphone)[3]
	Red Auerbach	(2)[1]	Chicago:	Jerry Sloan	(4)
	Dennis Johnson	(3)		Bob Love	(10)
	Bill Russell	(6)	Cleveland:	Bingo Smith	(7)
	Jo Jo White	(10)		Austin Carr	(34)
	Bob Cousy	(14)		Nate Thurmond	(42)[4]
	Tom Heinsohn	(15)	Dallas:	Brad Davis	(15)
	Tom Sanders	(16)	Denver:	Alex English	(2)
	John Havlicek	(17)		David Thompson	(33)
	Dave Cowens	(18)[2]		Byron Beck	(40)
	Don Nelson	(19)		Dan Issel	(44)
	Bill Sharman	(21)	Detroit:	Vinnie Johnson	(15)
	Ed Macauley	(22)		Bob Lanier	(16)[4]
	Frank Ramsey	(23)		Dave Bing	(21)
	Sam Jones	(24)	Golden State:	Tom Meschery	(14)

	Al Attles	(16)	Philadelphia:	Julius Erving	(6)[4]
	Rick Barry	(24)		Wilt Chamberlain	(13)[4]
	Nate Thurmond	(42)[4]		Hal Greer	(15)
Houston:	Calvin Murphy	(23)		Bobby Jones	(24)
	Rudy Tomjanovich	(45)		Billy Cunningham	(32)
Indiana:	George McGinnis	(30)		Dave Zinkoff	(microphone)[3]
	Mel Daniels	(34)	Phoenix:	Dick Van Arsdale	(5)
	Roger Brown	(35)		Walter Davis	(6)
L.A. Lakers:	Wilt Chamberlain	(13)[4]		Alvan Adams	(33)
	Elgin Baylor	(22)		Connie Hawkins	(42)
	Magic Johnson	(32)		Paul Westphal	(44)
	Kareem Abdul-Jabbar	(33)[4]	Portland:	Larry Weinberg	(1)[1]
	Jerry West	(44)		David Twardzik	(13)
Milwaukee:	Oscar Robertson	(1)[4]		Larry Steele	(15)
	Junior Bridgeman	(2)		Maurice Lucas	(20)
	Sidney Moncrief	(4)		Bill Walton	(32)
	Jon McGlocklin	(14)		Lloyd Neal	(36)
	Bob Lanier	(16)[4]		Geoff Petrie	(45)
	Brian Winters	(32)		Jack Ramsay	(77)[6]
	Kareem Abdul-Jabbar	(33)[4]	Sacramento:	Fans	(6)[7]
New Jersey:	Drazen Petrovic	(3)		Bob Davies	(11)
	Wendell Ladner	(4)		Maurice Stokes	(12)
	John Williamson	(23)		Oscar Robertson	(14)[4]
	Bill Melchionni	(25)		Jack Twyman	(27)
	Julius Erving	(32)[4]		Sam Lacey	(44)
New York:	Walt Frazier	(10)	San Antonio:	James Silas	(13)
	Dick Barnett	(12)		George Gervin	(44)
	Earl Monroe	(15)[5]	Seattle:	Lenny Wilkens	(19)
	Dick McGuire	(15)[5]		Fred Brown	(32)
	Willis Reed	(19)	Utah:	Frank Layden	(1)[8]
	Dave DeBusschere	(22)		Pete Maravich	(7)
	Bill Bradley	(24)		Darrell Griffith	(35)
	Red Holzman	(613)[6]	Washington:	Elvin Hayes	(11)
				Gus Johnson	(25)
				Wes Unseld	(41)

Note:

[1] Two owners are honored with the No. 1: Walter Brown of Boston and Larry Weinberg of Portland. With No. 1 having gone to Brown, Boston issued No. 2 to Red Auerbach, its longtime coach, general manager and team president.

[2] Boston retired No. 18 in honor of Dave Cowens and the nickname "Loscy" in honor of Jim Loscutoff, who also wore No. 18.

[3] Boston broadcaster Johnny Most and Philadelphia PA announcer Dave Zinkoff were honored with banners bearing microphones rather than numbers.

[4] Six players have had their numbers retired by more than one team: Kareem Abdul-Jabbar (No. 33 with Milwaukee and the Los Angeles Lakers), Oscar Robertson (No. 1 with Milwaukee and No. 14 with Sacramento), Bob Lanier (No. 16 with Detroit and Milwaukee), Julius Erving (No. 32 with New Jersey and No. 6 with Philadel-

phia), Wilt Chamberlain (No. 13 with Philadelphia and the Los Angeles Lakers), and Nate Thurmond (No. 42 with Cleveland and Golden State).

[5] New York retired No. 15 in honor of Earl Monroe and later retired the same number in honor of Dick McGuire.

[6] New York retired No. 613 in honor of Red Holzman, marking the number of coaching victories he compiled with the team, while Portland retired No. 77 in honor of Jack Ramsay, indicating the year (1977) Ramsay guided the Trail Blazers to their only NBA title.

[7] The Sacramento Kings retired No. 6 in recognition of their fans, who filled their arena to capacity after the team moved to Sacramento from Kansas City.

[8] The Utah Jazz retired No. 1 in honor of Frank Layden, who served as the team's coach, general manager and president.

CHAPTER FOUR

RED, WHITE AND BLUE: THE ABA

by Terry Pluto

Dennis Murphy, founder of the ABA, would have preferred to start a football league.

Terry Pluto, basketball writer for the Akron Beacon-Journal, *is a prolific author whose books include* Loose Balls, The Short, Wild Life of the American Basketball Association.

It was before Julius Erving, the slam-dunk sports contest and the three-point shot. George Gervin and George McGinnis were still in junior high and Doug Moe was playing basketball in Italy.

The year was 1967. The NBA had only 10 teams, and Wilt Chamberlain's Philadelphia 76ers were the defending champions, but pro basketball was primarily a game for the purists, a distant third among team sports in the race for the attention of most sports fans. Few games were nationally televised. Few were sellouts. In the mid-1960s, the average NBA player earned about $10,000 and had to buy his own sneakers.

About the last thing the world seemed to need was another pro basketball league.

"I knew that," said Dennis Murphy. "In the beginning, we didn't want a basketball league. We wanted a second football league, but somebody beat us to it and started the American Football League."

Dennis Murphy is one of those guys whose sports imagination never rests.

"If they ever put a sports league on Mars, you can be sure that Dennis started it," said former NBA referee John Vanak.

Murphy never had much money, but he knew some

people with cash. In the mid-1960s, he had some investors in line waiting to put their dollars down on pro sports. Since football was out, "and since we didn't want to fight baseball, that left basketball or hockey. I knew more about basketball than hockey, so we started a second basketball league," Murphy recalls.

And so the American Basketball Association was born in the spring of 1967. No surveys, no marketing research, no discussion among corporate titans regarding sponsorship and licensing opportunities. It was like a Judy Garland movie in which a bunch of kids got together and said, "Let's put on a show in our garage, sell tickets and see if anyone comes."

That was also why it was so hard for the NBA to take the new league seriously. You could hear them all saying, "Who is going to watch *their* games when we have so much trouble getting people to come to *our* games? So what if the ABA hired George Mikan as commissioner. If they could get Mikan to play, it would be something for us to worry about." But in 1967

Connie Hawkins, playground legend, led the Pittsburgh Pipers to the first ABA title in 1968.

Mikan was 43 years old, a lawyer and the owner of a travel agency in Minneapolis. No one pays a dime to watch a commissioner.

So that was how the NBA viewed the upstart ABA. Then came the ball. The red, white and blue ball. It was Mikan's idea and only Mikan's idea.

"The brown ball was really hard to see on TV or even if you were sitting in the balcony," said Mikan. "I wanted something to be the symbol of our league. We were the American Basketball Association. America's colors are red, white and blue. I'll tell you, we were going to have a red, white and blue ball or I wasn't going to be commissioner."

Since the ABA was desperate for a big name to give it legitimacy—the ABA needed Mikan more than Mikan needed the ABA—Mikan got his way with the ball . . . much to the delight of the NBA.

"It looks like something that belongs on the nose of a seal," said veteran NBA coach Alex Hannum.

And the early ABA was run like a circus.

There were 11 teams, and one of them was the Dallas Chaparrals, so named because the franchise's first ownership meeting was held at the Chaparral Room of the Dallas Sheraton. The team needed a nickname, somebody looked up at the name on the door and Chaparral seemed as good as any.

Where the Dallas franchise truly became a part of ABA lore was in the 1967 draft. The team's general manager was Max Williams, a former basketball star at SMU, and Williams put together a list of college prospects. Hoping to save travel expenses, Roland Speth, one of the owners, went to the draft by himself and took Williams's list.

"Roland thought it was done in order of talent," said Williams. "Instead, it was alphabetical order."

So Dallas's first five picks were Matt Aitch, Jim Burns, Gary Gray, Pat Riley and Jim Thompson—five guys in alphabetical order.

One of the owners of the New Orleans franchise was Morton Downey, Jr., who later became a controversial talk-show host. At the time, he was a salesman with American Can Company. He didn't survive the first

Rick Barry (24), here playing for the Oakland Oaks, is the only man to lead the NCAA, ABA and NBA in scoring.

Larry Brown led the ABA in assists three times before launching an outstanding coaching career.

moted" to public relations director. Amigos owner Art Kim explained, "Brightman has been our most effective PR man, so why not make him a PR man?"

Like the Statue of Liberty, Mikan opened the door to anyone who thought he could play. Connie Hawkins, Roger Brown and Moe had been banned from the NBA because their names had come up during the college basketball scandals of the early 1960s. So they came to the ABA. Hawkins would lead the Pittsburgh Pipers to the first ABA title in 1968 and eventually jump to Phoenix of the NBA for the 1969–70 season.

The ABA went to war with the NBA for talent and respect. Far more battles were fought *in* court than *on* the court; it appeared that the leagues and the players were constantly suing each other. For the first time, basketball players discovered that not every contract was a ball and chain and that being a free agent could make you a very expensive item.

season, but he did sign a point guard named Larry Brown and a forward named Doug Moe—two men who would become prominent NBA coaches. But first, they spent nine years in the ABA.

That initial 1967–68 season had some mind-boggling developments. The Anaheim Amigos had a player named Les Selvage. A former shipping clerk, Selvage made the Amigos as a walk-on and in one game launched 26 shots from beyond the three-point line, making 10.

Selvage's onslaught happened against the Denver Rockets, not Nuggets. The Rockets were named after Rocket Truck Lines, which owned the team. One of Denver's players was Lefty Thomas. "The only guy I've ever seen play with rings on his fingers," said Larry Brown. "I mean, 10 fingers, 10 rings."

Selvage's coach, Al Brightman, was fired after a 12–24 start. Actually, he wasn't fired, he was "pro-

Flamboyant, high-scoring Doug Moe is another ABA star who enjoyed coaching success in the NBA.

Consider the Oakland franchise, which hired Bruce Hale as its coach. You may not remember Bruce Hale, but you know his son-in-law, Rick Barry, whom he had coached in college. When Hale joined the Oakland Oaks, he inspired Barry to cross the bay from the San Francisco Warriors. The first of many lawsuits between the two leagues was filed—the only people who really got rich off the war between the ABA and NBA were the lawyers—and Barry was forced to sit out the ABA's first season while his case limped through the court system.

Ironically, when Barry was cleared to play in the ABA for the 1968–69 season, Hale was out as coach, replaced by Alex Hannum, the same coach who had ridiculed the ABA's red, white and blue ball. Barry's team won the 1969 title, with Larry Brown at point guard and Moe at forward. They had been traded by New Orleans, but don't even try to keep all of this straight.

Gates were small—the ABA claimed an average attendance of 2,804 for its first year, but many of those came disguised as empty seats. Franchises seemed to be constantly folding, moving or on the verge of one or the

Kentucky's Louie Dampier was one of the ABA's best guards, driving to the hoop or shooting the three.

other. Trades were made, players were sold and the NBA watched in absolute wonder. How did the amateurs in the ABA stay in business?

Part of the answer was that there was a lot of untapped basketball talent out there. When the ABA came into existence in 1967, there were only 120 pro basketball players. That meant a lot of guys who should have been pros were now presented the opportunity to show they belonged. Yes, Louie Dampier, Mel Daniels, Steve and Jimmy Jones, Hawkins, Moe and Brown were good players. So was Freddie Lewis, one of the most underrated players in basketball history, who signed with the Indiana Pacers for $15,000 and a used refrigerator. It seems his freezer was broken and his wife wouldn't let him play unless he got a new one, and since the Pacers were counting their pennies, they supplied a "nearly new" refrigerator as part of Lewis's contract.

In the late 1960s and early 1970s, the ABA's talent was not on a par with the NBA's, especially at the center position. But it was much closer than the NBA would dare to admit. Unfortunately for the junior league, only a small circle of friends knew it. The ABA had virtually no national TV exposure. Attempts to carve a niche in major cities such as New York, Los Angeles and Washington were failures. For one game in Oakland, the attendance was 98. For a game in Houston, the attendance was announced as 87. Teams regularly padded their gates and still couldn't reach triple digits on occasion!

To understand the entity that was the ABA, it is important to know something about the late 1960s and early 1970s. The Vietnam War, the civil rights movement, the ever-changing and questioning of values combined with a growing drug culture to rock America. The two basketball leagues were right in the midst of the upheaval; the players wore bell-bottoms, long hair, shoes with six-inch heels and Afros that reached to the heavens. When 7-2 Artis Gilmore signed with Kentucky, he measured 7-7 thanks to his hair. Larry Brown coached the Carolina Cougars while wearing farm overalls. Coaches no longer could be dictators. Some players even refused to acknowledge the National Anthem, much less blindly follow the orders of any authority figure. The San Diego Conquistadors even signed the free-spirited Wilt Chamberlain as a player-coach. As usual, lawsuits were filed as the Los Angeles Lakers successfully blocked Chamberlain from playing, although the judge allowed Wilt to coach in 1973. This led to a strange promotion, as San Diego billed itself as the team with "the world's tallest coach in the league's smallest arena"—not exactly "I love this game!" Chamberlain, whose record was 37-47, once received a memo

from the league office suggesting that it would be appreciated if his sideline attire could include shoes instead of sandals.

Agents also became major players in the basketball business, and nothing seemed sacred. Until the advent of the ABA, it was always assumed that a player would stay in college through his senior season before turning pro. Chamberlain quit the University of Kansas after his junior year in 1958, but the NBA would not accept him until his class graduated. So Chamberlain spent a year with the Harlem Globetrotters before coming to the Philadelphia Warriors in 1959.

"This was war," said Al Bianchi, the NBA veteran who coached the ABA's Virginia Squires. "We wanted to get to the players first. The NBA had the 'four-year rule,' that you couldn't sign a player until four years after he entered college. We knew it would never hold up in court, so we just went out and signed who we wanted."

The first was Spencer Haywood. A star on the 1968 U.S. Olympic team out of junior college, Haywood went to the University of Detroit in 1969 for his sophomore season. He clearly was too talented for college competi-

tion and very bored. The ABA hired an agent named Steve Arnold to approach underclassmen about turning pro, and he went to Haywood. Denver signed him to a three-year deal worth $450,000. Actually, it was $50,000 a year for three years, the remaining $300,000 to be paid out at $15,000 annually once he reached the age of 40. This was a typical ABA contract, worth far less than anyone dreamed because most of the money was deferred nearly into the next century, when the owners who gave the contract (and maybe the league itself) would be long gone.

"We knew that the Haywood signing would cause the basketball world to go crazy," said longtime ABA executive Mike Storen. "We didn't care. We were the underdog. We decided to legitimize it by calling Spencer a 'hardship case,' saying he had to support his mother and his nine brothers and sisters."

The NBA was enraged. So was the NCAA. For years, the NCAA had served as a farm system for future NBA players, and the NBA hadn't raided the college programs with early signings. All of that ended with the Haywood case. Then Bianchi and Johnny Kerr, general

Wilt Chamberlain, coach of the San Diego Conquistadors, could have used Wilt Chamberlain the player!

manager of the Virginia Squires, signed a couple of underclassmen named George Gervin and Julius Erving. The Indiana Pacers signed George McGinnis after his sophomore year at Indiana, and Jim Chones signed with the New York Nets following his junior year at Marquette. Naturally, the NBA and NCAA threatened legal action over the newly created hardship cases—no one in the basketball world could take a step in the nine-year history of the ABA without a lawyer filing a brief about it.

"What we tried to do was force a merger, just like the AFL did to the NFL," said Dick Tinkham, one of the owners of the Indiana Pacers. "That was the way we convinced guys to invest in our league. We told them to get in now for less than half of what it costs to buy an NBA team. Then, when the two leagues merged, your investment would double in value."

The ABA always was aware that the real enemy was the NBA. So the league would pool resources to make an offer to Kareem Abdul-Jabbar (then known as Lew Alcindor) and tell him he could play for any ABA team he wanted. They let Indiana have the draft rights to Purdue's Rick Mount because they figured he'd want to play near his home. When teams were on the verge of going under, the league would take over the franchise and search for a new owner.

Meanwhile, the NBA was growing weary of the young league, and it began to marshal its forces. Bidding

Spencer Haywood averaged 30.0 ppg and 19.5 ppg as a 20-year-old rookie for the Denver Rockets in 1969–70.

wars ensued, with the players (and their agents) the biggest winners. The ABA struck early, convincing Rick Barry and Zelmo Beaty to jump leagues. They even got veteran NBA officials Earl Strom, John Vanak, Joe Gushue and Norm Drucker to jump leagues in 1969. But the NBA hit back. Spencer Haywood played only one year for the Denver Rockets, then the NBA's Seattle SuperSonics snatched him in 1970. Western Kentucky star Jim McDaniels played part of the 1971–72 season with the ABA's Carolina Cougars, then jumped to Seattle. Barry spent four years in the ABA, then returned to the Golden State Warriors in 1972. The Phoenix Suns also got into the act, grabbing Charlie Scott from the Virginia Squires after Scott had led the ABA in scoring in 1972.

"What the ABA was really doing was forcing up the price of doing business, and it nearly put teams in both leagues out of business," said longtime agent Ron Grinker. "The ABA was paying in phony dollars, their contracts extended out 20 to 30 years. The NBA countered by paying real dollars, say over a five-year period. The two leagues were bleeding each other. "

The ABA had a wonderful source of revenue right in its hands, but had no commissioner such as David Stern to tap into this pot of gold. Remember the red, white and blue ball? You could find one at nearly every playground. Kids who never saw an ABA game played with its ball. But the ABA didn't patent the color scheme, just the league logo. So anyone could produce a red, white and blue ball and sell it without a dime going back to the ABA—and the ABA estimated that over 29 million of those red, white and blue balls were sold.

Sales of the basketball notwithstanding, few considered the early ABA to be on the same level with the NBA. Even those in the ABA knew that too many of the players were has-beens, never-gonna-bes or guys like

George McGinnis of the Indiana Pacers shared ABA Most Valuable Player honors in 1975 with Julius Erving.

Maurice McHartley, whose nickname was "Toothpick" because he played with one in the corner of his mouth.

Yes, the Indiana Pacers had terrific teams, winning titles in 1970, 1972 and 1973. In two other years, they lost in the ABA Finals. If any team could claim to be the Boston Celtics of the ABA, it was the Pacers, with Mel Daniels in the middle, Roger Brown and Bob Netolicky as forwards and Billy Keller and Freddie Lewis as guards. Later, George McGinnis and Billy Knight would join the mix. But these guys were more like the Bad Boys of Detroit. The coach was Bobby "Slick" Leonard, who would fine any player who *didn't* leave the bench during a fight. Leonard often led the charge himself, jumping onto a pile of bodies like a linebacker trying to recover a fumble. In one incident, a frustrated Leonard went after Netolicky with a hockey stick, taking a swing at his own player in an attempt to arouse the eccentric forward. The Pacers also fashioned themselves as cowboys, wearing western outfits (complete with pistols and holsters) to games. When one of the players accidentally shot a hole in the ceiling, Pacer trainer David Craig demanded that all players check their guns at the locker-room door. Maybe because of their outrageous personalities, the Pacers were not taken seriously by the older league. That's too bad because when they were on the court they could play ball with just about anyone.

Kentucky's 7-2 Artis Gilmore blocks a shot by Moses Malone, who jumped directly from high school to the pros.

But the player who probably allowed the ABA to last as long as it did, and perhaps even forced the two leagues to finally get together, was Julius Erving.

A 6-7 forward at the University of Massachusetts, Erving dominated the Yankee Conference. But in 1970, scouting was not nearly what it is today. Most NBA teams had a general manager, a coach and perhaps an assistant coach. Few had full-time scouts, so hardly anyone was aware what Erving was doing in the Yankee Conference. Furthermore, Erving played in the era when the NCAA had the no-dunk rule, which certainly inhibited his high-flying theatrics.

"We heard about Julius and asked for a tape of him," recalled the Squires' Johnny Kerr. "We got this grainy black-and-white film of the UMass–North Carolina game in the NIT. The quality was so bad that you could hardly tell what was going on, but we saw enough of Julius to sign him after his junior year."

The scouting report?

"Since we'd never seen him live before he wore a Squires uniform, we thought he'd help us on the boards and we hoped he'd be able to score some," said Kerr. "We had no idea what he'd become."

What Erving became was the ABA.

Center Mel Daniels helped make the Indiana Pacers one of the strongest franchises in the ABA.

"Players dunked before Julius Erving, but it was Julius Erving who made the dunk what it is today," said Rod Thorn, a former head coach of the Spirits of St. Louis, an assistant coach when Erving was with the New York Nets and now the NBA's vice president of operations.

Erving had enormous hands, with long fingers, and the dexterity of a pianist. He would palm that red, white and blue ball, waving it around to create a wonderful, rainbowlike illusion for the few fans who actually saw him play in the ABA. As a rookie in 1971–72, he averaged 27.3 points and 15.7 rebounds per game. He played two seasons for the Squires, and that meant two years of playing in Norfolk, Roanoke, Hampton and Richmond. The Squires were one of several "regional" franchises in the ABA, which meant they split their home games between several cities because no one city was big enough to support a full home schedule. The Squires also were always on the verge of bankruptcy and stayed in business by selling their top players. For half a season, they actually had Erving and Gervin on the same

Julius Erving launched his brilliant pro career in relative obscurity with the Virginia Squires.

court, but both were sent elsewhere to pay the bills— Gervin to San Antonio, Erving to the New York Nets.

Playing on Long Island, the Nets with Erving became the class of the ABA. Coached by a volatile Kevin Loughery—he once was whistled for six technicals in a game!—the Nets won ABA titles in 1974 and 1976. Playing close enough to the New York market, Erving invariably drew attention not just to himself but to the entire league. While some hard-core NBA types were skeptical (Red Auerbach once said, "Erving is a nice kid, but I don't know how well he'd do in our league"), most in the NBA who actually saw Erving knew that pro basketball had never quite seen anything like him before.

Even more impressive than his spectacular play was his demeanor. Erving was an eloquent and classy spokesman for the entire ABA.

The flip side of the Nets and Erving were the Spirits of St. Louis. This was the team of Movin' Marvin Barnes, a man who seldom was on time for anything. Barnes usually showed up about 20 minutes before a game wearing a full-length mink coat and carrying a bag of burgers from McDonald's. He would take off the coat and underneath would be his uniform. Then he would sit down and eat cheeseburgers while a trainer taped his ankles. Barnes had 13 telephones in his apartment. One of his famous quotes was "I'm a basketball player, not a monk. I play the women, I play the cars, I play everything I can . . . I'm 22, and a 22-year-old kid ain't no genius." That part was certainly true. One day Barnes was handed a travel schedule that showed the Spirits would leave Louisville by plane at 8:00 A.M. and arrive in St. Louis at 7:58 A.M. This baffled poor Marvin, who was unaware of the difference in time zones. "Oh, no," he said. "I ain't takin' no time machine. I ain't takin' no plane that takes me back in time." When Barnes managed to get to the games on time, he usually played well. According to his general manager, Harry Weltman, Barnes had "the worst shot selection in the Western Hemisphere," yet he still averaged 25 points and 15 rebounds.

Weltman assembled an intriguing collection of talent. The Spirits were around for only the final two years of the ABA, but their players included Maurice Lucas, Moses Malone, Don Chaney, Steve Jones, Freddie Lewis, M. L. Carr and Ron Boone. Their PR man was Rudy Martzke, now the sports TV columnist for *USA Today*. Telling the midwest about the team on 50,000-watt KMOX radio was Bobby Costas, a kid hired out of Syracuse University. "When I was first introduced at KMOX, I met Jack Buck, who asked me

how old I was," recalled Costas. "I said I was 22. He said, 'Kid, I have neckties older than you.' "

By the end of the 1975–76 season, it was clear that the ABA was on a life-support system. Teams in Utah, San Diego and Baltimore had gone under. Virginia was in such sad shape that it immediately shut down after the final game. That left the ABA with six surviving franchises—Indiana, Denver, New York, San Antonio, Kentucky and St. Louis. The ABA's commissioner was Dave DeBusschere, the former New York Knicks star who was hired to use his NBA contacts to get the leagues together. In charge of the NBA was Larry O'Brien, the former chairman of the Democratic party. These two men knew that it was time to combine forces before they drove each other to the brink of financial disaster. Here were the key parts of the deal:

• The NBA and O'Brien agreed to admit four ABA teams, which would raise the total teams in the NBA to 22 for the 1976–77 season. The four teams were Indiana, Denver, San Antonio and the New York Nets.

• Each ABA team would pay the NBA $3.2 million by September 15, 1976.

• The New York Nets had to pay the Knicks $4.8 million for the right to play in the Knicks' "territory."

• The four ABA teams were permitted to keep their players. The remaining ABA players would be spread across the NBA via a draft.

• The ABA would not take part in the 1976 college draft.

The ABA had to cut its own deals to satisfy the owners of Kentucky and St. Louis, teams that would be going out of business. John Y. Brown of Kentucky Fried Chicken fame owned the Colonels. He took a $3 million settlement, then bought the Buffalo Braves for $1.5 million and later engineered a franchise switch, trading Buffalo to become owner of the Boston Celtics.

The Spirits owners were even more creative. They took $2.2 million in cash and a share of the national television revenue from each of the four ABA teams heading into the NBA—which they get forever. In the 1980s, they reportedly made over $8 million from this TV money, which has grown tremendously over the past decade and keeps rolling in.

The terms created a nearly fatal financial squeeze for the Nets, who had to sell Erving to Philadelphia for $3 million to help pay for the right to get into the NBA. But without Erving, the Nets were not an NBA-caliber team.

Erving, meanwhile, led Philadelphia to the 1977 NBA Finals and a championship in 1983. He was an instant gate attraction and a spokesman for the entire league. It took a few years, but the NBA adopted the ABA's three-point shot in 1979. Another ABA innovation was the slam-dunk contest, called "the greatest

Kevin Loughery coached the New York Nets to ABA championships in 1974 and 1976.

halftime invention since the rest room" by *Sports Illustrated* after it was unveiled at the 1976 ABA All-Star Game in Denver. Naturally, Erving won it, and now the Gatorade Slam-Dunk Championship is a cornerstone (along with the AT&T Long Distance Shootout from three-point range) of the NBA All-Star Weekend.

Of the 84 players who competed in the ABA in its final season, 63 went on to play in the NBA and 10 of the NBA's 24 All-Stars in that first season spent at least part of their careers in the other league. The ABA also was a training ground for such coaches as Larry Brown, Hubie Brown and Kevin Loughery. And it was the first step for the man we now know as Bob Costas, a network star at NBC.

Although it only lasted for nine seasons, the free-wheeling ABA left an indelible mark on the growth chart of the sport of professional basketball.

Julius Erving soars in his famed court-length, take-off-from-the-foul-line dunk in 1976.

1967–68

There had been other attempts at competing professional basketball leagues throughout the NBA's 21-year history. But none would last as long, sign as many good players or create as much excitement as the American Basketball Association.

The league began play on Friday, October 13, when the Oakland Oaks defeated the Anaheim Amigos 134–129. The ABA competed as an 11-team league playing a 78-game schedule in its first season. The scoring star of the ABA's inaugural campaign was Connie Hawkins of the Pittsburgh Pipers, a 25-year-old New York playground legend who had been denied entry into the NBA after his name had come up in connection with college basketball betting scandals. Hawkins, a lithe 6-8, 215-

pounder, had huge hands and superior leaping ability and used both to average 26.8 ppg while adding 13.5 rpg. Other stars in the fledgling league included Minnesota's imposing Mel Daniels (22.2 ppg, league-leading 15.6 rpg), Doug Moe of New Orleans (24.2 ppg) and Darel Carrier of Kentucky (22.9 ppg).

Pittsburgh won the Eastern Division with a 54-24 record, while New Orleans (48-30) was the best in the West. Those two teams each won two playoff series to advance to the Finals, where Pittsburgh rebounded from a 3–2 deficit to capture the first ABA Championship. Hawkins was named the league's MVP, while Daniels was the Rookie of the Year.

ABA 1967-68

FINAL STANDINGS

Eastern Division

	W.	L.	PCT.
Pittsburgh	54	24	.692
Minnesota	50	28	.641
Indiana	38	40	.487
Kentucky *	36	42	.462
New Jersey	36	42	.462

* Qualified for playoffs via forfeit win over New Jersey

Western Division

	W.	L.	PCT.
New Orleans	48	30	.615
Dallas	46	32	.590
Denver	45	33	.577
Houston	29	49	.372
Anaheim	25	53	.321
Oakland	22	56	.282

PLAYOFFS

Eastern Division Semifinals

Minnesota 3, Kentucky 2
March 24—Minnesota 115, Kentucky 102
March 26—Kentucky 100, Minnesota 95
March 27—Minnesota 116, Kentucky 107
March 29—Kentucky 94, Minnesota 86
March 30—Minnesota 114, Kentucky 108

Pittsburgh 3, Indiana 0
March 25—Pittsburgh 146, Indiana 127
March 26—Pittsburgh 121, Indiana 108
March 27—Pittsburgh 133, Indiana 114

Western Division Semifinals

New Orleans 3, Denver 2
March 26—New Orleans 130, Denver 104
March 27—New Orleans 105, Denver 93
March 30—Denver 105, New Orleans 98
March 31—Denver 108, New Orleans 100
April 3—New Orleans 102, Denver 97

Dallas 3, Houston 0
March 23—Dallas 111, Houston 110
March 25—Dallas 115, Houston 97
March 26—Dallas 116, Houston 103

Eastern Division Finals

Pittsburgh 4, Minnesota 1
April 4—Pittsburgh 125, Minnesota 117
April 6—Minnesota 137, Pittsburgh 123
April 10—Pittsburgh 107, Minnesota 99
April 13—Pittsburgh 117, Minnesota 108
April 14—Pittsburgh 114, Minnesota 105

Western Division Finals

New Orleans 4, Dallas 1
April 5—New Orleans 104, Dallas 99
April 9—Dallas 112, New Orleans 109
April 10—New Orleans 110, Dallas 107
April 11—New Orleans 119, Dallas 103
April 13—New Orleans 108, Dallas 107

ABA Finals

Pittsburgh 4, New Orleans 3
April 18—Pittsburgh 120, New Orleans 112
April 20—New Orleans 109, Pittsburgh 100
April 24—New Orleans 109, Pittsburgh 101
April 25—Pittsburgh 106, New Orleans 105 (OT)
April 27—New Orleans 111, Pittsburgh 108
May 1—Pittsburgh 118, New Orleans 112
May 4—Pittsburgh 122, New Orleans 113

INDIVIDUAL LEADERS

Scoring

	G.	FG	FT	PTS.	AVG.
Hawkins, Pittsburgh	70	635	603	1875	26.8
Moe, New Orleans	78	665	551	1884	24.2
Tart, Oak.-N.J.	73	633	451	1718	23.5
Carrier, Kentucky	77	643	395	1765	22.9
Jones, Denver	76	602	530	1742	22.9
Daniels, Minnesota	78	669	390	1729	22.2
Somerset, Houston	61	467	359	1326	21.7
Williams, Pittsburgh	78	642	290	1625	20.8
Dampier, Kentucky	72	620	209	1487	20.7
Lewis, Indiana	76	542	465	1565	20.6

Field Goal Pct.

	FGM	FGA	PCT.
Washington, Pittsburgh	312	596	.523
Hawkins, Pittsburgh	635	1223	.519
Netolicky, Indiana	468	928	.504
Anderson, New Jersey	463	938	.494
C. Beasley, Dallas	374	758	.493

3-Pt. Field Goal Pct.

	FGM	FGA	PCT.
Carrier, Kentucky	84	235	.357
Perry, Minnesota	62	178	.348
Vaughn, Pittsburgh	137	410	.334
Rayl, Indiana	57	175	.326
Selvage, Anaheim	147	461	.319

Free Throw Pct.

	FTM	FTA	PCT.
C. Beasley, Dallas	285	327	.872
Lloyd, New Jersey	170	199	.854
J. Beasley, Dallas	271	322	.842
Jackson, New Jersey	450	543	.829
Nowell, New Jersey	176	213	.826

Assists

	G.	NO.	AVG.
Brown, New Orleans	78	506	6.5
Hagan, Dallas	56	276	4.9
Chubin, Anaheim	77	364	4.7
Hawkins, Pittsburgh	70	320	4.6
Brown, Indiana	76	327	4.3

Rebounds

	G.	OFF.	DEF.	TOT.	AVG.
Daniels, Minnesota	78	502	711	1213	15.6
Hawkins, Pittsburgh	70	368	577	945	13.5
J. Beasley, Dallas	77	278	704	982	12.8
Harge, Pit.-Oak.	82	357	681	1038	12.7
Robbins, New Orleans	73	366	528	894	12.2

Many thought it fitting that the ABA played its first game on Friday the 13th of October, 1967, the Oakland Oaks defeating the Anaheim Amigos 134–129 before 4,828 at the Oakland Coliseum. The league, which was to develop many outstanding players and coaches in its nine-year existence, never did achieve the off-court stability needed to survive.

An example of what people would come to refer to as the wacky world of the ABA came at the close of the initial regular season. The Kentucky Colonels and New Jersey Americans had tied for fourth place in the Eastern Division, and a one-game playoff was decreed to decide the final playoff berth. Since the Americans' regular home, the Teaneck Armory, was booked by the circus, the game was moved to the Commack Arena on Long Island. But when the two teams arrived, they found the basketball floor in a shambles, with loose nuts and bolts and chips of wood sticking up from the surface. Commissioner Mikan ruled the floor unplayable and forfeited the game to Kentucky, summarily ending the Americans' season and sending the Colonels into the playoffs.

To top it off, during the offseason, the New Jersey Americans became the New York Nets. Their home court for the following season? None other than the Commack Arena, site of the ultimate home-court disadvantage during the 1968 ABA Playoffs.

1968–69

The second year of the ABA ushered in what would become a trademark of the league: franchise movement. The Anaheim Amigos became the Los Angeles Stars, the New Jersey Americans became the New York Nets, the Minnesota Muskies became the Miami Floridians and the defending champion Pittsburgh Pipers became the Minnesota Pipers.

A dominant offensive force joined the league in Rick Barry, who had led the NBA in scoring in 1967 with 35.6 ppg. Barry was forced to sit out the ABA's first season due to a court order, but he helped a moribund Oakland team that had gone 22-56 to a league-best 60-18 record in 1969, leading the ABA in scoring with 34.0 ppg, shooting .511 from the field and a league-leading .888 from the free-throw line. The league also was developing stars who had never played in the NBA, like Hawkins (30.2 ppg, 11.4 rpg), ABA MVP Mel Daniels (24.0 ppg, league-best 16.5 rpg), Denver's Larry Jones (28.4 ppg) and James Jones of New Orleans (26.6 ppg, 5.7 apg).

Though Oakland lost Barry to knee surgery after just 35 games, the backcourt of Rookie of the Year Warren Armstrong (21.5 ppg) and playmaker Larry Brown, along with forwards Doug Moe (19.0 ppg) and Gary Bradds (18.7 ppg), picked up the slack for their missing teammate. Oakland defeated Denver in seven games in the first round of the playoffs, then roared by New Orleans and Indiana to take the title. Oakland averaged 131.6 ppg in the ABA Finals.

ABA 1968-69

FINAL STANDINGS

Eastern Division

	W.	L.	PCT.
Indiana	44	34	.564
Miami	43	35	.551
Kentucky	42	36	.538
Minnesota	36	42	.462
New York	17	61	.218

Western Division

	W.	L.	PCT.
Oakland	60	18	.769
New Orleans	46	32	.590
Denver	44	34	.564
Dallas	41	37	.526
Los Angeles	33	45	.423
Houston	23	55	.295

PLAYOFFS

Eastern Division Semifinals

Miami 4, Minnesota 3
April 7—Miami 119, Minnesota 110
April 9—Minnesota 106, Miami 99
April 10—Minnesota 109, Miami 93
April 12—Miami 116, Minnesota 109
April 13—Miami 122, Minnesota 107
April 15—Minnesota 105, Miami 100
April 19—Miami 137, Minnesota 128

Indiana 4, Kentucky 3
April 8—Kentucky 128, Indiana 118
April 9—Indiana 120, Kentucky 115
April 10—Kentucky 130, Indiana 111
April 13—Kentucky 105, Indiana 104 (OT)
April 14—Indiana 116, Kentucky 97
April 15—Indiana 107, Kentucky 89
April 17—Indiana 120, Kentucky 111

Western Division Semifinals

Oakland 4, Denver 3
April 5—Oakland 129, Denver 99
April 6—Denver 122, Oakland 119
April 8—Oakland 121, Denver 99
April 10—Denver 109, Oakland 108
April 12—Oakland 128, Denver 118
April 13—Denver 126, Oakland 115
April 16—Oakland 115, Denver 102

New Orleans 4, Dallas 3
April 5—New Orleans 129, Dallas 106
April 7—New Orleans 122, Dallas 108
April 10—Dallas 130, New Orleans 106
April 12—New Orleans 114, Dallas 107
April 14—Dallas 123, New Orleans 112
April 15—Dallas 136, New Orleans 118
April 17—New Orleans 101, Dallas 95

Eastern Division Finals

Indiana 4, Miami 1
April 20—Indiana 126, Miami 110
April 22—Indiana 131, Miami 116
April 23—Indiana 119, Miami 105
April 25—Miami 114, Indiana 110
April 26—Indiana 127, Miami 105

Western Division Finals

Oakland 4, New Orleans 0
April 19—Oakland 128, New Orleans 118
April 21—Oakland 135, New Orleans 124
April 23—Oakland 113, New Orleans 107
April 25—Oakland 128, New Orleans 114

ABA Finals

Oakland 4, Indiana 1
April 30—Oakland 123, Indiana 114
May 2—Indiana 150, Oakland 122
May 3—Oakland 134, Indiana 126 (OT)
May 5—Oakland 144, Indiana 117
May 7—Oakland 135, Indiana 131 (OT)

INDIVIDUAL LEADERS

Scoring

	G.	FG	FT	PTS.	AVG.
Barry, Oakland	35	392	403	1190	34.0
Hawkins, Minnesota	47	496	425	1420	30.2
Jones, Denver	75	759	591	2133	28.4
J. Jones, New Orleans	77	764	521	2050	26.6
Dampier, Kentucky	78	713	308	1933	24.8
Daniels, Indiana	76	712	400	1824	24.0
Somerset, Hou.-NY	74	619	484	1758	23.8
Carrier, Kentucky	73	559	447	1690	23.2
Freeman, Miami	78	651	420	1724	22.1
Armstrong, Oakland	71	573	373	1530	21.5

Field Goal Pct.

	FGM	FGA	PCT.
McGill, Denver	411	745	.552
Hammond, Denver	329	601	.547
Eakins, Oakland	351	646	.543
J. Jones, New Orleans	764	1429	.535
Barry, Oakland	392	767	.511

3-Pt. Field Goal Pct.

	FGM	FGA	PCT.
Carrier, Kentucky	125	330	.379
Combs, Dallas	84	233	.361
Dampier, Kentucky	199	552	.361
Lehmann, Los Angeles	48	137	.350
Johnson, NY-Hou.	64	183	.350

Free Throw Pct.

	FTM	FTA	PCT.
Barry, Oakland	403	454	.888
Jackson, NY-Min.-Hou.	299	337	.887
Lloyd, New York	218	246	.886
Becker, Houston	200	240	.833
Somerset, Hou.-NY	484	583	.830

Assists

	G.	NO.	AVG.
Brown, Oakland	77	544	7.1
Freeman, Miami	78	501	6.4
Dampier, Kentucky	78	456	5.8
J. Jones, New Orleans	77	437	5.7
Brown, Indiana	75	345	4.6

Rebounds

	G.	OFF.	DEF.	TOT.	AVG.
Daniels, Indiana	76	383	873	1256	16.5
Robbins, New Orleans	76	368	656	1024	13.5
Thoren, Miami	78	391	655	1046	13.4
Washington, Minnesota	69	367	501	868	12.6
Hawkins, Minnesota	47	167	367	534	11.4

The ABA received publicity for its red, white and blue ball, but an even more defining characteristic of the league, and one which lives on today, is the three-point field goal. The ABA's all-time top three-point shooter was Louie Dampier of the Kentucky Colonels, a six-foot guard who made 794 three-pointers in 2,217 attempts, a .358 percentage.

"Louie Dampier was a good player who used the three-pointer to make himself great," said Hubie Brown, who coached him at Kentucky. "He was one of those guys who would be a Mark Price type today, the smart six-foot guard who could beat you with the shot or the pass."

1969–70

More franchise movement occurred prior to the 1969–70 season. The Houston Mavericks became the Carolina Cougars, the Oakland Oaks became the Washington Capitols and the Minnesota Pipers moved back to Pittsburgh and once again were known as the Pittsburgh Pipers. The league also decided to expand the schedule so that each team would play 84 games, up from 78. The league suffered a big loss when Connie Hawkins gained entry into the NBA and also lost in the bidding for Kareem Abdul-Jabbar, who ended up in the NBA with the Milwaukee Bucks.

One bright new star in the ABA sky was power forward Spencer Haywood, who left college after just two years and led the league in scoring (30.0 ppg) and rebounding (19.5 rpg), becoming the ABA's Rookie of the Year and Most Valuable Player. The Indiana Pacers were the ABA's top team with a 59-25 record. Forwards Roger Brown (23.0 ppg) and Bob Netolicky (20.6 ppg) and center Mel Daniels (18.8 ppg, 17.6 rpg) gave Indiana the league's most productive frontcourt, while a small, quick backcourt of Freddie Lewis, John Barnhill and rookie Bill Keller shared minutes. Indiana swept past Carolina and Kentucky in the playoffs to reach the Finals against the Los Angeles Stars, coached by former Celtics great Bill Sharman and featuring quick guard Mack Calvin, forward George Stone and 6-11 center Craig Raymond. The Pacers won in six games behind the scoring of Brown, who hit for 53, 39 and 45 points in the final three games of the championship series.

ABA 1969-70

FINAL STANDINGS

Eastern Division

	W.	L.	PCT.
Indiana	59	25	.702
Kentucky	45	39	.536
Carolina	42	42	.500
New York	39	45	.464
Pittsburgh	29	55	.345
Miami	23	61	.274

Western Division

	W.	L.	PCT.
Denver	51	33	.607
Dallas	45	39	.536
Washington	44	40	.524
Los Angeles	43	41	.512
New Orleans	42	42	.500

PLAYOFFS

Eastern Division Semifinals

Indiana 4, Carolina 0
April 18—Indiana 123, Carolina 105
April 19—Indiana 103, Carolina 98
April 22—Indiana 115, Carolina 106
April 24—Indiana 110, Carolina 106

Kentucky 4, New York 3
April 17—New York 122, Kentucky 118 (OT)
April 18—Kentucky 113, New York 111
April 19—New York 107, Kentucky 99
April 22—Kentucky 128, New York 101
April 26—New York 127, Kentucky 112
April 28—Kentucky 116, New York 113
April 29—Kentucky 112, New York 101

Western Division Semifinals

Denver 4, Washington 3
April 17—Denver 130, Washington 111
April 18—Denver 143, Washington 133
April 19—Washington 125, Denver 120
April 22—Washington 131, Denver 114
April 23—Washington 132, Denver 110
April 25—Washington 116, Denver 111
April 28—Denver 143, Washington 119

Los Angeles 4, Dallas 2
April 17—Los Angeles 115, Dallas 103
April 18—Dallas 129, Los Angeles 121
April 20—Dallas 116, Los Angeles 104
April 22—Los Angeles 144, Dallas 138
April 24—Los Angeles 146, Dallas 139
April 26—Los Angeles 124, Dallas 123

Eastern Division Finals

Indiana 4, Kentucky 1
May 1—Kentucky 114, Indiana 110
May 2—Indiana 121, Kentucky 110
May 3—Indiana 114, Kentucky 110
May 5—Indiana 111, Kentucky 103
May 6—Indiana 117, Kentucky 103

Western Division Finals

Los Angeles 4, Denver 1
April 30—Denver 123, Los Angeles 113 (OT)
May 1—Los Angeles 114, Denver 105
May 4—Los Angeles 119, Denver 113
May 5—Los Angeles 114, Denver 110
May 9—Los Angeles 109, Denver 107

ABA Finals

Indiana 4, Los Angeles 2
May 15—Indiana 109, Los Angeles 93
May 17—Indiana 114, Los Angeles 111
May 18—Los Angeles 109, Indiana 106
May 19—Indiana 142, Los Angeles 120
May 23—Los Angeles 117, Indiana 113
May 25—Indiana 111, Los Angeles 107

INDIVIDUAL LEADERS

Scoring (Minimum 1200 points)

	G.	FG	FT	PTS.	AVG.
Haywood, Denver	84	986	547	2519	30.0
Barry, Washington	52	517	400	1442	27.7
Verga, Carolina	82	867	458	2258	27.5
Freeman, Miami	79	766	626	2163	27.4
Dampier, Kentucky	82	743	447	2131	26.0
Jones, Denver	75	625	579	1870	24.9
Tart, New York	80	756	412	1935	24.2
Carrier, Kentucky	77	608	454	1775	23.1
Brown, Indiana	84	719	457	1935	23.0
Combs, Dallas	84	640	458	1868	22.2

Field Goal Pct. (Minimum 300 FG made)

	FGM	FGA	PCT.
Washington, Pit.-LA	320	582	.550
Card, Washington	351	666	.527
Beck, Denver	440	841	.523
Becker, Indiana	309	593	.521
Ligon, Kentucky	507	1000	.507

3-Pt. Field Goal Pct. (Minimum 50 made)

	FGM	FGA	PCT.
Carrier, Kentucky	105	280	.375
Dampier, Kentucky	198	548	.361
Congdon, Denver	63	178	.354
Combs, Dallas	130	370	.351
Barrett, Washington	62	180	.344

Free Throw Pct. (Minimum 250 FT made)

	FTM	FTA	PCT.
Carrier, Kentucky	454	509	.892
Barry, Washington	400	463	.864
Combs, Dallas	458	548	.836
S. Jones, New Orleans	412	495	.832
Dampier, Kentucky	447	538	.831

Assists (Minimum 325)

	G.	NO.	AVG.
Brown, Washington	82	580	7.1
Melchionni, New York	80	457	5.7
Calvin, Los Angeles	84	478	5.7
Jones, Denver	75	426	5.7
Dampier, Kentucky	82	447	5.5

Rebounds (Minimum 750)

	G.	OFF.	DEF.	TOT.	AVG.
Haywood, Denver	84	533	1104	1637	19.5
Daniels, Indiana	83	423	1039	1462	17.6
Robbins, New Orleans	82	427	905	1332	16.2
Govan, New Orleans	84	285	932	1217	14.5
Harge, Washington	84	334	843	1177	14.0

Roger Brown, like Connie Hawkins, was a great talent who had been banned from the NBA because his name came up in a point-shaving scandal, though he was never convicted of a crime. Brown averaged 32.7 ppg in the 1970 ABA Finals.

"I grew up with Roger Brown in New York," said former Pacers guard Jerry Harkness. "Like Connie Hawkins, he was a legend when he was in high school. What made Roger so good on his one-on-one moves was that he'd fake you, then start to the basket, and you figured that since he was moving so fast, he was going all the way for the layup. But then he'd just stop and raise up with a jumper from 10 feet away. That was a killer move. I saw him beat guys on the playground with that move, and I saw him take apart teams in the ABA Finals doing the same thing."

1970-71

The changes continued as the ABA geared up for a fourth season. The New Orleans Buccaneers became the Memphis Pros, the Los Angeles Stars became the Utah Stars, the Washington Capitols became the Virginia Squires and the Pittsburgh Pipers were renamed the Condors. The Floridians and Chaparrals became regional franchises, playing at different sites around their respective states. Against the backdrop of all this movement was the possibility that the ABA and NBA would reach an agreement, an idea some people in both leagues subscribed to but one the players had lobbied successfully against. The competing leagues had helped drive up player salaries, and the players were in no hurry for it to end.

Another significant rookie came to the ABA as Dan Issel, a college star at the University of Kentucky, signed with the Colonels and enjoyed a tremendous rookie year, leading the ABA in scoring with 29.9 ppg and also averaging 13.2 rpg. Barry had been traded to the New York Nets, where he finished just behind Issel in scoring at 29.4 ppg. Zelmo Beaty, a powerful center who had played seven years in the NBA, signed with Utah and averaged 22.9 points and 15.7 rebounds per game. Charlie Scott, a collegiate star at North Carolina, averaged 27.1 ppg in his rookie year. Mack Calvin of the Floridians averaged 27.2 points and 7.6 assists per game. The Finals went to seven games, with Utah defeating Kentucky as the home team won each game. In Game 7, Beaty scored 36 points for Utah to offset a 41-point effort by Issel as the Stars won 131–121.

ABA 1970-71

FINAL STANDINGS

Eastern Division

	W.	L.	PCT.
Virginia	55	29	.655
Kentucky	44	40	.524
New York	40	44	.476
Floridians	37	47	.440
Pittsburgh	36	48	.429
Carolina	34	50	.405

Western Division

	W.	L.	PCT.
Indiana	58	26	.690
Utah	57	27	.679
Memphis	41	43	.488
Texas *	30	54	.357
Denver	30	54	.357

* Won special playoff for 4th place

PLAYOFFS

Eastern Division Semifinals

Kentucky 4, Floridians 2
April 2—Kentucky 116, Floridians 112
April 4—Kentucky 120, Floridians 110
April 6—Floridians 120, Kentucky 102
April 8—Floridians 129, Kentucky 117
April 10—Kentucky 118, Floridians 101
April 12—Kentucky 112, Floridians 103

Virginia 4, New York 2
April 2—Virginia 113, New York 105
April 4—Virginia 114, New York 108
April 6—New York 135, Virginia 131
April 7—New York 130, Virginia 127
April 9—Virginia 127, New York 124
April 10—Virginia 118, New York 114

Western Division Semifinals

Indiana 4, Memphis 0
April 2—Indiana 114, Memphis 98
April 3—Indiana 106, Memphis 104
April 5—Indiana 91, Memphis 90
April 7—Indiana 102, Memphis 101

Utah 4, Texas 0
April 2—Utah 125, Texas 115
April 3—Utah 137, Texas 107
April 4—Utah 113, Texas 101
April 6—Utah 128, Texas 107

Eastern Division Finals

Kentucky 4, Virginia 2
April 15—Kentucky 136, Virginia 132
April 17—Virginia 142, Kentucky 122
April 19—Virginia 150, Kentucky 137
April 21—Kentucky 128, Virginia 110
April 23—Kentucky 115, Virginia 107
April 24—Kentucky 129, Virginia 117

Western Division Finals

Utah 4, Indiana 3
April 12—Utah 120, Indiana 118
April 14—Indiana 120, Utah 107
April 17—Utah 121, Indiana 107
April 20—Utah 126, Indiana 99
April 22—Indiana 127, Utah 109
April 24—Indiana 105, Utah 102
April 28—Utah 108, Indiana 101

ABA Finals

Utah 4, Kentucky 3
May 3—Utah 136, Kentucky 117
May 5—Utah 138, Kentucky 125
May 7—Kentucky 116, Utah 110
May 8—Kentucky 129, Utah 125 (OT)
May 12—Utah 137, Kentucky 127
May 15—Kentucky 105, Utah 101
May 18—Utah 131, Kentucky 121

INDIVIDUAL LEADERS

Scoring
(Minimum 1000 points)

	G.	FG	FT	PTS.	AVG.
Issel, Kentucky	83	938	604	2480	29.9
Barry, New York	59	632	451	1734	29.4
Brisker, Pittsburgh	79	898	430	2315	29.3
Calvin, Floridians	81	744	696	2201	27.2
C. Scott, Virginia	84	902	456	2276	27.1
Cannon, Denver	80	751	606	2126	26.6
Jones, Floridians	84	764	471	2044	24.3
Freeman, Utah-Tex.	66	596	367	1559	23.6
Caldwell, Carolina	72	685	302	1678	23.3
Beaty, Utah	76	661	420	1744	22.9

Free Throw Pct.
(Minimum 225 FT made)

	FTM	FTA	PCT
Barry, New York	451	507	.890
Carrier, Kentucky	327	377	.867
Keller, Indiana	267	308	.867
Calvin, Floridians	696	805	.865
Dampier, Kentucky	320	376	.851

Field Goal Pct.
(Minimum 450 FG made)

	FGM	FGA	PCT.
Beaty, Utah	661	1192	.555
Paultz, New York	510	973	.524
Daniels, Indiana	698	1357	.514
Netolicky, Indiana	651	1305	.499
J. Beasley, Texas	532	1070	.497

3-Pt. Field Goal Pct.
(Minimum 35 made)

	FGM	FGA	PCT.
Lehmann, Carolina	154	382	.403
Carrier, Kentucky	63	161	.391
S. Jones, Memphis	40	108	.370
Dampier, Kentucky	103	280	.368
Combs, Tex.-Utah	77	210	.367

Assists
(Minimum 275)

	G.	NO.	AVG.
Melchionni, New York	81	672	8.3
Calvin, Floridians	81	619	7.6
J. Jones, Memphis	80	468	5.9
C. Scott, Virginia	84	472	5.6
Lehmann, Carolina	83	464	5.6

Rebounds
(Minimum 650)

	G.	OFF.	DEF.	TOT.	AVG.
Daniels, Indiana	82	394	1081	1475	18.0
Keye, Denver	83	370	1084	1454	17.5
Beaty, Utah	76	407	783	1190	15.7
Lewis, Pittsburgh	83	435	778	1213	14.6
Govan, Memphis	84	277	861	1138	13.5

Mack Calvin was just one example of a player who didn't get a chance in the NBA but became a star in the ABA, despite being a shade under six feet. Calvin had been drafted by the Lakers, but only in the 14th round. Extremely quick, he flourished in the ABA's up-tempo style.

"Mack was amazing," said Steve Jones, who scored more than 10,000 points in the ABA and is now a broadcaster for NBC Sports. "He was one of those guys who was faster while dribbling the basketball than most guys were when they sprinted. On defense, he was all over you, contesting every dribble. He was so competitive, so fiery."

1971–72

The ABA always seemed to be changing, with players, coaches and franchises moving year after year. But none of those changes would ultimately have as great an impact on the ABA as the arrival of a star who would sustain the league and eventually make an agreement between the ABA and NBA inevitable.

Julius Erving, a little-known forward who had played three years at the University of Massachusetts, was signed by the Virginia Squires. Massachusetts was not a highly ranked team, and Erving had existed there in relative anonymity. As a rookie with Virginia, Erving averaged an impressive 27.3 points and 15.7 rebounds. But it was the way Erving accomplished this—with style, grace and flair—that made him unique. He even had a catchy nickname—Dr. J, which he got from a high school buddy who admired Erving's skill and style

on the court. People who hadn't given the ABA a second thought suddenly heard about this aerial artist who soared above mere mortals.

While Erving was making a strong first impression, Kentucky had its own rookie star in 7-2 Artis Gilmore, who teamed with Issel to overmatch the competition. Kentucky won a league-record 68 games and Gilmore was named Rookie of the Year and MVP after averaging 23.8 points and 17.8 rebounds per game, leading the league in the latter category. Kentucky was shocked in the first round of the playoffs by New York, which was only 44-40 during the season. But the Nets made it all the way to the Finals behind the shooting of Barry and rookie guard John Roche. Indiana proved too strong and won the title in six games with a starting lineup of Roger Brown, George McGinnis, Mel Daniels, Freddie Lewis and Rick Mount.

ABA 1971-72

FINAL STANDINGS

Eastern Division

	W.	L.	PCT.
Kentucky	68	16	.810
Virginia	45	39	.536
New York	44	40	.524
Floridians	36	48	.429
Carolina	35	49	.417
Pittsburgh	25	59	.298

Western Division

	W.	L.	PCT.
Utah	60	24	.714
Indiana	47	37	.560
Dallas	42	42	.500
Denver	34	50	.405
Memphis	26	58	.310

PLAYOFFS

Eastern Division Semifinals

Virginia 4, Floridians 0
March 31—Virginia 114, Floridians 107 (OT)
April 1—Virginia 125, Floridians 100
April 4—Virginia 118, Floridians 113
April 6—Virginia 115, Floridians 106

New York 4, Kentucky 3
April 1—New York 122, Kentucky 108
April 4—New York 105, Kentucky 90
April 5—Kentucky 105, New York 99
April 7—New York 100, Kentucky 92
April 8—Kentucky 109, New York 103
April 10—New York 101, Kentucky 96

Western Division Semifinals

Indiana 4, Denver 3
March 31—Indiana 102, Denver 95
April 1—Denver 106, Indiana 105
April 4—Indiana 122, Denver 120 (OT)
April 6—Denver 112, Indiana 96
April 8—Indiana 91, Denver 79
April 9—Denver 106, Indiana 99
April 13—Indiana 91, Denver 89

Utah 4, Dallas 0
April 1—Utah 106, Dallas 96
April 3—Utah 113, Dallas 107
April 5—Utah 96, Dallas 89
April 7—Utah 103, Dallas 99

Eastern Division Finals

New York 4, Virginia 3
April 13—Virginia 138, New York 91
April 15—Virginia 115, New York 106
April 24—New York 119, Virginia 117
April 26—New York 118, Virginia 107
April 29—Virginia 116, New York 107
May 1—New York 146, Virginia 136
May 4—New York 94, Virginia 88

Western Division Finals

Indiana 4, Utah 3
April 15—Utah 108, Indiana 100
April 17—Utah 117, Indiana 109
April 19—Indiana 116, Utah 111
April 22—Indiana 118, Utah 108
April 24—Utah 139, Indiana 130
April 26—Indiana 105, Utah 99
May 1—Indiana 117, Utah 113

ABA Finals

Indiana 4, New York 2
May 6—Indiana 124, New York 103
May 9—New York 117, Indiana 115
May 12—Indiana 114, New York 108
May 15—New York 110, Indiana 105
May 18—Indiana 100, New York 99
May 20—Indiana 108, New York 105

INDIVIDUAL LEADERS

Scoring
(Minimum 1000 points)

	G.	FG	FT	PTS.	AVG.
C. Scott, Virginia	73	985	525	2524	34.6
Barry, New York	80	902	641	2518	31.5
Issel, Kentucky	83	972	591	2538	30.6
Brisker, Pittsburgh	49	563	248	1417	28.9
Simpson, Denver	84	920	457	2300	27.4
Erving, Virginia	84	910	467	2290	27.3
Thompson, Pittsburgh	70	696	455	1888	27.0
McDaniels, Carolina	58	659	234	1552	26.8
Freeman, Dallas	72	628	475	1733	24.1
Gilmore, Kentucky	84	806	391	2003	23.8

Field Goal Pct.
(Minimum 375 FG made)

	FGM	FGA	PCT.
Gilmore, Kentucky	806	1348	.598
Washington, New York	387	678	.571
Lewis, Pittsburgh	385	713	.540
Beaty, Utah	729	1353	.539
Jones, Floridians	423	797	.531

3-Pt. Field Goal Pct.
(Minimum 40 made)

	FGM	FGA	PCT.
Combs, Utah	103	254	.406
Dampier, Kentucky	84	233	.361
Jabali, Floridians	102	285	.358
Lehmann, Car.-Mem.	71	199	.357
Hamilton, Dallas	46	132	.348

Free Throw Pct.
(Minimum 300 FT made)

	FTM	FTA	PCT.
Barry, New York	641	730	.878
Calvin, Floridians	611	701	.872
S. Jones, Dallas	367	422	.870
Lewis, Indiana	341	396	.861
Combs, Utah	319	380	.839

Assists

(Minimum 335)

	G.	NO.	AVG.
Melchionni, New York	80	669	8.4
Lehmann, Car.-Mem.	53	411	7.8
Brown, Denver	76	549	7.2
Jones, Utah	78	485	6.2
Dampier, Kentucky	83	515	6.2

Rebounds

(Minimum 700)

	G.	OFF.	DEF.	TOT.	AVG.
Gilmore, Kentucky	84	421	1070	1491	17.8
Daniels, Indiana	79	383	914	1297	16.4
Erving, Virginia	84	476	843	1319	15.7
Govan, Memphis	83	310	872	1182	14.2
McDaniels, Carolina	58	249	565	814	14.0

The Virginia Squires signed Julius Erving before general manager Johnny Kerr or head coach Al Bianchi, two NBA veterans, had ever seen him play in person. After Erving signed, the Squires put him on the floor at a free-agent tryout camp.

"Julius was on the floor for a few minutes in that tryout camp, and then a shot banged against the back of the rim and went straight up," Kerr remembered. "It was one of those rebounds where it seems that all five players were jumping for it. Out of the middle of the pack came Julius . . . up . . . up . . . up. He cupped the rebound with one hand and then slammed it through the rim, all in one motion. The gym went silent. All the players stopped for a few seconds. This was a tryout camp, and I had just watched one of the best plays I had ever seen in my life."

1972–73

The ABA had seen franchises move around, but through the first five years of the league, all 11 of the original franchises—in one form or another—were still around. But prior to the 1972–73 season, the Pittsburgh Condors and the Floridians folded due to money troubles, with players from those teams dispersed throughout the league. The ABA then added the San Diego Conquistadors as its first expansion team.

Larry Brown, who had retired as a player as the ABA's all-time assist leader, took over as coach of the Carolina Cougars, who had secured four-time NBA All-Star forward Billy Cunningham. "The Kangaroo Kid," as Cunningham was called, was named ABA MVP, Brown was the ABA Coach of the Year and Carolina gave the Gilmore and Issel-led Colonels trouble before losing the Eastern Division Finals in seven games. Out west, Indiana dispatched Utah in six games to advance to the Finals.

The Finals proved to be another classic, the third ABA Finals in six seasons to go the full seven games. The series played before large crowds in both Kentucky and Indiana, something that had rarely happened in the league's six-year history. With the home team winning only in Games 2 and 4, Indiana took its third ABA title in four years as George McGinnis scored 27 points in a decisive Game 7 victory.

ABA 1972-73

FINAL STANDINGS

Eastern Division

	W.	L.	PCT.
Carolina	57	27	.679
Kentucky	56	28	.667
Virginia	42	42	.500
New York	30	54	.357
Memphis	24	60	.286

Western Division

	W.	L.	PCT.
Utah	55	29	.655
Indiana	51	33	.607
Denver	47	37	.560
San Diego	30	54	.357
Dallas	28	56	.333

PLAYOFFS

Eastern Division Semifinals

Kentucky 4, Virginia 1
March 30—Kentucky 129, Virginia 101
April 1—Virginia 109, Kentucky 94
April 3—Kentucky 115, Virginia 113
April 6—Kentucky 108, Virginia 90
April 7—Kentucky 114, Virginia 93

Carolina 4, New York 1
March 30—Carolina 104, New York 96
March 31—New York 114, Carolina 111
April 3—Carolina 101, New York 91
April 5—Carolina 112, New York 108
April 6—Carolina 136, New York 113

Western Division Semifinals

Indiana 4, Denver 1
March 31—Indiana 114, Denver 91
April 1—Indiana 106, Denver 93
April 3—Denver 105, Indiana 94
April 5—Indiana 97, Denver 95
April 7—Indiana 121, Denver 107

Utah 4, San Diego 0
April 2—Utah 107, San Diego 93
April 4—Utah 103, San Diego 92
April 7—Utah 97, San Diego 96
April 8—Utah 120, San Diego 98

Eastern Division Finals

Kentucky 4, Carolina 3
April 11—Kentucky 113, Carolina 103
April 14—Carolina 125, Kentucky 105
April 16—Kentucky 108, Carolina 94
April 18—Carolina 102, Kentucky 91
April 20—Carolina 112, Kentucky 107
April 21—Kentucky 119, Carolina 100
April 24—Kentucky 107, Carolina 96

Western Division Finals

Indiana 4, Utah 2
April 12—Utah 124, Indiana 107
April 14—Indiana 116, Utah 110
April 16—Indiana 118, Utah 108
April 18—Utah 104, Indiana 103
April 19—Indiana 104, Utah 102
April 21—Indiana 107, Utah 98

ABA Finals

Indiana 4, Kentucky 3
April 28—Indiana 111, Kentucky 107
April 30—Kentucky 114, Indiana 102
May 3—Kentucky 92, Indiana 88
May 5—Indiana 90, Kentucky 86
May 8—Indiana 89, Kentucky 86
May 10—Kentucky 109, Indiana 93
May 12—Indiana 88, Kentucky 81

INDIVIDUAL LEADERS

Scoring
(Minimum 1000 points)

	G.	FG	FT	PTS.	AVG.
Erving, Virginia	71	894	475	2268	31.9
McGinnis, Indiana	82	868	517	2261	27.6
Issel, Kentucky	84	902	485	2292	27.3
Cunningham, Carolina	84	771	472	2028	24.1
Simpson, Denver	81	732	421	1890	23.3
R. Jones, Dallas	67	564	324	1495	22.3
Johnson, San Diego	80	769	195	1770	22.1
Wise, Utah	83	672	476	1823	22.0
Thompson, Memphis	80	579	549	1727	21.6
Gilmore, Kentucky	84	687	368	1743	20.8

Field Goal Pct.
(Minimum 250 FG made)

	FGM	FGA	PCT.
Gilmore, Kentucky	687	1228	.559
Kennedy, Dallas	365	664	.550
Owens, Carolina	393	727	.541
Beck, Denver	466	879	.530
Irvine, Virginia	424	805	.527

3-Pt. Field Goal Pct.
(Minimum 28 made)

	FGM	FGA	PCT.
Combs, Utah	51	134	.381
Brown, Indiana	42	118	.356
Dampier, Kentucky	54	155	.348
Hamilton, Dallas	66	191	.346
Lewis, Indiana	38	110	.345

Free Throw Pct.
(Minimum 200 FT made)

	FTM	FTA	PCT.
Keller, Indiana	234	269	.870
Boone, Utah	415	479	.866
Warren, Car.-Dal.-Utah	236	274	.861
Calvin, Carolina	500	582	.859
Silas, Dallas	389	467	.833

Assists
(Minimum 250)

	G.	NO.	AVG.
Melchionni, New York	61	453	7.4
Williams, San Diego	83	582	7.0
Jabali, Denver	82	539	6.6
Dampier, Kentucky	80	521	6.5
Cunningham, Carolina	84	530	6.3

Rebounds
(Minimum 600)

	G.	OFF.	DEF.	TOT.	AVG.
Gilmore, Kentucky	84	449	1027	1476	17.6
Daniels, Indiana	81	348	899	1247	15.4
Paultz, New York	81	279	736	1015	12.5
McGinnis, Indiana	82	434	588	1022	12.5
Denton, Memphis	66	276	544	820	12.4

Billy Cunningham had been a star in the NBA, and when he signed with Carolina, some of the players were concerned that Cunningham might feel he was too good for the ABA.

"Once Billy came to the league and saw the competitiveness, he realized these guys could play," said Steve Jones. "He was the MVP, and he earned it because the guy had a knack for making the big plays, the plays that won games. He had a great year, but he didn't just walk out there and dominate the league. There were nights when he could control the game and other nights when he had his hands full, just like he did in the NBA."

1973–74

The wrangling between the two leagues for players had one important manifestation during the summer of 1973. Erving, who had played two years with Virginia, had attempted to jump to the Atlanta Hawks, who had offered him a superior contract. To complicate matters, Milwaukee had drafted Erving and held his NBA rights. The entire affair was destined to wind up in court, but Roy Boe, the new owner of the New York Nets, needed Erving to grab some attention in New York, so he worked a deal in which he would acquire Erving and Willie Sojourner for the Nets, send $1 million, the rights to Kermit Washington, and George Carter to Virginia, and pay another $500,000 to Atlanta; in turn, Atlanta would give Milwaukee $250,000 and two draft picks. Erving, meanwhile, received $250,000 from Atlanta and signed a five-year contract with the Nets for $2 million.

The acquisition of Erving couldn't have turned out any better for New York, which also signed rookies Larry Kenon and John Williamson to go along with center Billy Paultz and guard Brian Taylor. The Nets, behind Erving's second straight scoring title, won a league-high 55 games and blitzed Virginia and Kentucky to reach the Finals against Utah, which still had Willie Wise and Zelmo Beaty and had added Ron Boone, James Jones and Gerald Govan. The Nets won in five games, including a Game 5 clincher before 16,000 fans at Nassau Coliseum.

Prior to the season, Dallas had moved to San Antonio and become the San Antonio Spurs, who would develop into a successful ABA and NBA franchise.

ABA 1973-74

FINAL STANDINGS

Eastern Division

	W.	L.	PCT.
New York	55	29	.655
Kentucky	53	31	.631
Carolina	47	37	.560
Virginia	28	56	.333
Memphis	21	63	.250

Western Division

	W.	L.	PCT.
Utah	51	33	.607
Indiana	46	38	.548
San Antonio	45	39	.536
San Diego *	37	47	.440
Denver	37	47	.440

* Won special playoff for 4th place

PLAYOFFS

Eastern Division Semifinals

Kentucky 4, Carolina 0
April 1—Kentucky 118, Carolina 102
April 5—Kentucky 99, Carolina 96
April 6—Kentucky 120, Carolina 110
April 8—Kentucky 128, Carolina 119

New York 4, Virginia 1
March 29—New York 108, Virginia 96
April 1—New York 129, Virginia 110
April 4—Virginia 116, New York 115
April 7—New York 116, Virginia 88
April 8—New York 108, Virginia 96

Western Division Semifinals

Indiana 4, San Antonio 3
March 30—San Antonio 113, Indiana 109
April 1—Indiana 128, San Antonio 101
April 3—San Antonio 115, Indiana 96
April 4—Indiana 91, San Antonio 89
April 6—Indiana 105, San Antonio 100
April 10—San Antonio 102, Indiana 86
April 12—Indiana 97, San Antonio 86

Utah 4, San Diego 2
March 30—Utah 114, San Diego 99
April 1—Utah 119, San Diego 105
April 3—San Diego 97, Utah 96
April 4—San Diego 100, Utah 98
April 6—Utah 100, San Diego 93
April 8—Utah 110, San Diego 99

Eastern Division Finals

New York 4, Kentucky 0
April 13—New York 119, Kentucky 106
April 15—New York 99, Kentucky 80
April 17—New York 89, Kentucky 87
April 20—New York 103, Kentucky 90

Western Division Finals

Utah 4, Indiana 3
April 13—Utah 105, Indiana 96
April 15—Utah 106, Indiana 102
April 17—Utah 99, Indiana 90
April 18—Indiana 118, Utah 107
April 22—Indiana 110, Utah 101
April 25—Indiana 91, Utah 89
April 27—Utah 109, Indiana 87

ABA Finals

New York 4, Utah 1
April 30—New York 89, Utah 85
May 4—New York 118, Utah 94
May 6—New York 103, Utah 100 (OT)
May 8—Utah 97, New York 89
May 10—New York 111, Utah 100

INDIVIDUAL LEADERS

Scoring
(Minimum 1000 points)

	G.	FG	FT	PTS.	AVG.
Erving, New York	84	914	454	2299	27.4
McGinnis, Indiana	80	789	488	2071	25.9
Issel, Kentucky	83	829	457	2118	25.5
Gervin, Vir.-S.A.	74	672	378	1730	23.4
Wise, Utah	82	714	396	1826	22.3
Lamar, San Diego	84	686	272	1713	20.4
Johnson, San Diego	84	716	199	1690	20.1
Carter, Virginia	80	561	392	1546	19.3
Thompson, Memphis	78	539	410	1498	19.2
Simpson, Denver	75	597	208	1404	18.7

Field Goal Pct.
(Minimum 200 FG made)

	FGM	FGA	PCT.
Nater, Vir.-S.A.	467	846	.552
Jones, Utah	583	1060	.550
Owens, Carolina	444	843	.527
Chones, Carolina	535	1017	.526
Grant, San Diego	357	681	.524

3-Pt. Field Goal Pct.
(Minimum 20 made)

	FGM	FGA	PCT.
Dampier, Kentucky	48	124	.387
Keller, Indiana	50	131	.382
Jabali, Denver	45	123	.366
Brown, Indiana	56	155	.361
Combs, Utah-Mem.	52	147	.354

Free Throw Pct.
(Minimum 135 FT made)

	FTM	FTA	PCT.
Jones, Utah	229	259	.884
Calvin, Carolina	490	560	.875
Boone, Utah	300	343	.875
Johnson, San Diego	199	235	.847
Carter, Virginia	392	466	.841

Assists
(Minimum 200)

	G.	NO.	AVG.
Smith, Denver	76	619	8.1
Jabali, Denver	49	358	7.3
Williams, S.D.-Ken.	90	557	6.2
Dampier, Kentucky	84	473	5.6
Taylor, Virginia	80	416	5.2

Rebounds
(Minimum 500)

	G.	OFF.	DEF.	TOT.	AVG.
Gilmore, Kentucky	84	478	1060	1538	18.3
McGinnis, Indiana	80	422	775	1197	15.0
Jones, San Diego	79	322	773	1095	13.9
Nater, Vir.-S.A.	79	286	712	998	12.6
Daniels, Indiana	78	251	655	906	11.6

Steals

	G.	NO.	AVG.
McClain, Carolina	84	250	2.98
Taylor, Virginia	80	215	2.69
Erving, New York	84	190	2.26
Caldwell, Carolina	79	170	2.15
Gale, Ken.-NY	80	167	2.09

Blocked Shots

	G.	NO.	AVG.
Jones, San Diego	79	316	4.00
Gilmore, Kentucky	84	287	3.42
Erving, New York	84	204	2.43
Hillman, Indiana	83	177	2.13
Paultz, New York	77	147	1.91

Kevin Loughery had scored over 11,000 points in a successful NBA career, but he was just 33 years old when Boe hired him to coach the Nets. Loughery silenced critics who thought he was in over his head by leading the Nets to the ABA Championship.

"The growth of Kenon and Williamson into big-time players as rookies really made our season," said Rod Thorn, then Loughery's assistant coach, now the NBA's vice president of operations. "We also had a very colorful and aggressive team because that was Kevin Loughery's personality. A big factor was Julius's attitude. Kevin found that he could criticize Julius and Julius would not turn on him like most stars. In fact, sometimes Kevin would scream at Doc just to let the other guys know that Doc was no different than they were."

1974–75

The ABA had begun the practice of signing players out of college before their eligibility was completed, but prior to the 1974–75 season it went a step further when the Utah Stars signed Moses Malone, a 6-10, 19-year-old center from Petersburg High School in Virginia. While many thought it was an unwise move, Malone proved he was that rare player who could survive and even flourish in the professional ranks without college seasoning. In his rookie year, Malone averaged 18.8 points and 14.6 rebounds.

The league was signing prominent college players as well, including Marvin Barnes and Maurice Lucas, both of whom signed with the new St. Louis franchise, which had moved from Carolina. The Denver Nuggets, featuring Ralph Simpson, Mack Calvin and rookie Bobby Jones, won a league-high 65 games, but were defeated by the Pacers and ABA scoring champion George McGinnis (29.8 ppg) in the Western Division Finals. Kentucky, which had never won a title despite the presence of two of the game's top pivotmen, Artis Gilmore and Dan Issel, finally broke through. Kentucky defeated Memphis, St. Louis and Indiana, winning each series 4–1 to take its first ABA title. In 15 playoff games, Gilmore and Issel combined for more than 44 points and 25 rebounds per game.

ABA 1974-75

FINAL STANDINGS

Eastern Division

	W.	L.	PCT.
Kentucky *	58	26	.690
New York	58	26	.690
St. Louis	32	52	.381
Memphis	27	57	.321
Virginia	15	69	.179

* Won special playoff for 1st place

Western Division

	W.	L.	PCT.
Denver	65	19	.774
San Antonio	51	33	.607
Indiana	45	39	.536
Utah	38	46	.452
San Diego	31	53	.369

PLAYOFFS

Eastern Division Semifinals

Kentucky 4, Memphis 1
April 6—Kentucky 98, Memphis 91
April 8—Kentucky 119, Memphis 105
April 10—Kentucky 101, Memphis 80
April 11—Memphis 107, Kentucky 93
April 13—Kentucky 111, Memphis 99

St. Louis 4, New York 1
April 6—New York 111, St. Louis 105
April 9—St. Louis 115, New York 97
April 11—St. Louis 113, New York 108
April 13—St. Louis 100, New York 89
April 15—St. Louis 108, New York 107

Western Division Semifinals

Denver 4, Utah 2
April 6—Denver 122, Utah 107
April 7—Denver 126, Utah 120
April 9—Utah 122, Denver 108
April 11—Utah 132, Denver 110
April 12—Denver 130, Utah 119
April 14—Denver 115, Utah 113

Indiana 4, San Antonio 2
April 5—Indiana 122, San Antonio 119 (OT)
April 7—Indiana 98, San Antonio 93
April 10—Indiana 113, San Antonio 103
April 12—San Antonio 110, Indiana 109
April 14—San Antonio 123, Indiana 117
April 16—Indiana 115, San Antonio 100

Eastern Division Finals

Kentucky 4, St. Louis 1
April 21—Kentucky 112, St. Louis 109
April 23—Kentucky 108, St. Louis 103
April 25—St. Louis 103, Kentucky 97
April 27—Kentucky 117, St. Louis 98
April 28—Kentucky 123, St. Louis 103

Western Division Finals

Indiana 4, Denver 3
April 20—Denver 131, Indiana 128
April 22—Indiana 131, Denver 124
April 24—Indiana 118, Denver 112
April 25—Denver 126, Indiana 109
April 27—Indiana 109, Denver 90
April 30—Denver 104, Indiana 99
May 3—Indiana 104, Denver 96

ABA Finals

Kentucky 4, Indiana 1
May 13—Kentucky 120, Indiana 94
May 15—Kentucky 95, Indiana 93
May 17—Kentucky 109, Indiana 101
May 19—Indiana 94, Kentucky 86
May 22—Kentucky 110, Indiana 105

INDIVIDUAL LEADERS

Scoring
(Minimum 1000 points)

	G.	FG	FT	PTS.	AVG.
McGinnis, Indiana	79	873	545	2353	29.8
Erving, New York	84	914	486	2343	27.9
Boone, Utah	84	872	363	2117	25.2
Grant, San Diego	53	576	182	1335	25.2
Barnes, St. Louis	77	777	295	1849	24.0
Gilmore, Kentucky	84	784	412	1981	23.6
Gervin, San Antonio	84	784	380	1965	23.4
Lewis, Mem.-St.L.	69	579	355	1531	22.2
Lamar, San Diego	77	667	247	1606	20.9
Simpson, Denver	82	694	303	1692	20.6

Field Goal Pct.
(Minimum 250 FG made)

	FGM	FGA	PCT.
Jones, Denver	529	876	.604
Gilmore, Kentucky	784	1351	.580
Malone, Utah	591	1035	.571
Twardzik, Virginia	359	657	.546
Grant, San Diego	576	1058	.544

3-Pt. Field Goal Pct.
(Minimum 27 made)

	FGM	FGA	PCT.
Shepherd, Memphis	60	143	.420
Dampier, Kentucky	38	96	.396
Smith, Utah	34	94	.362
McGinnis, Indiana	62	175	.354
Brown, Mem.-Utah-Ind.	35	100	.350

Free Throw Pct.
(Minimum 200 FT made)

	FTM	FTA	PCT.
Calvin, Denver	475	530	.896
Silas, San Antonio	430	486	.885
Robisch, Denver	304	346	.879
Boone, Utah	363	422	.860
Lewis, Mem.-St.L.	355	421	.843

Assists
(Minimum 250)

	G.	NO.	AVG.
Calvin, Denver	74	570	7.7
Williams, Memphis	81	576	7.1
McGinnis, Indiana	79	495	6.3
Jabali, San Diego	62	358	5.8
O'Brien, San Diego	79	443	5.6

Rebounds
(Minimum 600)

	G.	OFF.	DEF.	TOT.	AVG.
Nater, San Antonio	78	369	910	1279	16.4
Gilmore, Kentucky	84	427	934	1361	16.2
Barnes, St. Louis	77	419	783	1202	15.6
Malone, Utah	83	455	754	1209	14.6
McGinnis, Indiana	79	396	730	1126	14.3

Steals
(Minimum 100)

	G.	NO.	AVG.
Taylor, New York	79	221	2.80
McGinnis, Indiana	79	206	2.61
Taylor, Denver	76	172	2.26
Erving, New York	84	186	2.21
Lewis, Mem.-St.L.	69	147	2.13

Blocked Shots
(Minimum 100)

	G.	NO.	AVG.
Jones, San Diego	76	246	3.24
Gilmore, Kentucky	84	258	3.07
Green, Denver	81	174	2.15
Erving, New York	84	157	1.87
Jones, Denver	84	153	1.82

Hubie Brown had been a respected NBA assistant coach under Larry Costello with the Milwaukee Bucks, who at the time had Kareem Abdul-Jabbar. Brown would go on to coach over 700 NBA games as a head coach, but he started as a head coach with the 1974–75 Kentucky Colonels.

"The 1975 Kentucky Colonels were the best team I have ever coached," Brown said. "No other team has even come close. They had perimeter scoring in Dampier and Issel, they had Gilmore at the low box. Teddy McClain could guard anybody in either league. Gene Littles was a hell of a defensive player. Wil Jones and Marvin Roberts combined for almost 20 points a game, and we never ran any plays for them."

1975–76

Just as the season was about to start, the two strongest teams in the ABA, New York and Denver, applied for entry into the NBA. While the application couldn't be acted upon until the players' antitrust suit was settled, an agreement between the two leagues seemed inevitable. While the ABA had a few strong teams, others were languishing badly. Memphis had become the Baltimore Claws, but the franchise folded before the season began. San Diego folded 11 games into the season, and Utah followed suit after 16 games. That left the league with only seven teams, so the two divisions were combined into one.

Erving won his third ABA scoring title and the Nets won 55 games, but the Denver Nuggets, who had acquired Issel, won a league-high 60 games. Denver also had an electrifying rookie, 6-4 David Thompson, who

was known for dunking over men nearly a foot taller on a regular basis. Thompson was named Rookie of the Year after averaging 26 points per game, third in the league behind Erving and Indiana's Billy Knight.

The playoffs consisted of two great semifinal rounds, New York defeating San Antonio in seven games and Denver taking Kentucky in seven, sweet revenge for Issel. But Erving averaged 34.7 ppg in 13 playoff games, and New York won its second ABA title in six games over Denver. Just as in the Nets' first championship season, Erving was named MVP of both the regular season and the playoffs.

On June 17, 1976, four ABA teams—New York, Indiana, San Antonio and Denver—were absorbed into the NBA, and the league of the red, white and blue ball passed into history.

ABA 1975-76

PLAYOFFS

FINAL STANDINGS

	W.	L.	PCT.
Denver	60	24	.714
New York	55	29	.655
San Antonio	50	34	.595
Kentucky	46	38	.548
Indiana	39	45	.464
St. Louis	35	49	.417
San Diego *	3	8	.273
Utah *	4	12	.250
Virginia	15	68	.181

* San Diego and Utah disbanded and did not finish the season

First Round

Kentucky 2, Indiana 1
April 8—Kentucky 120, Indiana 109
April 10—Indiana 109, Kentucky 95
April 12—Kentucky 100, Indiana 99

Semifinals

Denver 4, Kentucky 3
April 15—Denver 110, Kentucky 107
April 17—Kentucky 138, Denver 119
April 19—Kentucky 126, Denver 114
April 21—Denver 108, Kentucky 106
April 22—Denver 127, Kentucky 117
April 25—Kentucky 119, Denver 115
April 28—Denver 133, Kentucky 110

New York 4, San Antonio 3
April 9—New York 116, San Antonio 101
April 11—San Antonio 105, New York 79
April 14—San Antonio 111, New York 103
April 18—New York 110, San Antonio 108
April 19—New York 110, San Antonio 108
April 21—San Antonio 106, New York 105
April 24—New York 121, San Antonio 114

ABA Finals

New York 4, Denver 2
May 1—New York 120, Denver 118
May 4—Denver 127, New York 121
May 6—New York 117, Denver 111
May 8—New York 121, Denver 112
May 11—Denver 118, New York 110
May 13—New York 112, Denver 106

INDIVIDUAL LEADERS

Scoring
(Minimum 900 points)

	G.	FG	FT	PTS.	AVG.
Erving, New York	84	949	530	2462	29.3
Knight, Indiana	70	774	415	1969	28.1
Thompson, Denver	83	807	541	2158	26.0
Gilmore, Kentucky	84	773	521	2067	24.6
Barnes, St. Louis	67	681	251	1616	24.1
Silas, San Antonio	84	718	564	2000	23.8
Issel, Denver	84	752	425	1930	23.0
Boone, Utah-St.L.	78	713	277	1719	22.0
Gervin, San Antonio	81	706	342	1768	21.8
Burden, Virginia	71	561	283	1413	19.9

3-Pt. Field Goal Pct.
(Minimum 13 made)

	FGM	FGA	PCT.
Taylor, New York	32	76	.421
Boone, Utah-St.L.	16	43	.372
Dampier, Kentucky	32	87	.368
Keller, Indiana	123	349	.352
Buse, Indiana	72	208	.346

Field Goal Pct.
(Minimum 220 FG made)

	FGM	FGA	PCT.
Jones, Denver	510	878	.581
Gilmore, Kentucky	773	1401	.552
Hughes, New York	300	566	.530
Silas, San Antonio	718	1384	.519
Beck, Denver	334	646	.517

Free Throw Pct.
(Minimum 150 FT made)

	FTM	FTA	PCT.
Keller, Indiana	164	183	.896
Eakins, Utah-Vir.-NY	198	223	.888
Calvin, Virginia	253	285	.888
Silas, San Antonio	564	647	.872
Boone, Utah-St.L.	277	318	.871

Rebounds
(Minimum 550)

	G.	OFF.	DEF.	TOT.	AVG.
Gilmore, Kentucky	84	402	901	1303	15.5
Lucas, St.L.-Ken.	86	297	673	970	11.3
Jones, S.D.-Ken.-St.L.	76	246	607	853	11.2
Kenon, San Antonio	81	287	610	897	11.1
Erving, New York	84	337	588	925	11.0

Blocked Shots
(Minimum 110)

	G.	NO.	AVG.
Paultz, San Antonio	83	253	3.05
Jones, S.D.-Ken.-St.L.	76	218	2.87
Gilmore, Kentucky	84	205	2.44
Elmore, Indiana	76	178	2.34
Jones, Denver	83	184	2.22

Assists
(Minimum 225)

	G.	NO.	AVG.
Buse, Indiana	84	689	8.2
Simpson, Denver	84	597	7.1
Calvin, Virginia	45	271	6.0
Dampier, Kentucky	82	467	5.7
Silas, San Antonio	84	452	5.4

Steals
(Minimum 110)

	G.	NO.	AVG.
Buse, Indiana	84	346	4.12
Taylor, Virginia	76	206	2.71
Erving, New York	84	207	2.46
Taylor, New York	54	125	2.31
Jones, Denver	83	170	2.05

The top players from the ABA proved to be every bit as good as their brethren in the NBA. Julius Erving, Dan Issel, Artis Gilmore, George Gervin, Bobby Jones, David Thompson, Billy Knight, Don Buse, George McGinnis, Maurice Lucas, Moses Malone and many others became stars in the NBA. The very first year after the merger, the NBA Champion Portland Trail Blazers were guided by point guard Dave Twardzik, who had played four seasons in the ABA.

"Most of the players were excited because finally we were getting a chance to play the NBA teams," Issel said. "At first, the NBA players were very skeptical about us. We had to prove that we belonged, but we did that. The only thing I wished was that there were more survivors from the ABA instead of just four teams getting in."

ABA CHAMPIONS

Season	Champion
1967–68—Pittsburgh	
1968–69—Oakland	
1969–70—Indiana	
1970–71—Utah	
1971–72—Indiana	
1972–73—Indiana	
1973–74—New York	
1974–75—Kentucky	
1975–76—New York	

Eastern Division	W	L
Pittsburgh	54	24
Indiana	44	34
Indiana	59	25
Virginia	55	29
Kentucky	68	16
Carolina	57	27
New York	55	29
Kentucky	58	26
One division: Denver was first with 60		24

Western Division	W	L
New Orleans	48	30
Oakland	60	18
Denver	51	33
Indiana	58	26
Utah	60	24
Utah	55	29
Utah	51	33
Denver	65	19

ABA POSTSEASON AWARDS

ABA MOST VALUABLE PLAYER
1967–68—Connie Hawkins, Pittsburgh
1968–69—Mel Daniels, Indiana
1969–70—Spencer Haywood, Denver
1970–71—Mel Daniels, Indiana
1971–72—Artis Gilmore, Kentucky
1972–73—Billy Cunningham, Carolina
1973–74—Julius Erving, New York
1974–75—Julius Erving, New York, and
      George McGinnis, Indiana
1975–76—Julius Erving, New York

ABA ROOKIE OF THE YEAR
1967–68—Mel Daniels, Minnesota
1968–69—Warren Armstrong, Oakland
1969–70—Spencer Haywood, Denver
1970–71—Charlie Scott, Virginia, and
      Dan Issel, Kentucky
1971–72—Artis Gilmore, Kentucky
1972–73—Brian Taylor, New York
1973–74—Swen Nater, San Antonio
1974–75—Marvin Barnes, St. Louis
1975–76—David Thompson, Denver

ABA COACH OF THE YEAR
1967–68—Vince Cazetta, Pittsburgh
1968–69—Alex Hannum, Oakland
1969–70—Bill Sharman, Los Angeles, and
      Joe Belmont, Denver
1970–71—Al Bianchi, Virginia
1971–72—Tom Nissalke, Dallas
1972–73—Larry Brown, Carolina
1973–74—Babe McCarthy, Kentucky, and
      Joe Mullaney, Utah
1974–75—Larry Brown, Denver
1975–76—Larry Brown, Denver

INDIVIDUAL LEADERS

ABA 1967-68 LEADERS

SCORING

	G.	FG	FT	PTS.	AVG.
Hawkins, Pit.	70	635	603	1875	26.8
Moe, N.O.	78	665	551	1884	24.2
Tart, Oak.-N.J.	73	633	451	1718	23.5
Carrier, Ken.	77	643	395	1765	22.9
Jones, Den.	76	602	530	1742	22.9
Daniels, Min.	78	669	390	1729	22.2
Somerset, Hou.	61	467	359	1326	21.7
Williams, Pit.	78	642	290	1625	20.8
Dampier, Ken.	72	620	209	1487	20.7
Lewis, Ind.	76	542	465	1565	20.6

FIELD GOAL PCT.

	FGA	FGM	PCT.
Washington, Pit.	596	312	.523
Hawkins, Pit.	1223	635	.519
Netolicky, Ind.	928	468	.504
Anderson, N.J.	938	463	.494
C. Beasley, Dal.	758	374	.493

3-PT FIELD GOAL PCT.

	FGA	FGM	PCT.
Carrier, Ken.	235	84	.357
Perry, Min.	178	62	.348
Vaughn, Pit.	410	137	.334
Rayl, Ind.	175	57	.326
Selvage, Ana.	461	147	.319

FREE THROW PCT.

	FTA	FTM	PCT.
C. Beasley, Dal.	327	285	.872
Lloyd, N.J.	199	170	.854
J. Beasley, Dal.	322	271	.842
Jackson, N.J.	543	450	.829
Nowell, N.J.	213	176	.826

ASSISTS

	G.	AST.	AVG.
Brown, N.O.	78	506	6.5
Hagan, Dal.	56	276	4.9
Chubin, Ana.	77	364	4.7
Hawkins, Pit.	70	320	4.6
Brown, Ind.	76	327	4.3

REBOUNDS

	G.	OFF.	DEF.	TOT.	AVG.
Daniels, Min.	78	502	711	1213	15.6
Hawkins, Pit.	70	368	577	945	13.5
J. Beasley, Dal.	77	278	704	982	12.8
Harge, Pit.-Oak.	82	357	681	1038	12.7
Robbins, N.O.	73	366	528	894	12.2

ABA 1968-69 LEADERS

SCORING

	G.	FG	FT	PTS.	AVG.
Barry, Oak.	35	392	403	1190	34.0
Hawkins, Min.	47	496	425	1420	30.2
Jones, Den.	75	759	591	2133	28.4
Jones, N.O.	77	764	521	2050	26.6
Dampier, Ken.	78	713	308	1933	24.8
Daniels, Ind.	76	712	400	1824	24.0
Somerset, Hou.-N.Y.	74	619	484	1758	23.8
Carrier, Ken.	73	559	447	1690	23.2
Freeman, Mia.	78	651	420	1724	22.1
Armstrong, Oak.	71	573	373	1530	21.5

FIELD GOAL PCT.

	FGA	FGM	PCT.
McGill, Den.	745	411	.552
Hammond, Den.	601	329	.547
Eakins, Oak.	646	351	.543
Jones, N.O.	1429	764	.535
Barry, Oak.	767	392	.511

3-PT FIELD GOAL PCT.

	FGA	FGM	PCT.
Carrier, Ken.	330	125	.379
Combs, Dal.	233	84	.361
Dampier, Ken.	552	199	.361
Lehmann, L.A.	137	48	.350
Johnson, N.Y.-Hou.	183	64	.350

FREE THROW PCT.

	FTA	FTM	PCT.
Barry, Oak.	454	403	.888
Jackson, N.Y.-Min.-Hou.	337	299	.887
Lloyd, N.Y.	246	218	.886
Becker, Hou.	240	200	.833
Somerset, Hou.-N.Y.	583	484	.830

ASSISTS

	G.	AST.	AVG.
Brown, Oak.	77	544	7.1
Freeman, Mia.	78	501	6.4
Dampier, Ken.	78	456	5.8
J. Jones, N.O.	77	437	5.7
Brown, Ind.	75	345	4.6

REBOUNDS

	G.	OFF.	DEF.	TOT.	AVG.
Daniels, Ind.	76	383	873	1256	16.5
Robbins, N.O.	76	368	656	1024	13.5
Thoren, Mia.	78	391	655	1046	13.4
Washington, Min.	69	367	501	868	12.6
Hawkins, Min.	47	167	367	534	11.4

ABA 1969-70 LEADERS

SCORING

	G.	FG	FT	PTS.	AVG.
Haywood, Den.	84	986	547	2519	30.0
Barry, Was.	52	517	400	1442	27.7
Verga, Car.	82	867	458	2258	27.5
Freeman, Mia.	79	766	626	2163	27.4
Dampier, Ken.	82	743	447	2131	26.0
Jones, Den.	75	625	579	1870	24.9
Tart, N.Y.	80	756	412	1935	24.2
Carrier, Ken.	77	608	454	1775	23.1
Brown, Ind.	84	719	457	1935	23.0
Combs, Dal.	84	640	458	1868	22.2

FIELD GOAL PCT.

	FGA	FGM	PCT.
Card, Was.	666	351	.527
Beck, Den.	841	440	.523
Ligon, Ken.	1000	507	.507
Littles, Car.	817	414	.507
J. Beasley, Dal.	1254	626	.499

3-PT FIELD GOAL PCT.

	FGA	FGM	PCT.
Carrier, Ken.	280	105	.375
Dampier, Ken.	548	198	.361
Congdon, Den.	178	63	.354
Combs, Dal.	370	130	.351
Barrett, Was.	180	62	.344

FREE THROW PCT.

	FTA	FTM	PCT.
Carrier, Ken.	509	454	.892
Barry, Was.	463	400	.864
Combs, Dal.	548	458	.836
S. Jones, N.O.	495	412	.832
Dampier, Ken.	538	447	.831

ASSISTS

	G.	AST.	AVG.
Brown, Was.	82	580	7.1
Melchionni, N.Y.	80	457	5.7
Calvin, L.A.	84	478	5.7
Jones, Den.	75	426	5.7
Dampier, Ken.	82	447	5.5

REBOUNDS

	G.	OFF.	DEF.	TOT.	AVG.
Haywood, Den.	84	533	1104	1637	19.5
Daniels, Ind.	83	423	1039	1462	17.6
Robbins, N.O.	82	427	905	1332	16.2
Govan, N.O.	84	285	932	1217	14.5
Harge, Was.	84	334	843	1177	14.0

ABA 1970-71 LEADERS

SCORING

	G.	FG	FT	PTS.	AVG.
Issel, Ken.	83	938	604	2480	29.9
Barry, N.Y.	59	632	451	1734	29.4
Brisker, Pit.	79	898	430	2315	29.3
Calvin, Fla.	81	744	696	2201	27.2
Scott, Vir.	84	902	456	2276	27.1
Cannon, Den.	80	751	606	2126	26.6
Jones, Fla.	84	764	471	2044	24.3
Freeman, Utah-Tex.	66	596	367	1559	23.6
Caldwell, Car.	72	685	302	1678	23.3
Beaty, Utah	76	661	420	1744	22.9

FIELD GOAL PCT.

	FGA	FGM	PCT.
Beaty, Utah	1192	661	.555
Paultz, N.Y.	973	510	.524
Daniels, Ind.	1357	698	.514
Netolicky, Ind.	1305	651	.499
J. Beasley, Tex.	1070	532	.497

3-PT FIELD GOAL PCT.

	FGA	FGM	PCT.
Lehmann, Car.	382	154	.403
Carrier, Ken.	161	63	.391
S. Jones, Mem.	108	40	.370
Dampier, Ken.	280	103	.368
Combs, Tex.-Utah	210	77	.367

FREE THROW PCT.

	FTA	FTM	PCT.
Barry, N.Y.	507	451	.890
Carrier, Ken.	377	327	.867
Keller, Ind.	308	267	.867
Calvin, Fla.	805	696	.865
Dampier, Ken.	376	320	.851

ASSISTS

	G.	AST.	AVG.
Melchionni, N.Y.	81	672	8.3
Calvin, Fla.	81	619	7.6
J. Jones, Mem.	80	468	5.9
Scott, Vir.	84	472	5.6
Lehmann, Car.	83	464	5.6

REBOUNDS

	G.	OFF.	DEF.	TOT.	AVG.
Daniels, Ind.	82	394	1081	1475	18.0
Keye, Den.	83	370	1084	1454	17.5
Beaty, Utah	76	407	783	1190	15.7
Lewis, Pit.	83	435	778	1213	14.6
Govan, Mem.	84	277	861	1138	13.5

ABA 1971-72 LEADERS

SCORING

	G.	FG	FT	PTS.	AVG.
Scott, Vir.	73	985	525	2524	34.6
Barry, N.Y.	80	902	641	2518	31.5
Issel, Ken.	83	972	591	2538	30.6
Brisker, Pit.	49	563	248	1417	28.9
Simpson, Den.	84	920	457	2300	27.4
Erving, Vir.	84	910	467	2290	27.3
Thompson, Pit.	70	696	455	1888	27.0
McDaniels, Car.	58	659	234	1552	26.8
Freeman, Dal.	72	628	475	1733	24.1
Gilmore, Ken.	84	806	391	2003	23.8

FIELD GOAL PCT.

	FGA	FGM	PCT.
Gilmore, Ken.	1348	806	.598
Washington, N.Y.	678	387	.571
Lewis, Pit.	713	385	.540
Beaty, Utah	1353	729	.539
Jones, Fla.	797	423	.531

3-PT FIELD GOAL PCT.

	FGA	FGM	PCT.
Combs, Utah	254	103	.406
Dampier, Ken.	233	84	.361
Jabali, Fla.	285	102	.358
Lehmann, Car.-Mem.	199	71	.357
Hamilton, Dal.	132	46	.348

FREE THROW PCT.

	FTA	FTM	PCT.
Barry, N.Y.	730	641	.878
Calvin, Fla.	701	611	.872
S. Jones, Dal.	422	367	.870
Lewis, Ind.	396	341	.861
Combs, Utah	380	319	.839

ASSISTS

	G.	AST.	AVG.
Melchionni, N.Y.	80	669	8.4
Lehmann, Car.-Mem.	53	411	7.8
Brown, Den.	76	549	7.2
Jones, Utah	78	485	6.2
Dampier, Ken.	83	515	6.2

REBOUNDS

	G.	OFF.	DEF.	TOT.	AVG.
Gilmore, Ken.	84	421	1070	1491	17.8
Daniels, Ind.	79	383	914	1297	16.4
Erving, Vir.	84	476	843	1319	15.7
Govan, Mem.	83	310	872	1182	14.2
McDaniels, Car.	58	249	565	814	14.0

ABA 1972-73 LEADERS

SCORING

	G.	FG	FT	PTS.	AVG.
Erving, Vir.	71	894	475	2268	31.9
McGinnis, Ind.	82	868	517	2261	27.6
Issel, Ken.	84	902	485	2292	27.3
Cunningham, Car.	84	771	472	2028	24.1
Simpson, Den.	81	732	421	1890	23.3
R. Jones, Dal.	67	564	324	1495	22.3
Johnson, S.D.	80	769	195	1770	22.1
Wise, Utah	83	672	476	1823	22.0
Thompson, Mem.	80	579	549	1727	21.6
Gilmore, Ken.	84	687	368	1743	20.8

FIELD GOAL PCT.

	FGA	FGM	PCT.
Gilmore, Ken.	1228	687	.559
Kennedy, Dal.	664	365	.550
Owens, Car.	727	393	.541
Beck, Den.	879	466	.530
Irvine, Vir.	805	424	.527

3-PT FIELD GOAL PCT.

	FGA	FGM	PCT.
Combs, Utah	134	51	.381
Brown, Ind.	118	42	.356
Dampier, Ken.	155	54	.348
Hamilton, Dal.	191	66	.346
Lewis, Ind.	110	38	.345

FREE THROW PCT.

	FTA	FTM	PCT.
Keller, Ind.	269	234	.870
Boone, Utah	479	415	.866
Warren, Car.-Dal.-Utah	274	236	.861
Calvin, Car.	582	500	.859
Silas, Dal.	467	389	.833

ASSISTS

	G.	AST.	AVG.
Melchionni, N.Y.	61	453	7.4
Williams, S.D.	83	582	7.0
Jabali, Den.	82	539	6.6
Dampier, Ken.	80	521	6.5
Cunningham, Car.	84	530	6.3

REBOUNDS

	G.	OFF.	DEF.	TOT.	AVG.
Gilmore, Ken.	84	449	1027	1476	17.6
Daniels, Ind.	81	348	899	1247	15.4
Paultz, N.Y.	81	279	736	1015	12.5
McGinnis, Ind.	82	434	588	1022	12.5
Denton, Mem.	66	276	544	820	12.4

ABA 1973-74 LEADERS

SCORING

	G.	FG	FT	PTS.	AVG.
Erving, N.Y.	84	914	454	2299	27.4
McGinnis, Ind.	80	789	488	2071	25.9
Issel, Ken.	83	829	457	2118	25.5
Gervin, Vir.-S.A.	74	672	378	1730	23.4
Wise, Utah	82	714	396	1826	22.3
Lamar, S.D.	84	686	272	1713	20.4
Johnson, S.D.	84	716	199	1690	20.1
Carter, Vir.	80	561	392	1546	19.3
Thompson, Mem.	78	539	410	1498	19.2
Simpson, Den.	75	597	208	1404	18.7

FIELD GOAL PCT.

	FGA	FGM	PCT.
Nater, Vir.-S.A.	846	467	.552
Jones, Utah	1060	583	.550
Owens, Car.	843	444	.527
Chones, Car.	1017	535	.526
Grant, S.D.	681	357	.524

3-PT FIELD GOAL PCT.

	FGA	FGM	PCT.
Dampier, Ken.	124	48	.387
Keller, Ind.	131	50	.382
Jabali, Den.	123	45	.366
Brown, Ind.	155	56	.361
Combs, Utah-Mem.	147	52	.354

FREE THROW PCT.

	FTA	FTM	PCT.
Jones, Utah	259	229	.884
Calvin, Car.	560	490	.875
Boone, Utah	343	300	.875
Johnson, S.D.	235	199	.847
Carter, Vir.	466	392	.841

ASSISTS

	G.	AST.	AVG.
Smith, Den.	76	619	8.1
Jabali, Den.	49	358	7.3
Williams, S.D.-Ken.	90	557	6.2
Dampier, Ken.	84	473	5.6
Taylor, Vir.	80	416	5.2

REBOUNDS

	G.	OFF.	DEF.	TOT.	AVG.
Gilmore, Ken.	84	478	1060	1538	18.3
McGinnis, Ind.	80	422	775	1197	15.0
Jones, S.D.	79	322	773	1095	13.9
Nater, Vir.-S.A.	79	286	712	998	12.6
Daniels, Ind.	78	251	655	906	11.6

STEALS

	G.	STL.	AVG.
McClain, Car.	84	250	2.98
Taylor, Vir.	80	215	2.69
Erving, N.Y.	84	190	2.26
Caldwell, Car.	79	170	2.15
Gale, Ken.-N.Y.	80	167	2.09

BLOCKS

	G.	BLK.	AVG.
Jones, S.D.	79	316	4.00
Gilmore, Ken.	84	287	3.42
Erving, N.Y.	84	204	2.43
Hillman, Ind.	83	177	2.13
Paultz, N.Y.	77	147	1.91

ABA 1974-75 LEADERS

SCORING

	G.	FG	FT	PTS.	AVG.
McGinnis, Ind.	79	873	545	2353	29.8
Erving, N.Y.	84	914	486	2343	27.9
Boone, Utah	84	872	363	2117	25.2
Grant, S.D.	53	576	182	1335	25.2
Barnes, St.L.	77	777	295	1849	24.0
Gilmore, Ken.	84	784	412	1981	23.6
Gervin, S.A.	84	784	380	1965	23.4
Lewis, Mem.-St.L.	69	579	355	1531	22.2
Lamar, S.D.	77	667	247	1606	20.9
Simpson, Den.	82	694	303	1692	20.6

FIELD GOAL PCT.

	FGA	FGM	PCT.
Jones, Den.	876	529	.604
Gilmore, Ken.	1351	784	.580
Malone, Utah	1035	591	.571
Twardzik, Vir.	657	359	.546
Grant, S.D.	1058	576	.544

3-PT FIELD GOAL PCT.

	FGA	FGM	PCT.
Shepherd, Mem.	143	60	.420
Dampier, Ken.	96	38	.396
Smith, Utah	94	34	.362
McGinnis, Ind.	175	62	.354
Brown, Mem.-Utah-Ind.	100	35	.350

FREE THROW PCT.

	FTA	FTM	PCT.
Calvin, Den.	530	475	.896
Silas, S.A.	486	430	.885
Robisch, Den.	346	304	.879
Boone, Utah	422	363	.860
Lewis, Mem.-St.L.	421	355	.843

ASSISTS

	G.	AST.	AVG.
Calvin, Den.	74	570	7.7
Williams, Mem.	81	576	7.1
McGinnis, Ind.	79	495	6.3
Jabali, S.D.	62	358	5.8
O'Brien, S.D.	79	443	5.6

REBOUNDS

	G.	OFF.	DEF.	TOT.	AVG.
Nater, S.A.	78	369	910	1279	16.4
Gilmore, Ken.	84	427	934	1361	16.2
Barnes, St.L.	77	419	783	1202	15.6
Malone, Utah	83	455	754	1209	14.6
McGinnis, Ind.	79	396	730	1126	14.3

STEALS

	G.	STL.	AVG.
Taylor, N.Y.	79	221	2.80
McGinnis, Ind.	79	206	2.61
Taylor, Den.	76	172	2.26
Erving, N.Y.	84	186	2.21
Lewis, Mem.-St.L.	69	147	2.13

BLOCKS

	G.	BLK.	AVG.
Jones, S.D.	76	246	3.24
Gilmore, Ken.	84	258	3.07
Green, Den.	81	174	2.15
Erving, N.Y.	84	157	1.87
Jones, Den.	84	153	1.82

ABA 1975-76 LEADERS

SCORING

	G.	FG	FT	PTS.	AVG.
Erving, N.Y.	84	949	530	2462	29.3
Knight, Ind.	70	774	415	1969	28.1
Thompson, Den.	83	807	541	2158	26.0
Gilmore, Ken.	84	773	521	2067	24.6
Barnes, St.L.	67	681	251	1616	24.1
Silas, S.A.	84	718	564	2000	23.8
Issel, Den.	84	752	425	1930	23.0
Boone, Utah-St.L.	78	713	277	1719	22.0
Gervin, S.A.	81	706	342	1768	21.8
Burden, Vir.	71	561	283	1413	19.9

FIELD GOAL PCT.

	FGA	FGM	PCT.
Jones, Den.	878	510	.581
Gilmore, Ken.	1401	773	.552
Hughes, N.Y.	566	300	.530
Silas, S.A.	1384	718	.519
Beck, Den.	646	334	.517

3-PT FIELD GOAL PCT.

	FGA	FGM	PCT.
Taylor, N.Y.	76	32	.421
Boone, Utah-St.L.	43	16	.372
Dampier, Ken.	87	32	.368
Keller, Ind.	349	123	.352
Buse, Ind.	208	72	.346

FREE THROW PCT.

	FTA	FTM	PCT.
Keller, Ind.	183	164	.896
Eakins, Utah-Vir.-N.Y.	223	198	.888
Calvin, Vir.	285	253	.888
Silas, S.A.	647	564	.872
Boone, Utah-St.L.	318	277	.871

ASSISTS

	G.	AST.	AVG.
Buse, Ind.	84	689	8.2
Simpson, Den.	84	597	7.1
Calvin, Vir.	45	271	6.0
Dampier, Ken.	82	467	5.7
Silas, S.A.	84	452	5.4

REBOUNDS

	G.	OFF.	DEF.	TOT.	AVG.
Gilmore, Ken.	84	402	901	1303	15.5
Lucas, St.L.-Ken.	86	297	673	970	11.3
C.Jones, S.D.-Ken.-St.L.	76	246	607	853	11.2
Kenon, S.A.	81	287	610	897	11.1
Erving, N.Y.	84	337	588	925	11.0

STEALS

	G.	STL.	AVG.
Buse, Ind.	84	346	4.12
Taylor, Vir.	76	206	2.71
Erving, N.Y.	84	207	2.46
Taylor, N.Y.	54	125	2.31
Jones, Den.	83	170	2.05

BLOCKS

	G.	BLK.	AVG.
Paultz, S.A.	83	253	3.05
C.Jones, S.D.-Ken.-St.L.	76	218	2.87
Gilmore, Ken.	84	205	2.44
Elmore, Ind.	76	178	2.34
Jones, Den.	83	184	2.22

ALL-ABA TEAMS

First	Second
1967–68	
Connie Hawkins, Pittsburgh	Roger Brown, Indiana
Doug Moe, New Orleans	Cincy Powell, Dallas
Mel Daniels, Minnesota	John Beasley, Dallas
Larry Jones, Denver	Larry Brown, New Orleans
Charlie Williams, Pittsburgh	Louie Dampier, Kentucky
1968–69	
Connie Hawkins, Minnesota	John Beasley, Dallas
Rick Barry, Oakland	Doug Moe, Oakland
Mel Daniels, Indiana	Red Robbins, New Orleans
James Jones, New Orleans	Don Freeman, Miami
Larry Jones, Denver	Louie Dampier, Kentucky
1969–70	
Rick Barry, Washington	Roger Brown, Indiana
Spencer Haywood, Denver	Bob Netolicky, Indiana
Mel Daniels, Indiana	Red Robbins, New Orleans
Bob Verga, Carolina	Louie Dampier, Kentucky
Larry Jones, Denver	Don Freeman, Miami
1970–71	
Roger Brown, Indiana	John Brisker, Pittsburgh
Rick Barry, New York	Joe Caldwell, Carolina
Mel Daniels, Indiana	Zelmo Beaty, Utah
Mack Calvin, Floridians	Dan Issel, Kentucky
Charlie Scott, Virginia	Don Freeman, Texas
	Larry Cannon, Denver
1971–72	
Rick Barry, New York	Willie Wise, Utah
Dan Issel, Kentucky	Julius Erving, Virginia
Artis Gilmore, Kentucky	Zelmo Beaty, Utah
Don Freeman, Dallas	Ralph Simpson, Denver
Bill Melchionni, New York	Charlie Scott, Virginia

First	Second
1972–73	
Billy Cunningham, Carolina	George McGinnis, Indiana
Julius Erving, Virginia	Dan Issel, Kentucky
Artis Gilmore, Kentucky	Mel Daniels, Indiana
James Jones, Utah	Ralph Simpson, Denver
Warren Jabali, Denver	Mack Calvin, Carolina
1973–74	
Julius Erving, New York	Dan Issel, Kentucky
George McGinnis, Indiana	Willie Wise, Utah
Artis Gilmore, Kentucky	Swen Nater, San Antonio
James Jones, Utah	Ron Boone, Utah
Mack Calvin, Carolina	Louie Dampier, Kentucky
1974–75	
Julius Erving, New York	Marvin Barnes, St. Louis
George McGinnis, Indiana	George Gervin, San Antonio
Artis Gilmore, Kentucky	Swen Nater, San Antonio
Mack Calvin, Denver	Brian Taylor, New York
Ron Boone, Utah	James Silas, San Antonio
1975–76	
Julius Erving, New York	David Thompson, Denver
Billy Knight, Indiana	Bobby Jones, Denver
Artis Gilmore, Kentucky	Dan Issel, Denver
James Silas, San Antonio	Don Buse, Indiana
Ralph Simpson, Denver	George Gervin, San Antonio

ABA ALL-ROOKIE TEAMS

1968

Tom Washington, Pittsburgh
Bob Netolicky, Indiana
Mel Daniels, Minnesota
Louie Dampier, Kentucky
James Jones, New Orleans

1969

Larry Miller, Los Angeles
Watt Piatkowski, Denver
Gene Moore, Kentucky
Warren Armstrong, Oakland
Ron Boone, Dallas

1970

Willie Wise, Los Angeles
John Brisker, Pittsburgh
Spencer Haywood, Denver
Mike Barrett, Washington
Mack Calvin, Los Angeles

1971

Wendell Ladner, Memphis
Sam Robinson, Floridians
Dan Issel, Kentucky
Charlie Scott, Virginia
Joe Hamilton, Texas

1972

Julius Erving, Virginia
George McGinnis, Indiana
Artis Gilmore, Kentucky
John Roche, New York
Johnny Neumann, Memphis

1973

George Gervin, Virginia
Dennis Wuycik, Carolina
Jim Chones, New York
Brian Taylor, New York
James Silas, Dallas

1974

Larry Kenon, New York
Mike Green, Denver
Swen Nater, San Antonio
Dwight Lamar, San Antonio
John Williamson, New York

1975

Bobby Jones, Denver
Marvin Barnes, St. Louis
Moses Malone, Utah
Billy Knight, Indiana
Gus Gerard, St. Louis

1976

David Thompson, Denver
Mark Olberding, San Antonio
Kim Hughes, New York
M. L. Carr, St. Louis
Ticky Burden, Virginia

ABA REGULAR-SEASON RECORDS
Individual

GAMES
Most Games
728—Louie Dampier, Kentucky, 1967–76

MINUTES
Most Minutes, Career
27,770—Louie Dampier, Kentucky, 1967–76

SCORING
Most Points, Career
13,726—Louie Dampier, Kentucky, 1967–76

**Highest Average, Points per Game, Career
(minimum 250 games)**
28.7—Julius Erving, Virginia and New York, 1971–76

Most Points, Season
2,538—Dan Issel, Kentucky, 1971–72

Highest Average, Points per Game, Season
34.8—Charlie Scott, Virginia, 1971–72

FIELD GOALS
Most Field Goals, Career
5,290—Louie Dampier, Kentucky, 1967–68—1975–76

Most Field Goals, Season
986—Spencer Haywood, Denver, 1969–70

MOST FIELD GOAL ATTEMPTS
Most Field Goal Attempts, Career
12,047—Louis Dampier, Kentucky, 1967–68—1975–76

Most Field Goal Attempts, Season
2,302—Charlie Scott, Virginia, 1971–72

FIELD GOAL PERCENTAGE
**Highest Field Goal Percentage, Career
(minimum: 2,500 field goal attempts)**
.557—Artis Gilmore, Kentucky, 1971–72—1975–76 (3,671/6,588)

**Highest Field Goal Percentage, Season
(minimum: 500 field goal attempts)**
.604—Bobby Jones, Denver, 1974–75 (529/876)

THREE-POINT FIELD GOALS
Most Three-Point Field Goals, Career
794—Louie Dampier, Kentucky, 1967–76

Most Three-Point Field Goals, Season
199—Louie Dampier, Kentucky, 1968–69

Most Three-Point Field Goals, Game
10—Les Selvage, Anaheim at Denver, February 15, 1968

THREE-POINT FIELD GOAL PERCENTAGE
Highest Three-Point Field Goal Percentage, Career
.377—Darel Carrier, Kentucky and Memphis, 1967–68—1971–72 (398/1,055)

Highest Three-Point Field Goal Percentage, Season
.420—Billy Shepherd, Memphis, 1974–75 (60/143)

THREE-POINT FIELD GOAL ATTEMPTS
Most Three-Point Field Goal Attempts, Career
2,217—Louie Dampier, Kentucky, 1967–76

Most Three-Point Field Goal Attempts, Season
552—Louie Dampier, Kentucky, 1968–69

Most Three-Point Field Goal Attempts, Game
26—Les Selvage, Anaheim at Denver, February 15, 1968

FREE THROWS MADE
Most Free Throws Made, Career
3,554—Mack Calvin, Los Angeles, Miami, Carolina, Denver and Virginia, 1969–76

Most Free Throws Made, Season
696—Mack Calvin, Floridians, 1970–71

Most Free Throws Made, Game
24—Tony Jackson, New Jersey vs. Kentucky, at Louisville, November 27, 1967

ABA REGULAR-SEASON RECORDS
Individual

FREE THROWS ATTEMPTED
Most Free Throws Attempted, Career
4,105—Mack Calvin, Los Angeles, Miami, Carolina, Denver and Virginia, 1969–76

Most Free Throws Attempted, Season
805—Mack Calvin, Floridians, 1970–71

Most Free Throws Attempted, Game
30—George Thompson, Memphis at San Diego, October 14, 1972

FREE THROW PERCENTAGE
Highest Free Throw Percentage, Career
.866—Mack Calvin, Los Angeles, Miami, Carolina, Denver and Virginia, 1969–76 (4,105/3,554)

Highest Free Throw Percentage, Season
.896—Mack Calvin, Denver, 1974–75 (530/475)

PERSONAL FOULS
Most Personal Fouls, Career
1,348—Gene Moore, Kentucky, Texas, Dallas, New York, San Diego and St. Louis, 1968–75

Most Personal Fouls, Season
382—Gene Moore, Kentucky, 1969–70

DISQUALIFICATIONS
Most Times Disqualified, Career
43—Gene Moore, Kentucky, Texas, Dallas, New York, San Diego and St. Louis, 1968–74

STEALS
Steals were compiled since 1973–74

Most Steals, Career
658—Don Buse, Indiana, 1973–76

Most Steals, Season
346—Don Buse, Indiana, 1975–76

Most Steals, Game
12—Ted McClain, Carolina vs. New York, at Raleigh, N.C., December 26, 1973

BLOCKED SHOTS
Blocked Shots were compiled since 1973–74

Most Blocked Shots, Career
750—Artis Gilmore, Kentucky, 1973–76

Most Blocked Shots, Season
287—Artis Gilmore, Kentucky, 1973–74

Most Blocked Shots, Game
12—Julius Keye, Denver vs. Virginia, at Denver, December 14, 1972, and Caldwell Jones, San Diego vs. Carolina, at San Diego, January 6, 1974

REBOUNDS
Most Rebounds, Career
9,494—Mel Daniels, Minnesota, Indiana and Memphis, 1967–68—1974–75

Highest Average, Rebounds per Game, Career
15.1—Mel Daniels, Minnesota, Indiana and Memphis, 1967–75 (9,494/628)

Most Rebounds, Season
1,637—Spencer Haywood, Denver, 1969–70

Highest Average, Rebounds per Game, Season
19.5—Spencer Haywood, Denver, 1969–70

Most Rebounds, Game
40—Artis Gilmore, Kentucky at New York, February 3, 1974

ASSISTS
Most Assists, Career
4,084—Louie Dampier, Kentucky 1967–76

Most Assists, Season
689—Don Buse, Indiana, 1975–76

Most Assists, Game
23—Larry Brown, Denver vs. Pittsburgh, at Denver, February 20, 1972

Team

GAMES WON & LOST
Highest Winning Percentage, Season
.810—Kentucky, 1971–72 (68-16)

Lowest Winning Percentage, Season
.179—Virginia, 1974–75 (15-69)

Offense

SCORING
Most Points, Game
342—San Diego vs. New York, February 14, 1975 (4 OT)

Fewest Points, Game
158—San Antonio vs. Indiana, October 20, 1973

THE GLOBAL GAME

Prior to 1987, the relationship between the NBA and FIBA, the Fédération de Basketball International, the sport's international governing body, could be described as cordial at best. FIBA was about amateurs; the NBA was about professionals. FIBA believed amateurs represented the sanctity of sport; the NBA believed its professionals represented basketball played at its highest level.

Only when the two organizations finally came together, staging the first McDonald's Open in 1987, did the NBA truly begin to explore its fan following outside the United States. And what the league discovered was a global community hungry for the knowledge, skills and entertainment only the NBA and its athletes could provide.

Now members of the international basketball community find it hard to believe that was less than a decade ago. Since that first McDonald's Open, which featured the Milwaukee Bucks hosting the Soviet Union's National Team and the Italian club champion Tracer Milan in a groundbreaking tournament, the sport of basketball has enjoyed the fastest growth period in its history, a boom largely attributable to the NBA's presence on the global frontier.

In 1994 alone NBA teams played preseason games in France, Spain, Italy, Mexico, Canada and Puerto Rico, and the Los Angeles Clippers and Portland Trail Blazers were slated to open the 1994–95 regular season with a pair of games in Japan—the third time in this decade the NBA has played regular-season games in Japan. Fans in more than 140 countries watched NBA telecasts, whether they were regular-season games, highlights packages, the All-Star Weekend or the NBA

Playoffs and Finals. NBA-sponsored grassroots events, such as 3-on-3 tournaments and clinics for kids and coaches, stretched around the globe. Magazines and newspapers throughout the world cover the league on a regular basis, and some even devote their entire publications to the NBA. And children across the world have embraced NBA apparel and NBA-identified products as an integral part of global youth culture.

What was largely a dream for FIBA a decade ago has evolved into a realistic goal for both FIBA and the NBA. The two organizations have taken charge of a global movement to make basketball the most popular sport in the world. As the century winds to its close, basketball is making steady gains on soccer even in the farthest reaches of the world.

Every boom period generally has its watershed event, and the NBA's global growth spurt was no exception. The 1992 Summer Olympic Games in Barcelona proved a launching pad for the international popularity of basketball and the NBA, which to that point had been taxiing along the global runway. A landmark 1989 ruling by FIBA finally removed restrictions on NBA players' participating in FIBA's major international competitions, meaning that for the first time in history NBA players would be permitted to represent the United States—and other countries—in the Olympic Games.

The FIBA ruling also permitted the NBA to join USA Basketball, a federation of American basketball organizations previously limited to the amateur realm. And USAB set about assembling the Dream Team featuring NBA superstars that would represent the United States in Barcelona.

Charles Barkley (left) and Magic Johnson helped make USA
Basketball's 1992 Olympic Dream Team one for the ages.

But even as names like Michael Jordan, Magic Johnson, Larry Bird and Charles Barkley tumbled from the lips of Selection Committee members, even as the thought of those four on the same team turned pupils across America into gold medals, no one could anticipate the sweeping effect this team would have on the global community.

Magic Johnson likened it to a rock band with Bruce Springsteen, Madonna, Frank Sinatra and Sting all making music together, coexisting on a stage they usually dominated by themselves. Jordan, Bird and Johnson had become part of the American basketball lexicon. They had even ascended, through an increasing effort to distribute telecasts of NBA games outside the United States, to superstar status abroad. And the rest of the Dream Team—Barkley, Patrick Ewing, David Robinson, Chris Mullin, Scottie Pippen, Clyde Drexler, John Stockton, Karl Malone and college superstar Christian Laettner—had become icons in their respective communities.

The names individually signified excitement. The names together, on the same roster, signified an assemblage of excellence previously unknown in the sporting world. Because of its highly advanced basketball infrastructure, the United States had long been regarded as home of the world's best basketball and the world's best basketball players. Other countries had excellent players, even some who played and starred in the NBA. But few would deny that the Dream Team was made up of the best basketball players in the world. No other Olympic competition—or, for that matter, no other competition in history—had ever seen all of the world's top athletes in one sport on one team to such a degree.

As the Games approached, the concept began to sink in across the world, not only with basketball fans or Olympic fans, but even with the most casual observer. The Dream Team no longer belonged to the United States; it belonged to the world. With the winning of a gold medal all but a foregone conclusion, the focus of the competition centered upon its aesthetic value. Fans in Barcelona along with a global television audience simply wanted a glimpse of the team in action, if for no other reason than to see what was causing such a stir. Once attracted, they became hooked, captivated by the

This airport crowd in Barcelona shows why Coach Chuck Daly likened the Dream Team to a band of touring rock stars.

grace and style of the sport, the thrill of a Jordan dunk, the wizardry of a Johnson pass, the power of a Ewing block or the beauty of a Mullin jumper.

Members of the team became international celebrities. They traveled by motorcade wherever they went, cloaked by heavy security both inside and outside their hotel. Yet Barkley, ever the free spirit, abandoned the entourage and walked like the Pied Piper down Las Ramblas, Barcelona's picturesque downtown promenade, crowds jostling and moving with his every step. During the Opening Ceremonies, Dream Teamers marching with the U.S. contingent spent most of their time signing autographs for other athletes and team officials. Even during the competition itself, an opponent was seen waving to his bench while guarding Magic Johnson, making sure a teammate remembered to snap a picture.

Predictably, the United States had little trouble winning the gold. In its eight-game romp to the medal stand, the Dream Team won by an average margin of 44 points per game. In the medal round, the United States defeated Lithuania 127–76 despite a strong performance by the Golden State Warriors' Sarunas Marciulionis, who led the Lithuanian team. Two days later, on August 8, Jordan's 22 points led the charge for the gold in a 117–85 victory against Croatia and its NBA players, Toni Kukoc, Dino Radja and the late Drazen Petrovic.

It wasn't the first time an American team had dominated Olympic competition. In fact, in the history of its participation in Olympic basketball, the United States has posted a 93-2 record, winning every gold since 1936, with the exception of 1972, 1980 (when the United States boycotted the Moscow games) and 1988, when Team USA settled for the bronze behind the U.S.S.R. and Yugoslavia.

It also wasn't the first time NBA players had starred in the Olympics, although it was the first time they had done so while playing in the NBA. Legends such as Bill Russell (1956), K. C. Jones (1956), Oscar Robertson (1960), Jerry West (1960), Jerry Lucas (1960) and Bill Bradley (1964) all had represented the United States during or immediately after their college careers. Russell, in fact, postponed his debut with the Boston Celtics to play in the 1956 games in Melbourne, Australia. The Olympics were held from November 22 to December 1 that year, so Russell missed 24 of Boston's 72 games in the 1956–57 season. The choice served him well: Not only did the United States cruise to the gold behind a 53.5-point average victory margin and Russell's team-leading 14.1 points per game, but the Celtics also won the 1957 NBA Championship.

The difference between previous U.S. Olympic teams and the Dream Team was that the Dream Team boasted great basketball players in their prime, not at the very beginnings of what would become storied NBA

Charles Barkley gives international foes a taste of what NBA rivals had experienced for years.

On the Dream Team, Michael Jordan was the star of stars, blending in for the good of the team but elevating his game when it was needed most.

OLYMPIC MEDALISTS THROUGH THE YEARS

1992 Olympics—Barcelona, Spain

Gold	United States
Silver	Croatia
Bronze	Lithuania

1988 Olympics—Seoul, South Korea

Gold	Soviet Union
Silver	Yugoslavia
Bronze	United States

1984 Olympics—Los Angeles, USA

Gold	United States
Silver	Spain
Bronze	Yugoslavia

(Note: Soviet Union, among others, did not compete)

1980 Olympics—Moscow, Soviet Union

Gold	Yugoslavia
Silver	Italy
Bronze	Soviet Union

(Note: United States, among others, did not compete)

1976 Olympics—Montreal, Canada

Gold	United States
Silver	Yugoslavia
Bronze	Soviet Union

1972 Olympics—Munich, West Germany

Gold	Soviet Union
Silver	United States
Bronze	Cuba

careers. The Dream Team's average age was 29.1 years old. The average age of Team USA in 1988 was 21.6 years old. How good would the 1956 team have been if Russell and Jones were five years older, with five years of NBA experience? How good would the 1960 team have been if West, Robertson, Lucas and Walt Bellamy were all at the height of their NBA careers?

In the aftermath of the 1992 Olympic Games, a globalization process the NBA had set in motion in the late 1980s and early 1990s accelerated at a remarkable rate. Across the globe, demand skyrocketed for something, anything, associated with the NBA. Event promoters in other countries showered the league office with proposals to present NBA exhibition games. Television networks wanted to air NBA game telecasts and other NBA programming. Store owners clamored to sell NBA-licensed merchandise. And FIBA wanted the NBA's help in sponsoring grassroots programs to promote the sport throughout the world.

Suddenly, the NBA emerged at the forefront of the international basketball community. In 1990 the league office had a handful of employees working on international matters, most on a part-time basis and in addition to their domestic duties. By 1994 more than 45 NBA employees worked full-time on global projects and the NBA had regional offices in Geneva, Barcelona, Melbourne, Hong Kong and Tokyo.

The league's first mission on this new global frontier involved staging more NBA games outside the United States. Based on the success of the Dream Team, the NBA realized that nothing delivered its message better than presenting its players live to foreign audiences. At

1968 Olympics—Mexico City, Mexico

Gold	United States
Silver	Yugoslavia
Bronze	Soviet Union

1964 Olympics—Tokyo, Japan

Gold	United States
Silver	Soviet Union
Bronze	Brazil

1960 Olympics—Rome, Italy

Gold	United States
Silver	Soviet Union
Bronze	Brazil

1956 Olympics—Melbourne, Australia

Gold	United States
Silver	Soviet Union
Bronze	Uruguay

1952 Olympics—Helsinki, Finland

Gold	United States
Silver	Soviet Union
Bronze	Uruguay

1948 Olympics—London, England

Gold	United States
Silver	France
Bronze	Brazil

(Note: no Olympics were held in 1940 or 1944)

1936 Olympics—Berlin, Germany

Gold	United States
Silver	Canada
Bronze	Mexico

SUMMARY OF FINISHES

Country	Gold	Silver	Bronze
United States	10	1	1
Soviet Union	2	4	3
Yugoslavia	1	3	1
Canada	0	1	0
Croatia	0	1	0
France	0	1	0
Italy	0	1	0
Spain	0	1	0
Brazil	0	0	3
Uruguay	0	0	2
Cuba	0	0	1
Lithuania	0	0	1
Mexico	0	0	1

OLYMPIC, NCAA AND NBA CHAMPIONS

Dream Team member Magic Johnson became the seventh player in history to win an Olympic gold medal as well as NCAA and NBA championships. Following is the complete listing:

Clyde Lovellette
    Olympics: 1952
    NCAA: Kansas 1952
    NBA: Minneapolis 1954, Boston 1964

Bill Russell
    Olympics: 1956
    NCAA: San Francisco 1955, 1956
    NBA: Boston 1957, 1959, 1960, 1961, 1962,
        1963, 1964, 1965, 1966, 1968, 1969

K. C. Jones
    Olympics: 1956
    NCAA: San Francisco 1955, 1956
    NBA: Boston 1959, 1960, 1961, 1962, 1963,
        1964, 1965, 1966

Jerry Lucas
    Olympics: 1960
    NCAA: Ohio State 1960
    NBA: New York 1973

Quinn Buckner
    Olympics 1976
    NCAA: Indiana 1976
    NBA: Boston 1984

Michael Jordan
    Olympics: 1984, 1992
    NCAA: North Carolina 1982
    NBA: Chicago 1991, 1992, 1993

Magic Johnson
    Olympics: 1992
    NCAA: Michigan State 1979
    NBA: LA Lakers 1980, 1982, 1985, 1987, 1988

the time, the history of NBA exhibitions outside the United States was brief and certainly expandable.

Prior to the Olympics, the McDonald's Open served as the only forum in which NBA players could compete in front of global audiences and against international competition. A 1984 meeting between NBA Commissioner David J. Stern and FIBA Secretary Gen-eral Borislav Stankovic broke the ice between the two organizations and paved the way for the first McDonald's Open in 1987. Held at the Mecca in Milwaukee—the only time it has been staged in the United States—the McDonald's Open introduced the NBA to foreign competition, which had been steadily improving throughout the decade. It provided the league and its

Terry Cummings (34) led the Milwaukee Bucks to victory in the inaugural McDonald's Open in 1987.

players with a sampling of an entire realm the NBA had yet to discover.

In a round-robin format, each team played the other two, with the Bucks notching wins against both of their guests, 123–111 against Tracer Milan and 127–100 against the Soviet National Team, and the Soviets beating Tracer Milan 135–108. Milwaukee earned the tournament title, beginning a streak of NBA victories that continued through the 1993 tournament in Munich.

The 1988 McDonald's Open in Madrid marked the first time an NBA team participated in a FIBA-sanctioned event outside the United States. The NBA sent the Boston Celtics to Spain, showcasing Bird, Robert Parish and Kevin McHale in Madrid's Palacio de los Deportes. The Celtics won the title against a four-team field that included host club Real Madrid, the Yugoslavian National Team, and Italian club Scavolini Pesaro. Boston beat the Yugoslavian team 113–85 in the first round and downed Real Madrid 111–96 in the final.

The tournament moved to the Paleur in Rome in 1989, where the Denver Nuggets took on a club team from Barcelona, Jugoplastika Split from Yugoslavia, and Philips Milan from Italy. The Nuggets trounced Barcelona easily, 137–103, but had a more difficult time with Split, needing a second-half surge to pull out a 135–129 victory.

In 1990 the New York Knicks and Patrick Ewing carried the NBA's torch to Barcelona, where they nearly became the first NBA team to lose in foreign competition. Scavolini Pesaro forced New York into overtime in a semifinal before the Knicks won 119–115 at the Palau San Jordi. New York had an easier time in the final, beating Pop 84 Split, from Yugoslavia, 117–101. Host Barcelona filled out the four-team field.

Magic Johnson and his charismatic personality proved a perfect fit for Paris, host city of the 1991 McDonald's Open. Johnson and his Laker team triumphed again, but only after a scare in the final. After beating host team Limoges 132–101 in the first round, the Lakers survived a late run by Spanish club Joventut Badalona to win 116–114 in the championship game. Johnson dazzled sellout crowds at the Palais Omnisports de Bercy Arena with 38 assists in the two games.

With competition stiffening, it seemed only a matter of time before an NBA team would fall. The McDonald's Open moved to a biennial schedule after 1991, largely due to the fact that two major international events—the Olympics and the World Championship of Basketball in alternating even years—now were on the NBA's calendar. The league wanted attention focused on just one showcase event each year, so the McDonald's Open became an odd-year event.

The Phoenix Suns and Charles Barkley reasserted the NBA's dominance in 1993 at the sixth McDonald's Open in Munich. With the field expanded from four to

Earvin ''Magique'' Johnson brought extra sparkle to the City of Lights at the 1991 McDonald's Open in Paris.

six teams, the Suns received a bye to the semifinals, where they beat Real Madrid 145–115, notching the highest point total in tournament history. In the title game, Phoenix trounced Italy's Buckler Bologna 112–90. Barkley, who averaged 26.0 points per game over the two games, was awarded the Drazen Petrovic Trophy as the tournament's Most Valuable Player. The MVP award was named after the Croatian star who participated in the 1988 McDonald's Open with Real Madrid and went on to star in the NBA before being killed in an automobile accident in June 1993.

The five teams who joined the Suns in the 1993 tournament—Germany's Bayer Leverkusen, Brazil's All-Star Franca and France's Limoges filled out the field—had all won league championships in their respective countries. Phoenix had been the NBA's Western Conference Champion and finished runner-up to the Chicago Bulls in the 1993 NBA Finals. Stern and Stankovic vowed to take the next logical step and make the McDonald's Open a true world championship for club teams, they hope by its next appearance in 1995, with the NBA champion meeting the champions from the best leagues around the world.

The mystique surrounding the first Dream Team and the frenzied response to it throughout the world may never be duplicated. Talents like Johnson, Jordan and Bird may appear again in the NBA, but perhaps never again at the same time or in the same era. But the first Dream Team would pave the way for other equally impressive collections of NBA superstars. In each even

year after 1992, the NBA would send another Dream Team into national team competition, either at the Olympics or at the World Championship of Basketball.

Dream Team II, which included a formidable mix of NBA veterans and rising stars, won the gold medal for the United States at the 1994 World Championship of Basketball in Toronto and Hamilton, Ontario, and helped gain unprecedented attention for the tournament. Run by FIBA, the World Championship had an illustrious 44-year history, but like the Olympics it had never hosted current NBA players and as a result never captivated American audiences. The United States had won only two of the previous 11 tournaments leading up to the 1994 event, in 1954 and 1986, but sailed through the 1994 World Championship undefeated to capture the gold medal, beating Russia 137–91 in the final before a tournament record crowd of 32, 616 at Toronto's SkyDome.

The United States' entry in the 1994 World Championship of Basketball included established stars such as Dominique Wilkins, Joe Dumars, Mark Price, Kevin Johnson, Reggie Miller, Isiah Thomas and Tim Hardaway, the latter two unable to play due to injury. It also boasted young players headed for certain stardom, like Shaquille O'Neal, Shawn Kemp, Derrick Coleman, Larry Johnson, Steve Smith, Alonzo Mourning and Dan Majerle. The team certainly had a different look than its dreamy predecessor. USAB made it a policy not to put any members of the first Dream Team on Dream Team II, and what resulted was a hungry, feisty squad, with

Charles Barkley was a hit with fans of all ages at the 1993 McDonald's Open in Munich.

McDONALD'S OPENS RESULTS

McDonald's Open—Munich, Germany

/93   Buckler Bologna 129, All-Star Franca 88
        Real Madrid 85, Bayer Leverkusen 75
/93   All-Star Franca 104, Bayer Leverkusen 97
        Phoenix Suns 145, Real Madrid 115
        Buckler Bologna 101, Limoges 85
/93   Real Madrid 123, Limoges 119
        Phoenix Suns 112, Buckler Bologna 90
enix Suns win tournament.

McDonald's Open—Paris, France

/91   Los Angeles Lakers 132, Limoges 101
        Joventut Badalona 117, Slobodna Dalmacija Split 86
/91   Limoges 105, Slobodna Dalmacija Split 91
        Los Angeles Lakers 116, Joventut Badalona 114
Angeles Lakers win tournament.

McDonald's Open—Barcelona, Spain

/90   New York Knicks 119, Scavolini Pesaro 115, overtime
        POP 84 Split 102, Barcelona 97
/90   Barcelona 106, Scavolini Pesaro 105
        New York Knicks 117, POP 84 Split 101
York Knicks win tournament.

McDonald's Open—Rome, Italy

/89   Denver Nuggets 137, Barcelona 103
        Jugoplastika Split 102, Philips Milan 97
/89   Philips Milan 136, Barcelona 104
        Denver Nuggets 135, Jugoplastika Split 129
ver Nuggets win tournament.

McDonald's Open—Madrid, Spain

/88   Real Madrid 108, Scavolini Pesaro 96
        Boston Celtics 113, Yugoslavian National Team 85
/88   Yugoslavian National Team 100, Scavolini Pesaro 91
        Boston Celtics 111, Real Madrid 96
on Celtics win tournament.

McDonald's Open—Milwaukee, USA

/87   Milwaukee Bucks 123, Tracer Milan 111
/87   Soviet National Team 135, Tracer Milan 108
/87   Milwaukee Bucks 127, Soviet National Team 100
aukee Bucks win tournament.

players young and old looking to grab the same share of the global spotlight Magic, Jordan and the others had garnered two years earlier.

The 1994 World Championship of Basketball demonstrated the ultimate in basketball competition, with the best players from all over the world vying for the sport's highest honor in a basketball-only event. Stern compared it to soccer's World Cup, theorizing that as basketball grew in popularity outside the United States, so, too, would the World Championship of Basketball grow to World Cup proportions.

With the Olympics, the World Championship of Basketball and the McDonald's Open, the NBA had established a schedule that would send its athletes to a high-profile global tournament each year. The league supplements those major events annually with a slew of preseason and regular-season games in other countries.

In November 1990 NBA teams played against each other outside North America for the first time in the inaugural Opening Games in Japan. The NBA had wanted to expand its fan base in Japan, and research had shown that consumers would respond best to the real thing—actual regular-season games that counted on the NBA schedule. Never before had regular-season games in any major professional league—the NBA, NFL, NHL or Major League Baseball—been staged outside of North America. The games proved a tremendous success, as the Phoenix Suns and Utah Jazz dazzled capacity crowds at the Tokyo Metropolitan Gymnasium. The teams split their two games, with Phoenix winning the opener 119–96 and Utah taking the second game 102–101. The NBA returned to Japan in 1992 and 1994.

Building on the success of the first Opening Games in Japan, the NBA stepped up its efforts to bring more of its games to foreign countries. In October 1992 the league pushed across its northern and southern borders with three preseason games in Canada and one in Mexico. The following year NBA teams played to crowds in Canada, Mexico, Puerto Rico and London, in addition to the Suns' participation in Munich.

The 1993 NBA London Games, a preseason two-day event featuring two games between the Orlando Magic and the Atlanta Hawks, marked the first time two NBA teams had played each other in Europe. The Hawks and Magic did not disappoint two sellout crowds at London's Wembley Arena. Orlando won the first game, 120–95, while the Hawks took the second 113–101. Atlanta stars Dominique Wilkins and Kevin Willis thrilled British spectators in the second game with 36 and 33 points, respectively. Shaquille O'Neal made

his mark as well, leading the Magic with 31 points and 15 rebounds. A London audience some felt would never warm up to basketball had become hooked on the NBA.

The 1994 global preseason slate expanded even further, and sellout crowds were the rule at every arena. Fans who had diligently followed the NBA through television broadcasts or occasional magazine articles delighted at the opportunity to see their larger-than-life heroes in person.

As interest in the NBA exploded in the wake of the

Dream Team and the Barcelona Olympics, so, too, did a parallel interest in the sport of basketball. Throughout FIBA's 195-country membership, basketball federations reported dramatic increases in sign-ups for local clubs and leagues immediately following the Olympics. Newly enamored basketball fans outside the United States began to realize what the NBA and FIBA had felt all along—that, because of its simplicity and style, basketball had the potential to become a truly global game.

As the source of much of this global hoops excitement, the NBA shouldered the responsibility of bringing

WORLD CHAMPIONSHIP OF BASKETBALL MEDAL WINNERS

1994 World Championship—Toronto, Canada
Gold	United States
Silver	Russia
Bronze	Croatia

1990 World Championship—Buenos Aires, Argentina
Gold	Yugoslavia
Silver	Soviet Union
Bronze	United States

1986 World Championship—Madrid, Spain
Gold	United States
Silver	Soviet Union
Bronze	Yugoslavia

1982 World Championship—Cali, Colombia
Gold	Soviet Union
Silver	United States
Bronze	Yugoslavia

1978 World Championship—Manila, Philippines
Gold	Yugoslavia
Silver	Soviet Union
Bronze	Brazil

(Note: United States finished fifth)

1974 World Championship—San Juan, Puerto Rico
Gold	Soviet Union
Silver	Yugoslavia
Bronze	United States

1970 World Championship—Ljubljana, Yugoslavia
Gold	Yugoslavia
Silver	Brazil
Bronze	Soviet Union

(Note: United States finished fifth)

1967 World Championship—Montevideo, Uruguay
Gold	Soviet Union
Silver	Yugoslavia
Bronze	Brazil

(Note: United States finished fourth)

1963 World Championship—Rio de Janeiro, Brazil
Gold	Brazil
Silver	Yugoslavia
Bronze	Soviet Union

(Note: United States finished fourth)

1959 World Championship—Santiago, Chile
Gold	Brazil
Silver	United States
Bronze	Chile

1954 World Championship—Rio de Janeiro, Brazil
Gold	United States
Silver	Brazil
Bronze	Philippines

1950 World Championship—Buenos Aires, Argentina
Gold	Argentina
Silver	United States
Bronze	Chile

SUMMARY OF FINISHES

Country	Gold	Silver	Bronze
Soviet Union	3	3	2
United States	3	3	2
Yugoslavia	3	3	2
Brazil	2	2	2
Argentina	1	0	0
Russia	0	1	0
Chile	0	0	2
Croatia	0	0	1
Philippines	0	0	1

the sport to anyone who was interested. Prior to the Olympics, the NBA had teamed with FIBA to hold clinics for coaches in other countries. From 1990 to 1992, NBA players and coaches, past and present, traveled to 15 countries teaching the intricacies of the game to local coaches.

The Olympics caused FIBA and the NBA to move in a new direction. Rather than reaching out to a handful of coaches and hoping its message would trickle down, the NBA wanted to reach children, thousands of them, to stir up interest in the sport at the grassroots level. If the league could get kids to try the sport, to like it and to want to play it, the skills and coaching would follow in step.

Armed with this new philosophy, the league launched its cornerstone grassroots program in 1993. The NBA joined with Streetball Partners, Inc., to create the Converse/3-on-3 NBA World Tour. Best described

Wembley Arena in 1993 saw the first game in Europe to be played between two NBA teams, the Atlanta Hawks and Orlando Magic.

as a street basketball festival, the tour moves from city to city, attracting participants and spectators of all ages. The first tour in 1993 visited 13 cities and attracted 30,000 players for its 3-on-3 tournaments, along with an estimated 600,000 spectators. For 1994 the tour was expanded to 24 cities, and continued growth is anticipated in the years to come.

The World Tour's carnival-like atmosphere and the excitement of the sport tend to sell themselves. At the 1993 event in Paris, a spectacular tournament staged on the Trocadero plaza drew 2,000 participants. And because of the event's location in the shadow of the Eiffel Tower, some 180,000 spectators jammed the plaza just to get a glimpse of what was going on.

Spinning off the success of the tour and its capacity to reach thousands of potential fans, the NBA also went global with NBA Jam Session, an interactive fan event that made its debut at the 1993 All-Star Weekend in Salt Lake City. With skills contests, photo opportunities, entertainment and other participatory activities, NBA

Jam Session proved successful as a stand-alone attraction or as a perfect complement to an NBA event.

Elements of Jam Session appeared at an Australian basketball festival in August 1993, accompanied by several NBA players, including Hakeem Olajuwon and Muggsy Bogues, both of whom helped promote the event. Further activities, including exhibition games, are planned for Australia in years to come.

Jam Session took to the road in 1994, as a touring version moved across Canada during the summer to stir up interest in the 1994 World Championship of Basketball and another version accompanied the Converse/3-on-3 NBA World Tour.

In each case, with every basketball fan event or every street basketball festival, the sport demonstrated its ability as a societal catalyst. People came together to play basketball, irrespective of gender, race or creed. Much as it has across the United States, basketball proved it could break down nearly any societal barrier.

The NBA has taken that message abroad as well,

The Converse/3-on-3 World Tour, seen here in Seville, Spain, has won fans around the world.

particularly in visits to underdeveloped or politically troubled nations in Africa. NBA players have become an inspiration to children across the world, and the NBA's black players have become a symbol of hope for the children of Africa. In 1991 the league established a relationship with CARE, the worldwide relief and development organization. Largely at the urging of one of its players, Manute Bol, who grew up in Sudan, an NBA delegation traveled to Africa in the summer of 1991, visiting CARE projects and filming public service announcements to air back in the United States. Bol was a hero wherever he went, a symbol of success not in basketball but in life.

Denver Nuggets center Dikembe Mutombo took over as the NBA's spokesperson for CARE in 1992, and Mutombo led summer trips to Africa in 1992 and 1993. The NBA's 1993 Africa tour stopped in Kenya, Zambia and South Africa, and the NBA mixed its goodwill mission for CARE with its desire to bring basketball to the children of Africa. Mutombo and other NBA players and coaches conducted clinics for kids and coaches wherever they went, even in the desolate

townships of South Africa. Theirs was a message of hope, and their presence was a symbol of success. The NBA remains committed to delivering this message in Africa through its support for CARE and its power to bring happiness through sport.

The immediate goal of the NBA's grassroots efforts is clear: to increase the popularity of the sport on a global level. But the more far-reaching goal is more ambitious. In some distant era, the NBA would like to see European or South American or Asian teams playing the game at its highest level, making the Olympics or the World Championship of Basketball truly competitive tournaments. Grassroots programs can accomplish that goal by starting players young, putting basketballs in their hands and letting them discover the sport much the same way American youngsters do.

Along with establishing a higher level of competition around the world, more foreign talent would heighten the level of play in the NBA. The league has already hosted its share of foreign superstars, who travel to America to play with the best in the world. Olajuwon (Nigeria), Detlef Schrempf (Germany), Petrovic (Croa-

The Phoenix Suns' popular Gorilla entertains fans down under at the NBA Jam Session in Australia.

tia), Mutombo (Zaire), Kukoc (Croatia), Radja (Croatia), Divac (Serbia) and Marciulionis (Lithuania) not only have made NBA rosters but have succeeded and starred for their respective teams. In the future, the NBA will continue to attract these players and solidify its claim as home to the best basketball in the world.

What lies ahead on the NBA's global horizon? With all its grassroots programs, international tournaments and television distribution, the NBA certainly has demonstrated its desire to reach a global audience. The league presently harbors no intentions of expanding outside of North America, however, preferring instead to help leagues across the waters flourish on their own.

As the NBA moves into the 21st century, it will continue to walk a tightrope between its destiny as a global sports entity and its foundation as a domestic basketball league. Its route may be unclear, but its goal has not wavered. Don't be surprised if sometime in the 21st century basketball takes its place atop the sporting community as the most popular sport in the world.

Things have come a long way since 1987.

South African leader Nelson Mandela graciously accepts souvenirs from NBA Commissioner David J. Stern during the 1993 Africa friendship tour.

1993–94 NBA INTERNATIONAL TELEVISION DISTRIBUTION

Country	Licensee	Country	Licensee
ABU DHABI	STAR TV	KAZAKHSTAN	RUSSIAN TV
ADEN	STAR TV	KUWAIT	KUWAIT TV/STAR TV
AFGHANISTAN	STAR TV	KYRGYZSTAN	RUSSIAN TV
ARGENTINA	CH. 11/ESPN INT'L	LAOS	STAR TV
ARMENIA	RUSSIAN TV	LATVIA	TV LATVIJAS/RUSSIAN TV
ARUBA	TELE-ARUBA	LEBANON	MIDDLE EAST TV/STAR TV/MTV
AUSTRALIA	TEN NETWORK/ESPN INT'L	LITHUANIA	BALTIC TV
AUSTRIA	SAT 1/DSF	LUXEMBOURG	TBD
AZERBAIJAN	RUSSIAN TV	MADAGASCAR	STAR TV
AZORES	AFRTS	MALAYSIA	TV3/STAR TV
BAHAMAS	ZNS-13	MOLDIVES	STAR TV
BAHRAIN	STAR TV	MARTINIQUE	ATV
BANGLADESH	STAR TV	MAURITIUS	STAR TV
BARBADOS	ESPN INTERNATIONAL	MEXICO	CHANNEL 13/ESPN INT'L
BELGIUM	CANAL +/FILMNET	MOLDOVA	RUSSIAN TV
BERMUDA	ESPN INTERNATIONAL	MONACO	TELEMONTECARLO
BHUTAN	STAR TV	MONGOLIA	STAR TV
BOLIVIA	ESPN INTERNATIONAL	MOROCCO	2M
BOPHUTHATSWANA	BOP TV	NEPAL	STAR TV
BRAZIL	BANDEIRANTES/ESPN INT'L	NETHERLANDS	NOS/FILMNET
BRUNEI	STAR TV	NEW ZEALAND	TV3/SKY NETWORK/STAR TV/ESPN INT'L
BULGARIA	BTV	NICARAGUA	CH. 12/ESPN INTERNATIONAL
BURKINA FASO	TVB	NIGERIA	NTV
BURMA	STAR TV	NORTH KOREA	STAR TV
BYELORUSSIA	RUSSIAN TV	NORWAY	TVNORGE
CAMBODIA	STAR TV	OMAN	STAR TV
CANADA	TSN/RDS	PAKISTAN	STAR TV
CAPE VERDE	CVB	PANAMA	CHANNEL 2/CANAL 90/ESPN INT'L
CHILE	CH. 11/ESPN INT'L	PAPUA NEW GUINEA	ESPN INTERNATIONAL
CHINA	CCTV/STAR TV	PARAGUAY	ESPN INTERNATIONAL
COLOMBIA	TV INGENIOS/ESPN INT'L	PERU	CANAL 7/ESPN INTERNATIONAL
COSTA RICA	CH 2 & 29/ESPN INT'L	PHILIPPINES	RBS/STAR TV
CRETE	AFRTS	POLAND	CHANNEL 2
CROATIA	TV HRVATSKA	PORTUGAL	RTP
CUBA	AFRTS/ESPN INT'L	PUERTO RICO	WLII/TNT
CURAÇAO	ESPN INTERNATIONAL	QATAR	STAR TV/QATAR TV
CYPRUS	LUMIÈRE TV	REPUBLIC OF PALAU	ESPN INTERNATIONAL
CZECH REPUBLIC	CST	ROMANIA	RTI
DENMARK	DANRAD	RUSSIA	RUSSIAN TV
DOMINICA	ESPN INTERNATIONAL	SAINT KITTS	ESPN INTERNATIONAL
DOMINICAN REPUBLIC	RTVD/ESPN INT'L	SAINT LUCIA	HTS/ESPN INT'L
DUBAI	STAR TV	SAINT MARTIN	ESPN INTERNATIONAL
ECUADOR	CH. 11/ESPN INT'L	SÃO TOMÉ	STB
EGYPT	STAR TV	SAUDI ARABIA	ARAMCO/SAUDI TV/STAR TV
EL SALVADOR	CANAL DOS	SENEGAL	CANAL HORIZON
ESTONIA	RUSSIAN TV	SINGAPORE	SBC/STAR TV
FINLAND	TV1	SLOVAKIA	SLOVAK TV
FRANCE	CANAL +/TV SPORT	SLOVENIJA	TV SLOVENIJA
FRENCH GUIANA	ESPN INTERNATIONAL	SOUTH AFRICA	SABC/TSS
GABON	CANAL HORIZON	SOUTH KOREA	SBS/AFRTS/ESPN INT'L/STAR TV
GERMANY	SAT 1/DSF	SPAIN	TVE 2/TV 3
GREECE	MEGA CHANNEL	SRI LANKA	STAR TV
GREENLAND	AFRTS	SWEDEN	TV3
GUAM	ESPN INTERNATIONAL	SWITZERLAND	SAT 1/DSF
GUATEMALA	ESPN INTERNATIONAL	SYRIA	STAR TV
GUINEA-BISSAU	GBB	TADZHIKISTAN	RUSSIAN TV
HONDURAS	CANAL5/ESPN INT'L	TAIWAN	TAIWAN TV/STAR TV
HONG KONG	STAR TV/ESPN INT'L	THAILAND	IBC/CH 7/STAR TV/ESPN INT'L
HUNGARY	MTV	TORTOLA	ESPN INTERNATIONAL
ICELAND	CHANNEL 2	TRINIDAD	T&T TV
INDIA	STAR TV	TUNISIA	CANAL HORIZON
INDONESIA	RCTI/SCTV/STAR TV/ESPN INT'L	TURKEY	TRT/STAR TV
IRAN	STAR TV	TURKMENISTAN	RUSSIAN TV
IRAQ	STAR TV	UKRAINE	ICTV
IRELAND	RTE	UNITED ARAB EMIRATES	UAE TV/STAR TV
ISRAEL	ICP/2ND CH/STAR TV	UNITED KINGDOM	ITV
ITALY	TELEMONTECARLO	UNITED STATES	NBC/TNT
IVORY COAST	CANAL HORIZON/RTI	URUGUAY	CANAL 4
JAMAICA	CVM	UZBEKISTAN	RUSSIAN TV
JAPAN	NHK-DBS/JSC/STAR TV	VENEZUELA	VENEVISION/TELEVEN/ESPN INT'L
JORDAN	STAR TV/JORDAN TV	YEMEN	STAR TV

THE NBA ALL-STAR WEEKEND

The NBA All-Star Weekend celebration, which annually attracts fans, VIPs and media from around the world, evolved from a meeting that took place in the fall of 1950 on the 80th floor of the Empire State Building in New York, which at the time housed the league's small headquarters office.

Professional basketball was still in its formative stages and had not yet caught the fancy of American sports fans in the way that baseball and football had. Entering its fifth season, the NBA was looking for a shot in the arm, a vehicle to bring it into the public spotlight. NBA President (the title was changed in 1967 to Commissioner) Maurice Podoloff, NBA Public Relations Director Haskell Cohen and Boston Celtics President Walter Brown wanted something that would earn the league national exposure and recognition, both with fans and the media.

"The league wasn't doing very well back in 1951," recalled Podoloff. "The game had fallen into the doldrums. It had become sluggish. Something needed to be done to rescue us from this situation."

Cohen remembered Brown addressing Podoloff and saying, "We've got to come up with an idea or two that's going to bring our game before the public eye. We've got to do it quickly, and it's got to be something a little different from our regular type of operation."

Both looked to Cohen, whose idea was to emulate the success that baseball had enjoyed for years by establishing an NBA All-Star Game.

"I believed that if we had a break in the middle of the season and had an All-Star team selected from the Eastern Division and one from the Western Division to play against each other in an NBA All-Star Game, it would be a good idea and something radically different for us," Cohen said.

Brown and Podoloff backed the idea, and Brown donated his building, Boston Garden, free of charge to the NBA in order to ensure that the game would be

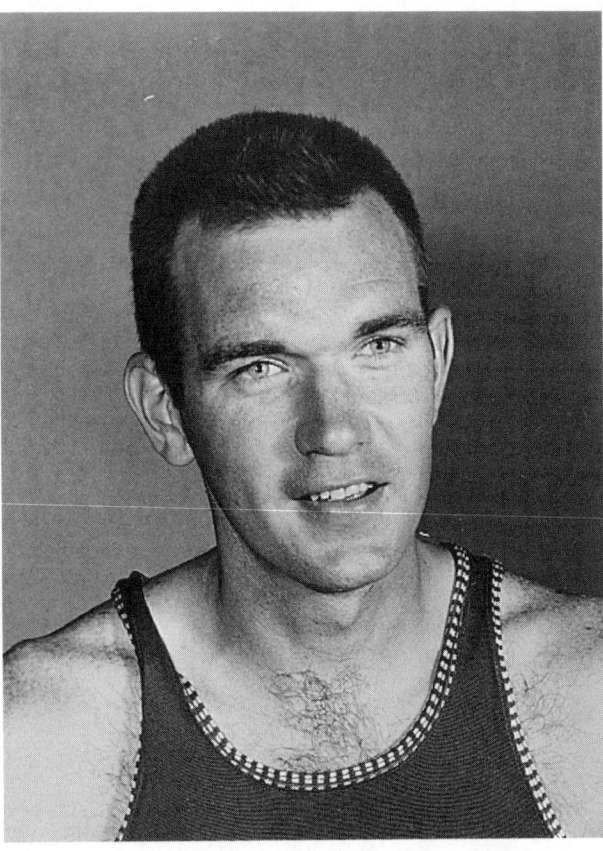

Ed Macauley of the host Boston Celtics scored 20 points to earn MVP honors in the first NBA All-Star Game.

played. So even though some other NBA owners remained skeptical, the inaugural NBA All-Star Game was planned for March 2, 1951, in Boston. The break-even attendance for the game was set at 10,000, considerably higher than most NBA clubs were drawing at the time.

Near the end of the first half of that first NBA All-Star Game, Podoloff's spirits were sky-high when he was told that 10,094 hoop fans in Beantown had passed through the turnstiles to watch East meet West.

Ed Macauley of the hometown Celtics scored a game-high 20 points and Joe Fulks of the Philadelphia Warriors added 19 to lead the East to a 111–94 win over the West, as the players put on an offensive showcase for the fans.

"It was a very electric feeling," recalled Dolph Schayes of the Syracuse Nationals, who scored 15 points for the East, "probably because it was the first All-Star Game. We East players were in our element. We were schoolyard players and didn't have to worry about plays in this game. It was like we were kids again, playing the city game. We ran them silly."

From those humble beginnings in 1951, the NBA All-Star Game has been transformed over more than four decades into the gala spectacle of the NBA All-Star Weekend, a four-day hoop-fest that has become a major event on the global sports calendar.

The NBA All-Star Game, while still the crown jewel

of All-Star Weekend, now shares the bill with three other major events—NBA Jam Session Presented by Fleer, the NBA All-Star Stay in School CELEBRATION and NBA All-Star Saturday. All play a part in giving the weekend a varied and distinct basketball flavor. And each event has created lasting memories of its own apart from the All-Star Game.

NBA All-Star Saturday, which began in 1984 in Denver when the league staged its first dunking contest, has grown into a sold-out, three-pronged event the night before the All-Star Game. Featured events are the Schick Rookie Game showcasing first-year NBA players and initially introduced in Minneapolis in 1994 (replacing the Schick Legends Classic, a contest played between two teams of retired NBA stars from 1984 to 1993); the Gatorade Slam-Dunk Championship, where high-flying NBA stars add their own personal touches to gravity-defying dunks; and the AT&T Long Distance Shootout, where sharpshooters from around the league compete against the clock and each other, to the delight of the cheering crowds.

A few memorable moments from the first decade of the Gatorade Slam-Dunk Championship include Larry Nance executing a windmill dunk with two balls to defeat Julius Erving and Dominique Wilkins in 1984's inaugural at McNichols Arena in Denver; the 5-7 Spud Webb flying above the rest of the field to capture the

Chris Webber controls a jump ball during the first Schick Rookie Game during the 1994 NBA All-Star Weekend.

contest at Reunion Arena in 1986 in his hometown of Dallas; the spectacular Michael Jordan winning the 1987 event in Seattle by following the amazing flight path of free-throw line to basket without touching the ground before slamming the ball home; and Cedric Ceballos, reaching into his bag of tricks for a "Hocus-Pocus" blindfolded dunk in Orlando in 1992.

The three-point contest has also entertained some grand performances, including Larry Bird winning his third straight shootout in 1988 at Chicago Stadium, narrowly defeating Dale Ellis and walking off the court with his finger extended in the No. 1 sign as his final shot ripped through the net, and Craig Hodges, en route to the second of his three shootout titles, holding 23,530 fans breathless while connecting on 19 straight treys in Charlotte in 1991.

The Stay in School CELEBRATION is the culmination of the NBA's yearlong Stay in School program,

Larry Nance soars to win the inaugural Gatorade Slam-Dunk Championship in Denver in 1984.

which emphasizes the importance of education to middle school students by stressing the "three A's" of attitude, attendance and achievement. Each year students in the All-Star city are rewarded for their efforts by getting the chance to be a part of the NBA All-Star Weekend by attending the nationally televised CELEBRATION, where they are entertained by NBA All-Stars and top-rated musical and television performers. Started in 1990 in Miami, the Stay in School program has had a positive effect in boosting attendance and achievement among middle school students, especially in cities hosting the All-Star Weekend.

The NBA Jam Session Presented by Fleer was unveiled at the 1993 All-Star Weekend in Salt Lake City and was a smashing success, as it was the following year at the Metrodome in Minneapolis. The four-day interactive basketball festival for fans includes interactive exhibits, slam-dunk and three-point contests, a 3-on-3

This "peek-a-boo" dunk by Dee Brown helped him win the 1991 Gatorade Slam-Dunk Championship in Charlotte.

tournament, an autograph session with NBA legends as well as current stars, officially licensed merchandise and much, much more, making it a hoop fan's dream come true.

The centerpiece of the weekend, however, remains the All-Star Game, where many of the greatest athletes in the world exhibit their multifaceted playing skills to the highest degree. The 1993 telecast on NBC from Utah drew a record 40 million viewers in the United States, millions more watched around the world, and the game was televised live to 55 countries in 23 languages. In total, 118 countries received the All-Star Game broadcast in 1993.

Julius Erving, who played in 11 NBA All-Star Games with the East team and was named MVP in 1977 and 1983, tells of his All-Star experiences.

"To be voted onto the All-Star team by the fans means they respect you, your abilities, your craft," Dr. J said. "You can exhibit your skills the way you know the majority of basketball fans want to see them. It's the one day you can cater completely to the fans who have made the game what it is. You perform simply for the love of the game of basketball."

Adrian Dantley, a six-time member of the West All-Star team, recalls what it was like growing up watching the games on TV.

"I'm pretty sure every kid has sat in front of a TV set and watched the All-Star Game and thought about

Even wearing a warm-up jacket, Larry Bird demonstrates uncanny accuracy from three-point range.

Craig Hodges hoists his third AT&T Long Distance Shootout trophy in 1992.

what it would be like to be there, in person, out on the court playing on television in a game that the whole country would be watching," he said. "That was me as a kid. That's what I used to do. I'd watch the All-Star Game and think what a great thrill it would be to actually be out there playing, on the court with the greatest players in the nation.

"When it finally did happen for me, it was in my hometown of Washington. It was certainly one of the greatest thrills of my entire life. Not many men have the chance to actually live out their greatest boyhood dream, but it happened to me."

Here are some highlights from the NBA All-Star series:

- The East topped the West 98–93 in overtime at Madison Square Garden in 1954, the first All-Star contest to go to an extra session. Bob Cousy scored 10 of the East's 14 overtime points.
- Rookie Wilt Chamberlain made his All-Star debut in front of the home fans at Philadelphia's Convention Hall in 1960, leading the East to a 125–115 victory after contributing 23 points and 25 rebounds.
- The West nipped the East 112–110 at the LA Forum in 1972, following a 20-foot jumper at the buzzer by Jerry West.
- Larry Bird drained the first three-point field goal in All-Star history with 1:40 left in overtime, and the East went on to defeat the West 144–136 in 1980 in Landover, Md.

Karl Malone kids around with Kid 'N Play during the 1993 All-Star Stay in School CELEBRATION.

Magic Johnson came out of retirement and put on quite a show at the 1992 All-Star Game in Orlando.

- In the highest-scoring All-Star Game ever, the East outgunned the West 154–145 in overtime at Denver's McNichols Arena in 1984. Julius Erving hit for a game-high 34 points for the East, but teammate Isiah Thomas copped MVP honors with 21 points and 15 assists.
- Michael Jordan thrilled the hometown fans at Chicago Stadium by scoring a game-high 40 points (the second-highest total in All-Star history, trailing only Wilt

Chamberlain's 42 points in 1962), leading the East to a 138–133 triumph in the 1988 matchup.
- Before an All-Star Game record crowd of 44,735 at Houston's Astrodome in 1989, MVP Karl Malone scored 28 points to lead the West, which scored a record 87 points in the first half, to a 143–134 victory.
- Magic Johnson made a triumphant one-game return from retirement in the 1992 All-Star Game in Orlando, leading the West to a 153–113 rout by scoring

RESULTS OF NBA ALL-STAR GAMES

Year	Result and Location	Most Valuable Player	Attendance
1951	East 111, West 94 at Boston	Ed Macauley, Boston	10,094
1952	East 108, West 91 at Boston	Paul Arizin, Philadelphia	10,211
1953	West 79, East 75 at Fort Wayne	George Mikan, Minneapolis	10,322
1954	East 98, West 93 (OT) at New York	Bob Cousy, Boston	16,487
1955	East 100, West 91 at New York	Bill Sharman, Boston	15,564
1956	West 108, East 94 at Rochester	Bob Pettit, St. Louis	8,517
1957	East 109, West 97 at Boston	Bob Cousy, Boston	11,178
1958	East 130, West 118 at St. Louis	Bob Pettit, St. Louis	12,854
1959	West 124, East 108 at Detroit	Elgin Baylor, Mn., & Bob Pettit, St. L.	10,541
1960	East 125, West 115 at Philadelphia	Wilt Chamberlain, Phil.	10,421
1961	West 153, East 131 at Syracuse	Oscar Robertson, Cincinnati	8,016
1962	West 150, East 130 at St. Louis	Bob Pettit, St. Louis	15,112
1963	East 115, West 108 at Los Angeles	Bill Russell, Boston	14,838
1964	East 111, West 107 at Boston	Oscar Robertson, Cincinnati	13,464
1965	East 124, West 123 at St. Louis	Jerry Lucas, Cincinnati	16,713
1966	East 137, West 94 at Cincinnati	Adrian Smith, Cincinnati	13,653
1967	West 135, East 120 at San Francisco	Rick Barry, San Francisco	13,972
1968	East 144, West 124 at New York	Hal Greer, Philadelphia	18,422
1969	East 123, West 112 at Baltimore	Oscar Robertson, Cincinnati	12,348
1970	East 142, West 135 at Philadelphia	Willis Reed, New York	15,244
1971	West 108, East 107 at San Diego	Lenny Wilkens, Seattle	14,378
1972	West 112, East 110 at Los Angeles	Jerry West, Los Angeles	17,214
1973	East 104, West 84 at Chicago	Dave Cowens, Boston	17,527
1974	West 134, East 123 at Seattle	Bob Lanier, Detroit	14,360
1975	East 108, West 102 at Phoenix	Walt Frazier, New York	12,885
1976	East 123, West 109 at Philadelphia	Dave Bing, Washington	17,511
1977	West 125, East 124 at Milwaukee	Julius Erving, Philadelphia	10,938
1978	East 133, West 125 at Atlanta	Randy Smith, Buffalo	15,491
1979	West 134, East 129 at Detroit	David Thompson, Denver	31,745
1980	East 144, West 136 (OT) at Landover	George Gervin, San Antonio	19,035
1981	East 123, West 120 at Cleveland	Nate Archibald, Boston	20,239
1982	East 120, West 118 at E. Rutherford	Larry Bird, Boston	20,149
1983	East 132, West 123 at Los Angeles	Julius Erving, Philadelphia	17,505
1984	East 154, West 145 (OT) at Denver	Isiah Thomas, Detroit	17,500
1985	West 140, East 129 at Indianapolis	Ralph Sampson, Houston	43,146
1986	East 139, West 132 at Dallas	Isiah Thomas, Detroit	16,573
1987	West 154, East 149 (OT) at Seattle	Tom Chambers, Seattle	34,275
1988	East 138, West 133 at Chicago	Michael Jordan, Chicago	18,403
1989	West 143, East 134 at Houston	Karl Malone, Utah	44,735
1990	East 130, West 113 at Miami	Magic Johnson, LA Lakers	14,810
1991	East 116, West 114 at Charlotte	Charles Barkley, Philadelphia	23,530
1992	West 153, East 113 at Orlando	Magic Johnson, LA Lakers	14,272
1993	West 135, East 132 (OT) at Salt Lake City	Karl Malone, Utah, & John Stockton, Utah	19,459
1994	East 127, West 118 at Minneapolis	Scottie Pippen, Chicago	17,096

The Admiral, David Robinson (50), steers his way to a rebound during the 1990 All-Star Game in Miami.

a game-high 25 points and dishing off for a game-high nine assists. For his efforts, Johnson was named MVP.

• John Stockton and Karl Malone of the Utah Jazz became the first players from the same NBA team to share the All-Star Game MVP Award after leading the West to a 135–132 overtime triumph at the Delta Center in Salt Lake City in 1993. Malone had 28 points and 10 rebounds, and Stockton chipped in with nine points and 15 assists.

Perhaps Dikembe Mutombo of the Denver Nuggets summed up the All-Star experience for NBA players best when he was asked to describe his appearance in the 1992 game in Orlando.

"Playing with the other All-Stars on the West team is something I will remember for the rest of my life," he said. "I can tell my kids that I played with some of the legends."

Not even an afternoon blizzard could keep fans from lining up to attend the inaugural NBA Jam Session Presented by Fleer at Salt Lake City in 1993.

NBA ALL-STAR SATURDAY RESULTS

AT&T LONG DISTANCE SHOOTOUT

1986—Larry Bird, Boston
1987—Larry Bird, Boston
1988—Larry Bird, Boston
1989—Dale Ellis, Seattle
1990—Craig Hodges, Chicago
1991—Craig Hodges, Chicago
1992—Craig Hodges, Chicago
1993—Mark Price, Cleveland
1994—Mark Price, Cleveland

GATORADE SLAM-DUNK CHAMPIONSHIP

1984—Larry Nance, Phoenix
1985—Dominique Wilkins, Atlanta
1986—Spud Webb, Atlanta
1987—Michael Jordan, Chicago
1988—Michael Jordan, Chicago
1989—Kenny Walker, New York
1990—Dominique Wilkins, Atlanta
1991—Dee Brown, Boston
1992—Cedric Ceballos, Phoenix
1993—Harold Miner, Miami
1994—Isaiah Rider, Minnesota

SCHICK ROOKIE GAME

1994—Phenoms 74, Sensations 68

SCHICK LEGENDS CLASSIC

1984—West 64, East 63
1985—East 63, West 53
1986—West 53, East 44
1987—West 54, East 43
1988—East 47, West 45 (OT)
1989—West 54, East 53
1990—East 37, West 36
1991—East 41, West 34
1992—West 46, East 38
1993—East 58, West 45

ALL-STAR GAME RECORDS

INDIVIDUALS

CAREER

Most games played
18—Kareem Abdul-Jabbar
13—Wilt Chamberlain
    Bob Cousy
    John Havlicek
12—Elvin Hayes
    Oscar Robertson
    Bill Russell
    Jerry West

Most minutes played
449—Kareem Abdul-Jabbar
388—Wilt Chamberlain
380—Oscar Robertson

Highest scoring average (minimum: 60 points)
22.1—Michael Jordan (177/8)
20.5—Oscar Robertson (246/12)
20.4—Bob Pettit (224/11)

Most field goals made
105—Kareem Abdul-Jabbar
88—Oscar Robertson
85—Julius Erving

Most field goal attempts
213—Kareem Abdul-Jabbar
193—Bob Pettit
178—Julius Erving

Highest field goal percentage (minimum: 15 field goals made)
.714—Larry Nance (15/21)
    Randy Smith (15/21)
.673—David Thompson (33/49)

Most free throws made
78—Elgin Baylor
70—Oscar Robertson
62—Bob Pettit

Most free throw attempts
98—Elgin Baylor
    Oscar Robertson
94—Wilt Chamberlain

Highest free throw percentage (minimum: 10 free throws made)
1.000—Archie Clark (11/11)
      Clyde Drexler (12/12)
.938—Larry Foust (15/16)

Most three-point field goals made
10—Magic Johnson
9—Mark Price
6—Isiah Thomas

Most three-point field goal attempts
21—Magic Johnson
19—Mark Price
15—Isiah Thomas

Most rebounds
197—Wilt Chamberlain
178—Bob Pettit
149—Kareem Abdul-Jabbar

CAREER

Most assists
127—Magic Johnson
97—Isiah Thomas
86—Bob Cousy

Most steals
31—Isiah Thomas
27—Michael Jordan
23—Larry Bird

Most blocked shots
31—Kareem Abdul-Jabbar
20—Hakeem Olajuwon
15—Patrick Ewing

Most personal fouls
57—Kareem Abdul-Jabbar
41—Oscar Robertson
37—Elvin Hayes
    Bill Russell

SINGLE GAME

Most minutes played
42—Oscar Robertson, 1964
    Bill Russell, 1964
    Jerry West, 1964
    Nate Thurmond, 1967

Most points scored
42—Wilt Chamberlain, 1962

Most field goals made
17—Wilt Chamberlain, 1962
    Michael Jordan, 1988

Most field goal attempts
27—Rick Barry, 1967

Most free throws made
12—Elgin Baylor, 1962
    Oscar Robertson, 1965

Most free throw attempts
16—Wilt Chamberlain, 1962

Most three-point field goals made
6—Mark Price, 1993 (ot)
5—Scottie Pippen, 1994

Most three-point field goal attempts
9—Mark Price, 1993 (ot)
    Scottie Pippen, 1994

Most rebounds
27—Bob Pettit, 1962

Most offensive rebounds
9—Dan Roundfield, 1980 (ot)
    Hakeem Olajuwon, 1990

Most defensive rebounds
14—Charles Barkley, 1991

Most assists
22—Magic Johnson, 1984 (ot)
19—Magic Johnson, 1988

Most steals
8—Rick Barry, 1975

SINGLE GAME

Most blocked shots
6—Kareem Abdul-Jabbar, 1980 (ot)
5—Patrick Ewing, 1990
    Hakeem Olajuwon, 1994

Most personal fouls
6—Bob Wanzer, 1954
    Paul Arizin, 1956
    Bob Cousy, 1956 and 1961
    Dolph Schayes, 1959
    Walt Bellamy, 1962
    Richie Guerin, 1962
    Bill Russell, 1965
    John Green, 1965
    Rick Barry, 1966 and 1978
    Kareem Abdul-Jabbar, 1970
    Willis Reed, 1970
    Hakeem Olajuwon, 1987

ONE HALF

Most points
23—Wilt Chamberlain, 1962
    Tom Chambers, 1987

Most field goals made
10—Wilt Chamberlain, 1962

Most field goal attempts
16—Dominique Wilkins, 1988

Most free throws made
10—Zelmo Beaty, 1966

Most free throw attempts
12—Zelmo Beaty, 1966

Most rebounds
16—Wilt Chamberlain, 1960
    Bob Pettit, 1962

Most assists
13—Magic Johnson, 1984

Most personal fouls
5—Randy Smith, 1978

ONE QUARTER

Most points
19—Hal Greer, 1968

Most field goals made
8—Dave DeBusschere, 1967

Most field goal attempts
12—Bill Sharman, 1960

Most free throws made
9—Zelmo Beaty, 1966
    Julius Erving, 1978

Most free throw attempts
11—Julius Erving, 1978

Most rebounds
10—Bob Pettit, 1962

Most assists
9—John Stockton, 1989

ONE QUARTER

Most personal fouls
4—Vern Mikkelsen, 1955
    Cliff Hagan, 1959
    Bob McAdoo, 1976
    Randy Smith, 1978
    David Robinson, 1991

ONE CLUB, FULL GAME

Most points
154—East, 1984 (ot)
      West, 1987 (ot)
153—West, 1961
      West, 1992

Most field goals made
64—West, 1992

Most field goal attempts
135—East, 1960

Most free throws made
40—East, 1959

Most free throw attempts
57—West, 1970

Most three-point field goals made
11—West, 1992

Most three-point field goal attempts
24—East, 1994

Most rebounds
83—East, 1965
79—West, 1955
    West, 1959
    West, 1961

Most offensive rebounds
33—East, 1985

Most defensive rebounds
44—East, 1982
    West, 1993 (ot)

Most assists
46—West, 1984 (ot)
45—West, 1986

Most steals
24—East, 1989

Most blocked shots
16—West, 1980 (ot)
12—West, 1994

Most personal fouls
36—East, 1965

Most disqualifications
2—East, 1956
    East, 1965
    East, 1970

ONE CLUB, ONE HALF

Most points
87—West, 1989

ALL-STAR GAME RECORDS

ONE CLUB, ONE HALF

Most field goals made
36—West, 1989

Most field goal attempts
73—East, 1960

Most free throws made
26—East, 1959

Most free throw attempts
31—East, 1959

Most rebounds
51—East, 1966

Most assists
28—West, 1984

Most personal fouls
18—West, 1954
    East, 1962
    East, 1970
    West, 1986
    East, 1987

Most disqualifications
2—East, 1956
    East, 1970

ONE CLUB, ONE QUARTER

Most points
50—West, 1970

Most field goals made
19—West, 1962
    West, 1979
    East, 1983
    West, 1989

Most field goal attempts
38—East, 1960

Most free throws made
19—East, 1986

Most free throw attempts
25—West, 1970

Most rebounds
29—West, 1962
    East, 1962

Most assists
15—West, 1977
    West, 1984

Most personal fouls
13—East, 1970

Most disqualifications
2—East, 1956
    East, 1970

BOTH CLUBS, FULL GAME

Most points
303—(West 154, East 149), 1987 (ot)
299—(East 154, West 145), 1984 (ot)
284—(West 153, East 131), 1961

Most field goals made
126—(East 63, West 63), 1984 (ot)
115—(West 61, East 54), 1988
    (West 64, East 51), 1991

Most field goal attempts
256—(East 135, West 121), 1960

Most free throws made
71—(West 39, East 32), 1987 (ot)
70—(West 37, East 33), 1961

Most free throw attempts
94—(West 47, East 47), 1961
    (West 52, East 42), 1993 (ot)

Most three-point field goals made
16—(East 9, West 7), 1993 (ot)
13—(West 11, East 2), 1992

Most three-point field goal attempts
41—(East 22, West 19), 1993 (ot)
33—(West 20, East 13), 1992

Most rebounds
175—(West 95, East 80), 1962

Most offensive rebounds
55—(East 31, West 24), 1980 (ot)
51—(West 28, East 23), 1987 (ot)
45—(West 24, East 21), 1994

Most defensive rebounds
81—(East 44, West 37), 1982

Most assists
85—(West 46, East 39), 1984 (ot)
77—(West 45, East 32), 1986

Most steals
40—(East 24, West 16), 1989

Most blocked shots
25—(West 16, East 9), 1980 (ot)
21—(West 12, East 9), 1994

Most personal fouls
64—(East 36, West 28), 1965

Most disqualifications
2—(East 2, West 0), 1956
    (East 1, West 1), 1962
    (East 2, West 0), 1970

BOTH CLUBS, ONE HALF

Most points
157—(West 79, East 78), 1988

Most field goals made
65—(West 35, East 30), 1962

Most field goal attempts
135—(East 73, West 62), 1960

Most free throws made
36—(West 20, East 16), 1961

Most free throw attempts
57—(West 29, East 28), 1962

Most rebounds
98—(East 50, West 48), 1962
    (East 51, West 47), 1966

Most assists
45—(West 28, East 17), 1984

Most personal fouls
37—(West 22, East 15), 1980

Most disqualifications
2—(East 2, West 0), 1956
    (East 1, West 1), 1962
    (East 2, West 0), 1970

BOTH CLUBS, ONE QUARTER

Most points
86—(West 50, East 36), 1970

Most field goals made
36—(West 19, East 17), 1962

Most field goal attempts
71—(East 37, West 34), 1962

Most free throws made
27—(East 19, West 8), 1986

Most free throw attempts
33—(East 20, West 13), 1962
    (West 21, East 12), 1993

Most rebounds
58—(West 30, East 28), 1966

Most assists
25—(West 15, East 10), 1984

Most personal fouls
20—(East 11, West 9), 1985
    (East 12, West 8), 1987

Most disqualifications
2—(East 2, West 0), 1956
    (East 1, West 1), 1962
    (East 2, West 0), 1970

Game 1: March 2, 1951—East 111, West 94 at Boston—Boston's "Easy" Ed Macauley scored a game-high 20 points and held George Mikan of Minneapolis to just four field goals in the first NBA All-Star Game.

Game 2: February 11, 1952—East 108, West 91 at Boston—Paul Arizin of Philadelphia shot 9-for-13 for 26 points, and the East pulled away with a 16–3 spurt in the fourth quarter.

Game 3: January 13, 1953—West 79, East 75 at Fort Wayne, Ind.—Rochester guard Bob Davies helped the West to its first All-Star victory with eight fourth-quarter points.

Game 4: January 21, 1954—East 98, West 93, OT, at New York—Before a sellout crowd at Madison Square Garden, Boston's Bob Cousy scored 10 of the East's 14 overtime points.

Game 5: January 18, 1955—East 100, West 91 at New York—Boston's Bill Sharman scored 10 of his 15 points in the fourth quarter, and Celtics teammate Bob Cousy had 20 points for the East.

Game 6: January 24, 1956—West 108, East 94 at Rochester, N.Y.—Bob Pettit of the St. Louis Hawks, in only his second pro season, chalked up a game-high 20 points and 24 rebounds to pace the West.

Game 7: January 15, 1957—East 109, West 97 at Boston—Boston's Bob Cousy controlled the game with his playmaking, and Celtics teammate Bill Sharman ended the first half with a 70-foot basket in the East's victory.

Game 8: January 21, 1958—East 130, West 118 at St. Louis—Philadelphia's Paul Arizin had 24 points for the East, but Bob Pettit of St. Louis became the first losing team member to gain MVP honors with 28 points and 26 rebounds.

Game 9: January 23, 1959—West 124, East 108 at Detroit—St. Louis veteran Bob Pettit and Minneapolis rookie Elgin Baylor became the first co-MVPs in the West's third All-Star triumph.

Game 10: January 22, 1960—East 125, West 115 at Philadelphia—Philadelphia's Wilt Chamberlain celebrated his rookie season by taking MVP honors with 23 points and 25 rebounds for the East.

Game 11: January 17, 1961—West 153, East 131 at Syracuse, N.Y.—Rookie Oscar Robertson of Cincinnati upstaged the veterans with 23 points and 14 assists in the West's high-scoring victory.

Game 12: January 16, 1962—West 150, East 130 at St. Louis—Four West players scored 23 points or more to offset an All-Star record 42-point outburst by Philadelphia's Wilt Chamberlain.

Game 13: January 16, 1963—East 115, West 108 at Los Angeles—Boston's Bill Russell outscored San Francisco's Wilt Chamberlain 19–17 and outrebounded him 24–19 in their first All-Star confrontation.

Game 14: January 14, 1964—East 111, West 107 at Boston—Cincinnati's Oscar Robertson gained MVP honors for the second time in four years in a game that was threatened by a possible players' strike until close to game time.

Game 15: January 13, 1965—East 124, West 123 at St. Louis—Jerry Lucas of Cincinnati gained MVP honors in a game overshadowed by the trade of superstar Wilt Chamberlain from San Francisco to Philadelphia.

Game 16: January 11, 1966—East 137, West 94 at Cincinnati—A late addition to the East team, Adrian Smith of the host Royals scored 24 points and was selected MVP.

Game 17: January 10, 1967—West 135, East 120 at San Francisco—The West ended four years of frustration as San Francisco's Rick Barry scored 38 points in 34 minutes.

Game 18: January 23, 1968—East 144, West 124 at New York—Philadelphia's Hal Greer shot 8-for-8 from the field and scored 21 points in only 17 minutes for the East.

Game 19: January 14, 1969—East 123, West 112 at Baltimore—Cincinnati's Oscar Robertson walked off with his third MVP trophy by scoring 24 points for the East.

Game 20: January 20, 1970—East 142, West 135 at Philadelphia—New York's Willis Reed and Cincinnati's Oscar Robertson scored 21 points apiece as the East won the 20th NBA All-Star Game.

Game 21: January 12, 1971—West 108, East 107 at San Diego—Milwaukee's Kareem Abdul-Jabbar (then known as Lew Alcindor) scored on a five-foot jumper and converted a free throw with 48 seconds left for the West.

Game 22: January 18, 1972—West 112, East 110 at Inglewood, Cal.—Laker Jerry West thrilled the hometown Forum fans by scoring the winning basket on a 20-foot jumper at the buzzer.

Game 23: January 23, 1973—East 104, West 84 at Chicago—Boston's Dave Cowens had 15 points and 13 rebounds as the East held the West to the fewest points since the advent of the shot clock.

Game 24: January 15, 1974—West 134, East 123 at Seattle—Detroit's Bob Lanier and Seattle's Spencer Haywood combined for 47 points, Lanier getting half his 24 in the fourth quarter for the West.

Game 25: January 14, 1975—East 108, West 102 at Phoenix—New York's Walt Frazier led all scorers with 30 points and dribbled off with the MVP Award for the East.

Game 26: February 3, 1976—East 123, West 109 at Philadelphia—Former Piston Dave Bing, now playing for the Washington Bullets near the end of his career, had 16 points and four assists and was voted MVP.

Game 27: February 13, 1977—West 125, East 124 at Milwaukee—Paul Westphal of Phoenix had two baskets and a steal in the closing minutes to clinch the West's victory, although Julius Erving of the East was voted MVP.

Game 28: February 5, 1978—East 133, West 125 at Atlanta—Buffalo's Randy Smith scored 27 points and shot 11-for-14 from the field, connecting on 30- and 40-foot jumpers at the buzzers ending the first and second quarters.

Game 29: February 4, 1979—West 134, East 129 at Pontiac, Mich.—Denver's David Thompson scored 25 points as the West jumped to an 80–58 halftime lead and held on to win before 31,745 at the Silverdome.

Game 30: February 4, 1980—East 144, West 136, OT, at Landover, Md.—George Gervin of San Antonio scored 34 points and Boston rookie Larry Bird scored the first All-Star three-pointer to put the East ahead to stay in overtime.

Game 31: February 1, 1981—East 123, West 120 at Richfield, Oh.—Boston's 6-1 Nate "Tiny" Archibald had nine points, nine assists and controlled play with his ballhandling down the stretch to gain MVP honors.

Game 32: January 31, 1982—East 120, West 118 at East Rutherford, N.J.—Boston's Larry Bird scored 12 of his team's last 15 points in the final 6½ minutes as the East edged the West.

Game 33: February 13, 1983—East 132, West 123 at Inglewood, Cal.—Julius Erving's dazzling dunks and drives led to a game-high 25 points for the Philadelphia forward in the East's victory.

Game 34: January 29, 1984—East 154, West 145, OT, at Denver—Detroit's Isiah Thomas scored all 21 of his points after halftime and Philadelphia's Julius Erving poured in a game-high 34 to offset Magic Johnson's record 22 assists.

Game 35: February 10, 1985—West 140, East 129 at Indianapolis—Before 43,146 at the Hoosier Dome, the West broke a five-game losing streak as 7-4 Ralph Sampson of Houston scored 24 points and grabbed 10 rebounds.

Game 36: February 9, 1986—East 139, West 132 at Dallas—Detroit's Isiah Thomas, used in a one-guard offense late in the game, finished with 30 points and 10 assists and won his second MVP Award in three years.

Game 37: February 8, 1987—West 154, East 149, OT, at Seattle—Late replacement Tom Chambers of Seattle tallied 34 points and Dallas' Rolando Blackman sent the game into overtime with two free throws after time had expired before 34,275 at the Kingdome.

Game 38: February 7, 1988—East 138, West 133 at Chicago—Michael Jordan scored 16 of his 40 points in the final 5:51 to clinch the East victory in a game in which Kareem Abdul-Jabbar of Los Angeles became the leading career All-Star scorer.

Game 39: February 12, 1989—West 143, East 134 at Houston—Before a record crowd of 44,735 at the Astrodome, Utah's Karl Malone had 28 points and nine rebounds and teammate John Stockton contributed 17 assists.

Game 40: February 11, 1990—East 130, West 113 at Miami—With seven players scoring in double figures, the East jumped ahead 40–23 in the first quarter and never trailed, shooting .543 for the game.

Game 41: February 10, 1991—East 116, West 114 at Charlotte, N.C.—Chicago's Michael Jordan scored 26 points and Philadelphia's Charles Barkley scored 17 points and hauled down 22 rebounds as the East edged the West.

Game 42: February 9, 1992—West 153, East 113 at Orlando—Magic Johnson came out of retirement with 25 points, nine assists and a dazzling all-around performance as the West routed the East.

Game 43: February 21, 1993—West 135, East 132, OT, at Salt Lake City—Utah teammates Karl Malone and John Stockton shared MVP honors, Malone tallying 28 points and Stockton handing out 15 assists.

Game 44: February 13, 1994—East 127, West 118 at Minneapolis—Chicago's Scottie Pippen gained MVP honors by scoring 29 points, including five three-point field goals, and grabbing 11 rebounds in the East's victory.

ABA ALL-STAR GAMES

RESULTS OF ABA ALL-STAR GAMES

Year	Result and Location	Most Valuable Player	Attendance
1968	East 126, West 120 at Indianapolis	Larry Brown, New Orleans	10,872
1969	West 133, East 127 at Louisville	John Beasley, Dallas	5,407
1970	West 128, East 98 at Indianapolis	Spencer Haywood, Denver	11,932
1971	East 126, West 122 at Greensboro	Mel Daniels, Indiana	14,407
1972	East 142, West 115 at Louisville	Dan Issel, Kentucky	15,738
1973	West 123, East 111 at Salt Lake City	Warren Jabali, Denver	12,556
1974	East 128, West 112 at Norfolk	Artis Gilmore, Kentucky	10,624
1975	East 151, West 124 at San Antonio	Freddie Lewis, St. Louis	10,449
1976	Denver 144, All-Stars 138 at Denver	David Thompson, Denver	17,798

Game 1: January 9, 1968—East 126, West 120 at Indianapolis—Minnesota's Mel Daniels, with 22 points and 15 rebounds, powered the East to victory in the first ABA All-Star Game.

Game 2: January 28, 1969—West 133, East 127 at Louisville—John Beasley of Dallas had 19 points and 14 rebounds and Alex Hannum, who had coached the NBA East All-Stars to victory a year earlier, led the West to the win.

Game 3: January 24, 1970—West 128, East 98 at Indianapolis—Denver rookie Spencer Haywood had 23 points, 19 rebounds and seven blocked shots and teammate Larry Jones scored 30 points in the West rout.

Game 4: January 23, 1971—East 126, West 122 at Greensboro, N.C.—Rick Barry of New York scored four points in the final 49 seconds as the East overcame an 18-point third-quarter deficit.

Game 5: January 29, 1972—East 142, West 115 at Louisville—Carolina's Jim McDaniels scored 18 of his 24 points in a 45-point fourth quarter as the East pulled away at the end.

Game 6: February 6, 1973—West 123, East 111 at Salt Lake City—Warren Jabali of Denver led the West to a 39–19 edge over the East in the final period for the victory.

Game 7: January 30, 1974—East 128, West 112 at Norfolk, Va.—Despite 29 points and 22 rebounds by San Antonio rookie Swen Nater for the West, the East shot .552 from the field to win.

Game 8: January 28, 1975—East 151, West 124 at San Antonio—Freddie Lewis of St. Louis scored 12 of his game-high 26 points in the first period as the East won easily.

Game 9: January 27, 1976—Denver 144, All-Stars 138 at Denver—The first-place Denver Nuggets, led by rookie David Thompson's 29 points, outscored a team of stars from the league's other six clubs.

NBA ALL-STAR GAMES

GAME 1, March 2, 1951, at Boston

Coaches—East, Joe Lapchick, New York/West, John Kundla, Minneapolis

MVP—Ed Macauley, Boston

WEST ALL-STARS (94)

PLAYER, TEAM	POS.	FGM	FGA	FTM	FTA	REB.	AST.	PF	PTS.
Groza, Indianapolis	F	8	16	1	1	13	1	4	17
Pollard, Minneapolis	F	2	11	0	0	4	5	1	4
Mikan, Minneapolis	C	4	17	4	6	11	3	2	12
Davies, Rochester	G	4	6	5	5	5	5	3	13
Beard, Indianapolis	G	3	8	0	3	3	2	1	6
Eddleman, Tri-Cities		2	9	3	5	0	3	3	7
Mikkelsen, Minneapolis		4	11	3	4	9	1	3	11
Foust, Fort Wayne		1	6	0	0	5	2	3	2
Brian, Tri-Cities		5	14	4	5	6	3	2	14
Schaus, Fort Wayne		2	9	4	4	4	2	3	8
TOTALS		35	107	24	33	60	27	25	94

EAST ALL-STARS (111)

PLAYER, TEAM	POS.	FGM	FGA	FTM	FTA	REB.	AST.	PF	PTS.
Fulks, Philadelphia	F	6	15	7	9	7	3	5	19
Schayes, Syracuse	F	7	10	1	2	14	3	1	15
Macauley, Boston	C	7	12	6	7	6	1	3	20
Cousy, Boston	G	2	12	4	5	9	8	3	8
Phillip, Philadelphia	G	3	8	0	0	10	8	1	6
Arizin, Philadelphia		7	12	1	2	7	0	2	15
Boryla, New York		4	6	1	1	2	2	3	9
Gallatin, New York		2	4	1	1	5	2	4	5
Rocha, Baltimore		2	10	4	4	2	3	2	8
McGuire, New York		3	4	0	0	5	10	2	6
TOTALS		43	93	25	31	67	40	26	111

Score by Periods:	1st	2nd	3rd	4th	Totals
East	31	22	30	28	111
West	22	20	22	30	94

Officials: Pat Kennedy and Charley Eckman.   Attendance: 10,094.

GAME 2, Feb. 11, 1952, at Boston

Coaches—East, Al Cervi, Syracuse/West, John Kundla, Minneapolis

MVP—Paul Arizin, Philadelphia

WEST ALL-STARS (91)

PLAYER, TEAM	POS.	MIN.	FGM	FGA	FTM	FTA	REB.	AST.	PF	PTS.
Pollard, Minneapolis	F	29	2	17	0	0	11	5	3	4
Barnhorst, Indianapolis	F	23	7	16	0	1	2	2	4	14
Mikan, Minneapolis	C	29	9	19	8	9	15	1	5	26
Davies, Rochester	G	27	4	11	0	0	5	4	4	8
Wanzer, Rochester	G	22	1	8	2	2	5	5	2	4
Brian, Fort Wayne		25	4	10	5	6	7	4	2	13
Mikkelsen, Minneapolis		23	5	8	2	2	10	0	2	12
Eddleman, Milwaukee		26	1	3	0	0	2	2	2	2
Risen, Rochester		19	3	7	0	1	5	1	3	6
Walther, Indianapolis		17	1	4	0	0	2	2	1	2
Foust, Fort Wayne		Injured								
TOTALS		240	37	103	17	21	59	27	28	91

EAST ALL-STARS (108)

PLAYER, TEAM	POS.	MIN.	FGM	FGA	FTM	FTA	REB.	AST.	PF	PTS.
Arizin, Philadelphia	F	32	9	13	8	8	6	0	1	26
Gallatin, New York	F	22	3	5	1	4	9	3	3	7
Macauley, Boston	C	28	3	7	9	9	7	3	2	15
Cousy, Boston	G	33	4	14	1	2	4	13	3	9
Phillip, Philadelphia	G	30	4	6	3	3	3	6	1	11
Fulks, Philadelphia		9	3	7	0	1	5	2	2	6
Rocha, Syracuse		28	5	11	2	2	5	2	4	12
Zaslofsky, New York		25	3	7	5	5	4	2	0	11
McGuire, New York		18	0	0	1	3	1	4	0	1
Scolari, Baltimore		15	5	9	0	0	0	2	0	10
Schayes, Syracuse		Injured								
TOTALS		240	39	79	30	37	44	37	16	108

Score by Periods:	1st	2nd	3rd	4th	Totals
East	26	23	33	26	108
West	22	22	27	20	91

Officials: Sid Borgia and Stan Stutz.   Attendance: 10,211.

GAME 3, Jan. 13, 1953, at Fort Wayne

Coaches—East, Joe Lapchick, New York/West, John Kundla, Minneapolis

MVP—George Mikan, Minneapolis

EAST ALL-STARS (75)

PLAYER, TEAM	POS.	MIN.	FGM	FGA	FTM	FTA	REB.	AST.	PF	PTS.
Gallatin, New York	F	19	1	4	1	2	3	2	1	3
Schayes, Syracuse	F	26	2	7	4	4	13	3	3	8
Macauley, Boston	C	35	5	12	8	8	7	3	2	18
Cousy, Boston	G	36	4	11	7	7	5	3	1	15
Sharman, Boston	G	26	5	8	1	1	4	0	2	11
Barksdale, Boston		11	0	1	1	3	3	2	0	1
Braun, New York		21	1	4	1	1	3	2	2	3
Johnston, Philadelphia		27	5	13	1	2	12	0	2	11
Seymour, Syracuse		14	2	3	1	2	3	2	1	5
Gabor, Syracuse		25	0	3	0	1	5	2	1	0
Scolari, Baltimore		Injured								
TOTALS		240	25	66	25	31	58	19	15	75
TEAM REBOUNDS: 8.										

WEST ALL-STARS (79)

PLAYER, TEAM	POS.	MIN.	FGM	FGA	FTM	FTA	REB.	AST.	PF	PTS.
Hutchins, Milwaukee	F	30	1	8	0	1	6	5	2	2
Mikkelsen, Minneapolis	F	19	3	13	0	0	6	3	3	6
Mikan, Minneapolis	C	40	9	26	4	4	16	2	2	22
Phillip, Fort Wayne	G	36	4	9	1	1	6	8	2	9
Wanzer, Rochester	G	22	4	7	1	1	2	2	1	9
Barnhorst, Indianapolis		13	1	2	0	1	3	2	0	2
Foust, Fort Wayne		18	5	7	0	0	6	0	4	10
Risen, Rochester		19	2	7	1	3	9	2	3	5
Davies, Rochester		17	3	7	3	6	3	2	2	9
Martin, Minneapolis		26	2	10	1	1	2	1	2	5
TOTALS		240	34	97	11	18	59	26	23	79
TEAM REBOUNDS: 3.										

SCORE BY PERIODS:	1st	2nd	3rd	4th	Totals
East	20	14	21	20	75
West	20	15	22	22	79

Officials: Sid Borgia and Bud Lowell.   Attendance: 10,322.

GAME 4, Jan. 21, 1954, at New York

Coaches—East, Joe Lapchick, New York/West, John Kundla, Minneapolis

MVP—Bob Cousy, Boston

WEST ALL-STARS (93)

PLAYER, TEAM	POS.	MIN.	FGM	FGA	FTM	FTA	REB.	AST.	PF	PTS.
Hutchins, Milwaukee	F	31	1	8	1	2	4	2	5	3
Pollard, Minneapolis	F	41	10	22	3	5	3	3	3	23
Mikan, Minneapolis	C	31	6	18	6	8	9	1	5	18
Martin, Minneapolis	G	23	1	5	0	0	0	3	3	2
Wanzer, Rochester	G	36	5	13	2	3	2	6	6	12
Risen, Rochester		20	4	10	0	1	7	0	5	8
Davies, Rochester		31	8	16	2	3	5	5	4	18
Sunderlage, Milwaukee		6	1	2	2	2	0	1	1	4
Foust, Fort Wayne		27	1	9	1	1	15	0	1	3
Phillip, Fort Wayne		19	1	4	0	1	3	3	1	2
TOTALS		265	38	97	17	25	48	24	24	93

TEAM REBOUNDS: 5.

EAST ALL-STARS (98)

PLAYER, TEAM	POS.	MIN.	FGM	FGA	FTM	FTA	REB.	AST.	PF	PTS.
Schayes, Syracuse	F	24	1	3	4	6	12	1	1	6
McGuire, New York	F	24	2	5	0	0	4	2	1	4
Felix, Baltimore	C	32	4	8	5	5	11	1	4	13
Macauley, Boston	G	25	4	11	5	6	1	3	2	13
Cousy, Boston	G	34	6	15	8	8	11	4	1	20
Braun, New York		29	4	8	1	1	4	2	3	9
Gallatin, New York		28	0	2	5	6	18	3	0	5
Johnston, Philadelphia		20	2	9	2	4	7	2	1	6
Sharman, Boston		30	6	9	2	4	2	3	3	14
Seymour, Syracuse		19	2	6	4	4	1	3	2	8
TOTALS		265	31	76	36	44	71	24	20	98

TEAM REBOUNDS: 7.

SCORE BY PERIODS:	1st	2nd	3rd	4th	OT	Totals
East	28	20	17	19	14	98
West	25	19	23	17	9	93

Officials: Mendy Rudolph and Sid Borgia.   Attendance: 16,487.

GAME 5, Jan. 18, 1955, at New York

Coaches—East, Al Cervi, Syracuse/West, Charley Eckman, Fort Wayne

MVP—Bill Sharman, Boston

WEST ALL-STARS (91)

PLAYER, TEAM	POS.	MIN.	FGM	FGA	FTM	FTA	REB.	AST.	PF	PTS.
Pollard, Minneapolis	F	27	7	19	3	3	4	0	1	17
Yardley, Fort Wayne	F	22	4	11	3	4	4	2	2	11
Foust, Fort Wayne	C	24	3	10	1	1	7	1	1	7
Phillip, Fort Wayne	G	28	3	4	0	0	3	6	3	6
Wanzer, Rochester	G	26	3	7	2	2	3	2	4	8
Pettit, Milwaukee		27	3	14	2	4	9	2	0	8
Coleman, Rochester		19	2	8	2	3	6	1	0	6
Mikkelsen, Minneapolis		25	7	15	2	3	9	1	5	16
Martin, Minneapolis		23	2	5	1	2	2	5	3	5
Selvy, Milwaukee		19	2	7	3	4	3	1	4	7
Risen, Rochester					Injured					
TOTALS		240	36	100	19	26	50	21	23	91

EAST ALL-STARS (100)

PLAYER, TEAM	POS.	MIN.	FGM	FGA	FTM	FTA	REB.	AST.	PF	PTS.
Gallatin, New York	F	36	4	7	5	5	14	3	2	13
Schayes, Syracuse	F	29	6	12	3	3	13	1	4	15
Macauley, Boston	C	27	1	5	4	5	4	2	1	6
Cousy, Boston	G	35	7	14	6	7	9	5	1	20
Seymour, Syracuse	G	16	3	8	2	2	3	1	1	8
Arizin, Philadelphia		23	4	9	1	2	2	2	5	9
Braun, New York		16	4	6	0	0	2	2	2	8
Johnston, Philadelphia		15	1	7	1	1	6	1	0	3
McGuire, New York		25	1	2	1	2	3	6	1	3
Sharman, Boston		18	5	10	5	5	4	2	4	15
TOTALS		240	36	80	28	32	60	25	21	100

Score by Periods	1st	2nd	3rd	4th	Totals
East	21	28	21	30	100
West	21	29	21	20	91

Officials: Phil Fox and Joe Serafin.   Attendance: 15,564.

Game 6, Jan. 24, 1956, at Rochester

Coaches—East, George Senesky, Philadelphia/West, Charley Eckman, Fort Wayne

MVP—Bob Pettit, St. Louis

WEST ALL-STARS (108)

PLAYER, TEAM	POS.	MIN.	FGM	FGA	FTM	FTA	REB.	AST.	PF	PTS.
Hutchins, Fort Wayne	F	27	5	11	1	2	4	0	0	11
Yardley, Fort Wayne	F	19	3	7	2	3	6	1	1	8
Foust, Fort Wayne	C	20	3	9	3	4	4	0	1	9
Martin, Minneapolis	G	29	3	7	3	3	1	7	5	9
Wanzer, Rochester	G	25	4	8	5	6	5	2	4	13
Stokes, Rochester		20	4	11	2	5	16	2	5	10
Pettit, St. Louis		31	7	17	6	7	24	7	4	20
Mikkelsen, Minneapolis		22	5	13	6	7	9	2	4	16
Lovellette, Minneapolis		20	3	10	1	3	10	0	4	7
Harrison, St. Louis		25	2	7	1	2	0	1	4	5
TOTALS		240	39	100	30	42	79	22	32	108

EAST ALL-STARS (94)

PLAYER, TEAM	POS.	MIN.	FGM	FGA	FTM	FTA	REB.	AST.	PF	PTS.
Arizin, Philadelphia	F	28	5	13	3	5	7	0	6	13
Schayes, Syracuse	F	25	4	8	6	10	4	2	2	14
Johnston, Philadelphia	C	25	5	9	7	11	10	1	3	17
Cousy, Boston	G	24	2	8	3	4	7	2	6	7
McGuire, New York	G	29	2	9	2	5	0	3	1	6
Kerr, Syracuse		16	2	4	0	1	8	0	2	4
Gallatin, New York		30	5	12	6	7	5	2	4	16
Macauley, Boston		20	1	9	2	4	2	3	3	4
George, Philadelphia		21	2	7	2	2	3	2	1	6
Sharman, Boston		24	2	8	3	4	7	2	6	7
Braun, New York					Injured					
TOTALS		240	30	87	34	53	53	18	34	94

Score by Periods:	1st	2nd	3rd	4th	Totals
West	17	26	41	24	108
East	24	16	24	30	94

Officials: Arnie Heft and Lou Eisenstein.   Attendance: 8,517.

GAME 7, Jan. 15, 1957, at Boston

Coaches—East, Red Auerbach, Boston/West, Bobby Wanzer, Rochester

MVP—Bob Cousy, Boston

WEST ALL-STARS (97)

PLAYER, TEAM	POS.	MIN.	FGM	FGA	FTM	FTA	REB.	AST.	PF	PTS.
Yardley, Fort Wayne	F	25	4	10	1	1	9	0	2	9
Pettit, St. Louis	F	31	8	18	5	6	11	2	2	21
Stokes, Rochester	C	31	8	19	3	3	12	7	1	19
Martin, St. Louis	G	31	4	11	0	0	2	3	1	8
Garmaker, Minneapolis	G	18	5	10	0	0	7	1	2	10
Macauley, St. Louis		19	3	6	1	2	5	3	0	7
Twyman, Rochester		17	1	8	1	3	0	1	1	3
Hutchins, Fort Wayne		26	4	12	2	3	7	0	0	10
Mikkelsen, Minneapolis		21	3	10	0	4	9	1	3	6
Regan, Rochester		21	2	7	0	0	4	1	0	4
TOTALS		240	42	111	13	22	66	19	12	97

TEAM REBOUNDS: 4.

EAST ALL-STARS (109)

PLAYER, TEAM	POS.	MIN.	FGM	FGA	FTM	FTA	REB.	AST.	PF	PTS.
Arizin, Philadelphia	F	26	6	13	1	2	5	1	2	13
Heinsohn, Boston	F	23	5	17	2	2	7	0	3	12
Gallatin, New York	C	24	4	7	0	2	11	1	3	8
Cousy, Boston	G	28	4	14	2	2	5	7	0	10
Sharman, Boston	G	23	5	17	2	2	6	5	1	12
Schayes, Syracuse		25	4	6	1	1	10	1	1	9
Johnston, Philadelphia		23	8	12	3	3	9	1	2	19
Clifton, New York		23	4	11	0	0	11	3	1	8
George, Philadelphia		21	3	6	2	2	1	5	1	8
Braun, New York		24	4	9	2	2	3	2	2	10
TOTALS		240	47	112	15	18	68	25	16	109

TEAM REBOUNDS: 2.

Score by Periods:	1st	2nd	3rd	4th	Totals
East	18	23	33	35	109
West	26	17	23	31	97

Officials: Mendy Rudolph and Sid Borgia. Attendance: 11,178.

GAME 8, Jan. 21, 1958, at St. Louis

Coaches—East, Red Auerbach, Boston/West, Alex Hannum, St. Louis

MVP—Bob Pettit, St. Louis

EAST ALL-STARS (130)

PLAYER, TEAM	POS.	MIN.	FGM	FGA	FTM	FTA	REB.	AST.	PF	PTS.
Schayes, Syracuse	F	39	6	15	6	6	9	2	4	18
Naulls, New York	F	15	3	9	2	2	3	0	0	8
Russell, Boston	C	26	5	12	1	3	11	2	5	11
Cousy, Boston	G	31	8	20	4	6	5	10	0	20
Sharman, Boston	G	25	6	19	3	4	4	3	2	15
Sears, New York		14	4	8	4	5	1	0	1	12
Arizin, Philadelphia		29	11	17	2	2	8	2	3	24
Johnston, Philadelphia		22	6	13	2	2	8	1	5	14
Guerin, New York		22	2	10	3	4	8	7	3	7
Costello, Syracuse		17	0	6	1	1	1	4	2	1
TOTALS		240	51	129	28	34	58	31	25	130

TEAM REBOUNDS: 9.

WEST ALL-STARS (118)

PLAYER, TEAM	POS.	MIN.	FGM	FGA	FTM	FTA	REB.	AST.	PF	PTS.
Yardley, Detroit	F	32	8	15	3	5	9	1	1	19
Twyman, Cincinnati	F	25	8	13	2	2	3	0	3	18
Pettit, St. Louis	C	38	10	21	8	10	26	1	1	28
Martin, St. Louis	G	26	2	9	2	4	2	8	3	6
Garmaker, Minneapolis	G	13	1	9	3	3	6	1	4	5
Stokes, Cincinnati		36	3	13	4	7	14	3	2	10
Foust, Minneapolis		13	1	4	8	8	3	0	3	10
Shue, Detroit		25	8	11	2	3	2	0	3	18
McGuire, Detroit		31	2	4	0	0	7	10	4	4
Hagan, St. Louis		Injured								
TOTALS		240	43	99	32	42	72	24	24	118

TEAM REBOUNDS: 7.

Score by Periods	1st	2nd	3rd	4th	Totals
East	30	31	31	38	130
West	31	35	25	25	118

Officials: Jim Duffy and Arnie Heft. Attendance: 12,854.

GAME 9, Jan. 23, 1959, at Detroit

Coaches—East, Red Auerbach, Boston/West, Ed Macauley, St. Louis

MVPs—Elgin Baylor, Minneapolis, and Bob Pettit, St. Louis

EAST ALL-STARS (108)

PLAYER, TEAM	POS.	MIN.	FGM	FGA	FTM	FTA	REB.	AST.	PF	PTS.
Sears, New York	F	26	5	9	5	5	8	1	4	15
Arizin, Philadelphia	F	30	4	15	8	9	8	0	2	16
Russell, Boston	C	27	3	10	1	1	9	1	4	7
Sharman, Boston	G	24	3	12	5	6	2	0	1	11
Cousy, Boston	G	32	4	8	5	6	5	4	0	13
Schayes, Syracuse		22	3	11	7	8	13	1	6	13
Sauldsberry, Philadelphia		18	5	11	4	4	2	3	2	14
Kerr, Syracuse		21	3	14	1	2	9	2	0	7
Costello, Syracuse		18	3	8	1	1	3	3	1	7
Guerin, New York		22	1	7	3	5	3	3	1	5
TOTALS		240	34	108	40	47	62	18	21	108

TEAM REBOUNDS: 8.

WEST ALL-STARS (124)

PLAYER, TEAM	POS.	MIN.	FGM	FGA	FTM	FTA	REB.	AST.	PF	PTS.
Hagan, St. Louis	F	22	6	12	3	3	8	3	5	15
Baylor, Minneapolis	F	32	10	20	4	5	11	1	3	24
Pettit, St. Louis	C	34	8	21	9	9	16	5	1	25
Shue, Detroit	G	31	6	11	1	2	4	3	4	13
Martin, St. Louis	G	22	2	6	1	2	6	1	2	5
Yardley, Detroit		17	2	8	2	2	4	0	3	6
Twyman, Cincinnati		23	8	12	2	4	8	3	4	18
Foust, Minneapolis		16	3	9	2	2	9	0	3	8
McGuire, Detroit		24	2	7	1	2	3	3	2	5
Garmaker, Minneapolis		19	2	6	1	1	2	1	2	5
TOTALS		240	49	112	26	32	71	20	29	124

TEAM REBOUNDS: 9.

Score by Periods:	1st	2nd	3rd	4th	Totals
West	27	34	30	33	124
East	31	21	32	24	108

Officials: Jim Duffy and Mendy Rudolph. Attendance: 10,541.

GAME 10, Jan. 22, 1960, at Philadelphia

Coaches—East, Red Auerbach, Boston/West, Ed Macauley, St. Louis
MVP—Wilt Chamberlain, Philadelphia

WEST ALL-STARS (115)

PLAYER, TEAM	POS.	MIN.	FGM	FGA	FTM	FTA	REB.	AST.	PF	PTS.
Pettit, St. Louis	F	28	4	15	3	6	14	2	2	11
Twyman, Cincinnati	F	28	11	17	5	8	5	1	4	27
Dukes, Detroit	C	26	2	10	0	1	15	1	3	4
Shue, Detroit	G	34	6	13	1	2	6	6	0	13
Baylor, Minneapolis	G	28	10	18	5	7	13	3	4	25
Hagan, St. Louis		21	1	9	0	0	3	2	1	1
Noble, Detroit		11	0	5	0	0	1	3	1	0
Lovellette, St. Louis		18	6	11	0	0	8	1	1	12
Hundley, Minneapolis		23	5	12	0	0	3	2	2	10
Garmaker, Minneapolis		23	5	11	1	2	4	3	1	11
TOTALS		240	50	121	15	26	72	24	19	115

TEAM REBOUNDS: 12.

EAST ALL-STARS (125)

PLAYER, TEAM	POS.	MIN.	FGM	FGA	FTM	FTA	REB.	AST.	PF	PTS.
Schayes, Syracuse	F	27	8	19	3	3	10	0	3	19
Russell, Boston	F	27	3	7	0	2	8	3	1	6
Chamberlain, Philadelphia	C	30	9	20	5	7	25	2	1	23
Cousy, Boston	G	26	1	7	0	0	5	8	2	2
Guerin, New York	G	22	5	11	2	2	4	4	4	12
Yardley, Syracuse		16	5	9	1	2	3	0	4	11
Gola, Philadelphia		20	5	13	2	3	4	2	3	12
Naulls, New York		26	5	19	3	4	10	0	1	13
Sharman, Boston		26	8	21	1	1	6	2	1	17
Costello, Syracuse		20	5	9	0	0	4	2	1	10
Arizin, Philadelphia					Injured					
TOTALS		240	54	135	17	24	79	23	21	125

TEAM REBOUNDS: 7.

Score by Periods:	1st	2nd	3rd	4th	Totals
East	25	33	33	34	125
West	26	25	30	34	115

Officials: Arnie Heft and Sid Borgia.   Attendance: 10,421.

GAME 11, Jan. 17, 1961, at Syracuse

Coaches—East, Red Auerbach, Boston/West, Paul Seymour, St. Louis
MVP—Oscar Robertson, Cincinnati

WEST ALL-STARS (153)

PLAYER, TEAM	POS.	MIN.	FGM	FGA	FTM	FTA	REB.	AST.	PF	PTS.
Baylor, Los Angeles	F	27	3	11	9	10	10	4	5	15
Lovellette, St. Louis	F	31	10	19	1	1	10	3	4	21
Pettit, St. Louis	C	32	13	22	3	7	9	0	2	29
Shue, Detroit	G	23	6	10	3	4	3	6	1	15
Robertson, Cincinnati	G	34	8	13	7	9	9	14	5	23
Embry, Cincinnati		8	2	4	0	0	3	0	0	4
Dukes, Detroit		17	3	6	2	2	4	1	4	8
Howell, Detroit		16	5	10	3	4	3	3	3	13
Hagan, St. Louis		13	0	2	2	2	2	0	1	2
West, Los Angeles		25	2	8	5	6	2	4	3	9
Hundley, Los Angeles		14	6	10	2	2	0	2	1	14
TOTALS		240	58	115	37	47	55	37	30	153

TEAM REBOUNDS: 16.

EAST ALL-STARS (131)

PLAYER, TEAM	POS.	MIN.	FGM	FGA	FTM	FTA	REB.	AST.	PF	PTS.
Heinsohn, Boston	F	19	2	16	0	0	6	1	4	4
Schayes, Syracuse	F	27	7	15	7	7	6	3	4	21
Chamberlain, Philadelphia	C	38	2	8	8	15	18	5	1	12
Cousy, Boston	G	33	2	11	0	0	3	8	6	4
Guerin, New York	G	15	3	8	5	6	0	2	2	11
Arizin, Philadelphia		17	6	12	5	6	2	1	4	17
Naulls, New York		16	4	6	0	1	6	2	2	8
Costello, Syracuse		5	1	2	0	0	0	0	2	2
Russell, Boston		28	9	15	6	8	11	1	2	24
Gola, Philadelphia		25	6	13	2	4	5	3	2	14
Greer, Syracuse		18	7	11	0	0	6	2	2	14
TOTALS		240	49	117	33	47	63	28	30	131

TEAM REBOUNDS: 15.

Score by Periods:	1st	2nd	3rd	4th	Totals
East	19	43	35	34	131
West	47	37	31	38	153

Officials: Norm Drucker and Richie Powers.   Attendance: 8,016.

GAME 12, Jan. 16, 1962, at St. Louis

Coaches—East, Red Auerbach, Boston/West, Fred Schaus, Los Angeles
MVP—Bob Pettit, St. Louis

EAST ALL-STARS (130)

PLAYER, TEAM	POS.	MIN.	FGM	FGA	FTM	FTA	REB.	AST.	PF	PTS.
Schayes, Syracuse	F	4	0	0	0	0	1	0	3	0
Heinsohn, Boston	F	13	4	11	2	2	2	1	4	10
Chamberlain, Philadelphia	C	37	17	23	8	16	24	1	4	42
Cousy, Boston	G	31	4	13	3	4	6	8	2	11
Guerin, New York	G	27	10	17	3	6	3	1	6	23
Russell, Boston		27	5	12	2	3	12	2	2	12
Green, New York		21	2	4	3	3	2	0	1	7
Naulls, New York		21	5	16	1	1	7	0	5	11
Greer, Syracuse		24	3	14	2	7	10	9	3	8
Arizin, Philadelphia		21	2	12	0	0	2	0	4	4
Jones, Boston		14	1	8	0	1	1	0	1	2
Gola, Philadelphia					Injured					
Costello, Syracuse					Injured					
TOTALS		240	53	130	24	43	70	22	35	130

TEAM REBOUNDS: 10.

WEST ALL-STARS (150)

PLAYER, TEAM	POS.	MIN.	FGM	FGA	FTM	FTA	REB.	AST.	PF	PTS.
Baylor, Los Angeles	F	37	10	23	12	14	9	4	2	32
Pettit, St. Louis	F	37	10	20	5	5	27	2	5	25
Bellamy, Chicago	C	29	10	18	3	8	17	1	6	23
Robertson, Cincinnati	G	37	9	20	8	14	7	13	3	26
West, Los Angeles	G	31	7	14	4	6	3	1	2	18
Embry, Cincinnati		16	2	6	0	0	4	1	4	4
Howell, Detroit		8	1	2	0	0	0	1	1	2
Twyman, Cincinnati		8	4	6	3	3	1	2	0	11
Hagan, St. Louis		9	1	3	0	0	2	1	1	2
Selvy, Los Angeles		11	0	3	0	0	4	1	1	0
Shue, Detroit		17	3	6	1	1	5	4	3	7
LaRusso, Los Angeles					Injured					
TOTALS		240	57	121	36	51	79	31	28	150

TEAM REBOUNDS: 16.

Score by Periods:	1st	2nd	3rd	4th	Totals
West	35	29	41	45	150
East	32	28	34	36	130

Officials: Sid Borgia and Willie Smith.   Attendance: 15,112.

GAME 13, Jan. 16, 1963, at Los Angeles

Coaches—East, Red Auerbach, Boston/West, Fred Schaus, Los Angeles

MVP—Bill Russell, Boston

EAST ALL-STARS (115)

PLAYER, TEAM	POS.	MIN.	FGM	FGA	FTM	FTA	REB.	AST.	PF	PTS.
Twyman, Cincinnati	F	16	6	12	0	0	4	1	2	12
Heinsohn, Boston	F	21	6	11	3	4	2	1	4	15
Russell, Boston	C	37	8	14	3	4	24	5	3	19
Robertson, Cincinnati	G	37	9	15	3	4	3	6	5	21
Cousy, Boston	G	25	4	11	0	0	4	6	2	8
Kerr, Syracuse		11	0	4	2	2	2	1	3	2
Shaffer, Syracuse		19	6	13	0	0	1	1	3	12
Green, New York		27	6	8	1	1	5	0	1	13
Gola, New York		18	1	3	0	0	2	1	3	2
Greer, Syracuse		15	3	7	0	0	3	2	4	6
Embry, Cincinnati		14	2	3	1	3	1	1	2	5
TOTALS		240	51	101	13	18	51	25	32	115

WEST ALL-STARS (108)

PLAYER, TEAM	POS.	MIN.	FGM	FGA	FTM	FTA	REB.	AST.	PF	PTS.
Bellamy, Chicago	F	14	1	4	0	2	1	2	3	2
Pettit, St. Louis	F	32	7	16	11	12	13	0	1	25
Chamberlain, San Francisco	C	35	7	11	3	7	19	0	2	17
West, Los Angeles	G	32	5	15	3	4	7	5	1	13
Baylor, Los Angeles	G	36	4	15	9	13	14	7	0	17
Meschery, San Francisco		8	1	3	1	2	1	1	1	3
Ohl, Detroit		12	1	4	1	1	0	2	2	3
Wilkens, St. Louis		25	2	7	0	1	2	3	0	4
Howell, Detroit		11	2	3	0	0	1	1	2	4
LaRusso, Los Angeles		11	3	3	0	0	1	2	1	6
Dischinger, Chicago		7	3	3	1	1	1	0	0	7
Rodgers, San Francisco		17	3	6	1	2	2	4	2	7
TOTALS		240	39	90	30	45	62	27	15	108

Score by Periods:	1st	2nd	3rd	4th	Totals
East	32	24	24	35	115
West	25	25	23	35	108

Officials: Sid Borgia and Earl Strom.   Attendance: 14,838.

GAME 14, Jan. 14, 1964, at Boston

Coaches—East, Red Auerbach, Boston/West, Fred Schaus, Los Angeles

MVP—Oscar Robertson, Cincinnati

WEST ALL-STARS (107)

PLAYER, TEAM	POS.	MIN.	FGM	FGA	FTM	FTA	REB.	AST.	PF	PTS.
Pettit, St. Louis	F	36	6	15	7	9	17	2	3	19
Baylor, Los Angeles	F	29	5	15	5	11	8	5	1	15
Bellamy, Baltimore	C	23	4	11	3	5	7	0	3	11
Rodgers, San Francisco	G	22	3	6	0	0	2	2	4	6
West, Los Angeles	G	42	8	20	1	1	4	5	3	17
Chamberlain, San Francisco		37	4	14	11	14	20	1	2	19
Dischinger, Baltimore		13	2	4	3	3	2	1	1	7
Howell, Detroit		6	1	3	0	0	2	0	0	2
Ohl, Detroit		18	3	9	2	2	2	0	2	8
Wilkens, St. Louis		14	1	5	1	1	0	0	3	3
TOTALS		240	37	102	33	46	64	16	22	107

TEAM REBOUNDS: 11.

EAST ALL-STARS (111)

PLAYER, TEAM	POS.	MIN.	FGM	FGA	FTM	FTA	REB.	AST.	PF	PTS.
Lucas, Cincinnati	F	36	3	6	5	6	8	0	5	11
Heinsohn, Boston	F	21	5	12	0	0	3	0	5	10
Russell, Boston	C	42	6	13	1	2	21	2	4	13
Robertson, Cincinnati	G	42	10	23	6	10	14	8	4	26
Greer, Philadelphia	G	20	5	10	3	4	3	4	1	13
Gola, New York		7	0	1	2	2	0	1	2	1
Walker, Philadelphia		12	2	5	0	0	0	0	1	4
Chappell, New York		12	1	5	2	2	1	2	2	4
Embry, Cincinnati		21	6	14	1	1	7	1	1	13
Jones, Boston		27	8	20	0	0	4	3	2	16
TOTALS		240	46	108	19	27	61	21	27	111

TEAM REBOUNDS: 16.

Score by Periods:	1st	2nd	3rd	4th	Totals
East	25	34	27	25	111
West	22	27	28	30	107

Officials: Sid Borgia and Mendy Rudolph.   Attendance: 13,464.

GAME 15, Jan. 13, 1965, at St. Louis

Coaches—East, Red Auerbach, Boston/West, Alex Hannum, San Francisco

MVP—Jerry Lucas, Cincinnati

EAST ALL-STARS (124)

PLAYER, TEAM	POS.	MIN.	FGM	FGA	FTM	FTA	REB.	AST.	PF	PTS.
Lucas, Cincinnati	F	35	12	19	1	1	10	1	2	25
Jackson, Philadelphia	F	15	2	5	1	2	1	1	4	5
Russell, Boston	C	33	7	12	3	9	13	5	6	17
Jones, Boston	G	24	2	12	2	2	5	3	2	6
Robertson, Cincinnati	G	40	8	18	12	13	6	8	5	28
Embry, Cincinnati		19	5	10	1	1	4	0	5	11
Green, New York		17	3	4	2	3	0	0	6	8
Reed, New York		25	3	11	1	2	5	1	2	7
Greer, Philadelphia		21	5	11	3	4	1	2	2	13
Costello, Philadelphia		11	2	7	0	0	1	2	2	4
Heinsohn, Boston					Injured					
TOTALS		240	49	109	26	37	49	22	36	124

TEAM REBOUNDS: 8.

WEST ALL-STARS (123)

PLAYER, TEAM	POS.	MIN.	FGM	FGA	FTM	FTA	REB.	AST.	PF	PTS.
Baylor, Los Angeles	F	27	5	13	8	8	7	0	4	18
Pettit, St. Louis	F	34	5	14	3	5	12	0	4	13
Chamberlain, San Francisco	C	31	9	15	2	8	16	1	4	20
Wilkens, St. Louis	G	20	2	6	4	4	3	3	3	8
West, Los Angeles	G	40	8	16	4	6	5	6	2	20
Thurmond, San Francisco		10	0	2	0	0	3	0	1	0
Bellamy, Baltimore		17	4	5	4	4	5	1	3	12
Ohl, Baltimore		12	0	1	2	2	2	1	1	2
Johnson, Baltimore		25	7	13	11	13	8	2	2	25
Dischinger, Detroit		24	2	8	1	2	5	1	4	5
TOTALS		240	42	93	39	52	66	15	28	123

TEAM REBOUNDS: 12.

Score by Periods:	1st	2nd	3rd	4th	Totals
West	27	34	30	32	123
East	36	39	32	17	124

Officials: Mendy Rudolph and Joe Gushue.   Attendance: 16,713.

GAME 16, Jan. 11, 1966, at Cincinnati

Coaches—East, Red Auerbach, Boston/West, Fred Schaus, Los Angeles
MVP—Adrian Smith, Cincinnati

WEST ALL-STARS (94)

PLAYER, TEAM	POS.	MIN.	FGM	FGA	FTM	FTA	REB.	AST.	PF	PTS.
Barry, San Francisco	F	17	4	10	2	4	2	2	6	10
Howell, Baltimore	F	26	3	11	1	2	2	2	4	7
Thurmond, San Francisco	C	33	3	16	1	3	16	1	1	7
Rodgers, San Francisco	G	34	3	11	0	0	7	11	4	8
West, Los Angeles	G	11	1	5	2	2	1	0	2	4
DeBusschere, Detroit		22	1	14	2	2	6	1	1	4
Miles, Detroit		28	8	16	1	5	1	0	1	17
Beaty, St. Louis		24	0	11	10	13	18	1	2	10
LaRusso, Los Angeles		22	4	10	3	7	3	2	2	11
Ohl, Baltimore		23	7	16	2	3	4	2	2	16
TOTALS		240	35	120	24	41	60	22	25	94

TEAM REBOUNDS: 8.

EAST ALL-STARS (137)

PLAYER, TEAM	POS.	MIN.	FGM	FGA	FTM	FTA	REB.	AST.	PF	PTS.
Lucas, Cincinnati	F	23	4	11	2	2	19	0	2	10
Havlicek, Boston	F	25	6	16	6	6	6	1	2	18
Chamberlain, Philadelphia	C	25	8	11	5	9	9	3	2	21
Robertson, Cincinnati	G	25	6	12	5	6	10	8	0	17
Jones, Boston	G	22	5	11	2	2	2	5	0	12
Walker, Philadelphia		25	3	10	2	3	6	4	2	8
Reed, New York		23	7	11	2	2	8	1	3	16
Russell, Boston		23	1	6	0	0	10	2	2	2
Greer, Philadelphia		23	4	13	1	1	5	1	4	9
Smith, Cincinnati		26	9	18	6	6	8	3	5	24
TOTALS		240	53	118	31	37	83	28	22	137

TEAM REBOUNDS:12.

Score by Periods:	1st	2nd	3rd	4th	Totals
East	33	30	38	36	137
West	18	18	32	26	94

Officials: Norm Drucker and John Vanak. Attendance: 13,653.

GAME 17, Jan. 10, 1967, at San Francisco

Coaches—East, Red Auerbach, Boston/West, Fred Schaus, Los Angeles
MVP—Rick Barry, San Francisco

EAST ALL-STARS (120)

PLAYER, TEAM	POS.	MIN.	FGM	FGA	FTM	FTA	REB.	AST.	PF	PTS.
Howell, Boston	F	14	1	4	2	2	2	1	1	4
Reed, New York	F	17	2	6	0	0	9	1	0	4
Chamberlain, Philadelphia	C	39	6	7	2	5	22	4	1	14
Robertson, Cincinnati	G	34	9	20	8	10	2	5	4	26
Greer, Philadelphia	G	31	5	16	7	8	4	1	5	17
Havlicek, Boston		17	7	14	0	0	2	1	1	14
Ohl, Baltimore		22	5	13	7	7	1	2	3	17
Russell, Boston		22	1	2	0	0	5	5	2	2
Walker, Philadelphia		22	6	9	3	4	4	2	2	15
Lucas, Cincinnati		22	3	5	1	1	7	2	3	7
TOTALS		240	45	96	30	37	58	24	22	120

TEAM REBOUNDS: 6.

WEST ALL-STARS (135)

PLAYER, TEAM	POS.	MIN.	FGM	FGA	FTM	FTA	REB.	AST.	PF	PTS.
Barry, San Francisco	F	34	16	27	6	8	6	3	5	38
Baylor, Los Angeles	F	20	8	14	4	4	5	5	2	20
Thurmond, San Francisco	C	42	7	16	2	4	18	0	1	16
Rodgers, Chicago	G	28	0	4	1	1	2	8	3	1
West, Los Angeles	G	30	6	11	4	4	3	6	3	16
Imhoff, Los Angeles		6	0	7	0	0	7	1	1	0
Sloan, Chicago		22	4	9	0	0	4	4	5	8
DeBusschere, Detroit		25	11	17	0	0	6	0	1	22
Bridges, St. Louis		17	4	5	0	2	3	3	1	8
Wilkens, St. Louis		16	2	6	2	3	2	6	2	6
TOTALS		240	58	116	19	26	56	36	24	135

TEAM REBOUNDS: 5.

Score by Periods:	1st	2nd	3rd	4th	Totals
East	33	34	28	25	120
West	39	38	27	31	135

Officials: Willie Smith and Earl Strom. Attendance: 13,972.

GAME 18, Jan. 23, 1968, at New York

Coaches—East, Alex Hannum, Philadelphia/West, Bill Sharman, Los Angeles
MVP—Hal Greer, Philadelphia

WEST ALL-STARS (124)

PLAYER, TEAM	POS.	MIN.	FGM	FGA	FTM	FTA	REB.	AST.	PF	PTS.
Boozer, Chicago	F	19	2	5	0	0	5	0	0	4
Baylor, Los Angeles	F	27	8	13	6	7	6	1	5	22
Beaty, St. Louis	C	30	2	11	2	2	10	1	4	6
Wilkens, St. Louis	G	22	4	10	6	8	3	3	1	14
West, Los Angeles	G	32	7	17	3	4	6	6	4	17
Bridges, St. Louis		21	7	9	1	4	7	1	4	15
LaRusso, San Francisco		19	3	8	0	2	7	0	0	6
Kojis, San Diego		10	2	5	0	0	2	1	0	4
Clark, Los Angeles		15	5	8	7	7	0	3	2	17
Lee, San Francisco		18	2	8	2	4	11	2	3	6
Hazzard, Seattle		20	4	12	1	1	3	3	3	9
King, San Francisco		7	1	4	2	3	1	2	3	4
Thurmond, San Francisco			Injured							
TOTALS		240	47	110	30	42	61	23	29	124

TEAM REBOUNDS: 7.

EAST ALL-STARS (144)

PLAYER, TEAM	POS.	MIN.	FGM	FGA	FTM	FTA	REB.	AST.	PF	PTS.
Lucas, Cincinnati	F	21	6	9	4	4	5	4	3	16
Reed, New York	F	25	7	14	2	3	8	1	4	16
Chamberlain, Philadelphia	C	25	3	4	1	4	7	6	2	7
Bing, Detroit	G	20	4	7	1	1	2	4	3	9
Robertson, Cincinnati	G	22	7	9	4	7	1	5	2	18
Barnett, New York		22	7	12	1	2	1	0	2	15
DeBusschere, Detroit		12	0	3	0	0	4	0	1	0
Havlicek, Boston		22	9	15	8	11	5	4	0	26
Russell, Boston		23	2	4	0	0	9	8	5	4
Johnson, Baltimore		16	3	9	1	2	6	1	2	7
Jones, Boston		15	2	5	1	1	2	4	1	5
Greer, Philadelphia		17	8	8	5	7	3	3	2	21
TOTALS		240	58	99	28	42	53	40	27	144

TEAM REBOUNDS: 9.

Score by Periods:	1st	2nd	3rd	4th	Totals
West	25	34	32	33	124
East	37	27	37	43	144

Officials: Mendy Rudolph and Don Murphy. Attendance: 18,422.

GAME 19, Jan. 14, 1969, at Baltimore

Coaches—East, Gene Shue, Baltimore/West, Richie Guerin, Atlanta

MVP—Oscar Robertson, Cincinnati

WEST ALL-STARS (112)

PLAYER, TEAM	POS.	MIN.	FGM	FGA	FTM	FTA	REB.	AST.	PF	PTS.
Baylor, Los Angeles	F	32	5	13	11	12	9	5	2	21
Kojis, San Diego	F	16	2	7	4	5	5	3	1	8
Hayes, San Diego	C	21	4	9	3	3	5	0	4	11
Sloan, Chicago	G	18	2	8	0	1	3	0	5	4
Wilkens, Seattle	G	24	3	15	4	5	7	5	3	10
Mullins, San Francisco		25	7	14	0	0	4	5	4	14
Chamberlain, Los Angeles		27	2	3	0	1	12	2	2	4
LaRusso, San Francisco		18	3	6	0	0	6	2	3	6
Van Arsdale, Phoenix		10	2	4	0	0	1	0	0	4
Hudson, Atlanta		20	6	13	1	1	1	1	0	13
Caldwell, Atlanta		23	6	9	0	1	4	3	5	12
Goodrich, Phoenix		6	2	4	1	2	1	1	1	5
West, Los Angeles					Injured						
TOTALS		240	44	105	24	31	58	27	30	112

TEAM REBOUNDS: 6.

EAST ALL-STARS (123)

PLAYER, TEAM	POS.	MIN.	FGM	FGA	FTM	FTA	REB.	AST.	PF	PTS.
Havlicek, Boston	F	31	6	14	2	2	7	2	2	14
Lucas, Cincinnati	F	17	2	5	4	5	6	1	3	8
Russell, Boston	C	28	1	4	1	2	6	3	1	3
Robertson, Cincinnati	G	32	8	16	8	8	6	5	3	24
Monroe, Baltimore	G	27	6	15	9	12	4	4	4	21
Johnson, Baltimore		18	4	10	5	8	10	0	3	13
Bing, Detroit		13	1	3	1	1	0	3	0	3
Cunningham, Philadelphia		22	5	10	0	0	5	1	3	10
Reed, New York		14	5	8	0	0	4	2	2	10
Unseld, Baltimore		14	5	7	1	3	8	1	3	11
Greer, Philadelphia		17	0	1	4	5	3	2	2	4
McGlocklin, Milwaukee		7	1	2	0	0	1	0	0	2
TOTALS		240	44	95	35	46	60	24	26	123

TEAM REBOUNDS: 6.

Score by Periods:	1st	2nd	3rd	4th	Totals
East	35	25	26	37	123
West	19	34	30	29	112

Officials: Joe Gushue and Norm Drucker. Attendance: 12,348.

GAME 20, Jan. 20, 1970, at Philadelphia

Coaches—East, Red Holzman, New York/West, Richie Guerin, Atlanta

MVP—Willis Reed, New York

WEST ALL-STARS (135)

PLAYER, TEAM	POS.	MIN.	FGM	FGA	FTM	FTA	REB.	AST.	PF	PTS.
Baylor, Los Angeles	F	26	2	9	5	7	7	3	3	9
Hawkins, Phoenix	F	19	2	4	6	6	4	2	3	10
Hayes, San Diego	C	35	9	21	6	12	15	1	1	24
Hudson, Atlanta	G	18	5	12	5	5	1	0	1	15
West, Los Angeles	G	31	7	12	8	12	5	5	3	22
Mullins, San Francisco		14	4	6	0	0	1	1	2	8
Rule, Seattle		13	2	6	1	1	4	0	2	5
Caldwell, Atlanta		19	5	11	3	4	7	1	2	13
Walker, Chicago		17	1	3	2	2	2	1	2	4
Bridges, Atlanta		15	2	2	1	5	4	2	1	5
Van Arsdale, Phoenix		16	4	8	0	0	2	2	0	8
Wilkens, Seattle		17	5	7	2	3	2	4	1	12
Thurmond, San Francisco					Injured						
TOTALS		240	48	101	39	57	54	22	21	135

TEAM REBOUNDS: 12.

EAST ALL-STARS (142)

PLAYER, TEAM	POS.	MIN.	FGM	FGA	FTM	FTA	REB.	AST.	PF	PTS.
Cunningham, Philadelphia	F	28	7	13	5	5	4	2	3	19
Havlicek, Boston	F	29	7	15	3	3	5	7	2	17
Reed, New York	C	30	9	18	3	3	11	0	6	21
Robertson, Cincinnati	G	29	9	11	3	4	6	4	3	21
Frazier, New York	G	24	3	7	1	2	3	4	2	7
Greer, Philadelphia		21	7	11	1	1	4	3	4	15
DeBusschere, New York		14	5	10	0	0	7	2	1	10
Abdul-Jabbar, Milwaukee		18	4	8	2	2	11	4	6	10
Johnson, Baltimore		17	5	12	0	0	7	1	2	10
Van Arsdale, Cincinnati		8	2	7	1	1	0	1	2	5
Walker, Detroit		14	0	3	1	1	1	0	2	1
Robinson, Milwaukee		8	3	4	0	0	1	2	2	6
TOTALS		240	61	119	20	22	60	30	35	142

TEAM REBOUNDS: 5.

Score by Periods:	1st	2nd	3rd	4th	Totals
East	36	35	35	36	142
West	21	38	26	50	135

Officials: Richie Powers and Jack Madden. Attendance: 15,244.

GAME 21, Jan. 12, 1971, at San Diego

Coaches—East, Red Holzman, New York/West, Larry Costello, Milwaukee

MVP—Lenny Wilkens, Seattle

EAST ALL-STARS (107)

PLAYER, TEAM	POS.	MIN.	FGM	FGA	FTM	FTA	REB.	AST.	PF	PTS.
Cunningham, Philadelphia	F	19	2	8	1	2	4	3	1	5
Havlicek, Boston	F	24	6	12	0	2	3	2	3	12
Reed, New York	C	27	5	16	4	6	13	1	3	14
Monroe, Baltimore	G	18	3	9	0	0	5	2	3	6
Frazier, New York	G	26	3	9	0	0	6	5	2	6
Green, Cincinnati		7	2	3	0	1	2	0	1	4
DeBusschere, New York		19	4	7	0	0	7	3	3	8
Hudson, Atlanta		17	6	13	2	3	3	1	3	14
Johnson, Baltimore		23	5	12	2	2	4	2	3	12
Johnson, Cleveland		2	0	0	0	0	0	1	0	0
Kauffman, Buffalo		4	0	2	0	0	0	0	0	0
Unseld, Baltimore		21	4	9	0	0	10	2	2	8
Van Arsdale, Cincinnati		11	4	8	0	0	2	1	1	8
White, Boston		22	5	10	0	0	9	2	2	10
TOTALS		240	49	118	9	18	68	25	27	107

WEST ALL-STARS (108)

PLAYER, TEAM	POS.	MIN.	FGM	FGA	FTM	FTA	REB.	AST.	PF	PTS.
Hawkins, Phoenix	F	1	0	0	0	0	0	0	0	0
Lucas, San Francisco	F	29	5	9	2	2	9	4	2	12
Abdul-Jabbar, Milwaukee	C	30	8	16	3	4	14	1	2	19
Bing, Detroit	G	19	2	7	0	0	2	2	1	4
West, Los Angeles	G	20	2	4	1	3	1	9	1	5
Hayes, San Diego		19	4	13	2	3	4	2	1	10
Love, Chicago		21	6	12	4	5	4	0	2	16
Chamberlain, Los Angeles		18	1	1	0	0	8	5	0	2
Mullins, San Francisco		3	0	0	0	0	0	0	0	0
Petrie, Portland		5	0	3	0	0	0	1	0	0
Robertson, Milwaukee		24	2	6	1	3	2	2	3	5
Van Arsdale, Phoenix		12	2	4	0	1	5	3	1	4
Walker, Chicago		19	3	9	4	5	3	1	1	10
Wilkens, Seattle		20	8	11	5	5	1	1	1	21
TOTALS		240	43	95	22	31	53	31	15	108

Score by Periods:	1st	2nd	3rd	4th	Totals
West	30	32	20	26	108
East	26	34	23	24	107

Officials: Mendy Rudolph and Ed Rush. Attendance: 14,378.

GAME 22, Jan. 18, 1972, at Los Angeles

Coaches—East, Tom Heinsohn, Boston/West, Bill Sharman, Los Angeles

MVP—Jerry West, Los Angeles

EAST ALL-STARS (110)

PLAYER, TEAM	POS.	MIN.	FGM	FGA	FTM	FTA	REB.	AST.	PF	PTS.
Havlicek, Boston	F	24	5	13	5	5	3	2	2	15
Cunningham, Philadelphia	F	24	4	13	6	8	10	3	4	14
Cowens, Boston	C	32	5	12	4	5	20	1	4	14
Hudson, Atlanta	G	18	2	7	2	2	3	3	3	6
Frazier, New York	G	25	7	11	1	2	3	5	2	15
Johnson, Cleveland		3	0	2	0	0	1	0	1	0
Kauffman, Buffalo		7	1	1	0	0	1	1	3	2
Marin, Baltimore		15	5	8	1	1	0	1	2	11
Unseld, Baltimore		16	1	5	0	0	7	1	3	2
Van Arsdale, Cincinnati		4	0	1	0	0	1	0	0	0
White, Boston		18	6	15	0	2	4	3	1	12
Beard, Cleveland		7	1	4	1	1	1	0	0	3
Clark, Baltimore		21	2	5	4	4	1	6	1	8
DeBusschere, New York		26	4	8	0	0	11	0	2	8
TOTALS		240	43	105	24	30	66	26	28	110

WEST ALL-STARS (112)

PLAYER, TEAM	POS.	MIN.	FGM	FGA	FTM	FTA	REB.	AST.	PF	PTS.
Love, Chicago	F	16	4	11	0	2	6	0	1	8
Haywood, Seattle	F	25	4	10	3	4	7	1	2	11
Abdul-Jabbar, Milwaukee	C	19	5	10	2	2	7	2	0	12
Goodrich, Los Angeles	G	14	2	7	0	0	1	2	2	4
West, Los Angeles	G	27	6	9	1	2	6	5	2	13
Robertson, Milwaukee		24	3	9	5	10	3	3	4	11
Russell, Golden State		20	4	13	2	2	1	0	1	10
Silas, Phoenix		15	0	6	2	3	9	1	1	2
Walker, Detroit		16	4	9	2	5	2	1	1	10
Hawkins, Phoenix		14	5	7	3	4	4	0	1	13
Hayes, Houston		11	1	6	2	2	2	0	2	4
Chamberlain, Los Angeles		24	3	3	2	8	10	3	2	8
Lanier, Detroit		5	0	2	2	3	3	0	0	2
Wicks, Portland		10	2	5	0	0	2	0	3	4
TOTALS		240	43	107	26	47	63	18	22	112

Score by Periods:	1st	2nd	3rd	4th	Totals
West	27	27	33	25	112
East	33	31	20	26	110

Officials: Darell Garretson and Manny Sokol. Attendance: 17,214.

GAME 23, Jan. 23, 1973, at Chicago

Coaches—East, Tom Heinsohn, Boston/West, Bill Sharman, Los Angeles

MVP—Dave Cowens, Boston

EAST ALL-STARS (104)

PLAYER, TEAM	POS.	MIN.	FGM	FGA	FTM	FTA	REB.	AST.	PF	PTS.
Havlicek, Boston	F	22	6	10	2	5	3	5	1	14
DeBusschere, New York	F	25	4	8	1	2	7	2	1	9
Cowens, Boston	C	30	7	15	1	1	13	1	2	15
Maravich, Atlanta	G	22	4	8	0	0	3	5	4	8
Frazier, New York	G	26	5	15	0	0	6	2	1	10
Hayes, Baltimore		16	4	13	2	2	12	0	0	10
Hudson, Atlanta		9	2	8	2	2	2	0	2	6
Kauffman, Buffalo		9	1	2	1	2	1	1	1	3
Block, Philadelphia		5	2	4	0	0	2	0	1	4
Bradley, New York		12	2	5	0	0	1	0	2	4
Marin, Houston		11	2	6	0	0	4	1	0	4
Unseld, Baltimore		11	2	4	0	0	5	1	0	4
White, Boston		18	3	7	0	0	5	5	0	6
Wilkens, Cleveland		24	3	8	1	2	2	1	1	7
TOTALS		240	47	113	10	16	66	24	16	104

WEST ALL-STARS (84)

PLAYER, TEAM	POS.	MIN.	FGM	FGA	FTM	FTA	REB.	AST.	PF	PTS.
Haywood, Seattle	F	22	5	10	2	2	10	0	5	12
Wicks, Portland	F	24	4	10	5	5	5	1	2	13
Chamberlain, Los Angeles	C	22	1	2	0	0	7	3	0	2
Archibald, KC-Omaha	G	27	6	12	5	5	1	5	1	17
West, Los Angeles	G	20	3	6	0	0	4	3	2	6
Bing, Detroit		19	0	4	2	2	3	0	1	2
Lanier, Detroit		12	5	9	0	0	6	0	1	10
Love, Chicago		12	2	4	2	2	3	0	1	6
Scott, Phoenix		14	0	5	0	0	2	2	1	0
Thurmond, Golden State		14	2	5	0	0	4	1	2	4
Walker, Chicago		16	1	5	2	2	1	0	2	4
Dandridge, Milwaukee		11	2	4	0	0	3	0	0	4
Goodrich, Los Angeles		16	1	7	0	0	2	1	2	2
Hawkins, Phoenix		11	1	5	0	0	2	3	1	2
Abdul-Jabbar, Milwaukee		Selected but did not play								
Barry, Golden State		Injured								
TOTALS		240	33	88	18	18	53	19	21	84

Score by Periods:	1st	2nd	3rd	4th	Totals
East	27	23	26	28	104
West	27	18	20	19	84

Officials: Richie Powers and Jake O'Donnell. Attendance: 17,527.

GAME 24, Jan. 15, 1974, at Seattle

Coaches—East, Tom Heinsohn, Boston/West, Larry Costello, Milwaukee

MVP—Bob Lanier, Detroit

EAST ALL-STARS (123)

PLAYER, TEAM	POS.	MIN.	FGM	FGA	FTM	FTA	REB.	AST.	PF	PTS.
Havlicek, Boston	F	18	5	10	0	2	0	2	2	10
Hudson, Atlanta	F	17	5	8	2	2	3	1	2	12
Cowens, Boston	C	26	5	10	1	3	12	1	3	11
Frazier, New York	G	28	5	12	2	2	2	5	1	12
Maravich, Atlanta	G	22	4	15	7	9	3	4	2	15
Hayes, Capital		35	5	13	2	3	15	6	4	12
McAdoo, Buffalo		13	3	4	5	8	3	1	4	11
White, Boston		22	6	12	1	3	6	4	1	13
DeBusschere, New York		24	8	14	0	0	3	3	2	16
Chenier, Capital		13	3	6	1	2	2	1	0	7
Tomjanovich, Houston		17	2	6	0	0	5	0	1	0
Carr, Cleveland		5	0	4	0	0	1	0	1	0
TOTALS		240	51	113	21	34	55	28	23	123

WEST ALL-STARS (134)

PLAYER, TEAM	POS.	MIN.	FGM	FGA	FTM	FTA	REB.	AST.	PF	PTS.
Barry, Golden State	F	19	3	6	2	2	4	3	3	8
Walker, Chicago	F	14	4	5	4	4	2	1	1	12
Abdul-Jabbar, Milwaukee	C	23	7	11	0	0	8	6	2	14
Goodrich, Los Angeles	G	26	9	16	0	0	4	6	2	18
Petrie, Portland	G	26	3	11	2	2	2	4	1	8
Wicks, Portland		24	5	6	6	10	1	1	4	16
Scott, Phoenix		19	0	4	2	2	1	4	2	2
Lanier, Detroit		26	11	15	2	2	10	2	1	24
Haywood, Seattle		33	10	17	3	3	11	5	5	23
Bing, Detroit		16	2	9	1	1	6	2	1	5
Van Lier, Chicago		9	0	0	0	0	1	2	1	0
Thurmond, Golden State		5	2	4	0	1	3	0	0	4
West, Los Angeles		Injured								
TOTALS		240	56	104	22	27	53	36	23	134

Score by Periods:	1st	2nd	3rd	4th	Totals
East	29	18	38	38	123
West	39	27	35	33	134

Blocked Shots: Cowens, Hayes, Hudson, McAdoo, White; Haywood 3, Lanier 2, Abdul-Jabbar, Scott. Officials: Don Murphy and Bob Rakel. Attendance: 14,360.

GAME 25, Jan. 14, 1975, at Phoenix

Coaches—East, K. C. Jones, Washington/West, Al Attles, Golden State
MVP—Walt Frazier, New York

EAST ALL-STARS (108)

PLAYER, TEAM	POS.	MIN.	FGM	FGA	FTM	FTA	REB.	AST.	PF	PTS.
Havlicek, Boston	F	31	7	12	2	2	6	1	2	16
Hayes, Washington	F	17	2	6	0	0	5	2	1	4
McAdoo, Buffalo	C	26	4	9	3	3	6	2	4	11
Frazier, New York	G	35	10	17	10	11	5	2	2	30
Monroe, New York	G	25	3	8	3	5	3	2	2	9
Tomjanovich, Houston		14	0	3	0	0	3	0	3	0
Unseld, Washington		15	2	3	2	2	6	1	2	6
Chenier, Washington		23	4	8	1	2	2	1	0	9
Cowens, Boston		15	3	7	0	0	6	3	4	6
Mix, Philadelphia		11	2	5	0	0	2	0	2	4
White, Boston		13	1	2	5	6	1	4	1	7
Silas, Boston		15	2	4	2	2	2	2	2	6
TOTALS		240	40	84	28	33	47	20	25	108

WEST ALL-STARS (102)

PLAYER, TEAM	POS.	MIN.	FGM	FGA	FTM	FTA	REB.	AST.	PF	PTS.
Barry, Golden State	F	38	11	20	0	0	5	8	4	22
Haywood, Seattle	F	17	1	9	0	0	3	0	1	2
Abdul-Jabbar, Milwaukee	C	19	3	10	1	2	10	3	2	7
Archibald, KC-Omaha	G	36	10	15	7	8	2	6	2	27
Goodrich, Los Angeles	G	15	2	4	0	0	1	4	1	4
Wicks, Portland		23	7	19	2	3	9	1	1	16
Lanier, Detroit		12	1	4	0	0	7	2	3	2
Scott, Phoenix		16	1	6	0	0	2	1	3	2
Bing, Detroit		12	0	2	2	2	0	1	0	2
Dandridge, Milwaukee		18	2	6	0	0	2	1	3	4
Lacey, KC-Omaha		17	2	6	2	2	7	1	2	6
Price, Milwaukee		17	3	9	2	2	2	0	4	8
TOTALS		240	43	110	16	19	50	28	26	102

Score by Periods:	1st	2nd	3rd	4th	Totals
East	29	22	32	25	108
West	29	17	27	29	102

Blocked Shots: Barry, Abdul-Jabbar, Archibald, Wicks, Lacey. Officials: Mendy Rudolph and Jerry Loeber. Attendance: 12,885.

GAME 26, Feb. 3, 1976, at Philadelphia

Coaches—East, Tom Heinsohn, Boston/West, Al Attles, Golden State
MVP—Dave Bing, Washington

WEST ALL-STARS (109)

PLAYER, TEAM	POS.	MIN.	FGM	FGA	FTM	FTA	REB.	AST.	PF	PTS.
Barry, Golden State	F	28	6	15	5	5	4	2	5	17
Dandridge, Milwaukee	F	27	5	10	0	0	6	0	4	10
Abdul-Jabbar, Los Angeles	C	36	9	16	4	4	15	3	3	22
Archibald, Kansas City	G	30	5	13	3	3	5	7	0	13
Winters, Milwaukee	G	16	1	5	0	0	2	1	2	2
Adams, Phoenix		11	2	4	0	0	3	0	1	4
Wilkes, Golden St.		14	3	9	2	2	4	2	0	8
Rowe, Detroit		8	0	2	1	2	2	0	2	1
Wedman, Kansas City		20	4	5	0	0	6	2	2	8
Van Lier, Chicago		14	1	4	1	2	1	0	2	3
Brown, Seattle		24	7	13	0	0		1	3	14
P. Smith, Golden State		12	3	7	1	4	1	0	1	7
TOTALS		240	46	103	17	22	49	18	25	109

EAST ALL-STARS (123)

PLAYER, TEAM	POS.	MIN.	FGM	FGA	FTM	FTA	REB.	AST.	PF	PTS.
Havlicek, Boston	F	21	3	10	3	3	2	2	0	9
Hayes, Washington	F	31	6	14	0	2	10	1	5	12
McAdoo, Buffalo	C	29	10	14	2	4	7	1	5	22
Frazier, New York	G	19	2	7	4	4	2	3	0	8
Bing, Washington	G	26	7	11	2	2	3	4	1	16
Cowens, Boston		23	6	13	4	5	16	1	3	16
McGinnis, Philadelphia		19	4	9	2	4	7	2	2	10
Tomjanovich, Houston		12	1	2	0	0	3	0	2	2
Drew, Atlanta		9	1	3	0	0	3	0	2	2
White, Boston		16	3	7	0	0	1	1	1	6
Collins, Philadelphia		20	5	10	2	2	6	3	3	12
R. Smith, Buffalo		15	4	7	0	0	1	3	0	8
TOTALS		240	52	107	19	26	61	21	24	123

Score by Periods:	1st	2nd	3rd	4th	Totals
East	28	17	38	40	123
West	23	27	30	29	109

Blocked Shots: R. Smith, Abdul-Jabbar 3, Van Lier. Officials: Paul Mihalak and Darell Garretson. Attendance: 17,511.

GAME 27, Feb. 13, 1977, at Milwaukee

Coaches—East, Gene Shue, Philadelphia/West, Larry Brown, Denver
MVP—Julius Erving, Philadelphia

EAST ALL-STARS (124)

PLAYER, TEAM	POS.	MIN.	FGM	FGA	FTM	FTA	REB.	AST.	PF	PTS.
Erving, Philadelphia	F	30	12	20	6	6	12	3	2	30
McGinnis, Philadelphia	F	26	2	9	0	2	7	2	3	4
McAdoo, Knicks	C	38	13	23	4	4	10	2	3	30
Collins, Philadelphia	G	21	3	6	2	2	2	6	2	8
Maravich, New Orleans	G	21	5	13	0	0	4	1	1	10
Havlicek, Boston		17	2	5	0	0	1	1	1	4
Monroe, Knicks		15	2	7	0	0	3	1		4
White, Boston		15	5	7	0	0	1	2	0	10
Hayes, Washington		11	6	6	0	0	2	1	5	12
Tomjanovich, Houston		22	3	9	0	0	10	1	1	6
Chenier, Washington		12	3	6	0	0	1	1	0	6
Gervin, San Antonio		12	0	6	0	0	1	0	1	0
Cowens, Boston					Injured					
TOTALS		240	56	117	12	14	47	26	20	124

WEST ALL-STARS (125)

PLAYER, TEAM	POS.	MIN.	FGM	FGA	FTM	FTA	REB.	AST.	PF	PTS.
Jones, Denver	F	14	1	4	0	0	0	3	0	2
Thompson, Denver	F	29	7	9	4	6	7	3	3	18
Issel, Denver	C	10	0	3	0	0	1	0	0	0
Westphal, Phoenix	G	31	10	16	0	0	1	6	2	20
Van Lier, Chicago	G	14	1	3	0	0	1	1	2	2
Abdul-Jabbar, Los Angeles		23	8	14	5	6	4	2	1	21
Barry, Golden State		29	7	16	4	4	4	8	1	18
Smith, Golden State		28	6	13	1	2	6	8	3	13
Buse, Indiana		19	2	4	0	0	2	5	0	4
Knight, Indiana		12	1	5	2	2	5	0	0	4
Lanier, Detroit		20	7	8	3	3	10	4	3	17
Lucas, Portland		11	3	9	0	0	4	2	2	6
Walton, Portland					Injured					
TOTALS		240	53	104	19	23	45	42	17	125

Score by Periods:	1st	2nd	3rd	4th	Totals
East	34	34	21	35	124
West	23	35	39	28	125

Blocked Shots: Erving, McAdoo, Tomjanovich, Gervin; Westphal 2, Jones, Abdul-Jabbar, Lanier, Lucas. Officials: Earl Strom and Lee Jones. Attendance: 10,938.

GAME 28, Feb. 5, 1978, at Atlanta

Coaches—East, Billy Cunningham, Philadelphia/West, Jack Ramsay, Portland

MVP—Randy Smith, Buffalo

WEST ALL-STARS (125)

PLAYER, TEAM	POS.	MIN.	FGM	FGA	FTM	FTA	REB.	AST.	PF	PTS.
Barry, Golden State	F	30	7	17	1	1	4	5	6	15
Lucas, Portland	F	33	6	13	0	0	13	4	2	12
Walton, Portland	C	31	6	14	3	3	10	2	3	15
Thompson, Denver	G	35	10	16	2	4	3	3	4	22
Westphal, Phoenix	G	24	9	14	2	5	0	5	4	20
Davis, Phoenix		15	3	6	4	4	1	6	1	10
Gilmore, Chicago		13	2	4	6	8	2	0	1	10
Hollins, Portland		23	3	8	4	5	0	8	2	10
Jones, Denver		18	1	3	0	0	6	2	4	2
Winters, Milwaukee		14	4	7	0	0	4	1	2	8
Lanier, Detroit		4	0	0	1	2	2	0	0	1
TOTALS		240	51	102	23	32	45	36	29	125

Turnovers: Barry 5, Walton 4, Thompson 4, Westphal 3, Winters 3, Hollins, Jones, Lanier. Total—23.

EAST ALL-STARS (133)

PLAYER, TEAM	POS.	MIN.	FGM	FGA	FTM	FTA	REB.	AST.	PF	PTS.
Erving, Philadelphia	F	27	3	14	10	12	8	3	1	16
Kenon, San Antonio	F	20	8	15	0	0	4	0	0	16
Cowens, Boston	C	28	7	9	0	0	14	5	5	14
Gervin, San Antonio	G	18	4	11	1	3	2	1	2	9
Havlicek, Boston	G	22	5	8	0	0	3	1	2	10
Collins, Philadelphia		27	3	8	8	11	5	8	3	14
Robinson, New Orleans		24	3	7	1	2	6	1	2	7
McAdoo, New York		20	7	14	0	0	4	0	2	14
Smith, Buffalo		29	11	14	5	6	7	6	5	27
Hayes, Washington		11	1	7	0	0	4	0	4	2
Malone, Houston		14	1	1	2	4	4	1	1	4
Maravich, New Orleans		Injured								
TOTALS		240	53	108	27	38	61	26	27	133

Turnovers: Havlicek 4, Collins 4, Robinson 3, McAdoo 3, Smith 3, Erving 2, Kenon 2, Cowens 2, Gervin 2, Hayes. Total—26.

Score by Periods:	1st	2nd	3rd	4th	Totals
West	39	27	34	25	125
East	28	29	35	41	133

Blocked Shots: Walton 2, Gilmore 2, Westphal, Jones, Erving, Gervin. Officials: Jake O'Donnell and Jim Capers. Attendance: 15,491.

GAME 29, Feb. 4, 1979, at Detroit

Coaches—East, Dick Motta, Washington/West, Lenny Wilkens, Seattle

MVP—David Thompson, Denver

WEST ALL-STARS (134)

PLAYER, TEAM	POS.	MIN.	FGM	FGA	FTM	FTA	REB.	AST.	PF	PTS.
M. Johnson, Milwaukee	F	20	3	11	4	6	6	2	1	10
McGinnis, Denver	F	25	5	12	6	11	6	3	4	16
Abdul-Jabbar, Los Angeles	C	28	5	12	1	2	8	3	4	11
Thompson, Denver	G	34	11	17	3	7	5	2	4	25
Westphal, Phoenix	G	21	8	12	1	2	1	5	0	17
Birdsong, Kansas City		14	4	6	1	2	2	0	1	9
Davis, Phoenix		19	4	9	0	0	4	4	0	8
Gilmore, Chicago		15	3	4	2	2	1	2	1	8
D. Johnson, Seattle		27	5	7	2	2	1	3	3	12
Lucas, Portland		19	4	10	2	2	7	1	5	10
Sikma, Seattle		18	4	5	0	0	4	0	1	8
TOTALS		240	56	105	33	36	45	25	24	134

Turnovers: Abdul-Jabbar 3, Lucas 3, Davis 2, Thompson, Westphal, Birdsong, Gilmore, Johnson. Total—13.

EAST ALL-STARS (129)

PLAYER, TEAM	POS.	MIN.	FGM	FGA	FTM	FTA	REB.	AST.	PF	PTS.
Erving, Philadelphia	F	39	10	22	9	12	8	5	4	29
Tomjanovich, Houston	F	24	6	13	0	0	6	1	2	12
Malone, Houston	C	17	2	2	4	5	7	1	0	8
Maravich, New Orleans	G	14	5	8	0	0	2	2	1	10
Gervin, San Antonio	G	34	8	16	10	11	6	2	4	26
Dandridge, Washington		18	3	5	2	3	3	1	2	8
Hayes, Washington		28	5	11	3	5	13	0	5	13
Kenon, San Antonio		7	1	3	1	2	2	1	0	3
Lanier, Detroit		31	5	10	0	0	4	4	4	10
Murphy, Houston		15	3	5	0	1	1	5	4	6
Russell, Cleveland		13	2	8	0	0	1	0	0	4
Collins, Philadelphia		Injured								
TOTALS		240	50	103	29	38	53	22	26	129

Turnovers: Maravich 4, Murphy 4, Gervin 3, Erving, Malone, Dandridge, Hayes, Russell. Total—16.

Score by Periods:	1st	2nd	3rd	4th	Totals
West	36	44	24	30	134
East	27	31	40	31	129

Blocked Shots: Abdul-Jabbar, Thompson, D. Johnson, Gervin, Hayes, Lanier. Officials: John Vanak, Jack Madden and Hugh Evans. Attendance: 31,745.

GAME 30, Feb. 4, 1980, at Landover, Md.

Coaches—East, Billy Cunningham, Philadelphia/West, Lenny Wilkens, Seattle

MVP—George Gervin, San Antonio

WEST ALL-STARS (136)

PLAYER, TEAM	POS.	MIN.	FGM	FGA	FTM	FTA	REB.	AST.	PF	PTS.
Dantley, Utah	F	30	8	15	7	8	5	2	1	23
M. Johnson, Milwaukee	F	34	1	6	2	4	4	1	2	4
Abdul-Jabbar, Los Angeles	C	30	6	17	5	6	16	9	5	17
Free, San Diego	G	21	7	13	0	1	3	5	1	14
E. Johnson, Los Angeles	G	24	5	8	2	2	4	4	3	12
D. Johnson, Seattle		20	7	13	5	6	4	1	3	19
Davis, Phoenix		23	5	10	2	2	4	2	2	12
Sikma, Seattle		28	4	10	0	0	8	4	5	8
Westphal, Phoenix		27	8	14	5	6	1	5	5	21
Washington, Portland		14	1	6	2	4	8	1	4	4
Birdsong, Kansas City		14	1	2	0	0	0	1	2	2
TOTALS		265	53	114	30	37	55	34	32	136

FG Pct.: .465   FT Pct.: .811.   Turnovers: Abdul-Jabbar 9, Free 5, Davis 3, Westphal 3, Dantley 2, E. Johnson 2, D. Johnson 2, Sikma, Washington, Birdsong. Total—29. Team Rebounds: 14.

EAST ALL-STARS (144)

PLAYER, TEAM	POS.	MIN.	FGM	FGA	FTM	FTA	REB.	AST.	PF	PTS.
Drew, Atlanta	F	15	0	4	4	5	3	0	5	4
Erving, Philadelphia	F	20	4	12	3	4	5	2	5	11
Malone, Houston	C	31	7	12	6	12	12	2	4	20
Gervin, San Antonio	G	40	14	26	6	9	10	3	2	34
E. Johnson, Atlanta	G	32	11	16	0	0	1	7	2	22
Roundfield, Atlanta		27	7	15	4	9	13	0	2	18
Archibald, Boston		21	0	8	2	3	3	6	1	2
Hayes, Washington		29	5	10	2	2	5	4	5	12
Richardson, New York		13	3	7	0	0	1	2	2	6
Cartwright, New York		14	4	8	0	0	3	1	1	8
Bird, Boston		23	3	6	0	0	6	7	1	7
TOTALS		265	58	124	27	44	62	34	30	144

FG Pct.: .468.   FT Pct.: .614.   Turnovers: Malone 5, Drew 3, Gervin 3, Roundfield 3, Hayes 3, Cartwright 3, Bird 3, Erving 2, E. Johnson 2, Archibald 2, Richardson 2. Total—31. Team Rebounds: 20.

GAME 30 (*Continued*)

Score by Periods:	1st	2nd	3rd	4th	OT	Totals
West	37	27	27	37	8	136
East	28	36	44	20	16	144

Blocked Shots: Abdul-Jabbar 6, Hayes 4, Sikma 3, Earvin Johnson 2, Malone 2, Roundfield 2, M. Johnson, Free, D. Johnson, Westphal, Washington, Erving.   3-Pt. Field Goals: Earvin Johnson 0-1, Bird 1-2.   Officials: Joe Gushue and Ed Rush.   Attendance: 19,035.

GAME 31, Feb. 1, 1981, at Richfield, Ohio

Coaches—East, Billy Cunningham, Philadelphia/West, John MacLeod, Phoenix

MVP—Nate Archibald, Boston

WEST ALL-STARS (120)

PLAYER, TEAM	POS.	MIN.	FGM	FGA	FTM	FTA	REB.	AST.	PF	PTS.
Davis, Phoenix	F	22	5	9	2	2	7	1	2	12
Dantley, Utah	F	21	3	9	2	2	5	0	1	12
Abdul-Jabbar, Los Angeles	C	23	6	9	3	3	6	4	3	15
Westphal, Seattle	G	25	8	12	3	3	4	3	3	19
Gervin, San Antonio	G	24	5	9	1	2	3	0	3	11
Wilkes, Los Angeles		25	6	12	3	3	8	3	3	15
Malone, Houston		22	3	8	2	4	6	3	3	8
Robinson, Phoenix		21	3	6	0	0	5	2	4	6
Sikma, Seattle		21	2	6	2	2	4	4	5	6
Johnson, Phoenix		24	5	8	9	10	2	1	1	19
Birdsong, Houston		12	0	3	1	2	1	1	0	1
TOTALS		240	46	91	28	33	51	22	28	120

FG Pct.: .505.   FT Pct.: .848.   Turnovers: Westphal 4, Robinson 4, Abdul-Jabbar 3, Gervin 2, Wilkes 2, Sikma 2, D. Johnson 2, Davis, Malone, Birdsong.   Total—22.

EAST ALL-STARS (123)

PLAYER, TEAM	POS.	MIN.	FGM	FGA	FTM	FTA	REB.	AST.	PF	PTS.
Bird, Boston	F	18	1	5	0	0	4	3	1	2
Erving, Philadelphia	F	29	6	15	6	7	3	2	2	18
Gilmore, Chicago	C	22	5	7	1	2	6	2	4	11
E. Johnson, Atlanta	G	28	7	12	2	3	2	2	1	16
Theus, Chicago	G	19	4	7	0	0	1	3	0	8
Archibald, Boston		25	4	7	1	3	5	9	3	9
Parish, Boston		25	5	18	6	6	10	2	3	16
Jones, Philadelphia		16	5	11	1	1	4	0	2	11
M. Johnson, Milwaukee		19	1	2	5	6	4	2	2	7
Richardson, New York		24	5	8	1	2	5	3	3	11
Mitchell, Cleveland		15	6	12	2	2	4	2	2	14
Roundfield, Atlanta						Injured				
TOTALS		240	49	104	25	32	48	30	23	123

FG Pct.: .471.   FT Pct.: .781.   Turnovers: Theus 4, E. Johnson 3, Bird 2, Erving 2, Archibald 2, Richardson 2, Parish, Mitchell.   Total—17.

Score by Periods:	1st	2nd	3rd	4th	Totals
West	27	31	30	32	120
East	23	38	36	26	123

Blocked Shots: Abdul-Jabbar 4, Parish 2, Gervin, Sikma, Erving, Gilmore, Jones.   Officials: Paul Mihalak and Darell Garretson.   Attendance: 20,239.

GAME 32, Jan. 31, 1982, at East Rutherford, N.J.

Coaches—East, Bill Fitch, Boston/West, Pat Riley, Los Angeles

MVP—Larry Bird, Boston

WEST ALL-STARS (118)

PLAYER, TEAM	POS.	MIN.	FGM	FGA	FTM	FTA	OFF.	DEF.	TOT.	AST.	PF	ST.	PTS.
Dantley, Utah	F	21	6	8	0	1	1	1	2	0	2	0	12
Shelton, Seattle	F	20	3	3	1	2	4	5	9	1	4	1	7
Abdul-Jabbar, Los Angeles	C	22	1	10	0	0	1	2	3	1	3	0	2
G. Williams, Seattle	G	26	9	19	4	4	2	0	2	9	1	1	22
Gervin, San Antonio	G	27	5	14	2	2	1	5	6	1	3	3	12
King, Golden State		14	2	7	2	2	0	4	4	1	2	3	6
Nixon, Los Angeles		19	7	14	0	0	0	0	0	2	0	1	14
E. Johnson, Los Angeles		23	5	9	6	7	3	1	4	7	5	0	16
Malone, Houston		20	5	11	2	6	5	6	11	0	2	1	12
Sikma, Seattle		21	5	11	0	0	2	7	9	1	2	2	10
English, Denver		12	2	6	0	0	2	3	5	1	2	1	4
D. Johnson, Phoenix		15	0	2	1	2	2	3	5	1	1	0	1
TOTALS		240	50	114	18	26	23	37	60	25	27	13	118

FG Pct.: .439.   FT Pct.: .692.   Turnovers: D. Johnson 3, Malone 3, King 2, Shelton 2, Williams 2, Abdul-Jabbar, Dantley, English, E. Johnson. Total—16.   Team Rebounds: 11.

EAST ALL-STARS (120)

PLAYER, TEAM	POS.	MIN.	FGM	FGA	FTM	FTA	OFF.	DEF.	TOT.	AST.	PF	ST.	PTS.
Erving, Philadelphia	F	32	7	16	2	4	3	5	8	2	4	1	16
Bird, Boston	F	28	7	12	5	8	0	12	12	5	3	1	19
Gilmore, Chicago	C	16	3	6	1	1	1	2	3	2	4	0	7
Archibald, Boston	G	23	2	5	2	2	1	1	2	7	3	1	6
Thomas, Detroit	G	17	5	7	2	4	1	0	1	4	1	3	12
Moncrief, Milwaukee		22	3	11	0	2	3	1	4	1	2	1	6
Lanier, Milwaukee		11	3	7	2	2	2	1	3	0	3	0	8
Richardson, New York		20	5	10	0	0	2	2	4	1	2	10	10
Jones, Philadelphia		14	2	5	1	2	1	3	4	1	2	1	5
B. Williams, New Jersey		22	2	7	0	2	1	9	10	1	3	0	4
Parish, Boston		20	9	12	3	4	0	7	7	1	2	0	21
Tripucka, Detroit		15	3	7	0	0	1	1	2	0	0	6	6
Roundfield, Atlanta						Injured							
TOTALS		240	51	105	18	31	13	44	57	30	28	10	120

FG Pct.: .486.   FT Pct.: .581.   Turnovers: Bird 4, Erving 4, Williams 3, Archibald 2, Gilmore 2, Lanier, Moncrief, Parish, Richardson, Thomas, Tripucka.   Total—21.   Team Rebounds: 11.

Score by Periods:	1st	2nd	3rd	4th	Totals
West	39	22	28	29	118
East	34	29	27	30	120

Blocked Shots: Gervin 3, Abdul-Jabbar 2, D. Johnson 2, King, Malone, Sikma; Erving 2, Parish 2, B. Williams 2, Bird, Gilmore, Lanier.   3-Pt. Field Goals: G. Williams 0-1.   Officials: Jake O'Donnell and Wally Rooney.   Attendance: 20,149.

GAME 33, Feb. 13, 1983, at Los Angeles

Coaches—East, Billy Cunningham, Philadelphia/West, Pat Riley, Los Angeles

MVP—Julius Erving, Philadelphia

EAST ALL-STARS (132)

PLAYER, TEAM	POS.	MIN.	FGM	FGA	FTM	FTA	OFF.	DEF.	TOT.	AST.	PF	ST.	PTS.
Bird, Boston	F	29	7	14	0	0	3	10	13	7	4	2	14
Erving, Philadelphia	F	28	11	19	3	3	3	3	6	3	1	1	25
Malone, Philadelphia	C	24	3	8	4	6	2	6	8	3	1	0	10
Cheeks, Philadelphia	G	18	3	8	0	0	0	1	1	1	0	0	6
Thomas, Detroit	G	29	9	14	1	1	3	1	4	7	0	4	19
Moncrief, Milwaukee		23	8	14	4	5	3	2	5	4	1	6	20
M. Johnson, Milwaukee		20	3	10	1	2	2	0	2	2	1	0	7
Parish, Boston		18	5	6	3	4	0	3	3	0	2	1	13
Toney, Philadelphia		18	4	5	0	0	0	1	1	7	3	2	8
Williams, New Jersey		19	3	4	2	4	3	4	7	1	0	1	8
Theus, Chicago		8	0	5	0	0	1	0	1	1	1	0	0
Laimbeer, Detroit		6	1	1	0	0	1	0	1	0	1	0	2
TOTALS		240	57	108	18	25	21	31	52	36	15	17	132

FG Pct.: .528.   FT Pct.: .720.   Turnovers: Bird 5, Thomas 5, Toney 4, Erving 2, Theus 2, Laimbeer 1, Malone 1, Moncrief 1, Parish 1.   Total—23.   Team Rebounds: 10.

WEST ALL-STARS (123)

PLAYER, TEAM	POS.	MIN.	FGM	FGA	FTM	FTA	OFF.	DEF.	TOT.	AST.	PF	ST.	PTS.
English, Denver	F	23	7	14	0	1	2	2	4	0	2	1	14
Lucas, Phoenix	F	27	3	8	0	1	1	6	7	1	1	0	6
Abdul-Jabbar, Los Angeles	C	32	9	12	2	3	2	4	6	5	1	1	20
E. Johnson, Los Angeles	G	33	7	16	3	4	3	2	5	16	2	5	17
Thompson, Seattle	G	17	5	7	0	0	1	1	2	2	2	1	10
Gervin, San Antonio		14	3	8	2	2	0	0	0	3	3	2	9
Wilkes, Los Angeles		15	4	6	2	2	1	1	2	2	0	1	10
Sikma, Seattle		17	4	6	0	0	1	2	3	1	2	1	8
Gilmore, San Antonio		16	2	4	1	2	1	4	5	1	4	1	5
Williams, Seattle		15	3	9	0	0	1	0	1	4	1	1	6
Paxson, Portland		17	5	7	1	2	0	0	0	1	0	2	11
Vandeweghe, Denver		14	3	4	1	2	0	3	3	1	0	1	7
TOTALS		240	55	101	12	19	12	25	37	37	18	17	123

FG Pct.: .545.   FT Pct.: .632.   Turnovers: E. Johnson 7, Paxson 4, Thompson 3, G. Williams 3, Wilkes 2, Abdul-Jabbar 1, English 1, Gilmore 1, Lucas 1, Sikma 1.   Total—24.   Team Rebounds: 12.

Score by Periods:	1st	2nd	3rd	4th	Totals
East	42	27	34	29	132
West	31	33	26	33	123

Blocked Shots: Erving 2, M. Johnson, Malone, Moncrief, Parish; Abdul-Jabbar 4, English 2, Sikma.   3-Pt. Field Goals: Bird 0-1, Toney 0-1; Gervin 1-1, E. Johnson 0-1.   Officials: Hugh Evans and Jess Kersey.   Attendance: 17,505.

GAME 34, Jan. 29, 1984, at Denver

Coaches—East, K. C. Jones, Boston/West, Frank Layden, Utah

MVP—Isiah Thomas, Detroit

EAST ALL-STARS (154)

PLAYER, TEAM	POS.	MIN.	FGM	FGA	FTM	FTA	OFF.	DEF.	TOT.	AST.	PF	ST.	PTS.
Erving, Philadelphia	F	36	14	22	6	8	4	4	8	5	4	2	34
Bird, Boston	F	33	6	18	4	4	1	6	7	3	1	2	16
Parish, Boston	C	28	5	11	2	4	4	11	15	2	1	3	12
Moncrief, Milwaukee	G	26	3	6	2	2	1	4	5	2	3	5	8
Thomas, Detroit	G	39	9	17	3	3	2	3	5	15	4	4	21
Toney, Philadelphia		22	6	11	1	1	0	0	0	3	0	2	13
Ruland, Washington		13	2	3	2	2	1	3	4	2	2	1	6
King, New York		22	8	13	2	5	2	1	3	4	2	0	18
Birdsong, New Jersey		12	1	5	0	0	2	1	3	1	1	0	2
McHale, Boston		11	3	7	4	6	2	3	5	0	1	0	10
Laimbeer, Detroit		17	6	8	1	1	1	4	5	0	3	1	13
Tripucka, Detroit		6	0	1	1	2	0	0	0	2	1	1	1
TOTALS		265	63	121	28	38	20	40	60	39	23	21	154

FG Pct.: .521.   FT Pct.: .737.   Turnovers: Thomas 6, Moncrief 4, Parish 4, Bird 2, McHale 2, Ruland 2, Tripucka 2, Erving.   Total—23.   Team Rebounds: 8.

WEST ALL-STARS (145)

PLAYER, TEAM	POS.	MIN.	FGM	FGA	FTM	FTA	OFF.	DEF.	TOT.	AST.	PF	ST.	PTS.
English, Denver	F	19	6	8	1	1	0	0	0	2	2	1	13
Dantley, Utah	F	18	1	8	0	0	0	2	2	1	4	1	2
Abdul-Jabbar, Los Angeles	C	37	11	19	3	4	5	8	13	2	5	0	25
Johnson, Los Angeles	G	37	6	13	2	2	4	5	9	22	3	3	15
Gervin, San Antonio	G	21	5	6	3	3	0	2	2	1	5	0	13
Vandeweghe, Denver		26	7	13	0	0	1	2	3	1	2	0	14
Sikma, Seattle		30	5	12	5	6	5	7	12	1	4	3	15
Sampson, Houston		16	4	7	1	2	1	4	5	0	4	0	9
Davis, Phoenix		15	5	9	0	0	0	2	2	1	0	1	10
Green, Utah		19	3	8	0	0	0	0	0	11	1	1	6
Aguirre, Dallas		13	5	8	3	4	1	0	1	2	1	1	13
Paxson, Portland		14	5	9	0	0	1	2	3	2	0	0	11
TOTALS		265	63	120	18	22	18	34	52	46	31	11	145

FG Pct.: .525.   FT Pct.: .818.   Turnovers: Gervin 6, Abdul-Jabbar 4, Green 4, Johnson 4, English 3, Sampson 3, Aguirre 2, Sikma 2, Dantley.   Total—29.   Team Rebounds: 9.

Score by Periods:	1st	2nd	3rd	4th	OT	Totals
East	32	30	37	33	22	154
West	40	36	31	25	13	145

Blocked Shots: Erving 2, Laimbeer 2, Johnson 2, Abdul-Jabbar, Aguirre, English, Gervin.   3-Pt. Field Goals: Thomas 0-2; Johnson 1-3.   Officials: Earl Strom and John Vanak.   Attendance: 17,500.

GAME 35, Feb. 10, 1985, at Indianapolis

Coaches—East, K. C. Jones, Boston/West, Pat Riley, L.A. Lakers

MVP—Ralph Sampson, Houston

WEST ALL-STARS (140)

PLAYER, TEAM	POS.	MIN.	FGM	FGA	FTM	FTA	OFF.	DEF.	TOT.	AST.	PF	ST.	PTS.
Dantley, Utah	F	23	2	6	6	6	0	2	2	1	4	1	10
Sampson, Houston	F	29	10	15	4	6	3	7	10	1	5	0	24
Abdul-Jabbar, L.A. Lakers	C	23	5	10	1	2	0	6	6	1	5	1	11
E. Johnson, L.A. Lakers	G	31	7	14	7	8	2	3	5	15	2	1	21
Gervin, San Antonio	G	25	10	12	3	4	0	3	3	1	2	3	23
English, Denver		14	0	3	0	0	1	1	2	1	1	0	0
Nixon, L.A. Clippers		19	5	7	1	2	0	2	2	8	0	1	11
Nance, Phoenix		15	7	8	2	2	1	4	5	0	5	0	16
Blackman, Dallas		23	7	14	1	2	1	2	3	2	1	1	15
Sikma, Seattle		12	0	2	0	0	2	2	2	0	1	0	0
Natt, Denver		11	1	3	1	2	0	3	3	1	1	0	3
Olajuwon, Houston		15	2	2	2	2	3	5	1	1	0	6	
TOTALS		240	56	96	28	40	10	38	48	32	28	8	140

FG Pct.: .583.   FT Pct.: .700.   Turnovers: Gervin 4, Johnson 3, Dantley 2, English 2, Nance 2, Abdul-Jabbar, Natt, Nixon, Sampson.   Total—17.   Team Rebounds: 11.

EAST ALL-STARS (129)

PLAYER, TEAM	POS.	MIN.	FGM	FGA	FTM	FTA	OFF.	DEF.	TOT.	AST.	PF	ST.	PTS.
Erving, Philadelphia	F	23	5	15	2	2	2	4	3	3	1	12	
Bird, Boston	F	31	8	16	5	6	5	3	8	2	3	0	21
Malone, Philadelphia	C	33	2	10	3	6	5	7	12	1	4	0	7
Thomas, Detroit	G	25	9	14	1	1	1	1	2	5	2	2	22
Jordan, Chicago	G	22	2	9	3	4	3	3	6	2	4	3	7
Richardson, New Jersey		13	2	8	1	2	2	0	2	1	3	2	5
Parish, Boston		10	2	5	0	3	3	6	1	0	0	4	
King, New York		22	6	10	1	2	4	3	7	1	5	0	13
Moncrief, Milwaukee		22	1	5	6	6	2	3	5	4	1	0	8
Cummings, Milwaukee		16	7	17	3	4	4	3	7	0	1	0	17
D. Johnson, Boston		12	3	7	2	2	1	5	6	3	2	0	8
Laimbeer, Detroit		11	2	4	1	2	1	2	3	1	1	0	5
TOTALS		240	49	120	28	37	33	35	68	24	29	8	129

FG Pct.: .408.   FT Pct.: .757.   Turnovers: Bird 4, Malone 3, Moncrief 2, Richardson 2, Erving, D. Johnson, Jordan, King, Thomas.   Total—16.   Team Rebounds: 5.

Score by Periods:	1st	2nd	3rd	4th	Totals
West	40	28	29	43	140
East	35	33	24	37	129

Blocked Shots: Nance 2, Olajuwon 2, Abdul-Jabbar, Blackman, Gervin, Sampson, Sikma, Bird, Cummings, Jordan.   3-Pt. Field Goals: Thomas 3-4, Bird 0-1, Jordan 0-1, Richardson 0-2.   Officials: Mike Mathis and Ed Rush.   Attendance: 43,146.

GAME 36, Feb. 9, 1986, at Dallas

Coaches—East, K. C. Jones, Boston/West, Pat Riley, L.A. Lakers

MVP—Isiah Thomas, Detroit

EAST ALL-STARS (139)

PLAYER, TEAM	POS.	MIN.	FGM	FGA	FTM	FTA	OFF.	DEF.	TOT.	AST.	PF	ST.	PTS.
Erving, Philadelphia	F	19	4	10	0	2	1	3	4	2	2	2	8
Bird, Boston	F	35	8	18	5	6	2	6	8	5	5	7	23
M. Malone, Philadelphia	C	34	5	12	6	9	5	8	13	0	4	1	16
Moncrief, Milwaukee	G	26	4	11	7	7	3	0	3	1	0	0	16
Thomas, Detroit	G	36	11	19	8	9	0	1	1	10	2	5	30
Williams, New Jersey		20	5	8	3	5	3	4	7	4	0	0	13
J. Malone, Washington		12	3	5	0	0	0	1	1	4	0	1	6
McHale, Boston		20	3	8	2	3	7	10	2	4	0	8	
Cheeks, Philadelphia		14	3	6	0	0	0	0	0	2	0	2	6
Parish, Boston		7	0	0	2	0	1	1	0	0	0	0	
Wilkins, Atlanta		17	6	15	1	2	2	1	3	2	2	0	13
Jordan, Chicago							Injured						
TOTALS		240	52	112	32	44	19	32	51	32	19	18	139

FG Pct.: .464.   FT Pct.: .727.   Turnovers: Thomas 5, Bird 4, Cheeks 3, Erving 2, M. Malone, Parish, Wilkins, Williams.   Total—18.   Team Rebounds: 14.

WEST ALL-STARS (132)

PLAYER, TEAM	POS.	MIN.	FGM	FGA	FTM	FTA	OFF.	DEF.	TOT.	AST.	PF	ST.	PTS.
Worthy, L.A. Lakers	F	28	10	19	0	0	2	1	3	2	3	0	20
Sampson, Houston	F	21	7	11	2	2	1	3	4	1	4	0	16
Abdul-Jabbar, L.A. Lakers	C	32	9	15	3	4	2	5	7	2	4	2	21
Robertson, San Antonio	G	20	2	6	0	0	1	8	9	5	1	0	4
E. Johnson, L.A. Lakers	G	28	1	3	4	4	0	4	4	15	4	1	6
Blackman, Dallas		22	6	11	0	0	1	3	4	8	1	2	12
Gilmore, San Antonio		13	3	4	4	4	1	1	2	1	4	2	10
English, Denver		16	8	12	0	0	1	0	1	2	0	0	16
Dantley, Utah		17	3	8	2	2	1	6	7	3	1	1	8
Drexler, Portland		15	5	7	0	0	4	4	4	3	3	0	10
Olajuwon, Houston		15	1	8	1	2	1	4	5	0	3	1	3
M. Johnson, L.A. Clippers		13	3	6	0	0	2	1	3	2	3	0	6
TOTALS		240	58	110	16	18	13	40	53	45	31	12	132

FG Pct.: .527.   FT Pct.: .889.   Turnovers: E. Johnson 9, Abdul-Jabbar 5, Robertson 4, Drexler 3, Sampson 2, Blackman, M. Johnson, Olajuwon, Worthy.   Total—27.   Team Rebounds: 8.

Score by Periods:	1st	2nd	3rd	4th	Totals
East	34	35	31	39	139
West	36	36	30	30	132

Blocked Shots: McHale 4, Abdul-Jabbar 2, Olajuwon 2, Worthy 2, Blackman, Drexler, English, Moncrief, Parish, Wilkins.   3-Pt. Field Goals: Bird 2-4, Moncrief 1-1, Drexler 0-1, E. Johnson 0-1, Thomas 0-1, Worthy 0-2.   Officials: Joe Crawford and Jack Madden.   Attendance: 16,573.

GAME 37, Feb. 8, 1987, at Seattle

Coaches—East, K. C. Jones, Boston/West, Pat Riley, L.A. Lakers

MVP—Tom Chambers, Seattle

EAST ALL-STARS (149)

PLAYER, TEAM	POS.	MIN.	FGM	FGA	FTM	FTA	OFF.	DEF.	TOT.	AST.	PF	ST.	PTS.
Bird, Boston	F	35	7	18	4	4	2	4	6	5	5	2	18
Wilkins, Atlanta	F	24	3	9	4	7	2	3	5	1	2	0	10
M. Malone, Washington	C	35	11	19	5	6	7	11	18	2	4	2	27
Erving, Philadelphia	G	33	9	13	3	3	3	1	4	5	3	1	22
Jordan, Chicago	G	28	5	12	1	2	0	0	0	4	2	2	11
Thomas, Detroit		24	4	6	8	9	2	1	3	9	3	0	16
McHale, Boston		30	7	11	2	2	4	3	7	2	5	0	16
Laimbeer, Detroit		11	4	7	0	0	0	2	2	1	2	1	8
J. Malone, Washington		13	3	5	0	0	1	1	2	1	0		6
Barkley, Philadelphia		16	2	6	3	6	1	3	4	1	2	1	7
Cheeks, Philadelphia		8	1	2	2	2	0	0	0	0	1	1	4
Parish, Boston		8	2	3	0	0	0	3	3	0	1	0	4
TOTALS		265	58	111	32	41	23	31	54	32	31	10	149

FG Pct.: .523.   FT Pct.: .780.   Turnovers: Jordan 5, Thomas 5, Bird 2, Erving 2, Wilkins 2, Cheeks, J. Malone, M. Malone.   Total—19.   Team Rebounds: 12.

WEST ALL-STARS (154)

PLAYER, TEAM	POS.	MIN.	FGM	FGA	FTM	FTA	OFF.	DEF.	TOT.	AST.	PF	ST.	PTS.
Chambers, Seattle	F	29	13	25	6	9	3	1	4	2	5	4	34
Worthy, L.A. Lakers	F	29	10	14	2	2	6	2	8	3	3	1	22
Olajuwon, Houston	C	26	2	6	6	8	4	9	13	2	6	0	10
Johnson, L.A. Lakers	G	34	4	10	1	2	1	6	7	13	2	4	9
Robertson, San Antonio	G	16	2	5	2	2	0	2	1	1	0	6	
Aguirre, Dallas		17	3	6	2	3	1	1	2	1	1	0	9
Abdul-Jabbar, L.A. Lakers		27	4	9	2	2	6	8	3	5	0	10	
Davis, Phoenix		15	3	12	0	0	2	0	2	1	0	0	7
Floyd, Golden State		19	4	7	5	7	2	3	5	1	2	1	14
Carroll, Golden State		18	1	7	2	4	2	6	0	4	0	4	
Blackman, Dallas		22	9	15	11	13	1	3	4	1	2	0	29
English, Denver		13	0	6	0	0	0	0	1	1	0	0	
Sampson, Houston							Injured						
TOTALS		265	55	122	39	50	28	33	61	29	32	10	154

FG Pct.: .451.   FT Pct.: .780.   Turnovers: Chambers 3, Aguirre 2, Blackman 2, English 2, Floyd 2, Worthy 2, Abdul-Jabbar, Carroll, Johnson, Olajuwon, Robertson.   Total—18.   Team Rebounds: 13.

Score by Periods:	1st	2nd	3rd	4th	OT	Totals
West	29	41	30	40	14	154
East	33	32	42	33	9	149

Blocked Shots: McHale 4, Erving, M. Malone, Parish, Wilkins; Olajuwon 3, Abdul-Jabbar 2, Carroll.   3-Pt. Field Goals: Erving 1-1, Jordan 0-1, J. Malone 0-1, Barkley 0-2, Bird 0-3; Chambers 2-3, Davis 1-1, Aguirre 1-2, Floyd 1-3.   Officials: Jess Kersey and Hue Hollins.   Attendance: 34,275.

GAME 38, Feb. 7, 1988, at Chicago

Coaches—East, Mike Fratello, Atlanta/West, Pat Riley, L.A. Lakers

MVP—Michael Jordan, Chicago

WEST ALL-STARS (133)

PLAYER, TEAM	POS.	MIN.	FGM	FGA	FTM	FTA	OFF.	DEF.	TOT.	AST.	PF	ST.	PTS.
English, Denver	F	22	5	10	0	0	2	1	3	4	0	1	10
K. Malone, Utah	F	33	9	19	4	5	4	6	10	2	4	2	22
Olajuwon, Houston	C	28	8	13	5	7	7	2	9	2	3	2	21
E. Johnson, L.A. Lakers	G	39	4	15	9	9	1	5	6	19	2	2	17
Lever, Denver	G	31	7	14	3	4	0	4	4	3	4	0	17
Aguirre, Dallas		12	5	10	3	3	0	1	1	1	3	1	14
Abdul-Jabbar, L.A. Lakers		14	4	9	2	2	2	4	0	3	0	10	
Robertson, San Antonio		12	1	3	0	0	0	0	0	1	1	2	2
McDaniel, Seattle		13	1	9	0	0	1	1	2	0	1	0	2
Drexler, Portland		15	3	5	6	6	2	3	5	0	3	1	12
Worthy, L.A. Lakers		13	2	8	0	1	1	2	3	1	0	4	
Donaldson, Dallas		8	0	0	2	2	1	5	6	1	2	0	2
TOTALS		240	49	115	34	39	21	32	53	34	27	11	133

FG Pct.: .426.   FT Pct.: .872.   Turnovers: E. Johnson 8, Olajuwon 4, Aguirre 3, K. Malone 3, Robertson 2, Drexler, McDaniel.   Total—22.   Team Rebounds: 12.

EAST ALL-STARS (138)

PLAYER, TEAM	POS.	MIN.	FGM	FGA	FTM	FTA	OFF.	DEF.	TOT.	AST.	PF	ST.	PTS.
Bird, Boston	F	32	2	8	2	2	0	7	7	1	4	4	6
Wilkins, Atlanta	F	30	12	22	5	6	1	4	5	0	3	0	29
M. Malone, Washington	C	22	2	6	3	6	5	4	9	2	2	0	7
Thomas, Detroit	G	28	4	10	0	0	1	1	2	15	1	1	8
Jordan, Chicago	G	29	17	23	6	6	3	5	8	3	5	4	40
Ewing, New York		16	4	8	1	1	1	5	6	0	1	0	9
Rivers, Atlanta		16	2	4	5	11	0	3	3	6	3	0	9
McHale, Boston		14	0	1	2	2	0	1	1	1	2	0	2
Barkley, Philadelphia		15	1	4	2	2	1	2	3	0	2	1	4
Ainge, Boston		19	4	11	1	2	1	2	3	2	1	1	12
Daugherty, Cleveland		15	6	7	0	0	3	3	1	4	0	12	
Cheeks, Philadelphia		4	0	0	0	0	2	2	1	1	0	0	
TOTALS		240	54	104	27	38	13	39	52	32	29	11	138

FG Pct.: .519.   FT Pct.: .711.   Turnovers: Thomas 6, Barkley 3, Rivers 3, Bird 2, Jordan 2, M. Malone 2, McHale 2, Ainge, Ewing.   Total—22.   Team Rebounds: 15.

Score by Periods:	1st	2nd	3rd	4th	Totals
East	27	33	39	39	138
West	32	22	35	44	133

Blocked Shots: Olajuwon 2, E. Johnson 2, Donaldson 2, Worthy; Jordan 4, McHale 2, Barkley, Bird, Daugherty, Ewing, Wilkins.   3-Pt. Field Goals: Aguirre 1-3, Drexler 0-1, E. Johnson 0-1; Ainge 3-4, Barkley 0-1, Bird 0-1.   Officials: Darell Garretson and Jake O'Donnell.   Attendance: 18,403.

GAME 39, Feb. 12, 1989, at Houston

Coaches—East, Lenny Wilkens, Cleveland/West, Pat Riley, L.A. Lakers

MVP—Karl Malone, Utah

EAST ALL-STARS (134)

PLAYER, TEAM	POS.	MIN.	FGM	FGA	FTM	FTA	OFF.	DEF.	TOT.	AST.	PF	ST.	PTS.
Barkley, Philadelphia	F	20	6	11	5	8	3	2	5	0	0	2	17
Wilkins, Atlanta	F	15	3	8	3	3	1	1	2	0	0	3	9
M. Malone, Atlanta	C	19	3	9	3	3	4	4	8	0	1	1	9
Jordan, Chicago	G	33	13	23	2	4	1	1	2	3	1	5	28
Thomas, Detroit	G	33	7	13	4	6	1	1	2	14	2	4	19
Ewing, New York		17	2	8	0	4	1	5	6	2	2	1	4
Cummings, Milwaukee		19	4	9	2	2	2	3	5	1	4	3	10
Nance, Cleveland		17	5	9	0	0	3	3	6	1	1	1	10
Price, Cleveland		20	3	9	2	1	2	3	1	2	2	9
Jackson, New York		16	3	5	2	4	1	1	2	4	1	1	9
Daugherty, Cleveland		15	0	3	0	2	1	3	0	0	1	0
McHale, Boston		16	5	7	0	1	2	3	0	3	0	10
TOTALS		240	54	114	23	36	21	26	47	26	17	24	134

FG Pct.: .474.   FT Pct.: .639.   Turnovers: Thomas 6, Jordan 4, Ewing 3, Jackson 2, Price 2, Wilkins 2, Barkley, Daugherty, Malone, McHale.   Total—23.   Team Rebounds: 17.

WEST ALL-STARS (143)

PLAYER, TEAM	POS.	MIN.	FGM	FGA	FTM	FTA	OFF.	DEF.	TOT.	AST.	PF	ST.	PTS.
English, Denver	F	29	8	13	0	0	1	2	3	4	0	2	16
K. Malone, Utah	F	26	12	17	4	6	4	5	9	3	3	2	28
Olajuwon, Houston	C	25	5	12	2	3	4	3	7	3	2	3	12
Ellis, Seattle	G	26	12	16	2	2	3	3	6	2	2	0	27
Stockton, Utah	G	32	5	6	0	0	2	2	17	4	5	11
Abdul-Jabbar, L.A. Lakers		13	1	6	2	2	0	3	3	0	3	0	4
Drexler, Portland		25	7	19	0	0	6	6	12	4	3	2	14
Chambers, Phoenix		16	4	8	6	6	2	3	5	1	3	0	14
Mullin, Golden State		14	1	4	2	2	0	2	2	0	0	4
Worthy, L.A. Lakers		18	4	7	0	0	2	2	2	0	2	8
Eaton, Utah		9	0	0	0	0	5	5	0	1	0	0
Duckworth, Portland		7	2	5	1	2	1	0	1	0	2	0	5
Johnson, L.A. Lakers						Injured							
TOTALS		240	61	113	19	23	23	34	57	38	23	16	143

FG Pct.: .540.   FT Pct.: .826.   Turnovers: Stockton 12, Drexler 6, English 3, Olajuwon 3, Chambers 2, Ellis 2, Malone 2, Mullin.   Total—31.   Team Rebounds: 8.

Score by Periods:

	1st	2nd	3rd	4th	Totals
East	31	28	37	38	134
West	47	40	24	32	143

Blocked Shots: Ewing 2, McHale 2, Barkley, Cummings, Jackson, M. Malone, Nance; Olajuwon 2, Abdul-Jabbar 2, Eaton 2.   3-Pt. Field Goals: Jackson 1-1, Thomas 1-3, Price 1-4, Jordan 0-1; Ellis 1-1, Stockton 1-1, Abdul-Jabbar 0-1, Worthy 0-1.   Officials: Hugh Evans, Dick Bavetta and Bill Saar.   Attendance: 44,735.

GAME 40, February 11, 1990, at Miami

Coaches—East—Chuck Daly, Detroit/West, Pat Riley, L.A. Lakers

MVP—Magic Johnson, L.A. Lakers

WEST ALL-STARS (113)

PLAYER, TEAM	POS.	MIN.	FGM	FGA	FTM	FTA	OFF.	DEF.	TOT.	AST.	PF	ST.	PTS.
Green, L.A. Lakers	F	12	0	3	0	0	0	3	3	1	1	0	0
Worthy, L.A. Lakers	F	19	1	11	0	0	3	1	4	0	1	1	2
Olajuwon, Houston	C	31	2	14	4	10	9	7	16	2	1	0	8
E. Johnson, L.A. Lakers	G	25	9	15	0	0	1	5	6	4	1	0	22
Stockton, Utah	G	15	1	4	0	0	0	0	0	6	1	1	2
Chambers, Phoenix		21	8	12	5	7	2	1	3	1	0	1	21
Drexler, Portland		19	2	6	2	2	4	0	4	2	1	1	7
Robinson, San Antonio		25	7	12	1	2	2	8	10	1	1	2	15
Mullin, Golden State		16	1	5	1	2	1	2	3	1	0	2	3
K. Johnson, Phoenix		14	1	1	0	0	0	0	0	4	2	0	2
Blackman, Dallas		21	7	9	1	1	1	1	2	2	1	2	15
Lever, Denver		22	7	13	2	2	0	3	3	2	0	2	16
Malone, Utah						Injured							
TOTALS		240	46	105	16	26	23	31	54	26	10	13	113

FG Pct.: .438.   FT Pct.: .615.   Team Rebounds: 8. Turnovers: Olajuwon 4, Chambers 3, E. Johnson 3, K. Johnson 3, Stockton 3, Blackman 2, Drexler 1, Green 1, Mullin 1, Robinson 1, Worthy 1. Total—23.

EAST ALL-STARS (130)

PLAYER, TEAM	POS.	MIN.	FGM	FGA	FTM	FTA	OFF.	DEF.	TOT.	AST.	PF	ST.	PTS.
Barkley, Philadelphia	F	22	7	12	2	3	2	2	4	0	1	1	17
Bird, Boston	F	23	3	8	2	2	2	6	8	3	1	3	8
Ewing, New York	C	27	5	9	2	2	1	9	10	1	5	1	12
Jordan, Chicago	G	29	8	17	0	0	1	4	5	2	1	5	17
Thomas, Detroit	G	27	7	12	0	0	1	3	4	9	0	3	15
McHale, Boston		20	6	11	0	0	2	6	8	1	4	0	13
Dumars, Detroit		18	3	4	1	2	0	1	1	5	0	0	9
Parish, Boston		21	7	11	0	1	2	2	4	2	4	0	14
Miller, Indiana		14	2	3	0	0	0	1	1	3	1	1	4
Wilkins, Atlanta		16	5	10	2	2	0	0	0	4	1	1	13
Rodman, Detroit		11	2	4	0	0	3	1	4	1	1	0	4
Pippen, Chicago		12	2	4	0	0	1	1	0	1	1	4
TOTALS		240	57	105	9	12	14	36	50	31	20	16	130

FG Pct.: .543.   FT Pct.: .750.   Team Rebounds: 8. Turnovers: Ewing 5, Jordan 5, Bird 3, Dumars 3, Barkley 2, Rodman 2, Parish 1, Pippen 1, Thomas 1. Total—23.

Score by Periods:

	1st	2nd	3rd	4th	Totals
West	23	29	31	30	113
East	40	25	35	30	130

Blocked Shots: Drexler 1, Green 1, E. Johnson 1, Mullin 1, Olajuwon 1, Robinson 1, Stockton 1; Ewing 5, Barkley 1, Jordan 1, Parish 1, Pippen 1, Rodman 1.   3-Pt. Field Goals: E. Johnson 4-6, Stockton 0-1, Chambers 0-1, Drexler 1-1, Lever 0-2; Barkley 1-1, Bird 0-1, Jordan 1-1, Thomas 1-1, McHale 1-1, Dumars 2-2, Miller 0-1, Wilkins 1-1, Pippen 0-1.   Officials: Earl Strom, Bill Oakes and Paul Mihalak.   Attendance: 14,810.

GAME 41, February 10, 1991, at Charlotte

Coaches—East, Chris Ford, Boston/West, Rick Adelman, Portland

MVP—Charles Barkley, Philadelphia

WEST ALL-STARS (114)

PLAYER, TEAM	POS.	MIN.	FGM	FGA	FTM	FTA	OFF.	DEF.	TOT.	AST.	PF	ST.	PTS.
Malone, Utah	F	31	6	11	4	6	4	7	11	4	1	1	16
Mullin, Golden State	F	24	4	8	4	4	0	2	2	2	2	2	13
Robinson, San Antonio	C	18	6	13	4	5	3	3	6	0	5	2	16
E. Johnson, L.A. Lakers	G	28	7	16	0	0	1	3	4	3	1	0	16
K. Johnson, Phoenix	G	23	2	5	1	2	1	1	2	7	2	3	5
Duckworth, Portland		19	2	3	2	2	2	2	4	0	3	1	6
Drexler, Portland		19	4	9	4	4	2	4	2	3	1		12
Worthy, L.A. Lakers		21	3	11	3	4	0	2	2	0	2	2	9
Porter, Portland		15	2	6	0	0	1	2	3	4	2	2	4
Chambers, Phoenix		18	4	11	0	0	2	2	4	1	3	1	8
Stockton, Utah		12	1	6	2	4	0	1	1	2	2	0	4
Hardaway, Golden State		12	2	7	0	0	2	1	3	4	1	2	5
TOTALS		240	43	106	24	31	18	28	46	29	27	17	114

FG Pct.: .406. FT Pct.: .774. Team Rebounds: 13. Turnovers: Chambers 4, E. Johnson 3, K. Johnson 3, Malone 3, Porter 3, Duckworth 2, Mullin 2, Robinson 2. Total—22.

EAST ALL-STARS (116)

PLAYER, TEAM	POS.	MIN.	FGM	FGA	FTM	FTA	OFF.	DEF.	TOT.	AST.	PF	ST.	PTS.
King, Washington	F	26	2	8	4	4	2	1	3	3	1	0	8
Barkley, Philadelphia	F	35	7	15	3	6	8	14	22	4	5	1	17
Ewing, New York	C	30	8	10	2	2	2	8	10	0	5	1	18
Dumars, Detroit	G	15	1	4	0	0	1	1	2	1	1	0	2
Jordan, Chicago	G	36	10	25	6	7	3	2	5	5	2	2	26
Robertson, Milwaukee		12	2	4	2	2	0	2	2	0	0	0	6
Wilkins, Atlanta		22	3	11	6	8	3	0	3	4	2	1	12
Parish, Boston		5	1	2	0	0	1	3	4	0	2	0	2
McHale, Boston		14	0	3	2	2	1	2	3	2	2	1	2
Pierce, Milwaukee		19	4	8	1	1	0	2	2	2	2	0	9
Daugherty, Cleveland		12	3	7	2	3	3	2	5	1	3	0	8
Hawkins, Philadelphia		14	3	5	0	0	0	0	0	1	1	0	6
Bird, Boston						Injured							
TOTALS		240	44	102	28	35	24	37	61	23	26	6	116

FG Pct.: .431. FT Pct.: .800. Team Rebounds: 15. Turnovers: Jordan 10, Dumars 4, Barkley 3, Robertson 3, Ewing 2, Pierce 2, Wilkins 2, Hawkins 1, King 1, Parish 1. Total—29.

Score by Periods:	1st	2nd	3rd	4th	Totals
West	23	35	34	22	114
East	22	45	27	22	116

Blocked Shots: Robinson 3, Drexler 1, K. Johnson 1, Malone 1, Porter 1, Worthy 1; Ewing 4, Barkley 1, King 1, Wilkins 1. 3-Pt. Field Goals: E. Johnson 2-5, Mullin 1-1, Hardaway 1-2, Chambers 0-1, Stockton 0-1, Porter 0-2; Dumars 0-1, Hawkins 0-1, McHale 0-1, Jordan 0-2, Wilkins 0-2. Officials: Ed T. Rush, Mike Mathis and Lee Jones. Attendance: 23,530.

GAME 42, February 9, 1992, at Orlando

Coaches—East, Phil Jackson, Chicago/West, Don Nelson, Golden State

MVP—Magic Johnson, L.A. Lakers

WEST ALL-STARS (153)

PLAYER, TEAM	POS.	MIN.	FGM	FGA	FTM	FTA	OFF.	DEF.	TOT.	AST.	PF	ST.	PTS.
Malone, Utah	F	19	5	7	1	2	0	7	7	3	1	1	11
Mullin, Golden State	F	24	6	7	0	0	1	1	3	0	0		13
Robinson, San Antonio	C	18	7	9	5	8	1	4	5	2	3	3	19
Drexler, Portland	G	28	10	15	0	0	2	7	9	6	2	0	22
Johnson, L.A. Lakers	G	29	9	12	4	4	3	2	5	9	0	2	25
Hardaway, Golden State		20	5	10	2	2	0	0	0	7	2	1	14
Olajuwon, Houston		20	3	6	1	2	0	4	4	3	2		7
Hornacek, Phoenix		24	5	7	0	0	1	1	2	3	0	1	11
Thorpe, Houston		4	1	1	0	0	0	0	0	0	0	0	2
Worthy, L.A. Lakers		14	4	7	1	2	0	4	4	1	0	1	9
Stockton, Utah		18	5	8	0	0	1	1	5	2	3		12
Majerle, Phoenix		12	2	5	0	0	3	3	2	0	0		4
Mutombo, Denver		10	2	7	0	0	1	1	2	1	0	1	4
TOTALS		240	64	98	14	20	8	35	43	44	13	15	153

FG Pct.: .653. FT Pct.: .700. Team Rebounds: 13. Turnovers: Johnson 7, Olajuwon 3, Stockton 3, Hardaway 2, Mutombo 2, Drexler 1, Majerle 1, Malone 1, Mullin 1. Total—21.

EAST ALL-STARS (113)

PLAYER, TEAM	POS.	MIN.	FGM	FGA	FTM	FTA	OFF.	DEF.	TOT.	AST.	PF	ST.	PTS.
Pippen, Chicago	F	21	6	13	2	3	4	0	4	1	0	2	14
Barkley, Philadelphia	F	28	6	14	0	0	2	7	9	1	3	0	12
Ewing, New York	C	17	4	7	2	5	2	2	4	0	3	2	10
Thomas, Detroit	G	28	7	14	0	0	1	1	5	0	3		15
Jordan, Chicago	G	31	9	17	0	1	0	1	5	2	2		18
Price, Cleveland		15	1	5	4	4	0	0	3	1	1		6
Daugherty, Cleveland		15	3	8	0	0	3	3	6	1	0	1	6
Dumars, Detroit		17	2	7	0	0	1	1	3	0	0		4
Rodman, Detroit		25	2	7	0	0	7	6	13	0	1	1	4
Lewis, Boston		15	3	7	1	2	4	0	4	2	3	0	7
Willis, Atlanta		14	4	10	0	0	4	0	4	0	1	0	8
Adams, Washington		14	4	8	0	0	1	0	1	1	1	4	9
Bird, Boston						Injured							
Wilkins, Atlanta						Injured							
TOTALS		240	51	117	9	14	28	20	48	22	15	16	113

FG Pct.: .436. FT Pct.: .643. Team Rebounds: 7. Turnovers: Barkley 3, Daugherty 3, Price 3, Thomas 3, Dumars 2, Ewing 2, Rodman 2, Adams 1, Jordan 1, Lewis 1, Pippen 1. Total—22.

Score by Periods:	1st	2nd	3rd	4th	Totals
West	44	35	36	38	153
East	31	24	28	30	113

Blocked Shots: Drexler 2, Malone 1, Olajuwon 1, Robinson 1; Ewing 1, Lewis 1, Pippen 1. 3-Pt. Field Goals: Johnson 3-3, Stockton 2-3, Drexler 2-4, Hardaway 2-5, Mullin 1-1, Hornacek 1-2, Majerle 0-2, Adams 1-3, Thomas 1-3, Barkley 0-2, Dumars 0-2, Price 0-3. Officials: Darell Garretson, Joe Crawford and Tommy Nunez. Attendance: 14,272.

GAME 43, February 21, 1993, at Salt Lake City

Coaches—East, Pat Riley, New York/West, Paul Westphal, Phoenix

MVP—Karl Malone, Utah, and John Stockton, Utah

EAST ALL-STARS (132)

PLAYER, TEAM	POS.	MIN.	FGM	FGA	FTM	FTA	OFF.	DEF.	TOT.	AST.	PF	ST.	PTS.
Johnson, Charlotte	F	16	2	6	0	0	3	1	4	0	1	0	4
Pippen, Chicago	F	29	4	14	2	3	2	3	5	4	4	5	10
O'Neal, Orlando	C	25	4	9	6	9	3	4	7	0	3	0	14
Thomas, Detroit	G	32	4	7	0	2	0	2	2	4	2	2	8
Jordan, Chicago	G	36	10	24	9	13	3	1	4	5	5	4	30
Nance, Cleveland		12	3	4	1	2	1	2	3	1	3	1	7
Ewing, New York		25	7	11	1	1	3	7	10	1	4	2	15
Dumars, Detroit		17	2	8	0	0	0	2	2	4	1	0	5
Price, Cleveland		23	6	11	1	2	0	1	1	4	5	1	19
Schrempf, Indiana		13	1	3	1	2	0	3	3	0	4	0	3
Daugherty, Cleveland		19	3	4	2	4	1	6	7	0	0	0	8
Wilkins, Atlanta		18	2	11	4	4	4	3	7	0	2	1	9
TOTALS		265	48	112	27	42	20	35	55	23	34	16	132

FG Pct.: .429.   FT Pct.: .643.   Team Rebounds: 11.   Turnovers: Jordan 6, Ewing 4, Price 3, Thomas 2, Dumars 1, Schrempf 1, Wilkins 1.   Total—18.

WEST ALL-STARS (135)

PLAYER, TEAM	POS.	MIN.	FGM	FGA	FTM	FTA	OFF.	DEF.	TOT.	AST.	PF	ST.	PTS.
Barkley, Phoenix	F	34	5	11	5	7	0	4	4	7	3	4	16
Malone, Utah	F	34	11	17	6	9	3	7	10	0	3	1	28
Robinson, San Antonio	C	26	7	10	7	12	2	8	10	1	4	0	21
Stockton, Utah	G	31	3	6	2	2	0	6	6	15	3	2	9
Drexler, Portland	G	11	1	3	0	0	1	0	1	1	3	0	2
Majerle, Phoenix		26	6	11	3	4	2	5	7	3	2	1	18
Kemp, Seattle		9	0	2	0	0	2	0	2	0	3	0	0
Manning, L.A. Clippers		18	5	5	0	0	1	3	4	1	1	0	10
Olajuwon, Houston		21	1	5	1	2	2	5	7	1	3	2	3
Porter, Portland		19	3	8	0	0	0	0	0	3	1	1	7
Elliott, San Antonio		15	1	6	3	4	1	1	2	0	1	0	5
Hardaway, Golden State		21	3	9	9	12	1	5	6	4	1	1	16
Mullin, Golden State						Injured							
Richmond, Sacramento						Injured							
TOTALS		265	46	93	36	52	15	44	59	36	28	12	135

FG Pct.: .495.   FT Pct.: .692.   Team Rebounds: 17.   Turnovers: Stockton 5, Barkley 4, Hardaway 3, Malone 3, Olajuwon 3, Drexler 2, Elliott 1, Porter 1, Robinson 1.   Total—23.

Score by Periods:	1st	2nd	3rd	4th	OT	Totals
East	26	26	32	35	13	132
West	27	30	29	33	16	135

Blocked Shots: Ewing 2, Pippen 2, Nance 1; Majerle 2, Malone 2, Olajuwon 2, Robinson 1.   3-Pt. Field Goals: Price 6-9, Jordan 1-2, Wilkins 1-3, Dumars 1-4, Thomas 0-1, Schrempf 0-1, Pippen 0-2; Majerle 3-6, Barkley 1-2, Stockton 1-2, Hardaway 1-3, Porter 1-5, Drexler 0-1.   Officials: Jack Madden, Hue Hollins and Bennett Salvatore.   Attendance: 19,459.

GAME 44, February 23, 1994, at Minneapolis

Coaches—East, Lenny Wilkens, Atlanta/West, George Karl, Seattle

MVP—Scottie Pippen, Chicago

EAST ALL-STARS (127)

PLAYER, TEAM	POS.	MIN.	FGM	FGA	FTM	FTA	OFF.	DEF.	TOT.	AST.	PF	ST.	PTS.
Pippen, Chicago	F	31	9	15	6	10	0	11	11	2	2	4	29
Coleman, New Jersey	F	18	1	6	0	0	1	2	3	1	3	1	2
O'Neal, Orlando	C	26	2	12	4	11	4	6	10	0	2	1	8
Anderson, New Jersey	G	16	3	10	0	0	1	3	4	3	2	0	6
Armstrong, Chicago	G	22	5	9	0	0	1	0	1	4	1	0	11
Starks, New York		20	4	9	0	0	1	2	3	3	1	1	9
Price, Cleveland		22	8	10	2	2	0	2	2	5	1	1	20
Ewing, New York		24	7	15	6	7	4	4	8	1	2	0	20
Oakley, New York		11	1	3	0	0	1	2	3	3	3	0	2
Wilkins, Atlanta		17	4	9	3	6	2	0	2	4	1	0	11
Blaylock, Atlanta		16	2	5	0	0	1	1	2	3	2	5	5
Grant, Chicago		17	2	8	0	6	2	8	8	2	0	1	4
Mourning, Charlotte						Injured							
TOTALS		240	48	111	21	36	21	35	56	30	21	11	127

FG Pct.: .432.   FT Pct.: .583.   Turnovers: Anderson 4, Pippen 2, Starks 2, O'Neal 1, Armstrong 1, Ewing 1, Blaylock 1, Grant 1.   Total—13.   Team Rebounds: 16.

WEST ALL-STARS (118)

PLAYER, TEAM	POS.	MIN.	FGM	FGA	FTM	FTA	OFF.	DEF.	TOT.	AST.	PF	ST.	PTS.
Malone, Utah	F	21	3	9	0	0	3	4	7	2	2	1	6
Kemp, Seattle	F	22	3	11	0	0	6	6	12	4	4	0	6
Olajuwon, Houston	C	30	8	15	3	6	4	7	11	2	4	2	19
Richmond, Sacramento	G	24	5	16	0	0	2	2	3	0	0	10
Drexler, Portland	G	15	3	7	0	0	3	3	1	1	1	6
Stockton, Utah		26	6	10	0	1	4	5	10	2	1	13
D. Robinson, San Antonio		21	6	13	7	10	3	2	5	0	2	0	19
Johnson, Phoenix		14	3	6	0	1	0	1	1	2	1	1	6
C. Robinson, Portland		18	5	8	0	0	1	1	2	5	0	1	10
Manning, L.A. Clippers		17	4	7	0	0	4	4	2	4	0	8
Payton, Seattle		17	3	4	0	0	2	4	6	9	2	0	6
Sprewell, Golden State		15	3	8	3	7	4	3	7	1	1	0	9
Barkley, Phoenix						Injured							
TOTALS		240	52	114	13	24	24	41	65	41	23	7	118

FG Pct.: .456.   FT Pct.: .542.   Turnovers: Kemp 6, Stockton 4, Olajuwon 3, Richmond 2, Johnson 2, Sprewell 2, Malone 1, Drexler 1, D. Robinson 1.   Total—22.   Team Rebounds: 14.

Score by Periods:	1st	2nd	3rd	4th	Totals
East	33	39	29	26	127
West	28	36	26	28	118

Blocked Shots: O'Neal 4, Grant 2, Pippen, Coleman, Price; Olajuwon 5, Kemp 3, D. Robinson 2, Drexler, Manning.   3-Pt. Field Goals: Pippen 5-9, Price 2-3, Armstrong 1-2, Blaylock 1-2, Starks 1-3, Anderson 0-1, Wilkins 0-2; Stockton 0-1, C. Robinson 0-1, Drexler 0-2, Sprewell 0-2.   Officials: Jake O'Donnell, Jess Kersey and Dan Crawford.   Attendance: 17,096.

ABA ALL-STAR GAMES

GAME 1, Jan. 9, 1968, at Indianapolis
Coaches—East, Jim Pollard, Minnesota/West, Babe McCarthy, New Orleans
MVP—Larry Brown, New Orleans

WEST ALL-STARS (120)

PLAYER, TEAM	POS.	MIN.	2-PT. FG-A	3-PT. FG-A	FT-A	REB.	A	PF	TP
Hagan, Dallas	F	24	4–11	0–0	2–2	0	5	2	10
Moe, New Orleans	F	29	7–12	0–1	3–5	7	5	4	17
Robbins, New Orleans	C	18	2–5	0–0	0–0	4	0	1	4
Tart, Oakland	G	27	4–12	0–0	5–5	3	3	0	13
Jones, Denver	G	28	6–10	0–0	2–3	13	2	3	14
Becker, Houston		19	5–13	0–0	1–1	5	0	1	11
Brown, New Orleans		22	5–7	2–2	1–1	3	5	2	17
Menyard, Houston		6	2–4	0–0	0–1	2	0	2	4
Jones, New Orleans		19	4–9	0–0	2–4	1	3	1	10
Warley, Anaheim		17	2–4	0–3	4–4	1	3	2	8
Beasley, Dallas		24	4–9	0–0	1–1	4	0	5	9
Bunce, Anaheim		7	1–2	0–0	1–1	0	0	0	3
Verga, Dallas				Military Service					
TOTALS		240	46–98	2–6	22–28	43	26	23	120

EAST ALL-STARS (126)

PLAYER, TEAM	POS.	MIN.	2-PT. FG-A	3-PT. FG-A	FT-A	REB.	A	PF	TP
Brown, Indiana	F	27	5–14	0–1	2–2	4	2	3	12
Hawkins, Pittsburgh	F	26	3–6	0–0	1–3	9	2	3	7
Daniels, Minnesota	C	29	9–18	0–0	4–11	15	0	1	22
Lewis, Indiana	G	18	3–9	0–0	0–0	0	3	1	6
Freeman, Minnesota	G	24	8–13	0–0	4–6	4	2	3	20
Hunter, Minnesota		21	2–7	0–0	3–5	8	1	4	7
Carrier, Kentucky		21	3–7	0–3	2–2	2	1	3	8
Mahaffey, Kentucky		7	1–2	0–0	2–6	4	0	0	4
Dampier, Kentucky		29	8–17	0–1	2–2	3	3	1	18
Netolicky, Indiana		19	4–8	0–0	4–4	11	1	1	12
Jackson, New Jersey		15	2–3	0–3	0–0	2	1	0	4
Vaughn, Pittsburgh		4	0–0	2–2	0–0	0	0	0	6
TOTALS		240	48–104	2–10	24–41	62	16	20	125

Score by Periods:	1st	2nd	3rd	4th	Totals
West	29	30	32	29	120
East	30	31	31	34	126

Officials: Joe Belmont and Ron Feiereisel. Attendance: 10,872.

GAME 2, Jan. 28, 1969, at Louisville
Coaches—East, Gene Rhodes, Kentucky/West, Alex Hannum, Oakland
MVP—John Beasley, Dallas

WEST ALL-STARS (133)

PLAYER, TEAM	POS.	MIN.	2-PT. FG-A	3-PT. FG-A	FT-A	REB.	A	PF	TP
Barry, Oakland	F	12	3–9	0–0	4–5	3	1	2	10
Beasley, Dallas	F	29	8–12	0–0	3–3	14	2	5	19
Beck, Denver	C	27	7–13	0–0	0–0	10	1	3	14
Jones, New Orleans	G	18	4–11	0–0	6–6	1	2	1	14
Jones, Denver	G	25	3–8	1–1	5–9	5	9	3	14
Moe, Oakland		25	6–13	0–0	5–8	6	6	3	17
Hightower, Denver		9	1–2	0–0	4–4	5	0	2	6
Davis, Los Angeles		20	3–8	0–0	0–0	7	2	2	6
Robbins, New Orleans		21	8–14	0–0	3–4	5	1	2	19
Somerset, Houston		17	2–7	0–0	2–2	3	3	3	6
Brown, Oakland		25	1–6	0–1	3–5	0	7	2	5
Jackson, Los Angeles		11	1–3	0–0	1–1	2	1	1	3
TOTALS		240	47–106	1–2	36–46	61	35	29	133

EAST ALL-STARS (127)

PLAYER, TEAM	POS.	MIN.	2-PT. FG-A	3-PT. FG-A	FT-A	REB.	A	PF	TP
Netolicky, Indiana	F	26	5–9	0–0	3–5	12	1	2	13
Simon, New York	F	21	8–11	0–0	2–3	4	1	3	18
Daniels, Indiana	C	31	5–16	0–0	7–10	10	2	3	17
Dampier, Kentucky	G	38	4–10	1–4	3–3	2	6	2	14
Carrier, Kentucky	G	26	4–8	1–4	8–10	4	5	3	19
Freeman, Miami		27	7–13	0–0	7–7	6	7	6	21
Williams, Minnesota		5	0–2	0–0	2–2	0	1	0	2
Thoren, Miami		17	1–4	0–0	0–0	5	2	3	2
Hunter, Miami		22	5–10	0–0	2–2	6	0	3	12
Ligon, Kentucky		12	0–2	0–0	3–4	3	0	2	3
Washington, Minnesota		15	2–5	0–0	2–2	5	1	3	6
Hawkins, Minnesota				Injured					
TOTALS		240	41–90	2–8	39–48	57	26	30	127

Score by Periods:	1st	2nd	3rd	4th	Totals
West	38	26	37	32	133
East	33	27	30	37	127

Officials: Andy Hershock and Ron Rakel. Attendance: 5,407.

GAME 3, Jan. 24, 1970, at Indianapolis
Coaches—East, Bob Leonard, Indiana/West, Babe McCarthy, New Orleans
MVP—Spencer Haywood, Denver

WEST ALL-STARS (128)

PLAYER, TEAM	POS.	MIN.	2-PT. FG-A	3-PT. FG-A	FT-A	REB.	A	PF	TP
Armstrong, Washington	F	15	1–3	0–0	2–2	2	1	2	4
Powell, Dallas	F	26	5–9	0–0	2–2	7	0	1	12
Haywood, Denver	C	39	10–19	0–0	3–4	19	2	4	23
Jones, Denver	G	36	10–20	0–2	10–13	6	5	3	30
Jones, New Orleans	G	14	0–3	0–0	0–0	3	0	1	0
Combs, Dallas		12	4–6	2–4	0–0	3	1	2	10
Brown, Washington		15	0–2	0–0	3–3	3	3	1	3
Govan, New Orleans		11	1–2	0–0	0–0	4	0	0	2
Jones, New Orleans		18	4–9	0–0	6–6	5	1	2	14
Barry, Washington		27	7–12	0–0	2–2	7	7	0	16
Beasley, Dallas		18	5–7	1–1	0–0	8	0	5	11
Davis, New Orleans		9	1–3	0–0	1–1	2	0	1	3
Robbins, New Orleans				Injured					
TOTALS		240	48–95	3–8	29–33	59	20	22	128

EAST ALL-STARS (98)

PLAYER, TEAM	POS.	MIN.	2-PT. FG-A	3-PT. FG-A	FT-A	REB.	A	PF	TP
Moe, Carolina	F	36	0–5	0–0	2–3	8	6	1	2
Netolicky, Indiana	F	33	7–18	0–0	1–4	8	2	2	15
Daniels, Indiana	C	26	6–14	0–0	1–3	12	1	4	13
Dampier, Kentucky	G	26	7–16	1–6	2–3	3	1	2	17
Freeman, Miami	G	24	4–16	0–0	2–3	4	5	2	10
Verga, Carolina		16	6–14	1–3	1–2	5	2	1	14
Lewis, Indiana		9	0–5	0–0	1–2	6	1	1	1
Tart, New York		13	1–8	1–2	0–0	3	1	2	3
Carrier, Kentucky		10	0–4	0–2	2–3	1	0	2	3
Brown, Indiana		28	5–10	0–0	5–6	6	2	4	15
Williams, Pittsburgh		7	1–5	0–2	0–0	0	1	2	2
Moore, Kentucky		12	2–6	0–1	0–0	4	0	1	4
TOTALS		240	39–121	3–16	17–29	60	22	24	98

Score by Periods:	1st	2nd	3rd	4th	Totals
West	34	27	25	42	128
East	18	23	33	24	98

Officials: Earl Strom and John Vanak. Attendance: 11,932.

GAME 4, Jan. 23, 1971, at Greensboro, N.C.
Coaches—East, Al Bianchi, Virginia/West, Bill Sharman, Utah
MVP—Mel Daniels, Indiana

WEST ALL-STARS (122)

PLAYER, TEAM	POS.	MIN.	2-PT. FG-A	3-PT. FG-A	FT-A	REB.	A	PF	TP
Brown, Indiana	F	28	3-9	0-2	6-8	3	3	4	12
Netolicky, Indiana	F	22	3-4	0-0	0-2	4	1	2	6
Beaty, Utah	C	27	5-11	0-0	2-3	8	3	4	12
Combs, Utah	G	17	1-5	0-2	0-2	1	2	2	2
Freeman, Texas	G	27	6-12	0-0	5-8	7	3	3	17
Robbins, Utah		14	2-6	0-0	0-0	2	1	2	4
Ladner, Memphis		20	6-11	0-0	0-0	7	0	3	12
Boone, Utah		4	2-4	0-0	2-3	2	0	0	6
Daniels, Indiana		30	12-19	0-0	5-7	13	3	3	29
J. Jones, Memphis		27	3-5	0-0	7-9	0	4	5	13
S. Jones, Memphis		21	4-8	0-1	1-1	3	0	4	9
Keye, Denver		7	0-1	0-0	0-0	4	0	1	0
TOTALS		240	47-95	0-5	28-43	54	20	33	122

EAST ALL-STARS (126)

PLAYER, TEAM	POS.	MIN.	2-PT. FG-A	3-PT. FG-A	FT-A	REB.	A	PF	TP
Caldwell, Carolina	F	32	10-19	0-0	1-3	8	3	3	21
Brisker, Pittsburgh	F	27	5-18	0-1	5-7	17	1	3	15
Issel, Kentucky	C	34	8-15	0-0	5-8	11	0	2	21
Calvin, Floridians	G	20	1-5	1-2	3-7	4	4	2	8
Scott, Virginia	G	21	2-6	0-0	3-6	2	3	4	7
Johnson, Virginia		4	0-3	0-0	0-0	1	0	1	0
Barry, New York		17	4-6	0-0	6-6	2	2	3	14
Powell, Kentucky		21	4-6	0-0	3-3	10	0	2	11
Carter, Virginia		8	2-3	0-0	0-2	2	0	2	4
Lewis, Pittsburgh		14	3-7	0-0	1-1	5	1	4	7
Jones, Floridians		18	2-3	0-0	2-2	2	1	2	6
Melchionni, New York		24	5-10	0-0	2-3	1	4	2	12
TOTALS		240	46-101	1-3	31-48	65	19	30	126

Score by Periods:	1st	2nd	3rd	4th	Totals
West	29	40	28	25	122
East	33	26	33	34	126

Officials: Norm Drucker and Joe Gushue. Attendance: 14,407.

GAME 5, Jan. 29, 1972, at Louisville
Coaches—East, Joe Mullaney, Kentucky/West, LaDell Andersen, Utah
MVP—Dan Issel, Kentucky

WEST ALL-STARS (115)

PLAYER, TEAM	POS.	MIN.	2-PT. FG-A	3-PT. FG-A	FT-A	REB.	A	PF	TP
Brown, Indiana	F	25	2-5	0-2	0-1	6	2	3	4
Wise, Utah	F	33	5-8	0-0	5-7	9	3	2	15
Beaty, Utah	C	27	7-11	0-0	1-1	7	0	4	15
Combs, Utah	G	18	1-5	0-3	0-0	0	3	0	2
Simpson, Denver	G	20	6-13	0-1	0-1	1	0	1	12
Jones, Memphis		10	1-3	0-0	0-0	3	0	2	2
Ladner, Memphis		14	2-4	0-1	0-0	6	1	2	4
Becker, Denver		9	0-2	0-0	0-0	1	0	0	0
Daniels, Indiana		26	8-14	0-0	5-8	9	1	4	21
Jones, Dallas		19	2-6	1-1	2-2	2	3	0	9
Freeman, Dallas		21	3-8	0-0	7-8	5	2	1	13
Lewis, Indiana		18	6-11	1-2	3-4	1	1	2	18
TOTALS		240	43-90	2-10	23-32	49	17	21	115

EAST ALL-STARS (142)

PLAYER, TEAM	POS.	MIN.	2-PT. FG-A	3-PT. FG-A	FT-A	REB.	A	PF	TP
Issel, Kentucky	F	23	9-13	0-0	3-4	9	5	2	21
Barry, New York	F	26	2-10	0-0	0-1	12	8	2	4
Gilmore, Kentucky	C	27	4-5	0-0	6-10	10	2	5	14
Melchionni, New York	G	18	2-4	0-0	1-1	2	2	1	5
Scott, Virginia	G	23	9-20	0-1	2-3	4	3	2	20
Erving, Virginia		25	9-15	0-0	2-2	6	3	3	20
Brisker, Pittsburgh		21	3-9	0-1	2-3	5	3	1	8
McDaniels, Carolina		20	11-15	0-0	2-3	11	1	3	24
Thompson, Pittsburgh		17	5-7	0-2	0-0	0	2	1	10
Calvin, Floridians		14	4-7	0-0	2-2	2	4	4	10
Jabali, Floridians		17	2-7	0-1	0-0	9	1	4	4
Dampier, Kentucky		9	1-2	0-2	0-0	1	3	0	2
TOTALS		240	61-114	0-7	20-29	71	37	28	142

Score by Periods:	1st	2nd	3rd	4th	Totals
West	31	35	23	26	115
East	36	29	32	45	142

Officials: John Vanak and Bob Serafin. Attendance: 15,738.

GAME 6, Feb. 6, 1973, at Salt Lake City
Coaches—East, Larry Brown, Carolina/West, LaDell Andersen, Utah
MVP—Warren Jabali, Denver

EAST ALL-STARS (111)

PLAYER, TEAM	POS.	MIN.	2-PT. FG-A	3-PT. FG-A	FT-A	REB.	A	PF	TP
Erving, Virginia	F	30	8-16	0-0	6-8	5	1	4	22
Cunningham, Carolina	F	20	9-11	0-1	0-0	6	4	6	18
Gilmore, Kentucky	C	31	3-8	0-0	4-8	16	0	5	10
Calvin, Carolina	G	23	3-8	0-0	7-7	2	8	5	13
Thompson, Memphis	G	22	4-10	0-0	2-2	1	0	1	10
Issel, Kentucky		29	6-14	0-0	2-2	7	4	0	14
Caldwell, Carolina		23	3-5	0-0	1-1	5	2	2	7
Paultz, New York		15	1-3	0-0	1-1	5	3	2	3
Dampier, Kentucky		23	5-12	0-1	0-0	1	0	3	10
Melchionni, New York		24	1-6	0-0	2-2	8	2	1	4
TOTALS		240	43-93	0-2	25-31	56	24	29	111

WEST ALL-STARS (123)

PLAYER, TEAM	POS.	MIN.	2-PT. FG-A	3-PT. FG-A	FT-A	REB.	A	PF	TP
McGinnis, Indiana	F	34	10-14	0-1	3-6	15	2	5	23
Wise, Utah	F	37	11-20	0-0	4-4	6	4	3	26
Daniels, Indiana	C	33	8-19	0-0	9-12	11	1	3	25
Jones, Utah	G	36	6-10	0-0	2-2	5	4	2	14
Simpson, Denver	G	13	2-6	0-2	2-3	3	2	1	6
Jones, Dallas		14	0-6	0-2	0-0	4	1	1	0
Johnson, San Diego		11	1-3	0-0	0-0	1	0	2	2
Beaty, Utah		15	3-6	0-0	0-0	4	1	1	6
Williams, San Diego		16	2-3	0-0	1-3	0	2	2	5
Jabali, Denver		31	6-11	1-1	1-3	4	7	2	16
TOTALS		240	49-98	1-4	22-33	53	24	22	123

Score by Periods:	1st	2nd	3rd	4th	Totals
West	28	24	32	39	123
East	28	37	27	19	111

Officials: Norm Drucker and Ed Middleton. Attendance: 12,556.

GAME 7, Jan. 30, 1974, at Norfolk, Va.

Coaches—East, Babe McCarthy, Kentucky/West, Joe Mullaney, Utah

MVP—Artis Gilmore, Kentucky

WEST ALL-STARS (112)

PLAYER, TEAM	POS.	MIN.	2-PT. FG-A	3-PT. FG-A	FT-A	REB.	A	PF	TP
Wise, Utah	F	25	4-12	0-0	0-0	7	0	1	8
McGinnis, Indiana	F	30	7-21	0-0	0-0	11	1	3	14
Daniels, Indiana	C	20	2-11	0-0	1-2	7	0	2	5
Jones, Utah	G	25	4-6	0-0	3-5	4	2	1	11
Jabali, Denver	G	24	3-10	0-5	0-1	2	3	2	6
Johnston, San Diego		22	3-7	0-2	2-2	4	0	2	8
Jones, San Antonio		19	2-10	0-1	0-0	8	2	4	4
Nater, San Antonio		28	13-24	0-0	3-4	22	0	2	29
Boone, Utah		24	6-11	1-2	0-0	3	5	1	15
Simpson, Denver		23	6-17	0-0	0-0	1	0	0	12
TOTALS		240	50-129	1-10	9-14	69	13	18	112

EAST ALL-STARS (128)

PLAYER, TEAM	POS.	MIN.	2-PT. FG-A	3-PT. FG-A	FT-A	REB.	A	PF	TP
Erving, New York	F	27	6-15	0-0	2-2	11	8	1	14
Issel, Kentucky	F	26	10-15	0-0	1-1	4	1	1	21
Gilmore, Kentucky	C	27	8-12	0-0	2-3	13	1	4	18
Dampier, Kentucky	G	23	8-12	0-0	0-0	2	1	0	16
Calvin, Carolina	G	27	3-10	0-0	2-3	2	11	3	8
Gervin, Virginia		21	3-8	0-1	3-4	5	3	1	9
Kenon, New York		22	3-12	0-0	2-3	6	0	1	8
Eakins, Virginia		21	1-4	0-0	0-0	4	4	2	2
McClain, Carolina		25	6-8	0-0	0-0	3	4	3	12
Thompson, Memphis		21	5-8	0-0	0-0	2	3	1	10
Paultz, New York				Injured					
TOTALS		240	58-104	0-1	12-16	52	36	17	128

Score by Periods:

	1st	2nd	3rd	4th	Totals
West	25	30	28	29	112
East	35	27	37	29	128

Officials: John Vanak and Wally Rooney. Attendance: 10,624.

GAME 8, Jan. 28, 1975, at San Antonio

Coaches—East, Kevin Loughery, N.Y. Nets/West, Larry Brown, Denver

MVP—Freddie Lewis, St. Louis

EAST ALL-STARS (151)

PLAYER, TEAM	POS.	MIN.	2-PT. FG-A	3-PT. FG-A	FT-A	REB.	A	PF	TP
Barnes, St. Louis	F	21	6-13	0-0	4-4	1	1	2	16
Erving, New York	F	27	5-11	1-1	8-10	7	7	4	21
Gilmore, Kentucky	C	28	4-8	0-0	3-7	13	2	3	11
Lewis, St. Louis	G	33	10-14	1-1	3-3	5	10	3	26
Dampier, Kentucky	G	27	4-6	1-2	0-0	3	1	4	11
Paultz, New York		18	2-7	0-0	0-0	4	4	2	4
Johnson, Memphis		14	4-10	0-1	0-0	3	2	2	8
Twardzik, Virginia		15	4-4	0-0	6-7	1	3	6	14
Taylor, New York		21	9-13	0-0	3-5	1	3	4	21
Kenon, New York		16	6-11	0-0	0-0	4	1	0	12
Issel, Kentucky		20	3-6	0-0	1-2	7	1	4	7
TOTALS		240	57-103	3-5	28-38	49	35	34	151

WEST ALL-STARS (124)

PLAYER, TEAM	POS.	MIN.	2-PT. FG-A	3-PT. FG-A	FT-A	REB.	A	PF	TP
McGinnis, Indiana	F	32	6-13	0-1	6-11	12	5	5	18
Gervin, San Antonio	F	30	8-14	0-1	7-8	6	3	2	23
Nater, San Antonio	C	26	5-13	0-0	2-2	5	1	3	12
Calvin, Denver	G	28	4-15	0-1	9-10	3	7	2	17
Boone, Utah	G	23	4-8	0-0	2-2	2	4	1	10
Jones, San Diego		15	2-4	0-0	1-1	4	0	4	5
Silas, San Antonio		23	5-7	0-0	11-11	3	5	3	21
Green, Denver		18	3-6	0-0	0-0	3	0	4	6
Malone, Utah		20	2-3	0-0	2-5	10	0	1	6
Simpson, Denver		25	3-10	0-0	0-0	3	0	1	6
TOTALS		240	42-93	0-3	40-50	51	23	29	124

Score by Periods:

	1st	2nd	3rd	4th	Totals
West	22	28	30	34	124
East	32	38	39	42	151

Officials: Jack Madden and Jess Kersey. Attendance: 10,449.

GAME 9, Jan. 27, 1976, at Denver

Coaches—All-Stars, Kevin Loughery, N.Y. Nets; Denver, Larry Brown

MVP—David Thompson, Denver

ALL-STARS (138)

PLAYER, TEAM	POS.	MIN.	2-PT. FG-A	3-PT. FG-A	FT-A	REB.	A	PF	TP
Knight, Indiana	F	23	9-14	0-1	2-2	10	2	3	20
Erving, New York	F	25	9-12	0-1	5-7	7	5	4	23
Gilmore, Kentucky	C	27	5-7	0-0	4-6	7	1	6	14
Silas, San Antonio	G	23	6-10	0-0	8-8	0	5	6	20
Taylor, New York	G	29	3-9	0-1	0-0	4	8	3	6
Boone, St. Louis		16	5-11	0-0	0-0	3	2	1	10
Paultz, San Antonio		20	4-6	0-0	2-2	2	1	1	10
Buse, Indiana		14	2-4	1-2	0-0	1	3	0	5
Lucas, St. Louis		14	2-5	0-0	1-1	5	3	1	5
Barnes, St. Louis		13	3-5	0-0	1-1	0	1	3	7
Kenon, San Antonio		20	5-7	0-0	0-0	6	2	5	10
Gervin, San Antonio		16	3-13	1-2	1-2	6	1	1	8
TOTALS		240	56-103	2-7	24-29	51	34	34	138

DENVER (144)

PLAYER, TEAM	POS.	MIN.	2-PT. FG-A	3-PT. FG-A	FT-A	REB.	A	PF	TP
Jones	F	29	8-12	0-0	8-11	10	3	2	24
Thompson	F	34	9-18	0-0	11-13	8	2	4	29
Issel	C	31	6-16	0-0	7-9	9	5	3	19
Williams	G	22	2-6	0-0	3-5	1	4	2	7
Simpson	G	37	8-15	0-0	3-3	7	5	0	19
Towe		11	1-3	0-0	0-0	0	2	0	2
Foster		5	0-3	0-0	0-0	1	0	1	0
Brown		9	2-2	0-0	0-0	3	1	4	4
Terry		25	5-12	1-3	3-5	3	3	2	14
Gerard		17	5-14	0-0	2-2	9	1	5	12
Beck		20	6-11	0-0	2-2	4	0	3	14
TOTALS		240	52-112	1-3	39-50	55	28	23	144

Score by Periods:

	1st	2nd	3rd	4th	Totals
Denver	32	23	37	52	144
All-Stars	31	25	41	41	138

Officials: Norm Drucker and Ed Middleton. Attendance: 17,798.

CHAPTER SEVEN

THE COACHES

Want to find a good coach? Try looking out on a limb.

From Red Auerbach to Pat Riley, the best coaches in the National Basketball Association have never been afraid to stand up and be counted, although Riley may have taken this to the extreme when, the day after his Los Angeles Lakers won the 1987 NBA Championship, he *guaranteed* they would repeat as titlists.

Most branded Riley's remark as foolish bravado. After all, 17 teams going back to 1969 had tried and failed to successfully defend their titles, including two coached by Riley. Was he not putting undue pressure on himself with a statement that would look foolish indeed if the Lakers fell short of their goal?

But such was not the case. Riley, a master motivator, had given his gifted athletes a goal and a challenge. For the next year, it was the players who were asked about Riley's guarantee and the pressure to produce. And ultimately, it was those players who won the 1988 NBA Championship, picking up the gauntlet Riley had thrown down before them.

It is said that the NBA is a players' league, but that can be a dangerous oversimplification. Would the Detroit Pistons of 1989 and 1990, a collection of talented but strong-willed and diverse individuals, have been able to win back-to-back NBA championships without the patience and persuasive powers of Chuck Daly? Not likely. It took Phil Jackson and his able assistants, Tex Winter, Johnny Bach and Jim Cleamons, to provide the structure in which the marvelous Michael Jordan and his teammates could blossom into three-time NBA Champions from 1991 to 1993.

With so many solid teams and so many great players, it is up to the coach to give his high-priced talent an edge. Riley's flat-out title guarantee did exactly that. And it was an example of how coaching had changed since the Celtics won eight consecutive titles and 11 championships in 13 years, ending in 1969.

Pat Riley, master motivator, guaranteed that the Lakers would repeat in 1988, and they did.

Coaching in the NBA in the 1990s no longer means devising a system for the players, imposing it on them and then motivating at least partially by fear and intimidation. Players in the modern era do not respond solely to discipline; free agency, multimillion-dollar salaries and guaranteed contracts have changed that. The old-school coaches have been phased out in favor of motivators who can "relate" to today's athletes and coax them to perform at their peak.

It's no longer enough simply to be a great basketball coach, a genius with Xs and Os, substitutions and timeouts. It's necessary to be at least a part-time psychologist as well, although Riley—forever clever with words—prefers a different description.

Dream Team Coach Chuck Daly says that to be a winner in today's game, a coach must be a people person.

"I don't like the word 'psychological,'" he said, "because when the players hear that, they think, 'Who does this guru think he is?' The word I like to use is 'communicate.' You have to communicate to your players and to yourself. I tell the players that all the time. What is important is how you communicate what we are and who we are to yourself. Then you can communicate it to everybody else."

Nice. But can anyone imagine Auerbach resorting to such tactics? Auerbach was a master psychologist in his own right, but he also was a dictator. In Boston, it was his way or the highway. Can anyone picture one of Auerbach's players stuffing a towel down Auerbach's mouth? That's what Kareem Abdul-Jabbar did to Riley on the podium, in front of the national television cameras, while champagne drenched Riley's hair, face and clothes moments after the Lakers got their second consecutive championship in 1988. That was Abdul-Jabbar's way of ensuring that his coach would not repeat his guarantee and place even more pressure on the Lakers to become three-time champions.

Riley's gleeful acceptance of Abdul-Jabbar's gesture was indicative of the modern-day coaching era, one in which the most successful coaches like Riley have learned to adapt.

"You have to handle and get the respect of the players," said Don Nelson, who played for Auerbach's Celtics before successful coaching stints at Milwaukee and Golden State. "It's so much more important than it ever was. Whatever important lessons you learn along the way, you'd better be able to use and be good at it."

Daly, who coached the USA Dream Team to the gold medal in Barcelona, calls himself a "lifer," a career coach who worked at the high school, college and pro levels before moving to the broadcast booth in 1944, at age 63. He reflected on the special challenge of coaching the best athletes in the world, today's NBA players.

"First of all, you have to look at your personnel and see what they are able to do offensively and defensively. That's No. 1 on the professional level," said Daly. "Systems are nice, but I think it's better to suit systems to personnel than vice versa. You have to learn to take advantage of the personnel that you are given.

"Also, in this day and age, the people aspect of coaching is paramount. A coach, to a great degree, has to be a people person. That doesn't mean he has to give up all his discipline, but he has to give up some of it. To be a successful coach in the NBA, you must understand the mentality of the players."

An example of the evolution of the NBA coach's role was seen in Boston in the mid-'80s, when K. C. Jones took over for Bill Fitch and led the Celtics to NBA championships in 1984 and 1986. Fitch had been part of a group of college coaches that included Jack Ramsay, Dick Motta and John MacLeod, who moved into the pro game during the late 1960s and early 1970s and enjoyed significant success. Fitch built the expansion Cleveland Cavaliers into a playoff team, then moved to Boston and led the Celtics to the 1981 NBA Championship.

Fitch was a throwback to the old school of coaching—a disciplinarian with a regimented system. Fitch's four Boston teams averaged more than 60 victories a season, but when the Celtics were swept by Nelson's Bucks in four games in a 1983 playoff series, Fitch resigned under pressure. Some of the players had expressed such unhappiness with the system that a mutiny was feared in Boston.

Jones quickly quelled that with his relaxed, low-key approach. He called upon his extensive experience as a Celtics player under Auerbach, the master, and his three years in Washington, where he had led the Bullets to an average of 52 victories a year. Jones had played on eight Celtic championship teams, so he understood that it took great players to win. He also understood that to win in the modern game, it took great players who were happy. He created an atmosphere that enabled the Celtics to advance to the NBA Finals four consecutive seasons and win two championships.

Jones continued a tradition that Auerbach had begun when he became the Celtics' coach in 1950. Indeed, in the next 38 years, Auerbach—the coach, general manager and president—was the one constant in the Celtics' brilliance. In terms of influence on the professional game, Auerbach was without peer. He not only molded the Celtics into the NBA's dominant franchise, he also was the league's dominant personality.

Auerbach the coach will be forever remembered for his agitating habit of lighting a victory cigar when it became obvious that the Celtics were in such command of the game that a win was guaranteed. One of the most famous cigar incidents occurred on April 25, 1965, during Game 5 of the NBA Finals against the Los Angeles Lakers in Boston Garden.

The Celtics, already leading the series 3–1, moved in front in Game 5 by 18 points at the end of the third period, then scored baskets on their first 10 possessions of the fourth quarter. As the crowd roared—as crowds must have roared in ancient Roman arenas when lions were savaging fallen, bleeding Christians—Auerbach reached inside his plaid sports coat for one of his trademark monogrammed cigars. With exaggerated care

and great puffs of blue smoke, which prompted a burst of raucous approval from the crowd, he lit up in affirmation of triumph assured.

As the fans continued to cheer hysterically, Auerbach reached into his pocket again, whirled dramatically, and flung a handful of his cigars into the stands. The Celtics went on to win the game 129–96, which gave them their seventh consecutive championship. They also won the next season to give them eight straight, a record considered as unreachable as Joe DiMaggio's 56-game hitting streak.

In his autobiography, *Go Up for Glory*, Bill Russell attempted to explain Auerbach's success:

"He knows exactly the right way to select a player—rookie or old pro—and move him onto a squad without disrupting the fluidity of the team," Russell wrote. "A tough kid who fought his way up from the streets of Brooklyn, he never deluded himself.

"Auerbach had a reason for everything—from yelling at a referee to selling out Boston Garden with a

K. C. Jones knew how to get the most from the talented veterans on the Boston Celtics of the mid-1980s.

promotion to bringing in a player who on the surface appears to be useless.

"Auerbach cannot stand the thought of losing. Neither can I. Anyone who has ever come to the Celtics had immediately been instilled with this philosophy. If you don't play to win, Auerbach has no place for you."

Auerbach agreed with that assessment. "I found players who wanted to win," he said. "They didn't have what we like to call 'Celtic pride' or tradition when they got here. They acquired it. It rubbed off on them. The learning was there if you wanted it. First and foremost, I considered myself a teacher. I taught basketball. If you were a Celtic, you learned to motivate and communicate."

There is little doubt that many of the Celtics learned well. What the NBA discovered after Auerbach's coaching career ended in 1966 was that Auerbach not only had an eye for talent and character, but he also had assembled a gifted group of men who were later to become successful coaches.

Bob Cousy, Bill Sharman, K. C. Jones, Frank Ramsey, Dave Cowens, Paul Silas, Tom Heinsohn, Tom Sanders, Bill Russell and Don Nelson all became pro coaches. And the list of successful college coaches includes more than a dozen, including Georgetown's John Thompson.

"Red just had so much to offer as far as handling men goes," Nelson said. "Not necessarily technical, but the management of time and effort and understanding to get the most out of one another. He was always a step ahead of everybody. About the time you thought he was going to give you hell, he patted you on the butt. And about the time you thought you just played your best game, he would ream you out for some little thing you didn't do defensively.

"Red Auerbach sought out dedicated people. You didn't play for him unless the game was really important to you and you were willing to make a lot of sacrifices, and that's what carries on into coaching."

Auerbach's influence was profound in several areas. The dedicated people he sought out learned from him and learned their lessons well. During the 1976–77 season, Nelson, then 36, became the Milwaukee head coach. Nelson was unsure of himself at the time, but through hard work and study he became one of the game's best head coaches. For seven consecutive years, Nelson's Bucks won 50 or more games. Nelson later enjoyed success with the Golden State Warriors and coached Dream Team II, the United States squad at the 1994 World Championship of Basketball.

Nelson refuted the notion that ex-players could not

technically match wits with former college coaches. No coach in the NBA was more creative at testing the limits of the illegal defense guidelines or utilizing unique lineups, including a "small" squad of four guards and one frontcourtman. Nelson's innovations proved he was as intellectually capable as any coach from any background.

Nelson's success had an effect on other ex-players, who began studying the game more seriously. When Riley was hired by the Lakers in 1981, he was less than two years removed from being the Lakers' radio-TV analyst. But, like Nelson, Riley set about making up for his lack of coaching experience by outworking other coaches.

"There's no question that that is what I had to do," Riley said. "When I got the job, I wasn't ready and I knew it. Thank God I had a year and a half as an assistant coach. But I didn't have a philosophy, so I had to dive in, work as hard as I could, do all the research that I could and develop a philosophy."

Riley also relied on veteran coaches as his top assistants, Bill Bertka in Los Angeles and Dick Harter in New York. Another ex-player, Billy Cunningham, did the same when he became coach of the Philadelphia 76ers, depending on Chuck Daly for his Xs and Os until he got accustomed to the coach's seat. And Phil Jackson, in building the Bulls' three-time champions in Chicago, tapped the resources of two outstanding tacticians, Tex Winter and Johnny Bach, who had more than 80 years of coaching experience between them.

With blacks such a significant presence on the court in the NBA, it's logical that this would extend to the coaching ranks as well, especially when the trend to hiring former players gained momentum. Contrary to popular notion, Russell was not the first black head coach of the modern era; that distinction belongs to John McLendon, who coached the Cleveland Pipers of the short-lived American Basketball League in 1961. But Russell was the first in the NBA, in 1966, and the first to win a championship when he guided the Celtics to titles in 1968 and 1969. Yes, it certainly helped that Russell the coach could start Russell the player at center.

The first black to win a championship without Russell was Al Attles, who directed the Golden State Warriors to the title in 1975, a significant year in the history of professional sports because of the matchup of two black coaches in the NBA Finals. Attles was praised for his leadership and innovations as he used as many as 12 players in a game during the series, which the Warriors swept in four games, defeating K. C. Jones's Washington Bullets.

The success of Attles and Russell and the dominance of black players led to more coaching and executive opportunities in the NBA for blacks, who had

The man who set the standard, Red Auerbach, celebrates a Boston championship with one of his star pupils, Bill Russell.

Don Nelson says getting and maintaining the respect of the players is one of the keys to coaching.

1993–94, his first season as coach of the Atlanta Hawks, Wilkens joined Auerbach as the only NBA coach with more than 900 regular-season victories.

"I always admired Red, and it will certainly be an achievement for me, but I couldn't care less about the recognition part," Wilkens said of his impending rise to the top spot on the list. "I had that recognition as a player. Now I like to focus in on helping players develop, knowing that if they're successful, I'm going to be, too."

Wilkens also is not one to dwell on past accomplishments, no matter how impressive. "You know how it is in our business," he mused. "You have to keep looking ahead. If you spend too much time dwelling on the past, you're going to get whipped by someone in the present."

Another special group that had impact on coaching in the NBA was college coaches. NBA teams began hiring these so-called coaching professionals in the mid-'60s. The two most successful were Jack Ramsay, who had a 234-72 record in 11 seasons at St. Joseph's (Pa.) before compiling 864 victories as coach of the Philadelphia 76ers, Buffalo Braves, Portland Trail Blazers and Indiana Pacers, and Dick Motta, who was hired from Weber State in Utah by the Chicago Bulls in 1968 and went on to post 856 career NBA victories and who

a more difficult time breaking down similar barriers in professional football and baseball. In basketball it was different, and one reason was the positive reinforcement owners received when black coaches proved to be successful. In 1979 Lenny Wilkens directed the Seattle SuperSonics to the NBA Championship, and Jones won two titles with the Celtics in the 1980s.

"What perpetuated the opportunity was black coaches winning championships," said Bernie Bickerstaff, the general manager of the Denver Nuggets. "People have come in and been successful, not as black coaches, but as coaches. And I think that's important."

Among the most successful has been Wilkens, who is poised to surpass Auerbach as the NBA's all-time winningest coach in 1994–95. An outstanding point guard who amassed Hall of Fame credentials in 15 NBA seasons, Wilkens served as a player-coach in both Seattle and Portland before hanging up his sneakers in 1975. The soft-spoken and gentlemanly Wilkens's teams have failed to make the playoffs only four times since 1978. In

Gentlemanly Lenny Wilkens is in his third decade as one of the NBA's finest coaches.

NBA'S ALL-TIME WINNINGEST COACHES
(Regular-season records through 1993–94 season)

COACH	WON-LOST	PCT.
1. Red Auerbach	938–479	.662
2. Lenny Wilkens	926–774	.545
3. Jack Ramsay	864–783	.525
4. Dick Motta	856–863	.498
5. Bill Fitch	845–877	.491
6. Cotton Fitzsimmons	805–745	.519
7. Don Nelson	803–573	.586
8. Gene Shue	784–861	.477
9. John MacLeod	707–657	.518
10. Pat Riley	701–272	.720

began his second stint as coach of the Dallas Mavericks in 1994–95. Each won one NBA title, Ramsay with Portland in 1977 and Motta with Washington in 1978.

The ex-college coaches reached their zenith in a five-year period beginning with the 1976–77 season. Of the next five championships, four were won by coaches whose primary training had been at the college level—Ramsay in 1977, Motta in 1978, the Lakers with Paul Westhead in 1980 and Boston with Fitch in 1981. Wilkens, who directed Seattle to the title in 1979, was the only ex-player to lead his team to the title during that span.

But in the next few years, the trend in hiring switched to either ex-players or pro assistant coaches. And by the 1990s, the trend most definitely was toward ex-players—preferably, but not necessarily, with experience as assistants. John Lucas (San Antonio) and Quinn Buckner (Dallas) became head coaches without any previous NBA coaching experience, although the more traditional route was to serve an apprenticeship as an assistant, as Phil Jackson (Chicago), Rudy Tomjanovich (Houston), Paul Westphal (Phoenix), Chris Ford (Boston), Mike Dunleavy (Milwaukee) and many others did.

At the championship level, ex-players clearly have dominated. From 1982 through 1994, teams coached by former players won 11 of 13 NBA championships, the exceptions being Daly's Detroit titlists in 1989 and 1990. And of the 26 coaches who coached teams in the NBA Finals during that period, 22 were ex-players.

Jackson guided the Chicago Bulls to three consecutive NBA championships from 1991 to 1993. A key reserve forward on the New York Knicks' 1973 championship team, Jackson spent five years coaching on the minor-league level, with the Albany Patroons of the Continental Basketball Association, and two seasons as an assistant coach with the Bulls before getting the head job. He believes the ability to motivate players is at least as important as diagramming Xs and Os.

"It's all-important," he said, "but general managers realize that you can hire assistant coaches that have been around basketball for 20 or 30 years to take teams through practices or teach skills. So it's really, basically, how you can motivate players and keep them interested in basketball that counts at this point."

"The best thing about Phil is he allows players freedom on the court," said Scottie Pippen, the Bulls' All-Star forward. "You need to be able to go out there and give yourself a lot of rope and see how far you can go just before you hang yourself."

Jackson agrees that he'll give his players a degree of freedom, saying, "Sometimes you've got to give the horse its reins and let it go. It knows how to run better than the rider—it's got its feet on the ground, and you're just on its back."

Which is not to say he lets the inmates run the asylum. There's no doubt that Jackson has his hold on the reins, it's just that he holds them with a light touch.

"I like to bring a player to a place where he can see things for himself, to guide him there rather than have a direct confrontation," Jackson explained. "I don't like to hit people over the head with a hammer."

Whether the personal style is a firm hand or a light touch, whether he comes from a college background or was a former player, today's NBA coach has found that simply to compete requires total commitment—more so than ever.

"You have to be a lifer," Nelson said, echoing Daly's description. "You have to be totally dedicated to your job and have it as one of your very, very high priorities. We're talking one-two-three here—family, religion and coaching. Coaching has got to be in your top three, otherwise you're not going to be successful."

"It has become more complicated," Bickerstaff said. "When I was an assistant in Washington [in the late '70s], I did all the scouting and everything. I was the only assistant coach. Now we've got two, three, even four assistants. You've also got a video man who breaks the tape down at halftime so we can see what we're doing and make adjustments for the second half. And then you've got the satellite dish so you can see every game that is played around the country."

Sophistication of this sort would have mystified the men who played the game in its early years. Men like Red Holzman, who played for Rochester in the 1940s and coached New York to championships in 1970 and

1973, or Joe Lapchick, a star player in the early 1920s who later was an outstanding coach at St. John's University and who led the Knicks in their early NBA years.

In his book *50 Years of Basketball*, Lapchick wrote: "Coaching, organization, discipline and regular practices are routine today. But in the early days, they were fairly loose. The 'coach' was either the oldest man on the club or the club owner who kept his office in his inside coat pocket. Just before the start of the game, the club owner would stick his head in the dressing room and say, 'This is no baloney, you guys. You've got to win!' Then he would slam the door for emphasis and go out to count the house. There was no coaching. Trial and error and advice from better players was the method used to improve."

Times may have changed and technology and staffing certainly have improved, but those old basics—"trial and error" and "advice from better players"—remain applicable today. Ask any good coach, even if you have to go out on a limb to find him.

BAA/NBA Coaches (1946–94)
(does not include interim head coaches)

Rick Adelman	Herb Brown
Richie Adubato	Hubie Brown
Stan Albeck	Larry Brown
Paul Armstrong	Phil Brownstein
Al Attles	Quinn Buckner
Red Auerbach	Bucky Buckwalter
John Bach	Walt Budko
Ed Badger	Donnie Butcher
Clif Barker	Fred Carter
Al Barthelme	Don Casey
Bob Bass	John Castellani
Elgin Baylor	Al Cervi
Clair Bee	Don Chaney
Carl Bennett	Roy Clifford
Al Bianchi	Neil Cohalan
Bernie Bickerstaff	Jerry Colangelo
Paul Birch	Doug Collins
Vince Boryla	Larry Costello
Carl Braun	Bob Cousy
Allan Bristow	

Paul Westphal is one of several former players who have enjoyed coaching success in the NBA.

Phil Jackson's light touch on the reins helped the Chicago Bulls to three consecutive titles.

Dave Cowens
Billy Cunningham
Glenn Curtis
Chuck Daly
Jim Darden
Dutch Dehnert
Dave DeBusschere
Don Delaney
Eddie Donovan
Mike Dunleavy
Charley Eckman
Johnny Egan
Mike Farmer
Bob Feerick
Bill Fitch
Cotton Fitzsimmons
Chris Ford
Mike Fratello
Burl Friddle
Harry Gallatin
Eddie Gottlieb
Matt Guokas

Ed Gregory
Richie Guerin
Bruce Hale
Frank Hamblen
Alex Hannum
Del Harris
Les Harrison
Dick Harter
Gar Heard
Tom Heinsohn
Nat Hickey
Bob Hill
Red Holzman
Bob Hopkins
Rex Hughes
George Irvine
Dan Issel
Phil Jackson
Stu Jackson
Buddy Jeannette
Earvin "Magic" Johnson

Phil Johnson
Neil Johnston
K. C. Jones
Wallace Jones
Ed Jucker
Alvin "Doggie" Julian
George Karl
Bob Kauffman
John Kerr
John Kundla
Joe Lapchick
Frank Layden
George Lee
Bob Leonard
Fuzzy Levane
Grady Lewis
Gene Littles
Earl Lloyd
Tates Locke
Ken Loeffler
Kevin Loughery
Sidney Lowe
John Lucas
Jim Lynam
Ed Macauley
Bob MacKinnon
John MacLeod
Tom Marshall
Johnny McCarthy
Jack McCloskey
Dick McGuire
Frank McGuire
Morris McHone
Bones McKinney
Jack McKinney
Jack McMahon
Dave McMillan
Murray Mendenhall
George Mikan
Doug Moe
Doxie Moore
Bob Morris
Dick Motta
Joe Mullaney
Bill Musselman
Don Nelson
Tom Nissalke
Harold Olsen
Randy Pfund
Andy Phillip
Rick Pitino
Jim Pollard
Roger Potter
Jack Ramsay

Willis Reed
Chick Reiser
Jerry Reynolds
Pat Riley
Scotty Robertson
Red Rocha
Jimmy Rodgers
Red Rolfe
Ron Rothstein
Roy Rubin
Bill Russell
Honey Russell
Cincy Sachs
Ed Sadowski
Garry St. Jean
Tom Sanders
Herm Schaefer
Fred Schaus
Dolph Schayes
Mike Schuler
Howie Schultz
Fred Scolari
Ray Scott
George Senesky
Paul Seymour
Bill Sharman
Charley Shipp
Gene Shue
Paul Silas
Jerry Sloan
Jack Smiley
Hank Soar
Ken Suesens
Jerry Tarkanian
Rod Thorn
Rolland Todd
Mike Todorovich
Rudy Tomjanovich
Wes Unseld
Butch van Breda Kolff
Dick Versace
Dick Vitale
Donnie Walsh
Bobby Wanzer
Bob Weiss
Jerry West
Paul Westhead
Paul Westphal
John Wetzel
Lenny Wilkens
Tex Winter
Dave Wohl
Charlie Wolf

ABA Coaches Only

LaDell Andersen	Vince Cazetta	Jim Harding	Gene Rhodes
Zelmo Beaty	Wilt Chamberlain	York Larese	Beryl Shipley
Joe Belmont	John Clark	Slater Martin	Larry Staverman
Mark Binstein	Rudy Davalos	Babe McCarthy	Jerry Steele
Bill Blakeley	Harry Dinnell	John McLendon	Jim Weaver
Hal Blitman	John Givens	Tom Meschery	Max Williams
Al Brightman	Alex Groza	Vern Mikkelsen	Gus Young
Lou Carnesecca	Cliff Hagan	Frank Ramsey	Max Zaslofsky

THE REFEREES

Officiating may be the only profession performed before crowds who pay tribute with their silence rather than with cheering and applause. The official does his job in front of thousands of critical eyes, all the while knowing that the best referee is the one who manages to appear the least conspicuous.

Officiating is, in other words, a challenging and often thankless occupation, and the job of the NBA referee is surely the most demanding of them all. NBA refs work a game that has become the fastest, quickest and most dynamic on the planet. In the 1980s and 1990s, the sport's soaring public appeal was equaled only by the ever-increasing size, strength and agility of the athletes who played it. The players are the show; the referees are the silent, anonymous arbitrators. And in the public's eye, these poor guys are wrong even when they're right—which is usually the case.

But do you know what? They wouldn't trade their jobs for the world.

"It's a good job," said Darell Garretson, an NBA referee from 1967 to 1994 and now the league's director of officiating. "It's not like the public's assumption. The media always likes to talk about the lonely nights on the road and so forth. The only thing I can say is there's a lot of people today who would like this job. You're only gone 16 days a month. Plus, it lasts only six and a half months, and all of a sudden you've got five months to do anything you want. I tell people not to be sorry for NBA officials because we have a hell of a job!"

Indeed, the referees have come a long way since the days when they were paid $30 and $40 a game to work in small, dimly lit arenas before often hostile and unruly crowds. Today's top officials earn six-figure salaries and also receive expenses for travel, hotels and transportation. Their union contract provides full health insurance, first-class air travel on flights exceeding two hours and first-class lodgings. It's not a bad lifestyle—the occasional fan abuse notwithstanding.

For obvious reasons, officials do not fly on the same flights with teams or stay in the same hotels. In the old days, they were encouraged to live as cheaply as possible to cut down on league expenses. Former referee Sid Borgia, one of the league's pioneer officials, recalled being chastised by the league for staying in a $6 hotel when a $4 room was available on the same street.

"And you had to travel on trains in those days," Borgia said. "I remember making a hop to St. Louis and spending 22 hours on a train. I would travel 5,000 and 6,000 miles a month by train.

"There was a method to my madness," Borgia explained. "The league allowed us to go first-class. I saved the difference and made more money on expenses than I did for the games. But in 1946 I was in the hospital for torn cartilage and had to pay for it myself. The league was struggling."

The league is certainly not struggling any longer. Under the stewardship of Commissioner David J. Stern, the NBA made tremendous strides, both financially and artistically, in the 1980s. And while the quality of officiating remained at a high level, Stern and the NBA Board of Governors realized that the game had become too swift and too potentially volatile to be handled by only a pair of officials.

So in 1988–89 the league went to a third official, a move that had been tried for a single year and then abandoned a decade earlier. After an exhaustive search

and a summer of intensive indoctrination, the league hired 18 new referees, ranging in age from 32 to 44, for the 1988–89 season.

"We picked up 14 college officials out of the 18," Garretson said, "and I think the roughest thing for them was realizing what kind of players they were refereeing. It's not how well they officiate. The biggest transition any official has is finding out just how fast, quick and strong NBA players are. College officials don't understand that until they get down on the floor."

What they find is a game that has become much more sophisticated defensively but at the same time more geared toward running and transition.

"In the old days, it was nothing more than a walk, walk, walk the ball up the floor game," Garretson said. "A guy could referee until he was 90. Now we're looking for athletic people, people who can flat-out run the floor. The days of the fat referee have long gone by the board. You're looking for a guy who, as the years go by, will maintain an athletic posture."

Former referee Darell Garretson now trains refs as the NBA's chief of officiating staff.

To assure that athletic standard, the league conducts physical exams for its referees each year during training camp and officials are required to run a distance in a prescribed time. Garretson said there are two essential rules for officials: Be in shape and know the rules. And the referees are fined when there is any breach of either.

Today's officials are studied and scrutinized more intensely than ever. The league office maintains a team of observers who attend games with one assignment: to watch the referees, see that they are in proper position to make the calls and generally perform their jobs up to the NBA's high standards. Referees are rated periodically on a variety of criteria, and those ratings go a long way toward determining playoff assignments and career advancement. The same scrutiny extends to the Continental Basketball Association, the minor league that is subsidized by the NBA and serves as a training ground for referees as well as a testing place for prospective NBA rules changes.

Garretson said his observational tasks have been advanced and improved immeasurably by the advent of videotape. In that way, he's much like the legion of NBA coaches, who have become increasingly dependent on videotape for scouting and game preparation.

"We do so much videotape work now," Garretson said. "I remember we used to go in once a year and sign a paper saying we'd looked at a 16-millimeter tape of one game. Now an official probably will see more than 30 games a year on tape. I watch better than 350 games a year on tape myself, plus I work 45 games and observe another 50 or 60 in person. Ten or 15 years ago, video just wasn't in."

Garretson will sit down with a young referee before a game and peruse the videotape of the official's most recent game to pinpoint his strengths and weaknesses. Then, after that night's game, they'll return to the hotel and play back a tape of that game. Garretson enlists the aid of other veteran officials, such as Hugh Evans and Ed Rush, to assist him in handling the videotape review.

Of course, no amount of training can produce three officials who all see a game the same way. Pairing up referees—or in this case, tripling them up—always has been a difficult task. "It's easy to pair them up ability-wise, but you also have to consider personalities," said Garretson.

John Nucatola, a former NBA supervisor of officials and a member of the Basketball Hall of Fame, agrees that compatibility is a vital ingredient in a refereeing team. "You've got to find out right away if guys don't like each other," he said. "Morale is important."

The NBA lifestyle can test a young official's morale.

Much like rookie players, they can find the adjustment to an arduous, 82-game schedule difficult, much more demanding than the shorter college or CBA schedule to which they'd been accustomed. "A young man can get lost," said Richie Powers, a retired official. "Even a rookie, though, must consider himself the best. He has to feel he is as good as anyone in the league. It will drive him to better his abilities. Unlike a rookie player, the referee is thrust into the meat grinder immediately."

Certainly consideration has never been one of the more evident qualities of the average American sports fan. In the formative years of the NBA, the only thing some fans considered was which expletive to hurl at the referees next. One night in Syracuse many years ago, Borgia and Nucatola had to be escorted off the court by a cordon of policemen because a number of unruly fans were trying to punch them. "We had to stay in the Knicks' locker room until everyone cleared out," Borgia said. "Then a detective pulled a car up to the back door and took us to the train station. We couldn't even go back to the hotel for our things."

On another occasion—again in Syracuse—a fan challenged Borgia to call a foul against the Boston Celtics. Borgia's reply brought the fan out of his seat and onto the floor, where they exchanged blows. The fan left without several of his teeth, and Borgia found himself with a $35,000 lawsuit on his hands. Nowadays, officials rarely get involved in exchanges with fans.

"The NBA has a whole Security Department now," Garretson said. "We're given police protection on and off the court, at halftime, before and after the game, even to your car if you so desire."

Actually, it is rare to see any physical outbursts by NBA fans these days. It's a tribute to the league's success at not only selling the game to the public but educating people as to its more subtle nuances. And that includes officiating.

"It amazes me how the fans are much more knowledgeable now," said Borgia. "A referee calls a technical, and there is no uproar. Fans will call goaltending before the official does. They understand the game."

It once was the prevailing notion that former players, who probably understand the game best of all, would make good referees. But surprisingly, that hasn't been the case. Only one ex-player, Bernie Fryer, is on the NBA officiating staff. Several former players—among them Ernie DiGregorio, Lucius Allen and Fred Foster—began to pursue refereeing careers but soon abandoned the vocation.

"Why aren't there more ex-players?" Garretson said. "We give every player who's ever come forward a

chance to officiate. We give them three years in the summer leagues to try it and see if they like it. They have to like it, first of all, and put in the work. Most of the time, they're not willing to put in the time and hard effort to be an official on every level. The other thing is, players themselves are tougher on an ex-player. He has a certain bit of knowledge that should work to his advantage . . . and yet, well, let's take Fryer, who's our only ex-player. The common thing he'll hear from players is, 'You couldn't play and that's why you're an official.' It's almost as if they don't want him to make it."

"Just because a man is a former player doesn't mean he will be a good referee," said Norm Drucker, another former referee and NBA supervisor of officials. "I think the better the player, the more difficult it will be to referee."

Drucker theorized that players have trouble making the transition to a profession in which their mistakes are so evident for the fan to see. And while referees are well paid for their labors, they still earn far less than the average NBA player—who is, after all, the star of the show.

Still, the officials command much more respect than in earlier times. Players and coaches are prohibited from criticizing referees publicly—a fine almost certainly will result—though that doesn't stop them from whining and complaining while the game is in progress. But again, it's nothing compared to the abuse of the old days, when confrontations between players and officials, or coaches and officials, were a commonplace, and even expected, part of the entertainment.

"The toughest thing about officiating years ago was containing the players," Borgia said. "It was different from the way it is today. You had to stand and fight them in those days. The owners were trying to sell the sport. They had to play doubleheaders and put the Globetrotters on the card to help draw a crowd. They had to try everything, so why spare the referee?"

Why indeed? "Fans who came to a game took a personal affront against every referee, no matter who he was," Borgia said. "In the smaller towns, they considered their teams their personal babies. In the league's infancy, the two cardinal sins were calling goaltending or a technical foul against the home team. It was like signing your life away if you blew your whistle and called it."

Borgia remembered a night when he and Max Tabacchi worked a game in St. Louis. Grady Lewis played for St. Louis, and it seemed every wrong move he made was spotted by Tabacchi. Finally, Lewis fouled out in the third quarter. On his way to the locker room, he

peeled off his jersey, tossed it to Tabacchi and said, "You took everything in the world, you might as well take this, too."

But the most consistently combative arena in those days was the Syracuse War Memorial. Al Bianchi, a hard-nosed Syracuse player of that era who later became a coach and general manager, carries some fond but frightful memories of those wars.

"Oh yeah, those were tough, tough pro crowds," he

Though only 5-7, Sid Borgia had no qualms about standing up to players like 6-9 Larry Foust.

said. "There's one story where Boston was going off the court with a police escort—there was always a police escort when we played Boston in those days. The cops are walking out with the Celtics and one of the players said, 'Hey, didn't you see that fan throw that thing at me?' The cop said, 'Yeah.' The player said, 'Well, aren't you going to do something about it?' And the cop said, 'Hell, no! You deserved it!'"

Drucker told of the time he was officiating a game in Syracuse with the late Mendy Rudolph in the 1950s.

"There was a long, winding path you had to take to get out of the place," Drucker said. "You had to go through the people. Syracuse was losing, so when it ended Mendy and I went through a tunnel the opposite way. There were times you literally had to fight your way off the court."

Technical fouls would inspire long, vicious protests by the spectators. One year, Maurice Podoloff, the first NBA president, issued a directive to officials instructing them to call "whispering fouls" to offset the inevitable crowd reaction. In other words, rather than call a technical foul when it occurred, the referee was told to wait until the next timeout. "We would go over to a team's huddle and sneak our hands in there and tell the offender he was being fined, say, $10 for an infraction," Borgia said. "Then we would get our heads right out of

Longtime referee and supervisor of officials Norm Drucker gets an earful from Red Auerbach.

there and call the teams out to play. No one would know except the player. We didn't even tell the scorekeepers until after the game.

"It used to be that when we called a technical against the home team, the public address announcer couldn't wait to tell everyone. We would be showered for 15 minutes. It was so bad that I must have had as many police escorts as the top scorers in the league."

Modern security has rendered such scenes rare, though there are still times when a referee can find himself nose to nose with an irate fan. During the historic triple-overtime fifth game of the 1976 NBA Finals between Phoenix and Boston, the crowd stormed the floor in Boston Garden, mistakenly thinking the game had ended. In the ensuing confusion, a fan attacked referee Richie Powers, at the time the league's senior official. Powers decided to fight back.

"I don't know why everyone made a big fuss," Borgia said. "We had one of those every night when I refereed. I think what disturbed Richie the most was that he punched the guy and didn't hurt him! When I worked, there was no money in the game. You had to be crazy and hungry to do it."

In fact, it really did help to be a little crazy in those days. The league was still struggling to survive, and if fans came out partly to see the wild, flamboyant antics of certain referees, all the better. Borgia was known for his animated style, but none could compare to Pat Kennedy, who gained renown for his shrill whistle, his finger-wagging style and his loud, resonant voice.

Kennedy, who was nicknamed the Hibernian from Hoboken, was frequently headlined over the game he was to officiate. Fans delighted in his style, watching gleefully as his neck would bulge, his face would turn purple and he'd blow his whistle several times before turning to the offending player and saying, "I caught you this time!"

As sports columnist Joe Williams once wrote, "You are told people went to Madison Square Garden first to see Mr. Kennedy officiate and second to watch the basketballers play. Mr. Kennedy does everything but throw himself through the hoop."

Kennedy's theatrics didn't always sit well with players, coaches or fellow referees, but his saving grace was that everyone conceded he was an outstanding official. Whatever his style, a referee above all has to be fair and consistent, and he has to keep his poise. Kennedy met these standards.

One of the best was Mendy Rudolph, who worked his first NBA game at the age of 25. When he retired 23 years later, Rudolph had officiated 2,113 games. Powers,

One of the most colorful officials of the modern era was
Earl Strom, who refereed for more than 30 years.

a contemporary, was another of the more expressive
officials of that generation. More recently, one of the
most demonstrative, and most easily recognizable, referees was Earl Strom, who officiated pro basketball
games for more than 30 years.

The notion of the referee as a marquee character is
something the NBA today feels it can do without. The
players are the unquestioned attractions in today's game,
although knowledgeable fans recognize the leading
current officials like Garretson, Jake O'Donnell, Hugh
Evans, Mike Mathis, Joe Crawford, Dick Bavetta, Ed
Rush, Jess Kersey, Jack Madden and Hue Hollins. Polls
repeatedly show that the NBA's players are the most
recognizable and popular of all pro athletes. They are
the show, and the league wants to keep it that way.

"We've advanced," Garretson said. "So much of
that earlier stuff, as far as I'm concerned, was vaudeville
as much as anything else. If any of my guys did that
today, there would be so much money taken out of their
pocket. You blew the whistle with reckless abandon
back then. You knew you could go out and get another
job that paid just as much money, but not today. And as
we pay them more money, of course, we turn around
and ask more things of them in return."

So don't pity the lot of the poor, unappreciated
NBA officials. As Garretson said, they love what they're
doing. In his expert judgment, there's nothing they'd
rather be doing. And as usual, the referee's judgment is
final.

Jake O'Donnell is consistently rated among today's top
officials for the way he keeps a game under control.

BAA/NBA REFEREES (1946–94)

Gene Agnes	Bob Delaney	Jim Harvey	Lou Moser	Sam Schoenfeld
John Anderson	Jay Dempsey	C. B. Hatcher	Harry Moskowitz	Dick Seidler
John Alderton	Tony DePhillips	Barney Hearn	Don Murphy	Joe Serafin
Bruce Alexander	Joe DeRosa	Arnie Heft	Chuck Newman	Glenn Shampel
Leroy Alexander	Charles Diehl	Rusty Herring	Bob Nichol	Dallas Shirley
Hagan Andersen	Hans Dienelt	Hue Hollins	Jack Nies	Bob Siembida
Howard Archer	Bob Dillard	Paul Holly	John Nucatola	Bob Sigholtz
Henry Armstrong	Mike DiTomasso	Bugg Horton	Tom Nunez	Jack Silverman
Morrie Arnovich	Lonnie Dixon	Ken Hudson	Ronnie Nunn	Bill Simmons
Howard Asher	Sylvester Dobson	Jim Huetter	Bill Oakes	Mike Smith
Bob Austin	Dick Dolack	Richard Jackson	Leo Oates	Willie Smith
Ken Balgeman	Bill Downes	Steve Javie	Jackie O'Brien	Manny Sokol
Gerry Bannan	Norm Drucker	Gary Johnson	Jake O'Donnell	Chuck Solodare
Al Barillari	Jim Duffy	Bill Jones	John O'Donnell	Frank Sowecke
Ed Batogowski	Terry Durham	David Jones	Ron Olesiak	Bill Spooner
Dick Bavetta	Don Durr	Lee Jones	Tom O'Neill	Derrick Stafford
Jim Beiersdorfer	Hank Dvorak	Cy Kaselman	John Pace	Dick Starzyk
Joe Belmont	Charley Eckman	Neal Kay	John Parker	Jerry Steiner
Gary Benson	Lou Eisenstein	Pat Kennedy	Pete Pavia	John Stevens
Ted Bernhardt	Jim Enright	Jess Kersey	John Payak	Red Strauthers
Dick Bestor	Hugh Evans	Terry Kilkenny	Dick Pearson	Earl Strom
Bill Biebel	Ken Falkner	Jim Kinsey	Sam Pecoraro	Stan Stutz
Tommy Birch	Frank Falzone	Tom Kouzmanoff	Oscar Peskoff	Lou Sugarman
Mike Boich	Bill Farrell	Mike Krom	Eddie Pimpton	Ken Sussman
Walt Bonham	Jack Feck	Bill Kunkel	Riley Pitkoff	Max Tabacchi
Joe Borgia	Dick Ferguson	Stan Landes	Richie Powers	Jack Taylor
John Borgia	Nolan Fine	Mike Lauerman	Vince Procter	Jess Thompson
Sid Borgia	Ed Flynn	Rube Lautenschlager	Sam Pulice	John Thompson
Phil Bova	Walter Foley	Hal Lebovits	Pete Quinn	Len Toff
Ed Boyle	Joe Forte	Ralph Lembo	Bob Rakel	George Toliver
Matt Braunstein	John Fox	Sol Levy	Ron Rakel	Cary Toone
Harold Bredemeier	Phil Fox	Jerry Loeber	Bob Reardon	Tony Tortorello
Alan Brunkhorst	Phil S. Fox	Bud Lowell	Rich Reels	Don Vaden
Joe Calandra	Tom Frangella	Jack Madden	Blaine Reichelt	John Vanak
Mike Callahan	Joe Frivaldsky	Mark Mano	Bob Rhodes	Houston Vaughn
Alex Campbell	Jim Gaffney	Charles Marino	Alex Robinson	Ellis Veach
Paul Campbell	Pete Gallo	Mike Mathis	Barry Rogan	Norris Ward
Chuck Camuso	Sonny Gamber	Kenny Mauer	Sam Rogolsky	Tom Ward
Jim Capers	Spike Garnish	Woody Mayfield	Fred Rohmann	Tom Washington
Cy Casper	Jess Garrett	Bob McAllister	Wally Rooney	Don Wedge
Chuck Chuckovits	Darell Garretson	Roger McCann	Paul Ruddy	Gene Weston
Jim Clark	Ron Garretson	Marty McCutcheon	Mendy Rudolph	Babe Wheeler
Jocko Collins	Wayne Garton	Charles McKenna	Ed T. Rush	Jackie White
Joe Conway	C. S. Gensicken	Dick McMahon	Eddie Rush	Mel Whitworth
Milt Cooper	Tony Gentile	Art McNally	Jim Russo	Mike Wiacek
Jim Cope	Ron Gibbs	Jim McNally	Jim Ryan	Greg Willard
Sean Corbin	Manny Gomes	Nate Messenger	Bill Saar	Don Wilson
Mike Costabile	Harry Greenberg	Vic Mettler	Bennett Salvatore	Paul Wilson
Ike Craig	Jon Greenberg	Julie Meyer	John Sammon	Len Wirtz
Danny Crawford	Luis Grillo	Ed Middleton	John Scalzi	Jim Wishmier
Joe Crawford	Joe Gushue	Paul Mihalak	Frank Scanlan	Tommie Wood
Marty Cribbins	Bruce Hale	Red Mihalik	Dick Schaper	Mark Wunderlich
Pete D'Ambrosio	Jesse Hall	Andy Mitchell	John Schick	Jewell Young
Hy Davis	Forrest Harris	Stan Mockford	Mark Schlafman	Leo Zatta
Lou Dehner	Christy Harrold	Max Mohr	Earl Schlupp	

ABA REFEREES ONLY (1967–76)

Harold Aldridge	Nat Childs	Andy Hershock	Len Loran	Mike Sgobba
Ott Anderson	George Conley	E. L. Hutton	Bill Miller	Dick Sheldon
Joe Bavetta	Pat Denoy	Howard Kinsbrunner	Dan Milusnic	Jim Smith
Lloyd Berg	Ron Feiereisel	Bud Kline	Gene Moyers	Ralph Stout
Harry Brooks	Tom Ferguson	Tom Knox	Charles Reed	William Walsh
Jim Burch	Bob Hartsfield	Dick Leber	Bob Serafin	Ron Zetcher
Guido Carosi	Doug Harvey			

SUPERVISORS OF REFEREES

BAA/NBA

Sid Borgia
Jocko Collins
Norm Drucker
Darell Garretson
Pat Kennedy
Doxie Moore
John Nucatola
Dolph Schayes

ABA ONLY

Bob Bass
Ed Mikan
Bud Olsen

THE OFFICIAL RULES OF THE NBA

(as of October 1, 1994)

RULES INDEX

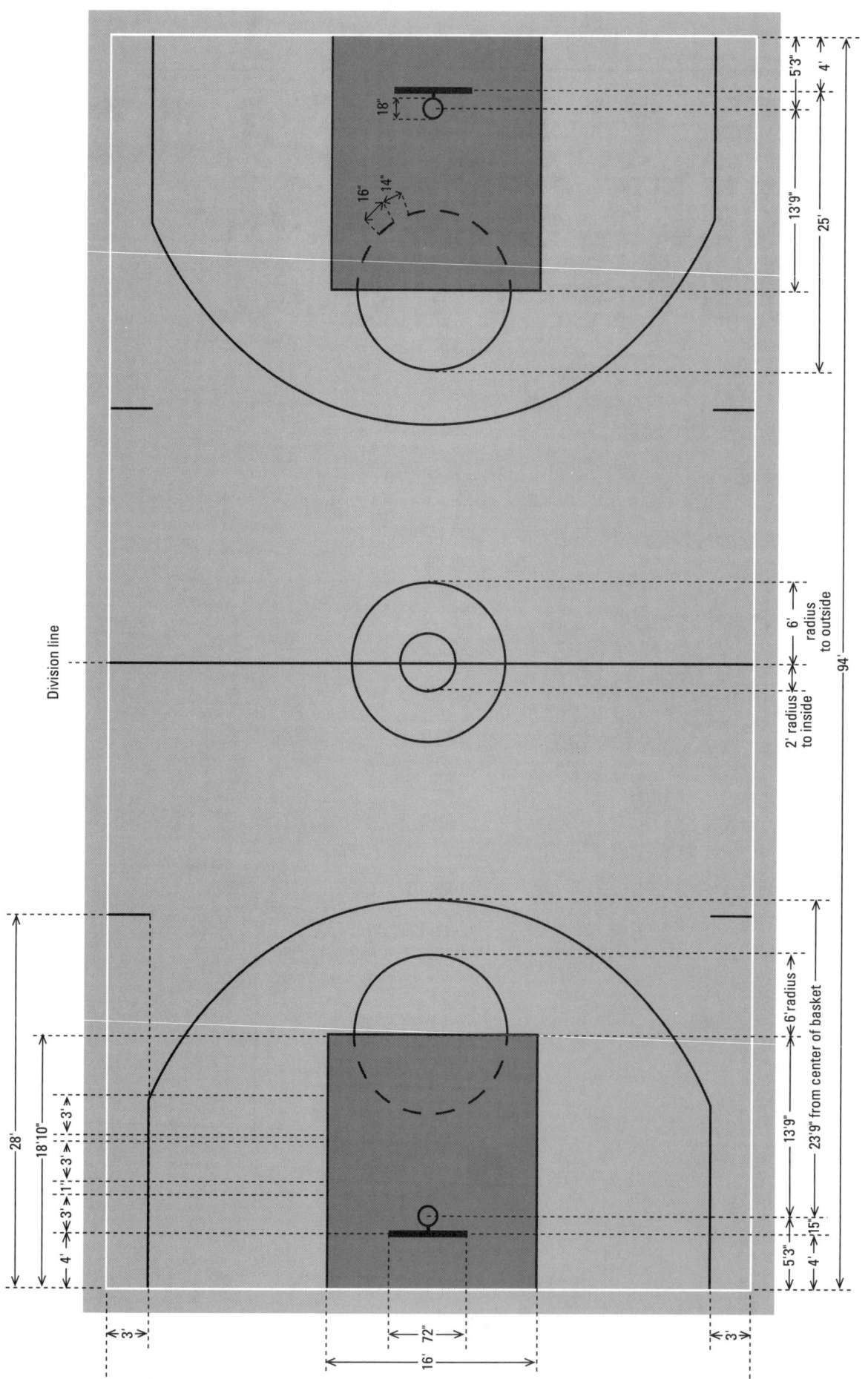

Division line

5'3"
4'
13'9"
25'
18"
16"
14"

6' radius to outside
2' radius to inside

94'

Optimal size is 94' by 50' to inside of sidelines

The color of the lane space marks and the neutral zones shall contrast with the color of the bounding lines

6' radius
23'9" from center of basket
13'9"
4'
15'
5'3"
4'

28'
18'10"
3'
3'
3'
3'-1"
3'
4'

72"
16'
3'
3'
50'

OFFICIAL RULES

RULE NO. 1—COURT DIMENSIONS— EQUIPMENT

SECTION I—COURT AND DIMENSIONS

a. The playing court shall be measured and marked as shown in the court diagram. (See page 280.)

b. A free throw lane shall be marked at each end of the court with dimensions and markings as shown on the court diagram. All boundary lines are part of the lane; lane space marks and neutral zone marks are not. The color of the lane space marks and neutral zones shall contrast with the color of the boundary lines. The areas identified by the lane space markings are 2″ by 8″ and the neutral zone marks are 12″ by 8″.

c. A free throw line shall be drawn (2″ wide) across each of the circles indicated in the court diagram. It shall be parallel to the end line and shall be 15′ from the plane of the face of the backboard.

d. The three-point field goal area has parallel lines 3′ from the sidelines, extending from the baseline, and an arc of 23′9″ from the middle of the basket which intersects the parallel lines.

e. Four hash marks shall be drawn (2″ wide) perpendicular to the sideline on each side of the court and 28′ from the baseline. These hash marks shall extend 3′ onto the court.

f. Four hash marks shall be drawn (2″ wide) perpendicular to the sideline on each side of the court and 25′ from the baseline. These hash marks shall extend 6″ onto the court.

g. Four hash marks shall be drawn (2″ wide) perpendicular to the baseline on each side of the free throw lane line. These hash marks shall be 3′ from the free throw lane line and extend 6″ onto the court.

h. Four hash marks shall be drawn (2″ wide) parallel to the baseline on each side of the free throw circle. These hash marks shall be 13′ from the baseline and 3′ from the free throw lane lines and shall be 6″ in length.

i. Two hash marks shall be drawn (2″ wide) perpendicular to the sideline, in front of the scorer's table, and 4′ on each side of the midcourt line. This will designate the Substitution Box area.

SECTION II—EQUIPMENT

a. The backboard shall be a rectangle measuring 6′ horizontally and 3½′ vertically. The front surface shall be flat and transparent.

b. A transparent backboard shall be marked with a 2″ white rectangle centered behind the ring. This rec-tangle shall have outside dimensions of 24″ horizontally and 18″ vertically.

c. Home management is required to have a spare board with supporting unit on hand for emergencies, and a steel tape or extension ruler and a level for use if necessary.

d. Each basket shall consist of a pressure-release NBA approved metal safety ring 18″ in inside diameter with a white cord net 15″ to 18″ in length. The cord of the net shall not be less than 30 thread nor more than 120 thread and shall be constructed to check the ball momentarily as it passes through the basket.

e. Each basket ring shall be securely attached to the backboard with its upper edge 10′ above and parallel to the floor and equidistant from the vertical edges of the board. The nearest point of the inside edge of the ring shall be 6″ from the plane of the face of the board. The ring shall be painted orange.

f. (1) The ball shall be an officially approved NBA ball between 7½ and 8½ pounds pressure.

(2) Six balls must be made available to each team for pre-game warmup.

g. At least one electric light is to be placed behind the backboard, obvious to officials and synchronized to light up when the horn sounds at the expiration of time for each period. The electric light is to be "red."

RULE NO. 2—OFFICIALS AND THEIR DUTIES

Section I—The Game Officials

a. The game officials shall be a crew chief, referee and umpire. They will be assisted by an official scorer and two trained timers. One timer will operate the game clock and the other will operate the 24-second clock. All officials shall be approved by the Operations Department.

b. The officials shall wear the uniform prescribed by the NBA.

Section II—Duties of the Officials

a. The officials shall, prior to the start of the game, inspect and approve all equipment, including court, baskets, balls, backboards, timers and scorer's equipment.

b. The officials shall not permit players to play with any type of hand, arm, face, nose, ear, head or neck jewelry.

c. The officials shall not permit any player to wear equipment which, in their judgment, is dangerous to other players. Any equipment which is of hard substance (casts, splints, guards and braces) must be

padded or foam covered and have no exposed sharp or cutting edge. All the face masks and eye or nose protectors must conform to the contour of the face and have no sharp or protruding edges. Approval is on a game-to-game basis.

d. All equipment used must be appropriate for basketball. Equipment that is unnatural and designed to increase a player's height or reach, or to gain an advantage, shall not be used.

e. The officials must check the three game balls to see that they are properly inflated. The recommended ball pressure should be between 7½ and 8½ pounds.

f. The crew chief shall be the official in charge.

g. If a coach desires to discuss a rule or interpretation of a rule prior to the start of a game or between periods, it will be mandatory for the officials to ask the other coach to be present during the discussion. The same procedure shall be followed if the officials wish to discuss a game situation with either coach.

h. The designated official shall toss the ball at the start of the game. The crew chief shall decide whether or not a goal shall count if the officials disagree, and he shall decide matters upon which scorers and timers disagree.

i. All officials shall be present during the 20-minute pre-game warm-up period to observe and report to the Operations Department any infractions of Rule 12A—Section VIII—j (hanging on the rim) and to review scoring and timing procedures with table personnel. Officials may await the on-court arrival of the first team.

j. Officials must meet with team captains prior to start of game.

k. Officials must report any atypical or unique incident to the Operations Department by datagram. Flagrant, punching, fighting fouls or a team's failure to have eight players to begin the game must also be reported.

Section III—Elastic Power

The officials shall have the power to make decisions on any point not specifically covered in the rules. The Operations Department will be advised of all such decisions at the earliest possible moment.

Section IV—Different Decisions by Officials

a. The crew chief shall have the authority to set aside or question decisions regarding rules made by the other officials.

b. It is the primary duty of the trail official to signal if goals count. If for any reason he does not know if the goal is made, he should ask the other officials. If none of them saw the goal made they should refer to the timer. If the timer saw the goal scored, it shall count.

EXCEPTION: Period Ending Score or No-Score in *Official's Manual*.

c. If the officials disagree as to who caused the ball to go out-of-bounds, a jump ball shall be called between the two players involved.

d. In the event that a violation and foul occur at the same time, the foul will take precedence.

e. Double Foul (See Rule 12-B—Section VI—f).

Section V—Time and Place for Decisions

a. The officials shall have the power to render decisions for infractions of rules committed either within or outside the boundary lines. This includes periods when the game may be stopped for any reason.

b. When a foul or violation occurs, an official shall blow his whistle to terminate play and signal the timer to stop the game clock. If it is a personal foul, he shall also designate the number of the offender to the scorer and indicate with his fingers the number of free throws to be attempted.

c. When a team is entitled to a throw-in, an official shall clearly signal the act which caused the ball to become dead, the throw-in spot and the team entitled to the throw-in, unless it follows a successful goal or an awarded goal.

Section VI—Correcting Errors

A. FREE THROWS

Officials may correct an error if a rule is inadvertently set aside and results in the following:

(1) A team not shooting a merited free throw
    EXCEPTION: If the offensive team scores or shoots earned free throws on the next possession which occurred due to not attempting a merited free throw, the error shall be ignored.

(2) A team shooting an unmerited free throw

(3) Permitting the wrong player to attempt a free throw

a. Officials shall be notified of a possible error at the first dead ball.

b. Errors which occur in the first, second or third periods must be discovered and rectified prior to the start of the next period.

c. Errors which occur in the fourth period or overtime(s) must be discovered and rectified prior to the end of the period.

d. The ball is not in play on corrected free throw attempt(s). Play is resumed at the same spot and under the same conditions as would have prevailed had the error not been discovered.

e. All play that occurs is to be nullified if the error is discovered within a 24-second time period. The game clock shall be reset to the time that the error occurred.

EXCEPTIONS

(1) Acts of unsportsmanlike conduct, and points scored therefrom, shall not be nullified.

(2) Free throw attempt resulting from an illegal defense violation.

(3) Free throw attempt(s) resulting from a personal foul which is a clear path to the basket, or a flagrant foul penalty (1).

NOTE: The game clock shall not be reset in (2) and (3) above.

B. LINEUP POSITIONS

If the first period or overtime(s) begins with jumpers lined up incorrectly, and the error is discovered:

(1) After more than 24 seconds has elapsed, the teams will continue to shoot for that basket.

(2) If 24 seconds or less has elapsed, all play shall be nullified.

EXCEPTION: Acts of unsportsmanlike conduct, and points scored therefrom, shall not be nullified.

a. The game clock shall be reset to 12:00 or 5:00, respectively.

b. The 24-second clock shall be reset to 24.
(EXAMPLE: 12:00 to 11:36 or 5:00 to 4:36—Restart; 12:00 to 11:35 or 5:00 to 4:35—Do not restart.)

C. START OF PERIOD—POSSESSION

If the second, third or fourth period begins with the wrong team being awarded possession, and the error is discovered:

(1) After 24 seconds has elapsed, the error cannot be corrected.

(2) With 24 seconds or less having elapsed, all play shall be nullified.

EXCEPTION: Acts of unsportsmanlike conduct, and points scored therefrom, shall not be nullified.

D. RECORD KEEPING

A record keeping error by the official scorer which involves the score, number of personal fouls and/or timeouts may be corrected by the officials at any time prior to the end of the fourth period. Any such error which occurs in overtime must be corrected prior to the end of that period.

Section VII—Duties of Scorers

a. The scorers shall record the field goals made, the free throws made and missed and shall keep a running summary of the points scored. They shall record the personal and technical fouls called on each player and shall notify the officials immediately when a sixth personal foul is called on any player. They shall record the timeouts charged to each team, shall notify a team and its coach through an official whenever that team takes a sixth and seventh charged timeout and shall notify the nearest official each time a team is granted a charged timeout in excess of the legal number. In case there is a question about an error in the scoring, the scorer shall check with the crew chief at once to find the discrepancy. If the error cannot be found, the official shall accept the record of the official scorer, unless he has knowledge that forces him to decide otherwise.

b. The scorers shall keep a record of the names, numbers and positions of the players who are to start the game and of all substitutes who enter the game. When there is an infraction of the rules pertaining to submission of the lineup, substitutions or numbers of players, they shall notify the nearest official immediately if the ball is dead, or as soon as it becomes dead if it is in play when the infraction is discovered. The scorer shall mark the time at which players are disqualified by reason of receiving six personal fouls, so that it may be easy to ascertain the order in which the players are eligible to go back into the game in accordance with Rule 3—Section I.

c. The scorers shall use a horn or other device unlike that used by the officials or timers to signal the officials. This may be used when the ball is dead or in certain specified situations when the ball is in control of a given team. The scorer shall signal the coach on the bench on every personal foul, designating the number of personal fouls a player has, and number of team fouls. NOTE: White paddles—team fouls; Red paddles—personal fouls.

d. When a player is disqualified from the game, or whenever a penalty free throw is being awarded, a buzzer, siren or some other clearly audible sound must be used by the scorer or timer to notify the game officials. It is the duty of the scorekeeper to be certain the officials have acknowledged the sixth personal foul buzzer and the penalty shot buzzer.

e. The scorer shall not signal the officials while the ball is in play, except to notify them of the necessity to correct an error.

f. Should the scorer sound the horn while the ball is in play, it shall be ignored by the players on the court. The officials must use their judgment in stopping play to consult with the scorer's table.

g. Scorers shall record on the scoreboard the number of team fouls up to a total of five, which will indicate that the team is in a penalty situation.

h. Scorers shall immediately record the name of the team which secures the first possession of the jump ball which opens the game.

i. Scorers shall record all illegal defense violations and notify the officials every time AFTER the first violation charged to each team.

Section VIII—Duties of Timers

a. The timers shall note when each half is to start and shall notify the crew chief and both coaches five minutes before this time, or cause them to be notified

at least five minutes before the half is to start. They shall signal the scorers two minutes before starting time. They shall record playing time and time of stoppages as provided in the rules. The timers shall be provided with an extra stopwatch to be used in timeouts, etc., other than the official game clock or watch. The official clock or scoreboard should show 12 minute periods.

b. At the beginning of the first period, any overtime period or whenever play is resumed by a jump ball, the game clock shall be started when the ball is legally tapped by either of the jumpers.

c. If, after time has been out, the ball is put in play by a throw-in or by a free throw, the game clock shall be started when the ball is legally touched by a player on the court.

d. During a jump ball, time may not be reduced from the 24-second clock or game clock if there is an illegal tap.

e. The game clock shall be stopped at the expiration of time for each period and when an official signals timeout. For a charged timeout, the timer shall start a timeout watch and shall signal the official when it is time to resume play.

f. The timer shall indicate with a controlled game horn the expiration of playing time. If the timer's signal fails to sound, or is not heard, the timer shall use other means to notify the officials immediately. If, in the meantime, a goal has been made or a foul has occurred, the crew chief shall consult the timer. If the timer agrees that time expired before the ball was in flight, the goal shall not count. If he agrees that the period ended before the foul occurred, the foul shall be disregarded unless it was unsportsmanlike. If there is a disagreement, the goal shall count or the foul shall be penalized unless the official has other knowledge.

g. In a dead ball situation, if the clock shows :00.0, the period or game is considered to have ended although the buzzer may not have sounded.

h. Record only the actual playing time in the last minute of the first, second and third periods.

i. Record only the actual playing time in the last two minutes of the fourth period and the last two minutes of any overtime period or periods.

j. Timers are responsible for contents in Comments on the Rules—II. Basic Principles—Section N.

RULE NO. 3—PLAYERS, SUBSTITUTES AND COACHES

Section I—Team

a. Each team shall consist of five players. No team may be reduced to fewer than five players. If a player in the game receives his sixth personal foul and all substi-

tutes have already been disqualified, said player shall remain in the game and shall be charged with a personal and team foul. A technical foul also shall be assessed against his team. All subsequent personal fouls, including offensive fouls, shall be treated similarly. All players who have six or more personal fouls and remain in the game shall be treated similarly.

b. In the event that there are only five eligible players remaining and one of these players is injured and must leave the game or is ejected, he must be replaced by the last player who was disqualified by reason of receiving six personal fouls. Each subsequent requirement to replace an injured or ejected player will be treated in this inverse order. Any such re-entry into a game by a disqualified player shall be penalized by a technical foul.

c. In the event that a player becomes ill and must leave the court while the ball is in play, the official will stop play immediately upon that team gaining new possession. The player will be immediately replaced and no technical foul will be assessed.

Section II—Starting Line-Ups

At least ten minutes before the game is scheduled to begin, the scorers shall be supplied with the name and number of each player who may participate in the game. Starting line-ups will be indicated. Failure to comply with this provision shall be reported to the Operations Department.

Section III—The Captain

a. A team may have a captain and a co-captain numbering a maximum of two. The designated captain may be anyone on the squad who is in uniform, except a player-coach.

b. The designated captain is the only player who may talk to an official during a regular or 20-second timeout charged to his team. He may discuss a rule interpretation, but not a judgment decision.

c. If the designated captain continues to sit on the bench, he remains the captain for the entire game.

d. In the event that the captain is absent from the court or bench, his coach shall immediately designate a new captain.

Section IV—The Coach and Others

a. The coach's position may be on or off the bench from the 28' hash mark to the baseline. All assistants and trainers must remain on the bench. Coaches and trainers may not leave this restricted 28' area unless specifically requested to do so by the officials. Coaches and trainers are not permitted to go to the scorer's table, for any reason, except during a timeout or between periods, and then only to check statistical information. The penalty for violation of this rule is a technical foul.

b. Coaches are not permitted to talk to an official during any timeout. (See Rule 3—Sec. III—b for captain's rights.)

c. A player-coach will have no special privileges. He is to conduct himself in the same manner as any other player.

d. Any club personnel not seated on the bench must conduct themselves in a manner that would reflect favorably on the dignity of the game or that of the officials. Violations by any of the personnel indicated shall require a written report to the Operations Department for subsequent action.

e. The bench shall be occupied only by a league-approved coach, assistant coaches, players and trainer.

f. If a player, coach or assistant coach is ejected or suspended from a game or games, he shall not at any time before, during or after such game or games appear in any part of the arena or stands where his team is playing. A player, coach or assistant coach may only remain in the dressing room of his team during such suspension, or leave the building. A violation of this rule shall call for an automatic fine of $500.

Section V—Substitutes

a. A substitute shall report to the scorer and position himself in the 8′ Substitution Box located in front of the scorer's table. He shall give his name, number and whom he is to replace. The scorer shall sound the horn as soon as the ball is dead to indicate a substitution. The horn does not have to be sounded if the substitution occurs between periods or during timeouts. No substitute may enter the game after a successful field goal by either team, unless the ball is dead due to a personal foul, technical foul, timeout or violation. He may enter the game after the first of multiple free throws, whether made or missed.

b. The substitute shall remain in the Substitution Box until he is beckoned onto the court by an official. If the ball is about to become live, the beckoning signal shall be withheld. Any player who enters the court prior to being beckoned by an official shall be assessed a technical foul.

c. A substitute must be ready to enter the game when beckoned. No delays for removal of warm-up clothing will be permitted.

d. The substitute shall not replace a free throw shooter or a player involved in a jump ball unless dictated to do so by an injury whereby he is selected by the opposing coach. At no time may he be allowed to attempt a free throw awarded as a result of a technical foul.

e. A substitute shall be considered as being in the game when he is beckoned onto the court or recognized as being in the game by an official. Once a player is in the game, he cannot be removed until the next dead ball.

EXCEPTION: Rule 3—Section V—f and Comments on the Rules—II. Basic Principles—P.

f. Any substitute may be removed after a successful free throw attempt which is to remain in play, if the offensive team requests and is granted a regular timeout.

g. A substitute may be recalled from the scorer's table prior to being beckoned onto the court by an official.

h. A player may be replaced and allowed to re-enter the game as a substitute during the same dead ball.

i. A player must be in the Substitution Box at the time a violation occurs if the throw-in is to be administered in the backcourt. If a substitute fails to meet this requirement, he may not enter the game until the next dead ball.

EXCEPTION: In the last two minutes of each period or overtime, a reasonable amount of time will be allowed for a substitution.

j. Notification of all above infractions and ensuing procedures shall be in accordance with Rule 2—Section VII.

k. No substitutes are allowed to enter the game during an official's suspension of play for (1) delay of game warning, (2) retrieving an errant ball or (3) any other unusual circumstance.

EXCEPTION: Suspension of play for a player bleeding. See Comments on the Rules—II. Basic Principles—P.

Section VI—Uniforms (Players' Jerseys)

a. Each player shall be numbered on the front and back of his jersey with a number of solid color contrasting with the color of the shirt.

b. Each number must be not less than ¾″ in width and not less than 6″ in height on both the front and back. Each player shall have his surname affixed to the back of his game jersey in letters at least 2″ in height. If a team has more than one player with the same surname, each such player's first initial must appear before the surname on the back of the game jersey.

c. The home team shall wear light colored jerseys, and the visitors dark jerseys. For neutral court games and doubleheaders, the second team named in the official schedule shall be regarded as the home team and shall wear the light colored jerseys.

RULE NO. 4—DEFINITIONS

Section I—Basket/Backboard

a. A team's own basket is the ring and net through which its players try to shoot the ball. The visiting team has the choice of baskets for the first half. The

basket selected by the visiting team when it first enters onto the court shall be its basket for the first half.

b. The teams change baskets for the second half. All overtime periods are considered extensions of the second half.

c. All parts of the backboard (front, sides, bottom and top) are considered in play when struck by the basketball except the back of the backboard, which is not in play.

Section II—Blocking

Blocking is illegal personal contact which impedes the progress of an opponent.

Section III—Dribble

A dribble is ball movement caused by a player in control, who throws or taps the ball into the air or to the floor, and then touches it once before it touches the floor.

a. The dribble ends when the dribbler:

(1) Touches the ball simultaneously with both hands

(2) Permits the ball to come to rest while he is in control of it

(3) Tries for a field goal

(4) Throws a pass

(5) Touches the ball more than once while dribbling, before it touches the floor

(6) Loses control

(7) Allows the ball to become dead

Section IV—Fouls

a. A personal foul is illegal physical contact which occurs with an opponent after the ball has become live.

b. A technical foul is the penalty for unsportsmanlike conduct or violations by team members on the floor or seated on the bench. It may be assessed for illegal contact which occurs with an opponent before the ball becomes live.

c. A double foul is a situation in which two opponents commit personal or technical fouls against each other at approximately the same time.

d. An offensive foul is illegal contact, committed by an offensive player, after the ball is live.

e. A loose ball foul is illegal contact, after the ball is alive, when team possession does not exist.

f. An elbow foul is making contact with the elbow in an unsportsmanlike manner.

g. A flagrant foul is unnecessary and/or excessive contact committed by a player against an opponent.

h. An away-from-the-play foul is illegal contact by the defense in the last two minutes of the game, which occurs (1) deliberately away from the immediate area

of the ball, and/or (2) prior to the ball being released on a throw-in.

Section V—Free Throw

A free throw is the privilege given a player to score one point by an unhindered attempt for the goal from a position directly behind the free throw line. This attempt must be made within 10 seconds.

Section VI—Frontcourt/Backcourt

a. A team's frontcourt consists of that part of the court between its endline and the nearer edge of the midcourt line, including the basket and inbounds part of the backboard.

b. A team's backcourt consists of the entire midcourt line and the rest of the court to include the opponent's basket and inbounds part of the backboard.

c. A ball which is in contact with a player or with the court is in the backcourt if either the ball or the player is touching the backcourt. It is in the frontcourt if neither the ball nor the player is touching the backcourt.

d. A ball which is not in contact with a player or the court retains the same status as when it was last in contact with a player or the court.
EXCEPTION: Rule 4—Section VI—f.

e. The team on the offense must bring the ball across the midcourt line within 10 seconds. No additional 10-second count is permitted in the backcourt.
EXCEPTIONS: (1) kicked ball, or (2) punched ball, or (3) technical foul on the defensive team or (4) delay of game warning on the defensive team.

f. The ball is considered in the frontcourt once it has broken the plane of the midcourt line and is not in player control.

g. The defensive team has no "frontcourt/backcourt."

Section VII—Held Ball

A held ball occurs when two opponents have one or both hands firmly on the ball.

a. A held ball should not be called until both players have both hands so firmly on the ball that neither can gain sole possession without undue roughness. If a player is lying or sitting on the floor while in possession, he should have an opportunity to throw the ball, but a held ball should be called if there is danger of injury.

Section VIII—Pivot

A pivot takes place when a player who is holding the ball steps once or more than once in any direction with the same foot, while the other foot—called the pivot foot—is being kept at its point of contact with the floor.

Section IX—Traveling

Traveling is progressing in any direction while in possession of the ball, which is in excess of pre-scribed limits as noted in Rule 10—Section XIV.

Section X—Screen

A screen is the legal action of a player who, without causing undue contact, delays or prevents an opponent from reaching a desired position.

Section XI—Field Goal Attempt

A field goal attempt is a player's attempt to shoot the ball into his basket for a field goal. The attempt starts when the player begins the motion which habitually precedes the actual shot. It continues until the shooting effort ceases and he returns to a normal floor position. The term is also used to include the movement of the ball in flight until it has become dead or has been touched by a player.

Section XII—Throw-In

A throw-in is a method of putting the ball in play from out-of-bounds in accordance with Rule 8—Section III. The throw-in begins when the ball is at the disposal of the team or player entitled to it and ends when the ball is released by the thrower-in.

Section XIII—Last Two Minutes

When the game clock shows 2:00, the game is considered to be in the two-minute period.

Section XIV—Disconcertion of Free Throw Shooter

Disconcertion of the free throw shooter is any of the following:

a. During the first of multiple free throw attempts, an opponent may not, while located on the lane lines, be allowed to raise his arms above his head.
b. During any free throw attempt, an opponent who is in the visual field of the free throw shooter, may not (1) wave his arms, (2) make a sudden dash upcourt, (3) talk to the free throw shooter, or (4) talk loudly to a teammate or coach.

Section XV—Live Ball

A live ball commences when the ball is placed at the disposal of a free throw shooter or thrower-in or is tossed by an official on a jump ball. A live ball becomes alive when it is released or legally tapped.

RULE NO. 5—SCORING AND TIMING

Section I—Scoring

a. A legal goal is made when a live ball enters the basket from above and remains in or passes through the net.
b. A successful field goal attempt from the area on or inside the three-point field goal line shall count two points.
c. A successful field goal attempt from the area outside the three-point field goal line shall count three points.
   (1) The shooter must have at least one foot on the floor outside the three-point field goal line prior to the attempt.
   (2) The shooter may not be touching the floor on or be inside the three-point field goal line.
   (3) The shooter may contact the three-point field goal line, or land in the two-point field goal area, after the ball is released.
d. A field goal accidentally scored in an opponent's basket shall be added to the opponent's score, credited to the opposing player nearest the shooter, and shall be mentioned in a footnote.
e. A field goal that, in the opinion of the officials, is intentionally scored in the wrong basket shall be disallowed. The ball shall be awarded to the opposing team out-of-bounds at the free throw line extended.
f. A successful free throw attempt shall count one point.
g. An unsuccessful free throw attempt which is tapped into the basket shall count two points and shall be credited to the player who tapped the ball in.
h. If there is a discrepancy in the score and it cannot be resolved, the running score shall be official.

Section II—Timing

a. All periods of regulation play in the NBA will be twelve minutes.
b. All overtime periods of play will be five minutes.
c. Fifteen minutes will be permitted between halves of all games.
d. 100 seconds will be permitted for regular timeouts and between the fourth period and/or any overtime periods. 130 seconds will be permitted between the first and second periods and the third and fourth periods.
e. A team is permitted 30 seconds to replace a disqualified player.
f. The game is considered to be in the two-minute part when the game clock shows 2:00 or less time remaining in the period.
g. The public address operator is required to announce that there are two minutes remaining in regulation and any overtime periods.
h. The game clock shall be equipped to show tenths of a second during the last minute of regulation or overtime periods.

Section III—End of Period

a. Each period ends when time expires.
   EXCEPTIONS:
   (1) If a live ball is in flight, the period ends when the

goal is made, missed or touched by an offensive player.

(2) If a personal or technical foul occurs at :00.0, but prior to the horn sounding, the period officially ends after the free throw(s) are attempted. The free throw(s) will be attempted immediately.

(3) If the ball is in the air when the buzzer sounds ending a period, and it subsequently is touched by: (a) a defensive player, the goal, if successful, shall count, or (b) an offensive player, the period has ended.

(4) If a timeout request is made at approximately the instant time expires for a period, the period ends and the timeout shall not be granted.

b. If the ball is dead and the game clock shows :00.0, the period has ended even though the buzzer may not have sounded.

Section IV—Tie Score—Overtime

If the score is tied at the end of the fourth period, play shall resume in 100 seconds without change of baskets for any of the overtime periods required. (See Rule 5—Section II—d for the amount of time between overtime periods.)

Section V—Stoppage of Timing Devices

a. The timing devices shall be stopped whenever the official's whistle sounds indicating one of the following:

(1) A foul (personal or technical)
(2) A jump ball
(3) A floor violation
(4) An unusual delay
(5) A timeout for any other emergency (official's time—no substitutions are permitted)
(6) A regular or 20-second timeout.

b. The timing devices shall be stopped:

(1) During the last minute of the first, second and third periods following a successful field goal attempt.

(2) During the last two minutes of regulation play and/or overtime(s) following a successful field goal attempt.

c. Officials may not use official time to permit a player to change or repair equipment.

Section VI—20-Second Timeout

A player's request for a 20-second timeout shall be granted only when the ball is dead or in control of the team making the request. A request at any other time shall be ignored.

EXCEPTION: The head coach may request a 20-second timeout if there is a suspension of play to administer Comments on the Rules—II. Basic Principles—P.

a. Each team is entitled to one (1) 20-second timeout

per half for a total of two (2) per game, including overtimes.

b. During a 20-second timeout a team may only substitute for one player. If the team calling the 20-second timeout replaces a player, the opposing team may also replace one player.

c. Only one player per team may be replaced during a 20-second timeout. If two players on the same team are injured at the same time and must be replaced, the coach must call a regular (100-second) timeout.

d. If a second 20-second timeout is requested during a half (including overtimes), it shall be granted. It will automatically become a charged regular timeout. Overtimes are considered to be an extension of the second half.

e. The official shall instruct the timer to record the 20 seconds and to inform him when the time has expired. An additional regular timeout will be charged if play is unable to resume at the expiration of that 20-second time limit.

EXCEPTION: No regular timeout remaining.

f. This rule may be used for any reason, including a request for a rule interpretation. If the correction is sustained, no timeout shall be charged.

g. Players should say "20-second timeout" when requesting this time.

h. A team is not entitled to any options during the last two minutes of the game or the overtime when a 20-second timeout is called.

i. If a 20-second timeout has been granted and a mandatory timeout by the same team is due, only the mandatory timeout will be charged.

j. A 20-second timeout shall not be granted to the defensive team during an official's suspension of play for (1) delay of game warning, (2) retrieving an errant ball, (3) any other unusual circumstance.

EXCEPTION: Suspension of play for a player bleeding, Comments on the Rules—II. Basic Principles—P.

Section VII—Regular Timeout—100 Seconds

A player's request for a timeout shall be granted only when the ball is dead or in control of the team making the request. A request at any other time shall be ignored.

A team is in control when one of its players has possession of the ball on the floor, in the air or following a successful field goal by the opposing team. A request at any other time is to be ignored. Timeouts are considered regular unless the player calls "20-second timeout."

EXCEPTION: The head coach may request a regular timeout if there is a suspension of play to administer Comments on the Rules—II. Basic Principles—P.

a. Each team is entitled to seven (7) charged timeouts

during regulation play. Each team is limited to no more than four (4) timeouts in the fourth period and no more than three (3) timeouts in the last two minutes of regulation play. (This is in addition to one 20-second timeout per half.)

b. In overtime periods each team shall be allowed three (3) timeouts regardless of the number of timeouts called or remaining during regulation play or previous overtimes. There is no restriction as to when a team must call its timeouts during any overtime period.

c. There must be two timeouts per period. If neither team has taken a timeout prior to 6:59 in each of the four regulation periods, it shall be mandatory for the Official Scorer to take it at the first dead ball, and to charge it to the home team.

If neither team has taken a second timeout prior to 2:59 in each of the four regulation periods, it shall be mandatory for the Official Scorer to take it at the first dead ball and charge it to the team not previously charged in that period.

The official scorer shall notify a team when it has been charged with a mandatory timeout.

No mandatory timeout shall be taken during an official's suspension of play for (1) a delay of game warning, (2) retrieving an errant ball, or (3) any other unusual circumstance.

d. If a regular or mandatory timeout is awarded the offensive team during the last two minutes of regulation play or overtime and (1) the ball is out of bounds in the backcourt, or (2) after securing the ball from a rebound and prior to any advance of the ball, or (3) after securing the ball from a change of possession and prior to any advance of the ball, the timeout shall be granted. Upon resumption of play, they shall have the option of putting the ball into play at the midcourt line, with the ball having to be passed into the frontcourt, or at the designated spot out-of-bounds.

However, once the ball is (1) thrown in from out-of-bounds, or (2) dribbled or passed after receiving it from a rebound or a change of possession, the timeout shall be granted, and, upon resumption of play, the ball shall be in-bounded at the spot nearest where the ball was when the timeout was called.

The time on the game clock and the 24-second clock shall remain as when the timeout was called. In order for the option to be available under the conditions in paragraph 2 above, the offensive team must call a 20-second timeout followed by a regular timeout, or call two successive regular timeouts.

EXCEPTION: Rule 12A—Section II—Excessive Timeouts.

In the last two minutes of the fourth period or overtime, the official shall ask the head coach the type of timeout desired (regular or 20-second) prior to notifying the scorer's table. This applies only to a requested timeout.

e. No timeout shall be charged if it is called to question a rule interpretation and the correction is sustained.

f. Additional timeouts may be granted at the expense of a technical foul and all privileges apply.

EXCEPTION: Rule 12A—Section II.

Section VIII—Timeout Requests

a. If an official, upon receiving a timeout request (regular or 20-second) by the defensive team, inadvertently signals while the play is in progress, play shall be suspended and the team in possession shall put the ball in play immediately at the sideline nearest where the ball was when the signal was given. The team in possession shall have only the time remaining of the original ten seconds in which to move the ball into the frontcourt. The 24-second clock shall remain the same.

b. If an official, upon receiving a timeout request (regular or 20-second) from the defensive team, inadvertently signals for a timeout during: (1) a successful field goal or free throw attempt, the point(s) shall be scored; (2) an unsuccessful field goal attempt, play shall be resumed with a jump ball at the center circle between any two opponents; (3) an unsuccessful free throw attempt, the official shall rule disconcerting and award a substitute free throw.

c. If an official inadvertently blows his whistle during (1) a successful field goal or free throw attempt, the points shall be scored, or (2) an unsuccessful field goal or free throw attempt, play shall be resumed with a jump ball at the center circle between any two opponents.

d. Whenever a team is granted a regular or 20-second timeout, play shall not resume until the full 100 seconds, or the full 20 seconds, have elapsed. The throw-in shall be nearest the spot where play was suspended.

Section IX—Time-In

a. After time has been out, the game clock shall be started when the official signals time-in. The timer is authorized to start the game clock if officials neglect to signal.

b. On a free throw that is unsuccessful and the ball continues in play, the clock shall be started when the missed free throw is touched by any player.

c. If play is resumed by a throw-in from out-of-bounds, the clock shall be started when the ball is legally touched by any player within the playing area of the court.

d. If play is resumed with a jump ball, the clock shall be started when the ball is legally tapped.

RULE NO. 6—PUTTING THE BALL IN PLAY—LIVE/DEAD BALL

Section I—Start of Games/Periods and Others

a. The game and overtimes shall be started with a jump ball in the center circle.

b. The team which gains possession after the opening tap will put the ball into play at its opponent's endline to begin the fourth period. The team losing the opening tap will put the ball into play at its opponent's endline at the beginning of the second and third periods.

c. In putting the ball into play, the thrower-in may run along the endline or pass it to a teammate who is also out-of-bounds at the endline—as after a score.

d. After any dead ball, play shall be resumed by a jump ball, a throw-in or by placing the ball at the disposal of a free thrower.

e. On the following floor violations, the ball shall be awarded to the opposing team out-of-bounds on the nearest sideline at the free throw line extended:

(1) Three seconds
(2) Ball entering basket from below
(3) Illegal assist in scoring
(4) Offensive screen set out-of-bounds
(5) Free throw violation by the offensive team
(6) Flagrant foul penalty (1) or (2)
(7) Illegal defense
(8) Jump ball at free throw circle
(9) Ball over backboard
(10) Offensive basket interference
(11) Ball hitting horizontal basket support
(12) Loose ball fouls which occur inside the free throw line extended

f. On the following floor violations, the ball shall be awarded to the opposing team on the baseline at the nearest spot:

(1) Ball out-of-bounds on baseline
(2) Ball hitting vertical basket support
(3) Defensive goaltending
(4) During a throw-in on the baseline
(5) Inadvertent whistle which is prior to a baseline throw-in

g. On the following floor violations, the ball shall be awarded to the opposing team on the sideline at the nearest spot:

(1) Where ball is out-of-bounds on sideline
(2) Traveling
(3) Double-dribble
(4) Striking or kicking the ball
(5) Swinging of elbows
(6) 24-second violation
(7) Inadvertent whistle when player control exists and the ball is in play

h. Upon resumption of play, the ball shall be awarded out-of-bounds at the nearest spot following a regular or 20-second timeout.

EXCEPTION: Rule 5—Section VII—d.

i. On a violation which requires putting the ball in play in the backcourt, the official will give the ball to the offensive player as soon as he is in a position out-of-bounds and ready to accept the ball.

EXCEPTION: In the last two minutes of each period or overtime, a reasonable amount of time shall be allowed for a substitution.

Section II—Live Ball

a. The ball becomes live when:

(1) It is tossed by an official on any jump ball.
(2) It is at the disposal of the offensive player for a throw-in.
(3) It is placed at the disposal of a free throw shooter.

Section III—Jump Balls in Center Circle

a. The ball shall be put into play in the center circle by a jump ball between two opponents:

(1) At the start of the game
(2) At the start of each overtime period
(3) For a double free throw violation
(4) For a double foul during a loose ball situation

(5) When the ball becomes dead when neither team is in control and no field goal or infraction is involved
(6) When the ball comes to rest on the basket flange or becomes lodged between the basket ring and the backboard
(7) When a double foul occurs as a result of a difference in opinion between officials
(8) When an inadvertent whistle occurs during a loose ball
(9) When a fighting foul occurs during a loose ball situation

b. In all cases above, the jump ball shall be between any two opponents in the game at that time. If injury, ejection or disqualification makes it necessary for any player to be replaced, his substitute may not participate in the jump ball.

Section IV—Other Jump Balls

a. The ball shall be put into play by a jump ball at the circle which is closest to the spot where:

(1) A held ball occurs
(2) A ball out-of-bounds is caused by both teams
(3) An official is in doubt as to who last touched the ball

b. The jump ball shall be between the two involved players unless injury or ejection precludes one of the jumpers from participation. If the injured or ejected player must leave the game, the coach of the opposing team shall select from his opponent's bench a

player who will replace the injured or ejected player. The injured player will not be permitted to re-enter the game.

Section V—Restrictions Governing Jump Balls

a. Each jumper must have at least one foot on or inside that half of the jumping circle which is farthest from his own basket. Each jumper must have both feet within the restraining circle.

b. The ball must be tapped by one or both of the players participating in the jump ball after it reaches its highest point. If the ball falls to the floor without being tapped by at least one of the jumpers, an official off the ball shall whistle the ball dead and signal another toss.

c. Neither jumper may tap the tossed ball before it reaches its highest point.

d. Neither jumper may leave the jumping circle until the ball has been tapped.

e. Neither jumper may catch the tossed ball nor tapped ball until such time as it has been touched by one of the eight non-jumpers, the floor, the basket or the backboard.

f. Neither jumper is permitted to tap the ball more than twice on any jump ball.

g. The eight non-jumpers will remain outside the restraining circle until the ball has been tapped. Teammates may not occupy adjacent positions around the restraining circle if an opponent desires one of the positions.

PENALTY for c, d, e, f, g: Ball awarded out-of-bounds to the opponent.

h. Player position on the restraining circle is determined by the direction of a player's basket. The player whose basket is nearest shall have first choice of position, with position being alternated thereafter.

Section VI—Dead Ball

a. The ball becomes dead and/or remains dead when the following occurs:
(1) Held ball
(2) Ball comes to rest on the basket flange or becomes lodged between the basket ring and the backboard
(3) Time expires for the end of any period
(4) Free throw attempt for a technical foul
(5) Personal foul (punching, away-from-the-play)
(6) Free throw which is the first of multiple attempts
(7) Floor violation (traveling, 3-second, 10-second, 24-second, etc.)
(8) Fighting foul
(9) Inadvertent whistle
(10) Prior to player possession out-of-bounds following a successful field goal or free throw,

whereby ball is going to be put into play by a throw-in. Contact which is not considered unsportsmanlike shall be ignored (Rule 12A—Section VI—i).

EXCEPTION: The ball does not become dead when (3) occurs with a live ball in flight.

Section VII—Ball Is Alive

a. The ball becomes alive when
(1) It is legally tapped by one of the participants of a jump ball.
(2) It is released by the thrower-in.
(3) It is released by the free throw shooter.

RULE NO. 7—24-SECOND CLOCK

Section I—Definition

For the purpose of clarification the 24-second device shall be referred to as "the 24-second clock."

Section II—Starting and Stopping of 24-Second Clock

a. The 24-second clock will start when a team gains new possession of a ball which is in play.

b. On a throw-in, the 24-second clock shall start when the ball is legally touched on the court by a player.

c. A team in possession of the ball must attempt a field goal within 24 seconds after gaining possession of the ball. To constitute a legal field goal attempt, the following conditions must be complied with:
(1) The ball must leave the player's hand(s) prior to the expiration of 24 seconds.
(2) After leaving the player's hand(s), the ball must make contact with the basket ring. If it fails to do so within 24 seconds, a 24-second violation has occurred.

d. A team is considered in possession of the ball when holding, passing or dribbling. The team is considered in possession of the ball even though the ball has been batted away but the opponent has not gained possession. No 3-second violation can occur under these conditions.

e. Team control ends when:
(1) There is a try for a field goal.
(2) The opponent gains possession.
(3) The ball becomes dead.

f. If a ball is touched by a defensive player who does not gain possession of the ball, the 24-second clock shall continue to run.

g. If a defensive player causes the ball to go out-of-bounds or causes the ball to enter the basket ring from below, the 24-second clock is stopped and the offensive team shall be awarded the ball on the sideline for a throw-in.

The offensive team shall have only the unexpired time remaining on the 24-second clock in which to

attempt a field goal. If the 24-second clock reads 0, a 24-second violation has occurred, even though the horn may not have sounded.

h. If during any period there are 24 seconds OR LESS left to play in the period, the 24-second clock shall not function.

i. If an official inadvertently blows his whistle and the 24-second clock buzzer sounds while the ball is in the air, play shall be suspended and play resumed by a jump ball between any two opponents at the center circle, if the shot is unsuccessful. If the shot is successful, the goal shall count and the whistle is ignored. It should be noted that even though the official blows his whistle, all provisions of the above rule apply.

j. If there is a question whether or not an attempt to score has been made within the 24 seconds allowed, the final decision shall be made by the officials.

k. Whenever the 24-second clock reads 0 and the ball is dead for any reason other than an Illegal Defense violation, kicking violation, punched ball violation, personal foul or a technical foul by the defensive team, the allotted 24 seconds have expired even though the horn may not have sounded.

Section III—Putting Ball in Play after Violation

If a team fails to attempt a field goal within the time allotted, a 24-second violation shall be called. The ball is awarded to the defensive team at the sideline, nearest the spot where play was suspended.

Section IV—Resetting 24-Second Clock

a. The 24-second clock shall be reset when a special situation occurs which warrants such action.

b. The 24-second clock shall remain the same as when play was stopped, or reset to 10 seconds, whichever is greater, on all technical fouls or delay of game warnings called on the defensive team.
EXCEPTION: Fighting foul

c. The 24-second clock is never reset on technical fouls called on the offensive team.
EXCEPTION: Fighting foul

d. The 24-second clock shall be reset to 24 seconds anytime the following occurs:
(1) Change of possession
(2) Illegal defense violation
(3) Personal foul
(4) Fighting foul
(5) Kicking the ball or blocking the ball with any part of the leg
(6) Punching the ball with fist
(7) Ball contacts the basket ring of the team which is in possession of it

RULE NO. 8—OUT-OF-BOUNDS AND THROW-IN

Section I—Player

The player is out-of-bounds when he touches the floor or any object on or outside a boundary. For location of a player in the air, his position is that from which he last touched the floor.

Section II—Ball

a. The ball is out-of-bounds when it touches a player who is out-of-bounds or any other person, the floor, or any object on, above or outside of a boundary or the supports or back of the backboard.

b. Any ball that rebounds or passes behind the backboard, in either direction, from any point is considered out-of-bounds.

c. The ball is caused to go out-of-bounds by the last player to touch it before it goes out, provided it is out-of-bounds because of touching something other than a player. If the ball is out-of-bounds because of touching a player who is on or outside a boundary, such player caused it to go out.

d. If the ball goes out-of-bounds and was last touched simultaneously by two opponents, both of whom are inbounds or out-of-bounds, or if the official is in doubt as to who last touched the ball, or if the officials disagree, play shall be resumed by a jump ball between the two involved players in the nearest restraining circle.

e. After the ball is out-of-bounds, the team shall designate a player to make the throw-in. He shall make the throw-in at the spot out-of-bounds nearest where the ball crossed the boundary. The designated thrower-in or his substitute shall not be changed except following a regular or 20-second timeout.

f. After any playing-floor violation, the ball is to be put into play on the sideline.

g. If the ball is interfered with by an opponent seated on the bench (Rule 12A—Section III—c), it shall be awarded to the offended team out-of-bounds at the free throw line extended.

Section III—The Throw-In

a. The throw-in starts when the ball is at the disposal of a player entitled to the throw-in. He shall release the ball inbounds within five (5) seconds from the time the throw-in starts. Until the passed ball has crossed the plane of the boundary, no player shall have any part of his person over the boundary line and teammates shall not occupy positions parallel or adjacent to the baseline if an opponent desires one of those positions. The defensive man shall have the right to be between his man and the basket.

b. On a throw-in which is not touched inbounds, the ball is returned to the original throw-in spot.

c. After a score—field goal or free throw, the latter coming as the result of a personal foul—any player of the team not credited with the score shall put the ball into play from any point out-of-bounds at the endline of the court where the point(s) were scored. He may pass the ball to a teammate behind the endline; however, the five-second throw-in rule applies.

d. After a free throw violation by the shooter or his teammate, the throw-in is made from out-of-bounds at either end of the free throw line extended.

e. Any ball out-of-bounds in a team's frontcourt or at the midcourt line cannot be passed into the backcourt. On all backcourt violations, and midcourt violations, the ball shall be given to the opposing team at the midcourt line and must be passed into the frontcourt.

f. A throw-in which touches the floor, or any object on or outside the boundary line, or touches anything above the playing surface is a violation. The ball must be thrown directly inbounds.

   EXCEPTION: Rule 8—Section III—c.

   PENALTY: Violation of this rule is loss of possession, and the ball must be inbounded at the previous spot of the throw-in.

RULE NO. 9—FREE THROW

Section I—Positions

a. When a free throw is awarded, an official shall put the ball in play by placing it at the disposal of the free throw shooter. The shooter shall be within the upper half of the free throw circle. The same procedure shall be followed each time a free throw is administered.

b. During a free throw for a personal foul, each of the spaces nearest the endline must be occupied by an opponent of the free throw shooter. Teammates of the free throw shooter must occupy the next adjacent spaces on each side. Only one of the third adjacent spaces may be occupied by an opponent of the free throw shooter. It is not mandatory that either of the third adjacent spaces be occupied. No teammates of the free throw shooter are permitted in these spaces.

c. All other players not stationed on the free throw lane must be at least six feet from the free throw lane lines and three feet from the free throw circle.

d. If the ball is to become dead after the last free throw, players shall not take positions along the free throw lane. No players shall be allowed inside the free throw line extended while a free throw is being attempted under these conditions.

   PENALTIES:

   (1) If the violation is by either team and the free throw attempt is successful or occurs on the first of multiple free throw attempts, it is ignored.

   (2) If the violation is by an opponent of the free throw shooter and the free throw attempt is unsuccessful, a substitute free throw attempt is awarded.

   (3) If the violation is by a teammate of the free throw shooter, it is a violation as soon as the free throw is attempted. The ball is awarded to his opponent at the free throw line extended.

Section II—Shooting of Free Throw

a. The free throw(s) awarded because of a personal foul shall be attempted by the offended player.

   EXCEPTIONS:

   (1) If the offended player is fouled and is subsequently ejected from the game before shooting the awarded free throw(s), he must immediately leave the court and another of the four players on the court will be designated by the opposing coach to shoot such free throw(s).

   (2) If the offended player is injured and cannot shoot the awarded free throw(s), the opposing coach shall select, from his opponent's bench, the player who will replace the injured player. That player will attempt the free throw(s) and the injured player will not be permitted to re-enter the game. The substitute must remain in the game until the next dead ball.

   (3) If the offended player is injured and unable to shoot the awarded free throw(s) due to any unsportsmanlike act, his coach may designate any eligible member of the squad to attempt the free throw(s). The injured player will be permitted to re-enter the game.

   (4) If the offended player is disqualified and unable to shoot the awarded free throw(s), his coach shall designate an eligible substitute from the bench. That substitute will attempt the free throw(s) and cannot be removed until the next dead ball.

   (5) Away from play foul (Rule 12B—Section X—a(1).

b. A free throw attempt, personal or technical, shall neither be legal nor count unless an official handles the ball and is also in the free throw area when the foul try is attempted.

c. A player awarded two free throws must attempt both even though the first attempt is nullified by a violation by an offensive player.

Section III—Time Limit

Each free throw attempt shall be made within 10 seconds after the ball has been placed at the disposal of the free thrower.

Section IV—Next Play

After a successful free throw which is not followed by another free throw, the ball shall be put into play by a throw-in, as after a field goal if the try is successful.

EXCEPTION: After a free throw for a foul which occurs during a dead ball which immediately precedes any period, the ball shall be put into play by the team entitled to the throw-in in the period which follows (See Rule 6—Section I—b).

RULE NO. 10—VIOLATIONS AND PENALTIES

Section I—Free Throw

a. After the ball is placed at the disposal of a free throw shooter, his attempt shall be within 10 seconds in such a way that the ball enters the basket or touches the ring before it is touched by a player. The free throw attempt shall be within that part of the free throw circle behind the free throw line.

b. A player shall not touch the ball or basket while the ball is on or within the basket.

c. A player who occupies a free throw lane space shall not touch the floor on or across the free throw lane line, nor shall any player "back out" more than 3' from the free throw lane line. A player who does not occupy a lane space must remain 6' from the free throw line and/or 3' from the free throw circle. This restriction applies until the ball leaves the free thrower's hands.

d. The free throw shooter may not cross the plane of the free throw line until the ball touches the basket ring or backboard or the free throw ends.

e. No player shall deflect or catch the ball before it reaches the basket or backboard on a free throw attempt.

f. The free throw shooter shall not purposely fake a free throw attempt.

g. An opponent shall not disconcert the free thrower in any way, once the ball has been placed at the disposal of the shooter.

h. No violation can occur if the ball is not released by the free throw shooter.

EXCEPTION: Rule 10—Section I—f.

PENALTIES:

(1) In (a–f) above, if the violation is by the offense, no point can be scored. The ball is awarded out-of-bounds to opponents at the free throw line extended.

(2) In (b), (c), and (g), if the violation is by the defense and the throw is successful, disregard violation; if the throw is unsuccessful, a substitute free throw shall be awarded.

(3) In (e), if the violation is by the defensive team, the point is scored and the same player receives another free throw attempt. The additional free throw attempt is considered a new play. This can only occur when the ball will remain in play after the free throw attempt. If it occurs on the first attempt of multiple free throws, only the single point is awarded, and the second free throw shall be attempted.

(4) If there is a free throw violation by each team, on a free throw which is to remain in play, the ball becomes dead, no point can be scored and play shall be resumed by a jump ball between any two opponents at the center circle.

(5) The "out-of-bounds" and "jump ball" provisions above do not apply if the free throw is to be followed by another free throw, or if there are free throws to be attempted by both teams.

(6) If a violation by the free thrower as in (a) above follows disconcertion, a substitute free throw shall be awarded.

Section II—Out of Bounds

a. A player shall not cause the ball to go out-of-bounds.

PENALTY: Loss of ball. The ball is awarded to opponents at boundary line nearest the spot of the violation.

EXCEPTION: On a throw-in which is not touched inbounds, the ball is returned to the original throw-in spot.

Section III—Dribble

a. A player shall not run with the ball without dribbling it.

b. A player in control of a dribble who steps on or outside a boundary line, even though not touching the ball while on or outside that boundary line, shall not be allowed to return inbounds and continue his dribble. He may not even be the first player to touch the ball after he has re-established a position inbounds.

c. A player may not dribble a second time after he has voluntarily ended his first dribble.

d. A player may dribble a second time if he lost control of the ball because of:

(1) A field goal attempt at his basket, provided the ball touches the backboard or basket ring

(2) An opponent touching the ball

(3) A pass or fumble which has then touched another player

PENALTY: Loss of ball. Ball is awarded to opponent at the sideline nearest the spot of the violation.

Section IV—Thrower-in

a. A thrower-in shall not (1) carry the ball onto the

court, (2) fail to release the ball within 5 seconds, (3) touch it on the court before it has touched another player, (4) leave the designated throw-in spot, (5) throw the ball so that it enters the basket before touching anyone on the court, (6) step over the boundary line while inbounding the ball, (7) cause the ball to go out-of-bounds without being touched inbounds, (8) leave the playing surface to gain an advantage on a throw-in.

b. After a team has designated a player to throw the ball in, there shall be no change of player (or his substitute) unless a regular or 20-second timeout has subsequently been called.

PENALTY: Loss of ball. The ball is awarded to the opponent at the original spot of the throw-in.

Section V—Strike the Ball

a. A player shall not kick the ball or strike it with his fist.

b. Kicking the ball or striking it with any part of the leg is a violation when it is an intentional act. The ball accidentally striking the foot, the leg or fist is not a violation.

PENALTIES:

(1) If the violation is by the offense, the ball is awarded to the opponent at the sideline nearest the spot of the violation.

(2) If the violation is by the defense, the offensive team retains possession of the ball at the sideline nearest the spot of the violation. The 24-second clock is reset to 24 seconds and if the violation occurred in the backcourt a new 10-second count is awarded.

Section VI—Jump Ball

a. A player shall not violate the jump ball rule (Rule 6—Section V).

b. A personal foul committed after the ball has become alive during a jump ball shall be ruled a "loose ball" foul.

PENALTIES:

(1) In (a) above, the ball is awarded to the opponent at the sideline nearest the spot of the violation.

(2) In (a) above, if there is a violation by each team, or if the official makes a bad toss, the toss shall be repeated.

(3) In (b) above, free throws may or may not be awarded, consistent with whether the penalty is in effect (Rule 12B—Section VIII).

In all violations of this rule, neither the game clock nor the 24-second clock shall be started.

Section VII—Three-Second Rule

a. A player shall not remain for more than 3 seconds in that part of his free throw lane between the endline

and extended 4′ (imaginary) off the court and the farther edge of the free throw line while the ball is in control of his team.

b. Allowance may be made for a player who, having been in the restricted area for less than 3 seconds, is in the act of shooting at the end of the third second. Under these conditions, the 3-second count is discontinued while his continuous motion is toward the basket. If that continuous motion ceases, the previous 3-second count is continued.

c. The 3-second count shall not begin until the ball is in control in the offensive team's frontcourt.

PENALTY: Loss of ball. The ball is awarded to the opponent at the sideline at the free throw line extended.

Section VIII—Ten-Second Rule

A team shall not be in continuous control of a ball which is in its backcourt for more than 10 consecutive seconds.

EXCEPTIONS:

(1) A new 10 seconds is awarded if the defense: (1) kicks or punches the ball, (2) is assessed a technical foul, or (3) is issued a delay of game warning.

(2) A new 10 seconds is awarded if play is suspended to administer Comments on the Rules—II. Basic Principles—P.

PENALTY: Loss of ball. The ball is awarded to the opponent at the midcourt line, with the ball having to be passed into the frontcourt.

Section IX—Ball in Backcourt

a. A player shall not be the first to touch a ball which he or a teammate caused to go from frontcourt to backcourt while his team was in control of the ball.

b. During a jump ball, a try for a goal or a situation in which a player taps the ball away from a congested area, as during rebounding, in an attempt to get the ball out where player control may be secured, the ball is not in control of either team. Hence, the restriction on first touching does not apply.

c. Following a jump ball, a player who secures a positive position and control of the ball in his frontcourt cannot pass the ball to a teammate or dribble the ball into the backcourt.

PENALTY: Loss of ball. The ball is awarded to the opponent at the midcourt line, with the ball having to be passed into the frontcourt. If the violation occurs on a throw-in, the game clock shall not start.

Section X—Swinging of Elbows

A player shall not be allowed excessive and/or vigorous swinging of the elbows in a swinging motion (no contact). When a defensive player is

nearby and the offensive player has the ball, it is considered a violation.

PENALTY: Loss of ball. The ball is awarded to the opponent at the sideline, nearest the spot of the violation. If the violation occurs on a throw-in, the game clock shall not be started.

Section XI—Entering Basket from Below

A player shall not cause the ball to enter the basket from below.

PENALTY: Loss of ball. The ball is awarded to the opponent at the sideline, at the free throw line extended.

Section XII—"Stick-um"

A player is not to use "Stick-um" or any similar substance.

PENALTY: Fine of $25 for the first violation, doubled for each subsequent violation upon notification to the Operations Department by an official.

Section XIII—Illegal Assist in Scoring

a. A player may not assist himself to score by using the ring or backboard to lift, hold or raise himself.

b. A player may not assist a teammate to gain height while attempting to score.

PENALTY: Loss of ball. The ball is awarded to the opponent at the free throw line extended.

Section XIV—Traveling

a. A player who receives the ball while standing still may pivot, using either foot as the pivot foot.

b. A player who receives the ball while he is progressing or upon completion of a dribble, may use a two-count rhythm in coming to a stop, passing or shooting the ball.

The first count occurs: (1) As he receives the ball, if either foot is touching the floor at the time he receives it. (2) As the foot touches the floor, or as both feet touch the floor simultaneously after he receives the ball if both feet are off the floor when he receives it. The second occurs: (1) After the count of one when either foot touches the floor or both feet touch the floor simultaneously.

c. A player who comes to a stop on the count of one may pivot, using either foot as the pivot foot.

d. A player who comes to a stop on the count of two, with one foot in advance of the other, may pivot using only the rear foot as the pivot foot.

e. A player who comes to a stop on the count of two, with neither foot in advance of the other, may use either foot as the pivot foot.

f. A player who receives the ball while standing still, or who comes to a legal stop while holding the ball, may lift the pivot foot or jump when he shoots for the goal or passes, but the ball must leave his hands before the pivot foot again touches the floor, or before either foot again touches the floor if the player has jumped.

g. In starting a dribble after receiving the ball while standing still, or after coming to a legal stop, a player may not jump before the ball leaves his hands, nor may he lift the pivot foot from the floor before the ball leaves his hands.

h. A player who leaves the floor with the ball must pass or shoot before he returns to the floor. If he drops the ball while in the air, he may not be the first to touch the ball.

i. A player who falls to the floor while holding the ball, or while coming to a stop, may not make progress by sliding.

j. A player who attempts a field goal may not be the first to touch the ball if it fails to touch the backboard, rim or another player.

PENALTY: Loss of ball. The ball is awarded to the opponent at the sideline, nearest the spot of the violation.

Section XV—Isolation

If the offensive team positions three or more players above the tip of the circle, on the weakside, a violation shall be called.

PENALTY: Loss of ball. The ball is awarded to the opponent at the tip of the circle extended.

Section XVI—Offensive Screen Set Out-of-Bounds

An offensive player shall not leave the playing area of the floor on the endline in the frontcourt for the purpose of setting a screen.

PENALTY: Loss of ball. The ball is awarded to the opponent at the sideline at the free-throw line extended.

RULE NO. 11—BASKETBALL INTERFERENCE—GOALTENDING

Section I—A Player Shall Not:

a. Touch the ball or the basket ring when the ball is on or within either basket.

b. Touch the ball when it is touching the cylinder having the basket ring as its lower base.

EXCEPTION: In (a) or (b) above if a player near his own basket has his hand legally in contact with the ball, it is not a violation if his contact with the ball continues after the ball enters the cylinder, or if, in such action, he touches the basket.

c. Touch the ball when it is above the basket ring and touching the imaginary cylinder.

d. Touch the ball when it is on its downward flight

during a field goal attempt, while the entire ball is above the basket ring level and before the ball has touched the basket ring or the attempt has ended.

e. For goaltending to occur, the ball, in the judgment of the official, must have a chance to score.

f. During a field goal attempt, touch a ball after it has touched any part of the backboard above ring level, whether the ball is considered on its upward or downward flight. The offensive player must have caused the ball to touch the backboard.

g. During a field goal attempt, touch a ball after it has touched the backboard below the ring level and while the ball is on its upward flight.

h. Trap the ball against the face of the backboard. (To be a trapped ball, three elements must exist simultaneously. The hand, the ball and the backboard must all occur at the same time. A batted ball against the backboard is not a trapped ball.)

i. Touch any live ball from within the playing area that is on its downward flight with an opportunity to touch the basket ring. This is considered to be a "field goal attempt" or trying for a goal (except a "tap" from a jump ball situation).

j. Touch the ball at any time with a hand which is through the basket ring.

PENALTY: If violation is at the opponent's basket, the offended team is awarded two points if the attempt is from the two point zone and three points if it is from the three point zone. The crediting of the score and subsequent procedure is the same as if the awarded score has resulted from the ball having gone through the basket, except that the official shall hand the ball to a player of the team entitled to the throw-in. If the violation is at a team's own basket, no points can be scored and the ball is awarded to the offended team at the out-of-bounds spot on the side at either end of the free throw line extended. If there is a violation by both teams, play shall be resumed by a jump ball between any two opponents at the center circle.

RULE NO. 12—FOULS AND PENALTIES

A. Technical Foul

Section I—Illegal Defenses

a. Illegal defenses which violate the rules and accepted guidelines set forth are not permitted in the NBA.

b. When the offensive team is in its backcourt with the ball, no illegal defense violation may occur.

(1) Penalties for Illegal Defenses.

On the first violation, the 24-second clock is reset to 24. On the second and succeeding violations, the clock is reset to 24 and one free throw (technical) is attempted. When a violation occurs during the last 24 seconds of any period (including overtime), regardless of the number of prior offenses, one free throw is awarded for the violation. (On all violations, the ball is awarded to the offended team out-of-bounds at the free throw line extended on either side of the court.)

EXCEPTION: If a field goal attempt is simultaneous with a whistle for an illegal violation, and that attempt is successful, the basket shall count and the violation is nullified.

(2) Guidelines for Defensive Coverage

a. Weakside defenders may be in a defensive position within the "outside lane" with no time limit, and within the "inside lane" for 2.9 seconds. The defensive player must re-establish a position with both feet out of the "inside-lane" to be considered as having legally cleared the restricted area.

b. When a defensive player is guarding an offensive player who is adjacent (posted-up) to the 3-second lane, the defensive player may be within the "inside lane" area with no time limitations.

An offensive player shall be ruled as "posted-up" when he is within 3' of the free throw lane line. A hash mark on the baseline denotes the 3' area.

c. An offensive player without the ball may not be double-teamed from the weakside. Only the player with the ball may be double-teamed by a weakside defensive player.

Weakside and strongside restrictions shall extend from the baseline to the midcourt line.

d. When an offensive player, with or without the ball, takes a position above the foul line, the defensive player may be no farther (toward the baseline) than the "middle defensive area." Defensive player(s) may enter and re-enter the "lower defensive area" as many times as desired, so long as he does not exceed 2.9 seconds.

e. When a weakside offensive player is above the free throw line extended, his defensive man may be no lower than the "middle defensive area" extended for more than 2.9 seconds.

When a weakside offensive player is below the free throw line extended, his defensive man must vacate the "inside lane" unless his man is positioned adjacent (posted up) to the three-second lane extended.

When a weakside offensive player is above the tip of the circle, his defensive man must be no lower than the "upper defensive area" for more than 2.9 seconds.

When a strongside offensive player is above the tip of the circle extended, his defensive man may be no lower than the free-throw line extended (upper defensive area) for more than 2.9 seconds.

When a strongside offensive player is above the free throw line extended "upper defensive area," his defensive man may be no lower than the "middle defensive area" for more than 2.9 seconds.

When an offensive player on the strongside is below the free throw line extended "middle defensive area," his defender must take a position below the free throw line extended immediately or double-team the ball as soon as the ball crosses midcourt. There is no 2.9 time limit.

If the offensive player relocates to a position above the free throw line extended, his defender may take a similar position no farther than one defensive area away within 2.9 seconds.

In all of the situations above, a defensive player may always aggressively double-team the ball regardless of his previous position on the floor.

f. When an offensive player takes a position above the tip of the circle, with or without the ball, the defensive player may be no farther (toward the baseline) from him than the "upper defensive area."

g. A defensive player must follow his weakside offensive man, switch to another man at an area of intersection, or double-team the ball. There is no 2.9-second time limit on this play. A defensive player must execute one of these three options or he is guilty of an illegal defense immediately.

h. A defensive player must follow his strongside offensive man, switch to another man at an area of intersection, or double-team the ball. There is a 2.9-second time limit on this play which commences when the defensive player reaches the weakside and "opens up."

i. A double team is when two or more defenders aggressively pursue a player with the ball to a position close enough for a held ball to occur.

Failure to comply with paragraphs (a) through (i) above will result in an Illegal Defense violation.

Section II—Excessive Timeouts

Requests for timeout in excess of the authorized number shall be granted. However, a technical foul penalty shall be assessed. A team is entitled to all regular timeout privileges.

EXCEPTION: During the last two minutes of the fourth period and/or overtime(s), the offensive team shall not have the option of putting the ball into play at the midcourt line.

Section III—Delay of Game

a. A player shall not delay the game by preventing the ball from being promptly put into play such as:
   (1) Attempting to gain an advantage by interfering with the ball after a goal.
   (2) Failing to immediately pass the ball to the nearest official when a violation is called.
   (3) Batting the ball away from an opponent before the player has the opportunity to inbound the ball.
   (4) Crossing the plane of the boundary line, as a defensive player, prior to the ball being inbounded.

b. A team shall not prevent play from commencing at any time.

c. Any person seated on the bench shall not interfere with a ball which is determined to be in play (Rule 8—Section II—g).

PENALTY: First offense is a warning, with each successive offense to be penalized by a technical foul which is charged to the team. Each offense will be announced by the Public Address Announcer. On each offense, the 24-second clock shall remain the same, or be reset to 10 seconds, whichever is greater. The offensive team shall be awarded a new 10 seconds if the ball is in the backcourt. If repeated acts become a travesty, the coach shall be held responsible upon being notified of same.

Section IV—Substitutions

a. A substitute (standing in the 8′ Box) shall not enter the court without reporting to the scorer and being beckoned by an official.

b. A substitute shall not be allowed to re-enter the game after having been disqualified.

EXCEPTION: Rule 3—Section I—b.

c. It is the responsibility of each team to have the proper number of players on the court at all times. Failure to do so, when the ball is alive, will result in a technical foul being assessed.

EXCEPTION: If the violation occurs on the first of multiple free throw attempts, it shall be ignored.

d. Penalty for failure to report to the scorer is a $25 fine. No technical foul is assessed.

Section V—Basket Ring, Backboard or Support

a. An offensive player who deliberately hangs on his

basket ring, net, backboard or support during the game shall be assessed a non-unsportsmanlike technical foul and a $100 fine.

EXCEPTION: A player may hang on the basket ring, backboard or support to prevent an injury to himself or another player, with no penalty.

b. A defensive player who deliberately hangs on his opponent's basket ring, net, backboard or support, in an attempt to touch a loose ball which may have an opportunity to score, shall be assessed an unsportsmanlike technical foul. The offensive team shall be awarded a successful field goal. The technical foul shall be assessed whether or not the ball is touched.

c. Should a defensive player deliberately hang on the basket ring, backboard or support to successfully touch a ball which is in possession of an opponent, an unsportsmanlike technical foul shall be assessed.

d. See Rule 10—Section XIII—a.

Section VI—Conduct

a. An official may assess a technical foul, without prior warning, at any time. A technical foul(s) may be assessed any player on the court or anyone seated on the bench for conduct which, in the opinion of an official, is detrimental to the game.

b. A maximum of two technicals for unsportsmanlike acts may be assessed any player, coach or trainer. Any of these offenders may be ejected for committing only one unsportsmanlike act, and they must be ejected for committing two unsportsmanlike acts.

c. A technical foul called for (1) delay of game, (2) coaches box violations, (3) illegal defensive violations, or (4) having a team total of fewer or more than five players when the ball is alive, or (5) hanging on the basket ring or backboard, is not considered an act of unsportsmanlike conduct.

EXCEPTION: Rule 12A—Section V—b and c.

d. A technical foul shall be assessed for unsportsmanlike tactics such as:
(1) Disrespectfully addressing an official
(2) Physically contacting an official
(3) Overt actions indicating resentment to a call
(4) Use of profanity
(5) A coach entering onto the court without permission of an official
(6) A deliberately thrown elbow or any attempted physical act with no contact involved

e. Cursing or blaspheming an official shall not be considered the only cause for imposing technical fouls. Running tirades, continuous criticism or griping may be sufficient cause to assess a technical. Excessive misconduct shall result in ejection from the game.

f. Assessment of a technical foul shall be avoided whenever and wherever possible; but, when they are necessary, they are to be assessed without delay or procrastination. Once a player has been ejected or the game is over, technicals cannot be assessed regardless of the provocation. Any additional unsportsmanlike conduct shall be reported by datagram immediately to the Operations Department.

g. If a technical foul is assessed on a team following a personal foul on the same team, the free throw attempt for the technical foul shall be administered first.

h. The ball shall be awarded to the team which had possession at the time the technical foul was assessed, whether the free-throw attempt is successful or not. Play shall be resumed by a throw-in nearest the spot where play was interrupted.

i. Anyone guilty of illegal contact which occurs during a dead ball may be assessed (1) a technical foul, if the contact is deemed to be unsportsmanlike in nature, or (2) a flagrant foul, if unnecessary and/or excessive contact occurs.

j. Free throws awarded for a technical foul must be attempted by a player in the game when the technical foul is assessed.
(1) If a substitute is beckoned into the game prior to the technical foul being assessed, he is eligible to attempt the free throw(s).
(2) If the technical foul is assessed before the opening tap, any player listed in the scorebook as a starter is eligible to attempt the free throw(s).
(3) If a technical foul is assessed before the starting lineup is indicated, any player on the squad may attempt the free throw(s).

k. A technical foul, unsportsmanlike act or flagrant foul must be called for a participant to be ejected. A player, coach or trainer may be ejected for:
(1) An elbow foul which makes contact shoulder level or below
(2) Any unsportsmanlike conduct where a technical foul is assessed
(3) A flagrant foul where unnecessary and/or excessive contact occurs
EXCEPTION: Rule 12A—Section VI—l(5)

l. A player, coach or trainer must be ejected for:
(1) A punching foul
(2) A fighting foul
(3) An elbow foul which makes contact above shoulder level
(4) An attempted punch which does not make contact
(5) Deliberately entering the stands other than as a continuance of play

m. Eye guarding (placing a hand in front of the opponent's eyes when guarding from the rear) a player

who does not have possession of the ball is illegal and an unsportsmanlike technical shall be assessed.

n. No free throw attempts are awarded when a double technical foul is called. A free throw attempt is awarded when all other technical fouls are assessed.

o. The deliberate act of throwing the ball or any object at an official by a player, coach or trainer is a technical foul and violators are subject to ejection from the game.

p. Punching fouls and elbow fouls, although recorded as both personal and team fouls, are unsportsmanlike acts and shall be counted toward a total of two for ejection. The player may be ejected immediately. (See Comments on the Rules—II. Basic Principles—M.)

Section VII—Fighting Fouls

a. Technical fouls shall be assessed players, coaches or trainers for fighting. No free throws will be attempted as in any other double foul situation. The participants will be ejected immediately.

b. This rule applies whether play is in progress or the ball is dead.

c. A fine not exceeding $20,000 and/or suspension may be imposed upon such person(s) by the commissioner at his sole discretion.

Section VIII—Fines

a. Recipients of technical fouls for unsportsmanlike conduct will be assessed a $100 fine for the first offense, and an additional $150 for the second offense in any one given game, for a minimum total of $250. If a player is ejected on (1) the first technical foul for unsportsmanlike conduct, (2) a punching foul, (3) a fighting foul, (4) an elbow foul, or (5) a flagrant foul, he shall be fined a minimum of $250.

b. Whether or not said player(s) are ejected, a fine not exceeding $20,000 and/or suspension may be imposed upon such player(s) by the Commissioner at his sole discretion.

c. During a fight all players not in the game must remain in the vicinity of their bench. Violators will be assessed a minimum of a $2,500 fine.

d. A player, coach or assistant coach, upon being notified by an official that he has been ejected from the game, must leave the playing area IMMEDI-ATELY and remain in the dressing room of his team during such suspension until completion of the game or leave the building. Violation of this rule shall call for an automatic fine of $500. A fine not to exceed $20,000 and possible forfeiture of the game may be imposed for any violation of this rule.

e. Any player who in the opinion of the officials has deliberately hung on the basket shall be assessed a technical foul and a fine of $100.

EXCEPTION: A player fouled in the act of dunking

or shooting may hang on the rim to prevent an injury to himself or to another player with no penalty.

f. Penalty for the use of "Stick-um" is a fine of $25 for the first violation, doubled for each subsequent violation. (Rule 10—Section XII).

g. Any player who fails to properly report to the scorer (Rule 3—Section V—a) shall be subject to a $25 fine on recommendation of the official scorer.

h. At halftime and the end of each game, the coach and his players are to leave the court and go directly to their dressing room, without pause or delay. There is to be absolutely no talking to game officials.
  PENALTY: $500 fine to be doubled for any additional violation.

i. Each player, when introduced prior to the start of the game, must be uniformly dressed.
  PENALTY: $100 fine.

j. A $250 fine shall be assessed to any player(s) hanging on the rim during pre-game warm-ups. Officials shall be present during warm-ups to observe violations.

k. Any player who is assessed a flagrant foul penalty (2) must be ejected and will be fined a minimum of $250. The incident will be reported to the Operations Department.

B. Personal Foul

Section I—Types

a. A player shall not hold, push, charge into or impede the progress of an opponent by extending an arm, leg or knee or by bending the body into a position that is not normal.

b. Contact caused by a defensive player approaching the ball holder from the rear is a form of pushing or holding.

c. Two free throw attempts are awarded for an elbow foul. It is also an unsportsmanlike act. If the elbow contact is above shoulder level, the player will be ejected. If the elbow contact is shoulder level or below, the player may be ejected at the discretion of the official.
  Contact must occur for an elbow foul to be called. (See Rule 12A—Section VI—d(6) for non-contact by an elbow.)

d. A defensive player is not permitted to retain hand contact with an offensive player when the player is in his "sights." Hand checking will be eliminated by rigid enforcement of this rule by all officials. The illegal use of hands will not be permitted.

e. Any player whose actions against an opponent cause illegal contact with yet another offensive player is guilty of a personal foul and will be penalized accordingly.

f. Contact which occurs on the shooting hand of the offensive player, while that hand is in contact with the ball, is not illegal.

Section II—By Dribbler

a. A dribbler shall not (1) charge into an opponent who has established a legal guarding position or (2) attempt to dribble between two opponents, or between an opponent and a boundary, where sufficient space is not available for contact to be avoided.

b. If a dribbler has sufficient space between two opponents, or between an opponent and a boundary, to have his head and shoulders in advance of them, the responsibility for illegal contact is on the opponent.

c. If a dribbler in his progress has established a straight line path, he may not be crowded out of that path.

d. If an opponent is able to establish a legal defensive position in that path, the dribbler must avoid contact by changing his direction or ending his dribble.

e. The dribbler must be in control of his body at all times.

f. A dribbler may not legally dribble again after a personal foul has been called.

Section III—By Screening

A player who sets a screen shall not (1) take a position closer than a normal step from an opponent, if that opponent is stationary and unaware of the screener's position, (2) make illegal contact with an opponent when he assumes a position at the side or front of an opponent, (3) take a position so close to a moving opponent that illegal contact cannot be avoided by that opponent without changing direction or stopping, or (4) move laterally or toward an opponent being screened after having assumed a legal screening position. The screener may move in the same direction and path of the opponent being screened.

In (3) above, the speed of the opponent being screened will determine what the screener's stationary position may be. This position will vary and may be one to two normal steps or strides from his opponent.

Section IV—Penalties for Sections I, II, III

The penalty for any violation of the sections above will be as follows:

a. The offender is charged with a personal foul. The offended team is awarded; (1) ball out-of-bounds if an offensive foul is assessed, (2) ball out-of-bounds if penalty situation is not in effect, (3) one free throw attempt if there is a successful field goal on the play, or (4) one free throw attempt plus a penalty free throw attempt if the offended player was not in the act of shooting.

b. If contact committed against a player, with or without the ball, is judged flagrant, the infraction shall be penalized as follows:

PENALTY:

(1) Two free throw attempts and possession of the ball out-of-bounds at the free throw line extended.

EXCEPTION: Rule 12B—Section V—Articles b and c.

(2) Offender may also be ejected if there is no apparent effort to play the ball, and/or if in the official's judgment, the contact was of such an excessive nature that an injury could have occurred.

(3) A personal foul is charged to the player and a team foul to the team.

(4) If the offended player is unable to attempt his free throws, his coach may select any player, on or off the floor, to do so. His coach will also select the substitute to replace the offended player. This penalty can be assessed only if the offender is ejected as in (2) above.

(5) The flagrant foul is considered an unsportsmanlike act if the player is ejected.

(6) The flagrant foul may be assessed whether the ball is dead or alive. Contact must occur.

c. A second free throw shall be awarded if the personal foul is:

(1) Committed against an offensive player attempting a field goal which is unsuccessful.

(2) For illegal contact with an elbow. Free throw attempt(s) are awarded whether the ball is dead, in possession, loose, or away from the play in the last two minutes of regulation or overtime(s). Contact must occur.

(3) Committed by a defensive player whose team has exceeded the limit for team fouls in the period.

(4) Committed by a defensive player prior to the ball being released on a throw-in from out-of-bounds.

EXCEPTION: Rule 12B—Section X.

(5) Committed against an offensive player in the frontcourt, if either he or a teammate has a clear path to the basket and thereby is deprived of the opportunity to score. The new possession must originate in the backcourt. There must be a minimum of one offensive player in the frontcourt.

(6) For intentionally undercutting an opponent.

d. If a personal foul is committed on a player who is subsequently ejected from the game before attempting any or all of the awarded free throw(s), the ejected player must leave the court immediately. The opposing coach will select one of the four remaining players on the floor to attempt the remaining free throw(s). The ejected player's coach will select the substitute.

e. When a personal foul is committed on an offensive player who, as part of a continuous motion which started before the illegal contact occurred, attempted

a field goal, that field goal shall be scored if successful, even if the ball leaves his hands after the whistle has sounded.

The offensive player must be attempting a field goal or starting his motion at the time the personal foul occurs. The field goal will not be scored if time on the game clock expires before the ball leaves the player's hand.

f. A personal foul committed by the offensive team during a throw-in shall be an offensive foul, regardless of whether the ball has been released or not.

EXCEPTION: Flagrant, elbow, and punching fouls.

Section V—Free Throw Penalty Situations

a. Each team shall be limited to four team fouls per regulation period without additional penalties. Common team fouls charged to a team in excess of four will be penalized by one free throw attempt plus an additional free throw attempt.

(1) The first four fouls committed by a team in any regulation period, if non-shooting, shall result in the ball being awarded to the opponent at the sideline nearest where the personal foul occurred. The ball shall be awarded no nearer to the baseline than the free throw line extended.

(2) The first three fouls committed by a team in any overtime period, if non-shooting, shall result in the ball being awarded to the opponent at the sideline nearest where the personal foul occurred. The ball shall be awarded no nearer to the baseline than the free throw line extended.

(3) If a team has not committed its quota of four team fouls during the first ten minutes of any regulation period, or its quota of three team fouls during the first three minutes of any overtime period, it shall be permitted to incur one team foul during the last two minutes without penalty.

(4) During each regulation or overtime period an additional penalty free throw will be awarded when the quota of team fouls has been reached.

(5) Personal fouls which are flagrant, punching, elbowing or away from the play will carry their own separate penalties and are included in the team foul total.

(6) Personal fouls committed against an offensive player in the act of shooting will result in two free throw attempts being awarded. No additional free throws shall be awarded if a penalty situation exists.

(7) Personal fouls committed during a successful field goal attempt, which result in one free throw attempt being awarded, will not result in an additional free throw attempt if the penalty situation exists.

b. A maximum of three points may be scored by the same team on a successful two-point field goal attempt.

c. A maximum of four points may be scored by the same team on a successful 3-point field goal attempt.

Section VI—Double Fouls

a. No free throw attempts will be awarded on double fouls, whether they are personal or technical.

b. Double personal fouls shall add to a player's total, but not to the team total.

c. If a double or fighting foul occurs, the team in possession of the ball at the time of the call shall retain possession. Play is resumed out-of-bounds on the sideline, nearest the point where play was interrupted. The 24-second clock is reset to 24 seconds.

d. If a double or fighting foul occurs with neither team in possession, or when the ball is in the air on an unsuccessful field goal attempt, play will be resumed with a jump ball at the center circle between any two opponents in the game at that time. If injury, ejection or disqualification makes it necessary for any player to be replaced, no substitute may participate in the jump ball.

e. If a double or fighting foul occurs on a successful field goal attempt, the team that has been scored upon will inbound the ball at the baseline as after any other score.

f. If a double foul occurs as a result of a difference in opinion by the officials, no points can be scored and play shall resume with a jump ball at the center circle between any two opponents in the game at that time. No substitute may participate in the jump ball.

Section VII—Offensive Fouls

A personal foul assessed against an offensive player which is neither an elbow, punching or flagrant foul shall be penalized in the following manner:

(1) No points can be scored by the offensive team.

(2) The offending player is charged with a personal foul.

(3) The offending team is not charged with a team foul.

EXCEPTION: Rule 3—Section I—a. No free throws are awarded.

Section VIII—Loose Ball Fouls

a. A personal foul, which is neither a punching, flagrant or an elbow foul, committed while there is no team possession, shall be administered in the following manner:

(1) Offending team is charged with a team foul.

(2) Offending player is charged with a personal foul.

(3) Offended team will be awarded possession at the sideline, nearest the spot of foul, if no penalty exists.

(4) Offended player is awarded one free throw at-

tempt plus a penalty free throw attempt if the offending team is in a penalty situation.

b. If a "loose ball" foul called against the defensive team is then followed by a successful field goal/free throw attempt, a free throw attempt will be awarded to the offended team, allowing for the three point or four point play. This interpretation applies:

(1) Regardless of which offensive player is fouled.

(2) Whether or not the penalty situation exists. The ball can never be awarded to the scoring team out-of-bounds following a personal foul which occurs on the same play.

c. If a "loose ball" foul called against the offensive team is then followed by a successful field goal attempt by an offensive player, no points may be scored.

Section IX—Punching Fouls

a. Illegal contact called on a player for punching is a personal foul and a team foul. One free-throw attempt shall be awarded, regardless of the number of previous fouls in the period. The ball shall be awarded to the offended team out-of-bounds at midcourt, whether the free throw is successful or unsuccessful.

b. Any player who throws a punch, whether it connects or not, has committed an unsportsmanlike act. He will be ejected immediately and suspended for a minimum of one game.

c. This rule applies whether play is in progress or the ball is dead.

d. In the case where one punching foul is followed by another, all aspects of the rule are applied in both cases, and the team last offended is awarded possession at midcourt.

e. A fine not exceeding $20,000 and/or suspension may be imposed upon such player(s) by the commissioner at his sole discretion. (See Rule 12A—Section VIII—c.)

Section X—Away-from-the-Play Foul

a. During the last two minutes of the fourth period or overtime period(s) with the offensive team in possession of the ball, all personal fouls which are assessed against the defensive team prior to the ball being released on a throw-in and/or away-from-the-play, shall be administered as follows:

(1) A personal foul and team foul shall be assessed and one free-throw attempt shall be awarded. The free throw may be attempted by any player in the game at the time the personal foul was committed.

(2) The offended team shall be awarded the ball at the nearest point where play was interrupted with all privileges remaining.

EXCEPTION: Rule 12-B—Section X-b.

b. In the event that the personal foul committed is an elbow foul, the play shall be administered as follows:

(1) A personal foul and team foul shall be assessed and the free throw shooter shall be awarded two free-throw attempts. The free throw(s) may be attempted by any player in the game at the time the personal foul was committed.

(2) In the event that the offended player is unable to participate in the game, the free throw shooter may be selected by his coach from any eligible player on the team. Any substitute must remain in the game until the next dead ball.

c. In the event that the personal foul committed is a flagrant foul, the play shall be administered as follows:

(1) A personal foul and team foul shall be assessed and the free throw shooter shall be awarded two free throw attempts. The free throws may be attempted by any player in the game at the time the flagrant foul was committed.

(2) If a flagrant foul penalty (1) is assessed and the offended player is unable to participate in the game, the substitute will be selected by his coach. The two free throws may be attempted by any of the four remaining players in the game. The ball will be awarded to the offended team at the free throw line extended in the frontcourt. The injured player may return to the game.

(3) If a flagrant foul penalty (2) is assessed and the offended player is unable to participate in the game, the substitute will be selected by his coach. The two free throws may be attempted by the substitute or any of the four remaining players in the game. The ball will be awarded to the offended team at the free throw line extended in the frontcourt. The injured player may return to the game.

COMMENTS ON THE RULES

I. GUIDES FOR ADMINISTRATION AND APPLICATION OF THE RULES

Each official should have a definite and clear conception of his overall responsibility to include the intent and purpose of each rule. If all officials possess the same conception there will be a guaranteed uniformity in the administration of all contests.

The restrictions placed upon the player by the rules are intended to create a balance of play, equal opportunity for the defense and the offense, to provide

reasonable safety and protection, and to emphasize cleverness and skill without unduly limiting freedom of action of player or team.

The primary purpose of penalties is to compensate a player who has been placed at a disadvantage through an illegal act of an opponent. A secondary purpose is to restrain players from committing acts which, if ignored, might lead to roughness even though they do not affect the immediate play. To implement this philosophy, many of the rules are written in general terms while the need for the rule may have been created by specific play situations. This practice eliminates the necessity for many additional rules and provides the officials the latitude and authority to adapt application of the rules to fit conditions of play in any particular game.

II. BASIC PRINCIPLES

A. CONTACT SITUATIONS

(1) Incidental Contact

a. The mere fact that contact occurs does not necessarily constitute a foul. Contact which is incidental to an effort by a player to play an opponent, reach a loose ball, or perform normal defensive or offensive movements, should not be considered illegal. If, however, a player attempts to play an opponent from a position where he has no reasonable chance to perform without making contact with his opponent, the responsibility is on the player in this position.

b. The hand is considered "part of the ball" when it is in contact with the ball. Therefore, contact on that hand by a defender while it is in contact with the ball is not illegal.

(2) Guarding an Opponent

In all guarding situations, a player is entitled to any spot on the court he desires, provided he gets to that spot first without contact with an opponent.

In all guarding situations during a live ball, a player is entitled to any spot on the court he desires, provided that he gets to the spot first without contact with an opponent.

In all guarding situations during a dead ball, the defensive player(s) must be allowed to take a position between his man and the basket.

a. In most guarding situations, the guard must be facing his opponent at the moment he assumes a guarding position after which no particular facing is required.

b. A player may continue to move after gaining a guarding position in the path of an opponent provided he is not moving directly or obliquely toward his opponent when contact occurs. A

player is never permitted to move into the path of an opponent after the opponent has jumped into the air.

c. A player who extends an arm, shoulder, hip or leg into the path of an opponent and thereby causes contact is not considered to have a legal position in the path of an opponent.

d. A player is entitled to an erect (vertical) position even to the extent of holding his arms above his shoulders, as in post play or when double-teaming in pressing tactics.

e. A player is not required to maintain any specific distance from an opponent.

f. Any player who conforms to the above is absolved from responsibility for any contact by an opponent which may dislodge or tend to dislodge such player from the position which he has attained and is maintaining legally. If contact occurs, the official must decide whether the contact is incidental or a foul has been committed.

The following are the usual situations to which the foregoing principles apply:

a. Guarding a player with the ball
b. Guarding a player who is trying for a goal
c. Switching to a player with the ball
d. Guarding a dribbler
e. Guarding a player without the ball
f. Guarding a post player with or without the ball
g. Guarding a rebounder

(3) Screening

When a player screens in front of or at the side of a stationary opponent, he may be as close as he desires providing he does not make contact. His opponent can see him and, therefore, is expected to detour around the screen.

If he screens behind a stationary opponent, the opponent must be able to take a normal step backward without contact. Because the opponent is not expected to see a screener behind him, the player screened is given latitude of movement.

To screen a moving opponent, the player must stop soon enough to permit his opponent to stop or change direction. The distance between the player screening and his opponent will depend upon the speed at which the players are moving.

If two opponents are moving in the same direction and path, the player who is behind is responsible for contact. The player in front may stop or slow his pace, but he may not move backward or sideward into his opponent. The player in front may or may not have the ball. This situation assumes the two players have been moving in identically the same direction and path before contact.

(4) The Dribble

If the dribbler's path is blocked, he is expected to pass or shoot; that is, he should not try to dribble by an opponent unless there is a reasonable chance of getting by without contact.

B. FIELD GOAL ATTEMPT

A player is attempting a field goal when he has the ball and is (in the judgment of the official) in the act of shooting or trying to attempt to shoot. It is not essential that the ball leave the shooter's hand. His arm(s) might be held so that he cannot actually make an attempt. He is thus deprived of an opportunity to score and is entitled to two free throw attempts.

If a player is fouled when tapping a tossed ball or a rebound toward or into the basket, he is not considered to be "trying for goal." If a live ball is in flight when time expires, the goal, if made, shall count.

C. FOULS: FLAGRANT/UNSPORTSMANLIKE

To be unsportsmanlike is to act in a manner unbecoming to the image of professional basketball. It consists of acts of deceit, disrespect for officials and profanity. The penalty for such action is a technical foul. Repeated acts shall result in expulsion from the game and a minimum fine of $250.

A flagrant foul penalty (1) is unnecessary contact committed by a player against an opponent.

A flagrant foul penalty (2) is unnecessary and excessive contact committed by a player against an opponent. It is an unsportsmanlike act and the offender is ejected immediately.

The offender will be subject to a fine not exceeding $20,000 and/or suspension by the Commissioner.

See Rule 12B—Section IV—b (1) for interpretation and penalties.

D. ILLEGAL DEFENSIVE ALIGNMENTS

The term Illegal Defense has replaced Zone Defense in NBA usage. The rule now in place, supported by guidelines, defines approved coverage by defensive players and teams. Violations of these rules and guidelines will be noted as Illegal Defense.

E. CHARGING/BLOCKING

A defensive player shall not be permitted to move into the path of an offensive player once he has picked up the ball in an effort to either pass or shoot.

If contact occurs on this play, and it is anything but negligible and/or incidental, a blocking foul shall be called on the defensive player. Any field goal attempt, if successful, shall count, as long as the ball has not been returned to the floor following the official's whistle.

If a defensive player acquires a position directly under the basket/backboard on anything but a "baseline drive," he shall be responsible if contact occurs. An offensive foul should never be called under these conditions. The offensive player remains a shooter until he has regained a normal playing position on the floor.

Many times this type of play is allowed to continue if the goal is successful.

The opposite is also true. If an offensive player causes contact with a defensive player who has established a legal position prior to the offensive player having picked up the ball in an effort to either pass or shoot, and it is anything but negligible and/or incidental, an offensive foul shall be called, and no points may be scored. A defensive player may turn slightly to protect himself, but is never allowed to bend over and submarine an opponent.

On a "drive-in" shot, if the defensive player has established a legal position in front of the basket/backboard, the offensive player shall be responsible for any illegal contact which occurs prior to his having regained his balance on the floor. An offensive foul shall be called and no points are to be awarded if the field goal is successful.

The mere fact that contact occurs on these types of plays, or any other similar play, does not necessarily mean that a personal foul has been committed. The officials must decide whether the contact is negligible and/or incidental, judging each situation separately.

In judging this play, the officials must be aware that if EITHER player has been placed at a disadvantage by the contact which has occurred, then a personal foul MUST be called on the player responsible for that contact.

F. GAME CANCELLATION

For the purpose of game cancellation, the officials' jurisdiction begins with the opening tipoff. Prior to this, it shall be the decision of the home management whether or not playing conditions are such to warrant postponement. However, once the game begins, if because of extremely hazardous playing conditions the question arises whether or not the game should be cancelled, the crew chief shall see that EVERY effort is made to continue the game before making the decision to terminate it.

G. PHYSICAL CONTACT/SUSPENSION

Any player or coach guilty of intentional physical contact with an official shall automatically be suspended without pay for one game. A fine and/or longer period of suspension will result if circumstances so dictate.

H. PROTEST

Protests are not permitted during the course of a game. In order to file a protest, the procedure, as set forth in the NBA constitution, is as follows: "In order to protest against or appeal from the result of a game, notice thereof must be given to the Commissioner within forty-eight (48) hours after the conclusion of said game, by telegram, stating therein the grounds for such protest. No protest may be filed in connection with any game played during the regular season after

midnight of the day of the last game of the regular schedule. A protest in connection with a playoff game must be filed not later than midnight of the day of the game protested. A game may be protested only by a Governor, Alternate Governor or Head Coach. The right of protest shall inure not only to the immediately allegedly aggrieved contestants, but to any other member who can show an interest in the grounds of protest and the results that might be attained if the protest were allowed. Each telegram of protest shall be immediately confirmed by letter and no protest shall be valid unless the letter of confirmation is accompanied by a check in the sum of $1,500 payable to the Association. If the member filing the protest prevails, the $1,500 is to be refunded. If the member does not prevail, the $1,500 is to be forfeited and retained in the Association treasury.

"Upon receipt of a protest, the Commissioner shall at once notify the member operating the opposing team in the game protested and require both of said members within five (5) days to file with him such evidence as he may desire bearing upon the issue. The Commissioner shall decide the question raised within five (5) days after receipt of such evidence."

I. SHATTERING BACKBOARDS

Any player whose contact with the basket ring or backboard causes the backboard to shatter will be penalized in the following manner:

(1) Pre-game and/or Half-time warm-ups—No penalty to be assessed by officials.

(2) During the game—Non-unsportsmanlike conduct technical foul. Under NO circumstances will that player be ejected from the game.

The Commissioner will review all actions and plays involved in the shattering of a backboard.

J. PLAYER/TEAM CONDUCT AND DRESS

(1) Each player when introduced, prior to the game, must be uniformly dressed.

(2) Players, coaches and trainers are to stand and line up in a dignified posture along the sidelines or on the foul line during the playing of the National Anthem.

(3) Coaches and assistant coaches must wear a sport coat or suit coat.

(4) While playing, players must keep their uniform shirts tucked into their pants, and no T-shirts are allowed.

(5) The only article bearing a commercial "logo" which can be worn by players is their shoes.

K. OFFENSIVE 3-SECONDS

The offensive player cannot be allowed in the 3-second lane for more than the allotted time. This causes the defensive player to "hand-check" because he cannot control the offensive player for that extended period of time.

If the offensive player is in the 3-second lane for less than three seconds and receives the ball, he must make a move toward the hoop for the official to discontinue his three-second count. If he attempts to back the defensive player down, attempting to secure a better position in relation to the basket, offensive three seconds or an offensive foul must be called. If he passes off and immediately makes a move out of the lane, there should be no whistle. The basic concern in this situation is that the offensive player not be allowed any advantage that is not allowed the defensive player by the illegal defensive guidelines.

L. PLAYER CONDUCT/SPECTATORS

Any coach, player or trainer who deliberately enters the spectator stands during the game will be automatically ejected and the incident reported by datagram to the Commissioner. Entering the stands to keep a ball in play by a player or the momentum which carries the player into the stands is not considered deliberate. The first row of seats is considered the beginning of the stands.

M. PUNCHING, FIGHTING AND ELBOW FOULS

Violent acts of any nature on the court will not be tolerated. Players involved in altercations will be ejected, fined and/or suspended.

Officials have been instructed to eject a player who throws a punch, whether or not it connects, or an elbow which makes contact above shoulder level. If elbow contact is shoulder level or below, it shall be left to the discretion of the official as to whether the player is ejected. Even if a punch or an elbow goes undetected by the officials during the game, but is detected during a review of a videotape, that player will be penalized.

There is absolutely no justification for fighting in an NBA game. The fact that a player may feel provoked by another player is not an acceptable excuse. If a player takes it upon himself to retaliate, he can expect to be subject to appropriate penalties.

N. EXPIRATION OF TIME

NO LESS THAN :00.3 must expire on the game clock when a ball is thrown inbounds and then hit instantly out-of-bounds. If less than :00.3 expires in such a situation, the timer will be instructed to deduct AT LEAST :00.3 from the game clock. If, in the judgment of the official, the play took longer than :00.3, he will instruct the timer to deduct more time. If less than :00.3 remain on the game clock when this situation occurs, the period is over.

NO LESS THAN :00.3 must expire on the game clock when a player secures possession of an inbounds pass and then attempts a field goal. If less than :00.3 expires in such a situation, the timer will be instructed

to deduct AT LEAST :00.3 from the game clock. If less than :00.3 remain on the game clock when this situation occurs, the period is over, and the field goal attempt will be disallowed immediately whether successful or unsuccessful.

This guideline shall apply to any field goal attempted by a player after he receives an inbounds pass, OTHER THAN what will be called, for this purpose, a "tip-in" or "alley-oop."

A "tip-in" is defined as any action in which the ball is deflected, not controlled, by a player and then enters the basket ring. This type of action shall be deemed legal if :00.1 or more remains in a period.

A "high lob" is defined as a pass which is received by an offensive player while in mid-air, and is followed instantaneously by a field goal attempt. If the reception of the pass and the subsequent "slam dunk" is immediately adjacent to the basket ring, this type of action shall be deemed legal if :00.1 or more remains in a period. However, if the "high lob" attempt is a distance from the basket ring whereby the ball must be controlled in mid-air, either one-handed or two-handed, a minimum of :00.3 is necessary for a field goal to score if successful.

NO LESS than :00.3 must expire on the game clock when a player secures possession of an unsuccessful free throw attempt and immediately requests a time-out. If LESS than :00.3 expires in such a circumstance, the time on the game clock shall be reduced by at least :00.3. Therefore, if :00.3 OR LESS remain on the game clock when the above situation exists, and a player requests a timeout upon securing possession of the ball, the period is over.

During ANY regular or 20-second timeout taken during the FINAL minute of ANY period, the crew chief must meet with his fellow officials to discuss possible timing scenarios, fouls being taken if either team is under the penalty limit, number of timeouts, assistance by all officials on 3-point field goal attempts, rotation or away-from-the-play foul.

Regardless of when the horn or red light operates to signify the end of a period, the officials will ultimately make the final decision whether to allow or disallow a successful field goal. THE CREW CHIEF MUST TAKE CHARGE OF THE SITUATION.

O. VERBAL FAN INTERFERENCE

Any spectator who verbally abuses players and/or coaches in a manner which, in the opinion of the game officials, interferes with the ability of a coach to communicate with his players during the game and/or huddles, will, at the direction of the crew chief, be given one warning by a building security officer. If the same spectator continues to behave in a like manner, the crew chief shall direct a building security officer to eject the spectator from the arena.

P. GUIDELINES FOR INFECTION CONTROL

If a player suffers a laceration or a wound where bleeding occurs, the officials shall suspend the game at the earliest appropriate time and remove the injured player from the game. The opposing team shall be allowed to substitute one player. The injured player may return to the game when he has received appropriate treatment by medical staff personnel.

If the player returns to the game, the officials shall make certain that any lesion, wound or dermatitis is covered with a dressing that will prevent contamination to and/or from other sources.

If the injured player is awarded a free throw attempt(s) as a result of a personal foul, play shall be suspended as soon as the final attempt is successful or unsuccessful. If the player is involved in a jump ball, play shall be suspended as soon as possession is gained by either team. Caution shall be used when suspending play, so as not to halt a fast break situation.

Mandatory timeouts shall not be granted at any time play is suspended. The offensive team may call a 20-second or regular timeout.

A 20-second or regular timeout may be granted upon request by the head coach after suspension of play.

If treatment is not completed within the allotted time, the head coach may call another timeout or substitute for the injured player. Substitutes are permitted consistent with existing rules on substitution.

If a team has no timeouts remaining when play is suspended, the officials will allow 20 seconds for appropriate treatment. If the treatment is not completed in accordance with paragraph two above, the injured player must be removed immediately. ONLY the injured player may be removed from the game under these circumstances.

No mandatory timeouts may be awarded if play is suspended for the defensive team.

The offensive team will receive a full 10 seconds to advance the ball into the frontcourt. The 24-second clock will remain as is or reset to 10, whichever is greater.

Q. DEAD BALL, LIVE BALL, BALL IS ALIVE

After the ball has been dead, it is put into play by a jump ball, throw-in, or a free throw attempt. The game clock does not start until the ball is legally touched on the court by a player. However, we wish to penalize any floor violation or personal foul which may occur.

Therefore, the ball is live when it is placed at the disposal of the thrower-in or free throw shooter, or is tossed on a jump ball. It is solely for the purpose of not having to assess a technical foul if illegal contact occurs.

CHAPTER TEN

THE HALL OF FAME

Dr. James Naismith, who invented basketball in 1891 in Springfield, Mass., never lived to see his game become one of the world's most popular sports. He passed away in 1939, three years after basketball became an official Olympic sport and 20 years before he became the first individual inducted into the Hall of Fame that bears his name.

Although Naismith would have been honored to become a charter member of the Hall of Fame in 1959, he would be completely overwhelmed that his name adorns the building. The unassuming Naismith also might find it humorous that the Hall of Fame didn't have a physical shrine to house its inductees until February 1968.

For 27 years, the Basketball Hall of Fame was a two-story, red-brick building on the campus of Springfield College. Since 1985 the Basketball Hall of Fame has become a major tourist attraction housed in an $11.5 million, three-story building located along Interstate 91, the major north-south highway through New England. The world's only Basketball Hall of Fame had humble beginnings, just like the game itself, but as basketball has broadened its worldwide horizons, so has the museum that pays tribute to every level of basketball

There's something for hoops fans of all ages at the Basketball Hall of Fame in Springfield, Mass.

—men and women, professional and amateur, domestic and international, coaches, referees, trainers, contributors and handicapped athletes.

The Basketball Hall of Fame was the brainchild of the National Association of Basketball Coaches. Basketball's earliest coaching organization had a strong desire to pay tribute to the game's inventor. The NABC launched its efforts at the 1936 Olympic Games in Berlin, and it took the organization 30 tireless years to see its dream become a reality. Hall of Fame discussion began in 1941, but World War II put the project on hold and it was not reapproached until 1949. Over the next 20 years, slow fund-raising, poor land plots and unanticipated expenditures slowed the building process. Despite these setbacks, the NABC collected artifacts and even started honoring the game's greatest players, coaches, referees and contributors. By the time the Hall of Fame officially opened its doors to the public in February 1968, it already had inducted 66 basketball legends and four entire teams—the First Team, Original Celtics, Buffalo Germans and New York Rens.

Within 10 years, the Hall of Fame outgrew its Springfield College location, and with local and state financing the new Hall of Fame opened its doors in June 1985. With state-of-the-art exhibits and memorabilia,

interactive videos, three movie theaters and a shooting and jumping arcade, the architecturally distinctive Naismith Memorial Basketball Hall of Fame had undergone a complete transformation.

In utilizing leading-edge technology to honor the game's greatest stars, the museum entertains over 170,000 visitors a year from all over the world. The 54,000-square-foot museum allows visitors to trace basketball's history from its origins in Springfield to present-day spectaculars such as the NBA All-Star Weekend, NBA Finals, NCAA Final Four, Olympic Games and World Championship of Basketball.

A focal point is the Honors Court, home to over 200 inductees. Any person affiliated with basketball is eligible for nomination into the Hall of Fame. Players and referees must be retired five years, and coaches must have coached at least 25 years or have been retired five years. Contributors are eligible any time after retirement.

Anyone may nominate a worthy basketball person. A candidate's nomination file is submitted to a seven-member Screening Committee and must receive at least five votes for presentation to the full 24-member Honors Committee. For election into the Basketball Hall of Fame, a candidate must receive 18 affirmative votes. Annual enshrinement ceremonies are held each May.

DIRECTORY OF MEMBERS
Individuals associated with the NBA appear in bold type. *Deceased

PLAYERS

Name	Year Elected				
Archibald, Nate "Tiny"	**1990**	DeBusschere, Dave	1982	Houbregs, Robert	1986
Arizin, Paul	**1977**	*Dehnert, Henry "Dutch"	1968	*Hyatt, Charles "Chuck"	1959
*Barlow, Thomas "Tarzan"	1980	Endacott, Paul	1971	**Issel, Dan**	**1992**
Barry, Rick	**1986**	**Erving, Julius "Dr. J"**	**1992**	**Jeannette, Harold E. "Buddy"**	**1993**
Baylor, Elgin	**1976**	Foster, Harold "Bud"	1964	*Johnson, William	1976
*Beckman, John	1972	**Frazier, Walt "Clyde"**	**1986**	*Johnston, Neil	1989
Bellamy, Walt	**1992**	*Friedman, Max "Marty"	1971	**Jones, K. C**	**1988**
Belov, Sergei	1991	*Fulks, Joe	1977	**Jones, Sam**	**1983**
Bing, Dave	**1989**	Gale, Lauren "Laddie"	1976	Krause, Edward "Moose"	1975
Blazejowski, Carol	1993	**Gallatin, Harry "The Horse"**	**1990**	Kurland, Bob	1961
*Borgmann, Bernhard "Bennie"	1961	**Gates, William "Pop"**	**1988**	**Lanier, Bob**	**1991**
Bradley, Bill	**1982**	Gola, Tom	1975	*Lapchick, Joe	1966
*Brennan, Joe	1974	**Greer, Hal**	**1981**	**Lovellette, Clyde**	**1987**
Cervi, Al	**1984**	*Gruenig, Robert "Ace"	1963	**Lucas, Jerry**	**1979**
Chamberlain, Wilt	**1978**	**Hagan, Cliff**	**1977**	Luisetti, Angelo "Hank"	1959
*Cooper, Charles "Tarzan"	1976	*Hanson, Victor	1960	**Macauley, Edward "Easy Ed"**	**1960**
Cousy, Bob	**1970**	Harris, Lusia	1991	*Maravich, Pete	1986
Cowens, Dave	**1990**	**Havlicek, John**	**1983**	**Martin, Slater**	**1981**
Cunningham, Billy	**1985**	**Hawkins, Connie**	**1991**	*McCracken, Branch	1960
*Davies, Bob	1969	**Hayes, Elvin "The Big E"**	**1989**	*McCracken, Jack	1962
*DeBarnardi, Forrest "Red"	1961	**Heinsohn, Tom**	**1985**	*McDermott, Bobby	1987
		Holman, Nat	1964	**McGuire, Dick**	**1992**

Meyers, Ann	1992
Mikan, George	**1959**
Monroe, Earl "The Pearl"	**1989**
Murphy, Calvin	**1992**
*Murphy, Charles "Stretch"	1960
*Page, Harlan "Pat"	1962
Pettit, Bob	**1970**
Phillip, Andy	**1961**
*Pollard, Jim	1977
Ramsey, Frank	**1981**
Reed, Willis	**1981**
Robertson, Oscar	**1979**
*Roosma, John	1961
Russell, Bill	**1974**
*Russell, John "Honey"	1964
Schayes, Dolph	**1972**
*Schmidt, Ernest	1973
*Schommer, John	1959
*Sedran, Barney	1962
Semenova, Juliana	1992
Sharman, Bill	**1975**
*Steinmetz, Christian	1961
*Thompson, John "Cat"	1962
Thurmond, Nate	**1984**
Twyman, Jack	**1982**
Unseld, Wes	**1987**
*Vandivier, Robert "Fuzzy"	1974
*Wachter, Edward	1961
Walton, Bill	**1992**
Wanzer, Bobby	**1986**
West, Jerry	**1979**
White, Nera	1991
Wilkens, Lenny	**1988**
Wooden, John	1960

COACHES

*Allen, Dr. Forrest "Phog"	1959
*Anderson, Harold	1984
Auerbach, Arnold "Red"	**1968**
*Barry, Justin "Sam"	1978
*Blood, Ernest	1960
*Cann, Howard "Jake"	1965
*Carlson, Dr. H. Clifford	1959
Carnesecca, Louie	1991
Carnevale, Ben	1969
*Case, Everett	1981
Crum, Denny	1993
Daly, Charles J. "Chuck"	**1993**
*Dean, Everett	1966
*Diddle, Ed	1971

*Drake, Bruce	1972
Gaines, Clarence "Big House"	1981
Gardner, Jack	1983
*Gill, Amory "Slats"	1967
Harshman, Marv	1984
*Hickey, Ed	1978
*Hobson, Howard	1965
Holzman, William "Red"	**1985**
*Iba, Henry "Hank"	1968
*Julian, Alvin "Doggie"	1967
*Keaney, Frank	1960
*Keogan, George	1961
Knight, Bobby	1990
*Lambert, Ward	1960
Litwack, Harry	**1975**
*Loeffler, Ken	1964
*Lonborg, Arthur "Dutch"	1972
*McCutchan, Arad	1980
McGuire, Al	**1991**
McGuire, Frank	**1976**
*Meanwell, Dr. Walter	1959
Meyer, Ray	1978
Miller, Ralph	1987
Ramsay, Jack	**1991**
Rubini, Cesare	1993
*Rupp, Adolph	1968
*Sachs, Leonard	1961
*Shelton, Everett	1979
Smith, Dean	1982
Taylor, Fred	1985
Wade, Margaret	1984
Watts, Stanley	1985
Wooden, John	1972
*Woolpert, Phil	1991

CONTRIBUTORS

*Abbott, Senda Berenson	1984
*Bee, Clair	1967
*Brown, Walter	1965
*Bunn, John	1964
*Douglas, Robert	1971
*Duer, Alva	1981
Fagan, Clifford	1983
*Fisher, Harry	1973
*Fleisher, Larry	1990
*Gottlieb, Eddie	1971
*Gulick, Dr. Luther	1959
Harrison, Lester	**1979**
*Hepp, Ferenc	1980
*Hickox, Edward	1959

*Hinkle, Paul "Tony"	1965
*Irish, Edward S. "Ned"	1964
*Jones, R. William	1964
*Kennedy, J. Walter	1980
*Liston, Emil	1974
McLendon, John	1978
*Mokray, Bill	1965
*Morgan, Ralph	1959
*Morgenweck, Frank	1962
*Naismith, Dr. James	1959
Newell, Pete	**1978**
*O'Brien, John	1961
*O'Brien, Larry	1990
*Olsen, Harold	1959
*Podoloff, Maurice	1973
*Porter, Henry	1960
*Reid, William	1963
*Ripley, Elmer	1972
*St. John, Lynn	1962
*Saperstein, Abe	1970
*Schabinger, Arthur	1961
*Stagg, Amos Alonzo	1959
Stankovic, Boris	1990
*Steitz, Edward	1983
*Taylor, Charles "Chuck"	1968
Teague, Bertha	1984
*Tower, Oswald	1959
*Trester, Arthur	1961
*Wells, Clifford	1971
*Wilke, Lou	1982

REFEREES

*Enright, Jim	1978
*Hepbron, George	1960
*Hoyt, George	1961
*Kennedy, Matthew "Pat"	1959
*Leith, Lloyd	1982
Mihalik, Zig "Red"	1985
Nucatola, John	**1977**
*Quigley, Ernest	1961
*Shirley, J. Dallas	1979
*Tobey, David	1961
*Walsh, David	1961

TEAMS

First Team	1959
Original Celtics	1959
Buffalo Germans	1961
New York Renaissance	1963

DIRECTORY OF MEMBERS ASSOCIATED WITH THE NBA

Members are listed alphabetically in their respective categories.
Date of nomination/election is next to their names.

PLAYERS

Nate Archibald (1990)—Only player ever to lead NBA in scoring and assists in the same season, 1973, when he averaged 34.0 ppg and 11.4 apg . . . Played 14 seasons, averaging 18.8 ppg and 7.4 apg . . . Six-time All-Star and MVP of 1981 contest . . . All-NBA First Team three times . . . Helped Boston Celtics to 1981 NBA Championship.

Paul Arizin (1977)—All-American and College Player of the Year at Villanova in 1950 . . . Averaged 17.2 ppg as Philadelphia Warrior rookie, more than 20 ppg for last nine pro seasons . . . Retired as third-highest NBA scorer with 16,266 points . . . A 10-time All-Star and Game's MVP in 1952 . . . Led league in scoring twice . . . Averaged 24.2 ppg while pacing Warriors to title in 1956.

Rick Barry (1986)—Led NCAA in scoring (37.4 ppg) in 1965 at Miami . . . NBA Rookie of the Year with San Francisco the next season . . . Had brilliant 14-year pro career—4 in ABA (Oakland, Washington, New York Nets) and 10 in NBA (San Francisco, Golden State and Houston) . . . Only player to lead both leagues in scoring (NBA 1967, ABA 1969) . . . Led Golden State to 1975 NBA crown and was NBA Finals MVP . . . Shot 90 percent from foul line using unorthodox underhand style . . . Scored 25,279 points in his career for a 24.8 average.

Elgin Baylor (1976)—All-American in 1958 at Seattle, averaging 32.5 ppg . . . NBA Rookie of the Year in 1959 . . . Selected to NBA All-Star team 11 times . . . All-Star co-MVP with Bob Pettit in 1959 . . . Scored LA Lakers' record 71 points in one game 1960 . . . Compiled 23,149 points and 27.4 average during 14-year career . . . Retired as third-leading all-time NBA scorer.

Walt Bellamy (1992)—Outstanding scorer and rebounder . . . Two-time All-American at Indiana and gold medal winner at 1960 Olympics . . . NBA Rookie of the Year in 1962 with Chicago, averaging 31.6 ppg and 19.0 rpg . . . Scored 20,941 points (20.1 ppg) and grabbed 14,241 rebounds (13.6 rpg) in 14 NBA seasons . . . Four-time NBA All-Star.

Dave Bing (1989)—All-American at Syracuse (1966) . . . Played 12 seasons in NBA, nine with Detroit Pistons . . . NBA Rookie of the Year in 1967 . . . Twice named to All-NBA First Team . . . Seven-time All-Star and MVP of 1976 contest . . . Averaged 20.3 ppg for career and led NBA with 27.1 ppg in

1968 . . . Founded Bing Steel in Detroit and has been honored for his business efforts.

Bill Bradley (1982)—Averaged 30 ppg and was a two-time All-American at Princeton . . . Established an NCAA tourney record of 58 points as a senior in 1965 when he was College Player of the Year . . . Member of U.S. Olympic gold medal team at Tokyo in 1964 . . . Spent two years as a Rhodes Scholar at Oxford before signing with New York Knicks . . . Noted for team play during 10-year career in which he helped Knicks to NBA championships in 1970 and 1973 . . . Elected to United States Senate from New Jersey in 1978.

Al Cervi (1984)—One of game's greatest backcourt players in late 1940s and early 1950s . . . Superb scorer and defensive player with Rochester Royals, he was MVP of NBL in 1946–47 . . . Became player-coach of Syracuse Nationals in NBL in 1948 and brought them into NBA the following year . . . One of his era's leading coaches, he retired as a player in 1953 and coached the Nats until the 1956–57 season.

Wilt Chamberlain (1978)—Considered by many as game's greatest offensive force . . . Starred at Kansas and played one year with Globetrotters before joining NBA . . . Holds NBA records for points in a season (4,029), points in a game (100 versus Knicks March 2, 1962), scoring average for season (50.4 in 1962), career rebounds (23,924), rebounds in a season (2,149) and rebounds in a game (55) . . . Led NBA in assists in 1967–68 . . . Played 47,859 minutes (including 48.5 mpg in 1962) and never fouled out in 1,045 games . . . Led 1967 Philadelphia 76ers and 1972 Los Angeles Lakers to NBA titles . . . NBA MVP four times . . . Played in 13 All-Star Games.

Bob Cousy (1970)—One of basketball's greatest playmakers . . . Three-time All-American at Holy Cross (1948–50) . . . Superb playmaker and court general, "The Cooz" led Boston Celtics to six NBA championships in seven years, including five in a row (1959–63) . . . All-NBA First Team 10 consecutive years . . . NBA MVP in 1957 . . . A 13-time All-Star, winning MVP honors in 1954 and 1957 . . . Once scored 50 points in an NBA playoff game . . . Had 6,959 career assists and 16,960 points.

Dave Cowens (1990)—Hardworking, competitive center who made up for lack of size (6-9) with tenacity . . . Led Boston Celtics to NBA championships in

1974 and 1976 . . . NBA co-Rookie of the Year (with Geoff Petrie) in 1971 . . . NBA MVP in 1973 . . . Played 10 seasons with Boston Celtics, including one as player-coach . . . Also played one-half season with Milwaukee . . . Averaged 17.6 ppg and 13.6 rpg for career.

Billy Cunningham (1985)—Two-time All-American at North Carolina, nicknamed "The Kangaroo Kid" for his jumping ability . . . Played nine years with Philadelphia 76ers, two with Carolina Cougars of ABA . . . Starred on Sixers' 1967 championship team and was MVP of ABA in 1973 . . . Averaged 21.2 ppg in 770 pro games . . . Coached Sixers from 1977 to 1985, compiling 454-196 record (.698) and winning NBA Championship in 1983 . . . Part-owner of Miami Heat.

Bob Davies (1969)—Two-time All-American at Seton Hall, leading team to 43 straight wins . . . Joined Rochester Royals in 1945 for a 10-year pro career in NBL and NBA . . . Outstanding playmaker . . . All-league seven times . . . MVP of NBL in 1947 . . . Led Royals to titles in 1946, 1947 (NBL) and 1951 (NBA) . . . Scored 7,771 points and annually ranked among league leaders in assists.

Dave DeBusschere (1982)—Three-time All-American at University of Detroit . . . At 24, became the youngest coach in NBA history when, early in the 1964–65 season, he became player-coach of Detroit Pistons . . . Coached them until late in the 1966–67 season . . . Also pitched for parts of two seasons for the Chicago White Sox (1962, 1963) . . . Helped New York Knicks to NBA titles in 1970 and 1973 . . . Outstanding shooter, also one of game's greatest defensive forwards . . . Later served as New York Nets' general manager, ABA commissioner and New York Knicks' executive vice president.

Julius Erving (1992)—At UMass, one of seven players in NCAA history to average over 20 ppg and 20 rpg for career . . . Played five seasons in ABA and 11 in NBA, making All-Star team every year . . . ABA MVP in 1974, 1975 and 1976, NBA MVP in 1981 . . . Led Nets to ABA titles in 1974 and 1976, Sixers to NBA title in 1983 . . . One of game's most exciting players, known for spectacular drives to the basket ending in dunks . . . With 30,026 points, ranks third behind only Kareem Abdul-Jabbar and Wilt Chamberlain on all-time NBA/ABA scoring list.

Walt "Clyde" Frazier (1986)—Led Southern Illinois to NIT title in 1967 and was named tourney MVP . . . One of the smoothest guards in the game, "Clyde" played for New York Knicks for 10 seasons (1968–77) . . . Outstanding at playing the passing lanes to come up with steals . . . Known for style and flair on and

off the court . . . Starred on 1970 and 1973 Knick championship teams . . . Had 36 points and 19 assists in Game 7 of 1970 NBA Finals against Lakers.

Joe Fulks (1977)—"Jumpin' Joe" was one of the first great jump shooters, scoring 1,560 NBA points for 26-point average in his third pro season after starring for Murray State . . . Scored 63 points for Philadelphia Warriors in 1949, an NBA record that stood for 10 years . . . Won scoring title with 23.2 average and led Philadelphia Warriors to championship in NBA's inaugural season, 1946–47 . . . Unanimous All-NBA First Team selection three times in eight-year career.

Harry Gallatin (1990)—One of the game's top players in the 1950s . . . Played 10 pro seasons, nine with New York and one with Detroit . . . Though only 6-6, played center for much of his career and led NBA in rebounding at 15.3 rpg in 1954 . . . "The Horse" averaged 11.9 rpg for eight seasons—rebounds were not kept as an official statistic during his first two years in the league . . . Coached St. Louis and New York, earning Coach of the Year honors in 1963.

Tom Gola (1975)—Four-time All-American at LaSalle . . . MVP in 1952 NIT and 1954 NCAA, leading LaSalle to both titles . . . Spent outstanding 10-year NBA career with Philadelphia and San Francisco Warriors and New York Knicks . . . All-NBA in 1958 . . . Versatile player who was always among league leaders in scoring, rebounds and assists.

Hal Greer (1981)—All-American at Marshall in 1958 . . . Spent 15-year pro career with the same franchise, joining Syracuse Nationals in 1958 and moving with them to Philadelphia in 1963 . . . Outstanding jump shooter . . . Averaged 22.1 ppg for 1966–67 Sixers, who are regarded as one of the NBA's greatest teams.

Cliff Hagan (1977)—Helped Kentucky win NCAA title in 1951 and go undefeated (25-0) in 1954 . . . After 10 seasons with St. Louis Hawks in which he averaged 18.0 ppg, he completed 13-year pro career as player-coach of ABA Dallas Chaparrals . . . Wound up with 14,870 points . . . One of the great all-time hook shooters . . . Played in five NBA All-Star Games . . . Key contributor as Hawks won five Western Division titles and NBA crown in 1958.

John Havlicek (1983)—Standout at Ohio State, leading Buckeyes to NCAA title and 78-6 record in three seasons . . . Boston Celtics' No. 1 pick in 1962 . . . At first known for his defense, later became outstanding scorer as well . . . "Hondo" began illustrious 16-year career as sixth man . . . Tireless, clutch, all-around performer . . . Played in 13 All-Star Games . . . Played in 1,270 games, scored 26,395 points for 20.8 ppg.

Connie Hawkins (1991)—One of the great leapers in

basketball history, a forerunner to Julius Erving and Michael Jordan at swooping to the basket . . . A playground legend in New York . . . Played seven NBA seasons with Phoenix, the LA Lakers and Atlanta . . . Four-time NBA All-Star . . . MVP of short-lived ABL with Pittsburgh Rens in 1961 . . . Led Pittsburgh Pipers to 1968 ABA championship and won league MVP honors . . . Also toured with Harlem Globetrotters.

Elvin Hayes (1989)—Among game's greatest scorers . . . Tallied 27,313 points (21.0 ppg), third-highest total in NBA history . . . All-American at Houston who played in famous Astrodome duel against Kareem Abdul-Jabbar's UCLA squad . . . Led NBA in scoring as a rookie with 28.4 ppg for San Diego Rockets in 1969 . . . Twelve-time All-Star and three-time All-NBA First Team . . . Twice led league in rebounding (1970, 1974) . . . Led Washington Bullets to 1978 NBA Championship.

Tom Heinsohn (1985)—All-American at Holy Cross in 1955 and 1956 . . . NBA Rookie of the Year in 1957, leading Boston Celtics to their first NBA title . . . Starting forward on eight NBA Championship teams . . . Averaged 18.6 ppg in nine-year career . . . Compiled 427-263 record as Celtics coach 1969–78, winning NBA crowns in 1974 and 1976 . . . An accomplished artist who has had many gallery exhibits.

Robert Houbregs (1986)—NCAA Player of the Year in 1953, leading Washington to best-ever 30-3 record . . . Ranks second in NCAA tournament history with 34.8 scoring average . . . Drafted by Milwaukee, "Houby" played five years in the NBA (1953–58) with Milwaukee, Baltimore, Boston, Fort Wayne and Detroit . . . Was Seattle SuperSonics general manager, 1970–73.

Dan Issel (1992)—Set 23 school records at Kentucky before starring in both ABA and NBA, averaging over 20 ppg in each league . . . Ranks fifth on combined ABA/NBA career scoring list with 27,482 points, a 22.6 average . . . ABA Rookie of the Year in 1971 and All-Star MVP in 1972 . . . Led Kentucky Colonels to ABA title in 1975 . . . NBA All-Star in 1977 . . . After serving as broadcaster for Denver Nuggets, became team's coach in 1992.

Buddy Jeannette (1993)—One of basketball's best backcourtmen of the 1940s . . . Won four MVP awards for his all-around skills, three in NBL and one in ABL . . . Helped Sheboygan to NBL championship in 1943 and Fort Wayne to NBL crown in 1944 and 1945 . . . Was player-coach of 1948 champion Baltimore Bullets in BAA, forerunner of NBA, and ranked among league leaders in assists.

Neil Johnston (1989)—High-scoring frontcourtman played eight seasons for Philadelphia Warriors in 1950s . . . Led NBA in scoring three consecutive years (1953–55) . . . Topped NBA in rebounding in 1955 . . . Averaged over 20 ppg in five of eight NBA seasons, two of them before the 24-second shot clock . . . Six-time All-Star . . . All-NBA First Team four times.

K. C. Jones (1988)—Teamed with Bill Russell for successive NCAA titles at the University of San Francisco in 1955 and 1956 and Olympic gold medal in 1956 . . . As a backcourtman with the Boston Celtics starting in 1958–59, he was known for tenacious defense during a nine-year career in which Celtics won eight consecutive NBA championships . . . Coached Brandeis University, San Diego (ABA), Washington, Boston and Seattle (NBA) . . . Guided Celtics to NBA titles in 1984 and 1986.

Sam Jones (1983)—One of NBA's all-time great shooters . . . Master of the bank shot, he scored 15,380 points for 17.7 ppg in fabulous 12-year career with Celtics . . . Played on 10 Celtic championship teams . . . A popular and supremely graceful player, teamed with K. C. Jones in great Celtics backcourt.

Bob Lanier (1991)—Two-time All-American and all-time scoring and rebounding leader at St. Bonaventure . . . Eight-time All-Star during 14-year NBA career with Detroit and Milwaukee . . . Led Bucks to five consecutive division titles . . . Retired with 19,248 points and 9,698 career rebounds, ranking among NBA's career Top 20 in both categories.

Joe Lapchick (1966)—Gained fame as first legitimate "star" center in game when he played for Original Celtics . . . Played pro ball from 1917 to 1936 . . . Later coached at St. John's University, where his teams won four NIT titles . . . Twice college Coach of the Year . . . Coached NBA's New York Knickerbockers (1947–56).

Clyde Lovellette (1987)—Three-time All-American at Kansas (1950–52) . . . Captained the 1952 Jayhawks squad that won NCAA title and was named MVP of the Final Four . . . Member of U.S. Olympic gold medal team in Helsinki in 1952 . . . Played on three NBA championship teams (Minneapolis Lakers in 1954 and Boston Celtics in 1963 and 1964) in 11-year pro career.

Jerry Lucas (1979)—Collegiate Player of the Year at Ohio State in 1961 and 1962 . . . His Buckeyes were 78-6, won three Big Ten titles and NCAA crown in 1960 . . . NBA Rookie of the Year with Cincinnati in 1964 . . . Great rebounder who also had soft outside shooting touch . . . NBA All-Star seven times, includ-

ing MVP in 1965 game . . . Helped New York to NBA Championship in 1973.

Ed Macauley (1960)—Two-time All-American at St. Louis University . . . "Easy Ed" led nation in field-goal percentage with .524 in 1948–49 . . . Played in seven NBA All-Star Games . . . Traded by Boston Celtics along with rights to Cliff Hagan for rights to Bill Russell in 1956 . . . Career high of 46 versus George Mikan and Minneapolis Lakers, March 6, 1953 . . . Coached St. Louis Hawks to Western Division titles 1959–60.

Pete Maravich (1986)—"Pistol Pete" set NCAA scoring records with 3,667 career points and 44.2 ppg at LSU . . . Known for his floppy socks and razzle-dazzle style of play, including no-look passes and fancy dribbling . . . Played 10 years in NBA with Atlanta, New Orleans, Utah and Boston . . . Led league in scoring in 1977 (31.1 ppg) . . . Five-time NBA All-Star . . . One of basketball's greatest showmen.

Slater Martin (1981)—All-American at Texas in 1949 . . . Playmaker on Minneapolis Laker teams that won NBA titles in 1950, 1952, 1953 and 1954 . . . Helped St. Louis Hawks to crown in 1958 . . . "Dugie" was voted All-Star seven times in 11-year career . . . At 5-10, he's considered one of greatest small men ever to play the game.

Dick McGuire (1992)—One of game's great early point guards . . . "Tricky Dick" starred at St. John's before 11-year NBA career, eight with New York Knicks . . . Ranked among league assist leaders every year . . . Later coached Detroit and New York . . . Currently is Knicks' director of scouting services.

George Mikan (1959)—Sport's first dominant big man . . . Three-time All-American center at DePaul . . . Voted AP Player of the Half Century in 1950 . . . One of all-time pro greats with Minneapolis Lakers . . . Led NBA in scoring three times, rebounding once . . . NBA All-Star Game MVP, 1953 . . . Led Lakers to five titles in six years as NBA's first dynasty . . . First commissioner of the American Basketball Association.

Earl Monroe (1989)—Crowd-pleasing showman with dazzling moves . . . Played 13 NBA seasons for Baltimore and New York . . . "The Pearl" first gained national attention by averaging 41.5 ppg as a senior at Winston-Salem State (1967) . . . NBA Rookie of the Year in 1968 and All-NBA First Team the following year . . . Blended his one-on-one moves into Knicks' team concept and helped team win 1973 NBA Championship . . . Averaged 18.8 ppg for pro career.

Calvin Murphy (1992)—One of game's great little men . . . Three-time All-American at Niagara, where

he averaged 33.1 ppg . . . Spent entire 13-year pro career with Rockets, first in San Diego and later in Houston . . . Team's all-time scoring leader with 17,949 points . . . Career free throw mark of .892 is among best in NBA history . . . Once held record with 78 consecutive free throws made . . . At 5-9, was one of sport's most popular players.

Bob Pettit (1970)—One of game's first great big forwards . . . Though 6-9, was mobile enough and shot well enough to play facing the basket . . . Three-time All-American at LSU . . . NBA Rookie of the Year in 1955 . . . All-NBA First Team 10 straight years for Milwaukee and St. Louis Hawks . . . NBA MVP 1956, 1959 . . . All-Star Game MVP three times and co-MVP once . . . Retired in 1965 as highest scorer in NBA history with 20,880 points.

Andy Phillip (1961)—One of the outstanding backcourtmen of his era, a solid scorer and playmaker . . . Leader of famed "Whiz Kids" team at Illinois, where he was a two-time All-American . . . Played 11 years in NBA with Chicago Stags, Philadelphia Warriors, Fort Wayne Pistons and Boston Celtics . . . Member of 1957 Boston Celtics NBA Championship team.

Jim Pollard (1977)—All-American as sophomore at Stanford, which won NCAA championship in 1942 . . . Smooth forward with great finesse moves . . . Played eight seasons with Minneapolis Lakers, one in NBL and seven in NBA . . . Four-time NBA All-Star . . . Helped Minneapolis to five NBA titles in six-year span from 1949 through 1954, as well as NBL title in 1948.

Frank Ramsey (1981)—All-American at Kentucky in 1952 and 1954 . . . Captained Adolph Rupp's NCAA champs in 1952 . . . Helped pioneer "sixth man" concept for the Boston Celtics . . . Played on seven NBA Championship teams in nine years, including six in a row (1959–64) . . . Versatile guard who could score or set up teammates.

Willis Reed (1981)—Led Grambling to NAIA championship in 1961 . . . Selected to all-time NAIA team in 1970 . . . NBA Rookie of the Year in 1965 with New York Knicks . . . Dominating and inspirational presence in 10-year Knick career . . . "The Captain" led Knicks to NBA titles in 1970 and 1973 . . . Only player ever selected as MVP for regular season, All-Star Game and NBA Finals in same season (1970) . . . Knicks' career rebound leader with 8,414 . . . Coached Knicks, Creighton University and New Jersey Nets and is now general manager of Nets.

Oscar Robertson (1979)—One of game's greatest all-around players . . . Two-time NCAA Player of the Year and three-time All-American at Cincinnati . . .

Set 14 NCAA records . . . Won Olympic gold medal in 1960 . . . Played 14 NBA seasons, 10 with Cincinnati and four with Milwaukee . . . NBA Rookie of the Year in 1961, MVP in 1964, All-Star MVP in 1961, 1964 and 1969 . . . "The Big O" averaged a triple-double in 1962 . . . Scored 26,710 points for a 25.7 average in 1,040 games, with then-record 9,887 assists.

Bill Russell (1974)—Brilliant shotblocker who revolutionized NBA defensive concepts and brought Boston Celtics eight straight titles, 11 in 13 seasons . . . Amassed 21,721 career rebounds and 15.1 scoring average . . . Appeared in 12 All-Star Games, winning MVP in 1963 . . . Five-time NBA MVP . . . Led San Francisco to NCAA titles in 1955 and 1956 and U.S. to gold medal at 1956 Olympics . . . Player-coach with Celtics for three seasons, winning NBA championships in 1968 and 1969 . . . Later coached Seattle and Sacramento and served as general manager of both clubs.

Dolph Schayes (1972)—All-American at NYU . . . High-scoring forward helped Syracuse Nats become one of NBA's top teams in 1950s . . . Owned outstanding shooting touch . . . A 12-time All-Star . . . Scored 19,249 points and played in a onetime record 1,059 games . . . Later coached Philadelphia and Buffalo . . . Also served as NBA supervisor of officials . . . Son Danny played in NBA in 1980s and 1990s.

Bill Sharman (1975)—Two-time All-American at Southern Cal . . . Broke into NBA with Washington in 1951, then on to 10 seasons with Boston Celtics . . . Teamed with Bob Cousy in great early Celtic backcourt . . . All-NBA seven times . . . 1955 NBA All-Star Game MVP . . . Scored 12,665 career points and ranks as one of top all-time foul shooters with 88 percent lifetime mark . . . Selected to NBA Silver Anniversary Team in 1971 . . . Only coach to win championships in three professional leagues—ABL (Cleveland, 1962) ABA (Utah, 1971) and NBA (LA Lakers, 1972) . . . Later served as Lakers' general manager and president.

Nate Thurmond (1984)—Outstanding all-around center who made presence felt with scoring, rebounding and defensive skills . . . All-American in 1963 at Bowling Green, where he set NCAA Tournament record for most rebounds (31) in one game . . . Averaged 15 points and 15 rebounds per game in 14-year NBA career with San Francisco–Golden State, Chicago and Cleveland . . . In 1974, posted first quadruple double in NBA history with 22 points, 14 rebounds, 13 assists and 12 blocked shots in one game.

Jack Twyman (1982)—All-American at Cincinnati in 1955 . . . One of NBA's greatest shooting forwards . . . Scored 15,840 points (19.2 ppg) in 11 seasons with Royals in Rochester and Cincinnati . . . Played in 609 consecutive games . . . Recognized for his humanitarianism, he was legal guardian for Maurice Stokes, Royals teammate who was paralyzed in 1958.

Wes Unseld (1987)—Although he was only 6-7, his strength and skills made him one of game's best centers . . . Outstanding rebounder who was known for his solid picks and outlet passing . . . All-American at Louisville . . . Played 13 NBA seasons with Bullets . . . Was Rookie of the Year and MVP in 1969, a feat achieved by only one other player, Wilt Chamberlain . . . Led team to NBA Playoffs 12 consecutive seasons and was MVP of the 1978 NBA Finals in which Washington won its only championship . . . Scored 10,624 points (10.8 ppg) and grabbed 13,769 rebounds (14.0 rpg) . . . Coached Bullets from 1987 to 1994.

Bill Walton (1992)—One of game's finest all-around centers, a brilliant passer, scorer and rebounder . . . Three-time All-American who led UCLA to 86-4 record, NCAA titles in 1972 and 1973 . . . Guided Portland to its only NBA Championship in 1977 . . . Was NBA's MVP in 1978 . . . Averaged 13.3 ppg and 10.5 rpg in injury-plagued NBA career . . . Came back to win NBA Sixth Man Award in 1986 when he helped Boston Celtics to championship.

Bobby Wanzer (1986)—Played 10 seasons with Rochester Royals after earning All-American honors at Seton Hall . . . Five-time NBA All-Star . . . An uncanny shooter, he ranked among league leaders in field-goal percentage four times . . . Sparked Rochester to NBA crown in 1951 . . . Led league in free-throw shooting (90.4 percent) in 1952 . . . Coached Royals for three years in Rochester and Cincinnati.

Jerry West (1979)—Among the greatest shooting guards in NBA history . . . Two-time All-American at West Virginia State and cocaptain of Olympic gold medalists in 1960 . . . Scored 25,192 points in 14 seasons with Los Angeles Lakers for an average of 27.0 ppg . . . "Mr. Clutch" scored then-record 4,457 NBA playoff points (29.1 in 153 games), including 40.6 ppg in 1965 . . . NBA Finals MVP in 1969 . . . Made All-NBA First Team 10 times and All-Defensive First Team four times . . . A 14-time All-Star . . . Later coached Lakers for three seasons and currently serves as team's general manager.

Lenny Wilkens (1988)—Brilliant playmaker . . . Handed out 7,211 career assists, an NBA record, when he retired in 1975 . . . After starring at Providence, played 15 NBA seasons with St. Louis, Seattle, Cleveland and Portland . . . Averaged 16.5 ppg and

6.7 apg . . . Nine-time All-Star, winning MVP honors in 1971 . . . Player-coach for three years at Seattle and one year at Portland . . . Became one of NBA's most successful coaches with over 900 career victories, second only to Red Auerbach on all-time list . . . On course to pass Auerbach's record of 938 coaching wins in 1994–95 season . . . Guided Seattle to 1979 NBA Championship.

COACHES

Arnold "Red" Auerbach (1968)—Winningest coach in NBA history with 938 regular-season victories, 1,037 overall . . . Coached Washington and Tri-Cities before forging basketball's greatest dynasty with Boston Celtics . . . Guided Celtics to nine NBA championships in 10 years, including eight in a row (1959–66) . . . Later served as general manager and president of the Celtics and still holds latter role . . . Coached East NBA All-Star team 11 years in a row . . . NBA's Coach of the Year trophy is named after him.

Chuck Daly (1993)—Coached Detroit Pistons to 1989 and 1990 NBA championships, then guided USA Basketball Dream Team to gold medal at 1992 Olympics in Barcelona . . . One of only 15 coaches in NBA history to win over 500 regular-season games . . . Coached eight seasons at Punxsutawney High School in Pennsylvania and eight seasons in college ranks at Boston College and Penn, in addition to 12 years in NBA . . . Winningest coach in Detroit Pistons history, having led team to NBA Playoffs in each of his nine seasons . . . Also coached one year at Cleveland and two at New Jersey.

William "Red" Holzman (1985)—Coached New York Knicks to 1970 and 1973 NBA championships, when "Dee-fense" was the popular chant . . . Compiled 696 regular-season victories (second-highest when he retired in 1982) and 58 playoff wins in 18 years as an NBA coach, 14 with New York and four with Milwaukee–St. Louis . . . Played nine pro seasons, eight with Rochester Royals in NBL and NBA . . . Typified the smarts and savvy of New York guards . . . Helped Rochester to NBL title in 1946 and NBA crown in 1951.

Alvin "Doggie" Julian (1967)—Coached Boston Celtics for two seasons prior to arrival of Red Auerbach in 1950 . . . Best known for college coaching success at Holy Cross, where he compiled 65-10 record and won 1947 NCAA title . . . Coached Bob Cousy, Joe Mullaney, George Kaftan, Frank Oftring and Bob Curran at Holy Cross . . . Also coached at Albright, Muhlenberg and Dartmouth.

Ken Loeffler (1964)—Coached St. Louis Bombers for two seasons and Providence Steamrollers for one in NBA's early years . . . Also coached at Geneva, Yale, LaSalle and Texas A&M, winning 310 games . . . Compiled 145-27 record at LaSalle, winning NIT in 1952 and NCAA Tournament in 1954 . . . Tom Gola was among his LaSalle players.

Frank McGuire (1976)—Coached Philadelphia Warriors to 49-31 record in 1962, the year Wilt Chamberlain averaged 50.4 ppg and scored 100 points in one game . . . First coach to compile 100 victories at three colleges—St. John's (103), North Carolina (164) and South Carolina (283) . . . Three-time NCAA Coach of the Year, led North Carolina to 32-0 mark and NCAA crown in 1957.

Jack Ramsay (1991)—Compiled 864 victories in 21-year NBA coaching career, the second-highest total in league history at the time he retired in 1988 . . . After compiling 234-72 record in 11 years at St. Joseph's, became general manager of Philadelphia 76ers in 1966 and coach of the team in 1968 . . . Guided Portland Trail Blazers to 1977 NBA Championship . . . Coached 10 years in Portland, four apiece at Philadelphia and Buffalo and three in Indiana.

CONTRIBUTORS

Clair Bee (1967)—Helped Danny Biasone in formulation of NBA's 24-second shot clock in 1954 . . . Instrumental in development of three-second rule . . . Coached for 29 years, including three with NBA Baltimore Bullets, 1952–54 . . . Highly successful college coach at Rider and LIU . . . Prolific author who wrote 21 instructional and nonfiction books and the 23-volume "Chip Hilton" fiction series for youth.

Walter Brown (1965)—One of the NBA's founding fathers . . . President of Boston Garden, organized the Boston Celtics as charter member of league . . . NBA's early championship trophy was named after

him . . . Served as chairman of the Hall of Fame board of directors, 1961–64.

Larry Fleisher (1990)—Served as general counsel of NBA Players Association for more than 25 years, from its inception in the early 1950s until his death in 1989 . . . Innovative leader who worked with NBA to raise level of popularity of basketball . . . Worked to improve player salaries, pensions and other benefits, including system of free agency.

Eddie Gottlieb (1971)—One of the NBA's founders . . . Coached the famed Philadelphia SPHAs beginning in 1918 . . . Teams enjoyed success barnstorm-

ing as well as in Eastern and American Basketball leagues . . . Coached Philadelphia Warriors to championship in 1947, first year of NBA (when it was known as BAA) . . . Coached team through 1954–55, then became owner . . . Subsequently served as NBA consultant and schedule maker.

Lester Harrison (1979)—Organized teams and games throughout 1930s and 1940s . . . Bought Rochester Pros in 1945, changed name to Royals and built them into one of the dominant teams of the late 1940s and early 1950s . . . As owner-coach, led Royals to NBL title in 1946 and NBA title in 1951 . . . Won 394 games before selling team in 1958.

Edward S. "Ned" Irish (1964)—One of the NBA's founders . . . Became basketball director of Madison Square Garden in 1934 and introduced popular college doubleheaders, which were a milestone in basketball's growth . . . New York and the Garden became mecca of basketball as the game, because of Irish, went intersectional . . . Founded New York Knickerbockers in 1946.

J. Walter Kennedy (1980)—Commissioner of NBA from 1963 to 1975, presiding over expansion from nine to 18 teams, a fourfold increase in attendance and acquisition of a national TV contract . . . Served as league's first publicity director under Maurice Podoloff . . . Was in second term as mayor of Stamford, Conn., when he was chosen as the NBA's second commissioner.

Bill Mokray (1965)—Edited *Official NBA Guide,* 1958–67 . . . Worked with Boston Celtics and Walter Brown for 21 years as scout and promotion director for Celtics and basketball director for Boston Garden . . . Author of *Basketball Encyclopedia* in 1963 . . . First chairman, Hall of Fame Honors Committee, 1959–64.

Pete Newell (1978)—Legendary coach won NIT title in 1949 with San Francisco, NCAA crown in 1959 with California and Olympic gold medal in 1960 . . . Runs highly regarded Big Man's Camp attended by many NBA centers and forwards each summer . . . Regarded as one of the game's outstanding teachers, has organized countless clinics around the world . . . Has served as personnel director and consultant to Golden State Warriors.

Larry O'Brien (1990)—NBA commissioner from 1975 to 1984 . . . An aide to presidents Kennedy and Johnson and former Democratic national committee chairman, was brought to NBA to negotiate an end to costly war with ABA, which he quickly accomplished . . . In his tenure NBA grew from 18 to 23 teams, attendance and TV revenues rose and the league formulated innovative and far-reaching collective bargaining and antidrug agreements with its players.

Harold Olsen (1959)—Coached Chicago Stags from 1946 to 1949, when league was known as BAA . . . Team won division title with 39-22 record and lost in championship series in league's first season . . . Coached at Ohio State 1922–46 . . . Was president of the National Association of Basketball Coaches and chairman NCAA rules committee, NCAA tournament committee and 1948 Olympic basketball committee . . . Helped introduce the 10-second rule.

Maurice Podoloff (1973)—Served as president of NBA from its founding in 1946 (as BAA) until 1963 . . . Oversaw absorption of surviving NBL teams in late 1940s and gradual movement of teams to larger markets in 1950s, including Lakers' move to Los Angeles in 1960 that made league truly national . . . Prior to heading basketball league, was president of the American Hockey League.

REFEREES

Jim Enright (1978)—Refereed in NBA, BAA and NBL . . . Also officiated for 24 years in Big Ten, Big Eight and Missouri Valley conferences . . . conducted officiating clinics in Europe . . . Also a highly regarded sportswriter who was president of U.S. Basketball Writers in 1967.

Matthew "Pat" Kennedy (1959)—Perhaps the most famous referee in basketball history . . . Renowned for his colorful, crowd-pleasing style of calling a game that made him a gate attraction in his own right . . . Served as high school, college and professional official from 1928 through 1952 . . . Was NBA supervisor of officials, 1946–50 . . . Toured with Harlem Globetrotters, 1950–57.

John Nucatola (1977)—Officiated more than 2,000 games, many of them while still coaching at his alma mater, Newtown (N.Y.) High School . . . Worked collegiate games in ECAC, ACC, Southern and Big 8 conferences, as well as NCAA Tournament and NIT . . . Refereed in pros in ABL, BAA and NBA until he hung up whistle in 1959 to concentrate on administrative career . . . Served as NBA's supervisor of officials, 1970–77.

J. Dallas Shirley (1979)—Worked games in Southern, ACC, ECAC, CBOA, Mason-Dixon conferences as well as NIT, NCAA tourneys, Sugar Bowl, Pan Am Games, Olympics and BAA during 32-year refereeing career . . . Also officiated in Colombia, Iceland, Puerto Rico and Libya . . . Received FIBA Award in 1979 for devoting lifetime to officiating development.

THE NBA DRAFT AND LOTTERY

From smoky back rooms to sold-out arenas, the NBA Draft has become both more and less than what it was when it first began prior to the start of the 1947–48 season.

While the draft is now only two rounds, down from the all-time high of 21 rounds in 1960, the event itself has become a major extravaganza, televised in prime time, held in a different city each year and attended by

The setting may be fancier these days, but team personnel still work the phones at the NBA Draft.

the top college players in the country as well as thousands of basketball enthusiasts.

It was all quite different in the beginning. The draft was no more than a conference call run out of league headquarters in New York, far away from cameras, lights and excitement and drawing little attention even from die-hard basketball fans. The top picks were the big college stars of the time, but by the time the later rounds came along, the names were unfamiliar and rarely ended up on an NBA roster.

Now there are fewer surprises in the draft. The increasing popularity of the college game, as well as extensive scouting, cable television and postseason all-star tournaments and predraft camps, all have combined to identify talented players from even the most obscure colleges, as well as leagues outside the United States. Yet the excitement and mystique of the draft remains because each year there are Top 10 picks whose best days were left in college and lower selections who become NBA All-Stars.

Draft drama is not limited to draft day, either. From Bob Cousy being the last of three players selected in a 1950 dispersal draft to the coin toss between Milwaukee and Phoenix in 1969 for the rights to select Kareem Abdul-Jabbar to Red Auerbach's picking future legend Larry Bird as a junior eligible in the 1978 draft to Orlando's coming up with the first draft pick in both 1992 and 1993, the excitement never ends.

For many years the NBA Draft was held in New York City, but beginning in 1992, it was decided to move the event around the country to a different site each year. Portland (Ore.) was the site of the 1992 NBA Draft, marking the first time since the draft had been opened to the public that it was held outside of New York City. As thousands of rabid fans await eagerly the host team's selections and the drafting of local college stars and hometown heroes, a number of those players expected to be early picks sit in a backstage green room with friends and family, anticipating the moment their name is called so they can begin that proud march

Larry Johnson (sitting) shakes hands with Dikembe Mutombo after both are selected in the first round at the 1990 NBA Draft.

through the crowds and onto the stage. For many, this is the realization of a lifetime of dreams and the crowning moment of their basketball careers. Rookie seasons will bring their share of trials and tribulations, but the draft supplies a magical moment that will never be taken away from them.

All players who have completed their college eligibility are eligible for the NBA Draft. Also, players with remaining college eligibility must notify the league office in writing at least 45 days prior to the draft for which they wish to become eligible. In addition, any foreign player who has his 22nd birthday during the calendar year in which the draft is held or any foreign player at least 18 years of age who has not played college basketball in the United States and has notified the league in writing 14 days prior to the draft is also eligible.

Beginning prior to the 1985 NBA Draft, a Draft

Shawn Bradley receives the traditional handshake from Commissioner David J. Stern at the 1993 NBA Draft.

Lottery was instituted in order to determine the order of selection for those teams not making the playoffs, thus eliminating any incentive for teams to lose games at the end of a season in order to improve their draft position. New York won the first Draft Lottery, and with it the right to draft Georgetown center Patrick Ewing in 1985.

The Draft Lottery gradually expanded from seven to nine to 11 teams by virtue of the NBA's expansion to Charlotte, Miami, Orlando and Minnesota in the late 1980s. With that growth, and the realization that the team finishing with the worst record in the NBA rightfully should have a better chance of receiving the first pick than the team that finishes 11th, just missing the playoffs, a weighted lottery system was introduced for the 1990 Draft Lottery and later modified for 1994.

From 1966 through 1984, a coin flip was held between the teams with the worst record in each conference (or division, when there were only two divisions) to determine which teams would pick first in the draft. The loser of the coin flip picked second, and the remaining teams picked in inverse order of their won-lost records.

In the early years, when the league was struggling to get established and teams were trying to build local fan bases, the draft included territorial picks. A team was permitted to select a player who played his college ball in the immediate area of the franchise before the regular draft began but forfeit its first-round pick. For example, in 1960 the Cincinnati Royals selected University of Cincinnati star Oscar Robertson as a territorial choice and gave up their first-round choice. The idea was to enable NBA teams to capitalize on the existing reputations of local college stars in their area. The Philadelphia Warriors took the concept one step further in 1959 when they petitioned the league and received permission to make Wilt Chamberlain their territorial pick, although Chamberlain had played college ball at Kansas, because he grew up in Philadelphia and was a star at Philadelphia's Overbrook High School. The concept of territorial picks was dropped after 1965.

Draft records for the league's early seasons are incomplete. Through 1956, players are listed in the order they were selected by each team. Starting in 1957, the draft is recorded round by round.

Also listed are the ABA draft selections, team by team through 1972 and round by round thereafter. Included as well are miscellaneous other NBA and ABA drafts, including the NBA dispersal draft of ABA players in 1976 and the various NBA expansion drafts.

After winning the 1992 NBA Lottery, Orlando President Pat Williams let everyone know who the Magic would pick for No. 1.

HISTORY OF THE NBA DRAFT LOTTERY

Beginning in 1985, the NBA held a lottery among all teams that failed to qualify for the playoffs to determine their order of selection in the first round of the NBA Draft. The lottery was later modified so as to determine only the order of the first three selections in the draft, with the remaining teams drafting in inverse order of their won-lost records, and weighted so as to give the teams with the worst records in the league a better chance at one of the top places. Following is a complete review of the NBA Draft Lottery:

1994

No.	Player, College	Team
1.	Glenn Robinson, Purdue	Milwaukee
2.	Jason Kidd, California	Dallas
3.	Grant Hill, Duke	Detroit
4.	Donyell Marshall, Connecticut	Minnesota
5.	Juwann Howard, Michigan	Washington
6.	Sharone Wright, Clemson	Philadelphia
7.	Lamond Murray, California	LA Clippers
8.	Brian Grant, Xavier	Sacramento
9.	Eric Montross, North Carolina	Boston
10.	Eddie Jones, Temple	LA Lakers
11.	Carlos Rogers, Tennessee State	Seattle (from Charlotte)

1993

1.	Chris Webber, Michigan	Orlando
2.	Shawn Bradley, Brigham Young	Philadelphia
3.	Anfernee Hardaway, Memphis State	Golden State
4.	Jamal Mashburn, Kentucky	Dallas
5.	Isaiah Rider, UNLV	Minnesota
6.	Calbert Cheaney, Indiana	Washington
7.	Bobby Hurley, Duke	Sacramento
8.	Vin Baker, Hartford	Milwaukee
9.	Rodney Rogers, Wake Forest	Denver
10.	Lindsey Hunter, Jackson State	Detroit (from Miami)
11.	Allen Houston, Tennessee	Detroit

1992

1.	Shaquille O'Neal, Louisiana State	Orlando
2.	Alonzo Mourning, Georgetown	Charlotte
3.	Christian Laettner, Duke	Minnesota
4.	Jimmy Jackson, Ohio State	Dallas
5.	LaPhonso Ellis, Notre Dame	Denver
6.	Tom Gugliotta, North Carolina State	Washington
7.	Walt Williams, Maryland	Sacramento
8.	Todd Day, Arkansas	Milwaukee
9.	Clarence Weatherspoon, Southern Mississippi	Philadelphia
10.	Adam Keefe, Stanford	Atlanta
11.	Robert Horry, Alabama	Houston

1991

1.	Larry Johnson, UNLV	Charlotte
2.	Kenny Anderson, Georgia Tech	New Jersey
3.	Billy Owens, Syracuse	Sacramento
4.	Dikembe Mutombo, Georgetown	Denver
5.	Steve Smith, Michigan State	Miami
6.	Doug Smith, Missouri	Dallas
7.	Luc Longley, New Mexico	Minnesota
8.	Mark Macon, Temple	Denver (from Washington)
9.	Stacey Augmon, UNLV	Atlanta (from LA Clippers)
10.	Brian Williams, Arizona	Orlando
11.	Terrell Brandon, Oregon	Cleveland

1990

1.	Derrick Coleman, Syracuse	New Jersey
2.	Gary Payton, Oregon State	Seattle
3.	Chris Jackson, LSU	Denver (from Miami)
4.	Dennis Scott, Georgia Tech	Orlando
5.	Kendall Gill, Illinois	Charlotte
6.	Felton Spencer, Louisville	Minnesota
7.	Lionel Simmons, La Salle	Sacramento
8.	Bo Kimble, Loyola Marymount	LA Clippers
9.	Willie Burton, Minnesota	Miami (from Washington via Dallas and Denver)
10.	Rumeal Robinson, Michigan	Atlanta (from Golden State)
11.	Tyrone Hill, Xavier	Golden State (from Atlanta)

1989

1.	Pervis Ellison, Louisville	Sacramento
2.	Danny Ferry, Duke	LA Clippers
3.	Sean Elliott, Arizona	San Antonio
4.	Glen Rice, Michigan	Miami
5.	J. R. Reid, North Carolina	Charlotte
6.	Stacey King, Oklahoma	Chicago (from New Jersey)
7.	George McCloud, Florida State	Indiana
8.	Randy White, Louisiana Tech	Dallas
9.	Tom Hammonds, Georgia Tech	Washington

1988

1.	Danny Manning, Kansas	LA Clippers
2.	Rik Smits, Marist	Indiana
3.	Charles Smith, Pittsburgh	Philadelphia
4.	Chris Morris, Auburn	New Jersey
5.	Mitch Richmond, Kansas State	Golden State
6.	Hersey Hawkins, Bradley	LA Clippers (from Sacramento)
7.	Tim Perry, Temple	Phoenix

1987

1.	David Robinson, Navy	San Antonio
2.	Armon Gilliam, UNLV	Phoenix
3.	Dennis Hopson, Ohio State	New Jersey
4.	Reggie Williams, Georgetown	LA Clippers
5.	Scottie Pippen, Central Arkansas	Seattle (from New York)
6.	Kenny Smith, North Carolina	Sacramento
7.	Kevin Johnson, California	Cleveland

1986

1.	Brad Daugherty, North Carolina	Cleveland (from LA Clippers via Philadelphia)
2.	Len Bias, Maryland	Boston (from Seattle)
3.	Chris Washburn, North Carolina State	Golden State
4.	Chuck Person, Auburn	Indiana
5.	Kenny Walker, Kentucky	New York
6.	William Bedford, Memphis State	Phoenix
7.	Roy Tarpley, Michigan	Dallas (from Cleveland)

1985

1.	Patrick Ewing, Georgetown	New York
2.	Wayman Tisdale, Oklahoma	Indiana
3.	Benoit Benjamin, Creighton	LA Clippers
4.	Xavier McDaniel, Wichita State	Seattle
5.	Jon Koncak, Southern Methodist	Atlanta
6.	Joe Kleine, Arkansas	Sacramento
7.	Chris Mullin, St. John's	Golden State

HISTORY OF THE NBA COIN FLIP

From 1966 through 1984, the NBA held a coin flip between the teams with the worst record in each conference to determine which team would choose first in the NBA Draft. Following are the complete results of the NBA coin flip:

Year	Flip Call	Result	First Two Picks
1984	Portland—Tails	Heads	Houston—Hakeem Olajuwon Portland—Sam Bowie (from Indiana)
1983	Houston—Heads	Heads	Houston—Ralph Sampson Indiana—Steve Stipanovich
1982	LA Lakers—Heads	Heads	LA Lakers—James Worthy (from Cleveland) San Diego—Terry Cummings
1981	Detroit—Heads	Tails	Dallas—Mark Aguirre Detroit—Isiah Thomas
1980	Utah—Heads	Tails	Golden State—Joe Barry Carroll (from Detroit via Boston) Utah—Darrell Griffith
1979	Chicago—Heads	Tails	LA Lakers—Magic Johnson (from New Orleans) Chicago—David Greenwood
1978	Kansas City—Heads	Tails	Portland—Mychal Thompson (from Indiana) Kansas City—Phil Ford (from New Jersey)
1977	Kansas City—Heads	Tails	Milwaukee—Kent Benson Kansas City—Otis Birdsong (from New Jersey)
1976	Houston—Heads	Heads	Houston—John Lucas (from Atlanta) Chicago—Scott May
1975	Atlanta—Tails	Tails	Atlanta—David Thompson LA Lakers—David Meyers
1974	Philadelphia—Heads	Tails	Portland—Bill Walton Philadelphia—Marvin Barnes
1973	Philadelphia—Tails	Tails	Philadelphia—Doug Collins Cleveland—Jim Brewer (from Portland)
1972	Portland—Tails	Tails	Portland—LaRue Martin Buffalo—Bob McAdoo
1971	Portland—Heads	Tails	Cleveland—Austin Carr Portland—Sidney Wicks
1970	San Diego—Heads	Tails	Detroit—Bob Lanier San Diego—Rudy Tomjanovich
1969	Phoenix—Heads	Tails	Milwaukee—Kareem Abdul-Jabbar Phoenix—Neal Walk
1968	San Diego—Heads	Heads	San Diego—Elvin Hayes Baltimore—Wes Unseld
1967	Baltimore—Tails	Heads	Detroit—Jimmy Walker Baltimore—Earl Monroe
1966	Detroit—Tails	Heads	New York—Cazzie Russell Detroit—Dave Bing

THE DRAFT

1947 (JULY 1, 1947)

BALTIMORE   Larry Killick, Vermont; Bob Jake, Vermont; John Rusinko, Penn State; Chick Gallatin, Missouri State Teachers; Charles Raynor, Houston. Negotiation list: Elmer Gainer, Scotty Hamilton, Hugh Hampton, Chick Reiser, Robert Belyard.

BOSTON   Ed Ehlers, Purdue; Hank Biasetti, LIU; Gene Stump, DePaul; George Felt, Northwestern. Negotiation list: Bob Alemeida, George Petrovick, John Ezersky, Jack Hewson, John Kelly.

CHICAGO   Paul Huston, Ohio State; Ben Shadler, Northwestern; Hank Decker, West Texas State; Gene Vance, Illinois; Andy Phillip, Illinois. Negotiation list: Ralph Bishop, Jim Darden, Jim Pollard, Don Smith, Jack Stone.

NEW YORK   Dick Holub, LIU; Tom Tomlinson, Southern Methodist; Garland Head, Texas Tech; Carl Reichert, Findlay; Ray Evans, Kansas. Negotiation list: Andy Duncan, Ed Golub, Ron Livingston, Dan Miller, Wat Misaka.

PHILADELPHIA   Francis Crossin, Penn; Ed Koffenberger, Duke; Norman Butz, St. Joseph's (Pa.); Jim Kaeding, York. Negotiation list: Jim Pollard.

PITTSBURGH   Clifton McNeeley, Texas Western; Bob Alamo, Santa Clara; Herman Knoche,. Washington & Jefferson; Dick Ives, Iowa; Jack Walton, DePauw. Negotiation list: Fritz Nagy, George Brown.

PROVIDENCE   Walt Dropo, Connecticut; Roy Lipscomb, St. Mary's; John Mills, Hofstra; Al Nichols, Rhode Island State. Negotiation list: Dick Furey, Robert Hubbard, Joe Barry, Bob Joyce.

ST. LOUIS   Jack Underman, Ohio State; Herb Wilkinson, Iowa; Jack Knopf, Louisville. Negotiation list: Bob Kurland, Paul Napolitano, Jim Pollard, Bill Strannigan.

TORONTO   Glen Selbo, Wisconsin; Red Rocha, Oregon State; Frank Broyles, Georgia Tech; Wimpy Quinn, Oregon; Paul Hoffman, Purdue. Negotiation list: None.

WASHINGTON   Dick O'Keefe, Santa Clara; Jack Tingle, Kentucky; Bill Burke, St. Mary's; Abel Rodriguez, San Francisco. Negotiation list: Paul Cloyd, Nat Zunice, John Mandic, Irwin Rothenberg, Saul Mariashin.

1948 (MAY 10, 1948)

BALTIMORE   Jim Black, Occidental; Darrell Brown, Humboldt State; Walter Budko, Columbia; Robert Carroll, West Virginia; Jake Carter, East Texas State; Marvin English, Newberry; Gene Fellmoth, Whittenberg; J. W. Fullerton, Arkansas State; Marshall Gemberling, Lebanon Valley; Vince Hansen, Washington State; Joe Holland, Kentucky; Dan Kraus, Georgetown; Wayne Jones, American International; Herbert Krautblatt, Rider; Paul Marcincin, Moravian.

BOSTON   John Bach, Fordham; Norman Carey, Oregon State; Bob Curran, Holy Cross; Neil Dooley, Colgate; George Hauptfuhrer, Harvard; Jack Hauser, Denver; Marshall Hawkins, Tennessee; Tom Kelley, NYU; Murray Mitchell, Sam Houston; Guinn Phillips, Texas Wesleyan; Ray Wehde, Iowa State.

CHICAGO   John Dillon, North Carolina; Ed Kachan, DePaul; Mickey Marty, Loras; Ed Mikan, DePaul; Ed Mills, Wisconsin; Don Reagan, Murray State; Joe Shafer, Wheaton; Odie Spears, Western Kentucky; Fred Weber, Siena.

FORT WAYNE   Bobby Cook, Wisconsin; Link Richmond, Arizona; Ken Rollins, Kentucky; Murray Wier, Iowa; Ward Williams, Indiana.

INDIANAPOLIS   Reede Berg, Oregon; Jack Coleman, LSU; Alex Hannum, USC; Norman Kohler, North Carolina; George Kok, Arkansas; Andy Kostecka, Georgetown; Ray Lumpp, NYU; Bob Paxton, North Carolina; Jack Phoenix, Idaho; Dick Wehr, Rice.

MINNEAPOLIS   Cliff Crandall, Oregon State; Arnold Ferrin, Utah; Earl Gardner, DePauw; Dee Gibson, Western Kentucky; Chuck Hanger, California; Ken Jastrow, Denver; Bob Lowther, LSU; Junior Skogland, Gustavus Adolphus; Quentin Stinson, Southern Illinois; Johnny Orr, Beloit.

NEW YORK   Gene Berce, Marquette; Leland Byrd, West Virginia; Harry Gallatin, Northeast Missouri; Keith Grimes, East Central State; Melvin McGaha, Arkansas; Ed Peterson, Cornell; Gobel Ritter, Western Kentucky; Adolph Schayes, NYU; Richard Shrider, Ohio U.; John Stanisch, UCLA.

PHILADELPHIA   William Brown, Maryland; Hugh Compton, Louisville; Joe Nelson, Brigham Young; Clint Pace, Pepperdine; Roy Pugh, Southern Methodist; Don Ray, Western Kentucky; Tom Short, Kansas Wesleyan; Joe Wahl, Akron; Andy Wolfe, California.

PROVIDENCE A. L. Bennett, Oklahoma A&M; Jack Coleman, Louisville; Ed Faber, Trinity; Verl Heap, Arizona State; Otto Snellbacher, Kansas; Andy Tonkovich, Marshall; Brady Walker, Brigham Young.

ROCHESTER Bill Gabor, Syracuse; Ed Keim, Niagara; Leo Kubiak, Bowling Green; Hank O'Keefe, Canisius; Whitey Macknowski, Seton Hall; Lionel Melamed, CCNY; Warren Stickel, Syracuse; Robert Wanzer, Seton Hall; Paul Yesavi, Niagara; Alex Athas, Tulane.

ST. LOUIS Jack Burmeister, Illinois; Gordon Flick, Drake; Robert Gale, Cornell; John Hoppin, Dickinson; Dan London, Washington U. (St. Louis); D. Miller, St. Louis; Easy Parham, Texas Wesleyan; D. C. Wilcutt, St. Louis.

WASHINGTON Fred Bartell, Oregon; Ed Hughes, San Jose State; Thorton Jenkins, Missouri; Leo Katkavek, North Carolina State; Jack Nichols, Washington; C. T. Parker, Louisiana Tech; John Parkinson, Kentucky; Don Walker, Sam Houston State; Al Williams, Arkansas.

1949 (MARCH 21, 1949)

BALTIMORE Ron Livingston, Wyoming; Roger Wiley, Oregon.

BOSTON Tony Lavelli, Yale; Joe Mullaney, Holy Cross; Bill Tom, Rice; Ed Little, Denver JC; Jim Simpson, Bates; Bill Vandenburgh, Washington; Duane Klueh, Indiana State; Emerson Speicher, Bowling Green; Bill Weight, Brigham Young; Russ Washburn, Colby.

CHICAGO Ralph Beard, Kentucky; Jack Kerris, Loyola (Ill.).

FORT WAYNE Bob Harris, Oklahoma A&M; John Oldham, Western Kentucky.

INDIANAPOLIS Alex Groza, Kentucky; Leo Barnhorst, Notre Dame; Mac Otten, Bowling Green; Bob Evans, Butler; Charlie Maas, Butler; Don Boven, Western Michigan; Jim O'Halloran, Notre Dame; J. L. Parks, Oklahoma A&M.

MINNEAPOLIS Vern Mikkelsen, Hamline; Bob Harrison, Michigan.

NEW YORK Dick McGuire, St. John's (N.Y.); Harry Donovan, Muhlenberg; Ernie Vandeweghe, Colgate; Bill Kleine, Missouri Valley; Don Bagley, Notre Dame; Bob Prewitt, Southern Methodist; Ken Kearns, Arkansas; Bill Litchfield, Emporia State.

PHILADELPHIA Vern Gardner, Utah; Jim Nolan, Georgia Tech.

PROVIDENCE Paul Courty, Oklahoma; Howie Shannon, Kansas State.

ROCHESTER Frank Saul, Seton Hall; Jack Coleman, Louisville.

ST. LOUIS Ed Macauley, St. Louis; John Orr, Beloit; Marv Schatzman, St. Louis; Preston Ward, Southwest Missouri; Earl Dodd, Northeast Missouri; Jack Davidson, Stanford; John Pritchard, Drake; Bob Retherford, Nebraska; Joe Crandall, Oregon State; Eddie Van Zant, Northwest Oklahoma.

WASHINGTON Wallace "Wah Wah" Jones, Kentucky; Jim Owens, Baylor.

1950 (APRIL 25, 1950)

BALTIMORE Don Rehfeldt, Wisconsin; John Pilch, Wyoming; Dick Dickey, North Carolina State; Jerry Reed, Wyoming; Norm Mager, CCNY; Rick Harman, Kansas State; Frank Comerford, LaSalle; George Bush, Toledo; Jack Laub, Cincinnati; Mike Zedalis, Loyola (Md.).

BOSTON Charlie Share, Bowling Green; Chuck Cooper, Duquesne; Bob Donham, Ohio State; Ken Reeves, Louisville; Jack Shelton, Oklahoma A&M; Fran Mahoney, Brown; Dale Barnstable, Kentucky; Frank Oftring, Holy Cross; Bob Cope, Montana State; Matt Forman, Holy Cross.

CHICAGO Larry Foust, LaSalle; Wally Osterkorn, Illinois; Lou Watson, Indiana; Ken Murray, St. Bonaventure; Don Stroot, Missouri; Stu Inman, San Jose State; Milt Whitehead, Nebraska; George King, Morris Harvey; John Brown, Georgetown; Bud Schaeffer, Wheaton.

FORT WAYNE George Yardley, Stanford; Jim Riffey, Tulane; Art Burris, Tennessee; Len Rzewszewski, Indiana State; Ed Thompson, Kent State; Bob Metcalf, Valparaiso; Ed Jones, Tennessee; Billy Joe Adcock, Vanderbilt; Al Henningsen, Northwest Missouri.

INDIANAPOLIS Bob Lavoy, Western Kentucky; Paul Unruh, Bradley; Charles Mrazovich, Eastern Kentucky; Jim Line, Kentucky; Sonny Allen, Morehead State; Ralph O'Brien, Butler; Leon Blevins, Arizona; Jerry Stuteville, Indiana; Gene Schmidt, Texas Christian; Colin Anderson, Georgia Tech; Jimmy Doyle, Butler.

MINNEAPOLIS Kevin O'Shea, Notre Dame; Hal Haskins, Hamline; Howie Williams, Purdue; Bud Grant, Minnesota; Ed Beach, West Virginia; Wayne Glasgow, Oklahoma; Joe Hutton Jr., Hamline; Newt Benson, River Falls Teachers; Jim Reilly, Swarthmore; Andy Butchko, Purdue.

NEW YORK Irwin Dambrot, CCNY; Herb Scherer, LIU; Stan Weber, Bowling Green; Joe Ossola, St. Louis; Dick Barnes, San Diego State; Don Parsons, Rutgers; Dan Bagley, Notre Dame; Charles Hope, Appalachian; Don Heathington, Baylor.

PHILADELPHIA Paul Arizin, Villanova; Ed Dahler, Duquesne; Buddy Cate, Western Kentucky; Paul Senesky, St. Joseph's (Pa.); Ike Borsavine, Temple; Dick Dallmer, Cincinnati; Charles Northrup, Siena; Brooks Ricca, Villanova; Joe Kaufman, NYU; Bernie Adams, Princeton; Leo Wolfe, Villanova; Ed Montgomery, Tennessee.

ROCHESTER Joe McNamee, San Francisco; George Stanich, UCLA; Bob Roper, John Carroll; Chet Giermak, William & Mary; Joe Nelson, Brigham Young; John Givens, Western Kentucky; Dan Kahler, Southwestern (Kan.); Carl Kraushaar, UCLA; Warren Switzer, Rice; Harry Foley, Niagara.

SYRACUSE Don Lofgran, San Francisco; Gerry Calabrese, St. John's (N.Y.); Stan Christie, Southern California; Paul Merchant, Oklahoma; Paul Hickey, Denver; Mack Suprunowicz, Michigan; Lou Arko, Akron; Bob Healey, Georgia; Bob Savage, Syracuse; Glenn Wilkes, Mercer.

TRI-CITIES Bob Cousy, Holy Cross; Ed Gayda, Washington State; Clarence Brannum, Kansas State; Paul Hicks, Eastern Kentucky; Cal Christensen, Toledo; Bob Anderson, Loyola (Md.); Bill Erickson, Illinois; Loy Doty, Wyoming; Nate DeLong, River Falls Teachers; Keith Bloom, Wyoming.

WASHINGTON Dick Schnittker, Ohio State; Bill Sharman, Southern California; Alan Sawyer, UCLA; Tom O'Keefe, Georgetown; Claude Overton, East Central Oklahoma; Warren Cartier, North Carolina State; Jim Cathcart, Arkansas; Joe Greenbach, Santa Clara; Earl Lloyd, West Virginia State; Joe Noertker, Virginia.

1951

BALTIMORE Gene Melchiorre, Bradley; Jack Stone, Kansas State; Bill Mann, Bradley; Bill Hagler, California; Leroy Ishman, American; Glen Duggins, Utah; Tom Riach, Southern California; Bill Harper, Oregon State; Bob Crowe, San Jose State; Dan Torrey, Oregon State; Clem Pavilonis, DePaul; John Burke, Springfield (Mass.).

BOSTON Ernie Barrett, Kansas State; Bill Garrett, Indiana; John Furlong, Pepperdine; Bob Barnett, Evansville; Rip Gish, Western Kentucky; Jim Luisi, St. Francis (N.Y.); John Azary, Columbia; Hugo Kappler, North Carolina State.

FORT WAYNE Zeke Sinicola, Niagara; Jack Kiley, Syracuse; Jake Fendley, Northwestern; Herb Hargett, Mississippi State; Leo Johnson, Arizona; Frank Clasbeek, Iowa; Jim Ramstead, Stanford; John Manning, Duquesne.

INDIANAPOLIS Marcus Freiberger, Oklahoma; Scotty Steagall, Millikin; Glenn Kammeyer, Central Missouri State; Bill Tosheff, Indiana; Bob Pierce, Nebraska; Marv Johnson, Wheaton; Ted Beach, Illinois; George Kelly, Vanderbilt.

MINNEAPOLIS Whitey Skoog, Minnesota; Lew Hitch, Kansas State; Bob Payne, Oregon State; Gale McArthur, Oklahoma A&M; Leo Vander Kuy, Michigan; Deward Dopson, Arkansas Polytechnic; Ed Head, Kansas State.

NEW YORK Ed Smith, Harvard; Roland Minson, Brigham Young; Joe Luchi, Cincinnati; Lloyd Sandstrom, St. Thomas; Tom Smith, St. Peter's; Al McGuire, St. John's (N.Y.); Sid Ryen, Denver.

PHILADELPHIA Don Sunderlage, Illinois; Mel Payton, Tulane; Bob Schloss, Georgia; Jud Milhon, Ohio Wesleyan; Mike Kearns, Princeton; Bob Swalls, Indiana Central; George Dempsey, King's; Jim Phelan, LaSalle; Hugh Faulkner, Pepperdine; Paul Gerwin, Cornell.

ROCHESTER Sam Ranzino, North Carolina State; Ray Ragelis, Northwestern; Fred Diute, St. Bonaventure; Elmer Behnke, Bradley; Dan Bagley, Notre Dame; Jim Ove, Valparaiso; John Brown, Southern Methodist; George Davidson, Lafayette.

SYRACUSE John McConathy, Northwestern Louisiana; Don Savage, LeMoyne; Bato Govedarica, DePaul; Paul Horvath, North Carolina State; Glen Anderson, Colorado A&M; Bob Wheeler, Idaho; Roy Reardon, St. Francis (N.Y.); Tom Jockle, Syracuse; Ray Kirkwasser, Ithaca.

TRI-CITIES Mel Hutchins, Brigham Young; Bill Gossett, Colorado A&M; Ron Bontemps, Beloit; Jim Slaughter, South Carolina; Bob Sakel, Evansville; John Rennicke, Drake; Bob Ambler, Arkansas; Aaron Pierce, Bradley; Wayne Tucker, Colorado; John DeWitt, Texas A&M.

1952

BALTIMORE Jim Baechtold, Eastern Kentucky; Blaine Denning, Lawrence Tech; Chuck Grigsby, Dayton; Frank Guisness, Washington; Bill Lea, Southwest Missouri; Art Press, Western Maryland; Bob Priddy, New Mexico A&M; Benny Purcell, Murray State; Bud Penwell, Oklahoma City; Mike Magula, Youngstown; Bob Peterson, Oregon; Jim Walsh, Stanford.

BOSTON   Bill Stauffer, Missouri; Jim Iverson, Kansas State; J. C. Maze, Southwest Texas; Herm Hedderick, Canisius; Don Johnson, Oklahoma State; Jim Buchanan, Nebraska; Fred Eydt, Cornell; Gordon Mungier, Spring Hill; Jim Dilling, Holy Cross; Gene Conley, Washington State.

FORT WAYNE   Bill Carlson, Fordham; Hal Cerra, Duquesne; Bob Clifton, Iowa; Leo Corkery, St. Bonaventure; Dick Groat, Duke; Don Meineke, Dayton; Lee Terrill, North Carolina State; Jim Ramstead, Stanford.

INDIANAPOLIS   Joe Dean, Louisiana State; Jay Handlan, Washington & Lee; Bill Harrell, Siena; Jim Hoverder, Central Missouri State; Gene Rhodes, Western Kentucky; Dale Toft, Denver; Lucian Whitaker, Kentucky; Bob Zawoluk, St. John's (N.Y.); Gordon Stauffer, Michigan State.

MILWAUKEE   Pete Brewster, Purdue; Roger Johnson, Arizona; Ed Miller, Syracuse; George McLeod, TCU; Ab Nicholas, Wisconsin; Dick Retherford, Baldwin-Wallace; John Snee, Clemson; Jim Tackett, New Mexico; Coyt Vance, Mississippi State; Bob Watson, Kentucky; Mark Workman, West Virginia.

MINNEAPOLIS   Tom Ackerman, West Liberty; Jim Bishop, Mississippi Southern; Rod Fletcher, Illinois; Cliff Haag, Wyoming; Jim Holstein, Cincinnati; Bob Holt, Tulane; Tom Katsimpalis, Eastern Illinois; Clyde Lovellette, Kansas; Dick Means, Minnesota; Dwight Morrison, Southern California; Carl McNulty, Purdue; Ed Ramiraz, Centenary; Don Schneider, Arizona; Gene Smith, Xavier (Ohio); Gene Smith, Huron; Homer Spain, Union (Tenn.); John Wallesea, Memphis State.

NEW YORK   Roy Belliveau, Seton Hall; Dick Bunt, NYU; Bert Cook, Utah State; Ben Gibson, St. Mary's (Cal.); Bud Julian, Southwest Missouri State; Ralph Polson, Whitworth; Paul Sullivan, Alabama; Dick Surhoff, LIU.

PHILADELPHIA   Tom Brennan, Villanova; Bob Brown, Louisville; Burr Carlson, Connecticut; Walter Davis, Texas A&M; Nick Kladis, Loyola (Ill.); Bill Mlkvy, Temple; Newt Jones, LaSalle; Moe Radovich, Wyoming; Don Scanlon, Pennsylvania; Glenn Smith, Utah; Ben Stewart, Villanova.

ROCHESTER   Chuck Darling, Iowa; Bryant Ivey, Alabama; Leroy Leslie, Notre Dame; Ronnie MacGilvray, St. John's (N.Y.); Jewell McDowell, Texas A&M; Jack McMahon, St. John's (N.Y.); Sam Miranda, Indiana; Jerry Romney, Brigham Young; Ray Royce, Houston; Arnold Smith, CCNY; Ray Sonnenberg, St. Louis; Ray Steiner, St. Louis; Bob Whitmer, Florida State.

SYRACUSE   Jim Brasco, NYU; Bud Donnelly, LaSalle; Jim Kennedy, Duquesne; Bob Lochmueller, Louisville; Ken McBride, Maryland State; Harry Moore, West Virginia; Bob Roche, Syracuse.

1953

BALTIMORE   Ray Felix, LIU; Bob Speight, North Carolina State; Bob Peterson, Illinois; Bill Schyman, DePaul; Paul Nolen, Texas Tech; Elmer Tolson, Eastern Kentucky; Herman Sledzik, Penn State; Connie Rea, Centenary; Dennis Murphy, Georgetown; Jack Carby, Kansas State; Bob Emmerick, Clarion State; Russ Johnson; Don Stemmerich; Bob Kraback; Joe Piorkowski; Edward Walsh.

BOSTON   Frank Ramsey, Kentucky; Chet Noe, Oregon; Cliff Hagan, Kentucky; Earle Markey, Holy Cross; John Holup, George Washington; Vernon Stokes, St. Francis (N.Y.); Lou Tsioropoulos, Kentucky; Ted Lallier, Colby; Lewis Gilcrease, Southwest Texas; Tom Lillis, St. Louis; Gil Reich, Kansas; Jim Dogerty, Whitworth.

FORT WAYNE   Jack Molinas, Columbia; George Glasgow, Fairleigh Dickinson; Jim Bredar, Illinois; Jim Bingham, Eastern Kentucky; Mike Bodnar, St. Bonaventure; Norb Lewinski, Notre Dame; William Hagan, Siena; Dean Kelley, Kansas; Dick White, Eastern Kentucky.

MILWAUKEE   Bob Houbregs, Washington; Bill Bolger, Georgetown; Irv Bemoras, Illinois; Gene Dyker, DePaul; Joe Cipriano, Washington; John O'Brien, Seattle; Eddie O'Brien, Seattle; Darrell Tucker, Utah State; Paul Brandt, Columbia; Bob Rousey, Kansas State.

MINNEAPOLIS   Jim Fritsche, Hamline; Ron Feiereisel, DePaul; Hartly Kruger, Idaho; Ken Flowers, Southern California; Zippy Morocco, Georgia; Pete Silas, Georgia Tech; Lloyd Olmstead, Cornell (Iowa); Joe Richey, Brigham Young; Hank Budde, Xavier (Oh.); Walt Kearns, Arkansas; Bill Chambers, William & Mary; Harold Christensen, Brigham Young; Bob Gelle, Minnesota; Lloyd Thorgaard, Hamline; Bob Gussner, Hamline; Chuck Wolfe, North Dakota; Doug Atkins, Tennessee; Roger Kuss, River Falls State.

NEW YORK   Walter Dukes, Seton Hall; Buddy Ackerman, LIU; Neil Gordon, Furman; Joe Smyth, Niagara; Allan Schutts, Springfield; Richard Atha, Indiana State; Forrest Hamilton, Southwest Missouri State; Robert Santini, Iona; Thomas Bishop, Mississippi Southern; Richard Prater, Kentucky; Bob Matheny, California; Larry O'Connor, Canisius; Delmar Diercks, Iowa State.

PHILADELPHIA   Ernie Beck, Pennsylvania; Larry Hennessy, Villanova; Norm Grekin, LaSalle; Fred Ihle, LaSalle; Eddie Solomon, West Virginia Tech; Don Eby, Southern California; Bob Marske, South Dakota; Bill Dodd, Colgate; Bob Sassone, St. Bonaventure; Toar Hester, Centenary; John Doogan, St. Joseph's (Pa.); Charles Duffley, St. Anselm's.

ROCHESTER   Richie Regan, Seton Hall; Norman Swanson, Detroit; Frank Reddout, Syracuse; Will Walls, Miami (Ohio); Hugh Beins, Georgetown; Kendall Sheets, Oklahoma A&M; Jim Sottile, West Virginia; Dick Gross, Wheaton; Jim Gerber, Bowling Green; Will Bales, Eastern Kentucky; Bill Edwards, St. Bonaventure; Bob Goss, North Carolina State; Paul Smaagard, Hamline; Ken Sears, Santa Clara; John Kurz, Loyola (Cal.); Ed Kohl, Regis; Gene Lambert Jr., Arkansas; Tex Silverman; Nick McGuire.

SYRACUSE   James Neal, Wofford; Dick Knostman, Kansas State; Bill Kenville, St. Bonaventure; Andy McGowan, Manhattan; Warren Shackelford, Tulsa; Bill Jenkins, LeMoyne; Bill Hull, Utah State; Joe Hughes, Denver; Gerald Nappy, Georgetown; Al Bailey, Duquesne; Glen Dille, Tulsa; Garrett Beshear, Murray State.

1954

BALTIMORE   Frank Selvy, Furman; Bob Leonard, Indiana; Werner Killen, Lawrence Tech; Burt Spice, Toledo; Lou Scott, Indiana; Bob Heim, Xavier (Ohio); Joe Pehanick, Seattle; Harry Brooks, Seton Hall; Ron Goerrs, Concordia (Mo.); Don Shivers, Houston; Elliott Karver, George Washington.

BOSTON   Togo Palazzi, Holy Cross; Dwight Morrison, Idaho; Henry Daubenschmidt, St. Francis (N.Y.); Ron Perry, Holy Cross; Troy Burris, West Texas; Otto Krieghauser, Washington (Mo.); Paul Estergaard, Bradley; Jim Young, Santa Clara; Tony Daukas, Boston College; Bill Johnson, Nebraska.

FORT WAYNE   Dick Rosenthal, Notre Dame; Arnold Short, Oklahoma City; B. H. Born, Kansas; Mel Thompson, North Carolina State; Dutch Burch, Pittsburgh; Charles Kraak, Indiana; Bernie Janicki, Duke; Don Bielke, Valparaiso; Joel Hittleman, Loyola (Md.); Phil Larson, Brigham Young; Forrest Jackson, Taylor.

MILWAUKEE   Bob Pettit, LSU; Bob Mattick, Oklahoma State; Walt Walowac, Marshall; Phil Martin, Toledo; Paul Ebert, Ohio State; Bob Carney, Bradley; Alan Kelley, Kansas; Dick Nunneley, Tulsa; Hal Cervini, Tulane; Joe Bertrand, Notre Dame; Jerry Domerschick, CCNY; Ron Weisner, Wisconsin.

MINNEAPOLIS   Ed Kalafat, Minnesota; Al Bianchi, Bowling Green; Don Lance, Rice; Gene Schwinger, Rice; Buzz Bennett, Minnesota; Nick Revon, Mississippi Southern; Dan Finch, Vanderbilt; Bob Hopkins, Pasadena; Dick Garmaker, Minnesota; John Blever, Northwestern.

NEW YORK   Jack Turner, Western Kentucky; Richie Guerin, Iona; Don Anielak, Southwest Missouri; Don Lange, Navy; Jesse Priscock, Kansas State; Ron Rivers, Wyoming; Solly Walker, St. John's (N.Y.); Cob Jarvis, Mississippi State; Henry Duckham, Brooklyn Poly; John Clune, Navy; Bob Walter, Oklahoma; Bill Stickel, Hastings.

PHILADELPHIA   Gene Shue, Maryland; Larry Costello, Niagara; Ben Peters, St. Benedict; Chuck Noble, Louisville; Rudy D'Emilio, Duke; Len Winograd, Brandeis; Bob Brady, San Diego State; Bob Hodges, East Carolina; Vince Leta, Lycoming; Bill Sullivan, Notre Dame; Frank O'Hara, LaSalle; John Glinski; John Holup, George Washington.

ROCHESTER   Tom Marshall, Western Kentucky; Boris Nachamkin, NYU; Lee Morton, Cornell; Art Spoelstra, Western Kentucky; Bo Erias, Niagara; Jim Davis, St. John's (N.Y.); Bill Hull, Utah State; Paul Morrow, Wisconsin; Roy Irvin, Southern California; Ed Parchinski, Fordham; John Paxson, Dayton.

SYRACUSE   John Kerr, Illinois; Dick Farley, Indiana; Jim Tucker, Duquesne; Don McLane, Duquesne; Paul Pottenburgh, Siena; Norman Pott, Wheaton; Gus Levett, Franklin & Marshall; Mel Besdin, Syracuse; Fletcher Johnson, Duquesne; Jack Davidson, UCLA.

1955

BOSTON   Jim Ahearn, Connecticut; Mark Davis, Marietta; Henry Dooley, Wiley; Carl Hartman, Alderson-Broaddus; Dick Hemric, Wake Forest; Bart Leach, Pennsylvania; Jim Loscutoff, Oregon; John Mahoney, William & Mary; John Moore, UCLA; Bob Patterson, Tulsa; Dean Parsons, Washington; Nick Romanoff, College of Pacific; Bob Scuddelari, Cooper Union; Buzz Wilkinson, Virginia.

FORT WAYNE   Jesse Arnelle, Penn State; Don Belcher, LSU; Ron Bennink, Washington State; Tom Harrold, Colorado; John Horan, Dayton; Dick Howard, Western Reserve; Cleo Littleton, Wichita State; Happy Mahfouz, Spring Hill; Tom Mock, Colorado; Tom Mixon, Mercer; Bob Reiter, Missouri; Ray Warren, TCU.

MILWAUKEE   Harvey Babetch, Bradley; Dick Cable, Wisconsin; Lynn Cole, Creighton; Al Ferrari, Michigan State; Joe Fitt; Burdette Haldorson, Colorado; Charles Hoxie, Niagara; Ed

O'Connor, Manhattan; Bill Reigel, McNeese; Dick Ricketts, Duquesne; Jack Stephens, Notre Dame; Dick Welsh, Southern California.

MINNEAPOLIS Bill Banks, Southwest Texas; Don Boldebuck, Houston; Dick Boushka, St. Louis; Don Bragg, UCLA; Dick Garmaker, Minnesota; K. C. Jones, San Francisco; Chuck Mencel, Minnesota; John Miller, Ohio State; Jim Scott, West Texas; Bill Warden, North Central (Ill.); O'Neal Weaver, Midwestern (Tex.).

NEW YORK Joe Beck, Northwest Missouri; Denver Brackeen, Mississippi; Ed Cole, Creighton; Joe Fay, St. Ambrose; Mickey Harrington, Southern Mississippi; Wally McCarvill, Iona; Jerry Mullen, San Francisco; Don Payne, Adelphi; Ken Sears, Santa Clara; Howard Sessums, Mississippi College; Guy Sparrow, Detroit; Charles Stickels, Hastings.

PHILADELPHIA Jack Devine, Villanova; Walt Devlin, George Washington; Al Didriksen, Temple; Tom Gola, LaSalle; Jerry Koch, St. Louis; Lester Lane, Oklahoma; Bob Schafer, Villanova; Harry Silcox, Temple; George Swyers, West Virginia Tech; Ed Wiener, Tennessee.

ROCHESTER Bob Armstrong, Michigan State; Bill Evans, Kentucky; Ed Fleming, Niagara; Harry Jorgensen, Wyoming; Jerry Jung, Kansas State; Jim McConnell, Niagara; Bob McKeen, California; John Prudhoe, Louisville; Art Quimby, Connecticut; Maurice Stokes, St. Francis (Pa.); Jack Twyman, Cincinnati; Tony Vlastelica, Oregon State.

SYRACUSE Ed Conlin, Fordham; Mal Duffy, St. Bonaventure; Frank Ehmann, Northwestern; Cliff Dwyer, North Carolina State; Ed Galvin, Loyola (La.); Stan Glowaski, Seattle; Russ Lawler, Stanford; Jack Sallee, Dayton; Don Schlundt, Indiana; Marty Satalino, St. John's (N.Y.); Ron Tomsic, Stanford.

1956 (APRIL 30, 1956)

TERRITORIAL CHOICE Boston—Tom Heinsohn, Holy Cross.

BOSTON K. C. Jones, San Francisco; George Linn, Alabama; Dan Swartz, Morehead State; Bill Logan, Iowa; Don Boldebuck, Houston; O'Neal Weaver, Midwestern (Tex.); Vic Molodet, North Carolina State; Jim Houston, Brandeis; Theophileus Lloyd, Maryland State.

FORT WAYNE Ron Sobieszczyk, DePaul; Bob Kessler, Maryland; Bill Thieben, Hofstra; Charles Slack, Marshall; Joe Lieber, Holy Cross; John Schlimm, John Carroll; Bruce Harris, Tennessee Poly.

MINNEAPOLIS Jim Paxson, Dayton; Terry Rand, Marquette; Jerry Bird, Kentucky; Lloyd Aubrey, Notre Dame; Bill Reigel, McNeese State; Phil Jordon, Whitworth; John Barber, Los Angeles State; Sam Jones, North Carolina College; Jim Springer, Gustavus Adolphus; Phil Grawmeyer, Kentucky; Robert Hodgson, Wichita; Carl Widseth, Tennessee; John Patzwald, Gustavus Adolphus; Elgin Baylor, Seattle.

NEW YORK Ronnie Shavlik, North Carolina State; Gary Bergen, Utah; Jerry Harper, Alabama; Ronnie Mayer, Duke; Joe Sexton, Purdue; Pat Dunn, Utah State; Jack Adams, Eastern Kentucky; Art Bunte, Utah; Dick Miller, Wisconsin; Howard Crittendon, Murray State Teachers; Dick Miani, Miami; Ed Petrie, Seton Hall; Tony Roybal, New Mexico.

PHILADELPHIA Hal Lear, Temple; Phil Rollins, Louisville; Bevo Francis, Rio Grande; Phil Wheeler, Cincinnati; Joe Belmont, Duke; Mickey Winograd, Duquesne; John Fannon, Notre Dame; Max Anderson, Oregon; Ronald Clark, Springfield.

ROCHESTER Si Green, Duquesne; Bob Burrow, Kentucky; Dave Piontek, Xavier (Ohio); John McCarthy, Canisius; Bill Uhl, Dayton; Kevin Thomas, Boston; Carl Cain, Iowa; Clayton Carter, Oklahoma A&M; Dan Mannix, St. Francis (N.Y.); Jerry Moreman, Louisville; Gene Carpenter, Texas Tech.

ST. LOUIS Bill Russell, San Francisco (traded to Boston); Willie Naulls, UCLA; Darrell Floyd, Furman; Robin Freeman, Ohio State; Norman Stewart, Missouri; Dave Plunkett, Cincinnati; Julius McCoy, Michigan State; Morris Taft, UCLA; Jim Reed, Texas Tech; Hershel Pederson, Brigham Young; Wally Choice, Indiana; Ed Huse, Wyoming; Arthur Helms, Houston; Junior Morgan, Duke.

SYRACUSE Joe Holup, George Washington; Paul Judson, Illinois; Forest Able, Western Kentucky; Wade Halbrook, Oregon State; Jim Ray, Toledo; Jim McLaughlin, St. Louis; Jess Roh, Idaho State; Chester Webb, Georgia State Teachers; Dick Julio, New Bedford State; Bob Hopkins, Grambling; Willie Bergines, West Virginia; Dick Kenyon, LeMoyne; Milt Graham, Colgate; Chuck Rolles, Cornell.

1957 (APRIL 17, 1957)

FIRST ROUND Cincinnati—Rod Hundley, West Virginia; Detroit—Charles Tyra, Louisville; Minneapolis—Jim Krebs, SMU; St. Louis—Win Wilfong, Memphis State; New York—Brendan McCann, St. Bonaventure; Philadelphia—Len Rosenbluth, North Carolina; Syracuse—George BonSalle, Illinois; Boston—Sam Jones, North Carolina Central.

SECOND ROUND Cincinnati—Dick Duckett, St. John's; Detroit—Bob McCoy, Grambling; Minneapolis—Harvey Schmidt, Illinois; St. Louis—Jim Palmer, Dayton; New York—Larry Friend, California; Philadelphia—Jack Sullivan, Mount St. Mary's; Syracuse—Jim Morgan, Louisville; Boston—Dick O'Neal, TCU.

THIRD ROUND Cincinnati—Jerry Paulson, Manhattan; Detroit—Bill Ebben, Detroit; Minneapolis—Jim Spivey, Southeast Oklahoma; St. Louis—John Smyth, Notre Dame; New York—Gary Clark, Syracuse; Philadelphia—Angelo Lombardo, Manhattan; Syracuse—Vince Cohen, Syracuse; Boston—Chuck Schramm, Western Illinois.

FOURTH ROUND Cincinnati—Jed Dormeyer, Minnesota; Detroit—Kurt Englebert, St. Joseph's (Pa.); Minneapolis—George Brown, Wayne State; St. Louis—Hank Nowak, Canisius; New York—Rayford Wells, Lenoir Rhyne; Philadelphia—Ray Radziszewski, St. Joseph's (Pa.); Syracuse—Jerry Mallett, Baylor; Boston—Jim Ashmore, Mississippi State.

FIFTH ROUND Cincinnati—Stewart Murray, Lafayette; Detroit—Ron Kramer, Michigan; Minneapolis—Gary Thompson, Iowa State; St. Louis—Al Rochelle, Vanderbilt; New York—Lee Marshall, Washington & Lee; Philadelphia—Jim Radcliffe, Lafayette; Syracuse—Frank Nimmo, Cincinnati; Boston—Grady Wallace, South Carolina.

SIXTH ROUND Cincinnati—John Maglio, North Carolina State; Detroit—Walt Adamushko, St. Francis (N.Y.); Minneapolis—Phil Murrell, Drake; St. Louis—Raymond Downs, Texas; New York—Jim Humphreys, St. Michael's; Philadelphia—Alonzo Lewis, LaSalle; Syracuse—Lyndon Lee, Oklahoma City; Boston—Maurice King, Kansas.

SEVENTH ROUND Cincinnati—Chet Forte, Columbia; Detroit—Carl Boldt, San Francisco; Minneapolis—George Ferguson, Michigan; St. Louis—Mason Pope, Kentucky Wesleyan; Philadelphia—Max Jameson, Kentucky State; Syracuse—Dick Gaines, Seton Hall; Boston—Dick Brott, Denver.

EIGHTH ROUND Cincinnati—Bob Daniels, Western Kentucky; Detroit—Doug Bolstorff, Minnesota; Minneapolis—John Haaven, North Dakota; St. Louis—Bill Darragh, Louisville; Philadelphia—Woody Sauldsberry, Texas Southern; Syracuse—Cebe Prince, Marshall; Boston—Bill Von Weyhe, Rhode Island.

NINTH ROUND Cincinnati—Dick Heise, DePaul; Detroit—Bob Lazor, Pittsburgh; Minneapolis—Jim Sutton, North Dakota State; St. Louis—Calvin Grosscup, Tulane; Philadelphia—Steve Hamilton, Morehead State; Syracuse—Jim Brown, Syracuse; Boston—Joe Gibbon, Mississippi.

TENTH ROUND Cincinnati—Mel Wright, Oklahoma A&M; Minneapolis—Gordon Fosness, Dakota Wesleyan; St. Louis—Bobby Mills, SMU; Philadelphia—Jerry Calvert, Kentucky; Syracuse—Jack Nichols, Colgate; Boston—Jack Butcher, Memphis State.

ELEVENTH ROUND Cincinnati—Cliff Hafer, North Carolina State; St. Louis—Gerald Dreier, Macalaster; Boston—Dick Neal, Indiana.

TWELFTH ROUND Cincinnati—Jim Boothe, Xavier (Ohio); St. Louis—Bob Seitz, North Carolina State; Syracuse—Jim Weeks, New York Tech.

THIRTEENTH ROUND St. Louis—Ed Romanoff.

FOURTEENTH ROUND St. Louis—Lavelle Langston, Northwestern State.

SUPPLEMENTAL PICKS Philadelphia—Jerry Gibson; Boston—Dan Tobin, Florida Southern.

1958

FIRST ROUND Minneapolis—Elgin Baylor, Seattle; Cincinnati—Archie Dees, Indiana; New York (from Detroit)—Mike Farmer, San Francisco; New York—Pete Brennan, North Carolina; Philadelphia—Guy Rodgers, Temple; Syracuse—Connie Dierking, Cincinnati; St. Louis—Dave Gambee, Oregon State; Boston—Ben Swain, Texas Southern.

SECOND ROUND Minneapolis—Steve Hamilton, Morehead State; Cincinnati—Vern Hatton, Kentucky; Detroit—Barney Cable, Bradley; New York—Joe Quigg, North Carolina; Philadelphia—Lamar Sharrar, West Virginia; Syracuse—Hal Greer, Marshall; Boston—Jimmy Smith, Steubenville.

THIRD ROUND Minneapolis—Alex Ellis, Niagara; Cincinnati—Arlen Bockhorn, Dayton; Detroit—Roy DeWitz, Kansas State; New York—John Lee, Yale; Philadelphia—Frank Howard, Ohio State; Syracuse—John Nacincik, Maryland; St. Louis—Hub Reed, Oklahoma City; Boston—Jim Cunningham, Fordham.

FOURTH ROUND Minneapolis—George Kline, Minnesota; Cincinnati—Phil Murrell, Drake; Detroit—Ralph Croswaite, Western Kentucky; New York—John Cox, Kentucky; Philadelphia—Temple Tucker, Rice; Syracuse—Tommy Kearns, North Carolina; St. Louis—Wayne Embry, Miami (Ohio); Boston—Don Flora, Washington & Lee.

FIFTH ROUND Minneapolis—Quitman Sullins, Murray State; Cincinnati—Jim Fulmer, Alabama; Detroit—Hank Morano, St. Peter's; New York—Don Lane, Dayton; Philadelphia—Don Ohl, Illinois; Syracuse—Fred Grim, Arkansas; St. Louis—Julius Peques, Pittsburgh; Boston—Gene Brown, San Francisco.

SIXTH ROUND Minneapolis—Al Inniss, St. Francis (N.Y.); Cincinnati—Jim McClennan, St. Francis (Pa.); Detroit—Shellie McMillon, Bradley; New York—Joe King, Oklahoma; Philadelphia—Bucky Allen, Duke; Syracuse—Jack Mimlitz, St. Louis; St. Louis—Rick Herrscher, SMU; Boston—Dave Keleher, Morehead State.

SEVENTH ROUND Minneapolis—Jim Bond, Pasadena; Cincinnati—Wayne Stevens, Cincinnati; Detroit—Ed Blair, Western Michigan; New York—Owen Lawson, Western Kentucky; Philadelphia—Jay Norman, Temple; Syracuse—Pete Tillotson, Michigan; St. Louis—John Crawford, Iowa State; Boston—Rudy Fenderson, Brandeis.

EIGHTH ROUND Minneapolis—Ed Brinkley, Clemson; Cincinnati—Bob Mantz, Lafayette; Detroit—Jack Quiggle, Michigan State; New York—Milt Kane, Utah; Philadelphia—Tom Brennan, Villanova; Syracuse—Ruel Tucker, Rockhurst; St. Louis—Ken Sidle, Ohio State.

NINTH ROUND Minneapolis—Joe Hobbs, Florida; Cincinnati—Larry Staverman, Villa Madonna; Detroit—Harry Marske, North Dakota State; New York—John McCarthy, Notre Dame; Philadelphia—Nick Davis, Maryland; St. Louis—Bruno Boin, Washington.

TENTH ROUND Minneapolis—Shorty Patterson, Gustavus Adolphus; Cincinnati—Jack Parr, Kansas State; Detroit—Pete Gaudin, Loyola (La.); Philadelphia—Larry Hedden, Michigan State; St. Louis—Tink Van Patton, Temple.

ELEVENTH ROUND Minneapolis—Hal Duffy, Oregon; Cincinnati—Frank Tartaton, Xavier (Ohio); Detroit—Herb Merritt, Tennessee Tech; St. Louis—James Purcell, Coe.

TWELFTH ROUND Minneapolis—Gary Simmons, Idaho; Cincinnati—Don Medsker, Iowa State; Detroit—Jim Dew, Alabama State; St. Louis—Don Klein, Rockhurst.

THIRTEENTH ROUND Minneapolis—Jerry Alcorn, Fresno State; Cincinnati—Jerry DuPont, Louisville; St. Louis—Joe Buckhalter, Tennessee A&I.

FOURTEENTH ROUND Cincinnati—Jim Newcomb, Duke.

FIFTEENTH ROUND Cincinnati—Bill Smith, Kentucky.

SIXTEENTH ROUND Cincinnati—Jack McCarthy, Dayton.

SEVENTEENTH ROUND Cincinnati—John Powell, Miami (Ohio).

1959

TERRITORIAL CHOICES Philadelphia—Wilt Chamberlain, Kansas (Overbrook HS, Pa.); St. Louis—Bob Ferry, St. Louis.

FIRST ROUND Cincinnati—Bob Boozer, Kansas State; Detroit—Bailey Howell, Mississippi State; Minneapolis—Tom Hawkins, Notre Dame; Syracuse—Dick Barnett, Tennessee State; New York—Johnny Green, Michigan State; Boston—John Richter, North Carolina State.

SECOND ROUND Detroit (from Cincinnati)—Tom Robitaille, Rice; Detroit—Don Goldstein, Louisville; Philadelphia—Joe Ruklick, Northwestern; Minneapolis—Rudy LaRusso, Dartmouth; Syracuse—Gene Tormohlen, Tennessee; St. Louis (from New York)—Alan Seiden, St. John's; St. Louis—Cal Ramsey, NYU; Boston—Gene Guarilla, George Washington.

THIRD ROUND Cincinnati—Mike Mendenhall, Cincinnati; Detroit—Gary Alcorn, Fresno State; Philadelphia—Jim Hockaday, Memphis State; Minneapolis—Bob Smith, West Virginia; Syracuse—Jon Cincebox, Syracuse; New York—Bob Anderegg, Michigan State; St. Louis—Hank Stein, Xavier (Ohio); Boston—Ralph Croswaite, Western Kentucky.

FOURTH ROUND Cincinnati—Leo Byrd, Marshall; Detroit—George Lee, Michigan; Philadelphia—Ron Stevenson, TCU; Minneapolis—Wilson Eison, Purdue; Syracuse—Paul Neumann, Stanford; New York—John Cox, Kentucky; St. Louis—Lee Harman, Oregon State; Boston—Ed Kazakavich, Stanford.

FIFTH ROUND Cincinnati—Harry Kirchner, TCU; Detroit—Tony Windis, Wyoming; Philadelphia—Bill Telasky, George Washington; Minneapolis—Bobby Joe Mason, Bradley; Syracuse—Roger Taylor, Illinois; New York—Herb Busch, Virginia; St. Louis—Nick Mantis, Northwestern; Boston—Don Lange, William & Mary.

SIXTH ROUND Cincinnati—Don Hennon, Pittsburgh; Detroit—Lou Jordan, Cornell; Philadelphia—Joe Spratt, St. Joseph's (Pa.); Minneapolis—Jim Henry, Vanderbilt; Syracuse—Bob Dalton, California; New York—Bucky McDonald, George Washington; St. Louis—Mike Moran, Marquette; Boston—Bob Cumings, Boston U.

SEVENTH ROUND Cincinnati—Dale Moore, Eastern Kentucky; Detroit—Doug Smart, Washington; Philadelphia—Joe Ryan, Villanova; Minneapolis—Charley Grote, Georgetown (Ky.); Syracuse—Darnell Haney, Navy; New York—Russ Robinson, Southwest Missouri; St. Louis—Orby Arnold, Memphis State.

EIGHTH ROUND Cincinnati—Don Matuszak, Kansas State; Detroit—Chuck Curtis, Pacific Lutheran; Philadelphia—Dave Gunther, Iowa; Minneapolis—Leon Hill, Texas Tech; New York—Walt Torrence, UCLA; St. Louis—Willie Merriweather, Purdue.

NINTH ROUND Cincinnati—Joe Billy McDade, Bradley; Detroit—Doyle Edmiston, Hardin-Simmons; Philadelphia—Carl Belz, Princeton; Minneapolis—Jim Mudd, North Texas State; New York—Jerry Shipp, Southeast Oklahoma; St. Louis—Lou Pucillo, North Carolina State.

TENTH ROUND Cincinnati—Joe Viviano, Xavier (Ohio); Detroit—Bruno Boin, Washington; Philadelphia—Tony Sellari, Lenoir Rhyne; Minneapolis—Roger Johnson, Minnesota; New York—Paul Wilcox, Davis & Elkins; St. Louis—Ron Loneski, Kansas.

ELEVENTH ROUND Cincinnati—Charley Brown, Seattle; Detroit—M. C. Burton, Michigan; Philadelphia—Phil Warren, Northwestern; Minneapolis—Jack Evans, Superior State; New York—Paul Benes, Hope; St. Louis—John Barnhill, Tennessee State.

TWELFTH ROUND Cincinnati—Roger Wendel, Tulsa; Minneapolis—Vern Baggenstoss, St. Cloud State; New York—Ed Blair, Western Michigan.

THIRTEENTH ROUND Minneapolis—Dwayne Smith, Gustavus Adolphus; New York—John Nicoll, Brigham Young.

FOURTEENTH ROUND New York—Jack Israel, Southwest Missouri.

1960

TERRITORIAL CHOICE Cincinnati—Oscar Robertson, Cincinnati.

FIRST ROUND Minneapolis—Jerry West, West Virginia; New York—Darrall Imhoff, California; Detroit—Jack Moreland, Louisiana Tech; Syracuse—Lee Shaffer, North Carolina; St. Louis—Lenny Wilkens, Providence; Philadelphia—Al Bunge, Maryland; Boston—Tom Sanders, NYU.

SECOND ROUND Cincinnati—Jay Arnette, Texas; New York (from Minneapolis)—Dave Budd, Wake Forest; New York—Kelly Coleman, Kentucky Wesleyan; Detroit—Ron Johnson, Minnesota; Syracuse—Wilbur Trosch, St. Francis (Pa.); St. Louis—Frank Radovich, Indiana; Philadelphia—Bill Kennedy, Temple; Boston—Leroy Wright, College of Pacific.

THIRD ROUND Cincinnati—Ralph Davis, Cincinnati; Minneapolis—Jim Hagan, Tennessee Tech; New York—Bob McNeill, St. Joseph's (Pa.); Detroit—Frank Case, Dayton; Syracuse—Joe Roberts, Ohio State; St. Louis—Fred LaCour, San Francisco; Philadelphia—Bob Mealy, Manhattan; Boston—Mike Graney, Notre Dame.

FOURTH ROUND Cincinnati—Dalen Showalter, Tennessee; Minneapolis—Wally Frank, Kansas State; Minneapolis (from New York)—Ben Warley, Tennessee A&I; Detroit—Ken Remley, West Virginia Wesleyan; Syracuse—Carl Cole, Eastern Kentucky; St. Louis—Horace Walker, Michigan State; Philadelphia—Charley Sharp, Southwest Texas; Boston—Sid Cohen, Kentucky.

FIFTH ROUND Cincinnati—Don Ogorek, Seattle; Minneapolis—George Farley, Cornell; New York—Charley McNeil, Maryland; Detroit—Willie Jones, Northwestern; Syracuse—Jim Mudd, North Texas State; St. Louis—Jim Darrow, Bowling Green; Philadelphia—Al Attles, North Carolina A&T; Boston—Wayne Lawrence, Texas A&M.

SIXTH ROUND Cincinnati—Bobby Joe Mason, Bradley; Minneapolis—Bobby Goodall, Tulsa; New York—David Denton, Georgia Tech; Detroit—Bill Lowery, Christian Brothers; Syracuse—Herschell Turner, Nebraska; St. Louis—York Larese, North Carolina; Philadelphia—Jim Brangan, Princeton; Boston—George Newman, Kentucky.

SEVENTH ROUND Cincinnati—Fred Sobrero, Santa Clara; Minneapolis—Howard Jolliff, Ohio; New York—Dick Doughty, California; Detroit—Doug Moe, North Carolina; Syracuse—Bernie Kauffman, Kentucky; St. Louis—Bob Sims, Pepperdine; Philadelphia—Bob Clarke, St. Joseph's (Pa.).

EIGHTH ROUND Cincinnati—Sam Stith, St. Bonaventure; Minneapolis—John Werhas, Southern California; New York—George Price, Memphis State; Detroit—Mike Yugovich, Youngstown; Syracuse—Don Lynch, LeMoyne; St. Louis—Don Curry, Mississippi Southern; Philadelphia—George Raveling, Villanova.

NINTH ROUND Cincinnati—Al Nealey, Arizona State; Minneapolis—Claude Lefevre, Gonzaga; New York—Tony Davis, Hawaii; Detroit—Martin Holland, Kentucky Wesleyan; Syracuse—Bernie Findlay, San Diego State; St. Louis—Bob Castanada, Rockhurst; Philadelphia—Joe Gallo, St. Joseph's.

TENTH ROUND Cincinnati—Lon Sizemore, West Virginia Tech; Minneapolis—Dick Harvey, Creighton; New York—Walter Mangham, Marquette; Detroit—Joe Kennelly, Dayton; St. Louis—Americas John-Lewis, Iowa.

ELEVENTH ROUND Cincinnati—Dennis Boone, Regis; Minneapolis—Sterling Forbes, Pepperdine; New York—Howard Willis, Grambling; Detroit—Mel Peterson, Wheaton; St. Louis—Dick Davies, Louisiana St.

TWELFTH ROUND Cincinnati—Ron Altenberg, Cornell (Iowa); Minneapolis—Will Jones, American; New York—Henry Hart, Auburn; Detroit—Don Dobbert, Wheaton; St. Louis—Bob Wilkinson, Indiana.

THIRTEENTH ROUND Cincinnati—John Milhoan, Marshall; New York—Dick Furry, Ohio State; Detroit—Lee Hopfenspirger, Hamline; St. Louis—Ed Smallwood, Evansville.

FOURTEENTH ROUND Cincinnati—Larry Chaney, Montana State; New York—Jim Hanna, Southern California.

FIFTEENTH ROUND Cincinnati—Ducky Potter, Moravian; New York—Jerry Bechtal, Maryland.

SIXTEENTH ROUND Cincinnati—Gene Jordan, Northwest Missouri; New York—Jerry Schofield, Utah State.

SEVENTEENTH ROUND Cincinnati—Ernie McCray, Arizona; New York—Tandy Gillis, California.

EIGHTEENTH ROUND Cincinnati—Don Mills, Kentucky; New York—George Krajack, Clemson.

NINETEENTH ROUND Cincinnati—Larry Willey, Cincinnati.

TWENTIETH ROUND Cincinnati—Tony Wilcox, Wittenberg.

TWENTY-FIRST ROUND Cincinnati—Jim McDonald, West Virginia Wesleyan.

1961

FIRST ROUND Chicago—Walt Bellamy, Indiana; New York—Tom Stith, St. Bonaventure; Cincinnati—Larry Siegfried, Ohio State; Detroit—Ray Scott, Portland; Los Angeles—Wayne Yates, Memphis State; Syracuse—Ben Warley, Tennessee A&I; Philadelphia—Tom Meschery, St. Mary's (Cal.); St. Louis—Cleo Hill, Winston-Salem; Boston—Gary Phillips, Houston.

SECOND ROUND New York—Whitey Martin, St. Bonaventure; Cincinnati—Bob Wiesenhahn, Cincinnati; Detroit—Johnny Egan, Providence; Los Angeles—Fred Sawyer, Louisville; Syracuse—Chris Smith, Virginia Tech; Philadelphia—Ted Luckenbill, Houston; St. Louis—Ron Horn, Indiana; Boston—Al Butler, Niagara; Chicago—John Turner, Louisville; Chicago—Jerry Graves, Mississippi State; Chicago—York Larese, North Carolina; Chicago—Don Kojis, Marquette; Chicago—Doug Moe, North Carolina; Chicago—Jeff Cohen, William & Mary.

THIRD ROUND New York—Tony Jackson, St. John's; Cincinnati—Bob Nordmann, St. Louis; Detroit—Doug Kistler, Duke; Los Angeles—Frank Burgess, Gonzaga; Syracuse—Charles Osborne, Western Kentucky; Philadelphia—Jack Egan, St. Joseph's (Pa.); St. Louis—Tom Chilton, East Tennessee; Boston—Bill Depp, Vanderbilt; Chicago—Bill Bridges, Kansas.

FOURTH ROUND New York—George Blaney, Holy Cross; Cincinnati—Lowery Kirk, Memphis State; Detroit—George Finley, Tennessee A&I; Los Angeles—Charles Henke, Missouri; Syracuse—Henry Whitney, Iowa State; Philadelphia—John Tidwell, Michigan; St. Louis—Gus Guydon, Drake; Boston—Carl Cole, Eastern Kentucky; Chicago—Roger Kaiser, Georgia Tech.

FIFTH ROUND New York—Bill Smith, St. Peter's; Cincinnati—Rossie Johnson, Tennessee A&I; Detroit—Dan Doyle, Belmont Abbey; Los Angeles—Bill Lickert, Kentucky; Syracuse—Don Jacobson, South Dakota; Philadelphia—Bruce Spraggins, Virginia Union; St. Louis—John Berberich, UCLA; Boston—Bob DiStefano, North Carolina State; Chicago—Howie Carl, DePaul.

SIXTH ROUND New York—Cleveland Buckner, Jackson State; Cincinnati—Bob Slobodnik, Duquesne; Detroit—Lee Patrone, West Virginia; Los Angeles—Bill McClintock, California; Syracuse—Billy Joe Price, New Mexico State; Philadelphia—Dick Goldberg, Mississippi Southern; St. Louis—Bob McDonald, Maryland; Boston—Ned Twyman, Duquesne; Chicago—Dave Voss, Tulsa.

SEVENTH ROUND New York—Donnis Butcher, Pikeville; Cincinnati—Dave Zeller, Miami (Ohio); Detroit—Burt Price, Wittenberg; Los Angeles—Albert Alamanza, Texas; Syracuse—Roger Newman, Kentucky; Philadelphia—Charles McNeil, Maryland; St. Louis—Charles Riley, Winston-Salem; Boston—Mel Klein, Aberdeen; Chicago—Ron Heller, Wichita.

EIGHTH ROUND New York—Cedrick Price, Kansas State; Cincinnati—Jerry Thelen, Villa Madonna; Detroit—Walter Ward, Hampton Institute; Los Angeles—Bill Ellis, UCLA; Syracuse—Dave Mills, Seattle; Philadelphia—Larry Swift, Northeast Missouri State; St. Louis—Gene Velloff, Doane; Chicago—John Wessels, Illinois.

NINTH ROUND New York—Charles Bowman, Wabash; Cincinnati—Larry Krueger, Ohio; Detroit—Peter Baltic, Penn State; Los Angeles—Carl Anderson, Oregon State; Syracuse—Rex Tippitt, Grambling; St. Louis—Herbert Gray, North Carolina A&T; Chicago—Steve Strange, SMU.

TENTH ROUND New York—Ron Debillous, Wisconsin State Teachers; Cincinnati—Jack Waters, Mississippi; Detroit—Wayne Monson, Northern Michigan; Los Angeles—Robert Williams, Hancock; Syracuse—Pete Chudy, Syracuse; Philadelphia—Leo Hill, Los Angeles State; St. Louis—Tom Faszholz, Concordia (Mo.); Chicago—Larry Comley, Kansas State.

ELEVENTH ROUND New York—Kevin Loughery, St. John's; Cincinnati—Carl Short, Newberry; Detroit—Richard Kraft, Brockport; Los Angeles—Howard Hurt, Duke; Syracuse—Dick Sammons, LeMoyne; Philadelphia—Corky Whitrow, Georgetown (Ky.); St. Louis—Dick Kepley, North Carolina.

TWELFTH ROUND New York—Earl Shultz, California; Cincinnati—George Patterson, Toledo; St. Louis—Jackie Crawford, Centenary.

THIRTEENTH ROUND New York—Ned Jennings, Kentucky; Cincinnati—Clair McRoberts, Monmouth; St. Louis—Howard Stacy, Louisville.

FOURTEENTH ROUND New York—Bill Engressor, LSU; Cincinnati—Carl Bouldin, Cincinnati.

FIFTEENTH ROUND New York—Vince Kempton, St. Joseph's (Pa.).

1962

TERRITORIAL CHOICES Detroit—Dave DeBusschere, Detroit; Cincinnati—Jerry Lucas, Ohio State.

FIRST ROUND Chicago—Bill McGill, Utah; New York—Paul Hogue, Cincinnati; St. Louis—Zelmo Beaty, Prairie View; Syracuse—Len Chappell, Wake Forest; Philadelphia—Wayne Hightower, Kansas; Los Angeles—Leroy Ellis, St. John's; Boston—John Havlicek, Ohio State.

SECOND ROUND Chicago—Terry Dischinger, Purdue; New York—John Rudometkin, Southern California; St. Louis—Bob Duffy, Colgate; Detroit—Kevin Loughery, St. John's; Syracuse—Chet Walker, Bradley; Cincinnati—Bud Olsen, Louisville; Philadelphia—Hubie White, Villanova; Los Angeles—Gene Wiley, Wichita State; Boston—Jack Foley, Holy Cross.

THIRD ROUND Chicago—Don Nelson, Iowa; New York—Bobby Rascoe, Western Kentucky; St. Louis—Charles Hardnett, Grambling; Detroit—Harold Hudgens, Texas Tech; Syracuse—Porter Meriwether, Tennessee State; Cincinnati—Chris Appel, Southern California; Philadelphia—Dave Fedor, Florida State; Los Angeles—John Green, UCLA; Boston—Jim Hadnot, Providence.

FOURTH ROUND St. Louis (from Chicago)—Charles Vaughn, Southern Illinois; New York—Cliff Luyk, Florida; St. Louis—Jerry Grote, Loyola (Cal.); Detroit—Reggie Harding, Detroit Eastern H.S.; Syracuse—Bob McCully, St. Bonaventure; Cincinnati—Jack Thobe, Xavier (Ohio); Philadelphia—Garry Roggenburk, Dayton; Los Angeles—Jan Loudermilk, SMU; Boston—Roger Strickland, Jacksonville.

FIFTH ROUND Chicago—Cornell Green, Utah State; New York—Bob Burgess, Marshall; St. Louis—Tom Hatton, Dayton; Detroit—Lindbergh Moody, South Carolina; Syracuse—John Windsor, Stanford; Cincinnati—Mike Wroblewski, Kansas State; Philadelphia—Jack Jackson, Virginia Union; Los Angeles—Art Whisnant, South Carolina; Boston—Gary Daniels, Citadel.

SIXTH ROUND Chicago—Bill Hanson, Washington; New York—Ken Stanley, Pacific; St. Louis—Jay Carty, Oregon State; Detroit—Ed Noe, Morehead State; Syracuse—Larry Van Eman, Wichita State; Cincinnati—Jerry Foster, Drake; Philadelphia—Jim Hudock, North Carolina; Los Angeles—Bucky Keller, Virginia Tech; Boston—Jim Hooley, Boston College.

SEVENTH ROUND Chicago—Jack Ardon, Tulane; New York—Richie Swartz, Hofstra; St. Louis—Bob McAteer, LaSalle; Detroit—John Bradley, Lawrence Tech; Syracuse—Bob Sharpenter, Georgetown; Cincinnati—Gary Cunningham, UCLA; Philadelphia—Howard Montgomery, Pan American; Boston—Clyde Arnold, Duquesne.

EIGHTH ROUND Chicago—Larry Pursiful, Kentucky; New York—Warren Fouts, Oklahoma; St. Louis—Terry Ball, Washington State; Detroit—Mike Rice, Duquesne; Syracuse—Jerry Harkness, Loyola (Ill.); Cincinnati—Ed Bento, Loyola (Cal.); Philadelphia—Bill Kirvin, Xavier (Ohio); Los Angeles—Bill Garner, Portland; Boston—Chuck Chevalier, Boston College.

NINTH ROUND Chicago—Carroll Broussard, Texas A&M; New York—Paul Benec, Duquesne; St. Louis—Marvin Trotman, Elizabeth City; Detroit—Bill Nelson, Hamline; Syracuse—Vince Brewer, Iowa State; Cincinnati—Chris Jones, Carson-Newman; Philadelphia—Tom Kiefer, St. Louis; Los Angeles—Bill Matson, Minnesota; Boston—Mike Cingiser, Brown.

TENTH ROUND　Chicago—Pete Campbell, Princeton; New York—Ralph Richardson, Eastern Kentucky; St. Louis—Charlie Sells, Washington State; Detroit—Glenn Moore, Oregon; Cincinnati—George Knighton, New Mexico State; Philadelphia—Ken McComb, North Carolina.

ELEVENTH ROUND　Chicago—Jeff Slade, Kenyon; New York—Ed Mazria, Pratt; St. Louis—Tom Chappelle, Maine; Cincinnati—Frank Pinchback, Xavier (Ohio); Philadelphia—Donnie Walsh, North Carolina.

TWELFTH ROUND　Chicago—Mel Nowell, Ohio State; St. Louis—John Caveny, LeMoyne; Philadelphia—Charles Warren, Oregon.

THIRTEENTH ROUND　Chicago—Tom Kennedy, Lewis; St. Louis—Jerry Carlton, Arkansas.

FOURTEENTH ROUND　Chicago—Bob Mahland, Williams; St. Louis—Wilky Gilmore, Colorado.

FIFTEENTH ROUND　Chicago—Pat McKenzie, Kansas State; St. Louis—Dave Ricerto, Rhode Island.

SIXTEENTH ROUND　Chicago—Norman Majors, Rockhurst (Mo.); St. Louis—Wally Roundsville, California Tech.

1963

TERRITORIAL CHOICE　Cincinnati—Tom Thacker, Cincinnati.

FIRST ROUND　New York—Art Heyman, Duke; Baltimore—Rod Thorn, West Virginia; San Francisco—Nate Thurmond, Bowling Green; Detroit—Ed Miles, Seattle; St. Louis—Gerry Ward, Boston College; Syracuse—Tom Hoover, Villanova; Los Angeles—Roger Strickland, Jacksonville; Boston—Bill Green, Colorado State.

SECOND ROUND　New York—Jerry Harkness, Loyola (Ill.); Baltimore—Gus Johnson, Idaho; San Francisco—Gary Hill, Oklahoma City; Detroit—Jerry Smith, Furman; Los Angeles (from Cincinnati)—Jim King, Tulsa; St. Louis—Leland Mitchell, Mississippi State; Syracuse—Hershell West, Grambling; Los Angeles—Mel Gibson, Western Carolina; St. Louis (from Boston)—Ken Saylors, Arkansas Tech.

THIRD ROUND　New York—Bill O'Connor, Canisius; Baltimore—Tom Bolyard, Indiana; San Francisco—Steve Gray, St. Mary's (Cal.); Detroit—Mike McCoy, Miami; Cincinnati—Jimmy Rayl, Indiana; St. Louis—Bill Burwell, Illinois; Syracuse—Jerry Greenspan, Maryland; Los Angeles—Lyle Harger, Houston; Boston—Chuck Kriston, Valparaiso.

FOURTH ROUND　New York—Nate Cloud, Delaware; Baltimore—Nolen Ellison, Kansas; San Francisco—Dave Downey, Illinois; Detroit—Dave Erickson, Marquette; Cincinnati—Ken Charlton, Colorado; St. Louis—Waite Bellamy, Florida A&M; Syracuse—Ray Flynn, Providence; Los Angeles—Layton Johns, Auburn; Boston—Connie McGuire, Southeast Oklahoma.

FIFTH ROUND　New York—Joe McDermott, Belmont Abbey; Baltimore—Ron Glaser, Marquette; San Francisco—Don Turner, Southwest Kansas; Detroit—Bill Small, Illinois; Cincinnati—Mac Herndon, Bradley; St. Louis—Tony Yates, Cincinnati; Syracuse—Tony Cerkvenik, Arizona State; Los Angeles—Larry Jones, Toledo; Boston—W. D. Stroud, Mississippi State.

SIXTH ROUND　New York—Jim Kerwin, Tulane; Baltimore—Ken Siebel, Wisconsin; San Francisco—Gene Shields, Santa Clara; Detroit—Reggie Harding, Detroit Eastern H.S.; Cincinnati—Jim McCormack, West Virginia; St. Louis—Al Santio, Maryland State; Syracuse—Vince Brewer, Iowa State; Los Angeles—Warren Salade, Westminster; Boston—Vinnie Ernst, Providence.

SEVENTH ROUND　New York—Bob Woollard, Wake Forest; Baltimore—Larry Brown, North Carolina; San Francisco—Don Clemetson, Stanford; Detroit—Ira Harge, New Mexico; Cincinnati—Hunter Beckman, Memphis State; St. Louis—Ken Rohloff, North Carolina State; Syracuse—Bill Brown, Howard Payne; Los Angeles—Gordie Martin, Southern California; Boston—Herb Magee, Philadelphia Textile.

EIGHTH ROUND　New York—Fred Crawford, St. Bonaventure; Baltimore—Dick Riesback, Iowa State; San Francisco—Harry Dinnel, Pepperdine; Detroit—Gary Silc, Northern Michigan; St. Louis—Harold Strothers, Texas A&M.

NINTH ROUND　New York—Ray Cronk, Lakeland; Baltimore—Ron Jackson, Wisconsin; San Francisco—Chuck White, Idaho; Detroit—Ernie Durston, Seattle; St. Louis—Frank Davis, Oklahoma Christian.

TENTH ROUND　New York—Gerald Glur, Furman; Baltimore—M. C. Thompson, DePaul; St. Louis—Carl Ritter, Southeast Missouri State.

ELEVENTH ROUND　New York—Orb Bowling, Tennessee; St. Louis—Marv Straw, Iowa State.

TWELFTH ROUND　New York—Bob Walters, Baldwin Wallace; St. Louis—Hugh Evans, North Carolina A&T.

THIRTEENTH ROUND　New York—Jerry Szachara, Cornell; St. Louis—Gary McFarland, Central Missouri State.

FOURTEENTH ROUND　New York—Bill Raftery, LaSalle.

FIFTEENTH ROUND　New York—Ron Pickett, Eastern Kentucky.

1964

TERRITORIAL CHOICES　Los Angeles—Walt Hazzard, UCLA; Cincinnati—George Wilson, Cincinnati.

FIRST ROUND　New York—Jim Barnes, Texas Western; Detroit—Joe Caldwell, Arizona State; Baltimore—Gary Bradds, Ohio State; Philadelphia—Lucious Jackson, Pan American; St. Louis—Jeff Mullins, Duke; San Francisco—Barry Kramer, NYU; Boston—Mel Counts, Oregon State.

SECOND ROUND　New York—Willis Reed, Grambling; Detroit—Les Hunter, Loyola (Ill.); St. Louis (from Baltimore)—Paul Silas, Creighton; Philadelphia—Ira Harge, New Mexico; Los Angeles—Cotton Nash, Kentucky; New York (from St. Louis)—Howard Komives, Bowling Green; San Francisco—Bud Koper, Oklahoma City; Cincinnati—Bill Chmielewski, Dayton; Boston—Ron Bonham, Cincinnati.

THIRD ROUND　New York—Brian Generalovich, Pittsburgh; Detroit—Wally Jones, Villanova; Baltimore—Jerry Sloan, Evansville; Philadelphia—Larry Jones, Toledo; Los Angeles—Tom Dose, Stanford; St. Louis—Art Becker, Arizona State; San Francisco—McCoy McLemore, Drake; Cincinnati—Steve Courtin, St. Joseph's (Pa.); Boston—John Thompson, Providence.

FOURTH ROUND　New York—Fred Crawford, St. Bonaventure; Detroit—Jim Davis, Colorado; Baltimore—Pete Spoden, State College of Iowa; Philadelphia—Frank Corace, LaSalle; Los Angeles—Henry Finkel, Dayton; St. Louis—Willie Murrell, Kansas State; San Francisco—Gene Elmore, SMU; Cincinnati—Happy Hairston, NYU; Boston—Joe Strawder, Bradley.

FIFTH ROUND　New York—Tony Gennari, Canisius; Detroit—Ray Wolford, Toledo; Baltimore—Bennie Lennox, Texas A&M; Philadelphia—Lou Skurcenski, Westminster; Los Angeles—John Savage, North Texas State; St. Louis—John Tresvant, Seattle; San Francisco—Roger Suttner, Kansas State; Cincinnati—George Kirk, Memphis State; Boston—Nick Werkman, Seton Hall.

SIXTH ROUND　New York—Tom Lavelle, Western Carolina; Detroit—Larry Phillips, Rice; Baltimore—Bobby Joe Edmonds, Tennessee State; Philadelphia—Ricky Kaminsky, Yale; Los Angeles—Troy Collier, Utah State; St. Louis—Ernest Brock, Virginia State; San Francisco—Ray Carey, Missouri; Cincinnati—Al Thresher, Wittenberg; Boston—Levern Tart, Bradley.

SEVENTH ROUND　New York—Emmette Bryant, DePaul; Detroit—Jerry Jackson, Ohio; Baltimore—Ron Miller, Loyola (Ill.); Philadelphia—Gordon Hatton, Dayton; Los Angeles—Steve Anstett, Portland; St. Louis—Maurice McHartley, North Carolina A&T; San Francisco—Dave Lee, San Francisco; Cincinnati—Vic Rouse, Loyola (Ill.); Boston—Rich Falk, Northwestern.

EIGHTH ROUND　New York—Jim Boutin, Lewis & Clark; Detroit—Ralph Telken, Rockhurst; Baltimore—Danny Schultz, Tennessee; Philadelphia—Bob Pelkington, Xavier (Ohio); Los Angeles—Jay Buckley, Duke; St. Louis—Kendall Rhine, Rice; San Francisco—Bob Garibaldi, Santa Clara; Cincinnati—Joe Gieger, Xavier (Ohio); Boston—Jeff Blue, Butler.

NINTH ROUND　New York—Jack Brens, Wisconsin; Baltimore—Tom Black, South Dakota State; Philadelphia—Jim Brennan, Clemson; St. Louis—Darel Carrier, Western Kentucky; San Francisco—Camden Wail, California; Cincinnati—Scotty Pierce, West Texas State; Boston—Charles Kelley, West Virginia Tech.

TENTH ROUND　New York—Jim Christie, Georgetown; Baltimore—Bill Kusleika, Tulsa; Philadelphia—Wally Briggs, North Carolina A&M; St. Louis—Frank Stephens, Virginia State; San Francisco—Jeff Cartwright, Chapman; Cincinnati—Bob Neumann, Memphis State; Boston—Duane Corribeau, Clark.

ELEVENTH ROUND　New York—Dennis Lynch, Yale; Baltimore—Fred Glover, Winston-Salem; Philadelphia—Thomas Lowry, West Virginia; St. Louis—Gerry Goran, St. Mary of the Plains; Cincinnati—Jim Reynolds, Abilene Christian.

TWELFTH ROUND　Baltimore—Frank Kamiaski, Randolph-Macon; Philadelphia—Julius Myers, Morris Brown; St. Louis—Warren Sutton, George Williams; Cincinnati—Fred Jones, Youngstown.

THIRTEENTH ROUND Baltimore—Doug Moon, Utah; St. Louis—Cecil Tuttle, Georgetown (Ky.).

FOURTEENTH ROUND Baltimore—Pete Gent, Michigan State; St. Louis—Bill Blair, Virginia Military.

FIFTEENTH ROUND Baltimore—Sandy Williams, St. Francis (Pa.); St. Louis—Al Cech, Detroit.

1965

TERRITORIAL CHOICES New York—Bill Bradley, Princeton; Detroit—Bill Buntin, Michigan; Los Angeles—Gail Goodrich, UCLA.

FIRST ROUND San Francisco—Fred Hetzel, Davidson; San Francisco—Rick Barry, Miami (bonus selection); New York—Dave Stallworth, Wichita (bonus selection); Philadelphia—Bill Cunningham, North Carolina; St. Louis—Jim Washington, Villanova; Cincinnati—Nate Bowman, Wichita State; Boston—Ollie Johnson, San Francisco.

SECOND ROUND Baltimore—Jerry Sloan, Evansville; Philadelphia—Jesse Branson, Elon; New York (from St. Louis)—Hal Blevins, Arkansas A&M; Cincinnati—Flynn Robinson, Wyoming; Los Angeles—John Fairchild, Brigham Young; Boston—Ronnie Watts, Wake Forest.

THIRD ROUND San Francisco—Wilbert Frazier, Grambling; New York—Dick Van Arsdale, Indiana; Detroit—Tom Van Arsdale, Indiana; Baltimore—Tal Brody, Illinois; Philadelphia—Bob Weiss, Penn State; St. Louis—Ken McIntyre, St. John's; Cincinnati—Jon McGlocklin, Indiana; Los Angeles—Jim Caldwell, Georgia Tech; Boston—Toby Kimball, Connecticut.

FOURTH ROUND San Francisco—Keith Erickson, UCLA; New York—Barry Clemens, Ohio Wesleyan; Detroit—Ron Reed, Notre Dame; Baltimore—Joe Newton, Auburn; Philadelphia—Henry Finkel, Dayton; St. Louis—Lynn Nance, Washington; Cincinnati—Bob Love, Southern; Los Angeles—Brooks Henderson, Florida; Boston—Richie Tarrant, St. Michael's (Vt.).

FIFTH ROUND San Francisco—Warren Rustand, Arizona; New York—Larry Lembo, Manhattan; Detroit—Jim King, Oklahoma State; Baltimore—Skip Thoren, Illinois; Philadelphia—Richie Moore, Villanova; St. Louis—Theodore Werner, Washington State; Cincinnati—Warren Isaac, Iona; Los Angeles—A. W. Davis, Tennessee; Boston—Don Davidson, Davidson.

SIXTH ROUND San Francisco—Eddie Jackson, Oklahoma City; New York—Steve Nisenson, Hofstra; Detroit—Ted Manning, North Carolina College; Baltimore—Charles Dinkens, Miami (Ohio); Philadelphia—Mitch Edwards, Pan American; St. Louis—John Rambo, Long Beach College; Cincinnati—Leon Clements, Ouachita Baptist; Los Angeles—Theo Cruz, Seattle; Boston—Haskell Tison, Duke.

SEVENTH ROUND San Francisco—Jim Jarvis, Oregon State; New York—Warren Davis, North Carolina A&T; Detroit—Barry Smith, High Point; Baltimore—Lavonne LeFlore, Jackson State; Philadelphia—John Young, Midwestern (Tex.); St. Louis—Terry Kunze, Minnesota; Cincinnati—Jeff Gehring, Miami (Ohio); Los Angeles—Dwayne Cruze, Idaho State; Boston—George Deehan, Lenoir Rhyne.

EIGHTH ROUND San Francisco—Dan Wolters, California; New York—Dale Neel, High Point; Baltimore—Willie Somerset, Duquesne; Philadelphia—Bob Barnek, St. Bonaventure; St. Louis—Cincy Powell, Portland; Cincinnati—Jim Fox, South Carolina; Los Angeles—George Unseld, Kansas.

NINTH ROUND San Francisco—Willie Cotton, Central State; New York—Frank Granat, Alliance; Baltimore—Jim Murphy, DePaul; Philadelphia—Gene West, Drake; St. Louis—Leroy Walker, Utah State; Cincinnati—Ron Krick, Cincinnati; Los Angeles—Marlbert Pradd, Dillard.

TENTH ROUND New York—Jay Neary, Wilmington (N.C.); Baltimore—John Wendelkin, Holy Cross; Philadelphia—Dean Church, Southwestern Louisiana; St. Louis—Spencer Carlson, Baylor; Cincinnati—Richie Dec, Seton Hall; Los Angeles—Don Rae, Montana State.

ELEVENTH ROUND New York—Wayne Molis, Lewis; Baltimore—Bogie Redmon, Illinois; Philadelphia—Curt Fromal, LaSalle; St. Louis—Weldon Kytle, Penn; Cincinnati—Dick Maile, LSU; Los Angeles—Bob Andrews, Alabama.

TWELFTH ROUND New York—Bill Meyer, Hiram; Baltimore—Thales McReynolds, Miles; Philadelphia—Dan Anderson, Augsburg; St. Louis—Elton McGriff, Creighton; Cincinnati—Robert McCollough, Benedict.

THIRTEENTH ROUND New York—Steve Trupin, Yale; Baltimore—Walt Sahm, Notre Dame; Philadelphia—Rich Parks, Tulsa; St. Louis—Mel Northway, Minnesota; Cincinnati—Oliver Jones, Albany State (Ga.).

FOURTEENTH ROUND New York—Dennis McGovern, Rhode Island; Baltimore—Joe Ramsey, Southern Illinois; Philadelphia—Jack Morgenthal, Houston; St. Louis—Terry Page, Detroit; Cincinnati—Larry Franks, Texas.

FIFTEENTH ROUND Baltimore—Jerry Rook, Arkansas State; Philadelphia—James Pitts, Georgia; St. Louis—George Pomey, Michigan; Cincinnati—Ronald Scharf, Georgia Tech.

SIXTEENTH ROUND Baltimore—Dave Hicks, New Haven H.S.; Philadelphia—Larry Rafferty, Fairfield; St. Louis—Bob Tolan, Eastern Kentucky; Cincinnati—Willie Porter, Tennessee State.

SEVENTEENTH ROUND Baltimore—Bunk Adams, Ohio.

EIGHTEENTH ROUND Baltimore—Roger Taylor, Illinois.

1966

FIRST ROUND New York—Cazzie Russell, Michigan; Detroit—Dave Bing, Syracuse; San Francisco—Clyde Lee, Vanderbilt; St. Louis—Lou Hudson, Minnesota; Baltimore—Jack Marin, Duke; Cincinnati—Walt Wesley, Kansas; Los Angeles—Jerry Chambers, Utah; Boston—Jim Barnett, Oregon; Philadelphia—Matt Guokas, St. Joseph's (Pa.); Chicago—Dave Schellhase, Purdue.

SECOND ROUND New York—Henry Akin, Morehead State; Detroit—Dorie Murrey, Detroit; San Francisco—Joe Ellis, San Francisco; St. Louis—Dick Snyder, Davidson; Baltimore—Neil Johnson, Creighton; Cincinnati—Jerry Lee Wells, Oklahoma City; Los Angeles (from Chicago)—Henry Finkel, Dayton; Boston—Leon Clark, Wyoming; Philadelphia—Bill Melchionni, Villanova; Chicago—Erwin Mueller, San Francisco.

THIRD ROUND New York—Stewart Johnson, Murray State; Detroit—Oliver Darden, Michigan; San Francisco—Steve Chubin, Rhode Island; St. Louis—Tommy Kron, Kentucky; Baltimore—Dave Wagnon, Idaho State; Cincinnati—James Ware, Oklahoma City; Los Angeles—John Block, Southern California; Boston—Gary Turner, TCU; Philadelphia—Don Freeman, Illinois; Chicago—Ed Bodkin, Eastern Kentucky.

FOURTH ROUND New York—Lee DeFore, Auburn; Detroit—Jeff Congdon, Brigham Young; San Francisco—Steve Vacendak, Duke; St. Louis—Bob McIntyre, St. John's; Baltimore—George Peeples, Iowa; Cincinnati—Charles Schmaus, Virginia Military; Los Angeles—Archie Clark, Minnesota; Boston—John Austin, Boston College; Philadelphia—Ken Wilburn, Central State (Ohio); Chicago—Jim Williams, Temple.

FIFTH ROUND New York—Ron Jackson, Clark; Detroit—William Pickens, Georgia Southern; San Francisco—Tom Kerwin, Centenary; St. Louis—Dick Nemelka, Brigham Young; Baltimore (from Boston)—John Beasley, Texas A&M; Baltimore—John Jones, LSU; Cincinnati—Rick Parks, St. Louis; Los Angeles—Stan Washington, Michigan State; Philadelphia—Tom Duff, St. Joseph's (Pa.); Chicago—Larry Humes, Evansville.

SIXTH ROUND New York—George Fisher, Utah; Detroit—Carroll Hooser, SMU; San Francisco—Jim Pitts, Northwestern; St. Louis—Lonnie Wright, Colorado State; Baltimore—Jeff Newman, Penn; Cincinnati—Steve Cunningham, Western Kentucky; Los Angeles—Keith Thomas, Vanderbilt; Boston—Charlie Hunter, Oklahoma City; Philadelphia—Red Robbins, Tennessee.

SEVENTH ROUND New York—Mike Dabich, New Mexico State; Detroit—Ted Manning, North Carolina College; San Francisco—Lon Hughey, Fresno State; St. Louis—Jay Neary, Wilmington (N.C.); Baltimore—Dave Mills, DePaul; Cincinnati—Gary Schull, Florida State; Los Angeles—Tab Jackson, Idaho College; Boston—Jerry Ward, Maryland; Chicago—John Comeaux, Grambling.

EIGHTH ROUND New York—Mike Silliman, Army; Detroit—George McNeil, Southern Illinois; San Francisco—Ken Washington, UCLA; St. Louis—Brian Williams, Xavier (Ohio); Baltimore—Roland West, Cincinnati; Cincinnati—Ron Krick, Cincinnati; Los Angeles—John Wetzel, Virginia Tech; Boston—Russ Gumina, San Francisco; Chicago—Stan Curtis, Northern Michigan.

NINTH ROUND New York—Bill Turner, Akron; St. Louis—Al Grant, LIU; Baltimore—Chuck Gardner, Colorado; Cincinnati—Billy Smith, Loyola (Ill.); Los Angeles—Julian Hammond, Tulsa; Philadelphia—Pat Caldwell, Rockhurst; Chicago—Gene Summers, Northern Michigan.

TENTH ROUND New York—Rich Moore, Hiram Scott; St. Louis—Don Yates, Minnesota; Baltimore—Guy Manning, Prairie View; Cincinnati—Freddie Lewis, Arizona State; Los Angeles—Mike Rooney, Oklahoma; Philadelphia—Bob Bedell, Stanford; Chicago—Don Swanson, DePaul.

ELEVENTH ROUND New York—Rich Dyer, NYU; St. Louis—Curt Gammell, Pacific Lutheran; Baltimore—Stan McKenzie, NYU; Cincinnati—R.B. Lynam, Oklahoma Baptist; Los Angeles—George Grams, Purdue; Chicago—Carver Clinton, Penn State.

TWELFTH ROUND New York—Dave Deutsch, Rochester; St. Louis—Lonnie Lynn, Wilberforce; Baltimore—Grant Simmons, Nebraska.

THIRTEENTH ROUND New York—Bob Bennett, North Carolina; St. Louis—Nick Aloi, Bowling Green; Baltimore—Al Lopes, Kansas.

FOURTEENTH ROUND St. Louis—Ollie Carter, San Francisco; Baltimore—Jim Harter, Pan American.

FIFTEENTH ROUND St. Louis—Paul Long, Wake Forest; Baltimore—Howard Bayne, Tennessee.

SIXTEENTH ROUND St. Louis—Eddie Jackson, Bradley; Baltimore—Ken Barnes, Wisconsin.

SEVENTEENTH ROUND Baltimore—Chris Pervall, Iowa.

EIGHTEENTH ROUND Baltimore—Jerry Trice, Weber State.

NINETEENTH ROUND Baltimore—Gene Visscher, Weber State.

NBA 1966 EXPANSION DRAFT

CHICAGO John Barnhill, Detroit; Al Bianchi, Philadelphia; Ron Bonham, Boston; Bob Boozer, Los Angeles; Nate Bowman, Cincinnati; Len Chappell, New York; Barry Clemens, New York; Keith Erickson, San Francisco; John Kerr, Baltimore; Jim King, Los Angeles; Don Kojis, Detroit; McCoy McLemore, San Francisco; Jeff Mullins, St. Louis; Jerry Sloan, Baltimore; Tom Thacker, Cincinnati; John Thompson, Boston; Gerry Ward, Philadelphia; Jim Washington, St. Louis.

NBA 1967

FIRST ROUND Detroit—Jimmy Walker, Providence; Baltimore—Earl Monroe, Winston-Salem; Chicago—Clem Haskins, Western Kentucky; Detroit (from Los Angeles)—Sonny Dove, St. John's; New York—Walt Frazier, Southern Illinois; Seattle—Al Tucker, Oklahoma Baptist; San Diego—Pat Riley, Kentucky; St. Louis—Tom Workman, Seattle; Cincinnati—Mel Daniels, New Mexico; San Francisco—Dave Lattin, Texas Western; Boston—Mal Graham, NYU; Philadelphia—Craig Raymond, Brigham Young.

SECOND ROUND Baltimore—James Jones, Grambling; Detroit—Steve Sullivan, Georgetown; Chicago—Byron Beck, Denver; Los Angeles—Randy Mahaffey, Clemson; New York—Phil Jackson, North Dakota; San Diego—Bob Netolicky, Drake; Seattle—Bob Rule, Colorado State.

THIRD ROUND Baltimore—Malkin Strong, Seattle; Detroit—Darrell Hardy, Baylor; Chicago—John Dickson, Arkansas State; Los Angeles—Dwight Smith, Western Kentucky; New York—Gary Gregor, South Carolina; St. Louis—Bob Verga, Duke; Cincinnati—Gary Gray, Oklahoma City; San Francisco—Bill Turner, Akron; Cincinnati (from Boston)—Sam Smith, Kentucky Wesleyan; San Diego (from Philadelphia)—Richie Moore, Hiram Scott; Seattle—Sam Singleton, Omaha; San Diego—Nick Jones, Oregon.

FOURTH ROUND Baltimore—Al Salvadori, South Carolina; Detroit—Ron Franz, Kansas; Chicago—Jim Burns, Northwestern; Los Angeles—Cliff Anderson, St. Joseph's; New York—Keith Swagerty, Pacific; St. Louis—Wes Bialosuknia, Connecticut; Cincinnati—Lou Dampier, Kentucky; San Francisco—Bob Lewis, North Carolina; Boston—Neville Shedd, Texas Western; San Diego (from Philadelphia)—Ron Kozlicki, Northwestern; San Diego—Craig Dill, Michigan; Seattle—Larry Bunce, Utah State.

FIFTH ROUND Baltimore—Dexter Westbrook, Providence; Detroit—Paul Long, Wake Forest; Chicago—Dick Pruet, Jacksonville; Los Angeles—Joe Allen, Bradley; New York—Barry Leibowitz, LIU; St. Louis—Mike Wittman, Miami (Fla.); Cincinnati—Tom Washington, Cheyney State; San Francisco—Mike Lynn, UCLA; Boston—Mike Redd, Kentucky Wesleyan; Philadelphia—James Reid, Winston-Salem; Seattle—Plummer Lott, Seattle; San Diego—Herb McPherson, Murray State.

SIXTH ROUND Baltimore—Bob Riedy, Duke; Detroit—Vaughn Harper, Syracuse; Chicago—Mal Pradd, Dillard; Los Angeles—Gary Keller, Florida; New York—Bob Benfield, West Virginia; St. Louis—John Morrison, Canisius; Cincinnati—Frank Stronczek, American International; San Francisco—Dale Schlueter, Colorado State; Boston—Ed Hummer, Princeton; Philadelphia—Tim Powers, Creighton; San Diego—Robert Cole, St. Louis; Seattle—Gordon Harris, Washington.

SEVENTH ROUND Baltimore—Ron Perry, VPI; Detroit—Bob Lloyd, Rutgers; Chicago—Bob Wolf, Marquette; Los Angeles—Jamie Thompson, Wichita State; New York—Butch Wade, Indiana State; St. Louis—Carl Fuller, Bethune-Cookman; Cincinnati—Charley Beasley, SMU; San Francisco—Sonny Bustion, Colorado State; Boston—Edgar Lacy, UCLA; Philadelphia—Frank Card, South Carolina State; Seattle—Dick Kolbert, Santa Barbara; San Diego—Elbert Miller, Nevada Southern.

EIGHTH ROUND Baltimore—Ed Manning, Jackson State Teachers; Detroit—George Carter, St. Bonaventure; Chicago—Leon Simon, Santa Fe; Los Angeles—Don Carlos, Otterbein; New York—Gil Radday, St. Francis; St. Louis—Arvesta Kelly, Lincoln (Mo.); Cincinnati—Frank Holloendoner, Georgetown; San Francisco—Bob Krulish, Pacific; Boston—Andy Anderson, Canisius; Philadelphia—Jim Conley, Virginia; San Diego—Al Grundy, St. Joseph's; Seattle—Willie Wolters, Boston College.

NINTH ROUND Baltimore—Robert Allen, Arkansas A&M; Chicago—Ernie Laurent, Albuquerque; Los Angeles—Jay McMillon, Maryland; New York—Ray Smith, Kansas State; St. Louis—Ed Biedenbach, North Carolina State; Cincinnati—Ron Sepic, Ohio State; San Francisco—Richard Dean, Syracuse; Boston—Henry Brown, Lowell Tech; Philadelphia—Ron Filipek, Tennessee Tech; Seattle—Rod McDonald, Whitworth; San Diego—Ron Coleman, Missouri.

TENTH ROUND Baltimore—Bill Gillespie, Montana State; Chicago—Jim Boshart, Wake Forest; Los Angeles—Don Kruze, Houston; New York—Bruce Kaplan, NYU; St. Louis—Rich Falkenbush, St. Michael's (Vt.); Cincinnati—Willie Davis, North Texas State; San Francisco—Joe Galbo, San Francisco State; Boston—Rick Weitzman, Northeastern; Philadelphia—Butch Ervin, Niagara; San Diego—John Duncan, Murray State; Seattle—Gary Lechman, Gonzaga.

ELEVENTH ROUND Baltimore—Bubba Smith, Michigan State; Chicago—Jim Andros, New Haven; Los Angeles—Nick Pino, Kansas State; New York—Mark Merkin, North Carolina; Cincinnati—Ken Callaway, Cincinnati; San Francisco—Bill Morgan, New Mexico; Boston—Joe Harrington, Maryland; Philadelphia—Ted Campbell, North Carolina A&T; Seattle—Randy Matson, Texas A&M; San Diego—Al Razutis, California Western.

TWELFTH ROUND Baltimore—Tony Eatmon, Pan American; Detroit—George Dalzell, Colgate College; Chicago—Ron Widby, Tennessee; Los Angeles—Ben Monroe, New Mexico; New York—Mike Riordan, Providence; Cincinnati—Frank Gadjunas, Villanova; San Francisco—David Fox, Pacific; Philadelphia—Hubie Marshall, LaSalle; San Diego—Martin Navia, New Mexico Highlands; Seattle—Rubin Russell, North Texas State.

THIRTEENTH ROUND Baltimore—Lyn Burkholder, South Carolina; Detroit—Matthew Aitch, Michigan State; Chicago—Tom Storm, Montana State; Los Angeles—Gary Jones, Iowa; Cincinnati—John Moates, Richmond; Philadelphia—George Mack, North Carolina A&T; Seattle—John Schroeder, Ohio; San Diego—Bob Chlupsa, Manhattan.

FOURTEENTH ROUND Baltimore—Paul Mickey, Penn State; Chicago—Don Whitehead, Erskine; Cincinnati—Jerry Pettway, Northwood Institute; Philadelphia—Wayne Brabender, Minnesota-Morris; San Diego—(first name unavailable) Toldar, South Carolina Trade School; Seattle—Jim Sutherland, Wake Forest.

FIFTEENTH ROUND Baltimore—Rich Peek, Louisiana Tech; Chicago—Jim Garza, Detroit Tech; Cincinnati—Earl Beechum, Midwestern; Philadelphia—Sherman Dillard, Tulsa; Seattle—Willie Campbell, Nebraska.

SIXTEENTH ROUND Baltimore—Gary Williams, Oklahoma; Chicago—Jim Dawson, Illinois; Cincinnati—John Vermelyea, Morningside; Philadelphia—Wayne Chapman, Western Kentucky.

SEVENTEENTH ROUND Baltimore—Loy Petersen, Oregon State; Cincinnati—Darryll Meachem, Edinboro State; Philadelphia—Gary Paulk, Oklahoma State.

EIGHTEENTH ROUND Baltimore—Jerry Southwood, Vanderbilt.

NINETEENTH ROUND Baltimore—George Spencer, Washington.

TWENTIETH ROUND Baltimore—Roland West, Cincinnati.

NBA 1967 EXPANSION DRAFT (MAY 1, 1967)

SAN DIEGO Jim Barnett, Boston; John Barnhill, Baltimore; John Block, Los Angeles; Henry Finkel, Los Angeles; Dave Gambee, Philadelphia; Johnny Green, Baltimore; Toby Kimball, Boston; Don Kojis, Chicago; Jon McGlocklin, Cincinnati; Jim Ware, Cincinnati.

SEATTLE Henry Akin, New York; Nate Bowman, Philadelphia; Dave Deutsch, New York; Richie Guerin, St. Louis; Walt Hazzard, Los Angeles; Tom Kron, St. Louis; Tom Meschery, San Francisco; Dorie Murrey, Detroit; Bud Olsen, San Francisco; Ron Reed, Detroit; Rod Thorn, St. Louis; Ben Warley, Baltimore; Ron Watts, Boston; Bob Weiss, Philadelphia; George Wilson, Chicago.

ABA 1967

ANAHEIM

FIRST FIVE ROUNDS—Darrell Hardy, Baylor; Bob Krulish, Pacific; Bob Lewis, North Carolina; Mike Lynn, UCLA; Tom Workman, Seattle.

ADDITIONAL ROUNDS—Jim Connolly, Virginia; Denny Holman, Southern Methodist; Edgar Lacy, UCLA; Les Powell, Utah State; Malcolm Strong, Seattle; Gary Williams, Oklahoma State; Mike Wittman, Miami (Fla.)

DALLAS

FIRST FIVE ROUNDS—Matt Aitch, Michigan State; Jim Burns, Northwestern; Gary Gray, Oklahoma City; Pat Riley, Kentucky; Jamie Thompson, Wichita State.
ADDITIONAL ROUNDS—Paul Brateris, Tennessee Wesleyan; Jeff Fitch, East Texas State; Ted Manning, North Carolina A&T; Duane Heckman, Dickinson; Gilbert McDowell, Tennessee Wesleyan; Jerry Southwood, Vanderbilt; Tom Storm, Montana State.

DENVER

FIRST FIVE ROUNDS—Byron Beck, Denver; Walt Frazier, Southern Illinois; Gary Keller, Florida; Bob Rule, Colorado State; Neville Shed, Texas Western.
ADDITIONAL ROUNDS—Vaughn Harper, Syracuse; Rick Dean, Syracuse; Neil Heskin, Georgetown; Dave Lattin, Texas Western; John Morrison, Canisius; Neil Roberts, Brigham Young; Bill Turner, Akron.

HOUSTON

FIRST FIVE ROUNDS—Bob Benfield, West Virginia; Tony Eatmon, Pan American; Bob Riedy, Duke; Frank Stronczek, American International; Keith Swagerty, Pacific.
ADDITIONAL ROUNDS—Don Carlos, Otterbein; Hal Hale, Utah State; Guy Manning, Prairie View; Jim Monahan, Notre Dame; Mike Nau, Oregon State; Jerry Pettway, Northwood Institute, Dale Schlueter, Colorado State.

INDIANA

FIRST FIVE ROUNDS—Charles Beasley, Southern Methodist; Jim Dawson, Illinois; Craig Dill, Michigan; Bob Netolicky, Drake; Jim Walker, Providence.
ADDITIONAL ROUNDS—Frank Gaidjunes, Villanova; Jerry Jones, Iowa; Ron Kozlicki, Northwestern; Hubie Marshall, LaSalle; Ed McKee, Rockhurst; Bill Russell, Indiana; Gene Washington, Michigan State.

KENTUCKY

FIRST FIVE ROUNDS—Louie Dampier, Kentucky; Clem Haskins, Western Kentucky; Dwight Smith; Western Kentucky; Willie Wolters, Boston College; Bob Verga, Duke.
ADDITIONAL ROUNDS—Earl Beechum, Midwestern; Mel Cox, Central Washington; Ken Gibbs, Vanderbilt; Pres Judy, Georgia Tech; Gwendell MacSwain, Valdosta State; Randy Mahaffey, Clemson; John Smith, Kent State.

MINNESOTA

FIRST FIVE ROUNDS—Mel Daniels, New Mexico; Phil Jackson, North Dakota; Bob Lloyd, Rutgers; Tim Powers, Creighton; Sam Smith, Kentucky Wesleyan.
ADDITIONAL ROUNDS—Al Clark, Eastern Kentucky; Gary Gregor, South Carolina; Erv Inniger, Indiana; Rich Jones, Illinois; Lindberg Moody, South Carolina State; Errol Palmer, DePaul; Ron Perry, Virginia Poly.

NEW ORLEANS

FIRST FIVE ROUNDS—Robert Allen, Arkansas AM&N; John Dickson, Arkansas State; James Jones, Grambling; Paul Long, Wake Forest; Ron Widby, Tennessee.
ADDITIONAL ROUNDS—Al Andrews, Tulane; George Carter, St. Bonaventure; Carl Head, West Virginia; Allan Parris, Utah; Jeff Ramsey, Florida; Bob Seagren, Southern California; Dexter Westbrook, Providence.

NEW YORK

FIRST FIVE ROUNDS—Sonny Dove, St. John's (N.Y.); Mal Graham, NYU; George Stone, Marshall; Dick Pruett, Jacksonville; Bob Wolf, Marquette.
ADDITIONAL ROUNDS—Tim Edwards, Amherst; Dan Hansard, St. Thomas, (Minn.); Frank Holloendoner, Georgetown; Harry Laurie, St. Peter's (N.J.).

OAKLAND

FIRST FIVE ROUNDS—Wes Bialosuknia, Connecticut; Gordy Harris, Washington; Richie Moore, Hiram Scott; Al Salvadori, South Carolina; Al Tucker, Oklahoma Baptist.
ADDITIONAL ROUNDS—Art Allen, Bethune-Cookman; Nate Branch, Nebraska; Mike Davis, Virginia Union; Dave Fox, Pacific; Ron Franz, Kansas; Bill Morgan, New Mexico; Marlbert Pradd, Dillard.

PITTSBURGH

FIRST FIVE ROUNDS—Cliff Anderson, St. Joseph's (Pa.); Barry Leibowitz, LIU; Earl Monroe, Winston-Salem; Craig Raymond, Brigham Young; Tom Washington, Cheyney State.
ADDITIONAL ROUNDS—Frank Card, North Carolina A&T; Ron Coleman, Missouri; Chris Kefalos, Temple; Mike Riordan, Providence; John Schroeder, Ohio University; Steve Sullivan, Georgetown; Jim Southerland, Clemson.

NBA 1968

FIRST ROUND   San Diego—Elvin Hayes, Houston; Baltimore—Wes Unseld, Louisville; Seattle—Bob Kauffman, Guilford; Chicago—Tom Boerwinkle, Tennessee; Cincinnati—Don Smith, Iowa State; Detroit—Otto Moore, Pan American; Milwaukee—Charles Paulk, Northeast Oklahoma; Phoenix—Gary Gregor, South Carolina; San Francisco—Ron Williams, West Virginia; New York—Bill Hosket, Ohio State; Los Angeles—Bill Hewitt, Southern California; Boston—Don Chaney, Houston; Atlanta—Skip Harlicka, South Carolina; Philadelphia—Shaler Halimon, Utah State.

SECOND ROUND   San Diego—John Q. Trapp, UNLV; Seattle—Art Harris, Stanford; Chicago—Loy Peterson, Oregon State; Baltimore—Bob Quick, Xavier (Ohio); Chicago (from Cincinnati)—Ron Dunlap, Illinois; Detroit—Manny Leaks, Niagara; Phoenix—Dick Cunningham, Murray State; Milwaukee—Eugene Moore, St. Louis.

THIRD ROUND   San Diego—Stu Lantz, Nebraska; Seattle—Jeff Ockel, Utah; Detroit (from Chicago)—Don Dee, St. Mary of the Plains; Baltimore—Ron Nelson, New Mexico; Cincinnati—Pat Frink, Colorado; Cincinnati (from Detroit)—Fred Foster, Miami (Ohio); San Francisco—Don Sidle, Oklahoma; New York—Don May, Dayton; Chicago (from Los Angeles)—Dave Newmark, Columbia; Boston—Garfield Smith, Eastern Kentucky; Baltimore (from Atlanta)—Jack Thompson, South Carolina; Seattle (from Philadelphia)—Ed Johnson, Tennessee State; Milwaukee—Sam Williams, Iowa; Phoenix—Art Beatty, American.

FOURTH ROUND   San Diego—Harry Barnes, Northeastern; Seattle—Henry Logan, Western Carolina; Chicago—Mike Lynn, UCLA; Baltimore—Dallas Thornton, Kentucky Wesleyan; Cincinnati—Dan Sparks, Weber State; Detroit—Rich Niemann, St. Louis; San Francisco—Edgar Lacy, UCLA; New York—Warren Armstrong, Wichita State; Los Angeles—Ed Biedenbach, North Carolina State; Boston—Rich Johnson, Grambling; Atlanta—Bob Warren, Vanderbilt; San Diego (from Philadelphia)—Darryl Jones, St. Benedict's; Phoenix—Rich Jones, Memphis State; Milwaukee—Greg Smith, Western Kentucky.

FIFTH ROUND   San Diego—Glenn Combs, Virginia Tech; Seattle—Al Hairston, Bowling Green; Chicago—Jim Tillman, Loyola (Ill.); Baltimore—Ed Chaplin, Voorhees; Cincinnati—Jim Kissane, Boston College; Detroit—Carl Fuller, Bethune-Cookman; San Francisco—Jim Eakins, Brigham Young; New York—Hal Booker, Cheyney State; Los Angeles—Lou Shepherd, Southwest Missouri State; Boston—Thad Jaracz, Kentucky; Atlanta—Rusty Parker, Miami (Fla.); Philadelphia—Larry Miller, North Carolina; Milwaukee—Joe Franklin, Wisconsin; Phoenix—Harry Hollines, Denver.

SIXTH ROUND   San Diego—Eldridge Webb, Tulsa; Seattle—Ron Guziak, Duquesne; Chicago—Ken Barnett, Delaware; Baltimore—Joe Heiser, Princeton; Cincinnati—Calvin Martin, Texas Southern; Detroit—Wally Anderzunas, Creighton; San Francisco—Bob Allen, Marshall; New York—Brian Brunkhorst, Marquette; Los Angeles—Nick Pino, Kansas State; Boston—Jerry Newsom, Indiana State; Atlanta—Phil Wagner, Georgia Tech; Philadelphia—Chuck Williams, Colorado; Phoenix—Rodney Knowles, Davidson; Milwaukee—Fred Smith, Hawaii.

SEVENTH ROUND   San Diego—Rick Adelman, Loyola (Cal.); Seattle—Jim McKean, Washington State; Chicago—Willie Davis, North Texas State; Baltimore—Jasper Wilson, Southern; Cincinnati—Rich Dumas, Northeast Oklahoma; Detroit—Larry Newbold, LIU; San Francisco—Dave Reasor, West Virginia; New York—Bob Waldal, Dickinson State; Los Angeles—Dennis Hrcka, Hillsdale; Boston—Mike Lewis, Duke; Atlanta—Oscar Smith, Elizabeth City; Philadelphia—Bill Jones, Fairfield; Milwaukee—Tom Kondla, Minnesota; Phoenix—Charles Parks, Idaho State.

EIGHTH ROUND   San Diego—Aaron Sellers, Jackson State; Seattle—Willie Rodgers, Oklahoma; Chicago—Lloyd Higgins, Pasadena College; Baltimore—Barry Orms, St. Louis; Cincinnati—Dave Williams, Mississippi State; Detroit—Harry Laurie, St. Peter's; San Francisco—Walt Piatkowski, Bowling Green; New York—Bob Hooper, Dayton; Los Angeles—John Smith, Southern Colorado; Boston—Julius Keye, Alcorn State; Atlanta—Martin Baietti, Manhattan; Philadelphia—Melvin Jones, Albany State; Phoenix—Brian Clare, Denver; Milwaukee—Elbert Miller, UNLV.

NINTH ROUND   San Diego—John Schetzsle, Ashland; Seattle—Jimmy Smith, Utah State; Chicago—Corky Bell, Loyola (Ill.); Baltimore—Wayne Chapman, Western Kentucky; Cincinnati—Butch Joyner, Indiana; Detroit—Vaughn Harper, Syracuse; San Francisco—Art Wilmore, San Francisco; New York—Roger Bohnenstiel, Kansas; Los Angeles—George Stone, Marshall; Boston—Bill Butler, St. Bonaventure; Atlanta—Mack Daughtry, Albany State; Philadelphia—Clarence Brookins, Temple; Milwaukee—Cliff Berger, Kentucky; Phoenix—Merv Jackson, Utah.

TENTH ROUND   San Diego—Mike Butler, Memphis State; Seattle—Joe Kennedy, Duke; Chicago—Mike Weaver, Northwestern; Baltimore—Steve Adelman, Boston College; Cincinnati—Robert Wyendanet, Vanderbilt; Detroit—Tom Baack, Nebraska; San Francisco—Bob Heaney, Santa Clara; New York—Sylvester Adams, North Carolina A&T; Los Angeles—Charles Alford, East Carolina; Boston—Ivan Leschinsky, LIU; Atlanta—Dwight Waller, Tennessee State; Philadelphia—Greg Cisson, Rider; Phoenix—Lee Davis, North Carolina College; Milwaukee—Eugene Jones, Missouri.

ELEVENTH ROUND San Diego—Leonardo Epps, Clark; Seattle—Jim Marsh, Southern California; Chicago—Jim McGonigle, Iowa State; Baltimore—Al Dixon, Bowling Green; Cincinnati—James Robinson, Rochester Institute; San Francisco—Jerry Chandler, UNLV; New York—Bob Redd, Marshall; Los Angeles—Harry Singletary, Presbyterian; Boston—Tom Neimeir, Evansville; Atlanta—Henry Watkins, Tennessee State; Philadelphia—Bill Soens, Miami (Fla.); Milwaukee—Brad Luchini, Marquette; Phoenix—Ron Boone, Idaho State.

TWELFTH ROUND San Diego—Roy Manning, Lane; Seattle—Walt Simon, Utah; Chicago—John Lallensack, Oshkosh State; Baltimore—Willie Cager, Texac Western; Cincinnati—Glynn Saulters, Western Louisiana; San Francisco—Bob Wolfe, California; New York—Pat Moriarty, Guilford; Los Angeles—Reggie Lacefield, Western Michigan; Boston—Bill Langheld, Fordham; Atlanta—Bill Harris, Texas Western; Philadelphia—Ted Campbell, North Carolina A&T; Milwaukee—Dave Miller, Florida; Phoenix—Bill Davis, Arizona.

THIRTEENTH ROUND San Diego—Marshall Evans, Lincoln; Seattle—Bud Ogden, Santa Clara; Chicago—Herm Gilliam, Purdue; Baltimore—Rudy Bogad, St. John's; Cincinnati—Jim Tindell, Massachusetts; New York—Ken Morehead, Hillside; Los Angeles—Harvey Mumford, Montana State; Boston—Art Stephenson, Rhode Island; Atlanta—Frank Standard, South Carolina; Philadelphia—Earl Seyfert, Kansas State; Phoenix—Pat Hobard, California State.

FOURTEENTH ROUND San Diego—Bobby Lewis, North Carolina State; Seattle—Mike Warren, UCLA; Chicago—Dave Carr, Washington; Baltimore—Ernest Sims, East Tennessee; Cincinnati—Charles Core, Southeastern Louisiana; New York—John Haarlow, Princeton; Los Angeles—John Godfrey, Abilene Christian; Boston—Keith Hockstein, Holy Cross; Atlanta—George Hicker, Syracuse; Philadelphia—Tom Youngdale, Davidson.

FIFTEENTH ROUND San Diego—Bill Gaines, East Texas State; Chicago—Mickey McCarthy, TCU; Baltimore—Joe Allen, Bradley; Cincinnati—Mike Drepling, Westminster; New York—Ed Fellers, Guilford; Los Angeles—John Baum, Temple; Atlanta—Bernie Foster, Pasadena; Philadelphia—George Mack, North Carolina A&T.

SIXTEENTH ROUND San Diego—Chuck Caldwell, Missouri-St. Louis; Chicago—Fred Holden, Louisville; Baltimore—Dennis Blace, San Francisco; Cincinnati—Dick Harris; New York—Bob Ferguson, Tennessee Wesleyan; Los Angeles—Mike Eberle, Wyoming; Atlanta—Terry Allerton, Baldwin-Wallace; Philadelphia—Joe Crews, Villanova.

SEVENTEENTH ROUND San Diego—Dave Miller, South Dakota State; Chicago—Tom Benedict, Central Washington State; Baltimore—Greg Morris, Cornell; Cincinnati—John Howard, Cincinnati; New York—Milt Williams, Lincoln; Philadelphia—Nate Ware, Tennessee State.

EIGHTEENTH ROUND San Diego—Harold Grant, Pepperdine; Chicago—Bob Zoretich, DePaul; Baltimore—Art Kenny, Fairfield; Cincinnati—Larry Humes, Evansville.

NINETEENTH ROUND San Diego—Bill Corley, Connecticut; Chicago—Rich Mason, Indiana State; Baltimore—Jim LaCour, Seattle; Cincinnati—Jay Refferds.

TWENTIETH ROUND Chicago—Rich Rirkendal, Norfolk State; Baltimore—Ron Woodruff, Midwestern.

TWENTY-FIRST ROUND Chicago—Willie Horton, Delaware.

NBA 1968 EXPANSION DRAFT (MAY 6, 1968)

MILWAUKEE Len Chappell, Detroit; Larry Costello, Philadelphia; John Egan, Baltimore; Wayne Embry, Boston; Dave Gambee, San Diego; Gary Gray, Cincinnati; Fred Hetzel, San Francisco; Johnny Jones, Boston; Bob Love, Cincinnati; Jon McGlocklin, San Diego; Jay Miller, St. Louis; Bud Olsen, Seattle; George Patterson, Detroit; Jim Reid, Philadelphia; Guy Rodgers, Cincinnati; Tom Thacker, Boston; Bob Warlick, San Francisco; Bob Weiss, Seattle.

PHOENIX John Barnhill, San Diego; Emmette Bryant, New York; Gail Goodrich, Los Angeles; Dennis Hamilton, Los Angeles; Neil Johnson, New York; David Lattin, San Francisco; Paul Long, Detroit; Stan McKenzie, Baltimore; McCoy McLemore, Chicago; Bill Melchionni, Philadelphia; David Schellhase, Chicago; Dick Snyder, Atlanta; Craig Spitzer, Chicago; Gene Tormohlen, Atlanta; Dick Van Arsdale, New York; Roland West, Baltimore; John Wetzel, Los Angeles; George Wilson, Seattle.

ABA 1968

DALLAS

FIRST FIVE ROUNDS—Shaler Halimon, Utah State; Rich Jones, Memphis State; Bob Lewis, South Carolina State; John Smith, Southern Colorado State; Jo Jo White, Kansas.
SECOND FIVE ROUNDS—Wally Anderzunas, Creighton; Ron Boone, Idaho State; Glen Combs, Virginia Tech; C. A. Core, Southeastern Louisiana; Roy Manning, Lane College.
THIRD FIVE ROUNDS—Billy Arnold, Texas; Gene Jones, Missouri; Gene Littles, High Point; Mickey McCarthy, Texas Christian; Calvin Pettit, Central Missouri.
ADDITIONAL ROUNDS—Willie Worsley, Texas-El Paso.

DENVER

FIRST FIVE ROUNDS—Tom Boerwinkle, Tennessee; Hal Booker, Cheyney State; Bill Hewitt, Southern California; Walt Piatkowski, Bowling Green.
SECOND FIVE ROUNDS—Harry Hollines, Denver; Charley Parks, Idaho State; Vernon Payne, Indiana; Willie Rodgers, Oklahoma; Glynn Saulters, Western Louisiana.
THIRD FIVE ROUNDS—Ken Hall, Westminster (Utah); Melvin Jones, Albany (Ga.) State; Julius Keye, Alcorn A&M; Mickey Smith, Memphis State; Oscar Smith, Elizabeth City.

HOUSTON

FIRST FIVE ROUNDS—Art Beatty, American University; Don Chaney, Houston; John Godfrey, Abilene Christian; Elvin Hayes, Houston; Aaron Sellers, Jackson State.
SECOND FIVE ROUNDS—Martin Baietti, Manhattan; Rich Dumas, Northeast Oklahoma; Calvin Martin, Texas Southern; Mike Nordholz, Alabama; Dan Smith, Howard-Payne.
THIRD FIVE ROUNDS—Sam Butler, Southern University; Warren Chapman, Duke; Bill Gaines, East Texas State; Jim Jones, Beloit; Frank Standard, South Carolina.

INDIANA

FIRST FIVE ROUNDS—Don Dee, St. Mary of the Plains; Mike Lewis, Duke; Don May, Dayton; Bob Quick, Xavier; Phil Wagner, Georgia Tech.
SECOND FIVE ROUNDS—Dave Benedict, Central Washington; Rudy Bogad, St. John's; Jerry Newsom, Indiana State; Rich Niemann, St. Louis; Jack Thompson, South Carolina.
THIRD FIVE ROUNDS—Greg Cisson, Rider; Bob Hooper, Dayton; Harry Joyner, Indiana; Tom Niemier, Evansville.

KENTUCKY

FIRST FIVE ROUNDS—Wayne Chapman, Western Kentucky; Willie Davis, North Texas State; Al Dixon, Bowling Green; Fred Foster, Miami (Ohio); Wes Unseld, Louisville.
SECOND FIVE ROUNDS—Joe Gallagher, Pembroke; Joe Kennedy, Duke; Manny Leaks, Niagara; Gene Moore, St. Louis; Greg Smith, Western Kentucky.
THIRD FIVE ROUNDS—Booker Brown, Middle Tennessee; Al Hairston, Bowling Green; Thad Jaracz, Kentucky; Reggie Lacefield, Western Michigan; Bob Zoretich, DePaul.
ADDITIONAL ROUNDS—Kermit Meystedt, Southeast Missouri; John Snipes, Elizabeth City; Butch Kaufman, Western Kentucky; Bo Wyenandt, Vanderbilt.

LOS ANGELES

FIRST FIVE ROUNDS—Mervin Jackson, Utah; Ed Johnson, Tennessee State; Larry Miller, North Carolina; George Stone, Marshall; Mike Warren, UCLA.
SECOND FIVE ROUNDS—Carl Fuller, Bethune-Cookman; Ed Leggett, Rocky Mountain; Lou Shepherd, Southwest Missouri State; Bob Warren, Vanderbilt; Eldridge Webb, Tulsa.
THIRD FIVE ROUNDS—Rick Adelman, Loyola (Cal.); Brian Brunkhorst, Marquette; Ben Foster, Pasadena; Phil Harris, Texas-El Paso; Lloyd Higgins, Pasadena.
ADDITIONAL ROUNDS—Mike LaRoche, Cal Poly-San Luis Obispo; Cary Smith, California State-Los Angeles.

MIAMI

FIRST FIVE ROUNDS—Tom Kondla, Minnesota; Ron Nelson, New Mexico; Don Sidle, Oklahoma; Dan Sparks, Weber State; Dallas Thornton, Kentucky Wesleyan.
SECOND FIVE ROUNDS—Ken Barnett, Delaware; Joe Franklin, Wisconsin; Darryl Jones, St. Benedict (Kan.); Al Knott, Cedarville (Ohio); Jerry Waugh, Northern Iowa.
THIRD FIVE ROUNDS—Lyndall Conway, Albuquerque; Jim Barza, Detroit Tech; Willie Iverson, Central Michigan; Terry Porter, St. Cloud; Jim Sterkin, Detroit.

MINNESOTA

FIRST FIVE ROUNDS—Bill Hosket, Ohio State; Larry Newbold, LIU; Dave Newmark, Columbia; Nick Pino, Kansas State; Sam Williams, Iowa.
SECOND FIVE ROUNDS—Roger Bohnenstiehl, Kansas; Clarence Brookins, Temple; John Haarlow, Princeton; Keith Hochstein, Holy Cross; Jeff Ockel, Utah.
THIRD FIVE ROUNDS—Willie Betts, Bradley; Greg Morris, Cornell; Billy Jones, Fairfield; Bob Redd, Marshall; Bill Tindall, Massachusetts.

NEW ORLEANS

FIRST FIVE ROUNDS—Mike Butler, Memphis State; Richard Johnson, Grambling; Mark LaMoreaux, Lenoir-Rhyne; Charles Paulk, Northeast Oklahoma; Ron Williams, West Virginia.
SECOND FIVE ROUNDS—Charles Alford, Eastern Carolina; Ted Campbell, North Carolina A&T; Lee Davis, North Carolina College; Dave Williams, Mississippi State; Jasper Wilson, Southern University.
THIRD FIVE ROUNDS—Passed.

NEW YORK

FIRST FIVE ROUNDS—Joe Allen, Bradley; Dick Cunningham, Murray State; Rodney Knowles, Davidson; Don Smith, Iowa State.

SECOND FIVE ROUNDS—Steve Adelman, Boston College; Eddie Biedenbach, North Carolina State; Ron Gruziak, Duquesne; Pete O'Dea, St. Peter's; Bill Soens, Miami (Fla.)
THIRD FIVE ROUNDS—Bill Butler, St. Bonaventure; John Chamberlain, C. W. Post; Anthony Koski, Providence; Bill Langheld, Fordham; Art Stephenson, Rhode Island.
ADDITIONAL ROUNDS—Harry Laurie, St. Peter's.

OAKLAND

FIRST FIVE ROUNDS—Warren Armstrong, Wichita; Jim Eakins, Brigham Young; Skip Harlicka, South Carolina; Bob Kauffman, Guilford; Stuart Lantz, Nebraska; Henry Logan, Western Carolina; Garfield Smith, Eastern Kentucky.
SECOND FIVE ROUNDS—Jim McKean, Washington State; Bud Ogden, Santa Clara; Rusty Parker, Miami (Fla.); Loy Petersen, Oregon State; John Trapp, UNLV.
THIRD FIVE ROUNDS—Russ Critchfield, California; Hal Grant, Pepperdine; Art Harris, Stanford; Bryan Phillips, Valdosta; Tony Sapit, Carroll (Mont.).

NBA 1969

FIRST ROUND Milwaukee—Kareem Abdul-Jabbar, UCLA; Phoenix—Neal Walk, Florida; Seattle—Lucius Allen, UCLA; Detroit—Terry Driscoll, Boston College; Chicago—Larry Cannon, LaSalle; San Diego—Bobby Smith, Tulsa; San Francisco—Bob Portman, Creighton; Cincinnati—Herm Gilliam, Purdue; Boston—Jo Jo White, Kansas; Atlanta—Butch Beard, Louisville; New York—John Warren, St. John's; Los Angeles—Willie McCarter, Drake; Philadelphia—Bud Ogden, Santa Clara; Baltimore—Mike Davis, Virginia Union; Los Angeles—Rick Roberson, Cincinnati.

SECOND ROUND Chicago (from Phoenix)—Simmie Hill, West Texas State; Milwaukee—Bob Greacen, Rutgers; Seattle—Ron Taylor, USC; Detroit—Willie Norwood, Alcorn A&M; Chicago—Kenny Spain, Houston; San Diego—Bernie Williams, LaSalle; San Francisco—Ed Siudet, Holy Cross; Chicago (from Cincinnati)—John Baum, Temple; Phoenix (from Boston)—Gene Williams, Kansas State; Atlanta—Wally Anderzunas, Creighton; New York—Bill Bunting, North Carolina; Los Angeles—Dick Garrett, Southern Illinois; Philadelphia—Willie Taylor, LeMoyne; Baltimore—Willie Scott, Alabama State.

THIRD ROUND Phoenix—Floyd Kerr, Colorado State; Milwaukee—Harley Swift, East Tennessee State; Seattle—Leroy Winfield, North Texas State; Phoenix (from Detroit)—Lamar Green, Morehead; Chicago—Norm Van Lier, St. Francis (Pa.); San Diego—Charles Bonaparte, Norfolk State; San Francisco—Tom Hagan, Vanderbilt; Cincinnati—Luther Rackley, Xavier (Ohio); Boston—Julius Keye, Alcorn A&M; Phoenix (from Atlanta)—Lloyd Kerr, Colorado State; New York—Ed Mast, Temple; Cincinnati (from Los Angeles)—Luther Green, LIU; Philadelphia—Mike Grosso, Louisville; Baltimore—Fred Carter, Mount St. Mary's.

FOURTH ROUND Phoenix—Dennis Stewart, Michigan; Milwaukee—Bob Dandridge, Norfolk State; Seattle—Hal Booker, Cheyney State; Detroit—Ted Wierman, Washington State; Chicago—Dave Nash, Kansas; San Diego—Johnny Allen, Bethune-Cookman; San Francisco—Lee Lafayette, Michigan State; Cincinnati—Ron Sanford, New Mexico; Boston—Steve Kuberski, Bradley; Atlanta—Billy Hann, Tennessee; New York—Elnardo Webster, St. Peter's; Atlanta (from Los Angeles)—Don Griffin, Stanford; Philadelphia—Dave Scholz, Illinois; Baltimore—Gene Ford, Western Michigan.

FIFTH ROUND Phoenix—Rich Jones, Memphis State; Milwaukee—Ken Heitz, UCLA; Seattle—Jerry King, Louisville; Detroit—Steve Mix, Toledo; Chicago—Chris Ellis, Virginia Tech; San Diego—Charles Hentz, Arkansas A&M; San Francisco—Willie Wise, Drake; Cincinnati—Jake Ford, Maryland State; Boston—George Thompson, Marquette; Atlanta—Mike Mitchell, West Texas State; New York—Gene Littles, High Point; Los Angeles—Wilbert Jones, Albany State; Philadelphia—Joe Cromer, Temple; Baltimore—Willie Jackson, Morehead State.

SIXTH ROUND Phoenix—Dan Sadlier, Dayton; Milwaukee—John Arthurs, Tulane; Seattle—Ben McGilmer, Iowa; Detroit—Larry Jeffries, Trinity; Chicago—George Tinsley, Kentucky Wesleyan; San Diego—Bob Tallent, George Washington; San Francisco—Dan Obravak, Dayton; Cincinnati—Mel Coleman, Stout State; Boston—Dolph Pulliam, Drake; Atlanta—Guy Mackner, South Dakota; New York—Dwight Durante, Catawba; Los Angeles—Dick Grubar, North Carolina; Philadelphia—John Jones, Villanova; Baltimore—Paul Loveday, California.

SEVENTH ROUND Phoenix—Bill Sweet, UCLA; Milwaukee—Bill Keller, Purdue; Seattle—Greg Wittman, Western Carolina; Detroit—Steve Vandenberg, Duke; Chicago—Frank Judge, Houston Tillotson; San Diego—Lynn Shackelford, UCLA; San Francisco—Pat Foley, Pacific; Cincinnati—L. C. Bowen, Bradley; Boston—Jim Johnson, Wisconsin; Atlanta—Bob Bundy, Vanderbilt; New York—Chris Thomforde, Princeton; Los Angeles—Kari Liimbo, Brigham Young; Philadelphia—Dave Hamilton, West Virginia State; Baltimore—Jeff Claypool, Grove City.

EIGHTH ROUND Phoenix—Bob Edwards, Arizona State; Milwaukee—John Schell, Wisconsin; Seattle—Theartis Wallace, Central Washington; Detroit—Bob Arnzen, Notre Dame; Chicago—Roger Moller, Westmar; San Diego—Bill DeHeer, Indiana; San Francisco—

Steve Rippe, Santa Barbara; Cincinnati—Merton Bancroft, Southwest Missouri State; Boston—Bob Whitmore, Notre Dame; Atlanta—Bob Christian, Grambling; New York—Jim Healey, Rockhurst; Los Angeles—Joe Smith, Oklahoma State; Philadelphia—Jim Bowles, Trinity (Tex.); Baltimore—Barry White, Hofstra.

NINTH ROUND Phoenix—Steve Jennings, Southern California; Milwaukee—Jim Satalin, St. Bonaventure; Seattle—Vince Fritz, Oregon State; Detroit—George Reynolds, Houston; Chicago—Sterling Burke, Northwestern; San Diego—Larry Cheatham, Tulsa; San Francisco—Greg Reed, Sacramento State; Cincinnati—James Hurley, Transylvania; Boston—Gordon Smith, Cincinnati; Atlanta—Pete Gayeska, Massachusetts; New York—Roger Walaszak, Columbia; Los Angeles—Jim Smith, Northern Illinois; Philadelphia—Larry Lewis, St. Francis (Pa.); Baltimore—Gary Major, Duquesne.

TENTH ROUND Phoenix—Rich Abrahamson, Oregon; Milwaukee—Willie Brown, Middle Tennessee; Seattle—Al Cueto, Tulsa; Detroit—Bill English, Winston-Salem; Chicago—Al Smith, Bradley; San Diego—Lee Sims, Ashland; San Francisco—Dick Chapman, San Francisco State; Cincinnati—Bill Bowes, Elon; Boston—Jim Picka, High Point; Atlanta—Dick Stewart, Rutgers; New York—Frank McLaughlin, Fordham; Los Angeles—Phil Argento, Kentucky; Philadelphia—Bill Justus, Tennessee; Baltimore—Frank Bartleson, Tennessee Tech.

ELEVENTH ROUND Phoenix—Fred Lind, Duke; Milwaukee—Bob Presley, California; Seattle—Jim Connolly, Bowling Green; Detroit—Rusty Clark, North Carolina; Chicago—Larry Bergh, Weber State; San Diego—Justus Thigpen, Weber State; San Francisco—Rich Holmberg, St. Mary's; Cincinnati—Jim Supple, Georgetown; Boston—Larry Frinston, Kenyon; Atlanta—Loran Bracci, San Fernando Valley State; New York—Marvin Lewis, Southampton; Los Angeles—Ron Peret, Texas A&M; Philadelphia—Bruce Sloan, Kansas; Baltimore—Gerald McKee, Ohio.

TWELFTH ROUND Phoenix—Bob Miller, Toledo; Milwaukee—Jack Lutz, Carthage; Seattle—John Smith, Puget Sound; Chicago—Harry Hall, Wyoming; San Diego—Raul Duarte, South Dakota State; San Francisco—Joe Callahan, San Francisco State; Cincinnati—Mike Davis, Colorado State; Boston—Rod Forbes, Boston State; Atlanta—Dave Jones, LaVerne; New York—Bill O'Rourke, St. John Fisher; Los Angeles—Jack Gillespie, Montana State; Philadelphia—Roland Taylor, LaSalle; Baltimore—Bob Washington, Tulsa.

THIRTEENTH ROUND Phoenix—Andy White, Texas-El Paso; Milwaukee—Lee Osgood, Northeastern; Seattle—Bob Burrow, Seattle Pacific; Chicago—Rick Kirkland, Norfolk State; San Diego—Joe McBride, Augusta; Cincinnati—Ted Johnson, Baldwin Wallace; Boston—Billy Evans, Boston College; Atlanta—Dick Barton, Riverside; New York—James Wyatt, Northwestern (La.); Los Angeles—Mallory Chestnutt, Tuskegee; Baltimore—Bill Thompson, Shephard.

FOURTEENTH ROUND Phoenix—Marv Schmitt, West Mexico; Milwaukee—Laymon Stewart, Lakeland; Seattle—Jerry Conley, Morehead; Chicago—Bill Voight, SMU; San Diego—Mike Heckman, California-Irvine; Atlanta—Mike Dahl, Oglethorpe; New York—Rich Travis, Oklahoma City; Los Angeles—Mack Calvin, Southern California; Baltimore—Perry Johnson, Robert Morris JC.

FIFTEENTH ROUND Phoenix—Bob Beamon, Texas-El Paso; Milwaukee—Stan Wlodarszek, LaSalle; Seattle—Ernie Powell, Southern California; San Diego—Jerry Nickens, Tougaloo; Atlanta—Norm Carmichael, Virginia; Baltimore—Jodie Harrison, Illinois.

SIXTEENTH ROUND Phoenix—Wayne Huckel, Davidson; Milwaukee—Bill Voight, SMU; Seattle—Danny Cornett, Morehead State; San Diego—Dick Groves, San Jose State; Atlanta—Buddy Cornelius, Jacksonville (Ala.); Baltimore—Phil Harris, Texas A&M.

SEVENTEENTH ROUND Phoenix—Howie Dickerman, Central Connecticut; Milwaukee—Lynn Phillips, SMU; Seattle—Steve Honeycutt, Kansas State; San Diego—Steve Howell, Ohio State; Atlanta—John Tolmie, Navy; Baltimore—Tom Haggart, Brandeis.

EIGHTEENTH ROUND Phoenix—Al Nuness, Minnesota; Milwaukee—Ken Hall, Westminster; San Diego—Joe Pridgen, North Carolina College; Atlanta—Cliff Parsons, Air Force; Baltimore—Chip Case, Virginia.

NINETEENTH ROUND Phoenix—Solomon Davis, Kentucky State; San Diego—Blaine Royer, Illinois State; Atlanta—Grady O'Malley, Manhattan; Baltimore—Brian Heaney, Acadia.

TWENTIETH ROUND Phoenix—Jim Plump, Northern Arizona; Atlanta—Carl Rodwell, California-Riverside; Baltimore—Stan McKain, Southern.

ABA 1969

CAROLINA

FIRST FIVE ROUNDS—L. C. Bowen, Bradley; Mel Coleman, Stout (Wis.); Steve Kuberski, Bradley; Steve Mix, Toledo; Jesse Price, Milliken; Neal Walk, Florida.
SECOND FIVE ROUNDS—Howie Dickerman, Central Connecticut; Gene Ford, Western

Michigan; Gene Littles, High Point; Jack Stenner, Missouri-St. Louis; Justus Thigpen, Weber State.
ADDITIONAL ROUNDS—Phil Argento, Kentucky; Rudy Bennett, New York Tech.

DALLAS

FIRST FIVE ROUNDS—Willie Brown, Middle Tennessee; Bobby Christian, Grambling; Tom Hagan, Vanderbilt; A.W. Holt, Jackson (Miss.) State; Cliff Shegogg, Colorado State.
SECOND FIVE ROUNDS—Butch Beard, Louisville; Jake Ford, Maryland State; Jud Roberts, Mercer (Ga.); Ron Sanford, New Mexico; Willie Scott, Troy (Ala.) State.

DENVER

FIRST FIVE ROUNDS—Isiah King, Hiram Scott; Jerry King, Louisville; Bob Portman, Creighton; Bob Presley, California; Bob Tallent, George Washington; Greg Wittman, Western Carolina.
SECOND FIVE ROUNDS—Harry Hall, Wyoming; Jim Healey, Rockhurst (Mo.); Larry Jeffries, Trinity (Tex.); Bill Justus, Tennessee; Elnardo Webster, St. Peter's (N.J.).

INDIANA

FIRST FIVE ROUNDS—Bob Arnzen, Notre Dame; Dick Grubar, North Carolina; Tony Masiello, Canisius; Willie McCarter, Drake.
SECOND FIVE ROUNDS—Bill Deher, Indiana; Dave Golden, Duke; Bill Keller, Purdue; Gerald McKee, Ohio; Ron Peret, Texas A&M.
ADDITIONAL ROUNDS—John Jamerson, Fairmont State; Jim Stephenson, Maine.

KENTUCKY

FIRST FIVE ROUNDS—Bob Dandridge, Norfolk State; Herm Gilliam, Purdue; Mike Grosso, Louisville; Dave Scholz, Illinois; Gene Williams, Kansas State.
SECOND FIVE ROUNDS—Chris Ellis, Virginia Tech; Dick Garrett, Southern Illinois; Willie Norwood, Alcorn A&M; Dan Sadlier, Dayton; Bobby Washington, Eastern Kentucky.
ADDITIONAL ROUNDS—Doug Brittelle, Rutgers; Gary Major, Duquesne.

LOS ANGELES

FIRST FIVE ROUNDS—John Baum, Temple; Simmie Hill, West Texas State; Bobby Smith, Tulsa; Dennis Stewart, Michigan; Ted Weirman, Washington State.
SECOND FIVE ROUNDS—Mack Calvin, Southern California; Mike Davis, Colorado State; Roger Moeler, Westmar (Iowa); Dan Obrovac, Dayton; Leroy Winfield, North Texas State.
ADDITIONAL ROUNDS—Vince Fritz, Oregon State; Floyd Kerr, Colorado State.

MIAMI

FIRST FIVE ROUNDS—Bill Bunting, North Carolina; Larry Cannon, LaSalle; Bob Greacen, Rutgers; John Jones, Villanova; Wilbert Jones, Albany (Ga.) State; Jim Smith, Northern Illinois.
SECOND FIVE ROUNDS—Johnny Allen, Bethune-Cookman; John Faircloth, Biscayne (Fla.); Luther Green, LIU; Larry Lewis, St. Francis (Pa.); Lynn Shackelford, UCLA.
ADDITIONAL ROUNDS—Ed Szczesny, LaSalle.

MINNESOTA

FIRST FIVE ROUNDS—Luther Rackley, Xavier (Ohio); George Thompson, Marquette; Bob Whitmore, Notre Dame.
SECOND FIVE ROUNDS—Charley Bonaparte, Norfolk (Va.) State; Charles Hentz, Arkansas A&M; Wilbur Kirkland, Cheyney State; Lee Lafayette, Michigan State; Kari Liimbo, Brigham Young.
ADDITIONAL ROUNDS—Mike Davis, Virginia Union; Bill English, Winston-Salem; Rich Tyler, Cheyney State.

NEW ORLEANS

FIRST FIVE ROUNDS—John Arthurs, Tulane; Rusty Clark, North Carolina; Dave Nash, Kansas; Harley Swift, East Tennessee State; Willie Taylor, Temple.
SECOND FIVE ROUNDS—Sammy Little, Delta State; Charley Powell, Loyola (La.); James Wyatt, Northwestern Louisiana. Passed in ninth and 10th rounds.

NEW YORK

FIRST FIVE ROUNDS—Kareem Abdul-Jabbar, UCLA; Terry Driscoll, Boston College; Rick Roberson, Cincinnati; Ed Siudet, Holy Cross; Chris Thomforde, Princeton; Norm Van Lier, St. Francis (Pa.).
SECOND FIVE ROUNDS—Bill Evans, Boston College; Tom Haggerty, Brandeis; Rob Washington, NYU.
ADDITIONAL ROUNDS—Jess Claypool, Grove City (Pa.); Marv Lewis, Southampton (N.Y.).

OAKLAND

FIRST FIVE ROUNDS—Jack Gillespie, Montana State; Lamar Green, Morehead State; Don Griffin, Stanford; Edward Mast, Temple; Ron Taylor, Southern California.
SECOND FIVE ROUNDS—Bill Bowes, Elon; Joe Comer, Temple; Lloyd Kerr, Colorado State; Ken Spain, Houston; George Tinsley, Kentucky Wesleyan.
ADDITIONAL ROUNDS—Jim Johnson, Wisconsin; Ron Teixeria, Holy Cross.

NBA 1970 (MARCH 20, 1970)

FIRST ROUND   Detroit—Bob Lanier, St. Bonaventure; San Diego—Rudy Tomjanovich, Michigan; Atlanta (from San Francisco)—Pete Maravich, LSU; Boston—Dave Cowens, Florida State; Cincinnati—Sam Lacey, New Mexico State; Seattle—Jim Ard, Cincinnati; Cleveland—John Johnson, Iowa; Portland—Geoff Petrie, Princeton; Baltimore (from Buffalo)—George Johnson, Stephen F. Austin; Phoenix—Greg Howard, New Mexico; Chicago—Jimmy Collins, New Mexico State; Philadelphia—Al Henry, Wisconsin; Los Angeles—Jim McMillian, Columbia; Atlanta—John Vallely, UCLA; Buffalo (from Baltimore)—John Hummer, Princeton; Milwaukee—Gary Freeman, Oregon State; New York—Mike Price, Illinois.

SECOND ROUND   San Diego—Calvin Murphy, Niagara; Cincinnati (from San Francisco)—Nate Archibald, Texas-El Paso; Seattle (from Detroit)—Jake Ford, Maryland State; Boston—Rex Morgan, Jacksonville; Cincinnati—Doug Cook, Davidson; Seattle—Pete Cross, San Francisco; Buffalo—Cornell Warner, Jackson State; Portland—Walt Gilmore, Fort Valley State; Cleveland—Dave Sorenson, Ohio State; Phoenix—Fred Taylor, Pan American; Chicago—Paul Ruffner, Brigham Young; Phoenix (from Philadelphia)—Joe DePre, St. John's; Los Angeles—Earnest Killum, Stetson; Atlanta—Dan Hester, LSU; Detroit (from Baltimore)—Ken Warzynski, DePaul; Milwaukee—Bill Zopf, Duquesne; New York—Howie Wright, Austin Peay.

THIRD ROUND   San Diego—Curtis Perry, Southwest Missouri; San Francisco—Earl Higgins, Eastern Michigan; Detroit—Bob St. Pierre, Hanover; Boston—Willie Williams, Florida State; Cincinnati—Greg Hyder, Eastern New Mexico; Seattle—Garfield Heard, Oklahoma; Cleveland—Surry Oliver, Stephen F. Austin; Portland—Bill Cain, Iowa State; Buffalo—Chip Case, Virginia; Phoenix—Greg McDivitt, Ohio; Chicago—Lou Herndon, Jackson State; Philadelphia—Dennis Awtrey, Santa Clara; Detroit (from Los Angeles)—Jim Hayes, Boston U.; Phoenix (from Atlanta)—Vann Williford, North Carolina State; Baltimore—Seaburn Hill, Arizona State; Milwaukee—Marvin Winkler, Southwest Louisiana; New York—Al Williams, Drake.

FOURTH ROUND   San Diego—Jody Finney, Ohio State; San Francisco—Ralph Ogden, Santa Clara; Baltimore (from Detroit)—Bill Stricker, Pacific; Boston—Jon McKinney, Norfolk State; Cincinnati—Wade Fuller, Loyola (Ill.); Chicago (from Seattle)—John Davis, Alabama State; Buffalo—Erwin Polnick, Stephen F. Austin; Portland—Jim Penix, Bowling Green; Cleveland—Glen Vidnovic, Iowa; Phoenix—Bob Lienhard, Georgia; Chicago—Jimmy Wilson, Cheyney State; Philadelphia—Dan Crenshaw, Alabama State; Los Angeles—Larry Mikan, Minnesota; Atlanta—Fred Davis, Howard Payne; Baltimore—Billy Jones, Louisiana College; Milwaukee—Virgle Fredricks, Drury; New York—John Marren, Manhattan.

FIFTH ROUND   San Diego—James Gilbert, Adams State; San Francisco—Levi Fontaine, Maryland State; Detroit—Bill Jankans, Long Beach State; Boston—Tom Carter, Paul Quinn; Cincinnati—Uluss Thompson, Wiley; Seattle—Boyd Lynch, Eastern Kentucky; Cleveland—Wayne Sokolowski, Ashland; Portland—Ron Knight, Los Angeles State; Buffalo—Robert Moore, Central State (Ohio); Phoenix—John Canine, Ohio; Chicago—George Johnson, Dillard; Philadelphia—Perry Wallace, Vanderbilt; Los Angeles—John Fultz, Rhode Island; Atlanta—Bob Riley, Mount St. Mary's; Baltimore—Gary Zeller, Drake; Milwaukee—Mike Grosso, Louisville; New York—Jim Oxley, Army.

SIXTH ROUND   San Diego—Mike Kretzer, East Tennessee; San Francisco—Vic Bartolome, Oregon State; Detroit—Sevira Brown, DePaul; Boston—Rod McIntyre, Jacksonville; Cincinnati—Charles Bishop, Louisiana Tech; Seattle—Sam Robinson, Long Beach State; Buffalo—Doug Hess, Toledo; Portland—George Janky, Dayton; Cleveland—Joe Cooke, Indiana; Phoenix—Joe Thomas, Marquette; Chicago—Lonny Kluttz, North Carolina A&T; Philadelphia—Jerry Venable, Kansas State; Los Angeles—Jerry Kroll, Davidson; Atlanta—Dave Parker, Windham; Baltimore—Marvin Polnick, Stephen F. Austin; Milwaukee—Willy Watson, Oklahoma City; New York—Jim Signorile, NYU.

SEVENTH ROUND   San Diego—Bill Paultz, St. John's; San Francisco—Joe Bergman, Creighton; Detroit—Marv Copeland, Michigan Lutheran; Boston—Charlie Scott, North Carolina; Cincinnati—Mike Bernard, Kentucky State; Seattle—James Morgan, Maryland State; Cleveland—Narvis Anderson, Stephen F. Austin; Portland—Claude English, Rhode Island; Buffalo—Cliff Shegogg, Colorado State; Phoenix—Heyward Dotson, Columbia; Chicago—Lou West, Seattle; Philadelphia—Carlton Poole, Philadelphia Textile; Los Angeles—Willie Woods, Eastern Kentucky; Atlanta—John Shinall, Jackson State; Baltimore—Charlie Wallace, Oklahoma City; Milwaukee—John Rinka, Kenyon; New York—Ray Hodge, Wagner.

EIGHTH ROUND   San Diego—Don Adams, Northwestern; San Francisco—Jeff Sewell, Marquette; Detroit—Dan Issel, Kentucky; Boston—Bob Croft, Tennessee; Cincinnati—Joel McBride, Augusta; Seattle—George Irvine, Washington; Buffalo—Larry Woods, West Virginia; Portland—Doug Boyd, TCU; Cleveland—Walter Robertson, Loyola (Ill.); Phoenix—Steve Patterson, UCLA; Chicago—Mike Casey, Kentucky; Philadelphia—Fran O'Hanlon, Villanova; Los Angeles—Rick Mount, Purdue; Atlanta—Herb White, Georgia; Baltimore—Tom Dyksera, Wheaton; Milwaukee—Jim Sarno, Northwestern; New York—Greg Fillmore, Cheyney State.

NINTH ROUND   San Diego—Jim Gottschall, Dayton; San Francisco—Lou Small, Nevada; Detroit—Alex Wynn, Dartmouth; Boston—Tom Little, Seattle; Cincinnati—Bob Mabry, Rio Grande; Seattle—Claude Virden, Murray State; Cleveland—Tom Lagodich, Kent State; Portland—Billy Gaskins, Oregon; Buffalo—Larry Duckworth, Henderson State; Phoenix—Carl Ashley, Wyoming; Chicago—Glen Johnson, Jackson State; Philadelphia—Mike Hauer, St. Joseph's; Los Angeles—Bobby Sands, Pepperdine; Atlanta—Larry Jackson, Sul Ross; Baltimore—Will Hetzel, Maryland; Milwaukee—Joe Hamilton, North Texas State; New York—Walter Banks, Western Kentucky.

TENTH ROUND   San Diego—Toke Coleman, Eastern Kentucky; San Francisco—Coby Dietrick, San Jose State; Detroit—Bruce Chapman, Nevada; Boston—Mike Maloy, Davidson; Cincinnati—Carl Johnson, Gustavus Adolphus; Seattle—Chuck Lloyd, Yankton; Buffalo—Joe Taylor, Dillard; Portland—Israel Oliver, Elizabeth City; Cleveland—Ken Johnson, Indiana; Phoenix—Gerhardus Schreur, Arizona State; Chicago—Dale Blaut, West Texas State; Philadelphia—Gordon Stiles, American; Los Angeles—Kindell Stephens, Fisk; Atlanta—Manuel Raga, Mexico; Baltimore—Ron Becker, New Mexico; Milwaukee—Bob Seemer, Georgia Tech; New York—Don Curnutt, Miami (Fla.).

ELEVENTH ROUND   San Diego—Ron Belton, Bellarmine; Detroit—Rick Anheuser, North Carolina State; Cincinnati—Ted Hillary, St. Joseph's (Ind.); Seattle—Andy Owens, Florida; Cleveland—Dave Schneider, Wayne State; Portland—Don McClemore, Bowling Green; Buffalo—Dick Walker, Wake Forest; Phoenix—Jim Walls, Clark; Chicago—Doug Howard, Brigham Young; Philadelphia—David Whitley, Tufts; Los Angeles—Bob Dukiet, Boston College; Atlanta—Dino Meneghin, Italy; Baltimore—Mel Bell, Houston.

TWELFTH ROUND   San Diego—Jim Brooks, Nebraska; Detroit—Don Ogletree, Cincinnati; Cincinnati—Reggie Roach, Virginia State; Seattle—John Brunson, Furman; Portland—Paul Adams, Central Washington; Cleveland—Ollie Taylor, Houston; Phoenix—Ric Cobb, Marquette; Chicago—Booker Brown, Middle Tennessee; Los Angeles—Dewey Varner, Tuskegee; Baltimore—Ben McGilmer, Iowa.

THIRTEENTH ROUND   San Diego—Harry Lozon, Old Dominion; Detroit—Ernest Hardy, Harvard; Cincinnati—Larry Gray, Huston-Pillotson; Seattle—Allen McManus, Winston-Salem; Cleveland—Kevin Wilson, Ashland; Portland—Alex Boyd, Nevada-Reno; Phoenix—Fred Carpenter, Hawaii; Chicago—Charles Bloodworth, Northwest Louisiana; Los Angeles—Garry Elliott, Washington; Baltimore—Dan Debardabi, Northern Arizona.

FOURTEENTH ROUND   San Diego—Clyde Oatis, Aurora; Detroit—Randy Smith, Buffalo State; Cincinnati—Andy Jennings, Alderson Broaddus; Seattle—Don Beenson, Linfield; Portland—Frank Loteridge, Pan American; Cleveland—Don Tomilson, Missouri; Phoenix—Chad Calabria, Iowa; Chicago—Paul Funkhouser, McKendree; Los Angeles—Ron Sanford, New Mexico State; Baltimore—Mike Williams, Northern Arizona.

FIFTEENTH ROUND   San Diego—Jay Bond, Washington; Detroit—Dennis Clark, Springfield (Mass.); Cincinnati—Mike Neer, Washington & Lee; Cleveland—Steve Wannamaker, Drake; Portland—John Canady, Miami (Fla.); Phoenix—Walt Williams, Miami (Ohio); Chicago—Paul Otay, Boise State; Los Angeles—Will Teague, Youngstown; Baltimore—Ted Rose, Northern Michigan.

SIXTEENTH ROUND   San Diego—Dean Olofson, Wayne State; Detroit—Harvey Marlatt, Eastern Michigan; Cincinnati—Paul Favorite, Georgetown; Portland—Doug Williams, St. Mary's (Texas); Cleveland—Steve Wilson, Hanover; Los Angeles—Pete Walthour, Fort Valley; Baltimore—Don Rather, Northern Arizona.

SEVENTEENTH ROUND   San Diego—Dennis Dickens, Azusa; Cleveland—Bob Peterson, Concordia; Portland—(first name unavailable) Borollas, Trinity; Los Angeles—Bob Thate, Occidental; Baltimore—Vince Fritz, Oregon State.

EIGHTEENTH ROUND   San Diego—Jeff Cunningham, California-Irvine; Portland—Bruce Butchko, Southern Illinois; Cleveland—John Cannon, Grambling.

NINETEENTH ROUND   San Diego—Rick Erickson, Washington State; Cleveland—Allen Waller, St. Mary's (Kansas); Portland—Mark Gabriel, Hanover.

NBA 1970 EXPANSION DRAFT (MAY 11, 1970)

BUFFALO   Emmette Bryant, Boston; Fred Crawford, Milwaukee; Dick Garrett, Los Angeles; Herm Gilliam, Cincinnati; Bill Hosket, New York; Bailey Howell, Boston; Paul Long, Detroit; Mike Lynn, Los Angeles; Don May, New York; Ray Scott, Baltimore; George Wilson, Philadelphia.

CLEVELAND   Butch Beard, Atlanta; Len Chappell, Milwaukee; Johnny Egan, Los Angeles; Bobby Lewis, San Francisco; McCoy McLemore, Detroit; Don Ohl, Atlanta; Loy Petersen, Chicago; Luther Rackley, Cincinnati; Bobby Smith, San Diego; John Warren, New York; Walt Wesley, Chicago.

PORTLAND   Rick Adelman, San Diego; Jerry Chambers, Phoenix; LeRoy Ellis, Baltimore; Fred Hetzel, Philadelphia; Joe Kennedy, Seattle; Ed Manning, Chicago; Stan McKenzie, Phoenix; Dorie Murrey, Seattle; Pat Riley, San Diego; Dale Schlueter, San Francisco; Larry Siegfried, Boston.

ABA 1970

CAROLINA

FIRST FIVE ROUNDS—Bob Leinhard, Georgia; Pete Maravich, Louisiana State; Greg McDivit, Ohio University; Vann Williford, North Carolina State.
SECOND FIVE ROUNDS—Paul Adams, Central Washington; Carl Johnson, Gustavus Adolphus; Earnest Killum, Stetson; Wayne Sokolowski, Ashland State.
THIRD FIVE ROUNDS—Don Adams, Northwestern; Norvis Anderson, Stephen F. Austin; John Fultz, Rhode Island; Chuck Lloyd, Yankton; Jim Signorile, NYU.

DENVER

FIRST FIVE ROUNDS—Greg Daust, Missouri-St. Louis; Spencer Haywood, Detroit; Dan Hester, Louisiana State; Greg Hyder, East New Mexico; John Marren, Manhattan; Ron St. Pierre, Hanover; John Vallely, UCLA.
SECOND FIVE ROUNDS—Ron Becker, New Mexico; Joe McBride, Augusta; Larry Mikan, Minnesota; Jim Penix, Bowling Green; Mike Price, Illinois.
THIRD FIVE ROUNDS—Fred Taylor, Pan American; Ken Warzyski, DePaul.

FLORIDIANS

FIRST FIVE ROUNDS—John Hummer, Princeton; Sam Robinson, Long Beach State.
SECOND FIVE ROUNDS—Clarence Ellis, Albany (Ga.) State; Levi Fontaine, Maryland State; Walt Gilmore, Fort Valley (Ga.) State; John McKinney, Norfolk State; Fran O'Hanlon, Villanova; Dan Sager, Kentucky State; Gary Zeller, Drake.
THIRD FIVE ROUNDS—Rubin Daniels, Cheyney State.

INDIANA

FIRST FIVE ROUNDS—Dennis Awtrey, Santa Clara; Vince Fritz, Oregon State; Rick Mount, Purdue; Surry Oliver, Stephen F. Austin.
SECOND FIVE ROUNDS—Don Curnutt, Miami; Rick Erickson, Washington State; Billy Jones, Louisiana College; Jerry Kroll, Davidson; Bob Riley, Mount St. Mary's.
THIRD FIVE ROUNDS—Heyward Dotson, Columbia; Mickey Foster, Arizona; Seaburn Hill, Arizona State; Ted Hillery, St. Joseph's (Ind.); Jeff Sewell, Marquette.

KENTUCKY

FIRST FIVE ROUNDS—Pete Cross, San Francisco; Dan Issel, Kentucky; Mike Pratt, Kentucky; Claude Virden, Murray State; Howard Wright, Austin Peay.
SECOND FIVE ROUNDS—Joe Bergman, Creighton; Mike Casey, Kentucky; Ted Rose, Northern Michigan; Charles Wallace, Oklahoma City; Al Williams, Drake.
THIRD FIVE ROUNDS—Skip Hess, Toledo; Perry Wallace, Vanderbilt; Lou West, Seattle; Willie Woods, Eastern Kentucky.

MEMPHIS

FIRST FIVE ROUNDS—Garfield Heard, Oklahoma; George Johnson, Stephen F. Austin; Sam Lacey, New Mexico State; Wendell Ladner, Mississippi Southern.
SECOND FIVE ROUNDS—Charles Bishop, Louisiana Tech; Coby Dietrick, San Jose State; George Johnson, Dillard; Robert Mabry, Rio Grande; Marvin Winkler, Southwestern Louisiana.
THIRD FIVE ROUNDS—Ron Coleman, Mississippi; Frank Lothridge, Pan American; Andy Owens, Florida.

NEW YORK

FIRST FIVE ROUNDS—Jim Ard, Cincinnati; Doug Cook, Davidson; Jim Hayes, Boston University; Bob Lanier, St. Bonaventure; Geoff Petrie, Princeton.
SECOND FIVE ROUNDS—Joe DePre, St. John's (N.Y.); Harvey Marlatt, Eastern Michigan; Rod McIntyre, Jacksonville; Carleton Poole, Philadelphia Textile; Ollie Taylor, Houston.
THIRD FIVE ROUNDS—Dale Kelley, Northwestern; Carl Macklin, Florida State; Erwin Polnick, Stephen F. Austin; Mike Switzer, Texas-El Paso; Jerry Venable, Kansas State.

PITTSBURGH

FIRST FIVE ROUNDS—Vic Bartolome, Oregon State; George Janky, Dayton; Mike Maloy, Davidson; Rex Morgan, Jacksonville; Calvin Murphy, Niagara; Doug Ogletree, Cincinnati; Cornell Warner, Jackson State.
SECOND FIVE ROUNDS—Lou Herndon, Jackson State; Lavern Howard, Grambling; Bill Jankins, Long Beach State.
THIRD FIVE ROUNDS—Robert Kornegay, Hampton Institute; Boyd Lynch, Eastern Kentucky; Willie Watson, Oklahoma City; Jimmy Wilson, Cheyney State; Billy Zopf, Duquesne.

TEXAS

FIRST FIVE ROUNDS—Nate Archibald, Texas-El Paso; Immanual Cannon, Grambling; Bob Croft, Tennessee; Joe Hamilton, North Texas State; John Johnson, Iowa; Stan Love, Oregon. SECOND FIVE ROUNDS—Michael Bernard, Kentucky State; Bill Cain, Iowa State; Randall Causey, McMurry; Al Henry, Wisconsin; Steve Patterson, UCLA; Glen Vidnovic, Iowa. THIRD FIVE ROUNDS—Paul Brown, Arkansas Tech; Ron Pitts, Wiley.

UTAH

FIRST FIVE ROUNDS—Carl Ashley, Wyoming; Jim Collins, New Mexico State; Dave Cowens, Florida State; Fred Davis, Howard Payne; Jim McMillian, Columbia; Dave Sorensen, Ohio State; Rudy Tomjanovich, Michigan. SECOND FIVE ROUNDS—Stan Dodds, Wyoming; Virgil Frederick, Drury; Ralph Ogden, Santa Clara; Israel Oliver, Elizabeth City; Bill Stricker, Pacific; Kevin Wilson, Ashland (Col.). THIRD FIVE ROUNDS—Bruce Chapman, Nevada-Las Vegas; Dennis Clark, Springfield; Ron Knight, California State-Los Angeles; Robert Moore, Central State (Ohio); Lou Small, Nevada-Las Vegas.

VIRGINIA

FIRST FIVE ROUNDS—Gary Freeman, Oregon State; James Gilbert, Adams State; Gregg Howard, New Mexico; George Irvine, Washington; Bill Paultz, St. John's; Charlie Scott, North Carolina. SECOND FIVE ROUNDS—Tommy Carter, Paul Quinn; Tom Everette, Carson-Newman; Curtis Perry, Southwest Missouri State; Paul Ruffner, Brigham Young; Will Teague, Youngstown. THIRD FIVE ROUNDS—Charles Bloodworth, Northwest Louisiana State; Leon Edmund, Portland; Andy Jennings, Alderson-Broaddus; George Jerman, West New England; Scott Warner, Brigham Young.

NBA 1971 (MARCH 29, 1971)

FIRST ROUND Cleveland—Austin Carr, Notre Dame; Portland—Sidney Wicks, UCLA; Buffalo—Elmore Smith, Kentucky State; Cincinnati—Ken Durrett, LaSalle; Atlanta—George Trapp, Long Beach State; Seattle—Fred Brown, Iowa; San Diego—Cliff Meely, Colorado; San Francisco—Darnell Hillman, San Jose State; Baltimore—Stan Love, Oregon; Boston—Clarence Glover, Western Kentucky; Detroit—Curtis Rowe, UCLA; Philadelphia—Dana Lewis, Tulsa; Los Angeles—Jim Cleamons, Ohio State; Phoenix—John Roche, South Carolina; Chicago—Kennedy McIntosh, Eastern Michigan; New York—Dean Meminger, Marquette; Milwaukee—Collis Jones, Notre Dame.

SECOND ROUND Cleveland—Steve Patterson, UCLA; Buffalo—Fred Hilton, Grambling; Chicago (from Portland)—Willie Sojourner, Weber State; Cincinnati—John Mengelt, Auburn; Atlanta—Ted McClain, Tennessee State; Seattle—Jim McDaniels, Western Kentucky; San Diego—Mike Newlin, Utah; Portland (from San Francisco)—Charles Yelverton, Fordham; Buffalo—Amos Thomas, Southwest Oklahoma State; Portland (from Baltimore)—Rick Fisher, Colorado State; Boston—Jim Rose, Western Kentucky; Detroit—Bunny Wilson, Baltimore; Buffalo (from Philadelphia)—Spencer Haywood, Detroit; Cincinnati (from Los Angeles)—Joe Bergman, Creighton; Chicago (from Phoenix)—Howard Porter, Villanova; Philadelphia (from Chicago)—Marvin Stewart, Nebraska; New York—Gregg Northington, Alabama State; Cleveland (from Milwaukee)—Willie Long, New Mexico.

THIRD ROUND Cleveland—Gerald Lockett, Arkansas AM&N; Portland—Larry Steele, Kentucky; Cincinnati—Rich Yunkus, Georgia Tech; Atlanta—Jeff Halliburton, Drake; Chicago (from Seattle)—Clifford Ray, Oklahoma; Cleveland (from San Diego)—Jackie Ridgle, California; Portland (from San Francisco)—Bill Smith, Syracuse; Baltimore—Rich Rinaldi, St. Peter's; Boston—Dave Robisch, Kansas; Detroit—Marv Roberts, Utah State; Philadelphia—Dave Wohl, Penn; Chicago (from Los Angeles)—Mike Gale, Elizabeth City; Phoenix—Dennis Layton, Southern California; Chicago—Dick Gibbs, Texas-El Paso; New York—Ken Mayfield, Tuskegee; Milwaukee—Gary Brell, Marquette.

FOURTH ROUND Cleveland—Cliff Harris, Hardin-Simmons; Buffalo—Jim O'Brien, Boston College; Portland—Bobby Fields, LaSalle; Cincinnati—Sid Catlett, Notre Dame; Atlanta—Jim Welch, Houston; Seattle—Pembrook Burrows, Jacksonville; San Diego—Tom Owens, South Carolina; San Francisco—Greg Gary, St. Bonaventure; Baltimore—Willie Allen, Miami (Ohio); Boston—Randy Denton, Duke; Detroit—Jarrett Durham, Duquesne; Philadelphia—Erwin Johnson, Augusta; Los Angeles—Roger Brown, Kansas; Phoenix—Walt Szczerbiak, George Washington; Chicago—Jim Irving, St. Louis; New York—Steve Niles, Texas A&M; Milwaukee—Henry Smith, Missouri.

FIFTH ROUND Cleveland—Brian Mahoney, Manhattan; Buffalo—Garry Nelson, Duquesne; Portland—Hector Blondet, Murray State; Cincinnati—Jim Guymond, Eastern New Mexico; Cincinnati (from Atlanta)—Tyrone Marioneaux, Loyola (La.); Seattle—Jeff Smith, New Mexico State; San Diego—Rudy Benjamin, Michigan State; San Francisco—Odis Allison, Nevada-Las Vegas; Baltimore—Don Johnson, Tennessee; San Diego (from Boston)—Greg Nelson, Jacksonville; Detroit—Vincent White, Savannah State; Philadelphia—Richard Hood, Phillips; Los Angeles—Lee Dedmon, North Carolina; Phoenix—Ken Gardner, Utah;

Chicago—Larry Weatherford, Purdue; Phoenix (from New York)—Bob Kissane, Holy Cross; Milwaukee—Barry Nelson, Duquesne.

SIXTH ROUND Cleveland—Mike Childress, Colorado State; Buffalo—Glen Summors, Gannon; Portland—Jim Day, Morehead; Cincinnati—Gil McGregor, Wake Forest; Atlanta—Willie Humes, Idaho State; Seattle—Mike Necaise, William Carey; San Diego—Garry Reist, Rice; San Francisco—Charlie Johnson, California; Baltimore—John Novey, Mount St. Mary's; Boston—Thorpe Weber, Vanderbilt; Detroit—Jim Larranaga, Providence; Philadelphia—Jake Jones, Assumption; Los Angeles—Bill Brickhouse, Montana State; Phoenix—William Graham, Kentucky State; Chicago—Jim England, Tennessee; New York—Bill Mainor, Fordham; Milwaukee—Ed Kemp, Adams State.

SEVENTH ROUND Cleveland—Tom Bush, Drake; Buffalo—Randy Smith, Buffalo State; Portland—Gene Knolle, Texas Tech; Cincinnati—Ollie Shannon, Minnesota; Atlanta—Mike Jordan, Savannah State; Seattle—John Duncan, Kentucky Wesleyan; San Diego—Eric Hill, Minnesota; San Francisco—Ken May, Dayton; Baltimore—Dennis Hogg, Washington State; Boston—Skip Young, Florida State; Detroit—Steve Kelly, Brigham Young; Philadelphia—Curtis Ford, Northeast Oklahoma State; Los Angeles—Gene Gathers, Bradley; Phoenix—Ralph Brateris, Trenton State; Chicago—Artis Gilmore, Jacksonville; New York—Danny Davis, Henderson State; Milwaukee—Gene Phillips, SMU.

EIGHTH ROUND Cleveland—Charlie Davis, Wake Forest; Buffalo—Craig Love, Ohio; Portland—John Sutter, Tulane; Cincinnati—Frank Fitzgerald, Boston College; Atlanta—Jim Smith, Kentucky Wesleyan; Seattle—Chuck Lowery, Puget Sound; San Diego—Rich Katherman, Duke; San Francisco—Jim Haderlein, Loyola (Cal.); Baltimore—Russell Golden, Jackson State; Boston—John Ribock, South Carolina; Detroit—Wayne Jones, Niagara; Philadelphia—Barry Yates, Maryland; Los Angeles—Luke Adams, Lamar Tech; Phoenix—Vernell Ellzy, Florida State; Chicago—Clarence Sherrod, Wisconsin; New York—Leroy Eldridge, Cheyney State; Milwaukee—Felix Thurston, Trinity (Tex.).

NINTH ROUND Cleveland—Rich Walker, Bowling Green; Buffalo—Gary Stewart, Canisius; Portland—Gene Kennedy, TCU; Atlanta—Ernie Fleming, Jacksonville; Seattle—Larry Holliday, Oregon; San Diego—Willie Kerry, Denver; San Francisco—Clarence Smith, Villanova; Baltimore—Ron Johnston, Murray State; Boston—Ray Green, California State (Pa.); Detroit—Paul Botts, Central Michigan; Philadelphia—Tom Lee, Arizona; Los Angeles—Bob Cheeks, Whittier; Phoenix—Mike Johnson, Kansas State; Chicago—Jackie Dinkins, Voorhees State; New York—Mike O'Brien, St. Leo's; Milwaukee—Rick Howat, Illinois.

TENTH ROUND Cleveland—Jim Meredith, Washington State; Buffalo—Don Ward, Colgate; Portland—Greg Starrick, Southern Illinois; Atlanta—Ron Rippicoe, David Lipscomb; Seattle—Ed Huston, Puget Sound; San Diego—Calvin Oliver, Pan American; San Francisco—Bill Drosdiak, Oregon; Baltimore—Eddie Myers, Arizona; Boston—Dale Dover, Harvard; Detroit—Steve Butcher, Pikeville; Philadelphia—Jim Dinwiddie, Kentucky; Los Angeles—Cliff Mosely, Quinnipiac; Phoenix—Tom Newell, Hawaii; Chicago—David Withers, Delaware State; New York—Andy Toth, Cheyney State; Milwaukee—Dan Fife, Michigan.

ELEVENTH ROUND Cleveland—Mike Casey, Kentucky; Buffalo—Bill Warner, Arizona; Portland—Howard Burford, Gonzaga; Atlanta—Levi Wyatt, Alcorn A&M; Seattle—Jerome Perry, Western Kentucky; San Diego—Doug Rex, California-Santa Barbara; Baltimore—Chuck Olowski, Baltimore; Boston—Reggie Brooks, New Hampshire College; Detroit—Larry Saunders, Duke; Philadelphia—Dana Pagett, USC; Phoenix—Paul Leitz, Western Carolina; Chicago—Al Smith, Bradley; New York—Ken Davis, Georgetown; Milwaukee—Blaine Henry, Marshall.

TWELFTH ROUND Cleveland—Doug Hess, Toledo; Buffalo—Butch Webster, LSU-New Orleans; Portland—Don Sechler, Delaware Valley; Atlanta—Roger Moore, Columbus College; San Diego—Chris Schrobilgen, Southern California; Baltimore—Bob Connor, Loyola (Md.); Boston—John Dalton, Suffolk; Detroit—Bob Horn, Drake; Philadelphia—Ken Kowall, Ohio; Phoenix—Floyd Mason, Alcorn A&M; Chicago—Ken Riley, Middle Tennessee; New York—Carl Greenfield, Eastern Kentucky; Milwaukee—Gene Mumford, Scranton.

THIRTEENTH ROUND Cleveland—Bobby Jones, Drake; Buffalo—Pete Smith, Valdosta State; Atlanta—Ed Jenkins, Michigan Lutheran; San Diego—Lee McCullough, Indiana; Baltimore—Ron Crosswhite, Dayton; Boston—Leroy Chalk, Nebraska; Detroit—Willie Roberson, Wyoming; Philadelphia—Hank Commodore, Northwest Oklahoma; Phoenix—Ron Dorsey, Tennessee State; Chicago—Ed Goode, DePaul; New York—Larry Duckworth, Henderson State; Milwaukee—Pierre Russell, Kansas.

FOURTEENTH ROUND Cleveland—James Harris, Indiana; Buffalo—Ray Lavender, Drury; San Diego—Gene Roberson, Canisius; Baltimore—Rudolph Peele, Norfolk State; Detroit—Art Davis, J.C. Smith; Phoenix—Ken Booker, UCLA; Chicago—Richard Dixon, Loyola (La.); New York—Jack O'Connor, Grant Falls; Milwaukee—George Jackson, Dayton.

FIFTEENTH ROUND Cleveland—Larry Baker, Wittenberg; Buffalo—William Chatmon, Baylor; San Diego—Terry Guigg, Gonzaga; Baltimore—James Morrell, Norfolk State; Detroit—James Fleming, Alcorn A&M; Phoenix—Curtis Carter, Bishop; Chicago—Liscio Thomas, Furman; Milwaukee—Lloyd King, Virginia Tech.

SIXTEENTH ROUND Cleveland—Vance Tyree, Wisconsin State; Buffalo—James Douglas, Memphis; San Diego—Leonard Jackson, Oregon; Detroit—Fred Smiley, Detroit; Chicago—Bob Bissant, Loyola (La.).

SEVENTEENTH ROUND Buffalo—Nelson Isley, LSU; San Diego—Steve Sims, Pepperdine; Detroit—Leroy Jenkins, Detroit.

EIGHTEENTH ROUND Buffalo—Joey Meyer, DePaul; San Diego—Carlos Quintar, Mexico; Detroit—Ike Bundy, Detroit Tech.

NINETEENTH ROUND San Diego—Gary Schneider, San Diego State; Detroit—Ed Jenkins, Shaw.

NBA 1971 HARDSHIP DRAFT

Following a lawsuit filed by Spencer Haywood, the NBA was required by the courts to grant admission to underclassmen even though their college classes had not yet graduated. Accordingly, in 1971 the league held a separate draft for underclassmen wishing to enter the NBA who displayed financial hardship. Beginning in 1972, such players were included in the regular NBA draft. In 1976, the hardship requirement was eliminated and the current early-entry procedure was adopted whereby any athlete with remaining college eligibility who desires to enter the NBA draft may do so by renouncing his college eligibility in a letter to the commissioner postmarked 45 days before the draft.

CINCINNATI Nate Williams, Utah State.

ATLANTA Tom Payne, Kentucky.

SAN FRANCISCO Cyril Baptiste, Creighton.

BALTIMORE Phil Chenier, California.

LOS ANGELES Joe Hammond, no college.

ABA 1971

CAROLINA

FIRST THREE ROUNDS—Ted McClain, Tennessee State; Gregg Northington, Alabama State; Elmore Smith, Kentucky State; Rich Yunkus, Georgia Tech.
ADDITIONAL ROUNDS—Luke Adams (5), Lamar Tech; Ron Rippicoe (6), David Lipscomb; Ed Kemp (7), Adams State; Kenny Davis (8), Georgetown (Ky.); Dave Wohl (9), Pennsylvania; Kendall Mayfield (10), Tuskegee; Robert McKenney (11), Pepperdine; Gregg Love (12), Ohio; Bob Wenzel (13), Rutgers; Ron Dorsey (14), Tennessee State; Hank Commodore (15), Northwest Oklahoma; Frank Lorthridge (16), Pan American; Dan Fife (17), Michigan; Cliff Harris (18), Hardin-Simmons; Steve Bilsky (19), Pennsylvania.

DALLAS

FIRST THREE ROUNDS—Roger Brown, Kansas; Stan Love, Oregon; Gary Nelson, Duquesne; Walt Szczerbiak, George Washington; Sidney Wicks, UCLA.
ADDITIONAL ROUNDS—Gene Phillips (4), SMU; Collis Jones (5), Notre Dame; George Trapp (6), Long Beach State; Sterling Quant (7), Central State (Ohio); Curtis Rowe (8), UCLA; Jimmy Guymon (9), E. New Mexico State; Gene Knolle (10), Texas Tech; Al Shumate (11), No. Texas State; Willie Hart (12), Grambling; Eugene Kennedy (13), TCU; Bill Brickhouse (14), Montana State; William Chatmon (15), Baylor; Harry Taylor (16), Los Angeles Baptist; Dan McGhee (17), Howard Payne.

DENVER

FIRST THREE ROUNDS—Cliff Meely, Colorado; Mike Newlin, Utah; Marv Roberts, Utah State.
ADDITIONAL ROUNDS—Al Smith (4), Bradley; Dave Robisch (5), Kansas; William Graham (6), Kentucky State; Ken Gardner (7), Utah; Tyrone Marioneaux (8), Loyola (La.); Mike Childress (9), Colorado State University; George Fasber (10), Purdue; John Ribock (11), South Carolina; Gary

Brell (12), Marquette; Glen Richels (13), Wisconsin; Jerry Hyder (14), East New Mexico; Richard Dixon (16), Loyola (Cal.); David Walls (17), Jackson State; Paul Botts (18), Central Michigan; Ron Smith (19), Wichita; Bobby Jones (20), Drake.

FLORIDIANS

FIRST THREE ROUNDS—Willie Long, New Mexico.
ADDITIONAL ROUNDS—Rich Rinaldi (5), St. Peter's (N.J.); Larry Holliday (6), Oregon; Gregg Starrick (7), Southern Illinois; Tom Lee (8), Arizona; Jim Haderlein (9), Loyola (Cal.); Doug Rex (10), Santa Barbara; Gerald Lockett (11), Arkansas AM&N; Willie Allen (12), Miami (Fla.); Jackie Ridgle (13), California; Pembrook Burrows (14), Jacksonville; Ken May (15), Dayton; Wayman Terrell (16), Oklahoma Baptist; Bill Drozdiak (17), Oregon; Eddie Myers (18), Arizona; Steve Sims (19), Pepperdine; Pat Biber (20), Tampa.

INDIANA

FIRST THREE ROUNDS—Darnell Hillman, San Jose State; John Mengelt, Auburn.
ADDITIONAL ROUNDS—Jim Cleamons (4), Ohio State; Clarence Glover (5), Western Kentucky; Jeff Halliburton (6), Drake; Dean Meminger (7), Marquette; Ken Booker (8), UCLA; Tom Crosswhite (9), Dayton; Larry Weatherford (10), Purdue; James England (11), Tennessee; Jeff Smith (12), New Mexico State; Rick Katherman (13), Duke; Clarence Smith (14), Villanova; Rich Walker (15), Bowling Green; Tom Bush (16), Drake; Jim Irving (17), St. Louis; Bob Bissant (18), Loyola (La.); Rudy Benjamin (19), Michigan State; Slick Pinkham (20), DePauw.

KENTUCKY

FIRST THREE ROUNDS—Artis Gilmore, Jacksonville; John Roche, South Carolina.
ADDITIONAL ROUNDS—Fred Brown (4), Iowa; Mike Gale (5), Elizabeth City (N.C.); James Welch (6), Houston; Larry Steele (7), Kentucky; Clarence Sherrod (8), Wisconsin; Mike O'Brien (9), St. Leo (Fla.); Larry Sanders (10), Duke; Sid Catlett (11), Notre Dame; James Dinwiddie (12), Kentucky; Pierre Russell (13), Kansas; Jerome Perry (14), Western Kentucky; Willie Cherry (15), Denver.

MEMPHIS

FIRST THREE ROUNDS—Randy Denton, Duke; Jim Rose, Western Kentucky; Thorpe Weber, Vanderbilt.
ADDITIONAL ROUNDS—Tom Owens (4), South Carolina; Amos Thomas (4), Southwest Oklahoma; Ken McIntosh (5), Eastern Michigan; Fred Hilton (6), Grambling; Loyd King (7), Virginia Tech; James Douglas (8), Memphis State; Henry Smith (9), Missouri; Jim Gregory (10), E. Carolina; Danny Davis (11), Henderson; Gary Reist (12), Rice; Edward Hoskins (13), Lemoyne; Ken Riley (14), Middle Tennessee State; Rod Behrens (15), Stanford; Don Johnson (16), Tennessee; Haywood Hill (17), Oral Roberts; Reggie Wood (18), Steubenville; Billy Barnes (19), Southern State; Alan Dalton (20), Suffolk (Mass.).

NEW YORK

FIRST THREE ROUNDS—Charles Davis, Wake Forest; Bob Kissane, Holy Cross; Marvin Stewart, Nebraska.
ADDITIONAL ROUNDS—Dick Gibbs (4), Texas-El Paso; Glen Summors (5), Gannon; Mike Necaise (6), William Carey; Odis Allison (7), UNLV; John Duncan (8), Kentucky Wesleyan; Jarrett Durham (9), Duquesne; Bill Warner (11), Arizona; Blain Henry (12), Marshall; Don Ward (13), Colgate; Skip Young (14), Florida State; George Sisk (15), Georgia Southern; Brian Mahoney (16), Manhattan; Ollie Sherman (17), Minnesota; Bobby Doyle (18), Texas-El Paso; Calvin Oliver (19), Pan American; Greg Cluess (20), St. John's (N.Y.).

PITTSBURGH

FIRST THREE ROUNDS—Jim O'Brien, Boston College; Howard Porter, Villanova; Levi Wyatt, Alcorn A&M.
ADDITIONAL ROUNDS—Bubba Jones (4), Ashland; Bill Smith (4), Syracuse; Mike Jordan (5), Savannah State; Barry Nelson (6), Duquesne; John Sutter (7), Tulane; Charles Yelverton (8), Fordham; Vincent White (9), Savannah State; James Fleming (10), Alcorn A&M; Eric Hill (10), Minnesota; Rayford McCambray (11), Miles; Bunny Wilson (12), Baltimore; Ray Green (13), California (Pa.) State; Gene Mumford (14), Scranton; Lee McCullough (15), Indiana (Pa.) State; Russell Golden (16), Jackson State; Harry James (17), Montclair State; Stan Novey (18), Mount St. Mary's.

UTAH

FIRST FIVE ROUNDS—Rick Fisher, Colorado State; Jim McDaniels, Western Kentucky.
ADDITIONAL ROUNDS—Dennis Layton (4), Southern California; Lee Dedmon (5), North Carolina; Bobby Fields (6), LaSalle; Erwin (Chip) Johnson (7), Augusta; Jim Day (8), Morehead State; Willy Humes (9), Idaho State; Jake Jones (10), Assumption (Mass.)

VIRGINIA

FIRST THREE ROUNDS—Austin Carr, Notre Dame; Ken Durrett, LaSalle; Dana Lewis, Tulsa; Willie Sojourner, Weber State.

ADDITIONAL ROUNDS—Dana Pagett (4), Southern California; Clifford Ray (7), Oklahoma; Bill Gerry (8), Virginia; Gilbert McGregor (10), Wake Forest; Hector Blondet (11), Murray State; Lou Grillo (12), Mount St. Mary's.

ABA 1971 HARDSHIP DRAFT

DENVER Mickey Davis, Duquesne.

NEW YORK NETS Ed Leftwich, North Carolina State.

CAROLINA Phil Chenier, California.

NBA 1972

FIRST ROUND Portland—LaRue Martin, Loyola (Ill.); Buffalo—Bob McAdoo, North Carolina; Cleveland—Dwight Davis, Houston; Phoenix (from Detroit)—Corky Calhoun, Penn; Philadelphia—Fred Boyd, Oregon State; Milwaukee (from Houston)—Russell Lee, Marshall; Seattle—Bud Stallworth, Kansas; New York—Tom Riker, South Carolina; Detroit (from Phoenix)—Bob Nash, Hawaii; Boston—Paul Westphal, Southern California; Chicago—Ralph Simpson, Michigan State; Milwaukee—Julius Erving, Massachusetts; Los Angeles—Travis Grant, Kentucky State.

SECOND ROUND Portland—Bob Davis, Weber State; Buffalo—Harold Fox, Jacksonville; Los Angeles (from Cleveland)—Jim Price, Louisville; Detroit—Chris Ford, Villanova; Seattle (from Philadelphia)—Joby Wright, Indiana; Cincinnati—Sam Sibert, Kentucky State; Houston—John Gianelli, Pacific; Atlanta—Steve Bracey, Tulsa; Los Angeles (from Baltimore)—Paul Stovall, Arizona State; Seattle—Brian Taylor, Princeton; Cleveland (from New York)—Steve Hawes, Washington; Baltimore (from Phoenix)—Tom Patterson, Ouachita Baptist; Portland (from Golden State)—Dave Twardzik, Old Dominion; Boston—Dennis Wuycik, North Carolina; Cincinnati (from Chicago)—Mike Ratliff, Eau Claire State; Milwaukee—Chuck Terry, Long Beach State; Portland (from Los Angeles)—Ollie Johnson, Temple.

THIRD ROUND Portland—Lloyd Neal, Tennessee State; Buffalo—Bob Morse, Penn; Phoenix (from Cleveland)—Scott English, Texas-El Paso; Phoenix (from Detroit)—Don Buse, Evansville; Chicago (from Cincinnati)—Frank Russell, Detroit; Philadelphia—Charlie Tharpe, Belhaven; Houston—Eric McWilliams, Long Beach State; Cincinnati (from Atlanta)—Ron Riley, Southern California; Baltimore—Kevin Porter, St. Francis (Pa.); Seattle—Jim Creighton, Colorado; New York—Ansley Truitt, California; Phoenix—Claude Terry, Stanford; Golden State—Bill Chamberlain, North Carolina; Boston—Wayne Grabiec, Michigan; Chicago—Chuck Jura, Nebraska; Milwaukee—George Adams, Gardner-Webb; Los Angeles—Gregg Northington, Alabama State.

FOURTH ROUND Portland—Gary Stewart, Canisius; Buffalo—George Bryant, Eastern Kentucky State; Cleveland—Hank Siemiontkowski, Villanova; Detroit—Ernie Fleming, Jacksonville; Philadelphia—Marshall Wingate, Niagara; Cincinnati—Frank Schade, Eau Claire State; Houston—Wil Robinson, West Virginia; Atlanta—Reggie Bird, Princeton; Baltimore—Al Saunders, LSU; Seattle—Joe Mackey, Southern California; New York—Henry Bibby, UCLA; Phoenix—Matt Gantt, St. Bonaventure; Golden State—John Tschogl, California-Santa Barbara; Boston—Nate Stephens, Long Beach State; Chicago—Ted Martiniuk, St. Peter's; Milwaukee—Art White, Georgetown.

FIFTH ROUND Portland—Mike Reid, California-Riverside; Buffalo—Arnie Berman, Brown; Cleveland—Sam Cash, California-Riverside; Detroit—Ernest Pettis, Western Michigan; Cincinnati—Dave Bustion, Denver; Philadelphia—Joe Bynes, Arkansas AM&N; Houston—James Silas, Stephen F. Austin; Atlanta—Bob Lackey, Marquette; Baltimore—Walter Jones, LIU; Seattle—Gary Ladd, Seattle; New York—Bob Ford, Purdue; Phoenix—Wardell Dyson, Shaw; Golden State—Charles Dudley, Washington; Boston—Bryan Adrian, Davidson; Chicago—Roland Garrett, Florida State; Milwaukee—Ron Harris, Wichita State; Los Angeles—Glen Summors, Gannon.

SIXTH ROUND Portland—Joe Gaines, Belmont; Buffalo—Ed Czernota, Sacred Heart; Cleveland—Tom Parker, Kentucky; Detroit—Terry Benton, Wichita State; Philadelphia—John Glover, Wiley; Cincinnati—Jerry Crocker, Guilford; Houston—Mike Collins, Seattle; Atlanta—Randy Knoll, Marshall; Baltimore—Wayne Dillard, Eastern Michigan; Seattle—Ron Thomas, Louisville; New York—Greg Cleuss, St. John's; Phoenix—Charles Edge, LeMoyne-Owen; Golden State—Henry Bacon, Louisville; Boston—Doug Holcomb, Memphis; Chicago—Mike Stewart, Santa Clara; Boston (from Milwaukee)—Wally Wright, PMC Colleges; Los Angeles—Sam Simmons, Bradley.

SEVENTH ROUND Portland—Bob Lynn, Long Beach State; Buffalo—Greg Kohls, Syracuse; Cleveland—Steve Davidson, West Texas State; Detroit—Bruce Anderson, Arizona; Cincinnati—Mike Sneed, Fayetteville; Philadelphia—Curtis Pritchett, St. Augustine; Houston—Mike Jackson, Los Angeles State; Atlanta—Billy Pleas, Detroit; Baltimore—Marvin Brown, Jackson State; Seattle—Jerry Dunn, Western Kentucky; New York—Tracy Tripucka,

Lafayette; Phoenix—Bernie Fryer, Brigham Young; Golden State—William Franklin, Purdue; Boston—Steve Previs, North Carolina; Chicago—Jerry Pender, Fresno State; Milwaukee—Mickey Davis, Duquesne.

EIGHTH ROUND Portland—Ruben Vance, Kent State; Buffalo—Andy Denny, South Alabama State; Cleveland—Roger Evans, Kent State; Detroit—Ben Kelso, Central Michigan; Philadelphia—Jim Kopp, Rockhurst; Cincinnati—Jerry Clack, Oklahoma; Houston—Henry Harris, Auburn; Atlanta—Oscar Evans, Butler; Baltimore—Jim Floyd, Shaw; Seattle—Willy Stoudamire, Portland State; New York—Tom Corde, Ohio; Phoenix—Russell Golden, Jackson State; Golden State—John Burks, San Francisco; Boston—Sam McCarney, Oral Roberts; Chicago—Cavin Anderson, Valley City; Milwaukee—Charles Kirkland, Cheyney.

NINTH ROUND Portland—Scott McCandlish, Virginia; Buffalo—John Collins, Brockport State; Cleveland—Greg Starrick, Southern Illinois; Detroit—Kessie Mangam, Ferris State; Cincinnati—Steve McMahon, Merrimack; Philadelphia—Rod Murray, Los Angeles State; Atlanta—Larry Strozier, Morehouse; Baltimore—Ruppert Breedlove, Oglethorpe; Seattle—Dwight Holliday, Hawaii; New York—Tom Sullivan, Fordham; Phoenix—Bill Kennedy, Arizona; Golden State—Bill Duey, California; Chicago—Ralph Houston, West Texas State; Milwaukee—Jim Regenold, Ball State.

TENTH ROUND Portland—Kresimir Cosic, Brigham Young; Cleveland—Kent Martens, Abilene Christian; Detroit—Kent Hollenbeck, Kentucky; Philadelphia—Gary Watson, Wisconsin; Cincinnati—David Hall, Kansas State; Atlanta—Jim Clesson, Tulsa; Baltimore—Will Loftin, Southwestern Louisiana; Seattle—Dan Stewart, Washington State; New York—Richie Garner, Manhattan; Phoenix—Al Vilcheck, Louisville; Boston—Marty Hunt, Kenyon; Chicago—Chuck Taylor, West Liberty State; Milwaukee—Jolly Spight, Santa Clara.

ELEVENTH ROUND Portland—Jimmy Wilkins, San Diego State; Buffalo—Jim Prokell, Edinboro State; Cincinnati—Floyd Mathew, Northern Arizona; Atlanta—Charles Allen, Texas Southern; Baltimore—Marvin Watkins, Jackson State; Seattle—Steve Turner, Vanderbilt; New York—Chic Downing, Benedictine; Phoenix—John Belcher, Arkansas State; Boston—Mark Minor, Ohio State; Chicago—Jackie Young, Rocky Mountain.

TWELFTH ROUND Buffalo—Frank Dewitt, Virginia; Cincinnati—Len Baltimore, George Washington; Atlanta—James Green, Paine College; Baltimore—Lloyd Adams, Rhode Island; Seattle—Gregg Daust, Missouri-St. Louis; Phoenix—Mark Soderberg, Utah; Boston—Phil Stephens, South Carolina State; Chicago—Al Cotler, Penn.

THIRTEENTH ROUND Portland—Larry Morris, Tulsa; Buffalo—Kim Huband, North Carolina; Cincinnati—Kent Scott, Pittsburgh; Baltimore—Mike Krawzyk, Loyola (Md.); Phoenix—Kelly Utley, Shaw; Chicago—Mike Barr, Duquesne.

FOURTEENTH ROUND Portland—Paul Kelly, Shaw; Buffalo—Greg Corson, North Carolina; Cincinnati—Bob Allen, Missouri; Baltimore—Aubrey Nash, Kansas; Seattle—Cleveland Hill, Nicholas State; Phoenix—Ray Golson, West Texas State; Chicago—Andrew Pettes, Oklahoma.

FIFTEENTH ROUND Portland—Rich Haubeggar, Wake Forest; Buffalo—Paul Hoffman, St. Bonaventure; Cincinnati—Mike Jefferies, Oklahoma State; Baltimore—Gary Handelman, Hopkins; Chicago—Greg Lowery, Texas Tech.

SIXTEENTH ROUND Portland—Mose Adolph, Los Angeles State; Buffalo—Norman Bounds, Brockport State; Cincinnati—Mike Peterson, Nebraska; Chicago—Charles Hall, West Montana.

SEVENTEENTH ROUND Chicago—John Thornton, South Carolina State.

EIGHTEENTH ROUND Chicago—Ron Manning, Manhattan.

ABA 1972

CAROLINA

FIRST FIVE ROUNDS—Tom Riker, South Carolina; Dennis Wuycik, North Carolina; Bill Chamberlain, North Carolina; Freddie Boyd, Oregon State.
ADDITIONAL ROUNDS—Steve Bracey, Tulsa; Don Holcomb, Memphis State; Henry Bibby, UCLA; Jerry Crocker, Guilford; Mike Collins, Seattle; Wilbur Loftin, Southwestern Louisiana; Charles Dudley, Washington; Mike Sneed, Fayetteville State; Steve Previs, North Carolina; Kent Martens, Abilene Christian; Nathan Cannady, Virginia Union; David Smith, Western Carolina; Curtis Pritchett, St. Augustine; Paul Coder, North Carolina State.

DALLAS

FIRST FIVE ROUNDS—LaRue Martin, Loyola (Ill.); Mike Ratliff, Eau Claire State; Bob Morse, Penn; Bill Walton, UCLA; Steve Hawes, Washington.
ADDITIONAL ROUNDS—Jim Creighton, Colorado; Frank Schade, Eau Claire State; Ansley Truitt, California; Wayne Grabiec, Michigan; Jerry Zelinski, Northern Illinois; Jeff Hickman, Houston; Stan Key, Kentucky; Don Wiese, Ripon; Rhea Taylor, Arizona State; Ron Williams, Murray State; Joe Reddick, Albany State (Ga.); Al Vilcheck, Louisville.

DENVER

FIRST FIVE ROUNDS—Bud Stallworth, Kansas; Paul Stovall, Arizona State; Paul Westphal, Southern California; Claude Terry, Stanford; Doug Collins, Illinois State; Dave Bustion, Denver. ADDITIONAL ROUNDS—Sam Sibert, Kentucky State; Ron Riley, Southern California; Ted Martiniuk, St. Peter's (N.J.); Bernie Fryer, Brigham Young; Jerry Pender, Fresno State; Gary Stewart, Canisius; Mike Reid, California-Riverside; John Burks, San Francisco; John Tschogl, Santa Barbara; Leon Huff, Drake; Larry Morris, Tulsa; Dave Hullman, Arizona State; Harold Little, New Mexico; Andy Knowles, Louisiana Tech; John Belcher, Arkansas State.

FLORIDIANS

FIRST FIVE ROUNDS—Dwight Davis, Houston; Mike Stewart, Santa Clara; Scott English, Texas-El Paso; Greg Starrick, Southern Illinois. ADDITIONAL ROUNDS—Charles Tharpe, Belhaven; Swen Nater, UCLA; Ron Thomas, Louisville; Ernie Fleming, Jacksonville; Sam Cash, California-Riverside; Tracy Tripucka, Lafayette; Jerry Brucks, Wyoming; Bobby Jack, Oklahoma; Gregg Flaker, Missouri; Ray Golson, West Texas State; Gregg Lowery, Texas Tech; Arnie Berman, Brown; Fred DeVaughn, Westmont; Bob Zinder, Kansas State; Al Davis, Hawaii.

INDIANA

FIRST FIVE ROUNDS—Ed Ratleff, Long Beach State; Nate Stephens, Long Beach State; Oscar Evans, Butler. ADDITIONAL ROUNDS—George Adams, Gardner-Webb; Rich Garner, Manhattan; Cavin Anderson, Valley City; Wardell Dyson, Shaw; Jolly Spight, Santa Clara; Bill Burton, Eastern Kentucky; Wally Rice, Penn Military; Lee Sims, Morehead State; Nate Williams, Utah State.

KENTUCKY

FIRST FIVE ROUNDS—Corky Calhoun, Penn. ADDITIONAL ROUNDS—Matt Gantt, St. Bonaventure; Bill Kennedy, Arizona State; Terry Benton, Wichita State; Ernest Pettis, Western Michigan; Cleveland Hill, Nicholls State; Andrew Pettes, Oklahoma; David Hall, Kansas State; Jerry Clack, Oklahoma State; Tom Parker, Kentucky; Jerry Dunn, Western Kentucky; Mike Bowling, Arizona State.

MEMPHIS

FIRST FIVE ROUNDS—David Brent, Jacksonville; Russell Lee, Marshall; Jim Price, Louisville; Rusty Blair, Oregon. ADDITIONAL ROUNDS—Bob Ford, Purdue; Rowland Garrett, Florida State; Sam Simmons, Bradley; Steve Davidson, West Texas State; Jackie Young, Rocky Mountain; Steve Turner, Vanderbilt; Henry Bacon, Louisville; Ruppert Breedlove, Oglethorpe; Sam McCarney, Oral Roberts; Gene Mack, Iowa State; Tom Arnholt, Vanderbilt; Steve Schmidt, South Alabama; Terry Hankton, Arkansas Tech.

NEW YORK

FIRST FIVE ROUNDS—Jim Chones, Marquette; Brian Taylor, Princeton; Joby Wright, Indiana; Bob Lackey, Marquette; Dwayne Dillard, Eastern Michigan; Art White, Georgetown. ADDITIONAL ROUNDS—Ron Harris, Wichita State; Hank Siemiontkowski, Villanova; Wally Jones, LIU; Ed Czernota, Sacred Heart; Randy Noll, Marshall; Quinas Brower, Hofstra; Bill Phillips, St. John's; Kelly Utley, Shaw; Paul Hoffman, St. Bonaventure; Ken Bradley, Nazarene.

PITTSBURGH

FIRST FIVE ROUNDS—John Gianelli, Pacific; Chuck Terry, Long Beach State; Bob Davis, Weber State; Wil Robinson, West Virginia; Harold Fox, Jacksonville. ADDITIONAL ROUNDS—James Silas, Stephen F. Austin; Joe Mackey, Southern California; Marshall Wingate, Niagara; Charles Edge, LeMoyne-Owen; Bryan Adrian, Davidson; Joe Gaines, Belmont; Chick Downing, St. Benedict's; Bill Pleas, Detroit; Dave Werthman, West Virginia; Henry Seawright, Manhattan; Steve McMahon, Merrimack; Harry Andersen, St. Peter's (N.J.); Manuel Raga, Mexico.

UTAH

FIRST FIVE ROUNDS—Chris Ford, Villanova; Travis Grant, Kentucky State; Chuck Jura, Nebraska; Bob Nash, Hawaii. ADDITIONAL ROUNDS—Tommy Patterson, Ouachita Baptist; Eric McWilliams, Long Beach State; Frank Russell, Detroit; Mike Jackson, Los Angeles State; Kevin Porter, St. Francis (Pa.); Willie Hart, Grambling; Lloyd Neal, Tennessee State; Simpson DeGrate, Texas Christian; Mose Adolph, California State; Harvey Catchings, Hardin-Simmons; Gary Ladd, Seattle; Henry Speele, Northeast Louisiana; Dwight Holliday, Hawaii; George Price, Colorado State; George Bryant, Eastern Kentucky.

VIRGINIA

FIRST FIVE ROUNDS—Bill Franklin, Purdue. ADDITIONAL ROUNDS—Reggie Bird, Princeton; Al Sanders, Louisiana State; Billy Shepherd, Butler; Mike Barr, Duquesne; Rick Aydlett, South Carolina; Kent Hollenbeck, Kentucky; Milton Adams, Portland; Ralph Houston, West Texas; Rudy Peele, Norfolk State; Scott McCandlish, Virginia; Jay Mottola, Lafayette.

ABA 1972 DISPERSAL DRAFT

Following is the list of veterans and rookies drafted on June 13, 1972, following the dissolution of the Floridians and Pittsburgh franchises.

FIRST ROUND

Memphis—George Thompson, Pittsburgh; Denver—Warren Jabali, Floridians; Carolina—Mike Lewis, Pittsburgh; Dallas—John Brisker, Pittsburgh; Dallas—Harley Swift, Pittsburgh; Carolina—Mack Calvin, Floridians; Denver—Willie Long, Floridians; Memphis—Ron Franz, Floridians; Virginia—Swen Nater (UCLA), Floridians; Utah—Larry Jones, Floridians; Kentucky—Walt Szczerbiak, Pittsburgh; New York—Chuck Terry (Long Beach State), Pittsburgh; Indiana—Dwight Davis (Houston), Floridians.

SECOND ROUND

Memphis—Dave Lattin, Pittsburgh; Denver—Scott English (Texas-El Paso), Floridians; Carolina—Mike Stewart (Santa Clara), Floridians; Dallas—John Gianelli (Pacific), Pittsburgh; Virginia—Joe Mackey (Southern California), Pittsburgh; Utah—Chick Downing (St. Benedict's), Pittsburgh; Kentucky—Ernie Fleming (Jacksonville), Floridians; Indiana—Dwight Jones (Houston), Floridians.

THIRD ROUND

Memphis—Sam Cash (California-Riverside), Floridians; Denver—Al Tucker, Floridians; Carolina—Mike Grosso, Pittsburgh; Dallas—Jerry Brucks (Wyoming), Floridians; Virginia—Craig Raymond, Floridians; Utah—Wil Robinson (West Virginia), Pittsburgh; Kentucky—Lonnie Wright, Floridians; New York—George Tinsley, Floridians; Indiana—Tracy Tripucka (Lafayette), Floridians.

FOURTH ROUND

Memphis—Ron Thomas (Louisville), Floridians; Carolina—Greg Starrick (Southern Illinois), Floridians; Dallas—Bobby Jack (Oklahoma), Floridians; Virginia—Jim Ligon, Pittsburgh; Utah—Henry Seawright (Manhattan), Pittsburgh; Kentucky—Gregg Flaker (Missouri), Floridians; Indiana—Bryan Adrian (Davidson), Pittsburgh.

FIFTH ROUND Memphis—Charles Edge (LeMoyne-Owen), Pittsburgh; Virginia—Greg Lowery (Texas Tech), Floridians; Utah—Bill Pleas (Detroit), Pittsburgh.

SIXTH ROUND Memphis—Ray Golson (West Texas State), Floridians; Virginia—Al Davis (Hawaii), Floridians.

ABA 1972 EXPANSION DRAFT

SAN DIEGO

FIRST ROUND—Stew Johnson, Carolina; George Johnson, Dallas; Art Becker, Denver; George Peeples, Indiana; Les Hunter, Kentucky; Don Sidle, Memphis; Ollie Taylor, New York; Red Robbins, Utah; Mike Barrett, Virginia. SECOND ROUND—Larry Miller, Carolina; Simmie Hill, Dallas; Chuck Williams, Denver; rights to Dwight Jones (Houston), Indiana; Lonnie Wright, Kentucky; Charlie Williams, Memphis; Gene Moore, New York; Mike Butler, Utah; Craig Raymond, Virginia.

NBA 1973 (APRIL 23, 1973)

FIRST ROUND Philadelphia—Doug Collins, Illinois State; Cleveland (from Portland)—Jim Brewer, Minnesota; Buffalo—Ernie DiGregorio, Providence; Seattle—Mike Green, Louisiana Tech; Los Angeles (from Cleveland)—Kermit Washington, American; Houston—Ed Ratleff, Long Beach State; KC-Omaha—Ron Behagen, Minnesota; Phoenix—Mike Bantom, St. Joseph's; Atlanta (from Detroit)—Dwight Jones, Houston; Atlanta—John Brown, Missouri; Golden State—Kevin Joyce, South Carolina; Chicago—Kevin Kunnert, Iowa; Capital—Nick Weatherspoon, Illinois; New York—Mel Davis, St. John's; Portland (from Los Angeles)—Barry Parkhill, Virginia; Milwaukee—Swen Nater, UCLA; Boston—Steve Downing, Indiana; Philadelphia (bonus selection)—Raymond Lewis, Los Angeles State.

SECOND ROUND Capital (from Philadelphia)—Louis Nelson, Washington; KC-Omaha (from Buffalo)—Mike D'Antoni, Marshall; Philadelphia (from Portland)—Allan Bristow, Virginia Tech; Philadelphia (from Seattle)—George McGinnis, Indiana; Los Angeles (from Cleveland)—Bill Schaeffer, St. John's; Chicago (from Houston)—Kevin Stacom, Providence; KC-Omaha—Larry McNeill, Marquette; Cleveland (from Phoenix)—Allan Hornyak, Ohio State; Atlanta (from Detroit)—Tom Inglesby, Villanova; New York (from Atlanta)—Pat McFarland, St. Joseph's; Golden State—Derrek Dickey, Cincinnati; Chicago—Wendell Hudson, Alabama; Los Angeles (from Capital)—Jim Chones, Marquette; Philadelphia (from New York)—Caldwell Jones, Albany State (Ga.); Phoenix (from Milwaukee)—Gary Melchionni, Duke; Los Angeles—John Perry, Pan American; Boston—Phil Hankinson, Penn.

THIRD ROUND Atlanta (from Philadelphia)—Ted Manakas, Princeton; Portland—Jim O'Brien, Maryland; Buffalo—Ken Charles, Fordham; Chicago (from Seattle)—Martin Terry, Arkansas; Cleveland—Ozzie Edwards, Oklahoma City; Cleveland (from Houston)—James Lister, Sam Houston; Phoenix (from KC-Omaha)—Joe Reaves, Bethel (Tenn.); Phoenix—Steve Mitchell, Kansas State; Detroit—Dwight Lamar, Southwestern Louisiana; Atlanta—Leonard Gray, Long Beach State; Golden State—Jim Retseck, Auburn; Chicago—Steve Newsome, Houston; Capital—Tom Kozelko, Toledo; New York—Allie McGuire, Marquette; Detroit (from Los Angeles)—Larry Kenon, Memphis State; Houston (from Milwaukee)—E. C. Coleman, Houston Baptist; Boston—Martinez Denmon, Iowa State.

FOURTH ROUND Philadelphia—Darrel Minniefield, New Mexico; Buffalo—Doug Little, Oregon; Portland—William Averitt, Pepperdine; Seattle—William Harris, North Carolina A&T; Cleveland—Luke Witte, Ohio State; Houston—Lee Colburn, South Dakota State; Milwaukee (from KC-Omaha)—Clyde Turner, Minnesota; Phoenix—Ron Robinson, Memphis State; Detroit—Ken Brady, Michigan; Atlanta—James Brown, Harvard; Golden State—Ron King, Florida State; Chicago—Mark Sibley, Northwestern; Capital—Aaron Stewart, Richmond; New York—George Karl, North Carolina; Milwaukee—Harry Rogers, St. Louis; Los Angeles—Larry Finch, Memphis State; Boston—Richie Fuqua, Oral Roberts.

FIFTH ROUND Philadelphia—Reggie Royals, Florida State; Portland—Fran Costello, Providence; Buffalo—Randy Knoll, Marshall; Seattle—Chuck Iverson, South Dakota; Cleveland—John Coughran, California; Houston—Gary Rhoades, Colorado State; KC-Omaha—M. L. Carr, Guilford; Phoenix—Clinton Harris, Iowa State; Detroit—Henry Wilmore, Michigan; Atlanta—Dave Winfield, Minnesota; Golden State—Nate Stephens, Long Beach State; Chicago—Ray Simpson, Furman; Capital—Danny Traylor, South Carolina; New York—Dennis Bell, Drake; Los Angeles—Kresimir Cosic, Brigham Young; Milwaukee—Larry Jackson, Northern Illinois; Boston—Byron Jones, San Francisco.

SIXTH ROUND Philadelphia—Sterling Wright, Lincoln; Buffalo—Mike Macaluso, Canisius; Portland—Neal Jurgensen, Oregon State; Seattle—Bill McCoy, Northern Iowa; Cleveland—Willie Calvert, Abilene Christian; Houston—Tom Peck, Eau Claire; KC-Omaha—Mike Quick, San Francisco; Phoenix—Gene Doyle, Holy Cross; Detroit—Dennis Johnson, Ferris State; Atlanta—John Williamson, New Mexico State; Golden State—Bob Lauriski, Utah State; Chicago—John Neumann, Mississippi; Capital—Mike Allocco, Stonehill; New York—Lawrence Lilly, Alabama State; Milwaukee—James Floyd, Shaw; Los Angeles—David Brent, Jacksonville; Boston—Joe Cafferty, North Carolina State.

SEVENTH ROUND Philadelphia—James Greene, Kentucky Wesleyan; Portland—Larry Hollyfield, UCLA; Buffalo—Tim Bassett, Georgia; Seattle—Jim Andrews, Kentucky; Cleveland—Larry Farmer, UCLA; Houston—Fred DeVaughn, Westmont; KC-Omaha—Mike Jeffries, Missouri; Phoenix—Jerry Bisbano, Southwestern Louisiana; Detroit—Fred Smiley, North-wood Michigan; Atlanta—Pete Harris, Stephen F. Austin; Golden State—Steve Smith, Loyola (Cal.); Chicago—Billy Harris, Northern Illinois; Capital—Ron Hogue, Georgia; New York—Mike Moore, Manhattan; Los Angeles—Nate Hawthorne, Southern Illinois; Milwaukee—Eddie Childress, Austin Peay; Boston—Mike Stewart, Santa Clara.

EIGHTH ROUND Philadelphia—Dave Langston, Drake; Buffalo—Carl Jackson, St. Bonaventure; Portland—Lindell Resson, Eastern Michigan; Seattle—Wardell Jeffries, Oklahoma Baptist; Cleveland—John Ritter, Indiana; Houston—John Thomas, Missouri Southern; KC-Omaha—Mike Williams, Kentucky Wesleyan; Phoenix—Jim Owens, Oregon State; Detroit—Ben Kelso, Central Michigan; Atlanta—Tim Dominey, Valdosta State; Golden State—Jeff Dawson, Illinois; Chicago—J. G. Brosterhos, Texas; Capital—Mark Jellison, Northeastern; New York—Steve Rowell, Rhode Island; Milwaukee—Walt McGrary, Tennessee-Chattanooga; Los Angeles—Roy McPipe, Eastern Montana; Boston—Robert White, Sam Houston State.

NINTH ROUND Philadelphia—Harvey Catchings, Hardin-Simmons; Portland—Mike Contreras, Arizona State; Buffalo—Bob Fullerton, Xavier (Ohio); Seattle—Greg Williams, Seattle; Cleveland—Les Taylor, Murray State; KC-Omaha—James Brown, Dartmouth; Phoenix—Sandy Smith, Winston-Salem; Detroit—Bill Kelgore, Michigan State; Golden State—Everett Fopma, Idaho State; Chicago—Rubin Montanez, Duquesne; Capital—Mike Boylan, Assumption; New York—Joe Wise, Bridgewater State; Milwaukee—Bob Bocca, Quinnipiac; Boston—Corky Taylor, Minnesota.

TENTH ROUND Philadelphia—Abe Steward, Jacksonville; Buffalo—Nick Connor, Illinois; Portland—Sam Whitehead, Oregon State; Seattle—Bob Bodell, Maryland; Cleveland—Dean Martin, Baldwin-Wallace; KC-Omaha—Ernie Kusyner, Kansas State; Phoenix—Claude White, Elmhurst; Detroit—Bob Solomon, Wayne State; Golden State—Fred Lavoroni, Santa Clara; Chicago—Russ Hunt, Furman; Capital—Dick Kelly, Bay College; New York—Ed Fields, C. W. Post; Milwaukee—Ron Battle, Sam Houston State; Boston—Steve Turner, Vanderbilt.

ELEVENTH ROUND Philadelphia—Rod Freeman, Vanderbilt; Portland—Ed Payne, Wake Forest; Buffalo—Mike Lee, Syracuse; Cleveland—Floyd Lewis, Harvard; Phoenix—Lynn Greer, Virginia State; Detroit—Len Paul, Akron; Capital—Dale Adams, St. Mary's (Md.); New York—Charles Edge, LeMoyne-Owen; Boston—Ed Hastings, Villanova.

TWELFTH ROUND Philadelphia—Connie Warren, Xavier (Ohio); Buffalo—Aaron Covington, Canisius; Portland—Rick Holdt, North Carolina State; Cleveland—Chris McMurray, San Diego State; Phoenix—Lyman Williamson, Samford; Detroit—Clarence Carlisle, Ferris State; Capital—Mike Battle, George Washington; Boston—Bruce Winkler, Santa Clara.

THIRTEENTH ROUND Philadelphia—Jim Crawford, LaSalle; Buffalo—Bob Vartanian, Buffalo; Cleveland—John Pennebacker, Hawaii; Phoenix—Kalevi Sarkalahti, Brigham Young; Capital—Chester Davis, Morgan State; Boston—Scott Koelzer, Montana State.

FOURTEENTH ROUND Philadelphia—Ernie Johnson, Michigan; Buffalo—Ron Gilliam, Brockport; Cleveland—Charles Mitchell, Eastern Kentucky; Capital—Howard White, Maryland; Boston—Rick Williams, Iowa.

FIFTEENTH ROUND Philadelphia—Lionel Harris, Cincinnati; Buffalo—John Fraley, Georgia; Cleveland—Reese Stovall, Pan American; Capital—W. Shorty Simmons, St. Mary's (Md.); Boston—James Gilchrist, Florida Southern.

SIXTEENTH ROUND Philadelphia—Larry Robinson, Tennessee; Buffalo—John Green, Oregon; Cleveland—Tom O'Connor, Iowa; Boston—Sam Barber, Bethune Cookman.

SEVENTEENTH ROUND Philadelphia—Tony Prince, St. John's; Buffalo—James Garvin, Boston U.; Cleveland—Phil Elderkin, Boston U.; Boston—Lamont King, Long Beach State.

EIGHTEENTH ROUND Buffalo—Don Johnston, North Carolina; Boston—Peter Gavitt, Maine.

NINETEENTH ROUND Buffalo—Ron Thornson, British Columbia; Boston—Tom Austin, Massachusetts.

TWENTIETH ROUND Buffalo—Phil Tollestrop, Brigham Young.

ABA 1973 SPECIAL CIRCUMSTANCE DRAFT

(Teams listed alphabetically)

FIRST ROUND Denver—Mike Bantom, St. Joseph's (Pa.); Indiana—Mike Green, Louisiana Tech; Kentucky—Ernie DiGregorio, Providence; Memphis—Larry Kenon, Memphis State; New York—Jim Brewer, Minnesota; San Antonio—Kevin Kunnert, Iowa; San Diego—David Vaughn, Oral Roberts; Utah—Robert Parish, Centenary, and Jim Baker, UNLV; Virginia—George Gervin, Eastern Michigan.

SECOND ROUND Carolina—Bobby Jones, North Carolina, and Tom Burleson, North Carolina State; Denver—Clyde Turner, Minnesota; Indiana—Louis Dunbar, Houston; Memphis—Ray Lewis, L.A. State; New York—Bill Schaeffer, St. John's; San Antonio—John Brown, Missouri; San Diego—Bird Averitt, Pepperdine; Utah—Alvan Adams, Oklahoma; Virginia—Barry Parkhill, Virginia.

ABA 1973

FIRST ROUND San Diego—Dwight Lamar, Southwest Louisiana; Memphis—Larry Finch, Memphis State; San Antonio—Mike D'Antoni, Marshall; New York—Doug Collins, Illinois State; Virginia—Allan Bristow, Virginia Tech; Denver—Ed Ratleff, Long Beach State; Indiana—Steve Downing, Indiana; Utah—Ronnie Robinson, Memphis State; Kentucky—Louis Nelson, Washington; Carolina—Mel Davis, St. John's.

SECOND ROUND Memphis—Wendell Hudson, Alabama; San Antonio—Kevin Joyce, South Carolina; San Diego—Tim Bassett, Georgia; Kentucky (from Utah-N.Y.)—Derrek Dickey, Cincinnati; Virginia—Allie McGuire, Marquette; Denver—Steve Mitchell, Kansas State; Indiana—Jim O'Brien, Maryland; Utah—Leonard Gray, Long Beach State; Kentucky—Ron King, Florida State; Carolina—Nick Weatherspoon, Illinois.

THIRD ROUND Memphis—David Langston, Drake; San Antonio—Tom Kozelko, Toledo; New York—Tom Ingelsby, Villanova; San Diego—Jim Lister, Sam Houston State; Virginia—Caldwell Jones, Albany State (Ga.); Denver—Kevin Stacom, Providence; Indiana—Jim Retseck, Auburn; Utah—Steve Newsome, Houston; Kentucky—M. L. Carr, Guilford State; Utah (from Carolina)—Ted Manakas, Princeton.

FOURTH ROUND Memphis—Harry Rogers, St. Louis; New York (from San Antonio)—Phil Hankinson, Penn; San Diego—Darrel Minniefield, New Mexico; New York—Kermit Washington, American; Virginia—Bob Lauriski, Utah State; Denver—Pat McFarland, St. Joseph's (Pa.); Indiana—John Ritter, Indiana; Utah—Martin Terry, Arkansas; Kentucky—Ron Behagen, Minnesota; Carolina—Kresimir Cosic, Brigham Young.

FIFTH ROUND Memphis—Dennis Bell, Drake; San Antonio—Luke Witte, Ohio State; New York—Reggie Royals, Florida State; San Diego—Ken Brady, Michigan; Virginia—John

Perry, Pan American; Denver—Larry Farmer, UCLA; Indiana—Alan Hornyak, Ohio State; Utah—Pete Harris, Stephen F. Austin; Kentucky—William Harris, North Carolina State; Carolina—Larry Hollyfield, UCLA.

SIXTH ROUND Memphis—George Karl, North Carolina; San Antonio—Gary Melchionni, Duke; San Diego—Jim Owens, Arizona State; New York—Neal Jorgenson, Oregon State; Virginia—Aaron Stewart, Richmond; Denver—Martinez Denmon, Iowa State; Indiana—Joe Wallace, Denver; Utah—David Winfield, Minnesota; Kentucky—Mike Boylan, Assumption (Mass.); Carolina—Joe Reaves, Bethel.

SEVENTH ROUND Memphis—E. C. Coleman, Houston Baptist; San Antonio—Richie Fuqua, Oral Roberts; New York—Kenny Charles, Fordham; San Diego—Nate Stevens, Long Beach State; Virginia—Rubin Montanez, Duquesne; Denver—James Brown, Harvard; Indiana—Jim Andrews, Kentucky; Utah—J. G. Brosterhos, Texas; Kentucky—Les Taylor, Murray State; Carolina—Ozzie Edwards, Oklahoma City.

EIGHTH ROUND Memphis—Rod Freeman, Vanderbilt; San Antonio—Henry Wilmore, Michigan; San Diego—Chris McMurray, San Diego State; New York—Gene Doyle, Holy Cross; Virginia—Walter McGary, Tennessee-Chattanooga; Denver—Gary Rhoades, Colorado State; Indiana—Mike Edwards, Tennessee; Utah—Mike Williams, Kentucky Wesleyan; Kentucky—James Greene, Kentucky Wesleyan; Carolina—Steve Becker, Yankton (S.D.).

NINTH ROUND Memphis—Charles Mitchell, Eastern Kentucky; San Antonio—Mark Sibley, Northwestern; New York—Russ Hunt, Furman; San Diego—Clint Harris, Iowa State; Virginia—Phil Chenier, California; Denver—Connie Warren, Xavier; Indiana—Robert Wilson, Wichita State; Utah—Roy McPipe, Eastern Montana; Kentucky—John Johnson, Denver; Carolina—Abe Stewart, Jacksonville.

TENTH ROUND Memphis—Chuck Iverson, South Dakota; San Antonio—Larry Lilly, Alabama State; San Diego—Nick Connor, Illinois; New York—Gene Armstead, Rutgers; Virginia—Joe Cafferky, North Carolina State; Denver—Jeff Dawson, Illinois; Indiana—Byron Jones, San Francisco; Utah—Melvin Russell, Centenary; Kentucky—Mike Macaluso, Canisius; Carolina—Gerald Smith, Detroit.

ABA 1973 UNDERGRADUATE DRAFT

FIRST ROUND San Diego—Bill Walton, UCLA; Memphis—David Thompson, North Carolina State; San Antonio—Dwight Jones, Houston; New York—Henry Williams, Jacksonville; Virginia—Phil Smith, San Francisco; Denver—Marvin Barnes, Providence; Indiana—Len Elmore, Maryland; Utah—Bruce Seals, Xavier (La.); Kentucky—Don Smith, Dayton; Carolina—Maurice Lucas, Marquette.

SECOND ROUND Memphis—Larry Robinson, Texas; San Antonio—Tom Henderson, Hawaii; San Diego—Jim Bradley, Northern Illinois; New York—Campy Russell, Michigan; Virginia—John Shumate, Notre Dame; Denver—Dennis DuVal, Syracuse; Indiana—Ruby Jackson, Hutchinson JC; Utah—Marvin Webster, Morgan State; Kentucky—James Forbes, Texas-El Paso; Carolina—Kevin Restani, San Francisco.

ABA 1973 SUPPLEMENTARY DRAFT

(Teams listed alphabetically)

FIRST ROUND Carolina—Cal Tatum, Southern Colorado State; Denver—Lamont King, Long Beach State; Kentucky—Steve Rowell, Rhode Island; Memphis—Wardell Jeffries, Oklahoma Baptist; San Antonio—Craig Littlepage, Penn; San Diego—Larry Moore, Texas-Arlington; Utah—Dennis Johnson, Ferris State; Virginia—Willie Calvert, Abilene Christian.

SECOND ROUND Carolina—Steve Smith, Loyola (Cal.); Denver—Tom Peck, Eau Claire; Kentucky—James Garvin, Boston U.; Memphis—Don Watts, Xavier (La.); San Antonio—John Coughran, California; San Diego—Mike Contreras, Arizona State; Utah—Bill McCoy, Northern Iowa; Virginia—Don Johnson, Lebanon Valley.

THIRD ROUND Carolina—Bill Bailey, Catawba; Denver—Lindell Reason, Eastern Michigan; Kentucky—Chuck Witt, Western Kentucky; Memphis—Roy Simpson, Furman; San Antonio—Bob Fullerton, Xavier; San Diego—Doug Little, Oregon; Utah—James Floyd, Shaw; Virginia—Gregg Hawkins, North Carolina State.

FOURTH ROUND Carolina—David Angel, Clemson; Kentucky—Fran Costello, Providence; Memphis—Norman Russell, Oklahoma; San Antonio—Bob Kilgore, Michigan State; San Diego—Ernie Kusyner, Kansas State; Utah—Charles Golson, Emporia; Virginia—Mike Allocco, Stonehill.

FIFTH ROUND Carolina—Carl Jackson, St Bonaventure; Kentucky—Ed Childress, Austin Peay; Memphis—Aaron Covington, Canisius; Utah—Mike Quick, San Francisco; San Antonio—Ron Hogue, Georgia; Virginia—Allan Shaw, Duke.

SIXTH ROUND Carolina—Lynn Greer, Virginia State; Kentucky—Jerry Clark, Skagit Valley JC (Wash.); Memphis—Fred Lavoroni, Santa Clara; San Antonio—John Lang, Augustana; San Diego—Jerry Brisbano, SW Louisiana; Utah—Lee Colburn, South Dakota State; Virginia—Howard White, Sam Houston State.

SEVENTH ROUND Carolina—Dale Adams, Mount St. Mary's; Memphis—John Wolfenberg, Valparaiso; San Antonio—Jeff Overhouse, Texas A&M; San Diego—Mark Beckwith, Montana State; Utah—Robert White, Sam Houston State; Virginia—Darryl Brown, Maryland.

EIGHTH ROUND Carolina—Terrance Murchinson, Fayetteville; Memphis—Jim Crawford, LaSalle; San Antonio—Tim Dominiz, Valdosta; San Diego—Wayne Pack, Tennessee Tech; Utah—Gary Watson, Wisconsin; Virginia—Linwood Johnson, Virginia State.

NINTH ROUND Memphis—Rick Williams, Iowa; San Antonio—Bill Harris, Northern Illinois; San Diego—Fred DeVaughn, Western Montana; Utah—Larry Davis, Centenary.

TENTH ROUND Memphis—Joe Wise, Bridgewater (Mass.) State; San Antonio—Bob Bodell, Maryland; Utah—Ben Kelso, Central Michigan.

ELEVENTH ROUND Memphis—Reed Johnson, Oklahoma Christian; San Antonio—Leon Howard, Wisconsin; Utah—Nate Hawthorne, Southern Illinois.

TWELFTH ROUND Memphis—Greg Juricisin, Cincinnati; San Antonio—Jeff Jellison, NE Massachusetts; Utah—John Thomas, Mississippi Southern.

THIRTEENTH ROUND Utah—Gary Black, Rocky Mountain; Utah—Sam Whitehead, Sam Houston State.

FOURTEENTH ROUND Utah—Harvey Catchings, Hardin-Simmons.

NBA 1974 (MAY 28, 1974)

FIRST ROUND Portland—Bill Walton, UCLA; Philadelphia—Marvin Barnes, Providence; Seattle (from Cleveland)—Tom Burleson, North Carolina State; Phoenix—John Shumate, Notre Dame; Houston—Bobby Jones, North Carolina; KC-Omaha—Scott Wedman, Colorado; Atlanta—Tom Henderson, Hawaii; Cleveland (from Seattle)—Campy Russell, Michigan; Buffalo—Tom McMillen, Maryland; Atlanta (from New Orleans)—Mike Sojourner, Utah; Golden State—Jamaal Wilkes, UCLA; Los Angeles—Brian Winters, South Carolina; Washington—Len Elmore, Maryland; Chicago (from New York)—Maurice Lucas, Marquette; Detroit—Al Eberhard, Missouri; Chicago—Cliff Pondexter, Long Beach State; Boston—Glenn McDonald, Long Beach State; Milwaukee—Gary Brokaw, Notre Dame.

SECOND ROUND Philadelphia—Don Smith, Dayton; Portland—Jan van Breda Kolff, Vanderbilt; Los Angeles (from Cleveland)—Billy Knight, Pittsburgh; Washington (from Phoenix)—Leonard Robinson, Tennessee State; Houston—Gus Bailey, Texas-El Paso; KC-Omaha—Len Kosmalski, Tennessee; Atlanta—John Drew, Gardner Webb; Seattle—Leonard Gray, Long Beach State; Chicago (from Buffalo)—Leon Benbow, Jacksonville; New Orleans—Aaron James, Grambling; Golden State—Phil Smith, San Francisco; Washington—Dennis DuVal, Syracuse; Phoenix (from Los Angeles)—Fred Saunders, Syracuse; New York—Jesse Dark, Virginia Commonwealth; Detroit—Eric Money, Arizona; Portland (from Chicago)—Phil Lumpkin, Miami (Ohio); Boston—Kevin Stacom, Providence; Portland (from Milwaukee)—Rubin Collins, Maryland-Eastern Shore.

THIRD ROUND Philadelphia—Coniel Norman, Arizona; Cleveland (from Portland)—Clarence Walker, West Georgia; Cleveland—Kevin Restani, San Francisco; Phoenix—George Gervin, Eastern Michigan; Houston—Robert Wilson, Iowa State; Philadelphia (from KC-Omaha)—Harvey Catchings, Hardin-Simmons; Atlanta—Darrell Elston, North Carolina; Seattle—Talvin Skinner, Maryland-Eastern Shore; Buffalo—Kim Hughes, Wisconsin; New Orleans—Bruce King, Pan American; Golden State—Frank Kendrick, Purdue; Los Angeles—Jim Bradley, Northern Illinois; Phoenix (from Washington)—Earl Williams, Winston-Salem; New York—Rudy Jackson, Hutchinson JC; Detroit—Roland Grant, New Mexico State; Chicago—Bob Wilson, Wichita State; Boston—Roscoe Pondexter, Long Beach State; Milwaukee—Greg McDougald, Oral Roberts.

FOURTH ROUND Philadelphia—Butch Taylor, Jacksonville; Portland—Mickey Johnson, Aurora; Cleveland—Jim Foster, Connecticut; Phoenix—Randy Allen, Indiana (Pa.); Houston—Larry Robinson, Texas; KC-Omaha—Lloyd Batts, Cincinnati; Atlanta—Ed Palubinskas, LSU; Seattle—William Gordon, Maryland-Eastern Shore; Buffalo—Bernard Harris, Virginia Commonwealth; New Orleans—Ray Price, Washington; Golden State—Willie Biles, Tulsa; Washington—Stan Washington, San Diego; Los Angeles—Ron de Vries, Illinois State; New York—Roy Ebron, Southwestern Louisiana; Detroit—Mickey Martin, Pittsburgh; Chicago—Jim Forbes, Texas-El Paso; Boston—Lerman Battle, Fairmont State; Milwaukee—Lionel Billingy, Duquesne.

FIFTH ROUND Philadelphia—Gary Crowthers, Hardin-Simmons; Portland—Bernard Hardin, New Mexico; Cleveland—Gary Novak, Notre Dame; Phoenix—Ralph Bobik, Creighton; Houston—Owen Wells, Detroit; KC-Omaha—Terry Compton, Vanderbilt; Atlanta—Tyrone Medley, Utah; Seattle—Dean Tolson, Arkansas; Buffalo—Tony Byers, Wake Forest;

New Orleans—Ed Searcy, St. John's; Golden State—Steve Erickson, Oregon; Los Angeles—Seymour Reed, Bradley; Washington—Gary Anderson, Wisconsin; New York—Greg Jackson, Guilford; Detroit—Joe Newman, Temple; Chicago—Randy Knowles, Texas A&M; Boston—Ben Clyde, Florida State; Milwaukee—John Johnson, Denver.

SIXTH ROUND Philadelphia—Mark Westra, Southern California; Portland—Dan Anderson, Southern California; Cleveland—Aron Stewart, Richmond; Phoenix—Collis Temple, LSU; Houston—Lawrence Johnson, Prairie View; KC-Omaha—Ron Kennedy, Arizona; Atlanta—Sam Hervey, SMU; Seattle—Wardell Jackson, Ohio State; Buffalo—Gary Link, Missouri; New Orleans—Lawrence McCray, Florida State; Golden State—John Errecart, Pacific; Washington—Roy McPipe, Eastern Michigan; Los Angeles—Billy Morris, St. Louis; New York—Terry Mikan, St. Thomas; Detroit—Mike Sylvester, Dayton; Chicago—Robert Rosier, St. Thomas; Boston—Gene Harmon, Creighton; Milwaukee—Larry Williams, Kansas State.

SEVENTH ROUND Philadelphia—Dave Stoczynski, Gannon; Portland—Doug Richards, Brigham Young; Cleveland—Mike Robinson, Michigan State; Phoenix—Clyde Dickey, Boise State; Houston—Kevin Fitzgerald, Oklahoma; KC-Omaha—Mark Browne, Missouri; Atlanta—Greg Lee, UCLA; Seattle—Jerry Faulkner, Western Georgia; Buffalo—Tommy Curtis, UCLA; New Orleans—Joel Copeland, Old Dominion; Golden State—Brady Allen, California; Los Angeles—Dennis Van Zant, Azusa Pacific; Washington—Tom Turner, Western Georgia, New York—Billy Smith, Mercer; Detroit—Sammy High, Tulsa; Chicago—Geoff Roberts, Missouri West; Boston—Ron Brown, Penn State; Milwaukee—Bob Hornstein, West Virginia.

EIGHTH ROUND Philadelphia—Jimmy Powell, Middle Tennessee; Portland—Eldridge Broussard, Pacific (Ore.); Cleveland—Kerry Hughes, Wisconsin; Phoenix—Tom Holland, Oklahoma; Houston—Steve Brooks, Arkansas State; KC-Omaha—Richie O'Connor, Fairfield; Atlanta—Bill Butler, Louisville; Seattle—Leonard Coulter, Morehead State; Buffalo—Glenn Price, St. Bonaventure; New Orleans—Jay Piccola, Roanoke; Golden State—Clarence Allen, California-Santa Barbara; Washington—Steve Platt, Huntington (Ind.); Los Angeles—Bob Florence, Nevada-Las Vegas; New York—Dennis McDermott, St. Francis; Detroit—Greg Newman, Drexel; Chicago—Sam McCants, Oral Roberts; Boston—Richard Wallace, Georgia Southern; Milwaukee—Ralph Palamar, Cameron.

NINTH ROUND Philadelphia—Perry Warbington, Georgia Southern; Portland—Lee Haven, Colorado; Cleveland—Jim Buskofsky, Upper Iowa; Phoenix—Ted Evans, Oklahoma; Houston—Ken Stalling, Missouri-Rolla; KC-Omaha—Jeff Dawson, Illinois; Atlanta—Lon Kruger, Kansas State; Seattle—Bertrand du Pont, Dillard; Buffalo—John Falconi, Davidson; New Orleans—Ken Boyd, Boston U.; Golden State—Carl Meier, California; Washington—Mark Raterink, Boston College; New York—Earl Brown, Lafayette, Detroit—Gary Deitelhoff, Millikin; Chicago—Jerry Davenport, Cameron; Boston—Al Skinner, Massachusetts; Milwaukee—Mike Deane, Potsdam State.

TENTH ROUND Philadelphia—Larry Witherspoon, Towson State; Portland—Ron Jones, Oregon State; Cleveland—Jim Kelly, Loras; Phoenix—Mark Wasley, Arizona State; Houston—Marcus Washington, Marquette; KC-Omaha—Dennis White, Arkansas; Atlanta—Brendy Lee, Nebraska; Seattle—Rod Derline, Seattle; Buffalo—Andy Rimol, Princeton; New Orleans—Walt McGary, Chattanooga; Golden State—Marvin Buckley, Nevada-Reno; Washington—Pete Collins, High Point; New York—John O'Donnell, North Carolina; Detroit—Bill Ligon, Vanderbilt; Chicago—Rick Hockenos, St. Francis (Pa.); Boston—Phil Rogers, Fairfield; Milwaukee—Bruce Featherston, Southwest Texas State.

NBA 1974 EXPANSION DRAFT (MAY 20, 1974)

NEW ORLEANS Dennis Awtrey, Chicago; Jim Barnett, Golden State; Walt Bellamy, Atlanta; John Block, KC-Omaha; Barry Clemens, Cleveland; E. C. Coleman, Houston; Lamar Green, Phoenix; Nate Hawthorne, Los Angeles; Ollie Johnson, Portland; Toby Kimball, Philadelphia; Steve Kuberski, Boston; Stu Lantz, Detroit; Dean Meminger, New York; Louie Nelson, Washington; Curtis Perry, Milwaukee; Bud Stallworth, Seattle; Bob Kauffman, Buffalo.

ABA 1974

FIRST ROUND Virginia—Tom McMillen, Maryland; Memphis—Scott Wedman, Colorado; San Diego—Major Jones, Albany State (Ga.); Denver—James "Fly" Williams, Austin Peay; Virginia (from San Antonio)—Jan van Breda Kolff, Vanderbilt; Indiana—Billy Knight, Pittsburgh; Carolina—John Lucas, Maryland; San Diego (from Kentucky)—Cliff Pondexter, Long Beach State; New York—Brian Winters, South Carolina; Utah—Joe Meriweather, Southern Illinois.

SECOND ROUND Memphis—Clarence "Foots" Walker, West Georgia State; Virginia—Jesse Dark, Virginia Commonwealth; San Diego—Gus Bailey, Texas-El Paso; Denver—Frank Kendrick, Purdue; San Antonio—Leonard Robinson, Tennessee State; Indiana—Bruce King, Pan American; New York (from Carolina)—Rich Kelley, Stanford; Kentucky—Al Eberhard, Missouri; Carolina (from New York)—Gus Gerard, Virginia; Utah—Len Kosmalski, Tennessee.

THIRD ROUND Memphis—Bob Wilson, Iowa State; Utah (from Virginia)—Moses Malone, Petersburg (Va.) H.S.; Denver—Mike Sojourner, Utah; Virginia (from San Diego)—

Lionel Billingy, Duquesne; Utah (from San Antonio)—Aaron James, Grambling; Indiana—Roland Grant, New Mexico State; Utah (from Carolina)—Tom Barker, Southern Idaho; Kentucky (from Utah)—Sammy High, Tulsa; San Antonio (from Kentucky)—Collis Temple, Louisiana State; New York—Tom Boswell, South Carolina.

FOURTH ROUND Memphis—Glenn McDonald, Long Beach State; Virginia—Lermon Battle, Fairmont State; San Diego—Richie O'Connor, Fairfield; Denver—Coniel Norman, Arizona; San Antonio—Fred Saunders, Syracuse; San Antonio (from Indiana)—Kim Hughes, Wisconsin; Carolina—Darrell Elston, North Carolina; Utah—Sam McCants, Oral Roberts; Kentucky—Lloyd Batts, Cincinnati; New York—Talvin Skinner, Maryland-Eastern Shore.

FIFTH ROUND Memphis—Tyrone Medley, Utah; Virginia—Bernard Harris, Virginia Commonwealth; Denver—Bernard Hardin, New Mexico; San Diego—Greg Lee, UCLA; San Antonio—Eugene Short, Jackson State; Indiana—Eddie Woods, Oral Roberts; Carolina—Mickey Johnson, Aurora (Ill.); Utah—Steve Brooks, Arkansas State; Kentucky—Seymour Reed, Bradley; New York—Eric Fernsten, San Francisco.

SIXTH ROUND Memphis—Wolfgang Fengler, Delaware; Virginia—Phil Lumpkin, Miami (Ohio); San Diego—Richard Wallace, Georgia Southern; Denver—Luther Burden, Utah; San Antonio—Gary Anderson, Wisconsin; Indiana—Ron De Vries, Illinois State; Carolina—Gary Novak, Notre Dame; Carolina (from Utah)—Harvey Catchings, Hardin-Simmons; Kentucky—Bill Ligon, Vanderbilt; New York—Gary Brokaw, Notre Dame.

SEVENTH ROUND Memphis—Lawrence Johnson, Prairie View; Virginia—Earl Williams, Winston-Salem; Denver—Eric Money, Arizona; San Diego—Leon Benbow, Jacksonville; San Antonio—Gerald Cunningham, Kentucky State; Indiana—Alex English, South Carolina; Carolina—Jim Foster, Connecticut; Utah—Ron Lee, Oregon; Kentucky—Bill Butler, Louisville; New York—Dean Tolson, Arkansas.

EIGHTH ROUND Memphis—Willie Biles, Tulsa; Virginia—John Drew, Gardner Webb; San Diego—Dan Anderson, Southern California; Denver—Larry Fogle, Canisius; San Antonio—Hercle Ivy, Iowa State; Indiana—Bobby Florence, Nevada-Las Vegas; Carolina—Tom Kivisto, Kansas; Utah—Ed Palubinskas, Louisiana State; Kentucky—Len Coulter, Morehead State; New York—Al Skinner, Massachusetts.

NINTH ROUND Memphis—Ron Brown, Penn State; Virginia—Bill Campion, Manhattan; Denver—Tony Byers, Wake Forest; San Diego—Stan Washington, San Diego; San Antonio—Walter Luckett, Ohio; Indiana—Kevin Fitzgerald, Oklahoma State; Carolina—Marcus Washington, Marquette; Utah—Lionel Hollins, Arizona State; Kentucky—Glenn Hansen, Louisiana State; New York—Bob Fleischer, Duke.

TENTH ROUND Memphis—Candy LaPrince, Iowa; Virginia—Mark Cartwright, Bowling Green; San Diego—Marques Johnson, UCLA; Denver—Roscoe Pondexter, Long Beach State; San Antonio—Charles McKinney, Baylor; Indiana—Mark Browne, Missouri Western; Carolina—Mike Sylvester, Dayton; Utah—Mike Westra, Southern California; Kentucky—Steve Walker, Kentucky Wesleyan; San Antonio (from New York)—Mike Ogan, Carson Newman.

ABA 1974 DRAFT OF NBA PLAYERS

FIRST ROUND Virginia—Bob Kauffman, Buffalo; Memphis—Rick Roberson, Portland; Denver—Nate Thurmond, Golden State; San Diego—Cazzie Russell, Golden State; San Antonio—Tom Boerwinkle, Chicago; Indiana—Clifford Ray, Chicago; Carolina—Pete Maravich, Atlanta; Utah—Bob Christian, Phoenix; Kentucky—Jim Price, Los Angeles; New York—Phil Chenier, Capital.

SECOND ROUND Memphis—Norm Van Lier, Chicago; Virginia—George Johnson, Golden State; San Diego—Sidney Wicks, Portland; Denver—Tom Van Arsdale, Philadelphia; San Antonio—Clyde Lee, Golden State; Indiana—Bill Bradley, New York; Carolina—Henry Bibby, New York; Utah—Geoff Petrie, Portland; Kentucky—Greg Smith, Portland; New York—Dave Cowens, Boston.

THIRD ROUND Virginia—Dick Snyder, Seattle; Memphis—Len Wilkens, Cleveland; Denver—Don Adams, Detroit; San Diego—Curtis Rowe, Detroit; San Antonio—Neal Walk, Phoenix; Indiana—Mel Counts, Los Angeles; Carolina—Phil Jackson, New York; Utah—Howard Porter, Chicago; Kentucky—Rowland Garrett, Chicago; New York—Jerry Sloan, Chicago.

FOURTH ROUND Memphis—Paul Silas, Boston; Virginia—Calvin Murphy, Houston; San Diego—Gale Goodrich, Los Angeles; Denver—Rick Adelman, Chicago; San Antonio—Steve Kuberski, Boston; Indiana—Pat Riley, Los Angeles; Carolina—Paul Westphal, Boston; Utah—Rudy Tomjanovich, Houston; Kentucky—Herm Gilliam, Atlanta; New York—Jim Fox, Seattle.

FIFTH ROUND Virginia—Barry Clemens, Cleveland; Memphis—Dave DeBusschere, New York; Denver—Lou Hudson, Atlanta; San Diego—Connie Hawkins, Los Angeles; San Antonio—Lloyd Neal, Portland; Indiana—Jim Davis, Detroit; Carolina—Jeff Mullins, Golden State; Utah—Bob McAdoo, Buffalo; Kentucky—Larry Steele, Portland; New York—Garfield Heard, Buffalo.

NBA 1975 (MAY 29, 1975)

FIRST ROUND Atlanta (from New Orleans)—David Thompson, North Carolina State; Los Angeles—David Meyers, UCLA; Atlanta—Marvin Webster, Morgan State; Phoenix—Alvan Adams, Oklahoma; Philadelphia—Darryl Dawkins, Maynard Evans H.S., (Orlando, Fla.); Portland—Lionel Hollins, Arizona State; New Orleans (from Milwaukee)—Rich Kelley, Stanford; Los Angeles (from Cleveland)—Junior Bridgeman, Louisville; New York—Eugene Short, Jackson State; KC-Omaha (from Detroit)—Bill Robinzine, DePaul; Houston—Joe Meriweather, Southern Illinois; Seattle—Frank Oleynick, Seattle; KC-Omaha—Bob Bigelow, Penn; Golden State (from Chicago)—Joe Bryant, LaSalle; Cleveland (from Golden State)—John Lambert, Southern California; Phoenix (from Buffalo)—Ricky Sobers, Nevada-Las Vegas; Boston—Tom Boswell, South Carolina; Washington—Kevin Grevey, Kentucky.

SECOND ROUND Atlanta (from New Orleans)—Bill Willoughby, Dwight Morrow H.S. (Englewood, N.J.); Golden State (from Los Angeles)—Gus Williams, Southern California; Seattle (from Atlanta)—Bruce Seals, Xavier (La.); Milwaukee (from Phoenix)—Clyde Mayes, Furman; Philadelphia—Lloyd Free, Guilford; Milwaukee—Cornelius Cash, Bowling Green; Portland—Bob Gross, Long Beach State; New York—Luther Burden, Utah; Detroit—Walter Luckett, Ohio; Cleveland—Dan Roundfield, Central Michigan; Houston—Jim Blanks, Gardner Webb; Chicago (from Seattle)—Steve Green, Indiana; KC-Omaha—Glen Hansen, LSU; Chicago—John Laskowski, Indiana; Cleveland (from Golden State)—Mel Utley, St. John's; New York (from Buffalo)—Larry Fogle, Canisius; Phoenix (from Washington)—Allen Murphy, Louisville; Phoenix (from Boston)—Jimmy Dan Conner, Kentucky.

THIRD ROUND New Orleans—Rudy Hackett, Syracuse; New Orleans (from Los Angeles)—Jim McElroy, Central Michigan; Philadelphia (from Atlanta)—Jim Baker, Hawaii; Golden State (from Phoenix)—Otis Johnson, Stetson; Philadelphia—Charles Cleveland, Alabama; Portland—Tom Roy, Maryland; Milwaukee—Brian Hammel, Bentley; Detroit—Pete Trgovich, UCLA; Cleveland—Ted Hathaway, Cleveland State; New York—John Ramsey, Seton Hall; Houston—Rudy White, Arizona State; Washington (from Seattle)—Tom Kropp, Kearney State; KC-Omaha—Bob Guyette, Kentucky; Portland (from Chicago)—Gus Gerard, Virginia; Golden State—Robert Hawkins, Illinois State; Buffalo—George Bucci, Manhattan; Boston—Jerome Anderson, West Virginia; Phoenix (from Washington)—Bayard Forrest, Grand Canyon.

FOURTH ROUND New Orleans—Mack Coleman, Houston Baptist; Los Angeles—C. J. Kupec, Michigan; Atlanta—Monte Towe, North Carolina State; Phoenix—Sam McCants, Oral Roberts; Philadelphia—Louis Dunbar, Houston; Milwaukee—Bill Campion, Manhattan; Portland—Phil Hicks, Tulane; Cleveland—Eric Fernsten, San Francisco; New York—David Vaughn, Oral Roberts; Detroit—Lindsay Hairston, Michigan State; Houston—Ken Smith, Tulsa; Seattle—Jim Moore, Utah State; KC-Omaha—Kevin Cleuss, St. John's; Chicago—Ron Haigler, Penn; Golden State—Billy Taylor, LaSalle; Buffalo—Bob Fleischer, Duke; Washington—Fessor Leonard, Furman; Boston—Cyrus Mann, Illinois State.

FIFTH ROUND New Orleans—Andre Hampton, Kentucky State; Los Angeles—Charles Russell, Alabama; Atlanta—Wilbur Holland, New Orleans; Phoenix—Joe Pace, Coppin State; Philadelphia—Ken Tyler, Gonzaga; Portland—Maurice Presley, Houston; Cleveland (from Milwaukee)—Jim Lee, Syracuse; New York—Don Washington, North Carolina; Detroit—Cliff Pratt, Shaw; Cleveland—Mike Odems, Western Kentucky; Houston—Rick Whitlow, Illinois State; Seattle—Dwain Govan, Bishop (Tex.); KC-Omaha—Ed Stahl, North Carolina; Chicago—Bob Iverson, North Texas State; Golden State—Larry Pounds, Washington; Buffalo—Sam Berry, Armstrong State; Boston—Darryl Brown, Fordham; Washington—Rich Jones, Virginia Commonwealth.

SIXTH ROUND New Orleans—Rich Schmidt, Illinois; Los Angeles—Don Ford, California-Santa Barbara; Atlanta—Danny Williams, Mississippi; Phoenix—Buff Burrell, Southern California; Philadelphia—Ken Alston, Valdosta State; Milwaukee—Oliver Purnell, Old Dominion; Portland—Gerald Willett, Oregon; Detroit—Allen Spruill, North Carolina A&T; Cleveland—Henry Ward, Jackson State; New York—Henry Williams, Jacksonville; Houston—William Johnson, Texas Tech; Seattle—Larry Smith, North Carolina A&T; KC-Omaha—Clint Chapman, Southern California; Chicago—Bill Andreas, Ohio State; Golden State—Tony Styles, San Francisco; Buffalo—Larry Jackson, North Carolina-Charlotte; Washington—John Garrett, Purdue; Boston—Rick Coleman, Jacksonville.

SEVENTH ROUND New Orleans—Bill Higgins, Ashland; Los Angeles—Rick Suttle, Kansas; Atlanta—Gus Johnson, Winona State; Phoenix—Dave Edmunds, Western Georgia; Philadelphia—Mike Flynn, Kentucky; Portland—Steve Fields, Miami (Ohio); Milwaukee—Wilbur Thomas, American; Cleveland—Shawn Leftwick, Jacksonville; New York—Peter Davis, Michigan State; Detroit—Ike Williams, Armstrong State; Houston—Nate Barnett, Akron; Seattle—Hollis Miller, Drury (Mo.); KC-Omaha—Wayne Croft, Clemson; Chicago—John Grochowalski, Assumption; Golden State—Stan Boyer, Wyoming; Buffalo—Mike Franklin, Cincinnati; Boston—Al Boswell, Oral Roberts; Washington—Fletcher Johnson, Randolph-Macon.

EIGHTH ROUND New Orleans—Harvey Carmichael, Kentucky State; Los Angeles—Mike Cashman, Willamette; Atlanta—Oscar Jackson, Duquesne; Phoenix—Jack Schrader, Arizona State; Philadelphia—Freeman Blade, Eastern Montana; Milwaukee—Bob McCurdy,

Richmond; Portland—Charley Neal, Oregon State; New York—Jerry Homan, Marquette; Detroit—John Kelley, Dillard; Cleveland—Andre McCarter, UCLA; Houston—Leon Johnson, Centenary; Seattle—Ken McKenzie, Montana; KC-Omaha—Jim Bostic, New Mexico State; Chicago—John Murphy, Massachusetts; Golden State—Mike Rozenski, St. Mary's (Cal.); Buffalo—Allen Jones, Pepperdine; Washington—Bruce Hamming, Augustana; Boston—Roger Morningstar, Kansas.

NINTH ROUND New Orleans—Fred Stokes, Barber Scotia; Atlanta—Dave Schlesser, Morningside; Phoenix—Owen Brown, Maryland; Philadelphia—Larry Harralson, Drake; Portland—Quintin Braxton, Portland; Milwaukee—Eric Hays, Montana; Detroit—Terry Thomas, Detroit; Cleveland—Skip Howard, Bowling Green; New York—Tim Van Blommesteyn, Princeton; Houston—Steve Storther, Providence; Seattle—Rich Haws, Utah State; Chicago—Gary Tomaszewski, St. Mary's (Tex.); Golden State—Scott Trobbe, Stanford; Buffalo—George Rautins, Niagara; Boston—Robert Rhodes, Albany State (Ga.); Washington—Doug Brookins, Creighton.

TENTH ROUND New Orleans—Aleksander Belov, Soviet Union; Atlanta—Vic Kelly, Hawaii; Phoenix—Mike Moon, Arizona State; Philadelphia—Rick Reed, Azusa Pacific; Milwaukee—Romy Thomas, Eau Claire; Portland—Tyree Foster, Portland; Cleveland—Eric Anderson, McAlister; New York—Mo Rivers, North Carolina State; Detroit—Mickey Fox, St. Mary's (N.S.); Seattle—Jerry Bellotti, Santa Clara; Golden State—Maurice Harper, St. Mary's (Cal.); Buffalo—Art Allen, Pepperdine; Washington—Mike Fahey, Brandeis; Boston—Bill Endicott, Massachusetts.

ABA 1975

BONUS CHOICE Denver—Marvin Webster, Morgan State

FIRST ROUND Virginia—David Thompson, North Carolina State; Memphis—Lonnie Shelton, Oregon State; San Diego—Kevin Grevey, Kentucky; St. Louis—Gus Williams, Southern California; Utah—Steve Green, Indiana; Indiana—Dan Roundfield, Central Michigan; San Antonio—Mark Olberding, Minnesota; New York—John Lucas, Maryland; Virginia (from Denver)—Melvin Bennett, Pittsburgh; Kentucky—Jim Baker, Hawaii.

SECOND ROUND Virginia—Jimmy Dan Conner, Kentucky; Memphis—Rich Kelley, Stanford; San Diego—Cornelius Cash, Bowling Green; St. Louis—Rudy White, Arizona State; Utah—Norman Cook, Kansas; Indiana—Charles Jordan, Canisius; Indiana (from San Antonio)—Jim Lee, Syracuse; New York—George Bucci, Manhattan; Denver—Bill Willoughby Dwight Morrow H.S., (Englewood, N.J.); San Antonio (from Kentucky)—Rich Suttle, Kansas.

THIRD ROUND Kentucky (from Virginia)—Allen Murphy, Kentucky; Memphis—Ron Haigler, Pennsylvania; San Diego—Bob Gross, Long Beach State; St. Louis—Rudy Hackett, Syracuse; Denver (from Utah)—Tom Kropp, Kearney State; Indiana—Ken Tyler, Gonzaga; San Antonio—Billy Taylor, LaSalle; New York—Leon Douglas, Alabama; Denver—Monte Towe, North Carolina State; Kentucky—Eric Fernsten, San Francisco.

FOURTH ROUND Virginia—Luther Burden, Utah; Memphis—Glenn Hansen, Louisiana State; San Diego—Pete Trgovich, UCLA; St. Louis—Tom Roy, Maryland; Virginia (from Utah)—Fessor Leonard, Furman; Indiana—Brian Hammel, Bentley; San Antonio—Ken Smith, Tulsa; New York—Bob Guyette, Kentucky; Denver—Bob Fleischer, Duke; Kentucky—John Laskowski, Indiana.

FIFTH ROUND Virginia—Rich Jones, Virginia Commonwealth; Memphis—Walter Luckett, Ohio; San Diego—Biff Burrell, Southern California; St. Louis—Larry Fogle, Canisius; St. Louis (from Utah through Denver)—C. J. Kupec, Michigan; Indiana—John Ramsey, Seton Hall; San Antonio—Robert Parish, Centenary; New York—Darryl Brown, Fordham; Denver—Jim Moore, Utah State; Kentucky—Charles Cleveland, Alabama.

SIXTH ROUND Virginia—Fletcher Johnson, Randolph-Macon; Memphis—Terry Furlow, Michigan State; San Diego—Louis Dunbar, Houston; St. Louis—Al Jones, San Diego; Utah—Otis Johnson, Stetson; Indiana—Mike Flynn, Kentucky; San Antonio—Bayard Forrest, Grand Canyon; New York—Mike Mitchell, Auburn; Denver—Charles Russell, Alabama; Kentucky—Mike Rozenski, St. Mary's (Cal.).

SEVENTH ROUND Virginia—Bill Bunton, Louisville; Memphis—Rich Whitlow, Illinois State; San Diego—Jerome Anderson, West Virginia; St. Louis—Al Spruill, North Carolina A&T; Utah—Tim Van Blommesteyn, Princeton; Indiana—Cliff Pratt, Shaw; San Antonio—Henry Ward, Jackson State; New York—Wayne Croft, Clemson; Denver—Mike Odems, Western Kentucky; Kentucky—Randy Meister, Penn State.

EIGHTH ROUND Virginia—Ricky Coleman, Jacksonville; Memphis—John Murphy, Massachusetts; San Diego—Mack Coleman, Houston Baptist; St. Louis—Ted Hathaway, Cleveland State; Utah—Kirk Bruce, Pittsburgh; Indiana—Bill Andreas, Ohio State; San Antonio—Gary Tomaszewski, St. Mary's (Tex.); New York—John Lambert, Southern California; Denver—Owen Brown, Maryland; Kentucky—Lou Silver, Harvard.

NBA 1976 (JUNE 8, 1976)

FIRST ROUND Houston (from Atlanta)—John Lucas, Maryland; Chicago—Scott May, Indiana; Kansas City—Richard Washington, UCLA; Detroit—Leon Douglas, Alabama; Portland—Wally Walker, Virginia; Buffalo (from New Orleans)—Adrian Dantley, Notre Dame; Milwaukee—Quinn Buckner, Indiana; Golden State (from Los Angeles)—Robert Parish, Centenary; Atlanta (from Houston)—Armond Hill, Princeton; Phoenix—Ron Lee, Oregon; Seattle—Bob Wilkerson, Indiana; Philadelphia—Terry Furlow, Michigan State; Washington (from Buffalo)—Mitch Kupchak, North Carolina; Washington—Larry Wright, Grambling; Cleveland—Chuckie Williams, Kansas State; Boston—Norman Cook, Kansas; Golden State—Sonny Parker, Texas A&M.

SECOND ROUND Chicago—Willie Smith, Missouri; Seattle (from Atlanta)—Bayard Forrest, Grand Canyon; Portland (from Kansas City)—Major Jones, Albany State (Ga.); Los Angeles (from Detroit)—Earl Tatum, Marquette; Portland—John Davis, Dayton; Milwaukee (from New Orleans)—Alex English, South Carolina; Milwaukee—Scott Lloyd, Arizona State; New York—Lonnie Shelton, Oregon State; New Orleans (from Los Angeles)—Jacky Dorsey, Georgia; Houston—Phil Hicks, Tulane; Atlanta (from Phoenix)—Bob Carrington, Boston College; Seattle—Dennis Johnson, Pepperdine; Phoenix (from Buffalo)—Al Fleming, Arizona; Washington—Joe Pace, Coppin State; Cleveland—Mo Howard, Maryland; Phoenix (from Boston)—Butch Feher, Vanderbilt; Golden State—Marshall Rogers, Pan American.

THIRD ROUND Chicago—Dallas Smith, West Texas State; Los Angeles (from Atlanta)—Mike Dabney, Rutgers; Chicago (from Kansas City)—Lars Hansen, Washington; Detroit—Phil Sellers, Rutgers; Portland—Jeff Tyson, Western Michigan; Milwaukee—Lloyd Walton, Marquette; New York—John McGill, Alcorn State; New Orleans—Steve Copp, San Diego State; Los Angeles—Tom Abernethy, Indiana; Houston—Barnes Hauptfuhrer, Princeton; Phoenix—Ira Terrell, SMU; Atlanta (from Seattle)—Larry Cooke, Virginia Tech; Philadelphia—Ron Norwood, DePaul; Buffalo—Gary Brewster, Texas-El Paso; Washington—Bill Cook, Memphis State; Cleveland—Gary Cole, Wisconsin-Parkside; Boston—Jerry Fort, Nebraska.

FOURTH ROUND Chicago—Keith Starr, Pittsburgh; Atlanta—Tom Barker, Hawaii; Kansas City—Clarence Ramsey, Washington; Detroit—Scott Thompson, Iowa; Portland—David Everett, Grand Canyon; New York—Rick Bullock, Texas Tech; New Orleans—John Service, California-Santa Barbara; Milwaukee—Dan Frost, Iowa; Los Angeles—Wayman Britt, Michigan; Houston—Hercle Ivy, Iowa State; Phoenix—Paul Miller, Oregon State; Seattle—Willie Parr, LeMoyne-Owen; Philadelphia—Freeman Blade, Eastern Montana; Washington—Marion Hillard, Memphis State; Cleveland—John Engles, Penn; Boston—Lewis Linder, Kentucky State; Golden State—Jeff Fosnes, Vanderbilt.

FIFTH ROUND Chicago—Nate Williams, Illinois; Atlanta—Ron Davis, Washington State; Kansas City—Willie Hodge, Duke; Detroit—Jim Hearns, Marymount; Portland—Gary Redding, Auburn; New Orleans—Paul Griffin, Western Michigan; Milwaukee—Tom Lockhart, Manhattan; New York—Beaver Smith, St. John's; Milwaukee (from Los Angeles)—James Rappis, Arizona; Houston—Dave Marrs, Houston; Phoenix—Ralph Walker, St. Mary's (Cal.); Seattle—Robert Gray, Wichita State; Philadelphia—Jeff Browne, Missouri Western; Atlanta (from Buffalo)—Connie White, California; Washington—L. C. Mason, Alabama State; Cleveland—Ed Lawrence, McNeese State; Boston—Lewis McKinney, St. Louis; Golden State—Carl Bird, California.

SIXTH ROUND Chicago—Tom Paulin, Winston-Salem; Atlanta—Pete Padgett, Nevada-Reno; Kansas City—Andre McCarter, UCLA; Detroit—Russell Davis, Virginia Tech; Golden State (from Portland)—Duane Barnett, Stanford; Milwaukee—Phil Spence, North Carolina State; New York—Joe Jones, Grambling; New Orleans—Bernard Tomlin, Hofstra; Los Angeles—Ed Schweitzer, Stanford; Houston—Robert Paige, Houston Baptist; Phoenix—Carl Brown, Eastern Kentucky; Seattle—Daryl Peterson, Wake Forest; Philadelphia—Mike Dunleavy, South Carolina; Buffalo—Danny Odums, Fairfield; Washington—Pat Tallent, George Washington; Cleveland—Harry Davis, Morris Brown; Boston—Art Collins, Biscayne; Golden State—Gene Cunningham, Norfolk State.

SEVENTH ROUND Chicago—Barry McLeod, Centenary; Atlanta—Carl Gerlach, Kansas State; Kansas City—Craig Prosser, Canisius; Detroit—Curt Peterson, Puget Sound; Portland—Al DeWitt, Weber State; New York—Boyd Batts, Nevada-Las Vegas; New Orleans—Andy Walker, Niagara; Milwaukee—Ron Barrow, Southern; Los Angeles—Tommie Lipsey, Los Angeles State; Houston—Barry Davis, Texas A&M; Phoenix—Brad Warble, East Illinois; Seattle—Mark Klein, Malone; Philadelphia—Phil Walker, Millersville; Buffalo—Frank Jones, Tennessee Tech; Washington—Ralph Vallott, Loyola (Ill.); Cleveland—Johnny Britt, Western Kentucky; Boston—Ralph Drollinger, UCLA; Golden State—Jesse Campbell, Mercyhurst.

EIGHTH ROUND Cleveland (from Chicago)—Dave Koehler, Wisconsin; Atlanta—Doug Terry, Utah; Kansas City—Mike Davis, Bradley; Detroit—Randy Henry, Illinois State; Portland—Brant Gibbler, Puget Sound; New Orleans—Richard Bryant, Southwest Texas State; Milwaukee—Bob Warner, Maine; New York—Rick McCutcheon, Arizona State; Los Angeles—Ed Gregg, Utah State; Houston—Dan Krueger, Texas; Phoenix—Tom DeBerry, Northern Arizona; Seattle—Norton Barnhill, Washington State; Philadelphia—Lee Dixon,

Hardin-Simmons; Buffalo—Mark McAndrew, Providence; Washington—Merlin Wilson, Georgetown; Cleveland—Tim Sisneros, Middle Tennessee; Boston—John Clark, Northeastern; Golden State—Stan Boskovich, West Virginia.

NINTH ROUND Chicago—John Thomas, Connecticut; Atlanta—Bob Kovach, San Diego State; Kansas City—Dave Logan, Colorado; Detroit—Bill Martin, Hartwick; Portland—Rob Torresdal, Linfield; Milwaukee—Benny Shaw, Florida Tech; New York—Archie Talley, Salem (W.Va.); New Orleans—Calvin Robinson, Mississippi Valley; Los Angeles—David Pickett, Northeastern Louisiana; Phoenix—John Irving, Hofstra; Seattle—Ron Johnson, North Carolina A&T; Philadelphia—Fly Williams, Austin Peay; Buffalo—Bob Rozyczko, St. Bonaventure; Washington—Clyde Agnew, Newberry; Cleveland—Bruce Parkinson, Purdue; Boston—Bill Collins, Boston College; Golden State—Howard Smith, San Francisco.

TENTH ROUND Chicago—John Hudson, Concord; Atlanta—Mike Dickerson, South Florida; Kansas City—Harry Bailey, North Texas State; Detroit—Bob Johnson, Wisconsin; Portland—Marcus Leite, Pepperdine; New York—Eugene Shy, Florida; New Orleans—Art Johnson, Iowa State; Milwaukee—Hugo Cabrera, East Texas State; Phoenix—Gary Jackson, Arizona State; Seattle—Ricky Lewis, Alcorn State; Philadelphia—Ed Stefanski, Penn; Buffalo—Tim Stokes, Canisius; Washington—Mike Beuscher, Seton Hall; Cleveland—Elisha McSweeney, Mankato State; Boston—Otho Tucker, Illinois; Golden State—Ken Smith, San Diego State.

1976 DISPERSAL DRAFT OF ABA PLAYERS

In 1976, four teams from the ABA were absorbed into the NBA. Players on ABA teams that were dissolved became available to NBA teams in a dispersal draft.

Chicago—Artis Gilmore, Kentucky; Portland (from Atlanta)—Maurice Lucas, Kentucky; Kansas City—Ron Boone, St. Louis; Detroit—Marvin Barnes, St. Louis; Portland—Moses Malone, St. Louis; N.Y. Knicks—Randy Denton, St. Louis; Buffalo (from Milwaukee)—William Averitt, Kentucky; Indiana—Wil Jones, Kentucky; Houston—Ron Thomas, Kentucky; San Antonio—Louie Dampier, Kentucky; N.Y. Nets—Jan van Breda Kolff, Kentucky; Kansas City—Mike Barr, St. Louis.

1977 (JUNE 10, 1977)

FIRST ROUND Milwaukee—Kent Benson, Indiana; Kansas City (from N.Y. Nets)—Otis Birdsong, Houston; Milwaukee (from Buffalo)—Marques Johnson, UCLA; Washington (from Atlanta)—Greg Ballard, Oregon; Phoenix—Walter Davis, North Carolina; Los Angeles (from New Orleans)—Kenny Carr, North Carolina State; N.Y. Nets (from Indiana)—Bernard King, Tennessee; Seattle—Jack Sikma, Illinois Wesleyan; Denver (from Kansas City)—Tom LaGarde, North Carolina; N.Y. Knicks—Ray Williams, Minnesota; Milwaukee (from Cleveland)—Ernie Grunfeld, Tennessee; Boston—Cedric Maxwell, North Carolina-Charlotte; Chicago—Tate Armstrong, Duke; Atlanta (from Detroit)—Wayne Rollins, Clemson; Los Angeles (from San Antonio)—Brad Davis, Maryland; Golden State—Rickey Green, Michigan; Washington—Bo Ellis, Marquette; Golden State (from Houston)—Wesley Cox, Louisville; Portland—Rich Laurel, Hofstra; Philadelphia—Glenn Mosley, Seton Hall; Denver—Anthony Roberts, Oral Roberts; Los Angeles—Norm Nixon, Duquesne.

SECOND ROUND Chicago (from N.Y. Nets)—Mike Glenn, Southern Illinois; Buffalo—Larry Johnson, Kentucky; Philadelphia (from Milwaukee)—Wilson Washington, Old Dominion; N.Y. Knicks (from Atlanta)—Glen Gondrezick, Nevada-Las Vegas; Milwaukee (from Phoenix)—Glenn Williams, St. John's; Portland (from New Orleans)—Kim Anderson, Missouri; Indiana—Alonzo Bradley, Texas Southern; Chicago (from Seattle)—Steve Sheppard, Maryland; Kansas City—Eddie Owens, Nevada-Las Vegas; N.Y. Knicks—Toby Knight, Notre Dame; Cleveland—Ed Jordan, Rutgers; Houston (from Boston)—Larry Moffett, Nevada-Las Vegas; Chicago—Mark Landsberger, Arizona State; Detroit—Ben Poquette, Central Michigan; San Antonio—Jeff Wilkins, Illinois State; Golden State—Ricky Love, Alabama-Huntsville; Washington—Phil Walker, Millersville; Houston—Robert Reid, St. Mary's (Tex.); Portland—T. R. Dunn, Alabama; Philadelphia—Bob Elliott, Arizona; Philadelphia (from Denver)—Herm Harris, Arizona; New Orleans (from Los Angeles)—Essie Hollis, St. Bonaventure.

THIRD ROUND Kansas City (from N.Y. Nets)—Bill Paterno, Notre Dame; Los Angeles (from Buffalo)—James Edwards, Washington; Milwaukee—Gary Yoder, Cincinnati; Atlanta—Sam Smith, Nevada-Las Vegas; Atlanta (from Phoenix)—Ed Johnson, Auburn; New Orleans—Tony Hansen, Connecticut; Indiana—Stan Mayhew, Weber State; Seattle—Joe Hassett, Providence; Kansas City—John Kuester, North Carolina; N.Y. Knicks—Lloyd McMillian, Long Beach State; Cleveland—Steve Grote, Michigan; Boston—Skip Brown, Wake Forest; Washington (from Chicago)—Steve Puidokas, Washington State; Detroit—John Irving, Hofstra; San Antonio—Dan Henderson, Arkansas State; Golden State—Marlon Redmond, San Francisco; Washington—Jerry Schellenberg, Wake Forest; Houston—Phil Bond, Louisville; Portland—Ricky Brown, Alabama; Philadelphia—Arnold Dugger, Oral Roberts; Denver—Robert Smith, Nevada-Las Vegas; Phoenix (from Los Angeles)—Mike Bratz, Stanford.

FOURTH ROUND N.Y. Nets—Bob Elmore, Wichita State; Buffalo—Melvin Watkins, North Carolina-Charlotte; Milwaukee—Lewis Brown, Nevada-Las Vegas; Atlanta—Dave Bormann, Gardner Webb; Phoenix—Greg Griffin, Idaho State; New Orleans—Dennis Boyd,

Detroit; Indiana—George Pendleton, Georgia State; Seattle—Jim Cooper, Alabama State; Kansas City—Larry Williams, Texas Southern; N.Y. Knicks—Steve Hayes, Idaho State; Cleveland—Melvin Jones, West Texas State; Boston—Jeff Cummings, Tulane; Chicago—Mike McConalthy, Louisiana Tech; Detroit—Bruce King, Iowa; San Antonio—Matt Hicks, Northern Illinois; Golden State—Roy Smith, Kentucky State; Washington—David Reavis, Georgia; Houston—Rocky Smith, Oregon State; Portland—Greg White, Southern California; Philadelphia—Jack Jonas, Utah; Golden State (from Denver)—Leartha Scott, Wisconsin-Parkside; Los Angeles—Tony Robertson, West Virginia.

FIFTH ROUND   N.Y. Nets—Gerald Cunningham, Kentucky State; Buffalo—Mike Hanley, Niagara; Milwaukee—Ron Norwood, DePaul; Atlanta—Bill Gordon, Tennessee-Chattanooga; Phoenix—Cecil Rellford, St. John's; New Orleans—Jim Grady, Gonzaga; Indiana—Marvin Jackson, Prairie View A&M; Seattle—Dale Haverman, McKendree; Kansas City—Bob Chapman, Michigan State; N.Y. Knicks—Bill Terry, Monmouth; Cleveland—Al Smith, Jackson State; Boston—Bill Langloh, Virginia; Chicago—Nate Davis, South Carolina; Detroit—Jim Kennedy, Missouri; San Antonio—Scott Sims, Missouri; Golden State—Ray Epps, Norfolk State; Washington—Bruce Parkinson, Purdue; Houston—Ed Thompson, Idaho State; Portland—Donn Wilber, LaSalle; Philadelphia—Teko Wynder, Tulsa; Denver—John Billups, Mississippi; Los Angeles—John Robinson, Michigan.

SIXTH ROUND   N.Y. Nets—Mark Crow, Duke; Buffalo—Curvan Lewis, Virginia Union; Milwaukee—Chuck Goodyear, Miami (Ohio); Atlanta—Calvin Crews, Southwestern Louisiana; Phoenix—Billy McKinney, Northwestern; New Orleans—Wayne Golden, Tennessee-Chattanooga; Indiana—Tom Scheffler, Pudue; Seattle—Bucky O'Brien, Seattle; Kansas City—Bob Cooper, Providence; N.Y. Knicks—Jerry Graycraft, Milligan; Cleveland—Ron Cox, East Washington State; Boston—Roy Pace, Rutgers-Camden; Chicago—Jay Chessman, Brigham Young; Detroit—Herb Nobles, Kansas; San Antonio—Bruce Buckley, North Carolina; Golden State—Jack Phelan, St. Francis (Pa.); Washington—Ernie Wansley, Virginia Tech; Portland—Myron Jordan. Pacific; Philadelphia—George Gibson, Winston-Salem; Denver—Jim Town, Massachusetts; Los Angeles—Grover Woolard, Murray State.

SEVENTH ROUND   N.Y. Nets—Scott Conant, Newberry; Buffalo—Mike Jackson, Tennessee; Milwaukee—Ron Bostic, Detroit; Atlanta—James Holliman, Arizona State; Phoenix—Alvin Scott, Oral Roberts; New Orleans—Lucy Harris, Delta State; Seattle—Billy Reynolds, Northwest Louisiana; Kansas City—Bruce Jenner, Graceland; N.Y. Knicks—Tom Weadock, St. John's; Cleveland—Bob Riddle, Eastern Michigan; Boston—Dave Kyle, Cleveland State; Chicago—Mike Smith, Evansville; Detroit—Robert Lewis, Johnson C. Smith; San Antonio—Richard Robinson, New Mexico; Golden State—Jerry Thurston, Mercer; Washington—Calvin Brown, American; Portland—Don Smith, Oregon State; Philadelphia—Dennis Forest, Nebraska-Omaha; Denver—Willie High, Alabama State; Los Angeles—Lars Hansen, Washington.

EIGHTH ROUND   N.Y. Nets—Ralph Drollinger, UCLA; Buffalo—Emery Sammons, Philadelphia Textile; Milwaukee—Larry Pikes, Wisconsin-Milwaukee; Atlanta—Vern Thompson, Brigham Young; Phoenix—Alvin Joseph, California-Riverside; New Orleans—Dave Speicher, Toledo; Seattle—Jeff Frey, Evansville; N.Y. Knicks—Ken Slappy, St. Peter's; Cleveland—Tom Cutter, Western Michigan; Boston—Tom Harris, Bowling Green; Chicago—Rich Rhodes, Eastern Illinois; Detroit—Tim Appleton, Kenyon; San Antonio—Jerome Gladney, Arizona; Golden State—Ricky Marsh, Manhattan; Washington—Pat McKinley, Towson State; Portland—Harold Rhodes, Washington; Philadelphia—John Olive, Villanova; Denver—Len Saunders, Florida; Los Angeles—Art Allen, Pepperdine.

1978 (JUNE 9, 1978)

FIRST ROUND   Portland (from Indiana)—Mychal Thompson, Minnesota; Kansas City (from New Jersey)—Phil Ford, North Carolina; Indiana (from Buffalo)—Rick Robey, Kentucky; New York (from Houston)—Micheal Ray Richardson, Montana; Golden State (from Kansas City)—Purvis Short, Jackson State; Boston—Larry Bird, Indiana State; Portland (from Detroit)—Ron Brewer, Arkansas; Boston (from New Orleans)—Freeman Williams, Portland State; Chicago—Reggie Theus, Nevada-Las Vegas; Atlanta—Butch Lee, Marquette; New Orleans (from Golden State)—James Hardy, San Francisco; Milwaukee (from Cleveland)—George Johnson, St. John's; New Jersey (from New York)—Winford Boynes, San Francisco; Washington—Roger Phegley, Bradley; Cleveland (from Milwaukee)—Mike Mitchell, Auburn; Atlanta (from Los Angeles)—Jack Givens, Kentucky; Denver (from Seattle)—Rod Griffin, Wake Forest; Washington (from Denver)—Dave Corzine, DePaul; Phoenix—Marty Byrnes, Syracuse; San Antonio—Frank Sanders, Southern; Denver (from Philadelphia)—Mike Evans, Kansas State; Golden State (from Portland)—Ray Townsend, UCLA.

SECOND ROUND   Detroit (from New Jersey)—Terry Tyler, Detroit; Portland (from Buffalo)—Keith Herron, Villanova; Atlanta (from Houston)—Rick Wilson, Louisville; Los Angeles (from Kansas City)—Ron Carter, VMI; Indiana—Wayne Radford, Indiana; Houston (from Boston)—Buster Matheney, Utah; Detroit—John Long, Detroit; Boston (from New Orleans)—Jeff Judkins, Utah; Chicago—Marvin Johnson, New Mexico; New York (from Atlanta)—John Rudd, McNeese State; Cleveland—Harry Davis, Florida State; New York—Greg Bunch, California State-Fullerton; New Orleans (from Golden State)—Tom Green, Southern; Philadelphia (from Milwaukee)—Maurice Cheeks, West Texas State; Washington—

Terry Sykes, Grambling; Los Angeles—Lew Massey, North Carolina-Charlotte; Seattle—James Lee, Kentucky; Golden State (from Denver)—Wayne Cooper, New Orleans; Buffalo (from Phoenix)—Jerome Whitehead, Marquette; Seattle (from San Antonio)—Kevin McDonald, Penn; Philadelphia—Glenn Hagan, St. Bonaventure; Portland—Clemon Johnson, Florida A&M.

THIRD ROUND   New Jersey—Mike Phillips, Kentucky; Denver (from Buffalo)—Hollis Copeland, Rutgers; Houston—Billy Ray Bates, Kentucky State; Buffalo (from Indiana)—Mike Santos, Utah State; Kansas City—Jeff Cook, Idaho State; Boston—Dana Skinner, Merrimack; Buffalo (from Detroit)—Ricky Gallon, Louisville; Kansas City (from New Orleans)—Mike Russell, Texas Tech; Chicago—Randy Ayers, Miami (Ohio); Atlanta—Steve Grant, Manhattan; New York—Mark Iavaroni, Virginia; Golden State—Steve Neff, Bethany Nazarene; Cleveland—Ken Higgs, LSU; Washington—Rick Apke, Creighton; Milwaukee—Pat Cummings, Cincinnati; Los Angeles—Michael Cooper, New Mexico; Seattle—Dave Baxter, Michigan; New Jersey (from Denver)—Dave Batton, Notre Dame; Phoenix—Joel Kramer, San Diego State; San Antonio—Gerald Henderson, Virginia Commonwealth; Buffalo (from Philadelphia)—Marvin Delph, Arkansas; Portland—Sterling Edmunds, Dartmouth.

FOURTH ROUND   Houston (from New Jersey)—Jackie Robinson, Nevada-Las Vegas; Buffalo—Jim Boylan, Marquette; Houston—Joel Thompson, Michigan; Kansas City—Geoff Crompton, North Carolina; Indiana—Ricky Lee, Oregon State; Boston—Dave Nelson, Bloomfield (N.J.); Buffalo (from Detroit)—Larry Harris, Pittsburgh; New Orleans—Mel Davis, North Texas State; New Orleans (from Chicago)—Jeff Covington, Youngstown State; Buffalo (from Atlanta)—Leroy McDonald, Wake Forest; Golden State—Derrick Jackson, Georgetown; Cleveland—Stan Rome, Clemson; New York—Erving Giddings, Dayton; Milwaukee—Otis Howard, Austin Peay; Washington—Larry Boston, Maryland; Los Angeles—Harold Robertson, Lincoln; Seattle—Billy Lewis, Illinois State; New Jersey (from Denver)—Walter Jordan, Purdue; Phoenix—Bob Miller, Cincinnati; San Antonio—Rich Adams, Illinois; Philadelphia—Brett Vroman, Nevada-Las Vegas; Phoenix (from Portland)—Wayne Smith, California-Irvine.

FIFTH ROUND   New Jersey—Cecile Rose, Houston; Buffalo—David Thompson, Florida State; Houston—Gary Goodner, Texas; Indiana—James Sparrow, North Carolina A&T; Kansas City—Derick Claiborne, Massachusetts; Boston—Greg Tynes, Seton Hall; Detroit—Dave Caligaris, Northeastern; New Orleans—Donald Williams, Notre Dame; Chicago—Ron Anthony, Jacksonville; Atlanta—Chris Potter, Holy Cross; Cleveland—Ken Koenigs, Kansas; New York—Greg Green, Southern; Golden State—Bubba Wilson, Western Carolina; Washington—Roger Dickens, Towson State; Milwaukee—Russ Coleman, Pacific; Los Angeles—Carlos Terry, Winston-Salem; Seattle—Ralph Drollinger, UCLA; Denver—Michael Edwards, Pan American; Phoenix—Andre Wakefield, Loyola (Ill.); San Antonio—Eugene Parker, Purdue; Philadelphia—Mark Haymore, Massachusetts; Portland—Clay Johnson, Missouri.

SIXTH ROUND   New Jersey—Golie Augustus, South Carolina; Buffalo—Bob Misevicius, Providence; Houston—Eddie Joe Chavez, Santa Clara; Kansas City—Jim Krivacs, Texas; Indiana—Sherman Dillard, James Madison; Boston—Dave Winey, Minnesota; Detroit—Audie Matthews, Illinois; New Orleans—John Douglas, Kansas; Chicago—John Shoemaker, Miami (Ohio); Atlanta—Gerald Glover, Howard; New York—Ed Warren, Briarcliff; Golden State—Buzz Hartnett, San Diego; Cleveland—Ron Bell, Virginia Tech; Milwaukee—Dave Kyle, Cleveland State; Washington—Archie Aldridge, Miami (Ohio); Los Angeles—Kim Stewart, Washington; Denver—Robert Heard, Columbus (Ga.); Phoenix—Charles Thompson, Houston; San Antonio—Harry Morgan, Indiana State; Philadelphia—Osborne Lockhart, Minnesota; Portland—Tim Evans, Puget Sound.

SEVENTH ROUND   New Jersey—Doug Jemison, San Francisco; Buffalo—Stan Pietkiewicz, Auburn; Houston—Stan Stewart, Loyola Marymount; Indiana—Ollie Matson Jr., Pepperdine; Kansas City—Charles McMillian, North Texas State; Boston—Steve Balkun, Fairfield; Detroit—Herb Entzminger, J. C. Smith; New Orleans—Willie Howard, New Mexico; Chicago—Jarvis Reynolds, West Georgia; Atlanta—Jim DeWeese, Gonzaga; Golden State—Rick Bernard, St. Mary's (Cal.); Cleveland—Tony Smith, Nevada-Las Vegas; New York—Gary Pember, Nasson; Washington—Ed Hopkins, Georgetown; Milwaukee—Kim Anderson, Missouri; Los Angeles—Larry Paige, Colorado State; Denver—Jack Gilloon, South Carolina; Phoenix—Steve Malovic, San Diego State; San Antonio—Hector Olivencia, Sacred Heart; Philadelphia—Anthony Murray, Alabama; Portland—Walter Reason, Pacific.

EIGHTH ROUND   New Jersey—Bruce Campbell, Providence; Buffalo—Felton Young, Jacksonville; Kansas City—Ron Hammye, Bowling Green; Boston—Kim Fisher, Fairfield; Detroit—Earl Evans, Nevada-Las Vegas; New Orleans—Carl Kilpatrick, Northeast Louisiana; Chicago—Chubby Cox, San Francisco; Atlanta—Ed Murphy, Merrimack; Cleveland—Roland Martin, Missouri Southern; New York—Greg Sanders, St. Bonaventure; Golden State—Tony Searcy, Appalachian State; Milwaukee—Tom Zaligaris, North Carolina; Washington—Nestor Cora, St. Francis (N.Y.); Denver—Larry Vaculik, Colorado; Phoenix—George Fowler, Pacific; San Antonio—Henry Taylor, Pan American; Philadelphia—Alan Cunningham, Colorado State; Portland—Mark Wickman, Linfield.

NINTH ROUND   New Jersey—Frank Sowinski, Princeton; Buffalo—Bobby White, Centenary; Boston—Les Anderson, George Washington; Detroit—Ulice Payne, Marquette; New Orleans—Chad Nelson, Drake; Chicago—Joe Ponsetto, DePaul; Atlanta—Maurice Robinson, West Virginia; New York—Danny Fields, North Carolina-Wilmington; Golden

State—Bobby Humbles, Bradley; Cleveland—Steve Bayless, Central State (Ohio); Washington—Tim Claxton, Temple; Milwaukee—Gary Rosenberger, Marquette; Denver—Tom Schneeberger, Air Force; Phoenix—Nate Stokes, Grand Canyon; San Antonio—Rick Taylor, Arizona State; Portland—Paul Cozens, George Fox.

TENTH ROUND New Jersey—Michael Vicens, Holy Cross; Boston—Walter Harrigan, Brandeis; Detroit—Dave Grauzer, Central Michigan; New Orleans—Rickey Williams, Long Beach State; Chicago—Mark Tucker, Oklahoma; Atlanta—Marshall Lester, Florida Southern; Golden State—Mike Muff, Murray State; Cleveland—Gary Winton, Army; New York—Ernest Simons, Pace; Milwaukee—Tom Anderson, Wisconsin-Green Bay; Washington—Steve Connor, Boise State; Denver—Phil Taylor, Arizona; Phoenix—Lewis Cohen, California Poly-San Luis Obispo; San Antonio—Larry Brewster, Florida; Philadelphia—Dennis James, Widener; Portland—Tim Workington, Biola.

1979 (JUNE 25, 1979)

FIRST ROUND Los Angeles (from Utah)—Earvin Johnson, Michigan State; Chicago—David Greenwood, UCLA; New York (from Boston)—Bill Cartwright, San Francisco; Detroit (from Cleveland)—Greg Kelser, Michigan State; Milwaukee (from Detroit)—Sidney Moncrief, Arkansas; Seattle (from New York)—James Bailey, Rutgers; Seattle (from New Jersey)—Vinnie Johnson, Baylor; New Jersey (from Indiana)—Calvin Natt, Northeast Louisiana; New York (from Golden State)—Larry Demic, Arizona; Detroit (from Milwaukee)—Roy Hamilton, UCLA; New Jersey (from San Diego)—Cliff Robinson, Southern California; Portland—Jim Paxson, Dayton; Indiana (from Atlanta)—Dudley Bradley, North Carolina; Los Angeles—Brad Holland, UCLA; Detroit (from Denver)—Phil Hubbard, Michigan; Philadelphia—Jim Spanarkel, Duke; Houston—Lee Johnson, East Texas State; Kansas City—Reggie King, Alabama; San Antonio—Wiley Peck, Mississippi State; Utah (from Phoenix)—Larry Knight, Loyola (Ill.); New York (from Seattle)—Sylvester Williams, Rhode Island; Phoenix (from Washington)—Kyle Macy, Kentucky.

SECOND ROUND Utah—Tico Brown, Georgia Tech; Phoenix (from Boston)—Johnny High, Nevada-Reno; Los Angeles (from Detroit)—Oliver Mack, East Carolina; Cleveland—Bruce Flowers, Notre Dame; New York—Reggie Carter, St. John's; Golden State (from Chicago)—Danny Salisbury, Pan American; Detroit (from New Jersey)—Tony Price, Penn; Denver (from Golden State)—Gary Garland, DePaul; Milwaukee—Edgar Jones, Nevada-Reno; Indiana—Tony Zeno, Arizona State; Chicago (from San Diego)—Lawrence Butler, Idaho State; New York (from Portland)—Kim Goetz, San Diego State; Atlanta—James Bradley, Memphis State; Philadelphia (from Denver)—Clint Richardson, Seattle; Philadelphia—Bernard Toone, Marquette; Atlanta (from Houston)—Larry Wilson, Nicholls State; Los Angeles—Victor King, Louisiana Tech; Portland (from San Antonio)—Andrew Fields, Cheyney State; Los Angeles (from Kansas City)—Mark Young, Fairfield; Houston (from Phoenix)—Paul Mokeski, Kansas; Seattle—John Moore, Texas; Washington—Joe DeSantis, Fairfield.

THIRD ROUND Utah—Arvid Kramer, Augustana (S.D.); Washington (from Boston)—Andrew Parker, Iowa State; Chicago (from Cleveland)—Calvin Garrett, Oral Roberts; Detroit—Terry Duerod, Detroit; Chicago—Cedric Hordges, South Carolina; New York—Geoff Huston, Texas Tech; New Jersey—John Gerdy, Davidson; Milwaukee—Larry Gibson, Maryland; Boston (from Indiana)—Wayne Kreklow, Drake; Golden State—Lynbert Johnson, Wichita State; San Diego—Tom Channel, Boston U.; Portland—Mickey Fox, St. Mary's (Canada); Atlanta—Don Marsh, Franklin & Marshall; Philadelphia—Earl Cureton, Detroit; Houston—Ricardo Brown, Pepperdine; Los Angeles—Walter Daniels, Georgia; Boston (from Denver)—Ernesto Malcolm, Briarcliff; Kansas City—Terry Crosby, Tennessee; San Antonio—Sylvester Norris, Jackson State; Phoenix—Al Green, LSU; Cleveland (from Seattle)—Bill Laimbeer, Notre Dame; Washington—Charles Floyd, High Point.

FOURTH ROUND Utah—Greg Deane, Utah; Boston—Nick Galis, Seton Hall; Milwaukee (from Detroit)—Eugene Robinson, Northeast Louisiana; Cleveland—Rick Swing, Citadel; New York—Larry Rogers, Southeast Missouri State; Chicago—George Maynor, East Carolina; Seattle (from New Jersey)—James Donaldson, Washington State; Indiana—Don Newman, Idaho; Golden State—Ron Ripley, Wisconsin-Green Bay; Houston (from Milwaukee)—Sammy Drummer, Georgia Tech; San Diego—Lionel Garrett, Southern; Portland—Daryll Robinson, Appalachian State; Los Angeles (from Atlanta)—Ray White, Mississippi State; Houston—Lionel Green, LSU; Los Angeles—Ricky Reed, Temple; Golden State (from Denver)—Jerry Sichting, Purdue; Philadelphia—Mike Niles, California State-Fullerton; San Antonio—Al Daniel, Furman; Kansas City—John McCollough, Oklahoma; Phoenix—Malcolm Cesare, Florida; Seattle—Richie Allen, Cal State-Dominguez Hills; Washington—Lamont Reid, Oral Roberts.

FIFTH ROUND Utah—Perry Wolfe, Stanford; Boston—Jimmy Allen, New Haven; Cleveland—Matt Simpkins, Georgia Southern; Detroit—Flintie Ray Williams, Nevada-Las Vegas; Chicago—Larry Washington, Drury (Mo.); New York—Johnny Green, California-Riverside; New Jersey—Joe Abramaitis, Connecticut; Golden State—George Lett, Centenary; Milwaukee—Jim Tillman, Eastern Kentucky; Indiana—Billy Reid, San Francisco; San Diego—Greg Joyner, Middle Tennessee State; Portland—Matt White, Penn; Atlanta—Tiny Pinder, North Carolina State; Denver—Larry Williams, Louisville; Philadelphia—Carl McPipe, Nebraska; Houston—Allen Leavell, Oklahoma City; Kansas City—Curtis Watkins, DePaul; San

Antonio—Steve Schall, Arkansas; Phoenix—Mark Eaton, Cypress JC; Washington—Marshall Ashford, Virginia Tech.

SIXTH ROUND Utah—Ernie Cobb, Boston U.; Boston—Marvin Delph, Arkansas; Detroit—Truman Claytor, Kentucky; Cleveland—Jon Manning, North Texas State; New York—Phil Abney, New Mexico; Chicago—Steve Smith, Southern California; New Jersey—Tony Smith, Nevada-Las Vegas; Milwaukee—Derrick Mayes, Illinois State; Indiana—Greg Guye, Stetson; Golden State—Jim Mitchem, DePaul; San Diego—Bob Bender, Duke; Portland—Ray Ellis, Pepperdine; Atlanta—Dwight Williams, Gardner-Webb; Denver—Odell Ball, Philadelphia—Dan Hartshorne, Oregon; Houston—Collie Davis, Southern; San Antonio—Terry Knight, Pittsburgh; Kansas City—Bob Roma, Princeton; Phoenix—Dale Shackelford, Syracuse; Washington—Garcia Hopkins, Morgan State.

SEVENTH ROUND Utah—Paul Poe, Louisiana; Boston—Steve Castellan, Virginia; Cleveland—Steve Skaggs, Ohio; Detroit—Ken Jones, St. Mary's (Cal.); Chicago—Mike Eversley, Chicago State; New York—Marc Coleman, Seton Hall; New Jersey—Jim Strickland, South Carolina; Indiana—Dirk Ewing, Stetson; Golden State—Ren Watson, Virginia Commonwealth; Milwaukee—Stan Ray, California State-Fullerton; San Diego—Jene Grey, LeMoyne; Portland—Jeff Tropf, Central Michigan; Atlanta—Tim Waterman, St. Bonaventure; Philadelphia—Bobby Willis, Penn; Houston—Rich Valavicius, Auburn; Denver—John Johnson, Creighton; Kansas City—Nick Daniels, Xavier (Ohio); San Antonio—Tyrone Branyan, Texas; Phoenix—Ollie Matson, Pepperdine.

EIGHTH ROUND Utah—Keith McDonald, Utah State; Boston—Glenn Sudhop, North Carolina State; Detroit—Rodney Lee, Memphis State; Cleveland—Mark Haymore, Massachusetts; New York—Billy Tucker, Tennessee State; Chicago—Tony Warren, North Carolina State; New Jersey—Henry Hollingsworth, Hofstra; Golden State—Mario Butler, Briarcliff; Milwaukee—Larry Spicer, Alabama-Birmingham; Indiana—Brian Magid, George Washington; San Diego—Renaldo Lawrence, Appalachian State; Portland—Willie Pounds, Chaminade; Atlanta—John Goedeke, Maryland-Baltimore County; Houston—Delbert Watson, East Tennessee State; Denver—Matt Teahan, Denver; Philadelphia—Rick Raivio, Portland; Kansas City—Tony Vann, Alabama-Huntsville; Phoenix—Charles Jones, Albany State; Washington—Jo Jo Walters, Manhattan.

NINTH ROUND Utah—Milt Huggins, Southern Illinois; Boston—Kevin Sinnett, Navy; Cleveland—Tim Joyce, Ohio; Detroit—Val Bracey, Central Michigan; Chicago—James Jackson, Minnesota; New York—Brett Wyatt, Jersey City State; New Jersey—Ricky Free, Columbia; Milwaukee—Roger Lapham, Maine; Golden State—Gene Ransom, California; San Diego—Mike Dodd, San Diego State; Portland—Stan Eckwood, Harding (Ark.); Atlanta—Cedric Oliver, Hamilton; Denver—Emmett Lewis, Colorado; Philadelphia—Coby Leavitt, Utah; Kansas City—Gary Wilson, Southern Illinois; San Antonio—Eddie McLeod, Nevada-Las Vegas; Phoenix—Hosea Champine, Robert Morris; Washington—Ray Hooker, Murray State.

TENTH ROUND Utah—Paul Dawkins, Northern Illinois; Boston—Alton Byrd, Columbia; Detroit—Willie Polk, Grand Canyon; Cleveland—Terry Peavy, Point Park; New York—Gordon Thomas, St. John's; Chicago—Marvin Thomas, UCLA; New Jersey—Eric Fleisher, Tulane; Golden State—Kevin Heenan, California State-Fullerton; Milwaukee—Chris Fahrbach, North Dakota; San Diego—Greg Hunter, Loyola Marymount; Portland—Kelvin Small, Oregon; Atlanta—Chad Nelson, Drake; Chicago (from Denver)—Cortez Collins, Indiana State-Evansville; Philadelphia—Keith McCord, Alabama-Birmingham; San Antonio—Glen Fine, Harvard; Kansas City—Russell Saunders, New Mexico; Phoenix—Korky Nelson, Santa Clara; Washington—Steve Martin, Georgetown.

1980 (JUNE 10, 1980)

FIRST ROUND Golden State (from Detroit)—Joe Barry Carroll, Purdue; Utah—Darrell Griffith, Louisville; Boston (from Golden State)—Kevin McHale, Minnesota; Chicago—Kelvin Ransey, Ohio State; Denver—James Ray, Jacksonville; New Jersey—Mike O'Koren, North Carolina; New Jersey (from San Diego)—Mike Gminski, Duke; Philadelphia (from Indiana)—Andrew Toney, Southwestern Louisiana; San Diego (from Cleveland)—Michael Brooks, LaSalle; Portland—Ronnie Lester, Iowa; Dallas—Kiki Vandeweghe, UCLA; New York—Mike Woodson, Indiana; Golden State (from Washington)—Rickey Brown, Mississippi State; Washington (from Houston)—Wes Matthews, Wisconsin; San Antonio—Reggie Johnson, Tennessee; Kansas City—Hawkeye Whitney, North Carolina State; Detroit (from Milwaukee)—Larry Drew, Missouri; Atlanta—Don Collins, Washington State; Utah (from Phoenix)—John Duren, Georgetown; Seattle—Bill Hanzlik, Notre Dame; Philadelphia—Monti Davis, Tennessee State; Cleveland (from Los Angeles)—Chad Kinch, North Carolina-Charlotte; Denver (from Boston)—Carl Nicks, Indiana State.

SECOND ROUND Golden State (from Detroit)—Larry Smith, Alcorn State; Golden State—Jeff Ruland, Iona; Chicago (from Utah)—Sam Worthen, Marquette; Houston (from Denver)—John Stroud, Mississippi; Atlanta (from Chicago)—Craig Shelton, Georgetown; Indiana (from New Jersey)—Louis Orr, Syracuse; Indiana (from San Diego)—Kenny Natt, Northeast Louisiana; Los Angeles (from Cleveland)—Wayne Robinson, Virginia Tech; Portland (from Indiana)—David Lawrence, McNeese State; Portland—Bruce Collins, Weber State; Dallas—Roosevelt Bouie, Syracuse; Washington—Ricky Mahorn, Hampton Institute; New

York—DeWayne Scales, LSU; Los Angeles (from San Antonio)—Butch Carter, Indiana; Houston—Terry Stotts, Oklahoma; San Antonio (from Kansas City)—Michael Wiley, Long Beach State; Indiana (from Milwaukee)—Dick Miller, Toledo; Denver (from Atlanta)—Jawaan Oldham, Seattle; Phoenix—Kimberly Belton, Stanford; Houston (from Seattle)—Billy Williams, Clemson; Philadelphia—Clyde Austin, North Carolina State; Detroit (from Los Angeles)—Brad Branson, SMU; Boston—Arnette Hallman, Purdue.

THIRD ROUND Denver (from Detroit)—Kurt Nimphius, Arizona State; Denver (from Utah)—Eddie Lee, Cincinnati; Golden State—John Virgil, North Carolina; Chicago—James Wilkes, UCLA; Denver—Ron Valentine, Old Dominion; New Jersey—Lowes Moore, West Virginia; Cleveland (from San Diego)—Stuart House, Washington State; Boston (from Indiana)—Ron Perry, Holy Cross; Cleveland—Wayne Abrams, Southern Illinois; Portland—Mike Harper, North Park; Dallas—Dave Britton, Texas A&M; New York—Kurt Rambis, Santa Clara; Phoenix (from Washington)—John Campbell, Clemson; San Antonio (from Houston)—Lavon Mercer, Georgia; San Antonio—Rich Yonakor, North Carolina; Kansas City—Tony Murphy, Southern; Milwaukee—Al Beal, Oklahoma; Detroit (from Atlanta)—Jonathan Moore, Furman; Phoenix—Doug True, California; Seattle—Carl Bailey, Tuskegee; Philadelphia—Reggie Gaines, Winston-Salem; Cleveland (from Los Angeles)—Ron Jones, Illinois State; Boston—Donald Newman, Idaho.

FOURTH ROUND Detroit—Darwin Cook, Portland; Golden State—Robert Scott, Alabama; Utah—Alan Taylor, Brigham Young; Denver—Sammie Ellis, Pittsburgh; Chicago—Ron Charles, Michigan State; New Jersey—Rory Sparrow, Villanova; San Diego—Ed Odom, Oklahoma State; Cleveland—Murray Brown, Florida State; Indiana—Rich Branning, Notre Dame; Portland—Kelvin Henderson, St. Louis; Dallas—David Johnson, Weber State; Washington—Francois Wise, Long Beach State; New York—Joseph Chrnelich, Wisconsin; San Antonio—Calvin Roberts, California State-Fullerton; Houston—Dean Hunger, Utah State; Philadelphia (from Kansas City)—Billy Bryant, Western Kentucky; Milwaukee—Jeff Wolf, North Carolina; Los Angeles (from Atlanta)—Tony Jackson, Florida State; Phoenix—Leroy Stampley, Loyola (Ill.); Seattle—Gary Ray Hooker, Murray State; Philadelphia—Harold Hubbard, Savannah State; Los Angeles—Ron Baxter, Texas; Boston—Kevin Hamilton, Iona.

FIFTH ROUND Detroit—Tony Fuller, Pepperdine; Utah—Wally West, Boston U.; Golden State—Don Carfino, Southern California; Chicago—Mike Campbell, Northwestern; Denver—James Patrick, Southwest Texas State; New Jersey—Aaron Curry, Oklahoma; San Diego—Wally Rank, San Jose State; Indiana—Joe Galvin, Illinois State; Cleveland—LaVon Williams, Kentucky; Portland—Larry Belin, New Mexico; Dallas—Darrell Allums, UCLA; New York—William Carey, Albright; Washington—Daryl Strickland, Rutgers; Houston—Albert Jones, New Mexico; San Antonio—Gib Hinz, Wisconsin-Eau Claire; Kansas City—Kevin Blakley, Eastern Michigan; Milwaukee—Ken Jones, Virginia Commonwealth; Atlanta—Mike Doyle, South Carolina; Phoenix—Mark Stevens, Northern Arizona; Seattle—Lenny Horton, Georgia Tech; Philadelphia—Jim Swaney, Toledo; Los Angeles—Rick Raivio, Portland; Boston—Rufus Harris, Maine.

SIXTH ROUND Detroit—Tony Turner, Alaska-Anchorage; Golden State—Neil Bresnahan, Illinois; Utah—Ken Cunningham, Western Michigan; Denver—Ernie Hill, Oklahoma City; Chicago—Bernard Rencher, St. John's; New Jersey—Rick Mattick, LSU; San Diego—Londale Theus, Santa Clara; Cleveland—Antonio Martin, Oral Roberts; Indiana—Randy Owens, Philadelphia Textile; Portland—Perry Mirkovich, Lethbridge (Canada); Dallas—Leroy Jackson, Cameron; Washington—Ken Dancy, Chicago State; New York—Kelvin Hicks, New York Tech; San Antonio—Dean Uthoff, Iowa State; Houston—Everette Jefferson, New Mexico; Kansas City—Trent Grooms, Kent State; Milwaukee—Alex Gilbert, Indiana State; Atlanta—Mike Zagardo, George Washington; Phoenix—Coby Leavitt, Utah; Seattle—Jim Strickland, South Carolina; Philadelphia—Donald Cooper, St. Augustine; Los Angeles—Odis Boddie, North Alabama; Boston—Kenny Evans, Norfolk State.

SEVENTH ROUND Detroit—Carl Pierce, Gonzaga; Utah—Dave Colescott, North Carolina; Golden State—Lorenzo Romar, Washington; Chicago—Robert Byrd, Marquette; Denver—Tommy Springer, Vanderbilt; New Jersey—Larry Spicer, Alabama-Birmingham; San Diego—Paul Anderson, Southern California College; Indiana—Charles Naddaff, Lafayette; Cleveland—Leroy Berry, Wilmington (Ohio); Portland—Gig Sims, UCLA; Dallas—Tony Forch, Midwestern; New York—Bobby Turner, Louisville; Washington—Karl Godine, Stephen F. Austin; Houston—Joe Nehls, Arizona; San Antonio—Allan Zahn, Arkansas; Kansas City—Arnold McDowell, Montana State; Milwaukee—Ron White, Furman; Atlanta—Charles Hightower, Dillard; Phoenix—Ron Williams, Western Montana; Seattle—Carl Ervin, Seattle; Philadelphia—Richard Smith, Weber State; Boston—Les Henson, Virginia Tech.

EIGHTH ROUND Detroit—Leroy Loggins, Fairmont State; Golden State—Kurt Kanaskie, LaSalle; Utah—Jim Brandon, St. Peter's; Chicago—Modzel Greer, North Park; New Jersey—Lloyd Terry, New Orleans; Cleveland—Jim Ellinghausen, Ohio State; Indiana—Steve Stielper, James Madison; Portland—John Stroeder, Montana; Dallas—Clarence Kea, Lamar; Washington—Rich Valavicius, Auburn; New York—James Salters, Penn; San Antonio—Bill Bailey, Pan American; Houston—Rosie Barnes, Bowling Green; Milwaukee—Keith Valentine, Virginia Union; Phoenix—Jim Connolly, LaSalle; Seattle—Al Dutch, Georgetown; Philadelphia—Martin Lemelle, Grambling; Los Angeles—Melvin Hooker, Edinboro State; Boston—Steve Wright, Boston U.

NINTH ROUND Detroit—Terry Dupris, Huron; Utah—Paul Renfro, Texas-Arlington; Golden State—Billy Reid, San Francisco; Chicago—Jay Shidler, Kentucky; Denver—Jim Graziano, South Carolina; New Jersey—Barry Young, Colorado State; Indiana—Scott Rogers, Kenyon; Cleveland—Melvin Crafter, Central State (Ohio); Portland—Rich Boucher, Maine; Dallas—Ken Williams, Houston; New York—Don Wiley, Monmouth; Washington—Clinton Wyatt, Alcorn State; San Antonio—Al Williams, North Texas State; Kansas City—Charley Cole, Delta State; Milwaukee—Del Yarbrough, Illinois State; Atlanta—Stanley Lamb, Steubenville; Phoenix—Keith French, North Park; Seattle—Jim Tillman, Eastern Kentucky; Philadelphia—Luke Griffin, St. Joseph's; Boston—Brian Jung, Northwestern.

TENTH ROUND Golden State—Tim Higgins, Kearney State; Utah—Leroy Coleman, Middle Tennessee; Denver—Earl Sango, Regis; Chicago—Billy Foster, Eastern Montana; Indiana—John Bates, West Virginia Wesleyan; Portland—Dave Kufeld, Yeshiva; Dallas—Tom Morgan, California State-Fullerton; Washington—Don Youman, Oklahoma State; New York—Gerald Ross, Grand Canyon; San Antonio—Steve Schall, Arkansas; Milwaukee—Melvin Crayton, Alabama State; Phoenix—Randy Carroll, Kansas; Seattle—Kent Williams, Texas Tech; Philadelphia—Joe Hand, Kings (Pa.); Boston—John Nolan, Providence.

1980 EXPANSION DRAFT

DALLAS Del Beshore, Chicago; Winford Boynes, New Jersey; Alonzo Bradley, Houston; Mike Bratz, Phoenix; Marty Byrnes, Los Angeles; Austin Carr, Cleveland; Jim Cleamons, Washington; Terry Duerod, Detroit; Jack Givens, Atlanta; Joe Hassett, Indiana; Geoff Huston, New York; Abdul Jeelani, Portland; Jeff Judkins, Boston; Arvid Kramer, Denver; Tom LaGarde, Seattle; Billy McKinney, Kansas City; Wiley Peck, San Antonio; Bingo Smith, San Diego; Jim Spanarkel, Philadelphia; Raymond Townsend, Golden State; Richard Washington, Milwaukee; Jerome Whitehead, Utah.

1981 (JUNE 9, 1981)

FIRST ROUND Dallas—Mark Aguirre, DePaul; Detroit—Isiah Thomas, Indiana; New Jersey—Buck Williams, Maryland; Atlanta (from Cleveland)—Al Wood, North Carolina; Seattle (from Utah)—Danny Vranes, Utah; Chicago (from Atlanta)—Orlando Woolridge, Notre Dame; Kansas City (from Seattle)—Steve Johnson, Oregon State; San Diego—Tom Chambers, Utah; Dallas (from Denver)—Rolando Blackman, Kansas State; New Jersey (from Golden State)—Albert King, Maryland; Washington—Frank Johnson, Wake Forest; Detroit (from Kansas City)—Kelly Tripucka, Notre Dame; Utah (from Houston)—Danny Schayes, Syracuse; Indiana—Herb Williams, Ohio State; Portland—Jeff Lamp, Virginia; Portland (from Chicago)—Darnell Valentine, Kansas; Kansas City (from New York)—Kevin Loder, Alabama State; New Jersey (from San Antonio)—Ray Tolbert, Indiana; Los Angeles—Mike McGee, Michigan; Phoenix—Larry Nance, Clemson; Milwaukee—Alton Lister, Arizona State; Philadelphia—Franklin Edwards, Cleveland State; Boston—Charles Bradley, Wyoming.

SECOND ROUND Dallas—Jay Vincent, Michigan State; Boston (from Detroit)—Tracy Jackson, Notre Dame; Portland (from New Jersey)—Brian Jackson, Utah State; Utah—Howard Wood, Tennessee; San Antonio (from Cleveland)—Gene Banks, Duke; Kansas City (from Atlanta)—Eddie Johnson, Illinois; San Antonio (from Seattle)—Ed Rains, South Alabama; Boston (from San Diego)—Danny Ainge, Brigham Young; Chicago (from Denver)—Mike Olliver, Lamar; Golden State (from Washington)—Sam Williams, Arizona State; Denver (from Golden State)—Kenneth Green, Pan American; Washington (from Houston)—Charles Davis, Vanderbilt; Indiana (from Kansas City)—Ray Blume, Oregon State; Indiana—Al Leslie, Bucknell; Atlanta (from Chicago)—Clyde Bradshaw, DePaul; Los Angeles (from Portland)—Harvey Knuckles, Toledo; New York—Greg Cook, LSU; Washington (from San Antonio)—Claude Gregory, Wisconsin; Los Angeles—Elvis Rolle, Florida State; Dallas (from Phoenix)—Elston Turner, Mississippi; Washington (from Milwaukee)—Steve Lingenfelter, South Dakota State; Houston (from Boston)—Ed Turner, Texas A&I; Philadelphia—Vernon Smith, Texas A&M.

THIRD ROUND Dallas—Art Housey, Kansas; Washington (from Detroit)—Mike Ferrara, Colgate; New Jersey—David Burns, St. Louis; Portland (from Cleveland)—Derek Holcomb, Illinois; Los Angeles (from Utah)—Zam Fredrick, South Carolina; Atlanta—Rudy Macklin, LSU; Seattle—Mark Radford, Oregon State; San Diego—Jim Smith, Ohio State; Cleveland (from Denver)—Mickey Dillard, Florida State; Golden State—Carlton Neverson, Pittsburgh; New York (from Washington)—Frank Brickowski, Penn State; Kansas City—Curtis Berry, Missouri; Cleveland (from Houston)—Russell Bowers, American; Indiana—Purvis Miller, Southern California; Portland—Petur Gudmundsson, Washington; Phoenix (from Chicago)—Sam Clancy, Pittsburgh; New York—Wayne McKoy, St. John's; San Antonio—Tom Baker, Eastern Kentucky; Los Angeles—Ron Cornelius, Pacific; Phoenix—Craig Dykema, Long Beach State; Milwaukee—Mark Smith, Illinois; Philadelphia—Ernest Graham, Maryland; Boston—John Johnson, Michigan.

FOURTH ROUND Dallas—Eddie Moss, Syracuse; Detroit—John May, South Alabama; New Jersey—Edmund Sherod, Virginia Commonwealth; Utah—George Torres, Bethany Nazarene; Cleveland—Ethan Martin, LSU; Atlanta—Kevin Figaro, Southwestern Louisiana; Golden State (from Seattle)—Lewis Lloyd, Drake; San Diego—Lee Raker, Virginia; Kansas

City (from Denver)—Kenny Dennard, Duke; Washington—Ron Davis, Arizona; Golden State—Terry Adolph, West Texas State; Houston—Larry Spriggs, Howard; Kansas City—B. B. Davis, Lamar; Indiana—Rolando Frazer, Briar Cliff; Chicago—Oliver Lee, Marquette; Portland—Peter Verhoeven, Fresno State; New York—Alex Bradley, Villanova; San Antonio—Earl Belcher, St. Bonaventure; Los Angeles—Kevin McKenna, Creighton; Detroit (from Phoenix)—Don Koonce, North Carolina-Charlotte; Milwaukee—Kris Anderson, Florida State; Boston—Stanley Williams, LaSalle; Philadelphia—Rynn Wright, Texas A&M.

FIFTH ROUND Dallas—Pete Budko, North Carolina; Detroit—George DeVone, North Carolina-Charlotte; New Jersey—Joe Cooper, Colorado; Cleveland—Ken Page, New Mexico; Utah—Mike Clark, Oregon; Atlanta—Steve Krafcisin, Iowa; Seattle—Andra Griffin, Washington; San Diego—Dennis Isbell, Memphis State; Denver—Willie Sims, LSU; Golden State—Hank McDowell, Memphis State; Washington—Garry Witts, Holy Cross; Kansas City—U. S. Reed, Arkansas; Houston—Hasan Houston, Bradley; Indiana—George Peterson, Jersey City State; Portland—Herb Andrew, South Alabama; Chicago—Johnny Nash, Arizona State; New York—Jim Wright, Rhode Island; San Antonio—Mike Rhodes, Vanderbilt; Los Angeles—Craig Watts, North Carolina State; Phoenix—Paul Heuerman, Michigan; Milwaukee—Kelvin Troy, Rutgers; Philadelphia—Steve Craig, Brigham Young; Boston—Glen Grunwald, Indiana.

SIXTH ROUND Dallas—Karl Bankowski, Utah; Detroit—Vince Brookins, Iowa; New Jersey—Kevin Lynam, LaSalle; Utah—Kevin Sprewer, Loyola (Ill.); Cleveland—Aaron Strayhorn, Hawaii; Atlanta—Darryl Warwick, Hampton Institute; Seattle—Earl Banks, Auburn; San Diego—Mike Pepper, North Carolina; Denver—Alonzo Weatherley, Denver; Washington—Robert Williams, Grambling; Golden State—Carter Scott, Ohio State; Houston—Fred Cowan, Kentucky; Kansas City—Brian Walker, Purdue; Indiana—Robert Fronk, Washington; Chicago—Roger Burkman, Louisville; Portland—Roshern Amie, Texas-El Paso; New York—John Blair, Monmouth; San Antonio—Doc Shavers, Jackson State; Los Angeles—Kevin Singleton, California; Phoenix—Pete Harris, Northeastern; Milwaukee—JoJo Hunter, Colorado; Boston—Steve Waite, Iowa; Philadelphia—Michael Thomas, North Park.

SEVENTH ROUND Dallas—Danny Davis, North Carolina-Wilmington; Detroit—Greg Nance, West Virginia; New Jersey—Rod Roberson, Northwestern; Cleveland—Andre Smith, Nebraska; Utah—Mike Robinson, Central Michigan; Atlanta—Kevin Vesey, Iona; Seattle—Tom Sienkiewicz, Villanova; San Diego—Randy Johnson, Southern Colorado; Denver—Greg Manning, Maryland; Golden State—Robby Dosty, Arizona; Washington—Randy Martell, Houston Baptist; Kansas City—Clinton Wheeler, William Paterson; Houston—Joe Faine, Bowling Green; Indiana—Larry McKinney, Boise State; Portland—Julius Wayne, Texas-El Paso; Chicago—Scott Williams, South Alabama; New York—Terry Cramer, Ripon; San Antonio—Mark Mindeman, Northern Michigan; Los Angeles—Larry Petty, Wisconsin; Phoenix—David Williams, Southern; Milwaukee—Lewis Latimore, Virginia; Philadelphia—John Crawford, Kansas; Boston—Tom Seaman, Holy Cross.

EIGHTH ROUND Dallas—David Kennedy, Cincinnati; Detroit—Joe Schoen, St. Francis (Pa.); New Jersey—Ken Webb, Fairleigh Dickinson; Utah—Bob Cattage, Auburn; Cleveland—Glen Marcus, Alabama-Birmingham; Atlanta—Gilbert Salinas, Notre Dame; San Diego—Todd Haynes, Davidson; Denver—Curtis Redding, St. John's; Washington—Mike Howard, Wofford; Golden State—Yasutaka Okayama, Japan; Houston—Stanley Brewer, Western Georgia; Kansas City—Randy Smithson, Wichita State; Indiana—Len Hatzenbeller, Drexel; Chicago—Ben Mitchell, Alabama-Huntsville; Portland—John Smith, St. Joseph's; New York—Brian O'Connor, Thomas More (Ky.); San Antonio—Bob Bartholomew, San Diego; Los Angeles—Jay Triano, Simon Fraser (Canada); Phoenix—Steve Risley, Indiana; Milwaukee—Mike Brkovich, Michigan State; Boston—George Morrow, Creighton; Philadelphia—Frank Gilroy, St. John's.

NINTH ROUND Dallas—John Hollinden, Indiana State-Evansville; Detroit—Eddie Baker, Alcorn State; New Jersey—Rudy Williams, Providence; Cleveland—Paul Roba, Cleveland State; Utah—Ken Ollie, Wyoming; Atlanta—Howard Thompkins, Wagner; San Diego—Art Jones, North Carolina State; Denver—Andrew Burton, Austin Peay; Golden State—Doug Murrey, San Jose State; Washington—Eddie Brown, Valdosta State; Kansas City—Mike Perry, Richmond; Indiana—Scott Whitley, William & Mary; Portland—Sid Williams, San Jose State; Chicago—Terry Martin, Lambuth (Tenn.); New York—Marty Headd, Syracuse; San Antonio—Leonel Marquetti, Hampton Institute; Phoenix—Brian Johnson, Colorado; Milwaukee—Chip Rucker, Northeastern; Philadelphia—Ron Wister, Temple; Boston—Greg McCray, Virginia Commonwealth.

TENTH ROUND Dallas—Scott Bosanko, Northern State College; Detroit—Melvin Maxwell, Western Michigan; New Jersey—Vic Sison, UCLA; Utah—Joe Merten, Wisconsin-Eau Claire; Cleveland—Greg Boone, Augsburg; Atlanta—Mike Frazier, Georgetown; San Diego—Tony Gwynn, San Diego State; Denver—Derrick Rowland, Potsdam State; Washington—Ralton May, Houston Baptist; Golden State—Barry Brooks, Southern California; Kansas City—Mark Wilson, Fort Hays State; Indiana—Rodney Benson, Wright State; Chicago—Kenny Easley, UCLA; Portland—Steve Cochran, Lewis & Clark; New York—Kevin Rogers, St. Peter's; San Antonio—Alvin Brooks, Lamar; Phoenix—Felton Sealey, Oregon; Milwaukee—Artie Green, Marquette; Boston—Ken Matthews, North Carolina State; Philadelphia—Pete Mullenberg, Delaware.

1982 (JUNE 29, 1982)

FIRST ROUND Los Angeles (from Cleveland)—James Worthy, North Carolina; San Diego—Terry Cummings, DePaul; Utah—Dominique Wilkins, Georgia; Dallas—Bill Garnett, Wyoming; Kansas City—LaSalle Thompson, Texas; New York—Trent Tucker, Minnesota; Chicago—Quintin Dailey, San Francisco; Indiana—Clark Kellogg, Ohio State; Detroit—Cliff Levingston, Wichita State; Atlanta—Keith Edmonson, Purdue; Portland—Lafayette Lever, Arizona State; Cleveland (from Washington)—John Bagley, Boston College; New Jersey—Eric Floyd, Georgetown; Golden State—Lester Conner, Oregon State; Phoenix (from Denver)—David Thirdkill, Bradley; Houston—Terry Teagle, Baylor; Kansas City (from Phoenix)—Brook Steppe, Georgia Tech; Detroit (from San Antonio)—Ricky Pierce, Rice; Denver (from Seattle)—Rob Williams, Houston; Milwaukee—Paul Pressey, Tulsa; New Jersey (from Los Angeles)—Eddie Phillips, Alabama; Philadelphia—Mark McNamara, California; Boston—Darren Tillis, Cleveland State.

SECOND ROUND San Antonio (from Cleveland)—Oliver Robinson, Alabama-Birmingham; Washington (from San Diego)—Bryan Warrick, St. Joseph's; Chicago (from Utah)—Ricky Frazier, Missouri; Milwaukee (from Dallas)—Fred Roberts, Brigham Young; Cleveland (from Kansas City)—David Magley, Kansas; New York—Scott Hastings, Arkansas; Chicago—Wallace Bryant, San Francisco; Chicago (from Indiana)—Rod Higgins, Fresno State; San Diego (from Detroit)—Richard Anderson, California-Santa Barbara; Portland—Linton Townes, James Madison; New York (from Atlanta)—Vince Taylor, Duke; Golden State (from Washington)—Derek Smith, Louisville; Philadelphia (from New Jersey)—Mitchell Anderson, Bradley; Portland (from Golden State)—Audie Norris, Jackson State; Golden State (from Houston)—Wayne Sappleton, Loyola (Ill.); Phoenix—Kevin Magee, California-Irvine; Indiana (from Denver)—Guy Morgan, Wake Forest; Washington (from San Antonio)—Dwight Anderson, Southern California; Houston (from Seattle)—Jeff Taylor, Texas Tech; Indiana (from Milwaukee)—Jose Slaughter, Portland; Washington (from Los Angeles)—Mike Gibson, South Carolina-Spartanburg; Philadelphia—Russ Schoene, Tennessee-Chattanooga; Boston—Tony Guy, Kansas.

THIRD ROUND Cleveland—Michael Wilson, Marquette; San Diego—Craig Hodges, Long Beach State; Utah—Steve Trumbo, Brigham Young; Dallas—Corny Thompson, Connecticut; Kansas City—Jim Johnstone, Wake Forest; New York—Dan Caldwell, Washington; Chicago—Tyrone Adams, Kansas State; Los Angeles (from Indiana)—Willie Jones, Vanderbilt; Utah (from Detroit)—Jerry Eaves, Louisville; Atlanta—Joe Kopicki, Detroit; New York (from Portland)—Craig Tucker, Illinois; Washington—Mike Largey, Upsala; New Jersey—Jimmy Black, North Carolina; Golden State—Chris Engler, Wyoming; Phoenix—Charles Pittman, Maryland; Denver—Roylin Bond, Pepperdine; Houston—Chuck Nevitt, North Carolina State; San Antonio—Willie Redden, South Florida; Seattle—John Greig, Oregon; Portland (from Milwaukee)—Phillip Lockett, Alabama; Los Angeles—Mike Hackett, Jacksonville; Philadelphia—Dale Solomon, Virginia Tech; Boston—Perry Moss, Northeastern.

FOURTH ROUND Cleveland—Reggie Hannah, South Alabama; San Diego—Darius Clemons, Loyola (Ill.); Utah—Mark Eaton, UCLA; Dallas—Rudy Woods, Texas A&M; Kansas City—Mike Sanders, UCLA; New York—Norm Anchrum, Alabama-Birmingham; Chicago—Chuck Aleksinas, Connecticut; Indiana—Jeff Jones, Virginia; Detroit—Walker Russell, Western Michigan; Portland—Eric Smith, Georgetown; New Jersey (from Atlanta)—James Griffin, Illinois; Washington—Dino Gregory, Long Beach State; New Jersey—Tony Brown, Arkansas; Golden State—Ken Stancell, Virginia Commonwealth; Denver—Alford Turner, Southwestern Louisiana; Houston—Andre Gaddy, George Mason; Phoenix—Rory White, South Alabama; San Antonio—Tony Grier, South Florida; Seattle—Ken Owens, Idaho; Milwaukee—Jerry Beck, Middle Tennessee; Los Angeles—Craig McCormick, Western Kentucky; Philadelphia—Bruce Atkins, Duquesne; Boston—Greg Stewart, Tulsa.

FIFTH ROUND Cleveland—Terry White, Texas-El Paso; San Diego—Gary Carter, Tennessee; Utah—Mike McKay, Connecticut; Dallas—Ken Arnold, Iowa; Kansas City—Ken Simpson, Grambling; New York—Aaron Howard, Villanova; Chicago—Rubin Jackson, Oklahoma City; Indiana—Rich DiBenedetto, Wisconsin-Eau Claire; Detroit—John Ebeling, Florida Southern; Atlanta—Mark Hall, Minnesota; Portland—Cherokee Rhone, Centenary; Washington—Clarence Dickerson, Hawaii; New Jersey—Chris Giles, Alabama-Birmingham; Golden State—Albert Irving, Alcorn State; Houston—Jeff Schneider, Virginia Tech; Phoenix—Marvin McCrary, Missouri; Denver—Bill Duffy, Santa Clara; San Antonio—Clarence Swannegan, Texas Tech; Seattle—Rod Camp, Southern Illinois; Washington (from Milwaukee)—Jerry Davis, Detroit; Los Angeles—Howard McNeil, Seton Hall; Philadelphia—Donald Mason, Fresno State; Boston—William Brown, St. Peter's.

SIXTH ROUND Cleveland—Vince Reynolds, South Florida; San Diego—Eric Marbury, Georgia; Utah—Alvin Jackson, Southern; Dallas—Wayne Waggoner, Northwest Louisiana; Kansas City—Poncho Wright, Louisville; New York—Mike Kanieski, Dayton; Chicago—B. B. Fontenet, Nevada-Reno; Indiana—Jeff Clark, St. Joseph's; Detroit—Gary Holmes, Minnesota; Portland—Leo Cunningham, Utah State; Atlanta—Jay Bruchak, Mount St. Mary's; Washington—Byron Williams, Idaho State; New Jersey—Mel Daniel, Furman; Golden State—David Vann, St. Mary's (Cal.); Phoenix—Jake Bethany, Hardin-Simmons; Denver—Chris Brust, North Carolina; Houston—Don Wilson, Northeast Louisiana; San Antonio—Jaime

Pena, New Mexico State; Seattle—Bobby Potts, North Carolina-Charlotte; Milwaukee—Tony Carr, Wisconsin-Eau Claire; Los Angeles—Lynden Rose, Houston; Philadelphia—Kevin Boyle, Iowa; Boston—John Schweitz, Richmond.

SEVENTH ROUND Cleveland—Randy Reed, Kansas State; San Diego—Ed Hughes, Colorado State; Utah—Thad Gardner, Michigan; Dallas—Bob Grady, Northwestern; Kansas City—Perry Range, Illinois; New York—Phil Seymore, Canisius; Chicago—Chuck Verderber, Kentucky; Indiana—Brad Leaf, Evansville; Detroit—Dean Marquardt, Marquette; Atlanta—Horace Wyatt, Clemson; Portland—Terry Long, Lamar; Washington—Wendell Gibson, South Carolina-Spartanburg; New Jersey—Tony Anderson, UCLA; Golden State—Matt Waldron, Pacific; Denver—Jeb Barlow, North Carolina; Houston—Mike Helms, Wake Forest; Phoenix—Phil Ward, North Carolina-Charlotte; San Antonio—Delonte Taylor, North Texas State; Seattle—Allen Rayhorn, Northern Illinois; Milwaukee—Bobby Austin, Cincinnati; Los Angeles—Maurice Williams, Southern California; Philadelphia—Keith Hilliard, Southwest Missouri State; Boston—Phil Collins, West Virginia.

EIGHTH ROUND Cleveland—Monty Knight, Virginia Commonwealth; San Diego—Jacques Tuz, Colorado; Utah—Rick Campbell, Middle Tennessee; Dallas—Keith Peterson, Arkansas; Kansas City—Ed Nealy, Kansas State; New York—Dan Terwilliger, Siena; Chicago—Mike Burns, Nevada-Las Vegas; Indiana—Donald Reese, Bradley; Detroit—Brian Nyenhuis, Marquette; Portland—Dave Porter, Western Oregon; Atlanta—James Ratiff, Howard; Washington—Ken Luck, Delaware; New Jersey—Otis Jackson, Memphis State; Golden State—Mark King, Florida Southern; Houston—Dan Callandrillo, Seton Hall; Phoenix—Rick Elrod, Georgetown (Ky.); Denver—Donny Speer, Alabama-Birmingham; San Antonio—Chris Faggi, Memphis State; Seattle—Steve Burks, Washington; Milwaukee—Bryan Leonard, Illinois; Los Angeles—Micah Blunt, Tulane; Philadelphia—Donald Seals, Jackson State; Boston—Ed Spriggs, Georgetown.

NINTH ROUND Cleveland—Tony Hafley, South Alabama; San Diego—John Hegwood, San Francisco; Utah—Riley Clarida, LIU; Dallas—Ralph McPherson, Texas-Arlington; Kansas City—Jack Moore, Nebraska; New York—Merle Scott, South Carolina State; Chicago—Skip Dillard, DePaul; Indiana—Mike Scearce, Purdue; Detroit—Kevin Smith, Michigan State; Atlanta—Pierre Bland, Elizabeth City; Portland—Mark Dearborn, St. Joseph's; Washington—James Terry, Howard; New Jersey—Gary Johnson, Oral Roberts; Golden State—Nick Morken, Tennessee; Phoenix—Ken Lyles, Washington; Denver—Dean Sears, UCLA; San Antonio—Harry O'Brien, St. Mary's (Tex.); Milwaukee—Robert Tate, Idaho State; Los Angeles—Tim Byrne, Rutgers; Philadelphia—George Melton, Cheyney State; Boston—Panayotis Giannakis, Hellenic.

TENTH ROUND Cleveland—Durand Walker, Marion; San Diego—Daryl Stovall, Creighton; Utah—Michael Edwards, New Orleans; Dallas—Albert Culton, Texas-Arlington; Kansas City—Robert Estes, Iowa State; New York—John Leonard, Manhattan; Chicago—Tony Britto, Campbell; Indiana—Craig Summers, Wisconsin-Stout; Detroit—David Coulthard, York (Canada); Portland—Grant Taylor, California-Irvine; Atlanta—Ronnie McAdoo, Old Dominion; Washington—Donald Sinclair, North Carolina Central; New Jersey—Sean Tuohy, Mississippi; Golden State—Randy Whieldon, California-Irvine; Denver—Mike Phillips, Niagara; Phoenix—Dale Wilkinson, Idaho State; San Antonio—Keith White, McMurry; Milwaukee—Bob Coenen, Wisconsin-Eau Claire; Philadelphia—Randy Burkert, Drexel; Boston—Landon Turner, Indiana.

1983 (JUNE 28, 1983)

FIRST ROUND Houston—Ralph Sampson, Virginia; Indiana—Steve Stipanovich, Missouri; Houston (from Cleveland)—Rodney McCray, Louisville; San Diego—Byron Scott, Arizona State; Chicago—Sidney Green, Nevada-Las Vegas; Golden State—Russell Cross, Purdue; Utah—Thurl Bailey, North Carolina State; Detroit—Antoine Carr, Wichita State; Dallas—Dale Ellis, Tennessee; Washington—Jeff Malone, Mississippi State; Dallas (from Atlanta)—Derek Harper, Illinois; New York—Darrell Walker, Arkansas; Kansas City—Ennis Whatley, Alabama; Portland (from Denver)—Clyde Drexler, Houston; Denver (from Portland)—Howard Carter, LSU; Seattle—Jon Sundvold, Missouri; Philadelphia (from New Jersey)—Leo Rautins, Syracuse; Milwaukee—Randy Breuer, Minnesota; San Antonio—John Paxson, Notre Dame; Cleveland (from Phoenix)—Roy Hinson, Rutgers; Boston—Greg Kite, Brigham Young; Washington (from Los Angeles)—Randy Wittman, Indiana; Indiana (from Philadelphia)—Mitchell Wiggins, Florida State; Cleveland—Stewart Granger, Villanova.

SECOND ROUND Chicago (from Houston)—Sidney Lowe, North Carolina State; Indiana—Leroy Combs, Oklahoma State; Cleveland—John Garris, Boston College; Phoenix (from San Diego)—Rod Foster, UCLA; Chicago—Larry Micheaux, Houston; Dallas (from Utah)—Mark West, Old Dominion; Atlanta (from Golden State)—Glenn Rivers, Marquette; Washington (from Detroit)—Michael Britt, District of Columbia; Dallas—Dirk Minniefield, Kentucky; Washington—Guy Williams, Washington State; San Antonio (from Atlanta)—Darrell Lockhart, Auburn; Seattle (from New York)—Scooter McCray, Louisville; Denver—David Russell, St. John's; Kansas City—Chris McNealy, San Jose State; Portland—Granville

Waiters, Ohio State; Indiana (from Seattle)—James Thomas, Indiana; Milwaukee (from New Jersey)—Ted Kitchel, Indiana; Milwaukee—Mike Davis, Alabama; Golden State (from Phoenix)—Pace Mannion, Utah; New Jersey (from San Antonio)—Horace Owens, Rhode Island; Phoenix (from Boston)—Paul Williams, Arizona State; San Antonio (from Los Angeles)—Kevin Williams, St. John's; Philadelphia—Ken Lyons, North Texas State.

THIRD ROUND Houston—Craig Ehlo, Washington State; Indiana—Greg Jones, West Virginia; Cleveland—Paul Thompson, Tulane; Phoenix (from San Diego)—Derek Whittenburg, North Carolina State; Boston (from Chicago)—Winfred King, East Tennessee; Golden State—Michael Holton, UCLA; Utah—Robert Hansen, Iowa; Detroit—Erich Santifer, Syracuse; Cleveland (from Dallas)—Larry Anderson, Nevada-Las Vegas; Washington—Darren Daye, UCLA; Atlanta—John Pinone, Villanova; New Jersey (from New York)—Bruce Kuczenski, Connecticut; Kansas City—Steve Harriel, Washington State; Denver—David Little, Oklahoma; Portland—Tom Piotrowski, LaSalle; Seattle—Frank Burnell, Stetson; Philadelphia (from New Jersey)—Claude Riley, Texas A&M; Milwaukee—Billy Goodwin, St. John's; Cleveland (from San Antonio)—Les Craft, Kansas State; Cleveland (from Phoenix)—Derrick Hord, Kentucky; Boston—Craig Robinson, Virginia; Los Angeles—Orlando Phillips, Pepperdine; Philadelphia—Dan Ruland, James Madison.

FOURTH ROUND Houston—Darrell Browder, TCU; Indiana—Terry Fair, Georgia; Cleveland—Dwight Jones, Cincinnati; Philadelphia (from San Diego)—Kalpatrick Wells, Mississippi State; Chicago—Ron Crevier, Boston College; Utah—Doug Arnold, TCU; Golden State—Pete Thibeaux, St. Mary's (Cal.); Detroit—Steve Bouchie, Indiana; Dallas—Johnny Martin, Northwestern Louisiana; Washington—Dan Gay, Southwestern Louisiana; Atlanta—Harry Kelly, Texas Southern; New York—Mark Jones, St. Bonaventure; Denver—York Gross, California-Santa Barbara; Kansas City—Mike Jackson, Wyoming; Portland—Tim Dunham, Chaminade; Seattle—Pete DeBisschop, Fairfield; New Jersey—Barney Mines, Bradley; Milwaukee—Mark Nickens, American; Phoenix—Sam Mosley, Nevada-Reno; San Antonio—Brant Weidner, William & Mary; Boston—Carlos Clark, Mississippi; Los Angeles—Terry Lewis, Mississippi State; Philadelphia—Craig Robinson, Princeton.

FIFTH ROUND Houston—Chuck Barnett, Oklahoma; Indiana—Roger Stieg, Mississippi; Cleveland—Chris Logan, Holy Cross; San Diego—Manute Bol, Sudan; Chicago—Tim Andree, Notre Dame; Golden State—Greg Hines, Hampton Institute; Utah—Matt Clark, Oklahoma State; Detroit—Ken Austin, Rice; Dallas—Jim Lampley, Arkansas-Little Rock; Washington—Robin Dixon, New Hampshire; Atlanta—Charles Jones, Oklahoma; New York—Troy Lee Mikell, East Tennessee; Kansas City—Lorenza Andrews, Oklahoma State; Denver—James Braddock, North Carolina; Portland—Gary Monroe, Wright State; Seattle—Brad Watson, Washington; New Jersey—Tyren Naulls, Texas A&M; Milwaukee—Mark Petteway, New Orleans; San Antonio—Jeff Pehl, Richmond; Phoenix—Rick Lamb, Illinois State; Boston—Bob Reitz, Stonehill; Los Angeles—Danny Dixon, Alabama A&M; Philadelphia—Mike Milligan, Tennessee State.

SIXTH ROUND Houston—Jim Stack, Northwestern; Indiana—Cliff Pruitt, Alabama-Birmingham; Cleveland—Mel McLaughlin, Central Michigan; Milwaukee (from San Diego)—Russell Todd, West Virginia; Chicago—Ernest Patterson, New Mexico State; Utah—Fred Gilliam, Clemson; Golden State—Tom Heywood, Weber State; Detroit—Derek Perry, Michigan State; Dallas—Billy Allen, Nevada-Reno; Washington—Donald Carroll, St. Augustine's; Atlanta—Tom Bethea, Richmond; New York—Tony Simms, Boston U.; Denver—Glenn Green, Murray State; Kansas City—Alvis Rogers, Wake Forest; Portland—Derrick Pope, Montana; Seattle—Tony Wilson, Western Kentucky; New Jersey—Oscar Taylor, New Orleans; Milwaukee—Charles Hurt, Kentucky; Phoenix—Edward Bona, Fordham; San Antonio—Ricky Hooker, St. Mary's (Tex.); Boston—Paul Atkins, Dallas Baptist; Los Angeles—Mark Steele, Colorado State; Philadelphia—Sedale Threatt, West Virginia Tech.

SEVENTH ROUND Houston—Brian Kellerman, Idaho; Indiana—Tony Brown, Indiana; Cleveland—John Columbo, John Carroll; San Diego—Dan Evans, Oregon State; Chicago—Jacque Hill, Southern California; Golden State—Peter Williams, Utah; Utah—Joe Kazanowski, Victoria (Canada); Detroit—Rob Gonzalez, Colorado; Dallas—Terrell Schlundt, Marquette; Washington—Danny Womack, Winston-Salem; Atlanta—Lex Drum, Alabama-Birmingham; New York—Desi Barmore, Fresno State; Kansas City—Dane Suttle, Pepperdine; Denver—Maurice McDaniel, Catawba; Portland—Paul Little, Penn; Seattle—Tony Gattis, Mercer; New Jersey—Keith Bennett, Sacred Heart; Milwaukee—Anthony Hicks, Xavier (Ohio); San Antonio—Keith Williams, Panhandle State; Phoenix—Fred Brown, Virginia Commonwealth; Boston—Ron Jackson, Providence; Los Angeles—Ricky Mixon, California State-Fullerton; Philadelphia—Tony Bruin, Syracuse.

EIGHTH ROUND Houston—Jeff Bolding, Arkansas State; Indiana—Ray McCallum, Ball State; Cleveland—Larry Tucker, Lewis (Ill.); San Diego—Mark Gannon, Iowa; Chicago—Terry Bradley, Chicago State; Utah—Michael McCombs, Santa Fe; Golden State—Doug Harris, Central Washington; Detroit—George Wenzel, Augustana; Dallas—Bill Sadler, Pepperdine; Washington—Bernard Perry, Howard; Atlanta—George Thomas, Georgia Tech; New York—Mike Lang, Penn State; Denver—Cliff Tribus, Davidson; Kansas City—Preston Neumayr, California-Davis; Portland—Frank Smith, Arizona; Seattle—Ray Smith, Armstrong State; New Jersey—Joe Myers, Duquesne; Milwaukee—Brett Burkholder, DePaul; Phoenix—Mike

Mulquin, Villanova; San Antonio—Norville Brown, Oklahoma Christian; Boston—Trent Johnson, Pittsburgh; Philadelphia—Gordon Austin, American.

NINTH ROUND   Houston—James Campbell, Oklahoma City; Indiana—Lynn Mitchem, Butler; Cleveland—Joe Brown, Georgia State; San Diego—David Maxwell, Fordham; Chicago—Ray Orange, Oklahoma Christian; Golden State—Greg Goorjian, Loyola Marymount; Utah—Ron Webb, Oklahoma Christian; Detroit—Marlow McLain, Eastern Michigan; Dallas—Sherrod Arnold, Chicago State; Washington—Ricky Moreland, Maryland-Baltimore; Atlanta—Wil Kotchery, Livingston State; New York—Charles Jones, Marshall; Kansas City—Bernard Hill, Panhandle State; Denver—Bobby Van Noy, Catawba; Portland—Phil Hopson, Idaho; Seattle—Tony Washington, Hampton Institute; New Jersey—Kevin Black, Rutgers; Milwaukee—Bill Varner, Notre Dame; San Antonio—Gary Gaspard, St. Mary's (Tex.); Phoenix—Joe Dykstra, Western Illinois; Boston—John Rice, Massachusetts-Boston; Philadelphia—Charles Fisher, James Madison.

TENTH ROUND   Indiana—Mark Smed, Augustana (S.D.); Cleveland—Jon Hanley, Xavier (Ohio); San Diego—Keith Smith, San Diego State; Chicago—Tom Emma, Duke; Utah—Odell Mosteller, Auburn; Golden State—Michael Zeno, Long Beach State; Detroit—Ike Person, Michigan; Dallas—Clyde Corley, Florida International; Washington—Isaiah Singletary, St. Louis; Atlanta—Ronnie Carr, Western Carolina; New York—Bernard Randolph, DePaul; Denver—Cleveland McCrae, Catawba; Kansas City—Aaron Haskins, Washington State; Portland—Russ Christianson, East Oregon State; Seattle—David Binion, North Carolina Central; New Jersey—Rich Simkus, Princeton; Milwaukee—Bob Kelly, St. John's; Phoenix—Bo Overton, Oklahoma; San Antonio—Lamar Heard, Georgia; Boston—Andy Kupec, Bentley.

1984 (JUNE 19, 1984)

FIRST ROUND   Houston—Hakeem Olajuwon, Houston; Portland (from Indiana)—Sam Bowie, Kentucky; Chicago—Michael Jordan, North Carolina; Dallas (from Cleveland)—Sam Perkins, North Carolina; Philadelphia (from LA Clippers)—Charles Barkley, Auburn; Washington—Melvin Turpin, Kentucky; San Antonio—Alvin Robertson, Arkansas; L.A. Clippers (from Golden State)—Lancaster Gordon, Louisville; Kansas City—Otis Thorpe, Providence; Philadelphia (from Denver)—Leon Wood, California State-Fullerton; Atlanta—Kevin Willis, Michigan State; Cleveland—Tim McCormick, Michigan (bonus selection); Phoenix—Jay Humphries, Colorado; LA Clippers (from Seattle)—Michael Cage, San Diego State; Dallas—Terence Stansbury, Temple; Utah—John Stockton, Gonzaga; New Jersey—Jeff Turner, Vanderbilt; Indiana (from New York)—Vern Fleming, Georgia; Portland—Bernard Thompson, Fresno State; Detroit—Tony Campbell, Ohio State; Milwaukee—Kenny Fields, UCLA; Philadelphia—Tom Sewell, Lamar; LA Lakers—Earl Jones, District of Columbia; Boston—Michael Young, Houston.

SECOND ROUND   Indiana—Devin Durrant, Brigham Young; Portland (from Chicago)—Victor Fleming, Xavier (Ohio); Cleveland—Ron Anderson, Fresno State; Seattle (from Houston)—Cory Blackwell, Wisconsin; Indiana (from LA Clippers)—Stuart Gray, UCLA; Golden State (from Washington)—Steve Burtt, Iona; Golden State—Jay Murphy, Boston College; Detroit (from San Antonio)—Eric Turner, Michigan; Portland (from Denver)—Steve Colter, New Mexico State; Washington (from Kansas City)—Tony Costner, St. Joseph's; Golden State (from Atlanta)—Othell Wilson, Virginia; Phoenix—Charles Jones, Louisville; Chicago (from Seattle)—Ben Coleman, Maryland; Dallas—Charles Sitton, Oregon State; Seattle (from New Jersey)—Danny Young, Wake Forest; Dallas (from Utah)—Anthony Teachey, Wake Forest; Dallas (from New York)—Tom Sluby, Notre Dame; Denver (from Portland)—Willie White, Tennessee-Chattanooga; Chicago (from Detroit)—Greg Wiltjer, Victoria (Canada); Washington (from Milwaukee)—Fred Reynolds, Texas-El Paso; Golden State (from Philadelphia)—Gary Plummer, Boston U.; Portland (from L.A. Lakers)—Jerome Kersey, Longwood (Va.); Boston—Ronnie Williams, Florida.

THIRD ROUND   Philadelphia (from Indiana)—James Banks, Georgia; Chicago—Tim Dillon, Northern Illinois; Cleveland—Ben McDonald, California-Irvine; Houston—Jim Petersen, Minnesota; Seattle (from LA Clippers)—Terry Williams, Alabama; Washington—Ricky Ross, Tulsa; Kansas City (from San Antonio)—Roosevelt Chapman, Dayton; Golden State—Lewis Jackson, Alabama State; Kansas City—Jeff Allen, St. John's; San Antonio (from Denver)—Joe Binion, North Carolina A&T; Atlanta—Bobby Parks, Memphis State; Phoenix—Murray Jarman, Clemson; Cleveland (from Seattle)—Leonard Mitchell, LSU; Dallas—Jeff Cross, Maine; Utah—David Pope, Norfolk State; New Jersey—Yommy Sangodeyi, Sam Houston State; New York—Curtis Green, Southern Mississippi; Portland—Tim Kearney, West Virginia; Detroit—Kevin Springman, St. Joseph's; Milwaukee—Vernon Delancy, Florida; Philadelphia—Butch Graves, Yale; LA Lakers—George Singleton, Furman; Boston—Rick Carlisle, Virginia.

FOURTH ROUND   Indiana—Ralph Jackson, UCLA; Chicago—Melvin Johnson, North Carolina-Charlotte; Cleveland—Art Aaron, Northwestern; Houston—Willie Jackson, Centenary; LA Clippers—Marc Glass, Montana; Washington—Jim Grandholm, South Florida; Chicago (from Golden State)—Mark Halsel, Northeastern; San Antonio—John Devereaux,

Ohio; Denver—Karl Tilleman, Calgary (Canada); Kansas City—Carl Henry, Kansas; Atlanta—Dickie Beal, Kentucky; Phoenix—Jeff Collins, Nevada-Las Vegas; Seattle—Jeff Jenkins, Xavier (Ohio); Dallas—John Horrocks, North Texas State; New Jersey—Hank Cornley, Illinois State; Utah—Jim Rowinski, Purdue; New York—Bob Thornton, California-Irvine; Portland—Brett Applegate, Brigham Young; Detroit—Phillip Smith, New Mexico; San Antonio (from Milwaukee)—Ozell Jones, California State-Fullerton; Philadelphia—Earl Harrison, Morehead State; LA Lakers—John Revelli, Stanford; Boston—Kevin Mullin, Princeton.

FIFTH ROUND   Indiana—Gene Smith, Georgetown; Chicago—Lamont Robinson, Lamar; Cleveland—Vince Hinchen, Boise State; Houston—Al McClain, New Hampshire; LA Clippers—Alonza Allen, Southwestern Louisiana; Washington—Colin Irish, Bowling Green; San Antonio—Eric Richardson, Alabama; Golden State—Steve Bartek, Doane; Kansas City—Jim Foster, South Carolina; Denver—Prince Bridges, Missouri; Atlanta—Terry Martin, Northeast Louisiana; Phoenix—Bill Flye, Richmond; Seattle—Elv Pasquale, Victoria (Canada); Dallas—Dave Williams, Illinois-Chicago; Utah—Marcus Gaither, Fairleigh Dickinson; New Jersey—Michael Gerren, South Alabama; Golden State (from New York)—Scott McCollum, Pepperdine; Portland—Mike Whitmarsh, San Diego; Detroit—Rick Doyle, Texas-San Antonio; Milwaukee—Ernie Floyd, Holy Cross; Philadelphia—Dan Federmann, Tennessee; LA Lakers—Lance Berwald, North Dakota State; Boston—Todd Orlando, Bentley.

SIXTH ROUND   Indiana—Clyde Vaughan, Pittsburgh; Chicago—Jeff Tipton, Morehead State; Cleveland—Matt Doherty, North Carolina; Milwaukee (from Houston)—McKinley Singleton, Alabama-Birmingham; LA Clippers—Phillip Haynes, Memphis State; Washington—Blaise Bugajeski, Illinois Wesleyan; Golden State—Tony Martin, Wyoming; San Antonio—Dion Brown, Southwestern Louisiana; Denver—Willie Burton, Tennessee; Kansas City—Bruce Vanley, Tulsa; Atlanta—Jim Master, Kentucky; Phoenix—Herman Veal, Maryland; Seattle—Graylin Warner, Southwestern Louisiana; Dallas—LaVerne Evans, Marshall; New Jersey—Oscar Schmidt, Brazil; Utah—Chris Harrison, West Virginia Wesleyan; New York—Eddie Wilkins, Gardner-Webb; Portland—Lance Ball, Western Oregon; Detroit—Rennie Bailey, Louisiana Tech; Milwaukee—Mike Reddick, Stetson; Philadelphia—Gary Springer, Iona; LA Lakers—Keith Jones, Stanford; Boston—Steve Carfino, Iowa.

SEVENTH ROUND   Indiana—Kenton Edelin, Virginia; Chicago—Butch Hays, California; Cleveland—Joe Jakubick, Akron; Houston—Joedy Gardner, California State-Long Beach; LA Clippers—David Brantley, Oregon; Washington—Tim Garrett, New Mexico; San Antonio—Michael Pitts, California; Golden State—Cliff Higgins, California State-Northridge; Kansas City—Chip Harris, Robert Morris; Denver—Mark Simpson, Catawba; Atlanta—Vince Martello, Florida State; Phoenix—Raymond Crenshaw, Oklahoma State; Seattle—Gary Gatewood, Oregon; Dallas—George Turner, California-Irvine; Utah—Bob Evans, Southern Utah State; New Jersey—Sean Kerins, Syracuse; New York—Ken Bannister, St. Augustine; Portland—Victor Anger, Pepperdine; Detroit—Barry Francisco, Bloomsburg State; Milwaukee—Tony William, Florida State; Philadelphia—Rich Congo, Drexel; LA Lakers—Richard Haenisch, Chaminade; Boston—Mark Van Valkenburg, Framingham State.

EIGHTH ROUND   Indiana—Tom Heitz, Kentucky; Chicago—Brett Crawford, U.S. International; Cleveland—Elliot Beard, Oberlin; Houston—Greg Wolff, Angelo State; LA Clippers—Jim McLoughlin, Temple; Washington—Darryl Odom, West Virginia Wesleyan; Golden State—Paul Brozovich, Nevada-Las Vegas; San Antonio—Dan Tarkanian, Nevada-Las Vegas; Denver—Bill Wendlandt, Texas; Kansas City—Nate Rollins, Fort Hays State; Atlanta—Robert Brown, Long Island; Phoenix—Mark Fothergill, Maryland; Seattle—Jerry McMillan, DePaul; Dallas—Leroy Sutton, Arkansas; New Jersey—Chris Winans, Utah; Utah—Eric Booker, Nevada-Las Vegas; New York—Ricky Tunstall, Youngstown State; Portland—Steve Flint, California-San Diego; Detroit—Dale Roberts, Appalachian State; Milwaukee—Brad Jergenson, South Carolina; Philadelphia—Frank Dobbs, Villanova; Boston—Champ Godboldt, Holy Cross.

NINTH ROUND   Indiana—Brian Martin, Kansas; Chicago—Calvin Pierce, Oklahoma; Cleveland—John Shimko, Xavier (Ohio); Houston—Bill Coon, Presbyterian; LA Clippers—Dave Schultz, Westmont; Washington—Mike Emanuel, Pembroke State; San Antonio—Melvin Roseboro, St. Mary's (Tex.); Golden State—Mitch Arnold, Fresno State; Kansas City—Greg Turner, Auburn; Denver—Cecil Exum, North Carolina; Atlanta—Fred Brown, Georgetown; Phoenix—Buddy Cox, Bellarmine; Seattle—Mike Williams, Idaho State; Dallas—John Tudor, LSU; Utah—Kelly Knight, Kansas; New Jersey—Billy Ryan, Princeton; New York—Marc Marotta, Marquette; Portland—Dennis Black, Portland; Detroit—Ben Tower, Michigan State; Milwaukee—Edwin Green, Massachusetts; Philadelphia—Michael Mitchell, Drexel; Boston—Joe Dixon, Merrimack.

TENTH ROUND   Indiana—Gary Carver, Western Kentucky; Chicago—Carl Lewis, Houston; Cleveland—Darrell Space, Northeast Illinois; Houston—Robert Turner, Canisius; LA Clippers—Dick Mumma, Penn State; Washington—Glynn Myrick, Stetson; Golden State—Tim Bell, California-Riverside; San Antonio—Frank Rodriguez, New Mexico State; Denver—Dexter Bailey, Xavier (Ohio); Kansas City—Victor Coleman, Northwest Missouri State; Atlanta—Doug Mills, Hofstra; Phoenix—Ezra Hill, Liberty Baptist; Seattle—Greg Brandon, Creighton; Dallas—Napoleon Johnson, Grambling; New Jersey—Phil Jamison, St. Peter's; Utah—Mike Curran, Niagara; New York—Mike Henderson, C. W. Post; Portland—Randy

Dunn, George Fox; Detroit—Dan Pelekoudas, Michigan; Milwaukee—Mike Toomer, Florida A&M; Philadelphia—Martin Clark, Boston College; Boston—Dan Trant, Clark.

1985 (JUNE 18, 1985)

FIRST ROUND New York—Patrick Ewing, Georgetown; Indiana—Wayman Tisdale, Oklahoma; L.A. Clippers—Benoit Benjamin, Creighton; Seattle—Xavier McDaniel, Wichita State; Atlanta—Jon Koncak, SMU; Sacramento—Joe Kleine, Arkansas; Golden State—Chris Mullin, St. John's; Dallas (from Cleveland)—Detlef Schrempf, Washington; Cleveland—Charles Oakley, Virginia Union (bonus selection); Phoenix—Ed Pinckney, Villanova; Chicago—Keith Lee, Memphis State; Washington—Kenny Green, Wake Forest; Utah—Karl Malone, Louisiana Tech; San Antonio—Alfredrick Hughes, Loyola (Ill.); Denver (from Portland)—Blair Rasmussen, Oregon; Dallas (from New Jersey)—Bill Wennington, St. John's; Dallas—Uwe Blab, Indiana; Detroit—Joe Dumars, McNeese State; Houston—Steve Harris, Tulsa; Boston (from Denver)—Sam Vincent, Michigan State; Philadelphia—Terry Catledge, South Alabama; Milwaukee—Jerry Reynolds, LSU; LA Lakers—A. C. Green, Oregon State; Portland (from Boston)—Terry Porter, Wisconsin-Stevens Point.

SECOND ROUND Portland (from Golden State)—Mike Smrek, Canisius; Indiana—Bill Martin, Georgetown; Indiana (from New York)—Dwayne McClain, Villanova; Chicago (from Seattle)—Ken Johnson, Michigan State; San Antonio (from Sacramento)—Mike Brittain, South Carolina; Cleveland (from LA Clippers)—Calvin Duncan, Virginia Commonwealth; Washington (from Atlanta)—Manute Bol, Bridgeport; Phoenix—Nick Vanos, Santa Clara; Philadelphia (from Cleveland)—Greg Stokes, Iowa; Chicago—Aubrey Sherrod, Wichita State; San Antonio (from Washington)—Tyrone Corbin, DePaul; New Jersey (from San Antonio)—Yvon Joseph, Georgia Tech; Utah—Carey Scurry, LIU; New Jersey—Fernando Martin, Spain; Portland—George Montgomery, Illinois; Dallas—Mark Acres, Oral Roberts; Atlanta (from Detroit)—Lorenzo Charles, North Carolina State; Golden State (from Houston)—Bobby Lee Hurt, Alabama; Denver—Barry Stevens, Iowa State; Philadelphia—Voise Winters, Bradley; Cleveland (from Milwaukee)—John Williams, Tulane; Chicago (from LA Lakers)—Adrian Branch, Maryland; New York (from Boston)—Gerald Wilkins, Tennessee-Chattanooga.

THIRD ROUND Indiana—Kenny Patterson, DePaul; Golden State—Brad Wright, UCLA; Dallas (from New York)—Leonard Allen, San Diego State; Sacramento—Charles Bradley, South Florida; LA Clippers—Anicet Lavodrama, Houston Baptist; Seattle—Rolando Lamb, Virginia Commonwealth; Houston (from Atlanta)—Sam Mitchell, Mercer; Cleveland—Herb Johnson, Tulsa; Phoenix—Jerry Everett, Lamar; Houston (from Chicago)—Michael Payne, Iowa; Washington—Vernon Moore, Creighton; Atlanta (from Utah)—Sedric Toney, Dayton; Detroit (from San Antonio)—Andre Goode, Northwestern; Portland—Perry Young, Virginia Tech; New Jersey—Nigel Manuel, UCLA; Dallas—Harold Keeling, Santa Clara; Detroit—Richie Johnson, Evansville; Washington (from Houston)—Ken Perry, Southern Illinois; Sacramento (from Denver)—Michael Adams, Boston College; Philadelphia—Steve Black, LaSalle; Milwaukee—Eugene McDowell, Florida; Chicago (from LA Lakers)—Mike Brown, George Washington; Boston—Andre Battle, Loyola (Ill.).

FOURTH ROUND Golden State—Luster Goodwin, Texas-El Paso; Indiana—Vince Hamilton, Clemson; New York—Fred Cofield, Eastern Michigan; LA Clippers—Jim Deines, Arizona State; Seattle—Alex Stivrins, Colorado; Sacramento—Willie Simmons, Louisiana Tech; Atlanta—Arvidas Sabonis, Soviet Union; Phoenix—Granger Hall, Temple; Cleveland—Mark Davis, Old Dominion; Chicago—Craig Beard, Samford; Washington—Richie Adams, Nevada-Las Vegas; San Antonio—Scott Roth, Wisconsin; Utah—Delaney Rudd, Wake Forest; Atlanta (from New Jersey)—John Battle, Rutgers; Portland—Joe Atkinson, Oklahoma State; Dallas—Bubba Jennings, Texas Tech; Detroit—Spud Webb, North Carolina State; Houston—Mike Brooks, Tennessee; Denver—Pete Williams, Arizona; Philadelphia—Derrick Gervin, Texas-San Antonio; Milwaukee—Cozell McQueen, North Carolina State; LA Lakers—Dexter Shouse, South Alabama; Boston—Cliff Webber, Liberty Baptist.

FIFTH ROUND Indiana—Kelvin Johnson, Richmond; Golden State—Greg Cavener, Missouri; New York—Mike Schlegel, Virginia Commonwealth; Seattle—Lou Stefanovic, Illinois State; Sacramento—Bob Lojewski, St. Joseph's; LA Clippers—Wayne Carlander, USC; Atlanta—Larry Hampton, Fairleigh Dickinson; Cleveland—Gunther Behnke, West Germany; Phoenix—Shawn Campbell, Weber State; Chicago—Reid Gettys, Houston; Washington—Dean Shaffer, Florida State; Utah—Ray Hall, Canisius; San Antonio—Clayton Olivier, Southern California; Portland—James Anderson, Union (Ky.); New Jersey—Kelly Blaine, South Alabama; Dallas—Tommy Davis, Minnesota; Detroit—Mike Lahm, Murray State; Indiana (from Houston)—Ivan Daniels, Illinois-Chicago; Denver—Kenny Brown, Texas A&M; Philadelphia—Carl Wright, SMU; Milwaukee—Ray Knight, Providence; LA Lakers—Timo Saarelainen, Brigham Young; Boston—Albert Butts, LaSalle.

SIXTH ROUND Golden State—Gerald Crosby, Georgia; Indiana—Stu Primus, Boston College; New York—Kent Lockhart, Texas-El Paso; Sacramento—Charles Balentine, Arkansas; LA Clippers—Malcolm Thomas, Missouri; Seattle—Earl Walker, Mercer; Atlanta—Tony Duckett, Lafayette; Phoenix—Charles Rayne, Temple; Cleveland—Ricky Johnson, Illinois State; Chicago—Dan Meagher, Duke; Washington—Matt England, Houston Baptist; San

Antonio—Chris Harper, Oregon; Utah—Jim Miller, Virginia; New Jersey—George Almones, Southwestern Louisiana; Portland—Curtis Moore, Nebraska; Dallas—Carlton Cooper, Texas; Detroit—Vincent Giles, Eastern Michigan; Houston—Sam Potter, Oral Roberts; Denver—Joe Carrabino, Harvard; Philadelphia—Daryl Lloyd, Drake; Milwaukee—Quentin Anderson, Texas Tech; LA Lakers—Tony Neal, California State-Fullerton; Boston—Ralph Lewis, LaSalle.

SEVENTH ROUND Indiana—Jeff Acres, Oral Roberts; Golden State—Eric Boyd, North Carolina A&T; New York—Ken Bantum, Cornell; LA Clippers—Gary Maloncon, UCLA; Seattle—Michael Phelps, Alcorn State; Sacramento—Alton Lee Gipson, Florida State; Atlanta—Bob Ferry, Jr., Harvard; Cleveland—Buzz Peterson, North Carolina; Phoenix—Georgi Glouckov, Bulgaria; Chicago—Jeff Adkins, Maryland; Washington—Keith Gray, Detroit; Utah—Mike Wacker, Texas; San Antonio—Al Young, Virginia Tech; Portland—Mark Owen, College of Idaho; New Jersey—Gary McLain, Villanova; Dallas—Ed Catchings, Nevada-Las Vegas; Detroit—Frank James, Nevada-Las Vegas; Houston—Don Turney, Marshall; Denver—Eddie Smith, Arizona; Philadelphia—Jaye Andrews, Bucknell; Milwaukee—Mario Elie, American International; LA Lakers—Keith Cieplicki, William & Mary; Boston—Chris Remly, Rutgers.

1986 (JUNE 17, 1986)

FIRST ROUND Cleveland (from L.A. Clippers)—Brad Daugherty, North Carolina; Boston (from Seattle)—Len Bias, Maryland; Golden State—Chris Washburn, North Carolina State; Indiana—Chuck Person, Auburn; New York—Kenny Walker, Kentucky; Phoenix—William Bedford, Memphis State; Dallas (from Cleveland)—Roy Tarpley, Michigan; Cleveland—Ron Harper, Miami (Ohio) (bonus selection); Chicago—Brad Sellers, Ohio State; San Antonio—Johnny Dawkins, Duke; Detroit (from Sacramento)—John Salley, Georgia Tech; Washington—John Williams, LSU; New Jersey—Dwayne Washington, Syracuse; Portland—Walter Berry, St. John's; Utah—Dell Curry, Virginia Tech; Denver (from Dallas)—Mo Martin, St. Joseph's; Sacramento (from Detroit)—Harold Pressley, Villanova; Denver—Mark Alarie, Duke; Atlanta—Billy Thompson, Louisville; Houston—Buck Johnson, Alabama; Washington (from Philadelphia)—Anthony Jones, Nevada-Las Vegas; Milwaukee—Scott Skiles, Michigan State; LA Lakers—Ken Barlow, Notre Dame; Portland (from Boston)—Arvidas Sabonis, Soviet Union.

SECOND ROUND Dallas (from New York)—Mark Price, Georgia Tech; Indiana—Greg Dreiling, Kansas; Detroit (from Cleveland)—Dennis Rodman, Southeastern Oklahoma State; Chicago—Larry Krystkowiak, Montana; Cleveland (from Golden State)—Johnny Newman, Richmond; Seattle—Nate McMillan, North Carolina State; Phoenix—Joe Ward, Georgia; Atlanta (from LA Clippers)—Cedric Henderson, Georgia; San Antonio—Kevin Duckworth, Eastern Illinois; Sacramento—Johnny Rogers, California-Irvine; Dallas (from New Jersey)—Milt Wagner, Louisville; Washington—Steve Mitchell, Alabama-Birmingham; Portland—Panayotis Fasoulas, North Carolina State; Seattle (from Utah)—Lemone Lampley, DePaul; Phoenix (from Dallas)—Rafael Addison, Syracuse; Atlanta (from Detroit)—Augusto Binelli, Italy; Denver—Otis Smith, Jacksonville; Atlanta—Ron Kellogg, Kansas; Houston—Dave Feitl, Texas-El Paso; Philadelphia—David Wingate, Georgetown; Milwaukee—Keith Smith, Loyola Marymount; Phoenix (from LA Lakers)—Jeff Hornacek, Iowa State; New York (from Boston)—Michael Jackson, Georgetown.

THIRD ROUND San Antonio (from New York)—Forrest McKenzie, Loyola Marymount; Portland (from Indiana)—Juden Smith, Texas-El Paso; Cleveland—Kevin Henderson, California State-Fullerton; Golden State—Mike Williams, Bradley; Chicago—Ricky Wilson, George Mason; Seattle—Tod Murphy, California-Irvine; LA Clippers—Dwayne Polee, Pepperdine; Phoenix—Ken Gattison, Old Dominion; Philadelphia (from San Antonio)—Keith Colbert, Virginia Tech; Sacramento—Bruce Douglas, Illinois; Washington—David Henderson, Duke; Golden State (from New Jersey)—Wendell Alexis, Syracuse; Portland—Drazen Petrovic, Yugoslavia; Utah—John Shasky, Minnesota; Dallas—Anthony Welch, Illinois; Utah (from Detroit)—Bill Breeding, Rocky Mountain; Denver—Don Redden, LSU; Atlanta—Dave Hoppen, Nebraska; Houston—Anthony Bowie, Oklahoma; Philadelphia—Ron Rowan, St. John's; Milwaukee—Baskerville Holmes, Memphis State; LA Lakers—Andre Turner, Memphis State; Atlanta (from Boston)—Jim Les, Bradley.

FOURTH ROUND New York—Calvin Thompson, Kansas; Indiana—Derrick Taylor, LSU; Cleveland—Warren Martin, North Carolina; Chicago—Scott Meents, Illinois; Golden State—Dan Bingenheimer, Missouri; Seattle—Michael Graham, Georgetown; Phoenix—Grant Gondrezick, Pepperdine; LA Clippers—John Brownlee, Texas; San Antonio—Carlos Briggs, Baylor; Sacramento—Alvin Franklin, Houston; New Jersey—Steve Hale, North Carolina; Washington—Barry Mungar, St. Bonaventure; Portland—David Shaffer, Florida State; Utah—Marty Embry, DePaul; Dallas—Myron Jackson, Arkansas-Little Rock; Detroit—Chauncey Robinson, Mississippi State; Denver—Anthony Watson, San Diego State; Atlanta—Efrem Winters, Illinois; Houston—Conner Henry, California-Santa Barbara; Philadelphia—Wes Stallings, East Tennessee State; Sacramento (from Milwaukee)—Bob Beecher, Virginia Tech; LA Lakers—Dale Blaney, West Virginia; Boston—Tony Benford, Texas Tech.

FIFTH ROUND New York—Jerome Mincey, Alabama-Birmingham; Indiana—Richard Rellford, Michigan; Cleveland—Ben Davis, Gardner-Webb; Golden State—Clinton Smith, Cleveland State; Chicago—Jimmy Gilbert, Texas A&M; Seattle—Dominic Pressley, Boston College; LA Clippers—Stefford Johnson, San Diego State; Phoenix—Greg Spurling, Carson-Newman; San Antonio—Earl Kelley, Connecticut; Sacramento—Keith Morrison, Washington State; Washington—Paul Fortier, Washington; New Jersey—Archie Johnson, Alabama-Birmingham; Portland—Jerry Adams, Oregon; Utah—Kerry Boagni, California State-Fullerton; Dallas—Jay Bilas, Duke; Detroit—Clarence Hanley, Old Dominion; Denver—Jon Collins, Eastern Illinois; Atlanta—Nicky Jones, Virginia Commonwealth; Houston—Andre Banks, Iowa; Philadelphia—Kevin Holmes, DePaul; Milwaukee—Bobby Deaton, Southwestern (Tex.); LA Lakers—Roger Harden, Kentucky; Boston—Dave Colbert, Dayton.

SIXTH ROUND New York—Butch Wade, Michigan; Indiana—Jeff Hall, Louisville; Cleveland—Gilbert Wilburn, New Mexico State; Chicago—Pete Myers, Arkansas-Little Rock; Golden State—Bobby Lee Hurt, Alabama; Seattle—Curtis Kitchen, South Florida; Phoenix—Jim McCaffrey, Holy Cross; LA Clippers—Tim Kempton, Notre Dame; San Antonio—Kevin Lewis, SMU; Sacramento—John Flowers, Nevada-Las Vegas; New Jersey—Troy Webster, George Washington; Washington—Lorenzo Duncan, Sam Houston State; Portland—Tony Hampton, Montana State; Utah—Chuck Everson, Villanova; Dallas—Greg Anderson, Lamar; Detroit—Greg Grant, Utah State; Denver—Anthony Frederick, Pepperdine; Atlanta—Aleksandr Volkov, Soviet Union; Houston—Robert Worthy, Dyke (Ohio); Philadelphia—Andre McCloud, Seton Hall; Milwaukee—John Kimbrell, David Lipscomb (Tenn.); LA Lakers—Walter Downing, Marquette; Boston—Greg Wendt, Detroit.

SEVENTH ROUND New York—Duane Kendall, South Carolina; Indiana—Steve Woodside, Oregon State; Cleveland—Ralph Dalton, Georgetown; Golden State—Steve Kenilvort, Santa Clara; Chicago—Robert Henderson, Michigan; Seattle—Glen McCants, Clemson; LA Clippers—Johnny Brown, New Mexico; Phoenix—Damon Goodwin, Dayton; San Antonio—Michael Anderson, Pan American; Sacramento—Ron Rankin, Southeast Missouri State; Washington—Joe Price, Notre Dame; New Jersey—Jim Dolan, Notre Dame; Portland—Randy Schiff, Linfield; Utah—Mark Mitchell, Hartford; Dallas—Kim Cooksey, Middle Tennessee State; Detroit—Larry Polec, Michigan State; Denver—Mike Marshall, McNeese State; Atlanta—Valerie Tikhonenko, Soviet Union; Houston—Rick Olson, Wisconsin; Philadelphia—Dan Palombizio, Ball State; Milwaukee—Jeff Strong, Missouri; LA Lakers—Mark Coleman, Mississippi Valley State; Boston—Tom Ivey, Boston U.

1987 (JUNE 22, 1987)

FIRST ROUND San Antonio—David Robinson, Navy; Phoenix—Armon Gilliam, Nevada-Las Vegas; New Jersey—Dennis Hopson, Ohio State; LA Clippers—Reggie Williams, Georgetown; Seattle (from New York)—Scottie Pippen, Central Arkansas; Sacramento—Kenny Smith, North Carolina; Cleveland—Kevin Johnson, California; Chicago (from Denver)—Olden Polynice, Virginia; Seattle—Derrick McKey, Alabama; Chicago—Horace Grant, Clemson; Indiana—Reggie Miller, UCLA; Washington—Tyrone Bogues, Wake Forest; LA Clippers (from Houston)—Joe Wolf, North Carolina; Golden State—Tellis Frank, Western Kentucky; Utah—Jose Ortiz, Oregon State; Philadelphia—Christian Welp, Washington; Portland—Ronnie Murphy, Jacksonville; New York (from Milwaukee)—Mark Jackson, St. John's; LA Clippers (from Detroit)—Ken Norman, Illinois; Dallas—Jim Farmer, Alabama; Atlanta—Dallas Comegys, DePaul; Boston—Reggie Lewis, Northeastern; San Antonio (from LA Lakers)—Greg Anderson, Houston.

SECOND ROUND Detroit (from LA Clippers)—Fred Banks, Nevada-Las Vegas; New York—Ron Moore, West Virginia State; Dallas (from New Jersey)—Steve Alford, Indiana; San Antonio—Nate Blackwell, Temple; Chicago (from Sacramento)—Ricky Winslow, Houston; Portland (from Cleveland)—Lester Fonville, Jackson State; Portland (from Phoenix)—Nikita Wilson, LSU; Denver—Andre Moore, Loyola (Ill.); Milwaukee (from Seattle)—Bob McCann, Morehead State; Chicago—Tony White, Tennessee; Indiana—Brian Rowsom, North Carolina-Wilmington; Houston—Doug Lee, Purdue; Washington (from Golden State)—Duane Washington, Middle Tennessee State; Washington—Derrick Dowell, Southern California; LA Clippers (from Utah)—Norris Coleman, Kansas State; Philadelphia—Vincent Askew, Memphis State; Milwaukee (from Portland)—Winston Garland, Southwest Missouri State; Cleveland (from Milwaukee)—Kannard Johnson, Western Kentucky; Atlanta (from Detroit)—Terrence Bailey, Wagner; Philadelphia (from Dallas)—Andrew Kennedy, Virginia; Atlanta—Terry Coner, Alabama; Boston—Brad Lohaus, Iowa; Phoenix (from LA Lakers)—Bruce Dalrymple, Georgia Tech.

THIRD ROUND LA Clippers—Tim McCalister, Oklahoma; New Jersey—Jamie Waller, Virginia Union; New York—Jerome Batiste, McNeese State; San Antonio—Phil Zevenbergen, Washington; Sacramento—Sven Meyer, Oregon; Cleveland—Donald Royal, Notre Dame; Phoenix—Winston Crite, Texas A&M; Denver—Tom Schafer, Iowa State; Seattle—Tommy Amaker, Duke; Chicago—John Fox, Millersville State; Philadelphia (from Indiana)—Hansi Gnad, Alaska-Anchorage; Golden State—Darryl Johnson, Michigan State; Washington—Danny Pearson, Jacksonville; Indiana (from Houston)—Sean Couch, Columbia; Utah—

Clarence Martin, Western Kentucky; Philadelphia—Eric Riggins, Rutgers; Portland—Kevin Gamble, Iowa; Milwaukee—J. J. Weber, Wisconsin; Detroit—Eric White, Pepperdine; Dallas—Mike Richmond, Texas-El Paso; Atlanta—Song Tao, China; Utah (from Boston)—Billy Donovan, Providence; LA Lakers—Willie Glass, St. John's.

FOURTH ROUND Boston (from LA Clippers)—Tom Sheehey, Virginia; New York—Mike Morgan, Drake; New Jersey—Andrew Moten, Florida; San Antonio—Todd May, Pikeville; Sacramento—Joe Arlauckas, Niagara; Cleveland—Chris Dudley, Yale; Phoenix—Steve Beck, Arizona State; Denver—David Boone, Marquette; Seattle—Todd Linder, Tampa; Chicago—Jack Haley, UCLA; Cleveland (from Indiana)—Carven Holcomb, Texas Christian; Washington—Scott Thompson, San Diego; Houston—Joe Niego, Lewis (Ill.); Golden State—Benny Bolton, North Carolina State; Utah—Reuben Holmes, Alabama State; Philadelphia—Brian Rahilly, Tulsa; Portland—Norwood Barber, Florida State; Milwaukee—Darryl Bedford, Austin Peay; Detroit—Dave Popson, North Carolina; Dallas—David Johnson, Oklahoma; Atlanta—Theofanis Christodoulou, Greece; Boston—Darryl Kennedy, Oklahoma; LA Lakers—Ralph Tally, Norfolk State.

FIFTH ROUND LA Clippers—Chad Kessler, Georgia; New Jersey—James Blackmon, Kentucky; New York—Glenn Clem, Vanderbilt; San Antonio—Dennis Williams, Georgia; Sacramento—Vernon Carr, Michigan State; Cleveland—Carl Lott, Texas Christian; Phoenix—Brent Counts, Pacific; Denver—Ron Grandison, New Orleans; Seattle—Michael Tait, Clemson; Chicago—Anthony Wilson, LSU; Indiana—Mike Milling, North Carolina-Charlotte; Houston—Andre LaFleur, Northeastern; Golden State—Terry Williams, SMU; Washington—Patrick Fairs, Texas; Utah—Bart Kofoed, Kearney State; Philadelphia—Frank Ross, American; Portland—David Moss, Tulsa; Milwaukee—Brian Vaughns, California-Santa Barbara; Detroit—Gerry Wright, Iowa; Dallas—Sam Hill, Iowa State; Atlanta—Jose Antonio Montero, Spain; Boston—Dave Butler, California.

SIXTH ROUND LA Lakers—Kenny Travis, New Mexico State; LA Clippers—Martin Nessley, Duke; New York—Howard Triche, Syracuse; New Jersey—Perry Bromwell, Penn; San Antonio—Ricky Brown, South Alabama; Sacramento—Darryl Thomas, Indiana; Cleveland—Harold Jensen, Villanova; Phoenix—Marcel Boyce, Akron; Denver—Kelvin Scarborough, New Mexico; Seattle—Tom Gneiting, Brigham Young; Chicago—Doug Altenberger, Illinois; Indiana—Gary Graham, Nevada-Las Vegas; Golden State—Sarunas Marciulionis, Soviet Union; Washington—Dwayne Scholten, Washington State; Houston—Fred Jenkins, Tennessee; Utah—Art Sabb, Bloomfield (N.J.); Philadelphia—Tracy Foster, Alabama-Birmingham; Portland—Bernard Jackson, Loyola (Ill.); Milwaukee—Gay Elmore, Virginia Military; Detroit—Antoine Joubert, Michigan; Dallas—Quintan Gates, Texas-El Paso; Atlanta—Riccardo Morandotti, Italy; Boston—Tim Naegeli, Wisconsin-Stevens Point; LA Lakers—Frank Ford, Auburn.

SEVENTH ROUND LA Clippers—Henry Carr, Wichita State; New Jersey—Frank Booker, Bowling Green; New York—Wayne Williams, St. Joseph's; San Antonio—Raynard Davis, Texas; Sacramento—Scott Adubato, Upsala; Cleveland—Michael Foster, South Carolina; Phoenix—Ron Singleton, Grand Canyon; Denver—Rowan Gomes, Hampton Institute; Seattle—Mike Giomi, North Carolina State; Chicago—Earvin Leavy, Central Michigan; Indiana—Montel Hatcher, UCLA; Washington—Jamie Dixon, Texas Christian; Houston—Clarence Grier, Campbell; Golden State—Ronnie Leggette, West Virginia State; Utah—Keith Webster, Harvard; Philadelphia—Eric Semisch, West Virginia; Portland—Kenny Stone, George Fox; Denver (from Milwaukee)—Curtis Hunter, North Carolina; Detroit—Mark Gottfried, Alabama; Dallas—Gerald White, Auburn; Atlanta—Franjo Arapovic, Yugoslavia; Boston—Jerry Corcoran, Northeastern; LA Lakers—Ron Vanderschaaf, Central Washington.

1988 (JUNE 28, 1988)

FIRST ROUND LA Clippers—Danny Manning, Kansas; Indiana—Rik Smits, Marist; Philadelphia—Charles Smith, Pittsburgh; New Jersey—Chris Morris, Auburn; Golden State—Mitch Richmond, Kansas State; LA Clippers (from Sacramento)—Hersey Hawkins, Bradley; Phoenix—Tim Perry, Temple; Charlotte—Rex Chapman, Kentucky; Miami—Rony Seikaly, Syracuse; San Antonio—Willie Anderson, Georgia; Chicago (from New York)—Will Perdue, Vanderbilt; Washington—Harvey Grant, Oklahoma; Milwaukee—Jeff Grayer, Iowa State; Phoenix (from Cleveland)—Dan Majerle, Central Michigan; Seattle—Gary Grant, Michigan; Houston—Derrick Chievous, Missouri; Utah—Eric Leckner, Wyoming; Sacramento (from Atlanta)—Ricky Berry, San Jose State; New York (from Chicago)—Rod Strickland, DePaul; Miami (from Dallas)—Kevin Edwards, DePaul; Portland—Mark Bryant, Seton Hall; Cleveland (from Detroit)—Randolph Keys, Southern Mississippi; Denver—Jerome Lane, Pittsburgh; Boston—Brian Shaw, California-Santa Barbara; LA Lakers—David Rivers, Notre Dame.

SECOND ROUND Portland (from LA Clippers)—Rolando Ferreira, Houston; San Antonio (from New Jersey)—Shelton Jones, St. John's; Phoenix (from Golden State)—Andrew Lang, Arkansas; Sacramento—Vinnie Del Negro, North Carolina State; Detroit (from Phoenix)—Fennis Dembo, Wyoming; Philadelphia (from San Antonio)—Everette Stephens, Purdue; New Jersey (from Philadelphia)—Charles Shackleford, North Carolina State; Miami—Grant Long,

Eastern Michigan; Charlotte—Tom Tolbert, Arizona; Miami (from New York)—Sylvester Gray, Memphis State; Washington—Ledell Eackles, New Orleans; New York (from Indiana)—Greg Butler, Stanford; Phoenix (from Cleveland)—Dean Garrett, Indiana; Milwaukee—Tito Horford, Miami (Fla.); Miami (from Seattle)—Orlando Graham, Auburn-Montgomery; Golden State (from Houston)—Keith Smart, Indiana; Utah—Jeff Moe, Iowa; Denver (from Chicago)—Todd Mitchell, Purdue; Atlanta—Anthony Taylor, Oregon; LA Clippers (from Portland)—Tom Garrick, Rhode Island; Dallas—Morlon Wiley, Long Beach State; Denver—Vernon Maxwell, Florida; Detroit—Michael Williams, Baylor; Dallas (from Boston)—Jose Vargas, LSU; Phoenix (from LA Lakers)—Steve Kerr, Arizona.

THIRD ROUND LA Clippers—Robert Lock, Kentucky; New Jersey—Derrek Hamilton, Southern Mississippi; Portland (from Golden State)—Anthony Mason, Tennessee State; Atlanta (from Sacramento)—Jorge Gonzalez, Argentina; Phoenix—Rodney Johns, Grand Canyon; San Antonio—Barry Sumpter, Austin Peay; Philadelphia—Hernan Montenegro, LSU; Charlotte—Jeff Moore, Auburn; Miami—Nate Johnston, Tampa; Washington—Ed Davender, Kentucky; Indiana—Herbert Crook, Louisville; Chicago (from New York)—Derrick Lewis, Maryland; Milwaukee—Mike Jones, Auburn; Cleveland—Winston Bennett, Kentucky; Seattle—Corey Gaines, Loyola Marymount; Denver (from Houston)—Dwight Boyd, Memphis State; Utah—Ricky Grace, Oklahoma; Atlanta—Darryl Middleton, Baylor; New York (from Chicago)—Phil Stinnie, Virginia Commonwealth; Dallas—Jerry Johnson, Florida Southern; Portland—Craig Neal, Georgia Tech; Detroit—Lee Johnson, Norfolk State; Indiana (from Denver)—Michael Anderson, Drexel; Boston—Gerald Paddio, Nevada-Las Vegas; San Antonio (from LA Lakers)—Archie Marshall, Kansas.

1988 EXPANSION DRAFT (JUNE 23, 1988)

CHARLOTTE Dell Curry, Cleveland; Dave Hoppen, Golden State; Tyrone Bogues, Washington; Mike Brown, Chicago; Rickey Green, Utah; Michael Holton, Portland; Michael Brooks, Denver; Bernard Thompson, Phoenix; Ralph Lewis, Detroit; Clinton Wheeler, Indiana; Sedric Toney, New York.

MIAMI Arvid Kramer, Dallas; Billy Thompson, LA Lakers; Fred Roberts, Boston; Scott Hastings, Atlanta; Jon Sundvold, San Antonio; Kevin Williams, Seattle; Hansi Gnad, Philadelphia; Darnell Valentine, LA Clippers; Dwayne Washington, New Jersey; Andre Turner, Houston; Conner Henry, Sacramento; John Stroeder, Milwaukee.

1989 (JUNE 27, 1989)

FIRST ROUND Sacramento—Pervis Ellison, Louisville; LA Clippers—Danny Ferry, Duke; San Antonio—Sean Elliott, Arizona; Miami—Glen Rice, Michigan; Charlotte—J. R. Reid, North Carolina; Chicago (from New Jersey)—Stacey King, Oklahoma; Indiana—George McCloud, Florida State; Dallas—Randy White, Louisiana Tech; Washington—Tom Hammonds, Georgia Tech; Minnesota—Pooh Richardson, UCLA; Orlando—Nick Anderson, Illinois; New Jersey (from Portland)—Mookie Blaylock, Oklahoma; Boston—Michael Smith, Brigham Young; Golden State—Tim Hardaway, Texas-El Paso; Denver—Todd Lichti, Stanford; Seattle (from Houston through Golden State)—Dana Barros, Boston College; Seattle (from Philadelphia)—Shawn Kemp, Trinity (Tex.) JC; Chicago (from Chicago through Seattle)—B. J. Armstrong, Iowa; Philadelphia (from Seattle)—Kenny Payne, Louisville; Chicago (from Milwaukee through Seattle)—Jeff Sanders, Georgia Southern; Utah—Blue Edwards, East Carolina; Portland (from New York)—Byron Irvin, Missouri; Atlanta—Roy Marble, Iowa; Phoenix—Anthony Cook, Arizona; Cleveland—John Morton, Seton Hall; LA Lakers—Vlade Divac, Yugoslavia; Detroit—Kenny Battle, Illinois.

SECOND ROUND Miami—Sherman Douglas, Syracuse; Charlotte—Dyron Nix, Tennessee; Milwaukee (from San Antonio)—Frank Kornet, Vanderbilt; LA Clippers—Jeff Martin, Murray State; New Jersey (from New Jersey through Chicago and Philadelphia)—Stanley Brundy, DePaul; LA Clippers (from Sacramento)—Jay Edwards, Indiana; Minnesota (from Indiana through Milwaukee)—Gary Leonard, Missouri; Dallas—Pat Durham, Colorado State; Portland—Cliff Robinson, Connecticut; Orlando—Michael Ansley, Alabama; Minnesota—Doug West, Villanova; Washington—Ed Horton, Iowa; Boston—Dino Radja, Yugoslavia; Washington (from Golden State)—Doug Roth, Tennessee; Denver—Michael Cutright, McNeese State; Cleveland (from Houston through LA Clippers and Chicago)—Chucky Brown, North Carolina State; Philadelphia—Reggie Cross, Hawaii; Miami (from Seattle through Milwaukee)—Scott Haffner, Evansville; Phoenix (from Chicago)—Ricky Blanton, Louisiana State; Denver (from Milwaukee through San Antonio)—Reggie Turner, Alabama-Birmingham; Utah—Junie Lewis, South Alabama; Atlanta—Haywoode Workman, Oral Roberts; New York—Brian Quinnett, Washington State; Phoenix—Mike Morrison, Loyola (Md.); Phoenix (from LA Lakers)—Greg Grant, Trenton State; Dallas (from Cleveland)—Jeff Hodge, South Alabama; Philadelphia (from Detroit)—Toney Mack, Georgia.

1989 EXPANSION DRAFT (JUNE 15, 1989)

ORLANDO Sidney Green, New York; Reggie Theus, Atlanta; Terry Catledge, Washington; Sam Vincent, Chicago; Otis Smith, Golden State; Scott Skiles, Indiana; Jerry Reynolds, Seattle; Mark Acres, Boston; Morlon Wiley, Dallas; Jim Farmer, Utah; Keith Lee, New Jersey; Frank Johnson, Houston.

MINNESOTA Rick Mahorn, Detroit; Tyrone Corbin, Phoenix; Steve Johnson, Portland; Brad Lohaus, Sacramento; David Rivers, LA Lakers; Mark Davis, Milwaukee; Scott Roth, San Antonio; Shelton Jones, Philadelphia; Eric White, LA Clippers; Maurice Martin, Denver; Gunther Behnke, Cleveland.

1990 (JUNE 27, 1990)

FIRST ROUND New Jersey—Derrick Coleman, Syracuse; Seattle—Gary Payton, Oregon State; Denver (from Miami)—Chris Jackson, LSU; Orlando—Dennis Scott, Georgia Tech; Charlotte—Kendall Gill, Illinois; Minnesota—Felton Spencer, Louisville; Sacramento—Lionel Simmons, LaSalle; LA Clippers—Bo Kimble, Loyola Marymount; Miami (from Washington via Dallas and Denver)—Willie Burton, Minnesota; Atlanta (from Golden State)—Rumeal Robinson, Michigan; Golden State (from Atlanta)—Tyrone Hill, Xavier; Houston—Alec Kessler, Georgia; LA Clippers (from Cleveland)—Loy Vaught, Michigan; Sacramento (from Indiana via Dallas)—Travis Mays, Texas; Miami (from Denver)—Dave Jamerson, Ohio; Milwaukee—Terry Mills, Michigan; New York—Jerrod Mustaf, Maryland; Sacramento (from Dallas)—Duane Causwell, Temple; Boston—Dee Brown, Jacksonville; Minnesota (from Philadelphia)—Gerald Glass, Mississippi; Phoenix—Jayson Williams, St. John's; New Jersey (from Chicago)—Tate George, Connecticut; Sacramento (from Utah)—Anthony Bonner, St. Louis; San Antonio—Dwayne Schintzius, Florida; Portland—Alaa Abdelnaby, Duke; Detroit—Lance Blanks, Texas; LA Lakers—Elden Campbell, Clemson.

SECOND ROUND Golden State (from New Jersey via Atlanta)—Les Jepsen, Iowa; Chicago (from Orlando)—Toni Kukoc, Yugoslavia; Miami—Carl Herrera, Houston; Phoenix (from Charlotte)—Negele Knight, Dayton; Philadelphia (from Minnesota)—Brian Oliver, Georgia Tech; Utah (from Sacramento)—Walter Palmer, Dartmouth; Golden State (from LA Clippers)—Kevin Pritchard, Kansas; Washington—Greg Foster, Texas-El Paso; Atlanta (from Golden State)—Trevor Wilson, UCLA; Washington (from Atlanta)—A. J. English, Virginia Union; Seattle—Jud Buechler, Arizona; Charlotte (from Houston)—Steve Scheffler, Purdue; Sacramento (from Indiana)—Bimbo Coles, Virginia Tech; Atlanta (from Cleveland via Miami and Golden State)—Steve Bardo, Illinois; Denver—Marcus Liberty, Illinois; San Antonio (from Milwaukee)—Tony Massenburg, Maryland; Milwaukee (from New York via Seattle)—Steve Henson, Kansas State; Indiana (from Dallas)—Antonio Davis, Texas-El Paso; Indiana (from Boston)—Kenny Williams, Elizabeth City State; Philadelphia—Derek Strong, Xavier; Phoenix—Cedric Ceballos, California-Fullerton; Dallas (from Utah via Sacramento)—Phil Henderson, Duke; Phoenix (from Chicago)—Milos Babic, Tennessee Tech; LA Lakers (from San Antonio)—Tony Smith, Marquette; Cleveland (from Detroit via Philadelphia)—Stefano Rusconi, Italy; Seattle (from Portland)—Abdul Shamsid-Deen, Providence; San Antonio (from LA Lakers)—Sean Higgins, Michigan.

1991 (JUNE 26, 1991)

FIRST ROUND Charlotte—Larry Johnson, UNLV; New Jersey—Kenny Anderson, Georgia Tech; Sacramento—Billy Owens, Syracuse; Denver—Dikembe Mutombo, Georgetown; Miami—Steve Smith, Michigan State; Dallas—Doug Smith, Missouri; Minnesota—Luc Longley, New Mexico; Denver (from Washington)—Mark Macon, Temple; Atlanta (from LA Clippers)—Stacey Augmon, UNLV; Orlando—Brian Williams, Arizona; Cleveland—Terrell Brandon, Oregon; New York—Greg Anthony, UNLV; Indiana—Dale Davis, Clemson; Seattle—Rich King, Nebraska; Atlanta—Anthony Avent, Seton Hall; Golden State (from Philadelphia)—Chris Gatling, Old Dominion; Golden State—Victor Alexander, Iowa State; Milwaukee—Kevin Brooks, Southwestern Louisiana; Washington (from Detroit, via Dallas and Denver)—LaBradford Smith, Louisville; Houston—John Turner, Phillips University; Utah—Eric Murdock, Providence; LA Clippers (from Phoenix via Seattle)—LeRon Ellis, Syracuse; Orlando (from San Antonio)—Stanley Roberts, LSU; Boston—Rick Fox, North Carolina; Golden State (from LA Lakers)—Shaun Vandiver, Colorado; Chicago—Mark Randall, Kansas; Sacramento (from Portland)—Pete Chilcutt, North Carolina.

SECOND ROUND Charlotte (from Denver)—Kevin Lynch, Minnesota; Miami—George Ackles, UNLV; Atlanta (from Sacramento)—Rodney Monroe, North Carolina State; Sacramento (from New Jersey)—Randy Brown, New Mexico State; Phoenix (from Charlotte)—Chad Gallagher, Creighton; Dallas—Donald Hodge, Temple; Minnesota—Myron Brown, Slippery Rock; Dallas (from Washington via Sacramento)—Mike Iuzzolino, St. Francis (Pa.); Orlando—Chris Corchiani, North Carolina State; LA Clippers—Elliot Perry, Memphis State; LA Clippers (from Cleveland)—Joe Wylie, Miami (Fla.); Cleveland (from New York via

Charlotte)—Jimmy Oliver, Purdue; Detroit (from Seattle)—Doug Overton, LaSalle; Indiana—Sean Green, Iona; Sacramento (from Atlanta)—Steve Hood, James Madison; Golden State—Lamont Strothers, Christopher Newport; Philadelphia—Alvaro Teheran, Houston; Milwaukee—Bobby Phills, Southern; Phoenix (from Detroit)—Richard Dumas, Oklahoma State; Houston—Keith Hughes, Rutgers; Utah—Isaac Austin, Arizona State; San Antonio—Greg Sutton, Oral Roberts; Phoenix—Joey Wright, Texas; Houston (from Boston, via New Jersey and Cleveland)—Zan Tabak, Yugoslavia; LA Lakers—Anthony Jones, Oral Roberts; New Jersey (from Chicago)—Von McDade, Wisconsin-Milwaukee; Portland—Marcus Kennedy, Eastern Michigan.

1992 (JUNE 24, 1992)

FIRST ROUND Orlando—Shaquille O'Neal, LSU; Charlotte—Alonzo Mourning, Georgetown; Minnesota—Christian Laettner, Duke; Dallas—Jimmy Jackson, Ohio State; Denver—LaPhonso Ellis, Notre Dame; Washington—Tom Gugliotta, North Carolina State; Sacramento—Walt Williams, Maryland; Milwaukee—Todd Day, Arkansas; Philadelphia—Clarence Weatherspoon, Southern Mississippi; Atlanta—Adam Keefe, Stanford; Houston—Robert Horry, Alabama; Miami—Harold Miner, USC; Denver (from New Jersey)—Bryant Stith, Virginia; Indiana—Malik Sealy, St. John's; LA Lakers—Anthony Peeler, Missouri; LA Clippers—Randy Woods, LaSalle; Seattle—Doug Christie, Pepperdine; San Antonio—Tracy Murray, UCLA; Detroit—Don MacLean, UCLA; New York—Hubert Davis, North Carolina; Boston—Jon Barry, Georgia Tech; Phoenix—Oliver Miller, Arkansas; Milwaukee (from Utah)—Lee Mayberry, Arkansas; Golden State—Latrell Sprewell, Alabama; LA Clippers (from Cleveland)—Elmore Spencer, UNLV; Portland—David Johnson, Syracuse; Chicago—Byron Houston, Oklahoma State.

SECOND ROUND Minnesota—Marlon Maxey, UTEP; New Jersey (from Orlando via Chicago)—P. J. Brown, Louisiana Tech; Dallas—Sean Rooks, Arizona; Portland (from Denver)—Reggie Smith, TCU; Washington—Brent Price, Oklahoma; Chicago (from Sacramento)—Corey Williams, Oklahoma State; Minnesota (from Milwaukee)—Chris Smith, Connecticut; Charlotte—Tony Bennett, Wisconsin-Green Bay; LA Lakers (from Philadelphia via Minnesota and Milwaukee)—Duane Cooper, USC; Miami—Isaiah Morris, Arkansas; Atlanta—Elmer Bennett, Notre Dame; Chicago (from Indiana)—Litterial Green, Georgia; New Jersey—Steve Rogers, Alabama State; Houston—Ronald "Popeye" Jones, Murray State; Miami (from LA Lakers)—Matt Geiger, Georgia Tech; Golden State (from LA Clippers)—Predrag Danilovic, Yugoslavia; San Antonio—Henry Williams, UNC-Charlotte; Seattle—Chris King, Wake Forest; Denver (from Detroit)—Robert Werdann, St. John's; Boston—Darren Morningstar, Pittsburgh; Phoenix (from New York)—Brian Davis, Duke; Phoenix—Ron Ellis, Louisiana Tech; Golden State—Matt Fish, UNC-Wilmington; Minnesota (from Utah)—Tim Burroughs, Jacksonville; Chicago (from Portland)—Matt Steigenga, Michigan State; Houston (from Cleveland)—Curtis Blair, Richmond; Sacramento (from Chicago via Portland)—Brett Roberts, Morehead State.

1993 (JUNE 30, 1993)

FIRST ROUND Orlando—Chris Webber, Michigan; Philadelphia—Shawn Bradley, Brigham Young; Golden State—Anfernee Hardaway, Memphis State; Dallas—Jamal Mashburn, Kentucky; Minnesota—J. R. Rider, UNLV; Washington—Calbert Cheaney, Indiana; Sacramento—Bobby Hurley, Duke; Milwaukee—Vin Baker, Hartford; Denver—Rodney Rogers, Wake Forest; Detroit (from Miami)—Lindsey Hunter, Jackson State; Detroit—Allan Houston, Tennessee; LA Lakers—George Lynch, North Carolina; LA Clippers—Terry Dehere, Seton Hall; Indiana—Scott Haskin, Oregon State; Atlanta—Doug Edwards, Florida State; New

Jersey—Rex Walters, Kansas; Charlotte—Greg Graham, Indiana; Utah—Luther Wright, Seton Hall; Boston—Acie Earl, Iowa; Charlotte (from San Antonio)—Scott Burrell, Connecticut; Portland—James Robinson, Alabama; Cleveland—Chris Mills, Arizona; Seattle—Ervin Johnson, New Orleans; Houston—Sam Cassell, Florida State; Chicago—Corie Blount, Cincinnati; Orlando (from New York)—Geert Hammink, LSU; Phoenix—Malcolm Mackey, Georgia Tech.

SECOND ROUND Dallas—Lucious Harris, Long Beach State; Minnesota—Sherron Mills; Virginia Commonwealth; Washington—Gheorge Muresan, Romania; Sacramento—Evers Burns, Maryland; Philadelphia—Alphonso Ford, Mississippi Valley State; Dallas (from Milwaukee)—Eric Riley, Michigan; Golden State—Darnell Mee, Western Kentucky; Miami—Ed Stokes, Arizona; New Jersey (from Denver via Washington)—John Best, Tennessee Tech; LA Lakers—Nick Van Exel, Cincinnati; Washington (from Detroit)—Conrad McRae, Syracuse; Indiana—Thomas Hill, Duke; Atlanta (from LA Clippers)—Richard Manning, Washington; Chicago (from Orlando)—Anthony Reed, Tulane; Seattle (from New Jersey via Orlando)—Adonis Jordan, Kansas; Denver (from Atlanta)—Josh Grant, Utah; Sacramento (from Charlotte)—Alex Holcombe, Baylor; Utah—Bryon Russell, Long Beach State; Houston (from Boston via New Jersey and Cleveland)—Richard Petruska, UCLA; San Antonio—Chris Whitney, Clemson; Portland (from Portland via Denver)—Kevin Thompson, North Carolina State; Phoenix (from Cleveland)—Mark Buford, Mississippi Valley State; Houston—Marcelo Nicola, Argentina; Indiana (from Seattle)—Spencer Dunkley, Delaware; Sacramento (from Chicago via Seattle)—Mike Peplowski, Michigan State; LA Clippers (from New York)—Leonard White, Southern; Phoenix—Byron Wilson, Utah.

1994 (JUNE 29, 1994)

FIRST ROUND Milwaukee—Glenn Robinson, Purdue; Dallas—Jason Kidd, California; Detroit—Grant Hill, Duke; Minnesota—Donyell Marshall, Connecticut; Washington—Juwan Howard, Michigan; Philadelphia—Sharone Wright, Clemson; LA Clippers—Lamond Murray, California; Sacramento—Brian Grant, Xavier; Boston—Eric Montross, North Carolina; LA Lakers—Eddie Jones, Temple; Seattle (from Charlotte)—Carlos Rogers, Tennessee State; Miami—Khalid Reeves, Arizona; Denver—Jalen Rose, Michigan; New Jersey—Yinka Dare, George Washington; Indiana—Eric Piatkowski, Nebraska; Golden State (from Cleveland)—Cliff Rozier, Louisville; Portland—Aaron McKie, Temple; Milwaukee (from Orlando)—Eric Mobley, Pittsburgh; Dallas (from Golden State)—Tony Dumas, Missouri-Kansas City; Philadelphia (from Utah)—B. J. Tyler, Texas; Chicago—Dickey Simpkins, Providence; San Antonio—Bill Curley, Boston College; Phoenix—Wesley Person, Auburn; New York—Monty Williams, Notre Dame; LA Clippers (from Atlanta)—Greg Minor, Louisville; New York (from Houston)—Charlie Ward, Florida State; Orlando (from Seattle)—Brooks Thompson, Oklahoma State.

SECOND ROUND Dallas—Deon Thomas, Illinois; Phoenix (from Detroit)—Antonio Lang, Duke; Minnesota—Howard Eisley, Boston College; Orlando (from Milwaukee)—Rodney Dent, Kentucky; Washington—Jim McIlvaine, Marquette; Philadelphia—Derrick Alston, Duquesne; Atlanta (from LA Clippers)—Gaylon Nickerson, NW Oklahoma State; Sacramento—Michael Smith, Providence; Boston—Andrei Fetisov, Russia; Seattle (from LA Lakers)—Dontonio Wingfield, Cincinnati; Charlotte—Darrin Hancock, Kansas; Golden State (from Denver)—Anthony Miller, Michigan State; Miami—Jeff Webster, Oklahoma; Indiana (from New Jersey)—William Njoku, St. Mary's (Canada); Cleveland—Gary Collier, Tulsa; Portland—Shawnelle Scott, St. John's; Indiana—Damon Bailey, Indiana; Golden State—Dwayne Morton, Louisville; Milwaukee (from Orlando)—Voshon Lenard, Minnesota; Utah—Jamie Watson, South Carolina; Detroit (from San Antonio)—Jevon Crudup, Missouri; Chicago—Kris Bruton, Benedict; Phoenix—Charles Claxton, Georgia; Sacramento (from Atlanta)—Lawrence Funderburke, Ohio State; Phoenix (from New York)—Anthony Goldwire, Houston; Houston—Albert Burditt, Texas; Seattle—Zeljko Rebraca, Serbia.

TEAM-BY-TEAM FIRST-ROUND DRAFT PICKS
*First player chosen overall in draft.

The following list of current NBA teams includes selections that reflect the previous cities in the history of a franchise. See ''The Family Tree'' on pages 24–25.

ATLANTA HAWKS

1947—Jack Underman, Ohio State
1948—Easy Parham, Texas Western
1949—Ed Macauley, St. Louis
1950—Bob Cousy, Holy Cross
1951—Mel Hutchins, Brigham Young
1952—Not available
1953—Bob Houbregs, Washington
1954—Bob Pettit, Louisiana State
1955—Not available
1956—Bill Russell, San Francisco
1957—Win Wilfong, Memphis State
1958—Dave Gambee, Oregon State
1959—Bob Ferry, St. Louis
1960—Lenny Wilkens, Providence
1961—Cleo Hill, Winston-Salem
1962—Zelmo Beaty, Prairie View
1963—Jerry Ward, Boston College
1964—Jeff Mullins, Duke
1965—Jim Washington, Villanova
1966—Lou Hudson, Minnesota
1967—Tim Workman, Seattle
1968—Skip Harlicka, South Carolina
1969—Butch Beard, Louisville
1970—Pete Maravich, Louisiana State
　　　John Vallely, UCLA
1971—George Trapp, Long Beach State
1972—(No first-round selection)
1973—Dwight Jones, Houston
　　　John Brown, Missouri
1974—Tom Henderson, Hawaii
　　　Mike Sojourner, Utah
1975—David Thompson, North Carolina State*
　　　Marvin Webster, Morgan State
1976—Armond Hill, Princeton
1977—Wayne Rollins, Clemson
1978—Butch Lee, Marquette
　　　Jack Givens, Kentucky
1979—(No first-round selection)
1980—Don Collins, Washington State
1981—Al Wood, North Carolina
1982—Keith Edmonson, Purdue
1983—(No first-round selection)
1984—Kevin Willis, Michigan State
1985—Jon Koncak, Southern Methodist
1986—Billy Thompson, Louisville
1987—Dallas Comegys, DePaul
1988—(No first-round selection)
1989—Roy Marble, Iowa
1990—Rumeal Robinson, Michigan
1991—Stacey Augmon, UNLV
　　　Anthony Avent, Seton Hall
1992—Adam Keefe, Stanford
1993—Doug Edwards, Florida State
1994—(No first-round selection)

BOSTON CELTICS

1947—Ed Ehlers, Purdue
1948—George Hauptfuehrer, Harvard
1949—Tony Lavelli, Yale
1950—Charlie Share, Bowling Green
1951—Ernie Barrett, Kansas State
1952—Bill Stauffer, Missouri
1953—Frank Ramsey, Kentucky
1954—Togo Palazzi, Holy Cross
1955—Jim Loscutoff, Oregon
1956—Tom Heinsohn, Holy Cross

1957—Sam Jones, North Carolina Central
1958—Ben Swain, Texas Southern
1959—John Richter, North Carolina State
1960—Tom Sanders, NYU
1961—Gary Phillips, Houston
1962—John Havlicek, Ohio State
1963—Bill Green, Colorado State
1964—Mel Counts, Oregon State
1965—Ollie Johnson, San Francisco
1966—Jim Barnett, Oregon
1967—Mal Graham, NYU
1968—Don Chaney, Houston
1969—Jo Jo White, Kansas
1970—Dave Cowens, Florida State
1971—Clarence Glover, Western Kentucky
1972—Paul Westphal, Southern California
1973—Steve Downing, Indiana
1974—Glenn McDonald, Long Beach State
1975—Tom Boswell, South Carolina
1976—Norm Cook, Kansas
1977—Cedric Maxwell, North Carolina-Charlotte
1978—Larry Bird, Indiana State
　　　Freeman Williams, Portland State
1979—(No first-round selection)
1980—Kevin McHale, Minnesota
1981—Charles Bradley, Wyoming
1982—Darren Tillis, Cleveland State
1983—Greg Kite, Brigham Young
1984—Michael Young, Houston
1985—Sam Vincent, Michigan State
1986—Len Bias, Maryland
1987—Reggie Lewis, Northeastern
1988—Brian Shaw, California-Santa Barbara
1989—Michael Smith, Brigham Young
1990—Dee Brown, Jacksonville
1991—Rick Fox, North Carolina
1992—Jon Barry, Georgia Tech
1993—Acie Earl, Iowa
1994—Eric Montross, North Carolina

CHARLOTTE HORNETS

1988—Rex Chapman, Kentucky
1989—J. R. Reid, North Carolina
1990—Kendall Gill, Illinois
1991—Larry Johnson, UNLV*
1992—Alonzo Mourning, Georgetown
1993—Greg Graham, Indiana
　　　Scott Burrell, Connecticut
1994—(No first-round selection)

CHICAGO BULLS

1966—Dave Schellhase, Purdue
1967—Clem Haskins, Western Kentucky
1968—Tom Boerwinkle, Tennessee
1969—Larry Cannon, LaSalle
1970—Jimmy Collins, New Mexico State
1971—Kennedy McIntosh, Eastern Michigan
1972—Ralph Simpson, Michigan State
1973—Kevin Kunnert, Iowa
1974—Maurice Lucas, Marquette
　　　Cliff Pondexter, Long Beach State
1975—(No first-round selection)
1976—Scott May, Indiana
1977—Tate Armstrong, Duke
1978—Reggie Theus, UNLV

1979—David Greenwood, UCLA
1980—Kelvin Ransey, Ohio State
1981—Orlando Woolridge, Notre Dame
1982—Quintin Dailey, San Francisco
1983—Sidney Green, UNLV
1984—Michael Jordan, North Carolina
1985—Keith Lee, Memphis State
1986—Brad Sellers, Ohio State
1987—Olden Polynice, Virginia
　　　Horace Grant, Clemson
1988—Will Perdue, Vanderbilt
1989—Stacey King, Oklahoma
　　　B.J. Armstrong, Iowa
　　　Jeff Sanders, Georgia Southern
1990—(No first-round selection)
1991—Mark Randall, Kansas
1992—Byron Houston, Oklahoma State
1993—Corie Blount, Cincinnati
1994—Dickey Simpkins, Providence

CLEVELAND CAVALIERS

1970—John Johnson, Iowa
1971—Austin Carr, Notre Dame*
1972—Dwight Davis, Houston
1973—Jim Brewer, Minnesota
1974—Campy Russell, Michigan
1975—John Lambert, Southern Cal
1976—Chuckie Williams, Kansas State
1977—(No first-round selection)
1978—Mike Mitchell, Auburn
1979—(No first-round selection)
1980—Chad Kinch, UNC-Charlotte
1981—(No first-round selection)
1982—John Bagley, Boston College
1983—Roy Hinson, Rutgers
　　　Stewart Granger, Villanova
1984—Tim McCormick, Michigan
1985—Charles Oakley, Virginia Union
1986—Brad Daugherty, North Carolina*
　　　Ron Harper, Miami (Ohio)
1987—Kevin Johnson, California
1988—Randolph Keys, Southern Mississippi
1989—John Morton, Seton Hall
1990—(No first-round selection)
1991—Terrell Brandon, Oregon
1992—(No first-round selection)
1993—Chris Mills, Arizona
1994—(No first-round selection)

DALLAS MAVERICKS

1980—Kiki Vandeweghe, UCLA
1981—Mark Aguirre, DePaul*
　　　Rolando Blackman, Kansas State
1982—Bill Garnett, Wyoming
1983—Dale Ellis, Tennessee
　　　Derek Harper, Illinois
1984—Sam Perkins, North Carolina
　　　Terence Stansbury, Temple
1985—Detlef Schrempf, Washington
　　　Bill Wennington, St. John's
　　　Uwe Blab, Indiana
1986—Roy Tarpley, Michigan
1987—Jim Farmer, Alabama

1988—(No first-round selection)
1989—Randy White, Louisiana Tech
1990—(No first-round selection)
1991—Doug Smith, Missouri
1992—Jimmy Jackson, Ohio State
1993—Jamal Mashburn, Kentucky
1994—Jason Kidd, California
       Tony Dumas, Missouri-Kansas City

DENVER NUGGETS

1967—Walt Frazier, Southern Illinois
1968—Tom Boerwinkle, Tennessee
1969—Bob Presley, California
1970—Spencer Haywood, Detroit
1971—Ralph Simpson, Michigan State
       Cliff Meely, Colorado
1972—Bud Stallworth, Kansas
1973—Ed Ratleff, Long Beach State
1974—James Williams, Austin Peay
1975—Marvin Webster, Morgan State
1976—(No first-round selection)
1977—Tom LaGarde, North Carolina
       Anthony Roberts, Oral Roberts
1978—Rod Griffin, Wake Forrest
       Mike Evans, Kansas State
1979—(No first-round selection)
1980—James Ray, Jacksonville
       Carl Nicks, Indiana State
1981—(No first-round selection)
1982—Rob Williams, Houston
1983—Howard Carter, Louisiana State
1984—(No first-round selection)
1985—Blair Rasmussen, Oregon
1986—Maurice Martin, St. Joseph's
       Mark Alarie, Duke
1987—(No first-round selection)
1988—Jerome Lane, Pittsburgh
1989—Todd Lichti, Stanford
1990—Chris Jackson, LSU
1991—Dikembe Mutombo, Georgetown
       Mark Macon, Temple
1992—LaPhonso Ellis, Notre Dame
       Bryant Stith, Virginia
1993—Rodney Rogers, Wake Forest
1994—Jalen Rose, Michigan

DETROIT PISTONS

1948—Dick Triptow, DePaul
1949—Bob Harris, Oklahoma A&M
1950—George Yardley, Stanford
1951—Zeke Sinicola, Niagara
1952—Not available
1953—Jack Molinas, Columbia
1954—Dick Rosenthal, Notre Dame
1955—Not available
1956—Ron Sobieszczk, DePaul
1957—Charles Tyra, Louisville
1958—(No first-round selection)
1959—Bailey Howell, Mississippi State
1960—Jackie Moreland, Louisiana Tech
1961—Ray Scott, Portland
1962—Dave DeBusschere, Detroit
1963—Eddie Miles, Seattle
1964—Joe Caldwell, Arizona State
1965—Bill Buntin, Michigan
1966—Dave Bing, Syracuse
1967—Jimmy Walker, Providence*
1968—Otto Moore, Pan American
1969—Terry Driscoll, Boston College
1970—Bob Lanier, St. Bonaventure*
1971—Curtis Rowe, UCLA
1972—Bob Nash, Hawaii

1973—(No first-round selection)
1974—Al Eberhard, Missouri
1975—(No first-round selection)
1976—Leon Douglas, Alabama
1977—(No first-round selection)
1978—(No first-round selection)
1979—Greg Kelser, Michigan State
       Roy Hamilton, UCLA
       Phil Hubbard, Michigan
1980—Larry Drew, Missouri
1981—Isiah Thomas, Indiana
       Kelly Tripucka, Notre Dame
1982—Cliff Levingston, Wichita State
       Ricky Pierce, Rice
1983—Antoine Carr, Wichita State
1984—Tony Campbell, Ohio State
1985—Joe Dumars, McNeese State
1986—John Salley, Georgia Tech
1987—(No first-round selection)
1988—(No first-round selection)
1989—Kenny Battle, Illinois
1990—Lance Blanks, Texas
1991—(No first-round selection)
1992—Don MacLean, UCLA
1993—Lindsey Hunter, Jackson State
       Allan Houston, Tennessee
1994—Grant Hill, Duke

GOLDEN STATE WARRIORS

1947—Francis Crossin, Pennsylvania
1948—Phil Farbman, CCNY
1949—Vern Gardner, Utah
1950—Paul Arizin, Villanova
1951—Don Sunderlage, Illinois
1952—Bill Mlkvy, Temple
1953—Ernie Beck, Pennsylvania
1954—Gene Shue, Maryland
1955—Tom Gola, LaSalle
1956—Hal Lear, Temple
1957—Len Rosenbluth, North Carolina
1958—Guy Rodgers, Temple
1959—Wilt Chamberlain, Kansas
1960—Al Bunge, Maryland
1961—Tom Meschery, St. Mary's (Cal.)
1962—Wayne Hightower, Kansas
1963—Nate Thurmond, Bowling Green
1964—Barry Kramer, NYU
1965—Fred Hetzel, Davidson
1966—Clyde Lee, Vanderbilt
1967—Dave Lattin, Texas Western
1968—Ron Williams, West Virginia
1969—Bob Portman, Creighton
1970—(No first-round selection)
1971—Darnell Hillman, San Jose State
1972—(No first-round selection)
1973—Kevin Joyce, South Carolina
1974—Jamaal Wilkes, UCLA
1975—Joe Bryant, LaSalle
1976—Robert Parish, Centenary
       Sonny Parker, Texas A&M
1977—Rickey Green, Michigan
       Wesley Cox, Louisville
1978—Purvis Short, Jackson State
       Raymond Townsend, UCLA
1979—(No first-round selection)
1980—Joe Barry Carroll, Purdue*
       Rickey Brown, Mississippi State
1981—(No first-round selection)
1982—Lester Conner, Oregon State
1983—Russell Cross, Purdue
1984—(No first-round selection)
1985—Chris Mullin, St. John's

1986—Chris Washburn, North Carolina State
1987—Tellis Frank, Western Kentucky
1988—Mitch Richmond, Kansas State
1989—Tim Hardaway, Texas-El Paso
1990—Tyrone Hill, Xavier
1991—Chris Gatling, Old Dominion
       Victor Alexander, Iowa State
       Shaun Vandiver, Colorado
1992—Latrell Sprewell, Alabama
1993—Anfernee Hardaway, Memphis State
1994—Cliff Rozier, Louisville

HOUSTON ROCKETS

1967—Pat Riley, Kentucky
1968—Elvin Hayes, Houston*
1969—Bobby Smith, Tulsa
1970—Rudy Tomjanovich, Michigan
1971—Cliff Meely, Colorado
1972—(No first-round selection)
1973—Ed Ratleff, Long Beach State
1974—Bobby Jones, North Carolina
1975—Joe Meriweather, Southern Illinois
1976—John Lucas, Maryland*
1977—(No first-round selection)
1978—(No first-round selection)
1979—Lee Johnson, East Texas State
1980—(No first-round selection)
1981—(No first-round selection)
1982—Terry Teagle, Baylor
1983—Ralph Sampson, Virginia*
       Rodney McCray, Louisville
1984—Hakeem Olajuwon, Houston*
1985—Steve Harris, Tulsa
1986—Buck Johnson, Alabama
1987—(No first-round selection)
1988—Derrick Chievous, Missouri
1989—(No first-round selection)
1990—Alec Kessler, Georgia
1991—John Turner, Phillips
1992—Robert Horry, Alabama
1993—Sam Cassell, Florida State
1994—(No first-round selection)

INDIANA PACERS

1967—Jimmy Walker, Providence
1968—Don May, Dayton
1969—(No first-round selection)
1970—Rick Mount, Purdue
1971—(No first-round selection)
1972—George McGinnis, Indiana
1973—Steve Downing, Indiana
1974—Billy Knight, Pittsburgh
1975—Dan Roundfield, Central Michigan
1976—(No first-round selection)
1977—(No first-round selection)
1978—Rick Robey, Kentucky
1979—Dudley Bradley, North Carolina
1980—(No first-round selection)
1981—Herb Williams, Ohio State
1982—Clark Kellogg, Ohio State
1983—Steve Stipanovich, Missouri
       Mitchell Wiggins, Florida State
1984—Vern Fleming, Georgia
1985—Wayman Tisdale, Oklahoma
1986—Chuck Person, Auburn
1987—Reggie Miller, UCLA
1988—Rik Smits, Marist
1989—George McCloud, Florida State
1990—(No first-round selection)
1991—Dale Davis, Clemson
1992—Malik Sealy, St. John's

1993—Scott Haskin, Oregon State
1994—Eric Piatkowski, Nebraska

LOS ANGELES CLIPPERS

1970—John Hummer, Princeton
1971—Elmore Smith, Kentucky State
1972—Bob McAdoo, North Carolina
1973—Ernie DiGregorio, Providence
1974—Tom McMillen, Maryland
1975—(No first-round selection)
1976—Adrian Dantley, Notre Dame
1977—(No first-round selection)
1978—(No first-round selection)
1979—(No first-round selection)
1980—Michael Brooks, LaSalle
1981—Tom Chambers, Utah
1982—Terry Cummings, DePaul
1983—Byron Scott, Arizona State
1984—Lancaster Gordon, Louisville
        Michael Cage, San Diego State
1985—Benoit Benjamin, Creighton
1986—(No first-round selection)
1987—Reggie Williams, Georgetown
        Joe Wolf, North Carolina
        Ken Norman, Illinois
1988—Danny Manning, Kansas*
        Hersey Hawkins, Bradley
1989—Danny Ferry, Duke
1990—Bo Kimble, Loyola Marymount
        Loy Vaught, Michigan
1991—LeRon Ellis, Syracuse
1992—Randy Woods, LaSalle
        Elmore Spencer, UNLV
1993—Terry Dehere, Seton Hall
1994—Lamond Murray, California
        Greg Minor, Louisville

LOS ANGELES LAKERS

1948—Arnie Ferrin, Utah
1949—Vern Mikkelsen, Hamline
1950—Kevin O'Shea, Notre Dame
1951—Whitey Skoog, Minnesota
1952—Not available
1953—Jim Fritsche, Hamline
1954—Ed Kalafat, Minnesota
1955—Not available
1956—Jim Paxson, Dayton
1957—Jim Krebs, Southern Methodist
1958—Elgin Baylor, Seattle*
1959—Tom Hawkins, Notre Dame
1960—Jerry West, West Virginia
1961—Wayne Yates, Memphis State
1962—LeRoy Ellis, St. John's
1963—Roger Strickland, Jacksonville
1964—Walt Hazzard, UCLA
1965—Gail Goodrich, UCLA
1966—Jerry Chambers, Utah
1967—(No first-round selection)
1968—Bill Hewitt, Southern Cal
1969—Willie McCarter, Drake
        Rick Roberson, Cincinnati
1970—Jim McMillian, Columbia
1971—Jim Cleamons, Ohio State
1972—Travis Grant, Kentucky State
1973—Kermit Washington, American
1974—Brian Winters, South Carolina
1975—David Meyers, UCLA
        Junior Bridgeman, Louisville
1976—(No first-round selection)
1977—Ken Carr, North Carolina State
        Brad Davis, Maryland
        Norm Nixon, Duquesne

1978—(No first-round selection)
1979—Earvin Johnson, Michigan State*
        Brad Holland, UCLA
1980—(No first-round selection)
1981—Mike McGee, Michigan
1982—James Worthy, North Carolina*
1983—(No first-round selection)
1984—Earl Jones, District of Columbia
1985—A. C. Green, Oregon State
1986—Ken Barlow, Notre Dame
1987—(No first-round selection)
1988—David Rivers, Notre Dame
1989—Vlade Divac, Yugoslavia
1990—Elden Campbell, Clemson
1991—(No first-round selection)
1992—Anthony Peeler, Missouri
1993—George Lynch, North Carolina
1994—Eddie Jones, Temple

MIAMI HEAT

1988—Rony Seikaly, Syracuse
        Kevin Edwards, DePaul
1989—Glen Rice, Michigan
1990—Willie Burton, Minnesota
        Dave Jamerson, Ohio
1991—Steve Smith, Michigan State
1992—Harold Miner, Southern Cal
1993—(No first-round selection)
1994—Khalid Reeves, Arizona

MILWAUKEE BUCKS

1968—Charlie Paulk, Northeastern Oklahoma
1969—Kareem Abdul-Jabbar, UCLA*
1970—Gary Freeman, Oregon State
1971—Collis Jones, Notre Dame
1972—Russell Lee, Marshall
        Julius Erving, Massachusetts
1973—Swen Nater, UCLA
1974—Gary Brokaw, Notre Dame
1975—(No first-round selection)
1976—Quinn Buckner, Indiana
1977—Kent Benson, Indiana*
        Marques Johnson, UCLA
        Ernie Grunfeld, Tennessee
1978—George Johnson, St. John's
1979—Sidney Moncrief, Arkansas
1980—(No first-round selection)
1981—Alton Lister, Arizona State
1982—Paul Pressey, Tulsa
1983—Randy Breuer, Minnesota
1984—Kenny Fields, UCLA
1985—Jerry Reynolds, Louisiana State
1986—Scott Skiles, Michigan State
1987—(No first-round selection)
1988—Jeff Grayer, Iowa State
1989—(No first-round selection)
1990—Terry Mills, Michigan
1991—Kevin Brooks, SW Louisiana
1992—Todd Day, Arkansas
        Lee Mayberry, Arkansas
1993—Vin Baker, Hartford
1994—Glenn Robinson, Purdue*
        Eric Mobley, Pittsburgh

MINNESOTA TIMBERWOLVES

1989—Pooh Richardson, UCLA
1990—Felton Spencer, Louisville
        Gerald Glass, Mississippi
1991—Luc Longley, New Mexico

1992—Christian Laettner, Duke
1993—J. R. Rider, UNLV
1994—Donyell Marshall, Connecticut

NEW JERSEY NETS

1967—Sonny Dove, St. John's
1968—Joe Allen, Bradley
1969—Kareem Abdul-Jabbar, UCLA
1970—Bob Lanier, St. Bonaventure
1971—Charles Davis, Wake Forest
1972—Jim Chones, Marquette
1973—Doug Collins, Illinois State
1974—Brian Winters, South Carolina
1975—John Lucas, Maryland
1976—(No first-round selection)
1977—Bernard King, Tennessee
1978—Winford Boynes, San Francisco
1979—Calvin Natt, Northeast Louisiana
        Cliff Robinson, Southern Cal
1980—Mike O'Koren, North Carolina
        Mike Gminski, Duke
1981—Buck Williams, Maryland
        Albert King, Maryland
        Ray Tolbert, Indiana
1982—Eric Floyd, Georgetown
        Eddie Phillips, Alabama
1983—(No first-round selection)
1984—Jeff Turner, Vanderbilt
1985—(No first-round selection)
1986—Dwayne Washington, Syracuse
1987—Dennis Hopson, Ohio State
1988—Chris Morris, Auburn
1989—Mookie Blaylock, Oklahoma
1990—Derrick Coleman, Syracuse*
        Tate George, Connecticut
1991—Kenny Anderson, Georgia Tech
1992—(No first-round selection)
1993—Rex Walters, Kansas
1994—Yinka Dare, George Washington

NEW YORK KNICKERBOCKERS

1947—Wat Misaka, Utah
1948—Harry Gallatin, NE Missouri State
1949—Dick McGuire, St. John's
1950—Not available
1951—Not available
1952—Ralph Polson, Whitworth
1953—Walter Dukes, Seton Hall
1954—Jack Turner, Western Kentucky
1955—Ken Sears, Santa Clara
1956—Ronnie Shavlik, North Carolina State
1957—Brendan McCann, St. Bonaventure
1958—Mike Farmer, San Francisco
1959—Johnny Green, Michigan State
1960—Darrall Imhoff, California
1961—Tom Stith, St. Bonaventure
1962—Paul Hogue, Cincinnati
1963—Art Heyman, Duke*
1964—Jim Barnes, Texas Western*
1965—Bill Bradley, Princeton*
1966—Cazzie Russell, Michigan*
1967—Walt Frazier, Southern Illinois
1968—Bill Hosket, Ohio State
1969—John Warren, St. John's
1970—Mike Price, Illinois
1971—Dean Meminger, Marquette
1972—Tom Riker, South Carolina
1973—Mel Davis, St. John's
1974—(No first-round selection)
1975—Eugene Short, Jackson State
1976—(No first-round selection)

1977—Ray Williams, Minnesota
1978—Micheal Ray Richardson, Montana
1979—Bill Cartwright, San Francisco
    Larry Demic, Arizona
    Sylvester Williams, Rhode Island
1980—Mike Woodson, Indiana
1981—(No first-round selection)
1982—Trent Tucker, Minnesota
1983—Darrell Walker, Arkansas
1984—(No first-round selection)
1985—Patrick Ewing, Georgetown*
1986—Kenny Walker, Kentucky
1987—Mark Jackson, St. John's
1988—Rod Strickland, DePaul
1989—(No first-round selection)
1990—Jerrod Mustaf, Maryland
1991—Greg Anthony, UNLV
1992—Hubert Davis, North Carolina
1993—(No first-round selection)
1994—Monty Williams, Notre Dame
    Charlie Ward, Florida State

ORLANDO MAGIC

1989—Nick Anderson, Illinois
1990—Dennis Scott, Georgia Tech
1991—Brian Williams, Arizona
    Stanley Roberts, LSU
1992—Shaquille O'Neal, LSU*
1993—Chris Webber, Michigan*
    Geert Hammink, LSU
1994—Brooks Thompson, Oklahoma State

PHILADELPHIA 76ERS

1950—Don Lofgran, San Francisco
1951—John McConathy, Northwestern Louisiana
1952—(unavailable)
1953—James Neal, Wolford
1954—John Kerr, Illinois
1955—(unavailable)
1956—Joe Holup, George Washington
1957—George BonSalle, Illinois
1958—Connie Dierking, Cincinnati
1959—Dick Barnett, Tennessee State
1960—Lee Shaffer, North Carolina
1961—Ben Warley, Tennessee A&I
1962—Len Chappell, Wake Forest
1963—Tom Hoover, Villanova
1964—Luke Jackson, Pan American
1965—Billy Cunningham, North Carolina
1966—Matt Guokas, St. Joseph's
1967—Craig Raymond, Brigham Young
1968—Shaler Halimon, Utah State
1969—Bud Ogden, Santa Clara
1970—Al Henry, Wisconsin
1971—Dana Lewis, Tulsa
1972—Fred Boyd, Oregon State
1973—Doug Collins, Illinois State*
    Raymond Lewis, Los Angeles State
1974—Marvin Barnes, Providence
1975—Darryl Dawkins, no college
1976—Terry Furlow, Michigan State
1977—Glenn Mosley, Seton Hall
1978—(No first-round selection)
1979—Jim Spanarkel, Duke
1980—Andrew Toney, Southwestern Louisiana
    Monti Davis, Tennessee State
1981—Franklin Edwards, Cleveland State
1982—Mark McNamara, California
1983—Leo Rautins, Syracuse

1984—Charles Barkley, Auburn
    Leon Wood, Cal State-Fullerton
    Tom Sewell, Lamar
1985—Terry Catledge, South Alabama
1986—(No first-round selection)
1987—Chris Welp, Washington
1988—Charles Smith, Pittsburgh
1989—Kenny Payne, Louisville
1990—(No first-round selection)
1991—(No first-round selection)
1992—Clarence Weatherspoon, Southern Mississippi
1993—Shawn Bradley, Brigham Young
1994—Sharone Wright, Clemson
    B. J. Tyler, Texas

PHOENIX SUNS

1968—Gary Gregor, South Carolina
1969—Neal Walk, Florida
1970—Greg Howard, New Mexico
1971—John Roche, South Carolina
1972—Corky Calhoun, Pennsylvania
1973—Mike Bantom, St. Joseph's
1974—John Shumate, Notre Dame
1975—Alvan Adams, Oklahoma
    Ricky Sobers, Nevada-Las Vegas
1976—Ron Lee, Oregon
1977—Walter Davis, North Carolina
1978—Marty Byrnes, Syracuse
1979—Kyle Macy, Kentucky
1980—(No first-round selection)
1981—Larry Nance, Clemson
1982—David Thirdkill, Bradley
1983—(No first-round selection)
1984—Jay Humphries, Colorado
1985—Ed Pinckney, Villanova
1986—William Bedford, Memphis State
1987—Armon Gilliam, UNLV
1988—Tim Perry, Temple
    Dan Majerle, Central Michigan
1989—Anthony Cook, Arizona
1990—Jayson Williams, St. John's
1991—(No first-round selection)
1992—Oliver Miller, Arkansas
1993—Malcolm Mackey, Georgia Tech
1994—Wesley Person, Auburn

PORTLAND TRAIL BLAZERS

1970—Geoff Petrie, Princeton
1971—Sidney Wicks, UCLA
1972—LaRue Martin, Loyola (Ill.)*
1973—Barry Parkhill, Virginia
1974—Bill Walton, UCLA*
1975—Lionel Hollins, Arizona State
1976—Wally Walker, Virginia
1977—Rich Laurel, Hofstra
1978—Mychal Thompson, Minnesota*
    Ron Brewer, Arkansas
1979—Jim Paxson, Dayton
1980—Ronnie Lester, Iowa
1981—Jeff Lamp, Virginia
    Darnell Valentine, Kansas
1982—Lafayette Lever, Arizona State
1983—Clyde Drexler, Houston
1984—Sam Bowie, Kentucky
    Bernard Thompson, Fresno State
1985—Terry Porter, Wisconsin-Stevens Point
1986—Walter Berry, St. John's
    Arvydas Sabonis, Soviet Union
1987—Ronnie Murphy, Jacksonville
1988—Mark Bryant, Seton Hall

1989—Byron Irvin, Missouri
1990—Alaa Abdelnaby, Duke
1991—(No first-round selection)
1992—David Johnson, Syracuse
1993—James Robinson, Alabama
1994—Aaron McKie, Temple

SACRAMENTO KINGS

1948—Bobby Wanzer, Seton Hall
1949—Frank Saul, Seton Hall
1950—Joe McNamee, San Francisco
1951—Sam Ranzino, North Carolina State
1952—Not available
1953—Richie Regan, Seton Hall
1954—Tom Marshall, Western Kentucky
1955—Not available
1956—Si Green, Duquesne
1957—Rod Hundley, West Virginia*
1958—Archie Dees, Indiana
1959—Bob Boozer, Kansas State*
1960—Oscar Robertson, Cincinnati*
1961—Larry Siegfried, Ohio State
1962—Jerry Lucas, Ohio State
1963—Tom Thacker, Cincinnati
1964—George Wilson, Cincinnati
1965—Nate Bowman, Wichita State
1966—Walt Wesley, Kansas
1967—Mel Daniels, New Mexico
1968—Don Smith, Iowa State
1969—Herm Gilliam, Purdue
1970—Sam Lacey, New Mexico State
1971—Ken Durrett, LaSalle
1972—Nate Williams, Utah State
1973—Ron Behagen, Minnesota
1974—Scott Wedman, Colorado
1975—Bill Robinzine, DePaul
    Bob Bigelow, Pennsylvania
1976—Richard Washington, UCLA
1977—Otis Birdsong, Houston
1978—Phil Ford, North Carolina
1979—Reggie King, Alabama
1980—Hawkeye Whitney, North Carolina State
1981—Steve Johnson, Oregon State
    Kevin Loder, Alabama State
1982—LaSalle Thompson, Texas
    Brook Steppe, Georgia Tech
1983—Ennis Whatley, Alabama
1984—Otis Thorpe, Providence
1985—Joe Kleine, Arkansas
1986—Harold Pressley, Villanova
1987—Kenny Smith, North Carolina
1988—Ricky Berry, San Jose State
1989—Pervis Ellison, Louisville*
1990—Lionel Simmons, La Salle
    Travis Mays, Texas
    Duane Causwell, Temple
    Anthony Bonner, St. Louis
1991—Billy Owens, Syracuse
    Pete Chilcutt, North Carolina
1992—Walt Williams, Maryland
1993—Bobby Hurley, Duke
1994—Brian Grant, Xavier

SAN ANTONIO SPURS

1967—Matt Aitch, Michigan State
1968—Shaler Halimon, Utah State
1969—Willie Brown, Middle Tennessee
1970—Nate Archibald, Texas-El Paso
1971—Stan Love, Oregon
1972—LaRue Martin, Loyola (Ill.)

1973—Kevin Kunnert, Iowa
1974—Leonard Robinson, Tennessee
1975—Mark Olberding, Minnesota
1976—(No first-round selection)
1977—(No first-round selection)
1978—Frankie Sanders, Southern
1979—Wiley Peck, Mississippi State
1980—Reggie Johnson, Tennessee
1981—(No first-round selection)
1982—(No first-round selection)
1983—John Paxson, Notre Dame
1984—Alvin Robertson, Arkansas
1985—Alfredrick Hughes, Loyola (Ill.)
1986—Johnny Dawkins, Duke
1987—David Robinson, Navy*
　　　Greg Anderson, Houston
1988—Willie Anderson, Georgia
1989—Sean Elliott, Arizona
1990—Dwayne Schintzius, Florida
1991—(No first-round selection)
1992—Tracy Murray, UCLA
1993—(No first-round selection)
1994—Bill Curley, Boston College

SEATTLE SUPERSONICS

1967—Al Tucker, Oklahoma Baptist
1968—Bob Kauffman, Guilford
1969—Lucius Allen, UCLA
1970—Jim Ard, Cincinnati
1971—Fred Brown, Iowa
1972—Bud Stallworth, Kansas
1973—Mike Green, Louisiana Tech
1974—Tom Burleson, North Carolina State
1975—Frank Oleynick, Seattle
1976—Bob Wilkerson, Indiana
1977—Jack Sikma, Illinois Wesleyan
1978—(No first-round selection)
1979—James Bailey, Rutgers
　　　Vinnie Johnson, Baylor
1980—Bill Hanzlik, Notre Dame

1981—Danny Vranes, Utah
1982—(No first-round selection)
1983—Jon Sundvold, Missouri
1984—(No first-round selection)
1985—Xavier McDaniel, Wichita State
1986—(No first-round selection)
1987—Scottie Pippen, Central Arkansas
　　　Derrick McKey, Alabama
1988—Gary Grant, Michigan
1989—Dana Barros, Boston College
　　　Shawn Kemp, Trinity JC
1990—Gary Payton, Oregon State
1991—Rich King, Nebraska
1992—Doug Christie, Pepperdine
1993—Ervin Johnson, New Orleans
1994—Carlos Rogers, Tennessee State

UTAH JAZZ

1974—(No first-round selection)
1975—Rich Kelley, Stanford
1976—(No first-round selection)
1977—(No first-round selection)
1978—James Hardy, San Francisco
1979—Larry Knight, Loyola (Ill.)
1980—Darrell Griffith, Louisville
　　　John Duren, Georgetown
1981—Danny Schayes, Syracuse
1982—Dominique Wilkins, Georgia
1983—Thurl Bailey, North Carolina State
1984—John Stockton, Gonzaga
1985—Karl Malone, Louisiana Tech
1986—Dell Curry, Virginia Tech
1987—Jose Ortiz, Oregon State
1988—Eric Leckner, Wyoming
1989—Blue Edwards, East Carolina
1990—(No first-round selection)
1991—Eric Murdock, Providence
1992—(No first-round selection)
1993—Luther Wright, Seton Hall
1994—(No first-round selection)

WASHINGTON BULLETS

1961—Walt Bellamy, Indiana*
1962—Billy McGill, Utah
1963—Rod Thorn, West Virginia
1964—Gary Bradds, Ohio State
1965—(No first-round selection)
1966—Jack Marin, Duke
1967—Earl Monroe, Winston-Salem
1968—Wes Unseld, Louisville
1969—Mike Davis, Virginia Union
1970—George Johnson, Stephen F. Austin
1971—Phil Chenier, California
　　　Stan Love, Oregon
1972—(No first-round selection)
1973—Nick Weatherspoon, Illinois
1974—Len Elmore, Maryland
1975—Kevin Grevey, Kentucky
1976—Mitch Kupchak, North Carolina
　　　Larry Wright, Grambling
1977—Greg Ballard, Oregon
　　　Bo Ellis, Marquette
1978—Roger Phegley, Bradley
　　　Dave Corzine, DePaul
1979—(No first-round selection)
1980—Wes Matthews, Wisconsin
1981—Frank Johnson, Wake Forest
1982—(No first-round selection)
1983—Jeff Malone, Mississippi State
　　　Randy Wittman, Indiana
1984—Melvin Turpin, Kentucky
1985—Kenny Green, Wake Forest
1986—John Williams, Louisiana State
　　　Anthony Jones, UNLV
1987—Tyrone Bogues, Wake Forest
1988—Harvey Grant, Oklahoma
1989—Tom Hammonds, Georgia Tech
1990—(No first-round selection)
1991—LaBradford Smith, Louisville
1992—Tom Gugliotta, North Carolina State
1993—Calbert Cheaney, Indiana
1994—Juwan Howard, Michigan

CHAPTER TWELVE

ALL-TIME RECORDS

NBA CHAMPIONS

SEASON	CHAMPION	EASTERN	W	L	WESTERN	W	L	SEASON	CHAMPION	EASTERN	W	L	WESTERN	W	L
1946–47	Philadelphia	Philadelphia	35	25	Chicago	39	22	1970–71	Milwaukee	Baltimore	42	40	Milwaukee	66	16
1947–48	Baltimore	Philadelphia	27	21	Baltimore	28	20	1971–72	Los Angeles	New York	48	34	Los Angeles	69	13
1948–49	Minneapolis	Washington	38	22	Minneapolis	44	16	1972–73	New York	New York	57	25	Los Angeles	60	22
1949–50	Minneapolis	Syracuse	51	13	Minneapolis	51	17	1973–74	Boston	Boston	56	26	Milwaukee	59	23
1950–51	Rochester	New York	36	3	Rochester	41	27	1974–75	Golden State	Washington	60	22	Golden State	48	34
1951–52	Minneapolis	New York	37	29	Minneapolis	40	28	1975–76	Boston	Boston	54	28	Phoenix	42	40
1952–53	Minneapolis	New York	47	23	Minneapolis	48	22	1976–77	Portland	Philadelphia	50	32	Portland	49	33
1953–54	Minneapolis	Syracuse	42	30	Minneapolis	46	26	1977–78	Washington	Washington	44	38	Seattle	47	35
1954–55	Syracuse	Syracuse	43	29	Fort Wayne	43	29	1978–79	Seattle	Washington	54	28	Seattle	52	30
1955–56	Philadelphia	Philadelphia	45	27	Fort Wayne	37	35	1979–80	Los Angeles	Philadelphia	59	23	Los Angeles	60	22
1956–57	Boston	Boston	44	28	St. Louis	34	38	1980–81	Boston	Boston	62	20	Houston	40	42
1957–58	St. Louis	Boston	49	23	St. Louis	41	31	1981–82	Los Angeles	Philadelphia	58	24	Los Angeles	57	25
1958–59	Boston	Boston	52	20	Minneapolis	33	39	1982–83	Philadelphia	Philadelphia	65	17	Los Angeles	58	24
1959–60	Boston	Boston	59	16	St. Louis	46	29	1983–84	Boston	Boston	62	20	Los Angeles	54	28
1960–61	Boston	Boston	57	22	St. Louis	51	28	1984–85	L.A. Lakers	Boston	63	19	L.A. Lakers	62	20
1961–62	Boston	Boston	60	20	Los Angeles	54	26	1985–86	Boston	Boston	67	15	Houston	51	31
1962–63	Boston	Boston	58	22	Los Angeles	53	27	1986–87	L.A. Lakers	Boston	59	23	L.A. Lakers	65	17
1963–64	Boston	Boston	59	21	San Francisco	48	32	1987–88	L.A. Lakers	Detroit	54	28	L.A. Lakers	62	20
1964–65	Boston	Boston	62	18	Los Angeles	49	31	1988–89	Detroit	Detroit	63	19	L.A. Lakers	57	25
1965–66	Boston	Boston	54	26	Los Angeles	45	35	1989–90	Detroit	Detroit	59	23	Portland	59	23
1966–67	Philadelphia	Philadelphia	68	13	San Francisco	44	37	1990–91	Chicago	Chicago	61	21	L.A. Lakers	58	24
1967–68	Boston	Boston	54	28	Los Angeles	52	30	1991–92	Chicago	Chicago	67	15	Portland	57	25
1968–69	Boston	Boston	48	34	Los Angeles	55	27	1992–93	Chicago	Chicago	57	25	Phoenix	62	20
1969–70	New York	New York	60	22	Los Angeles	46	36	1993–94	Houston	New York	57	25	Houston	58	24

ALL-TIME TEAM RECORDS

(Included are the year-by-year records and coaches of all NBA and ABA teams, and the pre-NBA records of NBL teams in the NBA.)

Season	Coach	Reg Sea W	L	Playoffs W	L
ANAHEIM AMIGOS (ABA)					
See Utah Stars					
ANDERSON PACKERS (NBL-NBA)					
1946–47	Murray Mendenhall	24	20	—	—
1947–48	Murray Mendenhall	42	18	4	2
1948–49	Murray Mendenhall	49	15	6	1

Season	Coach	Reg Sea W	L	Playoffs W	L
1949–50*	Howard Schultz (21–14)				
	Ike Duffy (1–2)				
	Doxie Moore (15–11)	37	27	4	4
	NBL TOTALS	115	53	10	3
	NBA TOTALS	37	27	4	4
* Joined NBA					

Season	Coach	Reg Sea W	L	Playoffs W	L
ATLANTA HAWKS (NBL-NBA)					
1946–47*	Matt Hickey	19	25	—	—
1947–48	Matt Hickey (9–12)				
	Bobby McDermott (21–18)	30	30	3	3
1948–49	Bobby McDermott (25–20)				
	Roger Potter (11–8)	36	28	3	3

Season	Coach	Reg Sea W	Reg Sea L	Playoffs W	Playoffs L
1949–50†	Roger Potter (1–6)				
	Red Auerbach (28–29)	29	35	1	2
1950–51	David McMillan (9–14)				
	John Logan (2–1)				
	Marko Todorovich (14–28)	25	43	—	—
1951–52‡	Doxie Moore	17	49	—	—
1952–53	Fuzzy Levane	27	44	—	—
1953–54	Fuzzy Levane (11–35)				
1954–54	Red Holtzman (10–16)	21	51	—	—
1954–55	Red Holtzman	26	46	—	—
1955–56§	Red Holtzman	33	39	4	4
1956–57	Red Holtzman (14–19)				
	Slater Martin (5–3)				
	Alex Hannum (15–16)	34	38	6	4
1957–58	Alex Hannum	41	31	8	3
1958–59	Andy Phillip (6–4)				
1958–59	Ed McCauley (43–19)	49	23	2	4
1959–60	Ed McCauley	46	29	7	7
1960–61	Paul Seymour	51	28	5	7
1961–62	Paul Seymour (5–9)				
	Fuzzy Levane (20–40)				
	Bob Petit (4–2)	29	51	—	—
1962–63	Harry Gallatin	48	32	6	5
1963–64	Harry Gallatin	46	34	6	6
1964–65	Harry Gallatin (17–16)				
	Richie Guerin (28–19)	45	35	1	3
1965–66	Richie Guerin	36	44	6	4
1966–67	Richie Guerin	39	42	5	4
1967–68	Richie Guerin	56	26	2	4
1968–69¶	Richie Guerin	48	34	5	6
1969–70	Richie Guerin	48	34	4	5
1970–71	Richie Guerin	36	46	1	4
1971–72	Richie Guerin	36	46	2	4
1972–73	Cotton Fitzsimmons	46	36	2	4
1973–74	Cotton Fitzsimmons	35	47	—	—
1974–75	Cotton Fitzsimmons	31	51	—	—
1975–76	Cotton Fitzsimmons (28–46)				
	Gene Tormohlen (1–7)	29	53	—	—
1976–77	Hubie Brown	31	51	—	—
1977–78	Hubie Brown	41	41	0	2
1978–79	Hubie Brown	46	36	5	4
1979–80	Hubie Brown	50	32	1	4
1980–81	Hubie Brown (31–48)				
	Mike Fratello (0–3)	31	51	—	—
1981–82	Kevin Loughery	42	40	0	2
1982–83	Kevin Loughery	43	39	1	2
1983–84	Mike Fratello	40	42	2	3
1984–85	Mike Fratello	34	48	—	—
1985–86	Mike Fratello	50	32	4	5
1986–87	Mike Fratello	57	25	4	5
1987–88	Mike Fratello	50	32	6	6
1988–89	Mike Fratello	52	30	2	3
1989–90	Mike Fratello	41	41	—	—
1990–91	Bob Weiss	43	39	2	3
1991–92	Bob Weiss	38	44	—	—
1992–93	Bob Weiss	43	39	0	3
1993–94	Lenny Wilkens	57	25	5	6
	NBL TOTALS	85	83	6	6
	NBA TOTALS	1796	1754	105	128

BALTIMORE BULLETS

Season	Coach	Reg Sea W	Reg Sea L	Playoffs W	Playoffs L
1947–48	Buddy Jeannette	28	20	8	3
1948–49	Buddy Jeannette	29	31	1	2
1949–50	Buddy Jeannette	25	43	—	—
1950–51	Buddy Jeannette (14–23)				
	Walt Budko (10–19)	24	42	—	—

* Started season as Buffalo Bisons, moved to Tri-Cities
† Joined NBA
‡ Moved from Tri-Cities to Milwaukee
§ Moved from Milwaukee to St. Louis
¶ Moved from St. Louis to Atlanta

Season	Coach	Reg Sea W	Reg Sea L	Playoffs W	Playoffs L
1951–52	Fred Scolari (12–27)				
	Joe Reiser (8–19)	20	46	—	—
1952–53	Joe Reiser (0–3)				
	Clair Bee (16–51)	16	54	—	2
1953–54	Clair Bee	16	56	—	2
1954–55*	Clair Bee (1–4)				
	Al Barthelme (2–7)	3	11	—	—
	TOTALS	161	303	9	7

* Disbanded Nov. 27, 1954

BALTIMORE BULLETS

See Washington Bullets

BOSTON CELTICS

Season	Coach	Reg Sea W	Reg Sea L	Playoffs W	Playoffs L
1946–47	John Russell	22	38	—	—
1947–48	John Russell	20	28	1	2
1948–49	Alvin Julian	25	35	—	—
1949–50	Alvin Julian	22	46	—	—
1950–51	Red Auerbach	39	30	0	2
1951–52	Red Auerbach	39	27	1	2
1952–53	Red Auerbach	46	25	3	3
1953–54	Red Auerbach	42	30	2	4
1954–55	Red Auerbach	36	36	3	4
1955–56	Red Auerbach	39	33	1	2
1956–57	Red Auerbach	44	28	7	3
1957–58	Red Auerbach	49	23	6	5
1958–59	Red Auerbach	52	20	8	3
1959–60	Red Auerbach	59	16	8	5
1960–61	Red Auerbach	57	22	8	2
1961–62	Red Auerbach	60	20	8	6
1962–63	Red Auerbach	58	22	8	5
1963–64	Red Auerbach	59	21	8	2
1964–65	Red Auerbach	62	18	8	4
1965–66	Red Auerbach	54	26	11	6
1966–67	Bill Russell	60	21	4	5
1967–68	Bill Russell	54	28	12	7
1968–69	Bill Russell	48	34	12	6
1969–70	Tom Heinsohn	34	48	—	—
1970–71	Tom Heinsohn	44	38	—	—
1971–72	Tom Heinsohn	56	26	5	6
1972–73	Tom Heinsohn	68	14	7	6
1973–74	Tom Heinsohn	56	26	12	6
1974–75	Tom Heinsohn	60	22	6	5
1975–76	Tom Heinsohn	54	28	12	6
1976–77	Tom Heinsohn	44	38	5	4
1977–78	Tom Heinsohn (11–23)				
	Tom Sanders (21–27)	32	50	—	—
1978–79	Tom Sanders (2–12)				
	Dave Cowens (27–41)	29	53	—	—
1979–80	Bill Fitch	61	21	5	4
1980–81	Bill Fitch	62	20	12	5
1981–82	Bill Fitch	63	19	7	5
1982–83	Bill Fitch	56	26	2	5
1983–84	K.C.Jones	62	20	15	8
1984–85	K.C.Jones	63	19	13	8
1985–86	K.C.Jones	67	15	15	3
1986–87	K.C.Jones	59	23	13	10
1987–88	K.C.Jones	57	25	9	8
1988–89	Jimmy Rodgers	42	40	0	3
1989–90	Jimmy Rodgers	52	30	2	3
1990–91	Chris Ford	56	26	5	6
1991–92	Chris Ford	51	31	6	4
1992–93	Chris Ford	48	34	1	3
1993–94	Chris Ford	32	50	—	—
	TOTALS	2354	1369	271	186

BUFFALO BISONS

See Atlanta Hawks

BUFFALO BRAVES

See Los Angeles Clippers

CAPITAL BULLETS

See Washington Bullets

CAROLINA COUGARS

See St. Louis Spirits

CHARLOTTE HORNETS

Season	Coach	Reg Sea W	Reg Sea L	Playoffs W	Playoffs L
1988–89	Dick Harter	20	62	—	—
1989–90	Dick Harter (8–32)				
	Gene Littles (11–31)	19	63	—	—
1990–91	Gene Littles	26	56	—	—
1991–92	Allan Bristow	31	51	—	—
1992–93	Allan Bristow	44	38	4	5
1993–94	Allan Bristow	41	41	—	—
	TOTALS	181	311	4	5

CHICAGO BULLS

Season	Coach	Reg Sea W	Reg Sea L	Playoffs W	Playoffs L
1966–67	John Kerr	33	48	0	3
1967–68	John Kerr	29	53	1	4
1968–69	Dick Motta	33	49	—	—
1969–70	Dick Motta	39	43	1	4
1970–71	Dick Motta	51	31	4	4
1971–72	Dick Motta	57	25	0	4
1972–73	Dick Motta	51	31	3	4
1973–74	Dick Motta	54	28	4	7
1974–75	Dick Motta	47	35	7	6
1975–76	Dick Motta	24	58	—	—
1976–77	Ed Badger	44	38	1	2
1977–78	Ed Badger	40	42	—	—
1978–79	Larry Costello (20–36)				
	Scotty Robertson (11–15)	31	51	—	—
1979–80	Jerry Sloan	30	52	—	—
1980–81	Jerry Sloan	45	37	2	4
1981–82	Jerry Sloan (19–32)				
	Phil Johnson (0–1)				
	Rod Thorn (15–15)	34	48	—	—
1982–83	Paul Westhead	28	54	—	—
1983–84	Kevin Loughery	27	55	—	—
1984–85	Kevin Loughery	38	44	1	3
1985–86	Stan Albeck	30	52	0	3
1986–87	Doug Collins	40	42	0	3
1987–88	Doug Collins	50	32	4	6
1988–89	Doug Collins	47	35	9	8
1989–90	Phil Jackson	55	27	10	6
1990–91	Phil Jackson	61	21	15	2
1991–92	Phil Jackson	67	15	15	7
1992–93	Phil Jackson	57	25	15	4
1993–94	Phil Jackson	55	27	6	4
	TOTALS	1197	1098	97	88

CHICAGO PACKERS

See Baltimore Bullets

CHICAGO STAGS

Season	Coach	Reg Sea W	Reg Sea L	Playoffs W	Playoffs L
1946–47	Harold Olsen	39	22	5	6
1947–48	Harold Olsen	28	20	2	3
1948–49	Harold Olsen (28–21)				
	Phillip Brownstein (10–1)	38	22	0	2
1949–50	Phillip Brownstein	40	28	0	2
	TOTALS	145	92	7	13

CHICAGO ZEPHYRS

See Washington Bullets

CINCINNATI ROYALS

See Sacramento Kings

CLEVELAND CAVALIERS

Season	Coach	Reg Sea W	Reg Sea L	Playoffs W	Playoffs L
1970–71	Bill Fitch	15	67	—	—
1971–72	Bill Fitch	23	59	—	—
1972–73	Bill Fitch	32	50	—	—
1973–74	Bill Fitch	29	53	—	—
1974–75	Bill Fitch	40	42	—	—

Season	Coach	Reg Sea W	L	Playoffs W	L
1975–76	Bill Fitch	49	33	6	7
1976–77	Bill Fitch	43	39	1	2
1977–78	Bill Fitch	43	39	0	2
1978–79	Bill Fitch	30	52	—	—
1979–80	Stan Albeck	37	45	—	—
1980–81	Bill Musselman (25–46)				
	Don Delaney (3–8)	28	54	—	—
1981–82	Don Delaney (4–11)				
	Bob Koppenburg (0–3)				
	Chuck Daly (9–32)				
	Bill Musselman (2–21)	15	67	—	—
1982–83	Tom Nissalke	23	59	—	—
1983–84	Tom Nissalke	28	54	—	—
1984–85	George Karl	36	46	1	3
1985–86	George Karl (25–42)				
	Gene Littles (4–11)	29	53	—	—
1986–87	Lenny Wilkens	31	51	—	—
1987–88	Lenny Wilkens	42	40	2	3
1988–89	Lenny Wilkens	57	25	2	3
1989–90	Lenny Wilkens	42	40	2	3
1990–91	Lenny Wilkens	33	49	—	—
1991–92	Lenny Wilkens	57	25	9	8
1992–93	Lenny Wilkens	54	28	3	6
1993–94	Mike Fratello	47	35	0	3
	TOTALS	863	1105	26	40

CLEVELAND REBELS

Season	Coach	Reg Sea W	L	Playoffs W	L
1946–47	Dutch Dehnert (17–20)				
	Roy Clifford (13–10)				
	TOTALS	30	30	1	2

DALLAS CHAPARRALS (ABA)

See San Antonio Spurs

DALLAS MAVERICKS

Season	Coach	Reg Sea W	L	Playoffs W	L
1980–81	Dick Motta	15	67	—	—
1981–82	Dick Motta	28	54	—	—
1982–83	Dick Motta	38	44	—	—
1983–84	Dick Motta	43	39	4	6
1984–85	Dick Motta	44	38	1	3
1985–86	Dick Motta	44	38	5	5
1986–87	Dick Motta	55	27	1	3
1987–88	John MacLeod	53	29	10	7
1988–89	John MacLeod	38	44	—	—
1989–90	John MacLeod (5–6)				
	Richie Adubato (42–29)	47	35	0	3
1990–91	Richie Adubato	28	54	—	—
1991–92	Richie Adubato	22	60	—	—
1992–93	Richie Adubato (2–27)				
	Gar Heard (9–44)	11	71	—	—
1993–94	Quinn Buckner	13	69	—	—
	TOTALS	479	669	21	27

DENVER NUGGETS (NBL–NBA)

Season	Coach	Reg Sea W	L	Playoffs W	L
1948–49	Ralph Bishop	18	44	—	—
1949–50*	James Darden	11	51	—	—
	NBL TOTALS	18	44	—	—
	NBA TOTALS	11	51	—	—

*Joined NBA

DENVER NUGGETS (ABA–NBA)

Season	Coach	Reg Sea W	L	Playoffs W	L
1967–68	Bob Bass	45	33	2	3
1968–69	Bob Bass	44	34	3	4
1969–70	John McClendon (9–19)				
	Joe Belmont (42–14)	51	33	5	7
1970–71	Joe Belmont (3–10)				
	Stan Albeck (27–44)	30	54	—	—
1971–72	Alex Hannum	34	50	3	4
1972–73	Alex Hannum	47	37	1	4
1973–74	Alex Hannum	37	47	—	—
1974–75*	Larry Brown	65	19	7	6
1975–76	Larry Brown	60	24	6	7

Season	Coach	Reg Sea W	L	Playoffs W	L
1976–77[†]	Larry Brown	50	32	2	4
1977–78	Larry Brown	48	34	6	7
1978–79	Larry Brown (28–25)				
	Donnie Walsh (19–10)	47	35	1	2
1979–80	Donnie Walsh	30	52	—	—
1980–81	Donnie Walsh (11–20)				
	Doug Moe (26–25)	37	45	—	—
1981–82	Doug Moe	46	36	1	2
1982–83	Doug Moe	45	37	3	5
1983–84	Doug Moe	38	44	2	3
1984–85	Doug Moe	52	30	8	7
1985–86	Doug Moe	47	35	5	5
1986–87	Doug Moe	37	45	0	3
1987–88	Doug Moe	54	28	5	6
1988–89	Doug Moe	44	38	0	3
1989–90	Doug Moe	43	39	0	3
1990–91	Paul Westhead	20	62	—	—
1991–92	Paul Westhead	24	58	—	—
1992–93	Dan Issel	36	46	—	—
1993–94	Dan Issel	42	40	6	6
	ABA TOTALS	413	331	27	35
	NBA TOTALS	740	736	39	56

* Changed name from Rockets to Nuggets
[†] Joined NBA

DETROIT FALCONS

Season	Coach	Reg Sea W	L	Playoffs W	L
1946–47	Glenn Curtis (13–26)				
	Philip Sachs (7–14)				
	TOTALS	20	40	—	—

DETROIT PISTONS (NBL–NBA)

Season	Coach	Reg Sea W	L	Playoffs W	L
1941–42	Carl Bennett	15	9	3	3
1942–43	Carl Bennett	17	6	3	3
1943–44	Bobby McDermott	18	4	5	0
1944–45	Bobby McDermott	25	5	5	2
1945–46	Carl Bennett	26	8	1	3
1946–47	Bobby McDermott (7–7)				
	Carl Bennett (18–12)	25	19	4	4
1947–48	Carl Bennett	40	20	1	3
1948–49*	Carl Bennett (0–6)				
	Paul Armstrong (22–32)	22	38	—	—
1949–50	Murray Mendenhall	40	28	2	2
1950–51	Murray Mendenhall	32	36	1	2
1951–52	Paul Birch	29	37	0	2
1952–53	Paul Birch	36	33	4	4
1953–54	Paul Birch	40	32	0	4
1954–55	Charles Eckman	43	29	6	5
1955–56	Charles Eckman	37	35	4	6
1956–57	Charles Eckman	34	38	0	2
1957–58[†]	Charles Eckman (9–16)				
	Red Rocha (24–23)	33	39	3	4
1958–59	Red Rocha	28	44	1	2
1959–60	Red Rocha (13–21)				
	Dick McGuire (17–24)	30	45	0	2
1960–61	Dick McGuire	34	45	2	3
1961–62	Dick McGuire	37	43	5	5
1962–63	Dick McGuire	34	46	1	3
1963–64	Charles Wolf	23	57	—	—
1964–65	Charles Wolf (2–9)				
	Dave DeBusschere (29–40)	31	49	—	—
1965–66	Dave DeBusschere	22	58	—	—
1966–67	Dave DeBusschere (28–45)				
	Donnis Butcher (2–6)	30	51	—	—
1967–68	Donnis Butcher	40	42	2	4
1968–69	Donnis Butcher (10–12)				
	Paul Seymour (22–38)	32	50	—	—
1969–70	Bill van Breda Kolff	31	51	—	—
1970–71	Bill van Breda Kolff	45	37	—	—
1971–72	Bill van Breda Kolff (6–4)				
	Terry Dischinger (0–2)				
	Earl Lloyd (20–50)	26	56	—	—

Season	Coach	Reg Sea W	L	Playoffs W	L
1972–73	Earl Lloyd (2–5)				
	Ray Scott (38–37)	40	42	—	—
1973–74	Ray Scott	52	30	3	4
1974–75	Ray Scott	40	42	1	2
1975–76	Ray Scott (17–25)				
	Herb Brown (19–21)	36	46	4	5
1976–77	Herb Brown	44	38	1	2
1977–78	Herb Brown (9–15)				
	Robert Kauffman (29–29)	38	44	—	—
1978–79	Dick Vitale	30	52	—	—
1979–80	Dick Vitale (4–8)				
	Richard Adubato (12–58)	16	66	—	—
1980–81	Scotty Robertson	21	61	—	—
1981–82	Scotty Robertson	39	43	—	—
1982–83	Scotty Robertson	37	45	—	—
1983–84	Chuck Daly	49	33	2	3
1984–85	Chuck Daly	46	36	5	4
1985–86	Chuck Daly	46	36	1	3
1986–87	Chuck Daly	52	30	10	5
1987–88	Chuck Daly	54	28	14	9
1988–89	Chuck Daly	63	19	15	2
1989–90	Chuck Daly	59	23	15	5
1990–91	Chuck Daly	50	32	7	8
1991–92	Chuck Daly	48	34	2	3
1992–93	Ron Rothstein	40	42	—	—
1993–94	Don Chaney	20	62	—	—
	NBL TOTALS	166	71	22	18
	NBA TOTALS	1709	1903	111	105

* Joined NBA
[†] Moved from Fort Wayne to Detroit

FORT WAYNE PISTONS (NBL–NBA)

See Detroit Pistons

GOLDEN STATE WARRIORS

Season	Coach	Reg Sea W	L	Playoffs W	L
1946–47	Eddie Gottlieb	35	25	8	2
1947–48	Eddie Gottlieb	27	21	6	7
1948–49	Eddie Gottlieb	28	32	0	2
1949–50	Eddie Gottlieb	26	42	0	2
1950–51	Eddie Gottlieb	40	26	0	2
1951–52	Eddie Gottlieb	33	33	1	2
1952–53	Eddie Gottlieb	12	57	—	—
1953–54	Eddie Gottlieb	29	43	—	—
1954–55	Eddie Gottlieb	33	39	—	—
1955–56	George Senesky	45	27	7	3
1956–57	George Senesky	37	35	0	2
1957–58	George Senesky	37	35	3	5
1958–59	Al Cervi	32	40	—	—
1959–60	Neil Johnston	49	26	4	5
1960–61	Neil Johnston	46	33	0	3
1961–62	Frank McGuire	49	31	6	6
1962–63*	Bob Feerick	31	49	—	—
1963–64	Alex Hannum	48	32	5	7
1964–65	Alex Hannum	17	63	—	—
1965–66	Alex Hannum	35	45	—	—
1966–67	Bill Sharman	44	37	9	6
1967–68	Bill Sharman	43	39	4	6
1968–69	George Lee	41	41	2	4
1969–70	George Lee (22–30)				
	Al Attles (8–22)	30	52	—	—
1970–71	Al Attles	41	41	1	4
1971–72[†]	Al Attles	51	31	1	4
1972–73	Al Attles	47	35	5	6
1973–74	Al Attles	44	38	—	—
1974–75	Al Attles	48	34	12	5
1975–76	Al Attles	59	23	7	6
1976–77	Al Attles	46	36	5	5
1977–78	Al Attles	43	39	—	—
1978–79	Al Attles	38	44	—	—
1979–80	Al Attles	24	58	—	—
1980–81	Al Attles	39	43	—	—
1981–82	Al Attles	45	37	—	—

Season	Coach	Reg Sea W	L	Playoffs W	L
1982–83	Al Attles	30	52	—	—
1983–84	John Bach	37	45	—	—
1984–85	John Bach	22	60	—	—
1985–86	John Bach	30	52	—	—
1986–87	George Karl	42	40	4	6
1987–88	George Karl (16–48)				
	Ed Gregory (4–14)	20	62	—	—
1988–89	Don Nelson	43	39	4	4
1989–90	Don Nelson	37	45	—	—
1990–91	Don Nelson	44	38	4	5
1991–92	Don Nelson	55	27	1	3
1992–93	Don Nelson	34	48	—	—
1993–94	Don Nelson	50	32	0	3
	TOTALS	1816	1902	99	115

* Moved from Philadelphia to San Francisco
† Moved to Oakland as Golden State Warriors

HOUSTON MAVERICKS (ABA)

See St. Louis Spirits

HOUSTON ROCKETS

Season	Coach	Reg Sea W	L	Playoffs W	L
1967–68	Jack McMahon	15	67	—	—
1968–69	Jack McMahon	37	45	2	4
1969–70	Jack McMahon (9–17)				
	Alex Hannum (18–38)	27	55	—	—
1970–71	Alex Hannum	40	42	—	—
1971–72*	Tex Winter	34	48	—	—
1972–73	Tex Winter (17–30)				
	John Egan (16–19)	33	49	—	—
1973–74	John Egan	32	50	—	—
1974–75	John Egan	41	41	3	5
1975–76	John Egan	40	42	—	—
1976–77	Tom Nissalke	49	33	6	6
1977–78	Tom Nissalke	28	54	—	—
1978–79	Tom Nissalke	47	35	0	2
1979–80	Del Harris	41	41	2	5
1980–81	Del Harris	40	42	12	9
1981–82	Del Harris	46	36	1	2
1982–83	Del Harris	14	68	—	—
1983–84	Bill Fitch	29	53	—	—
1984–85	Bill Fitch	48	34	2	3
1985–86	Bill Fitch	51	31	13	7
1986–87	Bill Fitch	42	40	5	5
1987–88	Bill Fitch	46	36	1	3
1988–89	Don Chaney	45	37	1	3
1989–90	Don Chaney	41	41	1	3
1990–91	Don Chaney	52	30	0	3
1991–92	Don Chaney (26–26)				
	Rudy Tomjanovich (16–14)	42	40	—	—
1992–93	Rudy Tomjanovich	55	27	6	6
1993–94	Rudy Tomjanovich	58	24	15	8
	TOTALS	1073	1141	70	74

*Moved from San Diego to Houston

INDIANA PACERS (ABA-NBA)

Season	Coach	Reg Sea W	L	Playoffs W	L
1967–68	Larry Staverman	38	40	0	3
1968–69	Larry Staverman (2–7)				
	Bob Leonard (42–27)	44	34	9	8
1969–70	Bob Leonard	59	25	12	3
1970–71	Bob Leonard	58	26	7	4
1971–72	Bob Leonard	47	37	12	8
1972–73	Bob Leonard	51	33	12	6
1973–74	Bob Leonard	46	38	7	7
1974–75	Bob Leonard	45	39	9	9
1975–76	Bob Leonard	39	45	1	2
1976–77*	Bob Leonard	36	46	—	—
1977–78	Bob Leonard	31	51	—	—
1978–79	Bob Leonard	38	44	—	—
1979–80	Bob Leonard	37	45	—	—
1980–81	Jack McKinney	44	38	0	2
1981–82	Jack McKinney	35	47	—	—
1982–83	Jack McKinney	20	62	—	—

Season	Coach	Reg Sea W	L	Playoffs W	L
1983–84	Jack McKinney	26	56	—	—
1984–85	George Irvine	22	60	—	—
1985–86	George Irvine	26	56	—	—
1986–87	Jack Ramsay	41	41	1	3
1987–88	Jack Ramsay	38	44	—	—
1988–89	Jack Ramsay (0–7)				
	Mel Daniels (0–2)				
	George Irvine (6–14)				
	Dick Versace (22–31)	28	54	—	—
1989–90	Dick Versace	42	40	0	3
1990–91	Dick Versace (9–16)				
	Bob Hill (32–25)	41	41	2	3
1991–92	Bob Hill	40	42	0	3
1992–93	Bob Hill	41	41	1	3
1993–94	Larry Brown	47	35	10	6
	ABA TOTALS	427	317	69	50
	NBA TOTALS	633	843	14	23

* Joined NBA

INDIANAPOLIS JETS (NBL-NBA)

Season	Coach	Reg Sea W	L	Playoffs W	L
1937–38*	Frank Kautsky	4	9	—	—
1938–39	Frank Kautsky	13	13	—	—
1939–40	Robert Nipper	9	19	—	—
1941–42	Frank Kautsky	12	11	0	2
1945–46	Matt Hickey	10	22	—	—
1946–47	Ernest Andres (21–13)				
	R. Dietz & H. Schaefer (6–4)	27	17	2	3
1947–48	Glenn Curtis (2–2)				
	Leo Klier (1–1)				
	Bruce Hale (21–32)	24	35	1	3
1948–49†	Bruce Hale (3–13)				
	Burl Friddle (15–29)	18	42	—	—
	NBL TOTALS	99	126	3	8
	NBA TOTALS	18	42	—	—

* Played as Indianapolis Kautskys
† Joined NBA and changed name to Jets

INDIANAPOLIS KAUTSKYS

See Indianapolis Jets

INDIANAPOLIS OLYMPIANS

Season	Coach	Reg Sea W	L	Playoffs W	L
1949–50	Clifford Barker	39	25	3	3
1950–51	Clifford Barker (24–32)				
	Wallace Jones (7–5)	31	37	1	2
1951–52	Herman Schaefer	34	32	0	2
1952–53	Herman Schaefer	28	43	0	2
	TOTALS	132	137	4	9

KANSAS CITY KINGS

See Sacramento Kings

KENTUCKY COLONELS (ABA)

Season	Coach	Reg Sea W	L	Playoffs W	L
1967–68	John Givens (5–12)				
	Gene Rhodes (32–30)	36	42	2	3
1968–69	Gene Rhodes	42	36	3	4
1969–70	Gene Rhodes	45	39	5	7
1970–71	Gene Rhodes (10–5)				
	Alex Groza (2–0)				
	Frank Ramsey (32–35)	44	40	11	8
1971–72	Joe Mullaney	68	16	2	4
1972–73	Joe Mullaney	56	28	11	8
1973–74	Babe McCarthy	53	31	4	4
1974–75	Hubie Brown	58	26	12	3
1975–76	Hubie Brown	46	38	5	5
	TOTALS	448	296	55	46

LOS ANGELES CLIPPERS

Season	Coach	Reg Sea W	L	Playoffs W	L
1970–71	Dolph Schayes	22	60	—	—
1971–72	Dolph Schayes (0–1)				
	Jack McCarthy (22–59)	22	60	—	—
1972–73	Jack Ramsay	21	61	—	—
1973–74	Jack Ramsay	42	40	2	4
1974–75	Jack Ramsay	49	33	3	4

Season	Coach	Reg Sea W	L	Playoffs W	L
1975–76	Jack Ramsay	46	36	4	5
1976–77	Tates Locke (16–30)				
	Bob MacKinnon (3–4)				
	Joe Mullaney (11–18)	30	52	—	—
1977–78	Cotton Fitzsimmons	27	55	—	—
1978–79*	Gene Shue	43	39	—	—
1979–80	Gene Shue	35	47	—	—
1980–81	Paul Silas	36	46	—	—
1981–82	Paul Silas	17	65	—	—
1982–83	Paul Silas	25	57	—	—
1983–84	Jim Lynam	30	52	—	—
1984–85†	Jim Lynam (22–39)				
	Don Chaney (9–12)	31	51	—	—
1985–86	Don Chaney	32	50	—	—
1986–87	Don Chaney	12	70	—	—
1987–88	Gene Shue	17	65	—	—
1988–89	Gene Shue (10–28)				
	Don Casey (11–33)	21	61	—	—
1989–90	Don Casey	30	52	—	—
1990–91	Mike Schuler	31	51	—	—
1991–92	Mike Schuler (21–24)				
	Mack Calvin (1–1)				
	Larry Brown (23–12)	45	37	2	3
1992–93	Larry Brown	41	41	2	3
1993–94	Bob Weiss	27	55	—	—
	TOTALS	732	1236	13	19

* Moved from Buffalo to San Diego
† Moved from San Diego to Los Angeles

LOS ANGELES LAKERS (NBL-NBA)

Season	Coach	Reg Sea W	L	Playoffs W	L
1947–48	John Kundla	43	17	8	2
1948–49*	John Kundla	44	16	8	2
1949–50	John Kundla	51	17	10	2
1950–51	John Kundla (43–24)				
	Herman Schaefer (1–0)	44	24	3	4
1951–52	John Kundla	40	26	9	4
1952–53	John Kundla	48	22	9	3
1953–54	John Kundla	46	26	9	4
1954–55	John Kundla	40	32	3	4
1955–56	John Kundla	33	39	1	2
1956–57	John Kundla	34	38	2	3
1957–58	George Mikan (9–30)				
	John Kundla (10–23)	19	53	—	—
1958–59	John Kundla	33	39	6	7
1959–60	John Castellani (11–25)				
	Jim Pollard (14–25)	25	50	5	4
1960–61†	Fred Schaus	36	43	6	6
1961–62	Fred Schaus	54	26	7	6
1962–63	Fred Schaus	53	27	6	7
1963–64	Fred Schaus	42	38	2	3
1964–65	Fred Schaus	49	31	5	6
1965–66	Fred Schaus	45	35	7	7
1966–67	Fred Schaus	36	45	0	3
1967–68	Bill van Breda Kolff	52	30	10	5
1968–69	Bill van Breda Kolff	55	27	11	7
1969–70	Joe Mullaney	46	36	11	7
1970–71	Joe Mullaney	48	34	5	7
1971–72	Bill Sharman	69	13	12	3
1972–73	Bill Sharman	60	22	9	8
1973–74	Bill Sharman	47	35	1	4
1974–75	Bill Sharman	30	52	—	—
1975–76	Bill Sharman	40	42	—	—
1976–77	Jerry West	53	29	4	7
1977–78	Jerry West	45	37	1	2
1978–79	Jerry West	47	35	3	5
1979–80	Jack McKinney (10–4)				
	Paul Westhead (50–18)	60	22	12	4
1980–81	Paul Westhead	54	28	1	2
1981–82	Paul Westhead (7–4)				
	Pat Riley (50–21)	57	25	12	2
1982–83	Pat Riley	58	24	8	7
1983–84	Pat Riley	54	28	14	7

Season	Coach	Reg Sea W	L	Playoffs W	L
1984–85	Pat Riley	62	20	15	4
1985–86	Pat Riley	62	20	8	6
1986–87	Pat Riley	65	17	15	3
1987–88	Pat Riley	62	20	15	9
1988–89	Pat Riley	57	25	11	4
1989–90	Pat Riley	63	19	4	5
1990–91	Mike Dunleavy	58	24	12	7
1991–92	Mike Dunleavy	43	39	1	3
1992–93	Randy Pfund	39	43	2	3
1993–94	Randy Pfund (27–37)				
	Bill Bertka (1–1)				
	Magic Johnson (5–11)	33	49	—	—
	NBL TOTALS	43	17	8	2
	NBA TOTALS	2191	1422	295	198

* Joined NBA
† Moved from Minneapolis to Los Angeles

LOS ANGELES STARS (ABA)

See Utah Stars

MEMPHIS SOUNDS (ABA)

Season	Coach	Reg Sea W	L	Playoffs W	L
1967–68*	Babe McCarthy	48	30	10	7
1968–69	Babe McCarthy	46	32	4	7
1969–70	Babe McCarthy	42	42	—	—
1970–71†	Babe McCarthy	41	43	0	4
1971–72	Babe McCarthy	26	58	—	—
1972–73‡	Bob Bass	24	60	—	—
1973–74	Bill van Breda Kolff	21	63	—	—
1974–75§	Joe Mullaney	27	57	1	4
	TOTALS	275	385	15	22

* Played in New Orleans as Buccaneers
† Moved from New Orleans to Memphis, changed name to Pros
‡ Changed name to Tams
§ Changed name to Sounds

MEMPHIS TAMS (ABA)

See Memphis Sounds

MIAMI FLORIDIANS (ABA)

Season	Coach	Reg Sea W	L	Playoffs W	L
1967–68*	Jim Pollard	50	28	4	6
1968–69†	Jim Pollard	43	35	5	7
1969–70	Jim Pollard (5–15)				
	Harold Blitman (18–46)	23	61	—	—
1970–71	Harold Blitman (18–30)				
	Bob Bass (19–17)	37	47	2	4
1971–72	Bob Bass	36	48	0	4
	TOTALS	189	219	11	21

* Played in Minneapolis as Muskies
† Moved from Minnesota to Miami, changed name to Floridians

MIAMI HEAT

Season	Coach	Reg Sea W	L	Playoffs W	L
1988–89	Ron Rothstein	15	67	—	—
1989–90	Ron Rothstein	18	64	—	—
1990–91	Ron Rothstein	24	58	—	—
1991–92	Kevin Loughery	38	44	0	3
1992–93	Kevin Loughery	36	46	—	—
1993–94	Kevin Loughery	42	40	2	3
	TOTALS	173	319	2	6

MILWAUKEE BUCKS

Season	Coach	Reg Sea W	L	Playoffs W	L
1968–69	Larry Costello	27	55	—	—
1969–70	Larry Costello	56	26	5	5
1970–71	Larry Costello	66	16	12	2
1971–72	Larry Costello	63	19	6	5
1972–73	Larry Costello	60	22	2	4
1973–74	Larry Costello	59	23	11	5
1974–75	Larry Costello	38	44	—	—
1975–76	Larry Costello	38	44	1	2
1976–77	Larry Costello (3–15)				
	Don Nelson (27–37)	30	52	—	—
1977–78	Don Nelson	44	38	5	4
1978–79	Don Nelson	38	44	—	—
1979–80	Don Nelson	49	33	3	4

Season	Coach	Reg Sea W	L	Playoffs W	L
1980–81	Don Nelson	60	22	3	4
1981–82	Don Nelson	55	27	2	4
1982–83	Don Nelson	51	31	5	4
1983–84	Don Nelson	50	32	8	8
1984–85	Don Nelson	59	23	3	5
1985–86	Don Nelson	57	25	7	7
1986–87	Don Nelson	50	32	6	6
1987–88	Del Harris	42	40	2	3
1988–89	Del Harris	49	33	3	6
1989–90	Del Harris	44	38	1	3
1990–91	Del Harris	48	34	0	3
1991–92	Del Harris (8–9)				
	Frank Hamblen (23–42)	31	51	—	—
1992–93	Mike Dunleavy	28	54	—	—
1993–94	Mike Dunleavy	20	62	—	—
	TOTALS	1212	920	85	84

MILWAUKEE HAWKS

See Atlanta Hawks

MINNEAPOLIS LAKERS (NBL-NBA)

See Los Angeles Lakers

MINNESOTA MUSKIES (ABA)

See Miami Floridians

MINNESOTA PIPERS (ABA)

See Pittsburgh Condors

MINNESOTA TIMBERWOLVES

Season	Coach	Reg Sea W	L	Playoffs W	L
1989–90	Bill Musselman	22	60	—	—
1990–91	Bill Musselman	29	53	—	—
1991–92	Jimmy Rodgers	15	67	—	—
1992–93	Jimmy Rodgers (6–23)				
	Sidney Lowe (13–40)	19	63	—	—
1993–94	Sidney Lowe	20	62	—	—
	TOTALS	105	305	—	—

NEW JERSEY AMERICANS (ABA)

See New Jersey Nets

NEW JERSEY NETS (ABA-NBA)

Season	Coach	Reg Sea W	L	Playoffs W	L
1967–68*	Max Zaslofsky	36	42	—	—
1968–69†	Max Zaslofsky	17	61	—	—
1969–70	York Larese	39	45	3	4
1970–71	Lou Carnesecca	40	44	2	4
1971–72	Lou Carnesecca	44	40	10	10
1972–73	Lou Carnesecca	30	54	1	4
1973–74	Kevin Loughery	55	29	12	2
1974–75	Kevin Loughery	58	26	1	4
1975–76	Kevin Loughery	55	29	8	5
1976–77‡	Kevin Loughery	22	60	—	—
1977–78§	Kevin Loughery	24	58	—	—
1978–79	Kevin Loughery	37	45	0	2
1979–80	Kevin Loughery	34	48	—	—
1980–81	Kevin Loughery (12–23)				
	Bob MacKinnon (12–35)	24	58	—	—
1981–82	Larry Brown	44	38	0	2
1982–83	Larry Brown (44–29)				
	Bill Blair (2–4)	49	33	0	2
1983–84	Stan Albeck	45	37	5	6
1984–85	Stan Albeck	42	40	0	3
1985–86	Dave Wohl	39	43	0	3
1986–87	Dave Wohl	24	58	—	—
1987–88	Dave Wohl (2–13)				
	Bob MacKinnon (10–29)				
	Willis Reed (7–21)	19	63	—	—
1988–89	Willis Reed	26	56	—	—
1989–90	Bill Fitch	17	65	—	—
1990–91	Bill Fitch	26	56	—	—
1991–92	Bill Fitch	40	42	1	3
1992–93	Chuck Daly	43	39	2	3

Season	Coach	Reg Sea W	L	Playoffs W	L
1993–94	Chuck Daly	45	37	1	3
	ABA TOTALS	374	370	37	33
	NBA TOTALS	600	876	9	27

* Played in New Jersey as New Jersey Americans
† Moved to New York, changed name to Nets
‡ Joined NBA
§ Moved from New York to New Jersey

NEW ORLEANS BUCCANEERS (ABA)

See Memphis Sounds

NEW ORLEANS JAZZ

See Utah Jazz

NEW YORK KNICKERBOCKERS

Season	Coach	Reg Sea W	L	Playoffs W	L
1946–47	Neil Cohalan	33	27	2	3
1947–48	Joe Lapchick	26	22	1	2
1948–49	Joe Lapchick	32	28	3	3
1949–50	Joe Lapchick	40	28	3	2
1950–51	Joe Lapchick	36	30	8	6
1951–52	Joe Lapchick	37	29	8	6
1952–53	Joe Lapchick	47	23	6	5
1953–54	Joe Lapchick	44	28	0	4
1954–55	Joe Lapchick	38	34	1	2
1955–56	Joe Lapchick (26–25)				
	Vince Boryla (9–12)	35	37	—	—
1956–57	Vince Boryla	36	36	—	—
1957–58	Vince Boryla	35	37	—	—
1958–59	Fuzzy Levane	40	32	0	2
1959–60	Fuzzy Levane (8–19)				
	Carl Braun (19–29)	27	48	—	—
1960–61	Carl Braun	21	58	—	—
1961–62	Eddie Donovan	29	51	—	—
1962–63	Eddie Donovan	21	59	—	—
1963–64	Eddie Donovan	22	58	—	—
1964–65	Eddie Donovan (12–26)				
	Harry Gallatin (19–23)	31	49	—	—
1965–66	Harry Gallatin (6–15)				
	Dick McGuire (24–35)	30	50	—	—
1966–67	Dick McGuire	36	45	1	3
1967–68	Dick McGuire (15–22)				
	Red Holzman (28–17)	43	39	2	4
1968–69	Red Holzman	54	28	6	4
1969–70	Red Holzman	60	22	12	7
1970–71	Red Holzman	52	30	7	5
1971–72	Red Holzman	48	34	9	7
1972–73	Red Holzman	57	25	12	5
1973–74	Red Holzman	49	33	5	7
1974–75	Red Holzman	40	42	1	2
1975–76	Red Holzman	38	44	—	—
1976–77	Red Holzman	40	42	—	—
1977–78	Willis Reed	43	39	2	4
1978–79	Willis Reed (6–8)				
	Red Holzman (25–43)	31	51	—	—
1979–80	Red Holzman	39	43	—	—
1980–81	Red Holzman	50	32	0	2
1981–82	Red Holzman	33	49	—	—
1982–83	Hubie Brown	44	38	2	4
1983–84	Hubie Brown	47	35	6	6
1984–85	Hubie Brown	24	58	—	—
1985–86	Hubie Brown	23	59	—	—
1986–87	Hubie Brown (4–12)				
	Bob Hill (20–46)	24	58	—	—
1987–88	Rick Pitino	38	44	1	3
1988–89	Rick Pitino	52	30	5	4
1989–90	Stu Jackson	45	37	4	6
1990–91	Stu Jackson (7–8)				
	John MacLeod (32–35)	39	43	0	3
1991–92	Pat Riley	51	31	6	6
1992–93	Pat Riley	60	22	9	6
1993–94	Pat Riley	57	25	14	11
	TOTALS	1877	1842	136	134

Season	Coach	Reg Sea W	L	Playoffs W	L

NEW YORK NETS
See New Jersey Nets

OAKLAND OAKS (ABA)
See Virginia Squires

ORLANDO MAGIC

Season	Coach	W	L	W	L
1989–90	Matt Guokas	18	64	—	—
1990–91	Matt Guokas	31	51	—	—
1991–92	Matt Guokas	21	61	—	—
1992–93	Matt Guokas	41	41	—	—
1993–94	Brian Hill	50	32	0	3
	TOTALS	161	249	0	3

PHILADELPHIA WARRIORS
See Golden State Warriors

PHILADELPHIA 76ERS (NBL-NBA)

Season	Coach	W	L	W	L
1946–47	George Mingin (2–0)				
	Benny Borgmann (19–23)	21	23	1	3
1947–48	Benny Borgmann	24	36	0	3
1948–49	Al Cervi	40	23	3	3
1949–50*	Al Cervi	51	13	6	5
1950–51	Al Cervi	32	34	4	3
1951–52	Al Cervi	40	26	3	4
1952–53	Al Cervi	47	24	0	2
1953–54	Al Cervi	42	30	9	4
1954–55	Al Cervi	43	29	7	4
1955–56	Al Cervi	35	37	4	4
1956–57	Al Cervi (4–8)				
	Paul Seymour (34–26)	38	34	2	3
1957–58	Paul Seymour	41	31	1	2
1958–59	Paul Seymour	35	37	5	4
1959–60	Paul Seymour	45	30	1	2
1960–61	Alex Hannum	38	41	4	4
1961–62	Alex Hannum	41	39	2	3
1962–63	Alex Hannum	48	32	2	3
1963–64†	Dolph Schayes	34	46	2	3
1964–65	Dolph Schayes	40	40	6	5
1965–66	Dolph Schayes	55	25	1	4
1966–67	Alex Hannum	68	13	11	4
1967–68	Alex Hannum	62	20	7	6
1968–69	Jack Ramsay	55	27	1	4
1969–70	Jack Ramsay	42	40	1	4
1970–71	Jack Ramsay	47	35	3	4
1971–72	Jack Ramsay	30	52	—	—
1972–73	Roy Rubin (4–47)				
	Kevin Loughery (5–26)	9	73	—	—
1973–74	Gene Shue	25	57	—	—
1974–75	Gene Shue	34	48	—	—
1975–76	Gene Shue	46	36	1	2
1976–77	Gene Shue	50	32	10	9
1977–78	Gene Shue (2–4)				
	Billy Cunningham (53–23)	55	27	6	4
1978–79	Billy Cunningham	47	35	5	4
1979–80	Billy Cunningham	59	23	12	6
1980–81	Billy Cunningham	62	20	9	7
1981–82	Billy Cunningham	58	24	12	9
1982–83	Billy Cunningham	65	17	12	1
1983–84	Billy Cunningham	52	30	2	3
1984–85	Billy Cunningham	58	24	8	5
1985–86	Matt Guokas	54	28	6	6
1986–87	Matt Guokas	45	37	2	3
1987–88	Matt Guokas (20–23)				
	Jim Lynam (16–23)	36	46	—	—
1988–89	Jim Lynam	46	36	0	3
1989–90	Jim Lynam	53	29	4	6
1990–91	Jim Lynam	44	38	4	4
1991–92	Jim Lynam	35	47	—	—
1992–93	Doug Moe (19–37)				
	Fred Carter (7–19)	26	56	—	—

Season	Coach	Reg Sea W	L	Playoffs W	L
1993–94	Fred Carter	25	57	—	—
	NBL TOTALS	85	82	4	9
	NBA TOTALS	1993	1555	175	153

* Joined NBA
† Moved from Syracuse to Philadelphia, changed name to 76ers

PHOENIX SUNS

Season	Coach	W	L	W	L
1968–69	John Kerr	16	66	—	—
1969–70	John Kerr (15–23)				
	Jerry Colangelo (24–20)	39	43	3	4
1970–71	Cotton Fitzsimmons	48	34	—	—
1971–72	Cotton Fitzsimmons	49	33	—	—
1972–73	Bill van Breda Kolff (3–4)				
	Jerry Colangelo (35–40)	38	44	—	—
1973–74	John MacLeod	30	52	—	—
1974–75	John MacLeod	32	50	—	—
1975–76	John MacLeod	42	40	10	9
1976–77	John MacLeod	34	48	—	—
1977–78	John MacLeod	49	33	0	2
1978–79	John MacLeod	50	32	9	6
1979–80	John MacLeod	55	27	3	5
1980–81	John MacLeod	57	25	3	4
1981–82	John MacLeod	46	36	2	5
1982–83	John MacLeod	53	29	1	2
1983–84	John MacLeod	41	41	9	8
1984–85	John MacLeod	36	46	0	3
1985–86	John MacLeod	32	50	—	—
1986–87	John MacLeod (22–34)				
	Dick Van Arsdale (14–12)	36	46	—	—
1987–88	John Wetzel	28	54	—	—
1988–89	Cotton Fitzsimmons	55	27	7	5
1989–90	Cotton Fitzsimmons	54	28	9	7
1990–91	Cotton Fitzsimmons	55	27	1	3
1991–92	Cotton Fitzsimmons	53	29	4	4
1992–93	Paul Westphal	62	20	13	11
1993–94	Paul Westphal	56	26	6	4
	TOTALS	1146	986	80	82

PITTSBURGH CONDORS (ABA)

Season	Coach	W	L	W	L
1967–68*	Vince Cazetta	54	24	11	4
1968–69†	Jim Harding (20–12)				
	Vern Mikkelsen (6–7)				
	Verl Young (10–23)	36	42	3	4
1969–70‡	John Clark (14–25)				
	Buddy Jeannette (15–30)	29	55	—	—
1970–71§	Jack McMahon	36	48	—	—
1971–72	Jack McMahon (4–6)				
	Mark Binstein (21–53)	25	59	—	—
	TOTALS	180	228	14	8

* Played as Pittsburgh Pipers
† Moved to Minnesota
‡ Moved to Pittsburgh
§ Changed name from Pipers to Condors

PITTSBURGH IRONMEN

Season	Coach	W	L	W	L
1946–47	Paul Birch	15	45	—	—
	TOTALS	15	45	—	—

PITTSBURGH PIPERS (ABA)
See Pittsburgh Condors

PORTLAND TRAIL BLAZERS

Season	Coach	W	L	W	L
1970–71	Rolland Todd	29	53	—	—
1971–72	Rolland Todd (12–44)				
	Stu Inman (6–20)	18	64	—	—
1972–73	Jack McCloskey	21	61	—	—
1973–74	Jack McCloskey	27	55	—	—
1974–75	Lenny Wilkens	38	44	—	—
1975–76	Lenny Wilkens	37	45	—	—
1976–77	Jack Ramsay	49	33	14	5
1977–78	Jack Ramsay	58	24	2	4
1978–79	Jack Ramsay	45	37	1	2

Season	Coach	Reg Sea W	L	Playoffs W	L
1979–80	Jack Ramsay	38	44	1	2
1980–81	Jack Ramsay	45	37	1	2
1981–82	Jack Ramsay	42	40	—	—
1982–83	Jack Ramsay	46	36	3	4
1983–84	Jack Ramsay	48	34	2	3
1984–85	Jack Ramsay	42	40	4	5
1985–86	Jack Ramsay	40	42	1	3
1986–87	Mike Schuler	49	33	1	3
1987–88	Mike Schuler	53	29	1	3
1988–89	Mike Schuler (25–22)				
	Rick Adelman (14–21)	39	43	0	3
1989–90	Rick Adelman	59	23	12	9
1990–91	Rick Adelman	63	19	9	7
1991–92	Rick Adelman	57	25	13	8
1992–93	Rick Adelman	51	31	1	3
1993–94	Rick Adelman	47	35	1	3
	TOTALS	1041	927	67	69

PROVIDENCE STEAMROLLERS

Season	Coach	W	L	W	L
1946–47	Robert Morris	28	32	—	—
1947–48	Albert Soar (2–17)				
	Matthew Hickey (4–25)	6	42	—	—
1948–49	Kenneth Loeffler	12	48	—	—
	TOTALS	46	122	—	—

ROCHESTER ROYALS (NBL-NBA)
See Sacramento Kings

SACRAMENTO KINGS (NBL-NBA)

Season	Coach	W	L	W	L
1945–46	Les Harrison	24	10	6	1
1946–47	Les Harrison	31	13	6	5
1947–48	Edmund Malanowicz	44	16	6	5
1948–49*	Les Harrison	45	15	2	2
1949–50	Les Harrison	51	17	0	2
1950–51	Les Harrison	41	27	9	5
1951–52	Les Harrison	41	25	3	3
1952–53	Les Harrison	44	26	1	2
1953–54	Les Harrison	44	28	3	3
1954–55	Les Harrison	29	43	1	2
1955–56	Bobby Wanzer	31	41	—	—
1956–57	Bobby Wanzer	31	41	—	—
1957–58†	Bobby Wanzer	33	39	0	2
1958–59	Bobby Wanzer (3–15)				
	Tom Marshall (16–38)	19	53	—	—
1959–60	Tom Marshall	19	56	—	—
1960–61	Charles Wolf	33	46	—	—
1961–62	Charles Wolf	43	37	1	3
1962–63	Charles Wolf	42	38	6	6
1963–64	Jack McMahon	55	25	4	6
1964–65	Jack McMahon	48	32	1	3
1965–66	Jack McMahon	45	35	2	3
1966–67	Jack McMahon	39	42	1	3
1967–68	Ed Jucker	39	43	—	—
1968–69	Ed Jucker	41	41	—	—
1969–70	Bob Cousy	36	46	—	—
1970–71	Bob Cousy	33	49	—	—
1971–72	Bob Cousy	30	52	—	—
1972–73‡	Bob Cousy	36	46	—	—
1973–74	Bob Cousy (6–16)				
	Draff Young (0–3)				
	Phil Johnson (27–30)	33	49	—	—
1974–75§	Phil Johnson	44	38	2	4
1975–76	Phil Johnson	31	51	—	—
1976–77	Phil Johnson	40	42	—	—
1977–78	Phil Johnson (13–24)				
	Larry Staverman (18–27)	31	51	—	—
1978–79	Cotton Fitzsimmons	48	34	1	4
1979–80	Cotton Fitzsimmons	47	35	1	2
1980–81	Cotton Fitzsimmons	40	42	7	8
1981–82	Cotton Fitzsimmons	30	52	—	—
1982–83	Cotton Fitzsimmons	45	37	—	—
1983–84	Cotton Fitzsimmons	38	44	0	3

Season	Coach	Reg Sea W	Reg Sea L	Playoffs W	Playoffs L
1984-85	Jack McKinney (1-8)				
	Phil Johnson (30-43)	31	51	—	—
1985-86§	Phil Johnson	37	45	0	3
1986-87	Phil Johnson (14-32)				
	Jerry Reynolds (15-21)	29	53	—	—
1987-88	Bill Russell (17-41)				
	Jerry Reynolds (7-17)	24	58	—	—
1988-89	Jerry Reynolds	27	55	—	—
1989-90	Jerry Reynolds (7-21)				
	Dick Motta (16-38)	23	59	—	—
1990-91	Dick Motta	25	57	—	—
1991-92	Dick Motta (7-18)				
	Rex Hughes (22-35)	29	53	—	—
1992-93	Garry St. Jean	25	57	—	—
1993-94	Garry St. Jean	28	54	—	—
	NBL TOTALS	99	39	18	11
	NBA TOTALS	1653	1960	45	69

* Joined NBA
† Moved from Rochester to Cincinnati
‡ Moved from Cincinnati to Kansas City-Omaha, changed name to Kings
§ Played in Kansas City
¶ Moved from Kansas City to Sacramento

ST. LOUIS BOMBERS

Season	Coach	Reg Sea W	Reg Sea L	Playoffs W	Playoffs L
1946-47	Kenneth Loeffler	38	23	1	2
1947-48	Kenneth Loeffler	29	19	3	4
1948-49	Grady Lewis	29	31	0	2
1949-50	Grady Lewis	26	42	—	—
	TOTALS	122	115	4	8

ST. LOUIS HAWKS

See Atlanta Hawks

ST. LOUIS SPIRITS (ABA)

Season	Coach	Reg Sea W	Reg Sea L	Playoffs W	Playoffs L
1967-68	Slater Martin	29	49	0	3
1968-69	Slater Martin (3-9)				
	James Weaver (20-46)	23	55	—	—
1969-70*	Bones McKinney	42	42	0	4
1970-71	Bones McKinney (17-25)				
	Jerry Steele (17-25)	34	50	—	—
1971-72	Tom Meschery	35	49	—	—
1972-73	Larry Brown	57	27	7	5
1973-74†	Larry Brown	47	37	0	4
1974-75	Bob MacKinnon	32	52	5	5
1975-76	Rod Thorn	35	49	—	—
	TOTALS	334	410	12	21

* Moved from Houston to Carolina, changed name to Cougars
† Moved from Carolina to St. Louis, changed name to Spirits

SAN ANTONIO SPURS (ABA-NBA)

Season	Coach	Reg Sea W	Reg Sea L	Playoffs W	Playoffs L
1967-68*	Cliff Hagen	46	32	4	4
1968-69	Cliff Hagen	41	37	3	4
1969-70	Cliff Hagen (22-21)				
	Max Williams (23-18)	45	39	2	4
1970-71†	Max Williams (5-14)				
	Bill Blakely (25-40)	30	54	0	4
1971-72	Tom Nissalke	42	42	0	4
1972-73	Babe McCarthy (24-48)				
	Dave Brown (4-8)	28	56	—	—
1973-74‡	Tom Nissalke	45	39	3	4
1974-75	Tom Nissalke (17-10)				
	Bob Bass (34-23)	51	33	2	4
1975-76	Bob Bass	50	34	3	4
1976-77§	Doug Moe	44	38	0	2
1977-78	Doug Moe	52	30	2	4
1978-79	Doug Moe	48	34	7	7
1979-80	Doug Moe (33-33)				
	Bob Bass (8-8)	41	41	1	2
1980-81	Stan Albeck	52	30	3	4
1981-82	Stan Albeck	48	34	4	5
1982-83	Stan Albeck	53	29	6	5

Season	Coach	Reg Sea W	Reg Sea L	Playoffs W	Playoffs L
1983-84	Morris McHone (11-20)				
	Bob Bass (26-25)	37	45	—	—
1984-85	Cotton Fitzsimmons	41	41	2	3
1985-86	Cotton Fitzsimmons	35	47	0	3
1986-87	Bob Weiss	28	54	—	—
1987-88	Bob Weiss	31	51	0	3
1988-89	Larry Brown	21	61	—	—
1989-90	Larry Brown	56	26	6	4
1990-91	Larry Brown	55	27	1	3
1991-92	Larry Brown (21-17)				
	Bob Bass (26-18)	47	35	0	3
1992-93	Jerry Tarkanian (9-11)				
	Rex Hughes (1-0)				
	John Lucas (39-22)	49	33	5	5
1993-94	John Lucas	55	27	1	3
	ABA TOTALS	378	366	17	32
	NBA TOTALS	793	683	38	56

* Played in Dallas as Dallas Chapparals
† Played season as Texas Chapparals
‡ Moved from Dallas to San Antonio, changed name to Spurs
§ Joined NBA

SAN DIEGO CLIPPERS

See Los Angeles Clippers

SAN DIEGO CONQUISTADORS (ABA)

Season	Coach	Reg Sea W	Reg Sea L	Playoffs W	Playoffs L
1972-73	K.C. Jones	30	54	0	4
1973-74	Wilt Chamberlain	37	47	2	4
1974-75	Alex Groza (15-23)				
	Beryl Shipley (16-30)	31	53	—	—
1975-76*	Bill Musselman	3	8	—	—
	TOTALS	101	162	2	8

* Changed name to Sails

SAN DIEGO ROCKETS

See Houston Rockets

SAN DIEGO SAILS (ABA)

See San Diego Conquistadors

SAN FRANCISCO WARRIORS

See Golden State Warriors

SEATTLE SUPERSONICS

Season	Coach	Reg Sea W	Reg Sea L	Playoffs W	Playoffs L
1968-69	Al Bianchi	30	52	—	—
1969-70	Lenny Wilkens	36	46	—	—
1970-71	Lenny Wilkens	38	44	—	—
1971-72	Lenny Wilkens	47	35	—	—
1972-73	Tom Nissalke (13-32)				
	Morris Buckwalter (13-24)	26	56	—	—
1973-74	Bill Russell	36	46	—	—
1974-75	Bill Russell	43	39	4	5
1975-76	Bill Russell	43	39	2	4
1976-77	Bill Russell	40	42	—	—
1977-78	Bob Hopkins (5-17)				
	Lenny Wilkens (42-18)	47	35	13	9
1978-79	Lenny Wilkens	52	30	12	5
1979-80	Lenny Wilkens	56	26	7	8
1980-81	Lenny Wilkens	34	48	—	—
1981-82	Lenny Wilkens	52	30	3	5
1982-83	Lenny Wilkens	48	34	0	2
1983-84	Lenny Wilkens	42	40	2	3
1984-85	Lenny Wilkens	31	51	—	—
1985-86	Bernie Bickerstaff	31	51	—	—
1986-87	Bernie Bickerstaff	39	43	7	7
1987-88	Bernie Bickerstaff	44	38	2	3
1988-89	Bernie Bickerstaff	47	35	3	5
1989-90	Bernie Bickerstaff	41	41	—	—
1990-91	K.C. Jones	41	41	2	3
1991-92	K.C. Jones (18-18)				
	Bob Kloppenburg (2-2)				
	George Karl (27-15)	47	35	4	5
1992-93	George Karl	55	27	10	9

Season	Coach	Reg Sea W	Reg Sea L	Playoffs W	Playoffs L
1993-94	George Karl	63	19	2	3
	TOTALS	1132	1082	73	76

SHEBOYGAN REDSKINS (NBL-NBA)

Season	Coach	Reg Sea W	Reg Sea L	Playoffs W	Playoffs L
1938-39	Edwin Schutte	11	17	—	—
1939-40	Francis Zummach	15	13	1	2
1940-41	Francis Zummach	13	11	2	4
1941-42	Francis Zummach	10	14	—	—
1942-43	Carl Roth	12	11	4	1
1943-44	Carl Roth	14	8	2	4
1944-45	Dutch Dehnert	19	11	4	4
1945-46	Dutch Dehnert	21	13	3	5
1946-47	Doxie Moore	26	18	2	3
1947-48	Doxie Moore (23-36)				
	Bobby McDermott (0-1)	23	37	—	—
1948-49	Ken Suesens	35	29	0	2
1949-50*	Ken Suesens	22	40	1	2
	NBL TOTALS	199	182	18	25
	NBA TOTALS	22	40	1	2

* Joined NBA

SYRACUSE NATIONALS (NBL-NBA)

See Philadelphia 76ers

TEXAS CHAPPARALS (ABA)

See San Antonio Spurs

TORONTO HUSKIES

Season	Coach	Reg Sea W	Reg Sea L	Playoffs W	Playoffs L
1946-47	Ed Sadowski (3-9)				
	Lew Hayman (0-1)				
	Dick Fitzgerald (2-1)				
	Bob Rolfe (17-27)	22	38	—	—
	TOTALS	22	38	—	—

TRI-CITIES BLACKHAWKS (NBL-NBA)

See Atlanta Hawks

UTAH JAZZ

Season	Coach	Reg Sea W	Reg Sea L	Playoffs W	Playoffs L
1974-75*	Scotty Robertson (1-14)				
	Elgin Baylor (0-1)				
	Bill van Breda Kolff (22-44)	23	59	—	—
1975-76	Bill van Breda Kolff	38	44	—	—
1976-77	Bill van Breda Kolff (14-12)				
	Elgin Baylor (21-35)	35	47	—	—
1977-78	Elgin Baylor	39	43	—	—
1978-79	Elgin Baylor	26	56	—	—
1979-80†	Tom Nissalke	24	58	—	—
1980-81	Tom Nissalke	28	54	—	—
1981-82	Tom Nissalke (8-12)				
	Frank Layden (17-45)	25	57	—	—
1982-83	Frank Layden	30	52	—	—
1983-84	Frank Layden	45	37	5	6
1984-85	Frank Layden	41	41	4	6
1985-86	Frank Layden	42	40	1	3
1986-87	Frank Layden	44	38	2	3
1987-88	Frank Layden	47	35	6	5
1988-89	Frank Layden (11-6)				
	Jerry Sloan (40-25)	51	31	0	3
1989-90	Jerry Sloan	55	27	2	3
1990-91	Jerry Sloan	54	28	4	5
1991-92	Jerry Sloan	55	27	9	7
1992-93	Jerry Sloan	47	35	2	3
1993-94	Jerry Sloan	53	29	8	8
	TOTALS	802	838	43	52

* Played in New Orleans as Jazz
† Moved from New Orleans to Utah

UTAH STARS (ABA)

Season	Coach	Reg Sea W	Reg Sea L	Playoffs W	Playoffs L
1967-68*	Al Brightman (12-24)				
	Harry Dinnell (13-29)	25	53	—	—
1968-69†	Bill Sharman	33	45	—	—
1969-70	Bill Sharman	43	41	10	7
1970-71‡	Bill Sharman	57	27	12	6

Season	Coach	Reg Sea W	L	Playoffs W	L
1971–72	LaDell Andersen	60	24	7	4
1972–73	LaDell Andersen	55	29	6	4
1973–74	Joe Mullaney	51	33	9	9
1974–75	Morris Buckwalter (24–32)				
	Tom Nissalke (14–14)	38	46	2	4
1975–76	Tom Nissalke	4	12	—	—
	TOTALS	366	310	46	34

* Played in Anaheim as Amigos
† Moved to Los Angeles, changed name to Stars
‡ Moved from Los Angeles to Utah

VIRGINIA SQUIRES (ABA)

Season	Coach	Reg Sea W	L	Playoffs W	L
1967–68*	Bruce Hale	22	56	—	—
1968–69	Alex Hannum	60	18	12	4
1969–70†	Al Bianchi	44	40	3	4
1970–71‡	Al Bianchi	55	29	6	6
1971–72	Al Bianchi	45	39	7	4
1972–73	Al Bianchi	42	42	1	4
1973–74	Al Bianchi	28	56	1	4
1974–75	Al Bianchi	15	69	—	—
1975–76	Al Bianchi (1–5)				
	Bill Musselman (4–26)				
	Mack Calvin (0–5)				
	Jim Ankerson (1–0)				
	Zelmo Beaty (9–32)	15	68	—	—
	TOTALS	326	417	30	26

* Played in Oakland as Oaks
† Moved from Oakland to Washington, D.C., changed name to Capitols
‡ Moved from Washington to Virginia, changed name to Squires

WASHINGTON BULLETS

Season	Coach	Reg Sea W	L	Playoffs W	L
1961–62*	Jim Pollard	18	62	—	—

Season	Coach	Reg Sea W	L	Playoffs W	L
1962–63†	Jack McMahon (12–26)				
	Bob Leonard (13–29)	25	55	—	—
1963–64‡	Bob Leonard	31	49	—	—
1964–65	Buddy Jeannette	37	43	5	5
1965–66	Paul Seymour	38	42	0	3
1966–67	Michael Farmer (1–8)				
	Buddy Jeannette (3–13)				
	Gene Shue (16–40)	20	61	—	—
1967–68	Gene Shue	36	46	—	—
1968–69	Gene Shue	57	25	0	4
1969–70	Gene Shue	50	32	3	4
1970–71	Gene Shue	42	40	8	10
1971–72	Gene Shue	38	44	2	4
1972–73	Gene Shue	52	30	1	4
1973–74§	K.C. Jones	47	35	3	4
1974–75¶	K.C. Jones	60	22	8	9
1975–76	K.C. Jones	48	34	3	4
1976–77	Dick Motta	48	34	4	5
1977–78	Dick Motta	44	38	14	7
1978–79	Dick Motta	54	28	9	10
1979–80	Dick Motta	39	43	0	2
1980–81	Gene Shue	39	43	—	—
1981–82	Gene Shue	43	39	3	4
1982–83	Gene Shue	42	40	—	—
1983–84	Gene Shue	35	47	1	3
1984–85	Gene Shue	40	42	1	3
1985–86	Gene Shue (32–37)				
	Kevin Loughery (7–6)	39	43	2	3
1986–87	Kevin Loughery	42	40	0	3
1987–88	Kevin Loughery (8–19)				
	Wes Unseld (30–25)	38	44	2	3
1988–89	Wes Unseld	40	42	—	—
1989–90	Wes Unseld	31	51	—	—

Season	Coach	Reg Sea W	L	Playoffs W	L
1990–91	Wes Unseld	30	52	—	—
1991–92	Wes Unseld	25	57	—	—
1992–93	Wes Unseld	22	60	—	—
1993–94	Wes Unseld	24	58	—	—
	TOTALS	1274	1421	69	94

* Played in Chicago as Packers
† Played in Chicago as Zephyrs
‡ Moved to Baltimore, changed name to Bullets
§ Played in Washington, D.C., as Capital Bullets
¶ Changed name to Washington Bullets

WASHINGTON CAPITOLS

Season	Coach	Reg Sea W	L	Playoffs W	L
1946–47	Red Auerbach	49	11	2	4
1947–48	Red Auerbach	28	20	—	—
1948–49	Red Auerbach	38	22	6	5
1949–50	Robert Feerick	32	36	0	2
1950–51*	Horace McKinney	10	25	—	—
	TOTALS	157	114	8	11

* Disbanded January 9, 1951

WASHINGTON CAPITOLS (ABA)

See Virginia Squires

WATERLOO HAWKS (NBL–NBA)

Season	Coach	Reg Sea W	L	Playoffs W	L
1948–49	Charles Shipp	30	32	—	—
1949–50*	Charles Shipp (8–27)				
	John Smiley (11–16)	19	43	—	—
	NBL TOTALS	30	32	—	—
	NBA TOTALS	19	43	—	—

*Joined NBA

NBA POSTSEASON AWARDS

NBA MOST VALUABLE PLAYER

(Maurice Podoloff Trophy)

Selected by vote of NBA players through 1979–80; by vote of writers and broadcasters since 1980–81

1955–56—Bob Pettit, St. Louis
1956–57—Bob Cousy, Boston
1957–58—Bill Russell, Boston
1958–59—Bob Pettit, St. Louis
1959–60—Wilt Chamberlain, Philadelphia
1960–61—Bill Russell, Boston
1961–62—Bill Russell, Boston
1962–63—Bill Russell, Boston
1963–64—Oscar Robertson, Cincinnati
1964–65—Bill Russell, Boston
1965–66—Wilt Chamberlain, Philadelphia
1966–67—Wilt Chamberlain, Philadelphia
1967–68—Wilt Chamberlain, Philadelphia

1968–69—Wes Unseld, Baltimore
1969–70—Willis Reed, New York
1970–71—Kareem Abdul-Jabbar, Milwaukee
1971–72—Kareem Abdul-Jabbar, Milwaukee
1972–73—Dave Cowens, Boston
1973–74—Kareem Abdul-Jabbar, Milwaukee
1974–75—Bob McAdoo, Buffalo
1975–76—Kareem Abdul-Jabbar, Los Angeles
1976–77—Kareem Abdul-Jabbar, Los Angeles
1977–78—Bill Walton, Portland
1978–79—Moses Malone, Houston
1979–80—Kareem Abdul-Jabbar, Los Angeles
1980–81—Julius Erving, Philadelphia

1981–82—Moses Malone, Houston
1982–83—Moses Malone, Philadelphia
1983–84—Larry Bird, Boston
1984–85—Larry Bird, Boston
1985–86—Larry Bird, Boston
1986–87—Magic Johnson, L.A. Lakers
1987–88—Michael Jordan, Chicago
1988–89—Magic Johnson, L.A. Lakers
1989–90—Magic Johnson, L.A. Lakers
1990–91—Michael Jordan, Chicago
1991–92—Michael Jordan, Chicago
1992–93—Charles Barkley, Phoenix
1993–94—Hakeem Olajuwon, Houston

NBA FINALS MVP AWARD

(Presented by Chrysler-Plymouth)

Selected by media panel

1969—Jerry West, Los Angeles
1970—Willis Reed, New York
1971—Kareem Abdul-Jabbar, Milwaukee
1972—Wilt Chamberlain, Los Angeles
1973—Willis Reed, New York
1974—John Havlicek, Boston
1975—Rick Barry, Golden State
1976—Jo Jo White, Boston
1977—Bill Walton, Portland

1978—Wes Unseld, Washington
1979—Dennis Johnson, Seattle
1980—Magic Johnson, Los Angeles
1981—Cedric Maxwell, Boston
1982—Magic Johnson, Los Angeles
1983—Moses Malone, Philadelphia
1984—Larry Bird, Boston
1985—Kareem Abdul-Jabbar, L.A. Lakers
1986—Larry Bird, Boston

1987—Magic Johnson, L.A. Lakers
1988—James Worthy, L.A. Lakers
1989—Joe Dumars, Detroit
1990—Isiah Thomas, Detroit
1991—Michael Jordan, Chicago
1992—Michael Jordan, Chicago
1993—Michael Jordan, Chicago
1994—Hakeem Olajuwon, Houston

IBM NBA COACH OF THE YEAR
(Red Auerbach Trophy)

Selected by writers and broadcasters

1962–63—Harry Gallatin, St. Louis	1973–74—Ray Scott, Detroit	1984–85—Don Nelson, Milwaukee
1963–64—Alex Hannum, San Francisco	1974–75—Phil Johnson, Kansas City-Omaha	1985–86—Mike Fratello, Atlanta
1964–65—Red Auerbach, Boston	1975–76—Bill Fitch, Cleveland	1986–87—Mike Schuler, Portland
1965–66—Dolph Schayes, Philadelphia	1976–77—Tom Nissalke, Houston	1987–88—Doug Moe, Denver
1966–67—Johnny Kerr, Chicago	1977–78—Hubie Brown, Atlanta	1988–89—Cotton Fitzsimmons, Phoenix
1967–68—Richie Guerin, St. Louis	1978–79—Cotton Fitzsimmons, Kansas City	1989–90—Pat Riley, L.A. Lakers
1968–69—Gene Shue, Baltimore	1979–80—Bill Fitch, Boston	1990–91—Don Chaney, Houston
1969–70—Red Holzman, New York	1980–81—Jack McKinney, Indiana	1991–92—Don Nelson, Golden State
1970–71—Dick Motta, Chicago	1981–82—Gene Shue, Washington	1992–93—Pat Riley, New York
1971–72—Bill Sharman, Los Angeles	1982–83—Don Nelson, Milwaukee	1993–94—Lenny Wilkens, Atlanta
1972–73—Tom Heinsohn, Boston	1983–84—Frank Layden, Utah	

COCA-COLA CLASSIC NBA ROOKIE OF THE YEAR
(Eddie Gottlieb Trophy)

Selected by writers and broadcasters

1947–48—Paul Hoffman, Baltimore	1963–64—Jerry Lucas, Cincinnati	1979–80—Larry Bird, Boston
1948–49—Howie Shannon, Providence	1964–65—Willis Reed, New York	1980–81—Darrell Griffith, Utah
1949–50—Alex Groza, Indianapolis	1965–66—Rick Barry, San Francisco	1981–82—Buck Williams, New Jersey
1950–51—Paul Arizin, Philadelphia	1966–67—Dave Bing, Detroit	1982–83—Terry Cummings, San Diego
1951–52—(tie) Bill Tosheff, Indianapolis	1967–68—Earl Monroe, Baltimore	1983–84—Ralph Sampson, Houston
Mel Hutchins, Milwaukee	1968–69—Wes Unseld, Baltimore	1984–85—Michael Jordan, Chicago
1952–53—Don Meineke, Fort Wayne	1969–70—Kareem Abdul-Jabbar, Milwaukee	1985–86—Patrick Ewing, New York
1953–54—Ray Felix, Baltimore	1970–71—(tie) Dave Cowens, Boston	1986–87—Chuck Person, Indiana
1954–55—Bob Pettit, Milwaukee	Geoff Petrie, Portland	1987–88—Mark Jackson, New York
1955–56—Maurice Stokes, Rochester	1971–72—Sidney Wicks, Portland	1988–89—Mitch Richmond, Golden State
1956–57—Tom Heinsohn, Boston	1972–73—Bob McAdoo, Buffalo	1989–90—David Robinson, San Antonio
1957–58—Woody Sauldsberry, Philadelphia	1973–74—Ernie DiGregorio, Buffalo	1990–91—Derrick Coleman, New Jersey
1958–59—Elgin Baylor, Minneapolis	1974–75—Jamaal Wilkes, Golden State	1991–92—Larry Johnson, Charlotte
1959–60—Wilt Chamberlain, Philadelphia	1975–76—Alvan Adams, Phoenix	1992–93—Shaquille O'Neal, Orlando
1960–61—Oscar Robertson, Cincinnati	1976–77—Adrian Dantley, Buffalo	1993–94—Chris Webber, Golden State
1961–62—Walt Bellamy, Chicago	1977–78—Walter Davis, Phoenix	
1962–63—Terry Dischinger, Chicago	1978–79—Phil Ford, Kansas City	

NBA DEFENSIVE PLAYER OF THE YEAR
Selected by writers and broadcasters

1982–83—Sidney Moncrief, Milwaukee	1986–87—Michael Cooper, L.A. Lakers	1990–91—Dennis Rodman, Detroit
1983–84—Sidney Moncrief, Milwaukee	1987–88—Michael Jordan, Chicago	1991–92—David Robinson, San Antonio
1984–85—Mark Eaton, Utah	1988–89—Mark Eaton, Utah	1992–93—Hakeem Olajuwon, Houston
1985–86—Alvin Robertson, San Antonio	1989–90—Dennis Rodman, Detroit	1993–94—Hakeem Olajuwon, Houston

MILLER GENUINE DRAFT NBA SIXTH MAN AWARD
Selected by writers and broadcasters

1982–83—Bobby Jones, Philadelphia	1986–87—Ricky Pierce, Milwaukee	1990–91—Detlef Schrempf, Indiana
1983–84—Kevin McHale, Boston	1987–88—Roy Tarpley, Dallas	1991–92—Detlef Schrempf, Indiana
1984–85—Kevin McHale, Boston	1988–89—Eddie Johnson, Phoenix	1992–93—Cliff Robinson, Portland
1985–86—Bill Walton, Boston	1989–90—Ricky Pierce, Milwaukee	1993–94—Dell Curry, Charlotte

IBM AWARD
Determined by computer formula

1983–84—Magic Johnson, Los Angeles	1987–88—Charles Barkley, Philadelphia	1991–92—Dennis Rodman, Detroit
1984–85—Michael Jordan, Chicago	1988–89—Michael Jordan, Chicago	1992–93—Hakeem Olajuwon, Houston
1985–86—Charles Barkley, Philadelphia	1989–90—David Robinson, San Antonio	1993–94—David Robinson, San Antonio
1986–87—Charles Barkley, Philadelphia	1990–91—David Robinson, San Antonio	

NBA MOST IMPROVED PLAYER
Selected by writers and broadcasters

1985–86—Alvin Robertson, San Antonio	1988–89—Kevin Johnson, Phoenix	1991–92—Pervis Ellison, Washington
1986–87—Dale Ellis, Seattle	1989–90—Rony Seikaly, Miami	1992–93—Mahmoud Abdul-Rauf, Denver
1987–88—Kevin Duckworth, Portland	1990–91—Scott Skiles, Orlando	1993–94—Don MacLean, Washington

BAUSCH & LOMB NBA COURT VISION AWARD
Awarded to assist leader

1992–93—John Stockton, Utah
1993–94—John Stockton, Utah

J. WALTER KENNEDY CITIZENSHIP AWARD
Selected by the Pro Basketball Writers Association of America

1974–75—Wes Unseld, Washington
1975–76—Slick Watts, Seattle
1976–77—Dave Bing, Washington
1977–78—Bob Lanier, Detroit
1978–79—Calvin Murphy, Houston
1979–80—Austin Carr, Cleveland
1980–81—Mike Glenn, New York

1981–82—Kent Benson, Detroit
1982–83—Julius Erving, Philadelphia
1983–84—Frank Layden, Utah
1984–85—Dan Issel, Denver
1985–86—(tie) Michael Cooper, L.A. Lakers
　　　　　　　Rory Sparrow, New York
1986–87—Isiah Thomas, Detroit

1987–88—Alex English, Denver
1988–89—Thurl Bailey, Utah
1989–90—Glenn Rivers, Atlanta
1990–91—Kevin Johnson, Phoenix
1991–92—Magic Johnson, L.A. Lakers
1992–93—Terry Porter, Portland
1993–94—Joe Dumars, Detroit

NBA EXECUTIVE OF THE YEAR
Selected by *The Sporting News*

1972–73—Joe Axelson, Kansas City-Omaha
1973–74—Eddie Donovan, Buffalo
1974–75—Dick Vertlieb, Golden State
1975–76—Jerry Colangelo, Phoenix
1976–77—Ray Patterson, Houston
1977–78—Angelo Drossos, San Antonio
1978–79—Bob Ferry, Washington
1979–80—Red Auerbach, Boston

1980–81—Jerry Colangelo, Phoenix
1981–82—Bob Ferry, Washington
1982–83—Zollie Volchok, Seattle
1983–84—Frank Layden, Utah
1984–85—Vince Boryla, Denver
1985–86—Stan Kasten, Atlanta
1986–87—Stan Kasten, Atlanta

1987–88—Jerry Krause, Chicago
1988–89—Jerry Colangelo, Phoenix
1989–90—Bob Bass, San Antonio
1990–91—Bucky Buckwalter, Portland
1991–92—Wayne Embry, Cleveland
1992–93—Jerry Colangelo, Phoenix
1993–94—Bob Whitsitt, Seattle

ALL-NBA TEAMS
Selected by writers and broadcasters

FIRST TEAM	SECOND TEAM	FIRST TEAM	SECOND TEAM
1946–47		**1951–52**	
Joe Fulks, Philadelphia	Ernie Calverley, Providence	George Mikan, Minneapolis	Larry Foust, Fort Wayne
Bob Feerick, Washington	Frank Baumholtz, Cleveland	Ed Macauley, Boston	Vern Mikkelsen, Minneapolis
Stan Miasek, Detroit	John Logan, St. Louis	Paul Arizin, Philadelphia	Jim Pollard, Minneapolis
Bones McKinney, Washington	Chuck Halbert, Chicago	Bob Cousy, Boston	Bob Wanzer, Rochester
Max Zaslofsky, Chicago	Fred Scolari, Washington	Bob Davies, Rochester	Andy Phillip, Philadelphia
		Dolph Schayes, Syracuse	
1947–48			
Joe Fulks, Philadelphia	John Logan, St. Louis	**1952–53**	
Max Zaslofsky, Chicago	Carl Braun, New York	George Mikan, Minneapolis	Bill Sharman, Boston
Ed Sadowski, Boston	Stan Miasek, Chicago	Bob Cousy, Boston	Vern Mikkelsen, Minneapolis
Howie Dallmar, Philadelphia	Fred Scolari, Washington	Neil Johnston, Philadelphia	Bob Wanzer, Rochester
Bob Feerick, Washington	Buddy Jeannette, Baltimore	Ed Macauley, Boston	Bob Davies, Rochester
		Dolph Schayes, Syracuse	Andy Phillip, Philadelphia
1948–49			
George Mikan, Minneapolis	Arnie Risen, Rochester	**1953–54**	
Joe Fulks, Philadelphia	Bob Feerick, Washington	Bob Cousy, Boston	Ed Macauley, Boston
Bob Davies, Rochester	Bones McKinney, Washington	Neil Johnston, Philadelphia	Jim Pollard, Minneapolis
Max Zaslofsky, Chicago	Ken Sailors, Providence	George Mikan, Minneapolis	Carl Braun, New York
Jim Pollard, Minneapolis	John Logan, St. Louis	Dolph Schayes, Syracuse	Bob Wanzer, Rochester
		Harry Gallatin, New York	Paul Seymour, Syracuse
1949–50			
George Mikan, Minneapolis	Frank Brian, Anderson	**1954–55**	
Jim Pollard, Minneapolis	Fred Schaus, Fort Wayne	Neil Johnston, Philadelphia	Vern Mikkelsen, Minneapolis
Alex Groza, Indianapolis	Dolph Schayes, Syracuse	Bob Cousy, Boston	Harry Gallatin, New York
Bob Davies, Rochester	Al Cervi, Syracuse	Dolph Schayes, Syracuse	Paul Seymour, Syracuse
Max Zaslofsky, Chicago	Ralph Beard, Indianapolis	Bob Pettit, Milwaukee	Slater Martin, Minneapolis
		Larry Foust, Fort Wayne	Bill Sharman, Boston
1950–51			
George Mikan, Minneapolis	Dolph Schayes, Syracuse	**1955–56**	
Alex Groza, Indianapolis	Frank Brian, Tri-Cities	Bob Pettit, St. Louis	Dolph Schayes, Syracuse
Ed Macauley, Boston	Vern Mikkelsen, Minneapolis	Paul Arizin, Philadelphia	Maurice Stokes, Rochester
Bob Davies, Rochester	Joe Fulks, Philadelphia	Neil Johnston, Philadelphia	Clyde Lovellette, Minneapolis
Ralph Beard, Indianapolis	Dick McGuire, New York	Bob Cousy, Boston	Slater Martin, Minneapolis
		Bill Sharman, Boston	Jack George, Philadelphia

FIRST TEAM	SECOND TEAM	FIRST TEAM	SECOND TEAM

1956-57

FIRST TEAM
Paul Arizin, Philadelphia
Dolph Schayes, Syracuse
Bob Pettit, St. Louis
Bob Cousy, Boston
Bill Sharman, Boston

SECOND TEAM
George Yardley, Fort Wayne
Maurice Stokes, Rochester
Neil Johnston, Philadelphia
Dick Garmaker, Minneapolis
Slater Martin, St. Louis

1957-58

FIRST TEAM
Dolph Schayes, Syracuse
George Yardley, Detroit
Bob Pettit, St. Louis
Bob Cousy, Boston
Bill Sharman, Boston

SECOND TEAM
Cliff Hagan, St. Louis
Maurice Stokes, Cincinnati
Bill Russell, Boston
Tom Gola, Philadelphia
Slater Martin, St. Louis

1958-59

FIRST TEAM
Bob Pettit, St. Louis
Elgin Baylor, Minneapolis
Bill Russell, Boston
Bob Cousy, Boston
Bill Sharman, Boston

SECOND TEAM
Paul Arizin, Philadelphia
Cliff Hagan, St. Louis
Dolph Schayes, Syracuse
Slater Martin, St. Louis
Richie Guerin, New York

1959-60

FIRST TEAM
Bob Pettit, St. Louis
Elgin Baylor, Minneapolis
Wilt Chamberlain, Philadelphia
Bob Cousy, Boston
Gene Shue, Detroit

SECOND TEAM
Jack Twyman, Cincinnati
Dolph Schayes, Syracuse
Bill Russell, Boston
Richie Guerin, New York
Bill Sharman, Boston

1960-61

FIRST TEAM
Elgin Baylor, Los Angeles
Bob Pettit, St. Louis
Wilt Chamberlain, Philadelphia
Bob Cousy, Boston
Oscar Robertson, Cincinnati

SECOND TEAM
Dolph Schayes, Syracuse
Tom Heinsohn, Boston
Bill Russell, Boston
Larry Costello, Syracuse
Gene Shue, Detroit

1961-62

FIRST TEAM
Bob Pettit, St. Louis
Elgin Baylor, Los Angeles
Wilt Chamberlain, Philadelphia
Jerry West, Los Angeles
Oscar Robertson, Cincinnati

SECOND TEAM
Tom Heinsohn, Boston
Jack Twyman, Cincinnati
Bill Russell, Boston
Richie Guerin, New York
Bob Cousy, Boston

1962-63

FIRST TEAM
Elgin Baylor, Los Angeles
Bob Pettit, St. Louis
Bill Russell, Boston
Oscar Robertson, Cincinnati
Jerry West, Los Angeles

SECOND TEAM
Tom Heinsohn, Boston
Bailey Howell, Detroit
Wilt Chamberlain, San Francisco
Bob Cousy, Boston
Hal Greer, Syracuse

1963-64

FIRST TEAM
Bob Pettit, St. Louis
Elgin Baylor, Los Angeles
Wilt Chamberlain, San Francisco
Oscar Robertson, Cincinnati
Jerry West, Los Angeles

SECOND TEAM
Tom Heinsohn, Boston
Jerry Lucas, Cincinnati
Bill Russell, Boston
John Havlicek, Boston
Hal Greer, Philadelphia

1964-65

FIRST TEAM
Elgin Baylor, Los Angeles
Jerry Lucas, Cincinnati
Bill Russell, Boston
Oscar Robertson, Cincinnati
Jerry West, Los Angeles

SECOND TEAM
Bob Pettit, St. Louis
Gus Johnson, Baltimore
Wilt Chamberlain, S.F.-Phil.
Sam Jones, Boston
Hal Greer, Philadelphia

1965-66

FIRST TEAM
Rick Barry, San Francisco
Jerry Lucas, Cincinnati
Wilt Chamberlain, Philadelphia
Oscar Robertson, Cincinnati
Jerry West, Los Angeles

SECOND TEAM
John Havlicek, Boston
Gus Johnson, Baltimore
Bill Russell, Boston
Sam Jones, Boston
Hal Greer, Philadelphia

1966-67

FIRST TEAM
Rick Barry, San Francisco
Elgin Baylor, Los Angeles
Wilt Chamberlain, Philadelphia
Jerry West, Los Angeles
Oscar Robertson, Cincinnati

SECOND TEAM
Willis Reed, New York
Jerry Lucas, Cincinnati
Bill Russell, Boston
Hal Greer, Philadelphia
Sam Jones, Boston

1967-68

FIRST TEAM
Elgin Baylor, Los Angeles
Jerry Lucas, Cincinnati
Wilt Chamberlain, Philadelphia
Dave Bing, Detroit
Oscar Robertson, Cincinnati

SECOND TEAM
Willis Reed, New York
John Havlicek, Boston
Bill Russell, Boston
Hal Greer, Philadelphia
Jerry West, Los Angeles

1968-69

FIRST TEAM
Billy Cunningham, Philadelphia
Elgin Baylor, Los Angeles
Wes Unseld, Baltimore
Earl Monroe, Baltimore
Oscar Robertson, Cincinnati

SECOND TEAM
John Havlicek, Boston
Dave DeBusschere, Det.-N.Y.
Willis Reed, New York
Hal Greer, Philadelphia
Jerry West, Los Angeles

1969-70

FIRST TEAM
Billy Cunningham, Philadelphia
Connie Hawkins, Phoenix
Willis Reed, New York
Jerry West, Los Angeles
Walt Frazier, New York

SECOND TEAM
John Havlicek, Boston
Gus Johnson, Baltimore
Kareem Abdul-Jabbar, Milwaukee
Lou Hudson, Atlanta
Oscar Robertson, Cincinnati

1970-71

FIRST TEAM
John Havlicek, Boston
Billy Cunningham, Philadelphia
Kareem Abdul-Jabbar, Milwaukee
Jerry West, Los Angeles
Dave Bing, Detroit

SECOND TEAM
Gus Johnson, Baltimore
Bob Love, Chicago
Willis Reed, New York
Walt Frazier, New York
Oscar Robertson, Milwaukee

1971-72

FIRST TEAM
John Havlicek, Boston
Spencer Haywood, Seattle
Kareem Abdul-Jabbar, Milwaukee
Jerry West, Los Angeles
Walt Frazier, New York

SECOND TEAM
Bob Love, Chicago
Billy Cunningham, Philadelphia
Wilt Chamberlain, Los Angeles
Nate Archibald, Cincinnati
Archie Clark, Phil.-Balt.

1972-73

FIRST TEAM
John Havlicek, Boston
Spencer Haywood, Seattle
Kareem Abdul-Jabbar, Milwaukee
Nate Archibald, Kansas City-Omaha
Jerry West, Los Angeles

SECOND TEAM
Elvin Hayes, Baltimore
Rick Barry, Golden State
Dave Cowens, Boston
Walt Frazier, New York
Pete Maravich, Atlanta

1973-74

FIRST TEAM
John Havlicek, Boston
Rick Barry, Golden State
Kareem Abdul-Jabbar, Milwaukee
Walt Frazier, New York
Gail Goodrich, Los Angeles

SECOND TEAM
Elvin Hayes, Capital
Spencer Haywood, Seattle
Bob McAdoo, Buffalo
Dave Bing, Detroit
Norm Van Lier, Chicago

1974-75

FIRST TEAM
Rick Barry, Golden State
Elvin Hayes, Washington
Bob McAdoo, Buffalo
Nate Archibald, Kansas City-Omaha
Walt Frazier, New York

SECOND TEAM
John Havlicek, Boston
Spencer Haywood, Seattle
Dave Cowens, Boston
Phil Chenier, Washington
Jo Jo White, Boston

1975-76

FIRST TEAM
Rick Barry, Golden State
George McGinnis, Philadelphia
Kareem Abdul-Jabbar, Los Angeles
Nate Archibald, Kansas City
Pete Maravich, New Orleans

SECOND TEAM
Elvin Hayes, Washington
John Havlicek, Boston
Dave Cowens, Boston
Randy Smith, Buffalo
Phil Smith, Golden State

FIRST TEAM	SECOND TEAM	FIRST TEAM	SECOND TEAM
1976-77		**1982-83**	
Elvin Hayes, Washington	Julius Erving, Philadelphia	Larry Bird, Boston	Alex English, Denver
David Thompson, Denver	George McGinnis, Philadelphia	Julius Erving, Philadelphia	Buck Williams, New Jersey
Kareem Abdul-Jabbar, Los Angeles	Bill Walton, Portland	Moses Malone, Philadelphia	Kareem Abdul-Jabbar, Los Angeles
Pete Maravich, New Orleans	George Gervin, San Antonio	Magic Johnson, Los Angeles	George Gervin, San Antonio
Paul Westphal, Phoenix	Jo Jo White, Boston	Sidney Moncrief, Milwaukee	Isiah Thomas, Detroit
1977-78		**1983-84**	
Leonard Robinson, New Orleans	Walter Davis, Phoenix	Larry Bird, Boston	Julius Erving, Philadelphia
Julius Erving, Philadelphia	Maurice Lucas, Portland	Bernard King, New York	Adrian Dantley, Utah
Bill Walton, Portland	Kareem Abdul-Jabbar, Los Angeles	Kareem Abdul-Jabbar, Los Angeles	Moses Malone, Philadelphia
George Gervin, San Antonio	Paul Westphal, Phoenix	Magic Johnson, Los Angeles	Sidney Moncrief, Milwaukee
David Thompson, Denver	Pete Maravich, New Orleans	Isiah Thomas, Detroit	Jim Paxson, Portland
1978-79		**1984-85**	
Marques Johnson, Milwaukee	Walter Davis, Phoenix	Larry Bird, Boston	Terry Cummings, Milwaukee
Elvin Hayes, Washington	Bobby Dandridge, Washington	Bernard King, New York	Ralph Sampson, Houston
Moses Malone, Houston	Kareem Abdul-Jabbar, Los Angeles	Moses Malone, Philadelphia	Kareem Abdul-Jabbar, L.A. Lakers
George Gervin, San Antonio	Lloyd Free, San Diego	Magic Johnson, L.A. Lakers	Michael Jordan, Chicago
Paul Westphal, Phoenix	Phil Ford, Kansas City	Isiah Thomas, Detroit	Sidney Moncrief, Milwaukee
1979-80		**1985-86**	
Julius Erving, Philadelphia	Dan Roundfield, Atlanta	Larry Bird, Boston	Charles Barkley, Philadelphia
Larry Bird, Boston	Marques Johnson, Milwaukee	Dominique Wilkins, Atlanta	Alex English, Denver
Kareem Abdul-Jabbar, Los Angeles	Moses Malone, Houston	Kareem Abdul-Jabbar, L.A. Lakers	Hakeem Olajuwon, Houston
George Gervin, San Antonio	Dennis Johnson, Seattle	Magic Johnson, L.A. Lakers	Sidney Moncrief, Milwaukee
Paul Westphal, Phoenix	Gus Williams, Seattle	Isiah Thomas, Detroit	Alvin Robertson, San Antonio
1980-81		**1986-87**	
Julius Erving, Philadelphia	Marques Johnson, Milwaukee	Larry Bird, Boston	Dominique Wilkins, Atlanta
Larry Bird, Boston	Adrian Dantley, Utah	Kevin McHale, Boston	Charles Barkley, Philadelphia
Kareem Abdul-Jabbar, Los Angeles	Moses Malone, Houston	Hakeem Olajuwon, Houston	Moses Malone, Washington
George Gervin, San Antonio	Otis Birdsong, Kansas City	Magic Johnson, L.A. Lakers	Isiah Thomas, Detroit
Dennis Johnson, Phoenix	Nate Archibald, Boston	Michael Jordan, Chicago	Lafayette Lever, Denver
1981-82		**1987-88**	
Larry Bird, Boston	Alex English, Denver	Larry Bird, Boston	Karl Malone, Utah
Julius Erving, Philadelphia	Bernard King, Golden State	Charles Barkley, Philadelphia	Dominique Wilkins, Atlanta
Moses Malone, Houston	Robert Parish, Boston	Hakeem Olajuwon, Houston	Patrick Ewing, New York
George Gervin, San Antonio	Magic Johnson, Los Angeles	Michael Jordan, Chicago	Clyde Drexler, Portland
Gus Williams, Seattle	Sidney Moncrief, Milwaukee	Magic Johnson, L.A. Lakers	John Stockton, Utah

FIRST TEAM	SECOND TEAM	THIRD TEAM	FIRST TEAM	SECOND TEAM	THIRD TEAM
1988-89			**1991-92**		
Karl Malone, Utah	Tom Chambers, Phoenix	Dominique Wilkins, Atlanta	Karl Malone, Utah	Scottie Pippen, Chicago	Dennis Rodman, Detroit
Charles Barkley, Phil.	Chris Mullin, Golden State	Terry Cummings, Milwaukee	Chris Mullin, Golden State	Charles Barkley, Phil.	Kevin Willis, Atlanta
Hakeem Olajuwon, Houston	Patrick Ewing, New York	Robert Parish, Boston	David Robinson, San Ant.	Patrick Ewing, New York	Brad Daugherty, Cleveland
Magic Johnson, L.A. Lakers	John Stockton, Utah	Dale Ellis, Seattle	Michael Jordan, Chicago	Tim Hardaway, Golden State	Mark Price, Cleveland
Michael Jordan, Chicago	Kevin Johnson, Phoenix	Mark Price, Cleveland	Clyde Drexler, Portland	John Stockton, Utah	Kevin Johnson, Phoenix
1989-90			**1992-93**		
Karl Malone, Utah	Larry Bird, Boston	James Worthy, L.A. Lakers	Charles Barkley, Phoenix	Dominique Wilkins, Atlanta	Scottie Pippen, Chicago
Charles Barkley, Phil.	Tom Chambers, Phoenix	Chris Mullin, Golden State	Karl Malone, Utah	Larry Johnson, Charlotte	Derrick Coleman, N.J.
Patrick Ewing, New York	Hakeem Olajuwon, Houston	David Robinson, San Ant.	Hakeem Olajuwon, Houston	Patrick Ewing, New York	David Robinson, San Ant.
Magic Johnson, L.A. Lakers	John Stockton, Utah	Clyde Drexler, Portland	Michael Jordan, Chicago	John Stockton, Utah	Tim Hardaway, Golden State
Michael Jordan, Chicago	Kevin Johnson, Phoenix	Joe Dumars, Detroit	Mark Price, Cleveland	Joe Dumars, Detroit	Drazen Petrovic, N.J.
1990-91			**1993-94**		
Karl Malone, Utah	Dominique Wilkins, Atlanta	James Worthy, L.A. Lakers	Scottie Pippen, Chicago	Shawn Kemp, Seattle	Derrick Coleman, N.J.
Charles Barkley, Phil.	Chris Mullin, Golden State	Bernard King, Washington	Karl Malone, Utah	Charles Barkley, Phoenix	Dominique Wilkins, LAC
David Robinson, San Ant.	Patrick Ewing, New York	Hakeem Olajuwon, Houston	Hakeem Olajuwon, Houston	David Robinson, S.A.	Shaquille O'Neal, Orlando
Michael Jordan, Chicago	Kevin Johnson, Phoenix	John Stockton, Utah	John Stockton, Utah	Mitch Richmond, Sacramento	Mark Price, Cleveland
Magic Johnson, L.A. Lakers	Clyde Drexler, Portland	Joe Dumars, Detroit	Latrell Sprewell, G.S.	Kevin Johnson, Phoenix	Gary Payton, Seattle

NBA ALL-ROOKIE TEAMS

Selected by NBA coaches

1962–63
Terry Dischinger, Chicago
Chet Walker, Syracuse
Zelmo Beaty, St. Louis
John Havlicek, Boston
Dave DeBusschere, Detroit

1963–64
Jerry Lucas, Cincinnati
Gus Johnson, Baltimore
Nate Thurmond, San Francisco
Art Heyman, New York
Rod Thorn, Baltimore

1964–65
Willis Reed, New York
Jim Barnes, New York
Howard Komives, New York
Lucious Jackson, Philadelphia
Wally Jones, Baltimore
Joe Caldwell, Detroit

1965–66
Rick Barry, San Francisco
Billy Cunningham, Philadelphia
Tom Van Arsdale, Detroit
Dick Van Arsdale, New York
Fred Hetzel, San Francisco

1966–67
Lou Hudson, St. Louis
Jack Marin, Baltimore
Erwin Mueller, Chicago
Cazzie Russell, New York
Dave Bing, Detroit

1967–68
Earl Monroe, Baltimore
Bob Rule, Seattle
Walt Frazier, New York
Al Tucker, Seattle
Phil Jackson, New York

1968–69
Wes Unseld, Baltimore
Elvin Hayes, San Diego
Bill Hewitt, Los Angeles
Art Harris, Seattle
Gary Gregor, Phoenix

1969–70
Kareem Abdul-Jabbar, Milwaukee
Bob Dandridge, Milwaukee
Jo Jo White, Boston
Mike Davis, Baltimore
Dick Garrett, Los Angeles

1970–71
Geoff Petrie, Portland
Dave Cowens, Boston
Pete Maravich, Atlanta
Calvin Murphy, San Diego
Bob Lanier, Detroit

1971–72
Elmore Smith, Buffalo
Sidney Wicks, Portland
Austin Carr, Cleveland
Phil Chenier, Baltimore
Clifford Ray, Chicago

1972–73
Bob McAdoo, Buffalo
Lloyd Neal, Portland
Fred Boyd, Philadelphia
Dwight Davis, Cleveland
Jim Price, Los Angeles

1973–74
Ernie DiGregorio, Buffalo
Ron Behagen, Kansas City-Omaha
Mike Bantom, Phoenix
John Brown, Atlanta
Nick Weatherspoon, Capital

1974–75
Jamaal Wilkes, Golden State
John Drew, Atlanta
Scott Wedman, Kansas City-Omaha
Tom Burleson, Seattle
Brian Winters, Los Angeles

1975–76
Alvan Adams, Phoenix
Gus Williams, Golden State
Joe Meriweather, Houston
John Shumate, Phoenix-Buffalo
Lionel Hollins, Portland

1976–77
Adrian Dantley, Buffalo
Scott May, Chicago
Mitch Kupchak, Washington
John Lucas, Houston
Ron Lee, Phoenix

1977–78
Walter Davis, Phoenix
Marques Johnson, Milwaukee
Bernard King, New Jersey
Jack Sikma, Seattle
Norm Nixon, Los Angeles

1978–79
Phil Ford, Kansas City
Mychal Thompson, Portland
Ron Brewer, Portland
Reggie Theus, Chicago
Terry Tyler, Detroit

1979–80
Larry Bird, Boston
Magic Johnson, Los Angeles
Bill Cartwright, New York
Calvin Natt, Portland
David Greenwood, Chicago

1980–81
Joe Barry Carroll, Golden State
Darrell Griffith, Utah
Larry Smith, Golden State
Kevin McHale, Boston
Kelvin Ransey, Portland

1981–82
Kelly Tripucka, Detroit
Jay Vincent, Dallas
Isiah Thomas, Detroit
Buck Williams, New Jersey
Jeff Ruland, Washington

1982–83
Terry Cummings, San Diego
Clark Kellogg, Indiana
Dominique Wilkins, Atlanta
James Worthy, Los Angeles
Quintin Dailey, Chicago

1983–84
Ralph Sampson, Houston
Steve Stipanovich, Indiana
Byron Scott, Los Angeles
Jeff Malone, Washington
Thurl Bailey, Utah (tie)
Darrell Walker, New York (tie)

1984–85
Michael Jordan, Chicago
Hakeem Olajuwon, Houston
Sam Bowie, Portland
Charles Barkley, Philadelphia
Sam Perkins, Dallas

1985–86
Xavier McDaniel, Seattle
Patrick Ewing, New York
Karl Malone, Utah
Joe Dumars, Detroit
Charles Oakley, Chicago

1986–87
Brad Daugherty, Cleveland
Ron Harper, Cleveland
Chuck Person, Indiana
Roy Tarpley, Dallas
John Williams, Cleveland

1987–88
Mark Jackson, New York
Armon Gilliam, Phoenix
Kenny Smith, Sacramento
Greg Anderson, San Antonio
Derrick McKey, Seattle

FIRST TEAM

Mitch Richmond, Golden State
Willie Anderson, San Antonio
Hersey Hawkins, Philadelphia
Rik Smits, Indiana
Charles Smith, L.A. Clippers

David Robinson, San Antonio
Tim Hardaway, Golden State
Vlade Divac, L.A. Lakers
Sherman Douglas, Miami
Pooh Richardson, Minnesota

Kendall Gill, Charlotte
Dennis Scott, Orlando
Dee Brown, Boston
Lionel Simmons, Sacramento
Derrick Coleman, New Jersey

SECOND TEAM

1988–89
Brian Shaw, Boston
Rex Chapman, Charlotte
Chris Morris, New Jersey
Rod Strickland, New York
Kevin Edwards, Miami

1989–90
J.R. Reid, Charlotte
Sean Elliott, San Antonio
Stacey King, Chicago
Blue Edwards, Utah
Glen Rice, Miami

1990–91
Mahmoud Abdul-Rauf, Denver
Gary Payton, Seattle
Felton Spencer, Minnesota
Travis Mays, Sacramento
Willie Burton, Miami

FIRST TEAM

Larry Johnson, Charlotte
Dikembe Mutombo, Denver
Billy Owens, Golden State
Steve Smith, Miami
Stacey Augmon, Atlanta

Shaquille O'Neal, Orlando
Alonzo Mourning, Charlotte
Christian Laettner, Minnesota
Tom Gugliotta, Washington
LaPhonso Ellis, Denver

Chris Webber, Golden State
Anfernee Hardaway, Orlando
Vin Baker, Milwaukee
Jamal Mashburn, Dallas
Isaiah Rider, Minnesota

SECOND TEAM

1991–92
Rick Fox, Boston
Terrell Brandon, Cleveland
Larry Stewart, Washington
Stanley Roberts, Orlando
Mark Macon, Denver

1992–93
Walt Williams, Sacramento
Robert Horry, Houston
Latrell Sprewell, Golden State
Clarence Weatherspoon, Philadelphia
Richard Dumas, Phoenix

1993–94
Dino Radja, Boston
Nick Van Exel, L.A. Lakers
Shawn Bradley, Philadelphia
Toni Kukoc, Chicago
Lindsey Hunter, Detroit

NBA ALL-DEFENSIVE TEAMS
Selected by NBA coaches

FIRST TEAM	SECOND TEAM
	1968-69
Dave DeBusschere, New York	Rudy LaRusso, San Francisco
Nate Thurmond, San Francisco	Tom Sanders, Boston
Bill Russell, Boston	John Havlicek, Boston
Walt Frazier, New York	Jerry West, Los Angeles
Jerry Sloan, Chicago	Bill Bridges, Atlanta
	1969-70
Dave DeBusschere, New York	John Havlicek, Boston
Gus Johnson, Baltimore	Bill Bridges, Atlanta
Willis Reed, New York	Kareem Abdul-Jabbar, Milwaukee
Walt Frazier, New York	Joe Caldwell, Atlanta
Jerry West, Los Angeles	Jerry Sloan, Chicago
	1970-71
Dave DeBusschere, New York	John Havlicek, Boston
Gus Johnson, Baltimore	Paul Silas, Phoenix
Nate Thurmond, San Francisco	Kareem Abdul-Jabbar, Milwaukee
Walt Frazier, New York	Jerry Sloan, Chicago
Jerry West, Los Angeles	Norm Van Lier, Cincinnati
	1971-72
Dave DeBusschere, New York	Paul Silas, Phoenix
John Havlicek, Boston	Bob Love, Chicago
Wilt Chamberlain, Los Angeles	Nate Thurmond, Golden State
Jerry West, Los Angeles	Norm Van Lier, Chicago
Walt Frazier, New York (tie)	Don Chaney, Boston
Jerry Sloan, Chicago (tie)	
	1972-73
Dave DeBusschere, New York	Paul Silas, Boston
John Havlicek, Boston	Mike Riordan, Baltimore
Wilt Chamberlain, Los Angeles	Nate Thurmond, Golden State
Jerry West, Los Angeles	Norm Van Lier, Chicago
Walt Frazier, New York	Don Chaney, Boston
	1973-74
Dave DeBusschere, New York	Elvin Hayes, Capital
John Havlicek, Boston	Bob Love, Chicago
Kareem Abdul-Jabbar, Milwaukee	Nate Thurmond, Golden State
Norm Van Lier, Chicago	Don Chaney, Boston
Walt Frazier, New York (tie)	Dick Van Arsdale, Phoenix (tie)
Jerry Sloan, Chicago (tie)	Jim Price, Los Angeles (tie)
	1974-75
John Havlicek, Boston	Elvin Hayes, Washington
Paul Silas, Boston	Bob Love, Chicago
Kareem Abdul-Jabbar, Milwaukee	Dave Cowens, Boston
Jerry Sloan, Chicago	Norm Van Lier, Chicago
Walt Frazier, New York	Don Chaney, Boston
	1975-76
Paul Silas, Boston	Jim Brewer, Cleveland
John Havlicek, Boston·	Jamaal Wilkes, Golden State
Dave Cowens, Boston	Kareem Abdul-Jabbar, Los Angeles
Norm Van Lier, Chicago	Jim Cleamons, Cleveland
Don Watts, Seattle	Phil Smith, Golden State
	1976-77
Bobby Jones, Denver	Jim Brewer, Cleveland
E.C. Coleman, New Orleans	Jamaal Wilkes, Golden State
Bill Walton, Portland	Kareem Abdul-Jabbar, Los Angeles
Don Buse, Indiana	Brian Taylor, Kansas City
Norm Van Lier, Chicago	Don Chaney, Los Angeles

FIRST TEAM	SECOND TEAM
	1977-78
Bobby Jones, Denver	E.C. Coleman, Golden State
Maurice Lucas, Portland	Bob Gross, Portland
Bill Walton, Portland	Kareem Abdul-Jabbar, Los Angeles (tie)
Lionel Hollins, Portland	Artis Gilmore, Chicago (tie)
Don Buse, Phoenix	Norm Van Lier, Chicago
	Quinn Buckner, Milwaukee
	1978-79
Bobby Jones, Philadelphia	Maurice Lucas, Portland
Bobby Dandridge, Washington	M.L. Carr, Detroit
Kareem Abdul-Jabbar, Los Angeles	Moses Malone, Houston
Dennis Johnson, Seattle	Lionel Hollins, Portland
Don Buse, Phoenix	Eddie Johnson, Atlanta
	1979-80
Bobby Jones, Philadelphia	Scott Wedman, Kansas City
Dan Roundfield, Atlanta	Kermit Washington, Portland
Kareem Abdul-Jabbar, Los Angeles	Dave Cowens, Boston
Dennis Johnson, Seattle	Quinn Buckner, Milwaukee
Don Buse, Phoenix (tie)	Eddie Johnson, Atlanta
Micheal Ray Richardson, New York (tie)	
	1980-81
Bobby Jones, Philadelphia	Dan Roundfield, Atlanta
Caldwell Jones, Philadelphia	Kermit Washington, Portland
Kareem Abdul-Jabbar, Los Angeles	George Johnson, San Antonio
Dennis Johnson, Phoenix	Quinn Buckner, Milwaukee
Micheal Ray Richardson, New York	Dudley Bradley, Indiana (tie)
	Michael Cooper, Los Angeles (tie)
	1981-82
Bobby Jones, Philadelphia	Larry Bird, Boston
Dan Roundfield, Atlanta	Lonnie Shelton, Seattle
Caldwell Jones, Philadelphia	Jack Sikma, Seattle
Michael Cooper, Los Angeles	Quinn Buckner, Milwaukee
Dennis Johnson, Phoenix	Sidney Moncrief, Milwaukee
	1982-83
Bobby Jones, Philadelphia	Larry Bird, Boston
Dan Roundfield, Atlanta	Kevin McHale, Boston
Moses Malone, Philadelphia	Wayne Rollins, Atlanta
Sidney Moncrief, Milwaukee	Michael Cooper, Los Angeles
Dennis Johnson, Phoenix (tie)	T.R. Dunn, Denver
Maurice Cheeks, Philadelphia (tie)	
	1983-84
Bobby Jones, Philadelphia	Larry Bird, Boston
Michael Cooper, Los Angeles	Dan Roundfield, Atlanta
Wayne Rollins, Atlanta	Kareem Abdul-Jabbar, Los Angeles
Maurice Cheeks, Philadelphia	Dennis Johnson, Boston
Sidney Moncrief, Milwaukee	T.R. Dunn, Denver
	1984-85
Sidney Moncrief, Milwaukee	Bobby Jones, Philadelphia
Paul Pressey, Milwaukee	Danny Vranes, Seattle
Mark Eaton, Utah	Hakeem Olajuwon, Houston
Michael Cooper, L.A. Lakers	Dennis Johnson, Boston
Maurice Cheeks, Philadelphia	T.R. Dunn, Denver
	1985-86
Paul Pressey, Milwaukee	Michael Cooper, L.A. Lakers
Kevin McHale, Boston	Bill Hanzlik, Denver
Mark Eaton, Utah	Manute Bol, Washington
Sidney Moncrief, Milwaukee	Alvin Robertson, San Antonio
Maurice Cheeks, Philadelphia	Dennis Johnson, Boston

FIRST TEAM

1986–87

Kevin McHale, Boston
Michael Cooper, L.A. Lakers
Hakeem Olajuwon, Houston
Alvin Robertson, San Antonio
Dennis Johnson, Boston

1987–88

Kevin McHale, Boston
Rodney McCray, Houston
Hakeem Olajuwon, Houston
Michael Cooper, L.A. Lakers
Michael Jordan, Chicago

1988–89

Dennis Rodman, Detroit
Larry Nance, Cleveland
Mark Eaton, Utah
Michael Jordan, Chicago
Joe Dumars, Detroit

1989–90

Dennis Rodman, Detroit
Buck Williams, Portland
Hakeem Olajuwon, Houston
Michael Jordan, Chicago
Joe Dumars, Detroit

SECOND TEAM

1986–87

Paul Pressey, Milwaukee
Rodney McCray, Houston
Mark Eaton, Utah
Maurice Cheeks, Philadelphia
Derek Harper, Dallas

1987–88

Buck Williams, New Jersey
Karl Malone, Utah
Mark Eaton, Utah (tie)
Patrick Ewing, New York (tie)
Alvin Robertson, San Antonio
Lafayette Lever, Denver

1988–89

Kevin McHale, Boston
A.C. Green, L.A. Lakers
Patrick Ewing, New York
John Stockton, Utah
Alvin Robertson, San Antonio

1989–90

Kevin McHale, Boston
Rick Mahorn, Philadelphia
David Robinson, San Antonio
Derek Harper, Dallas
Alvin Robertson, Milwaukee

FIRST TEAM

1990–91

Michael Jordan, Chicago
Alvin Robertson, Milwaukee
David Robinson, San Antonio
Dennis Rodman, Detroit
Buck Williams, Portland

(1991–92)

Dennis Rodman, Detroit
Scottie Pippen, Chicago
David Robinson, San Antonio
Michael Jordan, Chicago
Joe Dumars, Detroit

(1992–93)

Scottie Pippen, Chicago
Dennis Rodman, Detroit
Hakeem Olajuwon, Houston
Michael Jordan, Chicago
Joe Dumars, Detroit

(1993–94)

Scottie Pippen, Chicago
Charles Oakley, New York
Hakeem Olajuwon, Houston
Gary Payton, Seattle
Mookie Blaylock, Atlanta

SECOND TEAM

1990–91

Joe Dumars, Detroit
John Stockton, Utah
Hakeem Olajuwon, Houston
Scottie Pippen, Chicago
Dan Majerle, Phoenix

1991–92

Larry Nance, Cleveland
Buck Williams, Portland
Patrick Ewing, New York
John Stockton, Utah
Micheal Williams, Indiana

1992–93

Horace Grant, Chicago
Larry Nance, Cleveland
David Robinson, San Antonio
Dan Majerle, Phoenix
John Starks, New York

1993–94

Dennis Rodman, San Antonio
Horace Grant, Chicago
David Robinson, San Antonio
Nate McMillan, Seattle
Latrell Sprewell, Golden State

INDIVIDUAL LEADERS

SCORING

1946–47—Joe Fulks, Philadelphia	1389
1947–48—Max Zaslofsky, Chicago	1007
1948–49—George Mikan, Minneapolis	1698
1949–50—George Mikan, Minneapolis	1865
1950–51—George Mikan, Minneapolis	1932
1951–52—Paul Arizin, Philadelphia	1674
1952–53—Neil Johnston, Philadelphia	1564
1953–54—Neil Johnston, Philadelphia	1759
1954–55—Neil Johnston, Philadelphia	1631
1955–56—Bob Pettit, St. Louis	1849
1956–57—Paul Arizin, Philadelphia	1817
1957–58—George Yardley, Detroit	2001
1958–59—Bob Pettit, St. Louis	2105
1959–60—Wilt Chamberlain, Philadelphia	2707
1960–61—Wilt Chamberlain, Philadelphia	3033
1961–62—Wilt Chamberlain, Philadelphia	4029
1962–63—Wilt Chamberlain, San Francisco	3586
1963–64—Wilt Chamberlain, San Francisco	2948
1964–65—Wilt Chamberlain, S.F.-Phil.	2534
1965–66—Wilt Chamberlain, Philadelphia	2649
1966–67—Rick Barry, San Francisco	2775
1967–68—Dave Bing, Detroit	2142
1968–69—Elvin Hayes, San Diego	2327
1969–70—Jerry West, Los Angeles	*31.2
1970–71—Kareem Abdul-Jabbar, Milwaukee	31.7
1971–72—Kareem Abdul-Jabbar, Milwaukee	34.8
1972–73—Nate Archibald, K.C.-Omaha	34.0
1973–74—Bob McAdoo, Buffalo	30.6
1974–75—Bob McAdoo, Buffalo	34.5
1975–76—Bob McAdoo, Buffalo	31.1
1976–77—Pete Maravich, New Orleans	31.1
1977–78—George Gervin, San Antonio	27.2
1978–79—George Gervin, San Antonio	29.6
1979–80—George Gervin, San Antonio	33.1
1980–81—Adrian Dantley, Utah	30.7

1981–82—George Gervin, San Antonio	32.3
1982–83—Alex English, Denver	28.4
1983–84—Adrian Dantley, Utah	30.6
1984–85—Bernard King, New York	32.9
1985–86—Dominique Wilkins, Atlanta	30.3
1986–87—Michael Jordan, Chicago	37.1
1987–88—Michael Jordan, Chicago	35.0
1988–89—Michael Jordan, Chicago	32.5
1989–90—Michael Jordan, Chicago	33.6
1990–91—Michael Jordan, Chicago	31.5
1991–92—Michael Jordan, Chicago	30.1
1992–93—Michael Jordan, Chicago	32.6
1993–94—David Robinson, San Antonio	29.8

*Based on average starting in 1969–70

FIELD GOAL PERCENTAGE

1946–47—Bob Feerick, Washington	.401
1947–48—Bob Feerick, Washington	.340
1948–49—Arnie Risen, Rochester	.423
1949–50—Alex Groza, Indianapolis	.478
1950–51—Alex Groza, Indianapolis	.470
1951–52—Paul Arizin, Philadelphia	.448
1952–53—Neil Johnston, Philadelphia	.452
1953–54—Ed Macauley, Boston	.486
1954–55—Larry Foust, Fort Wayne	.487
1955–56—Neil Johnston, Philadelphia	.457
1956–57—Neil Johnston, Philadelphia	.447
1957–58—Jack Twyman, Cincinnati	.452
1958–59—Ken Sears, New York	.490
1959–60—Ken Sears, New York	.477
1960–61—Wilt Chamberlain, Philadelphia	.509
1961–62—Walt Bellamy, Chicago	.519
1962–63—Wilt Chamberlain, San Francisco	.528
1963–64—Jerry Lucas, Cincinnati	.527

1964–65—Wilt Chamberlain, S.F.-Phil.	.510
1965–66—Wilt Chamberlain, Philadelphia	.540
1966–67—Wilt Chamberlain, Philadelphia	.683
1967–68—Wilt Chamberlain, Philadelphia	.595
1968–69—Wilt Chamberlain, Los Angeles	.583
1969–70—Johnny Green, Cincinnati	.559
1970–71—Johnny Green, Cincinnati	.587
1971–72—Wilt Chamberlain, Los Angeles	.649
1972–73—Wilt Chamberlain, Los Angeles	.727
1973–74—Bob McAdoo, Buffalo	.547
1974–75—Don Nelson, Boston	.539
1975–76—Wes Unseld, Washington	.561
1976–77—Kareem Abdul-Jabbar, Los Angeles	.579
1977–78—Bobby Jones, Denver	.578
1978–79—Cedric Maxwell, Boston	.584
1979–80—Cedric Maxwell, Boston	.609
1980–81—Artis Gilmore, Chicago	.670
1981–82—Artis Gilmore, Chicago	.652
1982–83—Artis Gilmore, San Antonio	.626
1983–84—Artis Gilmore, San Antonio	.631
1984–85—James Donaldson, L.A. Clippers	.637
1985–86—Steve Johnson, San Antonio	.632
1986–87—Kevin McHale, Boston	.604
1987–88—Kevin McHale, Boston	.604
1988–89—Dennis Rodman, Detroit	.595
1989–90—Mark West, Phoenix	.625
1990–91—Buck Williams, Portland	.602
1991–92—Buck Williams, Portland	.604
1992–93—Cedric Ceballos, Phoenix	.576
1993–94—Shaquille O'Neal, Orlando	.599

THREE-POINT FIELD GOAL PERCENTAGE

1979–80—Fred Brown, Seattle	.443
1980–81—Brian Taylor, San Diego	.383
1981–82—Campy Russell, New York	.439

1982–83—Mike Dunleavy, San Antonio .345
1983–84—Darrell Griffith, Utah .361
1984–85—Byron Scott, L.A. Lakers .433
1985–86—Craig Hodges, Milwaukee .451
1986–87—Kiki Vandeweghe, Portland .481
1987–88—Craig Hodges, Milw.-Phoe. .491
1988–89—Jon Sundvold, Miami .522
1989–90—Steve Kerr, Cleveland .507
1990–91—Jim Les, Sacramento .461
1991–92—Dana Barros, Seattle .446
1992–93—B.J. Armstrong, Chicago .453
1993–94—Tracy Murray, Portland .459

FREE THROW PERCENTAGE

1946–47—Fred Scolari, Washington .811
1947–48—Bob Feerick, Washington .788
1948–49—Bob Feerick, Washington .859
1949–50—Max Zaslofsky, Chicago .843
1950–51—Joe Fulks, Philadelphia .855
1951–52—Bobby Wanzer, Rochester .904
1952–53—Bill Sharman, Boston .850
1953–54—Bill Sharman, Boston .844
1954–55—Bill Sharman, Boston .897
1955–56—Bill Sharman, Boston .867
1956–57—Bill Sharman, Boston .905
1957–58—Dolph Schayes, Syracuse .904
1958–59—Bill Sharman, Boston .932
1959–60—Dolph Schayes, Syracuse .892
1960–61—Bill Sharman, Boston .921
1961–62—Dolph Schayes, Syracuse .896
1962–63—Larry Costello, Syracuse .881
1963–64—Oscar Robertson, Cincinnati .853
1964–65—Larry Costello, Philadelphia .877
1965–66—Larry Siegfried, Boston .881
1966–67—Adrian Smith, Cincinnati .903
1967–68—Oscar Robertson, Cincinnati .873
1968–69—Larry Siegfried, Boston .864
1969–70—Flynn Robinson, Milwaukee .898
1970–71—Chet Walker, Chicago .859
1971–72—Jack Marin, Baltimore .894
1972–73—Rick Barry, Golden State .902
1973–74—Ernie DiGregorio, Buffalo .902
1974–75—Rick Barry, Golden State .904
1975–76—Rick Barry, Golden State .923
1976–77—Ernie DiGregorio, Buffalo .945
1977–78—Rick Barry, Golden State .924
1978–79—Rick Barry, Houston .947
1979–80—Rick Barry, Houston .935
1980–81—Calvin Murphy, Houston .958
1981–82—Kyle Macy, Phoenix .899
1982–83—Calvin Murphy, Houston .920
1983–84—Larry Bird, Boston .888
1984–85—Kyle Macy, Phoenix .907
1985–86—Larry Bird, Boston .896
1986–87—Larry Bird, Boston .910
1987–88—Jack Sikma, Milwaukee .922
1988–89—Magic Johnson, L.A. Lakers .911
1989–90—Larry Bird, Boston .930
1990–91—Reggie Miller, Indiana .918
1991–92—Mark Price, Cleveland .947
1992–93—Mark Price, Cleveland .948
1993–94—Mahmoud Abdul-Rauf, Denver .956

MINUTES PLAYED

1951–52—Paul Arizin, Philadelphia 2939
1952–53—Neil Johnston, Philadelphia 3166
1953–54—Neil Johnston, Philadelphia 3296
1954–55—Paul Arizin, Philadelphia 2953
1955–56—Slater Martin, Minneapolis 2838
1956–57—Dolph Schayes, Syracuse 2851
1957–58—Dolph Schayes, Syracuse 2918
1958–59—Bill Russell, Boston 2979
1959–60—Wilt Chamberlain, Philadelphia 3338
        Gene Shue, Detroit 3338

1960–61—Wilt Chamberlain, Philadelphia 3773
1961–62—Wilt Chamberlain, Philadelphia 3882
1962–63—Wilt Chamberlain, San Francisco 3806
1963–64—Wilt Chamberlain, San Francisco 3689
1964–65—Bill Russell, Boston 3466
1965–66—Wilt Chamberlain, Philadelphia 3737
1966–67—Wilt Chamberlain, Philadelphia 3682
1967–68—Wilt Chamberlain, Philadelphia 3836
1968–69—Elvin Hayes, San Diego 3695
1969–70—Elvin Hayes, San Diego 3665
1970–71—John Havlicek, Boston 3678
1971–72—John Havlicek, Boston 3698
1972–73—Nate Archibald, K.C.-Omaha 3681
1973–74—Elvin Hayes, Capital 3602
1974–75—Bob McAdoo, Buffalo 3539
1975–76—Kareem Abdul-Jabbar, Los Angeles 3379
1976–77—Elvin Hayes, Washington 3364
1977–78—Len Robinson, New Orleans 3638
1978–79—Moses Malone, Houston 3390
1979–80—Norm Nixon, Los Angeles 3226
1980–81—Adrian Dantley, Utah 3417
1981–82—Moses Malone, Houston 3398
1982–83—Isiah Thomas, Detroit 3093
1983–84—Jeff Ruland, Washington 3082
1984–85—Buck Williams, New Jersey 3182
1985–86—Maurice Cheeks, Philadelphia 3270
1986–87—Michael Jordan, Chicago 3281
1987–88—Michael Jordan, Chicago 3311
1988–89—Michael Jordan, Chicago 3255
1989–90—Rodney McCray, Sacramento 3238
1990–91—Chris Mullin, Golden State 3315
1991–92—Chris Mullin, Golden State 3346
1992–93—Larry Johnson, Charlotte 3323
1993–94—Latrell Sprewell, Golden State 3533

REBOUNDS

1950–51—Dolph Schayes, Syracuse 1080
1951–52—Larry Foust, Fort Wayne 880
        Mel Hutchins, Milwaukee 880
1952–53—George Mikan, Minneapolis 1007
1953–54—Harry Gallatin, New York 1098
1954–55—Neil Johnston, Philadelphia 1085
1955–56—Bob Pettit, St. Louis 1164
1956–57—Maurice Stokes, Rochester 1256
1957–58—Bill Russell, Boston 1564
1958–59—Bill Russell, Boston 1612
1959–60—Wilt Chamberlain, Philadelphia 1941
1960–61—Wilt Chamberlain, Philadelphia 2149
1961–62—Wilt Chamberlain, Philadelphia 2052
1962–63—Wilt Chamberlain, San Francisco 1946
1963–64—Bill Russell, Boston 1930
1964–65—Bill Russell, Boston 1878
1965–66—Wilt Chamberlain, Philadelphia 1943
1966–67—Wilt Chamberlain, Philadelphia 1957
1967–68—Wilt Chamberlain, Philadelphia 1952
1968–69—Wilt Chamberlain, Los Angeles 1712
1969–70—Elvin Hayes, San Diego *16.9
1970–71—Wilt Chamberlain, Los Angeles 18.2
1971–72—Wilt Chamberlain, Los Angeles 19.2
1972–73—Wilt Chamberlain, Los Angeles 18.6
1973–74—Elvin Hayes, Capital 18.1
1974–75—Wes Unseld, Washington 14.8
1975–76—Kareem Abdul-Jabbar, Los Angeles 16.9
1976–77—Bill Walton, Portland 14.4
1977–78—Len Robinson, New Orleans 15.7
1978–79—Moses Malone, Houston 17.6
1979–80—Swen Nater, San Diego 15.0
1980–81—Moses Malone, Houston 14.8
1981–82—Moses Malone, Houston 14.7
1982–83—Moses Malone, Philadelphia 15.3
1983–84—Moses Malone, Philadelphia 13.4
1984–85—Moses Malone, Philadelphia 13.1
1985–86—Bill Laimbeer, Detroit 13.1

1986–87—Charles Barkley, Philadelphia 14.6
1987–88—Michael Cage, L.A. Clippers 13.03
1988–89—Hakeem Olajuwon, Houston 13.5
1989–90—Hakeem Olajuwon, Houston 14.0
1990–91—David Robinson, San Antonio 13.0
1991–92—Dennis Rodman, Detroit 18.7
1992–93—Dennis Rodman, Detroit 18.3
1993–94—Dennis Rodman, San Antonio 17.3

*Based on average starting in 1969–70

ASSISTS

1946–47—Ernie Calverly, Providence 202
1947–48—Howie Dallmar, Philadelphia 120
1948–49—Bob Davies, Rochester 321
1949–50—Dick McGuire, New York 386
1950–51—Andy Phillip, Philadelphia 414
1951–52—Andy Phillip, Philadelphia 539
1952–53—Bob Cousy, Boston 547
1953–54—Bob Cousy, Boston 578
1954–55—Bob Cousy, Boston 557
1955–56—Bob Cousy, Boston 642
1956–57—Bob Cousy, Boston 478
1957–58—Bob Cousy, Boston 463
1958–59—Bob Cousy, Boston 557
1959–60—Bob Cousy, Boston 715
1960–61—Oscar Robertson, Cincinnati 690
1961–62—Oscar Robertson, Cincinnati 899
1962–63—Guy Rodgers, San Francisco 825
1963–64—Oscar Robertson, Cincinnati 868
1964–65—Oscar Robertson, Cincinnati 861
1965–66—Oscar Robertson, Cincinnati 847
1966–67—Guy Rodgers, Chicago 908
1967–68—Wilt Chamberlain, Philadelphia 702
1968–69—Oscar Robertson, Cincinnati 772
1969–70—Lenny Wilkens, Seattle *9.1
1970–71—Norm Van Lier, Cincinnati 10.1
1971–72—Jerry West, Los Angeles 9.7
1972–73—Nate Archibald, KC-Omaha 11.4
1973–74—Ernie DiGregorio, Buffalo 8.2
1974–75—Kevin Porter, Washington 8.0
1975–76—Don Watts, Seattle 8.1
1976–77—Don Buse, Indiana 8.5
1977–78—Kevin Porter, Det.-N.J. 10.2
1978–79—Kevin Porter, Detroit 13.4
1979–80—Micheal Richardson, New York 10.1
1980–81—Kevin Porter, Washington 9.1
1981–82—Johnny Moore, San Antonio 9.6
1982–83—Magic Johnson, Los Angeles 10.5
1983–84—Magic Johnson, Los Angeles 13.1
1984–85—Isiah Thomas, Detroit 13.98
1985–86—Magic Johnson, L.A. Lakers 12.6
1986–87—Magic Johnson, L.A. Lakers 12.2
1987–88—John Stockton, Utah 13.8
1988–89—John Stockton, Utah 13.6
1989–90—John Stockton, Utah 14.5
1990–91—John Stockton, Utah 14.2
1991–92—John Stockton, Utah 13.7
1992–93—John Stockton, Utah 12.0
1993–94—John Stockton, Utah 12.6

*Based on average starting in 1969–70

STEALS

1973–74—Larry Steele, Portland 2.68
1974–75—Rick Barry, Golden State 2.85
1975–76—Don Watts, Seattle 3.18
1976–77—Don Buse, Indiana 3.47
1977–78—Ron Lee, Phoenix 2.74
1978–79—M.L. Carr, Detroit 2.46
1979–80—Micheal Richardson, New York 3.23
1980–81—Magic Johnson, Los Angeles 3.43
1981–82—Magic Johnson, Los Angeles 2.67
1982–83—Micheal Richardson, G.S.-N.J. 2.84
1983–84—Rickey Green, Utah 2.65

1984–85—Micheal Richardson, New Jersey	2.96
1985–86—Alvin Robertson, San Antonio	3.67
1986–87—Alvin Robertson, San Antonio	3.21
1987–88—Michael Jordan, Chicago	3.16
1988–89—John Stockton, Utah	3.21
1989–90—Michael Jordan, Chicago	2.77
1990–91—Alvin Robertson, Milwaukee	3.04
1991–92—John Stockton, Utah	2.98
1992–93—Michael Jordan, Chicago	2.83
1993–94—Nate McMillan, Seattle	2.96

BLOCKED SHOTS

1973–74—Elmore Smith, Los Angeles	4.85
1974–75—Kareem Abdul-Jabbar, Milwaukee	3.26
1975–76—Kareem Abdul-Jabbar, Los Angeles	4.12
1976–77—Bill Walton, Portland	3.25
1977–78—George Johnson, New Jersey	3.38
1978–79—Kareem Abdul-Jabbar, Los Angeles	3.95
1979–80—Kareem Abdul-Jabbar, Los Angeles	3.41
1980–81—George Johnson, San Antonio	3.39
1981–82—George Johnson, San Antonio	3.12
1982–83—Wayne Rollins, Atlanta	4.29
1983–84—Mark Eaton, Utah	4.28
1984–85—Mark Eaton, Utah	5.56
1985–86—Manute Bol, Washington	4.96
1986–87—Mark Eaton, Utah	4.06
1987–88—Mark Eaton, Utah	3.71
1988–89—Manute Bol, Golden State	4.31
1989–90—Hakeem Olajuwon, Houston	4.59
1990–91—Hakeem Olajuwon, Houston	3.95
1991–92—David Robinson, San Antonio	4.49
1992–93—Hakeem Olajuwon, Houston	4.17
1993–94—Dikembe Mutombo, Denver	4.10

PERSONAL FOULS

1946–47—Stan Miasek, Detroit	208
1947–48—Charles Gilmur, Chicago	231
1948–49—Ed Sadowski, Philadelphia	273
1949–50—George Mikan, Minneapolis	297
1950–51—George Mikan, Minneapolis	308
1951–52—George Mikan, Minneapolis	286
1952–53—Don Meineke, Fort Wayne	334
1953–54—Earl Lloyd, Syracuse	303
1954–55—Vern Mikkelsen, Minneapolis	319
1955–56—Vern Mikkelsen, Minneapolis	319
1956–57—Vern Mikkelsen, Minneapolis	312
1957–58—Walt Dukes, Detroit	311
1958–59—Walt Dukes, Detroit	332

1959–60—Tom Gola, Philadelphia	311
1960–61—Paul Arizin, Philadelphia	335
1961–62—Tom Meschery, Philadelphia	330
1962–63—Zelmo Beaty, St. Louis	312
1963–64—Wayne Embry, Cincinnati	325
1964–65—Bailey Howell, Baltimore	345
1965–66—Zelmo Beaty, St. Louis	344
1966–67—Joe Strawder, Detroit	344
1967–68—Bill Bridges, St. Louis	366
1968–69—Billy Cunningham, Philadelphia	329
1969–70—Jim Davis, Atlanta	335
1970–71—Dave Cowens, Boston	350
1971–72—Dave Cowens, Boston	314
1972–73—Neal Walk, Phoenix	323
1973–74—Kevin Porter, Capital	319
1974–75—Bob Dandridge, Milwaukee	330
Phil Jackson, New York	330
1975–76—Charlie Scott, Boston	356
1976–77—Lonnie Shelton, N.Y. Knicks	363
1977–78—Lonnie Shelton, New York	350
1978–79—Bill Robinzine, Kansas City	367
1979–80—Darryl Dawkins, Philadelphia	328
1980–81—Ben Poquette, Utah	342
1981–82—Steve Johnson, Kansas City	372
1982–83—Darryl Dawkins, New Jersey	379
1983–84—Darryl Dawkins, New Jersey	386
1984–85—Hakeem Olajuwon, Houston	344
1985–86—Charles Barkley, Philadelphia	333
1986–87—Steve Johnson, Portland	340
1987–88—Patrick Ewing, New York	332
1988–89—Grant Long, Miami	337
1989–90—Rik Smits, Indiana	328
1990–91—Sam Mitchell, Minnesota	338
1991–92—Tyrone Hill, Golden State	315
1992–93—Stanley Roberts, L.A. Clippers	332
1993–94—Shawn Kemp, Seattle	312

DISQUALIFICATIONS

1950–51—Cal Christensen, Tri-Cities	19
1951–52—Don Boven, Milwaukee	18
1952–53—Don Meineke, Fort Wayne	26
1953–54—Earl Lloyd, Syracuse	12
1954–55—Charley Share, Milwaukee	17
1955–56—Vern Mikkelsen, Minneapolis	17
Arnie Risen, Boston	17
1956–57—Vern Mikkelsen, Minneapolis	18
1957–58—Vern Mikkelsen, Minneapolis	20

1958–59—Walt Dukes, Detroit	22
1959–60—Walt Dukes, Detroit	20
1960–61—Walt Dukes, Detroit	16
1961–62—Walt Dukes, Detroit	20
1962–63—Frank Ramsey, Boston	13
1963–64—Zelmo Beaty, St. Louis	11
Gus Johnson, Baltimore	11
1964–65—Tom Sanders, Boston	15
1965–66—Tom Sanders, Boston	19
1966–67—Joe Strawder, Detroit	19
1967–68—John Tresvant, Det.-Cinn.	18
Joe Strawder, Detroit	18
1968–69—Art Harris, Seattle	14
1969–70—Norm Van Lier, Cincinnati	18
1970–71—John Trapp, San Diego	16
1971–72—Curtis Perry, Hou.-Milw.	14
1972–73—Elmore Smith, Buffalo	16
1973–74—Mike Bantom, Phoenix	15
1974–75—Kevin Porter, Washington	12
1975–76—Bill Robinzine, Kansas City	19
1976–77—Joe Meriweather, Atlanta	21
1977–78—George Johnson, New Jersey	20
1978–79—John Drew, Atlanta	19
Wayne Rollins, Atlanta	19
1979–80—Wayne Rollins, Atlanta	12
James Edwards, Indiana	12
George McGinnis, Indiana	12
1980–81—Ben Poquette, Utah	18
1981–82—Steve Johnson, Kansas City	25
1982–83—Darryl Dawkins, New Jersey	23
1983–84—Darryl Dawkins, New Jersey	22
1984–85—Ken Bannister, New York	16
1985–86—Joe Barry Carroll, Golden State	13
Steve Johnson, San Antonio	13
1986–87—Steve Johnson, Portland	16
1987–88—Jack Sikma, Milwaukee	11
Frank Brickowski, San Antonio	11
1988–89—Rik Smits, Indiana	14
1989–90—Grant Long, Miami	11
Rik Smits, Indiana	11
LaSalle Thompson, Indiana	11
1990–91—Blair Rasmussen, Denver	15
1991–92—Shawn Kemp, Seattle	13
1992–93—Stanley Roberts, L.A. Clippers	15
1993–94—Shawn Kemp, Seattle	11
Rik Smits, Indiana	11

ALL-TIME TOP TENS

(Active 1993-1994 players in capital letters)

MOST GAMES PLAYED

Kareem Abdul-Jabbar	1,560
ROBERT PARISH	1,413
MOSES MALONE	1,312
Elvin Hayes	1,303
John Havlicek	1,270
Paul Silas	1,254
Alex English	1,193
Hal Greer	1,122
JAMES EDWARDS	1,112
Jack Sikma	1,107

MINUTES PLAYED

Kareem Abdul-Jabbar	57,446
Elvin Hayes	50,000
Wilt Chamberlain	47,859
John Havlicek	46,471

MOSES MALONE	44,922
Oscar Robertson	43,886
ROBERT PARISH	42,860
Bill Russell	40,726
Hal Greer	39,788
Walt Bellamy	38,940

FIELD GOALS MADE

Kareem Abdul-Jabbar	15,837
Wilt Chamberlain	12,681
Elvin Hayes	10,976
Alex English	10,659
John Havlicek	10,513
Oscar Robertson	9,508
MOSES MALONE	9,422
ROBERT PARISH	9,265
DOMINIQUE WILKINS	9,020
Jerry West	9,016

FIELD GOALS ATTEMPTED

Kareem Abdul-Jabbar	28,307
Elvin Hayes	24,272
John Havlicek	23,930
Wilt Chamberlain	23,497
Alex English	21,036
Elgin Baylor	20,171
Oscar Robertson	19,620
DOMINIQUE WILKINS	19,335
MOSES MALONE	19,190
Jerry West	19,032

HIGHEST FIELD GOAL PERCENTAGE

(2,000 FGM minimum)

	FGA	FGM	Pct.
Artis Gilmore	9,570	5,732	.599

MARK WEST	3,568	2,113	.592
Steve Johnson	4,965	2,841	.572
Darryl Dawkins	6,079	3,477	.572
James Donaldson	5,368	3,061	.570
Jeff Ruland	3,734	2,105	.564
CHARLES BARKLEY	11,144	6,259	.562
Kareem Abdul-Jabbar	28,307	15,837	.559
OTIS THORPE	8,834	4,898	.554
BUCK WILLIAMS	10,198	5,653	.554

MOST FREE THROWS MADE

MOSES MALONE	8,509
Oscar Robertson	7,694
Jerry West	7,160
Dolph Schayes	6,979
Adrian Dantley	6,832
Kareem Abdul-Jabbar	6,712
Bob Pettit	6,182
Wilt Chamberlain	6,057
Elgin Baylor	5,763
DOMINIQUE WILKINS	5,455

MOST FREE THROWS ATTEMPTED

Wilt Chamberlain	11,862
MOSES MALONE	11,058
Kareem Abdul-Jabbar	9,304
Oscar Robertson	9,185
Jerry West	8,801
Adrian Dantley	8,351
Dolph Schayes	8,273
Bob Pettit	8,119
Walt Bellamy	8,088
Elvin Hayes	7,999

HIGHEST FREE THROW PERCENTAGE
(1,200 FTM minimum)

	FTA	FTM	PCT.
MARK PRICE	1,916	1,735	.906
Rick Barry	4,243	3,818	.900
Calvin Murphy	3,864	3,445	.892
SCOTT SKILES	1,529	1,361	.890
Larry Bird	4,471	3,960	.886
Bill Sharman	3,559	3,143	.883
RICKY PIERCE	3,353	2,940	.877
REGGIE MILLER	3,197	2,803	.877
Kiki Vandeweghe	3,997	3,484	.872
JEFF MALONE	3,292	2,867	.871

MOST 3-PT. FIELD GOALS MADE

DALE ELLIS	1,013
DANNY AINGE	924
MICHAEL ADAMS	906
REGGIE MILLER	840
TERRY PORTER	729
MARK PRICE	699
CHUCK PERSON	684
DEREK HARPER	681
Larry Bird	649
VERNON MAXWELL	634

MOST 3-PT. FIELD GOALS ATTEMPTED

MICHAEL ADAMS	2,735
DALE ELLIS	2,520
DANNY AINGE	2,437
REGGIE MILLER	2,152
VERNON MAXWELL	1,981
DEREK HARPER	1,952
CHUCK PERSON	1,934
TERRY PORTER	1,892

Larry Bird	1,727
MARK PRICE	1,707

HIGHEST 3-POINT FIELD GOAL PERCENTAGE
(100 3FGM Minimum)

	3FGA	3FGM	PCT.
STEVE KERR	447	199	.445
B.J. ARMSTRONG	397	176	.443
Drazen Petrovic	583	255	.437
MARK PRICE	1,707	699	.409
Trent Tucker	1,410	575	.408
JIM LES	472	191	.405
Mike Iuzzolino	280	113	.404
DALE ELLIS	2,520	1,013	.402
Craig Hodges	1,408	563	.400
DANA BARROS	1,028	409	.398

MOST OFFENSIVE REBOUNDS

MOSES MALONE	6,711
ROBERT PARISH	4,374
BUCK WILLIAMS	3,872
Larry Smith	3,401
CHARLES BARKLEY	3,123
HAKEEM OLAJUWON	3,004
Kareem Abdul-Jabbar	2,975
DENNIS RODMAN	2,848
BILL LAIMBEER	2,819
Alex English	2,778
Elvin Hayes	2,778

MOST DEFENSIVE REBOUNDS

ROBERT PARISH	9,599
MOSES MALONE	9,455
Kareem Abdul-Jabbar	9,394
Jack Sikma	8,274
BILL LAIMBEER	7,581
BUCK WILLIAMS	7,492
Larry Bird	7,217
Elvin Hayes	6,973
Artis Gilmore	6,522
HAKEEM OLAJUWON	6,460

MOST TOTAL REBOUNDS

Wilt Chamberlain	23,924
Bill Russell	21,620
Kareem Abdul-Jabbar	17,440
Elvin Hayes	16,279
MOSES MALONE	16,166
Nate Thurmond	14,464
Walt Bellamy	14,241
ROBERT PARISH	13,973
Wes Unseld	13,769
Jerry Lucas	12,942

MOST ASSISTS

Magic Johnson	9,921
Oscar Robertson	9,887
JOHN STOCKTON	9,383
ISIAH THOMAS	9,061
Maurice Cheeks	7,392
Len Wilkens	7,211
Bob Cousy	6,955
Guy Rodgers	6,917
Nate Archibald	6,476
John Lucas	6,454

MOST PERSONAL FOULS

Kareem Abdul-Jabbar	4,657
Elvin Hayes	4,193
ROBERT PARISH	4,191

JAMES EDWARDS	3,937
Jack Sikma	3,879
Hal Greer	3,855
Dolph Schayes	3,664
BILL LAIMBEER	3,633
TOM CHAMBERS	3,553
Walt Bellamy	3,536

MOST DISQUALIFICATIONS

Vern Mikkelsen	127
Walter Dukes	121
Charlie Share	105
Paul Arizin	101
Darryl Dawkins	100
JAMES EDWARDS	95
Tom Gola	94
Tom Sanders	94
Steve Johnson	93
TREE ROLLINS	92

MOST STEALS

Maurice Cheeks	2,310
JOHN STOCKTON	2,031
ALVIN ROBERTSON	1,946
ISIAH THOMAS	1,861
Michael Jordan	1,815
CLYDE DREXLER	1,721
Magic Johnson	1,698
LAFAYETTE LEVER	1,666
Gus Williams	1,638
Larry Bird	1,556

MOST BLOCKED SHOTS

Kareem Abdul-Jabbar	3,189
MARK EATON	3,064
HAKEEM OLAJUWON	2,741
TREE ROLLINS	2,506
ROBERT PARISH	2,252
George T. Johnson	2,082
MANUTE BOL	2,077
LARRY NANCE	2,027
PATRICK EWING	1,984
Elvin Hayes	1,771

HIGHEST SCORING AVERAGE
(400 Games or 10,000 Points Minimum)

	G.	FGM	FTM	PTS.	AVG.
Michael Jordan	667	8,079	5,096	21,541	32.3
Wilt Chamberlain	1045	12,681	6,057	31,419	30.1
Elgin Baylor	846	8,693	5,763	23,149	27.4
Jerry West	932	9,016	7,160	25,192	27.0
DOMINIQUE WILKINS	907	9,020	5,455	24,019	26.5
Bob Pettit	792	7,349	6,182	20,880	26.4
George Gervin	791	8,045	4,541	20,708	26.2
KARL MALONE	734	7,027	4,956	19,050	26.0
Oscar Robertson	1040	9,508	7,694	26,710	25.7
Kareem Abdul-Jabbar	1560	15,837	6,712	38,387	24.6

POINTS

Kareem Abdul-Jabbar	38,387
Wilt Chamberlain	31,419
MOSES MALONE	27,360
Elvin Hayes	27,313
Oscar Robertson	26,710
John Havlicek	26,395
Alex English	25,613
Jerry West	25,192
DOMINIQUE WILKINS	24,019
Adrian Dantley	23,177

All-Time Regular-Season
NBA Records
Compiled by Elias Sports Bureau

Throughout this all-time NBA record section, records for 'fewest' and 'lowest' exclude games
and seasons before 1954–55, when the 24-second clock was introduced.

INDIVIDUAL

SEASONS

Most seasons
20—Kareem Abdul-Jabbar, Milwaukee, 1969–70—1974–75; L.A. Lakers, 1975–76—
1988–89
18—Moses Malone, Buffalo, 1976–77; Houston, 1976–77—1981–82; Philadelphia,
1982–83—1985–86; Washington, 1986–87—1987–88; Atlanta, 1988–89—1990–
91; Milwaukee, 1991–92—1992–93; Philadelphia, 1993–94
Robert Parish, Golden State, 1976–77—1979–80; Boston, 1980–81—1993–94
17—James Edwards, Los Angeles, 1977–78; Indiana, 1977–78—1980–81; Cleveland,
1981–82—1982–83; Phoenix, 1982–83—1987–88; Detroit, 1987–88—1990–
91; L.A. Clippers, 1991–92; L.A. Lakers, 1992–93—1993–94
Wayne Rollins, Atlanta, 1977–78—1987–88; Cleveland, 1988–89—1989–90;
Detroit, 1990–91; Houston, 1991–92—1992–93; Orlando, 1993–94
16—Dolph Schayes, Syracuse (NBL), 1948–49; Syracuse, 1949–50—1962–63; Philadelphia, 1963–64
John Havlicek, Boston, 1962–63—1977–78
Paul Silas, St. Louis, 1964–65—1967–68; Atlanta, 1968–69; Phoenix, 1969–70—
1971–1972; Boston, 1972- 73—1975–76; Denver, 1976–77; Seattle, 1977–78—
1979–80
Elvin Hayes, San Diego, 1968–69—1970–71; Houston, 1971–72; Baltimore,
1972–73; Capital, 1973–74; Washington, 1974–75—1980–81; Houston, 1981–82—
1983–84

GAMES

Most games, career
1,560—Kareem Abdul-Jabbar, Milwaukee, 1969–70—1974–75; L.A. Lakers, 1975–76—
1988–89
1,413—Robert Parish, Golden State, 1976–77—1979–80; Boston, 1980–81—1993–94
1,312—Moses Malone, Buffalo, 1976–77; Houston, 1976–77—1981–82; Philadelphia,
1982–83—1985–86; Washington, 1986–87—1987–88; Atlanta, 1988–89—
1990–91; Milwaukee, 1991–92—1992–93; Philadelphia, 1993–94
1,303—Elvin Hayes, San Diego, 1968–69—1970–71; Houston, 1971–72; Baltimore,
1972–73; Capital, 1973–74; Washington, 1974–75—1980–81; Houston,
1981–82—1983–84
1,270—John Havlicek, Boston, 1962–63—1977–78

Most consecutive games, career
906—Randy Smith, Buffalo, San Diego, Cleveland, New York, San Diego, February 18,
1972—March 13, 1983
844—John Kerr, Syracuse, Philadelphia, Baltimore, October 31, 1954—November 4, 1965
706—Dolph Schayes, Syracuse, February 17, 1952—December 26, 1961

Most games, season
88—Walt Bellamy, New York, Detroit, 1968–69
87—Tom Henderson, Atlanta, Washington, 1976–77
86—McCoy McLemore, Cleveland, Milwaukee, 1970–71

MINUTES

Minutes have been compiled since 1951–52

Most seasons leading league, minutes
8—Wilt Chamberlain, Philadelphia, 1959–60—1961–62; San Francisco, 1962–63—1963–
64; Philadelphia, 1965–66—1967–68
4—Elvin Hayes, San Diego, 1968–69—1969–70; Capital, 1973–74; Washington,
1976–77

Most consecutive seasons leading league, minutes
5—Wilt Chamberlain, Philadelphia, 1959–60—1961–62; San Francisco, 1962–63—1963–
64
3—Wilt Chamberlain, Philadelphia, 1965–66—1967–68
Michael Jordan, Chicago, 1986–87—1988–89

Most minutes, career
57,446—Kareem Abdul-Jabbar, Milwaukee, 1969–70—1974–75; L.A. Lakers, 1975–76—
1988–89
50,000—Elvin Hayes, San Diego, 1968–69—1970–71; Houston, 1971–72; Baltimore,
1972–73; Capital, 1973–74; Washington, 1974–75—1980–81; Houston,
1981–82—1983–84
47,859—Wilt Chamberlain, Philadelphia, 1959–60—1961–62; San Francisco, 1962–63—
1964–65; Philadelphia, 1964–65—1967–68; Los Angeles, 1968–69—1972–
73
46,471—John Havlicek, Boston, 1962–63—1977–78
44,922—Moses Malone, Buffalo, 1976–77; Houston, 1976–77—1981–82; Philadelphia,
1982–83—1985–86; Washington, 1986–87—1987–88; Atlanta, 1988–89—
1990–91; Milwaukee, 1991–92—1992–93; Philadelphia, 1993–94

Highest average, minutes per game, career (minimum: 400 games)
45.8—Wilt Chamberlain, Philadelphia, 1959–60—1961–62; San Francisco, 1962–63—
1964–65; Philadelphia, 1964–65—1967–68; Los Angeles, 1968–69—1972–73
(47,859/1,045)
42.3—Bill Russell, Boston, 1956–57—1968–69 (40,726/963)
42.2—Oscar Robertson, Cincinnati, 1960–61—1969–70; Milwaukee, 1970–71—1973–
74 (43,866/1,040)

Most minutes, season
3,882—Wilt Chamberlain, Philadelphia, 1961–62
3,836—Wilt Chamberlain, Philadelphia, 1967–68
3,806—Wilt Chamberlain, San Francisco, 1962–63
3,773—Wilt Chamberlain, Philadelphia, 1960–61
3,737—Wilt Chamberlain, Philadelphia, 1965–66
3,698—John Havlicek, Boston, 1971–72

Highest average, minutes per game, season
48.5—Wilt Chamberlain, Philadelphia, 1961–62 (3,882/80)
47.8—Wilt Chamberlain, Philadelphia, 1960–61 (3,773/79)
47.6—Wilt Chamberlain, San Francisco, 1962–63 (3,806/80)
47.3—Wilt Chamberlain, Philadelphia, 1965–66 (3,737/79)
46.8—Wilt Chamberlain, Philadelphia, 1967–68 (3,836/82)
46.4—Wilt Chamberlain, Philadelphia, 1959–60 (3,338/72)
46.1—Wilt Chamberlain, San Francisco, 1963–64 (3,689/80)
46.0—Nate Archibald, K.C.-Omaha, 1972–73 (3,681/80)

Most minutes, rookie, season
3,695—Elvin Hayes, San Diego, 1968–69
3,534—Kareem Abdul-Jabbar, Milwaukee, 1969–70
3,344—Walt Bellamy, Chicago, 1961–62

Most minutes, game
69—Dale Ellis, Seattle at Milwaukee, November 9, 1989 (5 ot)
68—Xavier McDaniel, Seattle at Milwaukee, November 9, 1989 (5 ot)
64—Norm Nixon, Los Angeles at Cleveland, January 29, 1980 (4 ot)
Eric Floyd, Golden State vs. New Jersey, February 1, 1987 (4 ot)

COMPLETE GAMES

Most complete games, season
79—Wilt Chamberlain, Philadelphia, 1961–62

Most consecutive complete games, season
47—Wilt Chamberlain, Philadelphia, January 5—March 14, 1962

SCORING

Most seasons leading league
7—Wilt Chamberlain, Philadelphia, 1959–60—1961–62; San Francisco, 1962–63—1963–

64; San Francisco, Philadelphia, 1964–65; Philadelphia, 1965–66
Michael Jordan, Chicago, 1986–87—1992–93
4—George Gervin, San Antonio, 1977–78—1979–80, 1981–82

Most consecutive seasons leading league

7—Wilt Chamberlain, Philadelphia, 1959–60—1961–62; San Francisco, 1962–63—1963–64; San Francisco, Philadelphia, 1964–65; Philadelphia, 1965–66
Michael Jordan, Chicago, 1986–87—1992–93
3—George Mikan, Minneapolis, 1948–49—1950–51
Neil Johnston, Philadelphia, 1952–53—1954–55
Bob McAdoo, Buffalo, 1973–74—1975–76
George Gervin, San Antonio, 1977–78—1979–80

Most points, lifetime

38,387—Kareem Abdul-Jabbar, Milwaukee, 1969–70—1974–75; L.A. Lakers, 1975–76—1988–89
31,419—Wilt Chamberlain, Philadelphia, 1959–60—1961–62; San Francisco, 1962–63—1964–65; Philadelphia, 1964–65—1967–68; Los Angeles, 1968–69—1972–73
27,360—Moses Malone, Buffalo, 1976–77; Houston, 1976–77—1981–82; Philadelphia, 1982–83—1985–86; Washington, 1986–87—1987–88; Atlanta, 1988–89—1990–91; Milwaukee, 1991–92—1992–93; Philadelphia, 1993–94
27,313—Elvin Hayes, San Diego, 1968–69—1970–71; Houston, 1971–72; Baltimore, 1972–73; Capital, 1973–74; Washington, 1974–75—1980–81; Houston, 1981–82—1983–84
26,710—Oscar Robertson, Cincinnati, 1960–61—1969–70; Milwaukee, 1970–71—1973–74

Highest average, points per game, career (minimum: 400 games)

32.3—Michael Jordan, Chicago, 1984–85—1992–93 (21,541/667)
30.1—Wilt Chamberlain, Philadelphia, 1959–60—1961–62; San Francisco, 1962–63—1964–65; Philadelphia, 1964–65—1967–68; Los Angeles, 1968–69—1972–73 (31,419/1,045)
27.4—Elgin Baylor, Minneapolis, 1958–59—1959–60; Los Angeles, 1960–61—1971–72 (23,149/846)
27.0—Jerry West, Los Angeles, 1960–61—1973–74 (25,192/932)
26.5—Dominique Wilkins, Atlanta, 1982–83—1993–94; L.A. Clippers, 1993–94 (24,019/907)

Most points, season

4,029—Wilt Chamberlain, Philadelphia, 1961–62
3,586—Wilt Chamberlain, San Francisco, 1962–63
3,041—Michael Jordan, Chicago, 1986–87
3,033—Wilt Chamberlain, Philadelphia, 1960–61
2,948—Wilt Chamberlain, San Francisco, 1963–64

Highest average, points per game, season (minimum: 70 games)

50.4—Wilt Chamberlain, Philadelphia, 1961–62 (4,029/80)
44.8—Wilt Chamberlain, San Francisco, 1962–63 (3,586/80)
38.4—Wilt Chamberlain, Philadelphia, 1960–61 (3,033/79)
37.6—Wilt Chamberlain, Philadelphia, 1959–60 (2,707/72)
37.1—Michael Jordan, Chicago, 1986–87 (3,041/82)
36.9—Wilt Chamberlain, San Francisco, 1963–64 (2,948/80)

Most points, rookie, season

2,707—Wilt Chamberlain, Philadelphia, 1959–60
2,495—Walt Bellamy, Chicago, 1961–62
2,361—Kareem Abdul-Jabbar, Milwaukee, 1969–70

Highest average, points per game, rookie, season

37.6—Wilt Chamberlain, Philadelphia, 1959–60 (2,707/72)
31.6—Walt Bellamy, Chicago, 1961–62 (2,495/79)
30.5—Oscar Robertson, Cincinnati, 1960–61 (2,165/71)

Most seasons, 2,000-or-more points

9—Kareem Abdul-Jabbar, Milwaukee, 1969–70—1973–74; Los Angeles, 1975–76—1976–77, 1979–80—1980–81
8—Alex English, Denver, 1981–82—1988–89
Michael Jordan, Chicago, 1984–85, 1986–87—1992–93
Dominique Wilkins, Atlanta, 1984–85—1990–91, 1992–93
7—Wilt Chamberlain, Philadelphia, 1959–60—1961–62; San Francisco, 1962–63—1963–64; San Francisco, Philadelphia, 1964–65; Philadelphia, 1965–66
Oscar Robertson, Cincinnati, 1960–61—1966–67
Karl Malone, Utah, 1987–88—1993–94

Most consecutive seasons, 2,000-or-more points

8—Alex English, Denver, 1981–82—1988–89
7—Wilt Chamberlain, Philadelphia, 1959–60—1961–62; San Francisco, 1962–63—1963–64; San Francisco, Philadelphia, 1964–65; Philadelphia, 1965–66
Oscar Robertson, Cincinnati, 1960–61—1966–67
Dominique Wilkins, Atlanta, 1984–85—1990–91
Michael Jordan, Chicago, 1986–87—1992–93
Karl Malone, Utah, 1987–88—1993–94
6—George Gervin, San Antonio, 1977–78—1982–83

Most seasons, 1,000-or-more points

19—Kareem Abdul-Jabbar, Milwaukee, 1969–70—1974–75; L.A. Lakers, 1975–76—1987–88
16—John Havlicek, Boston, 1962–63—1977–78
15—Elvin Hayes, San Diego, 1968–69—1970–71; Houston, 1971–72; Baltimore, 1972–73; Capital, 1973–74; Washington, 1974–75—1980–81; Houston, 1981–82—1982–83
Moses Malone, Buffalo, Houston, 1976–77; Houston, 1977–78—1981–82; Philadelphia, 1982–83—1985–86; Washington, 1986–87—1987–88; Atlanta, 1988–89—1989–90; Milwaukee, 1991–92
Robert Parish, Golden State, 1977–78—1979–80; Boston, 1980–81—1991–92

Most consecutive seasons, 1,000-or-more points

19—Kareem Abdul-Jabbar, Milwaukee, 1969–70—1974–75; L.A. Lakers, 1975–76—1987–88
16—John Havlicek, Boston, 1962–63—1977–78
15—Elvin Hayes, San Diego, 1968–69—1970–71; Houston, 1971–72; Baltimore, 1972–73; Capital, 1973–74; Washington, 1974–75—1980–81; Houston, 1981–82—1982–83
Robert Parish, Golden State, 1977–78—1979–80; Boston, 1980–81—1991–92

Most points, game

100—Wilt Chamberlain, Philadelphia vs. New York, at Hershey, Pa., March 2, 1962
78—Wilt Chamberlain, Philadelphia vs. Los Angeles, December 8, 1961 (3 ot)
73—Wilt Chamberlain, Philadelphia vs. Chicago, January 13, 1962
Wilt Chamberlain, San Francisco at New York, November 16, 1962
David Thompson, Denver at Detroit, April 9, 1978
72—Wilt Chamberlain, San Francisco at Los Angeles, November 3, 1962
71—Elgin Baylor, Los Angeles at New York, November 15, 1960
David Robinson, San Antonio at L.A. Clippers, April 24, 1994

Most points, rookie, game

58—Wilt Chamberlain, Philadelphia vs. Detroit, at Bethlehem, Pa., January 25, 1960
Wilt Chamberlain, Philadelphia at New York, February 21, 1960
57—Rick Barry, San Francisco at New York, December 14, 1965
56—Earl Monroe, Baltimore vs. Los Angeles, February 13, 1968 (ot)

Most games, 50-or-more points, career

118—Wilt Chamberlain, Philadelphia, 1959–60—1961–62; San Francisco, 1962–63—1964–65; Philadelphia, 1964–65—1967–68; Los Angeles, 1968–69—1972–73
26—Michael Jordan, Chicago, 1984–85—1992–93
17—Elgin Baylor, Minneapolis, 1958–59—1959–60; Los Angeles, 1960–61—1971–72
14—Rick Barry, San Francisco, 1965–66—1966–67; Golden State, 1972–73—1977–78; Houston, 1978–79—1979–80

Most games, 50-or-more points, season

45—Wilt Chamberlain, Philadelphia, 1961–62
30—Wilt Chamberlain, San Francisco, 1962–63
9—Wilt Chamberlain, San Francisco, 1963–64
Wilt Chamberlain, San Francisco, Philadelphia, 1964–65

Most consecutive games, 50-or-more points

7—Wilt Chamberlain, Philadelphia, December 16—December 29, 1961
6—Wilt Chamberlain, Philadelphia, January 11—January 19, 1962
5—Wilt Chamberlain, Philadelphia, December 8—December 13, 1961
Wilt Chamberlain, Philadelphia, February 25—March 4, 1962

Most games, 40-or-more points, career

271—Wilt Chamberlain, Philadelphia, 1959–60—1961–62; San Francisco, 1962–63—1964–65; Philadelphia, 1964–65—1967–68; Los Angeles, 1968–69—1972–73
135—Michael Jordan, Chicago, 1984–85—1992–93
87—Elgin Baylor, Minneapolis, 1958–59—1959–60; Los Angeles, 1960–61—1971–72

Most games, 40-or-more points, season

63—Wilt Chamberlain, Philadelphia, 1961–62

52—Wilt Chamberlain, San Francisco, 1962–63
37—Michael Jordan, Chicago, 1986–87

Most consecutive games, 40-or-more points
14—Wilt Chamberlain, Philadelphia, December 8—December 30, 1961
    Wilt Chamberlain, Philadelphia, January 11—February 1, 1962
10—Wilt Chamberlain, San Francisco, November 9—November 25, 1962
9—Michael Jordan, Chicago, November 28—December 12, 1986

Most consecutive games, 30-or-more points
65—Wilt Chamberlain, Philadelphia, November 4, 1961—February 22, 1962
31—Wilt Chamberlain, Philadelphia, San Francisco, February 25—December 8, 1962
25—Wilt Chamberlain, Philadelphia, November 11—December 27, 1960

Most consecutive games, 20-or-more points
126—Wilt Chamberlain, Philadelphia, San Francisco, October 19, 1961—January 19, 1963
92—Wilt Chamberlain, San Francisco, February 26, 1963—March 18, 1964
72—Michael Jordan, Chicago, December 29, 1987—December 6, 1988

Most consecutive games, 10-or-more points
787—Kareem Abdul-Jabbar, L.A. Lakers, December 4, 1977—December 2, 1987
577—Michael Jordan, Chicago, March 25, 1986—April 25, 1993 (current)
526—Moses Malone, Houston, Philadelphia, November 4, 1978—March 4, 1985

Most points, one half
59—Wilt Chamberlain, Philadelphia vs. New York, at Hershey, Pa., March 2, 1962 (2nd Half)
53—David Thompson, Denver at Detroit, April 9, 1978 (1st Half)
    George Gervin, San Antonio at New Orleans, April 9, 1978 (1st Half)
47—David Robinson, San Antonio at L.A. Clippers, April 24, 1994 (2nd Half)

Most points, one quarter
33—George Gervin, San Antonio at New Orleans, April 9, 1978 (2nd Qtr.)
32—David Thompson, Denver at Detroit, April 9, 1978 (1st Qtr.)
31—Wilt Chamberlain, Philadelphia vs. New York, at Hershey, Pa., March 2, 1962 (4th Qtr.)

Most points, overtime period
14—Butch Carter, Indiana vs. Boston, March 20, 1984
13—Earl Monroe, Baltimore vs. Detroit, February 6, 1970
    Joe Caldwell, Atlanta vs. Cincinnati, at Memphis, February 18, 1970

FIELD GOAL PERCENTAGE

Most seasons, leading league
9—Wilt Chamberlain, Philadelphia, 1960–61; San Francisco, 1962–63; San Francisco, Philadelphia, 1964–65; Philadelphia, 1965–66—1967–68; Los Angeles, 1968–69, 1971–72—1972–73
4—Artis Gilmore, Chicago, 1980–81—1981–82; San Antonio, 1982–83—1983–84
3—Neil Johnston, Philadelphia, 1952–53, 1955–56—1956–57

Most consecutive seasons leading league
5—Wilt Chamberlain, San Francisco, Philadelphia, 1964–65; Philadelphia, 1965–66—1967–68; Los Angeles, 1968–69
4—Artis Gilmore, Chicago, 1980–81—1981–82; San Antonio, 1982–83—1983–84

Highest field goal percentage, career (minimum: 2,000 field goals)
.599—Artis Gilmore, Chicago, 1976–77—1981–82; San Antonio, 1982–83—1986–87; Chicago, 1987–88; Boston, 1987–88
.592—Mark West, Dallas, 1983–84; Milwaukee, 1984–85; Cleveland, 1984–85—1987–88; Phoenix, 1987–88—1993–94
.5722—Steve Johnson, Kansas City, 1981–82—1983–84; Chicago, 1983–84—1984–85; San Antonio, 1985–86; Portland, 1986–87—1988–89; Minnesota, 1989–90; Seattle, 1989–90; Golden State, 1990–91
.5720—Darryl Dawkins, Philadelphia, 1975–76—1981–82; New Jersey, 1982–83—1986–87; Utah, 1987–88; Detroit, 1987–88—1988–89
.570—James Donaldson, Seattle, 1980–81—1982–83; San Diego, 1983–84; L.A. Clippers, 1984–85—1985–86; Dallas, 1985–86—1991–92; New York, 1991–92; Utah, 1992–93

Highest field goal percentage, season (qualifiers)
.727—Wilt Chamberlain, Los Angeles, 1972–73 (426/586)
.683—Wilt Chamberlain, Philadelphia, 1966–67 (785/1,150)
.670—Artis Gilmore, Chicago, 1980–81 (547/816)
.652—Artis Gilmore, Chicago, 1981–82 (546/837)
.649—Wilt Chamberlain, Los Angeles, 1971–72 (496/764)

Highest field goal percentage, rookie, season (qualifiers)
.613—Steve Johnson, Kansas City, 1981–82 (395/644)

.600—Otis Thorpe, Kansas City, 1984–85 (411/685)
.582—Buck Williams, New Jersey, 1981–82 (513/881)

Highest field goal percentage, game (minimum: 15 field goals)
1.000—Wilt Chamberlain, Philadelphia vs. Los Angeles, January 20, 1967 (15/15)
    Wilt Chamberlain, Philadelphia vs. Baltimore, at Pittsburgh, February 24, 1967 (18/18)
    Wilt Chamberlain, Philadelphia at Baltimore, March 19, 1967 (16/16)
.947—Wilt Chamberlain, San Francisco vs. New York, at Boston, November 27, 1963 (18/19)
.941—Wilt Chamberlain, Philadelphia at Baltimore, November 25, 1966 (16/17)
    Scottie Pippen, Chicago vs. Charlotte, February 23, 1991 (16/17)

Most field goals, no misses, game
18—Wilt Chamberlain, Philadelphia vs. Baltimore, at Pittsburgh, February 24, 1967
16—Wilt Chamberlain, Philadelphia at Baltimore, March 19, 1967
15—Wilt Chamberlain, Philadelphia vs. Los Angeles, January 20, 1967
14—Bailey Howell, Baltimore vs. San Francisco, January 3, 1965
    Wilt Chamberlain, Los Angeles vs. Detroit, March 11, 1969
    Billy McKinney, Kansas City vs. Boston, at St. Louis, December 27, 1978

Most field goal attempts, none made, game
17—Tim Hardaway, Golden State at San Antonio, December 27, 1991 (ot)
15—Howie Dallmar, Philadelphia vs. New York, November 27, 1947
    Howie Dallmar, Philadelphia vs. Washington, November 25, 1948
    Dick Ricketts, Rochester vs. St. Louis, March 7, 1956
    Corky Devlin, Ft. Wayne vs. Minneapolis, at Rochester, December 25, 1956
    Charlie Tyra, New York at Philadelphia, November 7, 1957
    Frank Ramsey, Boston vs. Cincinnati, at Philadelphia, December 8, 1960
    Ray Williams, New Jersey vs. Indiana, December 28, 1981
    Rodney McCray, Sacramento at Utah, November 9,1988
14—Ed Leede, Boston at Washington, December 13, 1950
    Jack George, Philadelphia at Syracuse, November 1, 1953
    Sihugo Green, St. Louis vs. Boston, at Philadelphia, December 14, 1961
    Bailey Howell, Detroit vs. St. Louis, January 4, 1963
    Bill Russell, Boston vs. Philadelphia, at Syracuse, January 23, 1965
    Adrian Smith, Cincinnati at New York, December 18, 1965
    Connie Dierking, Cincinnati at San Francisco, November 1, 1969
    Dino Radja, Boston at San Antonio, December 26, 1993

FIELD GOALS

Most seasons leading league
7—Wilt Chamberlain, Philadelphia, 1959–60—1961–62; San Francisco, 1962–63—1963–64; San Francisco, Philadelphia, 1964–65; Philadelphia, 1965–66
    Michael Jordan, Chicago, 1986–87—1992–93
5—Kareem Abdul-Jabbar, Milwaukee, 1969–70—1971–72, 1973–74; Los Angeles, 1976–77
4—George Gervin, San Antonio, 1977–78—1979–80, 1981–82

Most consecutive seasons leading league
7—Wilt Chamberlain, Philadelphia, 1959–60—1961–62; San Francisco, 1962–63—1963–64; San Francisco, Philadelphia, 1964–65; Philadelphia, 1965–66
    Michael Jordan, Chicago, 1986–87—1992–93
3—George Mikan, Minneapolis, 1948–49—1950–51
    Kareem Abdul-Jabbar, Milwaukee, 1969–70—1971–72
    George Gervin, San Antonio, 1977–78—1979–80

Most field goals, career
15,837—Kareem Abdul-Jabbar, Milwaukee, 1969–70—1974–75; L.A. Lakers, 1975–76—1988–89
12,681—Wilt Chamberlain, Philadelphia, 1959–60—1961–62; San Francisco, 1962–63—1964–65; Philadelphia, 1964–65—1967–68; Los Angeles, 1968–69—1972–73
10,976—Elvin Hayes, San Diego, 1968–69—1970–71; Houston, 1971–72; Baltimore, 1972–73; Capital, 1973–74; Washington, 1974–75—1980–81; Houston, 1981–82—1983–84

Most field goals, season
1,597—Wilt Chamberlain, Philadelphia, 1961–62
1,463—Wilt Chamberlain, San Francisco, 1962–63
1,251—Wilt Chamberlain, Philadelphia, 1960–61

Most consecutive field goals, no misses, season
35—Wilt Chamberlain, Philadelphia, February 17—February 28, 1967

Most field goals, game

36—Wilt Chamberlain, Philadelphia vs. New York, at Hershey, Pa., March 2, 1962
31—Wilt Chamberlain, Philadelphia vs. Los Angeles, December 8, 1961 (3 ot)
30—Wilt Chamberlain, Philadelphia at Chicago, December 16, 1967
   Rick Barry, Golden State vs. Portland, March 26, 1974

Most field goals, one half

22—Wilt Chamberlain, Philadelphia vs. New York, at Hershey, Pa., March 2, 1962 (2nd Half)
21—Rick Barry, Golden State vs. Portland, March 26, 1974 (2nd Half)
20—David Thompson, Denver at Detroit, April 9, 1978 (1st Half)

Most field goals, one quarter

13—David Thompson, Denver at Detroit, April 9, 1978 (1st Qtr.)
12—Cliff Hagan, St. Louis at New York, February 4, 1958 (4th Qtr.)
   Wilt Chamberlain, Philadelphia vs. New York, at Hershey, Pa., March 2, 1962 (4th Qtr.)
   George Gervin, San Antonio at New Orleans, April 9, 1978 (2nd Qtr.)
   Jeff Malone, Washington at Phoenix, February 27, 1988 (3rd Qtr.)

FIELD GOAL ATTEMPTS

Most seasons leading league

7—Wilt Chamberlain, Philadelphia, 1959-60—1961-62; San Francisco, 1962-63—1963-64; San Francisco, Philadelphia, 1964-65; Philadelphia, 1965-66
6—Michael Jordan, Chicago, 1986-87—1987-88, 1989-90—1992-93
3—Joe Fulks, Philadelphia, 1946-47—1948-49
   George Mikan, Minneapolis, 1949-50—1951-52
   Elvin Hayes, San Diego, 1968-69—1970-71
   George Gervin, San Antonio, 1978-79—1979-80, 1981-82

Most consecutive seasons leading league

7—Wilt Chamberlain, Philadelphia, 1959-60—1961-62; San Francisco, 1962-63—1963-64; San Francisco, Philadelphia, 1964-65; Philadelphia, 1965-66
4—Michael Jordan, Chicago, 1989-90—1992-93
3—Joe Fulks, Philadelphia, 1946-47—1948-49
   George Mikan, Minneapolis, 1949-50—1951-52
   Elvin Hayes, San Diego, 1968-69—1970-71

Most field goal attempts, career

28,307—Kareem Abdul-Jabbar, Milwaukee, 1969-70—1974-75; L.A. Lakers, 1975-76—1988-89
24,272—Elvin Hayes, San Diego, 1968-69—1970-71; Houston, 1971-72; Baltimore, 1972-73; Capital, 1973-74; Washington, 1974-75—1980-81; Houston, 1981-82—1983-84
23,930—John Havlicek, Boston, 1962-63—1977-78

Most field goal attempts, season

3,159—Wilt Chamberlain, Philadelphia, 1961-62
2,770—Wilt Chamberlain, San Francisco, 1962-63
2,457—Wilt Chamberlain, Philadelphia, 1960-61

Most field goal attempts, game

63—Wilt Chamberlain, Philadelphia vs. New York, at Hershey, Pa., March 2, 1962
62—Wilt Chamberlain, Philadelphia vs. Los Angeles, December 8, 1961 (3 ot)
60—Wilt Chamberlain, San Francisco at Cincinnati, October 28, 1962 (ot)

Most field goal attempts, one half

37—Wilt Chamberlain, Philadelphia vs. New York, at Hershey, Pa., March 2, 1962 (2nd Half)
34—George Gervin, San Antonio at New Orleans, April 9, 1978 (1st Half)
32—Wilt Chamberlain, Philadelphia vs. Chicago, at Boston, January 24, 1962

Most field goal attempts, one quarter

21—Wilt Chamberlain, Philadelphia vs. New York, at Hershey, Pa., March 2, 1962 (4th Qtr.)
20—Wilt Chamberlain, Philadelphia vs. Chicago, at Boston, January 24, 1962
   George Gervin, San Antonio at New Orleans, April 9, 1978 (2nd Qtr.)
19—Bob Pettit, St. Louis at Philadelphia, December 6, 1961

THREE-POINT FIELD GOAL PERCENTAGE

Most seasons leading league

2—Craig Hodges, Milwaukee, 1985-86; Milwaukee, Phoenix, 1987-88
1—Fred Brown, Seattle, 1979-80
   Brian Taylor, San Diego, 1980-81
   Campy Russell, New York, 1981-82
   Mike Dunleavy, San Antonio, 1982-83
   Darrell Griffith, Utah, 1983-84
   Byron Scott, L.A. Lakers, 1984-85

Kiki Vandeweghe, Portland, 1986-87
Jon Sundvold, Miami, 1988-89
Steve Kerr, Cleveland, 1989-90
Jim Les, Sacramento, 1990-91
Dana Barros, Seattle, 1991-92
B.J. Armstrong, Chicago, 1992-93
Tracy Murray, Portland, 1993-94

Highest three-point field goal percentage, career (minimum: 100 three-point FGs)

.445—Steve Kerr, Phoenix, 1988-89; Cleveland, 1989-90—1992-93, Orlando, 1992-93; Chicago, 1993-94 (199/447)
.443—B.J. Armstrong, Chicago, 1989-90—1993-94 (176/397)
.437—Drazen Petrovic, Portland, 1989-90—1990-91; New Jersey, 1990-91—1992-93 (255/583)

Highest three-point field goal percentage, season (qualifiers)

.522—Jon Sundvold, Miami, 1988-89 (48/92)
.507—Steve Kerr, Cleveland, 1989-90 (73/144)
.491—Craig Hodges, Milwaukee, Phoenix 1987-88 (86/175)

Most three-point field goals, no misses, game

7—Terry Porter, Portland at Golden State, November 14, 1992
   Sam Perkins, Seattle vs. Denver, November 9, 1993
6—Chuck Person, Indiana at Phoenix, February 11, 1987
   Danny Ainge, Boston at Utah, January 4, 1988
   Charles Barkley, Philadelphia at Miami, February 22, 1989
   Mark Price, Cleveland at Golden State, March 9, 1989
   Chuck Person, Minnesota vs. Miami, February 10, 1993
   Trent Tucker, Chicago vs. Atlanta, February 27, 1993
5—by many

Most three-point field goal attempts, none made, game

9—Isiah Thomas, Detroit vs. Milwaukee, November 6, 1992
8—Michael Adams, Denver vs. Washington, February 15, 1989
   Michael Adams, Denver vs. Indiana, March 17, 1991
   Vernon Maxwell, Houston at Orlando, March 30, 1991
   Reggie Miller, Indiana at New York, December 28, 1991
   Mookie Blaylock, Atlanta vs. Charlotte, April 17, 1993
   Nick Van Exel, L.A. Lakers vs. Philadelphia, February 20, 1994
7—by many

THREE-POINT FIELD GOALS

Most seasons leading league

2—Darrell Griffith, Utah, 1983-84—1984-85
   Larry Bird, Boston, 1985-86—1986-87
   Michael Adams, Denver, 1988-89—1989-90
   Vernon Maxwell, Houston, 1990-91—1991-92
   Dan Majerle, Phoenix, 1992-93—1993-94
1—Brian Taylor, San Diego, 1979-80
   Mike Bratz, Cleveland, 1980-81
   Don Buse, Indiana, 1981-82
   Mike Dunleavy, San Antonio, 1982-83
   Danny Ainge, Boston, 1987-88
   Reggie Miller, Indiana, 1992-93

Most three-point field goals, career

1,013—Dale Ellis, Dallas, 1983-84—1985-86; Seattle, 1986-87—1990-91; Milwaukee, 1990-91—1991-92; San Antonio, 1992-93—1993-94
924—Danny Ainge, Boston, 1981-82—1988-89; Sacramento, 1988-89—1989-90; Portland, 1990-91—1991-92; Phoenix, 1992-93—1993-94
906—Michael Adams, Sacramento, 1985-86; Washington, 1986-87; Denver, 1987-88—1990-91; Washington, 1991-92—1993-94

Most three-point field goals, season

192—Dan Majerle, Phoenix, 1993-94
172—Vernon Maxwell, Houston 1990-91
167—Michael Adams, Denver, 1990-91
   Dan Majerle, Phoenix, 1992-93
   Reggie Miller, Indiana, 1992-93

Most consecutive three-point field goals, no misses, season

11—Scott Wedman, Boston, December 21, 1984—March 31, 1985
10—Trent Tucker, New York, December 28, 1984—January 15, 1985

Brad Davis, Dallas, January 23—February 3, 1988
Kenny Smith, Houston, January 22—February 6, 1991
9—Craig Hodges, Chicago, February 3—February 8, 1990

Most three-point field goals, game

10—Brian Shaw, Miami at Milwaukee, April 8, 1993
9—Dale Ellis, Seattle vs. L.A. Clippers, April 20, 1990
Michael Adams, Denver at L.A. Clippers, April 12, 1991
Dennis Scott, Orlando vs. Milwaukee, April 13, 1993

Most consecutive games, three-point field goals made, season

43—Michael Adams, Denver, January 28—April 23, 1988
36—Michael Adams, Denver, November 4, 1988—January 23, 1989
34—Mark Price, Cleveland, December 5, 1989—February 17, 1990

Most three-point field goals, rookie, season

125—Dennis Scott, Orlando, 1990-91
95—Dana Barros, Seattle, 1989-90
73—Latrell Sprewell, Golden State, 1992-93

Most three-point field goals made, one half

7—John Roche, Denver vs. Seattle, January 9, 1982
Michael Adams, Denver vs. Milwaukee, January 21, 1989
John Starks, New York vs. Miami, November 22, 1993
6—by many

Most three-point field goals made, one quarter

7—John Roche, Denver vs. Seattle, January 9, 1982
6—Brian Shaw, Miami at Milwaukee, April 8, 1993

THREE-POINT FIELD GOAL ATTEMPTS

Most seasons leading league

4—Michael Adams, Denver, 1987-88—1990-91
2—Darrell Griffith, Utah, 1983-84—1984-85
Dan Majerle, Phoenix, 1992-93—1993-94
1—Brian Taylor, San Diego, 1979-80
Mike Bratz, Cleveland, 1980-81
Joey Hassett, Golden State, 1981-82
Mike Dunleavy, San Antonio, 1982-83
Larry Bird, Boston, 1985-86
Dale Ellis, Seattle, 1986-87
Vernon Maxwell, Houston, 1991-92

Most three-point field goal attempts, career

2,735—Michael Adams, Sacramento, 1985-86; Washington, 1986-87; Denver, 1987-88—1990-91; Washington, 1991-92—1993-94
2,520—Dale Ellis, Dallas, 1983-84—1985-86; Seattle, 1986-87—1990-91; Milwaukee, 1990-91—1991-92; San Antonio, 1992-93—1993-94
2,437—Danny Ainge, Boston, 1981-82—1988-89; Sacramento, 1988-89—1989-90; Portland, 1990-91—1991-92; Phoenix, 1992-93—1993-94

Most three-point field goal attempts, season

564—Michael Adams, Denver, 1990-91
510—Vernon Maxwell, Houston 1990-91
503—Dan Majerle, Phoenix, 1993-94

Most three-point field goal attempts, game

20—Michael Adams, Denver at L.A. Clippers, April 12, 1991
19—Dennis Scott, Orlando vs. Milwaukee, April 13, 1993
16—Michael Adams, Denver vs. Milwaukee, March 23, 1991 (ot)
Reggie Miller, Indiana at Milwaukee, April 18, 1993
Nick Van Exel, L.A. Lakers vs. Utah, April 24, 1994

Most three-point field goal attempts, one half

13—Michael Adams, Denver at L.A. Clippers, April 12, 1991
12—Manute Bol, Philadelphia at Phoenix, March 3, 1993
Dennis Scott, Orlando vs. Milwaukee, April 13, 1993

FREE THROW PERCENTAGE

Most seasons leading league

7—Bill Sharman, Boston, 1952-53—1956-57, 1958-59, 1960-61
6—Rick Barry, Golden State, 1972-73, 1974-75—1975-76, 1977-78; Houston, 1978-79—1979-80
4—Larry Bird, Boston, 1983-84, 1985-86—1986-87, 1989-90

Most consecutive seasons leading league

5—Bill Sharman, Boston, 1952-53—1956-57
3—Rick Barry, Golden State, 1977-78; Houston, 1978-79—1979-80
2—Bob Feerick, Washington, 1947-48—1948-49
Rick Barry, Golden State, 1974-75—1975-76
Larry Bird, Boston, 1985-86—1986-87
Mark Price, Cleveland, 1991-92—1992-93

Highest free throw percentage, career (minimum: 1,200 free throws made)

.906—Mark Price, Cleveland, 1986-87—1993-94 (1,916/1,735)
.900—Rick Barry, San Francisco, 1965-66—1966-67; Golden State, 1972-73—1977-78; Houston, 1978-79—1979-80 (3,818/4,243)
.892—Calvin Murphy, San Diego, 1970-71; Houston, 1971-72—1982-83 (3,445/3,864)
.890—Scott Skiles, Milwaukee, 1986-87; Indiana, 1987-88—1988-89; Orlando, 1989-90—1993-94 (1,361/1,529)

Highest free throw percentage, season (qualifiers)

.958—Calvin Murphy, Houston, 1980-81 (206/215)
.956—Mahmoud Abdul-Rauf, Denver, 1993-94 (219/229)
.948—Mark Price, Cleveland, 1992-93 (289/305)
.9473—Mark Price, Cleveland, 1991-92 (270/285)
.9467—Rick Barry, Houston, 1978-79 (160/169)

Highest free throw percentage, rookie, season (qualifiers)

.902—Ernie DiGregorio, Buffalo, 1973-74 (174/193)
.896—Chris Mullin, Golden State, 1985-86 (189/211)
.879—Winston Garland, Golden State, 1987-88 (138/157)

Most free throws made, no misses, game

23—Dominique Wilkins, Atlanta vs. Chicago, December 8, 1992
19—Bob Pettit, St. Louis at Boston, November 22, 1961
Bill Cartwright, New York vs. Kansas City, November 17, 1981
Adrian Dantley, Detroit vs. Chicago, December 15, 1987 (ot)

Most free throw attempts, none made, game

10—Wilt Chamberlain, Philadelphia vs. Detroit, November 4, 1960
9—Wilt Chamberlain, Philadelphia at St. Louis, February 19, 1967
8—Elvin Hayes, Houston vs. Portland, March 26, 1972
Jerome Lane, Cleveland at Atlanta, December 29, 1992
7—Connie Simmons, Rochester vs. Philadelphia, at New Haven, January 2, 1956
Frank Selvy, Los Angeles vs. New York, January 19, 1962
Jerome Lane, Denver vs. Houston, December 13, 1988

FREE THROWS MADE

Most seasons leading league

5—Adrian Dantley, Indiana, Los Angeles, 1977-78; Utah, 1980-81—1981-82; 1983-84, 1985-86
Karl Malone, Utah, 1988-89—1992-93
4—Oscar Robertson, Cincinnati, 1963-64—1964-65. 1967-68—1968-69
3—George Mikan, Minneapolis, 1948-49—1950-51
Neil Johnston, Philadelphia, 1952-53—1954-55
Bob Pettit, St. Louis, 1955-56, 1958-59, 1962-63
Nate Archibald, Cincinnati, 1971-72; K.C.-Omaha 1972-73, 1974-75

Most consecutive seasons leading league

5—Karl Malone, Utah, 1988-89—1992-93
3—George Mikan, Minneapolis, 1948-49—1950-51
Neil Johnston, Philadelphia, 1952-53—1954-55

Most free throws made, career

8,509—Moses Malone, Buffalo, 1976-77; Houston, 1976-77—1981-82; Philadelphia, 1982-83—1985-86; Washington, 1986-87—1987-88; Atlanta, 1988-89—1990-91; Milwaukee, 1991-92—1992-93; Philadelphia, 1993-94
7,694—Oscar Robertson, Cincinnati, 1960-61—1969-70; Milwaukee, 1970-71—1973-74
7,160—Jerry West, Los Angeles, 1960-61—1973-74

Most free throws made, season

840—Jerry West, Los Angeles, 1965-66
835—Wilt Chamberlain, Philadelphia, 1961-62
833—Michael Jordan, Chicago, 1986-87

Most consecutive free throws made, season

84—Micheal Williams, Minnesota, March 24, 1993—April 25, 1993

78—Calvin Murphy, Houston, December 27, 1980—February 28, 1981
77—Mark Price, Cleveland, February 5, 1993—April 2, 1993

Most free throws made, game

28—Wilt Chamberlain, Philadelphia vs. New York, at Hershey, Pa., March 2, 1962
   Adrian Dantley, Utah vs. Houston, at Las Vegas, January 4, 1984
27—Adrian Dantley, Utah vs. Denver, November 25, 1983
26—Adrian Dantley, Utah vs. Dallas, October 31, 1980
   Michael Jordan, Chicago vs. New Jersey, February 26, 1987

Most free throws made, one half

20—Michael Jordan, Chicago at Miami, December 30, 1992 (2nd Half)
19—Oscar Robertson, Cincinnati at Baltimore, December 27, 1964
18—Michael Jordan, Chicago vs. New York, January 21, 1990 (2nd Half)
   Detlef Schrempf, Indiana at Golden State, December 8, 1992 (2nd Half)

Most free throws made, one quarter

14—Rick Barry, San Francisco at New York, December 6, 1966 (3rd Qtr.)
   Pete Maravich, Atlanta vs. Buffalo, November 28, 1973 (3rd Qtr.)
   Adrian Dantley, Detroit vs. Sacramento, December 10, 1986 (4th Qtr.)
   Michael Jordan, Chicago at Utah, November 15, 1989 (4th Qtr.)
   Michael Jordan, Chicago at Miami, December 30, 1992 (4th Qtr.)
13—Ken Sears, New York at Boston, November 3, 1956
   Oscar Robertson, Cincinnati at Baltimore, December 27, 1964
   John Drew, Atlanta vs. New Orleans, January 20, 1979 (3rd Qtr.)

FREE THROW ATTEMPTS

Most seasons leading league

9—Wilt Chamberlain, Philadelphia, 1959-60—1961-62; San Francisco, 1962-63—1963-64; San Francisco, Philadelphia, 1964-65; Philadelphia, 1966-67—1967-68; Los Angeles, 1968-69
5—Moses Malone, Houston, 1979-80—1981-82; Philadelphia, 1982-83, 1984-85
   Karl Malone, Utah, 1988-89—1992-93

Most consecutive seasons leading league

6—Wilt Chamberlain, Philadelphia, 1959-60—1961-62; San Francisco, 1962-63—1963-64; San Francisco, Philadelphia, 1964-65
5—Karl Malone, Utah, 1988-89—1992-93
4—Moses Malone, Houston, 1979-80—1981-82; Philadelphia, 1982-83

Most free throw attempts, career

11,862—Wilt Chamberlain, Philadelphia, 1959-60—1961-62; San Francisco, 1962-63—1964-65; Philadelphia, 1964-65—1967-68; Los Angeles, 1968-69—1972-73
11,058—Moses Malone, Buffalo, 1976-77; Houston, 1976-77—1981-82; Philadelphia, 1982-83—1985-86; Washington, 1986-87—1987-88; Atlanta, 1988-89—1990-91; Milwaukee, 1991-92—1992-93; Philadelphia, 1993-94
9,304—Kareem Abdul-Jabbar, Milwaukee, 1969-70—1974-75; L.A. Lakers, 1975-76—1988-89

Most free throw attempts, season

1,363—Wilt Chamberlain, Philadelphia, 1961-62
1,113—Wilt Chamberlain, San Francisco, 1962-63
1,054—Wilt Chamberlain, Philadelphia, 1960-61

Most free throw attempts, game

34—Wilt Chamberlain, Philadelphia vs. St. Louis, February 22, 1962
32—Wilt Chamberlain, Philadelphia vs. New York, at Hershey, Pa., March 2, 1962
31—Adrian Dantley, Utah vs. Denver, November 25, 1983

Most free throw attempts, one half

23—Michael Jordan, Chicago at Miami, December 30, 1992
22—Oscar Robertson, Cincinnati at Baltimore, December 27, 1964
   Tony Campbell, Minnesota vs. L.A. Clippers, March 8, 1990
21—Adrian Dantley, Utah vs. New Jersey, February 25, 1981

Most free throw attempts, one quarter

16—Oscar Robertson, Cincinnati at Baltimore, December 27, 1964
   Stan McKenzie, Phoenix at Philadelphia, February 15, 1970
   Pete Maravich, Atlanta at Chicago, January 2, 1973 (2nd Qtr.)
   Michael Jordan, Chicago at Miami, December 30, 1992
15—George Yardley, Detroit vs. Minneapolis, December 25, 1957 (3rd Qtr.)
   Wilt Chamberlain, Philadelphia vs. Syracuse, November 9, 1961
   Wilt Chamberlain, Philadelphia at Cincinnati, February 13, 1962
   Rick Barry, San Francisco at New York, December 6, 1966 (3rd Qtr.)

Wilt Chamberlain, Philadelphia vs. Seattle, at New York, December 12, 1967
John Drew, Atlanta vs. New Orleans, January 20, 1979 (3rd Qtr.)
Adrian Dantley, Detroit vs. Sacramento, December 10, 1986 (4th Qtr.)
Shawn Kemp, Seattle at Phoenix, April 14, 1992 (4th Qtr.)

REBOUNDS

Rebounds have been compiled since 1950-51

Most seasons leading league

11—Wilt Chamberlain, Philadelphia, 1959-60—1961-62; San Francisco, 1962-63; Philadelphia, 1965-66—1967-68; Los Angeles, 1968-69, 1970-71—1972-73
6—Moses Malone, Houston, 1978-79, 1980-81—1981-82; Philadelphia, 1982-83—1984-85
4—Bill Russell, Boston, 1957-58—1958-59, 1963-64—1964-65

Most consecutive seasons leading league

5—Moses Malone, Houston, 1980-81—1981-82; Philadelphia, 1982-83—1984-85
4—Wilt Chamberlain, Philadelphia, 1959-60—1961-62; San Francisco, 1962-63
   Wilt Chamberlain, Philadelphia, 1965-66—1967-68; Los Angeles, 1968-69

Most rebounds, career

23,924—Wilt Chamberlain, Philadelphia, 1959-60—1961-62; San Francisco, 1962-63—1964-65; Philadelphia, 1964-65—1967-68; Los Angeles, 1968-69—1972-73
21,620—Bill Russell, Boston 1956-57—1968-69
17,440—Kareem Abdul-Jabbar, Milwaukee, 1969-70—1974-75; L.A. Lakers, 1975-76—1988-89
16,279—Elvin Hayes, San Diego, 1968-69—1970-71; Houston, 1971-72; Baltimore, 1972-73; Capital, 1973-74; Washington, 1974-75—1980-81; Houston, 1981-82—1983-84
16,166—Moses Malone, Buffalo, 1976-77; Houston, 1976-77—1981-82; Philadelphia, 1982-83—1985-86; Washington, 1986-87—1987-88; Atlanta, 1988-89—1990-91; Milwaukee, 1991-92—1992-93; Philadelphia, 1993-94

Highest average, rebounds per game, career (minimum: 400 games)

22.9—Wilt Chamberlain, Philadelphia, 1959-60—1961-62; San Francisco, 1962-63—1964-65; Philadelphia, 1964-65—1967-68; Los Angeles, 1968-69—1972-73 (23,924/1,045)
22.5—Bill Russell, Boston 1956-57—1968-69 (21,620/963)
16.2—Bob Pettit, Milwaukee, 1954-55; St. Louis, 1955-56—1964-65 (12,849/792)
15.6—Jerry Lucas, Cincinnati, 1963-64—1969-70; San Francisco, 1969-70—1970-71; New York, 1971- 72—1973-74 (12,942/829)
15.0—Nate Thurmond, San Francisco, 1963-64—1970-71; Golden State, 1971-72—1973-74; Chicago, 1974- 75—1975-76; Cleveland, 1975-76—1976-77 (14,464/964)

Most rebounds, season

2,149—Wilt Chamberlain, Philadelphia, 1960-61
2,052—Wilt Chamberlain, Philadelphia, 1961-62
1,957—Wilt Chamberlain, Philadelphia, 1966-67
1,952—Wilt Chamberlain, Philadelphia, 1967-68
1,946—Wilt Chamberlain, San Francisco, 1962-63
1,943—Wilt Chamberlain, Philadelphia, 1965-66
1,941—Wilt Chamberlain, Philadelphia, 1959-60
1,930—Bill Russell, Boston, 1963-64

Most rebounds, rookie, season

1,941—Wilt Chamberlain, Philadelphia, 1959-60
1,500—Walt Bellamy, Chicago, 1961-62
1,491—Wes Unseld, Baltimore, 1968-69

Most seasons, 1,000-or-more rebounds

13—Wilt Chamberlain, Philadelphia, 1959-60—1961-62; San Francisco, 1962-63—1963-64; San Francisco, Philadelphia, 1964-65; Philadelphia 1965-66—1967-68; Los Angeles, 1968-69, 1970-71—1972-73
12—Bill Russell, Boston, 1957-58—1968-69
9—Bob Pettit, St. Louis, 1955-56—1963-64
   Walt Bellamy, Chicago, 1961-62—1962-63; Baltimore, 1963-64—1964-65; Baltimore, New York, 1965-66; New York, 1966-67; New York, Detroit, 1968-69; Atlanta, 1970-71—1971-72
   Elvin Hayes, San Diego, 1968-69—1970-71; Houston, 1971-72; Baltimore, 1972-73; Capital, 1973-74; Washington, 1974-75, 1976-77—1977-78

Most consecutive seasons, 1,000-or-more rebounds

12—Bill Russell, Boston, 1957-58—1968-69
10—Wilt Chamberlain, Philadelphia, 1959-60—1961-62; San Francisco, 1962-63—
   1963-64; San Francisco, Philadelphia, 1964-65; Philadelphia 1965-66—1967-68;
   Los Angeles, 1968-69
9—Bob Pettit, St. Louis, 1955-56—1963-64

Highest average, rebounds per game, season

27.2—Wilt Chamberlain, Philadelphia, 1960-61 (2,149/79)
27.0—Wilt Chamberlain, Philadelphia, 1959-60 (1,941/72)
25.7—Wilt Chamberlain, Philadelphia, 1961-62 (2,052/80)
24.7—Bill Russell, Boston, 1963-64 (1,930/78)
24.6—Wilt Chamberlain, Philadelphia, 1965-66 (1,943/79)

Most rebounds, game

55—Wilt Chamberlain, Philadelphia vs. Boston, November 24, 1960
51—Bill Russell, Boston vs. Syracuse, February 5, 1960
49—Bill Russell, Boston vs. Philadelphia, November 16, 1957
   Bill Russell, Boston vs. Detroit, at Providence, March 11, 1965
45—Wilt Chamberlain, Philadelphia vs. Syracuse, February 6, 1960
   Wilt Chamberlain, Philadelphia vs. Los Angeles, January 21, 1961

Most rebounds, rookie, game

45—Wilt Chamberlain, Philadelphia vs. Syracuse, February 6, 1960
43—Wilt Chamberlain, Philadelphia vs. New York, November 10, 1959
42—Wilt Chamberlain, Philadelphia vs. Boston, January 15, 1960
   Wilt Chamberlain, Philadelphia vs. Detroit, at Bethlehem, Pa., January 25, 1960

Most rebounds, one half

32—Bill Russell, Boston vs. Philadelphia, November 16, 1957
31—Wilt Chamberlain, Philadelphia vs. Boston, November 24, 1960
28—Wilt Chamberlain, Philadelphia vs. Syracuse, February 6, 1960

Most rebounds, one quarter

18—Nate Thurmond, San Francisco at Baltimore, February 28, 1965
17—Bill Russell, Boston vs. Philadelphia, November 16, 1957
   Bill Russell, Boston vs. Cincinnati, December 12, 1958
   Bill Russell, Boston vs. Syracuse, February 5, 1960
   Wilt Chamberlain, Philadelphia vs. Syracuse, February 6, 1960

OFFENSIVE REBOUNDS

Offensive Rebounds have been compiled since 1973-74

Most seasons leading league

8—Moses Malone, Buffalo, Houston, 1976-77; Houston, 1977-78—1981-82; Philadelphia, 1982-83; Atlanta 1989-90
4—Dennis Rodman, Detroit, 1990-91—1992-93; San Antonio, 1993-94
3—Charles Barkley, Philadelphia, 1986-87—1988-89

Most consecutive seasons leading league

7—Moses Malone, Buffalo, Houston, 1976-77; Houston, 1977-78—1981-82; Philadelphia, 1982-83
4—Dennis Rodman, Detroit, 1990-91—1992-93; San Antonio, 1993-94
3—Charles Barkley, Philadelphia, 1986-87—1988-89

Most offensive rebounds, career

6,711—Moses Malone, Buffalo, 1976-77; Houston, 1976-77—1981-82; Philadelphia,
   1982-83—1985-86; Washington, 1986-87—1987-88; Atlanta, 1988-89—
   1990-91; Milwaukee, 1991-92—1992-93; Philadelphia, 1993-94
4,374—Robert Parish, Golden State, 1976-77—1979-80; Boston, 1980-81—1993-94
3,872—Buck Williams, New Jersey, 1981-82—1988-89; Portland, 1989-90—1993-94

Highest average, offensive rebounds per game, career (minimum: 400 games)

5.1—Moses Malone, Buffalo, 1976-77; Houston, 1976-77—1981-82; Philadelphia,
   1982-83—1985-86; Washington, 1986-87—1987-88; Atlanta, 1988-89—
   1990-91; Milwaukee, 1991-92—1992-93; Philadelphia, 1993-94 (6,711/1,312)
4.5—Dennis Rodman, Detroit, 1986-87—1992-93; San Antonio, 1993-94 (2,848/628)
4.2—Charles Barkley, Philadelphia, 1984-85—1991-92; Phoenix, 1992-93—1993-94
   (3,123/751)

Most offensive rebounds, season

587—Moses Malone, Houston, 1978-79
573—Moses Malone, Houston, 1979-80
558—Moses Malone, Houston, 1981-82

Most offensive rebounds, game

21—Moses Malone, Houston vs. Seattle, February 11, 1982
19—Moses Malone, Houston at New Orleans, February 9, 1979
18—Charles Oakley, Chicago vs. Milwaukee, March 15, 1986 (ot)
   Dennis Rodman, Detroit vs. Indiana, March 4, 1992 (ot)

Most offensive rebounds, one half

13—Charles Barkley, Philadelphia vs. New York, March 4, 1987
12—Moses Malone, Houston vs. San Antonio, February 10, 1978
   Larry Smith, Golden State vs. Denver, March 23, 1986
   Larry Smith, Houston vs. Phoenix, February 16, 1991

Most offensive rebounds, one quarter

11—Charles Barkley, Philadelphia vs. New York, March 4, 1987
   Larry Smith, Golden State vs. Denver, March 23, 1986
10—Moses Malone, Milwaukee vs. Sacramento, January 11, 1992

DEFENSIVE REBOUNDS

Defensive Rebounds have been compiled since 1973-74

Most seasons leading league

2—Kareem Abdul-Jabbar, Los Angeles, 1975-76—1976-77
   Swen Nater, San Diego, 1979-80—1980-81
   Moses Malone, Houston, 1978-79; Philadelphia, 1982-83
   Jack Sikma, Seattle, 1981-82, 1983-84
   Charles Oakley, Chicago, 1986-87—1987-88
   Hakeem Olajuwon, Houston, 1988-89—1989-90
   Dennis Rodman, Detroit, 1991-92; San Antonio, 1993-94

Most consecutive seasons leading league

2—Kareem Abdul-Jabbar, Los Angeles, 1975-76—1976-77
   Swen Nater, San Diego, 1979-80—1980-81
   Charles Oakley, Chicago, 1986-87—1987-88
   Hakeem Olajuwon, Houston, 1988-89—1989-90

Most defensive rebounds, career

9,599—Robert Parish, Golden State, 1976-77—1979-80; Boston, 1980-81—1993-94
9,455—Moses Malone, Buffalo, 1976-77; Houston, 1976-77—1981-82; Philadelphia,
   1982-83—1985-86; Washington, 1986-87—1987-88; Atlanta, 1988-89—
   1990-91; Milwaukee, 1991-92—1992-93; Philadelphia, 1993-94
9,394—Kareem Abdul-Jabbar, Milwaukee, 1973-74—1974-75; L.A. Lakers, 1975-76—
   1988-89

Highest average, defensive rebounds per game, career (minimum: 400 games)

9.8—Dave Cowens, Boston, 1973-74—1979-80; Milwaukee, 1982-83 (5,122/524)
8.5—Hakeem Olajuwon, Houston, 1984-85—1993-94 (6,460/756)
8.4—Wes Unseld, Capital, 1973-74; Washington, 1974-75—1980-81 (4,974/591)

Most defensive rebounds, season

1,111—Kareem Abdul-Jabbar, Los Angeles, 1975-76
1,109—Elvin Hayes, Capital, 1973-74
1,007—Dennis Rodman, Detroit, 1991-92

Most defensive rebounds, game

29—Kareem Abdul-Jabbar, Los Angeles vs. Detroit, December 14, 1975
28—Elvin Hayes, Capital at Atlanta, November 17, 1973
26—Rony Seikaly, Miami vs. Washington, March 3, 1993

Most defensive rebounds, one half

18—Swen Nater, San Diego vs. Denver, December 14, 1979
17—Marvin Webster, Seattle at Atlanta, November 1, 1977

Most defensive rebounds, one quarter

13—Happy Hairston, Los Angeles vs. Philadelphia, November 15, 1974
12—John Lambert, Cleveland vs. New Jersey, February 6, 1979
   Kevin Willis, Atlanta vs. Seattle, February 3, 1992

ASSISTS

Most seasons leading league

8—Bob Cousy, Boston, 1952-53—1959-60
7—John Stockton, Utah, 1987-88—1993-94
6—Oscar Robertson, Cincinnati, 1960-61—1961-62, 1963-64—1965-66, 1968-69

Most consecutive seasons leading league

8—Bob Cousy, Boston, 1952-53—1959-60
7—John Stockton, Utah, 1987-88—1993-94
3—Oscar Robertson, Cincinnati, 1963-64—1965-66

Most assists, career

9,921—Magic Johnson, L.A. Lakers, 1979-80—1990-91
9,887—Oscar Robertson, Cincinnati, 1960-61—1969-70; Milwaukee, 1970-71—1973-74
9,383—John Stockton, Utah, 1984-85—1993-94
9,061—Isiah Thomas, Detroit, 1981-82—1993-94
7,392—Maurice Cheeks, Philadelphia, 1978-79—1988-89; San Antonio, 1989-90; New York, 1989-90—1990-91; Atlanta, 1991-92; New Jersey, 1992-93

Highest average, assists per game, career (minimum: 400 games)

11.5—John Stockton, Utah, 1984-85—1993-94 (9,383/816)
11.4—Magic Johnson, L.A. Lakers, 1979-80—1990-91 (9,921/874)
9.7—Kevin Johnson, Cleveland, 1987-88; Phoenix, 1987-88—1993-94 (4,912/506)
9.5—Oscar Robertson, Cincinnati, 1960-61—1969-70; Milwaukee, 1970-71—1973-74 (9,887/1,040)
9.3—Isiah Thomas, Detroit, 1981-82—1993-94 (9,061/979)

Most assists, season

1,164—John Stockton, Utah, 1990-91
1,134—John Stockton, Utah, 1989-90
1,128—John Stockton, Utah, 1987-88

Most assists, rookie, season

868—Mark Jackson, New York, 1987-88
690—Oscar Robertson, Cincinnati, 1960-61
689—Tim Hardaway, Golden State, 1989-90

Highest average, assists per game, season (minimum: 70 games)

14.5—John Stockton, Utah, 1989-90 (1,134/78)
14.2—John Stockton, Utah, 1990-91 (1,164/82)
13.9—Isiah Thomas, Detroit, 1984-85 (1,123/81)
13.8—John Stockton, Utah, 1987-88 (1,128/82)

Most assists, game

30—Scott Skiles, Orlando vs. Denver, December 30, 1990
29—Kevin Porter, New Jersey vs. Houston, February 24, 1978
28—Bob Cousy, Boston vs. Minneapolis, February 27, 1959
    Guy Rodgers, San Francisco vs. St. Louis, March 14, 1963
    John Stockton, Utah vs. San Antonio, January 15, 1991

Most assists, rookie, game

25—Ernie DiGregorio, Buffalo at Portland, January 1, 1974
    Nate McMillan, Seattle vs. L.A. Clippers, February 23, 1987
22—Phil Ford, Kansas City vs. Milwaukee, February 21, 1979
    Ennis Whatley, Chicago vs. New York, January 14, 1984
    Ennis Whatley, Chicago vs. Atlanta, March 3, 1984
21—Phil Ford, Kansas City vs. Phoenix, February 23, 1979
    Nate McMillan, Seattle vs. Sacramento, March 31, 1987

Most assists, one half

19—Bob Cousy, Boston vs. Minneapolis, February 27, 1959
18—Magic Johnson, Los Angeles vs. Seattle, February 21, 1984 (1st Half)
17—Nate McMillan, Seattle vs. L.A. Clippers, February 23, 1987 (2nd Half)

Most assists, one quarter

14—John Lucas, San Antonio vs. Denver, April 15, 1984 (2nd Qtr.)
12—Bob Cousy, Boston vs. Minneapolis, February 27, 1959
    John Lucas, Houston vs. Milwaukee, October 27, 1977 (3rd Qtr.)
    John Lucas, Golden State vs. Chicago, November 17, 1978 (1st Qtr.)
    Magic Johnson, Los Angeles vs. Seattle, February 21, 1984 (1st Qtr.)
11—John McCarthy, St. Louis vs. Detroit, March 8, 1960 (1st Qtr.)
    Isiah Thomas, Detroit vs. Golden State, January 24, 1985 (1st Qtr.)
    Nate McMillan, Seattle vs. L.A. Clippers, February 23, 1987 (3rd Qtr.)
    John Stockton, Utah vs. Chicago, November 30, 1988 (2nd Qtr.)
    Michael Holton, Charlotte vs. Philadelphia, December 1, 1988 (1st Qtr.)
    Isiah Thomas, Detroit vs. Cleveland, November 24, 1989 (1st Qtr.)
    Avery Johnson, Seattle vs. Miami, January 5, 1990 (3rd Qtr.)
    John Stockton, Utah vs. Portland, March 1, 1990 (3rd Qtr.)
    Magic Johnson, L.A. Lakers at Charlotte, January 24, 1991 (1st Qtr.)

PERSONAL FOULS

Most seasons leading league

3—George Mikan, Minneapolis, 1949-50—1951-52
    Vern Mikkelsen, Minneapolis, 1954-55—1956-57
    Darryl Dawkins, Philadelphia, 1979-80; New Jersey, 1982-83—1983-84
2—Walter Dukes, Detroit, 1957-58—1958-59
    Zelmo Beaty, St. Louis, 1962-63—1965-66
    Dave Cowens, Boston, 1970-71—1971-72
    Lonnie Shelton, N.Y. Knicks, 1976-77—1977-78
    Steve Johnson, Kansas City, 1981-82; Portland, 1986-87

Most consecutive seasons leading league

3—George Mikan, Minneapolis, 1949-50—1951-52
    Vern Mikkelsen, Minneapolis, 1954-55—1956-57
2—Walter Dukes, Detroit, 1957-58—1958-59
    Dave Cowens, Boston, 1970-71—1971-72
    Lonnie Shelton, N.Y. Knicks, 1976-77—1977-78
    Darryl Dawkins, New Jersey, 1982-83—1983-84

Most personal fouls, career

4,657—Kareem Abdul-Jabbar, Milwaukee, 1969-70—1974-75; L.A. Lakers, 1975-76—1988-89
4,193—Elvin Hayes, San Diego, 1968-69—1970-71; Houston, 1971-72; Baltimore, 1972-73; Capital, 1973-74; Washington, 1974-75—1980-81; Houston, 1981-82—1983-84
4,191—Robert Parish, Golden State, 1976-77—1979-80; Boston, 1980-81—1993-94

Most personal fouls, season

386—Darryl Dawkins, New Jersey, 1983-84
379—Darryl Dawkins, New Jersey, 1982-83
372—Steve Johnson, Kansas City, 1981-82

Most personal fouls, game

8—Don Otten, Tri-Cities at Sheboygan, November 24, 1949
7—Alex Hannum, Syracuse at Boston, December 26, 1950
6—by many

Most personal fouls, one half

6—by many

Most personal fouls, one quarter

6—by many

DISQUALIFICATIONS

Disqualifications have been compiled since 1950–51

Most seasons leading league

4—Walter Dukes, Detroit, 1958-59—1961-62
3—Vern Mikkelsen, Minneapolis, 1955-56—1957-58
    Steve Johnson, Kansas City, 1981-82; San Antonio, 1985-86; Portland, 1986-87
    Rik Smits, Indiana, 1988-89—1989-90, 1993-94

Most consecutive seasons leading league

4—Walter Dukes, Detroit, 1958-59—1961-62
3—Vern Mikkelsen, Minneapolis, 1955-56—1957-58

Most disqualifications, career

127—Vern Mikkelsen, Minneapolis, 1950-51—1958-59
121—Walter Dukes, New York, 1955-56; Minneapolis, 1956-57; Detroit, 1957-58—1962-63
105—Charlie Share, Ft. Wayne, 1951-52—1953-54; Milwaukee, 1953-54—1954-55; St. Louis, 1955-56—1958-59; St. Louis, Minneapolis, 1959-60

Highest percentage, games disqualified, career (minimum: 400 games)

21.88—Walter Dukes, New York, 1955-56; Minneapolis, 1956-57; Detroit, 1957-58—1962-63 (121/553)
20.13—Vern Mikkelsen, Minneapolis, 1950-51—1958-59 (127/631)
18.14—Alex Hannum, Syracuse, 1950-51—Baltimore, 1951-52; Rochester, 1951-52—1953-54; Milwaukee, 1954-55; St. Louis, 1955-56; Ft. Wayne, 1956-57; St. Louis, 1956-57 (82/452)

Lowest percentage, games disqualified, career (minimum: 400 games)

0.00—Wilt Chamberlain, Philadelphia, 1959-60—1961-62; San Francisco, 1962-63—1964-65; Philadelphia, 1964-65—1967-68; Los Angeles, 1968-69—1972-73 (0/1,045)

Don Buse, Indiana, 1976-77; Phoenix, 1977-78—1979-80; Indiana, 1980-81—1981-82; Portland, 1982-83; Kansas City, 1983-84—1984-85 (0/648)

Jerry Sichting, Indiana, 1980-81—1984-85; Boston 1985-86—1987-88; Portland, 1987-88—1988-89; Charlotte, 1989-90; Milwaukee, 1989-90 (0/598)

John Battle, Atlanta, 1985-86—1990-91; Cleveland 1991-92—1993-94 (0/584)

Danny Young, Seattle, 1984-85—1987-88; Portland, 1988-89—1991-92; L.A. Clippers, 1991-92; Detroit, 1992-93 (0/567)

Randy Wittman, Atlanta, 1983-84—1987-88; Sacramento, 1988-89; Indiana, 1988-89—1991-92 (0/543)

Steve Colter, Portland, 1984-85—1985-86; Chicago, 1986-87; Philadelphia, 1986-87—1987-88; Washington, 1987-88—1989-90; Sacramento, 1990-91 (0/469)

Charlie Criss, Atlanta 1977-78—1981-82; San Diego, 1981-82; Milwaukee, 1982-83—1983-84; Atlanta, 1983-84—1984-85 (0/418)

0.102—Rolando Blackman, Dallas, 1981-82—1991-92; New York, 1992-93—1993-94 (1/980)

0.107—Mike Gminski, New Jersey, 1980-81—1987-88; Philadelphia, 1987-88—1990-91; Charlotte, 1990-91—1993-94; Milwaukee, 1993-94 (1/938)

Most consecutive games without disqualification, career

1,195—Moses Malone, Houston, Philadelphia, Washington, Atlanta, Milwaukee, Philadelphia, January 7, 1978—April 22, 1994 (current)

1,045—Wilt Chamberlain, Philadelphia, San Francisco, Philadelphia, Los Angeles, October 24, 1959—March 28, 1973

924—Mike Gminski, New Jersey, Philadelphia, Charlotte, Milwaukee, November 8, 1980—April 23, 1994 (current)

Most disqualifications, season

26—Don Meineke, Ft. Wayne, 1952-53
25—Steve Johnson, Kansas City, 1981-82
23—Darryl Dawkins, New Jersey, 1982-83

Fewest minutes, disqualified, game

5—Dick Farley, Syracuse at St. Louis, March 12, 1956
6—Bill Bridges, St. Louis at New York, October 29, 1963
Johnny Green, Baltimore vs. San Francisco, October 28, 1966
Jim Barnes, Los Angeles at Philadelphia, December 2, 1966
Leonard Gray, Washington at Philadelphia, April 9, 1977
Chris Engler, Golden State vs. Utah, March 5, 1983
Sam Mitchell, Minnesota vs. L.A. Lakers, March 17, 1990
Rik Smits, Indiana vs. Detroit, November 6, 1993

STEALS

Steals have been compiled since 1973-74

Most seasons leading league

3—Micheal Ray Richardson, New York, 1979-80; Golden State, New Jersey, 1982-83; New Jersey, 1984-85
Alvin Robertson, San Antonio, 1985-86—1986-87; Milwaukee, 1990-91
Michael Jordan, Chicago, 1987-88, 1989-90, 1992-93
2—Magic Johnson, Los Angeles, 1980-81—1981-82
John Stockton, Utah, 1988-89, 1991-92

Most consecutive seasons leading league

2—Magic Johnson, Los Angeles, 1980-81—1981-82
Alvin Robertson, San Antonio, 1985-86—1986-87

Most steals, career

2,310—Maurice Cheeks, Philadelphia, 1978-79—1988-89; San Antonio, 1989-90; New York, 1989-90—1990-91; Atlanta, 1991-92; New Jersey, 1992-93
2,031—John Stockton, Utah, 1984-85—1993-94
1,946—Alvin Robertson, San Antonio, 1984-85—1988-89; Milwaukee, 1989-90—1992-93; Detroit, 1992-93

Highest average, steals per game, career (minimum: 400 games)

2.77—Alvin Robertson, San Antonio, 1984-85—1988-89; Milwaukee, 1989-90—1992-93; Detroit, 1992-93 (1,946/702)
2.72—Michael Jordan, Chicago, 1984-85—1992-93 (1,815/667)

2.63—Micheal Ray Richardson, New York, 1978-79—1981-82; Golden State, New Jersey, 1982-83; New Jersey, 1983-84—1985-86 (1,463/556)

Most steals, season

301—Alvin Robertson, San Antonio, 1985-86
281—Don Buse, Indiana, 1976-77
265—Micheal Ray Richardson, New York, 1979-80

Highest average, steals per game, season (qualifiers)

3.67—Alvin Robertson, San Antonio, 1985-86 (301/82)
3.47—Don Buse, Indiana, 1976-77 (281/81)
3.43—Magic Johnson, Los Angeles, 1980-81 (127/37)

Most steals, rookie, season

211—Dudley Bradley, Indiana, 1979-80
209—Ron Harper, Cleveland, 1986-87
205—Mark Jackson, New York, 1987-88

Highest average, steals per game, rookie, season (qualifiers)

2.57—Dudley Bradley, Indiana, 1979-80 (211/82)
2.55—Ron Harper, Cleveland, 1986-87 (209/82)
2.50—Mark Jackson, New York, 1987-88 (205/82)

Most steals, game

11—Larry Kenon, San Antonio at Kansas City, December 26, 1976
10—Jerry West, Los Angeles vs. Seattle, December 7, 1973
Larry Steele, Portland vs. Los Angeles, November 16, 1974
Fred Brown, Seattle at Philadelphia, December 3, 1976
Gus Williams, Seattle at New Jersey, February 22, 1978
Eddie Jordan, New Jersey at Philadelphia, March 23, 1979
Johnny Moore, San Antonio vs. Indiana, March 6, 1985
Lafayette Lever, Denver vs. Indiana, March 9, 1985
Clyde Drexler, Portland at Milwaukee, January 10, 1986
Alvin Robertson, San Antonio vs. Phoenix, February 18, 1986
Alvin Robertson, San Antonio at L.A. Clippers, November 22, 1986
Ron Harper, Cleveland vs. Philadelphia, March 10, 1987
Michael Jordan, Chicago vs. New Jersey, January 29, 1988
Alvin Robertson, San Antonio vs. Houston, January 11, 1989 (ot)
Alvin Robertson, Milwaukee vs. Utah, November 19, 1990
Kevin Johnson, Phoenix vs. Washington, December 9, 1993

Most steals, one half

8—Quinn Buckner, Milwaukee vs. N.Y. Nets, November 27, 1976
Fred Brown, Seattle at Philadelphia, December 3, 1976
Gus Williams, Seattle at Washington, January 23, 1979
Eddie Jordan, New Jersey at Chicago, October 23, 1979
Dudley Bradley, Indiana at Utah, November 10, 1980
Rob Williams, Denver at New Jersey, February 17, 1983
Lafayette Lever, Denver vs. Indiana, March 9, 1985
Michael Jordan, Chicago at Boston, November 9, 1988

Most steals, one quarter

8—Lafayette Lever, Denver vs. Indiana, March 9, 1985
7—Quinn Buckner, Milwaukee vs. N.Y. Nets, November 27, 1976
Michael Adams, Washington at Atlanta, November 26, 1993

BLOCKED SHOTS

Blocked Shots have been compiled since 1973-74

Most seasons leading league

4—Kareem Abdul-Jabbar, Milwaukee, 1974-75; Los Angeles, 1975-76, 1978-79—1979-80
Mark Eaton, Utah, 1983-84—1984-85; 1986-87—1987-88
3—George T. Johnson, New Jersey, 1977-78; San Antonio, 1980-81—1981-82
Hakeem Olajuwon, Houston, 1989-90—1990-91, 1992-93

Most consecutive seasons leading league

2—Kareem Abdul-Jabbar, Milwaukee, 1974-75; Los Angeles, 1975-76
Kareem Abdul-Jabbar, Los Angeles, 1978-79—1979-80
George T. Johnson, San Antonio, 1980-81—1981-82
Mark Eaton, Utah, 1983-84—1984-85;
Mark Eaton, Utah, 1986-87—1987-88
Hakeem Olajuwon, Houston, 1989-90—1990-91

Most blocked shots, career

3,189—Kareem Abdul-Jabbar, Milwaukee, 1973-74—1974-75; L.A. Lakers, 1975-76—1988-89
3,064—Mark Eaton, Utah, 1982-83—1992-93
2,741—Hakeem Olajuwon, Houston, 1984-85—1993-94

Highest average, blocked shots per game, career (minimum: 400 games)

3.63—Hakeem Olajuwon, Houston, 1984-85—1993-94 (2,741/756)
3.50—Mark Eaton, Utah, 1982-83—1992-93 (3,064/875)
3.36—Manute Bol, Washington, 1985-86—1987-88; Golden State, 1988-89—1989-90; Philadelphia, 1990-91—1992-93; Miami, 1993-94; Washington, 1993-94; Philadelphia, 1993-94 (2,077/619)

Most blocked shots, season

456—Mark Eaton, Utah, 1984-85
397—Manute Bol, Washington, 1985-86
393—Elmore Smith, Los Angeles, 1973-74

Highest average, blocked shots per game, season (qualifiers)

5.56—Mark Eaton, Utah, 1984-85 (456/82)
4.97—Manute Bol, Washington, 1985-86 (397/80)
4.85—Elmore Smith, Los Angeles, 1973-74 (393/81)

Most blocked shots, rookie, season

397—Manute Bol, Washington, 1985-86
319—David Robinson, San Antonio, 1989-90
286—Shaquille O'Neal, Orlando, 1992-93

Highest average, blocked shots per game, rookie, season (qualifiers)

4.97—Manute Bol, Washington, 1985-86 (397/80)
3.89—David Robinson, San Antonio, 1989-90 (319/82)
3.53—Shaquille O'Neal, Orlando, 1992-93 (286/81)

Most blocked shots, game

17—Elmore Smith, Los Angeles vs. Portland, October 28, 1973
15—Manute Bol, Washington vs. Atlanta, January 25, 1986
    Manute Bol, Washington vs. Indiana, February 26, 1987
    Shaquille O'Neal, Orlando at New Jersey, November 20, 1993
14—Elmore Smith, Los Angeles vs. Detroit, October 26, 1973
    Elmore Smith, Los Angeles vs. Houston, November 4, 1973
    Mark Eaton, Utah vs. Portland, January 18, 1985
    Mark Eaton, Utah vs. San Antonio, February 18, 1989

Most blocked shots, one half

11—Elmore Smith, Los Angeles vs. Portland, October 28, 1973
    George Johnson, San Antonio vs. Golden State, February 24, 1981
    Manute Bol, Washington vs. Milwaukee, December 12, 1985
10—Harvey Catchings, Philadelphia vs. Atlanta, March 21, 1975
    Manute Bol, Washington vs. Indiana, February 26, 1987

Most blocked shots, one quarter

8—Manute Bol, Washington vs. Milwaukee, December 12, 1985
    Manute Bol, Washington vs. Indiana, February 26, 1987

TURNOVERS

Turnovers have been compiled since 1977-78

Most turnovers, career

3,793—Moses Malone, Houston, 1977-78—1981-82; Philadelphia, 1982-83—1985-86; Washington, 1986-87—1987-88; Atlanta, 1988-89—1990-91; Milwaukee, 1991-92—1992-93; Philadelphia, 1993-94
3,682—Isiah Thomas, Detroit, 1981-82—1993-94
3,493—Reggie Theus, Chicago, 1978-79—1983-84; Kansas City, 1983-84—1984-85; Sacramento, 1985-86—1987-88; Atlanta, 1988-89; Orlando, 1989-90; New Jersey, 1990-91

Most turnovers, season

366—Artis Gilmore, Chicago, 1977-78
360—Kevin Porter, Detroit, New Jersey, 1977-78
359—Micheal Ray Richardson, New York, 1979-80

Most turnovers, game

14—John Drew, Atlanta at New Jersey, March 1, 1978
13—Chris Mullin, Golden State at Utah, March 31, 1988
12—Kevin Porter, New Jersey at Philadelphia, November 9, 1977
    Artis Gilmore, Chicago vs. Atlanta, January 31, 1978 (ot)
    Kevin Porter, Detroit at Philadelphia, February 7, 1979
    Maurice Lucas, Portland vs. Phoenix, November 25, 1979
    Moses Malone, Houston at Phoenix, February 6, 1981
    Eric Floyd, Golden State vs. Denver, October 25, 1985
    Scottie Pippen, Chicago at New Jersey, February 25, 1990 (ot)

TEAM

GAMES WON & LOST

Highest winning percentage, season

.841—Los Angeles, 1971-72 (69-13)
.840—Philadelphia, 1966-67 (68-13)
.829—Boston, 1972-73 (68-14)
.8170—Boston, 1985-86 (67-15)
.8170—Chicago, 1991-92 (67-15)
.8167—Washington, 1946-47 (49-11)

Lowest winning percentage, season

.110—Philadelphia, 1972-73 (9-73)
.125—Providence, 1947-48 (6-42)
.134—Dallas, 1992-93 (11-71)

Most consecutive games won

33—Los Angeles, November 5, 1971—January 7, 1972
20—Washington, March 13—December 4, 1948 (5 games in 1947-48; 15 games in 1948-49)
    Milwaukee, February 6—March 8, 1971
18—Rochester, February 17—November 11, 1950 (15 games in 1949-50; 3 games in 1950-51)
    Philadelphia, March 3—November 4, 1966 (11 games in 1965-66; 7 games in 1966-67)
    New York, October 24—November 28, 1969
    Boston, February 24—March 26, 1982

Most consecutive games won, one season

33—Los Angeles, November 5, 1971—January 7, 1972

20—Milwaukee, February 6—March 8, 1971
18—New York, October 24—November 28, 1969
    Boston, February 24—March 26, 1982

Most consecutive games won, start of season

15—Washington, November 3—December 4, 1948
    Houston, November 5—December 2, 1993
14—Boston, October 22—November 27, 1957
12—Seattle, October 29—November 19, 1982

Most consecutive games won, end of season

15—Rochester, February 17—March 19, 1950
14—Milwaukee, February 28—March 27, 1973
11—Philadelphia, March 3—March 20, 1966

Most consecutive games lost

24—Cleveland, March 19—November 5, 1982 (19 games in 1981-82; 5 games in 1982-83)
21—Detroit, March 7—October 22, 1980 (14 games in 1979-80; 7 games in 1980-81)
20—Philadelphia, January 9—February 11, 1973
    Dallas, November 13—December 22, 1993
19—Philadelphia, March 21—November 10, 1972 (4 games in 1971-72; 15 games in 1972-73)
    San Diego, March 11—April 13, 1982
    L.A. Clippers, December 30, 1988—February 6, 1989
    Dallas, February 6—March 15, 1993

Most consecutive games lost, one season

20—Philadelphia, January 9—February 11, 1973
    Dallas, November 13—December 22, 1993
19—Cleveland, March 19—April 18, 1982
    San Diego, March 11—April 13, 1982
    L.A. Clippers, December 30, 1988—February 6, 1989
    Dallas, February 6—March 15, 1993
18—Utah, February 24—March 29, 1982

Most consecutive games lost, start of season

17—Miami, November 5—December 12, 1988
15—Denver, October 29—November 25, 1949
    Cleveland, October 14—November 10, 1970
    Philadelphia, October 10—November 10, 1972

Most consecutive games lost, end of season

19—Cleveland, March 19—April 18, 1982
15—San Diego, February 23—March 20, 1968
14—Detroit, March 7—March 30, 1980
    L.A. Clippers, March 27—April 19, 1987

Highest winning percentage, home games, season

.976—Boston, 1985–86 (40–1)
.971—Rochester, 1949–50 (33–1)
.969—Syracuse, 1949–50 (31–1)
.968—Minneapolis, 1949–50 (30–1)
.967—Washington, 1946–47 (29–1)

Lowest winning percentage, home games, season

.125—Providence, 1947–48 (3–21)
.146—Dallas, 1993–94 (6–35)
.161—Philadelphia, 1972–73 (5–26)

Most consecutive home games won

38—Boston, December 10, 1985—November 28, 1986 (31 games in 1985–86; 7 games in 1986–87)
36—Philadelphia, January 14, 1966—January 20, 1967 (14 games in 1965–66; 22 games in 1966–67)
34—Portland, March 5, 1977—February 3, 1978 (8 games in 1976–77; 26 games in 1977–78)

Most consecutive home games lost

19—Dallas, November 6, 1993—January 21, 1994
16—Orlando, March 1—November 6, 1990 (14 games in 1989–90; 2 games in 1990–91)
15—Cleveland, March 20—November 26, 1982 (9 games in 1981–82; 6 games in 1982–83)

Highest winning percentage, road games, season

.816—Los Angeles, 1971–72 (31–7)
.800—Boston, 1972–73 (32–8)
.780—Boston, 1974–75 (32–9)
.765—Philadelphia, 1966–67 (26–8)
.756—Chicago, 1991–92 (31–10)

Lowest winning percentage, road games, season

.000—Baltimore, 1953–54 (0–20)
.024—Sacramento, 1990–91 (1–40)
.034—Philadelphia, 1952–53 (1–28)

Most consecutive road games won

16—Los Angeles, November 6, 1971—January 7, 1972
13—Boston, December 5, 1964—January 20, 1965
12—New York, October 15—December 10, 1969
    Los Angeles, October 15—December 20, 1972
    Portland, April 10—December 8, 1990 (4 games in 1989–90; 8 games in 1990–91)

Most consecutive road games lost

43—Sacramento, November 21, 1990—November 22, 1991 (37 games in 1990–91; 6 games in 1991–92)
34—New Jersey, December 23, 1989—November 21, 1990 (28 games in 1989–90; 6 games in 1990–91)
32—Baltimore, January 2, 1953—March 14, 1954 (12 games in 1952–53; 20 games in 1953–54)

OVERTIME GAMES

Most overtime games, season

14—Philadelphia, 1990–91
13—New York, 1950–51
12—Baltimore, 1952–53
    Milwaukee, 1952–53
    Rochester, 1952–53

Most consecutive overtime games, season

3—Ft. Wayne, November 14–17–18, 1951
    Rochester, November 18–20–22, 1951
    San Francisco, October 26–27–28, 1962
    Houston, November 17–20–24, 1976
    Milwaukee, February 24–26–28, 1978
    Kansas City, March 2-4-7, 1979
    Phoenix, April 4-6-7, 1987
    L.A. Lakers, November 1–2-5, 1991
    Boston, March 24-27-29, 1994

Most overtime games won, season

8—Milwaukee, 1977–78
    Philadelphia, 1990–91
7—New York, 1949–50
    New York, 1955–56
    Boston, 1958–59
    Los Angeles, 1961–62
    Chicago, 1969–70
    New York, 1990–91

Most overtime games won, no losses, season

7—Los Angeles, 1961–62
5—New York, 1946–47
    Boston, 1966–67
    San Antonio, 1980–81
    Philadelphia, 1982–83
    Portland, 1986–87

Most consecutive overtime games won

11—San Antonio, November 13, 1979—February 8, 1983 (2 games in 1979–80; 5 games in 1980–81;
    1 game in 1981–82; 3 games in 1982–83)
10—Milwaukee, February 26, 1972—November 30, 1974 (3 games in 1971–72; 3 games in 1972–73;
    3 games in 1973–74; 1 game in 1974–75)
9—Boston, December 22, 1965—December 7, 1968 (1 game in 1965–66; 5 games in 1966–67; 1 game in 1967–68; 2 games in 1968–69)
    Boston, March 24, 1974—October 23, 1976 (1 game in 1973–74; 3 games in 1974–75; 3 games in 1975–76; 2 games in 1976–77)
    Houston, November 3, 1976—January 19, 1979 (4 games in 1976–77; 2 games in 1977–78; 3 games in 1978–79)
    New York, November 11, 1988—February 17, 1990 (4 games in 1988–89; 5 games in 1989–90)

Most overtime games lost, season

10—Baltimore, 1952–53
8—Milwaukee, 1952–53
    Golden State, 1979–80

Most overtime games lost, no wins, season

8—Golden State, 1979–80
6—Ft. Wayne, 1951–52
    Seattle, 1990–91
    Minnesota, 1992–93

Most consecutive overtime games lost

10—Golden State, October 13, 1979—March 15, 1981 (8 games in 1979–80; 2 games in 1980–81)
9—Baltimore, January 14, 1953—February 22, 1954 (6 games in 1952–53; 3 games in 1953–54)
    Syracuse, January 13, 1960—January 21, 1962 (2 games in 1959–60; 4 games in 1960–61; 3 games in 1961–62)
    New Jersey, March 18, 1986—April 19, 1988 (1 game in 1985–86; 4 games in 1986–87; 4 games in 1987–88)

Miami, January 2, 1992—February 14, 1993 (3 games in 1991–92; 6 games in 1992–93)

Most overtime periods, game

6—Indianapolis (75) at Rochester (73), January 6, 1951
5—Anderson (123) at Syracuse (125), November 24, 1949
    Seattle (154) at Milwaukee (155), November 9, 1989

4—New York (92) at Rochester (102), January 23, 1951
    Indianapolis (96) at Rochester (99), November 8, 1952
    Cleveland (129) at Portland (131), October 18, 1974
    Los Angeles (153) at Cleveland (154), January 29, 1980
    Atlanta (127) at Seattle (122), February 19, 1982
    Chicago (156) at Portland (155), March 16, 1984
    New Jersey (147) at Golden State (150), February 1, 1987

OFFENSE

SCORING

Highest average, points per game, season

126.5—Denver, 1981–82 (10,371/82)
125.4—Philadelphia, 1961–62 (10,035/80)
125.2—Philadelphia, 1966–67 (10,143/81)

Lowest average, points per game, season

87.4—Milwaukee, 1954–55 (6,291/72)
90.8—Rochester, 1954–55 (6,535/72)
91.1—Syracuse, 1954–55 (6,557/72)

Most consecutive games, 100-or-more points

136—Denver, January 21, 1981—December 8, 1982
129—San Antonio, December 12, 1978—March 14, 1980
81—Cincinnati, December 6, 1961—December 2, 1962

Most consecutive games, 100-or-more points, season

82—Denver, October 30, 1981—April 17, 1982 (entire season)
77—New York, October 23, 1966—March 19, 1967
73—Syracuse, November 4, 1961—March 14, 1962
    Philadelphia, November 8, 1966—March 19, 1967

Most consecutive games, fewer than 100 points, season

25—Milwaukee, December 18, 1954—January 30, 1955
15—Ft. Wayne, January 28—February 20, 1956
14—New York, November 27—December 19, 1954
    Ft. Wayne, December 11, 1955—January 5, 1956

Most points, game

186—Detroit at Denver, December 13, 1983 (3 ot)
184—Denver vs. Detroit, December 13, 1983 (3 ot)
173—Boston vs. Minneapolis, February 27, 1959
    Phoenix vs. Denver, November 10, 1990
171—San Antonio vs. Milwaukee, March 6, 1982 (3 ot)
169—Philadelphia vs. New York, at Hershey, Pa., March 2, 1962

Fewest points, game

57—Milwaukee vs. Boston, at Providence, February 27, 1955
59—Sacramento at Charlotte, January 10, 1991
61—New York at Detroit, April 12, 1992
    Indiana at Cleveland, March 22, 1994
62—Boston vs. Milwaukee, at Providence, February 27, 1955
63—Buffalo vs. Milwaukee, October 21, 1972

Most points, both teams, game

370—Detroit (186) at Denver (184), December 13, 1983 (3 ot)
337—San Antonio (171) vs. Milwaukee (166), March 6, 1982 (3 ot)
320—Golden State (162) at Denver (158), November 2, 1990
318—Denver (163) vs. San Antonio (155), January 11, 1984
316—Philadelphia (169) vs. New York (147), at Hershey, Pa., March 2, 1962
    Cincinnati (165) vs. San Diego (151), March 12, 1970
    Phoenix (173) vs. Denver (143), November 10, 1990

Fewest points, both teams, game

119—Milwaukee (57) vs. Boston (62), at Providence, February 27, 1955
133—New York (61) at Detroit (72), April 12, 1992
135—Syracuse (66) vs. Ft. Wayne (69), at Buffalo, January 25, 1955

Largest margin of victory, game

68—Cleveland vs. Miami, December 17, 1991 (148–80)
63—Los Angeles vs. Golden State, March 19, 1972 (162–99)

59—Golden State vs. Indiana, March 19, 1977 (150–91)
    Milwaukee vs. Detroit, December 26, 1978 (143–84)
58—Milwaukee vs. Sacramento, December 15, 1985 (140–82)
    Sacramento vs. Dallas, December 29, 1992 (139–81)

BY HALF

Most points, first half

107—Phoenix vs. Denver, November 10, 1990
90—Denver at San Antonio, November 7, 1990
89—Cincinnati vs. San Diego, March 12, 1970
    L.A. Lakers vs. Phoenix, January 2, 1987

Fewest points, first half

20—New Orleans at Seattle, January 4, 1975
22—Milwaukee vs. Syracuse, February 12, 1955
25—Rochester vs. Boston, at New York, February 26, 1957
    Philadelphia vs. Milwaukee, March 3, 1972
    Golden State vs. Chicago, January 1, 1974
    Detroit at Indiana, November 8, 1989
    Washington vs. Detroit, February 1, 1991
    Chicago vs. Miami, November 6, 1993
    L.A. Lakers vs. San Antonio, January 9, 1994

Most points, both teams, first half

174—Phoenix (107) vs. Denver (67), November 10, 1990
173—Denver (90) at San Antonio (83), November 7, 1990
170—Golden State (87) at Denver (83), November 2, 1990

Fewest points, both teams, first half

58—Syracuse (27) vs. Ft. Wayne (31), at Buffalo, January 25, 1955
61—Milwaukee (26) vs. Minneapolis (35), at Buffalo, November 6, 1954
    Rochester (30) vs. New York (31), December 15, 1956

Most points, second half

97—Atlanta at San Diego, February 11, 1970
95—Philadelphia at Seattle, December 20, 1967
94—Houston at Denver, January 10, 1991

Fewest points, second half

25—Boston vs. Milwaukee, at Providence, February 27, 1955
    St. Louis vs. Boston, December 26, 1964
    Golden State vs. Boston, February 14, 1978
    Washington vs. New York, December 22, 1985
    New Jersey at Seattle, November 21, 1989
26—Milwaukee vs. Boston, at Providence, February 27, 1955
    St. Louis vs. Rochester, November 23, 1955
    New York at Chicago, February 23, 1973
    Miami vs. Boston, November 15, 1988
    Houston at L.A. Lakers, November 15, 1991

Most points, both teams, second half

172—San Antonio (91) at Denver (81), January 11, 1984
170—Philadelphia (90) vs. Cincinnati (80), March 19, 1971
169—Philadelphia (90) vs. New York (79), at Hershey, Pa., March 2, 1962

Fewest points, both teams, second half

51—Boston (25) vs. Milwaukee (26), at Providence, February 27, 1955
58—St. Louis (26) vs. Rochester (32), November 23, 1955
60—Detroit (30) vs. New York (30), April 12, 1992
62—Syracuse vs. New York, December 25, 1960 (162–100)
    Golden State vs. Sacramento, November 2, 1991 (153–91)

BY QUARTER

Most points, first quarter
50—Syracuse at San Francisco, December 16, 1962
 Boston vs. Denver, February 5, 1982
 Utah vs. Denver, April 10, 1982
 Milwaukee vs. Orlando, November 16, 1989
 Phoenix vs. Denver, November 10, 1990
49—Atlanta vs. New Jersey, January 5, 1985
 Portland vs. San Antonio, November 25, 1990
48—Boston at San Diego, February 12, 1982
 Denver at Golden State, November 17, 1983
 Philadelphia vs. San Antonio, March 24, 1989
 Denver at San Antonio, November 7, 1990
 Washington vs. Denver, December 29, 1990
 Golden State vs. Sacramento, November 2, 1991

Fewest points, first quarter
4—Sacramento at L.A. Lakers, February 4, 1987
5—Syracuse at Milwaukee, November 13, 1954
 New York vs. Ft. Wayne, at Boston, November 21, 1956
 Cleveland at Chicago, December 15, 1990
6—Los Angeles vs. Chicago, November 20, 1977

Most points, both teams, first quarter
91—Utah (50) vs. Denver (41), April 10, 1982
87—Denver (47) vs. San Antonio (40), January 11, 1984
 Phoenix (50) vs. Denver (37), November 10, 1990
86—Denver (47) vs. San Antonio (39), November 20, 1987
 Houston (44) vs. Denver (42), November 6, 1990

Fewest points, both teams, first quarter
18—Ft. Wayne (9) at Syracuse (9), November 29, 1956
25—Minneapolis (11) at Rochester (14), December 11, 1954
 Boston (7) at Milwaukee (18), November 12, 1974
 L.A. Lakers (10) vs. Utah (15), February 6, 1994

Most points, second quarter
57—Phoenix vs. Denver, November 10, 1990
52—Baltimore vs. Detroit, December 18, 1965
50—San Diego vs. Utah, April 14, 1984
 San Antonio at Houston, November 17, 1984

Fewest points, second quarter
5—Utah at Los Angeles, December 1, 1981
6—Boston at New Jersey, January 9, 1990
 Chicago vs. Miami, November 6, 1993
7—Golden State at Portland, January 1, 1983
 Portland at Philadelphia, December 6, 1991

Most points, both teams, second quarter
91—Seattle (46) at Golden State (45), March 23, 1974
90—New York (47) at Philadelphia (43), November 18, 1988
88—Denver (45) at Dallas (44), January 14, 1983
 San Antonio (47) vs. Denver (42), November 7, 1990

Fewest points, both teams, second quarter
23—Rochester (10) at Milwaukee (13), January 4, 1955
24—Portland (7) at Philadelphia (17), December 6, 1991
 Chicago (6) vs. Miami (18), November 6, 1993

Most points, third quarter
57—Golden State vs. Sacramento, March 4, 1989
54—Atlanta at San Diego, February 11, 1970

Fewest points, third quarter
4—Buffalo vs. Milwaukee, October 21, 1972
6—New York at Milwaukee, December 29, 1974

Most points, both teams, third quarter
89—Atlanta (49) vs. Philadelphia (40), March 4, 1973
88—Los Angeles (44) vs. San Diego (44), March 23, 1979

Fewest points, both teams, third quarter
23—Houston (11) at Philadelphia (12), February 2, 1975
 Detroit (10) vs. New York (13), April 12, 1992

24—Rochester (10) vs. Philadelphia (14), at New Haven, Conn., February 17, 1955
 Charlotte (7) vs. Utah (17), February 8, 1990

Most points, fourth quarter
58—Buffalo at Boston, October 20, 1972
54—Boston vs. San Diego, February 25, 1970

Fewest points, fourth quarter
6—Detroit at Orlando, December 7, 1993
7—Houston at L.A. Lakers, November 15, 1991
 Washington vs. Golden State, February 6, 1994

Most points, both teams, fourth quarter
99—San Antonio (53) at Denver (46), January 11, 1984
96—Boston (52) vs. Minneapolis (44), February 27, 1959
 Detroit (53) vs. Cincinnati (43), January 7,1972

Fewest points, both teams, fourth quarter
23—Boston (10) vs. Philadelphia (13) November 21, 1956
 Miami (10) at New Jersey (13), April 1, 1993
 Orlando (11) vs. Boston (12), April 18, 1993
25—Milwaukee (12) vs. Boston (13), at Providence, February 27, 1955
 Minneapolis (10) at Ft. Wayne (15), February 12, 1956
 Dallas (9) at Minnesota (16), December 13, 1989

OVERTIME

Most points, overtime period
24—Sacramento vs. Utah, March 17, 1990
23—L.A. Clippers vs. Phoenix, November 12, 1988
 Dallas at L.A. Lakers, December 12, 1990
 Indiana vs. Golden State, March 31, 1991

Fewest points, overtime period
0—Houston vs. Portland, January 22, 1983
 L.A. Lakers vs. Detroit, December 1, 1989
 Seattle at Philadelphia, February 16, 1990
1—Washington at Atlanta, March 16, 1983
2—by many

Most points, both teams, overtime period
39—Indiana (23) vs. Golden State (16), March 31, 1991
38—Cleveland (21) at Washington (17), December 21, 1992
37—Los Angeles (21) at Baltimore (16), October 21, 1969

Fewest points, both teams, overtime period
4—Seattle (0) at Philadelphia (4), February 16, 1990
6—Philadelphia (3) vs. Washington (3), November 15, 1975 (2nd ot)
 Washington (2) vs. Philadelphia (4), March 24, 1990
 New York (2) at Milwaukee (4), December 26, 1992
 New York (2) at Orlando (4), February 14, 1993 (3rd ot)
 Cleveland (3) at Atlanta (3), April 13, 1993 (1st ot)

Largest margin of victory, overtime game
17—Portland at Houston, January 22, 1983 (113–96 game, 17–0 overtime)
16—Milwaukee vs. New Jersey, December 4, 1977 (134–118 game, 18–2 overtime)
15—Boston at San Francisco, January 2, 1963 (135–120 game, 21–6 overtime)
 Dallas at L.A. Lakers, December 12, 1990 (112–97 game, 23–8 overtime)

PLAYERS SCORING

Most players, 2,000-or-more points, season
2—Los Angeles, 1964–65 (West 2,292; Baylor 2,009)
 Atlanta, 1972–73 (Maravich 2,063; Hudson 2,029)
 Denver, 1982–83 (English 2,326; Vandeweghe 2,186)
 Denver, 1983–84 (Vandeweghe 2,295; English 2,167)
 Boston, 1986–87 (Bird 2,076; McHale 2,008)

Most players, 1,000-or-more points, season
6—Syracuse, 1960–61 (Schayes 1,868; Greer 1,551; Barnett 1,320; Gambee 1,085; Costello 1,084; Kerr 1,056)
 Denver, 1987–88 (English 2,000; Lever 1,546; Adams 1,137; Schayes 1,129; Vincent 1,124; Rasmussen 1,002)
 Boston, 1990–91 (Lewis 1,478; Gamble 1,281; McHale 1,251; Parish 1,207; Bird 1,164; Shaw 1,091)

Most players, 40-or-more points, game

2—Baltimore vs. Los Angeles, November 14, 1964 (Johnson 41, Bellamy 40)
   Los Angeles at San Francisco, February 11, 1970 (Baylor 43, West 43)
   New Orleans vs. Denver, April 10, 1977 (Maravich 45, Williams 41)
   Phoenix at Boston, January 5, 1978 (Westphal 43, Davis 40)
   San Antonio vs. Milwaukee, March 6, 1982 (3 ot) (Gervin 50, Mitchell 45)
   Detroit at Denver, December 13, 1983 (3 ot) (Thomas 47, Long 41)
   Denver vs. Detroit, December 13, 1983 (3 ot) (Vandeweghe 51, English 47)
   Utah vs. Detroit, March 19, 1984 (Dantley 43, Drew 42)

Most players, 40-or-more points, both teams, game

4—Denver vs. Detroit, December 13, 1983 (3 ot) (Detroit: Thomas 47, Long 41; Denver: Vandeweghe 51, English 47)
3—New Orleans (2) vs. Denver (1), April 10, 1977 (New Orleans: Maravich 45, Williams 41; Denver: Thompson 40)
   San Antonio (2) vs. Milwaukee (1), March 6, 1982 (3 ot) (San Antonio: Gervin 50, Mitchell 45; Milwaukee: Winters 42)

FIELD GOAL PERCENTAGE

Highest field goal percentage, season

.545—L.A. Lakers, 1984-85 (3,952/7,254)
.532—Los Angeles, 1983-84 (3,854/7,250)
.529—Los Angeles, 1979-80 (3,898/7,368)

Lowest field goal percentage, season

.362—Milwaukee, 1954-55 (2,187/6,041)
.3688—Syracuse, 1956-57 (2,550/6,915)
.3695—Rochester, 1956-57 (2,515/6,807)

Highest field goal percentage, game

.707—San Antonio at Dallas, April 16, 1983 (53/75)
.705—Chicago at Golden State, December 2, 1981 (43/61)
.699—Chicago vs. Detroit, January 22, 1980 (58/83)
.697—Portland vs. L.A. Clippers, February 1, 1986 (62/89)
.696—Phoenix at Golden State, March 12, 1980 (48/69)

Lowest field goal percentage, game

.229—Milwaukee vs. Minneapolis, at Buffalo, November 6, 1954 (22/96)
.235—New York vs. Milwaukee, at Providence, December 31, 1954 (24/102)
.238—Cleveland at San Francisco, November 10, 1970 (25/105)

Highest field goal percentage, both teams, game

.632—Boston (.650) vs. New Jersey (.615) at Hartford, December 11, 1984 (108/171)
.630—Portland (.697) vs. L.A. Clippers (.560), February 1, 1986 (109/173)
.628—New York (.642) vs. Denver (.612), December 8, 1981 (113/180)
.625—Chicago (.699) vs. Detroit (.559), January 22, 1980 (110/176)
   Phoenix (.696) at Golden State (.566), March 12, 1980 (95/152)

Lowest field goal percentage, both teams, game

.246—Milwaukee (.229) vs. Minneapolis (.263), at Buffalo, November 6, 1954 (48/195)
.260—Rochester (.250) at St. Louis (.270), November 23, 1955 (61/235)
.273—St. Louis (.239) vs. Syracuse (.315), November 12, 1955 (56/205)

FIELD GOALS

Most field goals per game, season

49.9—Boston, 1959-60 (3,744/75)
49.0—Philadelphia, 1961-62 (3,917/80)
48.5—Denver, 1981-82 (3,980/82)

Fewest field goals per game, season

30.4—Milwaukee, 1954-55 (2,187/72)
32.4—Ft. Wayne, 1954-55 (2,333/72)
32.8—Syracuse, 1954-55 (2,360/72)

Most field goals, game

74—Detroit at Denver, December 13, 1983 (3 ot)
72—Boston vs. Minneapolis, February 27, 1959
69—Syracuse vs. San Francisco, March 10, 1963
   Los Angeles vs. Golden State, March 19, 1972
   Detroit vs. Boston, March 9, 1979
   Milwaukee vs. New Orleans, March 14, 1979
   Los Angeles vs. Denver, April 9, 1982

Fewest field goals, game

19—Indiana at New York, December 10, 1985
20—Rochester vs. Milwaukee, February 19, 1955
21—Syracuse vs. Milwaukee, January 2, 1955

Most field goals, both teams, game

142—Detroit (74) at Denver (68), December 13, 1983 (3 ot)
136—Milwaukee (68) at San Antonio (68), March 6, 1982 (3 ot)
134—Cincinnati (67) vs. San Diego (67), March 12, 1970

Fewest field goals, both teams, game

46—Boston (23) vs. Milwaukee (23), at Providence, February 27, 1955
48—Milwaukee (22) vs. Minneapolis (26), at Buffalo, November 6, 1954
   Syracuse (21) vs. Milwaukee (27), January 2, 1955
   Philadelphia (23) at New York (25), December 27, 1955
   Minneapolis (23) vs. St. Louis (25), at Ft. Wayne, December 29, 1955

Most field goals, one half

43—Phoenix vs. Denver, November 10, 1990 (1st Half)

Most field goals, both teams, one half

71—Denver (37) at San Antonio (34), November 7, 1990 (1st Half)

Most field goals, one quarter

24—Phoenix vs. Denver, November 10, 1990 (2nd Qtr.)

Most field goals, both teams, one quarter

40—Boston (23) vs. Minneapolis (17), February 27, 1959 (4th Qtr.)

FIELD GOAL ATTEMPTS

Most field goal attempts per game, season

119.6—Boston, 1959-60 (8,971/75)
117.7—Boston, 1960-61 (9,295/79)
115.7—Philadelphia, 1959-60 (8,678/75)

Fewest field goal attempts per game, season

79.46—Indiana, 1993-94 (6,516/82)
79.62—Minnesota, 1992-93 (6,529/82)
79.69—Minnesota, 1993-94 (6,535/82)

Most field goal attempts, game

153—Philadelphia vs. Los Angeles, December 8, 1961 (3 ot)
150—Boston vs. Philadelphia, March 2, 1960
149—Boston vs. Detroit, January 27, 1961

Fewest field goal attempts, game

55—Ft. Wayne at Milwaukee, February 20, 1955
   Philadelphia vs. Atlanta, April 1, 1988
58—Chicago vs. Atlanta, February 14, 1989
   Utah at Minnesota, December 17, 1989
   Washington vs. Dallas, January 27, 1994

Most field goal attempts, both teams, game

291—Philadelphia (153) vs. Los Angeles (138), December 8, 1961 (3 ot)
274—Boston (149) vs. Detroit (125), January 27, 1961
   Philadelphia (141) at Boston (133), March 5, 1961

Fewest field goal attempts, both teams, game

132—Chicago (65) vs. New York (67), December 27, 1983
133—Minneapolis (66) vs. Milwaukee (67), at Huron, January 27, 1955
   Philadelphia (59) vs. Milwaukee (74), at Albany, N.Y., March 14, 1955
134—New Jersey (67) at New York (67), November 9, 1982
   Philadelphia (55) vs. Atlanta (79), April 1, 1988
   Indiana (66) at Chicago (68), March 26, 1994

Most field goal attempts, one half

83—Philadelphia vs. Syracuse, November 4, 1959
   Boston at Philadelphia, December 27, 1960

Most field goal attempts, both teams, one half

153—Boston (80) vs. Minneapolis (73), February 27, 1959 (2nd Half)

Most field goal attempts, one quarter

47—Boston vs. Minneapolis, February 27, 1959 (4th Qtr.)

Most field goal attempts, both teams, one quarter

86—Boston (47) vs. Minneapolis (39), February 27, 1959 (4th Qtr.)

THREE-POINT FIELD GOAL PERCENTAGE

Highest three-point field goal percentage, season

.407—Cleveland, 1989–90 (346/851)
.3844—Boston, 1987–88 (271/705)
.3838—Boston, 1979–80 (162/422)

Lowest three-point field goal percentage, season

.104—Los Angeles, 1982–83 (10/96)
.122—Atlanta, 1980–81 (10/82)
.138—Los Angeles, 1981–82 (13/94)

Most three-point field goals, no misses, game

6—Cleveland at Utah, January 24, 1985
 L.A. Lakers at Portland, January 1, 1987
 Houston vs. Denver, February 17, 1989
 San Antonio vs. Milwaukee, December 22, 1990
5—New York vs. Sacramento, January 10, 1987
 Utah at Denver, February 4, 1989
 Atlanta at L.A. Clippers, March 30, 1990
 San Antonio vs. Denver, April 22, 1993
4—by many

Most three-point field goals, no misses, both teams, game

5—San Antonio (4) at Philadelphia (1), December 19, 1984
4—Washington (4) at Kansas City (0), January 8, 1981
 Washington (3) vs. Atlanta (1), December 3, 1987

Most three-point field goal attempts, none made, game

15—Houston at Orlando, March 30, 1991
14—Philadelphia at Houston, February 22, 1988
 Cleveland at Golden State, November 12, 1992 (2 ot)
13—Portland at Philadelphia, March 1, 1991
 New York vs. Utah, November 20, 1993

THREE-POINT FIELD GOALS

Most three-point field goals per game, season

5.23—Houston, 1993–94 (429/82)
4.85—Phoenix, 1992–93 (398/82)
4.80—Orlando, 1993–94 (394/82)

Fewest three-point field goals per game, season

0.12—Atlanta, 1980–81 (10/82)
 Los Angeles, 1982–83 (10/82)
0.16—Atlanta, 1979–80 (13/82)
 Detroit, 1980–81 (13/82)
 Los Angeles, 1981–82 (13/82)

Most three-point field goals, game

16—Sacramento vs. Golden State, February 9, 1989
15—Miami at Milwaukee, April 8, 1993
14—Orlando at Detroit, December 9, 1992

Most three-point field goals, both teams, game

23—Miami (12) vs. L.A. Clippers (11), January 18, 1994
21—Milwaukee (12) vs. Portland (9), December 30, 1990
20—Sacramento (16) vs. Golden State (4), February 9, 1989
 Cleveland (10) at Orlando (10), January 12, 1994
 Orlando (11) at New York (9), April 11, 1994

Most three-point field goals, one half

10—New York vs. Miami, November 22, 1993
 Houston vs. Golden State, April 7, 1994

Most three-point field goals, one quarter

8—Denver vs. Seattle, January 9, 1982

THREE-POINT FIELD GOALS ATTEMPTS

Most three-point field goal attempts per game, season

15.67—Houston, 1993–94 (1,285/82)
13.98—New York, 1988–89 (1,147/82)
13.87—Orlando, 1993–94 (1,137/82)

Fewest three-point field goal attempts per game, season

0.91—Atlanta, 1979–80 (75/82)

1.00—Atlanta, 1980–81 (82/82)
1.02—Detroit, 1980–81 (84/82)
 Philadelphia, 1980–81 (84/82)

Most three-point field goal attempts, game

31—Sacramento vs. Golden State, February 9, 1989
30—Houston vs. Indiana, January 29, 1994
 Philadelphia vs. Charlotte, February 7, 1994
29—New York vs. Golden State, March 31, 1989
 Philadelphia at Phoenix, March 3, 1993

Most three-point field goal attempts, both teams, game

47—Orlando (24) at New York (23), April 11, 1994
46—Indiana (26) at Golden State (20), March 2, 1989 (ot)
45—Sacramento (31) vs. Golden State (14), February 9, 1989
 Philadelphia (29) at Phoenix (16), March 3, 1993

Most three-point field goal attempts, one half

21—Philadelphia at Phoenix, March 3, 1993

FREE THROW PERCENTAGE

Highest free throw percentage, season

.832—Boston, 1989–90 (1,791/2,153)
.824—Boston, 1990–91 (1,646/1,997)
.8207—Milwaukee, 1988–89 (1,955/2,382)
.8205—K.C.-Omaha, 1974–75 (1,797/2,190)

Lowest free throw percentage, season

.635—Philadelphia, 1967–68 (2,121/3,338)
.638—San Francisco, 1963–64 (1,800/2,821)
.640—San Francisco, 1964–65 (1,819/2,844)

Most free throws made, no misses, game

39—Utah at Portland, December 7, 1982
35—Boston vs. Miami, April 12, 1990
33—Boston vs. New Jersey, March 18, 1990
 Golden State vs. Houston, April 11, 1991
30—Buffalo vs. Los Angeles, November 18, 1975
 Utah vs. Boston, December 28, 1985
 Portland at Indiana, November 30, 1986
 Miami at Boston, March 24, 1993
29—Syracuse at Boston, November 2, 1957
 Utah at Boston, December 14, 1984

Lowest free throw percentage, game

.200—New Orleans at Houston, November 19, 1977 (1/5)
.214—Houston vs. Portland, February 22, 1983 (3/14)
.231—Miami at L.A. Lakers, April 5, 1991 (3/13)
.267—Detroit at Milwaukee, April 20, 1994 (4/15)
.308—Minnesota vs. Houston, November 25, 1990 (4/13)
 Detroit vs. Charlotte, March 25, 1994 (4/13)

Highest free throw percentage, both teams, game

.971—Boston (1.000) vs. Seattle (.947), March 20, 1987 (33/34)
.970—Phoenix (1.000) at Indiana (.929), January 7, 1983 (32/33)
.968—Milwaukee (1.000) at Detroit (.941), January 2, 1974 (30/31)

Lowest free throw percentage, both teams, game

.410—Los Angeles (.386) at Chicago (.471), December 7, 1968 (25/61)
.450—Milwaukee (.375) at Cleveland (.500), November 3, 1977 (9/20)
.465—Kansas City (.440) at Dallas (.500), March 26, 1982 (20/43)

FREE THROWS MADE

Most free throws made per game, season

31.9—New York, 1957–58 (2,300/72)
31.2—Minneapolis, 1957–58 (2,246/72)
30.9—Syracuse, 1952–53 (2,197/71)

Fewest free throws made per game, season

15.3—Detroit, 1993–94 (1,253/82)
15.5—Milwaukee, 1972–73 (1,271/82)
15.8—Baltimore, 1972–73 (1,294/82)

Most free throws made, game

61—Phoenix vs. Utah, April 9, 1990 (ot)

60—Washington vs. New York, November 13, 1987
59—Syracuse vs. Anderson, November 24, 1949 (5 ot)

Fewest free throws made, game

1—New Orleans at Houston, November 19, 1977
2—Chicago vs. Seattle, March 13, 1973
   N.Y. Knicks vs. Chicago, January 25, 1977
   Houston at Denver, January 27, 1978
   Los Angeles vs. San Diego, March 28, 1980
   Seattle vs. Dallas, January 7, 1985
   Detroit at Philadelphia, April 24, 1994

Most free throws made, both teams, game

116—Syracuse (59) vs. Anderson (57), November 24, 1949 (5 ot)
103—Boston (56) at Minneapolis (47), November 28, 1954
96—Philadelphia (48) vs. Minneapolis (48), November 2, 1957

Fewest free throws made, both teams, game

7—Milwaukee (3) vs. Baltimore (4), January 1, 1973
9—Milwaukee (3) at Cleveland (6), November 3, 1977
   Los Angeles (2) vs. San Diego (7), March 28, 1980

Most free throws made, one half

36—Chicago vs. Phoenix, January 8, 1970
   Golden State vs. Utah, March 29, 1990
   Seattle at Denver, April 7, 1991

Most free throws made, both teams, one half

58—Utah (34) at Minnesota (24), December 17, 1989

Most free throws made, one quarter

26—Atlanta at Milwaukee, March 3, 1991

Most free throws made, both teams, one quarter

39—Cincinnati (24) at Baltimore (15), December 27, 1964
   Chicago (22) vs. Denver (17), December 29, 1978

FREE THROW ATTEMPTS

Most free throw attempts per game, season

42.4—New York, 1957–58 (3,056/72)
42.3—St. Louis, 1957–58 (3,047/72)
42.1—Philadelphia, 1966–67 (3,411/81)

Fewest free throw attempts per game, season

20.6—Milwaukee, 1972–73 (1,687/82)
20.9—Detroit, 1993–94 (1,715/82)
21.2—New York, 1973–74 (1,738/82)

Most free throw attempts, game

86—Syracuse vs. Anderson, November 24, 1949 (5 ot)
80—Phoenix vs. Utah, April 9, 1990 (ot)
74—Anderson at Syracuse, November 24, 1949 (5 ot)
   San Francisco vs. New York, November 6, 1964 (2 ot)
71—Chicago vs. Phoenix, January 8, 1970

Fewest free throw attempts, game

3—Los Angeles vs. San Diego, March 28, 1980
4—New York at Atlanta, March 6, 1974
   Milwaukee at K.C.-Omaha, February 25, 1975
   Golden State vs. Chicago, March 6, 1977
   Houston at Denver, January 27, 1978
   Seattle vs. Dallas, January 7, 1985

Most free throw attempts, both teams, game

160—Syracuse (86) vs. Anderson (74), November 24, 1949 (5 ot)
136—Baltimore (70) vs. Syracuse (66), November 15, 1952 (ot)
127—Ft. Wayne (67) vs. Minneapolis (60), December 31, 1954

Fewest free throw attempts, both teams, game

12—Los Angeles (3) vs. San Diego (9), March 28, 1980
14—Milwaukee (6) vs. Baltimore (8), January 1, 1973
15—New Orleans (5) at Houston (10), November 19, 1977

Most free throw attempts, one half

48—Chicago vs. Phoenix, January 8, 1970

Most free throw attempts, both teams, one half

76—New York (40) at St. Louis (36), December 14, 1957

Most free throw attempts, one quarter

30—Boston at Chicago, January 9, 1963
   Seattle vs. Dallas, March 15, 1992

Most free throw attempts, both teams, one quarter

50—New York (26) at St. Louis (24), December 14, 1957
   Cincinnati (29) at Baltimore (21), December 27, 1964

REBOUNDS

Rebounds have been compiled since 1950–51
Team rebounds not included

Most rebounds per game, season

71.5—Boston, 1959–60 (5,365/75)
70.7—Boston, 1960–61 (5,582/79)

Fewest rebounds per game, season

38.3—Minnesota, 1992–93 (3,144/82)
38.6—Milwaukee, 1992–93 (3,163/82)
38.7—Charlotte, 1989–90 (3,173/82)

Most rebounds, game

109—Boston vs. Detroit, December 24, 1960
105—Boston vs. Minneapolis, February 26, 1960
104—Philadelphia vs. Syracuse, November 4, 1959
   Philadelphia vs. Cincinnati, November 8, 1959

Fewest rebounds, game

20—New York vs. Ft. Wayne, at Miami, February 14, 1955
   Buffalo at Houston, February 17, 1974
21—New York vs. Golden State, February 18, 1975

Most rebounds, both teams, game

188—Philadelphia (98) vs. Los Angeles (90), December 8, 1961 (3 ot)
177—Philadelphia (104) vs. Syracuse (73), November 4, 1959
   Boston (89) at Philadelphia (88), December 27, 1960

Fewest rebounds, both teams, game

48—New York (20) vs. Ft. Wayne (28), at Miami, February 14, 1955
53—Denver (26) vs. Indiana (27), February 2, 1992
55—Phoenix (25) at Philadelphia (30), January 7, 1985

Most rebounds, one half

65—Boston vs. Cincinnati, January 12, 1962

Most rebounds, one quarter

40—Philadelphia vs. Syracuse, November 9, 1961

OFFENSIVE REBOUNDS

Offensive rebounds have been compiled since 1973–74

Most offensive rebounds per game, season

18.5—Denver, 1990–91 (1,520/82)
18.4—New Jersey, 1991–92 (1,512/82)
17.8—Seattle, 1977–78 (1,456/82)

Fewest offensive rebounds per game, season

10.6—Utah, 1990–91 (867/82)
11.16—Golden State, 1989–90 (915/82)
11.21—San Antonio, 1992–93 (919/82)

Most offensive rebounds, game

39—Boston at Capital, October 20, 1973
37—Kansas City at Denver, January 4, 1983
   San Antonio at Golden State, February 28, 1990 (ot)
   New Jersey vs. Golden State, April 6, 1990
36—Detroit at Los Angeles, December 14, 1975

Fewest offensive rebounds, game

1—Cleveland vs. Houston, March 23, 1975
   New York vs. Boston, March 4, 1978

2—Houston at Cleveland, November 9, 1973
  Detroit vs. Portland, January 23, 1974
  Atlanta at K.C.-Omaha, March 18, 1975
  Phoenix vs. New Orleans, December 21, 1975
  Phoenix at Golden State, March 12, 1980
  San Antonio at Chicago, November 4, 1986
  L.A. Lakers vs. Chicago, February 2, 1988
  Houston at Portland, December 19, 1989
  L.A. Clippers vs. Seattle, January 24, 1993

Most offensive rebounds, both teams, game

57—Los Angeles (29) vs. Cleveland (28), January 22, 1974 (ot)
  Detroit (29) vs. Indiana (28), January 30, 1977
56—Los Angeles (30) vs. Utah (26), November 13, 1983
55—New Orleans (31) vs. Buffalo (24), November 6, 1974
  San Antonio (37) at Golden State (18), February 28, 1990 (ot)

Fewest offensive rebounds, both teams, game

8—Detroit (4) at Boston (4), November 11, 1988
9—Minnesota (4) at Washington (5), November 27, 1992
  Utah (4) at Minnesota (5), December 15, 1993
10—Detroit (5) at K.C.-Omaha (5), November 19, 1974
  Utah (3) vs. Portland (7), December 28, 1989

Most offensive rebounds, one half

23—Boston at Philadelphia, March 20, 1976
  Seattle vs. Boston, March 22, 1979
  Milwaukee vs. Utah, March 6, 1987
  Houston vs. Phoenix, February 16, 1991

DEFENSIVE REBOUNDS

Defensive rebounds have been compiled since 1973–74

Most defensive rebounds per game, season

37.5—Boston, 1973–74, (3,074/82)
37.0—Golden State, 1973–74 (3,035/82)
36.2—Boston, 1975–76 (2,972/82)

Fewest defensive rebounds per game, season

25.0—Minnesota, 1989–90 (2,053/82)
25.6—New York, 1984–85 (2,102/82)
25.7—San Diego, 1982–83 (2,108/82)

Most defensive rebounds, game

61—Boston vs. Capital, March 17, 1974
58—Los Angeles vs. Seattle, October 19, 1973
56—Portland vs. Cleveland, October 18, 1974 (4 ot)

Fewest defensive rebounds, game

10—Utah at L.A. Lakers, April 1, 1990
11—Charlotte vs. Indiana, February 2, 1994
12—Indiana at New Jersey, February 27, 1987
  Philadelphia at Boston, January 20, 1989

Most defensive rebounds, both teams, game

106—Portland (56) vs. Cleveland (50), October 18, 1974 (4 ot)
103—Philadelphia (54) vs. Washington (49), November 15, 1975 (3 ot)
101—Indiana (53) vs. Denver (48), January 23, 1989

Fewest defensive rebounds, both teams, game

31—Utah (10) at L.A. Lakers (21), April 1, 1990
33—Philadelphia (16) at Milwaukee (17), December 14, 1984
34—Philadelphia (16) vs. Phoenix (18), January 7, 1985
  New York (14) at Philadelphia (20), January 20, 1986
  New Jersey (15) at Miami (19), January 26, 1991

Most defensive rebounds, one half

36—Los Angeles vs. Seattle, October 19, 1973

ASSISTS

Most assists per game, season

31.4—L.A. Lakers, 1984–85 (2,575/82)
31.2—Milwaukee, 1978–79 (2,562/82)
30.7—Los Angeles, 1982–83 (2,519/82)

Fewest assists per game, season

16.6—Minneapolis, 1956–57 (1,195/72)
17.3—N.Y. Nets, 1976–77 (1,422/82)
17.6—Detroit, 1957–58 (1,264/72)

Most assists, game

53—Milwaukee vs. Detroit, December 26, 1978
52—Chicago vs. Atlanta, March 20, 1971
  Seattle vs. Denver, March 18, 1983
  Denver at Golden State, April 21, 1989
51—Sheboygan vs. Denver, March 10, 1950
  Phoenix vs. San Antonio, February 2, 1979
  Los Angeles vs. Denver, February 23, 1982

Fewest assists, game

3—Boston vs. Minneapolis, at Louisville, November 28, 1956
  Baltimore vs. Boston, October 16, 1963
  Cincinnati vs. Chicago, at Evansville, December 5, 1967
  New York at Boston, March 28, 1976

Most assists, both teams, game

93—Detroit (47) at Denver (46), December 13, 1983 (3 ot)
89—Detroit (48) at Cleveland (41), March 28, 1973 (ot)
88—Phoenix (47) vs. San Diego (41), at Tucson, March 15, 1969
  San Antonio (50) vs. Denver (38), April 15, 1984

Fewest assists, both teams, game

10—Boston (3) vs. Minneapolis (7), at Louisville, November 28, 1956
11—Baltimore (3) vs. Boston (8), October 16, 1963
12—Ft. Wayne (6) vs. New York (6), at Miami, February 17, 1955
  Chicago (6) vs. St. Louis (6), October 27, 1961

Most assists, one half

33—Phoenix vs. Denver, November 10, 1990

Most assists, both teams, one half

51—Denver (27) at San Antonio (24), November 7, 1990

Most assists, one quarter

19—Milwaukee vs. Detroit, December 26, 1978
  San Antonio vs. Denver, April 15, 1984 (2nd Qtr.)

Most assists, both teams, one quarter

28—Minnesota (15) vs. Charlotte (13), April 19, 1992

PERSONAL FOULS

Most personal fouls per game, season

32.1—Tri-Cities, 1949–50 (2,057/64)
31.6—Rochester, 1952–53 (2,210/70)
30.8—Tri-Cities, 1950–51 (2,092/68)

Since 1954–55 season

30.1—Atlanta, 1977–78 (2,470/82)

Fewest personal fouls per game, season

18.1—Philadelphia, 1993–94 (1,488/82)
18.6—L.A. Lakers, 1990–91 (1,524/82)
18.8—L.A. Lakers, 1991–92 (1,543/82)

Most personal fouls, game

66—Anderson at Syracuse, November 24, 1949 (5 ot)
60—Syracuse at Baltimore, November 15, 1952 (ot)
56—Syracuse vs. Anderson, November 24, 1949 (5 ot)
55—Milwaukee at Baltimore, November 12, 1952

Since 1954–55 season

52—Utah at Phoenix, April 9, 1990 (ot)

Since 1954–55 season (regulation game)

46—New York at Phoenix, December 3, 1987

Fewest personal fouls, game

7—San Antonio at Houston, April 13, 1984 (ot)
8—Detroit at Phoenix, March 27, 1975
  Indiana at New Jersey, November 3, 1984

Dallas at Seattle, January 7, 1985
Utah vs. Washington, December 4, 1991
9—by many

Most personal fouls, both teams, game
122—Anderson (66) at Syracuse (56), November 24, 1949 (5 ot)
114—Syracuse (60) at Baltimore (54), November 15, 1952 (ot)
97—Syracuse (50) vs. New York (47), February 15. 1953

Since 1954–55 season
87—Portland (44) vs. Chicago (43), March 16, 1984 (4 ot)

Since 1954–55 season (regulation game)
84—Indiana (44) vs. Kansas City (40), October 22, 1977

Fewest personal fouls, both teams, game
22—New Jersey (10) at Philadelphia (12), December 22, 1984
23—Detroit (8) at Phoenix (15), March 27, 1975
   Cleveland (10) at Washington (13), March 16, 1992
24—Philadelphia (9) at Rochester (15), January 5, 1957
   New York (12) at Philadelphia (12), February 25, 1960
   Washington (9) at L.A. Clippers (15), December 15, 1984
   Dallas (8) at Seattle (16), January 7, 1985
   Philadelphia (12) at Chicago (12), March 7, 1989
   Philadelphia (12) at Chicago (12), January 17, 1994

Most personal fouls, one half
30—Rochester at Syracuse, January 15, 1953

Most personal fouls, both teams, one half
51—Syracuse (28) at Boston (23), December 26, 1950

Most personal fouls, one quarter
19—Dallas at Denver, January 15, 1982

Most personal fouls, both teams, one quarter
32—Dallas (19) at Denver (13), January 15, 1982

DISQUALIFICATIONS

Disqualifications have been compiled since 1950–51

Most disqualifications per game, season
1.53—Rochester, 1952–53 (107/70)
1.41—Ft. Wayne, 1952–53 (97/69)
1.31—Baltimore, 1952–53 (93/71)
   Milwaukee, 1952–53 (93/71)

Since 1954–55 season
0.98—Atlanta, 1977–78 (80/82)

Fewest disqualifications per game, season
0.02—L.A. Lakers, 1988–89 (2/82)
0.03—Detroit, 1991–92 (3/82)
0.05—Chicago, 1991–92 (4/82)
   San Antonio, 1993–94 (4/82)

Most disqualifications, game
8—Syracuse at Baltimore, November 15, 1952 (ot)
6—Syracuse at Boston, December 26, 1950
5—Pittsburgh at Philadelphia, November 7, 1946
   Boston vs. Syracuse, December 26, 1950
   Baltimore vs. Syracuse, November 15, 1952 (ot)
   Rochester at Philadelphia, December 11, 1952
   Minneapolis vs. St. Louis, February 17, 1957 (ot)
   Indiana at New Jersey, February 8, 1978 (ot)
   Kansas City at Denver, November 11, 1978
   Chicago at Portland, March 16, 1984 (4 ot)
   Atlanta at Utah, February 19, 1986 (ot)

Most disqualifications, both teams, game
13—Syracuse (8) at Baltimore (5), November 15, 1952 (ot)
11—Syracuse (6) at Boston (5), December 26, 1950
9—Minneapolis (5) vs. St. Louis (4), February 17, 1957 (ot)

Since 1954–55 season (regulation game)
8—Kansas City (5) at Denver (3), November 11, 1978

STEALS

Steals have been compiled since 1973–74

Most steals per game, season
12.9—Phoenix, 1977–78 (1,059/82)
12.8—Seattle, 1993–94 (1,053/82)
11.9—Golden State, 1974–75 (972/82)

Fewest steals per game, season
5.94—Detroit, 1990–91 (487/82)
6.20—Boston, 1976–77 (506/82)
6.24—Detroit, 1989–90 (512/82)

Most steals, game
25—Golden State vs. Los Angeles, March 25, 1975
   Golden State vs. San Antonio, February 15, 1989
24—Golden State vs. Los Angeles, January 21, 1975
   Phoenix vs. San Antonio, November 20, 1977
   Philadelphia vs. Detroit, November 11, 1978
   Portland vs. Golden State, March 17, 1984
   Charlotte at Houston, November 30, 1989
   Milwaukee vs. Orlando, March 6, 1992

Fewest steals, game
0—Golden State at New York, November 24, 1973
   Seattle at Cleveland, November 27, 1973
   Cleveland vs. Philadelphia, March 15, 1975
   Chicago at Boston, March 24, 1976
   Denver at Atlanta, October 21, 1978
   Utah at Dallas, December 23, 1980
   Dallas at Phoenix, April 12, 1984
   Boston at Detroit, October 26, 1984
   Sacramento at Houston, January 23, 1986
   Sacramento vs. Portland, April 23, 1988
   Boston at Minnesota, February 2, 1990
   Utah vs. Sacramento, April 16, 1991
   Houston at Dallas, November 12, 1991

Most steals, both teams, game
40—Golden State (24) vs. Los Angeles (16), January 21, 1975
   Philadelphia (24) vs. Detroit (16), November 11, 1978
   Golden State (25) vs. San Antonio (15), February 15, 1989
39—Golden State (25) vs. Los Angeles (14), March 25, 1975
   Atlanta (22) vs. Detroit (17), January 3, 1978
   Phoenix (20) at New York (19), February 25, 1978

Fewest steals, both teams, game
2—Detroit (1) at New York (1), October 9, 1973
3—New York (1) vs. Chicago (2), October 20, 1973
   Golden State (0) at New York (3), November 24, 1973
   Cleveland (1) at Boston (2), January 30, 1974
   Phoenix (1) at Utah (2), March 5, 1981

Most steals, one half
17—Golden State vs. San Antonio, February 15, 1989

Most steals, one quarter
11—Los Angeles vs. Chicago, March 12, 1982
   New Jersey vs. L.A. Clippers, March 1, 1988
   Miami at L.A. Clippers, February 28, 1992
   Milwaukee vs. Orlando, March 6, 1992

BLOCKED SHOTS

Blocked shots have been compiled since 1973–74

Most blocked shots per game, season
8.7—Washington, 1985–86 (716/82)
8.5—Utah, 1984–85 (697/82)
8.4—Denver, 1993–94 (686/82)

Fewest blocked shots per game, season
2.6—Dallas, 1980–81 (214/82)
2.7—Philadelphia, 1973–74 (220/82)
2.8—Atlanta, 1974–75 (227/82)

Most blocked shots, game

22—New Jersey vs. Denver, December 12, 1991
21—Detroit vs. Atlanta, October 18, 1980 (2 ot)
     Los Angeles vs. Denver, April 9, 1982
     Cleveland vs. New York, January 7, 1989
20—San Antonio vs. Golden State, February 24, 1981
     Detroit vs. Chicago, November 3, 1982
     Philadelphia vs. Seattle, March 9, 1984
     Houston at Denver, November 16, 1984
     Washington vs. Indiana, February 26, 1987

Fewest blocked shots, game

0—by many

Most blocked shots, both teams, game

34—Detroit (19) vs. Washington (15), November 19, 1981
32—New Jersey (19) at New Orleans (13), March 21, 1978
     New Orleans (19) vs. Indiana (13), March 27, 1979
     Philadelphia (20) vs. Seattle (12), March 9, 1984
31—Houston (20) at Denver (11), November 16, 1984
     Washington (20) vs. Indiana (11), February 26, 1987

Fewest blocked shots, both teams, game

0—Seattle at Portland, November 22, 1973
     Atlanta at Phoenix, December 3, 1974
     Kansas City at New York, October 30, 1975
     Detroit at New York, November 29, 1975
     Houston at Los Angeles, January 22, 1978
     Buffalo at Atlanta, January 29, 1978
     Phoenix at Portland, November 25, 1979
     Washington at Dallas, February 10, 1982
     Miami at Detroit, January 2, 1994

Most blocked shots, one half

15—San Antonio vs. Golden State, February 24, 1981
     Detroit vs. Washington, November 19, 1981
     New Jersey vs. Seattle, February 1, 1994

TURNOVERS

Turnovers have been compiled since 1970–71

Most turnovers per game, season

24.5—Denver, 1976–77 (2,011/82)

24.4—Buffalo, 1972–73 (2,001/82)
23.4—Philadelphia, 1976–77 (1,915/82)

Fewest turnovers per game, season

13.0—Minnesota, 1990–91 (1,062/82)
13.1—Cleveland, 1991–92 (1,073/82)
13.3—Chicago, 1991–92 (1,088/82)

Most turnovers, game

43—Los Angeles vs. Seattle, February 15, 1974
41—New Jersey vs. Detroit, November 16, 1980
40—Boston vs. Portland, at Philadelphia, January 5, 1971
     Los Angeles vs. Atlanta, December 1, 1972 (ot)
     K.C.-Omaha at Detroit, February 18, 1973
     Buffalo at Detroit, March 16, 1973
     Portland at Phoenix, March 7, 1976
     San Antonio vs. Phoenix, November 3, 1977
     New York vs. Milwaukee, December 3, 1977
     San Antonio at Golden State, February 15, 1989

Fewest turnovers, game

3—Portland vs. Phoenix, February 22, 1991
4—New York vs. Milwaukee, January 3, 1972
     Washington at Utah, March 3, 1981
     Dallas vs. Utah, February 1, 1985
     Houston vs. Sacramento, January 23, 1986
     Dallas vs. Sacramento, November 26, 1986
     Washington vs. Boston, January 25, 1990
     Philadelphia at New York, January 21, 1991 (ot)
     Washington at Miami, March 3, 1993
     Boston vs. Phoenix, April 2, 1993
5—by many

Most turnovers, both teams, game

73—Philadelphia (38) vs. San Antonio (35), October 22, 1976
     Denver (38) vs. Phoenix (35), October 24, 1980
71—New Jersey (41) vs. Detroit (30), November 16, 1980

Fewest turnovers, both teams, game

12—Cleveland (6) at Boston (6), March 7, 1993
13—Detroit (6) vs. Philadelphia (7), April 21, 1989
     Washington (6) at Detroit (7), December 30, 1992
14—by many

DEFENSE

POINTS

Fewest points allowed per game, season

89.7—Syracuse, 1954–55 (6,457/72)
90.0—Ft. Wayne, 1954–55 (6,480/72)
90.4—Milwaukee, 1954–55 (6,510/72)

Most points allowed per game, season

130.8—Denver, 1990–91 (10,723/82)
126.0—Denver, 1981–82 (10,328/82)
125.1—Seattle, 1967–68 (10,261/82)

Most consecutive games, fewer than 100 points allowed, season

28—Ft. Wayne, October 30—December 30, 1954
20—Ft. Wayne, January 30—March 1, 1955
16—Philadelphia, November 13—December 15, 1954

Most consecutive games, 100-or-more points allowed, season

82—Denver, October 30, 1981—April 17, 1982 (entire season)
     Denver, November 2, 1990—April 21, 1991 (entire season)
80—Seattle, October 13, 1967—March 16, 1968

FIELD GOAL PERCENTAGE

Opponents' field goal percentage has been compiled since 1970–71

Lowest opponents' field goal percentage, season

.420—Milwaukee, 1971–72 (3,370/8,025)
.422—Milwaukee, 1972–73 (3,385/8,028)
.424—Milwaukee, 1970–71 (3,489/8,224)

Highest opponents' field goal percentage, season

.536—Golden State, 1984–85 (3,839/7,165)
.529—San Diego, 1982–83 (3,652/6,910)
.526—San Diego, 1981–82 (3,739/7,105)

TURNOVERS

Opponents' turnovers have been compiled since 1970–71

Most opponents' turnovers per game, season

24.1—Atlanta, 1977–78 (1,980/82)
24.0—Phoenix, 1977–78 (1,969/82)
23.7—Denver, 1976–77 (1,944/82)

Fewest opponents' turnovers per game, season

12.2—Boston, 1989–90 (1,003/82)
12.4—San Antonio, 1993–94 (1,020/82)
12.9—Dallas, 1991–92 (1,054/82)

ALL-TIME PLAYOFF RECORDS

INDIVIDUAL RECORDS

MINUTES

Most minutes, game

67—Red Rocha, Syracuse at Boston, March 21, 1953 (4 ot)
Paul Seymour, Syracuse at Boston, March 21, 1953 (4 ot)
66—Bob Cousy, Boston vs. Syracuse, March 21, 1953 (4 ot)

Highest average, minutes per game, one playoff series

49.33—Wilt Chamberlain, Philadelphia vs. New York, 1968 (296/6)
49.29—Kareem Abdul-Jabbar, Milwaukee vs. Boston, 1974 (345/7)
48.75—Wilt Chamberlain, Philadelphia vs. Cincinnati, 1965 (195/4)
Jerry Lucas, Cincinnati vs. Philadelphia, 1965 (195/4)
Oscar Robertson, Cincinnati vs. Philadelphia, 1965 (195/4)
Wilt Chamberlain, Los Angeles vs. Atlanta, 1970 (195/4)

SCORING

Highest scoring average, one playoff series

46.3—Jerry West, Los Angeles vs. Baltimore, 1965 (278/6)
45.2—Michael Jordan, Chicago vs. Cleveland, 1988 (226/5)
45.0—Michael Jordan, Chicago vs. Miami, 1992 (135/3)

Most points, game

63—Michael Jordan, Chicago at Boston, April 20, 1986 (2 ot)
61—Elgin Baylor, Los Angeles at Boston, April 14, 1962
56—Wilt Chamberlain, Philadelphia vs. Syracuse, March 22, 1962
Michael Jordan, Chicago at Miami, April 29, 1992
Charles Barkley, Phoenix at Golden State, May 4, 1994

Most points, rookie, game

53—Wilt Chamberlain, Philadelphia vs. Syracuse, March 14, 1960
50—Wilt Chamberlain, Philadelphia at Boston, March 22, 1960
46—Kareem Abdul-Jabbar, Milwaukee vs. Philadelphia, at Madison, Wis., April 3, 1970

Most consecutive games, 20-or-more points

60—Michael Jordan, Chicago, June 2, 1989—May 11, 1993
57—Kareem Abdul-Jabbar, Milwaukee, Los Angeles, April 13, 1973—April 5, 1981
49—Elgin Baylor, Minneapolis, Los Angeles, March 17, 1960—March 30, 1964

Most consecutive games, 30-or-more points

11—Elgin Baylor, Los Angeles, March 27, 1962—April 18, 1962
9—Kareem Abdul-Jabbar, Milwaukee, March 25, 1970—April 19, 1970
Bob McAdoo, Buffalo, April 12, 1974—April 15, 1976
8—Michael Jordan, Chicago, April 23, 1987—May 8, 1988

Most consecutive games, 40-or-more points

6—Jerry West, Los Angeles, April 3—April 13, 1965
4—Bernard King, New York, April 19—April 27, 1984
Michael Jordan, Chicago, June 11, 1993—June 18, 1993
3—Kareem Abdul-Jabbar, Los Angeles, April 26—May 1, 1977
Michael Jordan, Chicago, May 3—May 7, 1989
Michael Jordan, Chicago, May 9—May 13, 1990

Most points, one half

39—Eric Floyd, Golden State vs. L.A. Lakers, May 10, 1987
38—Charles Barkley, Phoenix at Golden State, May 4, 1994

Most points, one quarter

29—Eric Floyd, Golden State vs. L.A. Lakers, May 10, 1987
27—Mark Aguirre, Dallas at Houston, May 5, 1988
Charles Barkley, Phoenix at Golden State, May 4, 1994

Most points, overtime period

13—Clyde Drexler, Portland at L.A. Lakers, April 29, 1992

FIELD GOALS

Highest field goal percentage, game (minimum: 8 field goals)

1.000—Wilt Chamberlain, Los Angeles at Atlanta, April 17, 1969 (9/9)
Tom Kozelko, Capital at New York, April 12, 1974 (8/8)
Larry McNeill, K.C.-Omaha vs. Chicago, April 13, 1975 (12/12)

Scott Wedman, Boston vs. L.A. Lakers, May 27, 1985 (11/11)
Brad Davis, Dallas at Utah, April 25, 1986 (8/8)
Bob Hansen, Utah vs. Dallas, April 25, 1986 (9/9)
Robert Parish, Boston at Atlanta, May 16, 1988 (8/8)
John Paxson, Chicago vs. L.A. Lakers, June 5, 1991 (8/8)
Horace Grant, Chicago vs. Cleveland, May 13, 1993 (8/8)
.923—Wes Unseld, Washington vs. San Antonio, May 6, 1979 (12/13)
.917—Bill Bradley, New York at Los Angeles, April 26, 1972 (11/12)
James Worthy, Los Angeles at Boston, May 31, 1984 (ot) (11/12)
Clint Richardson, Philadelphia at Milwaukee, April 28, 1985 (11/12)
Larry Nance, Cleveland vs. Chicago, May 15, 1993 (11/12)

Most field goals, none missed, game

12—Larry McNeill, K.C.-Omaha vs. Chicago, April 13, 1975
11—Scott Wedman, Boston vs. L.A. Lakers, May 27, 1985
9—Wilt Chamberlain, Los Angeles at Atlanta, April 17, 1969
Bob Hansen, Utah vs. Dallas, April 25, 1986

Most field goals, game

24—Wilt Chamberlain, Philadelphia vs. Syracuse, March 14, 1960
John Havlicek, Boston vs. Atlanta, April 1, 1973
Michael Jordan, Chicago vs. Cleveland, May 1, 1988
23—Charles Barkley, Phoenix at Golden State, May 4, 1994

Most field goals, one half

15—Eric Floyd, Golden State vs. L.A. Lakers, May 10, 1987
Charles Barkley, Phoenix at Golden State, May 4, 1994
14—John Havlicek, Boston vs. Atlanta, April 1, 1973
Gus Williams, Seattle at Dallas, April 17, 1984
Michael Jordan, Chicago vs. Cleveland, May 1, 1988
Isiah Thomas, Detroit at L.A. Lakers, June 19, 1988
Michael Jordan, Chicago at Philadelphia, May 11, 1990
Michael Jordan, Chicago vs. Portland, June 3, 1992
Michael Jordan, Chicago vs. Phoenix, June 16, 1993

Most field goals, one quarter

12—Eric Floyd, Golden State vs. L.A. Lakers, May 10, 1987
11—Gus Williams, Seattle at Dallas, April 17, 1984
Isiah Thomas, Detroit at L.A. Lakers, June 19, 1988
Charles Barkley, Phoenix at Golden State, May 4, 1994

Most field goal attempts, game

48—Wilt Chamberlain, Philadelphia vs. Syracuse, March 22, 1962
Rick Barry, San Francisco vs. Philadelphia, April 18, 1967
46—Elgin Baylor, Los Angeles at Boston, April 14, 1962
45—Elgin Baylor, Los Angeles at St. Louis, March 27, 1961
Michael Jordan, Chicago vs. Cleveland, May 1, 1988

Most field goal attempts, none made, game

14—Chick Reiser, Baltimore at Philadelphia, April 10, 1948
Dennis Johnson, Seattle vs. Washington, June 7, 1978
12—Tom Gola, Philadelphia at Boston, March 23, 1958
Guy Rodgers, San Francisco at Boston, April 18, 1964
Paul Pressey, Milwaukee at Boston, May 5, 1987

Most field goal attempts, one half

25—Wilt Chamberlain, Philadelphia vs. Syracuse, March 22, 1962
Elgin Baylor, Los Angeles at Boston, April 14, 1962
Michael Jordan, Chicago vs. Cleveland, May 1, 1988

Most field goal attempts, one quarter

17—Rick Barry, San Francisco at Philadelphia, April 14, 1967

THREE-POINT FIELD GOALS

Most three-point field goals, none missed, game

5—Brad Davis, Dallas at Utah, April 25, 1986
Byron Scott, L.A. Lakers vs. Golden State, May 5, 1991
4—Kevin Grevey, Washington vs. New Jersey, April 23, 1982
Scott Wedman, Boston vs. L.A. Lakers, May 27, 1985
John Lucas, Milwaukee vs. Boston, May 8, 1987

Scottie Pippen, Chicago at Cleveland, April 28, 1989
Dale Ellis, Seattle at Houston, May 5, 1989
Scottie Pippen, Chicago vs. New York, May 19, 1989
Michael Cooper, L.A. Lakers at Phoenix, May 26, 1989
Craig Hodges, Chicago vs. Detroit, June 1, 1990
Chris Mullin, Golden State at L.A. Lakers, May 8, 1991
Byron Scott, L.A. Lakers at Portland, May 21, 1991
Steve Smith, Miami vs. Chicago, April 29, 1992

Most three-point field goals, game

8—Dan Majerle, Phoenix vs. Seattle, June 1, 1993
7—Chuck Person, Indiana at Boston, April 28, 1991
6—by many

Most three-point field goals, one half

6—Michael Jordan, Chicago vs. Portland, June 3, 1992
Reggie Miller, Indiana at New York, June 1, 1994

Most three-point field goals, one quarter

5—Reggie Miller, Indiana at New York, June 1, 1994

Most three-point field goal attempts, game

13—Vernon Maxwell, Houston at L.A. Lakers, April 27, 1991
Tim Hardaway, Golden State at Seattle, April 30, 1992
12—Michael Adams, Denver at Phoenix, April 30, 1989
Craig Hodges, Chicago at Detroit, June 3, 1990
Dennis Scott, Orlando at Indiana, May 2, 1994
Vernon Maxwell, Houston vs. Utah, May 31, 1994

Most three-point field goal attempts, one half

10—John Starks, New York at Houston, June 22, 1994

FREE THROWS

Most free throws made, none missed, game

17—Gail Goodrich, Los Angeles at Chicago, March 28, 1971
Bob Love, Chicago at Golden State, April 27, 1975
Reggie Miller, Indiana at New York, April 30, 1993
16—Dolph Schayes, Syracuse vs. Boston, March 25, 1959
Chet Walker, Chicago vs. Golden State, April 30, 1975
Tom Chambers, Phoenix at Utah, May 6, 1990
Kevin Johnson, Phoenix at Portland, May 7, 1992

Most free throws made, game

30—Bob Cousy, Boston vs. Syracuse, March 21, 1953 (4 ot)
23—Michael Jordan, Chicago vs. New York, May 14, 1989
22—Michael Jordan, Chicago vs. Cleveland, May 5, 1989 (ot)
Karl Malone, Utah at L.A. Clippers, May 3, 1992

Most free throws made, one half

19—Magic Johnson, L.A. Lakers vs. Golden State, May 8, 1991
Karl Malone, Utah at Portland, May 9, 1991
Charles Barkley, Phoenix vs. Seattle, June 5, 1993

Most free throws made, one quarter

13—Michael Jordan, Chicago vs. Detroit, May 21, 1991
12—Reggie Miller, Indiana at New York, April 30, 1993

Most free throw attempts, game

32—Bob Cousy, Boston vs. Syracuse, March 21, 1953 (4 ot)
28—Michael Jordan, Chicago vs. New York, May 14, 1989

Most free throw attempts, one half

21—Magic Johnson, L.A. Lakers vs. Golden State, May 8, 1991
20—Karl Malone, Utah at Portland, May 9, 1991
Charles Barkley, Phoenix vs. Seattle, June 5, 1993

Most free throw attempts, one quarter

14—Michael Jordan, Chicago vs. Detroit, May 21, 1991
13—Julius Erving, Philadelphia vs. Milwaukee, April 5, 1981
Charles Barkley, Philadelphia vs. Chicago, May 11, 1990

REBOUNDS

Highest average, rebounds per game, one playoff series

32.0—Wilt Chamberlain, Philadelphia vs. Boston, 1967 (160/5)

31.4—Wilt Chamberlain, Philadelphia vs. Boston, 1965 (200/7)
31.0—Bill Russell, Boston vs. Syracuse, 1961 (155/5)

Most rebounds, game

41—Wilt Chamberlain, Philadelphia vs. Boston, April 5, 1967
40—Bill Russell, Boston vs. Philadelphia, March 23, 1958
Bill Russell, Boston vs. St. Louis, March 29, 1960
Bill Russell, Boston vs. Los Angeles, April 18, 1962 (ot)

Most rebounds, rookie, game

35—Wilt Chamberlain, Philadelphia at Boston, March 22, 1960

Most rebounds, one half

26—Wilt Chamberlain, Philadelphia vs. San Francisco, April 16, 1967

Most rebounds, one quarter

19—Bill Russell, Boston vs. Los Angeles, April 18, 1962

Most offensive rebounds, game

15—Moses Malone, Houston vs. Washington, April 21, 1977 (ot)
13—Moses Malone, Houston at Atlanta, April 13, 1979
12—Moses Malone, Houston vs. Atlanta, April 11, 1979
Moses Malone, Houston at Seattle, April 23, 1982
Larry Smith, Golden State at L.A. Lakers, May 12, 1987
Charles Oakley, New York at Chicago, May 15, 1994

Most defensive rebounds, game

20—Dave Cowens, Boston at Houston, April 22, 1975
Dave Cowens, Boston at Philadelphia, May 1, 1977
Bill Walton, Portland at Philadelphia, June 3, 1977
Bill Walton, Portland vs. Philadelphia, June 5, 1977
19—Sam Lacey, K.C.-Omaha vs. Chicago, April 13, 1975
Dave Cowens, Boston at Buffalo, April 28, 1976
Elvin Hayes, Washington at Cleveland, April 15, 1977
Larry Bird, Boston at Philadelphia, April 23, 1980
Hakeem Olajuwon, Houston at Dallas, April 30, 1988

ASSISTS

Highest average, assists per game, one playoff series

17.0—Magic Johnson, L.A. Lakers vs. Portland, 1985 (85/5)
16.4—John Stockton, Utah vs. L.A. Lakers, 1988 (115/7)
16.2—Magic Johnson, L.A. Lakers vs. Houston, 1986 (81/5)

Most assists, game

24—Magic Johnson, Los Angeles vs. Phoenix, May 15, 1984
John Stockton, Utah at L.A. Lakers, May 17, 1988
23—Magic Johnson, L.A. Lakers at Portland, May 3, 1985
22—Doc Rivers, Atlanta vs. Boston, May 16, 1988

Most assists, rookie, game

18—Spud Webb, Atlanta vs. Detroit, April 19, 1986

Most assists, one half

15—Magic Johnson, L.A. Lakers at Portland, May 3, 1985
Doc Rivers, Atlanta vs. Boston, May 16, 1988

Most assists, one quarter

11—John Stockton, Utah vs. San Antonio, May 5, 1994

PERSONAL FOULS

Most personal fouls, game

8—Jack Toomay, Baltimore at New York, March 26, 1949 (ot)
7—Al Cervi, Syracuse at Boston, March 21, 1953 (4 ot)
6—by many

Most personal fouls, one half

6—by many

Most personal fouls, one quarter

6—Paul Mokeski, Milwaukee vs. Philadelphia, May 7, 1986
5—by many

Most minutes played, no personal fouls, game

59—Dan Majerle, Phoenix at Chicago, June 13, 1993 (3 ot)

54—Randy Wittman, Atlanta at Detroit, April 25, 1986 (2 ot)
50—Jo Jo White, Boston at Milwaukee, April 30, 1974 (ot)

DISQUALIFICATIONS

Fewest minutes played, diqualified player, game

7—Bob Lochmueller, Syracuse vs. Boston, March 19, 1953
   Will Perdue, Chicago at New York, May 14, 1992
8—Dick Schnittker, Minneapolis vs. Ft. Wayne, at Indianapolis, March 22, 1955
   Al Bianchi, Syracuse vs. Boston, March 25, 1959
   Jim Krebs, Los Angeles vs. Detroit, March 19, 1961
   Elston Turner, Denver vs. Portland, April 20, 1986
   Antoine Carr, Atlanta vs. Boston, May 15, 1988

STEALS

Most steals, game

8—Rick Barry, Golden State vs. Seattle, April 14, 1975
   Lionel Hollins, Portland at Los Angeles, May 8, 1977
   Maurice Cheeks, Philadelphia vs. New Jersey, April 11, 1979
   Craig Hodges, Milwaukee at Philadelphia, May 9, 1986
   Tim Hardaway, Golden State at L.A. Lakers, May 8, 1991
   Tim Hardaway, Golden State at Seattle, April 30, 1992
7—Rick Barry, Golden State at Chicago, May 11, 1975
   Rick Barry, Golden State vs. Detroit, April 28, 1976
   Bobby Jones, Denver at Portland, April 24, 1977
   Magic Johnson, Los Angeles vs. Portland, April 24, 1983
   Darrell Walker, New York at Detroit, April 17, 1984
   T.R. Dunn, Denver vs. Portland, April 20, 1986
   Dennis Johnson, Boston vs. Atlanta, April 29, 1986
   Derek Harper, Dallas at L.A. Lakers, April 30, 1986

Patrick Ewing, New York vs. Boston, May 4, 1990
Byron Scott, L.A. Lakers at Golden State, May 10, 1991
Charles Barkley, Phoenix vs. San Antonio, May 13, 1993
Haywoode Workman, Indiana at Orlando, April 28, 1994

BLOCKED SHOTS

Most blocked shots, game

10—Mark Eaton, Utah vs. Houston, April 26, 1985
    Hakeem Olajuwon, Houston at L.A. Lakers, April 29, 1990
9—Kareem Abdul-Jabbar, Los Angeles vs. Golden State, April 22, 1977
   Manute Bol, Washington at Philadelphia, April 18, 1986
   Hakeem Olajuwon, Houston vs. L.A. Clippers, April 29, 1993
   Derrick Coleman, New Jersey vs. Cleveland, May 7, 1993
8—by many

TURNOVERS

Most turnovers, game

11—John Williamson, New Jersey at Philadelphia, April 11, 1979
10—Quinn Buckner, Milwaukee vs. Phoenix, April 14, 1978
   Magic Johnson, Los Angeles vs. Philadelphia, May 14, 1980
   Larry Bird, Boston vs. Chicago, April 7, 1981
   Moses Malone, Philadelphia at New Jersey, April 24, 1984
   Kevin Johnson, Phoenix at L.A. Lakers, May 23, 1989
   Anfernee Hardaway, Orlando at Indiana, May 2, 1994

Most minutes played, no turnovers, game

59—Dan Majerle, Phoenix at Chicago, June 13, 1993 (3 ot)
51—Marques Johnson, Milwaukee at Seattle, April 8, 1980 (ot)
   Jeff Hornacek, Phoenix vs. Portland, May 11, 1992 (2 ot)
50—A.C. Green, L.A. Lakers at Phoenix, May 9, 1993 (ot)

ALL-TIME PLAYOFF RECORDS

NBA PLAYOFF RECORDS
Individuals (Series)

MOST POINTS

2-game series

68—Bob McAdoo, New York vs. Cleveland, 1978
65—Elgin Baylor, Minneapolis vs. Detroit, 1960
   Gus Williams, Seattle vs. Portland, 1983

3-game series

135—Michael Jordan, Chicago vs. Miami, 1992
131—Michael Jordan, Chicago vs. Boston, 1986

4-game series

150—Hakeem Olajuwon, Houston vs. Dallas, 1988
147—Michael Jordan, Chicago vs. Milwaukee, 1990

5-game series

226—Michael Jordan, Chicago vs. Cleveland, 1988
215—Michael Jordan, Chicago vs. Philadelphia, 1990

6-game series

278—Jerry West, Los Angeles vs. Baltimore, 1965
246—Michael Jordan, Chicago vs. Phoenix, 1993

7-game series

284—Elgin Baylor, Los Angeles vs. Boston, 1962
270—Wilt Chamberlain, San Francisco vs. St. Louis, 1964

MOST MINUTES PLAYED

2-game series

95—John Kerr, Syracuse vs. New York, 1959
92—John Williamson, New Jersey vs. Philadelphia, 1979
   Elvin Hayes, Washington vs. Philadelphia, 1980

3-game series

144—Wilt Chamberlain, Philadelphia vs. Syracuse, 1961

142—Wilt Chamberlain, Philadelphia vs. Syracuse, 1960
   Bill Bridges, St. Louis vs. Baltimore, 1966
   Bob McAdoo, Buffalo vs. Philadelphia, 1976
   Moses Malone, Houston vs. Los Angeles, 1981

4-game series

195—Wilt Chamberlain, Philadelphia vs. Cincinnati, 1965
   Jerry Lucas, Cincinnati vs. Philadelphia, 1965
   Oscar Robertson, Cincinnati vs. Philadelphia, 1965
   Wilt Chamberlain, Los Angeles vs. Atlanta, 1970
192—Wilt Chamberlain, Philadelphia vs. Cincinnati, 1967
   Wilt Chamberlain, Los Angeles vs. Chicago, 1972

5-game series

243—Oscar Robertson, Cincinnati vs. Syracuse, 1963
242—Kareem Abdul-Jabbar, Los Angeles vs. Seattle, 1979

6-game series

296—Wilt Chamberlain, Philadelphia vs. New York, 1968
292—Bill Russell, Boston vs. Los Angeles, 1968

7-game series

345—Kareem Abdul-Jabbar, Milwaukee vs. Boston, 1974
341—Wilt Chamberlain, Philadelphia vs. Boston, 1965

HIGHEST FIELD GOAL PERCENTAGE

(minimum: 4 FG per game)

2-game series

.773—Darryl Dawkins, New Jersey vs. New York, 1983
.750—Mike Bantom, Indiana vs. Philadelphia, 1981

3-game series

.778—Rick Mahorn, Philadelphia vs. Milwaukee, 1991
.750—Alton Lister, Milwaukee vs. New Jersey, 1986

4-game series

.739—Derrek Dickey, Golden State vs. Washington, 1975
.731—James Donaldson, Dallas vs. Houston, 1988

5-game series

.721—James Worthy, L.A. Lakers vs. Denver, 1985
.714—Bobby Jones, Philadelphia vs. Boston, 1985
   Robert Parish, Boston vs. Indiana, 1991

6-game series

.781—James Donaldson, Dallas vs. L.A. Lakers, 1986
.675—Clifford Ray, Golden State vs. Detroit, 1976

7-game series

.744—James Donaldson, Dallas vs. L.A. Lakers, 1988
.686—Robert Parish, Boston vs. Atlanta, 1988

MOST FIELD GOALS

2-game series

28—Bob McAdoo, New York vs. Cleveland, 1978
27—Jo Jo White, Boston vs. San Antonio, 1977

3-game series

53—Michael Jordan, Chicago vs. Miami, 1992
51—Wilt Chamberlain, Philadelphia vs. Syracuse, 1960

4-game series

65—Kareem Abdul-Jabbar, Milwaukee vs. Chicago, 1974
56—Hakeem Olajuwon, Houston vs. Dallas, 1988

5-game series

86—Michael Jordan, Chicago vs. Philadelphia, 1990
85—Michael Jordan, Chicago vs. Cleveland, 1988

6-game series

101—Michael Jordan, Chicago vs. Phoenix, 1993
96—Jerry West, Los Angeles vs. Baltimore, 1965

7-game series

113—Wilt Chamberlain, San Francisco vs. St. Louis, 1964
104—Bob McAdoo, Buffalo vs. Washington, 1975

MOST FIELD GOAL ATTEMPTS

2-game series

62—John Williamson, New Jersey vs. Philadelphia, 1979
53—Neil Johnston, Philadelphia vs. Syracuse, 1957
  George Yardley, Ft. Wayne vs. Minneapolis, 1957
  Elgin Baylor, Minneapolis vs. Detroit, 1960

3-game series

104—Wilt Chamberlain, Philadelphia vs. Syracuse, 1960
  96—Wilt Chamberlain, Philadelphia vs. Syracuse, 1961

4-game series

114—Earl Monroe, Baltimore vs. New York, 1969
  Dominique Wilkins, Atlanta vs. Detroit, 1986
108—Elgin Baylor, Los Angeles vs. San Francisco, 1968
  Dominique Wilkins, Atlanta vs. Indiana, 1987

5-game series

159—Wilt Chamberlain, Philadelphia vs. Syracuse, 1962
157—Michael Jordan, Chicago vs. Philadelphia, 1990

6-game series

235—Rick Barry, San Francisco vs. Philadelphia, 1967
212—Jerry West, Los Angeles vs. Baltimore, 1965

7-game series

235—Elgin Baylor, Los Angeles vs. Boston, 1962
216—Elgin Baylor, Los Angeles vs. St. Louis, 1961
  Bob McAdoo, Buffalo vs. Washington, 1975

MOST THREE-POINT FIELD GOALS MADE, NONE MISSED

2-game series

4—Kevin Grevey, Washington vs. New Jersey, 1982
1—Dudley Bradley, Indiana vs. Philadelphia, 1981
  Sly Williams, New York vs. New Jersey, 1983

3-game series

2—Mike McGee, L.A. Lakers vs. Phoenix, 1985
  Drazen Petrovic, Portland vs. Dallas, 1990
1—by many

4-game series

4—Dana Barros, Seattle vs. Golden State, 1992
2—Lafayette Lever, Denver vs. Portland, 1986
  B.J. Armstrong, Chicago vs. Detroit, 1991
  Mario Elie, Golden State vs. Seattle, 1992
  Mario Elie, Portland vs. San Antonio, 1993
  John Crotty, Utah vs. San Antonio, 1994

5-game series

4—Ricky Pierce, Milwaukee vs. Atlanta, 1989
3—Kiki Vandeweghe, New York vs. Detroit, 1992

6-game series

3—Norm Nixon, Los Angeles vs. San Antonio, 1983
  Lafayette Lever, Denver vs. Dallas, 1988
1—by many

7-game series

2—David Wingate, San Antonio vs. Portland, 1990
1—by many

MOST THREE-POINT FIELD GOALS MADE

2-game series

5—Kevin Grevey, Washington vs. Philadelphia, 1980
4—Kevin Grevey, Washington vs. New Jersey, 1982

3-game series

10—Michael Adams, Denver vs. Phoenix, 1989
  9—Byron Scott, L.A. Lakers vs. Portland, 1989
  Vernon Maxwell, Houston vs. L.A. Lakers, 1991

4-game series

10—Tim Hardaway, Golden State vs. Seattle, 1992
  Reggie Miller, Indiana vs. New York, 1993
  Vernon Maxwell, Houston vs. Portland, 1994
9—Larry Bird, Boston vs. Milwaukee, 1986
  Bob Hansen, Utah vs. Portland, 1988
  Michael Cooper, L.A. Lakers vs. Detroit, 1989
  Tim Hardaway, Golden State vs. San Antonio, 1991
  Terry Porter, Portland vs. L.A. Lakers, 1992

5-game series

17—Chuck Person, Indiana vs. Boston, 1991
16—Vernon Maxwell, Houston vs. Utah, 1994

6-game series

18—Terry Porter, Portland vs. Utah, 1992
17—Dan Majerle, Phoenix vs. Chicago, 1993

7-game series

20—Dan Majerle, Phoenix vs. Seattle, 1993
17—Derek Harper, New York vs. Houston, 1994

MOST THREE-POINT FIELD GOAL ATTEMPTS

2-game series

10—Kevin Grevey, Washington vs. Philadelphia, 1980
6—John Williamson, Washington vs. Philadelphia, 1980

3-game series

27—Vernon Maxwell, Houston vs. L.A. Lakers, 1991
23—Latrell Sprewell, Golden State vs. Phoenix, 1994

4-game series

29—Tim Hardaway, Golden State vs. Seattle, 1992
27—Michael Cooper, L.A. Lakers vs. Detroit, 1989

5-game series

39—Vernon Maxwell, Houston vs. Utah, 1994
35—Mookie Blaylock, Atlanta vs. Miami, 1994

6-game series

39—Dan Majerle, Phoenix vs. Chicago, 1993
37—Craig Hodges, Chicago vs. Detroit, 1989

7-game series

50—John Starks, New York vs. Houston, 1994
44—Dan Majerle, Phoenix vs. Houston, 1994

MOST FREE THROWS MADE, NONE MISSED

2-game series

8—Jo Jo White, Boston vs. Seattle, 1977
  Rick Barry, Houston vs. Atlanta, 1979
  Caldwell Jones, Philadelphia vs. New Jersey, 1979
  Mike Newlin, Houston vs. Atlanta, 1979
  Bobby Jones, Philadelphia vs. Washington, 1980

3-game series

18—Kiki Vandeweghe, Denver vs. Phoenix, 1982
15—Walter Davis, Denver vs. Phoenix, 1989

4-game series

32—Kiki Vandeweghe, Portland vs. Denver, 1986
27—Kevin Johnson, Phoenix vs. L.A. Lakers, 1989

5-game series

30—Mark Price, Cleveland vs. Philadelphia, 1990
25—Jeff Malone, Utah vs. Portland, 1991

6-game series

17—Bob Lanier, Milwaukee vs. New Jersey, 1984
14—Bobby Leonard, Minneapolis vs. St. Louis, 1959
  Dave Twardzik, Portland vs. Seattle, 1978

7-game series

35—Jack Sikma, Milwaukee vs. Boston, 1987
23—Calvin Murphy, Houston vs. San Antonio, 1981

MOST FREE THROWS MADE

2-game series

21—George Yardley, Detroit vs. Cincinnati, 1958
19—Larry Foust, Ft. Wayne vs. Minneapolis, 1957
  Reggie Theus, Chicago vs. New York, 1981

3-game series

43—Kevin Johnson, Phoenix vs. Denver, 1989
42—Dolph Schayes, Syracuse vs. Boston, 1957

4-game series

49—Jerry West, Los Angeles vs. Atlanta, 1970
48—Michael Jordan, Chicago vs. Milwaukee, 1985
  Sidney Moncrief, Milwaukee vs. Chicago, 1985

5-game series

62—Oscar Robertson, Cincinnati vs. Philadelphia, 1964
61—Oscar Robertson, Cincinnati vs. Boston, 1966
  Karl Malone, Utah vs. L.A. Clippers, 1992

6-game series

86—Jerry West, Los Angeles vs. Baltimore, 1965
68—Michael Jordan, Chicago vs. New York, 1989

7-game series

83—Dolph Schayes, Syracuse vs. Boston, 1959
82—Elgin Baylor, Los Angeles vs. Boston, 1962

MOST FREE THROW ATTEMPTS

2-game series

24—George Yardley, Detroit vs. Cincinnati, 1958
  Bernard King, New Jersey vs. Philadelphia, 1979
  Calvin Natt, Portland vs. Seattle, 1983
23—Larry Foust, Ft. Wayne vs. Minneapolis, 1957

3-game series

47—Dolph Schayes, Syracuse vs. Boston, 1957
46—Kevin Johnson, Phoenix vs. Denver, 1989

4-game series

58—Michael Jordan, Chicago vs. Milwaukee, 1985
57—Jerry West, Los Angeles vs. Atlanta, 1970

5-game series

79—Karl Malone, Utah vs. L.A. Clippers, 1992
72—Oscar Robertson, Cincinnati vs. Philadelphia, 1964

6-game series

95—Jerry West, Los Angeles vs. Baltimore, 1965
86—George Mikan, Minneapolis vs. Syracuse, 1950

7-game series

100—Charles Barkley, Philadelphia vs. Milwaukee, 1986
99—Elgin Baylor, Los Angeles vs. Boston, 1962

MOST REBOUNDS

2-game series

41—Moses Malone, Houston vs. Atlanta, 1979
39—John Kerr, Syracuse vs. Philadelphia, 1957

3-game series
84—Bill Russell, Boston vs. Syracuse, 1957
69—Wilt Chamberlain, Philadelphia vs. Syracuse, 1961

4-game series
118—Bill Russell, Boston vs. Minneapolis, 1959
106—Wilt Chamberlain, Philadelphia vs. Cincinnati, 1967

5-game series
160—Wilt Chamberlain, Philadelphia vs. Boston, 1967
155—Bill Russell, Boston vs. Syracuse, 1961

6-game series
171—Wilt Chamberlain, Philadelphia vs. San Francisco, 1967
165—Wilt Chamberlain, Philadelphia vs. Boston, 1960

7-game series
220—Wilt Chamberlain, Philadelphia vs. Boston, 1965
189—Bill Russell, Boston vs. Los Angeles, 1962

MOST OFFENSIVE REBOUNDS

2-game series
25—Moses Malone, Houston vs. Atlanta, 1979
13—Dan Roundfield, Atlanta vs. Houston, 1979
    Lonnie Shelton, Seattle vs. Portland, 1983

3-game series
28—Moses Malone, Houston vs. Seattle, 1982
22—Karl Malone, Utah vs. Golden State, 1989

4-game series
27—Moses Malone, Philadelphia vs. Los Angeles, 1983
25—Shawn Kemp, Seattle vs. Golden State, 1992

5-game series
36—Larry Smith, Golden State vs. L.A. Lakers, 1987
35—Charles Barkley, Philadelphia vs. Chicago, 1990

6-game series
46—Moses Malone, Houston vs. Boston, 1981
45—Moses Malone, Houston vs. Philadelphia, 1977

7-game series
45—Wes Unseld, Washington vs. San Antonio, 1979
44—Roy Tarpley, Dallas vs. L.A. Lakers, 1988

MOST DEFENSIVE REBOUNDS

2-game series
23—Wes Unseld, Washington vs. Atlanta, 1978
21—Wes Unseld, Washington vs. Philadelphia, 1980

3-game series
43—Bob McAdoo, Buffalo vs. Philadelphia, 1976
41—Elvin Hayes, Washington vs. Cleveland, 1977
    Tom Chambers, Phoenix vs. Denver, 1989

4-game series
62—Kareem Abdul-Jabbar, Milwaukee vs. Chicago, 1974
53—Wes Unseld, Washington vs. Golden State, 1975

5-game series
62—Jack Sikma, Seattle vs. Washington, 1979
    Karl Malone, Utah vs. Portland, 1991
61—Kareem Abdul-Jabbar, Milwaukee vs. Los Angeles, 1974

6-game series
91—Bill Walton, Portland vs. Philadelphia, 1977
79—Sam Lacey, K.C.-Omaha vs. Chicago, 1975

7-game series
95—Kareem Abdul-Jabbar, Los Angeles vs. Golden State, 1977
86—Dave Cowens, Boston vs. Philadelphia, 1977

MOST ASSISTS

2-game series
20—Frank Johnson, Washington vs. New Jersey, 1982
19—Paul Westphal, Phoenix vs. Milwaukee, 1978

3-game series
48—Magic Johnson, Los Angeles vs. San Antonio, 1986
47—Kevin Johnson, Phoenix vs. San Antonio, 1992

4-game series
57—Magic Johnson, L.A. Lakers vs. Phoenix, 1989
54—Magic Johnson, L.A. Lakers vs. Houston, 1990

5-game series
85—Magic Johnson, L.A. Lakers vs. Portland, 1985
81—Magic Johnson, L.A. Lakers vs. Houston, 1986

6-game series
90—Johnny Moore, San Antonio vs. Los Angeles, 1983
87—Magic Johnson, Los Angeles vs. Phoenix, 1984

7-game series
115—John Stockton, Utah vs. L.A. Lakers, 1988
96—Magic Johnson, L.A. Lakers vs. Dallas, 1988

MOST PERSONAL FOULS

2-game series
12—Bob Lochmueller, Syracuse vs. Boston, 1953
    Walter Dukes, Detroit vs. Cincinnati, 1958
    Ray Felix, New York vs. Syracuse, 1959
    Dave Cowens, Boston vs. San Antonio, 1977
    Dan Roundfield, Atlanta vs. Houston, 1979
    Albert King, New Jersey vs. New York, 1983
    Buck Williams, New Jersey vs. New York, 1983

3-game series
18—Charlie Share, St. Louis vs. Minneapolis, 1956
    Vern Mikkelsen, Minneapolis vs. St. Louis, 1957
17—Walter Dukes, Minneapolis vs. St. Louis, 1957
    Paul Arizin, Philadelphia vs. Syracuse, 1961
    Larry Costello, Syracuse vs. Philadelphia, 1961
    Kevin Duckworth, Portland vs. L.A. Lakers, 1989
    Sam Perkins, Dallas vs. Portland, 1990
    Jay Humphries, Milwaukee vs. Philadelphia, 1991

4-game series
22—Al Attles, San Francisco vs. Los Angeles, 1968
    Doc Rivers, Atlanta vs. Detroit, 1986
21—Hakeem Olajuwon, Houston vs. Portland, 1987
    Mark Eaton, Utah vs. Portland, 1988
    Roy Tarpley, Dallas vs. Houston, 1988

5-game series
27—George Mikan, Minneapolis vs. New York, 1953
    Red Rocha, Syracuse vs. Philadelphia, 1956
    Larry Costello, Syracuse vs. Cincinnati, 1963
26—Tom Gola, Philadelphia vs. Syracuse, 1962
    Bailey Howell, Boston vs. Philadelphia, 1969

6-game series
35—Charlie Scott, Boston vs. Phoenix, 1976
33—Tom Heinsohn, Boston vs. St. Louis, 1958
    Tom Meschery, San Francisco vs. Philadelphia, 1967

7-game series
37—Arnie Risen, Boston vs. St. Louis, 1957
    Tom Sanders, Boston vs. Philadelphia, 1965
36—Vern Mikkelsen, Minneapolis vs. New York, 1952
    Jack McMahon, St. Louis vs. Boston, 1957

MOST DISQUALIFICATIONS

2-game series
2—Bob Lochmueller, Syracuse vs. Boston, 1953
    Walter Dukes, Detroit vs. Cincinnati, 1958

Ray Felix, New York vs. Syracuse, 1959
Dave Cowens, Boston vs. San Antonio, 1977
Dan Roundfield, Atlanta vs. Houston, 1979
Albert King, New Jersey vs. New York, 1983
Buck Williams, New Jersey vs. New York, 1983

3-game series
3—Charlie Share, St. Louis vs. Minneapolis, 1956
    Vern Mikkelsen, Minneapolis vs. St. Louis, 1957

4-game series
2—Walter Dukes, Detroit vs. Cincinnati, 1962
    Zelmo Beaty, St. Louis vs. Detroit, 1963
    Al Attles, San Francisco vs. Los Angeles, 1968
    Lou Hudson, Atlanta vs. Los Angeles, 1970
    Dennis Johnson, Phoenix vs. Los Angeles, 1982
    Lonnie Shelton, Cleveland vs. Boston, 1985
    Ben Poquette, Cleveland vs. Boston, 1985
    Sam Bowie, Portland vs. Dallas, 1985
    Doc Rivers, Atlanta vs. Detroit, 1986
    Alton Lister, Seattle vs. L.A. Lakers, 1987
    Mark Eaton, Utah vs. Portland, 1988
    Greg Anderson, Milwaukee vs. Chicago, 1990
    Tyrone Hill, Golden State vs. San Antonio, 1991

5-game series
5—Art Hillhouse, Philadelphia vs. Chicago, 1947
4—Chuck Gilmur, Chicago vs. Philadelphia, 1947

6-game series
5—Charlie Scott, Boston vs. Phoenix, 1976

7-game series
5—Arnie Risen, Boston vs. St. Louis, 1957
4—Frank Ramsey, Boston vs. Syracuse, 1959
    Hal Greer, Philadelphia vs. Baltimore, 1971

MOST STEALS

2-game series
10—Maurice Cheeks, Philadelphia vs. New Jersey, 1979
    9—Maurice Cheeks, Philadelphia vs. Indiana, 1981

3-game series
13—Clyde Drexler, Portland vs. Dallas, 1990
    Hersey Hawkins, Philadelphia vs. Milwaukee, 1991
12—Alvin Robertson, San Antonio vs. L.A. Lakers, 1988

4-game series
17—Lionel Hollins, Portland vs. Los Angeles, 1977
15—Mookie Blaylock, New Jersey vs. Cleveland, 1992

5-game series
21—Micheal Ray Richardson, New Jersey vs. Philadelphia, 1984
20—Michael Jordan, Chicago vs. Philadelphia, 1990
    Isiah Thomas, Detroit vs. Washington, 1988

6-game series
19—Rick Barry, Golden State vs. Seattle, 1975
18—Slick Watts, Seattle vs. Golden State, 1975
    Gus Williams, Seattle vs. Portland, 1978

7-game series
28—John Stockton, Utah vs. L.A. Lakers, 1988
27—Maurice Cheeks, Philadelphia vs. San Antonio, 1979

MOST BLOCKED SHOTS

2-game series
10—Darryl Dawkins, Philadelphia vs. Atlanta, 1982
9—Artis Gilmore, Chicago vs. New York, 1981

3-game series
18—Manute Bol, Golden State vs. Utah, 1989
15—Kareem Abdul-Jabbar, Los Angeles vs. Denver, 1979

4-game series
23—Hakeem Olajuwon, Houston vs. L.A. Lakers, 1990
20—Hakeem Olajuwon, Houston vs. Portland, 1987

5-game series
31—Dikembe Mutombo, Denver vs. Seattle, 1994
29—Mark Eaton, Utah vs. Houston, 1985
Manute Bol, Washington vs. Philadelphia, 1986
Hakeem Olajuwon, Houston vs. L.A. Clippers, 1993

6-game series
27—Marvin Webster, Seattle vs. Denver, 1978
23—Kareem Abdul-Jabbar, Los Angeles vs. Philadelphia, 1980
Hakeem Olajuwon, Houston vs. Seattle, 1987

7-game series
38—Dikembe Mutombo, Denver vs. Utah, 1994
30—Hakeem Olajuwon, Houston vs. Seattle, 1993
Patrick Ewing, New York vs. Houston, 1994

MOST TURNOVERS
2-game series
14—John Williamson, New Jersey vs. Philadelphia, 1979
12—Wes Unseld, Washington vs. Atlanta, 1978
Frank Johnson, Washington vs. New Jersey, 1982

3-game series
20—Anfernee Hardaway, Orlando vs. Indiana, 1994
17—Walter Davis, Phoenix vs. Portland, 1979

4-game series
24—Magic Johnson, Los Angeles vs. Philadelphia, 1983
23—Jeff Ruland, Washington vs. Philadelphia, 1985

5-game series
29—Larry Bird, Boston vs. Milwaukee, 1984
28—Charles Barkley, Philadelphia vs. Washington, 1986

6-game series
30—Magic Johnson, Los Angeles vs. Philadelphia, 1980
Sidney Moncrief, Milwaukee vs. New Jersey, 1984
29—George McGinnis, Philadelphia vs. Washington, 1978

7-game series
37—Charles Barkley, Philadelphia vs. Milwaukee, 1986
34—John Johnson, Seattle vs. Phoenix, 1979

TEAM (SERIES)
MOST POINTS
2-game series
260—Syracuse vs. New York, 1959
241—Minneapolis vs. Ft. Wayne, 1957
New York vs. Cleveland, 1978

3-game series
408—L.A. Lakers vs. Phoenix, 1985
407—L.A. Lakers vs. Denver, 1987

4-game series
498—Philadelphia vs. New York, 1978
492—Portland vs. Dallas, 1985

5-game series
664—San Antonio vs. Denver, 1983
662—L.A. Lakers vs. Denver, 1985

6-game series
747—Philadelphia vs. San Francisco, 1967
735—Los Angeles vs. Detroit, 1962

7-game series
869—Boston vs. Syracuse, 1959
867—Boston vs. Cincinnati, 1963

FEWEST POINTS
2-game series
171—Atlanta vs. Philadelphia, 1982
175—New Jersey vs. Washington, 1982

3-game series
258—New York vs. Chicago, 1991
261—Houston vs. Seattle, 1982

4-game series
346—New Jersey vs. New York, 1994
352—San Antonio vs. Utah, 1994

5-game series
424—Detroit vs. New York, 1992
431—Kansas City vs. Houston, 1981

6-game series
511—Atlanta vs. Indiana, 1994
520—Houston vs. Boston, 1981

7-game series
603—Houston vs. New York, 1994
608—New York vs. Houston, 1994

HIGHEST FIELD GOAL PERCENTAGE
2-game series
.555—New York vs. Cleveland, 1978
.541—Philadelphia vs. Atlanta, 1982

3-game series
.600—L.A. Lakers vs. Phoenix, 1985
.596—L.A. Lakers vs. San Antonio, 1986

4-game series
.561—Milwaukee vs. Chicago, 1974
.554—Boston vs. Chicago, 1981

5-game series
.565—L.A. Lakers vs. Denver, 1985
.560—Los Angeles vs. Dallas, 1984

6-game series
.536—Los Angeles vs. Phoenix, 1984
.534—L.A. Lakers vs. Dallas, 1986

7-game series
.534—L.A. Lakers vs. Dallas, 1988
.526—Detroit vs. Boston, 1987

LOWEST FIELD GOAL PERCENTAGE
2-game series
.321—Cincinnati vs. Detroit, 1958
.355—Philadelphia vs. Syracuse, 1957

3-game series
.308—Syracuse vs. Boston, 1957
.324—Syracuse vs. Philadelphia, 1958

4-game series
.323—Minneapolis vs. Ft. Wayne, 1955
.357—New Jersey vs. New York, 1994

5-game series
.348—Syracuse vs. Boston, 1961
.352—Cincinnati vs. Boston, 1964

6-game series
.355—Boston vs. St. Louis, 1958
.363—San Francisco vs. Los Angeles, 1969

7-game series
.339—Syracuse vs. Ft. Wayne, 1955
.369—Boston vs. St. Louis, 1957

MOST FIELD GOALS
2-game series
101—New York vs. Cleveland, 1978
93—Minneapolis vs. Ft. Wayne, 1957

3-game series
165—L.A. Lakers vs. Phoenix, 1985
156—San Antonio vs. Denver, 1990

4-game series
206—Portland vs. Dallas, 1985
198—Milwaukee vs. Chicago, 1974

5-game series
274—San Antonio vs. Denver, 1983
L.A. Lakers vs. Denver, 1985
252—Los Angeles vs. Dallas, 1984

6-game series
293—Boston vs. Atlanta, 1972
292—Houston vs. Denver, 1986

7-game series
333—Boston vs. Cincinnati, 1963
332—New York vs. Los Angeles, 1970
Milwaukee vs. Denver, 1978

FEWEST FIELD GOALS
2-game series
63—Atlanta vs. Philadelphia, 1982
69—Cincinnati vs. Detroit, 1958

3-game series
88—Syracuse vs. Boston, 1957
93—St. Louis vs. Minneapolis, 1956

4-game series
107—New Jersey vs. New York, 1994
118—Minneapolis vs. Ft. Wayne, 1955

5-game series
155—St. Louis vs. Ft. Wayne, 1956
158—Detroit vs. New York, 1992

6-game series
194—Chicago vs. Detroit, 1989
200—Atlanta vs. Indiana, 1994

7-game series
207—Syracuse vs. Ft. Wayne, 1955
213—New York vs. Indiana, 1994

MOST FIELD GOAL ATTEMPTS
2-game series
248—New York vs. Syracuse, 1959
215—Cincinnati vs. Detroit, 1958
Detroit vs. Minneapolis, 1960

3-game series
349—Philadelphia vs. Syracuse, 1960
344—Minneapolis vs. St. Louis, 1957

4-game series
464—Minneapolis vs. Boston, 1959
463—Boston vs. Minneapolis, 1959

5-game series
568—Boston vs. Los Angeles, 1965
565—Boston vs. Philadelphia, 1967

6-game series

743—San Francisco vs. Philadelphia, 1967
712—Boston vs. Philadelphia, 1960

7-game series

835—Boston vs. Syracuse, 1959
799—Boston vs. St. Louis, 1957

FEWEST FIELD GOAL ATTEMPTS

2-game series

150—Atlanta vs. Philadelphia, 1982
157—Milwaukee vs. Phoenix, 1978
      Philadelphia vs. Atlanta, 1982

3-game series

219—New York vs. Chicago, 1991
228—Indiana vs. Detroit, 1990
      Chicago vs. Cleveland, 1994

4-game series

288—Indiana vs. Atlanta, 1987
293—Milwaukee vs. Chicago, 1990
      Chicago vs. Detroit, 1991

5-game series

366—Philadelphia vs. Chicago, 1991
368—Kansas City vs. Houston, 1981

6-game series

417—New York vs. Chicago, 1993
437—Chicago vs. Detroit, 1989

7-game series

499—New York vs. Indiana, 1994
504—Indiana vs. New York, 1994

MOST THREE-POINT FIELD GOALS MADE

2-game series

7—Washington vs. Philadelphia, 1980
4—Washington vs. New Jersey, 1992

3-game series

20—Indiana vs. Boston, 1992
      Orlando vs. Indiana, 1994
18—L.A. Lakers vs. Portland, 1989

4-game series

31—Houston vs. Portland, 1994
20—Golden State vs. San Antonio, 1991

5-game series

37—Houston vs. Utah, 1994
28—Denver vs. Seattle, 1994

6-game series

32—Portland vs. Utah, 1992
      Chicago vs. Phoenix, 1993
30—New York vs. Chicago, 1989
      Indiana vs. Atlanta, 1994

7-game series

49—Phoenix vs. Houston, 1994
44—Houston vs. Phoenix, 1994

MOST THREE-POINT FIELD GOAL ATTEMPTS

2-game series

19—Washington vs. Philadelphia, 1980
10—New York vs. Chicago, 1981

3-game series

55—Orlando vs. Indiana, 1994
45—Indiana vs. Boston, 1992

4-game series

71—Houston vs. Portland, 1994
52—Golden State vs. San Antonio, 1991

5-game series

98—Houston vs. Utah, 1994
71—Denver vs. Seattle, 1994

6-game series

81—New York vs. Chicago, 1989
79—Chicago vs. Detroit, 1989

7-game series

140—Phoenix vs. Houston, 1994
121—Houston vs. New York, 1994

HIGHEST FREE THROW PERCENTAGE

2-game series

.865—Syracuse vs. New York, 1959
.839—Chicago vs. New York, 1981

3-game series

.872—Denver vs. San Antonio, 1990
.852—Chicago vs. Boston, 1987

4-game series

.882—Houston vs. Boston, 1980
.869—Cincinnati vs. Philadelphia, 1965

5-game series

.894—Dallas vs. Seattle, 1984
.881—Utah vs. Portland, 1991

6-game series

.849—Boston vs. Detroit, 1985
.824—Los Angeles vs. Baltimore, 1965

7-game series

.840—Syracuse vs. Boston, 1959
.839—Cleveland vs. Boston, 1992

LOWEST FREE THROW PERCENTAGE

2-game series

.610—New Jersey vs. Washington, 1982
.629—San Antonio vs. Boston, 1977

3-game series

.611—Baltimore vs. St. Louis, 1966
.618—Kansas City vs. Phoenix, 1980

4-game series

.657—Seattle vs. L.A. Lakers, 1989
.667—Houston vs. L.A. Lakers, 1990

5-game series

.567—Houston vs. Utah, 1985
.613—Los Angeles vs. Milwaukee, 1971

6-game series

.603—Philadelphia vs. Boston, 1960
.613—Philadelphia vs. San Francisco, 1967

7-game series

.582—San Francisco vs. St. Louis, 1964
.606—Philadelphia vs. Boston, 1968

MOST FREE THROWS MADE

2-game series

90—Syracuse vs. New York, 1959
62—Detroit vs. Cincinnati, 1958

3-game series

131—Minneapolis vs. St. Louis, 1956
121—St. Louis vs. Minneapolis, 1956

4-game series

147—Los Angeles vs. San Francisco, 1968
144—L.A. Lakers vs. Seattle, 1987

5-game series

183—Philadelphia vs. Syracuse, 1956
176—Boston vs. Syracuse, 1961

6-game series

232—Boston vs. St. Louis, 1958
215—St. Louis vs. Boston, 1958

7-game series

244—St. Louis vs. Boston, 1957
239—Los Angeles vs. Boston, 1962

FEWEST FREE THROWS MADE

2-game series

25—New Jersey vs. Washington, 1982
31—Phoenix vs. Milwaukee, 1978
      Washington vs. Philadelphia, 1980

3-game series

37—Kansas City vs. Portland, 1981
38—Seattle vs. Detroit, 1975
      Portland vs. Chicago, 1977
      Houston vs. L.A. Lakers, 1991

4-game series

46—Milwaukee vs. Chicago, 1974
52—Baltimore vs. Milwaukee, 1971

5-game series

63—Seattle vs. Dallas, 1984
70—Baltimore vs. New York, 1973

6-game series

82—Chicago vs. Phoenix, 1993
84—Cleveland vs. Boston, 1976

7-game series

100—Milwaukee vs. Boston, 1974
102—New York vs. Capital, 1974
      Golden State vs. Chicago, 1975
      Boston vs. Cleveland, 1992

MOST FREE THROW ATTEMPTS

2-game series

104—Syracuse vs. New York, 1959
  82—Detroit vs. Cincinnati, 1958

3-game series

174—St. Louis vs. Minneapolis, 1956
173—Minnneapolis vs. St. Louis, 1956

4-game series

186—Syracuse vs. Boston, 1955
180—Minneapolis vs. Ft. Wayne, 1955

5-game series

238—Philadelphia vs. Syracuse, 1956
232—Boston vs. Syracuse, 1961

6-game series

298—Boston vs. St. Louis, 1958
292—St. Louis vs. Boston, 1958

7-game series
341—St. Louis vs. Boston, 1957
303—Cincinnati vs. Boston, 1963

FEWEST FREE THROW ATTEMPTS

2-game series
38—Phoenix vs. Milwaukee, 1978
40—Atlanta vs. Washington, 1978

3-game series
49—Houston vs. L.A. Lakers, 1991
51—Seattle vs. Detroit, 1975
    Kansas City vs. Portland, 1981

4-game series
57—Milwaukee vs. Chicago, 1974
69—Boston vs. Charlotte, 1993

5-game series
88—Seattle vs. Dallas, 1984
92—Milwaukee vs. Los Angeles, 1974
    Chicago vs. L.A. Lakers, 1991

6-game series
105—Boston vs. Buffalo, 1974
116—Houston vs. Washington, 1977

7-game series
128—New York vs. Capital, 1974
133—Boston vs. Cleveland, 1992

HIGHEST REBOUND PERCENTAGE

2-game series
.585—Boston vs. San Antonio, 1977
.559—Washington vs. Atlanta, 1978

3-game series
.652—L.A. Lakers vs. San Antonio, 1986
.590—Boston vs. Indiana, 1992

4-game series
.585—Portland vs. L.A. Lakers, 1992
.572—Detroit vs. Milwaukee, 1989

5-game series
.591—Boston vs. New York, 1974
.577—Seattle vs. Los Angeles, 1979

6-game series
.580—Los Angeles vs. Philadelphia, 1980
.570—Boston vs. Phoenix, 1976

7-game series
.5561—San Francisco vs. St. Louis, 1964
.5556—Seattle vs. Phoenix, 1979

MOST REBOUNDS

2-game series
137—New York vs. Syracuse, 1959
127—Cincinnati vs. Detroit, 1958
    Detroit vs. Cincinnati, 1958

3-game series
225—Philadelphia vs. Syracuse, 1960
212—San Francisco vs. Los Angeles, 1967

4-game series
295—Boston vs. Minneapolis, 1959
268—Minneapolis vs. Boston, 1959

5-game series
396—Boston vs. Syracuse, 1961
371—Boston vs. Philadelphia, 1958

6-game series
457—Boston vs. Philadelphia, 1960
435—San Francisco vs. Philadelphia, 1967

7-game series
525—Boston vs. Syracuse, 1959
517—Boston vs. Philadelphia, 1962

FEWEST REBOUNDS

2-game series
71—Atlanta vs. Philadelphia, 1982
76—San Antonio vs. Boston, 1977

3-game series
79—San Antonio vs. L.A. Lakers, 1986
99—Miami vs. Chicago, 1992

4-game series
134—Milwaukee vs. Chicago, 1990
135—L.A. Lakers vs. Portland, 1992

5-game series
176—Kansas City vs. Houston, 1981
    Seattle vs. Utah, 1992
178—L.A. Lakers vs. Chicago, 1991
    Philadelphia vs. Chicago, 1991

6-game series
201—Chicago vs. New York, 1993
214—L.A. Lakers vs. Portland, 1991

7-game series
248—Chicago vs. New York, 1992
250—Houston vs. San Antonio, 1981

MOST OFFENSIVE REBOUNDS

2-game series
51—Houston vs. Atlanta, 1979
43—Philadelphia vs. New Jersey, 1979

3-game series
72—Golden State vs. Detroit, 1977
65—Sacramento vs. Houston, 1986

4-game series
77—Seattle vs. L.A. Lakers, 1989
76—San Antonio vs. Los Angeles, 1982
    Seattle vs. L.A. Lakers, 1987
    Portland vs. Utah, 1988

5-game series
111—Phoenix vs. Golden State, 1989
110—Houston vs. Utah, 1985

6-game series
124—Golden State vs. Detroit, 1976
117—Washington vs. Philadelphia, 1978

7-game series
142—Washington vs. San Antonio, 1979
141—Boston vs. Philadelphia, 1982

FEWEST OFFENSIVE REBOUNDS

2-game series
19—Milwaukee vs. Phoenix, 1978
22—Portland vs. Seattle, 1983

3-game series
20—Milwaukee vs. Detroit, 1976

21—Portland vs. Chicago, 1977
    San Antonio vs. L.A. Lakers, 1986

4-game series
33—Utah vs. Portland, 1988
34—Golden State vs. San Antonio, 1991

5-game series
40—Los Angeles vs. Seattle, 1979
46—Cleveland vs. Philadelphia, 1990

6-game series
54—K.C.-Omaha vs. Chicago, 1975
    Phoenix vs. San Antonio, 1993
56—Buffalo vs. Boston, 1976

7-game series
62—Houston vs. Phoenix, 1994
66—Cleveland vs. Boston, 1992

MOST DEFENSIVE REBOUNDS

2-game series
79—Boston vs. San Antonio, 1977
77—Milwaukee vs. Phoenix, 1978

3-game series
119—L.A. Lakers vs. Denver, 1987
118—Phoenix vs. Denver, 1989
    San Antonio vs. Denver, 1990

4-game series
161—New York vs. Philadelphia, 1978
158—Milwaukee vs. Chicago, 1974

5-game series
208—San Antonio vs. Denver, 1983
197—Boston vs. New York, 1974

6-game series
240—Boston vs. Phoenix, 1976
234—Golden State vs. Phoenix, 1976

7-game series
246—Houston vs. Phoenix, 1994
245—Washington vs. Cleveland, 1976
    Washington vs. San Antonio, 1979

FEWEST DEFENSIVE REBOUNDS

2-game series
45—Atlanta vs. Philadelphia, 1982
49—Cleveland vs. New York, 1978

3-game series
58—San Antonio vs. L.A. Lakers, 1986
66—Miami vs. Chicago, 1992

4-game series
84—Detroit vs. Chicago, 1991
89—Seattle vs. L.A. Lakers, 1987

5-game series
108—Golden State vs. L.A. Lakers, 1987
112—Seattle vs. Utah, 1992

6-game series
134—Milwaukee vs. Philadelphia, 1982
138—Chicago vs. New York, 1993

7-game series
162—Dallas vs. L.A. Lakers, 1988
165—Chicago vs. New York, 1992

MOST ASSISTS

2-game series
62—New York vs. Cleveland, 1978
    Philadelphia vs. New Jersey, 1979
59—Boston vs. San Antonio, 1977

3-game series
107—L.A. Lakers vs. Denver, 1987
104—L.A. Lakers vs. Phoenix, 1985

4-game series
129—Los Angeles vs. San Antonio, 1982
123—Portland vs. Dallas, 1985

5-game series
181—San Antonio vs. Denver, 1983
179—L.A. Lakers vs. Denver, 1985

6-game series
197—Los Angeles vs. Phoenix, 1984
196—Los Angeles vs. San Antonio, 1983

7-game series
233—Milwaukee vs. Denver, 1978
218—Los Angeles vs. Phoenix, 1970

FEWEST ASSISTS

2-game series
24—Cincinnati vs. Detroit, 1958
30—Detroit vs. Cincinnati, 1958

3-game series
36—Syracuse vs. Philadelphia, 1958
39—Syracuse vs. Boston, 1957

4-game series
58—Minneapolis vs. Ft. Wayne, 1955
62—Baltimore vs. New York, 1969

5-game series
72—Miami vs. Atlanta, 1994
77—Chicago vs. Los Angeles, 1968

6-game series
93—Minneapolis vs. St. Louis, 1959
96—Detroit vs. Boston, 1968

7-game series
105—Washington vs. Cleveland, 1976
116—Denver vs. Utah, 1994

MOST PERSONAL FOULS

2-game series
70—New York vs. Syracuse, 1959
    Atlanta vs. Philadelphia, 1982

3-game series
99—Minneapolis vs. St. Louis, 1957
98—New Jersey vs. Milwaukee, 1986

4-game series
126—Detroit vs. Chicago, 1991
124—New York vs. Philadelphia, 1978
    Portland vs. Denver, 1986

5-game series
165—Syracuse vs. Boston, 1961
157—Los Angeles vs. Detroit, 1961

6-game series
197—Boston vs. Philadelphia, 1962
    Milwaukee vs. New Jersey, 1984

7-game series
221—Boston vs. St. Louis, 1957
216—Boston vs. Cincinnati, 1963

FEWEST PERSONAL FOULS

2-game series
40—Milwaukee vs. Phoenix, 1978
41—Philadelphia vs. Washington, 1980

3-game series
55—Chicago vs. New York, 1991
    L.A. Lakers vs. Houston, 1991
56—Phoenix vs. Golden State, 1994

4-game series
69—Chicago vs. Milwaukee, 1974
72—Philadelphia vs. Cincinnati, 1967

5-game series
89—Philadelphia vs. Boston, 1958
90—Los Angeles vs. Philadelphia, 1971

6-game series
108—Los Angeles vs. Milwaukee, 1972
116—L.A. Lakers vs. Portland, 1991

7-game series
124—Cleveland vs. Boston, 1992
133—Seattle vs. Houston, 1993

MOST DISQUALIFICATIONS

2-game series
4—New York vs. Syracuse, 1959
    New Jersey vs. New York, 1983
3—San Antonio vs. Boston, 1977
    Atlanta vs. Philadelphia, 1982

3-game series
8—Minneapolis vs. St. Louis, 1957
7—St. Louis vs. Minneapolis, 1956

4-game series
5—Minneapolis vs. Ft. Wayne, 1955
    Cleveland vs. Philadelphia, 1985
    Atlanta vs. Detroit, 1986
4—St. Louis vs. Detroit, 1963
    New York vs. Boston, 1967
    Milwaukee vs. Philadelphia, 1985
    Portland vs. Dallas, 1985
    Seattle vs. Dallas, 1987

5-game series
9—Chicago vs. Philadelphia, 1947
8—Philadelphia vs. Chicago, 1947

6-game series
11—Boston vs. St. Louis, 1958
10—Detroit vs. Los Angeles, 1962

7-game series
10—Boston vs. St. Louis, 1957
9—Minneapolis vs. New York, 1952
    St. Louis vs. Boston, 1957
    Boston vs. Los Angeles, 1962

MOST STEALS

2-game series
23—Philadelphia vs. Washington, 1980
22—Indiana vs. Philadelphia, 1981
    Philadelphia vs. Indiana, 1981

3-game series
38—Indiana vs. Orlando, 1994
37—Chicago vs. New York, 1991

MOST STEALS (continued)

4-game series
57—Portland vs. Los Angeles, 1977
55—Golden State vs. Washington, 1975

5-game series
66—Kansas City vs. Phoenix, 1979
59—Golden State vs. L.A. Lakers, 1987

6-game series
81—Golden State vs. Seattle, 1975
71—Philadelphia vs. Portland, 1977

7-game series
92—Golden State vs. Phoenix, 1976
78—Los Angeles vs. Golden State, 1977

FEWEST STEALS

2-game series
10—New York vs. Cleveland, 1978
    Atlanta vs. Washington, 1982
11—Portland vs. Seattle, 1983
    Seattle vs. Portland, 1983

3-game series
11—Indiana vs. Detroit, 1990
12—Denver vs. Phoenix, 1983

4-game series
10—Detroit vs. Milwaukee, 1989
16—Detroit vs. L.A. Lakers, 1989

5-game series
17—Dallas vs. Seattle, 1984
19—Boston vs. New York, 1974

6-game series
24—Detroit vs. Boston, 1991
26—Boston vs. Detroit, 1991

7-game series
21—Milwaukee vs. Boston, 1974
25—Detroit vs. Chicago, 1974

MOST BLOCKED SHOTS

2-game series
22—Philadelphia vs. Atlanta, 1982
20—Houston vs. Atlanta, 1979

3-game series
34—L.A. Lakers vs. Denver, 1987
    Golden State vs. Utah, 1989
32—Los Angeles vs. Kansas City, 1984

4-game series
35—Seattle vs. Houston, 1989
32—Golden State vs. Washington, 1975
    Los Angeles vs. San Antonio, 1982
    Philadelphia vs. Los Angeles, 1983
    Seattle vs. Dallas, 1987

5-game series
53—Boston vs. Washington, 1982
48—Denver vs. Seattle, 1994

6-game series
60—Philadelphia vs. Los Angeles, 1980
52—Phoenix vs. San Antonio, 1993

7-game series
71—Denver vs. Utah, 1994
62—Philadelphia vs. Milwaukee, 1981

FEWEST BLOCKED SHOTS

2-game series
4—New York vs. Chicago, 1981

5—Boston vs. San Antonio, 1977
  Indiana vs. Philadelphia, 1981
3-game series
3—Cleveland vs. Chicago, 1994
4—Seattle vs. Los Angeles, 1978
4-game series
6—Indiana vs. Atlanta, 1987
8—Boston vs. Milwaukee, 1983
  Milwaukee vs. Detroit, 1989
5-game series
10—Houston vs. Boston, 1975
11—New York vs. Boston, 1974
  Milwaukee vs. Atlanta, 1989
6-game series
10—Boston vs. Phoenix, 1976
11—Boston vs. Washington, 1975
7-game series
5—Boston vs. Milwaukee, 1974
21—Boston vs. Philadelphia, 1977
  L.A. Lakers vs. Detroit, 1988

MOST TURNOVERS
2-game series
47—Boston vs. San Antonio, 1977
46—Philadelphia vs. New Jersey, 1979
3-game series
82—Chicago vs. Portland, 1977
67—New York vs. Chicago, 1991
4-game series
94—Golden State vs. Washington, 1975
92—Milwaukee vs. Baltimore, 1971
5-game series
128—Phoenix vs. Kansas City, 1979
113—San Antonio vs. Denver, 1985
6-game series
149—Portland vs. Philadelphia, 1977
144—Boston vs. Phoenix, 1976
7-game series
147—Phoenix vs. Golden State, 1976
146—Seattle vs. Phoenix, 1979

FEWEST TURNOVERS
2-game series
23—Seattle vs. Portland, 1983
24—Portland vs. Seattle, 1983
3-game series
28—Houston vs. Seattle, 1982
31—Boston vs. Chicago, 1987
4-game series
36—Milwaukee vs. Detroit, 1989
44—Utah vs. Dallas, 1986
5-game series
52—Chicago vs. Philadelphia, 1991
55—Chicago vs. Los Angeles, 1972
6-game series
46—Detroit vs. Boston, 1991
60—Boston vs. Detroit, 1991
7-game series
76—Atlanta vs. Boston, 1988
77—Utah vs. Denver, 1994

ALL-TIME PLAYOFF RECORDS
TEAM RECORDS

WON-LOST

Most consecutive games won, all playoff series
13—L.A. Lakers, 1988-89
12—Detroit, 1989-90

Most consecutive games won, one year
11—L.A. Lakers, 1989
9—Los Angeles, 1982

Most consecutive games won at home, all playoff series
15—Chicago, 1990-91
14—Minneapolis, 1949-51
  Boston, 1986-87
  Detroit, 1989-90

Most consecutive games won at home, one year
10—Portland, 1977
  Boston, 1986
  L.A. Lakers, 1987
  Detroit, 1990
9—Boston, 1976
  Seattle, 1978
  Boston, 1984
  Boston, 1985
  Portland, 1990

Most consecutive games won on road, all playoff series
8—Chicago, 1991-92
5—Minneapolis, 1950
  Boston, 1968-69
  Los Angeles, 1982
  L.A. Lakers, 1989
  Detroit, 1989-90
  Chicago, 1993-94

Most consecutive games won on road, one year
6—Chicago, 1991

5—Minneapolis, 1950
  Los Angeles, 1982
  L.A. Lakers, 1989

Most consecutive games lost, all playoff series
11—Baltimore, 1965-66, 1969-70
  Denver, 1988-90, 1994
10—New Jersey, 1984-86, 1992

Most consecutive games lost at home, all playoff series
9—Philadelphia, 1968-71
6—Cincinnati, 1965-67
  Baltimore, 1965-66, 1968-69
  New Jersey, 1979, 1982-84

Most consecutive games lost at home, one year
3—New York, 1953
  Philadelphia, 1969
  San Francisco, 1969
  New Jersey, 1984
  Philadelphia, 1984
  Milwaukee, 1989
  Portland, 1990
  L.A. Lakers, 1991
  Phoenix, 1993

Most consecutive games lost on road, all playoff series
18—Chicago, 1967-68, 1970-73
14—Los Angeles, 1973-74, 1977-79
  Cleveland, 1976-78, 1985, 1988-89

Most consecutive games lost on road, one year
7—Boston, 1987
6—Los Angeles, 1971

Most games, one year
25—New York, 1994

24—L.A. Lakers, 1988
  Phoenix, 1993
23—Boston, 1984
  Boston, 1987
  Detroit, 1988
  Houston, 1994

Most home games, one year
14—L.A. Lakers, 1988
13—Boston, 1984
  Boston, 1987
  Phoenix, 1993
  Houston, 1994
  New York, 1994

Most road games, one year
12—Houston, 1981
  New York, 1994
11—Washington, 1978
  Detroit, 1988
  Phoenix, 1993

Most wins at home, one year
12—Boston, 1984
  L.A. Lakers, 1988
11—Boston, 1987
  New York, 1994

Most wins on road, one year
8—Houston, 1981
7—Boston, 1968
  Detroit, 1989
  Chicago, 1991
  Chicago, 1993

Most games lost, one year
11—Phoenix, 1993
  New York, 1994
10—Baltimore, 1971
  Washington, 1979
  Boston, 1987

Most games lost at home, one year

6—Phoenix, 1993
5—Washington, 1979
　　Houston, 1981

Most games lost on road, one year

9—New York, 1994
8—Boston, 1987

Most games won at home without a loss, one year

10—Portland, 1977
　　Boston, 1986
　　L.A. Lakers, 1987
9—Boston, 1976

Most games lost on road without a win, one year

6—Los Angeles, 1971
5—Cincinnati, 1964
　　Los Angeles, 1977
　　Philadelphia, 1990

Highest won-lost percentage, one year

.923—Philadelphia, 1983 (12–1)
.883—Detroit, 1989 (15–2)
　　Chicago, 1991 (15–2)

SCORING

Most points, game

157—Boston vs. New York, April 28, 1990
156—Milwaukee at Philadelphia, March 30, 1970
153—L.A. Lakers vs. Denver, May 22, 1985
　　Portland at Phoenix, May 11, 1992 (2 ot)

Fewest points, game

68—New York at Indiana, May 28, 1994
69—Indiana at Atlanta, May 12, 1994

Most points, both teams, game

304—Portland (153) at Phoenix (151), May 11, 1992 (2 ot)
285—San Antonio (152) vs. Denver (133), April 26, 1983
　　Boston (157) vs. New York (128), April 28, 1990
280—Dallas (151) vs. Seattle (129), April 23, 1987

Fewest points, both teams, game

145—Syracuse (71) vs. Ft. Wayne (74), at Indianapolis, April 7, 1955
156—New York (68) at Indiana (88), May 28, 1994
157—Phoenix (81) at Kansas City (76), April 17, 1981
　　Boston (79) at Detroit (78), May 30, 1988

Largest margin of victory, game

58—Minneapolis vs. St. Louis, March 19, 1956 (133–75)
56—Los Angeles at Golden State, April 21, 1973 (126–70)
50—Milwaukee vs. San Francisco, April 4, 1971 (136–86)

BY HALF

Most points, first half

82—San Antonio vs. Denver, April 26, 1983
　　L.A. Lakers vs. Denver, April 23, 1987
80—L.A. Lakers vs. Denver, May 11, 1985

Fewest points, first half

28—Los Angeles at Milwaukee, April 7, 1974
30—St. Louis at Minneapolis, March 19, 1956
　　Golden State at Los Angeles, April 22, 1977
　　Houston vs. Boston, May 9, 1981
　　Houston at Seattle, April 25, 1982
　　Seattle vs. Utah, May 8, 1993

Most points, both teams, first half

150—San Antonio (82) vs. Denver (68), April 26, 1983
147—L.A. Lakers (79) at Denver (68), May 17, 1985
　　Phoenix (74) at Golden State (73), May 4, 1994

Fewest points, both teams, first half

68—New Jersey (33) at New York (35), April 29, 1994
69—Syracuse (31) vs. Ft. Wayne (38), at Indianapolis, April 7, 1955
　　Seattle (30) vs. Utah (39), May 8, 1993
　　Utah (31) vs. Houston (38), May 29, 1994

Largest lead at halftime

40—Detroit vs. Washington, April 26, 1987 (led 76–36; won 128–85)
36—Milwaukee at Philadelphia, March 30, 1970 (led 77–41; won 156–120)

Largest deficit at halftime overcome to win a game

21—Baltimore at Philadelphia, April 13, 1948 (trailed 20–41; won 66–63)
18—Los Angeles at Seattle, April 27, 1980 (trailed 39–57; won 98–93)
　　Philadelphia vs. New York, April 27, 1983 (trailed 41–59; won 98–91)
　　Milwaukee at New Jersey, April 22, 1986 (trailed 55–73; won 118–113)
　　Phoenix at Denver, May 2, 1989 (trailed 54–72; won 130–121)
　　Portland vs. Phoenix, May 23, 1990 (trailed 41–59; won 108–107)

Most points, second half

87—Milwaukee vs. Denver, April 23, 1978
83—Houston vs. San Antonio, April 6, 1980
　　Detroit vs. Boston, May 24, 1987
　　Boston vs. New York, April 28, 1990

Fewest points, second half

27—Philadelphia vs. Boston, May 21, 1982
28—San Antonio vs. Portland, May 7, 1993

Most points, both teams, second half

158—Milwaukee (79) at Philadelphia (79), March 30, 1970
152—Boston (83) vs. New York (69), April 28, 1990

Fewest points, both teams, second half

63—Houston (31) vs. New York (32), June 8, 1994
65—Boston (32) at Philadelphia (33), May 1, 1977

BY QUARTER, OVERTIME PERIOD

Most points, first quarter

45—L.A. Lakers vs. Phoenix, April 18, 1985
　　Dallas vs. L.A. Lakers, May 4, 1986
43—Philadelphia vs. San Francisco, April 14, 1967
　　Philadelphia at San Francisco, April 24, 1967
　　Denver vs. Utah, May 7, 1985

Fewest points, first quarter

8—Utah at L.A. Lakers, May 8, 1988
9—Atlanta at Boston, May 13, 1988

Most points, both teams, first quarter

84—Philadelphia (43) at San Francisco (41), April 24, 1967
　　Phoenix (42) at Golden State (42), May 4, 1994
79—Boston (41) vs. New York (38), April 28, 1990

Fewest points, both teams, first quarter

26—Detroit (10) vs. Boston (16), May 30, 1988
30—Chicago (13) vs. Detroit (17), April 5, 1974
　　Denver (13) vs. Seattle (17), May 5, 1994

Largest lead, end of first quarter

26—Milwaukee at Philadelphia, March 30, 1970 (led 40–14; won 156–120)
22—Phoenix vs. Portland, May 25, 1990 (led 40–18; won 123–89)

Largest deficit end of first quarter overcome to win

20—L.A. Lakers at Seattle, May 14, 1989 (trailed 12–32; won 97–95)
18—San Francisco at St. Louis, April 12, 1967 (trailed 21–39; won 112–107)

Most points, second quarter

46—Boston vs. St. Louis, March 27, 1960
　　Boston vs. Detroit, March 24, 1968
45—New York vs. Boston, March 19, 1955
　　St. Louis vs. Ft. Wayne, March 14, 1957

Fewest points, second quarter

9—San Antonio vs. Utah, April 30, 1994
10—Houston at Seattle, April 25, 1982
　　Boston at Detroit, April 28, 1989
　　Utah vs. Houston, May 29, 1994

Most points, both teams, second quarter

76—Cincinnati (41) at Boston (35), March 31, 1963
　　Boston (39) vs. Milwaukee (37), May 6, 1987
75—Boston (46) vs. Detroit (29), March 24, 1968
　　Golden State (39) vs. Phoenix (36), May 13, 1989

Fewest points, both teams, second quarter

23—Utah (10) vs. Houston (13), May 29, 1994
25—Golden State (11) at Los Angeles (14), April 22, 1977

Most points, third quarter

49—L.A. Lakers vs. Golden State, May 5, 1987
47—Milwaukee at Philadelphia, March 30, 1970
　　Los Angeles vs. Boston, June 3, 1984

Fewest points, third quarter

6—Atlanta at Boston, May 6, 1986
8—Los Angeles vs. Milwaukee, April 9, 1972

Most points, both teams, third quarter

82—San Francisco (44) vs. St. Louis (38), April 1, 1967
80—Los Angeles (47) vs. Boston (33), June 3, 1984

Fewest points, both teams, third quarter

26—Capital (10) at New York (16), April 12, 1974
30—Capital (11) vs. New York (19), April 5, 1974

Largest lead end of third quarter

52—Milwaukee at Philadelphia, March 30, 1970 (led 124–72; won 156–120)
48—Milwaukee vs. San Francisco, April 4, 1971 (led 105–57; won 136–86)

Largest deficit end of third quarter overcome to win

18—Phoenix at Houston, May 11, 1994 (trailed 100–82; won 124–117 in ot)
16—New York vs. Boston, April 22, 1973 (trailed 56–72; won 117–110 in 2 ot)

Most points, fourth quarter

51—Los Angeles vs. Detroit, March 31, 1962
49—Golden State at San Antonio, April 25, 1991

Fewest points, fourth quarter

8—New Jersey vs. Cleveland, May 7, 1993
　　Houston vs. Phoenix, May 11, 1994
9—Boston vs. Milwaukee, April 29, 1983
　　New Jersey vs. New York, May 4, 1994

Most points, both teams, fourth quarter
86—Golden State (49) at San Antonio (37), April 25, 1991
83—Milwaukee (47) vs. Denver (36), April 23, 1978

Fewest points, both teams, fourth quarter
26—Philadelphia (12) vs. Boston (14), May 1, 1977
New Jersey (8) vs. Cleveland (18), May 7, 1993
28—Cleveland (12) vs. Chicago (16), May 3, 1994
Houston (13) vs. New York (15), June 8, 1994

Most points, overtime period
22—Los Angeles vs. New York, May 1, 1970
20—Portland vs. Utah, May 26, 1992

Fewest points, overtime period
1—Boston vs. Charlotte, May 1, 1993
2—Charlotte at Boston, May 1, 1993

Most points, both teams, overtime period
38—Los Angeles (22) vs. New York (16), May 1, 1970
36—L.A. Lakers (19) vs. Portland (17), April 29, 1992

Fewest points, both teams, overtime period
3—Boston (1) vs. Charlotte (2), May 1, 1993
8—Boston (4) vs. Milwaukee (4), May 10, 1974
Phoenix (4) at Chicago (4), June 13, 1993

PLAYERS SCORING

Most players, 30-or-more points, game
3—Denver at Utah, April 19, 1984
San Antonio vs. Golden State, April 25, 1991
2—by many

Most players, 30-or-more points, both teams, game
3—Accomplished 49 times. Most recent:
Phoenix (2) vs. Seattle (1), June 1, 1993

Most players, 20-or-more points, game
5—Boston vs. Los Angeles, April 19, 1965
Philadelphia vs. Boston, April 11, 1967
Phoenix at Los Angeles, May 23, 1984
Boston vs. Milwaukee, May 15, 1986
L.A. Lakers vs. Boston, June 4, 1987
Boston vs. L.A. Lakers, June 11, 1987

Most players, 20-or-more points, both teams, game
8—Cincinnati (4) at Detroit (4), March 16, 1962
Boston (4) at Los Angeles (4), April 26, 1966
Phoenix (5) at Los Angeles (3), May 23, 1984
Boston (5) vs. Milwaukee (3), May 15, 1986
L.A. Lakers (5) vs. Boston (3), June 4, 1987
Portland (4) at Phoenix (4), May 11, 1992 (2 ot)

Most players, 10-or-more points, game
10—Minneapolis vs. St. Louis, March 19, 1956
9—Cincinnati at Boston, March 31, 1963
Dallas vs. Seattle, April 23, 1987
Cleveland vs. New Jersey, April 29, 1993

Most players, 10-or-more points, both teams, game
15—Philadelphia (8) vs. Milwaukee (7), March 30, 1970
L.A. Lakers (8) vs. Phoenix (7), April 18, 1985
Dallas (9) vs. Seattle (6), April 23, 1987
Dallas (8) vs. Houston (7), April 28, 1988
14—Ft. Wayne (7) at Minneapolis (7), March 17, 1957
St. Louis (7) at Boston (7), March 27, 1960
Detroit (7) at Cincinnati (7), March 17, 1962
Boston (7) at Detroit (7), March 25, 1968
Philadelphia (7) at Washington (7), May 5, 1978
Phoenix (7) at L.A. Lakers (7), April 20, 1985

Denver (7) at L.A. Lakers (7), April 25, 1987
Boston (8) vs. New York (6), April 28, 1990

Fewest players, 10-or-more points, game
1—Golden State vs. Los Angeles, April 21, 1973
Utah at San Antonio, April 28, 1994
2—by many

Fewest players, 10-or-more points, both teams, game
5—Rochester (2) at Minneapolis (3), March 16, 1955
Ft. Wayne (2) vs. Philadelphia (3), April 1, 1956
Los Angeles (2) at Boston (3), April 29, 1969
Chicago (2) at Detroit (3), May 20, 1990
Indiana (2) at New York (3), May 26, 1994

FIELD GOAL PERCENTAGE

Highest field goal percentage, game
.670—Boston vs. New York, April 28, 1990 (63–94)
.663—L.A. Lakers vs. San Antonio, April 17, 1986 (57–86)

Lowest field goal percentage, game
.233—Golden State vs. Los Angeles, April 21, 1973 (27–116)
.242—St. Louis at Minneapolis, March 19, 1956 (22–91)

Highest field goal percentage, both teams, game
.591—L.A. Lakers (.640) vs. Denver (.543), May 11, 1985
.588—Boston (.608) vs. Atlanta (.571), May 22, 1988
Boston (.670) vs. New York (.510), April 28, 1990

Lowest field goal percentage, both teams, game
.277—Syracuse (.275) vs. Ft. Wayne (.280), at Indianapolis, April 7, 1955
.288—Minneapolis (.283) vs. Rochester (.293), March 16, 1955

FIELD GOALS

Most field goals, game
67—Milwaukee at Philadelphia, March 30, 1970
San Antonio vs. Denver, May 4, 1983
L.A. Lakers vs. Denver, May 22, 1985
64—Milwaukee vs. Denver, April 23, 1978

Fewest field goals, game
21—New Jersey at New York, May 1, 1994
22—St. Louis at Minneapolis, March 19, 1956
New York at Indiana, May 28, 1994

Most field goals, both teams, game
119—Milwaukee (67) at Philadelphia (52), March 30, 1970
114—San Antonio (62) vs. Denver (52), April 26, 1983
Boston (63) vs. New York (51), April 28, 1990

Fewest field goals, both teams, game
48—Ft. Wayne (23) vs. Syracuse (25), at Indianapolis, April 7, 1955
52—Boston (26) at Detroit (26), May 30, 1988

FIELD GOAL ATTEMPTS

Most field goal attempts, game
140—Boston vs. Syracuse, March 18, 1959
San Francisco at Philadelphia, April 14, 1967 (ot)
135—Boston vs. Syracuse, April 1, 1959
Boston vs. Philadelphia, March 22, 1960

Fewest field goal attempts, game
59—Chicago at Detroit, May 31, 1989
60—New York at Indiana, June 3, 1994

Most field goal attempts, both teams, game
257—Boston (135) vs. Philadelphia (122), March 22, 1960
256—San Francisco (140) at Philadelphia (116), April 14, 1967 (ot)

Fewest field goal attempts, both teams, game
129—New York (64) at Indiana (65), May 28, 1994
132—New York (60) at Indiana (72), June 3, 1994

THREE-POINT FIELD GOALS

Most three-point field goals, game
12—Phoenix at Houston, May 11, 1994 (ot)
11—Orlando vs. Indiana, April 30, 1994
Indiana vs. Atlanta, May 15, 1994

Most three-point field goals, both teams, game
22—Phoenix (12) at Houston (10), May 11, 1994 (ot)
15—Chicago (8) vs. New York (7), May 19, 1989
Seattle (9) vs. Houston (6), May 12, 1993
Houston (9) vs. Portland (6), April 29, 1994
Seattle (8) vs. Denver (7), April 30, 1994
Orlando (11) vs. Indiana (4), April 30, 1994

Most three-point field goals, none missed, game
5—Dallas at Utah, April 25, 1986
Dallas vs. L.A. Lakers, May 4, 1986
4—Washington vs. New Jersey, April 23, 1982
L.A. Lakers vs. Denver, May 11, 1985

Most three-point field goals, one half
7—Denver at Phoenix, April 30, 1989
Portland vs. San Antonio, May 15, 1990
L.A. Lakers vs. Houston, April 27, 1991
Houston vs. Seattle, May 20, 1993
Phoenix at Houston, May 11, 1994 (ot)

Most three-point field goals, one quarter
6—Chicago at Phoenix, June 20, 1993
Houston vs. Utah, May 31, 1994

THREE-POINT FIELD GOAL ATTEMPTS

Most three-point field goal attempts, game
28—Houston vs. Phoenix, May 11, 1994 (ot)
Phoenix at Houston,, May 11, 1994 (ot)
27—Phoenix at Houston, May 21, 1994

Most three-point field goal attempts, both teams, game
56—Phoenix (28) at Houston (28), May 11, 1994 (ot)
42—Phoenix (23) at Houston (19), May 8, 1994

Most three-point field goal attempts, one half
16—Denver at Houston, May 6, 1986
Denver vs. Dallas, May 12, 1988
New York at Houston, June 22, 1994

FREE THROW PERCENTAGE

Highest free throw percentage, game
1.000—Detroit at Milwaukee, April 18, 1976 (15–15)
Dallas vs. Seattle, April 19, 1984 (24–24)
Detroit vs. Chicago, May 18, 1988 (23–23)
Phoenix vs. Golden State, May 9, 1989 (28–28)
Chicago vs. Cleveland, May 19, 1992 (19–19)
Portland at Chicago, June 14, 1992 (21–21)
New Jersey vs. Cleveland, May 7, 1993 (3–3)
.971—Denver vs. San Antonio, May 1, 1990 (34–35)

Lowest free throw percentage, game

.261—Philadelphia at Boston, March 19, 1960 (6-23)
.429—New Jersey vs. Philadelphia, April 22, 1984 (9-21)
    Denver at L.A. Lakers, April 23, 1987 (9-21)

Highest free throw percentage, both teams, game

.957—Chicago (.964) at Boston (.947), April 23, 1987
.946—Phoenix (1.000) vs. Golden State (.893), May 9, 1989

Lowest free throw percentage, both teams, game

.500—Philadelphia (.261) at Boston (.762), March 19, 1960
    L.A. Lakers (.435) at Phoenix (.571), May 2, 1993
.523—New York (.455) at Detroit (.591), May 8, 1990

FREE THROWS MADE

Most free throws made, game

57—Boston vs. Syracuse, March 21, 1953 (4 ot)
    Phoenix vs. Seattle, June 5, 1993
54—St. Louis vs. Minneapolis, March 17, 1956

Fewest free throws made, game

3—Houston vs. Washington, April 19, 1977
    Los Angeles at Philadelphia, May 26, 1983
    New Jersey vs. Cleveland, May 7, 1993
4—Kansas City at Portland, April 1, 1981
    Boston at Cleveland, May 2, 1992
    Houston vs. Phoenix, May 8, 1994

Most free throws made, both teams, game

108—Boston (57) vs. Syracuse (51), March 21, 1953 (4 ot)
98—New York (51) vs. Baltimore (47), March 26, 1949 (ot)
91—St. Louis (54) vs. Minneapolis (37), March 17, 1956

Fewest free throws made, both teams, game

12—Boston (6) at Buffalo (6), April 6, 1974
14—Houston (4) vs. Phoenix (10), May 8, 1994

FREE THROW ATTEMPTS

Most free throw attempts, game

70—St. Louis vs. Minneapolis, March 17, 1956
68—Minneapolis vs. St. Louis, March 21, 1956

Fewest free throw attempts, game

3—New Jersey vs. Cleveland, May 7, 1993
5—Los Angeles at Philadelphia, May 26, 1983
    Boston at Cleveland, May 2, 1992

Most free throw attempts, both teams, game

128—Boston (64) vs. Syracuse (64), March 21, 1953 (4 ot)
122—St. Louis (70) vs. Minneapolis (52), March 17, 1956
    Minneapolis (68) vs. St. Louis (54), March 21, 1956

Fewest free throw attempts, both teams, game

16—New Jersey (3) vs. Cleveland (13), May 7, 1993
18—Boston (7) at Buffalo (11), April 6, 1974

TOTAL REBOUNDS

Highest rebound percentage, game

.723—L.A. Lakers vs. San Antonio, April 17, 1986 (47-65)
.689—Chicago vs. Atlanta, April 30, 1993 (62-90)

Most rebounds, game

97—Boston vs. Philadelphia, March 19, 1960
95—Boston vs. Syracuse, March 18, 1959

Fewest rebounds, game

18—San Antonio at L.A. Lakers, April 17, 1986
22—Golden State at Seattle, April 28, 1992

Most rebounds, both teams, game

169—Boston (89) vs. Philadelphia (80), March 22, 1960
    San Francisco (93) at Philadelphia (76), April 16, 1967
163—Boston (95) vs. Syracuse (68), March 18, 1959

Fewest rebounds, both teams, game

51—Milwaukee (25) vs. Philadelphia (26), May 1, 1982
57—Golden State (22) at Seattle (35), April 28, 1992

OFFENSIVE REBOUNDS

Highest offensive rebound percentage, game

.609—New York vs. Indiana, June 5, 1994 (28-46)
.583—Houston vs. Philadelphia, May 11, 1977 (28-48)

Most offensive rebounds, game

30—Seattle vs. Portland, April 23, 1978
29—Washington at Atlanta, April 26, 1979
    Kansas City at Phoenix, April 27, 1979

Fewest offensive rebounds, game

2—New York at Boston, April 19, 1974
    Golden State at Chicago, April 30, 1975
    Houston vs. L.A. Clippers, April 29, 1993
3—Boston at Buffalo, April 6, 1974
    K.C.-Omaha at Chicago, April 20, 1975
    Milwaukee at Detroit, April 15, 1976
    Boston vs. L.A. Lakers, May 30, 1985
    Atlanta at Indiana, April 29, 1987
    Phoenix at Utah, May 6, 1990
    Chicago vs. New York, April 28, 1991
    Boston at Detroit, May 13, 1991
    Houston vs. New York, June 22, 1994

Most offensive rebounds, both teams, game

51—Houston (27) vs. Atlanta (24), April 11, 1979
    Utah (27) at Houston (24), April 28, 1985
50—Washington (28) at San Antonio (22), May 11, 1979

Fewest offensive rebounds, both teams, game

13—Indiana (6) vs. Atlanta (7), May 1, 1987
    Cleveland (6) vs. Boston (7), May 4, 1992
    Phoenix (6) at Portland (7), May 14, 1992
14—Atlanta (3) at Indiana (11), April 29, 1987

DEFENSIVE REBOUNDS

Highest defensive rebound percentage, game

.952—Chicago vs. Golden State, April 30, 1975 (40-42)
.947—Boston vs. New York, April 19, 1974 (36-38)

Most defensive rebounds, game

56—San Antonio vs. Denver, May 4, 1983
49—Philadelphia vs. New York, April 16, 1978
    Denver vs. Portland, May 1, 1977 (ot)

Fewest defensive rebounds, game

12—Golden State at Seattle, April 28, 1992
13—San Antonio at L.A. Lakers, April 17, 1986

Most defensive rebounds, both teams, game

92—Denver (49) vs. Portland (43), May 1, 1977 (ot)
86—San Antonio (56) vs. Denver (30), May 4, 1983

Fewest defensive rebounds, both teams, game

34—Milwaukee (15) vs. Philadelphia (19), May 1, 1982
35—Golden State (12) at Seattle (23), April 28, 1992

ASSISTS

Most assists, game

51—San Antonio vs. Denver, May 4, 1983
46—Milwaukee at Philadelphia, March 30, 1970
    Milwaukee vs. Denver, April 23, 1978
    Boston vs. New York, April 28, 1990

Fewest assists, game

5—Boston at St. Louis, April 3, 1960
    Detroit at Chicago, April 5, 1974
6—Chicago vs. Los Angeles, March 29, 1968

Most assists, both teams, game

79—L.A. Lakers (44) vs. Boston (35), June 4, 1987
78—Denver (40) at San Antonio (38), April 26, 1983

Fewest assists, both teams, game

16—Chicago (6) vs. Los Angeles (10), March 29, 1968
17—Cincinnati (7) at Detroit (10), March 15, 1958

PERSONAL FOULS

Most personal fouls, game

55—Syracuse at Boston, March 21, 1953 (4 ot)
53—Baltimore at New York, March 26, 1949 (ot)
51—Boston vs. Syracuse, March 21, 1953 (4 ot)
47—New York vs. Baltimore, March 26, 1949 (ot)
45—Syracuse at New York, April 8, 1952

Fewest personal fouls, game

9—Cleveland vs. Boston, May 2, 1992
10—Cleveland at New Jersey, May 7, 1993

Most personal fouls, both teams, game

106—Syracuse (55) at Boston (51), March 21, 1953 (4 ot)
100—Baltimore (53) at New York (47), March 26, 1949 (ot)
82—Syracuse (45) at New York (37), April 8, 1952

Fewest personal fouls, both teams, game

25—Cleveland (10) at New Jersey (15), May 7, 1993
27—Philadelphia (12) at Boston (15), March 23, 1958
    Houston (13) vs. Utah (14), May 23, 1994

DISQUALIFICATIONS

Most disqualifications, game

7—Syracuse at Boston, March 21, 1953 (4 ot)
6—Baltimore at New York, March 26, 1949 (ot)
5—New York vs. Baltimore, March 26, 1949 (ot)
    Boston vs. Syracuse, March 21, 1953 (4 ot)
4—by many

Most disqualifications, both teams, game

12—Syracuse (7) at Boston (5), March 21, 1953 (4 ot)
11—Baltimore (6) at New York (5), March 26, 1949 (ot)
7—Los Angeles (4) at Detroit (3), April 3, 1962
    Boston (4) vs. Los Angeles (3), April 18, 1962 (ot)

STEALS

Most steals, game

22—Golden State vs. Seattle, April 14, 1975
20—Golden State vs. Phoenix, May 2, 1976

Fewest steals, game

0—Buffalo at Boston, March 30, 1974
    Phoenix at Seattle, April 15, 1976
1—Detroit at Chicago, March 30, 1974
    New York at Boston, April 14, 1974

Milwaukee at Boston, May 10, 1974 (2 ot)
Boston vs. Phoenix, May 23, 1976
Seattle at Portland, April 26, 1978
Dallas at Seattle, April 24, 1984
Chicago at Boston, April 26, 1987
Detroit vs. Milwaukee, May 10, 1989
Chicago at Detroit, May 31, 1989
Cleveland at Philadelphia, April 29, 1990
Phoenix at Portland, May 27, 1990
Detroit at Atlanta, April 30, 1991
Chicago vs. New York, May 5, 1992
Phoenix vs. San Antonio, May 18, 1993

Most steals, both teams, game

35—Golden State (22) vs. Seattle (13), April 14, 1975
32—Seattle (18) at Golden State (14), April 16, 1975
　Los Angeles (19) vs. Golden State (13), May 4, 1977
　Milwaukee (19) at Philadelphia (13), May 9, 1986

Fewest steals, both teams, game

2—Phoenix (0) at Seattle (2), April 15, 1976
3—New York (1) at Boston (2), April 14, 1974

BLOCKED SHOTS

Most blocked shots, game

20—Philadelphia vs. Milwaukee, April 5, 1981
16—Seattle at Utah, May 14, 1992
　Phoenix vs. Seattle, May 24, 1993
　Denver at Utah, May 17, 1994 (2 ot)

Fewest blocked shots, game

0—Accomplished 29 times. Most recent:
　Indiana at New York, June 1, 1994

Most blocked shots, both teams, game

29—Philadelphia (20) vs. Milwaukee (9), April 5, 1981
25—Washington (13) vs. Philadelphia (12), April 22, 1986
　Phoenix (16) vs. Seattle (9), May 24, 1993

Fewest blocked shots, both teams, game

1—Dallas (1) at Portland (0), April 25, 1985
2—New York (0) at Boston (2), April 19, 1974
　Philadelphia (1) at Milwaukee (1), April 12, 1981
　Boston (0) at Houston (2), May 14, 1981
　Boston (1) at Milwaukee (1), May 18, 1986
　Chicago (0) vs. New York (2), April 25, 1991

TURNOVERS

Most turnovers, game

36—Chicago at Portland, April 17, 1977
34—Portland at Philadelphia, May 22, 1977
31—Golden State at Washington, May 25, 1975
　Denver vs. Milwaukee, April 21, 1978
　Seattle at Phoenix, May 6, 1979

Fewest turnovers, game

4—Detroit at Boston, May 9, 1991
5—Chicago vs. Los Angeles, March 30, 1971
　Boston vs. Chicago, April 26, 1987
　Detroit vs. Milwaukee, May 12, 1989
　Boston at Detroit, May 13, 1991
　Chicago at L.A. Lakers, June 9, 1991

Most turnovers, both teams, game

60—Golden State (31) at Washington (29), May 25, 1975
55—Chicago (36) at Portland (19), April 17, 1977
　Denver (31) vs. Milwaukee (24), April 21, 1978
　Phoenix (29) vs. Kansas City (26), April 22, 1979

Fewest turnovers, both teams, game

13—Detroit (4) at Boston (9), May 9, 1991
14—Boston (5) at Detroit (9), May 13, 1991

NBA FINALS RECORDS

Individual Records

24.0—Tom Heinsohn, Boston vs. St. Louis, 1957 (168/7)
23.0—Alvan Adams, Phoenix vs. Boston, 1976 (138/6)

Most consecutive games, 20-or-more points

25—Jerry West, Los Angeles, April 20, 1966—May 8, 1970
19—Julius Erving, Philadelphia, May 22, 1977—May 22, 1983
18—Kareem Abdul-Jabbar, Milwaukee-Los Angeles, April 21, 1971—May 30, 1982

Most consecutive games, 30-or-more points

13—Elgin Baylor, Minneapolis-Los Angeles, April 9, 1959—April 21, 1963
9—Michael Jordan, Chicago, June 10, 1992—June 20, 1993 (current)
6—Rick Barry, San Francisco, April 14, 1967—April 24, 1967

Most consecutive games, 40-or-more points

4—Michael Jordan, June 11, 1993—June 18, 1993
2—Jerry West, Los Angeles, April 19, 1965—April 21, 1965
　Rick Barry, San Francisco, April 18, 1967—April 20, 1967
　Jerry West, Los Angeles, April 23, 1969—April 25, 1969

scoring 30-or-more points in all games in championship series

Elgin Baylor, Los Angeles vs. Boston, 1962 (7-game series)
Rick Barry, San Francisco vs. Philadelphia, 1967 (6-game series)
Michael Jordan, Chicago vs. Phoenix, 1993 (6-game series)

Scoring 20-or-more points in all games of 7-game championship series

Bob Pettit, St. Louis vs. Boston, 1960
Elgin Baylor, Los Angeles vs. Boston, 1962
Jerry West, Los Angeles vs. Boston, 1962

MINUTES

Most minutes, game

62—Kevin Johnson, Phoenix at Chicago, June 13, 1993 (3 ot)
61—Garfield Heard, Phoenix at Boston, June 4, 1976 (3 ot)
60—Jo Jo White, Boston vs. Phoenix, June 4, 1976 (3 ot)

Most minutes per game, one championship series

49.3—Kareem Abdul-Jabbar, Milwaukee vs. Boston, 1974 (345/7)
48.7—Bill Russell, Boston vs. Los Angeles, 1968 (292/6)
48.5—John Havlicek, Boston vs. Los Angeles, 1968 (291/6)

SCORING

Most points, game

61—Elgin Baylor, Los Angeles at Boston, April 14, 1962
55—Rick Barry, San Francisco vs. Philadelphia, April 18, 1967
　Michael Jordan, Chicago vs. Phoenix, June 16, 1993
53—Jerry West, Los Angeles vs. Boston, April 23, 1969

Most points, rookie, game

42—Magic Johnson, Los Angeles at Philadelphia, May 16, 1980
37—Joe Fulks, Philadelphia vs. Chicago, April 16, 1947
　Tom Heinsohn, Boston vs. St. Louis, April 13, 1957 (2 ot)
34—Joe Fulks, Philadelphia vs. Chicago, April 22, 1947
　Elgin Baylor, Minneapolis at Boston, April 4, 1959

Highest scoring average, one championship series

41.0—Michael Jordan, Chicago vs. Phoenix, 1993 (246/6)
40.8—Rick Barry, San Francisco vs. Philadelphia, 1967 (245/6)
40.6—Elgin Baylor, Los Angeles vs. Boston, 1962 (284/7)

Highest scoring average, rookie, one championship series

26.2—Joe Fulks, Philadelphia vs. Chicago, 1947 (131/5)

Jerry West, Los Angeles vs. Boston, 1969
Jerry West, Los Angeles vs. New York, 1970
Kareem Abdul-Jabbar, Milwaukee vs. Boston, 1974
Larry Bird, Boston vs. Los Angeles, 1984
Hakeem Olajuwon, Houston, 1994

Most points, one half

35—Michael Jordan, Chicago vs. Portland, June 3, 1992

Most points, one quarter

25—Isiah Thomas, Detroit at L.A. Lakers, June 19, 1988

Most points, overtime period

9—John Havlicek, Boston vs. Milwaukee, May 10, 1974
　Bill Laimbeer, Detroit vs. Portland, June 7, 1990
　Danny Ainge, Portland at Chicago, June 5, 1992

FIELD GOALS

Highest field goal percentage, game (minimum: 8 field goals)

1.000—Scott Wedman, Boston vs. L.A. Lakers, May 27, 1985 (11/11)
　John Paxson, Chicago vs. L.A. Lakers, June 5, 1991 (8/8)
.917—Bill Bradley, New York at Los Angeles, April 26, 1972 (11/12)
　James Worthy, Los Angeles at Boston, May 31, 1984 (11/12) (ot)

Most field goals, game

22—Elgin Baylor, Los Angeles at Boston, April 14, 1962
　Rick Barry, San Francisco vs. Philadelphia, April 18, 1967
21—Michael Jordan, Chicago vs. Phoenix, June 16, 1993

Most field goals, one half

14—Isiah Thomas, Detroit at L.A. Lakers, June 19, 1988
　Michael Jordan, Chicago vs. Portland, June 3, 1992
　Michael Jordan, Chicago vs. Phoenix, June 16, 1993

Most field goals, one quarter
11—Isiah Thomas, Detroit at L.A. Lakers, June 19, 1988

Most field goal attempts, game
48—Rick Barry, San Francisco vs. Philadelphia, April 18, 1967
46—Elgin Baylor, Los Angeles at Boston, April 14, 1962
43—Rick Barry, San Francisco at Philadelphia, April 14, 1967 (ot)
   Michael Jordan, Chicago vs. Phoenix, June 13, 1993 (3 ot)

Most field goal attempts, one half
25—Elgin Baylor, Los Angeles at Boston, April 14, 1962

Most field goal attempts, one quarter
17—Rick Barry, San Francisco at Philadelphia, April 14, 1967 (ot)

THREE-POINT FIELD GOALS

Most three-point field goals, none missed, game
4—Scott Wedman, Boston vs. L.A. Lakers, May 27, 1985
3—Danny Ainge, Boston at L.A. Lakers, June 2, 1987
   Isiah Thomas, Detroit at Portland, June 14, 1990
   Sam Cassell, Houston at New York, June 12, 1994

Most three-point field goals, game
6—Michael Cooper, L.A. Lakers vs. Boston, June 4, 1987
   Bill Laimbeer, Detroit vs. Portland, June 7, 1990 (ot)
   Michael Jordan, Chicago vs. Portland, June 3, 1992
   Dan Majerle, Phoenix at Chicago, June 13, 1993 (3 ot)
5—Danny Ainge, Boston vs. L.A. Lakers, June 11, 1987
   Derek Harper, New York vs. Houston, June 15, 1994
   John Starks, New York at Houston, June 19, 1994

Most three-point field goals, one half
6—Michael Jordan, Chicago vs. Portland, June 3, 1992

Most three-point field goals, one quarter
4—Danny Ainge, Boston vs. L.A. Lakers, June 11, 1987
   Isiah Thomas, Detroit at Portland, June 12, 1990

Most three-point field goal attempts, game
11—John Starks, New York at Houston, June 22, 1994
10—Michael Jordan, Chicago vs. Portland, June 3, 1992
   Derek Harper, New York vs. Houston, June 15, 1994

Most three-point field goal attempts, one half
10—John Starks, New York at Houston, June 22, 1994

FREE THROWS

Most free throws made, none missed, game
15—Terry Porter, Portland at Detroit, June 7, 1990 (ot)
14—Magic Johnson, Los Angeles at Philadelphia, May 16, 1980

Most free throws made, game
19—Bob Pettit, St. Louis at Boston, April 9, 1958
17—Cliff Hagan, St. Louis at Boston, March 30, 1958
   Elgin Baylor, Los Angeles at Boston, April 14, 1962
   Jerry West, Los Angeles vs. Boston, April 21, 1965
   Jerry West, Los Angeles vs. Boston, April 25, 1969

Most free throws made, one half
12—Rick Barry, San Francisco vs. Philadelphia, April 24, 1967
   Dennis Johnson, Boston vs. Los Angeles, June 12, 1984

Most free throws made, one quarter
9—Frank Ramsey, Boston vs. Minneapolis, April 4, 1959

Most free throw attempts, game
24—Bob Pettit, St. Louis at Boston, April 9, 1958
22—Bob Pettit, St. Louis vs. Boston, April 11, 1957
21—Elgin Baylor, Los Angeles at Boston, April 18, 1962 (ot)

Most free throw attempts, one half
15—Bill Russell, Boston vs. St. Louis, April 11, 1961

Most free throw attempts, one quarter
11—Bob Pettit, St. Louis at Boston, April 9, 1958
   Wilt Chamberlain, Philadelphia vs. San Francisco, April 16, 1967

REBOUNDS

Most rebounds, game
40—Bill Russell, Boston vs. St. Louis, March 29, 1960
   Bill Russell, Boston vs. Los Angeles, April 18, 1962 (ot)
38—Bill Russell, Boston vs. St. Louis, April 11, 1961
   Bill Russell, Boston vs. Los Angeles, April 16, 1963
   Wilt Chamberlain, San Francisco vs. Boston, April 24, 1964
   Wilt Chamberlain, Philadelphia vs. San Francisco, April 16, 1967

Most rebounds, rookie, game
32—Bill Russell, Boston vs. St. Louis, April 13, 1957 (2 ot)
25—Bill Russell, Boston vs. St. Louis, March 31, 1957
23—Bill Russell, Boston vs. St. Louis, April 9, 1957
   Bill Russell, Boston at St. Louis, April 11, 1957
   Tom Heinsohn, Boston vs. St. Louis, April 13, 1957 (2 ot)

Highest average, rebounds per game, one championship series
29.5—Bill Russell, Boston vs. Minneapolis, 1959 (118/4)
28.8—Bill Russell, Boston vs. St. Louis, 1961 (144/5)
28.5—Wilt Chamberlain, Philadelphia vs. San Francisco, 1967 (171/6)

Highest average, rebounds per game, rookie, one championship series
22.9—Bill Russell, Boston vs. St. Louis, 1957 (160/7)
13.0—Nate Thurmond, San Francisco vs. Boston, 1964 (65/5)
12.6—Tom Heinsohn, Boston vs. St. Louis, 1957 (88/7)

Most consecutive games, 20-or-more rebounds
15—Bill Russell, Boston, April 9, 1960—April 16, 1963
12—Wilt Chamberlain, San Francisco-Philadelphia-Los Angeles,
   April 18, 1964—April 23, 1969

Most consecutive games, 30-or-more rebounds
3—Bill Russell, Boston, April 5, 1959—April 9, 1959
2—Bill Russell, Boston, April 9, 1960—April 2, 1961
   Wilt Chamberlain, Philadelphia, April 14, 1967—April 16, 1967
   Wilt Chamberlain, Los Angeles, April 29, 1969—May 1, 1969

20-or-more rebounds in all championship series games
Bill Russell, Boston vs. Minneapolis, 1959 (4-game series)
Bill Russell, Boston vs. St. Louis, 1961 (5-game series)
Bill Russell, Boston vs. Los Angeles, 1962 (7-game series)
Wilt Chamberlain, San Francisco vs. Boston, 1964 (5-game series)
Wilt Chamberlain, Philadelphia vs. San Francisco, 1967 (6-game series)

Nate Thurmond, San Francisco vs. Philadelphia, 1967 (6-game series)

Most rebounds, one half
26—Wilt Chamberlain, Philadelphia vs. San Francisco, April 16, 1967

Most rebounds, one quarter
19—Bill Russell, Boston vs. Los Angeles, April 18, 1962

Most offensive rebounds, game
11—Elvin Hayes, Washington at Seattle, May 27, 1979
10—Marvin Webster, Seattle vs. Washington, June 7, 1978
   Robert Reid, Houston vs. Boston, May 10, 1981
   Moses Malone, Houston vs. Boston, May 14, 1981

Most defensive rebounds, game
20—Bill Walton, Portland at Philadelphia, June 3, 1977
   Bill Walton, Portland vs. Philadelphia, June 5, 1977
18—Dave Cowens, Boston vs. Phoenix, May 23, 1976

ASSISTS

Most assists, game
21—Magic Johnson, Los Angeles vs. Boston, June 3, 1984
20—Magic Johnson, L.A. Lakers vs. Boston, June 4, 1987
   Magic Johnson, L.A. Lakers vs. Chicago, June 12, 1991

Highest average, assists per game, one championship series
14.0—Magic Johnson, L.A. Lakers vs. Boston, 1985 (84/6)
13.6—Magic Johnson, Los Angeles vs. Boston, 1984 (95/7)

Most assists, rookie, game
11—Magic Johnson, Los Angeles vs. Philadelphia, May 7, 1980
10—Tom Gola, Philadelphia vs. Ft. Wayne, March 31, 1956
   Walt Hazzard, Los Angeles at Boston, April 25, 1965
   Magic Johnson, Los Angeles vs. Philadelphia, May 4, 1980
   Magic Johnson, Los Angeles vs. Philadelphia, May 14, 1980

Highest average, assists per game, rookie, one championship series
8.7—Magic Johnson, Los Angeles vs. Philadelphia, 1980 (52/6)
6.0—Tom Gola, Philadelphia vs. Ft. Wayne, 1956 (30/5)
5.2—Walt Hazzard, Los Angeles vs. Boston, 1965 (26/5)

Most consecutive games 10-or-more assists
13—Magic Johnson, L.A. Lakers, June 3, 1984—June 4, 1987
6—Magic Johnson, Los Angeles, June 8, 1982—May 27, 1984

Most assists, one half
14—Magic Johnson, L.A. Lakers vs. Detroit, June 19, 1988
13—Robert Reid, Houston vs. Boston, June 5, 1986
   Magic Johnson, L.A. Lakers vs. Boston, June 4, 1987

Most assists, one quarter
8—Bob Cousy, Boston vs. St. Louis, April 9, 1957
   Magic Johnson, Los Angeles vs. Boston, June 3, 1984
   Robert Reid, Houston vs. Boston, June 5, 1986
   Michael Cooper, L.A. Lakers vs. Boston, June 4, 1987
   Magic Johnson, L.A. Lakers vs. Boston, June 4, 1987
   Magic Johnson, L.A. Lakers at Detroit, June 16, 1988
   Magic Johnson, L.A. Lakers vs. Detroit, June 19, 1988

PERSONAL FOULS

Most minutes played, no personal fouls, game

59—Dan Majerle, Phoenix at Chicago, June 13, 1993 (3 ot)
50—Jo Jo White, Boston at Milwaukee, April 30, 1974 (ot)

DISQUALIFICATIONS

Most consecutive games, disqualified

5—Art Hillhouse, Philadelphia, 1947
   Charlie Scott, Boston, 1976
4—Arnie Risen, Boston, 1957

Fewest minutes played, disqualified player, game

9—Bob Harrison, Minneapolis vs. New York, April 13, 1952
10—Bob Harrison, Minneapolis vs. New York, April 4, 1953

MOST POINTS

4-game series

118—Rick Barry, Golden State, 1975
109—Joe Dumars, Detroit, 1989

5-game series

169—Jerry West, Los Angeles, 1965
156—Michael Jordan, Chicago, 1991

6-game series

246—Michael Jordan, Chicago, 1993
245—Rick Barry, San Francisco, 1967

7-game series

284—Elgin Baylor, Los Angeles, 1962
265—Jerry West, Los Angeles, 1969

MOST MINUTES PLAYED

4-game series

186—Bob Cousy, Boston, 1959
    Bill Russell, Boston, 1959
179—Magic Johnson, Los Angeles, 1983

5-game series

240—Wilt Chamberlain, Los Angeles, 1973
236—Wilt Chamberlain, Los Angeles, 1972

6-game series

292—Bill Russell, Boston, 1968
291—John Havlicek, Boston, 1968

7-game series

345—Kareem Abdul-Jabbar, Milwaukee, 1974
338—Bill Russell, Boston, 1962

HIGHEST FIELD GOAL PERCENTAGE

(minimum: 4 FG per game)

4-game series

.739—Derrek Dickey, Golden State, 1975
.605—Kareem Abdul-Jabbar, Milwaukee, 1971

5-game series

.702—Bill Russell, Boston, 1965
.653—John Paxson, Chicago, 1991

STEALS

Most steals, game

6—John Havlicek, Boston vs. Milwaukee, May 3, 1974
  Steve Mix, Philadelphia vs. Portland, May 22, 1977
  Maurice Cheeks, Philadelphia at Los Angeles, May 7, 1980
  Isiah Thomas, Detroit at L.A. Lakers, June 19, 1988

BLOCKED SHOTS

Most blocked shots, game

8—Bill Walton, Portland vs. Philadelphia, June 5, 1977
  Hakeem Olajuwon, Houston vs. Boston, June 5, 1986
  Patrick Ewing, New York vs. Houston, June 17, 1994
7—Dennis Johnson, Seattle at Washington, May 28, 1978
  Patrick Ewing, New York vs. Houston, June 12, 1994
  Hakeem Olajuwon, Houston at New York, June 12, 1994

NBA FINALS RECORDS

INDIVIDUAL (SERIES)

6-game series

.667—Bob Gross, Portland, 1977
.622—Bill Walton, Boston, 1986

7-game series

.638—James Worthy, Los Angeles, 1984
.625—Wilt Chamberlain, Los Angeles, 1970

MOST FIELD GOALS

4-game series

46—Kareem Abdul-Jabbar, Milwaukee, 1971
44—Rick Barry, Golden State, 1975

5-game series

63—Michael Jordan, Chicago, 1991
62—Wilt Chamberlain, San Francisco, 1964

6-game series

101—Michael Jordan, Chicago, 1993
94—Rick Barry, San Francisco, 1967

7-game series

101—Elgin Baylor, Los Angeles, 1962
97—Kareem Abdul-Jabbar, Milwaukee, 1974

MOST FIELD GOAL ATTEMPTS

4-game series

102—Elgin Baylor, Minneapolis, 1959
99—Rick Barry, Golden State, 1975

5-game series

139—Jerry West, Los Angeles, 1965
129—Paul Arizin, Philadelphia, 1956

6-game series

235—Rick Barry, San Francisco, 1967
199—Michael Jordan, Chicago, 1993

7-game series

235—Elgin Baylor, Los Angeles, 1962
196—Jerry West, Los Angeles, 1969

TURNOVERS

Most turnovers, game

10—Magic Johnson, Los Angeles vs. Philadelphia, May 14, 1980
9—Magic Johnson, Los Angeles vs. Philadelphia, May 31, 1983

Most minutes played, no turnovers, game

59—Dan Majerle, Phoenix at Chicago, June 13, 1993 (3 ot)
48—Rodney McCray, Houston vs. Boston, June 5, 1986
47—Wes Unseld, Washington at Seattle, May 27, 1979
  Michael Cooper, Los Angeles vs. Boston, June 6, 1984 (ot)

MOST THREE-POINT FIELD GOALS MADE

4-game series

9—Michael Cooper, L.A. Lakers, 1989
2—Bob McAdoo, Los Angeles, 1983
  Bill Laimbeer, Detroit, 1989
  Isiah Thomas, Detroit, 1989
  James Worthy, L.A. Lakers, 1989

5-game series

11—Isiah Thomas, Detroit, 1990
8—Bill Laimbeer, Detroit, 1990

6-game series

17—Dan Majerle, Phoenix, 1993
14—Michael Cooper, L.A. Lakers, 1987

7-game series

17—Derek Harper, New York, 1994
16—John Starks, New York, 1994

MOST THREE-POINT FIELD GOAL ATTEMPTS

4-game series

27—Michael Cooper, L.A. Lakers, 1989
6—Isiah Thomas, Detroit, 1989

5-game series

25—Terry Porter, Portland, 1990
22—Bill Laimbeer, Detroit, 1990

6-game series

39—Dan Majerle, Phoenix, 1993
28—Michael Jordan, Chicago, 1992

7-game series

50—John Starks, New York, 1994
40—Vernon Maxwell, Houston, 1994

HIGHEST FREE THROW PERCENTAGE

(minimum: 2 FTM per game)

4-game series

.944—Phil Chenier, Washington, 1975
.941—Bill Sharman, Boston, 1959

5-game series
1.000—Bill Laimbeer, Detroit, 1990
      Vlade Divac, L.A. Lakers, 1991
.957—Jim McMillian, Los Angeles, 1972

6-game series
.968—Bill Sharman, Boston, 1958
.960—Magic Johnson, L.A. Lakers, 1987

7-game series
.959—Bill Sharman, Boston, 1957
.947—Don Meineke, Ft. Wayne, 1955

MOST FREE THROWS MADE

4-game series
34—Phil Chenier, Washington, 1975
33—Joe Dumars, Detroit, 1989

5-game series
51—Jerry West, Los Angeles, 1965
48—Bob Pettit, St. Louis, 1961

6-game series
67—George Mikan, Minneapolis, 1950
61—Joe Fulks, Philadelphia, 1948

7-game series
82—Elgin Baylor, Los Angeles, 1962
75—Jerry West, Los Angeles, 1970

MOST FREE THROW ATTEMPTS

4-game series
47—Moses Malone, Philadelphia, 1983
38—Joe Dumars, Detroit, 1989

5-game series
60—Bob Pettit, St. Louis, 1961
59—Jerry West, Los Angeles, 1965

6-game series
86—George Mikan, Minneapolis, 1950
79—Bob Pettit, St. Louis, 1958

7-game series
99—Elgin Baylor, Los Angeles, 1962
97—Bob Pettit, St. Louis, 1957

MOST REBOUNDS

4-game series
118—Bill Russell, Boston, 1959
76—Wes Unseld, Baltimore, 1971

5-game series
144—Bill Russell, Boston, 1961
138—Wilt Chamberlain, San Francisco, 1964

6-game series
171—Wilt Chamberlain, Philadelphia, 1967
160—Nate Thurmond, San Francisco, 1967

7-game series
189—Bill Russell, Boston, 1962
175—Wilt Chamberlain, Los Angeles, 1969

MOST OFFENSIVE REBOUNDS

4-game series
27—Moses Malone, Philadelphia, 1983
16—George Johnson, Golden State, 1975

5-game series
21—Elvin Hayes, Washington, 1979
20—Wes Unseld, Washington, 1979

6-game series
46—Moses Malone, Houston, 1981
34—Cedric Maxwell, Boston, 1981

7-game series
33—Elvin Hayes, Washington, 1978
      Marvin Webster, Seattle, 1978
32—Patrick Ewing, New York, 1994

MOST DEFENSIVE REBOUNDS

4-game series
53—Wes Unseld, Washington, 1975
45—Moses Malone, Philadelphia, 1983

5-game series
62—Jack Sikma, Seattle, 1979
55—Bill Laimbeer, Detroit, 1990

6-game series
91—Bill Walton, Portland, 1977
76—Larry Bird, Boston, 1981

7-game series
72—Larry Bird, Boston, 1984
64—Marvin Webster, Seattle, 1978

MOST ASSISTS

4-game series
51—Bob Cousy, Boston, 1959
50—Magic Johnson, Los Angeles, 1983

5-game series
62—Magic Johnson, L.A. Lakers, 1991
57—Michael Jordan, Chicago, 1991

6-game series
84—Magic Johnson, L.A. Lakers, 1985
78—Magic Johnson, L.A. Lakers, 1987

7-game series
95—Magic Johnson, Los Angeles, 1984
91—Magic Johnson, L.A. Lakers, 1988

MOST PERSONAL FOULS

4-game series
20—Michael Cooper, Los Angeles, 1983
19—Kevin Porter, Washington, 1975
      Tony Campbell, L.A. Lakers, 1989

5-game series
27—George Mikan, Minneapolis, 1953
25—Art Hillhouse, Philadelphia, 1947
      Lonnie Shelton, Seattle, 1979
      Bill Laimbeer, Detroit, 1990

6-game series
35—Charlie Scott, Boston, 1976
33—Tom Heinsohn, Boston, 1958
      Tom Meschery, San Francisco, 1967

7-game series
37—Arnie Risen, Boston, 1957
36—Vern Mikkelsen, Minneapolis, 1952
      Jack McMahon, St. Louis, 1957

MOST DISQUALIFICATIONS

4-game series
1—John Tresvant, Baltimore, 1971
      Elvin Hayes, Washington, 1975
      George Johnson, Golden State, 1975
      Kevin Porter, Washington, 1975
      Marc Iavaroni, Philadelphia, 1983
      Michael Cooper, Los Angeles, 1983
      Tony Campbell, L.A. Lakers, 1989
      A.C. Green, L.A. Lakers, 1989
      Rick Mahorn, Detroit, 1989

5-game series
5—Art Hillhouse, Philadelphia, 1947
4—Chuck Gilmur, Chicago, 1947

6-game series
5—Charlie Scott, Boston, 1976

7-game series
5—Arnie Risen, Boston, 1957
3—Mel Hutchins, Ft. Wayne, 1955
      Jack McMahon, St. Louis, 1957

MOST STEALS

4-game series
14—Rick Barry, Golden State, 1975
11—Maurice Cheeks, Philadelphia, 1983

5-game series
14—Michael Jordan, Chicago, 1991
12—Scottie Pippen, Chicago, 1991

6-game series
16—Julius Erving, Philadelphia, 1977
      Magic Johnson, Los Angeles, 1980
      Larry Bird, Boston, 1986
15—Maurice Cheeks, Philadelphia, 1980
      Magic Johnson, Los Angeles, 1982
      Byron Scott, L.A. Lakers, 1985
      Danny Ainge, Boston, 1986

7-game series
20—Isiah Thomas, Detroit, 1988
17—Derek Harper, New York, 1994

MOST BLOCKED SHOTS

4-game series
11—Elvin Hayes, Washington, 1975
      George Johnson, Golden State, 1975
      Julius Erving, Philadelphia, 1983
      John Salley, Detroit, 1989
9—Kareem Abdul-Jabbar, Los Angeles, 1983
      Bobby Jones, Philadelphia, 1983

5-game series
16—Jack Sikma, Seattle, 1979
12—John Salley, Detroit, 1990
      Vlade Divac, L.A. Lakers, 1991

6-game series
23—Kareem Abdul-Jabbar, Los Angeles, 1980
22—Bill Walton, Portland, 1977

7-game series
30—Patrick Ewing, New York, 1994
27—Hakeem Olajuwon, Houston, 1994

MOST TURNOVERS

4-game series
24—Magic Johnson, Los Angeles, 1983
18—Andrew Toney, Philadelphia, 1983
14—Kareem Abdul-Jabbar, Los Angeles, 1983

5-game series
25—Isiah Thomas, Detroit, 1990
22—Terry Porter, Portland, 1990
      Magic Johnson, L.A. Lakers, 1991

6-game series
30—Magic Johnson, Los Angeles, 1980
26—Magic Johnson, Los Angeles, 1982
      Kevin Johnson, Phoenix, 1993
      Scottie Pippen, Chicago, 1993

7-game series
31—Magic Johnson, Los Angeles, 1984
26—Gus Williams, Seattle, 1978
      Isiah Thomas, Detroit, 1988

TEAM (SERIES)

MOST POINTS

4-game series
487—Boston vs. Minneapolis, 1959
446—Minneapolis vs. Boston, 1959

5-game series
617—Boston vs. Los Angeles, 1965
605—Boston vs. St. Louis, 1961

6-game series
747—Philadelphia vs. San Francisco, 1967
707—San Francisco vs. Philadelphia, 1967

7-game series
827—Boston vs. Los Angeles, 1966
824—Boston vs. Los Angeles, 1962

FEWEST POINTS

4-game series
376—Baltimore vs. Milwaukee, 1971
382—Washington vs. Golden State, 1975

5-game series
458—L.A. Lakers vs. Chicago, 1991
467—Ft. Wayne vs. Philadelphia, 1956

6-game series
520—Houston vs. Boston, 1981
579—Boston vs. Houston, 1981

7-game series
603—Houston vs. New York, 1994
608—New York vs. Houston, 1994

HIGHEST FIELD GOAL PERCENTAGE

4-game series
.527—Detroit vs. L.A. Lakers, 1989
.504—Milwaukee vs. Baltimore, 1971

5-game series
.527—Chicago vs. L.A. Lakers, 1991
.470—New York vs. Los Angeles, 1972

6-game series
.515—L.A. Lakers vs. Boston, 1987
.512—L.A. Lakers vs. Boston, 1985

7-game series
.515—Los Angeles vs. Boston, 1984
.494—Los Angeles vs. New York, 1970

LOWEST FIELD GOAL PERCENTAGE

4-game series
.384—Baltimore vs. Milwaukee, 1971
.388—Minneapolis vs. Boston, 1959

5-game series
.365—Ft. Wayne vs. Philadelphia, 1956
.372—St. Louis vs. Boston, 1961

6-game series
.355—Boston vs. St. Louis, 1958
.379—Houston vs. Boston, 1981

7-game series
.339—Syracuse vs. Ft. Wayne, 1955
.369—Boston vs. St. Louis, 1957

MOST FIELD GOALS

4-game series
188—Boston vs. Minneapolis, 1959
180—Minneapolis vs. Boston, 1959

MOST POINTS

5-game series
243—Boston vs. Los Angeles, 1965
238—Boston vs. St. Louis, 1961

6-game series
287—Philadelphia vs. San Francisco, 1967
    San Francisco vs. Philadelphia, 1967
280—L.A. Lakers vs. Boston, 1987

7-game series
332—New York vs. Los Angeles, 1970
327—Los Angeles vs. Boston, 1984

FEWEST FIELD GOALS

4-game series
144—L.A. Lakers vs. Detroit, 1989
147—Washington vs. Golden State, 1975

5-game series
163—Ft. Wayne vs. Philadelphia, 1956
167—L.A. Lakers vs. Chicago, 1991

6-game series
203—Houston vs. Boston, 1981
211—St. Louis vs. Boston, 1958

7-game series
207—Syracuse vs. Ft. Wayne, 1955
217—Ft. Wayne vs. Syracuse, 1955

MOST FIELD GOAL ATTEMPTS

4-game series
464—Minneapolis vs. Boston, 1959
463—Boston vs. Minneapolis, 1959

5-game series
568—Boston vs. Los Angeles, 1965
555—Boston vs. St. Louis, 1961

6-game series
743—San Francisco vs. Philadelphia, 1967
640—Boston vs. L.A. Lakers, 1963

7-game series
799—Boston vs. St. Louis, 1957
769—Boston vs. St. Louis, 1960

FEWEST FIELD GOAL ATTEMPTS

4-game series
310—L.A. Lakers vs. Detroit, 1989
317—Detroit vs. L.A. Lakers, 1989

5-game series
374—L.A. Lakers vs. Chicago, 1991
404—Chicago vs. L.A. Lakers, 1991

6-game series
478—Chicago vs. Portland, 1992
479—Portland vs. Chicago, 1992

7-game series
523—Houston vs. New York, 1994
531—L.A. Lakers vs. Detroit, 1988

MOST THREE-POINT FIELD GOALS MADE

4-game series
13—L.A. Lakers vs. Detroit, 1989
5—Detroit vs. L.A. Lakers, 1989

MOST THREE-POINT FIELD GOALS MADE

5-game series
25—Detroit vs. Portland, 1990
13—L.A. Lakers vs. Chicago, 1991

6-game series
32—Chicago vs. Phoenix, 1993
27—Phoenix vs. Chicago, 1993

7-game series
37—Houston vs. New York, 1994
36—New York vs. Houston, 1994

MOST THREE POINT FIELD GOAL ATTEMPTS

4-game series
43—L.A. Lakers vs. Detroit, 1989
20—Detroit vs. L.A. Lakers, 1989

5-game series
56—Detroit vs. Portland, 1990
47—Portland vs. Detroit, 1990

6-game series
69—Chicago vs. Phoenix, 1993
65—Chicago vs. Portland, 1992

7-game series
121—Houston vs. New York, 1994
105—New York vs. Houston, 1994

HIGHEST FREE THROW PERCENTAGE

4-game series
.785—Los Angeles vs. Philadelphia, 1983
.776—Detroit vs. L.A. Lakers, 1989

5-game series
.826—Chicago vs. L.A. Lakers, 1991
.810—L.A. Lakers vs. Chicago, 1991

6-game series
.821—Boston vs. Phoenix, 1976
.813—Los Angeles vs. Philadelphia, 1980

7-game series
.827—Boston vs. Los Angeles, 1966
.805—Los Angeles vs. Boston, 1962

LOWEST FREE THROW PERCENTAGE

4-game series
.675—Baltimore vs. Milwaukee, 1971
.698—Boston vs. Minneapolis, 1959

5-game series
.616—San Francisco vs. Boston, 1964
.647—Los Angeles vs. New York, 1973

6-game series
.613—Philadelphia vs. San Francisco, 1967
.631—Chicago vs. Phoenix, 1993

7-game series
.641—Los Angeles vs. Boston, 1969
.688—Los Angeles vs. New York, 1970

MOST FREE THROWS MADE

4-game series
111—Boston vs. Minneapolis, 1959
108—L.A. Lakers vs. Detroit, 1989

5-game series
146—Los Angeles vs. Boston, 1965
145—New York vs. Minneapolis, 1953

6-game series
232—Boston vs. St. Louis, 1958
215—St. Louis vs. Boston, 1958

7-game series
244—St. Louis vs. Boston, 1957
239—Los Angeles vs. Boston, 1962

FEWEST FREE THROWS MADE

4-game series
52—Baltimore vs. Milwuakee, 1971
72—Golden State vs. Washington, 1975

5-game series
73—New York vs. Los Angeles, 1973
76—Chicago vs. L.A. Lakers, 1991

6-game series
82—Chicago vs. Phoenix, 1993
94—Boston vs. Houston, 1981

7-game series
100—Milwaukee vs. Boston, 1974
108—New York vs. Houston, 1994

MOST FREE THROW ATTEMPTS

4-game series
159—Boston vs. Minneapolis, 1959
144—L.A. Lakers vs. Detroit, 1989

5-game series
211—San Francisco vs. Boston, 1964
199—New York vs. Minneapolis, 1953
       Los Angeles vs. Boston, 1965

6-game series
298—Boston vs. St. Louis, 1958
292—St. Louis vs. Boston, 1958

7-game series
341—St. Louis vs. Boston, 1957
299—Boston vs. St. Louis, 1957

FEWEST FREE THROW ATTEMPTS

4-game series
77—Baltimore vs. Milwaukee, 1971
93—Los Angeles vs. Philadelphia, 1983

5-game series
92—Chicago vs. L.A. Lakers, 1991
96—New York vs. Los Angeles, 1973

6-game series
129—Boston vs. Houston, 1981
130—Chicago vs. Phoenix, 1993

7-game series
137—Milwaukee vs. Boston, 1974
148—New York vs. Houston, 1994

HIGHEST REBOUND PERCENTAGE

4-game series
.557—Golden State vs. Washington, 1975
.533—Milwaukee vs. Baltimore, 1971

5-game series
.548—Boston vs. St. Louis, 1961
.542—Los Angeles vs. New York, 1972

6-game series
.580—Los Angeles vs. Philadelphia, 1980
.570—Boston vs. Phoenix, 1976

7-game series
.541—Rochester vs. New York, 1951
.538—Boston vs. Los Angeles, 1966

MOST REBOUNDS

4-game series
295—Boston vs. Minneapolis, 1959
268—Minneapolis vs. Boston, 1959

5-game series
369—Boston vs. St. Louis, 1961
316—Boston vs. Los Angeles, 1965

6-game series
435—San Francisco vs. Philadelphia, 1967
425—Philadelphia vs. San Francisco, 1967

7-game series
487—Boston vs. St. Louis, 1957
448—Boston vs. St. Louis, 1960

FEWEST REBOUNDS

4-game series
145—L.A. Lakers vs. Detroit, 1989
160—Detroit vs. L.A. Lakers, 1989

5-game series
178—L.A. Lakers vs. Chicago, 1991
196—Chicago vs. L.A. Lakers, 1991

6-game series
223—Philadelphia vs. Los Angeles, 1980
225—Chicago vs. Portland, 1992

7-game series
263—L.A. Lakers vs. Detroit, 1988
280—Houston vs. New York, 1994

HIGHEST OFFENSIVE REBOUND PERCENTAGE

4-game series
.396—Philadelphia vs. Los Angeles, 1983
.375—Golden State vs. Washington, 1975

5-game series
.336—Washington vs. Seattle, 1979
.332—Detroit vs. Portland, 1990

6-game series
.410—Boston vs. Houston, 1981
.407—Philadelphia vs. Los Angeles, 1982

7-game series
.384—Boston vs. Los Angeles, 1984
.366—Seattle vs. Washington, 1978

MOST OFFENSIVE REBOUNDS

4-game series
72—Golden State vs. Washington, 1975
     Philadelphia vs. Los Angeles, 1983

5-game series
82—Washington vs. Seattle, 1979
72—Detroit vs. Portland, 1990

6-game series
112—Houston vs. Boston, 1981
111—Houston vs. Boston, 1986

7-game series
131—Boston vs. Los Angeles, 1984
127—Seattle vs. Washington, 1978

FEWEST OFFENSIVE REBOUNDS

4-game series
45—Detroit vs. L.A. Lakers, 1989
47—L.A. Lakers vs. Detroit, 1989

5-game series
55—Chicago vs. L.A. Lakers, 1991
57—Portland vs. Detroit, 1990

6-game series
57—Philadelphia vs. Los Angeles, 1980
61—Chicago vs. Portland, 1992

7-game series
72—L.A. Lakers vs. Detroit, 1988
73—Houston vs. New York, 1994

HIGHEST DEFENSIVE REBOUND PERCENTAGE

4-game series
.737—Washington vs. Golden State, 1975
.710—Detroit vs. L.A. Lakers, 1989

5-game series
.718—Detroit vs. Portland, 1990
.705—Chicago vs. L.A. Lakers, 1991

6-game series
.782—Los Angeles vs. Philadelphia, 1980
.769—Boston vs. Phoenix, 1976

7-game series
.745—Detroit vs. L.A. Lakers, 1988
.735—Portland vs. Chicago, 1992

MOST DEFENSIVE REBOUNDS

4-game series
143—Golden State vs. Washington, 1975
120—Washington vs. Golden State, 1975
       Philadelphia vs. Los Angeles, 1983

5-game series
162—Seattle vs. Washington, 1979
151—Washington vs. Seattle, 1979

6-game series
240—Boston vs. Phoenix, 1976
228—Portland vs. Philadelphia, 1977

7-game series
223—Seattle vs. Washington, 1978
220—Milwaukee vs. Boston, 1974
       Washington vs. Seattle, 1978

FEWEST DEFENSIVE REBOUNDS

4-game series
98—L.A. Lakers vs. Detroit, 1989
110—Los Angeles vs. Philadelphia, 1983

5-game series
119—L.A. Lakers vs. Chicago, 1991
141—Chicago vs. L.A. Lakers, 1991

6-game series
144—Houston vs. Boston, 1981
160—Philadelphia vs. Los Angeles, 1982

7-game series
191—L.A. Lakers vs. Detroit, 1988
196—New York vs. Houston, 1994

MOST ASSISTS

4-game series
114—Boston vs. Minneapolis, 1959
104—Philadelphia vs. Los Angeles, 1983

5-game series
139—Chicago vs. L.A. Lakers, 1991
130—Boston vs. St. Louis, 1961

6-game series
192—L.A. Lakers vs. Boston, 1985
188—Los Angeles vs. Philadelphia, 1982

7-game series
198—Los Angeles vs. Boston, 1984
192—New York vs. Los Angeles, 1970

FEWEST ASSISTS

4-game series
78—Baltimore vs. Milwaukee, 1971
82—Golden State vs. Washington, 1975

5-game series
88—San Francisco vs. Boston, 1964
      Los Angeles vs. New York, 1973
94—Detroit vs. Portland, 1990

6-game series
105—Los Angeles vs. Boston, 1963
108—Houston vs. Boston, 1981

7-game series
121—Seattle vs. Washington, 1978
135—Los Angeles vs. Boston, 1962
      Boston vs. Los Angeles, 1969

MOST PERSONAL FOULS

4-game series
120—Los Angeles vs. Philadelphia, 1983
116—Golden State vs. Washington, 1975

5-game series
149—Portland vs. Detroit, 1990
146—Boston vs. San Francisco, 1964

6-game series
194—Boston vs. St. Louis, 1958
      St. Louis vs. Boston, 1958
182—San Francisco vs. Philadelphia, 1967
      Portland vs. Philadelphia, 1977

7-game series
221—Boston vs. St. Louis, 1957
210—Boston vs. Los Angeles, 1962

FEWEST PERSONAL FOULS

4-game series
84—Milwaukee vs. Baltimore, 1971
89—Philadelphia vs. Los Angeles, 1983

5-game series
96—L.A. Lakers vs. Chicago, 1991
106—Los Angeles vs. New York, 1972

6-game series
121—Houston vs. Boston, 1981
124—Boston vs. Houston, 1986

7-game series
149—Houston vs. New York, 1994
150—Los Angeles vs. New York, 1970

MOST DISQUALIFICATIONS

4-game series
2—Washington vs. Golden State, 1975
      L.A. Lakers vs. Detroit, 1989

1—Baltimore vs. Milwaukee, 1971
      Golden State vs. Washington, 1975
      Los Angeles vs. Philadelphia, 1983
      Philadelphia vs. Los Angeles, 1983
      Detroit vs. L.A. Lakers, 1989

5-game series
9—Chicago vs. Philadelphia, 1947
8—Philadelphia vs. Chicago, 1947

6-game series
11—Boston vs. St. Louis, 1958
9—Minneapolis vs. Syracuse, 1950

7-game series
10—Boston vs. St. Louis, 1957
9—Minneapolis vs. New York, 1952
      St. Louis vs. Boston, 1957
      Boston vs. Los Angeles, 1962

FEWEST DISQUALIFICATIONS

4-game series
0—Boston vs. Minneapolis, 1959
      Minneapolis vs. Boston, 1959
      Milwaukee vs. Baltimore, 1971

5-game series
0—Los Angeles vs. New York, 1972
1—New York vs. Los Angeles, 1972
      Chicago vs. L.A. Lakers, 1991

6-game series
0—Los Angeles vs. Philadelphia, 1980
      Boston vs. Houston, 1986
      Houston vs. Boston, 1986
1—by seven teams

7-game series
0—St. Louis vs. Boston, 1960
      L.A. Lakers vs. Detroit, 1988
1—Los Angeles vs. Boston, 1969
      Los Angeles vs. New York, 1970
      Houston vs. New York, 1994

MOST STEALS

4-game series
55—Golden State vs. Washington, 1975
45—Washington vs. Golden State, 1975

5-game series
49—Chicago vs. L.A. Lakers, 1991
38—Seattle vs. Washington, 1979

6-game series
71—Philadelphia vs. Portland, 1977
64—Portland vs. Philadelphia, 1977
      Los Angeles vs. Philadelphia, 1982

7-game series
65—Boston vs. Los Angeles, 1984
59—Los Angeles vs. Boston, 1984

FEWEST STEALS

4-game series
16—Detroit vs. L.A. Lakers, 1989
22—L.A. Lakers vs. Detroit, 1989

5-game series
28—Detroit vs. Portland, 1990
29—Washington vs. Seattle, 1979

6-game series
30—Boston vs. L.A. Lakers, 1987
40—Boston vs. Houston, 1981

7-game series
21—Milwaukee vs. Boston, 1974
40—Seattle vs. Washington, 1978

MOST BLOCKED SHOTS

4-game series
32—Golden State vs. Washington, 1975
      Philadelphia vs. Los Angeles, 1983
29—Los Angeles vs. Philadelphia, 1983

5-game series
39—Seattle vs. Washington, 1979
25—Detroit vs. Portland, 1990
      Chicago vs. L.A. Lakers, 1991

6-game series
60—Philadelphia vs. Los Angeles, 1980
51—Philadelphia vs. Los Angeles, 1982

7-game series
49—Seattle vs. Washington, 1978
43—New York vs. Houston, 1994

FEWEST BLOCKED SHOTS

4-game series
16—L.A. Lakers vs. Detroit, 1989
20—Washington vs. Golden State, 1975

5-game series
17—Portland vs. Detroit, 1990
22—L.A. Lakers vs. Chicago, 1991

6-game series
10—Boston vs. Phoenix, 1976
21—Phoenix vs. Boston, 1976

7-game series
5—Boston vs. Milwaukee, 1974
21—L.A. Lakers vs. Detroit, 1988

MOST TURNOVERS

4-game series
94—Golden State vs. Washington, 1975
92—Milwaukee vs. Baltimore, 1971

5-game series
104—Los Angeles vs. New York, 1973
88—New York vs. Los Angeles, 1972

6-game series
149—Portland vs. Philadelphia, 1977
144—Boston vs. Phoenix, 1976

7-game series
142—Milwaukee vs. Boston, 1974
126—Seattle vs. Washington, 1978

FEWEST TURNOVERS

4-game series
46—Detroit vs. L.A. Lakers, 1989
47—L.A. Lakers vs. Detroit, 1989

5-game series
66—Chicago vs. L.A. Lakers, 1991
74—New York vs. Los Angeles, 1973

6-game series
68—L.A. Lakers vs. Boston, 1987
76—L.A. Lakers vs. Boston, 1985

7-game series
87—Detroit vs. L.A. Lakers, 1988
92—New York vs. Houston, 1994

NBA FINALS RECORDS

Team Records

WON-LOST

**Most consecutive games won,
all championship series**

5—Minneapolis, 1953–54
  Boston, 1959–60
  Los Angeles, 1972–73
  Detroit, 1989–90
  Chicago, 1991–92

**Most consecutive games won,
one championship series**

4—Minneapolis vs. New York, 1953 (5-game series)
  Boston vs. Minneapolis, 1959 (4-game series)
  Milwaukee vs. Baltimore, 1971 (4-game series)
  Los Angeles vs. New York, 1972 (5-game series)
  New York vs. Los Angeles, 1973 (5-game series)
  Golden State vs. Washington, 1975 (4-game series)
  Portland vs. Philadelphia, 1977 (6-game series)
  Seattle vs. Washington, 1979 (5-game series)
  Philadelphia vs. Los Angeles, 1983 (4-game series)
  Detroit vs. L.A. Lakers, 1989 (4-game series)
  Chicago vs. L.A. Lakers, 1991 (5-game series)

**Most consecutive games won at home,
all championship series**

7—Minneapolis, 1949–52
6—Boston, 1960–62
  Boston, 1964–65
  Syracuse/Philadelphia, 1955–67

**Most consecutive games won at home,
one championship series**

4—Syracuse vs. Ft. Wayne, 1955 (7-game series)

**Most consecutive games won on road,
all championship series**

5—Detroit, 1989–90
4—Minneapolis, 1953–54
  Chicago, 1991–92
  Chicago, 1992–93 (current)

**Most consecutive games won on road,
one championship series**

3—Minneapolis vs. New York, 1953 (5-game series)
  Detroit vs. Portland, 1990 (5-game series)
  Chicago vs. L.A. Lakers, 1991 (5-game series)
  Chicago vs. Phoenix, 1993 (6-game series)

**Most consecutive games lost,
all championship series**

9—Baltimore/Washington, 1971–78
5—Minneapolis/Los Angeles, 1959–62
  New York, 1972–73
  Philadelphia, 1977–80

**Most consecutive games lost at home,
all championship series**

5—L.A. Lakers, 1989–91 (current)
4—Baltimore/Washington, 1971–75
  Portland, 1990–92
  Phoenix, 1976–93 (current)

**Most consecutive games lost on road,
all championship series**

7—Ft. Wayne, 1955–56
5—Philadelphia, 1947–56
  St. Louis, 1960–61

Syracuse/Philadelphia, 1954–67
Los Angeles, 1968–70
Baltimore/Washington, 1971–78

SCORING

Most points, game

148—Boston vs. L.A. Lakers (114), May 27, 1985
142—Boston vs. Los Angeles (110), April 18, 1965
141—Philadelphia vs. San Francisco (135), April 14, 1967
  (ot)
  L.A. Lakers vs. Boston (122), June 4, 1987

Fewest points, game

71—Syracuse vs. Ft. Wayne (74), at Indianapolis, April 7, 1955
  Houston vs. Boston (94), May 9, 1981
74—Ft. Wayne vs. Syracuse (71), at Indianapolis, April 7, 1955
78—New York at Houston (85), June 8, 1994

Most points, both teams, game

276—Philadelphia (141) vs. San Francisco (135), April 14, 1967 (ot)
263—L.A. Lakers (141) vs. Boston (122), June 4, 1987

Fewest points, both teams, game

145—Syracuse (71) vs. Ft. Wayne (74), at Indianapolis, April 7, 1955
163—New York (78) at Houston (85), June 8, 1994

Largest margin of victory, game

35—Washington vs. Seattle, June 4, 1978 (117–82)
34—Boston vs. St. Louis, April 2, 1961 (129–95)
  Boston vs. L.A. Lakers, May 27, 1985 (148–114)
33—Boston vs. Los Angeles, April 25, 1965 (129–96)
  Philadelphia vs. Los Angeles, June 6, 1982 (135–102)
  Los Angeles vs. Boston, June 3, 1984 (137–104)
  Chicago vs. Portland, June 3, 1992 (122–89)

BY HALF

Most points, first half

79—Boston vs. L.A. Lakers, May 27, 1985
76—Boston vs. St. Louis, March 27, 1960

Fewest points, first half

30—Houston vs. Boston, May 9, 1981
31—Syracuse vs. Ft. Wayne, at Indianapolis, April 7, 1955

Most points, both teams, first half

140—San Francisco (72) vs. Philadelphia (68), April 24, 1967
138—Philadelphia (73) vs. San Francisco (65), April 14, 1967

Fewest points, both teams, first half

69—Syracuse (31) vs. Ft. Wayne (38), at Indianapolis, April 7, 1955
71—Phoenix (33) vs. Boston (38), June 6, 1976
  Houston (30) vs. Boston (41), May 9, 1981

Largest lead at halftime

30—Boston vs. L.A. Lakers, May 27, 1985 (led 79–49; won 148–114)
27—New York vs. Los Angeles, May 8, 1970 (led 69–42; won 113–99)

**Largest deficit at halftime, overcome
to win**

21—Baltimore at Philadelphia, April 13, 1948 (trailed 20–41; won 66–63)
14—New York at Los Angeles, April 29, 1970 (trailed 42–56; won 111–108 in ot)
  Golden State at Washington, May 18, 1975 (trailed 40–54; won 101–95)
  Philadelphia at Los Angeles, May 31, 1983 (trailed 51–65; won 115–108)

Most points, second half

81—Philadelphia vs. Los Angeles, June 6, 1982
80—Los Angeles vs. Boston, June 3, 1984

Fewest points, second half

30—Washington vs. Seattle, May 24, 1979
31—St. Louis vs. Boston, April 2, 1960
  Houston vs. New York, June 8, 1994

Most points, both teams, second half

139—Boston (78) vs. Los Angeles (61), April 18, 1965
138—Los Angeles (71) at Boston (67), April 21, 1963
  Los Angeles (80) vs. Boston (58), June 3, 1984

Fewest points, both teams, second half

63—Houston (31) vs. New York (32), June 8, 1994
73—Washington (30) vs. Seattle (43), May 24, 1979

BY QUARTER, OVERTIME PERIOD

Most points, first quarter

43—Philadelphia vs. San Francisco, April 14, 1967
  Philadelphia at San Francisco, April 24, 1967
41—San Francisco vs. Philadelphia, April 24, 1967

Fewest points, first quarter

13—Ft. Wayne at Syracuse, April 2, 1955
  Milwaukee at Boston, May 3, 1974
14—Houston at New York, June 15, 1994

Most points, both teams, first quarter

84—Philadelphia (43) at San Francisco (41), April 24, 1967
73—Philadelphia (43) vs. San Francisco (30), April 14, 1967

Fewest points, both teams, first quarter

31—Los Angeles (15) at Boston (16), April 29, 1969
33—Ft. Wayne (13) at Syracuse (20), April 2, 1955
  Houston (14) at New York (19), June 15, 1994

Largest lead at end of first quarter

20—Los Angeles vs. New York, May 6, 1970 (led 36–16; won 135–113)
19—San Francisco vs. Boston, April 22, 1964 (led 40–21; won 115–91)
  Boston vs. Milwaukee, May 3, 1974 (led 32–13; won 95–83)

**Largest deficit at end of first quarter,
overcome to win**

14—Los Angeles at Boston, April 17, 1966 (trailed 20–34; won 133–129 in ot)
12—Detroit at L.A. Lakers, June 13, 1989 (trailed 23–35; won 105–97)

Most points, second quarter

46—Boston vs. St. Louis, March 27, 1960
43—Los Angeles at Boston, April 8, 1962

Fewest points, second quarter
12—Boston vs. Milwaukee, May 5, 1974
13—Syracuse vs. Ft. Wayne, at Indianapolis, April 7, 1955
   Phoenix vs. Boston, June 6, 1976
   Houston vs. Boston, May 9, 1981

Most points, both teams, second quarter
73—St. Louis (38) vs. Boston (35), April 8, 1961
   Boston (38) vs. Los Angeles (35), April 14, 1962
72—St. Louis (42) at Boston (30), March 29, 1958
   Boston (46) vs. St. Louis (26), March 27, 1960

Fewest points, both teams, second quarter
29—Syracuse (13) vs. Ft. Wayne (16), at Indianapolis, April 7, 1955
31—Phoenix (13) vs. Boston (18), June 6, 1976

Most points, third quarter
47—Los Angeles vs. Boston, June 3, 1984
41—Portland vs. Philadelphia, May 31, 1977
   Los Angeles at Philadelphia, May 27, 1982

Fewest points, third quarter
11—New York at Los Angeles, April 30, 1972
12—Boston at St. Louis, April 7, 1960
   Boston at L.A. Lakers, June 14, 1987

Most points, both teams, third quarter
80—Los Angeles (47) vs. Boston (33), June 3, 1984
75—Boston (40) vs. Los Angeles (35), April 21, 1963

Fewest points, both teams, third quarter
31—Portland (15) vs. Chicago (16), June 7, 1992
33—Washington (14) vs. Seattle (19), May 24, 1979

Largest lead at end of third quarter
36—Chicago vs. Portland, June 3, 1992 (led 104–68; won 122–89)
31—Portland vs. Philadelphia, May 31, 1977 (led 98–67; won 130–98)

Largest deficit at end of third quarter, overcome to win
15—Chicago vs. Portland, June 14, 1992 (trailed 64–79; won 97–93)
12—San Francisco at Philadelphia, April 23, 1967 (trailed 84–96; won 117–109)

Most points, fourth quarter
44—Philadelphia vs. Los Angeles, June 6, 1982
42—Boston vs. Los Angeles, April 25, 1965
   Portland vs. Philadelphia, May 29, 1977

Fewest points, fourth quarter
12—Chicago at Phoenix, June 20, 1993
13—Philadelphia vs. San Francisco, April 23, 1967
   Milwaukee vs. Boston, April 30, 1974
   L.A. Lakers at Detroit, June 8, 1989
   Houston vs. New York, June 8, 1994

Most points, both teams, fourth quarter
76—Philadelphia (38) at Los Angeles (38), June 1, 1982
75—Boston (40) vs. L.A. Lakers (35), May 27, 1985

Fewest points, both teams, fourth quarter
28—Houston (13) vs. New York (15), June 8, 1994
31—Chicago (12) at Phoenix (19), June 20, 1993

Most points, overtime period
22—Los Angeles vs. New York, May 1, 1970
18—Portland at Chicago, June 5, 1992

Fewest points, overtime period
4—Boston vs. Milwaukee, May 10, 1974
   Milwaukee at Boston, May 10, 1974
   L.A. Lakers vs. Chicago, June 7, 1991
   Chicago vs. Phoenix, June 13, 1993
   Phoenix at Chicago, June 13, 1993

6—Los Angeles vs. New York, April 29, 1970
   Boston at Milwaukee, April 30, 1974
   Boston vs. Phoenix, June 4, 1976
   Phoenix at Boston, June 4, 1976

Most points, both teams, overtime period
38—Los Angeles (22) vs. New York (16), May 1, 1970
30—Boston (16) vs. Phoenix (14), June 4, 1976

Fewest points, both teams, overtime period
8—Boston (4) vs. Milwaukee (4), May 10, 1974
   Chicago (4) vs. Phoenix (4), June 13, 1993
12—Boston (6) vs. Phoenix (6), June 4, 1976

100-POINT GAMES
Most consecutive games, 100-or-more points, all championship series
20—Minneapolis/Los Angeles, 1959–65
   L.A. Lakers, 1983–87
19—Boston, 1981–86
18—Philadelphia, 1977–83 (current)

Most consecutive games scoring fewer than 100 points, all championship series
8—Houston, 1986–94
7—New York, 1994
6—Houston, 1981

PLAYERS SCORING
Most players, 30-or-more points, game
2—Accomplished 25 times. Most recent:
   Chicago at L.A. Lakers, June 12, 1991

Most players, 30-or-more points, both teams, game
3—Los Angeles (2) vs. Boston (1), April 16, 1962
   Los Angeles (2) at Boston (1), April 18, 1962 (ot)
   Los Angeles (2) vs. Boston (1), April 17, 1963
   Los Angeles (2) at Boston (1), April 21, 1963
   Los Angeles (2) at Boston (1), April 24, 1966
   Philadelphia (2) vs. San Francisco (1), April 14, 1967 (ot)
   Philadelphia (2) at San Francisco (1), April 20, 1967
   Los Angeles (2) vs. Boston (1), April 25, 1969
   Portland (2) vs. Detroit (1), June 12, 1990

Most players, 20-or-more points, game
5—Boston vs. Los Angeles, April 19, 1965
   L.A. Lakers vs. Boston, June 4, 1987
   Boston vs. L.A. Lakers, June 11, 1987
4—by many

Most players, 20-or-more points, both teams, game
8—Boston (4) at Los Angeles (4), April 26, 1966
   L.A. Lakers (5) vs. Boston (3), June 4, 1987
7—Boston (5) vs. Los Angeles (2), April 19, 1965
   Philadelphia (4) vs. San Francisco (3), April 14, 1967 (ot)
   Boston (4) vs. Los Angeles (3), April 30, 1968 (ot)
   Philadelphia (4) at Los Angeles (3), May 31, 1983
   Los Angeles (4) vs. Boston (3), June 10, 1984
   Boston (4) at L.A. Lakers (3), June 7, 1985

Most players, 10-or-more points, game
8—Boston vs. Los Angeles, May 31, 1984 (ot)
7—Accomplished 17 times. Most recent:
   Phoenix at Chicago, June 13, 1993 (3 ot)

Most players, 10-or-more points, both teams, game
14—Boston (7) vs. St. Louis (7), March 27, 1960

13—Los Angeles (7) at Boston (6), April 19, 1966
   Boston (8) vs. Los Angeles (5), May 31, 1984 (ot)

Fewest players, 10-or-more points, game
2—Ft. Wayne vs. Philadelphia, April 1, 1956
   St. Louis at Boston, March 29, 1958
   St. Louis vs. Boston, April 12, 1958
   Los Angeles at Boston, April 29, 1969
   Chicago vs. L.A. Lakers, June 2, 1991
   Chicago at Portland, June 10, 1992

Fewest players, 10-or-more points, both teams, game
5—Ft. Wayne (2) vs. Philadelphia (3), April 1, 1956
   Los Angeles (2) at Boston (3), April 29, 1969
6—Boston (3) vs. Los Angeles (3), April 18, 1962 (ot)
   Boston (3) at Los Angeles (3), April 25, 1969
   Baltimore (3) at Milwaukee (3), April 21, 1971
   Golden State (3) vs. Washington (3), May 20, 1975
   Chicago (2) vs. L.A. Lakers (4), June 2, 1991
   Chicago (2) at Portland (4), June 10, 1992
   Chicago (3) at Phoenix (3), June 11, 1993

FIELD GOAL PERCENTAGE
Highest field goal percentage, game
.617—Chicago vs. L.A. Lakers, June 5, 1991 (50/81)
.615—L.A. Lakers vs. Boston, June 4, 1987 (56/91)
.608—Boston vs. L.A. Lakers, May 27, 1985 (62/102)

Lowest field goal percentage, game
.275—Syracuse vs. Ft. Wayne, at Indianapolis, April 7, 1955 (25/91)
.280—Ft. Wayne vs. Syracuse, at Indianapolis, April 7, 1955 (23/82)
.293—Boston at St. Louis, April 6, 1957 (29/99)
.295—San Francisco at Philadelphia, April 16, 1967 (38/129)
.302—Boston vs. St. Louis, April 9, 1958 (32/106)

Highest field goal percentage, both teams, game
.582—L.A. Lakers (.615) vs. Boston (.548), June 4, 1987 (107/184)
.553—L.A. Lakers (.556) vs. Boston (.549), June 2, 1987 (100/181)

Lowest field goal percentage, both teams, game
.277—Syracuse (.275) vs. Ft. Wayne (.280), at Indianapolis, April 7, 1955 (48/173)
.312—Boston (.304) at St. Louis (.320), April 11, 1957 (68/218)

Highest field goal percentage, one half
.706—Philadelphia vs. Los Angeles, June 6, 1982 (36/51)
.667—Philadelphia at Los Angeles, May 7, 1980 (26/39)
   Philadelphia at Los Angeles, June 8, 1982 (30/45)
   Los Angeles vs. Boston, June 6, 1984 (28/42)
.659—Chicago vs. L.A. Lakers, June 5, 1991 (27/41)

Highest field goal percentage, one quarter
.850—Chicago vs. L.A. Lakers, June 5, 1991 (17/20)
.824—Detroit vs. L.A. Lakers, June 6, 1989 (14/17)
.813—Los Angeles vs. Boston, June 6, 1984 (13/16)
   Boston at Houston, June 3, 1986 (13/16)

FIELD GOALS
Most field goals, game
62—Boston vs. L.A. Lakers, May 27, 1985
61—Boston vs. St. Louis, March 27, 1960

Fewest field goals, game
23—Ft. Wayne vs. Syracuse, at Indianapolis, April 7, 1955
25—Syracuse vs. Ft. Wayne, at Indianapolis, April 7, 1955

Most field goals, both teams, game

112—Philadelphia (57) vs. San Francisco (55), April 14, 1967 (ot)
111—Boston (62) vs. L.A. Lakers (49), May 27, 1985

Fewest field goals, both teams, game

48—Ft. Wayne (23) vs. Syracuse (25), at Indianapolis, April 7, 1955
57—Syracuse (26) vs. Ft. Wayne (31), at Indianapolis, April 3, 1955

FIELD GOAL ATTEMPTS

Most field goal attempts, game

140—San Francisco at Philadelphia, April 14, 1967 (ot)
133—Boston vs. St. Louis, March 27, 1960

Fewest field goal attempts, game

66—Los Angeles at New York, May 4, 1970
   L.A. Lakers at Chicago, June 2, 1991
   Houston vs. New York, June 19, 1994
69—New York at Houston, June 10, 1994

Most field goal attempts, both teams, game

256—San Francisco (140) at Philadelphia (116), April 14, 1967 (ot)
250—Boston (130) vs. Minneapolis (120), April 4, 1959

Fewest field goal attempts, both teams, game

146—L.A. Lakers (66) at Chicago (80), June 2, 1991
   Houston (66) vs. New York (80), June 19, 1994
149—Detroit (70) at L.A. Lakers (79), June 13, 1989

THREE-POINT FIELD GOALS MADE

Most three-point field goals made, game

10—Chicago at Phoenix, June 20, 1993
9—Phoenix at Chicago, June 13, 1993 (3 ot)

Most three-point field goals made, both teams, game

14—Phoenix (9) at Chicago (5), June 13, 1993 (3 ot)
   Chicago (10) at Phoenix (4), June 20, 1993
13—New York (7) at Houston (6), June 10, 1994
   New York (7) vs. Houston (6), June 15, 1994

Most three-point field goals made, one half

6—Chicago vs. Portland, June 3, 1992
   Chicago at Phoenix, June 20, 1993
   New York at Houston, June 10, 1994
   New York vs. Houston, June 15, 1994

Most three-point field goals made, one quarter

6—Chicago at Phoenix, June 20, 1993

THREE-POINT FIELD GOAL ATTEMPTS

Most three-point field goal attempts, game

22—Houston vs. New York, June 10, 1994
20—Houston at New York, June 15, 1994
   New York at Houston, June 22, 1994

Most three-point field goal attempts, both teams, game

37—Houston (20) at New York (17), June 15, 1994
36—New York (19) vs. Houston (17), June 12, 1994

Most three-point field goal attempts, one half

16—New York at Houston, June 22, 1994

FREE THROW PERCENTAGE

Highest free throw percentage, game

1.000—Portland at Chicago, June 14, 1992 (21/21)
.958—Boston vs. Houston, May 29, 1986 (23/24)

Lowest free throw percentage, game

.444—Philadelphia vs. San Francisco, April 16, 1967 (16/36)
   Golden State at Washington, May 25, 1975 (8/18)
.476—Baltimore at Milwaukee, April 21, 1971 (10/21)

Highest free throw percentage, both teams, game

.933—L.A. Lakers (.955) at Chicago (.875), June 5, 1991 (28/30)
.903—Boston (.926) vs. Los Angeles (.889), April 14, 1962 (65/72)

Lowest free throw percentage, both teams, game

.538—Philadelphia (.444) vs. San Francisco (.655), April 16, 1967 (35/65)
.541—San Francisco (.478) at Boston (.615), April 18, 1964 (46/85)

FREE THROWS MADE

Most free throws made, game

45—St. Louis at Boston, April 13, 1957 (2 ot)
44—St. Louis at Boston, April 9, 1958

Fewest free throws made, game

3—Los Angeles at Philadelphia, May 26, 1983
6—Chicago vs. Phoenix, June 13, 1993 (3 ot)

Most free throws made, both teams, game

80—St. Louis (44) at Boston (36), April 9, 1958
77—Syracuse (39) vs. Ft. Wayne (38), April 9, 1955
   Boston (43) at St. Louis (34), April 12, 1958

Fewest free throws made, both teams, game

21—Phoenix (10) vs. Chicago (11), June 9, 1993
23—Milwaukee (9) vs. Boston (14), April 28, 1974

FREE THROW ATTEMPTS

Most free throw attempts, game

64—Philadelphia at San Francisco, April 24, 1967
62—St. Louis at Boston, April 13, 1957 (2 ot)

Fewest free throw attempts, game

5—Los Angeles at Philadelphia, May 26, 1983
8—Chicago vs. L.A. Lakers, June 5, 1991

Most free throw attempts, both teams, game

116—St. Louis (62) at Boston (54), April 13, 1957 (2 ot)
107—Boston (60) at St. Louis (47), April 2, 1958
   St. Louis (57) at Boston (50), April 9, 1958

Fewest free throw attempts, both teams, game

30—Chicago (8) vs. L.A. Lakers (22), June 5, 1991
31—Milwaukee (13) vs. Boston (18), April 28, 1974

TOTAL REBOUNDS

Highest rebound percentage, game

.667—Boston vs. St. Louis, April 9, 1960 (78/117)
.632—Los Angeles vs. New York, May 7, 1972 (67/106)

Most rebounds, game

93—Philadelphia vs. San Francisco, April 16, 1967
86—Boston vs. Minneapolis, April 4, 1959

Fewest rebounds, game

29—L.A. Lakers vs. Chicago, June 7, 1991 (ot)
31—L.A. Lakers at Detroit, June 16, 1988
   Chicago at Portland, June 14, 1992

Most rebounds, both teams, game

169—Philadelphia (93) vs. San Francisco (76), April 16, 1967
159—San Francisco (80) at Philadelphia (79), April 14, 1967 (ot)

Fewest rebounds, both teams, game

69—Detroit (34) at L.A. Lakers (35), June 7, 1988
   Chicago (31) at Portland (38), June 14, 1992
70—L.A. Lakers (34) at Chicago (36), June 5, 1991

OFFENSIVE REBOUNDS

Highest offensive rebound percentage, game

.556—Detroit vs. L.A. Lakers, June 16, 1988 (20/36)
.529—Seattle vs. Washington, June 7, 1978 (27/51)

Most offensive rebounds, game

28—Houston vs. Boston, May 10, 1981
27—Seattle vs. Washington, June 7, 1978
   Boston at Los Angeles, June 6, 1984

Fewest offensive rebounds, game

3—Boston vs. L.A. Lakers, May 30, 1985
   Houston vs. New York, June 22, 1994
5—Philadelphia at Los Angeles, May 7, 1980
   Philadelphia vs. Los Angeles, May 11, 1980
   Boston at L.A. Lakers, June 2, 1987
   L.A. Lakers at Detroit, June 12, 1988
   Houston vs. New York, June 19, 1994

Most offensive rebounds, both teams, game

45—Houston (28) vs. Boston (17), May 10, 1981
44—Seattle (27) vs. Washington (17), June 7, 1978
   Boston (25) vs. Houston (19), May 5, 1981

Fewest offensive rebounds, both teams, game

15—L.A. Lakers (6) at Chicago (9), June 2, 1991
17—L.A. Lakers (14) at Boston (3), May 30, 1985
   L.A. Lakers (8) at Detroit (9), June 6, 1989
   Houston (3) vs. New York (14), June 22, 1994

DEFENSIVE REBOUNDS

Highest defensive rebound percentage, game

.921—L.A. Lakers at Boston, May 30, 1985 (35/38)
.897—New York at Houston, June 22, 1994 (26/29)

Most defensive rebounds, game

48—Portland at Philadelphia, June 3, 1977
46—Philadelphia vs. Portland, May 26, 1977

Fewest defensive rebounds, game

16—L.A. Lakers at Detroit, June 16, 1988
20—Philadelphia vs. Portland, May 22, 1977
   L.A. Lakers at Chicago, June 5, 1991
   L.A. Lakers vs. Chicago, June 7, 1991 (ot)

Most defensive rebounds, both teams, game

84—Portland (48) at Philadelphia (36), June 3, 1977
82—Philadelphia (46) vs. Portland (36), May 26, 1977

Fewest defensive rebounds, both teams, game

43—L.A. Lakers (21) at Detroit (22), June 8, 1989
45—L.A. Lakers (20) at Chicago (25), June 5, 1991

ASSISTS

Most assists, game
44—Los Angeles vs. New York, May 6, 1970
    L.A. Lakers vs. Boston, June 4, 1987
43—Boston vs. L.A. Lakers, May 27, 1985

Fewest assists, game
5—Boston at St. Louis, April 3, 1960
9—Los Angeles at Boston, April 28, 1966

Most assists, both teams, game
79—L.A. Lakers (44) vs. Boston (35), June 4, 1987
76—L.A. Lakers (40) vs. Boston (36), June 7, 1985

Fewest assists, both teams, game
21—Los Angeles (10) at Boston (11), April 29, 1969
24—Los Angeles (10) at Boston (14), May 3, 1969

PERSONAL FOULS

Most personal fouls, game
42—Minneapolis vs. Syracuse, April 23, 1950
40—Portland vs. Philadelphia, May 31, 1977

Fewest personal fouls, game
13—L.A. Lakers at Detroit, June 12, 1988
15—L.A. Lakers at Chicago, June 5, 1991

Most personal fouls, both teams, game
77—Minneapolis (42) vs. Syracuse (35), April 23, 1950
76—Minneapolis (39) at New York (37), April 18, 1952
    (ot)

Fewest personal fouls, both teams, game
35—Boston (17) at Milwaukee (18), April 28, 1974
    Boston (17) at Houston (18), June 3, 1986
    L.A. Lakers (15) at Chicago (20), June 5, 1991
36—Baltimore (17) vs. Milwaukee (19), April 25, 1971
    Boston (17) vs. Houston (19), May 26, 1986
    L.A. Lakers (13) at Detroit (23), June 12, 1988
    Phoenix (19) vs. Chicago (17), June 9, 1993

DISQUALIFICATIONS

Most disqualifications, game
4—Minneapolis vs. Syracuse, April 23, 1950
    Minneapolis vs. New York, April 4, 1953
    New York vs. Minneapolis, April 10, 1953

    St. Louis at Boston, April 13, 1957 (2 ot)
    Boston vs. Los Angeles, April 18, 1962 (ot)

Most disqualifications, both teams, game
7—Boston (4) vs. Los Angeles (3), April 18, 1962 (ot)
6—St. Louis (4) at Boston (2), April 13, 1957 (2 ot)

STEALS

Most steals, game
17—Golden State vs. Washington, May 23, 1975
16—Philadelphia vs. Portland, May 22, 1977

Fewest steals, game
1—Milwaukee at Boston, May 10, 1974 (2 ot)
    Boston vs. Phoenix, May 23, 1976
2—Milwaukee at Boston, May 3, 1974
    Milwaukee at Boston, May 5, 1974
    Milwaukee vs. Boston, May 12, 1974
    Detroit vs. L.A. Lakers, June 6, 1989
    Detroit vs. Portland, June 7, 1990 (ot)

Most steals, both teams, game
31—Golden State (17) vs. Washington (14), May 23, 1975
28—Golden State (15) at Washington (13), May 25, 1975

Fewest steals, both teams, game
6—Detroit (3) vs. L.A. Lakers (3), June 8, 1989
    L.A. Lakers (3) vs. Detroit (3), June 13, 1989
8—Milwaukee (2) at Boston (6), May 5, 1974
    Milwaukee (1) at Boston (7), May 10, 1974 (2 ot)
    Seattle (4) vs. Washington (4), June 2, 1978
    Seattle (4) vs. Washington (4), May 29, 1979 (ot)
    Chicago (4) at L.A. Lakers (4), June 9, 1991

BLOCKED SHOTS

Most blocked shots, game
13—Seattle at Washington, May 28, 1978
    Philadelphia at Los Angeles, May 4, 1980
    Philadelphia vs. Los Angeles, June 6, 1982
    Philadelphia at Los Angeles, May 22, 1983
    Houston vs. Boston, June 5, 1986
12—Golden State vs. Washington, May 20, 1975
    Phoenix vs. Chicago, June 11, 1993

Fewest blocked shots, game
0—Boston vs. Milwaukee, May 5, 1974
    Boston vs. Milwaukee, May 10, 1974 (2 ot)
    Boston vs. Phoenix, June 4, 1976 (3 ot)
    Philadelphia vs. Portland, May 22, 1977
    Washington at Seattle, May 21, 1978
    Boston at Houston, May 14, 1981
    L.A. Lakers vs. Boston, June 5, 1985
    L.A. Lakers vs. Detroit, June 7, 1988

Most blocked shots, both teams, game
22—Philadelphia (13) at Los Angeles (9), May 4, 1980
    Philadelphia (13) vs. Los Angeles (9), June 6, 1982
21—Philadelphia (13) vs. Los Angeles (8), May 22, 1983

Fewest blocked shots, both teams, game
2—Boston (0) at Houston (2), May 14, 1981
3—Boston (0) vs. Milwaukee (3), May 5, 1974
    Boston (0) vs. Milwaukee (3), May 10, 1974 (2 ot)
    Boston (1) vs. Phoenix (2), May 23, 1976
    L.A. Lakers (1) vs. Detroit (2), June 21, 1988
    Chicago (1) vs. L.A. Lakers (2), June 5, 1991

TURNOVERS

Most turnovers, game
34—Portland at Philadelphia, May 22, 1977
31—Golden State at Washington, May 25, 1975

Fewest turnovers, game
5—Chicago at L.A. Lakers, June 9, 1991
7—L.A. Lakers vs. Detroit, June 13, 1989

Most turnovers, both teams, game
60—Golden State (31) at Washington (29), May 25, 1975
54—Phoenix (29) at Boston (25), June 4, 1976 (3 ot)
    Portland (34) at Philadelphia (20), May 22, 1977

Fewest turnovers, both teams, game
15—Chicago (5) at L.A. Lakers (10), June 9, 1991
16—L.A. Lakers (7) vs. Detroit (9), June 13, 1989

ALL-TIME PLAYER DIRECTORY

The lifetime summaries and year-by-year records of everyone who played in the National Basketball Association, Basketball Association of America and American Basketball Association are contained in this section. Also included are National Basketball League players who appeared in the BAA or NBA.

Dashes indicate that no records were available or that records were not kept in some categories. Totals for offensive and defensive rebounds are not listed for those players who were active prior to 1973–74, the year that the NBA began recording those statistics. The letter "N" next to a team means NBL; "A" means ABA.

The following is a listing of all NBA, ABA and NBL franchises and their years of existence.

NBA TEAMS	SEASONS ACTIVE
Anderson Packers	1949–50
Atlanta Hawks	1968–69—Current
Baltimore Bullets	1947–48—1954–55
	1963–64—1972–73
Boston Celtics	1946–47—Current
Buffalo Braves	1970–71—1977–78
Capital Bullets	1973–74
Charlotte Hornets	1988–89—Current
Chicago Bulls	1966–67—Current
Chicago Packers	1961–62
Chicago Stags	1946–47—1949–50
Chicago Zephyrs	1962–63
Cincinnati Royals	1957–58—1971–72
Cleveland Cavaliers	1970–71—Current
Cleveland Rebels	1946–47
Dallas Mavericks	1980–81—Current
Denver Nuggets	1949–50
	1976–77—Current
Detroit Falcons	1946–47
Detroit Pistons	1957–58—Current
Fort Wayne Pistons	1948–49—1956–57
Golden State Warriors	1971–72—Current
Houston Rockets	1971–72—Current
Indiana Pacers	1976–77—Current
Indianapolis Jets	1948–49
Indianapolis Olympians	1949–50—1952–53
Kansas City Kings	1975–76—1984–85
Kansas City-Omaha Kings	1972–73—1974–75
Los Angeles Clippers	1984–85—Current
Los Angeles Lakers	1960–61—Current
Miami Heat	1988–89—Current
Milwaukee Bucks	1968–69—Current
Milwaukee Hawks	1951–52—1954–55
Minneapolis Lakers	1948–49—1959–60
Minnesota Timberwolves	1989–90—Current
New Jersey Nets	1977–78—Current
New Orleans Jazz	1974–75—1979–80
New York Knicks	1946–47—Current
New York Nets	1976–77
Orlando Magic	1989–90—Current
Philadelphia Warriors	1946–47—1961–62
Philadelphia 76ers	1963–64—Current
Phoenix Suns	1968–69—Current
Pittsburgh Ironmen	1946–47
Portland Trail Blazers	1970–71—Current
Providence Steamrollers	1946–47—1948–49
Rochester Royals	1948–49—1956–57

NBA TEAMS	SEASONS ACTIVE
St. Louis Bombers	1946–47—1949–50
St. Louis Hawks	1955–56—1967–68
Sacramento Kings	1985–86—Current
San Antonio Spurs	1976–77—Current
San Diego Clippers	1978–79—1983–84
San Diego Rockets	1967–68—1970–71
San Francisco Warriors	1962–63—1970–71
Seattle SuperSonics	1967–68—Current
Sheboygan Redskins	1949–50
Syracuse Nationals	1949–50—1962–63
Toronto Huskies	1946–47
Tri-Cities Blackhawks	1949–50—1950–51
Utah Jazz	1980–81—Current
Washington Bullets	1974–75—Current
Washington Capitols	1946–47—1950–51
Waterloo Hawks	1949–50

ABA TEAMS	SEASONS ACTIVE
Anaheim Amigos	1967–68
Carolina Cougars	1969–70—1973–74
Dallas Chaparrals	1967–68—1969–70
	1971–72—1972–73
Denver Nuggets	1974–75—1975–76
Denver Rockets	1967–68—1973–74
Floridians	1970–71—1971–72
Houston Mavericks	1967–68—1968–69
Indiana Pacers	1967–68—1975–76
Kentucky Colonels	1967–68—1975–76
Los Angeles Stars	1968–69—1969–70
Memphis Pros	1970–71—1971–72
Memphis Sounds	1974–75
Memphis Tams	1972–73—1973–74
Miami Floridians	1968–69—1969–70
Minnesota Muskies	1967–68
Minnesota Pipers	1968–69—1969–70
New Jersey Americans	1967–68
New York Nets	1968–69—1975–76
New Orleans Buccaneers	1967–68—1969–70
Oakland Oaks	1967–68—1968–69
Pittsburgh Condors	1970–71—1971–72
Pittsburgh Pipers	1967–68
St. Louis Spirits	1974–75—1975–76
San Antonio Spurs	1973–74—1975–76
San Diego Conquistadors	1972–73—1974–75
San Diego Sails	1975–76
Texas Chaparrals	1970–71

ABA TEAMS	SEASONS ACTIVE
Utah Stars	1970–71—1975–76
Virginia Squires	1970–71—1975–76
Washington Capitols	1969–70

NBL TEAMS	SEASONS ACTIVE
Akron Firestone Non-Skids	1937–38—1940–41
Akron Goodyear Wingfoots	1937–38—1941–42
Anderson Duffey Packers	1946–47—1948–49
Buffalo Bisons	1937–38
Buffalo Bisons-Tri-Cities Blackhawks	1946–47
Chicago American Gears	1944–45—1946–47
Chicago Bruins	1939–40—1941–42
Chicago Studebakers	1942–43
Cleveland Allmen Transfers	1944–45—1945–46
Cleveland Chase Brassmen	1943–44
Columbus Athletic Supply	1937–38
Dayton Metros	1937–38
Denver Nuggets	1948–49
Detroit Eagles	1939–40—1940–41
Detroit Gems	1946–47
Detroit Vagabond Kings-Dayton Rens	1948–49
Fort Wayne General Electrics	1937–38
Fort Wayne Zollner Pistons	1941–42—1947–48
Hammond Calumet Buccaneers	1948–49
Hammond Ciesar All-Americans	1938–39—1940–41
Indianapolis Kautskys	1937–38—1939–40,
	1941–42,
	1945–46—1947–48
Kankakee Gallagher Trojans	1937–38
Midland-Flint Dow A.C.'s	1947–48
Minneapolis Lakers	1947–48
Oshkosh All-Stars	1937–38—1948–49
Pittsburgh Pirates	1937–38—1938–39
Pittsburgh Raiders	1944–45
Richmond King Clothiers-Cincinnati Comellos	1937–38
Rochester Royals	1945–46—1947–48
Sheboygan Red Skins	1938–39—1948–49
Syracuse Nationals	1946–47—1948–49
Toledo Jeeps	1946–47—1947–48
Toledo Jim White Chevrolets	1941–42—1942–43
Tri-Cities Blackhawks	1947–48—1948–49
Warren Penns	1937–38
Warren Penns-Cleveland White Horses	1938–39
Waterloo Hawks	1948–49
Whiting Ciesar All-Americans	1937–38
Youngstown Bears	1945–46—1946–47

ABDELNABY, ALAA b. June 24, 1968 Ht. 6-10 Wt. 240 College—Duke

SEASON—TEAM	G	GS	MIN	FGM	FGA	PCT	3FGM	3FGA	PCT	FTM	FTA	PCT	O-RB	D-RB	TOT	AST	PF	DQ	STL	TO	BLK	PTS	RPG	APG	PPG
90-91—Portland	43	0	290	55	116	.474	0	0	—	25	44	.568	27	62	89	12	39	0	4	22	12	135	2.1	0.3	3.1
91-92—Portland	71	1	934	178	361	.493	0	0	—	76	101	.752	81	179	260	30	132	1	26	66	16	432	3.7	0.4	6.1
92-93—Milw.-Boston	75	52	1311	245	473	.518	0	1	.000	88	116	.759	126	211	337	27	189	0	25	97	26	578	4.5	0.4	7.7
93-94—Boston	13	0	159	24	55	.436	0	0	—	16	25	.640	12	34	46	3	20	0	2	17	3	64	3.5	0.2	4.9
REG. SEASON TOTALS	202	53	2694	502	1005	.500	0	1	.000	205	286	.717	246	486	732	72	380	1	56	202	57	1209	3.6	0.4	6.0
PLAYOFF TOTALS	17	4	106	18	40	.450	0	0	—	2	4	.500	3	17	20	3	11	0	0	11	1	38	1.2	0.2	2.2

ABDUL-AZIZ, ZAID (formerly Donald A. Smith) b. April 7, 1946 Ht. 6-9 Wt. 235 College—Iowa State

SEASON—TEAM	G	GS	MIN	FGM	FGA	PCT	3FGM	3FGA	PCT	FTM	FTA	PCT	O-RB	D-RB	TOT	AST	PF	DQ	STL	TO	BLK	PTS	RPG	APG	PPG
68-69—Cin.-Milw.	49	—	945	144	390	.369	.—	—	—	70	113	.619	—	—	409	37	115	3	—	—	—	358	8.3	0.8	7.3
69-70—Milwaukee	80	—	1637	237	546	.434	—	—	—	119	185	.643	—	—	603	62	167	2	—	—	—	593	7.5	0.8	7.4
70-71—Seattle	61	—	1276	263	597	.441	—	—	—	139	188	.739	—	—	468	42	118	0	—	—	—	665	7.7	0.7	10.9
71-72—Seattle	58	—	1780	322	751	.429	—	—	—	154	214	.720	—	—	654	124	178	1	—	—	—	798	11.3	2.1	13.8
72-73—Houston	48	—	900	149	375	.397	—	—	—	119	162	.735	—	—	304	53	108	2	—	—	—	417	6.3	1.1	8.7
73-74—Houston	79	—	2459	336	732	.459	—	—	—	193	240	.804	259	664	923	166	227	3	80	—	104	865	11.7	2.1	10.9
74-75—Houston	65	—	1450	235	538	.437	—	—	—	159	203	.783	154	334	488	84	128	1	37	—	74	629	7.5	1.3	9.7
75-76—Seattle	27	—	223	35	75	.467	—	—	—	16	29	.552	30	46	76	16	29	0	8	—	15	86	2.8	0.6	3.2
76-77—Buffalo	22	—	195	25	74	.338	—	—	—	33	43	.767	41	49	90	7	21	0	3	—	9	83	4.1	0.3	3.8
77-78—Boston-Houston	16	—	158	23	60	.383	—	—	—	17	23	.739	19	31	50	10	29	0	3	11	3	63	3.1	0.6	3.9
REG. SEASON TOTALS	505	—	11023	1769	4138	.428	—	—	—	1019	1400	.728	503	1124	4065	601	1120	12	131	11	205	4557	8.0	1.2	9.0
PLAYOFF TOTALS	18	—	210	37	70	.529	—	—	—	18	26	.692	11	27	64	9	12	0	1	—	8	92	3.6	0.5	5.1

ABDUL-JABBAR, KAREEM (formerly Ferdinand Lewis Alcindor Jr.) b. April 16, 1947 Ht. 7-2 Wt. 230 College—UCLA

SEASON—TEAM	G	GS	MIN	FGM	FGA	PCT	3FGM	3FGA	PCT	FTM	FTA	PCT	O-RB	D-RB	TOT	AST	PF	DQ	STL	TO	BLK	PTS	RPG	APG	PPG
69-70—Milwaukee	82	—	3534	938	1810	.518	—	—	—	485	743	.653	—	—	1190	337	283	8	—	—	—	2361	14.5	4.1	28.8
70-71—Milwaukee	82	—	3288	1063	1843	.577	—	—	—	470	681	.690	—	—	1311	272	264	4	—	—	—	2596	16.0	3.3	31.7
71-72—Milwaukee	81	—	3583	1159	2019	.574	—	—	—	504	732	.689	—	—	1346	370	235	1	—	—	—	2822	16.6	4.6	34.8
72-73—Milwaukee	76	—	3254	982	1772	.554	—	—	—	328	460	.713	—	—	1224	379	208	0	—	—	—	2292	16.1	5.0	30.2
73-74—Milwaukee	81	—	3548	948	1759	.539	—	—	—	295	420	.702	287	891	1178	386	238	2	112	—	283	2191	14.5	4.8	27.0
74-75—Milwaukee	65	—	2747	812	1584	.513	—	—	—	325	426	.763	194	718	912	264	205	2	65	—	212	1949	14.0	4.1	30.0
75-76—Los Angeles	82	—	3379	914	1728	.529	—	—	—	447	636	.703	272	1111	1383	413	292	6	119	—	338	2275	16.9	5.0	27.7
76-77—Los Angeles	82	—	3016	888	1533	.579	—	—	—	376	536	.701	266	824	1090	319	262	4	101	—	261	2152	13.3	3.9	26.2
77-78—Los Angeles	62	—	2265	663	1205	.550	—	—	—	274	350	.783	186	615	801	269	182	1	103	208	185	1600	12.9	4.3	25.8
78-79—Los Angeles	80	—	3157	777	1347	.577	—	—	—	349	474	.736	207	818	1025	431	230	3	76	282	316	1903	12.8	5.4	23.8
79-80—Los Angeles	82	—	3143	835	1383	.604	0	1	.000	364	476	.765	190	696	886	371	216	2	81	297	280	2034	10.8	4.5	24.8
80-81—Los Angeles	80	—	2976	836	1457	.574	0	1	.000	423	552	.766	197	624	821	272	244	4	59	249	228	2095	10.3	3.4	26.2
81-82—Los Angeles	76	76	2677	753	1301	.579	0	3	.000	312	442	.706	172	487	659	225	224	0	63	230	207	1818	8.7	3.0	23.9
82-83—Los Angeles	79	79	2554	722	1228	.588	0	2	.000	278	371	.749	167	425	592	200	220	1	61	200	170	1722	7.5	2.5	21.8
83-84—Los Angeles	80	80	2622	716	1238	.578	0	1	.000	285	394	.723	169	418	587	211	211	1	55	221	143	1717	7.3	2.6	21.5
84-85—L.A. Lakers	79	79	2630	723	1207	.599	0	1	.000	289	395	.732	162	460	622	249	238	3	63	197	162	1735	7.9	3.2	22.0
85-86—L.A. Lakers	79	79	2629	755	1338	.564	0	2	.000	336	439	.765	133	345	478	280	248	2	67	203	130	1846	6.1	3.5	23.4
86-87—L.A. Lakers	78	78	2441	560	993	.564	1	3	.333	245	343	.714	152	371	523	203	245	2	49	186	97	1366	6.7	2.6	17.5
87-88—L.A. Lakers	80	80	2308	480	903	.532	0	1	.000	205	269	.762	118	360	478	135	216	1	48	159	92	1165	6.0	1.7	14.6
88-89—L.A. Lakers	74	74	1695	313	659	.475	0	3	.000	122	165	.739	103	231	334	74	196	1	38	95	85	748	4.5	1.0	10.1
REG. SEASON TOTALS	1560	625	57446	15837	28307	.559	1	18	.056	6712	9304	.721	2975	9394	17440	5660	4657	48	1160	2527	3189	38387	11.2	3.6	24.6
PLAYOFF TOTALS	237	140	8851	2356	4422	.533	0	4	.000	1050	1419	.740	505	1273	2481	767	797	7	189	447	476	5762	10.5	3.2	24.3
ALL-STAR TOTALS	18	13	449	105	213	.493	0	1	.000	41	50	.820	33	84	149	51	57	1	6	28	31	251	8.3	2.8	13.9

ABDUL-RAHMAN, MAHDI (see Walter Raphael Hazzard Jr.)

ABDUL-RAUF, MAHMOUD (formerly Chris Wayne Jackson) b. March 9, 1969 Ht. 6-1 Wt. 165 College—Louisiana State

SEASON—TEAM	G	GS	MIN	FGM	FGA	PCT	3FGM	3FGA	PCT	FTM	FTA	PCT	O-RB	D-RB	TOT	AST	PF	DQ	STL	TO	BLK	PTS	RPG	APG	PPG
90-91—Denver	67	19	1505	417	1009	.413	24	100	.240	84	98	.857	34	87	121	206	149	2	55	110	4	942	1.8	3.1	14.1
91-92—Denver	81	11	1538	356	845	.421	31	94	.330	94	108	.870	22	92	114	192	130	0	44	117	4	837	1.4	2.4	10.3
92-93—Denver	81	81	2710	633	1407	.450	70	197	.355	217	232	.935	51	174	225	344	179	0	84	187	8	1553	2.8	4.2	19.2
93-94—Denver	80	78	2617	588	1279	.460	42	133	.316	219	229	.956	27	141	168	362	150	1	82	151	10	1437	2.1	4.5	18.0
REG. SEASON TOTALS	309	189	8370	1994	4540	.439	167	524	.319	614	667	.921	134	494	628	1104	608	3	265	565	26	4769	2.0	3.6	15.4
PLAYOFF TOTALS	12	12	339	57	154	.370	12	37	.324	29	31	.935	3	15	18	30	29	0	5	14	1	155	1.5	2.5	12.9

ABERNETHY, THOMAS CRAIG (Tom) b. May 6, 1954 Ht. 6-7 Wt. 220 College—Indiana

SEASON—TEAM	G	GS	MIN	FGM	FGA	PCT	3FGM	3FGA	PCT	FTM	FTA	PCT	O-RB	D-RB	TOT	AST	PF	DQ	STL	TO	BLK	PTS	RPG	APG	PPG
76-77—Los Angeles	70	—	1378	169	349	.484	—	—	—	101	134	.754	113	178	291	98	118	1	49	—	10	439	4.2	1.4	6.3
77-78—Los Angeles	73	—	1317	201	404	.498	—	—	—	91	111	.820	105	160	265	101	122	1	55	50	22	493	3.6	1.4	6.8
78-79—Golden State	70	—	1219	176	342	.515	—	—	—	70	94	.745	74	142	216	79	133	1	39	32	13	422	3.1	1.1	6.0
79-80—Golden State	67	—	1222	153	318	.481	0	1	.000	56	82	.683	62	129	191	87	118	0	35	39	12	362	2.9	1.3	5.4
80-81—G.S.-Indiana	39	—	298	25	59	.424	0	1	.000	13	22	.591	20	28	48	19	34	0	7	8	3	63	1.2	0.5	1.6
REG. SEASON TOTALS	319	—	5434	724	1472	.492	0	2	.000	331	443	.747	374	637	1011	384	525	3	185	129	60	1779	3.2	1.2	5.6
PLAYOFF TOTALS	13	—	226	22	54	.407	0	0	—	24	29	.828	14	28	42	23	18	0	7	0	2	68	3.2	1.8	5.2

ABLE, FOREST EDWARD (Frosty) b. July 27, 1932 Ht. 6-3 Wt. 180 College—Western Kentucky/Louisville

SEASON—TEAM	G	GS	MIN	FGM	FGA	PCT	3FGM	3FGA	PCT	FTM	FTA	PCT	O-RB	D-RB	TOT	AST	PF	DQ	STL	TO	BLK	PTS	RPG	APG	PPG
56-57—Syracuse	1	—	1	0	2	.000	—	—	—	0	0	—	—	—	1	1	1	0	—	—	—	0	1.0	1.0	0.0
REG. SEASON TOTALS	1	—	1	0	2	.000	—	—	—	0	0	—	—	—	1	1	1	0	—	—	—	0	1.0	1.0	0.0

ABRAMOVIC, JOHN JR. (Brooms) b. February 9, 1919 Ht. 6-3 Wt. 195 College—Salem

SEASON—TEAM	G	GS	MIN	FGM	FGA	PCT	3FGM	3FGA	PCT	FTM	FTA	PCT	O-RB	D-RB	TOT	AST	PF	DQ	STL	TO	BLK	PTS	RPG	APG	PPG
46-47—Pittsburgh	47	—	—	202	834	.242	—	—	—	123	178	.691	—	—	—	35	161	—	—	—	—	527	—	0.7	11.2
47-48—St. L.-Balt.	9	—	—	1	21	.048	—	—	—	4	7	.571	—	—	—	2	10	—	—	—	—	6	—	0.2	0.7
47-48—Syracuse (N)	35	—	—	72	—	—	—	—	—	42	54	.778	—	—	—	—	96	—	—	—	—	186	—	—	5.3
REG. NBA TOTALS	56	—	—	203	855	.237	—	—	—	127	185	.686	—	—	—	37	171	—	—	—	—	533	—	0.7	9.5
REG. NBL TOTALS	35	—	—	72	—	—	—	—	—	42	54	.778	—	—	—	—	96	—	—	—	—	186	—	—	5.3
NBL PLAYOFF TOTALS	3	—	—	5	—	—	—	—	—	2	3	.667	—	—	—	—	8	—	—	—	—	12	—	—	4.0

ACKERMAN, DONALD D. (Buddy) b. September 4, 1930 Ht. 6-0 Wt. 185 College—Long Island

SEASON—TEAM	G	GS	MIN	FGM	FGA	PCT	3FGM	3FGA	PCT	FTM	FTA	PCT	O-RB	D-RB	TOT	AST	PF	DQ	STL	TO	BLK	PTS	RPG	APG	PPG
53-54—New York	28	—	220	14	63	.222	—	—	—	15	28	.536	—	—	15	23	43	0	—	—	—	43	0.5	0.8	1.5
REG. SEASON TOTALS	28	—	220	14	63	.222	—	—	—	15	28	.536	—	—	15	23	43	0	—	—	—	43	0.5	0.8	1.5
PLAYOFF TOTALS	4	—	20	1	3	.333	—	—	—	0	0	—	—	—	4	1	7	0	—	—	—	2	1.3	0.3	0.5

ACRES, MARK RICHARD b. November 15, 1962 Ht. 6-11 Wt. 220 College—Oral Roberts

SEASON—TEAM	G	GS	MIN	FGM	FGA	PCT	3FGM	3FGA	PCT	FTM	FTA	PCT	O-RB	D-RB	TOT	AST	PF	DQ	STL	TO	BLK	PTS	RPG	APG	PPG
87-88—Boston	79	5	1151	108	203	.532	0	0	—	71	111	.640	105	165	270	42	198	2	29	54	27	287	3.4	0.5	3.6
88-89—Boston	62	0	632	55	114	.482	1	1	1.000	26	48	.542	59	87	146	19	94	0	19	23	6	137	2.4	0.3	2.2
89-90—Orlando	80	50	1691	138	285	.484	3	4	.750	83	120	.692	154	277	431	67	248	4	36	70	25	362	5.4	0.8	4.5
90-91—Orlando	68	0	1313	109	214	.509	1	3	.333	66	101	.653	140	219	359	25	218	4	25	42	25	285	5.3	0.4	4.2
91-92—Orlando	68	6	926	78	151	.517	1	3	.333	51	67	.761	97	155	252	22	140	1	25	33	15	208	3.7	0.3	3.1
92-93—Houston-Chicago-Wash.	18	7	269	26	49	.531	1	2	.500	11	16	.688	26	41	67	5	34	0	3	13	6	64	3.7	0.3	3.6
REG. SEASON TOTALS	375	68	5982	514	1016	.506	7	13	.538	308	463	.665	581	944	1525	180	932	11	137	235	104	1343	4.1	0.5	3.6
PLAYOFF TOTALS	19	0	160	14	27	.519	0	1	.000	9	18	.500	14	23	37	2	33	0	1	6	1	37	1.9	0.1	1.9

ACTON, CHARLES R. (Bud) b. January 11, 1942 Ht. 6-6 Wt. 210 College—Alma College/Hillsdale (Mich.)

SEASON—TEAM	G	GS	MIN	FGM	FGA	PCT	3FGM	3FGA	PCT	FTM	FTA	PCT	O-RB	D-RB	TOT	AST	PF	DQ	STL	TO	BLK	PTS	RPG	APG	PPG
67-68—San Diego	23	—	195	29	74	.392	—	—	—	19	29	.655	—	—	47	11	35	0	—	—	—	77	2.0	0.5	3.3
REG. SEASON TOTALS	23	—	195	29	74	.392	—	—	—	19	29	.655	—	—	47	11	35	0	—	—	—	77	2.0	0.5	3.3

ADAMS, ALVAN LEIGH (Double A) b. July 19, 1954 Ht. 6-9 Wt. 220 College—Oklahoma

SEASON—TEAM	G	GS	MIN	FGM	FGA	PCT	3FGM	3FGA	PCT	FTM	FTA	PCT	O-RB	D-RB	TOT	AST	PF	DQ	STL	TO	BLK	PTS	RPG	APG	PPG
75-76—Phoenix	80	—	2656	629	1341	.469	—	—	—	261	355	.735	215	512	727	450	274	6	121	—	116	1519	9.1	5.6	19.0
76-77—Phoenix	72	—	2278	522	1102	.474	—	—	—	252	334	.754	180	472	652	322	260	4	95	—	87	1296	9.1	4.5	18.0
77-78—Phoenix	70	—	1914	434	895	.485	—	—	—	214	293	.730	158	407	565	225	242	8	86	234	63	1082	8.1	3.2	15.5
78-79—Phoenix	77	—	2364	569	1073	.530	—	—	—	231	289	.799	220	485	705	360	246	4	110	279	63	1369	9.2	4.7	17.8
79-80—Phoenix	75	—	2168	465	875	.531	0	2	.000	188	236	.797	158	451	609	322	237	4	108	218	55	1118	8.1	4.3	14.9
80-81—Phoenix	75	—	2054	458	870	.526	0	0	—	199	259	.768	157	389	546	344	226	2	106	226	69	1115	7.3	4.6	14.9
81-82—Phoenix	79	75	2393	507	1027	.494	0	1	.000	182	233	.781	138	448	586	356	269	7	114	196	78	1196	7.4	4.5	15.1
82-83—Phoenix	80	75	2447	477	981	.486	1	3	.333	180	217	.829	161	387	548	376	287	7	114	242	74	1135	6.9	4.7	14.2
83-84—Phoenix	70	13	1452	269	582	.462	0	4	.000	132	160	.825	118	201	319	219	195	1	73	117	31	670	4.6	3.1	9.6
84-85—Phoenix	82	69	2136	476	915	.520	0	0	—	250	283	.883	153	347	500	308	254	2	115	197	48	1202	6.1	3.8	14.7
85-86—Phoenix	78	45	2005	341	679	.502	0	2	.000	159	203	.783	148	329	477	324	272	7	103	206	46	841	6.1	4.2	10.8
86-87—Phoenix	68	40	1690	311	618	.503	0	1	.000	134	170	.788	91	247	338	223	207	3	62	139	37	756	5.0	3.3	11.1
87-88—Phoenix	82	25	1646	251	506	.496	1	2	.500	108	128	.844	118	247	365	183	245	3	82	140	41	611	4.5	2.2	7.5
REG. SEASON TOTALS	988	342	27203	5709	11464	.498	2	15	.133	2490	3160	.788	2015	4922	6937	4012	3214	58	1289	2194	808	13910	7.0	4.1	14.1
PLAYOFF TOTALS	78	13	2288	440	930	.473	0	0	—	196	256	.766	169	419	588	320	251	3	88	154	71	1076	7.5	4.1	13.8
ALL-STAR TOTALS	1	0	11	2	4	.500	0	0	—	0	0	—	2	1	3	0	1	0	0	—	0	4	3.0	0.0	4.0

ADAMS, DONALD L. (Don) b. November 27, 1947 Ht. 6-7 Wt. 210 College—Northwestern

SEASON—TEAM	G	GS	MIN	FGM	FGA	PCT	3FGM	3FGA	PCT	FTM	FTA	PCT	O-RB	D-RB	TOT	AST	PF	DQ	STL	TO	BLK	PTS	RPG	APG	PPG
70-71—San Diego	82	—	2374	391	957	.409	—	—	—	155	212	.731	—	—	581	173	344	11	—	—	—	937	7.1	2.1	11.4
71-72—Houston-Atlanta	73	—	2071	313	798	.392	—	—	—	205	275	.745	—	—	502	140	266	6	—	—	—	831	6.9	1.9	11.4
72-73—Atlanta-Detroit	74	—	1874	265	678	.391	—	—	—	145	184	.788	—	—	441	117	231	2	—	—	—	675	6.0	1.6	9.1
73-74—Detroit	74	—	2298	303	742	.408	—	—	—	153	201	.761	133	315	448	141	242	2	110	—	12	759	6.1	1.9	10.3
74-75—Detroit	51	—	1376	127	315	.403	—	—	—	45	78	.577	63	181	244	75	179	1	69	—	20	299	4.8	1.5	5.9
74-75—St. Louis (A)	16	—	342	42	98	.429	0	1	.000	17	22	.773	21	47	68	54	38	1	13	27	2	101	4.3	3.4	6.3
75-76—Buffalo	56	—	704	67	170	.394	—	—	—	40	57	.702	38	107	145	73	128	1	30	—	7	174	2.6	1.3	3.1
75-76—St. Louis (A)	20	—	725	99	251	.394	0	2	.000	63	83	.759	44	72	116	88	80	—	38	52	7	261	5.8	4.4	13.1
76-77—Buffalo	77	—	1710	216	526	.411	—	—	—	129	173	.746	130	241	371	150	201	0	74	—	16	561	4.8	1.9	7.3
REG. NBA TOTALS	487	—	12407	1682	4186	.402	—	—	—	872	1180	.739	364	844	2732	869	1591	23	283	—	55	4236	5.6	1.8	8.7
REG. ABA TOTALS	36	—	1067	141	349	.404	0	3	.000	80	105	.762	65	119	184	142	118	—	51	79	9	362	5.1	3.9	10.1
NBA PLAYOFF TOTALS	22	—	566	63	165	.382	—	—	—	30	44	.682	25	53	116	45	74	1	8	—	1	156	5.3	2.0	7.1
ABA PLAYOFF TOTALS	10	—	301	35	82	.427	0	0	—	20	28	.714	12	35	47	46	32	—	17	28	11	90	4.7	4.6	9.0

ADAMS, GEORGE b. May 15, 1949 Ht. 6-5½ Wt. 210 College—Gardner-Webb

SEASON—TEAM	G	GS	MIN	FGM	FGA	PCT	3FGM	3FGA	PCT	FTM	FTA	PCT	O-RB	D-RB	TOT	AST	PF	DQ	STL	TO	BLK	PTS	RPG	APG	PPG
72-73—San Diego (A)	60	—	865	153	312	.490	2	7	.286	65	83	.783	75	130	205	64	97	0	—	67	—	373	3.4	1.1	6.2
73-74—San Diego (A)	80	—	1433	253	506	.500	1	7	.143	78	103	.757	124	217	341	127	111	—	44	119	23	585	4.3	1.6	7.3
74-75—San Diego (A)	75	—	1605	310	622	.498	1	3	.333	73	86	.849	114	213	327	126	164	—	44	106	36	694	4.4	1.7	9.3
REG. ABA TOTALS	215	—	3903	716	1440	.497	4	17	.235	216	272	.794	313	560	873	317	372	0	88	292	59	1652	4.1	1.5	7.7
ABA PLAYOFF TOTALS	9	—	184	34	66	.515	0	1	.000	12	16	.750	13	15	34	15	14	0	4	16	4	80	3.8	1.7	8.9

ADAMS, MICHAEL b. January 19, 1963 Ht. 5-11 Wt. 175 College—Boston College

SEASON—TEAM	G	GS	MIN	FGM	FGA	PCT	3FGM	3FGA	PCT	FTM	FTA	PCT	O-RB	D-RB	TOT	AST	PF	DQ	STL	TO	BLK	PTS	RPG	APG	PPG
85-86—Sacramento	18	0	139	16	44	.364	0	3	.000	8	12	.667	2	4	6	22	9	0	9	11	1	40	0.3	1.2	2.2
86-87—Washington	63	0	1303	160	393	.407	28	102	.275	105	124	.847	38	85	123	244	88	0	85	81	6	453	2.0	3.9	7.2
87-88—Denver	82	75	2778	416	927	.449	139	379	.367	166	199	.834	40	183	223	503	138	0	168	144	16	1137	2.7	6.1	13.9
88-89—Denver	77	77	2787	468	1082	.433	166	466	.356	322	393	.819	71	212	283	490	149	0	166	180	11	1424	3.7	6.4	18.5
89-90—Denver	79	74	2690	398	989	.402	158	432	.366	267	314	.850	49	176	225	495	133	0	121	141	3	1221	2.8	6.3	15.5
90-91—Denver	66	66	2346	560	1421	.394	167	564	.296	465	529	.879	58	198	256	693	162	1	147	240	6	1752	3.9	10.5	26.5
91-92—Washington	78	78	2795	485	1233	.393	125	386	.324	313	360	.869	58	252	310	594	162	1	145	212	9	1408	4.0	7.6	18.1
92-93—Washington	70	70	2499	365	831	.439	68	212	.321	237	277	.856	52	188	240	526	146	0	100	175	4	1035	3.4	7.5	14.8
93-94—Washington	70	67	2337	285	698	.408	55	191	.288	224	270	.830	37	146	183	480	140	0	96	167	6	849	2.6	6.9	12.1
REG. SEASON TOTALS	603	507	19674	3153	7618	.414	906	2735	.331	2107	2478	.850	405	1444	1849	4047	1127	2	1037	1351	62	9319	3.1	6.7	15.5
PLAYOFF TOTALS	19	16	668	83	225	.369	35	105	.333	51	60	.850	14	52	66	101	41	0	32	44	2	252	3.5	5.3	13.3
ALL-STAR TOTALS	1	0	14	4	8	.500	1	3	.333	0	0	—	1	0	1	1	1	0	4	1	0	9	1.0	1.0	9.0

ADDISON, RAFAEL b. July 22, 1964 Ht. 6-7 Wt. 225 College—Syracuse

SEASON—TEAM	G	GS	MIN	FGM	FGA	PCT	3FGM	3FGA	PCT	FTM	FTA	PCT	O-RB	D-RB	TOT	AST	PF	DQ	STL	TO	BLK	PTS	RPG	APG	PPG
86-87—Phoenix	62	12	711	146	331	.441	16	50	.320	51	64	.797	41	65	106	45	75	1	27	54	7	359	1.7	0.7	5.8
91-92—New Jersey	76	8	1175	187	432	.433	14	49	.286	56	76	.737	65	100	165	68	109	1	28	46	28	444	2.2	0.9	5.8
92-93—New Jersey	68	15	1164	182	411	.443	7	34	.206	57	70	.814	45	87	132	53	125	0	23	64	11	428	1.9	0.8	6.3
REG. SEASON TOTALS	206	35	3050	515	1174	.439	37	133	.278	164	210	.781	151	252	403	166	309	2	78	164	46	1231	2.0	0.8	6.0
PLAYOFF TOTALS	6	0	62	9	28	.321	1	2	.500	3	3	1.000	3	3	6	6	3	0	3	3	0	22	1.0	1.0	3.7

ADELMAN, RICHARD LEONARD (Rick) b. June 16, 1946 Ht. 6-1½ Wt. 180 College—Loyola Marymount

SEASON—TEAM	G	GS	MIN	FGM	FGA	PCT	3FGM	3FGA	PCT	FTM	FTA	PCT	O-RB	D-RB	TOT	AST	PF	DQ	STL	TO	BLK	PTS	RPG	APG	PPG
68-69—San Diego	77	—	1448	177	449	.394	—	—	—	131	204	.642	—	—	216	238	158	1	—	—	—	485	2.8	3.1	6.3
69-70—San Diego	35	—	717	96	247	.389	—	—	—	68	91	.747	—	—	81	113	90	0	—	—	—	260	2.3	3.2	7.4
70-71—Portland	81	—	2303	378	895	.422	—	—	—	267	369	.724	—	—	282	380	214	2	—	—	—	1023	3.5	4.7	12.6
71-72—Portland	80	—	2445	329	753	.437	—	—	—	151	201	.751	—	—	229	413	209	2	—	—	—	809	2.9	5.2	10.1
72-73—Portland	76	—	1822	214	525	.408	—	—	—	73	102	.716	—	—	157	294	155	2	—	—	—	501	2.1	3.9	6.6
73-74—Chicago	55	—	618	64	170	.376	—	—	—	54	76	.711	16	53	69	56	63	0	36	—	1	182	1.3	1.0	3.3
74-75—Chicago-N.O.-K.C.-Omaha	58	—	1074	123	291	.423	—	—	—	73	103	.709	25	70	95	112	101	1	70	—	8	319	1.6	1.9	5.5
REG. SEASON TOTALS	462	—	10427	1381	3330	.415	—	—	—	817	1146	.713	41	123	1129	1606	990	8	106	—	9	3579	2.4	3.5	7.7
PLAYOFF TOTALS	21	—	329	43	96	.448	—	—	—	35	56	.625	2	10	27	39	32	0	8	—	0	121	1.3	1.9	5.8

AGUIRRE, MARK ANTHONY b. December 10, 1959 Ht. 6-6 Wt. 235 College—DePaul

SEASON—TEAM	G	GS	MIN	FGM	FGA	PCT	3FGM	3FGA	PCT	FTM	FTA	PCT	O-RB	D-RB	TOT	AST	PF	DQ	STL	TO	BLK	PTS	RPG	APG	PPG
81-82—Dallas	51	20	1468	381	820	.465	25	71	.352	168	247	.680	89	160	249	164	152	0	37	135	22	955	4.9	3.2	18.7
82-83—Dallas	81	75	2784	767	1589	.483	16	76	.211	429	589	.728	191	317	508	332	247	5	80	261	26	1979	6.3	4.1	24.4
83-84—Dallas	79	79	2900	925	1765	.524	15	56	.268	465	621	.749	161	308	469	358	246	5	80	285	22	2330	5.9	4.5	29.5
84-85—Dallas	80	79	2699	794	1569	.506	27	85	.318	440	580	.759	188	289	477	249	250	3	60	253	24	2055	6.0	3.1	25.7
85-86—Dallas	74	73	2501	668	1327	.503	16	56	.286	318	451	.705	177	268	445	339	229	6	62	252	14	1670	6.0	4.6	22.6
86-87—Dallas	80	80	2663	787	1590	.495	53	150	.353	429	557	.770	181	246	427	254	243	4	84	217	30	2056	5.3	3.2	25.7
87-88—Dallas	77	77	2610	746	1571	.475	52	172	.302	388	504	.770	182	252	434	278	223	1	70	203	57	1932	5.6	3.6	25.1
88-89—Dallas-Detroit	80	76	2597	586	1270	.461	51	174	.293	288	393	.733	146	240	386	278	229	2	45	208	36	1511	4.8	3.5	18.9
89-90—Detroit	78	40	2005	438	898	.488	31	93	.333	192	254	.756	117	188	305	145	201	2	34	121	19	1099	3.9	1.9	14.1
90-91—Detroit	78	13	2006	420	909	.462	24	78	.308	240	317	.757	134	240	374	139	209	2	47	128	20	1104	4.8	1.8	14.2
91-92—Detroit	75	12	1582	339	787	.431	15	71	.211	158	230	.687	67	169	236	126	171	0	51	105	11	851	3.1	1.7	11.3
92-93—Detroit	51	15	1056	187	422	.443	30	83	.361	99	129	.767	43	109	152	105	101	1	16	68	7	503	3.0	2.1	9.9
93-94—L.A. Clippers	39	0	859	163	348	.468	37	93	.398	50	72	.694	28	88	116	104	98	2	21	70	8	413	3.0	2.7	10.6
REG. SEASON TOTALS	923	639	27730	7201	14865	.484	392	1258	.312	3664	4944	.741	1704	2874	4578	2871	2599	33	687	2306	296	18458	5.0	3.1	20.0
PLAYOFF TOTALS	102	66	2958	696	1435	.485	45	142	.317	310	417	.743	181	356	537	262	281	5	71	198	22	1747	5.3	2.6	17.1
ALL-STAR TOTALS	3	0	42	13	24	.542	2	5	.400	8	10	.800	2	2	4	4	5	0	2	7	1	36	1.3	1.3	12.0

AINGE, DANIEL RAE (**Danny**) b. March 17, 1959 Ht. 6-5 Wt. 185 College—Brigham Young

SEASON—TEAM	G	GS	MIN	FGM	FGA	PCT	3FGM	3FGA	PCT	FTM	FTA	PCT	O-RB	D-RB	TOT	AST	PF	DQ	STL	TO	BLK	PTS	RPG	APG	PPG
81-82—Boston	53	1	564	79	221	.357	5	17	.294	56	65	.862	25	31	56	87	86	1	37	53	3	219	1.1	1.6	4.1
82-83—Boston	80	76	2048	357	720	.496	5	29	.172	72	97	.742	83	131	214	251	259	2	109	98	6	791	2.7	3.1	9.9
83-84—Boston	71	3	1154	166	361	.460	6	22	.273	46	56	.821	29	87	116	162	143	2	41	70	4	384	1.6	2.3	5.4
84-85—Boston	75	73	2564	419	792	.529	15	56	.268	118	136	.868	76	192	268	399	228	4	122	149	6	971	3.6	5.3	12.9
85-86—Boston	80	78	2407	353	701	.504	26	73	.356	123	136	.904	47	188	235	405	204	4	94	129	7	855	2.9	5.1	10.7
86-87—Boston	71	66	2499	410	844	.486	85	192	.443	148	165	.897	49	193	242	400	189	3	101	141	14	1053	3.4	5.6	14.8
87-88—Boston	81	81	3018	482	982	.491	148	357	.415	158	180	.878	59	190	249	503	203	1	115	153	17	1270	3.1	6.2	15.7
88-89—Boston-Sac.	73	54	2377	480	1051	.457	116	305	.380	205	240	.854	71	184	255	402	186	1	93	145	8	1281	3.5	5.5	17.5
89-90—Sacramento	75	68	2727	506	1154	.438	108	289	.374	222	267	.831	69	257	326	453	238	2	113	185	18	1342	4.3	6.0	17.9
90-91—Portland	80	0	1710	337	714	.472	102	251	.406	114	138	.826	45	160	205	285	195	2	63	100	13	890	2.6	3.6	11.1
91-92—Portland	81	6	1595	299	676	.442	78	230	.339	108	131	.824	40	108	148	202	148	0	73	70	13	784	1.8	2.5	9.7
92-93—Phoenix	80	0	2163	337	730	.462	150	372	.403	123	145	.848	49	165	214	260	175	3	69	113	8	947	2.7	3.3	11.8
93-94—Phoenix	68	1	1555	224	537	.417	80	244	.328	78	94	.830	28	103	131	180	140	0	57	81	8	606	1.9	2.6	8.9
REG. SEASON TOTALS	968	507	26381	4449	9483	.469	924	2437	.379	1571	1850	.849	670	1989	2659	3989	2394	25	1087	1487	125	11393	2.7	4.1	11.8
PLAYOFF TOTALS	183	82	4901	698	1533	.455	160	407	.393	286	346	.827	118	315	433	646	518	4	167	251	19	1842	2.4	3.5	10.1
ALL-STAR TOTALS	1	0	19	4	11	.364	3	4	.750	1	2	.500	1	2	3	2	1	0	1	1	0	12	3.0	2.0	12.0

AITCH, MATTHEW ALEXANDER (**Matt**) b. September 21, 1944 Ht. 6-7 Wt. 230 College—Moberly Area CC/Michigan State

SEASON—TEAM	G	GS	MIN	FGM	FGA	PCT	3FGM	3FGA	PCT	FTM	FTA	PCT	O-RB	D-RB	TOT	AST	PF	DQ	STL	TO	BLK	PTS	RPG	APG	PPG
67-68—Indiana (A)	45	—	637	100	247	.405	0	2	.000	52	77	.675	—	—	160	18	69	1	—	37	—	252	3.6	0.4	5.6
REG. ABA TOTALS	45	—	637	100	247	.405	0	2	.000	52	77	.675	—	—	160	18	69	1	—	37	—	252	3.6	0.4	5.6
ABA PLAYOFF TOTALS	2	—	4	2	4	.500	0	0	—	0	0	—	—	—	—	0	0	0	—	1	—	4	0.0	0.0	2.0

AKIN, HENRY T. b. July 31, 1944 Ht. 6-10 Wt. 235 College—William Carey/Morehead State

SEASON—TEAM	G	GS	MIN	FGM	FGA	PCT	3FGM	3FGA	PCT	FTM	FTA	PCT	O-RB	D-RB	TOT	AST	PF	DQ	STL	TO	BLK	PTS	RPG	APG	PPG
66-67—New York	50	—	453	83	230	.361	—	—	—	26	37	.703	—	—	120	25	82	0	—	—	—	192	2.4	0.5	3.8
67-68—Seattle	36	—	259	46	137	.336	—	—	—	20	31	.645	—	—	57	14	48	1	—	—	—	112	1.6	0.4	3.1
68-69—Kentucky (A)	2	—	25	1	4	.250	0	2	.000	2	3	.667	—	—	4	1	0	0	—	4	—	4	2.0	0.5	2.0
REG. NBA TOTALS	86	—	712	129	367	.351	—	—	—	46	68	.676	—	—	177	39	130	1	—	—	—	304	2.1	0.5	3.5
REG. ABA TOTALS	2	—	25	1	4	.250	0	2	.000	2	3	.667	—	—	4	1	0	0	—	4	—	4	2.0	0.5	2.0
NBA PLAYOFF TOTALS	2	—	16	1	7	.143	—	—	—	1	2	.500	—	—	8	—	3	0	—	—	—	3	4.0	0.0	1.5

ALARIE, MARK STEVEN b. December 11, 1963 Ht. 6-8 Wt. 220 College—Duke

SEASON—TEAM	G	GS	MIN	FGM	FGA	PCT	3FGM	3FGA	PCT	FTM	FTA	PCT	O-RB	D-RB	TOT	AST	PF	DQ	STL	TO	BLK	PTS	RPG	APG	PPG
86-87—Denver	64	25	1110	217	443	.490	2	9	.222	67	101	.663	73	141	214	74	138	1	22	56	28	503	3.3	1.2	7.9
87-88—Washington	63	0	769	144	300	.480	4	18	.222	35	49	.714	70	90	160	39	107	1	10	50	12	327	2.5	0.6	5.2
88-89—Washington	74	5	1141	206	431	.478	13	38	.342	73	87	.839	103	152	255	63	160	1	25	62	22	498	3.4	0.9	6.7
89-90—Washington	82	10	1893	371	785	.473	10	49	.204	108	133	.812	151	223	.374	142	219	2	60	101	39	860	4.6	1.7	10.5
90-91—Washington	42	1	587	99	225	.440	5	21	.238	41	48	.854	41	76	117	45	88	1	15	40	8	244	2.8	1.1	5.8
REG. SEASON TOTALS	325	41	5500	1037	2184	.475	34	135	.252	324	418	.775	438	682	1120	363	712	6	132	309	109	2432	3.4	1.1	7.5
PLAYOFF TOTALS	4	0	45	10	17	.588	1	2	.500	2	2	1.000	0	6	6	1	9	0	2	4	2	23	1.5	0.3	5.8

ALCINDOR, FERDINAND LEWIS JR. (**Lew**), (see Kareem Abdul-Jabbar)

ALCORN, GARY R. b. October 8, 1936 Ht. 6-9 Wt. 225 College—Fresno City/Fresno State

SEASON—TEAM	G	GS	MIN	FGM	FGA	PCT	3FGM	3FGA	PCT	FTM	FTA	PCT	O-RB	D-RB	TOT	AST	PF	DQ	STL	TO	BLK	PTS	RPG	APG	PPG
59-60—Detroit	58	—	670	91	312	.292	—	—	—	48	84	.571	—	—	279	22	123	4	—	—	—	230	4.8	0.4	4.0
60-61—Los Angeles	20	—	174	12	40	.300	—	—	—	7	8	.875	—	—	50	2	47	1	—	—	—	31	2.5	0.1	1.6
REG. SEASON TOTALS	78	—	844	103	352	.293	—	—	—	55	92	.598	—	—	329	24	170	5	—	—	—	261	4.2	0.3	3.3

ALEKSINAS, CHARLES (**Chuck**) b. February 26, 1959 Ht. 6-11 Wt. 260 College—Kentucky/Connecticut

SEASON—TEAM	G	GS	MIN	FGM	FGA	PCT	3FGM	3FGA	PCT	FTM	FTA	PCT	O-RB	D-RB	TOT	AST	PF	DQ	STL	TO	BLK	PTS	RPG	APG	PPG
84-85—Golden State	74	4	1114	161	337	.478	0	1	.000	55	75	.733	87	183	270	36	171	1	15	72	15	377	3.6	0.5	5.1
REG. SEASON TOTALS	74	4	1114	161	337	.478	0	1	.000	55	75	.733	87	183	270	36	171	1	15	72	15	377	3.6	0.5	5.1

ALEXANDER, GARY b. November 1, 1969 Ht. 6-7 Wt. 240 College—South Florida

SEASON—TEAM	G	GS	MIN	FGM	FGA	PCT	3FGM	3FGA	PCT	FTM	FTA	PCT	O-RB	D-RB	TOT	AST	PF	DQ	STL	TO	BLK	PTS	RPG	APG	PPG
93-94—Miami-Clev.	11	0	55	8	14	.571	0	0	—	3	9	.333	7	8	15	2	10	0	3	8	0	19	1.4	0.2	1.7
REG. SEASON TOTALS	11	0	55	8	14	.571	0	0	—	3	9	.333	7	8	15	2	10	0	3	8	0	19	1.4	0.2	1.7

ALEXANDER, VICTOR JOE b. August 31, 1969 Ht. 6-9 Wt. 265 College—Iowa State

SEASON—TEAM	G	GS	MIN	FGM	FGA	PCT	3FGM	3FGA	PCT	FTM	FTA	PCT	O-RB	D-RB	TOT	AST	PF	DQ	STL	TO	BLK	PTS	RPG	APG	PPG
91-92—Golden State	80	28	1350	243	459	.529	0	1	.000	103	149	.691	106	230	336	32	176	0	45	91	62	589	4.2	0.4	7.4
92-93—Golden State	72	59	1753	344	667	.516	10	22	.455	111	162	.685	132	288	420	93	218	2	34	120	53	809	5.8	1.3	11.2
93-94—Golden State	69	39	1318	266	502	.530	2	13	.154	68	129	.527	114	194	308	66	168	0	28	86	32	602	4.5	1.0	8.7
REG. SEASON TOTALS	221	126	4421	853	1628	.524	12	36	.333	282	440	.641	352	712	1064	191	562	2	107	297	147	2000	4.8	0.9	9.0
PLAYOFF TOTALS	4	0	24	3	5	.600	0	0	—	1	1	1.000	1	5	6	1	8	0	2	2	0	7	1.5	0.3	1.8

ALFORD, STEPHEN TODD (**Steve**) b. November 23, 1964 Ht. 6-2 Wt. 185 College—Indiana

SEASON—TEAM	G	GS	MIN	FGM	FGA	PCT	3FGM	3FGA	PCT	FTM	FTA	PCT	O-RB	D-RB	TOT	AST	PF	DQ	STL	TO	BLK	PTS	RPG	APG	PPG
87-88—Dallas	28	0	197	21	55	.382	1	8	.125	16	17	.941	3	20	23	23	23	0	17	12	3	59	0.8	0.8	2.1
88-89—Dallas-G.S.	66	3	906	148	324	.457	20	55	.364	50	61	.820	10	62	72	92	57	0	45	45	3	366	1.1	1.4	5.5
89-90—Dallas	41	0	302	63	138	.457	7	22	.318	35	37	.946	2	23	25	39	22	0	15	16	3	168	0.6	1.0	4.1
90-91—Dallas	34	0	236	59	117	.504	7	23	.304	26	31	.839	10	14	24	22	11	0	8	16	1	151	0.7	0.6	4.4
REG. SEASON TOTALS	169	3	1641	291	634	.459	35	108	.324	127	146	.870	25	119	144	176	113	0	85	89	10	744	0.9	1.0	4.4
PLAYOFF TOTALS	13	0	106	20	48	.417	6	17	.353	8	9	.889	4	5	9	15	11	0	3	5	0	54	0.7	1.2	4.2

ALLEN, BILL b. 1945 Ht. 6-8 Wt. 205 College—New Mexico State

SEASON—TEAM	G	GS	MIN	FGM	FGA	PCT	3FGM	3FGA	PCT	FTM	FTA	PCT	O-RB	D-RB	TOT	AST	PF	DQ	STL	TO	BLK	PTS	RPG	APG	PPG
67-68—Anaheim (A)	38	—	857	120	280	.429	2	2	1.000	58	99	.586	—	—	269	23	121	5	—	38	—	300	7.1	0.6	7.9
REG. ABA TOTALS	38	—	857	120	280	.429	2	2	1.000	58	99	.586	—	—	269	23	121	5	—	38	—	300	7.1	0.6	7.9

ALLEN, JAMES RANDALL (**Randy**) b. January 26, 1965 Ht. 6-8 Wt. 220 College—Florida State

SEASON—TEAM	G	GS	MIN	FGM	FGA	PCT	3FGM	3FGA	PCT	FTM	FTA	PCT	O-RB	D-RB	TOT	AST	PF	DQ	STL	TO	BLK	PTS	RPG	APG	PPG
88-89—Sacramento	7	0	43	8	19	.421	0	1	.000	1	2	.500	3	4	7	0	7	0	1	2	1	17	1.0	0.0	2.4
89-90—Sacramento	63	6	746	106	239	.444	0	7	.000	23	43	.535	49	89	138	23	102	0	16	28	19	235	2.2	0.4	3.7
REG. SEASON TOTALS	70	6	789	114	258	.442	0	8	.000	24	45	.533	52	93	145	23	109	0	17	30	20	252	2.1	0.3	3.6

ALLEN, LUCIUS OLIVER JR. b. September 26, 1947 Ht. 6-2 Wt. 175 College—UCLA

SEASON—TEAM	G	GS	MIN	FGM	FGA	PCT	3FGM	3FGA	PCT	FTM	FTA	PCT	O-RB	D-RB	TOT	AST	PF	DQ	STL	TO	BLK	PTS	RPG	APG	PPG
69-70—Seattle	81	—	1817	306	692	.442	—	—	—	182	249	.731	—	—	211	342	201	0	—	—	—	794	2.6	4.2	9.8
70-71—Milwaukee	61	—	1162	178	398	.447	—	—	—	77	110	.700	—	—	152	161	108	0	—	—	—	433	2.5	2.6	7.1
71-72—Milwaukee	80	—	2316	441	874	.505	—	—	—	198	259	.764	—	—	254	333	214	2	—	—	—	1080	3.2	4.2	13.5
72-73—Milwaukee	80	—	2693	547	1130	.484	—	—	—	143	200	.715	—	—	279	426	188	1	—	—	—	1237	3.5	5.3	15.5
73-74—Milwaukee	72	—	2388	526	1062	.495	—	—	—	216	274	.788	89	202	291	374	215	2	137	—	22	1268	4.0	5.2	17.6
74-75—Milw.-L.A.	66	—	2353	511	1170	.437	—	—	—	238	306	.778	90	188	278	372	217	4	136	—	29	1260	4.2	5.6	19.1
75-76—Los Angeles	76	—	2388	461	1004	.459	—	—	—	197	254	.776	64	150	214	357	241	2	101	—	20	1119	2.8	4.7	14.7
76-77—Los Angeles	78	—	2482	472	1035	.456	—	—	—	195	252	.774	58	193	251	405	183	0	116	—	19	1139	3.2	5.2	14.6
77-78—Kansas City	77	—	2147	373	846	.441	—	—	—	174	220	.791	66	163	229	360	180	0	93	217	28	920	3.0	4.7	11.9
78-79—Kansas City	31	—	413	69	174	.397	—	—	—	19	33	.576	14	32	46	44	52	0	21	30	6	157	1.5	1.4	5.1
REG. SEASON TOTALS	702	—	20159	3884	8385	.463	—	—	—	1639	2157	.760	381	928	2205	3174	1799	11	604	247	124	9407	3.1	4.5	13.4
PLAYOFF TOTALS	43	—	1160	202	450	.449	—	—	—	102	135	.756	9	30	133	142	100	0	13	5	4	506	3.1	3.3	11.8

ALLEN, ROBERT J. (**Bob**) b. July 17, 1946 Ht. 6-9 Wt. 205 College—Marshall

SEASON—TEAM	G	GS	MIN	FGM	FGA	PCT	3FGM	3FGA	PCT	FTM	FTA	PCT	O-RB	D-RB	TOT	AST	PF	DQ	STL	TO	BLK	PTS	RPG	APG	PPG
68-69—San Francisco	27	—	232	14	43	.326	—	—	—	20	36	.556	—	—	56	10	27	0	—	—	—	48	2.1	0.4	1.8
REG. SEASON TOTALS	27	—	232	14	43	.326	—	—	—	20	36	.556	—	—	56	10	27	0	—	—	—	48	2.1	0.4	1.8
PLAYOFF TOTALS	3	—	19	0	4	.000	—	—	—	4	7	.571	—	—	6	—	2	0	—	—	—	4	2.0	0.0	1.3

ALLEN, WILLIE Ht. 6-6 Wt. 230 College—Miami

SEASON—TEAM	G	GS	MIN	FGM	FGA	PCT	3FGM	3FGA	PCT	FTM	FTA	PCT	O-RB	D-RB	TOT	AST	PF	DQ	STL	TO	BLK	PTS	RPG	APG	PPG
71-72—Floridians (A)	7	—	30	4	13	.308	0	0	—	5	6	.833	—	—	14	4	11	—	—	6	—	13	2.0	0.6	1.9
REG. ABA TOTALS	7	—	30	4	13	.308	0	0	—	5	6	.833	—	—	14	4	11	—	—	6	—	13	2.0	0.6	1.9

ALLISON, ODIS JR. b. October 2, 1949 Ht. 6-6 Wt. 195 College—Laney/Nevada-Las Vegas

SEASON—TEAM	G	GS	MIN	FGM	FGA	PCT	3FGM	3FGA	PCT	FTM	FTA	PCT	O-RB	D-RB	TOT	AST	PF	DQ	STL	TO	BLK	PTS	RPG	APG	PPG
71-72—Golden State	36	—	166	17	78	.218	—	—	—	33	61	.541	—	—	45	10	34	0	—	—	—	67	1.3	0.3	1.9
REG. SEASON TOTALS	36	—	166	17	78	.218	—	—	—	33	61	.541	—	—	45	10	34	0	—	—	—	67	1.3	0.3	1.9

ALLUMS, DARRELL WILBERT JR. b. September 12, 1958 Ht. 6-8½ Wt. 225 College—UCLA

SEASON—TEAM	G	GS	MIN	FGM	FGA	PCT	3FGM	3FGA	PCT	FTM	FTA	PCT	O-RB	D-RB	TOT	AST	PF	DQ	STL	TO	BLK	PTS	RPG	APG	PPG
80-81—Dallas	22	—	276	23	67	.343	0	1	.000	13	22	.591	19	46	65	25	51	2	5	23	8	59	3.0	1.1	2.7
REG. SEASON TOTALS	22	—	276	23	67	.343	0	1	.000	13	22	.591	19	46	65	25	51	2	5	23	8	59	3.0	1.1	2.7

ANDEREGG, ROBERT H. (Bob) b. August 24, 1937 Ht. 6-3 Wt. 200 College—Michigan State

SEASON—TEAM	G	GS	MIN	FGM	FGA	PCT	3FGM	3FGA	PCT	FTM	FTA	PCT	O-RB	D-RB	TOT	AST	PF	DQ	STL	TO	BLK	PTS	RPG	APG	PPG
59-60—New York	33	—	373	55	143	.385	—	—	—	23	42	.548	—	—	69	29	32	0	—	—	—	133	2.1	0.9	4.0
REG. SEASON TOTALS	33	—	373	55	143	.385	—	—	—	23	42	.548	—	—	69	29	32	0	—	—	—	133	2.1	0.9	4.0

ANDERSON, ANDREW EMIL (Andy) b. July 6, 1945 Ht. 6-2 Wt. 185 College—Canisius

SEASON—TEAM	G	GS	MIN	FGM	FGA	PCT	3FGM	3FGA	PCT	FTM	FTA	PCT	O-RB	D-RB	TOT	AST	PF	DQ	STL	TO	BLK	PTS	RPG	APG	PPG
67-68—Oakland (A)	77	—	1894	279	756	.369	9	44	.205	163	225	.724	—	—	167	118	190	1	—	120	—	730	2.2	1.5	9.5
68-69—Oakland-Miami (A)	36	—	742	123	272	.452	0	6	.000	98	123	.797	—	—	105	45	76	1	—	53	—	344	2.9	1.3	9.6
69-70—Miami-L.A. (A)	81	—	2150	401	930	.431	1	13	.077	204	268	.761	—	—	255	164	196	1	—	—	—	1007	3.1	2.0	12.4
REG. ABA TOTALS	194	—	4786	803	1958	.410	10	63	.159	465	616	.755	—	—	527	327	462	3	—	173	—	2081	2.7	1.7	10.7
ABA PLAYOFF TOTALS	28	—	551	85	215	.395	1	5	.200	54	66	.818	—	—	60	42	59	1	—	23	—	225	2.1	1.5	8.0

ANDERSON, CLIFFORD V. (Cliff) b. September 7, 1944 Ht. 6-5 Wt. 200 College—St. Joseph (Pa.)

SEASON—TEAM	G	GS	MIN	FGM	FGA	PCT	3FGM	3FGA	PCT	FTM	FTA	PCT	O-RB	D-RB	TOT	AST	PF	DQ	STL	TO	BLK	PTS	RPG	APG	PPG
67-68—Los Angeles	18	—	94	7	29	.241	—	—	—	12	28	.429	—	—	11	17	18	1	—	—	—	26	0.6	0.9	1.4
68-69—Los Angeles	35	—	289	44	108	.407	—	—	—	47	82	.573	—	—	44	31	58	0	—	—	—	135	1.3	0.9	3.9
69-70—Denver (A)	3	—	22	2	4	.500	0	0	—	2	6	.333	—	—	4	4	3	0	—	—	—	6	1.3	1.3	2.0
70-71—Clev.-Phil.	28	—	198	20	65	.308	—	—	—	46	67	.687	—	—	48	20	29	1	—	—	—	86	1.7	0.7	3.1
REG. NBA TOTALS	81	—	581	71	202	.351	—	—	—	105	177	.593	—	—	103	68	105	2	—	—	—	247	1.3	0.8	3.0
REG. ABA TOTALS	3	—	22	2	4	.500	0	0	—	2	6	.333	—	—	4	4	3	0	—	—	—	6	1.3	1.3	2.0
NBA PLAYOFF TOTALS	3	—	10	2	5	.400	—	—	—	0	0	—	—	—	1	—	1	0	—	—	—	4	0.3	0.0	1.3

ANDERSON, DANIEL EDWARD b. January 1, 1951 Ht. 6-2 Wt. 185 College—USC

SEASON—TEAM	G	GS	MIN	FGM	FGA	PCT	3FGM	3FGA	PCT	FTM	FTA	PCT	O-RB	D-RB	TOT	AST	PF	DQ	STL	TO	BLK	PTS	RPG	APG	PPG
74-75—Portland	43	—	453	47	105	.448	—	—	—	26	30	.867	8	21	29	81	44	0	16	—	1	120	0.7	1.9	2.8
75-76—Portland	52	—	614	88	181	.486	—	—	—	51	61	.836	15	47	62	85	58	0	20	—	2	227	1.2	1.6	4.4
REG. SEASON TOTALS	95	—	1067	135	286	.472	—	—	—	77	91	.846	23	68	91	166	102	0	36	—	3	347	1.0	1.7	3.7

ANDERSON, DANIEL W. b. February 15, 1943 Ht. 6-10 Wt. 230 College—Augsburg

SEASON—TEAM	G	GS	MIN	FGM	FGA	PCT	3FGM	3FGA	PCT	FTM	FTA	PCT	O-RB	D-RB	TOT	AST	PF	DQ	STL	TO	BLK	PTS	RPG	APG	PPG
67-68—New Jersey (A)	78	—	2626	463	938	.494	0	0	—	223	320	.697	303	553	856	92	329	10	—	131	—	1149	11.0	1.2	14.7
68-69—N.Y.-Ken.-Minn. (A)	62	—	1399	220	483	.455	0	0	—	118	149	.792	—	—	460	66	174	9	—	81	—	558	7.4	1.1	9.0
REG. ABA TOTALS	140	—	4025	683	1421	.481	0	0	—	341	469	.727	303	553	1316	158	503	19	—	212	—	1707	9.4	1.1	12.2
ABA PLAYOFF TOTALS	5	—	38	6	13	.462	0	0	—	3	4	.750	—	—	10	5	8	0	—	2	—	15	2.0	1.0	3.0

ANDERSON, DWIGHT ANTHONY b. December 28, 1960 Ht. 6-3 Wt. 185 College—Kentucky/USC

SEASON—TEAM	G	GS	MIN	FGM	FGA	PCT	3FGM	3FGA	PCT	FTM	FTA	PCT	O-RB	D-RB	TOT	AST	PF	DQ	STL	TO	BLK	PTS	RPG	APG	PPG
82-83—Denver	5	0	33	7	14	.500	0	0	—	7	10	.700	0	2	2	3	7	0	1	5	0	21	0.4	0.6	4.2
REG. SEASON TOTALS	5	0	33	7	14	.500	0	0	—	7	10	.700	0	2	2	3	7	0	1	5	0	21	0.4	0.6	4.2

ANDERSON, ERIC WALFRED b. May 26, 1970 Ht. 6-9 Wt. 230 College—Indiana

SEASON—TEAM	G	GS	MIN	FGM	FGA	PCT	3FGM	3FGA	PCT	FTM	FTA	PCT	O-RB	D-RB	TOT	AST	PF	DQ	STL	TO	BLK	PTS	RPG	APG	PPG
92-93—New York	16	0	44	5	18	.278	0	0	—	11	13	.846	6	8	14	3	14	0	3	5	1	21	0.9	0.2	1.3
93-94—New York	11	0	39	7	17	.412	2	2	1.000	5	14	.357	6	11	17	2	9	0	0	2	1	21	1.5	0.2	1.9
REG. SEASON TOTALS	27	0	83	12	35	.343	2	2	1.000	16	27	.593	12	19	31	5	23	0	3	7	2	42	1.1	0.2	1.6
PLAYOFF TOTALS	2	0	6	1	2	.500	0	0	—	0	0	—	0	1	1	—	2	0	1	0	0	2	0.5	0.0	1.0

ANDERSON, GREGORY WAYNE (Cadillac) b. June 22, 1964 Ht. 6-10 Wt. 230 College—Houston

SEASON—TEAM	G	GS	MIN	FGM	FGA	PCT	3FGM	3FGA	PCT	FTM	FTA	PCT	O-RB	D-RB	TOT	AST	PF	DQ	STL	TO	BLK	PTS	RPG	APG	PPG
87-88—San Antonio	82	41	1984	379	756	.501	1	5	.200	198	328	.604	161	352	513	79	228	1	54	143	122	957	6.3	1.0	11.7
88-89—San Antonio	82	56	2401	460	914	.503	0	3	.000	207	403	.514	255	421	676	61	221	2	102	180	103	1127	8.2	0.7	13.7
89-90—Milwaukee	60	28	1291	219	432	.507	0	0	—	91	170	.535	112	261	373	24	176	3	32	80	54	529	6.2	0.4	8.8
90-91—Milw.-N.J.-Denver	68	2	924	116	270	.430	0	1	.000	60	115	.522	97	221	318	16	140	3	35	84	45	292	4.7	0.2	4.3
91-92—Denver	82	82	2793	389	854	.456	0	4	.000	167	268	.623	337	604	941	78	263	3	88	201	65	945	11.5	1.0	11.5
93-94—Detroit	77	47	1624	201	370	.543	1	3	.333	88	154	.571	183	388	571	51	234	4	55	94	68	491	7.4	0.7	6.4
REG. SEASON TOTALS	451	260	11017	1764	3596	.491	2	16	.125	811	1438	.564	1145	2247	3392	309	1262	16	366	782	457	4341	7.5	0.7	9.6
PLAYOFF TOTALS	7	3	196	30	55	.545	0	0	—	11	23	.478	12	33	45	3	29	3	3	14	8	71	6.4	0.4	10.1

ANDERSON, JEROME b. October 9, 1953 Ht. 6-5½ Wt. 195 College—West Virginia

SEASON—TEAM	G	GS	MIN	FGM	FGA	PCT	3FGM	3FGA	PCT	FTM	FTA	PCT	O-RB	D-RB	TOT	AST	PF	DQ	STL	TO	BLK	PTS	RPG	APG	PPG
75-76—Boston	22	—	126	25	45	.556	—	—	—	11	16	.688	4	9	13	6	25	0	3	—	3	61	0.6	0.3	2.8
76-77—Indiana	27	—	164	26	59	.441	—	—	—	14	20	.700	9	3	12	10	26	0	6	—	2	66	0.4	0.4	2.4
REG. SEASON TOTALS	49	—	290	51	104	.490	—	—	—	25	36	.694	13	12	25	16	51	0	9	—	5	127	0.5	0.3	2.6
PLAYOFF TOTALS	4	—	5	1	3	.333	—	—	—	0	0	—	1	0	1	1	1	0	0	—	0	2	0.3	0.3	0.5

ANDERSON, KEITH KIM (Kim) b. May 12, 1955 Ht. 6-7 Wt. 200 College—Missouri

SEASON—TEAM	G	GS	MIN	FGM	FGA	PCT	3FGM	3FGA	PCT	FTM	FTA	PCT	O-RB	D-RB	TOT	AST	PF	DQ	STL	TO	BLK	PTS	RPG	APG	PPG
78-79—Portland	21	—	224	24	77	.312	—	—	—	15	28	.536	17	28	45	15	42	0	4	22	5	63	2.1	0.7	3.0
REG. SEASON TOTALS	21	—	224	24	77	.312	—	—	—	15	28	.536	17	28	45	15	42	0	4	22	5	63	2.1	0.7	3.0

ANDERSON, KENNETH (Kenny) b. October 9, 1970 Ht. 6-1 Wt. 170 College—Georgia Tech

SEASON—TEAM	G	GS	MIN	FGM	FGA	PCT	3FGM	3FGA	PCT	FTM	FTA	PCT	O-RB	D-RB	TOT	AST	PF	DQ	STL	TO	BLK	PTS	RPG	APG	PPG
91-92—New Jersey	64	13	1086	187	480	.390	3	13	.231	73	98	.745	38	89	127	203	68	0	67	97	9	450	2.0	3.2	7.0
92-93—New Jersey	55	55	2010	370	850	.435	7	25	.280	180	232	.776	51	175	226	449	140	1	96	153	11	927	4.1	8.2	16.9
93-94—New Jersey	82	82	3135	576	1381	.417	40	132	.303	346	423	.818	89	233	322	784	201	0	158	266	15	1538	3.9	9.6	18.8
REG. SEASON TOTALS	201	150	6231	1133	2711	.418	50	170	.294	599	753	.795	178	497	675	1436	409	1	321	516	35	2915	3.4	7.1	14.5
PLAYOFF TOTALS	7	4	205	22	63	.349	3	10	.300	24	35	.686	3	12	15	30	12	0	10	10	0	71	2.1	4.3	10.1
ALL-STAR TOTALS	1	1	16	3	10	.300	0	1	.000	0	0	—	1	3	4	3	2	0	0	4	0	6	4.0	3.0	6.0

ANDERSON, MICHAEL LEVIN b. March 23, 1966 Ht. 5-11 Wt. 185 College—Drexel

SEASON—TEAM	G	GS	MIN	FGM	FGA	PCT	3FGM	3FGA	PCT	FTM	FTA	PCT	O-RB	D-RB	TOT	AST	PF	DQ	STL	TO	BLK	PTS	RPG	APG	PPG
88-89—San Antonio	36	12	730	73	175	.417	1	7	.143	57	82	.695	44	45	89	153	64	0	44	84	3	204	2.5	4.3	5.7
REG. SEASON TOTALS	36	12	730	73	175	.417	1	7	.143	57	82	.695	44	45	89	153	64	0	44	84	3	204	2.5	4.3	5.7

ANDERSON, MITCHELL KEITH (J.J.) b. September 23, 1960 Ht. 6-8 Wt. 195 College—Bradley

SEASON—TEAM	G	GS	MIN	FGM	FGA	PCT	3FGM	3FGA	PCT	FTM	FTA	PCT	O-RB	D-RB	TOT	AST	PF	DQ	STL	TO	BLK	PTS	RPG	APG	PPG
82-83—Phil.-Utah	65	2	1202	190	379	.501	0	4	.000	100	175	.571	119	175	294	67	153	1	63	79	21	480	4.5	1.0	7.4
83-84—Utah	48	0	311	55	130	.423	0	3	.000	12	29	.414	38	25	63	22	28	0	15	20	9	122	1.3	0.5	2.5
84-85—Utah	44	0	457	61	149	.409	0	2	.000	27	45	.600	29	53	82	21	70	0	29	32	9	149	1.9	0.5	3.4
REG. SEASON TOTALS	157	2	1970	306	658	.465	0	9	.000	139	249	.558	186	253	439	110	251	1	107	131	39	751	2.8	0.7	4.8
PLAYOFF TOTALS	5	0	13	5	8	.625	1	1	1.000	0	0	—	3	1	4	—	2	0	0	1	1	11	0.8	0.0	2.2

ANDERSON, NELISON (Nick) b. January 20, 1968 Ht. 6-6 Wt. 205 College—Illinois

SEASON—TEAM	G	GS	MIN	FGM	FGA	PCT	3FGM	3FGA	PCT	FTM	FTA	PCT	O-RB	D-RB	TOT	AST	PF	DQ	STL	TO	BLK	PTS	RPG	APG	PPG
89-90—Orlando	81	9	1785	372	753	.494	1	17	.059	186	264	.705	107	209	316	124	140	0	69	138	34	931	3.9	1.5	11.5
90-91—Orlando	70	42	1971	400	857	.467	17	58	.293	173	259	.668	92	294	386	106	145	0	74	113	44	990	5.5	1.5	14.1
91-92—Orlando	60	59	2203	482	1042	.463	30	85	.353	202	303	.667	98	286	384	163	132	0	97	126	33	1196	6.4	2.7	19.9
92-93—Orlando	79	76	2920	594	1324	.449	88	249	.353	298	402	.741	122	355	477	265	200	1	128	164	56	1574	6.0	3.4	19.9
93-94—Orlando	81	81	2811	504	1054	.478	101	314	.322	168	250	.672	113	363	476	294	148	1	134	165	33	1277	5.9	3.6	15.8
REG. SEASON TOTALS	371	267	11690	2352	5030	.468	237	723	.328	1027	1478	.695	532	1507	2039	952	765	2	502	706	200	5968	5.5	2.6	16.1
PLAYOFF TOTALS	3	3	120	13	34	.382	8	20	.400	9	12	.750	2	8	10	8	8	0	5	5	2	43	3.3	3.3	14.3

ANDERSON, RICHARD ANDREW b. November 19, 1960 Ht. 6-10 Wt. 240 College—Cal-Santa Barbara

SEASON—TEAM	G	GS	MIN	FGM	FGA	PCT	3FGM	3FGA	PCT	FTM	FTA	PCT	O-RB	D-RB	TOT	AST	PF	DQ	STL	TO	BLK	PTS	RPG	APG	PPG
82-83—San Diego	78	5	1274	174	431	.404	7	19	.368	48	69	.696	111	161	272	120	170	2	57	93	26	403	3.5	1.5	5.2
83-84—Denver	78	17	1380	272	638	.426	3	19	.158	116	150	.773	136	270	406	193	183	0	46	109	28	663	5.2	2.5	8.5
86-87—Houston	51	0	312	59	139	.424	4	16	.250	22	29	.759	24	55	79	33	37	0	7	19	3	144	1.5	0.6	2.8
87-88—Houston-Port.	74	3	1350	171	439	.390	48	150	.320	58	77	.753	91	212	303	112	137	1	51	61	16	448	4.1	1.5	6.1
88-89—Portland	72	9	1082	145	348	.417	49	141	.348	32	38	.842	62	169	231	98	100	1	44	54	12	371	3.2	1.4	5.2
89-90—Charlotte	54	2	604	88	211	.417	37	100	.370	18	23	.783	33	94	127	55	64	0	20	26	9	231	2.4	1.0	4.3
REG. SEASON TOTALS	407	30	6002	909	2206	.412	148	445	.333	294	386	.762	457	961	1418	611	691	4	225	362	94	2260	3.5	1.5	5.6
PLAYOFF TOTALS	15	0	140	20	48	.417	8	21	.381	10	12	.833	7	19	26	10	20	0	2	4	3	58	1.7	0.7	3.9

ANDERSON, RONALD GENE (Ron) b. October 15, 1958 Ht. 6-7 Wt. 215 College—Santa Barbara CC/Fresno State

SEASON—TEAM	G	GS	MIN	FGM	FGA	PCT	3FGM	3FGA	PCT	FTM	FTA	PCT	O-RB	D-RB	TOT	AST	PF	DQ	STL	TO	BLK	PTS	RPG	APG	PPG
84-85—Cleveland	36	7	520	84	195	.431	1	2	.500	41	50	.820	39	49	88	34	40	0	9	34	7	210	2.4	0.9	5.8
85-86—Clev.-Indiana	77	30	1676	310	628	.494	2	9	.222	85	127	.669	130	144	274	144	125	0	56	82	6	707	3.6	1.9	9.2
86-87—Indiana	63	0	721	139	294	.473	0	5	.000	85	108	.787	73	78	151	54	65	0	31	55	3	363	2.4	0.9	5.8
87-88—Indiana	74	1	1097	217	436	.498	0	2	.000	108	141	.766	89	127	216	78	98	0	41	73	6	542	2.9	1.1	7.3
88-89—Philadelphia	82	12	2618	566	1152	.491	2	11	.182	196	229	.856	167	239	406	139	166	1	71	126	23	1330	5.0	1.7	16.2
89-90—Philadelphia	78	3	2089	379	841	.451	3	21	.143	165	197	.838	81	214	295	143	143	0	72	78	13	926	3.8	1.8	11.9
90-91—Philadelphia	82	13	2340	512	1055	.485	9	43	.209	165	198	.833	103	264	367	115	163	1	65	100	13	1198	4.5	1.4	14.6
91-92—Philadelphia	82	11	2432	469	1008	.465	42	127	.331	143	163	.877	96	182	278	135	128	0	86	109	11	1123	3.4	1.6	13.7
92-93—Philadelphia	69	0	1263	225	544	.414	39	120	.325	72	89	.809	62	122	184	93	75	0	31	63	5	561	2.7	1.3	8.1
93-94—N.J.-Wash.	21	2	356	35	86	.407	7	26	.269	19	23	.826	16	37	53	17	16	0	8	10	3	96	2.5	0.8	4.6
REG. SEASON TOTALS	664	79	15112	2936	6239	.471	105	366	.287	1079	1325	.814	856	1456	2312	952	1019	2	470	730	90	7056	3.5	1.4	10.6
PLAYOFF TOTALS	27	0	621	106	239	.444	4	11	.364	50	54	.926	25	55	80	46	58	0	11	29	2	266	3.0	1.7	9.9

ANDERSON, WILLIE LLOYD JR. (Chill) b. January 8, 1967 Ht. 6-8 Wt. 205 College—Georgia

SEASON—TEAM	G	GS	MIN	FGM	FGA	PCT	3FGM	3FGA	PCT	FTM	FTA	PCT	O-RB	D-RB	TOT	AST	PF	DQ	STL	TO	BLK	PTS	RPG	APG	PPG
88-89—San Antonio	81	79	2738	640	1285	.498	4	21	.190	224	289	.775	152	265	417	372	295	8	150	261	62	1508	5.1	4.6	18.6
89-90—San Antonio	82	81	2788	532	1082	.492	7	26	.269	217	290	.748	115	257	372	364	252	3	111	198	58	1288	4.5	4.4	15.7
90-91—San Antonio	75	75	2592	453	991	.457	7	35	.200	170	213	.798	68	283	351	358	226	4	79	167	46	1083	4.7	4.8	14.4
91-92—San Antonio	57	55	1889	312	685	.455	13	56	.232	107	138	.775	62	238	300	302	151	2	54	140	51	744	5.3	5.3	13.1
92-93—San Antonio	38	7	560	80	186	.430	1	8	.125	22	28	.786	7	50	57	79	52	0	14	44	6	183	1.5	2.1	4.8
93-94—San Antonio	80	79	2488	394	837	.471	22	68	.324	145	171	.848	68	174	242	347	187	1	71	153	46	955	3.0	4.3	11.9
REG. SEASON TOTALS	413	376	13055	2411	5066	.476	54	214	.252	885	1129	.784	472	1267	1739	1822	1163	18	479	963	269	5761	4.2	4.4	13.9
PLAYOFF TOTALS	28	18	859	171	355	.482	11	27	.407	56	73	.767	25	79	104	111	86	2	29	55	10	409	3.7	4.0	14.6

ANDERZUNAS, WALTER CHARLES (Wally) b. January 11, 1946 d. May 28, 1989 Ht. 6-7 Wt. 220 College—Creighton

SEASON—TEAM	G	GS	MIN	FGM	FGA	PCT	3FGM	3FGA	PCT	FTM	FTA	PCT	O-RB	D-RB	TOT	AST	PF	DQ	STL	TO	BLK	PTS	RPG	APG	PPG
69-70—Cincinnati	44	—	370	65	166	.392	—	—	—	29	46	.630	—	—	82	9	47	1	—	—	—	159	1.9	0.2	3.6
REG. SEASON TOTALS	44	—	370	65	166	.392	—	—	—	29	46	.630	—	—	82	9	47	1	—	—	—	159	1.9	0.2	3.6

ANIELAK, DONALD ROBERT (Don) b. November 1, 1930 Ht. 6-7½ Wt. 190 College—SW Missouri State/Bradley

SEASON—TEAM	G	GS	MIN	FGM	FGA	PCT	3FGM	3FGA	PCT	FTM	FTA	PCT	O-RB	D-RB	TOT	AST	PF	DQ	STL	TO	BLK	PTS	RPG	APG	PPG
54-55—New York	1	—	10	0	4	.000	—	—	—	3	4	.750	—	—	2	0	0	0	—	—	—	3	2.0	0.0	3.0
REG. SEASON TOTALS	1	—	10	0	4	.000	—	—	—	3	4	.750	—	—	2	0	0	0	—	—	—	3	2.0	0.0	3.0

ANSLEY, MICHAEL ANTONIO b. February 8, 1967 Ht. 6-7 Wt. 225 College—Alabama

SEASON—TEAM	G	GS	MIN	FGM	FGA	PCT	3FGM	3FGA	PCT	FTM	FTA	PCT	O-RB	D-RB	TOT	AST	PF	DQ	STL	TO	BLK	PTS	RPG	APG	PPG
89-90—Orlando	72	5	1221	231	465	.497	0	0	—	164	227	.722	187	175	362	40	152	0	24	50	17	626	5.0	0.6	8.7
90-91—Orlando	67	1	877	144	263	.548	0	0	—	91	127	.717	122	131	253	25	125	0	27	32	7	379	3.8	0.4	5.7
91-92—Phil.-Cha.	10	0	45	8	18	.444	0	0	—	5	6	.833	2	4	6	2	7	0	0	3	0	21	0.6	0.2	2.1
REG. SEASON TOTALS	149	6	2143	383	746	.513	0	0	—	260	360	.722	311	310	621	67	284	0	51	85	24	1026	4.2	0.4	6.9

ANTHONY, GREGORY C. (Greg) b. November 15, 1967 Ht. 6-2 Wt. 185 College—Portland/Nevada-Las Vegas

SEASON—TEAM	G	GS	MIN	FGM	FGA	PCT	3FGM	3FGA	PCT	FTM	FTA	PCT	O-RB	D-RB	TOT	AST	PF	DQ	STL	TO	BLK	PTS	RPG	APG	PPG
91-92—New York	82	1	1510	161	435	.370	8	55	.145	117	158	.741	33	103	136	314	170	0	59	98	9	447	1.7	3.8	5.5
92-93—New York	70	35	1699	174	419	.415	4	30	.133	107	159	.673	42	128	170	398	141	0	113	104	12	459	2.4	5.7	6.6
93-94—New York	80	36	1994	225	571	.394	48	160	.300	130	168	.774	43	146	189	365	163	1	114	127	13	628	2.4	4.6	7.9
REG. SEASON TOTALS	232	72	5203	560	1425	.393	60	245	.245	354	485	.730	118	377	495	1077	474	1	286	329	34	1534	2.1	4.6	6.6
PLAYOFF TOTALS	52	3	889	88	234	.376	26	87	.299	42	71	.592	17	57	74	152	109	0	48	55	10	244	1.4	2.9	4.7

ARCENEAUX, STACEY (formerly Robert L. Stacey) b. February 17, 1936 Ht. 6-4½ Wt. 220 College—Iowa State

SEASON—TEAM	G	GS	MIN	FGM	FGA	PCT	3FGM	3FGA	PCT	FTM	FTA	PCT	O-RB	D-RB	TOT	AST	PF	DQ	STL	TO	BLK	PTS	RPG	APG	PPG
61-62—St. Louis	7	—	110	22	56	.393	—	—	—	6	13	.462	—	—	32	4	10	0	—	—	—	50	4.6	0.6	7.1
REG. SEASON TOTALS	7	—	110	22	56	.393	—	—	—	6	13	.462	—	—	32	4	10	0	—	—	—	50	4.6	0.6	7.1

ARCHIBALD, NATHANIEL (Nate, Tiny) b. September 2, 1948 Ht. 6-1 Wt. 160 College—Arizona Western/Texas-El Paso

SEASON—TEAM	G	GS	MIN	FGM	FGA	PCT	3FGM	3FGA	PCT	FTM	FTA	PCT	O-RB	D-RB	TOT	AST	PF	DQ	STL	TO	BLK	PTS	RPG	APG	PPG
70-71—Cincinnati	82	—	2867	486	1095	.444	—	—	—	336	444	.757	—	—	242	450	218	2	—	—	—	1308	3.0	5.5	16.0
71-72—Cincinnati	76	—	3272	734	1511	.486	—	—	—	677	824	.822	—	—	222	701	198	3	—	—	—	2145	2.9	9.2	28.2
72-73—Kansas City-Omaha	80	—	3681	1028	2106	.488	—	—	—	663	783	.847	—	—	223	910	207	2	—	—	—	2719	2.8	11.4	34.0
73-74—Kansas City-Omaha	35	—	1272	222	492	.451	—	—	—	173	211	.820	21	64	85	266	76	0	56	—	7	617	2.4	7.6	17.6
74-75—Kansas City-Omaha	82	—	3244	759	1664	.456	—	—	—	652	748	.872	48	174	222	557	187	0	119	—	7	2170	2.7	6.8	26.5
75-76—Kansas City	78	—	3184	717	1583	.453	—	—	—	501	625	.802	67	146	213	615	169	0	126	—	15	1935	2.7	7.9	24.8
76-77—New York Nets	34	—	1277	250	560	.446	—	—	—	197	251	.785	22	58	80	254	77	1	59	—	11	697	2.4	7.5	20.5
78-79—Boston	69	—	1662	259	573	.452	—	—	—	242	307	.788	25	78	103	324	132	2	55	197	6	760	1.5	4.7	11.0
79-80—Boston	80	—	2864	383	794	.482	4	18	.222	361	435	.830	59	138	197	671	218	2	106	242	10	1131	2.5	8.4	14.1
80-81—Boston	80	—	2820	382	766	.499	0	9	.000	342	419	.816	36	140	176	618	201	1	75	265	18	1106	2.2	7.7	13.8
81-82—Boston	68	51	2167	308	652	.472	6	16	.375	236	316	.747	25	91	116	541	131	1	52	178	3	858	1.7	8.0	12.6
82-83—Boston	66	18	1811	235	553	.425	5	24	.208	220	296	.743	25	66	91	409	110	1	38	163	4	695	1.4	6.2	10.5
83-84—Milwaukee	46	46	1038	136	279	.487	4	18	.222	64	101	.634	16	60	76	160	78	0	33	78	0	340	1.7	3.5	7.4
REG. SEASON TOTALS	876	115	31159	5899	12628	.467	19	85	.224	4664	5760	.810	344	1015	2046	6476	2002	15	719	1123	81	16481	2.3	7.4	18.8
PLAYOFF TOTALS	47	8	1642	235	556	.423	2	17	.118	195	236	.826	15	62	77	306	118	1	34	122	2	667	1.6	6.5	14.2
ALL-STAR TOTALS	6	4	162	27	60	.450	0	0	—	20	24	.833	5	12	18	40	10	0	11	6	1	74	3.0	6.7	12.3

ARD, JIMMIE LEE (**Jim**) b. September 19, 1948   Ht. 6-9 Wt. 220 College—Cincinnati

SEASON—TEAM	G	GS	MIN	FGM	FGA	PCT	3FGM	3FGA	PCT	FTM	FTA	PCT	O-RB	D-RB	TOT	AST	PF	DQ	STL	TO	BLK	PTS	RPG	APG	PPG
70-71—New York (A)	73	—	1027	174	382	.455	0	3	.000	79	132	.598	—	—	337	40	119	—	—	—	—	427	4.6	0.5	5.8
71-72—New York (A)	71	—	1145	159	353	.450	2	8	.250	77	127	.606	—	—	368	34	150	—	—	98	—	397	5.2	0.5	5.6
72-73—New York (A)	42	—	426	53	140	.379	0	4	.000	34	50	.680	48	100	148	14	50	0	—	29	—	140	3.5	0.3	3.3
73-74—Memphis (A)	27	—	502	66	164	.402	2	2	1.000	40	51	.784	48	111	159	41	44	—	16	42	25	174	5.9	1.5	6.4
74-75—Boston	59	—	719	89	266	.335	—	—	—	48	65	.738	59	140	199	40	96	2	13	—	32	226	3.4	0.7	3.8
75-76—Boston	81	—	853	107	294	.364	—	—	—	71	100	.710	96	193	289	48	141	2	12	—	36	285	3.6	0.6	3.5
76-77—Boston	63	—	969	96	254	.378	—	—	—	49	76	.645	77	219	296	53	128	1	18	—	28	241	4.7	0.8	3.8
77-78—Boston-Chicago	15	—	125	8	17	.471	—	—	—	3	5	.600	9	27	36	8	19	0	0	14	0	19	2.4	0.5	1.3
REG. NBA TOTALS	218	—	2666	300	831	.361	—	—	—	171	246	.695	241	579	820	149	384	5	43	14	96	771	3.8	0.7	3.5
REG. ABA TOTALS	213	—	3100	452	1039	.435	4	17	.235	230	360	.639	96	211	1012	129	363	0	16	169	25	1138	4.8	0.6	5.3
NBA PLAYOFF TOTALS	21	—	124	14	37	.378	—	—	—	11	14	.786	12	16	28	9	34	0	1	—	4	39	1.3	0.4	1.9
ABA PLAYOFF TOTALS	19	—	215	30	61	.492	0	2	.000	18	32	.563	0	0	57	7	34	0	0	6	0	78	3.0	0.4	4.1

ARIZIN, PAUL JOSEPH b. April 9, 1928   Ht. 6-4 Wt. 200 College—Villanova

SEASON—TEAM	G	GS	MIN	FGM	FGA	PCT	3FGM	3FGA	PCT	FTM	FTA	PCT	O-RB	D-RB	TOT	AST	PF	DQ	STL	TO	BLK	PTS	RPG	APG	PPG
50-51—Philadelphia	65	—	—	352	864	.407	—	—	—	417	526	.793	—	—	640	138	284	18	—	—	—	1121	9.8	2.1	17.2
51-52—Philadelphia	66	—	2939	548	1222	.448	—	—	—	578	707	.818	—	—	745	170	250	5	—	—	—	1674	11.3	2.6	25.4
54-55—Philadelphia	72	—	2953	529	1325	.399	—	—	—	454	585	.776	—	—	675	210	270	5	—	—	—	1512	9.4	2.9	21.0
55-56—Philadelphia	72	—	2724	617	1378	.448	—	—	—	507	626	.810	—	—	539	189	282	11	—	—	—	1741	7.5	2.6	24.2
56-57—Philadelphia	71	—	2767	613	1451	.422	—	—	—	591	713	.829	—	—	561	150	274	13	—	—	—	1817	7.9	2.1	25.6
57-58—Philadelphia	68	—	2377	483	1229	.393	—	—	—	440	544	.809	—	—	503	135	235	7	—	—	—	1406	7.4	2.0	20.7
58-59—Philadelphia	70	—	2799	632	1466	.431	—	—	—	587	722	.813	—	—	637	119	264	7	—	—	—	1851	9.1	1.7	26.4
59-60—Philadelphia	72	—	2618	593	1400	.424	—	—	—	420	526	.798	—	—	621	165	263	6	—	—	—	1606	8.6	2.3	22.3
60-61—Philadelphia	79	—	2935	650	1529	.425	—	—	—	532	639	.833	—	—	681	188	335	18	—	—	—	1832	8.6	2.4	23.2
61-62—Philadelphia	78	—	2785	611	1490	.410	—	—	—	484	601	.805	—	—	527	201	307	18	—	—	—	1706	6.8	2.6	21.9
REG. SEASON TOTALS	713	—	24897	5628	13354	.421	—	—	—	5010	6189	.810	—	—	6129	1665	2764	101	—	—	—	16266	8.6	2.3	22.8
PLAYOFF TOTALS	49	—	1815	411	1001	.411	—	—	—	364	439	.829	—	—	404	128	177	8	—	—	—	1186	8.2	2.6	24.2
ALL-STAR TOTALS	9	—	206	54	116	.466	—	—	—	29	36	.806	—	—	47	6	29	1	—	—	—	137	5.2	0.7	15.2

ARLAUCKAS, JOSEPH (**Joe**) b. July 20, 1965   Ht. 6-9 Wt. 230 College—Niagara

SEASON—TEAM	G	GS	MIN	FGM	FGA	PCT	3FGM	3FGA	PCT	FTM	FTA	PCT	O-RB	D-RB	TOT	AST	PF	DQ	STL	TO	BLK	PTS	RPG	APG	PPG
87-88—Sacramento	9	0	85	14	43	.326	0	0	—	6	8	.750	6	7	13	8	16	0	3	4	4	34	1.4	0.9	3.8
REG. SEASON TOTALS	9	0	85	14	43	.326	0	0	—	6	8	.750	6	7	13	8	16	0	3	4	4	34	1.4	0.9	3.8

ARMSTRONG, BENJAMIN ROY JR. (**B.J.**) b. September 9, 1967   Ht. 6-2 Wt. 185 College—Iowa

SEASON—TEAM	G	GS	MIN	FGM	FGA	PCT	3FGM	3FGA	PCT	FTM	FTA	PCT	O-RB	D-RB	TOT	AST	PF	DQ	STL	TO	BLK	PTS	RPG	APG	PPG
89-90—Chicago	81	0	1291	190	392	.485	3	6	.500	69	78	.885	19	83	102	199	105	0	46	83	6	452	1.3	2.5	5.6
90-91—Chicago	82	0	1731	304	632	.481	15	30	.500	97	111	.874	25	124	149	301	118	0	70	107	4	720	1.8	3.7	8.8
91-92—Chicago	82	3	1875	335	697	.481	35	87	.402	104	129	.806	19	126	145	266	88	0	46	94	5	809	1.8	3.2	9.9
92-93—Chicago	82	74	2492	408	818	.499	63	139	.453	130	151	.861	27	122	149	330	169	0	66	83	6	1009	1.8	4.0	12.3
93-94—Chicago	82	82	2770	479	1007	.476	60	135	.444	194	227	.855	28	142	170	323	147	1	80	131	9	1212	2.1	3.9	14.8
REG. SEASON TOTALS	409	159	10159	1716	3546	.484	176	397	.443	594	696	.853	118	597	715	1419	627	1	308	498	30	4202	1.7	3.5	10.3
PLAYOFF TOTALS	84	29	1927	262	545	.481	36	79	.456	128	153	.837	18	105	123	206	138	0	70	66	3	688	1.5	2.5	8.2
ALL-STAR TOTALS	1	1	22	5	9	.556	1	2	.500	0	0	—	1	0	1	4	1	0	0	1	0	11	1.0	4.0	11.0

ARMSTRONG, MICHAEL TAYLOR (**Tate**) b. October 5, 1955   Ht. 6-3 Wt. 175 College—Duke

SEASON—TEAM	G	GS	MIN	FGM	FGA	PCT	3FGM	3FGA	PCT	FTM	FTA	PCT	O-RB	D-RB	TOT	AST	PF	DQ	STL	TO	BLK	PTS	RPG	APG	PPG
77-78—Chicago	66	—	716	131	280	.468	—	—	—	22	27	.815	24	44	68	74	42	0	23	58	0	284	1.0	1.1	4.3
78-79—Chicago	26	—	259	28	70	.400	—	—	—	10	13	.769	7	13	20	31	22	0	10	21	0	66	0.8	1.2	2.5
REG. SEASON TOTALS	92	—	975	159	350	.454	—	—	—	32	40	.800	31	57	88	105	64	0	33	79	0	350	1.0	1.1	3.8

ARMSTRONG, PAUL CARLYLE (**Curly**) b. November 1, 1918 d. June 6, 1983 Ht. 5-11 Wt. 170 College—Indiana

SEASON—TEAM	G	GS	MIN	FGM	FGA	PCT	3FGM	3FGA	PCT	FTM	FTA	PCT	O-RB	D-RB	TOT	AST	PF	DQ	STL	TO	BLK	PTS	RPG	APG	PPG
41-42—Fort Wayne (N)	24	—	—	69	—	—	—	—	—	60	—	—	—	—	—	—	—	—	—	—	—	198	—	—	8.3
42-43—Fort Wayne (N)	23	—	—	67	—	—	—	—	—	49	—	—	—	—	—	—	61	—	—	—	—	183	—	—	8.0
45-46—Fort Wayne (N)	6	—	—	3	—	—	—	—	—	1	—	—	—	—	—	—	—	—	—	—	—	7	—	—	1.2
46-47—Fort Wayne (N)	44	—	—	127	—	—	—	—	—	134	195	.687	—	—	—	—	145	—	—	—	—	388	—	—	8.8
47-48—Fort Wayne (N)	53	—	—	148	—	—	—	—	—	139	206	.675	—	—	—	—	180	—	—	—	—	435	—	—	8.2
48-49—Fort Wayne	52	—	—	131	428	.306	—	—	—	118	169	.698	—	—	—	105	152	—	—	—	—	380	—	2.0	7.3
49-50—Fort Wayne	63	—	—	144	516	.279	—	—	—	170	241	.705	—	—	—	176	217	—	—	—	—	458	—	2.8	7.3
50-51—Fort Wayne	38	—	—	72	232	.310	—	—	—	58	90	.644	—	—	89	77	87	2	—	—	—	202	2.3	2.0	5.3
REG. NBA TOTALS	153	—	—	347	1176	.295	—	—	—	346	500	.692	—	—	89	358	456	2	—	—	—	1040	2.3	2.3	6.8
REG. NBL TOTALS	150	—	—	414	—	—	—	—	—	383	401	.681	—	—	—	—	386	—	—	—	—	1211	—	—	8.1
NBA PLAYOFF TOTALS	6	—	—	11	41	.268	—	—	—	2	5	.400	—	—	7	11	14	0	—	—	—	24	2.3	1.8	4.0
NBL PLAYOFF TOTALS	27	—	—	87	—	—	—	—	—	75	49	.714	—	—	—	—	71	—	—	—	—	248	—	—	9.2

ARMSTRONG, T. ROBERT (**Bob**) b. June 17, 1933 Ht. 6-8 Wt. 220 College—Michigan State

SEASON—TEAM	G	GS	MIN	FGM	FGA	PCT	3FGM	3FGA	PCT	FTM	FTA	PCT	O-RB	D-RB	TOT	AST	PF	DQ	STL	TO	BLK	PTS	RPG	APG	PPG
56-57—Philadelphia	19	—	110	11	37	.297	—	—	—	6	12	.500	—	—	39	3	13	0	—	—	—	28	2.1	0.2	1.5
REG. SEASON TOTALS	19	—	110	11	37	.297	—	—	—	6	12	.500	—	—	39	3	13	0	—	—	—	28	2.1	0.2	1.5

ARMSTRONG, WARREN EDWARD (**see Warren Jabali**)

ARNELLE, HUGH JESSE (**Jesse**) b. December 30, 1933 Ht. 6-5 Wt. 225 College—Penn State

SEASON—TEAM	G	GS	MIN	FGM	FGA	PCT	3FGM	3FGA	PCT	FTM	FTA	PCT	O-RB	D-RB	TOT	AST	PF	DQ	STL	TO	BLK	PTS	RPG	APG	PPG
55-56—Fort Wayne	31	—	409	52	164	.317	—	—	—	43	69	.623	—	—	170	18	60	0	—	—	—	147	5.5	0.6	4.7
REG. SEASON TOTALS	31	—	409	52	164	.317	—	—	—	43	69	.623	—	—	170	18	60	0	—	—	—	147	5.5	0.6	4.7

ARNETTE, JAY HOYLAND b. December 19, 1938 Ht. 6-2 Wt. 175 College—Texas

SEASON—TEAM	G	GS	MIN	FGM	FGA	PCT	3FGM	3FGA	PCT	FTM	FTA	PCT	O-RB	D-RB	TOT	AST	PF	DQ	STL	TO	BLK	PTS	RPG	APG	PPG
63-64—Cincinnati	48	—	501	71	196	.362	—	—	—	42	54	.778	—	—	54	71	105	2	—	—	—	184	1.1	1.5	3.8
64-65—Cincinnati	63	—	662	91	245	.371	—	—	—	56	75	.747	—	—	62	68	125	1	—	—	—	238	1.0	1.1	3.8
65-66—Cincinnati	3	—	14	1	6	.167	—	—	—	0	0	—	—	—	0	0	3	0	—	—	—	2	0.0	0.0	0.7
REG. SEASON TOTALS	114	—	1177	163	447	.365	—	—	—	98	129	.760	—	—	116	139	233	3	—	—	—	424	1.0	1.2	3.7
PLAYOFF TOTALS	9	—	81	11	32	.344	—	—	—	7	8	.875	—	—	10	10	22	1	—	—	—	29	1.1	1.1	3.2

ARNZEN, ROBERT LOUIS (**Bob**) b. November 3, 1947 Ht. 6-6 Wt. 210 College—Notre Dame

SEASON—TEAM	G	GS	MIN	FGM	FGA	PCT	3FGM	3FGA	PCT	FTM	FTA	PCT	O-RB	D-RB	TOT	AST	PF	DQ	STL	TO	BLK	PTS	RPG	APG	PPG
69-70—New York (A)	13	—	98	19	48	.396	0	1	.000	2	6	.333	—	—	22	5	11	0	—	—	—	40	1.7	0.4	3.1
70-71—Cincinnati	55	—	594	128	277	.462	—	—	—	45	52	.865	—	—	152	24	54	0	—	—	—	301	2.8	0.4	5.5
72-73—Indiana (A)	23	—	111	20	38	.526	0	3	.000	6	8	.750	11	12	23	3	12	0	—	0	—	46	1.0	0.1	2.0
73-74—Indiana (A)	20	—	149	24	48	.500	1	1	1.000	7	9	.778	10	10	20	3	11	—	3	8	2	56	1.0	0.2	2.8
REG. NBA TOTALS	55	—	594	128	277	.462	—	—	—	45	52	.865	—	—	152	24	54	0	—	—	—	301	2.8	0.4	5.5
REG. ABA TOTALS	56	—	358	63	134	.470	1	5	.200	15	23	.652	21	22	65	11	34	0	3	8	2	142	1.2	0.2	2.5
ABA PLAYOFF TOTALS	7	—	13	3	6	.500	0	2	.000	1	1	1.000	0	0	0	0	1	0	0	0	0	7	0.0	0.0	1.0

ARTHURS, JOHN CHARLES b. August 15, 1947 Ht. 6-4 Wt. 185 College—Tulane

SEASON—TEAM	G	GS	MIN	FGM	FGA	PCT	3FGM	3FGA	PCT	FTM	FTA	PCT	O-RB	D-RB	TOT	AST	PF	DQ	STL	TO	BLK	PTS	RPG	APG	PPG
69-70—Milwaukee	11	—	86	12	35	.343	—	—	—	11	15	.733	—	—	14	17	15	0	—	—	—	35	1.3	1.5	3.2
REG. SEASON TOTALS	11	—	86	12	35	.343	—	—	—	11	15	.733	—	—	14	17	15	0	—	—	—	35	1.3	1.5	3.2

ASKEW, VINCENT JEROME b. February 28, 1966 Ht. 6-6 Wt. 235 College—Memphis State

SEASON—TEAM	G	GS	MIN	FGM	FGA	PCT	3FGM	3FGA	PCT	FTM	FTA	PCT	O-RB	D-RB	TOT	AST	PF	DQ	STL	TO	BLK	PTS	RPG	APG	PPG
87-88—Philadelphia	14	2	234	22	74	.297	0	0	—	8	11	.727	6	16	22	33	12	0	10	12	6	52	1.6	2.4	3.7
90-91—Golden State	7	0	85	12	25	.480	0	0	—	9	11	.818	7	4	11	13	21	1	2	6	0	33	1.6	1.9	4.7
91-92—Golden State	80	10	1496	193	379	.509	1	10	.100	111	160	.694	89	144	233	188	128	1	47	84	23	498	2.9	2.4	6.2
92-93—Sac.-Seattle	73	4	1129	152	309	.492	2	6	.333	105	149	.705	62	99	161	122	135	2	40	69	19	411	2.2	1.7	5.6
93-94—Seattle	80	3	1690	273	567	.481	6	31	.194	175	211	.829	60	124	184	194	145	0	73	70	19	727	2.3	2.4	9.1
REG. SEASON TOTALS	254	19	4634	652	1354	.482	9	47	.191	408	542	.753	224	387	611	550	441	4	172	241	67	1721	2.4	2.2	6.8
PLAYOFF TOTALS	27	0	269	40	92	.435	0	1	.000	35	48	.729	20	20	40	25	31	0	5	11	1	115	1.5	0.9	4.3

ASKINS, KEITH BERNARD b. December 15, 1967 Ht. 6-8 Wt. 215 College—Alabama

SEASON—TEAM	G	GS	MIN	FGM	FGA	PCT	3FGM	3FGA	PCT	FTM	FTA	PCT	O-RB	D-RB	TOT	AST	PF	DQ	STL	TO	BLK	PTS	RPG	APG	PPG
90-91—Miami	39	1	266	34	81	.420	6	25	.240	12	25	.480	30	38	68	19	46	0	16	11	13	86	1.7	0.5	2.2
91-92—Miami	59	4	843	84	205	.410	25	73	.342	26	37	.703	65	77	142	38	109	0	40	47	15	219	2.4	0.6	3.7
92-93—Miami	69	1	935	88	213	.413	22	65	.338	29	40	.725	74	124	198	31	141	2	31	37	29	227	2.9	0.4	3.3
93-94—Miami	37	0	319	36	88	.409	4	21	.190	9	10	.900	33	49	82	13	57	0	11	21	1	85	2.2	0.4	2.3
REG. SEASON TOTALS	204	6	2363	242	587	.412	57	184	.310	76	112	.679	202	288	490	101	353	2	98	116	58	617	2.4	0.5	3.0
PLAYOFF TOTALS	4	0	54	5	12	.417	3	5	.600	0	2	.000	5	5	10	3	7	0	1	3	0	13	2.5	0.8	3.3

ASMONGA, DONALD A. (**Don**) b. February 15, 1928 Ht. 6-2 Wt. 185 College—California (Pa.)/Alliance

SEASON—TEAM	G	GS	MIN	FGM	FGA	PCT	3FGM	3FGA	PCT	FTM	FTA	PCT	O-RB	D-RB	TOT	AST	PF	DQ	STL	TO	BLK	PTS	RPG	APG	PPG
53-54—Baltimore	7	—	46	2	15	.133	—	—	—	1	1	1.000	—	—	1	5	12	1	—	—	—	5	0.1	0.7	0.7
REG. SEASON TOTALS	7	—	46	2	15	.133	—	—	—	1	1	1.000	—	—	1	5	12	1	—	—	—	5	0.1	0.7	0.7

ATHA, RICHARD E. (**Dick**) b. September 21, 1931 Ht. 6-2 Wt. 195 College—Indiana State

SEASON—TEAM	G	GS	MIN	FGM	FGA	PCT	3FGM	3FGA	PCT	FTM	FTA	PCT	O-RB	D-RB	TOT	AST	PF	DQ	STL	TO	BLK	PTS	RPG	APG	PPG
55-56—New York	25	—	288	36	88	.409	—	—	—	21	27	.778	—	—	42	32	39	0	—	—	—	93	1.7	1.3	3.7
57-58—Detroit	18	—	160	17	47	.362	—	—	—	10	12	.833	—	—	24	19	24	0	—	—	—	44	1.3	1.1	2.4
REG. SEASON TOTALS	43	—	448	53	135	.393	—	—	—	31	39	.795	—	—	66	51	63	0	—	—	—	137	1.5	1.2	3.2

ATTLES, ALVIN A. JR. b. November 7, 1936   Ht. 6-1 Wt. 180 College—North Carolina A&T

SEASON—TEAM	G	GS	MIN	FGM	FGA	PCT	3FGM	3FGA	PCT	FTM	FTA	PCT	O-RB	D-RB	TOT	AST	PF	DQ	STL	TO	BLK	PTS	RPG	APG	PPG
60-61—Philadelphia	77	—	1544	222	543	.409	—	—	—	97	162	.599	—	—	214	174	235	5	—	—	—	541	2.8	2.3	7.0
61-62—Philadelphia	75	—	2468	343	724	.474	—	—	—	158	267	.592	—	—	355	333	279	8	—	—	—	844	4.7	4.4	11.3
62-63—San Francisco	71	—	1876	301	630	.478	—	—	—	133	206	.646	—	—	205	184	253	7	—	—	—	735	2.9	2.6	10.4
63-64—San Francisco	70	—	1883	289	640	.452	—	—	—	185	275	.673	—	—	236	197	249	4	—	—	—	763	3.4	2.8	10.9
64-65—San Francisco	73	—	1733	254	662	.384	—	—	—	171	274	.624	—	—	239	205	242	7	—	—	—	679	3.3	2.8	9.3
65-66—San Francisco	79	—	2053	364	724	.503	—	—	—	154	252	.611	—	—	322	225	265	7	—	—	—	882	4.1	2.8	11.2
66-67—San Francisco	69	—	1764	212	467	.454	—	—	—	88	151	.583	—	—	321	269	265	13	—	—	—	512	4.7	3.9	7.4
67-68—San Francisco	67	—	1992	252	540	.467	—	—	—	150	216	.694	—	—	276	390	284	9	—	—	—	654	4.1	5.8	9.8
68-69—San Francisco	51	—	1516	162	359	.451	—	—	—	95	149	.638	—	—	181	306	183	3	—	—	—	419	3.5	6.0	8.2
69-70—San Francisco	45	—	676	78	202	.386	—	—	—	75	113	.664	—	—	74	142	103	0	—	—	—	231	1.6	3.2	5.1
70-71—San Francisco	34	—	321	22	54	.407	—	—	—	24	41	.585	—	—	40	58	59	2	—	—	—	68	1.2	1.7	2.0
REG. SEASON TOTALS	711	—	17826	2499	5545	.451	—	—	—	1330	2106	.632	—	—	2463	2483	2417	65	—	—	—	6328	3.5	3.5	8.9
PLAYOFF TOTALS	62	—	1504	154	382	.403	—	—	—	86	158	.544	—	—	245	206	246	12	—	—	—	394	4.0	3.3	6.4

AUBUCHON, CHESTER J. JR. (**Chet**) b. May 8, 1916   Ht. 5-10 Wt. 145 College—Michigan State

SEASON—TEAM	G	GS	MIN	FGM	FGA	PCT	3FGM	3FGA	PCT	FTM	FTA	PCT	O-RB	D-RB	TOT	AST	PF	DQ	STL	TO	BLK	PTS	RPG	APG	PPG
46-47—Detroit	30	—	—	23	91	.253	—	—	—	19	35	.543	—	—	20	46	—	—	—	—	—	65	—	0.7	2.2
REG. SEASON TOTALS	30	—	—	23	91	.253	—	—	—	19	35	.543	—	—	20	46	—	—	—	—	—	65	—	0.7	2.2

AUGMON, STACEY ORLANDO b. August 1, 1968   Ht. 6-8 Wt. 205 College—Nevada-Las Vegas

SEASON—TEAM	G	GS	MIN	FGM	FGA	PCT	3FGM	3FGA	PCT	FTM	FTA	PCT	O-RB	D-RB	TOT	AST	PF	DQ	STL	TO	BLK	PTS	RPG	APG	PPG
91-92—Atlanta	82	82	2505	440	899	.489	1	6	.167	213	320	.666	191	229	420	201	161	0	124	181	27	1094	5.1	2.5	13.3
92-93—Atlanta	73	66	2112	397	792	.501	0	4	.000	227	307	.739	141	146	287	170	141	1	91	157	18	1021	3.9	2.3	14.0
93-94—Atlanta	82	82	2605	439	861	.510	1	7	.143	333	436	.764	178	216	394	187	179	0	149	147	45	1212	4.8	2.3	14.8
REG. SEASON TOTALS	237	230	7222	1276	2552	.500	2	17	.118	773	1063	.727	510	591	1101	558	481	1	364	485	90	3327	4.6	2.4	14.0
PLAYOFF TOTALS	14	14	417	60	120	.500	0	0	—	35	50	.700	16	21	37	33	33	0	11	19	2	155	2.6	2.4	11.1

AUSTIN, ISAAC EDWARD b. August 18, 1969   Ht. 6-10 Wt. 290 College—Kings River College/Arizona State

SEASON—TEAM	G	GS	MIN	FGM	FGA	PCT	3FGM	3FGA	PCT	FTM	FTA	PCT	O-RB	D-RB	TOT	AST	PF	DQ	STL	TO	BLK	PTS	RPG	APG	PPG
91-92—Utah	31	0	112	21	46	.457	0	0	—	19	30	.633	11	24	35	5	20	0	2	8	2	61	1.1	0.2	2.0
92-93—Utah	46	3	306	50	112	.446	0	1	.000	29	44	.659	38	41	79	6	60	1	8	23	14	129	1.7	0.1	2.8
93-94—Philadelphia	14	0	201	29	66	.439	0	1	.000	14	23	.609	25	44	69	17	29	0	5	17	10	72	4.9	1.2	5.1
REG. SEASON TOTALS	91	3	619	100	224	.446	0	2	.000	62	97	.639	74	109	183	28	109	1	15	48	26	262	2.0	0.3	2.9
PLAYOFF TOTALS	1	0	3	1	2	.500	0	0	—	0	0	—	0	1	1	—	1	0	0	0	1	2	1.0	0.0	2.0

AUSTIN, JOHN W. (**Johnny**) b. August 31, 1944   Ht. 6-0 Wt. 175 College—Boston College

SEASON—TEAM	G	GS	MIN	FGM	FGA	PCT	3FGM	3FGA	PCT	FTM	FTA	PCT	O-RB	D-RB	TOT	AST	PF	DQ	STL	TO	BLK	PTS	RPG	APG	PPG
66-67—Baltimore	4	—	61	5	22	.227	—	—	—	13	16	.813	—	—	7	4	12	0	—	—	—	23	1.8	1.0	5.8
67-68—New Jersey (A)	41	—	692	108	279	.387	0	11	.000	101	140	.721	—	—	64	58	110	0	—	57	—	317	1.6	1.4	7.7
REG. NBA TOTALS	4	—	61	5	22	.227	—	—	—	13	16	.813	—	—	7	4	12	0	—	—	—	23	1.8	1.0	5.8
REG. ABA TOTALS	41	—	692	108	279	.387	0	11	.000	101	140	.721	—	—	64	58	110	0	—	57	—	317	1.6	1.4	7.7

AUSTIN, KEN b. July 15, 1961   Ht. 6-9 Wt. 205 College—Rice

SEASON—TEAM	G	GS	MIN	FGM	FGA	PCT	3FGM	3FGA	PCT	FTM	FTA	PCT	O-RB	D-RB	TOT	AST	PF	DQ	STL	TO	BLK	PTS	RPG	APG	PPG
83-84—Detroit	7	0	28	6	13	.462	0	0	—	0	0	—	2	1	3	1	7	0	1	3	1	12	0.4	0.1	1.7
REG. SEASON TOTALS	7	0	28	6	13	.462	0	0	—	0	0	—	2	1	3	1	7	0	1	3	1	12	0.4	0.1	1.7

AVENT, ANTHONY b. October 18, 1969   Ht. 6-9 Wt. 235 College—Seton Hall

SEASON—TEAM	G	GS	MIN	FGM	FGA	PCT	3FGM	3FGA	PCT	FTM	FTA	PCT	O-RB	D-RB	TOT	AST	PF	DQ	STL	TO	BLK	PTS	RPG	APG	PPG
92-93—Milwaukee	82	78	2285	347	802	.433	0	2	.000	112	172	.651	180	332	512	91	237	0	57	140	73	806	6.2	1.1	9.8
93-94—Milw.-Orlando	74	40	1371	150	398	.377	0	0	—	89	123	.724	144	194	338	65	147	0	33	85	31	389	4.6	0.9	5.3
REG. SEASON TOTALS	156	118	3656	497	1200	.414	0	2	.000	201	295	.681	324	526	850	156	384	0	90	225	104	1195	5.4	1.0	7.7
PLAYOFF TOTALS	2	0	40	6	13	.462	0	0	—	7	8	.875	8	3	11	1	2	0	0	1	0	19	5.5	0.5	9.5

AVERITT, WILLIAM RODNEY (**Bird**) b. July 22, 1952   Ht. 6-2 Wt. 175 College—Pepperdine

SEASON—TEAM	G	GS	MIN	FGM	FGA	PCT	3FGM	3FGA	PCT	FTM	FTA	PCT	O-RB	D-RB	TOT	AST	PF	DQ	STL	TO	BLK	PTS	RPG	APG	PPG
73-74—San Antonio (A)	74	—	1639	343	912	.376	9	50	.180	156	224	.696	44	77	121	132	166	—	63	137	6	851	1.6	1.8	11.5
74-75—Kentucky (A)	84	—	2031	422	1014	.416	7	47	.149	249	320	.778	51	134	185	319	212	—	87	232	13	1100	2.2	3.8	13.1
75-76—Kentucky (A)	78	—	2272	546	1274	.429	40	128	.313	266	346	.769	55	158	213	297	208	—	106	221	22	1398	2.7	3.8	17.9
76-77—Buffalo	75	—	1136	234	619	.378	—	—	—	121	169	.716	20	58	78	134	127	2	30	—	5	589	1.0	1.8	7.9
77-78—N.J.-Buffalo	55	—	1085	198	484	.409	—	—	—	100	141	.709	17	66	83	196	123	3	39	143	9	496	1.5	3.6	9.0
REG. NBA TOTALS	130	—	2221	432	1103	.392	—	—	—	221	310	.713	37	124	161	330	250	5	69	143	14	1085	1.2	2.5	8.3
REG. ABA TOTALS	236	—	5942	1311	3200	.410	56	225	.249	671	890	.754	150	369	519	748	586	0	256	590	41	3349	2.2	3.2	14.2
ABA PLAYOFF TOTALS	30	—	727	155	403	.385	3	21	.143	77	92	.837	12	43	55	93	74	0	20	63	6	390	1.8	3.1	13.0

AWTREY, DENNIS WADE b. February 22, 1948   Ht. 6-10 Wt. 250 College—Santa Clara

SEASON—TEAM	G	GS	MIN	FGM	FGA	PCT	3FGM	3FGA	PCT	FTM	FTA	PCT	O-RB	D-RB	TOT	AST	PF	DQ	STL	TO	BLK	PTS	RPG	APG	PPG
70-71—Philadelphia	70	—	1292	200	421	.475	—	—	—	104	157	.662	—	—	430	89	211	7	—	—	—	504	6.1	1.3	7.2
71-72—Philadelphia	58	—	794	98	222	.441	—	—	—	49	76	.645	—	—	248	51	141	3	—	—	—	245	4.3	0.9	4.2
72-73—Phil.-Chicago	82	—	1687	146	305	.479	—	—	—	86	153	.562	—	—	447	224	234	6	—	—	—	378	5.5	2.7	4.6
73-74—Chicago	68	—	756	65	123	.528	—	—	—	54	94	.574	49	125	174	86	128	3	22	—	14	184	2.6	1.3	2.7
74-75—Phoenix	82	—	2837	339	722	.470	—	—	—	132	195	.677	242	462	704	342	227	2	60	—	52	810	8.6	4.2	9.9
75-76—Phoenix	74	—	1376	142	304	.467	—	—	—	75	109	.688	93	200	293	159	153	1	21	—	22	359	4.0	2.1	4.9
76-77—Phoenix	72	—	1760	160	373	.429	—	—	—	91	126	.722	111	245	356	182	170	1	23	—	31	411	4.9	2.5	5.7
77-78—Phoenix	81	—	1623	112	264	.424	—	—	—	69	109	.633	97	205	302	163	153	0	19	127	25	293	3.7	2.0	3.6
78-79—Boston-Seattle	63	—	746	44	107	.411	—	—	—	41	56	.732	42	109	151	69	106	0	16	52	13	129	2.4	1.1	2.0
79-80—Chicago	26	—	560	27	60	.450	0	0	—	32	50	.640	29	86	115	40	66	0	12	27	15	86	4.4	1.5	3.3
80-81—Seattle	47	—	607	44	93	.473	0	0	—	14	20	.700	33	75	108	54	85	0	12	33	8	102	2.3	1.1	2.2
81-82—Portland	10	3	121	5	15	.333	0	0	—	5	9	.556	7	7	14	8	28	1	1	6	2	15	1.4	0.8	1.5
REG. SEASON TOTALS	733	3	14159	1382	3009	.459	0	0	—	752	1154	.652	703	1514	3342	1467	1702	24	186	245	182	3516	4.6	2.0	4.8
PLAYOFF TOTALS	61	0	1033	91	177	.514	0	0	—	55	94	.585	45	102	251	88	144	3	17	10	15	237	4.1	1.4	3.9

BABIC, MILOS b. November 23, 1968   Ht. 7-0 Wt. 240 College—Tennessee Tech

SEASON—TEAM	G	GS	MIN	FGM	FGA	PCT	3FGM	3FGA	PCT	FTM	FTA	PCT	O-RB	D-RB	TOT	AST	PF	DQ	STL	TO	BLK	PTS	RPG	APG	PPG
90-91—Cleveland	12	0	52	6	19	.316	0	0	—	7	12	.583	6	3	9	4	7	0	1	5	1	19	0.8	0.3	1.6
91-92—Miami	9	0	35	6	13	.462	0	0	—	6	8	.750	2	9	11	6	0	0	1	5	0	18	1.2	0.7	2.0
REG. SEASON TOTALS	21	0	87	12	32	.375	0	0	—	13	20	.650	8	12	20	10	7	0	2	10	1	37	1.0	0.5	1.8

BACH, JOHN WILLIAM (**Johnny**) b. July 10, 1924   Ht. 6-2 Wt. 180 College—Rochester/Fordham/Brown

SEASON—TEAM	G	GS	MIN	FGM	FGA	PCT	3FGM	3FGA	PCT	FTM	FTA	PCT	O-RB	D-RB	TOT	AST	PF	DQ	STL	TO	BLK	PTS	RPG	APG	PPG
48-49—Boston	34	—	—	34	119	.286	—	—	—	51	75	.680	—	—	—	25	24	—	—	—	—	119	—	0.7	3.5
REG. SEASON TOTALS	34	—	—	34	119	.286	—	—	—	51	75	.680	—	—	—	25	24	—	—	—	—	119	—	0.7	3.5

BACON, WILLIAM HENRY (**Henry**) b. July 5, 1948   Ht. 6-3½ Wt. 205 College—Louisville

SEASON—TEAM	G	GS	MIN	FGM	FGA	PCT	3FGM	3FGA	PCT	FTM	FTA	PCT	O-RB	D-RB	TOT	AST	PF	DQ	STL	TO	BLK	PTS	RPG	APG	PPG
72-73—San Diego (A)	47	—	425	60	164	.366	2	10	.200	44	73	.603	40	42	82	38	72	1	—	64	—	166	1.7	0.8	3.5
REG. ABA TOTALS	47	—	425	60	164	.366	2	10	.200	44	73	.603	40	42	82	38	72	1	—	64	—	166	1.7	0.8	3.5
ABA PLAYOFF TOTALS	2	—	16	4	9	.444	2	3	.667	0	2	.000	—	—	6	1	0	0	—	2	—	10	3.0	0.5	5.0

BAECHTOLD, JAMES E. (**Jim**) b. December 9, 1927   Ht. 6-4 Wt. 205 College—Eastern Kentucky

SEASON—TEAM	G	GS	MIN	FGM	FGA	PCT	3FGM	3FGA	PCT	FTM	FTA	PCT	O-RB	D-RB	TOT	AST	PF	DQ	STL	TO	BLK	PTS	RPG	APG	PPG
52-53—Baltimore	64	—	1893	242	621	.390	—	—	—	177	240	.738	—	—	219	154	203	8	—	—	—	661	3.4	2.4	10.3
53-54—New York	70	—	1627	170	465	.366	—	—	—	134	177	.757	—	—	183	117	195	5	—	—	—	474	2.6	1.7	6.8
54-55—New York	72	—	2536	362	898	.403	—	—	—	279	339	.823	—	—	307	218	202	0	—	—	—	1003	4.3	3.0	13.9
55-56—New York	70	—	1738	268	695	.386	—	—	—	233	291	.801	—	—	220	163	156	2	—	—	—	769	3.1	2.3	11.0
56-57—New York	45	—	462	75	197	.381	—	—	—	66	88	.750	—	—	80	33	39	0	—	—	—	216	1.8	0.7	4.8
REG. SEASON TOTALS	321	—	8256	1117	2876	.388	—	—	—	889	1135	.783	—	—	1009	685	795	15	—	—	—	3123	3.1	2.1	9.7
PLAYOFF TOTALS	9	—	307	45	104	.433	—	—	—	31	39	.795	—	—	32	36	41	1	—	—	—	121	3.6	4.0	13.4

BAGLEY, JOHN EDWARD (**Bags**) b. April 23, 1960   Ht. 6-0 Wt. 195 College—Boston College

SEASON—TEAM	G	GS	MIN	FGM	FGA	PCT	3FGM	3FGA	PCT	FTM	FTA	PCT	O-RB	D-RB	TOT	AST	PF	DQ	STL	TO	BLK	PTS	RPG	APG	PPG
82-83—Cleveland	68	3	990	161	373	.432	0	14	.000	64	84	.762	17	79	96	167	74	0	54	118	5	386	1.4	2.5	5.7
83-84—Cleveland	76	19	1712	257	607	.423	2	17	.118	157	198	.793	49	107	156	333	113	1	78	170	4	673	2.1	4.4	8.9
84-85—Cleveland	81	65	2401	338	693	.488	3	26	.115	125	167	.749	54	237	291	697	132	0	129	207	5	804	3.6	8.6	9.9
85-86—Cleveland	78	77	2472	366	865	.423	9	37	.243	170	215	.791	76	199	275	735	165	1	122	239	10	911	3.5	9.4	11.7
86-87—Cleveland	72	67	2182	312	732	.426	31	103	.301	113	136	.831	55	197	252	379	114	0	91	163	7	768	3.5	5.3	10.7
87-88—New Jersey	82	74	2774	393	896	.439	47	161	.292	148	180	.822	61	196	257	479	162	0	110	201	10	981	3.1	5.8	12.0
88-89—New Jersey	68	20	1642	200	481	.416	11	54	.204	89	123	.724	36	108	144	391	117	0	72	159	5	500	2.1	5.8	7.4
89-90—Boston	54	1	1095	100	218	.459	1	18	.056	29	39	.744	26	63	89	296	77	0	40	90	4	230	1.6	5.5	4.3
91-92—Boston	73	59	1742	223	506	.441	10	42	.238	68	95	.716	38	123	161	480	123	1	57	148	4	524	2.2	6.6	7.2
92-93—Boston	10	0	97	9	25	.360	0	1	.000	5	6	.833	1	6	7	20	11	0	2	17	0	23	0.7	2.0	2.3
93-94—Atlanta	3	0	13	0	2	.000	0	0	—	2	2	1.000	0	1	1	3	2	0	0	0	0	2	0.3	1.0	0.7
REG. SEASON TOTALS	665	401	17120	2359	5398	.437	114	473	.241	970	1245	.779	413	1316	1729	3980	1090	3	755	1512	54	5802	2.6	6.0	8.7
PLAYOFF TOTALS	19	14	546	72	166	.434	1	8	.125	36	51	.706	12	35	47	142	33	0	23	61	2	181	2.5	7.5	9.5

BAILEY, AUGUSTUS (**Gus**) b. February 18, 1951 d. November 28, 1988 Ht. 6-5½ Wt. 185 College—Texas-El Paso

SEASON—TEAM	G	GS	MIN	FGM	FGA	PCT	3FGM	3FGA	PCT	FTM	FTA	PCT	O-RB	D-RB	TOT	AST	PF	DQ	STL	TO	BLK	PTS	RPG	APG	PPG
74-75—Houston	47	—	446	51	126	.405	—	—	—	20	41	.488	23	59	82	59	52	0	17	—	16	122	1.7	1.3	2.6
75-76—Houston	30	—	262	28	77	.364	—	—	—	14	28	.500	20	30	50	41	33	1	14	—	8	70	1.7	1.4	2.3
77-78—New Orleans	48	—	449	59	139	.424	—	—	—	37	67	.552	44	38	82	40	46	0	18	33	15	155	1.7	0.8	3.2
78-79—New Orleans	2	—	9	2	7	.286	—	—	—	0	0	—	2	0	2	2	1	0	1	0	4	4	1.0	1.0	2.0
79-80—Washington	20	—	180	16	35	.457	1	1	1.000	5	13	.385	6	22	28	26	18	0	7	11	4	38	1.4	1.3	1.9
REG. SEASON TOTALS	147	—	1346	156	384	.406	1	1	1.000	76	149	.510	95	149	244	168	150	1	56	45	43	389	1.7	1.1	2.6
PLAYOFF TOTALS	8	—	116	18	36	.500	0	0	—	9	10	.900	6	13	19	16	12	0	6	—	2	45	2.4	2.0	5.6

BAILEY, CARL b. April 23, 1958 Ht. 7-0 Wt. 210 College—Tuskegee

SEASON—TEAM	G	GS	MIN	FGM	FGA	PCT	3FGM	3FGA	PCT	FTM	FTA	PCT	O-RB	D-RB	TOT	AST	PF	DQ	STL	TO	BLK	PTS	RPG	APG	PPG
81-82—Portland	1	0	7	1	1	1.000	0	0	—	0	0	—	0	0	0	0	2	0	0	2	0	2	0.0	0.0	2.0
REG. SEASON TOTALS	1	0	7	1	1	1.000	0	0	—	0	0	—	0	0	0	0	2	0	0	2	0	2	0.0	0.0	2.0

BAILEY, AUGUSTUS (**Gus**) b. February 18, 1951 d. November 28, 1988 Ht. 6-5½ Wt. 185 College—Texas-El Paso

SEASON—TEAM	G	GS	MIN	FGM	FGA	PCT	3FGM	3FGA	PCT	FTM	FTA	PCT	O-RB	D-RB	TOT	AST	PF	DQ	STL	TO	BLK	PTS	RPG	APG	PPG
74-75—Houston	47	—	446	51	126	.405	—	—	—	20	41	.488	23	59	82	59	52	0	17	—	16	122	1.7	1.3	2.6
75-76—Houston	30	—	262	28	77	.364	—	—	—	14	28	.500	20	30	50	41	33	1	14	—	8	70	1.7	1.4	2.3
77-78—New Orleans	48	—	449	59	139	.424	—	—	—	37	67	.552	44	38	82	40	46	0	18	33	15	155	1.7	0.8	3.2
78-79—New Orleans	2	—	9	2	7	.286	—	—	—	0	0	—	2	0	2	2	1	0	0	1	0	4	1.0	1.0	2.0
79-80—Washington	20	—	180	16	35	.457	1	1	1.000	5	13	.385	6	22	28	26	18	0	7	11	4	38	1.4	1.3	1.9
REG. SEASON TOTALS	147	—	1346	156	384	.406	1	1	1.000	76	149	.510	95	149	244	168	150	1	56	45	43	389	1.7	1.1	2.6
PLAYOFF TOTALS	8	—	116	18	36	.500	0	0	—	9	10	.900	6	13	19	16	12	0	6	—	2	45	2.4	2.0	5.6

BAILEY, JAMES L. b. May 21, 1957 Ht. 6-9 Wt. 220 College—Rutgers

SEASON—TEAM	G	GS	MIN	FGM	FGA	PCT	3FGM	3FGA	PCT	FTM	FTA	PCT	O-RB	D-RB	TOT	AST	PF	DQ	STL	TO	BLK	PTS	RPG	APG	PPG
79-80—Seattle	67	—	726	122	271	.450	0	0	—	68	101	.673	71	126	197	28	116	1	21	79	54	312	2.9	0.4	4.7
80-81—Seattle	82	—	2539	444	889	.499	1	2	.500	256	361	.709	192	415	607	98	332	11	74	219	143	1145	7.4	1.2	14.0
81-82—Seattle-N.J.	77	0	1468	261	505	.517	0	0	—	137	224	.612	127	264	391	65	270	5	42	139	83	659	5.1	0.8	8.6
82-83—N.J.-Houston	75	39	1765	385	774	.497	0	1	.000	226	322	.702	171	303	474	67	271	7	43	196	60	996	6.3	0.9	13.3
83-84—Houston	73	0	1174	254	517	.491	0	1	.000	138	192	.719	104	190	294	79	197	8	33	101	40	646	4.0	1.1	8.8
84-85—New York	74	28	1297	156	349	.447	0	1	.000	73	108	.676	122	222	344	39	286	10	30	100	50	385	4.6	0.5	5.2
85-86—New York	48	36	1245	202	443	.456	0	4	.000	129	167	.772	102	232	334	50	207	12	33	99	40	533	7.0	1.0	11.1
86-87—New Jersey	34	2	542	112	239	.469	0	0	—	58	80	.725	48	89	137	20	119	5	12	54	23	282	4.0	0.6	8.3
87-88—Phoenix	65	0	869	109	241	.452	0	4	.000	70	89	.787	73	137	210	42	180	1	17	70	28	288	3.2	0.6	4.4
REG. SEASON TOTALS	595	105	11625	2045	4228	.484	1	13	.077	1155	1644	.703	1010	1978	2988	488	1978	60	305	1057	521	5246	5.0	0.8	8.8
PLAYOFF TOTALS	14	0	164	22	47	.468	0	0	—	15	22	.682	10	21	31	6	27	0	11	12	10	59	2.2	0.4	4.2

BAILEY, THURL LEE (**Big T.**) b. April 7, 1961 Ht. 6-11 Wt. 240 College—North Carolina State

SEASON—TEAM	G	GS	MIN	FGM	FGA	PCT	3FGM	3FGA	PCT	FTM	FTA	PCT	O-RB	D-RB	TOT	AST	PF	DQ	STL	TO	BLK	PTS	RPG	APG	PPG
83-84—Utah	81	54	2009	302	590	.512	0	0	—	88	117	.752	115	349	464	129	193	1	38	105	122	692	5.7	1.6	8.5
84-85—Utah	80	68	2481	507	1034	.490	1	1	1.000	197	234	.842	153	372	525	138	215	2	51	152	105	1212	6.6	1.7	15.2
85-86—Utah	82	13	2358	483	1077	.448	0	7	.000	230	277	.830	148	345	493	153	160	0	42	144	114	1196	6.0	1.9	14.6
86-87—Utah	81	2	2155	463	1036	.447	0	2	.000	190	236	.805	145	287	432	102	150	0	38	123	88	1116	5.3	1.3	13.8
87-88—Utah	82	10	2804	633	1286	.492	1	3	.333	337	408	.826	134	397	531	158	186	1	49	190	125	1604	6.5	1.9	19.6
88-89—Utah	82	3	2777	615	1272	.483	2	5	.400	363	440	.825	115	332	447	138	185	0	48	208	91	1595	5.5	1.7	19.5
89-90—Utah	82	33	2583	470	977	.481	0	8	.000	222	285	.779	116	294	410	137	175	2	32	139	100	1162	5.0	1.7	14.2
90-91—Utah	82	22	2486	399	872	.458	0	3	.000	219	271	.808	101	306	407	124	160	0	53	130	91	1017	5.0	1.5	12.4
91-92—Utah-Minn.	84	18	2104	368	836	.440	0	2	.000	215	270	.796	122	316	438	78	160	1	35	108	117	951	5.8	0.9	11.3
92-93—Minnesota	70	3	1276	203	446	.455	0	0	—	119	142	.838	53	162	215	61	88	0	20	60	47	525	3.1	0.9	7.5
93-94—Minnesota	79	3	1297	232	455	.510	0	2	.000	119	149	.799	66	149	215	54	93	0	20	58	58	583	2.7	0.7	7.4
REG. SEASON TOTALS	885	229	24330	4675	9881	.473	4	33	.121	2299	2829	.813	1268	3356	4624	1272	1765	7	426	1417	1058	11653	5.2	1.4	13.2
PLAYOFF TOTALS	58	31	2002	347	778	.446	0	4	.000	198	237	.835	111	256	367	96	177	3	27	101	76	892	6.3	1.7	15.4

BAKER, JIMMIE JR. b. December 25, 1953 Ht. 6-9 Wt. 220 College—Nevada-Las Vegas/Hawaii

SEASON—TEAM	G	GS	MIN	FGM	FGA	PCT	3FGM	3FGA	PCT	FTM	FTA	PCT	O-RB	D-RB	TOT	AST	PF	DQ	STL	TO	BLK	PTS	RPG	APG	PPG
75-76—Kentucky (A)	5	—	40	3	15	.200	0	0	—	0	2	.000	4	10	14	4	11	—	0	6	3	6	2.8	0.8	1.2
REG. ABA TOTALS	5	—	40	3	15	.200	0	0	—	0	2	.000	4	10	14	4	11	—	0	6	3	6	2.8	0.8	1.2

BAKER, NORMAN HENRY (**Norm**) b. February 17, 1923 Ht. 6-0 Wt. 180 College—None

SEASON—TEAM	G	GS	MIN	FGM	FGA	PCT	3FGM	3FGA	PCT	FTM	FTA	PCT	O-RB	D-RB	TOT	AST	PF	DQ	STL	TO	BLK	PTS	RPG	APG	PPG
46-47—Chicago	4	—	—	0	1	.000	—	—	—	0	0	—	—	—	—	0	0	—	—	—	—	0	—	0.0	0.0
REG. SEASON TOTALS	4	—	—	0	1	.000	—	—	—	0	0	—	—	—	—	0	0	—	—	—	—	0	—	0.0	0.0

BAKER, VINCENT LAMONT (**Vin**) b. November 23, 1971 Ht. 6-11 Wt. 235 College—Hartford

SEASON—TEAM	G	GS	MIN	FGM	FGA	PCT	3FGM	3FGA	PCT	FTM	FTA	PCT	O-RB	D-RB	TOT	AST	PF	DQ	STL	TO	BLK	PTS	RPG	APG	PPG
93-94—Milwaukee	82	63	2560	435	869	.501	1	5	.200	234	411	.569	277	344	621	163	231	3	60	162	114	1105	7.6	2.0	13.5
REG. SEASON TOTALS	82	63	2560	435	869	.501	1	5	.200	234	411	.569	277	344	621	163	231	3	60	162	114	1105	7.6	2.0	13.5

BALL, CEDRIC GLENN b. April 16, 1968 Ht. 6-8 Wt. 210 College—UNC-Charlotte

SEASON—TEAM	G	GS	MIN	FGM	FGA	PCT	3FGM	3FGA	PCT	FTM	FTA	PCT	O-RB	D-RB	TOT	AST	PF	DQ	STL	TO	BLK	PTS	RPG	APG	PPG
90-91—L.A. Clippers	7	0	26	3	8	.375	0	0	—	2	2	1.000	5	6	11	0	5	0	0	2	2	8	1.6	0.0	1.1
REG. SEASON TOTALS	7	0	26	3	8	.375	0	0	—	2	2	1.000	5	6	11	0	5	0	0	2	2	8	1.6	0.0	1.1

BALLARD, GREGORY (Greg) b. January 29, 1955 Ht. 6-7 Wt. 215 College—Shasta/Oregon

SEASON—TEAM	G	GS	MIN	FGM	FGA	PCT	3FGM	3FGA	PCT	FTM	FTA	PCT	O-RB	D-RB	TOT	AST	PF	DQ	STL	TO	BLK	PTS	RPG	APG	PPG
77-78—Washington	76	—	936	142	334	.425	—	—	—	88	114	.772	102	164	266	62	90	1	30	64	13	372	3.5	0.8	4.9
78-79—Washington	82	—	1552	260	559	.465	—	—	—	119	172	.692	143	307	450	116	167	3	58	97	30	639	5.5	1.4	7.8
79-80—Washington	82	—	2438	545	1101	.495	16	47	.340	171	227	.753	240	398	638	159	197	2	90	133	36	1277	7.8	1.9	15.6
80-81—Washington	82	—	2610	549	1186	.463	7	32	.219	166	196	.847	167	413	580	195	194	1	118	117	39	1271	7.1	2.4	15.5
81-82—Washington	79	79	2946	621	1307	.475	9	22	.409	235	283	.830	136	497	633	250	204	0	137	119	22	1486	8.0	3.2	18.8
82-83—Washington	78	78	2840	603	1274	.473	13	37	.351	182	233	.781	123	385	508	262	176	2	135	157	25	1401	6.5	3.4	18.0
83-84—Washington	82	82	2701	510	1061	.481	2	15	.133	166	208	.798	140	348	488	290	214	1	94	142	35	1188	6.0	3.5	14.5
84-85—Washington	82	77	2664	469	978	.480	14	46	.304	120	151	.795	150	381	531	208	221	0	100	106	33	1072	6.5	2.5	13.1
85-86—Golden State	75	14	1792	272	570	.477	17	35	.486	101	126	.802	132	285	417	83	174	0	65	54	8	662	5.6	1.1	8.8
86-87—Golden State	82	7	1579	248	564	.440	15	40	.375	68	91	.747	99	241	340	108	167	0	50	70	15	579	4.1	1.3	7.1
88-89—Seattle	2	0	15	1	8	.125	0	1	.000	4	4	1.000	2	5	7	3	0	0	0	0	0	6	3.5	0.0	3.0
REG. SEASON TOTALS	802	337	22073	4220	8942	.472	93	275	.338	1420	1805	.787	1434	3424	4858	1733	1807	10	877	1059	256	9953	6.1	2.2	12.4
PLAYOFF TOTALS	65	11	1308	183	423	.433	4	13	.308	111	140	.793	114	212	326	103	120	1	51	76	16	481	5.0	1.6	7.4

BALTIMORE, HERSCHEL DAVID (Herk) b. June 21, 1921 d. January 1, 1968 Ht. 6-4 Wt. 195 College—Penn State

SEASON—TEAM	G	GS	MIN	FGM	FGA	PCT	3FGM	3FGA	PCT	FTM	FTA	PCT	O-RB	D-RB	TOT	AST	PF	DQ	STL	TO	BLK	PTS	RPG	APG	PPG
46-47—St. Louis	58	—	—	53	263	.202	—	—	—	32	69	.464	—	—	—	16	98	—	—	—	—	138	—	0.3	2.4
REG. SEASON TOTALS	58	—	—	53	263	.202	—	—	—	32	69	.464	—	—	—	16	98	—	—	—	—	138	—	0.3	2.4
PLAYOFF TOTALS	3	—	—	2	10	.200	—	—	—	0	1	.000	—	—	—	—	3	—	—	—	—	4	—	0.0	1.3

BANKS, EUGENE LAVON (Gene) b. May 15, 1959 Ht. 6-7 Wt. 215 College—Duke

SEASON—TEAM	G	GS	MIN	FGM	FGA	PCT	3FGM	3FGA	PCT	FTM	FTA	PCT	O-RB	D-RB	TOT	AST	PF	DQ	STL	TO	BLK	PTS	RPG	APG	PPG
81-82—San Antonio	80	4	1700	311	652	.477	0	8	.000	145	212	.684	157	254	411	147	199	2	55	106	17	767	5.1	1.8	9.6
82-83—San Antonio	81	81	2722	505	919	.550	0	5	.000	196	278	.705	222	390	612	279	229	3	78	171	21	1206	7.6	3.4	14.9
83-84—San Antonio	80	66	2600	424	747	.568	1	6	.167	200	270	.741	204	378	582	254	256	5	105	166	23	1049	7.3	3.2	13.1
84-85—San Antonio	82	41	2091	289	493	.586	1	3	.333	199	257	.774	133	312	445	234	220	3	65	140	13	778	5.4	2.9	9.5
85-86—Chicago	82	33	2139	356	688	.517	0	19	.000	183	255	.718	178	182	360	251	212	4	81	139	10	895	4.4	3.1	10.9
86-87—Chicago	63	39	1822	249	462	.539	0	5	.000	112	146	.767	115	193	308	170	173	3	52	113	17	610	4.9	2.7	9.7
REG. SEASON TOTALS	468	264	13074	2134	3961	.539	2	46	.043	1035	1418	.730	1009	1709	2718	1335	1289	20	436	835	101	5305	5.8	2.9	11.3
PLAYOFF TOTALS	27	14	702	129	256	.504	0	3	.000	34	57	.596	55	82	137	67	63	2	16	35	4	292	5.1	2.5	10.8

BANKS, WALKER BURRELL JR. b. August 26, 1947 Ht. 6-10 Wt. 205 College—Western Kentucky

SEASON—TEAM	G	GS	MIN	FGM	FGA	PCT	3FGM	3FGA	PCT	FTM	FTA	PCT	O-RB	D-RB	TOT	AST	PF	DQ	STL	TO	BLK	PTS	RPG	APG	PPG
70-71—Pittsburgh (A)	16	—	154	17	34	.500	0	0	—	7	17	.412	—	—	49	8	34	—	—	—	—	41	3.1	0.5	2.6
REG. ABA TOTALS	16	—	154	17	34	.500	0	0	—	7	17	.412	—	—	49	8	34	—	—	—	—	41	3.1	0.5	2.6

BANNISTER, KENNETH (Ken, The Animal) b. April 1, 1960 Ht. 6-9 Wt. 235 College—Trinidad State JC/Indiana State/St. Augustine

SEASON—TEAM	G	GS	MIN	FGM	FGA	PCT	3FGM	3FGA	PCT	FTM	FTA	PCT	O-RB	D-RB	TOT	AST	PF	DQ	STL	TO	BLK	PTS	RPG	APG	PPG
84-85—New York	75	50	1404	209	445	.470	0	0	—	91	192	.474	108	222	330	39	279	16	38	141	40	509	4.4	0.5	6.8
85-86—New York	70	15	1405	235	479	.491	0	1	.000	131	249	.526	89	233	322	42	208	5	42	129	24	601	4.6	0.6	8.6
88-89—L.A. Clippers	9	2	130	22	36	.611	0	1	.000	30	53	.566	6	27	33	3	17	0	7	8	2	74	3.7	0.3	8.2
89-90—L.A. Clippers	52	1	589	77	161	.478	0	1	.000	52	110	.473	39	73	112	18	92	1	17	44	7	206	2.2	0.3	4.0
90-91—L.A. Clippers	47	3	339	43	81	.531	0	1	.000	25	65	.385	34	62	96	9	73	0	5	25	7	111	2.0	0.2	2.4
REG. SEASON TOTALS	253	71	3867	586	1202	.488	0	4	.000	329	669	.492	276	617	893	111	669	22	109	347	80	1501	3.5	0.4	5.9

BANTOM, MICHAEL ALLEN (Mike) b. December 3, 1951 Ht. 6-9 Wt. 200 College—St. Joseph's (Pa.)

SEASON—TEAM	G	GS	MIN	FGM	FGA	PCT	3FGM	3FGA	PCT	FTM	FTA	PCT	O-RB	D-RB	TOT	AST	PF	DQ	STL	TO	BLK	PTS	RPG	APG	PPG
73-74—Phoenix	76	—	1982	314	787	.399	—	—	—	141	213	.662	172	347	519	163	289	15	50	—	47	769	6.8	2.1	10.1
74-75—Phoenix	82	—	2239	418	907	.461	—	—	—	185	259	.714	211	342	553	159	273	8	62	—	47	1021	6.7	1.9	12.5
75-76—Phoenix-Seattle	73	—	1571	220	476	.462	—	—	—	136	199	.683	140	251	391	105	221	4	28	—	28	576	5.4	1.4	7.9
76-77—Seattle-N.Y.	77	—	1909	361	755	.478	—	—	—	224	310	.723	184	287	471	102	233	7	63	—	49	946	6.1	1.3	12.3
77-78—Indiana	82	—	2775	502	1047	.479	—	—	—	254	342	.743	184	426	610	238	333	13	100	218	50	1258	7.4	2.9	15.3
78-79—Indiana	81	—	2528	482	1036	.465	—	—	—	227	338	.672	225	425	650	223	316	8	99	193	62	1191	8.0	2.8	14.7
79-80—Indiana	77	—	2330	384	760	.505	1	3	.333	139	209	.665	192	264	456	279	268	7	85	189	49	908	5.9	3.6	11.8
80-81—Indiana	76	—	2375	431	882	.489	0	6	.000	199	281	.708	150	277	427	240	284	9	80	197	85	1061	5.6	3.2	14.0
81-82—Indiana-Phil.	82	38	2016	334	712	.469	2	6	.333	168	267	.629	174	266	440	114	272	5	63	149	61	838	5.4	1.4	10.2
REG. SEASON TOTALS	706	38	19725	3446	7362	.468	3	15	.200	1673	2418	.692	1632	2885	4517	1623	2489	76	630	946	478	8568	6.4	2.3	12.1
PLAYOFF TOTALS	29	0	564	70	145	.483	0	0	—	38	69	.551	53	55	108	33	97	2	20	30	12	178	3.7	1.1	6.1

BARBER, JOHN b. June 27, 1927 Ht. 6-6 Wt. 210 College—Cal State-Los Angeles

SEASON—TEAM	G	GS	MIN	FGM	FGA	PCT	3FGM	3FGA	PCT	FTM	FTA	PCT	O-RB	D-RB	TOT	AST	PF	DQ	STL	TO	BLK	PTS	RPG	APG	PPG
56-57—St. Louis	5	—	5	2	8	.250	—	—	—	3	6	.500	—	—	6	0	4	0	—	—	—	7	1.2	0.0	1.4
REG. SEASON TOTALS	5	—	5	2	8	.250	—	—	—	3	6	.500	—	—	6	0	4	0	—	—	—	7	1.2	0.0	1.4

BARDO, STEPHEN DEAN b. April 5, 1968   Ht. 6-6 Wt. 200 College—Illinois

SEASON—TEAM	G	GS	MIN	FGM	FGA	PCT	3FGM	3FGA	PCT	FTM	FTA	PCT	O-RB	D-RB	TOT	AST	PF	DQ	STL	TO	BLK	PTS	RPG	APG	PPG
91-92—San Antonio	1	0	1	0	0	—	0	0	—	0	0	—	1	0	1	0	0	0	0	0	0	0	1.0	0.0	0.0
92-93—Dallas	23	0	175	19	62	.306	1	6	.167	12	17	.706	10	27	37	29	28	0	8	17	3	51	1.6	1.3	2.2
REG. SEASON TOTALS	24	0	176	19	62	.306	1	6	.167	12	17	.706	11	27	38	29	28	0	8	17	3	51	1.6	1.2	2.1

BARKER, CLIFFORD E. b. January 15, 1921   Ht. 6-2 Wt. 185 College—Kentucky

SEASON—TEAM	G	GS	MIN	FGM	FGA	PCT	3FGM	3FGA	PCT	FTM	FTA	PCT	O-RB	D-RB	TOT	AST	PF	DQ	STL	TO	BLK	PTS	RPG	APG	PPG
49-50—Indianapolis	49	—	—	102	274	.372	—	—	—	75	106	.708	—	—	—	109	99	—	—	—	—	279	—	2.2	5.7
50-51—Indianapolis	56	—	—	51	202	.252	—	—	—	50	77	.649	—	—	100	115	98	0	—	—	—	152	1.8	2.1	2.7
51-52—Indianapolis	44	—	494	48	161	.298	—	—	—	30	51	.588	—	—	81	70	56	0	—	—	—	126	1.8	1.6	2.9
REG. SEASON TOTALS	149	—	494	201	637	.316	—	—	—	155	234	.662	—	—	181	294	253	0	—	—	—	557	1.8	2.0	3.7
PLAYOFF TOTALS	9	—	0	16	50	.320	—	—	—	10	18	.556	—	—	15	23	20	—	—	—	—	42	5.0	2.6	4.7

BARKER, THOMAS KEVIN (**Tom**) b. March 11, 1955   Ht. 6-11 Wt. 225 College—Minnesota/Southern Idaho/Hawaii

SEASON—TEAM	G	GS	MIN	FGM	FGA	PCT	3FGM	3FGA	PCT	FTM	FTA	PCT	O-RB	D-RB	TOT	AST	PF	DQ	STL	TO	BLK	PTS	RPG	APG	PPG
76-77—Atlanta	59	—	1354	182	436	.417	—	—	—	112	164	.683	111	290	401	60	223	11	33	—	41	476	6.8	1.0	8.1
78-79—Houston-Boston-N.Y.	39	—	476	68	156	.436	—	—	—	27	37	.730	45	74	119	15	76	0	10	34	11	163	3.1	0.4	4.2
REG. SEASON TOTALS	98	—	1830	250	592	.422	—	—	—	139	201	.692	156	364	520	75	299	11	43	34	52	639	5.3	0.8	6.5

BARKLEY, CHARLES WADE (**Sir Charles**) b. February 20, 1963   Ht. 6-5 Wt. 250 College—Auburn

SEASON—TEAM	G	GS	MIN	FGM	FGA	PCT	3FGM	3FGA	PCT	FTM	FTA	PCT	O-RB	D-RB	TOT	AST	PF	DQ	STL	TO	BLK	PTS	RPG	APG	PPG
84-85—Philadelphia	82	60	2347	427	783	.545	1	6	.167	293	400	.733	266	437	703	155	301	5	95	209	80	1148	8.6	1.9	14.0
85-86—Philadelphia	80	80	2952	595	1041	.572	17	75	.227	396	578	.685	354	672	1026	312	333	8	173	350	125	1603	12.8	3.9	20.0
86-87—Philadelphia	68	62	2740	557	937	.594	21	104	.202	429	564	.761	390	604	994	331	252	5	119	322	104	1564	14.6	4.9	23.0
87-88—Philadelphia	80	80	3170	753	1283	.587	44	157	.280	714	951	.751	385	566	951	254	278	6	100	304	103	2264	11.9	3.2	28.3
88-89—Philadelphia	79	79	3088	700	1208	.579	35	162	.216	602	799	.753	403	583	986	325	262	3	126	254	67	2037	12.5	4.1	25.8
89-90—Philadelphia	79	79	3085	706	1177	.600	20	92	.217	557	744	.749	361	548	909	307	250	2	148	243	50	1989	11.5	3.9	25.2
90-91—Philadelphia	67	67	2498	665	1167	.570	44	155	.284	475	658	.722	258	422	680	284	173	2	110	210	33	1849	10.1	4.2	27.6
91-92—Philadelphia	75	75	2881	622	1126	.552	32	137	.234	454	653	.695	271	559	830	308	196	2	136	235	44	1730	11.1	4.1	23.1
92-93—Phoenix	76	76	2859	716	1376	.520	67	220	.305	445	582	.765	237	691	928	385	196	0	119	233	74	1944	12.2	5.1	25.6
93-94—Phoenix	65	65	2298	518	1046	.495	48	178	.270	318	452	.704	198	529	727	296	160	1	101	206	37	1402	11.2	4.6	21.6
REG. SEASON TOTALS	751	723	27918	6259	11144	.562	329	1286	.256	4683	6381	.734	3123	5611	8734	2957	2401	34	1227	2566	717	17530	11.6	3.9	23.3
PLAYOFF TOTALS	85	74	3446	753	1424	.529	39	157	.248	513	726	.707	371	755	1126	362	289	2	146	265	84	2058	13.2	4.3	24.2
ALL-STAR TOTALS	7	5	170	34	73	.466	2	8	.250	20	32	.625	17	34	51	13	16	0	10	16	4	90	7.3	1.9	12.9

BARKSDALE, DON ANGELO b. March 31, 1923 d. March 8, 1993 Ht. 6-6 Wt. 200 College—Marin JC/UCLA

SEASON—TEAM	G	GS	MIN	FGM	FGA	PCT	3FGM	3FGA	PCT	FTM	FTA	PCT	O-RB	D-RB	TOT	AST	PF	DQ	STL	TO	BLK	PTS	RPG	APG	PPG
51-52—Baltimore	62	—	2014	272	804	.338	—	—	—	237	343	.691	—	—	601	137	230	13	—	—	—	781	9.7	2.2	12.6
52-53—Baltimore	65	—	2298	321	829	.387	—	—	—	257	401	.641	—	—	597	166	273	13	—	—	—	899	9.2	2.6	13.8
53-54—Boston	63	—	1358	156	415	.376	—	—	—	149	225	.662	—	—	345	117	213	4	—	—	—	461	5.5	1.9	7.3
54-55—Boston	72	—	1790	267	699	.382	—	—	—	220	338	.651	—	—	545	129	225	7	—	—	—	754	7.6	1.8	10.5
REG. SEASON TOTALS	262	—	7460	1016	2747	.370	—	—	—	863	1307	.660	—	—	2088	549	941	37	—	—	—	2895	8.0	2.1	11.0
PLAYOFF TOTALS	13	—	228	29	76	.382	—	—	—	26	32	.813	—	—	62	17	40	3	—	—	—	84	4.8	1.3	6.5
ALL-STAR TOTALS	1	—	11	0	1	.000	—	—	—	1	3	.333	—	—	3	2	0	0	—	—	—	1	3.0	2.0	1.0

BARNES, HARRY J. b. July 25, 1945   Ht. 6-3 Wt. 205 College—Northeastern

SEASON—TEAM	G	GS	MIN	FGM	FGA	PCT	3FGM	3FGA	PCT	FTM	FTA	PCT	O-RB	D-RB	TOT	AST	PF	DQ	STL	TO	BLK	PTS	RPG	APG	PPG
68-69—San Diego	22	—	126	18	64	.281	—	—	—	7	13	.538	—	—	26	5	25	0	—	—	—	43	1.2	0.2	2.0
REG. SEASON TOTALS	22	—	126	18	64	.281	—	—	—	7	13	.538	—	—	26	5	25	0	—	—	—	43	1.2	0.2	2.0

BARNES, MARVIN JEROME b. July 27, 1952   Ht. 6-9 Wt. 225 College—Providence

SEASON—TEAM	G	GS	MIN	FGM	FGA	PCT	3FGM	3FGA	PCT	FTM	FTA	PCT	O-RB	D-RB	TOT	AST	PF	DQ	STL	TO	BLK	PTS	RPG	APG	PPG
74-75—St. Louis (A)	77	—	3076	777	1561	.498	0	3	.000	295	440	.670	419	783	1202	250	328	—	96	307	137	1849	15.6	3.2	24.0
75-76—St. Louis (A)	67	—	2487	681	1355	.503	3	11	.273	251	339	.740	263	462	725	149	273	—	124	230	134	1616	10.8	2.2	24.1
76-77—Detroit	53	—	989	202	452	.447	—	—	—	106	156	.679	69	184	253	45	139	1	38	—	33	510	4.8	0.8	9.6
77-78—Detroit-Buffalo	60	—	1646	279	661	.422	—	—	—	128	182	.703	135	304	439	136	241	9	64	136	83	686	7.3	2.3	11.4
78-79—Boston	38	—	796	133	271	.491	—	—	—	43	66	.652	57	120	177	53	144	3	38	68	39	309	4.7	1.4	8.1
79-80—San Diego	20	—	287	24	60	.400	0	0	—	16	32	.500	34	43	77	18	52	0	5	18	12	64	3.9	0.9	3.2
REG. NBA TOTALS	171	—	3718	638	1444	.442	0	0	—	293	436	.672	295	651	946	252	576	13	145	222	167	1569	5.5	1.5	9.2
REG. ABA TOTALS	144	—	5563	1458	2916	.500	3	14	.214	546	779	.701	682	1245	1927	399	601	—	220	537	271	3465	13.4	2.8	24.1
ABA PLAYOFF TOTALS	10	—	444	124	249	.498	0	1	.000	60	77	.779	53	88	141	16	45	—	20	38	19	308	14.1	1.6	30.8
ABA ALL-STAR TOTALS	2	—	34	9	18	.500	0	0	—	5	5	1.000	1	1	2	5	—	0	2	0	2	23	0.5	1.0	11.5

BARNES, V. JAMES (Jim, Bad News) b. April 13, 1941 Ht. 6-8 Wt. 240 College—Cameron/Texas-El Paso

SEASON—TEAM	G	GS	MIN	FGM	FGA	PCT	3FGM	3FGA	PCT	FTM	FTA	PCT	O-RB	D-RB	TOT	AST	PF	DQ	STL	TO	BLK	PTS	RPG	APG	PPG
64-65—New York	75	—	2586	454	1070	.424	—	—	—	251	379	.662	—	—	729	93	312	8	—	—	—	1159	9.7	1.2	15.5
65-66—N.Y.-Balt.	73	—	2191	348	818	.425	—	—	—	212	310	.684	—	—	755	94	283	10	—	—	—	908	10.3	1.3	12.4
66-67—Los Angeles	80	—	1398	217	497	.437	—	—	—	128	187	.684	—	—	450	47	266	5	—	—	—	562	5.6	0.6	7.0
67-68—L.A.-Chicago	79	—	1425	221	499	.443	—	—	—	133	191	.696	—	—	415	55	262	7	—	—	—	575	5.3	0.7	7.3
68-69—Chicago-Boston	59	—	706	115	261	.441	—	—	—	75	111	.676	—	—	224	28	122	2	—	—	—	305	3.8	0.5	5.2
69-70—Boston	77	—	1049	178	434	.410	—	—	—	95	128	.742	—	—	350	52	229	4	—	—	—	451	4.5	0.7	5.9
70-71—Baltimore	11	—	100	15	28	.536	—	—	—	7	11	.636	—	—	16	8	23	0	—	—	—	37	1.5	0.7	3.4
REG. SEASON TOTALS	454	—	9455	1548	3607	.429	—	—	—	901	1317	.684	—	—	2939	377	1497	36	—	—	—	3997	6.5	0.8	8.8
PLAYOFF TOTALS	11	—	200	26	63	.413	—	—	—	12	18	.667	—	—	61	6	35	2	—	—	—	64	5.5	0.5	5.8

BARNETT, JAMES FRANKLIN (Jim) b. July 7, 1944 Ht. 6-4 Wt. 180 College—Oregon

SEASON—TEAM	G	GS	MIN	FGM	FGA	PCT	3FGM	3FGA	PCT	FTM	FTA	PCT	O-RB	D-RB	TOT	AST	PF	DQ	STL	TO	BLK	PTS	RPG	APG	PPG
66-67—Boston	48	—	383	78	211	.370	—	—	—	42	62	.677	—	—	53	41	61	0	—	—	—	198	1.1	0.9	4.1
67-68—San Diego	47	—	1068	179	456	.393	—	—	—	84	118	.712	—	—	155	134	101	0	—	—	—	442	3.3	2.9	9.4
68-69—San Diego	80	—	2346	465	1093	.425	—	—	—	233	310	.752	—	—	362	339	240	2	—	—	—	1163	4.5	4.2	14.5
69-70—San Diego	80	—	2105	450	998	.451	—	—	—	289	366	.790	—	—	305	287	222	3	—	—	—	1189	3.8	3.6	14.9
70-71—Portland	78	—	2371	559	1283	.436	—	—	—	326	402	.811	—	—	376	323	190	1	—	—	—	1444	4.8	4.1	18.5
71-72—Golden State	80	—	2200	374	915	.409	—	—	—	244	292	.836	—	—	250	309	189	0	—	—	—	992	3.1	3.9	12.4
72-73—Golden State	82	—	2215	394	844	.467	—	—	—	183	217	.843	—	—	255	301	150	1	—	—	—	971	3.1	3.7	11.8
73-74—Golden State	77	—	1689	350	755	.464	—	—	—	184	226	.814	76	146	222	209	146	1	56	—	11	884	2.9	2.7	11.5
74-75—N.O.-N.Y.	73	—	1776	285	652	.437	—	—	—	199	238	.836	60	119	179	176	160	1	47	—	16	769	2.5	2.4	10.5
75-76—New York	71	—	1026	164	371	.442	—	—	—	90	114	.789	48	40	88	90	86	0	24	—	3	418	1.2	1.3	5.9
76-77—Philadelphia	16	—	231	28	64	.438	—	—	—	10	18	.556	7	7	14	23	28	0	4	—	0	66	0.9	1.4	4.1
REG. SEASON TOTALS	732	—	17410	3326	7642	.435	—	—	—	1884	2363	.797	191	312	2259	2232	1573	9	131	—	30	8536	3.1	3.0	11.7
PLAYOFF TOTALS	30	—	669	127	303	.419	—	—	—	67	83	.807	5	3	74	78	64	0	1	—	1	321	2.5	2.6	10.7

BARNETT, NATHANIEL JR. (Nate) b. January 29, 1953 Ht. 6-4 Wt. 180 College—Akron

SEASON—TEAM	G	GS	MIN	FGM	FGA	PCT	3FGM	3FGA	PCT	FTM	FTA	PCT	O-RB	D-RB	TOT	AST	PF	DQ	STL	TO	BLK	PTS	RPG	APG	PPG
75-76—Indiana (A)	12	—	73	12	26	.462	0	1	.000	3	8	.375	3	5	8	8	22	—	3	8	1	27	0.7	0.7	2.3
REG. ABA TOTALS	12	—	73	12	26	.462	0	1	.000	3	8	.375	3	5	8	8	22	—	3	8	1	27	0.7	0.7	2.3

BARNETT, RICHARD (Dick) b. October 2, 1936 Ht. 6-4 Wt. 190 College—Tennessee State

SEASON—TEAM	G	GS	MIN	FGM	FGA	PCT	3FGM	3FGA	PCT	FTM	FTA	PCT	O-RB	D-RB	TOT	AST	PF	DQ	STL	TO	BLK	PTS	RPG	APG	PPG
59-60—Syracuse	57	—	1235	289	701	.412	—	—	—	128	180	.711	—	—	155	160	98	0	—	—	—	706	2.7	2.8	12.4
60-61—Syracuse	78	—	2070	540	1194	.452	—	—	—	240	337	.712	—	—	283	218	169	0	—	—	—	1320	3.6	2.8	16.9
62-63—Los Angeles	80	—	2544	547	1162	.471	—	—	—	343	421	.815	—	—	242	224	189	3	—	—	—	1437	3.0	2.8	18.0
63-64—Los Angeles	78	—	2620	541	1197	.452	—	—	—	351	454	.773	—	—	250	238	233	3	—	—	—	1433	3.2	3.1	18.4
64-65—Los Angeles	74	—	2026	375	908	.413	—	—	—	270	338	.799	—	—	200	159	209	1	—	—	—	1020	2.7	2.1	13.8
65-66—New York	75	—	2589	631	1344	.469	—	—	—	467	605	.772	—	—	310	259	235	6	—	—	—	1729	4.1	3.5	23.1
66-67—New York	67	—	1969	454	949	.478	—	—	—	231	295	.783	—	—	226	161	185	2	—	—	—	1139	3.4	2.4	17.0
67-68—New York	81	—	2488	559	1159	.482	—	—	—	343	440	.780	—	—	238	242	222	0	—	—	—	1461	2.9	3.0	18.0
68-69—New York	82	—	2953	565	1220	.463	—	—	—	312	403	.774	—	—	251	291	239	4	—	—	—	1442	3.1	3.5	17.6
69-70—New York	82	—	2772	494	1039	.475	—	—	—	232	325	.714	—	—	221	298	220	0	—	—	—	1220	2.7	3.6	14.9
70-71—New York	82	—	2843	540	1184	.456	—	—	—	193	278	.694	—	—	238	225	232	1	—	—	—	1273	2.9	2.7	15.5
71-72—New York	79	—	2256	401	918	.437	—	—	—	162	215	.753	—	—	153	198	229	4	—	—	—	964	1.9	2.5	12.2
72-73—New York	51	—	514	88	226	.389	—	—	—	16	30	.533	—	—	41	50	52	0	—	—	—	192	0.8	1.0	3.8
73-74—New York	5	—	58	10	26	.385	—	—	—	2	3	.667	1	3	4	6	2	0	1	—	0	22	0.8	1.2	4.4
REG. SEASON TOTALS	971	—	28937	6034	13227	.456	—	—	—	3290	4324	.761	1	3	2812	2729	2514	24	1	—	0	15358	2.9	2.8	15.8
PLAYOFF TOTALS	102	—	3027	603	1317	.458	—	—	—	333	445	.748	0	0	273	247	282	1	0	—	0	1539	2.7	2.4	15.1
ALL-STAR TOTALS	1	—	22	7	12	.583	—	—	—	1	2	.500	0	0	1	0	2	0	0	—	0	15	1.0	0.0	15.0

BARNHILL, JOHN ANTHONY (Rabbit) b. March 20, 1938 Ht. 6-1 Wt. 180 College—Tennessee State

SEASON—TEAM	G	GS	MIN	FGM	FGA	PCT	3FGM	3FGA	PCT	FTM	FTA	PCT	O-RB	D-RB	TOT	AST	PF	DQ	STL	TO	BLK	PTS	RPG	APG	PPG
62-63—St. Louis	77	—	2692	360	838	.430	—	—	—	181	255	.710	—	—	359	322	168	0	—	—	—	901	4.7	4.2	11.7
63-64—St. Louis	74	—	1367	208	505	.412	—	—	—	70	115	.609	—	—	157	145	107	0	—	—	—	486	2.1	2.0	6.6
64-65—St. Louis	41	—	777	121	312	.388	—	—	—	45	70	.643	—	—	91	76	56	0	—	—	—	287	2.2	1.9	7.0
65-66—St. L.-Detroit	76	—	1617	243	606	.401	—	—	—	113	184	.614	—	—	203	196	134	0	—	—	—	599	2.7	2.6	7.9
66-67—Baltimore	53	—	1214	187	447	.418	—	—	—	66	103	.641	—	—	157	136	80	0	—	—	—	440	3.0	2.6	8.3
67-68—San Diego	75	—	1883	295	700	.421	—	—	—	154	234	.658	—	—	173	259	143	1	—	—	—	744	2.3	3.5	9.9
68-69—Baltimore	30	—	504	76	175	.434	—	—	—	39	65	.600	—	—	53	71	63	0	—	—	—	191	1.8	2.4	6.4
69-70—Indiana (A)	77	—	2374	325	824	.394	71	272	.261	158	238	.664	—	—	173	312	196	2	—	—	—	879	2.2	4.1	11.4
70-71—Indiana-Denver (A)	67	—	1303	181	496	.365	32	147	.218	96	134	.716	—	—	116	160	106	—	—	—	—	490	1.7	2.4	7.3
71-72—Indiana (A)	19	—	194	28	87	.322	4	35	.114	8	15	.533	—	—	19	16	16	—	—	12	—	68	1.0	0.8	3.6
REG. NBA TOTALS	426	—	10054	1490	3583	.416	—	—	—	668	1026	.651	—	—	1193	1205	751	1	—	—	—	3648	2.8	2.8	8.6
REG. ABA TOTALS	163	—	3871	534	1407	.380	107	454	.236	262	387	.677	—	—	308	488	318	2	—	12	—	1437	1.9	3.0	8.8
NBA PLAYOFF TOTALS	21	—	421	46	113	.407	—	—	—	19	31	.613	—	—	41	44	42	0	—	—	—	111	2.0	2.1	5.3
ABA PLAYOFF TOTALS	14	—	317	28	88	.318	8	35	.229	21	41	.512	—	—	33	25	41	0	—	—	—	85	2.4	1.8	6.1

BARNHILL, NORTON b. July 15, 1953 Ht. 6-4 Wt. 205 College—Washington State

SEASON—TEAM	G	GS	MIN	FGM	FGA	PCT	3FGM	3FGA	PCT	FTM	FTA	PCT	O-RB	D-RB	TOT	AST	PF	DQ	STL	TO	BLK	PTS	RPG	APG	PPG
76-77—Seattle	4	—	10	2	6	.333	—	—	—	0	0	—	2	1	3	1	5	0	0	—	0	4	0.8	0.3	1.0
REG. SEASON TOTALS	4	—	10	2	6	.333	—	—	—	0	0	—	2	1	3	1	5	0	0	—	0	4	0.8	0.3	1.0

BARNHORST, LEO A. (Barney) b. May 11, 1924 Ht. 6-4 Wt. 195 College—Notre Dame

SEASON—TEAM	G	GS	MIN	FGM	FGA	PCT	3FGM	3FGA	PCT	FTM	FTA	PCT	O-RB	D-RB	TOT	AST	PF	DQ	STL	TO	BLK	PTS	RPG	APG	PPG
49-50—Chicago	67	—	—	174	499	.349	—	—	—	90	129	.698	—	—	—	140	192	—	—	—	—	438	—	2.1	6.5
50-51—Indianapolis	68	—	—	232	671	.346	—	—	—	82	119	.689	—	—	296	218	197	1	—	—	—	546	4.4	3.2	8.0
51-52—Indianapolis	66	—	2344	349	897	.389	—	—	—	122	187	.652	—	—	430	255	196	3	—	—	—	820	6.5	3.9	12.4
52-53—Indianapolis	71	—	2871	402	1034	.389	—	—	—	163	259	.629	—	—	483	277	245	8	—	—	—	967	6.8	3.9	13.6
53-54—Balt.-Ft.Wayne	72	—	2064	199	588	.338	—	—	—	63	88	.716	—	—	297	226	203	4	—	—	—	461	4.1	3.1	6.4
REG. SEASON TOTALS	344	—	7279	1356	3689	.368	—	—	—	520	782	.665	—	—	1506	1116	1033	16	—	—	—	3232	5.4	3.2	9.4
PLAYOFF TOTALS	13	—	224	57	146	.390	—	—	—	26	37	.703	—	—	45	35	44	1	—	—	—	140	4.1	2.7	10.8
ALL-STAR TOTALS	2	—	36	8	18	.444	—	—	—	0	2	.000	—	—	5	3	6	0	—	—	—	16	2.5	1.5	8.0

BARR, JOHN E. b. August 18, 1918 Ht. 6-3 Wt. 205 College—Penn State

SEASON—TEAM	G	GS	MIN	FGM	FGA	PCT	3FGM	3FGA	PCT	FTM	FTA	PCT	O-RB	D-RB	TOT	AST	PF	DQ	STL	TO	BLK	PTS	RPG	APG	PPG
46-47—St. Louis	58	—	—	124	438	.283	—	—	—	47	79	.595	—	—	—	54	164	—	—	—	—	295	—	0.9	5.1
REG. SEASON TOTALS	58	—	—	124	438	.283	—	—	—	47	79	.595	—	—	—	54	164	—	—	—	—	295	—	0.9	5.1

BARR, MICHAEL J. (Mike) b. October 19, 1950 Ht. 6-3 Wt. 180 College—Duquesne

SEASON—TEAM	G	GS	MIN	FGM	FGA	PCT	3FGM	3FGA	PCT	FTM	FTA	PCT	O-RB	D-RB	TOT	AST	PF	DQ	STL	TO	BLK	PTS	RPG	APG	PPG
72-73—Virginia (A)	79	—	2076	289	612	.472	1	4	.250	141	188	.750	—	—	227	254	220	0	—	185	—	720	2.9	3.2	9.1
73-74—Virginia (A)	45	—	652	82	171	.480	2	5	.400	33	43	.767	22	49	71	82	80	—	27	60	4	199	1.6	1.8	4.4
74-75—St. Louis (A)	54	—	1341	136	269	.506	0	2	.000	28	41	.683	20	75	95	176	117	—	67	100	14	300	1.8	3.3	5.6
75-76—St. Louis (A)	56	—	1048	124	240	.517	6	16	.375	46	55	.836	29	80	109	174	76	—	64	83	7	300	1.9	3.1	5.4
76-77—Kansas City	73	—	1224	122	279	.437	—	—	—	41	57	.719	33	97	130	175	96	0	52	—	18	285	1.8	2.4	3.9
REG. NBA TOTALS	73	—	1224	122	279	.437	—	—	—	41	57	.719	33	97	130	175	96	0	52	—	18	285	1.8	2.4	3.9
REG. ABA TOTALS	234	—	5117	631	1292	.488	9	27	.333	248	327	.758	71	204	502	686	493	0	158	428	25	1519	2.1	2.9	6.5
ABA PLAYOFF TOTALS	20	—	639	58	128	.453	1	1	1.000	19	24	.792	15	44	65	72	62	—	25	37	5	136	3.3	3.6	6.8

BARR, THOMAS L. (Moe) b. June 19, 1944 Ht. 6-4 Wt. 195 College—Duquesne

SEASON—TEAM	G	GS	MIN	FGM	FGA	PCT	3FGM	3FGA	PCT	FTM	FTA	PCT	O-RB	D-RB	TOT	AST	PF	DQ	STL	TO	BLK	PTS	RPG	APG	PPG
70-71—Cincinnati	31	—	145	25	62	.403	—	—	—	11	13	.846	—	—	20	28	27	0	—	—	—	61	0.6	0.9	2.0
REG. SEASON TOTALS	31	—	145	25	62	.403	—	—	—	11	13	.846	—	—	20	28	27	0	—	—	—	61	0.6	0.9	2.0

BARRETT, ERNIE DREW b. August 27, 1929 Ht. 6-3 Wt. 180 College—Kansas State

SEASON—TEAM	G	GS	MIN	FGM	FGA	PCT	3FGM	3FGA	PCT	FTM	FTA	PCT	O-RB	D-RB	TOT	AST	PF	DQ	STL	TO	BLK	PTS	RPG	APG	PPG
53-54—Boston	59	—	641	60	191	.314	—	—	—	14	25	.560	—	—	100	55	116	2	—	—	—	134	1.7	0.9	2.3
55-56—Boston	72	—	1451	207	533	.388	—	—	—	93	118	.788	—	—	243	174	184	4	—	—	—	507	3.4	2.4	7.0
REG. SEASON TOTALS	131	—	2092	267	724	.369	—	—	—	107	143	.748	—	—	343	229	300	6	—	—	—	641	2.6	1.7	4.9
PLAYOFF TOTALS	9	—	106	7	33	.212	—	—	—	5	5	1.000	—	—	13	8	21	0	—	—	—	19	1.4	0.9	2.1

BARRETT, MICHAEL THOMAS (Mike, Bird Man) b. September 5, 1943 Ht. 6-2 Wt. 160 College—West Virginia Tech

SEASON—TEAM	G	GS	MIN	FGM	FGA	PCT	3FGM	3FGA	PCT	FTM	FTA	PCT	O-RB	D-RB	TOT	AST	PF	DQ	STL	TO	BLK	PTS	RPG	APG	PPG
69-70—Washington (A)	84	—	2262	479	1126	.425	62	180	.344	232	305	.761	—	—	296	259	243	2	—	—	—	1252	3.5	3.1	14.9
70-71—Virginia (A)	84	—	2754	458	988	.464	28	103	.272	208	274	.759	—	—	272	425	202	—	—	—	—	1152	3.2	5.1	13.7
72-73—San Diego (A)	19	—	284	37	101	.366	4	20	.200	18	35	.514	8	16	24	46	28	0	—	39	—	96	1.3	2.4	5.1
REG. ABA TOTALS	187	—	5300	974	2215	.440	94	303	.310	458	614	.746	8	16	592	730	473	2	—	39	—	2500	3.2	3.9	13.4
ABA PLAYOFF TOTALS	20	—	727	143	328	.436	24	76	.316	77	92	.837	—	—	49	74	52	—	—	—	—	387	2.5	3.7	19.4

BARROS, DANA BRUCE b. April 13, 1967 Ht. 5-11 Wt. 165 College—Boston College

SEASON—TEAM	G	GS	MIN	FGM	FGA	PCT	3FGM	3FGA	PCT	FTM	FTA	PCT	O-RB	D-RB	TOT	AST	PF	DQ	STL	TO	BLK	PTS	RPG	APG	PPG
89-90—Seattle	81	25	1630	299	738	.405	95	238	.399	89	110	.809	35	97	132	205	97	0	53	123	1	782	1.6	2.5	9.7
90-91—Seattle	66	0	750	154	311	.495	32	81	.395	78	85	.918	17	54	71	111	40	0	23	54	1	418	1.1	1.7	6.3
91-92—Seattle	75	1	1331	238	493	.483	83	186	.446	60	79	.759	17	64	81	125	84	0	51	56	4	619	1.1	1.7	8.3
92-93—Seattle	69	2	1243	214	474	.451	64	169	.379	49	59	.831	18	89	107	151	78	0	63	58	3	541	1.6	2.2	7.8
93-94—Philadelphia	81	70	2519	412	878	.469	135	354	.381	116	145	.800	28	168	196	424	96	0	107	167	5	1075	2.4	5.2	13.3
REG. SEASON TOTALS	372	98	7473	1317	2894	.455	409	1028	.398	392	478	.820	115	472	587	1016	395	0	297	458	14	3435	1.6	2.7	9.2
PLAYOFF TOTALS	26	0	257	52	100	.520	17	38	.447	9	12	.750	2	21	23	25	18	0	12	17	0	130	0.9	1.0	5.0

BARRY, JON ALAN b. July 25, 1969 Ht. 6-5 Wt. 200 College—Pacific/Paris JC/Georgia Tech

SEASON—TEAM	G	GS	MIN	FGM	FGA	PCT	3FGM	3FGA	PCT	FTM	FTA	PCT	O-RB	D-RB	TOT	AST	PF	DQ	STL	TO	BLK	PTS	RPG	APG	PPG
92-93—Milwaukee	47	0	552	76	206	.369	21	63	.333	33	49	.673	10	33	43	68	57	0	35	42	3	206	0.9	1.4	4.4
93-94—Milwaukee	72	7	1242	158	382	.414	32	115	.278	97	122	.795	36	110	146	168	110	0	102	83	17	445	2.0	2.3	6.2
REG. SEASON TOTALS	119	7	1794	234	588	.398	53	178	.298	130	171	.760	46	143	189	236	167	0	137	125	20	651	1.6	2.0	5.5

BARRY, RICHARD FRANCIS DENNIS III (**Rick**) b. March 28, 1944 Ht. 6-7 Wt. 205 College—Miami

SEASON—TEAM	G	GS	MIN	FGM	FGA	PCT	3FGM	3FGA	PCT	FTM	FTA	PCT	O-RB	D-RB	TOT	AST	PF	DQ	STL	TO	BLK	PTS	RPG	APG	PPG
65-66—San Francisco	80	—	2990	745	1698	.439	—	—	—	569	660	.862	—	—	850	173	297	2	—	—	—	2059	10.6	2.2	25.7
66-67—San Francisco	78	—	3175	1011	2240	.451	—	—	—	753	852	.884	—	—	714	282	258	1	—	—	—	2775	9.2	3.6	35.6
68-69—Oakland (A)	35	—	1361	392	767	.511	3	10	.300	403	454	.888	—	—	329	136	124	1	—	141	—	1190	9.4	3.9	34.0
69-70—Washington (A)	52	—	1849	517	1036	.499	8	39	.205	400	463	.864	—	—	363	178	174	1	—	—	—	1442	7.0	3.4	27.7
70-71—New York (A)	59	—	2502	632	1348	.469	19	86	.221	451	507	.890	—	—	401	294	205	—	—	—	—	1734	6.8	5.0	29.4
71-72—New York (A)	80	—	3616	902	1969	.458	73	237	.308	641	730	.878	—	—	602	327	261	—	—	263	—	2518	7.5	4.1	31.5
72-73—Golden State	82	—	3075	737	1630	.452	—	—	—	358	397	.902	—	—	728	399	245	2	—	—	—	1832	8.9	4.9	22.3
73-74—Golden State	80	—	2918	796	1746	.456	—	—	—	417	464	.899	103	437	540	484	265	4	169	—	40	2009	6.8	6.1	25.1
74-75—Golden State	80	—	3235	1028	2217	.464	—	—	—	394	436	.904	92	364	456	492	225	0	228	—	33	2450	5.7	6.2	30.6
75-76—Golden State	81	—	3122	707	1624	.435	—	—	—	287	311	.923	74	422	496	496	215	1	202	—	27	1701	6.1	6.1	21.0
76-77—Golden State	79	—	2904	682	1551	.440	—	—	—	359	392	.916	73	349	422	475	194	2	172	—	58	1723	5.3	6.0	21.8
77-78—Golden State	82	—	3024	760	1686	.451	—	—	—	378	409	.924	75	374	449	446	188	1	158	224	45	1898	5.5	5.4	23.1
78-79—Houston	80	—	2566	461	1000	.461	—	—	—	160	169	.947	40	237	277	502	195	0	95	198	38	1082	3.5	6.3	13.5
79-80—Houston	72	—	1816	325	771	.422	73	221	.330	143	153	.935	53	183	236	268	182	0	80	152	28	866	3.3	3.7	12.0
REG. NBA TOTALS	794	—	28825	7252	16163	.449	73	221	.330	3818	4243	.900	510	2366	5168	4017	2264	13	1104	574	269	18395	6.5	5.1	23.2
REG. ABA TOTALS	226	—	9328	2443	5120	.477	103	372	.277	1895	2154	.880	—	—	1695	935	764	2	—	404	—	6884	7.5	4.1	30.5
NBA PLAYOFF TOTALS	74	—	2723	719	1688	.426	3	12	.250	392	448	.875	69	182	418	340	232	3	106	12	39	1833	5.6	4.6	24.8
ABA PLAYOFF TOTALS	31	—	1338	381	767	.497	40	97	.412	235	273	.861	17	53	257	116	118	0	—	61	—	1037	8.3	3.7	33.5
NBA ALL-STAR TOTALS	7	—	195	54	111	.486	0	0	—	20	24	.833	7	14	29	31	30	2	16	5	1	128	4.1	4.4	18.3
ABA ALL-STAR TOTALS	4	—	82	16	37	.432	0	0	—	12	14	.857	5	12	24	18	7	0	—	4	—	44	6.0	4.5	11.0

BARTELS, EDWARD JOHN (**Ed**) b. October 8, 1925 Ht. 6-5 Wt. 195 College—North Carolina State

SEASON—TEAM	G	GS	MIN	FGM	FGA	PCT	3FGM	3FGA	PCT	FTM	FTA	PCT	O-RB	D-RB	TOT	AST	PF	DQ	STL	TO	BLK	PTS	RPG	APG	PPG
49-50—Denver-N.Y.	15	—	—	22	86	.256	—	—	—	19	34	.559	—	—	20	29	—	—	—	—	—	63	—	1.3	4.2
50-51—Washington	17	—	—	24	97	.247	—	—	—	24	46	.522	—	—	84	12	54	0	—	—	—	72	4.9	0.7	4.2
REG. SEASON TOTALS	32	—	—	46	183	.251	—	—	—	43	80	.538	—	—	84	32	83	0	—	—	—	135	4.9	1.0	4.2

BARTOLOME, VICTOR (**Vic**) b. September 29, 1948 Ht. 7-0 Wt. 230 College—Oregon State

SEASON—TEAM	G	GS	MIN	FGM	FGA	PCT	3FGM	3FGA	PCT	FTM	FTA	PCT	O-RB	D-RB	TOT	AST	PF	DQ	STL	TO	BLK	PTS	RPG	APG	PPG
71-72—Golden State	38	—	165	15	59	.254	—	—	—	4	5	.800	—	—	60	3	22	0	—	—	—	34	1.6	0.1	0.9
REG. SEASON TOTALS	38	—	165	15	59	.254	—	—	—	4	5	.800	—	—	60	3	22	0	—	—	—	34	1.6	0.1	0.9

BASKERVILLE, JERRY W. b. November 10, 1951 Ht. 6-7 Wt. 190 College—Temple/Nevada-Las Vegas

SEASON—TEAM	G	GS	MIN	FGM	FGA	PCT	3FGM	3FGA	PCT	FTM	FTA	PCT	O-RB	D-RB	TOT	AST	PF	DQ	STL	TO	BLK	PTS	RPG	APG	PPG
75-76—Philadelphia	21	—	105	8	26	.308	—	—	—	10	16	.625	13	15	28	3	32	0	6	—	5	26	1.3	0.1	1.2
REG. SEASON TOTALS	21	—	105	8	26	.308	—	—	—	10	16	.625	13	15	28	3	32	0	6	—	5	26	1.3	0.1	1.2

BASSETT, EUGENE TIMOTHY (**Tim**) b. April 1, 1951 Ht. 6-8 Wt. 225 College—Southern Idaho/Georgia

SEASON—TEAM	G	GS	MIN	FGM	FGA	PCT	3FGM	3FGA	PCT	FTM	FTA	PCT	O-RB	D-RB	TOT	AST	PF	DQ	STL	TO	BLK	PTS	RPG	APG	PPG
73-74—San Diego (A)	82	—	1854	233	499	.467	0	4	.000	99	167	.593	252	343	595	109	185	—	57	87	35	565	7.3	1.3	6.9
74-75—San Diego (A)	72	—	1998	244	518	.471	3	4	.750	82	146	.562	210	316	526	117	159	—	45	97	36	573	7.3	1.6	8.0
75-76—New York (A)	84	—	1790	173	396	.437	1	6	.167	58	98	.592	185	346	531	65	247	—	47	97	41	405	6.3	0.8	4.8
76-77—New York Nets	76	—	2442	293	739	.396	—	—	—	101	177	.571	175	466	641	109	246	10	95	—	53	687	8.4	1.4	9.0
77-78—New Jersey	65	—	1474	149	384	.388	—	—	—	50	97	.515	142	262	404	63	181	5	62	80	33	348	6.2	1.0	5.4
78-79—New Jersey	82	—	1508	116	313	.371	—	—	—	89	131	.679	174	244	418	99	219	1	44	103	29	321	5.1	1.2	3.9
79-80—N.J.-S.A.	12	—	164	12	34	.353	0	0	—	10	15	.667	11	22	33	14	27	0	8	9	0	34	2.8	1.2	2.8
REG. NBA TOTALS	235	—	5588	570	1470	.388	0	0	—	250	420	.595	502	994	1496	285	673	16	209	192	115	1390	6.4	1.2	5.9
REG. ABA TOTALS	238	—	5642	650	1413	.460	4	14	.286	239	411	.582	647	1005	1652	291	591	0	149	281	112	1543	6.9	1.2	6.5
NBA PLAYOFF TOTALS	5	—	36	3	7	.429	0	0	—	2	2	1.000	3	0	3	—	11	0	0	2	0	8	0.6	0.0	1.6
ABA PLAYOFF TOTALS	19	—	556	77	158	.487	0	1	.000	16	23	.696	85	97	182	29	64	0	9	24	14	170	9.6	1.5	8.9

BATES, BILLY RAY (**Dunk**) b. May 31, 1956 Ht. 6-4 Wt. 210 College—Kentucky State

SEASON—TEAM	G	GS	MIN	FGM	FGA	PCT	3FGM	3FGA	PCT	FTM	FTA	PCT	O-RB	D-RB	TOT	AST	PF	DQ	STL	TO	BLK	PTS	RPG	APG	PPG
79-80—Portland	16	—	235	72	146	.493	8	19	.421	28	39	.718	13	16	29	31	26	0	14	20	2	180	1.8	1.9	11.3
80-81—Portland	77	—	1560	439	902	.487	14	54	.259	170	199	.854	71	86	157	196	120	0	82	149	6	1062	2.0	2.5	13.8
81-82—Portland	75	0	1229	327	692	.473	12	41	.293	166	211	.787	53	55	108	111	100	0	41	93	5	832	1.4	1.5	11.1
82-83—Wash.-L.A.	19	3	304	55	145	.379	2	5	.400	11	22	.500	11	8	19	14	19	0	14	12	3	123	1.0	0.7	6.5
REG. SEASON TOTALS	187	3	3328	893	1885	.474	36	119	.303	375	471	.796	148	165	313	352	265	0	151	274	16	2197	1.7	1.9	11.7
PLAYOFF TOTALS	6	0	219	66	121	.545	3	8	.375	25	31	.806	5	12	17	25	24	0	10	26	2	160	2.8	4.2	26.7

BATTLE, JOHN SIDNEY (Cricket, Pickle) b. November 9, 1962 Ht. 6-2 Wt. 190 College—Rutgers

SEASON—TEAM	G	GS	MIN	FGM	FGA	PCT	3FGM	3FGA	PCT	FTM	FTA	PCT	O-RB	D-RB	TOT	AST	PF	DQ	STL	TO	BLK	PTS	RPG	APG	PPG
85-86—Atlanta	64	0	639	101	222	.455	0	7	.000	75	103	.728	12	50	62	74	80	0	23	47	3	277	1.0	1.2	4.3
86-87—Atlanta	64	8	804	144	315	.457	0	10	.000	93	126	.738	16	44	60	124	76	0	29	60	5	381	0.9	1.9	6.0
87-88—Atlanta	67	1	1227	278	613	.454	16	41	.390	141	188	.750	26	87	113	158	84	0	31	75	5	713	1.7	2.4	10.6
88-89—Atlanta	82	0	1672	287	628	.457	11	34	.324	194	238	.815	30	110	140	197	125	0	42	104	9	779	1.7	2.4	9.5
89-90—Atlanta	60	48	1477	275	544	.506	2	13	.154	102	135	.756	27	72	99	154	115	0	28	89	3	654	1.7	2.6	10.9
90-91—Atlanta	79	2	1863	397	862	.461	14	49	.286	270	316	.854	34	125	159	217	145	0	45	113	6	1078	2.0	2.7	13.6
91-92—Cleveland	76	2	1637	316	659	.480	2	17	.118	145	171	.848	19	93	112	159	116	0	36	91	5	779	1.5	2.1	10.3
92-93—Cleveland	41	0	497	83	200	.415	1	6	.167	56	72	.778	4	25	29	54	39	0	9	22	5	223	0.7	1.3	5.4
93-94—Cleveland	51	1	814	130	273	.476	5	19	.263	73	97	.753	7	32	39	83	66	0	22	41	1	338	0.8	1.6	6.6
REG. SEASON TOTALS	584	62	10630	2011	4316	.466	51	196	.260	1149	1446	.795	175	638	813	1220	846	0	265	642	42	5222	1.4	2.1	8.9
PLAYOFF TOTALS	53	0	712	122	286	.427	4	21	.190	95	112	.848	17	55	72	79	69	0	13	55	1	343	1.4	1.5	6.5

BATTLE, KENNETH R. (Kenny) b. October 10, 1964 Ht. 6-6 Wt. 210 College—Northern Illinois/Illinois

SEASON—TEAM	G	GS	MIN	FGM	FGA	PCT	3FGM	3FGA	PCT	FTM	FTA	PCT	O-RB	D-RB	TOT	AST	PF	DQ	STL	TO	BLK	PTS	RPG	APG	PPG
89-90—Phoenix	59	8	729	93	170	.547	1	4	.250	55	82	.671	44	80	124	38	94	2	35	32	11	242	2.1	0.6	4.1
90-91—Phoenix-Denver	56	8	945	133	282	.472	3	24	.125	70	93	.753	83	93	176	62	108	0	60	53	18	339	3.1	1.1	6.1
91-92—Boston-G.S.	16	0	92	11	17	.647	0	1	.000	10	12	.833	4	12	16	4	10	0	2	4	2	32	1.0	0.3	2.0
92-93—Boston	3	1	29	6	13	.462	0	1	.000	2	2	1.000	7	4	11	2	2	0	1	2	0	14	3.7	0.7	4.7
REG. SEASON TOTALS	134	17	1795	243	482	.504	4	30	.133	137	189	.725	138	189	327	106	214	2	98	91	31	627	2.4	0.8	4.7
PLAYOFF TOTALS	8	0	34	4	13	.308	0	0	—	1	1	1.000	1	4	5	—	5	0	0	2	0	9	0.6	0.0	1.1

BATTON, DAVID ROBERT (Dave) b. March 26, 1956 Ht. 6-10 Wt. 240 College—Notre Dame

SEASON—TEAM	G	GS	MIN	FGM	FGA	PCT	3FGM	3FGA	PCT	FTM	FTA	PCT	O-RB	D-RB	TOT	AST	PF	DQ	STL	TO	BLK	PTS	RPG	APG	PPG
82-83—Washington	54	5	558	85	191	.445	0	3	.000	8	17	.471	45	74	119	29	56	0	15	28	13	178	2.2	0.5	3.3
83-84—San Antonio	4	0	31	5	10	.500	0	0	—	0	0	—	1	3	4	3	5	0	0	4	3	10	1.0	0.8	2.5
REG. SEASON TOTALS	58	5	589	90	201	.448	0	3	.000	8	17	.471	46	77	123	32	61	0	15	32	16	188	2.1	0.6	3.2

BATTS, LLOYD b. May 9, 1951 Ht. 6-4 Wt. 185 College—Cincinnati

SEASON—TEAM	G	GS	MIN	FGM	FGA	PCT	3FGM	3FGA	PCT	FTM	FTA	PCT	O-RB	D-RB	TOT	AST	PF	DQ	STL	TO	BLK	PTS	RPG	APG	PPG
74-75—Virginia (A)	58	—	1317	249	680	.366	42	147	.286	58	94	.617	71	126	197	106	104	—	73	89	6	598	3.4	1.8	10.3
REG. ABA TOTALS	58	—	1317	249	680	.366	42	147	.286	58	94	.617	71	126	197	106	104	—	73	89	6	598	3.4	1.8	10.3

BAUM, JOHN (Johnny) b. June 17, 1946 Ht. 6-5 Wt. 200 College—Pierce JC/Temple

SEASON—TEAM	G	GS	MIN	FGM	FGA	PCT	3FGM	3FGA	PCT	FTM	FTA	PCT	O-RB	D-RB	TOT	AST	PF	DQ	STL	TO	BLK	PTS	RPG	APG	PPG
69-70—Chicago	3	—	13	3	11	.273	—	—	—	0	0	—	—	—	4	0	1	0	—	—	—	6	1.3	0.0	2.0
70-71—Chicago	62	—	543	123	293	.420	—	—	—	40	58	.690	—	—	125	31	55	0	—	—	—	286	2.0	0.5	4.6
71-72—New York (A)	44	—	551	103	170	.606	0	0	—	41	52	.788	—	—	135	17	75	—	—	24	—	247	3.1	0.4	5.6
72-73—New York (A)	75	—	1071	221	438	.505	0	2	.000	107	143	.748	75	126	201	31	99	0	—	76	—	549	2.7	0.4	7.3
73-74—Memphis-Indiana (A)	60	—	1219	180	400	.450	0	0	—	50	61	.820	81	120	201	62	101	—	36	47	16	410	3.4	1.0	6.8
REG. NBA TOTALS	65	—	556	126	304	.414	—	—	—	40	58	.690	—	—	129	31	56	0	—	—	—	292	2.0	0.5	4.5
REG. ABA TOTALS	179	—	2841	504	1008	.500	0	2	.000	198	256	.773	156	246	537	110	275	0	36	147	16	1206	3.0	0.6	6.7
NBA PLAYOFF TOTALS	2	—	5	0	0	—	—	—	—	0	0	—	—	—	1	—	2	0	—	—	—	0	0.5	0.0	0.0
ABA PLAYOFF TOTALS	33	—	600	117	217	.539	0	0	—	28	39	.718	8	12	113	13	66	0	5	34	1	262	3.4	0.4	7.9

BAUMHOLTZ, FRANK CONRAD (Frankie) b. October 7, 1918 Ht. 5-10½ Wt. 170 College—Ohio

SEASON—TEAM	G	GS	MIN	FGM	FGA	PCT	3FGM	3FGA	PCT	FTM	FTA	PCT	O-RB	D-RB	TOT	AST	PF	DQ	STL	TO	BLK	PTS	RPG	APG	PPG
45-46—Youngstown (N)	26	—	—	99	—	—	—	—	—	76	107	.710	—	—	—	—	28	—	—	—	—	274	—	—	10.5
46-47—Cleveland	45	—	—	255	856	.298	—	—	—	121	156	.776	—	—	—	54	93	—	—	—	—	631	—	1.2	14.0
REG. NBA TOTALS	45	—	—	255	856	.298	—	—	—	121	156	.776	—	—	—	54	93	—	—	—	—	631	—	1.2	14.0
REG. NBL TOTALS	26	—	—	99	—	—	—	—	—	76	107	.710	—	—	—	—	28	—	—	—	—	274	—	—	10.5

BAYLOR, ELGIN GAY b. September 16, 1934 Ht. 6-5 Wt. 225 College—College of Idaho/Seattle

SEASON—TEAM	G	GS	MIN	FGM	FGA	PCT	3FGM	3FGA	PCT	FTM	FTA	PCT	O-RB	D-RB	TOT	AST	PF	DQ	STL	TO	BLK	PTS	RPG	APG	PPG
58-59—Minneapolis	70	—	2855	605	1482	.408	—	—	—	532	685	.777	—	—	1050	287	270	4	—	—	—	1742	15.0	4.1	24.9
59-60—Minneapolis	70	—	2873	755	1781	.424	—	—	—	564	770	.732	—	—	1150	243	234	2	—	—	—	2074	16.4	3.5	29.6
60-61—Los Angeles	73	—	3133	931	2166	.430	—	—	—	676	863	.783	—	—	1447	371	279	3	—	—	—	2538	19.8	5.1	34.8
61-62—Los Angeles	48	—	2129	680	1588	.428	—	—	—	476	631	.754	—	—	892	222	155	1	—	—	—	1836	18.6	4.6	38.3
62-63—Los Angeles	80	—	3370	1029	2273	.453	—	—	—	661	790	.837	—	—	1146	386	226	1	—	—	—	2719	14.3	4.8	34.0
63-64—Los Angeles	78	—	3164	756	1778	.425	—	—	—	471	586	.804	—	—	936	347	235	1	—	—	—	1983	12.0	4.4	25.4
64-65—Los Angeles	74	—	3056	763	1903	.401	—	—	—	483	610	.792	—	—	950	280	235	0	—	—	—	2009	12.8	3.8	27.1
65-66—Los Angeles	65	—	1975	415	1034	.401	—	—	—	249	337	.739	—	—	621	224	157	0	—	—	—	1079	9.6	3.4	16.6
66-67—Los Angeles	70	—	2706	711	1658	.429	—	—	—	440	541	.813	—	—	898	215	211	1	—	—	—	1862	12.8	3.1	26.6
67-68—Los Angeles	77	—	3029	757	1709	.443	—	—	—	488	621	.786	—	—	941	355	232	0	—	—	—	2002	12.2	4.6	26.0
68-69—Los Angeles	76	—	3064	730	1632	.447	—	—	—	421	567	.743	—	—	805	408	204	0	—	—	—	1881	10.6	5.4	24.8
69-70—Los Angeles	54	—	2213	511	1051	.486	—	—	—	276	357	.773	—	—	559	292	132	1	—	—	—	1298	10.4	5.4	24.0
70-71—Los Angeles	2	—	57	8	19	.421	—	—	—	4	6	.667	—	—	11	2	6	0	—	—	—	20	5.5	1.0	10.0
71-72—Los Angeles	9	—	239	42	97	.433	—	—	—	22	27	.815	—	—	57	18	20	0	—	—	—	106	6.3	2.0	11.8
REG. SEASON TOTALS	846	—	33863	8693	20171	.431	—	—	—	5763	7391	.780	—	—	11463	3650	2596	14	—	—	—	23149	13.5	4.3	27.4
PLAYOFF TOTALS	134	—	5510	1388	3161	.439	—	—	—	847	1098	.771	—	—	1724	541	435	3	—	—	—	3623	12.9	4.0	27.0
ALL-STAR TOTALS	11	—	321	70	164	.427	—	—	—	78	98	.796	—	—	99	38	31	0	—	—	—	218	9.0	3.5	19.8

BAYNE, HOWARD EDGAR b. July 28, 1942 Ht. 6-6½ Wt. 235 College—Tennessee

SEASON—TEAM	G	GS	MIN	FGM	FGA	PCT	3FGM	3FGA	PCT	FTM	FTA	PCT	O-RB	D-RB	TOT	AST	PF	DQ	STL	TO	BLK	PTS	RPG	APG	PPG
67-68—Kentucky (A)	69	—	1181	130	361	.360	1	7	.143	77	143	.538	—	—	456	71	199	6	—	117	—	338	6.6	1.0	4.9
REG. ABA TOTALS	69	—	1181	130	361	.360	1	7	.143	77	143	.538	—	—	456	71	199	6	—	117	—	338	6.6	1.0	4.9
ABA PLAYOFF TOTALS	5	—	85	3	19	.158	0	1	.000	6	11	.545	—	—	23	5	12	0	—	7	—	12	4.6	1.0	2.4

BEACH, EDWARD LEON JR. (Ed) b. January 25, 1929 Ht. 6-3 Wt. 200 College—West Virginia

SEASON—TEAM	G	GS	MIN	FGM	FGA	PCT	3FGM	3FGA	PCT	FTM	FTA	PCT	O-RB	D-RB	TOT	AST	PF	DQ	STL	TO	BLK	PTS	RPG	APG	PPG
50-51—Minn.-Tri-Cit	12	—	—	8	38	.211	—	—	—	6	9	.667	—	—	25	3	14	0	—	—	—	22	2.1	0.3	1.8
REG. SEASON TOTALS	12	—	—	8	38	.211	—	—	—	6	9	.667	—	—	25	3	14	0	—	—	—	22	2.1	0.3	1.8

BEARD, ALBERT (Al) b. April 27, 1942 Ht. 6-9½ Wt. 200 College—Norfolk State

SEASON—TEAM	G	GS	MIN	FGM	FGA	PCT	3FGM	3FGA	PCT	FTM	FTA	PCT	O-RB	D-RB	TOT	AST	PF	DQ	STL	TO	BLK	PTS	RPG	APG	PPG
67-68—New Jersey (A)	12	—	118	12	23	.522	0	0	—	6	11	.545	—	—	46	0	39	1	—	12	—	30	3.8	0.0	2.5
REG. ABA TOTALS	12	—	118	12	23	.522	0	0	—	6	11	.545	—	—	46	0	39	1	—	12	—	30	3.8	0.0	2.5

BEARD, ALFRED JR. (Butch) b. May 4, 1947 Ht. 6-3 Wt. 185 College—Louisville

SEASON—TEAM	G	GS	MIN	FGM	FGA	PCT	3FGM	3FGA	PCT	FTM	FTA	PCT	O-RB	D-RB	TOT	AST	PF	DQ	STL	TO	BLK	PTS	RPG	APG	PPG
69-70—Atlanta	72	—	941	183	392	.467	—	—	—	135	163	.828	—	—	140	121	124	0	—	—	—	501	1.9	1.7	7.0
71-72—Cleveland	68	—	2434	394	849	.464	—	—	—	260	342	.760	—	—	276	456	213	2	—	—	—	1048	4.1	6.7	15.4
72-73—Seattle	73	—	1403	191	435	.439	—	—	—	100	140	.714	—	—	174	247	139	0	—	—	—	482	2.4	3.4	6.6
73-74—Golden State	79	—	2134	316	617	.512	—	—	—	173	234	.739	136	253	389	300	241	11	105	—	9	805	4.9	3.8	10.2
74-75—Golden State	82	—	2521	408	773	.528	—	—	—	232	279	.832	116	200	316	345	297	9	132	—	11	1048	3.9	4.2	12.8
75-76—Clev.-N.Y.	75	—	1704	228	496	.460	—	—	—	144	192	.750	103	207	310	218	216	2	81	—	8	600	4.1	2.9	8.0
76-77—New York Knicks	70	—	1082	148	293	.505	—	—	—	75	109	.688	50	113	163	144	137	0	57	—	5	371	2.3	2.1	5.3
77-78—New York	79	—	1979	308	614	.502	—	—	—	129	160	.806	76	188	264	339	201	2	117	154	3	745	3.3	4.3	9.4
78-79—New York	7	—	85	11	26	.423	—	—	—	0	0	—	1	9	10	19	13	0	7	10	0	22	1.4	2.7	3.1
REG. SEASON TOTALS	605	—	14283	2187	4495	.487	—	—	—	1248	1619	.771	482	970	2042	2189	1581	26	499	164	36	5622	3.4	3.6	9.3
PLAYOFF TOTALS	32	—	754	115	259	.444	—	—	—	59	89	.663	30	63	119	88	105	1	34	11	4	289	3.7	2.8	9.0
ALL-STAR TOTALS	1	—	7	1	4	.250	—	—	—	1	1	1.000	0	1	1	0	0	0	0	—	0	3	1.0	0.0	3.0

BEARD, RALPH MILTON JR. b. December 2, 1927 Ht. 5-10 Wt. 175 College—Kentucky

SEASON—TEAM	G	GS	MIN	FGM	FGA	PCT	3FGM	3FGA	PCT	FTM	FTA	PCT	O-RB	D-RB	TOT	AST	PF	DQ	STL	TO	BLK	PTS	RPG	APG	PPG
49-50—Indianapolis	60	—	—	340	936	.363	—	—	—	215	282	.762	—	—	—	233	132	—	—	—	—	895	—	3.9	14.9
50-51—Indianapolis	66	—	—	409	1110	.368	—	—	—	293	378	.775	—	—	251	318	96	0	—	—	—	1111	3.8	4.8	16.8
REG. SEASON TOTALS	126	—	—	749	2046	.366	—	—	—	508	660	.770	—	—	251	551	228	0	—	—	—	2006	3.8	4.4	15.9
PLAYOFF TOTALS	8	—	—	49	131	.374	—	—	—	34	45	.756	—	—	12	35	17	0	—	—	—	132	4.0	4.4	16.5
ALL-STAR TOTALS	1	—	—	3	8	.375	—	—	—	0	3	.000	—	—	3	2	1	0	—	—	—	6	3.0	2.0	6.0

BEASLEY, CHARLES P. (Charlie) b. September 23, 1945 Ht. 6-5 Wt. 190 College—Southern Methodist

SEASON—TEAM	G	GS	MIN	FGM	FGA	PCT	3FGM	3FGA	PCT	FTM	FTA	PCT	O-RB	D-RB	TOT	AST	PF	DQ	STL	TO	BLK	PTS	RPG	APG	PPG
67-68—Dallas (A)	78	—	2969	374	758	.493	3	13	.231	285	327	.872	—	—	295	290	202	3	—	189	—	1036	3.8	3.7	13.3
68-69—Dallas (A)	75	—	1719	220	506	.435	1	15	.067	161	192	.839	—	—	158	208	158	0	—	129	—	602	2.1	2.8	8.0
69-70—Dallas (A)	80	—	2150	292	667	.438	19	72	.264	231	262	.882	—	—	205	280	222	2	—	—	—	834	2.6	3.5	10.4
70-71—Fla.-Texas (A)	48	—	509	57	136	.419	7	26	.269	40	49	.816	—	—	46	82	69	—	—	—	—	161	1.0	1.7	3.4
REG. ABA TOTALS	281	—	7347	943	2067	.456	30	126	.238	717	830	.864	—	—	704	860	651	5	—	318	—	2633	2.5	3.1	9.4
ABA PLAYOFF TOTALS	23	—	698	99	218	.454	3	18	.167	63	78	.808	—	—	50	80	66	1	—	41	—	264	2.2	3.5	11.5

BEASLEY, JOHN MICHAEL b. February 5, 1944   Ht. 6-9   Wt. 225   College—Texas A&M

SEASON—TEAM	G	GS	MIN	FGM	FGA	PCT	3FGM	3FGA	PCT	FTM	FTA	PCT	O-RB	D-RB	TOT	AST	PF	DQ	STL	TO	BLK	PTS	RPG	APG	PPG
67-68—Dallas (A)	77	—	2840	622	1264	.492	0	2	.000	271	322	.842	278	704	982	112	245	3	—	107	—	1515	12.8	1.5	19.7
68-69—Dallas (A)	78	—	3050	585	1200	.488	3	10	.300	332	402	.826	248	582	830	110	259	5	—	136	—	1505	10.6	1.4	19.3
69-70—Dallas (A)	84	—	3066	626	1254	.499	3	8	.375	284	347	.818	303	703	1006	132	278	4	—	—	—	1539	12.0	1.6	18.3
70-71—Texas (A)	83	—	2691	532	1070	.497	16	58	.276	236	285	.828	—	—	765	147	206	—	—	—	—	1316	9.2	1.8	15.9
71-72—Dallas-Utah (A)	70	—	885	132	284	.465	8	25	.320	61	75	.813	—	—	290	39	107	—	—	36	—	333	4.1	0.6	4.8
72-73—Utah (A)	71	—	934	214	417	.513	29	89	.326	62	70	.886	82	182	264	43	142	0	—	39	—	519	3.7	0.6	7.3
73-74—Utah (A)	43	—	481	75	181	.414	22	64	.344	10	11	.909	45	75	120	19	57	—	7	21	10	182	2.8	0.4	4.2
REG. ABA TOTALS	506	—	13947	2786	5670	.491	81	256	.316	1256	1512	.831	956	2246	4257	602	1294	12	7	339	10	6909	8.4	1.2	13.7
ABA PLAYOFF TOTALS	51	—	1274	228	465	.490	8	36	.222	96	112	.857	43	84	376	62	126	1	0	36	2	560	7.4	1.2	11.0
ABA ALL-STAR TOTALS	3	—	71	17	28	.607	1	1	1.000	4	4	1.000	6	12	26	2	15	0	0	2	0	39	8.7	0.7	13.0

BEATY, ZELMO JR. (Big Z) b. October 25, 1939   Ht. 6-9   Wt. 235   College—Prairie View A&M

SEASON—TEAM	G	GS	MIN	FGM	FGA	PCT	3FGM	3FGA	PCT	FTM	FTA	PCT	O-RB	D-RB	TOT	AST	PF	DQ	STL	TO	BLK	PTS	RPG	APG	PPG
62-63—St. Louis	80	—	1918	297	677	.439	—	—	—	220	307	.717	—	—	665	85	312	12	—	—	—	814	8.3	1.1	10.2
63-64—St. Louis	59	—	1922	287	647	.444	—	—	—	200	270	.741	—	—	633	79	262	11	—	—	—	774	10.7	1.3	13.1
64-65—St. Louis	80	—	2916	505	1047	.482	—	—	—	341	477	.715	—	—	966	111	328	11	—	—	—	1351	12.1	1.4	16.9
65-66—St. Louis	80	—	3072	616	1301	.473	—	—	—	424	559	.758	—	—	1086	125	344	15	—	—	—	1656	13.6	1.6	20.7
66-67—St. Louis	48	—	1661	328	694	.473	—	—	—	197	260	.758	—	—	515	60	189	3	—	—	—	853	10.7	1.3	17.8
67-68—St. Louis	82	—	3068	639	1310	.488	—	—	—	455	573	.794	—	—	959	174	295	6	—	—	—	1733	11.7	2.1	21.1
68-69—Atlanta	72	—	2578	588	1251	.470	—	—	—	370	506	.731	—	—	798	131	272	7	—	—	—	1546	11.1	1.8	21.5
70-71—Utah (A)	76	—	2915	661	1192	.555	2	4	.500	420	531	.791	407	783	1190	148	299	—	—	—	—	1744	15.7	1.9	22.9
71-72—Utah (A)	84	—	3133	729	1353	.539	0	7	.000	522	630	.829	355	755	1110	125	315	—	—	223	—	1980	13.2	1.5	23.6
72-73—Utah (A)	82	—	2804	521	1002	.520	0	1	.000	306	381	.803	261	540	801	125	269	3	—	197	79	1348	9.8	1.5	16.4
73-74—Utah (A)	77	—	2476	417	796	.524	0	1	.000	194	244	.795	170	445	615	128	229	—	62	110	64	1028	8.0	1.7	13.4
74-75—Los Angeles	69	—	1213	136	310	.439	—	—	—	108	135	.800	93	234	327	74	130	1	45	—	29	380	4.7	1.1	5.5
REG. NBA TOTALS	570	—	18348	3396	7237	.469	—	—	—	2315	3087	.750	93	234	5949	839	2132	66	45	—	29	9107	10.4	1.5	16.0
REG. ABA TOTALS	319	—	11328	2328	4343	.536	2	13	.154	1442	1786	.807	1193	2523	3716	526	1112	3	62	530	143	6100	11.6	1.6	19.1
NBA PLAYOFF TOTALS	63	—	2345	399	857	.466	—	—	—	273	370	.738	0	0	696	98	267	7	0	—	0	1071	11.0	1.6	17.0
ABA PLAYOFF TOTALS	52	—	2000	369	691	.534	0	0	—	253	303	.835	224	450	674	102	192	0	18	82	12	991	13.0	2.0	19.1
NBA ALL-STAR TOTALS	2	—	54	2	22	.091	—	—	—	12	15	.800	0	0	28	2	6	0	—	—	0	16	14.0	1.0	8.0
ABA ALL-STAR TOTALS	3	—	65	15	28	.536	0	0	—	3	4	.750	5	14	19	4	9	—	1	9	2	33	6.3	1.3	11.0

BECK, A. BYRON (Byron) b. January 25, 1945   Ht. 6-9   Wt. 235   College—Columbia Basin/Denver

SEASON—TEAM	G	GS	MIN	FGM	FGA	PCT	3FGM	3FGA	PCT	FTM	FTA	PCT	O-RB	D-RB	TOT	AST	PF	DQ	STL	TO	BLK	PTS	RPG	APG	PPG
67-68—Denver (A)	71	—	1623	275	570	.482	0	2	.000	119	159	.748	—	—	559	38	219	6	—	72	—	669	7.9	0.5	9.4
68-69—Denver (A)	71	—	2289	423	843	.502	2	3	.667	182	238	.765	272	507	779	77	248	9	—	92	—	1030	11.0	1.1	14.5
69-70—Denver (A)	79	—	2454	440	841	.523	0	2	.000	137	174	.787	—	—	764	112	293	12	—	—	—	1017	9.7	1.4	12.9
70-71—Denver (A)	84	—	2849	490	1033	.474	4	14	.286	158	182	.868	280	604	884	177	273	—	—	—	—	1142	10.5	2.1	13.6
71-72—Denver (A)	66	—	1816	337	669	.504	0	3	.000	140	166	.843	—	—	528	136	213	—	—	96	—	814	8.0	2.1	12.3
72-73—Denver (A)	77	—	2303	466	879	.530	2	7	.286	158	198	.798	203	334	537	107	267	9	—	126	—	1092	7.0	1.4	14.2
73-74—Denver (A)	82	—	1979	425	823	.516	0	1	.000	120	141	.851	164	253	417	76	233	—	48	83	8	970	5.1	0.9	11.8
74-75—Denver (A)	84	—	1818	384	745	.515	0	1	.000	81	97	.835	127	216	343	106	270	—	59	76	14	849	4.1	1.3	10.1
75-76—Denver (A)	80	—	1586	334	646	.517	5	11	.455	97	116	.836	123	231	354	116	192	—	48	91	20	770	4.4	1.5	9.6
76-77—Denver	53	—	480	107	246	.435	—	—	—	36	44	.818	45	51	96	33	59	1	15	—	1	250	1.8	0.6	4.7
REG. NBA TOTALS	53	—	480	107	246	.435	—	—	—	36	44	.818	45	51	96	33	59	1	15	—	1	250	1.8	0.6	4.7
REG. ABA TOTALS	694	—	18717	3574	7049	.507	13	44	.295	1192	1471	.810	1169	2145	5165	945	2208	36	155	636	42	8353	7.4	1.4	12.0
NBA PLAYOFF TOTALS	5	—	29	3	9	.333	—	—	—	2	2	1.000	2	4	6	1	5	0	—	0	0	8	1.2	0.2	1.6
ABA PLAYOFF TOTALS	61	—	1761	343	728	.471	2	10	.200	152	186	.817	104	218	479	81	215	1	8	81	4	840	7.9	1.3	13.8
ABA ALL-STAR TOTALS	2	—	47	13	24	.542	0	0	—	2	2	1.000	3	7	14	1	6	0	0	1	0	28	7.0	0.5	14.0

BECK, ERNEST JOSEPH (Ernie) b. December 11, 1931   Ht. 6-4   Wt. 190   College—Pennsylvania

SEASON—TEAM	G	GS	MIN	FGM	FGA	PCT	3FGM	3FGA	PCT	FTM	FTA	PCT	O-RB	D-RB	TOT	AST	PF	DQ	STL	TO	BLK	PTS	RPG	APG	PPG
53-54—Philadelphia	15	—	422	39	142	.275	—	—	—	34	43	.791	—	—	50	34	29	0	—	—	—	112	3.3	2.3	7.5
55-56—Philadelphia	67	—	1007	136	351	.387	—	—	—	76	106	.717	—	—	196	79	86	0	—	—	—	348	2.9	1.2	5.2
56-57—Philadelphia	72	—	1743	195	508	.384	—	—	—	111	157	.707	—	—	312	190	155	1	—	—	—	501	4.3	2.6	7.0
57-58—Philadelphia	71	—	1974	272	683	.398	—	—	—	170	203	.837	—	—	307	190	173	2	—	—	—	714	4.3	2.7	10.1
58-59—Philadelphia	70	—	1017	163	418	.390	—	—	—	43	65	.662	—	—	176	89	124	0	—	—	—	369	2.5	1.3	5.3
59-60—Philadelphia	66	—	809	114	294	.388	—	—	—	27	32	.844	—	—	127	72	90	0	—	—	—	255	1.9	1.1	3.9
60-61—St. L.-Syr.	10	—	82	10	29	.345	—	—	—	6	7	.857	—	—	23	15	10	0	—	—	—	26	2.3	1.5	2.6
REG. SEASON TOTALS	371	—	7054	929	2425	.383	—	—	—	467	613	.762	—	—	1191	669	667	3	—	—	—	2325	3.2	1.8	6.3
PLAYOFF TOTALS	24	—	517	72	180	.400	—	—	—	31	44	.705	—	—	99	43	53	1	—	—	—	175	4.1	1.8	7.3

BECKER, ARTHUR C. (**Art**) b. January 12, 1942 Ht. 6.6½ Wt. 210 College—Arizona State

SEASON—TEAM	G	GS	MIN	FGM	FGA	PCT	3FGM	3FGA	PCT	FTM	FTA	PCT	O-RB	D-RB	TOT	AST	PF	DQ	STL	TO	BLK	PTS	RPG	APG	PPG
67-68—Houston (A)	76	—	2689	563	1204	.468	4	12	.333	297	362	.820	252	461	713	95	321	12	—	154	—	1427	9.4	1.3	18.8
68-69—Houston (A)	78	—	2429	423	888	.476	0	3	.000	200	240	.833	—	—	597	103	304	9	—	156	—	1046	7.7	1.3	13.4
69-70—Indiana (A)	82	—	1504	309	593	.521	0	1	.000	111	137	.810	—	—	379	45	249	8	—	—	—	729	4.6	0.5	8.9
70-71—Indiana-Denver (A)	80	—	1643	370	741	.499	5	8	.625	135	156	.865	—	—	426	53	260	—	—	—	—	880	5.3	0.7	11.0
71-72—Denver (A)	84	—	2193	435	954	.456	0	3	.000	165	195	.846	—	—	471	113	271	—	—	132	—	1035	5.6	1.3	12.3
72-73—N.Y.-Dallas (A)	14	—	96	16	28	.571	0	1	.000	11	11	1.000	5	13	18	1	6	0	—	5	—	43	1.3	0.1	3.1
REG. ABA TOTALS	414	—	10554	2116	4408	.480	9	28	.321	919	1101	.835	257	474	2604	410	1411	29	—	447	—	5160	6.3	1.0	12.5
ABA PLAYOFF TOTALS	25	—	415	68	143	.476	0	1	.000	42	51	.824	—	—	86	14	64	1	—	9	—	178	3.4	0.6	7.1
ABA ALL-STAR TOTALS	2	—	28	5	15	.333	0	0	—	1	1	1.000	3	2	5	1	0	—	3	—	11	2.5	0.5	5.5

BECKER, MORRIS R. (**Moe**) b. February 24, 1917 Ht. 6-1 Wt. 185 College—Duquesne

SEASON—TEAM	G	GS	MIN	FGM	FGA	PCT	3FGM	3FGA	PCT	FTM	FTA	PCT	O-RB	D-RB	TOT	AST	PF	DQ	STL	TO	BLK	PTS	RPG	APG	PPG
45-46—Youngstown (N)	30	—	—	115	—	—	—	—	—	40	69	.580	—	—	—	114	—	—	—	—	270	—	—	9.0
46-47—Pitt.-Boston-Det. Falc.	43	—	—	70	358	.196	—	—	—	22	44	.500	—	—	—	30	98	—	—	—	—	162	—	0.7	3.8
REG. NBA TOTALS	43	—	—	70	358	.196	—	—	—	22	44	.500	—	—	—	30	98	—	—	—	—	162	—	0.7	3.8
REG. NBL TOTALS	30	—	—	115	—	—	—	—	—	40	69	.580	—	—	—	114	—	—	—	—	270	—	—	9.0

BEDELL, ROBERT GEORGE (**Bob**) b. June 26, 1944 Ht. 6-8 Wt. 205 College—Stanford

SEASON—TEAM	G	GS	MIN	FGM	FGA	PCT	3FGM	3FGA	PCT	FTM	FTA	PCT	O-RB	D-RB	TOT	AST	PF	DQ	STL	TO	BLK	PTS	RPG	APG	PPG
67-68—Anaheim (A)	76	—	1492	325	736	.442	0	4	.000	142	190	.747	—	—	506	79	203	5	—	111	—	792	6.7	1.0	10.4
68-69—Dallas (A)	42	—	479	92	221	.416	0	2	.000	48	84	.571	—	—	116	30	76	1	—	35	—	232	2.8	0.7	5.5
69-70—Dallas (A)	80	—	1536	285	677	.421	2	10	.200	207	246	.841	—	—	454	126	192	3	—	—	—	779	5.7	1.6	9.7
70-71—Texas (A)	71	—	970	176	441	.399	9	42	.214	93	113	.823	—	—	310	85	124	—	—	—	—	454	4.4	1.2	6.4
REG. ABA TOTALS	269	—	4477	878	2075	.423	11	58	.190	490	633	.774	—	—	1386	320	595	9	—	146	—	2257	5.2	1.2	8.4
ABA PLAYOFF TOTALS	16	—	250	50	114	.439	0	9	.000	25	32	.781	—	—	78	15	34	1	—	12	—	125	4.9	0.9	7.8

BEDFORD, WILLIAM b. December 14, 1963 Ht. 7-0 Wt. 235 College—Memphis State

SEASON—TEAM	G	GS	MIN	FGM	FGA	PCT	3FGM	3FGA	PCT	FTM	FTA	PCT	O-RB	D-RB	TOT	AST	PF	DQ	STL	TO	BLK	PTS	RPG	APG	PPG
86-87—Phoenix	50	18	979	142	358	.397	0	1	.000	50	86	.581	79	167	246	57	125	1	18	85	37	334	4.9	1.1	6.7
87-88—Detroit	38	0	298	44	101	.436	0	0	—	13	23	.565	27	38	65	4	47	0	8	19	17	101	1.7	0.1	2.7
89-90—Detroit	42	0	246	54	125	.432	1	6	.167	9	22	.409	15	43	58	4	39	0	3	21	17	118	1.4	0.1	2.8
90-91—Detroit	60	4	562	106	242	.438	5	13	.385	55	78	.705	55	76	131	32	76	0	2	32	36	272	2.2	0.5	4.5
91-92—Detroit	32	8	363	50	121	.413	0	1	.000	14	22	.636	24	39	63	12	56	0	6	15	18	114	2.0	0.4	3.6
92-93—San Antonio	16	0	66	9	27	.333	1	1	1.000	6	12	.500	1	9	10	0	15	0	0	1	1	25	0.6	0.0	1.6
REG. SEASON TOTALS	238	30	2514	405	974	.416	7	22	.318	147	243	.605	201	372	573	109	358	1	37	173	126	964	2.4	0.5	4.1
PLAYOFF TOTALS	14	3	93	9	36	.250	0	2	.000	11	16	.688	9	17	26	4	19	0	3	4	5	29	1.9	0.3	2.1

BEENDERS, HENRY G. (**Hank**) b. June 2, 1916 Ht. 6-5½ Wt. 185 College—Long Island University

SEASON—TEAM	G	GS	MIN	FGM	FGA	PCT	3FGM	3FGA	PCT	FTM	FTA	PCT	O-RB	D-RB	TOT	AST	PF	DQ	STL	TO	BLK	PTS	RPG	APG	PPG
46-47—Providence	58	—	—	266	1016	.262	—	—	—	181	257	.704	—	—	—	37	196	—	—	—	—	713	—	0.6	12.3
47-48—Prov.-Phil.	45	—	—	76	269	.283	—	—	—	51	82	.622	—	—	—	13	99	—	—	—	—	203	—	0.3	4.5
48-49—Boston	8	—	—	6	28	.214	—	—	—	7	9	.778	—	—	—	3	9	—	—	—	—	19	—	0.4	2.4
REG. SEASON TOTALS	111	—	—	348	1313	.265	—	—	—	239	348	.687	—	—	—	53	304	—	—	—	—	935	—	0.5	8.4
PLAYOFF TOTALS	12	—	—	8	35	.229	—	—	—	7	13	.538	—	—	—	4	15	—	—	—	—	23	—	0.3	1.9

BEHAGEN, RONALD MICHAEL (**Ron**) b. January 14, 1951 Ht. 6-9 Wt. 185 College—Southern Idaho/Minnesota

SEASON—TEAM	G	GS	MIN	FGM	FGA	PCT	3FGM	3FGA	PCT	FTM	FTA	PCT	O-RB	D-RB	TOT	AST	PF	DQ	STL	TO	BLK	PTS	RPG	APG	PPG
73-74—Kansas City-Omaha	80	—	2059	357	827	.432	—	—	—	162	212	.764	188	379	567	134	291	9	56	—	37	876	7.1	1.7	11.0
74-75—Kansas City-Omaha	81	—	2205	333	834	.399	—	—	—	199	264	.754	146	446	592	153	301	8	60	—	42	865	7.3	1.9	10.7
75-76—New Orleans	66	—	1733	308	691	.446	—	—	—	144	179	.804	190	363	553	139	222	6	67	—	26	760	8.4	2.1	11.5
76-77—New Orleans	60	—	1170	213	509	.418	—	—	—	90	126	.714	144	287	431	83	166	1	41	—	19	516	7.2	1.4	8.6
77-78—Atlanta-Houston-Indiana	80	—	1735	346	804	.430	—	—	—	179	247	.725	201	312	513	101	263	4	62	174	31	871	6.4	1.3	10.9
78-79—Detroit-N.Y.-K.C.	15	—	165	28	62	.452	—	—	—	10	13	.769	13	29	42	7	36	0	4	11	1	66	2.8	0.5	4.4
79-80—Washington	6	—	64	9	23	.391	0	0	—	5	6	.833	6	8	14	7	14	0	0	4	4	23	2.3	1.2	3.8
REG. SEASON TOTALS	388	—	9131	1594	3750	.425	0	0	—	789	1047	.754	888	1824	2712	624	1293	28	290	189	160	3977	7.0	1.6	10.3
PLAYOFF TOTALS	8	—	122	24	50	.480	0	0	—	3	3	1.000	5	26	31	9	32	2	1	1	2	51	3.9	1.1	6.4

BEHNKE, ELMER H. b. February 3, 1929 Ht. 6-7 Wt. 210 College—Bradley

SEASON—TEAM	G	GS	MIN	FGM	FGA	PCT	3FGM	3FGA	PCT	FTM	FTA	PCT	O-RB	D-RB	TOT	AST	PF	DQ	STL	TO	BLK	PTS	RPG	APG	PPG
51-52—Milwaukee	4	—	55	6	22	.273	—	—	—	4	7	.571	—	—	17	4	13	1	—	—	—	16	4.3	1.0	4.0
REG. SEASON TOTALS	4	—	55	6	22	.273	—	—	—	4	7	.571	—	—	17	4	13	1	—	—	—	16	4.3	1.0	4.0

BELL, DENNIS R. b. June 2, 1951   Ht. 6-5½ Wt. 210 College—Gulf Coast CC/Drake

SEASON—TEAM	G	GS	MIN	FGM	FGA	PCT	3FGM	3FGA	PCT	FTM	FTA	PCT	O-RB	D-RB	TOT	AST	PF	DQ	STL	TO	BLK	PTS	RPG	APG	PPG
73-74—New York	1	—	4	0	1	.000	—	—	—	0	0	—	0	0	0	0	0	0	0	—	0	0	0.0	0.0	0.0
74-75—New York	52	—	465	68	181	.376	—	—	—	20	36	.556	48	57	105	25	54	0	22	—	9	156	2.0	0.5	3.0
75-76—New York	10	—	76	8	21	.381	—	—	—	3	7	.429	4	10	14	3	11	0	6	—	1	19	1.4	0.3	1.9
REG. SEASON TOTALS	63	—	545	76	203	.374	—	—	—	23	43	.535	52	67	119	28	65	0	28	—	10	175	1.9	0.4	2.8
PLAYOFF TOTALS	3	—	27	1	8	.125	—	—	—	0	5	.000	0	4	4	—	6	0	0	—	0	2	1.3	0.0	0.7

BELL, WILLIAM HOYET (**Whitey**) b. September 13, 1932   Ht. 6-0 Wt. 180 College—North Carolina State

SEASON—TEAM	G	GS	MIN	FGM	FGA	PCT	3FGM	3FGA	PCT	FTM	FTA	PCT	O-RB	D-RB	TOT	AST	PF	DQ	STL	TO	BLK	PTS	RPG	APG	PPG
59-60—New York	31	—	449	70	185	.378	—	—	—	28	43	.651	—	—	87	55	59	0	—	—	—	168	2.8	1.8	5.4
60-61—New York	5	—	45	7	18	.389	—	—	—	1	3	.333	—	—	7	1	7	0	—	—	—	15	1.4	0.2	3.0
REG. SEASON TOTALS	36	—	494	77	203	.379	—	—	—	29	46	.630	—	—	94	56	66	0	—	—	—	183	2.6	1.6	5.1

BELLAMY, WALTER JONES (**Walt, Bells**) b. July 24, 1939   Ht. 6-10½ Wt. 245 College—Indiana

SEASON—TEAM	G	GS	MIN	FGM	FGA	PCT	3FGM	3FGA	PCT	FTM	FTA	PCT	O-RB	D-RB	TOT	AST	PF	DQ	STL	TO	BLK	PTS	RPG	APG	PPG
61-62—Chicago	79	—	3344	973	1875	.519	—	—	—	549	853	.644	—	—	1500	210	281	6	—	—	—	2495	19.0	2.7	31.6
62-63—Chicago	80	—	3306	840	1595	.527	—	—	—	553	821	.674	—	—	1309	233	283	7	—	—	—	2233	16.4	2.9	27.9
63-64—Baltimore	80	—	3394	811	1582	.513	—	—	—	537	825	.651	—	—	1361	126	300	7	—	—	—	2159	17.0	1.6	27.0
64-65—Baltimore	80	—	3301	733	1441	.509	—	—	—	515	752	.685	—	—	1166	191	260	2	—	—	—	1981	14.6	2.4	24.8
65-66—Balt.-N.Y.	80	—	3352	695	1373	.506	—	—	—	430	689	.624	—	—	1254	235	294	9	—	—	—	1820	15.7	2.9	22.8
66-67—New York	79	—	3010	565	1084	.521	—	—	—	369	580	.636	—	—	1064	206	275	5	—	—	—	1499	13.5	2.6	19.0
67-68—New York	82	—	2695	511	944	.541	—	—	—	350	529	.662	—	—	961	164	259	3	—	—	—	1372	11.7	2.0	16.7
68-69—N.Y.-Detroit	88	—	3159	563	1103	.510	—	—	—	401	618	.649	—	—	1101	176	320	5	—	—	—	1527	12.5	2.0	17.4
69-70—Detroit-Atlanta	79	—	2028	351	671	.523	—	—	—	215	373	.576	—	—	707	143	260	5	—	—	—	917	8.9	1.8	11.6
70-71—Atlanta	82	—	2908	433	879	.493	—	—	—	336	556	.604	—	—	1060	230	271	4	—	—	—	1202	12.9	2.8	14.7
71-72—Atlanta	82	—	3187	593	1089	.545	—	—	—	340	581	.585	—	—	1049	262	255	2	—	—	—	1526	12.8	3.2	18.6
72-73—Atlanta	74	—	2802	455	901	.505	—	—	—	283	526	.538	—	—	964	179	244	1	—	—	—	1193	13.0	2.4	16.1
73-74—Atlanta	77	—	2440	389	801	.486	—	—	—	233	383	.608	264	476	740	189	232	2	52	—	48	1011	9.6	2.5	13.1
74-75—New Orleans	1	—	14	2	2	1.000	—	—	—	2	2	1.000	0	5	5	0	2	0	0	—	0	6	5.0	0.0	6.0
REG. SEASON TOTALS	1043	—	38940	7914	15340	.516	—	—	—	5113	8088	.632	264	481	14241	2544	3536	58	52	—	48	20941	13.7	2.4	20.1
PLAYOFF TOTALS	46	—	1939	323	686	.471	—	—	—	204	318	.642	0	0	680	136	160	0	0	—	0	850	14.8	3.0	18.5
ALL-STAR TOTALS	4	—	83	19	38	.500	—	—	—	10	19	.526	0	0	30	4	15	1	0	—	0	48	7.5	1.0	12.0

BEMORAS, IRVING (**Irv**) b. November 18, 1930   Ht. 6-3 Wt. 185 College—Illinois

SEASON—TEAM	G	GS	MIN	FGM	FGA	PCT	3FGM	3FGA	PCT	FTM	FTA	PCT	O-RB	D-RB	TOT	AST	PF	DQ	STL	TO	BLK	PTS	RPG	APG	PPG
53-54—Milwaukee	69	—	1496	185	505	.366	—	—	—	139	208	.668	—	—	214	79	152	2	—	—	—	509	3.1	1.1	7.4
56-57—St. Louis	62	—	983	124	385	.322	—	—	—	70	103	.680	—	—	127	46	76	0	—	—	—	318	2.0	0.7	5.1
REG. SEASON TOTALS	131	—	2479	309	890	.347	—	—	—	209	311	.672	—	—	341	125	228	2	—	—	—	827	2.6	1.0	6.3
PLAYOFF TOTALS	3	—	20	3	8	.375	—	—	—	3	3	1.000	—	—	6	1	4	0	—	—	—	9	2.0	0.3	3.0

BENBOW, LEON b. July 23, 1950   Ht. 6-4 Wt. 185 College—Jacksonville

SEASON—TEAM	G	GS	MIN	FGM	FGA	PCT	3FGM	3FGA	PCT	FTM	FTA	PCT	O-RB	D-RB	TOT	AST	PF	DQ	STL	TO	BLK	PTS	RPG	APG	PPG
74-75—Chicago	39	—	252	35	94	.372	—	—	—	15	18	.833	14	24	38	25	41	0	11	—	6	85	1.0	0.6	2.2
75-76—Chicago	76	—	1586	219	551	.397	—	—	—	105	140	.750	65	111	176	158	186	1	62	—	11	543	2.3	2.1	7.1
REG. SEASON TOTALS	115	—	1838	254	645	.394	—	—	—	120	158	.759	79	135	214	183	227	1	73	—	17	628	1.9	1.6	5.5
PLAYOFF TOTALS	2	—	5	2	4	.500	—	—	—	1	2	.500	1	0	1	2	0	0	0	—	0	5	0.5	1.0	2.5

BENJAMIN, LENARD BENOIT (**Benoit**) b. November 22, 1964   Ht. 7-0 Wt. 265 College—Creighton

SEASON—TEAM	G	GS	MIN	FGM	FGA	PCT	3FGM	3FGA	PCT	FTM	FTA	PCT	O-RB	D-RB	TOT	AST	PF	DQ	STL	TO	BLK	PTS	RPG	APG	PPG
85-86—L.A. Clippers	79	37	2088	324	661	.490	1	3	.333	229	307	.746	161	439	600	79	286	5	64	145	206	878	7.6	1.0	11.1
86-87—L.A. Clippers	72	61	2230	320	713	.449	0	2	.000	188	263	.715	134	452	586	135	251	7	60	184	187	828	8.1	1.9	11.5
87-88—L.A. Clippers	66	59	2171	340	693	.491	0	8	.000	180	255	.706	112	418	530	172	203	2	50	223	225	860	8.0	2.6	13.0
88-89—L.A. Clippers	79	62	2585	491	907	.541	0	2	.000	317	426	.744	164	532	696	157	221	4	57	237	221	1299	8.8	2.0	16.4
89-90—L.A. Clippers	71	58	2313	362	688	.526	0	1	.000	235	321	.732	156	501	657	159	217	3	59	187	187	959	9.3	2.2	13.5
90-91—LAClips-Seattle	70	65	2236	386	778	.496	0	—	—	210	295	.712	157	566	723	119	184	1	54	235	145	982	10.3	1.7	14.0
91-92—Seattle	63	61	1941	354	740	.478	0	2	.000	171	249	.687	130	383	513	76	185	1	39	175	118	879	8.1	1.2	14.0
92-93—Seattle-Lakers	59	6	754	133	271	.491	0	0	—	69	104	.663	51	158	209	22	134	0	31	78	48	335	3.5	0.4	5.7
93-94—New Jersey	77	74	1817	283	589	.480	0	0	—	152	214	.710	135	364	499	44	198	0	35	97	90	718	6.5	0.6	9.3
REG. SEASON TOTALS	636	483	18135	2993	6040	.496	1	18	.056	1751	2434	.719	1200	3813	5013	963	1879	23	449	1561	1427	7738	7.9	1.5	12.2
PLAYOFF TOTALS	18	13	432	50	99	.505	0	1	.000	45	58	.776	22	78	100	7	53	1	10	24	34	145	5.6	0.4	8.1

BENNETT, ANTHONY GUY (**Tony**) b. June 1, 1969   Ht. 6-0 Wt. 175 College—Wisconsin-Green Bay

SEASON—TEAM	G	GS	MIN	FGM	FGA	PCT	3FGM	3FGA	PCT	FTM	FTA	PCT	O-RB	D-RB	TOT	AST	PF	DQ	STL	TO	BLK	PTS	RPG	APG	PPG
92-93—Charlotte	75	2	857	110	260	.423	26	80	.325	30	41	.732	12	51	63	136	110	0	30	50	0	276	0.8	1.8	3.7
93-94—Charlotte	74	5	983	105	263	.399	27	75	.360	11	15	.733	16	74	90	163	84	0	39	40	1	248	1.2	2.2	3.4
REG. SEASON TOTALS	149	7	1840	215	523	.411	53	155	.342	41	56	.732	28	125	153	299	194	0	69	90	1	524	1.0	2.0	3.5
PLAYOFF TOTALS	8	0	86	12	25	.480	4	8	.500	2	2	1.000	1	8	9	13	8	0	2	5	1	30	1.1	1.6	3.8

BENNETT, MELVIN P. (**Mel**) b. January 4, 1955 d. 1981 Ht. 6-7 Wt. 215 College—Pittsburgh

SEASON—TEAM	G	GS	MIN	FGM	FGA	PCT	3FGM	3FGA	PCT	FTM	FTA	PCT	O-RB	D-RB	TOT	AST	PF	DQ	STL	TO	BLK	PTS	RPG	APG	PPG
75-76—Virginia (A)	75	—	2193	329	819	.402	0	2	.000	246	403	.610	249	277	526	97	266	—	77	176	47	904	7.0	1.3	12.1
76-77—Indiana	67	—	911	101	294	.344	—	—	—	112	187	.599	110	127	237	70	155	0	37	—	33	314	3.5	1.0	4.7
77-78—Indiana	31	—	285	23	81	.284	—	—	—	28	45	.622	49	44	93	22	54	1	11	30	7	74	3.0	0.7	2.4
80-81—Utah	28	—	313	26	60	.433	0	2	.000	53	81	.654	33	60	93	15	56	0	3	31	11	105	3.3	0.5	3.8
81-82—Cleveland	3	0	23	2	4	.500	0	0	—	1	6	.167	1	2	3	0	2	0	1	4	0	5	1.0	0.0	1.7
REG. NBA TOTALS	129	0	1532	152	439	.346	0	2	.000	194	319	.608	193	233	426	107	267	1	52	65	51	498	3.3	0.8	3.9
REG. ABA TOTALS	75	—	2193	329	819	.402	0	2	.000	246	403	.610	249	277	526	97	266	—	77	176	47	904	7.0	1.3	12.1

BENNETT, WILLIS (**Spider**) b. August 4, 1943 Ht. 6-3 Wt. 190 College—Winston-Salem State

SEASON—TEAM	G	GS	MIN	FGM	FGA	PCT	3FGM	3FGA	PCT	FTM	FTA	PCT	O-RB	D-RB	TOT	AST	PF	DQ	STL	TO	BLK	PTS	RPG	APG	PPG
68-69—Dallas-Houston (A)	59	—	993	147	385	.382	6	25	.240	140	216	.648	—	—	147	84	165	9	—	145	—	440	2.5	1.4	7.5
REG. ABA TOTALS		59	—	993	147	385	.382	6	25	.240	140	216	.648	—	—	147	84	165	9	—	145	—	440	2.5	1.4	7.5

BENNETT, WINSTON GEORGE III (**Steady Bee**) b. February 9, 1965 Ht. 6-7 Wt. 220 College—Kentucky

SEASON—TEAM	G	GS	MIN	FGM	FGA	PCT	3FGM	3FGA	PCT	FTM	FTA	PCT	O-RB	D-RB	TOT	AST	PF	DQ	STL	TO	BLK	PTS	RPG	APG	PPG
89-90—Cleveland	55	34	990	137	286	.479	0	0	—	64	96	.667	84	104	188	54	133	1	23	62	10	338	3.4	1.0	6.1
90-91—Cleveland	27	13	334	40	107	.374	0	0	—	35	47	.745	30	34	64	28	50	0	8	20	2	115	2.4	1.0	4.3
91-92—Clev.-Miami	54	45	833	80	211	.379	0	1	.000	35	50	.700	63	99	162	38	122	1	19	33	9	195	3.0	0.7	3.6
REG. SEASON TOTALS	136	92	2157	257	604	.425	0	1	.000	134	193	.694	177	237	414	120	305	2	50	115	21	648	3.0	0.9	4.8
PLAYOFF TOTALS	5	5	135	23	47	.489	0	0	—	4	6	.667	14	7	21	5	11	0	3	4	1	50	4.2	1.0	10.0

BENOIT, DAVID b. May 9, 1968 Ht. 6-8 Wt. 220 College—Tyler JC/Alabama

SEASON—TEAM	G	GS	MIN	FGM	FGA	PCT	3FGM	3FGA	PCT	FTM	FTA	PCT	O-RB	D-RB	TOT	AST	PF	DQ	STL	TO	BLK	PTS	RPG	APG	PPG
91-92—Utah	77	2	1161	175	375	.467	3	14	.214	81	100	.810	105	191	296	34	124	0	19	71	44	434	3.8	0.4	5.6
92-93—Utah	82	27	1712	258	592	.436	34	98	.347	114	152	.750	116	276	392	43	201	2	45	90	43	664	4.8	0.5	8.1
93-94—Utah	55	18	1070	139	361	.385	12	59	.203	68	88	.773	89	171	260	23	115	0	23	37	37	358	4.7	0.4	6.5
REG. SEASON TOTALS	214	47	3943	572	1328	.431	49	171	.287	263	340	.774	310	638	948	100	440	2	87	198	124	1456	4.4	0.5	6.8
PLAYOFF TOTALS	34	19	750	97	247	.393	11	38	.289	36	49	.735	48	93	141	21	78	0	16	28	22	241	4.1	0.6	7.1

BENSON, MICHAEL KENT (**Kent**) b. December 27, 1954 Ht. 6-11 Wt. 245 College—Indiana

SEASON—TEAM	G	GS	MIN	FGM	FGA	PCT	3FGM	3FGA	PCT	FTM	FTA	PCT	O-RB	D-RB	TOT	AST	PF	DQ	STL	TO	BLK	PTS	RPG	APG	PPG
77-78—Milwaukee	69	—	1288	220	473	.465	—	—	—	92	141	.652	89	206	295	99	177	1	69	119	54	532	4.3	1.4	7.7
78-79—Milwaukee	82	—	2132	413	798	.518	—	—	—	180	245	.735	187	397	584	204	280	4	89	156	81	1006	7.1	2.5	12.3
79-80—Milw.-Detroit	73	—	1891	299	618	.484	1	5	.200	99	141	.702	126	327	453	178	246	4	73	157	92	698	6.2	2.4	9.6
80-81—Detroit	59	—	1956	364	770	.473	0	4	.000	196	254	.772	124	276	400	172	184	1	72	190	67	924	6.8	2.9	15.7
81-82—Detroit	75	72	2467	405	802	.505	3	11	.273	127	158	.804	219	434	653	159	214	2	66	160	98	940	8.7	2.1	12.5
82-83—Detroit	21	15	599	85	182	.467	0	1	.000	38	50	.760	53	102	155	49	61	0	14	35	17	208	7.4	2.3	9.9
83-84—Detroit	82	58	1734	248	451	.550	0	1	.000	83	101	.822	117	292	409	130	230	4	71	79	53	579	5.0	1.6	7.1
84-85—Detroit	72	35	1401	201	397	.506	0	3	.000	76	94	.809	103	221	324	93	207	4	53	68	44	478	4.5	1.3	6.6
85-86—Detroit	72	51	1344	201	415	.484	1	2	.500	66	83	.795	118	258	376	80	196	3	58	58	51	469	5.2	1.1	6.5
86-87—Utah	73	2	895	140	316	.443	2	7	.286	47	58	.810	80	151	231	39	138	0	39	45	28	329	3.2	0.5	4.5
87-88—Cleveland	2	0	12	2	2	1.000	0	0	—	1	2	.500	0	1	1	0	2	0	1	2	1	5	0.5	0.0	2.5
REG. SEASON TOTALS	680	233	15719	2578	5224	.493	7	34	.206	1005	1327	.757	1216	2665	3881	1203	1935	23	605	1069	586	6168	5.7	1.8	9.1
PLAYOFF TOTALS	29	6	432	56	116	.483	0	0	—	25	36	.694	26	68	94	14	72	0	18	17	14	137	3.2	0.5	4.7

BERCE, EUGENE D. (**Gene**) b. November 22, 1926 Ht. 5-11 Wt. 175 College—Cornell/Marquette

SEASON—TEAM	G	GS	MIN	FGM	FGA	PCT	3FGM	3FGA	PCT	FTM	FTA	PCT	O-RB	D-RB	TOT	AST	PF	DQ	STL	TO	BLK	PTS	RPG	APG	PPG
48-49—Oshkosh (N)	58	—	—	120	—	—	—	—	—	101	153	.660	—	—	—	—	137	—	—	—	—	341	—	—	5.9
49-50—Tri-Cities	3	—	—	5	16	.313	—	—	—	0	5	.000	—	—	—	2	6	—	—	—	—	10	—	0.7	3.3
REG. NBA TOTALS	3	—	—	5	16	.313	—	—	—	0	5	.000	—	—	—	2	6	—	—	—	—	10	—	0.7	3.3
REG. NBL TOTALS	58	—	—	120	—	—	—	—	—	101	153	.660	—	—	—	—	137	—	—	—	—	341	—	—	5.9
NBL PLAYOFF TOTALS	7	—	—	8	—	—	—	—	—	32	39	.821	—	—	—	—	16	—	—	—	—	48	—	—	6.9

BERGEN, GARY DEAN b. July 16, 1932 Ht. 6-8 Wt. 210 College—Utah/Kansas State

SEASON—TEAM	G	GS	MIN	FGM	FGA	PCT	3FGM	3FGA	PCT	FTM	FTA	PCT	O-RB	D-RB	TOT	AST	PF	DQ	STL	TO	BLK	PTS	RPG	APG	PPG
56-57—New York	6	—	40	3	11	.273	—	—	—	2	2	1.000	—	—	8	1	4	0	—	—	—	8	1.3	0.2	1.3
REG. SEASON TOTALS	6	—	40	3	11	.273	—	—	—	2	2	1.000	—	—	8	1	4	0	—	—	—	8	1.3	0.2	1.3

BERGH, LARRY CLIFFORD b. April 2, 1945 Ht. 6-7½ Wt. 210 College—Tuskegee/Weber State

SEASON—TEAM	G	GS	MIN	FGM	FGA	PCT	3FGM	3FGA	PCT	FTM	FTA	PCT	O-RB	D-RB	TOT	AST	PF	DQ	STL	TO	BLK	PTS	RPG	APG	PPG
69-70—Pittsburgh (A)	20	—	255	49	120	.408	0	1	.000	23	33	.697	—	—	85	18	52	2	—	—	—	121	4.3	0.9	6.1
REG. ABA TOTALS	20	—	255	49	120	.408	0	1	.000	23	33	.697	—	—	85	18	52	2	—	—	—	121	4.3	0.9	6.1

BERRY, RICKY ALAN b. October 6, 1964 d. August 14, 1989 Ht. 6-8 Wt. 205 College—Oregon State/San Jose State

SEASON—TEAM	G	GS	MIN	FGM	FGA	PCT	3FGM	3FGA	PCT	FTM	FTA	PCT	O-RB	D-RB	TOT	AST	PF	DQ	STL	TO	BLK	PTS	RPG	APG	PPG
88-89—Sacramento	64	21	1406	255	567	.450	65	160	.406	131	166	.789	57	140	197	80	197	4	37	82	22	706	3.1	1.3	11.0
REG. SEASON TOTALS	64	21	1406	255	567	.450	65	160	.406	131	166	.789	57	140	197	80	197	4	37	82	22	706	3.1	1.3	11.0

BERRY, WALTER b. May 14, 1964 Ht. 6-8 Wt. 215 College—San Jacinto/St. John's

SEASON—TEAM	G	GS	MIN	FGM	FGA	PCT	3FGM	3FGA	PCT	FTM	FTA	PCT	O-RB	D-RB	TOT	AST	PF	DQ	STL	TO	BLK	PTS	RPG	APG	PPG
86-87—Port.-S.A.	63	45	1586	407	766	.531	0	3	.000	187	288	.649	136	173	309	105	196	2	38	153	40	1001	4.9	1.7	15.9
87-88—San Antonio	73	56	1922	540	960	.563	0	0	—	192	320	.600	176	219	395	110	207	2	55	162	63	1272	5.4	1.5	17.4
88-89—N.J.-Houston	69	31	1355	254	501	.507	1	2	.500	100	143	.699	86	181	267	77	183	1	29	89	48	609	3.9	1.1	8.8
REG. SEASON TOTALS	205	132	4863	1201	2227	.539	1	5	.200	479	751	.638	398	573	971	292	586	5	122	404	151	2882	4.7	1.4	14.1
PLAYOFF TOTALS	7	0	151	40	76	.526	0	1	.000	19	23	.826	16	14	30	11	18	0	7	17	3	99	4.3	1.6	14.1

BESHORE, DELMER (**Del**) b. November 29, 1956 Ht. 6-0 Wt. 170 College—California (Pa.)

SEASON—TEAM	G	GS	MIN	FGM	FGA	PCT	3FGM	3FGA	PCT	FTM	FTA	PCT	O-RB	D-RB	TOT	AST	PF	DQ	STL	TO	BLK	PTS	RPG	APG	PPG
78-79—Milwaukee	1	—	1	0	0	—	—	—	—	0	0	—	0	0	0	0	0	0	0	0	0	0	0.0	0.0	0.0
79-80—Chicago	68	—	869	88	250	.352	10	26	.385	58	87	.667	16	47	63	139	105	0	58	104	5	244	0.9	2.0	3.6
REG. SEASON TOTALS	69	—	870	88	250	.352	10	26	.385	58	87	.667	16	47	63	139	105	0	58	104	5	244	0.9	2.0	3.5

BIALOSUKNIA, WESLEY JOHN (**Wes**) b. June 8, 1945 Ht. 6-2 Wt. 185 College—Connecticut

SEASON—TEAM	G	GS	MIN	FGM	FGA	PCT	3FGM	3FGA	PCT	FTM	FTA	PCT	O-RB	D-RB	TOT	AST	PF	DQ	STL	TO	BLK	PTS	RPG	APG	PPG
67-68—Oakland (A)	70	—	1224	238	570	.418	29	73	.397	103	132	.780	—	—	89	57	101	1	—	62	—	608	1.3	0.8	8.7
REG. ABA TOTALS	70	—	1224	238	570	.418	29	73	.397	103	132	.780	—	—	89	57	101	1	—	62	—	608	1.3	0.8	8.7

BIANCHI, ALFRED A. (**Al**) b. March 26, 1932 Ht. 6-3 Wt. 185 College—Bowling Green

SEASON—TEAM	G	GS	MIN	FGM	FGA	PCT	3FGM	3FGA	PCT	FTM	FTA	PCT	O-RB	D-RB	TOT	AST	PF	DQ	STL	TO	BLK	PTS	RPG	APG	PPG
56-57—Syracuse	68	—	1577	199	567	.351	—	—	—	165	239	.690	—	—	227	106	198	5	—	—	—	563	3.3	1.6	8.3
57-58—Syracuse	69	—	1421	215	625	.344	—	—	—	140	205	.683	—	—	221	114	188	4	—	—	—	570	3.2	1.7	8.3
58-59—Syracuse	72	—	1779	285	756	.377	—	—	—	149	206	.723	—	—	199	159	260	8	—	—	—	719	2.8	2.2	10.0
59-60—Syracuse	69	—	1256	211	576	.366	—	—	—	109	155	.703	—	—	179	169	231	5	—	—	—	531	2.6	2.4	7.7
60-61—Syracuse	52	—	667	118	342	.345	—	—	—	60	87	.690	—	—	105	93	137	5	—	—	—	296	2.0	1.8	5.7
61-62—Syracuse	80	—	1925	336	847	.397	—	—	—	154	221	.697	—	—	281	263	232	5	—	—	—	826	3.5	3.3	10.3
62-63—Syracuse	61	—	1159	202	476	.424	—	—	—	120	164	.732	—	—	134	170	165	2	—	—	—	524	2.2	2.8	8.6
63-64—Philadelphia	78	—	1437	257	684	.376	—	—	—	109	141	.773	—	—	147	149	248	6	—	—	—	623	1.9	1.9	8.0
64-65—Philadelphia	60	—	1116	175	486	.360	—	—	—	54	76	.711	—	—	95	140	178	10	—	—	—	404	1.6	2.3	6.7
65-66—Philadelphia	78	—	1312	214	560	.382	—	—	—	66	98	.673	—	—	134	134	232	4	—	—	—	494	1.7	1.7	6.3
REG. SEASON TOTALS	687	—	13649	2212	5919	.374	—	—	—	1126	1592	.707	—	—	1722	1497	2069	54	—	—	—	5550	2.5	2.2	8.1
PLAYOFF TOTALS	56	—	1135	184	471	.391	—	—	—	80	115	.696	—	—	125	101	193	9	—	—	—	448	2.2	1.8	8.0

BIASATTI, HENRY ARCADO (**Hank**) b. January 14, 1922 Ht. 6-0 Wt. 180 College—Assumption (Ont.)

SEASON—TEAM	G	GS	MIN	FGM	FGA	PCT	3FGM	3FGA	PCT	FTM	FTA	PCT	O-RB	D-RB	TOT	AST	PF	DQ	STL	TO	BLK	PTS	RPG	APG	PPG
46-47—Toronto	6	—	—	2	5	.400	—	—	—	2	4	.500	—	—	—	0	3	—	—	—	—	6	—	0.0	1.0
REG. SEASON TOTALS	6	—	—	2	5	.400	—	—	—	2	4	.500	—	—	—	0	3	—	—	—	—	6	—	0.0	1.0

BIBBY, CHARLES HENRY (**Henry**) b. November 24, 1949 Ht. 6-1 Wt. 185 College—UCLA

SEASON—TEAM	G	GS	MIN	FGM	FGA	PCT	3FGM	3FGA	PCT	FTM	FTA	PCT	O-RB	D-RB	TOT	AST	PF	DQ	STL	TO	BLK	PTS	RPG	APG	PPG
72-73—New York	55	—	475	78	205	.380	—	—	—	73	86	.849	—	—	82	64	67	0	—	—	—	229	1.5	1.2	4.2
73-74—New York	66	—	986	210	465	.452	—	—	—	73	88	.830	48	85	133	91	123	0	65	—	2	493	2.0	1.4	7.5
74-75—N.Y.-N.O.	75	—	1400	270	619	.436	—	—	—	137	189	.725	47	90	137	181	157	0	54	—	3	677	1.8	2.4	9.0
75-76—New Orleans	79	—	1772	266	622	.428	—	—	—	200	251	.797	58	121	179	225	165	0	62	—	3	732	2.3	2.8	9.3
76-77—Philadelphia	81	—	2639	302	702	.430	—	—	—	221	282	.784	86	187	273	356	200	2	108	—	5	825	3.4	4.4	10.2
77-78—Philadelphia	82	—	2518	286	659	.434	—	—	—	171	219	.781	62	189	251	464	207	0	91	153	6	743	3.1	5.7	9.1
78-79—Philadelphia	82	—	2538	368	869	.423	—	—	—	266	335	.794	72	172	244	371	199	7	72	197	7	1002	3.0	4.5	12.2
79-80—Philadelphia	82	—	2035	251	626	.401	11	52	.212	226	286	.790	65	143	208	307	161	0	62	147	6	739	2.5	3.7	9.0
80-81—San Diego	73	—	1112	118	306	.386	32	95	.337	67	98	.684	25	49	74	200	85	0	47	76	2	335	1.0	2.7	4.6
REG. SEASON TOTALS	675	—	15475	2149	5073	.424	43	147	.293	1434	1834	.782	463	1036	1581	2259	1364	2	561	573	34	5775	2.3	3.3	8.6
PLAYOFF TOTALS	72	—	1743	211	533	.396	5	13	.385	139	181	.768	65	109	176	231	165	0	50	71	2	566	2.4	3.2	7.9

BIEDENBACH, EDWARD JOSEPH (**Ed**) b. August 12, 1945 Ht. 6-1 Wt. 175 College—North Carolina State

SEASON—TEAM	G	GS	MIN	FGM	FGA	PCT	3FGM	3FGA	PCT	FTM	FTA	PCT	O-RB	D-RB	TOT	AST	PF	DQ	STL	TO	BLK	PTS	RPG	APG	PPG
68-69—Phoenix	7	—	18	0	6	.000	—	—	—	4	6	.667	—	—	2	3	1	0	—	—	—	4	0.3	0.4	0.6
REG. SEASON TOTALS	7	—	18	0	6	.000	—	—	—	4	6	.667	—	—	2	3	1	0	—	—	—	4	0.3	0.4	0.6

BIELKE, DONALD P. (Don)   Ht. 6-7 Wt. 240 College—Valparaiso

SEASON—TEAM	G	GS	MIN	FGM	FGA	PCT	3FGM	3FGA	PCT	FTM	FTA	PCT	O-RB	D-RB	TOT	AST	PF	DQ	STL	TO	BLK	PTS	RPG	APG	PPG
55-56—Fort Wayne	7	—	38	5	9	.556	—	—	—	4	7	.571	—	—	9	1	9	0	—	—	—	14	1.3	0.1	2.0
REG. SEASON TOTALS	7	—	38	5	9	.556	—	—	—	4	7	.571	—	—	9	1	9	0	—	—	—	14	1.3	0.1	2.0

BIGELOW, ROBERT S. (Bob) b. December 26, 1953 Ht. 6-7 Wt. 215 College—Pennsylvania

SEASON—TEAM	G	GS	MIN	FGM	FGA	PCT	3FGM	3FGA	PCT	FTM	FTA	PCT	O-RB	D-RB	TOT	AST	PF	DQ	STL	TO	BLK	PTS	RPG	APG	PPG
75-76—Kansas City	31	—	163	16	47	.340	—	—	—	24	33	.727	9	20	29	9	18	0	4	—	1	56	0.9	0.3	1.8
76-77—Kansas City	29	—	162	35	70	.500	—	—	—	15	17	.882	8	19	27	8	17	0	3	—	1	85	0.9	0.3	2.9
77-78—K.C.-Boston	5	—	24	4	13	.308	—	—	—	0	0	—	3	6	9	0	3	0	0	0	0	8	1.8	0.0	1.6
78-79—San Diego	29	—	413	36	90	.400	—	—	—	13	21	.619	15	31	46	25	37	0	12	18	2	85	1.6	0.9	2.9
REG. SEASON TOTALS	94	—	762	91	220	.414	—	—	—	52	71	.732	35	76	111	42	75	0	19	18	4	234	1.2	0.4	2.5

BILLINGY, LIONEL b. 1952 Ht. 6-9 Wt. 215 College—Duquesne

SEASON—TEAM	G	GS	MIN	FGM	FGA	PCT	3FGM	3FGA	PCT	FTM	FTA	PCT	O-RB	D-RB	TOT	AST	PF	DQ	STL	TO	BLK	PTS	RPG	APG	PPG
74-75—Virginia (A)	46	—	1022	150	351	.427	0	2	.000	93	143	.650	107	173	280	49	112	—	40	122	10	393	6.1	1.1	8.5
REG. ABA TOTALS	46	—	1022	150	351	.427	0	2	.000	93	143	.650	107	173	280	49	112	—	40	122	10	393	6.1	1.1	8.5

BING, DAVID (Dave) b. November 24, 1943 Ht. 6-3 Wt. 180 College—Syracuse

SEASON—TEAM	G	GS	MIN	FGM	FGA	PCT	3FGM	3FGA	PCT	FTM	FTA	PCT	O-RB	D-RB	TOT	AST	PF	DQ	STL	TO	BLK	PTS	RPG	APG	PPG
66-67—Detroit	80	—	2762	664	1522	.436	—	—	—	273	370	.738	—	—	359	330	217	2	—	—	—	1601	4.5	4.1	20.0
67-68—Detroit	79	—	3209	835	1893	.441	—	—	—	472	668	.707	—	—	373	509	254	2	—	—	—	2142	4.7	6.4	27.1
68-69—Detroit	77	—	3039	678	1594	.425	—	—	—	444	623	.713	—	—	382	546	256	3	—	—	—	1800	5.0	7.1	23.4
69-70—Detroit	70	—	2334	575	1295	.444	—	—	—	454	580	.783	—	—	299	418	196	0	—	—	—	1604	4.3	6.0	22.9
70-71—Detroit	82	—	3065	799	1710	.467	—	—	—	615	772	.797	—	—	364	408	228	4	—	—	—	2213	4.4	5.0	27.0
71-72—Detroit	45	—	1936	369	891	.414	—	—	—	278	354	.785	—	—	186	317	138	3	—	—	—	1016	4.1	7.0	22.6
72-73—Detroit	82	—	3361	692	1545	.448	—	—	—	456	560	.814	—	—	298	637	229	1	—	—	—	1840	3.6	7.8	22.4
73-74—Detroit	81	—	3124	582	1336	.436	—	—	—	356	438	.813	108	173	281	555	216	1	109	—	17	1520	3.5	6.9	18.8
74-75—Detroit	79	—	3222	578	1333	.434	—	—	—	343	424	.809	86	200	286	610	222	3	116	—	26	1499	3.6	7.7	19.0
75-76—Washington	82	—	2945	497	1113	.447	—	—	—	332	422	.787	94	143	237	492	262	0	118	—	23	1326	2.9	6.0	16.2
76-77—Washington	64	—	1516	271	597	.454	—	—	—	136	176	.773	54	89	143	275	150	1	61	—	5	678	2.2	4.3	10.6
77-78—Boston	80	—	2256	422	940	.449	—	—	—	244	296	.824	76	136	212	300	247	2	79	216	18	1088	2.7	3.8	13.6
REG. SEASON TOTALS	901	—	32769	6962	15769	.441	—	—	—	4403	5683	.775	418	741	3420	5397	2615	22	483	216	89	18327	3.8	6.0	20.3
PLAYOFF TOTALS	31	—	964	191	452	.423	—	—	—	95	127	.748	18	43	85	133	76	0	15	—	4	477	2.7	4.3	15.4
ALL-STAR TOTALS	7	—	125	16	43	.372	—	—	—	9	9	1.000	2	7	16	16	7	0	0	—	0	41	2.3	2.3	5.9

BINION, JOE b. March 26, 1961 Ht. 6-8 Wt. 235 College—North Carolina A&T

SEASON—TEAM	G	GS	MIN	FGM	FGA	PCT	3FGM	3FGA	PCT	FTM	FTA	PCT	O-RB	D-RB	TOT	AST	PF	DQ	STL	TO	BLK	PTS	RPG	APG	PPG
86-87—Portland	11	0	51	4	10	.400	0	0	—	6	10	.600	8	10	18	1	5	0	2	3	2	14	1.6	0.1	1.3
REG. SEASON TOTALS	11	0	51	4	10	.400	0	0	—	6	10	.600	8	10	18	1	5	0	2	3	2	14	1.6	0.1	1.3

BIRD, JERRY LEE b. February 2, 1935 Ht. 6-6 Wt. 215 College—Kentucky

SEASON—TEAM	G	GS	MIN	FGM	FGA	PCT	3FGM	3FGA	PCT	FTM	FTA	PCT	O-RB	D-RB	TOT	AST	PF	DQ	STL	TO	BLK	PTS	RPG	APG	PPG
58-59—New York	11	—	45	12	32	.375	—	—	—	1	1	1.000	—	—	12	4	7	0	—	—	—	25	1.1	0.4	2.3
REG. SEASON TOTALS	11	—	45	12	32	.375	—	—	—	1	1	1.000	—	—	12	4	7	0	—	—	—	25	1.1	0.4	2.3

BIRD, LARRY JOE b. December 7, 1956 Ht. 6-9 Wt. 220 College—Indiana/Northwood Institute/Indiana State

SEASON—TEAM	G	GS	MIN	FGM	FGA	PCT	3FGM	3FGA	PCT	FTM	FTA	PCT	O-RB	D-RB	TOT	AST	PF	DQ	STL	TO	BLK	PTS	RPG	APG	PPG
79-80—Boston	82	—	2955	693	1463	.474	58	143	.406	301	360	.836	216	636	852	370	279	4	143	263	53	1745	10.4	4.5	21.3
80-81—Boston	82	—	3239	719	1503	.478	20	74	.270	283	328	.863	191	704	895	451	239	2	161	289	63	1741	10.9	5.5	21.2
81-82—Boston	77	58	2923	711	1414	.503	11	52	.212	328	380	.863	200	637	837	447	244	0	143	254	66	1761	10.9	5.8	22.9
82-83—Boston	79	79	2982	747	1481	.504	22	77	.286	351	418	.840	193	677	870	458	197	0	148	240	71	1867	11.0	5.8	23.6
83-84—Boston	79	77	3028	758	1542	.492	18	73	.247	374	421	.888	181	615	796	520	197	0	144	237	69	1908	10.1	6.6	24.2
84-85—Boston	80	77	3161	918	1760	.522	56	131	.427	403	457	.882	164	678	842	531	208	0	129	248	98	2295	10.5	6.6	28.7
85-86—Boston	82	81	3113	796	1606	.496	82	194	.423	441	492	.896	190	615	805	557	182	0	166	266	51	2115	9.8	6.8	25.8
86-87—Boston	74	73	3005	786	1497	.525	90	225	.400	414	455	.910	124	558	682	566	185	3	135	240	70	2076	9.2	7.6	28.1
87-88—Boston	76	75	2965	881	1672	.527	98	237	.414	415	453	.916	108	595	703	467	157	0	125	213	57	2275	9.3	6.1	29.9
88-89—Boston	6	6	189	49	104	.471	0	0	—	18	19	.947	1	36	37	29	18	0	6	11	5	116	6.2	4.8	19.3
89-90—Boston	75	75	2944	718	1517	.473	65	195	.333	319	343	.930	90	622	712	562	173	2	106	243	61	1820	9.5	7.5	24.3
90-91—Boston	60	60	2277	462	1017	.454	77	198	.389	163	183	.891	53	456	509	431	118	0	108	187	58	1164	8.5	7.2	19.4
91-92—Boston	45	45	1662	353	758	.466	52	128	.406	150	162	.926	46	388	434	306	82	0	42	125	33	908	9.6	6.8	20.2
REG. SEASON TOTALS	897	706	34443	8591	17334	.496	649	1727	.376	3960	4471	.886	1757	7217	8974	5695	2279	11	1556	2816	755	21791	10.0	6.3	24.3
PLAYOFF TOTALS	164	136	6886	1458	3090	.472	80	249	.321	901	1012	.890	360	1323	1683	1062	466	1	296	506	145	3897	10.3	6.5	23.8
ALL-STAR TOTALS	10	9	287	52	123	.423	3	13	.231	27	32	.844	19	60	79	41	28	0	23	31	3	134	7.9	4.1	13.4

BIRDSONG, OTIS LEE b. December 9, 1955 Ht. 6-4 Wt. 195 College—Houston

SEASON—TEAM	G	GS	MIN	FGM	FGA	PCT	3FGM	3FGA	PCT	FTM	FTA	PCT	O-RB	D-RB	TOT	AST	PF	DQ	STL	TO	BLK	PTS	RPG	APG	PPG
77-78—Kansas City	73	—	1878	470	955	.492	—	—	—	216	310	.697	70	105	175	174	179	1	74	145	12	1156	2.4	2.4	15.8
78-79—Kansas City	82	—	2839	741	1456	.509	—	—	—	296	408	.725	176	178	354	281	255	2	125	200	17	1778	4.3	3.4	21.7
79-80—Kansas City	82	—	2885	781	1546	.505	10	36	.278	286	412	.694	170	161	331	202	226	2	136	179	22	1858	4.0	2.5	22.7
80-81—Kansas City	71	—	2593	710	1306	.544	10	35	.286	317	455	.697	119	139	258	233	172	2	93	173	18	1747	3.6	3.3	24.6
81-82—New Jersey	37	22	1025	225	480	.469	0	10	.000	74	127	.583	30	67	97	124	74	0	30	64	5	524	2.6	3.4	14.2
82-83—New Jersey	62	54	1885	426	834	.511	2	6	.333	82	145	.566	53	97	150	239	155	0	85	114	16	936	2.4	3.9	15.1
83-84—New Jersey	69	57	2168	583	1147	.508	5	20	.250	194	319	.608	74	96	170	266	180	2	86	170	17	1365	2.5	3.9	19.8
84-85—New Jersey	56	45	1842	495	968	.511	4	21	.190	161	259	.622	60	88	148	232	145	1	84	117	7	1155	2.6	4.1	20.6
85-86—New Jersey	77	74	2395	542	1056	.513	8	22	.364	122	210	.581	88	114	202	261	228	8	85	179	17	1214	2.6	3.4	15.8
86-87—New Jersey	7	6	127	19	42	.452	0	1	.000	6	9	.667	3	4	7	17	16	0	3	9	0	44	1.0	2.4	6.3
87-88—New Jersey	67	59	1882	337	736	.458	9	25	.360	47	92	.511	73	94	167	222	143	2	54	129	11	730	2.5	3.3	10.9
88-89—Boston	13	0	108	18	36	.500	1	3	.333	0	2	.000	4	9	13	9	10	0	3	12	1	37	1.0	0.7	2.8
REG. SEASON TOTALS	696	317	21627	5347	10562	.506	49	179	.274	1801	2748	.655	920	1152	2072	2260	1783	20	858	1491	143	12544	3.0	3.2	18.0
PLAYOFF TOTALS	35	15	1090	232	483	.480	1	11	.091	81	139	.583	40	64	104	104	89	1	56	71	5	546	3.0	3.0	15.6
ALL-STAR TOTALS	4	0	52	6	16	.375	0	0	—	2	4	.500	4	2	6	2	3	0	3	3	0	14	1.5	0.5	3.5

BISHOP, GALE b. June 4, 1922 Ht. 6-3 Wt. 195 College—Washington State

SEASON—TEAM	G	GS	MIN	FGM	FGA	PCT	3FGM	3FGA	PCT	FTM	FTA	PCT	O-RB	D-RB	TOT	AST	PF	DQ	STL	TO	BLK	PTS	RPG	APG	PPG
48-49—Philadelphia	56	—	—	170	523	.325	—	—	—	127	195	.651	—	—	—	92	137	—	—	—	—	467	—	1.6	8.3
REG. SEASON TOTALS	56	—	—	170	523	.325	—	—	—	127	195	.651	—	—	—	92	137	—	—	—	—	467	—	1.6	8.3
PLAYOFF TOTALS	2	—	—	7	26	.269	—	—	—	4	8	.500	—	—	—	2	3	—	—	—	—	18	—	1.0	9.0

BLAB, UWE KONSTANTINE b. March 26, 1962 Ht. 7-1 Wt. 255 College—Indiana

SEASON—TEAM	G	GS	MIN	FGM	FGA	PCT	3FGM	3FGA	PCT	FTM	FTA	PCT	O-RB	D-RB	TOT	AST	PF	DQ	STL	TO	BLK	PTS	RPG	APG	PPG
85-86—Dallas	48	0	409	44	94	.468	0	0	—	36	67	.537	25	66	91	17	65	0	3	28	12	124	1.9	0.4	2.6
86-87—Dallas	30	0	160	20	51	.392	0	0	—	13	28	.464	11	25	36	13	33	0	4	15	9	53	1.2	0.4	1.8
87-88—Dallas	73	1	658	58	132	.439	0	0	—	46	65	.708	52	82	134	35	108	1	8	49	29	162	1.8	0.5	2.2
88-89—Dallas	37	0	208	24	52	.462	0	0	—	20	25	.800	11	33	44	12	36	0	3	14	13	68	1.2	0.3	1.8
89-90—G.S.-S.A.	47	33	531	39	98	.398	0	0	—	20	37	.541	29	79	108	25	102	0	1	35	22	98	2.3	0.5	2.1
REG. SEASON TOTALS	235	34	1966	185	427	.433	0	0	—	135	222	.608	128	285	413	102	344	1	19	141	85	505	1.8	0.4	2.1
PLAYOFF TOTALS	7	0	29	3	7	.429	0	0	—	6	12	.500	2	5	7	1	6	0	1	3	1	12	1.0	0.1	1.7

BLACK, CHARLES BRADFORD JR. (**Charlie, Hawk**) b. June 15, 1921 d. December 22, 1992 Ht. 6-5 Wt. 200 College—Kansas

SEASON—TEAM	G	GS	MIN	FGM	FGA	PCT	3FGM	3FGA	PCT	FTM	FTA	PCT	O-RB	D-RB	TOT	AST	PF	DQ	STL	TO	BLK	PTS	RPG	APG	PPG
47-48—Anderson (N)	58	—	—	148			—	—		149	249	.598	—	—	—	—	196	—	—	—	—	445	—	—	7.7
48-49—Ind.-Ft. Wayne	58	—	—	203	691	.294	—	—	—	161	291	.553	—	—	—	140	247	—	—	—	—	567	—	2.4	9.8
49-50—Ft. Wayne-And.	65	—	—	226	813	.278	—	—	—	209	321	.651	—	—	—	163	273	—	—	—	—	661	—	2.5	10.2
51-52—Milwaukee	13	—	117	6	31	.194	—	—	—	5	12	.417	—	—	31	9	31	2	—	—	—	17	2.4	0.7	1.3
REG. NBA TOTALS	136	—	117	435	1535	.283	—	—	—	375	624	.601	—	—	31	312	551	2	—	—	—	1245	2.4	2.3	9.2
REG. NBL TOTALS	58	—	—	148	—	—	—	—	—	149	249	.598	—	—	—	—	196	—	—	—	—	445	—	—	7.7
NBA PLAYOFF TOTALS	8	—	0	18	61	.295	—	—	—	21	29	.724	—	—	—	17	38	4	—	—	—	57	—	2.1	7.1
NBL PLAYOFF TOTALS	6	—	—	28	—	—	—	—	—	10	22	.455	—	—	—	—	18	—	—	—	—	66	—	—	11.0

BLACK, NORMAN AUGUSTUS b. November 12, 1957 Ht. 6-5 Wt. 190 College—St. Joseph (Pa.)

SEASON—TEAM	G	GS	MIN	FGM	FGA	PCT	3FGM	3FGA	PCT	FTM	FTA	PCT	O-RB	D-RB	TOT	AST	PF	DQ	STL	TO	BLK	PTS	RPG	APG	PPG
80-81—Detroit	3	—	28	3	10	.300	0	0	—	2	8	.250	0	2	2	2	2	0	1	1	0	8	0.7	0.7	2.7
REG. SEASON TOTALS	3	—	28	3	10	.300	0	0	—	2	8	.250	0	2	2	2	2	0	1	1	0	8	0.7	0.7	2.7

BLACK, THOMAS DONALD (**Tom**) b. July 9, 1941 Ht. 6-10½ Wt. 240 College—Wisconsin/South Dakota State

SEASON—TEAM	G	GS	MIN	FGM	FGA	PCT	3FGM	3FGA	PCT	FTM	FTA	PCT	O-RB	D-RB	TOT	AST	PF	DQ	STL	TO	BLK	PTS	RPG	APG	PPG
70-71—Seattle-Cin.	71	—	873	121	301	.402	—	—	—	57	88	.648	—	—	259	44	136	1	—	—	—	299	3.6	0.6	4.2
REG. SEASON TOTALS	71	—	873	121	301	.402	—	—	—	57	88	.648	—	—	259	44	136	1	—	—	—	299	3.6	0.6	4.2

BLACKMAN, ROLANDO ANTONIO (**Ro**) b. February 26, 1959 Ht. 6-6 Wt. 205 College—Kansas State

SEASON—TEAM	G	GS	MIN	FGM	FGA	PCT	3FGM	3FGA	PCT	FTM	FTA	PCT	O-RB	D-RB	TOT	AST	PF	DQ	STL	TO	BLK	PTS	RPG	APG	PPG
81-82—Dallas	82	16	1979	439	855	.513	1	4	.250	212	276	.768	97	157	254	105	122	0	46	113	30	1091	3.1	1.3	13.3
82-83—Dallas	75	62	2349	513	1042	.492	3	15	.200	297	381	.780	108	185	293	185	116	0	37	118	29	1326	3.9	2.5	17.7
83-84—Dallas	81	81	3025	721	1320	.546	1	11	.091	372	458	.812	124	249	373	288	127	0	56	169	37	1815	4.6	3.6	22.4
84-85—Dallas	81	80	2834	625	1230	.508	6	20	.300	342	413	.828	107	193	300	289	96	0	61	162	16	1598	3.7	3.6	19.7
85-86—Dallas	82	81	2787	677	1318	.514	4	29	.138	404	483	.836	88	203	291	271	138	0	79	189	25	1762	3.5	3.3	21.5
86-87—Dallas	80	80	2758	626	1264	.495	5	15	.333	419	474	.884	96	182	278	266	142	0	64	174	21	1676	3.5	3.3	21.0
87-88—Dallas	71	69	2580	497	1050	.473	0	5	.000	331	379	.873	82	164	246	262	112	0	64	144	18	1325	3.5	3.7	18.7
88-89—Dallas	78	78	2946	594	1249	.476	30	85	.353	316	370	.854	70	203	273	288	137	0	65	165	20	1534	3.5	3.7	19.7
89-90—Dallas	80	80	2934	626	1256	.498	13	43	.302	287	340	.844	88	192	280	289	128	0	77	174	21	1552	3.5	3.6	19.4
90-91—Dallas	80	80	2965	634	1316	.482	40	114	.351	282	326	.865	63	193	256	301	153	0	69	159	19	1590	3.2	3.8	19.9
91-92—Dallas	75	74	2527	535	1161	.461	65	169	.385	239	266	.898	78	161	239	204	134	0	50	153	22	1374	3.2	2.7	18.3
92-93—New York	60	33	1434	239	539	.443	31	73	.425	71	90	.789	23	79	102	157	129	1	22	65	10	580	1.7	2.6	9.7
93-94—New York	55	1	969	161	369	.436	30	84	.357	48	53	.906	23	70	93	76	100	0	25	44	6	400	1.7	1.4	7.3
REG. SEASON TOTALS	980	815	32087	6887	13969	.493	229	667	.343	3620	4309	.840	1047	2231	3278	2981	1634	1	715	1829	274	17623	3.3	3.0	18.0
PLAYOFF TOTALS	69	48	2137	434	897	.484	9	31	.290	233	268	.869	78	122	200	217	119	1	42	126	14	1110	2.9	3.1	16.1
ALL-STAR TOTALS	4	0	88	29	49	.592	0	0	—	13	16	.813	4	9	13	13	5	0	5	5	2	71	3.3	3.3	17.8

BLACKWELL, CORY b. March 27, 1963 Ht. 6-6 Wt. 210 College—Wisconsin

SEASON—TEAM	G	GS	MIN	FGM	FGA	PCT	3FGM	3FGA	PCT	FTM	FTA	PCT	O-RB	D-RB	TOT	AST	PF	DQ	STL	TO	BLK	PTS	RPG	APG	PPG
84-85—Seattle	60	0	551	87	237	.367	0	2	.000	28	55	.509	42	54	96	26	55	0	25	44	3	202	1.6	0.4	3.4
REG. SEASON TOTALS	60	0	551	87	237	.367	0	2	.000	28	55	.509	42	54	96	26	55	0	25	44	3	202	1.6	0.4	3.4

BLACKWELL, NATHANIEL (**Nate**) b. February 15, 1965 Ht. 6-4 Wt. 170 College—Temple

SEASON—TEAM	G	GS	MIN	FGM	FGA	PCT	3FGM	3FGA	PCT	FTM	FTA	PCT	O-RB	D-RB	TOT	AST	PF	DQ	STL	TO	BLK	PTS	RPG	APG	PPG
87-88—San Antonio	10	0	112	15	41	.366	2	11	.182	5	6	.833	2	4	6	18	16	0	3	8	0	37	0.6	1.8	3.7
REG. SEASON TOTALS	10	0	112	15	41	.366	2	11	.182	5	6	.833	2	4	6	18	16	0	3	8	0	37	0.6	1.8	3.7

BLACKWELL, ROBERT ALEXANDER (**Alex**) b. June 27, 1970 Ht. 6-6 Wt. 255 College—Monmouth

SEASON—TEAM	G	GS	MIN	FGM	FGA	PCT	3FGM	3FGA	PCT	FTM	FTA	PCT	O-RB	D-RB	TOT	AST	PF	DQ	STL	TO	BLK	PTS	RPG	APG	PPG
92-93—L.A. Lakers	27	0	109	14	42	.333	0	3	.000	6	8	.750	10	13	23	7	14	0	4	5	2	34	0.9	0.3	1.3
REG. SEASON TOTALS	27	0	109	14	42	.333	0	3	.000	6	8	.750	10	13	23	7	14	0	4	5	2	34	0.9	0.3	1.3

BLANEY, GEORGE R. b. November 12, 1939 Ht. 6-1 Wt. 175 College—Holy Cross

SEASON—TEAM	G	GS	MIN	FGM	FGA	PCT	3FGM	3FGA	PCT	FTM	FTA	PCT	O-RB	D-RB	TOT	AST	PF	DQ	STL	TO	BLK	PTS	RPG	APG	PPG
61-62—New York	36	—	363	54	142	.380	—	—	—	9	17	.529	—	—	36	45	34	0	—	—	—	117	1.0	1.3	3.3
REG. SEASON TOTALS	36	—	363	54	142	.380	—	—	—	9	17	.529	—	—	36	45	34	0	—	—	—	117	1.0	1.3	3.3

BLANKS, LANCE b. September 9, 1966 Ht. 6-4 Wt. 195 College—Virginia/Texas

SEASON—TEAM	G	GS	MIN	FGM	FGA	PCT	3FGM	3FGA	PCT	FTM	FTA	PCT	O-RB	D-RB	TOT	AST	PF	DQ	STL	TO	BLK	PTS	RPG	APG	PPG
90-91—Detroit	38	0	214	26	61	.426	2	16	.125	10	14	.714	4	16	20	26	35	0	9	18	2	64	0.5	0.7	1.7
91-92—Detroit	43	0	189	25	55	.455	6	16	.375	8	11	.727	9	13	22	19	26	0	14	14	1	64	0.5	0.4	1.5
92-93—Detroit-Minn.	61	2	642	65	150	.433	11	43	.256	20	32	.625	18	50	68	72	61	1	16	31	5	161	1.1	1.2	2.6
REG. SEASON TOTALS	142	2	1045	116	266	.436	19	75	.253	38	57	.667	31	79	110	117	122	1	39	63	8	289	0.8	0.8	2.0
PLAYOFF TOTALS	1	0	10	1	2	.500	0	0	—	0	0	—	0	1	1	3	2	0	3	1	0	2	1.0	3.0	2.0

BLANTON, RICKY WAYNE b. April 21, 1966 Ht. 6-7 Wt. 215 College—Louisiana State

SEASON—TEAM	G	GS	MIN	FGM	FGA	PCT	3FGM	3FGA	PCT	FTM	FTA	PCT	O-RB	D-RB	TOT	AST	PF	DQ	STL	TO	BLK	PTS	RPG	APG	PPG
92-93—Chicago	2	0	13	3	7	.429	0	0	—	0	0	—	2	1	3	1	1	0	2	1	0	6	1.5	0.5	3.0
REG. SEASON TOTALS	2	0	13	3	7	.429	0	0	—	0	0	—	2	1	3	1	1	0	2	1	0	6	1.5	0.5	3.0

BLAYLOCK, DARON OSHAY (**Mookie**) b. March 20, 1967 Ht. 6-1 Wt. 185 College—Midland/Oklahoma

SEASON—TEAM	G	GS	MIN	FGM	FGA	PCT	3FGM	3FGA	PCT	FTM	FTA	PCT	O-RB	D-RB	TOT	AST	PF	DQ	STL	TO	BLK	PTS	RPG	APG	PPG
89-90—New Jersey	50	17	1267	212	571	.371	18	80	.225	63	81	.778	42	98	140	210	110	0	82	111	14	505	2.8	4.2	10.1
90-91—New Jersey	72	70	2585	432	1039	.416	14	91	.154	139	176	.790	67	182	249	441	180	0	169	207	40	1017	3.5	6.1	14.1
91-92—New Jersey	72	67	2548	429	993	.432	12	54	.222	126	177	.712	101	168	269	492	182	1	170	152	40	996	3.7	6.8	13.8
92-93—Atlanta	80	78	2820	414	964	.429	118	315	.375	123	169	.728	89	191	280	671	156	0	203	187	23	1069	3.5	8.4	13.4
93-94—Atlanta	81	81	2915	444	1079	.411	114	341	.334	116	159	.730	117	307	424	789	144	0	212	196	44	1118	5.2	9.7	13.8
REG. SEASON TOTALS	355	313	12135	1931	4646	.416	276	881	.313	567	762	.744	416	946	1362	2603	772	1	836	853	161	4705	3.8	7.3	13.3
PLAYOFF TOTALS	18	18	662	74	221	.335	27	82	.329	33	40	.825	23	61	84	142	47	0	42	50	11	208	4.7	7.9	11.6
ALL-STAR TOTALS	1	0	16	2	5	.400	1	2	.500	0	0	—	0	1	1	2	3	0	2	1	0	5	1.0	2.0	5.0

BLEVINS, LEON GRAVETTE b. June 25, 1926   Ht. 6-2 Wt. 160 College—Phoenix JC/Arizona

SEASON—TEAM	G	GS	MIN	FGM	FGA	PCT	3FGM	3FGA	PCT	FTM	FTA	PCT	O-RB	D-RB	TOT	AST	PF	DQ	STL	TO	BLK	PTS	RPG	APG	PPG
50-51—Indianapolis	3	—	—	1	4	.250	—	—	—	0	1	.000	—	—	2	1	3	0	—	—	—	2	0.7	0.3	0.7
REG. SEASON TOTALS	3	—	—	1	4	.250	—	—	—	0	1	.000	—	—	2	1	3	0	—	—	—	2	0.7	0.3	0.7

BLOCK, JOHN WILLIAM JR. b. April 16, 1944   Ht. 6-9½ Wt. 210 College—USC

SEASON—TEAM	G	GS	MIN	FGM	FGA	PCT	3FGM	3FGA	PCT	FTM	FTA	PCT	O-RB	D-RB	TOT	AST	PF	DQ	STL	TO	BLK	PTS	RPG	APG	PPG
66-67—Los Angeles	22	—	118	20	52	.385	—	—	—	24	34	.706	—	—	45	5	20	0	—	—	—	64	2.0	0.2	2.9
67-68—San Diego	52	—	1805	366	865	.423	—	—	—	316	394	.802	—	—	571	71	189	3	—	—	—	1048	11.0	1.4	20.2
68-69—San Diego	78	—	2489	448	1061	.422	—	—	—	299	400	.748	—	—	703	141	249	0	—	—	—	1195	9.0	1.8	15.3
69-70—San Diego	82	—	2152	453	1025	.442	—	—	—	287	367	.782	—	—	609	137	275	2	—	—	—	1193	7.4	1.7	14.5
70-71—San Diego	73	—	1464	245	584	.420	—	—	—	212	270	.785	—	—	442	98	193	2	—	—	—	702	6.1	1.3	9.6
71-72—Milwaukee	79	—	1524	233	530	.440	—	—	—	206	275	.749	—	—	410	95	213	4	—	—	—	672	5.2	1.2	8.5
72-73—Phil.-K.C.-Omaha	73	—	2041	391	886	.441	—	—	—	300	378	.794	—	—	562	113	242	5	—	—	—	1082	7.7	1.5	14.8
73-74—Kansas City-Omaha	82	—	1777	275	634	.434	—	—	—	164	206	.796	129	260	389	94	229	2	68	—	35	714	4.7	1.1	8.7
74-75—N.O.-Chicago	54	—	939	159	346	.460	—	—	—	114	144	.792	69	163	232	51	121	0	42	—	32	432	4.3	0.9	8.0
75-76—Chicago	2	—	7	2	4	.500	—	—	—	0	2	.000	0	2	2	0	2	0	1	—	0	4	1.0	0.0	2.0
REG. SEASON TOTALS	597	—	14316	2592	5987	.433	—	—	—	1922	2470	.778	198	425	3965	805	1733	18	111	—	67	7106	6.6	1.3	11.9
PLAYOFF TOTALS	21	—	288	50	112	.446	—	—	—	30	39	.769	2	4	75	9	38	0	4	—	0	130	3.6	0.4	6.2
ALL-STAR TOTALS	1	—	5	2	4	.500	—	—	—	0	0	—	0	0	2	0	1	0	0	—	0	4	2.0	0.0	4.0

BLOOM, MEYER (Mike) b. January 14, 1915 d. 1993 Ht. 6-6 Wt. 190 College—Temple

SEASON—TEAM	G	GS	MIN	FGM	FGA	PCT	3FGM	3FGA	PCT	FTM	FTA	PCT	O-RB	D-RB	TOT	AST	PF	DQ	STL	TO	BLK	PTS	RPG	APG	PPG
47-48—Balt.-Boston	48	—	—	174	640	.272	—	—	—	160	229	.699	—	—	—	38	116	—	—	—	—	508	—	0.8	10.6
48-49—Minn.-Chicago	45	—	—	35	181	.193	—	—	—	56	74	.757	—	—	—	32	53	—	—	—	—	126	—	0.7	2.8
REG. SEASON TOTALS	93	—	—	209	821	.255	—	—	—	216	303	.713	—	—	—	70	169	—	—	—	—	634	—	0.8	6.8
PLAYOFF TOTALS	4	—	—	11	48	.229	—	—	—	16	21	.762	—	—	—	2	10	—	—	—	—	38	—	0.5	9.5

BLOUNT, CORIE KASOUN b. January 4, 1969   Ht. 6-9 Wt. 240 College—Rancho Santiago CC/Cincinnati

SEASON—TEAM	G	GS	MIN	FGM	FGA	PCT	3FGM	3FGA	PCT	FTM	FTA	PCT	O-RB	D-RB	TOT	AST	PF	DQ	STL	TO	BLK	PTS	RPG	APG	PPG
93-94—Chicago	67	8	690	76	174	.437	0	0	—	46	75	.613	76	118	194	56	93	0	19	52	33	198	2.9	0.8	3.0
REG. SEASON TOTALS	67	8	690	76	174	.437	0	0	—	46	75	.613	76	118	194	56	93	0	19	52	33	198	2.9	0.8	3.0

BLUME, BERNARD RAY (Ray) b. September 23, 1958   Ht. 6-4 Wt. 185 College—Oregon State

SEASON—TEAM	G	GS	MIN	FGM	FGA	PCT	3FGM	3FGA	PCT	FTM	FTA	PCT	O-RB	D-RB	TOT	AST	PF	DQ	STL	TO	BLK	PTS	RPG	APG	PPG
81-82—Chicago	49	2	546	102	222	.459	4	18	.222	18	28	.643	14	27	41	68	57	0	23	54	2	226	0.8	1.4	4.6
REG. SEASON TOTALS	49	2	546	102	222	.459	4	18	.222	18	28	.643	14	27	41	68	57	0	23	54	2	226	0.8	1.4	4.6

BOBB, NELSON b. February 25, 1924   Ht. 6-0 Wt. 170 College—Temple

SEASON—TEAM	G	GS	MIN	FGM	FGA	PCT	3FGM	3FGA	PCT	FTM	FTA	PCT	O-RB	D-RB	TOT	AST	PF	DQ	STL	TO	BLK	PTS	RPG	APG	PPG
49-50—Philadelphia	57	—	—	80	248	.323	—	—	—	82	131	.626	—	—	—	46	97	—	—	—	—	242	—	0.8	4.2
50-51—Philadelphia	53	—	—	52	158	.329	—	—	—	44	79	.557	—	—	101	82	83	1	—	—	—	148	1.9	1.5	2.8
51-52—Philadelphia	62	—	1182	110	306	.359	—	—	—	99	167	.593	—	—	147	168	182	9	—	—	—	319	2.4	2.7	5.1
52-53—Philadelphia	55	—	1286	119	318	.374	—	—	—	105	162	.648	—	—	157	192	161	7	—	—	—	343	2.9	3.5	6.2
REG. SEASON TOTALS	227	—	2468	361	1030	.350	—	—	—	330	539	.612	—	—	405	488	523	17	—	—	—	1052	2.4	2.1	4.6
PLAYOFF TOTALS	6	—	29	2	6	.333	—	—	—	2	5	.400	—	—	2	4	9	0	—	—	—	6	0.5	0.7	1.0

BOCKHORN, ARLEN DALE (Bucky) b. July 8, 1933   Ht. 6-4 Wt. 200 College—Dayton

SEASON—TEAM	G	GS	MIN	FGM	FGA	PCT	3FGM	3FGA	PCT	FTM	FTA	PCT	O-RB	D-RB	TOT	AST	PF	DQ	STL	TO	BLK	PTS	RPG	APG	PPG
58-59—Cincinnati	71	—	2251	294	771	.381	—	—	—	138	196	.704	—	—	460	206	215	6	—	—	—	726	6.5	2.9	10.2
59-60—Cincinnati	75	—	2103	323	812	.398	—	—	—	145	194	.747	—	—	382	256	249	8	—	—	—	791	5.1	3.4	10.5
60-61—Cincinnati	79	—	2669	420	1059	.397	—	—	—	152	208	.731	—	—	434	338	282	9	—	—	—	992	5.5	4.3	12.6
61-62—Cincinnati	80	—	3062	531	1234	.430	—	—	—	198	251	.789	—	—	376	366	280	5	—	—	—	1260	4.7	4.6	15.8
62-63—Cincinnati	80	—	2612	375	954	.393	—	—	—	183	242	.756	—	—	322	261	260	6	—	—	—	933	4.0	3.3	11.7
63-64—Cincinnati	70	—	1670	242	587	.412	—	—	—	96	126	.762	—	—	205	173	227	4	—	—	—	580	2.9	2.5	8.3
64-65—Cincinnati	19	—	424	60	157	.382	—	—	—	28	39	.718	—	—	55	45	52	1	—	—	—	148	2.9	2.4	7.8
REG. SEASON TOTALS	474	—	14791	2245	5574	.403	—	—	—	940	1256	.748	—	—	2234	1645	1565	39	—	—	—	5430	4.7	3.5	11.5
PLAYOFF TOTALS	26	—	865	124	305	.407	—	—	—	52	67	.776	—	—	103	98	95	2	—	—	—	300	4.0	3.8	11.5

BOERWINKLE, THOMAS F. (**Tom**) b. August 23, 1945 Ht. 7-0 Wt. 265 College—Tennessee

SEASON—TEAM	G	GS	MIN	FGM	FGA	PCT	3FGM	3FGA	PCT	FTM	FTA	PCT	O-RB	D-RB	TOT	AST	PF	DQ	STL	TO	BLK	PTS	RPG	APG	PPG
68-69—Chicago	80	—	2365	318	831	.383	—	—	—	145	222	.653	—	—	889	178	317	11	—	—	—	781	11.1	2.2	9.8
69-70—Chicago	81	—	2335	348	775	.449	—	—	—	150	226	.664	—	—	1016	229	255	4	—	—	—	846	12.5	2.8	10.4
70-71—Chicago	82	—	2370	357	736	.485	—	—	—	168	232	.724	—	—	1133	397	275	3	—	—	—	882	13.8	4.8	10.8
71-72—Chicago	80	—	2022	219	500	.438	—	—	—	118	180	.656	—	—	897	281	253	4	—	—	—	556	11.2	3.5	7.0
72-73—Chicago	8	—	176	9	24	.375	—	—	—	12	20	.600	—	—	54	40	22	0	—	—	—	30	6.8	5.0	3.8
73-74—Chicago	46	—	602	58	119	.487	—	—	—	42	60	.700	53	160	213	94	80	0	16	—	18	158	4.6	2.0	3.4
74-75—Chicago	80	—	1175	132	271	.487	—	—	—	73	95	.768	105	275	380	272	163	0	25	—	45	337	4.8	3.4	4.2
75-76—Chicago	74	—	2045	265	530	.500	—	—	—	118	177	.667	263	529	792	283	263	9	47	—	52	648	10.7	3.8	8.8
76-77—Chicago	82	—	1070	134	273	.491	—	—	—	34	63	.540	101	211	312	189	147	0	19	—	19	302	3.8	2.3	3.7
77-78—Chicago	22	—	227	23	50	.460	—	—	—	10	13	.769	14	45	59	44	36	0	3	26	4	56	2.7	2.0	2.5
REG. SEASON TOTALS	635	—	14387	1863	4109	.453	—	—	—	870	1288	.675	536	1220	5745	2007	1811	31	110	26	138	4596	9.0	3.2	7.2
PLAYOFF TOTALS	35	—	785	107	233	.459	—	—	—	36	48	.750	58	118	330	123	94	2	4	—	11	250	9.4	3.5	7.1

BOGUES, TYRONE CURTIS (**Muggsy**) b. January 9, 1965 Ht. 5-3 Wt. 140 College—Wake Forest

SEASON—TEAM	G	GS	MIN	FGM	FGA	PCT	3FGM	3FGA	PCT	FTM	FTA	PCT	O-RB	D-RB	TOT	AST	PF	DQ	STL	TO	BLK	PTS	RPG	APG	PPG
87-88—Washington	79	14	1628	166	426	.390	3	16	.188	58	74	.784	35	101	136	404	138	1	127	101	3	393	1.7	5.1	5.0
88-89—Charlotte	79	21	1755	178	418	.426	1	13	.077	66	88	.750	53	112	165	620	141	1	111	124	7	423	2.1	7.8	5.4
89-90—Charlotte	81	65	2743	326	664	.491	5	26	.192	106	134	.791	48	159	207	867	168	1	166	146	3	763	2.6	10.7	9.4
90-91—Charlotte	81	46	2299	241	524	.460	0	12	.000	86	108	.796	58	158	216	669	160	2	137	120	3	568	2.7	8.3	7.0
91-92—Charlotte	82	69	2790	317	671	.472	2	27	.074	94	120	.783	58	177	235	743	156	0	170	156	6	730	2.9	9.1	8.9
92-93—Charlotte	81	80	2833	331	730	.453	6	26	.231	140	168	.833	51	247	298	711	179	0	161	154	5	808	3.7	8.8	10.0
93-94—Charlotte	77	77	2746	354	751	.471	2	12	.167	125	155	.806	78	235	313	780	147	1	133	171	2	835	4.1	10.1	10.8
REG. SEASON TOTALS	560	372	16794	1913	4184	.457	19	132	.144	675	847	.797	381	1189	1570	4794	1089	6	1005	972	29	4520	2.8	8.6	8.1
PLAYOFF TOTALS	10	9	348	39	82	.476	0	2	.000	10	14	.714	6	30	36	72	21	0	24	18	0	88	3.6	7.2	8.8

BOL, MANUTE b. October 16, 1962 Ht. 7-7 Wt. 225 College—Bridgeport

SEASON—TEAM	G	GS	MIN	FGM	FGA	PCT	3FGM	3FGA	PCT	FTM	FTA	PCT	O-RB	D-RB	TOT	AST	PF	DQ	STL	TO	BLK	PTS	RPG	APG	PPG
85-86—Washington	80	60	2090	128	278	.460	0	1	.000	42	86	.488	123	354	477	23	255	5	28	65	397	298	6.0	0.3	3.7
86-87—Washington	82	12	1552	103	231	.446	0	1	.000	45	67	.672	84	278	362	11	189	1	20	61	302	251	4.4	0.1	3.1
87-88—Washington	77	4	1136	75	165	.455	0	1	.000	26	49	.531	72	203	275	13	160	0	11	35	208	176	3.6	0.2	2.3
88-89—Golden State	80	4	1769	127	344	.369	20	91	.220	40	66	.606	116	346	462	27	226	2	11	79	345	314	5.8	0.3	3.9
89-90—Golden State	75	20	1310	56	169	.331	9	48	.188	25	49	.510	33	243	276	36	194	3	13	51	238	146	3.7	0.5	1.9
90-91—Philadelphia	82	6	1522	65	164	.396	1	14	.071	24	41	.585	66	284	350	20	184	0	16	63	247	155	4.3	0.2	1.9
91-92—Philadelphia	71	2	1267	49	128	.383	0	9	.000	12	26	.462	54	168	222	22	139	1	11	41	205	110	3.1	0.3	1.5
92-93—Philadelphia	58	23	855	52	127	.409	10	32	.313	12	19	.632	44	149	193	18	87	0	14	50	119	126	3.3	0.3	2.2
93-94—Miami-Wash.-Phil.	14	0	116	4	19	.211	0	3	.000	0	0	—	3	15	18	1	13	0	2	5	16	8	1.3	0.1	0.6
REG. SEASON TOTALS	619	131	11617	659	1625	.406	40	200	.200	226	403	.561	595	2040	2635	171	1447	12	126	450	2077	1584	4.3	0.3	2.6
PLAYOFF TOTALS	29	5	496	34	88	.386	2	23	.087	12	27	.444	37	72	109	3	61	0	6	13	77	82	3.8	0.1	2.8

BOLGER, WILLIAM J. (**Bill**) b. August 21, 1931 Ht. 6-5 Wt. 205 College—Georgetown

SEASON—TEAM	G	GS	MIN	FGM	FGA	PCT	3FGM	3FGA	PCT	FTM	FTA	PCT	O-RB	D-RB	TOT	AST	PF	DQ	STL	TO	BLK	PTS	RPG	APG	PPG
53-54—Baltimore	20	—	202	24	59	.407	—	—	—	8	13	.615	—	—	36	11	27	0	—	—	—	56	1.8	0.6	2.8
REG. SEASON TOTALS	20	—	202	24	59	.407	—	—	—	8	13	.615	—	—	36	11	27	0	—	—	—	56	1.8	0.6	2.8

BOLSTORFF, F. DOUGLAS (**Doug**) b. October 29, 1931 Ht. 6-4 Wt. 195 College—Minnesota

SEASON—TEAM	G	GS	MIN	FGM	FGA	PCT	3FGM	3FGA	PCT	FTM	FTA	PCT	O-RB	D-RB	TOT	AST	PF	DQ	STL	TO	BLK	PTS	RPG	APG	PPG
57-58—Detroit	3	—	21	2	5	.400	—	—	—	0	0	—	—	—	0	0	1	0	—	—	—	4	0.0	0.0	1.3
REG. SEASON TOTALS	3	—	21	2	5	.400	—	—	—	0	0	—	—	—	0	0	1	0	—	—	—	4	0.0	0.0	1.3

BOND, PHILLIP DAMONE (**Phil**) b. July 27, 1954 Ht. 6-2 Wt. 175 College—Louisville

SEASON—TEAM	G	GS	MIN	FGM	FGA	PCT	3FGM	3FGA	PCT	FTM	FTA	PCT	O-RB	D-RB	TOT	AST	PF	DQ	STL	TO	BLK	PTS	RPG	APG	PPG
77-78—Houston	7	—	21	2	6	.333	—	—	—	0	0	—	1	3	4	2	1	0	1	2	0	4	0.6	0.3	0.6
REG. SEASON TOTALS	7	—	21	2	6	.333	—	—	—	0	0	—	1	3	4	2	1	0	1	2	0	4	0.6	0.3	0.6

BOND, WALTER b. February 1, 1969 Ht. 6-5 Wt. 200 College—Minnesota

SEASON—TEAM	G	GS	MIN	FGM	FGA	PCT	3FGM	3FGA	PCT	FTM	FTA	PCT	O-RB	D-RB	TOT	AST	PF	DQ	STL	TO	BLK	PTS	RPG	APG	PPG
92-93—Dallas	74	38	1578	227	565	.402	7	42	.167	129	167	.772	52	144	196	122	223	3	75	112	18	590	2.6	1.6	8.0
93-94—Utah	56	4	559	63	156	.404	19	54	.352	31	40	.775	20	41	61	31	90	1	16	17	12	176	1.1	0.6	3.1
REG. SEASON TOTALS	130	42	2137	290	721	.402	26	96	.271	160	207	.773	72	185	257	153	313	4	91	129	30	766	2.0	1.2	5.9
PLAYOFF TOTALS	4	—	13	0	2	.000	0	1	.000	1	2	.500	0	1	1	—	4	0	1	0	0	1	0.3	0.0	0.3

BONHAM, RONALD D. (Ron) b. May 31, 1942 Ht. 6-5 Wt. 195 College—Cincinnati

SEASON—TEAM	G	GS	MIN	FGM	FGA	PCT	3FGM	3FGA	PCT	FTM	FTA	PCT	O-RB	D-RB	TOT	AST	PF	DQ	STL	TO	BLK	PTS	RPG	APG	PPG
64-65—Boston	37	—	369	91	220	.414	—	—	—	92	112	.821	—	—	78	19	33	0	—	—	—	274	2.1	0.5	7.4
65-66—Boston	39	—	312	76	207	.367	—	—	—	52	61	.852	—	—	35	11	29	0	—	—	—	204	0.9	0.3	5.2
67-68—Indiana (A)	42	—	426	80	210	.381	0	2	.000	85	105	.810	—	—	57	14	36	0	—	32	—	245	1.4	0.3	5.8
REG. NBA TOTALS	76	—	681	167	427	.391	—	—	—	144	173	.832	—	—	113	30	62	0	—	—	—	478	1.5	0.4	6.3
REG. ABA TOTALS	42	—	426	80	210	.381	0	2	.000	85	105	.810	—	—	57	14	36	0	—	32	—	245	1.4	0.3	5.8
NBA PLAYOFF TOTALS	9	—	29	12	23	.522	—	—	—	7	14	.500	—	—	4	—	3	0	—	—	—	31	0.4	0.0	3.4
ABA PLAYOFF TOTALS	3	—	30	4	15	.267	0	0	—	5	6	.833	—	—	6	3	4	0	—	2	—	13	2.0	1.0	4.3

BONNER, ANTHONY b. June 8, 1968 Ht. 6-8 Wt. 225 College—St. Louis

SEASON—TEAM	G	GS	MIN	FGM	FGA	PCT	3FGM	3FGA	PCT	FTM	FTA	PCT	O-RB	D-RB	TOT	AST	PF	DQ	STL	TO	BLK	PTS	RPG	APG	PPG
90-91—Sacramento	34	6	750	103	230	.448	0	0	—	44	76	.579	59	102	161	49	62	0	39	41	5	250	4.7	1.4	7.4
91-92—Sacramento	79	18	2287	294	658	.447	1	4	.250	151	241	.627	192	293	485	125	194	0	94	133	26	740	6.1	1.6	9.4
92-93—Sacramento	70	35	1764	229	497	.461	0	7	.000	143	241	.593	188	267	455	96	183	1	86	105	17	601	6.5	1.4	8.6
93-94—New York	73	38	1402	162	288	.563	0	0	—	50	105	.476	150	194	344	88	175	3	76	89	13	374	4.7	1.2	5.1
REG. SEASON TOTALS	256	97	6203	788	1673	.471	1	11	.091	388	663	.585	589	856	1445	358	614	4	295	368	61	1965	5.6	1.4	7.7
PLAYOFF TOTALS	13	7	118	10	22	.455	0	0	—	7	13	.538	15	13	28	2	22	0	5	13	0	27	2.2	0.2	2.1

BON SALLE, GEORGE H. b. July 1, 1935 Ht. 6-8 Wt. 230 College—Illinois

SEASON—TEAM	G	GS	MIN	FGM	FGA	PCT	3FGM	3FGA	PCT	FTM	FTA	PCT	O-RB	D-RB	TOT	AST	PF	DQ	STL	TO	BLK	PTS	RPG	APG	PPG
61-62—Chicago	3	—	9	2	8	.250	—	—	—	0	0	—	—	—	2	0	0	0	—	—	—	4	0.7	0.0	1.3
REG. SEASON TOTALS	3	—	9	2	8	.250	—	—	—	0	0	—	—	—	2	0	0	0	—	—	—	4	0.7	0.0	1.3

BOOKER, HAROLD (Butch) b. July 20, 1945 Ht. 6-10 Wt. 230 College—Cheyney State

SEASON—TEAM	G	GS	MIN	FGM	FGA	PCT	3FGM	3FGA	PCT	FTM	FTA	PCT	O-RB	D-RB	TOT	AST	PF	DQ	STL	TO	BLK	PTS	RPG	APG	PPG
69-70—Miami (A)	12	—	221	30	61	.492	0	1	.000	10	18	.556	—	—	91	6	23	0	—	—	—	70	7.6	0.5	5.8
REG. ABA TOTALS	12	—	221	30	61	.492	0	1	.000	10	18	.556	—	—	91	6	23	0	—	—	—	70	7.6	0.5	5.8

BOONE, RONALD BRUCE (Ron) b. September 6, 1946 Ht. 6-2 Wt. 200 College—Iowa Western CC/Idaho State

SEASON—TEAM	G	GS	MIN	FGM	FGA	PCT	3FGM	3FGA	PCT	FTM	FTA	PCT	O-RB	D-RB	TOT	AST	PF	DQ	STL	TO	BLK	PTS	RPG	APG	PPG
68-69—Dallas (A)	78	—	2682	520	1197	.434	2	15	.133	436	537	.812	—	—	394	279	303	8	—	355	—	1478	5.1	3.6	18.9
69-70—Dallas (A)	84	—	2340	423	980	.432	17	55	.309	300	382	.785	—	—	366	272	265	5	—	—	—	1163	4.4	3.2	13.8
70-71—Texas-Utah (A)	86	—	2476	610	1395	.437	49	138	.355	278	357	.779	—	—	564	256	298	—	—	—	—	1547	6.6	3.0	18.0
71-72—Utah (A)	84	—	2040	404	962	.420	13	65	.200	271	341	.795	—	—	393	233	274	—	215	—	—	1092	4.7	2.8	13.0
72-73—Utah (A)	84	—	2585	566	1136	.498	10	40	.250	415	479	.866	173	252	425	353	308	0	—	276	—	1557	5.1	4.2	18.5
73-74—Utah (A)	84	—	3098	587	1188	.494	6	26	.231	300	343	.875	157	278	435	417	289	—	123	316	22	1480	5.2	5.0	17.6
74-75—Utah (A)	84	—	3414	872	1776	.491	10	33	.303	363	422	.860	141	265	406	372	265	—	126	335	34	2117	4.8	4.4	25.2
75-76—Utah-St. L. (A)	78	—	2961	713	1467	.486	16	43	.372	277	318	.871	115	204	319	387	243	—	154	276	15	1719	4.1	5.0	22.0
76-77—Kansas City	82	—	3021	747	1577	.474	—	—	—	324	384	.844	128	193	321	338	258	1	119	—	19	1818	3.9	4.1	22.2
77-78—Kansas City	82	—	2653	563	1271	.443	—	—	—	322	377	.854	112	157	269	311	233	3	105	303	11	1448	3.3	3.8	17.7
78-79—Los Angeles	82	—	1583	259	569	.455	—	—	—	90	104	.865	53	92	145	154	171	1	66	147	11	608	1.8	1.9	7.4
79-80—L.A.-Utah	81	—	2392	405	915	.443	19	50	.380	175	196	.893	54	173	227	309	232	3	97	197	3	1004	2.8	3.8	12.4
80-81—Utah	52	—	1146	160	371	.431	11	39	.282	75	94	.798	17	67	84	161	126	0	33	111	8	406	1.6	3.1	7.8
REG. NBA TOTALS	379	—	10795	2134	4703	.454	30	89	.337	986	1155	.854	364	682	1046	1273	1020	8	420	758	52	5284	2.8	3.4	13.9
REG. ABA TOTALS	662	—	21596	4695	10101	.465	123	415	.296	2640	3179	.830	586	999	3302	2569	2245	13	403	1773	71	12153	5.0	3.9	18.4
NBA PLAYOFF TOTALS	8	—	226	37	77	.481	0	0	—	20	21	.952	7	8	15	14	28	0	9	14	0	94	1.9	1.8	11.8
ABA PLAYOFF TOTALS	76	—	2493	506	1094	.463	13	54	.241	236	270	.874	57	75	358	371	243	1	44	157	10	1261	4.7	4.9	16.6
ABA ALL-STAR TOTALS	4	—	67	18	36	.500	1	2	.500	4	5	.800	3	4	10	9	6	0	2	3	2	41	2.5	2.3	10.3

BOOZER, ROBERT LEWIS (Bob, Bullet Bob) b. April 26, 1937 Ht. 6-8 Wt. 220 College—Kansas State

SEASON—TEAM	G	GS	MIN	FGM	FGA	PCT	3FGM	3FGA	PCT	FTM	FTA	PCT	O-RB	D-RB	TOT	AST	PF	DQ	STL	TO	BLK	PTS	RPG	APG	PPG
60-61—Cincinnati	79	—	1573	250	603	.415	—	—	—	166	247	.672	—	—	488	109	193	1	—	—	—	666	6.2	1.4	8.4
61-62—Cincinnati	79	—	2488	410	936	.438	—	—	—	263	372	.707	—	—	804	130	275	3	—	—	—	1083	10.2	1.6	13.7
62-63—Cincinnati	79	—	2488	440	992	.444	—	—	—	252	353	.714	—	—	878	102	299	8	—	—	—	1132	11.1	1.3	14.3
63-64—Cin.-N.Y.	81	—	2379	468	1096	.427	—	—	—	272	376	.723	—	—	596	96	231	1	—	—	—	1208	7.4	1.2	14.9
64-65—New York	80	—	2139	424	963	.440	—	—	—	288	375	.768	—	—	604	108	183	0	—	—	—	1136	7.6	1.4	14.2
65-66—Los Angeles	78	—	1847	365	754	.484	—	—	—	225	289	.779	—	—	548	87	196	0	—	—	—	955	7.0	1.1	12.2
66-67—Chicago	80	—	2451	538	1104	.487	—	—	—	360	461	.781	—	—	679	90	212	0	—	—	—	1436	8.5	1.1	18.0
67-68—Chicago	77	—	2988	622	1265	.492	—	—	—	411	535	.768	—	—	756	121	229	1	—	—	—	1655	9.8	1.6	21.5
68-69—Chicago	79	—	2872	661	1375	.481	—	—	—	394	489	.806	—	—	614	156	218	2	—	—	—	1716	7.8	2.0	21.7
69-70—Seattle	82	—	2549	493	1005	.491	—	—	—	263	320	.822	—	—	717	110	237	2	—	—	—	1249	8.7	1.3	15.2
70-71—Milwaukee	80	—	1775	290	645	.450	—	—	—	148	181	.818	—	—	435	128	216	0	—	—	—	728	5.4	1.6	9.1
REG. SEASON TOTALS	874	—	25549	4961	10738	.462	—	—	—	3042	3998	.761	—	—	7119	1237	2489	18	—	—	—	12964	8.1	1.4	14.8
PLAYOFF TOTALS	48	—	1283	213	456	.467	—	—	—	130	176	.739	—	—	341	58	136	0	—	—	—	556	7.1	1.2	11.6
ALL-STAR TOTALS	1	—	19	2	5	.400	—	—	—	0	0	—	—	—	5	0	2	0	—	—	—	4	5.0	0.0	4.0

BORNHEIMER, JACOB (Jake) b. June 29, 1927 d. September 10, 1986 Ht. 6-5 Wt. 205 College—Muhlenberg

SEASON—TEAM	G	GS	MIN	FGM	FGA	PCT	3FGM	3FGA	PCT	FTM	FTA	PCT	O-RB	D-RB	TOT	AST	PF	DQ	STL	TO	BLK	PTS	RPG	APG	PPG
48-49—Philadelphia	15	—		34	109	.312	—	—	—	20	29	.690	—	—		13	47	—	—	—	—	88	—	0.9	5.9
49-50—Philadelphia	60	—		88	305	.289	—	—	—	78	117	.667	—	—		40	111	—	—	—	—	254	—	0.7	4.2
REG. SEASON TOTALS	75	—	—	122	414	.295	—	—	—	98	146	.671	—	—	—	53	158	—	—	—	—	342	—	0.7	4.6
PLAYOFF TOTALS	4	—	—	8	20	.400	—	—	—	6	9	.667	—	—	—	2	13	1	—	—	—	22	—	0.5	5.5

BORSAVAGE, COSTIC F. (Ike) b. July 25, 1924 Ht. 6-8 Wt. 220 College—Temple

SEASON—TEAM	G	GS	MIN	FGM	FGA	PCT	3FGM	3FGA	PCT	FTM	FTA	PCT	O-RB	D-RB	TOT	AST	PF	DQ	STL	TO	BLK	PTS	RPG	APG	PPG
50-51—Philadelphia	24	—	—	26	74	.351	—	—	—	12	18	.667	—	—	24	4	34	1	—	—	—	64	1.0	0.2	2.7
REG. SEASON TOTALS	24	—	—	26	74	.351	—	—	—	12	18	.667	—	—	24	4	34	1	—	—	—	64	1.0	0.2	2.7

BORYLA, VINCENT J. (Moose) b. March 11, 1927 Ht. 6-4½ Wt. 210 College—Notre Dame/Denver/Navy

SEASON—TEAM	G	GS	MIN	FGM	FGA	PCT	3FGM	3FGA	PCT	FTM	FTA	PCT	O-RB	D-RB	TOT	AST	PF	DQ	STL	TO	BLK	PTS	RPG	APG	PPG
49-50—New York	59	—	—	204	600	.340	—	—	—	204	267	.764	—	—	—	95	203	—	—	—	—	612	—	1.6	10.4
50-51—New York	66	—	—	352	867	.406	—	—	—	278	332	.837	—	—	249	182	244	6	—	—	—	982	3.8	2.8	14.9
51-52—New York	42	—	1440	202	522	.387	—	—	—	96	115	.835	—	—	219	90	121	2	—	—	—	500	5.2	2.1	11.9
52-53—New York	66	—	2200	254	686	.370	—	—	—	165	201	.821	—	—	233	166	226	8	—	—	—	673	3.5	2.5	10.2
53-54—New York	52	—	1522	175	525	.333	—	—	—	70	81	.864	—	—	130	77	128	0	—	—	—	420	2.5	1.5	8.1
REG. SEASON TOTALS	285	—	5162	1187	3200	.371	—	—	—	813	996	.816	—	—	831	610	922	16	—	—	—	3187	3.7	2.1	11.2
PLAYOFF TOTALS	33	—	463	158	375	.421	—	—	—	120	135	.889	—	—	89	65	114	5	—	—	—	436	3.2	2.0	13.2
ALL-STAR TOTALS	1	—	0	4	6	.667	—	—	—	1	1	1.000	—	—	2	2	3	0	—	—	—	9	2.0	2.0	9.0

BOSTIC, JAMES (Jim) b. January 28, 1953 Ht. 6-7 Wt. 225 College—New Mexico State

SEASON—TEAM	G	GS	MIN	FGM	FGA	PCT	3FGM	3FGA	PCT	FTM	FTA	PCT	O-RB	D-RB	TOT	AST	PF	DQ	STL	TO	BLK	PTS	RPG	APG	PPG
77-78—Detroit	4	—	48	12	22	.545	—	—	—	2	5	.400	8	8	16	3	5	0	0	3	0	26	4.0	0.8	6.5
REG. SEASON TOTALS	4	—	48	12	22	.545	—	—	—	2	5	.400	8	8	16	3	5	0	0	3	0	26	4.0	0.8	6.5

BOSTON, LAWRENCE D. b. May 18, 1956 Ht. 6-9 Wt. 225 College—Vincennes/Maryland

SEASON—TEAM	G	GS	MIN	FGM	FGA	PCT	3FGM	3FGA	PCT	FTM	FTA	PCT	O-RB	D-RB	TOT	AST	PF	DQ	STL	TO	BLK	PTS	RPG	APG	PPG
79-80—Washington	13	—	125	24	52	.462	0	0	—	8	13	.615	19	20	39	2	25	0	4	8	2	56	3.0	0.2	4.3
REG. SEASON TOTALS	13	—	125	24	52	.462	0	0	—	8	13	.615	19	20	39	2	25	0	4	8	2	56	3.0	0.2	4.3

BOSWELL, TOMMY G. (Tom) b. October 2, 1953 Ht. 6-8½ Wt. 220 College—South Carolina State/South Carolina

SEASON—TEAM	G	GS	MIN	FGM	FGA	PCT	3FGM	3FGA	PCT	FTM	FTA	PCT	O-RB	D-RB	TOT	AST	PF	DQ	STL	TO	BLK	PTS	RPG	APG	PPG
75-76—Boston	35	—	275	41	93	.441	—	—	—	14	24	.583	26	45	71	16	70	1	2	—	1	96	2.0	0.5	2.7
76-77—Boston	70	—	1083	175	340	.515	—	—	—	96	135	.711	111	195	306	85	237	9	27	—	8	446	4.4	1.2	6.4
77-78—Boston	65	—	1149	185	357	.518	—	—	—	93	123	.756	117	171	288	71	204	5	25	95	14	463	4.4	1.1	7.1
78-79—Denver	79	—	2201	321	603	.532	—	—	—	198	284	.697	248	290	538	242	263	4	50	185	51	840	6.8	3.1	10.6
79-80—Denver-Utah	79	—	2077	346	613	.564	5	10	.500	206	273	.755	146	296	442	161	270	9	29	181	37	903	5.6	2.0	11.4
83-84—Utah	38	0	261	28	52	.538	1	1	1.000	16	21	.762	28	36	64	16	58	1	9	13	0	73	1.7	0.4	1.9
REG. SEASON TOTALS	366	0	7046	1096	2058	.533	6	11	.545	623	860	.724	676	1033	1709	591	1102	29	142	474	111	2821	4.7	1.6	7.7
PLAYOFF TOTALS	20	0	259	33	59	.559	0	0	—	16	24	.667	26	28	54	25	42	0	4	10	6	82	2.7	1.3	4.1

BOVEN, DONALD E. (Don) b. March 6, 1925 Ht. 6-4 Wt. 210 College—Western Michigan

SEASON—TEAM	G	GS	MIN	FGM	FGA	PCT	3FGM	3FGA	PCT	FTM	FTA	PCT	O-RB	D-RB	TOT	AST	PF	DQ	STL	TO	BLK	PTS	RPG	APG	PPG
49-50—Waterloo	62	—	—	208	558	.373	—	—	—	240	349	.688	—	—	—	137	255	—	—	—	—	656	—	2.2	10.6
51-52—Milwaukee	66	—	1982	200	668	.299	—	—	—	256	350	.731	—	—	336	177	271	18	—	—	—	656	5.1	2.7	9.9
52-53—Milw.-Balt.-Ft. Wayne	67	—	1373	153	427	.358	—	—	—	145	209	.694	—	—	217	79	227	13	—	—	—	451	3.2	1.2	6.7
REG. SEASON TOTALS	195	—	3355	561	1653	.339	—	—	—	641	908	.706	—	—	553	393	753	31	—	—	—	1763	4.2	2.0	9.0
PLAYOFF TOTALS	8	—	111	7	28	.250	—	—	—	9	16	.563	—	—	16	2	22	0	—	—	—	23	2.0	0.3	2.9

BOWENS, TOMMIE LEE JR. (Tom) b. July 7, 1940 Ht. 6-7½ Wt. 220 College—Grambling State

SEASON—TEAM	G	GS	MIN	FGM	FGA	PCT	3FGM	3FGA	PCT	FTM	FTA	PCT	O-RB	D-RB	TOT	AST	PF	DQ	STL	TO	BLK	PTS	RPG	APG	PPG
67-68—Denver (A)	67	—	1287	177	453	.391	1	2	.500	55	90	.611	—	—	374	41	159	3	—	83	—	410	5.6	0.6	6.1
68-69—New York (A)	76	—	1550	186	453	.411	0	3	.000	83	128	.648	—	—	455	52	236	6	—	111	—	455	6.0	0.7	6.0
69-70—New Orleans (A)	68	—	753	110	251	.438	0	0	—	47	62	.758	—	—	178	41	147	2	—	—	—	267	2.6	0.6	3.9
REG. ABA TOTALS	211	—	3590	473	1157	.409	1	5	.200	185	280	.661	—	—	1007	134	542	11	—	194	—	1132	4.8	0.6	5.4
ABA PLAYOFF TOTALS	5	—	94	14	31	.452	0	1	.000	2	2	1.000	—	—	25	5	17	1	—	6	—	30	5.0	1.0	6.0

BOWIE, ANTHONY LEE b. November 9, 1963   Ht. 6-6 Wt. 190 College—Seminole JC/Oklahoma

SEASON—TEAM	G	GS	MIN	FGM	FGA	PCT	3FGM	3FGA	PCT	FTM	FTA	PCT	O-RB	D-RB	TOT	AST	PF	DQ	STL	TO	BLK	PTS	RPG	APG	PPG
88-89—San Antonio	18	5	438	72	144	.500	1	5	.200	10	15	.667	25	31	56	29	43	1	18	22	4	155	3.1	1.6	8.6
89-90—Houston	66	0	918	119	293	.406	6	21	.286	40	54	.741	36	82	118	96	80	0	42	59	5	284	1.8	1.5	4.3
91-92—Orlando	52	26	1721	312	633	.493	17	44	.386	117	136	.860	70	175	245	163	101	1	55	107	38	758	4.7	3.1	14.6
92-93—Orlando	77	45	1761	268	569	.471	15	48	.313	67	84	.798	36	158	194	175	131	0	54	84	14	618	2.5	2.3	8.0
93-94—Orlando	70	0	948	139	289	.481	1	18	.056	41	49	.837	29	91	120	102	81	0	32	58	12	320	1.7	1.5	4.6
REG. SEASON TOTALS	283	76	5786	910	1928	.472	40	136	.294	275	338	.814	196	537	733	565	436	2	201	330	73	2135	2.6	2.0	7.5
PLAYOFF TOTALS	4	0	17	0	2	.000	0	0	—	0	0	—	0	0	0	0	4	0	0	0	0	0	0.0	0.0	0.0

BOWIE, SAMUEL PAUL (**Sam**) b. March 17, 1961   Ht. 7-1 Wt. 260 College—Kentucky

SEASON—TEAM	G	GS	MIN	FGM	FGA	PCT	3FGM	3FGA	PCT	FTM	FTA	PCT	O-RB	D-RB	TOT	AST	PF	DQ	STL	TO	BLK	PTS	RPG	APG	PPG
84-85—Portland	76	62	2216	299	557	.537	0	0	—	160	225	.711	207	449	656	215	278	9	55	172	203	758	8.6	2.8	10.0
85-86—Portland	38	34	1132	167	345	.484	0	0	—	114	161	.708	93	234	327	99	142	4	21	88	96	448	8.6	2.6	11.8
86-87—Portland	5	5	163	30	66	.455	0	0	—	20	30	.667	14	19	33	9	19	0	1	15	10	80	6.6	1.8	16.0
88-89—Portland	20	0	412	69	153	.451	5	7	.714	28	49	.571	36	70	106	36	43	0	7	33	33	171	5.3	1.8	8.6
89-90—New Jersey	68	54	2207	347	834	.416	10	31	.323	294	379	.776	206	484	690	91	211	5	38	125	121	998	10.1	1.3	14.7
90-91—New Jersey	62	51	1916	314	723	.434	4	22	.182	169	231	.732	176	304	480	147	175	4	43	141	90	801	7.7	2.4	12.9
91-92—New Jersey	71	61	2179	421	947	.445	8	25	.320	212	280	.757	203	375	578	186	212	2	41	150	120	1062	8.1	2.6	15.0
92-93—New Jersey	79	65	2092	287	638	.450	2	6	.333	141	181	.779	158	398	556	127	226	3	32	120	128	717	7.0	1.6	9.1
93-94—L.A. Lakers	25	7	556	75	172	.436	1	4	.250	72	83	.867	27	104	131	47	65	0	4	43	28	223	5.2	1.9	8.9
REG. SEASON TOTALS	444	339	12873	2009	4435	.453	30	95	.316	1210	1619	.747	1120	2437	3557	957	1371	27	242	887	829	5258	8.0	2.2	11.8
PLAYOFF TOTALS	19	17	509	56	129	.434	2	4	.500	30	47	.638	36	91	127	35	72	2	13	24	32	144	6.7	1.8	7.6

BOWLING, ORBIE LEE (**Orb**) b. March 21, 1939   Ht. 6-10 Wt. 215 College—Tennessee

SEASON—TEAM	G	GS	MIN	FGM	FGA	PCT	3FGM	3FGA	PCT	FTM	FTA	PCT	O-RB	D-RB	TOT	AST	PF	DQ	STL	TO	BLK	PTS	RPG	APG	PPG
67-68—Kentucky (A)	11	—	90	9	28	.321	0	0	—	3	12	.250	—	—	29	1	16	0	—	6	—	21	2.6	0.1	1.9
REG. ABA TOTALS	11	—	90	9	28	.321	0	0	—	3	12	.250	—	—	29	1	16	0	—	6	—	21	2.6	0.1	1.9

BOWMAN, NATHANIEL (**Nate**) b. March 19, 1943 d. December 11, 1984   Ht. 6-10 Wt. 230 College—Wichita State

SEASON—TEAM	G	GS	MIN	FGM	FGA	PCT	3FGM	3FGA	PCT	FTM	FTA	PCT	O-RB	D-RB	TOT	AST	PF	DQ	STL	TO	BLK	PTS	RPG	APG	PPG
66-67—Chicago	9	—	65	8	21	.381	—	—	—	6	8	.750	—	—	28	2	18	0	—	—	—	22	3.1	0.2	2.4
67-68—New York	42	—	272	52	134	.388	—	—	—	10	15	.667	—	—	113	20	69	0	—	—	—	114	2.7	0.5	2.7
68-69—New York	67	—	607	82	226	.363	—	—	—	29	61	.475	—	—	220	53	142	4	—	—	—	193	3.3	0.8	2.9
69-70—New York	81	—	744	98	235	.417	—	—	—	41	79	.519	—	—	257	46	189	2	—	—	—	237	3.2	0.6	2.9
70-71—Buffalo	44	—	483	58	148	.392	—	—	—	20	38	.526	—	—	173	41	91	2	—	—	—	136	3.9	0.9	3.1
71-72—Pittsburgh (A)	18	—	217	19	53	.358	0	1	.000	5	9	.556	—	—	87	13	48	—	—	17	—	43	4.8	0.7	2.4
REG. NBA TOTALS	243	—	2171	298	764	.390	—	—	—	106	201	.527	—	—	791	162	509	8	—	—	—	702	3.3	0.7	2.9
REG. ABA TOTALS	18	—	217	19	53	.358	0	1	.000	5	9	.556	—	—	87	13	48	—	—	17	—	43	4.8	0.7	2.4
NBA PLAYOFF TOTALS	29	—	196	22	66	.333	—	—	—	10	13	.769	—	—	79	9	51	0	—	—	—	54	2.7	0.3	1.9

BOYD, DENNIS b. May 21, 1954   Ht. 6-1 Wt. 175 College—Detroit

SEASON—TEAM	G	GS	MIN	FGM	FGA	PCT	3FGM	3FGA	PCT	FTM	FTA	PCT	O-RB	D-RB	TOT	AST	PF	DQ	STL	TO	BLK	PTS	RPG	APG	PPG
78-79—Detroit	5	—	40	3	12	.250	—	—	—	0	0	—	0	2	2	7	5	0	0	6	0	6	0.4	1.4	1.2
REG. SEASON TOTALS	5	—	40	3	12	.250	—	—	—	0	0	—	0	2	2	7	5	0	0	6	0	6	0.4	1.4	1.2

BOYD, FRED L. (**Freddie**) b. June 13, 1950   Ht. 6-2 Wt. 180 College—Oregon State

SEASON—TEAM	G	GS	MIN	FGM	FGA	PCT	3FGM	3FGA	PCT	FTM	FTA	PCT	O-RB	D-RB	TOT	AST	PF	DQ	STL	TO	BLK	PTS	RPG	APG	PPG
72-73—Philadelphia	82	—	2351	362	923	.392	—	—	—	136	200	.680	—	—	210	301	184	1	—	—	—	860	2.6	3.7	10.5
73-74—Philadelphia	75	—	1818	286	712	.402	—	—	—	141	195	.723	16	77	93	249	173	1	60	—	9	713	1.2	3.3	9.5
74-75—Philadelphia	66	—	1362	205	495	.414	—	—	—	55	115	.478	16	73	89	161	134	0	43	—	4	465	1.3	2.4	7.0
75-76—Phil.-N.O.	36	—	617	74	171	.433	—	—	—	29	51	.569	4	28	32	80	59	0	28	—	7	177	0.9	2.2	4.9
76-77—New Orleans	47	—	1212	194	406	.478	—	—	—	79	98	.806	19	71	90	147	78	0	44	—	6	467	1.9	3.1	9.9
77-78—New Orleans	21	—	363	44	110	.400	—	—	—	14	22	.636	2	17	19	48	23	0	9	20	3	102	0.9	2.3	4.9
REG. SEASON TOTALS	327	—	7723	1165	2817	.414	—	—	—	454	681	.667	57	266	533	986	651	2	184	20	29	2784	1.6	3.0	8.5

BOYD, KEN b. March 25, 1952   Ht. 6-5 Wt. 195 College—Boston College

SEASON—TEAM	G	GS	MIN	FGM	FGA	PCT	3FGM	3FGA	PCT	FTM	FTA	PCT	O-RB	D-RB	TOT	AST	PF	DQ	STL	TO	BLK	PTS	RPG	APG	PPG
74-75—New Orleans	6	—	25	7	13	.538	—	—	—	5	11	.455	3	2	5	2	2	0	3	—	0	19	0.8	0.3	3.2
REG. SEASON TOTALS	6	—	25	7	13	.538	—	—	—	5	11	.455	3	2	5	2	2	0	3	—	0	19	0.8	0.3	3.2

BOYKOFF, HARRY J. (Big Hesh) b. July 24, 1922 Ht. 6-9½ Wt. 225 College—St. John's

SEASON—TEAM	G	GS	MIN	FGM	FGA	PCT	3FGM	3FGA	PCT	FTM	FTA	PCT	O-RB	D-RB	TOT	AST	PF	DQ	STL	TO	BLK	PTS	RPG	APG	PPG
47-48—Toledo (N)	59	—	—	225	—	—	—	—	—	124	161	.770	—	—	—	—	219	—	—	—	—	574	—	—	9.7
48-49—Waterloo (N)	61	—	—	293	—	—	—	—	—	191	265	.721	—	—	—	—	237	28	—	—	—	777	—	—	12.7
49-50—Waterloo	61	—	—	288	698	.413	—	—	—	203	262	.775	—	—	—	149	229	—	—	—	—	779	—	2.4	12.8
50-51—Boston-Tri-Cit	48	—	—	126	336	.375	—	—	—	74	100	.740	—	—	220	60	197	12	—	—	—	326	4.6	1.3	6.8
REG. NBA TOTALS	109	—	—	414	1034	.400	—	—	—	277	362	.765	—	—	220	209	426	12	—	—	—	1105	4.6	1.9	10.1
REG. NBL TOTALS	120	—	—	518	—	—	—	—	—	315	426	.739	—	—	—	—	456	28	—	—	—	1351	—	—	11.3

BOYNES, WINFORD GLADSTONE III b. May 17, 1957 Ht. 6-6½ Wt. 185 College—San Francisco

SEASON—TEAM	G	GS	MIN	FGM	FGA	PCT	3FGM	3FGA	PCT	FTM	FTA	PCT	O-RB	D-RB	TOT	AST	PF	DQ	STL	TO	BLK	PTS	RPG	APG	PPG
78-79—New Jersey	69	—	1176	256	595	.430	—	—	—	133	169	.787	60	95	155	75	117	1	43	119	7	645	2.2	1.1	9.3
79-80—New Jersey	64	—	1102	221	467	.473	0	4	.000	104	136	.765	51	82	133	95	132	1	59	96	19	546	2.1	1.5	8.5
80-81—Dallas	44	—	757	121	313	.387	0	0	—	45	55	.818	24	51	75	37	79	1	23	69	16	287	1.7	0.8	6.5
REG. SEASON TOTALS	177	—	3035	598	1375	.435	0	4	.000	282	360	.783	135	228	363	207	328	3	125	284	42	1478	2.1	1.2	8.4

BRACEY, STEPHEN HENRY (Steve) b. August 1, 1950 Ht. 6-1 Wt. 185 College—Kilgore/Tulsa

SEASON—TEAM	G	GS	MIN	FGM	FGA	PCT	3FGM	3FGA	PCT	FTM	FTA	PCT	O-RB	D-RB	TOT	AST	PF	DQ	STL	TO	BLK	PTS	RPG	APG	PPG
72-73—Atlanta	70	—	1050	192	395	.486	—	—	—	73	110	.664	—	—	107	125	125	0	—	—	—	457	1.5	1.8	6.5
73-74—Atlanta	75	—	1463	241	520	.463	—	—	—	69	96	.719	26	120	146	231	157	0	60	—	5	551	1.9	3.1	7.3
74-75—Golden State	42	—	340	54	130	.415	—	—	—	25	38	.658	10	28	38	52	41	0	14	—	1	133	0.9	1.2	3.2
REG. SEASON TOTALS	187	—	2853	487	1045	.466	—	—	—	167	244	.684	36	148	291	408	323	0	74	—	6	1141	1.6	2.2	6.1
PLAYOFF TOTALS	10	—	137	27	54	.500	—	—	—	15	20	.750	0	1	14	23	14	0	3	—	0	69	1.4	2.3	6.9

BRADDS, GARY LEE (Tex) b. July 26, 1942 d. July 15, 1983 Ht. 6-8 Wt. 220 College—Ohio State

SEASON—TEAM	G	GS	MIN	FGM	FGA	PCT	3FGM	3FGA	PCT	FTM	FTA	PCT	O-RB	D-RB	TOT	AST	PF	DQ	STL	TO	BLK	PTS	RPG	APG	PPG
64-65—Baltimore	41	—	335	46	111	.414	—	—	—	45	63	.714	—	—	84	19	36	0	—	—	—	137	2.0	0.5	3.3
65-66—Baltimore	3	—	15	2	6	.333	—	—	—	3	4	.750	—	—	8	1	1	0	—	—	—	7	2.7	0.3	2.3
67-68—Oakland (A)	49	—	1052	199	440	.452	0	4	.000	221	283	.781	—	—	289	51	131	1	—	81	—	619	5.9	1.0	12.6
68-69—Oakland (A)	75	—	2249	517	1041	.497	1	7	.143	364	444	.820	—	—	577	88	244	6	—	175	—	1399	7.7	1.2	18.7
69-70—Washington (A)	60	—	1239	292	608	.480	0	5	.000	217	262	.828	—	—	336	54	181	1	—	—	—	801	5.6	0.9	13.4
70-71—Car.-Texas (A)	26	—	321	52	127	.409	0	2	.000	39	58	.672	—	—	104	14	41	—	—	—	—	143	4.0	0.5	5.5
REG. NBA TOTALS	44	—	350	48	117	.410	—	—	—	48	67	.716	—	—	92	20	37	0	—	—	—	144	2.1	0.5	3.3
REG. ABA TOTALS	210	—	4861	1060	2216	.478	1	18	.056	841	1047	.803	—	—	1306	207	597	8	—	256	—	2962	6.2	1.0	14.1
NBA PLAYOFF TOTALS	1	—	5	2	3	.667	—	—	—	2	2	1.000	—	—	2	0	0	0	—	—	—	6	2.0	0.0	6.0
ABA PLAYOFF TOTALS	22	—	633	146	314	.465	1	1	1.000	92	115	.800	—	—	179	18	83	1	—	34	—	385	8.1	0.8	17.5

BRADLEY, ALEX III b. October 30, 1959 Ht. 6-7 Wt. 215 College—Villanova

SEASON—TEAM	G	GS	MIN	FGM	FGA	PCT	3FGM	3FGA	PCT	FTM	FTA	PCT	O-RB	D-RB	TOT	AST	PF	DQ	STL	TO	BLK	PTS	RPG	APG	PPG
81-82—New York	39	0	331	54	103	.524	0	1	.000	29	48	.604	31	34	65	11	37	0	12	28	5	137	1.7	0.3	3.5
REG. SEASON TOTALS	39	0	331	54	103	.524	0	1	.000	29	48	.604	31	34	65	11	37	0	12	28	5	137	1.7	0.3	3.5

BRADLEY, ALONZO b. October 16, 1953 Ht. 6-6 Wt. 195 College—Utica JC/Texas Southern

SEASON—TEAM	G	GS	MIN	FGM	FGA	PCT	3FGM	3FGA	PCT	FTM	FTA	PCT	O-RB	D-RB	TOT	AST	PF	DQ	STL	TO	BLK	PTS	RPG	APG	PPG
77-78—Houston	43	—	798	130	304	.428	—	—	—	43	59	.729	24	75	99	54	83	1	16	55	6	303	2.3	1.3	7.0
78-79—Houston	34	—	245	37	88	.420	—	—	—	22	33	.667	13	33	46	17	33	0	5	17	1	96	1.4	0.5	2.8
79-80—Houston	22	—	96	17	48	.354	1	1	1.000	6	9	.667	2	4	6	3	9	0	3	8	0	41	0.3	0.1	1.9
REG. SEASON TOTALS	99	—	1139	184	440	.418	1	1	1.000	71	101	.703	39	112	151	74	125	1	24	80	7	440	1.5	0.7	4.4
PLAYOFF TOTALS	5	—	16	6	9	.667	1	1	1.000	3	5	.600	1	2	3	1	2	0	1	0	0	16	0.6	0.2	3.2

BRADLEY, BILL b. 1941 Ht. 5-11 Wt. 165 College—Tennessee State

SEASON—TEAM	G	GS	MIN	FGM	FGA	PCT	3FGM	3FGA	PCT	FTM	FTA	PCT	O-RB	D-RB	TOT	AST	PF	DQ	STL	TO	BLK	PTS	RPG	APG	PPG
67-68—Kentucky (A)	58	—	521	82	258	.318	3	18	.167	51	56	.911	—	—	47	54	40	0	—	50	—	218	0.8	0.9	3.8
REG. ABA TOTALS	58	—	521	82	258	.318	3	18	.167	51	56	.911	—	—	47	54	40	0	—	50	—	218	0.8	0.9	3.8
ABA PLAYOFF TOTALS	2	—	9	2	2	1.000	0	0	—	2	2	1.000	—	—	1	1	3	0	—	—	—	6	0.5	0.5	3.0

BRADLEY, CHARLES WARNELL b. May 16, 1959 Ht. 6-5 Wt. 215 College—Wyoming

SEASON—TEAM	G	GS	MIN	FGM	FGA	PCT	3FGM	3FGA	PCT	FTM	FTA	PCT	O-RB	D-RB	TOT	AST	PF	DQ	STL	TO	BLK	PTS	RPG	APG	PPG
81-82—Boston	51	1	339	55	122	.451	0	1	.000	42	62	.677	12	26	38	22	61	0	14	37	6	152	0.7	0.4	3.0
82-83—Boston	51	5	532	69	176	.392	0	3	.000	46	90	.511	30	48	78	28	84	0	32	42	27	184	1.5	0.5	3.6
83-84—Seattle	8	0	39	3	7	.429	0	0	—	5	7	.714	0	3	3	5	6	0	0	8	1	11	0.4	0.6	1.4
REG. SEASON TOTALS	110	6	910	127	305	.416	0	4	.000	93	159	.585	42	77	119	55	151	0	46	87	34	347	1.1	0.5	3.2
PLAYOFF TOTALS	9	0	22	2	8	.250	0	0	—	0	2	.000	1	4	5	1	6	0	1	4	0	4	0.6	0.1	0.4

BRADLEY, DUDLEY LEROY b. March 19, 1957 Ht. 6-6 Wt. 195 College—North Carolina

SEASON—TEAM	G	GS	MIN	FGM	FGA	PCT	3FGM	3FGA	PCT	FTM	FTA	PCT	O-RB	D-RB	TOT	AST	PF	DQ	STL	TO	BLK	PTS	RPG	APG	PPG
79-80—Indiana	82	—	2027	275	609	.452	2	5	.400	136	174	.782	69	154	223	252	194	1	211	166	48	688	2.7	3.1	8.4
80-81—Indiana	82	—	1867	265	559	.474	2	16	.125	125	178	.702	70	123	193	188	236	2	186	122	37	657	2.4	2.3	8.0
81-82—Phoenix	64	3	937	125	281	.445	1	4	.250	74	100	.740	30	57	87	80	115	0	78	71	10	325	1.4	1.3	5.1
82-83—Chicago	58	11	683	82	159	.516	1	5	.200	36	45	.800	27	78	105	106	91	0	49	59	10	201	1.8	1.8	3.5
84-85—Washington	73	24	1232	142	299	.475	20	65	.308	54	79	.684	34	100	134	173	152	0	96	84	21	358	1.8	2.4	4.9
85-86—Washington	70	7	842	73	209	.349	17	68	.250	32	56	.571	24	71	95	107	101	0	85	44	3	195	1.4	1.5	2.8
86-87—Milwaukee	68	2	900	76	213	.357	13	50	.260	47	58	.810	31	71	102	66	118	2	105	34	8	212	1.5	1.0	3.1
87-88—Milw.-N.J.	65	15	1437	156	365	.427	37	102	.363	74	97	.763	25	102	127	151	172	1	114	88	43	423	2.0	2.3	6.5
88-89—Atlanta	38	0	267	28	86	.326	8	31	.258	8	16	.500	7	25	32	24	41	0	16	14	2	72	0.8	0.6	1.9
REG. SEASON TOTALS	600	62	10192	1222	2780	.440	101	346	.292	586	803	.730	317	781	1098	1147	1220	6	940	682	182	3131	1.8	1.9	5.2
PLAYOFF TOTALS	30	0	212	26	66	.394	5	22	.227	13	18	.722	5	9	14	22	35	0	13	23	1	70	0.5	0.7	2.3

BRADLEY, JAMES ARTHUR (Jim) b. March 16, 1952 d. February 20, 1982 Ht. 6-8 Wt. 225 College—Northern Illinois

SEASON—TEAM	G	GS	MIN	FGM	FGA	PCT	3FGM	3FGA	PCT	FTM	FTA	PCT	O-RB	D-RB	TOT	AST	PF	DQ	STL	TO	BLK	PTS	RPG	APG	PPG
73-74—Kentucky (A)	35	—	884	130	309	.421	0	2	.000	31	44	.705	67	147	214	49	106	—	37	55	27	291	6.1	1.4	8.3
74-75—Kentucky (A)	56	—	922	144	327	.440	0	4	.000	76	103	.738	101	183	284	68	112	—	27	73	30	364	5.1	1.2	6.5
75-76—Denver (A)	7	—	107	15	38	.395	0	0	—	2	3	.667	4	26	30	11	26	—	5	5	5	32	4.3	1.6	4.6
REG. ABA TOTALS	98	—	1913	289	674	.429	0	6	.000	109	150	.727	172	356	528	128	244	0	69	133	62	687	5.4	1.3	7.0
ABA PLAYOFF TOTALS	12	—	182	27	76	.355	0	0	—	7	13	.538	13	33	46	11	24	0	4	15	5	61	3.8	0.9	5.1

BRADLEY, JOSEPH L. (Joe) b. September 24, 1928 d. June 5, 1987 Ht. 6-3 Wt. 175 College—Oklahoma State

SEASON—TEAM	G	GS	MIN	FGM	FGA	PCT	3FGM	3FGA	PCT	FTM	FTA	PCT	O-RB	D-RB	TOT	AST	PF	DQ	STL	TO	BLK	PTS	RPG	APG	PPG
49-50—Chicago	46	—	—	36	134	.269	—	—	—	15	38	.395	—	—	—	36	51	—	—	—	—	87	—	0.8	1.9
REG. SEASON TOTALS	46	—	—	36	134	.269	—	—	—	15	38	.395	—	—	—	36	51	—	—	—	—	87	—	0.8	1.9

BRADLEY, SHAWN PAUL b. March 22, 1972 Ht. 7-6 Wt. 245 College—Brigham Young

SEASON—TEAM	G	GS	MIN	FGM	FGA	PCT	3FGM	3FGA	PCT	FTM	FTA	PCT	O-RB	D-RB	TOT	AST	PF	DQ	STL	TO	BLK	PTS	RPG	APG	PPG
93-94—Philadelphia	49	45	1385	201	491	.409	0	3	.000	102	168	.607	98	208	306	98	170	3	45	148	147	504	6.2	2.0	10.3
REG. SEASON TOTALS	49	45	1385	201	491	.409	0	3	.000	102	168	.607	98	208	306	98	170	3	45	148	147	504	6.2	2.0	10.3

BRADLEY, WILLIAM WARREN (Bill, Dollar Bill) b. July 28, 1943 Ht. 6-5 Wt. 205 College—Princeton

SEASON—TEAM	G	GS	MIN	FGM	FGA	PCT	3FGM	3FGA	PCT	FTM	FTA	PCT	O-RB	D-RB	TOT	AST	PF	DQ	STL	TO	BLK	PTS	RPG	APG	PPG
67-68—New York	45	—	874	142	341	.416	—	—	—	76	104	.731	—	—	113	137	138	2	—	—	—	360	2.5	3.0	8.0
68-69—New York	82	—	2413	407	948	.429	—	—	—	206	253	.814	—	—	350	302	295	4	—	—	—	1020	4.3	3.7	12.4
69-70—New York	67	—	2098	413	897	.460	—	—	—	145	176	.824	—	—	239	268	219	0	—	—	—	971	3.6	4.0	14.5
70-71—New York	78	—	2300	413	912	.453	—	—	—	144	175	.823	—	—	260	280	245	3	—	—	—	970	3.3	3.6	12.4
71-72—New York	78	—	2780	504	1085	.465	—	—	—	169	199	.849	—	—	250	315	254	4	—	—	—	1177	3.2	4.0	15.1
72-73—New York	82	—	2998	575	1252	.459	—	—	—	169	194	.871	—	—	301	367	273	5	—	—	—	1319	3.7	4.5	16.1
73-74—New York	82	—	2813	502	1112	.451	—	—	—	146	167	.874	59	194	253	242	278	2	42	—	21	1150	3.1	3.0	14.0
74-75—New York	79	—	2787	452	1036	.436	—	—	—	144	165	.873	65	186	251	247	283	5	74	—	18	1048	3.2	3.1	13.3
75-76—New York	82	—	2709	392	906	.433	—	—	—	130	148	.878	47	187	234	247	256	2	68	—	18	914	2.9	3.0	11.1
76-77—New York Knicks	67	—	1027	127	274	.464	—	—	—	34	42	.810	27	76	103	128	122	0	25	—	8	288	1.5	1.9	4.3
REG. SEASON TOTALS	742	—	22799	3927	8763	.448	—	—	—	1363	1623	.840	198	643	2354	2533	2363	27	209	—	65	9217	3.2	3.4	12.4
PLAYOFF TOTALS	95	—	3161	510	1165	.438	—	—	—	202	251	.805	12	25	333	263	313	5	9	—	3	1222	3.5	2.8	12.9
ALL-STAR TOTALS	1	—	12	2	5	.400	—	—	—	0	0	—	0	0	1	0	2	0	0	—	0	4	1.0	0.0	4.0

BRANCH, ADRIAN FRANCIS b. November 17, 1963 Ht. 6-8 Wt. 185 College—Maryland

SEASON—TEAM	G	GS	MIN	FGM	FGA	PCT	3FGM	3FGA	PCT	FTM	FTA	PCT	O-RB	D-RB	TOT	AST	PF	DQ	STL	TO	BLK	PTS	RPG	APG	PPG
86-87—L.A. Lakers	32	0	219	48	96	.500	0	2	.000	42	54	.778	23	30	53	16	39	0	16	24	3	138	1.7	0.5	4.3
87-88—New Jersey	20	3	308	56	134	.418	1	5	.200	20	23	.870	20	28	48	16	41	1	16	29	11	133	2.4	0.8	6.7
88-89—Portland	67	4	811	202	436	.463	7	31	.226	87	120	.725	63	69	132	60	99	0	45	64	3	498	2.0	0.9	7.4
89-90—Minnesota	11	0	91	25	61	.410	1	1	1.000	14	22	.636	8	12	20	4	14	0	6	8	0	65	1.8	0.4	5.9
REG. SEASON TOTALS	130	7	1429	331	727	.455	9	39	.231	163	219	.744	114	139	253	96	193	1	83	125	17	834	1.9	0.7	6.4
PLAYOFF TOTALS	12	0	47	4	24	.167	0	1	.000	8	14	.571	3	8	11	7	10	0	2	5	0	16	0.9	0.6	1.3

BRANDON, THOMAS TERRELL (Terrell) b. May 20, 1970 Ht. 6-0 Wt. 180 College—Oregon

SEASON—TEAM	G	GS	MIN	FGM	FGA	PCT	3FGM	3FGA	PCT	FTM	FTA	PCT	O-RB	D-RB	TOT	AST	PF	DQ	STL	TO	BLK	PTS	RPG	APG	PPG
91-92—Cleveland	82	9	1605	252	601	.419	1	23	.043	100	124	.806	49	113	162	316	107	0	81	136	22	605	2.0	3.9	7.4
92-93—Cleveland	82	8	1622	297	621	.478	13	42	.310	118	143	.825	37	142	179	302	122	1	79	107	27	725	2.2	3.7	8.8
93-94—Cleveland	73	10	1548	230	548	.420	7	32	.219	139	162	.858	38	121	159	277	108	0	84	111	16	606	2.2	3.8	8.3
REG. SEASON TOTALS	237	27	4775	779	1770	.440	21	97	.216	357	429	.832	124	376	500	895	337	1	244	354	65	1936	2.1	3.8	8.2
PLAYOFF TOTALS	23	0	345	54	120	.450	2	8	.250	14	16	.875	9	34	43	52	24	0	11	26	4	124	1.9	2.3	5.4

BRANNUM, ROBERT WARREN (**Bob, Beeb**) b. May 28, 1925   Ht. 6-5½ Wt. 215 College—Kentucky/Michigan State

SEASON—TEAM	G	GS	MIN	FGM	FGA	PCT	3FGM	3FGA	PCT	FTM	FTA	PCT	O-RB	D-RB	TOT	AST	PF	DQ	STL	TO	BLK	PTS	RPG	APG	PPG
48-49—Sheboygan (N)	64	—	—	169	—	—	—	—	—	169	261	.648	—	—	—	—	232	—	—	—	—	507	—	—	7.9
49-50—Sheboygan	59	—	—	234	718	.326	—	—	—	245	355	.690	—	—	—	205	279	—	—	—	—	713	—	3.5	12.1
51-52—Boston	66	—	1324	149	404	.369	—	—	—	107	171	.626	—	—	406	76	235	9	—	—	—	405	6.2	1.2	6.1
52-53—Boston	71	—	1900	188	541	.348	—	—	—	110	185	.595	—	—	537	147	287	17	—	—	—	486	7.6	2.1	6.8
53-54—Boston	71	—	1729	140	453	.309	—	—	—	129	206	.626	—	—	509	144	280	10	—	—	—	409	7.2	2.0	5.8
54-55—Boston	71	—	1623	176	465	.378	—	—	—	90	127	.709	—	—	492	127	232	6	—	—	—	442	6.9	1.8	6.2
REG. NBA TOTALS	338	—	6576	887	2581	.344	—	—	—	681	1044	.652	—	—	1944	699	1313	42	—	—	—	2455	7.0	2.1	7.3
REG. NBL TOTALS	64	—	—	169	—	—	—	—	—	169	261	.648	—	—	—	—	232	—	—	—	—	507	—	—	7.9
NBA PLAYOFF TOTALS	25	—	492	68	177	.384	—	—	—	38	67	.567	—	—	155	47	116	10	—	—	—	174	7.0	1.9	7.0
NBL PLAYOFF TOTALS	2	—	—	7	—	—	—	—	—	2	3	.667	—	—	—	—	10	—	—	—	—	16	—	—	8.0

BRANSON, BRADLEY ALEXANDER (**Brad**) b. September 24, 1958   Ht. 6-10 Wt. 220 College—Edison CC/Southern Methodist

SEASON—TEAM	G	GS	MIN	FGM	FGA	PCT	3FGM	3FGA	PCT	FTM	FTA	PCT	O-RB	D-RB	TOT	AST	PF	DQ	STL	TO	BLK	PTS	RPG	APG	PPG
81-82—Cleveland	10	3	176	21	52	.404	0	0	—	11	12	.917	14	19	33	6	17	0	5	13	4	53	3.3	0.6	5.3
82-83—Indiana	62	2	680	131	308	.425	0	1	.000	76	108	.704	73	100	173	46	81	0	27	45	26	338	2.8	0.7	5.5
REG. SEASON TOTALS	72	5	856	152	360	.422	0	1	.000	87	120	.725	87	119	206	52	98	0	32	58	30	391	2.9	0.7	5.4

BRANSON, HERMAN JESSE (**Jesse**) b. January 7, 1942   Ht. 6-7 Wt. 200 College—Elon

SEASON—TEAM	G	GS	MIN	FGM	FGA	PCT	3FGM	3FGA	PCT	FTM	FTA	PCT	O-RB	D-RB	TOT	AST	PF	DQ	STL	TO	BLK	PTS	RPG	APG	PPG
65-66—Philadelphia	5	—	14	1	6	.167	—	—	—	3	4	.750	—	—	9	1	4	0	—	—	—	5	1.8	0.2	1.0
67-68—New Orleans (A)	78	—	1892	376	877	.429	2	9	.222	332	473	.702	—	—	541	67	248	3	—	115	—	1086	6.9	0.9	13.9
REG. NBA TOTALS	5	—	14	1	6	.167	—	—	—	3	4	.750	—	—	9	1	4	0	—	—	—	5	1.8	0.2	1.0
REG. ABA TOTALS	78	—	1892	376	877	.429	2	9	.222	332	473	.702	—	—	541	67	248	3	—	115	—	1086	6.9	0.9	13.9
ABA PLAYOFF TOTALS	17	—	402	61	155	.394	0	3	.000	71	87	.816	—	—	102	20	62	0	—	31	—	193	6.0	1.2	11.4

BRASCO, JAMES J. (**Jim**) b. February 3, 1931   Ht. 6-1 Wt. 170 College—New York University

SEASON—TEAM	G	GS	MIN	FGM	FGA	PCT	3FGM	3FGA	PCT	FTM	FTA	PCT	O-RB	D-RB	TOT	AST	PF	DQ	STL	TO	BLK	PTS	RPG	APG	PPG
52-53—Syr.-Milw.	30	—	359	36	142	.254	—	—	—	38	48	.792	—	—	39	33	48	3	—	—	—	110	1.3	1.1	3.7
REG. SEASON TOTALS	30	—	359	36	142	.254	—	—	—	38	48	.792	—	—	39	33	48	3	—	—	—	110	1.3	1.1	3.7

BRATZ, MICHAEL LOUIS (**Mike**) b. October 17, 1955   Ht. 6-2 Wt. 185 College—Allan Hancock/Stanford

SEASON—TEAM	G	GS	MIN	FGM	FGA	PCT	3FGM	3FGA	PCT	FTM	FTA	PCT	O-RB	D-RB	TOT	AST	PF	DQ	STL	TO	BLK	PTS	RPG	APG	PPG
77-78—Phoenix	80	—	933	159	395	.403	—	—	—	56	68	.824	42	73	115	123	104	1	39	89	5	374	1.4	1.5	4.7
78-79—Phoenix	77	—	1297	242	533	.454	—	—	—	139	170	.818	55	86	141	179	151	0	64	135	7	623	1.8	2.3	8.1
79-80—Phoenix	82	—	1589	269	687	.392	21	86	.244	141	162	.870	50	117	167	223	165	0	93	135	9	700	2.0	2.7	8.5
80-81—Cleveland	80	—	2595	319	817	.390	57	169	.337	107	132	.811	66	132	198	452	194	1	136	162	17	802	2.5	5.7	10.0
81-82—San Antonio	81	3	1616	230	565	.407	46	138	.333	119	152	.783	40	126	166	438	183	0	65	139	11	625	2.0	5.4	7.7
82-83—Chicago	15	0	140	14	42	.333	1	8	.125	10	13	.769	3	16	19	23	20	0	7	14	0	39	1.3	1.5	2.6
83-84—Golden State	82	0	1428	213	521	.409	15	51	.294	120	137	.876	41	102	143	252	155	0	84	109	6	561	1.7	3.1	6.8
84-85—Golden State	56	6	746	106	250	.424	6	26	.231	69	82	.841	11	47	58	122	76	1	47	54	4	287	1.0	2.2	5.1
85-86—Sacramento	33	0	269	26	70	.371	4	14	.286	14	18	.778	2	21	23	39	43	0	13	17	0	70	0.7	1.2	2.1
REG. SEASON TOTALS	586	9	10613	1578	3880	.407	150	492	.305	775	934	.830	310	720	1030	1851	1091	3	548	854	59	4081	1.8	3.2	7.0
PLAYOFF TOTALS	37	0	666	119	262	.454	14	41	.341	63	80	.788	20	39	59	96	82	0	33	56	3	315	1.6	2.6	8.5

BRAUN, CARL AUGUST b. September 25, 1927   Ht. 6-5 Wt. 180 College—Colgate

SEASON—TEAM	G	GS	MIN	FGM	FGA	PCT	3FGM	3FGA	PCT	FTM	FTA	PCT	O-RB	D-RB	TOT	AST	PF	DQ	STL	TO	BLK	PTS	RPG	APG	PPG
47-48—New York	47	—	—	276	854	.323	—	—	—	119	183	.650	—	—	—	61	102	—	—	—	—	671	—	1.3	14.3
48-49—New York	57	—	—	299	906	.330	—	—	—	212	279	.760	—	—	—	173	144	—	—	—	—	810	—	3.0	14.2
49-50—New York	67	—	—	373	1024	.364	—	—	—	285	374	.762	—	—	—	247	188	—	—	—	—	1031	—	3.7	15.4
52-53—New York	70	—	2316	323	807	.400	—	—	—	331	401	.825	—	—	233	243	287	14	—	—	—	977	3.3	3.5	14.0
53-54—New York	72	—	2373	354	884	.400	—	—	—	354	429	.825	—	—	246	209	259	6	—	—	—	1062	3.4	2.9	14.8
54-55—New York	71	—	2479	400	1032	.388	—	—	—	274	342	.801	—	—	295	274	208	3	—	—	—	1074	4.2	3.9	15.1
55-56—New York	72	—	2316	396	1064	.372	—	—	—	320	382	.838	—	—	259	298	215	3	—	—	—	1112	3.6	4.1	15.4
56-57—New York	72	—	2345	378	993	.381	—	—	—	245	303	.809	—	—	259	256	195	1	—	—	—	1001	3.6	3.6	13.9
57-58—New York	71	—	2475	426	1018	.418	—	—	—	321	378	.849	—	—	330	393	183	2	—	—	—	1173	4.6	5.5	16.5
58-59—New York	72	—	1959	287	684	.420	—	—	—	180	218	.826	—	—	251	349	178	3	—	—	—	754	3.5	4.8	10.5
59-60—New York	54	—	1514	285	659	.432	—	—	—	129	154	.838	—	—	168	270	127	2	—	—	—	699	3.1	5.0	12.9
60-61—New York	15	—	218	37	79	.468	—	—	—	11	14	.786	—	—	31	48	29	0	—	—	—	85	2.1	3.2	5.7
61-62—Boston	48	—	414	78	207	.377	—	—	—	20	27	.741	—	—	50	71	49	0	—	—	—	176	1.0	1.5	3.7
REG. SEASON TOTALS	788	—	18409	3912	10211	.383	—	—	—	2801	3484	.804	—	—	2122	2892	2164	34	—	—	—	10625	3.4	3.7	13.5
PLAYOFF TOTALS	40	—	706	179	512	.350	—	—	—	203	250	.812	—	—	81	108	135	6	—	—	—	561	3.1	2.7	14.0
ALL-STAR TOTALS	4	—	90	13	27	.481	—	—	—	4	4	1.000	—	—	12	8	9	0	—	—	—	30	3.0	2.0	7.5

BRENNAN, PETER JOSEPH (**Pete**) b. September 23, 1936   Ht. 6-6 Wt. 205 College—North Carolina

SEASON—TEAM	G	GS	MIN	FGM	FGA	PCT	3FGM	3FGA	PCT	FTM	FTA	PCT	O-RB	D-RB	TOT	AST	PF	DQ	STL	TO	BLK	PTS	RPG	APG	PPG
58-59—New York	16	—	136	13	43	.302	—	—	—	14	25	.560	—	—	31	6	15	0	—	—	—	40	1.9	0.4	2.5
REG. SEASON TOTALS	16	—	136	13	43	.302	—	—	—	14	25	.560	—	—	31	6	15	0	—	—	—	40	1.9	0.4	2.5
PLAYOFF TOTALS	2	—	6	2	7	.286	—	—	—	0	1	.000	—	—	5	—	4	0	—	—	—	4	2.5	0.0	2.0

BRENNAN, THOMAS F. (**Tom**) b. August 6, 1930   Ht. 6-4 Wt. 200 College—Villanova

SEASON—TEAM	G	GS	MIN	FGM	FGA	PCT	3FGM	3FGA	PCT	FTM	FTA	PCT	O-RB	D-RB	TOT	AST	PF	DQ	STL	TO	BLK	PTS	RPG	APG	PPG
54-55—Philadelphia	11	—	52	5	11	.455	—	—	—	0	0	—	—	—	5	2	5	0	—	—	—	10	0.5	0.2	0.9
REG. SEASON TOTALS	11	—	52	5	11	.455	—	—	—	0	0	—	—	—	5	2	5	0	—	—	—	10	0.5	0.2	0.9

BREUER, RANDALL W. (**Randy**) b. October 11, 1960   Ht. 7-3 Wt. 260 College—Minnesota

SEASON—TEAM	G	GS	MIN	FGM	FGA	PCT	3FGM	3FGA	PCT	FTM	FTA	PCT	O-RB	D-RB	TOT	AST	PF	DQ	STL	TO	BLK	PTS	RPG	APG	PPG
83-84—Milwaukee	57	8	472	68	177	.384	0	0	—	32	46	.696	48	61	109	17	98	1	11	35	38	168	1.9	0.3	2.9
84-85—Milwaukee	78	0	1083	162	317	.511	0	0	—	89	127	.701	92	164	256	40	179	4	21	63	82	413	3.3	0.5	5.3
85-86—Milwaukee	82	63	1792	272	570	.477	0	1	.000	141	198	.712	159	299	458	114	214	2	50	122	116	685	5.6	1.4	8.4
86-87—Milwaukee	76	10	1467	241	497	.485	0	0	—	118	202	.584	129	221	350	47	229	9	56	100	61	600	4.6	0.6	7.9
87-88—Milwaukee	81	73	2258	390	788	.495	0	0	—	188	286	.657	191	360	551	103	198	3	46	107	107	968	6.8	1.3	12.0
88-89—Milwaukee	48	4	513	86	179	.480	0	0	—	28	51	.549	51	84	135	22	59	0	9	29	37	200	2.8	0.5	4.2
89-90—Milw.-Minn.	81	55	1879	298	696	.428	0	1	.000	126	193	.653	154	263	417	97	196	2	42	96	108	722	5.1	1.2	8.9
90-91—Minnesota	73	44	1505	197	435	.453	0	0	—	35	79	.443	114	231	345	73	132	1	35	69	80	429	4.7	1.0	5.9
91-92—Minnesota	67	25	1176	161	344	.468	0	1	.000	41	77	.532	98	183	281	89	117	0	27	41	99	363	4.2	1.3	5.4
92-93—Atlanta	12	0	107	15	31	.484	0	0	—	2	5	.400	10	18	28	6	12	0	2	5	3	32	2.3	0.5	2.7
93-94—Sacramento	26	3	247	8	26	.308	0	1	.000	3	14	.214	15	41	56	6	30	0	6	9	19	19	2.2	0.3	0.7
REG. SEASON TOTALS	681	285	12499	1898	4060	.467	0	4	.000	803	1278	.628	1061	1925	2986	616	1464	22	305	676	750	4599	4.4	0.9	6.8
PLAYOFF TOTALS	60	17	870	115	223	.516	0	0	—	57	95	.600	56	130	186	26	129	2	23	30	44	287	3.1	0.4	4.8

BREWER, JAMES TURNER (**Jim, Brew**) b. December 3, 1951   Ht. 6-9 Wt. 220 College—Minnesota

SEASON—TEAM	G	GS	MIN	FGM	FGA	PCT	3FGM	3FGA	PCT	FTM	FTA	PCT	O-RB	D-RB	TOT	AST	PF	DQ	STL	TO	BLK	PTS	RPG	APG	PPG
73-74—Cleveland	82	—	1862	210	548	.383	—	—	—	80	123	.650	207	317	524	149	192	1	46	—	35	500	6.4	1.8	6.1
74-75—Cleveland	82	—	1991	291	639	.455	—	—	—	103	159	.648	205	304	509	128	150	2	77	—	43	685	6.2	1.6	8.4
75-76—Cleveland	82	—	2913	400	874	.458	—	—	—	140	214	.654	298	593	891	209	214	0	94	—	89	940	10.9	2.5	11.5
76-77—Cleveland	81	—	2672	296	657	.451	—	—	—	97	178	.545	275	487	762	195	214	3	94	—	82	689	9.4	2.4	8.5
77-78—Cleveland	80	—	1798	175	390	.449	—	—	—	46	100	.460	182	313	495	98	178	1	60	103	48	396	6.2	1.2	5.0
78-79—Clev.-Detroit	80	—	1611	141	319	.442	0	5	.000	26	63	.413	159	316	475	87	174	2	61	97	66	308	5.9	1.1	3.9
79-80—Portland	67	—	1016	90	184	.489	0	5	.000	14	29	.483	101	156	257	75	129	2	42	47	43	194	3.8	1.1	2.9
80-81—Los Angeles	78	—	1107	101	197	.513	0	2	.000	15	40	.375	127	154	281	55	158	2	43	48	58	217	3.6	0.7	2.8
81-82—Los Angeles	71	9	966	81	175	.463	1	6	.167	7	19	.368	106	158	264	42	127	1	39	37	46	170	3.7	0.6	2.4
REG. SEASON TOTALS	703	9	15936	1785	3983	.448	1	13	.077	528	925	.571	1660	2798	4458	1038	1536	14	556	332	510	4099	6.3	1.5	5.8
PLAYOFF TOTALS	31	0	742	68	145	.469	0	0	—	28	54	.519	61	143	204	49	59	0	24	5	24	164	6.6	1.6	5.3

BREWER, RONALD CHARLES (**Ron**) b. September 16, 1955   Ht. 6-4 Wt. 180 College—Westark CC/Arkansas

SEASON—TEAM	G	GS	MIN	FGM	FGA	PCT	3FGM	3FGA	PCT	FTM	FTA	PCT	O-RB	D-RB	TOT	AST	PF	DQ	STL	TO	BLK	PTS	RPG	APG	PPG
78-79—Portland	81	—	2454	434	878	.494	—	—	—	210	256	.820	88	141	229	165	181	3	102	153	79	1078	2.8	2.0	13.3
79-80—Portland	82	—	2815	548	1182	.464	6	32	.188	184	219	.840	54	160	214	216	154	0	98	167	48	1286	2.6	2.6	15.7
80-81—Port.-S.A.	75	—	1452	275	631	.436	1	7	.143	91	114	.798	34	52	86	148	95	0	61	92	34	642	1.1	2.0	8.6
81-82—S.A.-Clev.	72	45	2319	569	1194	.477	8	31	.258	211	260	.812	55	106	161	188	151	0	82	125	30	1357	2.2	2.6	18.8
82-83—Clev.-G.S.	74	52	1964	344	807	.426	7	18	.389	142	170	.835	59	85	144	96	123	0	90	97	25	837	1.9	1.3	11.3
83-84—G.S.-S.A.	53	8	992	179	403	.444	3	14	.214	52	67	.776	22	41	63	50	64	0	24	40	21	413	1.2	0.9	7.8
84-85—S.A.-N.J.	20	0	326	62	118	.525	0	2	.000	23	25	.920	9	12	21	17	23	0	6	9	6	147	1.1	0.9	7.4
85-86—Chicago-Clev.	44	3	570	86	224	.384	5	17	.294	34	38	.895	14	39	53	40	44	0	17	23	6	211	1.2	0.9	4.8
REG. SEASON TOTALS	501	108	12892	2497	5437	.459	30	121	.248	947	1149	.824	335	636	971	920	835	3	480	706	249	5971	1.9	1.8	11.9
PLAYOFF TOTALS	16	0	411	92	191	.482	1	7	.143	41	59	.695	6	18	24	32	30	0	8	21	16	226	1.5	2.0	14.1

BRIAN, FRANK SANDS (**Flash**) b. May 1, 1923   Ht. 6-1½ Wt. 180 College—Louisiana State

SEASON—TEAM	G	GS	MIN	FGM	FGA	PCT	3FGM	3FGA	PCT	FTM	FTA	PCT	O-RB	D-RB	TOT	AST	PF	DQ	STL	TO	BLK	PTS	RPG	APG	PPG
47-48—Anderson (N)	59	—	—	248	—	—	—	—	—	155	210	.738	—	—	—	—	—	—	—	—	—	651	—	—	11.0
48-49—Anderson (N)	64	—	—	216	—	—	—	—	—	201	256	.785	—	—	—	—	—	—	—	—	—	633	—	—	9.9
49-50—Anderson	64	—	—	368	1156	.318	—	—	—	402	488	.824	—	—	—	189	192	—	—	—	—	1138	—	3.0	17.8
50-51—Tri-Cities	68	—	—	363	1127	.322	—	—	—	418	508	.823	—	—	244	266	215	4	—	—	—	1144	3.6	3.9	16.8
51-52—Fort Wayne	66	—	2672	342	972	.352	—	—	—	367	433	.848	—	—	232	233	220	6	—	—	—	1051	3.5	3.5	15.9
52-53—Fort Wayne	68	—	1910	245	699	.351	—	—	—	236	297	.795	—	—	133	142	205	8	—	—	—	726	2.0	2.1	10.7
53-54—Fort Wayne	64	—	973	132	352	.375	—	—	—	137	182	.753	—	—	79	92	100	2	—	—	—	401	1.2	1.4	6.3
54-55—Fort Wayne	71	—	1381	237	623	.380	—	—	—	217	255	.851	—	—	127	142	133	0	—	—	—	691	1.8	2.0	9.7
55-56—Fort Wayne	37	—	680	78	263	.297	—	—	—	72	88	.818	—	—	88	74	62	0	—	—	—	228	2.4	2.0	6.2
REG. NBA TOTALS	438	—	7616	1765	5192	.340	—	—	—	1849	2251	.821	—	—	903	1138	1127	20	—	—	—	5379	2.4	2.6	12.3
REG. NBL TOTALS	123	—	—	464	—	—	—	—	—	356	466	.764	—	—	—	—	—	—	—	—	—	1284	—	—	10.4
NBA PLAYOFF TOTALS	43	—	768	134	386	.347	—	—	—	126	154	.818	—	—	61	93	105	1	—	—	—	394	1.7	2.2	9.2
NBL PLAYOFF TOTALS	13	—	—	44	—	—	—	—	—	38	48	.792	—	—	—	35	—	—	—	—	—	126	—	—	9.7
NBA ALL-STAR TOTALS	2	—	25	9	24	.375	—	—	—	9	11	.818	—	—	13	7	4	0	—	—	—	27	6.5	3.5	13.5

BRICKOWSKI, FRANCIS ANTHONY (Frank, Brick) b. August 14, 1959 Ht. 6-9 Wt. 245 College—Penn State

SEASON—TEAM	G	GS	MIN	FGM	FGA	PCT	3FGM	3FGA	PCT	FTM	FTA	PCT	O-RB	D-RB	TOT	AST	PF	DQ	STL	TO	BLK	PTS	RPG	APG	PPG
84-85—Seattle	78	9	1115	150	305	.492	0	4	.000	85	127	.669	76	184	260	100	171	1	34	100	15	385	3.3	1.3	4.9
85-86—Seattle	40	2	311	30	58	.517	0	0	—	18	27	.667	16	38	54	21	74	2	11	23	7	78	1.4	0.5	2.0
86-87—Lakers-S.A.	44	0	487	63	124	.508	0	4	.000	50	70	.714	48	68	116	17	118	4	20	32	6	176	2.6	0.4	4.0
87-88—San Antonio	70	68	2227	425	805	.528	1	5	.200	268	349	.768	167	316	483	266	275	11	74	207	36	1119	6.9	3.8	16.0
88-89—San Antonio	64	60	1822	337	654	.515	0	2	.000	201	281	.715	148	258	406	131	252	10	102	165	35	875	6.3	2.0	13.7
89-90—San Antonio	78	12	1438	211	387	.545	0	2	.000	95	141	.674	89	238	327	105	226	4	66	93	37	517	4.2	1.3	6.6
90-91—Milwaukee	75	73	1912	372	706	.527	0	2	.000	198	248	.798	129	297	426	131	255	4	86	160	43	942	5.7	1.7	12.6
91-92—Milwaukee	65	60	1556	306	584	.524	3	6	.500	125	163	.767	97	247	344	122	223	11	60	112	23	740	5.3	1.9	11.4
92-93—Milwaukee	66	64	2075	456	836	.545	8	26	.308	195	268	.728	120	285	405	196	235	8	80	202	44	1115	6.1	3.0	16.9
93-94—Milw.-Cha.	71	46	2094	368	754	.488	4	20	.200	195	254	.768	85	319	404	222	242	6	80	181	27	935	5.7	3.1	13.2
REG. SEASON TOTALS	651	394	15037	2718	5213	.521	16	71	.225	1430	1928	.742	975	2250	3225	1311	2071	61	613	1275	273	6882	5.0	2.0	10.6
PLAYOFF TOTALS	16	6	384	77	143	.538	1	3	.333	37	59	.627	28	64	92	28	59	1	15	30	5	192	5.8	1.8	12.0

BRIDGEMAN, ULYSSES LEE (Junior) b. September 17, 1953 Ht. 6-5 Wt. 210 College—Louisville

SEASON—TEAM	G	GS	MIN	FGM	FGA	PCT	3FGM	3FGA	PCT	FTM	FTA	PCT	O-RB	D-RB	TOT	AST	PF	DQ	STL	TO	BLK	PTS	RPG	APG	PPG
75-76—Milwaukee	81	—	1646	286	651	.439	—	—	—	128	161	.795	113	181	294	157	235	3	52	—	21	700	3.6	1.9	8.6
76-77—Milwaukee	82	—	2410	491	1094	.449	—	—	—	197	228	.864	129	287	416	205	221	3	82	—	26	1179	5.1	2.5	14.4
77-78—Milwaukee	82	—	1876	476	947	.503	—	—	—	166	205	.810	114	176	290	175	202	1	72	176	30	1118	3.5	2.1	13.6
78-79—Milwaukee	82	—	1963	540	1067	.506	—	—	—	189	228	.829	113	184	297	163	184	2	88	138	41	1269	3.6	2.0	15.5
79-80—Milwaukee	81	—	2316	594	1243	.478	5	27	.185	230	266	.865	104	197	301	237	216	3	94	172	20	1423	3.7	2.9	17.6
80-81—Milwaukee	77	—	2215	537	1102	.487	3	21	.143	213	241	.884	78	211	289	234	182	2	88	150	28	1290	3.8	3.0	16.8
81-82—Milwaukee	41	4	924	209	433	.483	4	9	.444	89	103	.864	37	88	125	109	91	0	28	64	3	511	3.0	2.7	12.5
82-83—Milwaukee	70	5	1855	421	856	.492	1	13	.077	164	196	.837	44	202	246	207	155	0	40	122	9	1007	3.5	3.0	14.4
83-84—Milwaukee	81	10	2431	509	1094	.465	6	31	.194	196	243	.807	80	252	332	265	224	2	53	148	14	1220	4.1	3.3	15.1
84-85—L.A. Clippers	80	15	2042	460	990	.465	14	39	.359	181	206	.879	55	175	230	171	128	0	47	116	18	1115	2.9	2.1	13.9
85-86—L.A. Clippers	58	14	1161	199	451	.441	6	18	.333	106	119	.891	29	94	123	108	81	1	31	68	8	510	2.1	1.9	8.8
86-87—Milwaukee	34	4	418	79	171	.462	1	6	.167	16	20	.800	14	38	52	35	50	0	10	15	2	175	1.5	1.0	5.1
REG. SEASON TOTALS	849	52	21257	4801	10099	.475	40	164	.244	1875	2216	.846	910	2085	2995	2066	1969	17	685	1169	220	11517	3.5	2.4	13.6
PLAYOFF TOTALS	49	8	1359	264	581	.454	4	16	.250	118	145	.814	53	119	172	128	148	2	37	74	11	650	3.5	2.6	13.3

BRIDGES, WILLIAM C. (Bill) b. April 4, 1939 Ht. 6-5½ Wt. 230 College—Kansas

SEASON—TEAM	G	GS	MIN	FGM	FGA	PCT	3FGM	3FGA	PCT	FTM	FTA	PCT	O-RB	D-RB	TOT	AST	PF	DQ	STL	TO	BLK	PTS	RPG	APG	PPG
62-63—St. Louis	27	—	374	66	160	.413	—	—	—	32	51	.627	—	—	144	23	58	0	—	—	—	164	5.3	0.9	6.1
63-64—St. Louis	80	—	1949	268	675	.397	—	—	—	146	224	.652	—	—	680	181	269	6	—	—	—	682	8.5	2.3	8.5
64-65—St. Louis	79	—	2362	362	938	.386	—	—	—	186	275	.676	—	—	853	187	276	3	—	—	—	910	10.8	2.4	11.5
65-66—St. Louis	78	—	2677	377	927	.407	—	—	—	257	364	.706	—	—	951	208	333	11	—	—	—	1011	12.2	2.7	13.0
66-67—St. Louis	79	—	3130	503	1106	.455	—	—	—	367	523	.702	—	—	1190	222	325	12	—	—	—	1373	15.1	2.8	17.4
67-68—St. Louis	82	—	3197	466	1009	.462	—	—	—	347	484	.717	—	—	1102	253	366	12	—	—	—	1279	13.4	3.1	15.6
68-69—Atlanta	80	—	2930	351	775	.453	—	—	—	239	353	.677	—	—	1132	298	290	3	—	—	—	941	14.2	3.7	11.8
69-70—Atlanta	82	—	3269	443	932	.475	—	—	—	331	451	.734	—	—	1181	345	292	6	—	—	—	1217	14.4	4.2	14.8
70-71—Atlanta	82	—	3140	382	834	.458	—	—	—	211	330	.639	—	—	1233	240	317	7	—	—	—	975	15.0	2.9	11.9
71-72—Atlanta-Phil.	78	—	2756	379	779	.487	—	—	—	222	316	.703	—	—	1051	198	269	6	—	—	—	980	13.5	2.5	12.6
72-73—Phil.-L.A.	82	—	2867	333	722	.461	—	—	—	179	255	.702	—	—	904	219	296	3	—	—	—	845	11.0	2.7	10.3
73-74—Los Angeles	65	—	1812	216	513	.421	—	—	—	116	164	.707	193	306	499	148	219	3	58	—	31	548	7.7	2.3	8.4
74-75—L.A.-G.S.	32	—	415	35	93	.376	—	—	—	17	34	.500	64	70	134	31	65	1	11	—	5	87	4.2	1.0	2.7
REG. SEASON TOTALS	926	—	30878	4181	9463	.442	—	—	—	2650	3824	.693	257	376	11054	2553	3375	73	69	—	36	11012	11.9	2.8	11.9
PLAYOFF TOTALS	113	—	3521	475	1135	.419	—	—	—	235	349	.673	27	52	1305	219	408	10	16	—	4	1185	11.5	1.9	10.5
ALL-STAR TOTALS	3	—	53	13	16	.813	—	—	—	2	11	.182	0	0	14	6	6	0	—	—	0	28	4.7	2.0	9.3

BRIGHTMAN, HORACE ALBERT (Al) b. September 22, 1923 d. June 10, 1992 Ht. 6-2 Wt. 195 College—Charleston (West Va.)/Long Beach State

SEASON—TEAM	G	GS	MIN	FGM	FGA	PCT	3FGM	3FGA	PCT	FTM	FTA	PCT	O-RB	D-RB	TOT	AST	PF	DQ	STL	TO	BLK	PTS	RPG	APG	PPG
46-47—Boston	58	—	—	223	870	.256	—	—	—	121	193	.627	—	—	—	60	115	—	—	—	—	567	—	1.0	9.8
REG. SEASON TOTALS	58	—	—	223	870	.256	—	—	—	121	193	.627	—	—	—	60	115	—	—	—	—	567	—	1.0	9.8

BRINDLEY, AUDLEY (Aud) b. December 31, 1923 d. November 19, 1958 Ht. 6-4 Wt. 175 College—Dartmouth

SEASON—TEAM	G	GS	MIN	FGM	FGA	PCT	3FGM	3FGA	PCT	FTM	FTA	PCT	O-RB	D-RB	TOT	AST	PF	DQ	STL	TO	BLK	PTS	RPG	APG	PPG
46-47—New York	12	—	—	14	49	.286	—	—	—	6	7	.857	—	—	—	1	16	—	—	—	—	34	—	0.1	2.8
REG. SEASON TOTALS	12	—	—	14	49	.286	—	—	—	6	7	.857	—	—	—	1	16	—	—	—	—	34	—	0.1	2.8
PLAYOFF TOTALS	3	—	—	3	6	.500	—	—	—	4	6	.667	—	—	—	4	—	—	—	—	—	10	—	0.0	3.3

BRISKER, JOHN b. June 15, 1947 d. April 1978 Ht. 6-5 Wt. 210 College—Toledo

SEASON—TEAM	G	GS	MIN	FGM	FGA	PCT	3FGM	3FGA	PCT	FTM	FTA	PCT	O-RB	D-RB	TOT	AST	PF	DQ	STL	TO	BLK	PTS	RPG	APG	PPG
69-70—Pittsburgh (A)	77	—	2173	627	1361	.461	34	116	.293	329	398	.827	—	—	441	133	236	4	—	—	—	1617	5.7	1.7	21.0
70-71—Pittsburgh (A)	79	—	3089	898	1972	.455	89	264	.337	430	519	.829	—	—	766	226	273	—	—	—	—	2315	9.7	2.9	29.3
71-72—Pittsburgh (A)	49	—	2065	563	1228	.458	43	137	.314	248	286	.867	—	—	447	203	156	—	—	210	—	1417	9.1	4.1	28.9
72-73—Seattle	70	—	1633	352	809	.435	—	—	—	194	236	.822	—	—	319	150	169	1	—	—	—	898	4.6	2.1	12.8
73-74—Seattle	35	—	717	178	396	.449	—	—	—	82	100	.820	59	87	146	56	70	0	28	—	6	438	4.2	1.6	12.5
74-75—Seattle	21	—	276	60	141	.426	—	—	—	42	49	.857	15	18	33	19	33	0	7	—	3	162	1.6	0.9	7.7
REG. NBA TOTALS	126	—	2626	590	1346	.438	—	—	—	318	385	.826	74	105	498	225	272	1	35	—	9	1498	4.0	1.8	11.9
REG. ABA TOTALS	205	—	7327	2088	4561	.458	166	517	.321	1007	1203	.837	—	—	1654	562	665	4	—	210	—	5349	8.1	2.7	26.1
ABA ALL-STAR TOTALS	2	—	48	8	29	.276	0	2	.000	7	10	.700	9	13	22	4	4	0	—	3	—	23	11.0	2.0	11.5

BRISTOW, ALLAN MERCER JR. b. August 23, 1951 Ht. 6-7 Wt. 220 College—Toledo/Virginia Tech

SEASON—TEAM	G	GS	MIN	FGM	FGA	PCT	3FGM	3FGA	PCT	FTM	FTA	PCT	O-RB	D-RB	TOT	AST	PF	DQ	STL	TO	BLK	PTS	RPG	APG	PPG
73-74—Philadelphia	55	—	643	108	270	.400	—	—	—	42	57	.737	68	99	167	92	68	1	29	—	1	258	3.0	1.7	4.7
74-75—Philadelphia	72	—	1101	163	393	.415	—	—	—	121	153	.791	111	143	254	99	101	0	25	—	2	447	3.5	1.4	6.2
75-76—San Antonio (A)	47	—	882	125	271	.461	0	1	.000	78	92	.848	68	106	174	121	81	—	24	63	2	328	3.7	2.6	7.0
76-77—San Antonio	82	—	2017	365	747	.489	—	—	—	206	258	.798	119	229	348	240	195	1	89	—	2	936	4.2	2.9	11.4
77-78—San Antonio	82	—	1481	257	538	.478	—	—	—	152	208	.731	99	158	257	194	150	0	69	146	4	666	3.1	2.4	8.1
78-79—San Antonio	74	—	1324	174	354	.492	—	—	—	124	149	.832	80	167	247	231	154	0	56	108	15	472	3.3	3.1	6.4
79-80—Utah	82	—	2304	377	785	.480	2	7	.286	197	243	.811	170	342	512	341	211	2	88	179	6	953	6.2	4.2	11.6
80-81—Utah	82	—	2001	271	611	.444	5	18	.278	166	198	.838	103	327	430	383	190	1	63	171	3	713	5.2	4.7	8.7
81-82—Dallas	82	54	2035	218	499	.437	3	18	.167	134	164	.817	119	220	339	448	222	2	65	165	6	573	4.1	5.5	7.0
82-83—Dallas	37	0	371	44	99	.444	6	13	.462	10	14	.714	24	35	59	70	46	0	6	31	1	104	1.6	1.9	2.8
REG. NBA TOTALS	648	54	13277	1977	4296	.460	16	56	.286	1152	1444	.798	893	1720	2613	2098	1337	7	490	800	40	5122	4.0	3.2	7.9
REG. ABA TOTALS	47	—	882	125	271	.461	0	1	.000	78	92	.848	68	106	174	121	81	—	24	63	2	328	3.7	2.6	7.0
NBA PLAYOFF TOTALS	20	0	242	32	73	.438	0	0	—	22	36	.611	19	23	42	42	33	0	13	16	5	86	2.1	2.1	4.3
ABA PLAYOFF TOTALS	7	—	97	13	35	.371	0	1	.000	19	24	.792	9	5	14	12	14	—	5	8	0	45	2.0	1.7	6.4

BRITT, TYRONE b. April 18, 1944 Ht. 6-4½ Wt. 195 College—North Carolina Central/Johnson C. Smith

SEASON—TEAM	G	GS	MIN	FGM	FGA	PCT	3FGM	3FGA	PCT	FTM	FTA	PCT	O-RB	D-RB	TOT	AST	PF	DQ	STL	TO	BLK	PTS	RPG	APG	PPG
67-68—San Diego	11	—	84	13	34	.382	—	—	—	2	3	.667	—	—	15	12	10	0	—	—	—	28	1.4	1.1	2.5
REG. SEASON TOTALS	11	—	84	13	34	.382	—	—	—	2	3	.667	—	—	15	12	10	0	—	—	—	28	1.4	1.1	2.5

BRITT, WAYMAN P. b. August 31, 1952 Ht. 6-2 Wt. 185 College—Michigan

SEASON—TEAM	G	GS	MIN	FGM	FGA	PCT	3FGM	3FGA	PCT	FTM	FTA	PCT	O-RB	D-RB	TOT	AST	PF	DQ	STL	TO	BLK	PTS	RPG	APG	PPG
77-78—Detroit	7	—	16	3	10	.300	—	—	—	3	4	.750	1	3	4	2	3	0	1	1	0	9	0.6	0.3	1.3
REG. SEASON TOTALS	7	—	16	3	10	.300	—	—	—	3	4	.750	1	3	4	2	3	0	1	1	0	9	0.6	0.3	1.3

BRITTAIN, MICHAEL JAMES (**Mike**) b. June 21, 1963 Ht. 7-1 Wt. 235 College—South Carolina

SEASON—TEAM	G	GS	MIN	FGM	FGA	PCT	3FGM	3FGA	PCT	FTM	FTA	PCT	O-RB	D-RB	TOT	AST	PF	DQ	STL	TO	BLK	PTS	RPG	APG	PPG
85-86—San Antonio	32	2	219	22	43	.512	0	0	—	10	19	.526	10	39	49	5	54	1	3	20	12	54	1.5	0.2	1.7
86-87—San Antonio	6	0	29	4	9	.444	0	0	—	1	2	.500	2	2	4	2	3	0	1	2	0	9	0.7	0.3	1.5
REG. SEASON TOTALS	38	2	248	26	52	.500	0	0	—	11	21	.524	12	41	53	7	57	1	4	22	12	63	1.4	0.2	1.7
PLAYOFF TOTALS	1	0	2	1	2	.500	0	0	—	0	0	—	1	0	1	—	0	0	0	0	1	2	1.0	0.0	2.0

BRITTON, DAVID b. August 29, 1958 Ht. 6-4 Wt. 190 College—Potomac State/Texas A&M

SEASON—TEAM	G	GS	MIN	FGM	FGA	PCT	3FGM	3FGA	PCT	FTM	FTA	PCT	O-RB	D-RB	TOT	AST	PF	DQ	STL	TO	BLK	PTS	RPG	APG	PPG
80-81—Washington	2	—	9	2	3	.667	0	0	—	0	0	—	0	2	2	3	2	0	1	2	0	4	1.0	1.5	2.0
REG. SEASON TOTALS	2	—	9	2	3	.667	0	0	—	0	0	—	0	2	2	3	2	0	1	2	0	4	1.0	1.5	2.0

BROGAN, JAMES RILEY (**Jim**) b. February 24, 1958 Ht. 6-4 Wt. 185 College—West Virginia Wesleyan

SEASON—TEAM	G	GS	MIN	FGM	FGA	PCT	3FGM	3FGA	PCT	FTM	FTA	PCT	O-RB	D-RB	TOT	AST	PF	DQ	STL	TO	BLK	PTS	RPG	APG	PPG
81-82—San Diego	63	19	1027	165	364	.453	9	32	.281	61	84	.726	61	59	120	156	123	2	49	83	13	400	1.9	2.5	6.3
82-83—San Diego	58	0	466	91	213	.427	3	13	.231	34	43	.791	33	29	62	66	79	0	26	43	9	219	1.1	1.1	3.8
REG. SEASON TOTALS	121	19	1493	256	577	.444	12	45	.267	95	127	.748	94	88	182	222	202	2	75	126	22	619	1.5	1.8	5.1

BROKAW, GARY GEORGE b. January 11, 1954 Ht. 6-4 Wt. 180 College—Notre Dame

SEASON—TEAM	G	GS	MIN	FGM	FGA	PCT	3FGM	3FGA	PCT	FTM	FTA	PCT	O-RB	D-RB	TOT	AST	PF	DQ	STL	TO	BLK	PTS	RPG	APG	PPG
74-75—Milwaukee	73	—	1639	234	514	.455	—	—	—	126	184	.685	36	111	147	221	176	3	31	—	18	594	2.0	3.0	8.1
75-76—Milwaukee	75	—	1468	237	519	.457	—	—	—	159	227	.700	26	99	125	246	138	1	37	—	17	633	1.7	3.3	8.4
76-77—Milw.-Clev.	80	—	1487	242	564	.429	—	—	—	163	219	.744	22	101	123	228	164	2	36	—	36	647	1.5	2.9	8.1
77-78—Buffalo	13	—	130	18	43	.419	—	—	—	18	24	.750	3	9	12	20	11	0	3	12	5	54	0.9	1.5	4.2
REG. SEASON TOTALS	241	—	4724	731	1640	.446	—	—	—	466	654	.713	87	320	407	715	489	6	107	12	76	1928	1.7	3.0	8.0
PLAYOFF TOTALS	6	—	152	32	56	.571	—	—	—	19	24	.792	3	12	15	36	17	0	5	—	4	83	2.5	6.0	13.8

BROOKFIELD, EMERY PRICE (**Price**) b. May 11, 1920   Ht. 6-4½   Wt. 185   College—West Texas State/Iowa State

SEASON—TEAM	G	GS	MIN	FGM	FGA	PCT	3FGM	3FGA	PCT	FTM	FTA	PCT	O-RB	D-RB	TOT	AST	PF	DQ	STL	TO	BLK	PTS	RPG	APG	PPG
46-47—Chicago (N)	42	—	—	82	—	—	—	—	—	24	33	.727	—	—	—	—	53	—	—	—	—	188	—	—	4.5
47-48—Anderson (N)	49	—	—	82	—	—	—	—	—	27	40	.675	—	—	—	—	56	—	—	—	—	191	—	—	3.9
48-49—Indianapolis	54	—	—	176	638	.276	—	—	—	90	125	.720	—	—	—	136	145	—	—	—	—	442	—	2.5	8.2
49-50—Rochester	7	—	—	11	23	.478	—	—	—	12	13	.923	—	—	—	1	7	—	—	—	—	34	—	0.1	4.9
REG. NBA TOTALS	61	—	—	187	661	.283	—	—	—	102	138	.739	—	—	—	137	152	—	—	—	—	476	—	2.2	7.8
REG. NBL TOTALS	91	—	—	164	—	—	—	—	—	51	73	.699	—	—	—	—	109	—	—	—	—	379	—	—	4.2
NBL PLAYOFF TOTALS	17	—	—	46	—	—	—	—	—	12	19	.632	—	—	—	—	38	—	—	—	—	104	—	—	6.1

BROOKINS, CLARENCE b. 1946   Ht. 6-4   Wt. 190   College—Temple

SEASON—TEAM	G	GS	MIN	FGM	FGA	PCT	3FGM	3FGA	PCT	FTM	FTA	PCT	O-RB	D-RB	TOT	AST	PF	DQ	STL	TO	BLK	PTS	RPG	APG	PPG
70-71—Floridians (A)	8	—	59	8	26	.308	0	1	.000	5	12	.417	—	—	12	1	5	—	—	—	—	21	1.5	0.1	2.6
REG. ABA TOTALS	8	—	59	8	26	.308	0	1	.000	5	12	.417	—	—	12	1	5	—	—	—	—	21	1.5	0.1	2.6

BROOKS, KEVIN b. October 12, 1969   Ht. 6-8   Wt. 200   College—Southwestern Louisiana

SEASON—TEAM	G	GS	MIN	FGM	FGA	PCT	3FGM	3FGA	PCT	FTM	FTA	PCT	O-RB	D-RB	TOT	AST	PF	DQ	STL	TO	BLK	PTS	RPG	APG	PPG
91-92—Denver	37	0	270	43	97	.443	2	11	.182	17	21	.810	13	26	39	11	19	0	8	18	2	105	1.1	0.3	2.8
92-93—Denver	55	2	571	93	233	.399	6	26	.231	35	40	.875	22	59	81	34	46	0	10	39	2	227	1.5	0.6	4.1
93-94—Denver	34	0	190	36	99	.364	4	23	.174	9	10	.900	5	16	21	3	19	0	0	12	2	85	0.6	0.1	2.5
REG. SEASON TOTALS	126	2	1031	172	429	.401	12	60	.200	61	71	.859	40	101	141	48	84	0	18	69	6	417	1.1	0.4	3.3
PLAYOFF TOTALS	2	0	5	2	7	.286	0	1	.000	1	2	.500	1	1	2	—	0	0	0	0	0	5	1.0	0.0	2.5

BROOKS, MICHAEL ANTHONY b. August 17, 1958   Ht. 6-7   Wt. 220   College—La Salle

SEASON—TEAM	G	GS	MIN	FGM	FGA	PCT	3FGM	3FGA	PCT	FTM	FTA	PCT	O-RB	D-RB	TOT	AST	PF	DQ	STL	TO	BLK	PTS	RPG	APG	PPG
80-81—San Diego	82	—	2479	488	1018	.479	0	6	.000	226	320	.706	210	232	442	208	234	2	99	163	31	1202	5.4	2.5	14.7
81-82—San Diego	82	73	2750	537	1066	.504	0	7	.000	202	267	.757	207	417	624	236	285	7	113	197	39	1276	7.6	2.9	15.6
82-83—San Diego	82	26	2457	402	830	.484	5	15	.333	193	277	.697	239	282	521	262	297	6	112	177	39	1002	6.4	3.2	12.2
83-84—San Diego	47	30	1405	213	445	.479	0	5	.000	104	151	.689	142	200	342	88	125	1	50	78	14	530	7.3	1.9	11.3
86-87—Indiana	10	0	148	13	37	.351	0	0	—	7	10	.700	9	19	28	11	19	0	9	11	0	33	2.8	1.1	3.3
87-88—Denver	16	0	133	20	49	.408	0	0	—	3	4	.750	19	25	44	13	21	1	4	12	1	43	2.8	0.8	2.7
REG. SEASON TOTALS	319	129	9372	1673	3445	.486	5	33	.152	735	1029	.714	826	1175	2001	818	981	17	387	638	124	4086	6.3	2.6	12.8
PLAYOFF TOTALS	4	0	11	1	3	.333	1	2	.500	0	0	—	1	3	4	2	1	0	0	0	0	3	1.0	0.5	0.8

BROOKS, SCOTT WILLIAM b. July 31, 1965   Ht. 5-11   Wt. 165   College—Texas Christian/San Joaquin Delta/California-Irvine

SEASON—TEAM	G	GS	MIN	FGM	FGA	PCT	3FGM	3FGA	PCT	FTM	FTA	PCT	O-RB	D-RB	TOT	AST	PF	DQ	STL	TO	BLK	PTS	RPG	APG	PPG
88-89—Philadelphia	82	6	1372	156	371	.420	55	153	.359	61	69	.884	19	75	94	306	116	0	69	65	3	428	1.1	3.7	5.2
89-90—Philadelphia	72	1	975	119	276	.431	31	79	.392	50	57	.877	15	49	64	207	105	0	47	38	0	319	0.9	2.9	4.4
90-91—Minnesota	80	0	980	159	370	.430	45	135	.333	61	72	.847	28	44	72	204	122	1	53	51	5	424	0.9	2.6	5.3
91-92—Minnesota	82	0	1082	167	374	.447	32	90	.356	51	63	.810	27	72	99	205	82	0	66	51	7	417	1.2	2.5	5.1
92-93—Houston	82	0	1516	183	385	.475	41	99	.414	112	135	.830	22	77	99	243	136	0	79	72	3	519	1.2	3.0	6.3
93-94—Houston	73	0	1225	142	289	.491	23	61	.377	74	85	.871	10	92	102	149	98	0	51	55	2	381	1.4	2.0	5.2
REG. SEASON TOTALS	471	7	7150	926	2065	.448	227	617	.368	409	481	.850	121	409	530	1314	659	1	365	332	20	2488	1.1	2.8	5.3
PLAYOFF TOTALS	29	0	340	28	73	.384	10	23	.435	18	25	.720	4	20	24	55	41	0	12	21	0	84	0.8	1.9	2.9

BROWN, ANTHONY WILLIAM (**Tony**) b. July 29, 1960   Ht. 6-6   Wt. 200   College—Arkansas

SEASON—TEAM	G	GS	MIN	FGM	FGA	PCT	3FGM	3FGA	PCT	FTM	FTA	PCT	O-RB	D-RB	TOT	AST	PF	DQ	STL	TO	BLK	PTS	RPG	APG	PPG
84-85—Indiana	82	26	1586	214	465	.460	0	6	.000	116	171	.678	146	142	288	159	212	3	59	116	12	544	3.5	1.9	6.6
85-86—Chicago	10	0	132	18	41	.439	0	2	.000	9	13	.692	5	11	16	14	16	0	5	4	1	45	1.6	1.4	4.5
86-87—New Jersey	77	67	2339	358	810	.442	5	20	.250	152	206	.738	84	135	219	259	273	12	89	153	14	873	2.8	3.4	11.3
88-89—Houston-Milw.	43	0	365	50	118	.424	4	16	.250	24	31	.774	22	22	44	26	42	0	15	17	4	128	1.0	0.6	3.0
89-90—Milwaukee	61	10	635	88	206	.427	5	20	.250	38	56	.679	39	33	72	41	79	0	32	51	4	219	1.2	0.7	3.6
90-91—Lakers-Utah	30	0	294	30	80	.375	3	12	.250	20	23	.870	24	19	43	16	47	0	4	16	0	83	1.4	0.5	2.8
91-92—L.A. Clips-Seattle	56	2	654	102	249	.410	19	63	.302	48	66	.727	32	52	84	48	82	0	30	35	5	271	1.5	0.9	4.8
REG. SEASON TOTALS	359	105	6005	860	1969	.437	36	139	.259	407	566	.719	352	414	766	563	751	15	234	392	40	2163	2.1	1.6	6.0
PLAYOFF TOTALS	17	—	133	11	28	.393	3	8	.375	7	11	.636	4	8	12	9	17	1	4	2	0	32	0.7	0.5	1.9

BROWN, CLARENCE (**Chucky, Wild Thing**) b. February 29, 1968   Ht. 6-8   Wt. 215   College—North Carolina State

SEASON—TEAM	G	GS	MIN	FGM	FGA	PCT	3FGM	3FGA	PCT	FTM	FTA	PCT	O-RB	D-RB	TOT	AST	PF	DQ	STL	TO	BLK	PTS	RPG	APG	PPG
89-90—Cleveland	75	35	1339	210	447	.470	0	7	.000	125	164	.762	83	148	231	50	148	0	33	69	26	545	3.1	0.7	7.3
90-91—Cleveland	74	51	1485	263	502	.524	0	4	.000	101	144	.701	78	135	213	80	130	0	26	94	24	627	2.9	1.1	8.5
91-92—Clev.-Lakers	42	2	431	60	128	.469	0	3	.000	30	49	.612	31	51	82	26	48	0	12	29	7	150	2.0	0.6	3.6
92-93—New Jersey	77	20	1186	160	331	.483	0	5	.000	71	98	.724	88	144	232	51	112	0	20	56	24	391	3.0	0.7	5.1
93-94—Dallas	1	0	10	1	1	1.000	0	0	—	1	1	1.000	0	1	1	0	2	0	0	0	0	3	1.0	0.0	3.0
REG. SEASON TOTALS	269	108	4451	694	1409	.493	0	19	.000	328	456	.719	280	479	759	207	440	0	91	248	81	1716	2.8	0.8	6.4
PLAYOFF TOTALS	7	0	106	17	41	.415	0	1	.000	9	13	.692	6	14	20	3	5	0	3	3	5	43	2.9	0.4	6.1

BROWN, COLLIER JR. (**P.J.**) b. October 14, 1969   Ht. 6-11 Wt. 240 College—Louisiana Tech

SEASON—TEAM	G	GS	MIN	FGM	FGA	PCT	3FGM	3FGA	PCT	FTM	FTA	PCT	O-RB	D-RB	TOT	AST	PF	DQ	STL	TO	BLK	PTS	RPG	APG	PPG
93-94—New Jersey	79	54	1950	167	402	.415	1	6	.167	115	152	.757	188	305	493	93	177	1	71	72	93	450	6.2	1.2	5.7
REG. SEASON TOTALS	79	54	1950	167	402	.415	1	6	.167	115	152	.757	188	305	493	93	177	1	71	72	93	450	6.2	1.2	5.7
PLAYOFF TOTALS	4	1	56	2	9	.222	0	0	—	8	8	1.000	4	4	8	3	13	0	0	3	2	12	2.0	0.8	3.0

BROWN, DARRELL H. b. March 14, 1923   Ht. 6-2 Wt. 175 College—Humboldt State/Pacific

SEASON—TEAM	G	GS	MIN	FGM	FGA	PCT	3FGM	3FGA	PCT	FTM	FTA	PCT	O-RB	D-RB	TOT	AST	PF	DQ	STL	TO	BLK	PTS	RPG	APG	PPG
48-49—Baltimore	3	—	—	2	6	.333	—	—	—	0	2	.000	—	—	—	0	3	—	—	—	—	4	—	0.0	1.3
REG. SEASON TOTALS	3	—	—	2	6	.333	—	—	—	0	2	.000	—	—	—	0	3	—	—	—	—	4	—	0.0	1.3

BROWN, DeCOVAN KADELL (**Dee, Dee-lightful**) b. November 29, 1968   Ht. 6-1 Wt. 160 College—Jacksonville State

SEASON—TEAM	G	GS	MIN	FGM	FGA	PCT	3FGM	3FGA	PCT	FTM	FTA	PCT	O-RB	D-RB	TOT	AST	PF	DQ	STL	TO	BLK	PTS	RPG	APG	PPG
90-91—Boston	82	5	1945	284	612	.464	7	34	.206	137	157	.873	41	141	182	344	161	0	83	137	14	712	2.2	4.2	8.7
91-92—Boston	31	20	883	149	350	.426	5	22	.227	60	78	.769	15	64	79	164	74	0	33	59	7	363	2.5	5.3	11.7
92-93—Boston	80	48	2254	328	701	.468	26	82	.317	192	242	.793	45	201	246	461	203	2	138	136	32	874	3.1	5.8	10.9
93-94—Boston	77	76	2867	490	1021	.480	30	96	.313	182	219	.831	63	237	300	347	207	3	156	126	47	1192	3.9	4.5	15.5
REG. SEASON TOTALS	270	149	7949	1251	2684	.466	68	234	.291	571	696	.820	164	643	807	1316	645	5	410	458	100	3141	3.0	4.9	11.6
PLAYOFF TOTALS	21	3	537	90	193	.466	1	15	.067	46	54	.852	14	49	63	87	59	2	14	35	14	227	3.0	4.1	10.8

BROWN, FRED (**Downtown**) b. August 7, 1948   Ht. 6-3 Wt. 185 College—Southeastern CC/Iowa

SEASON—TEAM	G	GS	MIN	FGM	FGA	PCT	3FGM	3FGA	PCT	FTM	FTA	PCT	O-RB	D-RB	TOT	AST	PF	DQ	STL	TO	BLK	PTS	RPG	APG	PPG
71-72—Seattle	33	—	359	59	180	.328	—	—	—	22	29	.759	—	—	37	60	44	0	—	—	—	140	1.1	1.8	4.2
72-73—Seattle	79	—	2320	471	1035	.455	—	—	—	121	148	.818	—	—	318	438	226	5	—	—	—	1063	4.0	5.5	13.5
73-74—Seattle	82	—	2501	578	1226	.471	—	—	—	195	226	.863	114	287	401	414	276	6	136	—	18	1351	4.9	5.0	16.5
74-75—Seattle	81	—	2669	737	1537	.480	—	—	—	226	272	.831	113	230	343	284	227	2	187	—	14	1700	4.2	3.5	21.0
75-76—Seattle	76	—	2516	742	1522	.488	—	—	—	273	314	.869	111	206	317	207	186	0	143	—	18	1757	4.2	2.7	23.1
76-77—Seattle	72	—	2098	534	1114	.479	—	—	—	168	190	.884	68	164	232	176	140	1	124	—	19	1236	3.2	2.4	17.2
77-78—Seattle	72	—	1965	508	1042	.488	—	—	—	176	196	.898	61	127	188	240	145	0	110	164	25	1192	2.6	3.3	16.6
78-79—Seattle	77	—	1961	446	951	.469	—	—	—	183	206	.888	38	134	172	260	142	0	119	164	23	1075	2.2	3.4	14.0
79-80—Seattle	80	—	1701	404	843	.479	39	88	.443	113	135	.837	35	120	155	174	117	0	65	105	17	960	1.9	2.2	12.0
80-81—Seattle	78	—	1986	505	1035	.488	23	64	.359	173	208	.832	53	122	175	233	141	0	88	131	13	1206	2.2	3.0	15.5
81-82—Seattle	82	2	1785	393	863	.455	25	77	.325	111	129	.860	42	98	140	238	111	0	69	96	4	922	1.7	2.9	11.2
82-83—Seattle	80	1	1432	371	714	.520	14	32	.438	58	72	.806	32	65	97	242	98	0	59	110	13	814	1.2	3.0	10.2
83-84—Seattle	71	1	1129	258	506	.510	9	34	.265	77	86	.895	14	48	62	194	84	0	49	70	2	602	0.9	2.7	8.5
REG. SEASON TOTALS	963	4	24422	6006	12568	.478	110	295	.373	1896	2211	.858	681	1601	2637	3160	1937	14	1149	840	166	14018	2.7	3.3	14.6
PLAYOFF TOTALS	83	0	1900	499	1082	.461	13	42	.310	186	227	.819	72	124	196	193	144	0	74	82	8	1197	2.4	2.3	14.4
ALL-STAR TOTALS	1	0	24	7	13	.538	0	0	—	0	0	—	0	0	0	1	3	0	5	—	0	14	0.0	1.0	14.0

BROWN, GEORGE RAFF b. October 30, 1935   Ht. 6-6 Wt. 190 College—Wayne State (Mich.)

SEASON—TEAM	G	GS	MIN	FGM	FGA	PCT	3FGM	3FGA	PCT	FTM	FTA	PCT	O-RB	D-RB	TOT	AST	PF	DQ	STL	TO	BLK	PTS	RPG	APG	PPG
57-58—Minneapolis	1	—	6	0	2	.000	—	—	—	1	2	.500	—	—	1	0	1	0	—	—	—	1	1.0	0.0	1.0
REG. SEASON TOTALS	1	—	6	0	2	.000	—	—	—	1	2	.500	—	—	1	0	1	0	—	—	—	1	1.0	0.0	1.0

BROWN, HAROLD V. (**Brownie**) b. October 2, 1923 d. September 1980 Ht. 6-0 Wt. 155 College—Evansville

SEASON—TEAM	G	GS	MIN	FGM	FGA	PCT	3FGM	3FGA	PCT	FTM	FTA	PCT	O-RB	D-RB	TOT	AST	PF	DQ	STL	TO	BLK	PTS	RPG	APG	PPG
46-47—Detroit	54	—	—	95	383	.248	—	—	—	74	117	.632	—	—	—	39	122	—	—	—	—	264	—	0.7	4.9
REG. SEASON TOTALS	54	—	—	95	383	.248	—	—	—	74	117	.632	—	—	—	39	122	—	—	—	—	264	—	0.7	4.9

BROWN, JOHN YOUNG b. December 14, 1951   Ht. 6-7 Wt. 220 College—Missouri

SEASON—TEAM	G	GS	MIN	FGM	FGA	PCT	3FGM	3FGA	PCT	FTM	FTA	PCT	O-RB	D-RB	TOT	AST	PF	DQ	STL	TO	BLK	PTS	RPG	APG	PPG
73-74—Atlanta	77	—	1715	277	632	.438	—	—	—	163	217	.751	177	264	441	114	239	10	29	—	16	717	5.7	1.5	9.3
74-75—Atlanta	73	—	1986	315	684	.461	—	—	—	185	250	.740	180	254	434	133	228	7	54	—	15	815	5.9	1.8	11.2
75-76—Atlanta	75	—	1758	215	486	.442	—	—	—	162	209	.775	146	257	403	126	235	7	45	—	16	592	5.4	1.7	7.9
76-77—Atlanta	77	—	1405	160	350	.457	—	—	—	121	150	.807	75	161	236	103	217	7	46	—	7	441	3.1	1.3	5.7
77-78—Atlanta	75	—	1594	192	405	.474	—	—	—	165	200	.825	137	166	303	105	280	18	55	116	8	549	4.0	1.4	7.3
78-79—Chicago	77	—	1265	152	317	.479	—	—	—	84	98	.857	83	155	238	104	180	5	18	89	10	388	3.1	1.4	5.0
79-80—Utah-Atlanta	32	—	385	37	105	.352	0	0	—	38	48	.792	26	45	71	18	70	0	3	29	4	112	2.2	0.6	3.5
REG. SEASON TOTALS	486	—	10108	1348	2979	.453	0	0	—	918	1172	.783	824	1302	2126	703	1449	54	250	234	76	3614	4.4	1.4	7.4
PLAYOFF TOTALS	7	—	64	4	13	.308	0	1	.000	2	2	1.000	2	8	10	1	10	0	1	7	1	10	1.4	0.1	1.4

BROWN, JULIAN MYRON (**Myron**) b. November 3, 1969   Ht. 6-3 Wt. 180 College—Slippery Rock (Pa.)

SEASON—TEAM	G	GS	MIN	FGM	FGA	PCT	3FGM	3FGA	PCT	FTM	FTA	PCT	O-RB	D-RB	TOT	AST	PF	DQ	STL	TO	BLK	PTS	RPG	APG	PPG
91-92—Minnesota	4	0	23	4	6	.667	1	3	.333	0	0	—	0	3	3	6	2	0	1	4	0	9	0.8	1.5	2.3
REG. SEASON TOTALS	4	0	23	4	6	.667	1	3	.333	0	0	—	0	3	3	6	2	0	1	4	0	9	0.8	1.5	2.3

BROWN, LAWRENCE HARVEY (**Larry**) b. September 14, 1940   Ht. 5-9 Wt. 160 College—North Carolina

SEASON—TEAM	G	GS	MIN	FGM	FGA	PCT	3FGM	3FGA	PCT	FTM	FTA	PCT	O-RB	D-RB	TOT	AST	PF	DQ	STL	TO	BLK	PTS	RPG	APG	PPG
67-68—New Orleans (A)	78	—	2807	330	901	.366	19	89	.213	366	450	.813	—	—	249	506	220	1	—	355	—	1045	3.2	6.5	13.4
68-69—Oakland (A)	77	—	2381	308	706	.436	8	35	.229	301	379	.794	—	—	235	544	230	6	—	331	—	925	3.1	7.1	12.0
69-70—Washington (A)	82	—	2766	376	854	.440	10	39	.256	362	439	.825	—	—	246	580	257	4	—	—	—	1124	3.0	7.1	13.7
70-71—Vir.-Denver (A)	63	—	1343	127	340	.374	6	21	.286	186	225	.827	—	—	109	330	145	—	—	—	—	446	1.7	5.2	7.1
71-72—Denver (A)	76	—	2012	243	556	.437	5	25	.200	198	244	.811	—	—	166	549	207	—	—	217	—	689	2.2	7.2	9.1
REG. ABA TOTALS	376	—	11309	1384	3357	.412	48	209	.230	1413	1737	.813	—	—	1005	2509	1059	11	—	903	—	4229	2.7	6.7	11.2
ABA PLAYOFF TOTALS	47	—	1710	218	508	.429	5	29	.172	229	270	.848	—	—	156	320	158	1	—	150	—	670	3.3	6.8	14.3
ABA ALL-STAR TOTALS	3	—	62	8	18	.444	2	3	.667	7	9	.778	—	3	6	15	5	0	—	11	—	25	2.0	5.0	8.3

BROWN, LEON (**Stretch**) b. October 12, 1919   Ht. 6-3 Wt. 190 College—Wyoming

SEASON—TEAM	G	GS	MIN	FGM	FGA	PCT	3FGM	3FGA	PCT	FTM	FTA	PCT	O-RB	D-RB	TOT	AST	PF	DQ	STL	TO	BLK	PTS	RPG	APG	PPG
46-47—Cleveland	5	—	—	0	3	.000	—	—	—	0	0	—	—	—	—	0	2	—	—	—	—	0	—	0.0	0.0
REG. SEASON TOTALS	5	—	—	0	3	.000	—	—	—	0	0	—	—	—	—	0	2	—	—	—	—	0	—	0.0	0.0

BROWN, LEWIS b. February 19, 1955   Ht. 6-11 Wt. 230 College—Nevada-Las Vegas

SEASON—TEAM	G	GS	MIN	FGM	FGA	PCT	3FGM	3FGA	PCT	FTM	FTA	PCT	O-RB	D-RB	TOT	AST	PF	DQ	STL	TO	BLK	PTS	RPG	APG	PPG
80-81—Washington	2	—	5	0	3	.000	0	0	—	2	5	.400	1	1	2	0	2	0	0	1	0	2	1.0	0.0	1.0
REG. SEASON TOTALS	2	—	5	0	3	.000	0	0	—	2	5	.400	1	1	2	0	2	0	0	1	0	2	1.0	0.0	1.0

BROWN, MICHAEL (**Mike**) b. July 19, 1963   Ht. 6-10 Wt. 260 College—George Washington

SEASON—TEAM	G	GS	MIN	FGM	FGA	PCT	3FGM	3FGA	PCT	FTM	FTA	PCT	O-RB	D-RB	TOT	AST	PF	DQ	STL	TO	BLK	PTS	RPG	APG	PPG
86-87—Chicago	62	3	818	106	201	.527	0	0	—	46	72	.639	71	143	214	24	129	2	20	59	7	258	3.5	0.4	4.2
87-88—Chicago	46	27	591	78	174	.448	0	1	.000	41	71	.577	66	93	159	28	85	0	11	38	4	197	3.5	0.6	4.3
88-89—Utah	66	16	1051	104	248	.419	0	0	—	92	130	.708	92	166	258	41	133	0	25	77	17	300	3.9	0.6	4.5
89-90—Utah	82	0	1397	177	344	.515	1	2	.500	157	199	.789	111	262	373	47	187	0	32	88	28	512	4.5	0.6	6.2
90-91—Utah	82	2	1391	129	284	.454	0	0	—	132	178	.742	109	228	337	49	166	0	29	82	24	390	4.1	0.6	4.8
91-92—Utah	82	1	1783	221	488	.453	0	1	.000	190	285	.667	187	289	476	81	196	1	42	105	34	632	5.8	1.0	7.7
92-93—Utah	82	21	1551	176	409	.430	0	1	.000	113	164	.689	147	244	391	64	190	1	32	95	23	465	4.8	0.8	5.7
93-94—Minnesota	82	40	1921	111	260	.427	0	2	.000	77	118	.653	119	328	447	72	218	4	51	75	29	299	5.5	0.9	3.6
REG. SEASON TOTALS	584	110	10503	1102	2408	.458	1	7	.143	848	1217	.697	902	1753	2655	406	1304	8	242	619	166	3053	4.5	0.7	5.2
PLAYOFF TOTALS	39	1	675	77	174	.443	0	0	—	76	97	.784	51	108	159	22	103	1	8	39	5	230	4.1	0.6	5.9

BROWN, RANDY b. May 22, 1968   Ht. 6-3 Wt. 190 College—Houston/Howard County (Tex.)/New Mexico State

SEASON—TEAM	G	GS	MIN	FGM	FGA	PCT	3FGM	3FGA	PCT	FTM	FTA	PCT	O-RB	D-RB	TOT	AST	PF	DQ	STL	TO	BLK	PTS	RPG	APG	PPG
91-92—Sacramento	56	0	535	77	169	.456	0	6	.000	38	58	.655	26	43	69	59	68	0	35	42	12	192	1.2	1.1	3.4
92-93—Sacramento	75	34	1726	225	486	.463	2	6	.333	115	157	.732	75	137	212	196	206	4	108	120	34	567	2.8	2.6	7.6
93-94—Sacramento	61	2	1041	110	251	.438	0	4	.000	53	87	.609	40	72	112	133	132	2	63	75	14	273	1.8	2.2	4.5
REG. SEASON TOTALS	192	36	3302	412	906	.455	2	16	.125	206	302	.682	141	252	393	388	406	6	206	237	60	1032	2.0	2.0	5.4

BROWN, RAYMOND b. July 5, 1965   Ht. 6-8 Wt. 220 College—Mississippi State/Idaho

SEASON—TEAM	G	GS	MIN	FGM	FGA	PCT	3FGM	3FGA	PCT	FTM	FTA	PCT	O-RB	D-RB	TOT	AST	PF	DQ	STL	TO	BLK	PTS	RPG	APG	PPG
89-90—Utah	16	0	56	8	28	.286	0	0	—	0	2	.000	10	5	15	4	11	0	0	6	0	16	0.9	0.3	1.0
REG. SEASON TOTALS	16	0	56	8	28	.286	0	0	—	0	2	.000	10	5	15	4	11	0	0	6	0	16	0.9	0.3	1.0
PLAYOFF TOTALS	3	0	6	0	0	—	0	0	—	0	0	—	0	0	0	—	2	0	0	0	0	0	0.0	0.0	0.0

BROWN, RICKEY DARNELL b. August 20, 1958   Ht. 6-10 Wt. 220 College—Mississippi State

SEASON—TEAM	G	GS	MIN	FGM	FGA	PCT	3FGM	3FGA	PCT	FTM	FTA	PCT	O-RB	D-RB	TOT	AST	PF	DQ	STL	TO	BLK	PTS	RPG	APG	PPG
80-81—Golden State	45	—	580	83	162	.512	0	0	—	16	21	.762	52	114	166	21	103	4	9	31	14	182	3.7	0.5	4.0
81-82—Golden State	82	11	1260	192	418	.459	0	0	—	86	122	.705	136	228	364	19	243	4	36	84	29	470	4.4	0.2	5.7
82-83—G.S.-Atlanta	76	7	1048	167	349	.479	0	3	.000	65	105	.619	91	175	266	25	172	1	13	82	26	399	3.5	0.3	5.3
83-84—Atlanta	68	3	785	94	201	.468	0	0	—	48	65	.738	67	114	181	29	161	4	18	53	23	236	2.7	0.4	3.5
84-85—Atlanta	69	5	814	78	192	.406	0	0	—	39	68	.574	76	147	223	25	117	0	19	51	22	195	3.2	0.4	2.8
REG. SEASON TOTALS	340	26	4487	614	1322	.464	0	3	.000	254	381	.667	422	778	1200	119	796	13	95	301	114	1482	3.5	0.4	4.4
PLAYOFF TOTALS	7	0	98	11	24	.458	0	0	—	11	14	.786	5	17	22	2	22	0	0	5	1	33	3.1	0.3	4.7

BROWN, ROBERT EDWARD (**Bob**) b. November 12, 1923   Ht. 6-4 Wt. 205 College—Miami (Ohio)

SEASON—TEAM	G	GS	MIN	FGM	FGA	PCT	3FGM	3FGA	PCT	FTM	FTA	PCT	O-RB	D-RB	TOT	AST	PF	DQ	STL	TO	BLK	PTS	RPG	APG	PPG
48-49—Providence	20	—	—	37	111	.333	—	—	—	34	47	.723	—	—	—	14	67	—	—	—	—	108	—	0.7	5.4
49-50—Denver	62	—	—	276	764	.361	—	—	—	172	252	.683	—	—	—	101	269	—	—	—	—	724	—	1.6	11.7
REG. SEASON TOTALS	82	—	—	313	875	.358	—	—	—	206	299	.689	—	—	—	115	336	—	—	—	—	832	—	1.4	10.1

BROWN, ROGER A. b. May 22, 1942 Ht. 6-5 Wt. 205 College—Dayton

SEASON—TEAM	G	GS	MIN	FGM	FGA	PCT	3FGM	3FGA	PCT	FTM	FTA	PCT	O-RB	D-RB	TOT	AST	PF	DQ	STL	TO	BLK	PTS	RPG	APG	PPG
67-68—Indiana (A)	76	—	2974	544	1286	.423	14	54	.259	390	517	.754	—	—	647	327	296	10	—	265	—	1492	8.5	4.3	19.6
68-69—Indiana (A)	75	—	2658	563	1169	.482	5	16	.313	442	563	.785	—	—	510	345	281	11	—	215	—	1573	6.8	4.6	21.0
69-70—Indiana (A)	84	—	3495	719	1444	.498	40	120	.333	457	562	.813	—	—	620	392	308	3	—	—	—	1935	7.4	4.7	23.0
70-71—Indiana (A)	82	—	3364	610	1266	.482	63	223	.283	407	512	.795	—	—	569	395	289	—	—	—	—	1690	6.9	4.8	20.6
71-72—Indiana (A)	78	—	2987	532	1112	.478	57	185	.308	323	401	.805	—	—	502	306	227	—	—	214	—	1444	6.4	3.9	18.5
72-73—Indiana (A)	72	—	2177	332	700	.474	42	118	.356	203	247	.822	111	237	348	204	181	0	—	120	—	909	4.8	2.8	12.6
73-74—Indiana (A)	82	—	2527	379	829	.457	56	155	.361	155	200	.775	112	278	390	232	248	—	56	125	60	969	4.8	2.8	11.8
74-75—Mem.-Utah-Ind. (A)	56	—	1272	181	421	.430	35	100	.350	89	114	.781	56	116	172	114	99	—	47	94	21	486	3.1	2.0	8.7
REG. ABA TOTALS	605	—	21454	3860	8227	.469	312	971	.321	2466	3116	.791	279	631	3758	2315	1929	24	103	1033	81	10498	6.2	3.8	17.4
ABA PLAYOFF TOTALS	110	—	4030	765	1590	.481	68	190	.358	462	583	.792	72	180	705	405	391	8	13	137	35	2060	6.4	3.7	18.7
ABA ALL-STAR TOTALS	4	—	108	15	43	.349	0	5	.000	13	17	.765	4	9	19	9	14	0	0	9	0	43	4.8	2.3	10.8

BROWN, STANLEY (Stan) b. June 27, 1929 Ht. 6-3 Wt. 200 College—None

SEASON—TEAM	G	GS	MIN	FGM	FGA	PCT	3FGM	3FGA	PCT	FTM	FTA	PCT	O-RB	D-RB	TOT	AST	PF	DQ	STL	TO	BLK	PTS	RPG	APG	PPG
47-48—Philadelphia	19	—	—	19	71	.268	—	—	—	12	19	.632	—	—	—	1	16	—	—	—	—	50	—	0.1	2.6
51-52—Philadelphia	15	—	141	22	63	.349	—	—	—	10	18	.556	—	—	17	9	32	0	—	—	—	54	1.1	0.6	3.6
REG. SEASON TOTALS	34	—	141	41	134	.306	—	—	—	22	37	.595	—	—	17	10	48	0	—	—	—	104	1.1	0.3	3.1

BROWN, W. ROGER (Roger) b. February 23, 1950 Ht. 6-11 Wt. 230 College—Kansas

SEASON—TEAM	G	GS	MIN	FGM	FGA	PCT	3FGM	3FGA	PCT	FTM	FTA	PCT	O-RB	D-RB	TOT	AST	PF	DQ	STL	TO	BLK	PTS	RPG	APG	PPG
72-73—Los Angeles	1	—	5	0	0	—	—	—	—	1	3	.333	—	—	0	0	1	0	—	—	—	1	0.0	0.0	1.0
72-73—Carolina (A)	62	—	579	59	129	.457	0	0	—	28	51	.549	62	116	178	25	120	2	—	46	—	146	2.9	0.4	2.4
73-74—S.A.-Vir. (A)	63	—	990	98	260	.377	0	0	—	34	56	.607	145	207	352	46	129	—	23	80	62	230	5.6	0.7	3.7
75-76—Detroit	29	—	454	29	72	.403	—	—	—	14	18	.778	47	83	130	12	76	1	6	—	25	72	4.5	0.4	2.5
75-76—Denver (A)	37	—	291	28	61	.459	2	2	1.000	16	24	.667	25	50	75	22	63	—	8	17	22	74	2.0	0.6	2.0
76-77—Detroit	43	—	322	21	56	.375	—	—	—	18	26	.692	31	59	90	12	68	4	15	—	18	60	2.1	0.3	1.4
79-80—Chicago	4	—	37	1	3	.333	0	0	—	0	0	—	2	8	10	1	4	0	0	0	3	2	2.5	0.3	0.5
REG. NBA TOTALS	77	—	818	51	131	.389	0	0	—	33	47	.702	80	150	230	25	149	5	21	0	46	135	3.0	0.3	1.8
REG. ABA TOTALS	162	—	1860	185	450	.411	2	2	1.000	78	131	.595	232	373	605	93	312	2	31	143	84	450	3.7	0.6	2.8
NBA PLAYOFF TOTALS	11	—	56	4	10	.400	0	0	—	2	4	.500	7	7	14	2	10	0	0	—	2	10	1.3	0.2	0.9
ABA PLAYOFF TOTALS	12	—	90	14	26	.538	0	0	—	3	4	.750	8	6	25	3	12	0	4	4	2	31	2.1	0.3	2.6
ABA ALL-STAR TOTALS	1	—	9	2	2	1.000	0	0	—	0	0	—	0	0	3	3	1	—	0	0	0	4	3.0	3.0	4.0

BROWNE, JAMES (Jim) b. January 1, 1930 Ht. 6-10 Wt. 235 College—None

SEASON—TEAM	G	GS	MIN	FGM	FGA	PCT	3FGM	3FGA	PCT	FTM	FTA	PCT	O-RB	D-RB	TOT	AST	PF	DQ	STL	TO	BLK	PTS	RPG	APG	PPG
48-49—Chicago	4	—	—	1	2	.500	—	—	—	1	2	.500	—	—	—	0	4	—	—	—	—	3	—	0.0	0.8
49-50—Denver	31	—	—	17	48	.354	—	—	—	13	27	.481	—	—	—	8	16	—	—	—	—	47	—	0.3	1.5
REG. SEASON TOTALS	35	—	—	18	50	.360	—	—	—	14	29	.483	—	—	—	8	20	—	—	—	—	50	—	0.2	1.4

BRUNDY, STANLEY DWAYNE b. November 13, 1967 Ht. 6-6 Wt. 210 College—DePaul

SEASON—TEAM	G	GS	MIN	FGM	FGA	PCT	3FGM	3FGA	PCT	FTM	FTA	PCT	O-RB	D-RB	TOT	AST	PF	DQ	STL	TO	BLK	PTS	RPG	APG	PPG
89-90—New Jersey	16	0	128	15	30	.500	0	0	—	7	18	.389	15	11	26	3	24	0	6	6	5	37	1.6	0.2	2.3
REG. SEASON TOTALS	16	0	128	15	30	.500	0	0	—	7	18	.389	15	11	26	3	24	0	6	6	5	37	1.6	0.2	2.3

BRUNKHORST, BRIAN J. (Bronk) b. June 12, 1945 Ht. 6-6 Wt. 210 College—Marquette

SEASON—TEAM	G	GS	MIN	FGM	FGA	PCT	3FGM	3FGA	PCT	FTM	FTA	PCT	O-RB	D-RB	TOT	AST	PF	DQ	STL	TO	BLK	PTS	RPG	APG	PPG
68-69—Los Angeles (A)	3	—	56	6	11	.545	0	0	—	13	17	.765	—	—	13	3	8	0	—	5	—	25	4.3	1.0	8.3
REG. ABA TOTALS	3	—	56	6	11	.545	0	0	—	13	17	.765	—	—	13	3	8	0	—	5	—	25	4.3	1.0	8.3

BRUNS, GEORGE WILLIAM b. August 30, 1946 Ht. 6-0 Wt. 160 College—Manhattan

SEASON—TEAM	G	GS	MIN	FGM	FGA	PCT	3FGM	3FGA	PCT	FTM	FTA	PCT	O-RB	D-RB	TOT	AST	PF	DQ	STL	TO	BLK	PTS	RPG	APG	PPG
72-73—New York (A)	13	—	236	31	66	.470	2	4	.500	22	27	.815	1	7	8	36	26	0	—	20	—	86	0.6	2.8	6.6
REG. ABA TOTALS	13	—	236	31	66	.470	2	4	.500	22	27	.815	1	7	8	36	26	0	—	20	—	86	0.6	2.8	6.6
ABA PLAYOFF TOTALS	2	—	7	0	1	.000	0	0	—	1	2	.500	—	—	—	1	3	0	—	2	—	1	0.0	0.5	0.5

BRYANT, EMMETTE b. November 4, 1938 Ht. 6-1 Wt. 175 College—DePaul

SEASON—TEAM	G	GS	MIN	FGM	FGA	PCT	3FGM	3FGA	PCT	FTM	FTA	PCT	O-RB	D-RB	TOT	AST	PF	DQ	STL	TO	BLK	PTS	RPG	APG	PPG
64-65—New York	77	—	1332	145	436	.333	—	—	—	87	133	.654	—	—	167	167	212	3	—	—	—	377	2.2	2.2	4.9
65-66—New York	71	—	1193	212	449	.472	—	—	—	74	101	.733	—	—	170	216	215	4	—	—	—	498	2.4	3.0	7.0
66-67—New York	63	—	1593	236	577	.409	—	—	—	74	114	.649	—	—	273	218	231	4	—	—	—	546	4.3	3.5	8.7
67-68—New York	77	—	968	112	291	.385	—	—	—	59	86	.686	—	—	133	134	173	0	—	—	—	283	1.7	1.7	3.7
68-69—Boston	80	—	1388	197	488	.404	—	—	—	65	100	.650	—	—	192	176	264	9	—	—	—	459	2.4	2.2	5.7
69-70—Boston	71	—	1617	210	520	.404	—	—	—	135	181	.746	—	—	269	231	201	5	—	—	—	555	3.8	3.3	7.8
70-71—Buffalo	73	—	2137	288	684	.421	—	—	—	151	203	.744	—	—	262	352	266	7	—	—	—	727	3.6	4.8	10.0
71-72—Buffalo	54	—	1223	101	220	.459	—	—	—	75	125	.600	—	—	127	206	167	5	—	—	—	277	2.4	3.8	5.1
REG. SEASON TOTALS	566	—	11451	1501	3665	.410	—	—	—	720	1043	.690	—	—	1593	1700	1729	37	—	—	—	3722	2.8	3.0	6.6
PLAYOFF TOTALS	27	—	758	88	227	.388	—	—	—	55	69	.797	—	—	111	70	104	0	—	—	—	231	4.1	2.6	8.6

BRYANT, JOSEPH WASHINGTON (**Joe, Jellybean**) b. October 19, 1954 Ht. 6-9½ Wt. 200 College—La Salle

SEASON—TEAM	G	GS	MIN	FGM	FGA	PCT	3FGM	3FGA	PCT	FTM	FTA	PCT	O-RB	D-RB	TOT	AST	PF	DQ	STL	TO	BLK	PTS	RPG	APG	PPG
75-76—Philadelphia	75	—	1203	233	552	.422	—	—	—	92	147	.626	97	181	278	61	165	0	44	—	23	558	3.7	0.8	7.4
76-77—Philadelphia	61	—	612	107	240	.446	—	—	—	53	70	.757	45	72	117	48	84	1	36	—	13	267	1.9	0.8	4.4
77-78—Philadelphia	81	—	1236	190	436	.436	—	—	—	111	144	.771	103	177	280	129	185	1	56	115	24	491	3.5	1.6	6.1
78-79—Philadelphia	70	—	1064	205	478	.429	—	—	—	123	170	.724	96	163	259	103	171	1	49	114	9	533	3.7	1.5	7.6
79-80—San Diego	81	—	2328	294	682	.431	5	34	.147	161	217	.742	171	345	516	144	258	4	102	170	39	754	6.4	1.8	9.3
80-81—San Diego	82	—	2359	379	791	.479	2	15	.133	193	244	.791	146	294	440	189	264	4	72	176	34	953	5.4	2.3	11.6
81-82—San Diego	75	49	1988	341	701	.486	8	30	.267	194	247	.785	79	195	274	189	250	1	78	183	29	884	3.7	2.5	11.8
82-83—Houston	81	56	2055	344	768	.448	8	36	.222	116	165	.703	88	189	277	186	258	4	82	177	30	812	3.4	2.3	10.0
REG. SEASON TOTALS	606	105	12845	2093	4648	.450	23	115	.200	1043	1404	.743	825	1616	2441	1049	1635	16	519	935	201	5252	4.0	1.7	8.7
PLAYOFF TOTALS	30	0	274	52	116	.448	0	0	—	19	28	.679	12	42	54	21	54	1	14	7	4	123	1.8	0.7	4.1

BRYANT, MARK CRAIG b. April 25, 1965 Ht. 6-9 Wt. 245 College—Seton Hall

SEASON—TEAM	G	GS	MIN	FGM	FGA	PCT	3FGM	3FGA	PCT	FTM	FTA	PCT	O-RB	D-RB	TOT	AST	PF	DQ	STL	TO	BLK	PTS	RPG	APG	PPG
88-89—Portland	56	32	803	120	247	.486	0	0	—	40	69	.580	65	114	179	33	144	3	20	41	7	280	3.2	0.6	5.0
89-90—Portland	58	0	562	70	153	.458	0	0	—	28	50	.560	54	92	146	13	93	0	18	25	9	168	2.5	0.2	2.9
90-91—Portland	53	0	781	99	203	.488	0	1	.000	74	101	.733	65	125	190	27	120	0	15	33	12	272	3.6	0.5	5.1
91-92—Portland	56	0	800	95	198	.480	0	3	.000	40	60	.667	87	114	201	41	105	0	26	30	8	230	3.6	0.7	4.1
92-93—Portland	80	24	1396	186	370	.503	0	1	.000	104	148	.703	132	192	324	41	226	1	37	65	23	476	4.1	0.5	6.0
93-94—Portland	79	10	1441	185	384	.482	0	1	.000	72	104	.692	117	198	315	37	187	0	32	66	29	442	4.0	0.5	5.6
REG. SEASON TOTALS	382	66	5783	755	1555	.486	0	6	.000	358	532	.673	520	835	1355	192	875	4	148	260	88	1868	3.5	0.5	4.9
PLAYOFF TOTALS	47	5	560	60	138	.435	0	2	.000	28	33	.848	50	70	120	8	95	1	10	34	8	148	2.6	0.2	3.1

BRYANT, WALLACE GORDON JR. b. July 14, 1959 Ht. 7-0 Wt. 245 College—San Francisco

SEASON—TEAM	G	GS	MIN	FGM	FGA	PCT	3FGM	3FGA	PCT	FTM	FTA	PCT	O-RB	D-RB	TOT	AST	PF	DQ	STL	TO	BLK	PTS	RPG	APG	PPG
83-84—Chicago	29	0	317	52	133	.391	0	0	—	14	33	.424	37	43	80	13	48	0	9	16	11	118	2.8	0.4	4.1
84-85—Dallas	56	35	860	67	148	.453	0	0	—	30	44	.682	74	167	241	84	110	1	21	46	24	164	4.3	1.5	2.9
85-86—Dallas-L.A.-Clips	17	8	218	15	48	.313	0	0	—	11	19	.579	17	36	53	15	38	2	5	9	5	41	3.1	0.9	2.4
REG. SEASON TOTALS	102	43	1395	134	329	.407	0	0	—	55	96	.573	128	246	374	112	196	3	35	71	40	323	3.7	1.1	3.2
PLAYOFF TOTALS	2	1	36	0	1	.000	0	0	—	2	2	1.000	1	6	7	1	5	0	1	2	1	2	3.5	0.5	1.0

BRYN, TORGEIR b. August 8, 1964 Ht. 6-9 Wt. 250 College—Miracosta/SW Texas State

SEASON—TEAM	G	GS	MIN	FGM	FGA	PCT	3FGM	3FGA	PCT	FTM	FTA	PCT	O-RB	D-RB	TOT	AST	PF	DQ	STL	TO	BLK	PTS	RPG	APG	PPG
89-90—L.A. Clippers	3	0	10	0	2	.000	0	0	—	4	6	.667	0	2	2	0	5	0	2	1	1	4	0.7	0.0	1.3
REG. SEASON TOTALS	3	0	10	0	2	.000	0	0	—	4	6	.667	0	2	2	0	5	0	2	1	1	4	0.7	0.0	1.3

BUCCI, GEORGE P. JR. b. July 9, 1953 Ht. 6-3 Wt. 200 College—Manhattan

SEASON—TEAM	G	GS	MIN	FGM	FGA	PCT	3FGM	3FGA	PCT	FTM	FTA	PCT	O-RB	D-RB	TOT	AST	PF	DQ	STL	TO	BLK	PTS	RPG	APG	PPG
75-76—New York (A)	33	—	237	50	124	.403	0	4	.000	28	41	.683	15	22	37	15	19	—	12	22	3	128	1.1	0.5	3.9
REG. ABA TOTALS	33	—	237	50	124	.403	0	4	.000	28	41	.683	15	22	37	15	19	—	12	22	3	128	1.1	0.5	3.9
ABA PLAYOFF TOTALS	2	—	9	3	7	.429	1	1	1.000	1	2	.500	0	0	—	0	2	—	0	0	0	8	0.0	0.0	4.0

BUCKHALTER, JOSEPH (**Joe**) b. August 1, 1937 Ht. 6-7 Wt. 210 College—Tennessee State

SEASON—TEAM	G	GS	MIN	FGM	FGA	PCT	3FGM	3FGA	PCT	FTM	FTA	PCT	O-RB	D-RB	TOT	AST	PF	DQ	STL	TO	BLK	PTS	RPG	APG	PPG
61-62—Cincinnati	63	—	728	153	334	.458	—	—	—	67	108	.620	—	—	262	43	123	1	—	—	—	373	4.2	0.7	5.9
62-63—Cincinnati	2	—	12	0	5	.000	—	—	—	2	2	1.000	—	—	3	0	1	0	—	—	—	2	1.5	0.0	1.0
REG. SEASON TOTALS	65	—	740	153	339	.451	—	—	—	69	110	.627	—	—	265	43	124	1	—	—	—	375	4.1	0.7	5.8
PLAYOFF TOTALS	4	—	60	16	38	.421	—	—	—	2	3	.667	—	—	22	4	14	0	—	—	—	34	5.5	1.0	8.5

BUCKNALL, STEVEN LEE (**Steve**) b. March 17, 1966 Ht. 6-6 Wt. 215 College—North Carolina

SEASON—TEAM	G	GS	MIN	FGM	FGA	PCT	3FGM	3FGA	PCT	FTM	FTA	PCT	O-RB	D-RB	TOT	AST	PF	DQ	STL	TO	BLK	PTS	RPG	APG	PPG
89-90—L.A. Lakers	18	0	75	9	33	.273	0	1	.000	5	6	.833	5	2	7	10	10	0	2	11	1	23	0.4	0.6	1.3
REG. SEASON TOTALS	18	0	75	9	33	.273	0	1	.000	5	6	.833	5	2	7	10	10	0	2	11	1	23	0.4	0.6	1.3

BUCKNER, CLEVELAND b. August 17, 1938   Ht. 6-9 Wt. 210 College—Jackson State

SEASON—TEAM	G	GS	MIN	FGM	FGA	PCT	3FGM	3FGA	PCT	FTM	FTA	PCT	O-RB	D-RB	TOT	AST	PF	DQ	STL	TO	BLK	PTS	RPG	APG	PPG
61-62—New York	62	—	696	158	367	.431	—	—	—	83	133	.624	—	—	236	39	114	1	—	—	—	399	3.8	0.6	6.4
62-63—New York	6	—	27	5	10	.500	—	—	—	2	4	.500	—	—	4	5	6	0	—	—	—	12	0.7	0.8	2.0
REG. SEASON TOTALS	68	—	723	163	377	.432	—	—	—	85	137	.620	—	—	240	44	120	1	—	—	—	411	3.5	0.6	6.0

BUCKNER, WILLIAM QUINN (**Quinn**) b. August 20, 1954   Ht. 6-3 Wt. 205 College—Indiana

SEASON—TEAM	G	GS	MIN	FGM	FGA	PCT	3FGM	3FGA	PCT	FTM	FTA	PCT	O-RB	D-RB	TOT	AST	PF	DQ	STL	TO	BLK	PTS	RPG	APG	PPG
76-77—Milwaukee	79	—	2095	299	689	.434	—	—	—	83	154	.539	91	173	264	372	291	5	192	—	21	681	3.3	4.7	8.6
77-78—Milwaukee	82	—	2072	314	671	.468	—	—	—	131	203	.645	78	169	247	456	287	6	188	228	19	759	3.0	5.6	9.3
78-79—Milwaukee	81	—	1757	251	553	.454	—	—	—	79	125	.632	57	153	210	468	224	1	156	208	17	581	2.6	5.8	7.2
79-80—Milwaukee	67	—	1690	306	655	.467	2	5	.400	105	143	.734	69	169	238	383	202	1	135	149	4	719	3.6	5.7	10.7
80-81—Milwaukee	82	—	2384	471	956	.493	1	6	.167	149	203	.734	88	210	298	384	271	3	197	236	3	1092	3.6	4.7	13.3
81-82—Milwaukee	70	70	2156	396	822	.482	4	15	.267	110	168	.655	77	173	250	328	218	2	174	180	3	906	3.6	4.7	12.9
82-83—Boston	72	56	1565	248	561	.442	0	4	.000	74	117	.632	62	125	187	275	195	2	108	159	5	570	2.6	3.8	7.9
83-84—Boston	79	0	1249	138	323	.427	0	6	.000	48	74	.649	41	96	137	214	187	0	84	100	3	324	1.7	2.7	4.1
84-85—Boston	75	6	858	74	193	.383	0	1	.000	32	50	.640	26	61	87	148	142	0	63	67	2	180	1.2	2.0	2.4
85-86—Indiana	32	3	419	49	104	.471	0	1	.000	19	27	.704	9	42	51	86	80	0	40	55	3	117	1.6	2.7	3.7
REG. SEASON TOTALS	719	135	16245	2546	5527	.461	7	38	.184	830	1264	.657	598	1371	1969	3114	2097	20	1337	1382	80	5929	2.7	4.3	8.2
PLAYOFF TOTALS	68	0	1057	148	337	.439	0	4	.000	50	82	.610	29	86	115	170	170	2	64	95	1	346	1.7	2.5	5.1

BUDD, DAVID L. (**Dave**) b. October 28, 1938   Ht. 6-6 Wt. 210 College—Wake Forest

SEASON—TEAM	G	GS	MIN	FGM	FGA	PCT	3FGM	3FGA	PCT	FTM	FTA	PCT	O-RB	D-RB	TOT	AST	PF	DQ	STL	TO	BLK	PTS	RPG	APG	PPG
60-61—New York	61	—	1075	156	361	.432	—	—	—	87	134	.649	—	—	297	45	171	2	—	—	—	399	4.9	0.7	6.5
61-62—New York	79	—	1370	188	431	.436	—	—	—	138	231	.597	—	—	345	86	162	4	—	—	—	514	4.4	1.1	6.5
62-63—New York	78	—	1725	294	596	.493	—	—	—	151	202	.748	—	—	395	87	204	3	—	—	—	739	5.1	1.1	9.5
63-64—New York	73	—	1031	128	297	.431	—	—	—	84	115	.730	—	—	276	57	130	1	—	—	—	340	3.8	0.8	4.7
64-65—New York	62	—	1188	196	407	.482	—	—	—	121	170	.712	—	—	310	62	147	1	—	—	—	513	5.0	1.0	8.3
REG. SEASON TOTALS	353	—	6389	962	2092	.460	—	—	—	581	852	.682	—	—	1623	337	814	11	—	—	—	2505	4.6	1.0	7.1

BUDKO, WALTER JR. (**Walt**) b. June 30, 1925   Ht. 6-5 Wt. 220 College—Columbia

SEASON—TEAM	G	GS	MIN	FGM	FGA	PCT	3FGM	3FGA	PCT	FTM	FTA	PCT	O-RB	D-RB	TOT	AST	PF	DQ	STL	TO	BLK	PTS	RPG	APG	PPG
48-49—Baltimore	60	—	—	224	644	.348	—	—	—	244	309	.790	—	—	—	99	201	—	—	—	—	692	—	1.7	11.5
49-50—Baltimore	66	—	—	198	652	.304	—	—	—	199	263	.757	—	—	—	146	259	—	—	—	—	595	—	2.2	9.0
50-51—Baltimore	64	—	—	165	464	.356	—	—	—	166	223	.744	—	—	452	135	203	7	—	—	—	496	7.1	2.1	7.8
51-52—Philadelphia	63	—	1126	97	240	.404	—	—	—	60	89	.674	—	—	232	91	196	10	—	—	—	254	3.7	1.4	4.0
REG. SEASON TOTALS	253	—	1126	684	2000	.342	—	—	—	669	884	.757	—	—	684	471	859	17	—	—	—	2037	5.4	1.9	8.1
PLAYOFF TOTALS	6	—	58	17	40	.425	—	—	—	19	26	.731	—	—	12	9	27	2	—	—	—	53	4.0	1.5	8.8

BUECHLER, JUDSON DONALD (**Jud**) b. June 19, 1968   Ht. 6-6 Wt. 220 College—Arizona

SEASON—TEAM	G	GS	MIN	FGM	FGA	PCT	3FGM	3FGA	PCT	FTM	FTA	PCT	O-RB	D-RB	TOT	AST	PF	DQ	STL	TO	BLK	PTS	RPG	APG	PPG
90-91—New Jersey	74	10	859	94	226	.416	1	4	.250	43	66	.652	61	80	141	51	79	0	33	26	15	232	1.9	0.7	3.1
91-92—N.J.-S.A.-G.S.	28	0	290	29	71	.408	0	1	.000	12	21	.571	18	34	52	23	31	0	19	13	7	70	1.9	0.8	2.5
92-93—Golden State	70	9	1287	176	403	.437	20	59	.339	65	87	.747	81	114	195	94	98	0	47	55	19	437	2.8	1.3	6.2
93-94—Golden State	36	0	218	42	84	.500	12	29	.414	10	20	.500	13	19	32	16	24	0	8	12	1	106	0.9	0.4	2.9
REG. SEASON TOTALS	208	19	2654	341	784	.435	33	93	.355	130	194	.670	173	247	420	184	232	0	107	106	42	845	2.0	0.9	4.1

BULLARD, MATTHEW GORDON (**Matt**) b. June 5, 1967   Ht. 6-10 Wt. 235 College—Colorado/Iowa

SEASON—TEAM	G	GS	MIN	FGM	FGA	PCT	3FGM	3FGA	PCT	FTM	FTA	PCT	O-RB	D-RB	TOT	AST	PF	DQ	STL	TO	BLK	PTS	RPG	APG	PPG
90-91—Houston	18	0	63	14	31	.452	0	3	.000	11	17	.647	6	8	14	2	10	0	3	3	0	39	0.8	0.1	2.2
91-92—Houston	80	7	1278	205	447	.459	64	166	.386	38	50	.760	73	150	223	75	129	1	26	56	21	512	2.8	0.9	6.4
92-93—Houston	79	4	1356	213	494	.431	91	243	.374	58	74	.784	66	156	222	110	129	0	30	57	11	575	2.8	1.4	7.3
93-94—Houston	65	0	725	78	226	.345	50	154	.325	20	26	.769	23	61	84	64	67	0	14	28	6	226	1.3	1.0	3.5
REG. SEASON TOTALS	242	11	3422	510	1198	.426	205	566	.362	127	167	.760	168	375	543	251	335	1	73	144	38	1352	2.2	1.0	5.6
PLAYOFF TOTALS	22	0	224	24	61	.393	17	38	.447	12	14	.857	6	27	33	13	17	0	5	9	7	77	1.5	0.6	3.5

BUNCE, LAWRENCE MELVIN (**Larry**) b. July 29, 1945   Ht. 7-0 Wt. 245 College—Texas El Paso/Riverside CC/Utah State

SEASON—TEAM	G	GS	MIN	FGM	FGA	PCT	3FGM	3FGA	PCT	FTM	FTA	PCT	O-RB	D-RB	TOT	AST	PF	DQ	STL	TO	BLK	PTS	RPG	APG	PPG
67-68—Anaheim (A)	71	—	2266	300	716	.419	0	1	.000	256	352	.727	—	—	589	75	189	8	—	132	—	856	8.3	1.1	12.1
68-69—Den.-Dallas-Hous. (A)	58	—	804	86	203	.424	0	—	—	114	165	.691	—	—	232	19	128	3	—	60	—	286	4.0	0.3	4.9
REG. ABA TOTALS	129	—	3070	386	919	.420	0	1	.000	370	517	.716	—	—	821	94	317	11	—	192	—	1142	6.4	0.7	8.9
ABA ALL-STAR TOTALS	1	—	7	1	2	.500	0	0	—	1	1	1.000	—	—	0	0	0	0	—	0	—	3	0.0	0.0	3.0

BUNCH, DARNELL GREG (**Greg**) b. May 15, 1956   Ht. 6-6 Wt. 190 College—Cal State-Fullerton

SEASON—TEAM	G	GS	MIN	FGM	FGA	PCT	3FGM	3FGA	PCT	FTM	FTA	PCT	O-RB	D-RB	TOT	AST	PF	DQ	STL	TO	BLK	PTS	RPG	APG	PPG
78-79—New York	12	—	97	9	26	.346	—	—	—	10	12	.833	9	8	17	4	10	0	3	5	3	28	1.4	0.3	2.3
REG. SEASON TOTALS	12	—	97	9	26	.346	—	—	—	10	12	.833	9	8	17	4	10	0	3	5	3	28	1.4	0.3	2.3

BUNT, RICHARD J. (**Dick**) b. July 13, 1930 Ht. 6-0 Wt. 170 College—New York University

SEASON—TEAM	G	GS	MIN	FGM	FGA	PCT	3FGM	3FGA	PCT	FTM	FTA	PCT	O-RB	D-RB	TOT	AST	PF	DQ	STL	TO	BLK	PTS	RPG	APG	PPG
52-53—N.Y.-Balt.	26	—	271	29	107	.271	—	—	—	34	48	.708	—	—	28	17	40	0	—	—	—	92	1.1	0.7	3.5
REG. SEASON TOTALS	26	—	271	29	107	.271	—	—	—	34	48	.708	—	—	28	17	40	0	—	—	—	92	1.1	0.7	3.5
PLAYOFF TOTALS	1	—	1	0	0	—	—	—	—	0	0	—	—	—	0	1	0	0	—	—	—	0	0.0	1.0	0.0

BUNTIN, WILLIAM L. (**Bill**) b. May 5, 1942 d. May 9, 1968 Ht. 6-7 Wt. 250 College—Michigan

SEASON—TEAM	G	GS	MIN	FGM	FGA	PCT	3FGM	3FGA	PCT	FTM	FTA	PCT	O-RB	D-RB	TOT	AST	PF	DQ	STL	TO	BLK	PTS	RPG	APG	PPG
65-66—Detroit	42	—	713	118	299	.395	—	—	—	88	143	.615	—	—	252	36	119	4	—	—	—	324	6.0	0.9	7.7
REG. SEASON TOTALS	42	—	713	118	299	.395	—	—	—	88	143	.615	—	—	252	36	119	4	—	—	—	324	6.0	0.9	7.7

BUNTING, WILLIAM CARL (**Bill**) b. August 26, 1947 Ht. 6-8 Wt. 200 College—North Carolina

SEASON—TEAM	G	GS	MIN	FGM	FGA	PCT	3FGM	3FGA	PCT	FTM	FTA	PCT	O-RB	D-RB	TOT	AST	PF	DQ	STL	TO	BLK	PTS	RPG	APG	PPG
69-70—Carolina (A)	57	—	701	96	248	.387	0	0	—	79	106	.745	—	—	169	34	106	3	—	—	—	271	3.0	0.6	4.8
70-71—N.Y.-Vir. (A)	72	—	1123	114	245	.465	0	0	—	104	124	.839	—	—	233	58	157	—	—	—	—	332	3.2	0.8	4.6
71-72—Virginia (A)	16	—	115	4	15	.267	0	1	.000	12	17	.706	—	—	15	3	11	—	—	5	—	20	0.9	0.2	1.3
REG. ABA TOTALS	145	—	1939	214	508	.421	0	1	.000	195	247	.789	—	—	417	95	274	3	—	5	—	623	2.9	0.7	4.3
ABA PLAYOFF TOTALS	6	—	35	5	10	.500	0	0	—	8	12	.667	—	—	6	1	4	0	—	—	—	18	1.0	0.2	3.0

BURDEN, LUTHER D. (**Ticky**) b. February 28, 1953 Ht. 6-2 Wt. 190 College—Utah

SEASON—TEAM	G	GS	MIN	FGM	FGA	PCT	3FGM	3FGA	PCT	FTM	FTA	PCT	O-RB	D-RB	TOT	AST	PF	DQ	STL	TO	BLK	PTS	RPG	APG	PPG
75-76—Virginia (A)	71	—	2181	561	1247	.450	8	36	.222	283	369	.767	108	94	202	131	188	—	103	181	9	1413	2.8	1.8	19.9
76-77—New York Knicks	61	—	608	148	352	.420	—	—	—	51	85	.600	26	40	66	62	88	0	47	—	1	347	1.1	1.0	5.7
77-78—New York	2	—	15	1	2	.500	—	—	—	0	0	—	0	0	0	1	1	0	1	0	0	2	0.0	0.5	1.0
REG. NBA TOTALS	63	—	623	149	354	.421	—	—	—	51	85	.600	26	40	66	63	89	0	48	0	1	349	1.0	1.0	5.5
REG. ABA TOTALS	71	—	2181	561	1247	.450	8	36	.222	283	369	.767	108	94	202	131	188	—	103	181	9	1413	2.8	1.8	19.9

BURKMAN, ROGER ALLEN b. May 22, 1958 Ht. 6-5 Wt. 175 College—Louisville

SEASON—TEAM	G	GS	MIN	FGM	FGA	PCT	3FGM	3FGA	PCT	FTM	FTA	PCT	O-RB	D-RB	TOT	AST	PF	DQ	STL	TO	BLK	PTS	RPG	APG	PPG
81-82—Chicago	6	0	30	0	4	.000	0	1	.000	5	6	.833	2	4	6	5	6	0	6	3	2	5	1.0	0.8	0.8
REG. SEASON TOTALS	6	0	30	0	4	.000	0	1	.000	5	6	.833	2	4	6	5	6	0	6	3	2	5	1.0	0.8	0.8

BURLESON, THOMAS L. (**Tommy**) b. February 24, 1952 Ht. 7-2 Wt. 230 College—North Carolina State

SEASON—TEAM	G	GS	MIN	FGM	FGA	PCT	3FGM	3FGA	PCT	FTM	FTA	PCT	O-RB	D-RB	TOT	AST	PF	DQ	STL	TO	BLK	PTS	RPG	APG	PPG
74-75—Seattle	82	—	1888	322	772	.417	—	—	—	182	265	.687	155	417	572	115	221	1	64	—	153	826	7.0	1.4	10.1
75-76—Seattle	82	—	2647	496	1032	.481	—	—	—	291	388	.750	258	484	742	180	273	1	70	—	150	1283	9.0	2.2	15.6
76-77—Seattle	82	—	1803	288	652	.442	—	—	—	220	301	.731	184	367	551	93	259	1	74	—	117	796	6.7	1.1	9.7
77-78—Kansas City	76	—	1525	228	525	.434	—	—	—	197	248	.794	170	312	482	131	259	6	62	123	81	653	6.3	1.7	8.6
78-79—Kansas City	56	—	927	157	342	.459	—	—	—	121	169	.716	84	197	281	50	183	3	26	64	58	435	5.0	0.9	7.8
79-80—Kansas City	37	—	272	36	104	.346	0	3	.000	23	40	.575	23	49	72	20	49	0	8	25	13	95	1.9	0.5	2.6
80-81—Atlanta	31	—	363	41	99	.414	0	0	—	20	41	.488	44	50	94	12	73	2	8	24	19	102	3.0	0.4	3.3
REG. SEASON TOTALS	446	—	9425	1568	3526	.445	0	3	.000	1054	1452	.726	918	1876	2794	601	1317	14	312	236	591	4190	6.3	1.3	9.4
PLAYOFF TOTALS	15	—	572	123	227	.542	0	—	—	65	86	.756	45	108	153	23	54	1	13	—	26	311	10.2	1.5	20.7

BURMASTER, JOHN H. (**Jack**) b. December 23, 1926 Ht. 6-3 Wt. 190 College—Illinois

SEASON—TEAM	G	GS	MIN	FGM	FGA	PCT	3FGM	3FGA	PCT	FTM	FTA	PCT	O-RB	D-RB	TOT	AST	PF	DQ	STL	TO	BLK	PTS	RPG	APG	PPG
48-49—Oshkosh (N)	64	—	—	140	—	—	—	—	—	80	128	.625	—	—	—	—	168	—	—	—	—	360	—	—	5.6
49-50—Sheboygan	61	—	—	237	711	.333	—	—	—	124	182	.681	—	—	—	179	237	—	—	—	—	598	—	2.9	9.8
REG. NBA TOTALS	61	—	—	237	711	.333	—	—	—	124	182	.681	—	—	—	179	237	—	—	—	—	598	—	2.9	9.8
REG. NBL TOTALS	64	—	—	140	—	—	—	—	—	80	128	.625	—	—	—	—	168	—	—	—	—	360	—	—	5.6
NBA PLAYOFF TOTALS	3	—	—	16	31	.516	—	—	—	4	4	1.000	—	—	—	8	7	—	—	—	—	36	—	2.7	12.0
NBL PLAYOFF TOTALS	7	—	—	14	—	—	—	—	—	16	22	.727	—	—	—	—	21	—	—	—	—	44	—	—	6.3

BURNS, DAVID EARL b. July 3, 1958 Ht. 6-2 Wt. 180 College—Navarro/St. Louis

SEASON—TEAM	G	GS	MIN	FGM	FGA	PCT	3FGM	3FGA	PCT	FTM	FTA	PCT	O-RB	D-RB	TOT	AST	PF	DQ	STL	TO	BLK	PTS	RPG	APG	PPG
81-82—N.J.-Denver	9	1	87	7	16	.438	0	0	—	9	15	.600	1	4	5	15	17	0	3	13	0	23	0.6	1.7	2.6
REG. SEASON TOTALS	9	1	87	7	16	.438	0	0	—	9	15	.600	1	4	5	15	17	0	3	13	0	23	0.6	1.7	2.6

BURNS, EVERS ALLEN b. August 24, 1971 Ht. 6-8 Wt. 260 College—Maryland

SEASON—TEAM	G	GS	MIN	FGM	FGA	PCT	3FGM	3FGA	PCT	FTM	FTA	PCT	O-RB	D-RB	TOT	AST	PF	DQ	STL	TO	BLK	PTS	RPG	APG	PPG
93-94—Sacramento	23	0	143	22	55	.400	0	0	—	12	23	.522	13	17	30	9	33	0	6	7	3	56	1.3	0.4	2.4
REG. SEASON TOTALS	23	0	143	22	55	.400	0	0	—	12	23	.522	13	17	30	9	33	0	6	7	3	56	1.3	0.4	2.4

BURNS, JAMES B. (Jim) b. September 21, 1945 Ht. 6-3½ Wt. 195 College—Northwestern

SEASON—TEAM	G	GS	MIN	FGM	FGA	PCT	3FGM	3FGA	PCT	FTM	FTA	PCT	O-RB	D-RB	TOT	AST	PF	DQ	STL	TO	BLK	PTS	RPG	APG	PPG
67-68—Chicago	3	—	11	2	7	.286	—	—	—	0	0	—	—	—	2	1	1	0	—	—	—	4	0.7	0.3	1.3
67-68—Dallas (A)	33	—	392	52	137	.380	0	2	.000	51	89	.573	—	—	60	24	52	0	—	42	—	155	1.8	0.7	4.7
REG. NBA TOTALS	3	—	11	2	7	.286	—	—	—	0	0	—	—	—	2	1	1	0	—	—	—	4	0.7	0.3	1.3
REG. ABA TOTALS	33	—	392	52	137	.380	0	2	.000	51	89	.573	—	—	60	24	52	0	—	42	—	155	1.8	0.7	4.7

BURRELL, SCOTT DAVID b. January 12, 1971 Ht. 6-7 Wt. 220 College—Connecticut

SEASON—TEAM	G	GS	MIN	FGM	FGA	PCT	3FGM	3FGA	PCT	FTM	FTA	PCT	O-RB	D-RB	TOT	AST	PF	DQ	STL	TO	BLK	PTS	RPG	APG	PPG
93-94—Charlotte	51	16	767	98	234	.419	2	6	.333	46	70	.657	46	86	132	62	88	0	37	45	16	244	2.6	1.2	4.8
REG. SEASON TOTALS	51	16	767	98	234	.419	2	6	.333	46	70	.657	46	86	132	62	88	0	37	45	16	244	2.6	1.2	4.8

BURRIS, ARTHUR C. (Art) b. April 7, 1924 Ht. 6-5½ Wt. 225 College—Tennessee

SEASON—TEAM	G	GS	MIN	FGM	FGA	PCT	3FGM	3FGA	PCT	FTM	FTA	PCT	O-RB	D-RB	TOT	AST	PF	DQ	STL	TO	BLK	PTS	RPG	APG	PPG
50-51—Fort Wayne	33	—	—	28	113	.248	—	—	—	21	36	.583	—	—	106	27	51	0	—	—	—	77	3.2	0.8	2.3
51-52—Ft. Wayne-Milw.	41	—	514	42	156	.269	—	—	—	26	39	.667	—	—	99	27	49	3	—	—	—	110	2.4	0.7	2.7
REG. SEASON TOTALS	74	—	514	70	269	.260	—	—	—	47	75	.627	—	—	205	54	100	3	—	—	—	187	2.8	0.7	2.5

BURROW, ROBERT BRANTLEY (Bob) b. June 29, 1934 Ht. 6-7 Wt. 230 College—Lon Morris/Kentucky

SEASON—TEAM	G	GS	MIN	FGM	FGA	PCT	3FGM	3FGA	PCT	FTM	FTA	PCT	O-RB	D-RB	TOT	AST	PF	DQ	STL	TO	BLK	PTS	RPG	APG	PPG
56-57—Rochester	67	—	1028	137	366	.374	—	—	—	130	211	.616	—	—	293	41	165	2	—	—	—	404	4.4	0.6	6.0
57-58—Minneapolis	14	—	171	22	70	.314	—	—	—	11	33	.333	—	—	64	6	15	0	—	—	—	55	4.6	0.4	3.9
REG. SEASON TOTALS	81	—	1199	159	436	.365	—	—	—	141	244	.578	—	—	357	47	180	2	—	—	—	459	4.4	0.6	5.7

BURTON, EDWARD (Ed) b. August 13, 1939 Ht. 6-6½ Wt. 225 College—Michigan State

SEASON—TEAM	G	GS	MIN	FGM	FGA	PCT	3FGM	3FGA	PCT	FTM	FTA	PCT	O-RB	D-RB	TOT	AST	PF	DQ	STL	TO	BLK	PTS	RPG	APG	PPG
61-62—New York	8	—	28	7	14	.500	—	—	—	1	4	.250	—	—	5	1	3	0	—	—	—	15	0.6	0.1	1.9
64-65—St. Louis	7	—	42	7	20	.350	—	—	—	4	7	.571	—	—	13	2	13	0	—	—	—	18	1.9	0.3	2.6
REG. SEASON TOTALS	15	—	70	14	34	.412	—	—	—	5	11	.455	—	—	18	3	16	0	—	—	—	33	1.2	0.2	2.2

BURTON, WILLIE RICARDO b. May 26, 1968 Ht. 6-8 Wt. 215 College—Minnesota

SEASON—TEAM	G	GS	MIN	FGM	FGA	PCT	3FGM	3FGA	PCT	FTM	FTA	PCT	O-RB	D-RB	TOT	AST	PF	DQ	STL	TO	BLK	PTS	RPG	APG	PPG
90-91—Miami	76	26	1928	341	773	.441	4	30	.133	229	293	.782	111	151	262	107	275	6	72	144	24	915	3.4	1.4	12.0
91-92—Miami	68	50	1585	280	622	.450	6	15	.400	196	245	.800	76	168	244	123	186	2	46	119	37	762	3.6	1.8	11.2
92-93—Miami	26	8	451	54	141	.383	5	15	.333	91	127	.717	22	48	70	16	58	0	13	50	16	204	2.7	0.6	7.8
93-94—Miami	53	1	697	124	283	.438	3	15	.200	120	158	.759	50	86	136	39	96	0	18	54	20	371	2.6	0.7	7.0
REG. SEASON TOTALS	223	85	4661	799	1819	.439	18	75	.240	636	823	.773	259	453	712	285	615	8	149	367	97	2252	3.2	1.3	10.1
PLAYOFF TOTALS	2	0	11	1	4	.250	0	2	.000	0	0	—	0	0	0	—	3	0	0	1	0	2	0.0	0.0	1.0

BURTT, STEVEN DWAYNE (Steve) b. November 5, 1962 Ht. 6-2 Wt. 185 College—Iona

SEASON—TEAM	G	GS	MIN	FGM	FGA	PCT	3FGM	3FGA	PCT	FTM	FTA	PCT	O-RB	D-RB	TOT	AST	PF	DQ	STL	TO	BLK	PTS	RPG	APG	PPG
84-85—Golden State	47	0	418	72	188	.383	0	1	.000	53	77	.688	10	18	28	20	76	0	21	33	4	197	0.6	0.4	4.2
87-88—L.A. Clippers	19	0	312	62	138	.449	0	4	.000	47	69	.681	6	21	27	38	56	0	10	40	5	171	1.4	2.0	9.0
91-92—Phoenix	31	2	356	74	160	.463	1	6	.167	38	54	.704	10	24	34	59	58	0	16	33	4	187	1.1	1.9	6.0
92-93—Washington	4	0	35	10	26	.385	1	3	.333	8	10	.800	2	1	3	6	5	0	2	4	0	29	0.8	1.5	7.3
REG. SEASON TOTALS	101	2	1121	218	512	.426	2	14	.143	146	210	.695	28	64	92	123	195	0	49	110	13	584	0.9	1.2	5.8
PLAYOFF TOTALS	8	0	104	16	38	.421	0	2	.000	18	21	.857	3	9	12	14	18	0	5	8	0	50	1.5	1.8	6.3

BUSE, DONALD R. (Don, Boo) b. August 10, 1950 Ht. 6-4 Wt. 195 College—Evansville

SEASON—TEAM	G	GS	MIN	FGM	FGA	PCT	3FGM	3FGA	PCT	FTM	FTA	PCT	O-RB	D-RB	TOT	AST	PF	DQ	STL	TO	BLK	PTS	RPG	APG	PPG
72-73—Indiana (A)	77	—	1484	163	360	.453	5	24	.208	82	109	.752	96	114	210	223	143	0	—	66	—	413	2.7	2.9	5.4
73-74—Indiana (A)	77	—	1877	170	427	.398	36	107	.336	48	70	.686	85	169	254	258	109	—	146	75	20	424	3.3	3.4	5.5
74-75—Indiana (A)	80	—	2369	216	500	.432	38	123	.309	47	59	.797	84	188	272	335	149	—	166	95	15	517	3.4	4.2	6.5
75-76—Indiana (A)	84	—	3380	400	887	.451	72	208	.346	179	220	.814	90	232	322	689	194	—	346	159	31	1051	3.8	8.2	12.5
76-77—Indiana	81	—	2947	266	639	.416	—	—	—	114	145	.786	66	204	270	685	129	0	281	—	16	646	3.3	8.5	8.0
77-78—Phoenix	82	—	2547	287	626	.458	—	—	—	112	136	.824	59	190	249	391	144	0	185	124	14	686	3.0	4.8	8.4
78-79—Phoenix	82	—	2544	285	576	.495	—	—	—	70	91	.769	44	173	217	356	149	0	156	96	18	640	2.6	4.3	7.8
79-80—Phoenix	81	—	2499	261	589	.443	19	79	.241	85	128	.664	70	163	233	320	111	0	132	91	10	626	2.9	4.0	7.7
80-81—Indiana	58	—	1095	114	287	.397	19	58	.328	50	65	.769	19	65	84	140	61	0	74	38	8	297	1.4	2.4	5.1
81-82—Indiana	82	78	2529	312	685	.455	73	189	.386	100	123	.813	46	177	223	407	176	0	164	95	27	797	2.7	5.0	9.7
82-83—Portland	41	1	643	72	182	.396	9	35	.257	41	46	.891	19	35	54	115	60	0	44	25	2	194	1.3	2.8	4.7
83-84—Kansas City	76	10	1327	150	352	.426	18	59	.305	63	80	.788	29	87	116	303	62	0	86	87	1	381	1.5	4.0	5.0
84-85—Kansas City	65	14	939	82	203	.404	31	87	.356	23	30	.767	21	40	61	203	75	0	38	45	1	218	0.9	3.1	3.4
REG. NBA TOTALS	648	103	17070	1829	4139	.442	169	507	.333	658	844	.780	373	1134	1507	2920	967	0	1160	601	97	4485	2.3	4.5	6.9
REG. ABA TOTALS	318	—	9110	949	2174	.437	151	462	.327	356	458	.777	355	703	1058	1505	595	0	658	395	66	2405	3.3	4.7	7.6
NBA PLAYOFF TOTALS	35	0	940	89	223	.399	9	23	.391	40	56	.714	25	66	91	125	60	0	37	36	6	227	2.6	3.6	6.5
ABA PLAYOFF TOTALS	49	—	1208	100	249	.402	16	64	.250	39	64	.609	36	73	134	159	100	0	82	46	6	255	2.7	3.2	5.2
NBA ALL-STAR TOTALS	1	0	19	2	4	.500	0	0	—	0	0	—	0	2	2	5	0	0	4	—	0	4	2.0	5.0	4.0
ABA ALL-STAR TOTALS	1	0	14	2	4	.500	1	2	.500	0	0	—	0	1	3	0	—	0	0	0	5	1.0	3.0	5.0

BUSTION, DAVID C. (Dave) b. August 30, 1949 Ht. 6-8 Wt. 215 College—Northeastern JC/Denver

SEASON—TEAM	G	GS	MIN	FGM	FGA	PCT	3FGM	3FGA	PCT	FTM	FTA	PCT	O-RB	D-RB	TOT	AST	PF	DQ	STL	TO	BLK	PTS	RPG	APG	PPG
72-73—Denver (A)	47	—	355	58	133	.436	0	0	—	42	59	.712	39	62	101	21	82	0	—	54	—	158	2.1	0.4	3.4
REG. ABA TOTALS	47	—	355	58	133	.436	0	0	—	42	59	.712	39	62	101	21	82	0	—	54	—	158	2.1	0.4	3.4
ABA PLAYOFF TOTALS	1	—	11	2	7	.286	0	0	—	6	7	.857	—	—	1	1	3	0	—	1	—	10	1.0	1.0	10.0

BUTCHER, DONNIS (Donnie) b. February 8, 1936 Ht. 6-3 Wt. 200 College—Pikeville College

SEASON—TEAM	G	GS	MIN	FGM	FGA	PCT	3FGM	3FGA	PCT	FTM	FTA	PCT	O-RB	D-RB	TOT	AST	PF	DQ	STL	TO	BLK	PTS	RPG	APG	PPG
61-62—New York	47	—	479	48	155	.310	—	—	—	42	69	.609	—	—	79	51	63	0	—	—	—	138	1.7	1.1	2.9
62-63—New York	68	—	1193	172	424	.406	—	—	—	131	194	.675	—	—	180	138	164	1	—	—	—	475	2.6	2.0	7.0
63-64—N.Y.-Detroit	78	—	1971	202	507	.398	—	—	—	159	256	.621	—	—	329	244	249	4	—	—	—	563	4.2	3.1	7.2
64-65—Detroit	71	—	1157	143	353	.405	—	—	—	126	204	.618	—	—	200	122	183	4	—	—	—	412	2.8	1.7	5.8
65-66—Detroit	15	—	285	45	96	.469	—	—	—	18	34	.529	—	—	33	30	40	1	—	—	—	108	2.2	2.0	7.2
REG. SEASON TOTALS	279	—	5085	610	1535	.397	—	—	—	476	757	.629	—	—	821	585	699	10	—	—	—	1696	2.9	2.1	6.1

BUTLER, ELBERT J. (Al) b. July 9, 1938 Ht. 6-2 Wt. 175 College—Niagara

SEASON—TEAM	G	GS	MIN	FGM	FGA	PCT	3FGM	3FGA	PCT	FTM	FTA	PCT	O-RB	D-RB	TOT	AST	PF	DQ	STL	TO	BLK	PTS	RPG	APG	PPG
61-62—Boston-N.Y.	59	—	2016	349	754	.463	—	—	—	129	182	.709	—	—	337	205	156	0	—	—	—	827	5.7	3.5	14.0
62-63—New York	74	—	1488	297	676	.439	—	—	—	144	187	.770	—	—	170	156	145	3	—	—	—	738	2.3	2.1	10.0
63-64—New York	76	—	1379	260	616	.422	—	—	—	138	187	.738	—	—	168	157	167	3	—	—	—	658	2.2	2.1	8.7
64-65—Baltimore	25	—	172	24	73	.329	—	—	—	11	15	.733	—	—	21	12	25	0	—	—	—	59	0.8	0.5	2.4
REG. SEASON TOTALS	234	—	5055	930	2119	.439	—	—	—	422	571	.739	—	—	696	530	493	6	—	—	—	2282	3.0	2.3	9.8

BUTLER, GREGORY EDWARD (Greg) b. March 11, 1966 Ht. 6-11 Wt. 240 College—Stanford

SEASON—TEAM	G	GS	MIN	FGM	FGA	PCT	3FGM	3FGA	PCT	FTM	FTA	PCT	O-RB	D-RB	TOT	AST	PF	DQ	STL	TO	BLK	PTS	RPG	APG	PPG
88-89—New York	33	0	140	20	48	.417	0	3	.000	16	20	.800	9	19	28	2	28	0	1	17	2	56	0.8	0.1	1.7
89-90—New York	13	0	33	3	12	.250	0	0	—	0	2	.000	3	6	9	1	8	0	0	3	0	6	0.7	0.1	0.5
90-91—L.A. Clippers	9	0	37	5	19	.263	0	0	—	4	6	.667	8	8	16	1	9	0	0	4	0	14	1.8	0.1	1.6
REG. SEASON TOTALS	55	0	210	28	79	.354	0	3	.000	20	28	.714	20	33	53	4	45	0	1	24	2	76	1.0	0.1	1.4

BUTLER, MICHAEL EDWARD (Mike) b. October 22, 1946 Ht. 6-2 Wt. 175 College—Memphis State

SEASON—TEAM	G	GS	MIN	FGM	FGA	PCT	3FGM	3FGA	PCT	FTM	FTA	PCT	O-RB	D-RB	TOT	AST	PF	DQ	STL	TO	BLK	PTS	RPG	APG	PPG
68-69—New Orleans (A)	77	—	1315	207	528	.392	50	162	.309	112	133	.842	—	—	115	171	130	0	—	113	—	576	1.5	2.2	7.5
69-70—New Orleans (A)	83	—	1728	298	800	.373	87	300	.290	135	161	.839	—	—	119	134	193	1	—	—	—	818	1.4	1.6	9.9
70-71—Utah (A)	71	—	1414	271	646	.420	32	125	.256	153	168	.911	—	—	131	186	142	—	—	—	—	727	1.8	2.6	10.2
71-72—Utah (A)	14	—	97	14	36	.389	3	9	.333	6	7	.857	—	—	10	13	18	—	—	12	—	37	0.7	0.9	2.6
REG. ABA TOTALS	245	—	4554	790	2010	.393	172	596	.289	406	469	.866	—	—	375	504	483	1	—	125	—	2158	1.5	2.1	8.8
ABA PLAYOFF TOTALS	21	—	314	49	140	.350	16	61	.262	34	38	.895	—	—	40	23	34	0	—	14	—	148	1.9	1.1	7.0

BUTLER, MITCHELL LEON b. December 15, 1970 Ht. 6-5 Wt. 210 College—UCLA

SEASON—TEAM	G	GS	MIN	FGM	FGA	PCT	3FGM	3FGA	PCT	FTM	FTA	PCT	O-RB	D-RB	TOT	AST	PF	DQ	STL	TO	BLK	PTS	RPG	APG	PPG
93-94—Washington	75	19	1321	207	418	.495	0	5	.000	104	180	.578	106	119	225	77	131	1	54	87	20	518	3.0	1.0	6.9
REG. SEASON TOTALS	75	19	1321	207	418	.495	0	5	.000	104	180	.578	106	119	225	77	131	1	54	87	20	518	3.0	1.0	6.9

BYRD, WALTER (**Walt**) b. 1942 Ht. 6-7 Wt. 205 College—Temple

SEASON—TEAM	G	GS	MIN	FGM	FGA	PCT	3FGM	3FGA	PCT	FTM	FTA	PCT	O-RB	D-RB	TOT	AST	PF	DQ	STL	TO	BLK	PTS	RPG	APG	PPG
69-70—Miami (A)	22	—	109	14	43	.326	0	1	.000	5	17	.294	—	—	25	6	22	0	—	—	—	33	1.1	0.3	1.5
REG. ABA TOTALS	22	—	109	14	43	.326	0	1	.000	5	17	.294	—	—	25	6	22	0	—	—	—	33	1.1	0.3	1.5

BYRNES, MARTIN WILLIAM (**Marty**) b. April 30, 1956 Ht. 6-7 Wt. 220 College—Syracuse

SEASON—TEAM	G	GS	MIN	FGM	FGA	PCT	3FGM	3FGA	PCT	FTM	FTA	PCT	O-RB	D-RB	TOT	AST	PF	DQ	STL	TO	BLK	PTS	RPG	APG	PPG
78-79—Phoenix-N.O.	79	—	1264	187	389	.481	—	—	—	106	154	.688	90	101	191	104	111	0	27	119	10	480	2.4	1.3	6.1
79-80—Los Angeles	32	—	194	25	50	.500	0	0	—	13	15	.867	9	18	27	13	32	0	5	22	1	63	0.8	0.4	2.0
80-81—Dallas	72	—	1360	216	451	.479	9	20	.450	120	157	.764	74	103	177	113	126	0	29	61	17	561	2.5	1.6	7.8
82-83—Indiana	80	12	1436	157	374	.420	6	26	.231	71	95	.747	75	116	191	179	149	1	41	73	6	391	2.4	2.2	4.9
REG. SEASON TOTALS	263	12	4254	585	1264	.463	15	46	.326	310	421	.736	248	338	586	409	418	1	102	275	34	1495	2.2	1.6	5.7
PLAYOFF TOTALS	4	0	8	1	3	.333	0	0	—	4	6	.667	1	0	1	1	0	0	0	1	0	6	0.3	0.3	1.5

BYRNES, THOMAS P. (**Tommy**) b. February 19, 1923 d. January 9, 1981 Ht. 6-3 Wt. 175 College—Seton Hall

SEASON—TEAM	G	GS	MIN	FGM	FGA	PCT	3FGM	3FGA	PCT	FTM	FTA	PCT	O-RB	D-RB	TOT	AST	PF	DQ	STL	TO	BLK	PTS	RPG	APG	PPG
46-47—New York	60	—	—	175	583	.300	—	—	—	103	160	.644	—	—	—	35	90	—	—	—	—	453	—	0.6	7.6
47-48—New York	47	—	—	117	410	.285	—	—	—	65	103	.631	—	—	—	17	56	—	—	—	—	299	—	0.4	6.4
48-49—N.Y.-Ind.	57	—	—	160	525	.305	—	—	—	92	149	.617	—	—	—	102	84	—	—	—	—	412	—	1.8	7.2
49-50—Baltimore	53	—	—	120	397	.302	—	—	—	87	124	.702	—	—	—	88	76	—	—	—	—	327	—	1.7	6.2
50-51—Balt.-Wash.-Tri-Cit	48	—	—	83	275	.302	—	—	—	55	84	.655	—	—	72	69	86	0	—	—	—	221	1.5	1.4	4.6
REG. SEASON TOTALS	265	—	—	655	2190	.299	—	—	—	402	620	.648	—	—	72	311	392	0	—	—	—	1712	1.5	1.2	6.5
PLAYOFF TOTALS	8	—	—	22	73	.301	—	—	—	6	23	.261	—	—	—	2	9	—	—	—	—	50	—	0.3	6.3

BYTZURA, MICHAEL JOHN (**Mike**) b. June 18, 1922 d. January 24, 1989 Ht. 6-3 Wt. 175 College—Duquesne/Long Island University

SEASON—TEAM	G	GS	MIN	FGM	FGA	PCT	3FGM	3FGA	PCT	FTM	FTA	PCT	O-RB	D-RB	TOT	AST	PF	DQ	STL	TO	BLK	PTS	RPG	APG	PPG
44-45—Cleveland (N)	30	—	—	113	—	—	—	—	—	35	—	—	—	—	—	—	—	—	—	—	—	261	—	—	8.7
45-46—Cleveland (N)	33	—	—	78	—	—	—	—	—	35	65	.538	—	—	—	—	62	—	—	—	—	191	—	—	5.8
46-47—Pittsburgh	60	—	—	87	356	.244	—	—	—	36	72	.500	—	—	—	31	108	—	—	—	—	210	—	0.5	3.5
REG. NBA TOTALS	60	—	—	87	356	.244	—	—	—	36	72	.500	—	—	—	31	108	—	—	—	—	210	—	0.5	3.5
REG. NBL TOTALS	63	—	—	191	—	—	—	—	—	70	65	.538	—	—	—	—	62	—	—	—	—	452	—	—	7.2
NBL PLAYOFF TOTALS	2	—	—	4	—	—	—	—	—	3	—	—	—	—	—	—	3	—	—	—	—	11	—	—	5.5

CABLE, BYRUM WILLIAM (**Barney**) b. July 29, 1935 Ht. 6-7 Wt. 200 College—Bradley

SEASON—TEAM	G	GS	MIN	FGM	FGA	PCT	3FGM	3FGA	PCT	FTM	FTA	PCT	O-RB	D-RB	TOT	AST	PF	DQ	STL	TO	BLK	PTS	RPG	APG	PPG
58-59—Detroit	31	—	271	43	126	.341	—	—	—	23	29	.793	—	—	88	12	30	0	—	—	—	109	2.8	0.4	3.5
59-60—Detroit-Syr.	57	—	715	109	290	.376	—	—	—	44	67	.657	—	—	225	39	93	1	—	—	—	262	3.9	0.7	4.6
60-61—Syracuse	75	—	1642	266	574	.463	—	—	—	73	108	.676	—	—	469	85	246	1	—	—	—	605	6.3	1.1	8.1
61-62—Chicago-St. L.	67	—	1861	305	749	.407	—	—	—	118	181	.652	—	—	563	115	211	4	—	—	—	728	8.4	1.7	10.9
62-63—St. L.-Chicago	61	—	1200	173	380	.455	—	—	—	62	96	.646	—	—	242	82	136	0	—	—	—	408	4.0	1.3	6.7
63-64—Baltimore	71	—	1125	116	290	.400	—	—	—	28	42	.667	—	—	301	47	166	3	—	—	—	260	4.2	0.7	3.7
REG. SEASON TOTALS	362	—	6814	1012	2409	.420	—	—	—	348	523	.665	—	—	1888	380	882	9	—	—	—	2372	5.2	1.0	6.6
PLAYOFF TOTALS	11	—	248	31	79	.392	—	—	—	14	25	.560	—	—	89	8	41	1	—	—	—	76	8.1	0.7	6.9

CAGE, MICHAEL JEROME (**John Shaft**) b. January 28, 1962 Ht. 6-9 Wt. 235 College—San Diego State

SEASON—TEAM	G	GS	MIN	FGM	FGA	PCT	3FGM	3FGA	PCT	FTM	FTA	PCT	O-RB	D-RB	TOT	AST	PF	DQ	STL	TO	BLK	PTS	RPG	APG	PPG
84-85—L.A. Clippers	75	41	1610	216	398	.543	0	0	—	101	137	.737	126	266	392	51	164	1	41	81	32	533	5.2	0.7	7.1
85-86—L.A. Clippers	78	12	1566	204	426	.479	0	3	.000	113	174	.649	168	249	417	81	176	1	62	106	34	521	5.3	1.0	6.7
86-87—L.A. Clippers	80	76	2922	457	878	.521	0	3	.000	341	467	.730	354	568	922	131	221	1	99	171	67	1255	11.5	1.6	15.7
87-88—L.A. Clippers	72	70	2660	360	766	.470	0	1	.000	326	474	.688	371	567	938	110	184	1	91	160	58	1046	13.0	1.5	14.5
88-89—Seattle	80	71	2536	314	630	.498	0	4	.000	197	265	.743	276	489	765	126	184	1	92	124	52	825	9.6	1.6	10.3
89-90—Seattle	82	82	2595	325	645	.504	0	0	—	148	212	.698	306	515	821	70	232	1	79	94	45	798	10.0	0.9	9.7
90-91—Seattle	82	55	2141	226	445	.508	0	3	.000	70	112	.625	177	381	558	89	194	0	85	83	58	522	6.8	1.1	6.4
91-92—Seattle	82	69	2461	307	542	.566	0	5	.000	106	171	.620	266	462	728	92	237	0	99	78	55	720	8.9	1.1	8.8
92-93—Seattle	82	66	2156	219	416	.526	0	1	.000	61	130	.469	268	391	659	69	183	0	76	59	46	499	8.0	0.8	6.1
93-94—Seattle	82	42	1708	171	314	.545	0	1	.000	36	74	.486	164	280	444	45	179	0	77	51	38	378	5.4	0.5	4.6
REG. SEASON TOTALS	795	584	22355	2799	5460	.513	0	21	.000	1499	2216	.676	2476	4168	6644	864	1964	6	801	1007	485	7097	8.4	1.1	8.9
PLAYOFF TOTALS	46	11	923	97	184	.527	0	1	.000	32	64	.500	106	150	256	25	106	1	33	38	25	226	5.6	0.5	4.9

CALABRESE, GERALD A. (**Gerry**) b. February 4, 1925 Ht. 6-1 Wt. 175 College—St. John's

SEASON—TEAM	G	GS	MIN	FGM	FGA	PCT	3FGM	3FGA	PCT	FTM	FTA	PCT	O-RB	D-RB	TOT	AST	PF	DQ	STL	TO	BLK	PTS	RPG	APG	PPG
50-51—Syracuse	46	—	—	70	197	.355	—	—	—	61	88	.693	—	—	65	65	80	0	—	—	—	201	1.4	1.4	4.4
51-52—Syracuse	58	—	937	109	317	.344	—	—	—	73	103	.709	—	—	84	83	107	0	—	—	—	291	1.4	1.4	5.0
REG. SEASON TOTALS	104	—	937	179	514	.348	—	—	—	134	191	.702	—	—	149	148	187	0	—	—	—	492	1.4	1.4	4.7
PLAYOFF TOTALS	6	—	53	10	24	.417	—	—	—	4	4	1.000	—	—	8	4	18	—	—	—	—	24	1.3	0.7	4.0

CALDWELL, ADRIAN BERNARD b. July 4, 1966 Ht. 6-8 Wt. 265 College—Navarro College/Southern Methodist/Lamar

SEASON—TEAM	G	GS	MIN	FGM	FGA	PCT	3FGM	3FGA	PCT	FTM	FTA	PCT	O-RB	D-RB	TOT	AST	PF	DQ	STL	TO	BLK	PTS	RPG	APG	PPG
89-90—Houston	51	0	331	42	76	.553	0	0	—	13	28	.464	36	73	109	7	69	0	11	32	18	97	2.1	0.1	1.9
90-91—Houston	42	0	343	35	83	.422	0	1	.000	7	17	.412	43	57	100	8	35	0	19	30	10	77	2.4	0.2	1.8
REG. SEASON TOTALS	93	0	674	77	159	.484	0	1	.000	20	45	.444	79	130	209	15	104	0	30	62	28	174	2.2	0.2	1.9
PLAYOFF TOTALS	1	0	1	0	0	—	0	0	—	0	0	—	0	0	0	—	0	0	0	0	0	0	0.0	0.0	0.0

CALDWELL, JAMES W. JR. (**Jim**) b. January 28, 1943 Ht. 6-10 Wt. 240 College—Georgia Tech

SEASON—TEAM	G	GS	MIN	FGM	FGA	PCT	3FGM	3FGA	PCT	FTM	FTA	PCT	O-RB	D-RB	TOT	AST	PF	DQ	STL	TO	BLK	PTS	RPG	APG	PPG
67-68—New York	2	—	7	0	1	.000	—	—	—	0	0	—	—	—	1	1	1	0	—	—	—	0	0.5	0.5	0.0
67-68—N.J.-Ken. (A)	70	—	1843	223	535	.417	1	6	.167	99	166	.596	—	—	628	147	234	10	—	121	—	546	9.0	2.1	7.8
68-69—Kentucky (A)	65	—	1235	167	381	.438	1	9	.111	87	129	.674	—	—	423	130	211	3	—	97	—	422	6.5	2.0	6.5
REG. NBA TOTALS	2	—	7	0	1	.000	—	—	—	0	0	—	—	—	1	1	1	0	—	—	—	0	0.5	0.5	0.0
REG. ABA TOTALS	135	—	3078	390	916	.426	2	15	.133	186	295	.631	—	—	1051	277	445	13	—	218	—	968	7.8	2.1	7.2
ABA PLAYOFF TOTALS	12	—	238	26	66	.394	0	0	—	17	27	.630	—	—	80	19	36	0	—	13	—	69	6.7	1.6	5.8

CALDWELL, JOE (**Pogo**) b. November 1, 1941 Ht. 6-5 Wt. 195 College—Arizona State

SEASON—TEAM	G	GS	MIN	FGM	FGA	PCT	3FGM	3FGA	PCT	FTM	FTA	PCT	O-RB	D-RB	TOT	AST	PF	DQ	STL	TO	BLK	PTS	RPG	APG	PPG
64-65—Detroit	66	—	1543	290	776	.374	—	—	—	129	210	.614	—	—	441	118	171	3	—	—	—	709	6.7	1.8	10.7
65-66—Detroit-St. L.	79	—	1857	411	938	.438	—	—	—	179	254	.705	—	—	436	126	203	3	—	—	—	1001	5.5	1.6	12.7
66-67—St. Louis	81	—	2256	458	1076	.426	—	—	—	200	308	.649	—	—	442	166	230	4	—	—	—	1116	5.5	2.0	13.8
67-68—St. Louis	79	—	2641	564	1219	.463	—	—	—	165	290	.569	—	—	338	240	208	1	—	—	—	1293	4.3	3.0	16.4
68-69—Atlanta	81	—	2720	561	1106	.507	—	—	—	159	296	.537	—	—	303	320	231	1	—	—	—	1281	3.7	4.0	15.8
69-70—Atlanta	82	—	2857	674	1329	.507	—	—	—	379	551	.688	—	—	407	287	255	3	—	—	—	1727	5.0	3.5	21.1
70-71—Carolina (A)	72	—	3008	685	1528	.448	6	30	.200	302	541	.558	—	—	489	301	237	—	—	—	—	1678	6.8	4.2	23.3
71-72—Carolina (A)	61	—	2145	434	922	.471	5	20	.250	159	318	.500	—	—	343	259	208	—	—	164	—	1032	5.6	4.2	16.9
72-73—Carolina (A)	77	—	2739	555	1118	.496	1	6	.167	172	405	.425	189	206	395	352	252	4	166	246	—	1283	5.1	4.6	16.7
73-74—Carolina (A)	79	—	2654	502	1027	.489	3	17	.176	128	258	.496	177	235	412	350	255	—	170	242	35	1135	5.2	4.4	14.4
74-75—St. Louis (A)	25	—	841	161	326	.494	3	7	.429	39	87	.448	44	67	111	128	78	—	49	74	10	364	4.4	5.1	14.6
REG. NBA TOTALS	468	—	13874	2958	6444	.459	—	—	—	1211	1909	.634	—	—	2367	1257	1298	15	—	—	—	7127	5.1	2.7	15.2
REG. ABA TOTALS	314	—	11387	2337	4921	.475	18	80	.225	800	1609	.497	410	508	1750	1390	1030	4	385	726	45	5492	5.6	4.4	17.5
NBA PLAYOFF TOTALS	45	—	1477	293	652	.449	—	—	—	130	232	.560	—	—	215	119	140	3	—	—	—	716	4.8	2.6	15.9
ABA PLAYOFF TOTALS	16	—	572	96	197	.487	3	10	.300	30	62	.484	18	9	95	53	49	0	31	56	0	225	5.9	3.3	14.1
NBA ALL-STAR TOTALS	2	—	42	11	20	.550	—	—	—	3	5	.600	—	—	11	4	7	0	—	—	—	25	5.5	2.0	12.5
ABA ALL-STAR TOTALS	2	—	55	13	24	.542	0	0	—	2	4	.500	3	10	13	5	5	—	1	8	1	28	6.5	2.5	14.0

CALHOUN, DAVID L. (**Corky**) b. November 1, 1950 Ht. 6-7 Wt. 210 College—Pennsylvania

SEASON—TEAM	G	GS	MIN	FGM	FGA	PCT	3FGM	3FGA	PCT	FTM	FTA	PCT	O-RB	D-RB	TOT	AST	PF	DQ	STL	TO	BLK	PTS	RPG	APG	PPG
72-73—Phoenix	82	—	2025	211	450	.469	—	—	—	71	96	.740	—	—	338	76	214	2	—	—	—	493	4.1	0.9	6.0
73-74—Phoenix	77	—	2207	268	581	.461	—	—	—	98	129	.760	115	292	407	135	253	4	71	—	30	634	5.3	1.8	8.2
74-75—Phoenix-L.A.	70	—	1378	132	318	.415	—	—	—	58	77	.753	109	160	269	79	180	1	55	—	25	322	3.8	1.1	4.6
75-76—Los Angeles	76	—	1816	172	368	.467	—	—	—	65	83	.783	117	224	341	85	216	4	62	—	35	409	4.5	1.1	5.4
76-77—Portland	70	—	743	85	183	.464	—	—	—	66	85	.776	40	104	144	35	123	1	24	—	8	236	2.1	0.5	3.4
77-78—Portland	79	—	1370	175	365	.479	—	—	—	66	76	.868	73	142	215	87	141	3	42	64	15	416	2.7	1.1	5.3
78-79—Indiana	81	—	1332	153	335	.457	—	—	—	72	86	.837	64	174	238	104	189	1	37	56	19	378	2.9	1.3	4.7
79-80—Indiana	7	—	30	4	9	.444	0	0	—	0	2	.000	7	3	10	0	6	0	2	1	0	8	1.4	0.0	1.1
REG. SEASON TOTALS	542	—	10901	1200	2609	.460	0	0	—	496	634	.782	525	1099	1962	601	1322	16	293	121	132	2896	3.6	1.1	5.3
PLAYOFF TOTALS	18	—	203	28	54	.519	0	0	—	6	10	.600	12	16	28	7	22	0	6	3	3	62	1.6	0.4	3.4

CALHOUN, WILLIAM C. (**Bill**) b. November 4, 1927 Ht. 6-3 Wt. 180 College—San Francisco CC

SEASON—TEAM	G	GS	MIN	FGM	FGA	PCT	3FGM	3FGA	PCT	FTM	FTA	PCT	O-RB	D-RB	TOT	AST	PF	DQ	STL	TO	BLK	PTS	RPG	APG	PPG
47-48—Rochester (N)	42	—	—	31	—	—	—	—	—	18	34	.529	—	—	—	—	32	—	—	—	—	80	—	—	1.9
48-49—Rochester	56	—	—	146	408	.358	—	—	—	75	131	.573	—	—	—	125	97	—	—	—	—	367	—	2.2	6.6
49-50—Rochester	62	—	—	207	549	.377	—	—	—	146	203	.719	—	—	—	115	100	—	—	—	—	560	—	1.9	9.0
50-51—Rochester	66	—	—	175	506	.346	—	—	—	161	228	.706	—	—	199	99	87	1	—	—	—	511	3.0	1.5	7.7
51-52—Baltimore	55	—	1594	129	409	.315	—	—	—	125	183	.683	—	—	252	117	84	0	—	—	—	383	4.6	2.1	7.0
52-53—Syr.-Milw.	62	—	2148	180	534	.337	—	—	—	211	292	.723	—	—	277	156	136	4	—	—	—	571	4.5	2.5	9.2
53-54—Milwaukee	72	—	2370	190	545	.349	—	—	—	214	292	.733	—	—	274	189	151	3	—	—	—	594	3.8	2.6	8.3
54-55—Milwaukee	69	—	2109	144	480	.300	—	—	—	166	236	.703	—	—	290	235	181	4	—	—	—	454	4.2	3.4	6.6
REG. NBA TOTALS	442	—	8221	1171	3431	.341	—	—	—	1098	1565	.702	—	—	1292	1036	836	12	—	—	—	3440	4.0	2.3	7.8
REG. NBL TOTALS	42	—	—	31	—	—	—	—	—	18	34	.529	—	—	—	—	32	—	—	—	—	80	—	—	1.9
NBA PLAYOFF TOTALS	18	—	0	33	78	.423	—	—	—	34	46	.739	—	—	41	34	25	0	—	—	—	100	2.9	1.9	5.6
NBL PLAYOFF TOTALS	8	—	—	11	—	—	—	—	—	2	3	.667	—	—	—	—	8	—	—	—	—	24	—	—	3.0

CALIP, DEMETRIUS b. November 18, 1969 Ht. 6-1 Wt. 165 College—Michigan

SEASON—TEAM	G	GS	MIN	FGM	FGA	PCT	3FGM	3FGA	PCT	FTM	FTA	PCT	O-RB	D-RB	TOT	AST	PF	DQ	STL	TO	BLK	PTS	RPG	APG	PPG
91-92—L.A. Lakers	7	0	58	4	18	.222	1	5	.200	2	3	.667	1	4	5	12	8	0	1	5	0	11	0.7	1.7	1.6
REG. SEASON TOTALS	7	0	58	4	18	.222	1	5	.200	2	3	.667	1	4	5	12	8	0	1	5	0	11	0.7	1.7	1.6

CALLAHAN, THOMAS FRANCIS (**Tom**) b. June 2, 1921   Ht. 6-1 Wt. 180 College—Notre Dame/Rockhurst

SEASON—TEAM	G	GS	MIN	FGM	FGA	PCT	3FGM	3FGA	PCT	FTM	FTA	PCT	O-RB	D-RB	TOT	AST	PF	DQ	STL	TO	BLK	PTS	RPG	APG	PPG
46-47—Providence	13	—	—	6	29	.207	—	—	—	5	12	.417	—	—	—	4	9	—	—	—	—	17	—	0.3	1.3
REG. SEASON TOTALS	13	—	—	6	29	.207	—	—	—	5	12	.417	—	—	—	4	9	—	—	—	—	17	—	0.3	1.3

CALLOWAY, RICHARD MARLON (**Rick**) b. October 12, 1966   Ht. 6-6 Wt. 190 College—Indiana/Kansas

SEASON—TEAM	G	GS	MIN	FGM	FGA	PCT	3FGM	3FGA	PCT	FTM	FTA	PCT	O-RB	D-RB	TOT	AST	PF	DQ	STL	TO	BLK	PTS	RPG	APG	PPG
90-91—Sacramento	64	0	678	75	192	.391	0	2	.000	55	79	.696	25	53	78	61	98	1	22	51	7	205	1.2	1.0	3.2
REG. SEASON TOTALS	64	0	678	75	192	.391	0	2	.000	55	79	.696	25	53	78	61	98	1	22	51	7	205	1.2	1.0	3.2

CALVERLEY, ERNEST A. (**Ernie**) b. January 30, 1924   Ht. 5-10 Wt. 155 College—Rhode Island

SEASON—TEAM	G	GS	MIN	FGM	FGA	PCT	3FGM	3FGA	PCT	FTM	FTA	PCT	O-RB	D-RB	TOT	AST	PF	DQ	STL	TO	BLK	PTS	RPG	APG	PPG
46-47—Providence	59	—	—	323	1102	.293	—	—	—	199	283	.703	—	—	—	202	191	—	—	—	—	845	—	3.4	14.3
47-48—Providence	47	—	—	226	835	.271	—	—	—	107	161	.665	—	—	—	119	168	—	—	—	—	559	—	2.5	11.9
48-49—Providence	59	—	—	218	696	.313	—	—	—	121	160	.756	—	—	—	251	183	—	—	—	—	557	—	4.3	9.4
REG. SEASON TOTALS	165	—	—	767	2633	.291	—	—	—	427	604	.707	—	—	—	572	542	—	—	—	—	1961	—	3.5	11.9

CALVIN, MACK b. July 27, 1947   Ht. 6-0 Wt. 170 College—Long Beach CC/USC

SEASON—TEAM	G	GS	MIN	FGM	FGA	PCT	3FGM	3FGA	PCT	FTM	FTA	PCT	O-RB	D-RB	TOT	AST	PF	DQ	STL	TO	BLK	PTS	RPG	APG	PPG
69-70—Los Angeles (A)	84	—	2955	441	1047	.421	3	25	.120	529	642	.824	—	—	294	478	289	6	—	—	—	1414	3.5	5.7	16.8
70-71—Floridians (A)	81	—	3394	744	1728	.431	17	59	.288	696	805	.865	—	—	283	619	263	—	—	—	—	2201	3.5	7.6	27.2
71-72—Floridians (A)	82	—	2977	552	1253	.441	11	48	.229	611	701	.872	—	—	274	481	270	—	—	261	—	1726	3.3	5.9	21.0
72-73—Carolina (A)	84	—	2228	478	944	.506	11	28	.393	500	582	.859	97	118	215	301	219	3	—	247	—	1467	2.6	3.6	17.5
73-74—Carolina (A)	83	—	2592	498	1078	.462	10	43	.233	490	560	.875	78	165	243	347	244	—	135	234	7	1496	2.9	4.2	18.0
74-75—Denver (A)	74	—	2463	483	996	.485	3	16	.188	475	530	.896	36	174	210	570	206	—	140	279	8	1444	2.8	7.7	19.5
75-76—Virginia (A)	45	—	1658	306	717	.427	7	26	.269	253	285	.888	38	90	128	271	122	—	71	192	1	872	2.8	6.0	19.4
76-77—L.A.-S.A.-Denver	76	—	1438	220	544	.404	—	—	—	287	338	.849	36	60	96	240	127	0	61	—	3	727	1.3	3.2	9.6
77-78—Denver	77	—	988	147	333	.441	—	—	—	173	206	.840	11	73	84	148	87	0	46	108	5	467	1.1	1.9	6.1
79-80—Utah	48	—	772	100	227	.441	1	11	.091	105	117	.897	13	71	84	134	72	0	27	57	0	306	1.8	2.8	6.4
80-81—Cleveland	21	—	128	13	39	.333	1	5	.200	25	35	.714	2	10	12	28	13	0	5	17	0	52	0.6	1.3	2.5
REG. NBA TOTALS	222	—	3326	480	1143	.420	2	16	.125	590	696	.848	62	214	276	550	299	0	139	182	8	1552	1.2	2.5	7.0
REG. ABA TOTALS	533	—	18267	3502	7763	.451	62	245	.253	3554	4105	.866	249	547	1647	3067	1613	9	346	1213	16	10620	3.1	5.8	19.9
NBA PLAYOFF TOTALS	18	—	247	38	82	.463	0	0	—	51	58	.879	4	13	17	34	24	0	8	11	0	127	0.9	1.9	7.1
ABA PLAYOFF TOTALS	56	—	1959	405	870	.466	12	35	.343	367	437	.840	14	46	189	297	179	0	28	98	1	1189	3.4	5.3	21.2
ABA ALL-STAR TOTALS	5	—	112	16	48	.333	1	3	.333	23	29	.793	4	9	13	34	16	0	3	13	0	56	2.6	6.8	11.2

CAMBRIDGE, DEXTER RYAN b. January 29, 1970   Ht. 6-7 Wt. 225 College—Lon Morris/Texas

SEASON—TEAM	G	GS	MIN	FGM	FGA	PCT	3FGM	3FGA	PCT	FTM	FTA	PCT	O-RB	D-RB	TOT	AST	PF	DQ	STL	TO	BLK	PTS	RPG	APG	PPG
92-93—Dallas	53	13	885	151	312	.484	0	4	.000	68	99	.687	88	79	167	58	128	1	24	63	6	370	3.2	1.1	7.0
REG. SEASON TOTALS	53	13	885	151	312	.484	0	4	.000	68	99	.687	88	79	167	58	128	1	24	63	6	370	3.2	1.1	7.0

CAMPBELL, ANTHONY (**Tony**) b. May 7, 1962   Ht. 6-7 Wt. 215 College—Ohio State

SEASON—TEAM	G	GS	MIN	FGM	FGA	PCT	3FGM	3FGA	PCT	FTM	FTA	PCT	O-RB	D-RB	TOT	AST	PF	DQ	STL	TO	BLK	PTS	RPG	APG	PPG
84-85—Detroit	56	0	625	130	262	.496	0	1	.000	56	70	.800	41	48	89	24	107	1	28	69	3	316	1.6	0.4	5.6
85-86—Detroit	82	1	1292	294	608	.484	2	9	.222	58	73	.795	83	153	236	45	164	0	62	86	7	648	2.9	0.5	7.9
86-87—Detroit	40	0	332	57	145	.393	0	3	.000	24	39	.615	21	37	58	19	40	0	12	34	1	138	1.5	0.5	3.5
87-88—L.A. Lakers	13	1	242	57	101	.564	1	3	.333	28	39	.718	8	19	27	15	41	0	11	26	2	143	2.1	1.2	11.0
88-89—L.A. Lakers	63	2	787	158	345	.458	2	21	.095	70	83	.843	53	77	130	47	108	0	37	62	6	388	2.1	0.7	6.2
89-90—Minnesota	82	81	3164	723	1581	.457	9	54	.167	448	569	.787	209	242	451	213	260	7	111	251	31	1903	5.5	2.6	23.2
90-91—Minnesota	77	71	2893	652	1502	.434	16	61	.262	358	446	.803	161	185	346	214	204	0	121	190	46	1678	4.5	2.8	21.8
91-92—Minnesota	78	41	2441	527	1137	.464	13	37	.351	240	299	.803	141	145	286	229	206	1	84	165	31	1307	3.7	2.9	16.8
92-93—New York	58	13	1062	194	396	.490	2	5	.400	59	87	.678	59	96	155	62	150	0	34	51	5	449	2.7	1.1	7.7
93-94—N.Y.-Dallas	63	14	1214	227	512	.443	7	28	.250	94	120	.783	76	110	186	82	134	1	50	84	15	555	3.0	1.3	8.8
REG. SEASON TOTALS	612	224	14052	3019	6589	.458	52	222	.234	1435	1825	.786	852	1112	1964	950	1414	10	550	1018	149	7525	3.2	1.6	12.3
PLAYOFF TOTALS	34	1	271	49	102	.480	3	7	.429	36	50	.720	10	25	35	14	56	1	7	18	0	137	1.0	0.4	4.0

CAMPBELL, ELDEN JEROME (**Big E**) b. July 23, 1968   Ht. 6-11 Wt. 230 College—Clemson

SEASON—TEAM	G	GS	MIN	FGM	FGA	PCT	3FGM	3FGA	PCT	FTM	FTA	PCT	O-RB	D-RB	TOT	AST	PF	DQ	STL	TO	BLK	PTS	RPG	APG	PPG
90-91—L.A. Lakers	52	0	380	56	123	.455	0	0	—	32	49	.653	40	56	96	10	71	1	11	16	38	144	1.8	0.2	2.8
91-92—L.A. Lakers	81	47	1876	220	491	.448	0	2	.000	138	223	.619	155	268	423	59	203	1	53	73	159	578	5.2	0.7	7.1
92-93—L.A. Lakers	79	13	1551	238	520	.458	0	3	.000	130	204	.637	127	205	332	48	165	0	59	69	100	606	4.2	0.6	7.7
93-94—L.A. Lakers	76	74	2253	373	808	.462	0	2	.000	188	273	.689	167	352	519	86	241	2	64	98	146	934	6.8	1.1	12.3
REG. SEASON TOTALS	288	134	6060	887	1942	.457	0	7	.000	488	749	.652	489	881	1370	203	680	4	187	256	443	2262	4.8	0.7	7.9
PLAYOFF TOTALS	23	7	433	68	144	.472	0	0	—	31	57	.544	34	62	96	16	52	1	15	22	26	167	4.2	0.7	7.3

CANNON, LAWRENCE T. (Larry) b. April 12, 1947 Ht. 6-4½ Wt. 195 College—La Salle

SEASON—TEAM	G	GS	MIN	FGM	FGA	PCT	3FGM	3FGA	PCT	FTM	FTA	PCT	O-RB	D-RB	TOT	AST	PF	DQ	STL	TO	BLK	PTS	RPG	APG	PPG
69-70—Miami (A)	57	—	1503	253	660	.383	8	30	.267	158	232	.681	—	—	141	158	133	2	—	—	—	672	2.5	2.8	11.8
70-71—Denver (A)	80	—	3097	751	1722	.436	18	69	.261	606	763	.794	—	—	333	414	237	—	—	—	—	2126	4.2	5.2	26.6
71-72—Memphis-Indiana (A)	54	—	1171	228	610	.374	3	14	.214	164	221	.742	—	—	107	150	124	—	—	105	—	623	2.0	2.8	11.5
73-74—Indiana (A)	3	—	26	3	7	.429	0	0	—	1	3	.333	1	2	3	3	2	—	0	3	0	7	1.0	1.0	2.3
73-74—Philadelphia	19	—	335	49	127	.386	—	—	—	19	28	.679	16	20	36	52	48	0	7	—	4	117	1.9	2.7	6.2
REG. NBA TOTALS	19	—	335	49	127	.386	—	—	—	19	28	.679	16	20	36	52	48	0	7	—	4	117	1.9	2.7	6.2
REG. ABA TOTALS	194	—	5797	1235	2999	.412	29	113	.257	929	1219	.762	1	2	584	725	496	2	0	108	0	3428	3.0	3.7	17.7

CARD, FRANK HOWARD b. December 28, 1944 Ht. 6-7 Wt. 195 College—South Carolina State

SEASON—TEAM	G	GS	MIN	FGM	FGA	PCT	3FGM	3FGA	PCT	FTM	FTA	PCT	O-RB	D-RB	TOT	AST	PF	DQ	STL	TO	BLK	PTS	RPG	APG	PPG
68-69—Minnesota (A)	76	—	1596	222	537	.413	1	5	.200	146	244	.598	—	—	419	81	155	2	—	110	—	591	5.5	1.1	7.8
69-70—Washington (A)	74	—	1820	351	666	.527	1	5	.200	178	286	.622	—	—	480	92	216	3	—	—	—	881	6.5	1.2	11.9
70-71—Vir.-Car. (A)	70	—	1865	302	662	.456	1	5	.200	196	303	.647	—	—	457	113	216	—	—	—	—	801	6.5	1.6	11.4
71-72—Car.-Denver (A)	82	—	1584	235	543	.433	0	2	.000	130	197	.660	—	—	358	86	220	—	—	124	—	600	4.4	1.0	7.3
72-73—Denver (A)	4	—	36	6	15	.400	0	0	—	9	13	.692	4	3	7	0	4	0	—	3	—	21	1.8	0.0	5.3
REG. ABA TOTALS	306	—	6901	1116	2423	.461	3	17	.176	659	1043	.632	4	3	1721	372	811	5	—	237	—	2894	5.6	1.2	9.5
ABA PLAYOFF TOTALS	17	—	338	64	110	.582	0	1	.000	21	41	.512	—	—	84	22	56	2	—	11	—	149	4.9	1.3	8.8

CARL, HOWARD HERSHEY (Howie) b. June 7, 1938 Ht. 5-9½ Wt. 160 College—Illinois/DePaul

SEASON—TEAM	G	GS	MIN	FGM	FGA	PCT	3FGM	3FGA	PCT	FTM	FTA	PCT	O-RB	D-RB	TOT	AST	PF	DQ	STL	TO	BLK	PTS	RPG	APG	PPG
61-62—Chicago	31	—	382	67	201	.333	—	—	—	36	51	.706	—	—	39	57	41	1	—	—	—	170	1.3	1.8	5.5
REG. SEASON TOTALS	31	—	382	67	201	.333	—	—	—	36	51	.706	—	—	39	57	41	1	—	—	—	170	1.3	1.8	5.5

CARLISLE, CHESTER G. (Chet) b. November 2, 1916 d. August 1988 Ht. 6-5 Wt. 195 College—California

SEASON—TEAM	G	GS	MIN	FGM	FGA	PCT	3FGM	3FGA	PCT	FTM	FTA	PCT	O-RB	D-RB	TOT	AST	PF	DQ	STL	TO	BLK	PTS	RPG	APG	PPG
46-47—Chicago	51	—	—	100	373	.268	—	—	—	56	92	.609	—	—	—	17	136	—	—	—	—	256	—	0.3	5.0
REG. SEASON TOTALS	51	—	—	100	373	.268	—	—	—	56	92	.609	—	—	—	17	136	—	—	—	—	256	—	0.3	5.0
PLAYOFF TOTALS	10	—	—	20	88	.227	—	—	—	16	28	.571	—	—	—	2	33	2	—	—	—	56	—	0.2	5.6

CARLISLE, RICHARD PRESTON (Rick) b. October 27, 1959 Ht. 6-5 Wt. 210 College—Maine/Virginia

SEASON—TEAM	G	GS	MIN	FGM	FGA	PCT	3FGM	3FGA	PCT	FTM	FTA	PCT	O-RB	D-RB	TOT	AST	PF	DQ	STL	TO	BLK	PTS	RPG	APG	PPG
84-85—Boston	38	0	179	26	67	.388	0	2	.000	15	17	.882	8	13	21	25	21	0	3	19	0	67	0.6	0.7	1.8
85-86—Boston	77	1	760	92	189	.487	0	10	.000	15	23	.652	22	55	77	104	92	1	19	50	4	199	1.0	1.4	2.6
86-87—Boston	42	0	297	30	92	.326	5	16	.313	15	20	.750	8	22	30	35	28	0	8	25	0	80	0.7	0.8	1.9
87-88—New York	26	0	204	29	67	.433	6	17	.353	10	11	.909	6	7	13	32	39	1	11	22	4	74	0.5	1.2	2.8
89-90—New Jersey	5	0	21	1	7	.143	0	3	.000	0	0	—	0	0	0	5	7	0	1	4	1	2	0.0	1.0	0.4
REG. SEASON TOTALS	188	1	1461	178	422	.422	11	48	.229	55	71	.775	44	97	141	201	187	2	42	120	9	422	0.8	1.1	2.2
PLAYOFF TOTALS	12	0	62	9	19	.474	0	2	.000	3	4	.750	4	3	7	8	10	0	3	3	0	21	0.6	0.7	1.8

CARLOS, DON A. b. March 3, 1944 Ht. 6-4½ Wt. 210 College—Otterbein

SEASON—TEAM	G	GS	MIN	FGM	FGA	PCT	3FGM	3FGA	PCT	FTM	FTA	PCT	O-RB	D-RB	TOT	AST	PF	DQ	STL	TO	BLK	PTS	RPG	APG	PPG
68-69—Houston (A)	56	—	1527	207	505	.410	0	3	.000	214	283	.756	—	—	279	159	231	10	—	140	—	628	5.0	2.8	11.2
REG. ABA TOTALS	56	—	1527	207	505	.410	0	3	.000	214	283	.756	—	—	279	159	231	10	—	140	—	628	5.0	2.8	11.2

CARLSON, ALVIN HAROLD (Al) b. September 17, 1951 Ht. 6-11 Wt. 235 College—USC/Oregon

SEASON—TEAM	G	GS	MIN	FGM	FGA	PCT	3FGM	3FGA	PCT	FTM	FTA	PCT	O-RB	D-RB	TOT	AST	PF	DQ	STL	TO	BLK	PTS	RPG	APG	PPG
75-76—Seattle	28	—	279	27	79	.342	—	—	—	18	29	.621	30	43	73	13	39	1	7	—	11	72	2.6	0.5	2.6
REG. SEASON TOTALS	28	—	279	27	79	.342	—	—	—	18	29	.621	30	43	73	13	39	1	7	—	11	72	2.6	0.5	2.6

CARLSON, DON VERNON (Swede) b. March 22, 1921 Ht. 6-0 Wt. 170 College—Minnesota

SEASON—TEAM	G	GS	MIN	FGM	FGA	PCT	3FGM	3FGA	PCT	FTM	FTA	PCT	O-RB	D-RB	TOT	AST	PF	DQ	STL	TO	BLK	PTS	RPG	APG	PPG
46-47—Chicago	59	—	—	272	845	.322	—	—	—	86	159	.541	—	—	—	59	182	—	—	—	—	630	—	1.0	10.7
47-48—Minneapolis (N)	58	—	205	—	—	—	—	—	—	65	109	.596	—	—	—	—	177	—	—	—	—	475	—	—	8.2
48-49—Minneapolis	55	—	211	632	—	.334	—	—	—	86	130	.662	—	—	—	170	180	—	—	—	—	508	—	3.1	9.2
49-50—Minneapolis	57	—	99	290	.341	—	—	—	—	69	95	.726	—	—	—	76	126	—	—	—	—	267	—	1.3	4.7
50-51—Washington	9	—	17	46	.370	—	—	—	—	8	16	.500	—	—	15	19	23	0	—	—	—	42	1.7	2.1	4.7
REG. NBA TOTALS	180	—	—	599	1813	.330	—	—	—	249	400	.623	—	—	15	324	511	0	—	—	—	1447	1.7	1.8	8.0
REG. NBL TOTALS	58	—	205	—	—	—	—	—	—	65	109	.596	—	—	—	—	177	—	—	—	—	475	—	—	8.2
NBA PLAYOFF TOTALS	31	—	98	332	.295	—	—	—	—	53	84	.631	—	—	—	45	80	2	—	—	—	249	—	1.5	8.0
NBL PLAYOFF TOTALS	9	—	17	—	—	—	—	—	—	4	10	.400	—	—	—	—	27	—	—	—	—	38	—	—	4.2

CARNEY, ROBERT LEE (**Bob**) b. August 3, 1932 Ht. 6-3 Wt. 170 College—Bradley

SEASON—TEAM	G	GS	MIN	FGM	FGA	PCT	3FGM	3FGA	PCT	FTM	FTA	PCT	O-RB	D-RB	TOT	AST	PF	DQ	STL	TO	BLK	PTS	RPG	APG	PPG
54-55—Minneapolis	19	—	244	24	64	.375	—	—	—	21	40	.525	—	—	45	16	36	0	—	—	—	69	2.4	0.8	3.6
REG. SEASON TOTALS	19	—	244	24	64	.375	—	—	—	21	40	.525	—	—	45	16	36	0	—	—	—	69	2.4	0.8	3.6
PLAYOFF TOTALS	7	—	41	1	8	.125	—	—	—	8	9	.889	—	—	5	3	7	0	—	—	—	10	0.7	0.4	1.4

CARPENTER, ROBERT H. (**Bob**) b. November 6, 1917 Ht. 6-5 Wt. 200 College—East Texas State

SEASON—TEAM	G	GS	MIN	FGM	FGA	PCT	3FGM	3FGA	PCT	FTM	FTA	PCT	O-RB	D-RB	TOT	AST	PF	DQ	STL	TO	BLK	PTS	RPG	APG	PPG
40-41—Oshkosh (N)	24	—	—	40	—	—	—	—	—	41	—	—	—	—	—	—	37	—	—	—	—	121	—	—	5.0
45-46—Oshkosh (N)	34	—	—	186	—	—	—	—	—	101	144	.701	—	—	—	—	—	—	—	—	—	473	—	—	13.9
46-47—Oshkosh (N)	44	—	—	199	—	—	—	—	—	115	169	.680	—	—	—	—	—	—	—	—	—	513	—	—	11.7
47-48—Oshkosh (N)	60	—	—	211	—	—	—	—	—	160	213	.751	—	—	—	—	—	—	—	—	—	582	—	—	9.7
48-49—Hammond-Oshkosh (N)	47	—	—	160	—	—	—	—	—	131	180	.728	—	—	—	—	—	—	—	—	—	451	—	—	9.6
49-50—Fort Wayne	66	—	—	212	617	.344	—	—	—	190	256	.742	—	—	—	92	168	—	—	—	—	614	—	1.4	9.3
50-51—Ft. Wayne-Tri-Cit	56	—	—	109	355	.307	—	—	—	105	128	.820	—	—	229	79	115	2	—	—	—	323	4.1	1.4	5.8
REG. NBA TOTALS	122	—	—	321	972	.330	—	—	—	295	384	.768	—	—	229	171	283	2	—	—	—	937	4.1	1.4	7.7
REG. NBL TOTALS	209	—	—	796	—	—	—	—	—	548	706	.718	—	—	—	—	37	—	—	—	—	2140	—	—	10.2
NBA PLAYOFF TOTALS	4	—	—	11	30	.367	—	—	—	10	14	.714	—	—	—	2	6	0	—	—	—	32	—	0.5	8.0
NBL PLAYOFF TOTALS	28	—	—	82	—	—	—	—	—	91	88	.682	—	—	—	—	58	—	—	—	—	255	—	—	9.1

CARR, ANTOINE LABOTTE (**A.C.**) b. July 23, 1961 Ht. 6-9 Wt. 255 College—Wichita State

SEASON—TEAM	G	GS	MIN	FGM	FGA	PCT	3FGM	3FGA	PCT	FTM	FTA	PCT	O-RB	D-RB	TOT	AST	PF	DQ	STL	TO	BLK	PTS	RPG	APG	PPG
84-85—Atlanta	62	15	1195	198	375	.528	2	6	.333	101	128	.789	79	153	232	80	219	4	29	108	78	499	3.7	1.3	8.0
85-86—Atlanta	17	0	258	49	93	.527	0	0	—	18	27	.667	16	36	52	14	51	1	7	14	15	116	3.1	0.8	6.8
86-87—Atlanta	65	2	695	134	265	.506	1	3	.333	73	103	.709	60	96	156	34	146	1	14	40	48	342	2.4	0.5	5.3
87-88—Atlanta	80	2	1483	281	517	.544	1	4	.250	142	182	.780	94	195	289	103	272	7	38	116	83	705	3.6	1.3	8.8
88-89—Atlanta	78	12	1488	226	471	.480	0	1	.000	130	152	.855	106	168	274	91	221	0	31	82	62	582	3.5	1.2	7.5
89-90—Atlanta-Sac.	77	4	1727	356	721	.494	0	7	.000	237	298	.795	115	207	322	119	247	6	30	125	68	949	4.2	1.5	12.3
90-91—Sacramento	77	48	2527	628	1228	.511	0	3	.000	295	389	.758	163	257	420	191	315	14	45	171	101	1551	5.5	2.5	20.1
91-92—San Antonio	81	27	1867	359	732	.490	1	5	.200	162	212	.764	128	218	346	63	264	5	32	114	96	881	4.3	0.8	10.9
92-93—San Antonio	71	46	1947	379	705	.538	0	5	.000	174	224	.777	107	281	388	97	264	5	35	96	87	932	5.5	1.4	13.1
93-94—San Antonio	34	0	465	78	160	.488	0	1	.000	42	58	.724	12	39	51	15	75	0	9	15	22	198	1.5	0.4	5.8
REG. SEASON TOTALS	642	156	13652	2688	5267	.510	5	35	.143	1374	1773	.775	880	1650	2530	807	2074	43	270	881	660	6755	3.9	1.3	10.5
PLAYOFF TOTALS	40	11	770	156	274	.569	1	3	.333	67	92	.728	50	88	138	50	145	5	13	35	51	380	3.5	1.3	9.5

CARR, AUSTIN GEORGE b. March 10, 1948 Ht. 6-4 Wt. 200 College—Notre Dame

SEASON—TEAM	G	GS	MIN	FGM	FGA	PCT	3FGM	3FGA	PCT	FTM	FTA	PCT	O-RB	D-RB	TOT	AST	PF	DQ	STL	TO	BLK	PTS	RPG	APG	PPG
71-72—Cleveland	43	—	1539	381	894	.426	—	—	—	149	196	.760	—	—	150	148	99	0	—	—	—	911	3.5	3.4	21.2
72-73—Cleveland	82	—	3097	702	1575	.446	—	—	—	281	342	.822	—	—	369	279	185	1	—	—	—	1685	4.5	3.4	20.5
73-74—Cleveland	81	—	3100	748	1682	.445	—	—	—	279	326	.856	139	150	289	305	189	2	92	—	14	1775	3.6	3.8	21.9
74-75—Cleveland	41	—	1081	252	538	.468	—	—	—	89	106	.840	51	56	107	154	57	0	48	—	2	593	2.6	3.8	14.5
75-76—Cleveland	65	—	1282	276	625	.442	—	—	—	106	134	.791	67	65	132	122	92	0	37	—	2	658	2.0	1.9	10.1
76-77—Cleveland	82	—	2409	558	1221	.457	—	—	—	213	268	.795	120	120	240	220	221	3	57	—	10	1329	2.9	2.7	16.2
77-78—Cleveland	82	—	2186	414	945	.438	—	—	—	183	225	.813	76	111	187	225	168	1	68	146	19	1011	2.3	2.7	12.3
78-79—Cleveland	82	—	2714	551	1161	.475	—	—	—	292	358	.816	155	135	290	217	210	1	77	175	14	1394	3.5	2.6	17.0
79-80—Cleveland	77	—	1595	390	839	.465	2	6	.333	127	172	.738	81	84	165	150	120	0	39	108	3	909	2.1	1.9	11.8
80-81—Dallas-Wash.	47	—	657	87	234	.372	0	7	.000	34	54	.630	22	39	61	58	53	0	15	41	2	208	1.3	1.2	4.4
REG. SEASON TOTALS	682	—	19660	4359	9714	.449	2	13	.154	1753	2181	.804	711	760	1990	1878	1394	8	433	470	66	10473	2.9	2.8	15.4
PLAYOFF TOTALS	18	—	425	87	204	.426	0	0	—	38	55	.691	18	23	41	41	50	0	10	4	5	212	2.3	2.3	11.8
ALL-STAR TOTALS	1	—	5	0	4	.000	0	0	—	0	0	—	0	1	1	0	1	0	0	—	0	0	1.0	0.0	0.0

CARR, KENNETH ALAN (**Kenny**) b. August 15, 1955 Ht. 6-7 Wt. 220 College—North Carolina State

SEASON—TEAM	G	GS	MIN	FGM	FGA	PCT	3FGM	3FGA	PCT	FTM	FTA	PCT	O-RB	D-RB	TOT	AST	PF	DQ	STL	TO	BLK	PTS	RPG	APG	PPG
77-78—Los Angeles	52	—	733	134	302	.444	—	—	—	55	85	.647	53	155	208	26	127	0	18	89	14	323	4.0	0.5	6.2
78-79—Los Angeles	72	—	1149	225	450	.500	—	—	—	83	137	.606	70	222	292	60	152	0	38	116	31	533	4.1	0.8	7.4
79-80—L.A.-Clev.	79	—	1838	378	768	.492	0	4	.000	173	263	.658	199	389	588	77	246	3	66	154	52	929	7.4	1.0	11.8
80-81—Cleveland	81	—	2615	469	918	.511	0	4	.000	292	409	.714	260	575	835	192	296	3	76	231	42	1230	10.3	2.4	15.2
81-82—Clev.-Detroit	74	48	1926	348	692	.503	1	10	.100	198	302	.656	167	364	531	86	249	0	64	152	22	895	7.2	1.2	12.1
82-83—Portland	82	26	2331	362	717	.505	2	6	.333	255	366	.697	182	407	589	116	306	10	62	185	42	981	7.2	1.4	12.0
83-84—Portland	82	57	2455	518	923	.561	0	5	.000	247	367	.673	208	434	642	157	274	3	68	202	33	1283	7.8	1.9	15.6
84-85—Portland	48	30	1120	190	363	.523	0	3	.000	118	164	.720	90	233	323	56	141	0	25	100	17	498	6.7	1.2	10.4
85-86—Portland	55	31	1557	232	466	.498	0	4	.000	149	217	.687	146	346	492	70	203	5	38	106	30	613	8.9	1.3	11.1
86-87—Portland	49	43	1443	201	399	.504	0	2	.000	126	169	.746	131	368	499	83	159	1	29	103	13	528	10.2	1.7	10.8
REG. SEASON TOTALS	674	235	17167	3057	5998	.510	3	38	.079	1696	2479	.684	1506	3493	4999	923	2153	25	484	1438	296	7813	7.4	1.4	11.6
PLAYOFF TOTALS	35	18	893	153	299	.512	0	2	.000	62	85	.729	69	161	230	37	126	4	18	65	12	368	6.6	1.1	10.5

CARR, MICHAEL LEON (**M.L.**) b. January 9, 1951   Ht. 6-6   Wt. 205   College—Guilford

SEASON—TEAM	G	GS	MIN	FGM	FGA	PCT	3FGM	3FGA	PCT	FTM	FTA	PCT	O-RB	D-RB	TOT	AST	PF	DQ	STL	TO	BLK	PTS	RPG	APG	PPG
75-76—St. Louis (A)	74	—	2174	380	786	.483	9	24	.375	137	206	.665	171	288	459	224	225	—	127	162	44	906	6.2	3.0	12.2
76-77—Detroit	82	—	2643	443	931	.476	—	—	—	205	279	.735	211	420	631	181	287	8	165	—	58	1091	7.7	2.2	13.3
77-78—Detroit	79	—	2556	390	857	.455	—	—	—	200	271	.738	202	355	557	185	243	4	147	210	27	980	7.1	2.3	12.4
78-79—Detroit	80	—	3207	587	1143	.514	—	—	—	323	435	.743	219	370	589	262	279	2	197	255	46	1497	7.4	3.3	18.7
79-80—Boston	82	—	1994	362	763	.474	12	41	.293	178	241	.739	106	224	330	156	214	1	120	143	36	914	4.0	1.9	11.1
80-81—Boston	41	—	655	97	216	.449	1	14	.071	53	67	.791	26	57	83	56	74	0	30	47	18	248	2.0	1.4	6.0
81-82—Boston	56	27	1296	184	409	.450	5	17	.294	82	116	.707	56	94	150	128	136	2	67	63	21	455	2.7	2.3	8.1
82-83—Boston	77	0	883	135	315	.429	3	19	.158	60	81	.741	51	86	137	71	140	0	48	79	10	333	1.8	0.9	4.3
83-84—Boston	60	1	585	70	171	.409	3	15	.200	42	48	.875	26	49	75	49	67	0	17	46	4	185	1.3	0.8	3.1
84-85—Boston	47	0	397	62	149	.416	9	23	.391	17	17	1.000	21	22	43	24	44	0	21	24	6	150	0.9	0.5	3.2
REG. NBA TOTALS	604	28	14216	2330	4954	.470	33	129	.256	1160	1555	.746	918	1677	2595	1112	1484	17	812	867	226	5853	4.3	1.8	9.7
REG. ABA TOTALS	74	—	2174	380	786	.483	9	24	.375	137	206	.665	171	288	459	224	225	—	127	162	44	906	6.2	3.0	12.2
NBA PLAYOFF TOTALS	67	12	1005	142	372	.382	5	22	.227	65	91	.714	59	70	129	64	111	0	38	40	10	354	1.9	1.0	5.3

CARRIER, JAMES DAREL (**Darel**) b. October 26, 1940   Ht. 6-3   Wt. 185   College—Western Kentucky

SEASON—TEAM	G	GS	MIN	FGM	FGA	PCT	3FGM	3FGA	PCT	FTM	FTA	PCT	O-RB	D-RB	TOT	AST	PF	DQ	STL	TO	BLK	PTS	RPG	APG	PPG
67-68—Kentucky (A)	77	—	3192	643	1545	.416	84	235	.357	395	479	.825	—	—	352	172	263	7	—	228	—	1765	4.6	2.2	22.9
68-69—Kentucky (A)	73	—	2858	559	1376	.406	125	330	.379	447	545	.820	—	—	283	214	227	1	—	213	—	1690	3.9	2.9	23.2
69-70—Kentucky (A)	77	—	2805	608	1458	.417	105	280	.375	454	509	.892	—	—	249	212	268	8	—	—	—	1775	3.2	2.8	23.1
70-71—Kentucky (A)	84	—	2664	495	1140	.434	63	161	.391	327	377	.867	—	—	232	244	229	—	—	—	—	1380	2.8	2.9	16.4
71-72—Kentucky (A)	23	—	629	117	288	.406	16	37	.432	76	88	.864	—	—	57	44	64	—	—	38	—	326	2.5	1.9	14.2
72-73—Memphis (A)	16	—	190	23	60	.383	5	12	.417	24	26	.923	2	12	14	10	21	0	—	15	—	75	0.9	0.6	4.7
REG. ABA TOTALS	350	—	12338	2445	5867	.417	398	1055	.377	1723	2024	.851	2	12	1187	896	1072	16	—	494	—	7011	3.4	2.6	20.0
ABA PLAYOFF TOTALS	45	—	1693	309	733	.422	57	146	.390	241	277	.870	—	—	151	131	156	2	—	33	—	916	3.4	2.9	20.4
ABA ALL-STAR TOTALS	3	—	57	8	26	.308	1	9	.111	12	15	.800	2	4	7	6	8	0	—	5	—	29	2.3	2.0	9.7

CARRINGTON, ROBERT FREDERICK (**Bob**) b. July 3, 1953   Ht. 6-6   Wt. 195   College—Boston College

SEASON—TEAM	G	GS	MIN	FGM	FGA	PCT	3FGM	3FGA	PCT	FTM	FTA	PCT	O-RB	D-RB	TOT	AST	PF	DQ	STL	TO	BLK	PTS	RPG	APG	PPG
77-78—N.J.-Indiana	72	—	1653	253	589	.430	—	—	—	130	171	.760	70	104	174	117	205	6	65	118	23	636	2.4	1.6	8.8
79-80—San Diego	10	—	134	15	37	.405	0	2	.000	6	8	.750	6	7	13	3	18	0	4	5	1	36	1.3	0.3	3.6
REG. SEASON TOTALS	82	—	1787	268	626	.428	0	2	.000	136	179	.760	76	111	187	120	223	6	69	123	24	672	2.3	1.5	8.2

CARROLL, JOE BARRY (**Joe Barry, J.B.**) b. July 24, 1958   Ht. 7-0   Wt. 235   College—Purdue

SEASON—TEAM	G	GS	MIN	FGM	FGA	PCT	3FGM	3FGA	PCT	FTM	FTA	PCT	O-RB	D-RB	TOT	AST	PF	DQ	STL	TO	BLK	PTS	RPG	APG	PPG
80-81—Golden State	82	—	2919	616	1254	.491	0	2	.000	315	440	.716	274	485	759	117	313	10	50	243	121	1547	9.3	1.4	18.9
81-82—Golden State	76	75	2627	527	1016	.519	0	1	.000	235	323	.728	210	423	633	64	265	8	64	206	127	1289	8.3	0.8	17.0
82-83—Golden State	79	79	2988	785	1529	.513	0	3	.000	337	469	.719	220	468	688	169	260	7	108	285	155	1907	8.7	2.1	24.1
83-84—Golden State	80	80	2962	663	1390	.477	0	1	.000	313	433	.723	235	401	636	198	244	9	103	268	142	1639	8.0	2.5	20.5
85-86—Golden State	79	79	2801	650	1404	.463	0	2	.000	377	501	.752	193	477	670	176	277	13	101	275	144	1677	8.5	2.2	21.2
86-87—Golden State	81	81	2724	690	1461	.472	0	0	—	340	432	.787	173	416	589	214	255	2	92	226	123	1720	7.3	2.6	21.2
87-88—G.S.-Houston	77	30	2004	402	924	.435	0	2	.000	172	225	.764	131	358	489	113	195	1	50	164	106	976	6.4	1.5	12.7
88-89—New Jersey	64	62	1996	363	810	.448	0	0	—	176	220	.800	118	355	473	105	193	2	71	143	81	902	7.4	1.6	14.1
89-90—N.J.-Denver	76	47	1721	312	759	.411	0	2	.000	137	177	.774	133	310	443	97	192	4	47	142	115	761	5.8	1.3	10.0
90-91—Phoenix	11	0	96	13	36	.361	0	0	—	11	12	.917	3	21	24	11	18	0	1	12	8	37	2.2	1.0	3.4
REG. SEASON TOTALS	705	533	22838	5021	10583	.474	0	13	.000	2413	3232	.747	1690	3714	5404	1264	2212	56	687	1964	1122	12455	7.7	1.8	17.7
PLAYOFF TOTALS	19	17	511	105	234	.449	0	1	.000	51	64	.797	25	69	94	26	60	2	18	38	32	261	4.9	1.4	13.7
ALL-STAR TOTALS	1	0	18	1	7	.143	0	0	—	2	2	1.000	4	2	6	0	4	0	0	1	1	4	6.0	0.0	4.0

CARTER, CLARENCE EUGENE JR. (**Butch**) b. June 11, 1958   Ht. 6-5   Wt. 180   College—Indiana

SEASON—TEAM	G	GS	MIN	FGM	FGA	PCT	3FGM	3FGA	PCT	FTM	FTA	PCT	O-RB	D-RB	TOT	AST	PF	DQ	STL	TO	BLK	PTS	RPG	APG	PPG
80-81—Los Angeles	54	—	672	114	247	.462	3	10	.300	70	95	.737	34	31	65	52	99	0	23	50	1	301	1.2	1.0	5.6
81-82—Indiana	75	0	1035	188	402	.468	8	25	.320	58	70	.829	30	49	79	60	110	0	34	54	11	442	1.1	0.8	5.9
82-83—Indiana	81	28	1716	354	706	.501	17	51	.333	124	154	.805	62	88	150	194	207	5	78	118	13	849	1.9	2.4	10.5
83-84—Indiana	73	54	2045	413	862	.479	15	46	.326	136	178	.764	70	83	153	206	211	1	128	141	13	977	2.1	2.8	13.4
84-85—New York	69	11	1279	214	476	.450	11	43	.256	109	134	.813	36	59	95	167	151	1	57	109	5	548	1.4	2.4	7.9
85-86—N.Y.-Phil.	9	0	67	7	24	.292	0	1	.000	6	7	.857	2	2	4	4	14	0	1	7	0	20	0.4	0.4	2.2
REG. SEASON TOTALS	361	93	6814	1290	2717	.475	54	176	.307	503	638	.788	234	312	546	683	792	7	321	479	43	3137	1.5	1.9	8.7

CARTER, FREDERICK JAMES (**Fred, Mad Dog**) b. February 14, 1945   Ht. 6-3 Wt. 185 College—Mount St. Mary's

SEASON—TEAM	G	GS	MIN	FGM	FGA	PCT	3FGM	3FGA	PCT	FTM	FTA	PCT	O-RB	D-RB	TOT	AST	PF	DQ	STL	TO	BLK	PTS	RPG	APG	PPG
69-70—Baltimore	76	—	1219	157	439	.358	—	—	—	80	116	.690	—	—	192	121	137	0	—	—	—	394	2.5	1.6	5.2
70-71—Baltimore	77	—	1707	340	815	.417	—	—	—	119	183	.650	—	—	251	165	165	0	—	—	—	799	3.3	2.1	10.4
71-72—Balt.-Phil.	79	—	2215	446	1018	.438	—	—	—	182	293	.621	—	—	326	211	242	4	—	—	—	1074	4.1	2.7	13.6
72-73—Philadelphia	81	—	2993	679	1614	.421	—	—	—	259	368	.704	—	—	485	349	252	8	—	—	—	1617	6.0	4.3	20.0
73-74—Philadelphia	78	—	3044	706	1641	.430	—	—	—	254	358	.709	82	289	371	443	276	4	113	—	23	1666	4.8	5.7	21.4
74-75—Philadelphia	77	—	3046	715	1598	.447	—	—	—	256	347	.738	73	267	340	336	257	5	82	—	20	1686	4.4	4.4	21.9
75-76—Philadelphia	82	—	2992	665	1594	.417	—	—	—	219	312	.702	113	186	299	372	286	5	137	—	13	1549	3.6	4.5	18.9
76-77—Phil.-Milw.	61	—	1112	209	500	.418	—	—	—	68	96	.708	55	62	117	125	125	0	39	—	9	486	1.9	2.0	8.0
REG. SEASON TOTALS	611	—	18328	3917	9219	.425	—	—	—	1437	2073	.693	323	804	2381	2122	1740	26	371	—	65	9271	3.9	3.5	15.2
PLAYOFF TOTALS	28	—	975	178	434	.410	—	—	—	90	131	.687	4	6	123	75	102	1	4	—	1	446	4.4	2.7	15.9

CARTER, GEORGE b. January 10, 1944   Ht. 6-5 Wt. 220 College—St. Bonaventure

SEASON—TEAM	G	GS	MIN	FGM	FGA	PCT	3FGM	3FGA	PCT	FTM	FTA	PCT	O-RB	D-RB	TOT	AST	PF	DQ	STL	TO	BLK	PTS	RPG	APG	PPG
67-68—Detroit	1	—	5	1	2	.500	—	—	—	1	1	1.000	—	—	0	1	0	0	—	—	—	3	0.0	1.0	3.0
69-70—Washington (A)	67	—	1848	397	871	.456	7	13	.538	167	216	.773	—	—	425	94	203	1	—	—	—	968	6.3	1.4	14.4
70-71—Virginia (A)	81	—	2721	594	1255	.473	0	1	.000	346	437	.792	—	—	650	157	290	—	—	—	—	1534	8.0	1.9	18.9
71-72—Pitt.-Car. (A)	75	—	2623	538	1227	.438	0	10	.000	388	474	.819	—	—	506	128	220	—	—	190	—	1464	6.7	1.7	19.5
72-73—New York (A)	83	—	2976	569	1249	.456	0	9	.000	440	529	.832	205	310	515	173	308	7	—	255	—	1578	6.2	2.1	19.0
73-74—Virginia (A)	80	—	2815	561	1329	.422	32	93	.344	392	466	.841	189	346	535	136	308	—	67	229	12	1546	6.7	1.7	19.3
74-75—Memphis (A)	82	—	3066	590	1354	.436	10	37	.270	318	400	.795	232	349	581	255	276	—	92	198	33	1508	7.1	3.1	18.4
75-76—Utah (A)	10	—	180	25	65	.385	0	0	—	32	41	.780	11	20	31	15	27	—	5	16	3	82	3.1	1.5	8.2
REG. NBA TOTALS	1	—	5	1	2	.500	—	—	—	1	1	1.000	—	—	0	1	0	0	—	—	—	3	0.0	1.0	3.0
REG. ABA TOTALS	478	—	16229	3274	7350	.445	49	163	.301	2083	2563	.813	637	1025	3243	958	1632	8	164	888	48	8680	6.8	2.0	18.2
ABA PLAYOFF TOTALS	30	—	1119	215	461	.466	2	14	.143	138	166	.831	49	71	246	60	123	0	5	63	3	570	8.2	2.0	19.0
ABA ALL-STAR TOTALS	1	—	8	2	3	.667	0	0	—	0	2	.000	0	2	2	0	2	0	0	2	0	4	2.0	0.0	4.0

CARTER, HOWARD O'NEAL b. October 26, 1961   Ht. 6-5 Wt. 215 College—Louisiana State

SEASON—TEAM	G	GS	MIN	FGM	FGA	PCT	3FGM	3FGA	PCT	FTM	FTA	PCT	O-RB	D-RB	TOT	AST	PF	DQ	STL	TO	BLK	PTS	RPG	APG	PPG
83-84—Denver	55	5	688	145	316	.459	5	19	.263	47	61	.770	38	48	86	71	81	0	19	42	4	342	1.6	1.3	6.2
84-85—Dallas	11	0	66	4	23	.174	0	3	.000	1	1	1.000	1	2	3	4	4	0	1	8	0	9	0.3	0.4	0.8
REG. SEASON TOTALS	66	5	754	149	339	.440	5	22	.227	48	62	.774	39	50	89	75	85	0	20	50	4	351	1.3	1.1	5.3
PLAYOFF TOTALS	5	0	60	7	22	.318	1	5	.200	0	0	—	1	4	5	5	3	0	4	5	1	15	1.0	1.0	3.0

CARTER, JOHN D. (**Jake**) b. July 25, 1924   Ht. 6-5 Wt. 195 College—East Texas State

SEASON—TEAM	G	GS	MIN	FGM	FGA	PCT	3FGM	3FGA	PCT	FTM	FTA	PCT	O-RB	D-RB	TOT	AST	PF	DQ	STL	TO	BLK	PTS	RPG	APG	PPG
48-49—Hammond (N)	62	—	—	133	—	—	—	—	—	188	267	.704	—	—	—	—	201	—	—	—	—	454	—	—	7.3
49-50—Denver-And.	24	—	—	23	75	.307	—	—	—	36	53	.679	—	—	—	24	59	—	—	—	—	82	—	1.0	3.4
REG. NBA TOTALS	24	—	—	23	75	.307	—	—	—	36	53	.679	—	—	—	24	59	—	—	—	—	82	—	1.0	3.4
REG. NBL TOTALS	62	—	—	133	—	—	—	—	—	188	267	.704	—	—	—	—	201	—	—	—	—	454	—	—	7.3
NBA PLAYOFF TOTALS	8	—	—	3	21	.143	—	—	—	4	6	.667	—	—	—	3	12	—	—	—	—	10	—	0.4	1.3
NBL PLAYOFF TOTALS	2	—	—	7	—	—	—	—	—	5	12	.417	—	—	—	—	5	—	—	—	—	19	—	—	9.5

CARTER, REGINALD (**Reggie**) b. October 10, 1957   Ht. 6-3 Wt. 175 College—Hawaii/St. John's

SEASON—TEAM	G	GS	MIN	FGM	FGA	PCT	3FGM	3FGA	PCT	FTM	FTA	PCT	O-RB	D-RB	TOT	AST	PF	DQ	STL	TO	BLK	PTS	RPG	APG	PPG
80-81—New York	60	—	536	59	179	.330	0	3	.000	51	69	.739	30	39	69	76	68	0	22	38	2	169	1.2	1.3	2.8
81-82—New York	75	1	923	119	280	.425	0	0	—	64	80	.800	35	60	95	130	124	1	36	78	6	302	1.3	1.7	4.0
REG. SEASON TOTALS	135	1	1459	178	459	.388	0	3	.000	115	149	.772	65	99	164	206	192	1	58	116	8	471	1.2	1.5	3.5
PLAYOFF TOTALS	1	0	7	0	1	.000	0	0	—	0	0	—	1	1	2	—	4	0	0	1	0	0	2.0	0.0	0.0

CARTER, RONALD JR. (**Ron**) b. August 31, 1956   Ht. 6-5 Wt. 190 College—Virginia Military Institute

SEASON—TEAM	G	GS	MIN	FGM	FGA	PCT	3FGM	3FGA	PCT	FTM	FTA	PCT	O-RB	D-RB	TOT	AST	PF	DQ	STL	TO	BLK	PTS	RPG	APG	PPG
78-79—Los Angeles	46	—	332	54	124	.435	—	—	—	36	54	.667	21	24	45	25	54	1	17	40	7	144	1.0	0.5	3.1
79-80—Indiana	13	—	117	15	37	.405	0	0	—	2	7	.286	5	14	19	9	19	0	2	10	3	32	1.5	0.7	2.5
REG. SEASON TOTALS	59	—	449	69	161	.429	0	0	—	38	61	.623	26	38	64	34	73	1	19	50	10	176	1.1	0.6	3.0
PLAYOFF TOTALS	2	—	2	0	1	.000	0	0	—	0	0	—	0	0	0	—	0	0	0	0	0	0	0.0	0.0	0.0

CARTWRIGHT, JAMES WILLIAM (**Bill, Mr. Bill**) b. July 30, 1957 Ht. 7-1 Wt. 245 College—San Francisco

SEASON—TEAM	G	GS	MIN	FGM	FGA	PCT	3FGM	3FGA	PCT	FTM	FTA	PCT	O-RB	D-RB	TOT	AST	PF	DQ	STL	TO	BLK	PTS	RPG	APG	PPG
79-80—New York	82	—	3150	665	1215	.547	0	0	—	451	566	.797	194	532	726	165	279	2	48	222	101	1781	8.9	2.0	21.7
80-81—New York	82	—	2925	619	1118	.554	0	1	.000	408	518	.788	161	452	613	111	259	2	48	200	83	1646	7.5	1.4	20.1
81-82—New York	72	50	2060	390	694	.562	0	0	—	257	337	.763	116	305	421	87	208	2	48	166	65	1037	5.8	1.2	14.4
82-83—New York	82	82	2468	455	804	.566	0	0	—	380	511	.744	185	405	590	136	315	7	41	204	127	1290	7.2	1.7	15.7
83-84—New York	77	77	2487	453	808	.561	0	1	.000	404	502	.805	195	454	649	107	262	4	44	200	97	1310	8.4	1.4	17.0
85-86—New York	2	0	36	3	7	.429	0	0	—	6	10	.600	2	8	10	5	6	0	1	6	1	12	5.0	2.5	6.0
86-87—New York	58	50	1989	335	631	.531	0	0	—	346	438	.790	132	313	445	96	188	2	40	128	26	1016	7.7	1.7	17.5
87-88—New York	82	4	1676	287	528	.544	0	0	—	340	426	.798	127	257	384	85	234	4	43	135	43	914	4.7	1.0	11.1
88-89—Chicago	78	76	2333	365	768	.475	0	0	—	236	308	.766	152	369	521	90	234	2	21	190	41	966	6.7	1.2	12.4
89-90—Chicago	71	71	2160	292	598	.488	0	0	—	227	280	.811	137	328	465	145	243	6	38	123	34	811	6.5	2.0	11.4
90-91—Chicago	79	79	2273	318	649	.490	0	0	—	124	178	.697	167	319	486	126	167	0	32	113	15	760	6.2	1.6	9.6
91-92—Chicago	64	64	1471	208	445	.467	0	0	—	96	159	.604	93	231	324	87	131	0	22	75	14	512	5.1	1.4	8.0
92-93—Chicago	63	63	1253	141	343	.411	0	0	—	72	98	.735	83	150	233	83	154	1	20	62	10	354	3.7	1.3	5.6
93-94—Chicago	42	41	780	98	191	.513	0	0	—	39	57	.684	43	109	152	57	83	0	8	50	8	235	3.6	1.4	5.6
REG. SEASON TOTALS	934	657	27061	4629	8799	.526	0	2	.000	3386	4388	.772	1787	4232	6019	1380	2763	32	454	1874	665	12644	6.4	1.5	13.5
PLAYOFF TOTALS	124	117	3496	417	866	.482	0	0	—	266	367	.725	207	461	668	162	412	3	54	192	57	1100	5.4	1.3	8.9
ALL-STAR TOTALS	1	0	14	4	8	.500	0	0	—	0	0	—	1	2	3	1	1	0	0	2	0	8	3.0	1.0	8.0

CARTY, JAY J. JR. b. July 4, 1941 Ht. 6-7½ Wt. 220 College—Oregon State

SEASON—TEAM	G	GS	MIN	FGM	FGA	PCT	3FGM	3FGA	PCT	FTM	FTA	PCT	O-RB	D-RB	TOT	AST	PF	DQ	STL	TO	BLK	PTS	RPG	APG	PPG
68-69—Los Angeles	28	—	192	34	89	.382	—	—	—	8	11	.727	—	—	58	11	31	0	—	—	—	76	2.1	0.4	2.7
REG. SEASON TOTALS	28	—	192	34	89	.382	—	—	—	8	11	.727	—	—	58	11	31	0	—	—	—	76	2.1	0.4	2.7
PLAYOFF TOTALS	3	—	10	0	2	.000	—	—	—	1	3	.333	—	—	2	1	3	0	—	—	—	1	0.7	0.3	0.3

CASH, CORNELIUS JR. b. March 3, 1952 Ht. 6-8 Wt. 215 College—Bowling Green State

SEASON—TEAM	G	GS	MIN	FGM	FGA	PCT	3FGM	3FGA	PCT	FTM	FTA	PCT	O-RB	D-RB	TOT	AST	PF	DQ	STL	TO	BLK	PTS	RPG	APG	PPG
76-77—Detroit	6	—	49	9	23	.391	—	—	—	3	6	.500	8	8	16	1	8	0	2	—	1	21	2.7	0.2	3.5
REG. SEASON TOTALS	6	—	49	9	23	.391	—	—	—	3	6	.500	8	8	16	1	8	0	2	—	1	21	2.7	0.2	3.5

CASH, SAM b. November 13, 1950 Ht. 6-8 Wt. 230 College—San Bernardino Valley/Cal-Riverside

SEASON—TEAM	G	GS	MIN	FGM	FGA	PCT	3FGM	3FGA	PCT	FTM	FTA	PCT	O-RB	D-RB	TOT	AST	PF	DQ	STL	TO	BLK	PTS	RPG	APG	PPG
72-73—Memphis (A)	7	—	52	4	18	.222	0	0	—	12	17	.706	9	10	19	0	11	0	—	5	—	20	2.7	0.0	2.9
REG. ABA TOTALS	7	—	52	4	18	.222	0	0	—	12	17	.706	9	10	19	0	11	0	—	5	—	20	2.7	0.0	2.9

CASSELL, SAMUEL JAMES (**Sam**) b. November 18, 1969 Ht. 6-3 Wt. 195 College—San Jacinto/Florida State

SEASON—TEAM	G	GS	MIN	FGM	FGA	PCT	3FGM	3FGA	PCT	FTM	FTA	PCT	O-RB	D-RB	TOT	AST	PF	DQ	STL	TO	BLK	PTS	RPG	APG	PPG
93-94—Houston	66	6	1122	162	388	.418	26	88	.295	90	107	.841	25	109	134	192	136	1	59	94	7	440	2.0	2.9	6.7
REG. SEASON TOTALS	66	6	1122	162	388	.418	26	88	.295	90	107	.841	25	109	134	192	136	1	59	94	7	440	2.0	2.9	6.7
PLAYOFF TOTALS	22	0	478	63	160	.394	17	45	.378	64	74	.865	19	40	59	93	62	1	21	47	5	207	2.7	4.2	9.4

CATCHINGS, HARVEY LEE b. September 2, 1951 Ht. 6-10 Wt. 220 College—Weatherford/Hardin Simmons

SEASON—TEAM	G	GS	MIN	FGM	FGA	PCT	3FGM	3FGA	PCT	FTM	FTA	PCT	O-RB	D-RB	TOT	AST	PF	DQ	STL	TO	BLK	PTS	RPG	APG	PPG
74-75—Philadelphia	37	—	528	41	74	.554	—	—	—	16	25	.640	49	104	153	21	82	1	10	—	60	98	4.1	0.6	2.6
75-76—Philadelphia	75	—	1731	103	242	.426	—	—	—	58	96	.604	191	329	520	63	262	6	21	—	164	264	6.9	0.8	3.5
76-77—Philadelphia	53	—	864	62	123	.504	—	—	—	33	47	.702	64	170	234	30	130	1	23	—	78	157	4.4	0.6	3.0
77-78—Philadelphia	61	—	748	70	178	.393	—	—	—	34	55	.618	105	145	250	34	124	1	20	44	67	174	4.1	0.6	2.9
78-79—Phil.-N.J.	56	—	948	102	243	.420	—	—	—	60	78	.769	101	201	302	48	132	3	23	88	91	264	5.4	0.9	4.7
79-80—Milwaukee	72	—	1366	97	244	.398	0	1	.000	39	62	.629	164	246	410	82	191	1	23	68	162	233	5.7	1.1	3.2
80-81—Milwaukee	77	—	1635	134	300	.447	0	0	—	59	92	.641	154	319	473	99	284	7	33	105	184	327	6.1	1.3	4.2
81-82—Milwaukee	80	9	1603	94	224	.420	0	0	—	41	69	.594	129	227	356	97	237	3	42	94	134	229	4.5	1.2	2.9
82-83—Milwaukee	74	33	1554	90	197	.457	0	0	—	62	92	.674	132	276	408	77	224	4	26	83	148	242	5.5	1.0	3.3
83-84—Milwaukee	69	3	1156	61	153	.399	0	1	.000	22	42	.524	89	182	271	43	172	3	25	57	81	144	3.9	0.6	2.1
84-85—L.A. Clippers	70	14	1049	72	149	.483	0	1	.000	59	89	.663	89	173	262	14	162	0	15	55	57	203	3.7	0.2	2.9
REG. SEASON TOTALS	724	59	13182	926	2127	.435	0	3	.000	483	747	.647	1267	2372	3639	608	2000	30	261	594	1226	2335	5.0	0.8	3.2
PLAYOFF TOTALS	53	0	556	31	78	.397	0	0	—	12	24	.500	60	94	154	23	99	0	3	18	49	74	2.9	0.4	1.4

CATLEDGE, TERRY DeWAYNE (Cat Man) b. August 22, 1963 Ht. 6-8 Wt. 230 College—Itawamba CC/South Alabama

SEASON—TEAM	G	GS	MIN	FGM	FGA	PCT	3FGM	3FGA	PCT	FTM	FTA	PCT	O-RB	D-RB	TOT	AST	PF	DQ	STL	TO	BLK	PTS	RPG	APG	PPG
85-86—Philadelphia	64	7	1092	202	431	.469	0	4	.000	90	139	.647	107	165	272	21	127	0	31	69	8	494	4.3	0.3	7.7
86-87—Washington	78	77	2149	413	835	.495	0	4	.000	199	335	.594	248	312	560	56	195	1	43	145	14	1025	7.2	0.7	13.1
87-88—Washington	70	40	1610	296	585	.506	0	2	.000	154	235	.655	180	217	397	63	172	0	33	101	9	746	5.7	0.9	10.7
88-89—Washington	79	77	2077	334	681	.490	1	5	.200	153	254	.602	230	342	572	75	250	5	46	120	25	822	7.2	0.9	10.4
89-90—Orlando	74	72	2462	546	1152	.474	2	8	.250	341	486	.702	271	292	563	72	201	0	36	181	17	1435	7.6	1.0	19.4
90-91—Orlando	51	38	1459	292	632	.462	0	5	.000	161	258	.624	168	187	355	58	113	2	34	107	9	745	7.0	1.1	14.6
91-92—Orlando	78	67	2430	457	922	.496	0	4	.000	240	346	.694	257	292	549	109	196	2	58	138	16	1154	7.0	1.4	14.8
92-93—Orlando	21	1	262	36	73	.493	0	0	—	27	34	.794	18	28	46	5	31	1	4	25	1	99	2.2	0.2	4.7
REG. SEASON TOTALS	515	379	13541	2576	5311	.485	3	32	.094	1365	2087	.654	1479	1835	3314	459	1285	11	285	886	99	6520	6.4	0.9	12.7
PLAYOFF TOTALS	19	13	436	73	169	.432	0	1	.000	34	59	.576	46	60	106	7	48	0	9	23	9	180	5.6	0.4	9.5

CATLETT, SIDNY LEON (Sid) b. April 18, 1948 Ht. 6-6 Wt. 230 College—Notre Dame

SEASON—TEAM	G	GS	MIN	FGM	FGA	PCT	3FGM	3FGA	PCT	FTM	FTA	PCT	O-RB	D-RB	TOT	AST	PF	DQ	STL	TO	BLK	PTS	RPG	APG	PPG
71-72—Cincinnati	9	—	40	2	9	.222	—	—	—	2	9	.222	—	—	4	1	3	0	—	—	—	6	0.4	0.1	0.7
REG. SEASON TOTALS	9	—	40	2	9	.222	—	—	—	2	9	.222	—	—	4	1	3	0	—	—	—	6	0.4	0.1	0.7

CATTAGE, ROBERT LEWIS (Bobby) b. August 17, 1958 Ht. 6-9 Wt. 250 College—Auburn

SEASON—TEAM	G	GS	MIN	FGM	FGA	PCT	3FGM	3FGA	PCT	FTM	FTA	PCT	O-RB	D-RB	TOT	AST	PF	DQ	STL	TO	BLK	PTS	RPG	APG	PPG
81-82—Utah	49	0	337	60	135	.444	0	2	.000	30	41	.732	22	51	73	7	58	0	7	18	0	150	1.5	0.1	3.1
85-86—New Jersey	29	1	185	28	83	.337	1	5	.200	35	44	.795	15	19	34	4	23	0	6	13	0	92	1.2	0.1	3.2
REG. SEASON TOTALS	78	1	522	88	218	.404	1	7	.143	65	85	.765	37	70	107	11	81	0	13	31	0	242	1.4	0.1	3.1

CAUSWELL, DUANE b. May 31, 1968 Ht. 7-0 Wt. 240 College—Temple

SEASON—TEAM	G	GS	MIN	FGM	FGA	PCT	3FGM	3FGA	PCT	FTM	FTA	PCT	O-RB	D-RB	TOT	AST	PF	DQ	STL	TO	BLK	PTS	RPG	APG	PPG
90-91—Sacramento	76	55	1719	210	413	.508	0	0	—	105	165	.636	141	250	391	69	225	4	49	96	148	525	5.1	0.9	6.9
91-92—Sacramento	80	77	2291	250	455	.549	0	1	.000	136	222	.613	196	384	580	59	281	4	47	124	215	636	7.3	0.7	8.0
92-93—Sacramento	55	45	1211	175	321	.545	0	1	.000	103	165	.624	112	191	303	35	192	7	32	58	87	453	5.5	0.6	8.2
93-94—Sacramento	41	8	674	71	137	.518	0	0	—	40	68	.588	68	118	186	11	109	2	19	33	49	182	4.5	0.3	4.4
REG. SEASON TOTALS	252	185	5895	706	1326	.532	0	2	.000	384	620	.619	517	943	1460	174	807	17	147	311	499	1796	5.8	0.7	7.1

CAVENALL, RONNIE GOODALL (Ron) b. April 30, 1959 Ht. 7-1 Wt. 230 College—Texas Southern

SEASON—TEAM	G	GS	MIN	FGM	FGA	PCT	3FGM	3FGA	PCT	FTM	FTA	PCT	O-RB	D-RB	TOT	AST	PF	DQ	STL	TO	BLK	PTS	RPG	APG	PPG
84-85—New York	53	2	653	28	86	.326	0	0	—	22	39	.564	53	113	166	19	123	2	12	45	42	78	3.1	0.4	1.5
88-89—New Jersey	5	0	16	2	3	.667	0	0	—	2	5	.400	0	2	2	0	2	0	0	2	2	6	0.4	0.0	1.2
REG. SEASON TOTALS	58	2	669	30	89	.337	0	0	—	24	44	.545	53	115	168	19	125	2	12	47	44	84	2.9	0.3	1.4

CEBALLOS, CEDRIC Z. (Ice) b. August 2, 1969 Ht. 6-7 Wt. 225 College—Ventura College/Cal State-Fullerton

SEASON—TEAM	G	GS	MIN	FGM	FGA	PCT	3FGM	3FGA	PCT	FTM	FTA	PCT	O-RB	D-RB	TOT	AST	PF	DQ	STL	TO	BLK	PTS	RPG	APG	PPG
90-91—Phoenix	63	0	730	204	419	.487	1	6	.167	110	166	.663	77	73	150	35	70	0	22	69	5	519	2.4	0.6	8.2
91-92—Phoenix	64	4	725	176	365	.482	1	6	.167	109	148	.736	60	92	152	50	52	0	16	71	11	462	2.4	0.8	7.2
92-93—Phoenix	74	46	1607	381	662	.576	0	2	.000	187	258	.725	172	236	408	77	103	1	54	106	28	949	5.5	1.0	12.8
93-94—Phoenix	53	43	1602	425	795	.535	0	9	.000	160	221	.724	153	191	344	91	124	0	59	93	23	1010	6.5	1.7	19.1
REG. SEASON TOTALS	254	93	4664	1186	2241	.529	2	23	.087	566	793	.714	462	592	1054	253	349	1	151	339	67	2940	4.1	1.0	11.6
PLAYOFF TOTALS	37	19	609	134	255	.525	0	2	.000	53	76	.697	52	85	137	35	35	0	21	28	15	321	3.7	0.9	8.7

CERVI, ALFRED NICHOLAS (Al, Digger) b. February 12, 1917 Ht. 5-11½ Wt. 185 College—None

SEASON—TEAM	G	GS	MIN	FGM	FGA	PCT	3FGM	3FGA	PCT	FTM	FTA	PCT	O-RB	D-RB	TOT	AST	PF	DQ	STL	TO	BLK	PTS	RPG	APG	PPG
37-38—Buffalo (N)	9	—	—	19	—	—	—	—	—	6	—	—	—	—	—	—	—	—	—	—	—	44	—	—	4.9
45-46—Rochester (N)	28	—	—	112	—	—	—	—	—	76	108	.704	—	—	—	—	21	—	—	—	—	300	—	—	10.7
46-47—Rochester (N)	44	—	—	228	—	—	—	—	—	176	236	.746	—	—	—	—	127	—	—	—	—	632	—	—	14.4
47-48—Rochester (N)	49	—	—	234	—	—	—	—	—	187	242	.773	—	—	—	—	118	—	—	—	—	655	—	—	13.4
48-49—Syracuse (N)	57	—	—	204	—	—	—	—	—	287	382	.751	—	—	—	—	170	—	—	—	—	695	—	—	12.2
49-50—Syracuse	56	—	—	143	431	.332	—	—	—	287	346	.829	—	—	—	264	223	—	—	—	—	573	—	4.7	10.2
50-51—Syracuse	53	—	—	132	346	.382	—	—	—	194	237	.819	—	—	152	208	180	9	—	—	—	458	2.9	3.9	8.6
51-52—Syracuse	55	—	850	99	280	.354	—	—	—	219	248	.883	—	—	87	148	176	7	—	—	—	417	1.6	2.7	7.6
52-53—Syracuse	38	—	301	31	71	.437	—	—	—	81	100	.810	—	—	22	28	90	2	—	—	—	143	0.6	0.7	3.8
REG. NBA TOTALS	202	—	1151	405	1128	.359	—	—	—	781	931	.839	—	—	261	648	669	18	—	—	—	1591	1.8	3.2	7.9
REG. NBL TOTALS	187	—	—	797	—	—	—	—	—	732	968	.750	—	—	—	—	436	—	—	—	—	2326	—	—	12.4
NBA PLAYOFF TOTALS	27	—	116	50	159	.314	—	—	—	116	134	.866	—	—	43	106	102	5	—	—	—	216	2.7	3.9	8.0
NBL PLAYOFF TOTALS	30	—	102	—	—	—	—	—	—	110	146	.753	—	—	—	—	98	—	—	—	—	314	—	—	10.5

CHAMBERLAIN, WILLIAM MARTIN (Bill) b. December 16, 1949 Ht. 6-6 Wt. 195 College—North Carolina

SEASON—TEAM	G	GS	MIN	FGM	FGA	PCT	3FGM	3FGA	PCT	FTM	FTA	PCT	O-RB	D-RB	TOT	AST	PF	DQ	STL	TO	BLK	PTS	RPG	APG	PPG
72-73—Ken.-Memphis (A)	50	—	665	112	282	.397	2	8	.250	36	59	.610	61	57	118	76	98	1	—	58	—	262	2.4	1.5	5.2
73-74—Phoenix	28	—	367	57	130	.438	—	—	—	39	56	.696	33	47	80	37	74	2	20	—	12	153	2.9	1.3	5.5
REG. NBA TOTALS	28	—	367	57	130	.438	—	—	—	39	56	.696	33	47	80	37	74	2	20	—	12	153	2.9	1.3	5.5
REG. ABA TOTALS	50	—	665	112	282	.397	2	8	.250	36	59	.610	61	57	118	76	98	1	—	58	—	262	2.4	1.5	5.2

CHAMBERLAIN, WILTON NORMAN (Wilt, Wilt the Stilt, The Big Dipper) b. August 21, 1936 Ht. 7-1 Wt. 275 College—Kansas

SEASON—TEAM	G	GS	MIN	FGM	FGA	PCT	3FGM	3FGA	PCT	FTM	FTA	PCT	O-RB	D-RB	TOT	AST	PF	DQ	STL	TO	BLK	PTS	RPG	APG	PPG
59-60—Philadelphia	72	—	3338	1065	2311	.461	—	—	—	577	991	.582	—	—	1941	168	150	0	—	—	—	2707	27.0	2.3	37.6
60-61—Philadelphia	79	—	3773	1251	2457	.509	—	—	—	531	1054	.504	—	—	2149	148	130	0	—	—	—	3033	27.2	1.9	38.4
61-62—Philadelphia	80	—	3882	1597	3159	.506	—	—	—	835	1363	.613	—	—	2052	192	123	0	—	—	—	4029	25.7	2.4	50.4
62-63—San Francisco	80	—	3806	1463	2770	.528	—	—	—	660	1113	.593	—	—	1946	275	136	0	—	—	—	3586	24.3	3.4	44.8
63-64—San Francisco	80	—	3689	1204	2298	.524	—	—	—	540	1016	.531	—	—	1787	403	182	0	—	—	—	2948	22.3	5.0	36.9
64-65—S.F.-Phil.	73	—	3301	1063	2083	.510	—	—	—	408	880	.464	—	—	1673	250	146	0	—	—	—	2534	22.9	3.4	34.7
65-66—Philadelphia	79	—	3737	1074	1990	.540	—	—	—	501	976	.513	—	—	1943	414	171	0	—	—	—	2649	24.6	5.2	33.5
66-67—Philadelphia	81	—	3682	785	1150	.683	—	—	—	386	875	.441	—	—	1957	630	143	0	—	—	—	1956	24.2	7.8	24.1
67-68—Philadelphia	82	—	3836	819	1377	.595	—	—	—	354	932	.380	—	—	1952	702	160	0	—	—	—	1992	23.8	8.6	24.3
68-69—Los Angeles	81	—	3669	641	1099	.583	—	—	—	382	857	.446	—	—	1712	366	142	0	—	—	—	1664	21.1	4.5	20.5
69-70—Los Angeles	12	—	505	129	227	.568	—	—	—	70	157	.446	—	—	221	49	31	0	—	—	—	328	18.4	4.1	27.3
70-71—Los Angeles	82	—	3630	668	1226	.545	—	—	—	360	669	.538	—	—	1493	352	174	0	—	—	—	1696	18.2	4.3	20.7
71-72—Los Angeles	82	—	3469	496	764	.649	—	—	—	221	524	.422	—	—	1572	329	196	0	—	—	—	1213	19.2	4.0	14.8
72-73—Los Angeles	82	—	3542	426	586	.727	—	—	—	232	455	.510	—	—	1526	365	191	0	—	—	—	1084	18.6	4.5	13.2
REG. SEASON TOTALS	1045	—	47859	12681	23497	.540	—	—	—	6057	11862	.511	—	—	23924	4643	2075	0	—	—	—	31419	22.9	4.4	30.1
PLAYOFF TOTALS	160	—	7559	1425	2728	.522	—	—	—	757	1627	.465	—	—	3913	673	412	0	—	—	—	3607	24.5	4.2	22.5
ALL-STAR TOTALS	13	—	388	72	122	.590	—	—	—	47	94	.500	—	—	197	36	23	0	—	—	—	191	15.2	2.8	14.7

CHAMBERS, JEROME PURCELL (Jerry) b. July 18, 1943 Ht. 6-5 Wt. 185 College—Trinidad State JC/Utah

SEASON—TEAM	G	GS	MIN	FGM	FGA	PCT	3FGM	3FGA	PCT	FTM	FTA	PCT	O-RB	D-RB	TOT	AST	PF	DQ	STL	TO	BLK	PTS	RPG	APG	PPG
66-67—Los Angeles	68	—	1015	224	496	.452	—	—	—	68	93	.731	—	—	208	44	143	0	—	—	—	516	3.1	0.6	7.6
69-70—Phoenix	79	—	1139	283	658	.430	—	—	—	91	125	.728	—	—	219	54	162	3	—	—	—	657	2.8	0.7	8.3
70-71—Atlanta	65	—	1168	237	526	.451	—	—	—	106	134	.791	—	—	245	61	119	0	—	—	—	580	3.8	0.9	8.9
71-72—Buffalo	26	—	369	78	180	.433	—	—	—	22	32	.688	—	—	67	23	39	0	—	—	—	178	2.6	0.9	6.8
72-73—San Diego (A)	43	—	885	199	468	.425	2	10	.200	112	130	.862	83	107	190	46	102	0	—	55	—	512	4.4	1.1	11.9
73-74—San Antonio (A)	38	—	579	94	206	.456	0	0	—	36	48	.750	37	66	103	42	74	—	11	28	3	224	2.7	1.1	5.9
REG. NBA TOTALS	238	—	3691	822	1860	.442	—	—	—	287	384	.747	—	—	739	182	463	3	—	—	—	1931	3.1	0.8	8.1
REG. ABA TOTALS	81	—	1464	293	674	.435	2	10	.200	148	178	.831	120	173	293	88	176	0	11	83	3	736	3.6	1.1	9.1
NBA PLAYOFF TOTALS	14	—	139	29	69	.420	—	—	—	13	17	.765	—	—	30	8	17	0	—	—	—	71	2.1	0.6	5.1

CHAMBERS, THOMAS DOANE (Tom) b. June 21, 1959 Ht. 6-10 Wt. 230 College—Utah

SEASON—TEAM	G	GS	MIN	FGM	FGA	PCT	3FGM	3FGA	PCT	FTM	FTA	PCT	O-RB	D-RB	TOT	AST	PF	DQ	STL	TO	BLK	PTS	RPG	APG	PPG
81-82—San Diego	81	58	2682	554	1056	.525	0	2	.000	284	458	.620	211	350	561	146	341	17	58	220	46	1392	6.9	1.8	17.2
82-83—San Diego	79	79	2665	519	1099	.472	0	8	.000	353	488	.723	218	301	519	192	333	15	79	234	57	1391	6.6	2.4	17.6
83-84—Seattle	82	44	2570	554	1110	.499	0	12	.000	375	469	.800	219	313	532	133	309	8	47	192	51	1483	6.5	1.6	18.1
84-85—Seattle	81	60	2923	629	1302	.483	6	22	.273	475	571	.832	164	415	579	209	312	4	70	260	57	1739	7.1	2.6	21.5
85-86—Seattle	66	26	2019	432	928	.466	13	48	.271	346	414	.836	126	305	431	132	248	6	55	194	37	1223	6.5	2.0	18.5
86-87—Seattle	82	82	3018	660	1446	.456	54	145	.372	535	630	.849	163	382	545	245	307	9	81	268	50	1909	6.6	3.0	23.3
87-88—Seattle	82	82	2680	611	1364	.448	33	109	.303	419	519	.807	135	355	490	212	297	4	87	209	53	1674	6.0	2.6	20.4
88-89—Phoenix	81	81	3002	774	1643	.471	28	86	.326	509	598	.851	143	541	684	231	271	2	87	231	55	2085	8.4	2.9	25.7
89-90—Phoenix	81	81	3046	810	1617	.501	24	86	.279	557	647	.861	121	450	571	190	260	1	88	218	47	2201	7.0	2.3	27.2
90-91—Phoenix	76	75	2475	556	1271	.437	20	73	.274	379	459	.826	104	386	490	194	235	3	65	177	52	1511	6.4	2.6	19.9
91-92—Phoenix	69	66	1948	426	989	.431	18	49	.367	258	311	.830	86	315	401	142	196	1	57	103	37	1128	5.8	2.1	16.3
92-93—Phoenix	73	0	1723	320	716	.447	11	28	.393	241	288	.837	96	249	345	101	212	2	43	92	23	892	4.7	1.4	12.2
93-94—Utah	80	0	1838	329	748	.440	14	45	.311	221	281	.786	87	239	326	79	232	2	40	89	32	893	4.1	1.0	11.2
REG. SEASON TOTALS	1013	734	32589	7174	15289	.469	221	713	.310	4952	6133	.807	1873	4601	6474	2206	3553	74	857	2487	597	19521	6.4	2.2	19.3
PLAYOFF TOTALS	103	57	3001	596	1358	.439	26	86	.302	412	496	.831	135	421	556	181	341	4	60	205	68	1630	5.4	1.8	15.8
ALL-STAR TOTALS	4	1	84	29	56	.518	2	5	.400	17	22	.773	9	7	16	5	11	0	6	12	0	77	4.0	1.3	19.3

CHAMPION, MIKE O. b. April 5, 1964 Ht. 6-10 Wt. 230 College—Gonzaga

SEASON—TEAM	G	GS	MIN	FGM	FGA	PCT	3FGM	3FGA	PCT	FTM	FTA	PCT	O-RB	D-RB	TOT	AST	PF	DQ	STL	TO	BLK	PTS	RPG	APG	PPG
88-89—Seattle	2	0	4	0	3	.000	0	1	.000	0	0	—	0	0	0	0	2	0	0	1	0	0	0.0	0.0	0.0
REG. SEASON TOTALS	2	0	4	0	3	.000	0	1	.000	0	0	—	0	0	0	0	2	0	0	1	0	0	0.0	0.0	0.0

CHANEY, DONALD R. (**Don, Duck**) b. March 22, 1946   Ht. 6-5   Wt. 210   College—Houston

SEASON—TEAM	G	GS	MIN	FGM	FGA	PCT	3FGM	3FGA	PCT	FTM	FTA	PCT	O-RB	D-RB	TOT	AST	PF	DQ	STL	TO	BLK	PTS	RPG	APG	PPG
68-69—Boston	20	—	209	36	113	.319	—	—	—	8	20	.400	—	—	46	19	32	0	—	—	—	80	2.3	1.0	4.0
69-70—Boston	63	—	839	115	320	.359	—	—	—	82	109	.752	—	—	152	72	118	0	—	—	—	312	2.4	1.1	5.0
70-71—Boston	81	—	2289	348	766	.454	—	—	—	234	313	.748	—	—	463	235	288	11	—	—	—	930	5.7	2.9	11.5
71-72—Boston	79	—	2275	373	786	.475	—	—	—	197	255	.773	—	—	395	202	295	7	—	—	—	943	5.0	2.6	11.9
72-73—Boston	79	—	2488	414	859	.482	—	—	—	210	267	.787	—	—	449	221	276	6	—	—	—	1038	5.7	2.8	13.1
73-74—Boston	81	—	2258	348	750	.464	—	—	—	149	180	.828	210	168	378	176	247	7	83	—	62	845	4.7	2.2	10.4
74-75—Boston	82	—	2208	321	750	.428	—	—	—	133	165	.806	171	199	370	181	244	5	122	—	66	775	4.5	2.2	9.5
75-76—St. Louis (A)	48	—	1475	191	457	.418	1	4	.250	64	82	.780	113	121	234	169	170	—	66	119	36	447	4.9	3.5	9.3
76-77—Los Angeles	81	—	2408	213	522	.408	—	—	—	70	94	.745	120	210	330	308	224	4	140	—	33	496	4.1	3.8	6.1
77-78—L.A.-Boston	51	—	835	104	269	.387	—	—	—	38	45	.844	40	76	116	66	107	0	44	61	13	246	2.3	1.3	4.8
78-79—Boston	65	—	1074	174	414	.420	—	—	—	36	42	.857	63	78	141	75	167	3	72	65	11	384	2.2	1.2	5.9
79-80—Boston	60	—	523	67	189	.354	1	6	.167	32	42	.762	31	42	73	38	80	1	31	33	11	167	1.2	0.6	2.8
REG. NBA TOTALS	742	—	17406	2513	5738	.438	1	6	.167	1189	1532	.776	635	773	2913	1593	2078	44	492	159	196	6216	3.9	2.1	8.4
REG. ABA TOTALS	48	—	1475	191	457	.418	1	4	.250	64	82	.780	113	121	234	169	170	—	66	119	36	447	4.9	3.5	9.3
NBA PLAYOFF TOTALS	70	—	1835	230	511	.450	0	0	—	110	142	.775	85	82	250	156	229	3	66	—	17	570	3.6	2.2	8.1

CHANEY, JOHN LOUIE b. February 29, 1920   Ht. 6-3   Wt. 190   College—Louisiana State

SEASON—TEAM	G	GS	MIN	FGM	FGA	PCT	3FGM	3FGA	PCT	FTM	FTA	PCT	O-RB	D-RB	TOT	AST	PF	DQ	STL	TO	BLK	PTS	RPG	APG	PPG
46-47—Syracuse (N)	42	—	—	138	—	—	—	—	—	86	119	.723	—	—	—	—	119	—	—	—	—	362	—	—	8.6
47-48—Syracuse (N)	40	—	—	107	—	—	—	—	—	78	103	.757	—	—	—	—	112	—	—	—	—	292	—	—	7.3
48-49—Syracuse (N)	59	—	—	82	—	—	—	—	—	59	88	.670	—	—	—	—	84	—	—	—	—	223	—	—	3.8
49-50—Tri-Cit-She.	16	—	—	25	86	.291	—	—	—	20	29	.690	—	—	—	20	23	—	—	—	—	70	—	1.3	4.4
REG. NBA TOTALS	16	—	—	25	86	.291	—	—	—	20	29	.690	—	—	—	20	23	—	—	—	—	70	—	1.3	4.4
REG. NBL TOTALS	141	—	—	327	—	—	—	—	—	223	310	.719	—	—	—	315	—	—	—	—	877	—	—	6.2
NBL PLAYOFF TOTALS	13	—	—	31	—	—	—	—	—	14	26	.538	—	—	—	31	—	—	—	—	76	—	—	5.8

CHAPMAN, REX EVERETT b. October 5, 1967   Ht. 6-4   Wt. 205   College—Kentucky

SEASON—TEAM	G	GS	MIN	FGM	FGA	PCT	3FGM	3FGA	PCT	FTM	FTA	PCT	O-RB	D-RB	TOT	AST	PF	DQ	STL	TO	BLK	PTS	RPG	APG	PPG
88-89—Charlotte	75	44	2219	526	1271	.414	60	191	.314	155	195	.795	74	113	187	176	167	1	70	113	25	1267	2.5	2.3	16.9
89-90—Charlotte	54	52	1762	377	924	.408	47	142	.331	144	192	.750	52	127	179	132	113	0	46	100	6	945	3.3	2.4	17.5
90-91—Charlotte	70	68	2100	410	922	.445	48	148	.324	234	282	.830	45	146	191	250	167	1	73	131	16	1102	2.7	3.6	15.7
91-92—Cha.-Wash.	22	11	567	113	252	.448	8	29	.276	36	53	.679	10	48	58	89	51	0	15	45	8	270	2.6	4.0	12.3
92-93—Washington	60	23	1300	287	602	.477	43	116	.371	132	163	.810	19	69	88	116	119	1	38	79	10	749	1.5	1.9	12.5
93-94—Washington	60	59	2025	431	865	.498	64	165	.388	168	206	.816	57	89	146	185	83	0	59	117	8	1094	2.4	3.1	18.2
REG. SEASON TOTALS	341	257	9973	2144	4836	.443	270	791	.341	869	1091	.797	257	592	849	948	700	3	301	585	73	5427	2.5	2.8	15.9

CHAPMAN, WAYNE G. b. June 15, 1945   Ht. 6-6   Wt. 190   College—Western Kentucky

SEASON—TEAM	G	GS	MIN	FGM	FGA	PCT	3FGM	3FGA	PCT	FTM	FTA	PCT	O-RB	D-RB	TOT	AST	PF	DQ	STL	TO	BLK	PTS	RPG	APG	PPG
68-69—Kentucky (A)	48	—	458	68	202	.337	4	13	.308	54	72	.750	—	—	74	38	95	0	—	39	—	194	1.5	0.8	4.0
69-70—Kentucky (A)	82	—	1519	261	654	.399	8	37	.216	134	204	.657	—	—	252	139	250	7	—	—	—	664	3.1	1.7	8.1
70-71—Denver-Indiana (A)	69	—	1241	214	562	.381	15	57	.263	113	158	.715	—	—	174	128	158	—	—	—	—	556	2.5	1.9	8.1
71-72—Indiana (A)	7	—	76	7	18	.389	1	2	.500	3	6	.500	—	—	5	11	10	—	—	6	—	18	0.7	1.6	2.6
REG. ABA TOTALS	206	—	3294	550	1436	.383	28	109	.257	304	440	.691	—	—	505	316	513	7	—	45	—	1432	2.5	1.5	7.0
ABA PLAYOFF TOTALS	20	—	198	46	93	.495	2	9	.222	32	44	.727	—	—	33	16	40	0	—	—	—	126	1.7	0.8	6.3

CHAPPELL, LEONARD R. (**Len**) b. January 31, 1941   Ht. 6-8   Wt. 240   College—Wake Forest

SEASON—TEAM	G	GS	MIN	FGM	FGA	PCT	3FGM	3FGA	PCT	FTM	FTA	PCT	O-RB	D-RB	TOT	AST	PF	DQ	STL	TO	BLK	PTS	RPG	APG	PPG
62-63—Syracuse	80	—	1241	281	604	.465	—	—	—	148	238	.622	—	—	461	56	171	1	—	—	—	710	5.8	0.7	8.9
63-64—Phil.-N.Y.	79	—	2505	531	1185	.448	—	—	—	288	403	.715	—	—	771	83	214	1	—	—	—	1350	9.8	1.1	17.1
64-65—New York	43	—	655	145	367	.395	—	—	—	68	100	.680	—	—	140	15	73	0	—	—	—	358	3.3	0.3	8.3
65-66—New York	46	—	545	100	238	.420	—	—	—	46	78	.590	—	—	127	26	64	1	—	—	—	246	2.8	0.6	5.3
66-67—Chicago-Cin.	73	—	708	132	313	.422	—	—	—	53	81	.654	—	—	189	33	104	0	—	—	—	317	2.6	0.5	4.3
67-68—Cin.-Detroit	67	—	1064	235	458	.513	—	—	—	138	194	.711	—	—	361	53	119	1	—	—	—	608	5.4	0.8	9.1
68-69—Milwaukee	80	—	2207	459	1011	.454	—	—	—	250	339	.737	—	—	637	95	247	3	—	—	—	1168	8.0	1.2	14.6
69-70—Milwaukee	75	—	1134	243	523	.465	—	—	—	135	211	.640	—	—	276	56	127	1	—	—	—	621	3.7	0.7	8.3
70-71—Clev.-Atlanta	48	—	537	86	199	.432	—	—	—	71	88	.807	—	—	151	17	72	2	—	—	—	243	3.1	0.4	5.1
71-72—Dallas (A)	79	—	1403	231	511	.452	0	0	—	144	193	.746	—	—	318	69	158	—	—	63	—	606	4.0	0.9	7.7
REG. NBA TOTALS	591	—	10596	2212	4898	.452	—	—	—	1197	1732	.691	—	—	3113	434	1191	10	—	—	—	5621	5.3	0.7	9.5
REG. ABA TOTALS	79	—	1403	231	511	.452	0	0	—	144	193	.746	—	—	318	69	158	—	—	63	—	606	4.0	0.9	7.7
NBA PLAYOFF TOTALS	22	—	273	44	105	.419	—	—	—	31	45	.689	—	—	69	17	34	0	—	—	—	119	3.1	0.8	5.4
ABA PLAYOFF TOTALS	4	—	89	12	24	.500	0	0	—	5	8	.625	—	—	18	3	13	—	—	3	—	29	4.5	0.8	7.3

CHARLES, KENNETH M. (**Ken**) b. July 10, 1951   Ht. 6-3 Wt. 180 College—Fordham

SEASON—TEAM	G	GS	MIN	FGM	FGA	PCT	3FGM	3FGA	PCT	FTM	FTA	PCT	O-RB	D-RB	TOT	AST	PF	DQ	STL	TO	BLK	PTS	RPG	APG	PPG
73-74—Buffalo	59	—	693	88	185	.476	—	—	—	53	79	.671	25	40	65	54	91	0	31	—	10	229	1.1	0.9	3.9
74-75—Buffalo	79	—	1690	240	515	.466	—	—	—	120	146	.822	68	96	164	171	165	0	87	—	20	600	2.1	2.2	7.6
75-76—Buffalo	81	—	2247	328	719	.456	—	—	—	161	205	.785	58	161	219	204	257	5	123	—	48	817	2.7	2.5	10.1
76-77—Atlanta	82	—	2487	354	855	.414	—	—	—	205	256	.801	41	127	168	295	240	4	141	—	45	913	2.0	3.6	11.1
77-78—Atlanta	21	—	520	73	184	.397	—	—	—	42	50	.840	6	18	24	82	53	0	25	37	5	188	1.1	3.9	9.0
REG. SEASON TOTALS	322	—	7637	1083	2458	.441	—	—	—	581	736	.789	198	442	640	806	806	9	407	37	128	2747	2.0	2.5	8.5
PLAYOFF TOTALS	18	—	456	47	114	.412	—	—	—	17	24	.708	11	30	41	32	60	2	13	—	11	111	2.3	1.8	6.2

CHARLES, LORENZO EMILE b. November 25, 1963   Ht. 6-7 Wt. 225 College—North Carolina State

SEASON—TEAM	G	GS	MIN	FGM	FGA	PCT	3FGM	3FGA	PCT	FTM	FTA	PCT	O-RB	D-RB	TOT	AST	PF	DQ	STL	TO	BLK	PTS	RPG	APG	PPG
85-86—Atlanta	36	0	273	49	88	.557	0	0	—	24	36	.667	13	26	39	8	37	0	2	18	6	122	1.1	0.2	3.4
REG. SEASON TOTALS	36	0	273	49	88	.557	0	0	—	24	36	.667	13	26	39	8	37	0	2	18	6	122	1.1	0.2	3.4
PLAYOFF TOTALS	4	0	15	3	4	.750	0	0	—	1	1	1.000	0	2	2	2	1	0	0	0	0	7	0.5	0.5	1.8

CHEANEY, CALBERT NATHANIEL b. July 17, 1971   Ht. 6-7 Wt. 210 College—Indiana

SEASON—TEAM	G	GS	MIN	FGM	FGA	PCT	3FGM	3FGA	PCT	FTM	FTA	PCT	O-RB	D-RB	TOT	AST	PF	DQ	STL	TO	BLK	PTS	RPG	APG	PPG
93-94—Washington	65	21	1604	327	696	.470	1	23	.043	124	161	.770	88	102	190	126	148	0	63	108	10	779	2.9	1.9	12.0
REG. SEASON TOTALS	65	21	1604	327	696	.470	1	23	.043	124	161	.770	88	102	190	126	148	0	63	108	10	779	2.9	1.9	12.0

CHEEKS, MAURICE EDWARD (**Mo**) b. September 8, 1956   Ht. 6-1 Wt. 180 College—West Texas State

SEASON—TEAM	G	GS	MIN	FGM	FGA	PCT	3FGM	3FGA	PCT	FTM	FTA	PCT	O-RB	D-RB	TOT	AST	PF	DQ	STL	TO	BLK	PTS	RPG	APG	PPG
78-79—Philadelphia	82	—	2409	292	572	.510	—	—	—	101	140	.721	63	191	254	431	198	2	174	193	12	685	3.1	5.3	8.4
79-80—Philadelphia	79	—	2623	357	661	.540	4	9	.444	180	231	.779	75	199	274	556	197	1	183	216	32	898	3.5	7.0	11.4
80-81—Philadelphia	81	—	2415	310	581	.534	3	8	.375	140	178	.787	67	178	245	560	231	1	193	174	39	763	3.0	6.9	9.4
81-82—Philadelphia	79	79	2498	352	676	.521	6	22	.273	171	220	.777	51	197	248	667	247	0	209	184	33	881	3.1	8.4	11.2
82-83—Philadelphia	79	79	2465	404	745	.542	1	6	.167	181	240	.754	53	156	209	543	182	0	184	179	31	990	2.6	6.9	12.5
83-84—Philadelphia	75	75	2494	386	702	.550	8	20	.400	170	232	.733	44	161	205	478	196	1	171	182	20	950	2.7	6.4	12.7
84-85—Philadelphia	78	78	2616	422	741	.570	6	26	.231	175	199	.879	54	163	217	497	184	0	169	155	24	1025	2.8	6.4	13.1
85-86—Philadelphia	82	82	3270	490	913	.537	4	17	.235	282	335	.842	55	180	235	753	160	0	207	238	27	1266	2.9	9.2	15.4
86-87—Philadelphia	68	68	2624	415	788	.527	4	17	.235	227	292	.777	47	168	215	538	109	0	180	173	15	1061	3.2	7.9	15.6
87-88—Philadelphia	79	79	2871	428	865	.495	3	22	.136	227	275	.825	59	194	253	635	116	0	167	160	22	1086	3.2	8.0	13.7
88-89—Philadelphia	71	70	2298	336	696	.483	1	13	.077	151	195	.774	39	144	183	554	114	0	105	116	17	824	2.6	7.8	11.6
89-90—S.A.-N.Y.	81	62	2519	307	609	.504	4	16	.250	171	202	.847	50	190	240	453	78	0	124	121	10	789	3.0	5.6	9.7
90-91—New York	76	64	2147	241	483	.499	5	20	.250	105	129	.814	22	151	173	435	138	0	128	108	10	592	2.3	5.7	7.8
91-92—Atlanta	56	0	1086	115	249	.462	3	6	.500	26	43	.605	29	66	95	185	73	0	83	36	0	259	1.7	3.3	4.6
92-93—New Jersey	35	0	510	51	93	.548	0	2	.000	24	27	.889	5	37	42	107	35	0	33	33	2	126	1.2	3.1	3.6
REG. SEASON TOTALS	1101	736	34845	4906	9374	.523	52	204	.255	2331	2938	.793	713	2375	3088	7392	2258	5	2310	2268	294	12195	2.8	6.7	11.1
PLAYOFF TOTALS	133	85	4848	772	1509	.512	4	41	.098	362	466	.777	114	339	453	922	324	1	295	318	45	1910	3.4	6.9	14.4
ALL-STAR TOTALS	4	1	44	7	16	.438	0	0	—	2	2	1.000	0	3	3	4	2	0	3	4	0	16	0.8	1.0	4.0

CHENIER, PHILIP (**Phil**) b. October 30, 1950   Ht. 6-3 Wt. 180 College—California

SEASON—TEAM	G	GS	MIN	FGM	FGA	PCT	3FGM	3FGA	PCT	FTM	FTA	PCT	O-RB	D-RB	TOT	AST	PF	DQ	STL	TO	BLK	PTS	RPG	APG	PPG
71-72—Baltimore	81	—	2481	407	981	.415	—	—	—	182	247	.737	—	—	268	205	191	2	—	—	—	996	3.3	2.5	12.3
72-73—Baltimore	71	—	2776	602	1332	.452	—	—	—	194	244	.795	—	—	288	301	160	0	—	—	—	1398	4.1	4.2	19.7
73-74—Capital	76	—	2942	697	1607	.434	—	—	—	274	334	.820	114	274	388	239	135	0	155	—	67	1668	5.1	3.1	21.9
74-75—Washington	77	—	2869	690	1533	.450	—	—	—	301	365	.825	74	218	292	248	158	3	176	—	58	1681	3.8	3.2	21.8
75-76—Washington	80	—	2952	654	1355	.483	—	—	—	282	341	.827	84	236	320	255	186	2	158	—	45	1590	4.0	3.2	19.9
76-77—Washington	78	—	2842	654	1472	.444	—	—	—	270	321	.841	56	243	299	294	166	0	120	—	39	1578	3.8	3.8	20.2
77-78—Washington	36	—	937	200	451	.443	—	—	—	109	138	.790	15	87	102	73	54	0	36	67	9	509	2.8	2.0	14.1
78-79—Washington	27	—	385	69	158	.437	—	—	—	18	28	.643	3	17	20	31	28	0	4	31	5	156	0.7	1.1	5.8
79-80—Wash.-Indiana	43	—	850	136	349	.390	5	12	.417	49	67	.731	19	59	78	89	55	0	33	55	15	326	1.8	2.1	7.6
80-81—Golden State	9	—	82	11	33	.333	1	3	.333	6	6	1.000	1	7	8	7	10	0	4	4	0	29	0.9	0.8	3.2
REG. SEASON TOTALS	578	—	19116	4120	9271	.444	6	15	.400	1685	2091	.806	366	1141	2063	1742	1143	7	682	157	238	9931	3.6	3.0	17.2
PLAYOFF TOTALS	60	—	2088	438	974	.450	0	—	—	212	251	.845	41	152	230	131	152	1	59	6	26	1088	3.8	2.2	18.1
ALL-STAR TOTALS	3	—	48	10	20	.500	0	0	—	2	4	.500	3	2	5	3	0	0	2	—	0	22	1.7	1.0	7.3

CHIEVOUS, DERRICK JOSEPH (**Band-Aid**) b. July 3, 1967   Ht. 6-7 Wt. 195 College—Missouri

SEASON—TEAM	G	GS	MIN	FGM	FGA	PCT	3FGM	3FGA	PCT	FTM	FTA	PCT	O-RB	D-RB	TOT	AST	PF	DQ	STL	TO	BLK	PTS	RPG	APG	PPG
88-89—Houston	81	1	1539	277	634	.437	5	24	.208	191	244	.783	114	142	256	77	161	1	48	136	11	750	3.2	1.0	9.3
89-90—Houston-Clev.	55	0	591	105	220	.477	3	9	.333	80	111	.721	35	55	90	31	70	0	26	45	5	293	1.6	0.6	5.3
90-91—Cleveland	18	—	110	17	46	.370	0	0	—	9	16	.563	11	7	18	2	16	0	3	6	1	43	1.0	0.1	2.4
REG. SEASON TOTALS	154	1	2240	399	900	.443	8	33	.242	280	371	.755	160	204	364	110	247	1	77	187	17	1086	2.4	0.7	7.1
PLAYOFF TOTALS	7	0	68	11	27	.407	0	0	—	15	19	.789	7	2	9	4	9	0	2	6	1	37	1.3	0.6	5.3

CHILCUTT, PETER SHAWN (**Pete**) b. September 14, 1968   Ht. 6-10   Wt. 230   College—North Carolina

SEASON—TEAM	G	GS	MIN	FGM	FGA	PCT	3FGM	3FGA	PCT	FTM	FTA	PCT	O-RB	D-RB	TOT	AST	PF	DQ	STL	TO	BLK	PTS	RPG	APG	PPG
91-92—Sacramento	69	2	817	113	250	.452	2	2	1.000	23	28	.821	78	109	187	38	70	0	32	41	17	251	2.7	0.6	3.6
92-93—Sacramento	59	9	834	165	340	.485	0	0	—	32	46	.696	80	114	194	64	102	2	22	54	21	362	3.3	1.1	6.1
93-94—Sac.-Detroit	76	24	1365	203	448	.453	3	15	.200	41	65	.631	129	242	371	86	164	2	53	74	39	450	4.9	1.1	5.9
REG. SEASON TOTALS	204	35	3016	481	1038	.463	5	17	.294	96	139	.691	287	465	752	188	336	4	107	169	77	1063	3.7	0.9	5.2

CHOLLET, LEROY PATRICK b. March 5, 1925   Ht. 6-2   Wt. 190   College—Loyola (La.)/Canisius

SEASON—TEAM	G	GS	MIN	FGM	FGA	PCT	3FGM	3FGA	PCT	FTM	FTA	PCT	O-RB	D-RB	TOT	AST	PF	DQ	STL	TO	BLK	PTS	RPG	APG	PPG
49-50—Syracuse	49	—	—	61	179	.341	—	—	—	35	56	.625	—	—	—	37	52	—	—	—	—	157	—	0.8	3.2
50-51—Syracuse	14	—	—	6	51	.118	—	—	—	12	19	.632	—	—	15	12	29	0	—	—	—	24	1.1	0.9	1.7
REG. SEASON TOTALS	63	—	—	67	230	.291	—	—	—	47	75	.627	—	—	15	49	81	0	—	—	—	181	1.1	0.8	2.9
PLAYOFF TOTALS	15	—	—	11	49	.224	—	—	—	10	21	.476	—	—	16	13	27	1	—	—	—	32	2.3	0.9	2.1

CHONES, JAMES BERNETT (**Jim**) b. November 30, 1949   Ht. 6-11   Wt. 220   College—Marquette

SEASON—TEAM	G	GS	MIN	FGM	FGA	PCT	3FGM	3FGA	PCT	FTM	FTA	PCT	O-RB	D-RB	TOT	AST	PF	DQ	STL	TO	BLK	PTS	RPG	APG	PPG
72-73—New York (A)	82	—	2153	395	769	.514	0	1	.000	142	240	.592	143	443	586	95	291	7	—	213	—	932	7.1	1.2	11.4
73-74—Carolina (A)	83	—	2387	535	1017	.526	0	2	.000	155	252	.615	191	454	645	118	347	—	59	206	131	1225	7.8	1.4	14.8
74-75—Cleveland	72	—	2427	446	916	.487	—	—	—	152	224	.679	156	521	677	132	247	5	49	—	120	1044	9.4	1.8	14.5
75-76—Cleveland	82	—	2741	563	1258	.448	—	—	—	172	260	.662	197	542	739	163	241	2	42	—	93	1298	9.0	2.0	15.8
76-77—Cleveland	82	—	2378	450	972	.463	—	—	—	155	212	.731	208	480	688	104	258	3	32	—	77	1055	8.4	1.3	12.9
77-78—Cleveland	82	—	2906	525	1113	.472	—	—	—	180	250	.720	219	625	844	131	235	4	52	184	58	1230	10.3	1.6	15.0
78-79—Cleveland	82	—	2850	472	1073	.440	—	—	—	158	215	.735	260	582	842	181	278	4	47	187	102	1102	10.3	2.2	13.4
79-80—Los Angeles	82	—	2394	372	760	.489	0	2	.000	125	169	.740	143	421	564	151	271	5	56	175	65	869	6.9	1.8	10.6
80-81—Los Angeles	82	—	2562	378	751	.503	0	4	.000	126	193	.653	180	477	657	153	324	4	39	159	96	882	8.0	1.9	10.8
81-82—Washington	59	13	867	74	171	.433	0	0	—	36	46	.783	39	146	185	64	114	1	15	41	32	184	3.1	1.1	3.1
REG. NBA TOTALS	623	13	19125	3280	7014	.468	0	6	.000	1104	1569	.704	1402	3794	5196	1079	1968	28	332	746	643	7664	8.3	1.7	12.3
REG. ABA TOTALS	165	—	4540	930	1786	.521	0	3	.000	297	492	.604	334	897	1231	213	638	7	59	419	131	2157	7.5	1.3	13.1
NBA PLAYOFF TOTALS	36	0	959	136	312	.436	0	0	—	50	78	.641	67	156	223	47	116	0	13	40	20	322	6.2	1.3	8.9
ABA PLAYOFF TOTALS	9	—	170	29	70	.414	0	0	—	8	16	.500	6	18	51	8	25	0	2	8	4	66	5.7	0.9	7.3

CHRIST, FREDERICK L. (**Fred**) b. August 6, 1930   Ht. 6-4   Wt. 210   College—Fordham

SEASON—TEAM	G	GS	MIN	FGM	FGA	PCT	3FGM	3FGA	PCT	FTM	FTA	PCT	O-RB	D-RB	TOT	AST	PF	DQ	STL	TO	BLK	PTS	RPG	APG	PPG
54-55—New York	6	—	48	5	18	.278	—	—	—	10	11	.909	—	—	8	7	3	0	—	—	—	20	1.3	1.2	3.3
REG. SEASON TOTALS	6	—	48	5	18	.278	—	—	—	10	11	.909	—	—	8	7	3	0	—	—	—	20	1.3	1.2	3.3

CHRISTENSEN, CALVIN L. (**Cal**) b. June 8, 1927   Ht. 6-5   Wt. 220   College—Toledo

SEASON—TEAM	G	GS	MIN	FGM	FGA	PCT	3FGM	3FGA	PCT	FTM	FTA	PCT	O-RB	D-RB	TOT	AST	PF	DQ	STL	TO	BLK	PTS	RPG	APG	PPG
50-51—Tri-Cities	67	—	—	134	445	.301	—	—	—	175	245	.714	—	—	523	161	266	19	—	—	—	443	7.8	2.4	6.6
51-52—Milwaukee	24	—	374	29	96	.302	—	—	—	30	57	.526	—	—	82	34	47	2	—	—	—	88	3.4	1.4	3.7
52-53—Rochester	59	—	777	72	230	.313	—	—	—	68	114	.596	—	—	199	54	148	6	—	—	—	212	3.4	0.9	3.6
53-54—Rochester	70	—	1654	137	395	.347	—	—	—	138	261	.529	—	—	395	107	196	1	—	—	—	412	5.6	1.5	5.9
54-55—Rochester	71	—	1204	114	305	.374	—	—	—	124	206	.602	—	—	388	104	174	2	—	—	—	352	5.5	1.5	5.0
REG. SEASON TOTALS	291	—	4009	486	1471	.330	—	—	—	535	883	.606	—	—	1587	460	831	30	—	—	—	1507	5.5	1.6	5.2
PLAYOFF TOTALS	11	—	180	12	39	.308	—	—	—	18	32	.563	—	—	45	16	22	0	—	—	—	42	4.1	1.5	3.8

CHRISTIAN, BOB b. May 11, 1944   Ht. 6-11½   Wt. 255   College—Grambling State

SEASON—TEAM	G	GS	MIN	FGM	FGA	PCT	3FGM	3FGA	PCT	FTM	FTA	PCT	O-RB	D-RB	TOT	AST	PF	DQ	STL	TO	BLK	PTS	RPG	APG	PPG
69-70—N.Y.-Dallas (A)	2	—	11	1	3	.333	0	0	—	0	0	—	—	—	3	0	3	0	—	—	—	2	1.5	0.0	1.0
70-71—Atlanta	54	—	524	55	127	.433	—	—	—	40	64	.625	—	—	177	30	118	0	—	—	—	150	3.3	0.6	2.8
71-72—Atlanta	56	—	485	66	142	.465	—	—	—	44	61	.721	—	—	181	28	77	0	—	—	—	176	3.2	0.5	3.1
72-73—Atlanta	55	—	759	85	155	.548	—	—	—	60	79	.759	—	—	305	47	111	2	—	—	—	230	5.5	0.9	4.2
73-74—Phoenix	81	—	1244	140	288	.486	—	—	—	106	151	.702	85	254	339	98	191	3	19	—	32	386	4.2	1.2	4.8
REG. NBA TOTALS	246	—	3012	346	712	.486	—	—	—	250	355	.704	85	254	1002	203	497	5	19	—	32	942	4.1	0.8	3.8
REG. ABA TOTALS	2	—	11	1	3	.333	0	0	—	0	0	—	—	—	3	0	3	0	—	—	—	2	1.5	0.0	1.0
NBA PLAYOFF TOTALS	6	—	34	3	8	.375	—	—	—	1	1	1.000	0	0	7	—	10	0	0	—	0	7	1.2	0.0	1.2

CHRISTIE, DOUGLAS DALE (**Doug**) b. May 9, 1970   Ht. 6-6   Wt. 205   College—Pepperdine

SEASON—TEAM	G	GS	MIN	FGM	FGA	PCT	3FGM	3FGA	PCT	FTM	FTA	PCT	O-RB	D-RB	TOT	AST	PF	DQ	STL	TO	BLK	PTS	RPG	APG	PPG
92-93—L.A. Lakers	23	0	332	45	106	.425	2	12	.167	50	66	.758	24	27	51	53	53	0	22	50	5	142	2.2	2.3	6.2
93-94—L.A. Lakers	65	34	1515	244	562	.434	39	119	.328	145	208	.697	93	142	235	136	186	2	89	140	28	672	3.6	2.1	10.3
REG. SEASON TOTALS	88	34	1847	289	668	.433	41	131	.313	195	274	.712	117	169	286	189	239	2	111	190	33	814	3.3	2.1	9.3
PLAYOFF TOTALS	5	0	39	4	11	.364	1	3	.333	0	0	—	1	3	4	6	5	0	2	4	2	9	0.8	1.2	1.8

CHUBIN, STEPHEN (Steve, Chube)   Ht. 6-2 Wt. 200 College—Rhode Island

SEASON—TEAM	G	GS	MIN	FGM	FGA	PCT	3FGM	3FGA	PCT	FTM	FTA	PCT	O-RB	D-RB	TOT	AST	PF	DQ	STL	TO	BLK	PTS	RPG	APG	PPG
67-68—Anaheim (A)	77	—	2441	439	1057	.415	2	10	.200	518	639	.811	—	—	433	364	292	10	—	310	—	1398	5.6	4.7	18.2
68-69—L.A.-Minn.-Ind.-N.Y. (A)	77	—	2097	344	875	.393	3	27	.111	386	472	.818	—	—	291	354	287	6	—	286	—	1077	3.8	4.6	14.0
69-70—N.Y.-Pitt.-Ind.-Ken. (A)	72	—	1058	127	352	.361	5	14	.357	170	199	.854	—	—	137	117	174	3	—	—	—	429	1.9	1.6	6.0
REG. ABA TOTALS	226	—	5596	910	2284	.398	10	51	.196	1074	1310	.820	—	—	861	835	753	19	—	596	—	2904	3.8	3.7	12.8
ABA PLAYOFF TOTALS	11	—	55	8	17	.471	0	4	.000	12	14	.857	—	—	3	0	0	0	—	—	—	28	0.3	0.0	2.5

CLARK, ARCHIE L. b. July 15, 1941 Ht. 6-2 Wt. 175 College—Minnesota

SEASON—TEAM	G	GS	MIN	FGM	FGA	PCT	3FGM	3FGA	PCT	FTM	FTA	PCT	O-RB	D-RB	TOT	AST	PF	DQ	STL	TO	BLK	PTS	RPG	APG	PPG
66-67—Los Angeles	76	—	1763	331	732	.452	—	—	—	136	192	.708	—	—	218	205	193	1	—	—	—	798	2.9	2.7	10.5
67-68—Los Angeles	81	—	3039	628	1309	.480	—	—	—	356	481	.740	—	—	342	353	235	3	—	—	—	1612	4.2	4.4	19.9
68-69—Philadelphia	82	—	2144	444	928	.478	—	—	—	219	314	.697	—	—	265	296	188	1	—	—	—	1107	3.2	3.6	13.5
69-70—Philadelphia	76	—	2772	594	1198	.496	—	—	—	311	396	.785	—	—	301	380	201	2	—	—	—	1499	4.0	5.0	19.7
70-71—Philadelphia	82	—	3245	662	1334	.496	—	—	—	422	536	.787	—	—	391	440	217	2	—	—	—	1746	4.8	5.4	21.3
71-72—Phil.-Balt.	77	—	3285	712	1516	.470	—	—	—	514	667	.771	—	—	268	613	194	0	—	—	—	1938	3.5	8.0	25.2
72-73—Baltimore	39	—	1477	302	596	.507	—	—	—	111	137	.810	—	—	129	275	111	1	—	—	—	715	3.3	7.1	18.3
73-74—Capital	56	—	1786	315	675	.467	—	—	—	103	131	.786	44	97	141	285	122	0	59	—	6	733	2.5	5.1	13.1
74-75—Seattle	77	—	2481	455	919	.495	—	—	—	161	193	.834	59	176	235	433	188	4	110	—	5	1071	3.1	5.6	13.9
75-76—Detroit	79	—	1589	250	577	.433	—	—	—	100	116	.862	27	110	137	218	157	0	62	—	4	600	1.7	2.8	7.6
REG. SEASON TOTALS	725	—	23581	4693	9784	.480	—	—	—	2433	3163	.769	130	383	2427	3498	1806	14	231	—	15	11819	3.3	4.8	16.3
PLAYOFF TOTALS	71	—	2387	444	977	.454	—	—	—	237	307	.772	12	54	229	297	197	2	17	—	1	1125	3.2	4.2	15.8
ALL-STAR TOTALS	2	—	36	7	13	.538	—	—	—	11	11	1.000	0	0	1	9	3	0	0	—	0	25	0.5	4.5	12.5

CLARK, CARLOS R. b. August 10, 1960 Ht. 6-4 Wt. 210 College—Mississippi

SEASON—TEAM	G	GS	MIN	FGM	FGA	PCT	3FGM	3FGA	PCT	FTM	FTA	PCT	O-RB	D-RB	TOT	AST	PF	DQ	STL	TO	BLK	PTS	RPG	APG	PPG
83-84—Boston	31	0	127	19	52	.365	0	2	.000	16	18	.889	7	10	17	17	13	0	8	12	1	54	0.5	0.5	1.7
84-85—Boston	62	3	562	64	152	.421	0	5	.000	41	53	.774	29	40	69	48	66	0	35	42	2	169	1.1	0.8	2.7
REG. SEASON TOTALS	93	3	689	83	204	.407	0	7	.000	57	71	.803	36	50	86	65	79	0	43	54	3	223	0.9	0.7	2.4
PLAYOFF TOTALS	11	0	31	7	15	.467	0	0	—	3	4	.750	3	0	3	4	5	0	2	1	2	17	0.3	0.4	1.5

CLARK, RICHARD C. (Dick) b. January 5, 1944 Ht. 6-4 Wt. 195 College—Eastern Kentucky

SEASON—TEAM	G	GS	MIN	FGM	FGA	PCT	3FGM	3FGA	PCT	FTM	FTA	PCT	O-RB	D-RB	TOT	AST	PF	DQ	STL	TO	BLK	PTS	RPG	APG	PPG
67-68—Minnesota (A)	26	—	414	46	150	.307	0	10	.000	48	79	.608	—	—	52	33	49	0	—	33	—	140	2.0	1.3	5.4
68-69—Houston (A)	32	—	723	64	222	.288	1	8	.125	89	124	.718	—	—	88	68	99	0	—	73	—	218	2.8	2.1	6.8
REG. ABA TOTALS	58	—	1137	110	372	.296	1	18	.056	137	203	.675	—	—	140	101	148	0	—	106	—	358	2.4	1.7	6.2
ABA PLAYOFF TOTALS	10	—	231	17	65	.262	1	6	.167	21	28	.750	—	—	33	13	18	0	—	13	—	56	3.3	1.3	5.6

CLAWSON, JOHN RICHARD b. May 15, 1944 Ht. 6-4 Wt. 200 College—Michigan

SEASON—TEAM	G	GS	MIN	FGM	FGA	PCT	3FGM	3FGA	PCT	FTM	FTA	PCT	O-RB	D-RB	TOT	AST	PF	DQ	STL	TO	BLK	PTS	RPG	APG	PPG
68-69—Oakland (A)	70	—	1067	147	309	.476	0	0	—	37	54	.685	—	—	195	51	187	1	—	73	—	331	2.8	0.7	4.7
REG. ABA TOTALS	70	—	1067	147	309	.476	0	0	—	37	54	.685	—	—	195	51	187	1	—	73	—	331	2.8	0.7	4.7
ABA PLAYOFF TOTALS	16	—	313	42	95	.442	1	3	.333	15	24	.625	—	—	54	14	60	2	—	13	—	100	3.4	0.9	6.3

CLEAMONS, JAMES MITCHELL (Jim) b. September 13, 1949 Ht. 6-3½ Wt. 185 College—Ohio State

SEASON—TEAM	G	GS	MIN	FGM	FGA	PCT	3FGM	3FGA	PCT	FTM	FTA	PCT	O-RB	D-RB	TOT	AST	PF	DQ	STL	TO	BLK	PTS	RPG	APG	PPG
71-72—Los Angeles	38	—	201	35	100	.350	—	—	—	28	36	.778	—	—	39	35	21	0	—	—	—	98	1.0	0.9	2.6
72-73—Cleveland	80	—	1392	192	423	.454	—	—	—	75	101	.743	—	—	167	205	108	0	—	—	—	459	2.1	2.6	5.7
73-74—Cleveland	81	—	1642	236	545	.433	—	—	—	93	133	.699	63	167	230	227	152	1	61	—	17	565	2.8	2.8	7.0
74-75—Cleveland	74	—	2691	369	768	.480	—	—	—	144	181	.796	97	232	329	381	194	0	84	—	21	882	4.4	5.1	11.9
75-76—Cleveland	82	—	2835	413	887	.466	—	—	—	174	218	.798	124	230	354	428	214	2	124	—	20	1000	4.3	5.2	12.2
76-77—Cleveland	60	—	2045	257	592	.434	—	—	—	112	148	.757	99	174	273	308	126	0	66	—	23	626	4.6	5.1	10.4
77-78—New York	79	—	2009	215	448	.480	—	—	—	81	103	.786	69	143	212	283	142	1	68	113	17	511	2.7	3.6	6.5
78-79—New York	79	—	2390	311	657	.473	—	—	—	130	171	.760	65	160	225	376	147	1	73	142	11	752	2.8	4.8	9.5
79-80—N.Y.-Wash.	79	—	1789	214	450	.476	7	31	.226	84	113	.743	53	99	152	288	133	0	57	109	11	519	1.9	3.6	6.6
REG. SEASON TOTALS	652	—	16994	2242	4870	.460	7	31	.226	921	1204	.765	570	1205	1981	2531	1237	5	533	364	120	5412	3.0	3.9	8.3
PLAYOFF TOTALS	27	—	667	91	230	.396	0	0	—	39	46	.848	28	57	89	89	50	0	12	9	3	221	3.3	3.3	8.2

CLEMENS, JOHN BARRY (**Barry**) b. May 1, 1943 Ht. 6-6½ Wt. 215 College—Ohio Wesleyan

SEASON—TEAM	G	GS	MIN	FGM	FGA	PCT	3FGM	3FGA	PCT	FTM	FTA	PCT	O-RB	D-RB	TOT	AST	PF	DQ	STL	TO	BLK	PTS	RPG	APG	PPG
65-66—New York	70	—	877	161	391	.412	—	—	—	54	78	.692	—	—	183	67	113	0	—	—	—	376	2.6	1.0	5.4
66-67—Chicago	60	—	986	186	444	.419	—	—	—	68	90	.756	—	—	201	39	143	1	—	—	—	440	3.4	0.7	7.3
67-68—Chicago	78	—	1631	301	670	.449	—	—	—	123	170	.724	—	—	375	98	223	4	—	—	—	725	4.8	1.3	9.3
68-69—Chicago	75	—	1444	235	628	.374	—	—	—	82	125	.656	—	—	318	125	163	1	—	—	—	552	4.2	1.7	7.4
69-70—Seattle	78	—	1487	270	595	.454	—	—	—	111	140	.793	—	—	316	116	188	1	—	—	—	651	4.1	1.5	8.3
70-71—Seattle	78	—	1286	247	526	.470	—	—	—	83	114	.728	—	—	243	92	169	1	—	—	—	577	3.1	1.2	7.4
71-72—Seattle	82	—	1447	252	484	.521	—	—	—	76	90	.844	—	—	288	64	198	4	—	—	—	580	3.5	0.8	7.1
72-73—Cleveland	72	—	1119	209	405	.516	—	—	—	53	68	.779	—	—	211	115	136	0	—	—	—	471	2.9	1.6	6.5
73-74—Cleveland	71	—	913	163	346	.471	—	—	—	62	73	.849	42	124	166	80	136	2	36	—	2	388	2.3	1.1	5.5
74-75—Portland	77	—	952	168	355	.473	—	—	—	45	60	.750	33	128	161	76	139	0	68	—	2	381	2.1	1.0	4.9
75-76—Portland	49	—	443	70	143	.490	—	—	—	31	35	.886	27	43	70	33	57	0	27	—	7	171	1.4	0.7	3.5
REG. SEASON TOTALS	790	—	12585	2262	4987	.454	—	—	—	788	1043	.756	102	295	2532	905	1665	14	131	—	11	5312	3.2	1.1	6.7
PLAYOFF TOTALS	7	—	65	8	20	.400	—	—	—	10	11	.909	0	0	5	7	9	0	0	—	0	26	0.7	1.0	3.7

CLIFTON, NATHANIEL (**Nat, Sweetwater**) b. October 13, 1922 d. August 31, 1990 Ht. 6-7½ Wt. 235 College—Xavier (La.)

SEASON—TEAM	G	GS	MIN	FGM	FGA	PCT	3FGM	3FGA	PCT	FTM	FTA	PCT	O-RB	D-RB	TOT	AST	PF	DQ	STL	TO	BLK	PTS	RPG	APG	PPG
50-51—New York	65	—	—	211	656	.322	—	—	—	140	263	.532	—	—	491	162	269	13	—	—	—	562	7.6	2.5	8.6
51-52—New York	62	—	2101	244	729	.335	—	—	—	170	256	.664	—	—	731	209	227	8	—	—	—	658	11.8	3.4	10.6
52-53—New York	70	—	2496	272	794	.343	—	—	—	200	343	.583	—	—	761	231	274	6	—	—	—	744	10.9	3.3	10.6
53-54—New York	72	—	2179	257	699	.368	—	—	—	174	277	.628	—	—	528	176	215	0	—	—	—	688	7.3	2.4	9.6
54-55—New York	72	—	2390	360	932	.386	—	—	—	224	328	.683	—	—	612	198	221	2	—	—	—	944	8.5	2.8	13.1
55-56—New York	64	—	1537	213	541	.394	—	—	—	135	191	.707	—	—	386	151	189	4	—	—	—	561	6.0	2.4	8.8
56-57—New York	71	—	2231	308	818	.377	—	—	—	146	217	.673	—	—	557	164	243	5	—	—	—	762	7.8	2.3	10.7
57-58—Detroit	68	—	1435	217	597	.363	—	—	—	91	146	.623	—	—	403	76	202	3	—	—	—	525	5.9	1.1	7.7
REG. SEASON TOTALS	544	—	14369	2082	5766	.361	—	—	—	1280	2021	.633	—	—	4469	1367	1840	41	—	—	—	5444	8.2	2.5	10.0
PLAYOFF TOTALS	53	—	1176	170	489	.348	—	—	—	136	218	.624	—	—	495	142	215	9	—	—	—	476	9.3	2.7	9.0
ALL-STAR TOTALS	1	—	23	4	11	.364	—	—	—	0	0	—	—	—	11	3	1	0	—	—	—	8	11.0	3.0	8.0

CLOSS, WILLIAM THOMAS (**Bill**) b. January 8, 1922 Ht. 6-6 Wt. 205 College—Rice

SEASON—TEAM	G	GS	MIN	FGM	FGA	PCT	3FGM	3FGA	PCT	FTM	FTA	PCT	O-RB	D-RB	TOT	AST	PF	DQ	STL	TO	BLK	PTS	RPG	APG	PPG
46-47—Indianapolis (N)	44	—	—	119	—	—	—	—	—	34	63	.540	—	—	—	—	99	—	—	—	—	272	—	—	6.2
47-48—Indianapolis (N)	55	—	—	162	—	—	—	—	—	72	123	.585	—	—	—	—	139	—	—	—	—	396	—	—	7.2
48-49—Anderson (N)	64	—	—	203	—	—	—	—	—	110	166	.663	—	—	—	—	148	—	—	—	—	516	—	—	8.1
49-50—Anderson	64	—	—	283	898	.315	—	—	—	186	259	.718	—	—	—	160	190	—	—	—	—	752	—	2.5	11.8
50-51—Philadelphia	65	—	—	202	631	.320	—	—	—	166	223	.744	—	—	401	110	156	4	—	—	—	570	6.2	1.7	8.8
51-52—Fort Wayne	57	—	1120	120	389	.308	—	—	—	107	157	.682	—	—	204	76	125	2	—	—	—	347	3.6	1.3	6.1
REG. NBA TOTALS	186	—	1120	605	1918	.315	—	—	—	459	639	.718	—	—	605	346	471	6	—	—	—	1669	5.0	1.9	9.0
REG. NBL TOTALS	163	—	—	484	—	—	—	—	—	216	352	.614	—	—	—	—	386	—	—	—	—	1184	—	—	7.3
NBA PLAYOFF TOTALS	11	—	21	36	123	.293	—	—	—	31	38	.816	—	—	16	23	32	2	—	—	—	103	5.3	2.1	9.4
NBL PLAYOFF TOTALS	15	—	—	50	—	—	—	—	—	45	63	.698	—	—	—	—	41	—	—	—	—	145	—	—	9.7

CLOYD, PAUL V. b. June 13, 1920 Ht. 6-2 Wt. 180 College—Wisconsin

SEASON—TEAM	G	GS	MIN	FGM	FGA	PCT	3FGM	3FGA	PCT	FTM	FTA	PCT	O-RB	D-RB	TOT	AST	PF	DQ	STL	TO	BLK	PTS	RPG	APG	PPG
47-48—Sheboygan (N)	60	—	—	213	—	—	—	—	—	129	181	.713	—	—	—	—	123	—	—	—	—	555	—	—	9.3
48-49—Sheboygan (N)	56	—	—	119	—	—	—	—	—	98	137	.715	—	—	—	—	75	—	—	—	—	336	—	—	6.0
49-50—Balt.-Wat.	7	—	—	7	26	.269	—	—	—	5	8	.625	—	—	—	2	5	—	—	—	—	19	—	0.3	2.7
REG. NBA TOTALS	7	—	—	7	26	.269	—	—	—	5	8	.625	—	—	—	2	5	—	—	—	—	19	—	0.3	2.7
REG. NBL TOTALS	116	—	—	332	—	—	—	—	—	227	318	.714	—	—	—	—	198	—	—	—	—	891	—	—	7.7
NBL PLAYOFF TOTALS	2	—	—	3	—	—	—	—	—	2	3	.667	—	—	—	—	1	—	—	—	—	8	—	—	4.0

CLUGGISH, R. MARION (**Bob**) b. September 18, 1917 Ht. 6-10 Wt. 235 College—Kentucky

SEASON—TEAM	G	GS	MIN	FGM	FGA	PCT	3FGM	3FGA	PCT	FTM	FTA	PCT	O-RB	D-RB	TOT	AST	PF	DQ	STL	TO	BLK	PTS	RPG	APG	PPG
46-47—New York	54	—	—	93	356	.261	—	—	—	52	91	.571	—	—	—	22	113	—	—	—	—	238	—	0.4	4.4
REG. SEASON TOTALS	54	—	—	93	356	.261	—	—	—	52	91	.571	—	—	—	22	113	—	—	—	—	238	—	0.4	4.4
PLAYOFF TOTALS	5	—	—	4	27	.148	—	—	—	0	2	.000	—	—	—	—	12	1	—	—	—	8	—	0.0	1.6

CLYDE, BENNIE J. (**Ben**) b. June 10, 1951 Ht. 6-7 Wt. 200 College—Ellsworth CC/Florida State

SEASON—TEAM	G	GS	MIN	FGM	FGA	PCT	3FGM	3FGA	PCT	FTM	FTA	PCT	O-RB	D-RB	TOT	AST	PF	DQ	STL	TO	BLK	PTS	RPG	APG	PPG
74-75—Boston	25	—	157	31	72	.431	—	—	—	7	9	.778	15	26	41	5	34	1	5	—	3	69	1.6	0.2	2.8
REG. SEASON TOTALS	25	—	157	31	72	.431	—	—	—	7	9	.778	15	26	41	5	34	1	5	—	3	69	1.6	0.2	2.8

COFFEY, RICHARD LEE b. September 2, 1965 Ht. 6-6 Wt. 215 College—Minnesota

SEASON—TEAM	G	GS	MIN	FGM	FGA	PCT	3FGM	3FGA	PCT	FTM	FTA	PCT	O-RB	D-RB	TOT	AST	PF	DQ	STL	TO	BLK	PTS	RPG	APG	PPG
90-91—Minnesota	52	1	320	28	75	.373	0	1	.000	12	22	.545	42	37	79	3	45	0	6	5	4	68	1.5	0.1	1.3
REG. SEASON TOTALS	52	1	320	28	75	.373	0	1	.000	12	22	.545	42	37	79	3	45	0	6	5	4	68	1.5	0.1	1.3

COFIELD, FREDERICK (**Fred**) b. January 4, 1962 Ht. 6-3 Wt. 190 College—Oregon/Eastern Michigan

SEASON—TEAM	G	GS	MIN	FGM	FGA	PCT	3FGM	3FGA	PCT	FTM	FTA	PCT	O-RB	D-RB	TOT	AST	PF	DQ	STL	TO	BLK	PTS	RPG	APG	PPG
85-86—New York	45	1	469	75	184	.408	3	15	.200	12	20	.600	6	40	46	82	65	1	20	49	3	165	1.0	1.8	3.7
86-87—Chicago	5	0	27	2	11	.182	0	1	.000	0	0	—	1	4	5	4	1	0	2	1	0	4	1.0	0.8	0.8
REG. SEASON TOTALS	50	1	496	77	195	.395	3	16	.188	12	20	.600	7	44	51	86	66	1	22	50	3	169	1.0	1.7	3.4

COLE, GARY (**see Abdul Qadir Jeelani**)

COLEMAN, BENJAMIN (**Big Ben**) b. November 14, 1961 Ht. 6-9 Wt. 235 College—Minnesota/Maryland

SEASON—TEAM	G	GS	MIN	FGM	FGA	PCT	3FGM	3FGA	PCT	FTM	FTA	PCT	O-RB	D-RB	TOT	AST	PF	DQ	STL	TO	BLK	PTS	RPG	APG	PPG
86-87—New Jersey	68	7	1029	182	313	.581	0	1	.000	88	121	.727	99	189	288	37	200	7	32	94	31	452	4.2	0.5	6.6
87-88—N.J.-Phil.	70	24	1498	226	453	.499	0	3	.000	141	185	.762	116	234	350	62	230	5	43	127	41	593	5.0	0.9	8.5
88-89—Philadelphia	58	11	703	117	241	.485	0	0	—	61	77	.792	49	128	177	17	120	0	10	48	18	295	3.1	0.3	5.1
89-90—Milwaukee	22	0	305	46	97	.474	0	1	.000	34	41	.829	31	56	87	12	54	0	7	26	7	126	4.0	0.5	5.7
93-94—Detroit	9	0	77	12	25	.480	0	0	—	4	8	.500	10	16	26	0	9	0	2	7	2	28	2.9	0.0	3.1
REG. SEASON TOTALS	227	42	3612	583	1129	.516	0	5	.000	328	432	.759	305	623	928	128	613	12	94	302	99	1494	4.1	0.6	6.6
PLAYOFF TOTALS	3	0	23	6	8	.750	0	0	—	2	2	1.000	2	3	5	—	8	0	1	1	0	14	1.7	0.0	4.7

COLEMAN, DERRICK D. b. June 21, 1967 Ht. 6-10 Wt. 245 College—Syracuse

SEASON—TEAM	G	GS	MIN	FGM	FGA	PCT	3FGM	3FGA	PCT	FTM	FTA	PCT	O-RB	D-RB	TOT	AST	PF	DQ	STL	TO	BLK	PTS	RPG	APG	PPG
90-91—New Jersey	74	68	2602	514	1100	.467	13	38	.342	323	442	.731	269	490	759	163	217	3	71	217	99	1364	10.3	2.2	18.4
91-92—New Jersey	65	58	2207	483	958	.504	23	76	.303	300	393	.763	203	415	618	205	168	2	54	248	98	1289	9.5	3.2	19.8
92-93—New Jersey	76	73	2759	564	1226	.460	23	99	.232	421	521	.808	247	605	852	276	210	1	92	243	126	1572	11.2	3.6	20.7
93-94—New Jersey	77	77	2778	541	1209	.447	38	121	.314	439	567	.774	262	608	870	262	209	2	68	208	142	1559	11.3	3.4	20.2
REG. SEASON TOTALS	292	276	10346	2102	4493	.468	97	334	.290	1483	1923	.771	981	2118	3099	906	804	8	285	916	465	5784	10.6	3.1	19.8
PLAYOFF TOTALS	13	13	560	113	236	.479	11	27	.407	84	107	.785	45	124	169	54	42	0	15	42	22	321	13.0	4.2	24.7
ALL-STAR TOTALS	1	1	18	1	6	.167	0	2	.000	0	0	—	1	2	3	1	3	0	1	0	1	2	3.0	1.0	2.0

COLEMAN, E.C. JR. b. September 25, 1950 Ht. 6-8 Wt. 225 College—Houston Baptist

SEASON—TEAM	G	GS	MIN	FGM	FGA	PCT	3FGM	3FGA	PCT	FTM	FTA	PCT	O-RB	D-RB	TOT	AST	PF	DQ	STL	TO	BLK	PTS	RPG	APG	PPG
73-74—Houston	58	—	1075	128	250	.512	—	—	—	47	74	.635	81	171	252	76	162	4	37	—	20	303	4.3	1.3	5.2
74-75—New Orleans	77	—	2176	253	568	.445	—	—	—	116	166	.699	189	360	549	105	277	10	82	—	37	622	7.1	1.4	8.1
75-76—New Orleans	67	—	1850	216	479	.451	—	—	—	59	89	.663	124	295	419	87	227	3	56	—	30	491	6.3	1.3	7.3
76-77—New Orleans	77	—	2369	290	628	.462	—	—	—	82	112	.732	149	399	548	103	280	9	62	—	32	662	7.1	1.3	8.6
77-78—Golden State	72	—	1801	212	446	.475	—	—	—	40	55	.727	117	259	376	100	253	4	66	95	23	464	5.2	1.4	6.4
78-79—Houston	6	—	39	5	7	.714	—	—	—	1	1	1.000	1	6	7	1	11	0	2	0	0	11	1.2	0.2	1.8
REG. SEASON TOTALS	357	—	9310	1104	2378	.464	—	—	—	345	497	.694	661	1490	2151	472	1210	30	305	95	142	2553	6.0	1.3	7.2

COLEMAN, JACK L. b. May 23, 1924 Ht. 6-7 Wt. 230 College—Louisville

SEASON—TEAM	G	GS	MIN	FGM	FGA	PCT	3FGM	3FGA	PCT	FTM	FTA	PCT	O-RB	D-RB	TOT	AST	PF	DQ	STL	TO	BLK	PTS	RPG	APG	PPG
49-50—Rochester	68	—		250	663	.377	—	—	—	90	121	.744	—	—		153	223	—	—	—	—	590	—	2.3	8.7
50-51—Rochester	67	—	—	315	749	.421	—	—	—	134	172	.779	—	—	584	197	193	4	—	—	—	764	8.7	2.9	11.4
51-52—Rochester	66	—	2606	308	742	.415	—	—	—	120	169	.710	—	—	692	208	218	7	—	—	—	736	10.5	3.2	11.2
52-53—Rochester	70	—	2625	314	748	.420	—	—	—	135	208	.649	—	—	774	231	245	12	—	—	—	763	11.1	3.3	10.9
53-54—Rochester	71	—	2377	289	714	.405	—	—	—	108	181	.597	—	—	589	158	201	3	—	—	—	686	8.3	2.2	9.7
54-55—Rochester	72	—	2482	400	866	.462	—	—	—	124	183	.678	—	—	729	232	201	1	—	—	—	924	10.1	3.2	12.8
55-56—Roch.-St. L.	75	—	2738	390	946	.412	—	—	—	177	249	.711	—	—	688	294	242	2	—	—	—	957	9.2	3.9	12.8
56-57—St. Louis	72	—	2145	316	775	.408	—	—	—	123	161	.764	—	—	645	159	235	7	—	—	—	755	9.0	2.2	10.5
57-58—St. Louis	72	—	1506	231	560	.413	—	—	—	84	131	.641	—	—	485	117	169	3	—	—	—	546	6.7	1.6	7.6
REG. SEASON TOTALS	633	—	16479	2813	6763	.416	—	—	—	1095	1575	.695	—	—	5186	1749	1927	39	—	—	—	6721	9.2	2.8	10.6
PLAYOFF TOTALS	63	—	1573	249	646	.385	—	—	—	133	206	.646	—	—	621	216	224	4	—	—	—	631	10.2	3.4	10.0
ALL-STAR TOTALS	1	—	19	2	8	.250	—	—	—	2	3	.667	—	—	6	1	0	0	—	—	—	6	6.0	1.0	6.0

COLEMAN, NORRIS J. b. September 27, 1961 Ht. 6-8 Wt. 210 College—Kansas State

SEASON—TEAM	G	GS	MIN	FGM	FGA	PCT	3FGM	3FGA	PCT	FTM	FTA	PCT	O-RB	D-RB	TOT	AST	PF	DQ	STL	TO	BLK	PTS	RPG	APG	PPG
87-88—L.A. Clippers	29	11	431	66	191	.346	1	2	.500	20	36	.556	36	45	81	13	51	1	11	16	6	153	2.8	0.4	5.3
REG. SEASON TOTALS	29	11	431	66	191	.346	1	2	.500	20	36	.556	36	45	81	13	51	1	11	16	6	153	2.8	0.4	5.3

COLES, VERNELL EUFAYE (**Bimbo**) b. April 22, 1968 Ht. 6-2 Wt. 180 College—Virginia Tech

SEASON—TEAM	G	GS	MIN	FGM	FGA	PCT	3FGM	3FGA	PCT	FTM	FTA	PCT	O-RB	D-RB	TOT	AST	PF	DQ	STL	TO	BLK	PTS	RPG	APG	PPG
90-91—Miami	82	9	1355	162	393	.412	6	34	.176	71	95	.747	56	97	153	232	149	0	65	98	12	401	1.9	2.8	4.9
91-92—Miami	81	28	1976	295	649	.455	10	52	.192	216	262	.824	69	120	189	366	151	3	73	167	13	816	2.3	4.5	10.1
92-93—Miami	81	37	2232	318	686	.464	42	137	.307	177	220	.805	58	108	166	373	199	4	80	108	11	855	2.0	4.6	10.6
93-94—Miami	76	4	1726	233	519	.449	20	99	.202	102	131	.779	50	109	159	263	132	0	75	107	12	588	2.1	3.5	7.7
REG. SEASON TOTALS	320	78	7289	1008	2247	.449	78	322	.242	566	708	.799	233	434	667	1234	631	7	293	480	48	2660	2.1	3.9	8.3
PLAYOFF TOTALS	8	0	185	32	57	.561	2	5	.400	26	33	.788	4	17	21	23	20	0	10	16	1	92	2.6	2.9	11.5

COLLINS, ARTHUR **(Art)** b. April 14, 1954   Ht. 6-4½ Wt. 185 College—Biscayne

SEASON—TEAM	G	GS	MIN	FGM	FGA	PCT	3FGM	3FGA	PCT	FTM	FTA	PCT	O-RB	D-RB	TOT	AST	PF	DQ	STL	TO	BLK	PTS	RPG	APG	PPG
80-81—Atlanta	29	—	395	35	99	.354	0	2	.000	24	36	.667	19	22	41	25	35	0	11	32	1	94	1.4	0.9	3.2
REG. SEASON TOTALS	29	—	395	35	99	.354	0	2	.000	24	36	.667	19	22	41	25	35	0	11	32	1	94	1.4	0.9	3.2

COLLINS, DONALD **(Don)** b. November 28, 1958   Ht. 6-6 Wt. 190 College—Washington State

SEASON—TEAM	G	GS	MIN	FGM	FGA	PCT	3FGM	3FGA	PCT	FTM	FTA	PCT	O-RB	D-RB	TOT	AST	PF	DQ	STL	TO	BLK	PTS	RPG	APG	PPG
80-81—Atlanta-Wash.	81	—	1845	360	811	.444	0	6	.000	211	272	.776	129	139	268	190	259	6	104	174	25	931	3.3	2.3	11.5
81-82—Washington	79	18	1609	334	653	.511	1	12	.083	121	169	.716	101	95	196	148	195	3	89	135	24	790	2.5	1.9	10.0
82-83—Washington	65	21	1575	332	635	.523	0	6	.000	101	136	.743	116	94	210	132	166	1	87	146	30	765	3.2	2.0	11.8
83-84—Golden State	61	6	957	187	387	.483	1	5	.200	65	89	.730	62	67	129	67	119	1	43	80	14	440	2.1	1.1	7.2
84-85—Washington	11	0	91	12	34	.353	0	0	—	8	9	.889	10	9	19	7	5	0	7	8	4	32	1.7	0.6	2.9
86-87—Milwaukee	6	0	57	10	28	.357	0	0	—	5	7	.714	11	4	15	2	11	0	2	5	1	25	2.5	0.3	4.2
REG. SEASON TOTALS	303	45	6134	1235	2548	.485	2	29	.069	511	682	.749	429	408	837	546	755	11	332	548	98	2983	2.8	1.8	9.8
PLAYOFF TOTALS	8	6	151	19	44	.432	0	0	—	5	7	.714	9	13	22	6	25	1	4	11	1	43	2.8	0.8	5.4

COLLINS, JAMES E. **(Jimmy)** b. November 24, 1946   Ht. 6-2 Wt. 175 College—New Mexico State

SEASON—TEAM	G	GS	MIN	FGM	FGA	PCT	3FGM	3FGA	PCT	FTM	FTA	PCT	O-RB	D-RB	TOT	AST	PF	DQ	STL	TO	BLK	PTS	RPG	APG	PPG
70-71—Chicago	55	—	478	92	214	.430	—	—	—	35	45	.778	—	—	54	60	43	0	—	—	—	219	1.0	1.1	4.0
71-72—Chicago	19	—	134	26	71	.366	—	—	—	10	11	.909	—	—	12	10	11	0	—	—	—	62	0.6	0.5	3.3
REG. SEASON TOTALS	74	—	612	118	285	.414	—	—	—	45	56	.804	—	—	66	70	54	0	—	—	—	281	0.9	0.9	3.8
PLAYOFF TOTALS	2	—	8	0	1	.000	—	—	—	3	3	1.000	—	—	1	—	1	0	—	—	—	3	0.5	0.0	1.5

COLLINS, PAUL DOUGLAS **(Doug)** b. July 28, 1951   Ht. 6-6 Wt. 180 College—Illinois State

SEASON—TEAM	G	GS	MIN	FGM	FGA	PCT	3FGM	3FGA	PCT	FTM	FTA	PCT	O-RB	D-RB	TOT	AST	PF	DQ	STL	TO	BLK	PTS	RPG	APG	PPG
73-74—Philadelphia	25	—	436	72	194	.371	—	—	—	55	72	.764	7	39	46	40	65	1	13	—	2	199	1.8	1.6	8.0
74-75—Philadelphia	81	—	2820	561	1150	.488	—	—	—	331	392	.844	104	211	315	213	291	6	108	—	17	1453	3.9	2.6	17.9
75-76—Philadelphia	77	—	2995	614	1196	.513	—	—	—	372	445	.836	126	181	307	191	249	2	110	—	24	1600	4.0	2.5	20.8
76-77—Philadelphia	58	—	2037	426	823	.518	—	—	—	210	250	.840	64	131	195	271	174	2	70	—	15	1062	3.4	4.7	18.3
77-78—Philadelphia	79	—	2770	643	1223	.526	—	—	—	267	329	.812	87	143	230	320	228	2	128	250	25	1553	2.9	4.1	19.7
78-79—Philadelphia	47	—	1595	358	717	.499	—	—	—	201	247	.814	36	87	123	191	139	1	52	131	20	917	2.6	4.1	19.5
79-80—Philadelphia	36	—	963	191	410	.466	0	1	.000	113	124	.911	29	65	94	100	76	0	30	82	7	495	2.6	2.8	13.8
80-81—Philadelphia	12	—	329	62	126	.492	0	0	—	24	29	.828	6	23	29	42	23	0	7	22	4	148	2.4	3.5	12.3
REG. SEASON TOTALS	415	—	13945	2927	5839	.501	0	1	.000	1573	1888	.833	459	880	1339	1368	1245	14	518	485	114	7427	3.2	3.3	17.9
PLAYOFF TOTALS	32	—	1218	282	536	.526	0	0	—	123	159	.774	51	80	131	111	95	0	34	23	4	687	4.1	3.5	21.5
ALL-STAR TOTALS	3	—	68	11	24	.458	0	0	—	12	15	.800	7	6	13	17	8	0	6	4	0	34	4.3	5.7	11.3

COLONE, JOSEPH F. **(Joe, Bells)** b. January 23, 1926   Ht. 6-5 Wt. 210 College—Bloomsburg (Pa.)

SEASON—TEAM	G	GS	MIN	FGM	FGA	PCT	3FGM	3FGA	PCT	FTM	FTA	PCT	O-RB	D-RB	TOT	AST	PF	DQ	STL	TO	BLK	PTS	RPG	APG	PPG
48-49—New York	15	—	—	35	113	.310	—	—	—	13	19	.684	—	—	—	9	25	—	—	—	—	83	—	0.6	5.5
REG. SEASON TOTALS	15	—	—	35	113	.310	—	—	—	13	19	.684	—	—	—	9	25	—	—	—	—	83	—	0.6	5.5
PLAYOFF TOTALS	4	—	—	7	30	.233	—	—	—	3	6	.500	—	—	—	3	13	—	—	—	—	17	—	0.8	4.3

COLTER, STEVE b. July 24, 1962   Ht. 6-3 Wt. 175 College—New Mexico State

SEASON—TEAM	G	GS	MIN	FGM	FGA	PCT	3FGM	3FGA	PCT	FTM	FTA	PCT	O-RB	D-RB	TOT	AST	PF	DQ	STL	TO	BLK	PTS	RPG	APG	PPG
84-85—Portland	78	22	1462	216	477	.453	26	74	.351	98	130	.754	40	110	150	243	142	0	75	112	9	556	1.9	3.1	7.1
85-86—Portland	81	51	1868	272	597	.456	27	83	.325	135	164	.823	41	136	177	257	188	0	113	115	10	706	2.2	3.2	8.7
86-87—Chicago-Phil.	70	31	1322	169	397	.426	4	17	.235	82	107	.766	23	85	108	210	99	0	56	70	12	424	1.5	3.0	6.1
87-88—Phil.-Wash.	68	53	1513	203	441	.460	3	10	.300	75	95	.789	58	115	173	261	132	0	62	88	14	484	2.5	3.8	7.1
88-89—Washington	80	5	1425	203	457	.444	3	25	.120	125	167	.749	62	120	182	225	158	0	69	64	14	534	2.3	2.8	6.7
89-90—Washington	73	1	977	142	297	.478	0	5	.000	77	95	.811	55	121	176	148	98	0	47	38	10	361	2.4	2.0	4.9
90-91—Sacramento	19	0	251	23	56	.411	5	14	.357	7	10	.700	5	21	26	37	27	0	11	11	1	58	1.4	1.9	3.1
REG. SEASON TOTALS	469	163	8818	1228	2722	.451	68	228	.298	599	768	.780	284	708	992	1381	844	0	433	498	70	3123	2.1	2.9	6.7
PLAYOFF TOTALS	20	9	364	63	134	.470	3	12	.250	11	17	.647	12	34	46	75	47	1	13	21	4	140	2.3	3.8	7.0

COMBS, EDWIN LEROY **(Leroy)** b. January 1, 1961   Ht. 6-8 Wt. 210 College—Oklahoma State

SEASON—TEAM	G	GS	MIN	FGM	FGA	PCT	3FGM	3FGA	PCT	FTM	FTA	PCT	O-RB	D-RB	TOT	AST	PF	DQ	STL	TO	BLK	PTS	RPG	APG	PPG
83-84—Indiana	48	0	446	81	163	.497	0	3	.000	56	91	.615	19	37	56	38	49	0	23	46	18	218	1.2	0.8	4.5
REG. SEASON TOTALS	48	0	446	81	163	.497	0	3	.000	56	91	.615	19	37	56	38	49	0	23	46	18	218	1.2	0.8	4.5

COMBS, GLEN COURTNEY **(The Kentucky Rifle)** b. October 30, 1946 Ht. 6-2 Wt. 185 College—Virginia Tech

SEASON—TEAM	G	GS	MIN	FGM	FGA	PCT	3FGM	3FGA	PCT	FTM	FTA	PCT	O-RB	D-RB	TOT	AST	PF	DQ	STL	TO	BLK	PTS	RPG	APG	PPG
68-69—Dallas (A)	72	—	2241	364	868	.419	84	233	.361	300	394	.761	—	—	195	165	218	3	—	158	—	1112	2.7	2.3	15.4
69-70—Dallas (A)	84	—	3260	640	1474	.434	130	370	.351	458	548	.836	—	—	289	342	265	2	—	—	—	1868	3.4	4.1	22.2
70-71—Texas-Utah (A)	86	—	3204	610	1372	.445	77	210	.367	448	546	.821	—	—	292	361	286	—	—	—	—	1745	3.4	4.2	20.3
71-72—Utah (A)	84	—	2906	483	1109	.436	103	254	.406	319	380	.839	—	—	215	306	255	—	—	191	—	1388	2.6	3.6	16.5
72-73—Utah (A)	50	—	1488	228	535	.426	51	134	.381	154	189	.815	21	63	84	138	142	1	—	90	—	661	1.7	2.8	13.2
73-74—Utah-Memphis (A)	76	—	1986	304	696	.437	52	147	.354	156	212	.736	46	98	144	304	154	—	52	146	11	816	1.9	4.0	10.7
74-75—Virginia (A)	13	—	190	23	67	.343	6	21	.286	24	27	.889	5	6	11	23	13	—	4	16	2	76	0.8	1.8	5.8
REG. ABA TOTALS	465	—	15275	2652	6121	.433	503	1369	.367	1859	2296	.810	72	167	1230	1639	1333	6	56	601	13	7666	2.6	3.5	16.5
ABA PLAYOFF TOTALS	51	—	1545	286	678	.422	34	121	.281	163	207	.787	0	0	141	144	154	0	0	51	0	769	2.8	2.8	15.1
ABA ALL-STAR TOTALS	3	—	47	6	21	.286	2	9	.222	0	2	.000	0	1	4	6	4	0	0	2	0	14	1.3	2.0	4.7

COMEAUX, JOHN ROOSEVELT b. September 15, 1943 Ht. 6-5 Wt. 195 College—Grambling State

SEASON—TEAM	G	GS	MIN	FGM	FGA	PCT	3FGM	3FGA	PCT	FTM	FTA	PCT	O-RB	D-RB	TOT	AST	PF	DQ	STL	TO	BLK	PTS	RPG	APG	PPG
67-68—New Orleans (A)	23	—	189	27	63	.429	0	0	—	23	32	.719	—	—	28	11	27	0	—	15	—	77	1.2	0.5	3.3
REG. ABA TOTALS	23	—	189	27	63	.429	0	0	—	23	32	.719	—	—	28	11	27	0	—	15	—	77	1.2	0.5	3.3

COMEGYS, DALLAS ALONZO b. August 17, 1964 Ht. 6-9 Wt. 205 College—DePaul

SEASON—TEAM	G	GS	MIN	FGM	FGA	PCT	3FGM	3FGA	PCT	FTM	FTA	PCT	O-RB	D-RB	TOT	AST	PF	DQ	STL	TO	BLK	PTS	RPG	APG	PPG
87-88—New Jersey	75	17	1122	156	363	.430	0	1	.000	106	150	.707	54	164	218	65	175	3	36	116	70	418	2.9	0.9	5.6
88-89—San Antonio	67	10	1119	166	341	.487	0	2	.000	106	161	.658	112	122	234	30	160	2	42	85	63	438	3.5	0.4	6.5
REG. SEASON TOTALS	142	27	2241	322	704	.457	0	3	.000	212	311	.682	166	286	452	95	335	5	78	201	133	856	3.2	0.7	6.0

COMLEY, LAWRENCE ROBERT **(Larry)** b. August 17, 1939 Ht. 6-5½ Wt. 210 College—Kansas State

SEASON—TEAM	G	GS	MIN	FGM	FGA	PCT	3FGM	3FGA	PCT	FTM	FTA	PCT	O-RB	D-RB	TOT	AST	PF	DQ	STL	TO	BLK	PTS	RPG	APG	PPG
63-64—Baltimore	12	—	89	8	37	.216	—	—	—	9	16	.563	—	—	19	12	11	0	—	—	—	25	1.6	1.0	2.1
REG. SEASON TOTALS	12	—	89	8	37	.216	—	—	—	9	16	.563	—	—	19	12	11	0	—	—	—	25	1.6	1.0	2.1

CONGDON, JEFFREY D. **(Jeff)** b. October 17, 1943 Ht. 6-2 Wt. 180 College—Brigham Young

SEASON—TEAM	G	GS	MIN	FGM	FGA	PCT	3FGM	3FGA	PCT	FTM	FTA	PCT	O-RB	D-RB	TOT	AST	PF	DQ	STL	TO	BLK	PTS	RPG	APG	PPG
67-68—Anaheim-Denver (A)	64	—	1020	150	404	.371	13	54	.241	49	64	.766	—	—	106	133	84	1	—	119	—	362	1.7	2.1	5.7
68-69—Denver (A)	59	—	979	107	277	.386	5	31	.161	69	85	.812	—	—	93	135	104	1	—	97	—	288	1.6	2.3	4.9
69-70—Denver (A)	83	—	2461	299	775	.386	63	178	.354	151	192	.786	—	—	233	446	205	3	—	—	—	812	2.8	5.4	9.8
70-71—Utah-N.Y. (A)	80	—	1562	178	487	.366	18	88	.205	79	96	.823	—	—	143	252	126	—	—	—	—	453	1.8	3.2	5.7
71-72—Dallas (A)	20	—	261	30	86	.349	3	7	.429	17	20	.850	—	—	26	36	19	—	—	13	—	80	1.3	1.8	4.0
REG. ABA TOTALS	306	—	6283	764	2029	.377	102	358	.285	365	457	.799	—	—	601	1002	538	5	—	229	—	1995	2.0	3.3	6.5
ABA PLAYOFF TOTALS	26	—	607	78	202	.386	18	61	.295	54	66	.818	—	—	59	118	69	0	—	21	—	228	2.3	4.5	8.8

CONLEY, DONALD EUGENE **(Gene)** b. November 10, 1930 Ht. 6-8 Wt. 245 College—Washington State

SEASON—TEAM	G	GS	MIN	FGM	FGA	PCT	3FGM	3FGA	PCT	FTM	FTA	PCT	O-RB	D-RB	TOT	AST	PF	DQ	STL	TO	BLK	PTS	RPG	APG	PPG
52-53—Boston	39	—	461	35	108	.324	—	—	—	18	31	.581	—	—	171	19	74	1	—	—	—	88	4.4	0.5	2.3
58-59—Boston	50	—	663	86	262	.328	—	—	—	37	64	.578	—	—	276	19	117	2	—	—	—	209	5.5	0.4	4.2
59-60—Boston	71	—	1330	201	539	.373	—	—	—	76	114	.667	—	—	590	32	270	10	—	—	—	478	8.3	0.5	6.7
60-61—Boston	75	—	1242	183	495	.370	—	—	—	106	153	.693	—	—	550	40	275	15	—	—	—	472	7.3	0.5	6.3
62-63—New York	70	—	1544	254	651	.390	—	—	—	122	186	.656	—	—	469	70	263	10	—	—	—	630	6.7	1.0	9.0
63-64—New York	46	—	551	74	189	.392	—	—	—	44	65	.677	—	—	156	21	124	2	—	—	—	192	3.4	0.5	4.2
REG. SEASON TOTALS	351	—	5791	833	2244	.371	—	—	—	403	613	.657	—	—	2212	201	1123	40	—	—	—	2069	6.3	0.6	5.9
PLAYOFF TOTALS	33	—	482	70	187	.374	—	—	—	29	47	.617	—	—	222	11	119	4	—	—	—	169	6.7	0.3	5.1

CONLEY, GEORGE LARRY **(Larry)** b. January 22, 1944 Ht. 6-3 Wt. 175 College—Kentucky

SEASON—TEAM	G	GS	MIN	FGM	FGA	PCT	3FGM	3FGA	PCT	FTM	FTA	PCT	O-RB	D-RB	TOT	AST	PF	DQ	STL	TO	BLK	PTS	RPG	APG	PPG
67-68—Kentucky (A)	1	—	18	1	4	.250	0	0	—	0	0	—	—	—	0	0	0	0	—	3	—	2	0.0	0.0	2.0
REG. ABA TOTALS	1	—	18	1	4	.250	0	0	—	0	0	—	—	—	0	0	0	0	—	3	—	2	0.0	0.0	2.0

CONLIN, EDWARD JAMES **(Ed)** b. September 2, 1933 Ht. 6-6 Wt. 200 College—Fordham

SEASON—TEAM	G	GS	MIN	FGM	FGA	PCT	3FGM	3FGA	PCT	FTM	FTA	PCT	O-RB	D-RB	TOT	AST	PF	DQ	STL	TO	BLK	PTS	RPG	APG	PPG
55-56—Syracuse	66	—	1423	211	574	.368	—	—	—	121	178	.680	—	—	326	145	121	1	—	—	—	543	4.9	2.2	8.2
56-57—Syracuse	71	—	2250	335	896	.374	—	—	—	283	368	.769	—	—	430	205	170	0	—	—	—	953	6.1	2.9	13.4
57-58—Syracuse	60	—	1871	343	877	.391	—	—	—	215	270	.796	—	—	436	133	168	2	—	—	—	901	7.3	2.2	15.0
58-59—Syr.-Detroit	72	—	1955	329	891	.369	—	—	—	197	274	.719	—	—	394	132	188	6	—	—	—	855	5.5	1.8	11.9
59-60—Detroit	70	—	1636	300	831	.361	—	—	—	181	238	.761	—	—	346	126	158	2	—	—	—	781	4.9	1.8	11.2
60-61—Philadelphia	77	—	1294	216	599	.361	—	—	—	104	139	.748	—	—	262	123	153	1	—	—	—	536	3.4	1.6	7.0
61-62—Philadelphia	70	—	963	128	371	.345	—	—	—	66	89	.742	—	—	155	85	118	1	—	—	—	322	2.2	1.2	4.6
REG. SEASON TOTALS	486	—	11392	1862	5039	.370	—	—	—	1167	1556	.750	—	—	2349	949	1076	13	—	—	—	4891	4.8	2.0	10.1
PLAYOFF TOTALS	35	—	665	94	289	.325	—	—	—	65	96	.677	—	—	120	39	60	0	—	—	—	253	3.4	1.1	7.2

CONLON, MARTIN McBRIDE (**Marty**) b. January 19, 1968 Ht. 6-11 Wt. 245 College—Providence

SEASON—TEAM	G	GS	MIN	FGM	FGA	PCT	3FGM	3FGA	PCT	FTM	FTA	PCT	O-RB	D-RB	TOT	AST	PF	DQ	STL	TO	BLK	PTS	RPG	APG	PPG
91-92—Seattle	45	1	381	48	101	.475	0	0	—	24	32	.750	33	36	69	12	40	0	9	27	7	120	1.5	0.3	2.7
92-93—Sacramento	46	0	467	81	171	.474	0	4	.000	57	81	.704	48	75	123	37	43	0	13	28	5	219	2.7	0.8	4.8
93-94—Cha.-Wash.	30	9	579	95	165	.576	0	2	.000	43	53	.811	53	86	139	34	69	1	9	33	8	233	4.6	1.1	7.8
REG. SEASON TOTALS	121	10	1427	224	437	.513	0	6	.000	124	166	.747	134	197	331	83	152	1	31	88	20	572	2.7	0.7	4.7
PLAYOFF TOTALS	1	0	1	0	1	.000	0	0	—	2	2	1.000	0	1	1	—	0	0	0	0	0	2	1.0	0.0	2.0

CONNER, JIMMY DAN (**Jimmy Dan**) b. March 20, 1953 Ht. 6-4 Wt. 190 College—Kentucky

SEASON—TEAM	G	GS	MIN	FGM	FGA	PCT	3FGM	3FGA	PCT	FTM	FTA	PCT	O-RB	D-RB	TOT	AST	PF	DQ	STL	TO	BLK	PTS	RPG	APG	PPG
75-76—Kentucky (A)	24	—	240	42	86	.488	0	3	.000	22	29	.759	12	16	28	38	35	—	11	32	5	106	1.2	1.6	4.4
REG. ABA TOTALS	24	—	240	42	86	.488	0	3	.000	22	29	.759	12	16	28	38	35	—	11	32	5	106	1.2	1.6	4.4

CONNER, LESTER ALLEN b. September 17, 1959 Ht. 6-4 Wt. 185 College—Los Medanos/Chabot College/Oregon State

SEASON—TEAM	G	GS	MIN	FGM	FGA	PCT	3FGM	3FGA	PCT	FTM	FTA	PCT	O-RB	D-RB	TOT	AST	PF	DQ	STL	TO	BLK	PTS	RPG	APG	PPG
82-83—Golden State	75	10	1416	145	303	.479	0	4	.000	79	113	.699	69	152	221	253	141	1	116	99	7	369	2.9	3.4	4.9
83-84—Golden State	82	82	2573	360	730	.493	1	6	.167	186	259	.718	132	173	305	401	176	1	162	143	12	907	3.7	4.9	11.1
84-85—Golden State	79	49	2258	246	546	.451	4	20	.200	144	192	.750	87	159	246	369	136	1	161	138	13	640	3.1	4.7	8.1
85-86—Golden State	36	0	413	51	136	.375	2	7	.286	40	54	.741	25	37	62	43	23	0	24	15	1	144	1.7	1.2	4.0
87-88—Houston	52	3	399	50	108	.463	0	7	.000	32	41	.780	20	18	38	59	31	0	38	33	1	132	0.7	1.1	2.5
88-89—New Jersey	82	63	2532	309	676	.457	13	37	.351	212	269	.788	100	255	355	604	132	1	181	181	5	843	4.3	7.4	10.3
89-90—New Jersey	82	61	2355	237	573	.414	2	13	.154	172	214	.804	90	175	265	385	182	0	172	138	8	648	3.2	4.7	7.9
90-91—N.J.-Milw.	74	4	1008	96	207	.464	0	5	.000	68	94	.723	21	91	112	165	75	0	85	58	2	260	1.5	2.2	3.5
91-92—Milwaukee	81	9	1420	103	239	.431	0	7	.000	81	115	.704	63	121	184	294	86	0	97	79	10	287	2.3	3.6	3.5
92-93—L.A. Clippers	31	0	422	28	62	.452	0	0	—	18	19	.947	16	33	49	65	39	0	34	21	4	74	1.6	2.1	2.4
93-94—Indiana	11	0	169	14	38	.368	0	3	.000	3	6	.500	10	14	24	31	12	0	14	9	1	31	2.2	2.8	2.8
REG. SEASON TOTALS	685	281	14965	1639	3618	.453	22	109	.202	1035	1376	.752	633	1228	1861	2669	1033	4	1084	914	64	4335	2.7	3.9	6.3
PLAYOFF TOTALS	13	0	94	12	18	.667	1	1	1.000	6	7	.857	5	8	13	13	8	0	5	1	1	31	1.0	1.0	2.4

CONNORS, KEVIN JOSEPH ALOYSIUS (**Chuck**) b. April 10, 1921 d. November 10, 1992 Ht. 6-6 Wt. 205 College—Seton Hall

SEASON—TEAM	G	GS	MIN	FGM	FGA	PCT	3FGM	3FGA	PCT	FTM	FTA	PCT	O-RB	D-RB	TOT	AST	PF	DQ	STL	TO	BLK	PTS	RPG	APG	PPG
45-46—Rochester (N)	14	—	—	11	—	—	—	—	—	6	—	—	—	—	—	—	—	—	—	—	—	28	—	—	2.0
46-47—Boston	49	—	—	94	380	.247	—	—	—	39	84	.464	—	—	—	40	129	—	—	—	—	227	—	0.8	4.6
47-48—Boston	4	—	—	5	13	.385	—	—	—	2	3	.667	—	—	—	1	5	—	—	—	—	12	—	0.3	3.0
REG. NBA TOTALS	53	—	—	99	393	.252	—	—	—	41	87	.471	—	—	—	41	134	—	—	—	—	239	—	0.8	4.5
REG. NBL TOTALS	14	—	—	11	—	—	—	—	—	6	—	—	—	—	—	—	—	—	—	—	—	28	—	—	2.0

COOK, ANTHONY LACQUISE b. March 19, 1967 Ht. 6-9 Wt. 215 College—Arizona

SEASON—TEAM	G	GS	MIN	FGM	FGA	PCT	3FGM	3FGA	PCT	FTM	FTA	PCT	O-RB	D-RB	TOT	AST	PF	DQ	STL	TO	BLK	PTS	RPG	APG	PPG
90-91—Denver	58	25	1121	118	283	.417	0	3	.000	71	129	.550	134	192	326	26	100	1	35	50	72	307	5.6	0.4	5.3
91-92—Denver	22	0	115	15	25	.600	0	0	—	4	6	.667	13	21	34	2	10	0	5	3	4	34	1.5	0.1	1.5
93-94—Orlando-Milw.	25	0	203	26	54	.481	0	1	.000	10	25	.400	20	36	56	4	22	0	3	12	14	62	2.2	0.2	2.5
REG. SEASON TOTALS	105	25	1439	159	362	.439	0	4	.000	85	160	.531	167	249	416	32	132	1	43	65	90	403	4.0	0.3	3.8

COOK, BERT E. b. April 26, 1929 Ht. 6-3 Wt. 185 College—Utah State

SEASON—TEAM	G	GS	MIN	FGM	FGA	PCT	3FGM	3FGA	PCT	FTM	FTA	PCT	O-RB	D-RB	TOT	AST	PF	DQ	STL	TO	BLK	PTS	RPG	APG	PPG
54-55—New York	37	—	424	42	133	.316	—	—	—	34	50	.680	—	—	72	33	39	0	—	—	—	118	1.9	0.9	3.2
REG. SEASON TOTALS	37	—	424	42	133	.316	—	—	—	34	50	.680	—	—	72	33	39	0	—	—	—	118	1.9	0.9	3.2
PLAYOFF TOTALS	1	—	20	4	6	.667	—	—	—	0	2	.000	—	—	0	2	3	0	—	—	—	8	0.0	2.0	8.0

COOK, DARWIN LOUIS b. August 6, 1958 Ht. 6-3 Wt. 185 College—Portland

SEASON—TEAM	G	GS	MIN	FGM	FGA	PCT	3FGM	3FGA	PCT	FTM	FTA	PCT	O-RB	D-RB	TOT	AST	PF	DQ	STL	TO	BLK	PTS	RPG	APG	PPG
80-81—New Jersey	81	—	1980	383	819	.468	6	25	.240	132	180	.733	96	140	236	297	197	4	141	176	36	904	2.9	3.7	11.2
81-82—New Jersey	82	17	2090	387	803	.482	7	31	.226	118	162	.728	52	103	155	319	196	2	146	175	24	899	1.9	3.9	11.0
82-83—New Jersey	82	47	2625	443	986	.449	8	38	.211	186	242	.769	73	167	240	448	213	2	194	238	48	1080	2.9	5.5	13.2
83-84—New Jersey	82	31	1870	304	687	.443	11	46	.239	95	126	.754	51	105	156	356	184	3	164	142	36	714	1.9	4.3	8.7
84-85—New Jersey	58	9	1063	212	453	.468	2	23	.087	47	54	.870	21	71	92	160	96	0	74	75	10	473	1.6	2.8	8.2
85-86—New Jersey	79	33	1965	267	627	.426	11	53	.208	84	111	.757	51	126	177	390	172	0	156	132	22	629	2.2	4.9	8.0
86-87—Washington	82	2	1420	265	622	.426	2	23	.087	82	103	.796	46	99	145	151	136	0	98	96	17	614	1.8	1.8	7.5
88-89—S.A.-Denver	66	4	1143	218	478	.456	8	41	.195	63	78	.808	34	73	107	127	121	0	71	88	10	507	1.6	1.9	7.7
REG. SEASON TOTALS	612	143	14156	2479	5475	.453	55	280	.196	807	1056	.764	424	884	1308	2248	1315	11	1044	1122	203	5820	2.1	3.7	9.5
PLAYOFF TOTALS	25	7	525	86	223	.386	6	25	.240	30	46	.652	20	34	54	82	70	1	30	46	4	208	2.2	3.3	8.3

COOK, JEFFREY JAMES (**Jeff**) b. October 21, 1956 Ht. 6-10 Wt. 215 College—Idaho State

SEASON—TEAM	G	GS	MIN	FGM	FGA	PCT	3FGM	3FGA	PCT	FTM	FTA	PCT	O-RB	D-RB	TOT	AST	PF	DQ	STL	TO	BLK	PTS	RPG	APG	PPG
79-80—Phoenix	66	—	904	129	275	.469	0	3	.000	104	129	.806	90	151	241	84	102	0	28	71	18	362	3.7	1.3	5.5
80-81—Phoenix	79	—	2192	286	616	.464	0	5	.000	100	155	.645	170	297	467	201	236	3	82	146	54	672	5.9	2.5	8.5
81-82—Phoenix	76	22	1298	151	358	.422	0	2	.000	89	134	.664	112	189	301	100	174	1	37	80	23	391	4.0	1.3	5.1
82-83—Phoenix-Clev.	75	22	1333	148	304	.487	0	3	.000	79	104	.760	119	216	335	102	181	3	39	105	31	375	4.5	1.4	5.0
83-84—Cleveland	81	21	1950	188	387	.486	1	2	.500	94	130	.723	174	310	484	123	282	7	68	91	47	471	6.0	1.5	5.8
84-85—Clev.-S.A.	72	5	1288	138	279	.495	0	1	.000	47	64	.734	122	192	314	62	203	2	30	48	23	323	4.4	0.9	4.5
85-86—S.A.-Utah	36	0	373	31	73	.425	0	1	.000	27	42	.643	33	53	86	21	65	0	13	14	11	89	2.4	0.6	2.5
87-88—Phoenix	33	0	359	14	59	.237	0	1	.000	23	28	.821	37	69	106	14	64	1	9	14	8	51	3.2	0.4	1.5
REG. SEASON TOTALS	518	70	9697	1085	2351	.462	1	18	.056	563	786	.716	857	1477	2334	707	1307	17	306	569	215	2734	4.5	1.4	5.3
PLAYOFF TOTALS	30	0	468	55	108	.509	1	2	.500	56	74	.757	35	76	111	31	71	1	12	23	10	167	3.7	1.0	5.6

COOK, NORMAN (**Norm**) b. March 21, 1955 Ht. 6-8 Wt. 210 College—Kansas

SEASON—TEAM	G	GS	MIN	FGM	FGA	PCT	3FGM	3FGA	PCT	FTM	FTA	PCT	O-RB	D-RB	TOT	AST	PF	DQ	STL	TO	BLK	PTS	RPG	APG	PPG
76-77—Boston	25	—	138	27	72	.375	—	—	—	9	17	.529	10	17	27	5	27	0	10	—	3	63	1.1	0.2	2.5
77-78—Denver	2	—	10	1	3	.333	—	—	—	0	0	—	1	2	3	1	4	0	0	0	0	2	1.5	0.5	1.0
REG. SEASON TOTALS	27	—	148	28	75	.373	—	—	—	9	17	.529	11	19	30	6	31	0	10	0	3	65	1.1	0.2	2.4
PLAYOFF TOTALS	1	—	3	2	2	1.000	—	—	—	0	0	—	0	0	0	—	0	0	0	—	0	4	0.0	0.0	4.0

COOK, ROBERT BERNARD (**Bobby, Cookie**) b. April 1, 1923 Ht. 5-10½ Wt. 155 College—Wisconsin

SEASON—TEAM	G	GS	MIN	FGM	FGA	PCT	3FGM	3FGA	PCT	FTM	FTA	PCT	O-RB	D-RB	TOT	AST	PF	DQ	STL	TO	BLK	PTS	RPG	APG	PPG
48-49—Sheboygan (N)	64	—	—	172	—	—	—	—	—	98	136	.721	—	—	—	—	111	—	—	—	—	442	—	—	6.9
49-50—Sheboygan	51	—	—	222	620	.358	—	—	—	143	181	.790	—	—	—	158	114	—	—	—	—	587	—	3.1	11.5
REG. NBA TOTALS	51	—	—	222	620	.358	—	—	—	143	181	.790	—	—	—	158	114	—	—	—	—	587	—	3.1	11.5
REG. NBL TOTALS	64	—	—	172	—	—	—	—	—	98	136	.721	—	—	—	—	111	—	—	—	—	442	—	—	6.9
NBA PLAYOFF TOTALS	3	—	—	3	10	.300	—	—	—	3	6	.500	—	—	—	6	3	—	—	—	—	9	—	2.0	3.0
NBL PLAYOFF TOTALS	2	—	—	5	—	—	—	—	—	9	10	.900	—	—	—	—	6	—	—	—	—	19	—	—	9.5

COOKE, DAVID D. b. September 27, 1963 Ht. 6-8 Wt. 230 College—St. Mary's (Ca.)

SEASON—TEAM	G	GS	MIN	FGM	FGA	PCT	3FGM	3FGA	PCT	FTM	FTA	PCT	O-RB	D-RB	TOT	AST	PF	DQ	STL	TO	BLK	PTS	RPG	APG	PPG
85-86—Sacramento	6	0	38	2	11	.182	0	0	—	5	10	.500	5	5	10	1	5	0	4	2	0	9	1.7	0.2	1.5
REG. SEASON TOTALS	6	0	38	2	11	.182	0	0	—	5	10	.500	5	5	10	1	5	0	4	2	0	9	1.7	0.2	1.5

COOKE, JOSEPH (**Joe**) b. August 14, 1948 Ht. 6-3 Wt. 175 College—Indiana

SEASON—TEAM	G	GS	MIN	FGM	FGA	PCT	3FGM	3FGA	PCT	FTM	FTA	PCT	O-RB	D-RB	TOT	AST	PF	DQ	STL	TO	BLK	PTS	RPG	APG	PPG
70-71—Cleveland	73	—	725	134	341	.393	—	—	—	48	59	.814	—	—	114	93	135	2	—	—	—	316	1.6	1.3	4.3
REG. SEASON TOTALS	73	—	725	134	341	.393	—	—	—	48	59	.814	—	—	114	93	135	2	—	—	—	316	1.6	1.3	4.3

COOPER, ARTIS WAYNE (**Wayne, Coop**) b. November 16, 1956 Ht. 6-10 Wt. 220 College—New Orleans

SEASON—TEAM	G	GS	MIN	FGM	FGA	PCT	3FGM	3FGA	PCT	FTM	FTA	PCT	O-RB	D-RB	TOT	AST	PF	DQ	STL	TO	BLK	PTS	RPG	APG	PPG
78-79—Golden State	65	—	795	128	293	.437	—	—	—	41	61	.672	90	190	280	21	118	0	7	52	44	297	4.3	0.3	4.6
79-80—Golden State	79	—	1781	367	750	.489	1	4	.250	136	181	.751	202	305	507	42	246	5	20	140	79	871	6.4	0.5	11.0
80-81—Utah	71	—	1420	213	471	.452	1	3	.333	62	90	.689	166	274	440	52	219	8	18	77	51	489	6.2	0.7	6.9
81-82—Dallas	76	38	1818	281	669	.420	1	8	.125	119	160	.744	200	350	550	115	285	10	37	88	106	682	7.2	1.5	9.0
82-83—Portland	80	60	2099	320	723	.443	0	5	.000	135	197	.685	214	397	611	116	318	5	27	162	136	775	7.6	1.5	9.7
83-84—Portland	81	38	1662	304	663	.459	0	7	.000	185	230	.804	176	300	476	76	247	2	26	110	106	793	5.9	0.9	9.8
84-85—Denver	80	78	2031	404	856	.472	0	2	.000	161	235	.685	229	402	631	86	304	2	28	149	197	969	7.9	1.1	12.1
85-86—Denver	78	78	2112	422	906	.466	3	7	.429	174	219	.795	190	420	610	81	315	6	42	117	227	1021	7.8	1.0	13.1
86-87—Denver	69	64	1561	235	524	.448	0	3	.000	79	109	.725	162	311	473	68	257	5	13	78	101	549	6.9	1.0	8.0
87-88—Denver	45	32	865	118	270	.437	0	1	.000	50	67	.746	98	172	270	30	145	3	12	59	94	286	6.0	0.7	6.4
88-89—Denver	79	72	1864	220	444	.495	1	4	.250	79	106	.745	212	407	619	78	302	7	36	73	211	520	7.8	1.0	6.6
89-90—Portland	79	0	1176	138	304	.454	0	3	.000	25	39	.641	118	221	339	44	211	2	18	39	95	301	4.3	0.6	3.8
90-91—Portland	67	1	746	57	145	.393	0	1	.000	33	42	.786	54	134	188	22	120	0	7	22	61	147	2.8	0.3	2.2
91-92—Portland	35	0	344	35	82	.427	0	0	—	7	11	.636	38	63	101	21	57	0	4	15	27	77	2.9	0.6	2.2
REG. SEASON TOTALS	984	461	20274	3242	7100	.457	7	48	.146	1286	1747	.736	2149	3946	6095	852	3144	55	295	1181	1535	7777	6.2	0.9	7.9
PLAYOFF TOTALS	74	28	1276	178	400	.445	0	1	.000	78	110	.709	133	223	356	56	214	5	22	64	96	434	4.8	0.8	5.9

COOPER, CHARLES H. (**Chuck**) b. September 29, 1926 d. February 5, 1984 Ht. 6-5 Wt. 215 College—West Virginia State/Duquesne

SEASON—TEAM	G	GS	MIN	FGM	FGA	PCT	3FGM	3FGA	PCT	FTM	FTA	PCT	O-RB	D-RB	TOT	AST	PF	DQ	STL	TO	BLK	PTS	RPG	APG	PPG
50-51—Boston	66	—	—	207	601	.344	—	—	—	201	267	.753	—	—	562	174	219	7	—	—	—	615	8.5	2.6	9.3
51-52—Boston	66	—	1976	197	545	.361	—	—	—	149	201	.741	—	—	502	134	219	8	—	—	—	543	7.6	2.0	8.2
52-53—Boston	70	—	1994	157	466	.337	—	—	—	144	190	.758	—	—	439	112	258	11	—	—	—	458	6.3	1.6	6.5
53-54—Boston	70	—	1101	78	261	.299	—	—	—	78	116	.672	—	—	304	74	150	1	—	—	—	234	4.3	1.1	3.3
54-55—Milwaukee	70	—	1749	193	569	.339	—	—	—	187	249	.751	—	—	385	151	210	8	—	—	—	573	5.5	2.2	8.2
55-56—St. L.-Ft. Wayne	67	—	1144	101	308	.328	—	—	—	100	133	.752	—	—	239	89	140	0	—	—	—	302	3.6	1.3	4.5
REG. SEASON TOTALS	409	—	7964	933	2750	.339	—	—	—	859	1156	.743	—	—	2431	734	1196	35	—	—	—	2725	5.9	1.8	6.7
PLAYOFF TOTALS	26	—	490	44	127	.346	—	—	—	51	65	.785	—	—	116	27	78	5	—	—	—	139	4.5	1.0	5.3

COOPER, JOSEPH EDWARD (**Joe**) b. September 1, 1957   Ht. 6-10 Wt. 230 College—Howard (Tex.)/Tulsa/Colorado

SEASON—TEAM	G	GS	MIN	FGM	FGA	PCT	3FGM	3FGA	PCT	FTM	FTA	PCT	O-RB	D-RB	TOT	AST	PF	DQ	STL	TO	BLK	PTS	RPG	APG	PPG
81-82—New Jersey	1	0	11	1	2	.500	0	0	—	0	0	—	1	1	2	0	2	0	0	1	0	2	2.0	0.0	2.0
82-83—L.A.-Wash.-S.D.	20	4	333	37	72	.514	0	0	—	16	29	.552	42	44	86	17	49	0	9	32	20	90	4.3	0.9	4.5
84-85—Seattle	3	1	45	7	15	.467	0	0	—	3	6	.500	3	6	9	2	7	1	2	0	1	17	3.0	0.7	5.7
REG. SEASON TOTALS	24	5	389	45	89	.506	0	0	—	19	35	.543	46	51	97	19	58	1	11	33	21	109	4.0	0.8	4.5

COOPER, MICHAEL JEROME b. April 15, 1956   Ht. 6-7 Wt. 170 College—Pasadena CC/New Mexico

SEASON—TEAM	G	GS	MIN	FGM	FGA	PCT	3FGM	3FGA	PCT	FTM	FTA	PCT	O-RB	D-RB	TOT	AST	PF	DQ	STL	TO	BLK	PTS	RPG	APG	PPG
78-79—Los Angeles	3	—	7	3	6	.500	—		—	0	0	—	0	0	0	0	1	0	1	1	0	6	0.0	0.0	2.0
79-80—Los Angeles	82	—	1973	303	578	.524	5	20	.250	111	143	.776	101	128	229	221	215	3	86	142	38	722	2.8	2.7	8.8
80-81—Los Angeles	81	—	2625	321	654	.491	4	19	.211	117	149	.785	121	215	336	332	249	4	133	164	78	763	4.1	4.1	9.4
81-82—Los Angeles	76	14	2197	383	741	.517	2	17	.118	139	171	.813	84	185	269	230	216	1	120	151	61	907	3.5	3.0	11.9
82-83—Los Angeles	82	3	2148	266	497	.535	5	21	.238	102	130	.785	82	192	274	315	208	0	115	128	50	639	3.3	3.8	7.8
83-84—Los Angeles	82	9	2387	273	549	.497	38	121	.314	155	185	.838	53	209	262	482	267	3	113	148	67	739	3.2	5.9	9.0
84-85—L.A. Lakers	82	20	2189	276	593	.465	35	123	.285	115	133	.865	56	199	255	429	208	0	93	156	49	702	3.1	5.2	8.6
85-86—L.A. Lakers	82	15	2269	274	606	.452	63	163	.387	147	170	.865	44	200	244	466	238	2	89	151	43	758	3.0	5.7	9.2
86-87—L.A. Lakers	82	2	2253	322	736	.438	89	231	.385	126	148	.851	58	196	254	373	199	1	78	102	43	859	3.1	4.5	10.5
87-88—L.A. Lakers	61	8	1793	189	482	.392	57	178	.320	97	113	.858	50	178	228	289	136	1	66	101	26	532	3.7	4.7	8.7
88-89—L.A. Lakers	80	13	1943	213	494	.431	80	210	.381	81	93	.871	33	158	191	314	186	0	72	94	32	587	2.4	3.9	7.3
89-90—L.A. Lakers	80	10	1851	191	493	.387	50	157	.318	83	94	.883	59	168	227	215	206	1	67	91	36	515	2.8	2.7	6.4
REG. SEASON TOTALS	873	94	23635	3014	6429	.469	428	1260	.340	1273	1529	.833	741	2028	2769	3666	2329	16	1033	1429	523	7729	3.2	4.2	8.9
PLAYOFF TOTALS	168	26	4744	582	1244	.468	124	316	.392	293	355	.825	152	422	574	703	474	2	203	252	96	1581	3.4	4.2	9.4

COOPER, SAMUEL DUANE (**Duane**) b. June 25, 1969   Ht. 6-1 Wt. 185 College—USC

SEASON—TEAM	G	GS	MIN	FGM	FGA	PCT	3FGM	3FGA	PCT	FTM	FTA	PCT	O-RB	D-RB	TOT	AST	PF	DQ	STL	TO	BLK	PTS	RPG	APG	PPG
92-93—L.A. Lakers	65	0	645	62	158	.392	7	30	.233	25	35	.714	13	37	50	150	66	0	18	69	2	156	0.8	2.3	2.4
93-94—Phoenix	23	2	136	18	41	.439	1	7	.143	11	15	.733	2	7	9	28	12	0	3	20	0	48	0.4	1.2	2.1
REG. SEASON TOTALS	88	2	781	80	199	.402	8	37	.216	36	50	.720	15	44	59	178	78	0	21	89	2	204	0.7	2.0	2.3
PLAYOFF TOTALS	2	0	4	0	6	.000	0	3	.000	0	0	—	2	0	2	1	0	0	0	0	0	0	1.0	0.5	0.0

COPA, THOMAS JAMES (**Tom**) b. October 30, 1964   Ht. 6-10 Wt. 275 College—Marquette

SEASON—TEAM	G	GS	MIN	FGM	FGA	PCT	3FGM	3FGA	PCT	FTM	FTA	PCT	O-RB	D-RB	TOT	AST	PF	DQ	STL	TO	BLK	PTS	RPG	APG	PPG
91-92—San Antonio	33	1	132	22	40	.550	0	0	—	4	13	.308	14	22	36	3	29	0	2	8	6	48	1.1	0.1	1.5
REG. SEASON TOTALS	33	1	132	22	40	.550	0	0	—	4	13	.308	14	22	36	3	29	0	2	8	6	48	1.1	0.1	1.5

COPELAND, HOLLIS ALPHONSO JR. b. December 20, 1955   Ht. 6-6 Wt. 180 College—Rutgers

SEASON—TEAM	G	GS	MIN	FGM	FGA	PCT	3FGM	3FGA	PCT	FTM	FTA	PCT	O-RB	D-RB	TOT	AST	PF	DQ	STL	TO	BLK	PTS	RPG	APG	PPG
79-80—New York	75	—	1142	182	368	.495	0	2	.000	63	86	.733	70	86	156	80	154	0	61	84	25	427	2.1	1.1	5.7
81-82—New York	18	0	118	16	38	.421	0	0	—	5	6	.833	3	2	5	9	19	0	4	4	2	37	0.3	0.5	2.1
REG. SEASON TOTALS	93	0	1260	198	406	.488	0	2	.000	68	92	.739	73	88	161	89	173	0	65	88	27	464	1.7	1.0	5.0

COPELAND, LANARD b. July 16, 1965   Ht. 6-6 Wt. 210 College—Georgia State

SEASON—TEAM	G	GS	MIN	FGM	FGA	PCT	3FGM	3FGA	PCT	FTM	FTA	PCT	O-RB	D-RB	TOT	AST	PF	DQ	STL	TO	BLK	PTS	RPG	APG	PPG
89-90—Philadelphia	23	0	110	31	68	.456	1	5	.200	11	14	.786	4	6	10	9	12	0	1	19	1	74	0.4	0.4	3.2
91-92—L.A. Clippers	10	0	48	7	23	.304	0	2	.000	2	2	1.000	1	6	7	5	5	0	2	4	0	16	0.7	0.5	1.6
REG. SEASON TOTALS	33	0	158	38	91	.418	1	7	.143	13	16	.813	5	12	17	14	17	0	3	23	1	90	0.5	0.4	2.7
PLAYOFF TOTALS	4	0	9	2	6	.333	0	0	—	0	0	—	0	1	1	—	1	0	0	1	0	4	0.3	0.0	1.0

CORBIN, TYRONE KENNEDY b. December 31, 1962   Ht. 6-6 Wt. 220 College—DePaul

SEASON—TEAM	G	GS	MIN	FGM	FGA	PCT	3FGM	3FGA	PCT	FTM	FTA	PCT	O-RB	D-RB	TOT	AST	PF	DQ	STL	TO	BLK	PTS	RPG	APG	PPG
85-86—San Antonio	16	0	174	27	64	.422	0	1	.000	10	14	.714	11	14	25	11	21	0	11	12	2	64	1.6	0.7	4.0
86-87—S.A.-Clev.	63	15	1170	156	381	.409	1	4	.250	91	124	.734	88	127	215	97	129	0	55	66	5	404	3.4	1.5	6.4
87-88—Clev.-Phoenix	84	5	1739	257	525	.490	1	6	.167	110	138	.797	127	223	350	115	181	2	72	104	18	625	4.2	1.4	7.4
88-89—Phoenix	77	30	1655	245	454	.540	0	2	.000	141	179	.788	176	222	398	118	222	2	82	92	13	631	5.2	1.5	8.2
89-90—Minnesota	82	80	3011	521	1083	.481	0	11	.000	161	209	.770	219	385	604	216	288	5	175	143	41	1203	7.4	2.6	14.7
90-91—Minnesota	82	82	3196	587	1311	.448	2	10	.200	296	371	.798	185	404	589	347	257	3	162	209	53	1472	7.2	4.2	18.0
91-92—Minn.-Utah	80	9	2207	303	630	.481	0	4	.000	174	201	.866	163	309	472	140	193	1	82	97	20	780	5.9	1.8	9.8
92-93—Utah	82	58	2555	385	766	.503	0	5	.000	180	218	.826	194	325	519	173	252	3	108	108	32	950	6.3	2.1	11.6
93-94—Utah	82	17	2149	268	588	.456	6	29	.207	117	144	.813	150	239	389	122	212	0	99	92	24	659	4.7	1.5	8.0
REG. SEASON TOTALS	648	296	17856	2749	5802	.474	10	72	.139	1280	1598	.801	1313	2248	3561	1339	1755	16	846	923	208	6788	5.5	2.1	10.5
PLAYOFF TOTALS	50	23	1345	179	383	.467	4	14	.286	86	111	.775	123	168	291	68	128	0	60	49	11	448	5.8	1.4	9.0

CORCHIANI, CHRISTOPHER (**Chris**) b. March 28, 1968   Ht. 6-1 Wt. 185 College—North Carolina State

SEASON—TEAM	G	GS	MIN	FGM	FGA	PCT	3FGM	3FGA	PCT	FTM	FTA	PCT	O-RB	D-RB	TOT	AST	PF	DQ	STL	TO	BLK	PTS	RPG	APG	PPG
91-92—Orlando	51	1	741	77	193	.399	10	37	.270	91	104	.875	18	60	78	141	94	0	45	74	2	255	1.5	2.8	5.0
92-93—Orlando-Wash.	10	0	105	14	24	.583	0	3	.000	16	21	.762	1	6	7	16	18	0	6	8	0	44	0.7	1.6	4.4
93-94—Boston	51	0	467	40	94	.426	11	38	.289	26	38	.684	8	36	44	86	47	0	22	38	2	117	0.9	1.7	2.3
REG. SEASON TOTALS	112	1	1313	131	311	.421	21	78	.269	133	163	.816	27	102	129	243	159	0	73	120	4	416	1.2	2.2	3.7

CORLEY, KENNETH (**Ken**) b. 1921   Ht. 6-4½ Wt. 210 College—Oklahoma State

SEASON—TEAM	G	GS	MIN	FGM	FGA	PCT	3FGM	3FGA	PCT	FTM	FTA	PCT	O-RB	D-RB	TOT	AST	PF	DQ	STL	TO	BLK	PTS	RPG	APG	PPG
46-47—Cleveland	3	—	—	0	0	—	—	—	—	0	0	—	—	—	—	0	0	—	—	—	—	0	—	0.0	0.0
REG. SEASON TOTALS	3	—	—	0	0	—	—	—	—	0	0	—	—	—	—	0	0	—	—	—	—	0	—	0.0	0.0

CORLEY, RAYMOND CHARLES (**Ray**) b. January 1, 1928   Ht. 6-0 Wt. 180 College—Notre Dame/Georgetown

SEASON—TEAM	G	GS	MIN	FGM	FGA	PCT	3FGM	3FGA	PCT	FTM	FTA	PCT	O-RB	D-RB	TOT	AST	PF	DQ	STL	TO	BLK	PTS	RPG	APG	PPG
49-50—Syracuse	60	—	—	117	370	.316	—	—	—	75	122	.615	—	—	—	109	81	—	—	—	—	309	—	1.8	5.2
50-51—Tri-Cities	18	—	—	29	85	.341	—	—	—	16	29	.552	—	—	43	38	26	0	—	—	—	74	2.4	2.1	4.1
52-53—Fort Wayne	8	—	65	3	24	.125	—	—	—	5	6	.833	—	—	5	5	18	0	—	—	—	11	0.6	0.6	1.4
REG. SEASON TOTALS	86	—	65	149	479	.311	—	—	—	96	157	.611	—	—	48	152	125	0	—	—	—	394	1.8	1.8	4.6
PLAYOFF TOTALS	6	—	0	6	36	.167	—	—	—	5	11	.455	—	—	—	10	5	0	—	—	—	17	—	1.7	2.8

CORZINE, DAVID JOHN (**Dave**) b. April 25, 1956   Ht. 6-11 Wt. 255 College—DePaul

SEASON—TEAM	G	GS	MIN	FGM	FGA	PCT	3FGM	3FGA	PCT	FTM	FTA	PCT	O-RB	D-RB	TOT	AST	PF	DQ	STL	TO	BLK	PTS	RPG	APG	PPG
78-79—Washington	59	—	532	63	118	.534	—	—	—	49	63	.778	52	95	147	49	67	0	10	53	14	175	2.5	0.8	3.0
79-80—Washington	78	—	826	90	216	.417	0	0	—	45	68	.662	104	166	270	63	120	1	9	60	31	225	3.5	0.8	2.9
80-81—San Antonio	82	—	1960	366	747	.490	0	3	.000	125	175	.714	228	408	636	117	212	0	42	131	99	857	7.8	1.4	10.5
81-82—San Antonio	82	21	2189	336	648	.519	1	4	.250	159	213	.746	211	418	629	130	235	3	33	139	126	832	7.7	1.6	10.1
82-83—Chicago	82	71	2496	457	920	.497	0	2	.000	232	322	.720	243	474	717	154	242	4	47	228	109	1146	8.7	1.9	14.0
83-84—Chicago	82	82	2674	385	824	.467	3	9	.333	231	275	.840	169	406	575	202	227	3	58	175	120	1004	7.0	2.5	12.2
84-85—Chicago	82	50	2062	276	568	.486	0	1	.000	149	200	.745	130	292	422	140	189	2	32	124	64	701	5.1	1.7	8.5
85-86—Chicago	67	4	1709	255	519	.491	3	12	.250	127	171	.743	132	301	433	150	133	0	28	104	53	640	6.5	2.2	9.6
86-87—Chicago	82	39	2287	294	619	.475	0	5	.000	95	129	.736	199	341	540	209	202	1	38	114	87	683	6.6	2.5	8.3
87-88—Chicago	80	32	2328	344	715	.481	1	9	.111	115	153	.752	170	357	527	154	149	1	36	109	95	804	6.6	1.9	10.1
88-89—Chicago	81	7	1483	203	440	.461	2	8	.250	71	96	.740	92	223	315	103	134	0	29	93	45	479	3.9	1.3	5.9
89-90—Orlando	6	3	79	11	29	.379	0	0	—	0	2	.000	7	11	18	2	7	0	2	8	0	22	3.0	0.3	3.7
90-91—Seattle	28	0	147	17	38	.447	0	0	—	13	22	.591	10	23	33	4	18	0	5	2	5	47	1.2	0.1	1.7
REG. SEASON TOTALS	891	309	20772	3097	6401	.484	10	53	.189	1411	1889	.747	1747	3515	5262	1477	1935	15	369	1340	848	7615	5.9	1.7	8.5
PLAYOFF TOTALS	68	20	1332	180	396	.455	0	0	—	70	99	.707	115	215	330	71	137	0	23	79	37	430	4.9	1.0	6.3

COSTELLO, LAWRENCE RONALD (**Larry**) b. July 2, 1931   Ht. 6-1 Wt. 190 College—Niagara

SEASON—TEAM	G	GS	MIN	FGM	FGA	PCT	3FGM	3FGA	PCT	FTM	FTA	PCT	O-RB	D-RB	TOT	AST	PF	DQ	STL	TO	BLK	PTS	RPG	APG	PPG
54-55—Philadelphia	19	—	463	46	139	.331	—	—	—	26	32	.813	—	—	49	78	37	0	—	—	—	118	2.6	4.1	6.2
56-57—Philadelphia	72	—	2111	186	497	.374	—	—	—	175	222	.788	—	—	323	236	182	2	—	—	—	547	4.5	3.3	7.6
57-58—Syracuse	72	—	2746	378	888	.426	—	—	—	320	378	.847	—	—	378	317	246	3	—	—	—	1076	5.3	4.4	14.9
58-59—Syracuse	70	—	2750	414	948	.437	—	—	—	280	349	.802	—	—	365	379	263	7	—	—	—	1108	5.2	5.4	15.8
59-60—Syracuse	71	—	2469	372	822	.453	—	—	—	249	289	.862	—	—	388	449	234	4	—	—	—	993	5.5	6.3	14.0
60-61—Syracuse	75	—	2167	407	844	.482	—	—	—	270	338	.799	—	—	292	413	286	9	—	—	—	1084	3.9	5.5	14.5
61-62—Syracuse	63	—	1854	310	726	.427	—	—	—	247	295	.837	—	—	245	359	220	5	—	—	—	867	3.9	5.7	13.8
62-63—Syracuse	78	—	2066	285	660	.432	—	—	—	288	327	.881	—	—	237	334	263	4	—	—	—	858	3.0	4.3	11.0
63-64—Philadelphia	45	—	1137	191	408	.468	—	—	—	147	170	.865	—	—	105	167	150	3	—	—	—	529	2.3	3.7	11.8
64-65—Philadelphia	64	—	1967	309	695	.445	—	—	—	243	277	.877	—	—	169	275	242	10	—	—	—	861	2.6	4.3	13.5
66-67—Philadelphia	49	—	976	130	293	.444	—	—	—	120	133	.902	—	—	103	140	141	2	—	—	—	380	2.1	2.9	7.8
67-68—Philadelphia	28	—	492	67	148	.453	—	—	—	67	81	.827	—	—	51	68	62	0	—	—	—	201	1.8	2.4	7.2
REG. SEASON TOTALS	706	—	21198	3095	7068	.438	—	—	—	2432	2891	.841	—	—	2705	3215	2326	49	—	—	—	8622	3.8	4.6	12.2
PLAYOFF TOTALS	52	—	1471	198	476	.416	—	—	—	196	230	.852	—	—	171	218	210	11	—	—	—	592	3.3	4.2	11.4
ALL-STAR TOTALS	5	—	71	11	32	.344	—	—	—	2	2	1.000	—	—	9	11	8	0	—	—	—	24	1.8	2.2	4.8

COTTON, JOHN J. (**Jack**) b. October 15, 1924   Ht. 6-7 Wt. 205 College—Miles CC/Wyoming

SEASON—TEAM	G	GS	MIN	FGM	FGA	PCT	3FGM	3FGA	PCT	FTM	FTA	PCT	O-RB	D-RB	TOT	AST	PF	DQ	STL	TO	BLK	PTS	RPG	APG	PPG
48-49—Denver (N)	57	—	—	71	—	—	—	—	—	67	121	.554	—	—	—	—	110	—	—	—	—	209	—	—	3.7
49-50—Denver	54	—	—	97	332	.292	—	—	—	82	161	.509	—	—	65	—	184	—	—	—	—	276	—	1.2	5.1
REG. NBA TOTALS	54	—	—	97	332	.292	—	—	—	82	161	.509	—	—	65	—	184	—	—	—	—	276	—	1.2	5.1
REG. NBL TOTALS	57	—	—	71	—	—	—	—	—	67	121	.554	—	—	—	—	110	—	—	—	—	209	—	—	3.7

COUGHRAN, JOHN DOUGLAS b. September 12, 1951   Ht. 6-7 Wt. 225 College—California

SEASON—TEAM	G	GS	MIN	FGM	FGA	PCT	3FGM	3FGA	PCT	FTM	FTA	PCT	O-RB	D-RB	TOT	AST	PF	DQ	STL	TO	BLK	PTS	RPG	APG	PPG
79-80—Golden State	24	—	160	29	81	.358	2	9	.222	8	14	.571	2	17	19	12	24	0	7	13	1	68	0.8	0.5	2.8
REG. SEASON TOTALS	24	—	160	29	81	.358	2	9	.222	8	14	.571	2	17	19	12	24	0	7	13	1	68	0.8	0.5	2.8

COUNTS, MEL GRANT (Goose) b. October 16, 1941 Ht. 7-0 Wt. 230 College—Oregon State

SEASON—TEAM	G	GS	MIN	FGM	FGA	PCT	3FGM	3FGA	PCT	FTM	FTA	PCT	O-RB	D-RB	TOT	AST	PF	DQ	STL	TO	BLK	PTS	RPG	APG	PPG
64-65—Boston	54	—	572	100	272	.368	—	—	—	58	74	.784	—	—	265	19	134	1	—	—	—	258	4.9	0.4	4.8
65-66—Boston	67	—	1021	221	549	.403	—	—	—	120	145	.828	—	—	432	50	207	5	—	—	—	562	6.4	0.7	8.4
66-67—Balt.-L.A.	56	—	860	177	419	.422	—	—	—	69	94	.734	—	—	344	52	183	6	—	—	—	423	6.1	0.9	7.6
67-68—Los Angeles	82	—	1739	384	808	.475	—	—	—	190	254	.748	—	—	732	139	309	6	—	—	—	958	8.9	1.7	11.7
68-69—Los Angeles	77	—	1866	390	867	.450	—	—	—	178	221	.805	—	—	600	109	223	5	—	—	—	958	7.8	1.4	12.4
69-70—Los Angeles	81	—	2193	434	1017	.427	—	—	—	156	201	.776	—	—	683	160	304	7	—	—	—	1024	8.4	2.0	12.6
70-71—Phoenix	80	—	1669	365	799	.457	—	—	—	149	198	.753	—	—	503	136	279	8	—	—	—	879	6.3	1.7	11.0
71-72—Phoenix	76	—	906	147	344	.427	—	—	—	101	140	.721	—	—	257	96	159	2	—	—	—	395	3.4	1.3	5.2
72-73—Phil.-L.A.	66	—	658	132	294	.449	—	—	—	39	58	.672	—	—	253	65	106	1	—	—	—	303	3.8	1.0	4.6
73-74—Los Angeles	45	—	499	61	167	.365	—	—	—	24	33	.727	56	90	146	54	85	2	20	—	23	146	3.2	1.2	3.2
74-75—New Orleans	75	—	1421	217	495	.438	—	—	—	86	113	.761	102	339	441	182	196	0	49	—	43	520	5.9	2.4	6.9
75-76—New Orleans	30	—	319	37	91	.407	—	—	—	16	21	.762	27	73	100	38	74	1	16	—	8	90	3.3	1.3	3.0
REG. SEASON TOTALS	789	—	13723	2665	6122	.435	—	—	—	1186	1552	.764	185	502	4756	1100	2259	44	85	—	74	6516	6.0	1.4	8.3
PLAYOFF TOTALS	85	—	1462	255	599	.426	—	—	—	138	178	.775	2	4	519	100	263	5	2	—	2	648	6.1	1.2	7.6

COURTIN, STEPHEN EDWARD (Steve) b. September 21, 1942 Ht. 6-1 Wt. 190 College—St. Joseph's (Pa.)

SEASON—TEAM	G	GS	MIN	FGM	FGA	PCT	3FGM	3FGA	PCT	FTM	FTA	PCT	O-RB	D-RB	TOT	AST	PF	DQ	STL	TO	BLK	PTS	RPG	APG	PPG
64-65—Philadelphia	24	—	317	42	103	.408	—	—	—	17	21	.810	—	—	22	22	44	0	—	—	—	101	0.9	0.9	4.2
REG. SEASON TOTALS	24	—	317	42	103	.408	—	—	—	17	21	.810	—	—	22	22	44	0	—	—	—	101	0.9	0.9	4.2

COURTNEY, JOSEPH PIERRE (Joe) b. October 17, 1969 Ht. 6-8 Wt. 235 College—Mississippi State/Southern Mississippi

SEASON—TEAM	G	GS	MIN	FGM	FGA	PCT	3FGM	3FGA	PCT	FTM	FTA	PCT	O-RB	D-RB	TOT	AST	PF	DQ	STL	TO	BLK	PTS	RPG	APG	PPG
92-93—Chicago-G.S.	12	0	104	13	32	.406	0	0	—	7	9	.778	4	15	19	3	17	0	5	6	5	33	1.6	0.3	2.8
93-94—Phoenix-Milw.	52	1	345	67	148	.453	2	3	.667	32	47	.681	28	28	56	15	44	0	10	21	12	168	1.1	0.3	3.2
REG. SEASON TOTALS	64	1	449	80	180	.444	2	3	.667	39	56	.696	32	43	75	18	61	0	15	27	17	201	1.2	0.3	3.1

COUSY, ROBERT JOSEPH (Bob) b. August 9, 1928 Ht. 6-1½ Wt. 175 College—Holy Cross

SEASON—TEAM	G	GS	MIN	FGM	FGA	PCT	3FGM	3FGA	PCT	FTM	FTA	PCT	O-RB	D-RB	TOT	AST	PF	DQ	STL	TO	BLK	PTS	RPG	APG	PPG
50-51—Boston	69	—	—	401	1138	.352	—	—	—	276	365	.756	—	—	474	341	185	2	—	—	—	1078	6.9	4.9	15.6
51-52—Boston	66	—	2681	512	1388	.369	—	—	—	409	506	.808	—	—	421	441	190	5	—	—	—	1433	6.4	6.7	21.7
52-53—Boston	71	—	2945	464	1320	.352	—	—	—	479	587	.816	—	—	449	547	227	4	—	—	—	1407	6.3	7.7	19.8
53-54—Boston	72	—	2857	486	1262	.385	—	—	—	411	522	.787	—	—	394	518	201	3	—	—	—	1383	5.5	7.2	19.2
54-55—Boston	71	—	2747	522	1316	.397	—	—	—	460	570	.807	—	—	424	557	165	1	—	—	—	1504	6.0	7.8	21.2
55-56—Boston	72	—	2767	440	1223	.360	—	—	—	476	564	.844	—	—	492	642	206	2	—	—	—	1356	6.8	8.9	18.8
56-57—Boston	64	—	2364	478	1264	.378	—	—	—	363	442	.821	—	—	309	478	134	0	—	—	—	1319	4.8	7.5	20.6
57-58—Boston	65	—	2222	445	1262	.353	—	—	—	277	326	.850	—	—	322	463	136	1	—	—	—	1167	5.0	7.1	18.0
58-59—Boston	65	—	2403	484	1260	.384	—	—	—	329	385	.855	—	—	359	557	135	0	—	—	—	1297	5.5	8.6	20.0
59-60—Boston	75	—	2588	568	1481	.384	—	—	—	319	403	.792	—	—	352	715	146	2	—	—	—	1455	4.7	9.5	19.4
60-61—Boston	76	—	2468	513	1382	.371	—	—	—	352	452	.779	—	—	331	587	196	0	—	—	—	1378	4.4	7.7	18.1
61-62—Boston	75	—	2114	462	1181	.391	—	—	—	251	333	.754	—	—	261	584	135	0	—	—	—	1175	3.5	7.8	15.7
62-63—Boston	76	—	1975	392	988	.397	—	—	—	219	298	.735	—	—	193	515	175	0	—	—	—	1003	2.5	6.8	13.2
69-70—Cincinnati	7	—	34	1	3	.333	—	—	—	3	3	1.000	—	—	5	10	11	0	—	—	—	5	0.7	1.4	0.7
REG. SEASON TOTALS	924	—	30165	6168	16468	.375	—	—	—	4624	5756	.803	—	—	4786	6955	2242	20	—	—	—	16960	5.2	7.5	18.4
PLAYOFF TOTALS	109	—	4120	689	2016	.342	—	—	—	640	799	.801	—	—	546	937	314	4	—	—	—	2018	5.0	8.6	18.5
ALL-STAR TOTALS	13	—	368	52	158	.329	—	—	—	43	51	.843	—	—	78	86	27	2	—	—	—	147	6.0	6.6	11.3

COWENS, DAVID WILLIAM (Dave, Big Red) b. October 25, 1948 Ht. 6-9 Wt. 230 College—Florida State

SEASON—TEAM	G	GS	MIN	FGM	FGA	PCT	3FGM	3FGA	PCT	FTM	FTA	PCT	O-RB	D-RB	TOT	AST	PF	DQ	STL	TO	BLK	PTS	RPG	APG	PPG
70-71—Boston	81	—	3076	550	1302	.422	—	—	—	273	373	.732	—	—	1216	228	350	15	—	—	—	1373	15.0	2.8	17.0
71-72—Boston	79	—	3186	657	1357	.484	—	—	—	175	243	.720	—	—	1203	245	314	10	—	—	—	1489	15.2	3.1	18.8
72-73—Boston	82	—	3425	740	1637	.452	—	—	—	204	262	.779	—	—	1329	333	311	7	—	—	—	1684	16.2	4.1	20.5
73-74—Boston	80	—	3352	645	1475	.437	—	—	—	228	274	.832	264	993	1257	354	294	7	95	—	101	1518	15.7	4.4	19.0
74-75—Boston	65	—	2632	569	1199	.475	—	—	—	191	244	.783	229	729	958	296	243	7	87	—	73	1329	14.7	4.6	20.4
75-76—Boston	78	—	3101	611	1305	.468	—	—	—	257	340	.756	335	911	1246	325	314	10	94	—	71	1479	16.0	4.2	19.0
76-77—Boston	50	—	1888	328	756	.434	—	—	—	162	198	.818	147	550	697	248	181	7	46	—	49	818	13.9	5.0	16.4
77-78—Boston	77	—	3215	598	1220	.490	—	—	—	239	284	.842	248	830	1078	351	297	5	102	217	67	1435	14.0	4.6	18.6
78-79—Boston	68	—	2517	488	1010	.483	—	—	—	151	187	.807	152	500	652	242	263	16	76	174	51	1127	9.6	3.6	16.6
79-80—Boston	66	—	2159	422	932	.453	1	12	.083	95	122	.779	126	408	534	206	216	2	69	108	61	940	8.1	3.1	14.2
82-83—Milwaukee	40	34	1014	136	306	.444	0	2	.000	52	63	.825	73	201	274	82	137	4	30	44	15	324	6.9	2.1	8.1
REG. SEASON TOTALS	766	34	29565	5744	12499	.460	1	14	.071	2027	2590	.783	1574	5122	10444	2910	2920	90	599	543	488	13516	13.6	3.8	17.6
PLAYOFF TOTALS	89	0	3768	733	1627	.451	0	2	.000	218	293	.744	243	674	1285	333	398	15	78	8	56	1684	14.4	3.7	18.9
ALL-STAR TOTALS	6	4	154	33	66	.500	0	0	—	10	14	.714	20	28	81	12	21	0	4	2	1	76	13.5	2.0	12.7

COX, JOHN ARTHUR III (Chubby) b. December 29, 1955 Ht. 6-2 Wt. 180 College—Villanova/San Francisco

SEASON—TEAM	G	GS	MIN	FGM	FGA	PCT	3FGM	3FGA	PCT	FTM	FTA	PCT	O-RB	D-RB	TOT	AST	PF	DQ	STL	TO	BLK	PTS	RPG	APG	PPG
82-83—Washington	7	0	78	13	37	.351	0	2	.000	3	6	.500	7	3	10	6	16	0	0	9	1	29	1.4	0.9	4.1
REG. SEASON TOTALS	7	0	78	13	37	.351	0	2	.000	3	6	.500	7	3	10	6	16	0	0	9	1	29	1.4	0.9	4.1

COX, JOHNNY W. b. November 1, 1936 Ht. 6-4 Wt. 180 College—Kentucky

SEASON—TEAM	G	GS	MIN	FGM	FGA	PCT	3FGM	3FGA	PCT	FTM	FTA	PCT	O-RB	D-RB	TOT	AST	PF	DQ	STL	TO	BLK	PTS	RPG	APG	PPG
62-63—Chicago	73	—	1685	239	568	.421	—	—	—	95	135	.704	—	—	280	142	149	4	—	—	—	573	3.8	1.9	7.8
REG. SEASON TOTALS	73	—	1685	239	568	.421	—	—	—	95	135	.704	—	—	280	142	149	4	—	—	—	573	3.8	1.9	7.8

COX, WESLEY b. January 27, 1955 Ht. 6-6 Wt. 215 College—Louisville

SEASON—TEAM	G	GS	MIN	FGM	FGA	PCT	3FGM	3FGA	PCT	FTM	FTA	PCT	O-RB	D-RB	TOT	AST	PF	DQ	STL	TO	BLK	PTS	RPG	APG	PPG
77-78—Golden State	43	—	453	69	173	.399	—	—	—	58	100	.580	42	101	143	12	82	1	21	36	10	196	3.3	0.3	4.6
78-79—Golden State	31	—	360	53	123	.431	—	—	—	40	92	.435	18	45	63	11	68	0	13	44	5	146	2.0	0.4	4.7
REG. SEASON TOTALS	74	—	813	122	296	.412	—	—	—	98	192	.510	60	146	206	23	150	1	34	80	15	342	2.8	0.3	4.6

CRAWFORD, FREDERICK RUSSELL JR. (**Freddie**) b. December 23, 1940 Ht. 6-4 Wt. 195 College—St. Bonaventure

SEASON—TEAM	G	GS	MIN	FGM	FGA	PCT	3FGM	3FGA	PCT	FTM	FTA	PCT	O-RB	D-RB	TOT	AST	PF	DQ	STL	TO	BLK	PTS	RPG	APG	PPG
66-67—New York	19	—	192	44	116	.379	—	—	—	24	38	.632	—	—	48	12	39	0	—	—	—	112	2.5	0.6	5.9
67-68—N.Y.-L.A.	69	—	1182	224	507	.442	—	—	—	111	179	.620	—	—	195	141	171	1	—	—	—	559	2.8	2.0	8.1
68-69—Los Angeles	81	—	1690	211	454	.465	—	—	—	83	154	.539	—	—	215	154	224	1	—	—	—	505	2.7	1.9	6.2
69-70—Milwaukee	77	—	1331	243	506	.480	—	—	—	101	148	.682	—	—	184	225	181	1	—	—	—	587	2.4	2.9	7.6
70-71—Buffalo-Phil.	51	—	652	110	281	.391	—	—	—	48	98	.490	—	—	104	78	77	0	—	—	—	268	2.0	1.5	5.3
REG. SEASON TOTALS	297	—	5047	832	1864	.446	—	—	—	367	617	.595	—	—	746	610	692	3	—	—	—	2031	2.5	2.1	6.8
PLAYOFF TOTALS	35	—	606	105	252	.417	—	—	—	48	76	.632	—	—	97	73	89	2	—	—	—	258	2.8	2.1	7.4

CREIGHTON, JIM b. April 18, 1950 Ht. 6-8 Wt. 200 College—Colorado

SEASON—TEAM	G	GS	MIN	FGM	FGA	PCT	3FGM	3FGA	PCT	FTM	FTA	PCT	O-RB	D-RB	TOT	AST	PF	DQ	STL	TO	BLK	PTS	RPG	APG	PPG
75-76—Atlanta	32	—	172	12	43	.279	—	—	—	7	16	.438	13	32	45	4	23	0	2	—	9	31	1.4	0.1	1.0
REG. SEASON TOTALS	32	—	172	12	43	.279	—	—	—	7	16	.438	13	32	45	4	23	0	2	—	9	31	1.4	0.1	1.0

CREVIER, RONALD JOSEPH OSCAR CAMILLE (**Ron**) b. August 14, 1958 Ht. 7-0 Wt. 235 College—Boston College

SEASON—TEAM	G	GS	MIN	FGM	FGA	PCT	3FGM	3FGA	PCT	FTM	FTA	PCT	O-RB	D-RB	TOT	AST	PF	DQ	STL	TO	BLK	PTS	RPG	APG	PPG
85-86—G.S.-Detroit	3	0	4	0	3	.000	0	0	—	0	2	.000	1	0	1	0	2	0	0	0	0	0	0.3	0.0	0.0
REG. SEASON TOTALS	3	0	4	0	3	.000	0	0	—	0	2	.000	1	0	1	0	2	0	0	0	0	0	0.3	0.0	0.0

CRISLER, HAROLD JAMES (**Hal**) b. December 31, 1923 Ht. 6-3½ Wt. 215 College—San Jose State/Iowa State

SEASON—TEAM	G	GS	MIN	FGM	FGA	PCT	3FGM	3FGA	PCT	FTM	FTA	PCT	O-RB	D-RB	TOT	AST	PF	DQ	STL	TO	BLK	PTS	RPG	APG	PPG
46-47—Boston	4	—	—	2	6	.333	—	—	—	2	2	1.000	—	—	—	0	6	—	—	—	—	6	—	0.0	1.5
REG. SEASON TOTALS	4	—	—	2	6	.333	—	—	—	2	2	1.000	—	—	—	0	6	—	—	—	—	6	—	0.0	1.5

CRISS, CHARLES WASHINGTON JR. (**Charlie**) b. November 6, 1948 Ht. 5-8 Wt. 165 College—New Mexico JC/New Mexico State

SEASON—TEAM	G	GS	MIN	FGM	FGA	PCT	3FGM	3FGA	PCT	FTM	FTA	PCT	O-RB	D-RB	TOT	AST	PF	DQ	STL	TO	BLK	PTS	RPG	APG	PPG
77-78—Atlanta	77	—	1935	319	751	.425	—	—	—	236	296	.797	24	97	121	294	143	0	108	150	5	874	1.6	3.8	11.4
78-79—Atlanta	54	—	879	109	289	.377	—	—	—	67	86	.779	19	41	60	138	70	0	41	79	3	285	1.1	2.6	5.3
79-80—Atlanta	81	—	1794	249	578	.431	1	17	.059	172	212	.811	27	89	116	246	133	0	74	130	4	671	1.4	3.0	8.3
80-81—Atlanta	66	—	1708	220	485	.454	1	21	.048	185	214	.864	26	74	100	283	87	0	61	134	3	626	1.5	4.3	9.5
81-82—Atlanta-S.D.	55	20	1392	222	498	.446	10	29	.345	141	159	.887	13	69	82	187	96	0	44	82	6	595	1.5	3.4	10.8
82-83—Milwaukee	66	0	922	169	375	.451	6	31	.194	68	76	.895	14	65	79	127	44	0	27	44	0	412	1.2	1.9	6.2
83-84—Milw.-Atlanta	15	0	215	20	52	.385	1	6	.167	12	16	.750	5	15	20	38	11	0	8	10	0	53	1.3	2.5	3.5
84-85—Atlanta	4	2	115	7	17	.412	0	2	.000	4	6	.667	2	12	14	22	5	0	3	11	0	18	3.5	5.5	4.5
REG. SEASON TOTALS	418	22	8960	1315	3045	.432	19	106	.179	885	1065	.831	130	462	592	1335	589	0	366	640	21	3534	1.4	3.2	8.5
PLAYOFF TOTALS	25	0	432	66	146	.452	1	4	.250	44	49	.898	3	25	28	53	34	0	22	22	1	177	1.1	2.1	7.1

CRITCHFIELD, RUSSELL DEAN (**Rusty**) b. June 27, 1946 Ht. 5-10 Wt. 150 College—California

SEASON—TEAM	G	GS	MIN	FGM	FGA	PCT	3FGM	3FGA	PCT	FTM	FTA	PCT	O-RB	D-RB	TOT	AST	PF	DQ	STL	TO	BLK	PTS	RPG	APG	PPG
68-69—Oakland (A)	47	—	439	53	147	.361	0	3	.000	55	84	.655	—	—	29	54	41	0	—	33	—	161	0.6	1.1	3.4
REG. ABA TOTALS	47	—	439	53	147	.361	0	3	.000	55	84	.655	—	—	29	54	41	0	—	33	—	161	0.6	1.1	3.4
ABA PLAYOFF TOTALS	5	—	19	1	6	.167	0	0	—	2	6	.333	—	—	2	7	6	0	—	5	—	4	0.4	1.4	0.8

CRITE, WINSTON ARNEL b. June 20, 1965 Ht. 6-7 Wt. 235 College—Texas A&M

SEASON—TEAM	G	GS	MIN	FGM	FGA	PCT	3FGM	3FGA	PCT	FTM	FTA	PCT	O-RB	D-RB	TOT	AST	PF	DQ	STL	TO	BLK	PTS	RPG	APG	PPG
87-88—Phoenix	29	0	258	34	68	.500	0	0	—	19	25	.760	27	37	64	15	42	0	5	25	8	87	2.2	0.5	3.0
88-89—Phoenix	2	0	6	0	3	.000	0	0	—	0	0	—	1	0	1	0	1	0	0	1	0	0	0.5	0.0	0.0
REG. SEASON TOTALS	31	0	264	34	71	.479	0	0	—	19	25	.760	28	37	65	15	43	0	5	26	8	87	2.1	0.5	2.8

CROCKER, JAMES DILLARD (**Dillard**) b. January 19, 1925   Ht. 6-4 Wt. 205 College—Western Michigan

SEASON—TEAM	G	GS	MIN	FGM	FGA	PCT	3FGM	3FGA	PCT	FTM	FTA	PCT	O-RB	D-RB	TOT	AST	PF	DQ	STL	TO	BLK	PTS	RPG	APG	PPG
48-49—Detroit-And. (N)	51	—	—	101	—	—	—	—	—	95	131	.725	—	—	—	134	—	—	—	—	—	297	—	—	5.8
48-49—Fort Wayne	2	—	—	1	4	.250	—	—	—	4	6	.667	—	—	0	3	—	—	—	—	—	6	—	0.0	3.0
49-50—Denver	53	—	—	245	840	.292	—	—	—	233	317	.735	—	—	85	223	—	—	—	—	—	723	—	1.6	13.6
51-52—Ind.-Milw.	38	—	783	98	279	.351	—	—	—	97	145	.669	—	—	111	57	132	7	—	—	—	293	2.9	1.5	7.7
52-53—Milwaukee	61	—	776	100	284	.352	—	—	—	130	189	.688	—	—	104	63	199	11	—	—	—	330	1.7	1.0	5.4
REG. NBA TOTALS	154	—	1559	444	1407	.316	—	—	—	464	657	.706	—	—	215	205	557	18	—	—	—	1352	2.2	1.3	8.8
REG. NBL TOTALS	51	—	—	101	—	—	—	—	—	95	131	.725	—	—	—	134	—	—	—	—	—	297	—	—	5.8
NBL PLAYOFF TOTALS	6	—	—	5	—	—	—	—	—	3	8	.375	—	—	—	10	—	—	—	—	—	13	—	—	2.2

CROFT, ROBERT ALEXANDER (**Bobby**) b. August 10, 1947   Ht. 6-10½ Wt. 210 College—Tennessee

SEASON—TEAM	G	GS	MIN	FGM	FGA	PCT	3FGM	3FGA	PCT	FTM	FTA	PCT	O-RB	D-RB	TOT	AST	PF	DQ	STL	TO	BLK	PTS	RPG	APG	PPG
70-71—Ken.-Texas (A)	62	—	739	126	348	.362	0	2	.000	73	112	.652	—	—	206	41	137	—	—	—	—	325	3.3	0.7	5.2
REG. ABA TOTALS	62	—	739	126	348	.362	0	2	.000	73	112	.652	—	—	206	41	137	—	—	—	—	325	3.3	0.7	5.2
ABA PLAYOFF TOTALS	4	—	55	7	23	.304	1	1	1.000	5	7	.714	—	—	14	3	6	—	—	—	—	20	3.5	0.8	5.0

CROMPTON, JEFFREY (**Geoff**) b. July 4, 1955   Ht. 6-11½ Wt. 280 College—North Carolina

SEASON—TEAM	G	GS	MIN	FGM	FGA	PCT	3FGM	3FGA	PCT	FTM	FTA	PCT	O-RB	D-RB	TOT	AST	PF	DQ	STL	TO	BLK	PTS	RPG	APG	PPG
78-79—Denver	20	—	88	10	26	.385	—	—	—	6	12	.500	6	17	23	5	19	0	0	12	3	26	1.2	0.3	1.3
80-81—Portland	6	—	33	4	8	.500	0	0	—	1	5	.200	7	11	18	2	4	0	0	5	2	9	3.0	0.3	1.5
81-82—Milwaukee	35	1	203	11	32	.344	0	0	—	6	15	.400	10	31	41	13	39	0	6	17	12	28	1.2	0.4	0.8
82-83—San Antonio	14	0	148	14	34	.412	0	0	—	3	5	.600	18	30	48	7	25	0	3	5	5	31	3.4	0.5	2.2
83-84—Cleveland	7	0	23	1	8	.125	0	0	—	3	6	.500	6	3	9	1	4	0	1	4	1	5	1.3	0.1	0.7
REG. SEASON TOTALS	82	1	495	40	108	.370	0	0	—	19	43	.442	47	92	139	28	91	0	10	43	23	99	1.7	0.3	1.2

CROSBY, TERRY DALE b. January 4, 1957   Ht. 6-4 Wt. 195 College—Tennessee

SEASON—TEAM	G	GS	MIN	FGM	FGA	PCT	3FGM	3FGA	PCT	FTM	FTA	PCT	O-RB	D-RB	TOT	AST	PF	DQ	STL	TO	BLK	PTS	RPG	APG	PPG
79-80—Kansas City	4	—	28	2	4	.500	0	0	—	2	2	1.000	0	1	1	7	4	0	0	5	0	6	0.3	1.8	1.5
REG. SEASON TOTALS	4	—	28	2	4	.500	0	0	—	2	2	1.000	0	1	1	7	4	0	0	5	0	6	0.3	1.8	1.5

CROSS, JEFFREY A. (**Jeff**) b. September 1, 1961   Ht. 6-10 Wt. 240 College—Maine

SEASON—TEAM	G	GS	MIN	FGM	FGA	PCT	3FGM	3FGA	PCT	FTM	FTA	PCT	O-RB	D-RB	TOT	AST	PF	DQ	STL	TO	BLK	PTS	RPG	APG	PPG
85-86—L.A. Clippers	21	0	128	6	24	.250	0	0	—	14	25	.560	9	21	30	1	38	0	2	6	3	26	1.4	0.0	1.2
REG. SEASON TOTALS	21	0	128	6	24	.250	0	0	—	14	25	.560	9	21	30	1	38	0	2	6	3	26	1.4	0.0	1.2

CROSS, PETER MICHAEL (**Pete**) b. March 28, 1948 d. January 2, 1977 Ht. 6-9 Wt. 240 College—San Francisco

SEASON—TEAM	G	GS	MIN	FGM	FGA	PCT	3FGM	3FGA	PCT	FTM	FTA	PCT	O-RB	D-RB	TOT	AST	PF	DQ	STL	TO	BLK	PTS	RPG	APG	PPG
70-71—Seattle	79	—	2194	245	554	.442	—	—	—	140	203	.690	—	—	949	113	212	2	—	—	—	630	12.0	1.4	8.0
71-72—Seattle	74	—	1424	152	355	.428	—	—	—	103	140	.736	—	—	509	63	135	2	—	—	—	407	6.9	0.9	5.5
72-73—K.C.-Omaha-Seattle	29	—	157	6	25	.240	—	—	—	8	18	.444	—	—	61	11	29	0	—	—	—	20	2.1	0.4	0.7
REG. SEASON TOTALS	182	—	3775	403	934	.431	—	—	—	251	361	.695	—	—	1519	187	376	4	—	—	—	1057	8.3	1.0	5.8

CROSS, RUSSELL JR. b. September 5, 1961   Ht. 6-10 Wt. 215 College—Purdue

SEASON—TEAM	G	GS	MIN	FGM	FGA	PCT	3FGM	3FGA	PCT	FTM	FTA	PCT	O-RB	D-RB	TOT	AST	PF	DQ	STL	TO	BLK	PTS	RPG	APG	PPG
83-84—Golden State	45	0	354	64	112	.571	0	0	—	38	91	.418	35	47	82	22	58	0	12	19	7	166	1.8	0.5	3.7
REG. SEASON TOTALS	45	0	354	64	112	.571	0	0	—	38	91	.418	35	47	82	22	58	0	12	19	7	166	1.8	0.5	3.7

CROSSIN, FRANCIS P. (**Chink**) b. July 4, 1924 d. January 10, 1981 Ht. 6-1 Wt. 165 College—Pennsylvania

SEASON—TEAM	G	GS	MIN	FGM	FGA	PCT	3FGM	3FGA	PCT	FTM	FTA	PCT	O-RB	D-RB	TOT	AST	PF	DQ	STL	TO	BLK	PTS	RPG	APG	PPG
47-48—Philadelphia	39	—	—	29	121	.240	—	—	—	13	23	.565	—	—	—	20	28	—	—	—	—	71	—	0.5	1.8
48-49—Philadelphia	44	—	—	74	212	.349	—	—	—	26	42	.619	—	—	—	55	53	—	—	—	—	174	—	1.3	4.0
49-50—Philadelphia	64	—	—	185	574	.322	—	—	—	79	101	.782	—	—	—	148	139	—	—	—	—	449	—	2.3	7.0
REG. SEASON TOTALS	147	—	—	288	907	.318	—	—	—	118	166	.711	—	—	—	223	220	—	—	—	—	694	—	1.5	4.7
PLAYOFF TOTALS	14	—	—	38	107	.355	—	—	—	21	25	.840	—	—	—	17	24	—	—	—	—	97	—	1.2	6.9

CROTTY, JOHN KEVIN b. July 15, 1969   Ht. 6-1 Wt. 185 College—Virginia

SEASON—TEAM	G	GS	MIN	FGM	FGA	PCT	3FGM	3FGA	PCT	FTM	FTA	PCT	O-RB	D-RB	TOT	AST	PF	DQ	STL	TO	BLK	PTS	RPG	APG	PPG
92-93—Utah	40	0	243	37	72	.514	2	14	.143	26	38	.684	4	13	17	55	29	0	11	30	0	102	0.4	1.4	2.6
93-94—Utah	45	0	313	45	99	.455	11	24	.458	31	36	.861	11	20	31	77	36	0	15	27	1	132	0.7	1.7	2.9
REG. SEASON TOTALS	85	0	556	82	171	.480	13	38	.342	57	74	.770	15	33	48	132	65	0	26	57	1	234	0.6	1.6	2.8
PLAYOFF TOTALS	9	0	41	6	13	.462	2	2	1.000	2	2	1.000	1	3	4	10	6	0	1	1	0	16	0.4	1.1	1.8

CROW, MARK HARVEY b. October 22, 1954 Ht. 6-7 Wt. 210 College—Duke

SEASON—TEAM	G	GS	MIN	FGM	FGA	PCT	3FGM	3FGA	PCT	FTM	FTA	PCT	O-RB	D-RB	TOT	AST	PF	DQ	STL	TO	BLK	PTS	RPG	APG	PPG
77-78—New Jersey	15	—	154	35	80	.438	—	—	—	14	20	.700	14	13	27	8	24	0	5	12	1	84	1.8	0.5	5.6
REG. SEASON TOTALS	15	—	154	35	80	.438	—	—	—	14	20	.700	14	13	27	8	24	0	5	12	1	84	1.8	0.5	5.6

CROW, WILLIAM R. (Bill) b. December 9, 1940 Ht. 6-1 Wt. 180 College—Westminster (Utah)

SEASON—TEAM	G	GS	MIN	FGM	FGA	PCT	3FGM	3FGA	PCT	FTM	FTA	PCT	O-RB	D-RB	TOT	AST	PF	DQ	STL	TO	BLK	PTS	RPG	APG	PPG
67-68—Anaheim (A)	1	—	16	1	8	.125	0	0	—	1	4	.250	—	—	2	0	0	0	—	1	—	3	2.0	0.0	3.0
REG. ABA TOTALS	1	—	16	1	8	.125	0	0	—	1	4	.250	—	—	2	0	0	0	—	1	—	3	2.0	0.0	3.0

CROWDER, JONATHAN COREY (Corey) b. April 13, 1969 Ht. 6-5 Wt. 215 College—Kentucky Wesleyan

SEASON—TEAM	G	GS	MIN	FGM	FGA	PCT	3FGM	3FGA	PCT	FTM	FTA	PCT	O-RB	D-RB	TOT	AST	PF	DQ	STL	TO	BLK	PTS	RPG	APG	PPG
91-92—Utah	51	0	328	43	112	.384	13	30	.433	15	18	.833	16	25	41	17	35	0	7	13	2	114	0.8	0.3	2.2
REG. SEASON TOTALS	51	0	328	43	112	.384	13	30	.433	15	18	.833	16	25	41	17	35	0	7	13	2	114	0.8	0.3	2.2
PLAYOFF TOTALS	4	0	12	5	9	.556	0	2	.000	0	1	.000	1	1	2	1	1	0	1	2	0	10	0.5	0.3	2.5

CUETO, ALFONSO ANGEL (Al) b. August 2, 1946 Ht. 6-8 Wt. 230 College—St. Gregory's/Tulsa

SEASON—TEAM	G	GS	MIN	FGM	FGA	PCT	3FGM	3FGA	PCT	FTM	FTA	PCT	O-RB	D-RB	TOT	AST	PF	DQ	STL	TO	BLK	PTS	RPG	APG	PPG
69-70—Miami (A)	78	—	1265	182	449	.405	5	16	.313	102	144	.708	—	—	452	58	257	12	—	—	—	471	5.8	0.7	6.0
70-71—Memphis (A)	71	—	974	134	333	.402	0	5	.000	55	77	.714	—	—	279	86	166	—	—	—	—	323	3.9	1.2	4.5
REG. ABA TOTALS	149	—	2239	316	782	.404	5	21	.238	157	221	.710	—	—	731	144	423	12	—	—	—	794	4.9	1.0	5.3
ABA PLAYOFF TOTALS	4	—	51	6	14	.429	0	0	—	2	3	.667	—	—	18	3	7	0	—	—	—	14	4.5	0.8	3.5

CUMMINGS, PATRICK MICHAEL (Pat) b. July 11, 1956 Ht. 6-9½ Wt. 235 College—Cincinnati

SEASON—TEAM	G	GS	MIN	FGM	FGA	PCT	3FGM	3FGA	PCT	FTM	FTA	PCT	O-RB	D-RB	TOT	AST	PF	DQ	STL	TO	BLK	PTS	RPG	APG	PPG
79-80—Milwaukee	71	—	900	187	370	.505	0	0	—	94	123	.764	81	157	238	53	141	0	22	74	17	468	3.4	0.7	6.6
80-81—Milwaukee	74	—	1084	248	460	.539	0	2	.000	99	140	.707	97	195	292	62	192	4	31	114	19	595	3.9	0.8	8.0
81-82—Milwaukee	78	7	1132	219	430	.509	0	2	.000	67	91	.736	61	184	245	99	227	6	22	108	9	505	3.1	1.3	6.5
82-83—Dallas	81	71	2317	433	878	.493	0	1	.000	148	196	.755	225	443	668	144	296	9	57	162	35	1014	8.2	1.8	12.5
83-84—Dallas	80	80	2492	452	915	.494	0	2	.000	141	190	.742	151	507	658	158	282	2	64	146	23	1045	8.2	2.0	13.1
84-85—New York	63	63	2069	410	797	.514	0	4	.000	177	227	.780	139	379	518	109	247	6	50	166	17	997	8.2	1.7	15.8
85-86—New York	31	30	1007	195	408	.478	0	2	.000	97	139	.698	92	188	280	47	136	7	27	87	12	487	9.0	1.5	15.7
86-87—New York	49	11	1056	172	382	.450	0	0	—	79	110	.718	123	189	312	38	145	2	26	85	7	423	6.4	0.8	8.6
87-88—New York	62	9	946	140	307	.456	0	1	.000	59	80	.738	82	153	235	37	143	0	20	65	10	339	3.8	0.6	5.5
88-89—Miami	53	28	1096	197	394	.500	0	2	.000	72	97	.742	84	197	281	47	160	3	29	111	18	466	5.3	0.9	8.8
89-90—Miami	37	1	391	77	159	.484	0	0	—	21	37	.568	28	65	93	13	60	1	12	32	4	175	2.5	0.4	4.7
90-91—Utah	4	0	26	4	6	.667	0	0	—	7	10	.700	3	2	5	0	8	0	0	2	0	15	1.3	0.0	3.8
REG. SEASON TOTALS	683	300	14516	2734	5506	.497	0	16	.000	1061	1440	.737	1166	2659	3825	807	2037	40	360	1152	171	6529	5.6	1.2	9.6
PLAYOFF TOTALS	30	10	454	67	159	.421	0	0	—	26	31	.839	38	74	112	22	59	0	6	22	4	160	3.7	0.7	5.3

CUMMINGS, ROBERT TERRELL (Terry) b. March 15, 1961 Ht. 6-9 Wt. 250 College—DePaul

SEASON—TEAM	G	GS	MIN	FGM	FGA	PCT	3FGM	3FGA	PCT	FTM	FTA	PCT	O-RB	D-RB	TOT	AST	PF	DQ	STL	TO	BLK	PTS	RPG	APG	PPG
82-83—San Diego	70	69	2531	684	1309	.523	0	1	.000	292	412	.709	303	441	744	177	294	10	129	204	62	1660	10.6	2.5	23.7
83-84—San Diego	81	80	2907	737	1491	.494	0	3	.000	380	528	.720	323	454	777	139	298	6	92	218	57	1854	9.6	1.7	22.9
84-85—Milwaukee	79	78	2722	759	1532	.495	0	1	.000	343	463	.741	244	472	716	228	264	4	117	190	67	1861	9.1	2.9	23.6
85-86—Milwaukee	82	82	2669	681	1438	.474	0	2	.000	265	404	.656	222	472	694	193	283	4	121	191	51	1627	8.5	2.4	19.8
86-87—Milwaukee	82	77	2770	729	1426	.511	0	3	.000	249	376	.662	214	486	700	229	296	3	129	172	81	1707	8.5	2.8	20.8
87-88—Milwaukee	76	76	2629	675	1392	.485	1	3	.333	270	406	.665	184	369	553	181	274	6	78	170	46	1621	7.3	2.4	21.3
88-89—Milwaukee	80	78	2824	730	1563	.467	7	15	.467	362	460	.787	281	369	650	198	265	5	106	201	72	1829	8.1	2.5	22.9
89-90—San Antonio	81	78	2821	728	1532	.475	19	59	.322	343	440	.780	226	451	677	219	286	1	110	202	52	1818	8.4	2.7	22.4
90-91—San Antonio	67	62	2195	503	1039	.484	7	33	.212	164	240	.683	194	327	521	157	225	5	61	131	30	1177	7.8	2.3	17.6
91-92—San Antonio	70	67	2149	514	1053	.488	5	13	.385	177	249	.711	247	384	631	102	210	4	58	115	34	1210	9.0	1.5	17.3
92-93—San Antonio	8	0	76	11	29	.379	0	0	—	5	10	.500	6	13	19	4	17	0	1	2	1	27	2.4	0.5	3.4
93-94—San Antonio	59	29	1133	183	428	.428	0	2	.000	63	107	.589	132	165	297	50	137	0	31	59	13	429	5.0	0.8	7.3
REG. SEASON TOTALS	835	776	27426	6934	14232	.487	39	135	.289	2913	4095	.711	2576	4403	6979	1877	2849	48	1033	1855	566	16820	8.4	2.2	20.1
PLAYOFF TOTALS	75	59	2412	600	1177	.510	1	10	.100	267	373	.716	201	403	604	150	266	2	78	143	53	1468	8.1	2.0	19.6
ALL-STAR TOTALS	2	0	35	11	26	.423	0	0	—	5	6	.833	6	6	12	1	5	0	3	0	2	27	6.0	0.5	13.5

CUNNINGHAM, DICK b. July 11, 1946 Ht. 6-10 Wt. 245 College—Murray State (Ky.)

SEASON—TEAM	G	GS	MIN	FGM	FGA	PCT	3FGM	3FGA	PCT	FTM	FTA	PCT	O-RB	D-RB	TOT	AST	PF	DQ	STL	TO	BLK	PTS	RPG	APG	PPG
68-69—Milwaukee	77	—	1236	141	332	.425	—	—	—	69	106	.651	—	—	438	58	166	2	—	—	—	351	5.7	0.8	4.6
69-70—Milwaukee	60	—	416	52	141	.369	—	—	—	22	33	.667	—	—	160	28	70	0	—	—	—	126	2.7	0.5	2.1
70-71—Milwaukee	76	—	675	81	195	.415	—	—	—	39	59	.661	—	—	257	43	90	1	—	—	—	201	3.4	0.6	2.6
71-72—Houston	63	—	720	67	174	.385	—	—	—	37	53	.698	—	—	243	57	76	0	—	—	—	171	3.9	0.9	2.7
72-73—Milwaukee	74	—	692	64	156	.410	—	—	—	29	50	.580	—	—	208	34	94	0	—	—	—	157	2.8	0.5	2.1
73-74—Milwaukee	8	—	45	3	6	.500	—	—	—	0	7	.000	1	15	16	0	5	0	2	—	2	6	2.0	0.0	0.8
74-75—Milwaukee	2	—	8	0	0	—	—	—	—	0	0	—	0	2	2	1	1	0	0	—	0	0	1.0	0.5	0.0
REG. SEASON TOTALS	360	—	3792	408	1004	.406	—	—	—	196	308	.636	1	17	1324	221	502	3	2	—	2	1012	3.7	0.6	2.8
PLAYOFF TOTALS	27	—	151	20	40	.500	—	—	—	7	11	.636	0	0	39	5	22	0	0	—	0	47	1.4	0.2	1.7

CUNNINGHAM, WILLIAM JOHN (Billy, Kangaroo Kid) b. June 3, 1943   Ht. 6-6   Wt. 220   College—North Carolina

SEASON—TEAM	G	GS	MIN	FGM	FGA	PCT	3FGM	3FGA	PCT	FTM	FTA	PCT	O-RB	D-RB	TOT	AST	PF	DQ	STL	TO	BLK	PTS	RPG	APG	PPG
65-66—Philadelphia	80	—	2134	431	1011	.426	—	—	—	281	443	.634	—	—	599	207	301	12	—	—	—	1143	7.5	2.6	14.3
66-67—Philadelphia	81	—	2168	556	1211	.459	—	—	—	383	558	.686	—	—	589	205	260	2	—	—	—	1495	7.3	2.5	18.5
67-68—Philadelphia	74	—	2076	516	1178	.438	—	—	—	368	509	.723	—	—	562	187	260	3	—	—	—	1400	7.6	2.5	18.9
68-69—Philadelphia	82	—	3345	739	1736	.426	—	—	—	556	754	.737	—	1050	287	329	10	—	—	—		2034	12.8	3.5	24.8
69-70—Philadelphia	81	—	3194	802	1710	.469	—	—	—	510	700	.729	—	1101	352	331	15	—	—	—		2114	13.6	4.3	26.1
70-71—Philadelphia	81	—	3090	702	1519	.462	—	—	—	455	620	.734	—	946	395	328	5	—	—	—		1859	11.7	4.9	23.0
71-72—Philadelphia	75	—	2900	658	1428	.461	—	—	—	428	601	.712	—	918	443	295	12	—	—	—		1744	12.2	5.9	23.3
72-73—Carolina (A)	84	—	3248	771	1583	.487	14	49	.286	472	598	.789	240	772	1012	530	309	6	216	381	—	2028	12.0	6.3	24.1
73-74—Carolina (A)	32	—	1190	253	537	.471	1	8	.125	149	187	.797	86	245	331	150	105	—	59	127	21	656	10.3	4.7	20.5
74-75—Philadelphia	80	—	2859	609	1423	.428	—	—	—	345	444	.777	130	596	726	442	270	4	91	—	35	1563	9.1	5.5	19.5
75-76—Philadelphia	20	—	640	103	251	.410	—	—	—	68	88	.773	29	118	147	107	57	1	24	—	10	274	7.4	5.4	13.7
REG. NBA TOTALS	654	—	22406	5116	11467	.446	—	—	—	3394	4717	.720	159	714	6638	2625	2431	64	115	—	45	13626	10.1	4.0	20.8
REG. ABA TOTALS	116	—	4438	1024	2120	.483	15	57	.263	621	785	.791	326	1017	1343	680	414	6	275	508	21	2684	11.6	5.9	23.1
NBA PLAYOFF TOTALS	39	—	1217	289	677	.427	—	—	—	179	261	.686	0	0	356	125	151	3	0	—	0	757	9.1	3.2	19.4
ABA PLAYOFF TOTALS	15	—	533	121	254	.476	1	6	.167	61	88	.693	39	119	158	67	57	0	22	56	0	304	10.5	4.5	20.3
NBA ALL-STAR TOTALS	4	—	93	18	44	.409	—	—	—	12	15	.800	0	0	23	9	11	0	0	—	0	48	5.8	2.3	12.0
ABA ALL-STAR TOTALS	1	—	20	9	12	.750	0	1	.000	0	0	—	0	6	6	4	6	1	1	3	0	18	6.0	4.0	18.0

CURCIC, RADISAV b. September 26, 1965   Ht. 6-10   Wt. 275   College—None

SEASON—TEAM	G	GS	MIN	FGM	FGA	PCT	3FGM	3FGA	PCT	FTM	FTA	PCT	O-RB	D-RB	TOT	AST	PF	DQ	STL	TO	BLK	PTS	RPG	APG	PPG
92-93—Dallas	20	0	166	16	41	.390	0	0	—	26	36	.722	17	32	49	12	30	0	7	8	2	58	2.5	0.6	2.9
REG. SEASON TOTALS	20	0	166	16	41	.390	0	0	—	26	36	.722	17	32	49	12	30	0	7	8	2	58	2.5	0.6	2.9

CURE, ARMAND ARTHUR b. August 1, 1919   Ht. 6-1   Wt. 200   College—Rhode Island

SEASON—TEAM	G	GS	MIN	FGM	FGA	PCT	3FGM	3FGA	PCT	FTM	FTA	PCT	O-RB	D-RB	TOT	AST	PF	DQ	STL	TO	BLK	PTS	RPG	APG	PPG
46-47—Providence	12	—	—	4	15	.267	—	—	—	2	3	.667	—	—	—	0	5	—	—	—	—	10	—	0.0	0.8
REG. SEASON TOTALS	12	—	—	4	15	.267	—	—	—	2	3	.667	—	—	—	0	5	—	—	—	—	10	—	0.0	0.8

CURETON, EARL (The Twirl) b. September 3, 1957   Ht. 6-9   Wt. 210   College—Robert Morris/Detroit

SEASON—TEAM	G	GS	MIN	FGM	FGA	PCT	3FGM	3FGA	PCT	FTM	FTA	PCT	O-RB	D-RB	TOT	AST	PF	DQ	STL	TO	BLK	PTS	RPG	APG	PPG
80-81—Philadelphia	52	—	528	93	205	.454	0	1	.000	33	64	.516	51	104	155	25	68	0	20	29	23	219	3.0	0.5	4.2
81-82—Philadelphia	66	8	956	149	306	.487	0	2	.000	51	94	.543	90	180	270	32	142	0	31	44	27	349	4.1	0.5	5.3
82-83—Philadelphia	73	3	987	108	258	.419	0	0	—	33	67	.493	84	185	269	43	144	1	37	76	24	249	3.7	0.6	3.4
83-84—Detroit	73	0	907	81	177	.458	0	1	.000	31	59	.525	86	201	287	36	143	3	24	55	31	193	3.9	0.5	2.6
84-85—Detroit	81	1	1642	207	428	.484	0	3	.000	82	144	.569	169	250	419	83	216	1	56	114	42	496	5.2	1.0	6.1
85-86—Detroit	80	19	2017	285	564	.505	0	2	.000	117	211	.555	198	306	504	137	239	3	58	150	58	687	6.3	1.7	8.6
86-87—Chicago-L.A.Clips	78	47	1973	243	510	.476	0	2	.000	82	152	.539	212	240	452	122	188	2	33	80	56	568	5.8	1.6	7.3
87-88—L.A. Clippers	69	11	1128	133	310	.429	0	3	.000	33	63	.524	97	174	271	63	135	1	32	58	36	299	3.9	0.9	4.3
88-89—Charlotte	82	41	2047	233	465	.501	0	1	.000	66	123	.537	188	300	488	130	230	3	50	114	61	532	6.0	1.6	6.5
90-91—Charlotte	9	1	159	8	24	.333	0	1	.000	1	3	.333	6	30	36	3	16	0	0	6	3	17	4.0	0.3	1.9
93-94—Houston	2	0	30	2	8	.250	0	0	—	0	2	.000	4	8	12	0	4	0	0	1	0	4	6.0	0.0	2.0
REG. SEASON TOTALS	665	131	12374	1542	3255	.474	0	16	.000	529	982	.539	1185	1978	3163	674	1525	14	341	727	361	3613	4.8	1.0	5.4
PLAYOFF TOTALS	54	4	588	76	169	.450	0	3	.000	17	36	.472	55	118	173	22	83	0	19	26	8	169	3.2	0.4	3.1

CURRAN, FRANCIS HUGH (Fran) b. September 19, 1925   Ht. 6-0   Wt. 175   College—Notre Dame

SEASON—TEAM	G	GS	MIN	FGM	FGA	PCT	3FGM	3FGA	PCT	FTM	FTA	PCT	O-RB	D-RB	TOT	AST	PF	DQ	STL	TO	BLK	PTS	RPG	APG	PPG
47-48—Toledo (N)	58	—	—	129	—	—	—	—	—	119	156	.763	—	—	—	—	145	—	—	—	—	377	—	—	6.5
48-49—Rochester	57	—	—	61	168	.363	—	—	—	85	126	.675	—	—	—	78	118	—	—	—	—	207	—	1.4	3.6
49-50—Rochester	66	—	—	98	235	.417	—	—	—	199	241	.826	—	—	—	71	113	—	—	—	—	395	—	1.1	6.0
REG. NBA TOTALS	123	—	—	159	403	.395	—	—	—	284	367	.774	—	—	—	149	231	—	—	—	—	602	—	1.2	4.9
REG. NBL TOTALS	58	—	—	129	—	—	—	—	—	119	156	.763	—	—	—	—	145	—	—	—	—	377	—	—	6.5
NBA PLAYOFF TOTALS	6	—	—	3	12	.250	—	—	—	3	3	1.000	—	—	—	3	3	—	—	—	—	9	—	0.5	1.5

CURRY, MICHAEL b. August 12, 1968   Ht. 6-5   Wt. 220   College—Georgia Southern

SEASON—TEAM	G	GS	MIN	FGM	FGA	PCT	3FGM	3FGA	PCT	FTM	FTA	PCT	O-RB	D-RB	TOT	AST	PF	DQ	STL	TO	BLK	PTS	RPG	APG	PPG
93-94—Philadelphia	10	0	43	3	14	.214	0	2	.000	3	4	.750	0	1	1	1	6	0	1	3	0	9	0.1	0.1	0.9
REG. SEASON TOTALS	10	0	43	3	14	.214	0	2	.000	3	4	.750	0	1	1	1	6	0	1	3	0	9	0.1	0.1	0.9

CURRY, WARDELL STEPHEN (**Dell**) b. June 25, 1964 Ht. 6-5 Wt. 200 College—Virginia Tech

SEASON—TEAM	G	GS	MIN	FGM	FGA	PCT	3FGM	3FGA	PCT	FTM	FTA	PCT	O-RB	D-RB	TOT	AST	PF	DQ	STL	TO	BLK	PTS	RPG	APG	PPG
86-87—Utah	67	0	636	139	326	.426	17	60	.283	30	38	.789	30	48	78	58	86	0	27	44	4	325	1.2	0.9	4.9
87-88—Cleveland	79	8	1499	340	742	.458	28	81	.346	79	101	.782	43	123	166	149	128	0	94	108	22	787	2.1	1.9	10.0
88-89—Charlotte	48	0	813	256	521	.491	19	55	.345	40	46	.870	26	78	104	50	68	0	42	44	4	571	2.2	1.0	11.9
89-90—Charlotte	67	13	1860	461	990	.466	52	147	.354	96	104	.923	31	137	168	159	148	0	98	100	26	1070	2.5	2.4	16.0
90-91—Charlotte	76	14	1515	337	715	.471	32	86	.372	96	114	.842	47	152	199	166	125	0	75	80	25	802	2.6	2.2	10.6
91-92—Charlotte	77	0	2020	504	1038	.486	74	183	.404	127	152	.836	57	202	259	177	156	1	93	134	20	1209	3.4	2.3	15.7
92-93—Charlotte	80	0	2094	498	1102	.452	95	237	.401	136	157	.866	51	235	286	180	150	1	87	129	23	1227	3.6	2.3	15.3
93-94—Charlotte	82	0	2173	533	1171	.455	152	378	.402	117	134	.873	71	191	262	221	161	0	98	120	27	1335	3.2	2.7	16.3
REG. SEASON TOTALS	576	35	12610	3068	6605	.464	469	1227	.382	721	846	.852	356	1166	1522	1160	1022	2	614	759	151	7326	2.6	2.0	12.7
PLAYOFF TOTALS	13	0	243	43	104	.413	6	23	.261	9	11	.818	12	21	33	20	21	0	13	13	1	101	2.5	1.5	7.8

DABICH, MICHAEL LEE (**Mike, Dabbo**) b. December 27, 1942 Ht. 7-0 Wt. 255 College—New Mexico State

SEASON—TEAM	G	GS	MIN	FGM	FGA	PCT	3FGM	3FGA	PCT	FTM	FTA	PCT	O-RB	D-RB	TOT	AST	PF	DQ	STL	TO	BLK	PTS	RPG	APG	PPG
67-68—Oakland-Dallas (A)	10	—	49	8	12	.667	0	0	—	4	9	.444	—	—	13	2	12	0	—	5	—	20	1.3	0.2	2.0
REG. ABA TOTALS	10	—	49	8	12	.667	0	0	—	4	9	.444	—	—	13	2	12	0	—	5	—	20	1.3	0.2	2.0

DAHLER, EDWARD JR. (**Ed**) b. January 31, 1926 Ht. 6-5 Wt. 190 College—Duquesne

SEASON—TEAM	G	GS	MIN	FGM	FGA	PCT	3FGM	3FGA	PCT	FTM	FTA	PCT	O-RB	D-RB	TOT	AST	PF	DQ	STL	TO	BLK	PTS	RPG	APG	PPG
51-52—Philadelphia	14	—	112	14	38	.368	—	—	—	7	7	1.000	—	—	22	5	16	0	—	—	—	35	1.6	0.4	2.5
REG. SEASON TOTALS	14	—	112	14	38	.368	—	—	—	7	7	1.000	—	—	22	5	16	0	—	—	—	35	1.6	0.4	2.5

DAILEY, QUINTIN b. January 22, 1961 Ht. 6-3 Wt. 180 College—San Francisco

SEASON—TEAM	G	GS	MIN	FGM	FGA	PCT	3FGM	3FGA	PCT	FTM	FTA	PCT	O-RB	D-RB	TOT	AST	PF	DQ	STL	TO	BLK	PTS	RPG	APG	PPG
82-83—Chicago	76	32	2081	470	1008	.466	5	25	.200	206	282	.730	87	173	260	280	248	7	72	205	10	1151	3.4	3.7	15.1
83-84—Chicago	82	42	2449	583	1229	.474	4	32	.125	321	396	.811	61	174	235	254	218	4	109	220	11	1491	2.9	3.1	18.2
84-85—Chicago	79	0	2101	525	1111	.473	7	30	.233	205	251	.817	57	151	208	191	192	0	71	154	5	1262	2.6	2.4	16.0
85-86—Chicago	35	0	723	203	470	.432	0	8	.000	163	198	.823	20	48	68	67	86	0	22	67	5	569	1.9	1.9	16.3
86-87—L.A. Clippers	49	5	924	200	491	.407	1	10	.100	119	155	.768	34	49	83	79	113	4	43	71	8	520	1.7	1.6	10.6
87-88—L.A. Clippers	67	7	1282	328	755	.434	2	12	.167	243	313	.776	62	92	154	109	128	1	69	123	4	901	2.3	1.6	13.4
88-89—L.A. Clippers	69	51	1722	448	964	.465	1	9	.111	217	286	.759	69	135	204	154	152	0	90	122	6	1114	3.0	2.2	16.1
89-90—Seattle	30	2	491	97	240	.404	1	5	.200	52	66	.788	18	33	51	34	63	0	12	34	0	247	1.7	1.1	8.2
90-91—Seattle	30	0	299	73	155	.471	0	1	.000	38	62	.613	11	21	32	16	25	0	7	19	1	184	1.1	0.5	6.1
91-92—Seattle	11	1	98	9	37	.243	0	1	.000	13	16	.813	2	10	12	4	6	0	5	10	1	31	1.1	0.4	2.8
REG. SEASON TOTALS	528	140	12170	2936	6460	.454	21	133	.158	1577	2025	.779	421	886	1307	1188	1231	16	500	1025	51	7470	2.5	2.3	14.1
PLAYOFF TOTALS	4	0	129	26	62	.419	1	7	.143	8	11	.727	5	8	13	11	9	0	4	5	0	61	3.3	2.8	15.3

DALLMAR, HOWARD (**Howie**) b. May 24, 1922 d. December 19, 1991 Ht. 6-4½ Wt. 200 College—Stanford/Pennsylvania

SEASON—TEAM	G	GS	MIN	FGM	FGA	PCT	3FGM	3FGA	PCT	FTM	FTA	PCT	O-RB	D-RB	TOT	AST	PF	DQ	STL	TO	BLK	PTS	RPG	APG	PPG
46-47—Philadelphia	60	—	—	199	710	.280	—	—	—	130	203	.640	—	—	—	104	141	—	—	—	—	528	—	1.7	8.8
47-48—Philadelphia	48	—	—	215	781	.275	—	—	—	157	211	.744	—	—	—	120	141	—	—	—	—	587	—	2.5	12.2
48-49—Philadelphia	38	—	—	105	342	.307	—	—	—	83	116	.716	—	—	—	116	104	—	—	—	—	293	—	3.1	7.7
REG. SEASON TOTALS	146	—	—	519	1833	.283	—	—	—	370	530	.698	—	—	—	340	386	—	—	—	—	1408	—	2.3	9.6
PLAYOFF TOTALS	25	—	—	68	300	.227	—	—	—	65	95	.684	—	—	—	57	92	7	—	—	—	201	—	2.3	8.0

DAMPIER, LOUIE (**Lou**) b. November 20, 1944 Ht. 6-0 Wt. 175 College—Kentucky

SEASON—TEAM	G	GS	MIN	FGM	FGA	PCT	3FGM	3FGA	PCT	FTM	FTA	PCT	O-RB	D-RB	TOT	AST	PF	DQ	STL	TO	BLK	PTS	RPG	APG	PPG
67-68—Kentucky (A)	72	—	2961	620	1473	.421	38	142	.268	209	254	.823	—	—	333	256	143	0	—	163	—	1487	4.6	3.6	20.7
68-69—Kentucky (A)	78	—	3326	713	1696	.420	199	552	.361	308	380	.811	—	—	299	456	156	1	—	251	—	1933	3.8	5.8	24.8
69-70—Kentucky (A)	82	—	3353	743	1864	.399	198	548	.361	447	538	.831	—	—	310	447	235	2	—	—	—	2131	3.8	5.5	26.0
70-71—Kentucky (A)	84	—	3221	566	1353	.418	103	280	.368	320	376	.851	—	—	297	460	213	—	—	—	—	1555	3.5	5.5	18.5
71-72—Kentucky (A)	83	—	3214	477	1078	.442	84	233	.361	281	336	.836	—	—	259	515	237	—	—	211	—	1319	3.1	6.2	15.9
72-73—Kentucky (A)	80	—	3039	515	1143	.451	54	155	.348	262	334	.784	55	158	213	521	216	0	—	188	—	1346	2.7	6.5	16.8
73-74—Kentucky (A)	84	—	2942	603	1296	.465	48	124	.387	238	286	.832	46	155	201	473	152	—	84	230	18	1492	2.4	5.6	17.8
74-75—Kentucky (A)	83	—	2879	598	1195	.500	38	96	.396	161	199	.809	42	169	211	449	140	—	92	146	53	1395	2.5	5.4	16.8
75-76—Kentucky (A)	82	—	2835	455	949	.479	32	87	.368	126	146	.863	35	124	159	467	141	—	60	148	46	1068	1.9	5.7	13.0
76-77—San Antonio	80	—	1634	233	507	.460	—	—	—	64	86	.744	22	54	76	234	93	0	49	—	15	530	1.0	2.9	6.6
77-78—San Antonio	82	—	2037	336	660	.509	—	—	—	76	101	.752	24	98	122	285	84	0	87	95	13	748	1.5	3.5	9.1
78-79—San Antonio	70	—	760	123	251	.490	—	—	—	29	39	.744	15	48	63	124	42	0	35	39	8	275	0.9	1.8	3.9
REG. NBA TOTALS	232	—	4431	692	1418	.488	—	—	—	169	226	.748	61	200	261	643	219	0	171	134	36	1553	1.1	2.8	6.7
REG. ABA TOTALS	728	—	27770	5290	12047	.439	794	2217	.358	2352	2849	.825	178	606	2282	4044	1633	3	236	1337	117	13726	3.1	5.6	18.9
NBA PLAYOFF TOTALS	15	—	246	29	67	.433	—	—	—	9	15	.600	2	15	32	19	0	8	5	4	67	1.0	2.1	4.5
ABA PLAYOFF TOTALS	94	—	3788	598	1371	.436	119	325	.366	269	341	.789	15	50	286	617	195	0	36	142	12	1584	3.0	6.6	16.9
ABA ALL-STAR TOTALS	7	—	175	39	85	.459	3	16	.188	7	8	.875	1	11	15	15	12	0	2	9	0	88	2.1	2.1	12.6

DANDRIDGE, ROBERT L. JR. (Bob) b. November 15, 1947 Ht. 6-6 Wt. 195 College—Norfolk State

SEASON—TEAM	G	GS	MIN	FGM	FGA	PCT	3FGM	3FGA	PCT	FTM	FTA	PCT	O-RB	D-RB	TOT	AST	PF	DQ	STL	TO	BLK	PTS	RPG	APG	PPG
69-70—Milwaukee	81	—	2461	434	895	.485	—	—	—	199	264	.754	—	—	625	292	279	1	—	—	—	1067	7.7	3.6	13.2
70-71—Milwaukee	79	—	2862	594	1167	.509	—	—	—	264	376	.702	—	—	632	277	287	4	—	—	—	1452	8.0	3.5	18.4
71-72—Milwaukee	80	—	2957	630	1264	.498	—	—	—	215	291	.739	—	—	613	249	297	7	—	—	—	1475	7.7	3.1	18.4
72-73—Milwaukee	73	—	2852	638	1353	.472	—	—	—	198	251	.789	—	—	600	207	279	2	—	—	—	1474	8.2	2.8	20.2
73-74—Milwaukee	71	—	2521	583	1158	.503	—	—	—	175	214	.818	117	362	479	201	271	4	111	—	41	1341	6.7	2.8	18.9
74-75—Milwaukee	80	—	3031	691	1460	.473	—	—	—	211	262	.805	142	409	551	243	330	7	122	—	48	1593	6.9	3.0	19.9
75-76—Milwaukee	73	—	2735	650	1296	.502	—	—	—	271	329	.824	171	369	540	206	263	5	111	—	38	1571	7.4	2.8	21.5
76-77—Milwaukee	70	—	2501	585	1253	.467	—	—	—	283	367	.771	146	294	440	268	222	1	95	—	28	1453	6.3	3.8	20.8
77-78—Washington	75	—	2777	560	1190	.471	—	—	—	330	419	.788	137	305	442	287	262	6	101	241	44	1450	5.9	3.8	19.3
78-79—Washington	78	—	2629	629	1260	.499	—	—	—	331	401	.825	109	338	447	365	259	4	71	222	57	1589	5.7	4.7	20.4
79-80—Washington	45	—	1457	329	729	.451	2	11	.182	123	152	.809	63	183	246	178	112	1	29	123	36	783	5.5	4.0	17.4
80-81—Washington	23	—	545	101	237	.426	0	1	.000	28	39	.718	19	64	83	60	54	1	16	33	9	230	3.6	2.6	10.0
81-82—Milwaukee	11	0	174	21	55	.382	0	0	—	10	17	.588	4	13	17	13	25	0	5	11	2	52	1.5	1.2	4.7
REG. SEASON TOTALS	839	0	29502	6445	13317	.484	2	12	.167	2638	3382	.780	908	2337	5715	2846	2940	43	661	630	303	15530	6.8	3.4	18.5
PLAYOFF TOTALS	98	0	3882	823	1716	.480	0	0	—	321	422	.761	114	294	754	365	377	12	69	116	39	1967	7.7	3.7	20.1
ALL-STAR TOTALS	4	1	74	12	25	.480	0	0	—	2	3	.667	8	3	14	2	9	0	5	1	0	26	3.5	0.5	6.5

DANIELS, LLOYD b. September 4, 1967 Ht. 6-7 Wt. 205 College—Mount St. Antonio

SEASON—TEAM	G	GS	MIN	FGM	FGA	PCT	3FGM	3FGA	PCT	FTM	FTA	PCT	O-RB	D-RB	TOT	AST	PF	DQ	STL	TO	BLK	PTS	RPG	APG	PPG
92-93—San Antonio	77	10	1573	285	644	.443	59	177	.333	72	99	.727	86	130	216	148	144	0	38	102	30	701	2.8	1.9	9.1
93-94—San Antonio	65	5	980	140	372	.376	44	125	.352	46	64	.719	45	66	111	94	69	0	29	60	16	370	1.7	1.4	5.7
REG. SEASON TOTALS	142	15	2553	425	1016	.418	103	302	.341	118	163	.724	131	196	327	242	213	0	67	162	46	1071	2.3	1.7	7.5
PLAYOFF TOTALS	12	0	140	19	50	.380	5	15	.333	7	8	.875	11	13	24	5	12	0	3	7	1	50	2.0	0.4	4.2

DANIELS, MELVIN JOE (Mel) b. July 20, 1944 Ht. 6-9 Wt. 225 College—New Mexico

SEASON—TEAM	G	GS	MIN	FGM	FGA	PCT	3FGM	3FGA	PCT	FTM	FTA	PCT	O-RB	D-RB	TOT	AST	PF	DQ	STL	TO	BLK	PTS	RPG	APG	PPG
67-68—Minnesota (A)	78	—	2938	669	1640	.408	1	5	.200	390	678	.575	502	711	1213	109	268	11	—	232	—	1729	15.6	1.4	22.2
68-69—Indiana (A)	76	—	2934	712	1496	.476	0	4	.000	400	662	.604	383	873	1256	116	276	8	—	272	—	1824	16.5	1.5	24.0
69-70—Indiana (A)	83	—	3039	613	1295	.473	0	2	.000	330	489	.675	423	1039	1462	131	309	7	—	—	—	1556	17.6	1.6	18.7
70-71—Indiana (A)	82	—	3170	698	1357	.514	1	13	.077	326	480	.679	394	1081	1475	178	292	—	—	—	—	1723	18.0	2.2	21.0
71-72—Indiana (A)	79	—	2971	598	1184	.505	0	6	.000	317	451	.703	383	914	1297	176	289	—	—	239	—	1513	16.4	2.2	19.2
72-73—Indiana (A)	81	—	3103	587	1217	.482	1	4	.250	322	446	.722	348	899	1247	177	315	8	—	275	157	1497	15.4	2.2	18.5
73-74—Indiana (A)	78	—	2539	492	1117	.440	0	0	—	217	287	.756	251	655	906	122	283	—	56	215	92	1201	11.6	1.6	15.4
74-75—Memphis (A)	71	—	1646	290	644	.450	0	0	—	116	183	.634	186	452	638	125	248	—	40	141	102	696	9.0	1.8	9.8
76-77—New York Nets	11	—	126	13	35	.371	—	—	—	13	23	.565	10	24	34	6	29	0	3	—	11	39	3.1	0.5	3.5
REG. NBA TOTALS	11	—	126	13	35	.371	—	—	—	13	23	.565	10	24	34	6	29	0	3	—	11	39	3.1	0.5	3.5
REG. ABA TOTALS	628	—	22340	4659	9950	.468	3	34	.088	2418	3676	.658	2870	6624	9494	1134	2280	34	96	1374	351	11739	15.1	1.8	18.7
ABA PLAYOFF TOTALS	109	—	3901	740	1648	.449	0	5	.000	421	616	.683	435	1012	1608	168	433	2	12	218	51	1901	14.8	1.5	17.4
ABA ALL-STAR TOTALS	7	—	195	50	111	.450	0	0	—	32	53	.604	20	45	77	8	20	0	0	17	3	132	11.0	1.1	18.9

DANTLEY, ADRIAN DELANO b. February 28, 1956 Ht. 6-5 Wt. 208 College—Notre Dame

SEASON—TEAM	G	GS	MIN	FGM	FGA	PCT	3FGM	3FGA	PCT	FTM	FTA	PCT	O-RB	D-RB	TOT	AST	PF	DQ	STL	TO	BLK	PTS	RPG	APG	PPG
76-77—Buffalo	77	—	2816	544	1046	.520	—	—	—	476	582	.818	251	336	587	144	215	2	91	—	15	1564	7.6	1.9	20.3
77-78—Indiana-L.A.	79	—	2933	578	1128	.512	—	—	—	541	680	.796	265	355	620	253	233	2	118	228	24	1697	7.8	3.2	21.5
78-79—Los Angeles	60	—	1775	374	733	.510	—	—	—	292	342	.854	131	211	342	138	162	0	63	155	12	1040	5.7	2.3	17.3
79-80—Utah	68	—	2674	730	1267	.576	0	2	.000	443	526	.842	183	333	516	191	211	2	96	233	14	1903	7.6	2.8	28.0
80-81—Utah	80	—	3417	909	1627	.559	2	7	.286	632	784	.806	192	317	509	322	245	1	109	282	18	2452	6.4	4.0	30.7
81-82—Utah	81	81	3222	904	1586	.570	1	3	.333	648	818	.792	231	283	514	324	252	1	95	299	14	2457	6.3	4.0	30.3
82-83—Utah	22	22	887	233	402	.580	0	0	—	210	248	.847	58	82	140	105	62	2	20	81	0	676	6.4	4.8	30.7
83-84—Utah	79	79	2984	802	1438	.558	1	4	.250	813	946	.859	179	269	448	310	201	0	61	263	4	2418	5.7	3.9	30.6
84-85—Utah	55	46	1971	512	964	.531	0	0	—	438	545	.804	148	175	323	186	133	0	57	171	8	1462	5.9	3.4	26.6
85-86—Utah	76	75	2744	818	1453	.563	1	11	.091	630	796	.791	178	217	395	264	206	2	64	231	4	2267	5.2	3.5	29.8
86-87—Detroit	81	81	2736	601	1126	.534	1	6	.167	539	664	.812	104	228	332	162	193	1	63	181	7	1742	4.1	2.0	21.5
87-88—Detroit	69	50	2144	444	863	.514	0	2	.000	492	572	.860	84	143	227	171	144	0	39	135	10	1380	3.3	2.5	20.0
88-89—Detroit-Dallas	73	67	2422	470	954	.493	0	1	.000	460	568	.810	117	200	317	171	186	1	43	163	13	1400	4.3	2.3	19.2
89-90—Dallas	45	45	1300	231	484	.477	0	2	.000	200	254	.787	78	94	172	80	99	0	20	75	7	662	3.8	1.8	14.7
90-91—Milwaukee	10	—	126	19	50	.380	1	3	.333	18	26	.692	8	5	13	9	26	0	5	6	0	57	1.3	0.9	5.7
REG. SEASON TOTALS	955	546	34151	8169	15121	.540	7	41	.171	6832	8351	.818	2207	3248	5455	2830	2550	14	944	2503	150	23177	5.7	3.0	24.3
PLAYOFF TOTALS	73	59	2515	531	1012	.525	0	3	.000	496	623	.796	149	246	395	169	188	1	69	185	6	1558	5.4	2.3	21.3
ALL-STAR TOTALS	6	5	130	23	54	.426	0	0	—	17	19	.895	8	15	23	7	13	0	6	6	0	63	3.8	1.2	10.5

D'ANTONI, MICHAEL ANDREW (Mike) b. May 8, 1951 Ht. 6-3 Wt. 190 College—Marshall

SEASON—TEAM	G	GS	MIN	FGM	FGA	PCT	3FGM	3FGA	PCT	FTM	FTA	PCT	O-RB	D-RB	TOT	AST	PF	DQ	STL	TO	BLK	PTS	RPG	APG	PPG
73-74—Kansas City-Omaha	52	—	989	107	266	.402	—	—	—	33	47	.702	24	69	93	123	112	0	75	—	15	247	1.8	2.4	4.8
74-75—Kansas City-Omaha	67	—	759	69	173	.399	—	—	—	28	36	.778	13	64	77	107	106	0	67	—	12	166	1.1	1.6	2.5
75-76—Kansas City	9	—	101	7	27	.259	—	—	—	2	2	1.000	4	10	14	16	18	0	10	—	0	16	1.6	1.8	1.8
75-76—St. Louis (A)	50	—	798	77	162	.475	0	4	.000	19	26	.731	16	60	76	115	134	—	63	47	14	173	1.5	2.3	3.5
76-77—San Antonio	2	—	9	1	3	.333	—	—	—	1	2	.500	0	2	2	2	3	0	0	—	0	3	1.0	1.0	1.5
REG. NBA TOTALS	130	—	1858	184	469	.392	—	—	—	64	87	.736	41	145	186	248	239	0	152	—	27	432	1.4	1.9	3.3
REG. ABA TOTALS	50	—	798	77	162	.475	0	4	.000	19	26	.731	16	60	76	115	134	—	63	47	14	173	1.5	2.3	3.5
NBA PLAYOFF TOTALS	4	—	42	7	14	.500	—	—	—	4	4	1.000	2	5	7	1	6	0	4	—	1	18	1.8	0.3	4.5

DARCEY, HENRY J. (Pete) b. March 3, 1930 Ht. 6-9 Wt. 235 College—Oklahoma State

SEASON—TEAM	G	GS	MIN	FGM	FGA	PCT	3FGM	3FGA	PCT	FTM	FTA	PCT	O-RB	D-RB	TOT	AST	PF	DQ	STL	TO	BLK	PTS	RPG	APG	PPG
52-53—Milwaukee	12	—	90	3	18	.167	—	—	—	5	9	.556	—	—	10	2	29	2	—	—	—	11	0.8	0.2	0.9
REG. SEASON TOTALS	12	—	90	3	18	.167	—	—	—	5	9	.556	—	—	10	2	29	2	—	—	—	11	0.8	0.2	0.9

DARDEN, JAMES W. (Jimmy) b. June 19, 1922 d. April 29, 1994 Ht. 6-1 Wt. 170 College—Wyoming/Denver

SEASON—TEAM	G	GS	MIN	FGM	FGA	PCT	3FGM	3FGA	PCT	FTM	FTA	PCT	O-RB	D-RB	TOT	AST	PF	DQ	STL	TO	BLK	PTS	RPG	APG	PPG
48-49—Denver (N)	57	—	—	197	—	—	—	—	—	193	259	.745	—	—	—	149	—	—	—	—	—	587	—	—	10.3
49-50—Denver	26	—	—	78	243	.321	—	—	—	55	80	.688	—	—	—	67	67	—	—	—	—	211	—	2.6	8.1
REG. NBA TOTALS	26	—	—	78	243	.321	—	—	—	55	80	.688	—	—	—	67	67	—	—	—	—	211	—	2.6	8.1
REG. NBL TOTALS	57	—	—	197	—	—	—	—	—	193	259	.745	—	—	—	149	—	—	—	—	—	587	—	—	10.3

DARDEN, OLIVER (Ollie) b. July 28, 1944 Ht. 6-7 Wt. 240 College—Michigan

SEASON—TEAM	G	GS	MIN	FGM	FGA	PCT	3FGM	3FGA	PCT	FTM	FTA	PCT	O-RB	D-RB	TOT	AST	PF	DQ	STL	TO	BLK	PTS	RPG	APG	PPG
67-68—Indiana (A)	77	—	2045	371	831	.446	0	1	.000	180	270	.667	—	—	527	69	277	2	—	140	—	922	6.8	0.9	12.0
68-69—N.Y.-Ken. (A)	77	—	1947	318	714	.445	1	5	.200	178	240	.742	—	—	594	104	274	5	—	138	—	815	7.7	1.4	10.6
69-70—Ken.-Indiana (A)	69	—	819	126	327	.385	1	5	.200	57	87	.655	—	—	260	46	142	1	—	—	—	310	3.8	0.7	4.5
REG. ABA TOTALS	223	—	4811	815	1872	.435	2	11	.182	415	597	.695	—	—	1381	219	693	8	—	278	—	2047	6.2	1.0	9.2
ABA PLAYOFF TOTALS	18	—	183	44	83	.530	1	2	.500	13	20	.650	—	—	62	12	35	0	—	11	—	102	3.4	0.7	5.7

DARK, JESSE L. b. September 2, 1951 Ht. 6-4½ Wt. 210 College—Virginia Commonwealth

SEASON—TEAM	G	GS	MIN	FGM	FGA	PCT	3FGM	3FGA	PCT	FTM	FTA	PCT	O-RB	D-RB	TOT	AST	PF	DQ	STL	TO	BLK	PTS	RPG	APG	PPG
74-75—New York	47	—	401	74	157	.471	—	—	—	22	40	.550	15	22	37	30	48	0	3	—	1	170	0.8	0.6	3.6
REG. SEASON TOTALS	47	—	401	74	157	.471	—	—	—	22	40	.550	15	22	37	30	48	0	3	—	1	170	0.8	0.6	3.6
PLAYOFF TOTALS	2	—	11	1	6	.167	—	—	—	5	5	1.000	1	0	1	1	2	0	0	—	0	7	0.5	0.5	3.5

DARNELL, RICK b. January 1, 1953 Ht. 6-10 Wt. 215 College—San Jose State

SEASON—TEAM	G	GS	MIN	FGM	FGA	PCT	3FGM	3FGA	PCT	FTM	FTA	PCT	O-RB	D-RB	TOT	AST	PF	DQ	STL	TO	BLK	PTS	RPG	APG	PPG
75-76—Virginia (A)	11	—	120	11	30	.367	0	0	—	4	7	.571	12	24	36	9	30	—	5	14	3	26	3.3	0.8	2.4
REG. ABA TOTALS	11	—	120	11	30	.367	0	0	—	4	7	.571	12	24	36	9	30	—	5	14	3	26	3.3	0.8	2.4

DARROW, JAMES K. (Jimmy) b. September 25, 1937 d. June 8, 1987 Ht. 5-10 Wt. 170 College—Bowling Green

SEASON—TEAM	G	GS	MIN	FGM	FGA	PCT	3FGM	3FGA	PCT	FTM	FTA	PCT	O-RB	D-RB	TOT	AST	PF	DQ	STL	TO	BLK	PTS	RPG	APG	PPG
61-62—St. Louis	5	—	34	3	15	.200	—	—	—	6	7	.857	—	—	7	6	9	0	—	—	—	12	1.4	1.2	2.4
REG. SEASON TOTALS	5	—	34	3	15	.200	—	—	—	6	7	.857	—	—	7	6	9	0	—	—	—	12	1.4	1.2	2.4

DAUGHERTY, BRADLEY LEE (Brad, Big Dukie, Hooch) b. October 19, 1965 Ht. 7-0 Wt. 263 College—North Carolina

SEASON—TEAM	G	GS	MIN	FGM	FGA	PCT	3FGM	3FGA	PCT	FTM	FTA	PCT	O-RB	D-RB	TOT	AST	PF	DQ	STL	TO	BLK	PTS	RPG	APG	PPG
86-87—Cleveland	80	80	2695	487	905	.538	0	0	—	279	401	.696	152	495	647	304	248	3	49	248	63	1253	8.1	3.8	15.7
87-88—Cleveland	79	78	2957	551	1081	.510	0	2	.000	378	528	.716	151	514	665	333	235	2	48	267	56	1480	8.4	4.2	18.7
88-89—Cleveland	78	78	2821	544	1012	.538	1	3	.333	386	524	.737	167	551	718	285	175	1	63	230	40	1475	9.2	3.7	18.9
89-90—Cleveland	41	40	1438	244	509	.479	0	2	.000	202	287	.704	77	296	373	130	108	1	29	110	22	690	9.1	3.2	16.8
90-91—Cleveland	76	76	2946	605	1155	.524	0	3	.000	435	579	.751	177	653	830	253	191	2	74	211	46	1645	10.9	3.3	21.6
91-92—Cleveland	73	73	2643	576	1010	.570	0	2	.000	414	533	.777	191	569	760	262	190	1	65	185	78	1566	10.4	3.6	21.5
92-93—Cleveland	71	71	2691	520	911	.571	1	2	.500	391	492	.795	164	562	726	312	174	0	53	150	56	1432	10.2	4.4	20.2
93-94—Cleveland	50	50	1838	296	606	.488	0	0	—	256	326	.785	128	380	508	149	145	1	41	110	36	848	10.2	3.0	17.0
REG. SEASON TOTALS	548	546	20029	3823	7189	.532	2	14	.143	2741	3670	.747	1207	4020	5227	2028	1466	11	422	1511	397	10389	9.5	3.7	19.0
PLAYOFF TOTALS	41	41	1600	275	530	.519	0	2	.000	232	307	.756	89	330	419	137	113	1	27	98	40	782	10.2	3.3	19.1
ALL-STAR TOTALS	5	0	76	15	29	.517	0	0	—	4	7	.571	9	15	24	3	7	0	2	4	1	34	4.8	0.6	6.8

DAUGHTRY, MACK b. 1947 Ht. 6-3 Wt. 175 College—Albany State

SEASON—TEAM	G	GS	MIN	FGM	FGA	PCT	3FGM	3FGA	PCT	FTM	FTA	PCT	O-RB	D-RB	TOT	AST	PF	DQ	STL	TO	BLK	PTS	RPG	APG	PPG
70-71—Carolina (A)	4	—	43	4	10	.400	0	0	—	5	5	1.000	—	—	5	3	4	—	—	—	—	13	1.3	0.8	3.3
REG. ABA TOTALS	4	—	43	4	10	.400	0	0	—	5	5	1.000	—	—	5	3	4	—	—	—	—	13	1.3	0.8	3.3

DAVIES, ROBERT EDRIS (**Bob, Harrisburg Houdini**) b. January 15, 1920 d. April 22, 1990 Ht. 6-1 Wt. 175 College—Franklin & Marshall/Seton Hall

SEASON—TEAM	G	GS	MIN	FGM	FGA	PCT	3FGM	3FGA	PCT	FTM	FTA	PCT	O-RB	D-RB	TOT	AST	PF	DQ	STL	TO	BLK	PTS	RPG	APG	PPG
45-46—Rochester (N)	27	—	—	86	—	—	—	—	—	70	103	.680	—	—	—	—	85	—	—	—	—	242	—	—	9.0
46-47—Rochester (N)	32	—	—	166	—	—	—	—	—	130	166	.783	—	—	—	—	90	—	—	—	—	462	—	—	14.4
47-48—Rochester (N)	48	—	—	176	—	—	—	—	—	120	160	.750	—	—	—	—	111	—	—	—	—	472	—	—	9.8
48-49—Rochester	60	—	—	317	871	.364	—	—	—	270	348	.776	—	—	—	321	197	—	—	—	—	904	—	5.4	15.1
49-50—Rochester	64	—	—	317	887	.357	—	—	—	261	347	.752	—	—	—	294	187	—	—	—	—	895	—	4.6	14.0
50-51—Rochester	63	—	—	326	877	.372	—	—	—	303	381	.795	—	—	197	287	208	7	—	—	—	955	3.1	4.6	15.2
51-52—Rochester	65	—	2394	379	990	.383	—	—	—	294	379	.776	—	—	189	390	269	10	—	—	—	1052	2.9	6.0	16.2
52-53—Rochester	66	—	2216	339	880	.385	—	—	—	351	466	.753	—	—	195	280	261	7	—	—	—	1029	3.0	4.2	15.6
53-54—Rochester	72	—	2137	288	777	.371	—	—	—	311	433	.718	—	—	194	323	224	4	—	—	—	887	2.7	4.5	12.3
54-55—Rochester	72	—	1870	326	785	.415	—	—	—	220	293	.751	—	—	205	355	220	2	—	—	—	872	2.8	4.9	12.1
REG. NBA TOTALS	462	—	8617	2292	6067	.378	—	—	—	2010	2647	.759	—	—	980	2250	1566	30	—	—	—	6594	2.9	4.9	14.3
REG. NBL TOTALS	107	—	—	428	—	—	—	—	—	320	429	.746	—	—	—	—	286	—	—	—	—	1176	—	—	11.0
NBA PLAYOFF TOTALS	38	—	571	173	508	.341	—	—	—	160	203	.788	—	—	78	162	124	2	—	—	—	506	2.4	4.3	13.3
NBL PLAYOFF TOTALS	29	—	—	138	—	—	—	—	—	122	168	.726	—	—	—	—	71	—	—	—	—	398	—	—	13.7
NBA ALL-STAR TOTALS	4	—	75	19	40	.475	—	—	—	10	14	.714	—	—	13	17	13	0	—	—	—	48	3.3	4.3	12.0

DAVIS, ANTONIO LEE b. October 31, 1968 Ht. 6-9 Wt. 230 College—Texas El Paso

SEASON—TEAM	G	GS	MIN	FGM	FGA	PCT	3FGM	3FGA	PCT	FTM	FTA	PCT	O-RB	D-RB	TOT	AST	PF	DQ	STL	TO	BLK	PTS	RPG	APG	PPG
93-94—Indiana	81	4	1732	216	425	.508	0	1	.000	194	302	.642	190	315	505	55	189	1	45	107	84	626	6.2	0.7	7.7
REG. SEASON TOTALS	81	4	1732	216	425	.508	0	1	.000	194	302	.642	190	315	505	55	189	1	45	107	84	626	6.2	0.7	7.7
PLAYOFF TOTALS	16	0	401	48	89	.539	1	1	1.000	37	66	.561	37	69	106	7	47	0	11	22	18	134	6.6	0.4	8.4

DAVIS, AUBREY D. b. March 28, 1921 Ht. 6-2 Wt. 175 College—Oklahoma Baptist

SEASON—TEAM	G	GS	MIN	FGM	FGA	PCT	3FGM	3FGA	PCT	FTM	FTA	PCT	O-RB	D-RB	TOT	AST	PF	DQ	STL	TO	BLK	PTS	RPG	APG	PPG
46-47—St. Louis	59	—	—	107	381	.281	—	—	—	73	115	.635	—	—	—	14	136	—	—	—	—	287	—	0.2	4.9
48-49—Hammond (N)	8	—	—	3	—	—	—	—	—	3	7	.429	—	—	—	—	5	—	—	—	—	9	—	—	1.1
REG. NBA TOTALS	59	—	—	107	381	.281	—	—	—	73	115	.635	—	—	—	14	136	—	—	—	—	287	—	0.2	4.9
REG. NBL TOTALS	8	—	—	3	—	—	—	—	—	3	7	.429	—	—	—	—	5	—	—	—	—	9	—	—	1.1
NBA PLAYOFF TOTALS	3	—	—	2	6	.333	—	—	—	3	3	1.000	—	—	—	—	3	—	—	—	—	7	—	0.0	2.3

DAVIS, BRADLEY ERNEST (**Brad**) b. December 17, 1955 Ht. 6-3 Wt. 180 College—Maryland

SEASON—TEAM	G	GS	MIN	FGM	FGA	PCT	3FGM	3FGA	PCT	FTM	FTA	PCT	O-RB	D-RB	TOT	AST	PF	DQ	STL	TO	BLK	PTS	RPG	APG	PPG
77-78—Los Angeles	33	—	334	30	72	.417	—	—	—	22	29	.759	4	31	35	83	39	1	15	35	2	82	1.1	2.5	2.5
78-79—L.A.-Indiana	27	—	298	31	55	.564	—	—	—	16	23	.696	1	16	17	52	32	0	16	17	2	78	0.6	1.9	2.9
79-80—Indiana-Utah	18	—	268	35	63	.556	0	1	.000	13	16	.813	4	13	17	50	28	0	13	14	1	83	0.9	2.8	4.6
80-81—Dallas	56	—	1686	230	410	.561	3	17	.176	163	204	.799	29	122	151	385	156	2	52	123	11	626	2.7	6.9	11.2
81-82—Dallas	82	82	2614	397	771	.515	14	49	.286	185	230	.804	35	191	226	509	218	5	73	159	6	993	2.8	6.2	12.1
82-83—Dallas	79	78	2323	359	628	.572	11	43	.256	186	220	.845	34	164	198	565	176	2	80	143	11	915	2.5	7.2	11.6
83-84—Dallas	81	81	2665	345	651	.530	7	38	.184	199	238	.836	41	146	187	561	218	4	94	166	13	896	2.3	6.9	11.1
84-85—Dallas	82	82	2539	310	614	.505	47	115	.409	158	178	.888	39	154	193	581	219	1	91	123	10	825	2.4	7.1	10.1
85-86—Dallas	82	43	1971	267	502	.532	32	89	.360	198	228	.868	26	120	146	467	174	2	57	110	15	764	1.8	5.7	9.3
86-87—Dallas	82	6	1582	199	436	.456	32	106	.302	147	171	.860	27	87	114	373	159	0	63	114	10	577	1.4	4.5	7.0
87-88—Dallas	75	12	1480	208	415	.501	30	74	.405	91	108	.843	18	84	102	303	149	0	51	91	18	537	1.4	4.0	7.2
88-89—Dallas	78	4	1395	183	379	.483	32	102	.314	99	123	.805	14	94	108	242	151	0	48	92	18	497	1.4	3.1	6.4
89-90—Dallas	73	2	1292	179	365	.490	35	104	.337	77	100	.770	12	81	93	242	151	2	47	86	9	470	1.3	3.3	6.4
90-91—Dallas	80	6	1426	159	373	.426	22	85	.259	91	118	.771	13	105	118	230	212	1	45	77	17	431	1.5	2.9	5.4
91-92—Dallas	33	0	429	38	86	.442	5	18	.278	11	15	.733	4	29	33	66	57	0	11	27	3	92	1.0	2.0	2.8
REG. SEASON TOTALS	961	396	22302	2970	5820	.510	270	841	.321	1656	2001	.828	301	1437	1738	4709	2139	20	756	1377	146	7866	1.8	4.9	8.2
PLAYOFF TOTALS	45	14	950	125	236	.530	14	32	.438	77	91	.846	11	64	75	167	89	0	16	74	6	341	1.7	3.7	7.6

DAVIS, BRIAN KEITH b. June 21, 1970 Ht. 6-7 Wt. 200 College—Duke

SEASON—TEAM	G	GS	MIN	FGM	FGA	PCT	3FGM	3FGA	PCT	FTM	FTA	PCT	O-RB	D-RB	TOT	AST	PF	DQ	STL	TO	BLK	PTS	RPG	APG	PPG
93-94—Minnesota	68	3	374	40	126	.317	1	3	.333	50	68	.735	21	34	55	22	34	0	16	19	4	131	0.8	0.3	1.9
REG. SEASON TOTALS	68	3	374	40	126	.317	1	3	.333	50	68	.735	21	34	55	22	34	0	16	19	4	131	0.8	0.3	1.9

DAVIS, CHARLES EDWARD JR. (**Charlie**) b. October 5, 1958 Ht. 6-7 Wt. 215 College—Vanderbilt

SEASON—TEAM	G	GS	MIN	FGM	FGA	PCT	3FGM	3FGA	PCT	FTM	FTA	PCT	O-RB	D-RB	TOT	AST	PF	DQ	STL	TO	BLK	PTS	RPG	APG	PPG
81-82—Washington	54	10	575	88	184	.478	0	2	.000	30	37	.811	54	79	133	31	89	0	10	43	13	206	2.5	0.6	3.8
82-83—Washington	74	10	1161	251	534	.470	2	10	.200	56	89	.629	83	130	213	73	122	0	32	91	22	560	2.9	1.0	7.6
83-84—Washington	46	0	467	103	218	.472	1	9	.111	24	39	.615	34	69	103	30	58	1	14	36	10	231	2.2	0.7	5.0
84-85—Wash.-Milw.	61	2	774	153	356	.430	1	10	.100	51	62	.823	59	94	153	51	113	1	22	54	5	358	2.5	0.8	5.9
85-86—Milwaukee	57	7	873	188	397	.474	3	24	.125	61	75	.813	60	110	170	55	113	1	26	50	7	440	3.0	1.0	7.7
87-88—Milw.-S.A.	21	0	226	48	115	.417	1	17	.059	7	10	.700	16	25	41	20	29	0	2	18	4	104	2.0	1.0	5.0
88-89—Chicago	49	3	545	81	190	.426	4	15	.267	19	26	.731	47	67	114	31	58	1	11	22	5	185	2.3	0.6	3.8
89-90—Chicago	53	0	429	58	158	.367	7	25	.280	7	8	.875	25	56	81	18	52	0	10	20	8	130	1.5	0.3	2.5
REG. SEASON TOTALS	415	32	5050	970	2152	.451	19	112	.170	255	346	.737	378	630	1008	309	634	4	127	334	74	2214	2.4	0.7	5.3
PLAYOFF TOTALS	49	0	476	64	161	.398	1	11	.091	30	35	.857	36	53	89	19	70	1	9	38	2	159	1.8	0.4	3.2

DAVIS, CHARLES LAWRENCE (**Charlie**) b. September 7, 1949   Ht. 6-1½ Wt. 180 College—Wake Forest

SEASON—TEAM	G	GS	MIN	FGM	FGA	PCT	3FGM	3FGA	PCT	FTM	FTA	PCT	O-RB	D-RB	TOT	AST	PF	DQ	STL	TO	BLK	PTS	RPG	APG	PPG
71-72—Cleveland	61	—	1144	229	569	.402	—	—	—	142	169	.840	—	—	92	123	143	3	—	—	—	600	1.5	2.0	9.8
72-73—Clev.-Port.	75	—	1419	263	631	.417	—	—	—	130	168	.774	—	—	116	185	194	7	—	—	—	656	1.5	2.5	8.7
73-74—Portland	8	—	90	14	40	.350	—	—	—	3	4	.750	2	9	11	11	7	0	2	—	0	31	1.4	1.4	3.9
REG. SEASON TOTALS	144	—	2653	506	1240	.408	—	—	—	275	341	.806	2	9	219	319	344	10	2	—	0	1287	1.5	2.2	8.9

DAVIS, DAMON WILLIAM (**Monti**) b. July 26, 1958   Ht. 6-7½ Wt. 220 College—Tennessee State

SEASON—TEAM	G	GS	MIN	FGM	FGA	PCT	3FGM	3FGA	PCT	FTM	FTA	PCT	O-RB	D-RB	TOT	AST	PF	DQ	STL	TO	BLK	PTS	RPG	APG	PPG
80-81—Phil.-Dallas	2	—	10	1	5	.200	0	0	—	1	5	.200	2	2	4	0	0	0	0	0	1	3	2.0	0.0	1.5
REG. SEASON TOTALS	2	—	10	1	5	.200	0	0	—	1	5	.200	2	2	4	0	0	0	0	0	1	3	2.0	0.0	1.5

DAVIS, DWIGHT E. (**Double D**) b. October 28, 1949   Ht. 6-8 Wt. 220 College—Houston

SEASON—TEAM	G	GS	MIN	FGM	FGA	PCT	3FGM	3FGA	PCT	FTM	FTA	PCT	O-RB	D-RB	TOT	AST	PF	DQ	STL	TO	BLK	PTS	RPG	APG	PPG
72-73—Cleveland	81	—	2151	293	748	.392	—	—	—	176	222	.793	—	—	563	118	297	5	—	—	—	762	7.0	1.5	9.4
73-74—Cleveland	76	—	2477	376	862	.436	—	—	—	197	274	.719	174	470	644	186	291	6	63	—	74	949	8.5	2.4	12.5
74-75—Cleveland	78	—	1964	295	666	.443	—	—	—	176	245	.718	108	356	464	150	254	3	45	—	39	766	5.9	1.9	9.8
75-76—Golden State	72	—	866	111	269	.413	—	—	—	78	113	.690	86	139	225	46	141	0	20	—	28	300	3.1	0.6	4.2
76-77—Golden State	33	—	552	55	124	.444	—	—	—	49	72	.681	34	61	95	29	93	1	11	—	8	159	2.9	0.9	4.8
REG. SEASON TOTALS	340	—	8010	1130	2669	.423	—	—	—	676	926	.730	402	1026	1991	529	1076	15	139	—	149	2936	5.9	1.6	8.6
PLAYOFF TOTALS	11	—	142	16	37	.432	—	—	—	18	22	.818	9	19	28	10	28	1	3	—	4	50	2.5	0.9	4.5

DAVIS, EDWARD J. (**Mickey**) b. June 16, 1950   Ht. 6-7 Wt. 205 College—Duquesne

SEASON—TEAM	G	GS	MIN	FGM	FGA	PCT	3FGM	3FGA	PCT	FTM	FTA	PCT	O-RB	D-RB	TOT	AST	PF	DQ	STL	TO	BLK	PTS	RPG	APG	PPG
71-72—Pittsburgh (A)	23	—	126	25	63	.397	0	2	.000	14	20	.700	—	—	41	9	23	—	—	17	—	64	1.8	0.4	2.8
72-73—Milwaukee	74	—	1046	152	347	.438	—	—	—	76	92	.826	—	—	226	72	119	0	—	—	—	380	3.1	1.0	5.1
73-74—Milwaukee	73	—	1012	169	335	.504	—	—	—	93	112	.830	78	146	224	87	94	0	27	—	5	431	3.1	1.2	5.9
74-75—Milwaukee	75	—	1077	174	363	.479	—	—	—	78	88	.886	68	169	237	79	103	0	30	—	5	426	3.2	1.1	5.7
75-76—Milwaukee	45	—	411	55	152	.362	—	—	—	50	63	.794	25	59	84	37	36	0	13	—	2	160	1.9	0.8	3.6
76-77—Milwaukee	19	—	165	29	68	.426	—	—	—	23	25	.920	11	18	29	20	11	0	6	—	4	81	1.5	1.1	4.3
REG. NBA TOTALS	286	—	3711	579	1265	.458	—	—	—	320	380	.842	182	392	800	295	363	0	76	—	16	1478	2.8	1.0	5.2
REG. ABA TOTALS	23	—	126	25	63	.397	0	2	.000	14	20	.700	—	—	41	9	23	—	—	17	—	64	1.8	0.4	2.8
NBA PLAYOFF TOTALS	21	—	299	38	82	.463	—	—	—	24	26	.923	8	26	46	17	33	0	4	—	2	100	2.2	0.8	4.8

DAVIS, ELLIOTT LYDELL (**Dale**) b. March 25, 1969   Ht. 6-11 Wt. 230 College—Clemson

SEASON—TEAM	G	GS	MIN	FGM	FGA	PCT	3FGM	3FGA	PCT	FTM	FTA	PCT	O-RB	D-RB	TOT	AST	PF	DQ	STL	TO	BLK	PTS	RPG	APG	PPG
91-92—Indiana	64	23	1301	154	279	.552	0	1	.000	87	152	.572	158	252	410	30	191	2	27	49	74	395	6.4	0.5	6.2
92-93—Indiana	82	82	2264	304	535	.568	0	0	—	119	225	.529	291	432	723	69	274	5	63	79	148	727	8.8	0.8	8.9
93-94—Indiana	66	64	2292	308	582	.529	0	1	.000	155	294	.527	280	438	718	100	214	1	48	102	106	771	10.9	1.5	11.7
REG. SEASON TOTALS	212	169	5857	766	1396	.549	0	2	.000	361	671	.538	729	1122	1851	199	679	8	138	230	328	1893	8.7	0.9	8.9
PLAYOFF TOTALS	23	20	764	68	128	.531	0	1	.000	12	40	.300	72	138	210	17	75	0	22	34	26	148	9.1	0.7	6.4

DAVIS, HARRY A. b. January 27, 1956   Ht. 6-7 Wt. 220 College—Florida State

SEASON—TEAM	G	GS	MIN	FGM	FGA	PCT	3FGM	3FGA	PCT	FTM	FTA	PCT	O-RB	D-RB	TOT	AST	PF	DQ	STL	TO	BLK	PTS	RPG	APG	PPG
78-79—Cleveland	40	—	394	66	153	.431	—	—	—	30	43	.698	27	39	66	16	66	1	13	23	8	162	1.7	0.4	4.1
79-80—San Antonio	4	—	30	6	12	.500	0	0	—	1	2	.500	2	4	6	0	8	0	1	3	0	13	1.5	0.0	3.3
REG. SEASON TOTALS	44	—	424	72	165	.436	0	0	—	31	45	.689	29	43	72	16	74	1	14	26	8	175	1.6	0.4	4.0

DAVIS, HUBERT IRA JR. b. May 17, 1970   Ht. 6-5 Wt. 183 College—North Carolina

SEASON—TEAM	G	GS	MIN	FGM	FGA	PCT	3FGM	3FGA	PCT	FTM	FTA	PCT	O-RB	D-RB	TOT	AST	PF	DQ	STL	TO	BLK	PTS	RPG	APG	PPG
92-93—New York	50	2	815	110	251	.438	6	19	.316	43	54	.796	13	43	56	83	71	1	22	45	4	269	1.1	1.7	5.4
93-94—New York	56	27	1333	238	505	.471	53	132	.402	85	103	.825	23	44	67	165	118	0	40	76	4	614	1.2	2.9	11.0
REG. SEASON TOTALS	106	29	2148	348	756	.460	59	151	.391	128	157	.815	36	87	123	248	189	1	62	121	8	883	1.2	2.3	8.3
PLAYOFF TOTALS	30	7	492	58	146	.397	11	37	.297	25	35	.714	6	21	27	31	51	0	11	32	3	152	0.9	1.0	5.1

DAVIS, JAMES R. (**Red**) b. April 22, 1932   Ht. 6-7 Wt. 220 College—St. John's

SEASON—TEAM	G	GS	MIN	FGM	FGA	PCT	3FGM	3FGA	PCT	FTM	FTA	PCT	O-RB	D-RB	TOT	AST	PF	DQ	STL	TO	BLK	PTS	RPG	APG	PPG
55-56—Rochester	3	—	16	0	6	.000	—	—	—	2	2	1.000	—	—	4	1	2	0	—	—	—	2	1.3	0.3	0.7
REG. SEASON TOTALS	3	—	16	0	6	.000	—	—	—	2	2	1.000	—	—	4	1	2	0	—	—	—	2	1.3	0.3	0.7

DAVIS, JAMES W. (**Jim**) b. December 18, 1941 Ht. 6-9½ Wt. 230 College—Colorado

SEASON—TEAM	G	GS	MIN	FGM	FGA	PCT	3FGM	3FGA	PCT	FTM	FTA	PCT	O-RB	D-RB	TOT	AST	PF	DQ	STL	TO	BLK	PTS	RPG	APG	PPG
67-68—St. Louis	50	—	394	61	139	.439	—	—	—	25	64	.391	—	—	123	13	85	2	—	—	—	147	2.5	0.3	2.9
68-69—Atlanta	78	—	1367	265	568	.467	—	—	—	154	231	.667	—	—	529	97	239	6	—	—	—	684	6.8	1.2	8.8
69-70—Atlanta	82	—	2623	438	943	.464	—	—	—	240	318	.755	—	—	796	238	335	5	—	—	—	1116	9.7	2.9	13.6
70-71—Atlanta	82	—	1864	241	503	.479	—	—	—	195	288	.677	—	—	546	108	253	5	—	—	—	677	6.7	1.3	8.3
71-72—Atlanta-Houston-Detroit	75	—	983	147	338	.435	—	—	—	100	154	.649	—	—	276	51	138	1	—	—	—	394	3.7	0.7	5.3
72-73—Detroit	73	—	771	131	257	.510	—	—	—	72	114	.632	—	—	261	56	126	2	—	—	—	334	3.6	0.8	4.6
73-74—Detroit	78	—	947	117	283	.413	—	—	—	90	139	.647	102	191	293	86	158	1	39	—	30	324	3.8	1.1	4.2
74-75—Detroit	79	—	1078	118	260	.454	—	—	—	85	117	.726	96	189	285	90	129	2	50	—	36	321	3.6	1.1	4.1
REG. SEASON TOTALS	597	—	10027	1518	3291	.461	—	—	—	961	1425	.674	198	380	3109	739	1463	24	89	—	66	3997	5.2	1.2	6.7
PLAYOFF TOTALS	33	—	382	49	114	.430	—	—	—	44	63	.698	6	14	92	16	62	2	3	—	1	142	2.8	0.5	4.3

DAVIS, JOHNNY REGINALD (**J.D.**) b. October 21, 1955 Ht. 6-1½ Wt. 170 College—Dayton

SEASON—TEAM	G	GS	MIN	FGM	FGA	PCT	3FGM	3FGA	PCT	FTM	FTA	PCT	O-RB	D-RB	TOT	AST	PF	DQ	STL	TO	BLK	PTS	RPG	APG	PPG
76-77—Portland	79	—	1451	234	531	.441	—	—	—	166	209	.794	62	64	126	148	128	1	41	—	11	634	1.6	1.9	8.0
77-78—Portland	82	—	2188	343	756	.454	—	—	—	188	227	.828	65	108	173	217	173	0	81	151	14	874	2.1	2.6	10.7
78-79—Indiana	79	—	2971	565	1240	.456	—	—	—	314	396	.793	70	121	191	453	177	1	95	214	22	1444	2.4	5.7	18.3
79-80—Indiana	82	—	2912	496	1159	.428	4	42	.095	304	352	.864	102	124	226	440	178	0	110	202	23	1300	2.8	5.4	15.9
80-81—Indiana	76	—	2536	426	917	.465	4	33	.121	238	299	.796	56	114	170	480	179	2	95	167	14	1094	2.2	6.3	14.4
81-82—Indiana	82	70	2664	538	1153	.467	5	27	.185	315	394	.799	72	106	178	346	176	1	76	186	11	1396	2.2	4.2	17.0
82-83—Atlanta	53	33	1465	258	567	.455	5	18	.278	164	206	.796	37	91	128	315	100	0	43	114	7	685	2.4	5.9	12.9
83-84—Atlanta	75	72	2079	354	800	.443	0	8	.000	217	256	.848	53	86	139	326	146	0	62	134	6	925	1.9	4.3	12.3
84-85—Cleveland	76	30	1920	337	791	.426	12	46	.261	255	300	.850	35	84	119	426	136	1	43	152	4	941	1.6	5.6	12.4
85-86—Clev.-Atlanta	66	7	1014	148	344	.430	3	13	.231	118	138	.855	8	47	55	217	76	0	37	78	4	417	0.8	3.3	6.3
REG. SEASON TOTALS	750	212	21200	3699	8258	.448	33	187	.176	2279	2777	.821	560	945	1505	3368	1469	6	683	1398	116	9710	2.0	4.5	12.9
PLAYOFF TOTALS	43	8	1070	178	392	.454	0	3	.000	89	114	.781	21	57	78	157	80	0	39	28	5	445	1.8	3.7	10.3

DAVIS, LEE OMMIE b. October 11, 1945 Ht. 6-8½ Wt. 235 College—North Carolina Central

SEASON—TEAM	G	GS	MIN	FGM	FGA	PCT	3FGM	3FGA	PCT	FTM	FTA	PCT	O-RB	D-RB	TOT	AST	PF	DQ	STL	TO	BLK	PTS	RPG	APG	PPG
68-69—New Orleans (A)	65	—	570	88	227	.388	1	4	.250	45	90	.500	—	—	202	18	87	1	—	31	—	222	3.1	0.3	3.4
69-70—New Orleans (A)	16	—	128	16	36	.444	0	0	—	8	15	.533	—	—	40	2	31	0	—	—	—	40	2.5	0.1	2.5
70-71—Memphis (A)	75	—	925	197	431	.457	0	2	.000	63	117	.538	—	—	251	62	169	—	—	—	—	457	3.3	0.8	6.1
71-72—Memphis (A)	58	—	550	101	231	.437	1	8	.125	25	43	.581	—	—	178	21	90	—	—	25	—	228	3.1	0.4	3.9
72-73—Memphis (A)	78	—	2111	453	871	.520	0	3	.000	131	209	.627	223	385	608	82	266	7	—	96	—	1037	7.8	1.1	13.3
73-74—Memphis (A)	79	—	1632	266	590	.451	1	4	.250	98	152	.645	139	280	419	139	237	—	28	104	40	631	5.3	1.8	8.0
74-75—San Diego (A)	75	—	1838	387	733	.528	4	16	.250	113	169	.669	178	314	492	110	179	—	40	92	40	891	6.6	1.5	11.9
75-76—San Diego (A)	7	—	51	2	11	.182	0	0	—	1	2	.500	0	5	5	1	12	—	0	1	0	5	0.7	0.1	0.7
REG. ABA TOTALS	453	—	7805	1510	3130	.482	7	37	.189	484	797	.607	540	984	2195	435	1071	8	68	349	80	3511	4.8	1.0	7.8
ABA PLAYOFF TOTALS	9	—	71	13	35	.371	0	1	.000	8	13	.615	0	0	33	6	14	0	0	5	0	34	3.7	0.7	3.8

DAVIS, MARK GILES b. June 8, 1963 Ht. 6-5 Wt. 195 College—Old Dominion

SEASON—TEAM	G	GS	MIN	FGM	FGA	PCT	3FGM	3FGA	PCT	FTM	FTA	PCT	O-RB	D-RB	TOT	AST	PF	DQ	STL	TO	BLK	PTS	RPG	APG	PPG
88-89—Milw.-Phoenix	33	0	258	49	102	.480	1	10	.100	28	34	.824	16	21	37	14	39	0	13	12	5	127	1.1	0.4	3.8
REG. SEASON TOTALS	33	0	258	49	102	.480	1	10	.100	28	34	.824	16	21	37	14	39	0	13	12	5	127	1.1	0.4	3.8

DAVIS, MELVYN JEROME (**Mel, Killer**) b. November 9, 1950 Ht. 6-8 Wt. 220 College—St. John's

SEASON—TEAM	G	GS	MIN	FGM	FGA	PCT	3FGM	3FGA	PCT	FTM	FTA	PCT	O-RB	D-RB	TOT	AST	PF	DQ	STL	TO	BLK	PTS	RPG	APG	PPG
73-74—New York	30	—	167	33	95	.347	—	—	—	12	16	.750	17	37	54	8	36	0	3	—	4	78	1.8	0.3	2.6
74-75—New York	62	—	903	154	395	.390	—	—	—	48	70	.686	70	251	321	54	105	0	16	—	8	356	5.2	0.9	5.7
75-76—New York	42	—	408	76	193	.394	—	—	—	22	29	.759	43	105	148	31	56	0	16	—	5	174	3.5	0.7	4.1
76-77—N.Y.-K- N.Y.-N.	56	—	1094	168	464	.362	—	—	—	64	91	.703	98	195	293	71	130	0	31	—	5	400	5.2	1.3	7.1
REG. SEASON TOTALS	190	—	2572	431	1147	.376	—	—	—	146	206	.709	228	588	816	164	327	0	66	—	22	1008	4.3	0.9	5.3
PLAYOFF TOTALS	7	—	40	11	24	.458	—	—	—	2	2	1.000	2	7	9	2	3	0	—	—	0	24	1.3	0.3	3.4

DAVIS, MICHAEL b. August 2, 1956 Ht. 6-10 Wt. 230 College—Mercer County CC/Maryland

SEASON—TEAM	G	GS	MIN	FGM	FGA	PCT	3FGM	3FGA	PCT	FTM	FTA	PCT	O-RB	D-RB	TOT	AST	PF	DQ	STL	TO	BLK	PTS	RPG	APG	PPG
82-83—New York	8	0	28	4	10	.400	0	0	—	6	10	.600	3	7	10	0	4	0	0	0	4	14	1.3	0.0	1.8
REG. SEASON TOTALS	8	0	28	4	10	.400	0	0	—	6	10	.600	3	7	10	0	4	0	0	0	4	14	1.3	0.0	1.8
PLAYOFF TOTALS	1	0	1	0	0	—	0	0	—	0	0	—	0	0	0	0	0	0	0	0	0	0	0.0	0.0	0.0

DAVIS, MICHAEL A. (Mike, Crusher) b. July 26, 1946 Ht. 6-3 Wt. 185 College—Virginia Union

SEASON—TEAM	G	GS	MIN	FGM	FGA	PCT	3FGM	3FGA	PCT	FTM	FTA	PCT	O-RB	D-RB	TOT	AST	PF	DQ	STL	TO	BLK	PTS	RPG	APG	PPG
69-70—Baltimore	56	—	1330	260	586	.444	—	—	—	149	192	.776	—	—	128	111	174	1	—	—	—	669	2.3	2.0	11.9
70-71—Buffalo	73	—	1617	317	774	.410	—	—	—	199	262	.760	—	—	187	153	220	7	—	—	—	833	2.6	2.1	11.4
71-72—Buffalo	62	—	1068	213	501	.425	—	—	—	138	180	.767	—	—	120	82	141	5	—	—	—	564	1.9	1.3	9.1
72-73—Baltimore	13	—	283	50	118	.424	—	—	—	23	25	.920	—	—	35	19	45	4	—	—	—	123	2.7	1.5	9.5
72-73—Memphis (A)	38	—	553	93	222	.419	6	23	.261	62	87	.713	21	20	41	47	87	2	—	36	—	254	1.1	1.2	6.7
REG. NBA TOTALS	204	—	4298	840	1979	.424	—	—	—	509	659	.772	—	—	470	365	580	17	—	—	—	2189	2.3	1.8	10.7
REG. ABA TOTALS	38	—	553	93	222	.419	6	23	.261	62	87	.713	21	20	41	47	87	2	—	36	—	254	1.1	1.2	6.7

DAVIS, RALPH E. b. September 7, 1938 Ht. 6-4 Wt. 180 College—Cincinnati

SEASON—TEAM	G	GS	MIN	FGM	FGA	PCT	3FGM	3FGA	PCT	FTM	FTA	PCT	O-RB	D-RB	TOT	AST	PF	DQ	STL	TO	BLK	PTS	RPG	APG	PPG
60-61—Cincinnati	73	—	1210	181	451	.401	—	—	—	34	52	.654	—	—	86	177	127	1	—	—	—	396	1.2	2.4	5.4
61-62—Chicago	77	—	1992	364	881	.413	—	—	—	71	103	.689	—	—	162	247	187	1	—	—	—	799	2.1	3.2	10.4
REG. SEASON TOTALS	150	—	3202	545	1332	.409	—	—	—	105	155	.677	—	—	248	424	314	2	—	—	—	1195	1.7	2.8	8.0

DAVIS, ROBERT (Bob) b. April 2, 1950 Ht. 6-7 Wt. 215 College—Weber State

SEASON—TEAM	G	GS	MIN	FGM	FGA	PCT	3FGM	3FGA	PCT	FTM	FTA	PCT	O-RB	D-RB	TOT	AST	PF	DQ	STL	TO	BLK	PTS	RPG	APG	PPG
72-73—Portland	9	—	41	6	28	.214	—	—	—	4	6	.667	—	—	5	2	5	0	—	—	—	16	0.6	0.2	1.8
REG. SEASON TOTALS	9	—	41	6	28	.214	—	—	—	4	6	.667	—	—	5	2	5	0	—	—	—	16	0.6	0.2	1.8

DAVIS, RONALD HOWARD (Ron) b. May 1, 1954 Ht. 6-6½ Wt. 200 College—Glendale CC/Washington State

SEASON—TEAM	G	GS	MIN	FGM	FGA	PCT	3FGM	3FGA	PCT	FTM	FTA	PCT	O-RB	D-RB	TOT	AST	PF	DQ	STL	TO	BLK	PTS	RPG	APG	PPG
76-77—Atlanta	7	—	67	8	35	.229	—	—	—	4	13	.308	2	5	7	2	9	0	7	—	0	20	1.0	0.3	2.9
80-81—San Diego	64	—	817	139	314	.443	2	8	.250	94	158	.595	47	72	119	47	98	0	36	61	11	374	1.9	0.7	5.8
81-82—San Diego	7	0	67	10	25	.400	0	0	—	3	6	.500	7	6	13	4	8	0	0	5	0	23	1.9	0.6	3.3
REG. SEASON TOTALS	78	0	951	157	374	.420	2	8	.250	101	177	.571	56	83	139	53	115	0	43	66	11	417	1.8	0.7	5.3

DAVIS, TERRY RAYMOND b. June 17, 1967 Ht. 6-10 Wt. 250 College—Virginia Union

SEASON—TEAM	G	GS	MIN	FGM	FGA	PCT	3FGM	3FGA	PCT	FTM	FTA	PCT	O-RB	D-RB	TOT	AST	PF	DQ	STL	TO	BLK	PTS	RPG	APG	PPG
89-90—Miami	63	9	884	122	262	.466	0	1	.000	54	87	.621	93	136	229	25	171	2	25	68	28	298	3.6	0.4	4.7
90-91—Miami	55	17	996	115	236	.487	1	2	.500	69	124	.556	107	159	266	39	129	2	18	36	28	300	4.8	0.7	5.5
91-92—Dallas	68	67	2149	256	531	.482	0	5	.000	181	285	.635	228	444	672	57	202	1	26	117	29	693	9.9	0.8	10.2
92-93—Dallas	75	74	2462	393	863	.455	2	8	.250	167	281	.594	259	442	701	68	199	3	36	160	28	955	9.3	0.9	12.7
93-94—Dallas	15	5	286	24	59	.407	0	0	—	8	12	.667	30	44	74	6	27	0	9	5	1	56	4.9	0.4	3.7
REG. SEASON TOTALS	276	172	6777	910	1951	.466	3	16	.188	479	789	.607	717	1225	1942	195	728	8	114	386	114	2302	7.0	0.7	8.3

DAVIS, WALTER FRANCIS (Walt, Buddy) b. January 5, 1931 Ht. 6-8 Wt. 205 College—Texas A&M

SEASON—TEAM	G	GS	MIN	FGM	FGA	PCT	3FGM	3FGA	PCT	FTM	FTA	PCT	O-RB	D-RB	TOT	AST	PF	DQ	STL	TO	BLK	PTS	RPG	APG	PPG
53-54—Philadelphia	68	—	1568	167	455	.367	—	—	—	65	101	.644	—	—	435	58	207	9	—	—	—	399	6.4	0.9	5.9
54-55—Philadelphia	61	—	766	70	182	.385	—	—	—	35	48	.729	—	—	206	36	100	0	—	—	—	175	3.4	0.6	2.9
55-56—Philadelphia	70	—	1097	123	333	.369	—	—	—	77	112	.688	—	—	276	56	230	7	—	—	—	323	3.9	0.8	4.6
56-57—Philadelphia	65	—	1250	178	437	.407	—	—	—	74	106	.698	—	—	306	52	235	9	—	—	—	430	4.7	0.8	6.6
57-58—Phil.-St. L.	61	—	663	85	244	.348	—	—	—	61	82	.744	—	—	174	29	143	0	—	—	—	231	2.9	0.5	3.8
REG. SEASON TOTALS	325	—	5344	623	1651	.377	—	—	—	312	449	.695	—	—	1397	231	915	25	—	—	—	1558	4.3	0.7	4.8
PLAYOFF TOTALS	21	—	172	25	64	.391	—	—	—	17	22	.773	—	—	69	7	51	0	—	—	—	67	3.3	0.3	3.2

DAVIS, WALTER PAUL (Sweet D, Greyhound) b. September 9, 1954 Ht. 6-6 Wt. 193 College—North Carolina

SEASON—TEAM	G	GS	MIN	FGM	FGA	PCT	3FGM	3FGA	PCT	FTM	FTA	PCT	O-RB	D-RB	TOT	AST	PF	DQ	STL	TO	BLK	PTS	RPG	APG	PPG
77-78—Phoenix	81	—	2590	786	1494	.526	—	—	—	387	466	.830	158	326	484	273	242	2	113	283	20	1959	6.0	3.4	24.2
78-79—Phoenix	79	—	2437	764	1362	.561	—	—	—	340	409	.831	111	262	373	339	250	5	147	293	26	1868	4.7	4.3	23.6
79-80—Phoenix	75	—	2309	657	1166	.563	0	4	.000	299	365	.819	75	197	272	337	202	2	114	242	19	1613	3.6	4.5	21.5
80-81—Phoenix	78	—	2182	593	1101	.539	7	17	.412	209	250	.836	63	137	200	302	192	3	97	222	12	1402	2.6	3.9	18.0
81-82—Phoenix	55	12	1182	350	669	.523	3	16	.188	91	111	.820	21	82	103	162	104	1	46	112	3	794	1.9	2.9	14.4
82-83—Phoenix	80	79	2491	665	1289	.516	7	23	.304	184	225	.818	63	134	197	397	186	2	117	188	12	1521	2.5	5.0	19.0
83-84—Phoenix	78	70	2546	652	1274	.512	20	87	.230	233	270	.863	38	164	202	429	202	0	107	213	12	1557	2.6	5.5	20.0
84-85—Phoenix	23	9	570	139	309	.450	3	10	.300	64	73	.877	6	29	35	98	42	0	18	50	0	345	1.5	4.3	15.0
85-86—Phoenix	70	62	2239	624	1287	.485	18	76	.237	257	305	.843	54	149	203	361	153	1	99	219	3	1523	2.9	5.2	21.8
86-87—Phoenix	79	79	2646	779	1515	.514	21	81	.259	288	334	.862	90	154	244	364	184	1	96	226	5	1867	3.1	4.6	23.6
87-88—Phoenix	68	48	1951	488	1031	.473	36	96	.375	205	231	.887	32	127	159	278	131	0	86	126	3	1217	2.3	4.1	17.9
88-89—Denver	81	0	1857	536	1076	.498	20	69	.290	175	199	.879	41	110	151	190	187	1	72	132	5	1267	1.9	2.3	15.6
89-90—Denver	69	0	1635	497	1033	.481	6	46	.130	207	227	.912	46	133	179	155	160	1	59	102	9	1207	2.6	2.2	17.5
90-91—Denver-Port.	71	14	1483	403	862	.468	11	36	.306	107	117	.915	71	110	181	125	150	2	80	88	3	924	2.5	1.8	13.0
91-92—Denver	46	0	741	185	403	.459	5	16	.313	82	94	.872	20	50	70	68	69	0	29	45	1	457	1.5	1.5	9.9
REG. SEASON TOTALS	1033	373	28859	8118	15871	.511	157	577	.272	3128	3676	.851	889	2164	3053	3878	2454	21	1280	2541	133	19521	3.0	3.8	18.9
PLAYOFF TOTALS	78	20	2184	591	1192	.496	5	26	.192	263	317	.830	82	158	240	312	186	0	88	189	16	1450	3.1	4.0	18.6
ALL-STAR TOTALS	6	1	109	25	55	.455	1	1	1.000	8	8	1.000	6	14	20	15	5	0	7	6	0	59	3.3	2.5	9.8

DAVIS, WARREN LEE b. June 30, 1943 Ht. 6-6 Wt. 213 College—North Carolina A&T

SEASON—TEAM	G	GS	MIN	FGM	FGA	PCT	3FGM	3FGA	PCT	FTM	FTA	PCT	O-RB	D-RB	TOT	AST	PF	DQ	STL	TO	BLK	PTS	RPG	APG	PPG
67-68—Anaheim (A)	54	—	1816	343	758	.453	1	7	.143	229	353	.649	221	345	566	75	193	3	—	128	—	916	10.5	1.4	17.0
68-69—Los Angeles (A)	78	—	2406	356	711	.501	0	2	.000	282	433	.651	254	523	777	129	269	3	—	183	—	994	10.0	1.7	12.7
69-70—L.A.-Pitt. (A)	80	—	2647	428	861	.497	1	3	.333	304	418	.727	278	629	907	244	300	5	—	—	—	1161	11.3	3.1	14.5
70-71—Floridians (A)	76	—	1995	308	686	.449	0	2	.000	209	300	.697	—	—	639	170	254	—	—	—	—	825	8.4	2.2	10.9
71-72—Car.-Memphis (A)	86	—	2331	337	701	.481	0	2	.000	207	299	.692	—	—	693	180	279	—	—	187	—	881	8.1	2.1	10.2
72-73—Memphis (A)	73	—	1895	250	498	.502	0	0	—	172	227	.758	153	362	515	146	212	5	—	129	—	672	7.1	2.0	9.2
REG. ABA TOTALS	447	—	13090	2022	4215	.480	2	16	.125	1403	2030	.691	906	1859	4097	944	1507	16	—	627	—	5449	9.2	2.1	12.2
ABA PLAYOFF TOTALS	6	—	180	28	58	.483	0	0	—	22	29	.759	—	—	48	31	26	0	—	—	—	78	8.0	5.2	13.0
ABA ALL-STAR TOTALS	2	—	29	4	11	.364	0	1	.000	1	1	1.000	3	4	9	2	3	0	—	3	—	9	4.5	1.0	4.5

DAVIS, WILLIAM F. (Bill) b. October 3, 1921 Ht. 6-3 Wt. 215 College—Notre Dame

SEASON—TEAM	G	GS	MIN	FGM	FGA	PCT	3FGM	3FGA	PCT	FTM	FTA	PCT	O-RB	D-RB	TOT	AST	PF	DQ	STL	TO	BLK	PTS	RPG	APG	PPG
46-47—Chicago	47	—	—	35	146	.240	—	—	—	14	41	.341	—	—	—	11	92	—	—	—	—	84	—	0.2	1.8
REG. SEASON TOTALS	47	—	—	35	146	.240	—	—	—	14	41	.341	—	—	—	11	92	—	—	—	—	84	—	0.2	1.8
PLAYOFF TOTALS	7	—	—	2	14	.143	—	—	—	2	5	.400	—	—	—	—	10	—	—	—	—	6	0.0	0.0	0.9

DAVIS, WILLIE EDWARD b. August 9, 1945 Ht. 6-8 Wt. 234 College—North Texas

SEASON—TEAM	G	GS	MIN	FGM	FGA	PCT	3FGM	3FGA	PCT	FTM	FTA	PCT	O-RB	D-RB	TOT	AST	PF	DQ	STL	TO	BLK	PTS	RPG	APG	PPG
70-71—Texas (A)	8	—	29	7	15	.467	0	0	—	4	8	.500	—	—	13	2	10	—	—	—	—	18	1.6	0.3	2.3
REG. ABA TOTALS	8	—	29	7	15	.467	0	0	—	4	8	.500	—	—	13	2	10	—	—	—	—	18	1.6	0.3	2.3

DAWKINS, DARRYL (Chocolate Thunder) b. January 11, 1957 Ht. 6-11 Wt. 252 College—None

SEASON—TEAM	G	GS	MIN	FGM	FGA	PCT	3FGM	3FGA	PCT	FTM	FTA	PCT	O-RB	D-RB	TOT	AST	PF	DQ	STL	TO	BLK	PTS	RPG	APG	PPG
75-76—Philadelphia	37	—	165	41	82	.500	—	—	—	8	24	.333	15	34	49	3	40	1	2	—	9	90	1.3	0.1	2.4
76-77—Philadelphia	59	—	684	135	215	.628	—	—	—	40	79	.506	59	171	230	24	129	1	12	—	49	310	3.9	0.4	5.3
77-78—Philadelphia	70	—	1722	332	577	.575	—	—	—	156	220	.709	117	438	555	85	268	5	34	123	125	820	7.9	1.2	11.7
78-79—Philadelphia	78	—	2035	430	831	.517	—	—	—	158	235	.672	123	508	631	128	295	5	32	197	143	1018	8.1	1.6	13.1
79-80—Philadelphia	80	—	2541	494	946	.522	0	6	.000	190	291	.653	197	496	693	149	328	8	49	230	142	1178	8.7	1.9	14.7
80-81—Philadelphia	76	—	2088	423	697	.607	0	0	—	219	304	.720	106	439	545	109	316	9	38	220	112	1065	7.2	1.4	14.0
81-82—Philadelphia	48	36	1124	207	367	.564	0	2	.000	114	164	.695	68	237	305	55	193	5	19	96	55	528	6.4	1.1	11.0
82-83—New Jersey	81	81	2093	401	669	.599	0	0	—	166	257	.646	127	293	420	114	379	23	67	281	152	968	5.2	1.4	12.0
83-84—New Jersey	81	80	2417	507	855	.593	2	5	.400	341	464	.735	159	382	541	123	386	22	60	231	136	1357	6.7	1.5	16.8
84-85—New Jersey	39	30	972	192	339	.566	0	1	.000	143	201	.711	55	126	181	45	171	11	14	93	35	527	4.6	1.2	13.5
85-86—New Jersey	51	3	1207	284	441	.644	0	1	.000	210	297	.707	85	166	251	77	227	10	16	124	59	778	4.9	1.5	15.3
86-87—New Jersey	6	2	106	20	32	.625	0	0	—	17	24	.708	9	10	19	2	25	0	2	15	3	57	3.2	0.3	9.5
87-88—Utah-Detroit	6	0	33	2	9	.222	0	0	—	6	15	.400	2	3	5	2	14	0	0	7	2	10	0.8	0.3	1.7
88-89—Detroit	14	0	48	9	19	.474	0	0	—	9	18	.500	3	4	7	1	13	0	0	4	1	27	0.5	0.1	1.9
REG. SEASON TOTALS	726	232	17235	3477	6079	.572	2	15	.133	1777	2593	.685	1125	3307	4432	917	2784	100	345	1621	1023	8733	6.1	1.3	12.0
PLAYOFF TOTALS	109	25	2734	542	992	.546	0	7	.000	291	414	.703	160	505	665	119	438	16	47	200	165	1375	6.1	1.1	12.6

DAWKINS, JOHNNY EARL JR. b. September 28, 1963 Ht. 6-2 Wt. 170 College—Duke

SEASON—TEAM	G	GS	MIN	FGM	FGA	PCT	3FGM	3FGA	PCT	FTM	FTA	PCT	O-RB	D-RB	TOT	AST	PF	DQ	STL	TO	BLK	PTS	RPG	APG	PPG
86-87—San Antonio	81	14	1682	334	764	.437	14	47	.298	153	191	.801	56	113	169	290	118	0	67	120	3	835	2.1	3.6	10.3
87-88—San Antonio	65	61	2179	405	835	.485	19	61	.311	198	221	.896	66	138	204	480	95	0	88	154	2	1027	3.1	7.4	15.8
88-89—San Antonio	32	30	1083	177	400	.443	0	4	.000	100	112	.893	32	69	101	224	64	0	55	111	0	454	3.2	7.0	14.2
89-90—Philadelphia	81	81	2865	465	950	.489	22	66	.333	210	244	.861	48	199	247	601	159	1	121	214	9	1162	3.0	7.4	14.3
90-91—Philadelphia	4	4	124	26	41	.634	1	4	.250	10	11	.909	0	16	16	28	4	0	3	8	0	63	4.0	7.0	15.8
91-92—Philadelphia	82	82	2815	394	902	.437	36	101	.356	164	186	.882	42	185	227	567	158	0	89	183	5	988	2.8	6.9	12.0
92-93—Philadelphia	74	10	1598	258	590	.437	26	84	.310	113	142	.796	33	103	136	339	91	0	80	121	4	655	1.8	4.6	8.9
93-94—Philadelphia	72	12	1343	177	423	.418	37	105	.352	84	100	.840	28	95	123	263	74	0	63	111	5	475	1.7	3.7	6.6
REG. SEASON TOTALS	491	294	13689	2236	4905	.456	155	472	.328	1032	1207	.855	305	918	1223	2792	763	1	566	1022	28	5659	2.5	5.7	11.5
PLAYOFF TOTALS	13	10	439	59	138	.428	0	9	.000	39	47	.830	6	19	25	98	24	0	19	30	2	157	1.9	7.5	12.1

DAWKINS, PAUL LAMAR b. June 10, 1957 Ht. 6-5 Wt. 190 College—Northern Illinois

SEASON—TEAM	G	GS	MIN	FGM	FGA	PCT	3FGM	3FGA	PCT	FTM	FTA	PCT	O-RB	D-RB	TOT	AST	PF	DQ	STL	TO	BLK	PTS	RPG	APG	PPG
79-80—Utah	57	—	776	141	300	.470	1	5	.200	33	48	.688	42	83	125	77	112	0	33	76	9	316	2.2	1.4	5.5
REG. SEASON TOTALS	57	—	776	141	300	.470	1	5	.200	33	48	.688	42	83	125	77	112	0	33	76	9	316	2.2	1.4	5.5

DAWSON, JAMES C. (Jimmy) b. April 18, 1945 Ht. 6½ Wt. 175 College—Illinois

SEASON—TEAM	G	GS	MIN	FGM	FGA	PCT	3FGM	3FGA	PCT	FTM	FTA	PCT	O-RB	D-RB	TOT	AST	PF	DQ	STL	TO	BLK	PTS	RPG	APG	PPG
67-68—Indiana (A)	21	—	288	46	133	.346	1	7	.143	25	43	.581	—	—	21	32	16	0	—	16	—	118	1.0	1.5	5.6
REG. ABA TOTALS	21	—	288	46	133	.346	1	7	.143	25	43	.581	—	—	21	32	16	0	—	16	—	118	1.0	1.5	5.6

DAWSON, TONY b. August 25, 1967 Ht. 6-7 Wt. 215 College—Gulf Coast CC/Florida State

SEASON—TEAM	G	GS	MIN	FGM	FGA	PCT	3FGM	3FGA	PCT	FTM	FTA	PCT	O-RB	D-RB	TOT	AST	PF	DQ	STL	TO	BLK	PTS	RPG	APG	PPG
90-91—Sacramento	4	0	17	4	7	.571	1	1	1.000	0	0	—	2	0	2	0	0	0	0	1	0	9	0.5	0.0	2.3
REG. SEASON TOTALS	4	0	17	4	7	.571	1	1	1.000	0	0	—	2	0	2	0	0	0	0	1	0	9	0.5	0.0	2.3

DAY, TODD FITZGERALD b. January 7, 1970 Ht. 6-6 Wt. 200 College—Arkansas

SEASON—TEAM	G	GS	MIN	FGM	FGA	PCT	3FGM	3FGA	PCT	FTM	FTA	PCT	O-RB	D-RB	TOT	AST	PF	DQ	STL	TO	BLK	PTS	RPG	APG	PPG
92-93—Milwaukee	71	37	1931	358	828	.432	54	184	.293	213	297	.717	144	147	291	117	222	1	75	118	48	983	4.1	1.6	13.8
93-94—Milwaukee	76	39	2127	351	845	.415	33	148	.223	231	331	.698	115	195	310	138	221	4	103	129	52	966	4.1	1.8	12.7
REG. SEASON TOTALS	147	76	4058	709	1673	.424	87	332	.262	444	628	.707	259	342	601	255	443	5	178	247	100	1949	4.1	1.7	13.3

DAYE, DARREN KEEFE b. November 30, 1960 Ht. 6-8 Wt. 220 College—UCLA

SEASON—TEAM	G	GS	MIN	FGM	FGA	PCT	3FGM	3FGA	PCT	FTM	FTA	PCT	O-RB	D-RB	TOT	AST	PF	DQ	STL	TO	BLK	PTS	RPG	APG	PPG
83-84—Washington	75	0	1174	180	408	.441	0	6	.000	95	133	.714	90	98	188	176	154	0	38	96	12	455	2.5	2.3	6.1
84-85—Washington	80	8	1573	258	504	.512	1	7	.143	178	249	.715	93	179	272	240	164	1	53	134	19	695	3.4	3.0	8.7
85-86—Washington	64	4	1075	198	399	.496	1	3	.333	159	237	.671	71	112	183	109	121	0	46	98	11	556	2.9	1.7	8.7
86-87—Chicago-Boston	62	2	731	101	202	.500	0	0	—	34	65	.523	37	88	125	76	100	0	25	57	7	236	2.0	1.2	3.8
87-88—Boston	47	8	655	112	217	.516	0	1	.000	59	87	.678	30	46	76	71	68	0	29	44	4	283	1.6	1.5	6.0
REG. SEASON TOTALS	328	22	5208	849	1730	.491	2	17	.118	525	771	.681	321	523	844	672	607	1	191	429	53	2225	2.6	2.0	6.8
PLAYOFF TOTALS	34	5	372	64	119	.538	0	0	—	41	57	.719	20	32	52	28	46	1	12	30	4	169	1.5	0.8	5.0

DEANE, GREG STEVEN b. December 6, 1957 Ht. 6-4 Wt. 190 College—Utah

SEASON—TEAM	G	GS	MIN	FGM	FGA	PCT	3FGM	3FGA	PCT	FTM	FTA	PCT	O-RB	D-RB	TOT	AST	PF	DQ	STL	TO	BLK	PTS	RPG	APG	PPG
79-80—Utah	7	—	48	2	11	.182	1	1	1.000	5	7	.714	2	4	6	6	3	0	0	3	0	10	0.9	0.9	1.4
REG. SEASON TOTALS	7	—	48	2	11	.182	1	1	1.000	5	7	.714	2	4	6	6	3	0	0	3	0	10	0.9	0.9	1.4

DEANGELIS, WILLIAM R. (Billy) b. October 5, 1946 Ht. 6-1 Wt. 180 College—St. Joseph's (Pa.)

SEASON—TEAM	G	GS	MIN	FGM	FGA	PCT	3FGM	3FGA	PCT	FTM	FTA	PCT	O-RB	D-RB	TOT	AST	PF	DQ	STL	TO	BLK	PTS	RPG	APG	PPG
70-71—New York (A)	8	—	47	3	6	.500	0	0	—	4	6	.667	—	—	6	8	16	—	—	—	—	10	0.8	1.0	1.3
REG. ABA TOTALS	8	—	47	3	6	.500	0	0	—	4	6	.667	—	—	6	8	16	—	—	—	—	10	0.8	1.0	1.3

DEBUSSCHERE, DAVID ALBERT (Dave) b. October 16, 1940 Ht. 6-6 Wt. 225 College—Detroit

SEASON—TEAM	G	GS	MIN	FGM	FGA	PCT	3FGM	3FGA	PCT	FTM	FTA	PCT	O-RB	D-RB	TOT	AST	PF	DQ	STL	TO	BLK	PTS	RPG	APG	PPG
62-63—Detroit	80	—	2352	406	944	.430	—	—	—	206	287	.718	—	—	694	207	247	2	—	—	—	1018	8.7	2.6	12.7
63-64—Detroit	15	—	304	52	133	.391	—	—	—	25	43	.581	—	—	105	23	32	1	—	—	—	129	7.0	1.5	8.6
64-65—Detroit	79	—	2769	508	1196	.425	—	—	—	306	437	.700	—	—	874	253	242	5	—	—	—	1322	11.1	3.2	16.7
65-66—Detroit	79	—	2696	524	1284	.408	—	—	—	249	378	.659	—	—	916	209	252	5	—	—	—	1297	11.6	2.6	16.4
66-67—Detroit	78	—	2897	531	1278	.415	—	—	—	361	512	.705	—	—	924	216	297	7	—	—	—	1423	11.8	2.8	18.2
67-68—Detroit	80	—	3125	573	1295	.442	—	—	—	289	435	.664	—	—	1081	181	304	3	—	—	—	1435	13.5	2.3	17.9
68-69—Detroit-N.Y.	76	—	2943	506	1140	.444	—	—	—	229	328	.698	—	—	888	191	290	6	—	—	—	1241	11.7	2.5	16.3
69-70—New York	79	—	2627	488	1082	.451	—	—	—	176	256	.688	—	—	790	194	244	2	—	—	—	1152	10.0	2.5	14.6
70-71—New York	81	—	2891	523	1243	.421	—	—	—	217	312	.696	—	—	901	220	237	2	—	—	—	1263	11.1	2.7	15.6
71-72—New York	80	—	3072	520	1218	.427	—	—	—	193	265	.728	—	—	901	291	219	1	—	—	—	1233	11.3	3.6	15.4
72-73—New York	77	—	2827	532	1224	.435	—	—	—	194	260	.746	—	—	787	259	215	1	—	—	—	1258	10.2	3.4	16.3
73-74—New York	71	—	2699	559	1212	.461	—	—	—	164	217	.756	134	623	757	253	222	2	67	—	39	1282	10.7	3.6	18.1
REG. SEASON TOTALS	875	—	31202	5722	13249	.432	—	—	—	2609	3730	.699	134	623	9618	2497	2801	37	67	—	39	14053	11.0	2.9	16.1
PLAYOFF TOTALS	96	—	3682	634	1523	.416	—	—	—	268	384	.698	25	74	1155	253	327	5	7	—	4	1536	12.0	2.6	16.0
ALL-STAR TOTALS	8	—	167	37	81	.457	—	—	—	3	4	.750	2	1	51	11	12	0	1	—	0	77	6.4	1.4	9.6

DEE, DONALD M. (Don) b. August 9, 1943 Ht. 6-8 Wt. 210 College—St. Louis/St. Mary's of the Plains

SEASON—TEAM	G	GS	MIN	FGM	FGA	PCT	3FGM	3FGA	PCT	FTM	FTA	PCT	O-RB	D-RB	TOT	AST	PF	DQ	STL	TO	BLK	PTS	RPG	APG	PPG
68-69—Indiana (A)	58	—	989	138	387	.357	0	1	.000	56	75	.747	—	—	292	33	179	9	—	72	—	332	5.0	0.6	5.7
REG. ABA TOTALS	58	—	989	138	387	.357	0	1	.000	56	75	.747	—	—	292	33	179	9	—	72	—	332	5.0	0.6	5.7
ABA PLAYOFF TOTALS	12	—	41	4	13	.308	0	0	—	0	0	—	—	—	10	1	10	0	—	4	—	8	0.8	0.1	0.7

DEES, ARCHIE WILLIAM b. February 22, 1936 Ht. 6-8 Wt. 205 College—Indiana

SEASON—TEAM	G	GS	MIN	FGM	FGA	PCT	3FGM	3FGA	PCT	FTM	FTA	PCT	O-RB	D-RB	TOT	AST	PF	DQ	STL	TO	BLK	PTS	RPG	APG	PPG
58-59—Cincinnati	68	—	1252	200	562	.356	—	—	—	159	204	.779	—	—	339	56	114	0	—	—	—	559	5.0	0.8	8.2
59-60—Detroit	73	—	1244	271	617	.439	—	—	—	165	204	.809	—	—	397	43	188	3	—	—	—	707	5.4	0.6	9.7
60-61—Detroit	28	—	308	53	135	.393	—	—	—	39	47	.830	—	—	94	17	50	0	—	—	—	145	3.4	0.6	5.2
61-62—Chicago-St. L.	21	—	288	51	115	.443	—	—	—	35	46	.761	—	—	77	16	33	0	—	—	—	137	3.7	0.8	6.5
REG. SEASON TOTALS	190	—	3092	575	1429	.402	—	—	—	398	501	.794	—	—	907	132	385	3	—	—	—	1548	4.8	0.7	8.1
PLAYOFF TOTALS	2	—	18	4	12	.333	—	—	—	3	3	1.000	—	—	4	2	2	0	—	—	—	11	2.0	1.0	5.5

DEHERE, LENNOX DOMINIQUE (**Terry**) b. September 12, 1971   Ht. 6-4 Wt. 190 College—Seton Hall

SEASON—TEAM	G	GS	MIN	FGM	FGA	PCT	3FGM	3FGA	PCT	FTM	FTA	PCT	O-RB	D-RB	TOT	AST	PF	DQ	STL	TO	BLK	PTS	RPG	APG	PPG
93-94—L.A. Clippers	64	6	759	129	342	.377	23	57	.404	61	81	.753	25	43	68	78	69	0	28	61	3	342	1.1	1.2	5.3
REG. SEASON TOTALS	64	6	759	129	342	.377	23	57	.404	61	81	.753	25	43	68	78	69	0	28	61	3	342	1.1	1.2	5.3

DEHNERT, HENRY G. (**Red**) b. 1924   Ht. 6-2½ Wt. 175 College—Columbia

SEASON—TEAM	G	GS	MIN	FGM	FGA	PCT	3FGM	3FGA	PCT	FTM	FTA	PCT	O-RB	D-RB	TOT	AST	PF	DQ	STL	TO	BLK	PTS	RPG	APG	PPG
46-47—Providence	10	—	—	6	15	.400	—	—	—	2	6	.333	—	—	—	0	8	—	—	—	—	14	—	0.0	1.4
REG. SEASON TOTALS	10	—	—	6	15	.400	—	—	—	2	6	.333	—	—	—	0	8	—	—	—	—	14	—	0.0	1.4

DEL NEGRO, VINCENT JOSEPH (**Vinny**) b. August 9, 1966   Ht. 6-5 Wt. 200 College—North Carolina State

SEASON—TEAM	G	GS	MIN	FGM	FGA	PCT	3FGM	3FGA	PCT	FTM	FTA	PCT	O-RB	D-RB	TOT	AST	PF	DQ	STL	TO	BLK	PTS	RPG	APG	PPG
88-89—Sacramento	80	2	1556	239	503	.475	6	20	.300	85	100	.850	48	123	171	206	160	2	65	77	14	569	2.1	2.6	7.1
89-90—Sacramento	76	29	1858	297	643	.462	10	32	.313	135	155	.871	39	159	198	250	182	2	64	111	10	739	2.6	3.3	9.7
92-93—San Antonio	73	31	1526	218	430	.507	6	24	.250	101	117	.863	19	144	163	291	146	0	44	92	1	543	2.2	4.0	7.4
93-94—San Antonio	77	56	1949	309	634	.487	15	43	.349	140	170	.824	27	134	161	320	168	0	64	102	1	773	2.1	4.2	10.0
REG. SEASON TOTALS	306	118	6889	1063	2210	.481	37	119	.311	461	542	.851	133	560	693	1067	656	4	237	382	26	2624	2.3	3.5	8.6
PLAYOFF TOTALS	12	4	205	29	65	.446	4	13	.308	7	9	.778	7	19	26	42	19	0	2	9	1	69	2.2	3.5	5.8

DELONG, NATHAN J. (**Nate**) b. January 5, 1926   Ht. 6-6½ Wt. 220 College—Wisconsin River Falls

SEASON—TEAM	G	GS	MIN	FGM	FGA	PCT	3FGM	3FGA	PCT	FTM	FTA	PCT	O-RB	D-RB	TOT	AST	PF	DQ	STL	TO	BLK	PTS	RPG	APG	PPG
51-52—Milwaukee	17	—	132	20	42	.476	—	—	—	24	35	.686	—	—	31	14	47	3	—	—	—	64	1.8	0.8	3.8
REG. SEASON TOTALS	17	—	132	20	42	.476	—	—	—	24	35	.686	—	—	31	14	47	3	—	—	—	64	1.8	0.8	3.8

DEMBO, FENNIS MARX b. January 24, 1966   Ht. 6-6 Wt. 215 College—Wyoming

SEASON—TEAM	G	GS	MIN	FGM	FGA	PCT	3FGM	3FGA	PCT	FTM	FTA	PCT	O-RB	D-RB	TOT	AST	PF	DQ	STL	TO	BLK	PTS	RPG	APG	PPG
88-89—Detroit	31	0	74	14	42	.333	0	4	.000	8	10	.800	8	15	23	5	15	0	1	7	0	36	0.7	0.2	1.2
REG. SEASON TOTALS	31	0	74	14	42	.333	0	4	.000	8	10	.800	8	15	23	5	15	0	1	7	0	36	0.7	0.2	1.2
PLAYOFF TOTALS	2	0	4	1	1	1.000	0	0	—	0	0	—	0	0	0	—	1	0	0	1	0	2	0.0	0.0	1.0

DEMIC, LAWRENCE CURTIS (**Larry**) b. June 27, 1957   Ht. 6-9 Wt. 225 College—Arizona

SEASON—TEAM	G	GS	MIN	FGM	FGA	PCT	3FGM	3FGA	PCT	FTM	FTA	PCT	O-RB	D-RB	TOT	AST	PF	DQ	STL	TO	BLK	PTS	RPG	APG	PPG
79-80—New York	82	—	1872	230	528	.436	0	0	—	110	183	.601	195	288	483	64	306	10	56	168	30	570	5.9	0.8	7.0
80-81—New York	76	—	964	128	254	.504	0	2	.000	58	92	.630	114	129	243	28	153	0	12	58	13	314	3.2	0.4	4.1
81-82—New York	48	0	356	39	83	.470	0	1	.000	14	39	.359	29	50	79	14	65	1	4	26	6	92	1.6	0.3	1.9
REG. SEASON TOTALS	206	0	3192	397	865	.459	0	3	.000	182	314	.580	338	467	805	106	524	11	72	252	49	976	3.9	0.5	4.7
PLAYOFF TOTALS	2	0	37	4	5	.800	0	0	—	1	2	.500	5	2	7	—	3	0	0	0	1	9	3.5	0.0	4.5

DEMPS, DELL b. February 12, 1970   Ht. 6-4 Wt. 210 College—Pacific

SEASON—TEAM	G	GS	MIN	FGM	FGA	PCT	3FGM	3FGA	PCT	FTM	FTA	PCT	O-RB	D-RB	TOT	AST	PF	DQ	STL	TO	BLK	PTS	RPG	APG	PPG
93-94—Golden State	2	0	11	2	6	.333	0	0	—	0	2	.000	0	0	0	1	1	0	2	1	0	4	0.0	0.5	2.0
REG. SEASON TOTALS	2	0	11	2	6	.333	0	0	—	0	2	.000	0	0	0	1	1	0	2	1	0	4	0.0	0.5	2.0

DEMPSEY, GEORGE P. b. July 19, 1929   Ht. 6-3 Wt. 190 College—King's (Del.)

SEASON—TEAM	G	GS	MIN	FGM	FGA	PCT	3FGM	3FGA	PCT	FTM	FTA	PCT	O-RB	D-RB	TOT	AST	PF	DQ	STL	TO	BLK	PTS	RPG	APG	PPG
54-55—Philadelphia	48	—	1387	127	360	.353	—	—	—	98	141	.695	—	—	236	174	141	1	—	—	—	352	4.9	3.6	7.3
55-56—Philadelphia	72	—	1444	126	265	.475	—	—	—	88	139	.633	—	—	264	205	146	7	—	—	—	340	3.7	2.8	4.7
56-57—Philadelphia	71	—	1147	134	302	.444	—	—	—	55	102	.539	—	—	251	136	107	0	—	—	—	323	3.5	1.9	4.5
57-58—Philadelphia	67	—	1048	112	311	.360	—	—	—	70	105	.667	—	—	214	128	113	0	—	—	—	294	3.2	1.9	4.4
58-59—Phil.-Syr.	57	—	694	92	215	.428	—	—	—	81	106	.764	—	—	160	68	95	0	—	—	—	265	2.8	1.2	4.6
REG. SEASON TOTALS	315	—	5720	591	1453	.407	—	—	—	392	593	.661	—	—	1125	711	602	8	—	—	—	1574	3.6	2.3	5.0
PLAYOFF TOTALS	25	—	339	38	87	.437	—	—	—	29	49	.592	—	—	64	35	35	0	—	—	—	105	2.6	1.4	4.2

DENNARD, KENNETH STEPHEN (**Kenny**) b. October 18, 1958   Ht. 6-8 Wt. 220 College—Duke

SEASON—TEAM	G	GS	MIN	FGM	FGA	PCT	3FGM	3FGA	PCT	FTM	FTA	PCT	O-RB	D-RB	TOT	AST	PF	DQ	STL	TO	BLK	PTS	RPG	APG	PPG
81-82—Kansas City	30	3	607	62	121	.512	0	0	—	26	40	.650	47	86	133	42	81	0	35	35	8	150	4.4	1.4	5.0
82-83—Kansas City	22	0	224	11	34	.324	0	0	—	6	9	.667	20	32	52	6	27	0	16	5	1	28	2.4	0.3	1.3
83-84—Denver	43	0	413	36	99	.364	3	10	.300	15	24	.625	37	64	101	45	83	0	23	29	8	90	2.3	1.0	2.1
REG. SEASON TOTALS	95	3	1244	109	254	.429	3	10	.300	47	73	.644	104	182	286	93	191	0	74	69	17	268	3.0	1.0	2.8

DENNING, BLAINE b. September 19, 1930   Ht. 6-2 Wt. 175 College—Lawrence Tech

SEASON—TEAM	G	GS	MIN	FGM	FGA	PCT	3FGM	3FGA	PCT	FTM	FTA	PCT	O-RB	D-RB	TOT	AST	PF	DQ	STL	TO	BLK	PTS	RPG	APG	PPG
52-53—Baltimore	1	—	9	2	5	.400	—	—	—	1	1	1.000	—	—	4	0	3	0	—	—	—	5	4.0	0.0	5.0
REG. SEASON TOTALS	1	—	9	2	5	.400	—	—	—	1	1	1.000	—	—	4	0	3	0	—	—	—	5	4.0	0.0	5.0

DENTON, RANDALL DREW (Randy) b. February 18, 1949 Ht. 6-10½ Wt. 245 College—Duke

SEASON—TEAM	G	GS	MIN	FGM	FGA	PCT	3FGM	3FGA	PCT	FTM	FTA	PCT	O-RB	D-RB	TOT	AST	PF	DQ	STL	TO	BLK	PTS	RPG	APG	PPG
71-72—Car.-Memphis (A)	81	—	2039	430	935	.460	0	2	.000	135	168	.804	—	—	740	66	180	—	—	111	—	995	9.1	0.8	12.3
72-73—Memphis (A)	66	—	2205	472	979	.482	3	8	.375	177	237	.747	276	544	820	98	197	2	—	124	—	1124	12.4	1.5	17.0
73-74—Memphis (A)	79	—	2218	447	902	.496	0	3	.000	156	197	.792	255	522	777	152	225	—	55	164	35	1050	9.8	1.9	13.3
74-75—Utah (A)	75	—	1482	300	597	.503	0	0	—	92	120	.767	154	319	473	90	176	—	29	99	43	692	6.3	1.2	9.2
75-76—Utah-St. L. (A)	67	—	1540	283	634	.446	0	1	.000	83	99	.838	156	363	519	89	180	—	37	83	32	649	7.7	1.3	9.7
76-77—Atlanta	45	—	700	103	256	.402	—	—	—	33	47	.702	81	137	218	33	100	1	14	—	16	239	4.8	0.7	5.3
REG. NBA TOTALS	45	—	700	103	256	.402	—	—	—	33	47	.702	81	137	218	33	100	1	14	—	16	239	4.8	0.7	5.3
REG. ABA TOTALS	368	—	9484	1932	4047	.477	3	14	.214	643	821	.783	841	1748	3329	495	958	2	121	581	110	4510	9.0	1.3	12.3
ABA PLAYOFF TOTALS	6	—	236	49	92	.533	0	0	—	15	22	.682	28	52	80	11	18	0	4	15	2	113	13.3	1.8	18.8

DEPRE, JOE b. December 19, 1947 Ht. 6-3½ Wt. 190 College—St. John's

SEASON—TEAM	G	GS	MIN	FGM	FGA	PCT	3FGM	3FGA	PCT	FTM	FTA	PCT	O-RB	D-RB	TOT	AST	PF	DQ	STL	TO	BLK	PTS	RPG	APG	PPG
70-71—New York (A)	72	—	1707	250	488	.512	0	4	.000	132	172	.767	—	—	175	138	262	—	—	—	—	632	2.4	1.9	8.8
71-72—New York (A)	46	—	562	79	201	.393	2	6	.333	34	54	.630	—	—	49	45	80	—	—	66	—	194	1.1	1.0	4.2
72-73—New York (A)	1	—	12	2	5	.400	0	0	—	0	0	—	2	—	2	2	1	0	—	0	—	4	2.0	2.0	4.0
REG. ABA TOTALS	119	—	2281	331	694	.477	2	10	.200	166	226	.735	2	—	226	185	343	0	—	66	—	830	1.9	1.6	7.0
ABA PLAYOFF TOTALS	20	—	245	34	79	.430	1	3	.333	19	27	.704	—	—	26	19	45	0	—	6	—	88	1.3	1.0	4.4

DERLINE, RODNEY G. (Rod) b. March 11, 1952 Ht. 6-0 Wt. 175 College—Seattle

SEASON—TEAM	G	GS	MIN	FGM	FGA	PCT	3FGM	3FGA	PCT	FTM	FTA	PCT	O-RB	D-RB	TOT	AST	PF	DQ	STL	TO	BLK	PTS	RPG	APG	PPG
74-75—Seattle	58	—	666	142	332	.428	—	—	—	43	56	.768	12	47	59	45	47	0	23	—	4	327	1.0	0.8	5.6
75-76—Seattle	49	—	339	73	181	.403	—	—	—	45	56	.804	8	19	27	26	22	0	11	—	1	191	0.6	0.5	3.9
REG. SEASON TOTALS	107	—	1005	215	513	.419	—	—	—	88	112	.786	20	66	86	71	69	0	34	—	5	518	0.8	0.7	4.8
PLAYOFF TOTALS	10	—	105	20	43	.465	—	—	—	8	9	.889	2	15	17	8	10	0	3	—	0	48	1.7	0.8	4.8

DEUTSCH, DAVID (Dave) b. May 13, 1945 Ht. 6-1 Wt. 170 College—Rochester

SEASON—TEAM	G	GS	MIN	FGM	FGA	PCT	3FGM	3FGA	PCT	FTM	FTA	PCT	O-RB	D-RB	TOT	AST	PF	DQ	STL	TO	BLK	PTS	RPG	APG	PPG
66-67—New York	19	—	93	6	36	.167	—	—	—	9	20	.450	—	—	21	15	17	0	—	—	—	21	1.1	0.8	1.1
REG. SEASON TOTALS	19	—	93	6	36	.167	—	—	—	9	20	.450	—	—	21	15	17	0	—	—	—	21	1.1	0.8	1.1
PLAYOFF TOTALS	1	—	7	1	5	.200	—	—	—	0	0	—	—	—	3	1	0	0	—	—	—	2	3.0	1.0	2.0

DEVLIN, WALTER JAMES (Corky) b. December 21, 1931 Ht. 6-5 Wt. 195 College—George Washington

SEASON—TEAM	G	GS	MIN	FGM	FGA	PCT	3FGM	3FGA	PCT	FTM	FTA	PCT	O-RB	D-RB	TOT	AST	PF	DQ	STL	TO	BLK	PTS	RPG	APG	PPG
55-56—Fort Wayne	69	—	1535	200	541	.370	—	—	—	146	192	.760	—	—	171	138	119	0	—	—	—	546	2.5	2.0	7.9
56-57—Fort Wayne	71	—	1242	190	502	.378	—	—	—	97	143	.678	—	—	146	141	114	0	—	—	—	477	2.1	2.0	6.7
57-58—Minneapolis	70	—	1248	170	489	.348	—	—	—	133	172	.773	—	—	132	167	104	1	—	—	—	473	1.9	2.4	6.8
REG. SEASON TOTALS	210	—	4025	560	1532	.366	—	—	—	376	507	.742	—	—	449	446	337	1	—	—	—	1496	2.1	2.1	7.1
PLAYOFF TOTALS	11	—	300	47	109	.431	—	—	—	16	26	.615	—	—	26	28	26	0	—	—	—	110	2.4	2.5	10.0

DeZONIE, HENRY E. (Hank) b. February 12, 1922 Ht. 6-5½ Wt. 215 College—Clark (Ga.)

SEASON—TEAM	G	GS	MIN	FGM	FGA	PCT	3FGM	3FGA	PCT	FTM	FTA	PCT	O-RB	D-RB	TOT	AST	PF	DQ	STL	TO	BLK	PTS	RPG	APG	PPG
48-49—Dayton (N)	18	—	—	90	—	—	—	—	—	44	59	.746	—	—	—	—	—	—	—	—	—	224	—	—	12.4
50-51—Tri-Cities	5	—	—	6	25	.240	—	—	—	5	7	.714	—	—	18	9	6	0	—	—	—	17	3.6	1.8	3.4
REG. NBA TOTALS	5	—	—	6	25	.240	—	—	—	5	7	.714	—	—	18	9	6	0	—	—	—	17	3.6	1.8	3.4
REG. NBL TOTALS	18	—	—	90	—	—	—	—	—	44	59	.746	—	—	—	—	—	—	—	—	—	224	—	—	12.4

DICKERSON, HENRY b. November 27, 1951 Ht. 6-4 Wt. 190 College—Charleston (West Va.)

SEASON—TEAM	G	GS	MIN	FGM	FGA	PCT	3FGM	3FGA	PCT	FTM	FTA	PCT	O-RB	D-RB	TOT	AST	PF	DQ	STL	TO	BLK	PTS	RPG	APG	PPG
75-76—Detroit	17	—	112	9	29	.310	—	—	—	10	16	.625	3	0	3	8	17	1	2	—	1	28	0.2	0.5	1.6
76-77—Atlanta	6	—	63	6	12	.500	—	—	—	5	8	.625	0	2	2	11	13	0	1	—	0	17	0.3	1.8	2.8
REG. SEASON TOTALS	23	—	175	15	41	.366	—	—	—	15	24	.625	3	2	5	19	30	1	3	—	1	45	0.2	0.8	2.0
PLAYOFF TOTALS	5	—	15	4	9	.444	—	—	—	1	2	.500	4	0	4	3	1	0	1	—	0	9	0.8	0.6	1.8

DICKEY, CLYDE L. b. December 14, 1951 Ht. 6-3 Wt. 185 College—Cochise/Boston College/Boise State

SEASON—TEAM	G	GS	MIN	FGM	FGA	PCT	3FGM	3FGA	PCT	FTM	FTA	PCT	O-RB	D-RB	TOT	AST	PF	DQ	STL	TO	BLK	PTS	RPG	APG	PPG
74-75—Utah (A)	57	—	458	66	193	.342	2	15	.133	16	21	.762	12	42	54	46	45	—	14	45	0	150	0.9	0.8	2.6
REG. ABA TOTALS	57	—	458	66	193	.342	2	15	.133	16	21	.762	12	42	54	46	45	—	14	45	0	150	0.9	0.8	2.6
ABA PLAYOFF TOTALS	1	—	4	0	2	.000	0	0	—	0	0	—	0	1	1	0	0	—	0	1	0	0	1.0	0.0	0.0

DICKEY, DERREK b. March 20, 1951 Ht. 6-7 Wt. 220 College—Cincinnati

SEASON—TEAM	G	GS	MIN	FGM	FGA	PCT	3FGM	3FGA	PCT	FTM	FTA	PCT	O-RB	D-RB	TOT	AST	PF	DQ	STL	TO	BLK	PTS	RPG	APG	PPG
73-74—Golden State	66	—	930	115	233	.494	—	—	—	51	66	.773	123	216	339	54	112	1	17	—	15	281	5.1	0.8	4.3
74-75—Golden State	80	—	1859	274	569	.482	—	—	—	66	99	.667	190	360	550	125	199	0	52	—	19	614	6.9	1.6	7.7
75-76—Golden State	79	—	1207	220	473	.465	—	—	—	62	79	.785	114	235	349	83	141	1	26	—	11	502	4.4	1.1	6.4
76-77—Golden State	49	—	856	158	345	.458	—	—	—	45	61	.738	100	140	240	63	101	1	20	—	11	361	4.9	1.3	7.4
77-78—G.S.-Chicago	47	—	493	87	198	.439	—	—	—	30	36	.833	36	61	97	21	56	0	14	40	4	204	2.1	0.4	4.3
REG. SEASON TOTALS	321	—	5345	854	1818	.470	—	—	—	254	341	.745	563	1012	1575	346	609	3	129	40	60	1962	4.9	1.1	6.1
PLAYOFF TOTALS	27	—	430	78	140	.557	—	—	—	23	33	.697	38	77	115	17	55	1	10	—	1	179	4.3	0.6	6.6

DICKEY, RICHARD LEA (Dick) b. October 26, 1926 Ht. 6-1 Wt. 175 College—DePauw/St. Mary's (Ca.)

SEASON—TEAM	G	GS	MIN	FGM	FGA	PCT	3FGM	3FGA	PCT	FTM	FTA	PCT	O-RB	D-RB	TOT	AST	PF	DQ	STL	TO	BLK	PTS	RPG	APG	PPG
51-52—Boston	45	—	440	40	136	.294	—	—	—	47	69	.681	—	—	81	50	79	2	—	—	—	127	1.8	1.1	2.8
REG. SEASON TOTALS	45	—	440	40	136	.294	—	—	—	47	69	.681	—	—	81	50	79	2	—	—	—	127	1.8	1.1	2.8
PLAYOFF TOTALS	3	—	31	1	8	.125	—	—	—	6	7	.857	—	—	3	5	7	0	—	—	—	8	1.0	1.7	2.7

DICKSON, JOHN b. November 18, 1945 Ht. 6-10 Wt. 240 College—Arkansas State

SEASON—TEAM	G	GS	MIN	FGM	FGA	PCT	3FGM	3FGA	PCT	FTM	FTA	PCT	O-RB	D-RB	TOT	AST	PF	DQ	STL	TO	BLK	PTS	RPG	APG	PPG
67-68—New Orleans (A)	21	—	100	14	39	.359	0	0	—	8	13	.615	—	—	33	3	11	0	—	10	—	36	1.6	0.1	1.7
REG. ABA TOTALS	21	—	100	14	39	.359	0	0	—	8	13	.615	—	—	33	3	11	0	—	10	—	36	1.6	0.1	1.7
ABA PLAYOFF TOTALS	1	—	3	0	4	.000	0	0	—	0	0	—	—	—	2	0	0	0	—	1	—	0	2.0	0.0	0.0

DIERKING, CONRAD WILLIAM (Connie) b. October 2, 1936 Ht. 6-10 Wt. 230 College—Cincinnati

SEASON—TEAM	G	GS	MIN	FGM	FGA	PCT	3FGM	3FGA	PCT	FTM	FTA	PCT	O-RB	D-RB	TOT	AST	PF	DQ	STL	TO	BLK	PTS	RPG	APG	PPG
58-59—Syracuse	64	—	726	105	290	.362	—	—	—	83	140	.593	—	—	233	34	148	2	—	—	—	293	3.6	0.5	4.6
59-60—Syracuse	71	—	1119	192	526	.365	—	—	—	108	188	.574	—	—	456	54	168	4	—	—	—	492	6.4	0.8	6.9
63-64—Philadelphia	76	—	1286	191	514	.372	—	—	—	114	169	.675	—	—	422	50	221	3	—	—	—	496	5.6	0.7	6.5
64-65—Phil.-S.F.	68	—	1294	218	538	.405	—	—	—	100	168	.595	—	—	435	72	165	4	—	—	—	536	6.4	1.1	7.9
65-66—Cincinnati	57	—	782	134	322	.416	—	—	—	50	82	.610	—	—	245	43	113	0	—	—	—	318	4.3	0.8	5.6
66-67—Cincinnati	77	—	1905	291	729	.399	—	—	—	134	180	.744	—	—	603	158	251	7	—	—	—	716	7.8	2.1	9.3
67-68—Cincinnati	81	—	2637	544	1164	.467	—	—	—	237	310	.765	—	—	766	191	315	6	—	—	—	1325	9.5	2.4	16.4
68-69—Cincinnati	82	—	2540	546	1232	.443	—	—	—	243	319	.762	—	—	739	222	305	9	—	—	—	1335	9.0	2.7	16.3
69-70—Cincinnati	76	—	2448	521	1243	.419	—	—	—	230	306	.752	—	—	624	169	275	7	—	—	—	1272	8.2	2.2	16.7
70-71—Cin.-Phil.	54	—	737	125	322	.388	—	—	—	61	89	.685	—	—	234	60	114	1	—	—	—	311	4.3	1.1	5.8
REG. SEASON TOTALS	706	—	15474	2867	6880	.417	—	—	—	1360	1951	.697	—	—	4757	1053	2075	43	—	—	—	7094	6.7	1.5	10.0
PLAYOFF TOTALS	20	—	352	63	158	.399	—	—	—	27	35	.771	—	—	129	23	45	0	—	—	—	153	6.5	1.2	7.7

DIETRICK, COBY JOSEPH b. July 23, 1948 Ht. 6-10½ Wt. 230 College—San Jose State

SEASON—TEAM	G	GS	MIN	FGM	FGA	PCT	3FGM	3FGA	PCT	FTM	FTA	PCT	O-RB	D-RB	TOT	AST	PF	DQ	STL	TO	BLK	PTS	RPG	APG	PPG
70-71—Memphis (A)	37	—	357	61	160	.381	0	1	.000	21	34	.618	—	—	114	33	56	—	—	—	—	143	3.1	0.9	3.9
71-72—Memphis (A)	1	—	9	1	2	.500	0	0	—	0	2	.000	—	—	7	1	1	—	—	1	—	2	7.0	1.0	2.0
72-73—Dallas (A)	77	—	1347	205	489	.419	0	0	—	96	139	.691	133	244	377	136	224	5	—	93	88	506	4.9	1.8	6.6
73-74—San Antonio (A)	84	—	2142	251	569	.441	0	3	.000	81	114	.711	200	332	532	253	285	—	89	151	50	583	6.3	3.0	6.9
74-75—San Antonio (A)	82	—	1724	222	444	.500	2	4	.500	76	99	.768	191	333	524	168	266	—	82	117	55	522	6.4	2.0	6.4
75-76—San Antonio (A)	81	—	1467	200	403	.496	1	7	.143	68	82	.829	109	240	349	159	257	—	67	112	43	469	4.3	2.0	5.8
76-77—San Antonio	82	—	1772	285	620	.460	—	—	—	119	166	.717	111	261	372	148	267	8	88	—	57	689	4.5	1.8	8.4
77-78—San Antonio	79	—	1876	250	543	.460	—	—	—	89	114	.781	73	285	358	217	231	4	81	144	55	589	4.5	2.7	7.5
78-79—San Antonio	76	—	1487	209	400	.523	—	—	—	79	99	.798	88	227	315	198	206	7	72	92	38	497	4.1	2.6	6.5
79-80—Chicago	79	—	1830	227	500	.454	1	9	.111	90	118	.763	101	262	363	216	230	2	89	112	51	545	4.6	2.7	6.9
80-81—Chicago	82	—	1243	146	320	.456	2	6	.333	77	111	.694	79	186	265	118	176	1	48	88	53	371	3.2	1.4	4.5
81-82—Chicago	74	0	999	92	200	.460	0	1	.000	38	54	.704	63	125	188	87	131	1	49	44	30	222	2.5	1.2	3.0
82-83—San Antonio	8	0	34	1	5	.200	0	0	—	0	2	.000	2	6	8	6	6	0	1	1	0	2	1.0	0.8	0.3
REG. NBA TOTALS	480	0	9241	1210	2588	.468	3	16	.188	492	664	.741	517	1352	1869	990	1247	23	428	481	284	2915	3.9	2.1	6.1
REG. ABA TOTALS	362	—	7046	940	2067	.455	3	15	.200	342	470	.728	633	1149	1903	750	1089	5	238	474	236	2225	5.3	2.1	6.1
NBA PLAYOFF TOTALS	28	0	522	73	164	.445	0	3	.000	10	20	.500	41	73	114	39	82	1	20	29	11	156	4.1	1.4	5.6
ABA PLAYOFF TOTALS	22	—	534	71	133	.534	0	4	.000	27	38	.711	35	73	111	47	71	0	15	38	20	169	5.0	2.1	7.7

DiGREGORIO, ERNEST (Ernie, Ernie D.) b. January 15, 1951 Ht. 6-0 Wt. 180 College—Providence

SEASON—TEAM	G	GS	MIN	FGM	FGA	PCT	3FGM	3FGA	PCT	FTM	FTA	PCT	O-RB	D-RB	TOT	AST	PF	DQ	STL	TO	BLK	PTS	RPG	APG	PPG
73-74—Buffalo	81	—	2910	530	1260	.421	—	—	—	174	193	.902	48	171	219	663	242	2	59	—	9	1234	2.7	8.2	15.2
74-75—Buffalo	31	—	712	103	234	.440	—	—	—	35	45	.778	6	39	45	151	62	0	19	—	0	241	1.5	4.9	7.8
75-76—Buffalo	67	—	1364	182	474	.384	—	—	—	86	94	.915	15	97	112	265	158	1	37	—	1	450	1.7	4.0	6.7
76-77—Buffalo	81	—	2267	365	875	.417	—	—	—	138	146	.945	52	132	184	378	150	1	57	—	3	868	2.3	4.7	10.7
77-78—L.A.-Boston	52	—	606	88	209	.421	—	—	—	28	33	.848	7	43	50	137	44	0	18	93	1	204	1.0	2.6	3.9
REG. SEASON TOTALS	312	—	7859	1268	3052	.415	—	—	—	461	511	.902	128	482	610	1594	656	4	190	93	14	2997	2.0	5.1	9.6
PLAYOFF TOTALS	15	—	457	67	148	.453	—	—	—	16	17	.941	4	25	29	97	43	2	6	—	2	150	1.9	6.5	10.0

DILL, CRAIG H. b. December 17, 1944 Ht. 6-11 Wt. 220 College—Michigan

SEASON—TEAM	G	GS	MIN	FGM	FGA	PCT	3FGM	3FGA	PCT	FTM	FTA	PCT	O-RB	D-RB	TOT	AST	PF	DQ	STL	TO	BLK	PTS	RPG	APG	PPG
67-68—Pittsburgh (A)	65	—	1354	187	488	.383	0	3	.000	71	106	.670	—	—	378	31	164	3	—	64	—	445	5.8	0.5	6.8
REG. ABA TOTALS	65	—	1354	187	488	.383	0	3	.000	71	106	.670	—	—	378	31	164	3	—	64	—	445	5.8	0.5	6.8
ABA PLAYOFF TOTALS	6	—	15	3	8	.375	0	0	—	1	1	1.000	—	—	6	2	5	0	—	3	—	7	1.0	0.3	1.2

DILLARD, DAVE   College—None

SEASON—TEAM	G	GS	MIN	FGM	FGA	PCT	3FGM	3FGA	PCT	FTM	FTA	PCT	O-RB	D-RB	TOT	AST	PF	DQ	STL	TO	BLK	PTS	RPG	APG	PPG
75-76—Utah (A)	3	—	19	1	3	.333	0	0	—	2	2	1.000	2	7	9	2	7	—	2	5	2	4	3.0	0.7	1.3
REG. ABA TOTALS	3	—	19	1	3	.333	0	0	—	2	2	1.000	2	7	9	2	7	—	2	5	2	4	3.0	0.7	1.3

DILLARD, MICKEY ANTHONY b. October 15, 1958 Ht. 6-3 Wt. 170 College—Florida State

SEASON—TEAM	G	GS	MIN	FGM	FGA	PCT	3FGM	3FGA	PCT	FTM	FTA	PCT	O-RB	D-RB	TOT	AST	PF	DQ	STL	TO	BLK	PTS	RPG	APG	PPG
81-82—Cleveland	33	0	221	29	79	.367	0	4	.000	15	23	.652	6	9	15	34	40	0	8	17	2	73	0.5	1.0	2.2
REG. SEASON TOTALS	33	0	221	29	79	.367	0	4	.000	15	23	.652	6	9	15	34	40	0	8	17	2	73	0.5	1.0	2.2

DILLE, ROBERT ORVILLE (**Bob, Oscar**) b. July 2, 1917 Ht. 6-3 Wt. 200 College—Valparaiso

SEASON—TEAM	G	GS	MIN	FGM	FGA	PCT	3FGM	3FGA	PCT	FTM	FTA	PCT	O-RB	D-RB	TOT	AST	PF	DQ	STL	TO	BLK	PTS	RPG	APG	PPG
40-41—Hammond (N)	3	—	—	8	—	—	—	—	—	3	—	—	—	—	—	—	—	—	—	—	—	19	—	—	6.3
46-47—Detroit	57	—	—	111	563	.197	—	—	—	74	111	.667	—	—	—	40	92	—	—	—	—	296	—	0.7	5.2
REG. NBA TOTALS	57	—	—	111	563	.197	—	—	—	74	111	.667	—	—	—	40	92	—	—	—	—	296	—	0.7	5.2
REG. NBL TOTALS	3	—	—	8	—	—	—	—	—	3	—	—	—	—	—	—	—	—	—	—	—	19	—	—	6.3

DILLON, JOHN TURLEY (**Hooks**) b. January 8, 1924 Ht. 6-3 Wt. 180 College—Kentucky/North Carolina

SEASON—TEAM	G	GS	MIN	FGM	FGA	PCT	3FGM	3FGA	PCT	FTM	FTA	PCT	O-RB	D-RB	TOT	AST	PF	DQ	STL	TO	BLK	PTS	RPG	APG	PPG
49-50—Washington	22	—	—	10	55	.182	—	—	—	16	22	.727	—	—	—	5	19	—	—	—	—	36	—	0.2	1.6
REG. SEASON TOTALS	22	—	—	10	55	.182	—	—	—	16	22	.727	—	—	—	5	19	—	—	—	—	36	—	0.2	1.6
PLAYOFF TOTALS	1	—	—	1	1	1.000	—	—	—	2	2	1.000	—	—	—	2	—	—	—	—	—	4	—	0.0	4.0

DINKINS, BYRON STEWART b. June 15, 1967 Ht. 6-2 Wt. 170 College—UNC-Charlotte

SEASON—TEAM	G	GS	MIN	FGM	FGA	PCT	3FGM	3FGA	PCT	FTM	FTA	PCT	O-RB	D-RB	TOT	AST	PF	DQ	STL	TO	BLK	PTS	RPG	APG	PPG
89-90—Houston	33	0	362	44	109	.404	1	9	.111	26	30	.867	13	27	40	75	30	0	19	37	2	115	1.2	2.3	3.5
90-91—S.A.-Indiana	12	0	149	14	34	.412	0	0	—	8	9	.889	0	12	12	19	15	0	2	13	0	36	1.0	1.6	3.0
REG. SEASON TOTALS	45	0	511	58	143	.406	1	9	.111	34	39	.872	13	39	52	94	45	0	21	50	2	151	1.2	2.1	3.4

DINKINS, JACKIE b. January 22, 1950 d. March 1983 Ht. 6-5 Wt. 210 College—Voorhees College

SEASON—TEAM	G	GS	MIN	FGM	FGA	PCT	3FGM	3FGA	PCT	FTM	FTA	PCT	O-RB	D-RB	TOT	AST	PF	DQ	STL	TO	BLK	PTS	RPG	APG	PPG
71-72—Chicago	18	—	89	17	41	.415	—	—	—	11	20	.550	—	—	20	7	10	0	—	—	—	45	1.1	0.4	2.5
REG. SEASON TOTALS	18	—	89	17	41	.415	—	—	—	11	20	.550	—	—	20	7	10	0	—	—	—	45	1.1	0.4	2.5
PLAYOFF TOTALS	1	—	1	1	1	1.000	—	—	—	0	0	—	—	—	0	—	0	0	—	—	—	2	0.0	0.0	2.0

DINNEL, HARRY b. 1941 Ht. 6-4 Wt. 200 College—Pepperdine

SEASON—TEAM	G	GS	MIN	FGM	FGA	PCT	3FGM	3FGA	PCT	FTM	FTA	PCT	O-RB	D-RB	TOT	AST	PF	DQ	STL	TO	BLK	PTS	RPG	APG	PPG
67-68—Anaheim (A)	11	—	87	6	19	.316	0	0	—	7	8	.875	—	—	23	5	14	0	—	8	—	19	2.1	0.5	1.7
REG. ABA TOTALS	11	—	87	6	19	.316	0	0	—	7	8	.875	—	—	23	5	14	0	—	8	—	19	2.1	0.5	1.7

DINWIDDIE, WILLIAM E. (**Bill, Diamond Bill**) b. July 15, 1943 Ht. 6-7 Wt. 220 College—New Mexico Highlands

SEASON—TEAM	G	GS	MIN	FGM	FGA	PCT	3FGM	3FGA	PCT	FTM	FTA	PCT	O-RB	D-RB	TOT	AST	PF	DQ	STL	TO	BLK	PTS	RPG	APG	PPG
67-68—Cincinnati	67	—	871	141	358	.394	—	—	—	62	102	.608	—	—	237	31	122	2	—	—	—	344	3.5	0.5	5.1
68-69—Cincinnati	69	—	1028	124	352	.352	—	—	—	45	87	.517	—	—	242	55	146	0	—	—	—	293	3.5	0.8	4.2
70-71—Boston	61	—	717	123	328	.375	—	—	—	54	74	.730	—	—	209	34	90	1	—	—	—	300	3.4	0.6	4.9
71-72—Milwaukee	23	—	144	16	57	.281	—	—	—	5	9	.556	—	—	32	9	23	0	—	—	—	37	1.4	0.4	1.6
REG. SEASON TOTALS	220	—	2760	404	1095	.369	—	—	—	166	272	.610	—	—	720	129	381	3	—	—	—	974	3.3	0.6	4.4

DISCHINGER, TERRY GILBERT b. November 21, 1940 Ht. 6-7 Wt. 200 College—Purdue

SEASON—TEAM	G	GS	MIN	FGM	FGA	PCT	3FGM	3FGA	PCT	FTM	FTA	PCT	O-RB	D-RB	TOT	AST	PF	DQ	STL	TO	BLK	PTS	RPG	APG	PPG
62-63—Chicago	57	—	2294	525	1026	.512	—	—	—	402	522	.770	—	—	458	175	188	2	—	—	—	1452	8.0	3.1	25.5
63-64—Baltimore	80	—	2816	604	1217	.496	—	—	—	454	585	.776	—	—	667	157	321	10	—	—	—	1662	8.3	2.0	20.8
64-65—Detroit	80	—	2698	568	1153	.493	—	—	—	320	424	.755	—	—	479	198	253	5	—	—	—	1456	6.0	2.5	18.2
67-68—Detroit	78	—	1936	394	797	.494	—	—	—	237	311	.762	—	—	483	114	247	6	—	—	—	1025	6.2	1.5	13.1
68-69—Detroit	75	—	1456	264	513	.515	—	—	—	130	178	.730	—	—	323	93	230	5	—	—	—	658	4.3	1.2	8.8
69-70—Detroit	75	—	1754	342	650	.526	—	—	—	174	241	.722	—	—	369	106	213	5	—	—	—	858	4.9	1.4	11.4
70-71—Detroit	65	—	1855	304	568	.535	—	—	—	161	211	.763	—	—	339	113	189	2	—	—	—	769	5.2	1.7	11.8
71-72—Detroit	79	—	2062	295	574	.514	—	—	—	156	200	.780	—	—	338	92	289	7	—	—	—	746	4.3	1.2	9.4
72-73—Portland	63	—	970	161	338	.476	—	—	—	64	96	.667	—	—	190	103	125	1	—	—	—	386	3.0	1.6	6.1
REG. SEASON TOTALS	652	—	17841	3457	6836	.506	—	—	—	2098	2768	.758	—	—	3646	1151	2055	43	—	—	—	9012	5.6	1.8	13.8
PLAYOFF TOTALS	6	—	154	21	56	.375	—	—	—	14	19	.737	—	—	29	9	19	0	—	—	—	56	4.8	1.5	9.3
ALL-STAR TOTALS	3	—	44	7	15	.467	—	—	—	5	6	.833	—	—	8	2	5	0	—	—	—	19	2.7	0.7	6.3

DIUTE, FRED HOMER b. January 9, 1929 Ht. 6-3 Wt. 210 College—St. Bonaventure

SEASON—TEAM	G	GS	MIN	FGM	FGA	PCT	3FGM	3FGA	PCT	FTM	FTA	PCT	O-RB	D-RB	TOT	AST	PF	DQ	STL	TO	BLK	PTS	RPG	APG	PPG
54-55—Milwaukee	7	—	72	2	21	.095	—	—	—	7	12	.583	—	—	13	4	12	0	—	—	—	11	1.9	0.6	1.6
REG. SEASON TOTALS	7	—	72	2	21	.095	—	—	—	7	12	.583	—	—	13	4	12	0	—	—	—	11	1.9	0.6	1.6

DIVAC, VLADE b. February 3, 1968 Ht. 7-1 Wt. 260 College—None

SEASON—TEAM	G	GS	MIN	FGM	FGA	PCT	3FGM	3FGA	PCT	FTM	FTA	PCT	O-RB	D-RB	TOT	AST	PF	DQ	STL	TO	BLK	PTS	RPG	APG	PPG
89-90—L.A. Lakers	82	5	1611	274	549	.499	0	5	.000	153	216	.708	167	345	512	75	240	2	79	110	114	701	6.2	0.9	8.5
90-91—L.A. Lakers	82	81	2310	360	637	.565	5	14	.357	196	279	.703	205	461	666	92	247	3	106	146	127	921	8.1	1.1	11.2
91-92—L.A. Lakers	36	18	979	157	317	.495	5	19	.263	86	112	.768	87	160	247	60	114	3	55	88	35	405	6.9	1.7	11.3
92-93—L.A. Lakers	82	69	2525	397	819	.485	21	75	.280	235	341	.689	220	509	729	232	311	7	128	214	140	1050	8.9	2.8	12.8
93-94—L.A. Lakers	79	73	2685	453	895	.506	9	47	.191	208	303	.686	282	569	851	307	288	5	92	191	112	1123	10.8	3.9	14.2
REG. SEASON TOTALS	361	246	10110	1641	3217	.510	40	160	.250	878	1251	.702	961	2044	3005	766	1200	20	460	749	528	4200	8.3	2.1	11.6
PLAYOFF TOTALS	37	29	1094	181	333	.544	6	19	.316	95	122	.779	88	156	244	74	131	4	46	83	71	463	6.6	2.0	12.5

DODD, GLENN EARL (Earl) b. November 1, 1924 Ht. 6-5 Wt. 175 College—NE Missouri State

SEASON—TEAM	G	GS	MIN	FGM	FGA	PCT	3FGM	3FGA	PCT	FTM	FTA	PCT	O-RB	D-RB	TOT	AST	PF	DQ	STL	TO	BLK	PTS	RPG	APG	PPG
49-50—Denver	9	—	—	6	27	.222	—	—	—	3	5	.600	—	—	—	6	13	—	—	—	—	15	—	0.7	1.7
REG. SEASON TOTALS	9	—	—	6	27	.222	—	—	—	3	5	.600	—	—	—	6	13	—	—	—	—	15	—	0.7	1.7

DOLHON, JOSEPH (Joe) b. July 9, 1927 d. January 5, 1981 Ht. 6-0 Wt. 175 College—New York University

SEASON—TEAM	G	GS	MIN	FGM	FGA	PCT	3FGM	3FGA	PCT	FTM	FTA	PCT	O-RB	D-RB	TOT	AST	PF	DQ	STL	TO	BLK	PTS	RPG	APG	PPG
49-50—Baltimore	64	—	—	143	458	.312	—	—	—	157	214	.734	—	—	—	155	193	—	—	—	—	443	—	2.4	6.9
50-51—Baltimore	13	—	—	17	56	.304	—	—	—	17	23	.739	—	—	18	19	32	1	—	—	—	51	1.4	1.5	3.9
REG. SEASON TOTALS	77	—	—	160	514	.311	—	—	—	174	237	.734	—	—	18	174	225	1	—	—	—	494	1.4	2.3	6.4

DOLL, ROBERT W. (Bob) b. August 10, 1919 d. September 18, 1959 Ht. 6-4½ Wt. 195 College—Colorado

SEASON—TEAM	G	GS	MIN	FGM	FGA	PCT	3FGM	3FGA	PCT	FTM	FTA	PCT	O-RB	D-RB	TOT	AST	PF	DQ	STL	TO	BLK	PTS	RPG	APG	PPG
46-47—St. Louis	60	—	—	194	768	.253	—	—	—	134	206	.650	—	—	—	22	167	—	—	—	—	522	—	0.4	8.7
47-48—St. Louis	42	—	—	174	658	.264	—	—	—	98	148	.662	—	—	—	26	107	—	—	—	—	446	—	0.6	10.6
48-49—Boston	47	—	—	145	438	.331	—	—	—	80	117	.684	—	—	—	117	118	—	—	—	—	370	—	2.5	7.9
48-49—Denver (N)	9	—	—	16	—	—	—	—	—	13	28	.464	—	—	—	—	22	—	—	—	—	45	—	—	4.8
49-50—Boston	47	—	—	120	347	.346	—	—	—	75	114	.658	—	—	—	108	117	—	—	—	—	315	—	2.3	6.7
REG. NBA TOTALS	196	—	—	633	2211	.286	—	—	—	387	585	.662	—	—	—	273	509	—	—	—	—	1653	—	1.4	8.4
REG. NBL TOTALS	9	—	—	16	—	—	—	—	—	13	28	.464	—	—	—	—	22	—	—	—	—	45	—	—	5.0
NBA PLAYOFF TOTALS	10	—	—	24	130	.185	—	—	—	22	38	.579	—	—	—	5	29	—	—	—	—	70	—	0.5	7.0

DONALDSON, JAMES LEE III (J.D.) b. August 16, 1957 Ht. 7-2 Wt. 275 College—Washington State

SEASON—TEAM	G	GS	MIN	FGM	FGA	PCT	3FGM	3FGA	PCT	FTM	FTA	PCT	O-RB	D-RB	TOT	AST	PF	DQ	STL	TO	BLK	PTS	RPG	APG	PPG
80-81—Seattle	68	—	980	129	238	.542	0	0	—	101	170	.594	107	202	309	42	79	0	8	68	74	359	4.5	0.6	5.3
81-82—Seattle	82	1	1710	255	419	.609	0	0	—	151	240	.629	138	352	490	51	186	2	27	115	139	661	6.0	0.6	8.1
82-83—Seattle	82	11	1789	289	496	.583	0	0	—	150	218	.688	131	370	501	97	171	1	19	132	101	728	6.1	1.2	8.9
83-84—San Diego	82	67	2525	360	604	.596	0	0	—	249	327	.761	165	484	649	90	214	1	40	171	139	969	7.9	1.1	11.8
84-85—L.A. Clippers	82	58	2392	351	551	.637	0	0	—	227	303	.749	168	500	668	48	217	1	28	206	130	929	8.1	0.6	11.3
85-86—L.A. Clips-Dallas	83	78	2682	256	459	.558	0	0	—	204	254	.803	171	624	795	96	189	0	28	123	139	716	9.6	1.2	8.6
86-87—Dallas	82	82	3028	311	531	.586	0	0	—	267	329	.812	295	678	973	63	191	0	51	104	136	889	11.9	0.8	10.8
87-88—Dallas	81	81	2523	212	380	.558	0	0	—	147	189	.778	247	508	755	66	175	2	40	113	104	571	9.3	0.8	7.0
88-89—Dallas	53	53	1746	193	337	.573	0	0	—	95	124	.766	158	412	570	38	111	0	24	83	81	481	10.8	0.7	9.1
89-90—Dallas	73	73	2265	258	479	.539	0	0	—	149	213	.700	155	475	630	57	129	0	22	119	47	665	8.6	0.8	9.1
90-91—Dallas	82	82	2800	327	615	.532	0	0	—	165	229	.721	201	526	727	69	181	0	34	146	93	819	8.9	0.8	10.0
91-92—Dallas-N.Y.	58	32	1075	112	245	.457	0	0	—	61	86	.709	99	190	289	33	103	0	8	48	49	285	5.0	0.6	4.9
92-93—Utah	6	1	94	8	14	.571	0	0	—	5	9	.556	6	23	29	1	13	0	1	4	7	21	4.8	0.2	3.5
REG. SEASON TOTALS	914	619	25609	3061	5368	.570	0	0	—	1971	2691	.732	2041	5344	7385	751	1959	7	330	1432	1239	8093	8.1	0.8	8.9
PLAYOFF TOTALS	46	33	1303	148	238	.622	0	0	—	91	118	.771	115	276	391	35	103	0	18	57	39	387	8.5	0.8	8.4
ALL-STAR TOTALS	1	0	8	0	0	—	0	0	—	2	2	1.000	1	5	6	1	2	0	0	2	2	2	6.0	1.0	2.0

DONHAM, ROBERT E. (Bob) b. October 11, 1926 d. September 21, 1983 Ht. 6-2 Wt. 190 College—Ohio State

SEASON—TEAM	G	GS	MIN	FGM	FGA	PCT	3FGM	3FGA	PCT	FTM	FTA	PCT	O-RB	D-RB	TOT	AST	PF	DQ	STL	TO	BLK	PTS	RPG	APG	PPG
50-51—Boston	68	—	—	151	298	.507	—	—	—	114	229	.498	—	—	235	139	179	3	—	—	—	416	3.5	2.0	6.1
51-52—Boston	66	—	1980	201	413	.487	—	—	—	149	293	.509	—	—	330	228	223	9	—	—	—	551	5.0	3.5	8.3
52-53—Boston	71	—	1435	169	353	.479	—	—	—	113	240	.471	—	—	239	153	213	8	—	—	—	451	3.4	2.2	6.4
53-54—Boston	68	—	1451	141	315	.448	—	—	—	118	213	.554	—	—	267	186	235	11	—	—	—	400	3.9	2.7	5.9
REG. SEASON TOTALS	273	—	4866	662	1379	.480	—	—	—	494	975	.507	—	—	1071	706	850	31	—	—	—	1818	3.9	2.6	6.7
PLAYOFF TOTALS	17	—	348	31	81	.383	—	—	—	31	76	.408	—	—	54	38	81	9	—	—	—	93	3.2	2.2	5.5

DONOVAN, HENRY HARRY (Harry) b. September 10, 1926 Ht. 6-2 Wt. 190 College—Muhlenberg

SEASON—TEAM	G	GS	MIN	FGM	FGA	PCT	3FGM	3FGA	PCT	FTM	FTA	PCT	O-RB	D-RB	TOT	AST	PF	DQ	STL	TO	BLK	PTS	RPG	APG	PPG
49-50—New York	45	—	—	90	275	.327	—	—	—	73	106	.689	—	—	—	38	107	—	—	—	—	253	—	0.8	5.6
REG. SEASON TOTALS	45	—	—	90	275	.327	—	—	—	73	106	.689	—	—	—	38	107	—	—	—	—	253	—	0.8	5.6
PLAYOFF TOTALS	3	—	—	0	4	.000	—	—	—	2	2	1.000	—	—	—	—	4	—	—	—	—	2	—	0.0	0.7

DONOVAN, WILLIAM JOHN (Billy) b. May 30, 1965 Ht. 5-11 Wt. 171 College—Providence

SEASON—TEAM	G	GS	MIN	FGM	FGA	PCT	3FGM	3FGA	PCT	FTM	FTA	PCT	O-RB	D-RB	TOT	AST	PF	DQ	STL	TO	BLK	PTS	RPG	APG	PPG
87-88—New York	44	0	364	44	109	.404	0	7	.000	17	21	.810	5	20	25	87	33	0	16	42	1	105	0.6	2.0	2.4
REG. SEASON TOTALS	44	0	364	44	109	.404	0	7	.000	17	21	.810	5	20	25	87	33	0	16	42	1	105	0.6	2.0	2.4

DORSEY, JACKY b. December 18, 1954 Ht. 6-7 Wt. 230 College—Georgia

SEASON—TEAM	G	GS	MIN	FGM	FGA	PCT	3FGM	3FGA	PCT	FTM	FTA	PCT	O-RB	D-RB	TOT	AST	PF	DQ	STL	TO	BLK	PTS	RPG	APG	PPG
77-78—Denver-Port.	11	—	88	12	31	.387	—	—	—	10	16	.625	11	19	30	5	17	0	2	6	3	34	2.7	0.5	3.1
78-79—Houston	20	—	108	24	43	.558	—	—	—	8	16	.500	12	11	23	2	25	0	1	8	2	56	1.2	0.1	2.8
80-81—Seattle	29	—	253	20	70	.286	0	0	—	13	25	.520	23	65	88	9	47	0	9	14	1	53	3.0	0.3	1.8
REG. SEASON TOTALS	60	—	449	56	144	.389	0	0	—	31	57	.544	46	95	141	16	89	0	12	28	6	143	2.4	0.3	2.4
PLAYOFF TOTALS	1	—	1	0	0	—	0	0	—	0	0	—	0	0	0	0	0	0	0	0	0	0	0.0	0.0	0.0

DORSEY, RON b. October 10, 1948 Ht. 6-4 Wt. 200 College—Tennessee State

SEASON—TEAM	G	GS	MIN	FGM	FGA	PCT	3FGM	3FGA	PCT	FTM	FTA	PCT	O-RB	D-RB	TOT	AST	PF	DQ	STL	TO	BLK	PTS	RPG	APG	PPG
71-72—Carolina (A)	1	—	12	2	8	.250	0	1	.000	0	2	.000	—	—	5	0	2	—	—	1	—	4	5.0	0.0	4.0
REG. ABA TOTALS	1	—	12	2	8	.250	0	1	.000	0	2	.000	—	—	5	0	2	—	—	1	—	4	5.0	0.0	4.0

DOUGLAS, BRUCE b. April 9, 1964 Ht. 6-3 Wt. 195 College—Illinois

SEASON—TEAM	G	GS	MIN	FGM	FGA	PCT	3FGM	3FGA	PCT	FTM	FTA	PCT	O-RB	D-RB	TOT	AST	PF	DQ	STL	TO	BLK	PTS	RPG	APG	PPG
86-87—Sacramento	8	1	98	7	24	.292	0	1	.000	0	4	.000	5	9	14	17	9	0	9	9	0	14	1.8	2.1	1.8
REG. SEASON TOTALS	8	1	98	7	24	.292	0	1	.000	0	4	.000	5	9	14	17	9	0	9	9	0	14	1.8	2.1	1.8

DOUGLAS, JOHN DAVID b. June 12, 1956 Ht. 6-2 Wt. 175 College—John C. Calhoun State CC/Kansas

SEASON—TEAM	G	GS	MIN	FGM	FGA	PCT	3FGM	3FGA	PCT	FTM	FTA	PCT	O-RB	D-RB	TOT	AST	PF	DQ	STL	TO	BLK	PTS	RPG	APG	PPG
81-82—San Diego	64	9	1031	181	389	.465	18	59	.305	67	102	.657	27	63	90	146	147	2	48	92	9	447	1.4	2.3	7.0
82-83—San Diego	3	1	12	1	6	.167	1	2	.500	2	2	1.000	0	1	1	1	0	0	0	0	0	5	0.3	0.3	1.7
REG. SEASON TOTALS	67	10	1043	182	395	.461	19	61	.311	69	104	.663	27	64	91	147	147	2	48	92	9	452	1.4	2.2	6.7

DOUGLAS, LEON b. August 26, 1954 Ht. 6-10 Wt. 230 College—Alabama

SEASON—TEAM	G	GS	MIN	FGM	FGA	PCT	3FGM	3FGA	PCT	FTM	FTA	PCT	O-RB	D-RB	TOT	AST	PF	DQ	STL	TO	BLK	PTS	RPG	APG	PPG
76-77—Detroit	82	—	1626	245	512	.479	—	—	—	127	229	.555	181	345	526	68	294	10	44	—	81	617	6.4	0.8	7.5
77-78—Detroit	79	—	1993	321	667	.481	—	—	—	221	345	.641	181	401	582	112	295	6	57	197	48	863	7.4	1.4	10.9
78-79—Detroit	78	—	2215	342	698	.490	—	—	—	208	328	.634	248	416	664	74	319	13	39	190	55	892	8.5	0.9	11.4
79-80—Detroit	70	—	1782	221	455	.486	0	1	.000	125	185	.676	171	330	501	121	249	10	30	127	62	567	7.2	1.7	8.1
80-81—Kansas City	79	—	1356	185	323	.573	0	0	—	102	186	.548	150	234	384	69	251	2	25	90	38	472	4.9	0.9	6.0
81-82—Kansas City	63	17	1093	70	140	.500	0	0	—	32	80	.400	111	179	290	35	210	5	15	55	38	172	4.6	0.6	2.7
82-83—Kansas City	5	0	46	2	3	.667	0	0	—	0	2	.000	3	4	7	0	13	0	1	3	3	4	1.4	0.0	0.8
REG. SEASON TOTALS	456	17	10111	1386	2798	.495	0	1	.000	815	1355	.601	1045	1909	2954	479	1631	46	210	660	325	3587	6.5	1.1	7.9
PLAYOFF TOTALS	18	0	375	19	45	.422	0	0	—	17	42	.405	22	53	75	14	58	1	5	18	8	55	4.2	0.8	3.1

DOUGLAS, SHERMAN b. September 15, 1966 Ht. 6-1 Wt. 180 College—Syracuse

SEASON—TEAM	G	GS	MIN	FGM	FGA	PCT	3FGM	3FGA	PCT	FTM	FTA	PCT	O-RB	D-RB	TOT	AST	PF	DQ	STL	TO	BLK	PTS	RPG	APG	PPG
89-90—Miami	81	66	2470	463	938	.494	5	31	.161	224	326	.687	70	136	206	619	187	0	145	246	10	1155	2.5	7.6	14.3
90-91—Miami	73	73	2562	532	1055	.504	4	31	.129	284	414	.686	78	131	209	624	178	2	121	270	5	1352	2.9	8.5	18.5
91-92—Miami-Boston	42	2	752	117	253	.462	1	10	.100	73	107	.682	13	50	63	172	78	0	25	68	9	308	1.5	4.1	7.3
92-93—Boston	79	36	1932	264	530	.498	6	29	.207	84	150	.560	65	97	162	508	166	1	49	161	10	618	2.1	6.4	7.8
93-94—Boston	78	78	2789	425	919	.462	13	56	.232	177	276	.641	70	123	193	683	171	2	89	233	11	1040	2.5	8.8	13.3
REG. SEASON TOTALS	353	255	10505	1801	3695	.487	29	157	.185	842	1273	.661	296	537	833	2606	780	5	429	978	45	4473	2.4	7.4	12.7
PLAYOFF TOTALS	10	4	231	26	70	.371	0	5	.000	11	17	.647	13	17	30	48	18	0	4	16	0	63	3.0	4.8	6.3

DOVE, LLOYD (Sonny) b. August 16, 1945 d. February 14, 1983 Ht. 6-8 Wt. 200 College—St. John's

SEASON—TEAM	G	GS	MIN	FGM	FGA	PCT	3FGM	3FGA	PCT	FTM	FTA	PCT	O-RB	D-RB	TOT	AST	PF	DQ	STL	TO	BLK	PTS	RPG	APG	PPG
67-68—Detroit	28	—	162	22	75	.293	—	—	—	12	26	.462	—	—	52	11	27	0	—	—	—	56	1.9	0.4	2.0
68-69—Detroit	29	—	236	47	100	.470	—	—	—	24	36	.667	—	—	62	12	49	0	—	—	—	118	2.1	0.4	4.1
69-70—New York (A)	80	—	2284	456	987	.462	2	13	.154	240	379	.633	—	—	543	107	295	12	—	—	—	1154	6.8	1.3	14.4
70-71—New York (A)	83	—	2280	467	1006	.464	4	14	.286	186	273	.681	—	—	676	88	304	—	—	—	—	1124	8.1	1.1	13.5
71-72—New York (A)	2	—	9	2	5	.400	0	0	—	2	3	.667	—	—	1	1	4	—	—	2	—	6	0.5	0.5	3.0
REG. NBA TOTALS	57	—	398	69	175	.394	—	—	—	36	62	.581	—	—	114	23	76	0	—	—	—	174	2.0	0.4	3.1
REG. ABA TOTALS	165	—	4573	925	1998	.463	6	27	.222	428	655	.653	—	—	1220	196	603	12	—	2	—	2284	7.4	1.2	13.8
NBA PLAYOFF TOTALS	2	—	6	2	4	.500	—	—	—	0	0	—	—	—	2	—	0	0	—	—	—	4	1.0	0.0	2.0
ABA PLAYOFF TOTALS	12	—	313	53	107	.495	1	4	.250	27	43	.628	27	44	82	10	42	2	—	—	—	134	6.8	0.8	11.2

DOVER, JERRY L. b. October 16, 1949 Ht. 5-7 Wt. 155 College—LeMoyne-Owen

SEASON—TEAM	G	GS	MIN	FGM	FGA	PCT	3FGM	3FGA	PCT	FTM	FTA	PCT	O-RB	D-RB	TOT	AST	PF	DQ	STL	TO	BLK	PTS	RPG	APG	PPG
71-72—Memphis (A)	4	—	13	3	9	.333	2	5	.400	0	0	—	—	—	0	1	3	—	—	0	—	8	0.0	0.3	2.0
REG. ABA TOTALS	4	—	13	3	9	.333	2	5	.400	0	0	—	—	—	—	1	3	—	—	—	—	8	0.0	0.3	2.0

DOWNEY, WILLIAM K. (Bill) b. November 11, 1923 Ht. 6-6 Wt. 210 College—Marquette

SEASON—TEAM	G	GS	MIN	FGM	FGA	PCT	3FGM	3FGA	PCT	FTM	FTA	PCT	O-RB	D-RB	TOT	AST	PF	DQ	STL	TO	BLK	PTS	RPG	APG	PPG
47-48—Providence	3	—	—	0	2	.000	—	—	—	0	0	—	—	—	—	0	0	—	—	—	—	0	—	0.0	0.0
REG. SEASON TOTALS	3	—	—	0	2	.000	—	—	—	0	0	—	—	—	—	0	0	—	—	—	—	0	—	0.0	0.0

DOWNING, STEVE b. September 9, 1950 Ht. 6-8 Wt. 225 College—Indiana

SEASON—TEAM	G	GS	MIN	FGM	FGA	PCT	3FGM	3FGA	PCT	FTM	FTA	PCT	O-RB	D-RB	TOT	AST	PF	DQ	STL	TO	BLK	PTS	RPG	APG	PPG
73-74—Boston	24	—	137	21	64	.328	—	—	—	22	38	.579	14	25	39	11	33	0	5	—	0	64	1.6	0.5	2.7
74-75—Boston	3	—	9	0	2	.000	—	—	—	0	2	.000	0	2	2	0	0	0	0	—	0	0	0.7	0.0	0.0
REG. SEASON TOTALS	27	—	146	21	66	.318	—	—	—	22	40	.550	14	27	41	11	33	0	5	—	0	64	1.5	0.4	2.4
PLAYOFF TOTALS	1	—	4	1	2	.500	—	—	—	0	0	—	2	0	2	—	1	0	0	—	0	2	2.0	0.0	2.0

DOYLE, DANIEL F. (Danny) b. February 6, 1940 Ht. 6-8 Wt. 200 College—Belmont Abbey

SEASON—TEAM	G	GS	MIN	FGM	FGA	PCT	3FGM	3FGA	PCT	FTM	FTA	PCT	O-RB	D-RB	TOT	AST	PF	DQ	STL	TO	BLK	PTS	RPG	APG	PPG
62-63—Detroit	4	—	25	6	12	.500	—	—	—	4	5	.800	—	—	8	3	4	0	—	—	—	16	2.0	0.8	4.0
REG. SEASON TOTALS	4	—	25	6	12	.500	—	—	—	4	5	.800	—	—	8	3	4	0	—	—	—	16	2.0	0.8	4.0

DOZIER, TERRY LINNARD b. June 29, 1966 Ht. 6-9 Wt. 210 College—South Carolina

SEASON—TEAM	G	GS	MIN	FGM	FGA	PCT	3FGM	3FGA	PCT	FTM	FTA	PCT	O-RB	D-RB	TOT	AST	PF	DQ	STL	TO	BLK	PTS	RPG	APG	PPG
89-90—Charlotte	9	0	92	9	27	.333	0	1	.000	4	8	.500	7	8	15	3	10	0	6	7	2	22	1.7	0.3	2.4
REG. SEASON TOTALS	9	0	92	9	27	.333	0	1	.000	4	8	.500	7	8	15	3	10	0	6	7	2	22	1.7	0.3	2.4

DREILING, GREGORY ALAN (Greg) b. November 7, 1963 Ht. 7-1 Wt. 250 College—Wichita State/Kansas

SEASON—TEAM	G	GS	MIN	FGM	FGA	PCT	3FGM	3FGA	PCT	FTM	FTA	PCT	O-RB	D-RB	TOT	AST	PF	DQ	STL	TO	BLK	PTS	RPG	APG	PPG
86-87—Indiana	24	0	128	16	37	.432	0	0	—	10	12	.833	12	31	43	7	42	0	2	7	2	42	1.8	0.3	1.8
87-88—Indiana	20	0	74	8	17	.471	0	0	—	18	26	.692	3	14	17	5	19	0	2	11	4	34	0.9	0.3	1.7
88-89—Indiana	53	4	396	43	77	.558	0	0	—	43	64	.672	39	53	92	18	100	0	5	39	11	129	1.7	0.3	2.4
89-90—Indiana	49	0	307	20	53	.377	0	0	—	25	34	.735	21	66	87	8	69	0	4	19	14	65	1.8	0.2	1.3
90-91—Indiana	73	42	1031	98	194	.505	0	2	.000	63	105	.600	66	189	255	51	178	1	24	57	29	259	3.5	0.7	3.5
91-92—Indiana	60	23	509	43	87	.494	1	1	1.000	30	40	.750	22	74	96	25	123	1	10	31	16	117	1.6	0.4	2.0
92-93—Indiana	43	0	239	19	58	.328	0	4	.000	8	15	.533	26	40	66	8	60	0	5	9	8	46	1.5	0.2	1.1
93-94—Dallas	54	19	685	52	104	.500	1	1	1.000	27	38	.711	47	123	170	31	159	5	16	43	24	132	3.1	0.6	2.4
REG. SEASON TOTALS	376	88	3369	299	627	.477	2	8	.250	224	334	.671	236	590	826	153	750	7	68	216	108	824	2.2	0.4	2.2
PLAYOFF TOTALS	8	5	82	6	16	.375	1	1	1.000	4	6	.667	8	11	19	—	20	0	0	3	0	17	2.4	0.0	2.1

DREW, JOHN EDWARD (J.E.) b. September 30, 1954 Ht. 6-6 Wt. 205 College—Gardner-Webb

SEASON—TEAM	G	GS	MIN	FGM	FGA	PCT	3FGM	3FGA	PCT	FTM	FTA	PCT	O-RB	D-RB	TOT	AST	PF	DQ	STL	TO	BLK	PTS	RPG	APG	PPG
74-75—Atlanta	78	—	2289	527	1230	.428	—	—	—	388	544	.713	357	479	836	138	274	4	119	—	39	1442	10.7	1.8	18.5
75-76—Atlanta	77	—	2351	586	1168	.502	—	—	—	488	656	.744	286	374	660	150	261	11	138	—	30	1660	8.6	1.9	21.6
76-77—Atlanta	74	—	2688	689	1416	.487	—	—	—	412	577	.714	280	395	675	133	275	9	102	—	29	1790	9.1	1.8	24.2
77-78—Atlanta	70	—	2203	593	1236	.480	—	—	—	437	575	.760	213	298	511	141	247	8	119	210	27	1623	7.3	2.0	23.2
78-79—Atlanta	79	—	2410	650	1375	.473	—	—	—	495	677	.731	225	297	522	119	332	19	128	211	16	1795	6.6	1.5	22.7
79-80—Atlanta	80	—	2306	535	1182	.453	0	7	.000	489	646	.757	203	268	471	101	313	10	91	240	23	1559	5.9	1.3	19.5
80-81—Atlanta	67	—	2075	500	1096	.456	0	7	.000	454	577	.787	145	238	383	79	264	9	98	194	15	1454	5.7	1.2	21.7
81-82—Atlanta	70	51	2040	465	957	.486	4	12	.333	364	491	.741	169	206	375	96	250	6	64	178	3	1298	5.4	1.4	18.5
82-83—Utah	44	33	1206	318	671	.474	0	5	.000	296	392	.755	98	137	235	97	152	8	35	135	7	932	5.3	2.2	21.2
83-84—Utah	81	4	1797	511	1067	.479	6	22	.273	402	517	.778	146	192	338	135	208	1	88	192	2	1430	4.2	1.7	17.7
84-85—Utah	19	16	463	107	260	.412	0	4	.000	94	122	.770	36	46	82	35	65	0	22	42	2	308	4.3	1.8	16.2
REG. SEASON TOTALS	739	104	21828	5481	11658	.470	10	57	.175	4319	5774	.748	2158	2930	5088	1224	2641	85	1004	1402	193	15291	6.9	1.7	20.7
PLAYOFF TOTALS	29	2	735	151	350	.431	0	0	—	103	142	.725	55	85	140	24	103	3	21	48	5	405	4.8	0.8	14.0
ALL-STAR TOTALS	2	1	24	1	7	.143	0	0	—	4	5	.800	2	4	6	0	7	0	2	3	0	6	3.0	0.0	3.0

DREW, LARRY DONNELL b. April 2, 1958 Ht. 6-1½ Wt. 175 College—Missouri

SEASON—TEAM	G	GS	MIN	FGM	FGA	PCT	3FGM	3FGA	PCT	FTM	FTA	PCT	O-RB	D-RB	TOT	AST	PF	DQ	STL	TO	BLK	PTS	RPG	APG	PPG
80-81—Detroit	76	—	1581	197	484	.407	4	17	.235	106	133	.797	24	96	120	249	125	0	88	166	7	504	1.6	3.3	6.6
81-82—Kansas City	81	19	1973	358	757	.473	8	27	.296	150	189	.794	30	119	149	419	150	0	110	174	1	874	1.8	5.2	10.8
82-83—Kansas City	75	74	2690	599	1218	.492	2	16	.125	310	378	.820	44	163	207	610	207	1	126	272	10	1510	2.8	8.1	20.1
83-84—Kansas City	73	73	2363	474	1026	.462	3	10	.300	243	313	.776	33	113	146	558	170	0	121	194	10	1194	2.0	7.6	16.4
84-85—Kansas City	72	66	2373	457	913	.501	7	28	.250	154	194	.794	39	125	164	484	147	0	93	179	8	1075	2.3	6.7	14.9
85-86—Sacramento	75	31	1971	376	776	.485	10	31	.323	128	161	.795	25	100	125	338	134	0	66	133	2	890	1.7	4.5	11.9
86-87—L.A. Clippers	60	22	1566	295	683	.432	12	72	.167	139	166	.837	26	77	103	326	107	0	60	151	2	741	1.7	5.4	12.4
87-88—L.A. Clippers	74	51	2024	328	720	.456	26	90	.289	83	108	.769	21	98	119	383	114	0	65	152	0	765	1.6	5.2	10.3
89-90—L.A. Lakers	80	3	1333	170	383	.444	32	81	.395	46	60	.767	12	86	98	217	92	0	47	95	4	418	1.2	2.7	5.2
90-91—L.A. Lakers	48	2	496	54	125	.432	14	33	.424	17	22	.773	5	29	34	118	40	0	15	49	1	139	0.7	2.5	2.9
REG. SEASON TOTALS	714	341	18370	3308	7085	.467	118	405	.291	1376	1724	.798	259	1006	1265	3702	1286	1	791	1565	45	8110	1.8	5.2	11.4
PLAYOFF TOTALS	31	3	293	38	85	.447	5	18	.278	14	17	.824	0	15	15	50	33	0	11	18	0	95	0.5	1.6	3.1

DREXLER, CLYDE AUSTIN (**Clyde the Glide**) b. June 22, 1962 Ht. 6-7 Wt. 220 College—Houston

SEASON—TEAM	G	GS	MIN	FGM	FGA	PCT	3FGM	3FGA	PCT	FTM	FTA	PCT	O-RB	D-RB	TOT	AST	PF	DQ	STL	TO	BLK	PTS	RPG	APG	PPG
83-84—Portland	82	3	1408	252	559	.451	1	4	.250	123	169	.728	112	123	235	153	209	2	107	123	29	628	2.9	1.9	7.7
84-85—Portland	80	43	2555	573	1161	.494	8	37	.216	223	294	.759	217	259	476	441	265	3	177	223	68	1377	6.0	5.5	17.2
85-86—Portland	75	58	2576	542	1142	.475	12	60	.200	293	381	.769	171	250	421	600	270	8	197	282	46	1389	5.6	8.0	18.5
86-87—Portland	82	82	3114	707	1408	.502	11	47	.234	357	470	.760	227	291	518	566	281	7	204	253	71	1782	6.3	6.9	21.7
87-88—Portland	81	80	3060	849	1679	.506	11	52	.212	476	587	.811	261	272	533	467	250	2	203	236	52	2185	6.6	5.8	27.0
88-89—Portland	78	78	3064	829	1672	.496	27	104	.260	438	548	.799	289	326	615	450	269	2	213	250	54	2123	7.9	5.8	27.2
89-90—Portland	73	73	2683	670	1357	.494	30	106	.283	333	430	.774	208	299	507	432	222	1	145	191	51	1703	6.9	5.9	23.3
90-91—Portland	82	82	2852	645	1338	.482	61	191	.319	416	524	.794	212	334	546	493	226	2	144	232	60	1767	6.7	6.0	21.5
91-92—Portland	76	76	2751	694	1476	.470	114	338	.337	401	505	.794	166	334	500	512	229	2	138	240	70	1903	6.6	6.7	25.0
92-93—Portland	49	49	1671	350	816	.429	31	133	.233	245	292	.839	126	183	309	278	159	1	95	115	37	976	6.3	5.7	19.9
93-94—Portland	68	68	2334	473	1105	.428	71	219	.324	286	368	.777	154	291	445	333	202	2	98	167	34	1303	6.5	4.9	19.2
REG. SEASON TOTALS	826	692	28068	6584	13713	.480	377	1291	.292	3591	4568	.786	2143	2962	5105	4725	2582	32	1721	2312	572	17136	6.2	5.7	20.7
PLAYOFF TOTALS	94	89	3626	746	1659	.450	59	228	.259	464	586	.792	265	405	670	640	329	6	190	283	79	2015	7.1	6.8	21.4
ALL-STAR TOTALS	8	3	147	35	71	.493	3	10	.300	12	12	1.000	17	25	42	20	19	0	9	15	6	85	5.3	2.5	10.6

DRISCOLL, EDWARD CUTHBERT JR. (**Terry**) b. August 28, 1947 Ht. 6-7 Wt. 215 College—Boston College

SEASON—TEAM	G	GS	MIN	FGM	FGA	PCT	3FGM	3FGA	PCT	FTM	FTA	PCT	O-RB	D-RB	TOT	AST	PF	DQ	STL	TO	BLK	PTS	RPG	APG	PPG
70-71—Detroit	69	—	1255	132	318	.415	—	—	—	108	154	.701	—	—	402	54	212	2	—	—	—	372	5.8	0.8	5.4
71-72—Baltimore	40	—	313	40	104	.385	—	—	—	27	39	.692	—	—	109	23	53	0	—	—	—	107	2.7	0.6	2.7
72-73—Balt.-Milw.	60	—	964	140	327	.428	—	—	—	43	62	.694	—	—	300	55	144	3	—	—	—	323	5.0	0.9	5.4
73-74—Milwaukee	64	—	697	88	187	.471	—	—	—	30	46	.652	73	126	199	54	121	0	21	—	16	206	3.1	0.8	3.2
74-75—Milwaukee	11	—	52	3	13	.231	—	—	—	1	2	.500	7	9	16	3	7	0	1	—	0	7	1.5	0.3	0.6
74-75—St. Louis (A)	30	—	351	46	122	.377	0	0	—	20	27	.741	37	51	88	32	51	—	9	28	6	112	2.9	1.1	3.7
REG. NBA TOTALS	244	—	3281	403	949	.425	—	—	—	209	303	.690	80	135	1026	189	537	5	22	—	16	1015	4.2	0.8	4.2
REG. ABA TOTALS	30	—	351	46	122	.377	0	0	—	20	27	.741	37	51	88	32	51	—	9	28	6	112	2.9	1.1	3.7
NBA PLAYOFF TOTALS	16	—	47	6	15	.400	—	—	—	3	3	1.000	9	5	15	4	14	0	2	—	1	15	0.9	0.3	0.9

DROLLINGER, RALPH KIM b. April 20, 1954 Ht. 7-2 Wt. 250 College—UCLA

SEASON—TEAM	G	GS	MIN	FGM	FGA	PCT	3FGM	3FGA	PCT	FTM	FTA	PCT	O-RB	D-RB	TOT	AST	PF	DQ	STL	TO	BLK	PTS	RPG	APG	PPG
80-81—Dallas	6	—	67	7	14	.500	0	0	—	1	4	.250	5	14	19	14	16	0	1	13	2	15	3.2	2.3	2.5
REG. SEASON TOTALS	6	—	67	7	14	.500	0	0	—	1	4	.250	5	14	19	14	16	0	1	13	2	15	3.2	2.3	2.5

DUCKETT, RICHARD J. (**Dick**) b. March 25, 1933 Ht. 6-1 Wt. 185 College—St. John's

SEASON—TEAM	G	GS	MIN	FGM	FGA	PCT	3FGM	3FGA	PCT	FTM	FTA	PCT	O-RB	D-RB	TOT	AST	PF	DQ	STL	TO	BLK	PTS	RPG	APG	PPG
57-58—Cincinnati	34	—	424	54	158	.342	—	—	—	24	27	.889	—	—	56	47	60	0	—	—	—	132	1.6	1.4	3.9
REG. SEASON TOTALS	34	—	424	54	158	.342	—	—	—	24	27	.889	—	—	56	47	60	0	—	—	—	132	1.6	1.4	3.9

DUCKWORTH, KEVIN JEROME b. April 1, 1964 Ht. 7-0 Wt. 280 College—Eastern Illinois

SEASON—TEAM	G	GS	MIN	FGM	FGA	PCT	3FGM	3FGA	PCT	FTM	FTA	PCT	O-RB	D-RB	TOT	AST	PF	DQ	STL	TO	BLK	PTS	RPG	APG	PPG
86-87—S.A.-Port.	65	1	875	130	273	.476	0	1	.000	92	134	.687	76	147	223	29	192	3	21	78	21	352	3.4	0.4	5.4
87-88—Portland	78	50	2223	450	907	.496	0	0	—	331	430	.770	224	352	576	66	280	5	31	177	32	1231	7.4	0.8	15.8
88-89—Portland	79	79	2662	554	1161	.477	0	2	.000	324	428	.757	246	389	635	60	300	6	56	200	49	1432	8.0	0.8	18.1
89-90—Portland	82	82	2462	548	1146	.478	0	0	—	231	312	.740	184	325	509	91	271	2	36	171	34	1327	6.2	1.1	16.2
90-91—Portland	81	81	2511	521	1084	.481	0	2	.000	240	311	.772	177	354	531	89	251	5	33	186	34	1282	6.6	1.1	15.8
91-92—Portland	82	82	2222	362	786	.461	0	3	.000	156	226	.690	151	346	497	99	264	5	38	143	37	880	6.1	1.2	10.7
92-93—Portland	74	55	1762	301	688	.438	0	2	.000	127	174	.730	118	269	387	70	222	1	45	87	39	729	5.2	0.9	9.9
93-94—Washington	69	52	1485	184	441	.417	0	0	—	88	132	.667	103	222	325	56	223	2	37	101	35	456	4.7	0.8	6.6
REG. SEASON TOTALS	610	482	16202	3050	6486	.470	0	10	.000	1589	2147	.740	1279	2404	3683	560	2003	29	297	1143	281	7689	6.0	0.9	12.6
PLAYOFF TOTALS	67	59	1956	323	723	.447	0	1	.000	139	198	.702	143	250	393	84	246	6	30	155	34	785	5.9	1.3	11.7
ALL-STAR TOTALS	2	0	26	4	8	.500	0	0	—	3	4	.750	3	2	5	0	5	0	1	2	0	11	2.5	0.0	5.5

DUDLEY, CHARLES (**Grasshopper**) b. March 5, 1950   Ht. 6-2   Wt. 180   College—Washington

SEASON—TEAM	G	GS	MIN	FGM	FGA	PCT	3FGM	3FGA	PCT	FTM	FTA	PCT	O-RB	D-RB	TOT	AST	PF	DQ	STL	TO	BLK	PTS	RPG	APG	PPG
72-73—Seattle	12	—	99	10	23	.435	—	—	—	14	16	.875	—	—	6	16	15	0	—	—	—	34	0.5	1.3	2.8
74-75—Golden State	67	—	756	102	217	.470	—	—	—	70	97	.722	61	84	145	103	105	1	40	—	2	274	2.2	1.5	4.1
75-76—Golden State	82	—	1456	182	345	.528	—	—	—	157	245	.641	112	157	269	239	170	0	77	—	2	521	3.3	2.9	6.4
76-77—Golden State	79	—	1682	220	421	.523	—	—	—	129	203	.635	119	177	296	347	169	0	67	—	6	569	3.7	4.4	7.2
77-78—Golden State	78	—	1660	127	249	.510	—	—	—	138	195	.708	86	201	287	409	181	0	68	163	2	392	3.7	5.2	5.0
78-79—Chicago	43	—	684	45	125	.360	—	—	—	28	42	.667	25	61	86	116	82	0	32	64	1	118	2.0	2.7	2.7
REG. SEASON TOTALS	361	—	6337	686	1380	.497	—	—	—	536	798	.672	403	680	1089	1230	722	1	284	227	13	1908	3.0	3.4	5.3
PLAYOFF TOTALS	36	—	608	56	118	.475	—	—	—	55	84	.655	42	49	91	124	80	0	34	—	3	167	2.5	3.4	4.6

DUDLEY, CHRISTEN GUILFORD (**Chris**) b. February 22, 1965   Ht. 6-11   Wt. 235   College—Yale

SEASON—TEAM	G	GS	MIN	FGM	FGA	PCT	3FGM	3FGA	PCT	FTM	FTA	PCT	O-RB	D-RB	TOT	AST	PF	DQ	STL	TO	BLK	PTS	RPG	APG	PPG
87-88—Cleveland	55	1	513	65	137	.474	0	0	—	40	71	.563	74	70	144	23	87	2	13	31	19	170	2.6	0.4	3.1
88-89—Cleveland	61	2	544	73	168	.435	0	1	.000	39	107	.364	72	85	157	21	82	0	9	44	23	185	2.6	0.3	3.0
89-90—Clev.-N.J.	64	30	1356	146	355	.411	0	0	—	58	182	.319	174	249	423	39	164	2	41	84	72	350	6.6	0.6	5.5
90-91—New Jersey	61	25	1560	170	417	.408	0	0	—	94	176	.534	229	282	511	37	217	6	39	80	153	434	8.4	0.6	7.1
91-92—New Jersey	82	21	1902	190	472	.403	0	0	—	80	171	.468	343	396	739	58	275	5	38	79	179	460	9.0	0.7	5.6
92-93—New Jersey	71	16	1398	94	266	.353	0	0	—	57	110	.518	215	298	513	16	195	5	17	54	103	245	7.2	0.2	3.5
93-94—Portland	6	3	86	6	25	.240	0	0	—	2	4	.500	16	8	24	5	18	0	4	2	3	14	4.0	0.8	2.3
REG. SEASON TOTALS	400	98	7359	744	1840	.404	0	1	.000	370	821	.451	1123	1388	2511	199	1038	20	161	374	552	1858	6.3	0.5	4.6
PLAYOFF TOTALS	13	2	186	11	29	.379	0	0	—	6	12	.500	22	24	46	3	34	1	8	4	10	28	3.5	0.4	2.2

DUEROD, TERRY (**Sweet Due**) b. July 29, 1956   Ht. 6-2   Wt. 180   College—Detroit

SEASON—TEAM	G	GS	MIN	FGM	FGA	PCT	3FGM	3FGA	PCT	FTM	FTA	PCT	O-RB	D-RB	TOT	AST	PF	DQ	STL	TO	BLK	PTS	RPG	APG	PPG
79-80—Detroit	67	—	1331	282	598	.472	15	53	.283	45	66	.682	29	69	98	117	102	0	41	79	11	624	1.5	1.7	9.3
80-81—Dallas-Boston	50	—	451	104	234	.444	8	16	.500	31	41	.756	17	27	44	36	27	0	17	35	4	247	0.9	0.7	4.9
81-82—Boston	21	0	146	34	77	.442	0	1	.000	4	12	.333	6	9	15	12	9	0	3	2	1	72	0.7	0.6	3.4
82-83—Golden State	5	0	49	9	19	.474	0	0	—	0	0	—	0	3	3	5	5	0	2	9	1	18	0.6	1.0	3.6
REG. SEASON TOTALS	143	0	1977	429	928	.462	23	70	.329	80	119	.672	52	108	160	170	143	0	63	125	17	961	1.1	1.2	6.7
PLAYOFF TOTALS	10	0	12	4	10	.400	0	2	.000	0	0	—	0	0	0	—	0	0	1	1	0	8	0.0	0.0	0.8

DUFFY, ROBERT JOHN (**Bob John**) b. July 5, 1922   Ht. 6-4   Wt. 175   College—Tulane

SEASON—TEAM	G	GS	MIN	FGM	FGA	PCT	3FGM	3FGA	PCT	FTM	FTA	PCT	O-RB	D-RB	TOT	AST	PF	DQ	STL	TO	BLK	PTS	RPG	APG	PPG
46-47—Ch. Stags-Boston	17	—	—	7	32	.219	—	—	—	5	7	.714	—	—	—	0	17	—	—	—	—	19	—	0.0	1.1
REG. SEASON TOTALS	17	—	—	7	32	.219	—	—	—	5	7	.714	—	—	—	0	17	—	—	—	—	19	—	0.0	1.1

DUFFY, ROBERT JOSEPH (**Bob**) b. September 26, 1940   Ht. 6-3   Wt. 185   College—Colgate

SEASON—TEAM	G	GS	MIN	FGM	FGA	PCT	3FGM	3FGA	PCT	FTM	FTA	PCT	O-RB	D-RB	TOT	AST	PF	DQ	STL	TO	BLK	PTS	RPG	APG	PPG
62-63—St. Louis	42	—	435	66	174	.379	—	—	—	22	39	.564	—	—	39	83	42	0	—	—	—	154	0.9	2.0	3.7
63-64—St. L.-N.Y.-Detroit	48	—	662	94	229	.410	—	—	—	44	65	.677	—	—	61	79	48	0	—	—	—	232	1.3	1.6	4.8
64-65—Detroit	4	—	26	4	11	.364	—	—	—	6	7	.857	—	—	4	5	4	0	—	—	—	14	1.0	1.3	3.5
REG. SEASON TOTALS	94	—	1123	164	414	.396	—	—	—	72	111	.649	—	—	104	167	94	0	—	—	—	400	1.1	1.8	4.3
PLAYOFF TOTALS	5	—	24	6	15	.400	—	—	—	2	2	1.000	—	—	3	3	3	0	—	—	—	14	0.6	0.6	2.8

DUKES, WALTER F. b. June 23, 1930   Ht. 7-0   Wt. 220   College—Seton Hall

SEASON—TEAM	G	GS	MIN	FGM	FGA	PCT	3FGM	3FGA	PCT	FTM	FTA	PCT	O-RB	D-RB	TOT	AST	PF	DQ	STL	TO	BLK	PTS	RPG	APG	PPG
55-56—New York	60	—	1290	149	370	.403	—	—	—	167	236	.708	—	—	443	39	211	11	—	—	—	465	7.4	0.7	7.8
56-57—Minneapolis	71	—	1866	228	626	.364	—	—	—	264	383	.689	—	—	794	54	273	10	—	—	—	720	11.2	0.8	10.1
57-58—Detroit	72	—	2184	278	796	.349	—	—	—	247	366	.675	—	—	954	52	311	17	—	—	—	803	13.3	0.7	11.2
58-59—Detroit	72	—	2338	318	904	.352	—	—	—	297	452	.657	—	—	958	64	332	22	—	—	—	933	13.3	0.9	13.0
59-60—Detroit	66	—	2140	314	871	.361	—	—	—	376	508	.740	—	—	883	80	310	20	—	—	—	1004	13.4	1.2	15.2
60-61—Detroit	73	—	2044	286	706	.405	—	—	—	281	400	.703	—	—	1028	139	313	16	—	—	—	853	14.1	1.9	11.7
61-62—Detroit	77	—	1896	256	647	.396	—	—	—	208	291	.715	—	—	803	125	327	20	—	—	—	720	10.4	1.6	9.4
62-63—Detroit	62	—	913	83	255	.325	—	—	—	101	137	.737	—	—	360	55	183	5	—	—	—	267	5.8	0.9	4.3
REG. SEASON TOTALS	553	—	14671	1912	5175	.369	—	—	—	1941	2773	.700	—	—	6223	608	2260	121	—	—	—	5765	11.3	1.1	10.4
PLAYOFF TOTALS	35	—	1161	151	363	.416	—	—	—	145	204	.711	—	—	432	51	168	14	—	—	—	447	12.3	1.5	12.8
ALL-STAR TOTALS	2	—	43	5	16	.313	—	—	—	2	3	.667	—	—	19	2	7	0	—	—	—	12	9.5	1.0	6.0

DUMARS, JOE III b. May 24, 1963 Ht. 6-3 Wt. 195 College—McNeese State

SEASON—TEAM	G	GS	MIN	FGM	FGA	PCT	3FGM	3FGA	PCT	FTM	FTA	PCT	O-RB	D-RB	TOT	AST	PF	DQ	STL	TO	BLK	PTS	RPG	APG	PPG
85-86—Detroit	82	45	1957	287	597	.481	5	16	.313	190	238	.798	60	59	119	390	200	1	66	158	11	769	1.5	4.8	9.4
86-87—Detroit	79	75	2439	369	749	.493	9	22	.409	184	246	.748	50	117	167	352	194	1	83	171	5	931	2.1	4.5	11.8
87-88—Detroit	82	82	2732	453	960	.472	4	19	.211	251	308	.815	63	137	200	387	155	1	87	172	15	1161	2.4	4.7	14.2
88-89—Detroit	69	67	2408	456	903	.505	14	29	.483	260	306	.850	57	115	172	390	103	1	63	178	5	1186	2.5	5.7	17.2
89-90—Detroit	75	71	2578	508	1058	.480	22	55	.400	297	330	.900	60	152	212	368	129	1	63	145	2	1335	2.8	4.9	17.8
90-91—Detroit	80	80	3046	622	1292	.481	14	45	.311	371	417	.890	62	125	187	443	135	0	89	189	7	1629	2.3	5.5	20.4
91-92—Detroit	82	82	3192	587	1311	.448	49	120	.408	412	475	.867	82	106	188	375	145	0	71	193	12	1635	2.3	4.6	19.9
92-93—Detroit	77	77	3094	677	1454	.466	112	299	.375	343	397	.864	63	85	148	308	141	0	78	138	7	1809	1.9	4.0	23.5
93-94—Detroit	69	69	2591	505	1118	.452	124	320	.388	276	330	.836	35	116	151	261	118	0	63	159	4	1410	2.2	3.8	20.4
REG. SEASON TOTALS	695	648	24037	4464	9442	.473	353	925	.382	2584	3047	.848	532	1012	1544	3274	1320	5	663	1503	68	11865	2.2	4.7	17.1
PLAYOFF TOTALS	99	99	3607	589	1263	.466	32	92	.348	381	449	.849	87	141	228	478	204	2	84	183	6	1591	2.3	4.8	16.1
ALL-STAR TOTALS	4	1	67	8	23	.348	3	9	.333	1	2	.500	1	5	6	13	2	0	0	10	0	20	1.5	3.3	5.0

DUMAS, RICHARD (**Rich**) b. 1945 Ht. 6-3 Wt. 170 College—Northeastern State

SEASON—TEAM	G	GS	MIN	FGM	FGA	PCT	3FGM	3FGA	PCT	FTM	FTA	PCT	O-RB	D-RB	TOT	AST	PF	DQ	STL	TO	BLK	PTS	RPG	APG	PPG
68-69—Houston (A)	1	—	5	1	5	.200	0	0	—	0	0	—	—	—	1	0	1	0	—	1	—	2	1.0	0.0	2.0
REG. ABA TOTALS	1	—	5	1	5	.200	0	0	—	0	0	—	—	—	1	0	1	0	—	1	—	2	1.0	0.0	2.0

DUMAS, RICHARD WAYNE b. May 19, 1969 Ht. 6-7 Wt. 205 College—Oklahoma State

SEASON—TEAM	G	GS	MIN	FGM	FGA	PCT	3FGM	3FGA	PCT	FTM	FTA	PCT	O-RB	D-RB	TOT	AST	PF	DQ	STL	TO	BLK	PTS	RPG	APG	PPG
92-93—Phoenix	48	32	1320	302	576	.524	1	3	.333	152	215	.707	100	123	223	60	127	0	85	92	39	757	4.6	1.3	15.8
REG. SEASON TOTALS	48	32	1320	302	576	.524	1	3	.333	152	215	.707	100	123	223	60	127	0	85	92	39	757	4.6	1.3	15.8
PLAYOFF TOTALS	23	20	499	107	204	.525	0	2	.000	37	49	.755	36	29	65	24	52	0	21	27	13	251	2.8	1.0	10.9

DUNCAN, ANDREW (**Andy**) b. April 17, 1922 Ht. 6-6 Wt. 195 College—Kentucky/William & Mary

SEASON—TEAM	G	GS	MIN	FGM	FGA	PCT	3FGM	3FGA	PCT	FTM	FTA	PCT	O-RB	D-RB	TOT	AST	PF	DQ	STL	TO	BLK	PTS	RPG	APG	PPG
47-48—Rochester (N)	60	—	—	200	—	—	—	—	—	119	199	.598	—	—	—	—	183	—	—	—	—	519	—	—	8.7
48-49—Rochester	55	—	—	162	391	.414	—	—	—	83	135	.615	—	—	—	51	179	—	—	—	—	407	—	0.9	7.4
49-50—Rochester	67	—	—	125	289	.433	—	—	—	60	108	.556	—	—	—	42	160	—	—	—	—	310	—	0.6	4.6
50-51—Boston	14	—	—	7	40	.175	—	—	—	15	22	.682	—	—	30	8	27	0	—	—	—	29	2.1	0.6	2.1
REG. NBA TOTALS	136	—	—	294	720	.408	—	—	—	158	265	.596	—	—	30	101	366	0	—	—	—	746	2.1	0.7	5.5
REG. NBL TOTALS	60	—	—	200	—	—	—	—	—	119	199	.598	—	—	—	—	183	—	—	—	—	519	—	—	8.7
NBA PLAYOFF TOTALS	6	—	—	5	16	.313	—	—	—	2	3	.667	—	—	—	3	10	0	—	—	—	12	—	0.5	2.0
NBL PLAYOFF TOTALS	11	—	—	39	—	—	—	—	—	23	34	.676	—	—	—	—	25	—	—	—	—	101	—	—	9.2

DUNLEAVY, MICHAEL JOSEPH (**Mike**) b. March 21, 1954 Ht. 6-2½ Wt. 180 College—South Carolina

SEASON—TEAM	G	GS	MIN	FGM	FGA	PCT	3FGM	3FGA	PCT	FTM	FTA	PCT	O-RB	D-RB	TOT	AST	PF	DQ	STL	TO	BLK	PTS	RPG	APG	PPG
76-77—Philadelphia	32	—	359	60	145	.414	—	—	—	34	45	.756	10	24	34	56	64	1	13	—	2	154	1.1	1.8	4.8
77-78—Phil.-Houston	15	—	119	20	50	.400	—	—	—	13	18	.722	1	9	10	28	12	0	9	12	1	53	0.7	1.9	3.5
78-79—Houston	74	—	1486	215	425	.506	—	—	—	159	184	.864	28	100	128	324	168	2	56	130	5	589	1.7	4.4	8.0
79-80—Houston	51	—	1036	148	319	.464	3	20	.150	111	134	.828	26	74	100	210	120	2	40	110	4	410	2.0	4.1	8.0
80-81—Houston	74	—	1609	310	632	.491	1	16	.063	156	186	.839	28	90	118	268	165	1	64	137	2	777	1.6	3.6	10.5
81-82—Houston	70	15	1315	206	450	.458	33	86	.384	75	106	.708	24	80	104	227	161	0	45	80	3	520	1.5	3.2	7.4
82-83—San Antonio	79	9	1619	213	510	.418	67	194	.345	120	154	.779	18	116	134	437	210	1	74	160	4	613	1.7	5.5	7.8
83-84—Milwaukee	17	12	404	70	127	.551	19	45	.422	32	40	.800	6	22	28	78	51	0	12	36	1	191	1.6	4.6	11.2
84-85—Milwaukee	19	19	433	64	135	.474	16	47	.340	25	29	.862	6	25	31	85	55	1	15	40	3	169	1.6	4.5	8.9
88-89—Milwaukee	2	0	5	1	2	.500	1	2	.500	0	0	—	0	0	0	0	0	0	0	0	0	3	0.0	0.0	1.5
89-90—Milwaukee	5	0	43	4	14	.286	2	9	.222	7	8	.875	0	2	2	10	7	0	1	8	0	17	0.4	2.0	3.4
REG. SEASON TOTALS	438	55	8428	1311	2809	.467	142	419	.339	732	904	.810	147	542	689	1723	1013	8	329	713	25	3496	1.6	3.9	8.0
PLAYOFF TOTALS	67	15	1228	174	407	.428	32	101	.317	89	104	.856	25	78	103	194	173	3	51	86	2	469	1.5	2.9	7.0

DUNN, PATRICK L. (**Pat**) b. March 17, 1931 d. November 1975 Ht. 6-2 Wt. 170 College—Utah State

SEASON—TEAM	G	GS	MIN	FGM	FGA	PCT	3FGM	3FGA	PCT	FTM	FTA	PCT	O-RB	D-RB	TOT	AST	PF	DQ	STL	TO	BLK	PTS	RPG	APG	PPG
57-58—Philadelphia	28	—	206	28	90	.311	—	—	—	14	17	.824	—	—	31	28	20	0	—	—	—	70	1.1	1.0	2.5
REG. SEASON TOTALS	28	—	206	28	90	.311	—	—	—	14	17	.824	—	—	31	28	20	0	—	—	—	70	1.1	1.0	2.5
PLAYOFF TOTALS	3	—	8	0	4	.000	—	—	—	0	0	—	—	—	1	1	1	0	—	—	—	0	0.3	0.3	0.0

DUNN, THEODORE ROOSEVELT (**T.R.**) b. February 1, 1955   Ht. 6-4 Wt. 192 College—Alabama

SEASON—TEAM	G	GS	MIN	FGM	FGA	PCT	3FGM	3FGA	PCT	FTM	FTA	PCT	O-RB	D-RB	TOT	AST	PF	DQ	STL	TO	BLK	PTS	RPG	APG	PPG
77-78—Portland	63	—	768	100	240	.417	—	—	—	37	56	.661	63	84	147	45	74	0	46	35	8	237	2.3	0.7	3.8
78-79—Portland	80	—	1828	246	549	.448	—	—	—	122	158	.772	145	199	344	103	166	1	86	93	23	614	4.3	1.3	7.7
79-80—Portland	82	—	1841	240	551	.436	0	3	.000	84	111	.757	132	192	324	147	145	1	102	91	31	564	4.0	1.8	6.9
80-81—Denver	82	—	1427	146	354	.412	0	2	.000	79	121	.653	133	168	301	81	141	0	66	56	29	371	3.7	1.0	4.5
81-82—Denver	82	80	2519	258	504	.512	0	1	.000	153	215	.712	211	348	559	188	210	1	135	123	36	669	6.8	2.3	8.2
82-83—Denver	82	80	2640	254	527	.482	0	1	.000	119	163	.730	231	384	615	189	218	2	147	113	25	627	7.5	2.3	7.6
83-84—Denver	80	74	2705	174	370	.470	0	1	.000	106	145	.731	195	379	574	228	233	5	173	97	32	454	7.2	2.9	5.7
84-85—Denver	81	81	2290	175	358	.489	0	2	.000	84	116	.724	169	216	385	153	213	3	140	65	14	434	4.8	1.9	5.4
85-86—Denver	82	82	2401	172	379	.454	0	1	.000	68	88	.773	143	234	377	171	228	1	155	51	16	412	4.6	2.1	5.0
86-87—Denver	81	53	1932	118	276	.428	0	2	.000	36	55	.655	91	174	265	147	160	0	100	33	21	272	3.3	1.8	3.4
87-88—Denver	82	1	1534	70	156	.449	0	1	.000	40	52	.769	110	130	240	87	152	0	101	26	11	180	2.9	1.1	2.2
88-89—Phoenix	34	1	321	12	35	.343	0	0	—	9	12	.750	30	30	60	25	35	0	12	6	1	33	1.8	0.7	1.0
89-90—Denver	65	2	657	44	97	.454	0	2	.000	26	39	.667	56	82	138	43	67	1	41	19	4	114	2.1	0.7	1.8
90-91—Denver	17	3	217	21	47	.447	1	4	.250	9	10	.900	20	22	42	24	30	0	12	7	1	52	2.5	1.4	3.1
REG. SEASON TOTALS	993	457	23080	2030	4443	.457	1	20	.050	972	1341	.725	1729	2642	4371	1631	2072	15	1316	815	252	5033	4.4	1.6	5.1
PLAYOFF TOTALS	76	44	1634	109	244	.447	0	0	—	47	68	.691	130	187	317	104	180	1	95	51	13	265	4.2	1.4	3.5

DUREN, JOHN THOMAS b. October 30, 1958   Ht. 6-3 Wt. 195 College—Georgetown

SEASON—TEAM	G	GS	MIN	FGM	FGA	PCT	3FGM	3FGA	PCT	FTM	FTA	PCT	O-RB	D-RB	TOT	AST	PF	DQ	STL	TO	BLK	PTS	RPG	APG	PPG
80-81—Utah	40	—	458	33	101	.327	0	1	.000	5	9	.556	8	27	35	54	54	0	18	37	2	71	0.9	1.4	1.8
81-82—Utah	79	9	1056	121	268	.451	3	11	.273	27	37	.730	14	70	84	157	143	0	20	72	4	272	1.1	2.0	3.4
82-83—Indiana	82	24	1433	163	360	.453	0	13	.000	43	54	.796	38	69	107	200	203	2	66	96	5	369	1.3	2.4	4.5
REG. SEASON TOTALS	201	33	2947	317	729	.435	3	25	.120	75	100	.750	60	166	226	411	400	2	104	205	11	712	1.1	2.0	3.5

DURHAM, JARRETT M. b. August 22, 1949   Ht. 6-5 Wt. 190 College—Duquesne

SEASON—TEAM	G	GS	MIN	FGM	FGA	PCT	3FGM	3FGA	PCT	FTM	FTA	PCT	O-RB	D-RB	TOT	AST	PF	DQ	STL	TO	BLK	PTS	RPG	APG	PPG
71-72—New York (A)	1	—	1	0	0	—	0	0	—	0	0	—	—	—	0	0	0	—	—	1	—	0	0.0	0.0	0.0
REG. ABA TOTALS	1	—	1	0	0	—	0	0	—	0	0	—	—	—	0	0	0	—	—	1	—	0	0.0	0.0	0.0

DURHAM, PATRICK WAYNE (**Pat, Bull**) b. March 10, 1967   Ht. 6-7 Wt. 210 College—Colorado State

SEASON—TEAM	G	GS	MIN	FGM	FGA	PCT	3FGM	3FGA	PCT	FTM	FTA	PCT	O-RB	D-RB	TOT	AST	PF	DQ	STL	TO	BLK	PTS	RPG	APG	PPG
92-93—Golden State	5	1	78	6	25	.240	0	0	—	9	12	.750	5	9	14	4	6	0	1	7	1	21	2.8	0.8	4.2
REG. SEASON TOTALS	5	1	78	6	25	.240	0	0	—	9	12	.750	5	9	14	4	6	0	1	7	1	21	2.8	0.8	4.2

DURRANT, DEVIN GEORGE b. October 20, 1960   Ht. 6-7 Wt. 200 College—Brigham Young

SEASON—TEAM	G	GS	MIN	FGM	FGA	PCT	3FGM	3FGA	PCT	FTM	FTA	PCT	O-RB	D-RB	TOT	AST	PF	DQ	STL	TO	BLK	PTS	RPG	APG	PPG
84-85—Indiana	59	8	756	114	274	.416	0	3	.000	72	102	.706	49	75	124	80	106	0	19	77	10	300	2.1	1.4	5.1
85-86—Phoenix	4	0	51	8	21	.381	0	0	—	1	4	.250	2	6	8	5	10	0	3	4	0	17	2.0	1.3	4.3
REG. SEASON TOTALS	63	8	807	122	295	.414	0	3	.000	73	106	.689	51	81	132	85	116	0	22	81	10	317	2.1	1.3	5.0

DURRETT, KENNETH L. (**Ken**) b. December 8, 1948   Ht. 6-7½ Wt. 190 College—La Salle

SEASON—TEAM	G	GS	MIN	FGM	FGA	PCT	3FGM	3FGA	PCT	FTM	FTA	PCT	O-RB	D-RB	TOT	AST	PF	DQ	STL	TO	BLK	PTS	RPG	APG	PPG
71-72—Cincinnati	19	—	233	31	79	.392	—	—	—	21	28	.750	—	—	39	14	41	0	—	—	—	83	2.1	0.7	4.4
72-73—Kansas City-Omaha	8	—	65	8	21	.381	—	—	—	6	8	.750	—	—	14	3	16	0	—	—	—	22	1.8	0.4	2.8
73-74—Kansas City-Omaha	45	—	462	86	176	.489	—	—	—	42	69	.609	28	50	78	19	68	0	13	—	5	214	1.7	0.4	4.8
74-75—K.C.-Omaha-Phil.	48	—	445	67	166	.404	—	—	—	31	52	.596	35	67	102	18	72	0	9	—	8	165	2.1	0.4	3.4
REG. SEASON TOTALS	120	—	1205	192	442	.434	—	—	—	100	157	.637	63	117	233	54	197	0	22	—	13	484	1.9	0.5	4.0

DUVAL, DENNIS b. March 31, 1952   Ht. 6-3 Wt. 175 College—Syracuse

SEASON—TEAM	G	GS	MIN	FGM	FGA	PCT	3FGM	3FGA	PCT	FTM	FTA	PCT	O-RB	D-RB	TOT	AST	PF	DQ	STL	TO	BLK	PTS	RPG	APG	PPG
74-75—Washington	37	—	137	24	65	.369	—	—	—	12	18	.667	8	15	23	14	34	0	16	—	2	60	0.6	0.4	1.6
75-76—Atlanta	13	—	130	15	43	.349	—	—	—	6	9	.667	1	7	8	20	15	0	6	—	2	36	0.6	1.5	2.8
REG. SEASON TOTALS	50	—	267	39	108	.361	—	—	—	18	27	.667	9	22	31	34	49	0	22	—	4	96	0.6	0.7	1.9
PLAYOFF TOTALS	5	—	14	3	9	.333	—	—	—	1	2	.500	0	3	3	3	1	0	0	—	0	7	0.6	0.6	1.4

DWAN, JOHN (**Jack**) b. May 3, 1921 d. August 4, 1993 Ht. 6-4 Wt. 200 College—Loyola (Ill.)

SEASON—TEAM	G	GS	MIN	FGM	FGA	PCT	3FGM	3FGA	PCT	FTM	FTA	PCT	O-RB	D-RB	TOT	AST	PF	DQ	STL	TO	BLK	PTS	RPG	APG	PPG
47-48—Minneapolis (N)	55	—	—	128	—	—	—	—	—	50	73	.685	—	—	—	110	—	—	—	—	—	306	—	—	5.6
48-49—Minneapolis	60	—	—	121	380	.318	—	—	—	34	69	.493	—	—	—	129	157	—	—	—	—	276	—	2.2	4.6
REG. NBA TOTALS	60	—	—	121	380	.318	—	—	—	34	69	.493	—	—	—	129	157	—	—	—	—	276	—	2.2	4.6
REG. NBL TOTALS	55	—	—	128	—	—	—	—	—	50	73	.685	—	—	—	110	—	—	—	—	—	306	—	—	5.6
NBA PLAYOFF TOTALS	10	—	—	7	29	.241	—	—	—	4	9	.444	—	—	—	9	22	1	—	—	—	18	—	0.9	1.8
NBL PLAYOFF TOTALS	10	—	—	27	—	—	—	—	—	5	9	.556	—	—	—	28	—	—	—	—	—	59	—	—	5.9

DYKEMA, CRAIG b. June 11, 1959 Ht. 6-8 Wt. 190 College—Long Beach CC/Cal St.-Long Beach

SEASON—TEAM	G	GS	MIN	FGM	FGA	PCT	3FGM	3FGA	PCT	FTM	FTA	PCT	O-RB	D-RB	TOT	AST	PF	DQ	STL	TO	BLK	PTS	RPG	APG	PPG
81-82—Phoenix	32	0	103	17	37	.459	2	4	.500	7	9	.778	3	9	12	15	19	0	2	7	0	43	0.4	0.5	1.3
REG. SEASON TOTALS	32	0	103	17	37	.459	2	4	.500	7	9	.778	3	9	12	15	19	0	2	7	0	43	0.4	0.5	1.3
PLAYOFF TOTALS	6	0	12	1	6	.167	0	0	—	0	0	—	0	4	4	1	2	0	0	1	0	2	0.7	0.2	0.3

DYKER, EUGENE (**Gene**) b. February 17, 1930 d. January 1966 Ht. 6-6 Wt. 225 College—DePaul

SEASON—TEAM	G	GS	MIN	FGM	FGA	PCT	3FGM	3FGA	PCT	FTM	FTA	PCT	O-RB	D-RB	TOT	AST	PF	DQ	STL	TO	BLK	PTS	RPG	APG	PPG
53-54—Milwaukee	11	—	91	6	26	.231	—	—	—	4	8	.500	—	—	16	5	21	0	—	—	—	16	1.5	0.5	1.5
REG. SEASON TOTALS	11	—	91	6	26	.231	—	—	—	4	8	.500	—	—	16	5	21	0	—	—	—	16	1.5	0.5	1.5

EACKLES, LEDELL (**A-Train**) b. November 24, 1966 Ht. 6-5 Wt. 250 College—New Orleans

SEASON—TEAM	G	GS	MIN	FGM	FGA	PCT	3FGM	3FGA	PCT	FTM	FTA	PCT	O-RB	D-RB	TOT	AST	PF	DQ	STL	TO	BLK	PTS	RPG	APG	PPG
88-89—Washington	80	6	1459	318	732	.434	9	40	.225	272	346	.786	100	80	180	123	156	1	41	128	5	917	2.3	1.5	11.5
89-90—Washington	78	8	1696	413	940	.439	19	59	.322	210	280	.750	74	101	175	182	157	0	50	143	4	1055	2.2	2.3	13.5
90-91—Washington	67	17	1616	345	762	.453	14	59	.237	164	222	.739	47	81	128	136	121	0	47	115	10	868	1.9	2.0	13.0
91-92—Washington	65	25	1463	355	759	.468	7	35	.200	139	187	.743	39	139	178	125	145	1	47	75	7	856	2.7	1.9	13.2
REG. SEASON TOTALS	290	56	6234	1431	3193	.448	49	193	.254	785	1035	.758	260	401	661	566	579	2	185	461	26	3696	2.3	2.0	12.7

EAKINS, JAMES SCOTT (**Jim, Jimbo**) b. May 24, 1946 Ht. 6-11 Wt. 215 College—Brigham Young

SEASON—TEAM	G	GS	MIN	FGM	FGA	PCT	3FGM	3FGA	PCT	FTM	FTA	PCT	O-RB	D-RB	TOT	AST	PF	DQ	STL	TO	BLK	PTS	RPG	APG	PPG
68-69—Oakland (A)	78	—	1671	351	646	.543	0	1	.000	309	430	.719	—	—	563	53	234	4	—	141	—	1011	7.2	0.7	13.0
69-70—Washington (A)	82	—	1214	181	364	.497	0	0	—	166	224	.741	—	—	412	71	184	0	—	—	—	528	5.0	0.9	6.4
70-71—Virginia (A)	84	—	2235	332	645	.515	0	0	—	242	319	.759	—	—	778	160	282	—	—	—	—	906	9.3	1.9	10.8
71-72—Virginia (A)	84	—	2718	371	764	.486	0	0	—	288	377	.764	290	517	807	181	298	—	—	189	—	1030	9.6	2.2	12.3
72-73—Virginia (A)	83	—	2559	430	823	.522	0	1	.000	384	479	.802	234	499	733	262	287	5	—	233	131	1244	8.8	3.2	15.0
73-74—Virginia (A)	84	—	2649	445	856	.520	0	1	.000	339	432	.785	296	510	806	236	265	—	65	228	98	1229	9.6	2.8	14.6
74-75—Utah (A)	84	—	2566	380	756	.503	0	0	—	291	348	.836	210	394	604	146	259	—	57	173	85	1051	7.2	1.7	12.5
75-76—Utah-Vir.-N.Y. (A)	73	—	1667	215	477	.451	0	0	—	198	223	.888	167	272	439	88	220	—	34	114	70	628	6.0	1.2	8.6
76-77—Kansas City	82	—	1338	151	336	.449	—	—	—	188	222	.847	112	249	361	119	195	1	29	—	49	490	4.4	1.5	6.0
77-78—S.A.-Milw.	33	—	406	44	86	.512	—	—	—	50	60	.833	29	46	75	29	71	0	7	33	17	138	2.3	0.9	4.2
REG. NBA TOTALS	115	—	1744	195	422	.462	—	—	—	238	282	.844	141	295	436	148	266	1	36	33	66	628	3.8	1.3	5.5
REG. ABA TOTALS	652	—	17279	2705	5331	.507	0	3	.000	2217	2832	.783	1197	2192	5142	1197	2029	9	156	1078	384	7627	7.9	1.8	11.7
NBA PLAYOFF TOTALS	3	—	18	1	5	.200	—	—	—	0	0	—	1	0	1	1	2	0	1	1	0	2	0.3	0.3	0.7
ABA PLAYOFF TOTALS	75	—	1897	317	587	.540	0	1	.000	207	272	.761	153	289	558	117	257	0	22	123	22	841	7.4	1.6	11.2
ABA ALL-STAR TOTALS	1	—	21	1	4	.250	0	0	—	0	0	—	0	4	4	4	2	0	2	0	3	2	4.0	4.0	2.0

EARL, ACIE BOYD b. June 23, 1970 Ht. 6-10 Wt. 240 College—Iowa

SEASON—TEAM	G	GS	MIN	FGM	FGA	PCT	3FGM	3FGA	PCT	FTM	FTA	PCT	O-RB	D-RB	TOT	AST	PF	DQ	STL	TO	BLK	PTS	RPG	APG	PPG
93-94—Boston	74	8	1149	151	372	.406	0	1	.000	108	160	.675	85	162	247	12	178	5	24	72	53	410	3.3	0.2	5.5
REG. SEASON TOTALS	74	8	1149	151	372	.406	0	1	.000	108	160	.675	85	162	247	12	178	5	24	72	53	410	3.3	0.2	5.5

EARLE, EDWIN (**Ed**) b. April 28, 1927 Ht. 6-3 Wt. 190 College—Loyola (Ill.)

SEASON—TEAM	G	GS	MIN	FGM	FGA	PCT	3FGM	3FGA	PCT	FTM	FTA	PCT	O-RB	D-RB	TOT	AST	PF	DQ	STL	TO	BLK	PTS	RPG	APG	PPG
53-54—Syracuse	2	—	12	1	2	.500	—	—	—	2	4	.500	—	—	2	0	0	0	—	—	—	4	1.0	0.0	2.0
REG. SEASON TOTALS	2	—	12	1	2	.500	—	—	—	2	4	.500	—	—	2	0	0	0	—	—	—	4	1.0	0.0	2.0
PLAYOFF TOTALS	1	—	0	0	0	—	—	—	—	0	0	—	—	—	0	—	0	0	—	—	—	0	0.0	0.0	0.0

EATON, MARK E. b. January 24, 1957 Ht. 7-4 Wt. 290 College—Cypress College/UCLA

SEASON—TEAM	G	GS	MIN	FGM	FGA	PCT	3FGM	3FGA	PCT	FTM	FTA	PCT	O-RB	D-RB	TOT	AST	PF	DQ	STL	TO	BLK	PTS	RPG	APG	PPG
82-83—Utah	81	32	1528	146	353	.414	0	1	.000	59	90	.656	86	376	462	112	257	6	24	140	275	351	5.7	1.4	4.3
83-84—Utah	82	78	2139	194	416	.466	0	1	.000	73	123	.593	148	447	595	113	303	4	25	98	351	461	7.3	1.4	5.6
84-85—Utah	82	82	2813	302	673	.449	0	0	—	190	267	.712	207	720	927	124	312	5	36	206	456	794	11.3	1.5	9.7
85-86—Utah	80	80	2551	277	589	.470	0	0	—	122	202	.604	172	503	675	101	282	5	33	157	369	676	8.4	1.3	8.5
86-87—Utah	79	79	2505	234	585	.400	0	0	—	140	213	.657	211	486	697	105	273	5	43	142	321	608	8.8	1.3	7.7
87-88—Utah	82	82	2731	226	541	.418	0	0	—	119	191	.623	230	487	717	55	320	8	41	131	304	571	8.7	0.7	7.0
88-89—Utah	82	82	2914	188	407	.462	0	0	—	132	200	.660	227	616	843	83	290	6	40	142	315	508	10.3	1.0	6.2
89-90—Utah	82	82	2281	158	300	.527	0	0	—	79	118	.669	171	430	601	39	238	3	33	75	201	395	7.3	0.5	4.8
90-91—Utah	80	80	2580	169	292	.579	0	0	—	71	112	.634	182	485	667	51	298	6	39	99	188	409	8.3	0.6	5.1
91-92—Utah	81	81	2023	107	240	.446	0	0	—	52	87	.598	150	341	491	40	239	2	36	60	205	266	6.1	0.5	3.3
92-93—Utah	64	57	1104	71	130	.546	0	0	—	35	50	.700	73	191	264	17	143	0	18	43	79	177	4.1	0.3	2.8
REG. SEASON TOTALS	875	815	25169	2072	4526	.458	0	2	.000	1072	1653	.649	1857	5082	6939	840	2955	50	368	1293	3064	5216	7.9	1.0	6.0
PLAYOFF TOTALS	74	74	2295	180	368	.489	0	0	—	94	147	.639	169	388	557	52	250	5	35	81	210	454	7.5	0.7	6.1
ALL-STAR TOTALS	1	0	9	0	0	—	0	0	—	0	0	—	0	5	5	0	1	0	0	0	2	0	5.0	0.0	0.0

EAVES, JERRY LEE b. February 8, 1959   Ht. 6-4 Wt. 185 College—Louisville

SEASON—TEAM	G	GS	MIN	FGM	FGA	PCT	3FGM	3FGA	PCT	FTM	FTA	PCT	O-RB	D-RB	TOT	AST	PF	DQ	STL	TO	BLK	PTS	RPG	APG	PPG
82-83—Utah	82	7	1588	280	575	.487	1	8	.125	200	247	.810	34	88	122	210	116	0	51	152	3	761	1.5	2.6	9.3
83-84—Utah	80	1	1034	132	293	.451	0	6	.000	92	132	.697	29	56	85	200	90	0	33	93	5	356	1.1	2.5	4.5
84-85—Atlanta	3	0	37	3	6	.500	0	0	—	5	6	.833	0	0	0	4	6	0	0	4	0	11	0.0	1.3	3.7
86-87—Sacramento	3	0	26	1	8	.125	0	0	—	2	2	1.000	1	0	1	0	6	0	1	2	0	4	0.3	0.0	1.3
REG. SEASON TOTALS	168	8	2685	416	882	.472	1	14	.071	299	387	.773	64	144	208	414	218	0	85	251	8	1132	1.2	2.5	6.7
PLAYOFF TOTALS	11	0	132	22	46	.478	1	3	.333	10	13	.769	3	7	10	13	10	0	5	7	2	55	0.9	1.2	5.0

EBBEN, WILLIAM EDWARD (**Bill**) b. October 7, 1935   Ht. 6-4 Wt. 200 College—Detroit

SEASON—TEAM	G	GS	MIN	FGM	FGA	PCT	3FGM	3FGA	PCT	FTM	FTA	PCT	O-RB	D-RB	TOT	AST	PF	DQ	STL	TO	BLK	PTS	RPG	APG	PPG
57-58—Detroit	8	—	50	6	28	.214	—	—	—	3	4	.750	—	—	8	4	5	0	—	—	—	15	1.0	0.5	1.9
REG. SEASON TOTALS	8	—	50	6	28	.214	—	—	—	3	4	.750	—	—	8	4	5	0	—	—	—	15	1.0	0.5	1.9

EBERHARD, ALLEN DEAN (**Al**) b. May 10, 1952   Ht. 6-6 Wt. 225 College—Missouri

SEASON—TEAM	G	GS	MIN	FGM	FGA	PCT	3FGM	3FGA	PCT	FTM	FTA	PCT	O-RB	D-RB	TOT	AST	PF	DQ	STL	TO	BLK	PTS	RPG	APG	PPG
74-75—Detroit	34	—	277	31	85	.365	—	—	—	17	21	.810	18	29	47	16	33	0	13	—	1	79	1.4	0.5	2.3
75-76—Detroit	81	—	2066	283	683	.414	—	—	—	191	229	.834	139	251	390	83	250	5	87	—	15	757	4.8	1.0	9.3
76-77—Detroit	68	—	1219	181	380	.476	—	—	—	109	138	.790	76	145	221	50	197	4	45	—	15	471	3.3	0.7	6.9
77-78—Detroit	37	—	576	71	160	.444	—	—	—	41	61	.672	37	65	102	26	64	0	13	23	4	183	2.8	0.7	4.9
REG. SEASON TOTALS	220	—	4138	566	1308	.433	—	—	—	358	449	.797	270	490	760	175	544	9	158	23	35	1490	3.5	0.8	6.8
PLAYOFF TOTALS	11	—	224	18	48	.375	—	—	—	19	27	.704	13	22	35	9	20	0	9	—	4	55	3.2	0.8	5.0

EBRON, ROY LESTER b. August 31, 1951   Ht. 6-9 Wt. 225 College—Southwestern Louisiana

SEASON—TEAM	G	GS	MIN	FGM	FGA	PCT	3FGM	3FGA	PCT	FTM	FTA	PCT	O-RB	D-RB	TOT	AST	PF	DQ	STL	TO	BLK	PTS	RPG	APG	PPG
73-74—Utah (A)	40	—	529	103	211	.488	0	1	.000	43	84	.512	79	97	176	19	68	—	16	35	32	249	4.4	0.5	6.2
REG. ABA TOTALS	40	—	529	103	211	.488	0	1	.000	43	84	.512	79	97	176	19	68	0	16	35	32	249	4.4	0.5	6.2
ABA PLAYOFF TOTALS	7	—	41	6	19	.316	0	1	.000	5	10	.500	10	5	15	2	6	0	0	2	4	17	2.1	0.3	2.4

EDDIE, PATRICK b. December 27, 1967   Ht. 6-11 Wt. 240 College—Arkansas State/Mississippi

SEASON—TEAM	G	GS	MIN	FGM	FGA	PCT	3FGM	3FGA	PCT	FTM	FTA	PCT	O-RB	D-RB	TOT	AST	PF	DQ	STL	TO	BLK	PTS	RPG	APG	PPG
91-92—New York	4	0	13	2	9	.222	0	0	—	0	0	—	0	1	1	0	3	0	0	0	0	4	0.3	0.0	1.0
REG. SEASON TOTALS	4	0	13	2	9	.222	0	0	—	0	0	—	0	1	1	0	3	0	0	0	0	4	0.3	0.0	1.0

EDDLEMAN, THOMAS DWIGHT (**Dike**) b. December 27, 1922   Ht. 6-2½ Wt. 190 College—Illinois

SEASON—TEAM	G	GS	MIN	FGM	FGA	PCT	3FGM	3FGA	PCT	FTM	FTA	PCT	O-RB	D-RB	TOT	AST	PF	DQ	STL	TO	BLK	PTS	RPG	APG	PPG
49-50—Tri-Cities	64	—	—	332	906	.366	—	—	—	162	260	.623	—	—	—	142	254	—	—	—	—	826	—	2.2	12.9
50-51—Tri-Cities	68	—	—	398	1120	.355	—	—	—	244	349	.699	—	—	410	170	231	5	—	—	—	1040	6.0	2.5	15.3
51-52—Milw.-Ft. Wayne	65	—	1893	269	809	.333	—	—	—	202	329	.614	—	—	267	134	249	9	—	—	—	740	4.1	2.1	11.4
52-53—Fort Wayne	69	—	1571	241	687	.351	—	—	—	133	237	.561	—	—	236	104	220	5	—	—	—	615	3.4	1.5	8.9
REG. SEASON TOTALS	266	—	3464	1240	3522	.352	—	—	—	741	1175	.631	—	—	913	550	954	19	—	—	—	3221	4.5	2.1	12.1
PLAYOFF TOTALS	12	—	100	32	84	.381	—	—	—	23	47	.489	—	—	12	13	45	4	—	—	—	87	1.3	1.1	7.3
ALL-STAR TOTALS	1	—	0	2	9	.222	—	—	—	3	5	.600	—	—	0	3	3	0	—	—	—	7	0.0	3.0	7.0

EDELIN, KENTON SCOTT (**Kent**) b. May 24, 1962   Ht. 6-8 Wt. 205 College—Virginia

SEASON—TEAM	G	GS	MIN	FGM	FGA	PCT	3FGM	3FGA	PCT	FTM	FTA	PCT	O-RB	D-RB	TOT	AST	PF	DQ	STL	TO	BLK	PTS	RPG	APG	PPG
84-85—Indiana	10	1	143	4	13	.308	0	0	—	3	8	.375	8	18	26	10	39	1	5	3	4	11	2.6	1.0	1.1
REG. SEASON TOTALS	10	1	143	4	13	.308	0	0	—	3	8	.375	8	18	26	10	39	1	5	3	4	11	2.6	1.0	1.1

EDGE, CHARLES (**Charlie, Razor**) b. February 23, 1950   Ht. 6-6 Wt. 210 College—LeMoyne-Owen

SEASON—TEAM	G	GS	MIN	FGM	FGA	PCT	3FGM	3FGA	PCT	FTM	FTA	PCT	O-RB	D-RB	TOT	AST	PF	DQ	STL	TO	BLK	PTS	RPG	APG	PPG
73-74—Memphis (A)	78	—	1948	312	624	.500	0	1	.000	124	182	.681	250	391	641	70	137	—	64	130	70	748	8.2	0.9	9.6
74-75—Indiana (A)	77	—	1142	195	386	.505	0	3	.000	63	114	.553	164	176	340	39	103	—	53	82	35	453	4.4	0.5	5.9
REG. ABA TOTALS	155	—	3090	507	1010	.502	0	4	.000	187	296	.632	414	567	981	109	240	0	117	212	105	1201	6.3	0.7	7.7
ABA PLAYOFF TOTALS	7	—	42	2	8	.250	0	0	—	0	0	—	4	5	9	2	6	0	0	5	0	4	1.3	0.3	0.6

EDMONDS, BOBBY JOE b. March 8, 1941   d. November 12, 1991   Ht. 6-6 Wt. 220 College—Tennessee State

SEASON—TEAM	G	GS	MIN	FGM	FGA	PCT	3FGM	3FGA	PCT	FTM	FTA	PCT	O-RB	D-RB	TOT	AST	PF	DQ	STL	TO	BLK	PTS	RPG	APG	PPG
67-68—Indiana (A)	72	—	1338	213	488	.436	1	6	.167	150	229	.655	—	—	374	29	183	4	—	123	—	577	5.2	0.4	8.0
69-70—Indiana (A)	3	—	12	1	5	.200	0	0	—	1	3	.333	—	—	4	0	1	0	—	—	—	3	1.3	0.0	1.0
REG. ABA TOTALS	75	—	1350	214	493	.434	1	6	.167	151	232	.651	—	—	378	29	184	4	—	123	—	580	5.0	0.4	7.7
ABA PLAYOFF TOTALS	3	—	47	6	14	.429	1	2	.500	7	9	.778	—	—	18	2	12	1	—	5	—	20	6.0	0.7	6.7

EDMONSON, KEITH ANDRE b. September 28, 1960 Ht. 6-5 Wt. 205 College—Purdue

SEASON—TEAM	G	GS	MIN	FGM	FGA	PCT	3FGM	3FGA	PCT	FTM	FTA	PCT	O-RB	D-RB	TOT	AST	PF	DQ	STL	TO	BLK	PTS	RPG	APG	PPG
82-83—Atlanta	32	2	309	48	139	.345	0	2	.000	16	27	.593	20	19	39	22	41	0	11	20	6	112	1.2	0.7	3.5
83-84—S.A.-Denver	55	0	622	158	321	.492	0	0	—	94	126	.746	46	42	88	34	83	1	26	61	7	410	1.6	0.6	7.5
REG. SEASON TOTALS	87	2	931	206	460	.448	0	2	.000	110	153	.719	66	61	127	56	124	1	37	81	13	522	1.5	0.6	6.0
PLAYOFF TOTALS	1	0	2	1	1	1.000	0	0	—	0	0	—	1	0	1	1	0	0	0	0	0	2	1.0	1.0	2.0

EDWARDS, DOUGLAS (**Doug**) b. January 21, 1971 Ht. 6-7 Wt. 235 College—Florida State

SEASON—TEAM	G	GS	MIN	FGM	FGA	PCT	3FGM	3FGA	PCT	FTM	FTA	PCT	O-RB	D-RB	TOT	AST	PF	DQ	STL	TO	BLK	PTS	RPG	APG	PPG
93-94—Atlanta	16	0	107	17	49	.347	0	1	.000	9	16	.563	7	11	18	8	9	0	2	6	5	43	1.1	0.5	2.7
REG. SEASON TOTALS	16	0	107	17	49	.347	0	1	.000	9	16	.563	7	11	18	8	9	0	2	6	5	43	1.1	0.5	2.7
PLAYOFF TOTALS	1	0	3	0	0	—	0	0	—	0	0	—	0	0	0	—	0	0	0	0	1	0	0.0	0.0	0.0

EDWARDS, FRANKLIN DELANO b. February 2, 1959 Ht. 6-1 Wt. 190 College—Cleveland State

SEASON—TEAM	G	GS	MIN	FGM	FGA	PCT	3FGM	3FGA	PCT	FTM	FTA	PCT	O-RB	D-RB	TOT	AST	PF	DQ	STL	TO	BLK	PTS	RPG	APG	PPG
81-82—Philadelphia	42	3	291	65	150	.433	0	9	.000	20	27	.741	10	17	27	45	37	0	16	24	5	150	0.6	1.1	3.6
82-83—Philadelphia	81	3	1266	228	483	.472	0	8	.000	86	113	.761	23	62	85	221	119	0	81	110	6	542	1.0	2.7	6.7
83-84—Philadelphia	60	0	654	84	221	.380	0	1	.000	34	48	.708	12	47	59	90	78	1	31	46	5	202	1.0	1.5	3.4
84-85—L.A. Clippers	16	0	198	36	66	.545	0	0	—	19	24	.792	3	11	14	38	10	0	17	17	0	91	0.9	2.4	5.7
85-86—L.A. Clippers	73	19	1491	262	577	.454	1	9	.111	132	151	.874	24	62	86	259	87	0	89	137	4	657	1.2	3.5	9.0
86-87—Sacramento	8	0	122	9	32	.281	0	4	.000	10	14	.714	2	8	10	29	7	0	5	17	0	28	1.3	3.6	3.5
87-88—Sacramento	16	11	414	54	115	.470	0	2	.000	24	32	.750	4	15	19	92	10	0	10	47	1	132	1.2	5.8	8.3
REG. SEASON TOTALS	296	36	4436	738	1644	.449	1	33	.030	325	409	.795	78	222	300	774	348	1	249	398	21	1802	1.0	2.6	6.1
PLAYOFF TOTALS	21	0	133	25	52	.481	1	1	1.000	22	26	.846	4	10	14	22	7	0	8	8	0	73	0.7	1.0	3.5

EDWARDS, JAMES FRANKLIN b. November 22, 1955 Ht. 7½ Wt. 255 College—Washington

SEASON—TEAM	G	GS	MIN	FGM	FGA	PCT	3FGM	3FGA	PCT	FTM	FTA	PCT	O-RB	D-RB	TOT	AST	PF	DQ	STL	TO	BLK	PTS	RPG	APG	PPG
77-78—L.A.-Indiana	83	—	2405	495	1093	.453	—	—	—	272	421	.646	197	418	615	85	322	12	53	169	78	1262	7.4	1.0	15.2
78-79—Indiana	82	—	2546	534	1065	.501	—	—	—	298	441	.676	179	514	693	92	363	16	60	162	109	1366	8.5	1.1	16.7
79-80—Indiana	82	—	2314	528	1032	.512	0	1	.000	231	339	.681	179	399	578	127	324	12	55	131	104	1287	7.0	1.5	15.7
80-81—Indiana	81	—	2375	511	1004	.509	0	3	.000	244	347	.703	191	380	571	212	304	7	32	164	128	1266	7.0	2.6	15.6
81-82—Cleveland	77	75	2539	528	1033	.511	0	4	.000	232	339	.684	189	392	581	123	347	17	24	162	117	1288	7.5	1.6	16.7
82-83—Clev.-Phoenix	31	9	667	128	263	.487	0	0	—	69	108	.639	56	99	155	40	110	5	12	49	19	325	5.0	1.3	10.5
83-84—Phoenix	72	67	1897	438	817	.536	0	1	.000	183	254	.720	108	240	348	184	254	3	23	140	30	1059	4.8	2.6	14.7
84-85—Phoenix	70	58	1787	384	766	.501	0	3	.000	276	370	.746	95	292	387	153	237	5	26	162	52	1044	5.5	2.2	14.9
85-86—Phoenix	52	51	1314	318	587	.542	0	0	—	212	302	.702	79	222	301	74	200	5	23	128	29	848	5.8	1.4	16.3
86-87—Phoenix	14	9	304	57	110	.518	0	0	—	54	70	.771	20	40	60	19	42	1	6	15	7	168	4.3	1.4	12.0
87-88—Phoenix-Detroit	69	44	1705	302	643	.470	0	1	.000	210	321	.654	119	293	412	78	216	2	16	130	37	814	6.0	1.1	11.8
88-89—Detroit	76	1	1254	211	422	.500	0	2	.000	133	194	.686	68	163	231	49	226	1	11	72	31	555	3.0	0.6	7.3
89-90—Detroit	82	70	2283	462	928	.498	0	3	.000	265	354	.749	112	233	345	63	295	4	23	133	37	1189	4.2	0.8	14.5
90-91—Detroit	72	70	1903	383	792	.484	1	2	.500	215	295	.729	91	186	277	65	249	4	12	126	30	982	3.8	0.9	13.6
91-92—L.A. Clippers	72	11	1437	250	538	.465	0	1	.000	198	271	.731	55	147	202	53	236	1	24	72	33	698	2.8	0.7	9.7
92-93—L.A. Lakers	52	0	617	122	270	.452	0	0	—	84	118	.712	30	70	100	41	122	0	10	51	7	328	1.9	0.8	6.3
93-94—L.A. Lakers	45	2	469	78	168	.464	0	0	—	54	79	.684	11	54	65	22	90	0	4	30	3	210	1.4	0.5	4.7
REG. SEASON TOTALS	1112	467	27816	5729	11531	.497	1	21	.048	3230	4623	.699	1779	4142	5921	1480	3937	95	414	1896	851	14689	5.3	1.3	13.2
PLAYOFF TOTALS	104	50	2180	395	843	.469	0	3	.000	229	336	.682	110	240	350	84	315	3	17	125	46	1019	3.4	0.8	9.8

EDWARDS, JAY CHARLES b. January 3, 1969 Ht. 6-4 Wt. 185 College—Indiana

SEASON—TEAM	G	GS	MIN	FGM	FGA	PCT	3FGM	3FGA	PCT	FTM	FTA	PCT	O-RB	D-RB	TOT	AST	PF	DQ	STL	TO	BLK	PTS	RPG	APG	PPG
89-90—L.A. Clippers	4	0	26	3	7	.429	0	2	.000	1	3	.333	1	1	2	4	4	0	1	1	0	7	0.5	1.0	1.8
REG. SEASON TOTALS	4	0	26	3	7	.429	0	2	.000	1	3	.333	1	1	2	4	4	0	1	1	0	7	0.5	1.0	1.8

EDWARDS, KEVIN DURELL b. October 30, 1965 Ht. 6-3 Wt. 210 College—Lakeland CC/DePaul

SEASON—TEAM	G	GS	MIN	FGM	FGA	PCT	3FGM	3FGA	PCT	FTM	FTA	PCT	O-RB	D-RB	TOT	AST	PF	DQ	STL	TO	BLK	PTS	RPG	APG	PPG
88-89—Miami	79	62	2349	470	1105	.425	10	37	.270	144	193	.746	85	177	262	349	154	0	139	246	27	1094	3.3	4.4	13.8
89-90—Miami	78	54	2211	395	959	.412	9	30	.300	139	183	.760	77	205	282	252	149	1	125	180	33	938	3.6	3.2	12.0
90-91—Miami	79	16	2000	380	927	.410	24	84	.286	171	213	.803	80	125	205	240	151	2	129	163	46	955	2.6	3.0	12.1
91-92—Miami	81	1	1840	325	716	.454	7	32	.219	162	191	.848	56	155	211	170	138	1	99	120	20	819	2.6	2.1	10.1
92-93—Miami	40	30	1134	216	462	.468	5	17	.294	119	141	.844	48	73	121	120	69	0	68	75	12	556	3.0	3.0	13.9
93-94—New Jersey	82	82	2727	471	1028	.458	35	99	.354	167	217	.770	94	187	281	232	150	0	120	135	34	1144	3.4	2.8	14.0
REG. SEASON TOTALS	439	245	12261	2257	5197	.434	90	299	.301	902	1138	.793	440	922	1362	1363	811	4	680	919	172	5506	3.1	3.1	12.5
PLAYOFF TOTALS	7	4	203	23	63	.365	0	2	.000	18	22	.818	9	14	23	16	12	0	7	14	1	64	3.3	2.3	9.1

EDWARDS, THEODORE (**Blue**) b. October 31, 1965 Ht. 6-4 Wt. 225 College—Louisburg College/East Carolina

SEASON—TEAM	G	GS	MIN	FGM	FGA	PCT	3FGM	3FGA	PCT	FTM	FTA	PCT	O-RB	D-RB	TOT	AST	PF	DQ	STL	TO	BLK	PTS	RPG	APG	PPG
89-90—Utah	82	49	1889	286	564	.507	9	30	.300	146	203	.719	69	182	251	145	280	2	76	152	36	727	3.1	1.8	8.9
90-91—Utah	62	56	1611	244	464	.526	6	24	.250	82	117	.701	51	150	201	108	203	4	57	105	29	576	3.2	1.7	9.3
91-92—Utah	81	81	2283	433	830	.522	39	103	.379	113	146	.774	86	212	298	137	236	1	81	122	46	1018	3.7	1.7	12.6
92-93—Milwaukee	82	81	2729	554	1083	.512	37	106	.349	237	300	.790	123	259	382	214	242	1	129	175	45	1382	4.7	2.6	16.9
93-94—Milwaukee	82	64	2322	382	800	.478	38	106	.358	151	189	.799	104	225	329	171	235	1	83	146	27	953	4.0	2.1	11.6
REG. SEASON TOTALS	389	331	10834	1899	3741	.508	129	369	.350	729	955	.763	433	1028	1461	775	1196	9	426	700	183	4656	3.8	2.0	12.0
PLAYOFF TOTALS	30	16	689	103	214	.481	4	15	.267	46	60	.767	37	60	97	41	98	0	38	52	6	256	3.2	1.4	8.5

EDWARDS, WILLIAM ALLEN (**Bill**) b. September 22, 1971 Ht. 6-8 Wt. 215 College—Wright State

SEASON—TEAM	G	GS	MIN	FGM	FGA	PCT	3FGM	3FGA	PCT	FTM	FTA	PCT	O-RB	D-RB	TOT	AST	PF	DQ	STL	TO	BLK	PTS	RPG	APG	PPG
93-94—Philadelphia	3	0	44	2	18	.111	0	5	.000	2	5	.400	5	9	14	4	6	0	3	4	1	6	4.7	1.3	2.0
REG. SEASON TOTALS	3	0	44	2	18	.111	0	5	.000	2	5	.400	5	9	14	4	6	0	3	4	1	6	4.7	1.3	2.0

EGAN, JOHN FRANCIS (**Johnny**) b. January 31, 1939 Ht. 6-0 Wt. 180 College—Providence

SEASON—TEAM	G	GS	MIN	FGM	FGA	PCT	3FGM	3FGA	PCT	FTM	FTA	PCT	O-RB	D-RB	TOT	AST	PF	DQ	STL	TO	BLK	PTS	RPG	APG	PPG
61-62—Detroit	58	—	696	128	301	.425	—	—	—	64	84	.762	—	—	86	102	64	0	—	—	—	320	1.5	1.8	5.5
62-63—Detroit	46	—	752	110	296	.372	—	—	—	53	69	.768	—	—	59	114	70	0	—	—	—	273	1.3	2.5	5.9
63-64—Detroit-N.Y.	66	—	2325	334	758	.441	—	—	—	193	243	.794	—	—	191	358	181	3	—	—	—	861	2.9	5.4	13.0
64-65—New York	74	—	1664	258	529	.488	—	—	—	162	199	.814	—	—	143	252	139	0	—	—	—	678	1.9	3.4	9.2
65-66—N.Y.-Balt.	76	—	1644	259	574	.451	—	—	—	173	227	.762	—	—	183	273	167	1	—	—	—	691	2.4	3.6	9.1
66-67—Baltimore	71	—	1743	267	624	.428	—	—	—	185	219	.845	—	—	180	275	190	3	—	—	—	719	2.5	3.9	10.1
67-68—Baltimore	67	—	930	163	415	.393	—	—	—	142	183	.776	—	—	112	134	127	0	—	—	—	468	1.7	2.0	7.0
68-69—Los Angeles	82	—	1805	246	597	.412	—	—	—	204	240	.850	—	—	147	215	206	1	—	—	—	696	1.8	2.6	8.5
69-70—Los Angeles	72	—	1627	215	491	.438	—	—	—	99	121	.818	—	—	104	216	171	2	—	—	—	529	1.4	3.0	7.3
70-71—Clev.-S.D.	62	—	824	67	178	.376	—	—	—	42	51	.824	—	—	63	112	71	0	—	—	—	176	1.0	1.8	2.8
71-72—Houston	38	—	437	42	104	.404	—	—	—	26	32	.813	—	—	26	51	55	0	—	—	—	110	0.7	1.3	2.9
REG. SEASON TOTALS	712	—	14447	2089	4867	.429	—	—	—	1343	1668	.805	—	—	1294	2102	1441	10	—	—	—	5521	1.8	3.0	7.8
PLAYOFF TOTALS	42	—	947	165	369	.447	—	—	—	93	117	.795	—	—	67	131	97	1	—	—	—	423	1.6	3.1	10.1

EGGLESTON, LONNIE J. b. June 8, 1918 Ht. 6-1½ Wt. 170 College—Oklahoma State

SEASON—TEAM	G	GS	MIN	FGM	FGA	PCT	3FGM	3FGA	PCT	FTM	FTA	PCT	O-RB	D-RB	TOT	AST	PF	DQ	STL	TO	BLK	PTS	RPG	APG	PPG
48-49—St. Louis	2	—	—	1	4	.250	—	—	—	2	3	.667	—	—	—	1	3	—	—	—	—	4	—	0.5	2.0
REG. SEASON TOTALS	2	—	—	1	4	.250	—	—	—	2	3	.667	—	—	—	1	3	—	—	—	—	4	—	0.5	2.0

EHLERS, EDWIN S. (**Eddie, Bulbs**) b. March 10, 1923 Ht. 6-3 Wt. 200 College—Purdue

SEASON—TEAM	G	GS	MIN	FGM	FGA	PCT	3FGM	3FGA	PCT	FTM	FTA	PCT	O-RB	D-RB	TOT	AST	PF	DQ	STL	TO	BLK	PTS	RPG	APG	PPG
47-48—Boston	40	—	—	104	417	.249	—	—	—	78	144	.542	—	—	—	44	92	—	—	—	—	286	—	1.1	7.2
48-49—Boston	59	—	—	182	583	.312	—	—	—	150	225	.667	—	—	—	133	119	—	—	—	—	514	—	2.3	8.7
REG. SEASON TOTALS	99	—	—	286	1000	.286	—	—	—	228	369	.618	—	—	—	177	211	—	—	—	—	800	—	1.8	8.1

EHLO, JOEL CRAIG (**Craig, Mr. Everything**) b. August 11, 1961 Ht. 6-7 Wt. 205 College—Odessa College/Washington State

SEASON—TEAM	G	GS	MIN	FGM	FGA	PCT	3FGM	3FGA	PCT	FTM	FTA	PCT	O-RB	D-RB	TOT	AST	PF	DQ	STL	TO	BLK	PTS	RPG	APG	PPG
83-84—Houston	7	0	63	11	27	.407	0	0	—	1	1	1.000	4	5	9	6	13	0	3	3	0	23	1.3	0.9	3.3
84-85—Houston	45	0	189	34	69	.493	0	3	.000	19	30	.633	8	17	25	26	26	0	11	22	3	87	0.6	0.6	1.9
85-86—Houston	36	0	199	36	84	.429	3	9	.333	23	29	.793	17	29	46	29	22	0	11	15	4	98	1.3	0.8	2.7
86-87—Cleveland	44	15	890	99	239	.414	5	29	.172	70	99	.707	55	106	161	92	80	0	40	61	30	273	3.7	2.1	6.2
87-88—Cleveland	79	27	1709	226	485	.466	22	64	.344	89	132	.674	86	188	274	206	182	0	82	107	30	563	3.5	2.6	7.1
88-89—Cleveland	82	4	1867	249	524	.475	39	100	.390	71	117	.607	100	195	295	266	161	0	110	116	19	608	3.6	3.2	7.4
89-90—Cleveland	81	64	2894	436	940	.464	104	248	.419	126	185	.681	147	292	439	371	226	2	126	161	23	1102	5.4	4.6	13.6
90-91—Cleveland	82	68	2766	344	773	.445	49	149	.329	95	140	.679	142	246	388	376	209	0	121	160	34	832	4.7	4.6	10.1
91-92—Cleveland	63	62	2016	310	684	.453	69	167	.413	87	123	.707	94	213	307	238	150	0	78	104	22	776	4.9	3.8	12.3
92-93—Cleveland	82	73	2559	385	785	.490	93	244	.381	86	120	.717	113	290	403	254	170	0	104	124	22	949	4.9	3.1	11.6
93-94—Atlanta	82	0	2147	316	708	.446	77	221	.348	112	154	.727	71	208	279	273	161	0	136	130	26	821	3.4	3.3	10.0
REG. SEASON TOTALS	683	313	17299	2446	5318	.460	461	1234	.374	779	1130	.689	837	1789	2626	2137	1400	2	822	1003	213	6132	3.8	3.1	9.0
PLAYOFF TOTALS	64	30	1623	220	519	.424	49	137	.358	82	113	.726	56	141	197	210	140	0	66	80	11	571	3.1	3.3	8.9

EICHHORST, RICHARD A. (**Dick**) b. October 21, 1933 Ht. 6-3 Wt. 200 College—SE Missouri State

SEASON—TEAM	G	GS	MIN	FGM	FGA	PCT	3FGM	3FGA	PCT	FTM	FTA	PCT	O-RB	D-RB	TOT	AST	PF	DQ	STL	TO	BLK	PTS	RPG	APG	PPG
61-62—St. Louis	1	—	10	1	2	.500	—	—	—	0	0	—	—	—	1	3	1	0	—	—	—	2	1.0	3.0	2.0
REG. SEASON TOTALS	1	—	10	1	2	.500	—	—	—	0	0	—	—	—	1	3	1	0	—	—	—	2	1.0	3.0	2.0

ELIASON, DONALD CARLTON (**Don**) b. July 24, 1918 Ht. 6-2 Wt. 210 College—Hamline

SEASON—TEAM	G	GS	MIN	FGM	FGA	PCT	3FGM	3FGA	PCT	FTM	FTA	PCT	O-RB	D-RB	TOT	AST	PF	DQ	STL	TO	BLK	PTS	RPG	APG	PPG
46-47—Boston	1	—	—	0	1	.000	—	—	—	0	0	—	—	—	—	0	1	—	—	—	—	0	—	0.0	0.0
REG. SEASON TOTALS	1	—	—	0	1	.000	—	—	—	0	0	—	—	—	—	0	1	—	—	—	—	0	—	0.0	0.0

ELIE, MARIO ANTOINE b. November 26, 1963 Ht. 6-5 Wt. 210 College—American International

SEASON—TEAM	G	GS	MIN	FGM	FGA	PCT	3FGM	3FGA	PCT	FTM	FTA	PCT	O-RB	D-RB	TOT	AST	PF	DQ	STL	TO	BLK	PTS	RPG	APG	PPG
90-91—Phil.-G.S.	33	0	644	79	159	.497	4	10	.400	75	89	.843	46	64	110	45	85	1	19	30	10	237	3.3	1.4	7.2
91-92—Golden State	79	32	1677	221	424	.521	23	70	.329	155	182	.852	69	158	227	174	159	3	68	83	15	620	2.9	2.2	7.8
92-93—Portland	82	7	1757	240	524	.458	45	129	.349	183	214	.855	59	157	216	177	145	0	74	89	20	708	2.6	2.2	8.6
93-94—Houston	67	8	1606	208	466	.446	56	167	.335	154	179	.860	28	153	181	208	124	0	50	109	8	626	2.7	3.1	9.3
REG. SEASON TOTALS	261	47	5684	748	1573	.476	128	376	.340	567	664	.854	202	532	734	604	513	4	211	311	53	2191	2.8	2.3	8.4
PLAYOFF TOTALS	40	9	711	98	208	.471	15	37	.405	77	91	.846	39	61	100	65	74	1	20	42	5	288	2.5	1.6	7.2

ELLEFSON, E. RAY (**Ray**) b. November 18, 1922 Ht. 6-8 Wt. 230 College—Oklahoma State/Colorado/West Texas State

SEASON—TEAM	G	GS	MIN	FGM	FGA	PCT	3FGM	3FGA	PCT	FTM	FTA	PCT	O-RB	D-RB	TOT	AST	PF	DQ	STL	TO	BLK	PTS	RPG	APG	PPG
48-49—Minneapolis	3	—	—	1	5	.200	—	—	—	0	0	—	—	—	—	0	2	—	—	—	—	2	—	0.0	0.7
48-49—Waterloo (N)	7	—	—	4	—	—	—	—	—	8	11	.727	—	—	—	—	5	—	—	—	—	16	—	—	2.3
50-51—New York	3	—	—	0	4	.000	—	—	—	4	4	1.000	—	—	8	0	6	0	—	—	—	4	2.7	0.0	1.3
REG. NBA TOTALS	6	—	—	1	9	.111	—	—	—	4	4	1.000	—	—	8	0	8	0	—	—	—	6	2.7	0.0	1.0
REG. NBL TOTALS	7	—	—	4	—	—	—	—	—	8	11	.727	—	—	—	—	5	—	—	—	—	16	—	—	2.3

ELLIOTT, ROBERT ALAN (**Bob**) b. August 18, 1955 Ht. 6-9½ Wt. 225 College—Arizona

SEASON—TEAM	G	GS	MIN	FGM	FGA	PCT	3FGM	3FGA	PCT	FTM	FTA	PCT	O-RB	D-RB	TOT	AST	PF	DQ	STL	TO	BLK	PTS	RPG	APG	PPG
78-79—New Jersey	14	—	282	41	73	.562	—	—	—	41	56	.732	16	40	56	22	34	2	6	26	4	123	4.0	1.6	8.8
79-80—New Jersey	54	—	722	101	228	.443	1	4	.250	104	152	.684	67	118	185	53	97	0	29	88	14	307	3.4	1.0	5.7
80-81—New Jersey	73	—	1320	214	419	.511	1	2	.500	121	202	.599	104	157	261	129	175	3	34	119	16	550	3.6	1.8	7.5
REG. SEASON TOTALS	141	—	2324	356	720	.494	2	6	.333	266	410	.649	187	315	502	204	306	5	69	233	34	980	3.6	1.4	7.0

ELLIOTT, SEAN MICHAEL b. February 2, 1968 Ht. 6-8 Wt. 215 College—Arizona

SEASON—TEAM	G	GS	MIN	FGM	FGA	PCT	3FGM	3FGA	PCT	FTM	FTA	PCT	O-RB	D-RB	TOT	AST	PF	DQ	STL	TO	BLK	PTS	RPG	APG	PPG
89-90—San Antonio	81	69	2032	311	647	.481	1	9	.111	187	216	.866	127	170	297	154	172	0	45	112	14	810	3.7	1.9	10.0
90-91—San Antonio	82	82	3044	478	976	.490	20	64	.313	325	402	.808	142	314	456	238	190	2	69	147	33	1301	5.6	2.9	15.9
91-92—San Antonio	82	82	3120	514	1040	.494	25	82	.305	285	331	.861	143	296	439	214	149	0	84	152	29	1338	5.4	2.6	16.3
92-93—San Antonio	70	70	2604	451	918	.491	37	104	.356	268	337	.795	85	237	322	265	132	1	68	152	28	1207	4.6	3.8	17.2
93-94—Detroit	73	73	2409	360	791	.455	26	87	.299	139	173	.803	68	195	263	197	174	3	54	129	27	885	3.6	2.7	12.1
REG. SEASON TOTALS	388	376	13209	2114	4372	.484	109	346	.315	1204	1459	.825	565	1212	1777	1068	817	6	320	692	131	5541	4.6	2.8	14.3
PLAYOFF TOTALS	27	27	941	148	301	.492	8	26	.308	99	119	.832	31	93	124	78	74	0	24	52	14	403	4.6	2.9	14.9
ALL-STAR TOTALS	1	0	15	1	6	.167	0	0	—	3	4	.750	1	1	2	0	1	0	0	1	0	5	2.0	0.0	5.0

ELLIS, ALEXANDER (**Boo**) b. February 11, 1936 Ht. 6-5 Wt. 185 College—Niagara

SEASON—TEAM	G	GS	MIN	FGM	FGA	PCT	3FGM	3FGA	PCT	FTM	FTA	PCT	O-RB	D-RB	TOT	AST	PF	DQ	STL	TO	BLK	PTS	RPG	APG	PPG
58-59—Minneapolis	72	—	1202	163	379	.430	—	—	—	102	144	.708	—	—	380	59	137	0	—	—	—	428	5.3	0.8	5.9
59-60—Minneapolis	46	—	671	64	185	.346	—	—	—	51	76	.671	—	—	236	27	64	2	—	—	—	179	5.1	0.6	3.9
REG. SEASON TOTALS	118	—	1873	227	564	.402	—	—	—	153	220	.695	—	—	616	86	201	2	—	—	—	607	5.2	0.7	5.1
PLAYOFF TOTALS	16	—	291	37	90	.411	—	—	—	22	39	.564	—	—	105	18	37	0	—	—	—	96	6.6	1.1	6.0

ELLIS, DALE (**Lamar Mundane**) b. August 6, 1960 Ht. 6-7 Wt. 215 College—Tennessee

SEASON—TEAM	G	GS	MIN	FGM	FGA	PCT	3FGM	3FGA	PCT	FTM	FTA	PCT	O-RB	D-RB	TOT	AST	PF	DQ	STL	TO	BLK	PTS	RPG	APG	PPG
83-84—Dallas	67	2	1059	225	493	.456	12	29	.414	87	121	.719	106	144	250	56	118	0	41	78	9	549	3.7	0.8	8.2
84-85—Dallas	72	4	1314	274	603	.454	42	109	.385	77	104	.740	100	138	238	56	131	1	46	58	7	667	3.3	0.8	9.3
85-86—Dallas	72	1	1086	193	470	.411	63	173	.364	59	82	.720	86	82	168	37	78	0	40	38	9	508	2.3	0.5	7.1
86-87—Seattle	82	76	3073	785	1520	.516	86	240	.358	385	489	.787	187	260	447	238	267	2	104	238	32	2041	5.5	2.9	24.9
87-88—Seattle	75	73	2790	764	1519	.503	107	259	.413	303	395	.767	167	173	340	197	221	1	74	172	11	1938	4.5	2.6	25.8
88-89—Seattle	82	82	3190	857	1710	.501	162	339	.478	377	462	.816	156	186	342	164	197	0	108	218	22	2253	4.2	2.0	27.5
89-90—Seattle	55	49	2033	502	1011	.497	96	256	.375	193	236	.818	90	148	238	110	124	3	59	119	7	1293	4.3	2.0	23.5
90-91—Seattle-Milw.	51	24	1424	340	718	.474	57	157	.363	120	166	.723	66	107	173	95	112	1	49	81	8	857	3.4	1.9	16.8
91-92—Milwaukee	81	11	2191	485	1034	.469	138	329	.419	164	212	.774	92	161	253	104	151	0	57	119	18	1272	3.1	1.3	15.7
92-93—San Antonio	82	76	2731	545	1092	.499	119	297	.401	157	197	.797	81	231	312	107	179	0	78	111	18	1366	3.8	1.3	16.7
93-94—San Antonio	77	75	2590	478	967	.494	131	332	.395	83	107	.776	70	185	255	80	141	0	66	75	11	1170	3.3	1.0	15.2
REG. SEASON TOTALS	796	473	23481	5448	11137	.489	1013	2520	.402	2005	2571	.780	1201	1815	3016	1244	1719	8	722	1307	152	13914	3.8	1.6	17.5
PLAYOFF TOTALS	60	43	1738	373	828	.450	56	163	.344	117	152	.770	100	146	246	83	147	2	47	93	13	919	4.1	1.4	15.3
ALL-STAR TOTALS	1	1	26	12	16	.750	1	1	1.000	2	2	1.000	3	3	6	2	2	0	0	2	0	27	6.0	2.0	27.0

ELLIS, HAROLD b. October 7, 1970 Ht. 6-5 Wt. 210 College—Morehouse

SEASON—TEAM	G	GS	MIN	FGM	FGA	PCT	3FGM	3FGA	PCT	FTM	FTA	PCT	O-RB	D-RB	TOT	AST	PF	DQ	STL	TO	BLK	PTS	RPG	APG	PPG
93-94—L.A. Clippers	49	16	923	159	292	.545	0	4	.000	106	149	.711	94	59	153	31	97	0	73	43	2	424	3.1	0.6	8.7
REG. SEASON TOTALS	49	16	923	159	292	.545	0	4	.000	106	149	.711	94	59	153	31	97	0	73	43	2	424	3.1	0.6	8.7

ELLIS, JOSEPH FRANKLIN (**Joe**) b. May 3, 1944 Ht. 6-6 Wt. 175 College—San Francisco

SEASON—TEAM	G	GS	MIN	FGM	FGA	PCT	3FGM	3FGA	PCT	FTM	FTA	PCT	O-RB	D-RB	TOT	AST	PF	DQ	STL	TO	BLK	PTS	RPG	APG	PPG
66-67—San Francisco	41	—	333	67	164	.409	—	—	—	19	25	.760	—	—	112	27	45	0	—	—	—	153	2.7	0.7	3.7
67-68—San Francisco	51	—	624	111	302	.368	—	—	—	32	50	.640	—	—	195	37	83	2	—	—	—	254	3.8	0.7	5.0
68-69—San Francisco	74	—	1731	371	939	.395	—	—	—	147	201	.731	—	—	481	130	258	13	—	—	—	889	6.5	1.8	12.0
69-70—San Francisco	76	—	2380	501	1223	.410	—	—	—	200	270	.741	—	—	594	139	281	13	—	—	—	1202	7.8	1.8	15.8
70-71—San Francisco	80	—	2275	356	898	.396	—	—	—	151	203	.744	—	—	511	161	287	6	—	—	—	863	6.4	2.0	10.8
71-72—Golden State	78	—	1462	280	681	.411	—	—	—	95	132	.720	—	—	389	97	224	4	—	—	—	655	5.0	1.2	8.4
72-73—Golden State	74	—	1054	199	487	.409	—	—	—	69	93	.742	—	—	282	88	143	2	—	—	—	467	3.8	1.2	6.3
73-74—Golden State	50	—	515	61	190	.321	—	—	—	18	31	.581	37	85	122	37	76	2	33	—	9	140	2.4	0.7	2.8
REG. SEASON TOTALS	524	—	10374	1946	4884	.398	—	—	—	731	1005	.727	37	85	2686	716	1397	42	33	—	9	4623	5.1	1.4	8.8
PLAYOFF TOTALS	38	—	575	83	270	.307	—	—	—	36	52	.692	0	0	131	23	75	1	0	—	0	202	3.4	0.6	5.3

ELLIS, LAPHONSO DARNELL b. May 5, 1970 Ht. 6-8 Wt. 240 College—Notre Dame

SEASON—TEAM	G	GS	MIN	FGM	FGA	PCT	3FGM	3FGA	PCT	FTM	FTA	PCT	O-RB	D-RB	TOT	AST	PF	DQ	STL	TO	BLK	PTS	RPG	APG	PPG
92-93—Denver	82	82	2749	483	958	.504	2	13	.154	237	317	.748	274	470	744	151	293	8	72	153	111	1205	9.1	1.8	14.7
93-94—Denver	79	79	2699	483	963	.502	7	23	.304	242	359	.674	220	462	682	167	304	6	63	172	80	1215	8.6	2.1	15.4
REG. SEASON TOTALS	161	161	5448	966	1921	.503	9	36	.250	479	676	.709	494	932	1426	318	597	14	135	325	191	2420	8.9	2.0	15.0
PLAYOFF TOTALS	12	12	436	68	142	.479	3	6	.500	38	54	.704	27	70	97	26	46	2	9	19	11	177	8.1	2.2	14.8

ELLIS, LERON PERRY b. April 28, 1969 Ht. 6-11 Wt. 240 College—Kentucky/Syracuse

SEASON—TEAM	G	GS	MIN	FGM	FGA	PCT	3FGM	3FGA	PCT	FTM	FTA	PCT	O-RB	D-RB	TOT	AST	PF	DQ	STL	TO	BLK	PTS	RPG	APG	PPG
91-92—L.A. Clippers	29	0	103	17	50	.340	0	0	—	9	19	.474	12	12	24	1	11	0	6	11	9	43	0.8	0.0	1.5
93-94—Charlotte	50	1	680	88	182	.484	0	0	—	45	68	.662	70	118	188	24	83	1	17	21	25	221	3.8	0.5	4.4
REG. SEASON TOTALS	79	1	783	105	232	.453	0	0	—	54	87	.621	82	130	212	25	94	1	23	32	34	264	2.7	0.3	3.3
PLAYOFF TOTALS	1	0	2	0	0	—	0	0	—	0	0	—	0	0	0	0	0	0	0	0	0	0	0.0	0.0	0.0

ELLIS, LEROY b. March 10, 1940 Ht. 6-11 Wt. 210 College—St. John's

SEASON—TEAM	G	GS	MIN	FGM	FGA	PCT	3FGM	3FGA	PCT	FTM	FTA	PCT	O-RB	D-RB	TOT	AST	PF	DQ	STL	TO	BLK	PTS	RPG	APG	PPG
62-63—Los Angeles	80	—	1628	222	530	.419	—	—	—	133	202	.658	—	—	518	46	194	1	—	—	—	577	6.5	0.6	7.2
63-64—Los Angeles	78	—	1459	200	473	.423	—	—	—	112	170	.659	—	—	498	41	192	3	—	—	—	512	6.4	0.5	6.6
64-65—Los Angeles	80	—	2026	311	700	.444	—	—	—	198	284	.697	—	—	652	49	196	1	—	—	—	820	8.2	0.6	10.3
65-66—Los Angeles	80	—	2219	393	927	.424	—	—	—	186	256	.727	—	—	735	74	232	3	—	—	—	972	9.2	0.9	12.2
66-67—Baltimore	81	—	2938	496	1166	.425	—	—	—	211	286	.738	—	—	970	170	258	3	—	—	—	1203	12.0	2.1	14.9
67-68—Baltimore	78	—	2719	380	800	.475	—	—	—	207	286	.724	—	—	862	158	256	5	—	—	—	967	11.1	2.0	12.4
68-69—Baltimore	80	—	1603	229	527	.435	—	—	—	117	155	.755	—	—	510	73	168	0	—	—	—	575	6.4	0.9	7.2
69-70—Baltimore	72	—	1163	194	414	.469	—	—	—	86	116	.741	—	—	376	47	129	0	—	—	—	474	5.2	0.7	6.6
70-71—Portland	74	—	2581	485	1095	.443	—	—	—	209	261	.801	—	—	907	235	258	5	—	—	—	1179	12.3	3.2	15.9
71-72—Los Angeles	74	—	1081	138	300	.460	—	—	—	66	95	.695	—	—	310	46	115	0	—	—	—	342	4.2	0.6	4.6
72-73—L.A.-Phil.	79	—	2600	421	969	.434	—	—	—	129	161	.801	—	—	777	139	199	2	—	—	—	971	9.8	1.8	12.3
73-74—Philadelphia	81	—	2831	326	722	.452	—	—	—	147	196	.750	292	598	890	189	224	2	86	—	87	799	11.0	2.3	9.9
74-75—Philadelphia	82	—	2183	287	623	.461	—	—	—	72	99	.727	195	387	582	117	178	1	44	—	55	646	7.1	1.4	7.9
75-76—Philadelphia	29	—	489	61	132	.462	—	—	—	17	28	.607	47	75	122	21	62	0	16	—	9	139	4.2	0.7	4.8
REG. SEASON TOTALS	1048	—	27520	4143	9378	.442	—	—	—	1890	2595	.728	534	1060	8709	1405	2661	26	146	—	151	10176	8.3	1.3	9.7
PLAYOFF TOTALS	64	—	1487	175	424	.413	—	—	—	113	163	.693	0	0	462	44	152	1	0	—	0	463	7.2	0.7	7.2

ELLIS, MAURICE H. (**Bo**) b. August 8, 1954 Ht. 6-9 Wt. 200 College—Marquette

SEASON—TEAM	G	GS	MIN	FGM	FGA	PCT	3FGM	3FGA	PCT	FTM	FTA	PCT	O-RB	D-RB	TOT	AST	PF	DQ	STL	TO	BLK	PTS	RPG	APG	PPG
77-78—Denver	78	—	1213	133	320	.416	—	—	—	72	104	.692	114	190	304	73	208	2	49	99	47	338	3.9	0.9	4.3
78-79—Denver	42	—	269	42	92	.457	—	—	—	29	36	.806	17	45	62	10	45	0	10	22	13	113	1.5	0.2	2.7
79-80—Denver	48	—	502	61	136	.449	0	3	.000	40	53	.755	51	65	116	30	67	1	10	24	24	162	2.4	0.6	3.4
REG. SEASON TOTALS	168	—	1984	236	548	.431	0	3	.000	141	193	.731	182	300	482	113	320	3	69	145	84	613	2.9	0.7	3.6
PLAYOFF TOTALS	15	—	194	19	46	.413	0	0	—	14	17	.824	16	31	47	9	27	0	8	14	9	52	3.1	0.6	3.5

ELLISON, PERVIS (**Never Nervous Pervis**) b. April 3, 1967 Ht. 6-10 Wt. 225 College—Louisville

SEASON—TEAM	G	GS	MIN	FGM	FGA	PCT	3FGM	3FGA	PCT	FTM	FTA	PCT	O-RB	D-RB	TOT	AST	PF	DQ	STL	TO	BLK	PTS	RPG	APG	PPG
89-90—Sacramento	34	22	866	111	251	.442	0	2	.000	49	78	.628	64	132	196	65	132	4	16	62	57	271	5.8	1.9	8.0
90-91—Washington	76	30	1942	326	636	.513	0	6	.000	139	214	.650	224	361	585	102	268	6	49	146	157	791	7.7	1.3	10.4
91-92—Washington	66	64	2511	547	1014	.539	1	3	.333	227	312	.728	217	523	740	190	222	2	62	196	177	1322	11.2	2.9	20.0
92-93—Washington	49	48	1701	341	655	.521	0	4	.000	170	242	.702	138	295	433	117	154	3	45	110	108	852	8.8	2.4	17.4
93-94—Washington	47	24	1178	137	292	.469	0	3	.000	70	97	.722	77	165	242	70	140	3	25	73	50	344	5.1	1.5	7.3
REG. SEASON TOTALS	272	188	8198	1462	2848	.513	1	18	.056	655	943	.695	720	1476	2196	544	916	18	197	587	549	3580	8.1	2.0	13.2

ELMORE, LEONARD J. (Len) b. March 28, 1952 Ht. 6-10 Wt. 225 College—Maryland

SEASON—TEAM	G	GS	MIN	FGM	FGA	PCT	3FGM	3FGA	PCT	FTM	FTA	PCT	O-RB	D-RB	TOT	AST	PF	DQ	STL	TO	BLK	PTS	RPG	APG	PPG
74-75—Indiana (A)	77	—	1414	218	523	.417	1	1	1.000	72	93	.774	148	247	395	35	241	—	67	83	91	509	5.1	0.5	6.6
75-76—Indiana (A)	76	—	2591	480	1193	.402	0	3	.000	152	206	.738	242	577	819	122	310	—	136	175	178	1112	10.8	1.6	14.6
76-77—Indiana	6	—	46	7	17	.412	—	—	—	4	5	.800	7	8	15	2	11	0	0	—	4	18	2.5	0.3	3.0
77-78—Indiana	69	—	1327	142	386	.368	—	—	—	88	132	.667	139	281	420	80	174	4	74	73	71	372	6.1	1.2	5.4
78-79—Indiana	80	—	1264	139	342	.406	—	—	—	56	78	.718	115	287	402	75	183	3	62	73	79	334	5.0	0.9	4.2
79-80—Kansas City	58	—	915	104	242	.430	0	0	—	51	74	.689	74	183	257	64	154	0	41	67	39	259	4.4	1.1	4.5
80-81—Milwaukee	72	—	925	76	212	.358	0	0	—	54	75	.720	68	140	208	69	178	3	37	44	52	206	2.9	1.0	2.9
81-82—New Jersey	81	70	2100	300	652	.460	0	0	—	135	170	.794	167	274	441	100	280	6	92	136	92	735	5.4	1.2	9.1
82-83—New Jersey	74	0	975	97	244	.398	0	1	.000	54	84	.643	81	157	238	39	125	2	44	83	38	248	3.2	0.5	3.4
83-84—New York	65	5	832	64	157	.408	0	0	—	27	38	.711	62	103	165	30	153	3	29	46	30	155	2.5	0.5	2.4
REG. NBA TOTALS	505	75	8384	929	2252	.413	0	1	.000	469	656	.715	713	1433	2146	459	1258	21	379	522	405	2327	4.2	0.9	4.6
REG. ABA TOTALS	153	—	4005	698	1716	.407	1	4	.250	224	299	.749	390	824	1214	157	551	—	203	258	269	1621	7.9	1.0	10.6
NBA PLAYOFF TOTALS	11	2	146	15	35	.429	0	0	—	6	8	.750	12	24	36	4	16	0	5	8	3	36	3.3	0.4	3.3
ABA PLAYOFF TOTALS	21	—	633	92	220	.418	0	0	—	26	38	.684	55	105	160	20	84	—	26	28	41	210	7.6	1.0	10.0

ELSTON, DARRELL EUGENE b. August 15, 1952 Ht. 6-3½ Wt. 205 College—North Carolina

SEASON—TEAM	G	GS	MIN	FGM	FGA	PCT	3FGM	3FGA	PCT	FTM	FTA	PCT	O-RB	D-RB	TOT	AST	PF	DQ	STL	TO	BLK	PTS	RPG	APG	PPG
74-75—Virginia (A)	72	—	1869	250	613	.408	3	18	.167	93	123	.756	48	115	163	202	166	—	82	126	9	596	2.3	2.8	8.3
76-77—Indiana	5	—	40	2	14	.143	—	—	—	1	2	.500	1	5	6	2	6	0	1	—	0	5	1.2	0.4	1.0
REG. NBA TOTALS	5	—	40	2	14	.143	—	—	—	1	2	.500	1	5	6	2	6	0	1	—	0	5	1.2	0.4	1.0
REG. ABA TOTALS	72	—	1869	250	613	.408	3	18	.167	93	123	.756	48	115	163	202	166	—	82	126	9	596	2.3	2.8	8.3

EMBRY, WAYNE RICHARD (Goose) b. March 26, 1937 Ht. 6-8 Wt. 255 College—Miami (Ohio)

SEASON—TEAM	G	GS	MIN	FGM	FGA	PCT	3FGM	3FGA	PCT	FTM	FTA	PCT	O-RB	D-RB	TOT	AST	PF	DQ	STL	TO	BLK	PTS	RPG	APG	PPG
58-59—Cincinnati	66	—	1590	272	702	.387	—	—	—	206	314	.656	—	—	597	96	232	9	—	—	—	750	9.0	1.5	11.4
59-60—Cincinnati	73	—	1594	303	690	.439	—	—	—	167	325	.514	—	—	692	83	226	1	—	—	—	773	9.5	1.1	10.6
60-61—Cincinnati	79	—	2233	458	1015	.451	—	—	—	221	331	.668	—	—	864	127	286	7	—	—	—	1137	10.9	1.6	14.4
61-62—Cincinnati	75	—	2623	564	1210	.466	—	—	—	356	516	.690	—	—	977	182	286	6	—	—	—	1484	13.0	2.4	19.8
62-63—Cincinnati	76	—	2511	534	1165	.458	—	—	—	343	514	.667	—	—	936	177	286	7	—	—	—	1411	12.3	2.3	18.6
63-64—Cincinnati	80	—	2915	556	1213	.458	—	—	—	271	417	.650	—	—	925	113	325	7	—	—	—	1383	11.6	1.4	17.3
64-65—Cincinnati	74	—	2243	352	772	.456	—	—	—	239	371	.644	—	—	741	92	297	10	—	—	—	943	10.0	1.2	12.7
65-66—Cincinnati	80	—	1882	232	564	.411	—	—	—	141	234	.603	—	—	525	81	287	9	—	—	—	605	6.6	1.0	7.6
66-67—Boston	72	—	729	147	359	.409	—	—	—	82	144	.569	—	—	294	42	137	0	—	—	—	376	4.1	0.6	5.2
67-68—Boston	78	—	1088	193	483	.400	—	—	—	109	185	.589	—	—	321	52	174	1	—	—	—	495	4.1	0.7	6.3
68-69—Milwaukee	78	—	2355	382	894	.427	—	—	—	259	390	.664	—	—	672	149	302	8	—	—	—	1023	8.6	1.9	13.1
REG. SEASON TOTALS	831	—	21763	3993	9067	.440	—	—	—	2394	3741	.640	—	—	7544	1194	2838	65	—	—	—	10380	9.1	1.4	12.5
PLAYOFF TOTALS	56	—	1347	215	514	.418	—	—	—	136	211	.645	—	—	448	64	206	8	—	—	—	566	8.0	1.1	10.1
ALL-STAR TOTALS	4	—	64	15	34	.441	—	—	—	2	2	1.000	—	—	18	2	10	0	—	—	—	32	4.5	0.5	8.0

ENDRESS, NED R. b. March 2, 1918 Ht. 6-2 Wt. 200 College—Akron

SEASON—TEAM	G	GS	MIN	FGM	FGA	PCT	3FGM	3FGA	PCT	FTM	FTA	PCT	O-RB	D-RB	TOT	AST	PF	DQ	STL	TO	BLK	PTS	RPG	APG	PPG
43-44—Cleveland (N)	16	—	—	25	—	—	—	—	—	15	—	—	—	—	—	—	—	—	—	—	—	65	—	—	4.1
44-45—Cleveland (N)	29	—	—	62	—	—	—	—	—	46	—	—	—	—	—	—	—	—	—	—	—	170	—	—	5.9
45-46—Cleveland (N)	22	—	—	58	—	—	—	—	—	36	74	.486	—	—	—	—	41	—	—	—	—	152	—	—	6.9
46-47—Cleveland	16	—	—	3	25	.120	—	—	—	8	15	.533	—	—	—	4	13	—	—	—	—	14	—	0.3	0.9
REG. NBA TOTALS	16	—	—	3	25	.120	—	—	—	8	15	.533	—	—	—	4	13	—	—	—	—	14	—	0.3	0.9
REG. NBL TOTALS	67	—	—	145	—	—	—	—	—	97	74	.486	—	—	—	—	41	—	—	—	—	387	—	—	5.8
NBL PLAYOFF TOTALS	4	—	—	5	—	—	—	—	—	3	—	—	—	—	—	—	5	—	—	—	—	13	—	—	3.3

ENGLER, CHRISTOPHER AARON (Chris) b. March 1, 1959 Ht. 6-11 Wt. 250 College—Minnesota/Wyoming

SEASON—TEAM	G	GS	MIN	FGM	FGA	PCT	3FGM	3FGA	PCT	FTM	FTA	PCT	O-RB	D-RB	TOT	AST	PF	DQ	STL	TO	BLK	PTS	RPG	APG	PPG
82-83—Golden State	54	1	369	38	94	.404	0	0	—	5	16	.313	43	61	104	11	95	1	7	24	17	81	1.9	0.2	1.5
83-84—Golden State	46	1	360	33	83	.398	0	0	—	14	23	.609	27	70	97	11	68	0	9	24	3	80	2.1	0.2	1.7
84-85—N.J.-Chicago-Milw.	11	0	82	8	20	.400	0	0	—	5	9	.556	12	18	30	0	5	0	2	2	5	21	2.7	0.0	1.9
86-87—Port.-Milw.-N.J.	30	0	195	23	51	.451	0	0	—	12	16	.750	23	34	57	8	33	0	5	12	11	58	1.9	0.3	1.9
87-88—New Jersey	54	0	399	36	88	.409	0	0	—	31	35	.886	32	66	98	15	73	1	9	29	6	103	1.8	0.3	1.9
REG. SEASON TOTALS	195	2	1405	138	336	.411	0	0	—	67	99	.677	137	249	386	45	274	2	32	91	42	343	2.0	0.2	1.8
PLAYOFF TOTALS	1	0	6	1	1	1.000	0	0	—	0	0	—	0	2	2	—	2	0	0	0	0	2	2.0	0.0	2.0

ENGLESTAD, WAYNE EDWARD b. December 6, 1963 Ht. 6-8 Wt. 245 College—Cal State-Irvine

SEASON—TEAM	G	GS	MIN	FGM	FGA	PCT	3FGM	3FGA	PCT	FTM	FTA	PCT	O-RB	D-RB	TOT	AST	PF	DQ	STL	TO	BLK	PTS	RPG	APG	PPG
88-89—Denver	11	0	50	11	29	.379	0	0	—	6	10	.600	5	11	16	7	12	0	1	3	0	28	1.5	0.6	2.5
REG. SEASON TOTALS	11	0	50	11	29	.379	0	0	—	6	10	.600	5	11	16	7	12	0	1	3	0	28	1.5	0.6	2.5

ENGLISH, ALBERT JAY (A.J.) b. July 11, 1967 Ht. 6-5 Wt. 175 College—Virginia Union

SEASON—TEAM	G	GS	MIN	FGM	FGA	PCT	3FGM	3FGA	PCT	FTM	FTA	PCT	O-RB	D-RB	TOT	AST	PF	DQ	STL	TO	BLK	PTS	RPG	APG	PPG
90-91—Washington	70	12	1443	251	572	.439	3	31	.097	111	157	.707	66	81	147	177	127	1	25	114	15	616	2.1	2.5	8.8
91-92—Washington	81	6	1665	366	846	.433	6	34	.176	148	176	.841	74	94	168	143	160	1	32	89	9	886	2.1	1.8	10.9
REG. SEASON TOTALS	151	18	3108	617	1418	.435	9	65	.138	259	333	.778	140	175	315	320	287	2	57	203	24	1502	2.1	2.1	9.9

ENGLISH, ALEXANDER (Alex) b. January 5, 1954 Ht. 6-7½ Wt. 190 College—South Carolina

SEASON—TEAM	G	GS	MIN	FGM	FGA	PCT	3FGM	3FGA	PCT	FTM	FTA	PCT	O-RB	D-RB	TOT	AST	PF	DQ	STL	TO	BLK	PTS	RPG	APG	PPG
76-77—Milwaukee	60	—	648	132	277	.477	—	—	—	46	60	.767	68	100	168	25	78	0	17	—	18	310	2.8	0.4	5.2
77-78—Milwaukee	82	—	1552	343	633	.542	—	—	—	104	143	.727	144	251	395	129	178	1	41	137	55	790	4.8	1.6	9.6
78-79—Indiana	81	—	2696	563	1102	.511	—	—	—	173	230	.752	253	402	655	271	214	3	70	196	78	1299	8.1	3.3	16.0
79-80—Indiana-Denver	78	—	2401	553	1113	.497	2	6	.333	210	266	.789	269	336	605	224	206	0	73	214	62	1318	7.8	2.9	16.9
80-81—Denver	81	—	3093	768	1555	.494	3	5	.600	390	459	.850	273	373	646	290	255	2	106	241	100	1929	8.0	3.6	23.8
81-82—Denver	82	82	3015	855	1553	.551	0	8	.000	372	443	.840	210	348	558	433	261	2	87	261	120	2082	6.8	5.3	25.4
82-83—Denver	82	82	2988	959	1857	.516	2	12	.167	406	490	.829	263	338	601	397	235	1	116	263	126	2326	7.3	4.8	28.4
83-84—Denver	82	77	2870	907	1714	.529	1	7	.143	352	427	.824	216	248	464	406	252	3	83	222	95	2167	5.7	5.0	26.4
84-85—Denver	81	81	2924	939	1812	.518	1	5	.200	383	462	.829	203	255	458	344	259	1	101	251	46	2262	5.7	4.2	27.9
85-86—Denver	81	81	3024	951	1888	.504	1	5	.200	511	593	.862	192	213	405	320	235	1	73	249	29	2414	5.0	4.0	29.8
86-87—Denver	82	82	3085	965	1920	.503	4	15	.267	411	487	.844	146	198	344	422	216	0	73	214	21	2345	4.2	5.1	28.6
87-88—Denver	80	80	2818	843	1704	.495	0	6	.000	314	379	.828	166	207	373	377	193	1	70	181	23	2000	4.7	4.7	25.0
88-89—Denver	82	82	2990	924	1881	.491	2	8	.250	325	379	.858	148	178	326	383	174	0	66	198	12	2175	4.0	4.7	26.5
89-90—Denver	80	80	2211	635	1293	.491	2	5	.400	161	183	.880	119	167	286	225	130	0	51	93	23	1433	3.6	2.8	17.9
90-91—Dallas	79	26	1748	322	734	.439	0	1	.000	119	140	.850	108	146	254	105	141	0	40	101	25	763	3.2	1.3	9.7
REG. SEASON TOTALS	1193	753	38063	10659	21036	.507	18	83	.217	4277	5141	.832	2778	3760	6538	4351	3027	15	1067	2821	833	25613	5.5	3.6	21.5
PLAYOFF TOTALS	68	59	2427	668	1328	.503	0	8	.000	325	377	.862	166	205	371	293	188	2	47	142	32	1661	5.5	4.3	24.4
ALL-STAR TOTALS	8	4	148	36	72	.500	0	0	—	1	2	.500	9	9	18	15	8	0	6	12	4	73	2.3	1.9	9.1

ENGLISH, CLAUDE W. b. December 26, 1946 Ht. 6-4 Wt. 185 College—Christian College of the Southwest/Rhode Island

SEASON—TEAM	G	GS	MIN	FGM	FGA	PCT	3FGM	3FGA	PCT	FTM	FTA	PCT	O-RB	D-RB	TOT	AST	PF	DQ	STL	TO	BLK	PTS	RPG	APG	PPG
70-71—Portland	18	—	70	11	42	.262	—	—	—	5	7	.714	—	—	20	6	15	0	—	—	—	27	1.1	0.3	1.5
REG. SEASON TOTALS	18	—	70	11	42	.262	—	—	—	5	7	.714	—	—	20	6	15	0	—	—	—	27	1.1	0.3	1.5

ENGLISH, SCOTT GARRISON b. October 20, 1950 Ht. 6-6 Wt. 205 College—Texas-El Paso/North Carolina

SEASON—TEAM	G	GS	MIN	FGM	FGA	PCT	3FGM	3FGA	PCT	FTM	FTA	PCT	O-RB	D-RB	TOT	AST	PF	DQ	STL	TO	BLK	PTS	RPG	APG	PPG
72-73—Phoenix	29	—	196	36	93	.387	—	—	—	21	29	.724	—	—	44	15	38	0	—	—	—	93	1.5	0.5	3.2
73-74—Virginia (A)	5	—	48	3	15	.200	0	0	—	4	4	1.000	3	13	16	4	9	—	3	9	0	10	3.2	0.8	2.0
74-75—San Diego (A)	71	—	1316	210	494	.425	1	10	.100	69	89	.775	130	233	363	88	115	—	47	88	20	490	5.1	1.2	6.9
REG. NBA TOTALS	29	—	196	36	93	.387	—	—	—	21	29	.724	—	—	44	15	38	0	—	—	—	93	1.5	0.5	3.2
REG. ABA TOTALS	76	—	1364	213	509	.418	1	10	.100	73	93	.785	133	246	379	92	124	0	50	97	20	500	5.0	1.2	6.6

ENGLISH, STEPHEN (Jo-Jo) b. February 4, 1970 Ht. 6-4 Wt. 195 College—South Carolina

SEASON—TEAM	G	GS	MIN	FGM	FGA	PCT	3FGM	3FGA	PCT	FTM	FTA	PCT	O-RB	D-RB	TOT	AST	PF	DQ	STL	TO	BLK	PTS	RPG	APG	PPG
92-93—Chicago	6	0	31	3	10	.300	0	3	.000	0	2	.000	2	4	6	1	5	0	3	4	2	6	1.0	0.2	1.0
93-94—Chicago	36	0	419	56	129	.434	8	17	.471	10	21	.476	9	36	45	38	61	0	8	36	10	130	1.3	1.1	3.6
REG. SEASON TOTALS	42	0	450	59	139	.424	8	20	.400	10	23	.435	11	40	51	39	66	0	11	40	12	136	1.2	0.9	3.2
PLAYOFF TOTALS	7	0	58	5	12	.417	1	4	.250	3	6	.500	1	2	3	2	4	0	1	1	1	14	0.4	0.3	2.0

ENGLUND, GENE E. b. October 21, 1917 Ht. 6-5 Wt. 205 College—Wisconsin

SEASON—TEAM	G	GS	MIN	FGM	FGA	PCT	3FGM	3FGA	PCT	FTM	FTA	PCT	O-RB	D-RB	TOT	AST	PF	DQ	STL	TO	BLK	PTS	RPG	APG	PPG
41-42—Oshkosh (N)	22	—	—	61	—	—	—	—	—	42	—	—	—	—	—	—	44	—	—	—	—	164	—	—	7.5
42-43—Oshkosh (N)	17	—	—	41	—	—	—	—	—	48	65	.738	—	—	—	—	64	—	—	—	—	130	—	—	7.6
43-44—Oshkosh (N)	2	—	—	9	—	—	—	—	—	5	—	—	—	—	—	—	—	—	—	—	—	23	—	—	11.5
45-46—Oshkosh (N)	33	—	—	78	—	—	—	—	—	64	102	.627	—	—	—	—	92	—	—	—	—	220	—	—	6.7
46-47—Oshkosh (N)	43	—	—	187	—	—	—	—	—	105	151	.695	—	—	—	—	121	—	—	—	—	479	—	—	11.1
47-48—Oshkosh (N)	58	—	—	246	—	—	—	—	—	242	333	.727	—	—	—	—	204	—	—	—	—	734	—	—	12.7
48-49—Oshkosh (N)	63	—	—	284	—	—	—	—	—	282	393	.718	—	—	—	—	232	—	—	—	—	850	—	—	13.5
49-50—Boston-Tri-Cit	46	—	—	104	274	.380	—	—	—	152	192	.792	—	—	—	41	167	—	—	—	—	360	0.9	—	7.8
REG. NBA TOTALS	46	—	—	104	274	.380	—	—	—	152	192	.792	—	—	—	41	167	—	—	—	—	360	0.9	—	7.8
REG. NBL TOTALS	238	—	—	906	—	—	—	—	—	788	1044	.710	—	—	—	—	713	—	—	—	—	2600	—	—	10.9
NBA PLAYOFF TOTALS	2	—	—	1	5	.200	—	—	—	9	11	.818	—	—	—	1	6	—	—	—	—	11	0.5	—	5.5
NBL PLAYOFF TOTALS	29	—	—	120	—	—	—	—	—	89	93	.677	—	—	—	—	103	—	—	—	—	329	—	—	11.3

EPPS, RAYMOND EDWARD JR. (Ray) b. August 20, 1956 Ht. 6-6 Wt. 195 College—Norfolk State

SEASON—TEAM	G	GS	MIN	FGM	FGA	PCT	3FGM	3FGA	PCT	FTM	FTA	PCT	O-RB	D-RB	TOT	AST	PF	DQ	STL	TO	BLK	PTS	RPG	APG	PPG
78-79—Golden State	13	—	72	10	23	.435	—	—	—	6	8	.750	0	5	5	2	7	0	1	2	0	26	0.4	0.2	2.0
REG. SEASON TOTALS	13	—	72	10	23	.435	—	—	—	6	8	.750	0	5	5	2	7	0	1	2	0	26	0.4	0.2	2.0

ERIAS, BALTICO S. (**Bo**) b. July 30, 1932 Ht. 6-3½ Wt. 220 College—Niagara

SEASON—TEAM	G	GS	MIN	FGM	FGA	PCT	3FGM	3FGA	PCT	FTM	FTA	PCT	O-RB	D-RB	TOT	AST	PF	DQ	STL	TO	BLK	PTS	RPG	APG	PPG
57-58—Minneapolis	18	—	401	59	170	.347	—	—	—	30	47	.638	—	—	83	26	52	1	—	—	—	148	4.6	1.4	8.2
REG. SEASON TOTALS	18	—	401	59	170	.347	—	—	—	30	47	.638	—	—	83	26	52	1	—	—	—	148	4.6	1.4	8.2

ERICKSON, KEITH RAYMOND b. April 19, 1944 Ht. 6-5 Wt. 195 College—UCLA

SEASON—TEAM	G	GS	MIN	FGM	FGA	PCT	3FGM	3FGA	PCT	FTM	FTA	PCT	O-RB	D-RB	TOT	AST	PF	DQ	STL	TO	BLK	PTS	RPG	APG	PPG
65-66—San Francisco	64	—	646	95	267	.356	—	—	—	43	65	.662	—	—	162	38	91	1	—	—	—	233	2.5	0.6	3.6
66-67—Chicago	76	—	1454	235	641	.367	—	—	—	117	159	.736	—	—	338	119	199	2	—	—	—	587	4.4	1.6	7.7
67-68—Chicago	78	—	2257	377	940	.401	—	—	—	194	257	.755	—	—	423	267	276	15	—	—	—	948	5.4	3.4	12.2
68-69—Los Angeles	77	—	1974	264	629	.420	—	—	—	120	175	.686	—	—	308	194	222	6	—	—	—	648	4.0	2.5	8.4
69-70—Los Angeles	68	—	1755	258	563	.458	—	—	—	91	122	.746	—	—	304	209	175	3	—	—	—	607	4.5	3.1	8.9
70-71—Los Angeles	73	—	2272	369	783	.471	—	—	—	85	112	.759	—	—	404	223	241	4	—	—	—	823	5.5	3.1	11.3
71-72—Los Angeles	15	—	262	40	83	.482	—	—	—	6	7	.857	—	—	39	35	26	0	—	—	—	86	2.6	2.3	5.7
72-73—Los Angeles	76	—	1920	299	696	.430	—	—	—	89	110	.809	—	—	337	242	190	3	—	—	—	687	4.4	3.2	9.0
73-74—Phoenix	66	—	2033	393	824	.477	—	—	—	177	221	.801	94	320	414	205	193	3	63	—	20	963	6.3	3.1	14.6
74-75—Phoenix	49	—	1469	237	557	.425	—	—	—	130	156	.833	70	173	243	170	150	3	50	—	12	604	5.0	3.5	12.3
75-76—Phoenix	74	—	1850	305	649	.470	—	—	—	134	157	.854	106	226	332	185	196	4	79	—	6	744	4.5	2.5	10.1
76-77—Phoenix	50	—	949	142	294	.483	—	—	—	37	50	.740	36	108	144	104	122	0	30	—	7	321	2.9	2.1	6.4
REG. SEASON TOTALS	766	—	18841	3014	6926	.435	—	—	—	1223	1591	.769	306	827	3448	1991	2081	44	222	—	45	7251	4.5	2.6	9.5
PLAYOFF TOTALS	87	—	2393	364	806	.452	—	—	—	144	189	.762	15	52	386	216	286	7	11	—	4	872	4.4	2.5	10.0

ERVING, JULIUS WINFIELD II (**Dr. J**) b. February 22, 1950 Ht. 6-6½ Wt. 200 College—Massachusetts

SEASON—TEAM	G	GS	MIN	FGM	FGA	PCT	3FGM	3FGA	PCT	FTM	FTA	PCT	O-RB	D-RB	TOT	AST	PF	DQ	STL	TO	BLK	PTS	RPG	APG	PPG
71-72—Virginia (A)	84	—	3513	910	1826	.498	3	16	.188	467	627	.745	476	843	1319	335	264	—	—	342	—	2290	15.7	4.0	27.3
72-73—Virginia (A)	71	—	2993	894	1804	.496	5	24	.208	475	612	.776	262	605	867	298	197	0	181	326	127	2268	12.2	4.2	31.9
73-74—New York (A)	84	—	3398	914	1785	.512	17	43	.395	454	593	.766	263	636	899	434	270	—	190	341	204	2299	10.7	5.2	27.4
74-75—New York (A)	84	—	3402	914	1806	.506	29	87	.333	486	608	.799	284	630	914	462	256	—	186	301	157	2343	10.9	5.5	27.9
75-76—New York (A)	84	—	3244	949	1873	.507	34	103	.330	530	662	.801	337	588	925	423	221	—	207	307	160	2462	11.0	5.0	29.3
76-77—Philadelphia	82	—	2940	685	1373	.499	—	—	—	400	515	.777	192	503	695	306	251	1	159	—	113	1770	8.5	3.7	21.6
77-78—Philadelphia	74	—	2429	611	1217	.502	—	—	—	306	362	.845	179	302	481	279	207	0	135	238	97	1528	6.5	3.8	20.6
78-79—Philadelphia	78	—	2802	715	1455	.491	—	—	—	373	501	.745	198	366	564	357	207	0	133	315	100	1803	7.2	4.6	23.1
79-80—Philadelphia	78	—	2812	838	1614	.519	4	20	.200	420	534	.787	215	361	576	355	208	0	170	284	140	2100	7.4	4.6	26.9
80-81—Philadelphia	82	—	2874	794	1524	.521	4	18	.222	422	536	.787	244	413	657	364	233	0	173	266	147	2014	8.0	4.4	24.6
81-82—Philadelphia	81	81	2789	780	1428	.546	3	11	.273	411	539	.763	220	337	557	319	229	1	161	214	141	1974	6.9	3.9	24.4
82-83—Philadelphia	72	72	2421	605	1170	.517	2	7	.286	330	435	.759	173	318	491	263	202	1	112	196	131	1542	6.8	3.7	21.4
83-84—Philadelphia	77	77	2683	678	1324	.512	7	21	.333	364	483	.754	190	342	532	309	217	3	141	230	139	1727	6.9	4.0	22.4
84-85—Philadelphia	78	78	2535	610	1236	.494	3	14	.214	338	442	.765	172	242	414	233	199	0	135	208	109	1561	5.3	3.0	20.0
85-86—Philadelphia	74	74	2474	521	1085	.480	9	32	.281	289	368	.785	169	201	370	248	196	3	113	214	82	1340	5.0	3.4	18.1
86-87—Philadelphia	60	60	1918	400	850	.471	14	53	.264	191	235	.813	115	149	264	191	137	0	76	158	94	1005	4.4	3.2	16.8
REG. NBA TOTALS	836	442	28677	7237	14276	.507	46	176	.261	3844	4950	.777	2067	3534	5601	3224	2286	9	1508	2323	1293	18364	6.7	3.9	22.0
REG. ABA TOTALS	407	—	16550	4581	9094	.504	88	273	.322	2412	3102	.778	1622	3302	4924	1952	1208	0	764	1617	648	11662	12.1	4.8	28.7
NBA PLAYOFF TOTALS	141	69	5288	1187	2441	.486	7	36	.194	707	908	.779	360	634	994	594	403	1	235	396	239	3088	7.0	4.2	21.9
ABA PLAYOFF TOTALS	48	—	2064	582	1122	.519	10	40	.250	318	400	.795	199	418	617	247	141	0	52	181	54	1492	12.9	5.1	31.1
NBA ALL-STAR TOTALS	11	11	316	85	178	.478	1	1	1.000	50	63	.794	34	36	70	35	31	0	18	19	11	221	6.4	3.2	20.1
ABA ALL-STAR TOTALS	5	4	134	38	70	.543	1	2	.500	23	29	.793	11	18	36	24	16	—	2	8	5	100	7.2	4.8	20.0

ESKRIDGE, JOHN I. (**Jack**) b. January 21, 1924 Ht. 6-5 Wt. 200 College—Kansas

SEASON—TEAM	G	GS	MIN	FGM	FGA	PCT	3FGM	3FGA	PCT	FTM	FTA	PCT	O-RB	D-RB	TOT	AST	PF	DQ	STL	TO	BLK	PTS	RPG	APG	PPG
48-49—Chicago-Ind.	23	—	—	25	69	.362	—	—	—	14	20	.700	—	—	—	14	25	—	—	—	—	64	—	0.6	2.8
REG. SEASON TOTALS	23	—	—	25	69	.362	—	—	—	14	20	.700	—	—	—	14	25	—	—	—	—	64	—	0.6	2.8

EVANS, EARL JOSEPH II b. November 11, 1955 Ht. 6-8 Wt. 205 College—USC/Nevada-Las Vegas

SEASON—TEAM	G	GS	MIN	FGM	FGA	PCT	3FGM	3FGA	PCT	FTM	FTA	PCT	O-RB	D-RB	TOT	AST	PF	DQ	STL	TO	BLK	PTS	RPG	APG	PPG
79-80—Detroit	36	—	381	63	140	.450	7	18	.389	24	42	.571	26	49	75	37	64	0	14	36	1	157	2.1	1.0	4.4
REG. SEASON TOTALS	36	—	381	63	140	.450	7	18	.389	24	42	.571	26	49	75	37	64	0	14	36	1	157	2.1	1.0	4.4

EVANS, MICHAEL LEEROYALL (**Mike**) b. April 19, 1955 Ht. 6-1 Wt. 170 College—Kansas State

SEASON—TEAM	G	GS	MIN	FGM	FGA	PCT	3FGM	3FGA	PCT	FTM	FTA	PCT	O-RB	D-RB	TOT	AST	PF	DQ	STL	TO	BLK	PTS	RPG	APG	PPG
79-80—San Antonio	79	—	1246	208	464	.448	12	42	.286	58	85	.682	29	78	107	230	194	2	60	128	9	486	1.4	2.9	6.2
80-81—Milwaukee	71	—	911	134	291	.460	2	14	.143	50	64	.781	22	65	87	167	114	0	34	72	4	320	1.2	2.4	4.5
81-82—Milw.-Clev.	22	0	270	35	86	.407	0	6	.000	13	20	.650	5	17	22	42	36	1	13	26	0	83	1.0	1.9	3.8
82-83—Denver	42	5	695	115	243	.473	0	9	.000	33	41	.805	4	54	58	113	94	3	23	71	3	263	1.4	2.7	6.3
83-84—Denver	78	5	1687	243	564	.431	32	89	.360	111	131	.847	23	115	138	288	175	2	61	117	4	629	1.8	3.7	8.1
84-85—Denver	81	0	1437	323	661	.489	57	157	.363	113	131	.863	26	93	119	231	174	2	65	130	12	816	1.5	2.9	10.1
85-86—Denver	81	1	1389	304	715	.425	39	176	.222	126	149	.846	30	71	101	177	159	1	61	124	1	773	1.2	2.2	9.5
86-87—Denver	81	4	1567	334	729	.458	53	169	.314	96	123	.780	36	92	128	185	149	1	79	107	12	817	1.6	2.3	10.1
87-88—Denver	56	0	656	139	307	.453	36	91	.396	30	37	.811	9	39	48	81	78	0	34	43	6	344	0.9	1.4	6.1
REG. SEASON TOTALS	591	15	9858	1835	4060	.452	231	753	.307	630	781	.807	184	624	808	1514	1173	12	430	818	51	4531	1.4	2.6	7.7
PLAYOFF TOTALS	58	2	1071	201	485	.414	44	155	.284	80	97	.825	20	86	106	160	127	0	43	97	7	526	1.8	2.8	9.1

EVANS, ROBERT W. (**Bob**) b. May 31, 1925 Ht. 6-2 Wt. 175 College—Indiana/Butler

SEASON—TEAM	G	GS	MIN	FGM	FGA	PCT	3FGM	3FGA	PCT	FTM	FTA	PCT	O-RB	D-RB	TOT	AST	PF	DQ	STL	TO	BLK	PTS	RPG	APG	PPG
49-50—Indianapolis	47	—	—	56	200	.280	—	—	—	30	44	.682	—	—	—	55	99	—	—	—	—	142	—	1.2	3.0
REG. SEASON TOTALS	47	—	—	56	200	.280	—	—	—	30	44	.682	—	—	—	55	99	—	—	—	—	142	—	1.2	3.0
PLAYOFF TOTALS	2	—	—	1	4	.250	—	—	—	0	0	—	—	—	—	—	3	—	—	—	—	2	0.0	0.0	1.0

EVANS, WILLIAM D. (**Billy**) b. March 3, 1947 Ht. 6-0 Wt. 170 College—Boston College

SEASON—TEAM	G	GS	MIN	FGM	FGA	PCT	3FGM	3FGA	PCT	FTM	FTA	PCT	O-RB	D-RB	TOT	AST	PF	DQ	STL	TO	BLK	PTS	RPG	APG	PPG
69-70—New York (A)	53	—	602	32	87	.368	0	2	.000	38	70	.543	—	—	39	100	89	1	—	—	—	102	0.7	1.9	1.9
REG. ABA TOTALS	53	—	602	32	87	.368	0	2	.000	38	70	.543	—	—	39	100	89	1	—	—	—	102	0.7	1.9	1.9
ABA PLAYOFF TOTALS	6	—	27	1	2	.500	0	1	.000	1	3	.333	—	—	3	1	7	0	—	—	—	3	0.5	0.2	0.5

EWING, PATRICK ALOYSIUS b. August 5, 1962 Ht. 7-0 Wt. 240 College—Georgetown

SEASON—TEAM	G	GS	MIN	FGM	FGA	PCT	3FGM	3FGA	PCT	FTM	FTA	PCT	O-RB	D-RB	TOT	AST	PF	DQ	STL	TO	BLK	PTS	RPG	APG	PPG
85-86—New York	50	50	1771	386	814	.474	0	5	.000	226	306	.739	124	327	451	102	191	7	54	172	103	998	9.0	2.0	20.0
86-87—New York	63	63	2206	530	1053	.503	0	7	.000	296	415	.713	157	398	555	104	248	5	89	229	147	1356	8.8	1.7	21.5
87-88—New York	82	82	2546	656	1183	.555	0	3	.000	341	476	.716	245	431	676	125	332	5	104	287	245	1653	8.2	1.5	20.2
88-89—New York	80	80	2896	727	1282	.567	0	6	.000	361	484	.746	213	527	740	188	311	5	117	266	281	1815	9.3	2.4	22.7
89-90—New York	82	82	3165	922	1673	.551	1	4	.250	502	648	.775	235	658	893	182	325	7	78	278	327	2347	10.9	2.2	28.6
90-91—New York	81	81	3104	845	1645	.514	0	6	.000	464	623	.745	194	711	905	244	287	3	80	291	258	2154	11.2	3.0	26.6
91-92—New York	82	82	3150	796	1525	.522	1	6	.167	377	511	.738	228	693	921	156	277	2	88	209	245	1970	11.2	1.9	24.0
92-93—New York	81	81	3003	779	1550	.503	1	7	.143	400	556	.719	191	789	980	151	286	2	74	265	161	1959	12.1	1.9	24.2
93-94—New York	79	79	2972	745	1503	.496	4	14	.286	445	582	.765	219	666	885	179	275	3	90	260	217	1939	11.2	2.3	24.5
REG. SEASON TOTALS	680	680	24813	6386	12228	.522	7	58	.121	3412	4601	.742	1806	5200	7006	1431	2532	39	774	2257	1984	16191	10.3	2.1	23.8
PLAYOFF TOTALS	78	78	3116	714	1507	.474	6	16	.375	365	487	.749	226	640	866	195	308	4	85	209	194	1799	11.1	2.5	23.1
ALL-STAR TOTALS	7	3	156	37	68	.544	0	0	—	14	22	.636	14	40	54	5	22	0	7	18	15	88	7.7	0.7	12.6

EZERSKY, JOHN J. (**Johnny**) b. 1921 Ht. 6-3 Wt. 175 College—Rhode Island

SEASON—TEAM	G	GS	MIN	FGM	FGA	PCT	3FGM	3FGA	PCT	FTM	FTA	PCT	O-RB	D-RB	TOT	AST	PF	DQ	STL	TO	BLK	PTS	RPG	APG	PPG
47-48—Tri-Cities (N)	5	—	—	9	—	—	—	—	—	5	8	.625	—	—	—	—	—	—	—	—	—	23	—	—	4.6
47-48—Providence	25	—	—	95	376	.253	—	—	—	63	104	.606	—	—	—	16	62	—	—	—	—	253	—	0.6	10.1
48-49—Prov.-Boston-Balt.	56	—	—	128	407	.314	—	—	—	109	160	.681	—	—	—	67	98	—	—	—	—	365	—	1.2	6.5
49-50—Balt.-Boston	54	—	—	143	487	.294	—	—	—	127	183	.694	—	—	—	86	139	—	—	—	—	413	—	1.6	7.6
REG. NBA TOTALS	135	—	—	366	1270	.288	—	—	—	299	447	.669	—	—	—	169	299	—	—	—	—	1031	—	1.3	7.6
REG. NBL TOTALS	5	—	—	9	—	—	—	—	—	5	8	.625	—	—	—	—	—	—	—	—	—	23	—	—	4.6

FABEL, JOSEPH (**Joe**) b. September 4, 1913 d. January 1967 Ht. 6-1 Wt. 190 College—Pittsburgh

SEASON—TEAM	G	GS	MIN	FGM	FGA	PCT	3FGM	3FGA	PCT	FTM	FTA	PCT	O-RB	D-RB	TOT	AST	PF	DQ	STL	TO	BLK	PTS	RPG	APG	PPG
38-39—Pittsburgh (N)	1	—	—	3	—	—	—	—	—	0	—	—	—	—	—	—	—	—	—	—	—	6	—	—	6.0
46-47—Pittsburgh	30	—	—	25	96	.260	—	—	—	13	26	.500	—	—	—	2	64	—	—	—	—	63	—	0.1	2.1
REG. NBA TOTALS	30	—	—	25	96	.260	—	—	—	13	26	.500	—	—	—	2	64	—	—	—	—	63	—	0.1	2.1
REG. NBL TOTALS	1	—	—	3	—	—	—	—	—	0	—	—	—	—	—	—	—	—	—	—	—	6	—	—	6.0

FAIRCHILD, JOHN RUSSELL b. April 28, 1943 Ht. 6-7½ Wt. 205 College—Palomar/Brigham Young

SEASON—TEAM	G	GS	MIN	FGM	FGA	PCT	3FGM	3FGA	PCT	FTM	FTA	PCT	O-RB	D-RB	TOT	AST	PF	DQ	STL	TO	BLK	PTS	RPG	APG	PPG
65-66—Los Angeles	30	—	171	23	89	.258	—	—	—	14	20	.700	—	—	45	11	33	0	—	—	—	60	1.5	0.4	2.0
67-68—Anaheim (A)	62	—	1311	271	620	.437	1	4	.250	135	200	.675	—	—	332	63	155	0	—	103	—	678	5.4	1.0	10.9
68-69—Denver-Indiana (A)	63	—	717	113	294	.384	10	29	.345	89	127	.701	—	—	129	37	98	1	—	74	—	325	2.0	0.6	5.2
69-70—Indiana-Ken. (A)	10	—	78	7	23	.304	3	5	.600	5	10	.500	—	—	17	4	18	0	—	—	—	22	1.7	0.4	2.2
REG. NBA TOTALS	30	—	171	23	89	.258	—	—	—	14	20	.700	—	—	45	11	33	0	—	—	—	60	1.5	0.4	2.0
REG. ABA TOTALS	135	—	2106	391	937	.417	14	38	.368	229	337	.680	—	—	478	104	271	1	—	177	—	1025	3.5	0.8	7.6
ABA PLAYOFF TOTALS	9	—	85	19	44	.432	4	10	.400	4	6	.667	—	—	21	3	13	0	—	4	—	46	2.3	0.3	5.1

FARBMAN, PHILIP M. (**Phil**) b. April 3, 1924 Ht. 6-4 Wt. 185 College—City College of New York/Brooklyn

SEASON—TEAM	G	GS	MIN	FGM	FGA	PCT	3FGM	3FGA	PCT	FTM	FTA	PCT	O-RB	D-RB	TOT	AST	PF	DQ	STL	TO	BLK	PTS	RPG	APG	PPG
48-49—Phil.-Boston	48	—	—	50	163	.307	—	—	—	55	81	.679	—	—	—	36	86	—	—	—	—	155	—	0.8	3.2
REG. SEASON TOTALS	48	—	—	50	163	.307	—	—	—	55	81	.679	—	—	—	36	86	—	—	—	—	155	—	0.8	3.2

FARLEY, RICHARD L. (**Dick**) b. April 13, 1932 d. October 1, 1969 Ht. 6-4 Wt. 190 College—Indiana

SEASON—TEAM	G	GS	MIN	FGM	FGA	PCT	3FGM	3FGA	PCT	FTM	FTA	PCT	O-RB	D-RB	TOT	AST	PF	DQ	STL	TO	BLK	PTS	RPG	APG	PPG
54-55—Syracuse	69	—	1113	136	353	.385	—	—	—	136	201	.677	—	—	167	111	145	1	—	—	—	408	2.4	1.6	5.9
55-56—Syracuse	72	—	1429	168	451	.373	—	—	—	143	207	.691	—	—	165	151	154	2	—	—	—	479	2.3	2.1	6.7
58-59—Detroit	70	—	1280	177	448	.395	—	—	—	137	186	.737	—	—	195	124	130	2	—	—	—	491	2.8	1.8	7.0
REG. SEASON TOTALS	211	—	3822	481	1252	.384	—	—	—	416	594	.700	—	—	527	386	429	5	—	—	—	1378	2.5	1.8	6.5
PLAYOFF TOTALS	22	—	370	58	140	.414	—	—	—	34	57	.596	—	—	40	51	66	2	—	—	—	150	1.8	2.3	6.8

FARMER, DON MICHAEL (Mike) b. September 26, 1936   Ht. 6-7   Wt. 210   College—San Francisco

SEASON—TEAM	G	GS	MIN	FGM	FGA	PCT	3FGM	3FGA	PCT	FTM	FTA	PCT	O-RB	D-RB	TOT	AST	PF	DQ	STL	TO	BLK	PTS	RPG	APG	PPG
58-59—New York	72	—	1545	176	498	.353	—	—	—	83	99	.838	—	—	315	66	152	1	—	—	—	435	4.4	0.9	6.0
59-60—New York	67	—	1536	212	568	.373	—	—	—	70	83	.843	—	—	385	57	130	1	—	—	—	494	5.7	0.9	7.4
60-61—N.Y.-Cin.	59	—	1301	180	461	.390	—	—	—	69	94	.734	—	—	380	81	130	1	—	—	—	429	6.4	1.4	7.3
62-63—St. Louis	80	—	1724	239	562	.425	—	—	—	117	139	.842	—	—	369	143	155	0	—	—	—	595	4.6	1.8	7.4
63-64—St. Louis	76	—	1361	178	438	.406	—	—	—	68	83	.819	—	—	225	109	140	0	—	—	—	424	3.0	1.4	5.6
64-65—St. Louis	60	—	1272	167	408	.409	—	—	—	75	94	.798	—	—	258	88	123	0	—	—	—	409	4.3	1.5	6.8
65-66—St. Louis	9	—	79	13	30	.433	—	—	—	4	5	.800	—	—	18	6	10	0	—	—	—	30	2.0	0.7	3.3
REG. SEASON TOTALS	423	—	8818	1165	2965	.393	—	—	—	486	597	.814	—	—	1950	550	840	3	—	—	—	2816	4.6	1.3	6.7
PLAYOFF TOTALS	25	—	412	53	129	.411	—	—	—	23	32	.719	—	—	79	36	45	0	—	—	—	129	3.2	1.4	5.2

FARMER, JAMES HUBERT III (Jim) b. September 23, 1964   Ht. 6-4   Wt. 190   College—Alabama

SEASON—TEAM	G	GS	MIN	FGM	FGA	PCT	3FGM	3FGA	PCT	FTM	FTA	PCT	O-RB	D-RB	TOT	AST	PF	DQ	STL	TO	BLK	PTS	RPG	APG	PPG
87-88—Dallas	30	0	157	26	69	.377	0	6	.000	9	10	.900	9	9	18	16	18	0	3	22	1	61	0.6	0.5	2.0
88-89—Utah	37	0	412	57	142	.401	9	20	.450	29	41	.707	22	33	55	28	41	0	9	26	0	152	1.5	0.8	4.1
89-90—Seattle	38	0	400	89	203	.438	8	27	.296	57	80	.713	17	26	43	25	44	0	17	27	1	243	1.1	0.7	6.4
90-91—Phil.-Denver	27	1	456	101	223	.453	5	23	.217	48	65	.738	29	39	68	38	58	0	13	38	2	255	2.5	1.4	9.4
93-94—Denver	4	0	29	2	6	.333	0	2	.000	0	0	—	0	2	2	4	3	0	0	5	0	4	0.5	1.0	1.0
REG. SEASON TOTALS	136	1	1454	275	643	.428	22	78	.282	143	196	.730	77	109	186	111	164	0	42	118	4	715	1.4	0.8	5.3
PLAYOFF TOTALS	5	0	14	2	8	.250	0	1	.000	0	0	—	3	1	4	1	2	0	0	2	0	4	0.8	0.2	0.8

FAUGHT, ROBERT EDWARD (Bob) b. September 2, 1921   Ht. 6-5   Wt. 185   College—Notre Dame

SEASON—TEAM	G	GS	MIN	FGM	FGA	PCT	3FGM	3FGA	PCT	FTM	FTA	PCT	O-RB	D-RB	TOT	AST	PF	DQ	STL	TO	BLK	PTS	RPG	APG	PPG
46-47—Cleveland	51	—	—	141	478	.295	—	—	—	61	106	.575	—	—	—	33	97	—	—	—	—	343	—	0.6	6.7
REG. SEASON TOTALS	51	—	—	141	478	.295	—	—	—	61	106	.575	—	—	—	33	97	—	—	—	—	343	—	0.6	6.7
PLAYOFF TOTALS	3	—	—	11	32	.344	—	—	—	3	3	1.000	—	—	—	1	10	1	—	—	—	25	—	0.3	8.3

FEDOR, SAMUEL DAVID (Dave) b. December 10, 1940   Ht. 6-6   Wt. 190   College—Florida State

SEASON—TEAM	G	GS	MIN	FGM	FGA	PCT	3FGM	3FGA	PCT	FTM	FTA	PCT	O-RB	D-RB	TOT	AST	PF	DQ	STL	TO	BLK	PTS	RPG	APG	PPG
62-63—San Francisco	7	—	27	3	10	.300	—	—	—	0	1	.000	—	—	6	1	4	0	—	—	—	6	0.9	0.1	0.9
REG. SEASON TOTALS	7	—	27	3	10	.300	—	—	—	0	1	.000	—	—	6	1	4	0	—	—	—	6	0.9	0.1	0.9

FEERICK, ROBERT JOSEPH (Bob) b. January 2, 1920   d. June 8, 1976   Ht. 6-3   Wt. 190   College—Santa Clara

SEASON—TEAM	G	GS	MIN	FGM	FGA	PCT	3FGM	3FGA	PCT	FTM	FTA	PCT	O-RB	D-RB	TOT	AST	PF	DQ	STL	TO	BLK	PTS	RPG	APG	PPG
45-46—Oshkosh (N)	21	—	—	81	—	—	—	—	—	36	44	.818	—	—	—	—	44	—	—	—	—	198	—	—	9.4
46-47—Washington	55	—	—	364	908	.401	—	—	—	198	260	.762	—	—	—	69	142	—	—	—	—	926	—	1.3	16.8
47-48—Washington	48	—	—	293	861	.340	—	—	—	189	240	.788	—	—	—	56	139	—	—	—	—	775	—	1.2	16.1
48-49—Washington	58	—	—	248	708	.350	—	—	—	256	298	.859	—	—	—	188	171	—	—	—	—	752	—	3.2	13.0
49-50—Washington	60	—	—	172	500	.344	—	—	—	139	174	.799	—	—	—	127	140	—	—	—	—	483	—	2.1	8.1
REG. NBA TOTALS	221	—	—	1077	2977	.362	—	—	—	782	972	.805	—	—	—	440	592	—	—	—	—	2936	—	2.0	13.3
REG. NBL TOTALS	21	—	—	81	—	—	—	—	—	36	44	.818	—	—	—	—	44	—	—	—	—	198	—	—	9.4
NBA PLAYOFF TOTALS	9	—	—	38	122	.311	—	—	—	25	33	.758	—	—	—	13	33	2	—	—	—	101	—	1.4	11.2
NBL PLAYOFF TOTALS	5	—	—	16	—	—	—	—	—	10	—	—	—	—	—	—	6	—	—	—	—	42	—	—	8.4

FEHER, RAYMOND G. (Butch) b. May 19, 1954   Ht. 6-4   Wt. 185   College—Vanderbilt

SEASON—TEAM	G	GS	MIN	FGM	FGA	PCT	3FGM	3FGA	PCT	FTM	FTA	PCT	O-RB	D-RB	TOT	AST	PF	DQ	STL	TO	BLK	PTS	RPG	APG	PPG
76-77—Phoenix	48	—	487	86	162	.531	—	—	—	76	99	.768	18	56	74	36	46	0	11	—	7	248	1.5	0.8	5.2
REG. SEASON TOTALS	48	—	487	86	162	.531	—	—	—	76	99	.768	18	56	74	36	46	0	11	—	7	248	1.5	0.8	5.2

FEIEREISEL, RONALD E. (Ron) b. August 6, 1931   Ht. 6-3   Wt. 185   College—DePaul

SEASON—TEAM	G	GS	MIN	FGM	FGA	PCT	3FGM	3FGA	PCT	FTM	FTA	PCT	O-RB	D-RB	TOT	AST	PF	DQ	STL	TO	BLK	PTS	RPG	APG	PPG
55-56—Minneapolis	10	—	59	8	28	.286	—	—	—	14	16	.875	—	—	6	6	9	0	—	—	—	30	0.6	0.6	3.0
REG. SEASON TOTALS	10	—	59	8	28	.286	—	—	—	14	16	.875	—	—	6	6	9	0	—	—	—	30	0.6	0.6	3.0

FEIGENBAUM, GEORGE b. July 2, 1929   Ht. 6-1   Wt. 185   College—Long Island University/Kentucky

SEASON—TEAM	G	GS	MIN	FGM	FGA	PCT	3FGM	3FGA	PCT	FTM	FTA	PCT	O-RB	D-RB	TOT	AST	PF	DQ	STL	TO	BLK	PTS	RPG	APG	PPG
49-50—Baltimore	12	—	—	14	57	.246	—	—	—	8	18	.444	—	—	—	10	15	—	—	—	—	36	—	0.8	3.0
52-53—Milwaukee	5	—	79	4	22	.182	—	—	—	8	15	.533	—	—	7	9	14	1	—	—	—	16	1.4	1.8	3.2
REG. SEASON TOTALS	17	—	79	18	79	.228	—	—	—	16	33	.485	—	—	7	19	29	1	—	—	—	52	1.4	1.1	3.1

FEITL, DAVE SCOTT b. June 8, 1962   Ht. 6-11 Wt. 240 College—Texas-El Paso

SEASON—TEAM	G	GS	MIN	FGM	FGA	PCT	3FGM	3FGA	PCT	FTM	FTA	PCT	O-RB	D-RB	TOT	AST	PF	DQ	STL	TO	BLK	PTS	RPG	APG	PPG
86-87—Houston	62	1	498	88	202	.436	0	1	.000	53	71	.746	39	78	117	22	83	0	9	38	4	229	1.9	0.4	3.7
87-88—Golden State	70	19	1128	182	404	.450	0	4	.000	94	134	.701	83	252	335	53	146	1	15	87	9	458	4.8	0.8	6.5
88-89—Washington	57	36	828	116	266	.436	0	1	.000	54	65	.831	69	133	202	36	136	0	17	65	18	286	3.5	0.6	5.0
90-91—Houston	52	2	372	52	140	.371	0	3	.000	33	44	.750	29	71	100	8	52	0	3	25	12	137	1.9	0.2	2.6
91-92—New Jersey	34	0	175	33	77	.429	0	0	—	16	19	.842	21	40	61	6	22	0	2	19	3	82	1.8	0.2	2.4
REG. SEASON TOTALS	275	58	3001	471	1089	.433	0	9	.000	250	333	.751	241	574	815	125	439	1	46	234	46	1192	3.0	0.5	4.3
PLAYOFF TOTALS	7	0	11	1	2	.500	0	0	—	2	2	1.000	0	2	2	—	0	0	0	1	0	4	0.3	0.0	0.6

FELIX, RAYMOND DARLINGTON (**Ray**) b. December 10, 1930 d. July 28, 1991 Ht. 6-11 Wt. 220 College—Long Island University

SEASON—TEAM	G	GS	MIN	FGM	FGA	PCT	3FGM	3FGA	PCT	FTM	FTA	PCT	O-RB	D-RB	TOT	AST	PF	DQ	STL	TO	BLK	PTS	RPG	APG	PPG
53-54—Baltimore	72	—	2672	410	983	.417	—	—	—	449	704	.638	—	—	958	82	253	5	—	—	—	1269	13.3	1.1	17.6
54-55—New York	72	—	2024	364	832	.438	—	—	—	310	498	.622	—	—	818	67	286	11	—	—	—	1038	11.4	0.9	14.4
55-56—New York	72	—	1702	277	668	.415	—	—	—	331	469	.706	—	—	623	47	293	13	—	—	—	885	8.7	0.7	12.3
56-57—New York	72	—	1622	295	709	.416	—	—	—	277	371	.747	—	—	587	36	284	8	—	—	—	867	8.2	0.5	12.0
57-58—New York	72	—	1709	304	688	.442	—	—	—	271	389	.697	—	—	747	52	283	12	—	—	—	879	10.4	0.7	12.2
58-59—New York	72	—	1588	260	700	.371	—	—	—	229	321	.713	—	—	569	49	275	9	—	—	—	749	7.9	0.7	10.4
59-60—N.Y.-Minn.	47	—	883	136	355	.383	—	—	—	70	112	.625	—	—	338	23	177	5	—	—	—	342	7.2	0.5	7.3
60-61—Los Angeles	78	—	1510	189	508	.372	—	—	—	135	193	.699	—	—	539	37	302	12	—	—	—	513	6.9	0.5	6.6
61-62—Los Angeles	80	—	1478	171	398	.430	—	—	—	90	130	.692	—	—	473	55	266	6	—	—	—	432	5.9	0.7	5.4
REG. SEASON TOTALS	637	—	15188	2406	5841	.412	—	—	—	2162	3187	.678	—	—	5652	448	2419	81	—	—	—	6974	8.9	0.7	10.9
PLAYOFF TOTALS	38	—	836	106	248	.427	—	—	—	89	127	.701	—	—	290	29	143	6	—	—	—	301	7.6	0.8	7.9
ALL-STAR TOTALS	1	—	32	4	8	.500	—	—	—	5	5	1.000	—	—	11	1	4	0	—	—	—	13	11.0	1.0	13.0

FENDLEY, JOHN PHILLIP (**Jake**) b. June 12, 1929 Ht. 6-1 Wt. 180 College—Northwestern

SEASON—TEAM	G	GS	MIN	FGM	FGA	PCT	3FGM	3FGA	PCT	FTM	FTA	PCT	O-RB	D-RB	TOT	AST	PF	DQ	STL	TO	BLK	PTS	RPG	APG	PPG
51-52—Fort Wayne	58	—	651	54	170	.318	—	—	—	75	95	.789	—	—	80	58	118	3	—	—	—	183	1.4	1.0	3.2
52-53—Fort Wayne	45	—	380	32	80	.400	—	—	—	40	60	.667	—	—	46	36	82	3	—	—	—	104	1.0	0.8	2.3
REG. SEASON TOTALS	103	—	1031	86	250	.344	—	—	—	115	155	.742	—	—	126	94	200	6	—	—	—	287	1.2	0.9	2.8
PLAYOFF TOTALS	2	—	6	1	4	.250	—	—	—	0	0	—	—	—	2	1	3	0	—	—	—	2	1.0	0.5	1.0

FENLEY, WILLIAM WARREN (**Bill**) b. February 8, 1922 Ht. 6-3½ Wt. 190 College—Manhattan

SEASON—TEAM	G	GS	MIN	FGM	FGA	PCT	3FGM	3FGA	PCT	FTM	FTA	PCT	O-RB	D-RB	TOT	AST	PF	DQ	STL	TO	BLK	PTS	RPG	APG	PPG
46-47—Boston	33	—	—	31	138	.225	—	—	—	23	45	.511	—	—	—	16	59	—	—	—	—	85	—	0.5	2.6
REG. SEASON TOTALS	33	—	—	31	138	.225	—	—	—	23	45	.511	—	—	—	16	59	—	—	—	—	85	—	0.5	2.6

FERNSTEN, ERIC ROBERT b. November 1, 1953 Ht. 6-10 Wt. 205 College—San Francisco

SEASON—TEAM	G	GS	MIN	FGM	FGA	PCT	3FGM	3FGA	PCT	FTM	FTA	PCT	O-RB	D-RB	TOT	AST	PF	DQ	STL	TO	BLK	PTS	RPG	APG	PPG
75-76—Clev.-Chicago	37	—	268	33	86	.384	—	—	—	26	37	.703	25	45	70	19	21	0	7	—	14	92	1.9	0.5	2.5
76-77—Chicago	5	—	61	3	15	.200	—	—	—	8	11	.727	9	7	16	6	9	0	1	—	3	14	3.2	1.2	2.8
79-80—Boston	56	—	431	71	153	.464	0	0	—	33	52	.635	40	56	96	28	43	0	17	20	12	175	1.7	0.5	3.1
80-81—Boston	45	—	279	38	79	.481	0	0	—	20	30	.667	29	33	62	10	29	0	6	20	7	96	1.4	0.2	2.1
81-82—Boston	43	0	202	19	49	.388	0	0	—	19	30	.633	12	30	42	8	23	0	5	13	7	57	1.0	0.2	1.3
83-84—New York	32	0	402	29	52	.558	0	0	—	25	34	.735	29	57	86	11	49	0	16	19	8	83	2.7	0.3	2.6
REG. SEASON TOTALS	218	0	1643	193	434	.445	0	0	—	131	194	.675	144	228	372	82	174	0	52	72	51	517	1.7	0.4	2.4
PLAYOFF TOTALS	20	0	46	4	13	.308	0	0	—	5	8	.625	6	5	11	1	4	0	1	2	4	13	0.6	0.1	0.7

FERRARI, ALBERT R. (**Al**) b. July 6, 1933 Ht. 6-4 Wt. 190 College—Michigan State

SEASON—TEAM	G	GS	MIN	FGM	FGA	PCT	3FGM	3FGA	PCT	FTM	FTA	PCT	O-RB	D-RB	TOT	AST	PF	DQ	STL	TO	BLK	PTS	RPG	APG	PPG
55-56—St. Louis	68	—	1611	191	534	.358	—	—	—	164	236	.695	—	—	186	163	192	3	—	—	—	546	2.7	2.4	8.0
58-59—St. Louis	72	—	1189	134	385	.348	—	—	—	145	199	.729	—	—	142	122	155	1	—	—	—	413	2.0	1.7	5.7
59-60—St. Louis	71	—	1567	216	523	.413	—	—	—	176	225	.782	—	—	162	188	205	7	—	—	—	608	2.3	2.6	8.6
60-61—St. Louis	63	—	1031	117	328	.357	—	—	—	95	116	.819	—	—	115	143	157	4	—	—	—	329	1.8	2.3	5.2
61-62—St. Louis	79	—	2046	208	582	.357	—	—	—	175	219	.799	—	—	213	313	278	9	—	—	—	591	2.7	4.0	7.5
62-63—Chicago	18	—	138	12	37	.324	—	—	—	14	17	.824	—	—	12	14	21	0	—	—	—	38	0.7	0.8	2.1
REG. SEASON TOTALS	371	—	7582	878	2389	.368	—	—	—	769	1012	.760	—	—	830	943	1008	24	—	—	—	2525	2.2	2.5	6.8
PLAYOFF TOTALS	33	—	736	81	207	.391	—	—	—	94	130	.723	—	—	79	75	97	2	—	—	—	256	2.4	2.3	7.8

FERREIRA, ROLANDO JR. b. May 24, 1964 Ht. 7-1 Wt. 240 College—Houston

SEASON—TEAM	G	GS	MIN	FGM	FGA	PCT	3FGM	3FGA	PCT	FTM	FTA	PCT	O-RB	D-RB	TOT	AST	PF	DQ	STL	TO	BLK	PTS	RPG	APG	PPG
88-89—Portland	12	0	34	1	18	.056	0	0	—	7	8	.875	4	9	13	1	7	0	0	6	1	9	1.1	0.1	0.8
REG. SEASON TOTALS	12	0	34	1	18	.056	0	0	—	7	8	.875	4	9	13	1	7	0	0	6	1	9	1.1	0.1	0.8

FERRELL, DUANE b. February 28, 1965 Ht. 6-7 Wt. 215 College—Georgia Tech

SEASON—TEAM	G	GS	MIN	FGM	FGA	PCT	3FGM	3FGA	PCT	FTM	FTA	PCT	O-RB	D-RB	TOT	AST	PF	DQ	STL	TO	BLK	PTS	RPG	APG	PPG
88-89—Atlanta	41	0	231	35	83	.422	0	0	—	30	44	.682	19	22	41	10	33	0	7	12	6	100	1.0	0.2	2.4
89-90—Atlanta	14	0	29	5	14	.357	0	1	.000	2	6	.333	3	4	7	2	3	0	1	2	0	12	0.5	0.1	0.9
90-91—Atlanta	78	2	1165	174	356	.489	2	3	.667	125	156	.801	97	82	179	55	151	3	33	78	27	475	2.3	0.7	6.1
91-92—Atlanta	66	12	1598	331	632	.524	11	33	.333	166	218	.761	105	105	210	92	134	0	49	99	17	839	3.2	1.4	12.7
92-93—Atlanta	82	15	1736	327	696	.470	9	36	.250	176	226	.779	97	94	191	132	160	1	59	103	17	839	2.3	1.6	10.2
93-94—Atlanta	72	13	1155	184	379	.485	1	9	.111	144	184	.783	62	67	129	65	85	0	44	64	16	513	1.8	0.9	7.1
REG. SEASON TOTALS	353	42	5914	1056	2160	.489	23	82	.280	643	834	.771	383	374	757	356	566	4	193	358	83	2778	2.1	1.0	7.9
PLAYOFF TOTALS	19	0	314	47	104	.452	2	7	.286	39	53	.736	29	24	53	21	40	0	5	11	3	135	2.8	1.1	7.1

FERRIN, C. ARNOLD JR. (**Arnie**) b. July 29, 1925 Ht. 6-4 Wt. 180 College—Utah

SEASON—TEAM	G	GS	MIN	FGM	FGA	PCT	3FGM	3FGA	PCT	FTM	FTA	PCT	O-RB	D-RB	TOT	AST	PF	DQ	STL	TO	BLK	PTS	RPG	APG	PPG
48-49—Minneapolis	47	—	—	130	378	.344	—	—	—	85	128	.664	—	—	—	76	142	—	—	—	—	345	—	1.6	7.3
49-50—Minneapolis	63	—	—	132	396	.333	—	—	—	76	109	.697	—	—	—	95	147	—	—	—	—	340	—	1.5	5.4
50-51—Minneapolis	68	—	—	119	373	.319	—	—	—	114	164	.695	—	—	271	107	220	8	—	—	—	352	4.0	1.6	5.2
REG. SEASON TOTALS	178	—	—	381	1147	.332	—	—	—	275	401	.686	—	—	271	278	509	8	—	—	—	1037	4.0	1.6	5.8
PLAYOFF TOTALS	29	—	—	71	210	.338	—	—	—	63	92	.685	—	—	33	67	113	7	—	—	—	205	4.7	2.3	7.1

FERRY, DANIEL JOHN WILLARD (**Danny**) b. October 17, 1966 Ht. 6-10 Wt. 245 College—Duke

SEASON—TEAM	G	GS	MIN	FGM	FGA	PCT	3FGM	3FGA	PCT	FTM	FTA	PCT	O-RB	D-RB	TOT	AST	PF	DQ	STL	TO	BLK	PTS	RPG	APG	PPG
90-91—Cleveland	81	2	1661	275	643	.428	23	77	.299	124	152	.816	99	187	286	142	230	1	43	120	25	697	3.5	1.8	8.6
91-92—Cleveland	68	1	937	134	328	.409	17	48	.354	61	73	.836	53	160	213	75	135	0	22	46	15	346	3.1	1.1	5.1
92-93—Cleveland	76	1	1461	220	459	.479	34	82	.415	99	113	.876	81	198	279	137	171	1	29	83	49	573	3.7	1.8	7.5
93-94—Cleveland	70	1	965	149	334	.446	14	51	.275	38	43	.884	47	94	141	74	113	0	28	41	22	350	2.0	1.1	5.0
REG. SEASON TOTALS	295	5	5024	778	1764	.441	88	258	.341	322	381	.845	280	639	919	428	649	2	122	290	111	1966	3.1	1.5	6.7
PLAYOFF TOTALS	18	0	177	20	49	.408	5	12	.417	13	14	.929	11	30	41	16	22	0	5	10	4	58	2.3	0.9	3.2

FERRY, ROBERT DEAN (**Bob**) b. May 31, 1937 Ht. 6-8 Wt. 230 College—St. Louis

SEASON—TEAM	G	GS	MIN	FGM	FGA	PCT	3FGM	3FGA	PCT	FTM	FTA	PCT	O-RB	D-RB	TOT	AST	PF	DQ	STL	TO	BLK	PTS	RPG	APG	PPG
59-60—St. Louis	62	—	875	144	338	.426	—	—	—	76	119	.639	—	—	233	40	132	2	—	—	—	364	3.8	0.6	5.9
60-61—Detroit	79	—	1657	350	776	.451	—	—	—	189	255	.741	—	—	500	129	205	1	—	—	—	889	6.3	1.6	11.3
61-62—Detroit	80	—	1918	411	939	.438	—	—	—	286	422	.678	—	—	503	145	199	2	—	—	—	1108	6.3	1.8	13.9
62-63—Detroit	79	—	2479	426	984	.433	—	—	—	220	339	.649	—	—	537	170	246	1	—	—	—	1072	6.8	2.2	13.6
63-64—Detroit	74	—	1522	298	670	.445	—	—	—	186	279	.667	—	—	428	94	174	2	—	—	—	782	5.8	1.3	10.6
64-65—Baltimore	77	—	1280	143	338	.423	—	—	—	122	199	.613	—	—	355	60	156	2	—	—	—	408	4.6	0.8	5.3
65-66—Baltimore	66	—	1229	188	457	.411	—	—	—	105	157	.669	—	—	334	111	134	1	—	—	—	481	5.1	1.7	7.3
66-67—Baltimore	51	—	991	132	315	.419	—	—	—	70	110	.636	—	—	258	92	97	0	—	—	—	334	5.1	1.8	6.5
67-68—Baltimore	59	—	841	128	311	.412	—	—	—	73	117	.624	—	—	186	61	92	0	—	—	—	329	3.2	1.0	5.6
68-69—Baltimore	7	—	36	5	14	.357	—	—	—	3	6	.500	—	—	9	4	3	0	—	—	—	13	1.3	0.6	1.9
REG. SEASON TOTALS	634	—	12828	2225	5142	.433	—	—	—	1330	2003	.664	—	—	3343	906	1438	11	—	—	—	5780	5.3	1.4	9.1
PLAYOFF TOTALS	42	—	681	115	255	.451	—	—	—	89	145	.614	—	—	198	46	70	0	—	—	—	319	4.7	1.1	7.6

FIELDS, KENNETH HENRY (**Kenny**) b. February 9, 1962 Ht. 6-5 Wt. 240 College—UCLA

SEASON—TEAM	G	GS	MIN	FGM	FGA	PCT	3FGM	3FGA	PCT	FTM	FTA	PCT	O-RB	D-RB	TOT	AST	PF	DQ	STL	TO	BLK	PTS	RPG	APG	PPG
84-85—Milwaukee	51	1	535	84	191	.440	0	0	—	27	36	.750	41	43	84	38	84	2	9	32	10	195	1.6	0.7	3.8
85-86—Milwaukee	78	3	1120	204	398	.513	0	4	.000	91	132	.689	59	144	203	79	170	3	51	77	15	499	2.6	1.0	6.4
86-87—Milw.-L.A.-Clips	48	17	883	159	352	.452	3	12	.250	73	94	.777	63	85	148	61	123	2	32	53	11	394	3.1	1.3	8.2
87-88—L.A. Clippers	7	0	154	16	36	.444	0	0	—	20	26	.769	13	16	29	10	17	0	5	19	2	52	4.1	1.4	7.4
REG. SEASON TOTALS	184	21	2692	463	977	.474	3	16	.188	211	288	.733	176	288	464	188	394	7	97	181	38	1140	2.5	1.0	6.2
PLAYOFF TOTALS	12	4	158	38	69	.551	1	3	.333	12	23	.522	7	21	28	10	23	0	8	16	0	89	2.3	0.8	7.4

FIELDS, ROBERT L. (**Bobby**) b. October 20, 1949 Ht. 6-2½ Wt. 175 College—Brandywine/La Salle

SEASON—TEAM	G	GS	MIN	FGM	FGA	PCT	3FGM	3FGA	PCT	FTM	FTA	PCT	O-RB	D-RB	TOT	AST	PF	DQ	STL	TO	BLK	PTS	RPG	APG	PPG
71-72—Utah (A)	22	—	124	22	48	.458	2	7	.286	8	13	.615	—	—	30	20	33	—	—	21	—	54	1.4	0.9	2.5
REG. ABA TOTALS	22	—	124	22	48	.458	2	7	.286	8	13	.615	—	—	30	20	33	—	—	21	—	54	1.4	0.9	2.5

FILIPEK, RONALD STANLEY (**Ron**) b. February 5, 1944 Ht. 6-5 Wt. 210 College—Tennessee Tech

SEASON—TEAM	G	GS	MIN	FGM	FGA	PCT	3FGM	3FGA	PCT	FTM	FTA	PCT	O-RB	D-RB	TOT	AST	PF	DQ	STL	TO	BLK	PTS	RPG	APG	PPG
67-68—Philadelphia	19	—	73	18	47	.383	—	—	—	7	14	.500	—	—	25	7	12	0	—	—	—	43	1.3	0.4	2.3
REG. SEASON TOTALS	19	—	73	18	47	.383	—	—	—	7	14	.500	—	—	25	7	12	0	—	—	—	43	1.3	0.4	2.3

FILLMORE, GREGORY PAUL (**Greg**) b. March 7, 1947 Ht. 7-1 Wt. 250 College—Fort Dodge CC/Cheyney State

SEASON—TEAM	G	GS	MIN	FGM	FGA	PCT	3FGM	3FGA	PCT	FTM	FTA	PCT	O-RB	D-RB	TOT	AST	PF	DQ	STL	TO	BLK	PTS	RPG	APG	PPG
70-71—New York	39	—	271	45	102	.441	—	—	—	13	27	.481	—	—	93	17	80	0	—	—	—	103	2.4	0.4	2.6
71-72—New York	10	—	67	7	27	.259	—	—	—	1	3	.333	—	—	15	3	17	0	—	—	—	15	1.5	0.3	1.5
REG. SEASON TOTALS	49	—	338	52	129	.403	—	—	—	14	30	.467	—	—	108	20	97	0	—	—	—	118	2.2	0.4	2.4
PLAYOFF TOTALS	8	—	24	0	4	.000	—	—	—	0	0	—	—	—	8	1	9	0	—	—	—	0	1.0	0.1	0.0

FINCH, LARRY O. b. February 16, 1951   Ht. 6-2 Wt. 195 College—Memphis State

SEASON—TEAM	G	GS	MIN	FGM	FGA	PCT	3FGM	3FGA	PCT	FTM	FTA	PCT	O-RB	D-RB	TOT	AST	PF	DQ	STL	TO	BLK	PTS	RPG	APG	PPG
73-74—Memphis (A)	65	—	1154	164	399	.411	7	26	.269	108	136	.794	24	50	74	111	162	—	26	95	1	443	1.1	1.7	6.8
74-75—Memphis (A)	63	—	1888	264	593	.445	20	53	.377	115	133	.865	44	99	143	190	164	—	52	90	6	663	2.3	3.0	10.5
REG. ABA TOTALS	128	—	3042	428	992	.431	27	79	.342	223	269	.829	68	149	217	301	326	0	78	185	7	1106	1.7	2.4	8.6

FINKEL, HENRY J. (**Hank**) b. April 20, 1942   Ht. 7-0 Wt. 240 College—St. Peter's/Dayton

SEASON—TEAM	G	GS	MIN	FGM	FGA	PCT	3FGM	3FGA	PCT	FTM	FTA	PCT	O-RB	D-RB	TOT	AST	PF	DQ	STL	TO	BLK	PTS	RPG	APG	PPG
66-67—Los Angeles	27	—	141	17	47	.362	—	—	—	7	12	.583	—	—	64	5	39	1	—	—	—	41	2.4	0.2	1.5
67-68—San Diego	53	—	1116	242	492	.492	—	—	—	131	191	.686	—	—	375	72	175	5	—	—	—	615	7.1	1.4	11.6
68-69—San Diego	35	—	332	49	111	.441	—	—	—	31	41	.756	—	—	107	21	53	1	—	—	—	129	3.1	0.6	3.7
69-70—Boston	80	—	1866	310	683	.454	—	—	—	156	233	.670	—	—	613	103	292	13	—	—	—	776	7.7	1.3	9.7
70-71—Boston	80	—	1234	214	489	.438	—	—	—	93	127	.732	—	—	343	79	196	5	—	—	—	521	4.3	1.0	6.5
71-72—Boston	78	—	736	103	254	.406	—	—	—	43	74	.581	—	—	251	61	118	4	—	—	—	249	3.2	0.8	3.2
72-73—Boston	76	—	496	78	173	.451	—	—	—	28	52	.538	—	—	151	26	83	0	—	—	—	184	2.0	0.3	2.4
73-74—Boston	60	—	427	60	130	.462	—	—	—	28	43	.651	41	94	135	27	62	1	3	—	7	148	2.3	0.5	2.5
74-75—Boston	62	—	518	52	129	.403	—	—	—	23	43	.535	33	79	112	32	72	0	1	—	3	127	1.8	0.5	2.0
REG. SEASON TOTALS	551	—	6866	1125	2508	.449	—	—	—	540	816	.662	74	173	2151	426	1090	30	10	—	10	2790	3.9	0.8	5.1
PLAYOFF TOTALS	33	—	175	27	59	.458	—	—	—	4	6	.667	8	8	53	13	29	0	1	—	0	58	1.6	0.4	1.8

FINN, DANIEL LAWRENCE JR. (**Danny**) b. May 27, 1928   Ht. 6-1 Wt. 185 College—St. John's

SEASON—TEAM	G	GS	MIN	FGM	FGA	PCT	3FGM	3FGA	PCT	FTM	FTA	PCT	O-RB	D-RB	TOT	AST	PF	DQ	STL	TO	BLK	PTS	RPG	APG	PPG
52-53—Philadelphia	31	—	1015	135	409	.330	—	—	—	99	182	.544	—	—	175	146	124	9	—	—	—	369	5.6	4.7	11.9
53-54—Philadelphia	68	—	1562	170	495	.343	—	—	—	126	196	.643	—	—	216	265	215	7	—	—	—	466	3.2	3.9	6.9
54-55—Philadelphia	43	—	820	77	265	.291	—	—	—	53	86	.616	—	—	157	155	114	3	—	—	—	207	3.7	3.6	4.8
REG. SEASON TOTALS	142	—	3397	382	1169	.327	—	—	—	278	464	.599	—	—	548	566	453	19	—	—	—	1042	3.9	4.0	7.3

FISHER, RICHARD B. (**Rick**) b. October 27, 1948   Ht. 6-5 Wt. 220 College—Colorado State

SEASON—TEAM	G	GS	MIN	FGM	FGA	PCT	3FGM	3FGA	PCT	FTM	FTA	PCT	O-RB	D-RB	TOT	AST	PF	DQ	STL	TO	BLK	PTS	RPG	APG	PPG
71-72—Utah-Fla. (A)	12	—	66	18	34	.529	0	0	—	1	1	1.000	—	—	32	5	9	—	—	4	—	37	2.7	0.4	3.1
REG. ABA TOTALS	12	—	66	18	34	.529	0	0	—	1	1	1.000	—	—	32	5	9	—	—	4	—	37	2.7	0.4	3.1

FITZGERALD, RICHARD (**Dick**) b. November 18, 1920 d. April 13, 1968 Ht. 6-5 Wt. 175 College—Seton Hall

SEASON—TEAM	G	GS	MIN	FGM	FGA	PCT	3FGM	3FGA	PCT	FTM	FTA	PCT	O-RB	D-RB	TOT	AST	PF	DQ	STL	TO	BLK	PTS	RPG	APG	PPG
46-47—Toronto	60	—	—	118	495	.238	—	—	—	41	60	.683	—	—	—	40	89	—	—	—	—	277	—	0.7	4.6
47-48—Providence	1	—	—	0	3	.000	—	—	—	0	0	—	—	—	0	1	—	—	—	—	—	0	—	0.0	0.0
REG. SEASON TOTALS	61	—	—	118	498	.237	—	—	—	41	60	.683	—	—	—	40	90	—	—	—	—	277	—	0.7	4.5

FITZGERALD, ROBERT (**Bob**) b. March 14, 1923 d. July 1983 Ht. 6-5 Wt. 190 College—Fordham

SEASON—TEAM	G	GS	MIN	FGM	FGA	PCT	3FGM	3FGA	PCT	FTM	FTA	PCT	O-RB	D-RB	TOT	AST	PF	DQ	STL	TO	BLK	PTS	RPG	APG	PPG
45-46—Rochester (N)	10	—	—	9	—	—	—	—	—	15	—	—	—	—	—	—	—	—	—	—	—	33	—	—	3.3
46-47—Toronto-N.Y.	60	—	—	70	362	.193	—	—	—	81	130	.623	—	—	—	35	153	—	—	—	—	221	—	0.6	3.7
47-48—Syracuse (N)	1	—	—	0	—	—	—	—	—	0	1	.000	—	—	—	0	—	—	—	—	—	0	—	—	0.0
48-49—Rochester	18	—	—	6	29	.207	—	—	—	7	10	.700	—	—	—	12	26	—	—	—	—	19	—	0.7	1.1
REG. NBA TOTALS	78	—	—	76	391	.194	—	—	—	88	140	.629	—	—	—	47	179	—	—	—	—	240	—	0.6	3.1
REG. NBL TOTALS	11	—	—	9	—	—	—	—	—	15	1	.000	—	—	—	—	—	—	—	—	—	33	—	—	3.0
NBA PLAYOFF TOTALS	6	—	—	1	10	.100	—	—	—	3	4	.750	—	—	—	1	4	—	—	—	—	5	—	0.2	0.8
NBL PLAYOFF TOTALS	6	—	—	2	—	—	—	—	—	6	8	.750	—	—	—	—	6	—	—	—	—	10	—	—	1.7

FLEISHMAN, JEROME (**Jerry**) b. February 14, 1922   Ht. 6-2 Wt. 190 College—New York University/Long Island University

SEASON—TEAM	G	GS	MIN	FGM	FGA	PCT	3FGM	3FGA	PCT	FTM	FTA	PCT	O-RB	D-RB	TOT	AST	PF	DQ	STL	TO	BLK	PTS	RPG	APG	PPG
46-47—Philadelphia	59	—	—	97	372	.261	—	—	—	69	127	.543	—	—	—	40	101	—	—	—	—	263	—	0.7	4.5
47-48—Philadelphia	46	—	—	119	501	.238	—	—	—	95	138	.688	—	—	—	43	122	—	—	—	—	333	—	0.9	7.2
48-49—Philadelphia	59	—	—	123	424	.290	—	—	—	77	118	.653	—	—	—	120	137	—	—	—	—	323	—	2.0	5.5
49-50—Philadelphia	65	—	—	102	353	.289	—	—	—	93	151	.616	—	—	—	118	129	—	—	—	—	297	—	1.8	4.6
52-53—Phil.-N.Y.	33	—	882	100	303	.330	—	—	—	96	140	.686	—	—	152	108	118	7	—	—	—	296	4.6	3.3	9.0
REG. SEASON TOTALS	262	—	882	541	1953	.277	—	—	—	430	674	.638	—	—	152	429	607	7	—	—	—	1512	4.6	1.6	5.8
PLAYOFF TOTALS	22	—	26	37	131	.282	—	—	—	31	49	.633	—	—	5	19	45	3	—	—	—	105	2.5	0.9	4.8

FLEMING, ALBERT JR. (**Al**) b. April 5, 1954   Ht. 6-7 Wt. 215 College—Arizona

SEASON—TEAM	G	GS	MIN	FGM	FGA	PCT	3FGM	3FGA	PCT	FTM	FTA	PCT	O-RB	D-RB	TOT	AST	PF	DQ	STL	TO	BLK	PTS	RPG	APG	PPG
77-78—Seattle	20	—	97	15	31	.484	—	—	—	10	17	.588	13	17	30	7	16	0	0	16	5	40	1.5	0.4	2.0
REG. SEASON TOTALS	20	—	97	15	31	.484	—	—	—	10	17	.588	13	17	30	7	16	0	0	16	5	40	1.5	0.4	2.0
PLAYOFF TOTALS	5	—	21	2	6	.333	—	—	—	3	4	.750	1	3	4	2	5	0	1	2	0	7	0.8	0.4	1.4

FLEMING, EDWARD R. (Ed) b. July 25, 1933   Ht. 6-3   Wt. 190   College—Niagara

SEASON—TEAM	G	GS	MIN	FGM	FGA	PCT	3FGM	3FGA	PCT	FTM	FTA	PCT	O-RB	D-RB	TOT	AST	PF	DQ	STL	TO	BLK	PTS	RPG	APG	PPG
55-56—Rochester	71	—	2028	306	824	.371	—	—	—	277	372	.745	—	—	489	197	178	1	—	—	—	889	6.9	2.8	12.5
56-57—Rochester	51	—	927	109	364	.299	—	—	—	139	191	.728	—	—	183	81	94	0	—	—	—	357	3.6	1.6	7.0
57-58—Minneapolis	72	—	1686	226	655	.345	—	—	—	181	255	.710	—	—	492	139	222	5	—	—	—	633	6.8	1.9	8.8
58-59—Minneapolis	71	—	1132	162	419	.387	—	—	—	137	190	.721	—	—	281	89	148	1	—	—	—	461	4.0	1.3	6.5
59-60—Minneapolis	27	—	413	59	141	.418	—	—	—	53	69	.768	—	—	87	38	46	0	—	—	—	171	3.2	1.4	6.3
REG. SEASON TOTALS	292	—	6186	862	2403	.359	—	—	—	787	1077	.731	—	—	1532	544	688	7	—	—	—	2511	5.2	1.9	8.6
PLAYOFF TOTALS	13	—	178	27	77	.351	—	—	—	22	25	.880	—	—	39	18	32	0	—	—	—	76	3.0	1.4	5.8

FLEMING, VERN b. February 4, 1962   Ht. 6-5   Wt. 185   College—Georgia

SEASON—TEAM	G	GS	MIN	FGM	FGA	PCT	3FGM	3FGA	PCT	FTM	FTA	PCT	O-RB	D-RB	TOT	AST	PF	DQ	STL	TO	BLK	PTS	RPG	APG	PPG
84-85—Indiana	80	65	2486	433	922	.470	0	4	.000	260	339	.767	148	175	323	247	232	4	99	197	8	1126	4.0	3.1	14.1
85-86—Indiana	80	77	2870	436	862	.506	1	6	.167	263	353	.745	102	284	386	505	230	3	131	208	5	1136	4.8	6.3	14.2
86-87—Indiana	82	82	2549	370	727	.509	2	10	.200	238	302	.788	109	225	334	473	222	3	109	167	18	980	4.1	5.8	12.0
87-88—Indiana	80	80	2733	442	845	.523	0	13	.000	227	283	.802	106	258	364	568	225	0	115	175	11	1111	4.6	7.1	13.9
88-89—Indiana	76	69	2552	419	814	.515	3	23	.130	243	304	.799	85	225	310	494	212	4	77	192	12	1084	4.1	6.5	14.3
89-90—Indiana	82	82	2876	467	919	.508	12	34	.353	230	294	.782	118	204	322	610	213	1	92	206	10	1176	3.9	7.4	14.3
90-91—Indiana	69	45	1929	356	671	.531	4	18	.222	161	221	.729	83	131	214	369	116	0	76	137	13	877	3.1	5.3	12.7
91-92—Indiana	82	6	1737	294	610	.482	6	27	.222	132	179	.737	69	140	209	266	134	0	56	140	7	726	2.5	3.2	8.9
92-93—Indiana	75	8	1503	280	554	.505	7	36	.194	143	197	.726	63	106	169	224	126	1	63	121	9	710	2.3	3.0	9.5
93-94—Indiana	55	5	1053	147	318	.462	0	4	.000	64	87	.736	27	96	123	173	98	1	40	87	6	358	2.2	3.1	6.5
REG. SEASON TOTALS	761	519	22288	3644	7242	.503	35	175	.200	1961	2559	.766	910	1844	2754	3929	1808	17	858	1630	99	9284	3.6	5.2	12.2
PLAYOFF TOTALS	34	11	747	108	231	.468	2	13	.154	64	80	.800	36	48	84	112	69	1	22	57	7	282	2.5	3.3	8.3

FLOWERS, BRUCE DOUGLAS b. June 13, 1957   Ht. 6-8   Wt. 225   College—Notre Dame

SEASON—TEAM	G	GS	MIN	FGM	FGA	PCT	3FGM	3FGA	PCT	FTM	FTA	PCT	O-RB	D-RB	TOT	AST	PF	DQ	STL	TO	BLK	PTS	RPG	APG	PPG
82-83—Cleveland	53	5	699	110	206	.534	0	2	.000	41	53	.774	71	109	180	47	99	2	19	43	12	261	3.4	0.9	4.9
REG. SEASON TOTALS	53	5	699	110	206	.534	0	2	.000	41	53	.774	71	109	180	47	99	2	19	43	12	261	3.4	0.9	4.9

FLOYD, ERIC AUGUSTUS (Sleepy) b. March 6, 1960   Ht. 6-3   Wt. 185   College—Georgetown

SEASON—TEAM	G	GS	MIN	FGM	FGA	PCT	3FGM	3FGA	PCT	FTM	FTA	PCT	O-RB	D-RB	TOT	AST	PF	DQ	STL	TO	BLK	PTS	RPG	APG	PPG
82-83—N.J.-G.S.	76	17	1248	226	527	.429	10	25	.400	150	180	.833	56	81	137	138	134	3	58	106	17	612	1.8	1.8	8.1
83-84—Golden State	77	73	2555	484	1045	.463	8	45	.178	315	386	.816	87	184	271	269	216	0	103	196	31	1291	3.5	3.5	16.8
84-85—Golden State	82	82	2873	610	1372	.445	42	143	.294	336	415	.810	62	140	202	406	226	1	134	251	41	1598	2.5	5.0	19.5
85-86—Golden State	82	82	2764	510	1007	.506	39	119	.328	351	441	.796	76	221	297	746	199	2	157	290	16	1410	3.6	9.1	17.2
86-87—Golden State	82	82	3064	503	1030	.488	73	190	.384	462	537	.860	56	212	268	848	199	1	146	280	18	1541	3.3	10.3	18.8
87-88—G.S.-Houston	77	73	2514	420	969	.433	14	72	.194	301	354	.850	77	219	296	544	190	1	95	223	12	1155	3.8	7.1	15.0
88-89—Houston	82	82	2788	396	893	.443	109	292	.373	261	309	.845	48	258	306	709	196	1	124	253	11	1162	3.7	8.6	14.2
89-90—Houston	82	73	2630	362	803	.451	89	234	.380	187	232	.806	46	152	198	600	159	0	94	204	11	1000	2.4	7.3	12.2
90-91—Houston	82	4	1850	386	939	.411	48	176	.273	185	246	.752	52	107	159	317	122	0	95	140	17	1005	1.9	3.9	12.3
91-92—Houston	82	3	1662	286	704	.406	37	123	.301	135	170	.794	34	116	150	239	128	0	57	128	21	744	1.8	2.9	9.1
92-93—Houston	52	10	867	124	305	.407	16	56	.286	81	102	.794	14	72	86	132	59	0	32	68	6	345	1.7	2.5	6.6
93-94—San Antonio	53	2	737	70	209	.335	8	36	.222	52	78	.667	10	60	70	101	71	0	12	61	8	200	1.3	1.9	3.8
REG. SEASON TOTALS	909	583	25552	4377	9803	.446	493	1511	.326	2816	3450	.816	618	1822	2440	5049	1899	9	1107	2200	209	12063	2.7	5.6	13.3
PLAYOFF TOTALS	36	22	1038	171	374	.457	29	70	.414	96	118	.814	23	54	77	219	58	0	43	92	5	467	2.1	6.1	13.0
ALL-STAR TOTALS	1	0	19	4	7	.571	1	3	.333	5	7	.714	2	3	5	1	2	0	1	2	0	14	5.0	1.0	14.0

FLYNN, MICHAEL DAVID (Mike) b. July 31, 1953   Ht. 6-3   Wt. 190   College—Kentucky

SEASON—TEAM	G	GS	MIN	FGM	FGA	PCT	3FGM	3FGA	PCT	FTM	FTA	PCT	O-RB	D-RB	TOT	AST	PF	DQ	STL	TO	BLK	PTS	RPG	APG	PPG
75-76—Indiana (A)	67	—	1097	166	439	.378	25	99	.253	64	111	.577	63	70	133	133	112	—	44	81	9	421	2.0	2.0	6.3
76-77—Indiana	73	—	1324	250	573	.436	—	—	—	101	142	.711	76	111	187	179	106	0	57	—	6	601	2.6	2.5	8.2
77-78—Indiana	71	—	955	120	267	.449	—	—	—	55	97	.567	47	70	117	142	52	0	41	75	10	295	1.6	2.0	4.2
REG. NBA TOTALS	144	—	2279	370	840	.440	—	—	—	156	239	.653	123	181	304	321	158	0	98	75	16	896	2.1	2.2	6.2
REG. ABA TOTALS	67	—	1097	166	439	.378	25	99	.253	64	111	.577	63	70	133	133	112	—	44	81	9	421	2.0	2.0	6.3
ABA PLAYOFF TOTALS	3	—	83	15	30	.500	3	8	.375	8	11	.727	5	5	10	10	6	—	3	5	0	41	3.3	3.3	13.7

FOGLE, LARRY b. March 19, 1953   Ht. 6-5   Wt. 205   College—Southwestern Lousiana/Canisius

SEASON—TEAM	G	GS	MIN	FGM	FGA	PCT	3FGM	3FGA	PCT	FTM	FTA	PCT	O-RB	D-RB	TOT	AST	PF	DQ	STL	TO	BLK	PTS	RPG	APG	PPG
75-76—New York	2	—	14	1	5	.200	—	—	—	0	0	—	1	2	3	0	4	0	1	—	0	2	1.5	0.0	1.0
REG. SEASON TOTALS	2	—	14	1	5	.200	—	—	—	0	0	—	1	2	3	0	4	0	1	—	0	2	1.5	0.0	1.0

FOLEY, JOHN E. (Jack, Jack the Shot) b. April 19, 1939   Ht. 6-5   Wt. 185   College—Holy Cross

SEASON—TEAM	G	GS	MIN	FGM	FGA	PCT	3FGM	3FGA	PCT	FTM	FTA	PCT	O-RB	D-RB	TOT	AST	PF	DQ	STL	TO	BLK	PTS	RPG	APG	PPG
62-63—Boston-N.Y.	11	—	83	20	51	.392	—	—	—	13	15	.867	—	—	16	5	8	0	—	—	—	53	1.5	0.5	4.8
REG. SEASON TOTALS	11	—	83	20	51	.392	—	—	—	13	15	.867	—	—	16	5	8	0	—	—	—	53	1.5	0.5	4.8

FONTAINE, LEVI b. November 1, 1948 Ht. 6-4 Wt. 190 College—Maryland State

SEASON—TEAM	G	GS	MIN	FGM	FGA	PCT	3FGM	3FGA	PCT	FTM	FTA	PCT	O-RB	D-RB	TOT	AST	PF	DQ	STL	TO	BLK	PTS	RPG	APG	PPG
70-71—San Francisco	35	—	210	53	145	.366	—	—	—	28	37	.757	—	—	15	22	27	0	—	—	—	134	0.4	0.6	3.8
REG. SEASON TOTALS	35	—	210	53	145	.366	—	—	—	28	37	.757	—	—	15	22	27	0	—	—	—	134	0.4	0.6	3.8
PLAYOFF TOTALS	2	—	9	2	3	.667	—	—	—	1	3	.333	—	—	0	—	2	0	—	—	—	5	0.0	0.0	2.5

FORD, ALPHONSO GENE b. October 31, 1971 Ht. 6-2 Wt. 190 College—Mississippi Valley

SEASON—TEAM	G	GS	MIN	FGM	FGA	PCT	3FGM	3FGA	PCT	FTM	FTA	PCT	O-RB	D-RB	TOT	AST	PF	DQ	STL	TO	BLK	PTS	RPG	APG	PPG
93-94—Seattle	6	0	16	7	13	.538	1	1	1.000	1	2	.500	0	0	0	1	2	0	2	1	0	16	0.0	0.2	2.7
REG. SEASON TOTALS	6	0	16	7	13	.538	1	1	1.000	1	2	.500	0	0	0	1	2	0	2	1	0	16	0.0	0.2	2.7

FORD, CHRISTOPHER JOSEPH (**Chris**) b. January 11, 1949 Ht. 6-5 Wt. 190 College—Villanova

SEASON—TEAM	G	GS	MIN	FGM	FGA	PCT	3FGM	3FGA	PCT	FTM	FTA	PCT	O-RB	D-RB	TOT	AST	PF	DQ	STL	TO	BLK	PTS	RPG	APG	PPG
72-73—Detroit	74	—	1537	208	434	.479	—	—	—	60	93	.645	—	—	266	194	133	1	—	—	—	476	3.6	2.6	6.4
73-74—Detroit	82	—	2059	264	595	.444	—	—	—	57	77	.740	109	195	304	279	159	1	148	—	14	585	3.7	3.4	7.1
74-75—Detroit	80	—	1962	206	435	.474	—	—	—	63	95	.663	93	176	269	230	187	0	113	—	26	475	3.4	2.9	5.9
75-76—Detroit	82	—	2198	301	707	.426	—	—	—	83	115	.722	80	211	291	272	222	0	178	—	24	685	3.5	3.3	8.4
76-77—Detroit	82	—	2539	437	918	.476	—	—	—	131	170	.771	96	174	270	337	192	1	179	—	26	1005	3.3	4.1	12.3
77-78—Detroit	82	—	2582	374	777	.481	—	—	—	113	154	.734	117	151	268	381	182	2	166	232	17	861	3.3	4.6	10.5
78-79—Detroit-Boston	81	—	2737	538	1142	.471	—	—	—	172	227	.758	124	150	274	374	209	3	115	210	25	1248	3.4	4.6	15.4
79-80—Boston	73	—	2115	330	709	.465	70	164	.427	86	114	.754	77	104	181	215	178	0	111	105	27	816	2.5	2.9	11.2
80-81—Boston	82	—	2723	314	707	.444	36	109	.330	64	87	.736	72	91	163	295	212	2	100	127	23	728	2.0	3.6	8.9
81-82—Boston	76	53	1591	188	450	.418	20	63	.317	39	56	.696	52	56	108	142	143	0	42	52	10	435	1.4	1.9	5.7
REG. SEASON TOTALS	794	53	22043	3160	6874	.460	126	336	.375	868	1188	.731	820	1308	2394	2719	1817	10	1152	726	192	7314	3.0	3.4	9.2
PLAYOFF TOTALS	58	0	1477	185	420	.440	11	45	.244	53	77	.688	48	120	168	151	159	2	52	35	15	434	2.9	2.6	7.5

FORD, DONALD J. (**Don**) b. December 31, 1952 Ht. 6-8½ Wt. 215 College—New Mexico/Santa Barbara CC/Cal-Santa Barbara

SEASON—TEAM	G	GS	MIN	FGM	FGA	PCT	3FGM	3FGA	PCT	FTM	FTA	PCT	O-RB	D-RB	TOT	AST	PF	DQ	STL	TO	BLK	PTS	RPG	APG	PPG
75-76—Los Angeles	76	—	1838	311	710	.438	—	—	—	104	139	.748	118	215	333	111	186	3	50	—	14	726	4.4	1.5	9.6
76-77—Los Angeles	82	—	1782	262	570	.460	—	—	—	73	102	.716	105	248	353	133	170	0	60	—	21	597	4.3	1.6	7.3
77-78—Los Angeles	79	—	1945	272	576	.472	—	—	—	68	90	.756	106	247	353	142	210	1	68	88	46	612	4.5	1.8	7.7
78-79—Los Angeles	79	—	1540	228	450	.507	—	—	—	72	89	.809	83	185	268	101	177	2	51	93	25	528	3.4	1.3	6.7
79-80—L.A.-Clev.	73	—	999	131	274	.478	1	3	.333	45	53	.849	44	141	185	65	131	0	22	51	21	308	2.5	0.9	4.2
80-81—Cleveland	64	—	996	100	224	.446	0	3	.000	22	24	.917	74	90	164	84	100	1	15	49	12	222	2.6	1.3	3.5
81-82—Cleveland	21	1	201	9	24	.375	0	1	.000	5	6	.833	14	21	35	11	30	0	8	15	0	23	1.7	0.5	1.1
REG. SEASON TOTALS	474	1	9301	1313	2828	.464	1	7	.143	389	503	.773	544	1147	1691	647	1004	7	274	296	139	3016	3.6	1.4	6.4
PLAYOFF TOTALS	20	0	481	58	131	.443	0	0	—	28	39	.718	26	59	85	44	50	0	21	5	6	144	4.3	2.2	7.2

FORD, JAKE b. April 29, 1946 Ht. 6-3 Wt. 180 College—Maryland State

SEASON—TEAM	G	GS	MIN	FGM	FGA	PCT	3FGM	3FGA	PCT	FTM	FTA	PCT	O-RB	D-RB	TOT	AST	PF	DQ	STL	TO	BLK	PTS	RPG	APG	PPG
70-71—Seattle	5	—	68	9	25	.360	—	—	—	16	22	.727	—	—	9	9	11	0	—	—	—	34	1.8	1.8	6.8
71-72—Seattle	26	—	181	33	66	.500	—	—	—	26	33	.788	—	—	11	26	21	0	—	—	—	92	0.4	1.0	3.5
REG. SEASON TOTALS	31	—	249	42	91	.462	—	—	—	42	55	.764	—	—	20	35	32	0	—	—	—	126	0.6	1.1	4.1

FORD, PHIL JACKSON JR. b. February 9, 1956 Ht. 6-2 Wt. 175 College—North Carolina

SEASON—TEAM	G	GS	MIN	FGM	FGA	PCT	3FGM	3FGA	PCT	FTM	FTA	PCT	O-RB	D-RB	TOT	AST	PF	DQ	STL	TO	BLK	PTS	RPG	APG	PPG
78-79—Kansas City	79	—	2723	467	1004	.465	—	—	—	326	401	.813	33	149	182	681	245	3	174	323	6	1260	2.3	8.6	15.9
79-80—Kansas City	82	—	2621	489	1058	.462	4	23	.174	346	423	.818	29	143	172	610	208	0	136	282	4	1328	2.1	7.4	16.2
80-81—Kansas City	66	—	2287	424	887	.478	11	36	.306	294	354	.831	26	102	128	580	190	3	99	241	6	1153	1.9	8.8	17.5
81-82—Kansas City	72	65	1952	285	649	.439	7	32	.219	136	166	.819	24	81	105	451	160	0	63	194	1	713	1.5	6.3	9.9
82-83—N.J.-Milw.	77	63	1610	213	445	.479	1	9	.111	97	123	.789	18	85	103	290	190	2	52	134	3	524	1.3	3.8	6.8
83-84—Houston	81	55	2020	236	470	.502	2	15	.133	98	117	.838	28	109	137	410	243	7	59	135	8	572	1.7	5.1	7.1
84-85—Houston	25	1	290	14	47	.298	0	4	.000	16	18	.889	3	24	27	61	33	0	6	17	1	44	1.1	2.4	1.8
REG. SEASON TOTALS	482	184	13503	2128	4560	.467	25	119	.210	1313	1602	.820	161	693	854	3083	1269	15	589	1326	29	5594	1.8	6.4	11.6
PLAYOFF TOTALS	15	0	416	50	137	.365	3	5	.600	33	46	.717	9	23	26	85	30	0	22	44	0	136	1.7	5.7	9.1

FORD, ROBERT ALAN (**Bob**) b. January 26, 1950 Ht. 6-7 Wt. 230 College—Purdue

SEASON—TEAM	G	GS	MIN	FGM	FGA	PCT	3FGM	3FGA	PCT	FTM	FTA	PCT	O-RB	D-RB	TOT	AST	PF	DQ	STL	TO	BLK	PTS	RPG	APG	PPG
72-73—Memphis (A)	9	—	74	5	17	.294	0	0	—	4	5	.800	2	10	12	4	8	0	—	4	—	14	1.3	0.4	1.6
REG. ABA TOTALS	9	—	74	5	17	.294	0	0	—	4	5	.800	2	10	12	4	8	0	—	4	—	14	1.3	0.4	1.6

FORMAN, DONALD J. (**Donnie**) b. January 17, 1926 Ht. 6-1 Wt. 175 College—New York University

SEASON—TEAM	G	GS	MIN	FGM	FGA	PCT	3FGM	3FGA	PCT	FTM	FTA	PCT	O-RB	D-RB	TOT	AST	PF	DQ	STL	TO	BLK	PTS	RPG	APG	PPG
48-49—Minneapolis	44	—	—	68	231	.294	—	—	—	43	67	.642	—	—	74	94	—	—	—	—	—	179	—	1.7	4.1
REG. SEASON TOTALS	44	—	—	68	231	.294	—	—	—	43	67	.642	—	—	74	94	—	—	—	—	—	179	—	1.7	4.1
PLAYOFF TOTALS	9	—	—	3	20	.150	—	—	—	7	11	.636	—	—	7	15	—	—	—	—	—	13	—	0.8	1.4

FORREST, BAYARD b. July 8, 1954 Ht. 6-10 Wt. 235 College—Grand Canyon College

SEASON—TEAM	G	GS	MIN	FGM	FGA	PCT	3FGM	3FGA	PCT	FTM	FTA	PCT	O-RB	D-RB	TOT	AST	PF	DQ	STL	TO	BLK	PTS	RPG	APG	PPG
77-78—Phoenix	64	—	887	111	238	.466	—	—	—	49	103	.476	84	166	250	129	105	0	23	84	34	271	3.9	2.0	4.2
78-79—Phoenix	75	—	1243	118	272	.434	—	—	—	62	115	.539	110	205	315	167	151	1	29	107	37	298	4.2	2.2	4.0
REG. SEASON TOTALS	139	—	2130	229	510	.449	—	—	—	111	218	.509	194	371	565	296	256	1	52	191	71	569	4.1	2.1	4.1
PLAYOFF TOTALS	15	—	113	11	19	.579	—	—	—	2	10	.200	9	20	29	11	21	0	4	10	2	24	1.9	0.7	1.6

FOSTER, FRED J. b. March 18, 1946 d. October 4, 1985 Ht. 6-5½ Wt. 215 College—Miami (Ohio)

SEASON—TEAM	G	GS	MIN	FGM	FGA	PCT	3FGM	3FGA	PCT	FTM	FTA	PCT	O-RB	D-RB	TOT	AST	PF	DQ	STL	TO	BLK	PTS	RPG	APG	PPG
68-69—Cincinnati	56	—	497	74	193	.383	—	—	—	43	66	.652	—	—	61	36	49	0	—	—	—	191	1.1	0.6	3.4
69-70—Cincinnati	73	—	2077	461	1026	.449	—	—	—	176	243	.724	—	—	310	107	209	2	—	—	—	1098	4.2	1.5	15.0
70-71—Cin.-Phil.	67	—	909	148	368	.402	—	—	—	73	106	.689	—	—	151	61	115	3	—	—	—	369	2.3	0.9	5.5
71-72—Philadelphia	74	—	1699	347	837	.415	—	—	—	185	243	.761	—	—	276	90	184	3	—	—	—	879	3.7	1.2	11.9
72-73—Detroit	63	—	1460	243	627	.388	—	—	—	61	87	.701	—	—	183	94	150	0	—	—	—	547	2.9	1.5	8.7
73-74—Cleveland	58	—	649	112	288	.389	—	—	—	54	64	.844	43	65	108	62	79	0	19	—	6	278	1.9	1.1	4.8
74-75—Cleveland	73	—	1136	217	521	.417	—	—	—	69	97	.711	56	54	110	103	130	1	22	—	2	503	1.5	1.4	6.9
76-77—Buffalo	59	—	689	99	247	.401	—	—	—	30	44	.682	33	43	76	48	92	0	16	—	0	228	1.3	0.8	3.9
REG. SEASON TOTALS	523	—	9116	1701	4107	.414	—	—	—	691	950	.727	132	162	1275	601	1008	9	57	—	8	4093	2.4	1.1	7.8
PLAYOFF TOTALS	5	—	49	8	19	.421	—	—	—	2	2	1.000	0	0	12	5	6	0	0	—	0	18	2.4	1.0	3.6

FOSTER, GREGORY CLINTON (Greg) b. October 3, 1968 Ht. 6-11 Wt. 250 College—UCLA/Texas-El Paso

SEASON—TEAM	G	GS	MIN	FGM	FGA	PCT	3FGM	3FGA	PCT	FTM	FTA	PCT	O-RB	D-RB	TOT	AST	PF	DQ	STL	TO	BLK	PTS	RPG	APG	PPG
90-91—Washington	54	3	606	97	211	.460	0	5	.000	42	61	.689	52	99	151	37	112	1	12	45	22	236	2.8	0.7	4.4
91-92—Washington	49	3	548	89	193	.461	0	1	.000	35	49	.714	43	102	145	35	83	0	6	36	12	213	3.0	0.7	4.3
92-93—Wash.-Atlanta	43	0	298	55	120	.458	0	4	.000	15	21	.714	32	51	83	21	58	0	3	25	14	125	1.9	0.5	2.9
93-94—Milwaukee	3	0	19	4	7	.571	0	0	—	2	2	1.000	0	3	3	0	3	0	0	1	1	10	1.0	0.0	3.3
REG. SEASON TOTALS	149	6	1471	245	531	.461	0	10	.000	94	133	.707	127	255	382	93	256	1	21	107	49	584	2.6	0.6	3.9
PLAYOFF TOTALS	1	0	5	1	3	.333	0	0	—	3	4	.750	0	1	1	—	0	0	0	0	0	5	1.0	0.0	5.0

FOSTER, JAMES (Jimmy) b. December 16, 1951 Ht. 6-1 Wt. 175 College—Connecticut

SEASON—TEAM	G	GS	MIN	FGM	FGA	PCT	3FGM	3FGA	PCT	FTM	FTA	PCT	O-RB	D-RB	TOT	AST	PF	DQ	STL	TO	BLK	PTS	RPG	APG	PPG
74-75—St. Louis (A)	41	—	806	78	209	.373	0	6	.000	27	34	.794	19	56	75	143	118	—	39	88	5	183	1.8	3.5	4.5
75-76—Denver (A)	48	—	352	54	145	.372	1	8	.125	39	64	.609	19	23	42	47	78	—	19	63	4	148	0.9	1.0	3.1
REG. ABA TOTALS	89	—	1158	132	354	.373	1	14	.071	66	98	.673	38	79	117	190	196	—	58	151	9	331	1.3	2.1	3.7
ABA PLAYOFF TOTALS	9	—	65	11	24	.458	0	1	.000	7	15	.467	4	4	8	7	13	—	4	8	0	29	0.9	0.8	3.2
ABA ALL-STAR TOTALS	1	—	5	0	3	.000	0	0	—	0	0	—	0	0	1	0	1	—	0	0	0	0	1.0	0.0	0.0

FOSTER, RODERICK ALLEN (Rod) b. October 10, 1960 Ht. 6-1 Wt. 160 College—UCLA

SEASON—TEAM	G	GS	MIN	FGM	FGA	PCT	3FGM	3FGA	PCT	FTM	FTA	PCT	O-RB	D-RB	TOT	AST	PF	DQ	STL	TO	BLK	PTS	RPG	APG	PPG
83-84—Phoenix	80	34	1424	260	580	.448	22	84	.262	122	155	.787	39	81	120	172	193	0	54	108	9	664	1.5	2.2	8.3
84-85—Phoenix	79	1	1318	286	636	.450	41	126	.325	83	110	.755	27	53	80	186	171	1	61	117	0	696	1.0	2.4	8.8
85-86—Phoenix	48	0	704	85	218	.390	9	32	.281	23	32	.719	9	49	58	121	77	0	22	61	1	202	1.2	2.5	4.2
REG. SEASON TOTALS	207	35	3446	631	1434	.440	72	242	.298	228	297	.768	75	183	258	479	441	1	137	286	10	1562	1.2	2.3	7.5
PLAYOFF TOTALS	19	0	184	17	64	.266	0	9	.000	15	17	.882	6	10	16	25	25	0	10	18	1	49	0.8	1.3	2.6

FOUST, LAWRENCE MICHAEL (Larry) b. June 24, 1928 d. October 27, 1984 Ht. 6-9 Wt. 250 College—La Salle

SEASON—TEAM	G	GS	MIN	FGM	FGA	PCT	3FGM	3FGA	PCT	FTM	FTA	PCT	O-RB	D-RB	TOT	AST	PF	DQ	STL	TO	BLK	PTS	RPG	APG	PPG
50-51—Fort Wayne	68	—	—	327	944	.346	—	—	—	261	396	.659	—	—	681	90	247	6	—	—	—	915	10.0	1.3	13.5
51-52—Fort Wayne	66	—	2615	390	989	.394	—	—	—	267	394	.678	—	—	880	200	245	10	—	—	—	1047	13.3	3.0	15.9
52-53—Fort Wayne	67	—	2303	311	865	.360	—	—	—	336	465	.723	—	—	769	151	267	16	—	—	—	958	11.5	2.3	14.3
53-54—Fort Wayne	72	—	2693	376	919	.409	—	—	—	338	475	.712	—	—	967	161	258	4	—	—	—	1090	13.4	2.2	15.1
54-55—Fort Wayne	70	—	2264	398	818	.487	—	—	—	393	513	.766	—	—	700	118	264	9	—	—	—	1189	10.0	1.7	17.0
55-56—Fort Wayne	72	—	2024	367	821	.447	—	—	—	432	555	.778	—	—	648	127	263	7	—	—	—	1166	9.0	1.8	16.2
56-57—Fort Wayne	61	—	1533	243	617	.394	—	—	—	273	380	.718	—	—	555	71	221	7	—	—	—	759	9.1	1.2	12.4
57-58—Minneapolis	72	—	2200	391	982	.398	—	—	—	428	566	.756	—	—	876	108	299	11	—	—	—	1210	12.2	1.5	16.8
58-59—Minneapolis	72	—	1933	301	771	.390	—	—	—	280	366	.765	—	—	627	91	233	5	—	—	—	882	8.7	1.3	12.3
59-60—Minn.-St. L.	72	—	1964	312	766	.407	—	—	—	253	320	.791	—	—	621	96	241	7	—	—	—	877	8.6	1.3	12.2
60-61—St. Louis	68	—	1208	194	489	.397	—	—	—	164	208	.788	—	—	389	77	185	0	—	—	—	552	5.7	1.1	8.1
61-62—St. Louis	57	—	1153	204	433	.471	—	—	—	145	178	.815	—	—	328	78	186	3	—	—	—	553	5.8	1.4	9.7
REG. SEASON TOTALS	817	—	21890	3814	9414	.405	—	—	—	3570	4816	.741	—	—	8041	1368	2909	85	—	—	—	11198	9.8	1.7	13.7
PLAYOFF TOTALS	73	—	1920	301	763	.394	—	—	—	300	384	.781	—	—	707	94	255	9	—	—	—	902	9.7	1.3	12.4
ALL-STAR TOTALS	7	—	118	17	54	.315	—	—	—	15	16	.938	—	—	49	3	16	0	—	—	—	49	7.0	0.4	7.0

FOWLER, CALVIN BERNARD (Cal) b. February 11, 1940 Ht. 6-1½ Wt. 175 College—St. Francis (Pa.)

SEASON—TEAM	G	GS	MIN	FGM	FGA	PCT	3FGM	3FGA	PCT	FTM	FTA	PCT	O-RB	D-RB	TOT	AST	PF	DQ	STL	TO	BLK	PTS	RPG	APG	PPG
69-70—Carolina (A)	78	—	1234	131	288	.455	7	17	.412	74	119	.622	—	—	170	126	156	2	—	—	—	343	2.2	1.6	4.4
REG. ABA TOTALS	78	—	1234	131	288	.455	7	17	.412	74	119	.622	—	—	170	126	156	2	—	—	—	343	2.2	1.6	4.4
ABA PLAYOFF TOTALS	4	—	76	6	14	.429	0	1	.000	7	10	.700	—	—	6	8	11	0	—	—	—	19	1.5	2.0	4.8

FOWLER, JERRY A. b. June 20, 1927 Ht. 6-7½ Wt. 230 College—Missouri

SEASON—TEAM	G	GS	MIN	FGM	FGA	PCT	3FGM	3FGA	PCT	FTM	FTA	PCT	O-RB	D-RB	TOT	AST	PF	DQ	STL	TO	BLK	PTS	RPG	APG	PPG
51-52—Milwaukee	6	—	41	4	13	.308	—	—	—	1	4	.250	—	—	10	2	9	0	—	—	—	9	1.7	0.3	1.5
REG. SEASON TOTALS	6	—	41	4	13	.308	—	—	—	1	4	.250	—	—	10	2	9	0	—	—	—	9	1.7	0.3	1.5

FOX, HAROLD b. August 29, 1949 Ht. 6-2 Wt. 175 College—Brevard CC/Jacksonville

SEASON—TEAM	G	GS	MIN	FGM	FGA	PCT	3FGM	3FGA	PCT	FTM	FTA	PCT	O-RB	D-RB	TOT	AST	PF	DQ	STL	TO	BLK	PTS	RPG	APG	PPG
72-73—Buffalo	10	—	84	12	32	.375	—	—	—	7	8	.875	—	—	8	10	7	0	—	—	—	31	0.8	1.0	3.1
REG. SEASON TOTALS	10	—	84	12	32	.375	—	—	—	7	8	.875	—	—	8	10	7	0	—	—	—	31	0.8	1.0	3.1

FOX, JAMES L. (**Jim**) b. April 7, 1943 Ht. 6-10 Wt. 230 College—Gordon Military/South Carolina

SEASON—TEAM	G	GS	MIN	FGM	FGA	PCT	3FGM	3FGA	PCT	FTM	FTA	PCT	O-RB	D-RB	TOT	AST	PF	DQ	STL	TO	BLK	PTS	RPG	APG	PPG
67-68—Cin.-Detroit	55	—	624	66	161	.410	—	—	—	66	108	.611	—	—	230	29	85	0	—	—	—	198	4.2	0.5	3.6
68-69—Detroit-Phoenix	76	—	2354	318	677	.470	—	—	—	191	267	.715	—	—	818	166	266	6	—	—	—	827	10.8	2.2	10.9
69-70—Phoenix	81	—	2041	413	788	.524	—	—	—	218	283	.770	—	—	570	93	261	7	—	—	—	1044	7.0	1.1	12.9
70-71—Chicago	82	—	1628	280	611	.458	—	—	—	239	321	.745	—	—	598	196	213	0	—	—	—	799	7.3	2.4	9.7
71-72—Chicago-Cin.	81	—	2180	354	788	.449	—	—	—	227	297	.764	—	—	713	86	257	8	—	—	—	935	8.8	1.1	11.5
72-73—Seattle	74	—	2439	316	613	.515	—	—	—	214	265	.808	—	—	827	176	239	6	—	—	—	846	11.2	2.4	11.4
73-74—Seattle	78	—	2179	322	673	.478	—	—	—	241	293	.823	244	470	714	227	247	5	56	—	21	885	9.2	2.9	11.3
74-75—Seattle	75	—	1766	253	540	.469	—	—	—	170	212	.802	128	363	491	137	168	1	48	—	17	676	6.5	1.8	9.0
75-76—Milwaukee	70	—	918	105	203	.517	—	—	—	62	79	.785	82	153	235	42	129	1	27	—	16	272	3.4	0.6	3.9
76-77—New York Nets	71	—	1165	184	398	.462	—	—	—	95	114	.833	100	229	329	49	158	1	20	—	25	463	4.6	0.7	6.5
REG. SEASON TOTALS	743	—	17294	2611	5452	.479	—	—	—	1723	2239	.770	554	1215	5525	1201	2023	35	151	—	79	6945	7.4	1.6	9.3
PLAYOFF TOTALS	30	—	504	72	183	.393	—	—	—	51	71	.718	6	10	183	33	62	2	0	—	2	195	6.1	1.1	6.5

FOX, ULRICH ALEXANDER (**Rick**) b. July 24, 1969 Ht. 6-7 Wt. 230 College—North Carolina

SEASON—TEAM	G	GS	MIN	FGM	FGA	PCT	3FGM	3FGA	PCT	FTM	FTA	PCT	O-RB	D-RB	TOT	AST	PF	DQ	STL	TO	BLK	PTS	RPG	APG	PPG
91-92—Boston	81	5	1535	241	525	.459	23	70	.329	139	184	.755	73	147	220	126	230	3	78	123	30	644	2.7	1.6	8.0
92-93—Boston	71	14	1082	184	380	.484	4	23	.174	81	101	.802	55	104	159	113	133	1	61	77	21	453	2.2	1.6	6.4
93-94—Boston	82	53	2096	340	728	.467	33	100	.330	174	230	.757	105	250	355	217	244	4	81	158	52	887	4.3	2.6	10.8
REG. SEASON TOTALS	234	72	4713	765	1633	.468	60	193	.311	394	515	.765	233	501	734	456	607	8	220	358	103	1984	3.1	1.9	8.5
PLAYOFF TOTALS	12	0	138	18	48	.375	4	9	.444	6	6	1.000	11	14	25	9	18	0	4	6	3	46	2.1	0.8	3.8

FRANK, TELLIS JOSEPH JR. b. April 26, 1965 Ht. 6-10 Wt. 230 College—Western Kentucky

SEASON—TEAM	G	GS	MIN	FGM	FGA	PCT	3FGM	3FGA	PCT	FTM	FTA	PCT	O-RB	D-RB	TOT	AST	PF	DQ	STL	TO	BLK	PTS	RPG	APG	PPG
87-88—Golden State	78	29	1597	242	565	.428	0	1	.000	150	207	.725	95	235	330	111	267	5	53	109	23	634	4.2	1.4	8.1
88-89—Golden State	32	2	245	34	91	.374	0	1	.000	39	51	.765	26	35	61	15	59	1	14	29	6	107	1.9	0.5	3.3
89-90—Miami	77	39	1762	278	607	.458	0	0	—	179	234	.765	151	234	385	85	282	6	51	134	27	735	5.0	1.1	9.5
91-92—Minnesota	10	0	140	18	33	.545	0	0	—	10	15	.667	8	18	26	8	24	0	5	5	4	46	2.6	0.8	4.6
93-94—Minnesota	67	11	959	67	160	.419	0	2	.000	54	76	.711	83	137	220	57	163	1	35	49	35	188	3.3	0.9	2.8
REG. SEASON TOTALS	264	81	4703	639	1456	.439	0	4	.000	432	583	.741	363	659	1022	276	795	13	158	326	95	1710	3.9	1.0	6.5

FRANKEL, NATHAN (**Nat**) b. November 3, 1913 Ht. 6-2 Wt. 195 College—Brooklyn

SEASON—TEAM	G	GS	MIN	FGM	FGA	PCT	3FGM	3FGA	PCT	FTM	FTA	PCT	O-RB	D-RB	TOT	AST	PF	DQ	STL	TO	BLK	PTS	RPG	APG	PPG
39-40—Detroit (N)	27	—	—	73	—	—	—	—	—	55	86	.640	—	—	—	31	—	—	—	—	—	201	—	—	7.4
46-47—Pittsburgh	6	—	—	4	27	.148	—	—	—	8	12	.667	—	—	—	3	6	—	—	—	—	16	—	0.5	2.7
REG. NBA TOTALS	6	—	—	4	27	.148	—	—	—	8	12	.667	—	—	—	3	6	—	—	—	—	16	—	0.5	2.7
REG. NBL TOTALS	27	—	—	73	—	—	—	—	—	55	86	.640	—	—	—	31	—	—	—	—	—	201	—	—	7.4
NBL PLAYOFF TOTALS	3	—	—	10	—	—	—	—	—	4	2	.000	—	—	—	9	—	—	—	—	—	24	—	—	8.0

FRANKLIN, WILLIAM THOMAS (**Will**) b. October 19, 1949 Ht. 6-7 Wt. 225 College—Purdue

SEASON—TEAM	G	GS	MIN	FGM	FGA	PCT	3FGM	3FGA	PCT	FTM	FTA	PCT	O-RB	D-RB	TOT	AST	PF	DQ	STL	TO	BLK	PTS	RPG	APG	PPG
72-73—Virginia (A)	73	—	990	218	524	.416	2	7	.286	107	179	.598	123	166	289	50	157	0	—	123	—	545	4.0	0.7	7.5
74-75—San Antonio (A)	24	—	179	32	85	.376	0	1	.000	15	23	.652	39	43	82	10	37	—	3	18	2	79	3.4	0.4	3.3
75-76—San Antonio (A)	10	—	95	12	22	.545	0	0	—	9	16	.563	12	17	29	5	16	—	3	5	3	33	2.9	0.5	3.3
REG. ABA TOTALS	107	—	1264	262	631	.415	2	8	.250	131	218	.601	174	226	400	65	210	0	6	146	5	657	3.7	0.6	6.1
ABA PLAYOFF TOTALS	2	—	10	2	5	.400	0	0	—	0	0	—	3	2	5	0	2	0	0	0	0	4	2.5	0.0	2.0

FRANZ, RONALD STEPHEN (**Ron**) b. October 20, 1945 Ht. 6-7 Wt. 210 College—Kansas

SEASON—TEAM	G	GS	MIN	FGM	FGA	PCT	3FGM	3FGA	PCT	FTM	FTA	PCT	O-RB	D-RB	TOT	AST	PF	DQ	STL	TO	BLK	PTS	RPG	APG	PPG
67-68—Oakland (A)	74	—	2080	354	903	.392	25	97	.258	197	285	.691	—	—	469	129	249	11	—	173	—	930	6.3	1.7	12.6
68-69—New Orleans (A)	73	—	2195	381	850	.448	11	31	.355	286	388	.737	—	—	518	189	233	5	—	174	—	1059	7.1	2.6	14.5
69-70—New Orleans (A)	55	—	1305	231	547	.422	7	25	.280	163	259	.629	—	—	287	91	139	3	—	—	—	632	5.2	1.7	11.5
70-71—Floridians (A)	67	—	1596	309	637	.485	7	22	.318	188	259	.726	—	—	320	97	178	—	—	—	—	813	4.8	1.4	12.1
71-72—Floridians (A)	74	—	1822	342	705	.485	2	11	.182	171	243	.704	—	—	342	94	209	—	—	97	—	857	4.6	1.3	11.6
72-73—Memphis-Dallas (A)	60	—	914	148	303	.488	1	4	.250	145	201	.721	67	125	192	68	112	0	—	78	—	442	3.2	1.1	7.4
REG. ABA TOTALS	403	—	9912	1765	3945	.447	53	190	.279	1150	1635	.703	67	125	2128	668	1120	19	—	522	—	4733	5.3	1.7	11.7
ABA PLAYOFF TOTALS	17	—	389	57	169	.337	1	9	.111	31	53	.585	—	—	82	24	42	0	—	28	—	146	4.8	1.4	8.6

FRAZIER, WALTER JR. (**Walt, Clyde**) b. March 29, 1945   Ht. 6-4 Wt. 200 College—Southern Illinois

SEASON—TEAM	G	GS	MIN	FGM	FGA	PCT	3FGM	3FGA	PCT	FTM	FTA	PCT	O-RB	D-RB	TOT	AST	PF	DQ	STL	TO	BLK	PTS	RPG	APG	PPG
67-68—New York	74	—	1588	256	568	.451	—	—	—	154	235	.655	—	—	313	305	199	2	—	—	—	666	4.2	4.1	9.0
68-69—New York	80	—	2949	531	1052	.505	—	—	—	341	457	.746	—	—	499	635	245	2	—	—	—	1403	6.2	7.9	17.5
69-70—New York	77	—	3040	600	1158	.518	—	—	—	409	547	.748	—	—	465	629	203	1	—	—	—	1609	6.0	8.2	20.9
70-71—New York	80	—	3455	651	1317	.494	—	—	—	434	557	.779	—	—	544	536	240	1	—	—	—	1736	6.8	6.7	21.7
71-72—New York	77	—	3126	669	1307	.512	—	—	—	450	557	.808	—	—	513	446	185	0	—	—	—	1788	6.7	5.8	23.2
72-73—New York	78	—	3181	681	1389	.490	—	—	—	286	350	.817	—	—	570	461	186	0	—	—	—	1648	7.3	5.9	21.1
73-74—New York	80	—	3338	674	1429	.472	—	—	—	295	352	.838	120	416	536	551	212	2	161	—	15	1643	6.7	6.9	20.5
74-75—New York	78	—	3204	672	1391	.483	—	—	—	331	400	.828	90	375	465	474	205	2	190	—	14	1675	6.0	6.1	21.5
75-76—New York	59	—	2427	470	969	.485	—	—	—	186	226	.823	79	321	400	351	163	1	106	—	9	1126	6.8	5.9	19.1
76-77—New York Knicks	76	—	2687	532	1089	.489	—	—	—	259	336	.771	52	241	293	403	194	0	132	—	9	1323	3.9	5.3	17.4
77-78—Cleveland	51	—	1664	336	714	.471	—	—	—	153	180	.850	54	155	209	209	124	1	77	113	9	825	4.1	4.1	16.2
78-79—Cleveland	12	—	279	54	122	.443	—	—	—	21	27	.778	7	13	20	32	22	0	13	22	2	129	1.7	2.7	10.8
79-80—Cleveland	3	—	27	4	11	.364	0	1	.000	2	2	1.000	1	2	3	8	2	0	2	4	1	10	1.0	2.7	3.3
REG. SEASON TOTALS	825	—	30965	6130	12516	.490	0	1	.000	3321	4226	.786	403	1523	4830	5040	2180	12	681	139	59	15581	5.9	6.1	18.9
PLAYOFF TOTALS	93	—	3953	767	1500	.511	0	0	—	393	523	.751	24	91	666	599	285	2	32	—	4	1927	7.2	6.4	20.7
ALL-STAR TOTALS	7	—	183	35	78	.449	0	0	—	18	21	.857	1	8	27	26	10	0	9	—	0	88	3.9	3.7	12.6

FRAZIER, WILBERT B. (**Will**) b. August 24, 1942   Ht. 6-7 Wt. 210 College—Grambling State

SEASON—TEAM	G	GS	MIN	FGM	FGA	PCT	3FGM	3FGA	PCT	FTM	FTA	PCT	O-RB	D-RB	TOT	AST	PF	DQ	STL	TO	BLK	PTS	RPG	APG	PPG
65-66—San Francisco	2	—	9	0	4	.000	—	—	—	1	2	.500	—	—	5	1	1	0	—	—	—	1	2.5	0.5	0.5
67-68—Houston (A)	76	—	2125	358	870	.411	1	2	.500	228	376	.606	—	—	666	104	219	3	—	146	—	945	8.8	1.4	12.4
68-69—New York (A)	75	—	1370	217	512	.424	0	0	—	120	194	.619	—	—	416	66	200	1	—	75	—	554	5.5	0.9	7.4
REG. NBA TOTALS	2	—	9	0	4	.000	—	—	—	1	2	.500	—	—	5	1	1	0	—	—	—	1	2.5	0.5	0.5
REG. ABA TOTALS	151	—	3495	575	1382	.416	1	2	.500	348	570	.611	—	—	1082	170	419	4	—	221	—	1499	7.2	1.1	9.9
ABA PLAYOFF TOTALS	3	—	85	13	29	.448	0	1	.000	3	7	.429	—	—	12	4	11	0	—	5	—	29	4.0	1.3	9.7

FREDERICK, ANTHONY b. December 7, 1964   Ht. 6-7 Wt. 205 College—Santa Monica/Pepperdine

SEASON—TEAM	G	GS	MIN	FGM	FGA	PCT	3FGM	3FGA	PCT	FTM	FTA	PCT	O-RB	D-RB	TOT	AST	PF	DQ	STL	TO	BLK	PTS	RPG	APG	PPG
88-89—Indiana	46	0	313	63	125	.504	2	5	.400	24	34	.706	26	26	52	20	59	0	14	34	6	152	1.1	0.4	3.3
90-91—Sacramento	35	3	475	67	168	.399	0	0	—	43	60	.717	36	48	84	44	50	0	22	40	13	177	2.4	1.3	5.1
91-92—Charlotte	66	26	852	161	370	.435	4	17	.235	63	92	.685	75	69	144	71	91	0	40	58	26	389	2.2	1.1	5.9
REG. SEASON TOTALS	147	29	1640	291	663	.439	6	22	.273	130	186	.699	137	143	280	135	200	0	76	132	45	718	1.9	0.9	4.9

FREE, LLOYD B. (**see World B. Free**)

FREE, WORLD B. (**formerly Lloyd B. Free**) b. December 9, 1953   Ht. 6-3 Wt. 185 College—Guilford

SEASON—TEAM	G	GS	MIN	FGM	FGA	PCT	3FGM	3FGA	PCT	FTM	FTA	PCT	O-RB	D-RB	TOT	AST	PF	DQ	STL	TO	BLK	PTS	RPG	APG	PPG
75-76—Philadelphia	71	—	1121	239	533	.448	—	—	—	112	186	.602	64	61	125	104	107	0	37	—	6	590	1.8	1.5	8.3
76-77—Philadelphia	78	—	2253	467	1022	.457	—	—	—	334	464	.720	97	140	237	266	207	2	75	—	25	1268	3.0	3.4	16.3
77-78—Philadelphia	76	—	2050	390	857	.455	—	—	—	411	562	.731	92	120	212	306	199	0	68	200	41	1191	2.8	4.0	15.7
78-79—San Diego	78	—	2954	795	1653	.481	—	—	—	654	865	.756	127	174	301	340	253	8	111	297	35	2244	3.9	4.4	28.8
79-80—San Diego	68	—	2585	737	1556	.474	9	25	.360	572	760	.753	129	109	238	283	195	0	81	228	32	2055	3.5	4.2	30.2
80-81—Golden State	65	—	2370	516	1157	.446	5	31	.161	528	649	.814	48	111	159	361	183	1	85	195	11	1565	2.4	5.6	24.1
81-82—Golden State	78	78	2796	650	1452	.448	10	56	.179	479	647	.740	118	130	248	419	222	1	71	208	8	1789	3.2	5.4	22.9
82-83—G.S.-Clev.	73	69	2638	649	1423	.456	15	45	.333	430	583	.738	92	109	201	290	241	4	97	209	15	1743	2.8	4.0	23.9
83-84—Cleveland	75	71	2375	626	1407	.445	22	69	.319	395	504	.784	89	128	217	226	214	2	94	154	8	1669	2.9	3.0	22.3
84-85—Cleveland	71	50	2249	609	1328	.459	71	193	.368	308	411	.749	61	150	211	320	163	0	75	139	16	1597	3.0	4.5	22.5
85-86—Cleveland	75	75	2535	652	1433	.455	71	169	.420	379	486	.780	72	146	218	314	186	1	91	172	19	1754	2.9	4.2	23.4
86-87—Philadelphia	20	2	285	39	123	.317	2	9	.222	36	47	.766	5	14	19	30	26	0	5	18	4	116	1.0	1.5	5.8
87-88—Houston	58	0	682	143	350	.409	8	35	.229	80	100	.800	14	30	44	60	74	2	20	49	3	374	0.8	1.0	6.4
REG. SEASON TOTALS	886	345	26893	6512	14294	.456	213	632	.337	4718	6264	.753	1008	1422	2430	3319	2270	21	910	1869	223	17955	2.7	3.7	20.3
PLAYOFF TOTALS	34	4	773	166	417	.398	0	5	.000	145	196	.740	26	50	76	103	79	0	25	35	14	477	2.2	3.0	14.0
ALL-STAR TOTALS	1	1	21	7	13	.538	0	0	—	0	1	.000	1	2	3	5	1	0	0	5	1	14	3.0	5.0	14.0

FREEMAN, DONALD E. (Donnie) b. July 18, 1944 Ht. 6-3 Wt. 185 College—Illinois

SEASON—TEAM	G	GS	MIN	FGM	FGA	PCT	3FGM	3FGA	PCT	FTM	FTA	PCT	O-RB	D-RB	TOT	AST	PF	DQ	STL	TO	BLK	PTS	RPG	APG	PPG
67-68—Minnesota (A)	69	—	2431	414	1013	.409	0	6	.000	296	414	.715	—	—	326	190	185	5	—	187	—	1124	4.7	2.8	16.3
68-69—Miami (A)	78	—	2874	651	1346	.484	2	23	.087	420	534	.787	—	—	285	501	229	7	—	230	—	1724	3.7	6.4	22.1
69-70—Miami (A)	79	—	3164	766	1684	.455	5	19	.263	626	762	.822	—	—	400	291	253	5	—	—	—	2163	5.1	3.7	27.4
70-71—Utah-Texas (A)	66	—	2414	596	1235	.483	0	7	.000	367	459	.800	—	—	324	332	192	—	—	—	—	1559	4.9	5.0	23.6
71-72—Dallas (A)	72	—	2377	628	1336	.470	2	5	.400	475	576	.825	—	—	206	245	177	—	—	176	—	1733	2.9	3.4	24.1
72-73—Indiana (A)	77	—	2170	412	933	.442	2	6	.333	277	343	.808	103	116	219	195	225	0	—	160	—	1103	2.8	2.5	14.3
73-74—Indiana (A)	66	—	1735	383	839	.456	0	2	.000	177	222	.797	91	77	168	165	174	—	48	132	22	943	2.5	2.5	14.3
74-75—San Antonio (A)	77	—	2381	453	1012	.448	0	5	.000	289	352	.821	107	77	184	202	169	—	65	131	15	1195	2.4	2.6	15.5
75-76—Los Angeles	64	—	1480	263	606	.434	—	—	—	163	199	.819	72	108	180	171	160	1	57	—	11	689	2.8	2.7	10.8
REG. NBA TOTALS	64	—	1480	263	606	.434	—	—	—	163	199	.819	72	108	180	171	160	1	57	—	11	689	2.8	2.7	10.8
REG. ABA TOTALS	584	—	19546	4303	9398	.458	11	73	.151	2927	3662	.799	301	270	2112	2121	1604	17	113	1016	37	11544	3.6	3.6	19.8
ABA PLAYOFF TOTALS	60	—	1968	405	913	.444	0	10	.000	230	300	.767	13	11	218	198	176	4	6	132	0	1040	3.6	3.3	17.3
ABA ALL-STAR TOTALS	5	—	123	28	62	.452	0	0	—	25	32	.781	9	13	26	19	15	1	0	13	0	81	5.2	3.8	16.2

FREEMAN, GARY C. b. July 25, 1948 Ht. 6-9 Wt. 210 College—Oregon State

SEASON—TEAM	G	GS	MIN	FGM	FGA	PCT	3FGM	3FGA	PCT	FTM	FTA	PCT	O-RB	D-RB	TOT	AST	PF	DQ	STL	TO	BLK	PTS	RPG	APG	PPG
70-71—Milw.-Clev.	52	—	382	69	134	.515	—	—	—	29	40	.725	—	—	106	35	67	0	—	—	—	167	2.0	0.7	3.2
REG. SEASON TOTALS	52	—	382	69	134	.515	—	—	—	29	40	.725	—	—	106	35	67	0	—	—	—	167	2.0	0.7	3.2

FREEMAN, RODNEY LEE (Rod) b. November 5, 1950 Ht. 6-7 Wt. 225 College—Vanderbilt

SEASON—TEAM	G	GS	MIN	FGM	FGA	PCT	3FGM	3FGA	PCT	FTM	FTA	PCT	O-RB	D-RB	TOT	AST	PF	DQ	STL	TO	BLK	PTS	RPG	APG	PPG
73-74—Philadelphia	35	—	265	39	103	.379	—	—	—	28	41	.683	22	32	54	14	42	0	12	—	1	106	1.5	0.4	3.0
REG. SEASON TOTALS	35	—	265	39	103	.379	—	—	—	28	41	.683	22	32	54	14	42	0	12	—	1	106	1.5	0.4	3.0

FREY, FRIDO b. October 26, 1921 Ht. 6-2 Wt. 195 College—St. John's/Long Island University

SEASON—TEAM	G	GS	MIN	FGM	FGA	PCT	3FGM	3FGA	PCT	FTM	FTA	PCT	O-RB	D-RB	TOT	AST	PF	DQ	STL	TO	BLK	PTS	RPG	APG	PPG
46-47—New York	23	—	—	28	97	.289	—	—	—	32	56	.571	—	—	—	14	37	—	—	—	—	88	—	0.6	3.8
REG. SEASON TOTALS	23	—	—	28	97	.289	—	—	—	32	56	.571	—	—	—	14	37	—	—	—	—	88	—	0.6	3.8
PLAYOFF TOTALS	5	—	—	3	19	.158	—	—	—	4	11	.364	—	—	—	7	11	—	—	—	—	10	—	1.4	2.0

FRIEND, LAWRENCE (Larry) b. April 14, 1935 Ht. 6-4 Wt. 195 College—Los Angeles CC/California

SEASON—TEAM	G	GS	MIN	FGM	FGA	PCT	3FGM	3FGA	PCT	FTM	FTA	PCT	O-RB	D-RB	TOT	AST	PF	DQ	STL	TO	BLK	PTS	RPG	APG	PPG
57-58—New York	44	—	569	74	226	.327	—	—	—	27	41	.659	—	—	106	47	54	0	—	—	—	175	2.4	1.1	4.0
REG. SEASON TOTALS	44	—	569	74	226	.327	—	—	—	27	41	.659	—	—	106	47	54	0	—	—	—	175	2.4	1.1	4.0

FRINK, PATRICK EDWARD (Pat) b. February 18, 1945 Ht. 6-4 Wt. 195 College—Colorado

SEASON—TEAM	G	GS	MIN	FGM	FGA	PCT	3FGM	3FGA	PCT	FTM	FTA	PCT	O-RB	D-RB	TOT	AST	PF	DQ	STL	TO	BLK	PTS	RPG	APG	PPG
68-69—Cincinnati	48	—	363	50	147	.340	—	—	—	23	29	.793	—	—	41	55	54	1	—	—	—	123	0.9	1.1	2.6
REG. SEASON TOTALS	48	—	363	50	147	.340	—	—	—	23	29	.793	—	—	41	55	54	1	—	—	—	123	0.9	1.1	2.6

FRITSCHE, JAMES A. (Jim) b. December 10, 1931 Ht. 6-8 Wt. 210 College—Hamline

SEASON—TEAM	G	GS	MIN	FGM	FGA	PCT	3FGM	3FGA	PCT	FTM	FTA	PCT	O-RB	D-RB	TOT	AST	PF	DQ	STL	TO	BLK	PTS	RPG	APG	PPG
53-54—Minn.-Balt.	68	—	1221	116	379	.306	—	—	—	49	68	.721	—	—	217	73	103	0	—	—	—	281	3.2	1.1	4.1
54-55—Fort Wayne	16	—	151	16	48	.333	—	—	—	13	16	.813	—	—	32	4	28	0	—	—	—	45	2.0	0.3	2.8
REG. SEASON TOTALS	84	—	1372	132	427	.309	—	—	—	62	84	.738	—	—	249	77	131	0	—	—	—	326	3.0	0.9	3.9

FRYER, BERNIE W. b. December 25, 1949 Ht. 6-3 Wt. 185 College—Brigham Young

SEASON—TEAM	G	GS	MIN	FGM	FGA	PCT	3FGM	3FGA	PCT	FTM	FTA	PCT	O-RB	D-RB	TOT	AST	PF	DQ	STL	TO	BLK	PTS	RPG	APG	PPG
73-74—Portland	80	—	1674	226	491	.460	—	—	—	107	135	.793	60	99	159	279	187	1	92	—	10	559	2.0	3.5	7.0
74-75—New Orleans	31	—	432	47	106	.443	—	—	—	33	43	.767	16	30	46	52	54	0	22	—	0	127	1.5	1.7	4.1
74-75—St. Louis (A)	9	—	264	24	68	.353	0	1	.000	22	28	.786	5	17	22	26	28	—	6	17	0	70	2.4	2.9	7.8
REG. NBA TOTALS	111	—	2106	273	597	.457	—	—	—	140	178	.787	76	129	205	331	241	1	114	—	10	686	1.8	3.0	6.2
REG. ABA TOTALS	9	—	264	24	68	.353	0	1	.000	22	28	.786	5	17	22	26	28	—	6	17	0	70	2.4	2.9	7.8

FUCARINO, FRANK A. b. July 24, 1920 Ht. 6-2 Wt. 175 College—Long Island University

SEASON—TEAM	G	GS	MIN	FGM	FGA	PCT	3FGM	3FGA	PCT	FTM	FTA	PCT	O-RB	D-RB	TOT	AST	PF	DQ	STL	TO	BLK	PTS	RPG	APG	PPG
46-47—Toronto	28	—	—	53	198	.268	—	—	—	34	60	.567	—	—	—	8	38	—	—	—	—	140	—	0.3	5.0
REG. SEASON TOTALS	28	—	—	53	198	.268	—	—	—	34	60	.567	—	—	—	8	38	—	—	—	—	140	—	0.3	5.0

FUETSCH, HERMAN JOSEPH (Herm, Dutch) b. July 6, 1918 Ht. 6-0 Wt. 170 College—None

SEASON—TEAM	G	GS	MIN	FGM	FGA	PCT	3FGM	3FGA	PCT	FTM	FTA	PCT	O-RB	D-RB	TOT	AST	PF	DQ	STL	TO	BLK	PTS	RPG	APG	PPG
45-46—Cleveland (N)	27	—	—	82	—	—	—	—	—	61	75	.813	—	—	—	—	36	—	—	—	—	225	—	—	8.3
47-48—Baltimore	42	—	—	42	140	.300	—	—	—	25	40	.625	—	—	—	17	39	—	—	—	—	109	—	0.4	2.6
REG. NBA TOTALS	42	—	—	42	140	.300	—	—	—	25	40	.625	—	—	—	17	39	—	—	—	—	109	—	0.4	2.6
REG. NBL TOTALS	27	—	—	82	—	—	—	—	—	61	75	.813	—	—	—	—	36	—	—	—	—	225	—	—	8.3
NBA PLAYOFF TOTALS	9	—	—	3	7	.429	—	—	—	6	8	.750	—	—	—	—	13	—	—	—	—	12	—	0.0	1.3

FULKS, JOSEPH FRANKLIN (Joe, Jumpin' Joe) b. October 26, 1921 d. March 21, 1976 Ht. 6-5 Wt. 190 College—Millsaps College/Murray State

SEASON—TEAM	G	GS	MIN	FGM	FGA	PCT	3FGM	3FGA	PCT	FTM	FTA	PCT	O-RB	D-RB	TOT	AST	PF	DQ	STL	TO	BLK	PTS	RPG	APG	PPG
46-47—Philadelphia	60	—	—	475	1557	.305	—	—	—	439	601	.730	—	—	—	25	199	—	—	—	—	1389	—	0.4	23.2
47-48—Philadelphia	43	—	—	326	1258	.259	—	—	—	297	390	.762	—	—	—	26	162	—	—	—	—	949	—	0.6	22.1
48-49—Philadelphia	60	—	—	529	1689	.313	—	—	—	502	638	.787	—	—	—	74	262	—	—	—	—	1560	—	1.2	26.0
49-50—Philadelphia	68	—	—	336	1209	.278	—	—	—	293	421	.696	—	—	—	56	240	—	—	—	—	965	—	0.8	14.2
50-51—Philadelphia	66	—	—	429	1358	.316	—	—	—	378	442	.855	—	—	523	117	247	8	—	—	—	1236	7.9	1.8	18.7
51-52—Philadelphia	61	—	1904	336	1078	.312	—	—	—	250	303	.825	—	—	368	123	255	13	—	—	—	922	6.0	2.0	15.1
52-53—Philadelphia	70	—	2085	332	960	.346	—	—	—	168	231	.727	—	—	387	138	319	20	—	—	—	832	5.5	2.0	11.9
53-54—Philadelphia	61	—	501	61	229	.266	—	—	—	28	49	.571	—	—	101	28	90	0	—	—	—	150	1.7	0.5	2.5
REG. SEASON TOTALS	489	—	4490	2824	9338	.302	—	—	—	2355	3075	.766	—	—	1379	587	1774	41	—	—	—	8003	5.3	1.2	16.4
PLAYOFF TOTALS	31	—	70	192	745	.258	—	—	—	204	261	.782	—	—	28	11	120	5	—	—	—	588	5.6	0.4	19.0
ALL-STAR TOTALS	2	—	9	9	22	.409	—	—	—	7	10	.700	—	—	12	5	7	0	—	—	—	25	6.0	2.5	12.5

FULLER, ANTHONY IKE (Tony) b. September 4, 1958 Ht. 6-4 Wt. 180 College—Vincennes/Pepperdine

SEASON—TEAM	G	GS	MIN	FGM	FGA	PCT	3FGM	3FGA	PCT	FTM	FTA	PCT	O-RB	D-RB	TOT	AST	PF	DQ	STL	TO	BLK	PTS	RPG	APG	PPG
80-81—Detroit	15	—	248	24	66	.364	0	1	.000	12	16	.750	13	29	42	28	25	0	10	23	1	60	2.8	1.9	4.0
REG. SEASON TOTALS	15	—	248	24	66	.364	0	1	.000	12	16	.750	13	29	42	28	25	0	10	23	1	60	2.8	1.9	4.0

FULLER, CARL b. January 10, 1946 Ht. 6-9½ Wt. 225 College—Bethune-Cookman

SEASON—TEAM	G	GS	MIN	FGM	FGA	PCT	3FGM	3FGA	PCT	FTM	FTA	PCT	O-RB	D-RB	TOT	AST	PF	DQ	STL	TO	BLK	PTS	RPG	APG	PPG
70-71—Floridians (A)	70	—	1151	170	372	.457	0	1	.000	72	120	.600	—	—	330	54	209	—	—	—	—	412	4.7	0.8	5.9
71-72—Floridians (A)	6	—	63	6	14	.429	0	0	—	9	15	.600	—	—	28	6	11	—	—	7	—	21	4.7	1.0	3.5
REG. ABA TOTALS	76	—	1214	176	386	.456	0	1	.000	81	135	.600	—	—	358	60	220	—	—	7	—	433	4.7	0.8	5.7
ABA PLAYOFF TOTALS	6	—	43	6	22	.273	0	2	.000	4	6	.667	—	—	15	4	11	—	—	—	—	16	2.5	0.7	2.7

FURLOW, TERRY L. b. October 18, 1954 d. May 23, 1980 Ht. 6-5 Wt. 200 College—Michigan State

SEASON—TEAM	G	GS	MIN	FGM	FGA	PCT	3FGM	3FGA	PCT	FTM	FTA	PCT	O-RB	D-RB	TOT	AST	PF	DQ	STL	TO	BLK	PTS	RPG	APG	PPG
76-77—Philadelphia	32	—	174	34	100	.340	—	—	—	16	18	.889	18	21	39	19	11	0	7	—	2	84	1.2	0.6	2.6
77-78—Cleveland	53	—	827	192	443	.433	—	—	—	88	99	.889	47	60	107	72	67	0	21	77	14	472	2.0	1.4	8.9
78-79—Clev.-Atlanta	78	—	1686	388	804	.483	—	—	—	163	195	.836	76	91	167	184	122	1	58	134	30	939	2.1	2.4	12.0
79-80—Atlanta-Utah	76	—	2122	430	926	.464	24	82	.293	171	196	.872	70	124	194	293	98	0	73	163	23	1055	2.6	3.9	13.9
REG. SEASON TOTALS	239	—	4809	1044	2273	.459	24	82	.293	438	508	.862	211	296	507	568	298	1	159	374	69	2550	2.1	2.4	10.7
PLAYOFF TOTALS	16	—	310	74	151	.490	0	0	—	36	38	.947	17	25	42	34	18	0	8	15	2	184	2.6	2.1	11.5

GABOR, WILLIAM A. (Billy, The Human Projectile) b. May 13, 1922 Ht. 5-11½ Wt. 180 College—Syracuse

SEASON—TEAM	G	GS	MIN	FGM	FGA	PCT	3FGM	3FGA	PCT	FTM	FTA	PCT	O-RB	D-RB	TOT	AST	PF	DQ	STL	TO	BLK	PTS	RPG	APG	PPG
48-49—Syracuse (N)	58	—	—	115	—	—	—	—	—	125	169	.740	—	—	—	—	163	—	—	—	—	355	—	—	6.1
49-50—Syracuse	56	—	—	226	671	.337	—	—	—	157	228	.689	—	—	—	108	198	—	—	—	—	609	—	1.9	10.9
50-51—Syracuse	61	—	—	255	745	.342	—	—	—	179	242	.740	—	—	150	125	213	7	—	—	—	689	2.5	2.0	11.3
51-52—Syracuse	57	—	1085	173	538	.322	—	—	—	142	183	.776	—	—	93	86	188	5	—	—	—	488	1.6	1.5	8.6
52-53—Syracuse	69	—	1337	215	614	.350	—	—	—	217	284	.764	—	—	104	134	262	11	—	—	—	647	1.5	1.9	9.4
53-54—Syracuse	61	—	1211	204	551	.370	—	—	—	139	194	.716	—	—	96	162	183	4	—	—	—	547	1.6	2.7	9.0
54-55—Syracuse	3	—	47	7	22	.318	—	—	—	3	5	.600	—	—	5	11	6	0	—	—	—	17	1.7	3.7	5.7
REG. NBA TOTALS	307	—	3680	1080	3141	.344	—	—	—	837	1136	.737	—	—	448	626	1050	27	—	—	—	2997	1.8	2.0	9.8
REG. NBL TOTALS	58	—	—	115	—	—	—	—	—	125	169	.740	—	—	—	—	163	—	—	—	—	355	—	—	6.1
NBA PLAYOFF TOTALS	36	—	304	92	297	.310	—	—	—	83	114	.728	—	—	57	74	115	6	—	—	—	267	2.2	2.1	7.4
NBL PLAYOFF TOTALS	6	—	—	12	—	—	—	—	—	12	15	.800	—	—	—	—	25	—	—	—	—	36	—	—	6.0
NBA ALL-STAR TOTALS	1	—	25	0	3	.000	—	—	—	0	1	.000	—	—	5	2	1	0	—	—	—	0	5.0	2.0	0.0

GAINER, ELMER R. b. 1919 Ht. 6-6½ Wt. 205 College—DePaul

SEASON—TEAM	G	GS	MIN	FGM	FGA	PCT	3FGM	3FGA	PCT	FTM	FTA	PCT	O-RB	D-RB	TOT	AST	PF	DQ	STL	TO	BLK	PTS	RPG	APG	PPG
41-42—Fort Wayne (N)	24	—	—	36	—	—	—	—	—	28	—	—	—	—	—	—	—	—	—	—	—	100	—	—	4.2
43-44—Sheboygan (N)	22	—	—	15	—	—	—	—	—	20	—	—	—	—	—	—	—	—	—	—	—	50	—	—	2.3
44-45—Chicago (N)	29	—	—	44	—	—	—	—	—	38	—	—	—	—	—	—	—	—	—	—	—	126	—	—	4.3
45-46—Chicago (N)	5	—	—	2	—	—	—	—	—	2	—	—	—	—	—	—	—	—	—	—	—	6	—	—	1.2
46-47—Anderson (N)	43	—	—	77	—	—	—	—	—	59	79	.747	—	—	—	—	87	—	—	—	—	213	—	—	5.0
47-48—Baltimore	5	—	—	1	9	.111	—	—	—	3	6	.500	—	—	—	3	8	—	—	—	—	5	—	0.6	1.0
48-49—Waterloo (N)	36	—	—	33	—	—	—	—	—	30	39	.769	—	—	—	—	64	—	—	—	—	96	—	—	2.7
49-50—Waterloo	15	—	—	9	35	.257	—	—	—	6	8	.750	—	—	—	7	28	—	—	—	—	24	—	0.5	1.6
REG. NBA TOTALS	20	—	—	10	44	.227	—	—	—	9	14	.643	—	—	—	10	36	—	—	—	—	29	—	0.5	1.5
REG. NBL TOTALS	159	—	—	207	—	—	—	—	—	177	118	.754	—	—	—	—	151	—	—	—	—	591	—	—	3.7
NBL PLAYOFF TOTALS	15	—	—	13	—	—	—	—	—	15	7	.286	—	—	—	—	28	—	—	—	—	41	—	—	2.7

GAINES, COREY YASUTO b. June 1, 1965 Ht. 6-3 Wt. 195 College—UCLA/Loyola Marymount

SEASON—TEAM	G	GS	MIN	FGM	FGA	PCT	3FGM	3FGA	PCT	FTM	FTA	PCT	O-RB	D-RB	TOT	AST	PF	DQ	STL	TO	BLK	PTS	RPG	APG	PPG
88-89—New Jersey	32	0	337	27	64	.422	1	5	.200	12	16	.750	3	16	19	67	27	0	15	20	1	67	0.6	2.1	2.1
89-90—Philadelphia	9	0	81	4	12	.333	1	2	.500	1	4	.250	1	4	5	26	11	0	4	10	0	10	0.6	2.9	1.1
90-91—Denver	10	2	226	28	70	.400	5	21	.238	22	26	.846	4	10	14	91	25	0	10	23	2	83	1.4	9.1	8.3
93-94—New York	18	0	78	9	20	.450	2	5	.400	13	15	.867	3	10	13	30	12	0	2	5	0	33	0.7	1.7	1.8
REG. SEASON TOTALS	69	2	722	68	166	.410	9	33	.273	48	61	.787	11	40	51	214	75	0	31	58	3	193	0.7	3.1	2.8
PLAYOFF TOTALS	4	0	28	0	4	.000	0	1	.000	0	0	—	0	2	2	2	4	0	0	0	0	0	0.5	0.5	0.0

GAINES, DAVID (Dave, Smokey) b. February 27, 1942 Ht. 6-1½ Wt. 175 College—LeMoyne-Owen

SEASON—TEAM	G	GS	MIN	FGM	FGA	PCT	3FGM	3FGA	PCT	FTM	FTA	PCT	O-RB	D-RB	TOT	AST	PF	DQ	STL	TO	BLK	PTS	RPG	APG	PPG
67-68—Kentucky (A)	3	—	36	4	16	.250	1	1	1.000	1	2	.500	—	—	10	0	4	0	—	0	—	10	3.3	0.0	3.3
REG. ABA TOTALS	3	—	36	4	16	.250	1	1	1.000	1	2	.500	—	—	10	0	4	0	—	—	—	10	3.3	0.0	3.3

GAINES, WILLIAM ROOSEVELT (Bill) b. March 10, 1946 Ht. 6-4 Wt. 185 College—East Texas State

SEASON—TEAM	G	GS	MIN	FGM	FGA	PCT	3FGM	3FGA	PCT	FTM	FTA	PCT	O-RB	D-RB	TOT	AST	PF	DQ	STL	TO	BLK	PTS	RPG	APG	PPG
68-69—Houston (A)	1	—	5	1	2	.500	0	0	—	0	0	—	—	—	1	0	0	0	—	1	—	2	1.0	0.0	2.0
REG. ABA TOTALS	1	—	5	1	2	.500	0	0	—	0	0	—	—	—	1	0	0	0	—	1	—	2	1.0	0.0	2.0

GALE, MICHAEL EUGENE (Mike) b. July 18, 1950 Ht. 6-4 Wt. 190 College—Elizabeth City

SEASON—TEAM	G	GS	MIN	FGM	FGA	PCT	3FGM	3FGA	PCT	FTM	FTA	PCT	O-RB	D-RB	TOT	AST	PF	DQ	STL	TO	BLK	PTS	RPG	APG	PPG
71-72—Kentucky (A)	78	—	1701	201	447	.450	0	3	.000	95	140	.679	—	—	271	200	206	—	—	113	—	497	3.5	2.6	6.4
72-73—Kentucky (A)	81	—	1854	218	463	.471	1	6	.167	100	143	.699	78	163	241	248	207	0	131	108	—	537	3.0	3.1	6.6
73-74—Ken.-N.Y. (A)	80	—	2495	314	720	.436	2	17	.118	105	140	.750	107	261	368	324	242	—	167	178	81	735	4.6	4.1	9.2
74-75—New York (A)	72	—	1624	228	492	.463	7	23	.304	72	91	.791	97	139	236	165	131	—	88	111	47	535	3.3	2.3	7.4
75-76—San Antonio (A)	78	—	1782	230	506	.455	3	17	.176	64	80	.800	49	158	207	244	145	—	123	143	40	527	2.7	3.1	6.8
76-77—San Antonio	82	—	2598	353	754	.468	—	—	—	137	167	.820	54	219	273	473	224	3	191	—	50	843	3.3	5.8	10.3
77-78—San Antonio	70	—	2091	275	581	.473	—	—	—	87	100	.870	57	166	223	376	170	2	159	176	25	637	3.2	5.4	9.1
78-79—San Antonio	82	—	2121	284	612	.464	—	—	—	91	108	.843	40	146	186	374	192	1	152	153	40	659	2.3	4.6	8.0
79-80—San Antonio	67	—	1474	171	377	.454	2	13	.154	97	120	.808	34	118	152	312	134	2	123	115	13	441	2.3	4.7	6.6
80-81—S.A.-Port.	77	—	1112	157	309	.508	2	7	.286	55	68	.809	16	83	99	169	117	0	94	77	7	371	1.3	2.2	4.8
81-82—Golden State	75	70	1793	185	373	.496	0	5	.000	51	65	.785	37	152	189	261	173	1	121	126	28	421	2.5	3.5	5.6
REG. NBA TOTALS	453	70	11189	1425	3006	.474	4	25	.160	518	628	.825	238	884	1122	1965	1010	9	840	647	163	3372	2.5	4.3	7.4
REG. ABA TOTALS	389	—	9456	1191	2628	.453	13	66	.197	436	594	.734	330	722	1323	1181	931	0	509	653	168	2831	3.4	3.0	7.3
NBA PLAYOFF TOTALS	28	0	690	84	202	.416	1	4	.250	29	40	.725	25	50	75	122	65	1	37	38	10	198	2.7	4.4	7.1
ABA PLAYOFF TOTALS	38	—	1048	128	299	.428	3	11	.273	55	66	.833	20	83	137	162	100	0	70	64	34	314	3.6	4.3	8.3

GALLAGHER, CHAD AUSTIN b. May 30, 1969 Ht. 6-10 Wt. 255 College—Creighton

SEASON—TEAM	G	GS	MIN	FGM	FGA	PCT	3FGM	3FGA	PCT	FTM	FTA	PCT	O-RB	D-RB	TOT	AST	PF	DQ	STL	TO	BLK	PTS	RPG	APG	PPG
93-94—Utah	2	0	3	3	3	1.000	0	0	—	0	0	—	0	0	0	0	2	0	0	0	0	6	0.0	0.0	3.0
REG. SEASON TOTALS	2	0	3	3	3	1.000	0	0	—	0	0	—	0	0	0	0	2	0	0	0	0	6	0.0	0.0	3.0

GALLATIN, HARRY J. (The Horse) b. April 26, 1927 Ht. 6-6 Wt. 215 College—NE Missouri State

SEASON—TEAM	G	GS	MIN	FGM	FGA	PCT	3FGM	3FGA	PCT	FTM	FTA	PCT	O-RB	D-RB	TOT	AST	PF	DQ	STL	TO	BLK	PTS	RPG	APG	PPG
48-49—New York	52	—	—	157	479	.328	—	—	—	120	169	.710	—	—	—	63	127	—	—	—	—	434	—	1.2	8.3
49-50—New York	68	—	—	263	664	.396	—	—	—	277	366	.757	—	—	—	56	215	—	—	—	—	803	—	0.8	11.8
50-51—New York	66	—	—	293	705	.416	—	—	—	259	354	.732	—	—	800	180	244	4	—	—	—	845	12.1	2.7	12.8
51-52—New York	66	—	1931	233	527	.442	—	—	—	275	341	.806	—	—	661	115	223	5	—	—	—	741	10.0	1.7	11.2
52-53—New York	70	—	2333	282	635	.444	—	—	—	301	430	.700	—	—	916	126	224	5	—	—	—	865	13.1	1.8	12.4
53-54—New York	72	—	2690	258	639	.404	—	—	—	433	552	.784	—	—	1098	153	208	2	—	—	—	949	15.3	2.1	13.2
54-55—New York	72	—	2548	330	859	.384	—	—	—	393	483	.814	—	—	995	176	206	5	—	—	—	1053	13.8	2.4	14.6
55-56—New York	72	—	2378	322	834	.386	—	—	—	358	455	.787	—	—	740	168	220	6	—	—	—	1002	10.3	2.3	13.9
56-57—New York	72	—	1943	332	817	.406	—	—	—	415	519	.800	—	—	725	85	202	1	—	—	—	1079	10.1	1.2	15.0
57-58—Detroit	72	—	1990	340	898	.379	—	—	—	392	498	.787	—	—	749	86	217	5	—	—	—	1072	10.4	1.2	14.9
REG. SEASON TOTALS	682	—	15813	2810	7057	.398	—	—	—	3223	4167	.773	—	—	6684	1208	2086	34	—	—	—	8843	11.9	1.8	13.0
PLAYOFF TOTALS	64	—	1215	242	620	.390	—	—	—	284	373	.761	—	—	592	100	235	9	—	—	—	768	11.2	1.6	12.0
ALL-STAR TOTALS	7	—	159	19	41	.463	—	—	—	19	27	.704	—	—	65	16	17	0	—	—	—	57	9.3	2.3	8.1

GAMBEE, DAVID P. (Dave) b. April 16, 1937 Ht. 6-6 Wt. 215 College—Oregon State

SEASON—TEAM	G	GS	MIN	FGM	FGA	PCT	3FGM	3FGA	PCT	FTM	FTA	PCT	O-RB	D-RB	TOT	AST	PF	DQ	STL	TO	BLK	PTS	RPG	APG	PPG
58-59—St. Louis	2	—	7	1	1	1.000	—	—	—	0	0	—	—	—	2	0	2	0	—	—	—	2	1.0	0.0	1.0
59-60—St. L.-Cin.	61	—	656	117	291	.402	—	—	—	69	106	.651	—	—	229	38	83	1	—	—	—	303	3.8	0.6	5.0
60-61—Syracuse	79	—	2090	397	947	.419	—	—	—	291	352	.827	—	—	581	101	276	6	—	—	—	1085	7.4	1.3	13.7
61-62—Syracuse	80	—	2301	477	1126	.424	—	—	—	384	470	.817	—	—	631	114	275	10	—	—	—	1338	7.9	1.4	16.7
62-63—Syracuse	60	—	1234	235	537	.438	—	—	—	199	238	.836	—	—	289	48	190	2	—	—	—	669	4.8	0.8	11.2
63-64—Philadelphia	41	—	927	149	378	.394	—	—	—	151	185	.816	—	—	256	35	161	6	—	—	—	449	6.2	0.9	11.0
64-65—Philadelphia	80	—	1993	356	864	.412	—	—	—	299	368	.813	—	—	468	113	277	7	—	—	—	1011	5.9	1.4	12.6
65-66—Philadelphia	72	—	1068	168	437	.384	—	—	—	159	187	.850	—	—	273	71	189	3	—	—	—	495	3.8	1.0	6.9
66-67—Philadelphia	63	—	757	150	345	.435	—	—	—	107	125	.856	—	—	197	42	143	5	—	—	—	407	3.1	0.7	6.5
67-68—San Diego	80	—	1755	375	853	.440	—	—	—	321	379	.847	—	—	464	93	253	5	—	—	—	1071	5.8	1.2	13.4
68-69—Milw.-Detroit	59	—	926	210	465	.452	—	—	—	159	195	.815	—	—	257	47	159	4	—	—	—	579	4.4	0.8	9.8
69-70—San Francisco	73	—	951	185	464	.399	—	—	—	156	186	.839	—	—	244	55	172	0	—	—	—	526	3.3	0.8	7.2
REG. SEASON TOTALS	750	—	14665	2820	6708	.420	—	—	—	2295	2791	.822	—	—	3891	757	2180	49	—	—	—	7935	5.2	1.0	10.6
PLAYOFF TOTALS	43	—	840	118	331	.356	—	—	—	131	157	.834	—	—	188	36	143	3	—	—	—	367	4.4	0.8	8.5

GAMBLE, KEVIN DOUGLAS b. November 13, 1965 Ht. 6-6 Wt. 210 College—Lincoln (Ill.)/Iowa

SEASON—TEAM	G	GS	MIN	FGM	FGA	PCT	3FGM	3FGA	PCT	FTM	FTA	PCT	O-RB	D-RB	TOT	AST	PF	DQ	STL	TO	BLK	PTS	RPG	APG	PPG
87-88—Portland	9	0	19	0	3	.000	0	1	.000	0	0	—	2	1	3	1	2	0	2	2	0	0	0.3	0.1	0.0
88-89—Boston	44	6	375	75	136	.551	2	11	.182	35	55	.636	11	31	42	34	40	0	14	19	3	187	1.0	0.8	4.3
89-90—Boston	71	10	990	137	301	.455	3	18	.167	85	107	.794	42	70	112	119	77	1	28	44	8	362	1.6	1.7	5.1
90-91—Boston	82	76	2706	548	933	.587	0	7	.000	185	227	.815	85	182	267	256	237	6	100	148	34	1281	3.3	3.1	15.6
91-92—Boston	82	77	2496	480	908	.529	9	31	.290	139	157	.885	80	206	286	219	200	2	75	97	37	1108	3.5	2.7	13.5
92-93—Boston	82	58	2541	459	906	.507	52	139	.374	123	149	.826	46	200	246	226	185	1	86	81	37	1093	3.0	2.8	13.3
93-94—Boston	75	28	1880	368	804	.458	25	103	.243	103	126	.817	41	118	159	149	134	0	57	77	22	864	2.1	2.0	11.5
REG. SEASON TOTALS	445	255	11007	2067	3991	.518	91	310	.294	670	821	.816	307	808	1115	1004	875	10	362	468	141	4895	2.5	2.3	11.0
PLAYOFF TOTALS	29	26	752	121	249	.486	5	15	.333	24	33	.727	21	45	66	56	63	0	23	23	9	271	2.3	1.9	9.3

GANTT, ROBERT M. JR. (Bob) b. June 22, 1922 Ht. 6-4 Wt. 205 College—Duke

SEASON—TEAM	G	GS	MIN	FGM	FGA	PCT	3FGM	3FGA	PCT	FTM	FTA	PCT	O-RB	D-RB	TOT	AST	PF	DQ	STL	TO	BLK	PTS	RPG	APG	PPG
46-47—Washington	23	—	—	29	89	.326	—	—	—	13	28	.464	—	—	—	5	45	—	—	—	—	71	—	0.2	3.1
REG. SEASON TOTALS	23	—	—	29	89	.326	—	—	—	13	28	.464	—	—	—	5	45	—	—	—	—	71	—	0.2	3.1
PLAYOFF TOTALS	2	—	—	1	3	.333	—	—	—	0	1	.000	—	—	—	—	0	—	—	—	—	2	0.0	0.0	1.0

GARDNER, CHARLES RUTLAND (Chuck) b. September 30, 1944 Ht. 6-8 Wt. 205 College—Colorado

SEASON—TEAM	G	GS	MIN	FGM	FGA	PCT	3FGM	3FGA	PCT	FTM	FTA	PCT	O-RB	D-RB	TOT	AST	PF	DQ	STL	TO	BLK	PTS	RPG	APG	PPG
67-68—Denver (A)	42	—	487	71	175	.406	0	4	.000	55	79	.696	—	—	136	13	74	1	—	52	—	197	3.2	0.3	4.7
REG. ABA TOTALS	42	—	487	71	175	.406	0	4	.000	55	79	.696	—	—	136	13	74	1	—	52	—	197	3.2	0.3	4.7

GARDNER, EARL BAKER (Red) b. September 18, 1923 Ht. 6-3 Wt. 195 College—Wabash/DePauw

SEASON—TEAM	G	GS	MIN	FGM	FGA	PCT	3FGM	3FGA	PCT	FTM	FTA	PCT	O-RB	D-RB	TOT	AST	PF	DQ	STL	TO	BLK	PTS	RPG	APG	PPG
48-49—Minneapolis	50	—	—	38	101	.376	—	—	—	13	28	.464	—	—	—	19	50	—	—	—	—	89	—	0.4	1.8
REG. SEASON TOTALS	50	—	—	38	101	.376	—	—	—	13	28	.464	—	—	—	19	50	—	—	—	—	89	—	0.4	1.8
PLAYOFF TOTALS	7	—	—	1	9	.111	—	—	—	2	4	.500	—	—	—	1	3	—	—	—	—	4	—	0.1	0.6

GARDNER, KENNETH KAY (Kenny) b. September 27, 1949 Ht. 6-5 Wt. 205 College—Utah

SEASON—TEAM	G	GS	MIN	FGM	FGA	PCT	3FGM	3FGA	PCT	FTM	FTA	PCT	O-RB	D-RB	TOT	AST	PF	DQ	STL	TO	BLK	PTS	RPG	APG	PPG
75-76—Utah (A)	9	—	51	6	18	.333	0	0	—	2	2	1.000	8	5	13	3	9	—	2	1	1	14	1.4	0.3	1.6
REG. ABA TOTALS	9	—	51	6	18	.333	0	0	—	2	2	1.000	8	5	13	3	9	—	2	1	1	14	1.4	0.3	1.6

GARDNER, VERN B. b. May 14, 1925 d. August 26, 1987 Ht. 6-5 Wt. 200 College—Wyoming/Utah

SEASON—TEAM	G	GS	MIN	FGM	FGA	PCT	3FGM	3FGA	PCT	FTM	FTA	PCT	O-RB	D-RB	TOT	AST	PF	DQ	STL	TO	BLK	PTS	RPG	APG	PPG
49-50—Philadelphia	63	—	—	313	916	.342	—	—	—	227	296	.767	—	—	—	119	236	—	—	—	—	853	—	1.9	13.5
50-51—Philadelphia	61	—	—	129	383	.337	—	—	—	69	97	.711	—	—	237	89	149	6	—	—	—	327	3.9	1.5	5.4
51-52—Philadelphia	27	—	507	72	194	.371	—	—	—	15	23	.652	—	—	112	37	60	2	—	—	—	159	4.1	1.4	5.9
REG. SEASON TOTALS	151	—	507	514	1493	.344	—	—	—	311	416	.748	—	—	349	245	445	8	—	—	—	1339	4.0	1.6	8.9
PLAYOFF TOTALS	7	—	77	26	71	.366	—	—	—	19	23	.826	—	—	18	5	33	2	—	—	—	71	3.6	0.7	10.1

GARFINKEL, JACK (Dutch) b. June 13, 1918 Ht. 6-0 Wt. 190 College—St. John's

SEASON—TEAM	G	GS	MIN	FGM	FGA	PCT	3FGM	3FGA	PCT	FTM	FTA	PCT	O-RB	D-RB	TOT	AST	PF	DQ	STL	TO	BLK	PTS	RPG	APG	PPG
45-46—Rochester (N)	18	—	—	14	—	—	—	—	—	6	—	—	—	—	—	—	—	—	—	—	—	34	—	—	1.9
46-47—Rochester (N)	10	—	—	5	—	—	—	—	—	3	6	.500	—	—	—	—	—	—	—	—	—	13	—	—	1.3
46-47—Boston	40	—	—	81	304	.266	—	—	—	17	28	.607	—	—	—	58	62	—	—	—	—	179	—	1.5	4.5
47-48—Boston	43	—	—	114	380	.300	—	—	—	35	46	.761	—	—	—	59	78	—	—	—	—	263	—	1.4	6.1
48-49—Boston	9	—	—	12	70	.171	—	—	—	10	14	.714	—	—	—	17	19	—	—	—	—	34	—	1.9	3.8
REG. NBA TOTALS	92	—	—	207	754	.275	—	—	—	62	88	.705	—	—	—	134	159	—	—	—	—	476	—	1.5	5.2
REG. NBL TOTALS	28	—	—	19	—	—	—	—	—	9	6	.500	—	—	—	—	—	—	—	—	—	47	—	—	1.7
NBA PLAYOFF TOTALS	3	—	—	7	23	.304	—	—	—	8	10	.800	—	—	—	7	15	—	—	—	—	22	—	2.3	7.3
NBL PLAYOFF TOTALS	6	—	—	1	—	—	—	—	—	1	3	.333	—	—	—	—	1	—	—	—	—	3	—	—	0.5

GARLAND, GARY J. b. October 12, 1957 Ht. 6-4 Wt. 180 College—DePaul

SEASON—TEAM	G	GS	MIN	FGM	FGA	PCT	3FGM	3FGA	PCT	FTM	FTA	PCT	O-RB	D-RB	TOT	AST	PF	DQ	STL	TO	BLK	PTS	RPG	APG	PPG
79-80—Denver	78	—	1106	155	356	.435	6	19	.316	18	26	.692	50	88	138	145	80	1	54	73	4	334	1.8	1.9	4.3
REG. SEASON TOTALS	78	—	1106	155	356	.435	6	19	.316	18	26	.692	50	88	138	145	80	1	54	73	4	334	1.8	1.9	4.3

GARLAND, WINSTON KINNARD b. December 19, 1964 Ht. 6-2 Wt. 170 College—Southeastern CC (La.)/SW Missouri State

SEASON—TEAM	G	GS	MIN	FGM	FGA	PCT	3FGM	3FGA	PCT	FTM	FTA	PCT	O-RB	D-RB	TOT	AST	PF	DQ	STL	TO	BLK	PTS	RPG	APG	PPG
87-88—Golden State	67	62	2122	340	775	.439	13	39	.333	138	157	.879	68	159	227	429	188	2	116	167	7	831	3.4	6.4	12.4
88-89—Golden State	79	79	2661	466	1074	.434	10	43	.233	203	251	.809	101	227	328	505	216	2	175	187	14	1145	4.2	6.4	14.5
89-90—G.S.-L.A. Clips	79	19	1762	230	573	.401	12	36	.333	102	122	.836	51	163	214	303	152	1	78	158	10	574	2.7	3.8	7.3
90-91—L.A. Clippers	69	26	1702	221	519	.426	4	26	.154	118	157	.752	46	152	198	317	189	3	97	116	10	564	2.9	4.6	8.2
91-92—Denver	78	67	2209	333	750	.444	9	28	.321	171	199	.859	67	123	190	411	206	1	98	175	22	846	2.4	5.3	10.8
92-93—Houston	66	4	1004	152	343	.443	6	13	.462	81	89	.910	32	76	108	138	116	0	39	67	4	391	1.6	2.1	5.9
REG. SEASON TOTALS	438	257	11460	1742	4034	.432	54	185	.292	813	975	.834	365	900	1265	2103	1067	9	603	870	67	4351	2.9	4.8	9.9
PLAYOFF TOTALS	20	13	516	71	172	.413	1	4	.250	41	45	.911	20	46	66	60	58	2	29	37	2	184	3.3	3.0	9.2

GARMAKER, RICHARD EUGENE (Dick) b. October 29, 1932 Ht. 6-3½ Wt. 205 College—Hibbing CC/Minnesota

SEASON—TEAM	G	GS	MIN	FGM	FGA	PCT	3FGM	3FGA	PCT	FTM	FTA	PCT	O-RB	D-RB	TOT	AST	PF	DQ	STL	TO	BLK	PTS	RPG	APG	PPG
55-56—Minneapolis	68	—	870	138	373	.370	—	—	—	112	139	.806	—	—	132	104	127	0	—	—	—	388	1.9	1.5	5.7
56-57—Minneapolis	72	—	2406	406	1015	.400	—	—	—	365	435	.839	—	—	336	190	199	1	—	—	—	1177	4.7	2.6	16.3
57-58—Minneapolis	68	—	2216	390	988	.395	—	—	—	314	411	.764	—	—	365	183	190	2	—	—	—	1094	5.4	2.7	16.1
58-59—Minneapolis	72	—	2493	350	885	.395	—	—	—	284	368	.772	—	—	325	211	226	3	—	—	—	984	4.5	2.9	13.7
59-60—Minn.-N.Y.	70	—	1932	323	815	.396	—	—	—	203	263	.772	—	—	313	206	186	4	—	—	—	849	4.5	2.9	12.1
60-61—New York	71	—	2238	415	943	.440	—	—	—	275	358	.768	—	—	277	220	240	2	—	—	—	1105	3.9	3.1	15.6
REG. SEASON TOTALS	421	—	12155	2022	5019	.403	—	—	—	1553	1974	.787	—	—	1748	1114	1168	12	—	—	—	5597	4.2	2.6	13.3
PLAYOFF TOTALS	21	—	668	96	253	.379	—	—	—	92	112	.821	—	—	98	67	71	2	—	—	—	284	4.7	3.2	13.5
ALL-STAR TOTALS	4	—	73	13	36	.361	—	—	—	5	6	.833	—	—	19	6	9	0	—	—	—	31	4.8	1.5	7.8

GARNER, WILLIAM (Bill) b. June 17, 1940 Ht. 6-11 Wt. 225 College—Portland

SEASON—TEAM	G	GS	MIN	FGM	FGA	PCT	3FGM	3FGA	PCT	FTM	FTA	PCT	O-RB	D-RB	TOT	AST	PF	DQ	STL	TO	BLK	PTS	RPG	APG	PPG
67-68—Anaheim (A)	53	—	514	28	103	.272	0	1	.000	25	50	.500	—	—	119	24	101	4	—	47	—	81	2.2	0.5	1.5
REG. ABA TOTALS	53	—	514	28	103	.272	0	1	.000	25	50	.500	—	—	119	24	101	4	—	47	—	81	2.2	0.5	1.5

GARNETT, WILLIAM PATRICK (Bill) b. April 22, 1960 Ht. 6-9 Wt. 225 College—Wyoming

SEASON—TEAM	G	GS	MIN	FGM	FGA	PCT	3FGM	3FGA	PCT	FTM	FTA	PCT	O-RB	D-RB	TOT	AST	PF	DQ	STL	TO	BLK	PTS	RPG	APG	PPG
82-83—Dallas	75	13	1411	170	319	.533	0	3	.000	129	174	.741	141	265	406	103	245	3	48	81	70	469	5.4	1.4	6.3
83-84—Dallas	80	34	1529	141	299	.472	0	2	.000	129	176	.733	123	208	331	128	217	4	44	68	66	411	4.1	1.6	5.1
84-85—Indiana	65	13	1123	149	310	.481	0	2	.000	120	174	.690	98	188	286	67	196	3	28	92	15	418	4.4	1.0	6.4
85-86—Indiana	80	2	1197	112	239	.469	0	2	.000	116	162	.716	106	169	275	95	174	0	39	91	22	340	3.4	1.2	4.3
REG. SEASON TOTALS	300	62	5260	572	1167	.490	0	9	.000	494	686	.720	468	830	1298	393	832	10	159	332	173	1638	4.3	1.3	5.5
PLAYOFF TOTALS	8	0	74	15	30	.500	1	1	1.000	7	8	.875	10	12	22	4	10	0	0	1	2	38	2.8	0.5	4.8

GARRETT, CALVIN EUGENE b. July 11, 1956 Ht. 6-7 Wt. 190 College—Austin Peay/Oral Roberts

SEASON—TEAM	G	GS	MIN	FGM	FGA	PCT	3FGM	3FGA	PCT	FTM	FTA	PCT	O-RB	D-RB	TOT	AST	PF	DQ	STL	TO	BLK	PTS	RPG	APG	PPG
80-81—Houston	70	—	1638	188	415	.453	1	3	.333	50	62	.806	85	179	264	132	167	0	50	90	10	427	3.8	1.9	6.1
81-82—Houston	51	22	858	105	242	.434	3	10	.300	17	26	.654	27	67	94	76	94	0	32	38	6	230	1.8	1.5	4.5
82-83—Houston	4	0	34	4	11	.364	0	1	.000	2	2	1.000	3	4	7	3	4	0	0	3	0	10	1.8	0.8	2.5
83-84—Los Angeles	41	0	478	78	152	.513	2	6	.333	30	39	.769	24	47	71	31	62	2	12	34	2	188	1.7	0.8	4.6
REG. SEASON TOTALS	166	22	3008	375	820	.457	6	20	.300	99	129	.767	139	297	436	242	327	2	94	165	18	855	2.6	1.5	5.2
PLAYOFF TOTALS	14	0	118	9	22	.409	0	1	.000	7	8	.875	3	12	15	6	10	0	5	6	1	25	1.1	0.4	1.8

GARRETT, ELDO (Dick) b. January 31, 1947 Ht. 6-3 Wt. 185 College—Southern Illinois

SEASON—TEAM	G	GS	MIN	FGM	FGA	PCT	3FGM	3FGA	PCT	FTM	FTA	PCT	O-RB	D-RB	TOT	AST	PF	DQ	STL	TO	BLK	PTS	RPG	APG	PPG
69-70—Los Angeles	73	—	2318	354	816	.434	—	—	—	138	162	.852	—	—	235	180	236	5	—	—	—	846	3.2	2.5	11.6
70-71—Buffalo	75	—	2375	373	902	.414	—	—	—	218	251	.869	—	—	295	264	290	9	—	—	—	964	3.9	3.5	12.9
71-72—Buffalo	73	—	1905	325	735	.442	—	—	—	136	157	.866	—	—	225	165	225	5	—	—	—	786	3.1	2.3	10.8
72-73—Buffalo	78	—	1805	341	813	.419	—	—	—	96	110	.873	—	—	209	217	217	4	—	—	—	778	2.7	2.8	10.0
73-74—N.Y.-Milw.	40	—	326	43	126	.341	—	—	—	15	19	.789	15	25	40	23	56	0	10	—	1	101	1.0	0.6	2.5
REG. SEASON TOTALS	339	—	8729	1436	3392	.423	—	—	—	603	699	.863	15	25	1004	849	1024	23	10	—	1	3475	3.0	2.5	10.3
PLAYOFF TOTALS	26	—	641	103	205	.502	—	—	—	30	36	.833	1	2	55	46	75	2	2	—	0	236	2.1	1.8	9.1

GARRETT, ROWLAND G. b. July 16, 1950 Ht. 6-6½ Wt. 210 College—Florida State

SEASON—TEAM	G	GS	MIN	FGM	FGA	PCT	3FGM	3FGA	PCT	FTM	FTA	PCT	O-RB	D-RB	TOT	AST	PF	DQ	STL	TO	BLK	PTS	RPG	APG	PPG
72-73—Chicago	35	—	211	52	118	.441	—	—	—	21	31	.677	—	—	61	8	29	0	—	—	—	125	1.7	0.2	3.6
73-74—Chicago	41	—	373	68	184	.370	—	—	—	21	32	.656	31	39	70	11	43	0	5	—	9	157	1.7	0.3	3.8
74-75—Chicago	70	—	1183	228	474	.481	—	—	—	77	97	.794	80	167	247	43	124	0	24	—	13	533	3.5	0.6	7.6
75-76—Chicago-Clev.	55	—	540	108	258	.419	—	—	—	53	65	.815	45	72	117	17	68	0	25	—	7	269	2.1	0.3	4.9
76-77—Clev.-Milw.	62	—	598	106	239	.444	—	—	—	41	51	.804	37	75	112	27	80	0	21	—	10	253	1.8	0.4	4.1
REG. SEASON TOTALS	263	—	2905	562	1273	.441	—	—	—	213	276	.772	193	353	607	106	344	0	75	—	39	1337	2.3	0.4	5.1
PLAYOFF TOTALS	19	—	155	21	60	.350	—	—	—	4	8	.500	8	22	30	3	28	0	4	—	4	46	1.6	0.2	2.4

GARRICK, THOMAS S. (Tom, Chief) b. July 7, 1966 Ht. 6-2 Wt. 195 College—Rhode Island

SEASON—TEAM	G	GS	MIN	FGM	FGA	PCT	3FGM	3FGA	PCT	FTM	FTA	PCT	O-RB	D-RB	TOT	AST	PF	DQ	STL	TO	BLK	PTS	RPG	APG	PPG
88-89—L.A. Clippers	71	20	1499	176	359	.490	0	13	.000	102	127	.803	37	119	156	243	141	1	78	116	9	454	2.2	3.4	6.4
89-90—L.A. Clippers	73	22	1721	208	421	.494	4	21	.190	88	114	.772	34	128	162	289	151	4	90	117	7	508	2.2	4.0	7.0
90-91—L.A. Clippers	67	0	949	100	236	.424	0	22	.000	60	79	.759	40	87	127	223	101	0	62	66	2	260	1.9	3.3	3.9
91-92—S.A.-Minn.-Dallas	40	5	549	59	143	.413	1	4	.250	18	26	.692	12	44	56	98	54	0	36	44	4	137	1.4	2.5	3.4
REG. SEASON TOTALS	251	47	4718	543	1159	.469	5	60	.083	268	346	.775	123	378	501	853	447	5	266	343	22	1359	2.0	3.4	5.4

GARRIS, JOHN BRASKER b. June 6, 1959 Ht. 6-8 Wt. 205 College—Michigan/Boston College

SEASON—TEAM	G	GS	MIN	FGM	FGA	PCT	3FGM	3FGA	PCT	FTM	FTA	PCT	O-RB	D-RB	TOT	AST	PF	DQ	STL	TO	BLK	PTS	RPG	APG	PPG
83-84—Cleveland	33	1	267	52	102	.510	0	0	—	27	34	.794	35	42	77	10	40	0	8	11	6	131	2.3	0.3	4.0
REG. SEASON TOTALS	33	1	267	52	102	.510	0	0	—	27	34	.794	35	42	77	10	40	0	8	11	6	131	2.3	0.3	4.0

GARVIN, JAMES D. (Jim) b. February 5, 1950 Ht. 6-7 Wt. 210 College—Boston

SEASON—TEAM	G	GS	MIN	FGM	FGA	PCT	3FGM	3FGA	PCT	FTM	FTA	PCT	O-RB	D-RB	TOT	AST	PF	DQ	STL	TO	BLK	PTS	RPG	APG	PPG
73-74—Buffalo	6	—	11	1	4	.250	—	—	—	0	0	—	1	4	5	0	1	0	0	—	0	2	0.8	0.0	0.3
REG. SEASON TOTALS	6	—	11	1	4	.250	—	—	—	0	0	—	1	4	5	0	1	0	0	—	0	2	0.8	0.0	0.3

GATES, BEN FRANK (Frank, Needle) b. April 12, 1920 d. July 26, 1978 Ht. 6-0 Wt. 165 College—Sam Houston State

SEASON—TEAM	G	GS	MIN	FGM	FGA	PCT	3FGM	3FGA	PCT	FTM	FTA	PCT	O-RB	D-RB	TOT	AST	PF	DQ	STL	TO	BLK	PTS	RPG	APG	PPG
46-47—And.-Ft. Wayne (N)	32	—	—	68	—	—	—	—	—	30	52	.577	—	—	—	—	78	—	—	—	—	166	—	—	5.2
48-49—Anderson (N)	64	—	—	150	—	—	—	—	—	78	123	.634	—	—	—	—	166	—	—	—	—	378	—	—	5.9
49-50—Anderson	64	—	—	113	402	.281	—	—	—	61	98	.622	—	—	—	91	147	—	—	—	—	287	—	1.4	4.5
REG. NBA TOTALS	64	—	—	113	402	.281	—	—	—	61	98	.622	—	—	—	91	147	—	—	—	—	287	—	1.4	4.5
REG. NBL TOTALS	96	—	—	218	—	—	—	—	—	108	175	.617	—	—	—	—	244	—	—	—	—	544	—	—	5.7
NBA PLAYOFF TOTALS	7	—	—	9	37	.243	—	—	—	7	10	.700	—	—	—	9	15	1	—	—	—	25	—	1.3	3.6
NBL PLAYOFF TOTALS	14	—	—	22	—	—	—	—	—	14	23	.609	—	—	—	—	33	—	—	—	—	58	—	—	4.1

GATLING, CHRIS RAYMOND b. September 3, 1967 Ht. 6-10 Wt. 225 College—Pittsburgh/Old Dominion

SEASON—TEAM	G	GS	MIN	FGM	FGA	PCT	3FGM	3FGA	PCT	FTM	FTA	PCT	O-RB	D-RB	TOT	AST	PF	DQ	STL	TO	BLK	PTS	RPG	APG	PPG
91-92—Golden State	54	1	612	117	206	.568	0	4	.000	72	109	.661	75	107	182	16	101	0	31	44	36	306	3.4	0.3	5.7
92-93—Golden State	70	11	1248	249	462	.539	0	6	.000	150	207	.725	129	191	320	40	197	2	44	102	53	648	4.6	0.6	9.3
93-94—Golden State	82	23	1296	271	461	.588	0	1	.000	129	208	.620	143	254	397	41	223	5	40	84	63	671	4.8	0.5	8.2
REG. SEASON TOTALS	206	35	3156	637	1129	.564	0	11	.000	351	524	.670	347	552	899	97	521	7	115	230	152	1625	4.4	0.5	7.9
PLAYOFF TOTALS	7	1	135	26	42	.619	0	0	—	24	35	.686	16	26	42	4	24	0	4	3	11	76	6.0	0.6	10.9

GATTISON, KENNETH CLAY (Kenny) b. May 23, 1964 Ht. 6-8 Wt. 245 College—Old Dominion

SEASON—TEAM	G	GS	MIN	FGM	FGA	PCT	3FGM	3FGA	PCT	FTM	FTA	PCT	O-RB	D-RB	TOT	AST	PF	DQ	STL	TO	BLK	PTS	RPG	APG	PPG
86-87—Phoenix	77	14	1104	148	311	.476	0	3	.000	108	171	.632	87	183	270	36	178	1	24	88	33	404	3.5	0.5	5.2
88-89—Phoenix	2	0	9	0	1	.000	0	0	—	1	2	.500	0	1	1	0	2	0	0	0	0	1	0.5	0.0	0.5
89-90—Charlotte	63	2	941	148	269	.550	1	1	1.000	75	110	.682	75	122	197	39	150	1	35	67	31	372	3.1	0.6	5.9
90-91—Charlotte	72	6	1552	243	457	.532	0	2	.000	164	248	.661	136	243	379	44	211	3	48	102	67	650	5.3	0.6	9.0
91-92—Charlotte	82	71	2223	423	799	.529	0	2	.000	196	285	.688	177	403	580	131	273	4	59	140	69	1042	7.1	1.6	12.7
92-93—Charlotte	75	5	1475	203	384	.529	0	3	.000	102	169	.604	108	245	353	68	237	3	48	64	55	508	4.7	0.9	6.8
93-94—Charlotte	77	18	1644	233	445	.524	0	0	—	126	195	.646	105	253	358	95	229	3	59	79	46	592	4.6	1.2	7.7
REG. SEASON TOTALS	448	116	8948	1398	2666	.524	1	11	.091	772	1180	.654	688	1450	2138	413	1280	15	273	540	301	3569	4.8	0.9	8.0
PLAYOFF TOTALS	9	0	187	22	46	.478	0	0	—	9	21	.429	19	20	39	11	18	0	5	7	1	53	4.3	1.2	5.9

GAYDA, EDWARD C. (Ed) b. May 11, 1927 Ht. 6-4 Wt. 210 College—Washington State

SEASON—TEAM	G	GS	MIN	FGM	FGA	PCT	3FGM	3FGA	PCT	FTM	FTA	PCT	O-RB	D-RB	TOT	AST	PF	DQ	STL	TO	BLK	PTS	RPG	APG	PPG
50-51—Tri-Cities	14	—	—	18	42	.429	—	—	—	18	23	.783	—	—	38	13	32	0	—	—	—	54	2.7	0.9	3.9
REG. SEASON TOTALS	14	—	—	18	42	.429	—	—	—	18	23	.783	—	—	38	13	32	0	—	—	—	54	2.7	0.9	3.9

GAZE, ANDREW b. July 24, 1965 Ht. 6-7 Wt. 205 College—Seton Hall

SEASON—TEAM	G	GS	MIN	FGM	FGA	PCT	3FGM	3FGA	PCT	FTM	FTA	PCT	O-RB	D-RB	TOT	AST	PF	DQ	STL	TO	BLK	PTS	RPG	APG	PPG
93-94—Washington	7	0	70	8	17	.471	4	8	.500	2	2	1.000	1	6	7	5	9	0	2	3	1	22	1.0	0.7	3.1
REG. SEASON TOTALS	7	0	70	8	17	.471	4	8	.500	2	2	1.000	1	6	7	5	9	0	2	3	1	22	1.0	0.7	3.1

GEIGER, MATTHEW ALLEN (Matt) b. September 10, 1969 Ht. 7-0 Wt. 245 College—Auburn/Georgia Tech

SEASON—TEAM	G	GS	MIN	FGM	FGA	PCT	3FGM	3FGA	PCT	FTM	FTA	PCT	O-RB	D-RB	TOT	AST	PF	DQ	STL	TO	BLK	PTS	RPG	APG	PPG
92-93—Miami	48	2	554	76	145	.524	0	4	.000	62	92	.674	46	74	120	14	123	6	15	36	18	214	2.5	0.3	4.5
93-94—Miami	72	0	1199	202	352	.574	1	5	.200	116	149	.779	119	184	303	32	201	2	36	61	29	521	4.2	0.4	7.2
REG. SEASON TOTALS	120	2	1753	278	497	.559	1	9	.111	178	241	.739	165	258	423	46	324	8	51	97	47	735	3.5	0.4	6.1
PLAYOFF TOTALS	2	0	11	0	2	.000	0	0	—	1	2	.500	0	4	4	—	1	0	0	0	0	1	2.0	0.0	0.5

GEORGE, JOHN EDWIN JR. (Jack) b. November 13, 1928 d. January 30, 1989 Ht. 6-2½ Wt. 190 College—Notre Dame/La Salle

SEASON—TEAM	G	GS	MIN	FGM	FGA	PCT	3FGM	3FGA	PCT	FTM	FTA	PCT	O-RB	D-RB	TOT	AST	PF	DQ	STL	TO	BLK	PTS	RPG	APG	PPG
53-54—Philadelphia	71	—	2648	259	736	.352	—	—	—	157	266	.590	—	—	386	312	210	4	—	—	—	675	5.4	4.4	9.5
54-55—Philadelphia	68	—	2480	291	756	.385	—	—	—	192	291	.660	—	—	302	359	191	2	—	—	—	774	4.4	5.3	11.4
55-56—Philadelphia	72	—	2840	352	940	.374	—	—	—	296	391	.757	—	—	313	457	202	1	—	—	—	1000	4.3	6.3	13.9
56-57—Philadelphia	67	—	2229	253	750	.337	—	—	—	200	293	.683	—	—	318	307	165	3	—	—	—	706	4.7	4.6	10.5
57-58—Philadelphia	72	—	1910	232	627	.370	—	—	—	178	242	.736	—	—	288	234	140	1	—	—	—	642	4.0	3.3	8.9
58-59—Phil.-N.Y.	71	—	1881	233	674	.346	—	—	—	153	203	.754	—	—	293	221	149	0	—	—	—	619	4.1	3.1	8.7
59-60—New York	69	—	1604	250	650	.385	—	—	—	155	202	.767	—	—	197	240	148	1	—	—	—	655	2.9	3.5	9.5
60-61—New York	16	—	268	31	93	.333	—	—	—	20	30	.667	—	—	32	39	37	0	—	—	—	82	2.0	2.4	5.1
REG. SEASON TOTALS	506	—	15860	1901	5226	.364	—	—	—	1351	1918	.704	—	—	2129	2169	1242	12	—	—	—	5153	4.2	4.3	10.2
PLAYOFF TOTALS	22	—	776	87	226	.385	—	—	—	64	85	.753	—	—	96	92	60	2	—	—	—	238	4.4	4.2	10.8
ALL-STAR TOTALS	2	—	42	5	13	.385	—	—	—	4	4	1.000	—	—	4	7	2	0	—	—	—	14	2.0	3.5	7.0

GEORGE, TATE CLAUDE b. May 29, 1968 Ht. 6-5 Wt. 200 College—Connecticut

SEASON—TEAM	G	GS	MIN	FGM	FGA	PCT	3FGM	3FGA	PCT	FTM	FTA	PCT	O-RB	D-RB	TOT	AST	PF	DQ	STL	TO	BLK	PTS	RPG	APG	PPG
90-91—New Jersey	56	11	594	80	193	.415	0	2	.000	32	40	.800	19	28	47	104	58	0	25	42	5	192	0.8	1.9	3.4
91-92—New Jersey	70	2	1037	165	386	.427	1	6	.167	87	106	.821	36	69	105	162	98	0	41	82	3	418	1.5	2.3	6.0
92-93—New Jersey	48	1	380	51	135	.378	0	5	.000	20	24	.833	9	18	27	59	25	0	10	31	3	122	0.6	1.2	2.5
REG. SEASON TOTALS	174	14	2011	296	714	.415	1	13	.077	139	170	.818	64	115	179	325	181	0	76	155	11	732	1.0	1.9	4.2
PLAYOFF TOTALS	6	0	66	9	30	.300	0	0	—	1	3	.333	1	2	3	14	9	0	4	5	1	19	0.5	2.3	3.2

GERARD, DANIEL JAMES (Gus) b. July 27, 1953 Ht. 6-8 Wt. 200 College—Virginia

SEASON—TEAM	G	GS	MIN	FGM	FGA	PCT	3FGM	3FGA	PCT	FTM	FTA	PCT	O-RB	D-RB	TOT	AST	PF	DQ	STL	TO	BLK	PTS	RPG	APG	PPG
74-75—St. Louis (A)	84	—	2702	554	1220	.454	1	6	.167	206	279	.738	282	373	655	189	274	—	63	207	111	1315	7.8	2.3	15.7
75-76—St. L.-Denver (A)	82	—	1727	332	795	.418	4	9	.444	175	238	.735	141	296	437	147	238	—	69	186	72	843	5.3	1.8	10.3
76-77—Denver-Buffalo	65	—	1048	201	454	.443	—	—	—	78	117	.667	89	128	217	92	164	1	44	—	62	480	3.3	1.4	7.4
77-78—Buffalo-Detroit	57	—	890	170	395	.430	—	—	—	75	108	.694	55	105	160	53	109	1	36	61	25	415	2.8	0.9	7.3
78-79—Detroit-K.C.	58	—	465	84	194	.433	—	—	—	50	91	.549	40	58	98	21	74	1	20	36	13	218	1.7	0.4	3.8
79-80—Kansas City	73	—	869	159	348	.457	1	3	.333	66	100	.660	77	100	177	43	96	1	41	49	26	385	2.4	0.6	5.3
80-81—K.C.-S.A.	27	—	252	41	111	.369	0	4	.000	27	40	.675	30	37	67	15	41	0	10	15	9	109	2.5	0.6	4.0
REG. NBA TOTALS	280	—	3524	655	1502	.436	1	7	.143	296	456	.649	291	428	719	224	484	4	151	161	135	1607	2.6	0.8	5.7
REG. ABA TOTALS	166	—	4429	886	2015	.440	5	15	.333	381	517	.737	423	669	1092	336	512	—	132	393	183	2158	6.6	2.0	13.0
NBA PLAYOFF TOTALS	8	—	50	8	19	.421	0	0	—	4	8	.500	6	10	16	2	8	0	1	5	1	20	2.0	0.3	2.5
ABA PLAYOFF TOTALS	23	—	410	59	150	.393	0	1	.000	25	38	.658	30	53	83	28	58	—	14	47	14	143	3.6	1.2	6.2
ABA ALL-STAR TOTALS	1	—	17	5	14	.357	0	0	—	2	2	1.000	—	—	9	1	5	—	0	0	0	12	9.0	1.0	12.0

GERVIN, DERRICK EUGENE b. March 28, 1963 Ht. 6-8 Wt. 205 College—Texas-San Antonio

SEASON—TEAM	G	GS	MIN	FGM	FGA	PCT	3FGM	3FGA	PCT	FTM	FTA	PCT	O-RB	D-RB	TOT	AST	PF	DQ	STL	TO	BLK	PTS	RPG	APG	PPG
89-90—New Jersey	21	0	339	93	197	.472	0	3	.000	65	89	.730	29	36	65	8	47	0	20	12	7	251	3.1	0.4	12.0
90-91—New Jersey	56	4	743	164	394	.416	7	28	.250	90	114	.789	40	70	110	30	88	0	19	45	19	425	2.0	0.5	7.6
REG. SEASON TOTALS	77	4	1082	257	591	.435	7	31	.226	155	203	.764	69	106	175	38	135	0	39	57	26	676	2.3	0.5	8.8

GERVIN, GEORGE (Iceman) b. April 27, 1952 Ht. 6-7 Wt. 185 College—Long Beach State/Eastern Michigan

SEASON—TEAM	G	GS	MIN	FGM	FGA	PCT	3FGM	3FGA	PCT	FTM	FTA	PCT	O-RB	D-RB	TOT	AST	PF	DQ	STL	TO	BLK	PTS	RPG	APG	PPG
72-73—Virginia (A)	30	—	689	161	341	.472	6	26	.231	96	118	.814	34	94	128	34	72	0	—	54	—	424	4.3	1.1	14.1
73-74—Vir.-S.A. (A)	74	—	2511	672	1426	.471	8	56	.143	378	464	.815	170	454	624	142	264	—	101	252	120	1730	8.4	1.9	23.4
74-75—San Antonio (A)	84	—	3113	784	1655	.474	17	55	.309	380	458	.830	247	450	697	207	295	—	131	249	138	1965	8.3	2.5	23.4
75-76—San Antonio (A)	81	—	2748	706	1414	.499	14	55	.255	342	399	.857	179	367	546	201	288	—	110	217	119	1768	6.7	2.5	21.8
76-77—San Antonio	82	—	2705	726	1335	.544	—	—	—	443	532	.833	134	320	454	238	286	12	105	—	104	1895	5.5	2.9	23.1
77-78—San Antonio	82	—	2857	864	1611	.536	—	—	—	504	607	.830	118	302	420	302	255	3	136	306	110	2232	5.1	3.7	27.2
78-79—San Antonio	80	—	2888	947	1749	.541	—	—	—	471	570	.826	142	258	400	219	275	5	137	286	91	2365	5.0	2.7	29.6
79-80—San Antonio	78	—	2934	1024	1940	.528	32	102	.314	505	593	.852	154	249	403	202	208	0	110	254	79	2585	5.2	2.6	33.1
80-81—San Antonio	82	—	2765	850	1729	.492	9	35	.257	512	620	.826	126	293	419	260	212	4	94	251	56	2221	5.1	3.2	27.1
81-82—San Antonio	79	79	2817	993	1987	.500	10	36	.278	555	642	.864	138	254	392	187	215	2	77	210	45	2551	5.0	2.4	32.3
82-83—San Antonio	78	78	2830	757	1553	.487	12	33	.364	517	606	.853	111	246	357	264	243	5	88	247	67	2043	4.6	3.4	26.2
83-84—San Antonio	76	76	2584	765	1561	.490	10	24	.417	427	507	.842	106	207	313	220	219	3	79	224	47	1967	4.1	2.9	25.9
84-85—San Antonio	72	69	2091	600	1182	.508	0	10	.000	324	384	.844	79	155	234	178	208	2	66	198	48	1524	3.3	2.5	21.2
85-86—Chicago	82	75	2065	519	1100	.472	4	19	.211	283	322	.879	78	137	215	144	210	4	49	161	23	1325	2.6	1.8	16.2
REG. NBA TOTALS	791	377	26536	8045	15747	.511	77	259	.297	4541	5383	.844	1186	2421	3607	2214	2331	40	941	2137	670	20708	4.6	2.8	26.2
REG. ABA TOTALS	269	—	9061	2323	4836	.480	45	192	.234	1196	1439	.831	630	1365	1995	584	919	0	342	772	377	5887	7.4	2.2	21.9
NBA PLAYOFF TOTALS	59	25	2202	622	1225	.508	0	13	.000	348	424	.821	110	231	341	186	207	5	69	187	51	1592	5.8	3.2	27.0
ABA PLAYOFF TOTALS	25	—	990	237	491	.483	5	21	.238	152	186	.817	78	122	238	54	87	0	15	65	30	631	9.5	2.2	25.2
NBA ALL-STAR TOTALS	9	7	215	54	108	.500	1	1	1.000	28	36	.778	9	24	33	12	25	0	16	20	9	137	3.7	1.3	15.2
ABA ALL-STAR TOTALS	3	1	67	14	37	.378	1	4	.250	11	14	.786	3	8	17	7	4	—	6	4	5	40	5.7	2.3	13.3

GETCHELL, CHARLES GORHAM (Gorham) b. August 14, 1920 d. July 1980 Ht. 6-6 Wt. 215 College—Temple

SEASON—TEAM	G	GS	MIN	FGM	FGA	PCT	3FGM	3FGA	PCT	FTM	FTA	PCT	O-RB	D-RB	TOT	AST	PF	DQ	STL	TO	BLK	PTS	RPG	APG	PPG
46-47—Pittsburgh	16	—	—	0	8	.000	—	—	—	5	5	1.000	—	—	—	0	5	—	—	—	—	5	—	0.0	0.3
REG. SEASON TOTALS	16	—	—	0	8	.000	—	—	—	5	5	1.000	—	—	—	0	5	—	—	—	—	5	—	0.0	0.3

GIANELLI, JOHN AREC b. June 10, 1950 Ht. 6-10 Wt. 220 College—Pacific

SEASON—TEAM	G	GS	MIN	FGM	FGA	PCT	3FGM	3FGA	PCT	FTM	FTA	PCT	O-RB	D-RB	TOT	AST	PF	DQ	STL	TO	BLK	PTS	RPG	APG	PPG
72-73—New York	52	—	516	79	175	.451	—	—	—	23	33	.697	—	—	150	25	72	0	—	—	—	181	2.9	0.5	3.5
73-74—New York	70	—	1423	208	434	.479	—	—	—	92	121	.760	110	233	343	77	159	1	23	—	42	508	4.9	1.1	7.3
74-75—New York	80	—	2797	343	726	.472	—	—	—	135	195	.692	214	475	689	163	263	3	38	—	118	821	8.6	2.0	10.3
75-76—New York	82	—	2332	325	687	.473	—	—	—	114	160	.713	187	365	552	115	194	1	25	—	62	764	6.7	1.4	9.3
76-77—N.Y.-K-Buffalo	76	—	1913	257	579	.444	—	—	—	90	125	.720	154	321	475	83	171	0	35	—	98	604	6.3	1.1	7.9
77-78—Milwaukee	82	—	2327	307	629	.488	—	—	—	79	123	.642	166	343	509	192	189	4	54	147	92	693	6.2	2.3	8.5
78-79—Milwaukee	82	—	2057	256	527	.486	—	—	—	72	102	.706	122	286	408	160	196	4	44	106	57	584	5.0	2.0	7.1
79-80—Utah	17	—	285	23	66	.348	0	0	—	9	16	.563	14	48	62	17	26	0	6	22	7	55	3.6	1.0	3.2
REG. SEASON TOTALS	541	—	13650	1798	3823	.470	0	0	—	614	875	.702	967	2071	3188	832	1270	13	225	275	476	4210	5.9	1.5	7.8
PLAYOFF TOTALS	31	—	776	82	189	.434	0	0	—	44	61	.721	60	100	173	40	81	0	12	13	21	208	5.6	1.3	6.7

GIBBS, DICK b. December 20, 1948 Ht. 6-5 Wt. 210 College—Burlington CC/Texas-El Paso

SEASON—TEAM	G	GS	MIN	FGM	FGA	PCT	3FGM	3FGA	PCT	FTM	FTA	PCT	O-RB	D-RB	TOT	AST	PF	DQ	STL	TO	BLK	PTS	RPG	APG	PPG
71-72—Houston	64	—	757	90	265	.340	—	—	—	55	66	.833	—	—	140	51	127	0	—	—	—	235	2.2	0.8	3.7
72-73—Houston-K.C.-Omaha	67	—	735	80	222	.360	—	—	—	47	63	.746	—	—	94	62	114	1	—	—	—	207	1.4	0.9	3.1
73-74—Seattle	71	—	1528	302	700	.431	—	—	—	162	201	.806	91	132	223	79	195	1	39	—	18	766	3.1	1.1	10.8
74-75—Washington	59	—	424	74	190	.389	—	—	—	48	64	.750	26	35	61	19	60	0	12	—	3	196	1.0	0.3	3.3
75-76—Buffalo	72	—	866	129	301	.429	—	—	—	77	93	.828	42	64	106	49	133	2	16	—	14	335	1.5	0.7	4.7
REG. SEASON TOTALS	333	—	4310	675	1678	.402	—	—	—	389	487	.799	159	231	624	260	629	4	67	—	35	1739	1.9	0.8	5.2
PLAYOFF TOTALS	11	—	40	7	19	.368	—	—	—	4	4	1.000	0	2	2	4	10	0	3	—	0	18	0.2	0.4	1.6

GIBSON, DEE JR. (Gibby) b. August 25, 1923 Ht. 5-11 Wt. 175 College—Western Kentucky

SEASON—TEAM	G	GS	MIN	FGM	FGA	PCT	3FGM	3FGA	PCT	FTM	FTA	PCT	O-RB	D-RB	TOT	AST	PF	DQ	STL	TO	BLK	PTS	RPG	APG	PPG
48-49—Tri-Cities (N)	64	—	—	94	—	—	—	—	—	113	177	.638	—	—	—	—	137	—	—	—	—	301	—	—	4.7
49-50—Tri-Cities	44	—	—	77	245	.314	—	—	—	127	177	.718	—	—	—	126	113	—	—	—	—	281	—	2.9	6.4
REG. NBA TOTALS	44	—	—	77	245	.314	—	—	—	127	177	.718	—	—	—	126	113	—	—	—	—	281	—	2.9	6.4
REG. NBL TOTALS	64	—	—	94	—	—	—	—	—	113	177	.638	—	—	—	—	137	—	—	—	—	301	—	—	4.7
NBA PLAYOFF TOTALS	3	—	—	4	11	.364	—	—	—	3	5	.600	—	—	—	2	11	—	—	—	—	11	—	0.7	3.7
NBL PLAYOFF TOTALS	6	—	—	19	—	—	—	—	—	19	32	.594	—	—	—	—	19	—	—	—	—	57	—	—	9.5

GIBSON, MELVIN L. (Mel) b. December 30, 1940 Ht. 6-3 Wt. 180 College—Western Carolina

SEASON—TEAM	G	GS	MIN	FGM	FGA	PCT	3FGM	3FGA	PCT	FTM	FTA	PCT	O-RB	D-RB	TOT	AST	PF	DQ	STL	TO	BLK	PTS	RPG	APG	PPG
63-64—Los Angeles	9	—	53	6	20	.300	—	—	—	1	2	.500	—	—	4	6	10	0	—	—	—	13	0.4	0.7	1.4
REG. SEASON TOTALS	9	—	53	6	20	.300	—	—	—	1	2	.500	—	—	4	6	10	0	—	—	—	13	0.4	0.7	1.4

GIBSON, MICHAEL JEROME (Mike) b. October 27, 1960 Ht. 6-11 Wt. 215 College—South Carolina-Spartanburg

SEASON—TEAM	G	GS	MIN	FGM	FGA	PCT	3FGM	3FGA	PCT	FTM	FTA	PCT	O-RB	D-RB	TOT	AST	PF	DQ	STL	TO	BLK	PTS	RPG	APG	PPG
83-84—Washington	32	0	229	21	55	.382	0	0	—	11	17	.647	29	37	66	9	30	1	5	14	7	53	2.1	0.3	1.7
85-86—Detroit	32	0	161	20	51	.392	0	0	—	8	11	.727	15	25	40	5	35	0	8	6	4	48	1.3	0.2	1.5
REG. SEASON TOTALS	64	0	390	41	106	.387	0	0	—	19	28	.679	44	62	106	14	65	1	13	20	11	101	1.7	0.2	1.6

GIBSON, WARD B. JR. (Hoot) b. December 5, 1921 d. February 1, 1958 Ht. 6-5 Wt. 215 College—Creighton

SEASON—TEAM	G	GS	MIN	FGM	FGA	PCT	3FGM	3FGA	PCT	FTM	FTA	PCT	O-RB	D-RB	TOT	AST	PF	DQ	STL	TO	BLK	PTS	RPG	APG	PPG
48-49—Denver-Tri-Cit (N)	62	—	—	291	—	—	—	—	—	223	334	.668	—	—	—	180	—	—	—	—	—	805	—	—	13.0
49-50—Boston-Wat.	32	—	—	67	195	.344	—	—	—	42	64	.656	—	—	37	106	—	—	—	—	—	176	—	1.2	5.5
REG. NBA TOTALS	32	—	—	67	195	.344	—	—	—	42	64	.656	—	—	37	106	—	—	—	—	—	176	—	1.2	5.5
REG. NBL TOTALS	62	—	—	291	—	—	—	—	—	223	334	.668	—	—	—	180	—	—	—	—	—	805	—	—	13.0
NBL PLAYOFF TOTALS	6	—	—	9	—	—	—	—	—	6	9	.667	—	—	—	16	—	—	—	—	—	24	—	—	4.0

GILL, KENDALL CEDRIC (K.G.) b. May 25, 1968 Ht. 6-5 Wt. 200 College—Illinois

SEASON—TEAM	G	GS	MIN	FGM	FGA	PCT	3FGM	3FGA	PCT	FTM	FTA	PCT	O-RB	D-RB	TOT	AST	PF	DQ	STL	TO	BLK	PTS	RPG	APG	PPG
90-91—Charlotte	82	36	1944	376	836	.450	2	14	.143	152	182	.835	105	158	263	303	186	0	104	163	39	906	3.2	3.7	11.0
91-92—Charlotte	79	79	2906	666	1427	.467	6	25	.240	284	381	.745	165	237	402	329	237	1	154	180	46	1622	5.1	4.2	20.5
92-93—Charlotte	69	67	2430	463	1032	.449	17	62	.274	224	290	.772	120	220	340	268	191	2	98	174	36	1167	4.9	3.9	16.9
93-94—Seattle	79	77	2435	429	969	.443	38	120	.317	215	275	.782	91	177	268	275	194	1	151	143	32	1111	3.4	3.5	14.1
REG. SEASON TOTALS	309	259	9715	1934	4264	.454	63	221	.285	875	1128	.776	481	792	1273	1175	808	4	507	660	153	4806	4.1	3.8	15.6
PLAYOFF TOTALS	14	14	506	91	222	.410	3	15	.200	38	56	.679	33	37	70	36	41	0	27	25	7	223	5.0	2.6	15.9

GILLERY, BENJAMIN (Ben) b. September 19, 1965 Ht. 7-0 Wt. 235 College—Hutchinson CC/Georgetown

SEASON—TEAM	G	GS	MIN	FGM	FGA	PCT	3FGM	3FGA	PCT	FTM	FTA	PCT	O-RB	D-RB	TOT	AST	PF	DQ	STL	TO	BLK	PTS	RPG	APG	PPG
88-89—Sacramento	24	0	84	6	19	.316	0	0	—	13	23	.565	7	16	23	2	29	0	2	5	4	25	1.0	0.1	1.0
REG. SEASON TOTALS	24	0	84	6	19	.316	0	0	—	13	23	.565	7	16	23	2	29	0	2	5	4	25	1.0	0.1	1.0

GILLESPIE, JACK A. b. October 1, 1947 Ht. 6-9 Wt. 220 College—Montana State

SEASON—TEAM	G	GS	MIN	FGM	FGA	PCT	3FGM	3FGA	PCT	FTM	FTA	PCT	O-RB	D-RB	TOT	AST	PF	DQ	STL	TO	BLK	PTS	RPG	APG	PPG
69-70—New York (A)	2	—	27	0	5	.000	0	0	—	2	2	1.000	—	—	7	0	3	0	—	—	—	2	3.5	0.0	1.0
REG. ABA TOTALS	2	—	27	0	5	.000	0	0	—	2	2	1.000	—	—	7	0	3	0	—	—	—	2	3.5	0.0	1.0

GILLETTE, GENE b. 1921 Ht. 6-2 Wt. 205 College—St. Mary's (Ca.)

SEASON—TEAM	G	GS	MIN	FGM	FGA	PCT	3FGM	3FGA	PCT	FTM	FTA	PCT	O-RB	D-RB	TOT	AST	PF	DQ	STL	TO	BLK	PTS	RPG	APG	PPG
46-47—Washington	14	—	—	1	11	.091	—	—	—	6	9	.667	—	—	2	13	—	—	—	—	—	8	—	0.1	0.6
REG. SEASON TOTALS	14	—	—	1	11	.091	—	—	—	6	9	.667	—	—	2	13	—	—	—	—	—	8	—	0.1	0.6

GILLIAM, ARMON LOUIS (The Hammer) b. May 28, 1964 Ht. 6-9 Wt. 250 College—Independence JC/Nevada-Las Vegas

SEASON—TEAM	G	GS	MIN	FGM	FGA	PCT	3FGM	3FGA	PCT	FTM	FTA	PCT	O-RB	D-RB	TOT	AST	PF	DQ	STL	TO	BLK	PTS	RPG	APG	PPG
87-88—Phoenix	55	53	1807	342	720	.475	0	0	—	131	193	.679	134	300	434	72	143	1	58	123	29	815	7.9	1.3	14.8
88-89—Phoenix	74	60	2120	468	930	.503	0	0	—	240	323	.743	165	376	541	52	176	2	54	140	27	1176	7.3	0.7	15.9
89-90—Phoenix-Cha.	76	66	2426	484	940	.515	0	2	.000	303	419	.723	211	388	599	99	212	4	69	183	51	1271	7.9	1.3	16.7
90-91—Cha.-Phil.	75	75	2644	487	1001	.487	0	2	.000	268	329	.815	220	378	598	105	185	2	69	174	53	1242	8.0	1.4	16.6
91-92—Philadelphia	81	81	2771	512	1001	.511	0	2	.000	343	425	.807	234	426	660	118	176	1	51	166	85	1367	8.1	1.5	16.9
92-93—Philadelphia	80	26	1742	359	774	.464	0	1	.000	274	325	.843	136	336	472	116	123	0	37	157	54	992	5.9	1.5	12.4
93-94—New Jersey	82	5	1969	348	682	.510	0	1	.000	274	361	.759	197	303	500	69	129	0	38	106	61	970	6.1	0.8	11.8
REG. SEASON TOTALS	523	366	15479	3000	6048	.496	0	8	.000	1833	2375	.772	1297	2507	3804	631	1144	10	376	1049	360	7833	7.3	1.2	15.0
PLAYOFF TOTALS	21	8	525	90	189	.476	0	1	.000	70	84	.833	33	89	122	13	34	0	8	28	15	250	5.8	0.6	11.9

GILLIAM, HERMAN L. JR. (Herm) b. May 5, 1946 Ht. 6-3 Wt. 190 College—Purdue

SEASON—TEAM	G	GS	MIN	FGM	FGA	PCT	3FGM	3FGA	PCT	FTM	FTA	PCT	O-RB	D-RB	TOT	AST	PF	DQ	STL	TO	BLK	PTS	RPG	APG	PPG
69-70—Cincinnati	57	—	1161	179	441	.406	—	—	—	68	91	.747	—	—	215	178	163	6	—	—	—	426	3.8	3.1	7.5
70-71—Buffalo	80	—	2082	378	896	.422	—	—	—	142	189	.751	—	—	334	291	246	4	—	—	—	898	4.2	3.6	11.2
71-72—Atlanta	82	—	2337	345	774	.446	—	—	—	145	173	.838	—	—	335	377	232	3	—	—	—	835	4.1	4.6	10.2
72-73—Atlanta	76	—	2741	471	1007	.468	—	—	—	123	150	.820	—	—	399	482	257	8	—	—	—	1065	5.3	6.3	14.0
73-74—Atlanta	62	—	2003	384	846	.454	—	—	—	106	134	.791	61	206	267	355	190	5	134	—	18	874	4.3	5.7	14.1
74-75—Atlanta	60	—	1393	314	736	.427	—	—	—	94	113	.832	76	128	204	170	124	1	77	—	13	722	3.4	2.8	12.0
75-76—Seattle	81	—	1644	299	676	.442	—	—	—	90	116	.776	56	164	220	202	139	0	82	—	12	688	2.7	2.5	8.5
76-77—Portland	80	—	1665	326	744	.438	—	—	—	92	120	.767	64	137	201	170	168	1	76	—	6	744	2.5	2.1	9.3
REG. SEASON TOTALS	578	—	15026	2696	6120	.441	—	—	—	860	1086	.792	257	635	2175	2225	1519	28	369	—	49	6252	3.8	3.8	10.8
PLAYOFF TOTALS	36	—	751	120	302	.397	—	—	—	29	36	.806	10	21	93	108	73	1	19	—	1	269	2.6	3.0	7.5

GILMORE, ARTIS b. September 21, 1949 Ht. 7-2 Wt. 240 College—Gardner-Webb/Jacksonville

SEASON—TEAM	G	GS	MIN	FGM	FGA	PCT	3FGM	3FGA	PCT	FTM	FTA	PCT	O-RB	D-RB	TOT	AST	PF	DQ	STL	TO	BLK	PTS	RPG	APG	PPG
71-72—Kentucky (A)	84	—	3666	806	1348	.598	0	0	—	391	605	.646	421	1070	1491	230	280	—	—	335	422	2003	17.8	2.7	23.8
72-73—Kentucky (A)	84	—	3502	687	1228	.559	1	2	.500	368	572	.643	449	1027	1476	295	302	0	—	286	259	1743	17.6	3.5	20.8
73-74—Kentucky (A)	84	—	3502	621	1260	.493	0	3	.000	326	489	.667	478	1060	1538	329	302	—	57	319	287	1568	18.3	3.9	18.7
74-75—Kentucky (A)	84	—	3493	784	1351	.580	1	2	.500	412	592	.696	427	934	1361	208	318	—	63	344	258	1981	16.2	2.5	23.6
75-76—Kentucky (A)	84	—	3286	773	1401	.552	0	0	—	521	764	.682	402	901	1303	211	341	—	58	295	205	2067	15.5	2.5	24.6
76-77—Chicago	82	—	2877	570	1091	.522	—	—	—	387	586	.660	313	757	1070	199	266	4	44	—	203	1527	13.0	2.4	18.6
77-78—Chicago	82	—	3067	704	1260	.559	—	—	—	471	669	.704	318	753	1071	263	261	4	42	366	181	1879	13.1	3.2	22.9
78-79—Chicago	82	—	3265	753	1310	.575	—	—	—	434	587	.739	293	750	1043	274	280	2	50	310	156	1940	12.7	3.3	23.7
79-80—Chicago	48	—	1568	305	513	.595	0	0	—	245	344	.712	108	324	432	133	167	5	29	133	59	855	9.0	2.8	17.8
80-81—Chicago	82	—	2832	547	816	.670	0	0	—	375	532	.705	220	608	828	172	295	2	47	236	198	1469	10.1	2.1	17.9
81-82—Chicago	82	82	2796	546	837	.652	1	1	1.000	424	552	.768	224	611	835	136	287	4	49	227	220	1517	10.2	1.7	18.5
82-83—San Antonio	82	82	2797	556	888	.626	0	6	.000	367	496	.740	299	685	984	126	273	4	40	254	192	1479	12.0	1.5	18.0
83-84—San Antonio	64	59	2034	351	556	.631	0	3	.000	280	390	.718	213	449	662	70	229	4	36	149	132	982	10.3	1.1	15.3
84-85—San Antonio	81	81	2756	532	854	.623	0	2	.000	484	646	.749	231	615	846	131	306	4	40	241	173	1548	10.4	1.6	19.1
85-86—San Antonio	71	71	2395	423	684	.618	0	1	.000	338	482	.701	166	434	600	102	239	3	39	186	108	1184	8.5	1.4	16.7
86-87—San Antonio	82	74	2405	346	580	.597	0	0	—	242	356	.680	185	394	579	150	235	2	39	178	95	934	7.1	1.8	11.4
87-88—Chicago-Boston	71	27	893	99	181	.547	0	0	—	67	128	.523	69	142	211	21	148	0	15	67	30	265	3.0	0.3	3.7
REG. NBA TOTALS	909	476	29685	5732	9570	.599	1	13	.077	4114	5768	.713	2639	6522	9161	1777	2986	38	470	2347	1747	15579	10.1	2.0	17.1
REG. ABA TOTALS	420	—	17449	3671	6588	.557	2	7	.286	2018	3022	.668	2177	4992	7169	1273	1543	0	178	1579	1431	9362	17.1	3.0	22.3
NBA PLAYOFF TOTALS	42	19	1152	179	315	.568	0	0	—	134	197	.680	97	239	336	47	113	1	27	81	71	492	8.0	1.1	11.7
ABA PLAYOFF TOTALS	58	—	2478	490	877	.559	0	1	.000	296	428	.692	284	647	931	185	213	0	33	224	162	1276	16.1	3.2	22.0
NBA ALL-STAR TOTALS	6	2	95	18	29	.621	0	0	—	15	19	.789	5	14	19	8	18	0	4	5	4	51	3.2	1.3	8.5
ABA ALL-STAR TOTALS	5	5	140	24	40	.600	0	0	—	19	34	.559	14	38	59	6	23	—	2	15	7	67	11.8	1.2	13.4

GILMORE, WALT b. February 27, 1947 Ht. 6-6 Wt. 225 College—Fort Valley State

SEASON—TEAM	G	GS	MIN	FGM	FGA	PCT	3FGM	3FGA	PCT	FTM	FTA	PCT	O-RB	D-RB	TOT	AST	PF	DQ	STL	TO	BLK	PTS	RPG	APG	PPG
70-71—Portland	27	—	261	23	54	.426	—	—	—	12	26	.462	—	—	73	12	49	1	—	—	—	58	2.7	0.4	2.1
REG. SEASON TOTALS	27	—	261	23	54	.426	—	—	—	12	26	.462	—	—	73	12	49	1	—	—	—	58	2.7	0.4	2.1

GILMUR, CHARLES E. JR. (Chuck) b. August 13, 1922 Ht. 6-4 Wt. 225 College—Washington

SEASON—TEAM	G	GS	MIN	FGM	FGA	PCT	3FGM	3FGA	PCT	FTM	FTA	PCT	O-RB	D-RB	TOT	AST	PF	DQ	STL	TO	BLK	PTS	RPG	APG	PPG
46-47—Chicago	51	—	—	76	253	.300	—	—	—	26	66	.394	—	—	—	21	139	—	—	—	—	178	—	0.4	3.5
47-48—Chicago	48	—	—	181	597	.303	—	—	—	97	148	.655	—	—	—	77	231	—	—	—	—	459	—	1.6	9.6
48-49—Chicago	56	—	—	110	281	.391	—	—	—	66	121	.545	—	—	—	125	194	—	—	—	—	286	—	2.2	5.1
49-50—Washington	68	—	—	127	379	.335	—	—	—	164	241	.680	—	—	—	108	275	—	—	—	—	418	—	1.6	6.1
50-51—Washington	16	—	—	17	61	.279	—	—	—	17	32	.531	—	—	75	17	57	3	—	—	—	51	4.7	1.1	3.2
REG. SEASON TOTALS	239	—	—	511	1571	.325	—	—	—	370	608	.609	—	—	75	348	896	3	—	—	—	1392	4.7	1.5	5.8
PLAYOFF TOTALS	19	—	—	43	182	.236	—	—	—	25	39	.641	—	—	—	14	80	6	—	—	—	111	—	0.7	5.8

GIVENS, JACK (Goose) b. September 21, 1956 Ht. 6-5 Wt. 205 College—Kentucky

SEASON—TEAM	G	GS	MIN	FGM	FGA	PCT	3FGM	3FGA	PCT	FTM	FTA	PCT	O-RB	D-RB	TOT	AST	PF	DQ	STL	TO	BLK	PTS	RPG	APG	PPG
78-79—Atlanta	74	—	1347	234	564	.415	—	—	—	102	135	.756	98	116	214	83	121	0	72	75	17	570	2.9	1.1	7.7
79-80—Atlanta	82	—	1254	182	473	.385	0	2	.000	106	128	.828	114	128	242	59	132	1	51	59	19	470	3.0	0.7	5.7
REG. SEASON TOTALS	156	—	2601	416	1037	.401	0	2	.000	208	263	.791	212	244	456	142	253	1	123	134	36	1040	2.9	0.9	6.7
PLAYOFF TOTALS	13	—	117	13	44	.295	0	0	—	3	3	1.000	8	18	26	6	16	0	3	8	2	29	2.0	0.5	2.2

GLAMACK, GEORGE GREGORY (Blind Bomber) b. June 7, 1919 d. March 10, 1987 Ht. 6-9 Wt. 230 College—North Carolina

SEASON—TEAM	G	GS	MIN	FGM	FGA	PCT	3FGM	3FGA	PCT	FTM	FTA	PCT	O-RB	D-RB	TOT	AST	PF	DQ	STL	TO	BLK	PTS	RPG	APG	PPG
41-42—Akron (N)	24	—	—	87	—	—	—	—	—	82	—	—	—	—	—	—	—	—	—	—	—	256	—	—	10.7
45-46—Rochester (N)	34	—	—	151	—	—	—	—	—	115	184	.625	—	—	—	108	—	—	—	—	—	417	—	—	12.3
46-47—Rochester (N)	44	—	—	141	—	—	—	—	—	90	135	.667	—	—	—	139	—	—	—	—	—	372	—	—	8.5
47-48—Indianapolis (N)	57	—	—	215	—	—	—	—	—	162	244	.664	—	—	—	151	—	—	—	—	—	592	—	—	10.4
48-49—Hammond (N)	43	—	—	169	—	—	—	—	—	163	216	.755	—	—	—	120	—	—	—	—	—	501	—	—	11.7
48-49—Indianapolis	11	—	—	30	121	.248	—	—	—	42	55	.764	—	—	—	19	28	—	—	—	—	102	—	1.7	9.3
REG. NBA TOTALS	11	—	—	30	121	.248	—	—	—	42	55	.764	—	—	—	19	28	—	—	—	—	102	—	1.7	9.3
REG. NBL TOTALS	202	—	—	763	—	—	—	—	—	612	779	.680	—	—	—	518	—	—	—	—	—	2138	—	—	10.6
NBL PLAYOFF TOTALS	26	—	—	109	—	—	—	—	—	88	97	.753	—	—	—	77	—	—	—	—	—	306	—	—	11.8

GLASS, GERALD DAMON (**World Class**) b. November 12, 1967 Ht. 6-6 Wt. 225 College—Delta State/Mississippi

SEASON—TEAM	G	GS	MIN	FGM	FGA	PCT	3FGM	3FGA	PCT	FTM	FTA	PCT	O-RB	D-RB	TOT	AST	PF	DQ	STL	TO	BLK	PTS	RPG	APG	PPG
90-91—Minnesota	51	3	606	149	340	.438	2	17	.118	52	76	.684	54	48	102	42	76	2	28	41	9	352	2.0	0.8	6.9
91-92—Minnesota	75	41	1822	383	871	.440	16	54	.296	77	125	.616	107	153	260	175	171	0	66	103	30	859	3.5	2.3	11.5
92-93—Minn.-Detroit	60	5	848	142	339	.419	7	33	.212	25	39	.641	61	81	142	77	104	1	33	35	18	316	2.4	1.3	5.3
REG. SEASON TOTALS	186	49	3276	674	1550	.435	25	104	.240	154	240	.642	222	282	504	294	351	3	127	179	57	1527	2.7	1.6	8.2

GLENN, MIKE THEODORE (**Stinger**) b. September 10, 1955 Ht. 6-3 Wt. 175 College—Southern Illinois

SEASON—TEAM	G	GS	MIN	FGM	FGA	PCT	3FGM	3FGA	PCT	FTM	FTA	PCT	O-RB	D-RB	TOT	AST	PF	DQ	STL	TO	BLK	PTS	RPG	APG	PPG
77-78—Buffalo	56	—	947	195	370	.527	—	—	—	51	65	.785	14	65	79	78	98	0	35	50	5	441	1.4	1.4	7.9
78-79—New York	75	—	1171	263	486	.541	—	—	—	57	63	.905	28	54	82	136	113	0	37	64	6	583	1.1	1.8	7.8
79-80—New York	75	—	800	188	364	.516	2	10	.200	63	73	.863	21	45	66	85	79	0	35	38	7	441	0.9	1.1	5.9
80-81—New York	82	—	1506	285	511	.558	4	11	.364	98	110	.891	27	61	88	108	126	0	72	62	5	672	1.1	1.3	8.2
81-82—Atlanta	49	0	833	158	291	.543	1	2	.500	59	67	.881	5	56	61	87	80	0	26	27	3	376	1.2	1.8	7.7
82-83—Atlanta	73	4	1124	230	444	.518	0	1	.000	74	89	.831	16	74	90	125	132	0	30	52	9	534	1.2	1.7	7.3
83-84—Atlanta	81	0	1503	312	554	.563	1	2	.500	56	70	.800	17	87	104	171	146	1	46	63	5	681	1.3	2.1	8.4
84-85—Atlanta	60	5	1126	228	388	.588	0	2	.000	62	76	.816	20	61	81	122	74	0	27	55	0	518	1.4	2.0	8.6
85-86—Milwaukee	38	1	573	94	190	.495	0	0	—	47	49	.959	4	53	57	39	42	0	9	18	3	235	1.5	1.0	6.2
86-87—Milwaukee	4	0	34	5	13	.385	0	0	—	5	7	.714	0	2	2	1	3	0	1	0	0	15	0.5	0.3	3.8
REG. SEASON TOTALS	593	10	9617	1958	3611	.542	8	28	.286	572	669	.855	152	558	710	952	893	1	318	429	43	4496	1.2	1.6	7.6
PLAYOFF TOTALS	22	0	295	39	86	.453	0	2	.000	19	21	.905	5	21	26	19	28	0	9	16	0	97	1.2	0.9	4.4

GLICK, NORMAN STANLEY (**Normie**) b. November 10, 1927 Ht. 6-6½ Wt. 205 College—Loyola Marymount

SEASON—TEAM	G	GS	MIN	FGM	FGA	PCT	3FGM	3FGA	PCT	FTM	FTA	PCT	O-RB	D-RB	TOT	AST	PF	DQ	STL	TO	BLK	PTS	RPG	APG	PPG
49-50—Minneapolis	1	—	—	1	1	1.000	—	—	—	0	0	—	—	—	—	0	1	—	—	—	—	2	—	0.0	2.0
REG. SEASON TOTALS	1	—	—	1	1	1.000	—	—	—	0	0	—	—	—	—	0	1	—	—	—	—	2	—	0.0	2.0

GLOUCHKOV, GEORGI NIKOLOV b. January 10, 1960 Ht. 6-8 Wt. 235 College—Akademik Varna (Bulgaria)

SEASON—TEAM	G	GS	MIN	FGM	FGA	PCT	3FGM	3FGA	PCT	FTM	FTA	PCT	O-RB	D-RB	TOT	AST	PF	DQ	STL	TO	BLK	PTS	RPG	APG	PPG
85-86—Phoenix	49	16	772	84	209	.402	1	1	1.000	70	122	.574	31	132	163	32	124	0	26	76	25	239	3.3	0.7	4.9
REG. SEASON TOTALS	49	16	772	84	209	.402	1	1	1.000	70	122	.574	31	132	163	32	124	0	26	76	25	239	3.3	0.7	4.9

GLOVER, CLARENCE b. November 1, 1947 Ht. 6-8 Wt. 210 College—Western Kentucky

SEASON—TEAM	G	GS	MIN	FGM	FGA	PCT	3FGM	3FGA	PCT	FTM	FTA	PCT	O-RB	D-RB	TOT	AST	PF	DQ	STL	TO	BLK	PTS	RPG	APG	PPG
71-72—Boston	25	—	119	25	55	.455	—	—	—	15	32	.469	—	—	46	4	26	0	—	—	—	65	1.8	0.2	2.6
REG. SEASON TOTALS	25	—	119	25	55	.455	—	—	—	15	32	.469	—	—	46	4	26	0	—	—	—	65	1.8	0.2	2.6
PLAYOFF TOTALS	3	—	10	2	6	.333	—	—	—	2	2	1.000	—	—	3	—	1	0	—	—	—	6	1.0	0.0	2.0

GMINSKI, MICHAEL THOMAS (**Mike, G-Man**) b. August 3, 1959 Ht. 6-11 Wt. 255 College—Duke

SEASON—TEAM	G	GS	MIN	FGM	FGA	PCT	3FGM	3FGA	PCT	FTM	FTA	PCT	O-RB	D-RB	TOT	AST	PF	DQ	STL	TO	BLK	PTS	RPG	APG	PPG
80-81—New Jersey	56	—	1579	291	688	.423	0	1	.000	155	202	.767	137	282	419	72	127	1	54	128	100	737	7.5	1.3	13.2
81-82—New Jersey	64	6	740	119	270	.441	0	0	—	97	118	.822	70	116	186	41	69	0	17	56	48	335	2.9	0.6	5.2
82-83—New Jersey	80	1	1255	213	426	.500	0	1	.000	175	225	.778	154	228	382	61	118	0	35	126	116	601	4.8	0.8	7.5
83-84—New Jersey	82	2	1655	237	462	.513	0	3	.000	147	184	.799	161	272	433	92	162	0	37	120	70	621	5.3	1.1	7.6
84-85—New Jersey	81	54	2418	380	818	.465	0	1	.000	276	328	.841	229	404	633	158	135	0	38	136	92	1036	7.8	2.0	12.8
85-86—New Jersey	81	78	2525	491	949	.517	0	1	.000	351	393	.893	206	462	668	133	163	0	56	140	71	1333	8.2	1.6	16.5
86-87—New Jersey	72	66	2272	433	947	.457	0	0	—	313	370	.846	192	438	630	99	159	0	52	129	69	1179	8.8	1.4	16.4
87-88—N.J.-Phil.	81	81	2961	505	1126	.448	0	2	.000	355	392	.906	245	569	814	139	176	0	64	177	118	1365	10.0	1.7	16.9
88-89—Philadelphia	82	82	2739	556	1166	.477	0	6	.000	297	341	.871	213	556	769	138	142	0	46	129	106	1409	9.4	1.7	17.2
89-90—Philadelphia	81	81	2659	458	1002	.457	3	17	.176	193	235	.821	196	491	687	128	136	0	43	98	102	1112	8.5	1.6	13.7
90-91—Phil.-Cha.	80	79	2196	357	808	.442	2	14	.143	128	158	.810	186	396	582	93	99	0	40	85	56	844	7.3	1.2	10.6
91-92—Charlotte	35	10	499	90	199	.452	1	3	.333	21	28	.750	37	81	118	31	37	0	11	20	16	202	3.4	0.9	5.8
92-93—Charlotte	34	0	251	42	83	.506	0	0	—	9	10	.900	34	51	85	7	28	0	1	11	9	93	2.5	0.2	2.7
93-94—Cha.-Milw.	29	7	309	36	103	.350	0	0	—	14	18	.778	22	52	74	11	23	0	13	13	16	86	2.6	0.4	3.0
REG. SEASON TOTALS	938	547	24058	4208	9047	.465	6	49	.122	2531	3002	.843	2082	4398	6480	1203	1574	1	507	1368	989	10953	6.9	1.3	11.7
PLAYOFF TOTALS	35	16	917	148	305	.485	0	5	.000	97	122	.795	55	138	193	29	72	0	22	48	57	393	5.5	0.8	11.2

GODFREAD, DANIEL JOSEPH (**Dan**) b. June 14, 1967 Ht. 6-10 Wt. 250 College—Evansville

SEASON—TEAM	G	GS	MIN	FGM	FGA	PCT	3FGM	3FGA	PCT	FTM	FTA	PCT	O-RB	D-RB	TOT	AST	PF	DQ	STL	TO	BLK	PTS	RPG	APG	PPG
90-91—Minnesota	10	0	20	5	12	.417	0	1	.000	3	4	.750	0	2	2	0	5	0	1	0	4	13	0.2	0.0	1.3
91-92—Houston	1	0	2	0	0	—	0	0	—	0	0	—	0	0	0	0	0	0	0	0	0	0	0.0	0.0	0.0
REG. SEASON TOTALS	11	0	22	5	12	.417	0	1	.000	3	4	.750	0	2	2	0	5	0	1	0	4	13	0.2	0.0	1.2

GOLA, THOMAS JOSEPH (Tom) b. January 13, 1933 Ht. 6-6 Wt. 205 College—La Salle

SEASON—TEAM	G	GS	MIN	FGM	FGA	PCT	3FGM	3FGA	PCT	FTM	FTA	PCT	O-RB	D-RB	TOT	AST	PF	DQ	STL	TO	BLK	PTS	RPG	APG	PPG
55-56—Philadelphia	68	—	2346	244	592	.412	—	—	—	244	333	.733	—	—	616	404	272	11	—	—	—	732	9.1	5.9	10.8
57-58—Philadelphia	59	—	2126	295	711	.415	—	—	—	223	299	.746	—	—	639	327	225	11	—	—	—	813	10.8	5.5	13.8
58-59—Philadelphia	64	—	2333	310	773	.401	—	—	—	281	357	.787	—	—	710	269	243	7	—	—	—	901	11.1	4.2	14.1
59-60—Philadelphia	75	—	2870	426	983	.433	—	—	—	270	340	.794	—	—	779	409	311	9	—	—	—	1122	10.4	5.5	15.0
60-61—Philadelphia	74	—	2712	420	940	.447	—	—	—	210	281	.747	—	—	692	292	321	13	—	—	—	1050	9.4	3.9	14.2
61-62—Philadelphia	60	—	2462	322	765	.421	—	—	—	176	230	.765	—	—	587	295	267	16	—	—	—	820	9.8	4.9	13.7
62-63—S.F.-N.Y.	73	—	2670	363	791	.459	—	—	—	170	219	.776	—	—	517	298	295	9	—	—	—	896	7.1	4.1	12.3
63-64—New York	74	—	2156	258	602	.429	—	—	—	154	212	.726	—	—	469	257	278	7	—	—	—	670	6.3	3.5	9.1
64-65—New York	77	—	1727	204	455	.448	—	—	—	133	180	.739	—	—	319	220	269	8	—	—	—	541	4.1	2.9	7.0
65-66—New York	74	—	1127	122	271	.450	—	—	—	82	105	.781	—	—	289	191	207	3	—	—	—	326	3.9	2.6	4.4
REG. SEASON TOTALS	698	—	22529	2964	6883	.431	—	—	—	1943	2556	.760	—	—	5617	2962	2688	94	—	—	—	7871	8.0	4.2	11.3
PLAYOFF TOTALS	39	—	1470	142	422	.336	—	—	—	148	192	.771	—	—	391	179	164	8	—	—	—	432	10.0	4.6	11.1
ALL-STAR TOTALS	4	—	70	12	29	.414	—	—	—	5	9	.556	—	—	11	7	10	0	—	—	—	29	2.8	1.8	7.3

GOLDFADEN, BENJAMIN PAUL (Ben) b. September 6, 1913 Ht. 6-3 Wt. 185 College—George Washington

SEASON—TEAM	G	GS	MIN	FGM	FGA	PCT	3FGM	3FGA	PCT	FTM	FTA	PCT	O-RB	D-RB	TOT	AST	PF	DQ	STL	TO	BLK	PTS	RPG	APG	PPG
46-47—Washington	2	—	—	0	2	.000	—	—	—	2	4	.500	—	—	—	0	3	—	—	—	—	2	—	0.0	1.0
REG. SEASON TOTALS	2	—	—	0	2	.000	—	—	—	2	4	.500	—	—	—	0	3	—	—	—	—	2	—	0.0	1.0

GONDREZICK, GLEN MICHAEL b. August 30, 1955 Ht. 6-6½ Wt. 220 College—Nevada-Las Vegas

SEASON—TEAM	G	GS	MIN	FGM	FGA	PCT	3FGM	3FGA	PCT	FTM	FTA	PCT	O-RB	D-RB	TOT	AST	PF	DQ	STL	TO	BLK	PTS	RPG	APG	PPG
77-78—New York	72	—	1017	131	339	.386	—	—	—	83	121	.686	92	158	250	83	181	0	56	82	18	345	3.5	1.2	4.8
78-79—New York	75	—	1602	161	326	.494	—	—	—	55	97	.567	147	277	424	106	226	1	98	95	18	377	5.7	1.4	5.0
79-80—Denver	59	—	1020	148	286	.517	2	6	.333	92	121	.760	107	152	259	81	119	0	68	58	16	390	4.4	1.4	6.6
80-81—Denver	73	—	1077	155	329	.471	0	2	.000	112	137	.818	136	171	307	83	185	2	91	69	20	422	4.2	1.1	5.8
81-82—Denver	80	0	1699	250	495	.505	0	3	.000	160	217	.737	140	283	423	152	229	0	92	100	36	660	5.3	1.9	8.3
82-83—Denver	76	2	1130	134	294	.456	0	3	.000	82	114	.719	108	193	301	100	161	0	80	49	9	350	4.0	1.3	4.6
REG. SEASON TOTALS	435	2	7545	979	2069	.473	2	14	.143	584	807	.724	730	1234	1964	605	1101	3	485	453	117	2544	4.5	1.4	5.8
PLAYOFF TOTALS	15	0	187	25	58	.431	0	1	.000	8	13	.615	22	23	45	19	27	0	7	7	2	58	3.0	1.3	3.9

GONDREZICK, GRANT b. January 19, 1963 Ht. 6-5 Wt. 205 College—Pepperdine

SEASON—TEAM	G	GS	MIN	FGM	FGA	PCT	3FGM	3FGA	PCT	FTM	FTA	PCT	O-RB	D-RB	TOT	AST	PF	DQ	STL	TO	BLK	PTS	RPG	APG	PPG
86-87—Phoenix	64	1	836	135	300	.450	4	17	.235	75	107	.701	47	63	110	81	91	0	25	56	4	349	1.7	1.3	5.5
88-89—L.A. Clippers	27	0	244	38	95	.400	3	11	.273	26	40	.650	15	21	36	34	36	0	13	17	1	105	1.3	1.3	3.9
REG. SEASON TOTALS	91	1	1080	173	395	.438	7	28	.250	101	147	.687	62	84	146	115	127	0	38	73	5	454	1.6	1.3	5.0

GOODRICH, GAIL CHARLES JR. b. April 23, 1943 Ht. 6-1 Wt. 170 College—UCLA

SEASON—TEAM	G	GS	MIN	FGM	FGA	PCT	3FGM	3FGA	PCT	FTM	FTA	PCT	O-RB	D-RB	TOT	AST	PF	DQ	STL	TO	BLK	PTS	RPG	APG	PPG
65-66—Los Angeles	65	—	1008	203	503	.404	—	—	—	103	149	.691	—	—	130	103	103	1	—	—	—	509	2.0	1.6	7.8
66-67—Los Angeles	77	—	1780	352	776	.454	—	—	—	253	337	.751	—	—	251	210	194	3	—	—	—	957	3.3	2.7	12.4
67-68—Los Angeles	79	—	2057	395	812	.486	—	—	—	302	392	.770	—	—	199	205	228	2	—	—	—	1092	2.5	2.6	13.8
68-69—Phoenix	81	—	3236	718	1746	.411	—	—	—	495	663	.747	—	—	437	518	253	3	—	—	—	1931	5.4	6.4	23.8
69-70—Phoenix	81	—	3234	568	1251	.454	—	—	—	488	604	.808	—	—	340	605	251	3	—	—	—	1624	4.2	7.5	20.0
70-71—Los Angeles	79	—	2808	558	1174	.475	—	—	—	264	343	.770	—	—	260	380	258	3	—	—	—	1380	3.3	4.8	17.5
71-72—Los Angeles	82	—	3040	826	1695	.487	—	—	—	475	559	.850	—	—	295	365	210	0	—	—	—	2127	3.6	4.5	25.9
72-73—Los Angeles	76	—	2697	750	1615	.464	—	—	—	314	374	.840	—	—	263	332	193	1	—	—	—	1814	3.5	4.4	23.9
73-74—Los Angeles	82	—	3061	784	1773	.442	—	—	—	508	588	.864	95	155	250	427	227	3	126	—	12	2076	3.0	5.2	25.3
74-75—Los Angeles	72	—	2668	656	1429	.459	—	—	—	318	378	.841	96	123	219	420	214	1	102	—	6	1630	3.0	5.8	22.6
75-76—Los Angeles	75	—	2646	583	1321	.441	—	—	—	293	346	.847	94	120	214	421	238	3	123	—	17	1459	2.9	5.6	19.5
76-77—New Orleans	27	—	609	136	305	.446	—	—	—	68	86	.806	25	36	61	74	43	0	22	—	2	340	2.3	2.7	12.6
77-78—New Orleans	81	—	2553	520	1050	.495	—	—	—	264	332	.795	75	102	177	388	186	0	82	205	22	1304	2.2	4.8	16.1
78-79—New Orleans	74	—	2130	382	850	.449	—	—	—	174	204	.853	68	115	183	357	177	1	90	185	13	938	2.5	4.8	12.7
REG. SEASON TOTALS	1031	—	33527	7431	16300	.456	—	—	—	4319	5354	.807	453	651	3279	4805	2775	24	545	390	72	19181	3.2	4.7	18.6
PLAYOFF TOTALS	80	—	2622	542	1227	.442	—	—	—	366	447	.819	7	9	250	333	219	1	7	—	1	1450	3.1	4.2	18.1
ALL-STAR TOTALS	5	—	77	16	38	.421	—	—	—	1	2	.500	1	4	9	14	8	0	1	—	0	33	1.8	2.8	6.6

GOODWIN, WILFRED R. (Pop, Bill) b. December 22, 1920 Ht. 6-2 Wt. 205 College—None

SEASON—TEAM	G	GS	MIN	FGM	FGA	PCT	3FGM	3FGA	PCT	FTM	FTA	PCT	O-RB	D-RB	TOT	AST	PF	DQ	STL	TO	BLK	PTS	RPG	APG	PPG
45-46—Sheboygan (N)	2	—	—	1	—	—	—	—	—	1	—	—	—	—	—	—	—	—	—	—	—	3	—	—	1.5
46-47—Providence	55	—	—	98	348	.282	—	—	—	60	75	.800	—	—	—	15	94	—	—	—	—	256	—	0.3	4.7
47-48—Providence	24	—	—	36	155	.232	—	—	—	19	27	.704	—	—	—	7	36	—	—	—	—	91	—	0.3	3.8
REG. NBA TOTALS	79	—	—	134	503	.266	—	—	—	79	102	.775	—	—	—	22	130	—	—	—	—	347	—	0.3	4.4
REG. NBL TOTALS	2	—	—	1	—	—	—	—	—	1	—	—	—	—	—	—	—	—	—	—	—	3	—	—	1.5

GORDON, LANCASTER b. June 24, 1962 Ht. 6-3 Wt. 195 College—Louisville

SEASON—TEAM	G	GS	MIN	FGM	FGA	PCT	3FGM	3FGA	PCT	FTM	FTA	PCT	O-RB	D-RB	TOT	AST	PF	DQ	STL	TO	BLK	PTS	RPG	APG	PPG
84-85—L.A. Clippers	63	1	682	110	287	.383	2	9	.222	37	49	.755	26	35	61	88	61	0	33	69	6	259	1.0	1.4	4.1
85-86—L.A. Clippers	60	1	704	130	345	.377	7	28	.250	45	56	.804	24	44	68	60	91	1	33	62	10	312	1.1	1.0	5.2
86-87—L.A. Clippers	70	4	1130	221	545	.406	14	48	.292	70	95	.737	64	62	126	139	106	1	61	102	13	526	1.8	2.0	7.5
87-88—L.A. Clippers	8	0	65	11	31	.355	0	0	—	6	6	1.000	2	2	4	7	8	0	1	4	2	28	0.5	0.9	3.5
REG. SEASON TOTALS	201	6	2581	472	1208	.391	23	85	.271	158	206	.767	116	143	259	294	266	2	128	237	31	1125	1.3	1.5	5.6

GORDON, PAUL C. JR. b. April 8, 1927 Ht. 6-3 Wt. 195 College—Baltimore CC/Notre Dame

SEASON—TEAM	G	GS	MIN	FGM	FGA	PCT	3FGM	3FGA	PCT	FTM	FTA	PCT	O-RB	D-RB	TOT	AST	PF	DQ	STL	TO	BLK	PTS	RPG	APG	PPG
49-50—Baltimore	4	—	—	0	6	.000	—	—	—	3	5	.600	—	—	—	3	3	—	—	—	—	3	—	0.8	0.8
REG. SEASON TOTALS	4	—	—	0	6	.000	—	—	—	3	5	.600	—	—	—	3	3	—	—	—	—	3	—	0.8	0.8

GOTTLIEB, LEO (Ace) b. November 28, 1920 d. August 1972 Ht. 5-11 Wt. 180 College—None

SEASON—TEAM	G	GS	MIN	FGM	FGA	PCT	3FGM	3FGA	PCT	FTM	FTA	PCT	O-RB	D-RB	TOT	AST	PF	DQ	STL	TO	BLK	PTS	RPG	APG	PPG
46-47—New York	57	—	—	149	494	.302	—	—	—	36	55	.655	—	—	—	24	71	—	—	—	—	334	—	0.4	5.9
47-48—New York	27	—	—	59	228	.259	—	—	—	13	21	.619	—	—	—	12	36	—	—	—	—	131	—	0.4	4.9
REG. SEASON TOTALS	84	—	—	208	722	.288	—	—	—	49	76	.645	—	—	—	36	107	—	—	—	—	465	—	0.4	5.5
PLAYOFF TOTALS	4	—	—	10	39	.256	—	—	—	4	6	.667	—	—	—	1	6	—	—	—	—	24	—	0.3	6.0

GOVAN, GERALD b. January 2, 1942 Ht. 6-10 Wt. 220 College—St. Mary's of the Plains

SEASON—TEAM	G	GS	MIN	FGM	FGA	PCT	3FGM	3FGA	PCT	FTM	FTA	PCT	O-RB	D-RB	TOT	AST	PF	DQ	STL	TO	BLK	PTS	RPG	APG	PPG
67-68—New Orleans (A)	78	—	1587	156	390	.400	1	1	1.000	79	131	.603	—	—	596	95	156	2	—	100	—	392	7.6	1.2	5.0
68-69—New Orleans (A)	77	—	1902	211	537	.393	1	4	.250	134	208	.644	—	—	701	150	238	4	—	162	—	557	9.1	1.9	7.2
69-70—New Orleans (A)	84	—	3701	422	1044	.404	1	11	.091	208	285	.730	285	932	1217	385	273	5	—	—	—	1053	14.5	4.6	12.5
70-71—Memphis (A)	84	—	3698	296	794	.373	1	4	.250	119	191	.623	277	861	1138	407	284	—	—	—	—	712	13.5	4.8	8.5
71-72—Memphis (A)	83	—	3414	277	719	.385	0	0	—	162	230	.704	310	872	1182	348	260	—	—	241	—	716	14.2	4.2	8.6
72-73—Utah (A)	84	—	2408	229	530	.432	0	0	—	81	135	.600	175	620	795	250	279	0	—	168	—	539	9.5	3.0	6.4
73-74—Utah (A)	83	—	2766	255	541	.471	0	2	.000	73	106	.689	142	586	728	245	260	—	60	156	50	583	8.8	3.0	7.0
74-75—Utah (A)	84	—	2791	239	602	.397	1	2	.500	83	105	.790	121	480	601	230	217	—	72	195	36	562	7.2	2.7	6.7
75-76—Virginia (A)	24	—	658	57	131	.435	0	0	—	23	28	.821	44	117	161	54	65	—	7	47	11	137	6.7	2.3	5.7
REG. ABA TOTALS	681	—	22925	2142	5288	.405	5	24	.208	962	1419	.678	1354	4468	7119	2164	2032	11	139	1069	97	5251	10.5	3.2	7.7
ABA PLAYOFF TOTALS	66	—	1930	189	497	.380	1	2	.500	76	109	.697	98	335	657	190	223	2	19	138	26	455	10.0	2.9	6.9
ABA ALL-STAR TOTALS	1	—	11	1	2	.500	0	0	—	0	0	—	0	0	4	0	0	0	0	0	0	2	4.0	0.0	2.0

GOVEDARICA, BATO ZDRAVKO b. April 17, 1928 Ht. 5-11 Wt. 185 College—DePaul

SEASON—TEAM	G	GS	MIN	FGM	FGA	PCT	3FGM	3FGA	PCT	FTM	FTA	PCT	O-RB	D-RB	TOT	AST	PF	DQ	STL	TO	BLK	PTS	RPG	APG	PPG
53-54—Syracuse	23	—	258	25	79	.316	—	—	—	25	37	.676	—	—	18	24	44	1	—	—	—	75	0.8	1.0	3.3
REG. SEASON TOTALS	23	—	258	25	79	.316	—	—	—	25	37	.676	—	—	18	24	44	1	—	—	—	75	0.8	1.0	3.3

GRABOSKI, JOSEPH W. (Joe, Grabbo) b. January 15, 1930 Ht. 6-8 Wt. 230 College—None

SEASON—TEAM	G	GS	MIN	FGM	FGA	PCT	3FGM	3FGA	PCT	FTM	FTA	PCT	O-RB	D-RB	TOT	AST	PF	DQ	STL	TO	BLK	PTS	RPG	APG	PPG
48-49—Chicago	45	—	—	54	157	.344	—	—	—	17	49	.347	—	—	—	18	86	—	—	—	—	125	—	0.4	2.8
49-50—Chicago	57	—	—	75	247	.304	—	—	—	53	89	.596	—	—	—	37	95	—	—	—	—	203	—	0.6	3.6
51-52—Indianapolis	66	—	2439	320	827	.387	—	—	—	264	396	.667	—	—	655	130	254	10	—	—	—	904	9.9	2.0	13.7
52-53—Indianapolis	69	—	2769	272	799	.340	—	—	—	350	513	.682	—	—	687	156	303	18	—	—	—	894	10.0	2.3	13.0
53-54—Philadelphia	71	—	2759	354	1000	.354	—	—	—	236	350	.674	—	—	670	163	223	4	—	—	—	944	9.4	2.3	13.3
54-55—Philadelphia	70	—	2515	373	1096	.340	—	—	—	208	303	.686	—	—	636	182	259	8	—	—	—	954	9.1	2.6	13.6
55-56—Philadelphia	72	—	2375	397	1075	.369	—	—	—	240	340	.706	—	—	642	190	272	5	—	—	—	1034	8.9	2.6	14.4
56-57—Philadelphia	72	—	2501	390	1118	.349	—	—	—	252	322	.783	—	—	614	140	244	5	—	—	—	1032	8.5	1.9	14.3
57-58—Philadelphia	72	—	2077	341	1017	.335	—	—	—	227	303	.749	—	—	570	125	249	3	—	—	—	909	7.9	1.7	12.6
58-59—Philadelphia	72	—	2482	394	1116	.353	—	—	—	270	360	.750	—	—	751	148	249	5	—	—	—	1058	10.4	2.1	14.7
59-60—Philadelphia	73	—	1269	217	583	.372	—	—	—	131	174	.753	—	—	358	111	147	1	—	—	—	565	4.9	1.5	7.7
60-61—Philadelphia	68	—	1011	169	507	.333	—	—	—	127	183	.694	—	—	262	74	148	2	—	—	—	465	3.9	1.1	6.8
61-62—St. L.-Chicago-Syr.	38	—	468	77	221	.348	—	—	—	39	65	.600	—	—	154	28	62	0	—	—	—	193	4.1	0.7	5.1
REG. SEASON TOTALS	845	—	22665	3433	9763	.352	—	—	—	2414	3447	.700	—	—	5999	1502	2591	61	—	—	—	9280	8.1	1.8	11.0
PLAYOFF TOTALS	40	—	982	157	473	.332	—	—	—	75	102	.735	—	—	271	73	104	2	—	—	—	389	7.1	1.9	9.7

GRACE, RICKY b. August 20, 1967 Ht. 6-1 Wt. 180 College—Midland/Oklahoma

SEASON—TEAM	G	GS	MIN	FGM	FGA	PCT	3FGM	3FGA	PCT	FTM	FTA	PCT	O-RB	D-RB	TOT	AST	PF	DQ	STL	TO	BLK	PTS	RPG	APG	PPG
93-94—Atlanta	3	0	8	2	3	.667	0	0	—	0	2	.000	0	1	1	1	3	0	0	0	0	4	0.3	0.3	1.3
REG. SEASON TOTALS	3	0	8	2	3	.667	0	0	—	0	2	.000	0	1	1	1	3	0	0	0	0	4	0.3	0.3	1.3

GRAHAM, CALVIN J. (Cal) b. June 7, 1944 Ht. 6-2½ Wt. 195 College—Gannon

SEASON—TEAM	G	GS	MIN	FGM	FGA	PCT	3FGM	3FGA	PCT	FTM	FTA	PCT	O-RB	D-RB	TOT	AST	PF	DQ	STL	TO	BLK	PTS	RPG	APG	PPG
67-68—Pittsburgh (A)	8	—	52	4	14	.286	0	0	—	5	8	.625	—	—	10	0	12	0	—	1	—	13	1.3	0.0	1.6
REG. ABA TOTALS	8	—	52	4	14	.286	0	0	—	5	8	.625	—	—	10	0	12	0	—	1	—	13	1.3	0.0	1.6

GRAHAM, GREGORY LAWRENCE (Greg) b. November 26, 1970 Ht. 6-4 Wt. 190 College—Indiana

SEASON—TEAM	G	GS	MIN	FGM	FGA	PCT	3FGM	3FGA	PCT	FTM	FTA	PCT	O-RB	D-RB	TOT	AST	PF	DQ	STL	TO	BLK	PTS	RPG	APG	PPG
93-94—Philadelphia	70	6	889	122	305	.400	2	25	.080	92	110	.836	21	65	86	66	54	0	61	65	4	338	1.2	0.9	4.8
REG. SEASON TOTALS	70	6	889	122	305	.400	2	25	.080	92	110	.836	21	65	86	66	54	0	61	65	4	338	1.2	0.9	4.8

GRAHAM, ORLANDO b. May 5, 1965 Ht. 6-8 Wt. 230 College—West Texas State/Auburn-Montgomery

SEASON—TEAM	G	GS	MIN	FGM	FGA	PCT	3FGM	3FGA	PCT	FTM	FTA	PCT	O-RB	D-RB	TOT	AST	PF	DQ	STL	TO	BLK	PTS	RPG	APG	PPG
88-89—Golden State	7	0	22	3	10	.300	0	0	—	2	4	.500	8	3	11	0	6	0	0	2	0	8	1.6	0.0	1.1
REG. SEASON TOTALS	7	0	22	3	10	.300	0	0	—	2	4	.500	8	3	11	0	6	0	0	2	0	8	1.6	0.0	1.1
PLAYOFF TOTALS	2	0	8	1	2	.500	0	0	—	1	2	.500	0	1	1	—	0	0	0	1	0	3	0.5	0.0	1.5

GRAHAM, PAUL (Snoop) b. November 28, 1967 Ht. 6-6 Wt. 200 College—Ohio

SEASON—TEAM	G	GS	MIN	FGM	FGA	PCT	3FGM	3FGA	PCT	FTM	FTA	PCT	O-RB	D-RB	TOT	AST	PF	DQ	STL	TO	BLK	PTS	RPG	APG	PPG
91-92—Atlanta	78	9	1718	305	682	.447	55	141	.390	126	170	.741	72	159	231	175	193	3	96	91	21	791	3.0	2.2	10.1
92-93—Atlanta	80	11	1508	256	560	.457	42	141	.298	96	131	.733	61	129	190	164	185	0	86	120	6	650	2.4	2.1	8.1
93-94—Atlanta	21	0	128	21	57	.368	3	13	.231	13	17	.765	4	8	12	13	11	0	4	5	5	58	0.6	0.6	2.8
REG. SEASON TOTALS	179	20	3354	582	1299	.448	100	295	.339	235	318	.739	137	296	433	352	389	3	186	216	32	1499	2.4	2.0	8.4
PLAYOFF TOTALS	3	0	29	3	10	.300	0	3	.000	0	0	—	1	2	3	2	2	0	4	2	0	6	1.0	0.7	2.0

GRAHAM, ROBERT MALCOLM (Mal) b. February 23, 1945 Ht. 6-1 Wt. 185 College—New York University

SEASON—TEAM	G	GS	MIN	FGM	FGA	PCT	3FGM	3FGA	PCT	FTM	FTA	PCT	O-RB	D-RB	TOT	AST	PF	DQ	STL	TO	BLK	PTS	RPG	APG	PPG
67-68—Boston	78	—	786	117	272	.430	—	—	—	56	88	.636	—	—	94	61	123	0	—	—	—	290	1.2	0.8	3.7
68-69—Boston	22	—	103	13	55	.236	—	—	—	11	14	.786	—	—	24	14	27	0	—	—	—	37	1.1	0.6	1.7
REG. SEASON TOTALS	100	—	889	130	327	.398	—	—	—	67	102	.657	—	—	118	75	150	0	—	—	—	327	1.2	0.8	3.3
PLAYOFF TOTALS	7	—	25	2	7	.286	—	—	—	1	3	.333	—	—	4	2	3	0	—	—	—	5	0.6	0.3	0.7

GRANDHOLM, JAMES THOMAS (Jim) b. October 4, 1960 Ht. 7-0 Wt. 235 College—Florida/South Florida

SEASON—TEAM	G	GS	MIN	FGM	FGA	PCT	3FGM	3FGA	PCT	FTM	FTA	PCT	O-RB	D-RB	TOT	AST	PF	DQ	STL	TO	BLK	PTS	RPG	APG	PPG
90-91—Dallas	26	0	168	30	58	.517	9	17	.529	10	21	.476	20	30	50	8	33	0	2	11	8	79	1.9	0.3	3.0
REG. SEASON TOTALS	26	0	168	30	58	.517	9	17	.529	10	21	.476	20	30	50	8	33	0	2	11	8	79	1.9	0.3	3.0

GRANDISON, RONNIE CALVIN b. July 9, 1964 Ht. 6-8 Wt. 215 College—New Orleans

SEASON—TEAM	G	GS	MIN	FGM	FGA	PCT	3FGM	3FGA	PCT	FTM	FTA	PCT	O-RB	D-RB	TOT	AST	PF	DQ	STL	TO	BLK	PTS	RPG	APG	PPG
88-89—Boston	72	0	528	59	142	.415	0	10	.000	59	80	.738	47	45	92	42	71	0	18	36	3	177	1.3	0.6	2.5
91-92—Charlotte	3	0	25	2	4	.500	0	0	—	6	10	.600	3	8	11	1	4	0	1	3	1	10	3.7	0.3	3.3
REG. SEASON TOTALS	75	0	553	61	146	.418	0	10	.000	65	90	.722	50	53	103	43	75	0	19	39	4	187	1.4	0.6	2.5

GRANGER, STEWART FRANCIS b. October 27, 1961 Ht. 6-3 Wt. 190 College—Villanova

SEASON—TEAM	G	GS	MIN	FGM	FGA	PCT	3FGM	3FGA	PCT	FTM	FTA	PCT	O-RB	D-RB	TOT	AST	PF	DQ	STL	TO	BLK	PTS	RPG	APG	PPG
83-84—Cleveland	56	13	738	97	226	.429	4	13	.308	53	70	.757	8	47	55	134	97	0	24	57	0	251	1.0	2.4	4.5
84-85—Atlanta	9	1	92	6	17	.353	0	1	.000	4	8	.500	1	5	6	12	13	0	2	12	0	16	0.7	1.3	1.8
86-87—New York	15	0	166	20	54	.370	0	3	.000	9	11	.818	6	11	17	27	17	0	7	22	1	49	1.1	1.8	3.3
REG. SEASON TOTALS	80	14	996	123	297	.414	4	17	.235	66	89	.742	15	63	78	173	127	0	33	91	1	316	1.0	2.2	4.0

GRANT, GARY (The General) b. April 21, 1965 Ht. 6-3 Wt. 195 College—Michigan

SEASON—TEAM	G	GS	MIN	FGM	FGA	PCT	3FGM	3FGA	PCT	FTM	FTA	PCT	O-RB	D-RB	TOT	AST	PF	DQ	STL	TO	BLK	PTS	RPG	APG	PPG
88-89—L.A. Clippers	71	48	1924	361	830	.435	5	22	.227	119	162	.735	80	158	238	506	170	1	144	258	9	846	3.4	7.1	11.9
89-90—L.A. Clippers	44	44	1529	241	517	.466	5	21	.238	88	113	.779	59	136	195	442	120	1	108	206	5	575	4.4	10.0	13.1
90-91—L.A. Clippers	68	65	2105	265	587	.451	9	39	.231	51	74	.689	69	140	209	587	192	4	103	210	12	590	3.1	8.6	8.7
91-92—L.A. Clippers	78	53	2049	275	595	.462	15	51	.294	44	54	.815	34	150	184	538	181	4	138	187	14	609	2.4	6.9	7.8
92-93—L.A. Clippers	74	8	1624	210	476	.441	11	42	.262	55	74	.743	27	112	139	353	168	2	106	129	9	486	1.9	4.8	6.6
93-94—L.A. Clippers	78	8	1533	253	563	.449	17	62	.274	65	76	.855	42	100	142	291	139	1	119	136	12	588	1.8	3.7	7.5
REG. SEASON TOTALS	413	226	10764	1605	3568	.450	62	237	.262	422	553	.763	311	796	1107	2717	970	13	718	1126	61	3694	2.7	6.6	8.9
PLAYOFF TOTALS	10	1	178	20	52	.385	0	2	.000	3	4	.750	1	5	6	41	23	0	6	15	2	43	0.6	4.1	4.3

GRANT, GREGORY ALAN (Greg, Waterbug) b. August 29, 1966 Ht. 5-7 Wt. 140 College—Morris Brown/Trenton State

SEASON—TEAM	G	GS	MIN	FGM	FGA	PCT	3FGM	3FGA	PCT	FTM	FTA	PCT	O-RB	D-RB	TOT	AST	PF	DQ	STL	TO	BLK	PTS	RPG	APG	PPG
89-90—Phoenix	67	3	678	83	216	.384	3	16	.188	39	59	.661	16	43	59	168	58	0	36	77	1	208	0.9	2.5	3.1
90-91—New York	22	0	107	10	27	.370	1	3	.333	5	6	.833	1	9	10	20	12	0	9	10	0	26	0.5	0.9	1.2
91-92—Cha.-Phil.	68	0	891	99	225	.440	7	18	.389	20	24	.833	14	55	69	217	76	0	45	46	2	225	1.0	3.2	3.3
92-93—Philadelphia	72	0	996	77	220	.350	20	68	.294	20	31	.645	24	43	67	206	73	0	43	54	1	194	0.9	2.9	2.7
REG. SEASON TOTALS	229	3	2672	269	688	.391	31	105	.295	84	120	.700	55	150	205	611	219	0	133	187	4	653	0.9	2.7	2.9
PLAYOFF TOTALS	7	0	47	9	20	.450	1	3	.333	0	0	—	2	4	6	10	2	0	2	5	0	19	0.9	1.4	2.7

GRANT, HARRY PETER (Bud) b. May 20, 1927 Ht. 6-3 Wt. 195 College—Minnesota

SEASON—TEAM	G	GS	MIN	FGM	FGA	PCT	3FGM	3FGA	PCT	FTM	FTA	PCT	O-RB	D-RB	TOT	AST	PF	DQ	STL	TO	BLK	PTS	RPG	APG	PPG
49-50—Minneapolis	35	—	—	42	115	.365	—	—	—	7	17	.412	—	—	—	19	36	—	—	—	—	91	—	0.5	2.6
50-51—Minneapolis	61	—	—	53	184	.288	—	—	—	52	83	.627	—	—	115	71	106	0	—	—	—	158	1.9	1.2	2.6
REG. SEASON TOTALS	96	—	—	95	299	.318	—	—	—	59	100	.590	—	—	115	90	142	0	—	—	—	249	1.9	0.9	2.6
PLAYOFF TOTALS	17	—	—	22	56	.393	—	—	—	10	17	.588	—	—	—	5	7	37	0	—	—	54	1.0	0.4	3.2

GRANT, HARVEY (The General) b. July 4, 1965 Ht. 6-9 Wt. 230 College—Clemson/Independence JC/Oklahoma

SEASON—TEAM	G	GS	MIN	FGM	FGA	PCT	3FGM	3FGA	PCT	FTM	FTA	PCT	O-RB	D-RB	TOT	AST	PF	DQ	STL	TO	BLK	PTS	RPG	APG	PPG
88-89—Washington	71	1	1193	181	390	.464	0	1	.000	34	57	.596	75	88	163	79	147	2	35	28	29	396	2.3	1.1	5.6
89-90—Washington	81	25	1846	284	601	.473	0	8	.000	96	137	.701	138	204	342	131	194	1	52	85	43	664	4.2	1.6	8.2
90-91—Washington	77	76	2842	609	1224	.498	2	15	.133	185	249	.743	179	378	557	204	232	2	91	125	61	1405	7.2	2.6	18.2
91-92—Washington	64	60	2388	489	1022	.478	1	8	.125	176	220	.800	157	275	432	170	178	1	74	109	27	1155	6.8	2.7	18.0
92-93—Washington	72	72	2667	560	1149	.487	1	10	.100	218	300	.727	133	279	412	205	168	0	72	90	44	1339	5.7	2.8	18.6
93-94—Portland	77	73	2112	356	774	.460	2	7	.286	84	131	.641	109	242	351	107	179	1	70	56	49	798	4.6	1.4	10.4
REG. SEASON TOTALS	442	307	13048	2479	5160	.480	6	49	.122	793	1094	.725	791	1466	2257	896	1098	7	394	493	253	5757	5.1	2.0	13.0
PLAYOFF TOTALS	4	1	76	17	33	.515	0	0	—	0	0	—	5	4	9	3	2	0	1	1	2	34	2.3	0.8	8.5

GRANT, HORACE JUNIOR b. July 4, 1965 Ht. 6-10 Wt. 225 College—Clemson

SEASON—TEAM	G	GS	MIN	FGM	FGA	PCT	3FGM	3FGA	PCT	FTM	FTA	PCT	O-RB	D-RB	TOT	AST	PF	DQ	STL	TO	BLK	PTS	RPG	APG	PPG
87-88—Chicago	81	6	1827	254	507	.501	0	2	.000	114	182	.626	155	292	447	89	221	3	51	86	53	622	5.5	1.1	7.7
88-89—Chicago	79	79	2809	405	781	.519	0	5	.000	140	199	.704	240	441	681	168	251	1	86	128	62	950	8.6	2.1	12.0
89-90—Chicago	80	80	2753	446	853	.523	0	0	—	179	256	.699	236	393	629	227	230	1	92	110	84	1071	7.9	2.8	13.4
90-91—Chicago	78	76	2641	401	733	.547	1	6	.167	197	277	.711	266	393	659	178	203	2	95	92	69	1000	8.4	2.3	12.8
91-92—Chicago	81	81	2859	457	790	.578	0	2	.000	235	317	.741	344	463	807	217	196	0	100	98	131	1149	10.0	2.7	14.2
92-93—Chicago	77	77	2745	421	829	.508	1	5	.200	174	281	.619	341	388	729	201	218	4	89	110	96	1017	9.5	2.6	13.2
93-94—Chicago	70	69	2570	460	878	.524	0	6	.000	137	230	.596	306	463	769	236	164	0	74	109	84	1057	11.0	3.4	15.1
REG. SEASON TOTALS	546	468	18204	2844	5371	.530	2	26	.077	1176	1742	.675	1888	2833	4721	1316	1483	11	587	733	579	6866	8.6	2.4	12.6
PLAYOFF TOTALS	111	101	4106	537	990	.542	1	6	.167	245	350	.700	374	584	958	265	350	7	115	132	122	1320	8.6	2.4	11.9
ALL-STAR TOTALS	1	0	17	2	8	.250	0	0	—	0	0	—	6	2	8	2	0	0	1	1	2	4	8.0	2.0	4.0

GRANT, JOSHUA DAVID (Josh) b. August 7, 1967 Ht. 6-10 Wt. 225 College—Utah

SEASON—TEAM	G	GS	MIN	FGM	FGA	PCT	3FGM	3FGA	PCT	FTM	FTA	PCT	O-RB	D-RB	TOT	AST	PF	DQ	STL	TO	BLK	PTS	RPG	APG	PPG
93-94—Golden State	53	0	382	59	146	.404	17	61	.279	22	29	.759	27	62	89	24	62	0	18	30	8	157	1.7	0.5	3.0
REG. SEASON TOTALS	53	0	382	59	146	.404	17	61	.279	22	29	.759	27	62	89	24	62	0	18	30	8	157	1.7	0.5	3.0
PLAYOFF TOTALS	1	0	1	0	0	—	0	0	—	0	0	—	0	0	0	0	0	0	0	0	0	0	0.0	0.0	0.0

GRANT, TRAVIS (Machine Gun) b. January 1, 1950 Ht. 6-8 Wt. 215 College—Kentucky State

SEASON—TEAM	G	GS	MIN	FGM	FGA	PCT	3FGM	3FGA	PCT	FTM	FTA	PCT	O-RB	D-RB	TOT	AST	PF	DQ	STL	TO	BLK	PTS	RPG	APG	PPG
72-73—Los Angeles	33	—	153	51	116	.440	—	—	—	23	26	.885	—	—	52	7	19	0	—	—	—	125	1.6	0.2	3.8
73-74—Los Angeles	3	—	6	1	4	.250	—	—	—	1	3	.333	0	1	1	0	1	0	0	—	0	3	0.3	0.0	1.0
73-74—San Diego (A)	56	—	1324	357	681	.524	1	4	.250	141	176	.801	106	192	298	63	118	—	46	88	12	856	5.3	1.1	15.3
74-75—San Diego (A)	53	—	1998	576	1058	.544	1	2	.500	182	218	.835	117	211	328	98	160	—	44	118	21	1335	6.2	1.8	25.2
75-76—Ken.-Indiana (A)	56	—	828	198	398	.497	0	0	—	52	69	.754	61	79	140	43	98	—	16	55	18	448	2.5	0.8	8.0
REG. NBA TOTALS	36	—	159	52	120	.433	—	—	—	24	29	.828	0	1	53	7	20	0	0	—	0	128	1.5	0.2	3.6
REG. ABA TOTALS	165	—	4150	1131	2137	.529	2	6	.333	375	463	.810	284	482	766	204	376	0	106	261	51	2639	4.6	1.2	16.0
NBA PLAYOFF TOTALS	2	—	11	4	6	.667	—	—	—	0	0	—	0	0	4	—	1	0	0	—	0	8	2.0	0.0	4.0
ABA PLAYOFF TOTALS	1	—	1	0	1	.000	0	0	—	0	0	—	0	0	0	0	0	0	0	0	0	0	0.0	0.0	0.0

GRATE, DONALD (Don) b. August 27, 1923 Ht. 6-2½ Wt. 185 College—Ohio State

SEASON—TEAM	G	GS	MIN	FGM	FGA	PCT	3FGM	3FGA	PCT	FTM	FTA	PCT	O-RB	D-RB	TOT	AST	PF	DQ	STL	TO	BLK	PTS	RPG	APG	PPG
47-48—Indianapolis (N)	11	—	—	14	—	—	—	—	—	3	6	.500	—	—	—	—	—	—	—	—	—	31	—	—	2.8
49-50—Sheboygan	2	—	—	1	6	.167	—	—	—	2	2	1.000	—	—	—	3	3	—	—	—	—	4	—	1.5	2.0
REG. NBA TOTALS	2	—	—	1	6	.167	—	—	—	2	2	1.000	—	—	—	3	3	—	—	—	—	4	—	1.5	2.0
REG. NBL TOTALS	11	—	—	14	—	—	—	—	—	3	6	.500	—	—	—	—	—	—	—	—	—	31	—	—	2.8

GRAVES, EARL G. JR. (Butch) b. January 5, 1962 Ht. 6-3 Wt. 200 College—Yale

SEASON—TEAM	G	GS	MIN	FGM	FGA	PCT	3FGM	3FGA	PCT	FTM	FTA	PCT	O-RB	D-RB	TOT	AST	PF	DQ	STL	TO	BLK	PTS	RPG	APG	PPG
84-85—Cleveland	4	0	11	2	6	.333	0	1	.000	1	5	.200	0	2	2	1	4	0	1	1	0	5	0.5	0.3	1.3
REG. SEASON TOTALS	4	0	11	2	6	.333	0	1	.000	1	5	.200	0	2	2	1	4	0	1	1	0	5	0.5	0.3	1.3

GRAY, GARY MICHAEL b. February 23, 1945 Ht. 6-1 Wt. 185 College—Oklahoma City

SEASON—TEAM	G	GS	MIN	FGM	FGA	PCT	3FGM	3FGA	PCT	FTM	FTA	PCT	O-RB	D-RB	TOT	AST	PF	DQ	STL	TO	BLK	PTS	RPG	APG	PPG
67-68—Cincinnati	44	—	276	49	134	.366	—	—	—	7	10	.700	—	—	23	26	48	0	—	—	—	105	0.5	0.6	2.4
REG. SEASON TOTALS	44	—	276	49	134	.366	—	—	—	7	10	.700	—	—	23	26	48	0	—	—	—	105	0.5	0.6	2.4

GRAY, LEONARD EARL b. December 19, 1951 Ht. 6-8 Wt. 240 College—Kansas/Long Beach State

SEASON—TEAM	G	GS	MIN	FGM	FGA	PCT	3FGM	3FGA	PCT	FTM	FTA	PCT	O-RB	D-RB	TOT	AST	PF	DQ	STL	TO	BLK	PTS	RPG	APG	PPG
74-75—Seattle	75	—	2280	378	773	.489	—	—	—	104	144	.722	133	345	478	163	292	9	63	—	24	860	6.4	2.2	11.5
75-76—Seattle	66	—	2139	394	831	.474	—	—	—	126	169	.746	109	289	398	203	260	10	75	—	36	914	6.0	3.1	13.8
76-77—Seattle-Wash.	83	—	1639	258	592	.436	—	—	—	118	158	.747	84	209	293	124	273	9	58	—	31	634	3.5	1.5	7.6
REG. SEASON TOTALS	224	—	6058	1030	2196	.469	—	—	—	348	471	.739	326	843	1169	490	825	28	196	—	91	2408	5.2	2.2	10.8
PLAYOFF TOTALS	17	—	315	45	101	.446	—	—	—	11	13	.846	13	41	54	21	53	0	14	—	5	101	3.2	1.2	5.9

GRAY, STUART ALLAN b. May 27, 1963 Ht. 7-0 Wt. 245 College—UCLA

SEASON—TEAM	G	GS	MIN	FGM	FGA	PCT	3FGM	3FGA	PCT	FTM	FTA	PCT	O-RB	D-RB	TOT	AST	PF	DQ	STL	TO	BLK	PTS	RPG	APG	PPG
84-85—Indiana	52	0	391	35	92	.380	0	0	—	32	47	.681	29	94	123	15	82	1	9	51	14	102	2.4	0.3	2.0
85-86—Indiana	67	3	423	54	108	.500	0	0	—	47	74	.635	45	73	118	15	94	0	8	32	11	155	1.8	0.2	2.3
86-87—Indiana	55	1	456	41	101	.406	0	0	—	28	39	.718	39	90	129	26	93	0	10	36	28	110	2.3	0.5	2.0
87-88—Indiana	74	0	807	90	193	.466	0	1	.000	44	73	.603	70	180	250	44	152	1	11	50	32	224	3.4	0.6	3.0
88-89—Indiana	72	0	783	72	153	.471	0	1	.000	44	64	.688	84	161	245	29	128	0	11	48	21	188	3.4	0.4	2.6
89-90—Cha.-N.Y.	58	1	560	42	99	.424	0	5	.000	32	47	.681	40	105	145	19	90	0	15	24	26	116	2.5	0.3	2.0
90-91—New York	8	0	37	4	12	.333	0	0	—	3	3	1.000	2	8	10	0	6	0	0	2	1	11	1.3	0.0	1.4
REG. SEASON TOTALS	386	5	3457	338	758	.446	0	7	.000	230	347	.663	309	711	1020	148	645	2	64	243	133	906	2.6	0.4	2.3
PLAYOFF TOTALS	7	0	26	2	6	.333	0	0	—	2	4	.500	5	10	15	—	6	0	1	3	0	6	2.1	0.0	0.9

GRAY, SYLVESTER b. July 8, 1967 Ht. 6-6 Wt. 240 College—Memphis State

SEASON—TEAM	G	GS	MIN	FGM	FGA	PCT	3FGM	3FGA	PCT	FTM	FTA	PCT	O-RB	D-RB	TOT	AST	PF	DQ	STL	TO	BLK	PTS	RPG	APG	PPG
88-89—Miami	55	15	1220	167	398	.420	1	4	.250	105	156	.673	117	169	286	117	144	1	36	102	25	440	5.2	2.1	8.0
REG. SEASON TOTALS	55	15	1220	167	398	.420	1	4	.250	105	156	.673	117	169	286	117	144	1	36	102	25	440	5.2	2.1	8.0

GRAY, WYNDOL WOODROW b. March 20, 1922 d. January 30, 1994 Ht. 6-1 Wt. 175 College—Harvard/Bowling Green

SEASON—TEAM	G	GS	MIN	FGM	FGA	PCT	3FGM	3FGA	PCT	FTM	FTA	PCT	O-RB	D-RB	TOT	AST	PF	DQ	STL	TO	BLK	PTS	RPG	APG	PPG
46-47—Boston	55	—		139	476	.292	—	—	—	72	124	.581	—	—	—	47	105	—	—	—	—	350	—	0.9	6.4
47-48—Toledo (N)	2	—		2	—	—	—	—	—	2	4	.500	—	—	—	—	4	—	—	—	—	6	—	—	3.0
47-48—Prov.-St. L.	12	—		6	37	.162	—	—	—	1	4	.250	—	—	—	3	16	—	—	—	—	13	—	0.3	1.1
REG. NBA TOTALS	67	—		145	513	.283	—	—	—	73	128	.570	—	—	—	50	121	—	—	—	—	363	—	0.7	5.4
REG. NBL TOTALS	2	—		2	—	—	—	—	—	2	4	.500	—	—	—	—	4	—	—	—	—	6	—	—	3.0

GRAYER, JEFFREY (Jeff) b. December 17, 1965 Ht. 6-5 Wt. 210 College—Iowa State

SEASON—TEAM	G	GS	MIN	FGM	FGA	PCT	3FGM	3FGA	PCT	FTM	FTA	PCT	O-RB	D-RB	TOT	AST	PF	DQ	STL	TO	BLK	PTS	RPG	APG	PPG
88-89—Milwaukee	11	2	200	32	73	.438	0	2	.000	17	20	.850	14	21	35	22	15	0	10	19	1	81	3.2	2.0	7.4
89-90—Milwaukee	71	40	1427	224	487	.460	1	8	.125	99	152	.651	94	123	217	107	125	0	48	82	10	548	3.1	1.5	7.7
90-91—Milwaukee	82	7	1422	210	485	.433	0	3	.000	101	147	.687	111	135	246	123	98	0	48	86	9	521	3.0	1.5	6.4
91-92—Milwaukee	82	11	1659	309	689	.448	19	66	.288	102	153	.667	129	128	257	150	142	0	64	105	13	739	3.1	1.8	9.0
92-93—Golden State	48	12	1025	165	353	.467	2	14	.143	91	136	.669	71	86	157	70	120	1	31	54	8	423	3.3	1.5	8.8
93-94—Golden State	67	4	1096	191	363	.526	2	12	.167	71	118	.602	76	115	191	62	103	0	33	63	13	455	2.9	0.9	6.8
REG. SEASON TOTALS	361	76	6829	1131	2450	.462	24	105	.229	481	726	.663	495	608	1103	534	603	1	234	409	54	2767	3.1	1.5	7.7
PLAYOFF TOTALS	10	0	95	16	33	.485	0	0	—	7	9	.778	4	10	14	8	10	0	2	6	1	39	1.4	0.8	3.9

GREACEN, ROBERT ALEXANDER (Bob) b. September 15, 1947 Ht. 6-7 Wt. 210 College—Rutgers

SEASON—TEAM	G	GS	MIN	FGM	FGA	PCT	3FGM	3FGA	PCT	FTM	FTA	PCT	O-RB	D-RB	TOT	AST	PF	DQ	STL	TO	BLK	PTS	RPG	APG	PPG
69-70—Milwaukee	41	—	292	44	109	.404	—	—	—	18	28	.643	—	—	59	27	49	0	—	—	—	106	1.4	0.7	2.6
70-71—Milwaukee	2	—	43	1	12	.083	—	—	—	3	7	.429	—	—	6	13	7	0	—	—	—	5	3.0	6.5	2.5
71-72—New York (A)	4	—	20	1	2	.500	0	0	—	0	0	—	—	—	2	1	1	—	—	2	—	2	0.5	0.3	0.5
REG. NBA TOTALS	43	—	335	45	121	.372	—	—	—	21	35	.600	—	—	65	40	56	0	—	—	—	111	1.5	0.9	2.6
REG. ABA TOTALS	4	—	20	1	2	.500	0	0	—	0	0	—	—	—	2	1	1	—	—	2	—	2	0.5	0.3	0.5
NBA PLAYOFF TOTALS	8	—	24	5	15	.333	—	—	—	4	5	.800	—	—	7	3	4	0	—	—	—	14	0.9	0.4	1.8

GREEN, A.C. JR. b. October 4, 1963 Ht. 6-9 Wt. 230 College—Oregon State

SEASON—TEAM	G	GS	MIN	FGM	FGA	PCT	3FGM	3FGA	PCT	FTM	FTA	PCT	O-RB	D-RB	TOT	AST	PF	DQ	STL	TO	BLK	PTS	RPG	APG	PPG
85-86—L.A. Lakers	82	1	1542	209	388	.539	1	6	.167	102	167	.611	160	221	381	54	229	2	49	99	49	521	4.6	0.7	6.4
86-87—L.A. Lakers	79	72	2240	316	587	.538	0	5	.000	220	282	.780	210	405	615	84	171	0	70	102	80	852	7.8	1.1	10.8
87-88—L.A. Lakers	82	64	2636	322	640	.503	0	2	.000	293	379	.773	245	465	710	93	204	0	87	120	45	937	8.7	1.1	11.4
88-89—L.A. Lakers	82	82	2510	401	758	.529	4	17	.235	282	359	.786	258	481	739	103	172	0	94	119	55	1088	9.0	1.3	13.3
89-90—L.A. Lakers	82	82	2709	385	806	.478	13	46	.283	278	370	.751	262	450	712	90	207	0	66	116	50	1061	8.7	1.1	12.9
90-91—L.A. Lakers	82	21	2164	258	542	.476	11	55	.200	223	302	.738	201	315	516	71	117	0	59	99	23	750	6.3	0.9	9.1
91-92—L.A. Lakers	82	53	2902	382	803	.476	12	56	.214	340	457	.744	306	456	762	117	141	0	91	111	36	1116	9.3	1.4	13.6
92-93—L.A. Lakers	82	55	2819	379	706	.537	16	46	.348	277	375	.739	287	424	711	116	149	0	88	116	39	1051	8.7	1.4	12.8
93-94—Phoenix	82	55	2825	465	926	.502	8	35	.229	266	362	.735	275	478	753	137	142	0	70	100	38	1204	9.2	1.7	14.7
REG. SEASON TOTALS	735	485	22347	3117	6156	.506	65	268	.243	2281	3053	.747	2204	3695	5899	865	1532	2	674	982	415	8580	8.0	1.2	11.7
PLAYOFF TOTALS	113	72	3214	375	770	.487	11	33	.333	314	437	.719	302	544	846	100	263	2	78	124	41	1075	7.5	0.9	9.5
ALL-STAR TOTALS	1	1	12	0	3	.000	0	0	—	0	0	—	0	3	3	1	1	0	0	1	0	0	3.0	1.0	0.0

GREEN, JOHN M. (Johnny) b. December 8, 1933 Ht. 6-5 Wt. 200 College—Michigan State

SEASON—TEAM	G	GS	MIN	FGM	FGA	PCT	3FGM	3FGA	PCT	FTM	FTA	PCT	O-RB	D-RB	TOT	AST	PF	DQ	STL	TO	BLK	PTS	RPG	APG	PPG
59-60—New York	69	—	1232	209	468	.447	—	—	—	63	155	.406	—	—	539	52	195	3	—	—	—	481	7.8	0.8	7.0
60-61—New York	78	—	1784	326	758	.430	—	—	—	145	278	.522	—	—	838	97	194	3	—	—	—	797	10.7	1.2	10.2
61-62—New York	80	—	2789	507	1164	.436	—	—	—	261	434	.601	—	—	1066	191	265	4	—	—	—	1275	13.3	2.4	15.9
62-63—New York	80	—	2553	582	1261	.462	—	—	—	280	439	.638	—	—	964	152	243	5	—	—	—	1444	12.1	1.9	18.1
63-64—New York	80	—	2134	482	1026	.470	—	—	—	195	392	.497	—	—	799	157	246	4	—	—	—	1159	10.0	2.0	14.5
64-65—New York	78	—	1720	346	737	.469	—	—	—	165	301	.548	—	—	545	129	194	3	—	—	—	857	7.0	1.7	11.0
65-66—N.Y.-Balt.	79	—	1645	358	668	.536	—	—	—	202	388	.521	—	—	645	107	183	3	—	—	—	918	8.2	1.4	11.6
66-67—Baltimore	61	—	948	203	437	.465	—	—	—	96	207	.464	—	—	394	57	139	7	—	—	—	502	6.5	0.9	8.2
67-68—S.D.-Phil.	77	—	1440	310	676	.459	—	—	—	139	295	.471	—	—	545	80	163	3	—	—	—	759	7.1	1.0	9.9
68-69—Philadelphia	74	—	795	146	282	.518	—	—	—	57	125	.456	—	—	330	47	110	1	—	—	—	349	4.5	0.6	4.7
69-70—Cincinnati	78	—	2278	481	860	.559	—	—	—	254	429	.592	—	—	841	112	268	6	—	—	—	1216	10.8	1.4	15.6
70-71—Cincinnati	75	—	2147	502	855	.587	—	—	—	248	402	.617	—	—	656	89	233	7	—	—	—	1252	8.7	1.2	16.7
71-72—Cincinnati	82	—	1914	331	582	.569	—	—	—	141	250	.564	—	—	560	120	238	5	—	—	—	803	6.8	1.5	9.8
72-73—Kansas City-Omaha	66	—	1245	190	317	.599	—	—	—	89	131	.679	—	—	361	59	185	7	—	—	—	469	5.5	0.9	7.1
REG. SEASON TOTALS	1057	—	24624	4973	10091	.493	—	—	—	2335	4226	.553	—	—	9083	1449	2856	61	—	—	—	12281	8.6	1.4	11.6
PLAYOFF TOTALS	20	—	359	67	115	.583	—	—	—	26	60	.433	—	—	107	13	40	1	—	—	—	160	5.4	0.7	8.0
ALL-STAR TOTALS	4	—	72	13	19	.684	—	—	—	6	8	.750	—	—	9	0	9	1	—	—	—	32	2.3	0.0	8.0

GREEN, KENNETH (Apple) b. September 19, 1959 Ht. 6-8 Wt. 220 College—Ranger JC/Texas-Pan American

SEASON—TEAM	G	GS	MIN	FGM	FGA	PCT	3FGM	3FGA	PCT	FTM	FTA	PCT	O-RB	D-RB	TOT	AST	PF	DQ	STL	TO	BLK	PTS	RPG	APG	PPG
85-86—New York	7	0	72	13	27	.481	0	0	—	5	9	.556	12	15	27	2	8	0	4	1	0	31	3.9	0.3	4.4
REG. SEASON TOTALS	7	0	72	13	27	.481	0	0	—	5	9	.556	12	15	27	2	8	0	4	1	0	31	3.9	0.3	4.4

GREEN, KENNETH LEROY (Kenny) b. October 11, 1964 Ht. 6-7 Wt. 215 College—Wake Forest

SEASON—TEAM	G	GS	MIN	FGM	FGA	PCT	3FGM	3FGA	PCT	FTM	FTA	PCT	O-RB	D-RB	TOT	AST	PF	DQ	STL	TO	BLK	PTS	RPG	APG	PPG
85-86—Wash.-Phil.	41	0	453	83	192	.432	0	1	.000	35	49	.714	27	46	73	9	53	0	5	35	9	201	1.8	0.2	4.9
86-87—Philadelphia	19	0	172	25	70	.357	0	0	—	14	19	.737	6	22	28	7	8	0	4	15	2	64	1.5	0.4	3.4
REG. SEASON TOTALS	60	0	625	108	262	.412	0	1	.000	49	68	.721	33	68	101	16	61	0	9	50	11	265	1.7	0.3	4.4

GREEN, LAMAR ANTHONY b. March 22, 1947 Ht. 6-7½ Wt. 215 College—Morehead State

SEASON—TEAM	G	GS	MIN	FGM	FGA	PCT	3FGM	3FGA	PCT	FTM	FTA	PCT	O-RB	D-RB	TOT	AST	PF	DQ	STL	TO	BLK	PTS	RPG	APG	PPG
69-70—Phoenix	58	—	700	101	234	.432	—	—	—	41	70	.586	—	—	276	17	115	2	—	—	—	243	4.8	0.3	4.2
70-71—Phoenix	68	—	1326	167	369	.453	—	—	—	64	106	.604	—	—	466	53	202	5	—	—	—	398	6.9	0.8	5.9
71-72—Phoenix	67	—	991	133	298	.446	—	—	—	66	90	.733	—	—	348	45	134	1	—	—	—	332	5.2	0.7	5.0
72-73—Phoenix	80	—	2048	224	520	.431	—	—	—	89	118	.754	—	—	746	89	263	10	—	—	—	537	9.3	1.1	6.7
73-74—Phoenix	72	—	1103	129	317	.407	—	—	—	38	68	.559	85	265	350	43	150	1	32	—	38	296	4.9	0.6	4.1
74-75—New Orleans	15	—	280	24	70	.343	—	—	—	9	20	.450	28	81	109	16	38	0	4	—	5	57	7.3	1.1	3.8
74-75—Virginia (A)	51	—	856	115	270	.426	0	0	—	40	54	.741	86	169	255	47	139	—	13	60	25	270	5.0	0.9	5.3
REG. NBA TOTALS	360	—	6448	778	1808	.430	—	—	—	307	472	.650	113	346	2295	263	902	19	36	—	43	1863	6.4	0.7	5.2
REG. ABA TOTALS	51	—	856	115	270	.426	0	0	—	40	54	.741	86	169	255	47	139	—	13	60	25	270	5.0	0.9	5.3
NBA PLAYOFF TOTALS	6	—	69	8	28	.286	—	—	—	2	5	.400	0	0	23	5	8	0	0	—	0	18	3.8	0.8	3.0

GREEN, LITTERIAL b. March 7, 1970 Ht. 6-1 Wt. 185 College—Georgia

SEASON—TEAM	G	GS	MIN	FGM	FGA	PCT	3FGM	3FGA	PCT	FTM	FTA	PCT	O-RB	D-RB	TOT	AST	PF	DQ	STL	TO	BLK	PTS	RPG	APG	PPG
92-93—Orlando	52	4	626	87	198	.439	1	10	.100	60	96	.625	11	23	34	116	70	0	23	42	4	235	0.7	2.2	4.5
93-94—Orlando	29	0	126	22	57	.386	1	4	.250	28	37	.757	6	6	12	9	16	0	6	13	1	73	0.4	0.3	2.5
REG. SEASON TOTALS	81	4	752	109	255	.427	2	14	.143	88	133	.662	17	29	46	125	86	0	29	55	5	308	0.6	1.5	3.8

GREEN, LUTHER b. November 13, 1946 Ht. 6-7 Wt. 190 College—Long Island University

SEASON—TEAM	G	GS	MIN	FGM	FGA	PCT	3FGM	3FGA	PCT	FTM	FTA	PCT	O-RB	D-RB	TOT	AST	PF	DQ	STL	TO	BLK	PTS	RPG	APG	PPG
69-70—New York (A)	59	—	739	114	303	.376	0	3	.000	55	97	.567	—	—	263	27	117	2	—	—	—	283	4.5	0.5	4.8
70-71—New York (A)	26	—	164	40	88	.455	0	4	.000	18	44	.409	—	—	55	3	19	—	—	—	—	98	2.1	0.1	3.8
72-73—Philadelphia	5	—	32	0	11	.000	—	—	—	3	9	.333	—	—	3	0	3	0	—	—	—	3	0.6	0.0	0.6
REG. NBA TOTALS	5	—	32	0	11	.000	—	—	—	3	9	.333	—	—	3	0	3	0	—	—	—	3	0.6	0.0	0.6
REG. ABA TOTALS	85	—	903	154	391	.394	0	7	.000	73	141	.518	—	—	318	30	136	2	—	—	—	381	3.7	0.4	4.5
ABA PLAYOFF TOTALS	7	—	82	11	29	.379	1	2	.500	10	15	.667	—	—	28	3	22	0	—	—	—	33	4.0	0.4	4.7

GREEN, MICHAEL KENNETH (Mike) b. August 6, 1951 Ht. 6-10 Wt. 200 College—Louisiana Tech

SEASON—TEAM	G	GS	MIN	FGM	FGA	PCT	3FGM	3FGA	PCT	FTM	FTA	PCT	O-RB	D-RB	TOT	AST	PF	DQ	STL	TO	BLK	PTS	RPG	APG	PPG
73-74—Denver (A)	79	—	1648	367	799	.459	1	2	.500	169	226	.748	225	359	584	64	191	—	47	128	126	904	7.4	0.8	11.4
74-75—Denver (A)	81	—	2557	593	1095	.542	0	4	.000	225	305	.738	282	467	749	101	271	—	85	203	174	1411	9.2	1.2	17.4
75-76—Virginia (A)	54	—	1719	385	832	.463	0	4	.000	154	198	.778	196	323	519	82	187	—	68	136	80	924	9.6	1.5	17.1
76-77—Seattle	76	—	1928	290	658	.441	—	—	—	166	235	.706	191	312	503	120	201	1	45	—	129	746	6.6	1.6	9.8
77-78—Seattle-S.A.	72	—	1382	238	514	.463	—	—	—	107	142	.754	130	229	359	76	193	1	30	105	100	583	5.0	1.1	8.1
78-79—San Antonio	76	—	1641	235	477	.493	—	—	—	101	144	.701	131	223	354	116	230	3	37	89	122	571	4.7	1.5	7.5
79-80—Kansas City	21	—	459	69	159	.434	0	2	.000	24	42	.571	35	78	113	28	55	0	13	36	21	162	5.4	1.3	7.7
REG. NBA TOTALS	245	—	5410	832	1808	.460	0	2	.000	398	563	.707	487	842	1329	340	679	5	125	230	372	2062	5.4	1.4	8.4
REG. ABA TOTALS	214	—	5924	1345	2726	.493	1	10	.100	548	729	.752	703	1149	1852	247	649	0	200	467	380	3239	8.7	1.2	15.1
NBA PLAYOFF TOTALS	20	—	524	76	172	.442	0	0	—	23	31	.742	52	65	117	22	80	3	18	26	52	175	5.9	1.1	8.8
ABA PLAYOFF TOTALS	13	—	487	112	226	.496	0	1	.000	53	60	.883	54	67	121	14	51	0	10	27	21	277	9.3	1.1	21.3
ABA ALL-STAR TOTALS	1	—	18	3	6	.500	0	0	—	0	0	—	0	3	3	0	4	—	0	1	0	6	3.0	0.0	6.0

GREEN, RICKEY b. August 18, 1954 Ht. 6-1½ Wt. 170 College—Vincennes/Michigan

SEASON—TEAM	G	GS	MIN	FGM	FGA	PCT	3FGM	3FGA	PCT	FTM	FTA	PCT	O-RB	D-RB	TOT	AST	PF	DQ	STL	TO	BLK	PTS	RPG	APG	PPG
77-78—Golden State	76	—	1098	143	375	.381	—	—	—	54	90	.600	49	67	116	149	95	0	58	79	1	340	1.5	2.0	4.5
78-79—Detroit	27	—	431	67	177	.379	—	—	—	45	67	.672	15	25	40	63	37	0	25	44	1	179	1.5	2.3	6.6
80-81—Utah	47	—	1307	176	366	.481	0	1	.000	70	97	.722	30	86	116	235	123	2	75	83	1	422	2.5	5.0	9.0
81-82—Utah	81	73	2822	500	1015	.493	0	8	.000	202	264	.765	85	158	243	630	183	0	185	198	9	1202	3.0	7.8	14.8
82-83—Utah	78	78	2783	464	942	.493	2	13	.154	185	232	.797	62	161	223	697	154	0	220	222	4	1115	2.9	8.9	14.3
83-84—Utah	81	81	2768	439	904	.486	2	17	.118	192	234	.821	56	174	230	748	155	1	215	172	13	1072	2.8	9.2	13.2
84-85—Utah	77	77	2431	381	798	.477	6	20	.300	232	267	.869	37	152	189	597	131	0	132	177	3	1000	2.5	7.8	13.0
85-86—Utah	80	44	2012	357	758	.471	5	29	.172	213	250	.852	32	103	135	411	130	0	106	132	6	932	1.7	5.1	11.7
86-87—Utah	81	80	2090	301	644	.467	7	19	.368	172	208	.827	38	125	163	541	108	0	110	133	2	781	2.0	6.7	9.6
87-88—Utah	81	3	1116	157	370	.424	4	19	.211	75	83	.904	14	66	80	300	83	0	57	94	1	393	1.0	3.7	4.9
88-89—Cha.-Milw.	63	2	871	129	264	.489	3	11	.273	30	33	.909	11	58	69	187	35	0	40	61	2	291	1.1	3.0	4.6
89-90—Indiana	69	0	927	100	231	.433	1	11	.091	43	51	.843	9	45	54	182	60	0	51	62	1	244	0.8	2.6	3.5
90-91—Philadelphia	79	75	2248	334	722	.463	8	36	.222	117	141	.830	33	104	137	413	130	0	57	108	6	793	1.7	5.2	10.0
91-92—Boston	26	0	367	46	103	.447	1	4	.250	13	18	.722	3	21	24	68	28	0	17	18	1	106	0.9	2.6	4.1
REG. SEASON TOTALS	946	513	23271	3594	7669	.469	39	188	.207	1643	2035	.807	474	1345	1819	5221	1452	3	1348	1583	51	8870	1.9	5.5	9.4
PLAYOFF TOTALS	55	36	1275	192	422	.455	7	20	.350	94	111	.847	24	81	105	294	71	0	50	83	4	485	1.9	5.3	8.8
ALL-STAR TOTALS	1	0	19	3	8	.375	0	0	—	0	0	—	0	0	0	11	1	0	1	4	0	6	0.0	11.0	6.0

GREEN, SEAN CURTIS b. February 2, 1970 Ht. 6-5 Wt. 210 College—North Carolina State/Iona

SEASON—TEAM	G	GS	MIN	FGM	FGA	PCT	3FGM	3FGA	PCT	FTM	FTA	PCT	O-RB	D-RB	TOT	AST	PF	DQ	STL	TO	BLK	PTS	RPG	APG	PPG
91-92—Indiana	35	0	256	62	158	.392	2	10	.200	15	28	.536	22	20	42	22	31	0	13	27	6	141	1.2	0.6	4.0
92-93—Indiana	13	0	81	28	55	.509	3	10	.300	3	4	.750	4	5	9	7	11	0	2	9	1	62	0.7	0.5	4.8
93-94—Phil.-Utah	36	0	334	63	183	.344	10	41	.244	13	18	.722	10	24	34	16	21	0	18	27	6	149	0.9	0.4	4.1
REG. SEASON TOTALS	84	0	671	153	396	.386	15	61	.246	31	50	.620	36	49	85	45	63	0	33	63	13	352	1.0	0.5	4.2
PLAYOFF TOTALS	1	0	3	0	0	—	0	0	—	0	0	—	0	0	0	—	0	0	0	0	0	0	0.0	0.0	0.0

GREEN, SIDNEY b. January 4, 1961 Ht. 6-9 Wt. 225 College—Nevada-Las Vegas

SEASON—TEAM	G	GS	MIN	FGM	FGA	PCT	3FGM	3FGA	PCT	FTM	FTA	PCT	O-RB	D-RB	TOT	AST	PF	DQ	STL	TO	BLK	PTS	RPG	APG	PPG
83-84—Chicago	49	0	667	100	228	.439	0	0	—	55	77	.714	58	116	174	25	128	1	18	60	17	255	3.6	0.5	5.2
84-85—Chicago	48	1	740	108	250	.432	0	4	.000	79	98	.806	72	174	246	29	102	0	11	68	11	295	5.1	0.6	6.1
85-86—Chicago	80	68	2307	407	875	.465	0	8	.000	262	335	.782	208	450	658	139	292	5	70	220	37	1076	8.2	1.7	13.5
86-87—Detroit	80	69	1792	256	542	.472	0	2	.000	119	177	.672	196	457	653	62	197	0	41	127	50	631	8.2	0.8	7.9
87-88—New York	82	65	2049	258	585	.441	0	2	.000	126	190	.663	221	421	642	93	318	9	65	148	32	642	7.8	1.1	7.8
88-89—New York	82	0	1277	194	422	.460	0	3	.000	129	170	.759	157	237	394	76	172	0	47	125	18	517	4.8	0.9	6.3
89-90—Orlando	73	31	1860	312	667	.468	1	3	.333	136	209	.651	166	422	588	99	231	4	50	119	26	761	8.1	1.4	10.4
90-91—San Antonio	66	7	1099	177	384	.461	0	3	.000	89	105	.848	98	215	313	52	172	0	32	89	13	443	4.7	0.8	6.7
91-92—San Antonio	80	1	1127	147	344	.427	0	3	.000	73	89	.820	92	250	342	36	148	0	29	62	11	367	4.3	0.5	4.6
92-93—S.A.-Cha.	39	0	329	34	89	.382	0	2	.000	25	31	.806	32	86	118	24	37	1	6	20	5	93	3.0	0.6	2.4
REG. SEASON TOTALS	679	242	13247	1993	4386	.454	1	27	.037	1093	1481	.738	1300	2828	4128	635	1797	20	369	1038	220	5080	6.1	0.9	7.5
PLAYOFF TOTALS	43	4	506	58	135	.430	0	0	—	34	52	.654	56	93	149	18	80	0	5	28	7	150	3.5	0.4	3.5

GREEN, SIHUGO (Si) b. August 20, 1933 d. October 4, 1980 Ht. 6-2 Wt. 185 College—Duquesne

SEASON—TEAM	G	GS	MIN	FGM	FGA	PCT	3FGM	3FGA	PCT	FTM	FTA	PCT	O-RB	D-RB	TOT	AST	PF	DQ	STL	TO	BLK	PTS	RPG	APG	PPG
56-57—Rochester	13	—	423	50	143	.350	—	—	—	49	69	.710	—	—	67	47	36	1	—	—	—	149	5.2	3.6	11.5
58-59—Cin.-St. L.	46	—	1109	146	415	.352	—	—	—	104	160	.650	—	—	252	113	127	1	—	—	—	396	5.5	2.5	8.6
59-60—St. Louis	70	—	1354	159	427	.372	—	—	—	111	175	.634	—	—	257	133	150	3	—	—	—	429	3.7	1.9	6.1
60-61—St. Louis	76	—	1968	263	718	.366	—	—	—	174	247	.704	—	—	380	258	234	2	—	—	—	700	5.0	3.4	9.2
61-62—St. L.-Chicago	71	—	2388	341	905	.377	—	—	—	218	311	.701	—	—	399	318	226	3	—	—	—	900	5.6	4.5	12.7
62-63—Chicago	73	—	2648	322	783	.411	—	—	—	209	306	.683	—	—	335	422	274	5	—	—	—	853	4.6	5.8	11.7
63-64—Baltimore	75	—	2064	287	691	.415	—	—	—	198	290	.683	—	—	282	215	224	5	—	—	—	772	3.8	2.9	10.3
64-65—Baltimore	70	—	1086	152	368	.413	—	—	—	101	161	.627	—	—	169	140	134	5	—	—	—	405	2.4	2.0	5.8
65-66—Boston	10	—	92	12	31	.387	—	—	—	8	16	.500	—	—	11	9	16	0	—	—	—	32	1.1	0.9	3.2
REG. SEASON TOTALS	504	—	13132	1732	4481	.387	—	—	—	1172	1735	.676	—	—	2152	1655	1421	21	—	—	—	4636	4.3	3.3	9.2
PLAYOFF TOTALS	41	—	1111	156	360	.433	—	—	—	76	124	.613	—	—	222	165	121	3	—	—	—	388	5.4	4.0	9.5

GREEN, STEVEN MICHAEL (**Steve**) b. October 4, 1953 Ht. 6-7 Wt. 220 College—Indiana

SEASON—TEAM	G	GS	MIN	FGM	FGA	PCT	3FGM	3FGA	PCT	FTM	FTA	PCT	O-RB	D-RB	TOT	AST	PF	DQ	STL	TO	BLK	PTS	RPG	APG	PPG
75-76—Utah-St. L. (A)	52	—	1068	195	438	.445	0	5	.000	84	108	.778	84	110	194	64	150	—	31	72	10	474	3.7	1.2	9.1
76-77—Indiana	70	—	918	183	424	.432	—	—	—	84	113	.743	79	98	177	46	157	2	46	—	12	450	2.5	0.7	6.4
77-78—Indiana	44	—	449	56	128	.438	—	—	—	39	56	.696	31	40	71	30	67	0	14	23	2	151	1.6	0.7	3.4
78-79—Indiana	39	—	265	42	89	.472	—	—	—	20	34	.588	22	30	52	21	39	0	11	17	3	104	1.3	0.5	2.7
REG. NBA TOTALS	153	—	1632	281	641	.438	—	—	—	143	203	.704	132	168	300	97	263	2	71	40	17	705	2.0	0.6	4.6
REG. ABA TOTALS	52	—	1068	195	438	.445	0	5	.000	84	108	.778	84	110	194	64	150	—	31	72	10	474	3.7	1.2	9.1

GREEN, TOMMIE L. (**Tommy**) b. April 8, 1956 Ht. 6-2 Wt. 185 College—Southern

SEASON—TEAM	G	GS	MIN	FGM	FGA	PCT	3FGM	3FGA	PCT	FTM	FTA	PCT	O-RB	D-RB	TOT	AST	PF	DQ	STL	TO	BLK	PTS	RPG	APG	PPG
78-79—New Orleans	59	—	809	92	237	.388	—	—	—	48	63	.762	20	48	68	140	111	0	61	89	6	232	1.2	2.4	3.9
REG. SEASON TOTALS	59	—	809	92	237	.388	—	—	—	48	63	.762	20	48	68	140	111	0	61	89	6	232	1.2	2.4	3.9

GREENSPAN, GERALD (**Jerry**) b. November 22, 1941 Ht. 6-5 Wt. 195 College—Maryland

SEASON—TEAM	G	GS	MIN	FGM	FGA	PCT	3FGM	3FGA	PCT	FTM	FTA	PCT	O-RB	D-RB	TOT	AST	PF	DQ	STL	TO	BLK	PTS	RPG	APG	PPG
63-64—Philadelphia	20	—	280	32	90	.356	—	—	—	34	50	.680	—	—	72	11	54	0	—	—	—	98	3.6	0.6	4.9
64-65—Philadelphia	5	—	49	8	13	.615	—	—	—	8	8	1.000	—	—	11	0	12	0	—	—	—	24	2.2	0.0	4.8
REG. SEASON TOTALS	25	—	329	40	103	.388	—	—	—	42	58	.724	—	—	83	11	66	0	—	—	—	122	3.3	0.4	4.9

GREENWOOD, DAVID KASIM b. May 27, 1957 Ht. 6-9½ Wt. 230 College—UCLA

SEASON—TEAM	G	GS	MIN	FGM	FGA	PCT	3FGM	3FGA	PCT	FTM	FTA	PCT	O-RB	D-RB	TOT	AST	PF	DQ	STL	TO	BLK	PTS	RPG	APG	PPG
79-80—Chicago	82	—	2791	498	1051	.474	1	7	.143	337	416	.810	223	550	773	182	313	8	60	210	129	1334	9.4	2.2	16.3
80-81—Chicago	82	—	2710	481	989	.486	0	2	.000	217	290	.748	243	481	724	218	282	5	77	192	124	1179	8.8	2.7	14.4
81-82—Chicago	82	82	2914	480	1014	.473	0	3	.000	240	291	.825	192	594	786	262	292	1	70	180	93	1200	9.6	3.2	14.6
82-83—Chicago	79	61	2355	312	686	.455	0	4	.000	165	233	.708	217	548	765	151	261	5	54	154	90	789	9.7	1.9	10.0
83-84—Chicago	78	76	2718	369	753	.490	0	1	.000	213	289	.737	214	572	786	139	265	9	67	149	72	951	10.1	1.8	12.2
84-85—Chicago	61	28	1523	152	332	.458	0	1	.000	67	94	.713	108	280	388	78	190	1	34	63	21	371	6.4	1.3	6.1
85-86—San Antonio	68	24	1910	198	388	.510	0	1	.000	142	184	.772	151	380	531	90	207	3	37	113	52	538	7.8	1.3	7.9
86-87—San Antonio	79	78	2587	336	655	.513	3	6	.500	241	307	.785	256	527	783	237	248	3	71	161	50	916	9.9	3.0	11.6
87-88—San Antonio	45	40	1236	151	328	.460	0	2	.000	83	111	.748	92	208	300	97	134	2	33	74	22	385	6.7	2.2	8.6
88-89—S.A.-Denver	67	18	1403	167	395	.423	0	0	—	132	176	.750	140	262	402	96	201	5	47	91	52	466	6.0	1.4	7.0
89-90—Detroit	37	0	205	22	52	.423	0	0	—	16	29	.552	24	54	78	12	40	0	4	16	9	60	2.1	0.3	1.6
90-91—San Antonio	63	11	1018	85	169	.503	0	2	.000	69	94	.734	61	160	221	52	172	3	29	71	25	239	3.5	0.8	3.8
REG. SEASON TOTALS	823	418	23370	3251	6812	.477	4	29	.138	1922	2514	.765	1921	4616	6537	1614	2605	45	583	1474	739	8428	7.9	2.0	10.2
PLAYOFF TOTALS	22	7	538	83	149	.557	0	2	.000	21	36	.583	32	83	115	22	70	0	21	26	11	187	5.2	1.0	8.5

GREER, HAROLD EVERETT (**Hal**) b. June 26, 1936 Ht. 6-2 Wt. 175 College—Marshall

SEASON—TEAM	G	GS	MIN	FGM	FGA	PCT	3FGM	3FGA	PCT	FTM	FTA	PCT	O-RB	D-RB	TOT	AST	PF	DQ	STL	TO	BLK	PTS	RPG	APG	PPG
58-59—Syracuse	68	—	1625	308	679	.454	—	—	—	137	176	.778	—	—	196	101	189	1	—	—	—	753	2.9	1.5	11.1
59-60—Syracuse	70	—	1979	388	815	.476	—	—	—	148	189	.783	—	—	303	188	208	4	—	—	—	924	4.3	2.7	13.2
60-61—Syracuse	79	—	2763	623	1381	.451	—	—	—	305	394	.774	—	—	455	302	242	4	—	—	—	1551	5.8	3.8	19.6
61-62—Syracuse	71	—	2705	644	1442	.447	—	—	—	331	404	.819	—	—	524	313	252	2	—	—	—	1619	7.4	4.4	22.8
62-63—Syracuse	80	—	2631	600	1293	.464	—	—	—	362	434	.834	—	—	457	275	286	4	—	—	—	1562	5.7	3.4	19.5
63-64—Philadelphia	80	—	3157	715	1611	.444	—	—	—	435	525	.829	—	—	484	374	291	6	—	—	—	1865	6.1	4.7	23.3
64-65—Philadelphia	70	—	2600	539	1245	.433	—	—	—	335	413	.811	—	—	355	313	254	7	—	—	—	1413	5.1	4.5	20.2
65-66—Philadelphia	80	—	3326	703	1580	.445	—	—	—	413	514	.804	—	—	473	384	315	6	—	—	—	1819	5.9	4.8	22.7
66-67—Philadelphia	80	—	3086	699	1524	.459	—	—	—	367	466	.788	—	—	422	303	302	5	—	—	—	1765	5.3	3.8	22.1
67-68—Philadelphia	82	—	3263	777	1626	.478	—	—	—	422	549	.769	—	—	444	372	289	6	—	—	—	1976	5.4	4.5	24.1
68-69—Philadelphia	82	—	3311	732	1595	.459	—	—	—	432	543	.796	—	—	435	414	294	8	—	—	—	1896	5.3	5.0	23.1
69-70—Philadelphia	80	—	3024	705	1551	.455	—	—	—	352	432	.815	—	—	376	405	300	8	—	—	—	1762	4.7	5.1	22.0
70-71—Philadelphia	81	—	3060	591	1371	.431	—	—	—	326	405	.805	—	—	364	369	289	4	—	—	—	1508	4.5	4.6	18.6
71-72—Philadelphia	81	—	2410	389	866	.449	—	—	—	181	234	.774	—	—	271	316	268	10	—	—	—	959	3.3	3.9	11.8
72-73—Philadelphia	38	—	848	91	232	.392	—	—	—	32	39	.821	—	—	106	111	76	1	—	—	—	214	2.8	2.9	5.6
REG. SEASON TOTALS	1122	—	39788	8504	18811	.452	—	—	—	4578	5717	.801	—	—	5665	4540	3855	72	—	—	—	21586	5.0	4.0	19.2
PLAYOFF TOTALS	92	—	3642	705	1657	.425	—	—	—	466	574	.812	—	—	505	393	357	13	—	—	—	1876	5.5	4.3	20.4
ALL-STAR TOTALS	10	—	207	47	102	.461	—	—	—	26	37	.703	—	—	45	28	29	0	—	—	—	120	4.5	2.8	12.0

GREGOR, GARY W. b. August 13, 1945 Ht. 6-7 Wt. 235 College—South Carolina

SEASON—TEAM	G	GS	MIN	FGM	FGA	PCT	3FGM	3FGA	PCT	FTM	FTA	PCT	O-RB	D-RB	TOT	AST	PF	DQ	STL	TO	BLK	PTS	RPG	APG	PPG
68-69—Phoenix	80	—	2182	400	963	.415	—	—	—	85	131	.649	—	—	711	96	249	2	—	—	—	885	8.9	1.2	11.1
69-70—Atlanta	81	—	1603	286	661	.433	—	—	—	88	113	.779	—	—	397	63	159	5	—	—	—	660	4.9	0.8	8.1
70-71—Portland	44	—	1153	181	421	.430	—	—	—	59	89	.663	—	—	334	81	120	2	—	—	—	421	7.6	1.8	9.6
71-72—Portland	82	—	2371	399	884	.451	—	—	—	114	151	.755	—	—	591	187	201	2	—	—	—	912	7.2	2.3	11.1
72-73—Milwaukee	9	—	88	11	33	.333	—	—	—	5	7	.714	—	—	32	9	9	0	—	—	—	27	3.6	1.0	3.0
72-73—New York (A)	40	—	595	99	204	.485	1	1	1.000	32	39	.821	40	110	150	31	84	0	—	41	—	231	3.8	0.8	5.8
73-74—New York (A)	25	—	313	40	85	.471	2	3	.667	9	11	.818	22	49	71	15	48	—	4	10	1	91	2.8	0.6	3.6
REG. NBA TOTALS	296	—	7397	1277	2962	.431	—	—	—	351	491	.715	—	—	2065	436	738	11	—	—	—	2905	7.0	1.5	9.8
REG. ABA TOTALS	65	—	908	139	289	.481	3	4	.750	41	50	.820	62	159	221	46	132	0	4	51	1	322	3.4	0.7	5.0
NBA PLAYOFF TOTALS	7	—	67	6	21	.286	—	—	—	4	6	.667	—	—	17	2	14	0	—	—	—	16	2.4	0.3	2.3
ABA PLAYOFF TOTALS	1	—	12	1	6	.167	0	0	—	2	2	1.000	0	0	4	0	3	0	0	0	0	4	4.0	0.0	4.0

GREGORY, CLAUDE ANDRE b. December 26, 1958   Ht. 6-9   Wt. 235   College—Wisconsin

SEASON—TEAM	G	GS	MIN	FGM	FGA	PCT	3FGM	3FGA	PCT	FTM	FTA	PCT	O-RB	D-RB	TOT	AST	PF	DQ	STL	TO	BLK	PTS	RPG	APG	PPG
85-86—Washington	2	0	2	1	2	.500	0	0	—	0	0	—	2	0	2	0	1	0	1	2	0	2	1.0	0.0	1.0
87-88—L.A. Clippers	23	2	313	61	134	.455	0	1	.000	12	36	.333	37	58	95	16	37	0	9	22	13	134	4.1	0.7	5.8
REG. SEASON TOTALS	25	2	315	62	136	.456	0	1	.000	12	36	.333	39	58	97	16	38	0	10	24	13	136	3.9	0.6	5.4

GREIG, JOHN W. b. April 28, 1961   Ht. 6-7   Wt. 215   College—Wenatchee Valley/Oregon

SEASON—TEAM	G	GS	MIN	FGM	FGA	PCT	3FGM	3FGA	PCT	FTM	FTA	PCT	O-RB	D-RB	TOT	AST	PF	DQ	STL	TO	BLK	PTS	RPG	APG	PPG
82-83—Seattle	9	0	26	7	13	.538	0	0	—	5	6	.833	2	4	6	0	4	0	0	2	1	19	0.7	0.0	2.1
REG. SEASON TOTALS	9	0	26	7	13	.538	0	0	—	5	6	.833	2	4	6	0	4	0	0	2	1	19	0.7	0.0	2.1

GREKIN, NORMAN (Norm) b. June 22, 1930   d. September 29, 1981   Ht. 6-5   Wt. 180   College—La Salle

SEASON—TEAM	G	GS	MIN	FGM	FGA	PCT	3FGM	3FGA	PCT	FTM	FTA	PCT	O-RB	D-RB	TOT	AST	PF	DQ	STL	TO	BLK	PTS	RPG	APG	PPG
53-54—Philadelphia	1	—	1	0	0	—	—	—	—	0	0	—	—	—	—	0	0	1	0	—	—	—	0	0.0	0.0	0.0
REG. SEASON TOTALS	1	—	1	0	0	—	—	—	—	0	0	—	—	—	—	0	0	1	0	—	—	—	0	0.0	0.0	0.0

GREVEY, KEVIN MICHAEL b. May 12, 1953   Ht. 6-5   Wt. 210   College—Kentucky

SEASON—TEAM	G	GS	MIN	FGM	FGA	PCT	3FGM	3FGA	PCT	FTM	FTA	PCT	O-RB	D-RB	TOT	AST	PF	DQ	STL	TO	BLK	PTS	RPG	APG	PPG
75-76—Washington	56	—	504	79	213	.371	—	—	—	52	58	.897	24	36	60	27	65	0	13	—	3	210	1.1	0.5	3.8
76-77—Washington	76	—	1306	224	530	.423	—	—	—	79	119	.664	73	105	178	68	148	1	29	—	9	527	2.3	0.9	6.9
77-78—Washington	81	—	2121	505	1128	.448	—	—	—	243	308	.789	124	166	290	155	203	4	61	159	17	1253	3.6	1.9	15.5
78-79—Washington	65	—	1856	418	922	.453	—	—	—	173	224	.772	90	142	232	153	159	1	46	120	14	1009	3.6	2.4	15.5
79-80—Washington	65	—	1818	331	804	.412	34	92	.370	216	249	.867	80	107	187	177	158	0	56	102	16	912	2.9	2.7	14.0
80-81—Washington	75	—	2616	500	1103	.453	45	136	.331	244	290	.841	67	152	219	300	161	1	68	144	17	1289	2.9	4.0	17.2
81-82—Washington	71	62	2164	376	857	.439	28	82	.341	165	193	.855	57	138	195	149	151	1	44	96	23	945	2.7	2.1	13.3
82-83—Washington	41	11	756	114	294	.388	15	38	.395	54	69	.783	18	31	49	49	61	0	18	27	7	297	1.2	1.2	7.2
83-84—Milwaukee	64	3	923	178	395	.451	15	53	.283	75	84	.893	30	51	81	75	95	0	27	45	4	446	1.3	1.2	7.0
84-85—Milwaukee	78	6	1182	190	424	.448	8	33	.242	88	107	.822	27	76	103	94	85	1	30	55	2	476	1.3	1.2	6.1
REG. SEASON TOTALS	672	82	15246	2915	6670	.437	145	434	.334	1389	1701	.817	590	1004	1594	1247	1286	9	392	748	112	7364	2.4	1.9	11.0
PLAYOFF TOTALS	70	1	1625	310	738	.420	9	18	.500	156	199	.784	65	80	145	102	181	4	38	95	18	785	2.1	1.5	11.2

GREY, DENNIS b. August 26, 1947   Ht. 6-8½   Wt. 215   College—California Western

SEASON—TEAM	G	GS	MIN	FGM	FGA	PCT	3FGM	3FGA	PCT	FTM	FTA	PCT	O-RB	D-RB	TOT	AST	PF	DQ	STL	TO	BLK	PTS	RPG	APG	PPG
68-69—Los Angeles (A)	58	—	1317	184	439	.419	0	1	.000	157	292	.538	—	—	320	52	196	11	—	129	—	525	5.5	0.9	9.1
69-70—New York (A)	4	—	74	6	24	.250	0	0	—	6	12	.500	—	—	25	0	15	1	—	—	—	18	6.3	0.0	4.5
REG. ABA TOTALS	62	—	1391	190	463	.410	0	1	.000	163	304	.536	—	—	345	52	211	12	—	129	—	543	5.6	0.8	8.8

GRIFFIN, GREG b. September 6, 1952   Ht. 6-7   Wt. 190   College—Pasadena CC/Idaho State

SEASON—TEAM	G	GS	MIN	FGM	FGA	PCT	3FGM	3FGA	PCT	FTM	FTA	PCT	O-RB	D-RB	TOT	AST	PF	DQ	STL	TO	BLK	PTS	RPG	APG	PPG
77-78—Phoenix	36	—	422	61	169	.361	—	—	—	23	36	.639	44	59	103	24	56	0	16	39	0	145	2.9	0.7	4.0
REG. SEASON TOTALS	36	—	422	61	169	.361	—	—	—	23	36	.639	44	59	103	24	56	0	16	39	0	145	2.9	0.7	4.0
PLAYOFF TOTALS	2	—	25	3	7	.429	—	—	—	0	0	—	2	2	4	3	5	0	1	2	1	6	2.0	1.5	3.0

GRIFFIN, PAUL ARTHUR b. January 20, 1954   Ht. 6-9   Wt. 205   College—Western Michigan

SEASON—TEAM	G	GS	MIN	FGM	FGA	PCT	3FGM	3FGA	PCT	FTM	FTA	PCT	O-RB	D-RB	TOT	AST	PF	DQ	STL	TO	BLK	PTS	RPG	APG	PPG
76-77—New Orleans	81	—	1645	140	256	.547	—	—	—	145	201	.721	167	328	495	167	241	6	50	—	43	425	6.1	2.1	5.2
77-78—New Orleans	82	—	1853	160	358	.447	—	—	—	112	157	.713	157	353	510	172	228	6	88	150	45	432	6.2	2.1	5.3
78-79—New Orleans	77	—	1398	106	223	.475	—	—	—	91	147	.619	126	265	391	138	198	3	54	117	36	303	5.1	1.8	3.9
79-80—San Antonio	82	—	1812	173	313	.553	0	0	—	174	240	.725	154	284	438	250	306	9	81	131	53	520	5.3	3.0	6.3
80-81—San Antonio	82	—	1930	166	325	.511	0	0	—	170	253	.672	184	321	505	249	207	3	77	132	38	502	6.2	3.0	6.1
81-82—San Antonio	23	0	459	32	66	.485	0	0	—	24	37	.649	29	66	95	54	67	0	20	40	8	88	4.1	2.3	3.8
82-83—San Antonio	53	0	956	60	116	.517	0	0	—	53	76	.697	77	139	216	86	153	0	33	68	25	173	4.1	1.6	3.3
REG. SEASON TOTALS	480	0	10053	837	1657	.505	0	0	—	769	1111	.692	894	1756	2650	1116	1400	27	403	638	248	2443	5.5	2.3	5.1
PLAYOFF TOTALS	10	0	252	21	38	.553	0	0	—	15	26	.577	19	36	55	35	37	2	6	16	6	57	5.5	3.5	5.7

GRIFFITH, DARRELL STEVEN (Dr. Dunkenstein) b. June 16, 1958   Ht. 6-4   Wt. 190   College—Louisville

SEASON—TEAM	G	GS	MIN	FGM	FGA	PCT	3FGM	3FGA	PCT	FTM	FTA	PCT	O-RB	D-RB	TOT	AST	PF	DQ	STL	TO	BLK	PTS	RPG	APG	PPG
80-81—Utah	81	—	2867	716	1544	.464	10	52	.192	229	320	.716	79	209	288	194	219	0	106	231	40	1671	3.6	2.4	20.6
81-82—Utah	80	79	2597	689	1429	.482	15	52	.288	189	271	.697	128	177	305	187	213	0	95	193	34	1582	3.8	2.3	19.8
82-83—Utah	77	76	2787	752	1554	.484	38	132	.288	167	246	.679	100	204	304	270	184	0	138	252	33	1709	3.9	3.5	22.2
83-84—Utah	82	82	2650	697	1423	.490	91	252	.361	151	217	.696	95	243	338	283	202	1	114	243	23	1636	4.1	3.5	20.0
84-85—Utah	78	78	2776	728	1593	.457	92	257	.358	216	298	.725	124	220	344	243	178	1	133	247	30	1764	4.4	3.1	22.6
86-87—Utah	76	10	1843	463	1038	.446	67	200	.335	149	212	.703	81	146	227	129	167	0	97	135	29	1142	3.0	1.7	15.0
87-88—Utah	52	11	1052	251	585	.429	28	102	.275	59	92	.641	36	91	127	91	102	0	52	67	5	589	2.4	1.8	11.3
88-89—Utah	82	73	2382	466	1045	.446	61	196	.311	142	182	.780	77	253	330	130	175	0	86	141	22	1135	4.0	1.6	13.8
89-90—Utah	82	1	1444	301	649	.464	80	215	.372	51	78	.654	43	123	166	63	149	0	68	75	19	733	2.0	0.8	8.9
90-91—Utah	75	2	1005	174	445	.391	48	138	.348	34	45	.756	17	73	90	37	100	1	42	48	7	430	1.2	0.5	5.7
REG. SEASON TOTALS	765	412	21403	5237	11305	.463	530	1596	.332	1387	1961	.707	780	1739	2519	1627	1689	3	931	1632	242	12391	3.3	2.1	16.2
PLAYOFF TOTALS	37	21	1038	221	504	.438	46	124	.371	69	97	.711	37	104	141	77	60	0	47	77	11	557	3.8	2.1	15.1

GRIGSBY, CHARLES L. (**Chuck**) b. August 15, 1928   Ht. 6-5 Wt. 190 College—Dayton

SEASON—TEAM	G	GS	MIN	FGM	FGA	PCT	3FGM	3FGA	PCT	FTM	FTA	PCT	O-RB	D-RB	TOT	AST	PF	DQ	STL	TO	BLK	PTS	RPG	APG	PPG
54-55—New York	7	—	45	7	19	.368	—	—	—	2	8	.250	—	—	11	7	9	0	—	—	—	16	1.6	1.0	2.3
REG. SEASON TOTALS	7	—	45	7	19	.368	—	—	—	2	8	.250	—	—	11	7	9	0	—	—	—	16	1.6	1.0	2.3

GRIMSHAW, GEORGE W. (**Woodie**) b. September 24, 1919 d. October 1974 Ht. 6-1 Wt. 185 College—Brown

SEASON—TEAM	G	GS	MIN	FGM	FGA	PCT	3FGM	3FGA	PCT	FTM	FTA	PCT	O-RB	D-RB	TOT	AST	PF	DQ	STL	TO	BLK	PTS	RPG	APG	PPG
46-47—Providence	21	—	—	20	56	.357	—	—	—	21	44	.477	—	—	—	1	25	—	—	—	—	61	—	0.0	2.9
REG. SEASON TOTALS	21	—	—	20	56	.357	—	—	—	21	44	.477	—	—	—	1	25	—	—	—	—	61	—	0.0	2.9

GROAT, RICHARD MORROW (**Dick**) b. November 4, 1930   Ht. 6-1 Wt. 185 College—Duke

SEASON—TEAM	G	GS	MIN	FGM	FGA	PCT	3FGM	3FGA	PCT	FTM	FTA	PCT	O-RB	D-RB	TOT	AST	PF	DQ	STL	TO	BLK	PTS	RPG	APG	PPG
52-53—Fort Wayne	26	—	663	100	272	.368	—	—	—	109	138	.790	—	—	86	69	90	7	—	—	—	309	3.3	2.7	11.9
REG. SEASON TOTALS	26	—	663	100	272	.368	—	—	—	109	138	.790	—	—	86	69	90	7	—	—	—	309	3.3	2.7	11.9

GROSS, ROBERT EDWIN (**Bob**) b. August 3, 1953   Ht. 6-6 Wt. 200 College—Seattle/Los Angeles Harbor/Long Beach State

SEASON—TEAM	G	GS	MIN	FGM	FGA	PCT	3FGM	3FGA	PCT	FTM	FTA	PCT	O-RB	D-RB	TOT	AST	PF	DQ	STL	TO	BLK	PTS	RPG	APG	PPG
75-76—Portland	76	—	1474	209	400	.523	—	—	—	97	142	.683	138	169	307	163	186	3	91	—	43	515	4.0	2.1	6.8
76-77—Portland	82	—	2232	376	711	.529	—	—	—	183	215	.851	173	221	394	242	255	7	107	—	57	935	4.8	3.0	11.4
77-78—Portland	72	—	2163	381	720	.529	—	—	—	152	190	.800	180	220	400	254	234	5	100	179	52	914	5.6	3.5	12.7
78-79—Portland	53	—	1441	209	443	.472	—	—	—	96	119	.807	106	144	250	184	161	4	70	121	47	514	4.7	3.5	9.7
79-80—Portland	62	—	1581	221	472	.468	1	10	.100	95	114	.833	84	165	249	228	179	3	60	166	47	538	4.0	3.7	8.7
80-81—Portland	82	—	1934	253	479	.528	0	9	.000	135	159	.849	126	202	328	251	238	5	90	151	67	641	4.0	3.1	7.8
81-82—Portland	59	24	1377	173	322	.537	3	6	.500	78	104	.750	101	158	259	125	162	2	75	88	41	427	4.4	2.1	7.2
82-83—San Diego	27	3	373	35	82	.427	1	3	.333	12	19	.632	32	34	66	34	69	1	22	24	7	83	2.4	1.3	3.1
REG. SEASON TOTALS	513	27	12575	1857	3629	.512	5	28	.179	848	1062	.798	940	1313	2253	1481	1484	30	615	729	361	4567	4.4	2.9	8.9
PLAYOFF TOTALS	25	0	694	122	209	.584	0	0	—	63	74	.851	55	69	124	89	101	5	35	8	17	307	5.0	3.6	12.3

GROSSO, MICHAEL JAMES (**Mike**) b. September 7, 1947   Ht. 6-9 Wt. 230 College—Louisville/South Carolina

SEASON—TEAM	G	GS	MIN	FGM	FGA	PCT	3FGM	3FGA	PCT	FTM	FTA	PCT	O-RB	D-RB	TOT	AST	PF	DQ	STL	TO	BLK	PTS	RPG	APG	PPG
71-72—Pittsburgh (A)	25	—	335	45	102	.441	0	0	—	13	23	.565	—	—	123	11	64	—	—	20	—	103	4.9	0.4	4.1
REG. ABA TOTALS	25	—	335	45	102	.441	0	0	—	13	23	.565	—	—	123	11	64	—	—	20	—	103	4.9	0.4	4.1

GROTE, JERRY C. b. December 28, 1940   Ht. 6-4 Wt. 215 College—Loyola Marymount

SEASON—TEAM	G	GS	MIN	FGM	FGA	PCT	3FGM	3FGA	PCT	FTM	FTA	PCT	O-RB	D-RB	TOT	AST	PF	DQ	STL	TO	BLK	PTS	RPG	APG	PPG
64-65—Los Angeles	11	—	33	6	11	.545	—	—	—	2	2	1.000	—	—	4	4	5	0	—	—	—	14	0.4	0.4	1.3
REG. SEASON TOTALS	11	—	33	6	11	.545	—	—	—	2	2	1.000	—	—	4	4	5	0	—	—	—	14	0.4	0.4	1.3

GROZA, ALEX JOHN b. October 7, 1926   Ht. 6-7 Wt. 220 College—Kentucky

SEASON—TEAM	G	GS	MIN	FGM	FGA	PCT	3FGM	3FGA	PCT	FTM	FTA	PCT	O-RB	D-RB	TOT	AST	PF	DQ	STL	TO	BLK	PTS	RPG	APG	PPG
49-50—Indianapolis	64	—	—	521	1090	.478	—	—	—	454	623	.729	—	—	—	162	221	—	—	—	—	1496	—	2.5	23.4
50-51—Indianapolis	66	—	—	492	1046	.470	—	—	—	445	566	.786	—	—	709	156	237	8	—	—	—	1429	10.7	2.4	21.7
REG. SEASON TOTALS	130	—	—	1013	2136	.474	—	—	—	899	1189	.756	—	—	709	318	458	8	—	—	—	2925	10.7	2.4	22.5
PLAYOFF TOTALS	9	—	—	80	147	.544	—	—	—	74	92	.804	—	—	42	14	35	1	—	—	—	234	14.0	1.6	26.0
ALL-STAR TOTALS	1	—	—	8	16	.500	—	—	—	1	1	1.000	—	—	13	1	4	0	—	—	—	17	13.0	1.0	17.0

GRUBAR, RICHARD ARTHUR (**Dick**) b. July 26, 1947   Ht. 6-4 Wt. 185 College—North Carolina

SEASON—TEAM	G	GS	MIN	FGM	FGA	PCT	3FGM	3FGA	PCT	FTM	FTA	PCT	O-RB	D-RB	TOT	AST	PF	DQ	STL	TO	BLK	PTS	RPG	APG	PPG
69-70—Indiana (A)	2	—	8	2	3	.667	0	0	—	0	0	—	—	—	0	1	1	0	—	—	—	4	0.0	0.5	2.0
REG. ABA TOTALS	2	—	8	2	3	.667	0	0	—	0	0	—	—	—	—	1	1	0	—	—	—	4	0.0	0.5	2.0

GRUNFELD, ERNEST (**Ernie**) b. April 24, 1955   Ht. 6-6 Wt. 215 College—Tennessee

SEASON—TEAM	G	GS	MIN	FGM	FGA	PCT	3FGM	3FGA	PCT	FTM	FTA	PCT	O-RB	D-RB	TOT	AST	PF	DQ	STL	TO	BLK	PTS	RPG	APG	PPG
77-78—Milwaukee	73	—	1261	204	461	.443	—	—	—	94	143	.657	70	124	194	145	150	1	54	98	19	502	2.7	2.0	6.9
78-79—Milwaukee	82	—	1778	326	661	.493	—	—	—	191	251	.761	124	236	360	216	220	3	58	141	15	843	4.4	2.6	10.3
79-80—Kansas City	80	—	1397	186	420	.443	1	2	.500	101	131	.771	87	145	232	109	151	1	56	81	9	474	2.9	1.4	5.9
80-81—Kansas City	79	—	1584	260	486	.535	0	0	—	75	101	.743	31	175	206	205	155	1	60	88	15	595	2.6	2.6	7.5
81-82—Kansas City	81	11	1892	420	822	.511	2	14	.143	188	229	.821	55	127	182	276	191	0	72	148	39	1030	2.2	3.4	12.7
82-83—New York	77	0	1422	167	377	.443	0	4	.000	81	98	.827	42	121	163	136	172	1	40	84	10	415	2.1	1.8	5.4
83-84—New York	76	6	1119	166	362	.459	2	9	.222	64	83	.771	24	97	121	108	151	0	43	71	7	398	1.6	1.4	5.2
84-85—New York	69	0	1061	188	384	.490	2	8	.250	77	104	.740	41	110	151	105	129	2	50	40	7	455	2.2	1.5	6.6
85-86—New York	76	0	1402	148	355	.417	26	61	.426	90	108	.833	42	164	206	119	192	2	39	50	13	412	2.7	1.6	5.4
REG. SEASON TOTALS	693	17	12916	2065	4328	.477	33	98	.337	961	1248	.770	516	1299	1815	1419	1511	11	472	801	134	5124	2.6	2.0	7.4
PLAYOFF TOTALS	42	0	944	146	299	.488	2	4	.500	81	98	.827	19	73	92	121	89	1	43	63	12	375	2.2	2.9	8.9

GUARILIA, EUGENE MICHAEL (Gene) b. September 13, 1937 Ht. 6-5 Wt. 220 College—Potomac State/George Washington

SEASON—TEAM	G	GS	MIN	FGM	FGA	PCT	3FGM	3FGA	PCT	FTM	FTA	PCT	O-RB	D-RB	TOT	AST	PF	DQ	STL	TO	BLK	PTS	RPG	APG	PPG
59-60—Boston	48	—	423	58	154	.377	—	—	—	29	41	.707	—	—	85	18	57	1	—	—	—	145	1.8	0.4	3.0
60-61—Boston	25	—	209	38	94	.404	—	—	—	3	10	.300	—	—	71	5	28	0	—	—	—	79	2.8	0.2	3.2
61-62—Boston	45	—	367	61	161	.379	—	—	—	41	64	.641	—	—	124	11	56	0	—	—	—	163	2.8	0.2	3.6
62-63—Boston	11	—	83	11	38	.289	—	—	—	4	11	.364	—	—	14	2	5	0	—	—	—	26	1.3	0.2	2.4
REG. SEASON TOTALS	129	—	1082	168	447	.376	—	—	—	77	126	.611	—	—	294	36	146	1	—	—	—	413	2.3	0.3	3.2
PLAYOFF TOTALS	12	—	67	6	26	.231	—	—	—	8	11	.727	—	—	23	4	10	0	—	—	—	20	1.9	0.3	1.7

GUDMUNDSSON, KARL PETUR (Petur) b. October 30, 1958 Ht. 7-2 Wt. 260 College—Washington

SEASON—TEAM	G	GS	MIN	FGM	FGA	PCT	3FGM	3FGA	PCT	FTM	FTA	PCT	O-RB	D-RB	TOT	AST	PF	DQ	STL	TO	BLK	PTS	RPG	APG	PPG
81-82—Portland	68	6	845	83	166	.500	1	1	1.000	52	76	.684	51	135	186	59	163	2	13	73	30	219	2.7	0.9	3.2
85-86—L.A. Lakers	8	2	128	20	37	.541	0	0	—	18	27	.667	17	21	38	3	25	1	3	11	4	58	4.8	0.4	7.3
87-88—San Antonio	69	9	1017	139	280	.496	0	1	.000	117	145	.807	93	230	323	86	197	5	18	103	61	395	4.7	1.2	5.7
88-89—San Antonio	5	3	70	9	25	.360	0	0	—	3	4	.750	5	11	16	5	15	0	1	8	1	21	3.2	1.0	4.2
REG. SEASON TOTALS	150	20	2060	251	508	.494	1	2	.500	190	252	.754	166	397	563	153	400	8	35	195	96	693	3.8	1.0	4.6
PLAYOFF TOTALS	14	0	117	16	29	.552	0	2	.000	10	15	.667	8	18	26	4	23	1	3	13	4	42	1.9	0.3	3.0

GUERIN, RICHARD V. (Richie) b. May 29, 1932 Ht. 6-4 Wt. 210 College—Iona

SEASON—TEAM	G	GS	MIN	FGM	FGA	PCT	3FGM	3FGA	PCT	FTM	FTA	PCT	O-RB	D-RB	TOT	AST	PF	DQ	STL	TO	BLK	PTS	RPG	APG	PPG
56-57—New York	72	—	1793	257	699	.368	—	—	—	181	292	.620	—	—	334	182	186	3	—	—	—	695	4.6	2.5	9.7
57-58—New York	63	—	2368	344	973	.354	—	—	—	353	511	.691	—	—	489	317	202	3	—	—	—	1041	7.8	5.0	16.5
58-59—New York	71	—	2558	443	1046	.424	—	—	—	405	505	.802	—	—	518	364	255	1	—	—	—	1291	7.3	5.1	18.2
59-60—New York	74	—	2429	579	1379	.420	—	—	—	457	591	.773	—	—	505	468	242	3	—	—	—	1615	6.8	6.3	21.8
60-61—New York	79	—	3023	612	1545	.396	—	—	—	496	626	.792	—	—	628	503	310	3	—	—	—	1720	7.9	6.4	21.8
61-62—New York	78	—	3348	839	1897	.442	—	—	—	625	762	.820	—	—	501	539	299	3	—	—	—	2303	6.4	6.9	29.5
62-63—New York	79	—	2712	596	1380	.432	—	—	—	509	600	.848	—	—	331	348	228	2	—	—	—	1701	4.2	4.4	21.5
63-64—N.Y.-St. L.	80	—	2366	351	846	.415	—	—	—	347	424	.818	—	—	256	375	276	4	—	—	—	1049	3.2	4.7	13.1
64-65—St. Louis	57	—	1678	295	662	.446	—	—	—	231	301	.767	—	—	149	271	193	1	—	—	—	821	2.6	4.8	14.4
65-66—St. Louis	80	—	2363	414	998	.415	—	—	—	362	446	.812	—	—	314	388	256	4	—	—	—	1190	3.9	4.9	14.9
66-67—St. Louis	80	—	2275	394	904	.436	—	—	—	304	416	.731	—	—	192	345	247	2	—	—	—	1092	2.4	4.3	13.7
68-69—Atlanta	27	—	472	47	111	.423	—	—	—	57	74	.770	—	—	59	99	66	0	—	—	—	151	2.2	3.7	5.6
69-70—Atlanta	8	—	64	3	11	.273	—	—	—	1	1	1.000	—	—	2	12	9	0	—	—	—	7	0.3	1.5	0.9
REG. SEASON TOTALS	848	—	27449	5174	12451	.416	—	—	—	4328	5549	.780	—	—	4278	4211	2769	29	—	—	—	14676	5.0	5.0	17.3
PLAYOFF TOTALS	42	—	1345	231	539	.429	—	—	—	192	239	.803	—	—	149	214	157	2	—	—	—	654	3.5	5.1	15.6
ALL-STAR TOTALS	6	—	122	23	56	.411	—	—	—	17	26	.654	—	—	19	18	17	1	—	—	—	63	3.2	3.0	10.5

GUGLIOTTA, THOMAS JAMES (Tom) b. December 19, 1969 Ht. 6-10 Wt. 240 College—North Carolina State

SEASON—TEAM	G	GS	MIN	FGM	FGA	PCT	3FGM	3FGA	PCT	FTM	FTA	PCT	O-RB	D-RB	TOT	AST	PF	DQ	STL	TO	BLK	PTS	RPG	APG	PPG
92-93—Washington	81	81	2795	484	1135	.426	38	135	.281	181	281	.644	219	562	781	306	195	0	134	230	35	1187	9.6	3.8	14.7
93-94—Washington	78	78	2795	540	1159	.466	40	148	.270	213	311	.685	189	539	728	276	174	0	172	247	51	1333	9.3	3.5	17.1
REG. SEASON TOTALS	159	159	5590	1024	2294	.446	78	283	.276	394	592	.666	408	1101	1509	582	369	0	306	477	86	2520	9.5	3.7	15.8

GUIBERT, ANDRES b. October 28, 1968 Ht. 6-10 Wt. 242 College—None

SEASON—TEAM	G	GS	MIN	FGM	FGA	PCT	3FGM	3FGA	PCT	FTM	FTA	PCT	O-RB	D-RB	TOT	AST	PF	DQ	STL	TO	BLK	PTS	RPG	APG	PPG
93-94—Minnesota	5	0	33	6	20	.300	0	0	—	3	6	.500	10	6	16	2	6	0	0	6	1	15	3.2	0.4	3.0
REG. SEASON TOTALS	5	0	33	6	20	.300	0	0	—	3	6	.500	10	6	16	2	6	0	0	6	1	15	3.2	0.4	3.0

GUIDINGER, JAY PATRICK b. August 18, 1969 Ht. 6-10 Wt. 255 College—Minnesota-Duluth

SEASON—TEAM	G	GS	MIN	FGM	FGA	PCT	3FGM	3FGA	PCT	FTM	FTA	PCT	O-RB	D-RB	TOT	AST	PF	DQ	STL	TO	BLK	PTS	RPG	APG	PPG
92-93—Cleveland	32	5	215	19	55	.345	0	0	—	13	25	.520	26	38	64	17	48	0	9	10	10	51	2.0	0.5	1.6
93-94—Cleveland	32	0	131	16	32	.500	0	0	—	15	21	.714	15	18	33	3	23	0	4	16	5	47	1.0	0.1	1.5
REG. SEASON TOTALS	64	5	346	35	87	.402	0	0	—	28	46	.609	41	56	97	20	71	0	13	26	15	98	1.5	0.3	1.5
PLAYOFF TOTALS	4	0	15	1	3	.333	0	0	—	0	2	.000	1	0	1	—	1	0	0	2	1	2	0.3	0.0	0.5

GUNTHER, COULBY b. February 5, 1923 Ht. 6-4 Wt. 190 College—Boston College/St. John's

SEASON—TEAM	G	GS	MIN	FGM	FGA	PCT	3FGM	3FGA	PCT	FTM	FTA	PCT	O-RB	D-RB	TOT	AST	PF	DQ	STL	TO	BLK	PTS	RPG	APG	PPG
46-47—Pittsburgh	52	—	—	254	756	.336	—	—	—	226	351	.644	—	—	—	32	117	—	—	—	—	734	—	0.6	14.1
48-49—St. Louis	32	—	—	57	181	.315	—	—	—	45	71	.634	—	—	—	33	64	—	—	—	—	159	—	1.0	5.0
REG. SEASON TOTALS	84	—	—	311	937	.332	—	—	—	271	422	.642	—	—	—	65	181	—	—	—	—	893	—	0.8	10.6
PLAYOFF TOTALS	1	—	—	0	1	.000	—	—	—	0	0	—	—	—	—	0	—	—	—	—	—	0	—	0.0	0.0

GUNTHER, DAVID C. (Dave) b. July 22, 1937 Ht. 6-7 Wt. 220 College—Iowa

SEASON—TEAM	G	GS	MIN	FGM	FGA	PCT	3FGM	3FGA	PCT	FTM	FTA	PCT	O-RB	D-RB	TOT	AST	PF	DQ	STL	TO	BLK	PTS	RPG	APG	PPG
62-63—San Francisco	1	—	5	1	2	.500	—	—	—	0	0	—	—	—	3	3	1	0	—	—	—	2	3.0	3.0	2.0
REG. SEASON TOTALS	1	—	5	1	2	.500	—	—	—	0	0	—	—	—	3	3	1	0	—	—	—	2	3.0	3.0	2.0

GUOKAS, ALBERT G. (Al, Gook) b. August 7, 1925 d. 1990 Ht. 6-5½ Wt. 200 College—St. Joseph's (Pa.)

SEASON—TEAM	G	GS	MIN	FGM	FGA	PCT	3FGM	3FGA	PCT	FTM	FTA	PCT	O-RB	D-RB	TOT	AST	PF	DQ	STL	TO	BLK	PTS	RPG	APG	PPG
48-49—Denver (N)	60	—	—	146	—	—	—	—	—	81	129	.628	—	—	—	—	182	—	—	—	—	373	—	—	6.2
49-50—Denver-Phil.	57	—	—	93	299	.311	—	—	—	28	50	.560	—	—	—	95	143	—	—	—	—	214	—	1.7	3.8
REG. NBA TOTALS	57	—	—	93	299	.311	—	—	—	28	50	.560	—	—	—	95	143	—	—	—	—	214	—	1.7	3.8
REG. NBL TOTALS	60	—	—	146	—	—	—	—	—	81	129	.628	—	—	—	—	182	—	—	—	—	373	—	—	6.2
NBA PLAYOFF TOTALS	2	—	—	2	4	.500	—	—	—	2	6	.333	—	—	—	5	3	—	—	—	—	6	—	2.5	3.0

GUOKAS, MATTHEW GEORGE JR. (Matt) b. February 25, 1944 Ht. 6-5½ Wt. 185 College—Miami/St. Joseph (Pa.)

SEASON—TEAM	G	GS	MIN	FGM	FGA	PCT	3FGM	3FGA	PCT	FTM	FTA	PCT	O-RB	D-RB	TOT	AST	PF	DQ	STL	TO	BLK	PTS	RPG	APG	PPG
66-67—Philadelphia	69	—	808	79	203	.389	—	—	—	49	81	.605	—	—	83	105	82	0	—	—	—	207	1.2	1.5	3.0
67-68—Philadelphia	82	—	1612	190	393	.483	—	—	—	118	152	.776	—	—	185	191	172	0	—	—	—	498	2.3	2.3	6.1
68-69—Philadelphia	72	—	838	92	216	.426	—	—	—	54	81	.667	—	—	94	104	121	1	—	—	—	238	1.3	1.4	3.3
69-70—Philadelphia	80	—	1558	189	416	.454	—	—	—	106	149	.711	—	—	216	222	201	0	—	—	—	484	2.7	2.8	6.1
70-71—Phil.-Chicago	79	—	2213	206	418	.493	—	—	—	101	138	.732	—	—	158	342	189	1	—	—	—	513	2.0	4.3	6.5
71-72—Cincinnati	61	—	1975	191	385	.496	—	—	—	64	83	.771	—	—	142	321	150	0	—	—	—	446	2.3	5.3	7.3
72-73—Kansas City-Omaha	79	—	2846	322	565	.570	—	—	—	74	90	.822	—	—	245	403	190	0	—	—	—	718	3.1	5.1	9.1
73-74—K.C.-Oma.-Hou.-Buf.	75	—	1871	195	396	.492	—	—	—	39	60	.650	31	90	121	238	150	3	54	—	21	429	1.6	3.2	5.7
74-75—Chicago	82	—	2089	255	500	.510	—	—	—	78	103	.757	24	115	139	178	154	1	45	—	17	588	1.7	2.2	7.2
75-76—Chicago-K.C.	56	—	793	73	173	.422	—	—	—	18	27	.667	22	41	63	70	76	0	18	—	3	164	1.1	1.3	2.9
REG. SEASON TOTALS	735	—	16603	1792	3665	.489	—	—	—	701	964	.727	77	246	1446	2174	1485	6	117	—	41	4285	2.0	3.0	5.8
PLAYOFF TOTALS	60	—	1072	101	242	.417	—	—	—	52	67	.776	7	15	118	98	121	0	7	—	2	254	2.0	1.6	4.2

GUOKAS, MATTHEW GEORGE SR. (Matt) b. November 11, 1915 d. December 9, 1993 Ht. 6-3 Wt. 195 College—St. Joseph (Pa.)

SEASON—TEAM	G	GS	MIN	FGM	FGA	PCT	3FGM	3FGA	PCT	FTM	FTA	PCT	O-RB	D-RB	TOT	AST	PF	DQ	STL	TO	BLK	PTS	RPG	APG	PPG
46-47—Philadelphia	47	—	—	28	104	.269	—	—	—	26	47	.553	—	—	—	9	70	—	—	—	—	82	—	0.2	1.7
REG. SEASON TOTALS	47	—	—	28	104	.269	—	—	—	26	47	.553	—	—	—	9	70	—	—	—	—	82	—	0.2	1.7
PLAYOFF TOTALS	8	—	—	1	9	.111	—	—	—	2	5	.400	—	—	—	—	11	—	—	—	—	4	—	0.0	0.5

HACKETT, RUDOLPH (Rudy) b. May 10, 1953 Ht. 6-9 Wt. 215 College—Syracuse

SEASON—TEAM	G	GS	MIN	FGM	FGA	PCT	3FGM	3FGA	PCT	FTM	FTA	PCT	O-RB	D-RB	TOT	AST	PF	DQ	STL	TO	BLK	PTS	RPG	APG	PPG
75-76—St. Louis (A)	22	—	414	55	131	.420	0	0	—	31	49	.633	20	58	78	28	48	—	15	24	8	141	3.5	1.3	6.4
76-77—N.Y.-Indiana	6	—	46	3	10	.300	—	—	.—	8	14	.571	4	9	13	3	8	0	0	—	1	14	2.2	0.5	2.3
REG. NBA TOTALS	6	—	46	3	10	.300	—	—	—	8	14	.571	4	9	13	3	8	0	0	—	1	14	2.2	0.5	2.3
REG. ABA TOTALS	22	—	414	55	131	.420	0	0	—	31	49	.633	20	58	78	28	48	—	15	24	8	141	3.5	1.3	6.4

HADNOT, JAMES WELDON (Jim) b. January 15, 1940 Ht. 6-10 Wt. 235 College—Providence

SEASON—TEAM	G	GS	MIN	FGM	FGA	PCT	3FGM	3FGA	PCT	FTM	FTA	PCT	O-RB	D-RB	TOT	AST	PF	DQ	STL	TO	BLK	PTS	RPG	APG	PPG
67-68—Oakland (A)	77	—	3004	488	1045	.467	0	2	.000	368	551	.668	303	633	936	135	279	9	—	169	—	1344	12.2	1.8	17.5
REG. ABA TOTALS	77	—	3004	488	1045	.467	0	2	.000	368	551	.668	303	633	936	135	279	9	—	169	—	1344	12.2	1.8	17.5

HAFFNER, SCOTT RICHARD b. February 2, 1966 Ht. 6-3 Wt. 180 College—Illinois/Evansville

SEASON—TEAM	G	GS	MIN	FGM	FGA	PCT	3FGM	3FGA	PCT	FTM	FTA	PCT	O-RB	D-RB	TOT	AST	PF	DQ	STL	TO	BLK	PTS	RPG	APG	PPG
89-90—Miami	43	6	559	88	217	.406	3	21	.143	17	25	.680	7	44	51	80	53	0	13	33	2	196	1.2	1.9	4.6
90-91—Charlotte	7	0	50	8	21	.381	0	2	.000	1	2	.500	2	2	4	9	4	0	3	4	1	17	0.6	1.3	2.4
REG. SEASON TOTALS	50	6	609	96	238	.403	3	23	.130	18	27	.667	9	46	55	89	57	0	16	37	3	213	1.1	1.8	4.3

HAGAN, CLIFFORD OLDHAM (Cliff, Li'l Abner) b. December 9, 1931 Ht. 6-4 Wt. 215 College—Kentucky

SEASON—TEAM	G	GS	MIN	FGM	FGA	PCT	3FGM	3FGA	PCT	FTM	FTA	PCT	O-RB	D-RB	TOT	AST	PF	DQ	STL	TO	BLK	PTS	RPG	APG	PPG
56-57—St. Louis	67	—	971	134	371	.361	—	—	—	100	145	.690	—	—	247	86	165	3	—	—	—	368	3.7	1.3	5.5
57-58—St. Louis	70	—	2190	503	1135	.443	—	—	—	385	501	.768	—	—	707	175	267	9	—	—	—	1391	10.1	2.5	19.9
58-59—St. Louis	72	—	2702	646	1417	.456	—	—	—	415	536	.774	—	—	783	245	275	10	—	—	—	1707	10.9	3.4	23.7
59-60—St. Louis	75	—	2798	719	1549	.464	—	—	—	421	524	.803	—	—	803	299	270	4	—	—	—	1859	10.7	4.0	24.8
60-61—St. Louis	77	—	2701	661	1490	.444	—	—	—	383	467	.820	—	—	715	381	286	9	—	—	—	1705	9.3	4.9	22.1
61-62—St. Louis	77	—	2784	701	1490	.470	—	—	—	362	439	.825	—	—	633	370	282	8	—	—	—	1764	8.2	4.8	22.9
62-63—St. Louis	79	—	1716	491	1055	.465	—	—	—	244	305	.800	—	—	341	193	211	2	—	—	—	1226	4.3	2.4	15.5
63-64—St. Louis	77	—	2279	572	1280	.447	—	—	—	269	331	.813	—	—	377	193	273	4	—	—	—	1413	4.9	2.5	18.4
64-65—St. Louis	77	—	1739	393	901	.436	—	—	—	214	268	.799	—	—	276	136	182	0	—	—	—	1000	3.6	1.8	13.0
65-66—St. Louis	74	—	1851	419	942	.445	—	—	—	176	206	.854	—	—	234	164	177	1	—	—	—	1014	3.2	2.2	13.7
67-68—Dallas (A)	56	—	1737	371	759	.489	0	3	.000	277	351	.789	—	—	334	276	202	6	—	216	—	1019	6.0	4.9	18.2
68-69—Dallas (A)	35	—	579	132	259	.510	0	1	.000	123	144	.854	—	—	102	122	73	2	—	74	—	387	2.9	3.5	11.1
69-70—Dallas (A)	3	—	27	8	13	.615	0	1	.000	1	2	.500	—	—	13	6	2	0	—	—	—	17	1.0	2.0	5.7
REG. NBA TOTALS	745	—	21731	5239	11630	.450	—	—	—	2969	3722	.798	—	—	5116	2242	2388	50	—	—	—	13447	6.9	3.0	18.0
REG. ABA TOTALS	94	—	2343	511	1031	.496	0	5	.000	401	497	.807	—	—	439	404	277	8	—	290	—	1423	4.7	4.3	15.1
NBA PLAYOFF TOTALS	90	—	2965	701	1544	.454	—	—	—	432	540	.800	—	—	744	305	320	12	—	—	—	1834	8.3	3.4	20.4
ABA PLAYOFF TOTALS	5	—	115	19	51	.373	0	0	—	17	23	.739	—	—	19	23	16	1	—	12	—	55	3.8	4.6	11.0
NBA ALL-STAR TOTALS	4	—	65	8	26	.308	—	—	—	5	5	1.000	—	—	15	6	8	0	—	—	—	21	3.8	1.5	5.3
ABA ALL-STAR TOTALS	1	—	24	4	11	.364	0	0	—	2	2	1.000	—	—	0	5	2	0	—	3	—	10	0.0	5.0	10.0

HAGAN, GLENN KASSABIN b. June 25, 1955 Ht. 6-0 Wt. 170 College—St. Bonaventure

SEASON—TEAM	G	GS	MIN	FGM	FGA	PCT	3FGM	3FGA	PCT	FTM	FTA	PCT	O-RB	D-RB	TOT	AST	PF	DQ	STL	TO	BLK	PTS	RPG	APG	PPG
81-82—Detroit	4	0	25	3	7	.429	0	0	—	1	1	1.000	2	2	4	8	7	0	3	1	0	7	1.0	2.0	1.8
REG. SEASON TOTALS	4	0	25	3	7	.429	0	0	—	1	1	1.000	2	2	4	8	7	0	3	1	0	7	1.0	2.0	1.8

HAGAN, THOMAS MEDARD (**Tom**) b. January 29, 1947 Ht. 6-3½ Wt. 185 College—Vanderbilt

SEASON—TEAM	G	GS	MIN	FGM	FGA	PCT	3FGM	3FGA	PCT	FTM	FTA	PCT	O-RB	D-RB	TOT	AST	PF	DQ	STL	TO	BLK	PTS	RPG	APG	PPG
69-70—Dallas (A)	24	—	226	37	81	.457	7	17	.412	22	29	.759	—	—	30	29	42	0	—	—	—	103	1.3	1.2	4.3
70-71—Texas-Ken. (A)	49	—	690	100	246	.407	12	41	.293	43	63	.683	—	—	83	106	78	—	—	—	—	255	1.7	2.2	5.2
REG. ABA TOTALS	73	—	916	137	327	.419	19	58	.328	65	92	.707	—	—	113	135	120	0	—	—	—	358	1.5	1.8	4.9

HAHN, ROBERT B. (**Bob**) b. August 25, 1925 Ht. 6-10 Wt. 240 College—North Carolina State

SEASON—TEAM	G	GS	MIN	FGM	FGA	PCT	3FGM	3FGA	PCT	FTM	FTA	PCT	O-RB	D-RB	TOT	AST	PF	DQ	STL	TO	BLK	PTS	RPG	APG	PPG
49-50—Chicago	10	—	—	4	13	.308	—	—	—	2	7	.286	—	—	—	1	17	—	—	—	—	10	—	0.1	1.0
REG. SEASON TOTALS	10	—	—	4	13	.308	—	—	—	2	7	.286	—	—	—	1	17	—	—	—	—	10	—	0.1	1.0

HAIRSTON, ALAN LEROY (**Al**) b. December 11, 1945 Ht. 6-1 Wt. 170 College—Port Huron/Bowling Green

SEASON—TEAM	G	GS	MIN	FGM	FGA	PCT	3FGM	3FGA	PCT	FTM	FTA	PCT	O-RB	D-RB	TOT	AST	PF	DQ	STL	TO	BLK	PTS	RPG	APG	PPG
68-69—Seattle	39	—	274	38	114	.333	—	—	—	8	14	.571	—	—	36	38	35	0	—	—	—	84	0.9	1.0	2.2
69-70—Seattle	3	—	20	3	8	.375	—	—	—	1	1	1.000	—	—	5	6	3	0	—	—	—	7	1.7	2.0	2.3
REG. SEASON TOTALS	42	—	294	41	122	.336	—	—	—	9	15	.600	—	—	41	44	38	0	—	—	—	91	1.0	1.0	2.2

HAIRSTON, HAROLD (**Happy**) b. May 31, 1942 Ht. 6-7 Wt. 225 College—New York University

SEASON—TEAM	G	GS	MIN	FGM	FGA	PCT	3FGM	3FGA	PCT	FTM	FTA	PCT	O-RB	D-RB	TOT	AST	PF	DQ	STL	TO	BLK	PTS	RPG	APG	PPG
64-65—Cincinnati	61	—	736	131	351	.373	—	—	—	110	165	.667	—	—	293	27	95	0	—	—	—	372	4.8	0.4	6.1
65-66—Cincinnati	72	—	1794	398	814	.489	—	—	—	220	321	.685	—	—	546	44	216	3	—	—	—	1016	7.6	0.6	14.1
66-67—Cincinnati	79	—	2442	461	962	.479	—	—	—	252	382	.660	—	—	631	62	273	5	—	—	—	1174	8.0	0.8	14.9
67-68—Cin.-Detroit	74	—	2517	481	987	.487	—	—	—	365	522	.699	—	—	617	95	199	1	—	—	—	1327	8.3	1.3	17.9
68-69—Detroit	81	—	2889	530	1131	.469	—	—	—	404	553	.731	—	—	959	109	255	3	—	—	—	1464	11.8	1.3	18.1
69-70—Detroit-L.A.	70	—	2427	483	973	.496	—	—	—	326	413	.789	—	—	775	121	230	9	—	—	—	1292	11.1	1.7	18.5
70-71—Los Angeles	80	—	2921	574	1233	.466	—	—	—	337	431	.782	—	—	797	168	256	2	—	—	—	1485	10.0	2.1	18.6
71-72—Los Angeles	80	—	2748	368	798	.461	—	—	—	311	399	.779	—	—	1045	193	251	2	—	—	—	1047	13.1	2.4	13.1
72-73—Los Angeles	28	—	939	158	328	.482	—	—	—	140	178	.787	—	—	370	68	77	0	—	—	—	456	13.2	2.4	16.3
73-74—Los Angeles	77	—	2634	385	759	.507	—	—	—	343	445	.771	335	705	1040	208	264	2	64	—	17	1113	13.5	2.7	14.5
74-75—Los Angeles	74	—	2283	271	536	.506	—	—	—	217	271	.801	304	642	946	173	218	2	52	—	11	759	12.8	2.3	10.3
REG. SEASON TOTALS	776	—	24330	4240	8872	.478	—	—	—	3025	4080	.741	639	1347	8019	1268	2334	29	116	—	28	11505	10.3	1.6	14.8
PLAYOFF TOTALS	69	—	2020	307	690	.445	—	—	—	187	255	.733	15	37	559	121	185	4	5	—	1	801	8.1	1.8	11.6

HAIRSTON, LINDSAY (**Spider**) b. December 8, 1951 Ht. 6-7½ Wt. 190 College—Michigan State

SEASON—TEAM	G	GS	MIN	FGM	FGA	PCT	3FGM	3FGA	PCT	FTM	FTA	PCT	O-RB	D-RB	TOT	AST	PF	DQ	STL	TO	BLK	PTS	RPG	APG	PPG
75-76—Detroit	47	—	651	104	228	.456	—	—	—	65	112	.580	65	114	179	21	84	2	21	—	32	273	3.8	0.4	5.8
REG. SEASON TOTALS	47	—	651	104	228	.456	—	—	—	65	112	.580	65	114	179	21	84	2	21	—	32	273	3.8	0.4	5.8

HALBERT, CHARLES P. (**Chuck**) b. February 27, 1919 Ht. 6-9½ Wt. 225 College—West Texas State

SEASON—TEAM	G	GS	MIN	FGM	FGA	PCT	3FGM	3FGA	PCT	FTM	FTA	PCT	O-RB	D-RB	TOT	AST	PF	DQ	STL	TO	BLK	PTS	RPG	APG	PPG
46-47—Chicago	61	—	—	280	915	.306	—	—	—	213	356	.598	—	—	—	46	161	—	—	—	—	773	—	0.8	12.7
47-48—Chicago-Phil.	46	—	—	156	605	.258	—	—	—	140	220	.636	—	—	—	32	126	—	—	—	—	452	—	0.7	9.8
48-49—Boston-Prov.	60	—	—	202	647	.312	—	—	—	214	345	.620	—	—	—	113	175	—	—	—	—	618	—	1.9	10.3
49-50—Washington	68	—	—	108	284	.380	—	—	—	112	175	.640	—	—	—	89	136	—	—	—	—	328	—	1.3	4.8
50-51—Wash.-Balt.	68	—	—	164	449	.365	—	—	—	172	248	.694	—	—	539	158	216	7	—	—	—	500	7.9	2.3	7.4
REG. SEASON TOTALS	303	—	—	910	2900	.314	—	—	—	851	1344	.633	—	—	539	438	814	7	—	—	—	2671	7.9	1.4	8.8
PLAYOFF TOTALS	26	—	—	106	399	.266	—	—	—	111	184	.603	—	—	—	10	84	2	—	—	—	323	—	0.4	12.4

HALBROOK, HARVEY WADE (**Swede**) b. January 30, 1933 d. April 5, 1988 Ht. 7-3 Wt. 235 College—Oregon State

SEASON—TEAM	G	GS	MIN	FGM	FGA	PCT	3FGM	3FGA	PCT	FTM	FTA	PCT	O-RB	D-RB	TOT	AST	PF	DQ	STL	TO	BLK	PTS	RPG	APG	PPG
60-61—Syracuse	79	—	1131	155	463	.335	—	—	—	76	140	.543	—	—	550	31	262	9	—	—	—	386	7.0	0.4	4.9
61-62—Syracuse	64	—	908	152	422	.360	—	—	—	96	151	.636	—	—	399	33	179	7	—	—	—	400	6.2	0.5	6.3
REG. SEASON TOTALS	143	—	2039	307	885	.347	—	—	—	172	291	.591	—	—	949	64	441	16	—	—	—	786	6.6	0.4	5.5
PLAYOFF TOTALS	8	—	176	24	78	.308	—	—	—	15	22	.682	—	—	85	12	25	1	—	—	—	63	10.6	1.5	7.9

HALE, HAL RIES b. September 21, 1945 Ht. 6-1 Wt. 185 College—Utah State

SEASON—TEAM	G	GS	MIN	FGM	FGA	PCT	3FGM	3FGA	PCT	FTM	FTA	PCT	O-RB	D-RB	TOT	AST	PF	DQ	STL	TO	BLK	PTS	RPG	APG	PPG
67-68—Houston (A)	72	—	1706	133	408	.326	35	112	.313	60	89	.674	—	—	206	144	143	1	—	91	—	361	2.9	2.0	5.0
REG. ABA TOTALS	72	—	1706	133	408	.326	35	112	.313	60	89	.674	—	—	206	144	143	1	—	91	—	361	2.9	2.0	5.0
ABA PLAYOFF TOTALS	3	—	103	6	16	.375	3	3	1.000	7	7	1.000	—	—	8	3	10	0	—	—	—	22	2.7	1.0	7.3

HALE, WILLIAM BRUCE (**Bruce**) b. August 30, 1918 d. December 30, 1980 Ht. 6-1 Wt. 170 College—Cal State-Santa Clara

SEASON—TEAM	G	GS	MIN	FGM	FGA	PCT	3FGM	3FGA	PCT	FTM	FTA	PCT	O-RB	D-RB	TOT	AST	PF	DQ	STL	TO	BLK	PTS	RPG	APG	PPG
46-47—Chicago (N)	41	—	—	156	—	—	—	—	—	116	141	.823	—	—	—	—	103	—	—	—	—	428	—	—	10.4
47-48—Indianapolis (N)	48	—	—	196	—	—	—	—	—	155	215	.721	—	—	—	—	136	—	—	—	—	547	—	—	11.4
48-49—Ind.-Ft. Wayne	52	—	—	187	585	.320	—	—	—	172	228	.754	—	—	—	156	112	—	—	—	—	546	—	3.0	10.5
49-50—Indianapolis	64	—	—	217	614	.353	—	—	—	223	285	.782	—	—	—	226	143	—	—	—	—	657	—	3.5	10.3
50-51—Indianapolis	26	—	—	40	135	.296	—	—	—	14	23	.609	—	—	49	42	30	0	—	—	—	94	1.9	1.6	3.6
REG. NBA TOTALS	142	—	—	444	1334	.333	—	—	—	409	536	.763	—	—	49	424	285	0	—	—	—	1297	1.9	3.0	9.1
REG. NBL TOTALS	89	—	—	352	—	—	—	—	—	271	356	.761	—	—	—	—	239	—	—	—	—	975	—	—	11.0
NBA PLAYOFF TOTALS	7	—	—	14	40	.350	—	—	—	15	17	.882	—	—	—	17	11	0	—	—	—	43	—	2.8	6.1
NBL PLAYOFF TOTALS	15	—	—	56	—	—	—	—	—	44	53	.792	—	—	—	—	28	—	—	—	—	156	—	—	10.4

HALEY, JACK KEVIN b. January 27, 1964 Ht. 6-10 Wt. 240 College—Golden West College/UCLA

SEASON—TEAM	G	GS	MIN	FGM	FGA	PCT	3FGM	3FGA	PCT	FTM	FTA	PCT	O-RB	D-RB	TOT	AST	PF	DQ	STL	TO	BLK	PTS	RPG	APG	PPG
88-89—Chicago	51	1	289	37	78	.474	0	0	—	36	46	.783	21	50	71	10	56	0	11	26	0	110	1.4	0.2	2.2
89-90—Chicago-N.J.	67	26	1084	138	347	.398	0	1	.000	85	125	.680	115	185	300	26	170	1	18	72	12	361	4.5	0.4	5.4
90-91—New Jersey	78	18	1178	161	343	.469	0	0	—	112	181	.619	140	216	356	31	199	0	20	63	21	434	4.6	0.4	5.6
91-92—L.A. Lakers	49	9	394	31	84	.369	0	0	—	14	29	.483	31	64	95	7	75	0	7	25	8	76	1.9	0.1	1.6
93-94—San Antonio	28	0	94	21	48	.438	0	0	—	17	21	.810	6	18	24	1	18	0	0	10	0	59	0.9	0.0	2.1
REG. SEASON TOTALS	273	54	3039	388	900	.431	0	1	.000	264	402	.657	313	533	846	75	518	1	56	196	41	1040	3.1	0.3	3.8
PLAYOFF TOTALS	10	0	30	7	15	.467	0	0	—	6	8	.750	4	5	9	4	8	0	0	0	0	20	0.9	0.4	2.0

HALIMON, SHALER JR. b. March 30, 1945 Ht. 6-6 Wt. 200 College—Imperial Valley CC/Utah State

SEASON—TEAM	G	GS	MIN	FGM	FGA	PCT	3FGM	3FGA	PCT	FTM	FTA	PCT	O-RB	D-RB	TOT	AST	PF	DQ	STL	TO	BLK	PTS	RPG	APG	PPG
68-69—Philadelphia	50	—	350	88	196	.449	—	—	—	10	32	.313	—	—	86	18	34	0	—	—	—	186	1.7	0.4	3.7
69-70—Chicago	38	—	517	96	244	.393	—	—	—	49	73	.671	—	—	68	69	58	0	—	—	—	241	1.8	1.8	6.3
70-71—Chicago-Port.	81	—	1652	301	783	.384	—	—	—	107	162	.660	—	—	417	215	183	1	—	—	—	709	5.1	2.7	8.8
71-72—Atlanta	1	—	4	0	0	—	—	—	—	0	0	—	—	—	0	0	1	0	—	—	—	0	0.0	0.0	0.0
71-72—Dallas (A)	55	—	770	123	294	.418	0	2	.000	62	86	.721	—	—	156	72	89	—	—	46	—	308	2.8	1.3	5.6
72-73—Dallas (A)	29	—	355	59	149	.396	1	7	.143	23	37	.622	16	38	54	49	53	—	—	43	—	142	1.9	1.7	4.9
REG. NBA TOTALS	170	—	2523	485	1223	.397	—	—	—	166	267	.622	—	—	571	302	276	1	—	—	—	1136	3.4	1.8	6.7
REG. ABA TOTALS	84	—	1125	182	443	.411	1	9	.111	85	123	.691	16	38	210	121	142	—	—	89	—	450	2.5	1.4	5.4
NBA PLAYOFF TOTALS	6	—	108	22	63	.349	—	—	—	2	3	.667	—	—	20	18	13	0	—	—	—	46	3.3	3.0	7.7
ABA PLAYOFF TOTALS	4	—	55	9	17	.529	0	0	—	4	7	.571	—	—	13	7	4	0	—	5	—	22	3.3	1.8	5.5

HALLIBURTON, JEFFREY (**Jeff**) b. July 3, 1949 Ht. 6-5 Wt. 195 College—San Jacinto/Drake

SEASON—TEAM	G	GS	MIN	FGM	FGA	PCT	3FGM	3FGA	PCT	FTM	FTA	PCT	O-RB	D-RB	TOT	AST	PF	DQ	STL	TO	BLK	PTS	RPG	APG	PPG
71-72—Atlanta	37	—	288	61	133	.459	—	—	—	25	30	.833	—	—	37	20	50	1	—	—	—	147	1.0	0.5	4.0
72-73—Atlanta-Phil.	55	—	787	172	396	.434	—	—	—	71	88	.807	—	—	108	96	107	1	—	—	—	415	2.0	1.7	7.5
REG. SEASON TOTALS	92	—	1075	233	529	.440	—	—	—	96	118	.814	—	—	145	116	157	2	—	—	—	562	1.6	1.3	6.1
PLAYOFF TOTALS	1	—	2	0	1	.000	—	—	—	0	0	—	—	—	0	0	0	0	—	—	—	0	0.0	0.0	0.0

HAMILTON, DALE B. b. August 16, 1919 Ht. 6-1 Wt. 200 College—Franklin (Ind.)

SEASON—TEAM	G	GS	MIN	FGM	FGA	PCT	3FGM	3FGA	PCT	FTM	FTA	PCT	O-RB	D-RB	TOT	AST	PF	DQ	STL	TO	BLK	PTS	RPG	APG	PPG
39-40—Hammond (N)	7	—	—	5	—	—	—	—	—	1	—	—	—	—	—	—	—	—	—	—	—	11	—	—	1.6
41-42—Fort Wayne (N)	16	—	—	10	—	—	—	—	—	16	—	—	—	—	—	—	—	—	—	—	—	36	—	—	2.3
42-43—Fort Wayne (N)	18	—	—	8	—	—	—	—	—	1	—	—	—	—	—	—	—	—	—	—	—	17	—	—	0.9
43-44—Fort Wayne (N)	11	—	—	2	—	—	—	—	—	0	—	—	—	—	—	—	—	—	—	—	—	4	—	—	0.4
44-45—Fort Wayne (N)	2	—	—	0	—	—	—	—	—	0	—	—	—	—	—	—	—	—	—	—	—	0	—	—	0.0
46-47—Toledo (N)	44	—	—	114	—	—	—	—	—	67	131	.511	—	—	—	—	94	—	—	—	—	295	—	—	6.7
47-48—Toledo (N)	53	—	—	93	—	—	—	—	—	62	133	.466	—	—	—	—	130	—	—	—	—	248	—	—	4.7
48-49—Waterloo (N)	62	—	—	78	—	—	—	—	—	94	179	.525	—	—	—	—	194	—	—	—	—	250	—	—	4.0
49-50—Waterloo	14	—	—	8	33	.242	—	—	—	9	19	.474	—	—	17	—	30	—	—	—	—	25	1.2	—	1.8
REG. NBA TOTALS	14	—	—	8	33	.242	—	—	—	9	19	.474	—	—	17	—	30	—	—	—	—	25	1.2	—	1.8
REG. NBL TOTALS	213	—	—	310	—	—	—	—	—	241	443	.503	—	—	—	—	418	—	—	—	—	861	—	—	4.0
NBL PLAYOFF TOTALS	15	—	—	8	—	—	—	—	—	10	20	.350	—	—	—	—	15	—	—	—	—	26	—	—	1.7

HAMILTON, DENNIS EUGENE b. May 8, 1944 Ht. 6-8 Wt. 210 College—Arizona State

SEASON—TEAM	G	GS	MIN	FGM	FGA	PCT	3FGM	3FGA	PCT	FTM	FTA	PCT	O-RB	D-RB	TOT	AST	PF	DQ	STL	TO	BLK	PTS	RPG	APG	PPG
67-68—Los Angeles	44	—	378	54	108	.500	—	—	—	13	13	1.000	—	—	72	30	46	0	—	—	—	121	1.6	0.7	2.8
68-69—Atlanta	25	—	141	37	67	.552	—	—	—	2	5	.400	—	—	29	8	19	0	—	—	—	76	1.2	0.3	3.0
69-70—Pittsburgh (A)	72	—	1331	190	375	.507	0	1	.000	76	100	.760	—	—	340	73	144	0	—	—	—	456	4.7	1.0	6.3
70-71—Kentucky (A)	3	—	11	1	2	.500	0	0	—	1	1	1.000	—	—	1	1	1	0	—	—	—	3	0.3	0.3	1.0
REG. NBA TOTALS	69	—	519	91	175	.520	—	—	—	15	18	.833	—	—	101	38	65	0	—	—	—	197	1.5	0.6	2.9
REG. ABA TOTALS	75	—	1342	191	377	.507	0	1	.000	77	101	.762	—	—	341	74	145	0	—	—	—	459	4.5	1.0	6.1
NBA PLAYOFF TOTALS	2	—	11	1	3	.333	—	—	—	0	0	—	—	—	2	1	0	0	—	—	—	2	1.0	0.5	1.0

HAMILTON, JAMES JR. (Joe) b. July 5, 1948 Ht. 5-10½ Wt. 180 College—Christian JC of the Southwest/North Texas

SEASON—TEAM	G	GS	MIN	FGM	FGA	PCT	3FGM	3FGA	PCT	FTM	FTA	PCT	O-RB	D-RB	TOT	AST	PF	DQ	STL	TO	BLK	PTS	RPG	APG	PPG
70-71—Texas (A)	84	—	2564	500	1184	.422	85	285	.298	233	279	.835	—	—	285	365	279	—	—	—	—	1318	3.4	4.3	15.7
71-72—Dallas (A)	82	—	1959	317	791	.401	46	132	.348	201	256	.785	—	—	194	240	202	—	—	110	—	881	2.4	2.9	10.7
72-73—Dallas (A)	83	—	2359	370	902	.410	66	191	.346	209	262	.798	46	169	215	325	247	0	—	143	—	1015	2.6	3.9	12.2
73-74—S.A.-Ken. (A)	73	—	1961	331	834	.397	37	144	.257	117	143	.818	40	125	165	242	154	—	76	112	5	816	2.3	3.3	11.2
74-75—Kentucky (A)	9	—	124	15	40	.375	3	5	.600	5	6	.833	2	9	11	21	13	—	4	9	0	38	1.2	2.3	4.2
75-76—Utah (A)	13	—	131	31	78	.397	6	21	.286	9	13	.692	5	9	14	15	12	—	8	6	0	77	1.1	1.2	5.9
REG. ABA TOTALS	344	—	9098	1564	3829	.408	243	778	.312	774	959	.807	93	312	884	1208	907	0	88	380	5	4145	2.6	3.5	12.0
ABA PLAYOFF TOTALS	15	—	319	48	145	.331	12	37	.324	27	33	.818	3	20	54	49	38	0	4	19	0	135	3.6	3.3	9.0

HAMILTON, RALPH ALBERT (Ham) b. June 10, 1921 d. June 3, 1993 Ht. 6-1 Wt. 190 College—Indiana

SEASON—TEAM	G	GS	MIN	FGM	FGA	PCT	3FGM	3FGA	PCT	FTM	FTA	PCT	O-RB	D-RB	TOT	AST	PF	DQ	STL	TO	BLK	PTS	RPG	APG	PPG
47-48—Fort Wayne (N)	49	—	—	143	—	—	—	—	—	101	135	.748	—	—	—	74	—	—	—	—	—	387	—	—	7.9
48-49—Ft. Wayne-Ind.	48	—	—	114	447	.255	—	—	—	61	91	.670	—	—	—	83	67	—	—	—	—	289	—	1.7	6.0
REG. NBA TOTALS	48	—	—	114	447	.255	—	—	—	61	91	.670	—	—	—	83	67	—	—	—	—	289	—	1.7	6.0
REG. NBL TOTALS	49	—	—	143	—	—	—	—	—	101	135	.748	—	—	—	74	—	—	—	—	—	387	—	—	7.9
NBL PLAYOFF TOTALS	2	—	—	1	—	—	—	—	—	2	4	.500	—	—	—	1	—	—	—	—	—	4	—	—	2.0

HAMILTON, ROY LEE (Roy Lee) b. July 20, 1957 Ht. 6-2 Wt. 180 College—UCLA

SEASON—TEAM	G	GS	MIN	FGM	FGA	PCT	3FGM	3FGA	PCT	FTM	FTA	PCT	O-RB	D-RB	TOT	AST	PF	DQ	STL	TO	BLK	PTS	RPG	APG	PPG
79-80—Detroit	72	—	1116	115	287	.401	0	2	.000	103	150	.687	45	62	107	192	82	0	48	118	5	333	1.5	2.7	4.6
80-81—Portland	1	—	5	1	3	.333	0	0	—	1	2	.500	2	1	3	0	1	0	0	1	0	3	3.0	0.0	3.0
REG. SEASON TOTALS	73	—	1121	116	290	.400	0	2	.000	104	152	.684	47	63	110	192	83	0	48	119	5	336	1.5	2.6	4.6

HAMILTON, STEVE ABSHER b. November 30, 1935 Ht. 6-7 Wt. 190 College—Purdue/Morehead State

SEASON—TEAM	G	GS	MIN	FGM	FGA	PCT	3FGM	3FGA	PCT	FTM	FTA	PCT	O-RB	D-RB	TOT	AST	PF	DQ	STL	TO	BLK	PTS	RPG	APG	PPG
58-59—Minneapolis	67	—	847	109	294	.371	—	—	—	74	109	.679	—	—	220	36	144	2	—	—	—	292	3.3	0.5	4.4
59-60—Minneapolis	15	—	247	29	77	.377	—	—	—	18	23	.783	—	—	58	7	39	1	—	—	—	76	3.9	0.5	5.1
REG. SEASON TOTALS	82	—	1094	138	371	.372	—	—	—	92	132	.697	—	—	278	43	183	3	—	—	—	368	3.4	0.5	4.5
PLAYOFF TOTALS	10	—	87	12	43	.279	—	—	—	8	10	.800	—	—	35	5	14	0	—	—	—	32	3.5	0.5	3.2

HAMMINK, GEERT HENDRIK b. July 12, 1969 Ht. 7-0 Wt. 262 College—Louisiana State

SEASON—TEAM	G	GS	MIN	FGM	FGA	PCT	3FGM	3FGA	PCT	FTM	FTA	PCT	O-RB	D-RB	TOT	AST	PF	DQ	STL	TO	BLK	PTS	RPG	APG	PPG
93-94—Orlando	1	0	3	1	3	.333	0	0	—	0	0	—	1	0	1	1	1	0	0	0	0	2	1.0	1.0	2.0
REG. SEASON TOTALS	1	0	3	1	3	.333	0	0	—	0	0	—	1	0	1	1	1	0	0	0	0	2	1.0	1.0	2.0

HAMMOND, JULIAN (Julie) b. May 27, 1943 Ht. 6-5 Wt. 210 College—Tulsa

SEASON—TEAM	G	GS	MIN	FGM	FGA	PCT	3FGM	3FGA	PCT	FTM	FTA	PCT	O-RB	D-RB	TOT	AST	PF	DQ	STL	TO	BLK	PTS	RPG	APG	PPG
67-68—Denver (A)	74	—	1364	224	458	.489	0	0	—	143	209	.684	—	—	327	62	112	0	—	98	—	591	4.4	0.8	8.0
68-69—Denver (A)	78	—	2335	329	601	.547	0	0	—	165	253	.652	—	—	600	124	213	3	—	152	—	823	7.7	1.6	10.6
69-70—Denver (A)	69	—	1847	329	660	.498	0	1	.000	169	243	.695	—	—	471	109	183	2	—	—	—	827	6.8	1.6	12.0
70-71—Denver (A)	83	—	2082	435	834	.522	0	0	—	273	375	.728	—	—	523	97	189	—	—	—	—	1143	6.3	1.2	13.8
71-72—Denver (A)	25	—	411	66	140	.471	0	0	—	31	50	.620	—	—	115	29	47	—	—	30	—	163	4.6	1.2	6.5
REG. ABA TOTALS	329	—	8039	1383	2693	.514	0	1	.000	781	1130	.691	—	—	2036	421	744	5	—	280	—	3547	6.2	1.3	10.8
ABA PLAYOFF TOTALS	24	—	739	140	272	.515	0	0	—	63	93	.677	—	—	157	46	92	3	—	25	—	343	6.5	1.9	14.3

HAMMONDS, TOM EDWARD (The Terminator) b. March 27, 1967 Ht. 6-9 Wt. 225 College—Georgia Tech

SEASON—TEAM	G	GS	MIN	FGM	FGA	PCT	3FGM	3FGA	PCT	FTM	FTA	PCT	O-RB	D-RB	TOT	AST	PF	DQ	STL	TO	BLK	PTS	RPG	APG	PPG
89-90—Washington	61	8	805	129	295	.437	0	1	.000	63	98	.643	61	107	168	51	98	0	11	46	14	321	2.8	0.8	5.3
90-91—Washington	70	7	1023	155	336	.461	0	4	.000	57	79	.722	58	148	206	43	108	0	15	54	7	367	2.9	0.6	5.2
91-92—Wash.-Cha.	37	19	984	195	400	.488	0	1	.000	50	82	.610	49	136	185	36	118	1	22	58	13	440	5.0	1.0	11.9
92-93—Cha.-Denver	54	5	713	105	221	.475	0	1	.000	38	62	.613	38	89	127	24	77	0	18	34	12	248	2.4	0.4	4.6
93-94—Denver	74	2	877	115	230	.500	0	0	—	71	104	.683	62	137	199	34	91	0	20	41	12	301	2.7	0.5	4.1
REG. SEASON TOTALS	296	41	4402	699	1482	.472	0	7	.000	279	425	.656	268	617	885	188	492	1	86	233	58	1677	3.0	0.6	5.7
PLAYOFF TOTALS	8	0	49	2	9	.222	0	0	—	5	6	.833	5	8	13	2	6	0	0	1	0	9	1.6	0.3	1.1

HAMOOD, JOSEPH (Joe) b. September 7, 1943 d. August 19, 1970 Ht. 6-0 Wt. 185 College—Houston

SEASON—TEAM	G	GS	MIN	FGM	FGA	PCT	3FGM	3FGA	PCT	FTM	FTA	PCT	O-RB	D-RB	TOT	AST	PF	DQ	STL	TO	BLK	PTS	RPG	APG	PPG
67-68—Houston (A)	76	—	1839	274	819	.335	16	78	.205	186	252	.738	—	—	217	227	200	2	—	126	—	750	2.9	3.0	9.9
REG. ABA TOTALS	76	—	1839	274	819	.335	16	78	.205	186	252	.738	—	—	217	227	200	2	—	126	—	750	2.9	3.0	9.9
ABA PLAYOFF TOTALS	3	—	42	3	17	.176	0	3	.000	1	2	.500	—	—	5	2	8	0	—	1	—	7	1.7	0.7	2.3

HANKINS, CECIL O. b. January 6, 1922 Ht. 6-1 Wt. 175 College—Oklahoma State

SEASON—TEAM	G	GS	MIN	FGM	FGA	PCT	3FGM	3FGA	PCT	FTM	FTA	PCT	O-RB	D-RB	TOT	AST	PF	DQ	STL	TO	BLK	PTS	RPG	APG	PPG
46-47—St. Louis	55	—	—	117	391	.299	—	—	—	90	150	.600	—	—	—	14	49	—	—	—	—	324	—	0.3	5.9
47-48—Boston	25	—	—	23	116	.198	—	—	—	24	35	.686	—	—	—	8	28	—	—	—	—	70	—	0.3	2.8
47-48—Sheboygan (N)	1	—	—	0	—	—	—	—	—	1	1	1.000	—	—	—	—	2	—	—	—	—	1	—	—	1.0
REG. NBA TOTALS	80	—	—	140	507	.276	—	—	—	114	185	.616	—	—	—	22	77	—	—	—	—	394	—	0.3	4.9
REG. NBL TOTALS	1	—	—	0	—	—	—	—	—	1	1	1.000	—	—	—	—	2	—	—	—	—	1	—	—	1.0
NBA PLAYOFF TOTALS	2	—	—	2	7	.286	—	—	—	1	2	.500	—	—	—	—	1	—	—	—	—	5	—	0.0	2.5

HANKINSON, PHIL b. July 26, 1951 Ht. 6-8 Wt. 195 College—Pennsylvania

SEASON—TEAM	G	GS	MIN	FGM	FGA	PCT	3FGM	3FGA	PCT	FTM	FTA	PCT	O-RB	D-RB	TOT	AST	PF	DQ	STL	TO	BLK	PTS	RPG	APG	PPG
73-74—Boston	28	—	163	50	103	.485	—	—	—	10	13	.769	22	28	50	4	18	0	3	—	1	110	1.8	0.1	3.9
74-75—Boston	3	—	24	6	11	.545	—	—	—	0	0	—	1	6	7	2	3	0	1	—	0	12	2.3	0.7	4.0
REG. SEASON TOTALS	31	—	187	56	114	.491	—	—	—	10	13	.769	23	34	57	6	21	0	4	—	1	122	1.8	0.2	3.9
PLAYOFF TOTALS	4	—	8	3	7	.429	—	—	—	2	2	1.000	2	1	3	—	0	0	0	—	1	8	0.8	0.0	2.0

HANNUM, ALEXANDER MURRAY (Alex) b. July 19, 1923 Ht. 6-7 Wt. 225 College—USC

SEASON—TEAM	G	GS	MIN	FGM	FGA	PCT	3FGM	3FGA	PCT	FTM	FTA	PCT	O-RB	D-RB	TOT	AST	PF	DQ	STL	TO	BLK	PTS	RPG	APG	PPG
48-49—Oshkosh (N)	64	—	—	126	—	—	—	—	—	113	191	.592	—	—	—	—	188	—	—	—	—	365	—	—	5.7
49-50—Syracuse	64	—	—	177	488	.363	—	—	—	128	186	.688	—	—	—	129	264	—	—	—	—	482	—	2.0	7.5
50-51—Syracuse	63	—	—	182	494	.368	—	—	—	107	197	.543	—	—	301	119	271	16	—	—	—	471	4.8	1.9	7.5
51-52—Balt.-Roch.	66	—	1508	170	462	.368	—	—	—	98	137	.715	—	—	336	133	271	16	—	—	—	438	5.1	2.0	6.6
52-53—Rochester	68	—	1288	129	360	.358	—	—	—	88	133	.662	—	—	279	81	258	18	—	—	—	346	4.1	1.2	5.1
53-54—Rochester	72	—	1707	175	503	.348	—	—	—	102	164	.622	—	—	350	105	279	11	—	—	—	452	4.9	1.5	6.3
54-55—Milwaukee	53	—	1088	126	358	.352	—	—	—	61	107	.570	—	—	245	105	206	9	—	—	—	313	4.6	2.0	5.9
55-56—St. Louis	71	—	1480	146	453	.322	—	—	—	93	154	.604	—	—	344	157	271	10	—	—	—	385	4.8	2.2	5.4
56-57—Ft. Wayne-St. L.	59	—	642	77	223	.345	—	—	—	37	56	.661	—	—	158	28	135	2	—	—	—	191	2.7	0.5	3.2
REG. NBA TOTALS	516	—	7713	1182	3341	.354	—	—	—	714	1134	.630	—	—	2013	857	1955	82	—	—	—	3078	4.5	1.7	6.0
REG. NBL TOTALS	64	—	—	126	—	—	—	—	—	113	191	.592	—	—	—	—	188	—	—	—	—	365	—	—	5.7
NBA PLAYOFF TOTALS	43	—	470	108	274	.394	—	—	—	70	124	.565	—	—	128	52	199	16	—	—	—	286	4.0	1.2	6.7
NBL PLAYOFF TOTALS	7	—	—	12	—	—	—	—	—	16	26	.615	—	—	—	—	26	—	—	—	—	40	—	—	5.7

HANRAHAN, DONALD (Don) b. February 6, 1929 Ht. 6-7 Wt. 200 College—Loyola (Ill.)

SEASON—TEAM	G	GS	MIN	FGM	FGA	PCT	3FGM	3FGA	PCT	FTM	FTA	PCT	O-RB	D-RB	TOT	AST	PF	DQ	STL	TO	BLK	PTS	RPG	APG	PPG
52-53—Indianapolis	18	—	121	11	32	.344	—	—	—	11	15	.733	—	—	30	11	24	1	—	—	—	33	1.7	0.6	1.8
REG. SEASON TOTALS	18	—	121	11	32	.344	—	—	—	11	15	.733	—	—	30	11	24	1	—	—	—	33	1.7	0.6	1.8

HANS, ROLLEN F. (Rolly) b. April 13, 1931 Ht. 6-2 Wt. 210 College—Los Angeles CC/Long Island University

SEASON—TEAM	G	GS	MIN	FGM	FGA	PCT	3FGM	3FGA	PCT	FTM	FTA	PCT	O-RB	D-RB	TOT	AST	PF	DQ	STL	TO	BLK	PTS	RPG	APG	PPG
53-54—Baltimore	67	—	1556	191	515	.371	—	—	—	101	180	.561	—	—	160	181	172	1	—	—	—	483	2.4	2.7	7.2
54-55—Baltimore	13	—	178	30	67	.448	—	—	—	13	25	.520	—	—	16	26	20	0	—	—	—	73	1.2	2.0	5.6
REG. SEASON TOTALS	80	—	1734	221	582	.380	—	—	—	114	205	.556	—	—	176	207	192	1	—	—	—	556	2.2	2.6	7.0

HANSEN, GLENN R. b. April 21, 1952 Ht. 6-4 Wt. 205 College—Utah State/Louisiana State

SEASON—TEAM	G	GS	MIN	FGM	FGA	PCT	3FGM	3FGA	PCT	FTM	FTA	PCT	O-RB	D-RB	TOT	AST	PF	DQ	STL	TO	BLK	PTS	RPG	APG	PPG
75-76—Kansas City	66	—	1145	173	420	.412	—	—	—	85	117	.726	77	110	187	67	144	1	47	—	13	431	2.8	1.0	6.5
76-77—Kansas City	41	—	289	67	155	.432	—	—	—	23	32	.719	28	31	59	25	44	0	13	—	3	157	1.4	0.6	3.8
77-78—Chicago-K.C.	5	—	13	0	7	.000	—	—	—	0	0	—	1	0	1	1	3	0	1	1	0	0	0.2	0.2	0.0
REG. SEASON TOTALS	112	—	1447	240	582	.412	—	—	—	108	149	.725	106	141	247	93	191	1	61	1	16	588	2.2	0.8	5.3

HANSEN, LARS b. September 14, 1954 Ht. 6-10 Wt. 225 College—Washington

SEASON—TEAM	G	GS	MIN	FGM	FGA	PCT	3FGM	3FGA	PCT	FTM	FTA	PCT	O-RB	D-RB	TOT	AST	PF	DQ	STL	TO	BLK	PTS	RPG	APG	PPG
78-79—Seattle	15	—	205	29	57	.509	—	—	—	18	31	.581	22	37	59	14	28	0	1	9	1	76	3.9	0.9	5.1
REG. SEASON TOTALS	15	—	205	29	57	.509	—	—	—	18	31	.581	22	37	59	14	28	0	1	9	1	76	3.9	0.9	5.1

HANSEN, ROBERT LOUIS II (Bob) b. January 18, 1961 Ht. 6-6 Wt. 195 College—Iowa

SEASON—TEAM	G	GS	MIN	FGM	FGA	PCT	3FGM	3FGA	PCT	FTM	FTA	PCT	O-RB	D-RB	TOT	AST	PF	DQ	STL	TO	BLK	PTS	RPG	APG	PPG
83-84—Utah	55	0	419	65	145	.448	0	8	.000	18	28	.643	13	35	48	44	62	0	15	35	4	148	0.9	0.8	2.7
84-85—Utah	54	4	646	110	225	.489	1	7	.143	40	72	.556	20	50	70	75	88	0	25	49	1	261	1.3	1.4	4.8
85-86—Utah	82	82	2032	299	628	.476	17	50	.340	95	132	.720	82	162	244	193	205	1	74	126	9	710	3.0	2.4	8.7
86-87—Utah	72	72	1453	272	601	.453	16	45	.356	136	179	.760	84	119	203	102	146	0	44	77	6	696	2.8	1.4	9.7
87-88—Utah	81	51	1796	316	611	.517	32	97	.330	113	152	.743	64	123	187	175	193	2	65	91	5	777	2.3	2.2	9.6
88-89—Utah	46	9	964	140	300	.467	19	54	.352	42	75	.560	29	99	128	50	105	0	37	43	6	341	2.8	1.1	7.4
89-90—Utah	81	81	2174	265	568	.467	54	154	.351	33	64	.516	66	163	229	149	194	2	52	79	11	617	2.8	1.8	7.6
90-91—Sacramento	36	24	811	96	256	.375	19	69	.275	18	36	.500	33	63	96	90	72	1	20	34	5	229	2.7	2.5	6.4
91-92—Sac.-Chicago	68	2	809	79	178	.444	7	27	.259	8	22	.364	17	60	77	69	134	0	27	28	3	173	1.1	1.0	2.5
REG. SEASON TOTALS	575	325	11104	1642	3512	.468	165	511	.323	503	760	.662	408	874	1282	947	1199	6	359	562	50	3952	2.2	1.6	6.9
PLAYOFF TOTALS	49	28	1079	160	336	.476	38	76	.500	57	78	.731	40	83	123	81	121	1	19	58	4	415	2.5	1.7	8.5

HANZLIK, WILLIAM HENRY (Bill) b. December 6, 1957 Ht. 6-7 Wt. 200 College—Notre Dame

SEASON—TEAM	G	GS	MIN	FGM	FGA	PCT	3FGM	3FGA	PCT	FTM	FTA	PCT	O-RB	D-RB	TOT	AST	PF	DQ	STL	TO	BLK	PTS	RPG	APG	PPG
80-81—Seattle	74	—	1259	138	289	.478	1	5	.200	119	150	.793	67	86	153	111	168	1	58	84	20	396	2.1	1.5	5.4
81-82—Seattle	81	76	1974	167	357	.468	0	4	.000	138	176	.784	99	167	266	183	250	3	81	106	30	472	3.3	2.3	5.8
82-83—Denver	82	8	1547	187	437	.428	1	7	.143	125	160	.781	80	156	236	268	220	0	75	144	15	500	2.9	3.3	6.1
83-84—Denver	80	14	1469	132	306	.431	3	12	.250	167	207	.807	66	139	205	252	255	6	68	109	19	434	2.6	3.2	5.4
84-85—Denver	80	1	1673	220	522	.421	1	15	.067	180	238	.756	88	119	207	210	291	5	84	115	26	621	2.6	2.6	7.8
85-86—Denver	79	0	1982	331	741	.447	8	41	.195	318	405	.785	88	176	264	316	277	2	107	165	16	988	3.3	4.0	12.5
86-87—Denver	73	10	1990	307	746	.412	22	80	.275	316	402	.786	79	177	256	280	245	3	87	132	28	952	3.5	3.8	13.0
87-88—Denver	77	0	1334	109	287	.380	3	16	.188	129	163	.791	39	132	171	166	185	1	64	95	17	350	2.2	2.2	4.5
88-89—Denver	41	0	701	66	151	.437	1	5	.200	68	87	.782	18	75	93	86	82	1	25	53	5	201	2.3	2.1	4.9
89-90—Denver	81	0	1605	179	396	.452	6	31	.194	136	183	.743	67	140	207	186	249	7	78	87	29	500	2.6	2.3	6.2
REG. SEASON TOTALS	748	109	15534	1836	4232	.434	46	216	.213	1696	2171	.781	691	1367	2058	2058	2222	29	727	1090	205	5414	2.8	2.8	7.2
PLAYOFF TOTALS	62	15	1327	154	354	.435	5	26	.192	127	165	.770	64	118	182	167	209	5	49	80	29	440	2.9	2.7	7.1

HARDAWAY, ANFERNEE DEON b. July 18, 1972 Ht. 6-7 Wt. 200 College—Memphis State

SEASON—TEAM	G	GS	MIN	FGM	FGA	PCT	3FGM	3FGA	PCT	FTM	FTA	PCT	O-RB	D-RB	TOT	AST	PF	DQ	STL	TO	BLK	PTS	RPG	APG	PPG
93-94—Orlando	82	82	3015	509	1092	.466	50	187	.267	245	330	.742	192	247	439	544	205	2	190	292	51	1313	5.4	6.6	16.0
REG. SEASON TOTALS	82	82	3015	509	1092	.466	50	187	.267	245	330	.742	192	247	439	544	205	2	190	292	51	1313	5.4	6.6	16.0
PLAYOFF TOTALS	3	3	133	22	50	.440	5	11	.455	7	10	.700	8	12	20	21	10	0	5	20	6	56	6.7	7.0	18.7

HARDAWAY, TIMOTHY DUANE (Tim) b. September 1, 1966 Ht. 6-0 Wt. 195 College—Texas-El Paso

SEASON—TEAM	G	GS	MIN	FGM	FGA	PCT	3FGM	3FGA	PCT	FTM	FTA	PCT	O-RB	D-RB	TOT	AST	PF	DQ	STL	TO	BLK	PTS	RPG	APG	PPG
89-90—Golden State	79	78	2663	464	985	.471	23	84	.274	211	276	.764	57	253	310	689	232	6	165	260	12	1162	3.9	8.7	14.7
90-91—Golden State	82	82	3215	739	1551	.476	97	252	.385	306	381	.803	87	245	332	793	228	7	214	270	12	1881	4.0	9.7	22.9
91-92—Golden State	81	81	3332	734	1592	.461	127	376	.338	298	389	.766	81	229	310	807	208	1	164	267	13	1893	3.8	10.0	23.4
92-93—Golden State	66	66	2609	522	1168	.447	102	309	.330	273	367	.744	60	203	263	699	152	0	116	220	12	1419	4.0	10.6	21.5
REG. SEASON TOTALS	308	307	11819	2459	5296	.464	349	1021	.342	1088	1413	.770	285	930	1215	2988	820	14	659	1017	49	6355	3.9	9.7	20.6
PLAYOFF TOTALS	13	13	572	122	265	.460	27	77	.351	54	75	.720	11	37	48	130	36	0	41	39	7	325	3.7	10.0	25.0
ALL-STAR TOTALS	3	0	53	10	26	.385	4	10	.400	11	14	.786	3	6	9	15	4	0	4	5	0	35	3.0	5.0	11.7

HARDING, REGINALD (Reggie) b. May 4, 1942 d. September 2, 1972 Ht. 7-0 Wt. 255 College—None

SEASON—TEAM	G	GS	MIN	FGM	FGA	PCT	3FGM	3FGA	PCT	FTM	FTA	PCT	O-RB	D-RB	TOT	AST	PF	DQ	STL	TO	BLK	PTS	RPG	APG	PPG
63-64—Detroit	39	—	1158	184	460	.400	—	—	—	61	98	.622	—	—	410	52	119	1	—	—	—	429	10.5	1.3	11.0
64-65—Detroit	78	—	2699	405	987	.410	—	—	—	128	209	.612	—	—	906	179	258	5	—	—	—	938	11.6	2.3	12.0
66-67—Detroit	74	—	1367	172	383	.449	—	—	—	63	103	.612	—	—	455	94	164	2	—	—	—	407	6.1	1.3	5.5
67-68—Chicago	14	—	305	24	71	.338	—	—	—	17	33	.515	—	—	94	18	35	0	—	—	—	65	6.7	1.3	4.6
67-68—Indiana (A)	25	—	840	142	314	.452	0	1	.000	52	90	.578	—	—	334	53	59	0	—	77	—	336	13.4	2.1	13.4
REG. NBA TOTALS	205	—	5529	785	1901	.413	—	—	—	269	443	.607	—	—	1865	343	576	8	—	—	—	1839	9.1	1.7	9.0
REG. ABA TOTALS	25	—	840	142	314	.452	0	1	.000	52	90	.578	—	—	334	53	59	0	—	77	—	336	13.4	2.1	13.4

HARDNETT, CHARLES (Charlie) b. September 13, 1938 Ht. 6-8 Wt. 230 College—Grambling State

SEASON—TEAM	G	GS	MIN	FGM	FGA	PCT	3FGM	3FGA	PCT	FTM	FTA	PCT	O-RB	D-RB	TOT	AST	PF	DQ	STL	TO	BLK	PTS	RPG	APG	PPG
62-63—Chicago	78	—	1657	301	683	.441	—	—	—	225	349	.645	—	—	602	74	225	4	—	—	—	827	7.7	0.9	10.6
63-64—Baltimore	66	—	617	107	260	.412	—	—	—	84	125	.672	—	—	251	27	114	1	—	—	—	298	3.8	0.4	4.5
64-65—Baltimore	20	—	200	25	80	.313	—	—	—	23	39	.590	—	—	77	2	37	0	—	—	—	73	3.9	0.1	3.7
REG. SEASON TOTALS	164	—	2474	433	1023	.423	—	—	—	332	513	.647	—	—	930	103	376	5	—	—	—	1198	5.7	0.6	7.3
PLAYOFF TOTALS	5	—	22	4	10	.400	—	—	—	2	5	.400	—	—	6	2	2	0	—	—	—	10	1.2	0.4	2.0

HARDY, ALAN TIMOTHY b. May 25, 1957 Ht. 6-6.5 Wt. 195 College—Michigan

SEASON—TEAM	G	GS	MIN	FGM	FGA	PCT	3FGM	3FGA	PCT	FTM	FTA	PCT	O-RB	D-RB	TOT	AST	PF	DQ	STL	TO	BLK	PTS	RPG	APG	PPG
80-81—Los Angeles	22	—	111	22	59	.373	0	0	—	7	10	.700	8	11	19	3	13	0	1	11	9	51	0.9	0.1	2.3
81-82—Detroit	38	0	310	62	136	.456	0	5	.000	18	29	.621	14	20	34	20	32	0	9	20	4	142	0.9	0.5	3.7
REG. SEASON TOTALS	60	0	421	84	195	.431	0	5	.000	25	39	.641	22	31	53	23	45	0	10	31	13	193	0.9	0.4	3.2

HARDY, DARRELL GENE b. 1944 Ht. 6-7 Wt. 220 College—Baylor

SEASON—TEAM	G	GS	MIN	FGM	FGA	PCT	3FGM	3FGA	PCT	FTM	FTA	PCT	O-RB	D-RB	TOT	AST	PF	DQ	STL	TO	BLK	PTS	RPG	APG	PPG
67-68—Houston (A)	17	—	172	32	74	.432	0	1	.000	25	35	.714	—	—	56	8	23	0	—	12	—	89	3.3	0.5	5.2
REG. ABA TOTALS	17	—	172	32	74	.432	0	1	.000	25	35	.714	—	—	56	8	23	0	—	12	—	89	3.3	0.5	5.2

HARDY, JAMES PERCIVAL b. December 1, 1956 Ht. 6-8.5 Wt. 220 College—San Francisco

SEASON—TEAM	G	GS	MIN	FGM	FGA	PCT	3FGM	3FGA	PCT	FTM	FTA	PCT	O-RB	D-RB	TOT	AST	PF	DQ	STL	TO	BLK	PTS	RPG	APG	PPG
78-79—New Orleans	68	—	1456	196	426	.460	—	—	—	61	88	.693	121	189	310	65	133	1	52	93	61	453	4.6	1.0	6.7
79-80—Utah	76	—	1600	184	363	.507	1	2	.500	51	66	.773	124	275	399	104	207	4	47	105	87	420	5.3	1.4	5.5
80-81—Utah	23	—	509	52	111	.468	0	0	—	11	20	.550	39	94	133	36	58	2	21	23	20	115	5.8	1.6	5.0
81-82—Utah	82	17	1814	179	369	.485	0	1	.000	64	93	.688	153	317	470	110	192	2	58	78	67	422	5.7	1.3	5.1
REG. SEASON TOTALS	249	17	5379	611	1269	.481	1	3	.333	187	267	.700	437	875	1312	315	590	9	178	299	235	1410	5.3	1.3	5.7

HARGE, IRA LEE b. March 14, 1941 Ht. 6-9 Wt. 225 College—Burlington CC/Bowling Green State/New Mexico

SEASON—TEAM	G	GS	MIN	FGM	FGA	PCT	3FGM	3FGA	PCT	FTM	FTA	PCT	O-RB	D-RB	TOT	AST	PF	DQ	STL	TO	BLK	PTS	RPG	APG	PPG
67-68—Pitt.-Oakland (A)	82	—	2699	311	781	.398	0	0	—	202	298	.678	357	681	1038	99	294	7	—	182	—	824	12.7	1.2	10.0
68-69—Oakland (A)	78	—	2095	269	578	.465	0	0	—	123	200	.615	269	547	816	96	245	1	—	222	—	661	10.5	1.2	8.5
69-70—Washington (A)	84	—	2991	415	886	.468	0	0	—	196	289	.678	334	843	1177	200	328	8	—	—	—	1026	14.0	2.4	12.2
70-71—Car.-Fla. (A)	82	—	2934	460	999	.460	2	5	.400	197	306	.644	328	757	1085	202	291	—	—	—	—	1119	13.2	2.5	13.6
71-72—Fla.-Utah (A)	84	—	2264	314	679	.462	0	1	.000	104	150	.693	—	—	780	130	267	—	—	163	—	732	9.3	1.5	8.7
72-73—Utah-Car. (A)	17	—	177	14	40	.350	0	0	—	6	10	.600	15	44	59	9	43	0	—	17	—	34	3.5	0.5	2.0
REG. ABA TOTALS	427	—	13160	1783	3963	.450	2	6	.333	828	1253	.661	1303	2872	4955	736	1468	16	—	584	—	4396	11.6	1.7	10.3
ABA PLAYOFF TOTALS	39	—	1051	132	282	.468	0	3	.000	51	83	.614	112	273	425	61	90	1	—	39	—	315	10.9	1.6	8.1

HARGIS, JOHN ARLINGTON (**Shotgun**) b. August 20, 1920 d. January 2, 1986 Ht. 6-2 Wt. 185 College—Texas

SEASON—TEAM	G	GS	MIN	FGM	FGA	PCT	3FGM	3FGA	PCT	FTM	FTA	PCT	O-RB	D-RB	TOT	AST	PF	DQ	STL	TO	BLK	PTS	RPG	APG	PPG
47-48—Anderson (N)	59	—	—	235	—	—	—	—	—	172	329	.523	—	—	—	149	—	—	—	—	—	642	—	—	10.9
48-49—Anderson (N)	57	—	—	169	—	—	—	—	—	106	173	.613	—	—	—	129	—	—	—	—	—	444	—	—	7.8
49-50—Anderson	60	—	—	223	550	.405	—	—	—	197	277	.711	—	—	102	170	—	—	—	—	—	643	—	1.7	10.7
50-51—Ft. Wayne-Tri-Cit	14	—	—	25	66	.379	—	—	—	17	24	.708	—	—	30	9	26	0	—	—	—	67	2.1	0.6	4.8
REG. NBA TOTALS	74	—	—	248	616	.403	—	—	—	214	301	.711	—	—	30	111	196	0	—	—	—	710	2.1	1.5	9.6
REG. NBL TOTALS	116	—	—	404	—	—	—	—	—	278	502	.554	—	—	—	278	—	—	—	—	—	1086	—	—	9.4
NBA PLAYOFF TOTALS	8	—	—	32	89	.360	—	—	—	35	47	.745	—	—	13	26	1	—	—	—	—	99	—	1.6	12.4
NBL PLAYOFF TOTALS	13	—	—	52	—	—	—	—	—	53	81	.654	—	—	—	31	—	—	—	—	—	157	—	—	12.1

HARKNESS, JERALD B. (**Jerry**) b. May 7, 1940 Ht. 6-2 Wt. 180 College—Loyola (Ill.)

SEASON—TEAM	G	GS	MIN	FGM	FGA	PCT	3FGM	3FGA	PCT	FTM	FTA	PCT	O-RB	D-RB	TOT	AST	PF	DQ	STL	TO	BLK	PTS	RPG	APG	PPG
63-64—New York	5	—	59	13	30	.433	—	—	—	3	8	.375	—	—	6	6	4	0	—	—	—	29	1.2	1.2	5.8
67-68—Indiana (A)	71	—	1241	172	394	.437	1	5	.200	152	223	.682	—	—	193	129	109	1	—	77	—	497	2.7	1.8	7.0
68-69—Indiana (A)	10	—	272	31	67	.463	0	0	—	30	47	.638	—	—	34	21	27	0	—	20	—	92	3.4	2.1	9.2
REG. NBA TOTALS	5	—	59	13	30	.433	—	—	—	3	8	.375	—	—	6	6	4	0	—	—	—	29	1.2	1.2	5.8
REG. ABA TOTALS	81	—	1513	203	461	.440	1	5	.200	182	270	.674	—	—	227	150	136	1	—	97	—	589	2.8	1.9	7.3
ABA PLAYOFF TOTALS	3	—	32	4	12	.333	0	0	—	2	2	1.000	—	—	5	5	6	0	—	3	—	10	1.7	1.7	3.3

HARLICKA, JULES PETER (**Skip**) b. October 14, 1946 Ht. 6-1½ Wt. 185 College—South Carolina

SEASON—TEAM	G	GS	MIN	FGM	FGA	PCT	3FGM	3FGA	PCT	FTM	FTA	PCT	O-RB	D-RB	TOT	AST	PF	DQ	STL	TO	BLK	PTS	RPG	APG	PPG
68-69—Atlanta	26	—	218	41	90	.456	—	—	—	24	31	.774	—	—	16	37	29	0	—	—	—	106	0.6	1.4	4.1
REG. SEASON TOTALS	26	—	218	41	90	.456	—	—	—	24	31	.774	—	—	16	37	29	0	—	—	—	106	0.6	1.4	4.1
PLAYOFF TOTALS	1	—	1	0	0	—	—	—	—	0	0	—	—	—	0	—	1	0	—	—	—	0	0.0	0.0	0.0

HARPER, DEREK RICARDO b. October 13, 1961 Ht. 6-4 Wt. 205 College—Illinois

SEASON—TEAM	G	GS	MIN	FGM	FGA	PCT	3FGM	3FGA	PCT	FTM	FTA	PCT	O-RB	D-RB	TOT	AST	PF	DQ	STL	TO	BLK	PTS	RPG	APG	PPG
83-84—Dallas	82	1	1712	200	451	.443	3	26	.115	66	98	.673	53	119	172	239	143	0	95	111	21	469	2.1	2.9	5.7
84-85—Dallas	82	1	2218	329	633	.520	21	61	.344	111	154	.721	47	152	199	360	194	1	144	123	37	790	2.4	4.4	9.6
85-86—Dallas	79	39	2150	390	730	.534	12	51	.235	171	229	.747	75	151	226	416	166	1	153	144	23	963	2.9	5.3	12.2
86-87—Dallas	77	76	2556	497	993	.501	76	212	.358	160	234	.684	51	148	199	609	195	0	167	138	25	1230	2.6	7.9	16.0
87-88—Dallas	82	82	3032	536	1167	.459	60	192	.313	261	344	.759	71	175	246	634	164	0	168	190	35	1393	3.0	7.7	17.0
88-89—Dallas	81	81	2968	538	1127	.477	99	278	.356	229	284	.806	46	182	228	570	219	3	172	205	41	1404	2.8	7.0	17.3
89-90—Dallas	82	82	3007	567	1161	.488	89	240	.371	250	315	.794	54	190	244	609	224	1	187	207	26	1473	3.0	7.4	18.0
90-91—Dallas	77	77	2879	572	1226	.467	89	246	.362	286	391	.731	59	174	233	548	222	1	147	177	14	1519	3.0	7.1	19.7
91-92—Dallas	65	64	2252	448	1011	.443	58	186	.312	198	261	.759	44	121	170	373	150	0	101	154	17	1152	2.6	5.7	17.7
92-93—Dallas	62	60	2108	393	939	.419	101	257	.393	239	316	.756	42	81	123	334	145	1	80	136	16	1126	2.0	5.4	18.2
93-94—Dallas-N.Y.	82	55	2204	303	744	.407	73	203	.360	112	163	.687	20	121	141	334	163	0	125	135	8	791	1.7	4.1	9.6
REG. SEASON TOTALS	851	618	27086	4773	10182	.469	681	1952	.349	2083	2789	.747	567	1614	2181	5026	1985	8	1539	1720	263	12310	2.6	5.9	14.5
PLAYOFF TOTALS	71	56	2300	317	703	.451	57	171	.333	136	191	.712	50	118	168	398	182	1	125	123	9	827	2.4	5.6	11.6

HARPER, MICHAEL EDWARD (**Mike**) b. December 9, 1957 Ht. 6-10 Wt. 200 College—North Park

SEASON—TEAM	G	GS	MIN	FGM	FGA	PCT	3FGM	3FGA	PCT	FTM	FTA	PCT	O-RB	D-RB	TOT	AST	PF	DQ	STL	TO	BLK	PTS	RPG	APG	PPG
80-81—Portland	55	—	461	56	136	.412	0	3	.000	37	85	.435	28	65	93	17	73	0	23	32	20	149	1.7	0.3	2.7
81-82—Portland	68	38	1433	184	370	.497	0	1	.000	96	153	.627	127	212	339	54	229	7	55	92	82	464	5.0	0.8	6.8
REG. SEASON TOTALS	123	38	1894	240	506	.474	0	4	.000	133	238	.559	155	277	432	71	302	7	78	124	102	613	3.5	0.6	5.0
PLAYOFF TOTALS	1	0	6	1	1	1.000	0	0	—	1	1	1.000	0	0	1	1	—	0	0	0	0	3	1.0	0.0	3.0

HARPER, RONALD (Ron, Hollywood) b. January 20, 1964 Ht. 6-6 Wt. 205 College—Miami (Ohio)

SEASON—TEAM	G	GS	MIN	FGM	FGA	PCT	3FGM	3FGA	PCT	FTM	FTA	PCT	O-RB	D-RB	TOT	AST	PF	DQ	STL	TO	BLK	PTS	RPG	APG	PPG
86-87—Cleveland	82	82	3064	734	1614	.455	20	94	.213	386	564	.684	169	223	392	394	247	3	209	345	84	1874	4.8	4.8	22.9
87-88—Cleveland	57	52	1830	340	732	.464	3	20	.150	196	278	.705	64	159	223	281	157	3	122	158	52	879	3.9	4.9	15.4
88-89—Cleveland	82	82	2851	587	1149	.511	29	116	.250	323	430	.751	122	287	409	434	224	1	185	230	74	1526	5.0	5.3	18.6
89-90—Clev.-L.A. Clips	35	35	1367	301	637	.473	14	51	.275	182	231	.788	74	132	206	182	105	1	81	100	41	798	5.9	5.2	22.8
90-91—L.A. Clippers	39	34	1383	285	729	.391	48	148	.324	145	217	.668	58	130	188	209	111	0	66	129	35	763	4.8	5.4	19.6
91-92—L.A. Clippers	82	82	3144	569	1292	.440	64	211	.303	293	398	.736	120	327	447	417	199	0	152	252	72	1495	5.5	5.1	18.2
92-93—L.A. Clippers	80	77	2970	542	1203	.451	52	186	.280	307	399	.769	117	308	425	360	212	1	177	222	73	1443	5.3	4.5	18.0
93-94—L.A. Clippers	75	75	2856	569	1335	.426	71	236	.301	299	418	.715	129	331	460	344	167	0	144	242	54	1508	6.1	4.6	20.1
REG. SEASON TOTALS	532	519	19465	3927	8691	.452	301	1062	.283	2131	2935	.726	853	1897	2750	2621	1422	9	1136	1678	485	10286	5.2	4.9	19.3
PLAYOFF TOTALS	19	19	703	145	297	.488	6	23	.261	53	73	.726	25	68	93	74	49	1	42	44	22	349	4.9	3.9	18.4

HARRIS, ARTHUR CARLOS JR. (Art) b. January 13, 1947 Ht. 6-4 Wt. 185 College—Stanford

SEASON—TEAM	G	GS	MIN	FGM	FGA	PCT	3FGM	3FGA	PCT	FTM	FTA	PCT	O-RB	D-RB	TOT	AST	PF	DQ	STL	TO	BLK	PTS	RPG	APG	PPG
68-69—Seattle	80	—	2556	416	1054	.395	—	—	—	161	251	.641	—	—	301	258	326	14	—	—	—	993	3.8	3.2	12.4
69-70—Seattle-Phoenix	81	—	1553	285	723	.394	—	—	—	86	134	.642	—	—	161	231	220	—	—	—	—	656	2.0	2.9	8.1
70-71—Phoenix	56	—	952	199	484	.411	—	—	—	69	113	.611	—	—	100	132	137	0	—	—	—	467	1.8	2.4	8.3
71-72—Phoenix	21	—	145	23	70	.329	—	—	—	9	21	.429	—	—	13	18	26	0	—	—	—	55	0.6	0.9	2.6
REG. SEASON TOTALS	238	—	5206	923	2331	.396	—	—	—	325	519	.626	—	—	575	639	709	14	—	—	—	2171	2.4	2.7	9.1
PLAYOFF TOTALS	7	—	89	15	42	.357	—	—	—	0	2	.000	—	—	13	12	13	0	—	—	—	30	1.9	1.7	4.3

HARRIS, BILLY b. November 12, 1951 Ht. 6-2 Wt. 190 College—Northern Illinois

SEASON—TEAM	G	GS	MIN	FGM	FGA	PCT	3FGM	3FGA	PCT	FTM	FTA	PCT	O-RB	D-RB	TOT	AST	PF	DQ	STL	TO	BLK	PTS	RPG	APG	PPG
74-75—San Diego (A)	76	—	1221	264	664	.398	16	73	.219	65	96	.677	58	64	122	111	166	—	55	79	6	609	1.6	1.5	8.0
REG. ABA TOTALS	76	—	1221	264	664	.398	16	73	.219	65	96	.677	58	64	122	111	166	—	55	79	6	609	1.6	1.5	8.0

HARRIS, C. BERNARD (Bernie) b. November 26, 1950 Ht. 6-10 Wt. 200 College—Virginia Commonwealth

SEASON—TEAM	G	GS	MIN	FGM	FGA	PCT	3FGM	3FGA	PCT	FTM	FTA	PCT	O-RB	D-RB	TOT	AST	PF	DQ	STL	TO	BLK	PTS	RPG	APG	PPG
74-75—Buffalo	11	—	25	2	11	.182	—	—	—	1	2	.500	2	6	8	1	0	0	0	0	—	1	5	0.7	0.1	0.5
REG. SEASON TOTALS	11	—	25	2	11	.182	—	—	—	1	2	.500	2	6	8	1	0	0	0	0	—	1	5	0.7	0.1	0.5

HARRIS, CHRISTOPHER R. (Chris) b. August 11, 1933 Ht. 6-3 Wt. 190 College—Dayton

SEASON—TEAM	G	GS	MIN	FGM	FGA	PCT	3FGM	3FGA	PCT	FTM	FTA	PCT	O-RB	D-RB	TOT	AST	PF	DQ	STL	TO	BLK	PTS	RPG	APG	PPG
55-56—St. L.-Roch.	41	—	420	37	149	.248	—	—	—	27	45	.600	—	—	44	44	43	0	—	—	—	101	1.1	1.1	2.5
REG. SEASON TOTALS	41	—	420	37	149	.248	—	—	—	27	45	.600	—	—	44	44	43	0	—	—	—	101	1.1	1.1	2.5

HARRIS, LUCIOUS H. JR. b. December 18, 1970 Ht. 6-5 Wt. 190 College—Long Beach State

SEASON—TEAM	G	GS	MIN	FGM	FGA	PCT	3FGM	3FGA	PCT	FTM	FTA	PCT	O-RB	D-RB	TOT	AST	PF	DQ	STL	TO	BLK	PTS	RPG	APG	PPG
93-94—Dallas	77	0	1165	162	385	.421	7	33	.212	87	119	.731	45	112	157	106	117	0	49	78	10	418	2.0	1.4	5.4
REG. SEASON TOTALS	77	0	1165	162	385	.421	7	33	.212	87	119	.731	45	112	157	106	117	0	49	78	10	418	2.0	1.4	5.4

HARRIS, ROBERT AZZEL (Bob) b. March 16, 1927 Ht. 6-7 Wt. 195 College—Murray State (Okla.)/Oklahoma State

SEASON—TEAM	G	GS	MIN	FGM	FGA	PCT	3FGM	3FGA	PCT	FTM	FTA	PCT	O-RB	D-RB	TOT	AST	PF	DQ	STL	TO	BLK	PTS	RPG	APG	PPG
49-50—Fort Wayne	62	—	—	168	465	.361	—	—	—	140	223	.628	—	—	—	129	190	—	—	—	—	476	—	2.1	7.7
50-51—Ft. Wayne-Boston	56	—	—	98	295	.332	—	—	—	86	127	.677	—	—	291	64	157	4	—	—	—	282	5.2	1.1	5.0
51-52—Boston	66	—	1899	190	463	.410	—	—	—	134	209	.641	—	—	531	120	194	5	—	—	—	514	8.0	1.8	7.8
52-53—Boston	70	—	1971	192	459	.418	—	—	—	133	226	.588	—	—	485	95	238	6	—	—	—	517	6.9	1.4	7.4
53-54—Boston	71	—	1898	156	409	.381	—	—	—	108	172	.628	—	—	517	94	224	8	—	—	—	420	7.3	1.3	5.9
REG. SEASON TOTALS	325	—	5768	804	2091	.385	—	—	—	601	957	.628	—	—	1824	502	1003	23	—	—	—	2209	6.9	1.5	6.8
PLAYOFF TOTALS	21	—	430	51	123	.415	—	—	—	56	79	.709	—	—	120	32	88	5	—	—	—	158	7.1	1.5	7.5

HARRIS, STEVEN DWAYNE (Steve) b. October 15, 1963 Ht. 6-5 Wt. 195 College—Tulsa

SEASON—TEAM	G	GS	MIN	FGM	FGA	PCT	3FGM	3FGA	PCT	FTM	FTA	PCT	O-RB	D-RB	TOT	AST	PF	DQ	STL	TO	BLK	PTS	RPG	APG	PPG
85-86—Houston	57	0	482	103	233	.442	1	5	.200	50	54	.926	25	32	57	50	55	0	21	34	4	257	1.0	0.9	4.5
86-87—Houston	74	3	1174	251	599	.419	0	8	.000	111	130	.854	71	99	170	100	111	1	37	74	16	613	2.3	1.4	8.3
87-88—Houston-G.S.	58	26	1084	223	487	.458	0	7	.000	89	113	.788	53	73	126	87	89	0	50	56	8	535	2.2	1.5	9.2
88-89—Detroit	3	0	7	1	4	.250	0	0	—	2	2	1.000	0	2	2	0	1	0	1	0	0	4	0.7	0.0	1.3
89-90—L.A. Clippers	15	0	93	14	40	.350	0	0	—	3	4	.750	5	5	10	1	9	0	7	5	1	31	0.7	0.1	2.1
REG. SEASON TOTALS	207	29	2840	592	1363	.434	1	20	.050	255	303	.842	154	211	365	238	265	1	116	169	29	1440	1.8	1.1	7.0
PLAYOFF TOTALS	24	0	174	30	72	.417	0	1	.000	7	11	.636	8	9	17	7	18	0	7	5	3	67	0.7	0.3	2.8

HARRIS, TONY DWAYNE b. May 13, 1967   Ht. 6-3 Wt. 190 College—Lamar/Johnson County CC/Delgado/SW Mississippi JC/New Orleans

SEASON—TEAM	G	GS	MIN	FGM	FGA	PCT	3FGM	3FGA	PCT	FTM	FTA	PCT	O-RB	D-RB	TOT	AST	PF	DQ	STL	TO	BLK	PTS	RPG	APG	PPG
90-91—Philadelphia	6	0	41	4	16	.250	0	2	.000	2	4	.500	0	1	1	0	5	0	1	3	0	10	0.2	0.0	1.7
93-94—Boston	5	0	88	9	31	.290	3	9	.333	23	25	.920	3	7	10	8	8	0	4	6	0	44	2.0	1.6	8.8
REG. SEASON TOTALS	11	0	129	13	47	.277	3	11	.273	25	29	.862	3	8	11	8	13	0	5	9	0	54	1.0	0.7	4.9

HARRISON, ROBERT WILLIAM (Bob, Tiger) b. August 12, 1927   Ht. 6-1 Wt. 190 College—Michigan

SEASON—TEAM	G	GS	MIN	FGM	FGA	PCT	3FGM	3FGA	PCT	FTM	FTA	PCT	O-RB	D-RB	TOT	AST	PF	DQ	STL	TO	BLK	PTS	RPG	APG	PPG
49-50—Minneapolis	66	—	—	125	348	.359	—	—	—	50	74	.676	—	—	—	131	175	—	—	—	—	300	—	2.0	4.5
50-51—Minneapolis	68	—	—	150	432	.347	—	—	—	101	128	.789	—	—	172	195	218	—	—	—	—	401	2.5	2.9	5.9
51-52—Minneapolis	65	—	1712	156	487	.320	—	—	—	89	124	.718	—	—	160	188	203	9	—	—	—	401	2.5	2.9	6.2
52-53—Minneapolis	70	—	1643	195	518	.376	—	—	—	107	165	.648	—	—	153	160	264	16	—	—	—	497	2.2	2.3	7.1
53-54—Minn.-Milw.	64	—	1443	144	449	.321	—	—	—	94	158	.595	—	—	130	139	218	9	—	—	—	382	2.0	2.2	6.0
54-55—Milwaukee	72	—	2300	299	875	.342	—	—	—	126	185	.681	—	—	226	252	291	14	—	—	—	724	3.1	3.5	10.1
55-56—St. Louis	72	—	2219	260	725	.359	—	—	—	97	146	.664	—	—	195	277	246	6	—	—	—	617	2.7	3.8	8.6
56-57—St. L.-Syr.	66	—	1810	243	629	.386	—	—	—	93	130	.715	—	—	156	161	220	5	—	—	—	579	2.4	2.4	8.8
57-58—Syracuse	72	—	1799	210	604	.348	—	—	—	97	122	.795	—	—	166	169	200	1	—	—	—	517	2.3	2.3	7.2
REG. SEASON TOTALS	615	—	12926	1782	5067	.352	—	—	—	854	1232	.693	—	—	1358	1672	2035	65	—	—	—	4418	2.5	2.7	7.2
PLAYOFF TOTALS	59	—	871	138	358	.385	—	—	—	62	90	.689	—	—	113	118	189	10	—	—	—	338	2.4	2.0	5.7
ALL-STAR TOTALS	1	—	25	2	7	.286	—	—	—	1	2	.500	—	—	0	1	4	—	—	—	—	5	0.0	1.0	5.0

HARVEY, ANTONIO b. July 9, 1970   Ht. 6-11 Wt. 225 College—Southern Illinois/Georgia/Pfeiffer

SEASON—TEAM	G	GS	MIN	FGM	FGA	PCT	3FGM	3FGA	PCT	FTM	FTA	PCT	O-RB	D-RB	TOT	AST	PF	DQ	STL	TO	BLK	PTS	RPG	APG	PPG
93-94—L.A. Lakers	27	6	247	29	79	.367	0	0	—	12	26	.462	26	33	59	5	39	0	8	17	19	70	2.2	0.2	2.6
REG. SEASON TOTALS	27	6	247	29	79	.367	0	0	—	12	26	.462	26	33	59	5	39	0	8	17	19	70	2.2	0.2	2.6

HASKIN, SCOTT RUSSELL b. September 19, 1970   Ht. 6-11 Wt. 250 College—Oregon State

SEASON—TEAM	G	GS	MIN	FGM	FGA	PCT	3FGM	3FGA	PCT	FTM	FTA	PCT	O-RB	D-RB	TOT	AST	PF	DQ	STL	TO	BLK	PTS	RPG	APG	PPG
93-94—Indiana	27	2	186	21	45	.467	0	0	—	13	19	.684	17	38	55	6	33	0	2	13	15	55	2.0	0.2	2.0
REG. SEASON TOTALS	27	2	186	21	45	.467	0	0	—	13	19	.684	17	38	55	6	33	0	2	13	15	55	2.0	0.2	2.0

HASKINS, CLEM SMITH (The Gem) b. July 11, 1943   Ht. 6-3 Wt. 195 College—Western Kentucky

SEASON—TEAM	G	GS	MIN	FGM	FGA	PCT	3FGM	3FGA	PCT	FTM	FTA	PCT	O-RB	D-RB	TOT	AST	PF	DQ	STL	TO	BLK	PTS	RPG	APG	PPG
67-68—Chicago	76	—	1477	273	650	.420	—	—	—	133	202	.658	—	—	227	165	175	1	—	—	—	679	3.0	2.2	8.9
68-69—Chicago	79	—	2874	537	1275	.421	—	—	—	282	361	.781	—	—	359	306	230	0	—	—	—	1356	4.5	3.9	17.2
69-70—Chicago	82	—	3214	668	1486	.450	—	—	—	332	424	.783	—	—	378	624	237	0	—	—	—	1668	4.6	7.6	20.3
70-71—Phoenix	82	—	2764	562	1277	.440	—	—	—	338	431	.784	—	—	324	383	207	2	—	—	—	1462	4.0	4.7	17.8
71-72—Phoenix	79	—	2453	509	1054	.483	—	—	—	220	258	.853	—	—	270	290	194	1	—	—	—	1238	3.4	3.7	15.7
72-73—Phoenix	77	—	1581	339	731	.464	—	—	—	130	156	.833	—	—	173	203	143	2	—	—	—	808	2.2	2.6	10.5
73-74—Phoenix	81	—	1822	364	792	.460	—	—	—	171	203	.842	78	144	222	250	166	1	81	—	16	899	2.7	3.2	11.1
74-75—Washington	70	—	702	115	290	.397	—	—	—	53	63	.841	29	51	80	79	73	0	23	—	6	283	1.1	1.1	4.0
75-76—Washington	55	—	737	148	269	.550	—	—	—	54	65	.831	12	42	54	73	79	2	23	—	8	350	1.0	1.3	6.4
REG. SEASON TOTALS	681	—	17624	3515	7824	.449	—	—	—	1713	2163	.792	119	237	2087	2382	1504	9	127	—	30	8743	3.1	3.5	12.8
PLAYOFF TOTALS	28	—	322	68	145	.469	—	—	—	28	38	.737	6	6	37	38	41	0	2	—	1	164	1.3	1.4	5.9

HASSETT, JOSEPH PATRICK JR. (Joey) b. September 11, 1955   Ht. 6-5 Wt. 180 College—Providence

SEASON—TEAM	G	GS	MIN	FGM	FGA	PCT	3FGM	3FGA	PCT	FTM	FTA	PCT	O-RB	D-RB	TOT	AST	PF	DQ	STL	TO	BLK	PTS	RPG	APG	PPG
77-78—Seattle	48	—	404	91	205	.444	—	—	—	10	12	.833	14	22	36	41	45	0	21	34	0	192	0.8	0.9	4.0
78-79—Seattle	55	—	463	100	211	.474	—	—	—	23	23	1.000	13	32	45	42	58	0	14	32	4	223	0.8	0.8	4.1
79-80—Indiana	74	—	1135	215	509	.422	69	198	.348	24	29	.828	35	59	94	104	85	0	46	45	8	523	1.3	1.4	7.1
80-81—Dallas-G.S.	41	—	714	143	340	.421	53	156	.340	17	21	.810	24	44	68	74	65	0	13	22	2	356	1.7	1.8	8.7
81-82—Golden State	68	2	787	144	382	.377	71	214	.332	31	37	.838	13	40	53	104	94	1	30	36	3	390	0.8	1.5	5.7
82-83—Golden State	6	2	139	19	44	.432	1	9	.111	0	0	—	3	8	11	21	14	0	2	9	0	39	1.8	3.5	6.5
REG. SEASON TOTALS	292	4	3642	712	1691	.421	194	577	.336	105	122	.861	102	205	307	386	361	1	126	178	17	1723	1.1	1.3	5.9
PLAYOFF TOTALS	16	0	37	10	20	.500	0	0	—	0	0	—	0	3	3	1	1	0	1	3	0	20	0.2	0.1	1.3

HASSETT, WILLIAM JOSEPH (Billy) b. October 21, 1921 d. November 15, 1992 Ht. 6-1 Wt. 180 College—Georgetown/Notre Dame

SEASON—TEAM	G	GS	MIN	FGM	FGA	PCT	3FGM	3FGA	PCT	FTM	FTA	PCT	O-RB	D-RB	TOT	AST	PF	DQ	STL	TO	BLK	PTS	RPG	APG	PPG
46-47—Tri-Cities (N)	27	—	—	73	—	—	—	—	—	66	101	.653	—	—	—	—	58	—	—	—	—	212	—	—	7.9
47-48—Tri-Cities (N)	56	—	—	199	—	—	—	—	—	203	269	.755	—	—	—	—	145	—	—	—	—	601	—	—	10.7
48-49—Tri-Cities (N)	64	—	—	125	—	—	—	—	—	106	156	.679	—	—	—	—	152	—	—	—	—	356	—	—	5.6
49-50—Tri-Cit.-Minn.	60	—	—	84	302	.278	—	—	—	104	161	.646	—	—	—	137	136	—	—	—	—	272	—	2.3	4.5
50-51—Baltimore	31	—	—	45	160	.281	—	—	—	43	63	.683	—	—	35	47	72	1	—	—	—	133	1.1	1.5	4.3
REG. NBA TOTALS	91	—	—	129	462	.279	—	—	—	147	224	.656	—	—	35	184	208	1	—	—	—	405	1.1	2.0	4.5
REG. NBL TOTALS	147	—	—	397	—	—	—	—	—	375	526	.713	—	—	—	355	—	—	—	—	—	1169	—	—	8.0
NBA PLAYOFF TOTALS	7	—	—	3	12	.250	—	—	—	3	10	.300	—	—	4	8	0	—	—	—	—	9	0.6	1.3	
NBL PLAYOFF TOTALS	11	—	—	29	—	—	—	—	—	34	47	.723	—	—	—	27	—	—	—	—	—	92	—	—	8.4

HASTINGS, SCOTT ALAN b. June 3, 1960 Ht. 6-10 Wt. 235 College—Arkansas

SEASON—TEAM	G	GS	MIN	FGM	FGA	PCT	3FGM	3FGA	PCT	FTM	FTA	PCT	O-RB	D-RB	TOT	AST	PF	DQ	STL	TO	BLK	PTS	RPG	APG	PPG
82-83—N.Y.-Atlanta	31	0	140	13	38	.342	0	3	.000	11	20	.550	15	26	41	3	34	0	6	9	1	37	1.3	0.1	1.2
83-84—Atlanta	68	8	1135	111	237	.468	1	4	.250	82	104	.788	96	174	270	46	220	7	40	66	36	305	4.0	0.7	4.5
84-85—Atlanta	64	1	825	89	188	.473	0	0	—	63	81	.778	59	100	159	46	135	1	24	50	23	241	2.5	0.7	3.8
85-86—Atlanta	62	0	650	65	159	.409	3	4	.750	60	70	.857	44	80	124	26	118	2	14	40	8	193	2.0	0.4	3.1
86-87—Atlanta	40	0	256	23	68	.338	2	12	.167	23	29	.793	16	54	70	13	35	0	10	13	7	71	1.8	0.3	2.0
87-88—Atlanta	55	0	403	40	82	.488	5	12	.417	25	27	.926	27	70	97	16	67	1	8	14	10	110	1.8	0.3	2.0
88-89—Miami	75	6	1206	143	328	.436	9	28	.321	91	107	.850	72	159	231	59	203	5	32	68	42	386	3.1	0.8	5.1
89-90—Detroit	40	0	166	10	33	.303	3	12	.250	19	22	.864	7	25	32	8	31	0	3	7	3	42	0.8	0.2	1.1
90-91—Detroit	27	0	113	16	28	.571	3	4	.750	13	13	1.000	14	14	28	7	23	0	0	7	0	48	1.0	0.3	1.8
91-92—Denver	40	4	421	17	50	.340	0	9	.000	24	28	.857	30	68	98	26	56	0	10	22	15	58	2.5	0.7	1.5
92-93—Denver	76	0	670	57	112	.509	2	8	.250	40	55	.727	44	93	137	34	115	1	12	29	8	156	1.8	0.4	2.1
REG. SEASON TOTALS	578	19	5985	584	1323	.441	28	96	.292	451	556	.811	424	863	1287	284	1037	17	159	325	153	1647	2.2	0.5	2.8
PLAYOFF TOTALS	44	0	256	28	50	.560	3	12	.250	18	25	.720	15	32	47	9	51	1	8	13	3	77	1.1	0.2	1.8

HATTON, WALTER VERNON (Vern) b. January 13, 1936 Ht. 6-3 Wt. 195 College—Kentucky

SEASON—TEAM	G	GS	MIN	FGM	FGA	PCT	3FGM	3FGA	PCT	FTM	FTA	PCT	O-RB	D-RB	TOT	AST	PF	DQ	STL	TO	BLK	PTS	RPG	APG	PPG
58-59—Cin.-Phil.	64	—	1109	149	418	.356	—	—	—	77	105	.733	—	—	178	70	111	0	—	—	—	375	2.8	1.1	5.9
59-60—Philadelphia	67	—	1049	127	356	.357	—	—	—	53	87	.609	—	—	159	82	61	0	—	—	—	307	2.4	1.2	4.6
60-61—Philadelphia	54	—	610	97	304	.319	—	—	—	46	56	.821	—	—	92	59	59	0	—	—	—	240	1.7	1.1	4.4
61-62—Chicago-St. L.	40	—	898	112	331	.338	—	—	—	98	125	.784	—	—	102	99	63	0	—	—	—	322	2.6	2.5	8.1
REG. SEASON TOTALS	225	—	3666	485	1409	.344	—	—	—	274	373	.735	—	—	531	310	294	0	—	—	—	1244	2.4	1.4	5.5
PLAYOFF TOTALS	6	—	17	4	13	.308	—	—	—	1	3	.333	—	—	3	1	3	0	—	—	—	9	0.5	0.2	1.5

HAVLICEK, JOHN J. (Hondo) b. April 8, 1940 Ht. 6-5 Wt. 205 College—Ohio State

SEASON—TEAM	G	GS	MIN	FGM	FGA	PCT	3FGM	3FGA	PCT	FTM	FTA	PCT	O-RB	D-RB	TOT	AST	PF	DQ	STL	TO	BLK	PTS	RPG	APG	PPG
62-63—Boston	80	—	2200	483	1085	.445	—	—	—	174	239	.728	—	—	534	179	189	2	—	—	—	1140	6.7	2.2	14.3
63-64—Boston	80	—	2587	640	1535	.417	—	—	—	315	422	.746	—	—	428	238	227	1	—	—	—	1595	5.4	3.0	19.9
64-65—Boston	75	—	2169	570	1420	.401	—	—	—	235	316	.744	—	—	371	199	200	2	—	—	—	1375	4.9	2.7	18.3
65-66—Boston	71	—	2175	530	1328	.399	—	—	—	274	349	.785	—	—	423	210	158	1	—	—	—	1334	6.0	3.0	18.8
66-67—Boston	81	—	2602	684	1540	.444	—	—	—	365	441	.828	—	—	532	278	210	0	—	—	—	1733	6.6	3.4	21.4
67-68—Boston	82	—	2921	666	1551	.429	—	—	—	368	453	.812	—	—	546	384	237	2	—	—	—	1700	6.7	4.7	20.7
68-69—Boston	82	—	3174	692	1709	.405	—	—	—	387	496	.780	—	—	570	441	247	0	—	—	—	1771	7.0	5.4	21.6
69-70—Boston	81	—	3369	736	1585	.464	—	—	—	488	578	.844	—	—	635	550	211	1	—	—	—	1960	7.8	6.8	24.2
70-71—Boston	81	—	3678	892	1982	.450	—	—	—	554	677	.818	—	—	730	607	200	0	—	—	—	2338	9.0	7.5	28.9
71-72—Boston	82	—	3698	897	1957	.458	—	—	—	458	549	.834	—	—	672	614	183	1	—	—	—	2252	8.2	7.5	27.5
72-73—Boston	80	—	3367	766	1704	.450	—	—	—	370	431	.858	—	—	567	529	195	1	—	—	—	1902	7.1	6.6	23.8
73-74—Boston	76	—	3091	685	1502	.456	—	—	—	346	416	.832	138	349	487	447	196	1	95	—	32	1716	6.4	5.9	22.6
74-75—Boston	82	—	3132	642	1411	.455	—	—	—	289	332	.870	154	330	484	432	231	2	110	—	16	1573	5.9	5.3	19.2
75-76—Boston	76	—	2598	504	1121	.450	—	—	—	281	333	.844	116	198	314	278	204	1	97	—	29	1289	4.1	3.7	17.0
76-77—Boston	79	—	2913	580	1283	.452	—	—	—	235	288	.816	109	273	382	400	208	4	84	—	18	1395	4.8	5.1	17.7
77-78—Boston	82	—	2797	546	1217	.449	—	—	—	230	269	.855	93	239	332	328	185	2	90	204	22	1322	4.0	4.0	16.1
REG. SEASON TOTALS	1270	—	46471	10513	23930	.439	—	—	—	5369	6589	.815	610	1389	8007	6114	3281	21	476	204	117	26395	6.3	4.8	20.8
PLAYOFF TOTALS	172	—	6860	1451	3329	.436	—	—	—	874	1046	.836	79	199	1186	825	527	9	60	—	16	3776	6.9	4.8	22.0
ALL-STAR TOTALS	13	—	303	74	154	.481	—	—	—	31	41	.756	2	10	46	31	20	0	4	4	0	179	3.5	2.4	13.8

HAWES, STEVEN SHERBURNE (Steve) b. May 26, 1950 Ht. 6-9 Wt. 220 College—Washington

SEASON—TEAM	G	GS	MIN	FGM	FGA	PCT	3FGM	3FGA	PCT	FTM	FTA	PCT	O-RB	D-RB	TOT	AST	PF	DQ	STL	TO	BLK	PTS	RPG	APG	PPG
74-75—Houston	55	—	897	140	279	.502	—	—	—	45	55	.818	80	195	275	88	99	1	36	—	36	325	5.0	1.6	5.9
75-76—Houston-Port.	72	—	1411	199	403	.494	—	—	—	87	120	.725	171	326	497	115	169	5	44	—	25	485	6.9	1.6	6.7
76-77—Atlanta	44	—	945	147	305	.482	—	—	—	67	88	.761	78	183	261	63	141	4	36	—	24	361	5.9	1.4	8.2
77-78—Atlanta	75	—	2325	387	854	.453	—	—	—	175	214	.818	180	510	690	190	230	4	78	148	57	949	9.2	2.5	12.7
78-79—Atlanta	81	—	2205	372	756	.492	—	—	—	108	132	.818	190	401	591	184	264	1	79	145	47	852	7.3	2.3	10.5
79-80—Atlanta	82	—	1853	304	605	.502	3	8	.375	150	182	.824	148	348	496	144	205	4	74	121	29	761	6.0	1.8	9.3
80-81—Atlanta	74	—	2309	333	637	.523	1	4	.250	222	278	.799	165	396	561	168	289	13	73	161	32	889	7.6	2.3	12.0
81-82—Atlanta	49	42	1317	178	370	.481	4	10	.400	96	126	.762	89	231	320	142	156	4	36	87	34	456	6.5	2.9	9.3
82-83—Atlanta-Seattle	77	4	1416	163	390	.418	5	21	.238	69	94	.734	81	280	361	95	189	2	38	107	14	400	4.7	1.2	5.2
83-84—Seattle	79	0	1153	114	237	.481	1	4	.250	61	78	.782	50	170	220	99	144	2	24	52	16	290	2.8	1.3	3.7
REG. SEASON TOTALS	688	46	15831	2337	4836	.483	14	47	.298	1080	1367	.790	1232	3040	4272	1288	1886	40	518	821	314	5768	6.2	1.9	8.4
PLAYOFF TOTALS	32	0	712	96	207	.464	1	2	.500	42	51	.824	58	117	175	71	86	3	23	24	9	235	5.5	2.2	7.3

HAWKINS, CORNELIUS L. (Connie, Hawk) b. July 17, 1942 Ht. 6-8 Wt. 215 College—Iowa

SEASON—TEAM	G	GS	MIN	FGM	FGA	PCT	3FGM	3FGA	PCT	FTM	FTA	PCT	O-RB	D-RB	TOT	AST	PF	DQ	STL	TO	BLK	PTS	RPG	APG	PPG
67-68—Pittsburgh (A)	70	—	3146	635	1223	.519	2	9	.222	603	789	.764	368	577	945	320	248	2	—	200	—	1875	13.5	4.6	26.8
68-69—Minnesota (A)	47	—	1852	496	971	.511	3	22	.136	425	554	.767	167	367	534	184	166	3	—	155	—	1420	11.4	3.9	30.2
69-70—Phoenix	81	—	3312	709	1447	.490	—	—	—	577	741	.779	—	—	846	391	287	4	—	—	—	1995	10.4	4.8	24.6
70-71—Phoenix	71	—	2662	512	1181	.434	—	—	—	457	560	.816	—	—	643	322	197	2	—	—	—	1481	9.1	4.5	20.9
71-72—Phoenix	76	—	2798	571	1244	.459	—	—	—	456	565	.807	—	—	633	296	235	2	—	—	—	1598	8.3	3.9	21.0
72-73—Phoenix	75	—	2768	441	920	.479	—	—	—	322	404	.797	—	—	641	304	229	5	—	—	—	1204	8.5	4.1	16.1
73-74—Phoenix-L.A.	79	—	2761	404	807	.501	—	—	—	191	251	.761	176	389	565	407	223	1	113	—	81	999	7.2	5.2	12.6
74-75—Los Angeles	43	—	1026	139	324	.429	—	—	—	68	99	.687	54	144	198	120	116	1	51	—	23	346	4.6	2.8	8.0
75-76—Atlanta	74	—	1907	237	530	.447	—	—	—	136	191	.712	102	343	445	212	172	2	80	—	46	610	6.0	2.9	8.2
REG. NBA TOTALS	499	—	17234	3013	6453	.467	—	—	—	2207	2811	.785	332	876	3971	2052	1459	17	244	—	150	8233	8.0	4.1	16.5
REG. ABA TOTALS	117	—	4998	1131	2194	.515	5	31	.161	1028	1343	.765	535	944	1479	504	414	5	—	355	—	3295	12.6	4.3	28.2
NBA PLAYOFF TOTALS	12	—	500	83	210	.395	—	—	—	66	81	.815	14	26	137	57	35	0	7	—	1	232	11.4	4.8	19.3
ABA PLAYOFF TOTALS	21	—	936	210	416	.505	4	8	.500	169	239	.707	39	47	258	91	83	4	—	67	—	593	12.3	4.3	28.2
NBA ALL-STAR TOTALS	4	—	45	8	16	.500	—	—	—	9	10	.900	0	0	10	5	5	0	0	—	0	25	2.5	1.3	6.3
ABA ALL-STAR TOTALS	1	—	26	3	6	.500	0	0	—	1	3	.333	4	5	9	2	3	0	—	0	—	7	9.0	2.0	7.0

HAWKINS, HERSEY R. JR. b. September 29, 1966 Ht. 6-3 Wt. 190 College—Bradley

SEASON—TEAM	G	GS	MIN	FGM	FGA	PCT	3FGM	3FGA	PCT	FTM	FTA	PCT	O-RB	D-RB	TOT	AST	PF	DQ	STL	TO	BLK	PTS	RPG	APG	PPG
88-89—Philadelphia	79	79	2577	442	971	.455	71	166	.428	241	290	.831	51	174	225	239	184	0	120	158	37	1196	2.8	3.0	15.1
89-90—Philadelphia	82	82	2856	522	1136	.460	84	200	.420	387	436	.888	85	219	304	261	217	2	130	185	28	1515	3.7	3.2	18.5
90-91—Philadelphia	80	80	3110	590	1251	.472	108	270	.400	479	550	.871	48	262	310	299	182	0	178	213	39	1767	3.9	3.7	22.1
91-92—Philadelphia	81	81	3013	521	1127	.462	91	229	.397	403	461	.874	53	218	271	248	174	0	157	189	43	1536	3.3	3.1	19.0
92-93—Philadelphia	81	81	2977	551	1172	.470	122	307	.397	419	487	.860	91	255	346	317	189	0	137	180	30	1643	4.3	3.9	20.3
93-94—Charlotte	82	82	2648	395	859	.460	78	235	.332	312	362	.862	89	288	377	216	167	2	135	158	22	1180	4.6	2.6	14.4
REG. SEASON TOTALS	485	485	17181	3021	6516	.464	554	1407	.394	2241	2586	.867	417	1416	1833	1580	1113	4	857	1083	199	8837	3.8	3.3	18.2
PLAYOFF TOTALS	21	21	816	131	288	.455	28	67	.418	120	128	.938	17	65	82	67	60	1	35	50	18	410	3.9	3.2	19.5
ALL-STAR TOTALS	1	0	14	3	5	.600	0	1	.000	0	0	—	0	0	0	1	1	0	0	1	0	6	0.0	1.0	6.0

HAWKINS, JAMES MARSHALL (Marshall) b. August 3, 1924 Ht. 6-3 Wt. 210 College—Tennessee

SEASON—TEAM	G	GS	MIN	FGM	FGA	PCT	3FGM	3FGA	PCT	FTM	FTA	PCT	O-RB	D-RB	TOT	AST	PF	DQ	STL	TO	BLK	PTS	RPG	APG	PPG
48-49—Oshkosh (N)	64	—	—	200	—	—	—	—	—	116	160	.725	—	—	—	—	149	—	—	—	—	516	—	—	8.1
49-50—Indianapolis	39	—	—	55	195	.282	—	—	—	42	61	.689	—	—	—	—	51	87	—	—	—	152	—	1.3	3.9
REG. NBA TOTALS	39	—	—	55	195	.282	—	—	—	42	61	.689	—	—	—	—	51	87	—	—	—	152	—	1.3	3.9
REG. NBL TOTALS	64	—	—	200	—	—	—	—	—	116	160	.725	—	—	—	—	149	—	—	—	—	516	—	—	8.1
NBA PLAYOFF TOTALS	2	—	—	0	1	.000	—	—	—	0	0	—	—	—	—	—	1	—	—	—	—	0	0.0	0.0	0.0
NBL PLAYOFF TOTALS	7	—	—	25	—	—	—	—	—	20	27	.741	—	—	—	—	28	—	—	—	—	70	—	—	10.0

HAWKINS, ROBERT (Bubbles) b. June 30, 1954 d. November 28, 1993 Ht. 6-4 Wt. 190 College—Illinois State

SEASON—TEAM	G	GS	MIN	FGM	FGA	PCT	3FGM	3FGA	PCT	FTM	FTA	PCT	O-RB	D-RB	TOT	AST	PF	DQ	STL	TO	BLK	PTS	RPG	APG	PPG
75-76—Golden State	32	—	153	53	104	.510	—	—	—	20	31	.645	16	14	30	16	31	0	10	—	8	126	0.9	0.5	3.9
76-77—New York Nets	52	—	1481	406	909	.447	—	—	—	194	282	.688	67	87	154	93	163	2	77	—	26	1006	3.0	1.8	19.3
77-78—New Jersey	15	—	343	69	150	.460	—	—	—	25	29	.862	21	29	50	37	51	1	22	43	13	163	3.3	2.5	10.9
78-79—Detroit	4	—	28	6	16	.375	—	—	—	6	6	1.000	3	3	6	4	7	0	5	2	0	18	1.5	1.0	4.5
REG. SEASON TOTALS	103	—	2005	534	1179	.453	—	—	—	245	348	.704	107	133	240	150	252	3	114	45	47	1313	2.3	1.5	12.7
PLAYOFF TOTALS	5	—	12	4	5	.800	—	—	—	2	2	1.000	0	0	0	2	6	0	1	—	0	10	0.0	0.4	2.0

HAWKINS, THOMAS JEROME (Tom, Hawk) b. December 22, 1936 Ht. 6-5 Wt. 210 College—Notre Dame

SEASON—TEAM	G	GS	MIN	FGM	FGA	PCT	3FGM	3FGA	PCT	FTM	FTA	PCT	O-RB	D-RB	TOT	AST	PF	DQ	STL	TO	BLK	PTS	RPG	APG	PPG
59-60—Minneapolis	69	—	1467	220	579	.380	—	—	—	106	164	.646	—	—	428	54	188	3	—	—	—	546	6.2	0.8	7.9
60-61—Los Angeles	78	—	1846	310	719	.431	—	—	—	140	235	.596	—	—	479	88	209	2	—	—	—	760	6.1	1.1	9.7
61-62—Los Angeles	79	—	1903	289	704	.411	—	—	—	143	222	.644	—	—	514	95	244	7	—	—	—	721	6.5	1.2	9.1
62-63—Cincinnati	79	—	1721	299	635	.471	—	—	—	147	241	.610	—	—	543	100	197	2	—	—	—	745	6.9	1.3	9.4
63-64—Cincinnati	73	—	1770	256	580	.441	—	—	—	113	188	.601	—	—	435	74	198	4	—	—	—	625	6.0	1.0	8.6
64-65—Cincinnati	79	—	1864	220	538	.409	—	—	—	116	204	.569	—	—	475	80	240	4	—	—	—	556	6.0	1.0	7.0
65-66—Cincinnati	79	—	2126	273	604	.452	—	—	—	116	209	.555	—	—	575	99	274	4	—	—	—	662	7.3	1.3	8.4
66-67—Los Angeles	76	—	1798	275	572	.481	—	—	—	82	173	.474	—	—	434	83	207	1	—	—	—	632	5.7	1.1	8.3
67-68—Los Angeles	78	—	2463	389	779	.499	—	—	—	125	229	.546	—	—	458	117	289	7	—	—	—	903	5.9	1.5	11.6
68-69—Los Angeles	74	—	1507	230	461	.499	—	—	—	62	151	.411	—	—	266	81	168	1	—	—	—	522	3.6	1.1	7.1
REG. SEASON TOTALS	764	—	18465	2761	6171	.447	—	—	—	1150	2016	.570	—	—	4607	871	2214	35	—	—	—	6672	6.0	1.1	8.7
PLAYOFF TOTALS	96	—	2099	311	677	.459	—	—	—	145	235	.617	—	—	537	106	310	8	—	—	—	767	5.6	1.1	8.0

HAWTHORNE, NATE b. January 15, 1950 Ht. 6-4 Wt. 190 College—Southern Illinois

SEASON—TEAM	G	GS	MIN	FGM	FGA	PCT	3FGM	3FGA	PCT	FTM	FTA	PCT	O-RB	D-RB	TOT	AST	PF	DQ	STL	TO	BLK	PTS	RPG	APG	PPG
73-74—Los Angeles	33	—	229	38	93	.409	—	—	—	30	48	.625	16	16	32	23	33	1	9	—	6	106	1.0	0.7	3.2
74-75—Phoenix	50	—	618	118	287	.411	—	—	—	61	94	.649	34	58	92	39	94	0	30	—	21	297	1.8	0.8	5.9
75-76—Phoenix	79	—	1144	182	423	.430	—	—	—	115	170	.676	86	123	209	46	147	0	33	—	15	479	2.6	0.6	6.1
REG. SEASON TOTALS	162	—	1991	338	803	.421	—	—	—	206	312	.660	136	197	333	108	274	1	72	—	42	882	2.1	0.7	5.4
PLAYOFF TOTALS	18	—	95	10	33	.303	—	—	—	12	16	.750	7	11	18	6	20	0	6	—	2	32	1.0	0.3	1.8

HAYES, ELVIN ERNEST (Big E.) b. November 17, 1945 Ht. 6-9 Wt. 235 College—Houston

SEASON—TEAM	G	GS	MIN	FGM	FGA	PCT	3FGM	3FGA	PCT	FTM	FTA	PCT	O-RB	D-RB	TOT	AST	PF	DQ	STL	TO	BLK	PTS	RPG	APG	PPG
68-69—San Diego	82	—	3695	930	2082	.447	—	—	—	467	746	.626	—	—	1406	113	266	2	—	—	—	2327	17.1	1.4	28.4
69-70—San Diego	82	—	3665	914	2020	.452	—	—	—	428	622	.688	—	—	1386	162	270	5	—	—	—	2256	16.9	2.0	27.5
70-71—San Diego	82	—	3633	948	2215	.428	—	—	—	454	676	.672	—	—	1362	186	225	1	—	—	—	2350	16.6	2.3	28.7
71-72—Houston	82	—	3461	832	1918	.434	—	—	—	399	615	.649	—	—	1197	270	233	1	—	—	—	2063	14.6	3.3	25.2
72-73—Baltimore	81	—	3347	713	1607	.444	—	—	—	291	434	.671	—	—	1177	127	232	3	—	—	—	1717	14.5	1.6	21.2
73-74—Capital	81	—	3602	689	1627	.423	—	—	—	357	495	.721	354	1109	1463	163	252	1	86	—	240	1735	18.1	2.0	21.4
74-75—Washington	82	—	3465	739	1668	.443	—	—	—	409	534	.766	221	783	1004	206	238	0	158	—	187	1887	12.2	2.5	23.0
75-76—Washington	80	—	2975	649	1381	.470	—	—	—	287	457	.628	210	668	878	121	293	5	104	—	202	1585	11.0	1.5	19.8
76-77—Washington	82	—	3364	760	1516	.501	—	—	—	422	614	.687	289	740	1029	158	312	1	87	—	220	1942	12.5	1.9	23.7
77-78—Washington	81	—	3246	636	1409	.451	—	—	—	326	514	.634	335	740	1075	149	313	7	96	229	159	1598	13.3	1.8	19.7
78-79—Washington	82	—	3105	720	1477	.487	—	—	—	349	534	.654	312	682	994	143	308	5	75	235	190	1789	12.1	1.7	21.8
79-80—Washington	81	—	3183	761	1677	.454	3	13	.231	334	478	.699	269	627	896	129	309	9	62	215	189	1859	11.1	1.6	23.0
80-81—Washington	81	—	2931	584	1296	.451	0	10	.000	271	439	.617	235	554	789	98	300	6	68	189	171	1439	9.7	1.2	17.8
81-82—Houston	82	82	3032	519	1100	.472	0	5	.000	280	422	.664	267	480	747	144	287	4	62	208	104	1318	9.1	1.8	16.1
82-83—Houston	81	43	2302	424	890	.476	2	4	.500	196	287	.683	199	417	616	158	232	2	50	200	81	1046	7.6	2.0	12.9
83-84—Houston	81	4	994	158	389	.406	0	2	.000	86	132	.652	87	173	260	71	123	1	16	82	28	402	3.2	0.9	5.0
REG. SEASON TOTALS	1303	129	50000	10976	24272	.452	5	34	.147	5356	7999	.670	2778	6973	16279	2398	4193	53	864	1358	1771	27313	12.5	1.8	21.0
PLAYOFF TOTALS	96	3	4160	883	1901	.464	0	0	—	428	656	.652	336	768	1244	185	378	8	97	124	222	2194	13.0	1.9	22.9
ALL-STAR TOTALS	12	4	264	52	129	.403	0	0	—	22	34	.647	16	38	92	17	37	0	5	5	6	126	7.7	1.4	10.5

HAYES, JIM b. February 18, 1948 Ht. 6-3 Wt. 200 College—Boston

SEASON—TEAM	G	GS	MIN	FGM	FGA	PCT	3FGM	3FGA	PCT	FTM	FTA	PCT	O-RB	D-RB	TOT	AST	PF	DQ	STL	TO	BLK	PTS	RPG	APG	PPG
70-71—New York (A)	47	—	494	46	109	.422	0	0	—	52	67	.776	—	—	45	47	73	—	—	—	—	144	1.0	1.0	3.1
REG. ABA TOTALS	47	—	494	46	109	.422	0	0	—	52	67	.776	—	—	45	47	73	—	—	—	—	144	1.0	1.0	3.1

HAYES, STEVEN LEONARD (Steve) b. August 2, 1955 Ht. 7-0 Wt. 205 College—Idaho State

SEASON—TEAM	G	GS	MIN	FGM	FGA	PCT	3FGM	3FGA	PCT	FTM	FTA	PCT	O-RB	D-RB	TOT	AST	PF	DQ	STL	TO	BLK	PTS	RPG	APG	PPG
81-82—S.A.-Detroit	35	0	487	54	111	.486	0	0	—	32	53	.604	39	78	117	28	71	0	4	19	20	140	3.3	0.8	4.0
82-83—Cleveland	65	3	1058	104	217	.479	0	1	.000	29	51	.569	102	134	236	36	215	9	17	49	41	237	3.6	0.6	3.6
83-84—Seattle	43	0	253	26	50	.520	0	0	—	5	14	.357	19	43	62	13	52	0	5	13	18	57	1.4	0.3	1.3
84-85—Philadelphia	11	0	101	10	18	.556	0	0	—	2	4	.500	11	23	34	1	19	0	1	2	4	22	3.1	0.1	2.0
85-86—Utah	58	0	397	39	87	.448	0	0	—	11	36	.306	32	45	77	7	81	0	5	16	19	89	1.3	0.1	1.5
REG. SEASON TOTALS	212	3	2296	233	483	.482	0	1	.000	79	158	.500	203	323	526	85	438	9	32	99	102	545	2.5	0.4	2.6
PLAYOFF TOTALS	1	0	1	1	1	1.000	0	0	—	0	0	—	0	1	1	—	0	0	0	0	0	2	1.0	0.0	2.0

HAYWOOD, SPENCER b. April 22, 1949 Ht. 6-8 Wt. 225 College—Trinidad State JC/Detroit

SEASON—TEAM	G	GS	MIN	FGM	FGA	PCT	3FGM	3FGA	PCT	FTM	FTA	PCT	O-RB	D-RB	TOT	AST	PF	DQ	STL	TO	BLK	PTS	RPG	APG	PPG
69-70—Denver (A)	84	—	3808	986	1998	.493	0	11	.000	547	705	.776	533	1104	1637	190	221	1	—	—	—	2519	19.5	2.3	30.0
70-71—Seattle	33	—	1162	260	579	.449	—	—	—	160	218	.734	—	—	396	48	84	1	—	—	—	680	12.0	1.5	20.6
71-72—Seattle	73	—	3167	717	1557	.461	—	—	—	480	586	.819	—	—	926	148	208	0	—	—	—	1914	12.7	2.0	26.2
72-73—Seattle	77	—	3259	889	1868	.476	—	—	—	473	564	.839	—	—	995	196	213	2	—	—	—	2251	12.9	2.5	29.2
73-74—Seattle	75	—	3039	694	1520	.457	—	—	—	373	458	.814	318	689	1007	240	198	2	65	—	106	1761	13.4	3.2	23.5
74-75—Seattle	68	—	2529	608	1325	.459	—	—	—	309	381	.811	198	432	630	137	173	1	54	—	108	1525	9.3	2.0	22.4
75-76—New York	78	—	2892	605	1360	.445	—	—	—	339	448	.757	234	644	878	92	255	1	53	—	80	1549	11.3	1.2	19.9
76-77—New York Knicks	31	—	1021	202	449	.450	—	—	—	109	131	.832	77	203	280	50	72	0	14	—	29	513	9.0	1.6	16.5
77-78—New York	67	—	1765	412	852	.484	—	—	—	96	135	.711	141	301	442	126	188	1	37	140	72	920	6.6	1.9	13.7
78-79—N.Y.-N.O.	68	—	2361	595	1205	.494	—	—	—	231	292	.791	172	361	533	127	236	8	40	200	82	1421	7.8	1.9	20.9
79-80—Los Angeles	76	—	1544	288	591	.487	1	4	.250	159	206	.772	132	214	346	93	197	2	35	134	57	736	4.6	1.2	9.7
81-82—Washington	76	63	2086	395	829	.476	0	3	.000	219	260	.842	144	278	422	64	249	6	45	175	68	1009	5.6	0.8	13.3
82-83—Washington	38	25	775	125	312	.401	0	1	.000	63	87	.724	77	106	183	30	94	2	12	67	27	313	4.8	0.8	8.2
REG. NBA TOTALS	760	88	25600	5790	12447	.465	1	8	.125	3011	3766	.800	1493	3228	7038	1351	2167	26	355	716	629	14592	9.3	1.8	19.2
REG. ABA TOTALS	84	—	3808	986	1998	.493	0	11	.000	547	705	.776	533	1104	1637	190	221	1	—	—	—	2519	19.5	2.3	30.0
NBA PLAYOFF TOTALS	33	7	890	172	384	.448	0	1	.000	97	123	.789	69	119	188	41	98	2	13	45	36	441	5.7	1.2	13.4
ABA PLAYOFF TOTALS	12	—	568	185	362	.511	1	5	.200	69	83	.831	79	158	237	39	31	0	—	—	—	440	19.8	3.3	36.7
NBA ALL-STAR TOTALS	4	3	97	20	46	.435	—	—	—	8	9	.889	3	11	31	6	13	0	0	—	3	48	7.8	1.5	12.0
ABA ALL-STAR TOTALS	1	1	39	10	19	.526	0	0	—	3	4	.750	—	—	19	2	4	0	—	—	—	23	19.0	2.0	23.0

HAZEN, JOHN W. b. March 2, 1927   Ht. 6-2 Wt. 175 College—Indiana State

SEASON—TEAM	G	GS	MIN	FGM	FGA	PCT	3FGM	3FGA	PCT	FTM	FTA	PCT	O-RB	D-RB	TOT	AST	PF	DQ	STL	TO	BLK	PTS	RPG	APG	PPG
48-49—Boston	6	—	—	6	17	.353	—	—	—	6	7	.857	—	—	—	3	10	—	—	—	—	18	—	0.5	3.0
REG. SEASON TOTALS	6	—	—	6	17	.353	—	—	—	6	7	.857	—	—	—	3	10	—	—	—	—	18	—	0.5	3.0

HAZZARD, WALTER RAPHAEL JR. (**Walt, formerly Mahdi Abdul-Rahman**) b. April 15, 1942   Ht. 6-2 Wt. 190 College—UCLA

SEASON—TEAM	G	GS	MIN	FGM	FGA	PCT	3FGM	3FGA	PCT	FTM	FTA	PCT	O-RB	D-RB	TOT	AST	PF	DQ	STL	TO	BLK	PTS	RPG	APG	PPG
64-65—Los Angeles	66	—	919	117	306	.382	—	—	—	46	71	.648	—	—	111	140	132	0	—	—	—	280	1.7	2.1	4.2
65-66—Los Angeles	80	—	2198	458	1003	.457	—	—	—	182	257	.708	—	—	219	393	224	0	—	—	—	1098	2.7	4.9	13.7
66-67—Los Angeles	79	—	1642	301	706	.426	—	—	—	129	177	.729	—	—	231	323	203	1	—	—	—	731	2.9	4.1	9.3
67-68—Seattle	79	—	2666	733	1662	.441	—	—	—	428	553	.774	—	—	332	493	246	3	—	—	—	1894	4.2	6.2	24.0
68-69—Atlanta	80	—	2420	345	869	.397	—	—	—	208	294	.707	—	—	266	474	264	6	—	—	—	898	3.3	5.9	11.2
69-70—Atlanta	82	—	2757	493	1056	.467	—	—	—	267	330	.809	—	—	329	561	264	3	—	—	—	1253	4.0	6.8	15.3
70-71—Atlanta	82	—	2877	517	1126	.459	—	—	—	315	415	.759	—	—	300	514	276	2	—	—	—	1349	3.7	6.3	16.5
71-72—Buffalo	72	—	2389	450	998	.451	—	—	—	237	303	.782	—	—	213	406	230	2	—	—	—	1137	3.0	5.6	15.8
72-73—Buffalo-G.S.	55	—	763	107	256	.418	—	—	—	47	57	.825	—	—	88	129	110	1	—	—	—	261	1.6	2.3	4.7
73-74—Seattle	49	—	571	76	180	.422	—	—	—	34	45	.756	18	39	57	122	78	0	26	—	6	186	1.2	2.5	3.8
REG. SEASON TOTALS	724	—	19202	3597	8162	.441	—	—	—	1893	2502	.757	18	39	2146	3555	2027	18	26	—	6	9087	3.0	4.9	12.6
PLAYOFF TOTALS	58	—	1576	268	649	.413	—	—	—	149	202	.738	0	0	169	242	176	1	0	—	0	685	2.9	4.2	11.8
ALL-STAR TOTALS	1	—	20	4	12	.333	—	—	—	1	1	1.000	0	0	3	3	3	0	0	—	0	9	3.0	3.0	9.0

HEANEY, BRIAN PATRICK b. September 3, 1946   Ht. 6-2 Wt. 180 College—Acadia

SEASON—TEAM	G	GS	MIN	FGM	FGA	PCT	3FGM	3FGA	PCT	FTM	FTA	PCT	O-RB	D-RB	TOT	AST	PF	DQ	STL	TO	BLK	PTS	RPG	APG	PPG
69-70—Baltimore	14	—	70	13	24	.542	—	—	—	2	4	.500	—	—	4	6	17	0	—	—	—	28	0.3	0.4	2.0
REG. SEASON TOTALS	14	—	70	13	24	.542	—	—	—	2	4	.500	—	—	4	6	17	0	—	—	—	28	0.3	0.4	2.0
PLAYOFF TOTALS	6	—	7	0	2	.000	—	—	—	0	0	—	—	—	1	1	0	0	—	—	—	0	0.2	0.2	0.0

HEARD, GARFIELD b. May 3, 1948   Ht. 6-7 Wt. 220 College—Oklahoma

SEASON—TEAM	G	GS	MIN	FGM	FGA	PCT	3FGM	3FGA	PCT	FTM	FTA	PCT	O-RB	D-RB	TOT	AST	PF	DQ	STL	TO	BLK	PTS	RPG	APG	PPG
70-71—Seattle	65	—	1027	152	399	.381	—	—	—	82	125	.656	—	—	328	45	126	0	—	—	—	386	5.0	0.7	5.9
71-72—Seattle	58	—	1499	190	474	.401	—	—	—	79	128	.617	—	—	442	55	126	2	—	—	—	459	7.6	0.9	7.9
72-73—Seattle-Chicago	81	—	1552	350	824	.425	—	—	—	116	178	.652	—	—	453	60	171	1	—	—	—	816	5.6	0.7	10.1
73-74—Buffalo	81	—	2889	524	1205	.435	—	—	—	191	294	.650	270	677	947	180	300	3	136	—	230	1239	11.7	2.2	15.3
74-75—Buffalo	67	—	2148	318	819	.388	—	—	—	106	188	.564	185	481	666	190	242	2	106	—	120	742	9.9	2.8	11.1
75-76—Buffalo-Phoenix	86	—	2747	392	901	.435	—	—	—	158	248	.637	247	622	869	190	303	2	117	—	96	942	10.1	2.2	11.0
76-77—Phoenix	46	—	1363	173	457	.379	—	—	—	100	138	.725	120	320	440	89	139	2	55	—	55	446	9.6	1.9	9.7
77-78—Phoenix	80	—	2099	265	625	.424	—	—	—	90	147	.612	166	486	652	132	213	0	129	120	101	620	8.2	1.7	7.8
78-79—Phoenix	63	—	1213	162	367	.441	—	—	—	71	103	.689	98	253	351	60	141	1	53	60	57	395	5.6	1.0	6.3
79-80—Phoenix	82	—	1403	171	410	.417	0	2	.000	64	86	.744	118	262	380	97	177	0	84	88	49	406	4.6	1.2	5.0
80-81—San Diego	78	—	1631	149	396	.376	0	7	.000	79	101	.782	120	228	348	122	196	0	104	81	72	377	4.5	1.6	4.8
REG. SEASON TOTALS	787	—	19571	2846	6877	.414	0	9	.000	1136	1736	.654	1324	3329	5876	1220	2134	13	784	349	780	6828	7.5	1.6	8.7
PLAYOFF TOTALS	59	—	1825	247	589	.419	0	0	—	108	166	.651	146	388	537	96	174	0	80	31	98	602	9.1	1.6	10.2

HEDDERICK, HERMAN ARTHUR (**Herm**) b. January 1, 1930   Ht. 6-5 Wt. 170 College—Canisius

SEASON—TEAM	G	GS	MIN	FGM	FGA	PCT	3FGM	3FGA	PCT	FTM	FTA	PCT	O-RB	D-RB	TOT	AST	PF	DQ	STL	TO	BLK	PTS	RPG	APG	PPG
54-55—New York	5	—	23	2	9	.222	—	—	—	0	1	.000	—	—	4	2	3	0	—	—	—	4	0.8	0.4	0.8
REG. SEASON TOTALS	5	—	23	2	9	.222	—	—	—	0	1	.000	—	—	4	2	3	0	—	—	—	4	0.8	0.4	0.8

HEINSOHN, THOMAS WILLIAM (**Tom, Ack-Ack**) b. August 26, 1934   Ht. 6-7 Wt. 220 College—Holy Cross

SEASON—TEAM	G	GS	MIN	FGM	FGA	PCT	3FGM	3FGA	PCT	FTM	FTA	PCT	O-RB	D-RB	TOT	AST	PF	DQ	STL	TO	BLK	PTS	RPG	APG	PPG
56-57—Boston	72	—	2150	446	1123	.397	—	—	—	271	343	.790	—	—	705	117	304	12	—	—	—	1163	9.8	1.6	16.2
57-58—Boston	69	—	2206	468	1226	.382	—	—	—	294	394	.746	—	—	705	125	274	6	—	—	—	1230	10.2	1.8	17.8
58-59—Boston	66	—	2089	465	1192	.390	—	—	—	312	391	.798	—	—	638	164	271	11	—	—	—	1242	9.7	2.5	18.8
59-60—Boston	75	—	2420	673	1590	.423	—	—	—	283	386	.733	—	—	794	171	275	8	—	—	—	1629	10.6	2.3	21.7
60-61—Boston	74	—	2256	627	1566	.400	—	—	—	325	424	.767	—	—	732	141	260	7	—	—	—	1579	9.9	1.9	21.3
61-62—Boston	79	—	2383	692	1613	.429	—	—	—	358	437	.819	—	—	747	165	280	2	—	—	—	1742	9.5	2.1	22.1
62-63—Boston	76	—	2004	550	1300	.423	—	—	—	340	407	.835	—	—	569	95	270	4	—	—	—	1440	7.5	1.3	18.9
63-64—Boston	76	—	2040	487	1223	.398	—	—	—	283	342	.827	—	—	460	183	268	3	—	—	—	1257	6.1	2.4	16.5
64-65—Boston	67	—	1706	365	954	.383	—	—	—	182	229	.795	—	—	399	157	252	5	—	—	—	912	6.0	2.3	13.6
REG. SEASON TOTALS	654	—	19254	4773	11787	.405	—	—	—	2648	3353	.790	—	—	5749	1318	2454	58	—	—	—	12194	8.8	2.0	18.6
PLAYOFF TOTALS	104	—	3223	818	2035	.402	—	—	—	422	568	.743	—	—	954	215	417	14	—	—	—	2058	9.2	2.1	19.8
ALL-STAR TOTALS	5	—	97	22	67	.328	—	—	—	7	8	.875	—	—	20	3	20	—	—	—	—	51	4.0	0.6	10.2

HEMRIC, NED DIXON (Dick) b. August 29, 1933 Ht. 6-6 Wt. 220 College—Wake Forest

SEASON—TEAM	G	GS	MIN	FGM	FGA	PCT	3FGM	3FGA	PCT	FTM	FTA	PCT	O-RB	D-RB	TOT	AST	PF	DQ	STL	TO	BLK	PTS	RPG	APG	PPG
55-56—Boston	71	—	1329	161	400	.403	—	—	—	177	273	.648	—	—	399	60	142	2	—	—	—	499	5.6	0.8	7.0
56-57—Boston	67	—	1055	109	317	.344	—	—	—	146	210	.695	—	—	304	42	98	0	—	—	—	364	4.5	0.6	5.4
REG. SEASON TOTALS	138	—	2384	270	717	.377	—	—	—	323	483	.669	—	—	703	102	240	2	—	—	—	863	5.1	0.7	6.3
PLAYOFF TOTALS	5	—	73	6	31	.194	—	—	—	9	16	.563	—	—	31	2	8	0	—	—	—	21	6.2	0.4	4.2

HENDERSON, CEDRIC b. October 3, 1965 Ht. 6-8 Wt. 210 College—Georgia

SEASON—TEAM	G	GS	MIN	FGM	FGA	PCT	3FGM	3FGA	PCT	FTM	FTA	PCT	O-RB	D-RB	TOT	AST	PF	DQ	STL	TO	BLK	PTS	RPG	APG	PPG
86-87—Atlanta-Milw.	8	0	16	4	8	.500	0	0	—	3	3	1.000	3	5	8	0	2	0	0	4	0	11	1.0	0.0	1.4
REG. SEASON TOTALS	8	0	16	4	8	.500	0	0	—	3	3	1.000	3	5	8	0	2	0	0	4	0	11	1.0	0.0	1.4

HENDERSON, DAVID McKINLEY (Dave) b. July 21, 1964 Ht. 6-5 Wt. 195 College—Duke

SEASON—TEAM	G	GS	MIN	FGM	FGA	PCT	3FGM	3FGA	PCT	FTM	FTA	PCT	O-RB	D-RB	TOT	AST	PF	DQ	STL	TO	BLK	PTS	RPG	APG	PPG
87-88—Philadelphia	22	1	351	47	116	.405	0	1	.000	32	47	.681	11	24	35	34	41	0	12	40	5	126	1.6	1.5	5.7
REG. SEASON TOTALS	22	1	351	47	116	.405	0	1	.000	32	47	.681	11	24	35	34	41	0	12	40	5	126	1.6	1.5	5.7

HENDERSON, JEROME D. b. October 5, 1959 Ht. 6-11 Wt. 230 College—Wabash Valley/New Mexico

SEASON—TEAM	G	GS	MIN	FGM	FGA	PCT	3FGM	3FGA	PCT	FTM	FTA	PCT	O-RB	D-RB	TOT	AST	PF	DQ	STL	TO	BLK	PTS	RPG	APG	PPG
85-86—L.A. Lakers	1	0	3	2	3	.667	0	0	—	0	0	—	0	1	1	0	1	0	0	0	0	4	1.0	0.0	4.0
86-87—Milwaukee	6	0	36	4	13	.308	0	0	—	4	4	1.000	2	5	7	0	12	0	1	6	1	12	1.2	0.0	2.0
REG. SEASON TOTALS	7	0	39	6	16	.375	0	0	—	4	4	1.000	2	6	8	0	13	0	1	6	1	16	1.1	0.0	2.3
PLAYOFF TOTALS	1	0	1	0	0	—	0	0	—	0	0	—	0	0	0	—	1	0	0	0	0	0	0.0	0.0	0.0

HENDERSON, JEROME McKINLEY (Gerald) b. January 16, 1956 Ht. 6-2 Wt. 175 College—Virginia Commonwealth

SEASON—TEAM	G	GS	MIN	FGM	FGA	PCT	3FGM	3FGA	PCT	FTM	FTA	PCT	O-RB	D-RB	TOT	AST	PF	DQ	STL	TO	BLK	PTS	RPG	APG	PPG
79-80—Boston	76	—	1061	191	382	.500	2	6	.333	89	129	.690	37	46	83	147	96	0	45	109	15	473	1.1	1.9	6.2
80-81—Boston	82	—	1608	261	579	.451	1	16	.063	113	157	.720	43	89	132	213	177	0	79	160	12	636	1.6	2.6	7.8
81-82—Boston	82	31	1844	353	705	.501	2	12	.167	125	172	.727	47	105	152	252	199	3	82	150	11	833	1.9	3.1	10.2
82-83—Boston	82	9	1551	286	618	.463	3	16	.188	96	133	.722	57	67	124	195	190	6	95	128	3	671	1.5	2.4	8.2
83-84—Boston	78	78	2088	376	718	.524	20	57	.351	136	177	.768	68	79	147	300	209	1	117	161	14	908	1.9	3.8	11.6
84-85—Seattle	79	78	2648	427	891	.479	9	38	.237	199	255	.780	71	119	190	559	196	1	140	231	9	1062	2.4	7.1	13.4
85-86—Seattle	82	82	2568	434	900	.482	18	52	.346	185	223	.830	89	98	187	487	230	2	138	184	12	1071	2.3	5.9	13.1
86-87—Seattle-N.Y.	74	59	2045	298	674	.442	19	77	.247	190	230	.826	50	125	175	471	208	1	101	172	11	805	2.4	6.4	10.9
87-88—N.Y.-Phil.	75	5	1505	194	453	.428	69	163	.423	138	170	.812	27	80	107	231	187	0	69	133	5	595	1.4	3.1	7.9
88-89—Philadelphia	65	0	986	144	348	.414	33	107	.308	104	127	.819	17	51	68	140	121	1	42	73	3	425	1.0	2.2	6.5
89-90—Milw.-Detroit	57	0	464	53	109	.486	17	38	.447	12	15	.800	11	32	43	74	50	0	16	24	2	135	0.8	1.3	2.4
90-91—Detroit	23	10	392	50	117	.427	7	21	.333	16	21	.762	8	29	37	62	43	0	12	28	2	123	1.6	2.7	5.3
91-92—Houston-Detroit	16	0	96	12	32	.375	3	8	.375	9	11	.818	1	7	8	10	12	0	3	8	0	36	0.5	0.6	2.3
REG. SEASON TOTALS	871	352	18856	3079	6526	.472	203	611	.332	1412	1820	.776	526	927	1453	3141	1918	15	939	1561	99	7773	1.7	3.6	8.9
PLAYOFF TOTALS	88	35	1570	259	584	.443	5	32	.156	108	155	.697	63	74	137	229	182	1	78	105	7	631	1.6	2.6	7.2

HENDERSON, KEVIN DWAYNE b. March 22, 1964 Ht. 6-4 Wt. 195 College—Cal State-Fullerton

SEASON—TEAM	G	GS	MIN	FGM	FGA	PCT	3FGM	3FGA	PCT	FTM	FTA	PCT	O-RB	D-RB	TOT	AST	PF	DQ	STL	TO	BLK	PTS	RPG	APG	PPG
86-87—Golden State	5	0	45	3	8	.375	0	0	—	2	2	1.000	1	2	3	11	9	0	1	4	0	8	0.6	2.2	1.6
87-88—G.S.-Clev.	17	2	190	21	53	.396	0	1	.000	15	26	.577	9	12	21	23	26	0	8	17	0	57	1.2	1.4	3.4
REG. SEASON TOTALS	22	2	235	24	61	.393	0	1	.000	17	28	.607	10	14	24	34	35	0	9	21	0	65	1.1	1.5	3.0

HENDERSON, THOMAS EDWARD (Tom) b. January 26, 1952 Ht. 6-3 Wt. 190 College—San Jacinto/Hawaii

SEASON—TEAM	G	GS	MIN	FGM	FGA	PCT	3FGM	3FGA	PCT	FTM	FTA	PCT	O-RB	D-RB	TOT	AST	PF	DQ	STL	TO	BLK	PTS	RPG	APG	PPG
74-75—Atlanta	79	—	2131	367	893	.411	—	—	—	168	241	.697	51	161	212	314	149	0	105	—	7	902	2.7	4.0	11.4
75-76—Atlanta	81	—	2900	469	1136	.413	—	—	—	216	305	.708	58	207	265	374	195	1	137	—	10	1154	3.3	4.6	14.2
76-77—Atlanta-Wash.	87	—	2791	371	826	.449	—	—	—	233	313	.744	43	196	239	598	148	0	138	—	17	975	2.7	6.9	11.2
77-78—Washington	75	—	2315	339	784	.432	—	—	—	179	240	.746	66	127	193	406	131	0	93	195	15	857	2.6	5.4	11.4
78-79—Washington	70	—	2081	299	641	.466	—	—	—	156	195	.800	51	112	163	419	123	0	87	148	10	754	2.3	6.0	10.8
79-80—Houston	66	—	1551	154	323	.477	0	2	.000	56	77	.727	34	77	111	274	107	1	55	102	4	364	1.7	4.2	5.5
80-81—Houston	66	—	1411	137	332	.413	0	3	.000	78	95	.821	30	74	104	307	111	1	53	93	4	352	1.6	4.7	5.3
81-82—Houston	75	23	1721	183	403	.454	0	2	.000	105	150	.700	33	105	138	306	120	0	55	105	2	471	1.8	4.1	6.3
82-83—Houston	51	2	789	107	263	.407	0	2	.000	45	57	.789	18	51	69	138	57	0	37	50	2	259	1.4	2.7	5.1
REG. SEASON TOTALS	650	25	17690	2426	5601	.433	0	9	.000	1236	1673	.739	384	1110	1494	3136	1141	3	760	693	76	6088	2.3	4.8	9.4
PLAYOFF TOTALS	80	3	2364	270	650	.415	0	2	.000	161	214	.752	64	117	181	431	168	2	79	120	18	701	2.3	5.4	8.8

HENNESSY, LAWRENCE E. (Larry) b. May 20, 1929 Ht. 6-3 Wt. 185 College—Villanova

SEASON—TEAM	G	GS	MIN	FGM	FGA	PCT	3FGM	3FGA	PCT	FTM	FTA	PCT	O-RB	D-RB	TOT	AST	PF	DQ	STL	TO	BLK	PTS	RPG	APG	PPG
55-56—Philadelphia	53	—	444	85	247	.344	—	—	—	26	32	.813	—	—	49	46	37	0	—	—	—	196	0.9	0.9	3.7
56-57—Syracuse	21	—	373	56	175	.320	—	—	—	23	32	.719	—	—	45	27	28	0	—	—	—	135	2.1	1.3	6.4
REG. SEASON TOTALS	74	—	817	141	422	.334	—	—	—	49	64	.766	—	—	94	73	65	0	—	—	—	331	1.3	1.0	4.5
PLAYOFF TOTALS	3	—	11	0	9	.000	—	—	—	0	0	—	—	—	1	2	1	0	—	—	—	0	0.3	0.7	0.0

HENRIKSEN, DONALD ANTON (Don) b. October 10, 1929 Ht. 6-7 Wt. 225 College—California

SEASON—TEAM	G	GS	MIN	FGM	FGA	PCT	3FGM	3FGA	PCT	FTM	FTA	PCT	O-RB	D-RB	TOT	AST	PF	DQ	STL	TO	BLK	PTS	RPG	APG	PPG
52-53—Baltimore	68	—	2263	199	475	.419	—	—	—	176	281	.626	—	—	506	129	242	12	—	—	—	574	7.4	1.9	8.4
54-55—Balt.-Roch.	70	—	1664	139	406	.342	—	—	—	137	195	.703	—	—	484	111	190	2	—	—	—	415	6.9	1.6	5.9
REG. SEASON TOTALS	138	—	3927	338	881	.384	—	—	—	313	476	.658	—	—	990	240	432	14	—	—	—	989	7.2	1.7	7.2
PLAYOFF TOTALS	5	—	164	13	27	.481	—	—	—	12	19	.632	—	—	40	11	16	1	—	—	—	38	8.0	2.2	7.6

HENRY, ALBERT J. JR. (Al, The Tree) b. February 9, 1949 Ht. 6-9 Wt. 190 College—Wisconsin

SEASON—TEAM	G	GS	MIN	FGM	FGA	PCT	3FGM	3FGA	PCT	FTM	FTA	PCT	O-RB	D-RB	TOT	AST	PF	DQ	STL	TO	BLK	PTS	RPG	APG	PPG
70-71—Philadelphia	6	—	26	1	6	.167	—	—	—	5	7	.714	—	—	11	0	1	0	—	—	—	7	1.8	0.0	1.2
71-72—Philadelphia	43	—	421	68	156	.436	—	—	—	51	73	.699	—	—	137	8	42	0	—	—	—	187	3.2	0.2	4.3
REG. SEASON TOTALS	49	—	447	69	162	.426	—	—	—	56	80	.700	—	—	148	8	43	0	—	—	—	194	3.0	0.2	4.0

HENRY, CARL J. b. August 16, 1960 Ht. 6-6 Wt. 205 College—Oklahoma City/Kansas

SEASON—TEAM	G	GS	MIN	FGM	FGA	PCT	3FGM	3FGA	PCT	FTM	FTA	PCT	O-RB	D-RB	TOT	AST	PF	DQ	STL	TO	BLK	PTS	RPG	APG	PPG
85-86—Sacramento	28	0	149	31	67	.463	4	10	.400	12	17	.706	8	11	19	4	11	0	5	9	0	78	0.7	0.1	2.8
REG. SEASON TOTALS	28	0	149	31	67	.463	4	10	.400	12	17	.706	8	11	19	4	11	0	5	9	0	78	0.7	0.1	2.8
PLAYOFF TOTALS	1	0	2	1	1	1.000	1	1	1.000	0	0	—	0	0	0	—	0	0	0	0	0	3	0.0	0.0	3.0

HENRY, CONNER b. July 21, 1963 Ht. 6-7 Wt. 195 College—Cal-Santa Barbara

SEASON—TEAM	G	GS	MIN	FGM	FGA	PCT	3FGM	3FGA	PCT	FTM	FTA	PCT	O-RB	D-RB	TOT	AST	PF	DQ	STL	TO	BLK	PTS	RPG	APG	PPG
86-87—Houston-Boston	54	0	323	46	136	.338	13	42	.310	17	27	.630	7	27	34	35	34	0	9	26	1	122	0.6	0.6	2.3
87-88—Boston-Milw.-Sac.	39	2	433	62	150	.413	20	45	.444	39	47	.830	13	36	49	67	37	0	12	39	5	183	1.3	1.7	4.7
REG. SEASON TOTALS	93	2	756	108	286	.378	33	87	.379	56	74	.757	20	63	83	102	71	0	21	65	6	305	0.9	1.1	3.3
PLAYOFF TOTALS	11	0	35	8	16	.500	1	5	.200	5	10	.500	3	3	6	—	3	0	0	4	0	22	0.5	0.0	2.0

HENRY, HERMAN (Skeeter) b. December 8, 1967 Ht. 6-7 Wt. 190 College—Oklahoma

SEASON—TEAM	G	GS	MIN	FGM	FGA	PCT	3FGM	3FGA	PCT	FTM	FTA	PCT	O-RB	D-RB	TOT	AST	PF	DQ	STL	TO	BLK	PTS	RPG	APG	PPG
93-94—Phoenix	4	0	15	1	5	.200	0	2	.000	2	4	.500	0	2	2	4	1	0	0	1	0	4	0.5	1.0	1.0
REG. SEASON TOTALS	4	0	15	1	5	.200	0	2	.000	2	4	.500	0	2	2	4	1	0	0	1	0	4	0.5	1.0	1.0
PLAYOFF TOTALS	3	0	16	1	6	.167	0	2	.000	0	0	—	1	2	3	3	1	0	0	1	0	2	1.0	1.0	0.7

HENRY, WILLIAM GAMBRELL (Bill, Big Bill) b. December 27, 1924 d. December 1985 Ht. 6-9 Wt. 215 College—Rice

SEASON—TEAM	G	GS	MIN	FGM	FGA	PCT	3FGM	3FGA	PCT	FTM	FTA	PCT	O-RB	D-RB	TOT	AST	PF	DQ	STL	TO	BLK	PTS	RPG	APG	PPG
48-49—Fort Wayne	32	—	—	96	300	.320	—	—	—	125	203	.616	—	—	—	55	110	—	—	—	—	317	—	1.7	9.9
49-50—Ft. Wayne-Tri-Cit	63	—	—	89	278	.320	—	—	—	118	176	.670	—	—	—	48	122	—	—	—	—	296	—	0.8	4.7
REG. SEASON TOTALS	95	—	—	185	578	.320	—	—	—	243	379	.641	—	—	—	103	232	—	—	—	—	613	—	1.1	6.5
PLAYOFF TOTALS	3	—	—	2	17	.118	—	—	—	5	9	.556	—	—	—	5	14	1	—	—	—	9	—	1.7	3.0

HENSON, STEVEN MICHAEL (Steve) b. February 2, 1968 Ht. 6-1 Wt. 180 College—Kansas State

SEASON—TEAM	G	GS	MIN	FGM	FGA	PCT	3FGM	3FGA	PCT	FTM	FTA	PCT	O-RB	D-RB	TOT	AST	PF	DQ	STL	TO	BLK	PTS	RPG	APG	PPG
90-91—Milwaukee	68	0	690	79	189	.418	18	54	.333	38	42	.905	14	37	51	131	83	0	32	43	0	214	0.8	1.9	3.1
91-92—Milwaukee	50	1	386	52	144	.361	23	48	.479	23	29	.793	17	24	41	82	50	0	15	40	1	150	0.8	1.6	3.0
92-93—Atlanta	53	2	719	71	182	.390	37	80	.463	34	40	.850	12	43	55	155	85	0	30	52	1	213	1.0	2.9	4.0
93-94—Charlotte	3	0	17	1	2	.500	1	1	1.000	0	0	—	0	1	1	5	3	0	0	1	0	3	0.3	1.7	1.0
REG. SEASON TOTALS	174	3	1812	203	517	.393	79	183	.432	95	111	.856	43	105	148	373	221	0	77	136	2	580	0.9	2.1	3.3
PLAYOFF TOTALS	6	0	87	9	21	.429	4	8	.500	3	4	.750	1	6	7	8	7	0	5	8	0	25	1.2	1.3	4.2

HENTZ, CHARLES (Charlie, Helicopter) b. September 13, 1947 Ht. 6-6 Wt. 235 College—Arkansas-Pine Bluff

SEASON—TEAM	G	GS	MIN	FGM	FGA	PCT	3FGM	3FGA	PCT	FTM	FTA	PCT	O-RB	D-RB	TOT	AST	PF	DQ	STL	TO	BLK	PTS	RPG	APG	PPG
70-71—Pittsburgh (A)	57	—	1075	142	303	.469	0	4	.000	57	98	.582	—	—	386	31	114	—	—	—	—	341	6.8	0.5	6.0
REG. ABA TOTALS	57	—	1075	142	303	.469	0	4	.000	57	98	.582	—	—	386	31	114	—	—	—	—	341	6.8	0.5	6.0

HERMAN, WILLIAM R. (Bill) b. May 17, 1924 Ht. 6-3 Wt. 170 College—Mount Union

SEASON—TEAM	G	GS	MIN	FGM	FGA	PCT	3FGM	3FGA	PCT	FTM	FTA	PCT	O-RB	D-RB	TOT	AST	PF	DQ	STL	TO	BLK	PTS	RPG	APG	PPG
49-50—Denver	13	—	—	25	65	.385	—	—	—	6	11	.545	—	—	—	15	13	—	—	—	—	56	—	1.2	4.3
REG. SEASON TOTALS	13	—	—	25	65	.385	—	—	—	6	11	.545	—	—	—	15	13	—	—	—	—	56	—	1.2	4.3

HERMSEN, CLARENCE HENRY (Kleggie) b. March 12, 1923 d. March 2, 1994 Ht. 6-8½ Wt. 235 College—Minnesota

SEASON—TEAM	G	GS	MIN	FGM	FGA	PCT	3FGM	3FGA	PCT	FTM	FTA	PCT	O-RB	D-RB	TOT	AST	PF	DQ	STL	TO	BLK	PTS	RPG	APG	PPG
43-44—Sheboygan (N)	12	—	—	3	—	—	—	—	—	5	—	—	—	—	—	—	—	—	—	—	—	11	—	—	0.9
45-46—Sheboygan (N)	21	—	—	19	—	—	—	—	—	17	—	—	—	—	—	—	—	—	—	—	—	55	—	—	2.6
46-47—Clev.-Toronto	32	—	—	113	394	.287	—	—	—	71	112	.634	—	—	—	—	25	86	—	—	—	297	—	0.8	9.3
47-48—Baltimore	48	—	—	212	765	.277	—	—	—	151	227	.665	—	—	—	—	48	154	—	—	—	575	—	1.0	12.0
48-49—Washington	60	—	—	248	794	.312	—	—	—	212	311	.682	—	—	—	—	99	257	—	—	—	708	—	1.7	11.8
49-50—Chicago	67	—	—	196	615	.319	—	—	—	153	247	.619	—	—	—	—	98	267	—	—	—	545	—	1.5	8.1
50-51—Tri-Cit-Boston	71	—	—	189	644	.293	—	—	—	155	237	.654	—	—	448	92	261	8	—	—	—	533	6.3	1.3	7.5
52-53—Boston-Ind.	10	—	62	4	31	.129	—	—	—	3	5	.600	—	—	19	4	18	0	—	—	—	11	1.9	0.4	1.1
REG. NBA TOTALS	288	—	62	962	3243	.297	—	—	—	745	1139	.654	—	—	467	366	1043	8	—	—	—	2669	5.8	1.3	9.3
REG. NBL TOTALS	33	—	—	22	—	—	—	—	—	22	—	—	—	—	—	—	—	—	—	—	—	66	—	—	2.0
NBA PLAYOFF TOTALS	26	—	0	86	330	.261	—	—	—	104	151	.689	—	—	3	29	116	6	—	—	—	276	1.5	1.1	10.6
NBL PLAYOFF TOTALS	5	—	—	4	—	—	—	—	—	5	8	.625	—	—	—	—	5	—	—	—	—	13	—	—	2.6

HERRERA, CARL VICTOR b. December 14, 1966 Ht. 6-9 Wt. 225 College—Jacksonville (Tex.)/Houston

SEASON—TEAM	G	GS	MIN	FGM	FGA	PCT	3FGM	3FGA	PCT	FTM	FTA	PCT	O-RB	D-RB	TOT	AST	PF	DQ	STL	TO	BLK	PTS	RPG	APG	PPG
91-92—Houston	43	7	566	83	161	.516	0	1	.000	25	44	.568	33	66	99	27	60	0	16	37	25	191	2.3	0.6	4.4
92-93—Houston	81	12	1800	240	444	.541	0	2	.000	125	176	.710	148	306	454	61	190	1	47	92	35	605	5.6	0.8	7.5
93-94—Houston	75	0	1292	142	310	.458	0	0	—	69	97	.711	101	184	285	37	159	0	32	69	26	353	3.8	0.5	4.7
REG. SEASON TOTALS	199	19	3658	465	915	.508	0	3	.000	219	317	.691	282	556	838	125	409	1	95	198	86	1149	4.2	0.6	5.8
PLAYOFF TOTALS	28	0	443	53	115	.461	0	2	.000	25	36	.694	30	60	90	10	73	2	8	18	5	131	3.2	0.4	4.7

HERRON, KEITH ORLANDO b. June 14, 1956 Ht. 6-6 Wt. 195 College—Villanova

SEASON—TEAM	G	GS	MIN	FGM	FGA	PCT	3FGM	3FGA	PCT	FTM	FTA	PCT	O-RB	D-RB	TOT	AST	PF	DQ	STL	TO	BLK	PTS	RPG	APG	PPG
78-79—Atlanta	14	—	81	14	48	.292	—	—	—	12	13	.923	4	6	10	3	11	0	6	5	2	40	0.7	0.2	2.9
80-81—Detroit	80	—	2270	432	954	.453	2	11	.182	228	267	.854	98	113	211	148	154	1	91	153	26	1094	2.6	1.9	13.7
81-82—Cleveland	30	0	269	39	106	.368	0	1	.000	7	8	.875	10	11	21	23	25	0	8	12	2	85	0.7	0.8	2.8
REG. SEASON TOTALS	124	0	2620	485	1108	.438	2	12	.167	247	288	.858	112	130	242	174	190	1	105	170	30	1219	2.0	1.4	9.8

HERTZBERG, SIDNEY (Sonny) b. July 29, 1922 Ht. 5-10 Wt. 185 College—CCNY

SEASON—TEAM	G	GS	MIN	FGM	FGA	PCT	3FGM	3FGA	PCT	FTM	FTA	PCT	O-RB	D-RB	TOT	AST	PF	DQ	STL	TO	BLK	PTS	RPG	APG	PPG
46-47—New York	59	—	—	201	695	.289	—	—	—	113	149	.758	—	—	—	37	109	—	—	—	—	515	—	0.6	8.7
47-48—N.Y.-Wash.	41	—	—	110	414	.266	—	—	—	58	73	.795	—	—	—	23	61	—	—	—	—	278	—	0.6	6.8
48-49—Washington	60	—	—	154	541	.285	—	—	—	134	164	.817	—	—	—	114	140	—	—	—	—	442	—	1.9	7.4
49-50—Boston	68	—	—	275	865	.318	—	—	—	143	191	.749	—	—	—	200	153	—	—	—	—	693	—	2.9	10.2
50-51—Boston	65	—	—	206	651	.316	—	—	—	223	270	.826	—	—	260	244	156	4	—	—	—	635	4.0	3.8	9.8
REG. SEASON TOTALS	293	—	—	946	3166	.299	—	—	—	671	847	.792	—	—	260	618	619	4	—	—	—	2563	4.0	2.1	8.7
PLAYOFF TOTALS	18	—	—	57	194	.294	—	—	—	50	60	.833	—	—	2	35	55	1	—	—	—	164	1.0	1.9	9.1

HESTER, DAN W. b. November 8, 1948 Ht. 6-8 Wt. 220 College—Murray State (Okla.)/Louisiana State

SEASON—TEAM	G	GS	MIN	FGM	FGA	PCT	3FGM	3FGA	PCT	FTM	FTA	PCT	O-RB	D-RB	TOT	AST	PF	DQ	STL	TO	BLK	PTS	RPG	APG	PPG
70-71—Denver-Ken. (A)	42	—	555	97	245	.396	5	12	.417	49	60	.817	—	—	234	35	82	—	—	—	—	248	5.6	0.8	5.9
REG. ABA TOTALS	42	—	555	97	245	.396	5	12	.417	49	60	.817	—	—	234	35	82	—	—	—	—	248	5.6	0.8	5.9
ABA PLAYOFF TOTALS	7	—	42	4	14	.286	0	0	—	8	9	.889	—	—	13	1	9	—	—	—	—	16	1.9	0.1	2.3

HETZEL, FRED W. b. July 21, 1942 Ht. 6-8 Wt. 230 College—Davidson

SEASON—TEAM	G	GS	MIN	FGM	FGA	PCT	3FGM	3FGA	PCT	FTM	FTA	PCT	O-RB	D-RB	TOT	AST	PF	DQ	STL	TO	BLK	PTS	RPG	APG	PPG
65-66—San Francisco	56	—	722	160	401	.399	—	—	—	63	92	.685	—	—	290	27	121	2	—	—	—	383	5.2	0.5	6.8
66-67—San Francisco	77	—	2123	373	932	.400	—	—	—	192	237	.810	—	—	639	111	228	3	—	—	—	938	8.3	1.4	12.2
67-68—San Francisco	77	—	2394	533	1287	.414	—	—	—	395	474	.833	—	—	546	131	262	7	—	—	—	1461	7.1	1.7	19.0
68-69—Milw.-Cin.	84	—	2276	456	1047	.436	—	—	—	299	357	.838	—	—	613	112	287	9	—	—	—	1211	7.3	1.3	14.4
69-70—Philadelphia	63	—	757	156	323	.483	—	—	—	71	85	.835	—	—	207	44	110	3	—	—	—	383	3.3	0.7	6.1
70-71—Los Angeles	59	—	613	111	256	.434	—	—	—	60	77	.779	—	—	149	37	99	3	—	—	—	282	2.5	0.6	4.8
REG. SEASON TOTALS	416	—	8885	1789	4246	.421	—	—	—	1080	1322	.817	—	—	2444	462	1107	27	—	—	—	4658	5.9	1.1	11.2
PLAYOFF TOTALS	35	—	742	138	323	.427	—	—	—	83	102	.814	—	—	184	44	95	3	—	—	—	359	5.3	1.3	10.3

HEWITT, WILLIAM SEVERLYN (Bill) b. August 8, 1944 Ht. 6-7 Wt. 210 College—USC

SEASON—TEAM	G	GS	MIN	FGM	FGA	PCT	3FGM	3FGA	PCT	FTM	FTA	PCT	O-RB	D-RB	TOT	AST	PF	DQ	STL	TO	BLK	PTS	RPG	APG	PPG
68-69—Los Angeles	75	—	1455	239	528	.453	—	—	—	61	106	.575	—	—	332	76	139	1	—	—	—	539	4.4	1.0	7.2
69-70—L.A.-Detroit	65	—	1279	110	298	.369	—	—	—	54	94	.574	—	—	354	64	130	1	—	—	—	274	5.4	1.0	4.2
70-71—Detroit	62	—	1725	203	435	.467	—	—	—	69	120	.575	—	—	454	124	189	5	—	—	—	475	7.3	2.0	7.7
71-72—Detroit	68	—	1203	131	277	.473	—	—	—	41	82	.500	—	—	370	71	134	1	—	—	—	303	5.4	1.0	4.5
72-73—Buffalo	73	—	1332	152	364	.418	—	—	—	41	74	.554	—	—	368	110	154	3	—	—	—	345	5.0	1.5	4.7
74-75—Chicago	18	—	467	56	129	.434	—	—	—	14	23	.609	30	86	116	24	46	1	9	—	10	126	6.4	1.3	7.0
REG. SEASON TOTALS	361	—	7461	891	2031	.439	—	—	—	280	499	.561	30	86	1994	469	792	12	9	—	10	2062	5.5	1.3	5.7
PLAYOFF TOTALS	15	—	412	61	151	.404	—	—	—	18	29	.621	0	0	78	17	40	0	—	—	0	140	5.2	1.1	9.3

HEWSON, JOHN G. (**Jack**) b. September 7, 1924   Ht. 6-6 Wt. 195 College—Bucknell/Muhlenberg/Temple

SEASON—TEAM	G	GS	MIN	FGM	FGA	PCT	3FGM	3FGA	PCT	FTM	FTA	PCT	O-RB	D-RB	TOT	AST	PF	DQ	STL	TO	BLK	PTS	RPG	APG	PPG
47-48—Boston	24	—	—	22	89	.247	—	—	—	21	30	.700	—	—	—	1	39	—	—	—	—	65	—	0.0	2.7
REG. SEASON TOTALS	24	—	—	22	89	.247	—	—	—	21	30	.700	—	—	—	1	39	—	—	—	—	65	—	0.0	2.7

HEYMAN, ARTHUR BRUCE (**Art**) b. June 24, 1941   Ht. 6-5 Wt. 205 College—Duke

SEASON—TEAM	G	GS	MIN	FGM	FGA	PCT	3FGM	3FGA	PCT	FTM	FTA	PCT	O-RB	D-RB	TOT	AST	PF	DQ	STL	TO	BLK	PTS	RPG	APG	PPG
63-64—New York	75	—	2236	432	1003	.431	—	—	—	289	422	.685	—	—	298	256	229	2	—	—	—	1153	4.0	3.4	15.4
64-65—New York	55	—	663	114	267	.427	—	—	—	88	132	.667	—	—	99	79	96	0	—	—	—	316	1.8	1.4	5.7
65-66—Cin.-Phil.	17	—	120	18	52	.346	—	—	—	14	22	.636	—	—	17	11	23	0	—	—	—	50	1.0	0.6	2.9
67-68—N.J.-Pitt. (A)	73	—	2555	457	1058	.432	35	134	.261	400	547	.731	—	—	496	276	188	0	—	239	—	1349	6.8	3.8	18.5
68-69—Minnesota (A)	71	—	2362	350	832	.421	37	118	.314	285	409	.697	—	—	494	217	195	2	—	163	—	1022	7.0	3.1	14.4
69-70—Pitt.-Miami (A)	19	—	310	47	106	.443	0	4	.000	46	65	.708	—	—	57	20	32	1	—	—	—	140	3.0	1.1	7.4
REG. NBA TOTALS	147	—	3019	564	1322	.427	—	—	—	391	576	.679	—	—	414	346	348	2	—	—	—	1519	2.8	2.4	10.3
REG. ABA TOTALS	163	—	5227	854	1996	.428	72	256	.281	731	1021	.716	—	—	1047	513	415	3	—	402	—	2511	6.4	3.1	15.4
ABA PLAYOFF TOTALS	22	—	828	135	286	.472	21	55	.382	126	180	.700	—	—	158	78	68	1	—	71	—	417	7.2	3.5	19.0

HICKEY, MATTHEW (**Nat**) b. January 30, 1902 d. September 1979 Ht. 5-11½ Wt. 180 College—None

SEASON—TEAM	G	GS	MIN	FGM	FGA	PCT	3FGM	3FGA	PCT	FTM	FTA	PCT	O-RB	D-RB	TOT	AST	PF	DQ	STL	TO	BLK	PTS	RPG	APG	PPG
44-45—Pittsburgh (N)	2	—	—	3	—	—	—	—	—	2	—	—	—	—	—	—	—	—	—	—	—	8	—	—	4.0
45-46—Indianapolis (N)	13	—	—	30	—	—	—	—	—	13	—	—	—	—	—	—	—	—	—	—	—	73	—	—	5.6
46-47—Tri-Cities (N)	8	—	—	9	—	—	—	—	—	6	12	.500	—	—	—	—	—	—	—	—	—	24	—	—	3.0
47-48—Tri-Cities (N)	3	—	—	1	—	—	—	—	—	1	1	1.000	—	—	—	—	—	—	—	—	—	3	—	—	1.0
47-48—Providence	1	—	—	0	6	.000	—	—	—	2	3	.667	—	—	—	0	5	—	—	—	—	2	—	0.0	2.0
REG. NBA TOTALS	1	—	—	0	6	.000	—	—	—	2	3	.667	—	—	—	0	5	—	—	—	—	2	—	0.0	2.0
REG. NBL TOTALS	26	—	—	43	—	—	—	—	—	22	13	.538	—	—	—	—	—	—	—	—	—	108	—	—	4.2

HICKS, PHILLIP JAMES (**Phil**) b. January 31, 1953   Ht. 6-7 Wt. 205 College—Tulane

SEASON—TEAM	G	GS	MIN	FGM	FGA	PCT	3FGM	3FGA	PCT	FTM	FTA	PCT	O-RB	D-RB	TOT	AST	PF	DQ	STL	TO	BLK	PTS	RPG	APG	PPG
76-77—Houston-Chicago	37	—	262	41	89	.461	—	—	—	11	13	.846	26	40	66	24	37	0	8	—	0	93	1.8	0.6	2.5
78-79—Denver	20	—	128	18	43	.419	—	—	—	3	5	.600	13	15	28	8	20	0	5	13	0	39	1.4	0.4	2.0
REG. SEASON TOTALS	57	—	390	59	132	.447	—	—	—	14	18	.778	39	55	94	32	57	0	13	13	0	132	1.6	0.6	2.3
PLAYOFF TOTALS	1	—	4	0	2	.000	—	—	—	0	0	—	1	2	3	—	1	0	0	—	0	0	3.0	0.0	0.0

HIGGINS, EARLE BRENT (**Sticks**) b. December 30, 1946   Ht. 6-8 Wt. 200 College—Casper/Eastern Michigan

SEASON—TEAM	G	GS	MIN	FGM	FGA	PCT	3FGM	3FGA	PCT	FTM	FTA	PCT	O-RB	D-RB	TOT	AST	PF	DQ	STL	TO	BLK	PTS	RPG	APG	PPG
70-71—Indiana (A)	53	—	467	104	223	.466	3	17	.176	20	30	.667	—	—	128	35	109	—	—	—	—	231	2.4	0.7	4.4
REG. ABA TOTALS	53	—	467	104	223	.466	3	17	.176	20	30	.667	—	—	128	35	109	—	—	—	—	231	2.4	0.7	4.4
ABA PLAYOFF TOTALS	5	—	31	6	20	.300	0	2	.000	6	7	.857	—	—	13	2	5	—	—	—	—	18	2.6	0.4	3.6

HIGGINS, MICHAEL S. (**Mike**) b. February 17, 1967   Ht. 6-9 Wt. 220 College—Northern Colorado

SEASON—TEAM	G	GS	MIN	FGM	FGA	PCT	3FGM	3FGA	PCT	FTM	FTA	PCT	O-RB	D-RB	TOT	AST	PF	DQ	STL	TO	BLK	PTS	RPG	APG	PPG
89-90—Lakers-Denver	11	0	50	3	8	.375	0	0	—	8	10	.800	2	2	4	3	5	0	2	1	2	14	0.4	0.3	1.3
90-91—Sacramento	7	0	61	6	10	.600	0	0	—	4	7	.571	4	1	5	2	16	1	0	4	2	16	0.7	0.3	2.3
REG. SEASON TOTALS	18	0	111	9	18	.500	0	0	—	12	17	.706	6	3	9	5	21	1	2	5	4	30	0.5	0.3	1.7

HIGGINS, RODERICK DWAYNE (**Rod**) b. January 31, 1960   Ht. 6-7 Wt. 205 College—Fresno State

SEASON—TEAM	G	GS	MIN	FGM	FGA	PCT	3FGM	3FGA	PCT	FTM	FTA	PCT	O-RB	D-RB	TOT	AST	PF	DQ	STL	TO	BLK	PTS	RPG	APG	PPG
82-83—Chicago	82	42	2196	313	698	.448	13	41	.317	209	264	.792	159	207	366	175	248	3	66	127	65	848	4.5	2.1	10.3
83-84—Chicago	78	6	1577	193	432	.447	1	22	.045	113	156	.724	87	119	206	116	161	0	49	76	29	500	2.6	1.5	6.4
84-85—Chicago	68	5	942	119	270	.441	10	37	.270	60	90	.667	55	92	147	73	91	0	21	49	13	308	2.2	1.1	4.5
85-86—Seat.-S.A.-N.J.-Chi.	30	0	332	39	106	.368	1	9	.111	19	27	.704	14	37	51	24	49	0	9	13	11	98	1.7	0.8	3.3
86-87—Golden State	73	28	1497	214	412	.519	3	17	.176	200	240	.833	72	165	237	96	145	0	40	76	21	631	3.2	1.3	8.6
87-88—Golden State	68	67	2188	381	725	.526	19	39	.487	273	322	.848	94	199	293	188	188	2	70	111	31	1054	4.3	2.8	15.5
88-89—Golden State	81	1	1887	301	633	.476	66	168	.393	188	229	.821	111	265	376	160	172	2	39	76	42	856	4.6	2.0	10.6
89-90—Golden State	82	22	1993	304	632	.481	67	193	.347	234	285	.821	120	302	422	129	184	0	47	93	53	909	5.1	1.6	11.1
90-91—Golden State	82	9	2024	259	559	.463	73	220	.332	185	226	.819	109	245	354	113	198	2	52	65	37	776	4.3	1.4	9.5
91-92—Golden State	25	6	535	87	211	.412	33	95	.347	48	59	.814	30	55	85	22	75	2	15	15	13	255	3.4	0.9	10.2
92-93—Sacramento	69	4	1425	199	483	.412	43	133	.323	130	151	.861	66	127	193	119	141	0	51	63	29	571	2.8	1.7	8.3
93-94—Cleveland	36	11	547	71	163	.436	22	50	.440	31	42	.738	25	57	82	36	53	1	25	21	14	195	2.3	1.0	5.4
REG. SEASON TOTALS	774	201	17143	2480	5324	.466	351	1024	.343	1690	2091	.808	942	1870	2812	1251	1705	12	484	785	358	7001	3.6	1.6	9.0
PLAYOFF TOTALS	33	22	733	90	205	.439	21	71	.296	61	75	.813	39	74	113	55	78	0	28	23	22	262	3.4	1.7	7.9

HIGGINS, SEAN MARIELLE (**The Dean**) b. December 30, 1968 Ht. 6-9 Wt. 215 College—Michigan

SEASON—TEAM	G	GS	MIN	FGM	FGA	PCT	3FGM	3FGA	PCT	FTM	FTA	PCT	O-RB	D-RB	TOT	AST	PF	DQ	STL	TO	BLK	PTS	RPG	APG	PPG
90-91—San Antonio	50	0	464	97	212	.458	3	19	.158	28	33	.848	18	45	63	35	53	0	8	49	1	225	1.3	0.7	4.5
91-92—S.A.-Orlando	38	12	616	127	277	.458	6	25	.240	31	36	.861	29	73	102	41	58	0	16	41	6	291	2.7	1.1	7.7
92-93—Golden State	29	4	591	96	215	.447	13	37	.351	35	47	.745	23	45	68	66	54	0	13	64	5	240	2.3	2.3	8.3
REG. SEASON TOTALS	117	16	1671	320	704	.455	22	81	.272	94	116	.810	70	163	233	142	165	0	37	154	12	756	2.0	1.2	6.5
PLAYOFF TOTALS	3	0	13	0	2	.000	0	0	—	0	0	—	0	0	0	1	1	0	0	0	0	0	0.0	0.3	0.0

HIGGINS, WILLIAM (**Bill**) b. December 15, 1952 Ht. 6-2 Wt. 185 College—Ashland

SEASON—TEAM	G	GS	MIN	FGM	FGA	PCT	3FGM	3FGA	PCT	FTM	FTA	PCT	O-RB	D-RB	TOT	AST	PF	DQ	STL	TO	BLK	PTS	RPG	APG	PPG
74-75—Virginia (A)	15	—	348	61	139	.439	1	5	.200	15	23	.652	5	16	21	32	41	—	8	40	1	138	1.4	2.1	9.2
REG. ABA TOTALS	15	—	348	61	139	.439	1	5	.200	15	23	.652	5	16	21	32	41	—	8	40	1	138	1.4	2.1	9.2

HIGGS, KENNETH LEE JR. (**Kenny**) b. January 31, 1955 Ht. 6½ Wt. 180 College—Louisiana State

SEASON—TEAM	G	GS	MIN	FGM	FGA	PCT	3FGM	3FGA	PCT	FTM	FTA	PCT	O-RB	D-RB	TOT	AST	PF	DQ	STL	TO	BLK	PTS	RPG	APG	PPG
78-79—Cleveland	68	—	1050	127	279	.455	—	—	—	85	111	.766	18	84	102	141	176	2	66	47	11	339	1.5	2.1	5.0
80-81—Denver	72	—	1689	209	474	.441	4	34	.118	140	172	.814	24	121	145	408	243	5	101	166	6	562	2.0	5.7	7.8
81-82—Denver	76	49	1696	202	468	.432	4	21	.190	161	197	.817	23	121	144	395	263	8	72	156	6	569	1.9	5.2	7.5
REG. SEASON TOTALS	216	49	4435	538	1221	.441	8	55	.145	386	480	.804	65	326	391	944	682	15	239	369	23	1470	1.8	4.4	6.8
PLAYOFF TOTALS	3	0	54	8	21	.381	0	2	.000	7	12	.583	1	2	3	6	12	0	3	5	0	23	1.0	2.0	7.7

HIGH, JOHNNY HAROLD (**Sky**) b. April 25, 1957 d. June 13, 1987 Ht. 6-3 Wt. 185 College—Lawson State CC/Nevada Reno

SEASON—TEAM	G	GS	MIN	FGM	FGA	PCT	3FGM	3FGA	PCT	FTM	FTA	PCT	O-RB	D-RB	TOT	AST	PF	DQ	STL	TO	BLK	PTS	RPG	APG	PPG
79-80—Phoenix	82	—	1121	144	323	.446	1	7	.143	120	178	.674	69	104	173	119	172	1	71	123	15	409	2.1	1.5	5.0
80-81—Phoenix	81	—	1750	246	576	.427	2	24	.083	183	264	.693	89	139	228	202	251	2	129	188	26	677	2.8	2.5	8.4
82-83—Phoenix	82	2	1155	100	217	.461	1	5	.200	63	136	.463	45	105	150	153	205	0	85	106	34	264	1.8	1.9	3.2
83-84—Phoenix	29	9	512	18	52	.346	0	2	.000	10	29	.345	16	50	66	51	84	1	40	38	11	46	2.3	1.8	1.6
REG. SEASON TOTALS	274	11	4538	508	1168	.435	4	38	.105	376	607	.619	219	398	617	525	712	4	325	455	86	1396	2.3	1.9	5.1
PLAYOFF TOTALS	18	0	282	31	75	.413	0	3	.000	17	32	.531	26	28	54	32	51	0	15	14	5	79	3.0	1.8	4.4

HIGHTOWER, WAYNE A. b. January 14, 1940 Ht. 6-8½ Wt. 200 College—Kansas/Madrid (Spain)

SEASON—TEAM	G	GS	MIN	FGM	FGA	PCT	3FGM	3FGA	PCT	FTM	FTA	PCT	O-RB	D-RB	TOT	AST	PF	DQ	STL	TO	BLK	PTS	RPG	APG	PPG
62-63—San Francisco	66	—	1387	192	543	.354	—	—	—	105	157	.669	—	—	354	51	181	5	—	—	—	489	5.4	0.8	7.4
63-64—San Francisco	79	—	2536	393	1022	.385	—	—	—	260	329	.790	—	—	566	133	269	7	—	—	—	1046	7.2	1.7	13.2
64-65—S.F.-Balt.	75	—	1547	196	570	.344	—	—	—	195	254	.768	—	—	420	54	204	2	—	—	—	587	5.6	0.7	7.8
65-66—Baltimore	24	—	460	63	186	.339	—	—	—	57	78	.731	—	—	131	35	61	2	—	—	—	183	5.5	1.5	7.6
66-67—Balt.-Detroit	72	—	1310	195	567	.344	—	—	—	153	210	.729	—	—	405	64	190	6	—	—	—	543	5.6	0.9	7.5
67-68—Denver (A)	74	—	2459	431	1126	.383	0	6	.000	420	543	.773	—	—	536	143	237	5	—	165	—	1282	7.2	1.9	17.3
68-69—Denver (A)	67	—	2318	311	762	.408	0	2	.000	311	426	.730	—	—	641	203	241	5	—	176	—	933	9.6	3.0	13.9
69-70—Los Angeles (A)	27	—	961	180	403	.447	0	2	.000	129	170	.759	—	—	255	71	101	4	—	—	—	489	9.4	2.6	18.1
70-71—Utah-Texas (A)	68	—	2355	339	848	.400	0	3	.000	268	361	.742	—	—	615	194	204	—	—	—	—	946	9.0	2.9	13.9
71-72—Carolina (A)	13	—	141	20	64	.313	0	2	.000	30	36	.833	—	—	43	11	19	—	—	12	—	70	3.3	0.8	5.4
REG. NBA TOTALS	316	—	7240	1039	2888	.360	—	—	—	770	1028	.749	—	—	1876	337	905	22	—	—	—	2848	5.9	1.1	9.0
REG. ABA TOTALS	249	—	8234	1281	3203	.400	0	15	.000	1158	1536	.754	—	—	2090	622	802	14	—	353	—	3720	8.4	2.5	14.9
NBA PLAYOFF TOTALS	22	—	482	56	176	.318	—	—	—	37	55	.673	—	—	107	26	67	1	—	—	—	149	4.9	1.2	6.8
ABA PLAYOFF TOTALS	16	—	522	71	197	.360	0	1	.000	90	116	.776	—	—	123	34	59	3	—	40	—	232	7.7	2.1	14.5
ABA ALL-STAR TOTALS	1	—	9	1	2	.500	0	0	—	4	4	1.000	1	4	5	0	2	0	—	0	—	6	5.0	0.0	6.0

HILL, ARMOND G. b. March 31, 1953 Ht. 6-4 Wt. 190 College—Princeton

SEASON—TEAM	G	GS	MIN	FGM	FGA	PCT	3FGM	3FGA	PCT	FTM	FTA	PCT	O-RB	D-RB	TOT	AST	PF	DQ	STL	TO	BLK	PTS	RPG	APG	PPG
76-77—Atlanta	81	—	1825	175	439	.399	—	—	—	139	174	.799	39	104	143	403	245	8	85	—	6	489	1.8	5.0	6.0
77-78—Atlanta	82	—	2530	304	732	.415	—	—	—	189	223	.848	59	172	231	427	302	15	151	240	15	797	2.8	5.2	9.7
78-79—Atlanta	82	—	2527	296	682	.434	—	—	—	246	288	.854	41	123	164	480	292	8	102	202	16	838	2.0	5.9	10.2
79-80—Atlanta	79	—	2092	177	431	.411	1	4	.250	124	146	.849	31	107	138	424	261	7	107	171	8	479	1.7	5.4	6.1
80-81—Atlanta-Seattle	75	—	1738	117	335	.349	0	7	.000	141	172	.820	41	118	159	292	207	3	66	127	11	375	2.1	3.9	5.0
81-82—Seattle-S.D.	40	18	723	53	126	.421	0	2	.000	39	55	.709	12	40	52	106	88	0	21	66	5	145	1.3	2.7	3.6
82-83—Milwaukee	14	3	169	14	26	.538	0	0	—	18	22	.818	5	15	20	27	20	0	9	13	0	46	1.4	1.9	3.3
83-84—Atlanta	15	2	181	14	46	.304	0	0	—	17	21	.810	2	8	10	35	30	1	7	14	0	45	0.7	2.3	3.0
REG. SEASON TOTALS	468	23	11785	1150	2817	.408	1	13	.077	913	1101	.829	230	687	917	2194	1445	42	548	833	61	3214	2.0	4.7	6.9
PLAYOFF TOTALS	16	0	437	47	116	.405	0	1	.000	23	28	.821	4	22	26	72	54	1	18	39	2	117	1.6	4.5	7.3

HILL, CLEO b. May 24, 1938 Ht. 6-1 Wt. 185 College—Winston-Salem State

SEASON—TEAM	G	GS	MIN	FGM	FGA	PCT	3FGM	3FGA	PCT	FTM	FTA	PCT	O-RB	D-RB	TOT	AST	PF	DQ	STL	TO	BLK	PTS	RPG	APG	PPG
61-62—St. Louis	58	—	1050	107	309	.346	—	—	—	106	137	.774	—	—	178	114	98	1	—	—	—	320	3.1	2.0	5.5
REG. SEASON TOTALS	58	—	1050	107	309	.346	—	—	—	106	137	.774	—	—	178	114	98	1	—	—	—	320	3.1	2.0	5.5

HILL, GARY W. b. October 7, 1941 Ht. 6-4 Wt. 185 College—Oklahoma City

SEASON—TEAM	G	GS	MIN	FGM	FGA	PCT	3FGM	3FGA	PCT	FTM	FTA	PCT	O-RB	D-RB	TOT	AST	PF	DQ	STL	TO	BLK	PTS	RPG	APG	PPG
63-64—San Francisco	67	—	1015	146	384	.380	—	—	—	51	77	.662	—	—	114	103	165	2	—	—	—	343	1.7	1.5	5.1
64-65—S.F.-Balt.	12	—	103	10	36	.278	—	—	—	7	14	.500	—	—	16	7	11	0	—	—	—	27	1.3	0.6	2.3
REG. SEASON TOTALS	79	—	1118	156	420	.371	—	—	—	58	91	.637	—	—	130	110	176	2	—	—	—	370	1.6	1.4	4.7
PLAYOFF TOTALS	9	—	69	12	24	.500	—	—	—	4	13	.308	—	—	6	8	13	0	—	—	—	28	0.7	0.9	3.1

HILL, SIMMIE JR. b. November 14, 1946 Ht. 6-7 Wt. 235 College—El Centro/Cameron JC/West Texas State/Wichita State/Texas Baptist

SEASON—TEAM	G	GS	MIN	FGM	FGA	PCT	3FGM	3FGA	PCT	FTM	FTA	PCT	O-RB	D-RB	TOT	AST	PF	DQ	STL	TO	BLK	PTS	RPG	APG	PPG
69-70—L.A.-Miami (A)	53	—	1499	297	709	.419	5	30	.167	126	167	.754	—	—	401	47	201	10	—	—	—	725	7.6	0.9	13.7
71-72—Dallas (A)	70	—	1845	281	629	.447	4	13	.308	129	164	.787	—	—	406	94	234	—	—	125	—	695	5.8	1.3	9.9
72-73—San Diego (A)	69	—	1658	315	743	.424	27	69	.391	103	135	.763	126	225	351	131	221	0	—	150	—	760	5.1	1.9	11.0
73-74—San Antonio (A)	60	—	837	112	244	.459	0	11	.000	45	62	.726	59	113	172	62	145	—	13	63	16	269	2.9	1.0	4.5
REG. ABA TOTALS	252	—	5839	1005	2325	.432	36	123	.293	403	528	.763	185	338	1330	334	801	10	13	338	16	2449	5.3	1.3	9.7
ABA PLAYOFF TOTALS	12	—	226	32	79	.405	0	4	.000	8	12	.667	0	0	39	16	28	0	0	17	0	72	3.3	1.3	6.0

HILL, TYRONE b. March 17, 1968 Ht. 6-9 Wt. 245 College—Xavier (Ohio)

SEASON—TEAM	G	GS	MIN	FGM	FGA	PCT	3FGM	3FGA	PCT	FTM	FTA	PCT	O-RB	D-RB	TOT	AST	PF	DQ	STL	TO	BLK	PTS	RPG	APG	PPG
90-91—Golden State	74	22	1192	147	299	.492	0	0	—	96	152	.632	157	226	383	19	264	8	33	72	30	390	5.2	0.3	5.3
91-92—Golden State	82	75	1886	254	487	.522	0	1	.000	163	235	.694	182	411	593	47	315	7	73	106	43	671	7.2	0.6	8.2
92-93—Golden State	74	66	2070	251	494	.508	0	4	.000	138	221	.624	255	499	754	68	320	8	41	92	40	640	10.2	0.9	8.6
93-94—Cleveland	57	20	1447	216	398	.543	0	2	.000	171	256	.668	184	315	499	46	193	5	53	78	35	603	8.8	0.8	10.6
REG. SEASON TOTALS	287	183	6595	868	1678	.517	0	7	.000	568	864	.657	778	1451	2229	180	1092	28	200	348	148	2304	7.8	0.6	8.0
PLAYOFF TOTALS	16	4	250	23	48	.479	0	1	.000	24	45	.533	24	38	62	7	51	3	6	13	5	70	3.9	0.4	4.4

HILLHOUSE, ARTHUR SHERWOOD (Art) b. June 12, 1916 d. October 1980 Ht. 6-7 Wt. 220 College—Rutgers/Long Island University

SEASON—TEAM	G	GS	MIN	FGM	FGA	PCT	3FGM	3FGA	PCT	FTM	FTA	PCT	O-RB	D-RB	TOT	AST	PF	DQ	STL	TO	BLK	PTS	RPG	APG	PPG
46-47—Philadelphia	60	—	—	120	412	.291	—	—	—	120	166	.723	—	—	—	41	139	—	—	—	—	360	—	0.7	6.0
47-48—Philadelphia	11	—	—	14	71	.197	—	—	—	30	37	.811	—	—	—	3	30	—	—	—	—	58	—	0.3	5.3
REG. SEASON TOTALS	71	—	—	134	483	.277	—	—	—	150	203	.739	—	—	—	44	169	—	—	—	—	418	—	0.6	5.9
PLAYOFF TOTALS	10	—	—	24	91	.264	—	—	—	39	46	.848	—	—	—	8	41	6	—	—	—	87	—	0.8	8.7

HILLMAN, DARNELL (Dr. Dunk) b. August 29, 1949 Ht. 6-9 Wt. 215 College—San Jose State

SEASON—TEAM	G	GS	MIN	FGM	FGA	PCT	3FGM	3FGA	PCT	FTM	FTA	PCT	O-RB	D-RB	TOT	AST	PF	DQ	STL	TO	BLK	PTS	RPG	APG	PPG
71-72—Indiana (A)	73	—	1386	200	410	.488	1	5	.200	114	177	.644	—	—	478	49	210	—	—	84	—	515	6.5	0.7	7.1
72-73—Indiana (A)	84	—	2541	328	735	.446	0	9	.000	148	252	.587	218	517	735	128	291	0	—	154	116	804	8.8	1.5	9.6
73-74—Indiana (A)	83	—	2319	328	658	.498	3	8	.375	99	191	.518	198	478	676	96	295	—	70	177	177	758	8.1	1.2	9.1
74-75—Indiana (A)	81	—	2603	486	923	.527	0	4	.000	152	202	.752	296	451	747	131	330	—	73	209	132	1124	9.2	1.6	13.9
75-76—Indiana (A)	74	—	2166	375	828	.453	1	4	.250	243	336	.723	248	422	670	147	306	—	80	196	80	994	9.1	2.0	13.4
76-77—Indiana	82	—	2302	359	811	.443	—	—	—	161	244	.660	228	465	693	166	353	15	95	—	106	879	8.5	2.0	10.7
77-78—N.J.-Denver	78	—	1966	340	710	.479	—	—	—	167	286	.584	199	378	577	102	290	11	63	175	81	847	7.4	1.3	10.9
78-79—Kansas City	78	—	1618	211	428	.493	—	—	—	125	224	.558	138	293	431	91	288	11	50	134	66	547	5.5	1.2	7.0
79-80—Golden State	49	—	708	82	179	.458	0	0	—	34	68	.500	59	121	180	47	128	2	21	59	24	198	3.7	1.0	4.0
REG. NBA TOTALS	287	—	6594	992	2128	.466	0	0	—	487	822	.592	624	1257	1881	406	1059	39	229	368	277	2471	6.6	1.4	8.6
REG. ABA TOTALS	395	—	11015	1717	3554	.483	5	30	.167	756	1158	.653	960	1868	3306	551	1432	0	223	820	505	4195	8.4	1.4	10.6
NBA PLAYOFF TOTALS	18	—	372	41	111	.369	0	0	—	20	32	.625	44	69	113	26	66	1	10	34	10	102	6.3	1.4	5.7
ABA PLAYOFF TOTALS	72	—	1757	232	466	.498	0	3	.000	107	179	.598	90	174	509	62	222	0	22	103	67	571	7.1	0.9	7.9

HILTON, FRED b. January 15, 1948 Ht. 6-3 Wt. 185 College—Grambling State

SEASON—TEAM	G	GS	MIN	FGM	FGA	PCT	3FGM	3FGA	PCT	FTM	FTA	PCT	O-RB	D-RB	TOT	AST	PF	DQ	STL	TO	BLK	PTS	RPG	APG	PPG
71-72—Buffalo	61	—	1349	309	795	.389	—	—	—	90	122	.738	—	—	156	116	145	0	—	—	—	708	2.6	1.9	11.6
72-73—Buffalo	59	—	731	191	494	.387	—	—	—	41	53	.774	—	—	98	74	100	0	—	—	—	423	1.7	1.3	7.2
REG. SEASON TOTALS	120	—	2080	500	1289	.388	—	—	—	131	175	.749	—	—	254	190	245	0	—	—	—	1131	2.1	1.6	9.4

HINSON, ROY MANUS JR. b. May 2, 1961 Ht. 6-9 Wt. 215 College—Rutgers

SEASON—TEAM	G	GS	MIN	FGM	FGA	PCT	3FGM	3FGA	PCT	FTM	FTA	PCT	O-RB	D-RB	TOT	AST	PF	DQ	STL	TO	BLK	PTS	RPG	APG	PPG
83-84—Cleveland	80	61	1858	184	371	.496	0	0	—	69	117	.590	175	324	499	69	306	11	31	109	145	437	6.2	0.9	5.5
84-85—Cleveland	76	75	2344	465	925	.503	0	3	.000	271	376	.721	186	410	596	68	311	13	51	171	173	1201	7.8	0.9	15.8
85-86—Cleveland	82	82	2834	621	1167	.532	0	4	.000	364	506	.719	167	472	639	102	316	7	62	188	112	1606	7.8	1.2	19.6
86-87—Philadelphia	76	58	2489	393	823	.478	0	1	.000	273	360	.758	150	338	488	60	281	4	45	149	161	1059	6.4	0.8	13.9
87-88—Phil.-N.J.	77	57	2592	453	930	.487	0	2	.000	272	351	.775	159	358	517	99	275	6	69	169	140	1178	6.7	1.3	15.3
88-89—New Jersey	82	39	2542	495	1027	.482	0	2	.000	318	420	.757	152	370	522	71	298	3	34	165	121	1308	6.4	0.9	16.0
89-90—New Jersey	25	19	793	145	286	.507	0	0	—	86	99	.869	61	111	172	22	87	0	14	52	27	376	6.9	0.9	15.0
90-91—New Jersey	9	0	91	20	39	.513	0	0	—	1	3	.333	6	13	19	4	14	0	0	6	3	41	2.1	0.4	4.6
REG. SEASON TOTALS	507	391	15543	2776	5568	.499	0	12	.000	1654	2232	.741	1056	2396	3452	495	1888	44	306	1009	882	7206	6.8	1.0	14.2
PLAYOFF TOTALS	9	4	279	57	100	.570	0	0	—	39	61	.639	16	37	53	6	36	1	7	10	19	153	5.9	0.7	17.0

HIRSCH, MELVIN M. (Mel) b. July 31, 1921 d. December 1968 Ht. 5-8 Wt. 165 College—Brooklyn

SEASON—TEAM	G	GS	MIN	FGM	FGA	PCT	3FGM	3FGA	PCT	FTM	FTA	PCT	O-RB	D-RB	TOT	AST	PF	DQ	STL	TO	BLK	PTS	RPG	APG	PPG
46-47—Boston	13	—	—	9	45	.200	—	—	—	1	2	.500	—	—	—	10	18	—	—	—	—	19	—	0.8	1.5
REG. SEASON TOTALS	13	—	—	9	45	.200	—	—	—	1	2	.500	—	—	—	10	18	—	—	—	—	19	—	0.8	1.5

HITCH, LEWIS RUFUS (Lew) b. July 16, 1929 Ht. 6-8 Wt. 200 College—Kansas State

SEASON—TEAM	G	GS	MIN	FGM	FGA	PCT	3FGM	3FGA	PCT	FTM	FTA	PCT	O-RB	D-RB	TOT	AST	PF	DQ	STL	TO	BLK	PTS	RPG	APG	PPG
51-52—Minneapolis	61	—	849	77	215	.358	—	—	—	63	94	.670	—	—	243	50	89	3	—	—	—	217	4.0	0.8	3.6
52-53—Minneapolis	70	—	1027	89	255	.349	—	—	—	83	136	.610	—	—	275	66	122	2	—	—	—	261	3.9	0.9	3.7
53-54—Milwaukee	72	—	2452	221	603	.367	—	—	—	133	208	.639	—	—	691	141	176	3	—	—	—	575	9.6	2.0	8.0
54-55—Milw.-Minn.	74	—	1774	167	417	.400	—	—	—	115	169	.680	—	—	438	125	110	0	—	—	—	449	5.9	1.7	6.1
55-56—Minneapolis	69	—	1129	94	235	.400	—	—	—	100	132	.758	—	—	283	77	85	0	—	—	—	288	4.1	1.1	4.2
56-57—Minn.-Phil.	68	—	1133	111	296	.375	—	—	—	63	88	.716	—	—	253	40	103	0	—	—	—	285	3.7	0.6	4.2
REG. SEASON TOTALS	414	—	8364	759	2021	.376	—	—	—	557	827	.674	—	—	2183	499	685	8	—	—	—	2075	5.3	1.2	5.0
PLAYOFF TOTALS	37	—	535	45	125	.360	—	—	—	55	94	.585	—	—	167	32	64	1	—	—	—	145	4.5	0.9	3.9

HODGE, DONALD JEROME b. February 25, 1969 Ht. 7-0 Wt. 230 College—Temple

SEASON—TEAM	G	GS	MIN	FGM	FGA	PCT	3FGM	3FGA	PCT	FTM	FTA	PCT	O-RB	D-RB	TOT	AST	PF	DQ	STL	TO	BLK	PTS	RPG	APG	PPG
91-92—Dallas	51	27	1058	163	328	.497	0	0	—	100	150	.667	118	157	275	39	128	2	25	75	23	426	5.4	0.8	8.4
92-93—Dallas	79	8	1267	161	400	.403	0	0	—	71	104	.683	93	201	294	75	204	2	33	90	37	393	3.7	0.9	5.0
93-94—Dallas	50	0	428	46	101	.455	0	0	—	44	52	.846	46	49	95	32	66	1	15	30	13	136	1.9	0.6	2.7
REG. SEASON TOTALS	180	35	2753	370	829	.446	0	0	—	215	306	.703	257	407	664	146	398	5	73	195	73	955	3.7	0.8	5.3

HODGES, CRAIG ANTHONY b. June 27, 1960 Ht. 6-3 Wt. 195 College—Long Beach State

SEASON—TEAM	G	GS	MIN	FGM	FGA	PCT	3FGM	3FGA	PCT	FTM	FTA	PCT	O-RB	D-RB	TOT	AST	PF	DQ	STL	TO	BLK	PTS	RPG	APG	PPG
82-83—San Diego	76	48	2022	318	704	.452	20	90	.222	94	130	.723	53	69	122	275	192	3	82	161	4	750	1.6	3.6	9.9
83-84—San Diego	76	28	1571	258	573	.450	10	46	.217	66	88	.750	22	64	86	116	166	2	58	85	1	592	1.1	1.5	7.8
84-85—Milwaukee	82	63	2496	359	733	.490	47	135	.348	106	130	.815	74	112	186	349	262	8	96	135	1	871	2.3	4.3	10.6
85-86—Milwaukee	66	66	1739	284	568	.500	73	162	.451	75	86	.872	39	78	117	229	157	3	74	89	2	716	1.8	3.5	10.8
86-87—Milwaukee	78	43	2147	315	682	.462	85	228	.373	131	147	.891	48	92	140	240	189	3	76	124	7	846	1.8	3.1	10.8
87-88—Milw.-Phoenix	66	0	1445	242	523	.463	86	175	.491	59	71	.831	19	59	78	153	118	1	46	77	2	629	1.2	2.3	9.5
88-89—Phoenix-Chicago	59	6	1204	203	430	.472	75	180	.417	48	57	.842	23	66	89	146	90	0	43	57	4	529	1.5	2.5	9.0
89-90—Chicago	63	0	1055	145	331	.438	87	181	.481	30	33	.909	11	42	53	110	87	1	30	30	2	407	0.8	1.7	6.5
90-91—Chicago	73	0	843	146	344	.424	44	115	.383	26	27	.963	10	32	42	97	74	0	34	35	2	362	0.6	1.3	5.0
91-92—Chicago	56	2	555	93	242	.384	36	96	.375	16	17	.941	7	17	24	54	33	0	14	22	1	238	0.4	1.0	4.3
REG. SEASON TOTALS	695	256	15077	2363	5130	.461	563	1408	.400	651	786	.828	306	631	937	1769	1368	21	553	815	26	5940	1.3	2.5	8.5
PLAYOFF TOTALS	101	40	2056	292	669	.436	90	248	.363	58	74	.784	39	72	111	203	206	5	95	102	8	732	1.1	2.0	7.2

HOEFER, ADOLPH CHARLES (Dutch, Charlie) b. July 12, 1917 Ht. 5-9 Wt. 160 College—Queens College

SEASON—TEAM	G	GS	MIN	FGM	FGA	PCT	3FGM	3FGA	PCT	FTM	FTA	PCT	O-RB	D-RB	TOT	AST	PF	DQ	STL	TO	BLK	PTS	RPG	APG	PPG
46-47—Toronto-Boston	58	—	—	130	514	.253	—	—	—	91	139	.655	—	—	—	33	142	—	—	—	—	351	—	0.6	6.1
47-48—Boston	7	—	—	3	19	.158	—	—	—	4	8	.500	—	—	—	3	17	—	—	—	—	10	—	0.4	1.4
REG. SEASON TOTALS	65	—	—	133	533	.250	—	—	—	95	147	.646	—	—	—	36	159	—	—	—	—	361	—	0.6	5.6

HOFFMAN, PAUL JAMES (Bear, The Body) b. May 5, 1925 Ht. 6-2 Wt. 205 College—Indiana/Purdue

SEASON—TEAM	G	GS	MIN	FGM	FGA	PCT	3FGM	3FGA	PCT	FTM	FTA	PCT	O-RB	D-RB	TOT	AST	PF	DQ	STL	TO	BLK	PTS	RPG	APG	PPG
47-48—Baltimore	37	—	—	142	408	.348	—	—	—	104	157	.662	—	—	—	23	123	—	—	—	—	388	—	0.6	10.5
49-50—Baltimore	60	—	—	312	914	.341	—	—	—	242	364	.665	—	—	—	161	234	—	—	—	—	866	—	2.7	14.4
50-51—Baltimore	41	—	—	127	399	.318	—	—	—	105	156	.673	—	—	202	111	135	2	—	—	—	359	4.9	2.7	8.8
52-53—Baltimore	69	—	1955	240	656	.366	—	—	—	224	342	.655	—	—	317	237	282	13	—	—	—	704	4.6	3.4	10.2
53-54—Baltimore	72	—	2505	253	761	.332	—	—	—	217	303	.716	—	—	486	285	271	10	—	—	—	723	6.8	4.0	10.0
54-55—Balt.-N.Y.-Phil.	38	—	670	65	216	.301	—	—	—	64	93	.688	—	—	124	94	93	0	—	—	—	194	3.3	2.5	5.1
REG. SEASON TOTALS	317	—	5130	1139	3354	.340	—	—	—	956	1415	.676	—	—	1129	911	1138	25	—	—	—	3234	5.1	2.9	10.2
PLAYOFF TOTALS	13	—	81	49	169	.290	—	—	—	48	74	.649	—	—	7	18	49	1	—	—	—	146	3.5	1.4	11.2

HOGSETT, ROBERT L. (Bob) b. January 29, 1941 d. December 5, 1984 Ht. 6-7½ Wt. 230 College—Tennessee

SEASON—TEAM	G	GS	MIN	FGM	FGA	PCT	3FGM	3FGA	PCT	FTM	FTA	PCT	O-RB	D-RB	TOT	AST	PF	DQ	STL	TO	BLK	PTS	RPG	APG	PPG
66-67—Detroit	7	—	22	5	16	.313	—	—	—	6	6	1.000	—	—	3	1	5	0	—	—	—	16	0.4	0.1	2.3
67-68—Pittsburgh (A)	13	—	119	7	20	.350	0	0	—	7	17	.412	—	—	23	1	11	0	—	4	—	21	1.8	0.1	1.6
REG. NBA TOTALS	7	—	22	5	16	.313	—	—	—	6	6	1.000	—	—	3	1	5	0	—	—	—	16	0.4	0.1	2.3
REG. ABA TOTALS	13	—	119	7	20	.350	0	0	—	7	17	.412	—	—	23	1	11	0	—	4	—	21	1.8	0.1	1.6

HOGUE, PAUL H. (Duke) b. April 28, 1940 Ht. 6-9 Wt. 240 College—Cincinnati

SEASON—TEAM	G	GS	MIN	FGM	FGA	PCT	3FGM	3FGA	PCT	FTM	FTA	PCT	O-RB	D-RB	TOT	AST	PF	DQ	STL	TO	BLK	PTS	RPG	APG	PPG
62-63—New York	50	—	1340	152	419	.363	—	—	—	79	174	.454	—	—	430	42	220	12	—	—	—	383	8.6	0.8	7.7
63-64—N.Y.-Balt.	15	—	147	12	30	.400	—	—	—	2	7	.286	—	—	31	6	35	1	—	—	—	26	2.1	0.4	1.7
REG. SEASON TOTALS	65	—	1487	164	449	.365	—	—	—	81	181	.448	—	—	461	48	255	13	—	—	—	409	7.1	0.7	6.3

HOLCOMB, DOUGLAS M. (**Doug**) b. February 9, 1925   Ht. 6-4   Wt. 200   College—Wisconsin

SEASON—TEAM	G	GS	MIN	FGM	FGA	PCT	3FGM	3FGA	PCT	FTM	FTA	PCT	O-RB	D-RB	TOT	AST	PF	DQ	STL	TO	BLK	PTS	RPG	APG	PPG
48-49—Baltimore	3	—	—	3	12	.250	—	—	—	9	14	.643	—	—	—	5	5	—	—	—	—	15	—	1.7	5.0
REG. SEASON TOTALS	3	—	—	3	12	.250	—	—	—	9	14	.643	—	—	—	5	5	—	—	—	—	15	—	1.7	5.0

HOLLAND, JOHN BRADLEY (**Brad**) b. December 6, 1956   Ht. 6-3   Wt. 180   College—UCLA

SEASON—TEAM	G	GS	MIN	FGM	FGA	PCT	3FGM	3FGA	PCT	FTM	FTA	PCT	O-RB	D-RB	TOT	AST	PF	DQ	STL	TO	BLK	PTS	RPG	APG	PPG
79-80—Los Angeles	38	—	197	44	104	.423	3	15	.200	15	16	.938	4	13	17	22	24	0	15	13	1	106	0.4	0.6	2.8
80-81—Los Angeles	41	—	295	47	111	.423	1	3	.333	35	49	.714	9	20	29	23	44	0	21	31	1	130	0.7	0.6	3.2
81-82—Wash.-Milw.	14	3	194	27	78	.346	0	3	.000	3	6	.500	6	7	13	18	13	0	11	8	1	57	0.9	1.3	4.1
REG. SEASON TOTALS	93	3	686	118	293	.403	4	21	.190	53	71	.746	19	40	59	63	81	0	47	52	3	293	0.6	0.7	3.2
PLAYOFF TOTALS	11	0	36	6	11	.545	0	0	—	4	4	1.000	2	3	5	4	8	0	5	4	0	16	0.5	0.4	1.5

HOLLAND, JOSEPH BURNETT b. September 26, 1925   Ht. 6-4   Wt. 185   College—Berea/Murray State (Ky.)/Iowa/Kentucky

SEASON—TEAM	G	GS	MIN	FGM	FGA	PCT	3FGM	3FGA	PCT	FTM	FTA	PCT	O-RB	D-RB	TOT	AST	PF	DQ	STL	TO	BLK	PTS	RPG	APG	PPG
49-50—Indianapolis	64	—	—	145	453	.320	—	—	—	98	142	.690	—	—	—	130	220	—	—	—	—	388	—	2.0	6.1
50-51—Indianapolis	67	—	—	196	594	.330	—	—	—	78	137	.569	—	—	344	150	228	8	—	—	—	470	5.1	2.2	7.0
51-52—Indianapolis	55	—	737	93	265	.351	—	—	—	40	69	.580	—	—	166	47	90	0	—	—	—	226	3.0	0.9	4.1
REG. SEASON TOTALS	186	—	737	434	1312	.331	—	—	—	216	348	.621	—	—	510	327	538	8	—	—	—	1084	4.2	1.8	5.8
PLAYOFF TOTALS	9	—	0	38	36	.472	—	—	—	7	19	.368	—	—	12	11	38	3	—	—	—	83	4.0	3.7	9.2

HOLLAND, WILBUR b. November 8, 1951   Ht. 6-0   Wt. 175   College—New Orleans

SEASON—TEAM	G	GS	MIN	FGM	FGA	PCT	3FGM	3FGA	PCT	FTM	FTA	PCT	O-RB	D-RB	TOT	AST	PF	DQ	STL	TO	BLK	PTS	RPG	APG	PPG
75-76—Atlanta	33	—	351	85	213	.399	—	—	—	22	34	.647	15	26	41	26	48	0	20	—	2	192	1.2	0.8	5.8
76-77—Chicago	79	—	2453	509	1120	.454	—	—	—	158	192	.823	78	175	253	253	201	3	169	—	16	1176	3.2	3.2	14.9
77-78—Chicago	82	—	2884	569	1285	.443	—	—	—	223	279	.799	105	189	294	313	258	4	164	223	14	1361	3.6	3.8	16.6
78-79—Chicago	82	—	2483	445	940	.473	—	—	—	141	176	.801	78	176	254	330	240	9	122	185	12	1031	3.1	4.0	12.6
REG. SEASON TOTALS	276	—	8171	1608	3558	.452	—	—	—	544	681	.799	276	566	842	922	747	16	475	408	44	3760	3.1	3.3	13.6
PLAYOFF TOTALS	3	—	84	17	34	.500	—	—	—	10	10	1.000	5	4	9	3	8	0	1	—	0	44	3.0	1.0	14.7

HOLLINS, LIONEL EUGENE b. October 19, 1953   Ht. 6-3   Wt. 185   College—Dixie/Arizona State

SEASON—TEAM	G	GS	MIN	FGM	FGA	PCT	3FGM	3FGA	PCT	FTM	FTA	PCT	O-RB	D-RB	TOT	AST	PF	DQ	STL	TO	BLK	PTS	RPG	APG	PPG
75-76—Portland	74	—	1891	311	738	.421	—	—	—	178	247	.721	39	136	175	306	235	5	131	—	28	800	2.4	4.1	10.8
76-77—Portland	76	—	2224	452	1046	.432	—	—	—	215	287	.749	52	158	210	313	265	5	166	—	38	1119	2.8	4.1	14.7
77-78—Portland	81	—	2741	531	1202	.442	—	—	—	223	300	.743	81	196	277	380	268	4	157	241	29	1285	3.4	4.7	15.9
78-79—Portland	64	—	1967	402	886	.454	—	—	—	172	221	.778	32	117	149	325	199	3	114	223	24	976	2.3	5.1	15.3
79-80—Port.-Phil.	47	—	1209	212	526	.403	3	20	.150	101	140	.721	29	60	89	162	103	0	76	128	10	528	1.9	3.4	11.2
80-81—Philadelphia	82	—	2154	327	696	.470	2	15	.133	125	171	.731	47	144	191	352	205	2	104	207	18	781	2.3	4.3	9.5
81-82—Philadelphia	81	81	2257	380	797	.477	2	16	.125	132	188	.702	35	152	187	316	198	1	103	146	20	894	2.3	3.9	11.0
82-83—San Diego	56	54	1844	313	717	.437	3	21	.143	129	179	.721	30	98	128	373	155	2	111	198	14	758	2.3	6.7	13.5
83-84—Detroit	32	—	216	24	63	.381	0	2	.000	11	13	.846	4	18	22	62	26	0	13	24	1	59	0.7	1.9	1.8
84-85—Houston	80	60	1950	249	540	.461	3	13	.231	108	136	.794	33	140	173	417	187	1	78	170	10	609	2.2	5.2	7.6
REG. SEASON TOTALS	673	195	18453	3201	7211	.444	13	87	.149	1394	1882	.741	382	1219	1601	3006	1841	23	1053	1337	192	7809	2.4	4.5	11.6
PLAYOFF TOTALS	77	3	2293	369	897	.411	0	12	.000	173	236	.733	46	161	207	344	221	4	114	113	11	911	2.7	4.5	11.8
ALL-STAR TOTALS	1	0	23	3	8	.375	0	0	—	4	5	.800	0	0	0	8	2	0	2	1	0	10	0.0	8.0	10.0

HOLLIS, ESSIE B. b. May 16, 1955   Ht. 6-6   Wt. 195   College—St. Bonaventure

SEASON—TEAM	G	GS	MIN	FGM	FGA	PCT	3FGM	3FGA	PCT	FTM	FTA	PCT	O-RB	D-RB	TOT	AST	PF	DQ	STL	TO	BLK	PTS	RPG	APG	PPG
78-79—Detroit	25	—	154	30	75	.400	—	—	—	9	12	.750	21	24	45	6	28	0	11	14	1	69	1.8	0.2	2.8
REG. SEASON TOTALS	25	—	154	30	75	.400	—	—	—	9	12	.750	21	24	45	6	28	0	11	14	1	69	1.8	0.2	2.8

HOLMAN, DENNIS R. (**Denny**) b. October 8, 1945   Ht. 6-3   Wt. 175   College—Southern Methodist

SEASON—TEAM	G	GS	MIN	FGM	FGA	PCT	3FGM	3FGA	PCT	FTM	FTA	PCT	O-RB	D-RB	TOT	AST	PF	DQ	STL	TO	BLK	PTS	RPG	APG	PPG
67-68—Dallas (A)	46	—	554	55	153	.359	4	9	.444	62	103	.602	—	—	78	73	85	1	—	40	—	176	1.7	1.6	3.8
REG. ABA TOTALS	46	—	554	55	153	.359	4	9	.444	62	103	.602	—	—	78	73	85	1	—	40	—	176	1.7	1.6	3.8
ABA PLAYOFF TOTALS	8	—	128	9	31	.290	1	2	.500	12	12	1.000	—	—	16	15	19	0	—	9	—	31	2.0	1.9	3.9

HOLSTEIN, JAMES H. (**Jim**) b. September 24, 1930   Ht. 6-3   Wt. 180   College—Cincinnati

SEASON—TEAM	G	GS	MIN	FGM	FGA	PCT	3FGM	3FGA	PCT	FTM	FTA	PCT	O-RB	D-RB	TOT	AST	PF	DQ	STL	TO	BLK	PTS	RPG	APG	PPG
52-53—Minneapolis	66	—	989	98	274	.358	—	—	—	70	105	.667	—	—	173	74	128	1	—	—	—	266	2.6	1.1	4.0
53-54—Minneapolis	70	—	1155	88	288	.306	—	—	—	64	112	.571	—	—	204	79	140	0	—	—	—	240	2.9	1.1	3.4
54-55—Minneapolis	62	—	980	107	330	.324	—	—	—	67	94	.713	—	—	206	58	107	0	—	—	—	281	3.3	0.9	4.5
55-56—Fort Wayne	27	—	352	24	89	.270	—	—	—	24	37	.649	—	—	76	38	51	1	—	—	—	72	2.8	1.4	2.7
REG. SEASON TOTALS	225	—	3476	317	981	.323	—	—	—	225	348	.647	—	—	659	249	426	2	—	—	—	859	2.9	1.1	3.8
PLAYOFF TOTALS	32	—	497	51	129	.395	—	—	—	36	55	.655	—	—	95	28	66	0	—	—	—	138	3.0	0.9	4.3

HOLT, ALVIN WILLIAM (**A.W.**) b. August 26, 1946 Ht. 6-7½ Wt. 210 College—Jackson State

SEASON—TEAM	G	GS	MIN	FGM	FGA	PCT	3FGM	3FGA	PCT	FTM	FTA	PCT	O-RB	D-RB	TOT	AST	PF	DQ	STL	TO	BLK	PTS	RPG	APG	PPG
70-71—Chicago	6	—	14	1	8	.125	—	—	—	2	3	.667	—	—	4	0	1	0	—	—	—	4	0.7	0.0	0.7
REG. SEASON TOTALS	6	—	14	1	8	.125	—	—	—	2	3	.667	—	—	4	0	1	0	—	—	—	4	0.7	0.0	0.7

HOLTON, MICHAEL DAVID b. August 4, 1961 Ht. 6-4 Wt. 185 College—UCLA

SEASON—TEAM	G	GS	MIN	FGM	FGA	PCT	3FGM	3FGA	PCT	FTM	FTA	PCT	O-RB	D-RB	TOT	AST	PF	DQ	STL	TO	BLK	PTS	RPG	APG	PPG
84-85—Phoenix	74	59	1761	257	576	.446	14	45	.311	96	118	.814	30	102	132	198	141	0	59	123	6	624	1.8	2.7	8.4
85-86—Phoenix-Chicago	28	0	512	77	175	.440	1	12	.083	28	44	.636	11	22	33	55	47	1	25	27	0	183	1.2	2.0	6.5
86-87—Portland	58	1	479	70	171	.409	7	23	.304	44	55	.800	9	29	38	73	51	0	16	41	2	191	0.7	1.3	3.3
87-88—Portland	82	2	1279	163	353	.462	3	15	.200	107	129	.829	50	99	149	211	154	0	41	86	10	436	1.8	2.6	5.3
88-89—Charlotte	67	60	1696	215	504	.427	3	14	.214	120	143	.839	30	75	105	424	165	0	66	119	12	553	1.6	6.3	8.3
89-90—Charlotte	16	0	109	14	26	.538	0	0	—	1	2	.500	1	1	2	16	19	0	1	13	0	29	0.1	1.0	1.8
REG. SEASON TOTALS	325	122	5836	796	1805	.441	28	109	.257	396	491	.807	131	328	459	977	577	1	208	409	30	2016	1.4	3.0	6.2
PLAYOFF TOTALS	9	0	98	13	34	.382	0	5	.000	4	4	1.000	1	7	8	15	15	0	2	4	0	30	0.9	1.7	3.3

HOLUB, RICHARD W. (**Dick**) b. October 29, 1921 Ht. 6-6 Wt. 205 College—Long Island University

SEASON—TEAM	G	GS	MIN	FGM	FGA	PCT	3FGM	3FGA	PCT	FTM	FTA	PCT	O-RB	D-RB	TOT	AST	PF	DQ	STL	TO	BLK	PTS	RPG	APG	PPG
47-48—New York	48	—	—	195	662	.295	—	—	—	114	180	.633	—	—	—	37	159	—	—	—	—	504	—	0.8	10.5
REG. SEASON TOTALS	48	—	—	195	662	.295	—	—	—	114	180	.633	—	—	—	37	159	—	—	—	—	504	—	0.8	10.5
PLAYOFF TOTALS	3	—	—	9	36	.250	—	—	—	8	14	.571	—	—	—	12	—	—	—	—	—	26	—	0.0	8.7

HOLUP, JOSEPH J. (**Joe**) b. February 26, 1934 Ht. 6-6 Wt. 215 College—George Washington

SEASON—TEAM	G	GS	MIN	FGM	FGA	PCT	3FGM	3FGA	PCT	FTM	FTA	PCT	O-RB	D-RB	TOT	AST	PF	DQ	STL	TO	BLK	PTS	RPG	APG	PPG
56-57—Syracuse	71	—	1284	160	487	.329	—	—	—	204	253	.806	—	—	279	84	177	5	—	—	—	524	3.9	1.2	7.4
57-58—Syr.-Detroit	53	—	740	91	278	.327	—	—	—	71	94	.755	—	—	221	36	99	2	—	—	—	253	4.2	0.7	4.8
58-59—Detroit	68	—	1502	209	580	.360	—	—	—	152	200	.760	—	—	352	73	239	12	—	—	—	570	5.2	1.1	8.4
REG. SEASON TOTALS	192	—	3526	460	1345	.342	—	—	—	427	547	.781	—	—	852	193	515	19	—	—	—	1347	4.4	1.0	7.0
PLAYOFF TOTALS	15	—	258	24	85	.282	—	—	—	26	35	.743	—	—	64	7	30	0	—	—	—	74	4.3	0.5	4.9

HOLZMAN, WILLIAM (**Red**) b. August 10, 1920 Ht. 5-10 Wt. 175 College—Balitmore/CCNY

SEASON—TEAM	G	GS	MIN	FGM	FGA	PCT	3FGM	3FGA	PCT	FTM	FTA	PCT	O-RB	D-RB	TOT	AST	PF	DQ	STL	TO	BLK	PTS	RPG	APG	PPG
45-46—Rochester (N)	34	—	—	143	—	—	—	—	—	77	115	.670	—	—	—	—	54	—	—	—	—	363	—	—	10.7
46-47—Rochester (N)	44	—	—	227	—	—	—	—	—	74	139	.532	—	—	—	—	68	—	—	—	—	528	—	—	12.0
47-48—Rochester (N)	60	—	—	246	—	—	—	—	—	117	182	.643	—	—	—	—	58	—	—	—	—	609	—	—	10.2
48-49—Rochester	60	—	—	225	691	.326	—	—	—	96	157	.611	—	—	—	149	93	—	—	—	—	546	—	2.5	9.1
49-50—Rochester	68	—	—	206	625	.330	—	—	—	144	210	.686	—	—	—	200	67	—	—	—	—	556	—	2.9	8.2
50-51—Rochester	68	—	—	183	561	.326	—	—	—	130	179	.726	—	—	152	147	94	0	—	—	—	496	2.2	2.2	7.3
51-52—Rochester	65	—	1065	104	372	.280	—	—	—	61	85	.718	—	—	106	115	95	1	—	—	—	269	1.6	1.8	4.1
52-53—Rochester	46	—	392	38	149	.255	—	—	—	27	38	.711	—	—	40	35	56	2	—	—	—	103	0.9	0.8	2.2
53-54—Milwaukee	51	—	649	74	224	.330	—	—	—	48	73	.658	—	—	46	75	73	1	—	—	—	196	0.9	1.5	3.8
REG. NBA TOTALS	358	—	2106	830	2622	.317	—	—	—	506	742	.682	—	—	344	721	478	4	—	—	—	2166	1.5	2.0	6.1
REG. NBL TOTALS	138	—	—	616	—	—	—	—	—	268	436	.615	—	—	—	—	180	—	—	—	—	1500	—	—	10.9
NBA PLAYOFF TOTALS	28	—	79	56	145	.386	—	—	—	31	52	.596	—	—	26	36	27	0	—	—	—	143	1.2	1.3	5.1
NBL PLAYOFF TOTALS	28	—	—	107	—	—	—	—	—	53	73	.726	—	—	—	—	39	—	—	—	—	267	—	—	9.5

HOOPER, BOBBY JOE b. December 22, 1946 Ht. 6-0 Wt. 190 College—Dayton

SEASON—TEAM	G	GS	MIN	FGM	FGA	PCT	3FGM	3FGA	PCT	FTM	FTA	PCT	O-RB	D-RB	TOT	AST	PF	DQ	STL	TO	BLK	PTS	RPG	APG	PPG
68-69—Indiana (A)	54	—	955	112	271	.413	4	32	.125	43	59	.729	—	—	109	142	91	0	—	52	—	271	2.0	2.6	5.0
REG. ABA TOTALS	54	—	955	112	271	.413	4	32	.125	43	59	.729	—	—	109	142	91	0	—	52	—	271	2.0	2.6	5.0
ABA PLAYOFF TOTALS	16	—	288	25	74	.338	4	16	.250	22	26	.846	—	—	38	45	41	0	—	13	—	76	2.4	2.8	4.8

HOOSER, CARROLL L. b. March 5, 1944 Ht. 6-7 Wt. 230 College—Southern Methodist

SEASON—TEAM	G	GS	MIN	FGM	FGA	PCT	3FGM	3FGA	PCT	FTM	FTA	PCT	O-RB	D-RB	TOT	AST	PF	DQ	STL	TO	BLK	PTS	RPG	APG	PPG
67-68—Dallas (A)	56	—	720	128	297	.431	1	1	1.000	59	83	.711	—	—	216	29	139	6	—	49	—	316	3.9	0.5	5.6
REG. ABA TOTALS	56	—	720	128	297	.431	1	1	1.000	59	83	.711	—	—	216	29	139	6	—	49	—	316	3.9	0.5	5.6
ABA PLAYOFF TOTALS	3	—	6	1	2	.500	0	0	—	0	0	—	—	—	2	0	3	0	—	2	—	2	0.7	0.0	0.7

HOOVER, THOMAS LEE JR. (Tom) b. January 23, 1941   Ht. 6-10 Wt. 240 College—Villanova

SEASON—TEAM	G	GS	MIN	FGM	FGA	PCT	3FGM	3FGA	PCT	FTM	FTA	PCT	O-RB	D-RB	TOT	AST	PF	DQ	STL	TO	BLK	PTS	RPG	APG	PPG
63-64—New York	59	—	988	102	247	.413	—	—	—	81	132	.614	—	—	331	36	185	4	—	—	—	285	5.6	0.6	4.8
64-65—New York	24	—	153	13	32	.406	—	—	—	8	14	.571	—	—	58	12	37	0	—	—	—	34	2.4	0.5	1.4
66-67—St. Louis	17	—	129	13	31	.419	—	—	—	5	13	.385	—	—	36	8	35	1	—	—	—	31	2.1	0.5	1.8
67-68—Denver (A)	70	—	1588	161	357	.451	4	10	.400	128	206	.621	—	—	491	64	268	8	—	139	—	454	7.0	0.9	6.5
68-69—Houston-Minn.-N.Y. (A)	53	—	1419	191	408	.468	0	2	.000	125	189	.661	—	—	472	117	223	13	—	172	—	507	8.9	2.2	9.6
REG. NBA TOTALS	100	—	1270	128	310	.413	—	—	—	94	159	.591	—	—	425	56	257	5	—	—	—	350	4.3	0.6	3.5
REG. ABA TOTALS	123	—	3007	352	765	.460	4	12	.333	253	395	.641	—	—	963	181	491	21	—	311	—	961	7.8	1.5	7.8
NBA PLAYOFF TOTALS	3	—	11	2	3	.667	—	—	—	0	0	—	—	—	3	1	3	0	—	—	—	4	1.0	0.3	1.3
ABA PLAYOFF TOTALS	2	—	16	4	7	.571	0	0	—	5	7	.714	—	—	4	1	6	0	—	2	—	13	2.0	0.5	6.5

HOPKINS, ROBERT M. (Bob) b. November 3, 1934   Ht. 6-8 Wt. 205 College—Grambling State

SEASON—TEAM	G	GS	MIN	FGM	FGA	PCT	3FGM	3FGA	PCT	FTM	FTA	PCT	O-RB	D-RB	TOT	AST	PF	DQ	STL	TO	BLK	PTS	RPG	APG	PPG
56-57—Syracuse	62	—	764	130	343	.379	—	—	—	94	126	.746	—	—	233	22	106	0	—	—	—	354	3.8	0.4	5.7
57-58—Syracuse	69	—	1224	221	554	.399	—	—	—	123	161	.764	—	—	392	45	162	5	—	—	—	565	5.7	0.7	8.2
58-59—Syracuse	67	—	1518	246	611	.403	—	—	—	176	234	.752	—	—	436	67	181	5	—	—	—	668	6.5	1.0	10.0
59-60—Syracuse	75	—	1616	257	660	.389	—	—	—	136	174	.782	—	—	465	55	193	4	—	—	—	650	6.2	0.7	8.7
REG. SEASON TOTALS	273	—	5122	854	2168	.394	—	—	—	529	695	.761	—	—	1526	189	642	14	—	—	—	2237	5.6	0.7	8.2
PLAYOFF TOTALS	18	—	334	38	117	.325	—	—	—	45	58	.776	—	—	99	11	57	2	—	—	—	121	5.5	0.6	6.7

HOPPEN, DAVID DIRK (Dave) b. March 13, 1964   Ht. 6-11 Wt. 235 College—Nebraska

SEASON—TEAM	G	GS	MIN	FGM	FGA	PCT	3FGM	3FGA	PCT	FTM	FTA	PCT	O-RB	D-RB	TOT	AST	PF	DQ	STL	TO	BLK	PTS	RPG	APG	PPG
87-88—Milw.-G.S.	39	8	642	84	183	.459	0	1	.000	54	62	.871	58	116	174	32	87	1	13	37	6	222	4.5	0.8	5.7
88-89—Charlotte	77	36	1419	199	353	.564	1	2	.500	101	139	.727	123	261	384	57	239	4	25	77	21	500	5.0	0.7	6.5
89-90—Charlotte	10	2	135	16	41	.390	0	0	—	8	10	.800	19	17	36	6	26	0	2	8	1	40	3.6	0.6	4.0
90-91—Cha.-Phil.	30	0	155	24	44	.545	0	2	.000	16	22	.727	18	21	39	3	29	0	3	13	1	64	1.3	0.1	2.1
91-92—Philadelphia	11	0	40	2	7	.286	0	0	—	5	10	.500	1	9	10	2	6	0	0	3	0	9	0.9	0.2	0.8
92-93—New Jersey	2	0	10	1	1	1.000	0	0	—	0	2	.000	1	3	4	0	2	0	0	0	0	2	2.0	0.0	1.0
REG. SEASON TOTALS	169	46	2401	326	629	.518	1	5	.200	184	245	.751	220	427	647	100	389	5	43	138	29	837	3.8	0.6	5.0
PLAYOFF TOTALS	3	0	9	3	3	1.000	0	0	—	0	2	.000	0	3	3	—	1	0	0	0	0	6	1.0	0.0	2.0

HOPSON, DENNIS b. April 22, 1965   Ht. 6-5 Wt. 200 College—Ohio State

SEASON—TEAM	G	GS	MIN	FGM	FGA	PCT	3FGM	3FGA	PCT	FTM	FTA	PCT	O-RB	D-RB	TOT	AST	PF	DQ	STL	TO	BLK	PTS	RPG	APG	PPG
87-88—New Jersey	61	19	1365	222	549	.404	12	45	.267	131	177	.740	63	80	143	118	145	0	57	119	25	587	2.3	1.9	9.6
88-89—New Jersey	62	36	1551	299	714	.419	4	27	.148	186	219	.849	91	111	202	103	150	0	70	102	30	788	3.3	1.7	12.7
89-90—New Jersey	79	64	2551	474	1093	.434	32	101	.317	271	342	.792	113	166	279	151	183	1	100	168	51	1251	3.5	1.9	15.8
90-91—Chicago	61	0	728	104	244	.426	1	5	.200	55	83	.663	49	60	109	65	79	0	25	59	14	264	1.8	1.1	4.3
91-92—Chicago-Sac.	71	0	1314	276	593	.465	12	47	.255	179	253	.708	105	101	206	102	115	0	67	100	39	743	2.9	1.4	10.5
REG. SEASON TOTALS	334	119	7509	1375	3193	.431	61	225	.271	822	1074	.765	421	518	939	539	672	1	319	548	159	3633	2.8	1.6	10.9
PLAYOFF TOTALS	5	0	18	2	6	.333	0	0	—	4	9	.444	2	2	4	1	2	0	0	1	1	8	0.8	0.2	1.6

HORAN, JOHN F. (Johnny, The Vertical Hyphen) b. November 24, 1932 d. November 14, 1980 Ht. 6-8 Wt. 190 College—Dayton

SEASON—TEAM	G	GS	MIN	FGM	FGA	PCT	3FGM	3FGA	PCT	FTM	FTA	PCT	O-RB	D-RB	TOT	AST	PF	DQ	STL	TO	BLK	PTS	RPG	APG	PPG
55-56—Ft. Wayne-Minn.	19	—	93	12	42	.286	—	—	—	10	11	.909	—	—	10	2	21	0	—	—	—	34	0.5	0.1	1.8
REG. SEASON TOTALS	19	—	93	12	42	.286	—	—	—	10	11	.909	—	—	10	2	21	0	—	—	—	34	0.5	0.1	1.8

HORDGES, CEDRICK TYRONE b. January 8, 1957   Ht. 6-8½ Wt. 220 College—Auburn/South Carolina

SEASON—TEAM	G	GS	MIN	FGM	FGA	PCT	3FGM	3FGA	PCT	FTM	FTA	PCT	O-RB	D-RB	TOT	AST	PF	DQ	STL	TO	BLK	PTS	RPG	APG	PPG
80-81—Denver	68	—	1599	221	480	.460	0	3	.000	130	186	.699	120	338	458	104	226	4	33	120	19	572	6.7	1.5	8.4
81-82—Denver	77	1	1372	204	414	.493	3	13	.231	116	199	.583	119	276	395	65	230	1	26	111	19	527	5.1	0.8	6.8
REG. SEASON TOTALS	145	1	2971	425	894	.475	3	16	.188	246	385	.639	239	614	853	169	456	5	59	231	38	1099	5.9	1.2	7.6
PLAYOFF TOTALS	3	0	45	8	19	.421	0	1	.000	3	4	.750	2	11	13	2	4	0	1	4	0	19	4.3	0.7	6.3

HORFORD, ALFREDO WILLIAM (Tito) b. January 19, 1966   Ht. 7-1 Wt. 245 College—Louisiana State/Miami

SEASON—TEAM	G	GS	MIN	FGM	FGA	PCT	3FGM	3FGA	PCT	FTM	FTA	PCT	O-RB	D-RB	TOT	AST	PF	DQ	STL	TO	BLK	PTS	RPG	APG	PPG
88-89—Milwaukee	25	0	112	15	46	.326	0	0	—	12	19	.632	9	13	22	3	14	0	1	15	7	42	0.9	0.1	1.7
89-90—Milwaukee	35	0	236	18	62	.290	0	0	—	15	24	.625	19	40	59	2	33	0	5	14	16	51	1.7	0.1	1.5
93-94—Washington	3	0	28	0	2	.000	0	0	—	0	0	—	1	2	3	0	3	0	1	1	3	0	1.0	0.0	0.0
REG. SEASON TOTALS	63	0	376	33	110	.300	0	0	—	27	43	.628	29	55	84	5	50	0	7	30	26	93	1.3	0.1	1.5
PLAYOFF TOTALS	2	0	2	1	1	1.000	0	0	—	0	0	—	0	0	0	—	0	0	0	0	0	2	0.0	0.0	1.0

HORN, RONALD LEROY (Ron) b. May 24, 1938 Ht. 6-7 Wt. 225 College—Indiana

SEASON—TEAM	G	GS	MIN	FGM	FGA	PCT	3FGM	3FGA	PCT	FTM	FTA	PCT	O-RB	D-RB	TOT	AST	PF	DQ	STL	TO	BLK	PTS	RPG	APG	PPG
61-62—St. Louis	3	—	25	1	12	.083	—	—	—	1	2	.500	—	—	6	1	4	0	—	—	—	3	2.0	0.3	1.0
62-63—Los Angeles	28	—	289	27	82	.329	—	—	—	20	29	.690	—	—	71	10	46	0	—	—	—	74	2.5	0.4	2.6
67-68—Denver (A)	1	—	6	0	2	.000	0	0	—	2	2	1.000	—	—	1	0	0	0	—	1	—	2	1.0	0.0	2.0
REG. NBA TOTALS	31	—	314	28	94	.298	—	—	—	21	31	.677	—	—	77	11	50	0	—	—	—	77	2.5	0.4	2.5
REG. ABA TOTALS	1	—	6	0	2	.000	0	0	—	2	2	1.000	—	—	1	0	0	0	—	1	—	2	1.0	0.0	2.0
NBA PLAYOFF TOTALS	7	—	55	4	12	.333	—	—	—	4	5	.800	—	—	11	2	13	0	—	—	—	12	1.6	0.3	1.7

HORNACEK, JEFFREY JOHN (Jeff) b. May 3, 1963 Ht. 6-4 Wt. 190 College—Iowa State

SEASON—TEAM	G	GS	MIN	FGM	FGA	PCT	3FGM	3FGA	PCT	FTM	FTA	PCT	O-RB	D-RB	TOT	AST	PF	DQ	STL	TO	BLK	PTS	RPG	APG	PPG
86-87—Phoenix	80	3	1561	159	350	.454	12	43	.279	94	121	.777	41	143	184	361	130	0	70	153	5	424	2.3	4.5	5.3
87-88—Phoenix	82	49	2243	306	605	.506	17	58	.293	152	185	.822	71	191	262	540	151	0	107	156	10	781	3.2	6.6	9.5
88-89—Phoenix	78	73	2487	440	889	.495	27	81	.333	147	178	.826	75	191	266	465	188	0	129	111	8	1054	3.4	6.0	13.5
89-90—Phoenix	67	60	2278	483	901	.536	40	98	.408	173	202	.856	86	227	313	337	144	2	117	125	14	1179	4.7	5.0	17.6
90-91—Phoenix	80	77	2733	544	1051	.518	61	146	.418	201	224	.897	74	247	321	409	185	1	111	130	16	1350	4.0	5.1	16.9
91-92—Phoenix	81	81	3078	635	1240	.512	83	189	.439	279	315	.886	106	301	407	411	218	1	158	170	31	1632	5.0	5.1	20.1
92-93—Philadelphia	79	78	2860	582	1239	.470	97	249	.390	250	289	.865	84	258	342	548	203	2	131	222	21	1511	4.3	6.9	19.1
93-94—Phil.-Utah	80	62	2820	472	1004	.470	70	208	.337	260	296	.878	60	219	279	419	186	0	127	171	13	1274	3.5	5.2	15.9
REG. SEASON TOTALS	627	483	20060	3621	7279	.497	407	1072	.380	1556	1810	.860	597	1777	2374	3490	1405	6	950	1238	118	9205	3.8	5.6	14.7
PLAYOFF TOTALS	56	56	2003	355	726	.489	32	88	.364	208	228	.912	64	182	246	249	158	1	81	102	13	950	4.4	4.4	17.0
ALL-STAR TOTALS	1	0	24	5	7	.714	1	2	.500	0	0	—	1	1	2	3	0	0	1	0	0	11	2.0	3.0	11.0

HORRY, ROBERT K. b. August 25, 1970 Ht. 6-10 Wt. 220 College—Alabama

SEASON—TEAM	G	GS	MIN	FGM	FGA	PCT	3FGM	3FGA	PCT	FTM	FTA	PCT	O-RB	D-RB	TOT	AST	PF	DQ	STL	TO	BLK	PTS	RPG	APG	PPG
92-93—Houston	79	79	2330	323	682	.474	12	47	.255	143	200	.715	113	279	392	191	210	1	80	156	83	801	5.0	2.4	10.1
93-94—Houston	81	81	2370	322	702	.459	44	136	.324	115	157	.732	128	312	440	231	186	0	119	137	75	803	5.4	2.9	9.9
REG. SEASON TOTALS	160	160	4700	645	1384	.466	56	183	.306	258	357	.723	241	591	832	422	396	1	199	293	158	1604	5.2	2.6	10.0
PLAYOFF TOTALS	35	35	1152	145	327	.443	43	119	.361	59	78	.756	54	149	203	120	98	1	53	55	36	392	5.8	3.4	11.2

HORTON, EDWARD C. (Ed) b. December 17, 1967 Ht. 6-8 Wt. 230 College—Iowa

SEASON—TEAM	G	GS	MIN	FGM	FGA	PCT	3FGM	3FGA	PCT	FTM	FTA	PCT	O-RB	D-RB	TOT	AST	PF	DQ	STL	TO	BLK	PTS	RPG	APG	PPG
89-90—Washington	45	10	374	80	162	.494	0	4	.000	42	69	.609	59	49	108	19	63	1	9	39	5	202	2.4	0.4	4.5
REG. SEASON TOTALS	45	10	374	80	162	.494	0	4	.000	42	69	.609	59	49	108	19	63	1	9	39	5	202	2.4	0.4	4.5

HOSKET, WILMER FREDERICK (Bill) b. December 20, 1946 Ht. 6-8 Wt. 225 College—Ohio State

SEASON—TEAM	G	GS	MIN	FGM	FGA	PCT	3FGM	3FGA	PCT	FTM	FTA	PCT	O-RB	D-RB	TOT	AST	PF	DQ	STL	TO	BLK	PTS	RPG	APG	PPG
68-69—New York	50	—	351	53	123	.431	—	—	—	24	42	.571	—	—	94	19	77	0	—	—	—	130	1.9	0.4	2.6
69-70—New York	36	—	235	46	91	.505	—	—	—	26	33	.788	—	—	63	17	36	0	—	—	—	118	1.8	0.5	3.3
70-71—Buffalo	13	—	217	47	90	.522	—	—	—	11	17	.647	—	—	75	20	27	1	—	—	—	105	5.8	1.5	8.1
71-72—Buffalo	44	—	592	89	181	.492	—	—	—	42	52	.808	—	—	123	38	79	0	—	—	—	220	2.8	0.9	5.0
REG. SEASON TOTALS	143	—	1395	235	485	.485	—	—	—	103	144	.715	—	—	355	94	219	1	—	—	—	573	2.5	0.7	4.0
PLAYOFF TOTALS	9	—	51	7	16	.438	—	—	—	3	5	.600	—	—	12	4	9	0	—	—	—	17	1.3	0.4	1.9

HOUBREGS, ROBERT J. (Bob, Houby) b. March 12, 1932 Ht. 6-8 Wt. 225 College—Washington

SEASON—TEAM	G	GS	MIN	FGM	FGA	PCT	3FGM	3FGA	PCT	FTM	FTA	PCT	O-RB	D-RB	TOT	AST	PF	DQ	STL	TO	BLK	PTS	RPG	APG	PPG
53-54—Milw.-Balt.	70	—	1970	209	562	.372	—	—	—	190	266	.714	—	—	375	123	209	2	—	—	—	608	5.4	1.8	8.7
54-55—Balt.-Boston-Ft. Wayne	64	—	1326	148	386	.383	—	—	—	129	182	.709	—	—	297	86	180	5	—	—	—	425	4.6	1.3	6.6
55-56—Fort Wayne	70	—	1535	247	575	.430	—	—	—	283	383	.739	—	—	414	159	147	0	—	—	—	777	5.9	2.3	11.1
56-57—Fort Wayne	60	—	1592	253	585	.432	—	—	—	167	234	.714	—	—	401	113	118	2	—	—	—	673	6.7	1.9	11.2
57-58—Detroit	17	—	302	49	137	.358	—	—	—	30	43	.698	—	—	65	19	36	0	—	—	—	128	3.8	1.1	7.5
REG. SEASON TOTALS	281	—	6725	906	2245	.404	—	—	—	799	1108	.721	—	—	1552	500	690	9	—	—	—	2611	5.5	1.8	9.3
PLAYOFF TOTALS	23	—	468	67	158	.424	—	—	—	68	92	.739	—	—	135	36	55	1	—	—	—	202	5.9	1.6	8.8

HOUSTON, ALLAN WADE b. April 4, 1971 Ht. 6-6 Wt. 200 College—Tennessee

SEASON—TEAM	G	GS	MIN	FGM	FGA	PCT	3FGM	3FGA	PCT	FTM	FTA	PCT	O-RB	D-RB	TOT	AST	PF	DQ	STL	TO	BLK	PTS	RPG	APG	PPG
93-94—Detroit	79	20	1519	272	671	.405	35	117	.299	89	108	.824	19	101	120	100	165	2	34	99	13	668	1.5	1.3	8.5
REG. SEASON TOTALS	79	20	1519	272	671	.405	35	117	.299	89	108	.824	19	101	120	100	165	2	34	99	13	668	1.5	1.3	8.5

HOUSTON, BYRON DWIGHT b. November 22, 1969 Ht. 6-5 Wt. 250 College—Oklahoma State

SEASON—TEAM	G	GS	MIN	FGM	FGA	PCT	3FGM	3FGA	PCT	FTM	FTA	PCT	O-RB	D-RB	TOT	AST	PF	DQ	STL	TO	BLK	PTS	RPG	APG	PPG
92-93—Golden State	79	8	1274	145	325	.446	2	7	.286	129	194	.665	119	196	315	69	253	12	44	87	43	421	4.0	0.9	5.3
93-94—Golden State	71	2	866	81	177	.458	1	7	.143	33	54	.611	67	127	194	32	181	4	33	49	31	196	2.7	0.5	2.8
REG. SEASON TOTALS	150	10	2140	226	502	.450	3	14	.214	162	248	.653	186	323	509	101	434	16	77	136	74	617	3.4	0.7	4.1
PLAYOFF TOTALS	3	2	46	6	8	.750	0	0	—	3	5	.600	2	3	5	3	9	0	1	0	2	15	1.7	1.0	5.0

HOWARD, BRIAN EUGENE b. October 19, 1967 Ht. 6-6 Wt. 210 College—North Carolina State

SEASON—TEAM	G	GS	MIN	FGM	FGA	PCT	3FGM	3FGA	PCT	FTM	FTA	PCT	O-RB	D-RB	TOT	AST	PF	DQ	STL	TO	BLK	PTS	RPG	APG	PPG
91-92—Dallas	27	0	318	54	104	.519	1	2	.500	22	31	.710	17	34	51	14	55	2	11	15	8	131	1.9	0.5	4.9
92-93—Dallas	68	22	1295	183	414	.442	1	7	.143	72	94	.766	66	146	212	67	217	8	55	68	34	439	3.1	1.0	6.5
REG. SEASON TOTALS	95	22	1613	237	518	.458	2	9	.222	94	125	.752	83	180	263	81	272	10	66	83	42	570	2.8	0.9	6.0

HOWARD, GREGORY DARRYLE (Greg, Stretch) b. January 8, 1948 Ht. 6-9 Wt. 215 College—Hartnell CC/New Mexico

SEASON—TEAM	G	GS	MIN	FGM	FGA	PCT	3FGM	3FGA	PCT	FTM	FTA	PCT	O-RB	D-RB	TOT	AST	PF	DQ	STL	TO	BLK	PTS	RPG	APG	PPG
70-71—Phoenix	44	—	426	68	173	.393	—	—	—	37	58	.638	—	—	119	26	67	0	—	—	—	173	2.7	0.6	3.9
71-72—Cleveland	48	—	426	50	131	.382	—	—	—	39	51	.765	—	—	108	27	50	0	—	—	—	139	2.3	0.6	2.9
REG. SEASON TOTALS	92	—	852	118	304	.388	—	—	—	76	109	.697	—	—	227	53	117	0	—	—	—	312	2.5	0.6	3.4

HOWARD, MAURICE (Mo) b. August 24, 1954 Ht. 6-2 Wt. 175 College—Maryland

SEASON—TEAM	G	GS	MIN	FGM	FGA	PCT	3FGM	3FGA	PCT	FTM	FTA	PCT	O-RB	D-RB	TOT	AST	PF	DQ	STL	TO	BLK	PTS	RPG	APG	PPG
76-77—Clev.-N.O.	32	—	345	64	132	.485	—	—	—	24	35	.686	17	22	39	42	51	0	17	—	8	152	1.2	1.3	4.8
REG. SEASON TOTALS	32	—	345	64	132	.485	—	—	—	24	35	.686	17	22	39	42	51	0	17	—	8	152	1.2	1.3	4.8

HOWARD, STEPHEN CHRISTOPHER b. July 15, 1970 Ht. 6-9 Wt. 225 College—DePaul

SEASON—TEAM	G	GS	MIN	FGM	FGA	PCT	3FGM	3FGA	PCT	FTM	FTA	PCT	O-RB	D-RB	TOT	AST	PF	DQ	STL	TO	BLK	PTS	RPG	APG	PPG
92-93—Utah	49	0	260	35	93	.376	0	0	—	34	53	.642	26	34	60	10	58	0	15	23	12	104	1.2	0.2	2.1
93-94—Utah	9	0	53	10	17	.588	0	0	—	11	16	.688	10	6	16	1	13	0	1	6	3	31	1.8	0.1	3.4
REG. SEASON TOTALS	58	0	313	45	110	.409	0	0	—	45	69	.652	36	40	76	11	71	0	16	29	15	135	1.3	0.2	2.3
PLAYOFF TOTALS	10	0	27	3	11	.273	0	0	—	8	11	.727	3	7	10	—	11	0	0	2	0	14	1.0	0.0	1.4

HOWARD, W. OTIS b. November 5, 1956 Ht. 6-7 Wt. 220 College—Austin Peay

SEASON—TEAM	G	GS	MIN	FGM	FGA	PCT	3FGM	3FGA	PCT	FTM	FTA	PCT	O-RB	D-RB	TOT	AST	PF	DQ	STL	TO	BLK	PTS	RPG	APG	PPG
78-79—Milw.-Detroit	14	—	113	24	56	.429	—	—	—	11	23	.478	18	23	41	5	24	0	2	7	2	59	2.9	0.4	4.2
REG. SEASON TOTALS	14	—	113	24	56	.429	—	—	—	11	23	.478	18	23	41	5	24	0	2	7	2	59	2.9	0.4	4.2

HOWELL, BAILEY E. b. January 20, 1937 Ht. 6-7 Wt. 220 College—Mississippi State

SEASON—TEAM	G	GS	MIN	FGM	FGA	PCT	3FGM	3FGA	PCT	FTM	FTA	PCT	O-RB	D-RB	TOT	AST	PF	DQ	STL	TO	BLK	PTS	RPG	APG	PPG
59-60—Detroit	75	—	2346	510	1119	.456	—	—	—	312	422	.739	—	—	790	63	282	13	—	—	—	1332	10.5	0.8	17.8
60-61—Detroit	77	—	2952	607	1293	.469	—	—	—	601	798	.753	—	—	1111	196	297	10	—	—	—	1815	14.4	2.5	23.6
61-62—Detroit	79	—	2857	553	1193	.464	—	—	—	470	612	.768	—	—	996	186	317	10	—	—	—	1576	12.6	2.4	19.9
62-63—Detroit	79	—	2971	637	1235	.516	—	—	—	519	650	.798	—	—	910	232	300	9	—	—	—	1793	11.5	2.9	22.7
63-64—Detroit	77	—	2700	598	1267	.472	—	—	—	470	581	.809	—	—	776	205	290	9	—	—	—	1666	10.1	2.7	21.6
64-65—Baltimore	80	—	2975	515	1040	.495	—	—	—	504	629	.801	—	—	869	208	345	10	—	—	—	1534	10.9	2.6	19.2
65-66—Baltimore	78	—	2328	481	986	.488	—	—	—	402	551	.730	—	—	773	155	306	12	—	—	—	1364	9.9	2.0	17.5
66-67—Boston	81	—	2503	636	1242	.512	—	—	—	349	471	.741	—	—	677	103	296	4	—	—	—	1621	8.4	1.3	20.0
67-68—Boston	82	—	2801	643	1336	.481	—	—	—	335	461	.727	—	—	805	133	285	4	—	—	—	1621	9.8	1.6	19.8
68-69—Boston	78	—	2527	612	1257	.487	—	—	—	313	426	.735	—	—	685	137	285	3	—	—	—	1537	8.8	1.8	19.7
69-70—Boston	82	—	2078	399	931	.429	—	—	—	235	308	.763	—	—	550	120	261	4	—	—	—	1033	6.7	1.5	12.6
70-71—Philadelphia	82	—	1589	324	686	.472	—	—	—	230	315	.730	—	—	441	115	234	2	—	—	—	878	5.4	1.4	10.7
REG. SEASON TOTALS	950	—	30627	6515	13585	.480	—	—	—	4740	6224	.762	—	—	9383	1853	3498	90	—	—	—	17770	9.9	2.0	18.7
PLAYOFF TOTALS	86	—	2712	542	1165	.465	—	—	—	317	433	.732	—	—	697	130	376	21	—	—	—	1401	8.1	1.5	16.3
ALL-STAR TOTALS	6	—	81	13	33	.394	—	—	—	6	8	.750	—	—	10	8	12	0	—	—	—	32	1.7	1.3	5.3

HUBBARD, PHILLIP GREGORY (Phil) b. December 13, 1956 Ht. 6-8 Wt. 215 College—Michigan

SEASON—TEAM	G	GS	MIN	FGM	FGA	PCT	3FGM	3FGA	PCT	FTM	FTA	PCT	O-RB	D-RB	TOT	AST	PF	DQ	STL	TO	BLK	PTS	RPG	APG	PPG
79-80—Detroit	64	—	1189	210	451	.466	0	2	.000	165	220	.750	114	206	320	70	202	9	48	120	10	585	5.0	1.1	9.1
80-81—Detroit	80	—	2289	433	880	.492	1	3	.333	294	426	.690	236	350	586	150	317	14	80	229	20	1161	7.3	1.9	14.5
81-82—Detroit-Clev.	83	40	1839	326	665	.490	0	4	.000	191	280	.682	187	286	473	91	292	3	65	161	19	843	5.7	1.1	10.2
82-83—Cleveland	82	38	1953	288	597	.482	0	2	.000	204	296	.689	222	249	471	89	271	11	87	158	8	780	5.7	1.1	9.5
83-84—Cleveland	80	6	1799	321	628	.511	0	1	.000	221	299	.739	172	208	380	86	244	3	71	115	6	863	4.8	1.1	10.8
84-85—Cleveland	76	55	2249	415	822	.505	0	4	.000	371	494	.751	214	265	479	114	258	8	81	178	9	1201	6.3	1.5	15.8
85-86—Cleveland	23	21	640	93	198	.470	0	1	.000	76	112	.679	48	72	120	29	78	2	20	66	3	262	5.2	1.3	11.4
86-87—Cleveland	68	68	2083	321	605	.531	0	4	.000	162	272	.596	178	210	388	136	224	6	66	156	7	804	5.7	2.0	11.8
87-88—Cleveland	78	59	1631	237	485	.489	0	5	.000	182	243	.749	117	164	281	81	167	1	50	118	7	656	3.6	1.0	8.4
88-89—Cleveland	31	0	191	28	63	.444	0	0	—	17	25	.680	14	26	40	11	20	0	6	9	0	73	1.3	0.4	2.4
REG. SEASON TOTALS	665	287	15863	2672	5394	.495	1	26	.038	1883	2667	.706	1502	2036	3538	857	2073	57	574	1310	89	7228	5.3	1.3	10.9
PLAYOFF TOTALS	8	4	123	25	51	.490	1	1	1.000	13	18	.722	12	11	23	3	17	0	3	8	0	64	2.9	0.4	8.0

HUBBARD, ROBERT CECIL (**Bob**) b. December 27, 1922 Ht. 6-6 Wt. 215 College—Springfield College

SEASON—TEAM	G	GS	MIN	FGM	FGA	PCT	3FGM	3FGA	PCT	FTM	FTA	PCT	O-RB	D-RB	TOT	AST	PF	DQ	STL	TO	BLK	PTS	RPG	APG	PPG
47-48—Tri-Cities (N)	20	—	—	27	—	—	—	—	—	22	26	.846	—	—	—	—	—	—	—	—	—	76	—	—	3.8
47-48—Providence	28	—	—	58	199	.291	—	—	—	36	52	.692	—	—	—	11	34	—	—	—	—	152	—	0.4	5.4
48-49—Providence	34	—	—	25	135	.185	—	—	—	22	34	.647	—	—	—	18	39	—	—	—	—	72	—	0.5	2.1
REG. NBA TOTALS	62	—	—	83	334	.249	—	—	—	58	86	.674	—	—	—	29	73	—	—	—	—	224	—	0.5	3.6
REG. NBL TOTALS	20	—	—	27	—	—	—	—	—	22	26	.846	—	—	—	—	—	—	—	—	—	76	—	—	3.8

HUDSON, LOUIS CLYDE (**Lou, Super Lou**) b. July 11, 1944 Ht. 6-4½ Wt. 215 College—Minnesota

SEASON—TEAM	G	GS	MIN	FGM	FGA	PCT	3FGM	3FGA	PCT	FTM	FTA	PCT	O-RB	D-RB	TOT	AST	PF	DQ	STL	TO	BLK	PTS	RPG	APG	PPG
66-67—St. Louis	80	—	2446	620	1328	.467	—	—	—	231	327	.706	—	—	435	95	277	3	—	—	—	1471	5.4	1.2	18.4
67-68—St. Louis	46	—	966	227	500	.454	—	—	—	120	164	.732	—	—	193	65	113	2	—	—	—	574	4.2	1.4	12.5
68-69—Atlanta	81	—	2869	716	1455	.492	—	—	—	338	435	.777	—	—	533	216	248	0	—	—	—	1770	6.6	2.7	21.9
69-70—Atlanta	80	—	3091	830	1564	.531	—	—	—	371	450	.824	—	—	373	276	225	1	—	—	—	2031	4.7	3.5	25.4
70-71—Atlanta	76	—	3113	829	1713	.484	—	—	—	381	502	.759	—	—	386	257	186	0	—	—	—	2039	5.1	3.4	26.8
71-72—Atlanta	77	—	3042	775	1540	.503	—	—	—	349	430	.812	—	—	385	309	225	0	—	—	—	1899	5.0	4.0	24.7
72-73—Atlanta	75	—	3027	816	1710	.477	—	—	—	397	481	.825	—	—	467	258	197	1	—	—	—	2029	6.2	3.4	27.1
73-74—Atlanta	65	—	2588	678	1356	.500	—	—	—	295	353	.836	126	224	350	213	205	3	160	—	29	1651	5.4	3.3	25.4
74-75—Atlanta	11	—	380	97	225	.431	—	—	—	48	57	.842	14	33	47	40	33	1	13	—	2	242	4.3	3.6	22.0
75-76—Atlanta	81	—	2558	569	1205	.472	—	—	—	237	291	.814	104	196	300	214	241	3	124	—	17	1375	3.7	2.6	17.0
76-77—Atlanta	58	—	1745	413	905	.456	—	—	—	142	169	.840	48	81	129	155	160	2	67	—	19	968	2.2	2.7	16.7
77-78—Los Angeles	82	—	2283	493	992	.497	—	—	—	137	177	.774	80	108	188	193	196	0	94	150	14	1123	2.3	2.4	13.7
78-79—Los Angeles	78	—	1686	329	636	.517	—	—	—	110	124	.887	64	76	140	141	133	1	58	99	17	768	1.8	1.8	9.8
REG. SEASON TOTALS	890	—	29794	7392	15129	.489	—	—	—	3156	3960	.797	436	718	3926	2432	2439	17	516	249	98	17940	4.4	2.7	20.2
PLAYOFF TOTALS	61	—	2199	519	1164	.446	—	—	—	262	326	.804	8	5	318	164	196	4	6	10	0	1300	5.2	2.7	21.3
ALL-STAR TOTALS	6	—	99	26	61	.426	—	—	—	14	15	.933	1	2	13	6	11	0	0	—	1	66	2.2	1.0	11.0

HUGHES, ALFREDRICK b. July 19, 1962 Ht. 6-5 Wt. 215 College—Loyola (Ill.)

SEASON—TEAM	G	GS	MIN	FGM	FGA	PCT	3FGM	3FGA	PCT	FTM	FTA	PCT	O-RB	D-RB	TOT	AST	PF	DQ	STL	TO	BLK	PTS	RPG	APG	PPG
85-86—San Antonio	68	0	866	152	372	.409	3	17	.176	49	84	.583	49	64	113	61	79	0	26	63	5	356	1.7	0.9	5.2
REG. SEASON TOTALS	68	0	866	152	372	.409	3	17	.176	49	84	.583	49	64	113	61	79	0	26	63	5	356	1.7	0.9	5.2
PLAYOFF TOTALS	3	0	18	4	9	.444	0	0	—	0	0	—	0	0	0	1	3	0	1	1	0	8	0.0	0.3	2.7

HUGHES, EDDIE b. May 26, 1960 Ht. 5-10 Wt. 165 College—Colorado State

SEASON—TEAM	G	GS	MIN	FGM	FGA	PCT	3FGM	3FGA	PCT	FTM	FTA	PCT	O-RB	D-RB	TOT	AST	PF	DQ	STL	TO	BLK	PTS	RPG	APG	PPG
87-88—Utah	11	0	42	5	13	.385	1	6	.167	6	6	1.000	3	1	4	8	5	0	6	0	0	17	0.4	0.7	1.5
88-89—Denver	26	1	224	28	64	.438	7	22	.318	7	12	.583	6	13	19	35	30	0	17	11	2	70	0.7	1.3	2.7
89-90—Denver	60	7	892	83	202	.411	20	49	.408	23	34	.676	15	55	70	116	87	0	48	39	1	209	1.2	1.9	3.5
REG. SEASON TOTALS	97	8	1158	116	279	.416	28	77	.364	36	52	.692	24	69	93	159	122	0	65	56	3	296	1.0	1.6	3.1
PLAYOFF TOTALS	7	0	16	2	7	.286	1	3	.333	0	0	—	0	0	0	1	1	0	1	1	0	5	0.0	0.1	0.7

HUGHES, KIM GALEN b. June 4, 1952 Ht. 6-11 Wt. 220 College—Wisconsin

SEASON—TEAM	G	GS	MIN	FGM	FGA	PCT	3FGM	3FGA	PCT	FTM	FTA	PCT	O-RB	D-RB	TOT	AST	PF	DQ	STL	TO	BLK	PTS	RPG	APG	PPG
75-76—New York (A)	84	—	2162	300	566	.530	0	0	—	92	202	.455	341	434	775	55	292	—	98	102	120	692	9.2	0.7	8.2
76-77—New York Nets	81	—	2081	151	354	.427	—	—	—	19	69	.275	189	375	564	98	308	9	122	—	119	321	7.0	1.2	4.0
77-78—New Jersey	56	—	854	57	160	.356	—	—	—	9	29	.310	95	145	240	38	163	9	49	57	49	123	4.3	0.7	2.2
78-79—Denver	81	—	1086	98	182	.538	—	—	—	18	45	.400	112	223	335	74	215	2	56	78	102	214	4.1	0.9	2.6
79-80—Denver	70	—	1208	102	202	.505	0	0	—	15	41	.366	125	201	326	74	184	3	66	50	77	219	4.7	1.1	3.1
80-81—Denver-Clev.	53	—	490	27	70	.386	0	0	—	1	2	.500	48	79	127	35	106	2	28	44	35	55	2.4	0.7	1.0
REG. NBA TOTALS	341	—	5719	435	968	.449	0	0	—	62	186	.333	569	1023	1592	319	976	25	321	229	382	932	4.7	0.9	2.7
REG. ABA TOTALS	84	—	2162	300	566	.530	0	0	—	92	202	.455	341	434	775	55	292	—	98	102	120	692	9.2	0.7	8.2
NBA PLAYOFF TOTALS	3	—	35	1	2	.500	0	0	—	1	2	.500	3	8	11	—	8	0	2	3	0	3	3.7	0.0	1.0
ABA PLAYOFF TOTALS	12	—	266	29	57	.509	0	0	—	2	5	.400	34	38	72	9	53	—	10	9	13	60	6.0	0.8	5.0

HUMMER, JOHN R. b. May 4, 1948 Ht. 6-9 Wt. 230 College—Princeton

SEASON—TEAM	G	GS	MIN	FGM	FGA	PCT	3FGM	3FGA	PCT	FTM	FTA	PCT	O-RB	D-RB	TOT	AST	PF	DQ	STL	TO	BLK	PTS	RPG	APG	PPG
70-71—Buffalo	81	—	2637	339	764	.444	—	—	—	235	405	.580	—	—	717	163	284	10	—	—	—	913	8.9	2.0	11.3
71-72—Buffalo	55	—	1186	113	290	.390	—	—	—	58	124	.468	—	—	229	72	178	4	—	—	—	284	4.2	1.3	5.2
72-73—Buffalo	66	—	1546	206	464	.444	—	—	—	115	205	.561	—	—	323	138	185	5	—	—	—	527	4.9	2.1	8.0
73-74—Chicago-Seattle	53	—	1119	144	305	.472	—	—	—	59	124	.476	84	199	283	107	119	0	28	—	22	347	5.3	2.0	6.5
74-75—Seattle	43	—	568	41	108	.380	—	—	—	14	51	.275	28	76	104	38	63	0	8	—	7	96	2.4	0.9	2.2
75-76—Seattle	29	—	364	32	67	.478	—	—	—	17	41	.415	21	56	77	25	71	5	6	—	9	81	2.7	0.9	2.8
REG. SEASON TOTALS	327	—	7420	875	1998	.438	—	—	—	498	950	.524	133	331	1733	543	900	24	42	—	38	2248	5.3	1.7	6.9
PLAYOFF TOTALS	9	—	84	2	10	.200	—	—	—	0	0	—	2	8	10	4	10	0	2	—	0	4	1.1	0.4	0.4

HUMPHRIES, JOHN JAY (**Jay**) b. October 17, 1962 Ht. 6-3 Wt. 185 College—Colorado

SEASON—TEAM	G	GS	MIN	FGM	FGA	PCT	3FGM	3FGA	PCT	FTM	FTA	PCT	O-RB	D-RB	TOT	AST	PF	DQ	STL	TO	BLK	PTS	RPG	APG	PPG
84-85—Phoenix	80	39	2062	279	626	.446	4	20	.200	141	170	.829	32	132	164	350	209	2	107	167	8	703	2.1	4.4	8.8
85-86—Phoenix	82	82	2733	352	735	.479	4	29	.138	197	257	.767	56	204	260	526	222	1	132	190	9	905	3.2	6.4	11.0
86-87—Phoenix	82	82	2579	359	753	.477	5	27	.185	200	260	.769	62	198	260	632	239	1	112	195	9	923	3.2	7.7	11.3
87-88—Phoenix-Milw.	68	33	1809	284	538	.528	3	18	.167	112	153	.732	49	125	174	395	177	1	81	127	5	683	2.6	5.8	10.0
88-89—Milwaukee	73	50	2220	345	714	.483	25	94	.266	129	158	.816	70	119	189	405	187	1	142	160	5	844	2.6	5.5	11.6
89-90—Milwaukee	81	81	2818	496	1005	.494	21	70	.300	224	285	.786	80	189	269	472	253	2	156	151	11	1237	3.3	5.8	15.3
90-91—Milwaukee	80	80	2726	482	960	.502	60	161	.373	191	239	.799	57	163	220	538	237	2	129	151	7	1215	2.8	6.7	15.2
91-92—Milwaukee	71	71	2261	377	803	.469	42	144	.292	195	249	.783	44	140	184	466	210	2	119	148	13	991	2.6	6.6	14.0
92-93—Utah	78	20	2034	287	659	.436	15	75	.200	101	130	.777	40	103	143	317	236	3	101	132	11	690	1.8	4.1	8.8
93-94—Utah	75	19	1619	233	535	.436	38	96	.396	57	76	.750	35	92	127	219	168	0	65	95	11	561	1.7	2.9	7.5
REG. SEASON TOTALS	770	557	22861	3494	7328	.477	217	734	.296	1547	1977	.782	525	1465	1990	4320	2138	15	1144	1516	89	8752	2.6	5.6	11.4
PLAYOFF TOTALS	41	17	1104	151	323	.467	15	56	.268	79	101	.782	26	67	93	187	123	2	32	57	5	396	2.3	4.6	9.7

HUNDLEY, RODNEY CLARK (**Rod, Hot Rod**) b. October 26, 1934 Ht. 6-4 Wt. 185 College—West Virginia

SEASON—TEAM	G	GS	MIN	FGM	FGA	PCT	3FGM	3FGA	PCT	FTM	FTA	PCT	O-RB	D-RB	TOT	AST	PF	DQ	STL	TO	BLK	PTS	RPG	APG	PPG
57-58—Minneapolis	65	—	1154	174	548	.318	—	—	—	104	162	.642	—	—	186	121	99	0	—	—	—	452	2.9	1.9	7.0
58-59—Minneapolis	71	—	1664	259	719	.360	—	—	—	164	218	.752	—	—	250	205	139	0	—	—	—	682	3.5	2.9	9.6
59-60—Minneapolis	73	—	2279	365	1019	.358	—	—	—	203	273	.744	—	—	390	338	194	0	—	—	—	933	5.3	4.6	12.8
60-61—Los Angeles	79	—	2179	323	921	.351	—	—	—	223	296	.753	—	—	289	350	144	0	—	—	—	869	3.7	4.4	11.0
61-62—Los Angeles	78	—	1492	173	509	.340	—	—	—	83	127	.654	—	—	199	290	129	1	—	—	—	429	2.6	3.7	5.5
62-63—Los Angeles	65	—	785	88	262	.336	—	—	—	84	119	.706	—	—	106	151	81	0	—	—	—	260	1.6	2.3	4.0
REG. SEASON TOTALS	431	—	9553	1382	3978	.347	—	—	—	861	1195	.721	—	—	1420	1455	786	1	—	—	—	3625	3.3	3.4	8.4
PLAYOFF TOTALS	53	—	1020	101	316	.320	—	—	—	68	95	.716	—	—	149	157	80	0	—	—	—	270	2.8	3.0	5.1
ALL-STAR TOTALS	2	—	37	11	22	.500	—	—	—	2	2	1.000	—	—	3	4	3	0	—	—	—	24	1.5	2.0	12.0

HUNTER, CEDRIC R. b. January 16, 1965 Ht. 6-0 Wt. 180 College—Kansas

SEASON—TEAM	G	GS	MIN	FGM	FGA	PCT	3FGM	3FGA	PCT	FTM	FTA	PCT	O-RB	D-RB	TOT	AST	PF	DQ	STL	TO	BLK	PTS	RPG	APG	PPG
91-92—Charlotte	1	0	1	0	0	—	0	0	—	0	0	—	0	0	0	0	0	0	0	0	0	0	0.0	0.0	0.0
REG. SEASON TOTALS	1	0	1	0	0	—	0	0	—	0	0	—	0	0	0	0	0	0	0	0	0	0	0.0	0.0	0.0

HUNTER, LESLIE (**Les, Big Game**) b. August 16, 1942 Ht. 6-7 Wt. 210 College—Loyola (Ill.)

SEASON—TEAM	G	GS	MIN	FGM	FGA	PCT	3FGM	3FGA	PCT	FTM	FTA	PCT	O-RB	D-RB	TOT	AST	PF	DQ	STL	TO	BLK	PTS	RPG	APG	PPG
64-65—Baltimore	24	—	114	18	64	.281	—	—	—	6	14	.429	—	—	50	11	16	0	—	—	—	42	2.1	0.5	1.8
67-68—Minnesota (A)	75	—	2552	513	1207	.425	2	17	.118	290	468	.620	332	406	738	116	297	7	—	204	—	1318	9.8	1.5	17.6
68-69—Miami (A)	77	—	2537	476	1073	.444	0	5	.000	335	448	.748	—	—	743	127	311	14	—	220	—	1287	9.6	1.6	16.7
69-70—New York (A)	79	—	2859	486	1122	.433	6	41	.146	317	432	.734	—	—	673	215	335	15	—	—	—	1295	8.5	2.7	16.4
70-71—N.Y.-Ken. (A)	80	—	1525	288	645	.447	10	49	.204	159	223	.713	—	—	493	95	253	—	—	—	—	745	6.2	1.2	9.3
71-72—Kentucky (A)	70	—	967	183	383	.478	5	16	.313	101	144	.701	—	—	225	93	154	—	—	93	—	472	3.2	1.3	6.7
72-73—Memphis (A)	63	—	1333	236	474	.498	9	33	.273	95	135	.704	94	208	302	95	183	0	—	95	—	576	4.8	1.5	9.1
REG. NBA TOTALS	24	—	114	18	64	.281	—	—	—	6	14	.429	—	—	50	11	16	0	—	—	—	42	2.1	0.5	1.8
REG. ABA TOTALS	444	—	11773	2182	4904	.445	32	161	.199	1297	1850	.701	426	614	3174	741	1533	36	—	612	—	5693	7.1	1.7	12.8
ABA PLAYOFF TOTALS	52	—	1302	250	613	.408	8	28	.286	167	253	.660	—	—	349	89	177	5	—	55	—	675	6.7	1.7	13.0
ABA ALL-STAR TOTALS	2	—	43	7	17	.412	0	0	—	5	7	.714	8	6	14	1	7	0	—	6	—	19	7.0	0.5	9.5

HUNTER, LINDSEY BENSON JR. b. December 3, 1970 Ht. 6-2 Wt. 195 College—Alcorn State/Jackson State

SEASON—TEAM	G	GS	MIN	FGM	FGA	PCT	3FGM	3FGA	PCT	FTM	FTA	PCT	O-RB	D-RB	TOT	AST	PF	DQ	STL	TO	BLK	PTS	RPG	APG	PPG
93-94—Detroit	82	26	2172	335	893	.375	69	207	.333	104	142	.732	47	142	189	390	174	1	121	184	10	843	2.3	4.8	10.3
REG. SEASON TOTALS	82	26	2172	335	893	.375	69	207	.333	104	142	.732	47	142	189	390	174	1	121	184	10	843	2.3	4.8	10.3

HURLEY, ROBERT MATTHEW (**Bobby**) b. June 28, 1971 Ht. 6-0 Wt. 165 College—Duke

SEASON—TEAM	G	GS	MIN	FGM	FGA	PCT	3FGM	3FGA	PCT	FTM	FTA	PCT	O-RB	D-RB	TOT	AST	PF	DQ	STL	TO	BLK	PTS	RPG	APG	PPG
93-94—Sacramento	19	19	499	54	146	.370	2	16	.125	24	30	.800	6	28	34	115	28	0	13	48	1	134	1.8	6.1	7.1
REG. SEASON TOTALS	19	19	499	54	146	.370	2	16	.125	24	30	.800	6	28	34	115	28	0	13	48	1	134	1.8	6.1	7.1

HURLEY, ROY LEONARD b. August 12, 1922 d. October 14, 1993 Ht. 6-2½ Wt. 170 College—Indiana/Murray State (Ky.)

SEASON—TEAM	G	GS	MIN	FGM	FGA	PCT	3FGM	3FGA	PCT	FTM	FTA	PCT	O-RB	D-RB	TOT	AST	PF	DQ	STL	TO	BLK	PTS	RPG	APG	PPG
45-46—Indianapolis (N)	30	—	—	76	—	—	—	—	—	24	38	.632	—	—	—	68	—	—	—	—	—	176	—	—	5.9
46-47—Toronto	46	—	—	100	447	.224	—	—	—	39	64	.609	—	—	—	34	85	—	—	—	—	239	—	0.7	5.2
47-48—Tri-Cit.-Syr. (N)	16	—	—	19	—	—	—	—	—	13	21	.619	—	—	—	—	—	—	—	—	—	51	—	—	3.2
REG. NBA TOTALS	46	—	—	100	447	.224	—	—	—	39	64	.609	—	—	—	34	85	—	—	—	—	239	—	0.7	5.2
REG. NBL TOTALS	46	—	—	95	—	—	—	—	—	37	59	.627	—	—	—	68	—	—	—	—	—	227	—	—	4.9

HUSTON, GEOFFREY ANGIER (**Geoff**) b. November 8, 1957 Ht. 6-2 Wt. 175 College—Texas Tech

SEASON—TEAM	G	GS	MIN	FGM	FGA	PCT	3FGM	3FGA	PCT	FTM	FTA	PCT	O-RB	D-RB	TOT	AST	PF	DQ	STL	TO	BLK	PTS	RPG	APG	PPG
79-80—New York	71	—	923	94	241	.390	3	17	.176	28	38	.737	14	44	58	159	83	0	39	73	5	219	0.8	2.2	3.1
80-81—Dallas-Clev.	81	—	2434	461	942	.489	1	5	.200	150	212	.708	45	93	138	394	148	1	58	179	7	1073	1.7	4.9	13.2
81-82—Cleveland	78	43	2409	325	672	.484	3	10	.300	153	200	.765	53	97	150	590	169	1	70	171	11	806	1.9	7.6	10.3
82-83—Cleveland	80	79	2716	401	832	.482	4	12	.333	168	245	.686	41	118	159	487	215	1	74	195	4	974	2.0	6.1	12.2
83-84—Cleveland	77	56	2041	348	699	.498	2	11	.182	110	154	.714	32	64	96	413	126	0	38	145	1	808	1.2	5.4	10.5
84-85—Cleveland	8	0	93	12	25	.480	0	0	—	2	3	.667	0	1	1	23	8	0	0	8	0	26	0.1	2.9	3.3
85-86—Golden State	82	0	1208	140	273	.513	2	6	.333	63	92	.685	10	55	65	342	67	0	38	83	4	345	0.8	4.2	4.2
86-87—L.A. Clippers	19	8	428	55	121	.455	1	2	.500	18	34	.529	6	11	17	101	28	0	14	45	0	129	0.9	5.3	6.8
REG. SEASON TOTALS	496	186	12252	1836	3805	.483	16	63	.254	692	978	.708	201	483	684	2509	844	3	331	899	32	4380	1.4	5.1	8.8

HUSTON, PAUL F. (**Shad**) b. June 2, 1925 Ht. 6-3 Wt. 175 College—Ohio State

SEASON—TEAM	G	GS	MIN	FGM	FGA	PCT	3FGM	3FGA	PCT	FTM	FTA	PCT	O-RB	D-RB	TOT	AST	PF	DQ	STL	TO	BLK	PTS	RPG	APG	PPG
47-48—Chicago	46	—	—	51	215	.237	—	—	—	62	89	.697	—	—	—	27	82	—	—	—	—	164	—	0.6	3.6
REG. SEASON TOTALS	46	—	—	51	215	.237	—	—	—	62	89	.697	—	—	—	27	82	—	—	—	—	164	—	0.6	3.6
PLAYOFF TOTALS	5	—	—	3	19	.158	—	—	—	7	13	.538	—	—	—	2	14	—	—	—	—	13	—	0.4	2.6

HUTCHINS, MELVIN R. (**Mel, Hutch**) b. November 22, 1928 Ht. 6-6 Wt. 200 College—Brigham Young

SEASON—TEAM	G	GS	MIN	FGM	FGA	PCT	3FGM	3FGA	PCT	FTM	FTA	PCT	O-RB	D-RB	TOT	AST	PF	DQ	STL	TO	BLK	PTS	RPG	APG	PPG
51-52—Milwaukee	66	—	2618	231	633	.365	—	—	—	145	225	.644	—	—	880	190	192	5	—	—	—	607	13.3	2.9	9.2
52-53—Milwaukee	71	—	2891	319	842	.379	—	—	—	193	295	.654	—	—	793	227	214	5	—	—	—	831	11.2	3.2	11.7
53-54—Fort Wayne	72	—	2934	295	736	.401	—	—	—	151	223	.677	—	—	695	210	229	4	—	—	—	741	9.7	2.9	10.3
54-55—Fort Wayne	72	—	2860	341	903	.378	—	—	—	182	257	.708	—	—	665	247	232	0	—	—	—	864	9.2	3.4	12.0
55-56—Fort Wayne	66	—	2240	325	764	.425	—	—	—	142	221	.643	—	—	496	180	166	1	—	—	—	792	7.5	2.7	12.0
56-57—Fort Wayne	72	—	2647	369	953	.387	—	—	—	152	206	.738	—	—	571	210	182	0	—	—	—	890	7.9	2.9	12.4
57-58—New York	18	—	384	51	131	.389	—	—	—	24	43	.558	—	—	86	34	31	0	—	—	—	126	4.8	1.9	7.0
REG. SEASON TOTALS	437	—	16574	1931	4962	.389	—	—	—	989	1470	.673	—	—	4186	1298	1246	15	—	—	—	4851	9.6	3.0	11.1
PLAYOFF TOTALS	27	—	1024	118	332	.355	—	—	—	80	121	.661	—	—	237	70	100	5	—	—	—	316	8.8	2.6	11.7
ALL-STAR TOTALS	4	—	114	11	39	.282	—	—	—	4	8	.500	—	—	21	7	7	0	—	—	—	26	5.3	1.8	6.5

HUTTON, JOSEPH W. JR. (**Joe**) b. October 6, 1928 Ht. 6-1 Wt. 170 College—Hamline

SEASON—TEAM	G	GS	MIN	FGM	FGA	PCT	3FGM	3FGA	PCT	FTM	FTA	PCT	O-RB	D-RB	TOT	AST	PF	DQ	STL	TO	BLK	PTS	RPG	APG	PPG
50-51—Minneapolis	60	—	—	59	180	.328	—	—	—	29	43	.674	—	—	102	53	89	1	—	—	—	147	1.7	0.9	2.5
51-52—Minneapolis	60	—	723	53	158	.335	—	—	—	49	70	.700	—	—	85	62	110	1	—	—	—	155	1.4	1.0	2.6
REG. SEASON TOTALS	120	—	723	112	338	.331	—	—	—	78	113	.690	—	—	187	115	199	2	—	—	—	302	1.6	1.0	2.5
PLAYOFF TOTALS	19	—	139	12	32	.375	—	—	—	11	18	.611	—	—	16	13	22	0	—	—	—	35	1.0	0.8	1.8

HYDER, GREGORY PECK (**Greg**) b. June 21, 1948 Ht. 6-6 Wt. 215 College—Eastern New Mexico

SEASON—TEAM	G	GS	MIN	FGM	FGA	PCT	3FGM	3FGA	PCT	FTM	FTA	PCT	O-RB	D-RB	TOT	AST	PF	DQ	STL	TO	BLK	PTS	RPG	APG	PPG
70-71—Cincinnati	77	—	1359	183	409	.447	—	—	—	51	71	.718	—	—	332	48	187	2	—	—	—	417	4.3	0.6	5.4
REG. SEASON TOTALS	77	—	1359	183	409	.447	—	—	—	51	71	.718	—	—	332	48	187	2	—	—	—	417	4.3	0.6	5.4

IAVARONI, MARCUS JOHN (**Marc**) b. September 15, 1956 Ht. 6-10 Wt. 225 College—Virginia

SEASON—TEAM	G	GS	MIN	FGM	FGA	PCT	3FGM	3FGA	PCT	FTM	FTA	PCT	O-RB	D-RB	TOT	AST	PF	DQ	STL	TO	BLK	PTS	RPG	APG	PPG
82-83—Philadelphia	80	77	1612	163	353	.462	0	2	.000	78	113	.690	117	212	329	83	238	0	32	133	44	404	4.1	1.0	5.1
83-84—Philadelphia	78	71	1532	149	322	.463	0	2	.000	97	131	.740	91	219	310	95	222	1	36	124	55	395	4.0	1.2	5.1
84-85—Phil.-S.A.	69	43	1334	162	354	.458	0	4	.000	87	128	.680	95	209	304	119	217	5	35	119	35	411	4.4	1.7	6.0
85-86—S.A.-Utah	68	9	1014	110	244	.451	0	2	.000	76	115	.661	63	146	209	82	163	0	32	72	17	296	3.1	1.2	4.4
86-87—Utah	78	0	845	100	215	.465	0	4	.000	78	116	.672	64	109	173	36	154	0	16	56	11	278	2.2	0.5	3.6
87-88—Utah	81	71	1238	143	308	.464	0	2	.000	78	99	.788	94	174	268	67	162	1	23	83	25	364	3.3	0.8	4.5
88-89—Utah	77	50	796	72	163	.442	0	1	.000	36	44	.818	41	91	132	32	99	0	11	52	13	180	1.7	0.4	2.3
REG. SEASON TOTALS	531	321	8371	899	1959	.459	0	17	.000	530	746	.710	565	1160	1725	514	1255	7	185	639	200	2328	3.2	1.0	4.4
PLAYOFF TOTALS	43	31	721	76	151	.503	1	4	.250	48	67	.716	50	82	132	59	126	3	17	49	15	201	3.1	1.4	4.7

IMHOFF, DARRALL TUCKER (**Big D**) b. October 11, 1938   Ht. 6-10 Wt. 220 College—California

SEASON—TEAM	G	GS	MIN	FGM	FGA	PCT	3FGM	3FGA	PCT	FTM	FTA	PCT	O-RB	D-RB	TOT	AST	PF	DQ	STL	TO	BLK	PTS	RPG	APG	PPG
60-61—New York	62	—	994	122	310	.394	—	—	—	49	96	.510	—	—	296	51	143	2	—	—	—	293	4.8	0.8	4.7
61-62—New York	76	—	1481	186	482	.386	—	—	—	80	139	.576	—	—	470	82	230	10	—	—	—	452	6.2	1.1	5.9
62-63—Detroit	45	—	458	48	153	.314	—	—	—	24	50	.480	—	—	155	28	66	1	—	—	—	120	3.4	0.6	2.7
63-64—Detroit	58	—	871	104	251	.414	—	—	—	69	114	.605	—	—	283	56	167	5	—	—	—	277	4.9	1.0	4.8
64-65—Los Angeles	76	—	1521	145	311	.466	—	—	—	88	154	.571	—	—	500	87	238	7	—	—	—	378	6.6	1.1	5.0
65-66—Los Angeles	77	—	1413	151	337	.448	—	—	—	77	136	.566	—	—	509	113	234	7	—	—	—	379	6.6	1.5	4.9
66-67—Los Angeles	81	—	2725	370	780	.474	—	—	—	127	207	.614	—	—	1080	222	281	7	—	—	—	867	13.3	2.7	10.7
67-68—Los Angeles	82	—	2271	293	613	.478	—	—	—	177	286	.619	—	—	893	206	264	3	—	—	—	763	10.9	2.5	9.3
68-69—Philadelphia	82	—	2360	279	593	.470	—	—	—	194	325	.597	—	—	792	218	310	12	—	—	—	752	9.7	2.7	9.2
69-70—Philadelphia	79	—	2474	430	796	.540	—	—	—	215	331	.650	—	—	754	211	294	7	—	—	—	1075	9.5	2.7	13.6
70-71—Cincinnati	34	—	826	119	258	.461	—	—	—	37	73	.507	—	—	233	79	120	5	—	—	—	275	6.9	2.3	8.1
71-72—Cin.-Port.	49	—	480	52	132	.394	—	—	—	24	43	.558	—	—	134	52	98	2	—	—	—	128	2.7	1.1	2.6
REG. SEASON TOTALS	801	—	17874	2299	5016	.458	—	—	—	1161	1954	.594	—	—	6099	1405	2445	68	—	—	—	5759	7.6	1.8	7.2
PLAYOFF TOTALS	54	—	1251	139	291	.478	—	—	—	76	131	.580	—	—	442	101	179	2	—	—	—	354	8.2	1.9	6.6
ALL-STAR TOTALS	1	—	6	0	7	.000	—	—	—	0	0	—	—	—	7	1	1	0	—	—	—	0	7.0	1.0	0.0

INGELSBY, TOM b. February 12, 1951   Ht. 6-3 Wt. 185 College—Villanova

SEASON—TEAM	G	GS	MIN	FGM	FGA	PCT	3FGM	3FGA	PCT	FTM	FTA	PCT	O-RB	D-RB	TOT	AST	PF	DQ	STL	TO	BLK	PTS	RPG	APG	PPG
73-74—Atlanta	48	—	398	50	131	.382	—	—	—	29	37	.784	10	34	44	37	43	0	19	—	4	129	0.9	0.8	2.7
74-75—St. Louis (A)	22	—	344	44	90	.489	1	5	.200	20	27	.741	22	28	50	38	19	—	14	17	1	109	2.3	1.7	5.0
75-76—San Diego (A)	5	—	14	1	3	.333	0	0	—	2	2	1.000	1	2	3	0	1	—	0	0	0	4	0.6	0.0	0.8
REG. NBA TOTALS	48	—	398	50	131	.382	—	—	—	29	37	.784	10	34	44	37	43	0	19	—	4	129	0.9	0.8	2.7
REG. ABA TOTALS	27	—	358	45	93	.484	1	5	.200	22	29	.759	23	30	53	38	20	—	14	17	1	113	2.0	1.4	4.2

INGRAM, JOEL McCOY (**McCoy**) b. August 31, 1931   Ht. 6-0 Wt. 210 College—Jackson State

SEASON—TEAM	G	GS	MIN	FGM	FGA	PCT	3FGM	3FGA	PCT	FTM	FTA	PCT	O-RB	D-RB	TOT	AST	PF	DQ	STL	TO	BLK	PTS	RPG	APG	PPG
57-58—Minneapolis	24	—	267	27	103	.262	—	—	—	13	28	.464	—	—	116	20	44	1	—	—	—	67	4.8	0.8	2.8
REG. SEASON TOTALS	24	—	267	27	103	.262	—	—	—	13	28	.464	—	—	116	20	44	1	—	—	—	67	4.8	0.8	2.8

INNIGER, ERVIN LEE JR. (**Irv**) b. January 16, 1945   Ht. 6-4 Wt. 190 College—Indiana

SEASON—TEAM	G	GS	MIN	FGM	FGA	PCT	3FGM	3FGA	PCT	FTM	FTA	PCT	O-RB	D-RB	TOT	AST	PF	DQ	STL	TO	BLK	PTS	RPG	APG	PPG
67-68—Minnesota (A)	75	—	1993	345	790	.437	5	35	.143	99	137	.723	—	—	325	115	201	2	—	94	—	794	4.3	1.5	10.6
68-69—Miami (A)	34	—	484	73	182	.401	3	13	.231	21	25	.840	—	—	60	41	59	0	—	30	—	170	1.8	1.2	5.0
REG. ABA TOTALS	109	—	2477	418	972	.430	8	48	.167	120	162	.741	—	—	385	156	260	2	—	124	—	964	3.5	1.4	8.8
ABA PLAYOFF TOTALS	10	—	364	55	140	.393	2	11	.182	26	32	.813	—	—	57	35	36	0	—	15	—	138	5.7	3.5	13.8

IRVIN, BYRON EDWARD b. December 2, 1966   Ht. 6-6 Wt. 195 College—Arkansas/Missouri

SEASON—TEAM	G	GS	MIN	FGM	FGA	PCT	3FGM	3FGA	PCT	FTM	FTA	PCT	O-RB	D-RB	TOT	AST	PF	DQ	STL	TO	BLK	PTS	RPG	APG	PPG
89-90—Portland	50	2	488	96	203	.473	5	14	.357	61	91	.670	30	44	74	47	40	0	28	39	1	258	1.5	0.9	5.2
90-91—Washington	33	4	316	60	129	.465	1	5	.200	50	61	.820	24	21	45	24	32	0	15	16	2	171	1.4	0.7	5.2
92-93—Washington	4	2	45	9	18	.500	1	1	1.000	3	6	.500	2	2	4	2	5	0	1	4	0	22	1.0	0.5	5.5
REG. SEASON TOTALS	87	8	849	165	350	.471	7	20	.350	114	158	.722	56	67	123	73	77	0	44	59	3	451	1.4	0.8	5.2
PLAYOFF TOTALS	4	0	47	5	22	.227	0	0	—	5	6	.833	4	4	8	5	7	0	2	3	0	15	2.0	1.3	3.8

IRVINE, GEORGE R. (**Hawkeye**) b. February 1, 1948   Ht. 6-6 Wt. 200 College—Washington

SEASON—TEAM	G	GS	MIN	FGM	FGA	PCT	3FGM	3FGA	PCT	FTM	FTA	PCT	O-RB	D-RB	TOT	AST	PF	DQ	STL	TO	BLK	PTS	RPG	APG	PPG
70-71—Virginia (A)	34	—	338	83	149	.557	2	8	.250	26	35	.743	—	—	65	25	67	—	—	—	—	194	1.9	0.7	5.7
71-72—Virginia (A)	75	—	1362	200	397	.504	3	10	.300	54	75	.720	—	—	217	70	202	—	—	74	—	457	2.9	0.9	6.1
72-73—Virginia (A)	79	—	2075	424	805	.527	7	33	.212	169	203	.833	108	188	296	149	267	0	—	138	—	1024	3.7	1.9	13.0
73-74—Virginia (A)	75	—	1140	254	516	.492	12	46	.261	120	138	.870	56	121	177	76	134	—	28	67	16	640	2.4	1.0	8.5
74-75—Virginia (A)	59	—	1522	311	589	.528	13	37	.351	139	164	.848	73	130	203	108	171	—	32	94	12	774	3.4	1.8	13.1
75-76—Denver (A)	3	—	14	2	6	.333	0	1	.000	0	0	—	1	0	1	0	1	—	0	1	0	4	0.3	0.0	1.3
REG. ABA TOTALS	325	—	6451	1274	2462	.517	37	135	.274	508	615	.826	238	439	959	428	842	0	60	374	28	3093	3.0	1.3	9.5
ABA PLAYOFF TOTALS	28	—	472	89	162	.549	1	10	.100	41	47	.872	3	8	48	27	73	0	3	29	1	220	1.7	1.0	7.9

ISSEL, DANIEL PAUL (**Dan**) b. October 25, 1948 Ht. 6-9 Wt. 240 College—Kentucky

SEASON—TEAM	G	GS	MIN	FGM	FGA	PCT	3FGM	3FGA	PCT	FTM	FTA	PCT	O-RB	D-RB	TOT	AST	PF	DQ	STL	TO	BLK	PTS	RPG	APG	PPG
70-71—Kentucky (A)	83	—	3274	938	1924	.488	0	5	.000	604	748	.807	421	672	1093	162	323	—	—	—	—	2480	13.2	2.0	29.9
71-72—Kentucky (A)	83	—	3570	972	2001	.486	3	11	.273	591	753	.785	353	578	931	195	242	—	—	244	—	2538	11.2	2.3	30.6
72-73—Kentucky (A)	84	—	3531	902	1757	.513	3	15	.200	485	635	.764	329	593	922	220	255	0	—	216	—	2292	11.0	2.6	27.3
73-74—Kentucky (A)	83	—	3347	829	1726	.480	3	17	.176	457	581	.787	346	501	847	137	199	—	69	171	32	2118	10.2	1.7	25.5
74-75—Kentucky (A)	83	—	2864	614	1303	.471	0	5	.000	237	321	.738	258	452	710	188	197	—	76	157	48	1465	8.6	2.3	17.7
75-76—Denver (A)	84	—	2856	752	1472	.511	1	4	.250	425	521	.816	303	620	923	201	266	—	100	200	56	1930	11.0	2.4	23.0
76-77—Denver	79	—	2507	660	1282	.515	—	—	—	445	558	.797	211	485	696	177	246	7	91	—	29	1765	8.8	2.2	22.3
77-78—Denver	82	—	2851	659	1287	.512	—	—	—	428	547	.782	253	577	830	304	279	5	100	259	41	1746	10.1	3.7	21.3
78-79—Denver	81	—	2742	532	1030	.517	—	—	—	316	419	.754	240	498	738	255	233	6	61	171	46	1380	9.1	3.1	17.0
79-80—Denver	82	—	2938	715	1416	.505	4	12	.333	517	667	.775	236	483	719	198	190	1	88	163	54	1951	8.8	2.4	23.8
80-81—Denver	80	—	2641	614	1220	.503	2	12	.167	519	684	.759	229	447	676	158	249	6	83	130	53	1749	8.5	2.0	21.9
81-82—Denver	81	81	2472	651	1236	.527	4	6	.667	546	655	.834	174	434	608	179	245	4	67	169	55	1852	7.5	2.2	22.9
82-83—Denver	80	80	2431	661	1296	.510	4	19	.211	400	479	.835	151	445	596	223	227	0	83	174	43	1726	7.5	2.8	21.6
83-84—Denver	76	66	2076	569	1153	.493	4	19	.211	364	428	.850	112	401	513	173	182	2	60	122	44	1506	6.8	2.3	19.8
84-85—Denver	77	9	1684	363	791	.459	1	7	.143	257	319	.806	80	251	331	137	171	1	65	93	31	984	4.3	1.8	12.8
REG. NBA TOTALS	718	236	22342	5424	10711	.506	19	75	.253	3792	4756	.797	1686	4021	5707	1804	2022	32	698	1281	396	14659	7.9	2.5	20.4
REG. ABA TOTALS	500	—	19442	5007	10183	.492	10	57	.175	2799	3559	.786	2010	3416	5426	1103	1482	0	245	988	136	12823	10.9	2.2	25.6
NBA PLAYOFF TOTALS	53	20	1599	402	810	.496	2	4	.500	223	269	.829	111	282	393	145	157	1	42	93	24	1029	7.4	2.7	19.4
ABA PLAYOFF TOTALS	80	—	3119	744	1543	.482	1	8	.125	416	508	.819	278	584	862	136	308	0	51	148	37	1905	10.8	1.7	23.8
NBA ALL-STAR TOTALS	1	1	10	0	3	.000	0	0	—	0	0	—	1	0	1	0	0	0	0	—	0	0	1.0	0.0	0.0
ABA ALL-STAR TOTALS	6	4	163	42	79	.532	0	0	—	19	26	.731	17	21	47	16	12	—	1	10	1	103	7.8	2.7	17.2

IUZZOLINO, MICHAEL ALAN (**Mike**) b. January 22, 1968 Ht. 5-11 Wt. 175 College—Penn State/St. Francis (Pa.)

SEASON—TEAM	G	GS	MIN	FGM	FGA	PCT	3FGM	3FGA	PCT	FTM	FTA	PCT	O-RB	D-RB	TOT	AST	PF	DQ	STL	TO	BLK	PTS	RPG	APG	PPG
91-92—Dallas	52	21	1280	160	355	.451	59	136	.434	107	128	.836	27	71	98	194	79	0	33	92	1	486	1.9	3.7	9.3
92-93—Dallas	70	23	1769	221	478	.462	54	144	.375	114	149	.765	31	109	140	328	101	0	49	129	6	610	2.0	4.7	8.7
REG. SEASON TOTALS	122	44	3049	381	833	.457	113	280	.404	221	277	.798	58	180	238	522	180	0	82	221	7	1096	2.0	4.3	9.0

IVERSON, WILLIE b. October 8, 1945 Ht. 6-0 Wt. 180 College—Central Michigan

SEASON—TEAM	G	GS	MIN	FGM	FGA	PCT	3FGM	3FGA	PCT	FTM	FTA	PCT	O-RB	D-RB	TOT	AST	PF	DQ	STL	TO	BLK	PTS	RPG	APG	PPG
68-69—Miami (A)	28	—	531	50	146	.342	0	2	.000	36	60	.600	—	—	46	80	47	0	—	55	—	136	1.6	2.9	4.9
REG. ABA TOTALS	28	—	531	50	146	.342	0	2	.000	36	60	.600	—	—	46	80	47	0	—	55	—	136	1.6	2.9	4.9

IVORY, ELVIN DENNIS (**Little E.**) b. July 2, 1948 Ht. 6-7½ Wt. 215 College—Louisiana

SEASON—TEAM	G	GS	MIN	FGM	FGA	PCT	3FGM	3FGA	PCT	FTM	FTA	PCT	O-RB	D-RB	TOT	AST	PF	DQ	STL	TO	BLK	PTS	RPG	APG	PPG
68-69—Los Angeles (A)	20	—	188	38	87	.437	1	4	.250	11	17	.647	—	—	166	9	38	0	—	14	—	88	8.3	0.5	4.4
REG. ABA TOTALS	20	—	188	38	87	.437	1	4	.250	11	17	.647	—	—	166	9	38	0	—	14	—	88	8.3	0.5	4.4

JABALI, WARREN (**formerly Warren Edward Armstrong**) b. August 29, 1946 Ht. 6-2 Wt. 200 College—Wichita State

SEASON—TEAM	G	GS	MIN	FGM	FGA	PCT	3FGM	3FGA	PCT	FTM	FTA	PCT	O-RB	D-RB	TOT	AST	PF	DQ	STL	TO	BLK	PTS	RPG	APG	PPG
68-69—Oakland (A)	71	—	2545	573	1276	.449	11	44	.250	373	545	.684	—	—	688	252	263	4	—	307	—	1530	9.7	3.5	21.5
69-70—Washington (A)	40	—	1510	342	768	.445	19	62	.306	210	293	.717	—	—	416	173	143	5	—	—	—	913	10.4	4.3	22.8
70-71—Indiana (A)	62	—	1586	227	554	.410	47	163	.288	181	238	.761	—	—	298	214	205	—	—	—	—	682	4.8	3.5	11.0
71-72—Floridians (A)	81	—	3313	569	1304	.436	102	285	.358	375	496	.756	—	—	656	495	298	—	—	332	—	1615	8.1	6.1	19.9
72-73—Denver (A)	82	—	2738	441	974	.453	36	140	.257	480	596	.805	129	295	424	539	280	0	—	302	—	1398	5.2	6.6	17.0
73-74—Denver (A)	49	—	1711	257	657	.391	45	123	.366	220	274	.803	82	164	246	358	167	—	97	195	10	779	5.0	7.3	15.9
74-75—San Diego (A)	62	—	1861	254	648	.392	62	193	.321	179	227	.789	72	185	257	358	188	—	112	184	19	749	4.1	5.8	12.1
REG. ABA TOTALS	447	—	15264	2663	6181	.431	322	1010	.319	2018	2669	.756	283	644	2985	2389	1544	9	209	1320	29	7666	6.7	5.3	17.1
ABA PLAYOFF TOTALS	36	—	1209	221	532	.415	11	66	.167	198	282	.702	81	178	306	115	111	1	0	109	0	651	8.5	3.2	18.1
ABA ALL-STAR TOTALS	4	—	87	13	38	.342	1	7	.143	3	6	.500	5	10	17	12	10	0	4	7	0	30	4.3	3.0	7.5

JACKSON, ALVIN (**Al**) b. July 29, 1943 Ht. 6-1½ Wt. 185 College—Wilberforce

SEASON—TEAM	G	GS	MIN	FGM	FGA	PCT	3FGM	3FGA	PCT	FTM	FTA	PCT	O-RB	D-RB	TOT	AST	PF	DQ	STL	TO	BLK	PTS	RPG	APG	PPG
67-68—Cincinnati	2	—	17	0	3	.000	—	—	—	0	0	—	—	—	0	1	6	0	—	—	—	0	0.0	0.5	0.0
REG. SEASON TOTALS	2	—	17	0	3	.000	—	—	—	0	0	—	—	—	0	1	6	0	—	—	—	0	0.0	0.5	0.0

JACKSON, ANTHONY EUGENE (**Tony**) b. January 17, 1958 Ht. 6-0 Wt. 170 College—Florida State

SEASON—TEAM	G	GS	MIN	FGM	FGA	PCT	3FGM	3FGA	PCT	FTM	FTA	PCT	O-RB	D-RB	TOT	AST	PF	DQ	STL	TO	BLK	PTS	RPG	APG	PPG
80-81—Los Angeles	2	—	14	1	3	.333	0	0	—	0	0	—	0	2	2	2	1	0	2	0	0	2	1.0	1.0	1.0
REG. SEASON TOTALS	2	—	14	1	3	.333	0	0	—	0	0	—	0	2	2	2	1	0	2	0	0	2	1.0	1.0	1.0

JACKSON, CHRIS WAYNE (**see Mahmoud Abdul-Rauf**)

JACKSON, GREGORY (Greg) b. August 2, 1952   Ht. 6-0 Wt. 185 College—Guilford

SEASON—TEAM	G	GS	MIN	FGM	FGA	PCT	3FGM	3FGA	PCT	FTM	FTA	PCT	O-RB	D-RB	TOT	AST	PF	DQ	STL	TO	BLK	PTS	RPG	APG	PPG
74-75—N.Y.-Phoenix	49	—	802	73	176	.415	—	—	—	36	62	.581	19	50	69	96	130	5	23	—	9	182	1.4	2.0	3.7
REG. SEASON TOTALS	49	—	802	73	176	.415	—	—	—	36	62	.581	19	50	69	96	130	5	23	—	9	182	1.4	2.0	3.7

JACKSON, JAMES ARTHUR (Jim) b. October 14, 1970   Ht. 6-6 Wt. 220 College—Ohio State

SEASON—TEAM	G	GS	MIN	FGM	FGA	PCT	3FGM	3FGA	PCT	FTM	FTA	PCT	O-RB	D-RB	TOT	AST	PF	DQ	STL	TO	BLK	PTS	RPG	APG	PPG
92-93—Dallas	28	28	938	184	466	.395	21	73	.288	68	92	.739	42	80	122	131	80	0	40	115	11	457	4.4	4.7	16.3
93-94—Dallas	82	82	3066	637	1432	.445	17	60	.283	285	347	.821	169	219	388	374	161	0	87	334	25	1576	4.7	4.6	19.2
REG. SEASON TOTALS	110	110	4004	821	1898	.433	38	133	.286	353	439	.804	211	299	510	505	241	0	127	449	36	2033	4.6	4.6	18.5

JACKSON, JAREN b. October 27, 1967   Ht. 6-6 Wt. 190 College—Georgetown

SEASON—TEAM	G	GS	MIN	FGM	FGA	PCT	3FGM	3FGA	PCT	FTM	FTA	PCT	O-RB	D-RB	TOT	AST	PF	DQ	STL	TO	BLK	PTS	RPG	APG	PPG
89-90—New Jersey	28	0	160	25	69	.362	0	3	.000	17	21	.810	16	8	24	13	16	0	13	18	1	67	0.9	0.5	2.4
91-92—Golden State	5	0	54	11	23	.478	0	0	—	4	6	.667	5	5	10	3	7	1	2	4	0	26	2.0	0.6	5.2
92-93—L.A. Clippers	34	0	350	53	128	.414	2	5	.400	23	27	.852	19	20	39	35	45	1	19	17	5	131	1.1	1.0	3.9
93-94—Portland	29	0	187	34	87	.391	0	6	.000	12	14	.857	6	11	17	27	20	0	4	14	2	80	0.6	0.9	2.8
REG. SEASON TOTALS	96	0	751	123	307	.401	2	14	.143	56	68	.824	46	44	90	78	88	2	38	53	8	304	0.9	0.8	3.2
PLAYOFF TOTALS	5	0	29	5	13	.385	0	1	.000	0	0	—	4	1	5	2	6	0	2	3	0	10	1.0	0.4	2.0

JACKSON, LUCIOUS B. (Luke) b. October 31, 1941   Ht. 6-9 Wt. 250 College—Quincy College/Texas Southern/Texas-Pan American

SEASON—TEAM	G	GS	MIN	FGM	FGA	PCT	3FGM	3FGA	PCT	FTM	FTA	PCT	O-RB	D-RB	TOT	AST	PF	DQ	STL	TO	BLK	PTS	RPG	APG	PPG
64-65—Philadelphia	76	—	2590	419	1013	.414	—	—	—	288	404	.713	—	—	980	93	251	4	—	—	—	1126	12.9	1.2	14.8
65-66—Philadelphia	79	—	1966	246	614	.401	—	—	—	158	214	.738	—	—	676	132	216	2	—	—	—	650	8.6	1.7	8.2
66-67—Philadelphia	81	—	2377	386	882	.438	—	—	—	198	261	.759	—	—	724	114	276	6	—	—	—	970	8.9	1.4	12.0
67-68—Philadelphia	82	—	2570	401	927	.433	—	—	—	166	231	.719	—	—	872	139	287	6	—	—	—	968	10.6	1.7	11.8
68-69—Philadelphia	25	—	840	145	332	.437	—	—	—	69	97	.711	—	—	286	54	102	3	—	—	—	359	11.4	2.2	14.4
69-70—Philadelphia	37	—	583	71	181	.392	—	—	—	60	81	.741	—	—	198	50	80	0	—	—	—	202	5.4	1.4	5.5
70-71—Philadelphia	79	—	1774	199	529	.376	—	—	—	131	189	.693	—	—	568	148	211	3	—	—	—	529	7.2	1.9	6.7
71-72—Philadelphia	63	—	1083	137	346	.396	—	—	—	92	133	.692	—	—	309	88	141	1	—	—	—	366	4.9	1.4	5.8
REG. SEASON TOTALS	522	—	13783	2004	4824	.415	—	—	—	1162	1610	.722	—	—	4613	818	1564	25	—	—	—	5170	8.8	1.6	9.9
PLAYOFF TOTALS	56	—	1692	216	555	.389	—	—	—	113	152	.743	—	—	508	92	186	7	—	—	—	545	9.1	1.6	9.7
ALL-STAR TOTALS	1	—	15	2	5	.400	—	—	—	1	2	.500	—	—	1	1	4	0	—	—	—	5	1.0	1.0	5.0

JACKSON, MARK A. b. April 1, 1965   Ht. 6-3 Wt. 195 College—St. John's

SEASON—TEAM	G	GS	MIN	FGM	FGA	PCT	3FGM	3FGA	PCT	FTM	FTA	PCT	O-RB	D-RB	TOT	AST	PF	DQ	STL	TO	BLK	PTS	RPG	APG	PPG
87-88—New York	82	80	3249	438	1013	.432	32	126	.254	206	266	.774	120	276	396	868	244	2	205	258	6	1114	4.8	10.6	13.6
88-89—New York	72	72	2477	479	1025	.467	81	240	.338	180	258	.698	106	235	341	619	163	1	139	226	7	1219	4.7	8.6	16.9
89-90—New York	82	69	2428	327	749	.437	35	131	.267	120	165	.727	106	212	318	604	121	0	109	211	4	809	3.9	7.4	9.9
90-91—New York	72	21	1595	250	508	.492	13	51	.255	117	160	.731	62	135	197	452	81	0	60	135	9	630	2.7	6.3	8.8
91-92—New York	81	81	2461	367	747	.491	11	43	.256	171	222	.770	95	210	305	694	153	0	112	211	13	916	3.8	8.6	11.3
92-93—L.A. Clippers	82	81	3117	459	945	.486	22	82	.268	241	300	.803	129	259	388	724	158	0	136	220	12	1181	4.7	8.8	14.4
93-94—L.A. Clippers	79	79	2711	331	732	.452	36	127	.283	167	211	.791	107	241	348	678	115	0	120	232	6	865	4.4	8.6	10.9
REG. SEASON TOTALS	550	483	18038	2651	5719	.464	230	800	.288	1202	1582	.760	725	1568	2293	4639	1035	3	881	1493	57	6734	4.2	8.4	12.2
PLAYOFF TOTALS	42	30	1180	152	350	.434	21	65	.323	76	99	.768	34	77	111	283	62	0	41	97	5	401	2.6	6.7	9.5
ALL-STAR TOTALS	1	0	16	3	5	.600	1	1	1.000	2	4	.500	1	1	2	4	1	0	1	2	1	9	2.0	4.0	9.0

JACKSON, MERVIN P. JR. (Merv, The Magician) b. August 15, 1946   Ht. 6-3 Wt. 175 College—Utah

SEASON—TEAM	G	GS	MIN	FGM	FGA	PCT	3FGM	3FGA	PCT	FTM	FTA	PCT	O-RB	D-RB	TOT	AST	PF	DQ	STL	TO	BLK	PTS	RPG	APG	PPG
68-69—Los Angeles (A)	71	—	2314	423	1000	.423	19	62	.306	249	302	.825	—	—	299	237	262	9	—	191	—	1114	4.2	3.3	15.7
69-70—Los Angeles (A)	52	—	1118	169	475	.356	16	44	.364	92	114	.807	—	—	138	114	145	4	—	—	—	446	2.7	2.2	8.6
70-71—Utah (A)	65	—	1902	351	836	.420	7	20	.350	196	244	.803	—	—	262	225	207	—	—	—	—	905	4.0	3.5	13.9
71-72—Utah (A)	52	—	1136	185	412	.449	5	15	.333	92	109	.844	—	—	123	155	150	—	—	88	—	467	2.4	3.0	9.0
72-73—Memphis (A)	22	—	420	34	103	.330	4	11	.364	28	35	.800	9	29	38	82	61	1	—	35	—	100	1.7	3.7	4.5
REG. ABA TOTALS	262	—	6890	1162	2826	.411	51	152	.336	657	804	.817	9	29	860	813	825	14	—	314	—	3032	3.3	3.1	11.6
ABA PLAYOFF TOTALS	46	—	1391	250	543	.460	12	30	.400	97	120	.808	—	—	179	188	144	0	—	16	—	609	3.9	4.1	13.2
ABA ALL-STAR TOTALS	1	—	11	1	3	.333	0	0	—	1	1	1.000	1	1	2	1	0	—	0	—	3	2.0	1.0	3.0

JACKSON, MICHAEL b. July 13, 1964   Ht. 6-2 Wt. 185 College—Georgetown

SEASON—TEAM	G	GS	MIN	FGM	FGA	PCT	3FGM	3FGA	PCT	FTM	FTA	PCT	O-RB	D-RB	TOT	AST	PF	DQ	STL	TO	BLK	PTS	RPG	APG	PPG
87-88—Sacramento	58	0	760	64	171	.374	6	25	.240	23	32	.719	17	42	59	179	81	0	20	58	5	157	1.0	3.1	2.7
88-89—Sacramento	14	0	70	9	24	.375	2	6	.333	1	2	.500	1	3	4	11	12	0	3	4	0	21	0.3	0.8	1.5
89-90—Sacramento	17	0	58	3	11	.273	1	2	.500	3	6	.500	2	5	7	8	3	0	5	4	0	10	0.4	0.5	0.6
REG. SEASON TOTALS	89	0	888	76	206	.369	9	33	.273	27	40	.675	20	50	70	198	96	0	28	66	5	188	0.8	2.2	2.1

JACKSON, MICHAEL (Mike) b. July 31, 1949 Ht. 6-7 Wt. 230 College—Allan Hancock/Cal State-Los Angeles

SEASON—TEAM	G	GS	MIN	FGM	FGA	PCT	3FGM	3FGA	PCT	FTM	FTA	PCT	O-RB	D-RB	TOT	AST	PF	DQ	STL	TO	BLK	PTS	RPG	APG	PPG
72-73—Utah (A)	30	—	191	36	83	.434	0	0	—	28	46	.609	24	38	62	2	46	0	—	27	—	100	2.1	0.1	3.3
73-74—Utah-Memphis (A)	72	—	1474	247	489	.505	3	7	.429	110	152	.724	140	240	380	57	222	—	25	109	15	607	5.3	0.8	8.4
74-75—Virginia (A)	82	—	2023	382	724	.528	1	3	.333	232	295	.786	183	274	457	82	308	—	47	212	19	997	5.6	1.0	12.2
75-76—Virginia (A)	80	—	2230	390	781	.499	0	5	.000	199	250	.796	209	398	607	113	306	—	45	190	29	979	7.6	1.4	12.2
REG. ABA TOTALS	264	—	5918	1055	2077	.508	4	15	.267	569	743	.766	556	950	1506	254	882	0	117	538	63	2683	5.7	1.0	10.2
ABA PLAYOFF TOTALS	1	—	2	0	0	—	0	0	—	0	0	—	0	0	—	0	2	0	0	0	0	0	0.0	0.0	0.0

JACKSON, MYRON b. May 6, 1964 Ht. 6-3 Wt. 185 College—Arkansas-Little Rock

SEASON—TEAM	G	GS	MIN	FGM	FGA	PCT	3FGM	3FGA	PCT	FTM	FTA	PCT	O-RB	D-RB	TOT	AST	PF	DQ	STL	TO	BLK	PTS	RPG	APG	PPG
86-87—Dallas	8	0	22	2	9	.222	0	0	—	7	8	.875	1	2	3	6	1	0	1	5	0	11	0.4	0.8	1.4
REG. SEASON TOTALS	8	0	22	2	9	.222	0	0	—	7	8	.875	1	2	3	6	1	0	1	5	0	11	0.4	0.8	1.4

JACKSON, PHILIP D. (Phil) b. September 17, 1945 Ht. 6-8 Wt. 220 College—North Dakota

SEASON—TEAM	G	GS	MIN	FGM	FGA	PCT	3FGM	3FGA	PCT	FTM	FTA	PCT	O-RB	D-RB	TOT	AST	PF	DQ	STL	TO	BLK	PTS	RPG	APG	PPG
67-68—New York	75	—	1093	182	455	.400	—	—	—	99	168	.589	—	—	338	55	212	3	—	—	—	463	4.5	0.7	6.2
68-69—New York	47	—	924	126	294	.429	—	—	—	80	119	.672	—	—	246	43	168	6	—	—	—	332	5.2	0.9	7.1
70-71—New York	71	—	771	118	263	.449	—	—	—	95	133	.714	—	—	238	31	169	4	—	—	—	331	3.4	0.4	4.7
71-72—New York	80	—	1273	205	466	.440	—	—	—	167	228	.732	—	—	326	72	224	4	—	—	—	577	4.1	0.9	7.2
72-73—New York	80	—	1393	245	553	.443	—	—	—	154	195	.790	—	—	344	94	218	2	—	—	—	644	4.3	1.2	8.1
73-74—New York	82	—	2050	361	757	.477	—	—	—	191	246	.776	123	355	478	134	277	7	42	—	67	913	5.8	1.6	11.1
74-75—New York	78	—	2285	324	712	.455	—	—	—	193	253	.763	137	463	600	136	330	10	84	—	53	841	7.7	1.7	10.8
75-76—New York	80	—	1461	185	387	.478	—	—	—	110	150	.733	80	263	343	105	275	3	41	—	20	480	4.3	1.3	6.0
76-77—New York Knicks	76	—	1033	102	232	.440	—	—	—	51	71	.718	75	154	229	85	184	4	33	—	18	255	3.0	1.1	3.4
77-78—New York	63	—	654	55	115	.478	—	—	—	43	56	.768	29	81	110	46	106	0	31	47	15	153	1.7	0.7	2.4
78-79—New Jersey	59	—	1070	144	303	.475	—	—	—	86	105	.819	59	119	178	85	168	7	45	78	22	374	3.0	1.4	6.3
79-80—New Jersey	16	—	194	29	46	.630	0	2	.000	7	10	.700	12	12	24	12	35	1	5	9	4	65	1.5	0.8	4.1
REG. SEASON TOTALS	807	—	14201	2076	4583	.453	0	2	.000	1276	1734	.736	515	1447	3454	898	2366	51	281	134	199	5428	4.3	1.1	6.7
PLAYOFF TOTALS	67	—	1223	200	437	.458	0	0	—	115	147	.782	26	69	284	63	208	4	18	4	8	515	4.2	0.9	7.7

JACKSON, RALPH A. III b. October 26, 1962 Ht. 6-2 Wt. 190 College—UCLA

SEASON—TEAM	G	GS	MIN	FGM	FGA	PCT	3FGM	3FGA	PCT	FTM	FTA	PCT	O-RB	D-RB	TOT	AST	PF	DQ	STL	TO	BLK	PTS	RPG	APG	PPG
84-85—Indiana	1	0	12	1	3	.333	0	0	—	0	0	—	1	0	1	4	1	0	2	1	0	2	1.0	4.0	2.0
REG. SEASON TOTALS	1	0	12	1	3	.333	0	0	—	0	0	—	1	0	1	4	1	0	2	1	0	2	1.0	4.0	2.0

JACKSON, STANLEY LEON b. October 10, 1970 Ht. 6-3 Wt. 185 College—Alabama-Birmingham

SEASON—TEAM	G	GS	MIN	FGM	FGA	PCT	3FGM	3FGA	PCT	FTM	FTA	PCT	O-RB	D-RB	TOT	AST	PF	DQ	STL	TO	BLK	PTS	RPG	APG	PPG
93-94—Minnesota	17	0	92	17	33	.515	1	5	.200	3	3	1.000	12	15	27	16	13	0	5	10	0	38	1.6	0.9	2.2
REG. SEASON TOTALS	17	0	92	17	33	.515	1	5	.200	3	3	1.000	12	15	27	16	13	0	5	10	0	38	1.6	0.9	2.2

JACKSON, TONY B. b. November 7, 1942 Ht. 6-4 Wt. 200 College—St. John's

SEASON—TEAM	G	GS	MIN	FGM	FGA	PCT	3FGM	3FGA	PCT	FTM	FTA	PCT	O-RB	D-RB	TOT	AST	PF	DQ	STL	TO	BLK	PTS	RPG	APG	PPG
67-68—New Jersey (A)	74	—	2638	449	1171	.383	91	302	.301	450	543	.829	—	—	500	140	184	1	—	144	—	1439	6.8	1.9	19.4
68-69—N.Y.-Minn.-Houston (A)	64	—	1453	210	588	.357	32	145	.221	299	337	.887	—	—	241	139	147	2	—	153	—	751	3.8	2.2	11.7
REG. ABA TOTALS	138	—	4091	659	1759	.375	123	447	.275	749	880	.851	—	—	741	279	331	3	—	297	—	2190	5.4	2.0	15.9
ABA ALL-STAR TOTALS	1	—	15	2	6	.333	0	3	.000	0	0	—	—	2	2	1	0	0	—	2	—	4	2.0	1.0	4.0

JACKSON, TRACY CORDELL b. April 21, 1959 Ht. 6-6 Wt. 215 College—Notre Dame

SEASON—TEAM	G	GS	MIN	FGM	FGA	PCT	3FGM	3FGA	PCT	FTM	FTA	PCT	O-RB	D-RB	TOT	AST	PF	DQ	STL	TO	BLK	PTS	RPG	APG	PPG
81-82—Boston-Chicago	49	0	478	79	172	.459	0	0	—	38	49	.776	35	28	63	27	48	0	14	24	3	196	1.3	0.6	4.0
82-83—Chicago	78	3	1309	199	426	.467	2	13	.154	92	126	.730	87	92	179	105	132	0	64	83	11	492	2.3	1.3	6.3
83-84—Indiana	2	0	10	1	4	.250	0	0	—	4	4	1.000	1	0	1	0	3	0	0	1	0	6	0.5	0.0	3.0
REG. SEASON TOTALS	129	3	1797	279	602	.463	2	13	.154	134	179	.749	123	120	243	132	183	0	78	108	14	694	1.9	1.0	5.4

JACKSON, WARDELL b. July 18, 1951 Ht. 6-7 Wt. 200 College—Ohio State

SEASON—TEAM	G	GS	MIN	FGM	FGA	PCT	3FGM	3FGA	PCT	FTM	FTA	PCT	O-RB	D-RB	TOT	AST	PF	DQ	STL	TO	BLK	PTS	RPG	APG	PPG
74-75—Seattle	56	—	939	96	242	.397	—	—	—	51	71	.718	53	80	133	30	126	2	26	—	5	243	2.4	0.5	4.3
REG. SEASON TOTALS	56	—	939	96	242	.397	—	—	—	51	71	.718	53	80	133	30	126	2	26	—	5	243	2.4	0.5	4.3

JACOBS, WINFRED O. (Fred) b. December 2, 1922 Ht. 6-3 Wt. 175 College—Denver

SEASON—TEAM	G	GS	MIN	FGM	FGA	PCT	3FGM	3FGA	PCT	FTM	FTA	PCT	O-RB	D-RB	TOT	AST	PF	DQ	STL	TO	BLK	PTS	RPG	APG	PPG
46-47—St. Louis	18	—	—	19	69	.275	—	—	—	12	25	.480	—	—	—	5	25	—	—	—	—	50	—	0.3	2.8
REG. SEASON TOTALS	18	—	—	19	69	.275	—	—	—	12	25	.480	—	—	—	5	25	—	—	—	—	50	—	0.3	2.8

JAMERSON, JOHN DAVID (**Dave**) b. August 13, 1967 Ht. 6-5 Wt. 190 College—Ohio

SEASON—TEAM	G	GS	MIN	FGM	FGA	PCT	3FGM	3FGA	PCT	FTM	FTA	PCT	O-RB	D-RB	TOT	AST	PF	DQ	STL	TO	BLK	PTS	RPG	APG	PPG
90-91—Houston	37	0	202	43	113	.381	5	19	.263	22	27	.815	9	21	30	27	24	0	6	20	1	113	0.8	0.7	3.1
91-92—Houston	48	0	378	79	191	.414	8	28	.286	25	27	.926	22	21	43	33	39	0	17	24	0	191	0.9	0.7	4.0
93-94—Utah-N.J.	5	0	14	0	7	.000	0	0	—	2	3	.667	0	4	4	1	0	0	0	1	0	2	0.8	0.2	0.4
REG. SEASON TOTALS	90	0	594	122	311	.392	13	47	.277	49	57	.860	31	46	77	61	63	0	23	45	1	306	0.9	0.7	3.4
PLAYOFF TOTALS	2	0	21	5	13	.385	0	1	.000	6	6	1.000	1	2	3	4	4	0	1	1	0	16	1.5	2.0	8.0

JAMES, AARON (**A.J.**) b. October 5, 1952 Ht. 6-8 Wt. 210 College—Grambling State

SEASON—TEAM	G	GS	MIN	FGM	FGA	PCT	3FGM	3FGA	PCT	FTM	FTA	PCT	O-RB	D-RB	TOT	AST	PF	DQ	STL	TO	BLK	PTS	RPG	APG	PPG
74-75—New Orleans	76	—	1731	370	776	.477	—	—	—	147	189	.778	140	226	366	66	217	4	41	—	15	887	4.8	0.9	11.7
75-76—New Orleans	75	—	1346	262	594	.441	—	—	—	153	204	.750	93	156	249	59	172	1	33	—	6	677	3.3	0.8	9.0
76-77—New Orleans	52	—	1059	238	486	.490	—	—	—	89	114	.781	56	130	186	55	127	1	20	—	5	565	3.6	1.1	10.9
77-78—New Orleans	80	—	2118	428	861	.497	—	—	—	117	157	.745	163	258	421	112	254	5	36	130	22	973	5.3	1.4	12.2
78-79—New Orleans	73	—	1417	311	630	.494	—	—	—	105	140	.750	97	151	248	78	202	1	28	111	21	727	3.4	1.1	10.0
REG. SEASON TOTALS	356	—	7671	1609	3347	.481	—	—	—	611	804	.760	549	921	1470	370	972	12	158	241	69	3829	4.1	1.0	10.8

JAMES, HAROLD GENE (**Gene, Goose**) b. February 15, 1925 Ht. 6-4½ Wt. 180 College—Marshall

SEASON—TEAM	G	GS	MIN	FGM	FGA	PCT	3FGM	3FGA	PCT	FTM	FTA	PCT	O-RB	D-RB	TOT	AST	PF	DQ	STL	TO	BLK	PTS	RPG	APG	PPG
48-49—New York	11	—	—	18	48	.375	—	—	—	6	12	.500	—	—	5	20	—	—	—	—	—	42	—	0.5	3.8
49-50—New York	29	—	—	19	64	.297	—	—	—	14	31	.452	—	—	20	53	—	—	—	—	—	52	—	0.7	1.8
50-51—N.Y.-Balt.	48	—	—	79	235	.336	—	—	—	44	71	.620	—	—	141	70	118	2	—	—	—	202	2.9	1.5	4.2
REG. SEASON TOTALS	88	—	—	116	347	.334	—	—	—	64	114	.561	—	—	141	95	191	2	—	—	—	296	2.9	1.1	3.4
PLAYOFF TOTALS	4	—	—	1	9	.111	—	—	—	2	4	.500	—	—	2	6	0	—	—	—	—	4	—	0.5	1.0

JAMES, HENRY CHARLES b. July 29, 1965 Ht. 6-8 Wt. 220 College—South Plains/St. Mary's (Tex.)

SEASON—TEAM	G	GS	MIN	FGM	FGA	PCT	3FGM	3FGA	PCT	FTM	FTA	PCT	O-RB	D-RB	TOT	AST	PF	DQ	STL	TO	BLK	PTS	RPG	APG	PPG
90-91—Cleveland	37	4	505	112	254	.441	24	60	.400	52	72	.722	26	53	79	32	59	1	15	37	5	300	2.1	0.9	8.1
91-92—Cleveland	65	5	866	164	403	.407	29	90	.322	61	76	.803	35	77	112	25	94	1	16	43	11	418	1.7	0.4	6.4
92-93—Sac.-Utah	10	0	88	21	51	.412	3	13	.231	22	26	.846	7	4	11	1	9	0	3	7	0	67	1.1	0.1	6.7
93-94—L.A. Clippers	12	0	75	16	42	.381	4	18	.222	5	5	1.000	6	8	14	1	9	0	2	2	0	41	1.2	0.1	3.4
REG. SEASON TOTALS	124	9	1534	313	750	.417	60	181	.331	140	179	.782	74	142	216	59	171	2	36	89	16	826	1.7	0.5	6.7
PLAYOFF TOTALS	8	0	22	1	10	.100	0	3	.000	2	4	.500	1	1	2	2	2	0	1	1	0	4	0.3	0.3	0.5

JAMES, MACK WILLIAM (**Billy**) b. February 11, 1950 Ht. 6-3 Wt. 185 College—Marshall

SEASON—TEAM	G	GS	MIN	FGM	FGA	PCT	3FGM	3FGA	PCT	FTM	FTA	PCT	O-RB	D-RB	TOT	AST	PF	DQ	STL	TO	BLK	PTS	RPG	APG	PPG
73-74—Kentucky (A)	1	—	10	1	3	.333	0	0	—	0	0	—	0	0	0	1	3	—	0	1	0	2	0.0	1.0	2.0
REG. ABA TOTALS	1	—	10	1	3	.333	0	0	—	0	0	—	0	0	—	1	3	0	0	1	0	2	0.0	1.0	2.0

JANISCH, JOHN ALBERT b. March 15, 1920 d. August 25, 1992 Ht. 6-3 Wt. 200 College—Valparaiso

SEASON—TEAM	G	GS	MIN	FGM	FGA	PCT	3FGM	3FGA	PCT	FTM	FTA	PCT	O-RB	D-RB	TOT	AST	PF	DQ	STL	TO	BLK	PTS	RPG	APG	PPG
46-47—Detroit	60	—	—	283	983	.288	—	—	—	131	198	.662	—	—	—	49	132	—	—	—	—	697	—	0.8	11.6
47-48—Boston-Prov.	10	—	—	14	50	.280	—	—	—	9	16	.563	—	—	—	2	5	—	—	—	—	37	—	0.2	3.7
47-48—Flint (N)	36	—	—	36	—	—	—	—	—	21	28	.750	—	—	—	—	38	—	—	—	—	93	—	—	2.6
REG. NBA TOTALS	70	—	—	297	1033	.288	—	—	—	140	214	.654	—	—	—	51	137	—	—	—	—	734	—	0.7	10.5
REG. NBL TOTALS	36	—	—	36	—	—	—	—	—	21	28	.750	—	—	—	—	38	—	—	—	—	93	—	—	2.6

JANOTTA, HOWARD (**Howie**) b. October 19, 1924 Ht. 6-3 Wt. 185 College—Seton Hall

SEASON—TEAM	G	GS	MIN	FGM	FGA	PCT	3FGM	3FGA	PCT	FTM	FTA	PCT	O-RB	D-RB	TOT	AST	PF	DQ	STL	TO	BLK	PTS	RPG	APG	PPG
49-50—Baltimore	9	—	—	9	30	.300	—	—	—	13	16	.813	—	—	—	4	10	—	—	—	—	31	—	0.4	3.4
REG. SEASON TOTALS	9	—	—	9	30	.300	—	—	—	13	16	.813	—	—	—	4	10	—	—	—	—	31	—	0.4	3.4

JAROS, ANTHONY JOSEPH (**Tony**) b. February 22, 1920 Ht. 6-3 Wt. 185 College—Minnesota

SEASON—TEAM	G	GS	MIN	FGM	FGA	PCT	3FGM	3FGA	PCT	FTM	FTA	PCT	O-RB	D-RB	TOT	AST	PF	DQ	STL	TO	BLK	PTS	RPG	APG	PPG
46-47—Chicago	59	—	—	177	613	.289	—	—	—	128	181	.707	—	—	—	28	156	—	—	—	—	482	—	0.5	8.2
47-48—Minneapolis (N)	58	—	—	95	—	—	—	—	—	83	114	.728	—	—	—	—	90	—	—	—	—	273	—	—	4.7
48-49—Minneapolis	59	—	—	132	385	.343	—	—	—	79	110	.718	—	—	—	58	114	—	—	—	—	343	—	1.0	5.8
49-50—Minneapolis	61	—	—	84	289	.291	—	—	—	72	96	.750	—	—	—	60	106	—	—	—	—	240	—	1.0	3.9
50-51—Minneapolis	63	—	—	88	287	.307	—	—	—	65	103	.631	—	—	131	72	131	0	—	—	—	241	2.1	1.1	3.8
REG. NBA TOTALS	242	—	—	481	1574	.306	—	—	—	344	490	.702	—	—	131	218	507	0	—	—	—	1306	2.1	0.9	5.4
REG. NBL TOTALS	58	—	—	95	—	—	—	—	—	83	114	.728	—	—	—	—	90	—	—	—	—	273	—	—	4.7
NBA PLAYOFF TOTALS	30	—	—	66	230	.287	—	—	—	49	67	.731	—	—	—	7	21	73	2	—	—	—	181	1.0	0.7	6.0
NBL PLAYOFF TOTALS	10	—	—	29	—	—	—	—	—	22	33	.667	—	—	—	—	29	—	—	—	—	80	—	—	8.0

JARVIS, JAMES C. (Jim) b. March 3, 1943 Ht. 6-1 Wt. 175 College—Oregon State

SEASON—TEAM	G	GS	MIN	FGM	FGA	PCT	3FGM	3FGA	PCT	FTM	FTA	PCT	O-RB	D-RB	TOT	AST	PF	DQ	STL	TO	BLK	PTS	RPG	APG	PPG
67-68—Pittsburgh (A)	63	—	818	132	343	.385	12	48	.250	53	64	.828	—	—	106	72	103	0	—	48	—	329	1.7	1.1	5.2
68-69—Minn.-L.A. (A)	62	—	911	147	402	.366	19	47	.404	86	109	.789	—	—	129	80	137	1	—	71	—	399	2.1	1.3	6.4
REG. ABA TOTALS	125	—	1729	279	745	.374	31	95	.326	139	173	.803	—	—	235	152	240	1	—	119	—	728	1.9	1.2	5.8
ABA PLAYOFF TOTALS	15	—	211	39	89	.438	0	2	.000	16	20	.800	—	—	21	15	29	0	—	11	—	94	1.4	1.0	6.3

JEANNETTE, HARRY EDWARD (Buddy) b. September 15, 1917 Ht. 5-11 Wt. 175 College—Washington & Jefferson

SEASON—TEAM	G	GS	MIN	FGM	FGA	PCT	3FGM	3FGA	PCT	FTM	FTA	PCT	O-RB	D-RB	TOT	AST	PF	DQ	STL	TO	BLK	PTS	RPG	APG	PPG
38-39—Cleveland (N)	26	—	—	54	—	—	—	—	—	65	—	—	—	—	—	—	57	—	—	—	—	173	—	—	6.7
39-40—Detroit (N)	25	—	—	45	—	—	—	—	—	52	80	.650	—	—	—	—	62	—	—	—	—	142	—	—	5.7
40-41—Detroit (N)	23	—	—	75	—	—	—	—	—	54	86	.628	—	—	—	—	56	—	—	—	—	204	—	—	8.9
42-43—Sheboygan (N)	4	—	—	24	—	—	—	—	—	14	17	.824	—	—	—	—	8	—	—	—	—	62	—	—	15.5
43-44—Fort Wayne (N)	22	—	—	68	—	—	—	—	—	48	65	.738	—	—	—	—	46	—	—	—	—	184	—	—	8.4
44-45—Fort Wayne (N)	27	—	—	85	—	—	—	—	—	82	111	.739	—	—	—	—	67	—	—	—	—	252	—	—	9.3
45-46—Fort Wayne (N)	34	—	—	99	—	—	—	—	—	105	136	.772	—	—	—	—	184	—	—	—	—	303	—	—	8.9
47-48—Baltimore	46	—	—	150	430	.349	—	—	—	191	252	.758	—	—	—	70	147	—	—	—	—	491	—	1.5	10.7
48-49—Baltimore	56	—	—	73	199	.367	—	—	—	167	213	.784	—	—	—	124	157	—	—	—	—	313	—	2.2	5.6
49-50—Baltimore	37	—	—	42	148	.284	—	—	—	109	133	.820	—	—	—	93	82	—	—	—	—	193	—	2.5	5.2
REG. NBA TOTALS	139	—	—	265	777	.341	—	—	—	467	598	.781	—	—	—	287	386	—	—	—	—	997	—	2.1	7.2
REG. NBL TOTALS	161	—	—	450	—	—	—	—	—	420	495	.717	—	—	—	—	480	—	—	—	—	1320	—	—	8.2
NBA PLAYOFF TOTALS	14	—	—	32	74	.432	—	—	—	41	46	.891	—	—	—	17	56	1	—	—	—	105	—	1.2	7.5
NBL PLAYOFF TOTALS	27	—	—	71	—	—	—	—	—	68	32	.781	—	—	—	—	69	—	—	—	—	210	—	—	7.8

JEELANI, ABDUL QADIR (formerly Gary Cole) b. February 10, 1954 Ht. 6-8 Wt. 210 College—Wisconsin-Parkside

SEASON—TEAM	G	GS	MIN	FGM	FGA	PCT	3FGM	3FGA	PCT	FTM	FTA	PCT	O-RB	D-RB	TOT	AST	PF	DQ	STL	TO	BLK	PTS	RPG	APG	PPG
79-80—Portland	77	—	1286	288	565	.510	0	6	.000	161	204	.789	114	156	270	95	155	0	40	117	40	737	3.5	1.2	9.6
80-81—Dallas	66	—	1108	187	440	.425	0	1	.000	179	220	.814	83	147	230	65	123	2	44	87	31	553	3.5	1.0	8.4
REG. SEASON TOTALS	143	—	2394	475	1005	.473	0	7	.000	340	424	.802	197	303	500	160	278	2	84	204	71	1290	3.5	1.1	9.0

JENNINGS, KEITH RUSSELL (Mister) b. November 2, 1968 Ht. 5-7 Wt. 160 College—East Tennessee State

SEASON—TEAM	G	GS	MIN	FGM	FGA	PCT	3FGM	3FGA	PCT	FTM	FTA	PCT	O-RB	D-RB	TOT	AST	PF	DQ	STL	TO	BLK	PTS	RPG	APG	PPG
92-93—Golden State	8	0	136	25	42	.595	5	9	.556	14	18	.778	2	9	11	23	18	0	4	7	0	69	1.4	2.9	8.6
93-94—Golden State	76	2	1097	138	342	.404	56	151	.371	100	120	.833	16	73	89	218	62	0	65	74	0	432	1.2	2.9	5.7
REG. SEASON TOTALS	84	2	1233	163	384	.424	61	160	.381	114	138	.826	18	82	100	241	80	0	69	81	0	501	1.2	2.9	6.0
PLAYOFF TOTALS	3	0	39	4	13	.308	1	5	.200	6	7	.857	1	4	5	4	11	0	1	4	0	15	1.7	1.3	5.0

JENT, CHRIS b. January 11, 1970 Ht. 6-7 Wt. 220 College—Ohio State

SEASON—TEAM	G	GS	MIN	FGM	FGA	PCT	3FGM	3FGA	PCT	FTM	FTA	PCT	O-RB	D-RB	TOT	AST	PF	DQ	STL	TO	BLK	PTS	RPG	APG	PPG
93-94—Houston	3	0	78	13	26	.500	4	11	.364	1	2	.500	4	11	15	7	13	1	0	5	0	31	5.0	2.3	10.3
REG. SEASON TOTALS	3	0	78	13	26	.500	4	11	.364	1	2	.500	4	11	15	7	13	1	0	5	0	31	5.0	2.3	10.3
PLAYOFF TOTALS	11	0	62	5	20	.250	3	13	.231	0	0	—	1	8	9	7	7	0	2	3	0	13	0.8	0.6	1.2

JEPSEN, LESLIE BURNELL (Les, Big Boy) b. June 24, 1967 Ht. 7-0 Wt. 240 College—Iowa

SEASON—TEAM	G	GS	MIN	FGM	FGA	PCT	3FGM	3FGA	PCT	FTM	FTA	PCT	O-RB	D-RB	TOT	AST	PF	DQ	STL	TO	BLK	PTS	RPG	APG	PPG
90-91—Golden State	21	0	105	11	36	.306	0	1	.000	6	9	.667	17	20	37	1	16	0	1	3	3	28	1.8	0.0	1.3
91-92—Sacramento	31	0	87	9	24	.375	0	1	.000	7	11	.636	12	18	30	1	17	0	1	3	5	25	1.0	0.0	0.8
REG. SEASON TOTALS	52	0	192	20	60	.333	0	2	.000	13	20	.650	29	38	67	2	33	0	2	6	8	53	1.3	0.0	1.0

JETER, HAROLD (Hal) b. May 17, 1945 Ht. 6-3 Wt. 195 College—Drake

SEASON—TEAM	G	GS	MIN	FGM	FGA	PCT	3FGM	3FGA	PCT	FTM	FTA	PCT	O-RB	D-RB	TOT	AST	PF	DQ	STL	TO	BLK	PTS	RPG	APG	PPG
69-70—Washington (A)	5	—	19	1	4	.250	0	0	—	0	0	—	—	—	1	0	8	0	—	—	—	2	0.2	0.0	0.4
REG. ABA TOTALS	5	—	19	1	4	.250	0	0	—	0	0	—	—	—	1	0	8	0	—	—	—	2	0.2	0.0	0.4

JOHNSON, ALFONSO JR. (Buck) b. January 3, 1964 Ht. 6-7 Wt. 200 College—Alabama-Birmingham

SEASON—TEAM	G	GS	MIN	FGM	FGA	PCT	3FGM	3FGA	PCT	FTM	FTA	PCT	O-RB	D-RB	TOT	AST	PF	DQ	STL	TO	BLK	PTS	RPG	APG	PPG
86-87—Houston	60	3	520	94	201	.468	0	1	.000	40	58	.690	38	50	88	40	81	0	17	37	15	228	1.5	0.7	3.8
87-88—Houston	70	2	879	155	298	.520	1	8	.125	67	91	.736	77	91	168	49	127	0	30	54	26	378	2.4	0.7	5.4
88-89—Houston	67	51	1850	270	515	.524	1	9	.111	101	134	.754	114	172	286	126	213	4	64	110	35	642	4.3	1.9	9.6
89-90—Houston	82	82	2832	504	1019	.495	2	17	.118	205	270	.759	113	268	381	252	321	8	104	167	62	1215	4.6	3.1	14.8
90-91—Houston	73	70	2279	416	873	.477	2	15	.133	157	216	.727	108	222	330	142	240	5	81	122	47	991	4.5	1.9	13.6
91-92—Houston	80	69	2202	290	633	.458	1	9	.111	104	143	.727	95	217	312	158	234	2	72	104	49	685	3.9	2.0	8.6
92-93—Washington	73	19	1287	193	403	.479	0	3	.000	92	126	.730	78	117	195	89	187	2	36	70	18	478	2.7	1.2	6.5
REG. SEASON TOTALS	505	296	11849	1922	3942	.488	7	62	.113	766	1038	.738	623	1137	1760	856	1403	21	404	664	252	4617	3.5	1.7	9.1
PLAYOFF TOTALS	20	11	382	53	125	.424	0	2	.000	24	33	.727	20	28	48	29	46	0	12	21	5	130	2.4	1.5	6.5

JOHNSON, ANDREW JR. (Andy) b. November 8, 1932 Ht. 6-5 Wt. 215 College—Portland

SEASON—TEAM	G	GS	MIN	FGM	FGA	PCT	3FGM	3FGA	PCT	FTM	FTA	PCT	O-RB	D-RB	TOT	AST	PF	DQ	STL	TO	BLK	PTS	RPG	APG	PPG
58-59—Philadelphia	67	—	1158	174	466	.373	—	—	—	115	191	.602	—	—	212	90	176	4	—	—	—	463	3.2	1.3	6.9
59-60—Philadelphia	75	—	1421	245	648	.378	—	—	—	125	208	.601	—	—	282	152	196	5	—	—	—	615	3.8	2.0	8.2
60-61—Philadelphia	79	—	2000	299	834	.359	—	—	—	157	275	.571	—	—	345	205	249	3	—	—	—	755	4.4	2.6	9.6
61-62—Chicago	71	—	2193	365	814	.448	—	—	—	284	452	.628	—	—	351	228	247	5	—	—	—	1014	4.9	3.2	14.3
REG. SEASON TOTALS	292	—	6772	1083	2762	.392	—	—	—	681	1126	.605	—	—	1190	675	868	17	—	—	—	2847	4.1	2.3	9.8
PLAYOFF TOTALS	12	—	233	35	89	.393	—	—	—	30	56	.536	—	—	55	22	37	2	—	—	—	100	4.6	1.8	8.3

JOHNSON, ARNITZ L. (Arnie) b. May 17, 1920 Ht. 6-5 Wt. 240 College—Bemidji State

SEASON—TEAM	G	GS	MIN	FGM	FGA	PCT	3FGM	3FGA	PCT	FTM	FTA	PCT	O-RB	D-RB	TOT	AST	PF	DQ	STL	TO	BLK	PTS	RPG	APG	PPG
46-47—Rochester (N)	32	—	—	68	—	—	—	—	—	68	98	.694	—	—	—	—	74	—	—	—	—	204	—	—	6.4
47-48—Rochester (N)	57	—	—	101	—	—	—	—	—	97	147	.660	—	—	—	—	153	—	—	—	—	299	—	—	5.2
48-49—Rochester	60	—	—	156	375	.416	—	—	—	199	284	.701	—	—	—	80	247	—	—	—	—	511	—	1.3	8.5
49-50—Rochester	68	—	—	149	376	.396	—	—	—	200	294	.680	—	—	—	141	260	—	—	—	—	498	—	2.1	7.3
50-51—Rochester	68	—	—	185	403	.459	—	—	—	269	371	.725	—	—	449	175	290	11	—	—	—	639	6.6	2.6	9.4
51-52—Rochester	66	—	2158	178	411	.433	—	—	—	301	387	.778	—	—	404	182	259	9	—	—	—	657	6.1	2.8	10.0
52-53—Rochester	70	—	1984	140	369	.379	—	—	—	303	405	.748	—	—	419	153	282	14	—	—	—	583	6.0	2.2	8.3
REG. NBA TOTALS	332	—	4142	808	1934	.418	—	—	—	1272	1741	.731	—	—	1272	731	1338	34	—	—	—	2888	6.2	2.2	8.7
REG. NBL TOTALS	89	—	—	169	—	—	—	—	—	165	245	.673	—	—	—	—	227	—	—	—	—	503	—	—	5.7
NBA PLAYOFF TOTALS	29	—	253	77	201	.383	—	—	—	124	165	.752	—	—	175	82	137	5	—	—	—	278	7.6	2.8	9.6
NBL PLAYOFF TOTALS	11	—	—	23	—	—	—	—	—	20	24	.833	—	—	—	—	21	—	—	—	—	66	—	—	6.0

JOHNSON, AVERY (Taz) b. March 25, 1965 Ht. 5-10 Wt. 175 College—New Mexico JC/Cameron/Southern

SEASON—TEAM	G	GS	MIN	FGM	FGA	PCT	3FGM	3FGA	PCT	FTM	FTA	PCT	O-RB	D-RB	TOT	AST	PF	DQ	STL	TO	BLK	PTS	RPG	APG	PPG
88-89—Seattle	43	0	291	29	83	.349	1	9	.111	9	16	.563	11	13	24	73	34	0	21	18	3	68	0.6	1.7	1.6
89-90—Seattle	53	10	575	55	142	.387	1	4	.250	29	40	.725	21	22	43	162	55	0	26	48	1	140	0.8	3.1	2.6
90-91—Denver-S.A.	68	14	959	130	277	.469	1	9	.111	59	87	.678	22	55	77	230	62	0	47	74	4	320	1.1	3.4	4.7
91-92—S.A.-Houston	69	15	1235	158	330	.479	4	15	.267	66	101	.653	13	67	80	266	89	1	61	110	9	386	1.2	3.9	5.6
92-93—San Antonio	75	49	2030	256	510	.502	0	8	.000	144	182	.791	20	126	146	561	141	0	85	145	16	656	1.9	7.5	8.7
93-94—Golden State	82	70	2332	356	724	.492	0	12	.000	178	253	.704	41	135	176	433	160	0	113	172	8	890	2.1	5.3	10.9
REG. SEASON TOTALS	390	158	7422	984	2066	.476	7	57	.123	485	679	.714	128	418	546	1725	541	1	353	567	41	2460	1.4	4.4	6.3
PLAYOFF TOTALS	22	10	405	50	104	.481	0	7	.000	13	18	.722	10	28	38	100	33	0	19	26	2	113	1.7	4.5	5.1

JOHNSON, CHARLES (Charlie, C.J.) b. March 31, 1949 Ht. 6-0 Wt. 170 College—California

SEASON—TEAM	G	GS	MIN	FGM	FGA	PCT	3FGM	3FGA	PCT	FTM	FTA	PCT	O-RB	D-RB	TOT	AST	PF	DQ	STL	TO	BLK	PTS	RPG	APG	PPG
72-73—Golden State	70	—	887	171	400	.428	—	—	—	33	46	.717	—	—	132	118	105	0	—	—	—	375	1.9	1.7	5.4
73-74—Golden State	59	—	1051	194	468	.415	—	—	—	38	55	.691	49	126	175	102	111	1	62	—	7	426	3.0	1.7	7.2
74-75—Golden State	79	—	2171	394	957	.412	—	—	—	75	102	.735	134	177	311	233	204	2	138	—	8	863	3.9	2.9	10.9
75-76—Golden State	81	—	1549	342	732	.467	—	—	—	60	79	.759	77	125	202	122	178	1	100	—	7	744	2.5	1.5	9.2
76-77—Golden State	79	—	1196	255	583	.437	—	—	—	49	69	.710	50	91	141	91	134	1	77	—	7	559	1.8	1.2	7.1
77-78—G.S.-Wash.	71	—	1299	237	581	.408	—	—	—	49	61	.803	43	112	155	130	129	1	62	73	5	523	2.2	1.8	7.4
78-79—Washington	82	—	1819	342	786	.435	—	—	—	67	79	.848	70	132	202	177	161	0	95	87	6	751	2.5	2.2	9.2
REG. SEASON TOTALS	521	—	9972	1935	4507	.429	—	—	—	371	491	.756	423	763	1318	973	1022	5	534	160	40	4241	2.5	1.9	8.1
PLAYOFF TOTALS	85	—	1723	321	806	.398	—	—	—	80	107	.748	71	126	207	142	201	1	88	37	10	722	2.4	1.7	8.5

JOHNSON, CLARENCE STEPHEN (Steve) b. November 3, 1957 Ht. 6-10 Wt. 235 College—Oregon State

SEASON—TEAM	G	GS	MIN	FGM	FGA	PCT	3FGM	3FGA	PCT	FTM	FTA	PCT	O-RB	D-RB	TOT	AST	PF	DQ	STL	TO	BLK	PTS	RPG	APG	PPG
81-82—Kansas City	78	50	1741	395	644	.613	0	0	—	212	330	.642	152	307	459	91	372	25	39	197	89	1002	5.9	1.2	12.8
82-83—Kansas City	79	21	1544	371	595	.624	0	0	—	186	324	.574	140	258	398	95	323	9	40	180	82	928	5.0	1.2	11.7
83-84—K.C.-Chicago	81	21	1487	302	540	.559	0	0	—	165	287	.575	162	256	418	81	307	15	37	164	69	769	5.2	1.0	9.5
84-85—Chicago	74	54	1659	281	516	.545	0	3	.000	181	252	.718	146	291	437	64	265	7	37	151	62	743	5.9	0.9	10.0
85-86—San Antonio	71	55	1828	362	573	.632	0	0	—	259	373	.694	143	319	462	95	291	13	44	191	66	983	6.5	1.3	13.8
86-87—Portland	79	74	2345	494	889	.556	0	0	—	342	490	.698	194	372	566	155	340	16	49	276	76	1330	7.2	2.0	16.8
87-88—Portland	43	33	1050	258	488	.529	0	1	.000	146	249	.586	84	158	242	57	151	4	17	122	32	662	5.6	1.3	15.4
88-89—Portland	72	11	1477	296	565	.524	0	0	—	129	245	.527	135	223	358	105	254	3	20	140	44	721	5.0	1.5	10.0
89-90—Minn.-Seattle	25	0	259	48	92	.522	0	0	—	21	35	.600	19	34	53	17	56	0	3	31	5	117	2.1	0.7	4.7
90-91—Golden State	24	8	228	34	63	.540	0	0	—	22	37	.595	18	39	57	17	50	1	4	25	4	90	2.4	0.7	3.8
REG. SEASON TOTALS	626	327	13618	2841	4965	.572	0	4	.000	1663	2622	.634	1193	2257	3450	777	2409	93	290	1477	530	7345	5.5	1.2	11.7
PLAYOFF TOTALS	13	4	246	37	91	.407	0	0	—	37	59	.627	23	34	57	6	40	1	4	20	2	111	4.4	0.5	8.5

JOHNSON, CLAYTON H. (Clay) b. July 18, 1956 Ht. 6-4 Wt. 175 College—Penn Valley CC/Missouri

SEASON—TEAM	G	GS	MIN	FGM	FGA	PCT	3FGM	3FGA	PCT	FTM	FTA	PCT	O-RB	D-RB	TOT	AST	PF	DQ	STL	TO	BLK	PTS	RPG	APG	PPG
81-82—Los Angeles	7	0	65	11	20	.550	0	0	—	3	6	.500	8	4	12	7	13	0	3	7	3	25	1.7	1.0	3.6
82-83—Los Angeles	48	0	447	53	135	.393	0	2	.000	38	48	.792	40	29	69	24	62	0	22	25	4	144	1.4	0.5	3.0
83-84—Seattle	25	0	176	20	50	.400	1	1	1.000	14	22	.636	6	6	12	14	24	0	8	12	2	55	0.5	0.6	2.2
REG. SEASON TOTALS	80	0	688	84	205	.410	1	3	.333	55	76	.724	54	39	93	45	99	0	33	44	9	224	1.2	0.6	2.8
PLAYOFF TOTALS	17	0	67	11	20	.550	0	2	.000	2	2	1.000	4	4	8	3	12	0	3	2	0	24	0.5	0.2	1.4

JOHNSON, CLEMON b. September 12, 1956 Ht. 6-10 Wt. 240 College—Florida A&M

SEASON—TEAM	G	GS	MIN	FGM	FGA	PCT	3FGM	3FGA	PCT	FTM	FTA	PCT	O-RB	D-RB	TOT	AST	PF	DQ	STL	TO	BLK	PTS	RPG	APG	PPG
78-79—Portland	74	—	794	102	217	.470	—			36	74	.486	83	143	226	78	121	1	23	65	36	240	3.1	1.1	3.2
79-80—Indiana	79	—	1541	199	396	.503	0	0	—	74	117	.632	145	249	394	115	211	2	48	78	121	472	5.0	1.5	6.0
80-81—Indiana	81	—	1643	235	466	.504	0	1	.000	112	189	.593	173	295	468	144	185	1	44	121	119	582	5.8	1.8	7.2
81-82—Indiana	79	42	1979	312	641	.487	0	0	—	123	189	.651	184	387	571	127	241	3	60	138	110	747	7.2	1.6	9.5
82-83—Indiana-Phil.	83	11	1914	299	581	.515	0	1	.000	111	180	.617	190	334	524	139	221	3	67	124	92	709	6.3	1.7	8.5
83-84—Philadelphia	80	10	1721	193	412	.468	0	0	—	69	113	.611	131	267	398	55	205	1	35	95	65	455	5.0	0.7	5.7
84-85—Philadelphia	58	0	875	117	235	.498	0	1	.000	36	49	.735	92	129	221	33	112	0	15	43	44	270	3.8	0.6	4.7
85-86—Philadelphia	75	2	1069	105	223	.471	0	0	—	51	81	.630	106	149	255	15	129	0	23	38	62	261	3.4	0.2	3.5
86-87—Seattle	78	7	1051	88	178	.494	0	2	.000	70	110	.636	106	171	277	21	137	0	21	36	42	246	3.6	0.3	3.2
87-88—Seattle	74	26	723	49	105	.467	0	0	—	22	32	.688	66	108	174	17	104	0	13	29	24	120	2.4	0.2	1.6
REG. SEASON TOTALS	761	98	13310	1699	3454	.492	0	5	.000	704	1134	.621	1276	2232	3508	744	1666	11	349	767	715	4102	4.6	1.0	5.4
PLAYOFF TOTALS	66	9	1118	107	230	.465	0	1	.000	56	92	.609	104	134	238	26	139	0	33	52	52	270	3.6	0.4	4.1

JOHNSON, DAVE M. b. November 16, 1970 Ht. 6-7 Wt. 210 College—Syracuse

SEASON—TEAM	G	GS	MIN	FGM	FGA	PCT	3FGM	3FGA	PCT	FTM	FTA	PCT	O-RB	D-RB	TOT	AST	PF	DQ	STL	TO	BLK	PTS	RPG	APG	PPG
92-93—Portland	42	0	356	57	149	.383	3	14	.214	40	59	.678	18	30	48	13	23	0	8	28	1	157	1.1	0.3	3.7
93-94—Chicago	17	0	119	17	54	.315	0	1	.000	13	21	.619	9	7	16	4	7	0	4	9	0	47	0.9	0.2	2.8
REG. SEASON TOTALS	59	0	475	74	203	.365	3	15	.200	53	80	.663	27	37	64	17	30	0	12	37	1	204	1.1	0.3	3.5

JOHNSON, DAVID RALPH (**Boag, Ralph**) b. December 6, 1921 Ht. 5-11 Wt. 170 College—Huntington College

SEASON—TEAM	G	GS	MIN	FGM	FGA	PCT	3FGM	3FGA	PCT	FTM	FTA	PCT	O-RB	D-RB	TOT	AST	PF	DQ	STL	TO	BLK	PTS	RPG	APG	PPG
47-48—Anderson (N)	57	—		84	—		—			31	53	.585	—	—			99	—	—			199	—	—	3.5
48-49—Anderson (N)	64	—		218	—		—			85	129	.659	—	—			178	—	—			521	—	—	8.1
49-50—And.-Ft. Wayne	67	—		243	779	.312	—			104	129	.806	—	—		171	207	—	—			590	—	2.6	8.8
50-51—Fort Wayne	68	—		235	737	.319	—			114	162	.704	—	—	275	183	247	11	—			584	4.0	2.7	8.6
51-52—Fort Wayne	66	—	2265	211	592	.356	—			101	140	.721	—	—	222	210	243	6	—			523	3.4	3.2	7.9
52-53—Fort Wayne	3	—	30	3	9	.333	—			2	3	.667	—	—	1	5	6	0	—			8	0.3	1.7	2.7
REG. NBA TOTALS	204	—	2295	692	2117	.327	—			321	434	.740	—	—	498	569	703	17	—			1705	3.6	2.8	8.4
REG. NBL TOTALS	121	—	302	—	—		—			116	182	.637	—	—	—	277	—	—	—			720	—	—	6.0
NBA PLAYOFF TOTALS	9	—	70	28	87	.322	—			14	19	.737	—	—	13	22	41	3	—			70	2.6	2.4	7.8
NBL PLAYOFF TOTALS	13	—		49	—		—			21	27	.778	—	—	—	33	—	—	—			119	—	—	9.2

JOHNSON, DENNIS WAYNE (**D.J.**) b. September 18, 1954 Ht. 6-4 Wt. 200 College—Los Angeles Harbor/Pepperdine

SEASON—TEAM	G	GS	MIN	FGM	FGA	PCT	3FGM	3FGA	PCT	FTM	FTA	PCT	O-RB	D-RB	TOT	AST	PF	DQ	STL	TO	BLK	PTS	RPG	APG	PPG
76-77—Seattle	81	—	1667	285	566	.504	—		—	179	287	.624	161	141	302	123	221	3	123	—	57	749	3.7	1.5	9.2
77-78—Seattle	81	—	2209	367	881	.417	—		—	297	406	.732	152	142	294	230	213	2	118	164	51	1031	3.6	2.8	12.7
78-79—Seattle	80	—	2717	482	1110	.434	—		—	306	392	.781	146	228	374	280	209	2	100	191	97	1270	4.7	3.5	15.9
79-80—Seattle	81	—	2937	574	1361	.422	12	58	.207	380	487	.780	173	241	414	332	267	6	144	227	82	1540	5.1	4.1	19.0
80-81—Phoenix	79	—	2615	532	1220	.436	11	51	.216	411	501	.820	160	203	363	291	244	2	136	208	61	1486	4.6	3.7	18.8
81-82—Phoenix	80	77	2937	577	1228	.470	8	42	.190	399	495	.806	142	268	410	369	253	6	105	233	55	1561	5.1	4.6	19.5
82-83—Phoenix	77	74	2551	398	861	.462	5	31	.161	292	369	.791	92	243	335	388	204	1	97	204	39	1093	4.4	5.0	14.2
83-84—Boston	80	78	2665	384	878	.437	4	32	.125	281	330	.852	87	193	280	338	251	6	93	172	57	1053	3.5	4.2	13.2
84-85—Boston	80	77	2976	493	1066	.462	7	26	.269	261	306	.853	91	226	317	543	224	2	96	212	39	1254	4.0	6.8	15.7
85-86—Boston	78	78	2732	482	1060	.455	6	42	.143	243	297	.818	69	199	268	456	206	3	110	173	35	1213	3.4	5.8	15.6
86-87—Boston	79	78	2933	423	953	.444	7	62	.113	209	251	.833	45	216	261	594	201	0	87	177	38	1062	3.3	7.5	13.4
87-88—Boston	77	74	2670	352	803	.438	12	46	.261	255	298	.856	62	178	240	598	204	0	93	195	29	971	3.1	7.8	12.6
88-89—Boston	72	72	2309	277	638	.434	7	50	.140	160	195	.821	31	159	190	472	211	3	94	175	21	721	2.6	6.6	10.0
89-90—Boston	75	65	2036	206	475	.434	1	24	.042	118	140	.843	48	153	201	485	179	2	81	117	14	531	2.7	6.5	7.1
REG. SEASON TOTALS	1100	673	35954	5832	13100	.445	80	464	.172	3791	4754	.797	1459	2790	4249	5499	3087	38	1477	2448	675	15535	3.9	5.0	14.1
PLAYOFF TOTALS	180	117	6994	1167	2661	.439	26	110	.236	756	943	.802	262	519	781	1006	575	8	247	480	113	3116	4.3	5.6	17.3
ALL-STAR TOTALS	5	0	98	20	37	.541	0	0	—	19	22	.864	7	11	18	9	10	0	5	9	4	59	3.6	1.8	11.8

JOHNSON, EARVIN JR. (**Magic**) b. August 14, 1959 Ht. 6-9 Wt. 220 College—Michigan State

SEASON—TEAM	G	GS	MIN	FGM	FGA	PCT	3FGM	3FGA	PCT	FTM	FTA	PCT	O-RB	D-RB	TOT	AST	PF	DQ	STL	TO	BLK	PTS	RPG	APG	PPG
79-80—Los Angeles	77	—	2795	503	949	.530	7	31	.226	374	462	.810	166	430	596	563	218	1	187	305	41	1387	7.7	7.3	18.0
80-81—Los Angeles	37	—	1371	312	587	.532	3	17	.176	171	225	.760	101	219	320	317	100	0	127	143	27	798	8.6	8.6	21.6
81-82—Los Angeles	78	77	2991	556	1036	.537	6	29	.207	329	433	.760	252	499	751	743	223	1	208	286	34	1447	9.6	9.5	18.6
82-83—Los Angeles	79	79	2907	511	933	.548	0	21	.000	304	380	.800	214	469	683	829	200	1	176	301	47	1326	8.6	10.5	16.8
83-84—Los Angeles	67	66	2567	441	780	.565	6	29	.207	290	358	.810	99	392	491	875	169	1	150	306	49	1178	7.3	13.1	17.6
84-85—L.A. Lakers	77	77	2781	504	899	.561	7	37	.189	391	464	.843	90	386	476	968	155	0	113	305	25	1406	6.2	12.6	18.3
85-86—L.A. Lakers	72	70	2578	483	918	.526	10	43	.233	378	434	.871	85	341	426	907	133	0	113	273	16	1354	5.9	12.6	18.8
86-87—L.A. Lakers	80	80	2904	683	1308	.522	8	39	.205	535	631	.848	122	382	504	977	168	0	138	300	36	1909	6.3	12.2	23.9
87-88—L.A. Lakers	72	70	2637	490	996	.492	11	56	.196	417	489	.853	88	361	449	858	147	0	114	269	13	1408	6.2	11.9	19.6
88-89—L.A. Lakers	77	77	2886	579	1137	.509	59	188	.314	513	563	.911	111	496	607	988	172	0	138	312	22	1730	7.9	12.8	22.5
89-90—L.A. Lakers	79	79	2937	546	1138	.480	106	276	.384	567	637	.890	128	394	522	907	167	1	132	289	34	1765	6.6	11.5	22.3
90-91—L.A. Lakers	79	79	2933	466	976	.477	80	250	.320	519	573	.906	105	446	551	989	150	0	102	314	17	1531	7.0	12.5	19.4
REG. SEASON TOTALS	874	754	32287	6074	11657	.521	303	1016	.298	4788	5649	.848	1561	4815	6376	9921	2002	5	1698	3403	361	17239	7.3	11.4	19.7
PLAYOFF TOTALS	186	167	7403	1276	2513	.508	48	203	.236	1040	1241	.838	341	1090	1431	2320	521	3	358	684	64	3640	7.7	12.5	19.6
ALL-STAR TOTALS	11	10	331	64	131	.489	10	21	.476	38	42	.905	21	36	57	127	25	0	21	48	7	176	5.2	11.5	16.0

JOHNSON, ED L. b. June 17, 1944 Ht. 6-9 Wt. 205 College—Tennessee State

SEASON—TEAM	G	GS	MIN	FGM	FGA	PCT	3FGM	3FGA	PCT	FTM	FTA	PCT	O-RB	D-RB	TOT	AST	PF	DQ	STL	TO	BLK	PTS	RPG	APG	PPG
68-69—Los Angeles (A)	58	—	1662	263	548	.480	0	1	.000	156	303	.515	—	—	539	58	281	18	—	127	—	682	9.3	1.0	11.8
69-70—New York (A)	74	—	2486	405	848	.478	1	2	.500	226	404	.559	328	551	879	88	305	18	—	—	—	1037	11.9	1.2	14.0
70-71—N.Y.-Texas (A)	34	—	751	119	265	.449	0	0	—	82	130	.631	—	—	270	34	101	—	—	—	—	320	7.9	1.0	9.4
REG. ABA TOTALS	166	—	4899	787	1661	.474	1	3	.333	464	837	.554	328	551	1688	180	687	36	—	127	—	2039	10.2	1.1	12.3
ABA PLAYOFF TOTALS	7	—	216	32	69	.464	0	0	—	30	52	.577	—	—	67	5	31	4	—	—	—	94	9.6	0.7	13.4

JOHNSON, EDWARD ARNET (**Eddie**) b. May 1, 1959 Ht. 6-8 Wt. 215 College—Illinois

SEASON—TEAM	G	GS	MIN	FGM	FGA	PCT	3FGM	3FGA	PCT	FTM	FTA	PCT	O-RB	D-RB	TOT	AST	PF	DQ	STL	TO	BLK	PTS	RPG	APG	PPG
81-82—Kansas City	74	27	1517	295	643	.459	1	11	.091	99	149	.664	128	194	322	109	210	6	50	97	14	690	4.4	1.5	9.3
82-83—Kansas City	82	82	2933	677	1370	.494	20	71	.282	247	317	.779	191	310	501	216	259	3	70	181	20	1621	6.1	2.6	19.8
83-84—Kansas City	82	82	2920	753	1552	.485	20	64	.313	268	331	.810	165	290	455	296	266	4	76	213	21	1794	5.5	3.6	21.9
84-85—Kansas City	82	81	3029	769	1565	.491	13	54	.241	325	373	.871	151	256	407	273	237	2	83	225	22	1876	5.0	3.3	22.9
85-86—Sacramento	82	30	2514	623	1311	.475	4	20	.200	280	343	.816	173	246	419	214	237	0	54	191	17	1530	5.1	2.6	18.7
86-87—Sacramento	81	30	2457	606	1309	.463	37	118	.314	267	322	.829	146	207	353	251	218	4	42	163	19	1516	4.4	3.1	18.7
87-88—Phoenix	73	59	2177	533	1110	.480	24	94	.255	204	240	.850	121	197	318	180	190	0	33	139	9	1294	4.4	2.5	17.7
88-89—Phoenix	70	7	2043	608	1224	.497	71	172	.413	217	250	.868	91	215	306	162	198	0	47	122	7	1504	4.4	2.3	21.5
89-90—Phoenix	64	4	1811	411	907	.453	70	184	.380	188	205	.917	69	177	246	107	174	4	32	108	10	1080	3.8	1.7	16.9
90-91—Phoenix-Seattle	81	27	2085	543	1122	.484	39	120	.325	229	257	.891	107	164	271	111	181	0	58	122	9	1354	3.3	1.4	16.7
91-92—Seattle	81	19	2366	534	1164	.459	27	107	.252	291	338	.861	118	174	292	161	199	0	55	130	11	1386	3.6	2.0	17.1
92-93—Seattle	82	0	1869	463	991	.467	17	56	.304	234	257	.911	124	148	272	135	173	0	36	134	4	1177	3.3	1.6	14.4
93-94—Charlotte	73	27	1460	339	738	.459	59	150	.393	99	127	.780	80	144	224	125	143	2	36	84	8	836	3.1	1.7	11.5
REG. SEASON TOTALS	1007	475	29181	7154	15006	.477	402	1221	.329	2948	3509	.840	1664	2722	4386	2340	2685	25	672	1909	171	17658	4.4	2.3	17.5
PLAYOFF TOTALS	67	9	1732	395	905	.436	50	157	.318	167	196	.852	94	174	268	90	172	3	41	88	13	1007	4.0	1.3	15.0

JOHNSON, EDWARD JR. (**Eddie, Fast Eddie**) b. February 24, 1955 Ht. 6-2 Wt. 180 College—Auburn

SEASON—TEAM	G	GS	MIN	FGM	FGA	PCT	3FGM	3FGA	PCT	FTM	FTA	PCT	O-RB	D-RB	TOT	AST	PF	DQ	STL	TO	BLK	PTS	RPG	APG	PPG
77-78—Atlanta	79	—	1875	332	686	.484	—	—	—	164	201	.816	51	102	153	235	232	4	100	168	4	828	1.9	3.0	10.5
78-79—Atlanta	78	—	2413	501	982	.510	—	—	—	243	292	.832	65	105	170	360	241	6	121	213	11	1245	2.2	4.6	16.0
79-80—Atlanta	79	—	2622	590	1212	.487	5	13	.385	280	338	.828	95	105	200	370	216	2	120	189	24	1465	2.5	4.7	18.5
80-81—Atlanta	75	—	2693	573	1136	.504	6	20	.300	279	356	.784	60	119	179	407	188	2	126	197	11	1431	2.4	5.4	19.1
81-82—Atlanta	68	57	2314	455	1011	.450	7	30	.233	294	385	.764	63	128	191	358	188	1	102	186	16	1211	2.8	5.3	17.8
82-83—Atlanta	61	57	1813	389	858	.453	14	41	.341	186	237	.785	26	98	124	318	138	2	61	156	6	978	2.0	5.2	16.0
83-84—Atlanta	67	43	1893	353	798	.442	16	43	.372	164	213	.770	31	115	146	374	155	2	58	173	7	886	2.2	5.6	13.2
84-85—Atlanta	73	66	2367	453	946	.479	22	72	.306	265	332	.798	38	154	192	566	184	1	43	244	7	1193	2.6	7.8	16.3
85-86—Atlanta-Clev.	71	9	1477	284	621	.457	29	85	.341	112	155	.723	30	91	121	333	128	1	18	150	2	709	1.7	4.7	10.0
86-87—Seattle	24	0	508	85	186	.457	5	15	.333	42	55	.764	11	35	46	115	36	0	12	41	1	217	1.9	4.8	9.0
REG. SEASON TOTALS	675	232	19975	4015	8436	.476	104	319	.326	2029	2564	.791	470	1052	1522	3436	1706	21	761	1717	89	10163	2.3	5.1	15.1
PLAYOFF TOTALS	37	3	885	174	359	.485	3	11	.273	91	117	.778	20	56	76	150	79	1	31	58	6	442	2.1	4.1	11.9
ALL-STAR TOTALS	2	2	60	18	28	.643	0	0	—	2	3	.667	2	1	3	9	3	0	7	5	0	38	1.5	4.5	19.0

JOHNSON, ERIC b. February 7, 1966 Ht. 6-2 Wt. 205 College—Baylor/Nebraska

SEASON—TEAM	G	GS	MIN	FGM	FGA	PCT	3FGM	3FGA	PCT	FTM	FTA	PCT	O-RB	D-RB	TOT	AST	PF	DQ	STL	TO	BLK	PTS	RPG	APG	PPG
89-90—Utah	48	2	272	20	84	.238	1	6	.167	13	17	.765	8	20	28	64	49	1	17	26	2	54	0.6	1.3	1.1
REG. SEASON TOTALS	48	2	272	20	84	.238	1	6	.167	13	17	.765	8	20	28	64	49	1	17	26	2	54	0.6	1.3	1.1
PLAYOFF TOTALS	1	0	3	0	0	—	0	0	—	0	0	—	0	0	0	0	0	0	0	0	0	0	0.0	0.0	0.0

JOHNSON, ERVIN JR. b. December 21, 1967 Ht. 6-11 Wt. 245 College—New Orleans

SEASON—TEAM	G	GS	MIN	FGM	FGA	PCT	3FGM	3FGA	PCT	FTM	FTA	PCT	O-RB	D-RB	TOT	AST	PF	DQ	STL	TO	BLK	PTS	RPG	APG	PPG
93-94—Seattle	45	3	280	44	106	.415	0	0	—	29	46	.630	48	70	118	7	45	0	10	24	22	117	2.6	0.2	2.6
REG. SEASON TOTALS	45	3	280	44	106	.415	0	0	—	29	46	.630	48	70	118	7	45	0	10	24	22	117	2.6	0.2	2.6
PLAYOFF TOTALS	2	0	8	0	1	.000	0	0	—	0	0	—	0	4	4	—	1	0	0	1	0	0	2.0	0.0	0.0

JOHNSON, FRANKLIN LENARD (**Frank**) b. November 23, 1958 Ht. 6-3 Wt. 185 College—Wake Forest

SEASON—TEAM	G	GS	MIN	FGM	FGA	PCT	3FGM	3FGA	PCT	FTM	FTA	PCT	O-RB	D-RB	TOT	AST	PF	DQ	STL	TO	BLK	PTS	RPG	APG	PPG
81-82—Washington	79	29	2027	336	812	.414	17	79	.215	153	204	.750	34	113	147	380	196	1	76	160	7	842	1.9	4.8	10.7
82-83—Washington	68	65	2324	321	786	.408	14	61	.230	196	261	.751	46	132	178	549	170	1	110	238	6	852	2.6	8.1	12.5
83-84—Washington	82	81	2686	392	840	.467	11	43	.256	187	252	.742	58	126	184	567	174	1	96	191	6	982	2.2	6.9	12.0
84-85—Washington	46	1	925	175	358	.489	6	17	.353	72	96	.750	23	40	63	143	72	0	43	59	3	428	1.4	3.1	9.3
85-86—Washington	14	9	402	69	154	.448	0	3	.000	38	54	.704	7	21	28	76	30	0	11	29	1	176	2.0	5.4	12.6
86-87—Washington	18	10	399	59	128	.461	0	1	.000	35	49	.714	10	20	30	58	31	0	21	31	0	153	1.7	3.2	8.5
87-88—Washington	75	17	1258	216	498	.434	1	9	.111	121	149	.812	39	82	121	188	120	0	70	99	4	554	1.6	2.5	7.4
88-89—Houston	67	0	879	109	246	.443	1	6	.167	75	93	.806	22	57	79	181	91	0	42	102	0	294	1.2	2.7	4.4
92-93—Phoenix	77	0	1122	136	312	.436	1	12	.083	59	76	.776	41	72	113	186	112	0	60	80	8	332	1.5	2.4	4.3
93-94—Phoenix	70	5	875	134	299	.448	2	12	.167	54	69	.783	29	53	82	148	120	0	41	65	1	324	1.2	2.1	4.6
REG. SEASON TOTALS	596	217	12897	1947	4433	.439	53	243	.218	990	1303	.760	309	716	1025	2476	1116	3	570	1054	36	4937	1.7	4.2	8.3
PLAYOFF TOTALS	54	11	801	102	257	.397	8	29	.276	78	91	.857	20	43	63	126	87	0	31	60	0	290	1.2	2.3	5.4

JOHNSON, GEORGE E. b. June 19, 1947 Ht. 6-11 Wt. 245 College—Stephen F. Austin State

SEASON—TEAM	G	GS	MIN	FGM	FGA	PCT	3FGM	3FGA	PCT	FTM	FTA	PCT	O-RB	D-RB	TOT	AST	PF	DQ	STL	TO	BLK	PTS	RPG	APG	PPG
70-71—Baltimore	24	—	337	41	100	.410				11	30	.367	—	—	114	10	63	1	—	—	—	93	4.8	0.4	3.9
71-72—Dallas (A)	67	—	1477	128	282	.454	0	0	—	61	103	.592	—	—	464	59	209	—	—	84	—	317	6.9	0.9	4.7
72-73—Houston	19	—	169	20	39	.513	—	—	—	3	4	.750	—	—	45	3	33	0	—	—	—	43	2.4	0.2	2.3
73-74—Houston	26	—	238	23	51	.451	—	—	—	8	17	.471	20	41	61	9	46	1	8	—	8	54	2.3	0.3	2.1
REG. NBA TOTALS	69	—	744	84	190	.442				22	51	.431	20	41	220	22	142	2	8	—	8	190	3.2	0.3	2.8
REG. ABA TOTALS	67	—	1477	128	282	.454	0	0	—	61	103	.592	—	—	464	59	209	—	—	84	—	317	6.9	0.9	4.7
NBA PLAYOFF TOTALS	11	—	35	7	13	.538				1	2	.500	0	0	11	2	9	0	0	—	0	15	1.0	0.2	1.4
ABA PLAYOFF TOTALS	4	—	96	3	9	.333	0	0	—	0	0	—	—	—	24	9	16	—	—	6	—	6	6.0	2.3	1.5

JOHNSON, GEORGE L. b. December 8, 1956 Ht. 6-7 Wt. 210 College—St. John's

SEASON—TEAM	G	GS	MIN	FGM	FGA	PCT	3FGM	3FGA	PCT	FTM	FTA	PCT	O-RB	D-RB	TOT	AST	PF	DQ	STL	TO	BLK	PTS	RPG	APG	PPG
78-79—Milwaukee	67	—	1157	165	342	.482	—	—	—	84	117	.718	106	254	360	81	187	5	75	100	49	414	5.4	1.2	6.2
79-80—Denver	75	—	1938	309	649	.476	2	9	.222	148	189	.783	190	394	584	157	260	4	84	148	67	768	7.8	2.1	10.2
80-81—Indiana	43	—	930	182	394	.462	0	5	.000	93	122	.762	99	179	278	86	120	1	47	85	23	457	6.5	2.0	10.6
81-82—Indiana	59	4	720	120	291	.412	0	2	.000	60	80	.750	72	145	217	40	147	2	36	68	27	300	3.7	0.7	5.1
82-83—Indiana	82	64	2297	409	858	.477	7	38	.184	126	172	.733	176	369	545	220	279	6	77	242	53	951	6.6	2.7	11.6
83-84—Indiana	81	20	2073	411	884	.465	11	47	.234	223	270	.826	139	321	460	195	256	3	82	186	46	1056	5.7	2.4	13.0
84-85—Philadelphia	55	3	756	107	263	.407	1	10	.100	49	56	.875	48	116	164	38	99	0	31	49	16	264	3.0	0.7	4.8
85-86—Washington	2	0	7	1	3	.333	0	0	—	2	2	1.000	1	1	2	0	1	0	0	1	0	4	1.0	0.0	2.0
REG. SEASON TOTALS	464	91	9878	1704	3684	.463	21	111	.189	785	1008	.779	831	1779	2610	817	1349	21	432	879	284	4214	5.6	1.8	9.1
PLAYOFF TOTALS	7	0	47	10	16	.625	1	1	1.000	0	0	—	4	7	11	1	3	0	0	3	0	21	1.6	0.1	3.0

JOHNSON, GEORGE THOMAS b. December 18, 1948 Ht. 6-11 Wt. 205 College—Dillard

SEASON—TEAM	G	GS	MIN	FGM	FGA	PCT	3FGM	3FGA	PCT	FTM	FTA	PCT	O-RB	D-RB	TOT	AST	PF	DQ	STL	TO	BLK	PTS	RPG	APG	PPG
72-73—Golden State	56	—	349	41	100	.410	—	—	—	7	17	.412	—	—	138	8	40	0	—	—	—	89	2.5	0.1	1.6
73-74—Golden State	66	—	1291	173	358	.483	—	—	—	59	107	.551	190	332	522	73	176	3	35	—	124	405	7.9	1.1	6.1
74-75—Golden State	82	—	1439	152	319	.476	—	—	—	60	91	.659	217	357	574	67	206	1	32	—	136	364	7.0	0.8	4.4
75-76—Golden State	82	—	1745	165	341	.484	—	—	—	70	104	.673	200	427	627	82	275	6	51	—	174	400	7.6	1.0	4.9
76-77—G.S.-Buffalo	78	—	1652	198	429	.462	—	—	—	71	98	.724	204	407	611	104	246	8	37	—	177	467	7.8	1.3	6.0
77-78—New Jersey	81	—	2411	285	721	.395	—	—	—	133	185	.719	245	534	779	111	339	20	78	221	274	703	9.6	1.4	8.7
78-79—New Jersey	78	—	2058	206	483	.427	—	—	—	105	138	.761	201	415	616	88	315	8	68	178	253	517	7.9	1.1	6.6
79-80—New Jersey	81	—	2119	248	543	.457	0	1	.000	89	126	.706	192	410	602	173	312	7	53	199	258	585	7.4	2.1	7.2
80-81—San Antonio	82	—	1935	164	347	.473	0	0	—	80	109	.734	215	387	602	92	273	3	47	110	278	408	7.3	1.1	5.0
81-82—San Antonio	75	62	1578	91	195	.467	0	0	—	43	64	.672	152	302	454	79	259	6	20	92	234	225	6.1	1.1	3.0
82-83—Atlanta	37	0	461	25	57	.439	0	0	—	14	19	.737	44	73	117	17	69	0	10	19	59	64	3.2	0.5	1.7
84-85—New Jersey	65	0	800	42	79	.532	1	1	1.000	22	27	.815	74	111	185	22	151	2	19	39	78	107	2.8	0.3	1.6
85-86—Seattle	41	0	264	12	23	.522	0	0	—	11	16	.688	26	34	60	13	46	0	6	14	37	35	1.5	0.3	0.9
REG. SEASON TOTALS	904	62	18102	1802	3995	.451	1	2	.500	764	1101	.694	1960	3789	5887	929	2707	64	456	872	2082	4369	6.5	1.0	4.8
PLAYOFF TOTALS	59	9	1043	103	187	.551	0	0	—	42	68	.618	136	211	361	55	165	2	34	15	101	248	6.1	0.9	4.2

JOHNSON, GUS JR. (Honeycomb) b. December 13, 1935 d. April 28, 1987 Ht. 6-5½ Wt. 230 College—Boise JC/Akron/Idaho

SEASON—TEAM	G	GS	MIN	FGM	FGA	PCT	3FGM	3FGA	PCT	FTM	FTA	PCT	O-RB	D-RB	TOT	AST	PF	DQ	STL	TO	BLK	PTS	RPG	APG	PPG
63-64—Baltimore	78	—	2847	571	1329	.430	—	—	—	210	319	.658	—	—	1064	169	321	11	—	—	—	1352	13.6	2.2	17.3
64-65—Baltimore	76	—	2899	577	1379	.418	—	—	—	261	386	.676	—	—	988	270	258	4	—	—	—	1415	13.0	3.6	18.6
65-66—Baltimore	41	—	1284	273	661	.413	—	—	—	131	178	.736	—	—	546	114	136	3	—	—	—	677	13.3	2.8	16.5
66-67—Baltimore	73	—	2626	620	1377	.450	—	—	—	271	383	.708	—	—	855	194	281	7	—	—	—	1511	11.7	2.7	20.7
67-68—Baltimore	60	—	2271	482	1033	.467	—	—	—	180	270	.667	—	—	782	159	223	7	—	—	—	1144	13.0	2.7	19.1
68-69—Baltimore	49	—	1671	359	782	.459	—	—	—	160	223	.717	—	—	568	97	176	1	—	—	—	878	11.6	2.0	17.9
69-70—Baltimore	78	—	2919	578	1282	.451	—	—	—	197	272	.724	—	—	1086	264	269	6	—	—	—	1353	13.9	3.4	17.3
70-71—Baltimore	66	—	2538	494	1090	.453	—	—	—	214	290	.738	—	—	1128	192	227	4	—	—	—	1202	17.1	2.9	18.2
71-72—Baltimore	39	—	668	103	269	.383	—	—	—	43	63	.683	—	—	226	51	91	0	—	—	—	249	5.8	1.3	6.4
72-73—Phoenix	21	—	417	69	181	.381	—	—	—	25	36	.694	—	—	136	31	55	0	—	—	—	163	6.5	1.5	7.8
72-73—Indiana (A)	50	—	753	132	299	.441	4	21	.190	31	42	.738	85	160	245	62	113	1	—	70	—	299	4.9	1.2	6.0
REG. NBA TOTALS	581	—	20140	4126	9383	.440	—	—	—	1692	2420	.699	—	—	7379	1541	2037	43	—	—	—	9944	12.7	2.7	17.1
REG. ABA TOTALS	50	—	753	132	299	.441	4	21	.190	31	42	.738	85	160	245	62	113	1	—	70	—	299	4.9	1.2	6.0
NBA PLAYOFF TOTALS	34	—	1125	177	446	.397	—	—	—	98	129	.760	—	—	330	76	110	1	—	—	—	452	9.7	2.2	13.3
ABA PLAYOFF TOTALS	17	—	184	15	59	.254	0	3	.000	12	16	.750	—	—	69	15	27	0	—	18	—	42	4.1	0.9	2.5
NBA ALL-STAR TOTALS	5	—	99	24	56	.429	—	—	—	19	25	.760	—	—	35	6	12	0	—	—	—	67	7.0	1.2	13.4

JOHNSON, HAROLD H. b. January 20, 1920 Ht. 6-6 Wt. 240 College—Indiana State

SEASON—TEAM	G	GS	MIN	FGM	FGA	PCT	3FGM	3FGA	PCT	FTM	FTA	PCT	O-RB	D-RB	TOT	AST	PF	DQ	STL	TO	BLK	PTS	RPG	APG	PPG
46-47—Detroit	27	—	—	4	20	.200	—	—	—	7	14	.500	—	—	—	11	13	—	—	—	—	15	—	0.4	0.6
REG. SEASON TOTALS	27	—	—	4	20	.200	—	—	—	7	14	.500	—	—	—	11	13	—	—	—	—	15	—	0.4	0.6

JOHNSON, JOHN HOWARD GETTY (**J.J.**) b. October 18, 1947   Ht. 6-7   Wt. 200   College—Northwest CC/Iowa

SEASON—TEAM	G	GS	MIN	FGM	FGA	PCT	3FGM	3FGA	PCT	FTM	FTA	PCT	O-RB	D-RB	TOT	AST	PF	DQ	STL	TO	BLK	PTS	RPG	APG	PPG
70-71—Cleveland	67	—	2310	435	1032	.422	—	—	—	240	298	.805	—	—	453	323	251	3	—	—	—	1110	6.8	4.8	16.6
71-72—Cleveland	82	—	3041	557	1286	.433	—	—	—	277	353	.785	—	—	631	415	268	2	—	—	—	1391	7.7	5.1	17.0
72-73—Cleveland	82	—	2815	492	1143	.430	—	—	—	199	271	.734	—	—	552	309	246	3	—	—	—	1183	6.7	3.8	14.4
73-74—Portland	69	—	2287	459	990	.464	—	—	—	212	261	.812	160	355	515	284	221	1	69	—	29	1130	7.5	4.1	16.4
74-75—Portland	80	—	2540	527	1082	.487	—	—	—	236	301	.784	162	339	501	240	249	3	75	—	39	1290	6.3	3.0	16.1
75-76—Port.-Houston	76	—	1697	316	697	.453	—	—	—	120	155	.774	94	238	332	217	194	1	57	—	36	752	4.4	2.9	9.9
76-77—Houston	79	—	1738	319	696	.458	—	—	—	94	132	.712	75	191	266	163	199	1	47	—	24	732	3.4	2.1	9.3
77-78—Houston-Seattle	77	—	1823	342	824	.415	—	—	—	133	177	.751	102	208	310	211	197	0	43	169	19	817	4.0	2.7	10.6
78-79—Seattle	82	—	2386	356	821	.434	—	—	—	190	250	.760	127	285	412	358	245	2	59	254	25	902	5.0	4.4	11.0
79-80—Seattle	81	—	2533	377	772	.488	0	0	—	161	201	.801	163	263	426	424	213	1	76	247	35	915	5.3	5.2	11.3
80-81—Seattle	80	—	2324	373	866	.431	0	1	.000	173	214	.808	135	227	362	312	202	2	57	230	25	919	4.5	3.9	11.5
81-82—Seattle	14	1	187	22	45	.489	0	0	—	15	20	.750	3	15	18	29	20	1	4	17	3	59	1.3	2.1	4.2
REG. SEASON TOTALS	869	1	25681	4575	10254	.446	0	1	.000	2050	2633	.779	1021	2121	4778	3285	2505	19	487	917	235	11200	5.5	3.8	12.9
PLAYOFF TOTALS	73	0	2002	295	656	.450	0	1	.000	121	173	.699	133	226	359	275	195	1	43	184	12	711	4.9	3.8	9.7
ALL-STAR TOTALS	2	0	5	0	2	.000	0	0	—	0	0	—	0	0	1	1	1	0	0	—	0	0	0.5	0.5	0.0

JOHNSON, KANNARD b. June 24, 1965   Ht. 6-9   Wt. 220   College—Western Kentucky

SEASON—TEAM	G	GS	MIN	FGM	FGA	PCT	3FGM	3FGA	PCT	FTM	FTA	PCT	O-RB	D-RB	TOT	AST	PF	DQ	STL	TO	BLK	PTS	RPG	APG	PPG
87-88—Cleveland	4	0	12	1	3	.333	0	0	—	0	0	—	0	0	0	0	1	0	1	2	0	2	0.0	0.0	0.5
REG. SEASON TOTALS	4	0	12	1	3	.333	0	0	—	0	0	—	0	0	0	0	1	0	1	2	0	2	0.0	0.0	0.5

JOHNSON, KENNETH H. (**Ken**) b. November 7, 1962   Ht. 6-8   Wt. 240   College—USC/Michigan State

SEASON—TEAM	G	GS	MIN	FGM	FGA	PCT	3FGM	3FGA	PCT	FTM	FTA	PCT	O-RB	D-RB	TOT	AST	PF	DQ	STL	TO	BLK	PTS	RPG	APG	PPG
85-86—Portland	64	0	815	113	214	.528	0	0	—	37	85	.435	90	153	243	19	147	1	13	59	22	263	3.8	0.3	4.1
REG. SEASON TOTALS	64	0	815	113	214	.528	0	0	—	37	85	.435	90	153	243	19	147	1	13	59	22	263	3.8	0.3	4.1
PLAYOFF TOTALS	2	0	11	0	0	—	0	0	—	0	0	—	0	2	2	—	1	0	2	1	0	0	1.0	0.0	0.0

JOHNSON, KEVIN MAURICE b. March 4, 1966   Ht. 6-1   Wt. 180   College—California

SEASON—TEAM	G	GS	MIN	FGM	FGA	PCT	3FGM	3FGA	PCT	FTM	FTA	PCT	O-RB	D-RB	TOT	AST	PF	DQ	STL	TO	BLK	PTS	RPG	APG	PPG
87-88—Clev.-Phoenix	80	28	1917	275	596	.461	5	24	.208	177	211	.839	36	155	191	437	155	1	103	146	24	732	2.4	5.5	9.2
88-89—Phoenix	81	81	3179	570	1128	.505	2	22	.091	508	576	.882	46	294	340	991	226	1	135	322	24	1650	4.2	12.2	20.4
89-90—Phoenix	74	74	2782	578	1159	.499	8	41	.195	501	598	.838	42	228	270	846	143	0	95	263	14	1665	3.6	11.4	22.5
90-91—Phoenix	77	76	2772	591	1145	.516	9	44	.205	519	616	.843	54	217	271	781	174	0	163	269	11	1710	3.5	10.1	22.2
91-92—Phoenix	78	78	2899	539	1125	.479	10	46	.217	448	555	.807	61	231	292	836	180	0	116	272	23	1536	3.7	10.7	19.7
92-93—Phoenix	49	47	1643	282	565	.499	1	8	.125	226	276	.819	30	74	104	384	100	0	85	151	19	791	2.1	7.8	16.1
93-94—Phoenix	67	67	2449	477	980	.487	6	27	.222	380	464	.819	55	112	167	637	127	1	125	235	10	1340	2.5	9.5	20.0
REG. SEASON TOTALS	506	451	17641	3312	6698	.494	41	212	.193	2759	3296	.837	324	1311	1635	4912	1105	3	822	1658	125	9424	3.2	9.7	18.6
PLAYOFF TOTALS	73	73	2898	531	1130	.470	12	47	.255	467	561	.832	51	196	247	727	169	2	103	272	22	1541	3.4	10.0	21.1
ALL-STAR TOTALS	3	1	51	6	12	.500	0	0	—	1	3	.333	1	2	3	13	5	0	4	8	1	13	1.0	4.3	4.3

JOHNSON, LARRY b. November 28, 1954   Ht. 6-3   Wt. 205   College—Kentucky

SEASON—TEAM	G	GS	MIN	FGM	FGA	PCT	3FGM	3FGA	PCT	FTM	FTA	PCT	O-RB	D-RB	TOT	AST	PF	DQ	STL	TO	BLK	PTS	RPG	APG	PPG
77-78—Buffalo	4	—	38	3	13	.231	—	—	—	0	2	.000	1	4	5	7	3	0	5	3	2	6	1.3	1.8	1.5
REG. SEASON TOTALS	4	—	38	3	13	.231	—	—	—	0	2	.000	1	4	5	7	3	0	5	3	2	6	1.3	1.8	1.5

JOHNSON, LARRY DEMETRIC b. March 14, 1969   Ht. 6-7   Wt. 250   College—Odessa JC/Nevada-Las Vegas

SEASON—TEAM	G	GS	MIN	FGM	FGA	PCT	3FGM	3FGA	PCT	FTM	FTA	PCT	O-RB	D-RB	TOT	AST	PF	DQ	STL	TO	BLK	PTS	RPG	APG	PPG
91-92—Charlotte	82	77	3047	616	1258	.490	5	22	.227	339	409	.829	323	576	899	292	225	3	81	160	51	1576	11.0	3.6	19.2
92-93—Charlotte	82	82	3323	728	1385	.526	18	71	.254	336	438	.767	281	583	864	353	187	0	53	227	27	1810	10.5	4.3	22.1
93-94—Charlotte	51	51	1757	346	672	.515	5	21	.238	137	197	.695	143	305	448	184	131	0	29	116	14	834	8.8	3.6	16.4
REG. SEASON TOTALS	215	210	8127	1690	3315	.510	28	114	.246	812	1044	.778	747	1464	2211	829	543	3	163	503	92	4220	10.3	3.9	19.6
PLAYOFF TOTALS	9	9	348	68	122	.557	1	4	.250	41	52	.788	19	43	62	30	27	0	5	19	2	178	6.9	3.3	19.8
ALL-STAR TOTALS	1	1	16	2	6	.333	0	0	—	0	0	—	3	1	4	0	1	0	0	0	0	4	4.0	0.0	4.0

JOHNSON, LEE b. June 16, 1957   Ht. 6-11   Wt. 205   College—McCook JC/Montana/East Texas State

SEASON—TEAM	G	GS	MIN	FGM	FGA	PCT	3FGM	3FGA	PCT	FTM	FTA	PCT	O-RB	D-RB	TOT	AST	PF	DQ	STL	TO	BLK	PTS	RPG	APG	PPG
80-81—Houston-Detroit	12	—	90	7	25	.280	0	0	—	3	5	.600	6	16	22	1	18	0	0	7	5	17	1.8	0.1	1.4
REG. SEASON TOTALS	12	—	90	7	25	.280	0	0	—	3	5	.600	6	16	22	1	18	0	0	7	5	17	1.8	0.1	1.4

JOHNSON, LYNBERT R. (**Cheese**) b. September 7, 1957   Ht. 6-5½   Wt. 195   College—Wichita State

SEASON—TEAM	G	GS	MIN	FGM	FGA	PCT	3FGM	3FGA	PCT	FTM	FTA	PCT	O-RB	D-RB	TOT	AST	PF	DQ	STL	TO	BLK	PTS	RPG	APG	PPG
79-80—Golden State	9	—	53	12	30	.400	0	0	—	3	5	.600	6	8	14	2	11	0	1	4	0	27	1.6	0.2	3.0
REG. SEASON TOTALS	9	—	53	12	30	.400	0	0	—	3	5	.600	6	8	14	2	11	0	1	4	0	27	1.6	0.2	3.0

JOHNSON, MARQUES KEVIN b. February 8, 1956 Ht. 6-7 Wt. 220 College—UCLA

SEASON—TEAM	G	GS	MIN	FGM	FGA	PCT	3FGM	3FGA	PCT	FTM	FTA	PCT	O-RB	D-RB	TOT	AST	PF	DQ	STL	TO	BLK	PTS	RPG	APG	PPG
77-78—Milwaukee	80	—	2765	628	1204	.522	—	—	—	301	409	.736	292	555	847	190	221	3	92	175	103	1557	10.6	2.4	19.5
78-79—Milwaukee	77	—	2779	820	1491	.550	—	—	—	332	437	.760	212	374	586	234	186	1	116	170	89	1972	7.6	3.0	25.6
79-80—Milwaukee	77	—	2686	689	1267	.544	2	9	.222	291	368	.791	217	349	566	273	173	0	100	185	70	1671	7.4	3.5	21.7
80-81—Milwaukee	76	—	2542	636	1153	.552	0	9	.000	269	381	.706	225	293	518	346	196	1	115	190	41	1541	6.8	4.6	20.3
81-82—Milwaukee	60	52	1900	404	760	.532	0	4	.000	182	260	.700	153	211	364	213	142	1	59	145	35	990	6.1	3.6	16.5
82-83—Milwaukee	80	80	2853	723	1420	.509	4	20	.200	264	359	.735	196	366	562	363	211	0	100	196	56	1714	7.0	4.5	21.4
83-84—Milwaukee	74	74	2715	646	1288	.502	2	13	.154	241	340	.709	173	307	480	315	194	1	115	180	45	1535	6.5	4.3	20.7
84-85—L.A. Clippers	72	68	2448	494	1094	.452	3	13	.231	190	260	.731	184	244	428	248	193	2	72	176	30	1181	5.9	3.4	16.4
85-86—L.A. Clippers	75	75	2605	613	1201	.510	1	15	.067	298	392	.760	156	260	416	283	214	2	107	183	50	1525	5.5	3.8	20.3
86-87—L.A. Clippers	10	10	302	68	155	.439	0	6	.000	30	42	.714	9	24	33	28	24	0	12	17	5	166	3.3	2.8	16.6
89-90—Golden State	10	0	99	12	32	.375	2	3	.667	14	17	.824	8	9	17	9	12	0	0	10	1	40	1.7	0.9	4.0
REG. SEASON TOTALS	691	359	23694	5733	11065	.518	14	92	.152	2412	3265	.739	1825	2992	4817	2502	1766	11	888	1627	525	13892	7.0	3.6	20.1
PLAYOFF TOTALS	54	31	2112	471	964	.489	3	13	.231	218	311	.701	173	254	427	198	156	0	56	111	45	1163	7.9	3.7	21.5
ALL-STAR TOTALS	5	2	106	11	35	.314	0	0	—	12	16	.750	9	10	19	9	9	0	1	1	2	34	3.8	1.8	6.8

JOHNSON, NEIL A. b. April 17, 1943 Ht. 6-7 Wt. 220 College—Tulsa/Creighton

SEASON—TEAM	G	GS	MIN	FGM	FGA	PCT	3FGM	3FGA	PCT	FTM	FTA	PCT	O-RB	D-RB	TOT	AST	PF	DQ	STL	TO	BLK	PTS	RPG	APG	PPG
66-67—New York	51	—	522	59	171	.345	—	—	—	57	86	.663	—	—	167	38	102	0	—	—	—	175	3.3	0.7	3.4
67-68—New York	43	—	286	44	106	.415	—	—	—	23	48	.479	—	—	75	33	63	0	—	—	—	111	1.7	0.8	2.6
68-69—Phoenix	80	—	1319	177	368	.481	—	—	—	110	177	.621	—	—	396	134	214	3	—	—	—	464	5.0	1.7	5.8
69-70—Phoenix	28	—	136	20	60	.333	—	—	—	8	12	.667	—	—	47	12	38	0	—	—	—	48	1.7	0.4	1.7
70-71—Virginia (A)	78	—	1838	398	758	.525	0	2	.000	194	259	.749	—	—	668	179	295	—	—	—	—	990	8.6	2.3	12.7
71-72—Virginia (A)	31	—	874	128	273	.469	1	3	.333	65	94	.691	—	—	286	78	123	—	—	67	—	322	9.2	2.5	10.4
72-73—Virginia (A)	69	—	1442	210	429	.490	0	1	.000	103	156	.660	156	208	364	158	232	5	—	131	—	523	5.3	2.3	7.6
REG. NBA TOTALS	202	—	2263	300	705	.426	—	—	—	198	323	.613	—	—	685	217	417	3	—	—	—	798	3.4	1.1	4.0
REG. ABA TOTALS	178	—	4154	736	1460	.504	1	6	.167	362	509	.711	156	208	1318	415	650	5	—	198	—	1835	7.4	2.3	10.3
NBA PLAYOFF TOTALS	8	—	77	11	34	.324	—	—	—	7	8	.875	—	—	30	5	13	0	—	—	—	29	3.8	0.6	3.6
ABA PLAYOFF TOTALS	17	—	351	54	118	.458	1	1	1.000	35	52	.673	—	—	121	37	70	0	—	7	—	144	7.1	2.2	8.5
ABA ALL-STAR TOTALS	1	—	4	0	3	.000	0	0	—	0	0	—	—	1	1	0	1	—	—	0	—	0	1.0	0.0	0.0

JOHNSON, OLLIE b. May 11, 1949 Ht. 6-6 Wt. 200 College—Philadelphia CC/Temple

SEASON—TEAM	G	GS	MIN	FGM	FGA	PCT	3FGM	3FGA	PCT	FTM	FTA	PCT	O-RB	D-RB	TOT	AST	PF	DQ	STL	TO	BLK	PTS	RPG	APG	PPG
72-73—Portland	78	—	2138	308	620	.497	—	—	—	156	206	.757	—	—	417	200	166	0	—	—	—	772	5.3	2.6	9.9
73-74—Portland	79	—	1718	209	434	.482	—	—	—	77	94	.819	116	208	324	167	179	2	60	—	30	495	4.1	2.1	6.3
74-75—N.O.-K.C.-Omaha	73	—	1667	203	429	.473	—	—	—	95	114	.833	87	156	243	110	172	1	59	—	33	501	3.3	1.5	6.9
75-76—Kansas City	81	—	2150	348	678	.513	—	—	—	125	149	.839	116	241	357	146	217	4	67	—	42	821	4.4	1.8	10.1
76-77—Kansas City	81	—	1386	218	446	.489	—	—	—	101	115	.878	68	144	212	105	169	1	43	—	21	537	2.6	1.3	6.6
77-78—Atlanta	82	—	1704	292	619	.472	—	—	—	111	130	.854	89	171	260	120	180	2	80	107	36	695	3.2	1.5	8.5
78-79—Chicago	71	—	1734	281	540	.520	—	—	—	88	110	.800	58	169	227	163	182	2	54	114	33	650	3.2	2.3	9.2
79-80—Chicago	79	—	1535	262	527	.497	1	11	.091	82	93	.882	50	113	163	161	165	0	59	96	24	607	2.1	2.0	7.7
80-81—Philadelphia	40	—	372	87	158	.551	1	6	.167	27	31	.871	8	47	55	30	45	0	20	25	2	202	1.4	0.8	5.1
81-82—Philadelphia	26	0	150	27	54	.500	1	3	.333	6	7	.857	7	15	22	10	28	0	13	13	3	61	0.8	0.4	2.3
REG. SEASON TOTALS	690	0	14554	2235	4505	.496	3	20	.150	868	1049	.827	599	1264	2280	1212	1503	12	455	355	224	5341	3.3	1.8	7.7
PLAYOFF TOTALS	16	0	209	33	77	.429	0	1	.000	12	12	1.000	13	18	31	10	21	0	10	2	6	78	1.9	0.6	4.9

JOHNSON, REGINALD (Reggie) b. June 25, 1957 Ht. 6-9 Wt. 210 College—Tennessee

SEASON—TEAM	G	GS	MIN	FGM	FGA	PCT	3FGM	3FGA	PCT	FTM	FTA	PCT	O-RB	D-RB	TOT	AST	PF	DQ	STL	TO	BLK	PTS	RPG	APG	PPG
80-81—San Antonio	79	—	1716	340	682	.499	0	1	.000	128	193	.663	132	226	358	78	283	8	45	130	48	808	4.5	1.0	10.2
81-82—S.A.-Clev.-K.C.	75	48	1904	351	662	.530	0	1	.000	118	156	.756	140	311	451	73	257	5	33	100	60	820	6.0	1.0	10.9
82-83—K.C.-Phil.	79	8	1541	247	509	.485	1	4	.250	95	130	.731	107	184	291	71	232	3	26	104	43	590	3.7	0.9	7.5
83-84—New Jersey	72	4	818	127	256	.496	0	1	.000	92	126	.730	53	85	138	40	141	1	24	59	18	346	1.9	0.6	4.8
REG. SEASON TOTALS	305	60	5979	1065	2109	.505	1	7	.143	433	605	.716	432	806	1238	262	913	17	128	393	169	2564	4.1	0.9	8.4
PLAYOFF TOTALS	19	0	273	37	81	.457	0	0	—	26	33	.788	16	23	39	19	34	2	5	17	6	100	2.1	1.0	5.3

JOHNSON, RICHARD LEWIS (Rich) b. December 18, 1946 Ht. 6-9 Wt. 210 College—Grambling State

SEASON—TEAM	G	GS	MIN	FGM	FGA	PCT	3FGM	3FGA	PCT	FTM	FTA	PCT	O-RB	D-RB	TOT	AST	PF	DQ	STL	TO	BLK	PTS	RPG	APG	PPG
68-69—Boston	31	—	163	29	76	.382	—	—	—	11	23	.478	—	—	52	7	40	0	—	—	—	69	1.7	0.2	2.2
69-70—Boston	65	—	898	167	361	.463	—	—	—	46	70	.657	—	—	208	32	155	3	—	—	—	380	3.2	0.5	5.8
70-71—Boston	1	—	13	4	5	.800	—	—	—	0	0	—	—	—	5	0	3	0	—	—	—	8	5.0	0.0	8.0
70-71—Fla.-Car.-Pitt. (A)	38	—	542	92	191	.482	0	0	—	36	54	.667	—	—	152	19	83	—	—	—	—	220	4.0	0.5	5.8
REG. NBA TOTALS	97	—	1074	200	442	.452	—	—	—	57	93	.613	—	—	265	39	198	3	—	—	—	457	2.7	0.4	4.7
REG. ABA TOTALS	38	—	542	92	191	.482	0	0	—	36	54	.667	—	—	152	19	83	—	—	—	—	220	4.0	0.5	5.8
NBA PLAYOFF TOTALS	2	—	4	1	1	1.000	—	—	—	0	0	—	—	—	2	—	0	0	—	—	—	2	1.0	0.0	1.0

JOHNSON, RONALD F. (**Ron**) b. July 20, 1938 Ht. 6-8 Wt. 215 College—Minnesota

SEASON—TEAM	G	GS	MIN	FGM	FGA	PCT	3FGM	3FGA	PCT	FTM	FTA	PCT	O-RB	D-RB	TOT	AST	PF	DQ	STL	TO	BLK	PTS	RPG	APG	PPG
60-61—Detroit-L.A.	14	—	92	13	43	.302	—	—	—	11	17	.647	—	—	29	2	10	0	—	—	—	37	2.1	0.1	2.6
REG. SEASON TOTALS	14	—	92	13	43	.302	—	—	—	11	17	.647	—	—	29	2	10	0	—	—	—	37	2.1	0.1	2.6

JOHNSON, STEFFOND O'SHEA b. November 4, 1962 Ht. 6-8 Wt. 240 College—Louisiana State/San Diego State

SEASON—TEAM	G	GS	MIN	FGM	FGA	PCT	3FGM	3FGA	PCT	FTM	FTA	PCT	O-RB	D-RB	TOT	AST	PF	DQ	STL	TO	BLK	PTS	RPG	APG	PPG
86-87—L.A. Clippers	29	0	234	27	64	.422	0	3	.000	20	38	.526	15	28	43	5	55	2	9	18	2	74	1.5	0.2	2.6
REG. SEASON TOTALS	29	0	234	27	64	.422	0	3	.000	20	38	.526	15	28	43	5	55	2	9	18	2	74	1.5	0.2	2.6

JOHNSON, STEWART (**Stew**) b. August 19, 1944 Ht. 6-9 Wt. 225 College—Murray State (Ky.)

SEASON—TEAM	G	GS	MIN	FGM	FGA	PCT	3FGM	3FGA	PCT	FTM	FTA	PCT	O-RB	D-RB	TOT	AST	PF	DQ	STL	TO	BLK	PTS	RPG	APG	PPG
67-68—Ken.-N.J. (A)	72	—	1475	255	743	.343	25	79	.316	69	113	.611	—	—	415	49	147	2	—	89	—	604	5.8	0.7	8.4
68-69—N.Y.-Houston (A)	78	—	2484	616	1444	.427	64	183	.350	199	253	.787	—	—	604	142	178	1	—	172	—	1495	7.7	1.8	19.2
69-70—Pittsburgh (A)	81	—	2347	544	1337	.407	15	55	.273	137	176	.778	—	—	547	120	210	2	—	—	—	1240	6.8	1.5	15.3
70-71—Pittsburgh (A)	84	—	2595	593	1350	.439	12	40	.300	144	171	.842	—	—	646	123	221	—	—	—	—	1342	7.7	1.5	16.0
71-72—Pitt.-Car. (A)	67	—	1534	368	874	.421	16	47	.340	73	99	.737	—	—	382	88	159	—	—	91	—	825	5.7	1.3	12.3
72-73—San Diego (A)	80	—	2952	769	1748	.440	37	133	.278	195	238	.819	178	419	597	174	258	6	—	161	—	1770	7.5	2.2	22.1
73-74—San Diego (A)	84	—	2652	716	1668	.429	59	190	.311	199	235	.847	181	350	531	127	162	—	72	136	13	1690	6.3	1.5	20.1
74-75—S.D.-Memphis (A)	81	—	2812	664	1493	.445	40	132	.303	63	86	.733	138	355	493	138	228	—	97	118	28	1431	6.1	1.7	17.7
75-76—S.D.-S.A. (A)	20	—	350	61	197	.310	1	13	.077	18	22	.818	22	26	48	23	35	—	8	13	1	141	2.4	1.2	7.1
REG. ABA TOTALS	647	—	19201	4586	10854	.423	269	872	.308	1097	1393	.788	519	1150	4263	984	1598	11	177	780	42	10538	6.6	1.5	16.3
ABA PLAYOFF TOTALS	15	—	569	103	264	.390	12	30	.400	20	25	.800	20	48	93	33	32	0	16	23	7	238	6.2	2.2	15.9
ABA ALL-STAR TOTALS	3	—	47	8	23	.348	0	3	.000	2	2	1.000	3	5	8	2	6	0	1	1	0	18	2.7	0.7	6.0

JOHNSON, VINCENT (**Vinnie, Microwave**) b. September 1, 1956 Ht. 6-2 Wt. 200 College—McLennan CC/Baylor

SEASON—TEAM	G	GS	MIN	FGM	FGA	PCT	3FGM	3FGA	PCT	FTM	FTA	PCT	O-RB	D-RB	TOT	AST	PF	DQ	STL	TO	BLK	PTS	RPG	APG	PPG
79-80—Seattle	38	—	325	45	115	.391	0	1	.000	31	39	.795	19	36	55	54	40	0	19	42	4	121	1.4	1.4	3.2
80-81—Seattle	81	—	2311	419	785	.534	1	5	.200	214	270	.793	193	173	366	341	198	0	78	216	20	1053	4.5	4.2	13.0
81-82—Seattle-Detroit	74	15	1295	217	444	.489	3	12	.250	107	142	.754	82	77	159	171	101	0	56	96	25	544	2.1	2.3	7.4
82-83—Detroit	82	51	2511	520	1013	.513	11	40	.275	245	315	.778	167	186	353	301	263	2	93	152	49	1296	4.3	3.7	15.8
83-84—Detroit	82	0	1909	426	901	.473	4	19	.211	207	275	.753	130	107	237	271	196	1	44	135	19	1063	2.9	3.3	13.0
84-85—Detroit	82	16	2093	428	942	.454	5	27	.185	190	247	.769	134	118	252	325	205	2	71	135	20	1051	3.1	4.0	12.8
85-86—Detroit	79	12	1978	465	996	.467	2	13	.154	165	214	.771	119	107	226	269	180	2	80	88	23	1097	2.9	3.4	13.9
86-87—Detroit	78	8	2166	533	1154	.462	4	14	.286	158	201	.786	123	134	257	300	159	0	92	133	16	1228	3.3	3.8	15.7
87-88—Detroit	82	1	1935	425	959	.443	5	24	.208	147	217	.677	90	141	231	267	164	0	58	152	18	1002	2.8	3.3	12.2
88-89—Detroit	82	21	2073	462	996	.464	13	44	.295	193	263	.734	109	146	255	242	155	0	74	105	17	1130	3.1	3.0	13.8
89-90—Detroit	82	12	1972	334	775	.431	5	34	.147	131	196	.668	108	148	256	255	143	0	71	123	13	804	3.1	3.1	9.8
90-91—Detroit	82	28	2390	406	936	.434	11	34	.324	135	209	.646	110	170	280	271	166	0	75	118	15	958	3.4	3.3	11.7
91-92—San Antonio	60	23	1350	202	499	.405	19	60	.317	55	85	.647	67	115	182	145	93	0	41	74	14	478	3.0	2.4	8.0
REG. SEASON TOTALS	984	187	24308	4882	10515	.464	83	327	.254	1978	2673	.740	1451	1658	3109	3212	2063	7	852	1569	253	11825	3.2	3.3	12.0
PLAYOFF TOTALS	116	3	2671	578	1275	.453	17	62	.274	214	284	.754	167	197	364	306	234	0	65	142	22	1387	3.1	2.6	12.0

JOHNSON, WALLACE EDGAR (**Mickey**) b. August 31, 1952 Ht. 6-10 Wt. 190 College—Aurora

SEASON—TEAM	G	GS	MIN	FGM	FGA	PCT	3FGM	3FGA	PCT	FTM	FTA	PCT	O-RB	D-RB	TOT	AST	PF	DQ	STL	TO	BLK	PTS	RPG	APG	PPG
74-75—Chicago	38	—	291	53	118	.449	—	—	—	37	58	.638	32	62	94	20	57	1	10	—	11	143	2.5	0.5	3.8
75-76—Chicago	81	—	2390	478	1033	.463	—	—	—	283	360	.786	279	479	758	130	292	8	93	—	66	1239	9.4	1.6	15.3
76-77—Chicago	81	—	2847	538	1205	.446	—	—	—	324	407	.796	297	531	828	195	315	10	103	—	64	1400	10.2	2.4	17.3
77-78—Chicago	81	—	2870	561	1215	.462	—	—	—	362	446	.812	218	520	738	267	317	8	92	270	68	1484	9.1	3.3	18.3
78-79—Chicago	82	—	2594	496	1105	.449	—	—	—	273	329	.830	193	434	627	380	286	9	88	312	59	1265	7.6	4.6	15.4
79-80—Indiana	82	—	2647	588	1271	.463	5	32	.156	385	482	.799	258	423	681	344	291	11	153	286	112	1566	8.3	4.2	19.1
80-81—Milwaukee	82	—	2118	379	846	.448	3	18	.167	262	332	.789	183	362	545	286	256	4	94	230	71	1023	6.6	3.5	12.5
81-82—Milwaukee	76	71	1934	372	757	.491	1	7	.143	233	291	.801	133	321	454	215	240	4	72	191	45	978	6.0	2.8	12.9
82-83—Milw.-N.J.-G.S.	78	16	2053	391	921	.425	3	36	.083	312	380	.821	163	331	494	255	288	10	82	238	46	1097	6.3	3.3	14.1
83-84—Golden State	78	25	2122	359	852	.421	5	29	.172	339	432	.785	198	320	518	219	290	3	101	216	30	1062	6.6	2.8	13.6
84-85—Golden State	66	9	1565	304	714	.426	7	30	.233	260	316	.823	149	247	396	149	221	5	70	142	35	875	6.0	2.3	13.3
85-86—New Jersey	79	4	1574	214	507	.422	5	24	.208	183	233	.785	98	234	332	217	248	1	67	165	25	616	4.2	2.7	7.8
REG. SEASON TOTALS	904	125	25005	4733	10544	.449	29	176	.165	3253	4066	.800	2201	4264	6465	2677	3101	74	1025	2050	632	12748	7.2	3.0	14.1
PLAYOFF TOTALS	22	1	559	109	234	.466	0	4	.000	84	101	.832	55	74	129	40	74	1	24	37	13	302	5.9	1.8	13.7

JOHNSTON, DONALD NEIL (Neil, Gabby) b. February 4, 1929 d. September 28, 1978 Ht. 6-8 Wt. 215 College—Ohio State

SEASON—TEAM	G	GS	MIN	FGM	FGA	PCT	3FGM	3FGA	PCT	FTM	FTA	PCT	O-RB	D-RB	TOT	AST	PF	DQ	STL	TO	BLK	PTS	RPG	APG	PPG
51-52—Philadelphia	64	—	993	141	299	.472	—	—	—	100	151	.662	—	—	342	39	154	5	—	—	—	382	5.3	0.6	6.0
52-53—Philadelphia	70	—	3166	504	1114	.452	—	—	—	556	794	.700	—	—	976	197	248	6	—	—	—	1564	13.9	2.8	22.3
53-54—Philadelphia	72	—	3296	591	1317	.449	—	—	—	577	772	.747	—	—	797	203	259	7	—	—	—	1759	11.1	2.8	24.4
54-55—Philadelphia	72	—	2917	521	1184	.440	—	—	—	589	769	.766	—	—	1085	215	255	4	—	—	—	1631	15.1	3.0	22.7
55-56—Philadelphia	70	—	2594	499	1092	.457	—	—	—	549	685	.801	—	—	872	225	251	8	—	—	—	1547	12.5	3.2	22.1
56-57—Philadelphia	69	—	2531	520	1163	.447	—	—	—	535	648	.826	—	—	855	203	231	2	—	—	—	1575	12.4	2.9	22.8
57-58—Philadelphia	71	—	2408	473	1102	.429	—	—	—	442	540	.819	—	—	790	166	233	4	—	—	—	1388	11.1	2.3	19.5
58-59—Philadelphia	28	—	393	54	164	.329	—	—	—	69	88	.784	—	—	139	21	50	0	—	—	—	177	5.0	0.8	6.3
REG. SEASON TOTALS	516	—	18298	3303	7435	.444	—	—	—	3417	4447	.768	—	—	5856	1269	1681	36	—	—	—	10023	11.3	2.5	19.4
PLAYOFF TOTALS	23	—	702	121	310	.390	—	—	—	102	139	.734	—	—	257	75	76	0	—	—	—	344	11.2	3.3	15.0
ALL-STAR TOTALS	6	—	132	27	63	.429	—	—	—	16	23	.696	—	—	52	6	13	0	—	—	—	70	8.7	1.0	11.7

JOHNSTON, NATE b. December 18, 1966 Ht. 6-8 Wt. 210 College—Tampa

SEASON—TEAM	G	GS	MIN	FGM	FGA	PCT	3FGM	3FGA	PCT	FTM	FTA	PCT	O-RB	D-RB	TOT	AST	PF	DQ	STL	TO	BLK	PTS	RPG	APG	PPG
89-90—Utah-Port.	21	0	87	18	48	.375	1	4	.250	9	13	.692	13	10	23	1	11	1	3	6	8	46	1.1	0.0	2.2
REG. SEASON TOTALS	21	0	87	18	48	.375	1	4	.250	9	13	.692	13	10	23	1	11	1	3	6	8	46	1.1	0.0	2.2
PLAYOFF TOTALS	3	0	19	6	11	.545	0	0	—	1	1	1.000	2	4	6	1	5	0	1	0	1	13	2.0	0.3	4.3

JOHNSTONE, JAMES ROBERT (Jim) b. September 20, 1960 Ht. 6-11 Wt. 245 College—Wake Forest

SEASON—TEAM	G	GS	MIN	FGM	FGA	PCT	3FGM	3FGA	PCT	FTM	FTA	PCT	O-RB	D-RB	TOT	AST	PF	DQ	STL	TO	BLK	PTS	RPG	APG	PPG
82-83—S.A.-Detroit	23	0	191	11	30	.367	0	0	—	9	20	.450	15	31	46	11	33	0	3	15	7	31	2.0	0.5	1.3
REG. SEASON TOTALS	23	0	191	11	30	.367	0	0	—	9	20	.450	15	31	46	11	33	0	3	15	7	31	2.0	0.5	1.3

JOLLIFF, HOWARD (Howie) b. July 20, 1938 Ht. 6-7 Wt. 220 College—Ohio

SEASON—TEAM	G	GS	MIN	FGM	FGA	PCT	3FGM	3FGA	PCT	FTM	FTA	PCT	O-RB	D-RB	TOT	AST	PF	DQ	STL	TO	BLK	PTS	RPG	APG	PPG
60-61—Los Angeles	46	—	352	46	141	.326	—	—	—	11	23	.478	—	—	141	16	53	0	—	—	—	103	3.1	0.3	2.2
61-62—Los Angeles	64	—	1094	104	253	.411	—	—	—	41	78	.526	—	—	383	76	175	4	—	—	—	249	6.0	1.2	3.9
62-63—Los Angeles	28	—	293	15	55	.273	—	—	—	6	9	.667	—	—	62	20	49	1	—	—	—	36	2.2	0.7	1.3
REG. SEASON TOTALS	138	—	1739	165	449	.367	—	—	—	58	110	.527	—	—	586	112	277	5	—	—	—	388	4.2	0.8	2.8
PLAYOFF TOTALS	13	—	112	8	22	.364	—	—	—	8	8	1.000	—	—	53	15	21	1	—	—	—	24	4.1	1.2	1.8

JONES, ANTHONY HAMILTON b. September 13, 1962 Ht. 6-6 Wt. 195 College—Georgetown/Nevada-Las Vegas

SEASON—TEAM	G	GS	MIN	FGM	FGA	PCT	3FGM	3FGA	PCT	FTM	FTA	PCT	O-RB	D-RB	TOT	AST	PF	DQ	STL	TO	BLK	PTS	RPG	APG	PPG
86-87—Wash.-S.A.	65	4	858	133	322	.413	7	20	.350	50	65	.769	40	64	104	73	79	0	42	49	19	323	1.6	1.1	5.0
88-89—Chicago-Dallas	33	0	196	29	79	.367	4	16	.250	14	16	.875	14	14	28	17	20	0	11	5	3	76	0.8	0.5	2.3
89-90—Dallas	66	0	650	72	194	.371	4	13	.308	47	69	.681	33	49	82	29	77	0	32	42	16	195	1.2	0.4	3.0
REG. SEASON TOTALS	164	4	1704	234	595	.393	15	49	.306	111	150	.740	87	127	214	119	176	0	85	96	38	594	1.3	0.7	3.6
PLAYOFF TOTALS	1	0	3	0	0	—	0	0	—	0	0	—	0	0	0	0	0	—	0	0	0	0	0.0	0.0	0.0

JONES, CALDWELL b. August 4, 1950 Ht. 6-11 Wt. 230 College—Albany State

SEASON—TEAM	G	GS	MIN	FGM	FGA	PCT	3FGM	3FGA	PCT	FTM	FTA	PCT	O-RB	D-RB	TOT	AST	PF	DQ	STL	TO	BLK	PTS	RPG	APG	PPG
73-74—San Diego (A)	79	—	2929	507	1091	.465	2	8	.250	171	230	.743	322	773	1095	144	319	—	64	155	316	1187	13.9	1.8	15.0
74-75—San Diego (A)	76	—	3004	606	1240	.489	3	11	.273	264	335	.788	311	763	1074	162	269	—	60	192	246	1479	14.1	2.1	19.5
75-76—S.D.-Ken.-St. L. (A)	76	—	2674	423	900	.470	0	7	.000	140	186	.753	246	607	853	147	321	—	81	166	218	986	11.2	1.9	13.0
76-77—Philadelphia	82	—	2023	215	424	.507	—	—	—	64	116	.552	190	476	666	92	301	3	43	—	200	494	8.1	1.1	6.0
77-78—Philadelphia	80	—	1636	169	359	.471	—	—	—	96	153	.627	165	405	570	92	281	4	26	128	127	434	7.1	1.2	5.4
78-79—Philadelphia	78	—	2171	302	637	.474	—	—	—	121	162	.747	177	570	747	151	303	10	39	156	157	725	9.6	1.9	9.3
79-80—Philadelphia	80	—	2771	232	532	.436	0	2	.000	124	178	.697	219	731	950	164	298	5	43	218	162	588	11.9	2.1	7.4
80-81—Philadelphia	81	—	2639	218	485	.449	0	0	—	148	193	.767	200	613	813	122	271	2	53	168	134	584	10.0	1.5	7.2
81-82—Philadelphia	81	47	2446	231	465	.497	0	3	.000	179	219	.817	164	544	708	100	301	3	38	155	146	641	8.7	1.2	7.9
82-83—Houston	82	82	2440	307	677	.453	0	2	.000	162	206	.786	222	446	668	138	278	2	46	171	131	776	8.1	1.7	9.5
83-84—Houston	81	73	2506	318	633	.502	1	3	.333	164	196	.837	168	414	582	156	335	7	46	158	80	801	7.2	1.9	9.9
84-85—Chicago	42	32	885	53	115	.461	0	2	.000	36	47	.766	49	162	211	34	125	3	12	40	31	142	5.0	0.8	3.4
85-86—Portland	80	19	1437	126	254	.496	0	7	.000	124	150	.827	105	250	355	74	244	2	38	102	61	376	4.4	0.9	4.7
86-87—Portland	78	37	1578	111	224	.496	0	2	.000	97	124	.782	114	341	455	64	227	5	23	87	77	319	5.8	0.8	4.1
87-88—Portland	79	77	1778	128	263	.487	0	4	.000	78	106	.736	105	303	408	81	251	0	29	82	99	334	5.2	1.0	4.2
88-89—Portland	72	40	1279	77	183	.421	0	1	.000	48	61	.787	88	212	300	59	166	2	24	83	85	202	4.2	0.8	2.8
89-90—San Antonio	72	2	885	67	144	.465	1	5	.200	38	54	.704	76	154	230	20	146	2	20	48	27	173	3.2	0.3	2.4
REG. NBA TOTALS	1068	409	26474	2554	5395	.473	2	31	.065	1479	1965	.753	2042	5621	7663	1347	3527	48	480	1596	1517	6589	7.2	1.3	6.2
REG. ABA TOTALS	231	—	8607	1536	3231	.475	5	26	.192	575	751	.766	879	2143	3022	453	909	0	205	513	780	3652	13.1	2.0	15.8
NBA PLAYOFF TOTALS	119	30	3466	322	665	.484	0	4	.000	170	224	.759	267	732	999	147	426	9	51	157	223	814	8.4	1.2	6.8
ABA PLAYOFF TOTALS	6	—	277	36	88	.409	0	0	—	11	16	.688	21	73	94	15	19	0	6	9	14	83	15.7	2.5	13.8
ABA ALL-STAR TOTALS	1	0	15	2	4	.500	0	0	—	1	1	1.000	2	2	4	0	4	—	0	3	1	5	4.0	0.0	5.0

JONES, CHARLES (C.J., Gadget) b. April 3, 1957 Ht. 6-9 Wt. 220 College—Albany State

SEASON—TEAM	G	GS	MIN	FGM	FGA	PCT	3FGM	3FGA	PCT	FTM	FTA	PCT	O-RB	D-RB	TOT	AST	PF	DQ	STL	TO	BLK	PTS	RPG	APG	PPG
83-84—Philadelphia	1	0	3	0	1	.000	0	0	—	1	4	.250	0	0	0	0	1	0	0	0	0	1	0.0	0.0	1.0
84-85—Chicago-Wash.	31	4	667	67	127	.528	0	0	—	40	58	.690	71	113	184	26	107	3	22	25	79	174	5.9	0.8	5.6
85-86—Washington	81	58	1609	129	254	.508	0	2	.000	54	86	.628	122	199	321	76	235	2	57	71	133	312	4.0	0.9	3.9
86-87—Washington	79	64	1609	118	249	.474	0	1	.000	48	76	.632	144	212	356	80	252	2	67	77	165	284	4.5	1.0	3.6
87-88—Washington	69	49	1313	72	177	.407	0	1	.000	53	75	.707	106	219	325	59	226	5	53	57	113	197	4.7	0.9	2.9
88-89—Washington	53	45	1154	60	125	.480	0	1	.000	16	25	.640	77	180	257	42	187	4	39	39	76	136	4.8	0.8	2.6
89-90—Washington	81	81	2240	94	185	.508	0	0	—	68	105	.648	145	359	504	139	296	10	50	76	197	256	6.2	1.7	3.2
90-91—Washington	62	54	1499	67	124	.540	0	0	—	29	50	.580	119	240	359	48	199	2	51	46	124	163	5.8	0.8	2.6
91-92—Washington	75	32	1365	33	90	.367	0	0	—	20	40	.500	105	212	317	62	214	0	43	39	92	86	4.2	0.8	1.1
92-93—Washington	67	21	1206	33	63	.524	0	1	.000	22	38	.579	87	190	277	42	144	1	38	38	77	88	4.1	0.6	1.3
93-94—Detroit	42	0	877	36	78	.462	0	1	.000	19	34	.559	89	146	235	29	136	3	14	12	43	91	5.6	0.7	2.2
REG. SEASON TOTALS	641	408	13542	709	1473	.481	0	7	.000	370	591	.626	1065	2070	3135	603	1997	32	434	480	1099	1788	4.9	0.9	2.8
PLAYOFF TOTALS	17	9	333	18	40	.450	0	0	—	14	22	.636	23	37	60	11	56	0	9	12	21	50	3.5	0.6	2.9

JONES, CHARLES ALEXANDER b. January 12, 1962 Ht. 6-8 Wt. 215 College—Louisville

SEASON—TEAM	G	GS	MIN	FGM	FGA	PCT	3FGM	3FGA	PCT	FTM	FTA	PCT	O-RB	D-RB	TOT	AST	PF	DQ	STL	TO	BLK	PTS	RPG	APG	PPG
84-85—Phoenix	78	14	1565	236	454	.520	0	4	.000	182	281	.648	139	255	394	128	149	0	45	143	61	654	5.1	1.6	8.4
85-86—Phoenix	43	18	742	75	164	.457	0	1	.000	50	98	.510	65	128	193	52	87	0	32	57	25	200	4.5	1.2	4.7
87-88—Portland	37	0	186	16	40	.400	0	1	.000	19	33	.576	11	20	31	8	28	0	3	12	6	51	0.8	0.2	1.4
88-89—Washington	43	0	516	38	82	.463	1	3	.333	33	53	.623	54	86	140	18	49	0	18	22	16	110	3.3	0.4	2.6
REG. SEASON TOTALS	201	32	3009	365	740	.493	1	9	.111	284	465	.611	269	489	758	206	313	0	98	234	108	1015	3.8	1.0	5.0
PLAYOFF TOTALS	4	0	36	3	6	.500	0	0	—	6	6	1.000	1	3	4	3	4	0	0	3	3	12	1.0	0.8	3.0

JONES, CLARENCE WILLIAM (Bill) b. March 18, 1966 Ht. 6-7 Wt. 185 College—Iowa

SEASON—TEAM	G	GS	MIN	FGM	FGA	PCT	3FGM	3FGA	PCT	FTM	FTA	PCT	O-RB	D-RB	TOT	AST	PF	DQ	STL	TO	BLK	PTS	RPG	APG	PPG
88-89—New Jersey	37	0	307	50	102	.490	0	1	.000	29	43	.674	20	27	47	20	38	0	17	18	6	129	1.3	0.5	3.5
REG. SEASON TOTALS	37	0	307	50	102	.490	0	1	.000	29	43	.674	20	27	47	20	38	0	17	18	6	129	1.3	0.5	3.5

JONES, DWIGHT E. b. February 27, 1952 Ht. 6-10 Wt. 210 College—Houston

SEASON—TEAM	G	GS	MIN	FGM	FGA	PCT	3FGM	3FGA	PCT	FTM	FTA	PCT	O-RB	D-RB	TOT	AST	PF	DQ	STL	TO	BLK	PTS	RPG	APG	PPG
73-74—Atlanta	74	—	1448	238	502	.474	—	—	—	116	156	.744	145	309	454	86	197	3	29	—	64	592	6.1	1.2	8.0
74-75—Atlanta	75	—	2086	323	752	.430	—	—	—	132	183	.721	236	461	697	152	226	1	51	—	51	778	9.3	2.0	10.4
75-76—Atlanta	66	—	1762	251	542	.463	—	—	—	163	219	.744	171	353	524	83	214	8	52	—	61	665	7.9	1.3	10.1
76-77—Houston	74	—	1239	167	338	.494	—	—	—	101	126	.802	98	186	284	48	175	1	38	—	19	435	3.8	0.6	5.9
77-78—Houston	82	—	2476	346	777	.445	—	—	—	181	233	.777	215	426	641	109	265	2	77	165	39	873	7.8	1.3	10.6
78-79—Houston	81	—	1215	181	395	.458	—	—	—	96	132	.727	110	218	328	57	204	1	34	102	26	458	4.0	0.7	5.7
79-80—Houston-Chicago	74	—	1448	257	506	.508	0	0	—	146	201	.726	114	254	368	101	207	0	28	122	42	660	5.0	1.4	8.9
80-81—Chicago	81	—	1574	245	507	.483	0	0	—	125	161	.776	127	274	401	99	200	1	40	126	36	615	5.0	1.2	7.6
81-82—Chicago	78	18	2040	303	572	.530	1	1	1.000	172	238	.723	156	351	507	114	217	0	49	155	36	779	6.5	1.5	10.0
82-83—Chicago-L.A.	81	2	1164	148	325	.455	0	1	.000	79	123	.642	84	225	309	62	172	0	31	101	23	375	3.8	0.8	4.6
REG. SEASON TOTALS	766	20	16452	2459	5216	.471	1	2	.500	1311	1772	.740	1456	3057	4513	911	2077	17	429	771	397	6230	5.9	1.2	8.1
PLAYOFF TOTALS	27	0	555	69	153	.451	0	0	—	43	51	.843	39	95	134	29	67	2	15	27	10	181	5.0	1.1	6.7

JONES, EARL b. January 13, 1961 Ht. 7-0 Wt. 230 College—District of Columbia

SEASON—TEAM	G	GS	MIN	FGM	FGA	PCT	3FGM	3FGA	PCT	FTM	FTA	PCT	O-RB	D-RB	TOT	AST	PF	DQ	STL	TO	BLK	PTS	RPG	APG	PPG
84-85—L.A. Lakers	2	0	7	0	1	.000	0	0	—	0	0	—	0	0	0	0	0	0	0	1	0	0	0.0	0.0	0.0
85-86—Milwaukee	12	0	43	5	12	.417	0	0	—	3	4	.750	4	6	10	4	13	0	0	7	1	13	0.8	0.3	1.1
REG. SEASON TOTALS	14	0	50	5	13	.385	0	0	—	3	4	.750	4	6	10	4	13	0	0	8	1	13	0.7	0.3	0.9

JONES, EDGAR JR. (E.J.) b. June 17, 1956 Ht. 6-10 Wt. 225 College—Nevada-Reno

SEASON—TEAM	G	GS	MIN	FGM	FGA	PCT	3FGM	3FGA	PCT	FTM	FTA	PCT	O-RB	D-RB	TOT	AST	PF	DQ	STL	TO	BLK	PTS	RPG	APG	PPG
80-81—New Jersey	60	—	950	189	357	.529	0	4	.000	146	218	.670	92	171	263	43	185	4	36	101	81	524	4.4	0.7	8.7
81-82—Detroit	48	19	802	142	259	.548	1	2	.500	90	129	.698	70	137	207	40	149	3	28	66	92	375	4.3	0.8	7.8
82-83—Detroit-S.A.	77	28	1658	237	479	.495	2	9	.222	201	286	.703	136	312	448	89	267	10	42	146	108	677	5.8	1.2	8.8
83-84—San Antonio	81	33	1770	322	644	.500	6	19	.316	176	242	.727	143	306	449	85	298	7	64	125	107	826	5.5	1.0	10.2
84-85—S.A.-Clev.	44	5	769	130	275	.473	0	4	.000	82	111	.739	50	121	171	29	123	2	20	61	29	342	3.9	0.7	7.8
85-86—Cleveland	53	6	1011	187	370	.505	7	23	.304	132	178	.742	71	136	207	45	142	0	30	64	38	513	3.9	0.8	9.7
REG. SEASON TOTALS	363	91	6960	1207	2384	.506	16	61	.262	827	1164	.710	562	1183	1745	331	1164	26	220	563	455	3257	4.8	0.9	9.0
PLAYOFF TOTALS	15	0	238	37	80	.463	0	3	.000	26	41	.634	25	36	61	20	50	1	8	20	14	100	4.1	1.3	6.7

JONES, J. COLLIS (Collis) b. July 3, 1949 Ht. 6-7 Wt. 205 College—Notre Dame

SEASON—TEAM	G	GS	MIN	FGM	FGA	PCT	3FGM	3FGA	PCT	FTM	FTA	PCT	O-RB	D-RB	TOT	AST	PF	DQ	STL	TO	BLK	PTS	RPG	APG	PPG
71-72—Dallas (A)	78	—	1428	163	372	.438	1	4	.250	98	154	.636	—	—	334	78	200	—	—	83	—	425	4.3	1.0	5.4
72-73—Dallas (A)	81	—	2204	357	768	.465	0	6	.000	227	318	.714	262	260	522	143	230	3	—	145	—	941	6.4	1.8	11.6
73-74—Kentucky (A)	58	—	719	102	263	.388	0	3	.000	51	78	.654	94	90	184	36	91	—	21	38	13	255	3.2	0.6	4.4
74-75—Memphis (A)	81	—	1880	333	702	.474	5	15	.333	134	177	.757	150	219	369	81	186	—	105	69	33	805	4.6	1.0	9.9
REG. ABA TOTALS	298	—	6231	955	2105	.454	6	28	.214	510	727	.702	506	569	1409	338	707	3	126	335	46	2426	4.7	1.1	8.1
ABA PLAYOFF TOTALS	12	—	256	28	73	.384	0	1	.000	15	26	.577	15	20	49	4	28	0	9	11	1	71	4.1	0.3	5.9

JONES, JACOB (Jake) b. May 9, 1949 Ht. 6-3 Wt. 180 College—Assumption

SEASON—TEAM	G	GS	MIN	FGM	FGA	PCT	3FGM	3FGA	PCT	FTM	FTA	PCT	O-RB	D-RB	TOT	AST	PF	DQ	STL	TO	BLK	PTS	RPG	APG	PPG
71-72—Phil.-Cin.	17	—	202	28	72	.389	—	—	—	20	31	.645	—	—	26	12	22	0	—	—	—	76	1.5	0.7	4.5
REG. SEASON TOTALS	17	—	202	28	72	.389	—	—	—	20	31	.645	—	—	26	12	22	0	—	—	—	76	1.5	0.7	4.5

JONES, JAMES (Jimmy) b. January 1, 1945 Ht. 6-4 Wt. 190 College—Grambling State

SEASON—TEAM	G	GS	MIN	FGM	FGA	PCT	3FGM	3FGA	PCT	FTM	FTA	PCT	O-RB	D-RB	TOT	AST	PF	DQ	STL	TO	BLK	PTS	RPG	APG	PPG
67-68—New Orleans (A)	78	—	3255	551	1181	.467	2	9	.222	360	508	.709	—	—	443	179	243	6	—	241	—	1464	5.7	2.3	18.8
68-69—New Orleans (A)	77	—	3188	764	1429	.535	1	7	.143	521	647	.805	—	—	441	437	225	4	—	198	—	2050	5.7	5.7	26.6
69-70—New Orleans (A)	70	—	2513	533	1072	.497	2	9	.222	380	469	.810	—	—	315	340	238	5	—	—	—	1448	4.5	4.9	20.7
70-71—Memphis (A)	80	—	3004	593	1220	.486	4	7	.571	374	481	.778	—	—	386	468	240	—	—	—	—	1564	4.8	5.9	19.6
71-72—Utah (A)	78	—	2903	462	903	.512	1	6	.167	282	362	.779	—	—	377	485	252	—	—	270	—	1207	4.8	6.2	15.5
72-73—Utah (A)	80	—	2848	496	948	.523	0	1	.000	345	432	.799	72	263	335	448	271	5	—	267	—	1337	4.2	5.6	16.7
73-74—Utah (A)	83	—	3162	583	1060	.550	0	1	.000	229	259	.884	103	258	361	429	205	—	154	238	32	1395	4.3	5.2	16.8
74-75—Washington	73	—	1424	207	400	.518	—	—	—	103	142	.725	36	101	137	162	190	0	76	—	10	517	1.9	2.2	7.1
75-76—Washington	64	—	1133	153	308	.497	—	—	—	72	94	.766	32	99	131	120	127	1	33	—	5	378	2.0	1.9	5.9
76-77—Washington	3	—	33	2	9	.222	—	—	—	2	4	.500	1	3	4	1	4	0	2	—	0	6	1.3	0.3	2.0
REG. NBA TOTALS	140	—	2590	362	717	.505	—	—	—	177	240	.738	69	203	272	283	321	1	111	—	15	901	1.9	2.0	6.4
REG. ABA TOTALS	546	—	20873	3982	7813	.510	10	40	.250	2491	3158	.789	175	521	2658	2786	1674	20	154	1214	32	10465	4.9	5.1	19.2
NBA PLAYOFF TOTALS	18	—	371	51	109	.468	—	—	—	28	32	.875	7	32	39	31	36	0	26	—	1	130	2.2	1.7	7.2
ABA PLAYOFF TOTALS	71	—	2853	602	1155	.521	0	7	.000	336	448	.750	30	57	371	340	244	2	27	188	5	1540	5.2	4.8	21.7
ABA ALL-STAR TOTALS	6	—	139	21	44	.477	0	—	—	20	26	.769	4	7	14	15	11	0	1	7	0	62	2.3	2.5	10.3

JONES, JOHN (Johnny) b. March 12, 1943 Ht. 6-7½ Wt. 205 College—Cal State-Los Angeles

SEASON—TEAM	G	GS	MIN	FGM	FGA	PCT	3FGM	3FGA	PCT	FTM	FTA	PCT	O-RB	D-RB	TOT	AST	PF	DQ	STL	TO	BLK	PTS	RPG	APG	PPG
67-68—Boston	51	—	475	86	253	.340	—	—	—	42	68	.618	—	—	114	26	60	0	—	—	—	214	2.2	0.5	4.2
68-69—Kentucky (A)	29	—	449	81	213	.380	0	3	.000	41	71	.577	—	—	117	34	53	0	—	39	—	203	4.0	1.2	7.0
REG. NBA TOTALS	51	—	475	86	253	.340	—	—	—	42	68	.618	—	—	114	26	60	0	—	—	—	214	2.2	0.5	4.2
REG. ABA TOTALS	29	—	449	81	213	.380	0	3	.000	41	71	.577	—	—	117	34	53	0	—	39	—	203	4.0	1.2	7.0
NBA PLAYOFF TOTALS	5	—	10	3	6	.500	—	—	—	0	0	—	—	—	4	—	2	0	—	—	—	6	0.8	0.0	1.2

JONES, K.C. b. May 25, 1932 Ht. 6-1 Wt. 200 College—San Francisco

SEASON—TEAM	G	GS	MIN	FGM	FGA	PCT	3FGM	3FGA	PCT	FTM	FTA	PCT	O-RB	D-RB	TOT	AST	PF	DQ	STL	TO	BLK	PTS	RPG	APG	PPG
58-59—Boston	49	—	609	65	192	.339	—	—	—	41	68	.603	—	—	127	70	58	0	—	—	—	171	2.6	1.4	3.5
59-60—Boston	74	—	1274	169	414	.408	—	—	—	128	170	.753	—	—	199	189	109	1	—	—	—	466	2.7	2.6	6.3
60-61—Boston	78	—	1605	203	601	.338	—	—	—	186	280	.664	—	—	279	253	190	3	—	—	—	592	3.6	3.2	7.6
61-62—Boston	80	—	2054	294	724	.406	—	—	—	147	232	.634	—	—	298	343	206	1	—	—	—	735	3.7	4.3	9.2
62-63—Boston	79	—	1945	230	591	.389	—	—	—	112	177	.633	—	—	263	317	221	3	—	—	—	572	3.3	4.0	7.2
63-64—Boston	80	—	2424	283	722	.392	—	—	—	88	168	.524	—	—	372	407	253	0	—	—	—	654	4.7	5.1	8.2
64-65—Boston	78	—	2434	253	639	.396	—	—	—	143	227	.630	—	—	318	437	263	5	—	—	—	649	4.1	5.6	8.3
65-66—Boston	80	—	2710	240	619	.388	—	—	—	209	303	.690	—	—	304	503	243	4	—	—	—	689	3.8	6.3	8.6
66-67—Boston	78	—	2446	182	459	.397	—	—	—	119	189	.630	—	—	239	389	273	7	—	—	—	483	3.1	5.0	6.2
REG. SEASON TOTALS	676	—	17501	1919	4961	.387	—	—	—	1173	1814	.647	—	—	2399	2908	1816	24	—	—	—	5011	3.5	4.3	7.4
PLAYOFF TOTALS	105	—	2499	241	656	.367	—	—	—	186	269	.691	—	—	320	396	335	4	—	—	—	668	3.0	3.8	6.4

JONES, MAJOR JAMES BROOKS b. July 9, 1953 Ht. 6-9 Wt. 225 College—Albany State

SEASON—TEAM	G	GS	MIN	FGM	FGA	PCT	3FGM	3FGA	PCT	FTM	FTA	PCT	O-RB	D-RB	TOT	AST	PF	DQ	STL	TO	BLK	PTS	RPG	APG	PPG
79-80—Houston	82	—	1545	188	392	.480	1	3	.333	61	108	.565	147	234	381	67	186	0	50	112	67	438	4.6	0.8	5.3
80-81—Houston	68	—	1003	117	252	.464	0	1	.000	64	101	.634	96	138	234	41	112	0	18	57	23	298	3.4	0.6	4.4
81-82—Houston	60	6	746	113	213	.531	0	3	.000	42	77	.545	80	122	202	25	100	0	20	50	29	268	3.4	0.4	4.5
82-83—Houston	60	4	878	142	311	.457	0	2	.000	56	102	.549	114	149	263	39	104	0	22	83	22	340	4.4	0.7	5.7
83-84—Houston	57	5	473	70	130	.538	0	0	—	30	49	.612	33	82	115	28	63	0	14	30	14	170	2.0	0.5	3.0
84-85—Detroit	47	0	418	48	87	.552	0	0	—	33	51	.647	48	80	128	15	58	0	9	35	14	129	2.7	0.3	2.7
REG. SEASON TOTALS	374	15	5063	678	1385	.490	1	9	.111	286	488	.586	518	805	1323	215	623	0	133	367	169	1643	3.5	0.6	4.4
PLAYOFF TOTALS	19	0	162	22	40	.550	0	0	—	8	14	.571	15	25	40	9	23	0	3	6	4	52	2.1	0.5	2.7

JONES, MARK ANTHONY b. April 10, 1961 Ht. 6-1 Wt. 175 College—St. Bonaventure

SEASON—TEAM	G	GS	MIN	FGM	FGA	PCT	3FGM	3FGA	PCT	FTM	FTA	PCT	O-RB	D-RB	TOT	AST	PF	DQ	STL	TO	BLK	PTS	RPG	APG	PPG
83-84—New Jersey	6	0	16	3	6	.500	0	1	.000	1	2	.500	0	2	2	5	2	0	0	2	0	7	0.3	0.8	1.2
REG. SEASON TOTALS	6	0	16	3	6	.500	0	1	.000	1	2	.500	2	0	2	5	2	0	0	2	0	7	0.3	0.8	1.2

JONES, OZELL b. November 20, 1960 Ht. 6-11 Wt. 235 College—Wichita State/Fullerton State

SEASON—TEAM	G	GS	MIN	FGM	FGA	PCT	3FGM	3FGA	PCT	FTM	FTA	PCT	O-RB	D-RB	TOT	AST	PF	DQ	STL	TO	BLK	PTS	RPG	APG	PPG
84-85—San Antonio	67	6	888	106	180	.589	0	1	.000	33	83	.398	65	173	238	56	139	1	30	61	57	245	3.6	0.8	3.7
85-86—L.A. Clippers	3	0	18	0	2	.000	0	0	—	0	0	—	0	2	2	0	5	0	2	3	1	0	0.7	0.0	0.0
REG. SEASON TOTALS	70	6	906	106	182	.582	0	1	.000	33	83	.398	65	175	240	56	144	1	32	64	58	245	3.4	0.8	3.5
PLAYOFF TOTALS	5	0	73	8	11	.727	0	0	—	1	6	.167	5	12	17	4	18	1	1	7	4	17	3.4	0.8	3.4

JONES, RICHARD WESLEY (**Rich, House**) b. December 27, 1946 Ht. 6-8 Wt. 230 College—Illinois/Memphis State

SEASON—TEAM	G	GS	MIN	FGM	FGA	PCT	3FGM	3FGA	PCT	FTM	FTA	PCT	O-RB	D-RB	TOT	AST	PF	DQ	STL	TO	BLK	PTS	RPG	APG	PPG
69-70—Dallas (A)	2	—	50	9	20	.450	0	0	—	10	11	.909	—	—	23	1	11	1	—	—	—	28	11.5	0.5	14.0
70-71—Texas (A)	79	—	2074	371	910	.408	33	95	.347	175	230	.761	—	—	525	182	246	—	—	—	—	950	6.6	2.3	12.0
71-72—Dallas (A)	82	—	2932	475	1053	.451	14	47	.298	212	279	.760	—	—	696	222	298	—	152	—	—	1176	8.5	2.7	14.3
72-73—Dallas (A)	67	—	2691	564	1364	.413	43	127	.339	324	414	.783	174	493	667	274	240	5	—	225	—	1495	10.0	4.1	22.3
73-74—San Antonio (A)	78	—	2843	510	1175	.434	13	46	.283	186	241	.772	170	411	581	268	273	—	70	145	13	1219	7.4	3.4	15.6
74-75—San Antonio (A)	83	—	3097	649	1480	.439	13	50	.260	287	374	.767	247	398	645	270	297	—	88	210	32	1598	7.8	3.3	19.3
75-76—New York (A)	83	—	2427	441	1153	.382	15	67	.224	199	261	.762	103	325	428	131	294	—	81	159	21	1096	5.2	1.6	13.2
76-77—New York Nets	34	—	877	134	348	.385	—	—	—	92	121	.760	48	146	194	46	109	2	38	—	11	360	5.7	1.4	10.6
REG. NBA TOTALS	34	—	877	134	348	.385	—	—	—	92	121	.760	48	146	194	46	109	2	38	—	11	360	5.7	1.4	10.6
REG. ABA TOTALS	474	—	16114	3019	7155	.422	131	432	.303	1393	1810	.770	694	1627	3565	1348	1659	6	239	891	66	7562	7.5	2.8	16.0
ABA PLAYOFF TOTALS	39	—	1177	195	502	.388	7	38	.184	62	92	.674	48	130	255	90	145	0	33	62	14	459	6.5	2.3	11.8
ABA ALL-STAR TOTALS	2	—	33	2	19	.105	0	3	.000	0	0	—	4	8	12	3	5	0	0	4	1	4	6.0	1.5	2.0

JONES, ROBERT CLYDE (**Bobby**) b. December 18, 1951 Ht. 6-9 Wt. 210 College—North Carolina

SEASON—TEAM	G	GS	MIN	FGM	FGA	PCT	3FGM	3FGA	PCT	FTM	FTA	PCT	O-RB	D-RB	TOT	AST	PF	DQ	STL	TO	BLK	PTS	RPG	APG	PPG
74-75—Denver (A)	84	—	2706	529	876	.604	0	1	.000	187	269	.695	230	462	692	303	263	—	167	234	153	1245	8.2	3.6	14.8
75-76—Denver (A)	83	—	2845	510	878	.581	0	0	—	215	308	.698	241	550	791	331	253	—	170	232	184	1235	9.5	4.0	14.9
76-77—Denver	82	—	2419	501	879	.570	—	—	—	236	329	.717	174	504	678	264	238	3	186	—	162	1238	8.3	3.2	15.1
77-78—Denver	75	—	2440	440	761	.578	—	—	—	208	277	.751	164	472	636	252	221	2	137	194	126	1088	8.5	3.4	14.5
78-79—Philadelphia	80	—	2304	378	704	.537	—	—	—	209	277	.755	199	332	531	201	245	2	107	165	96	965	6.6	2.5	12.1
79-80—Philadelphia	81	—	2125	398	748	.532	0	3	.000	257	329	.781	152	298	450	146	223	3	102	146	118	1053	5.6	1.8	13.0
80-81—Philadelphia	81	—	2046	407	755	.539	0	3	.000	282	347	.813	142	293	435	226	226	2	95	149	74	1096	5.4	2.8	13.5
81-82—Philadelphia	76	73	2181	416	737	.564	0	3	.000	263	333	.790	109	284	393	189	211	3	99	145	112	1095	5.2	2.5	14.4
82-83—Philadelphia	74	0	1749	250	460	.543	0	1	.000	165	208	.793	102	242	344	142	199	4	85	109	91	665	4.6	1.9	9.0
83-84—Philadelphia	75	0	1761	226	432	.523	0	1	.000	167	213	.784	92	231	323	187	199	1	107	101	103	619	4.3	2.5	8.3
84-85—Philadelphia	80	8	1633	207	385	.538	0	4	.000	186	216	.861	105	192	297	155	183	2	84	118	50	600	3.7	1.9	7.5
85-86—Philadelphia	70	42	1519	189	338	.559	0	1	.000	114	145	.786	49	120	169	126	159	0	48	90	50	492	2.4	1.8	7.0
REG. NBA TOTALS	774	123	20177	3412	6199	.550	0	16	.000	2087	2674	.780	1288	2968	4256	1888	2104	22	1050	1217	982	8911	5.5	2.4	11.5
REG. ABA TOTALS	167	—	5551	1039	1754	.592	0	1	.000	402	577	.697	471	1012	1483	634	516	—	337	466	337	2480	8.9	3.8	14.9
NBA PLAYOFF TOTALS	125	31	3431	553	1034	.535	0	3	.000	347	429	.809	219	395	614	284	400	4	132	187	156	1453	4.9	2.3	11.6
ABA PLAYOFF TOTALS	26	—	859	143	256	.559	0	1	.000	61	81	.753	76	147	223	97	102	—	28	65	32	347	8.6	3.7	13.3
NBA ALL-STAR TOTALS	4	1	62	9	23	.391	0	0	—	2	3	.667	3	11	14	6	8	0	2	1	3	20	3.5	1.5	5.0
ABA ALL-STAR TOTALS	1	1	29	8	12	.667	0	0	—	8	11	.727	0	0	10	3	2	—	0	0	0	24	10.0	3.0	24.0

JONES, ROBIN DALE b. February 2, 1954 Ht. 6-9 Wt. 225 College—St. Louis

SEASON—TEAM	G	GS	MIN	FGM	FGA	PCT	3FGM	3FGA	PCT	FTM	FTA	PCT	O-RB	D-RB	TOT	AST	PF	DQ	STL	TO	BLK	PTS	RPG	APG	PPG
76-77—Portland	63	—	1065	139	299	.465	—	—	—	66	109	.606	103	193	296	80	124	3	37	—	38	344	4.7	1.3	5.5
77-78—Houston	12	—	66	11	20	.550	—	—	—	4	10	.400	5	9	14	2	16	0	1	7	1	26	1.2	0.2	2.2
REG. SEASON TOTALS	75	—	1131	150	319	.470	—	—	—	70	119	.588	108	202	310	82	140	3	38	7	39	370	4.1	1.1	4.9
PLAYOFF TOTALS	19	—	105	15	32	.469	—	—	—	6	9	.667	8	15	23	9	24	0	4	—	4	36	1.2	0.5	1.9

JONES, RONALD JEROME (**Popeye**) b. June 17, 1970 Ht. 6-8 Wt. 250 College—Murray State (Ky.)

SEASON—TEAM	G	GS	MIN	FGM	FGA	PCT	3FGM	3FGA	PCT	FTM	FTA	PCT	O-RB	D-RB	TOT	AST	PF	DQ	STL	TO	BLK	PTS	RPG	APG	PPG
93-94—Dallas	81	47	1773	195	407	.479	0	1	.000	78	107	.729	299	306	605	99	246	2	61	94	31	468	7.5	1.2	5.8
REG. SEASON TOTALS	81	47	1773	195	407	.479	0	1	.000	78	107	.729	299	306	605	99	246	2	61	94	31	468	7.5	1.2	5.8

JONES, RYAN NICHOLAS (**Nick**) b. March 28, 1945 Ht. 6-2 Wt. 190 College—Oregon

SEASON—TEAM	G	GS	MIN	FGM	FGA	PCT	3FGM	3FGA	PCT	FTM	FTA	PCT	O-RB	D-RB	TOT	AST	PF	DQ	STL	TO	BLK	PTS	RPG	APG	PPG
67-68—San Diego	42	—	603	86	232	.371	—	—	—	55	69	.797	—	—	67	89	84	0	—	—	—	227	1.6	2.1	5.4
68-69—Dallas-Miami (A)	7	—	81	9	28	.321	0	2	.000	2	6	.333	—	—	8	6	14	0	—	6	—	20	1.1	0.9	2.9
70-71—San Francisco	81	—	1183	225	523	.430	—	—	—	111	151	.735	—	—	110	113	192	2	—	—	—	561	1.4	1.4	6.9
71-72—Golden State	65	—	478	82	196	.418	—	—	—	51	61	.836	—	—	39	45	109	0	—	—	—	215	0.6	0.7	3.3
72-73—Dallas (A)	3	—	16	3	8	.375	0	0	—	2	3	.667	1	—	1	1	4	0	—	2	—	8	0.3	0.3	2.7
REG. NBA TOTALS	188	—	2264	393	951	.413	—	—	—	217	281	.772	—	—	216	247	385	2	—	—	—	1003	1.1	1.3	5.3
REG. ABA TOTALS	10	—	97	12	36	.333	0	2	.000	4	9	.444	1	—	9	7	18	0	—	8	—	28	0.9	0.7	2.8
NBA PLAYOFF TOTALS	7	—	84	8	28	.286	—	—	—	17	20	.850	—	—	5	7	9	0	—	—	—	33	0.7	1.0	4.7

JONES, SAMUEL (Sam) b. June 24, 1933 Ht. 6-4 Wt. 205 College—North Carolina Central

SEASON—TEAM	G	GS	MIN	FGM	FGA	PCT	3FGM	3FGA	PCT	FTM	FTA	PCT	O-RB	D-RB	TOT	AST	PF	DQ	STL	TO	BLK	PTS	RPG	APG	PPG
57-58—Boston	56	—	594	100	233	.429	—	—	—	60	84	.714	—	—	160	37	42	0	—	—	—	260	2.9	0.7	4.6
58-59—Boston	71	—	1466	305	703	.434	—	—	—	151	196	.770	—	—	428	101	102	0	—	—	—	761	6.0	1.4	10.7
59-60—Boston	74	—	1512	355	782	.454	—	—	—	168	220	.764	—	—	375	125	101	1	—	—	—	878	5.1	1.7	11.9
60-61—Boston	78	—	2028	480	1069	.449	—	—	—	211	268	.787	—	—	421	217	148	1	—	—	—	1171	5.4	2.8	15.0
61-62—Boston	78	—	2388	596	1284	.464	—	—	—	243	297	.818	—	—	458	232	149	0	—	—	—	1435	5.9	3.0	18.4
62-63—Boston	76	—	2323	621	1305	.476	—	—	—	257	324	.793	—	—	396	241	162	1	—	—	—	1499	5.2	3.2	19.7
63-64—Boston	76	—	2381	612	1359	.450	—	—	—	249	318	.783	—	—	349	202	192	1	—	—	—	1473	4.6	2.7	19.4
64-65—Boston	80	—	2885	821	1818	.452	—	—	—	428	522	.820	—	—	411	223	176	0	—	—	—	2070	5.1	2.8	25.9
65-66—Boston	67	—	2155	626	1335	.469	—	—	—	325	407	.799	—	—	347	216	170	0	—	—	—	1577	5.2	3.2	23.5
66-67—Boston	72	—	2325	638	1406	.454	—	—	—	318	371	.857	—	—	338	217	191	1	—	—	—	1594	4.7	3.0	22.1
67-68—Boston	73	—	2408	621	1348	.461	—	—	—	311	376	.827	—	—	357	216	181	0	—	—	—	1553	4.9	3.0	21.3
68-69—Boston	70	—	1820	496	1103	.450	—	—	—	148	189	.783	—	—	265	182	121	0	—	—	—	1140	3.8	2.6	16.3
REG. SEASON TOTALS	871	—	24285	6271	13745	.456	—	—	—	2869	3572	.803	—	—	4305	2209	1735	5	—	—	—	15411	4.9	2.5	17.7
PLAYOFF TOTALS	154	—	4654	1149	2571	.447	—	—	—	611	753	.811	—	—	718	358	391	5	—	—	—	2909	4.7	2.3	18.9
ALL-STAR TOTALS	5	—	102	18	56	.321	—	—	—	5	6	.833	—	—	14	15	6	0	—	—	—	41	2.8	3.0	8.2

JONES, SHELTON b. April 6, 1966 Ht. 6-9 Wt. 210 College—St. John's

SEASON—TEAM	G	GS	MIN	FGM	FGA	PCT	3FGM	3FGA	PCT	FTM	FTA	PCT	O-RB	D-RB	TOT	AST	PF	DQ	STL	TO	BLK	PTS	RPG	APG	PPG
88-89—S.A.-G.S.-Phil.	51	34	682	93	209	.445	0	1	.000	58	80	.725	32	81	113	42	58	0	21	47	15	244	2.2	0.8	4.8
REG. SEASON TOTALS	51	34	682	93	209	.445	0	1	.000	58	80	.725	32	81	113	42	58	0	21	47	15	244	2.2	0.8	4.8

JONES, STEPHEN HOWARD (Steve, Snapper) b. October 17, 1942 Ht. 6-5 Wt. 205 College—Oregon

SEASON—TEAM	G	GS	MIN	FGM	FGA	PCT	3FGM	3FGA	PCT	FTM	FTA	PCT	O-RB	D-RB	TOT	AST	PF	DQ	STL	TO	BLK	PTS	RPG	APG	PPG
67-68—Oakland (A)	76	—	1950	278	665	.418	23	54	.426	186	233	.798	—	—	343	111	239	7	—	135	—	765	4.5	1.5	10.1
68-69—New Orleans (A)	78	—	3024	576	1372	.420	52	151	.344	348	437	.796	—	—	393	226	280	4	—	192	—	1552	5.0	2.9	19.9
69-70—New Orleans (A)	84	—	3116	689	1558	.442	15	66	.227	412	495	.832	—	—	388	195	290	3	—	—	—	1805	4.6	2.3	21.5
70-71—Memphis (A)	83	—	2923	732	1556	.470	40	108	.370	332	400	.830	—	—	299	182	234	—	—	—	—	1836	3.6	2.2	22.1
71-72—Dallas (A)	84	—	3091	572	1343	.426	26	78	.333	367	422	.870	—	—	317	237	268	—	—	205	—	1537	3.8	2.8	18.3
72-73—Dallas-Car. (A)	80	—	2129	430	883	.487	13	31	.419	200	247	.810	56	168	224	119	220	3	—	150	—	1073	2.8	1.5	13.4
73-74—Car.-Denver (A)	86	—	2092	400	899	.445	13	43	.302	128	168	.762	62	172	234	185	223	—	26	175	15	941	2.7	2.2	10.9
74-75—St. Louis (A)	69	—	1884	287	654	.439	4	19	.211	171	206	.830	43	151	194	197	131	—	53	147	7	749	2.8	2.9	10.9
75-76—Portland	64	—	819	168	380	.442	—	—	—	78	94	.830	13	62	75	63	96	0	17	—	6	414	1.2	1.0	6.5
REG. NBA TOTALS	64	—	819	168	380	.442	—	—	—	78	94	.830	13	62	75	63	96	0	17	—	6	414	1.2	1.0	6.5
REG. ABA TOTALS	640	—	20209	3964	8930	.444	186	550	.338	2144	2608	.822	161	491	2392	1452	1885	17	79	1004	22	10258	3.7	2.3	16.0
ABA PLAYOFF TOTALS	37	—	1224	224	505	.444	8	30	.267	111	141	.787	1	13	144	61	132	0	2	78	3	567	3.9	1.6	15.3
NBA ALL-STAR TOTALS	2	—	40	7	16	.438	1	2	.500	3	3	1.000	1	4	5	3	4	0	0	2	0	18	2.5	1.5	9.0
ABA ALL-STAR TOTALS	3	—	58	11	25	.440	1	2	.500	9	9	1.000	1	4	10	4	6	0	0	2	0	32	3.3	1.3	10.7

JONES, WALI (formerly Walter Jones) b. February 14, 1942 Ht. 6-2 Wt. 180 College—Villanova

SEASON—TEAM	G	GS	MIN	FGM	FGA	PCT	3FGM	3FGA	PCT	FTM	FTA	PCT	O-RB	D-RB	TOT	AST	PF	DQ	STL	TO	BLK	PTS	RPG	APG	PPG
64-65—Baltimore	77	—	1250	154	411	.375	—	—	—	99	136	.728	—	—	140	200	196	1	—	—	—	407	1.8	2.6	5.3
65-66—Philadelphia	80	—	2196	296	799	.370	—	—	—	128	172	.744	—	—	169	273	250	6	—	—	—	720	2.1	3.4	9.0
66-67—Philadelphia	81	—	2249	423	982	.431	—	—	—	223	266	.838	—	—	265	303	246	6	—	—	—	1069	3.3	3.7	13.2
67-68—Philadelphia	77	—	2058	413	1040	.397	—	—	—	159	202	.787	—	—	219	245	225	5	—	—	—	985	2.8	3.2	12.8
68-69—Philadelphia	81	—	2340	432	1005	.430	—	—	—	207	256	.809	—	—	251	292	280	5	—	—	—	1071	3.1	3.6	13.2
69-70—Philadelphia	78	—	1740	366	851	.430	—	—	—	190	226	.841	—	—	173	276	210	2	—	—	—	922	2.2	3.5	11.8
70-71—Philadelphia	41	—	962	168	418	.402	—	—	—	79	101	.782	—	—	64	128	110	1	—	—	—	415	1.6	3.1	10.1
71-72—Milwaukee	48	—	1030	144	354	.407	—	—	—	74	90	.822	—	—	75	141	112	0	—	—	—	362	1.6	2.9	7.5
72-73—Milwaukee	27	—	419	59	145	.407	—	—	—	16	18	.889	—	—	29	56	39	0	—	—	—	134	1.1	2.1	5.0
74-75—Utah (A)	71	—	1339	212	524	.405	6	25	.240	102	124	.823	15	62	77	152	147	—	42	76	3	532	1.1	2.1	7.5
75-76—Detroit-Phil.	17	—	176	23	49	.469	—	—	—	9	13	.692	0	9	9	33	27	0	6	—	0	55	0.5	1.9	3.2
REG. NBA TOTALS	607	—	14420	2478	6054	.409	—	—	—	1184	1480	.800	0	9	1394	1947	1695	26	6	—	0	6140	2.3	3.2	10.1
REG. ABA TOTALS	71	—	1339	212	524	.405	6	25	.240	102	124	.823	15	62	77	152	147	—	42	76	3	532	1.1	2.1	7.5
NBA PLAYOFF TOTALS	70	—	1761	333	821	.406	—	—	—	167	215	.777	0	1	166	202	234	5	0	—	0	833	2.4	2.9	11.9
ABA PLAYOFF TOTALS	5	—	46	8	21	.381	0	0	—	6	6	1.000	1	1	2	4	6	—	4	7	0	22	0.4	0.8	4.4

JONES, WALLACE C. (Wah Wah) b. July 14, 1926 Ht. 6-4 Wt. 225 College—Kentucky

SEASON—TEAM	G	GS	MIN	FGM	FGA	PCT	3FGM	3FGA	PCT	FTM	FTA	PCT	O-RB	D-RB	TOT	AST	PF	DQ	STL	TO	BLK	PTS	RPG	APG	PPG
49-50—Indianapolis	60	—	—	264	706	.374	—	—	—	223	297	.751	—	—	—	194	241	—	—	—	—	751	—	3.2	12.5
50-51—Indianapolis	22	—	—	93	237	.392	—	—	—	61	77	.792	—	—	125	85	74	4	—	—	—	247	5.7	3.9	11.2
51-52—Indianapolis	58	—	1320	164	524	.313	—	—	—	102	136	.750	—	—	283	150	137	3	—	—	—	430	4.9	2.6	7.4
REG. SEASON TOTALS	140	—	1320	521	1467	.355	—	—	—	386	510	.757	—	—	408	429	452	7	—	—	—	1428	5.1	3.1	10.2
PLAYOFF TOTALS	6	—	8	23	76	.303	—	—	—	29	34	.853	—	—	0	22	28	3	—	—	—	75	0.0	3.7	12.5

JONES, WALTER (see Wali Jones)

JONES, WALTER (Larry) b. September 22, 1942 Ht. 6-2½ Wt. 180 College—Toledo

SEASON—TEAM	G	GS	MIN	FGM	FGA	PCT	3FGM	3FGA	PCT	FTM	FTA	PCT	O-RB	D-RB	TOT	AST	PF	DQ	STL	TO	BLK	PTS	RPG	APG	PPG
64-65—Philadelphia	23	—	359	47	153	.307	—	—	—	37	52	.712	—	—	57	40	46	2	—	—	—	131	2.5	1.7	5.7
67-68—Denver (A)	76	—	3085	602	1409	.427	8	42	.190	530	683	.776	—	—	599	270	268	4	—	232	—	1742	7.9	3.6	22.9
68-69—Denver (A)	75	—	3042	759	1631	.465	24	100	.240	591	760	.778	—	—	493	258	273	3	—	218	—	2133	6.6	3.4	28.4
69-70—Denver (A)	75	—	3027	625	1441	.434	41	165	.248	579	732	.791	—	—	391	426	228	1	—	—	—	1870	5.2	5.7	24.9
70-71—Floridians (A)	84	—	3611	764	1636	.467	45	124	.363	471	587	.802	—	—	453	390	269	—	—	—	—	2044	5.4	4.6	24.3
71-72—Floridians (A)	66	—	2255	423	797	.531	18	60	.300	300	373	.804	—	—	309	210	203	—	—	135	—	1164	4.7	3.2	17.6
72-73—Utah-Dallas (A)	80	—	1701	240	521	.461	16	57	.281	202	244	.828	88	151	239	206	184	2	—	104	—	698	3.0	2.6	8.7
73-74—Philadelphia	72	—	1876	263	622	.423	—	—	—	197	235	.838	71	113	184	230	116	0	85	—	18	723	2.6	3.2	10.0
REG. NBA TOTALS	95	—	2235	310	775	.400	—	—	—	234	287	.815	71	113	241	270	162	2	85	—	18	854	2.5	2.8	9.0
REG. ABA TOTALS	456	—	16721	3413	7435	.459	152	548	.277	2673	3379	.791	88	151	2484	1760	1425	10	—	689	—	9651	5.4	3.9	21.2
NBA PLAYOFF TOTALS	5	—	25	5	12	.417	—	—	—	7	11	.636	0	0	4	2	5	0	0	—	0	17	0.8	0.4	3.4
ABA PLAYOFF TOTALS	30	—	1189	220	485	.454	10	37	.270	195	238	.819	—	—	160	158	99	0	—	26	—	645	5.3	5.3	21.5
ABA ALL-STAR TOTALS	4	—	107	22	42	.524	1	3	.333	19	26	.731	4	16	26	17	11	0	—	6	—	64	6.5	4.3	16.0

JONES, WILBERT (Wil) b. February 27, 1947 Ht. 6-8 Wt. 205 College—Albany State

SEASON—TEAM	G	GS	MIN	FGM	FGA	PCT	3FGM	3FGA	PCT	FTM	FTA	PCT	O-RB	D-RB	TOT	AST	PF	DQ	STL	TO	BLK	PTS	RPG	APG	PPG
69-70—Miami (A)	74	—	1697	243	616	.394	2	11	.182	118	162	.728	—	—	565	48	207	5	—	—	—	606	7.6	0.6	8.2
70-71—Memphis (A)	84	—	2234	391	812	.482	1	13	.077	174	258	.674	—	—	680	152	249	—	—	—	—	957	8.1	1.8	11.4
71-72—Memphis (A)	84	—	3098	506	1078	.469	2	16	.125	240	320	.750	371	505	876	154	322	—	—	160	—	1254	10.4	1.8	14.9
72-73—Memphis (A)	76	—	2316	344	722	.476	1	7	.143	146	198	.737	245	359	604	117	281	9	—	130	—	835	7.9	1.5	11.0
73-74—Memphis (A)	81	—	2842	453	997	.454	3	26	.115	163	220	.741	205	460	665	205	276	—	105	184	82	1072	8.2	2.5	13.2
74-75—Kentucky (A)	84	—	2689	458	948	.483	0	5	.000	139	189	.735	198	409	607	256	353	—	108	199	70	1055	7.2	3.0	12.6
75-76—Kentucky (A)	83	—	2635	483	1015	.476	3	6	.500	158	204	.775	243	382	625	209	326	—	84	200	54	1127	7.5	2.5	13.6
76-77—Indiana	80	—	2709	438	1019	.430	—	—	—	166	223	.744	218	386	604	189	305	10	102	—	80	1042	7.6	2.4	13.0
77-78—Buffalo	79	—	1711	226	514	.440	—	—	—	84	119	.706	106	228	334	116	255	7	70	137	43	536	4.2	1.5	6.8
REG. NBA TOTALS	159	—	4420	664	1533	.433	—	—	—	250	342	.731	324	614	938	305	560	17	172	137	123	1578	5.9	1.9	9.9
REG. ABA TOTALS	566	—	17511	2878	6188	.465	12	84	.143	1138	1551	.734	1262	2115	4622	1141	2014	14	297	873	206	6906	8.2	2.0	12.2
ABA PLAYOFF TOTALS	29	—	936	142	306	.464	0	2	.000	39	47	.830	95	121	216	81	118	0	28	51	12	323	7.4	2.8	11.1
ABA ALL-STAR TOTALS	1	—	10	1	3	.333	0	0	—	0	0	—	—	1	2	3	0	2	0	0	0	2	3.0	0.0	2.0

JONES, WILLIAM A. (Willie) b. June 29, 1936 Ht. 6-3½ Wt. 185 College—Northwestern

SEASON—TEAM	G	GS	MIN	FGM	FGA	PCT	3FGM	3FGA	PCT	FTM	FTA	PCT	O-RB	D-RB	TOT	AST	PF	DQ	STL	TO	BLK	PTS	RPG	APG	PPG
60-61—Detroit	35	—	452	78	216	.361	—	—	—	40	63	.635	—	—	94	63	90	2	—	—	—	196	2.7	1.8	5.6
61-62—Detroit	69	—	1006	177	475	.373	—	—	—	64	101	.634	—	—	177	115	137	1	—	—	—	418	2.6	1.7	6.1
62-63—Detroit	79	—	1470	305	730	.418	—	—	—	118	164	.720	—	—	233	188	207	4	—	—	—	728	2.9	2.4	9.2
63-64—Detroit	77	—	1539	265	680	.390	—	—	—	100	141	.709	—	—	253	172	211	5	—	—	—	630	3.3	2.2	8.2
64-65—Detroit	12	—	101	21	52	.404	—	—	—	2	6	.333	—	—	10	7	13	0	—	—	—	44	0.8	0.6	3.7
REG. SEASON TOTALS	272	—	4568	846	2153	.393	—	—	—	324	475	.682	—	—	767	545	658	12	—	—	—	2016	2.8	2.0	7.4
PLAYOFF TOTALS	16	—	287	66	158	.418	—	—	—	25	29	.862	—	—	37	43	43	2	—	—	—	157	2.3	2.7	9.8

JONES, WILLIE D. (Hutch) b. September 1, 1959 Ht. 6-8 Wt. 195 College—Buffalo/Vanderbilt

SEASON—TEAM	G	GS	MIN	FGM	FGA	PCT	3FGM	3FGA	PCT	FTM	FTA	PCT	O-RB	D-RB	TOT	AST	PF	DQ	STL	TO	BLK	PTS	RPG	APG	PPG
82-83—San Diego	9	0	85	17	37	.459	0	0	—	6	6	1.000	10	7	17	4	14	0	3	6	0	40	1.9	0.4	4.4
83-84—San Diego	4	0	18	0	3	.000	0	0	—	1	4	.250	0	0	0	0	0	0	1	2	0	1	0.0	0.0	0.3
REG. SEASON TOTALS	13	0	103	17	40	.425	0	0	—	7	10	.700	10	7	17	4	14	0	4	8	0	41	1.3	0.3	3.2

JORDAN, ADONIS ADELECINO b. August 21, 1970 Ht. 5-11 Wt. 170 College—Kansas

SEASON—TEAM	G	GS	MIN	FGM	FGA	PCT	3FGM	3FGA	PCT	FTM	FTA	PCT	O-RB	D-RB	TOT	AST	PF	DQ	STL	TO	BLK	PTS	RPG	APG	PPG
93-94—Denver	6	0	79	6	23	.261	3	10	.300	0	0	—	3	3	6	19	6	0	0	6	1	15	1.0	3.2	2.5
REG. SEASON TOTALS	6	0	79	6	23	.261	3	10	.300	0	0	—	3	3	6	19	6	0	0	6	1	15	1.0	3.2	2.5

JORDAN, CHARLES C. b. January 31, 1954 Ht. 6-8 Wt. 220 College—Canisius

SEASON—TEAM	G	GS	MIN	FGM	FGA	PCT	3FGM	3FGA	PCT	FTM	FTA	PCT	O-RB	D-RB	TOT	AST	PF	DQ	STL	TO	BLK	PTS	RPG	APG	PPG
75-76—Indiana (A)	71	—	855	162	373	.434	2	10	.200	43	72	.597	94	122	216	53	184	—	33	84	13	369	3.0	0.7	5.2
REG. ABA TOTALS	71	—	855	162	373	.434	2	10	.200	43	72	.597	94	122	216	53	184	—	33	84	13	369	3.0	0.7	5.2
ABA PLAYOFF TOTALS	2	—	18	1	6	.167	0	0	—	0	0	—	0	5	5	2	9	—	2	1	0	2	2.5	1.0	1.0

JORDAN, EDWARD MONTGOMERY (Eddie, Fast Eddie) b. January 29, 1955 Ht. 6-1 Wt. 170 College—Rutgers

SEASON—TEAM	G	GS	MIN	FGM	FGA	PCT	3FGM	3FGA	PCT	FTM	FTA	PCT	O-RB	D-RB	TOT	AST	PF	DQ	STL	TO	BLK	PTS	RPG	APG	PPG
77-78—Clev.-N.J.	73	—	1213	215	538	.400	—	—	—	131	167	.784	35	84	119	177	94	0	126	106	19	561	1.6	2.4	7.7
78-79—New Jersey	82	—	2260	401	960	.418	—	—	—	213	274	.777	74	141	215	365	209	0	201	244	40	1015	2.6	4.5	12.4
79-80—New Jersey	82	—	2657	437	1017	.430	12	48	.250	201	258	.779	62	208	270	557	238	7	223	258	27	1087	3.3	6.8	13.3
80-81—N.J.-L.A.	74	—	1226	150	352	.426	6	22	.273	87	127	.685	30	68	98	241	165	0	98	143	8	393	1.3	3.3	5.3
81-82—Los Angeles	58	0	608	89	208	.428	1	9	.111	43	54	.796	4	39	43	131	98	0	62	66	1	222	0.7	2.3	3.8
82-83—Los Angeles	35	0	333	40	132	.303	3	16	.188	11	17	.647	8	18	26	80	52	0	31	54	1	94	0.7	2.3	2.7
83-84—Port.-L.A.	16	0	210	17	49	.347	0	3	.000	8	12	.667	3	14	17	44	37	0	25	26	0	42	1.1	2.8	2.6
REG. SEASON TOTALS	420	0	8507	1349	3256	.414	22	98	.224	694	909	.763	216	572	788	1595	893	7	766	897	96	3414	1.9	3.8	8.1
PLAYOFF TOTALS	7	—	93	15	40	.375	0	1	.000	8	9	.889	6	9	15	23	6	0	10	7	3	38	2.1	3.3	5.4

JORDAN, MICHAEL JEFFREY (Air) b. February 17, 1963 Ht. 6-6 Wt. 195 College—North Carolina

SEASON—TEAM	G	GS	MIN	FGM	FGA	PCT	3FGM	3FGA	PCT	FTM	FTA	PCT	O-RB	D-RB	TOT	AST	PF	DQ	STL	TO	BLK	PTS	RPG	APG	PPG
84-85—Chicago	82	82	3144	837	1625	.515	9	52	.173	630	746	.845	167	367	534	481	285	4	196	291	69	2313	6.5	5.9	28.2
85-86—Chicago	18	7	451	150	328	.457	3	18	.167	105	125	.840	23	41	64	53	46	0	37	45	21	408	3.6	2.9	22.7
86-87—Chicago	82	82	3281	1098	2279	.482	12	66	.182	833	972	.857	166	264	430	377	237	0	236	272	125	3041	5.2	4.6	37.1
87-88—Chicago	82	82	3311	1069	1998	.535	7	53	.132	723	860	.841	139	310	449	485	270	2	259	252	131	2868	5.5	5.9	35.0
88-89—Chicago	81	81	3255	966	1795	.538	27	98	.276	674	793	.850	149	503	652	650	247	2	234	290	65	2633	8.0	8.0	32.5
89-90—Chicago	82	82	3197	1034	1964	.526	92	245	.376	593	699	.848	143	422	565	519	241	0	227	247	54	2753	6.9	6.3	33.6
90-91—Chicago	82	82	3034	990	1837	.539	29	93	.312	571	671	.851	118	374	492	453	229	1	223	202	83	2580	6.0	5.5	31.5
91-92—Chicago	80	80	3102	943	1818	.519	27	100	.270	491	590	.832	91	420	511	489	201	1	182	200	75	2404	6.4	6.1	30.1
92-93—Chicago	78	78	3067	992	2003	.495	81	230	.352	476	569	.837	135	387	522	428	188	0	221	207	61	2541	6.7	5.5	32.6
REG. SEASON TOTALS	667	656	25842	8079	15647	.516	287	955	.301	5096	6025	.846	1131	3088	4219	3935	1944	10	1815	2006	684	21541	6.3	5.9	32.3
PLAYOFF TOTALS	111	111	4645	1411	2818	.501	86	244	.352	942	1129	.834	179	562	741	738	369	3	258	369	109	3850	6.7	6.6	34.7
ALL-STAR TOTALS	8	8	244	74	150	.493	2	8	.250	27	36	.750	15	16	31	29	22	0	27	34	6	177	3.9	3.6	22.1

JORDAN, REGINALD (Reggie) b. January 26, 1968 Ht. 6-4 Wt. 195 College—New Mexico State

SEASON—TEAM	G	GS	MIN	FGM	FGA	PCT	3FGM	3FGA	PCT	FTM	FTA	PCT	O-RB	D-RB	TOT	AST	PF	DQ	STL	TO	BLK	PTS	RPG	APG	PPG
93-94—L.A. Lakers	23	0	259	44	103	.427	2	4	.500	35	51	.686	46	21	67	26	26	0	14	14	5	125	2.9	1.1	5.4
REG. SEASON TOTALS	23	0	259	44	103	.427	2	4	.500	35	51	.686	46	21	67	26	26	0	14	14	5	125	2.9	1.1	5.4

JORDAN, THOMAS b. May 23, 1968 Ht. 6-10 Wt. 220 College—Oklahoma State

SEASON—TEAM	G	GS	MIN	FGM	FGA	PCT	3FGM	3FGA	PCT	FTM	FTA	PCT	O-RB	D-RB	TOT	AST	PF	DQ	STL	TO	BLK	PTS	RPG	APG	PPG
92-93—Philadelphia	4	0	106	18	41	.439	0	0	—	8	17	.471	5	14	19	3	14	0	3	12	5	44	4.8	0.8	11.0
REG. SEASON TOTALS	4	0	106	18	41	.439	0	0	—	8	17	.471	5	14	19	3	14	0	3	12	5	44	4.8	0.8	11.0

JORDAN, WALTER LEE b. February 19, 1956 Ht. 6-7½ Wt. 205 College—Purdue

SEASON—TEAM	G	GS	MIN	FGM	FGA	PCT	3FGM	3FGA	PCT	FTM	FTA	PCT	O-RB	D-RB	TOT	AST	PF	DQ	STL	TO	BLK	PTS	RPG	APG	PPG
80-81—Cleveland	30	—	207	29	75	.387	0	0	—	10	17	.588	23	19	42	11	35	0	11	17	5	68	1.4	0.4	2.3
REG. SEASON TOTALS	30	—	207	29	75	.387	0	0	—	10	17	.588	23	19	42	11	35	0	11	17	5	68	1.4	0.4	2.3

JORDON, PHIL b. September 12, 1933 d. June 7, 1965 Ht. 6-10 Wt. 205 College—Whitworth

SEASON—TEAM	G	GS	MIN	FGM	FGA	PCT	3FGM	3FGA	PCT	FTM	FTA	PCT	O-RB	D-RB	TOT	AST	PF	DQ	STL	TO	BLK	PTS	RPG	APG	PPG
56-57—New York	9	—	91	18	49	.367	—	—	—	8	12	.667	—	—	34	2	15	0	—	—	—	44	3.8	0.2	4.9
57-58—N.Y.-Detroit	58	—	898	193	467	.413	—	—	—	64	93	.688	—	—	301	37	108	1	—	—	—	450	5.2	0.6	7.8
58-59—Detroit	72	—	2058	399	967	.413	—	—	—	231	303	.762	—	—	594	83	193	1	—	—	—	1029	8.3	1.2	14.3
59-60—Cincinnati	75	—	2066	381	970	.393	—	—	—	242	338	.716	—	—	624	207	227	7	—	—	—	1004	8.3	2.8	13.4
60-61—Cin.-N.Y.	79	—	2064	360	932	.386	—	—	—	208	297	.700	—	—	674	181	273	5	—	—	—	928	8.5	2.3	11.7
61-62—New York	76	—	2195	403	1028	.392	—	—	—	96	168	.571	—	—	482	156	258	7	—	—	—	902	6.3	2.1	11.9
62-63—St. Louis	73	—	1420	211	527	.400	—	—	—	56	101	.554	—	—	319	103	172	3	—	—	—	478	4.4	1.4	6.5
REG. SEASON TOTALS	442	—	10792	1965	4940	.398	—	—	—	905	1312	.690	—	—	3028	769	1246	24	—	—	—	4835	6.9	1.7	10.9
PLAYOFF TOTALS	16	—	243	36	99	.364	—	—	—	33	42	.786	—	—	51	14	34	0	—	—	—	105	3.2	0.9	6.6

JORGENSEN, JOHN J. (Johnny) b. December 28, 1921 d. January 19, 1973 Ht. 6-2 Wt. 185 College—William & Mary/DePaul

SEASON—TEAM	G	GS	MIN	FGM	FGA	PCT	3FGM	3FGA	PCT	FTM	FTA	PCT	O-RB	D-RB	TOT	AST	PF	DQ	STL	TO	BLK	PTS	RPG	APG	PPG
47-48—Chicago-Balt.	3	—	—	4	9	.444	—	—	—	1	1	1.000	—	—	0	2	—	—	—	—	—	9	—	0.0	3.0
47-48—Minneapolis (N)	38	—	—	37	—	—	—	—	—	27	49	.551	—	—	—	52	—	—	—	—	—	101	—	—	2.7
48-49—Minneapolis	48	—	—	41	114	.360	—	—	—	24	33	.727	—	—	33	68	—	—	—	—	—	106	—	0.7	2.2
REG. NBA TOTALS	51	—	—	45	123	.366	—	—	—	25	34	.735	—	—	33	70	—	—	—	—	—	115	—	0.6	2.3
REG. NBL TOTALS	38	—	—	37	—	—	—	—	—	27	49	.551	—	—	—	52	—	—	—	—	—	101	—	—	2.7
NBA PLAYOFF TOTALS	6	—	—	3	7	.429	—	—	—	1	1	1.000	—	—	—	4	—	—	—	—	—	7	—	0.0	1.2
NBL PLAYOFF TOTALS	10	—	—	11	—	—	—	—	—	4	8	.500	—	—	—	20	—	—	—	—	—	26	—	—	2.6

JORGENSEN, NOBLE GORDON (Jorgy) b. May 18, 1925 d. November 1982 Ht. 6-9 Wt. 230 College—Iowa/Westminster

SEASON—TEAM	G	GS	MIN	FGM	FGA	PCT	3FGM	3FGA	PCT	FTM	FTA	PCT	O-RB	D-RB	TOT	AST	PF	DQ	STL	TO	BLK	PTS	RPG	APG	PPG
46-47—Pittsburgh	15	—	—	25	112	.223	—	—	—	16	25	.640	—	—	—	4	40	—	—	—	—	66	—	0.3	4.4
48-49—Sheboygan (N)	63	—	—	218	—	—	—	—	—	194	255	.761	—	—	—	—	189	—	—	—	—	630	—	—	10.0
49-50—Sheboygan	54	—	—	218	618	.353	—	—	—	268	350	.766	—	—	—	90	201	—	—	—	—	704	—	1.7	13.0
50-51—Tri-Cit-Syr.	63	—	—	223	600	.372	—	—	—	182	265	.687	—	—	—	338	91	237	8	—	—	—	628	5.4	1.4	10.0
51-52—Syracuse	66	—	1318	190	460	.413	—	—	—	149	187	.797	—	—	—	288	63	190	2	—	—	—	529	4.4	1.0	8.0
52-53—Syracuse	70	—	1355	145	436	.333	—	—	—	146	199	.734	—	—	—	236	76	247	7	—	—	—	436	3.4	1.1	6.2
REG. NBA TOTALS	268	—	2673	801	2226	.360	—	—	—	761	1026	.742	—	—	862	324	915	17	—	—	—	2363	4.3	1.2	8.8
REG. NBL TOTALS	63	—	—	218	—	—	—	—	—	194	255	.761	—	—	—	—	189	—	—	—	—	630	—	—	10.0
NBA PLAYOFF TOTALS	19	—	194	59	148	.399	—	—	—	59	89	.663	—	—	58	23	75	4	—	—	—	177	3.6	1.2	9.3
NBL PLAYOFF TOTALS	2	—	—	11	—	—	—	—	—	7	8	.875	—	—	—	—	7	—	—	—	—	29	—	—	14.5

JORGENSEN, ROGER KENNEDY b. September 2, 1920 Ht. 6-5 Wt. 200 College—Pittsburgh/Ohio State

SEASON—TEAM	G	GS	MIN	FGM	FGA	PCT	3FGM	3FGA	PCT	FTM	FTA	PCT	O-RB	D-RB	TOT	AST	PF	DQ	STL	TO	BLK	PTS	RPG	APG	PPG
46-47—Pittsburgh	28	—	—	14	54	.259	—	—	—	13	19	.684	—	—	—	1	36	—	—	—	—	41	—	0.0	1.5
REG. SEASON TOTALS	28	—	—	14	54	.259	—	—	—	13	19	.684	—	—	—	1	36	—	—	—	—	41	—	0.0	1.5

JOSEPH, YVON b. October 31, 1957 Ht. 6-11 Wt. 245 College—Miami-Dade CC North/Georgia Tech

SEASON—TEAM	G	GS	MIN	FGM	FGA	PCT	3FGM	3FGA	PCT	FTM	FTA	PCT	O-RB	D-RB	TOT	AST	PF	DQ	STL	TO	BLK	PTS	RPG	APG	PPG
85-86—New Jersey	1	0	5	0	0	—	0	0	—	2	2	1.000	0	0	0	0	1	0	0	0	0	2	0.0	0.0	2.0
REG. SEASON TOTALS	1	0	5	0	0	—	0	0	—	2	2	1.000	0	0	0	0	1	0	0	0	0	2	0.0	0.0	2.0

JOYCE, KEVIN F. b. June 27, 1951 Ht. 6-3 Wt. 190 College—South Carolina

SEASON—TEAM	G	GS	MIN	FGM	FGA	PCT	3FGM	3FGA	PCT	FTM	FTA	PCT	O-RB	D-RB	TOT	AST	PF	DQ	STL	TO	BLK	PTS	RPG	APG	PPG
73-74—Indiana (A)	56	—	987	171	432	.396	5	27	.185	64	78	.821	33	59	92	128	86	—	32	80	8	411	1.6	2.3	7.3
74-75—Indiana (A)	81	—	2828	530	1245	.426	8	42	.190	142	180	.789	60	103	163	322	259	—	107	151	23	1210	2.0	4.0	14.9
75-76—S.D.-Ken. (A)	43	—	916	114	311	.367	2	12	.167	55	74	.743	7	42	49	130	96	—	31	91	3	285	1.1	3.0	6.6
REG. ABA TOTALS	180	—	4731	815	1988	.410	15	81	.185	261	332	.786	100	204	304	580	441	0	170	322	34	1906	1.7	3.2	10.6
ABA PLAYOFF TOTALS	37	—	846	115	300	.383	7	20	.350	50	63	.794	7	36	43	87	89	0	24	58	11	287	1.2	2.4	7.8

JOYNER, HARRY C. (Butch) b. April 26, 1945 Ht. 6-5 Wt. 200 College—Indiana

SEASON—TEAM	G	GS	MIN	FGM	FGA	PCT	3FGM	3FGA	PCT	FTM	FTA	PCT	O-RB	D-RB	TOT	AST	PF	DQ	STL	TO	BLK	PTS	RPG	APG	PPG
68-69—Indiana (A)	2	—	5	0	0	—	0	0	—	0	0	—	—	—	1	0	1	0	—	0	—	0	0.5	0.0	0.0
REG. ABA TOTALS	2	—	5	0	0	—	0	0	—	0	0	—	—	—	1	0	1	0	—	0	—	0	0.5	0.0	0.0

JUDKINS, JEFFREY REED (Jeff) b. March 23, 1956 Ht. 6-6 Wt. 185 College—Utah

SEASON—TEAM	G	GS	MIN	FGM	FGA	PCT	3FGM	3FGA	PCT	FTM	FTA	PCT	O-RB	D-RB	TOT	AST	PF	DQ	STL	TO	BLK	PTS	RPG	APG	PPG
78-79—Boston	81	—	1521	295	587	.503	—	—	—	119	146	.815	70	121	191	145	184	1	81	109	12	709	2.4	1.8	8.8
79-80—Boston	65	—	674	139	276	.504	11	27	.407	62	76	.816	32	34	66	47	91	0	29	49	5	351	1.0	0.7	5.4
80-81—Utah	62	—	666	92	216	.426	9	28	.321	45	51	.882	29	64	93	59	84	0	16	30	2	238	1.5	1.0	3.8
81-82—Detroit	30	0	251	31	81	.383	1	10	.100	16	26	.615	14	20	34	14	33	0	6	9	5	79	1.1	0.5	2.6
82-83—Portland	34	0	309	39	88	.443	2	8	.250	25	30	.833	18	25	43	17	39	0	15	17	2	105	1.3	0.5	3.1
REG. SEASON TOTALS	272	0	3421	596	1248	.478	23	73	.315	267	329	.812	163	264	427	282	431	1	147	214	26	1482	1.6	1.0	5.4
PLAYOFF TOTALS	7	0	10	4	8	.500	1	3	.333	0	0	—	3	1	4	—	0	0	1	0	0	9	0.6	0.0	1.3

KACHAN, EDWIN JOHN (Whitey) b. September 15, 1925 Ht. 6-2 Wt. 175 College—DePaul

SEASON—TEAM	G	GS	MIN	FGM	FGA	PCT	3FGM	3FGA	PCT	FTM	FTA	PCT	O-RB	D-RB	TOT	AST	PF	DQ	STL	TO	BLK	PTS	RPG	APG	PPG
48-49—Chicago-Minn.	52	—	—	38	142	.268	—	—	—	36	56	.643	—	—	—	37	81	—	—	—	—	112	—	0.7	2.2
REG. SEASON TOTALS	52	—	—	38	142	.268	—	—	—	36	56	.643	—	—	—	37	81	—	—	—	—	112	—	0.7	2.2
PLAYOFF TOTALS	8	—	—	2	5	.400	—	—	—	0	0	—	—	—	—	2	3	—	—	—	—	4	—	0.3	0.5

KAFTAN, GEORGE A. (The Golden Greek) b. February 22, 1928 Ht. 6-3 Wt. 190 College—Holy Cross

SEASON—TEAM	G	GS	MIN	FGM	FGA	PCT	3FGM	3FGA	PCT	FTM	FTA	PCT	O-RB	D-RB	TOT	AST	PF	DQ	STL	TO	BLK	PTS	RPG	APG	PPG
48-49—Boston	21	—	—	116	315	.368	—	—	—	72	115	.626	—	—	—	61	28	—	—	—	—	304	—	2.9	14.5
49-50—Boston	55	—	—	199	535	.372	—	—	—	136	208	.654	—	—	—	145	92	—	—	—	—	534	—	2.6	9.7
50-51—New York	61	—	—	111	286	.388	—	—	—	78	125	.624	—	—	153	74	102	1	—	—	—	300	2.5	1.2	4.9
51-52—New York	52	—	955	115	307	.375	—	—	—	92	134	.687	—	—	196	88	107	0	—	—	—	322	3.8	1.7	6.2
52-53—Baltimore	23	—	380	45	142	.317	—	—	—	44	67	.657	—	—	75	31	59	2	—	—	—	134	3.3	1.3	5.8
REG. SEASON TOTALS	212	—	1335	586	1585	.370	—	—	—	422	649	.650	—	—	424	399	388	3	—	—	—	1594	3.1	1.9	7.5
PLAYOFF TOTALS	21	—	232	32	84	.381	—	—	—	29	45	.644	—	—	36	24	48	3	—	—	—	93	1.8	1.2	4.4

KALAFAT, EDWARD L. (Ed) b. October 13, 1932 Ht. 6-6 Wt. 245 College—Minnesota

SEASON—TEAM	G	GS	MIN	FGM	FGA	PCT	3FGM	3FGA	PCT	FTM	FTA	PCT	O-RB	D-RB	TOT	AST	PF	DQ	STL	TO	BLK	PTS	RPG	APG	PPG
54-55—Minneapolis	72	—	1102	118	375	.315	—	—	—	111	168	.661	—	—	317	75	205	9	—	—	—	347	4.4	1.0	4.8
55-56—Minneapolis	72	—	1639	194	540	.359	—	—	—	186	252	.738	—	—	440	130	236	2	—	—	—	574	6.1	1.8	8.0
56-57—Minneapolis	65	—	1617	178	507	.351	—	—	—	197	298	.661	—	—	425	105	243	9	—	—	—	553	6.5	1.6	8.5
REG. SEASON TOTALS	209	—	4358	490	1422	.345	—	—	—	494	718	.688	—	—	1182	310	684	20	—	—	—	1474	5.7	1.5	7.1
PLAYOFF TOTALS	15	—	235	32	79	.405	—	—	—	39	60	.650	—	—	63	11	49	3	—	—	—	103	4.2	0.7	6.9

KAPLOWITZ, RALPH (Kappy) b. May 18, 1919 Ht. 6-2 Wt. 170 College—New York University

SEASON—TEAM	G	GS	MIN	FGM	FGA	PCT	3FGM	3FGA	PCT	FTM	FTA	PCT	O-RB	D-RB	TOT	AST	PF	DQ	STL	TO	BLK	PTS	RPG	APG	PPG
46-47—N.Y.-Phil.	57	—	—	146	532	.274	—	—	—	111	151	.735	—	—	—	38	122	—	—	—	—	403	—	0.7	7.1
47-48—Philadelphia	48	—	—	71	292	.243	—	—	—	47	60	.783	—	—	—	19	100	—	—	—	—	189	—	0.4	3.9
REG. SEASON TOTALS	105	—	—	217	824	.263	—	—	—	158	211	.749	—	—	—	57	222	—	—	—	—	592	—	0.5	5.6
PLAYOFF TOTALS	23	—	—	54	191	.283	—	—	—	44	56	.786	—	—	—	13	47	—	—	—	—	152	—	0.6	6.6

KAPPEN, ANTHONY GEORGE (Tony) b. April 13, 1919 d. December 18, 1993 Ht. 5-10 Wt. 165 College—None

SEASON—TEAM	G	GS	MIN	FGM	FGA	PCT	3FGM	3FGA	PCT	FTM	FTA	PCT	O-RB	D-RB	TOT	AST	PF	DQ	STL	TO	BLK	PTS	RPG	APG	PPG
46-47—Pitt.-Boston	59	—	—	128	537	.238	—	—	—	128	161	.795	—	—	—	28	78	—	—	—	—	384	—	0.5	6.5
REG. SEASON TOTALS	59	—	—	128	537	.238	—	—	—	128	161	.795	—	—	—	28	78	—	—	—	—	384	—	0.5	6.5

KARL, GEORGE MATTHEW b. May 12, 1951 Ht. 6-2 Wt. 185 College—North Carolina

SEASON—TEAM	G	GS	MIN	FGM	FGA	PCT	3FGM	3FGA	PCT	FTM	FTA	PCT	O-RB	D-RB	TOT	AST	PF	DQ	STL	TO	BLK	PTS	RPG	APG	PPG
73-74—San Antonio (A)	74	—	1339	236	502	.470	8	22	.364	94	113	.832	41	85	126	160	161	—	65	92	10	574	1.7	2.2	7.8
74-75—San Antonio (A)	82	—	1629	261	534	.489	4	23	.174	137	177	.774	47	108	155	334	207	—	96	158	7	663	1.9	4.1	8.1
75-76—San Antonio (A)	75	—	1200	150	334	.449	0	9	.000	81	106	.764	13	53	66	250	149	—	60	108	3	381	0.9	3.3	5.1
76-77—San Antonio	29	—	251	25	73	.342	—	—	—	29	42	.690	4	13	17	46	36	0	10	—	0	79	0.6	1.6	2.7
77-78—San Antonio	4	—	30	2	6	.333	—	—	—	2	2	1.000	0	5	5	5	6	0	1	4	0	6	1.3	1.3	1.5
REG. NBA TOTALS	33	—	281	27	79	.342	—	—	—	31	44	.705	4	18	22	51	42	0	11	4	0	85	0.7	1.5	2.6
REG. ABA TOTALS	231	—	4168	647	1370	.472	12	54	.222	312	396	.788	101	246	347	744	517	0	221	358	20	1618	1.5	3.2	7.0
NBA PLAYOFF TOTALS	1	—	1	0	0	—	—	—	—	0	0	—	0	0	0	0	0	0	0	—	0	0	0.0	0.0	0.0
ABA PLAYOFF TOTALS	17	—	245	24	58	.414	0	3	.000	11	18	.611	4	18	22	45	36	0	16	19	0	59	1.3	2.6	3.5

KASID, EDWARD (Ed) b. August 13, 1923 Ht. 5-11 Wt. 185 College—None

SEASON—TEAM	G	GS	MIN	FGM	FGA	PCT	3FGM	3FGA	PCT	FTM	FTA	PCT	O-RB	D-RB	TOT	AST	PF	DQ	STL	TO	BLK	PTS	RPG	APG	PPG
46-47—Toronto	8	—	—	6	21	.286	—	—	—	0	6	.000	—	—	—	6	8	—	—	—	—	12	—	0.8	1.5
REG. SEASON TOTALS	8	—	—	6	21	.286	—	—	—	0	6	.000	—	—	—	6	8	—	—	—	—	12	—	0.8	1.5

KATKAVECK, LEO FRANK b. April 17, 1923 Ht. 6-0 Wt. 185 College—North Carolina State

SEASON—TEAM	G	GS	MIN	FGM	FGA	PCT	3FGM	3FGA	PCT	FTM	FTA	PCT	O-RB	D-RB	TOT	AST	PF	DQ	STL	TO	BLK	PTS	RPG	APG	PPG
48-49—Washington	53	—	—	84	253	.332	—	—	—	53	71	.746	—	—	—	68	110	—	—	—	—	221	—	1.3	4.2
49-50—Washington	54	—	—	101	330	.306	—	—	—	34	56	.607	—	—	—	68	102	—	—	—	—	236	—	1.3	4.4
REG. SEASON TOTALS	107	—	—	185	583	.317	—	—	—	87	127	.685	—	—	—	136	212	—	—	—	—	457	—	1.3	4.3
PLAYOFF TOTALS	11	—	—	9	42	.214	—	—	—	8	11	.727	—	—	—	13	20	—	—	—	—	26	—	1.2	2.4

KAUFFMAN, ROBERT (Bob, Horse) b. July 13, 1946 Ht. 6-8 Wt. 240 College—Guilford

SEASON—TEAM	G	GS	MIN	FGM	FGA	PCT	3FGM	3FGA	PCT	FTM	FTA	PCT	O-RB	D-RB	TOT	AST	PF	DQ	STL	TO	BLK	PTS	RPG	APG	PPG
68-69—Seattle	82	—	1660	219	496	.442	—	—	—	203	289	.702	—	—	484	83	252	8	—	—	—	641	5.9	1.0	7.8
69-70—Chicago	64	—	775	94	221	.425	—	—	—	88	123	.715	—	—	211	76	117	1	—	—	—	276	3.3	1.2	4.3
70-71—Buffalo	78	—	2778	616	1309	.471	—	—	—	359	485	.740	—	—	837	354	263	8	—	—	—	1591	10.7	4.5	20.4
71-72—Buffalo	77	—	3205	558	1123	.497	—	—	—	341	429	.795	—	—	787	297	273	7	—	—	—	1457	10.2	3.9	18.9
72-73—Buffalo	77	—	3049	535	1059	.505	—	—	—	280	359	.780	—	—	855	396	211	1	—	—	—	1350	11.1	5.1	17.5
73-74—Buffalo	74	—	1304	171	366	.467	—	—	—	107	150	.713	97	229	326	142	155	0	37	—	18	449	4.4	1.9	6.1
74-75—Atlanta	73	—	797	113	261	.433	—	—	—	59	84	.702	67	115	182	81	103	1	19	—	4	285	2.5	1.1	3.9
REG. SEASON TOTALS	525	—	13568	2306	4835	.477	—	—	—	1437	1919	.749	164	344	3682	1429	1374	26	56	—	22	6049	7.0	2.7	11.5
PLAYOFF TOTALS	5	—	24	2	6	.333	—	—	—	2	5	.400	1	0	7	6	5	0	0	—	0	6	1.4	1.2	1.2
ALL-STAR TOTALS	3	—	20	2	5	.400	—	—	—	1	2	.500	0	0	2	2	4	0	0	—	0	5	0.7	0.7	1.7

KAUTZ, WILBERT (Wibs) b. September 7, 1915 d. May 1979 Ht. 5-11½ Wt. 180 College—Loyola (Ill.)

SEASON—TEAM	G	GS	MIN	FGM	FGA	PCT	3FGM	3FGA	PCT	FTM	FTA	PCT	O-RB	D-RB	TOT	AST	PF	DQ	STL	TO	BLK	PTS	RPG	APG	PPG
39-40—Chicago (N)	28	—	—	105	—	—	—	—	—	63	116	.543	—	—	—	—	55	—	—	—	—	273	—	—	9.8
40-41—Chicago (N)	21	—	—	94	—	—	—	—	—	39	63	.619	—	—	—	—	31	—	—	—	—	227	—	—	10.8
41-42—Chicago (N)	20	—	—	85	—	—	—	—	—	40	—	—	—	—	—	—	—	—	—	—	—	210	—	—	10.5
46-47—Chicago	50	—	—	107	420	.255	—	—	—	39	73	.534	—	—	—	37	114	—	—	—	—	253	—	0.7	5.1
REG. NBA TOTALS	50	—	—	107	420	.255	—	—	—	39	73	.534	—	—	—	37	114	—	—	—	—	253	—	0.7	5.1
REG. NBL TOTALS	69	—	—	284	—	—	—	—	—	142	179	.570	—	—	—	—	86	—	—	—	—	710	—	—	10.3
NBA PLAYOFF TOTALS	9	—	—	10	45	.222	—	—	—	2	6	.333	—	—	—	—	14	—	—	—	—	22	0.0	0.0	2.4

KEA, CLARENCE LEROY b. February 2, 1959   Ht. 6-7 Wt. 220 College—Lamar

SEASON—TEAM	G	GS	MIN	FGM	FGA	PCT	3FGM	3FGA	PCT	FTM	FTA	PCT	O-RB	D-RB	TOT	AST	PF	DQ	STL	TO	BLK	PTS	RPG	APG	PPG
80-81—Dallas	16	—	199	37	81	.457	0	1	.000	43	62	.694	28	39	67	5	44	2	6	16	1	117	4.2	0.3	7.3
81-82—Dallas	35	0	248	26	49	.531	0	0	—	29	42	.690	26	35	61	14	55	0	4	16	3	81	1.7	0.4	2.3
REG. SEASON TOTALS	51	0	447	63	130	.485	0	1	.000	72	104	.692	54	74	128	19	99	2	10	32	4	198	2.5	0.4	3.9

KEARNS, MICHAEL JOSEPH b. June 18, 1929   Ht. 6-2 Wt. 180 College—Princeton

SEASON—TEAM	G	GS	MIN	FGM	FGA	PCT	3FGM	3FGA	PCT	FTM	FTA	PCT	O-RB	D-RB	TOT	AST	PF	DQ	STL	TO	BLK	PTS	RPG	APG	PPG
54-55—Philadelphia	6	—	25	0	5	.000	—	—	—	1	4	.250	—	—	3	5	1	0	—	—	—	1	0.5	0.8	0.2
REG. SEASON TOTALS	6	—	25	0	5	.000	—	—	—	1	4	.250	—	—	3	5	1	0	—	—	—	1	0.5	0.8	0.2

KEARNS, THOMAS FRANCIS JR. (Tommy) b. October 6, 1936   Ht. 5-11 Wt. 185 College—North Carolina

SEASON—TEAM	G	GS	MIN	FGM	FGA	PCT	3FGM	3FGA	PCT	FTM	FTA	PCT	O-RB	D-RB	TOT	AST	PF	DQ	STL	TO	BLK	PTS	RPG	APG	PPG
58-59—Syracuse	1	—	7	1	1	1.000	—	—	—	0	0	—	—	—	0	0	1	0	—	—	—	2	0.0	0.0	2.0
REG. SEASON TOTALS	1	—	7	1	1	1.000	—	—	—	0	0	—	—	—	0	0	1	0	—	—	—	2	0.0	0.0	2.0

KEEFE, ADAM THOMAS b. February 22, 1970   Ht. 6-9 Wt. 240 College—Stanford

SEASON—TEAM	G	GS	MIN	FGM	FGA	PCT	3FGM	3FGA	PCT	FTM	FTA	PCT	O-RB	D-RB	TOT	AST	PF	DQ	STL	TO	BLK	PTS	RPG	APG	PPG
92-93—Atlanta	82	6	1549	188	376	.500	0	1	.000	166	237	.700	171	261	432	80	195	1	57	100	16	542	5.3	1.0	6.6
93-94—Atlanta	63	1	763	96	213	.451	0	0	—	81	111	.730	77	124	201	34	80	0	20	60	9	273	3.2	0.5	4.3
REG. SEASON TOTALS	145	7	2312	284	589	.482	0	1	.000	247	348	.710	248	385	633	114	275	1	77	160	25	815	4.4	0.8	5.6
PLAYOFF TOTALS	10	0	115	13	23	.565	0	0	—	8	15	.533	7	19	26	8	16	0	2	7	1	34	2.6	0.8	3.4

KEELING, HAROLD A. b. September 18, 1963   Ht. 6-4 Wt. 185 College—Cal State-Santa Clara

SEASON—TEAM	G	GS	MIN	FGM	FGA	PCT	3FGM	3FGA	PCT	FTM	FTA	PCT	O-RB	D-RB	TOT	AST	PF	DQ	STL	TO	BLK	PTS	RPG	APG	PPG
85-86—Dallas	20	0	75	17	39	.436	0	0	—	10	14	.714	3	3	6	10	9	0	7	7	0	44	0.3	0.5	2.2
REG. SEASON TOTALS	20	0	75	17	39	.436	0	0	—	10	14	.714	3	3	6	10	9	0	7	7	0	44	0.3	0.5	2.2
PLAYOFF TOTALS	1	0	1	0	0	—	0	0	—	0	0	—	0	0	0	—	0	0	0	0	0	0	0.0	0.0	0.0

KELLER, GARY J. b. June 13, 1944   Ht. 6-9 Wt. 220 College—Florida

SEASON—TEAM	G	GS	MIN	FGM	FGA	PCT	3FGM	3FGA	PCT	FTM	FTA	PCT	O-RB	D-RB	TOT	AST	PF	DQ	STL	TO	BLK	PTS	RPG	APG	PPG
67-68—Minnesota (A)	69	—	1211	184	483	.381	0	2	.000	139	214	.650	—	—	383	39	168	7	—	87	—	507	5.6	0.6	7.3
68-69—Miami (A)	53	—	503	78	192	.406	0	3	.000	72	120	.600	—	—	167	8	102	2	—	41	—	228	3.2	0.2	4.3
REG. ABA TOTALS	122	—	1714	262	675	.388	0	5	.000	211	334	.632	—	—	550	47	270	9	—	128	—	735	4.5	0.4	6.0
ABA PLAYOFF TOTALS	16	—	199	37	88	.420	0	0	—	19	33	.576	—	—	73	11	39	0	—	17	—	93	4.6	0.7	5.8

KELLER, KENNETH W. (Ken) b. 1922 d. February 24, 1983 Ht. 6-1½ Wt. 180 College—Vermont/St. John's

SEASON—TEAM	G	GS	MIN	FGM	FGA	PCT	3FGM	3FGA	PCT	FTM	FTA	PCT	O-RB	D-RB	TOT	AST	PF	DQ	STL	TO	BLK	PTS	RPG	APG	PPG
46-47—Wash.-Prov.	28	—	—	10	30	.333	—	—	—	2	5	.400	—	—	—	1	15	—	—	—	—	22	—	0.0	0.8
REG. SEASON TOTALS	28	—	—	10	30	.333	—	—	—	2	5	.400	—	—	—	1	15	—	—	—	—	22	—	0.0	0.8

KELLER, WILLIAM CURRY (Billy) b. August 30, 1947   Ht. 5-10 Wt. 180 College—Purdue

SEASON—TEAM	G	GS	MIN	FGM	FGA	PCT	3FGM	3FGA	PCT	FTM	FTA	PCT	O-RB	D-RB	TOT	AST	PF	DQ	STL	TO	BLK	PTS	RPG	APG	PPG
69-70—Indiana (A)	82	—	1482	252	634	.397	42	154	.273	164	193	.850	—	—	174	235	153	0	—	—	—	710	2.1	2.9	8.7
70-71—Indiana (A)	83	—	2490	417	980	.426	84	230	.365	267	308	.867	—	—	240	437	170	—	—	—	—	1185	2.9	5.3	14.3
71-72—Indiana (A)	76	—	1729	264	619	.426	56	169	.331	153	174	.879	—	—	164	264	118	—	—	131	—	737	2.2	3.5	9.7
72-73—Indiana (A)	83	—	2251	421	973	.433	71	222	.320	234	269	.870	82	122	204	361	162	1	—	171	—	1147	2.5	4.3	13.8
73-74—Indiana (A)	75	—	1428	279	615	.454	50	131	.382	107	123	.870	44	84	128	172	83	—	37	100	3	715	1.7	2.3	9.5
74-75—Indiana (A)	79	—	1918	397	908	.437	80	240	.333	113	128	.883	90	121	211	204	101	—	59	109	3	987	2.7	2.6	12.5
75-76—Indiana (A)	78	—	2311	410	1011	.406	123	349	.352	164	183	.896	81	147	228	307	116	—	59	148	5	1107	2.9	3.9	14.2
REG. ABA TOTALS	556	—	13609	2440	5740	.425	506	1495	.338	1202	1378	.872	297	474	1349	1980	903	1	155	659	11	6588	2.4	3.6	11.8
ABA PLAYOFF TOTALS	95	—	2504	415	975	.426	87	255	.341	222	255	.871	17	28	225	334	184	0	13	82	0	1139	2.4	3.5	12.0

KELLEY, RICHARD RYLAND (Rich) b. March 23, 1953   Ht. 7-0 Wt. 235 College—Stanford

SEASON—TEAM	G	GS	MIN	FGM	FGA	PCT	3FGM	3FGA	PCT	FTM	FTA	PCT	O-RB	D-RB	TOT	AST	PF	DQ	STL	TO	BLK	PTS	RPG	APG	PPG
75-76—New Orleans	75	—	1346	184	379	.485	—	—	—	159	205	.776	193	335	528	155	209	5	52	—	60	527	7.0	2.1	7.0
76-77—New Orleans	76	—	1505	184	386	.477	—	—	—	156	197	.792	210	377	587	208	244	7	45	—	63	524	7.7	2.7	6.9
77-78—New Orleans	82	—	2119	304	602	.505	—	—	—	225	289	.779	249	510	759	233	293	6	89	225	129	833	9.3	2.8	10.2
78-79—New Orleans	80	—	2705	440	870	.506	—	—	—	373	458	.814	303	723	1026	285	309	8	126	288	166	1253	12.8	3.6	15.7
79-80—N.J.-Phoenix	80	—	1839	229	484	.473	0	3	.000	244	310	.787	200	315	515	178	273	5	78	198	96	702	6.4	2.2	8.8
80-81—Phoenix	81	—	1686	196	387	.506	0	2	.000	175	231	.758	131	310	441	282	210	0	79	209	63	567	5.4	3.5	7.0
81-82—Phoenix	81	39	1892	236	505	.467	0	1	.000	167	223	.749	168	329	497	293	292	14	64	244	71	639	6.1	3.6	7.9
82-83—Denver-Utah	70	23	1345	130	293	.444	0	0	—	142	175	.811	131	273	404	138	221	4	54	118	39	402	5.8	2.0	5.7
83-84—Utah	75	30	1674	132	264	.500	0	0	—	124	162	.765	140	350	490	157	273	6	55	148	29	388	6.5	2.1	5.2
84-85—Utah	77	34	1276	103	216	.477	0	2	.000	84	112	.750	118	232	350	120	227	5	42	124	30	290	4.5	1.6	3.8
85-86—Sacramento	37	0	324	28	49	.571	0	2	.000	18	22	.818	29	52	81	43	62	0	10	22	3	74	2.2	1.2	2.0
REG. SEASON TOTALS	814	126	17711	2166	4435	.488	0	10	.000	1867	2384	.783	1872	3806	5678	2092	2613	60	694	1576	749	6199	7.0	2.6	7.6
PLAYOFF TOTALS	45	12	860	92	197	.467	0	2	.000	75	94	.798	95	151	246	105	133	2	39	69	24	259	5.5	2.3	5.8

KELLOGG, CLARK CLIFTON JR. b. July 2, 1961 Ht. 6-7 Wt. 225 College—Ohio State

SEASON—TEAM	G	GS	MIN	FGM	FGA	PCT	3FGM	3FGA	PCT	FTM	FTA	PCT	O-RB	D-RB	TOT	AST	PF	DQ	STL	TO	BLK	PTS	RPG	APG	PPG
82-83—Indiana	81	81	2761	680	1420	.479	4	18	.222	261	352	.741	340	520	860	223	298	6	141	217	43	1625	10.6	2.8	20.1
83-84—Indiana	79	79	2676	619	1193	.519	7	21	.333	261	340	.768	230	489	719	234	242	2	121	218	28	1506	9.1	3.0	19.1
84-85—Indiana	77	65	2449	562	1112	.505	7	14	.500	301	396	.760	224	500	724	244	247	2	86	231	26	1432	9.4	3.2	18.6
85-86—Indiana	19	12	568	139	294	.473	4	13	.308	53	69	.768	51	117	168	57	59	2	28	61	8	335	8.8	3.0	17.6
86-87—Indiana	4	4	60	8	22	.364	1	2	.500	3	4	.750	7	4	11	6	12	0	5	4	0	20	2.8	1.5	5.0
REG. SEASON TOTALS	260	241	8514	2008	4041	.497	23	68	.338	879	1161	.757	852	1630	2482	764	858	12	381	731	105	4918	9.5	2.9	18.9

KELLY, ARVESTA b. November 20, 1945 Ht. 6-3 Wt. 195 College—Lincoln (Mo.)

SEASON—TEAM	G	GS	MIN	FGM	FGA	PCT	3FGM	3FGA	PCT	FTM	FTA	PCT	O-RB	D-RB	TOT	AST	PF	DQ	STL	TO	BLK	PTS	RPG	APG	PPG
67-68—Pittsburgh (A)	16	—	146	26	76	.342	3	13	.231	8	13	.615	—	—	33	13	34	0	—	10	—	63	2.1	0.8	3.9
68-69—Minnesota (A)	68	—	1066	155	425	.365	25	105	.238	63	103	.612	—	—	157	61	141	0	—	89	—	398	2.3	0.9	5.9
69-70—Pittsburgh (A)	70	—	2391	384	778	.494	21	74	.284	168	257	.654	—	—	267	226	195	4	—	—	—	957	3.8	3.2	13.7
70-71—Car.-Pitt. (A)	22	—	180	20	35	.571	0	3	.000	18	31	.581	—	—	25	17	34	—	—	—	—	58	1.1	0.8	2.6
71-72—Pitt.-Indiana (A)	12	—	112	13	29	.448	1	3	.333	3	4	.750	—	—	15	14	20	—	—	8	—	30	1.3	1.2	2.5
REG. ABA TOTALS	188	—	3895	598	1343	.445	50	198	.253	260	408	.637	—	—	497	331	424	4	—	107	—	1506	2.6	1.8	8.0
ABA PLAYOFF TOTALS	13	—	77	13	36	.361	7	18	.389	7	8	.875	—	—	16	5	22	0	—	6	—	40	1.2	0.4	3.1

KELLY, GERARD ALLAN (Jerry) b. June 14, 1918 Ht. 6-3 Wt. 185 College—Marshall

SEASON—TEAM	G	GS	MIN	FGM	FGA	PCT	3FGM	3FGA	PCT	FTM	FTA	PCT	O-RB	D-RB	TOT	AST	PF	DQ	STL	TO	BLK	PTS	RPG	APG	PPG
46-47—Boston	43	—	—	91	313	.291	—	—	—	74	111	.667	—	—	—	21	128	—	—	—	—	256	—	0.5	6.0
47-48—Providence	3	—	—	3	10	.300	—	—	—	0	1	.000	—	—	—	0	3	—	—	—	—	6	—	0.0	2.0
REG. SEASON TOTALS	46	—	—	94	323	.291	—	—	—	74	112	.661	—	—	—	21	131	—	—	—	—	262	—	0.5	5.7

KELLY, THOMAS EDWARD (Tom) b. March 5, 1924 Ht. 6-2 Wt. 170 College—New York University

SEASON—TEAM	G	GS	MIN	FGM	FGA	PCT	3FGM	3FGA	PCT	FTM	FTA	PCT	O-RB	D-RB	TOT	AST	PF	DQ	STL	TO	BLK	PTS	RPG	APG	PPG
48-49—Boston	27	—	—	73	218	.335	—	—	—	45	73	.616	—	—	—	38	73	—	—	—	—	191	—	1.4	7.1
REG. SEASON TOTALS	27	—	—	73	218	.335	—	—	—	45	73	.616	—	—	—	38	73	—	—	—	—	191	—	1.4	7.1

KELSER, GREGORY (Greg, Special K) b. September 17, 1957 Ht. 6-7 Wt. 195 College—Michigan State

SEASON—TEAM	G	GS	MIN	FGM	FGA	PCT	3FGM	3FGA	PCT	FTM	FTA	PCT	O-RB	D-RB	TOT	AST	PF	DQ	STL	TO	BLK	PTS	RPG	APG	PPG
79-80—Detroit	50	—	1231	280	593	.472	3	15	.200	146	203	.719	124	152	276	108	176	5	60	140	34	709	5.5	2.2	14.2
80-81—Detroit	25	—	654	120	285	.421	0	2	.000	68	106	.642	53	67	120	45	89	0	34	78	29	308	4.8	1.8	12.3
81-82—Detroit-Seattle	60	10	741	116	271	.428	0	3	.000	105	160	.656	80	113	193	57	131	0	18	84	21	337	3.2	1.0	5.6
82-83—Seattle	80	9	1507	247	450	.549	0	3	.000	173	257	.673	158	245	403	97	243	5	52	149	35	667	5.0	1.2	8.3
83-84—San Diego	80	21	1783	313	603	.519	2	6	.333	250	356	.702	188	203	391	91	249	3	68	195	31	878	4.9	1.1	11.0
84-85—Indiana	10	0	114	21	53	.396	0	1	.000	20	28	.714	6	13	19	13	16	0	7	12	0	62	1.9	1.3	6.2
REG. SEASON TOTALS	305	40	6030	1097	2255	.486	5	30	.167	762	1110	.686	609	793	1402	411	904	13	239	658	150	2961	4.6	1.3	9.7
PLAYOFF TOTALS	5	0	25	2	7	.286	0	0	—	4	4	1.000	4	5	9	2	6	0	1	2	0	8	1.8	0.4	1.6

KELSO, BEN b. April 11, 1949 Ht. 6-3 Wt. 195 College—Central Michigan

SEASON—TEAM	G	GS	MIN	FGM	FGA	PCT	3FGM	3FGA	PCT	FTM	FTA	PCT	O-RB	D-RB	TOT	AST	PF	DQ	STL	TO	BLK	PTS	RPG	APG	PPG
73-74—Detroit	46	—	298	35	96	.365	—	—	—	15	22	.682	15	16	31	18	45	0	12	—	1	85	0.7	0.4	1.8
REG. SEASON TOTALS	46	—	298	35	96	.365	—	—	—	15	22	.682	15	16	31	18	45	0	12	—	1	85	0.7	0.4	1.8
PLAYOFF TOTALS	1	—	1	0	2	.000	—	—	—	0	0	—	0	1	1	1	0	0	0	—	0	0	1.0	1.0	0.0

KEMP, SHAWN T. b. November 26, 1969 Ht. 6-10 Wt. 245 College—Kentucky/Trinity Valley CC

SEASON—TEAM	G	GS	MIN	FGM	FGA	PCT	3FGM	3FGA	PCT	FTM	FTA	PCT	O-RB	D-RB	TOT	AST	PF	DQ	STL	TO	BLK	PTS	RPG	APG	PPG
89-90—Seattle	81	1	1120	203	424	.479	2	12	.167	117	159	.736	146	200	346	26	204	5	47	107	70	525	4.3	0.3	6.5
90-91—Seattle	81	66	2442	462	909	.508	2	12	.167	288	436	.661	267	412	679	144	319	11	77	202	123	1214	8.4	1.8	15.0
91-92—Seattle	64	23	1808	362	718	.504	0	3	.000	270	361	.748	264	401	665	86	261	13	70	156	124	994	10.4	1.3	15.5
92-93—Seattle	78	68	2582	515	1047	.492	0	4	.000	358	503	.712	287	546	833	155	327	13	119	217	146	1388	10.7	2.0	17.8
93-94—Seattle	79	73	2597	533	990	.538	1	4	.250	364	491	.741	312	539	851	207	312	11	142	259	166	1431	10.8	2.6	18.1
REG. SEASON TOTALS	383	231	10549	2075	4088	.508	5	35	.143	1397	1950	.716	1276	2098	3374	618	1423	53	455	941	629	5552	8.8	1.6	14.5
PLAYOFF TOTALS	38	38	1356	206	443	.465	0	1	.000	198	255	.776	160	225	385	76	157	3	47	111	70	610	10.1	2.0	16.1
ALL-STAR TOTALS	2	1	31	3	13	.231	0	0	—	0	0	—	8	6	14	4	7	0	0	6	3	6	7.0	2.0	3.0

KEMPTON, TIMOTHY JOSEPH (Tim) b. January 25, 1964 Ht. 6-10 Wt. 255 College—Notre Dame

SEASON—TEAM	G	GS	MIN	FGM	FGA	PCT	3FGM	3FGA	PCT	FTM	FTA	PCT	O-RB	D-RB	TOT	AST	PF	DQ	STL	TO	BLK	PTS	RPG	APG	PPG
86-87—L.A. Clippers	66	6	936	97	206	.471	0	1	.000	95	137	.693	70	124	194	53	162	6	38	49	12	289	2.9	0.8	4.4
88-89—Charlotte	79	0	1341	171	335	.510	0	1	.000	142	207	.686	91	213	304	102	215	3	41	121	14	484	3.8	1.3	6.1
89-90—Denver	71	14	1061	153	312	.490	0	1	.000	77	114	.675	51	167	218	118	144	2	30	80	9	383	3.1	1.7	5.4
92-93—Phoenix	30	0	167	19	48	.396	0	0	—	18	31	.581	12	27	39	19	30	0	4	16	4	56	1.3	0.6	1.9
93-94—Phoenix-Cha.-Clev.	13	0	136	15	38	.395	0	0	—	9	16	.563	10	14	24	9	33	0	6	11	2	39	1.8	0.7	3.0
REG. SEASON TOTALS	259	20	3641	455	939	.485	0	3	.000	341	505	.675	234	545	779	301	584	11	119	277	41	1251	3.0	1.2	4.8
PLAYOFF TOTALS	6	2	121	17	34	.500	0	0	—	10	10	1.000	11	10	21	12	17	0	3	6	0	44	3.5	2.0	7.3

KENDRICK, FRANK EDWARD b. September 11, 1950 Ht. 6-6 Wt. 200 College—Purdue

SEASON—TEAM	G	GS	MIN	FGM	FGA	PCT	3FGM	3FGA	PCT	FTM	FTA	PCT	O-RB	D-RB	TOT	AST	PF	DQ	STL	TO	BLK	PTS	RPG	APG	PPG
74-75—Golden State	24	—	121	31	77	.403	—	—	—	18	22	.818	19	17	36	6	22	0	11	—	3	80	1.5	0.3	3.3
REG. SEASON TOTALS	24	—	121	31	77	.403	—	—	—	18	22	.818	19	17	36	6	22	0	11	—	3	80	1.5	0.3	3.3

KENNEDY, EUGENE (Goo) b. August 23, 1949 Ht. 6-6 Wt. 205 College—Texas Christian

SEASON—TEAM	G	GS	MIN	FGM	FGA	PCT	3FGM	3FGA	PCT	FTM	FTA	PCT	O-RB	D-RB	TOT	AST	PF	DQ	STL	TO	BLK	PTS	RPG	APG	PPG
71-72—Dallas (A)	65	—	1453	234	406	.576	0	0	—	88	133	.662	—	—	485	65	262	—	—	75	—	556	7.5	1.0	8.6
72-73—Dallas (A)	70	—	1809	365	664	.550	0	0	—	148	232	.638	167	323	490	75	275	8	—	113	—	878	7.0	1.1	12.5
73-74—San Antonio (A)	76	—	1440	194	352	.551	0	0	—	60	87	.690	121	266	387	83	240	—	59	79	15	448	5.1	1.1	5.9
74-75—St. Louis (A)	74	—	1532	281	536	.524	1	1	1.000	129	178	.725	171	202	373	59	190	—	64	92	10	692	5.0	0.8	9.4
75-76—Utah (A)	16	—	271	38	69	.551	0	0	—	24	37	.649	30	50	80	11	43	—	10	12	2	100	5.0	0.7	6.3
76-77—Houston	32	—	277	31	58	.534	—	—	—	3	8	.375	14	37	51	6	45	1	7	—	5	65	1.6	0.2	2.0
REG. NBA TOTALS	32	—	277	31	58	.534	—	—	—	3	8	.375	14	37	51	6	45	1	7	—	5	65	1.6	0.2	2.0
REG. ABA TOTALS	301	—	6505	1112	2027	.549	1	1	1.000	449	667	.673	489	841	1815	293	1010	8	133	371	27	2674	6.0	1.0	8.9
NBA PLAYOFF TOTALS	6	—	35	5	10	.500	—	—	—	2	2	1.000	4	8	12	—	6	0	0	—	0	12	2.0	0.0	2.0
ABA PLAYOFF TOTALS	16	—	165	29	62	.468	0	1	.000	15	20	.750	15	21	42	6	31	0	1	9	1	73	2.6	0.4	4.6

KENNEDY, JOSEPH A. (Joe) b. January 12, 1947 Ht. 6-6 Wt. 210 College—Duke

SEASON—TEAM	G	GS	MIN	FGM	FGA	PCT	3FGM	3FGA	PCT	FTM	FTA	PCT	O-RB	D-RB	TOT	AST	PF	DQ	STL	TO	BLK	PTS	RPG	APG	PPG
68-69—Seattle	72	—	1241	174	441	.395	—	—	—	98	124	.790	—	—	241	60	158	2	—	—	—	446	3.3	0.8	6.2
69-70—Seattle	14	—	82	3	34	.088	—	—	—	2	2	1.000	—	—	20	7	7	0	—	—	—	8	1.4	0.5	0.6
70-71—Pittsburgh (A)	82	—	1382	189	498	.380	0	2	.000	130	160	.813	—	—	341	73	156	—	—	—	—	508	4.2	0.9	6.2
REG. NBA TOTALS	86	—	1323	177	475	.373	—	—	—	100	126	.794	—	—	261	67	165	2	—	—	—	454	3.0	0.8	5.3
REG. ABA TOTALS	82	—	1382	189	498	.380	0	2	.000	130	160	.813	—	—	341	73	156	—	—	—	—	508	4.2	0.9	6.2

KENNEDY, WILLIAM R. (Pickles) b. May 17, 1938 Ht. 5-11 Wt. 180 College—Temple

SEASON—TEAM	G	GS	MIN	FGM	FGA	PCT	3FGM	3FGA	PCT	FTM	FTA	PCT	O-RB	D-RB	TOT	AST	PF	DQ	STL	TO	BLK	PTS	RPG	APG	PPG
60-61—Philadelphia	7	—	52	4	21	.190	—	—	—	4	6	.667	—	—	8	9	6	0	—	—	—	12	1.1	1.3	1.7
REG. SEASON TOTALS	7	—	52	4	21	.190	—	—	—	4	6	.667	—	—	8	9	6	0	—	—	—	12	1.1	1.3	1.7

KENON, LARRY JOE (Special K) b. December 13, 1952 Ht. 6-9 Wt. 210 College—Amarillo/Memphis State

SEASON—TEAM	G	GS	MIN	FGM	FGA	PCT	3FGM	3FGA	PCT	FTM	FTA	PCT	O-RB	D-RB	TOT	AST	PF	DQ	STL	TO	BLK	PTS	RPG	APG	PPG
73-74—New York (A)	84	—	2908	589	1274	.462	0	1	.000	156	222	.703	375	587	962	112	251	—	79	250	19	1334	11.5	1.3	15.9
74-75—New York (A)	84	—	3165	676	1327	.509	1	2	.500	217	282	.770	279	621	900	122	229	—	107	206	30	1570	10.7	1.5	18.7
75-76—San Antonio (A)	81	—	2920	647	1344	.481	0	1	.000	221	283	.781	287	610	897	151	165	—	91	243	43	1515	11.1	1.9	18.7
76-77—San Antonio	78	—	2936	706	1435	.492	—	—	—	293	356	.823	282	597	879	229	190	0	167	—	60	1705	11.3	2.9	21.9
77-78—San Antonio	81	—	2869	698	1426	.489	—	—	—	276	323	.854	245	528	773	268	209	2	115	279	24	1672	9.5	3.3	20.6
78-79—San Antonio	81	—	2947	748	1484	.504	—	—	—	295	349	.845	260	530	790	335	192	1	154	300	19	1791	9.8	4.1	22.1
79-80—San Antonio	78	—	2798	647	1333	.485	1	9	.111	270	345	.783	258	517	775	231	192	0	111	232	18	1565	9.9	3.0	20.1
80-81—Chicago	77	—	2161	454	946	.480	0	0	—	180	245	.735	179	219	398	120	160	2	75	161	18	1088	5.2	1.6	14.1
81-82—Chicago	60	30	1036	192	412	.466	0	0	—	50	88	.568	72	108	180	65	71	0	30	82	7	434	3.0	1.1	7.2
82-83—Chicago-G.S.-Clev.	48	7	770	119	257	.463	0	1	.000	42	57	.737	66	81	147	39	64	0	23	47	9	280	3.1	0.8	5.8
REG. NBA TOTALS	503	37	15517	3564	7293	.489	1	10	.100	1406	1763	.798	1362	2580	3942	1287	1078	5	675	1101	155	8535	7.8	2.6	17.0
REG. ABA TOTALS	249	—	8993	1912	3945	.485	1	4	.250	594	787	.755	941	1818	2759	385	645	0	277	699	92	4419	11.1	1.5	17.7
NBA PLAYOFF TOTALS	31	0	1031	218	508	.429	0	1	.000	65	93	.699	99	171	270	82	84	1	34	58	5	501	8.7	2.6	16.2
ABA PLAYOFF TOTALS	26	—	946	209	423	.494	1	3	.333	59	78	.756	118	189	307	46	66	0	30	90	6	478	11.8	1.8	18.4
NBA ALL-STAR TOTALS	2	1	27	9	18	.500	0	0	—	1	2	.500	3	3	6	1	0	0	0	2	0	19	3.0	0.5	9.5
ABA ALL-STAR TOTALS	3	0	58	19	30	.633	0	0	—	2	3	.667	1	9	16	3	6	—	0	4	0	40	5.3	1.0	13.3

KENVILLE, WILLIAM McGILL (Billy, The Kid) b. December 1, 1930 Ht. 6-2 Wt. 190 College—St. Bonaventure

SEASON—TEAM	G	GS	MIN	FGM	FGA	PCT	3FGM	3FGA	PCT	FTM	FTA	PCT	O-RB	D-RB	TOT	AST	PF	DQ	STL	TO	BLK	PTS	RPG	APG	PPG
53-54—Syracuse	72	—	1405	149	388	.384	—	—	—	136	182	.747	—	—	247	122	138	0	—	—	—	434	3.4	1.7	6.0
54-55—Syracuse	70	—	1380	172	482	.357	—	—	—	154	201	.766	—	—	247	150	132	1	—	—	—	498	3.5	2.1	7.1
55-56—Syracuse	72	—	1278	170	448	.379	—	—	—	195	257	.759	—	—	215	159	132	0	—	—	—	535	3.0	2.2	7.4
56-57—Fort Wayne	71	—	1701	204	608	.336	—	—	—	174	218	.798	—	—	324	172	169	3	—	—	—	582	4.6	2.4	8.2
57-58—Detroit	35	—	649	106	280	.379	—	—	—	46	75	.613	—	—	102	66	68	0	—	—	—	258	2.9	1.9	7.4
59-60—Detroit	25	—	365	47	131	.359	—	—	—	33	41	.805	—	—	71	46	31	0	—	—	—	127	2.8	1.8	5.1
REG. SEASON TOTALS	345	—	6778	848	2337	.363	—	—	—	738	974	.758	—	—	1206	715	670	4	—	—	—	2434	3.5	2.1	7.1
PLAYOFF TOTALS	41	—	761	89	224	.397	—	—	—	106	153	.693	—	—	116	60	103	2	—	—	—	284	2.8	1.5	6.9

KERR, JOHN G. **(Johnny, Red)** b. August 17, 1932 Ht. 6-9 Wt. 230 College—Illinois

SEASON—TEAM	G	GS	MIN	FGM	FGA	PCT	3FGM	3FGA	PCT	FTM	FTA	PCT	O-RB	D-RB	TOT	AST	PF	DQ	STL	TO	BLK	PTS	RPG	APG	PPG
54-55—Syracuse	72	—	1529	301	718	.419	—	—	—	152	223	.682	—	—	474	80	165	2	—	—	—	754	6.6	1.1	10.5
55-56—Syracuse	72	—	2114	377	935	.403	—	—	—	207	316	.655	—	—	607	84	168	3	—	—	—	961	8.4	1.2	13.3
56-57—Syracuse	72	—	2191	333	827	.403	—	—	—	225	313	.719	—	—	807	90	190	3	—	—	—	891	11.2	1.3	12.4
57-58—Syracuse	72	—	2384	407	1020	.399	—	—	—	280	422	.664	—	—	963	88	197	4	—	—	—	1094	13.4	1.2	15.2
58-59—Syracuse	72	—	2671	502	1139	.441	—	—	—	281	367	.766	—	—	1008	142	183	1	—	—	—	1285	14.0	2.0	17.8
59-60—Syracuse	75	—	2372	436	1111	.392	—	—	—	233	310	.752	—	—	913	167	207	4	—	—	—	1105	12.2	2.2	14.7
60-61—Syracuse	79	—	2676	419	1056	.397	—	—	—	218	299	.729	—	—	951	199	230	4	—	—	—	1056	12.0	2.5	13.4
61-62—Syracuse	80	—	2768	541	1220	.443	—	—	—	222	302	.735	—	—	1176	243	272	7	—	—	—	1304	14.7	3.0	16.3
62-63—Syracuse	80	—	2561	507	1069	.474	—	—	—	241	320	.753	—	—	1039	214	208	3	—	—	—	1255	13.0	2.7	15.7
63-64—Philadelphia	80	—	2938	536	1250	.429	—	—	—	268	357	.751	—	—	1017	275	187	2	—	—	—	1340	12.7	3.4	16.8
64-65—Philadelphia	80	—	1810	264	714	.370	—	—	—	126	181	.696	—	—	551	197	132	1	—	—	—	654	6.9	2.5	8.2
65-66—Baltimore	71	—	1770	286	692	.413	—	—	—	209	272	.768	—	—	586	225	148	0	—	—	—	781	8.3	3.2	11.0
REG. SEASON TOTALS	905	—	27784	4909	11751	.418	—	—	—	2662	3682	.723	—	—	10092	2004	2287	34	—	—	—	12480	11.2	2.2	13.8
PLAYOFF TOTALS	76	—	2275	370	959	.386	—	—	—	193	281	.687	—	—	827	152	173	0	—	—	—	933	10.9	2.0	12.3
ALL-STAR TOTALS	3	—	48	5	22	.227	—	—	—	3	5	.600	—	—	19	3	5	0	—	—	—	13	6.3	1.0	4.3

KERR, STEPHEN DOUGLAS **(Steve)** b. September 27, 1965 Ht. 6-3 Wt. 180 College—Arizona

SEASON—TEAM	G	GS	MIN	FGM	FGA	PCT	3FGM	3FGA	PCT	FTM	FTA	PCT	O-RB	D-RB	TOT	AST	PF	DQ	STL	TO	BLK	PTS	RPG	APG	PPG
88-89—Phoenix	26	0	157	20	46	.435	8	17	.471	6	9	.667	3	14	17	24	12	0	7	6	0	54	0.7	0.9	2.1
89-90—Cleveland	78	5	1664	192	432	.444	73	144	.507	63	73	.863	12	86	98	248	59	0	45	74	7	520	1.3	3.2	6.7
90-91—Cleveland	57	4	905	99	223	.444	28	62	.452	45	53	.849	5	32	37	131	52	0	29	40	4	271	0.6	2.3	4.8
91-92—Cleveland	48	20	847	121	237	.511	32	74	.432	45	54	.833	14	64	78	110	29	0	27	31	10	319	1.6	2.3	6.6
92-93—Clev.-Orlando	52	0	481	53	122	.434	6	26	.231	22	24	.917	5	40	45	70	36	0	10	27	1	134	0.9	1.3	2.6
93-94—Chicago	82	0	2036	287	577	.497	52	124	.419	83	97	.856	26	105	131	210	97	0	75	57	3	709	1.6	2.6	8.6
REG. SEASON TOTALS	343	29	6090	772	1637	.472	199	447	.445	264	310	.852	65	341	406	793	285	0	193	235	25	2007	1.2	2.3	5.9
PLAYOFF TOTALS	27	3	408	35	91	.385	9	30	.300	8	8	1.000	4	22	26	30	31	0	16	7	0	87	1.0	1.1	3.2

KERRIS, JOHN E. **(Jack)** b. January 30, 1925 Ht. 6-6 Wt. 215 College—Loyola (Ill.)

SEASON—TEAM	G	GS	MIN	FGM	FGA	PCT	3FGM	3FGA	PCT	FTM	FTA	PCT	O-RB	D-RB	TOT	AST	PF	DQ	STL	TO	BLK	PTS	RPG	APG	PPG
49-50—Tri-Cit.-Ft. Wayne	68	—	—	157	481	.326	—	—	—	169	260	.650	—	—	—	118	175	—	—	—	—	483	—	1.7	7.1
50-51—Fort Wayne	68	—	—	255	689	.370	—	—	—	201	295	.681	—	—	477	181	253	12	—	—	—	711	7.0	2.7	10.5
51-52—Fort Wayne	66	—	2148	186	480	.388	—	—	—	217	325	.668	—	—	514	212	265	16	—	—	—	589	7.8	3.2	8.9
52-53—Ft. Wayne-Balt.	69	—	1424	93	256	.363	—	—	—	88	140	.629	—	—	295	156	165	7	—	—	—	274	4.3	2.3	4.0
REG. SEASON TOTALS	271	—	3572	691	1906	.363	—	—	—	675	1020	.662	—	—	1286	667	858	35	—	—	—	2057	6.3	2.5	7.6
PLAYOFF TOTALS	11	—	94	30	86	.349	—	—	—	32	55	.582	—	—	40	24	47	3	—	—	—	92	5.7	2.2	8.4

KERSEY, JEROME b. June 26, 1962 Ht. 6-7 Wt. 220 College—Longwood College

SEASON—TEAM	G	GS	MIN	FGM	FGA	PCT	3FGM	3FGA	PCT	FTM	FTA	PCT	O-RB	D-RB	TOT	AST	PF	DQ	STL	TO	BLK	PTS	RPG	APG	PPG
84-85—Portland	77	0	958	178	372	.478	0	3	.000	117	181	.646	95	111	206	63	147	1	49	66	29	473	2.7	0.8	6.1
85-86—Portland	79	2	1217	258	470	.549	0	6	.000	156	229	.681	137	156	293	83	208	2	85	113	32	672	3.7	1.1	8.5
86-87—Portland	82	8	2088	373	733	.509	1	23	.043	262	364	.720	201	295	496	194	328	5	122	149	77	1009	6.0	2.4	12.3
87-88—Portland	79	75	2888	611	1225	.499	3	15	.200	291	396	.735	211	446	657	243	302	8	127	161	65	1516	8.3	3.1	19.2
88-89—Portland	76	76	2716	533	1137	.469	6	21	.286	258	372	.694	246	383	629	243	277	6	137	167	84	1330	8.3	3.2	17.5
89-90—Portland	82	82	2843	519	1085	.478	3	20	.150	269	390	.690	251	439	690	188	304	7	121	144	63	1310	8.4	2.3	16.0
90-91—Portland	73	72	2359	424	887	.478	4	13	.308	232	327	.709	169	312	481	227	251	4	101	149	76	1084	6.6	3.1	14.8
91-92—Portland	77	76	2553	398	852	.467	1	8	.125	174	262	.664	241	392	633	243	254	1	114	151	71	971	8.2	3.2	12.6
92-93—Portland	65	50	1719	281	642	.438	8	28	.286	116	183	.634	126	280	406	121	181	2	80	84	41	686	6.2	1.9	10.6
93-94—Portland	78	6	1276	203	469	.433	1	8	.125	101	135	.748	130	201	331	75	213	1	71	63	49	508	4.2	1.0	6.5
REG. SEASON TOTALS	768	447	20617	3778	7872	.480	27	145	.186	1976	2839	.696	1807	3015	4822	1680	2465	37	1007	1247	587	9559	6.3	2.2	12.4
PLAYOFF TOTALS	88	66	2731	519	1092	.475	1	11	.091	315	437	.721	238	349	587	202	326	7	138	140	61	1354	6.7	2.3	15.4

KERWIN, THOMAS VINCENT **(Tom)** b. July 7, 1944 Ht. 6-7 Wt. 210 College—Centenary (La.)

SEASON—TEAM	G	GS	MIN	FGM	FGA	PCT	3FGM	3FGA	PCT	FTM	FTA	PCT	O-RB	D-RB	TOT	AST	PF	DQ	STL	TO	BLK	PTS	RPG	APG	PPG
67-68—Pittsburgh (A)	13	—	68	7	22	.318	0	0	—	0	2	.000	—	—	20	1	5	0	—	2	—	14	1.5	0.1	1.1
REG. ABA TOTALS	13	—	68	7	22	.318	0	0	—	0	2	.000	—	—	20	1	5	0	—	2	—	14	1.5	0.1	1.1

KESSLER, ALEC CHRISTOPHER b. January 13, 1967 Ht. 6-11 Wt. 240 College—Georgia

SEASON—TEAM	G	GS	MIN	FGM	FGA	PCT	3FGM	3FGA	PCT	FTM	FTA	PCT	O-RB	D-RB	TOT	AST	PF	DQ	STL	TO	BLK	PTS	RPG	APG	PPG
90-91—Miami	78	18	1259	199	468	.425	0	4	.000	88	131	.672	115	221	336	31	189	1	17	108	26	486	4.3	0.4	6.2
91-92—Miami	77	4	1197	158	383	.413	0	0	—	94	115	.817	114	200	314	34	185	3	17	58	32	410	4.1	0.4	5.3
92-93—Miami	40	2	415	57	122	.467	5	11	.455	36	47	.766	25	66	91	14	63	0	4	21	12	155	2.3	0.4	3.9
93-94—Miami	15	0	66	11	25	.440	5	9	.556	6	8	.750	4	6	10	2	14	0	1	5	1	33	0.7	0.1	2.2
REG. SEASON TOTALS	210	24	2937	425	998	.426	10	24	.417	224	301	.744	258	493	751	81	451	4	39	192	71	1084	3.6	0.4	5.2
PLAYOFF TOTALS	2	0	12	0	2	.000	0	0	—	2	2	1.000	0	1	1	—	1	0	0	1	0	2	0.5	0.0	1.0

KEYE, JULIUS b. September 5, 1946 d. September 13, 1984 Ht. 6-10 Wt. 225 College—Alcorn A&M/South Carolina State

SEASON—TEAM	G	GS	MIN	FGM	FGA	PCT	3FGM	3FGA	PCT	FTM	FTA	PCT	O-RB	D-RB	TOT	AST	PF	DQ	STL	TO	BLK	PTS	RPG	APG	PPG
69-70—Denver (A)	77	—	1641	245	618	.396	0	7	.000	116	193	.601	—	—	530	47	209	2	—	—	—	606	6.9	0.6	7.9
70-71—Denver (A)	83	—	3634	505	1182	.427	0	5	.000	212	317	.669	370	1084	1454	140	317	—	—	—	—	1222	17.5	1.7	14.7
71-72—Denver (A)	84	—	2557	192	476	.403	0	2	.000	108	174	.621	315	667	982	153	346	—	—	139	—	492	11.7	1.8	5.9
72-73—Denver (A)	83	—	3016	163	375	.435	3	8	.375	130	233	.558	275	617	892	180	269	3	—	134	—	459	10.7	2.2	5.5
73-74—Denver (A)	79	—	2595	147	329	.447	1	5	.200	57	84	.679	225	464	689	135	240	—	40	87	149	352	8.7	1.7	4.5
74-75—Memphis (A)	12	—	233	12	47	.255	0	0	—	6	8	.750	16	39	55	2	26	—	4	8	5	30	4.6	0.2	2.5
REG. ABA TOTALS	418	—	13676	1264	3027	.418	4	27	.148	629	1009	.623	1201	2871	4602	657	1407	5	44	368	154	3161	11.0	1.6	7.6
ABA PLAYOFF TOTALS	19	—	643	57	135	.422	0	2	.000	15	31	.484	73	108	210	42	62	0	0	21	17	129	11.1	2.2	6.8
ABA ALL-STAR TOTALS	1	—	7	0	1	.000	0	0	—	0	0	—	2	2	4	0	1	0	0	0	0	0	4.0	0.0	0.0

KEYS, RANDOLPH (**Rudy**) b. April 19, 1966 Ht. 6-7 Wt. 195 College—Southern Mississippi

SEASON—TEAM	G	GS	MIN	FGM	FGA	PCT	3FGM	3FGA	PCT	FTM	FTA	PCT	O-RB	D-RB	TOT	AST	PF	DQ	STL	TO	BLK	PTS	RPG	APG	PPG
88-89—Cleveland	42	0	331	74	172	.430	1	10	.100	20	29	.690	23	33	56	19	51	0	12	21	6	169	1.3	0.5	4.0
89-90—Clev.-Cha.	80	18	1615	293	678	.432	14	43	.326	101	140	.721	100	153	253	88	224	1	68	84	8	701	3.2	1.1	8.8
90-91—Charlotte	44	0	473	59	145	.407	3	14	.214	19	33	.576	40	60	100	18	93	0	22	35	15	140	2.3	0.4	3.2
REG. SEASON TOTALS	166	18	2419	426	995	.428	18	67	.269	140	202	.693	163	246	409	125	368	1	102	140	29	1010	2.5	0.8	6.1
PLAYOFF TOTALS	1	0	12	0	3	.000	0	1	.000	0	0	—	0	3	3	1	1	0	0	2	0	0	3.0	1.0	0.0

KIDD, WARREN LYNN b. September 9, 1970 Ht. 6-9 Wt. 235 College—Middle Tennessee State

SEASON—TEAM	G	GS	MIN	FGM	FGA	PCT	3FGM	3FGA	PCT	FTM	FTA	PCT	O-RB	D-RB	TOT	AST	PF	DQ	STL	TO	BLK	PTS	RPG	APG	PPG
93-94—Philadelphia	68	14	884	100	169	.592	0	0	—	47	86	.547	76	157	233	19	129	0	19	44	23	247	3.4	0.3	3.6
REG. SEASON TOTALS	68	14	884	100	169	.592	0	0	—	47	86	.547	76	157	233	19	129	0	19	44	23	247	3.4	0.3	3.6

KIFFIN, IRVIN A. JR. b. August 8, 1951 Ht. 6-9 Wt. 225 College—Virginia Union/Oklahoma Baptist

SEASON—TEAM	G	GS	MIN	FGM	FGA	PCT	3FGM	3FGA	PCT	FTM	FTA	PCT	O-RB	D-RB	TOT	AST	PF	DQ	STL	TO	BLK	PTS	RPG	APG	PPG
79-80—San Antonio	26	—	212	32	96	.333	0	0	—	18	25	.720	12	28	40	19	43	0	10	30	2	82	1.5	0.7	3.2
REG. SEASON TOTALS	26	—	212	32	96	.333	0	0	—	18	25	.720	12	28	40	19	43	0	10	30	2	82	1.5	0.7	3.2

KILEY, JOHN F. (**Jack**) b. January 5, 1929 d. February 16, 1982 Ht. 6-1 Wt. 170 College—Syracuse

SEASON—TEAM	G	GS	MIN	FGM	FGA	PCT	3FGM	3FGA	PCT	FTM	FTA	PCT	O-RB	D-RB	TOT	AST	PF	DQ	STL	TO	BLK	PTS	RPG	APG	PPG
51-52—Fort Wayne	47	—	477	44	193	.228	—	—	—	30	54	.556	—	—	49	62	54	2	—	—	—	118	1.0	1.3	2.5
52-53—Fort Wayne	6	—	27	2	10	.200	—	—	—	2	2	1.000	—	—	2	3	7	0	—	—	—	6	0.3	0.5	1.0
REG. SEASON TOTALS	53	—	504	46	203	.227	—	—	—	32	56	.571	—	—	51	65	61	2	—	—	—	124	1.0	1.2	2.3
PLAYOFF TOTALS	1	—	2	1	3	.333	—	—	—	0	0	—	—	—	0	1	0	0	—	—	—	2	0.0	1.0	2.0

KILLUM, EARNEST (**Ernie**) b. June 11, 1948 Ht. 6-3 Wt. 185 College—Stetson

SEASON—TEAM	G	GS	MIN	FGM	FGA	PCT	3FGM	3FGA	PCT	FTM	FTA	PCT	O-RB	D-RB	TOT	AST	PF	DQ	STL	TO	BLK	PTS	RPG	APG	PPG
70-71—Los Angeles	4	—	12	0	4	.000	—	—	—	1	1	1.000	—	—	2	0	1	0	—	—	—	1	0.5	0.0	0.3
REG. SEASON TOTALS	4	—	12	0	4	.000	—	—	—	1	1	1.000	—	—	2	0	1	0	—	—	—	1	0.5	0.0	0.3
PLAYOFF TOTALS	2	—	4	1	1	1.000	—	—	—	2	3	.667	—	—	0	—	1	0	—	—	—	4	0.0	0.0	2.0

KILPATRICK, CARL b. May 16, 1956 Ht. 6-10 Wt. 230 College—Kilgore/NE Louisiana

SEASON—TEAM	G	GS	MIN	FGM	FGA	PCT	3FGM	3FGA	PCT	FTM	FTA	PCT	O-RB	D-RB	TOT	AST	PF	DQ	STL	TO	BLK	PTS	RPG	APG	PPG
79-80—Utah	2	—	6	1	2	.500	0	0	—	1	2	.500	1	3	4	0	1	0	0	0	0	3	2.0	0.0	1.5
REG. SEASON TOTALS	2	—	6	1	2	.500	0	0	—	1	2	.500	1	3	4	0	1	0	0	0	0	3	2.0	0.0	1.5

KIMBALL, THOMAS (**Toby**) b. September 7, 1942 Ht. 6-8 Wt. 220 College—Connecticut

SEASON—TEAM	G	GS	MIN	FGM	FGA	PCT	3FGM	3FGA	PCT	FTM	FTA	PCT	O-RB	D-RB	TOT	AST	PF	DQ	STL	TO	BLK	PTS	RPG	APG	PPG
66-67—Boston	38	—	222	35	97	.361	—	—	—	27	40	.675	—	—	146	13	42	0	—	—	—	97	3.8	0.3	2.6
67-68—San Diego	81	—	2519	354	894	.396	—	—	—	181	306	.592	—	—	947	147	273	3	—	—	—	889	11.7	1.8	11.0
68-69—San Diego	76	—	1680	239	537	.445	—	—	—	117	250	.468	—	—	669	90	216	6	—	—	—	595	8.8	1.2	7.8
69-70—San Diego	77	—	1622	218	508	.429	—	—	—	107	185	.578	—	—	621	95	187	1	—	—	—	543	8.1	1.2	7.1
70-71—San Diego	80	—	1100	111	287	.387	—	—	—	51	108	.472	—	—	406	62	128	1	—	—	—	273	5.1	0.8	3.4
71-72—Milwaukee	74	—	971	107	229	.467	—	—	—	44	81	.543	—	—	312	60	137	0	—	—	—	258	4.2	0.8	3.5
72-73—Kansas City-Omaha	67	—	643	96	220	.436	—	—	—	44	67	.657	—	—	191	27	86	2	—	—	—	236	2.9	0.4	3.5
73-74—Philadelphia	75	—	1592	216	456	.474	—	—	—	127	185	.686	185	367	552	73	199	1	49	—	23	559	7.4	1.0	7.5
74-75—New Orleans	3	—	90	7	23	.304	—	—	—	6	7	.857	8	18	26	4	12	0	2	—	0	20	8.7	1.3	6.7
REG. SEASON TOTALS	571	—	10439	1383	3251	.425	—	—	—	704	1229	.573	193	385	3870	571	1280	14	51	—	23	3470	6.8	1.0	6.1
PLAYOFF TOTALS	14	—	237	28	67	.418	—	—	—	15	27	.556	0	0	83	6	21	0	—	—	0	71	5.9	0.4	5.1

KIMBLE, GREGORY KEVIN (Bo) b. April 9, 1966 Ht. 6-4 Wt. 190 College—USC/Loyola Marymount

SEASON—TEAM	G	GS	MIN	FGM	FGA	PCT	3FGM	3FGA	PCT	FTM	FTA	PCT	O-RB	D-RB	TOT	AST	PF	DQ	STL	TO	BLK	PTS	RPG	APG	PPG
90-91—L.A. Clippers	62	22	1004	159	418	.380	19	65	.292	92	119	.773	42	77	119	76	158	2	30	77	8	429	1.9	1.2	6.9
91-92—L.A. Clippers	34	0	277	44	111	.396	4	13	.308	20	31	.645	13	19	32	17	37	0	10	15	6	112	0.9	0.5	3.3
92-93—New York	9	0	55	14	33	.424	2	8	.250	3	8	.375	3	8	11	5	10	0	1	6	0	33	1.2	0.6	3.7
REG. SEASON TOTALS	105	22	1336	217	562	.386	25	86	.291	115	158	.728	58	104	162	98	205	2	41	98	14	574	1.5	0.9	5.5
PLAYOFF TOTALS	3	0	5	0	1	.000	0	0	—	0	0	—	0	0	0	1	2	0	0	1	0	0	0.0	0.3	0.0

KIMBROUGH, STAN b. April 24, 1966 Ht. 5-11 Wt. 155 College—Central Florida/Xavier (Ohio)

SEASON—TEAM	G	GS	MIN	FGM	FGA	PCT	3FGM	3FGA	PCT	FTM	FTA	PCT	O-RB	D-RB	TOT	AST	PF	DQ	STL	TO	BLK	PTS	RPG	APG	PPG
89-90—Detroit	10	0	50	7	16	.438	0	0	—	2	2	1.000	4	3	7	5	4	0	4	4	0	16	0.7	0.5	1.6
92-93—Sacramento	3	0	15	2	6	.333	1	2	.500	0	0	—	0	0	0	1	1	0	1	0	0	5	0.0	0.3	1.7
REG. SEASON TOTALS	13	0	65	9	22	.409	1	2	.500	2	2	1.000	4	3	7	6	5	0	5	4	0	21	0.5	0.5	1.6

KINCH, CHADWICK OLIVER (Chad) b. May 22, 1958 d. April 3, 1994 Ht. 6-4 Wt. 190 College—UNC-Charlotte

SEASON—TEAM	G	GS	MIN	FGM	FGA	PCT	3FGM	3FGA	PCT	FTM	FTA	PCT	O-RB	D-RB	TOT	AST	PF	DQ	STL	TO	BLK	PTS	RPG	APG	PPG
80-81—Clev.-Dallas	41	—	353	52	141	.369	0	0	—	14	18	.778	7	26	33	45	33	0	11	30	6	118	0.8	1.1	2.9
REG. SEASON TOTALS	41	—	353	52	141	.369	0	0	—	14	18	.778	7	26	33	45	33	0	11	30	6	118	0.8	1.1	2.9

KING, ALBERT b. December 17, 1959 Ht. 6-6 Wt. 215 College—Maryland

SEASON—TEAM	G	GS	MIN	FGM	FGA	PCT	3FGM	3FGA	PCT	FTM	FTA	PCT	O-RB	D-RB	TOT	AST	PF	DQ	STL	TO	BLK	PTS	RPG	APG	PPG
81-82—New Jersey	76	52	1694	391	812	.482	3	13	.231	133	171	.778	105	207	312	142	261	4	64	180	36	918	4.1	1.9	12.1
82-83—New Jersey	79	75	2447	582	1226	.475	6	23	.261	176	227	.775	157	299	456	291	278	5	95	245	41	1346	5.8	3.7	17.0
83-84—New Jersey	79	53	2103	465	946	.492	3	22	.136	232	295	.786	125	263	388	203	258	6	91	208	33	1165	4.9	2.6	14.7
84-85—New Jersey	42	7	860	226	460	.491	0	8	.000	85	104	.817	70	89	159	58	110	0	41	65	9	537	3.8	1.4	12.8
85-86—New Jersey	73	69	1998	438	961	.456	4	23	.174	167	203	.823	116	250	366	181	205	4	58	181	24	1047	5.0	2.5	14.3
86-87—New Jersey	61	15	1291	244	573	.426	13	32	.406	81	100	.810	82	132	214	103	177	5	34	103	28	582	3.5	1.7	9.5
87-88—Philadelphia	72	44	1593	211	540	.391	17	49	.347	78	103	.757	71	145	216	109	219	4	39	93	18	517	3.0	1.5	7.2
88-89—San Antonio	46	11	791	141	327	.431	8	32	.250	37	48	.771	33	107	140	79	97	2	27	74	7	327	3.0	1.7	7.1
91-92—Washington	6	0	59	11	30	.367	2	7	.286	7	8	.875	1	10	11	5	7	0	3	2	0	31	1.8	0.8	5.2
REG. SEASON TOTALS	534	326	12836	2709	5875	.461	56	209	.268	996	1259	.791	760	1502	2262	1171	1612	30	452	1151	196	6470	4.2	2.2	12.1
PLAYOFF TOTALS	21	10	624	135	298	.453	3	9	.333	54	74	.730	44	66	110	49	81	3	26	47	8	327	5.2	2.3	15.6

KING, BERNARD b. December 4, 1956 Ht. 6-7 Wt. 205 College—Tennessee

SEASON—TEAM	G	GS	MIN	FGM	FGA	PCT	3FGM	3FGA	PCT	FTM	FTA	PCT	O-RB	D-RB	TOT	AST	PF	DQ	STL	TO	BLK	PTS	RPG	APG	PPG
77-78—New Jersey	79	—	3092	798	1665	.479	—	—	—	313	462	.677	265	486	751	193	302	5	122	311	36	1909	9.5	2.4	24.2
78-79—New Jersey	82	—	2859	710	1359	.522	—	—	—	349	619	.564	251	418	669	295	326	10	118	323	39	1769	8.2	3.6	21.6
79-80—Utah	19	—	419	71	137	.518	0	0	—	34	63	.540	24	64	88	52	66	3	7	50	4	176	4.6	2.7	9.3
80-81—Golden State	81	—	2914	731	1244	.588	2	6	.333	307	437	.703	178	373	551	287	304	5	72	265	34	1771	6.8	3.5	21.9
81-82—Golden State	79	77	2861	740	1307	.566	1	5	.200	352	499	.705	140	329	469	282	285	6	78	267	23	1833	5.9	3.6	23.2
82-83—New York	68	68	2207	603	1142	.528	0	6	.000	280	388	.722	99	227	326	195	233	5	90	197	13	1486	4.8	2.9	21.9
83-84—New York	77	76	2667	795	1391	.572	0	4	.000	437	561	.779	123	271	394	164	273	2	75	197	17	2027	5.1	2.1	26.3
84-85—New York	55	55	2063	691	1303	.530	1	10	.100	426	552	.772	114	203	317	204	191	3	71	204	15	1809	5.8	3.7	32.9
86-87—New York	6	4	214	52	105	.495	0	0	—	32	43	.744	13	19	32	19	14	0	2	15	0	136	5.3	3.2	22.7
87-88—Washington	69	38	2044	470	938	.501	1	6	.167	247	324	.762	86	194	280	192	202	3	49	211	10	1188	4.1	2.8	17.2
88-89—Washington	81	81	2559	654	1371	.477	5	30	.167	361	441	.819	133	251	384	294	219	1	64	227	13	1674	4.7	3.6	20.7
89-90—Washington	82	82	2687	711	1459	.487	3	23	.130	412	513	.803	129	275	404	376	230	1	51	248	7	1837	4.9	4.6	22.4
90-91—Washington	64	64	2401	713	1511	.472	8	37	.216	383	485	.790	114	205	319	292	187	1	56	255	16	1817	5.0	4.6	28.4
92-93—New Jersey	32	2	430	91	177	.514	2	7	.286	39	57	.684	35	41	76	18	53	0	11	21	3	223	2.4	0.6	7.0
REG. SEASON TOTALS	874	547	29417	7830	15109	.518	23	134	.172	3972	5444	.730	1704	3356	5060	2863	2885	45	866	2791	230	19655	5.8	3.3	22.5
PLAYOFF TOTALS	28	23	934	269	481	.559	1	4	.250	148	203	.729	45	76	121	65	94	0	24	62	6	687	4.3	2.3	24.5
ALL-STAR TOTALS	4	1	84	18	38	.474	0	0	—	9	13	.692	8	9	17	9	10	0	3	4	2	45	4.3	2.3	11.3

KING, CHRISTOPHER DONNELL (Chris) b. July 24, 1969 Ht. 6-8 Wt. 215 College—Wake Forest

SEASON—TEAM	G	GS	MIN	FGM	FGA	PCT	3FGM	3FGA	PCT	FTM	FTA	PCT	O-RB	D-RB	TOT	AST	PF	DQ	STL	TO	BLK	PTS	RPG	APG	PPG
93-94—Seattle	15	0	86	19	48	.396	2	7	.286	15	26	.577	5	10	15	11	12	0	4	12	0	55	1.0	0.7	3.7
REG. SEASON TOTALS	15	0	86	19	48	.396	2	7	.286	15	26	.577	5	10	15	11	12	0	4	12	0	55	1.0	0.7	3.7
PLAYOFF TOTALS	2	0	7	0	1	.000	0	0	—	0	2	.000	0	0	0	—	1	0	1	0	0	0	0.0	0.0	0.0

KING, DANIEL (Dan) b. January 7, 1931 Ht. 6-6 Wt. 220 College—Western Kentucky

SEASON—TEAM	G	GS	MIN	FGM	FGA	PCT	3FGM	3FGA	PCT	FTM	FTA	PCT	O-RB	D-RB	TOT	AST	PF	DQ	STL	TO	BLK	PTS	RPG	APG	PPG
54-55—Baltimore	12	—	103	7	22	.318	—	—	—	5	10	.500	—	—	25	3	5	0	—	—	—	19	2.1	0.3	1.6
REG. SEASON TOTALS	12	—	103	7	22	.318	—	—	—	5	10	.500	—	—	25	3	5	0	—	—	—	19	2.1	0.3	1.6

KING, GEORGE SMITH JR. b. August 16, 1928   Ht. 6-0 Wt. 185 College—Charleston (West Va.)

SEASON—TEAM	G	GS	MIN	FGM	FGA	PCT	3FGM	3FGA	PCT	FTM	FTA	PCT	O-RB	D-RB	TOT	AST	PF	DQ	STL	TO	BLK	PTS	RPG	APG	PPG
51-52—Syracuse	66	—	1889	235	579	.406	—	—	—	188	264	.712	—	—	274	244	199	6	—	—	—	658	4.2	3.7	10.0
52-53—Syracuse	71	—	2519	255	635	.402	—	—	—	284	442	.643	—	—	281	364	244	2	—	—	—	794	4.0	5.1	11.2
53-54—Syracuse	72	—	2370	280	744	.376	—	—	—	257	410	.627	—	—	268	272	179	2	—	—	—	817	3.7	3.8	11.3
54-55—Syracuse	67	—	2015	228	605	.377	—	—	—	140	229	.611	—	—	227	331	148	0	—	—	—	596	3.4	4.9	8.9
55-56—Syracuse	72	—	2343	284	763	.372	—	—	—	176	275	.640	—	—	250	410	150	2	—	—	—	744	3.5	5.7	10.3
57-58—Cincinnati	63	—	2272	235	645	.364	—	—	—	140	227	.617	—	—	306	337	124	0	—	—	—	610	4.9	5.3	9.7
REG. SEASON TOTALS	411	—	13408	1517	3971	.382	—	—	—	1185	1847	.642	—	—	1606	1958	1044	12	—	—	—	4219	3.9	4.8	10.3
PLAYOFF TOTALS	39	—	1327	142	382	.372	—	—	—	144	212	.679	—	—	149	180	113	3	—	—	—	428	3.8	4.6	11.0

KING, JAMES LEONARD (**Jim, Country**) b. February 7, 1941   Ht. 6-2 Wt. 175 College—Tulsa

SEASON—TEAM	G	GS	MIN	FGM	FGA	PCT	3FGM	3FGA	PCT	FTM	FTA	PCT	O-RB	D-RB	TOT	AST	PF	DQ	STL	TO	BLK	PTS	RPG	APG	PPG
63-64—Los Angeles	60	—	762	84	198	.424	—	—	—	66	101	.653	—	—	113	110	99	0	—	—	—	234	1.9	1.8	3.9
64-65—Los Angeles	77	—	1671	184	469	.392	—	—	—	118	151	.781	—	—	214	178	193	2	—	—	—	486	2.8	2.3	6.3
65-66—Los Angeles	76	—	1499	238	545	.437	—	—	—	94	115	.817	—	—	204	223	181	1	—	—	—	570	2.7	2.9	7.5
66-67—San Francisco	67	—	1667	286	685	.418	—	—	—	174	221	.787	—	—	319	240	193	5	—	—	—	746	4.8	3.6	11.1
67-68—San Francisco	54	—	1743	340	800	.425	—	—	—	217	268	.810	—	—	243	226	172	1	—	—	—	897	4.5	4.2	16.6
68-69—San Francisco	46	—	1010	137	394	.348	—	—	—	78	108	.722	—	—	120	123	99	1	—	—	—	352	2.6	2.7	7.7
69-70—S.F.-Cin.	34	—	391	53	129	.411	—	—	—	33	41	.805	—	—	62	52	47	0	—	—	—	139	1.8	1.5	4.1
70-71—Chicago	55	—	645	100	228	.439	—	—	—	64	79	.810	—	—	68	78	55	0	—	—	—	264	1.2	1.4	4.8
71-72—Chicago	73	—	1014	162	356	.455	—	—	—	89	113	.788	—	—	81	101	103	0	—	—	—	413	1.1	1.4	5.7
72-73—Chicago	65	—	785	116	263	.441	—	—	—	44	52	.846	—	—	76	81	76	0	—	—	—	276	1.2	1.2	4.2
REG. SEASON TOTALS	607	—	11187	1700	4067	.418	—	—	—	977	1249	.782	—	—	1500	1412	1218	10	—	—	—	4377	2.5	2.3	7.2
PLAYOFF TOTALS	73	—	1452	246	564	.436	—	—	—	110	151	.728	—	—	246	182	196	4	—	—	—	602	3.4	2.5	8.2
ALL-STAR TOTALS	1	—	7	1	4	.250	—	—	—	2	3	.667	—	—	1	2	3	0	—	—	—	4	1.0	2.0	4.0

KING, LOYD HAROLD b. May 29, 1949   Ht. 6-2 Wt. 180 College—Virginia Tech

SEASON—TEAM	G	GS	MIN	FGM	FGA	PCT	3FGM	3FGA	PCT	FTM	FTA	PCT	O-RB	D-RB	TOT	AST	PF	DQ	STL	TO	BLK	PTS	RPG	APG	PPG
71-72—Memphis (A)	74	—	1153	185	494	.374	21	87	.241	96	119	.807	—	—	113	103	168	—	—	76	—	487	1.5	1.4	6.6
72-73—Memphis (A)	10	—	102	6	29	.207	0	3	.000	7	8	.875	2	10	12	14	20	0	—	4	—	19	1.2	1.4	1.9
REG. ABA TOTALS	84	—	1255	191	523	.365	21	90	.233	103	127	.811	2	10	125	117	188	0	—	80	—	506	1.5	1.4	6.0

KING, MAURICE E. (**Maury**) b. March 12, 1935   Ht. 6-2 Wt. 195 College—Kansas

SEASON—TEAM	G	GS	MIN	FGM	FGA	PCT	3FGM	3FGA	PCT	FTM	FTA	PCT	O-RB	D-RB	TOT	AST	PF	DQ	STL	TO	BLK	PTS	RPG	APG	PPG
59-60—Boston	1	—	19	5	8	.625	—	—	—	0	1	.000	—	—	4	2	3	0	—	—	—	10	4.0	2.0	10.0
62-63—Chicago	37	—	954	94	241	.390	—	—	—	28	34	.824	—	—	102	142	87	0	—	—	—	216	2.8	3.8	5.8
REG. SEASON TOTALS	38	—	973	99	249	.398	—	—	—	28	35	.800	—	—	106	144	90	0	—	—	—	226	2.8	3.8	5.9

KING, REGINALD BIDDINGS (**Reggie**) b. February 14, 1957   Ht. 6-6 Wt. 240 College—Alabama

SEASON—TEAM	G	GS	MIN	FGM	FGA	PCT	3FGM	3FGA	PCT	FTM	FTA	PCT	O-RB	D-RB	TOT	AST	PF	DQ	STL	TO	BLK	PTS	RPG	APG	PPG
79-80—Kansas City	82	—	2052	257	499	.515	0	1	.000	159	219	.726	184	382	566	106	230	2	69	100	31	673	6.9	1.3	8.2
80-81—Kansas City	81	—	2743	472	867	.544	0	0	—	264	386	.684	235	551	786	122	227	2	102	164	41	1208	9.7	1.5	14.9
81-82—Kansas City	80	76	2609	383	752	.509	0	0	—	201	285	.705	162	361	523	173	221	6	84	155	29	967	6.5	2.2	12.1
82-83—Kansas City	58	5	995	104	225	.462	0	0	—	73	96	.760	91	149	240	58	94	1	28	65	11	281	4.1	1.0	4.8
83-84—Seattle	77	42	2086	233	448	.520	0	2	.000	136	206	.660	134	336	470	179	159	2	54	127	24	602	6.1	2.3	7.8
84-85—Seattle	60	5	860	63	149	.423	0	0	—	41	59	.695	44	78	122	53	74	1	28	42	11	167	2.0	0.9	2.8
REG. SEASON TOTALS	438	128	11345	1512	2940	.514	0	3	.000	874	1251	.699	850	1857	2707	691	1005	14	365	653	147	3898	6.2	1.6	8.9
PLAYOFF TOTALS	23	0	788	137	281	.488	0	1	.000	80	111	.721	69	122	191	35	73	0	21	44	13	354	8.3	1.5	15.4

KING, RICHARD THOMAS (**Rich**) b. April 4, 1969   Ht. 7-2 Wt. 260 College—Nebraska

SEASON—TEAM	G	GS	MIN	FGM	FGA	PCT	3FGM	3FGA	PCT	FTM	FTA	PCT	O-RB	D-RB	TOT	AST	PF	DQ	STL	TO	BLK	PTS	RPG	APG	PPG
91-92—Seattle	40	2	213	27	71	.380	0	1	.000	34	45	.756	20	29	49	12	42	0	4	18	5	88	1.2	0.3	2.2
92-93—Seattle	3	0	12	2	5	.400	0	0	—	2	2	1.000	1	4	5	1	1	0	0	3	0	6	1.7	0.3	2.0
93-94—Seattle	27	0	78	15	34	.441	0	1	.000	11	22	.500	9	11	20	8	18	0	1	7	2	41	0.7	0.3	1.5
REG. SEASON TOTALS	70	2	303	44	110	.400	0	2	.000	47	69	.681	30	44	74	21	61	0	5	28	7	135	1.1	0.3	1.9

KING, RON b. 1951   Ht. 6-4 Wt. 195 College—Florida State

SEASON—TEAM	G	GS	MIN	FGM	FGA	PCT	3FGM	3FGA	PCT	FTM	FTA	PCT	O-RB	D-RB	TOT	AST	PF	DQ	STL	TO	BLK	PTS	RPG	APG	PPG
73-74—Kentucky (A)	9	—	126	24	70	.343	2	6	.333	14	17	.824	8	11	19	14	14	—	5	7	2	64	2.1	1.6	7.1
REG. ABA TOTALS	9	—	126	24	70	.343	2	6	.333	14	17	.824	8	11	19	14	14	0	5	7	2	64	2.1	1.6	7.1

KING, RONALD STACEY (**Stacey**) b. January 29, 1967 Ht. 6-11 Wt. 235 College—Oklahoma

SEASON—TEAM	G	GS	MIN	FGM	FGA	PCT	3FGM	3FGA	PCT	FTM	FTA	PCT	O-RB	D-RB	TOT	AST	PF	DQ	STL	TO	BLK	PTS	RPG	APG	PPG
89-90—Chicago	82	2	1777	267	530	.504	0	1	.000	194	267	.727	169	215	384	87	215	0	38	119	58	728	4.7	1.1	8.9
90-91—Chicago	76	6	1198	156	334	.467	0	2	.000	107	152	.704	72	136	208	65	134	0	24	91	42	419	2.7	0.9	5.5
91-92—Chicago	79	12	1268	215	425	.506	2	5	.400	119	158	.753	87	118	205	77	129	0	21	76	25	551	2.6	1.0	7.0
92-93—Chicago	76	3	1059	160	340	.471	2	6	.333	86	122	.705	105	102	207	71	128	0	26	70	20	408	2.7	0.9	5.4
93-94—Chicago-Minn.	49	30	1053	146	341	.428	0	2	.000	93	136	.684	90	151	241	58	121	1	31	83	42	385	4.9	1.2	7.9
REG. SEASON TOTALS	362	53	6355	944	1970	.479	4	16	.250	599	835	.717	523	722	1245	358	727	1	140	439	187	2491	3.4	1.0	6.9
PLAYOFF TOTALS	60	2	707	89	224	.397	2	4	.500	83	112	.741	53	80	133	30	97	0	21	50	15	263	2.2	0.5	4.4

KING, THOMAS VAN DYKE (**Tom**) b. March 9, 1924 Ht. 6-1 Wt. 165 College—Michigan

SEASON—TEAM	G	GS	MIN	FGM	FGA	PCT	3FGM	3FGA	PCT	FTM	FTA	PCT	O-RB	D-RB	TOT	AST	PF	DQ	STL	TO	BLK	PTS	RPG	APG	PPG
46-47—Detroit	58	—	—	97	410	.237	—	—	—	101	160	.631	—	—	—	32	102	—	—	—	—	295	—	0.6	5.1
REG. SEASON TOTALS	58	—	—	97	410	.237	—	—	—	101	160	.631	—	—	—	32	102	—	—	—	—	295	—	0.6	5.1

KINNEY, ROBERT PAUL (**Bob, Hi-Pocket**) b. September 16, 1920 d. September 2, 1985 Ht. 6-6½ Wt. 215 College—Rice

SEASON—TEAM	G	GS	MIN	FGM	FGA	PCT	3FGM	3FGA	PCT	FTM	FTA	PCT	O-RB	D-RB	TOT	AST	PF	DQ	STL	TO	BLK	PTS	RPG	APG	PPG
45-46—Fort Wayne (N)	13	—	—	16	—	—	—	—	—	2	—	—	—	—	—	—	—	—	—	—	—	34	—	—	2.6
46-47—Fort Wayne (N)	44	—	—	102	—	—	—	—	—	42	84	.500	—	—	—	—	129	—	—	—	—	246	—	—	5.6
47-48—Fort Wayne (N)	58	—	—	149	—	—	—	—	—	92	147	.626	—	—	—	—	192	—	—	—	—	390	—	—	6.7
48-49—Ft. Wayne-Boston	58	—	—	161	495	.325	—	—	—	136	234	.581	—	—	—	77	224	—	—	—	—	458	—	1.3	7.9
49-50—Boston	60	—	—	233	621	.375	—	—	—	201	320	.628	—	—	—	100	251	—	—	—	—	667	—	1.7	11.1
REG. NBA TOTALS	118	—	—	394	1116	.353	—	—	—	337	554	.608	—	—	—	177	475	—	—	—	—	1125	—	1.5	9.5
REG. NBL TOTALS	115	—	—	267	—	—	—	—	—	136	231	.580	—	—	—	—	321	—	—	—	—	670	—	—	5.8
NBL PLAYOFF TOTALS	15	—	—	43	—	—	—	—	—	21	32	.656	—	—	—	—	44	—	—	—	—	107	—	—	7.1

KIRK, WALTON JR. (**Walt, Junior**) b. September 3, 1924 Ht. 6-3 Wt. 175 College—Illinois

SEASON—TEAM	G	GS	MIN	FGM	FGA	PCT	3FGM	3FGA	PCT	FTM	FTA	PCT	O-RB	D-RB	TOT	AST	PF	DQ	STL	TO	BLK	PTS	RPG	APG	PPG
47-48—Fort Wayne (N)	45	—	—	62	—	—	—	—	—	44	90	.489	—	—	—	—	—	—	—	—	—	168	—	—	3.7
48-49—Ft. Wayne-Ind.	49	—	—	140	406	.345	—	—	—	167	231	.723	—	—	—	118	127	—	—	—	—	447	—	2.4	9.1
49-50—And.-Tri-Cit	58	—	—	97	361	.269	—	—	—	155	216	.718	—	—	—	103	155	—	—	—	—	349	—	1.8	6.0
51-52—Milwaukee	11	—	396	28	101	.277	—	—	—	55	78	.705	—	—	44	28	47	3	—	—	—	111	4.0	2.5	10.1
REG. NBA TOTALS	118	—	396	265	868	.305	—	—	—	377	525	.718	—	—	44	249	329	3	—	—	—	907	4.0	2.1	7.7
REG. NBL TOTALS	45	—	—	62	—	—	—	—	—	44	90	.489	—	—	—	—	—	—	—	—	—	168	—	—	3.7
NBA PLAYOFF TOTALS	3	—	0	2	7	.286	—	—	—	1	6	.167	—	—	—	1	8	0	—	—	—	5	—	0.3	1.7
NBL PLAYOFF TOTALS	3	—	—	3	—	—	—	—	—	1	6	.167	—	—	—	—	8	—	—	—	—	7	—	—	2.3

KIRKLAND, WILBER b. 1947 Ht. 6-7 Wt. 195 College—Cheyney

SEASON—TEAM	G	GS	MIN	FGM	FGA	PCT	3FGM	3FGA	PCT	FTM	FTA	PCT	O-RB	D-RB	TOT	AST	PF	DQ	STL	TO	BLK	PTS	RPG	APG	PPG
69-70—Pittsburgh (A)	2	—	27	3	7	.429	0	0	—	0	0	—	—	—	11	1	5	0	—	—	—	6	5.5	0.5	3.0
REG. ABA TOTALS	2	—	27	3	7	.429	0	0	—	0	0	—	—	—	11	1	5	0	—	—	—	6	5.5	0.5	3.0

KISSANE, JAMES J. JR. (**Jim**) b. August 17, 1946 Ht. 6-7 Wt. 210 College—Boston College

SEASON—TEAM	G	GS	MIN	FGM	FGA	PCT	3FGM	3FGA	PCT	FTM	FTA	PCT	O-RB	D-RB	TOT	AST	PF	DQ	STL	TO	BLK	PTS	RPG	APG	PPG
68-69—Minnesota (A)	2	—	15	2	6	.333	0	0	—	2	2	1.000	—	—	3	0	3	0	—	1	—	6	1.5	0.0	3.0
REG. ABA TOTALS	2	—	15	2	6	.333	0	0	—	2	2	1.000	—	—	3	0	3	0	—	1	—	6	1.5	0.0	3.0

KISTLER, DOUGLAS C. (**Doug**) b. March 21, 1938 d. February 29, 1980 Ht. 6-9 Wt. 210 College—Duke

SEASON—TEAM	G	GS	MIN	FGM	FGA	PCT	3FGM	3FGA	PCT	FTM	FTA	PCT	O-RB	D-RB	TOT	AST	PF	DQ	STL	TO	BLK	PTS	RPG	APG	PPG
61-62—New York	5	—	13	3	6	.500	—	—	—	2	4	.500	—	—	1	0	2	0	—	—	—	8	0.2	0.0	1.6
REG. SEASON TOTALS	5	—	13	3	6	.500	—	—	—	2	4	.500	—	—	1	0	2	0	—	—	—	8	0.2	0.0	1.6

KITCHEN, CURTIS b. January 30, 1964 Ht. 6-9 Wt. 235 College—South Florida

SEASON—TEAM	G	GS	MIN	FGM	FGA	PCT	3FGM	3FGA	PCT	FTM	FTA	PCT	O-RB	D-RB	TOT	AST	PF	DQ	STL	TO	BLK	PTS	RPG	APG	PPG
86-87—Seattle	6	0	31	3	6	.500	0	1	.000	3	4	.750	4	5	9	1	4	0	2	0	3	9	1.5	0.2	1.5
REG. SEASON TOTALS	6	0	31	3	6	.500	0	1	.000	3	4	.750	4	5	9	1	4	0	2	0	3	9	1.5	0.2	1.5
PLAYOFF TOTALS	8	0	23	1	2	.500	0	0	—	0	4	.000	2	4	6	—	7	0	0	0	2	2	0.8	0.0	0.3

KITE, GREGORY FULLER (Greg) b. August 5, 1961   Ht. 6-11 Wt. 260 College—Brigham Young

SEASON—TEAM	G	GS	MIN	FGM	FGA	PCT	3FGM	3FGA	PCT	FTM	FTA	PCT	O-RB	D-RB	TOT	AST	PF	DQ	STL	TO	BLK	PTS	RPG	APG	PPG
83-84—Boston	35	1	197	30	66	.455	0	0	—	5	16	.313	27	35	62	7	42	0	1	20	5	65	1.8	0.2	1.9
84-85—Boston	55	4	424	33	88	.375	0	0	—	22	32	.688	38	51	89	17	84	3	3	29	10	88	1.6	0.3	1.6
85-86—Boston	64	2	464	34	91	.374	0	1	.000	15	39	.385	35	93	128	17	81	1	3	32	28	83	2.0	0.3	1.3
86-87—Boston	74	1	745	47	110	.427	0	1	.000	29	76	.382	61	108	169	27	148	2	17	34	46	123	2.3	0.4	1.7
87-88—Boston-L.A. Clips	53	19	1063	92	205	.449	0	1	.000	40	79	.506	85	179	264	47	153	1	19	73	58	224	5.0	0.9	4.2
88-89—L.A. Clips-Cha.	70	24	942	65	151	.430	0	0	—	20	41	.488	81	162	243	36	161	1	27	58	54	150	3.5	0.5	2.1
89-90—Sacramento	71	47	1515	101	234	.432	1	1	1.000	27	54	.500	131	246	377	76	201	2	31	76	51	230	5.3	1.1	3.2
90-91—Orlando	82	82	2225	166	338	.491	0	0	—	63	123	.512	189	399	588	59	298	4	25	102	81	395	7.2	0.7	4.8
91-92—Orlando	72	44	1479	94	215	.437	0	1	.000	40	68	.588	156	246	402	44	212	2	30	61	57	228	5.6	0.6	3.2
92-93—Orlando	64	1	640	38	84	.452	0	1	.000	13	24	.542	66	127	193	10	133	1	13	35	12	89	3.0	0.2	1.4
93-94—Orlando	29	0	309	13	35	.371	0	0	—	8	22	.364	22	48	70	4	61	0	2	17	12	34	2.4	0.1	1.2
REG. SEASON TOTALS	669	225	10003	713	1617	.441	1	6	.167	282	574	.491	891	1694	2585	344	1574	17	171	537	414	1709	3.9	0.5	2.6
PLAYOFF TOTALS	53	1	351	20	50	.400	0	0	—	13	22	.591	30	60	90	17	85	1	5	15	13	53	1.7	0.3	1.0

KLEINE, JOSEPH WILLIAM (Joe) b. January 4, 1962   Ht. 7-0 Wt. 270 College—Notre Dame/Arkansas

SEASON—TEAM	G	GS	MIN	FGM	FGA	PCT	3FGM	3FGA	PCT	FTM	FTA	PCT	O-RB	D-RB	TOT	AST	PF	DQ	STL	TO	BLK	PTS	RPG	APG	PPG
85-86—Sacramento	80	18	1180	160	344	.465	0	0	—	94	130	.723	113	260	373	46	224	1	24	107	34	414	4.7	0.6	5.2
86-87—Sacramento	79	31	1658	256	543	.471	0	1	.000	110	140	.786	173	310	483	71	213	2	35	90	30	622	6.1	0.9	7.9
87-88—Sacramento	82	60	1999	324	686	.472	0	0	—	153	188	.814	179	400	579	93	228	1	28	107	59	801	7.1	1.1	9.8
88-89—Sac.-Boston	75	13	1411	175	432	.405	0	2	.000	134	152	.882	124	254	378	67	192	2	33	104	23	484	5.0	0.9	6.5
89-90—Boston	81	4	1365	176	367	.480	0	4	.000	83	100	.830	117	238	355	46	170	0	15	64	27	435	4.4	0.6	5.4
90-91—Boston	72	1	850	102	218	.468	0	2	.000	54	69	.783	71	173	244	21	108	0	15	53	14	258	3.4	0.3	3.6
91-92—Boston	70	3	991	144	293	.491	4	8	.500	34	48	.708	94	202	296	32	99	1	23	27	14	326	4.2	0.5	4.7
92-93—Boston	78	3	1129	108	267	.404	0	6	.000	41	58	.707	113	233	346	39	123	0	17	37	17	257	4.4	0.5	3.3
93-94—Phoenix	74	4	848	125	256	.488	5	11	.455	30	39	.769	50	143	193	45	118	1	14	35	19	285	2.6	0.6	3.9
REG. SEASON TOTALS	691	137	11431	1570	3406	.461	9	34	.265	733	924	.793	1034	2213	3247	460	1475	7	204	624	237	3882	4.7	0.7	5.6
PLAYOFF TOTALS	37	1	412	52	105	.495	0	3	.000	23	29	.793	31	69	100	10	66	0	4	19	11	127	2.7	0.3	3.4

KLIER, LEO ANTHONY (Crystal) b. May 21, 1923   Ht. 6-2 Wt. 170 College—Notre Dame

SEASON—TEAM	G	GS	MIN	FGM	FGA	PCT	3FGM	3FGA	PCT	FTM	FTA	PCT	O-RB	D-RB	TOT	AST	PF	DQ	STL	TO	BLK	PTS	RPG	APG	PPG
46-47—Indianapolis (N)	44	—	—	162	—	—	—	—	—	93	128	.727	—	—	—	97	—	—	—	—	—	417	—	—	9.5
47-48—Indianapolis (N)	56	—	—	227	—	—	—	—	—	152	223	.682	—	—	—	159	—	—	—	—	—	606	—	—	10.8
48-49—Fort Wayne	47	—	—	125	492	.254	—	—	—	97	137	.708	—	—	—	56	124	—	—	—	—	347	—	1.2	7.4
49-50—Fort Wayne	66	—	—	157	516	.304	—	—	—	141	190	.742	—	—	—	121	177	—	—	—	—	455	—	1.8	6.9
REG. NBA TOTALS	113	—	—	282	1008	.280	—	—	—	238	327	.728	—	—	—	177	301	—	—	—	—	802	—	1.6	7.1
REG. NBL TOTALS	100	—	—	389	—	—	—	—	—	245	351	.698	—	—	—	—	256	—	—	—	—	1023	—	—	10.2
NBA PLAYOFF TOTALS	2	—	—	0	3	.000	—	—	—	1	1	1.000	—	—	—	3	1	—	—	—	—	1	—	1.5	0.5
NBL PLAYOFF TOTALS	9	—	—	32	—	—	—	—	—	26	34	.735	—	—	—	—	22	—	—	—	—	90	—	—	10.0

KLOTZ, LOUIS HERMAN (Herm, Red) b. October 21, 1921   Ht. 5-7 Wt. 150 College—Villanova

SEASON—TEAM	G	GS	MIN	FGM	FGA	PCT	3FGM	3FGA	PCT	FTM	FTA	PCT	O-RB	D-RB	TOT	AST	PF	DQ	STL	TO	BLK	PTS	RPG	APG	PPG
47-48—Baltimore	11	—	—	7	31	.226	—	—	—	1	3	.333	—	—	—	7	3	—	—	—	—	15	—	0.6	1.4
REG. SEASON TOTALS	11	—	—	7	31	.226	—	—	—	1	3	.333	—	—	—	7	3	—	—	—	—	15	—	0.6	1.4
PLAYOFF TOTALS	6	—	—	2	9	.222	—	—	—	2	3	.667	—	—	—	1	3	—	—	—	—	6	—	0.2	1.0

KLUEH, DUANE M. b. January 6, 1926   Ht. 6-3 Wt. 175 College—Indiana State

SEASON—TEAM	G	GS	MIN	FGM	FGA	PCT	3FGM	3FGA	PCT	FTM	FTA	PCT	O-RB	D-RB	TOT	AST	PF	DQ	STL	TO	BLK	PTS	RPG	APG	PPG
49-50—Denver-Ft. Wayne	52	—	—	159	414	.384	—	—	—	157	222	.707	—	—	—	91	111	—	—	—	—	475	—	1.8	9.1
50-51—Fort Wayne	61	—	—	157	458	.343	—	—	—	135	184	.734	—	—	—	183	82	143	5	—	—	—	449	3.0	1.3	7.4
REG. SEASON TOTALS	113	—	—	316	872	.362	—	—	—	292	406	.719	—	—	—	183	173	254	5	—	—	—	924	3.0	1.5	8.2
PLAYOFF TOTALS	4	—	—	3	16	.188	—	—	—	5	5	1.000	—	—	—	3	6	10	1	—	—	—	11	1.5	1.5	2.8

KLUTTZ, LONNIE GENE (Gene) b. September 17, 1945   Ht. 6-7 Wt. 220 College—North Carolina A&T

SEASON—TEAM	G	GS	MIN	FGM	FGA	PCT	3FGM	3FGA	PCT	FTM	FTA	PCT	O-RB	D-RB	TOT	AST	PF	DQ	STL	TO	BLK	PTS	RPG	APG	PPG
70-71—Carolina (A)	3	—	8	0	4	.000	0	0	—	0	0	—	—	—	5	0	3	—	—	—	—	0	1.7	0.0	0.0
REG. ABA TOTALS	3	—	8	0	4	.000	0	0	—	0	0	—	—	—	5	0	3	—	—	—	—	0	1.7	0.0	0.0

KNIGHT, NEGELE OSCAR b. March 6, 1967   Ht. 6-1 Wt. 175 College—Dayton

SEASON—TEAM	G	GS	MIN	FGM	FGA	PCT	3FGM	3FGA	PCT	FTM	FTA	PCT	O-RB	D-RB	TOT	AST	PF	DQ	STL	TO	BLK	PTS	RPG	APG	PPG
90-91—Phoenix	64	6	792	131	308	.425	6	25	.240	71	118	.602	20	51	71	191	83	0	20	76	7	339	1.1	3.0	5.3
91-92—Phoenix	42	1	631	103	217	.475	4	13	.308	33	48	.688	16	30	46	112	58	0	24	58	3	243	1.1	2.7	5.8
92-93—Phoenix	52	35	888	124	317	.391	0	7	.000	67	86	.779	28	36	64	145	66	1	23	73	4	315	1.2	2.8	6.1
93-94—Phoenix-S.A.	65	18	1438	225	475	.474	4	21	.190	141	174	.810	28	75	103	197	121	0	34	94	11	595	1.6	3.0	9.2
REG. SEASON TOTALS	223	60	3749	583	1317	.443	14	66	.212	312	426	.732	92	192	284	645	328	1	101	301	25	1492	1.3	2.9	6.7
PLAYOFF TOTALS	17	1	198	35	83	.422	1	6	.167	16	19	.842	5	8	13	28	17	0	4	14	1	87	0.8	1.6	5.1

KNIGHT, ROBERT (Bob) b. 1931 Ht. 6-2 Wt. 185 College—None

SEASON—TEAM	G	GS	MIN	FGM	FGA	PCT	3FGM	3FGA	PCT	FTM	FTA	PCT	O-RB	D-RB	TOT	AST	PF	DQ	STL	TO	BLK	PTS	RPG	APG	PPG
54-55—New York	2	—	29	3	7	.429	—	—	—	1	1	1.000	—	—	1	8	6	0	—	—	—	7	0.5	4.0	3.5
REG. SEASON TOTALS	2	—	29	3	7	.429	—	—	—	1	1	1.000	—	—	1	8	6	0	—	—	—	7	0.5	4.0	3.5

KNIGHT, RONALD EUGENE (Ron) b. August 4, 1947 Ht. 6-7 Wt. 215 College—Cal State-Los Angeles

SEASON—TEAM	G	GS	MIN	FGM	FGA	PCT	3FGM	3FGA	PCT	FTM	FTA	PCT	O-RB	D-RB	TOT	AST	PF	DQ	STL	TO	BLK	PTS	RPG	APG	PPG
70-71—Portland	52	—	662	99	230	.430	—	—	—	19	38	.500	—	—	167	50	99	1	—	—	—	217	3.2	1.0	4.2
71-72—Portland	49	—	483	112	257	.436	—	—	—	31	62	.500	—	—	116	33	52	0	—	—	—	255	2.4	0.7	5.2
REG. SEASON TOTALS	101	—	1145	211	487	.433	—	—	—	50	100	.500	—	—	283	83	151	1	—	—	—	472	2.8	0.8	4.7

KNIGHT, TOBY THOMAS b. May 3, 1955 Ht. 6-9 Wt. 210 College—Notre Dame

SEASON—TEAM	G	GS	MIN	FGM	FGA	PCT	3FGM	3FGA	PCT	FTM	FTA	PCT	O-RB	D-RB	TOT	AST	PF	DQ	STL	TO	BLK	PTS	RPG	APG	PPG
77-78—New York	80	—	1169	222	465	.477	—	—	—	63	97	.649	121	200	321	38	211	1	50	97	28	507	4.0	0.5	6.3
78-79—New York	82	—	2667	609	1174	.519	—	—	—	145	206	.704	201	347	548	124	309	7	61	163	60	1363	6.7	1.5	16.6
79-80—New York	81	—	2945	669	1265	.529	0	2	.000	211	261	.808	201	292	493	150	302	4	117	163	86	1549	6.1	1.9	19.1
81-82—New York	40	0	550	102	183	.557	0	0	—	17	25	.680	33	49	82	23	74	0	14	21	11	221	2.1	0.6	5.5
REG. SEASON TOTALS	283	0	7331	1602	3087	.519	0	2	.000	436	589	.740	556	888	1444	335	896	12	242	444	185	3640	5.1	1.2	12.9
PLAYOFF TOTALS	6	0	48	6	20	.300	0	0	—	4	8	.500	9	10	19	1	9	0	1	3	4	16	3.2	0.2	2.7

KNIGHT, WILLIAM R. (Billy) b. June 9, 1952 Ht. 6-6½ Wt. 200 College—Pittsburgh

SEASON—TEAM	G	GS	MIN	FGM	FGA	PCT	3FGM	3FGA	PCT	FTM	FTA	PCT	O-RB	D-RB	TOT	AST	PF	DQ	STL	TO	BLK	PTS	RPG	APG	PPG
74-75—Indiana (A)	80	—	2559	580	1087	.534	4	16	.250	207	259	.799	284	348	632	168	194	—	115	236	29	1371	7.9	2.1	17.1
75-76—Indiana (A)	70	—	2775	774	1567	.494	6	15	.400	415	501	.828	294	414	708	259	206	—	92	299	23	1969	10.1	3.7	28.1
76-77—Indiana	78	—	3117	831	1687	.493	—	—	—	413	506	.816	223	359	582	260	197	0	117	—	19	2075	7.5	3.3	26.6
77-78—Buffalo	53	—	2155	457	926	.494	—	—	—	301	372	.809	126	257	383	161	137	0	82	167	13	1215	7.2	3.0	22.9
78-79—Boston-Indiana	79	—	2095	441	835	.528	—	—	—	249	296	.841	94	253	347	152	160	1	63	225	8	1131	4.4	1.9	14.3
79-80—Indiana	75	—	1910	385	722	.533	4	15	.267	212	262	.809	136	225	361	155	96	0	82	132	9	986	4.8	2.1	13.1
80-81—Indiana	82	—	2385	546	1025	.533	3	19	.158	341	410	.832	191	219	410	157	155	1	84	177	12	1436	5.0	1.9	17.5
81-82—Indiana	81	19	1803	378	764	.495	9	32	.281	233	282	.826	97	160	257	118	132	0	63	137	14	998	3.2	1.5	12.3
82-83—Indiana	80	54	2262	512	984	.520	3	19	.158	343	408	.841	152	172	324	192	143	0	66	193	8	1370	4.1	2.4	17.1
83-84—Kansas City	75	39	1885	358	729	.491	4	14	.286	243	283	.859	89	166	255	160	122	0	54	155	6	963	3.4	2.1	12.8
84-85—K.C.-S.A.	68	1	800	156	354	.441	11	25	.440	64	73	.877	50	68	118	80	62	0	16	70	2	387	1.7	1.2	5.7
REG. NBA TOTALS	671	113	18412	4064	8026	.506	34	124	.274	2399	2892	.830	1158	1879	3037	1435	1204	2	627	1256	91	10561	4.5	2.1	15.7
REG. ABA TOTALS	150	—	5334	1354	2654	.510	10	31	.323	622	760	.818	578	762	1340	427	400	—	207	535	52	3340	8.9	2.8	22.3
NBA PLAYOFF TOTALS	10	0	153	32	69	.464	0	4	.000	7	10	.700	11	10	21	10	9	0	3	9	0	71	2.1	1.0	7.1
ABA PLAYOFF TOTALS	21	—	906	217	384	.565	0	3	.000	101	119	.849	74	118	192	55	54	—	19	75	1	535	9.1	2.6	25.5
NBA ALL-STAR TOTALS	1	0	12	1	5	.200	0	0	—	2	2	1.000	1	4	5	0	0	0	2	—	0	4	5.0	0.0	4.0
ABA ALL-STAR TOTALS	1	1	23	9	14	.643	0	1	.000	2	2	1.000	0	10	10	2	3	0	0	0	0	20	10.0	2.0	20.0

KNOREK, LEE J. b. July 15, 1921 Ht. 6-7 Wt. 215 College—DeSales/Denison/Detroit

SEASON—TEAM	G	GS	MIN	FGM	FGA	PCT	3FGM	3FGA	PCT	FTM	FTA	PCT	O-RB	D-RB	TOT	AST	PF	DQ	STL	TO	BLK	PTS	RPG	APG	PPG
46-47—New York	22	—	—	62	219	.283	—	—	—	47	72	.653	—	—	—	21	64	—	—	—	—	171	—	1.0	7.8
47-48—New York	48	—	—	99	369	.268	—	—	—	61	120	.508	—	—	—	50	171	—	—	—	—	259	—	1.0	5.4
48-49—New York	60	—	—	156	457	.341	—	—	—	131	183	.716	—	—	—	135	258	—	—	—	—	443	—	2.3	7.4
49-50—Baltimore	1	—	—	0	2	.000	—	—	—	0	0	—	—	—	—	0	4	—	—	—	—	0	—	0.0	0.0
REG. SEASON TOTALS	131	—	—	317	1047	.303	—	—	—	239	375	.637	—	—	—	206	497	—	—	—	—	873	—	1.6	6.7
PLAYOFF TOTALS	14	—	—	50	129	.388	—	—	—	30	48	.625	—	—	—	23	57	6	—	—	—	130	—	1.6	9.3

KNOSTMAN, RICHARD W. (Dick) b. August 9, 1931 Ht. 6-6 Wt. 215 College—Kansas State

SEASON—TEAM	G	GS	MIN	FGM	FGA	PCT	3FGM	3FGA	PCT	FTM	FTA	PCT	O-RB	D-RB	TOT	AST	PF	DQ	STL	TO	BLK	PTS	RPG	APG	PPG
53-54—Syracuse	5	—	47	3	10	.300	—	—	—	7	11	.636	—	—	17	6	9	0	—	—	—	13	3.4	1.2	2.6
REG. SEASON TOTALS	5	—	47	3	10	.300	—	—	—	7	11	.636	—	—	17	6	9	0	—	—	—	13	3.4	1.2	2.6

KNOWLES, W. RODNEY (Rod) b. February 27, 1946 Ht. 6-9 Wt. 215 College—Davidson

SEASON—TEAM	G	GS	MIN	FGM	FGA	PCT	3FGM	3FGA	PCT	FTM	FTA	PCT	O-RB	D-RB	TOT	AST	PF	DQ	STL	TO	BLK	PTS	RPG	APG	PPG
68-69—Phoenix	8	—	40	4	14	.286	—	—	—	1	3	.333	—	—	9	0	10	0	—	—	—	9	1.1	0.0	1.1
68-69—New York (A)	1	—	3	0	0	—	0	0	—	0	0	—	—	—	0	0	1	0	—	—	—	0	0.0	0.0	0.0
REG. NBA TOTALS	8	—	40	4	14	.286	—	—	—	1	3	.333	—	—	9	0	10	0	—	—	—	9	1.1	0.0	1.1
REG. ABA TOTALS	1	—	3	0	0	—	0	0	—	0	0	—	—	—	0	0	1	0	—	—	—	0	0.0	0.0	0.0

KOFOED, BART b. March 24, 1964 Ht. 6-4 Wt. 210 College—Hastings/Nebraska-Kearney

SEASON—TEAM	G	GS	MIN	FGM	FGA	PCT	3FGM	3FGA	PCT	FTM	FTA	PCT	O-RB	D-RB	TOT	AST	PF	DQ	STL	TO	BLK	PTS	RPG	APG	PPG
87-88—Utah	36	0	225	18	48	.375	2	7	.286	8	13	.615	4	11	15	23	42	0	6	18	1	46	0.4	0.6	1.3
88-89—Utah	19	0	176	12	33	.364	0	1	.000	6	11	.545	4	7	11	20	22	0	9	13	0	30	0.6	1.1	1.6
90-91—Golden State	5	0	21	0	3	.000	0	0	—	3	6	.500	2	1	3	4	4	0	0	2	0	3	0.6	0.8	0.6
91-92—Seattle	44	0	239	25	53	.472	1	7	.143	15	26	.577	6	20	26	51	26	0	2	20	2	66	0.6	1.2	1.5
92-93—Boston	7	0	41	3	13	.231	0	1	.000	11	14	.786	0	1	1	10	1	0	2	3	1	17	0.1	1.4	2.4
REG. SEASON TOTALS	111	0	702	58	150	.387	3	16	.188	43	70	.614	16	40	56	108	95	0	19	56	4	162	0.5	1.0	1.5
PLAYOFF TOTALS	10	0	109	9	23	.391	1	5	.200	2	2	1.000	3	11	14	11	18	0	1	9	0	21	1.4	1.1	2.1

KOJIS, DONALD R. (Don) b. July 15, 1939 Ht. 6-3 Wt. 215 College—Marquette

SEASON—TEAM	G	GS	MIN	FGM	FGA	PCT	3FGM	3FGA	PCT	FTM	FTA	PCT	O-RB	D-RB	TOT	AST	PF	DQ	STL	TO	BLK	PTS	RPG	APG	PPG
63-64—Baltimore	78	—	1148	203	484	.419	—	—	—	82	146	.562	—	—	309	57	123	0	—	—	—	488	4.0	0.7	6.3
64-65—Detroit	65	—	836	180	416	.433	—	—	—	62	98	.633	—	—	243	63	115	1	—	—	—	422	3.7	1.0	6.5
65-66—Detroit	60	—	783	182	439	.415	—	—	—	76	141	.539	—	—	260	42	94	0	—	—	—	440	4.3	0.7	7.3
66-67—Chicago	78	—	1655	329	773	.426	—	—	—	134	222	.604	—	—	479	70	204	3	—	—	—	792	6.1	0.9	10.2
67-68—San Diego	69	—	2548	530	1189	.446	—	—	—	300	413	.726	—	—	710	176	259	5	—	—	—	1360	10.3	2.6	19.7
68-69—San Diego	81	—	3130	687	1582	.434	—	—	—	446	596	.748	—	—	776	214	303	6	—	—	—	1820	9.6	2.6	22.5
69-70—San Diego	56	—	1578	338	756	.447	—	—	—	181	241	.751	—	—	388	78	135	1	—	—	—	857	6.9	1.4	15.3
70-71—Seattle	79	—	2143	454	1018	.446	—	—	—	249	320	.778	—	—	435	130	220	3	—	—	—	1157	5.5	1.6	14.6
71-72—Seattle	73	—	1857	322	687	.469	—	—	—	188	237	.793	—	—	335	82	168	1	—	—	—	832	4.6	1.1	11.4
72-73—Kansas City-Omaha	77	—	1240	276	575	.480	—	—	—	106	137	.774	—	—	198	80	128	0	—	—	—	658	2.6	1.0	8.5
73-74—Kansas City-Omaha	77	—	2091	400	836	.478	—	—	—	210	272	.772	126	257	383	110	157	2	77	—	15	1010	5.0	1.4	13.1
74-75—Kansas City-Omaha	21	—	232	46	98	.469	—	—	—	20	30	.667	14	25	39	10	31	0	12	—	1	112	1.9	0.5	5.3
REG. SEASON TOTALS	814	—	19241	3947	8853	.446	—	—	—	2054	2853	.720	140	282	4555	1112	1937	22	89	—	16	9948	5.6	1.4	12.2
PLAYOFF TOTALS	13	—	358	72	163	.442	—	—	—	35	45	.778	1	3	85	26	35	1	1	—	0	179	6.5	2.0	13.8
ALL-STAR TOTALS	2	—	26	4	12	.333	—	—	—	4	5	.800	0	0	7	4	1	0	0	—	0	12	3.5	2.0	6.0

KOMENICH, MILAN (Milo, Miles) b. June 22, 1920 d. May 25, 1977 Ht. 6-7 Wt. 220 College—Wyoming

SEASON—TEAM	G	GS	MIN	FGM	FGA	PCT	3FGM	3FGA	PCT	FTM	FTA	PCT	O-RB	D-RB	TOT	AST	PF	DQ	STL	TO	BLK	PTS	RPG	APG	PPG
46-47—Fort Wayne (N)	36	—	—	50	—	—	—	—	—	23	50	.460	—	—	—	—	59	—	—	—	—	123	—	—	3.4
47-48—Ft. Wayne-And. (N)	50	—	—	127	—	—	—	—	—	44	95	.463	—	—	—	—	119	—	—	—	—	298	—	—	6.0
48-49—Anderson (N)	64	—	—	243	—	—	—	—	—	124	217	.571	—	—	—	—	209	—	—	—	—	610	—	—	9.5
49-50—Anderson	64	—	—	244	861	.283	—	—	—	146	250	.584	—	—	—	124	246	—	—	—	—	634	—	1.9	9.9
REG. NBA TOTALS	64	—	—	244	861	.283	—	—	—	146	250	.584	—	—	—	124	246	—	—	—	—	634	—	1.9	9.9
REG. NBL TOTALS	150	—	—	420	—	—	—	—	—	191	362	.528	—	—	—	—	387	—	—	—	—	1031	—	—	6.9
NBA PLAYOFF TOTALS	8	—	—	26	107	.243	—	—	—	16	28	.571	—	—	—	14	36	1	—	—	—	68	—	1.8	8.5
NBL PLAYOFF TOTALS	21	—	—	50	—	—	—	—	—	39	69	.565	—	—	—	—	49	—	—	—	—	139	—	—	6.6

KOMIVES, HOWARD K. (Howie, Butch) b. May 9, 1941 Ht. 6-1 Wt. 185 College—Bowling Green

SEASON—TEAM	G	GS	MIN	FGM	FGA	PCT	3FGM	3FGA	PCT	FTM	FTA	PCT	O-RB	D-RB	TOT	AST	PF	DQ	STL	TO	BLK	PTS	RPG	APG	PPG
64-65—New York	80	—	2378	381	1020	.374	—	—	—	212	254	.835	—	—	195	265	246	2	—	—	—	974	2.4	3.3	12.2
65-66—New York	80	—	2612	436	1116	.391	—	—	—	241	280	.861	—	—	281	425	278	5	—	—	—	1113	3.5	5.3	13.9
66-67—New York	65	—	2282	402	995	.404	—	—	—	217	253	.858	—	—	183	401	213	1	—	—	—	1021	2.8	6.2	15.7
67-68—New York	78	—	1660	233	631	.369	—	—	—	132	161	.820	—	—	168	246	170	1	—	—	—	598	2.2	3.2	7.7
68-69—N.Y.-Detroit	85	—	2562	379	974	.389	—	—	—	211	264	.799	—	—	299	403	274	1	—	—	—	969	3.5	4.7	11.4
69-70—Detroit	82	—	2418	363	878	.413	—	—	—	190	234	.812	—	—	193	312	247	2	—	—	—	916	2.4	3.8	11.2
70-71—Detroit	82	—	1932	275	715	.385	—	—	—	121	151	.801	—	—	152	262	184	0	—	—	—	671	1.9	3.2	8.2
71-72—Detroit	79	—	2071	262	702	.373	—	—	—	164	203	.808	—	—	172	291	196	0	—	—	—	688	2.2	3.7	8.7
72-73—Buffalo	67	—	1468	163	429	.380	—	—	—	85	98	.867	—	—	118	239	155	1	—	—	—	411	1.8	3.6	6.1
73-74—Kansas City-Omaha	44	—	830	78	192	.406	—	—	—	33	38	.868	10	33	43	97	83	0	32	—	3	189	1.0	2.2	4.3
REG. SEASON TOTALS	742	—	20213	2972	7652	.388	—	—	—	1606	1936	.830	10	33	1804	2941	2046	13	32	—	3	7550	2.4	4.0	10.2
PLAYOFF TOTALS	10	—	263	31	103	.301	—	—	—	14	19	.737	0	0	25	38	35	1	0	—	0	76	2.5	3.8	7.6

KONCAK, JON FRANCIS (Kak) b. May 17, 1963 Ht. 7-0 Wt. 250 College—Southern Methodist

SEASON—TEAM	G	GS	MIN	FGM	FGA	PCT	3FGM	3FGA	PCT	FTM	FTA	PCT	O-RB	D-RB	TOT	AST	PF	DQ	STL	TO	BLK	PTS	RPG	APG	PPG
85-86—Atlanta	82	15	1695	263	519	.507	0	1	.000	156	257	.607	171	296	467	55	296	10	37	111	69	682	5.7	0.7	8.3
86-87—Atlanta	82	19	1684	169	352	.480	0	1	.000	125	191	.654	153	340	493	31	262	2	52	92	76	463	6.0	0.4	5.6
87-88—Atlanta	49	22	1073	98	203	.483	0	2	.000	83	136	.610	103	230	333	19	161	1	36	53	56	279	6.8	0.4	5.7
88-89—Atlanta	74	22	1531	141	269	.524	0	3	.000	63	114	.553	147	306	453	56	238	4	54	60	98	345	6.1	0.8	4.7
89-90—Atlanta	54	28	977	78	127	.614	0	1	.000	42	79	.532	58	168	226	23	182	4	38	47	34	198	4.2	0.4	3.7
90-91—Atlanta	77	61	1931	140	321	.436	1	8	.125	32	54	.593	101	274	375	124	265	6	74	50	76	313	4.9	1.6	4.1
91-92—Atlanta	77	14	1489	111	284	.391	0	12	.000	19	29	.655	62	199	261	132	207	2	50	54	67	241	3.4	1.7	3.1
92-93—Atlanta	78	65	1975	124	267	.464	3	8	.375	24	50	.480	100	327	427	140	264	6	75	52	100	275	5.5	1.8	3.5
93-94—Atlanta	82	78	1823	159	369	.431	0	3	.000	24	36	.667	83	282	365	102	236	1	63	44	125	342	4.5	1.2	4.2
REG. SEASON TOTALS	655	324	14178	1283	2711	.473	4	39	.103	568	946	.600	978	2422	3400	682	2111	36	479	563	701	3138	5.2	1.0	4.8
PLAYOFF TOTALS	41	24	888	71	161	.441	0	0	—	67	101	.663	49	135	184	36	132	3	22	26	43	209	4.5	0.9	5.1

KONDLA, THOMAS A. **(Tom)** b. November 30, 1946 Ht. 6-8 Wt. 225 College—Minnesota

SEASON—TEAM	G	GS	MIN	FGM	FGA	PCT	3FGM	3FGA	PCT	FTM	FTA	PCT	O-RB	D-RB	TOT	AST	PF	DQ	STL	TO	BLK	PTS	RPG	APG	PPG
68-69—Minn.-Houston (A)	42	—	353	58	145	.400	0	1	.000	22	46	.478	—	—	125	13	56	0	—	23	—	138	3.0	0.3	3.3
REG. ABA TOTALS	42	—	353	58	145	.400	0	1	.000	22	46	.478	—	—	125	13	56	0	—	23	—	138	3.0	0.3	3.3

KOPER, HERBERT L. **(Bud)** b. August 9, 1942 Ht. 6-6 Wt. 210 College—Oklahoma City

SEASON—TEAM	G	GS	MIN	FGM	FGA	PCT	3FGM	3FGA	PCT	FTM	FTA	PCT	O-RB	D-RB	TOT	AST	PF	DQ	STL	TO	BLK	PTS	RPG	APG	PPG
64-65—San Francisco	56	—	631	106	241	.440	—	—	—	35	42	.833	—	—	61	43	59	1	—	—	—	247	1.1	0.8	4.4
REG. SEASON TOTALS	56	—	631	106	241	.440	—	—	—	35	42	.833	—	—	61	43	59	1	—	—	—	247	1.1	0.8	4.4

KOPICKI, JOSEPH GERARD **(Joe)** b. June 12, 1960 Ht. 6-9 Wt. 240 College—Detroit

SEASON—TEAM	G	GS	MIN	FGM	FGA	PCT	3FGM	3FGA	PCT	FTM	FTA	PCT	O-RB	D-RB	TOT	AST	PF	DQ	STL	TO	BLK	PTS	RPG	APG	PPG
82-83—Washington	17	1	201	23	51	.451	0	1	.000	21	25	.840	18	44	62	9	21	0	9	8	2	67	3.6	0.5	3.9
83-84—Washington	59	2	678	64	132	.485	1	7	.143	91	112	.813	64	102	166	46	71	0	15	39	5	220	2.8	0.8	3.7
84-85—Denver	42	0	308	50	95	.526	2	3	.667	43	54	.796	29	57	86	29	58	0	13	28	1	145	2.0	0.7	3.5
REG. SEASON TOTALS	118	3	1187	137	278	.493	3	11	.273	155	191	.812	111	203	314	84	150	0	37	75	8	432	2.7	0.7	3.7
PLAYOFF TOTALS	10	0	57	9	22	.409	0	0	—	9	17	.529	2	16	18	4	11	0	1	3	1	27	1.8	0.4	2.7

KORNET, FRANCIS MILTON **(Frank)** b. January 27, 1967 Ht. 6-9 Wt. 225 College—Vanderbilt

SEASON—TEAM	G	GS	MIN	FGM	FGA	PCT	3FGM	3FGA	PCT	FTM	FTA	PCT	O-RB	D-RB	TOT	AST	PF	DQ	STL	TO	BLK	PTS	RPG	APG	PPG
89-90—Milwaukee	57	0	438	42	114	.368	5	20	.250	24	39	.615	25	46	71	21	54	0	14	23	3	113	1.2	0.4	2.0
90-91—Milwaukee	32	0	157	23	62	.371	5	18	.278	7	13	.538	10	14	24	9	28	0	5	11	1	58	0.8	0.3	1.8
REG. SEASON TOTALS	89	0	595	65	176	.369	10	38	.263	31	52	.596	35	60	95	30	82	0	19	34	4	171	1.1	0.3	1.9
PLAYOFF TOTALS	2	0	4	0	1	.000	0	1	.000	0	0	—	0	1	1	—	1	0	0	1	0	0	0.5	0.0	0.0

KOSKI, ANTHONY P. **(Tony)** b. June 26, 1946 Ht. 6-8½ Wt. 215 College—Providence

SEASON—TEAM	G	GS	MIN	FGM	FGA	PCT	3FGM	3FGA	PCT	FTM	FTA	PCT	O-RB	D-RB	TOT	AST	PF	DQ	STL	TO	BLK	PTS	RPG	APG	PPG
68-69—New York (A)	5	—	30	2	7	.286	0	0	—	2	2	1.000	—	—	7	4	9	0	—	2	—	6	1.4	0.8	1.2
REG. ABA TOTALS	5	—	30	2	7	.286	0	0	—	2	2	1.000	—	—	7	4	9	0	—	2	—	6	1.4	0.8	1.2

KOSMALSKI, LEONARD J. **(Len)** b. November 29, 1951 Ht. 6-11½ Wt. 245 College—Tennessee

SEASON—TEAM	G	GS	MIN	FGM	FGA	PCT	3FGM	3FGA	PCT	FTM	FTA	PCT	O-RB	D-RB	TOT	AST	PF	DQ	STL	TO	BLK	PTS	RPG	APG	PPG
74-75—Kansas City-Omaha	67	—	413	33	83	.398	—	—	—	24	29	.828	31	88	119	41	64	0	6	—	6	90	1.8	0.6	1.3
75-76—Kansas City	9	—	93	8	20	.400	—	—	—	4	7	.571	9	16	25	12	11	0	3	—	4	20	2.8	1.3	2.2
REG. SEASON TOTALS	76	—	506	41	103	.398	—	—	—	28	36	.778	40	104	144	53	75	0	9	—	10	110	1.9	0.7	1.4
PLAYOFF TOTALS	6	—	29	2	3	.667	—	—	—	2	3	.667	1	9	10	5	4	0	1	—	0	6	1.7	0.8	1.0

KOSTECKA, ANDREW **(Andy)** b. February 10, 1921 Ht. 6-3 Wt. 205 College—Georgetown

SEASON—TEAM	G	GS	MIN	FGM	FGA	PCT	3FGM	3FGA	PCT	FTM	FTA	PCT	O-RB	D-RB	TOT	AST	PF	DQ	STL	TO	BLK	PTS	RPG	APG	PPG
48-49—Indianapolis	21	—	—	46	110	.418	—	—	—	43	70	.614	—	—	—	14	48	—	—	—	—	135	—	0.7	6.4
REG. SEASON TOTALS	21	—	—	46	110	.418	—	—	—	43	70	.614	—	—	—	14	48	—	—	—	—	135	—	0.7	6.4

KOTTMAN, HAROLD M. b. August 22, 1922 Ht. 6-8 Wt. 220 College—Culver-Stockton

SEASON—TEAM	G	GS	MIN	FGM	FGA	PCT	3FGM	3FGA	PCT	FTM	FTA	PCT	O-RB	D-RB	TOT	AST	PF	DQ	STL	TO	BLK	PTS	RPG	APG	PPG
46-47—Boston	53	—	—	59	188	.314	—	—	—	47	101	.465	—	—	—	17	58	—	—	—	—	165	—	0.3	3.1
REG. SEASON TOTALS	53	—	—	59	188	.314	—	—	—	47	101	.465	—	—	—	17	58	—	—	—	—	165	—	0.3	3.1

KOZELKO, THOMAS WILLIAM **(Tom)** b. July 1, 1951 Ht. 6-8 Wt. 220 College—Toledo

SEASON—TEAM	G	GS	MIN	FGM	FGA	PCT	3FGM	3FGA	PCT	FTM	FTA	PCT	O-RB	D-RB	TOT	AST	PF	DQ	STL	TO	BLK	PTS	RPG	APG	PPG
73-74—Capital	49	—	573	59	133	.444	—	—	—	23	32	.719	52	72	124	25	82	3	21	—	7	141	2.5	0.5	2.9
74-75—Washington	73	—	754	60	167	.359	—	—	—	31	36	.861	50	90	140	41	125	4	28	—	5	151	1.9	0.6	2.1
75-76—Washington	67	—	584	48	99	.485	—	—	—	19	30	.633	19	63	82	33	74	0	19	—	4	115	1.2	0.5	1.7
REG. SEASON TOTALS	189	—	1911	167	399	.419	—	—	—	73	98	.745	121	225	346	99	281	7	68	—	16	407	1.8	0.5	2.2
PLAYOFF TOTALS	25	—	126	15	25	.600	—	—	—	9	11	.818	9	8	17	2	18	1	0	—	1	39	0.7	0.1	1.6

KOZLICKI, RONALD F. **(Ron, Koz)** b. December 12, 1944 Ht. 6-7 Wt. 215 College—Northwestern

SEASON—TEAM	G	GS	MIN	FGM	FGA	PCT	3FGM	3FGA	PCT	FTM	FTA	PCT	O-RB	D-RB	TOT	AST	PF	DQ	STL	TO	BLK	PTS	RPG	APG	PPG
67-68—Indiana (A)	37	—	354	41	121	.339	6	29	.207	21	34	.618	—	—	69	14	31	0	—	19	—	109	1.9	0.4	2.9
REG. ABA TOTALS	37	—	354	41	121	.339	6	29	.207	21	34	.618	—	—	69	14	31	0	—	19	—	109	1.9	0.4	2.9
ABA PLAYOFF TOTALS	2	—	5	0	2	.000	0	1	.000	0	0	—	—	—	1	0	1	0	—	1	—	0	0.5	0.0	0.0

KRAMER, ARVID b. October 2, 1956 Ht. 6-9 Wt. 220 College—Augustana (S.D.)

SEASON—TEAM	G	GS	MIN	FGM	FGA	PCT	3FGM	3FGA	PCT	FTM	FTA	PCT	O-RB	D-RB	TOT	AST	PF	DQ	STL	TO	BLK	PTS	RPG	APG	PPG
79-80—Denver	8	—	45	7	22	.318	0	0	—	2	2	1.000	6	6	12	3	8	0	0	5	5	16	1.5	0.4	2.0
REG. SEASON TOTALS	8	—	45	7	22	.318	0	0	—	2	2	1.000	6	6	12	3	8	0	0	5	5	16	1.5	0.4	2.0

KRAMER, BARRY D. b. November 10, 1942 Ht. 6-4 Wt. 200 College—New York University

SEASON—TEAM	G	GS	MIN	FGM	FGA	PCT	3FGM	3FGA	PCT	FTM	FTA	PCT	O-RB	D-RB	TOT	AST	PF	DQ	STL	TO	BLK	PTS	RPG	APG	PPG
64-65—S.F.-N.Y.	52	—	507	63	186	.339	—	—	—	60	84	.714	—	—	100	41	67	1	—	—	—	186	1.9	0.8	3.6
69-70—New York (A)	7	—	56	10	31	.323	0	1	.000	7	8	.875	—	—	13	3	10	0	—	—	—	27	1.9	0.4	3.9
REG. NBA TOTALS	52	—	507	63	186	.339	—	—	—	60	84	.714	—	—	100	41	67	1	—	—	—	186	1.9	0.8	3.6
REG. ABA TOTALS	7	—	56	10	31	.323	0	1	.000	7	8	.875	—	—	13	3	10	0	—	—	—	27	1.9	0.4	3.9

KRAMER, JOEL BRUCE b. November 30, 1955 Ht. 6-7 Wt. 205 College—San Diego State

SEASON—TEAM	G	GS	MIN	FGM	FGA	PCT	3FGM	3FGA	PCT	FTM	FTA	PCT	O-RB	D-RB	TOT	AST	PF	DQ	STL	TO	BLK	PTS	RPG	APG	PPG
78-79—Phoenix	82	—	1401	181	370	.489	—	—	—	125	176	.710	134	203	337	92	224	2	45	98	23	487	4.1	1.1	5.9
79-80—Phoenix	54	—	711	67	143	.469	0	1	.000	56	70	.800	49	102	151	75	104	0	26	51	5	190	2.8	1.4	3.5
80-81—Phoenix	82	—	1065	136	258	.527	0	1	.000	63	91	.692	77	155	232	88	132	0	35	67	17	335	2.8	1.1	4.1
81-82—Phoenix	56	0	549	55	133	.414	0	0	—	33	42	.786	36	72	108	51	62	0	19	26	11	143	1.9	0.9	2.6
82-83—Phoenix	54	4	458	44	104	.423	0	1	.000	14	16	.875	41	47	88	37	63	0	15	22	6	102	1.6	0.7	1.9
REG. SEASON TOTALS	328	4	4184	483	1008	.479	0	3	.000	291	395	.737	337	579	916	343	585	2	140	264	62	1257	2.8	1.0	3.8
PLAYOFF TOTALS	28	0	384	50	93	.538	0	0	—	29	41	.707	25	53	78	24	64	2	12	18	9	129	2.8	0.9	4.6

KRAMER, STEVEN P. (**Steve**) b. January 1, 1945 Ht. 6-5 Wt. 205 College—Brigham Young

SEASON—TEAM	G	GS	MIN	FGM	FGA	PCT	3FGM	3FGA	PCT	FTM	FTA	PCT	O-RB	D-RB	TOT	AST	PF	DQ	STL	TO	BLK	PTS	RPG	APG	PPG
67-68—Anaheim (A)	50	—	1140	218	497	.439	1	5	.200	129	165	.782	—	—	173	85	149	3	—	96	—	566	3.5	1.7	11.3
68-69—Houston (A)	23	—	701	113	281	.402	0	1	.000	95	117	.812	—	—	85	112	96	4	—	69	—	321	3.7	4.9	14.0
69-70—Carolina (A)	51	—	447	49	107	.458	0	2	.000	63	86	.733	—	—	52	39	70	0	—	—	—	161	1.0	0.8	3.2
REG. ABA TOTALS	124	—	2288	380	885	.429	1	8	.125	287	368	.780	—	—	310	236	315	7	—	165	—	1048	2.5	1.9	8.5
ABA PLAYOFF TOTALS	2	—	20	2	5	.400	0	0	—	3	3	1.000	—	—	4	2	3	0	—	—	—	7	2.0	1.0	3.5

KRAUS, DANIEL JOSEPH (**Dan**) b. February 13, 1923 Ht. 6-0 Wt. 195 College—Georgetown

SEASON—TEAM	G	GS	MIN	FGM	FGA	PCT	3FGM	3FGA	PCT	FTM	FTA	PCT	O-RB	D-RB	TOT	AST	PF	DQ	STL	TO	BLK	PTS	RPG	APG	PPG
48-49—Baltimore	13	—	—	5	35	.143	—	—	—	11	24	.458	—	—	—	7	24	—	—	—	—	21	—	0.5	1.6
REG. SEASON TOTALS	13	—	—	5	35	.143	—	—	—	11	24	.458	—	—	—	7	24	—	—	—	—	21	—	0.5	1.6

KRAUTBLATT, HERBERT (**Herb**) b. November 19, 1926 Ht. 6-1 Wt. 190 College—Rider

SEASON—TEAM	G	GS	MIN	FGM	FGA	PCT	3FGM	3FGA	PCT	FTM	FTA	PCT	O-RB	D-RB	TOT	AST	PF	DQ	STL	TO	BLK	PTS	RPG	APG	PPG
48-49—Baltimore	10	—	—	4	18	.222	—	—	—	5	11	.455	—	—	—	4	14	—	—	—	—	13	—	0.4	1.3
REG. SEASON TOTALS	10	—	—	4	18	.222	—	—	—	5	11	.455	—	—	—	4	14	—	—	—	—	13	—	0.4	1.3

KREBS, JAMES (**Jim, Red**) b. September 8, 1935 d. May 6, 1965 Ht. 6-8 Wt. 230 College—Southern Methodist

SEASON—TEAM	G	GS	MIN	FGM	FGA	PCT	3FGM	3FGA	PCT	FTM	FTA	PCT	O-RB	D-RB	TOT	AST	PF	DQ	STL	TO	BLK	PTS	RPG	APG	PPG
57-58—Minneapolis	68	—	1259	199	527	.378	—	—	—	135	176	.767	—	—	502	27	182	4	—	—	—	533	7.4	0.4	7.8
58-59—Minneapolis	72	—	1578	271	679	.399	—	—	—	92	123	.748	—	—	491	50	212	4	—	—	—	634	6.8	0.7	8.8
59-60—Minneapolis	75	—	1269	237	605	.392	—	—	—	98	136	.721	—	—	327	38	210	2	—	—	—	572	4.4	0.5	7.6
60-61—Los Angeles	75	—	1655	271	692	.392	—	—	—	75	93	.806	—	—	456	68	223	2	—	—	—	617	6.1	0.9	8.2
61-62—Los Angeles	78	—	2012	312	701	.445	—	—	—	156	208	.750	—	—	616	110	290	9	—	—	—	780	7.9	1.4	10.0
62-63—Los Angeles	79	—	1913	272	627	.434	—	—	—	115	154	.747	—	—	502	87	256	2	—	—	—	659	6.4	1.1	8.3
63-64—Los Angeles	68	—	975	134	357	.375	—	—	—	65	85	.765	—	—	283	49	166	6	—	—	—	333	4.2	0.7	4.9
REG. SEASON TOTALS	515	—	10661	1696	4188	.405	—	—	—	736	975	.755	—	—	3177	429	1539	29	—	—	—	4128	6.2	0.8	8.0
PLAYOFF TOTALS	62	—	1129	127	341	.372	—	—	—	75	96	.781	—	—	348	53	211	12	—	—	—	329	5.6	0.9	5.3

KREKLOW, WAYNE R. b. January 4, 1957 Ht. 6-4 Wt. 180 College—Drake

SEASON—TEAM	G	GS	MIN	FGM	FGA	PCT	3FGM	3FGA	PCT	FTM	FTA	PCT	O-RB	D-RB	TOT	AST	PF	DQ	STL	TO	BLK	PTS	RPG	APG	PPG
80-81—Boston	25	—	100	11	47	.234	1	4	.250	7	10	.700	2	10	12	9	20	0	2	10	1	30	0.5	0.4	1.2
REG. SEASON TOTALS	25	—	100	11	47	.234	1	4	.250	7	10	.700	2	10	12	9	20	0	2	10	1	30	0.5	0.4	1.2

KRON, THOMAS M. (**Tommy**) b. February 28, 1943 Ht. 6-5 Wt. 200 College—Kentucky

SEASON—TEAM	G	GS	MIN	FGM	FGA	PCT	3FGM	3FGA	PCT	FTM	FTA	PCT	O-RB	D-RB	TOT	AST	PF	DQ	STL	TO	BLK	PTS	RPG	APG	PPG
66-67—St. Louis	32	—	221	27	87	.310	—	—	—	13	19	.684	—	—	36	46	35	0	—	—	—	67	1.1	1.4	2.1
67-68—Seattle	76	—	1794	277	699	.396	—	—	—	184	233	.790	—	—	355	281	231	4	—	—	—	738	4.7	3.7	9.7
68-69—Seattle	76	—	1124	146	372	.392	—	—	—	96	137	.701	—	—	212	191	179	2	—	—	—	388	2.8	2.5	5.1
69-70—Kentucky (A)	40	—	493	55	147	.374	7	19	.368	41	46	.891	—	—	69	87	80	1	—	—	—	158	1.7	2.2	4.0
REG. NBA TOTALS	184	—	3139	450	1158	.389	—	—	—	293	389	.753	—	—	603	518	445	6	—	—	—	1193	3.3	2.8	6.5
REG. ABA TOTALS	40	—	493	55	147	.374	7	19	.368	41	46	.891	—	—	69	87	80	1	—	—	—	158	1.7	2.2	4.0
NBA PLAYOFF TOTALS	1	—	1	0	1	.000	—	—	—	0	0	—	—	—	0	1	0	—	—	—	—	0	0.0	0.0	0.0

KROPP, THOMAS CARL (**Tom**) b. February 12, 1953 Ht. 6-3 Wt. 205 College—Nebraska-Kearney

SEASON—TEAM	G	GS	MIN	FGM	FGA	PCT	3FGM	3FGA	PCT	FTM	FTA	PCT	O-RB	D-RB	TOT	AST	PF	DQ	STL	TO	BLK	PTS	RPG	APG	PPG
75-76—Washington	25	—	72	7	30	.233	—	—	—	5	6	.833	5	10	15	8	20	0	2	—	0	19	0.6	0.3	0.8
76-77—Chicago	53	—	480	73	152	.480	—	—	—	28	41	.683	21	26	47	39	77	1	18	—	1	174	0.9	0.7	3.3
REG. SEASON TOTALS	78	—	552	80	182	.440	—	—	—	33	47	.702	26	36	62	47	97	1	20	—	1	193	0.8	0.6	2.5
PLAYOFF TOTALS	2	—	4	1	1	1.000	—	—	—	0	0	—	0	0	0	—	3	0	0	—	0	2	0.0	0.0	1.0

KRYSTKOWIAK, LARRY BRETT (**Special K**) b. September 23, 1964 Ht. 6-9 Wt. 240 College—Montana

SEASON—TEAM	G	GS	MIN	FGM	FGA	PCT	3FGM	3FGA	PCT	FTM	FTA	PCT	O-RB	D-RB	TOT	AST	PF	DQ	STL	TO	BLK	PTS	RPG	APG	PPG
86-87—San Antonio	68	2	1004	170	373	.456	1	12	.083	110	148	.743	77	162	239	85	141	1	22	67	12	451	3.5	1.3	6.6
87-88—Milwaukee	50	7	1050	128	266	.481	0	3	.000	103	127	.811	88	143	231	50	137	0	18	57	8	359	4.6	1.0	7.2
88-89—Milwaukee	80	77	2472	362	766	.473	4	12	.333	289	351	.823	198	412	610	107	219	0	93	147	9	1017	7.6	1.3	12.7
89-90—Milwaukee	16	7	381	43	118	.364	0	2	.000	26	33	.788	16	60	76	25	41	0	10	19	2	112	4.8	1.6	7.0
91-92—Milwaukee	79	16	1848	293	660	.444	0	5	.000	128	169	.757	131	298	429	114	218	2	54	115	12	714	5.4	1.4	9.0
92-93—Utah	71	0	1362	198	425	.466	0	1	.000	117	147	.796	74	205	279	68	181	1	42	62	13	513	3.9	1.0	7.2
93-94—Orlando	34	11	682	71	148	.480	0	1	.000	31	39	.795	38	85	123	35	74	0	14	29	4	173	3.6	1.0	5.1
REG. SEASON TOTALS	398	120	8799	1265	2756	.459	5	36	.139	804	1014	.793	622	1365	1987	484	1011	4	253	496	60	3339	5.0	1.2	8.4
PLAYOFF TOTALS	20	16	527	50	122	.410	0	2	.000	47	53	.887	35	74	109	30	53	0	10	24	3	147	5.5	1.5	7.4

KUBERSKI, STEPHEN PAUL (**Steve**) b. November 6, 1947 Ht. 6-8 Wt. 215 College—Illinois/Bradley

SEASON—TEAM	G	GS	MIN	FGM	FGA	PCT	3FGM	3FGA	PCT	FTM	FTA	PCT	O-RB	D-RB	TOT	AST	PF	DQ	STL	TO	BLK	PTS	RPG	APG	PPG
69-70—Boston	51	—	797	130	335	.388	—	—	—	64	92	.696	—	—	257	29	87	0	—	—	—	324	5.0	0.6	6.4
70-71—Boston	82	—	1867	313	745	.420	—	—	—	133	183	.727	—	—	538	58	198	1	—	—	—	759	6.6	1.0	9.3
71-72—Boston	71	—	1128	185	444	.417	—	—	—	80	102	.784	—	—	320	46	130	1	—	—	—	450	4.5	0.6	6.3
72-73—Boston	78	—	762	140	347	.403	—	—	—	65	84	.774	—	—	197	26	92	0	—	—	—	345	2.5	0.3	4.4
73-74—Boston	78	—	985	157	368	.427	—	—	—	86	111	.775	96	141	237	38	125	0	7	—	7	400	3.0	0.5	5.1
74-75—Milwaukee	59	—	517	62	159	.390	—	—	—	44	56	.786	52	71	123	35	59	0	11	—	3	168	2.1	0.6	2.8
75-76—Buffalo-Boston	70	—	967	135	291	.464	—	—	—	71	79	.899	90	169	259	47	133	1	12	—	13	341	3.7	0.7	4.9
76-77—Boston	76	—	860	131	312	.420	—	—	—	63	83	.759	76	133	209	39	89	0	7	—	5	325	2.8	0.5	4.3
77-78—Boston	3	—	14	1	4	.250	—	—	—	0	0	—	1	5	6	0	2	0	1	2	0	2	2.0	0.0	0.7
REG. SEASON TOTALS	568	—	7897	1254	3005	.417	—	—	—	606	790	.767	315	519	2146	338	915	3	38	2	28	3114	3.8	0.6	5.5
PLAYOFF TOTALS	50	—	614	110	239	.460	—	—	—	65	84	.774	24	47	148	24	85	0	1	—	4	285	3.0	0.5	5.7

KUBIAK, LEO R. b. December 25, 1927 Ht. 5-11 Wt. 175 College—Bowling Green State

SEASON—TEAM	G	GS	MIN	FGM	FGA	PCT	3FGM	3FGA	PCT	FTM	FTA	PCT	O-RB	D-RB	TOT	AST	PF	DQ	STL	TO	BLK	PTS	RPG	APG	PPG
48-49—Waterloo (N)	62	—	—	177	—	—	—	—	—	108	142	.761	—	—	—	177	—	—	—	—	—	462	—	—	7.5
49-50—Waterloo	62	—	—	259	794	.326	—	—	—	192	236	.814	—	—	—	201	250	—	—	—	—	710	—	3.2	11.5
REG. NBA TOTALS	62	—	—	259	794	.326	—	—	—	192	236	.814	—	—	—	201	250	—	—	—	—	710	—	3.2	11.5
REG. NBL TOTALS	62	—	—	177	—	—	—	—	—	108	142	.761	—	—	—	177	—	—	—	—	—	462	—	—	7.5

KUCZENSKI, BRUCE JOHN b. February 3, 1961 Ht. 6-10 Wt. 230 College—Connecticut

SEASON—TEAM	G	GS	MIN	FGM	FGA	PCT	3FGM	3FGA	PCT	FTM	FTA	PCT	O-RB	D-RB	TOT	AST	PF	DQ	STL	TO	BLK	PTS	RPG	APG	PPG
83-84—N.J.-Phil.-Indiana	15	2	119	10	37	.270	0	0	—	8	12	.667	7	16	23	8	18	0	1	15	1	28	1.5	0.5	1.9
REG. SEASON TOTALS	15	2	119	10	37	.270	0	0	—	8	12	.667	7	16	23	8	18	0	1	15	1	28	1.5	0.5	1.9

KUDELKA, FRANK CARL (**Apples**) b. June 25, 1925 d. May 4, 1993 Ht. 6-2 Wt. 195 College—St. Mary's (Ca.)

SEASON—TEAM	G	GS	MIN	FGM	FGA	PCT	3FGM	3FGA	PCT	FTM	FTA	PCT	O-RB	D-RB	TOT	AST	PF	DQ	STL	TO	BLK	PTS	RPG	APG	PPG
49-50—Chicago	65	—	—	172	528	.326	—	—	—	89	140	.636	—	—	—	132	198	—	—	—	—	433	—	2.0	6.7
50-51—Wash.-Boston	62	—	—	179	518	.346	—	—	—	83	119	.697	—	—	158	105	211	8	—	—	—	441	2.5	1.7	7.1
51-52—Baltimore	65	—	1583	204	614	.332	—	—	—	198	258	.767	—	—	275	183	220	11	—	—	—	606	4.2	2.8	9.3
52-53—Balt.-Phil.	36	—	567	59	193	.306	—	—	—	44	68	.647	—	—	88	70	109	2	—	—	—	162	2.4	1.9	4.5
REG. SEASON TOTALS	228	—	2150	614	1853	.331	—	—	—	414	585	.708	—	—	521	490	738	21	—	—	—	1642	3.2	2.1	7.2
PLAYOFF TOTALS	3	—	0	4	14	.286	—	—	—	1	5	.200	—	—	5	6	7	0	—	—	—	9	5.0	2.0	3.0

KUESTER, JOHN DeWITT JR. b. February 6, 1955 Ht. 6-2½ Wt. 180 College—North Carolina

SEASON—TEAM	G	GS	MIN	FGM	FGA	PCT	3FGM	3FGA	PCT	FTM	FTA	PCT	O-RB	D-RB	TOT	AST	PF	DQ	STL	TO	BLK	PTS	RPG	APG	PPG
77-78—Kansas City	78	—	1215	145	319	.455	—	—	—	87	105	.829	19	95	114	252	143	1	58	97	1	377	1.5	3.2	4.8
78-79—Denver	33	—	212	16	52	.308	—	—	—	13	14	.929	5	8	13	37	29	0	18	20	1	45	0.4	1.1	1.4
79-80—Indiana	24	—	100	12	34	.353	0	1	.000	5	7	.714	3	11	14	16	8	0	7	5	1	29	0.6	0.7	1.2
REG. SEASON TOTALS	135	—	1527	173	405	.427	0	1	.000	105	126	.833	27	114	141	305	180	1	83	122	3	451	1.0	2.3	3.3

KUKA, RAPHAEL EUGENE **(Ray)** b. February 17, 1922 d. March 27, 1990 Ht. 6-3 Wt. 200 College—Montana State/Notre Dame

SEASON—TEAM	G	GS	MIN	FGM	FGA	PCT	3FGM	3FGA	PCT	FTM	FTA	PCT	O-RB	D-RB	TOT	AST	PF	DQ	STL	TO	BLK	PTS	RPG	APG	PPG
47-48—New York	44	—	—	89	273	.326	—	—	—	50	84	.595	—	—	—	27	117	—	—	—	—	228	—	0.6	5.2
48-49—New York	8	—	—	10	36	.278	—	—	—	5	9	.556	—	—	—	11	16	—	—	—	—	25	—	1.4	3.1
REG. SEASON TOTALS	52	—	—	99	309	.320	—	—	—	55	93	.591	—	—	—	38	133	—	—	—	—	253	—	0.7	4.9
PLAYOFF TOTALS	3	—	—	3	10	.300	—	—	—	2	2	1.000	—	—	—	—	12	—	—	—	—	8	—	0.0	2.7

KUKOC, TONI b. September 18, 1968 Ht. 6-11 Wt. 230 College—None

SEASON—TEAM	G	GS	MIN	FGM	FGA	PCT	3FGM	3FGA	PCT	FTM	FTA	PCT	O-RB	D-RB	TOT	AST	PF	DQ	STL	TO	BLK	PTS	RPG	APG	PPG
93-94—Chicago	75	8	1808	313	726	.431	32	118	.271	156	210	.743	98	199	297	252	122	0	81	167	33	814	4.0	3.4	10.9
REG. SEASON TOTALS	75	8	1808	313	726	.431	32	118	.271	156	210	.743	98	199	297	252	122	0	81	167	33	814	4.0	3.4	10.9
PLAYOFF TOTALS	10	0	194	30	67	.448	8	19	.421	25	34	.735	11	29	40	36	15	0	5	17	3	93	4.0	3.6	9.3

KUNNERT, KEVIN ROBERT b. November 11, 1951 Ht. 7-0 Wt. 230 College—Iowa

SEASON—TEAM	G	GS	MIN	FGM	FGA	PCT	3FGM	3FGA	PCT	FTM	FTA	PCT	O-RB	D-RB	TOT	AST	PF	DQ	STL	TO	BLK	PTS	RPG	APG	PPG
73-74—Buffalo-Houston	64	—	701	105	215	.488	—	—	—	21	33	.636	83	134	217	43	151	1	10	—	54	231	3.4	0.7	3.6
74-75—Houston	75	—	1801	346	676	.512	—	—	—	116	169	.686	214	417	631	108	223	2	34	—	84	808	8.4	1.4	10.8
75-76—Houston	80	—	2335	465	954	.487	—	—	—	102	156	.654	267	520	787	155	315	14	57	—	105	1032	9.8	1.9	12.9
76-77—Houston	81	—	2050	333	685	.486	—	—	—	93	126	.738	210	459	669	154	361	17	35	—	105	759	8.3	1.9	9.4
77-78—Houston	80	—	2152	368	842	.437	—	—	—	93	135	.689	262	431	693	97	315	13	44	141	90	829	8.7	1.2	10.4
78-79—San Diego	81	—	1684	234	501	.467	—	—	—	56	85	.659	202	367	569	113	309	7	45	144	118	524	7.0	1.4	6.5
79-80—Portland	18	—	302	50	114	.439	0	0	—	26	43	.605	37	75	112	29	59	1	7	41	22	126	6.2	1.6	7.0
80-81—Portland	55	—	842	101	216	.468	0	0	—	42	54	.778	98	189	287	67	143	1	17	50	32	244	5.2	1.2	4.4
81-82—Portland	21	0	237	20	48	.417	0	0	—	9	17	.529	20	46	66	18	51	1	3	18	6	49	3.1	0.9	2.3
REG. SEASON TOTALS	555	0	12104	2022	4251	.476	0	0	—	558	818	.682	1393	2638	4031	784	1927	57	252	391	616	4602	7.3	1.4	8.3
PLAYOFF TOTALS	23	0	615	91	195	.467	0	1	.000	30	53	.566	61	115	176	27	95	3	7	3	21	212	7.7	1.2	9.2

KUNZE, TERRY D. b. March 11, 1943 Ht. 6-4 Wt. 210 College—Minnesota

SEASON—TEAM	G	GS	MIN	FGM	FGA	PCT	3FGM	3FGA	PCT	FTM	FTA	PCT	O-RB	D-RB	TOT	AST	PF	DQ	STL	TO	BLK	PTS	RPG	APG	PPG
67-68—Minnesota (A)	46	—	662	83	245	.339	5	11	.455	59	102	.578	—	—	75	47	77	0	—	58	—	230	1.6	1.0	5.0
REG. ABA TOTALS	46	—	662	83	245	.339	5	11	.455	59	102	.578	—	—	75	47	77	0	—	58	—	230	1.6	1.0	5.0

KUPCHAK, MITCHELL **(Mitch)** b. May 24, 1954 Ht. 6-9½ Wt. 230 College—North Carolina

SEASON—TEAM	G	GS	MIN	FGM	FGA	PCT	3FGM	3FGA	PCT	FTM	FTA	PCT	O-RB	D-RB	TOT	AST	PF	DQ	STL	TO	BLK	PTS	RPG	APG	PPG
76-77—Washington	82	—	1513	341	596	.572	—	—	—	170	246	.691	183	311	494	62	204	3	22	—	34	852	6.0	0.8	10.4
77-78—Washington	67	—	1759	393	768	.512	—	—	—	280	402	.697	162	298	460	71	196	1	28	184	42	1066	6.9	1.1	15.9
78-79—Washington	66	—	1604	369	685	.539	—	—	—	223	300	.743	152	278	430	88	141	0	23	120	23	961	6.5	1.3	14.6
79-80—Washington	40	—	451	67	160	.419	0	2	.000	52	75	.693	32	73	105	16	49	1	8	40	8	186	2.6	0.4	4.7
80-81—Washington	82	—	1934	392	747	.525	0	1	.000	240	340	.706	198	371	569	62	195	1	36	161	26	1024	6.9	0.8	12.5
81-82—Los Angeles	26	26	821	153	267	.573	0	0	—	65	98	.663	64	146	210	33	80	1	12	43	10	371	8.1	1.3	14.3
83-84—Los Angeles	34	3	324	41	108	.380	0	0	—	22	34	.647	35	52	87	7	46	0	4	22	6	104	2.6	0.2	3.1
84-85—L.A. Lakers	58	3	716	123	244	.504	0	0	—	60	91	.659	68	116	184	21	104	0	19	48	20	306	3.2	0.4	5.3
85-86—L.A. Lakers	55	0	783	124	257	.482	0	1	.000	84	112	.750	69	122	191	17	102	0	12	64	7	332	3.5	0.3	6.0
REG. SEASON TOTALS	510	32	9905	2003	3832	.523	0	4	.000	1196	1698	.704	963	1767	2730	377	1117	7	164	682	176	5202	5.4	0.7	10.2
PLAYOFF TOTALS	68	0	1215	202	426	.474	0	1	.000	120	185	.649	121	200	321	44	164	1	13	66	15	524	4.7	0.6	7.7

KUPEC, CHARLES J. **(C.J.)** b. January 16, 1953 Ht. 6-6 Wt. 220 College—Michigan

SEASON—TEAM	G	GS	MIN	FGM	FGA	PCT	3FGM	3FGA	PCT	FTM	FTA	PCT	O-RB	D-RB	TOT	AST	PF	DQ	STL	TO	BLK	PTS	RPG	APG	PPG
75-76—Los Angeles	16	—	55	10	40	.250	—	—	—	7	11	.636	4	19	23	5	7	0	3	—	0	27	1.4	0.3	1.7
76-77—Los Angeles	82	—	908	153	342	.447	—	—	—	78	101	.772	76	123	199	53	113	0	18	—	4	384	2.4	0.6	4.7
77-78—Houston	49	—	626	84	197	.426	—	—	—	27	33	.818	27	64	91	50	54	0	10	24	3	195	1.9	1.0	4.0
REG. SEASON TOTALS	147	—	1589	247	579	.427	—	—	—	112	145	.772	107	206	313	108	174	0	31	24	7	606	2.1	0.7	4.1
PLAYOFF TOTALS	11	—	57	8	18	.444	—	—	—	5	7	.714	3	13	16	4	7	0	3	—	0	21	1.5	0.4	1.9

LACEFIELD, REGGIE b. April 10, 1945 Ht. 6-6 Wt. 230 College—Western Michigan

SEASON—TEAM	G	GS	MIN	FGM	FGA	PCT	3FGM	3FGA	PCT	FTM	FTA	PCT	O-RB	D-RB	TOT	AST	PF	DQ	STL	TO	BLK	PTS	RPG	APG	PPG
68-69—Kentucky (A)	8	—	48	11	22	.500	0	1	.000	2	4	.500	—	—	11	0	9	0	—	3	—	24	1.4	0.0	3.0
REG. ABA TOTALS	8	—	48	11	22	.500	0	1	.000	2	4	.500	—	—	11	0	9	0	—	3	—	24	1.4	0.0	3.0

LACEY, SAMUEL (Sam) b. March 28, 1948 Ht. 6-10 Wt. 235 College—New Mexico State

SEASON—TEAM	G	GS	MIN	FGM	FGA	PCT	3FGM	3FGA	PCT	FTM	FTA	PCT	O-RB	D-RB	TOT	AST	PF	DQ	STL	TO	BLK	PTS	RPG	APG	PPG
70-71—Cincinnati	81	—	2648	467	1117	.418	—	—	—	156	227	.687	—	—	913	117	270	8	—	—	—	1090	11.3	1.4	13.5
71-72—Cincinnati	81	—	2832	410	972	.422	—	—	—	119	169	.704	—	—	968	173	284	6	—	—	—	939	12.0	2.1	11.6
72-73—Kansas City-Omaha	79	—	2930	471	994	.474	—	—	—	126	178	.708	—	—	933	189	283	6	—	—	—	1068	11.8	2.4	13.5
73-74—Kansas City-Omaha	79	—	3107	467	982	.476	—	—	—	185	247	.749	293	762	1055	299	254	3	126	—	184	1119	13.4	3.8	14.2
74-75—Kansas City-Omaha	81	—	3378	392	917	.427	—	—	—	144	191	.754	228	921	1149	428	274	4	139	—	168	928	14.2	5.3	11.5
75-76—Kansas City	81	—	3083	409	1019	.401	—	—	—	217	286	.759	218	806	1024	378	286	7	132	—	134	1035	12.6	4.7	12.8
76-77—Kansas City	82	—	2595	327	774	.422	—	—	—	215	282	.762	189	545	734	386	292	9	119	—	133	869	9.0	4.7	10.6
77-78—Kansas City	77	—	2131	265	590	.449	—	—	—	134	187	.717	155	487	642	300	264	7	120	186	108	664	8.3	3.9	8.6
78-79—Kansas City	82	—	2627	350	697	.502	—	—	—	167	226	.739	179	523	702	430	309	11	106	245	141	867	8.6	5.2	10.6
79-80—Kansas City	81	—	2412	303	677	.448	0	1	.000	137	185	.741	172	473	645	460	307	8	111	211	109	743	8.0	5.7	9.2
80-81—Kansas City	82	—	2228	237	536	.442	1	5	.200	92	117	.786	131	453	584	399	302	5	95	182	120	567	7.1	4.9	6.9
81-82—K.C.-N.J.	56	7	670	67	154	.435	0	1	.000	27	37	.730	20	87	107	77	139	1	22	56	38	161	1.9	1.4	2.9
82-83—Cleveland	60	33	1232	111	264	.420	2	9	.222	29	37	.784	62	169	231	118	209	3	29	98	25	253	3.9	2.0	4.2
REG. SEASON TOTALS	1002	40	31873	4276	9693	.441	3	16	.188	1748	2369	.738	1647	5226	9687	3754	3473	78	999	978	1160	10303	9.7	3.7	10.3
PLAYOFF TOTALS	29	0	1074	107	267	.401	1	4	.250	59	76	.776	68	219	287	144	113	5	56	66	44	274	9.9	5.0	9.4
ALL-STAR TOTALS	1	0	17	2	6	.333	0	0	—	2	2	1.000	3	4	7	1	2	0	2	—	1	6	7.0	1.0	6.0

LACKEY, ROBERT (Bob) b. April 4, 1949 Ht. 6-6 Wt. 210 College—Casper/Marquette

SEASON—TEAM	G	GS	MIN	FGM	FGA	PCT	3FGM	3FGA	PCT	FTM	FTA	PCT	O-RB	D-RB	TOT	AST	PF	DQ	STL	TO	BLK	PTS	RPG	APG	PPG
72-73—New York (A)	68	—	1185	153	355	.431	2	5	.400	99	167	.593	60	100	160	136	170	0	—	120	—	407	2.4	2.0	6.0
73-74—New York (A)	3	—	15	3	7	.429	0	0	—	0	0	—	3	1	4	1	2	—	1	1	0	6	1.3	0.3	2.0
REG. ABA TOTALS	71	—	1200	156	362	.431	2	5	.400	99	167	.593	63	101	164	137	172	0	1	121	0	413	2.3	1.9	5.8
ABA PLAYOFF TOTALS	5	—	60	4	8	.500	0	2	.000	4	11	.364	0	0	8	5	10	0	0	7	0	12	1.6	1.0	2.4

LACOUR, FRED b. February 7, 1938 d. August 1972 Ht. 6-5 Wt. 210 College—San Francisco

SEASON—TEAM	G	GS	MIN	FGM	FGA	PCT	3FGM	3FGA	PCT	FTM	FTA	PCT	O-RB	D-RB	TOT	AST	PF	DQ	STL	TO	BLK	PTS	RPG	APG	PPG
60-61—St. Louis	55	—	722	123	295	.417	—	—	—	63	84	.750	—	—	178	84	73	0	—	—	—	309	3.2	1.5	5.6
61-62—St. Louis	73	—	1507	230	536	.429	—	—	—	106	130	.815	—	—	272	166	168	3	—	—	—	566	3.7	2.3	7.8
62-63—San Francisco	16	—	171	28	73	.384	—	—	—	9	16	.563	—	—	24	19	27	0	—	—	—	65	1.5	1.2	4.1
REG. SEASON TOTALS	144	—	2400	381	904	.421	—	—	—	178	230	.774	—	—	474	269	268	3	—	—	—	940	3.3	1.9	6.5
PLAYOFF TOTALS	5	—	47	7	21	.333	—	—	—	6	7	.857	—	—	6	4	6	0	—	—	—	20	1.2	0.8	4.0

LACY, EDGAR EDDIE b. August 2, 1944 Ht. 6-6 Wt. 190 College—UCLA

SEASON—TEAM	G	GS	MIN	FGM	FGA	PCT	3FGM	3FGA	PCT	FTM	FTA	PCT	O-RB	D-RB	TOT	AST	PF	DQ	STL	TO	BLK	PTS	RPG	APG	PPG
68-69—Los Angeles (A)	46	—	609	98	219	.447	0	2	.000	38	67	.567	—	—	180	30	92	1	—	63	—	234	3.9	0.7	5.1
REG. ABA TOTALS	46	—	609	98	219	.447	0	2	.000	38	67	.567	—	—	180	30	92	1	—	63	—	234	3.9	0.7	5.1

LADNER, WENDALL b. October 6, 1948 d. June 24, 1975 Ht. 6-5 Wt. 220 College—Southern Mississippi

SEASON—TEAM	G	GS	MIN	FGM	FGA	PCT	3FGM	3FGA	PCT	FTM	FTA	PCT	O-RB	D-RB	TOT	AST	PF	DQ	STL	TO	BLK	PTS	RPG	APG	PPG
70-71—Memphis (A)	77	—	2504	572	1308	.437	8	29	.276	154	219	.703	337	538	875	160	334	—	—	—	—	1306	11.4	2.1	17.0
71-72—Memphis-Car. (A)	82	—	2446	491	1287	.382	61	236	.258	122	159	.767	244	589	833	166	347	—	—	215	—	1165	10.2	2.0	14.2
72-73—Memphis-Ken. (A)	52	—	932	146	446	.327	12	53	.226	55	73	.753	94	183	277	107	186	4	—	78	—	359	5.3	2.1	6.9
73-74—Ken.-N.Y. (A)	64	—	1565	244	670	.364	24	90	.267	29	53	.547	110	318	428	149	233	—	108	128	6	541	6.7	2.3	8.5
74-75—New York (A)	25	—	436	45	173	.260	7	36	.194	6	10	.600	21	47	68	39	68	—	32	23	1	103	2.7	1.6	4.1
REG. ABA TOTALS	300	—	7883	1498	3884	.386	112	444	.252	366	514	.712	806	1675	2481	621	1168	4	140	444	7	3474	8.3	2.1	11.6
ABA PLAYOFF TOTALS	40	—	718	131	359	.365	23	86	.267	20	33	.606	19	56	171	69	145	0	56	45	0	305	4.3	1.7	7.6
ABA ALL-STAR TOTALS	2	—	34	8	16	.500	0	1	.000	0	0	—	3	10	13	1	5	—	0	2	0	16	6.5	0.5	8.0

LAETTNER, CHRISTIAN DONALD b. August 17, 1969 Ht. 6-11 Wt. 245 College—Duke

SEASON—TEAM	G	GS	MIN	FGM	FGA	PCT	3FGM	3FGA	PCT	FTM	FTA	PCT	O-RB	D-RB	TOT	AST	PF	DQ	STL	TO	BLK	PTS	RPG	APG	PPG
92-93—Minnesota	81	81	2823	503	1061	.474	4	40	.100	462	553	.835	171	537	708	223	290	4	105	275	83	1472	8.7	2.8	18.2
93-94—Minnesota	70	67	2428	396	883	.448	6	25	.240	375	479	.783	160	442	602	307	264	6	87	259	86	1173	8.6	4.4	16.8
REG. SEASON TOTALS	151	148	5251	899	1944	.462	10	65	.154	837	1032	.811	331	979	1310	530	554	10	192	534	169	2645	8.7	3.5	17.5

LAGARDE, THOMAS JOSEPH (Tom) b. February 10, 1955 Ht. 6-10 Wt. 220 College—North Carolina

SEASON—TEAM	G	GS	MIN	FGM	FGA	PCT	3FGM	3FGA	PCT	FTM	FTA	PCT	O-RB	D-RB	TOT	AST	PF	DQ	STL	TO	BLK	PTS	RPG	APG	PPG
77-78—Denver	77	—	868	96	237	.405	—	—	—	114	150	.760	75	139	214	47	146	1	17	101	17	306	2.8	0.6	4.0
78-79—Seattle	23	—	575	98	181	.541	—	—	—	57	95	.600	61	129	190	32	75	2	6	47	18	253	8.3	1.4	11.0
79-80—Seattle	82	—	1164	146	306	.477	0	0	—	90	137	.657	127	185	312	91	206	2	19	97	34	382	3.8	1.1	4.7
80-81—Dallas	82	—	2670	417	888	.470	0	0	—	288	444	.649	177	488	665	237	293	6	35	206	45	1122	8.1	2.9	13.7
81-82—Dallas	47	28	909	113	269	.420	0	2	.000	86	166	.518	63	147	210	49	138	3	17	82	17	312	4.5	1.0	6.6
84-85—New Jersey	1	0	8	0	1	.000	0	0	—	2	2	.500	1	1	2	0	2	0	0	1	0	2	2.0	0.0	1.0
REG. SEASON TOTALS	312	28	6194	870	1882	.462	0	2	.000	636	994	.640	504	1089	1593	456	860	14	94	534	131	2376	5.1	1.5	7.6
PLAYOFF TOTALS	23	0	240	27	65	.415	0	0	—	14	18	.778	22	36	58	19	37	0	2	16	2	68	2.5	0.8	3.0

LAIMBEER, WILLIAM JR. (**Bill**) b. May 19, 1957   Ht. 6-11 Wt. 255 College—Owens Tech/Notre Dame

SEASON—TEAM	G	GS	MIN	FGM	FGA	PCT	3FGM	3FGA	PCT	FTM	FTA	PCT	O-RB	D-RB	TOT	AST	PF	DQ	STL	TO	BLK	PTS	RPG	APG	PPG
80-81—Cleveland	81	—	2460	337	670	.503	0	0	—	117	153	.765	266	427	693	216	332	14	56	132	78	791	8.6	2.7	9.8
81-82—Clev.-Detroit	80	34	1829	265	536	.494	4	13	.308	184	232	.793	234	383	617	100	296	5	39	121	64	718	7.7	1.3	9.0
82-83—Detroit	82	82	2871	436	877	.497	2	13	.154	245	310	.790	282	711	993	263	320	9	51	176	118	1119	12.1	3.2	13.6
83-84—Detroit	82	82	2864	553	1044	.530	0	11	.000	316	365	.866	329	674	1003	149	273	4	49	151	84	1422	12.2	1.8	17.3
84-85—Detroit	82	82	2892	595	1177	.506	4	18	.222	244	306	.797	295	718	1013	154	308	4	69	129	71	1438	12.4	1.9	17.5
85-86—Detroit	82	82	2891	545	1107	.492	4	14	.286	266	319	.834	305	770	1075	146	291	4	59	133	65	1360	13.1	1.8	16.6
86-87—Detroit	82	82	2854	506	1010	.501	6	21	.286	245	274	.894	243	712	955	151	283	4	72	120	69	1263	11.6	1.8	15.4
87-88—Detroit	82	82	2897	455	923	.493	13	39	.333	187	214	.874	165	667	832	199	284	6	66	136	78	1110	10.1	2.4	13.5
88-89—Detroit	81	81	2640	449	900	.499	30	86	.349	178	212	.840	138	638	776	177	259	2	51	129	100	1106	9.6	2.2	13.7
89-90—Detroit	81	81	2675	380	785	.484	57	158	.361	164	192	.854	166	614	780	171	278	4	57	98	84	981	9.6	2.1	12.1
90-91—Detroit	82	81	2668	372	778	.478	37	125	.296	123	147	.837	173	564	737	157	242	3	38	98	56	904	9.0	1.9	11.0
91-92—Detroit	81	46	2234	342	727	.470	32	85	.376	67	75	.893	104	347	451	160	225	0	51	102	54	783	5.6	2.0	9.7
92-93—Detroit	79	41	1933	292	574	.509	10	27	.370	93	104	.894	110	309	419	127	212	4	46	59	40	687	5.3	1.6	8.7
93-94—Detroit	11	5	248	47	90	.522	3	9	.333	11	13	.846	9	47	56	14	30	0	6	10	4	108	5.1	1.3	9.8
REG. SEASON TOTALS	1068	861	33956	5574	11198	.498	202	619	.326	2440	2916	.837	2819	7581	10400	2184	3633	63	710	1594	965	13790	9.7	2.0	12.9
PLAYOFF TOTALS	113	112	3735	549	1174	.468	44	137	.321	212	259	.819	257	840	1097	195	408	13	84	143	83	1354	9.7	1.7	12.0
ALL-STAR TOTALS	4	0	45	13	20	.650	0	0	—	2	3	.667	3	8	11	2	7	0	2	1	2	28	2.8	0.5	7.0

LALICH, PETER T. (**Pete**) b. June 23, 1920   Ht. 6-2 Wt. 190 College—Ohio

SEASON—TEAM	G	GS	MIN	FGM	FGA	PCT	3FGM	3FGA	PCT	FTM	FTA	PCT	O-RB	D-RB	TOT	AST	PF	DQ	STL	TO	BLK	PTS	RPG	APG	PPG
42-43—Sheboygan (N)	1	—	—	0	—	—	—	—	—	0	—	—	—	—	—	—	—	—	—	—	—	0	—	—	0.0
43-44—Cleveland (N)	17	—	—	44	—	—	—	—	—	21	—	—	—	—	—	—	—	—	—	—	—	109	—	—	6.4
44-45—Pittsburgh (N)	9	—	—	8	—	—	—	—	—	4	—	—	—	—	—	—	—	—	—	—	—	20	—	—	2.2
45-46—Youngstown (N)	11	—	—	2	—	—	—	—	—	3	—	—	—	—	—	—	—	—	—	—	—	7	—	—	0.6
46-47—Cleveland	1	—	—	0	1	.000	—	—	—	0	0	—	—	—	—	0	1	—	—	—	—	0	—	0.0	0.0
REG. NBA TOTALS	1	—	—	0	1	.000	—	—	—	0	0	—	—	—	—	0	1	—	—	—	—	0	—	0.0	0.0
REG. NBL TOTALS	38	—	—	54	—	—	—	—	—	28	—	—	—	—	—	—	—	—	—	—	—	136	—	—	3.6
NBL PLAYOFF TOTALS	2	—	—	1	—	—	—	—	—	2	—	—	—	—	—	5	—	—	—	—	—	4	—	—	2.0

LAMAR, DWIGHT (**Bo**) b. April 7, 1951   Ht. 6-1 Wt. 180 College—Southwestern Louisiana

SEASON—TEAM	G	GS	MIN	FGM	FGA	PCT	3FGM	3FGA	PCT	FTM	FTA	PCT	O-RB	D-RB	TOT	AST	PF	DQ	STL	TO	BLK	PTS	RPG	APG	PPG
73-74—San Diego (A)	84	—	2824	686	1726	.397	69	247	.279	272	350	.777	105	187	292	288	155	—	129	183	13	1713	3.5	3.4	20.4
74-75—San Diego (A)	77	—	2917	667	1571	.425	25	109	.229	247	315	.784	88	151	239	427	150	—	129	238	12	1606	3.1	5.5	20.9
75-76—S.D.-Indiana (A)	41	—	1130	277	668	.415	24	86	.279	79	106	.745	46	70	116	171	58	—	42	95	2	657	2.8	4.2	16.0
76-77—Los Angeles	71	—	1165	228	561	.406	—	—	—	46	68	.676	30	62	92	177	73	0	59	—	3	502	1.3	2.5	7.1
REG. NBA TOTALS	71	—	1165	228	561	.406	—	—	—	46	68	.676	30	62	92	177	73	0	59	—	3	502	1.3	2.5	7.1
REG. ABA TOTALS	202	—	6871	1630	3965	.411	118	442	.267	598	771	.776	239	408	647	886	363	0	300	516	27	3976	3.2	4.4	19.7
NBA PLAYOFF TOTALS	10	—	109	12	41	.293	—	—	—	9	10	.900	0	9	9	14	12	0	3	—	0	33	0.9	1.4	3.3
ABA PLAYOFF TOTALS	6	—	241	71	161	.441	7	17	.412	16	19	.842	7	17	24	21	19	0	11	22	2	165	4.0	3.5	27.5

LAMBERT, JOHN EDWARD b. January 14, 1953   Ht. 6-10 Wt. 225 College—USC

SEASON—TEAM	G	GS	MIN	FGM	FGA	PCT	3FGM	3FGA	PCT	FTM	FTA	PCT	O-RB	D-RB	TOT	AST	PF	DQ	STL	TO	BLK	PTS	RPG	APG	PPG
75-76—Cleveland	54	—	333	49	110	.445	—	—	—	25	37	.676	37	65	102	16	54	0	8	—	12	123	1.9	0.3	2.3
76-77—Cleveland	63	—	555	67	157	.427	—	—	—	25	36	.694	62	92	154	31	75	0	16	—	18	159	2.4	0.5	2.5
77-78—Cleveland	76	—	1075	142	336	.423	—	—	—	27	48	.563	125	199	324	38	169	0	27	62	50	311	4.3	0.5	4.1
78-79—Cleveland	70	—	1030	148	329	.450	—	—	—	35	55	.636	116	174	290	43	163	0	25	65	29	331	4.1	0.6	4.7
79-80—Cleveland	74	—	1324	165	400	.413	0	3	.000	73	101	.723	138	214	352	56	203	4	47	64	42	403	4.8	0.8	5.4
80-81—Clev.-K.C.	46	—	483	68	165	.412	0	2	.000	18	23	.783	28	65	93	27	76	0	12	19	5	154	2.0	0.6	3.3
81-82—K.C.-S.A.	63	7	764	86	197	.437	1	7	.143	34	42	.810	55	123	178	37	123	0	18	48	16	207	2.8	0.6	3.3
REG. SEASON TOTALS	446	7	5564	725	1694	.428	1	12	.083	237	342	.693	561	932	1493	248	863	4	153	258	172	1688	3.3	0.6	3.8
PLAYOFF TOTALS	28	0	250	30	75	.400	0	4	.000	8	10	.800	25	35	60	11	35	0	8	6	6	68	2.1	0.4	2.4

LAMP, JEFFREY ALAN (**Jeff**) b. March 9, 1959   Ht. 6-6 Wt. 195 College—Virginia

SEASON—TEAM	G	GS	MIN	FGM	FGA	PCT	3FGM	3FGA	PCT	FTM	FTA	PCT	O-RB	D-RB	TOT	AST	PF	DQ	STL	TO	BLK	PTS	RPG	APG	PPG
81-82—Portland	54	0	617	100	196	.510	0	1	.000	50	61	.820	24	40	64	28	83	0	16	45	1	250	1.2	0.5	4.6
82-83—Portland	59	1	690	107	252	.425	1	6	.167	42	52	.808	25	51	76	58	67	0	20	38	3	257	1.3	1.0	4.4
83-84—Portland	64	0	660	128	261	.490	2	13	.154	60	67	.896	23	40	63	51	67	0	22	52	4	318	1.0	0.8	5.0
85-86—Milw.-S.A.	74	2	1321	245	514	.477	7	30	.233	111	133	.835	53	147	200	117	155	1	39	68	4	608	2.7	1.6	8.2
87-88—L.A. Lakers	3	0	7	0	0	—	0	0	—	2	2	1.000	0	0	0	1	0	0	0	0	0	2	0.0	0.3	0.7
88-89—L.A. Lakers	37	0	176	27	69	.391	2	4	.500	4	5	.800	6	28	34	15	27	0	8	16	2	60	0.9	0.4	1.6
REG. SEASON TOTALS	291	3	3471	607	1292	.470	12	54	.222	269	320	.841	131	306	437	269	400	1	105	219	14	1495	1.5	0.9	5.1
PLAYOFF TOTALS	12	0	79	13	32	.406	1	3	.333	1	2	.500	3	1	4	8	10	0	1	6	0	28	0.3	0.7	2.3

LAMPLEY, JIMMY D. b. July 2, 1960   Ht. 6-11 Wt. 230 College—Vanderbilt/Arkansas-Lttle Rock

SEASON—TEAM	G	GS	MIN	FGM	FGA	PCT	3FGM	3FGA	PCT	FTM	FTA	PCT	O-RB	D-RB	TOT	AST	PF	DQ	STL	TO	BLK	PTS	RPG	APG	PPG
86-87—Philadelphia	1	0	16	1	3	.333	0	0	—	1	2	.500	1	4	5	0	0	0	1	1	0	3	5.0	0.0	3.0
REG. SEASON TOTALS	1	0	16	1	3	.333	0	0	—	1	2	.500	1	4	5	0	0	0	1	1	0	3	5.0	0.0	3.0

LANDSBERGER, MARK WALTER b. May 21, 1955 Ht. 6-8 Wt. 225 College—Allan Hancock/Minnesota/Arizona State

SEASON—TEAM	G	GS	MIN	FGM	FGA	PCT	3FGM	3FGA	PCT	FTM	FTA	PCT	O-RB	D-RB	TOT	AST	PF	DQ	STL	TO	BLK	PTS	RPG	APG	PPG
77-78—Chicago	62	—	926	127	251	.506	—	—	—	91	157	.580	110	191	301	41	78	0	21	69	6	345	4.9	0.7	5.6
78-79—Chicago	80	—	1959	278	585	.475	—	—	—	91	194	.469	292	450	742	68	125	0	27	149	22	647	9.3	0.9	8.1
79-80—Chicago-L.A.	77	—	1510	249	483	.516	0	0	—	116	222	.523	226	387	613	46	140	1	33	100	22	614	8.0	0.6	8.0
80-81—Los Angeles	69	—	1086	164	327	.502	0	1	.000	62	116	.534	152	225	377	27	135	0	19	65	6	390	5.5	0.4	5.7
81-82—Los Angeles	75	1	1134	144	329	.438	0	2	.000	33	65	.508	164	237	401	32	134	0	10	49	7	321	5.3	0.4	4.3
82-83—Los Angeles	39	4	356	43	102	.422	0	0	—	12	25	.480	55	73	128	12	48	0	8	20	4	98	3.3	0.3	2.5
83-84—Atlanta	35	0	335	19	51	.373	0	0	—	15	26	.577	42	77	119	10	32	0	6	21	3	53	3.4	0.3	1.5
REG. SEASON TOTALS	437	5	7306	1024	2128	.481	0	3	.000	420	805	.522	1041	1640	2681	236	692	1	124	473	70	2468	6.1	0.5	5.6
PLAYOFF TOTALS	41	0	433	42	114	.368	0	2	.000	12	20	.600	65	86	151	7	77	0	4	21	4	96	3.7	0.2	2.3

LANE, JEROME b. December 4, 1966 Ht. 6-6 Wt. 230 College—Pittsburgh

SEASON—TEAM	G	GS	MIN	FGM	FGA	PCT	3FGM	3FGA	PCT	FTM	FTA	PCT	O-RB	D-RB	TOT	AST	PF	DQ	STL	TO	BLK	PTS	RPG	APG	PPG
88-89—Denver	54	1	550	109	256	.426	0	7	.000	43	112	.384	87	113	200	60	105	1	20	50	4	261	3.7	1.1	4.8
89-90—Denver	67	46	956	145	309	.469	0	5	.000	44	120	.367	144	217	361	105	189	1	53	85	17	334	5.4	1.6	5.0
90-91—Denver	62	25	1383	202	461	.438	1	4	.250	58	141	.411	280	298	578	123	192	1	51	105	14	463	9.3	2.0	7.5
91-92—Denver-Indiana-Milw.	14	5	177	14	46	.304	0	0	—	9	27	.333	32	34	66	17	28	0	2	14	1	37	4.7	1.2	2.6
92-93—Cleveland	21	2	149	27	54	.500	0	0	—	5	20	.250	24	29	53	17	32	0	12	7	3	59	2.5	0.8	2.8
REG. SEASON TOTALS	218	79	3215	497	1126	.441	1	16	.063	159	420	.379	567	691	1258	322	546	3	138	261	39	1154	5.8	1.5	5.3
PLAYOFF TOTALS	4	2	35	2	10	.200	0	1	.000	3	4	.750	1	6	7	4	8	0	0	2	0	7	1.8	1.0	1.8

LANG, ANDREW CHARLES JR. b. June 28, 1966 Ht. 6-11 Wt. 250 College—Arkansas

SEASON—TEAM	G	GS	MIN	FGM	FGA	PCT	3FGM	3FGA	PCT	FTM	FTA	PCT	O-RB	D-RB	TOT	AST	PF	DQ	STL	TO	BLK	PTS	RPG	APG	PPG
88-89—Phoenix	62	25	526	60	117	.513	0	0	—	39	60	.650	54	93	147	9	112	1	17	28	48	159	2.4	0.1	2.6
89-90—Phoenix	74	0	1011	97	174	.557	0	0	—	64	98	.653	83	188	271	21	171	1	22	41	133	258	3.7	0.3	3.5
90-91—Phoenix	63	18	1152	109	189	.577	0	1	.000	93	130	.715	113	190	303	27	168	2	17	45	127	311	4.8	0.4	4.9
91-92—Phoenix	81	71	1965	248	475	.522	0	1	.000	126	164	.768	170	376	546	43	306	8	48	87	201	622	6.7	0.5	7.7
92-93—Philadelphia	73	59	1861	149	351	.425	1	5	.200	87	114	.763	136	300	436	79	261	4	46	89	141	386	6.0	1.1	5.3
93-94—Atlanta	82	0	1608	215	458	.469	1	4	.250	73	106	.689	126	187	313	51	192	2	38	81	87	504	3.8	0.6	6.1
REG. SEASON TOTALS	435	173	8123	878	1764	.498	2	11	.182	482	672	.717	682	1334	2016	230	1210	18	188	371	737	2240	4.6	0.5	5.1
PLAYOFF TOTALS	39	8	582	56	125	.448	0	1	.000	50	65	.769	41	82	123	11	100	3	13	33	48	162	3.2	0.3	4.2

LANIER, ROBERT JERRY JR. (Bob) b. September 10, 1948 Ht. 6-11 Wt. 260 College—St. Bonaventure

SEASON—TEAM	G	GS	MIN	FGM	FGA	PCT	3FGM	3FGA	PCT	FTM	FTA	PCT	O-RB	D-RB	TOT	AST	PF	DQ	STL	TO	BLK	PTS	RPG	APG	PPG
70-71—Detroit	82	—	2017	504	1108	.455	—	—	—	273	376	.726	—	—	665	146	272	4	—	—	—	1281	8.1	1.8	15.6
71-72—Detroit	80	—	3092	834	1690	.493	—	—	—	388	505	.768	—	—	1132	248	297	6	—	—	—	2056	14.2	3.1	25.7
72-73—Detroit	81	—	3150	810	1654	.490	—	—	—	307	397	.773	—	—	1205	260	278	4	—	—	—	1927	14.9	3.2	23.8
73-74—Detroit	81	—	3047	748	1483	.504	—	—	—	326	409	.797	269	805	1074	343	273	7	110	—	247	1822	13.3	4.2	22.5
74-75—Detroit	76	—	2987	731	1433	.510	—	—	—	361	450	.802	225	689	914	350	237	1	75	—	172	1823	12.0	4.6	24.0
75-76—Detroit	64	—	2363	541	1017	.532	—	—	—	284	370	.768	217	529	746	217	203	2	79	—	86	1366	11.7	3.4	21.3
76-77—Detroit	64	—	2446	678	1269	.534	—	—	—	260	318	.818	200	545	745	214	174	0	70	—	126	1616	11.6	3.3	25.3
77-78—Detroit	63	—	2311	622	1159	.537	—	—	—	298	386	.772	197	518	715	216	185	2	82	225	93	1542	11.3	3.4	24.5
78-79—Detroit	53	—	1835	489	950	.515	—	—	—	275	367	.749	164	330	494	140	181	5	50	175	75	1253	9.3	2.6	23.6
79-80—Detroit-Milw.	63	—	2131	466	867	.537	1	6	.167	277	354	.782	152	400	552	184	200	3	74	162	89	1210	8.8	2.9	19.2
80-81—Milwaukee	67	—	1753	376	716	.525	1	1	1.000	208	277	.751	128	285	413	179	184	0	73	139	81	961	6.2	2.7	14.3
81-82—Milwaukee	74	72	1986	407	729	.558	0	2	.000	182	242	.752	92	296	388	219	211	3	72	166	56	996	5.2	3.0	13.5
82-83—Milwaukee	39	35	978	163	332	.491	0	1	.000	91	133	.684	58	142	200	105	125	2	34	82	24	417	5.1	2.7	10.7
83-84—Milwaukee	72	72	2007	392	685	.572	0	3	.000	194	274	.708	141	314	455	186	228	8	58	163	51	978	6.3	2.6	13.6
REG. SEASON TOTALS	959	179	32103	7761	15092	.514	2	13	.154	3724	4858	.767	1843	4853	9698	3007	3048	47	777	1112	1100	19248	10.1	3.1	20.1
PLAYOFF TOTALS	67	31	2361	508	955	.532	0	1	.000	228	297	.768	179	466	645	235	233	7	62	105	99	1244	9.6	3.5	18.6
ALL-STAR TOTALS	8	0	121	32	55	.582	0	0	—	10	12	.833	14	22	45	12	15	0	4	2	5	74	5.6	1.5	9.3

LANTZ, STUART BURRELL (Stu) b. July 13, 1946 Ht. 6-3 Wt. 180 College—Nebraska

SEASON—TEAM	G	GS	MIN	FGM	FGA	PCT	3FGM	3FGA	PCT	FTM	FTA	PCT	O-RB	D-RB	TOT	AST	PF	DQ	STL	TO	BLK	PTS	RPG	APG	PPG
68-69—San Diego	73	—	1378	220	482	.456	—	—	—	129	167	.772	—	—	236	99	178	0	—	—	—	569	3.2	1.4	7.8
69-70—San Diego	82	—	2471	455	1027	.443	—	—	—	278	361	.770	—	—	255	287	238	2	—	—	—	1188	3.1	3.5	14.5
70-71—San Diego	82	—	3102	585	1305	.448	—	—	—	519	644	.806	—	—	406	344	230	3	—	—	17	1689	5.0	4.2	20.6
71-72—Houston	81	—	3097	557	1279	.435	—	—	—	387	462	.838	—	—	345	337	211	2	—	—	—	1501	4.3	4.2	18.5
72-73—Detroit	51	—	1603	185	455	.407	—	—	—	120	150	.800	—	—	172	138	117	0	—	—	—	490	3.4	2.7	9.6
73-74—Detroit	50	—	980	154	361	.427	—	—	—	139	164	.848	34	79	113	97	79	0	38	—	3	447	2.3	1.9	8.9
74-75—N.O.-L.A.	75	—	1783	228	561	.406	—	—	—	192	229	.838	88	106	194	188	162	1	56	—	12	648	2.6	2.5	8.6
75-76—Los Angeles	53	—	853	85	204	.417	—	—	—	80	89	.899	28	71	99	76	105	1	27	—	3	250	1.9	1.4	4.7
REG. SEASON TOTALS	547	—	15267	2469	5674	.435	—	—	—	1844	2266	.814	150	256	1820	1566	1320	9	121	—	18	6782	3.3	2.9	12.4
PLAYOFF TOTALS	13	—	435	58	128	.453	—	—	—	49	59	.831	10	19	50	24	41	0	2	—	0	165	3.8	1.8	12.7

LARESE, YORK BRUNO b. July 18, 1938 Ht. 6-4 Wt. 185 College—North Carolina

SEASON—TEAM	G	GS	MIN	FGM	FGA	PCT	3FGM	3FGA	PCT	FTM	FTA	PCT	O-RB	D-RB	TOT	AST	PF	DQ	STL	TO	BLK	PTS	RPG	APG	PPG
61-62—Chicago-Phil.	59	—	703	122	327	.373	—	—	—	58	72	.806	—	—	77	94	104	0	—	—	—	302	1.3	1.6	5.1
REG. SEASON TOTALS	59	—	703	122	327	.373	—	—	—	58	72	.806	—	—	77	94	104	0	—	—	—	302	1.3	1.6	5.1
PLAYOFF TOTALS	9	—	78	11	35	.314	—	—	—	8	12	.667	—	—	15	5	14	0	—	—	—	30	1.7	0.6	3.3

LARUSSO, RUDOLPH A. (**Rudy**) b. November 11, 1937 Ht. 6-8 Wt. 220 College—Dartmouth

SEASON—TEAM	G	GS	MIN	FGM	FGA	PCT	3FGM	3FGA	PCT	FTM	FTA	PCT	O-RB	D-RB	TOT	AST	PF	DQ	STL	TO	BLK	PTS	RPG	APG	PPG
59-60—Minneapolis	71	—	2092	355	913	.389	—	—	—	265	357	.742	—	—	679	83	222	8	—	—	—	975	9.6	1.2	13.7
60-61—Los Angeles	79	—	2593	416	992	.419	—	—	—	323	409	.790	—	—	781	135	280	8	—	—	—	1155	9.9	1.7	14.6
61-62—Los Angeles	80	—	2754	516	1108	.466	—	—	—	342	448	.763	—	—	828	179	255	5	—	—	—	1374	10.4	2.2	17.2
62-63—Los Angeles	75	—	2505	321	761	.422	—	—	—	282	393	.718	—	—	747	187	255	5	—	—	—	924	10.0	2.5	12.3
63-64—Los Angeles	79	—	2746	337	776	.434	—	—	—	298	397	.751	—	—	800	190	268	5	—	—	—	972	10.1	2.4	12.3
64-65—Los Angeles	77	—	2588	381	827	.461	—	—	—	321	415	.773	—	—	725	198	258	3	—	—	—	1083	9.4	2.6	14.1
65-66—Los Angeles	76	—	2316	410	897	.457	—	—	—	350	445	.787	—	—	660	165	261	9	—	—	—	1170	8.7	2.2	15.4
66-67—Los Angeles	45	—	1292	211	509	.415	—	—	—	156	224	.696	—	—	351	78	149	6	—	—	—	578	7.8	1.7	12.8
67-68—San Francisco	79	—	2819	602	1389	.433	—	—	—	522	661	.790	—	—	741	182	337	14	—	—	—	1726	9.4	2.3	21.8
68-69—San Francisco	75	—	2782	553	1349	.410	—	—	—	444	559	.794	—	—	624	159	268	9	—	—	—	1550	8.3	2.1	20.7
REG. SEASON TOTALS	736	—	24487	4102	9521	.431	—	—	—	3303	4308	.767	—	—	6936	1556	2553	72	—	—	—	11507	9.4	2.1	15.6
PLAYOFF TOTALS	93	—	3188	467	1152	.405	—	—	—	410	546	.751	—	—	779	194	366	13	—	—	—	1344	8.4	2.1	14.5
ALL-STAR TOTALS	4	—	70	13	27	.481	—	—	—	3	9	.333	—	—	17	6	6	0	—	—	—	29	4.3	1.5	7.3

LASKOWSKI, JOHN b. June 7, 1953 Ht. 6-6 Wt. 190 College—Indiana

SEASON—TEAM	G	GS	MIN	FGM	FGA	PCT	3FGM	3FGA	PCT	FTM	FTA	PCT	O-RB	D-RB	TOT	AST	PF	DQ	STL	TO	BLK	PTS	RPG	APG	PPG
75-76—Chicago	71	—	1570	284	690	.412	—	—	—	87	120	.725	52	167	219	55	90	0	56	—	10	655	3.1	0.8	9.2
76-77—Chicago	47	—	562	75	212	.354	—	—	—	27	30	.900	16	47	63	44	22	0	32	—	2	177	1.3	0.9	3.8
REG. SEASON TOTALS	118	—	2132	359	902	.398	—	—	—	114	150	.760	68	214	282	99	112	0	88	—	12	832	2.4	0.8	7.1

LATTIN, DAVID (**Dave, Big Daddy**) b. December 23, 1943 Ht. 6-7 Wt. 230 College—Texas-El Paso

SEASON—TEAM	G	GS	MIN	FGM	FGA	PCT	3FGM	3FGA	PCT	FTM	FTA	PCT	O-RB	D-RB	TOT	AST	PF	DQ	STL	TO	BLK	PTS	RPG	APG	PPG
67-68—San Francisco	44	—	257	37	102	.363	—	—	—	23	33	.697	—	—	104	14	94	4	—	—	—	97	2.4	0.3	2.2
68-69—Phoenix	68	—	987	150	366	.410	—	—	—	109	172	.634	—	—	323	48	163	5	—	—	—	409	4.8	0.7	6.0
70-71—Pittsburgh (A)	71	—	1135	177	377	.469	0	1	.000	108	177	.610	—	—	467	64	215	—	—	—	—	462	6.6	0.9	6.5
71-72—Pittsburgh (A)	64	—	1482	329	605	.544	0	1	.000	148	242	.612	—	—	375	51	178	—	—	108	—	806	5.9	0.8	12.6
72-73—Memphis (A)	16	—	296	48	104	.462	0	1	.000	34	45	.756	21	42	63	7	45	0	—	32	—	130	3.9	0.4	8.1
REG. NBA TOTALS	112	—	1244	187	468	.400	—	—	—	132	205	.644	—	—	427	62	257	9	—	—	—	506	3.8	0.6	4.5
REG. ABA TOTALS	151	—	2913	554	1086	.510	0	3	.000	290	464	.625	21	42	905	122	438	0	—	140	—	1398	6.0	0.8	9.3
NBA PLAYOFF TOTALS	5	—	27	1	5	.200	—	—	—	5	6	.833	—	—	5	1	9	0	—	—	—	7	1.0	0.2	1.4

LAUREL, RICHARD (**Rich**) b. July 11, 1954 Ht. 6-7 Wt. 195 College—Hofstra

SEASON—TEAM	G	GS	MIN	FGM	FGA	PCT	3FGM	3FGA	PCT	FTM	FTA	PCT	O-RB	D-RB	TOT	AST	PF	DQ	STL	TO	BLK	PTS	RPG	APG	PPG
77-78—Milwaukee	10	—	57	10	31	.323	—	—	—	4	4	1.000	6	4	10	3	10	0	3	4	1	24	1.0	0.3	2.4
REG. SEASON TOTALS	10	—	57	10	31	.323	—	—	—	4	4	1.000	6	4	10	3	10	0	3	4	1	24	1.0	0.3	2.4

LAURIE, HARRY b. November 2, 1944 Ht. 6-1 Wt. 180 College—Loyola (Ill.)/St. Peter's

SEASON—TEAM	G	GS	MIN	FGM	FGA	PCT	3FGM	3FGA	PCT	FTM	FTA	PCT	O-RB	D-RB	TOT	AST	PF	DQ	STL	TO	BLK	PTS	RPG	APG	PPG
70-71—Pittsburgh (A)	9	—	57	3	12	.250	0	0	—	7	11	.636	—	—	15	8	16	—	—	—	—	13	1.7	0.9	1.4
REG. ABA TOTALS	9	—	57	3	12	.250	0	0	—	7	11	.636	—	—	15	8	16	—	—	—	—	13	1.7	0.9	1.4

LAUTENBACH, WALTER HENRY (**Walt**) b. November 17, 1922 Ht. 6-2 Wt. 190 College—Wisconsin

SEASON—TEAM	G	GS	MIN	FGM	FGA	PCT	3FGM	3FGA	PCT	FTM	FTA	PCT	O-RB	D-RB	TOT	AST	PF	DQ	STL	TO	BLK	PTS	RPG	APG	PPG
47-48—Oshkosh (N)	60	—	—	159	—	—	—	—	—	36	60	.600	—	—	—	130	—	—	—	—	—	354	—	—	5.9
48-49—Oshkosh (N)	61	—	—	104	—	—	—	—	—	26	45	.578	—	—	—	84	—	—	—	—	—	234	—	—	3.8
49-50—Sheboygan	55	—	—	100	332	.301	—	—	—	38	55	.691	—	—	73	122	—	—	—	—	—	238	—	1.3	4.3
REG. NBA TOTALS	55	—	—	100	332	.301	—	—	—	38	55	.691	—	—	73	122	—	—	—	—	—	238	—	1.3	4.3
REG. NBL TOTALS	121	—	—	263	—	—	—	—	—	62	105	.590	—	—	—	214	—	—	—	—	—	588	—	—	4.9
NBL PLAYOFF TOTALS	11	—	—	26	—	—	—	—	—	11	18	.611	—	—	—	28	—	—	—	—	—	63	—	—	5.7

LAVELLI, ANTHONY (**Tony**) b. July 11, 1926 Ht. 6-3 Wt. 185 College—Yale

SEASON—TEAM	G	GS	MIN	FGM	FGA	PCT	3FGM	3FGA	PCT	FTM	FTA	PCT	O-RB	D-RB	TOT	AST	PF	DQ	STL	TO	BLK	PTS	RPG	APG	PPG
49-50—Boston	56	—	—	162	436	.372	—	—	—	168	197	.853	—	—	—	40	107	—	—	—	—	492	—	0.7	8.8
50-51—New York	30	—	—	32	93	.344	—	—	—	35	41	.854	—	—	59	23	56	1	—	—	—	99	2.0	0.8	3.3
REG. SEASON TOTALS	86	—	—	194	529	.367	—	—	—	203	238	.853	—	—	59	63	163	1	—	—	—	591	2.0	0.7	6.9
PLAYOFF TOTALS	2	—	—	1	5	.200	—	—	—	2	2	1.000	—	—	1	1	2	0	—	—	—	4	0.5	0.5	2.0

LAVOY, ROBERT WILLIAM (**Bob**) b. June 29, 1926 Ht. 6-7 Wt. 185 College—Illinois/Western Kentucky

SEASON—TEAM	G	GS	MIN	FGM	FGA	PCT	3FGM	3FGA	PCT	FTM	FTA	PCT	O-RB	D-RB	TOT	AST	PF	DQ	STL	TO	BLK	PTS	RPG	APG	PPG
50-51—Indianapolis	63	—	—	221	619	.357	—	—	—	84	133	.632	—	—	310	76	190	2	—	—	—	526	4.9	1.2	8.3
51-52—Indianapolis	63	—	1829	240	604	.397	—	—	—	168	223	.753	—	—	479	107	210	5	—	—	—	648	7.6	1.7	10.3
52-53—Indianapolis	70	—	2327	225	560	.402	—	—	—	168	242	.694	—	—	528	130	274	18	—	—	—	618	7.5	1.9	8.8
53-54—Milw.-Syr.	68	—	1277	135	356	.379	—	—	—	94	129	.729	—	—	317	78	215	2	—	—	—	364	4.7	1.1	5.4
REG. SEASON TOTALS	264	—	5433	821	2139	.384	—	—	—	514	727	.707	—	—	1634	391	889	27	—	—	—	2156	6.2	1.5	8.2
PLAYOFF TOTALS	20	—	483	50	145	.345	—	—	—	55	73	.753	—	—	121	30	74	2	—	—	—	155	6.1	1.5	7.8

LAWRENCE, EDMUND (**Ed**) b. December 8, 1952 Ht. 6-11½ Wt. 240 College—McNeese State

SEASON—TEAM	G	GS	MIN	FGM	FGA	PCT	3FGM	3FGA	PCT	FTM	FTA	PCT	O-RB	D-RB	TOT	AST	PF	DQ	STL	TO	BLK	PTS	RPG	APG	PPG
80-81—Detroit	3	—	19	5	8	.625	0	0	—	2	4	.500	2	2	4	1	6	0	1	1	0	12	1.3	0.3	4.0
REG. SEASON TOTALS	3	—	19	5	8	.625	0	0	—	2	4	.500	2	2	4	1	6	0	1	1	0	12	1.3	0.3	4.0

LAYTON, DENNIS (**Mo**) b. December 24, 1948 Ht. 6-1 Wt. 180 College—Phoenix/USC

SEASON—TEAM	G	GS	MIN	FGM	FGA	PCT	3FGM	3FGA	PCT	FTM	FTA	PCT	O-RB	D-RB	TOT	AST	PF	DQ	STL	TO	BLK	PTS	RPG	APG	PPG
71-72—Phoenix	80	—	1849	304	717	.424	—	—	—	122	165	.739	—	—	164	247	219	0	—	—	—	730	2.1	3.1	9.1
72-73—Phoenix	65	—	990	187	434	.431	—	—	—	90	119	.756	—	—	77	139	127	2	—	—	—	464	1.2	2.1	7.1
73-74—Portland	22	—	327	55	112	.491	—	—	—	14	26	.538	7	26	33	51	45	0	9	—	1	124	1.5	2.3	5.6
73-74—Memphis (A)	3	—	65	8	17	.471	0	0	—	3	3	1.000	1	3	4	7	4	—	0	7	1	19	1.3	2.3	6.3
76-77—New York Knicks	56	—	765	134	277	.484	—	—	—	58	73	.795	11	36	47	154	87	0	21	—	6	326	0.8	2.8	5.8
77-78—San Antonio	41	—	498	85	168	.506	—	—	—	12	13	.923	4	28	32	108	51	0	21	59	4	182	0.8	2.6	4.4
REG. NBA TOTALS	264	—	4429	765	1708	.448	—	—	—	296	396	.747	22	90	353	699	529	2	51	59	11	1826	1.3	2.6	6.9
REG. ABA TOTALS	3	—	65	8	17	.471	0	0	—	3	3	1.000	1	3	4	7	4	0	0	7	1	19	1.3	2.3	6.3

LEAKS, EMANUEL (**Manny**) b. November 27, 1945 Ht. 6-8 Wt. 230 College—Niagara

SEASON—TEAM	G	GS	MIN	FGM	FGA	PCT	3FGM	3FGA	PCT	FTM	FTA	PCT	O-RB	D-RB	TOT	AST	PF	DQ	STL	TO	BLK	PTS	RPG	APG	PPG
68-69—Ken.-N.Y.-Dallas (A)	78	—	2089	299	756	.396	0	1	.000	160	229	.699	—	—	763	92	253	4	—	97	—	758	9.8	1.2	9.7
69-70—Dallas (A)	84	—	3086	636	1287	.494	0	2	.000	305	428	.713	427	620	1047	100	283	11	—	—	—	1577	12.5	1.2	18.8
70-71—Texas-N.Y. (A)	80	—	2614	510	1080	.472	0	1	.000	279	381	.732	317	538	855	104	211	—	—	—	—	1299	10.7	1.3	16.2
71-72—N.Y.-Utah-Fla. (A)	69	—	1443	240	580	.414	0	1	.000	74	121	.612	—	—	412	55	136	—	—	73	—	554	6.0	0.8	8.0
72-73—Philadelphia	82	—	2530	377	933	.404	—	—	—	144	200	.720	—	—	677	95	191	5	—	—	—	898	8.3	1.2	11.0
73-74—Capital	53	—	845	79	232	.341	—	—	—	58	83	.699	94	150	244	25	95	1	10	—	39	216	4.6	0.5	4.1
REG. NBA TOTALS	135	—	3375	456	1165	.391	—	—	—	202	283	.714	94	150	921	120	286	6	10	—	39	1114	6.8	0.9	8.3
REG. ABA TOTALS	311	—	9232	1685	3703	.455	0	5	.000	818	1159	.706	744	1158	3077	351	883	15	—	170	—	4188	9.9	1.1	13.5
NBA PLAYOFF TOTALS	2	—	5	1	2	.500	—	—	—	0	0	—	1	1	2	—	1	0	0	—	0	2	1.0	0.0	1.0
ABA PLAYOFF TOTALS	19	—	640	111	236	.470	0	0	—	46	65	.708	23	63	196	20	58	—	—	15	—	268	10.3	1.1	14.1

LEAR, HAROLD C. JR. (**Hal, King**) b. January 31, 1935 Ht. 5-11½ Wt. 165 College—Temple

SEASON—TEAM	G	GS	MIN	FGM	FGA	PCT	3FGM	3FGA	PCT	FTM	FTA	PCT	O-RB	D-RB	TOT	AST	PF	DQ	STL	TO	BLK	PTS	RPG	APG	PPG
56-57—Philadelphia	3	—	14	2	6	.333	—	—	—	0	0	—	—	—	1	1	3	0	—	—	—	4	0.3	0.3	1.3
REG. SEASON TOTALS	3	—	14	2	6	.333	—	—	—	0	0	—	—	—	1	1	3	0	—	—	—	4	0.3	0.3	1.3

LEAVELL, ALLEN FRAZIER b. May 27, 1957 Ht. 6-1 Wt. 170 College—Oklahoma City

SEASON—TEAM	G	GS	MIN	FGM	FGA	PCT	3FGM	3FGA	PCT	FTM	FTA	PCT	O-RB	D-RB	TOT	AST	PF	DQ	STL	TO	BLK	PTS	RPG	APG	PPG
79-80—Houston	77	—	2123	330	656	.503	3	19	.158	180	221	.814	57	127	184	417	197	1	127	205	28	843	2.4	5.4	10.9
80-81—Houston	79	—	1686	258	548	.471	2	17	.118	124	149	.832	30	104	134	384	160	1	97	189	15	642	1.7	4.9	8.1
81-82—Houston	79	61	2150	370	793	.467	9	31	.290	115	135	.852	49	119	168	457	182	2	150	153	15	864	2.1	5.8	10.9
82-83—Houston	79	76	2602	439	1059	.415	42	175	.240	247	297	.832	64	131	195	530	215	0	165	198	14	1167	2.5	6.7	14.8
83-84—Houston	82	27	2009	349	731	.477	11	71	.155	238	286	.832	31	86	117	459	199	2	107	184	12	947	1.4	5.6	11.5
84-85—Houston	42	0	536	88	209	.421	8	37	.216	44	57	.772	8	29	37	102	61	0	23	51	4	228	0.9	2.4	5.4
85-86—Houston	74	12	1190	212	458	.463	24	67	.358	135	158	.854	6	61	67	234	126	1	58	88	8	583	0.9	3.2	7.9
86-87—Houston	53	11	1175	147	358	.411	18	57	.316	100	119	.840	14	47	61	224	126	1	53	64	10	412	1.2	4.2	7.8
87-88—Houston	80	54	2150	291	666	.437	19	88	.216	218	251	.869	22	126	148	405	162	1	124	130	9	819	1.9	5.1	10.2
88-89—Houston	55	3	627	65	188	.346	5	41	.122	44	60	.733	13	40	53	127	61	0	25	62	5	179	1.0	2.3	3.3
REG. SEASON TOTALS	700	244	16248	2549	5666	.450	141	603	.234	1445	1733	.834	294	870	1164	3339	1489	9	929	1324	120	6684	1.7	4.8	9.5
PLAYOFF TOTALS	63	13	1072	138	377	.366	13	44	.295	113	131	.863	18	62	80	203	109	2	58	74	8	402	1.3	3.2	6.4

LEBO, JEFFREY BRIAN (**Jeff**) b. October 5, 1966 Ht. 6-2 Wt. 180 College—North Carolina

SEASON—TEAM	G	GS	MIN	FGM	FGA	PCT	3FGM	3FGA	PCT	FTM	FTA	PCT	O-RB	D-RB	TOT	AST	PF	DQ	STL	TO	BLK	PTS	RPG	APG	PPG
89-90—San Antonio	4	0	32	2	7	.286	0	0	—	2	2	1.000	2	2	4	3	7	0	2	1	0	6	1.0	0.8	1.5
REG. SEASON TOTALS	4	0	32	2	7	.286	0	0	—	2	2	1.000	2	2	4	3	7	0	2	1	0	6	1.0	0.8	1.5

LECKNER, ERIC CHARLES b. May 27, 1966 Ht. 6-11 Wt. 265 College—Wyoming

SEASON—TEAM	G	GS	MIN	FGM	FGA	PCT	3FGM	3FGA	PCT	FTM	FTA	PCT	O-RB	D-RB	TOT	AST	PF	DQ	STL	TO	BLK	PTS	RPG	APG	PPG
88-89—Utah	75	0	779	120	220	.545	0	0	—	79	113	.699	48	151	199	16	174	1	8	69	22	319	2.7	0.2	4.3
89-90—Utah	77	0	764	125	222	.563	0	0	—	81	109	.743	48	144	192	19	157	0	15	63	23	331	2.5	0.2	4.3
90-91—Sac.-Cha.	72	2	1122	131	294	.446	0	0	—	62	111	.559	82	213	295	39	192	4	14	69	22	324	4.1	0.5	4.5
91-92—Charlotte	59	2	716	79	154	.513	0	1	.000	38	51	.745	49	157	206	31	114	1	9	39	18	196	3.5	0.5	3.3
93-94—Philadelphia	71	36	1163	139	286	.486	0	2	.000	84	130	.646	75	207	282	86	190	2	18	86	34	362	4.0	1.2	5.1
REG. SEASON TOTALS	354	40	4544	594	1176	.505	0	3	.000	344	514	.669	302	872	1174	191	827	8	64	326	119	1532	3.3	0.5	4.3
PLAYOFF TOTALS	6	0	38	7	14	.500	1	1	1.000	5	9	.556	3	7	10	2	10	0	0	4	0	20	1.7	0.3	3.3

LEE, ALFRED (Butch) b. December 5, 1956 Ht. 6-0 Wt. 185 College—Marquette

SEASON—TEAM	G	GS	MIN	FGM	FGA	PCT	3FGM	3FGA	PCT	FTM	FTA	PCT	O-RB	D-RB	TOT	AST	PF	DQ	STL	TO	BLK	PTS	RPG	APG	PPG
78-79—Atlanta-Clev.	82	—	1779	290	634	.457	—	—	—	175	230	.761	33	93	126	295	146	0	86	154	1	755	1.5	3.6	9.2
79-80—Clev.-L.A.	14	—	55	6	24	.250	0	0	—	6	8	.750	7	4	11	12	2	0	1	10	0	18	0.8	0.9	1.3
REG. SEASON TOTALS	96	—	1834	296	658	.450	0	0	—	181	238	.761	40	97	137	307	148	0	87	164	1	773	1.4	3.2	8.1
PLAYOFF TOTALS	3	—	6	0	0	—	0	0	—	2	2	1.000	0	1	1	—	2	0	0	3	0	2	0.3	0.0	0.7

LEE, CLYDE WAYNE b. March 14, 1944 Ht. 6-10 Wt. 215 College—Vanderbilt

SEASON—TEAM	G	GS	MIN	FGM	FGA	PCT	3FGM	3FGA	PCT	FTM	FTA	PCT	O-RB	D-RB	TOT	AST	PF	DQ	STL	TO	BLK	PTS	RPG	APG	PPG
66-67—San Francisco	74	—	1247	205	503	.408	—	—	—	105	166	.633	—	—	551	77	168	5	—	—	—	515	7.4	1.0	7.0
67-68—San Francisco	82	—	2699	373	894	.417	—	—	—	229	335	.684	—	—	1141	135	331	10	—	—	—	975	13.9	1.6	11.9
68-69—San Francisco	65	—	2237	268	674	.398	—	—	—	160	256	.625	—	—	897	82	225	1	—	—	—	696	13.8	1.3	10.7
69-70—San Francisco	82	—	2641	362	822	.440	—	—	—	178	300	.593	—	—	929	80	263	5	—	—	—	902	11.3	1.0	11.0
70-71—San Francisco	82	—	1392	194	428	.453	—	—	—	111	199	.558	—	—	570	63	137	0	—	—	—	499	7.0	0.8	6.1
71-72—Golden State	78	—	2674	256	544	.471	—	—	—	120	222	.541	—	—	1132	85	244	4	—	—	—	632	14.5	1.1	8.1
72-73—Golden State	66	—	1476	170	365	.466	—	—	—	74	131	.565	—	—	598	34	183	5	—	—	—	414	9.1	0.5	6.3
73-74—Golden State	54	—	1642	129	284	.454	—	—	—	62	107	.579	188	410	598	68	179	3	27	—	17	320	11.1	1.3	5.9
74-75—Atlanta-Phil.	80	—	2456	176	427	.412	—	—	—	119	177	.672	288	469	757	105	285	9	30	—	20	471	9.5	1.3	5.9
75-76—Philadelphia	79	—	1421	123	282	.436	—	—	—	63	95	.663	164	289	453	59	188	0	23	—	27	309	5.7	0.7	3.9
REG. SEASON TOTALS	742	—	19885	2256	5223	.432	—	—	—	1221	1988	.614	640	1168	7626	788	2203	42	80	—	64	5733	10.3	1.1	7.7
PLAYOFF TOTALS	51	—	1398	146	368	.397	—	—	—	68	116	.586	4	12	519	61	157	3	0	—	1	360	10.2	1.2	7.1
ALL-STAR TOTALS	1	—	18	2	8	.250	—	—	—	2	4	.500	0	0	11	2	3	0	0	—	0	6	11.0	2.0	6.0

LEE, DAVID G. (Dave) b. March 31, 1942 Ht. 6-7½ Wt. 225 College—San Francisco

SEASON—TEAM	G	GS	MIN	FGM	FGA	PCT	3FGM	3FGA	PCT	FTM	FTA	PCT	O-RB	D-RB	TOT	AST	PF	DQ	STL	TO	BLK	PTS	RPG	APG	PPG
67-68—Oakland (A)	54	—	753	125	276	.453	2	6	.333	120	140	.857	—	—	184	20	83	2	—	42	—	372	3.4	0.4	6.9
68-69—New Orleans (A)	4	—	16	1	9	.111	0	0	—	0	0	—	—	—	3	0	0	0	—	2	—	2	0.8	0.0	0.5
REG. ABA TOTALS	58	—	769	126	285	.442	2	6	.333	120	140	.857	—	—	187	20	83	2	—	44	—	374	3.2	0.3	6.4

LEE, DOUGLAS EDWARD (Doug) b. October 24, 1964 Ht. 6-6 Wt. 200 College—Texas A&M/Purdue

SEASON—TEAM	G	GS	MIN	FGM	FGA	PCT	3FGM	3FGA	PCT	FTM	FTA	PCT	O-RB	D-RB	TOT	AST	PF	DQ	STL	TO	BLK	PTS	RPG	APG	PPG
91-92—New Jersey	46	0	307	50	116	.431	10	37	.270	10	19	.526	17	18	35	22	39	0	11	12	1	120	0.8	0.5	2.6
92-93—New Jersey	5	0	33	2	7	.286	1	3	.333	0	0	—	0	2	2	5	7	0	0	3	1	5	0.4	1.0	1.0
REG. SEASON TOTALS	51	0	340	52	123	.423	11	40	.275	10	19	.526	17	20	37	27	46	0	11	15	2	125	0.7	0.5	2.5
PLAYOFF TOTALS	2	0	6	0	3	.000	0	2	.000	0	0	—	0	0	0	1	1	0	0	0	1	0	0.0	0.5	0.0

LEE, GEORGE C. b. November 23, 1936 Ht. 6-4 Wt. 200 College—Michigan

SEASON—TEAM	G	GS	MIN	FGM	FGA	PCT	3FGM	3FGA	PCT	FTM	FTA	PCT	O-RB	D-RB	TOT	AST	PF	DQ	STL	TO	BLK	PTS	RPG	APG	PPG
60-61—Detroit	74	—	1735	310	776	.399	—	—	—	276	394	.701	—	—	490	89	158	1	—	—	—	896	6.6	1.2	12.1
61-62—Detroit	75	—	1351	179	500	.358	—	—	—	213	280	.761	—	—	349	64	128	1	—	—	—	571	4.7	0.9	7.6
62-63—San Francisco	64	—	1192	149	394	.378	—	—	—	152	193	.788	—	—	217	64	113	0	—	—	—	450	3.4	1.0	7.0
63-64—San Francisco	54	—	522	64	169	.379	—	—	—	47	71	.662	—	—	97	25	67	0	—	—	—	175	1.8	0.5	3.2
64-65—San Francisco	19	—	247	27	77	.351	—	—	—	38	52	.731	—	—	55	12	22	0	—	—	—	92	2.9	0.6	4.8
66-67—San Francisco	1	—	5	3	4	.750	—	—	—	6	7	.857	—	—	0	0	0	0	—	—	—	12	0.0	0.0	12.0
67-68—San Francisco	10	—	106	8	35	.229	—	—	—	17	24	.708	—	—	27	4	16	0	—	—	—	33	2.7	0.4	3.3
REG. SEASON TOTALS	297	—	5158	740	1955	.379	—	—	—	749	1021	.734	—	—	1235	258	504	2	—	—	—	2229	4.2	0.9	7.5
PLAYOFF TOTALS	21	—	262	48	110	.436	—	—	—	38	54	.704	—	—	58	19	32	0	—	—	—	134	2.8	0.9	6.4

LEE, GREGORY SCOTT (Greg) b. December 12, 1951 Ht. 6-3½ Wt. 195 College—UCLA

SEASON—TEAM	G	GS	MIN	FGM	FGA	PCT	3FGM	3FGA	PCT	FTM	FTA	PCT	O-RB	D-RB	TOT	AST	PF	DQ	STL	TO	BLK	PTS	RPG	APG	PPG
74-75—San Diego (A)	5	—	63	8	15	.533	0	0	—	2	2	1.000	1	2	3	13	6	—	4	6	0	18	0.6	2.6	3.6
75-76—Portland	5	—	35	2	4	.500	—	—	—	2	2	1.000	0	2	2	11	6	0	2	—	0	6	0.4	2.2	1.2
REG. NBA TOTALS	5	—	35	2	4	.500	—	—	—	2	2	1.000	0	2	2	11	6	0	2	—	0	6	0.4	2.2	1.2
REG. ABA TOTALS	5	—	63	8	15	.533	0	0	—	2	2	1.000	1	2	3	13	6	—	4	6	0	18	0.6	2.6	3.6

LEE, KEITH DeWAYNE b. December 28, 1962 Ht. 6-10 Wt. 220 College—Memphis State

SEASON—TEAM	G	GS	MIN	FGM	FGA	PCT	3FGM	3FGA	PCT	FTM	FTA	PCT	O-RB	D-RB	TOT	AST	PF	DQ	STL	TO	BLK	PTS	RPG	APG	PPG
85-86—Cleveland	58	38	1197	177	380	.466	2	9	.222	75	96	.781	116	235	351	67	204	9	29	78	37	431	6.1	1.2	7.4
86-87—Cleveland	67	1	870	170	374	.455	0	1	.000	72	101	.713	93	158	251	69	147	0	25	85	40	412	3.7	1.0	6.1
88-89—New Jersey	57	4	840	109	258	.422	0	2	.000	53	71	.746	73	186	259	42	138	1	20	53	33	271	4.5	0.7	4.8
REG. SEASON TOTALS	182	43	2907	456	1012	.451	2	12	.167	200	268	.746	282	579	861	178	489	10	74	216	110	1114	4.7	1.0	6.1

LEE, KURK b. June 3, 1967 Ht. 6-3 Wt. 190 College—Western Kentucky/Townson State

SEASON—TEAM	G	GS	MIN	FGM	FGA	PCT	3FGM	3FGA	PCT	FTM	FTA	PCT	O-RB	D-RB	TOT	AST	PF	DQ	STL	TO	BLK	PTS	RPG	APG	PPG
90-91—New Jersey	48	0	265	19	71	.268	3	15	.200	25	28	.893	7	23	30	34	39	0	11	20	2	66	0.6	0.7	1.4
REG. SEASON TOTALS	48	0	265	19	71	.268	3	15	.200	25	28	.893	7	23	30	34	39	0	11	20	2	66	0.6	0.7	1.4

LEE, RICHARD (Dick) College—None

SEASON—TEAM	G	GS	MIN	FGM	FGA	PCT	3FGM	3FGA	PCT	FTM	FTA	PCT	O-RB	D-RB	TOT	AST	PF	DQ	STL	TO	BLK	PTS	RPG	APG	PPG
67-68—Anaheim (A)	2	—	2	0	0	—	0	0	—	0	0	—	—	—	1	1	0	0	—	0	—	0	0.5	0.5	0.0
REG. ABA TOTALS	2	—	2	0	0	—	0	0	—	0	0	—	—	—	1	1	0	0	—	—	—	0	0.5	0.5	0.0

LEE, ROCK ALAN b. May 1, 1955 Ht. 6-10 Wt. 220 College—California/San Diego State

SEASON—TEAM	G	GS	MIN	FGM	FGA	PCT	3FGM	3FGA	PCT	FTM	FTA	PCT	O-RB	D-RB	TOT	AST	PF	DQ	STL	TO	BLK	PTS	RPG	APG	PPG
81-82—San Diego	2	0	10	1	2	.500	0	0	—	0	4	.000	0	1	1	2	3	0	0	0	0	2	0.5	1.0	1.0
REG. SEASON TOTALS	2	0	10	1	2	.500	0	0	—	0	4	.000	0	1	1	2	3	0	0	0	0	2	0.5	1.0	1.0

LEE, RONALD HENRY (Ron) b. November 2, 1952 Ht. 6-3½ Wt. 195 College—Oregon

SEASON—TEAM	G	GS	MIN	FGM	FGA	PCT	3FGM	3FGA	PCT	FTM	FTA	PCT	O-RB	D-RB	TOT	AST	PF	DQ	STL	TO	BLK	PTS	RPG	APG	PPG
76-77—Phoenix	82	—	1849	347	786	.441	—	—	—	142	210	.676	99	200	299	263	276	10	156	—	33	836	3.6	3.2	10.2
77-78—Phoenix	82	—	1928	417	950	.439	—	—	—	170	228	.746	95	159	254	305	257	3	225	221	17	1004	3.1	3.7	12.2
78-79—Phoenix-N.O.	60	—	1346	218	507	.430	—	—	—	98	141	.695	63	105	168	205	182	3	107	165	6	534	2.8	3.4	8.9
79-80—Atlanta-Detroit	61	—	1167	113	305	.370	22	59	.373	44	70	.629	40	83	123	241	172	5	99	101	17	292	2.0	4.0	4.8
80-81—Detroit	82	—	1829	113	323	.350	2	13	.154	113	156	.724	65	155	220	362	260	4	166	173	29	341	2.7	4.4	4.2
81-82—Detroit	81	7	1467	88	246	.358	18	59	.305	84	119	.706	35	120	155	312	221	3	116	123	20	278	1.9	3.9	3.4
REG. SEASON TOTALS	448	7	9586	1296	3117	.416	42	131	.321	651	924	.705	397	822	1219	1688	1368	28	869	783	122	3285	2.7	3.8	7.3
PLAYOFF TOTALS	2	0	41	5	16	.313	0	0	—	2	2	1.000	2	4	6	3	7	0	4	4	0	12	3.0	1.5	6.0

LEE, RUSSELL E. b. January 27, 1950 Ht. 6-5 Wt. 185 College—Marshall

SEASON—TEAM	G	GS	MIN	FGM	FGA	PCT	3FGM	3FGA	PCT	FTM	FTA	PCT	O-RB	D-RB	TOT	AST	PF	DQ	STL	TO	BLK	PTS	RPG	APG	PPG
72-73—Milwaukee	46	—	277	49	127	.386	—	—	—	32	43	.744	—	—	43	38	36	0	—	—	—	130	0.9	0.8	2.8
73-74—Milwaukee	36	—	166	38	94	.404	—	—	—	11	16	.688	16	24	40	20	29	0	11	—	0	87	1.1	0.6	2.4
74-75—New Orleans	15	—	139	29	76	.382	—	—	—	7	14	.500	15	16	31	7	17	1	11	—	3	65	2.1	0.5	4.3
REG. SEASON TOTALS	97	—	582	116	297	.391	—	—	—	50	73	.685	31	40	114	65	82	1	22	—	3	282	1.2	0.7	2.9
PLAYOFF TOTALS	11	—	25	13	22	.591	—	—	—	1	4	.250	1	2	7	3	1	0	3	—	1	27	0.6	0.3	2.5

LEEDE, EDWARD HORST (Ed) b. July 17, 1927 Ht. 6-3 Wt. 185 College—Dartmouth

SEASON—TEAM	G	GS	MIN	FGM	FGA	PCT	3FGM	3FGA	PCT	FTM	FTA	PCT	O-RB	D-RB	TOT	AST	PF	DQ	STL	TO	BLK	PTS	RPG	APG	PPG
49-50—Boston	64	—	—	174	507	.343	—	—	—	223	316	.706	—	—	—	130	167	—	—	—	—	571	—	2.0	8.9
50-51—Boston	57	—	—	119	370	.322	—	—	—	140	189	.741	—	—	118	95	144	3	—	—	—	378	2.1	1.7	6.6
REG. SEASON TOTALS	121	—	—	293	877	.334	—	—	—	363	505	.719	—	—	118	225	311	3	—	—	—	949	2.1	1.9	7.8
PLAYOFF TOTALS	2	—	—	1	7	.143	—	—	—	1	1	1.000	—	—	0	2	3	0	—	—	—	3	0.0	1.0	1.5

LEFKOWITZ, HENRY A. (Hank) b. August 31, 1923 Ht. 6-2 Wt. 190 College—Western Reserve

SEASON—TEAM	G	GS	MIN	FGM	FGA	PCT	3FGM	3FGA	PCT	FTM	FTA	PCT	O-RB	D-RB	TOT	AST	PF	DQ	STL	TO	BLK	PTS	RPG	APG	PPG
46-47—Cleveland	24	—	—	22	114	.193	—	—	—	7	13	.538	—	—	—	4	35	—	—	—	—	51	—	0.2	2.1
REG. SEASON TOTALS	24	—	—	22	114	.193	—	—	—	7	13	.538	—	—	—	4	35	—	—	—	—	51	—	0.2	2.1
PLAYOFF TOTALS	3	—	—	4	18	.222	—	—	—	1	1	1.000	—	—	—	—	4	—	—	—	—	9	—	0.0	3.0

LEGLER, TIMOTHY EUGENE (Tim) b. December 26, 1966 Ht. 6-4 Wt. 205 College—La Salle

SEASON—TEAM	G	GS	MIN	FGM	FGA	PCT	3FGM	3FGA	PCT	FTM	FTA	PCT	O-RB	D-RB	TOT	AST	PF	DQ	STL	TO	BLK	PTS	RPG	APG	PPG
89-90—Phoenix	11	0	83	11	29	.379	0	1	.000	6	6	1.000	4	4	8	6	12	0	2	4	0	28	0.7	0.5	2.5
90-91—Denver	10	0	148	25	72	.347	3	12	.250	5	6	.833	8	10	18	12	20	0	2	4	0	58	1.8	1.2	5.8
92-93—Utah-Dallas	33	0	635	105	241	.436	22	65	.338	57	71	.803	25	34	59	46	63	0	24	28	6	289	1.8	1.4	8.8
93-94—Dallas	79	0	1322	231	528	.438	52	139	.374	142	169	.840	36	92	128	120	133	0	52	60	13	656	1.6	1.5	8.3
REG. SEASON TOTALS	133	0	2188	372	870	.428	77	217	.355	210	252	.833	73	140	213	184	228	0	80	96	19	1031	1.6	1.4	7.8

LEHMANN, GEORGE b. May 1, 1942 Ht. 6-2 Wt. 185 College—Campbell

SEASON—TEAM	G	GS	MIN	FGM	FGA	PCT	3FGM	3FGA	PCT	FTM	FTA	PCT	O-RB	D-RB	TOT	AST	PF	DQ	STL	TO	BLK	PTS	RPG	APG	PPG
67-68—St. Louis	55	—	497	59	172	.343	—	—	—	35	43	.814	—	—	44	93	54	0	—	—	—	153	0.8	1.7	2.8
68-69—Atlanta	11	—	138	26	67	.388	—	—	—	8	12	.667	—	—	9	27	18	0	—	—	—	60	0.8	2.5	5.5
68-69—Los Angeles (A)	32	—	937	212	511	.415	48	137	.350	132	164	.805	—	—	73	159	96	1	—	122	—	604	2.3	5.0	18.9
69-70—L.A.-N.Y.-Miami (A)	81	—	1994	318	847	.375	92	286	.322	180	211	.853	—	—	121	256	189	0	—	—	—	908	1.5	3.2	11.2
70-71—Carolina (A)	83	—	2918	535	1186	.451	154	382	.403	214	256	.836	—	—	203	464	221	—	—	—	—	1438	2.4	5.6	17.3
71-72—Car.-Memphis (A)	53	—	1921	303	663	.457	71	199	.357	169	192	.880	—	—	98	411	155	—	—	210	—	846	1.8	7.8	16.0
72-73—Memphis (A)	28	—	753	95	240	.396	26	67	.388	61	74	.824	7	27	34	150	74	1	—	65	—	277	1.2	5.4	9.9
73-74—Memphis (A)	33	—	554	68	177	.384	18	50	.360	18	19	.947	8	29	37	117	52	—	13	53	4	172	1.1	3.5	5.2
REG. NBA TOTALS	66	—	635	85	239	.356	—	—	—	43	55	.782	—	—	53	120	72	0	—	—	—	213	0.8	1.8	3.2
REG. ABA TOTALS	310	—	9077	1531	3624	.422	409	1121	.365	774	916	.845	15	56	566	1557	787	2	13	450	4	4245	1.8	5.0	13.7
NBA PLAYOFF TOTALS	1	—	2	0	1	.000	—	—	—	0	0	—	—	—	0	2	1	0	—	—	—	0	0.0	2.0	0.0

LENTZ, LEARY LEE b. February 23, 1945 Ht. 6-6 Wt. 200 College—Houston

SEASON—TEAM	G	GS	MIN	FGM	FGA	PCT	3FGM	3FGA	PCT	FTM	FTA	PCT	O-RB	D-RB	TOT	AST	PF	DQ	STL	TO	BLK	PTS	RPG	APG	PPG
67-68—Houston (A)	78	—	2504	343	845	.406	0	3	.000	147	221	.665	—	—	648	89	175	0	—	97	—	833	8.3	1.1	10.7
68-69—Houston-N.Y. (A)	70	—	1129	135	334	.404	0	1	.000	76	117	.650	—	—	271	31	103	1	—	52	—	346	3.9	0.4	4.9
REG. ABA TOTALS	148	—	3633	478	1179	.405	0	4	.000	223	338	.660	—	—	919	120	278	1	—	149	—	1179	6.2	0.8	8.0
ABA PLAYOFF TOTALS	3	—	73	12	26	.462	0	0	—	1	3	.333	—	—	19	3	6	0	—	2	—	25	6.3	1.0	8.3

LEONARD, GARY FRANCIS b. February 16, 1967 Ht. 7-1 Wt. 255 College—Missouri

SEASON—TEAM	G	GS	MIN	FGM	FGA	PCT	3FGM	3FGA	PCT	FTM	FTA	PCT	O-RB	D-RB	TOT	AST	PF	DQ	STL	TO	BLK	PTS	RPG	APG	PPG
89-90—Minnesota	22	0	127	13	31	.419	0	1	.000	6	14	.429	10	17	27	1	26	0	3	8	9	32	1.2	0.0	1.5
90-91—Atlanta	4	0	9	0	0	—	0	0	—	2	4	.500	0	2	2	0	2	0	0	0	1	2	0.5	0.0	0.5
91-92—Atlanta	5	0	13	4	6	.667	0	0	—	2	2	1.000	3	2	5	1	3	0	1	1	0	10	1.0	0.2	2.0
REG. SEASON TOTALS	31	0	149	17	37	.459	0	1	.000	10	20	.500	13	21	34	2	31	0	4	9	10	44	1.1	0.1	1.4
PLAYOFF TOTALS	2	0	5	2	2	1.000	0	0	—	0	0	—	0	2	2	—	0	0	0	0	0	4	1.0	0.0	2.0

LEONARD, WILLIAM ROBERT (Bob, Slick) b. July 17, 1932 Ht. 6-3 Wt. 185 College—Indiana

SEASON—TEAM	G	GS	MIN	FGM	FGA	PCT	3FGM	3FGA	PCT	FTM	FTA	PCT	O-RB	D-RB	TOT	AST	PF	DQ	STL	TO	BLK	PTS	RPG	APG	PPG
56-57—Minneapolis	72	—	1943	303	867	.349	—	—	—	186	241	.772	—	—	220	169	140	0	—	—	—	792	3.1	2.3	11.0
57-58—Minneapolis	66	—	2074	266	794	.335	—	—	—	205	268	.765	—	—	237	218	145	0	—	—	—	737	3.6	3.3	11.2
58-59—Minneapolis	58	—	1598	206	552	.373	—	—	—	120	160	.750	—	—	178	186	119	0	—	—	—	532	3.1	3.2	9.2
59-60—Minneapolis	73	—	2074	231	717	.322	—	—	—	136	193	.705	—	—	245	252	171	3	—	—	—	598	3.4	3.5	8.2
60-61—Los Angeles	55	—	600	61	207	.295	—	—	—	71	100	.710	—	—	70	81	70	0	—	—	—	193	1.3	1.5	3.5
61-62—Chicago	70	—	2464	423	1128	.375	—	—	—	279	371	.752	—	—	199	378	186	0	—	—	—	1125	2.8	5.4	16.1
62-63—Chicago	32	—	879	84	245	.343	—	—	—	59	85	.694	—	—	68	143	84	1	—	—	—	227	2.1	4.5	7.1
REG. SEASON TOTALS	426	—	11632	1574	4510	.349	—	—	—	1056	1418	.745	—	—	1217	1427	915	4	—	—	—	4204	2.9	3.3	9.9
PLAYOFF TOTALS	34	—	924	130	364	.357	—	—	—	74	98	.755	—	—	90	165	77	0	—	—	—	334	2.6	4.9	9.8

LES, JAMES ALLEN (Jim) b. August 18, 1963 Ht. 5-11 Wt. 165 College—Cleveland State/Bradley

SEASON—TEAM	G	GS	MIN	FGM	FGA	PCT	3FGM	3FGA	PCT	FTM	FTA	PCT	O-RB	D-RB	TOT	AST	PF	DQ	STL	TO	BLK	PTS	RPG	APG	PPG
88-89—Utah	82	0	781	40	133	.301	1	14	.071	57	73	.781	23	64	87	215	88	0	27	88	5	138	1.1	2.6	1.7
89-90—Utah-L.A. Clips	7	0	92	5	14	.357	0	1	.000	13	17	.765	3	4	7	21	9	0	3	10	0	23	1.0	3.0	3.3
90-91—Sacramento	55	8	1399	119	268	.444	71	154	.461	86	103	.835	18	93	111	299	141	0	57	75	4	395	2.0	5.4	7.2
91-92—Sacramento	62	5	712	74	192	.385	45	131	.344	38	47	.809	11	52	63	143	58	0	31	42	3	231	1.0	2.3	3.7
92-93—Sacramento	73	0	881	110	259	.425	66	154	.429	42	50	.840	20	69	89	169	81	0	40	48	7	328	1.2	2.3	4.5
93-94—Sacramento	18	0	169	13	34	.382	8	18	.444	11	13	.846	5	8	13	39	16	0	7	11	1	45	0.7	2.2	2.5
REG. SEASON TOTALS	297	13	4034	361	900	.401	191	472	.405	247	303	.815	80	290	370	886	393	0	165	274	20	1160	1.2	3.0	3.9
PLAYOFF TOTALS	3	0	5	0	0	—	0	0	—	0	0	—	0	0	0	1	2	0	0	1	0	0	0.0	0.3	0.0

LESTER, RONNIE b. January 1, 1959 Ht. 6-2 Wt. 175 College—Iowa

SEASON—TEAM	G	GS	MIN	FGM	FGA	PCT	3FGM	3FGA	PCT	FTM	FTA	PCT	O-RB	D-RB	TOT	AST	PF	DQ	STL	TO	BLK	PTS	RPG	APG	PPG
80-81—Chicago	8	—	83	10	24	.417	0	0	—	10	11	.909	3	3	6	7	5	0	2	9	0	30	0.8	0.9	3.8
81-82—Chicago	75	74	2252	329	657	.501	4	8	.500	208	256	.813	75	138	213	362	158	2	80	185	14	870	2.8	4.8	11.6
82-83—Chicago	65	38	1437	202	446	.453	0	5	.000	124	171	.725	46	126	172	332	121	2	51	134	6	528	2.6	5.1	8.1
83-84—Chicago	43	3	687	78	188	.415	1	5	.200	75	87	.862	20	26	46	168	59	1	30	72	6	232	1.1	3.9	5.4
84-85—L.A. Lakers	32	1	278	34	82	.415	0	1	.000	21	31	.677	4	22	26	80	25	0	15	32	3	89	0.8	2.5	2.8
85-86—L.A. Lakers	27	0	222	26	52	.500	0	3	.000	15	19	.789	0	10	10	54	27	0	9	42	3	67	0.4	2.0	2.5
REG. SEASON TOTALS	250	116	4959	679	1449	.469	5	22	.227	453	575	.788	148	325	473	1003	395	5	187	474	32	1816	1.9	4.0	7.3
PLAYOFF TOTALS	14	0	96	13	33	.394	0	1	.000	12	16	.750	7	7	14	13	11	0	2	9	0	38	1.0	0.9	2.7

LETT, CLIFFORD EARL b. December 23, 1965 Ht. 6-3 Wt. 170 College—Florida

SEASON—TEAM	G	GS	MIN	FGM	FGA	PCT	3FGM	3FGA	PCT	FTM	FTA	PCT	O-RB	D-RB	TOT	AST	PF	DQ	STL	TO	BLK	PTS	RPG	APG	PPG
89-90—Chicago	4	0	28	2	8	.250	0	0	—	0	0	—	0	1	1	8	0	0	2	0	0	4	0.0	0.3	1.0
90-91—San Antonio	7	0	99	14	29	.483	0	1	.000	6	9	.667	1	6	7	9	0	2	8	1	34	1.0	1.0	4.9
REG. SEASON TOTALS	11	0	127	16	37	.432	0	1	.000	6	9	.667	1	6	7	8	17	0	2	10	1	38	0.6	0.7	3.5

LEVANE, ANDREW JOSEPH (Fuzzy) b. April 11, 1920 Ht. 6-2 Wt. 190 College—St. John's

SEASON—TEAM	G	GS	MIN	FGM	FGA	PCT	3FGM	3FGA	PCT	FTM	FTA	PCT	O-RB	D-RB	TOT	AST	PF	DQ	STL	TO	BLK	PTS	RPG	APG	PPG
45-46—Rochester (N)	22	—	—	52	—	—	—	—	—	8	19	.421	—	—	—	—	23	—	—	—	—	112	—	—	5.1
46-47—Rochester (N)	39	—	—	133	—	—	—	—	—	49	87	.563	—	—	—	—	83	—	—	—	—	315	—	—	8.1
47-48—Rochester (N)	54	—	—	147	—	—	—	—	—	45	62	.726	—	—	—	100	—	—	—	—	—	339	—	—	6.3
48-49—Rochester	36	—	—	55	193	.285	—	—	—	13	21	.619	—	—	—	39	37	—	—	—	—	123	—	1.1	3.4
49-50—Syracuse	60	—	—	139	418	.333	—	—	—	54	85	.635	—	—	—	156	106	—	—	—	—	332	—	2.6	5.5
52-53—Milwaukee	7	—	68	3	24	.125	—	—	—	2	3	.667	—	—	9	9	15	0	—	—	—	8	1.3	1.3	1.1
REG. NBA TOTALS	103	—	68	197	635	.310	—	—	—	69	109	.633	—	—	9	204	158	0	—	—	—	463	1.3	2.0	4.5
REG. NBL TOTALS	115	—	—	332	—	—	—	—	—	102	168	.607	—	—	—	—	206	—	—	—	—	766	—	—	6.7
NBA PLAYOFF TOTALS	9	—	0	13	37	.351	—	—	—	5	5	1.000	—	—	—	13	11	0	—	—	—	31	—	1.4	3.4
NBL PLAYOFF TOTALS	23	—	—	57	—	—	—	—	—	22	32	.688	—	—	—	—	43	—	—	—	—	136	—	—	5.9

LEVER, LAFAYETTE (Fat) b. August 18, 1960 Ht. 6-3 Wt. 180 College—Arizona State

SEASON—TEAM	G	GS	MIN	FGM	FGA	PCT	3FGM	3FGA	PCT	FTM	FTA	PCT	O-RB	D-RB	TOT	AST	PF	DQ	STL	TO	BLK	PTS	RPG	APG	PPG
82-83—Portland	81	45	2020	256	594	.431	5	15	.333	116	159	.730	85	140	225	426	179	2	153	137	15	633	2.8	5.3	7.8
83-84—Portland	81	22	2010	313	701	.447	3	15	.200	159	214	.743	96	122	218	372	178	1	135	125	31	788	2.7	4.6	9.7
84-85—Denver	82	82	2559	424	985	.430	6	24	.250	197	256	.770	147	264	411	613	226	1	202	203	30	1051	5.0	7.5	12.8
85-86—Denver	78	77	2616	468	1061	.441	12	38	.316	132	182	.725	136	284	420	584	204	3	178	210	15	1080	5.4	7.5	13.8
86-87—Denver	82	82	3054	643	1370	.469	22	92	.239	244	312	.782	216	513	729	654	219	1	201	167	34	1552	8.9	8.0	18.9
87-88—Denver	82	82	3061	643	1360	.473	12	57	.211	248	316	.785	203	462	665	639	214	0	223	182	21	1546	8.1	7.8	18.9
88-89—Denver	71	71	2745	558	1221	.457	23	66	.348	270	344	.785	187	475	662	559	178	1	195	157	20	1409	9.3	7.9	19.8
89-90—Denver	79	79	2832	568	1283	.443	36	87	.414	271	337	.804	230	504	734	517	172	1	168	156	13	1443	9.3	6.5	18.3
90-91—Dallas	4	0	86	9	23	.391	0	3	.000	11	14	.786	3	12	15	12	5	0	6	10	3	29	3.8	3.0	7.3
91-92—Dallas	31	5	884	135	349	.387	17	52	.327	60	80	.750	56	105	161	107	73	0	46	36	12	347	5.2	3.5	11.2
93-94—Dallas	81	54	1947	227	557	.408	26	74	.351	75	98	.765	83	200	283	213	155	1	159	88	15	555	3.5	2.6	6.9
REG. SEASON TOTALS	752	599	23814	4244	9504	.447	162	523	.310	1783	2312	.771	1442	3081	4523	4696	1803	11	1666	1471	209	10433	6.0	6.2	13.9
PLAYOFF TOTALS	48	33	1441	227	548	.414	18	44	.409	124	160	.775	85	191	276	297	118	0	89	81	9	596	5.8	6.2	12.4
ALL-STAR TOTALS	2	1	53	14	27	.519	0	2	.000	5	6	.833	0	7	7	5	4	0	2	0	0	33	3.5	2.5	16.5

LEVINGSTON, CLIFFORD EUGENE (Cliff) b. January 4, 1961 Ht. 6-8 Wt. 220 College—Wichita State

SEASON—TEAM	G	GS	MIN	FGM	FGA	PCT	3FGM	3FGA	PCT	FTM	FTA	PCT	O-RB	D-RB	TOT	AST	PF	DQ	STL	TO	BLK	PTS	RPG	APG	PPG
82-83—Detroit	62	5	879	131	270	.485	0	1	.000	84	147	.571	104	128	232	52	125	2	23	73	36	346	3.7	0.8	5.6
83-84—Detroit	80	24	1746	229	436	.525	0	3	.000	125	186	.672	234	311	545	109	281	7	44	77	78	583	6.8	1.4	7.3
84-85—Atlanta	74	53	2017	291	552	.527	0	2	.000	145	222	.653	230	336	566	104	231	3	70	133	69	727	7.6	1.4	9.8
85-86—Atlanta	81	35	1945	294	551	.534	0	1	.000	164	242	.678	193	341	534	72	260	5	76	113	39	752	6.6	0.9	9.3
86-87—Atlanta	82	10	1848	251	496	.506	0	3	.000	155	212	.731	219	314	533	40	261	4	48	72	68	657	6.5	0.5	8.0
87-88—Atlanta	82	32	2135	314	564	.557	1	2	.500	190	246	.772	228	276	504	71	287	5	52	94	84	819	6.1	0.9	10.0
88-89—Atlanta	80	52	2184	300	568	.528	1	5	.200	133	191	.696	194	304	498	75	270	4	97	105	70	734	6.2	0.9	9.2
89-90—Atlanta	75	5	1706	216	424	.509	1	5	.200	83	122	.680	113	206	319	80	216	2	55	49	41	516	4.3	1.1	6.9
90-91—Chicago	78	0	1013	127	282	.450	1	4	.250	59	91	.648	99	126	225	56	143	0	29	50	43	314	2.9	0.7	4.0
91-92—Chicago	79	0	1020	125	251	.498	1	6	.167	60	96	.625	109	118	227	66	134	0	27	42	45	311	2.9	0.8	3.9
REG. SEASON TOTALS	773	216	16493	2278	4394	.518	5	32	.156	1198	1755	.683	1723	2460	4183	725	2208	32	521	808	573	5759	5.4	0.9	7.5
PLAYOFF TOTALS	79	0	1012	117	233	.502	2	4	.500	69	103	.670	97	127	224	32	158	0	24	40	35	305	2.8	0.4	3.9

LEWIS, FREDERICK B. JR. (Fred) b. January 6, 1921 Ht. 6-2½ Wt. 195 College—Long Island University/Eastern Kentucky

SEASON—TEAM	G	GS	MIN	FGM	FGA	PCT	3FGM	3FGA	PCT	FTM	FTA	PCT	O-RB	D-RB	TOT	AST	PF	DQ	STL	TO	BLK	PTS	RPG	APG	PPG
46-47—Sheboygan (N)	44	—	—	230	—	—	—	—	—	125	170	.735	—	—	—	—	106	—	—	—	—	585	—	—	13.3
47-48—She.-Ind. (N)	44	—	—	169	—	—	—	—	—	101	137	.737	—	—	—	—	100	—	—	—	—	439	—	—	10.0
48-49—Ind.-Balt.	61	—	—	272	834	.326	—	—	—	138	181	.762	—	—	—	107	167	—	—	—	—	682	—	1.8	11.2
49-50—Balt.-Phil.	34	—	—	46	184	.250	—	—	—	25	32	.781	—	—	—	25	40	—	—	—	—	117	—	0.7	3.4
REG. NBA TOTALS	95	—	—	318	1018	.312	—	—	—	163	213	.765	—	—	—	132	207	—	—	—	—	799	—	1.4	8.4
REG. NBL TOTALS	88	—	—	399	—	—	—	—	—	226	307	.736	—	—	—	—	206	—	—	—	—	1024	—	—	11.6
NBA PLAYOFF TOTALS	3	—	—	15	35	.429	—	—	—	7	10	.700	—	—	—	3	13	—	—	—	—	37	—	1.0	12.3
NBL PLAYOFF TOTALS	9	—	—	41	—	—	—	—	—	14	18	.611	—	—	—	—	14	—	—	—	—	96	—	—	10.7

LEWIS, FREDERICK L. (**Freddie**) b. July 1, 1943 Ht. 6-0 Wt. 180 College—Eastern Arizona/Arizona State

SEASON—TEAM	G	GS	MIN	FGM	FGA	PCT	3FGM	3FGA	PCT	FTM	FTA	PCT	O-RB	D-RB	TOT	AST	PF	DQ	STL	TO	BLK	PTS	RPG	APG	PPG
66-67—Cincinnati	32	—	334	60	153	.392	—	—	—	29	41	.707	—	—	44	40	49	1	—	—	—	149	1.4	1.3	4.7
67-68—Indiana (A)	76	—	2921	542	1287	.421	16	74	.216	465	583	.798	—	—	440	183	217	2	—	209	—	1565	5.8	2.4	20.6
68-69—Indiana (A)	78	—	3055	572	1300	.440	22	83	.265	419	510	.822	—	—	374	346	289	5	—	224	—	1585	4.8	4.4	20.3
69-70—Indiana (A)	81	—	2877	448	1065	.421	47	177	.266	383	485	.790	—	—	277	289	294	5	—	—	—	1326	3.4	3.6	16.4
70-71—Indiana (A)	81	—	3034	547	1241	.441	59	194	.304	372	461	.807	—	—	336	433	249	—	—	—	—	1525	4.1	5.3	18.8
71-72—Indiana (A)	77	—	2714	405	947	.428	31	100	.310	341	396	.861	—	—	327	362	230	—	—	194	—	1182	4.2	4.7	15.4
72-73—Indiana (A)	72	—	2217	375	860	.436	38	110	.345	287	349	.822	97	131	228	288	204	4	—	173	—	1075	3.2	4.0	14.9
73-74—Indiana (A)	78	—	2164	290	728	.398	13	72	.181	182	219	.831	84	117	201	322	189	—	99	169	11	775	2.6	4.1	9.9
74-75—Memphis-St. L. (A)	69	—	2790	579	1232	.470	18	67	.269	355	421	.843	111	154	265	367	161	—	147	206	3	1531	3.8	5.3	22.2
75-76—St. Louis (A)	74	—	2266	403	953	.423	31	106	.292	259	317	.817	67	146	213	293	183	—	109	193	7	1096	2.9	4.0	14.8
76-77—Indiana	32	—	552	81	199	.407	—	—	—	62	77	.805	17	30	47	56	58	0	18	—	2	224	1.5	1.8	7.0
REG. NBA TOTALS	64	—	886	141	352	.401	—	—	—	91	118	.771	17	30	91	96	107	1	18	—	2	373	1.4	1.5	5.8
REG. ABA TOTALS	686	—	24038	4161	9613	.433	275	983	.280	3063	3741	.819	359	548	2661	2883	2016	16	355	1368	21	11660	3.9	4.2	17.0
NBA PLAYOFF TOTALS	3	—	9	4	9	.444	—	—	—	0	0	—	0	0	4	—	1	0	0	—	0	8	1.3	0.0	2.7
ABA PLAYOFF TOTALS	106	—	4151	712	1679	.424	43	175	.246	548	643	.852	41	55	437	458	348	2	56	203	2	2015	4.1	4.3	19.0
ABA ALL-STAR TOTALS	4	—	78	21	42	.500	2	3	.667	7	9	.778	0	6	12	15	7	0	2	9	0	51	3.0	3.8	12.8

LEWIS, GRADY W. b. March 25, 1917 Ht. 6-7 Wt. 215 College—Southwestern Oklahoma State/Oklahoma

SEASON—TEAM	G	GS	MIN	FGM	FGA	PCT	3FGM	3FGA	PCT	FTM	FTA	PCT	O-RB	D-RB	TOT	AST	PF	DQ	STL	TO	BLK	PTS	RPG	APG	PPG
46-47—Detroit	60	—	—	106	520	.204	—	—	—	75	138	.543	—	—	—	54	166	—	—	—	—	287	—	0.9	4.8
47-48—St. L.-Balt.	45	—	—	114	425	.268	—	—	—	87	135	.644	—	—	—	41	151	—	—	—	—	315	—	0.9	7.0
48-49—St. Louis	34	—	—	53	137	.387	—	—	—	42	70	.600	—	—	—	37	104	—	—	—	—	148	—	1.1	4.4
REG. SEASON TOTALS	139	—	—	273	1082	.252	—	—	—	204	343	.595	—	—	—	132	421	—	—	—	—	750	—	0.9	5.4
PLAYOFF TOTALS	11	—	—	23	109	.211	—	—	—	22	29	.759	—	—	—	9	49	4	—	—	—	68	—	0.8	6.2

LEWIS, MICHAEL J. (**Mike**) b. March 18, 1946 Ht. 6-8 Wt. 225 College—Duke

SEASON—TEAM	G	GS	MIN	FGM	FGA	PCT	3FGM	3FGA	PCT	FTM	FTA	PCT	O-RB	D-RB	TOT	AST	PF	DQ	STL	TO	BLK	PTS	RPG	APG	PPG
68-69—Indiana-Minn. (A)	76	—	1617	247	566	.436	0	2	.000	153	235	.651	—	—	632	107	246	8	—	138	—	647	8.3	1.4	8.5
69-70—Pittsburgh (A)	78	—	2698	499	1006	.496	0	0	—	269	356	.756	370	684	1054	268	306	7	—	—	—	1267	13.5	3.4	16.2
70-71—Pittsburgh (A)	83	—	2741	420	825	.509	0	0	—	235	306	.768	435	778	1213	268	332	—	—	—	—	1075	14.6	3.2	13.0
71-72—Pittsburgh (A)	82	—	2618	385	713	.540	0	0	—	165	226	.730	357	639	996	316	315	—	—	237	—	935	12.1	3.9	11.4
72-73—Carolina (A)	15	—	430	59	119	.496	0	0	—	33	41	.805	44	78	122	41	48	1	—	27	—	151	8.1	2.7	10.1
73-74—Carolina (A)	3	—	14	3	8	.375	0	0	—	0	0	—	3	2	5	0	2	—	0	1	0	6	1.7	0.0	2.0
REG. ABA TOTALS	337	—	10118	1613	3237	.498	0	2	.000	855	1164	.735	1209	2181	4022	1000	1249	16	0	403	0	4081	11.9	3.0	12.1
ABA PLAYOFF TOTALS	7	—	131	20	52	.385	0	0	—	10	19	.526	0	0	47	11	28	2	0	5	0	50	6.7	1.6	7.1
ABA ALL-STAR TOTALS	1	—	14	3	7	.429	0	0	—	1	1	1.000	1	4	5	1	4	0	0	1	0	7	5.0	1.0	7.0

LEWIS, RALPH ADOLPHUS b. March 28, 1963 Ht. 6-6 Wt. 200 College—La Salle

SEASON—TEAM	G	GS	MIN	FGM	FGA	PCT	3FGM	3FGA	PCT	FTM	FTA	PCT	O-RB	D-RB	TOT	AST	PF	DQ	STL	TO	BLK	PTS	RPG	APG	PPG
87-88—Detroit	50	0	310	27	87	.310	0	1	.000	29	48	.604	17	34	51	14	36	0	13	19	4	83	1.0	0.3	1.7
88-89—Charlotte	42	0	336	58	121	.479	1	3	.333	19	39	.487	35	26	61	15	28	0	11	24	3	136	1.5	0.4	3.2
89-90—Detroit-Cha.	7	0	26	4	7	.571	0	0	—	2	2	1.000	4	2	6	0	3	0	1	2	0	10	0.9	0.0	1.4
REG. SEASON TOTALS	99	0	672	89	215	.414	1	4	.250	50	89	.562	56	62	118	29	67	0	25	45	7	229	1.2	0.3	2.3
PLAYOFF TOTALS	10	0	17	2	6	.333	0	1	.000	0	0	—	3	5	8	1	2	0	0	0	0	4	0.8	0.1	0.4

LEWIS, REGGIE b. November 21, 1965 d. July 27, 1993 Ht. 6-7 Wt. 195 College—Northeastern

SEASON—TEAM	G	GS	MIN	FGM	FGA	PCT	3FGM	3FGA	PCT	FTM	FTA	PCT	O-RB	D-RB	TOT	AST	PF	DQ	STL	TO	BLK	PTS	RPG	APG	PPG
87-88—Boston	49	0	405	90	193	.466	0	4	.000	40	57	.702	28	35	63	26	54	0	16	30	15	220	1.3	0.5	4.5
88-89—Boston	81	57	2657	604	1242	.486	3	22	.136	284	361	.787	116	261	377	218	258	5	124	142	72	1495	4.7	2.7	18.5
89-90—Boston	79	54	2522	540	1089	.496	4	15	.267	256	317	.808	109	238	347	225	216	2	88	120	63	1340	4.4	2.8	17.0
90-91—Boston	79	79	2878	598	1219	.491	1	13	.077	281	340	.826	119	291	410	201	234	1	98	147	85	1478	5.2	2.5	18.7
91-92—Boston	82	82	3070	703	1397	.503	5	21	.238	292	343	.851	117	277	394	185	258	4	125	136	105	1703	4.8	2.3	20.8
92-93—Boston	80	80	3144	663	1410	.470	14	60	.233	326	376	.867	88	259	347	298	248	1	118	133	77	1666	4.3	3.7	20.8
REG. SEASON TOTALS	450	352	14676	3198	6550	.488	27	135	.200	1479	1794	.824	577	1361	1938	1153	1268	13	569	708	417	7902	4.3	2.6	17.6
PLAYOFF TOTALS	42	30	1278	293	575	.510	2	15	.133	146	188	.777	54	121	175	109	110	3	51	57	19	734	4.2	2.6	17.5
ALL-STAR TOTALS	1	0	15	3	7	.429	0	0	—	1	2	.500	4	0	4	2	3	0	0	1	1	7	4.0	2.0	7.0

LEWIS, ROBERT FRANKLIN (**Bobby**) b. March 20, 1945 Ht. 6-3 Wt. 185 College—North Carolina

SEASON—TEAM	G	GS	MIN	FGM	FGA	PCT	3FGM	3FGA	PCT	FTM	FTA	PCT	O-RB	D-RB	TOT	AST	PF	DQ	STL	TO	BLK	PTS	RPG	APG	PPG
67-68—San Francisco	41	—	342	59	151	.391	—	—	—	61	79	.772	—	—	56	41	40	0	—	—	—	179	1.4	1.0	4.4
68-69—San Francisco	62	—	756	113	290	.390	—	—	—	83	113	.735	—	—	114	76	117	0	—	—	—	309	1.8	1.2	5.0
69-70—San Francisco	73	—	1353	213	557	.382	—	—	—	100	152	.658	—	—	157	194	170	0	—	—	—	526	2.2	2.7	7.2
70-71—Cleveland	79	—	1852	179	484	.370	—	—	—	109	152	.717	—	—	206	244	176	1	—	—	—	467	2.6	3.1	5.9
REG. SEASON TOTALS	255	—	4303	564	1482	.381	—	—	—	353	496	.712	—	—	533	555	503	1	—	—	—	1481	2.1	2.2	5.8
PLAYOFF TOTALS	6	—	63	13	31	.419	—	—	—	1	3	.333	—	—	5	6	12	0	—	—	—	27	0.8	1.0	4.5

LIBERTY, MARCUS (Doc) b. October 27, 1968 Ht. 6-8 Wt. 205 College—Illinois

SEASON—TEAM	G	GS	MIN	FGM	FGA	PCT	3FGM	3FGA	PCT	FTM	FTA	PCT	O-RB	D-RB	TOT	AST	PF	DQ	STL	TO	BLK	PTS	RPG	APG	PPG
90-91—Denver	76	18	1171	216	513	.421	17	57	.298	58	92	.630	117	104	221	64	153	2	48	71	19	507	2.9	0.8	6.7
91-92—Denver	75	13	1527	275	621	.443	17	50	.340	131	180	.728	144	164	308	58	165	3	66	90	29	698	4.1	0.8	9.3
92-93—Denver	78	32	1585	252	620	.406	22	59	.373	102	156	.654	131	204	335	105	143	0	64	79	21	628	4.3	1.3	8.1
93-94—Denver-Detroit	38	0	285	40	123	.325	10	28	.357	19	39	.487	26	35	61	17	34	0	11	24	4	109	1.6	0.4	2.9
REG. SEASON TOTALS	267	63	4568	783	1877	.417	66	194	.340	310	467	.664	418	507	925	244	495	5	189	264	73	1942	3.5	0.9	7.3

LICHTI, TODD SAMUEL b. January 8, 1967 Ht. 6-4 Wt. 205 College—Stanford

SEASON—TEAM	G	GS	MIN	FGM	FGA	PCT	3FGM	3FGA	PCT	FTM	FTA	PCT	O-RB	D-RB	TOT	AST	PF	DQ	STL	TO	BLK	PTS	RPG	APG	PPG
89-90—Denver	79	4	1326	250	514	.486	0	14	.000	130	174	.747	49	102	151	116	145	1	55	95	13	630	1.9	1.5	8.0
90-91—Denver	29	25	860	166	378	.439	14	47	.298	59	69	.855	49	63	112	72	65	1	46	33	8	405	3.9	2.5	14.0
91-92—Denver	68	10	1176	173	376	.460	1	9	.111	99	118	.839	36	82	118	74	131	0	43	72	12	446	1.7	1.1	6.6
92-93—Denver	48	12	752	124	276	.449	2	6	.333	81	102	.794	35	67	102	52	60	0	28	49	11	331	2.1	1.1	6.9
93-94—Orlando-G.S.-Boston	13	0	126	20	51	.392	2	2	1.000	16	25	.640	8	14	22	11	16	0	7	5	1	58	1.7	0.8	4.5
REG. SEASON TOTALS	237	51	4240	733	1595	.460	19	78	.244	385	488	.789	177	328	505	325	417	2	179	254	45	1870	2.1	1.4	7.9
PLAYOFF TOTALS	3	0	70	15	29	.517	0	1	.000	14	19	.737	5	13	18	9	6	0	1	8	0	44	6.0	3.0	14.7

LIEBOWITZ, BARRY b. 1943 Ht. 6-2 Wt. 180 College—Long Island University

SEASON—TEAM	G	GS	MIN	FGM	FGA	PCT	3FGM	3FGA	PCT	FTM	FTA	PCT	O-RB	D-RB	TOT	AST	PF	DQ	STL	TO	BLK	PTS	RPG	APG	PPG
67-68—Pitt.-N.J.-Oakland (A)	82	—	2168	320	873	.367	6	39	.154	248	308	.805	—	—	170	301	208	1	—	224	—	894	2.1	3.7	10.9
REG. ABA TOTALS	82	—	2168	320	873	.367	6	39	.154	248	308	.805	—	—	170	301	208	1	—	224	—	894	2.1	3.7	10.9

LIGON, JIM (Goose) b. February 22, 1944 Ht. 6-7 Wt. 215 College—None

SEASON—TEAM	G	GS	MIN	FGM	FGA	PCT	3FGM	3FGA	PCT	FTM	FTA	PCT	O-RB	D-RB	TOT	AST	PF	DQ	STL	TO	BLK	PTS	RPG	APG	PPG
67-68—Kentucky (A)	78	—	2801	428	942	.454	1	4	.250	405	595	.681	370	559	929	143	307	6	—	188	—	1262	11.9	1.8	16.2
68-69—Kentucky (A)	75	—	2815	391	879	.445	1	5	.200	337	510	.661	328	491	819	172	312	6	—	193	—	1120	10.9	2.3	14.9
69-70—Kentucky (A)	84	—	3130	507	1000	.507	0	2	.000	287	445	.645	399	695	1094	190	360	13	—	—	—	1301	13.0	2.3	15.5
70-71—Kentucky (A)	84	—	2753	429	795	.540	0	6	.000	214	391	.547	312	677	989	211	331	—	—	—	—	1072	11.8	2.5	12.8
71-72—Ken.-Pitt. (A)	82	—	2341	213	428	.498	1	6	.167	141	217	.650	—	—	700	163	265	—	—	126	—	568	8.5	2.0	6.9
72-73—Virginia (A)	12	—	360	58	103	.563	0	0	—	28	43	.651	36	58	94	20	40	0	—	21	—	144	7.8	1.7	12.0
73-74—Virginia (A)	19	—	360	37	85	.435	0	1	.000	19	25	.760	45	50	95	11	43	—	9	24	9	93	5.0	0.6	4.9
REG. ABA TOTALS	434	—	14560	2063	4232	.487	3	24	.125	1431	2226	.643	1490	2530	4720	910	1658	25	9	552	9	5560	10.9	2.1	12.8
ABA PLAYOFF TOTALS	46	—	1521	211	439	.481	0	3	.000	166	249	.667	163	295	516	76	129	1	0	41	1	588	11.2	1.7	12.8
ABA ALL-STAR TOTALS	1	—	12	0	2	.000	0	0	—	3	4	.750	1	2	3	0	2	0	0	1	0	3	3.0	0.0	3.0

LIGON, WILLIAM N. (Bill) b. May 19, 1952 Ht. 6-4 Wt. 180 College—Vanderbilt

SEASON—TEAM	G	GS	MIN	FGM	FGA	PCT	3FGM	3FGA	PCT	FTM	FTA	PCT	O-RB	D-RB	TOT	AST	PF	DQ	STL	TO	BLK	PTS	RPG	APG	PPG
74-75—Detroit	38	—	272	55	143	.385	—	—	—	16	25	.640	14	12	26	25	31	0	8	—	9	126	0.7	0.7	3.3
REG. SEASON TOTALS	38	—	272	55	143	.385	—	—	—	16	25	.640	14	12	26	25	31	0	8	—	9	126	0.7	0.7	3.3
PLAYOFF TOTALS	2	—	7	1	1	1.000	—	—	—	0	0	—	0	0	0	—	1	0	0	—	0	2	0.0	0.0	1.0

LINGENFELTER, STEVEN RODNEY (Steve) b. June 10, 1958 Ht. 6-9 Wt. 225 College—Minnesota/South Dakota State

SEASON—TEAM	G	GS	MIN	FGM	FGA	PCT	3FGM	3FGA	PCT	FTM	FTA	PCT	O-RB	D-RB	TOT	AST	PF	DQ	STL	TO	BLK	PTS	RPG	APG	PPG
82-83—Washington	7	0	53	4	6	.667	0	0	—	0	4	.000	1	11	12	4	16	1	1	5	3	8	1.7	0.6	1.1
83-84—San Antonio	3	0	14	1	1	1.000	0	0	—	0	2	.000	3	1	4	1	6	0	0	1	0	2	1.3	0.3	0.7
REG. SEASON TOTALS	10	0	67	5	7	.714	0	0	—	0	6	.000	4	12	16	5	22	1	1	6	3	10	1.6	0.5	1.0

LISTER, ALTON LAVELLE b. October 1, 1958 Ht. 7-0 Wt. 240 College—San Jacinto/Arizona State

SEASON—TEAM	G	GS	MIN	FGM	FGA	PCT	3FGM	3FGA	PCT	FTM	FTA	PCT	O-RB	D-RB	TOT	AST	PF	DQ	STL	TO	BLK	PTS	RPG	APG	PPG
81-82—Milwaukee	80	23	1186	149	287	.519	0	0	—	64	123	.520	108	279	387	84	239	4	18	129	118	362	4.8	1.1	4.5
82-83—Milwaukee	80	37	1885	272	514	.529	0	0	—	130	242	.537	168	400	568	111	328	18	50	186	177	674	7.1	1.4	8.4
83-84—Milwaukee	82	72	1955	256	512	.500	0	0	—	114	182	.626	156	447	603	110	327	11	41	153	140	626	7.4	1.3	7.6
84-85—Milwaukee	81	80	2091	322	598	.538	0	1	.000	154	262	.588	219	428	647	127	287	5	49	183	167	798	8.0	1.6	9.9
85-86—Milwaukee	81	19	1812	318	577	.551	0	2	.000	160	266	.602	199	393	592	101	300	8	49	161	142	796	7.3	1.2	9.8
86-87—Seattle	75	75	2288	346	687	.504	0	1	.000	179	265	.675	223	482	705	110	289	11	32	169	180	871	9.4	1.5	11.6
87-88—Seattle	82	55	1812	173	343	.504	1	2	.500	114	188	.606	200	427	627	58	319	8	27	90	141	461	7.6	0.7	5.6
88-89—Seattle	82	82	1806	271	543	.499	0	0	—	115	178	.646	207	338	545	54	310	3	28	117	180	657	6.6	0.7	8.0
89-90—Golden State	3	0	40	4	8	.500	0	1	.000	4	7	.571	5	3	8	2	8	0	1	0	0	12	2.7	0.7	4.0
90-91—Golden State	77	65	1552	188	393	.478	0	1	.000	115	202	.569	121	362	483	93	282	4	20	106	90	491	6.3	1.2	6.4
91-92—Golden State	26	12	293	44	79	.557	0	0	—	14	33	.424	21	71	92	14	61	0	5	20	16	102	3.5	0.5	3.9
92-93—Golden State	20	9	174	19	42	.452	0	0	—	7	13	.538	15	29	44	5	40	0	0	18	9	45	2.2	0.3	2.3
REG. SEASON TOTALS	769	529	16894	2362	4583	.515	1	8	.125	1170	1961	.597	1642	3659	5301	869	2790	72	320	1332	1359	5895	6.9	1.1	7.7
PLAYOFF TOTALS	85	59	1786	240	474	.506	0	2	.000	135	211	.640	178	326	504	70	314	10	39	124	141	615	5.9	0.8	7.2

LITTLE, SAMUEL RAY (**Sammy**) b. March 29, 1946 Ht. 6-0 Wt. 180 College—Delta State

SEASON—TEAM	G	GS	MIN	FGM	FGA	PCT	3FGM	3FGA	PCT	FTM	FTA	PCT	O-RB	D-RB	TOT	AST	PF	DQ	STL	TO	BLK	PTS	RPG	APG	PPG
69-70—Kentucky (A)	3	—	11	2	4	.500	0	1	.000	1	1	1.000	—	—	1	2	4	0	—	—	—	5	0.3	0.7	1.7
REG. ABA TOTALS	3	—	11	2	4	.500	0	1	.000	1	1	1.000	—	—	1	2	4	0	—	—	—	5	0.3	0.7	1.7

LITTLES, EUGENE SCAPE (**Gene**) b. June 29, 1943 Ht. 6-1½ Wt. 180 College—High Point

SEASON—TEAM	G	GS	MIN	FGM	FGA	PCT	3FGM	3FGA	PCT	FTM	FTA	PCT	O-RB	D-RB	TOT	AST	PF	DQ	STL	TO	BLK	PTS	RPG	APG	PPG
69-70—Carolina (A)	82	—	2832	414	817	.507	0	3	.000	197	254	.776	—	—	415	282	255	0	—	—	—	1025	5.1	3.4	12.5
70-71—Carolina (A)	70	—	1495	223	501	.445	4	14	.286	117	168	.696	—	—	205	173	175	—	—	—	—	567	2.9	2.5	8.1
71-72—Carolina (A)	69	—	2006	280	605	.463	7	26	.269	178	237	.751	—	—	276	237	180	—	—	104	—	745	4.0	3.4	10.8
72-73—Carolina (A)	84	—	2060	310	622	.498	8	30	.267	179	246	.728	104	158	262	245	198	0	—	125	—	807	3.1	2.9	9.6
73-74—Carolina (A)	84	—	2017	294	626	.470	4	23	.174	115	161	.714	87	144	231	280	159	—	105	122	17	707	2.8	3.3	8.4
74-75—Kentucky (A)	61	—	900	85	202	.421	2	8	.250	43	58	.741	30	56	86	119	81	—	52	62	4	215	1.4	2.0	3.5
REG. ABA TOTALS	450	—	11310	1606	3373	.476	25	104	.240	829	1124	.738	221	358	1475	1336	1048	0	157	413	21	4066	3.3	3.0	9.0
ABA PLAYOFF TOTALS	28	—	492	65	143	.455	4	9	.444	29	49	.592	8	8	70	52	43	1	26	16	0	163	2.5	1.9	5.8

LIVINGSTONE, GEORGE RONALD (**Ron**) b. October 9, 1925 Ht. 6-10 Wt. 220 College—Modesto JC/Wyoming/St. Mary's (Ca.)

SEASON—TEAM	G	GS	MIN	FGM	FGA	PCT	3FGM	3FGA	PCT	FTM	FTA	PCT	O-RB	D-RB	TOT	AST	PF	DQ	STL	TO	BLK	PTS	RPG	APG	PPG
49-50—Balt.-Phil.	54	—	—	163	579	.282	—	—	—	122	177	.689	—	—	—	141	260	—	—	—	—	448	—	2.6	8.3
50-51—Philadelphia	63	—	—	104	353	.295	—	—	—	76	109	.697	—	—	297	76	220	10	—	—	—	284	4.7	1.2	4.5
REG. SEASON TOTALS	117	—	—	267	932	.286	—	—	—	198	286	.692	—	—	297	217	480	10	—	—	—	732	4.7	1.9	6.3
PLAYOFF TOTALS	4	—	—	8	19	.421	—	—	—	4	7	.571	—	—	2	5	13	2	—	—	—	20	1.0	1.3	5.0

LLOYD, CHARLES P. JR. (**Chuck**) b. May 22, 1947 Ht. 6-8 Wt. 220 College—Yankton

SEASON—TEAM	G	GS	MIN	FGM	FGA	PCT	3FGM	3FGA	PCT	FTM	FTA	PCT	O-RB	D-RB	TOT	AST	PF	DQ	STL	TO	BLK	PTS	RPG	APG	PPG
70-71—Carolina (A)	14	—	118	23	51	.451	0	0	—	20	30	.667	—	—	25	6	25	—	—	—	—	—	66	1.8	0.4	4.7
REG. ABA TOTALS	14	—	118	23	51	.451	0	0	—	20	30	.667	—	—	25	6	25	—	—	—	—	—	66	1.8	0.4	4.7

LLOYD, EARL FRANCIS (**Big Cat**) b. April 3, 1928 Ht. 6-6 Wt. 220 College—West Virginia State

SEASON—TEAM	G	GS	MIN	FGM	FGA	PCT	3FGM	3FGA	PCT	FTM	FTA	PCT	O-RB	D-RB	TOT	AST	PF	DQ	STL	TO	BLK	PTS	RPG	APG	PPG
50-51—Washington	7	—	—	16	35	.457	—	—	—	11	13	.846	—	—	47	11	26	0	—	—	—	43	6.7	1.6	6.1
52-53—Syracuse	64	—	1806	156	453	.344	—	—	—	160	231	.693	—	—	444	64	241	6	—	—	—	472	6.9	1.0	7.4
53-54—Syracuse	72	—	2206	249	666	.374	—	—	—	156	209	.746	—	—	529	115	303	12	—	—	—	654	7.3	1.6	9.1
54-55—Syracuse	72	—	2212	286	784	.365	—	—	—	159	212	.750	—	—	553	151	283	4	—	—	—	731	7.7	2.1	10.2
55-56—Syracuse	72	—	1837	213	636	.335	—	—	—	186	241	.772	—	—	492	116	267	6	—	—	—	612	6.8	1.6	8.5
56-57—Syracuse	72	—	1965	256	687	.373	—	—	—	134	179	.749	—	—	435	114	282	10	—	—	—	646	6.0	1.6	9.0
57-58—Syracuse	61	—	1045	119	359	.331	—	—	—	79	106	.745	—	—	287	60	179	3	—	—	—	317	4.7	1.0	5.2
58-59—Detroit	72	—	1796	234	670	.349	—	—	—	137	182	.753	—	—	500	90	291	15	—	—	—	605	6.9	1.3	8.4
59-60—Detroit	68	—	1610	237	665	.356	—	—	—	128	160	.800	—	—	322	89	226	1	—	—	—	602	4.7	1.3	8.9
REG. SEASON TOTALS	560	—	14477	1766	4955	.356	—	—	—	1150	1533	.750	—	—	3609	810	2098	57	—	—	—	4682	6.4	1.4	8.4
PLAYOFF TOTALS	44	—	1115	131	389	.337	—	—	—	96	129	.744	—	—	254	82	171	2	—	—	—	358	5.8	1.9	8.1

LLOYD, LEWIS KEVIN b. February 22, 1959 Ht. 6-6 Wt. 205 College—New Mexico Military Institute/Drake

SEASON—TEAM	G	GS	MIN	FGM	FGA	PCT	3FGM	3FGA	PCT	FTM	FTA	PCT	O-RB	D-RB	TOT	AST	PF	DQ	STL	TO	BLK	PTS	RPG	APG	PPG
81-82—Golden State	16	0	95	25	45	.556	0	0	—	7	11	.636	9	7	16	6	20	0	5	14	1	57	1.0	0.4	3.6
82-83—Golden State	73	24	1350	293	566	.518	1	4	.250	100	139	.719	77	183	260	130	109	0	61	118	31	687	3.6	1.8	9.4
83-84—Houston	82	82	2578	610	1182	.516	3	13	.231	235	298	.789	128	167	295	321	211	4	102	245	44	1458	3.6	3.9	17.8
84-85—Houston	82	58	2128	457	869	.526	2	8	.250	161	220	.732	98	133	231	280	196	1	73	177	28	1077	2.8	3.4	13.1
85-86—Houston	82	82	2444	592	1119	.529	3	14	.214	199	236	.843	155	169	324	300	216	0	102	194	24	1386	4.0	3.7	16.9
86-87—Houston	32	14	688	165	310	.532	1	7	.143	65	86	.756	13	35	48	90	69	0	19	52	5	396	1.5	2.8	12.4
89-90—Phil.-Houston	21	0	123	30	53	.566	0	0	—	9	16	.563	8	10	18	11	12	0	3	20	0	69	0.9	0.5	3.3
REG. SEASON TOTALS	388	260	9406	2172	4144	.524	10	46	.217	776	1006	.771	488	704	1192	1138	833	5	365	820	133	5130	3.1	2.9	13.2
PLAYOFF TOTALS	25	25	763	154	318	.484	2	5	.400	57	72	.792	49	46	95	111	59	0	23	57	14	367	3.8	4.4	14.7

LLOYD, ROBERT E. (**Bobby**) b. January 3, 1946 Ht. 6-2 Wt. 185 College—Rutgers

SEASON—TEAM	G	GS	MIN	FGM	FGA	PCT	3FGM	3FGA	PCT	FTM	FTA	PCT	O-RB	D-RB	TOT	AST	PF	DQ	STL	TO	BLK	PTS	RPG	APG	PPG
67-68—New Jersey (A)	58	—	995	147	349	.421	3	8	.375	170	199	.854	—	—	108	93	114	1	—	74	—	467	1.9	1.6	8.1
68-69—New York (A)	67	—	1358	215	541	.397	12	31	.387	218	246	.886	—	—	112	136	176	1	—	95	—	660	1.7	2.0	9.9
REG. ABA TOTALS	125	—	2353	362	890	.407	15	39	.385	388	445	.872	—	—	220	229	290	2	—	169	—	1127	1.8	1.8	9.0

LLOYD, SCOTT G. b. December 19, 1952 Ht. 6-10 Wt. 230 College—Arizona State

SEASON—TEAM	G	GS	MIN	FGM	FGA	PCT	3FGM	3FGA	PCT	FTM	FTA	PCT	O-RB	D-RB	TOT	AST	PF	DQ	STL	TO	BLK	PTS	RPG	APG	PPG
76-77—Milwaukee	69	—	1025	153	324	.472	—	—	—	95	126	.754	81	129	210	33	158	5	21	—	13	401	3.0	0.5	5.8
77-78—Milw.-Buffalo	70	—	678	80	193	.415	—	—	—	49	68	.721	52	93	145	44	105	1	14	43	14	209	2.1	0.6	3.0
78-79—S.D.-Chicago	72	—	496	42	122	.344	—	—	—	27	47	.574	49	47	96	32	92	0	10	51	8	111	1.3	0.4	1.5
80-81—Dallas	72	—	2186	245	547	.448	0	2	.000	147	205	.717	161	293	454	159	269	8	34	145	25	637	6.3	2.2	8.8
81-82—Dallas	74	17	1047	108	285	.379	2	4	.500	69	91	.758	60	103	163	67	175	6	15	59	7	287	2.2	0.9	3.9
82-83—Dallas	15	0	206	19	50	.380	0	1	.000	11	17	.647	19	27	46	21	24	0	6	6	6	49	3.1	1.4	3.3
REG. SEASON TOTALS	372	17	5638	647	1521	.425	2	7	.286	398	554	.718	422	692	1114	356	823	20	100	304	73	1694	3.0	1.0	4.6

LOCHMANN, REINHOLD D. **(Riney)** b. May 26, 1944 Ht. 6-6 Wt. 215 College—Kansas

SEASON—TEAM	G	GS	MIN	FGM	FGA	PCT	3FGM	3FGA	PCT	FTM	FTA	PCT	O-RB	D-RB	TOT	AST	PF	DQ	STL	TO	BLK	PTS	RPG	APG	PPG
67-68—Dallas (A)	63	—	808	108	285	.379	1	4	.250	49	79	.620	—	—	166	44	113	2	—	40	—	266	2.6	0.7	4.2
68-69—Dallas (A)	60	—	950	115	279	.412	1	4	.250	60	97	.619	—	—	204	59	138	4	—	50	—	291	3.4	1.0	4.9
69-70—Dallas (A)	47	—	447	73	166	.440	3	8	.375	25	45	.556	—	—	96	40	61	0	—	—	—	174	2.0	0.9	3.7
REG. ABA TOTALS	170	—	2205	296	730	.405	5	16	.313	134	221	.606	—	—	466	143	312	6	—	90	—	731	2.7	0.8	4.3
ABA PLAYOFF TOTALS	8	—	51	5	14	.357	0	0	—	3	3	1.000	—	—	7	1	7	0	—	—	—	13	0.9	0.1	1.6

LOCHMUELLER, ROBERT L. **(Bob)** b. June 5, 1927 Ht. 6-5 Wt. 185 College—Louisville

SEASON—TEAM	G	GS	MIN	FGM	FGA	PCT	3FGM	3FGA	PCT	FTM	FTA	PCT	O-RB	D-RB	TOT	AST	PF	DQ	STL	TO	BLK	PTS	RPG	APG	PPG
52-53—Syracuse	62	—	802	79	245	.322	—	—	—	74	122	.607	—	—	162	47	143	1	—	—	—	232	2.6	0.8	3.7
REG. SEASON TOTALS	62	—	802	79	245	.322	—	—	—	74	122	.607	—	—	162	47	143	1	—	—	—	232	2.6	0.8	3.7
PLAYOFF TOTALS	2	—	21	2	10	.200	—	—	—	1	4	.250	—	—	5	2	12	2	—	—	—	5	2.5	1.0	2.5

LOCK, ROBERT ALAN **(Rob)** b. May 22, 1966 Ht. 6-9 Wt. 235 College—Kentucky

SEASON—TEAM	G	GS	MIN	FGM	FGA	PCT	3FGM	3FGA	PCT	FTM	FTA	PCT	O-RB	D-RB	TOT	AST	PF	DQ	STL	TO	BLK	PTS	RPG	APG	PPG
88-89—L.A. Clippers	20	0	110	9	32	.281	0	0	—	12	15	.800	14	18	32	4	15	0	3	13	4	30	1.6	0.2	1.5
REG. SEASON TOTALS	20	0	110	9	32	.281	0	0	—	12	15	.800	14	18	32	4	15	0	3	13	4	30	1.6	0.2	1.5

LOCKHART, DARRELL b. September 14, 1960 Ht. 6-9 Wt. 245 College—Auburn

SEASON—TEAM	G	GS	MIN	FGM	FGA	PCT	3FGM	3FGA	PCT	FTM	FTA	PCT	O-RB	D-RB	TOT	AST	PF	DQ	STL	TO	BLK	PTS	RPG	APG	PPG
83-84—San Antonio	2	0	14	2	2	1.000	0	0	—	0	0	—	0	3	3	0	5	0	0	2	0	4	1.5	0.0	2.0
REG. SEASON TOTALS	2	0	14	2	2	1.000	0	0	—	0	0	—	0	3	3	0	5	0	0	2	0	4	1.5	0.0	2.0

LOCKHART, IAN DeWITT b. June 25, 1967 Ht. 6-8 Wt. 240 College—Tennessee

SEASON—TEAM	G	GS	MIN	FGM	FGA	PCT	3FGM	3FGA	PCT	FTM	FTA	PCT	O-RB	D-RB	TOT	AST	PF	DQ	STL	TO	BLK	PTS	RPG	APG	PPG
90-91—Phoenix	1	0	2	1	1	1.000	0	0	—	2	2	1.000	0	0	0	0	0	0	0	0	0	4	0.0	0.0	4.0
REG. SEASON TOTALS	1	0	2	1	1	1.000	0	0	—	2	2	1.000	0	0	0	0	0	0	0	0	0	4	0.0	0.0	4.0

LODER, KEVIN ALLEN b. March 15, 1959 Ht. 6-6 Wt. 205 College—Kentucky State/Alabama State

SEASON—TEAM	G	GS	MIN	FGM	FGA	PCT	3FGM	3FGA	PCT	FTM	FTA	PCT	O-RB	D-RB	TOT	AST	PF	DQ	STL	TO	BLK	PTS	RPG	APG	PPG
81-82—Kansas City	71	13	1139	208	448	.464	0	11	.000	77	107	.720	69	126	195	88	147	0	35	68	30	493	2.7	1.2	6.9
82-83—Kansas City	66	13	818	138	300	.460	5	9	.556	53	80	.663	37	88	125	72	98	0	29	64	8	334	1.9	1.1	5.1
83-84—K.C.-S.D.	11	0	137	19	43	.442	1	3	.333	9	13	.692	7	11	18	14	16	0	3	11	5	48	1.6	1.3	4.4
REG. SEASON TOTALS	148	26	2094	365	791	.461	6	23	.261	139	200	.695	113	225	338	174	261	0	67	143	43	875	2.3	1.2	5.9

LOFGRAN, DONALD b. November 18, 1928 d. June 1976 Ht. 6-5 Wt. 200 College—Grant Tech/San Francisco

SEASON—TEAM	G	GS	MIN	FGM	FGA	PCT	3FGM	3FGA	PCT	FTM	FTA	PCT	O-RB	D-RB	TOT	AST	PF	DQ	STL	TO	BLK	PTS	RPG	APG	PPG
50-51—Syr.-Ind.	61	—	—	79	270	.293	—	—	—	79	127	.622	—	—	157	36	132	4	—	—	—	237	2.6	0.6	3.9
51-52—Indianapolis	63	—	1254	149	417	.357	—	—	—	156	219	.712	—	—	257	48	147	3	—	—	—	454	4.1	0.8	7.2
52-53—Philadelphia	64	—	1788	173	525	.330	—	—	—	126	173	.728	—	—	339	106	178	6	—	—	—	472	5.3	1.7	7.4
53-54—Milwaukee	21	—	380	35	112	.313	—	—	—	32	49	.653	—	—	64	26	34	0	—	—	—	102	3.0	1.2	4.9
REG. SEASON TOTALS	209	—	3422	436	1324	.329	—	—	—	393	568	.692	—	—	817	216	491	13	—	—	—	1265	3.9	1.0	6.1
PLAYOFF TOTALS	3	—	10	2	9	.222	—	—	—	1	1	1.000	—	—	1	—	6	0	—	—	—	5	0.3	0.0	1.7

LOGAN, HENRY LEE b. March 14, 1946 Ht. 6-0 Wt. 185 College—Western Carolina

SEASON—TEAM	G	GS	MIN	FGM	FGA	PCT	3FGM	3FGA	PCT	FTM	FTA	PCT	O-RB	D-RB	TOT	AST	PF	DQ	STL	TO	BLK	PTS	RPG	APG	PPG
68-69—Oakland (A)	76	—	1751	339	694	.488	1	4	.250	268	382	.702	—	—	287	185	226	4	—	188	—	947	3.8	2.4	12.5
69-70—Washington (A)	32	—	659	110	269	.409	0	3	.000	91	127	.717	—	—	89	59	93	3	—	—	—	311	2.8	1.8	9.7
REG. ABA TOTALS	108	—	2410	449	963	.466	1	7	.143	359	509	.705	—	—	376	244	319	7	—	188	—	1258	3.5	2.3	11.6
ABA PLAYOFF TOTALS	17	—	381	75	176	.426	0	0	—	68	101	.673	—	—	40	34	50	3	—	36	—	218	2.4	2.0	12.8

LOGAN, JOHN ARNOLD (**Johnny**) b. January 1, 1921 d. September 16, 1977 Ht. 6-2 Wt. 175 College—Indiana

SEASON—TEAM	G	GS	MIN	FGM	FGA	PCT	3FGM	3FGA	PCT	FTM	FTA	PCT	O-RB	D-RB	TOT	AST	PF	DQ	STL	TO	BLK	PTS	RPG	APG	PPG
46-47—St. Louis	61	—	—	290	1043	.278	—	—	—	190	254	.748	—	—	—	78	136	—	—	—	—	770	—	1.3	12.6
47-48—St. Louis	48	—	—	221	734	.301	—	—	—	202	272	.743	—	—	—	62	141	—	—	—	—	644	—	1.3	13.4
48-49—St. Louis	57	—	—	282	816	.346	—	—	—	239	302	.791	—	—	—	276	191	—	—	—	—	803	—	4.8	14.1
49-50—St. Louis	62	—	—	251	759	.331	—	—	—	253	323	.783	—	—	—	240	206	—	—	—	—	755	—	3.9	12.2
50-51—Tri-Cities	29	—	—	81	257	.315	—	—	—	62	83	.747	—	—	134	127	66	2	—	—	—	224	4.6	4.4	7.7
REG. SEASON TOTALS	257	—	—	1125	3609	.312	—	—	—	946	1234	.767	—	—	134	783	740	2	—	—	—	3196	4.6	3.0	12.4
PLAYOFF TOTALS	10	—	—	34	123	.276	—	—	—	39	52	.750	—	—	—	19	36	0	—	—	—	107	—	1.9	10.7

LOHAUS, BRAD ALLEN b. September 29, 1964 Ht. 7-0 Wt. 235 College—Iowa

SEASON—TEAM	G	GS	MIN	FGM	FGA	PCT	3FGM	3FGA	PCT	FTM	FTA	PCT	O-RB	D-RB	TOT	AST	PF	DQ	STL	TO	BLK	PTS	RPG	APG	PPG
87-88—Boston	70	4	718	122	246	.496	3	13	.231	50	62	.806	46	92	138	49	123	1	20	59	41	297	2.0	0.7	4.2
88-89—Boston-Sac.	77	25	1214	210	486	.432	1	11	.091	81	103	.786	84	172	256	66	161	1	30	77	56	502	3.3	0.9	6.5
89-90—Minn.-Milw.	80	41	1943	305	663	.460	47	137	.343	75	103	.728	98	300	398	168	211	3	58	109	88	732	5.0	2.1	9.2
90-91—Milwaukee	81	3	1219	179	415	.431	33	119	.277	37	54	.685	59	158	217	75	170	3	50	60	74	428	2.7	0.9	5.3
91-92—Milwaukee	70	8	1081	162	360	.450	57	144	.396	27	41	.659	65	184	249	74	144	5	40	46	71	408	3.6	1.1	5.8
92-93—Milwaukee	80	24	1766	283	614	.461	85	230	.370	73	101	.723	59	217	276	127	178	1	47	93	74	724	3.5	1.6	9.1
93-94—Milwaukee	67	2	962	102	281	.363	46	134	.343	20	29	.690	33	117	150	62	142	3	30	58	55	270	2.2	0.9	4.0
REG. SEASON TOTALS	525	107	8903	1363	3065	.445	272	788	.345	363	493	.736	444	1240	1684	621	1129	17	275	502	459	3361	3.2	1.2	6.4
PLAYOFF TOTALS	16	4	214	29	67	.433	9	26	.346	1	2	.500	9	31	40	6	27	1	8	13	10	68	2.5	0.4	4.3

LONG, GRANT ANDREW b. March 12, 1966 Ht. 6-9 Wt. 245 College—Eastern Michigan

SEASON—TEAM	G	GS	MIN	FGM	FGA	PCT	3FGM	3FGA	PCT	FTM	FTA	PCT	O-RB	D-RB	TOT	AST	PF	DQ	STL	TO	BLK	PTS	RPG	APG	PPG
88-89—Miami	82	73	2435	336	692	.486	0	5	.000	304	406	.749	240	306	546	149	337	13	122	201	48	976	6.7	1.8	11.9
89-90—Miami	81	31	1856	257	532	.483	0	3	.000	172	241	.714	156	246	402	96	300	11	91	139	38	686	5.0	1.2	8.5
90-91—Miami	80	66	2514	276	561	.492	1	6	.167	181	230	.787	225	343	568	176	295	10	119	156	43	734	7.1	2.2	9.2
91-92—Miami	82	82	3063	440	890	.494	6	22	.273	326	404	.807	259	432	691	225	248	2	139	185	40	1212	8.4	2.7	14.8
92-93—Miami	76	62	2728	397	847	.469	6	26	.231	261	341	.765	197	371	568	182	264	8	104	133	31	1061	7.5	2.4	14.0
93-94—Miami	69	59	2201	300	672	.446	1	6	.167	187	238	.786	190	305	495	170	244	5	89	125	26	788	7.2	2.5	11.4
REG. SEASON TOTALS	470	373	14797	2006	4194	.478	14	68	.206	1431	1860	.769	1267	2003	3270	998	1688	49	664	939	226	5457	7.0	2.1	11.6
PLAYOFF TOTALS	7	5	230	29	72	.403	0	4	.000	28	37	.757	17	16	33	15	27	1	8	15	2	86	4.7	2.1	12.3

LONG, JOHN EDDIE b. August 28, 1956 Ht. 6-5 Wt. 200 College—Detroit

SEASON—TEAM	G	GS	MIN	FGM	FGA	PCT	3FGM	3FGA	PCT	FTM	FTA	PCT	O-RB	D-RB	TOT	AST	PF	DQ	STL	TO	BLK	PTS	RPG	APG	PPG
78-79—Detroit	82	—	2498	581	1240	.469	—	—	—	157	190	.826	127	139	266	121	224	1	102	137	19	1319	3.2	1.5	16.1
79-80—Detroit	69	—	2364	588	1164	.505	1	12	.083	160	194	.825	152	185	337	206	221	4	129	206	26	1337	4.9	3.0	19.4
80-81—Detroit	59	—	1750	441	957	.461	2	11	.182	160	184	.870	95	102	197	106	164	3	95	151	22	1044	3.3	1.8	17.7
81-82—Detroit	69	66	2211	637	1294	.492	2	15	.133	238	275	.865	95	162	257	148	173	0	65	167	25	1514	3.7	2.1	21.9
82-83—Detroit	70	30	1485	312	692	.451	2	7	.286	111	146	.760	56	124	180	105	130	1	44	144	12	737	2.6	1.5	10.5
83-84—Detroit	82	82	2514	545	1155	.472	1	5	.200	243	275	.884	139	150	289	205	199	1	93	143	18	1334	3.5	2.5	16.3
84-85—Detroit	66	55	1820	431	885	.487	5	15	.333	106	123	.862	81	109	190	130	139	0	71	98	14	973	2.9	2.0	14.7
85-86—Detroit	62	30	1176	264	548	.482	3	16	.188	89	104	.856	47	51	98	82	92	0	41	59	13	620	1.6	1.3	10.0
86-87—Indiana	80	68	2265	490	1170	.419	19	67	.284	219	246	.890	75	142	217	258	167	1	96	153	8	1218	2.7	3.2	15.2
87-88—Indiana	81	81	2022	417	879	.474	34	77	.442	166	183	.907	72	157	229	173	164	1	84	127	11	1034	2.8	2.1	12.8
88-89—Indiana-Detroit	68	1	919	147	359	.409	8	20	.400	70	76	.921	18	59	77	80	84	1	29	57	3	372	1.1	1.2	5.5
89-90—Atlanta	48	19	1030	174	384	.453	10	29	.345	46	55	.836	26	57	83	85	66	0	45	75	5	404	1.7	1.8	8.4
90-91—Detroit	25	0	256	35	85	.412	2	6	.333	24	25	.960	9	23	32	18	17	0	9	14	2	96	1.3	0.7	3.8
REG. SEASON TOTALS	861	432	22310	5062	10812	.468	89	280	.318	1789	2076	.862	992	1460	2452	1717	1840	13	903	1531	178	12002	2.8	2.0	13.9
PLAYOFF TOTALS	23	18	534	87	218	.399	2	11	.182	47	49	.959	19	16	35	24	54	0	28	28	2	223	1.5	1.0	9.7

LONG, PAUL RICHARD b. February 8, 1944 Ht. 6-2 Wt. 180 College—Wake Forest/Virginia Tech

SEASON—TEAM	G	GS	MIN	FGM	FGA	PCT	3FGM	3FGA	PCT	FTM	FTA	PCT	O-RB	D-RB	TOT	AST	PF	DQ	STL	TO	BLK	PTS	RPG	APG	PPG
67-68—Detroit	16	—	93	23	51	.451	—	—	—	11	15	.733	—	—	15	12	13	0	—	—	—	57	0.9	0.8	3.6
68-69—Kentucky (A)	9	—	82	9	40	.225	0	0	—	17	21	.810	—	—	9	12	21	0	—	15	—	35	1.0	1.3	3.9
69-70—Detroit	25	—	130	28	62	.452	—	—	—	27	38	.711	—	—	11	17	22	0	—	—	—	83	0.4	0.7	3.3
70-71—Buffalo	30	—	213	57	120	.475	—	—	—	20	24	.833	—	—	31	25	23	0	—	—	—	134	1.0	0.8	4.5
REG. NBA TOTALS	71	—	436	108	233	.464	—	—	—	58	77	.753	—	—	57	54	58	0	—	—	—	274	0.8	0.8	3.9
REG. ABA TOTALS	9	—	82	9	40	.225	0	0	—	17	21	.810	—	—	9	12	21	0	—	15	—	35	1.0	1.3	3.9
NBA PLAYOFF TOTALS	1	—	4	3	3	1.000	—	—	—	0	0	—	—	—	0	1	1	0	—	—	—	6	0.0	1.0	6.0

LONG, WILLIE b. March 1, 1950 Ht. 6-8 Wt. 230 College—New Mexico

SEASON—TEAM	G	GS	MIN	FGM	FGA	PCT	3FGM	3FGA	PCT	FTM	FTA	PCT	O-RB	D-RB	TOT	AST	PF	DQ	STL	TO	BLK	PTS	RPG	APG	PPG
71-72—Floridians (A)	75	—	1925	336	761	.442	0	1	.000	206	291	.708	—	—	513	66	215	—	—	137	—	878	6.8	0.9	11.7
72-73—Denver (A)	56	—	1050	183	458	.400	0	2	.000	138	177	.780	99	191	290	43	147	3	—	95	—	504	5.2	0.8	9.0
73-74—Denver (A)	82	—	2058	383	925	.414	0	2	.000	270	325	.831	197	269	466	100	244	—	54	157	13	1036	5.7	1.2	12.6
REG. ABA TOTALS	213	—	5033	902	2144	.421	0	5	.000	614	793	.774	296	460	1269	209	606	3	54	389	13	2418	6.0	1.0	11.4
ABA PLAYOFF TOTALS	8	—	209	29	77	.377	0	0	—	23	31	.742	14	26	49	5	29	0	0	20	0	81	6.1	0.6	10.1

LONGLEY, LUCIEN JAMES (Luc) b. January 19, 1969 Ht. 7-2 Wt. 265 College—New Mexico

SEASON—TEAM	G	GS	MIN	FGM	FGA	PCT	3FGM	3FGA	PCT	FTM	FTA	PCT	O-RB	D-RB	TOT	AST	PF	DQ	STL	TO	BLK	PTS	RPG	APG	PPG
91-92—Minnesota	66	3	991	114	249	.458	0	0	—	53	80	.663	67	190	257	53	157	0	35	83	64	281	3.9	0.8	4.3
92-93—Minnesota	55	25	1045	133	292	.455	0	0	—	53	74	.716	71	169	240	51	169	4	47	88	77	319	4.4	0.9	5.8
93-94—Minn.-Chicago	76	46	1502	219	465	.471	0	1	.000	90	125	.720	129	304	433	109	216	3	45	119	79	528	5.7	1.4	6.9
REG. SEASON TOTALS	197	74	3538	466	1006	.463	0	1	.000	196	279	.703	267	663	930	213	542	7	127	290	220	1128	4.7	1.1	5.7
PLAYOFF TOTALS	10	2	170	25	50	.500	0	0	—	13	18	.722	13	32	45	18	38	0	6	21	8	63	4.5	1.8	6.3

LOSCUTOFF, JAMES JR. (Jim, Jungle Jim) b. February 4, 1930 Ht. 6-5 Wt. 230 College—Sacramento CC/Grant Tech/Oregon

SEASON—TEAM	G	GS	MIN	FGM	FGA	PCT	3FGM	3FGA	PCT	FTM	FTA	PCT	O-RB	D-RB	TOT	AST	PF	DQ	STL	TO	BLK	PTS	RPG	APG	PPG
55-56—Boston	71	—	1582	226	628	.360	—	—	—	139	207	.671	—	—	622	65	213	4	—	—	—	591	8.8	0.9	8.3
56-57—Boston	70	—	2220	306	888	.345	—	—	—	132	187	.706	—	—	730	89	244	5	—	—	—	744	10.4	1.3	10.6
57-58—Boston	5	—	56	11	31	.355	—	—	—	1	3	.333	—	—	20	1	8	0	—	—	—	23	4.0	0.2	4.6
58-59—Boston	66	—	1680	242	686	.353	—	—	—	62	84	.738	—	—	460	60	285	15	—	—	—	546	7.0	0.9	8.3
59-60—Boston	28	—	536	66	205	.322	—	—	—	22	36	.611	—	—	108	12	108	6	—	—	—	154	3.9	0.4	5.5
60-61—Boston	76	—	1153	144	478	.301	—	—	—	49	76	.645	—	—	291	25	238	5	—	—	—	337	3.8	0.3	4.4
61-62—Boston	79	—	1146	188	519	.362	—	—	—	45	84	.536	—	—	329	51	185	3	—	—	—	421	4.2	0.6	5.3
62-63—Boston	63	—	607	94	251	.375	—	—	—	22	42	.524	—	—	157	25	126	1	—	—	—	210	2.5	0.4	3.3
63-64—Boston	53	—	451	56	182	.308	—	—	—	18	31	.581	—	—	131	25	90	1	—	—	—	130	2.5	0.5	2.5
REG. SEASON TOTALS	511	—	9431	1333	3868	.345	—	—	—	490	750	.653	—	—	2848	353	1497	40	—	—	—	3156	5.6	0.7	6.2
PLAYOFF TOTALS	57	—	997	136	420	.324	—	—	—	48	79	.608	—	—	299	32	219	8	—	—	—	320	5.2	0.6	5.6

LOTT, PLUMMER E. b. December 11, 1945 Ht. 6-5 Wt. 210 College—Seattle

SEASON—TEAM	G	GS	MIN	FGM	FGA	PCT	3FGM	3FGA	PCT	FTM	FTA	PCT	O-RB	D-RB	TOT	AST	PF	DQ	STL	TO	BLK	PTS	RPG	APG	PPG
67-68—Seattle	44	—	478	46	148	.311	—	—	—	19	31	.613	—	—	93	36	65	1	—	—	—	111	2.1	0.8	2.5
68-69—Seattle	23	—	160	17	66	.258	—	—	—	2	5	.400	—	—	30	7	9	0	—	—	—	36	1.3	0.3	1.6
REG. SEASON TOTALS	67	—	638	63	214	.294	—	—	—	21	36	.583	—	—	123	43	74	1	—	—	—	147	1.8	0.6	2.2

LOUGHERY, KEVIN MICHAEL (Murph) b. March 28, 1940 Ht. 6-3 Wt. 190 College—St. John's/Boston College

SEASON—TEAM	G	GS	MIN	FGM	FGA	PCT	3FGM	3FGA	PCT	FTM	FTA	PCT	O-RB	D-RB	TOT	AST	PF	DQ	STL	TO	BLK	PTS	RPG	APG	PPG
62-63—Detroit	57	—	845	146	397	.368	—	—	—	71	100	.710	—	—	109	104	135	1	—	—	—	363	1.9	1.8	6.4
63-64—Detroit-Balt.	66	—	1459	236	631	.374	—	—	—	126	177	.712	—	—	138	182	175	2	—	—	—	598	2.1	2.8	9.1
64-65—Baltimore	80	—	2417	406	957	.424	—	—	—	212	281	.754	—	—	235	296	320	13	—	—	—	1024	2.9	3.7	12.8
65-66—Baltimore	74	—	2455	526	1264	.416	—	—	—	297	358	.830	—	—	227	356	273	8	—	—	—	1349	3.1	4.8	18.2
66-67—Baltimore	76	—	2577	520	1306	.398	—	—	—	340	412	.825	—	—	349	288	294	10	—	—	—	1380	4.6	3.8	18.2
67-68—Baltimore	77	—	2297	458	1127	.406	—	—	—	305	392	.778	—	—	247	256	301	13	—	—	—	1221	3.2	3.3	15.9
68-69—Baltimore	80	—	3135	717	1636	.438	—	—	—	372	463	.803	—	—	266	384	299	3	—	—	—	1806	3.3	4.8	22.6
69-70—Baltimore	55	—	2037	477	1082	.441	—	—	—	253	298	.849	—	—	168	292	183	3	—	—	—	1207	3.1	5.3	21.9
70-71—Baltimore	82	—	2260	481	1193	.403	—	—	—	275	331	.831	—	—	219	301	246	2	—	—	—	1237	2.7	3.7	15.1
71-72—Balt.-Phil.	76	—	1771	341	809	.422	—	—	—	263	320	.822	—	—	183	196	213	3	—	—	—	945	2.4	2.6	12.4
72-73—Philadelphia	32	—	955	169	427	.396	—	—	—	107	130	.823	—	—	113	148	104	0	—	—	—	445	3.5	4.6	13.9
REG. SEASON TOTALS	755	—	22208	4477	10829	.413	—	—	—	2621	3262	.803	—	—	2254	2803	2543	58	—	—	—	11575	3.0	3.7	15.3
PLAYOFF TOTALS	43	—	1176	196	522	.375	—	—	—	140	186	.753	—	—	107	116	140	2	—	—	—	532	2.5	2.7	12.4

LOVE, ROBERT (Bob) b. December 8, 1942 Ht. 6-8 Wt. 215 College—Southern

SEASON—TEAM	G	GS	MIN	FGM	FGA	PCT	3FGM	3FGA	PCT	FTM	FTA	PCT	O-RB	D-RB	TOT	AST	PF	DQ	STL	TO	BLK	PTS	RPG	APG	PPG
66-67—Cincinnati	66	—	1074	173	403	.429	—	—	—	93	147	.633	—	—	257	49	153	3	—	—	—	439	3.9	0.7	6.7
67-68—Cincinnati	72	—	1068	193	455	.424	—	—	—	78	114	.684	—	—	209	55	141	1	—	—	—	464	2.9	0.8	6.4
68-69—Milw.-Chicago	49	—	542	108	272	.397	—	—	—	71	96	.740	—	—	150	17	59	0	—	—	—	287	3.1	0.3	5.9
69-70—Chicago	82	—	3123	640	1373	.466	—	—	—	442	525	.842	—	—	712	148	260	2	—	—	—	1722	8.7	1.8	21.0
70-71—Chicago	81	—	3482	765	1710	.447	—	—	—	513	619	.829	—	—	690	185	259	0	—	—	—	2043	8.5	2.3	25.2
71-72—Chicago	79	—	3108	819	1854	.442	—	—	—	399	509	.784	—	—	518	125	235	2	—	—	—	2037	6.6	1.6	25.8
72-73—Chicago	82	—	3033	774	1794	.431	—	—	—	347	421	.824	—	—	532	119	240	1	—	—	—	1895	6.5	1.5	23.1
73-74—Chicago	82	—	3292	731	1752	.417	—	—	—	323	395	.818	183	309	492	130	221	1	84	—	28	1785	6.0	1.6	21.8
74-75—Chicago	61	—	2401	539	1256	.429	—	—	—	264	318	.830	99	286	385	102	209	3	63	—	12	1342	6.3	1.7	22.0
75-76—Chicago	76	—	2823	543	1391	.390	—	—	—	362	452	.801	191	319	510	145	233	3	63	—	10	1448	6.7	1.9	19.1
76-77—Chicago-N.Y.-Seattle	59	—	1174	162	428	.379	—	—	—	109	132	.826	79	119	198	48	120	1	22	—	6	433	3.4	0.8	7.3
REG. SEASON TOTALS	789	—	25120	5447	12688	.429	—	—	—	3001	3728	.805	552	1033	4653	1123	2130	17	232	—	56	13895	5.9	1.4	17.6
PLAYOFF TOTALS	47	—	2061	441	1023	.431	—	—	—	194	250	.776	58	103	352	87	144	1	24	—	10	1076	7.5	1.9	22.9
ALL-STAR TOTALS	3	—	49	12	27	.444	—	—	—	6	9	.667	0	0	13	0	4	0	0	—	0	30	4.3	0.0	10.0

LOVE, STANLEY S. (**Stan**) b. April 9, 1949 Ht. 6-9 Wt. 215 College—Oregon

SEASON—TEAM	G	GS	MIN	FGM	FGA	PCT	3FGM	3FGA	PCT	FTM	FTA	PCT	O-RB	D-RB	TOT	AST	PF	DQ	STL	TO	BLK	PTS	RPG	APG	PPG
71-72—Baltimore	74	—	1327	242	536	.451	—	—	—	103	140	.736	—	—	338	52	202	0	—	—	—	587	4.6	0.7	7.9
72-73—Baltimore	72	—	995	190	436	.436	—	—	—	79	100	.790	—	—	300	46	175	0	—	—	—	459	4.2	0.6	6.4
73-74—Los Angeles	51	—	698	119	278	.428	—	—	—	49	64	.766	54	116	170	48	132	3	28	—	20	287	3.3	0.9	5.6
74-75—Los Angeles	30	—	431	85	194	.438	—	—	—	47	66	.712	31	66	97	26	69	1	16	—	13	217	3.2	0.9	7.2
74-75—San Antonio (A)	12	—	64	13	30	.433	0	0	—	3	4	.750	6	18	24	9	16	—	0	6	4	29	2.0	0.8	2.4
REG. NBA TOTALS	227	—	3451	636	1444	.440	—	—	—	278	370	.751	85	182	905	172	578	4	44	—	33	1550	4.0	0.8	6.8
REG. ABA TOTALS	12	—	64	13	30	.433	0	0	—	3	4	.750	6	18	24	9	16	—	0	6	4	29	2.0	0.8	2.4
NBA PLAYOFF TOTALS	7	—	30	3	10	.300	—	—	—	2	3	.667	1	2	10	2	4	0	1	—	0	8	1.4	0.3	1.1

LOVELLETTE, CLYDE EDWARD b. September 7, 1929 Ht. 6-9 Wt. 235 College—Kansas

SEASON—TEAM	G	GS	MIN	FGM	FGA	PCT	3FGM	3FGA	PCT	FTM	FTA	PCT	O-RB	D-RB	TOT	AST	PF	DQ	STL	TO	BLK	PTS	RPG	APG	PPG
53-54—Minneapolis	72	—	1255	237	560	.423	—	—	—	114	164	.695	—	—	419	51	210	2	—	—	—	588	5.8	0.7	8.2
54-55—Minneapolis	70	—	2361	519	1192	.435	—	—	—	273	398	.686	—	—	802	100	262	6	—	—	—	1311	11.5	1.4	18.7
55-56—Minneapolis	71	—	2518	594	1370	.434	—	—	—	338	469	.721	—	—	992	164	245	5	—	—	—	1526	14.0	2.3	21.5
56-57—Minneapolis	69	—	2492	574	1348	.426	—	—	—	286	399	.717	—	—	932	139	251	4	—	—	—	1434	13.5	2.0	20.8
57-58—Cincinnati	71	—	2589	679	1540	.441	—	—	—	301	405	.743	—	—	862	134	236	3	—	—	—	1659	12.1	1.9	23.4
58-59—St. Louis	70	—	1599	402	885	.454	—	—	—	205	250	.820	—	—	605	91	216	1	—	—	—	1009	8.6	1.3	14.4
59-60—St. Louis	68	—	1953	550	1174	.468	—	—	—	316	385	.821	—	—	721	127	248	6	—	—	—	1416	10.6	1.9	20.8
60-61—St. Louis	67	—	2111	599	1321	.453	—	—	—	273	329	.830	—	—	677	172	248	4	—	—	—	1471	10.1	2.6	22.0
61-62—St. Louis	40	—	1192	341	724	.471	—	—	—	155	187	.829	—	—	350	68	136	4	—	—	—	837	8.8	1.7	20.9
62-63—Boston	61	—	568	161	376	.428	—	—	—	73	98	.745	—	—	177	27	137	0	—	—	—	395	2.9	0.4	6.5
63-64—Boston	45	—	437	128	305	.420	—	—	—	45	57	.789	—	—	126	24	100	0	—	—	—	301	2.8	0.5	6.7
REG. SEASON TOTALS	704	—	19075	4784	10795	.443	—	—	—	2379	3141	.757	—	—	6663	1097	2289	35	—	—	—	11947	9.5	1.6	17.0
PLAYOFF TOTALS	69	—	1642	371	892	.416	—	—	—	221	323	.684	—	—	557	89	232	4	—	—	—	963	8.1	1.3	14.0
ALL-STAR TOTALS	3	—	71	19	40	.475	—	—	—	2	4	.500	—	—	28	4	9	0	—	—	—	40	9.3	1.3	13.3

LOWE, SIDNEY ROCHELL b. January 21, 1960 Ht. 6-0 Wt. 195 College—North Carolina State

SEASON—TEAM	G	GS	MIN	FGM	FGA	PCT	3FGM	3FGA	PCT	FTM	FTA	PCT	O-RB	D-RB	TOT	AST	PF	DQ	STL	TO	BLK	PTS	RPG	APG	PPG
83-84—Indiana	78	2	1238	107	259	.413	2	18	.111	108	139	.777	30	92	122	269	112	0	93	106	5	324	1.6	3.4	4.2
84-85—Detroit-Atlanta	21	0	190	10	27	.370	0	1	.000	8	8	1.000	4	12	16	50	28	0	11	13	0	28	0.8	2.4	1.3
88-89—Charlotte	14	0	250	8	25	.320	0	2	.000	7	11	.636	6	28	34	93	28	0	14	9	0	23	2.4	6.6	1.6
89-90—Minnesota	80	38	1744	73	229	.319	2	9	.222	39	54	.722	41	122	163	337	114	0	73	63	4	187	2.0	4.2	2.3
REG. SEASON TOTALS	193	40	3422	198	540	.367	4	30	.133	162	212	.764	81	254	335	749	282	0	191	191	9	562	1.7	3.9	2.9

LOWERY, CHARLES P. (**Chuck**) b. November 12, 1949 Ht. 6-3 Wt. 185 College—Puget Sound

SEASON—TEAM	G	GS	MIN	FGM	FGA	PCT	3FGM	3FGA	PCT	FTM	FTA	PCT	O-RB	D-RB	TOT	AST	PF	DQ	STL	TO	BLK	PTS	RPG	APG	PPG
71-72—Milwaukee	20	—	134	17	38	.447	—	—	—	11	18	.611	—	—	19	14	16	1	—	—	—	45	1.0	0.7	2.3
REG. SEASON TOTALS	20	—	134	17	38	.447	—	—	—	11	18	.611	—	—	19	14	16	1	—	—	—	45	1.0	0.7	2.3
PLAYOFF TOTALS	7	—	26	2	8	.250	—	—	—	2	3	.667	—	—	3	1	4	0	—	—	—	6	0.4	0.1	0.9

LUCAS, ALBERT THOMAS (**Al, Lukey**) b. July 4, 1922 Ht. 6-3 Wt. 195 College—Fordham

SEASON—TEAM	G	GS	MIN	FGM	FGA	PCT	3FGM	3FGA	PCT	FTM	FTA	PCT	O-RB	D-RB	TOT	AST	PF	DQ	STL	TO	BLK	PTS	RPG	APG	PPG
44-45—Sheboygan (N)	26	—	—	57	—	—	—	—	—	36	—	—	—	—	—	—	—	—	—	—	—	150	—	—	5.8
45-46—Sheboygan (N)	32	—	—	75	—	—	—	—	—	24	38	.632	—	—	—	—	66	—	—	—	—	174	—	—	5.4
46-47—Sheboygan (N)	42	—	—	87	—	—	—	—	—	32	60	.533	—	—	—	—	74	—	—	—	—	206	—	—	4.9
47-48—Sheboygan (N)	58	—	—	98	—	—	—	—	—	39	56	.696	—	—	—	—	135	—	—	—	—	235	—	—	4.1
48-49—Boston	2	—	—	1	3	.333	—	—	—	0	0	—	—	—	2	—	—	—	—	—	—	2	—	1.0	1.0
REG. NBA TOTALS	2	—	—	1	3	.333	—	—	—	0	0	—	—	—	2	0	—	—	—	—	—	2	—	1.0	1.0
REG. NBL TOTALS	158	—	—	317	—	—	—	—	—	131	154	.617	—	—	—	275	—	—	—	—	—	765	—	—	4.8
NBL PLAYOFF TOTALS	17	—	—	31	—	—	—	—	—	15	22	.636	—	—	—	29	—	—	—	—	—	77	—	—	4.5

LUCAS, JERRY RAY (**Luke**) b. March 30, 1940 Ht. 6-8 Wt. 230 College—Ohio State

SEASON—TEAM	G	GS	MIN	FGM	FGA	PCT	3FGM	3FGA	PCT	FTM	FTA	PCT	O-RB	D-RB	TOT	AST	PF	DQ	STL	TO	BLK	PTS	RPG	APG	PPG
63-64—Cincinnati	79	—	3273	545	1035	.527	—	—	—	310	398	.779	—	—	1375	204	300	6	—	—	—	1400	17.4	2.6	17.7
64-65—Cincinnati	66	—	2864	558	1121	.498	—	—	—	298	366	.814	—	—	1321	157	214	1	—	—	—	1414	20.0	2.4	21.4
65-66—Cincinnati	79	—	3517	690	1523	.453	—	—	—	317	403	.787	—	—	1668	213	274	5	—	—	—	1697	21.1	2.7	21.5
66-67—Cincinnati	81	—	3558	577	1257	.459	—	—	—	284	359	.791	—	—	1547	268	280	2	—	—	—	1438	19.1	3.3	17.8
67-68—Cincinnati	82	—	3619	707	1361	.519	—	—	—	346	445	.778	—	—	1560	251	243	3	—	—	—	1760	19.0	3.1	21.5
68-69—Cincinnati	74	—	3075	555	1007	.551	—	—	—	247	327	.755	—	—	1360	306	206	0	—	—	—	1357	18.4	4.1	18.3
69-70—Cin.-S.F.	67	—	2420	405	799	.507	—	—	—	200	255	.784	—	—	951	173	166	2	—	—	—	1010	14.2	2.6	15.1
70-71—San Francisco	80	—	3251	623	1250	.498	—	—	—	289	367	.787	—	—	1265	293	197	0	—	—	—	1535	15.8	3.7	19.2
71-72—New York	77	—	2926	543	1060	.512	—	—	—	197	249	.791	—	—	1011	318	218	1	—	—	—	1283	13.1	4.1	16.7
72-73—New York	71	—	2001	312	608	.513	—	—	—	80	100	.800	—	—	510	317	157	0	—	—	—	704	7.2	4.5	9.9
73-74—New York	73	—	1627	194	420	.462	—	—	—	67	96	.698	62	312	374	230	134	0	28	—	24	455	5.1	3.2	6.2
REG. SEASON TOTALS	829	—	32131	5709	11441	.499	—	—	—	2635	3365	.783	62	312	12942	2730	2389	20	28	—	24	14053	15.6	3.3	17.0
PLAYOFF TOTALS	72	—	2370	367	786	.467	—	—	—	162	206	.786	6	16	717	214	197	2	4	—	0	896	10.0	3.0	12.4
ALL-STAR TOTALS	7	—	183	35	64	.547	—	—	—	19	21	.905	0	0	64	12	20	0	0	—	0	89	9.1	1.7	12.7

LUCAS, JOHN HARDING JR. b. October 31, 1953 Ht. 6-2½ Wt. 180 College—Maryland

SEASON—TEAM	G	GS	MIN	FGM	FGA	PCT	3FGM	3FGA	PCT	FTM	FTA	PCT	O-RB	D-RB	TOT	AST	PF	DQ	STL	TO	BLK	PTS	RPG	APG	PPG
76-77—Houston	82	—	2531	388	814	.477	—	—	—	135	171	.789	55	164	219	463	174	0	125	—	19	911	2.7	5.6	11.1
77-78—Houston	82	—	2933	412	947	.435	—	—	—	193	250	.772	51	204	255	768	208	1	160	213	9	1017	3.1	9.4	12.4
78-79—Golden State	82	—	3095	530	1146	.462	—	—	—	264	321	.822	65	182	247	762	229	1	152	255	9	1324	3.0	9.3	16.1
79-80—Golden State	80	—	2763	388	830	.467	12	42	.286	222	289	.768	61	159	220	602	196	2	138	184	3	1010	2.8	7.5	12.6
80-81—Golden State	66	—	1919	222	506	.439	4	24	.167	107	145	.738	34	120	154	464	140	1	83	185	2	555	2.3	7.0	8.4
81-82—Washington	79	53	1940	263	618	.426	2	22	.091	138	176	.784	40	126	166	551	105	0	95	156	6	666	2.1	7.0	8.4
82-83—Washington	35	0	386	62	131	.473	0	5	.000	21	42	.500	8	21	29	102	18	0	25	47	1	145	0.8	2.9	4.1
83-84—San Antonio	63	39	1807	275	595	.462	19	69	.275	120	157	.764	23	157	180	673	123	1	92	147	5	689	2.9	10.7	10.9
84-85—Houston	47	21	1158	206	446	.462	21	66	.318	103	129	.798	21	64	85	318	78	0	62	102	2	536	1.8	6.8	11.4
85-86—Houston	65	65	2120	365	818	.446	45	146	.308	231	298	.775	33	110	143	571	124	0	77	149	5	1006	2.2	8.8	15.5
86-87—Milwaukee	43	40	1358	285	624	.457	46	126	.365	137	174	.787	29	96	125	290	82	0	71	89	6	753	2.9	6.7	17.5
87-88—Milwaukee	81	22	1766	281	631	.445	51	151	.338	130	162	.802	29	130	159	392	102	1	88	125	3	743	2.0	4.8	9.2
88-89—Seattle	74	8	842	119	299	.398	18	68	.265	54	77	.701	22	57	79	260	53	0	60	66	1	310	1.1	3.5	4.2
89-90—Houston	49	18	938	109	291	.375	26	87	.299	42	55	.764	19	71	90	238	59	0	45	85	2	286	1.8	4.9	5.8
REG. SEASON TOTALS	928	266	25556	3905	8696	.449	244	806	.303	1897	2446	.776	490	1661	2151	6454	1691	7	1273	1803	73	9951	2.3	7.0	10.7
PLAYOFF TOTALS	45	16	1135	198	439	.451	18	69	.261	88	118	.746	20	76	96	219	80	1	52	39	6	502	2.1	4.9	11.2

LUCAS, MAURICE D. (Luke) b. February 18, 1952 Ht. 6-9 Wt. 215 College—Marquette

SEASON—TEAM	G	GS	MIN	FGM	FGA	PCT	3FGM	3FGA	PCT	FTM	FTA	PCT	O-RB	D-RB	TOT	AST	PF	DQ	STL	TO	BLK	PTS	RPG	APG	PPG
74-75—St. Louis (A)	80	—	2464	438	937	.467	2	9	.222	180	229	.786	282	534	816	287	301	—	89	208	64	1058	10.2	3.6	13.2
75-76—St. L.-Ken. (A)	86	—	2861	620	1346	.461	3	18	.167	217	283	.767	297	673	970	224	332	—	75	298	57	1460	11.3	2.6	17.0
76-77—Portland	79	—	2863	632	1357	.466	—	—	—	335	438	.765	271	628	899	229	294	6	83	—	56	1599	11.4	2.9	20.2
77-78—Portland	68	—	2119	453	989	.458	—	—	—	207	270	.767	186	435	621	173	221	3	61	192	56	1113	9.1	2.5	16.4
78-79—Portland	69	—	2462	568	1208	.470	—	—	—	270	345	.783	192	524	716	215	254	3	66	233	81	1406	10.4	3.1	20.4
79-80—Port.-N.J.	63	—	1884	371	813	.456	2	9	.222	179	239	.749	143	394	537	208	223	2	42	218	62	923	8.5	3.3	14.7
80-81—New Jersey	68	—	2162	404	835	.484	0	2	.000	191	254	.752	153	422	575	173	260	3	57	176	59	999	8.5	2.5	14.7
81-82—New York	80	74	2671	505	1001	.504	0	3	.000	253	349	.725	274	629	903	179	309	4	68	173	70	1263	11.3	2.2	15.8
82-83—Phoenix	77	71	2586	495	1045	.474	1	3	.333	278	356	.781	201	598	799	219	274	5	56	221	43	1269	10.4	2.8	16.5
83-84—Phoenix	75	69	2309	451	908	.497	0	5	.000	293	383	.765	208	517	725	203	235	2	55	177	39	1195	9.7	2.7	15.9
84-85—Phoenix	63	22	1670	346	727	.476	0	4	.000	150	200	.750	138	419	557	145	183	0	39	151	17	842	8.8	2.3	13.4
85-86—L.A. Lakers	77	8	1750	302	653	.462	1	2	.500	180	230	.783	164	402	566	84	253	1	45	121	24	785	7.4	1.1	10.2
86-87—Seattle	63	0	1120	175	388	.451	0	5	.000	150	187	.802	88	219	307	65	171	1	34	75	21	500	4.9	1.0	7.9
87-88—Portland	73	0	1191	168	373	.450	0	3	.000	109	148	.736	101	214	315	94	188	0	33	73	10	445	4.3	1.3	6.1
REG. NBA TOTALS	855	244	24787	4870	10297	.473	4	36	.111	2595	3399	.763	2119	5401	7520	1987	2865	30	639	1810	538	12339	8.8	2.3	14.4
REG. ABA TOTALS	166	—	5325	1058	2283	.463	5	27	.185	397	512	.775	579	1207	1786	511	633	—	164	506	121	2518	10.8	3.1	15.2
NBA PLAYOFF TOTALS	82	18	2426	472	975	.484	0	1	.000	215	289	.744	180	510	690	225	310	6	71	107	46	1159	8.4	2.7	14.1
ABA PLAYOFF TOTALS	20	—	705	143	305	.469	0	1	.000	42	60	.700	89	166	255	72	92	—	20	49	20	328	12.8	3.6	16.4
NBA ALL-STAR TOTALS	4	2	90	16	40	.400	0	0	—	2	3	.667	10	21	31	8	10	0	2	4	1	34	7.8	2.0	8.5
ABA ALL-STAR TOTALS	1	0	14	2	5	.400	0	0	—	1	1	1.000	0	0	5	3	1	—	0	0	0	5	5.0	3.0	5.0

LUCKENBILL, THEODORE (Ted) b. July 27, 1939 Ht. 6-6 Wt. 205 College—Houston

SEASON—TEAM	G	GS	MIN	FGM	FGA	PCT	3FGM	3FGA	PCT	FTM	FTA	PCT	O-RB	D-RB	TOT	AST	PF	DQ	STL	TO	BLK	PTS	RPG	APG	PPG
61-62—Philadelphia	67	—	396	43	120	.358	—	—	—	49	76	.645	—	—	110	27	67	0	—	—	—	135	1.6	0.4	2.0
62-63—San Francisco	20	—	201	26	68	.382	—	—	—	9	20	.450	—	—	56	8	34	0	—	—	—	61	2.8	0.4	3.1
REG. SEASON TOTALS	87	—	597	69	188	.367	—	—	—	58	96	.604	—	—	166	35	101	0	—	—	—	196	1.9	0.4	2.3
PLAYOFF TOTALS	4	—	17	0	5	.000	—	—	—	2	5	.400	—	—	3	1	3	0	—	—	—	2	0.8	0.3	0.5

LUISI, JAMES A. (Jim) b. November 2, 1928 Ht. 6-2 Wt. 180 College—St. Francis (N.Y.)

SEASON—TEAM	G	GS	MIN	FGM	FGA	PCT	3FGM	3FGA	PCT	FTM	FTA	PCT	O-RB	D-RB	TOT	AST	PF	DQ	STL	TO	BLK	PTS	RPG	APG	PPG
53-54—Baltimore	31	—	367	31	95	.326	—	—	—	27	41	.659	—	—	25	35	45	0	—	—	—	89	0.8	1.1	2.9
REG. SEASON TOTALS	31	—	367	31	95	.326	—	—	—	27	41	.659	—	—	25	35	45	0	—	—	—	89	0.8	1.1	2.9

LUJACK, ALOYSIUS R. (Al) b. October 5, 1921 Ht. 6-3 Wt. 220 College—Georgetown

SEASON—TEAM	G	GS	MIN	FGM	FGA	PCT	3FGM	3FGA	PCT	FTM	FTA	PCT	O-RB	D-RB	TOT	AST	PF	DQ	STL	TO	BLK	PTS	RPG	APG	PPG
46-47—Washington	5	—	—	1	8	.125	—	—	—	2	5	.400	—	—	0	6	—	—	—	—	4	—	0.0	0.8	
REG. SEASON TOTALS	5	—	—	1	8	.125	—	—	—	2	5	.400	—	—	0	6	—	—	—	—	4	—	0.0	0.8	

LUMPKIN, PHIL b. December 20, 1951 Ht. 6-0 Wt. 165 College—Miami (Ohio)

SEASON—TEAM	G	GS	MIN	FGM	FGA	PCT	3FGM	3FGA	PCT	FTM	FTA	PCT	O-RB	D-RB	TOT	AST	PF	DQ	STL	TO	BLK	PTS	RPG	APG	PPG
74-75—Portland	48	—	792	86	190	.453	—	—	—	30	39	.769	10	49	59	177	80	1	20	—	3	202	1.2	3.7	4.2
75-76—Phoenix	34	—	370	22	65	.338	—	—	—	26	30	.867	7	16	23	48	26	0	15	—	0	70	0.7	1.4	2.1
REG. SEASON TOTALS	82	—	1162	108	255	.424	—	—	—	56	69	.812	17	65	82	225	106	1	35	—	3	272	1.0	2.7	3.3
PLAYOFF TOTALS	17	—	136	10	30	.333	—	—	—	11	14	.786	5	8	13	21	8	0	2	—	0	31	0.8	1.2	1.8

LUMPP, RAYMOND G. (Ray) b. July 11, 1923   Ht. 6-1 Wt. 180 College—New York University

SEASON—TEAM	G	GS	MIN	FGM	FGA	PCT	3FGM	3FGA	PCT	FTM	FTA	PCT	O-RB	D-RB	TOT	AST	PF	DQ	STL	TO	BLK	PTS	RPG	APG	PPG
48-49—Ind.-N.Y.	61	—	—	279	800	.349	—	—	—	219	283	.774	—	—	—	158	173	—	—	—	—	777	—	2.6	12.7
49-50—New York	58	—	—	91	283	.322	—	—	—	86	108	.796	—	—	—	90	117	—	—	—	—	268	—	1.6	4.6
50-51—New York	64	—	—	153	379	.404	—	—	—	124	160	.775	—	—	125	115	160	2	—	—	—	430	2.0	1.8	6.7
51-52—New York	62	—	1317	184	476	.387	—	—	—	90	119	.756	—	—	125	123	165	4	—	—	—	458	2.0	2.0	7.4
52-53—N.Y.-Balt.	55	—	1422	188	506	.372	—	—	—	153	206	.743	—	—	141	168	178	5	—	—	—	529	2.6	3.1	9.6
REG. SEASON TOTALS	300	—	2739	895	2444	.366	—	—	—	672	876	.767	—	—	391	654	793	11	—	—	—	2462	2.2	2.2	8.2
PLAYOFF TOTALS	38	—	269	75	244	.307	—	—	—	79	96	.823	—	—	47	57	119	5	—	—	—	229	1.7	1.5	6.0

LYNAM, ROBERT BRACEY (R.B.) b. 1944   Ht. 6-1 Wt. 190 College—Oklahoma Baptist

SEASON—TEAM	G	GS	MIN	FGM	FGA	PCT	3FGM	3FGA	PCT	FTM	FTA	PCT	O-RB	D-RB	TOT	AST	PF	DQ	STL	TO	BLK	PTS	RPG	APG	PPG
67-68—Denver (A)	7	—	39	5	17	.294	0	1	.000	7	8	.875	—	—	5	0	10	0	—	5	—	17	0.7	0.0	2.4
REG. ABA TOTALS	7	—	39	5	17	.294	0	1	.000	7	8	.875	—	—	5	0	10	0	—	5	—	17	0.7	0.0	2.4

LYNCH, GEORGE DeWITT III b. September 3, 1970   Ht. 6-8 Wt. 220 College—North Carolina

SEASON—TEAM	G	GS	MIN	FGM	FGA	PCT	3FGM	3FGA	PCT	FTM	FTA	PCT	O-RB	D-RB	TOT	AST	PF	DQ	STL	TO	BLK	PTS	RPG	APG	PPG
93-94—L.A. Lakers	71	46	1762	291	573	.508	0	5	.000	99	166	.596	220	190	410	96	177	1	102	87	27	681	5.8	1.4	9.6
REG. SEASON TOTALS	71	46	1762	291	573	.508	0	5	.000	99	166	.596	220	190	410	96	177	1	102	87	27	681	5.8	1.4	9.6

LYNCH, KEVIN JOSEPH b. December 24, 1968   Ht. 6-5 Wt. 195 College—Minnesota

SEASON—TEAM	G	GS	MIN	FGM	FGA	PCT	3FGM	3FGA	PCT	FTM	FTA	PCT	O-RB	D-RB	TOT	AST	PF	DQ	STL	TO	BLK	PTS	RPG	APG	PPG
91-92—Charlotte	55	3	819	93	223	.417	3	8	.375	35	46	.761	30	55	85	83	107	0	37	44	9	224	1.5	1.5	4.1
92-93—Charlotte	40	8	324	30	59	.508	0	1	.000	26	38	.684	12	23	35	25	44	0	11	24	6	86	0.9	0.6	2.2
REG. SEASON TOTALS	95	11	1143	123	282	.436	3	9	.333	61	84	.726	42	78	120	108	151	0	48	68	15	310	1.3	1.1	3.3
PLAYOFF TOTALS	1	0	3	0	0	—	0	0	—	0	0	—	0	0	0	1	0	0	0	0	0	0	0.0	1.0	0.0

LYNN, LONNIE b. May 24, 1943   Ht. 6-7½ Wt. 215 College—Upper Iowa/Wilberforce

SEASON—TEAM	G	GS	MIN	FGM	FGA	PCT	3FGM	3FGA	PCT	FTM	FTA	PCT	O-RB	D-RB	TOT	AST	PF	DQ	STL	TO	BLK	PTS	RPG	APG	PPG
69-70—Denver-Pitt. (A)	52	—	779	112	275	.407	0	3	.000	36	74	.486	—	—	258	43	120	1	—	—	—	260	5.0	0.8	5.0
REG. ABA TOTALS	52	—	779	112	275	.407	0	3	.000	36	74	.486	—	—	258	43	120	1	—	—	—	260	5.0	0.8	5.0

LYNN, MICHAEL EDWARD (Mike) b. November 25, 1945   Ht. 6-7 Wt. 215 College—UCLA

SEASON—TEAM	G	GS	MIN	FGM	FGA	PCT	3FGM	3FGA	PCT	FTM	FTA	PCT	O-RB	D-RB	TOT	AST	PF	DQ	STL	TO	BLK	PTS	RPG	APG	PPG
69-70—Los Angeles	44	—	403	44	133	.331	—	—	—	31	48	.646	—	—	64	30	87	4	—	—	—	119	1.5	0.7	2.7
70-71—Buffalo	5	—	25	2	7	.286	—	—	—	3	3	1.000	—	—	4	1	9	0	—	—	—	7	0.8	0.2	1.4
REG. SEASON TOTALS	49	—	428	46	140	.329	—	—	—	34	51	.667	—	—	68	31	96	4	—	—	—	126	1.4	0.6	2.6
PLAYOFF TOTALS	3	—	6	2	3	.667	—	—	—	0	0	—	—	—	2	1	1	0	—	—	—	4	0.7	0.3	1.3

MACALUSO, MICHAEL EMILIUS (Mike) b. July 20, 1951   Ht. 6-5 Wt. 210 College—Canisius

SEASON—TEAM	G	GS	MIN	FGM	FGA	PCT	3FGM	3FGA	PCT	FTM	FTA	PCT	O-RB	D-RB	TOT	AST	PF	DQ	STL	TO	BLK	PTS	RPG	APG	PPG
73-74—Buffalo	30	—	112	19	44	.432	—	—	—	10	17	.588	10	15	25	3	31	0	7	—	1	48	0.8	0.1	1.6
REG. SEASON TOTALS	30	—	112	19	44	.432	—	—	—	10	17	.588	10	15	25	3	31	0	7	—	1	48	0.8	0.1	1.6

MACAULEY, CHARLES EDWARD JR. (Ed, Easy Ed) b. March 22, 1928   Ht. 6-8 Wt. 190 College—St. Louis

SEASON—TEAM	G	GS	MIN	FGM	FGA	PCT	3FGM	3FGA	PCT	FTM	FTA	PCT	O-RB	D-RB	TOT	AST	PF	DQ	STL	TO	BLK	PTS	RPG	APG	PPG
49-50—St. Louis	67	—	—	351	882	.398	—	—	—	379	528	.718	—	—	—	200	221	—	—	—	—	1081	—	3.0	16.1
50-51—Boston	68	—	—	459	985	.466	—	—	—	466	614	.759	—	—	616	252	205	4	—	—	—	1384	9.1	3.7	20.4
51-52—Boston	66	—	2631	384	888	.432	—	—	—	496	621	.799	—	—	529	232	174	0	—	—	—	1264	8.0	3.5	19.2
52-53—Boston	69	—	2902	451	997	.452	—	—	—	500	667	.750	—	—	629	280	188	0	—	—	—	1402	9.1	4.1	20.3
53-54—Boston	71	—	2792	462	950	.486	—	—	—	420	554	.758	—	—	571	271	168	1	—	—	—	1344	8.0	3.8	18.9
54-55—Boston	71	—	2706	403	951	.424	—	—	—	442	558	.792	—	—	600	275	171	0	—	—	—	1248	8.5	3.9	17.6
55-56—Boston	71	—	2354	420	995	.422	—	—	—	400	504	.794	—	—	422	211	158	2	—	—	—	1240	5.9	3.0	17.5
56-57—St. Louis	72	—	2582	414	987	.419	—	—	—	359	479	.749	—	—	440	202	206	2	—	—	—	1187	6.1	2.8	16.5
57-58—St. Louis	72	—	1908	376	879	.428	—	—	—	267	369	.724	—	—	478	143	156	2	—	—	—	1019	6.6	2.0	14.2
58-59—St. Louis	14	—	196	22	75	.293	—	—	—	21	35	.600	—	—	40	13	20	—	—	—	—	65	2.9	0.9	4.6
REG. SEASON TOTALS	641	—	18071	3742	8589	.436	—	—	—	3750	4929	.761	—	—	4325	2079	1667	12	—	—	—	11234	7.5	3.2	17.5
PLAYOFF TOTALS	47	—	1414	218	499	.437	—	—	—	212	291	.729	—	—	321	138	141	6	—	—	—	648	6.8	2.9	13.8
ALL-STAR TOTALS	7	—	154	24	62	.387	—	—	—	35	41	.854	—	—	32	18	13	0	—	—	—	83	4.6	2.6	11.9

MACGILVRAY, RONALD (Ronnie) b. July 20, 1930   Ht. 6-2 Wt. 185 College—St. John's

SEASON—TEAM	G	GS	MIN	FGM	FGA	PCT	3FGM	3FGA	PCT	FTM	FTA	PCT	O-RB	D-RB	TOT	AST	PF	DQ	STL	TO	BLK	PTS	RPG	APG	PPG
54-55—Milwaukee	6	—	57	2	12	.167	—	—	—	4	7	.571	—	—	9	11	5	0	—	—	—	8	1.5	1.8	1.3
REG. SEASON TOTALS	6	—	57	2	12	.167	—	—	—	4	7	.571	—	—	9	11	5	0	—	—	—	8	1.5	1.8	1.3

MACK, OLIVER (**Ollie**) b. June 6, 1957   Ht. 6-3   Wt. 195   College—San Jacinto/East Carolina

SEASON—TEAM	G	GS	MIN	FGM	FGA	PCT	3FGM	3FGA	PCT	FTM	FTA	PCT	O-RB	D-RB	TOT	AST	PF	DQ	STL	TO	BLK	PTS	RPG	APG	PPG
79-80—L.A.-Chicago	50	—	681	98	199	.492	0	5	.000	38	51	.745	32	39	71	53	50	0	24	35	3	234	1.4	1.1	4.7
80-81—Chicago-Dallas	65	—	1682	279	606	.460	0	9	.000	80	125	.640	92	138	230	163	117	0	56	70	7	638	3.5	2.5	9.8
81-82—Dallas	13	3	150	19	59	.322	0	2	.000	6	8	.750	8	10	18	14	6	0	5	4	1	44	1.4	1.1	3.4
REG. SEASON TOTALS	128	3	2513	396	864	.458	0	16	.000	124	184	.674	132	187	319	230	173	0	85	109	11	916	2.5	1.8	7.2

MACK, SAM b. May 26, 1970   Ht. 6-7   Wt. 220   College—Iowa State/Arizona State/Tyler JC/Houston

SEASON—TEAM	G	GS	MIN	FGM	FGA	PCT	3FGM	3FGA	PCT	FTM	FTA	PCT	O-RB	D-RB	TOT	AST	PF	DQ	STL	TO	BLK	PTS	RPG	APG	PPG
92-93—San Antonio	40	0	267	47	118	.398	3	22	.136	45	58	.776	18	30	48	15	44	0	14	22	5	142	1.2	0.4	3.6
REG. SEASON TOTALS	40	0	267	47	118	.398	3	22	.136	45	58	.776	18	30	48	15	44	0	14	22	5	142	1.2	0.4	3.6

MACKEY, MALCOLM MALIK b. July 11, 1970   Ht. 6-10   Wt. 250   College—Georgia Tech

SEASON—TEAM	G	GS	MIN	FGM	FGA	PCT	3FGM	3FGA	PCT	FTM	FTA	PCT	O-RB	D-RB	TOT	AST	PF	DQ	STL	TO	BLK	PTS	RPG	APG	PPG
93-94—Phoenix	22	0	69	14	37	.378	0	2	.000	4	8	.500	12	12	24	1	9	0	0	2	3	32	1.1	0.0	1.5
REG. SEASON TOTALS	22	0	69	14	37	.378	0	2	.000	4	8	.500	12	12	24	1	9	0	0	2	3	32	1.1	0.0	1.5

MACKLIN, DURAND (**Rudy**) b. February 19, 1958   Ht. 6-7   Wt. 215   College—Louisiana State

SEASON—TEAM	G	GS	MIN	FGM	FGA	PCT	3FGM	3FGA	PCT	FTM	FTA	PCT	O-RB	D-RB	TOT	AST	PF	DQ	STL	TO	BLK	PTS	RPG	APG	PPG
81-82—Atlanta	79	32	1516	210	484	.434	0	3	.000	134	173	.775	113	150	263	47	225	5	40	112	20	554	3.3	0.6	7.0
82-83—Atlanta	73	20	1171	170	360	.472	0	4	.000	101	131	.771	85	105	190	71	189	4	41	89	10	441	2.6	1.0	6.0
83-84—New York	8	0	65	12	30	.400	0	0	—	11	13	.846	5	6	11	3	17	0	1	6	0	35	1.4	0.4	4.4
REG. SEASON TOTALS	160	52	2752	392	874	.449	0	7	.000	246	317	.776	203	261	464	121	431	9	82	207	30	1030	2.9	0.8	6.4
PLAYOFF TOTALS	5	3	108	15	32	.469	0	1	.000	14	16	.875	7	11	18	3	18	1	2	7	2	44	3.6	0.6	8.8

MACKNOWSKI, JOHN ANDREW (**Johnny, Whitey**) b. January 7, 1923   Ht. 6-1   Wt. 185   College—Seton Hall

SEASON—TEAM	G	GS	MIN	FGM	FGA	PCT	3FGM	3FGA	PCT	FTM	FTA	PCT	O-RB	D-RB	TOT	AST	PF	DQ	STL	TO	BLK	PTS	RPG	APG	PPG
48-49—Syracuse (N)	62	—	—	146	—	—	—	—	—	128	178	.719	—	—	—	—	128	—	—	—	—	420	—	—	6.8
49-50—Syracuse	59	—	—	154	463	.333	—	—	—	131	178	.736	—	—	—	65	128	—	—	—	—	439	—	1.1	7.4
50-51—Syracuse	58	—	—	131	435	.301	—	—	—	122	170	.718	—	—	110	69	134	3	—	—	—	384	1.9	1.2	6.6
REG. NBA TOTALS	117	—	—	285	898	.317	—	—	—	253	348	.727	—	—	110	134	262	3	—	—	—	823	1.9	1.1	7.0
REG. NBL TOTALS	62	—	—	146	—	—	—	—	—	128	178	.719	—	—	—	—	128	—	—	—	—	420	—	—	6.8
NBA PLAYOFF TOTALS	13	—	—	45	113	.398	—	—	—	40	54	.741	—	—	7	25	23	0	—	—	—	130	3.5	1.9	10.0
NBL PLAYOFF TOTALS	6	—	—	3	—	—	—	—	—	7	9	.778	—	—	—	—	7	—	—	—	—	13	—	—	2.2

MACLEAN, DONALD JAMES (**Don**) b. January 16, 1970   Ht. 6-10   Wt. 235   College—UCLA

SEASON—TEAM	G	GS	MIN	FGM	FGA	PCT	3FGM	3FGA	PCT	FTM	FTA	PCT	O-RB	D-RB	TOT	AST	PF	DQ	STL	TO	BLK	PTS	RPG	APG	PPG
92-93—Washington	62	4	674	157	361	.435	3	6	.500	90	111	.811	33	89	122	39	82	0	11	42	4	407	2.0	0.6	6.6
93-94—Washington	75	69	2487	517	1030	.502	3	21	.143	328	398	.824	140	327	467	160	169	0	47	152	22	1365	6.2	2.1	18.2
REG. SEASON TOTALS	137	73	3161	674	1391	.485	6	27	.222	418	509	.821	173	416	589	199	251	0	58	194	26	1772	4.3	1.5	12.9

MACON, MARK L. b. April 14, 1969   Ht. 6-5   Wt. 185   College—Temple

SEASON—TEAM	G	GS	MIN	FGM	FGA	PCT	3FGM	3FGA	PCT	FTM	FTA	PCT	O-RB	D-RB	TOT	AST	PF	DQ	STL	TO	BLK	PTS	RPG	APG	PPG
91-92—Denver	76	67	2304	333	889	.375	4	30	.133	135	185	.730	80	140	220	168	242	4	154	155	14	805	2.9	2.2	10.6
92-93—Denver	48	27	1141	158	381	.415	0	6	.000	42	60	.700	33	70	103	126	135	2	69	72	3	358	2.1	2.6	7.5
93-94—Denver-Detroit	42	1	496	69	184	.375	2	10	.200	23	34	.676	18	23	41	51	73	0	39	40	1	163	1.0	1.2	3.9
REG. SEASON TOTALS	166	95	3941	560	1454	.385	6	46	.130	200	279	.717	131	233	364	345	450	6	262	267	18	1326	2.2	2.1	8.0

MACY, KYLE ROBERT b. April 9, 1957   Ht. 6-3   Wt. 175   College—Purdue/Kentucky

SEASON—TEAM	G	GS	MIN	FGM	FGA	PCT	3FGM	3FGA	PCT	FTM	FTA	PCT	O-RB	D-RB	TOT	AST	PF	DQ	STL	TO	BLK	PTS	RPG	APG	PPG
80-81—Phoenix	82	—	1469	272	532	.511	12	51	.235	107	119	.899	44	88	132	160	120	0	76	95	5	663	1.6	2.0	8.1
81-82—Phoenix	82	72	2845	486	945	.514	39	100	.390	152	169	.899	78	183	261	384	185	1	143	125	9	1163	3.2	4.7	14.2
82-83—Phoenix	82	9	1836	328	634	.517	23	76	.303	129	148	.872	41	124	165	278	130	0	64	90	8	808	2.0	3.4	9.9
83-84—Phoenix	82	45	2402	357	713	.501	23	70	.329	95	114	.833	49	137	186	353	181	0	123	116	6	832	2.3	4.3	10.1
84-85—Phoenix	65	52	2018	282	582	.485	23	85	.271	127	140	.907	33	146	179	380	128	0	85	111	3	714	2.8	5.8	11.0
85-86—Chicago	82	79	2426	286	592	.483	58	140	.414	73	90	.811	41	137	178	446	201	1	81	117	11	703	2.2	5.4	8.6
86-87—Indiana	76	0	1250	164	341	.481	14	46	.304	34	41	.829	25	88	113	197	136	0	59	58	7	376	1.5	2.6	4.9
REG. SEASON TOTALS	551	257	14246	2175	4339	.501	192	568	.338	717	821	.873	311	903	1214	2198	1081	2	631	712	49	5259	2.2	4.0	9.5
PLAYOFF TOTALS	44	28	1258	169	363	.466	20	53	.377	44	53	.830	34	78	112	170	99	0	44	56	3	402	2.5	3.9	9.1

MADDOX, JACK C. b. December 10, 1921 Ht. 6-3½ Wt. 190 College—West Texas State

SEASON—TEAM	G	GS	MIN	FGM	FGA	PCT	3FGM	3FGA	PCT	FTM	FTA	PCT	O-RB	D-RB	TOT	AST	PF	DQ	STL	TO	BLK	PTS	RPG	APG	PPG
46-47—Oshkosh (N)	43	—	—	102	—	—	—	—	—	33	39	.846	—	—	—	—	53	—	—	—	—	237	—	—	5.5
47-48—Oshkosh (N)	60	—	—	146	—	—	—	—	—	59	90	.656	—	—	—	—	112	—	—	—	—	351	—	—	5.9
48-49—Hammond (N)	17	—	—	39	—	—	—	—	—	18	29	.621	—	—	—	—	28	—	—	—	—	96	—	—	5.6
48-49—Indianapolis	1	—	—	0	0	—	—	—	—	0	0	—	—	—	—	1	0	—	—	—	—	0	—	1.0	0.0
REG. NBA TOTALS	1	—	—	0	0	—	—	—	—	0	0	—	—	—	—	1	0	—	—	—	—	0	—	1.0	0.0
REG. NBL TOTALS	120	—	—	287	—	—	—	—	—	110	158	.696	—	—	—	—	193	—	—	—	—	684	—	—	5.7
NBL PLAYOFF TOTALS	10	—	—	7	—	—	—	—	—	2	4	.500	—	—	—	—	5	—	—	—	—	16	—	—	1.6

MADKINS, GERALD JR. b. April 18, 1969 Ht. 6-4 Wt. 200 College—UCLA

SEASON—TEAM	G	GS	MIN	FGM	FGA	PCT	3FGM	3FGA	PCT	FTM	FTA	PCT	O-RB	D-RB	TOT	AST	PF	DQ	STL	TO	BLK	PTS	RPG	APG	PPG
93-94—Cleveland	22	0	149	11	31	.355	5	15	.333	8	10	.800	1	10	11	19	16	0	9	13	0	35	0.5	0.9	1.6
REG. SEASON TOTALS	22	0	149	11	31	.355	5	15	.333	8	10	.800	1	10	11	19	16	0	9	13	0	35	0.5	0.9	1.6

MAGER, NORMAN CLIFFORD (Norm) b. March 23, 1926 Ht. 6-5 Wt. 185 College—St. John's/City College of New York

SEASON—TEAM	G	GS	MIN	FGM	FGA	PCT	3FGM	3FGA	PCT	FTM	FTA	PCT	O-RB	D-RB	TOT	AST	PF	DQ	STL	TO	BLK	PTS	RPG	APG	PPG
50-51—Baltimore	24	—	—	40	142	.282	—	—	—	44	56	.786	—	—	47	22	68	3	—	—	—	124	2.0	0.9	5.2
REG. SEASON TOTALS	24	—	—	40	142	.282	—	—	—	44	56	.786	—	—	47	22	68	3	—	—	—	124	2.0	0.9	5.2

MAGLEY, DAVID JOHN (Dave) b. November 24, 1959 Ht. 6-8 Wt. 210 College—Kansas

SEASON—TEAM	G	GS	MIN	FGM	FGA	PCT	3FGM	3FGA	PCT	FTM	FTA	PCT	O-RB	D-RB	TOT	AST	PF	DQ	STL	TO	BLK	PTS	RPG	APG	PPG
82-83—Cleveland	14	0	56	4	16	.250	0	1	.000	4	8	.500	2	8	10	2	5	0	2	2	0	12	0.7	0.1	0.9
REG. SEASON TOTALS	14	0	56	4	16	.250	0	1	.000	4	8	.500	2	8	10	2	5	0	2	2	0	12	0.7	0.1	0.9

MAHAFFEY, RANDOLPH (Randy) b. September 28, 1945 Ht. 6-7 Wt. 210 College—Clemson

SEASON—TEAM	G	GS	MIN	FGM	FGA	PCT	3FGM	3FGA	PCT	FTM	FTA	PCT	O-RB	D-RB	TOT	AST	PF	DQ	STL	TO	BLK	PTS	RPG	APG	PPG
67-68—Kentucky (A)	75	—	2325	373	875	.426	0	2	.000	281	411	.684	259	425	684	129	278	15	—	224	—	1027	9.1	1.7	13.7
68-69—Ken.-N.Y. (A)	79	—	2353	351	828	.424	0	2	.000	232	329	.705	—	—	571	99	261	8	—	243	—	934	7.2	1.3	11.8
69-70—Carolina (A)	84	—	2558	367	821	.447	0	4	.000	194	283	.686	—	—	681	164	275	7	—	—	—	928	8.1	2.0	11.0
70-71—Carolina (A)	83	—	2353	385	791	.487	0	8	.000	156	239	.653	—	—	618	115	304	—	—	—	—	926	7.4	1.4	11.2
REG. ABA TOTALS	321	—	9589	1476	3315	.445	0	16	.000	863	1262	.684	259	425	2554	507	1118	30	—	467	—	3815	8.0	1.6	11.9
ABA PLAYOFF TOTALS	9	—	238	43	91	.473	0	0	—	27	38	.711	—	—	50	11	16	1	—	16	—	113	5.6	1.2	12.6
ABA ALL-STAR TOTALS	1	—	7	1	2	.500	0	0	—	2	6	.333	2	2	4	0	0	0	—	1	—	4	4.0	0.0	4.0

MAHNKEN, JOHN E. (Long John) b. June 16, 1922 Ht. 6-8 Wt. 220 College—Lafayette/Georgetown

SEASON—TEAM	G	GS	MIN	FGM	FGA	PCT	3FGM	3FGA	PCT	FTM	FTA	PCT	O-RB	D-RB	TOT	AST	PF	DQ	STL	TO	BLK	PTS	RPG	APG	PPG
45-46—Rochester (N)	16	—	—	50	—	—	—	—	—	23	39	.590	—	—	—	—	56	—	—	—	—	123	—	—	7.7
46-47—Washington	60	—	—	223	876	.255	—	—	—	111	163	.681	—	—	—	60	181	—	—	—	—	557	—	1.0	9.3
47-48—Washington	48	—	—	131	526	.249	—	—	—	54	88	.614	—	—	—	31	151	—	—	—	—	316	—	0.6	6.6
48-49—Balt.-Ind.-Ft. Wayne	57	—	—	215	830	.259	—	—	—	104	167	.623	—	—	—	125	215	—	—	—	—	534	—	2.2	9.4
49-50—Ft. Wayne-Tri-Cit-Boston	62	—	—	132	495	.267	—	—	—	77	115	.670	—	—	—	108	231	—	—	—	—	341	—	1.7	5.5
50-51—Boston-Ind.	58	—	—	111	351	.316	—	—	—	45	70	.643	—	—	219	77	164	6	—	—	—	267	3.8	1.3	4.6
51-52—Boston	60	—	581	78	227	.344	—	—	—	26	43	.605	—	—	132	63	91	2	—	—	—	182	2.2	1.1	3.0
52-53—Boston	69	—	771	76	252	.302	—	—	—	39	56	.696	—	—	182	75	110	1	—	—	—	191	2.6	1.1	2.8
REG. NBA TOTALS	414	—	1352	966	3557	.272	—	—	—	456	702	.650	—	—	533	539	1143	9	—	—	—	2388	2.9	1.3	5.8
REG. NBL TOTALS	16	—	—	50	—	—	—	—	—	23	39	.590	—	—	—	—	56	—	—	—	—	123	—	—	7.7
NBA PLAYOFF TOTALS	18	—	122	27	128	.211	—	—	—	24	30	.800	—	—	40	19	63	6	—	—	—	78	3.3	1.1	4.3
NBL PLAYOFF TOTALS	7	—	—	19	—	—	—	—	—	8	11	.727	—	—	—	—	24	—	—	—	—	46	—	—	6.6

MAHONEY, BRIAN C. b. December 17, 1948 Ht. 6-3 Wt. 175 College—Manhattan

SEASON—TEAM	G	GS	MIN	FGM	FGA	PCT	3FGM	3FGA	PCT	FTM	FTA	PCT	O-RB	D-RB	TOT	AST	PF	DQ	STL	TO	BLK	PTS	RPG	APG	PPG
72-73—New York (A)	19	—	181	17	57	.298	0	2	.000	24	40	.600	4	10	14	12	35	1	—	17	—	58	0.7	0.6	3.1
REG. ABA TOTALS	19	—	181	17	57	.298	0	2	.000	24	40	.600	4	10	14	12	35	1	—	17	—	58	0.7	0.6	3.1

MAHONEY, FRANCIS H. (Mo) b. November 20, 1927 Ht. 6-3 Wt. 205 College—Brown

SEASON—TEAM	G	GS	MIN	FGM	FGA	PCT	3FGM	3FGA	PCT	FTM	FTA	PCT	O-RB	D-RB	TOT	AST	PF	DQ	STL	TO	BLK	PTS	RPG	APG	PPG
52-53—Boston	6	—	34	4	10	.400	—	—	—	4	5	.800	—	—	7	1	7	0	—	—	—	12	1.2	0.2	2.0
53-54—Baltimore	2	—	11	0	2	.000	—	—	—	0	0	—	—	—	2	1	0	0	—	—	—	0	1.0	0.5	0.0
REG. SEASON TOTALS	8	—	45	4	12	.333	—	—	—	4	5	.800	—	—	9	2	7	0	—	—	—	12	1.1	0.3	1.5
PLAYOFF TOTALS	4	—	45	3	14	.214	—	—	—	3	5	.600	—	—	7	2	14	0	—	—	—	9	1.8	0.5	2.3

MAHORN, DERRICK ALLEN (Rick) b. September 21, 1958 Ht. 6-10 Wt. 260 College—Hampton

SEASON—TEAM	G	GS	MIN	FGM	FGA	PCT	3FGM	3FGA	PCT	FTM	FTA	PCT	O-RB	D-RB	TOT	AST	PF	DQ	STL	TO	BLK	PTS	RPG	APG	PPG
80-81—Washington	52	—	696	111	219	.507	0	0	—	27	40	.675	67	148	215	25	134	3	21	38	44	249	4.1	0.5	4.8
81-82—Washington	80	80	2664	414	816	.507	0	3	.000	148	234	.632	149	555	704	150	349	12	57	162	138	976	8.8	1.9	12.2
82-83—Washington	82	82	3023	376	768	.490	0	3	.000	146	254	.575	171	608	779	115	335	13	86	170	148	898	9.5	1.4	11.0
83-84—Washington	82	82	2701	307	605	.507	0	0	—	125	192	.651	169	569	738	131	358	14	62	142	123	739	9.0	1.6	9.0
84-85—Washington	77	63	2072	206	413	.499	0	0	—	71	104	.683	150	458	608	121	308	11	59	133	104	483	7.9	1.6	6.3
85-86—Detroit	80	12	1442	157	345	.455	0	1	.000	81	119	.681	121	291	412	64	261	4	40	109	61	395	5.2	0.8	4.9
86-87—Detroit	63	6	1278	144	322	.447	0	0	—	96	117	.821	93	282	375	38	221	4	32	73	50	384	6.0	0.6	6.1
87-88—Detroit	67	64	1963	276	481	.574	1	2	.500	164	217	.756	159	406	565	60	262	4	43	119	42	717	8.4	0.9	10.7
88-89—Detroit	72	61	1795	203	393	.517	0	2	.000	116	155	.748	141	355	496	59	206	1	40	97	66	522	6.9	0.8	7.3
89-90—Philadelphia	75	66	2271	313	630	.497	2	9	.222	183	256	.715	167	401	568	98	251	2	44	104	103	811	7.6	1.3	10.8
90-91—Philadelphia	80	74	2439	261	559	.467	0	9	.000	189	240	.788	151	470	621	118	276	6	79	127	56	711	7.8	1.5	8.9
92-93—New Jersey	74	9	1077	101	214	.472	1	3	.333	88	110	.800	93	186	279	33	156	0	19	58	31	291	3.8	0.4	3.9
93-94—New Jersey	28	0	226	23	47	.489	0	1	.000	13	20	.650	16	38	54	5	38	0	3	7	5	59	1.9	0.2	2.1
REG. SEASON TOTALS	912	599	23647	2892	5812	.498	4	33	.121	1447	2058	.703	1647	4767	6414	1017	3155	74	585	1339	971	7235	7.0	1.1	7.9
PLAYOFF TOTALS	99	85	2382	247	520	.475	0	3	.000	113	150	.753	147	423	570	71	337	6	41	92	63	607	5.8	0.7	6.1

MAJERLE, DANIEL LEWIS (Dan, Thunder) b. September 9, 1965 Ht. 6-6 Wt. 220 College—Central Michigan

SEASON—TEAM	G	GS	MIN	FGM	FGA	PCT	3FGM	3FGA	PCT	FTM	FTA	PCT	O-RB	D-RB	TOT	AST	PF	DQ	STL	TO	BLK	PTS	RPG	APG	PPG
88-89—Phoenix	54	5	1354	181	432	.419	27	82	.329	78	127	.614	62	147	209	130	139	1	63	48	14	467	3.9	2.4	8.6
89-90—Phoenix	73	23	2244	296	698	.424	19	80	.238	198	260	.762	144	286	430	188	177	5	100	82	32	809	5.9	2.6	11.1
90-91—Phoenix	77	7	2281	397	821	.484	30	86	.349	227	298	.762	168	250	418	216	162	0	106	114	40	1051	5.4	2.8	13.6
91-92—Phoenix	82	15	2853	551	1153	.478	87	228	.382	229	303	.756	148	335	483	274	158	0	131	102	43	1418	5.9	3.3	17.3
92-93—Phoenix	82	82	3199	509	1096	.464	167	438	.381	203	261	.778	120	263	383	311	180	0	138	133	33	1388	4.7	3.8	16.9
93-94—Phoenix	80	76	3207	476	1138	.418	192	503	.382	176	238	.739	120	229	349	275	153	0	129	137	43	1320	4.4	3.4	16.5
REG. SEASON TOTALS	448	208	15138	2410	5338	.451	522	1417	.368	1111	1487	.747	762	1510	2272	1394	969	6	667	616	205	6453	5.1	3.1	14.4
PLAYOFF TOTALS	73	34	2688	376	875	.430	99	280	.354	187	243	.770	115	265	380	187	165	0	92	86	39	1038	5.2	2.6	14.2
ALL-STAR TOTALS	2	0	38	8	16	.500	3	8	.375	3	4	.750	2	8	10	5	2	0	1	1	2	22	5.0	2.5	11.0

MALAMED, LIONEL b. November 15, 1924 d. September 17, 1989 Ht. 5-9 Wt. 150 College—City College of New York

SEASON—TEAM	G	GS	MIN	FGM	FGA	PCT	3FGM	3FGA	PCT	FTM	FTA	PCT	O-RB	D-RB	TOT	AST	PF	DQ	STL	TO	BLK	PTS	RPG	APG	PPG
48-49—Ind.-Roch.	44	—	—	97	290	.334	—	—	—	64	77	.831	—	—	—	61	53	—	—	—	—	258	—	1.4	5.9
REG. SEASON TOTALS	44	—	—	97	290	.334	—	—	—	64	77	.831	—	—	—	61	53	—	—	—	—	258	—	1.4	5.9

MALONE, JEFFREY NIGEL (Jeff) b. June 28, 1961 Ht. 6-4 Wt. 205 College—Mississippi State

SEASON—TEAM	G	GS	MIN	FGM	FGA	PCT	3FGM	3FGA	PCT	FTM	FTA	PCT	O-RB	D-RB	TOT	AST	PF	DQ	STL	TO	BLK	PTS	RPG	APG	PPG
83-84—Washington	81	2	1976	408	918	.444	24	74	.324	142	172	.826	57	98	155	151	162	1	23	110	13	982	1.9	1.9	12.1
84-85—Washington	76	61	2613	605	1213	.499	15	72	.208	211	250	.844	60	146	206	184	176	1	52	107	9	1436	2.7	2.4	18.9
85-86—Washington	80	80	2992	735	1522	.483	3	17	.176	322	371	.868	66	222	288	191	180	2	70	168	12	1795	3.6	2.4	22.4
86-87—Washington	80	79	2763	689	1509	.457	4	26	.154	376	425	.885	50	168	218	298	154	0	75	182	13	1758	2.7	3.7	22.0
87-88—Washington	80	80	2655	648	1360	.476	10	24	.417	335	380	.882	44	162	206	237	198	1	51	172	13	1641	2.6	3.0	20.5
88-89—Washington	76	75	2418	677	1410	.480	1	19	.053	296	340	.871	55	124	179	219	155	0	39	165	14	1651	2.4	2.9	21.7
89-90—Washington	75	74	2567	781	1592	.491	1	6	.167	257	293	.877	54	152	206	243	116	1	48	125	6	1820	2.7	3.2	24.3
90-91—Utah	69	69	2466	525	1034	.508	1	6	.167	231	252	.917	36	170	206	143	128	0	50	108	6	1282	3.0	2.1	18.6
91-92—Utah	81	81	2922	691	1353	.511	1	12	.083	256	285	.898	49	184	233	180	126	1	56	140	5	1639	2.9	2.2	20.2
92-93—Utah	79	59	2558	595	1205	.494	3	9	.333	236	277	.852	31	142	173	128	117	0	42	125	4	1429	2.2	1.6	18.1
93-94—Utah-Phil.	77	73	2560	525	1081	.486	7	12	.583	205	247	.830	51	148	199	125	123	0	40	85	5	1262	2.6	1.6	16.4
REG. SEASON TOTALS	854	733	28490	6879	14197	.485	70	277	.253	2867	3292	.871	553	1716	2269	2099	1635	7	546	1487	100	16695	2.7	2.5	19.5
PLAYOFF TOTALS	51	47	1809	382	812	.470	2	12	.167	190	223	.852	35	106	141	110	123	1	39	90	12	956	2.8	2.2	18.7
ALL-STAR TOTALS	2	0	25	6	10	.600	0	1	.000	0	0	—	1	2	3	6	1	0	1	1	0	12	1.5	3.0	6.0

MALONE, KARL (The Mailman) b. July 24, 1963 Ht. 6-9 Wt. 255 College—Louisiana Tech

SEASON—TEAM	G	GS	MIN	FGM	FGA	PCT	3FGM	3FGA	PCT	FTM	FTA	PCT	O-RB	D-RB	TOT	AST	PF	DQ	STL	TO	BLK	PTS	RPG	APG	PPG
85-86—Utah	81	76	2475	504	1016	.496	0	2	.000	195	405	.481	174	544	718	236	295	2	105	279	44	1203	8.9	2.9	14.9
86-87—Utah	82	82	2857	728	1422	.512	0	7	.000	323	540	.598	278	577	855	158	323	6	104	237	60	1779	10.4	1.9	21.7
87-88—Utah	82	82	3198	858	1650	.520	0	5	.000	552	789	.700	277	709	986	199	296	2	117	325	50	2268	12.0	2.4	27.7
88-89—Utah	80	80	3126	809	1559	.519	5	16	.313	703	918	.766	259	594	853	219	286	3	144	285	70	2326	10.7	2.7	29.1
89-90—Utah	82	82	3122	914	1627	.562	16	43	.372	696	913	.762	232	679	911	226	259	1	121	304	50	2540	11.1	2.8	31.0
90-91—Utah	82	82	3302	847	1608	.527	4	14	.286	684	888	.770	236	731	967	270	268	2	89	244	79	2382	11.8	3.3	29.0
91-92—Utah	81	81	3054	798	1516	.526	3	17	.176	673	865	.778	225	684	909	241	226	2	108	248	51	2272	11.2	3.0	28.0
92-93—Utah	82	82	3099	797	1443	.552	4	20	.200	619	836	.740	227	692	919	308	261	2	124	240	85	2217	11.2	3.8	27.0
93-94—Utah	82	82	3329	772	1552	.497	8	32	.250	511	736	.694	235	705	940	328	268	2	125	234	126	2063	11.5	4.0	25.2
REG. SEASON TOTALS	734	729	27562	7027	13393	.525	40	156	.256	4956	6890	.719	2143	5915	8058	2185	2482	22	1037	2396	615	19050	11.0	3.0	26.0
PLAYOFF TOTALS	74	74	3167	722	1514	.477	1	18	.056	573	750	.764	222	637	859	177	283	6	106	213	62	2018	11.6	2.4	27.3
ALL-STAR TOTALS	6	6	164	46	80	.575	0	0	—	19	28	.679	18	36	54	14	14	0	8	13	4	111	9.0	2.3	18.5

MALONE, MOSES EUGENE b. March 23, 1955 Ht. 6-10 Wt. 255 College—None

SEASON—TEAM	G	GS	MIN	FGM	FGA	PCT	3FGM	3FGA	PCT	FTM	FTA	PCT	O-RB	D-RB	TOT	AST	PF	DQ	STL	TO	BLK	PTS	RPG	APG	PPG
74-75—Utah (A)	83	—	3205	591	1035	.571	0	1	.000	375	591	.635	455	754	1209	82	288	—	85	320	128	1557	14.6	1.0	18.8
75-76—St. Louis (A)	43	—	1168	251	490	.512	0	2	.000	112	183	.612	196	217	413	58	113	—	25	140	28	614	9.6	1.3	14.3
76-77—Buffalo-Houston	82	—	2506	389	810	.480	—	—	—	305	440	.693	437	635	1072	89	275	3	67	—	181	1083	13.1	1.1	13.2
77-78—Houston	59	—	2107	413	828	.499	—	—	—	318	443	.718	380	506	886	31	179	2	48	220	76	1144	15.0	0.5	19.4
78-79—Houston	82	—	3390	716	1325	.540	—	—	—	599	811	.739	587	857	1444	147	223	0	79	326	119	2031	17.6	1.8	24.8
79-80—Houston	82	—	3140	778	1549	.502	0	6	.000	563	783	.719	573	617	1190	147	210	0	80	300	107	2119	14.5	1.8	25.8
80-81—Houston	80	—	3245	806	1545	.522	1	3	.333	609	804	.757	474	706	1180	141	223	0	83	308	150	2222	14.8	1.8	27.8
81-82—Houston	81	81	3398	945	1822	.519	0	6	.000	630	827	.762	558	630	1188	142	208	0	76	294	125	2520	14.7	1.8	31.1
82-83—Philadelphia	78	78	2922	654	1305	.501	0	1	.000	600	788	.761	445	749	1194	101	206	0	89	264	157	1908	15.3	1.3	24.5
83-84—Philadelphia	71	71	2613	532	1101	.483	0	4	.000	545	727	.750	352	598	950	96	188	0	71	250	110	1609	13.4	1.4	22.7
84-85—Philadelphia	79	79	2957	602	1284	.469	0	2	.000	737	904	.815	385	646	1031	130	216	0	67	286	123	1941	13.1	1.6	24.6
85-86—Philadelphia	74	74	2706	571	1246	.458	0	1	.000	617	784	.787	339	533	872	90	194	0	67	261	71	1759	11.8	1.2	23.8
86-87—Washington	73	70	2488	595	1311	.454	0	11	.000	570	692	.824	340	484	824	120	139	0	59	202	92	1760	11.3	1.6	24.1
87-88—Washington	79	78	2692	531	1090	.487	2	7	.286	543	689	.788	372	512	884	112	160	0	59	249	72	1607	11.2	1.4	20.3
88-89—Atlanta	81	80	2878	538	1096	.491	0	12	.000	561	711	.789	386	570	956	112	154	0	79	245	100	1637	11.8	1.4	20.2
89-90—Atlanta	81	81	2735	517	1077	.480	1	9	.111	493	631	.781	364	448	812	130	158	0	47	232	84	1528	10.0	1.6	18.9
90-91—Atlanta	82	15	1912	280	598	.468	0	7	.000	309	372	.831	271	396	667	68	134	0	30	137	74	869	8.1	0.8	10.6
91-92—Milwaukee	82	77	2511	440	929	.474	3	8	.375	396	504	.786	320	424	744	93	136	0	74	150	64	1279	9.1	1.1	15.6
92-93—Milwaukee	11	0	104	13	42	.310	0	0	—	24	31	.774	22	24	46	7	6	0	1	10	8	50	4.2	0.6	4.5
93-94—Philadelphia	55	0	618	102	232	.440	0	1	.000	90	117	.769	106	120	226	34	52	0	11	59	17	294	4.1	0.6	5.3
REG. NBA TOTALS	1312	784	44922	9422	19190	.491	7	78	.090	8509	11058	.769	6711	9455	16166	1790	3061	5	1087	3793	1730	27360	12.3	1.4	20.9
REG. ABA TOTALS	126	—	4373	842	1525	.552	0	3	.000	487	774	.629	651	971	1622	140	401	—	110	460	156	2171	12.9	1.1	17.2
NBA PLAYOFF TOTALS	94	47	3796	750	1566	.479	1	7	.143	576	756	.762	510	785	1295	136	244	0	84	215	151	2077	13.8	1.4	22.1
ABA PLAYOFF TOTALS	6	—	235	51	80	.638	0	0	—	34	51	.667	47	58	105	9	21	—	0	13	9	136	17.5	1.5	22.7
NBA ALL-STAR TOTALS	11	8	271	44	98	.449	0	0	—	40	67	.597	44	64	108	15	26	0	9	19	6	128	9.8	1.4	11.6
ABA ALL-STAR TOTALS	1	0	20	2	3	.667	0	0	—	2	5	.400	3	7	10	0	1	—	0	1	1	6	10.0	0.0	6.0

MALOVIC, STEPHEN L. (**Steve**) b. July 21, 1956 Ht. 6-10 Wt. 230 College—USC/San Diego State

SEASON—TEAM	G	GS	MIN	FGM	FGA	PCT	3FGM	3FGA	PCT	FTM	FTA	PCT	O-RB	D-RB	TOT	AST	PF	DQ	STL	TO	BLK	PTS	RPG	APG	PPG
79-80—Wash.-S.D.-Detroit	39	—	445	31	67	.463	0	0	—	18	27	.667	36	50	86	26	51	0	8	23	6	80	2.2	0.7	2.1
REG. SEASON TOTALS	39	—	445	31	67	.463	0	0	—	18	27	.667	36	50	86	26	51	0	8	23	6	80	2.2	0.7	2.1

MALOY, MICHAEL ALVIN (**Mike**) b. May 10, 1949 Ht. 6-7 Wt. 230 College—Davidson

SEASON—TEAM	G	GS	MIN	FGM	FGA	PCT	3FGM	3FGA	PCT	FTM	FTA	PCT	O-RB	D-RB	TOT	AST	PF	DQ	STL	TO	BLK	PTS	RPG	APG	PPG
70-71—Virginia (A)	55	—	725	149	334	.446	0	1	.000	98	139	.705	—	—	236	43	125	—	—	—	—	396	4.3	0.8	7.2
71-72—Virginia (A)	7	—	73	12	35	.343	0	0	—	2	2	1.000	—	—	17	2	14	—	—	9	—	26	2.4	0.3	3.7
72-73—Dallas (A)	9	—	63	7	27	.259	0	0	—	6	10	.600	6	9	15	3	14	0	—	4	—	20	1.7	0.3	2.2
REG. ABA TOTALS	71	—	861	168	396	.424	0	1	.000	106	151	.702	6	9	268	48	153	0	—	13	—	442	3.8	0.7	6.2
ABA PLAYOFF TOTALS	1	—	2	1	3	.333	0	0	—	0	0	—	—	—	1	0	0	0	—	—	—	2	1.0	0.0	2.0

MANAKAS, THEODORE (**Ted**) b. February 22, 1951 Ht. 6-2 Wt. 180 College—Princeton

SEASON—TEAM	G	GS	MIN	FGM	FGA	PCT	3FGM	3FGA	PCT	FTM	FTA	PCT	O-RB	D-RB	TOT	AST	PF	DQ	STL	TO	BLK	PTS	RPG	APG	PPG
73-74—Kansas City-Omaha	5	—	45	4	10	.400	—	—	—	4	4	1.000	0	3	3	2	4	0	1	—	0	12	0.6	0.4	2.4
REG. SEASON TOTALS	5	—	45	4	10	.400	—	—	—	4	4	1.000	0	3	3	2	4	0	1	—	0	12	0.6	0.4	2.4

MANDIC, JOHN J. b. October 3, 1919 Ht. 6-4 Wt. 205 College—Oregon State

SEASON—TEAM	G	GS	MIN	FGM	FGA	PCT	3FGM	3FGA	PCT	FTM	FTA	PCT	O-RB	D-RB	TOT	AST	PF	DQ	STL	TO	BLK	PTS	RPG	APG	PPG
47-48—Rochester (N)	33	—	—	32	—	—	—	—	—	13	23	.565	—	—	—	—	57	—	—	—	—	77	—	—	2.3
48-49—Indianapolis	56	—	—	97	302	.321	—	—	—	75	115	.652	—	—	—	80	151	—	—	—	—	269	—	1.4	4.8
49-50—Wash.-Balt.	25	—	—	22	75	.293	—	—	—	22	32	.688	—	—	—	8	54	—	—	—	—	66	—	0.3	2.6
REG. NBA TOTALS	81	—	—	119	377	.316	—	—	—	97	147	.660	—	—	—	88	205	—	—	—	—	335	—	1.1	4.1
REG. NBL TOTALS	33	—	—	32	—	—	—	—	—	13	23	.565	—	—	—	—	57	—	—	—	—	77	—	—	2.3
NBL PLAYOFF TOTALS	5	—	—	2	—	—	—	—	—	2	4	.500	—	—	—	—	9	—	—	—	—	6	—	—	1.2

MANGIAPANE, FRANCIS E. (**Frank**) b. August 25, 1925 Ht. 5-10 Wt. 195 College—New York University

SEASON—TEAM	G	GS	MIN	FGM	FGA	PCT	3FGM	3FGA	PCT	FTM	FTA	PCT	O-RB	D-RB	TOT	AST	PF	DQ	STL	TO	BLK	PTS	RPG	APG	PPG
46-47—New York	6	—	—	2	13	.154	—	—	—	1	3	.333	—	—	—	0	6	—	—	—	—	5	—	0.0	0.8
REG. SEASON TOTALS	6	—	—	2	13	.154	—	—	—	1	3	.333	—	—	—	0	6	—	—	—	—	5	—	0.0	0.8

MANNING, DANIEL RICARDO (Danny, D.) b. May 17, 1966 Ht. 6-10 Wt. 230 College—Kansas

SEASON—TEAM	G	GS	MIN	FGM	FGA	PCT	3FGM	3FGA	PCT	FTM	FTA	PCT	O-RB	D-RB	TOT	AST	PF	DQ	STL	TO	BLK	PTS	RPG	APG	PPG
88-89—L.A. Clippers	26	18	950	177	358	.494	1	5	.200	79	103	.767	70	101	171	81	89	1	44	93	25	434	6.6	3.1	16.7
89-90—L.A. Clippers	71	42	2269	440	826	.533	0	5	.000	274	370	.741	142	280	422	187	261	4	91	188	39	1154	5.9	2.6	16.3
90-91—L.A. Clippers	73	47	2197	470	905	.519	0	3	.000	219	306	.716	169	257	426	196	281	5	117	188	62	1159	5.8	2.7	15.9
91-92—L.A. Clippers	82	82	2904	650	1199	.542	0	5	.000	279	385	.725	229	335	564	285	293	5	135	210	122	1579	6.9	3.5	19.3
92-93—L.A. Clippers	79	77	2761	702	1379	.509	8	30	.267	388	484	.802	198	322	520	207	323	8	108	230	101	1800	6.6	2.6	22.8
93-94—L.A. Clips-Atlanta	68	66	2520	586	1201	.488	3	17	.176	228	341	.669	131	334	465	261	260	2	99	233	82	1403	6.8	3.8	20.6
REG. SEASON TOTALS	399	332	13601	3025	5868	.516	12	65	.185	1467	1989	.738	939	1629	2568	1217	1507	25	594	1142	431	7529	6.4	3.1	18.9
PLAYOFF TOTALS	21	21	791	165	338	.488	1	5	.200	93	123	.756	55	86	141	59	79	1	27	52	18	424	6.7	2.8	20.2
ALL-STAR TOTALS	2	0	35	9	12	.750	0	0	—	0	0	—	1	7	8	3	5	0	0	0	1	18	4.0	1.5	9.0

MANNING, EDWARD R. (Ed) b. January 2, 1944 Ht. 6-7½ Wt. 215 College—Jackson State

SEASON—TEAM	G	GS	MIN	FGM	FGA	PCT	3FGM	3FGA	PCT	FTM	FTA	PCT	O-RB	D-RB	TOT	AST	PF	DQ	STL	TO	BLK	PTS	RPG	APG	PPG
67-68—Baltimore	71	—	951	112	259	.432	—	—	—	60	99	.606	—	—	375	32	153	3	—	—	—	284	5.3	0.5	4.0
68-69—Baltimore	63	—	727	129	288	.448	—	—	—	35	54	.648	—	—	246	21	120	0	—	—	—	293	3.9	0.3	4.7
69-70—Balt.-Chicago	67	—	777	119	321	.371	—	—	—	42	56	.750	—	—	232	36	122	1	—	—	—	280	3.5	0.5	4.2
70-71—Portland	79	—	1558	243	559	.435	—	—	—	75	93	.806	—	—	411	111	198	3	—	—	—	561	5.2	1.4	7.1
71-72—Carolina (A)	77	—	1648	228	499	.457	0	3	.000	95	114	.833	—	—	441	58	227	—	—	83	—	551	5.7	0.8	7.2
72-73—Carolina (A)	83	—	1631	263	554	.475	0	1	.000	64	84	.762	110	283	393	64	247	4	—	84	—	590	4.7	0.8	7.1
73-74—Carolina (A)	82	—	1816	297	609	.488	1	2	.500	86	101	.851	105	265	370	100	210	—	93	95	16	681	4.5	1.2	8.3
74-75—New York (A)	70	—	992	103	243	.424	0	2	.000	35	42	.833	59	153	212	58	144	—	40	57	9	241	3.0	0.8	3.4
75-76—Indiana (A)	12	—	134	24	60	.400	0	0	—	12	17	.706	15	22	37	14	18	—	4	7	2	60	3.1	1.2	5.0
REG. NBA TOTALS	280	—	4013	603	1427	.423	—	—	—	212	302	.702	—	—	1264	200	593	7	—	—	—	1418	4.5	0.7	5.1
REG. ABA TOTALS	324	—	6221	915	1965	.466	1	8	.125	292	358	.816	289	723	1453	294	846	4	137	326	27	2123	4.5	0.9	6.6
NBA PLAYOFF TOTALS	6	—	92	12	28	.429	—	—	—	1	2	.500	—	—	32	4	13	0	—	—	—	25	5.3	0.7	4.2
ABA PLAYOFF TOTALS	19	—	361	64	126	.508	1	2	.500	24	29	.828	4	10	71	8	53	0	0	18	1	153	3.7	0.4	8.1

MANNING, GUY R. b. February 4, 1944 Ht. 6-6½ Wt. 205 College—Prairie View A&M

SEASON—TEAM	G	GS	MIN	FGM	FGA	PCT	3FGM	3FGA	PCT	FTM	FTA	PCT	O-RB	D-RB	TOT	AST	PF	DQ	STL	TO	BLK	PTS	RPG	APG	PPG
67-68—Houston (A)	59	—	1107	206	502	.410	2	6	.333	115	199	.578	—	—	311	37	151	4	—	53	—	529	5.3	0.6	9.0
68-69—Houston (A)	14	—	167	27	95	.284	0	2	.000	21	37	.568	—	—	42	2	20	0	—	12	—	75	3.0	0.1	5.4
REG. ABA TOTALS	73	—	1274	233	597	.390	2	8	.250	136	236	.576	—	—	353	39	171	4	—	65	—	604	4.8	0.5	8.3
ABA PLAYOFF TOTALS	3	—	66	15	34	.441	0	0	—	11	19	.579	—	—	19	2	11	0	—	5	—	41	6.3	0.7	13.7

MANNION, PACE SHEWAN b. September 22, 1960 Ht. 6-7 Wt. 190 College—Utah

SEASON—TEAM	G	GS	MIN	FGM	FGA	PCT	3FGM	3FGA	PCT	FTM	FTA	PCT	O-RB	D-RB	TOT	AST	PF	DQ	STL	TO	BLK	PTS	RPG	APG	PPG
83-84—Golden State	57	0	469	50	126	.397	3	13	.231	18	23	.783	23	36	59	47	63	0	25	23	2	121	1.0	0.8	2.1
84-85—Utah	34	0	190	27	63	.429	0	1	.000	16	23	.696	12	11	23	27	17	0	16	18	3	70	0.7	0.8	2.1
85-86—Utah	57	0	673	97	214	.453	8	42	.190	53	82	.646	26	56	82	55	68	0	32	41	5	255	1.4	1.0	4.5
86-87—New Jersey	23	3	284	31	94	.330	3	9	.333	18	31	.581	10	29	39	45	32	0	18	23	4	83	1.7	2.0	3.6
87-88—Milwaukee	35	1	477	48	118	.407	2	12	.167	25	37	.676	17	34	51	55	53	0	13	24	7	123	1.5	1.6	3.5
88-89—Detroit-Atlanta	10	0	32	4	8	.500	0	2	.000	0	0	—	0	5	5	2	5	0	3	3	0	8	0.5	0.2	0.8
REG. SEASON TOTALS	216	4	2125	257	623	.413	16	79	.203	130	196	.663	88	171	259	231	238	0	107	132	21	660	1.2	1.1	3.1
PLAYOFF TOTALS	8	0	41	4	12	.333	0	1	.000	10	12	.833	3	4	7	4	5	0	1	7	2	18	0.9	0.5	2.3

MANTIS, NICHOLAS (Nick) b. December 7, 1935 Ht. 6-3 Wt. 190 College—Northwestern

SEASON—TEAM	G	GS	MIN	FGM	FGA	PCT	3FGM	3FGA	PCT	FTM	FTA	PCT	O-RB	D-RB	TOT	AST	PF	DQ	STL	TO	BLK	PTS	RPG	APG	PPG
59-60—Minneapolis	10	—	71	10	39	.256	—	—	—	1	2	.500	—	—	6	9	8	0	—	—	—	21	0.6	0.9	2.1
62-63—St. L.-Chicago	32	—	684	94	244	.385	—	—	—	27	49	.551	—	—	85	83	94	0	—	—	—	215	2.7	2.6	6.7
REG. SEASON TOTALS	42	—	755	104	283	.367	—	—	—	28	51	.549	—	—	91	92	102	0	—	—	—	236	2.2	2.2	5.6

MARAVICH, PETER (Press) b. August 20, 1920 d. April 15, 1987 Ht. 6-0 Wt. 185 College—Davis & Elkins

SEASON—TEAM	G	GS	MIN	FGM	FGA	PCT	3FGM	3FGA	PCT	FTM	FTA	PCT	O-RB	D-RB	TOT	AST	PF	DQ	STL	TO	BLK	PTS	RPG	APG	PPG
45-46—Youngstown (N)	32	—	—	72	—	—	—	—	—	34	51	.667	—	—	—	—	76	—	—	—	—	178	—	—	5.6
46-47—Pittsburgh	51	—	—	102	375	.272	—	—	—	30	58	.517	—	—	—	6	102	—	—	—	—	234	—	0.1	4.6
REG. NBA TOTALS	51	—	—	102	375	.272	—	—	—	30	58	.517	—	—	—	6	102	—	—	—	—	234	—	0.1	4.6
REG. NBL TOTALS	32	—	—	72	—	—	—	—	—	34	51	.667	—	—	—	—	76	—	—	—	—	178	—	—	5.6

MARAVICH, PETER PRESS (**Pete, Pistol Pete**) b. June 22, 1947 d. January 5, 1988 Ht. 6-5 Wt. 200 College—Louisiana State

SEASON—TEAM	G	GS	MIN	FGM	FGA	PCT	3FGM	3FGA	PCT	FTM	FTA	PCT	O-RB	D-RB	TOT	AST	PF	DQ	STL	TO	BLK	PTS	RPG	APG	PPG
70-71—Atlanta	81	—	2926	738	1613	.458	—	—	—	404	505	.800	—	—	298	355	238	1	—	—	—	1880	3.7	4.4	23.2
71-72—Atlanta	66	—	2302	460	1077	.427	—	—	—	355	438	.811	—	—	256	393	207	0	—	—	—	1275	3.9	6.0	19.3
72-73—Atlanta	79	—	3089	789	1788	.441	—	—	—	485	606	.800	—	—	346	546	245	1	—	—	—	2063	4.4	6.9	26.1
73-74—Atlanta	76	—	2903	819	1791	.457	—	—	—	469	568	.826	98	276	374	396	261	4	111	—	13	2107	4.9	5.2	27.7
74-75—New Orleans	79	—	2853	655	1562	.419	—	—	—	390	481	.811	93	329	422	488	227	4	120	—	18	1700	5.3	6.2	21.5
75-76—New Orleans	62	—	2373	604	1316	.459	—	—	—	396	488	.811	46	254	300	332	197	3	87	—	23	1604	4.8	5.4	25.9
76-77—New Orleans	73	—	3041	886	2047	.433	—	—	—	501	600	.835	90	284	374	392	191	1	84	—	22	2273	5.1	5.4	31.1
77-78—New Orleans	50	—	2041	556	1253	.444	—	—	—	240	276	.870	49	129	178	335	116	1	101	248	8	1352	3.6	6.7	27.0
78-79—New Orleans	49	—	1824	436	1035	.421	—	—	—	233	277	.841	33	88	121	243	104	2	60	200	18	1105	2.5	5.0	22.6
79-80—Utah-Boston	43	—	964	244	543	.449	10	15	.667	91	105	.867	17	61	78	83	79	1	24	82	6	589	1.8	1.9	13.7
REG. SEASON TOTALS	658	—	24316	6187	14025	.441	10	15	.667	3564	4344	.820	426	1421	2747	3563	1865	18	587	530	108	15948	4.2	5.4	24.2
PLAYOFF TOTALS	26	—	756	190	449	.423	2	6	.333	105	134	.784	0	8	95	98	74	1	3	9	0	487	3.7	3.8	18.7
ALL-STAR TOTALS	4	—	79	18	44	.409	0	0	—	7	9	.778	1	4	8	15	8	0	4	4	0	43	2.0	3.8	10.8

MARBLE, ROY LANE JR. b. December 13, 1966 Ht. 6-6 Wt. 190 College—Iowa

SEASON—TEAM	G	GS	MIN	FGM	FGA	PCT	3FGM	3FGA	PCT	FTM	FTA	PCT	O-RB	D-RB	TOT	AST	PF	DQ	STL	TO	BLK	PTS	RPG	APG	PPG
89-90—Atlanta	24	0	162	16	58	.276	0	2	.000	19	29	.655	15	9	24	11	16	0	7	14	1	51	1.0	0.5	2.1
93-94—Denver	5	0	32	2	12	.167	0	0	—	0	3	.000	3	5	8	1	1	0	0	3	2	4	1.6	0.2	0.8
REG. SEASON TOTALS	29	0	194	18	70	.257	0	2	.000	19	32	.594	18	14	32	12	17	0	7	17	3	55	1.1	0.4	1.9

MARCIULIONIS, RAIMONDAS SARUNAS (**Sarunas, Rooney**) b. June 13, 1964 Ht. 6-5 Wt. 215 College—Vilnius State (Lithuania)

SEASON—TEAM	G	GS	MIN	FGM	FGA	PCT	3FGM	3FGA	PCT	FTM	FTA	PCT	O-RB	D-RB	TOT	AST	PF	DQ	STL	TO	BLK	PTS	RPG	APG	PPG
89-90—Golden State	75	3	1695	289	557	.519	10	39	.256	317	403	.787	84	137	221	121	230	5	94	137	7	905	2.9	1.6	12.1
90-91—Golden State	50	10	987	183	365	.501	1	6	.167	178	246	.724	51	67	118	85	136	4	62	75	4	545	2.4	1.7	10.9
91-92—Golden State	72	5	2117	491	912	.538	3	10	.300	376	477	.788	68	140	208	243	237	4	116	193	10	1361	2.9	3.4	18.9
92-93—Golden State	30	8	836	178	328	.543	3	15	.200	162	213	.761	40	57	97	105	92	1	51	76	2	521	3.2	3.5	17.4
REG. SEASON TOTALS	227	26	5635	1141	2162	.528	17	70	.243	1033	1339	.771	243	401	644	554	695	14	323	481	23	3332	2.8	2.4	14.7
PLAYOFF TOTALS	13	0	339	67	131	.511	1	3	.333	69	80	.863	11	21	32	47	36	1	14	18	2	204	2.5	3.6	15.7

MARIASCHIN, SAUL GEORGE b. September 1, 1924 Ht. 5-11 Wt. 165 College—Bloomsburg/Syracuse/Harvard

SEASON—TEAM	G	GS	MIN	FGM	FGA	PCT	3FGM	3FGA	PCT	FTM	FTA	PCT	O-RB	D-RB	TOT	AST	PF	DQ	STL	TO	BLK	PTS	RPG	APG	PPG
47-48—Boston	43	—	—	125	463	.270	—	—	—	83	117	.709	—	—	—	60	121	—	—	—	—	333	—	1.4	7.7
REG. SEASON TOTALS	43	—	—	125	463	.270	—	—	—	83	117	.709	—	—	—	60	121	—	—	—	—	333	—	1.4	7.7
PLAYOFF TOTALS	3	—	—	10	42	.238	—	—	—	9	14	.643	—	—	—	1	12	—	—	—	—	29	—	0.3	9.7

MARIN, JOHN WARREN (**Jack**) b. October 12, 1944 Ht. 6-6.5 Wt. 200 College—Duke

SEASON—TEAM	G	GS	MIN	FGM	FGA	PCT	3FGM	3FGA	PCT	FTM	FTA	PCT	O-RB	D-RB	TOT	AST	PF	DQ	STL	TO	BLK	PTS	RPG	APG	PPG
66-67—Baltimore	74	—	1323	283	632	.448	—	—	—	145	187	.775	—	—	313	75	199	6	—	—	—	711	4.2	1.0	9.6
67-68—Baltimore	82	—	2037	429	932	.460	—	—	—	250	314	.796	—	—	473	110	246	4	—	—	—	1108	5.8	1.3	13.5
68-69—Baltimore	82	—	2710	505	1109	.455	—	—	—	292	352	.830	—	—	608	231	275	4	—	—	—	1302	7.4	2.8	15.9
69-70—Baltimore	82	—	2947	666	1363	.489	—	—	—	286	339	.844	—	—	537	217	248	6	—	—	—	1618	6.5	2.6	19.7
70-71—Baltimore	82	—	2920	626	1360	.460	—	—	—	290	342	.848	—	—	513	217	261	3	—	—	—	1542	6.3	2.6	18.8
71-72—Baltimore	78	—	2927	690	1444	.478	—	—	—	356	398	.894	—	—	528	169	240	2	—	—	—	1736	6.8	2.2	22.3
72-73—Houston	81	—	3019	624	1334	.468	—	—	—	248	292	.849	—	—	499	291	247	4	—	—	—	1496	6.2	3.6	18.5
73-74—Houston-Buffalo	74	—	1782	355	709	.501	—	—	—	153	179	.855	59	169	228	167	213	5	46	—	26	863	3.1	2.3	11.7
74-75—Buffalo	81	—	2147	380	836	.455	—	—	—	193	222	.869	104	259	363	133	238	7	51	—	16	953	4.5	1.6	11.8
75-76—Buffalo-Chicago	79	—	1909	343	812	.422	—	—	—	161	188	.856	69	183	252	141	164	0	45	—	11	847	3.2	1.8	10.7
76-77—Chicago	54	—	869	167	359	.465	—	—	—	31	39	.795	27	64	91	62	85	0	13	—	6	365	1.7	1.1	6.8
REG. SEASON TOTALS	849	—	24590	5068	10890	.465	—	—	—	2405	2852	.843	259	675	4405	1813	2416	41	155	—	59	12541	5.2	2.1	14.8
PLAYOFF TOTALS	51	—	1679	292	649	.450	—	—	—	173	210	.824	10	27	283	120	151	2	9	—	1	757	5.5	2.4	14.8
ALL-STAR TOTALS	2	—	26	7	14	.500	—	—	—	1	1	1.000	0	0	4	2	2	0	0	—	0	15	2.0	1.0	7.5

MARLATT, HARVEY W. b. August 26, 1948 Ht. 6-3 Wt. 185 College—Eastern Michigan

SEASON—TEAM	G	GS	MIN	FGM	FGA	PCT	3FGM	3FGA	PCT	FTM	FTA	PCT	O-RB	D-RB	TOT	AST	PF	DQ	STL	TO	BLK	PTS	RPG	APG	PPG
70-71—Detroit	23	—	214	25	80	.313	—	—	—	15	18	.833	—	—	23	30	27	0	—	—	—	65	1.0	1.3	2.8
71-72—Detroit	31	—	506	60	149	.403	—	—	—	36	42	.857	—	—	62	60	64	1	—	—	—	156	2.0	1.9	5.0
72-73—Detroit	7	—	26	2	4	.500	—	—	—	0	0	—	—	—	1	4	1	0	—	—	—	4	0.1	0.6	0.6
REG. SEASON TOTALS	61	—	746	87	233	.373	—	—	—	51	60	.850	—	—	86	94	92	1	—	—	—	225	1.4	1.5	3.7

MARSH, ERIC CLIFTON (**Ricky**) b. March 10, 1954 Ht. 6-3 Wt. 200 College—Nebraska/Manhattan

SEASON—TEAM	G	GS	MIN	FGM	FGA	PCT	3FGM	3FGA	PCT	FTM	FTA	PCT	O-RB	D-RB	TOT	AST	PF	DQ	STL	TO	BLK	PTS	RPG	APG	PPG
77-78—Golden State	60	—	851	123	289	.426	—	—	—	23	33	.697	16	59	75	90	111	0	29	50	19	269	1.3	1.5	4.5
REG. SEASON TOTALS	60	—	851	123	289	.426	—	—	—	23	33	.697	16	59	75	90	111	0	29	50	19	269	1.3	1.5	4.5

MARSH, JAMES (**Jim**) b. April 26, 1946 Ht. 6-7 Wt. 215 College—USC

SEASON—TEAM	G	GS	MIN	FGM	FGA	PCT	3FGM	3FGA	PCT	FTM	FTA	PCT	O-RB	D-RB	TOT	AST	PF	DQ	STL	TO	BLK	PTS	RPG	APG	PPG
71-72—Portland	39	—	375	39	117	.333	—	—	—	41	59	.695	—	—	84	30	50	0	—	—	—	119	2.2	0.8	3.1
REG. SEASON TOTALS	39	—	375	39	117	.333	—	—	—	41	59	.695	—	—	84	30	50	0	—	—	—	119	2.2	0.8	3.1

MARSHALL, JOHN THOMAS (**Tom**) b. January 6, 1931 Ht. 6-4 Wt. 215 College—Western Kentucky

SEASON—TEAM	G	GS	MIN	FGM	FGA	PCT	3FGM	3FGA	PCT	FTM	FTA	PCT	O-RB	D-RB	TOT	AST	PF	DQ	STL	TO	BLK	PTS	RPG	APG	PPG
54-55—Rochester	72	—	1337	223	505	.442	—	—	—	131	194	.675	—	—	256	111	99	0	—	—	—	577	3.6	1.5	8.0
56-57—Rochester	40	—	460	56	163	.344	—	—	—	47	58	.810	—	—	83	31	33	0	—	—	—	159	2.1	0.8	4.0
57-58—Detroit-Cin.	38	—	518	52	166	.313	—	—	—	48	63	.762	—	—	101	19	43	0	—	—	—	152	2.7	0.5	4.0
58-59—Cincinnati	18	—	272	23	79	.291	—	—	—	18	29	.621	—	—	52	27	22	0	—	—	—	64	2.9	1.5	3.6
REG. SEASON TOTALS	168	—	2587	354	913	.388	—	—	—	244	344	.709	—	—	492	188	197	0	—	—	—	952	2.9	1.1	5.7
PLAYOFF TOTALS	5	—	83	10	37	.270	—	—	—	7	10	.700	—	—	33	4	2	0	—	—	—	27	6.6	0.8	5.4

MARSHALL, VESTER b. December 22, 1948 Ht. 6-7 Wt. 200 College—Oklahoma

SEASON—TEAM	G	GS	MIN	FGM	FGA	PCT	3FGM	3FGA	PCT	FTM	FTA	PCT	O-RB	D-RB	TOT	AST	PF	DQ	STL	TO	BLK	PTS	RPG	APG	PPG
73-74—Seattle	13	—	174	7	29	.241	—	—	—	3	7	.429	14	23	37	4	20	0	4	—	3	17	2.8	0.3	1.3
REG. SEASON TOTALS	13	—	174	7	29	.241	—	—	—	3	7	.429	14	23	37	4	20	0	4	—	3	17	2.8	0.3	1.3

MARTIN, BRIAN b. August 18, 1962 Ht. 6-9 Wt. 215 College—Hutchinson CC/Kansas

SEASON—TEAM	G	GS	MIN	FGM	FGA	PCT	3FGM	3FGA	PCT	FTM	FTA	PCT	O-RB	D-RB	TOT	AST	PF	DQ	STL	TO	BLK	PTS	RPG	APG	PPG
85-86—Seattle-Port.	8	0	21	3	7	.429	0	0	—	0	2	.000	1	3	4	0	7	0	0	2	1	6	0.5	0.0	0.8
REG. SEASON TOTALS	8	0	21	3	7	.429	0	0	—	0	2	.000	1	3	4	0	7	0	0	2	1	6	0.5	0.0	0.8

MARTIN, DONALD E. (**Dino**) b. May 25, 1920 Ht. 5-9 Wt. 160 College—Georgetown

SEASON—TEAM	G	GS	MIN	FGM	FGA	PCT	3FGM	3FGA	PCT	FTM	FTA	PCT	O-RB	D-RB	TOT	AST	PF	DQ	STL	TO	BLK	PTS	RPG	APG	PPG
46-47—Providence	60	—	—	311	1022	.304	—	—	—	111	168	.661	—	—	—	59	98	—	—	—	—	733	—	1.0	12.2
47-48—Providence	32	—	—	46	193	.238	—	—	—	9	20	.450	—	—	—	14	17	—	—	—	—	101	—	0.4	3.2
REG. SEASON TOTALS	92	—	—	357	1215	.294	—	—	—	120	188	.638	—	—	—	73	115	—	—	—	—	834	—	0.8	9.1

MARTIN, FERNANDO b. March 25, 1962 d. December 3, 1989 Ht. 6-10 Wt. 240 College—None

SEASON—TEAM	G	GS	MIN	FGM	FGA	PCT	3FGM	3FGA	PCT	FTM	FTA	PCT	O-RB	D-RB	TOT	AST	PF	DQ	STL	TO	BLK	PTS	RPG	APG	PPG
86-87—Portland	24	0	146	9	31	.290	0	1	.000	4	11	.364	8	20	28	9	24	0	7	20	1	22	1.2	0.4	0.9
REG. SEASON TOTALS	24	0	146	9	31	.290	0	1	.000	4	11	.364	8	20	28	9	24	0	7	20	1	22	1.2	0.4	0.9
PLAYOFF TOTALS	1	0	1	0	1	.000	0	0	—	0	0	—	0	0	0	—	0	0	0	0	0	0	0.0	0.0	0.0

MARTIN, JAMES DONALD (**Don**) b. February 7, 1920 Ht. 6-7 Wt. 210 College—Central Missouri State

SEASON—TEAM	G	GS	MIN	FGM	FGA	PCT	3FGM	3FGA	PCT	FTM	FTA	PCT	O-RB	D-RB	TOT	AST	PF	DQ	STL	TO	BLK	PTS	RPG	APG	PPG
46-47—St. Louis	54	—	—	89	304	.293	—	—	—	13	31	.419	—	—	—	9	75	—	—	—	—	191	—	0.2	3.5
47-48—St. Louis	39	—	—	35	150	.233	—	—	—	15	33	.455	—	—	—	2	61	—	—	—	—	85	—	0.1	2.2
48-49—St. L.-Balt.	44	—	—	52	170	.306	—	—	—	30	47	.638	—	—	—	25	115	—	—	—	—	134	—	0.6	3.0
REG. SEASON TOTALS	137	—	—	176	624	.282	—	—	—	58	111	.523	—	—	—	36	251	—	—	—	—	410	—	0.3	3.0
PLAYOFF TOTALS	8	—	—	9	56	.161	—	—	—	3	3	1.000	—	—	—	2	16	1	—	—	—	21	0.0	0.3	2.6

MARTIN, JEFFERY ALLEN (**Jeff**) b. January 14, 1967 Ht. 6-5 Wt. 195 College—Murray State (Ky.)

SEASON—TEAM	G	GS	MIN	FGM	FGA	PCT	3FGM	3FGA	PCT	FTM	FTA	PCT	O-RB	D-RB	TOT	AST	PF	DQ	STL	TO	BLK	PTS	RPG	APG	PPG
89-90—L.A. Clippers	69	23	1351	170	414	.411	2	15	.133	91	129	.705	78	81	159	44	97	0	41	47	16	433	2.3	0.6	6.3
90-91—L.A. Clippers	74	26	1334	214	507	.422	27	88	.307	68	100	.680	53	78	131	65	104	0	37	49	31	523	1.8	0.9	7.1
REG. SEASON TOTALS	143	49	2685	384	921	.417	29	103	.282	159	229	.694	131	159	290	109	201	0	78	96	47	956	2.0	0.8	6.7

MARTIN, LARUE b. March 30, 1950 Ht. 6-11 Wt. 210 College—Loyola (Ill.)

SEASON—TEAM	G	GS	MIN	FGM	FGA	PCT	3FGM	3FGA	PCT	FTM	FTA	PCT	O-RB	D-RB	TOT	AST	PF	DQ	STL	TO	BLK	PTS	RPG	APG	PPG
72-73—Portland	77	—	996	145	366	.396	—	—	—	50	77	.649	—	—	358	42	162	0	—	—	—	340	4.6	0.5	4.4
73-74—Portland	50	—	538	101	232	.435	—	—	—	42	66	.636	74	107	181	20	90	0	7	—	26	244	3.6	0.4	4.9
74-75—Portland	81	—	1372	236	522	.452	—	—	—	99	142	.697	136	272	408	69	239	5	33	—	49	571	5.0	0.9	7.0
75-76—Portland	63	—	889	109	302	.361	—	—	—	57	77	.740	68	243	311	72	126	1	6	—	23	275	4.9	1.1	4.4
REG. SEASON TOTALS	271	—	3795	591	1422	.416	—	—	—	248	362	.685	278	622	1258	203	617	6	46	—	98	1430	4.6	0.7	5.3

MARTIN, MAURICE (**Mo**) b. July 2, 1964 Ht. 6-6 Wt. 200 College—St. Joseph (Pa.)

SEASON—TEAM	G	GS	MIN	FGM	FGA	PCT	3FGM	3FGA	PCT	FTM	FTA	PCT	O-RB	D-RB	TOT	AST	PF	DQ	STL	TO	BLK	PTS	RPG	APG	PPG
86-87—Denver	43	0	286	51	135	.378	3	15	.200	42	66	.636	12	29	41	35	48	0	13	33	6	147	1.0	0.8	3.4
87-88—Denver	26	0	136	23	61	.377	1	4	.250	10	21	.476	13	11	24	14	21	0	6	10	3	57	0.9	0.5	2.2
REG. SEASON TOTALS	69	0	422	74	196	.378	4	19	.211	52	87	.598	25	40	65	49	69	0	19	43	9	204	0.9	0.7	3.0
PLAYOFF TOTALS	6	0	63	13	34	.382	0	2	.000	12	18	.667	4	6	10	10	13	0	6	2	0	38	1.7	1.7	6.3

MARTIN, PHILLIP ROGER (**Phil**) b. April 2, 1928 Ht. 6-3 Wt. 190 College—Toledo

SEASON—TEAM	G	GS	MIN	FGM	FGA	PCT	3FGM	3FGA	PCT	FTM	FTA	PCT	O-RB	D-RB	TOT	AST	PF	DQ	STL	TO	BLK	PTS	RPG	APG	PPG
54-55—Milwaukee	7	—	47	5	19	.263	—	—	—	2	2	1.000	—	—	10	6	7	0	—	—	—	12	1.4	0.9	1.7
REG. SEASON TOTALS	7	—	47	5	19	.263	—	—	—	2	2	1.000	—	—	10	6	7	0	—	—	—	12	1.4	0.9	1.7

MARTIN, ROBERT W. (**Bob**) b. October 7, 1969 Ht. 7-0 Wt. 255 College—Minnesota

SEASON—TEAM	G	GS	MIN	FGM	FGA	PCT	3FGM	3FGA	PCT	FTM	FTA	PCT	O-RB	D-RB	TOT	AST	PF	DQ	STL	TO	BLK	PTS	RPG	APG	PPG
93-94—L.A. Clippers	53	1	535	40	88	.455	0	0	—	31	51	.608	36	81	117	17	106	1	8	29	33	111	2.2	0.3	2.1
REG. SEASON TOTALS	53	1	535	40	88	.455	0	0	—	31	51	.608	36	81	117	17	106	1	8	29	33	111	2.2	0.3	2.1

MARTIN, RONALD BARRY (**Whitey**) b. April 11, 1939 Ht. 6-2 Wt. 185 College—St. Bonaventure

SEASON—TEAM	G	GS	MIN	FGM	FGA	PCT	3FGM	3FGA	PCT	FTM	FTA	PCT	O-RB	D-RB	TOT	AST	PF	DQ	STL	TO	BLK	PTS	RPG	APG	PPG
61-62—New York	66	—	1018	95	292	.325	—	—	—	37	55	.673	—	—	158	115	158	4	—	—	—	227	2.4	1.7	3.4
REG. SEASON TOTALS	66	—	1018	95	292	.325	—	—	—	37	55	.673	—	—	158	115	158	4	—	—	—	227	2.4	1.7	3.4

MARTIN, SLATER NELSON JR. (**Dugie**) b. October 22, 1925 Ht. 5-10 Wt. 170 College—Texas

SEASON—TEAM	G	GS	MIN	FGM	FGA	PCT	3FGM	3FGA	PCT	FTM	FTA	PCT	O-RB	D-RB	TOT	AST	PF	DQ	STL	TO	BLK	PTS	RPG	APG	PPG
49-50—Minneapolis	67	—	—	106	302	.351	—	—	—	59	93	.634	—	—	—	148	162	—	—	—	—	271	—	2.2	4.0
50-51—Minneapolis	68	—	—	227	627	.362	—	—	—	121	177	.684	—	—	246	235	199	3	—	—	—	575	3.6	3.5	8.5
51-52—Minneapolis	66	—	2480	237	632	.375	—	—	—	142	190	.747	—	—	228	249	226	9	—	—	—	616	3.5	3.8	9.3
52-53—Minneapolis	70	—	2556	260	634	.410	—	—	—	224	287	.780	—	—	186	250	246	4	—	—	—	744	2.7	3.6	10.6
53-54—Minneapolis	69	—	2472	254	654	.388	—	—	—	176	243	.724	—	—	166	253	198	3	—	—	—	684	2.4	3.7	9.9
54-55—Minneapolis	72	—	2784	350	919	.381	—	—	—	276	359	.769	—	—	260	427	221	7	—	—	—	976	3.6	5.9	13.6
55-56—Minneapolis	72	—	2838	309	863	.358	—	—	—	329	395	.833	—	—	260	445	202	2	—	—	—	947	3.6	6.2	13.2
56-57—N.Y.-St. L.	66	—	2401	244	736	.332	—	—	—	230	291	.790	—	—	288	269	193	1	—	—	—	718	4.4	4.1	10.9
57-58—St. Louis	60	—	2098	258	768	.336	—	—	—	206	276	.746	—	—	228	218	187	0	—	—	—	722	3.8	3.6	12.0
58-59—St. Louis	71	—	2504	245	706	.347	—	—	—	197	254	.776	—	—	253	336	230	8	—	—	—	687	3.6	4.7	9.7
59-60—St. Louis	64	—	1756	142	383	.371	—	—	—	113	155	.729	—	—	187	330	174	2	—	—	—	397	2.9	5.2	6.2
REG. SEASON TOTALS	745	—	21889	2632	7224	.364	—	—	—	2073	2720	.762	—	—	2302	3160	2238	39	—	—	—	7337	3.4	4.2	9.8
PLAYOFF TOTALS	92	—	2876	304	867	.351	—	—	—	316	442	.715	—	—	270	354	342	10	—	—	—	924	3.4	3.8	10.0
ALL-STAR TOTALS	7	—	180	16	53	.302	—	—	—	8	12	.667	—	—	15	28	19	0	—	—	—	40	2.1	4.0	5.7

MARTIN, WILLIAM (**Bill**) b. August 16, 1962 Ht. 6-7 Wt. 205 College—Georgetown

SEASON—TEAM	G	GS	MIN	FGM	FGA	PCT	3FGM	3FGA	PCT	FTM	FTA	PCT	O-RB	D-RB	TOT	AST	PF	DQ	STL	TO	BLK	PTS	RPG	APG	PPG
85-86—Indiana	66	0	691	143	298	.480	0	8	.000	46	54	.852	42	60	102	52	108	1	21	58	7	332	1.5	0.8	5.0
86-87—New York	8	0	68	9	25	.360	0	0	—	7	8	.875	2	5	7	0	5	0	4	7	2	25	0.9	0.0	3.1
87-88—Phoenix	10	0	101	16	51	.314	0	1	.000	8	13	.615	9	18	27	6	16	0	5	9	0	40	2.7	0.6	4.0
REG. SEASON TOTALS	84	0	860	168	374	.449	0	9	.000	61	75	.813	53	83	136	58	129	1	30	74	9	397	1.6	0.7	4.7

MASHBURN, JAMAL b. November 29, 1972 Ht. 6-8 Wt. 240 College—Kentucky

SEASON—TEAM	G	GS	MIN	FGM	FGA	PCT	3FGM	3FGA	PCT	FTM	FTA	PCT	O-RB	D-RB	TOT	AST	PF	DQ	STL	TO	BLK	PTS	RPG	APG	PPG
93-94—Dallas	79	73	2896	561	1382	.406	85	299	.284	306	438	.699	107	246	353	266	205	0	89	245	14	1513	4.5	3.4	19.2
REG. SEASON TOTALS	79	73	2896	561	1382	.406	85	299	.284	306	438	.699	107	246	353	266	205	0	89	245	14	1513	4.5	3.4	19.2

MASINO, ALFRED ALBERT (**Al**) b. February 5, 1928 Ht. 5-11 Wt. 175 College—Canisius

SEASON—TEAM	G	GS	MIN	FGM	FGA	PCT	3FGM	3FGA	PCT	FTM	FTA	PCT	O-RB	D-RB	TOT	AST	PF	DQ	STL	TO	BLK	PTS	RPG	APG	PPG
52-53—Milwaukee	72	—	1773	134	400	.335	—	—	—	128	204	.627	—	—	177	160	252	12	—	—	—	396	2.5	2.2	5.5
53-54—Roch.-Syr.	27	—	181	26	62	.419	—	—	—	30	49	.612	—	—	28	22	44	0	—	—	—	82	1.0	0.8	3.0
REG. SEASON TOTALS	99	—	1954	160	462	.346	—	—	—	158	253	.625	—	—	205	182	296	12	—	—	—	478	2.1	1.8	4.8
PLAYOFF TOTALS	13	—	96	7	20	.350	—	—	—	7	15	.467	—	—	6	7	23	0	—	—	—	21	0.5	0.5	1.6

MASON, ANTHONY GEORGE DOUGLAS b. December 14, 1966 Ht. 6-7 Wt. 250 College—Tennessee State

SEASON—TEAM	G	GS	MIN	FGM	FGA	PCT	3FGM	3FGA	PCT	FTM	FTA	PCT	O-RB	D-RB	TOT	AST	PF	DQ	STL	TO	BLK	PTS	RPG	APG	PPG
89-90—New Jersey	21	0	108	14	40	.350	0	0	—	9	15	.600	11	23	34	7	20	0	2	11	2	37	1.6	0.3	1.8
90-91—Denver	3	0	21	2	4	.500	0	0	—	6	8	.750	3	2	5	0	6	0	1	0	0	10	1.7	0.0	3.3
91-92—New York	82	0	2198	203	399	.509	0	0	—	167	260	.642	216	357	573	106	229	0	46	101	20	573	7.0	1.3	7.0
92-93—New York	81	0	2482	316	629	.502	0	0	—	199	292	.682	231	409	640	170	240	2	43	137	19	831	7.9	2.1	10.3
93-94—New York	73	12	1903	206	433	.476	0	1	.000	116	161	.720	158	269	427	151	190	2	31	107	9	528	5.8	2.1	7.2
REG. SEASON TOTALS	260	12	6712	741	1505	.492	0	1	.000	497	736	.675	619	1060	1679	434	685	4	123	356	50	1979	6.5	1.7	7.6
PLAYOFF TOTALS	52	0	1458	158	302	.523	0	0	—	120	173	.694	136	195	331	97	150	2	27	70	19	436	6.4	1.9	8.4

MASSENBURG, TONY ARNEL b. July 31, 1967 Ht. 6-9 Wt. 220 College—Maryland

SEASON—TEAM	G	GS	MIN	FGM	FGA	PCT	3FGM	3FGA	PCT	FTM	FTA	PCT	O-RB	D-RB	TOT	AST	PF	DQ	STL	TO	BLK	PTS	RPG	APG	PPG
90-91—San Antonio	35	0	161	27	60	.450	0	0	—	28	45	.622	23	35	58	4	26	0	4	13	9	82	1.7	0.1	2.3
91-92—S.A.-Cha.-Boston-G.S.	18	0	90	10	25	.400	0	0	—	9	15	.600	7	18	25	0	21	0	1	9	1	29	1.4	0.0	1.6
REG. SEASON TOTALS	53	0	251	37	85	.435	0	0	—	37	60	.617	30	53	83	4	47	0	5	22	10	111	1.6	0.1	2.1
PLAYOFF TOTALS	1	0	1	0	0	—	0	0	—	0	0	—	0	0	0	—	0	0	0	0	0	0	0.0	0.0	0.0

MAST, EDWARD (Eddie) b. October 3, 1948 Ht. 6-9 Wt. 220 College—Temple

SEASON—TEAM	G	GS	MIN	FGM	FGA	PCT	3FGM	3FGA	PCT	FTM	FTA	PCT	O-RB	D-RB	TOT	AST	PF	DQ	STL	TO	BLK	PTS	RPG	APG	PPG
70-71—New York	30	—	164	25	66	.379	—	—	—	11	20	.550	—	—	56	4	25	0	—	—	—	61	1.9	0.1	2.0
71-72—New York	40	—	270	39	112	.348	—	—	—	25	41	.610	—	—	73	10	39	0	—	—	—	103	1.8	0.3	2.6
72-73—Atlanta	42	—	447	50	118	.424	—	—	—	19	30	.633	—	—	136	37	50	0	—	—	—	119	3.2	0.9	2.8
REG. SEASON TOTALS	112	—	881	114	296	.385	—	—	—	55	91	.604	—	—	265	51	114	0	—	—	—	283	2.4	0.5	2.5
PLAYOFF TOTALS	16	—	49	11	17	.647	—	—	—	1	5	.200	—	—	15	2	7	0	—	—	—	23	0.9	0.1	1.4

MATHIS, JOHNNY C. b. July 14, 1943 Ht. 6-6½ Wt. 220 College—Savannah State

SEASON—TEAM	G	GS	MIN	FGM	FGA	PCT	3FGM	3FGA	PCT	FTM	FTA	PCT	O-RB	D-RB	TOT	AST	PF	DQ	STL	TO	BLK	PTS	RPG	APG	PPG
67-68—New Jersey (A)	51	—	656	69	186	.371	0	2	.000	35	55	.636	—	—	194	28	102	3	—	42	—	173	3.8	0.5	3.4
REG. ABA TOTALS	51	—	656	69	186	.371	0	2	.000	35	55	.636	—	—	194	28	102	3	—	42	—	173	3.8	0.5	3.4

MATTHEWS, WESLEY JOEL (Wes) b. August 24, 1959 Ht. 6-1 Wt. 170 College—Wisconsin

SEASON—TEAM	G	GS	MIN	FGM	FGA	PCT	3FGM	3FGA	PCT	FTM	FTA	PCT	O-RB	D-RB	TOT	AST	PF	DQ	STL	TO	BLK	PTS	RPG	APG	PPG
80-81—Wash.-Atlanta	79	—	2266	385	779	.494	5	21	.238	202	252	.802	46	93	139	411	242	2	107	261	17	977	1.8	5.2	12.4
81-82—Atlanta	47	5	837	131	298	.440	2	8	.250	60	79	.759	19	39	58	139	129	3	53	63	2	324	1.2	3.0	6.9
82-83—Atlanta	64	0	1187	171	424	.403	14	48	.292	86	112	.768	25	66	91	249	129	0	60	123	8	442	1.4	3.9	6.9
83-84—Atlanta-Phil.	20	5	388	61	131	.466	1	8	.125	27	36	.750	7	20	27	83	45	0	16	40	3	150	1.4	4.2	7.5
84-85—Chicago	78	38	1523	191	386	.495	2	16	.125	59	85	.694	16	51	67	354	133	0	73	124	12	443	0.9	4.5	5.7
85-86—San Antonio	75	46	1853	320	603	.531	4	25	.160	173	211	.820	30	101	131	476	168	1	87	232	32	817	1.7	6.3	10.9
86-87—L.A. Lakers	50	0	532	89	187	.476	1	3	.333	29	36	.806	13	34	47	100	53	0	23	51	4	208	0.9	2.0	4.2
87-88—L.A. Lakers	51	8	706	114	248	.460	7	30	.233	54	65	.831	16	50	66	138	65	0	25	69	3	289	1.3	2.7	5.7
89-90—Atlanta	1	0	13	1	3	.333	0	1	.000	2	2	1.000	0	0	0	5	0	0	0	0	0	4	0.0	5.0	4.0
REG. SEASON TOTALS	465	102	9305	1463	3059	.478	36	160	.225	692	878	.788	172	454	626	1955	964	6	444	963	81	3654	1.3	4.2	7.9
PLAYOFF TOTALS	38	7	384	68	141	.482	1	9	.111	36	45	.800	3	15	18	66	43	0	14	43	2	173	0.5	1.7	4.6

MAUGHAN, ARIEL LEISHMAN (Ace) b. February 23, 1923 Ht. 6-4 Wt. 190 College—Utah State

SEASON—TEAM	G	GS	MIN	FGM	FGA	PCT	3FGM	3FGA	PCT	FTM	FTA	PCT	O-RB	D-RB	TOT	AST	PF	DQ	STL	TO	BLK	PTS	RPG	APG	PPG
46-47—Detroit	59	—	—	224	929	.241	—	—	—	84	114	.737	—	—	—	57	180	—	—	—	—	532	—	1.0	9.0
47-48—Prov.-St. L.	42	—	—	76	256	.297	—	—	—	32	53	.604	—	—	—	6	89	—	—	—	—	184	—	0.1	4.4
48-49—St. Louis	55	—	—	206	650	.317	—	—	—	184	285	.646	—	—	—	99	134	—	—	—	—	596	—	1.8	10.8
49-50—St. Louis	68	—	—	160	574	.279	—	—	—	157	205	.766	—	—	—	101	174	—	—	—	—	477	—	1.5	7.0
50-51—Washington	35	—	—	78	250	.312	—	—	—	101	120	.842	—	—	141	48	91	2	—	—	—	257	4.0	1.4	7.3
REG. SEASON TOTALS	259	—	—	744	2659	.280	—	—	—	558	777	.718	—	—	141	311	668	2	—	—	—	2046	4.0	1.2	7.9
PLAYOFF TOTALS	9	—	—	32	128	.250	—	—	—	18	26	.692	—	—	—	4	25	1	—	—	—	82	—	0.4	9.1

MAXEY, MARLON LEE b. February 19, 1969 Ht. 6-8 Wt. 250 College—Minnesota/Texas-El Paso

SEASON—TEAM	G	GS	MIN	FGM	FGA	PCT	3FGM	3FGA	PCT	FTM	FTA	PCT	O-RB	D-RB	TOT	AST	PF	DQ	STL	TO	BLK	PTS	RPG	APG	PPG
92-93—Minnesota	43	3	520	93	169	.550	0	1	.000	45	70	.643	66	98	164	12	75	0	11	38	18	231	3.8	0.3	5.4
93-94—Minnesota	55	2	626	89	167	.533	0	2	.000	70	98	.714	75	124	199	10	113	1	16	40	33	248	3.6	0.2	4.5
REG. SEASON TOTALS	98	5	1146	182	336	.542	0	3	.000	115	168	.685	141	222	363	22	188	1	27	78	51	479	3.7	0.2	4.9

MAXWELL, CEDRIC BRYAN (Cornbread) b. November 21, 1955 Ht. 6-8 Wt. 205 College—UNC-Charlotte

SEASON—TEAM	G	GS	MIN	FGM	FGA	PCT	3FGM	3FGA	PCT	FTM	FTA	PCT	O-RB	D-RB	TOT	AST	PF	DQ	STL	TO	BLK	PTS	RPG	APG	PPG
77-78—Boston	72	—	1213	170	316	.538	—	—	—	188	250	.752	138	241	379	68	151	2	53	122	48	528	5.3	0.9	7.3
78-79—Boston	80	—	2969	472	808	.584	—	—	—	574	716	.802	272	519	791	228	266	4	98	273	74	1518	9.9	2.9	19.0
79-80—Boston	80	—	2744	457	750	.609	0	0	—	436	554	.787	284	420	704	199	266	6	76	230	61	1350	8.8	2.5	16.9
80-81—Boston	81	—	2730	441	750	.588	0	1	.000	352	450	.782	222	303	525	219	256	5	79	180	68	1234	6.5	2.7	15.2
81-82—Boston	78	73	2590	397	724	.548	0	3	.000	357	478	.747	218	281	499	183	263	6	79	174	49	1151	6.4	2.3	14.8
82-83—Boston	79	72	2252	331	663	.499	0	1	.000	280	345	.812	185	237	422	186	202	3	65	165	39	942	5.3	2.4	11.9
83-84—Boston	80	78	2502	317	596	.532	1	6	.167	320	425	.753	201	260	461	205	224	4	63	203	24	955	5.8	2.6	11.9
84-85—Boston	57	51	1495	201	377	.533	0	2	.000	231	278	.831	98	144	242	102	140	2	36	98	15	633	4.2	1.8	11.1
85-86—L.A. Clippers	76	72	2458	314	661	.475	0	3	.000	447	562	.795	241	383	624	215	252	2	61	206	29	1075	8.2	2.8	14.1
86-87—L.A. Clips-Houston	81	31	1968	253	477	.530	0	1	.000	303	391	.775	175	260	435	197	178	1	39	136	14	809	5.4	2.4	10.0
87-88—Houston	71	0	848	80	171	.468	0	2	.000	110	143	.769	74	105	179	60	75	0	22	54	12	270	2.5	0.8	3.8
REG. SEASON TOTALS	835	377	23769	3433	6293	.546	1	19	.053	3598	4592	.784	2108	3153	5261	1862	2273	35	671	1841	433	10465	6.3	2.2	12.5
PLAYOFF TOTALS	102	42	2731	375	688	.545	0	2	.000	366	471	.777	233	320	553	194	260	2	74	172	50	1116	5.4	1.9	10.9

MAXWELL, VERNON **(Hawk)** b. September 12, 1965 Ht. 6-4 Wt. 185 College—Florida

SEASON—TEAM	G	GS	MIN	FGM	FGA	PCT	3FGM	3FGA	PCT	FTM	FTA	PCT	O-RB	D-RB	TOT	AST	PF	DQ	STL	TO	BLK	PTS	RPG	APG	PPG
88-89—San Antonio	79	36	2065	357	827	.432	32	129	.248	181	243	.745	49	153	202	301	136	0	86	178	8	927	2.6	3.8	11.7
89-90—S.A.-Houston	79	12	1987	275	627	.439	28	105	.267	136	211	.645	50	178	228	296	148	0	84	143	10	714	2.9	3.7	9.0
90-91—Houston	82	79	2870	504	1247	.404	172	510	.337	217	296	.733	41	197	238	303	179	2	127	171	15	1397	2.9	3.7	17.0
91-92—Houston	80	80	2700	502	1216	.413	162	473	.342	206	267	.772	37	206	243	326	200	3	104	178	28	1372	3.0	4.1	17.2
92-93—Houston	71	68	2251	349	858	.407	120	361	.332	164	228	.719	29	192	221	297	124	1	86	140	8	982	3.1	4.2	13.8
93-94—Houston	75	73	2571	380	976	.389	120	403	.298	143	191	.749	42	187	229	380	143	0	125	185	20	1023	3.1	5.1	13.6
REG. SEASON TOTALS	466	348	14444	2367	5751	.412	634	1981	.320	1047	1436	.729	248	1113	1361	1903	930	6	612	995	89	6415	2.9	4.1	13.8
PLAYOFF TOTALS	39	37	1460	218	568	.384	73	237	.308	70	101	.693	21	102	123	154	92	1	38	79	5	579	3.2	3.9	14.8

MAY, DONALD JOHN **(Don)** b. January 3, 1946 Ht. 6-4 Wt. 220 College—Dayton

SEASON—TEAM	G	GS	MIN	FGM	FGA	PCT	3FGM	3FGA	PCT	FTM	FTA	PCT	O-RB	D-RB	TOT	AST	PF	DQ	STL	TO	BLK	PTS	RPG	APG	PPG
68-69—New York	48	—	560	81	223	.363	—	—	—	42	58	.724	—	—	114	35	64	0	—	—	—	204	2.4	0.7	4.3
69-70—New York	37	—	238	39	101	.386	—	—	—	18	19	.947	—	—	52	17	42	0	—	—	—	96	1.4	0.5	2.6
70-71—Buffalo	76	—	2666	629	1336	.471	—	—	—	277	350	.791	—	—	567	150	219	4	—	—	—	1535	7.5	2.0	20.2
71-72—Atlanta	75	—	1285	234	476	.492	—	—	—	126	164	.768	—	—	217	55	133	0	—	—	—	594	2.9	0.7	7.9
72-73—Atlanta-Phil.	58	—	919	189	424	.446	—	—	—	75	93	.806	—	—	210	64	135	1	—	—	—	453	3.6	1.1	7.8
73-74—Philadelphia	56	—	812	152	367	.414	—	—	—	89	102	.873	25	111	136	63	137	0	25	—	8	393	2.4	1.1	7.0
74-75—Kansas City-Omaha	29	—	139	27	54	.500	—	—	—	10	12	.833	4	9	13	5	21	0	4	—	2	64	0.4	0.2	2.2
REG. SEASON TOTALS	379	—	6619	1351	2981	.453	—	—	—	637	798	.798	29	120	1309	389	751	5	29	—	10	3339	3.5	1.0	8.8
PLAYOFF TOTALS	14	—	126	14	42	.333	—	—	—	13	17	.765	0	0	31	9	12	0	0	—	0	41	2.2	0.6	2.9

MAY, SCOTT GLENN b. March 19, 1954 Ht. 6-6½ Wt. 215 College—Indiana

SEASON—TEAM	G	GS	MIN	FGM	FGA	PCT	3FGM	3FGA	PCT	FTM	FTA	PCT	O-RB	D-RB	TOT	AST	PF	DQ	STL	TO	BLK	PTS	RPG	APG	PPG
76-77—Chicago	72	—	2369	431	955	.451	—	—	—	188	227	.828	141	296	437	145	185	2	78	—	17	1050	6.1	2.0	14.6
77-78—Chicago	55	—	1802	280	617	.454	—	—	—	175	216	.810	118	214	332	114	170	4	50	125	6	735	6.0	2.1	13.4
78-79—Chicago	37	—	403	59	136	.434	—	—	—	30	40	.750	14	50	64	39	51	0	22	51	1	148	1.7	1.1	4.0
79-80—Chicago	54	—	1298	264	587	.450	0	4	.000	144	172	.837	78	140	218	104	126	2	45	77	5	672	4.0	1.9	12.4
80-81—Chicago	63	—	815	165	338	.488	0	0	—	113	149	.758	62	93	155	63	83	0	35	71	7	443	2.5	1.0	7.0
81-82—Milwaukee	65	7	1187	212	417	.508	0	4	.000	159	193	.824	85	133	218	133	151	2	50	92	6	583	3.4	2.0	9.0
82-83—Detroit	9	1	155	21	50	.420	—	—	—	17	21	.810	10	16	26	12	24	1	5	13	2	59	2.9	1.3	6.6
REG. SEASON TOTALS	355	8	8029	1432	3100	.462	0	8	.000	826	1018	.811	508	942	1450	610	790	11	285	429	44	3690	4.1	1.7	10.4
PLAYOFF TOTALS	7	0	147	14	46	.304	0	0	—	21	29	.724	13	12	25	13	16	0	6	2	49	3.6	1.9	7.0	

MAYBERRY, ORVA LEE JR. **(Lee)** b. June 12, 1970 Ht. 6-1 Wt. 175 College—Arkansas

SEASON—TEAM	G	GS	MIN	FGM	FGA	PCT	3FGM	3FGA	PCT	FTM	FTA	PCT	O-RB	D-RB	TOT	AST	PF	DQ	STL	TO	BLK	PTS	RPG	APG	PPG
92-93—Milwaukee	82	4	1503	171	375	.456	43	110	.391	39	68	.574	26	92	118	273	148	1	59	85	7	424	1.4	3.3	5.2
93-94—Milwaukee	82	6	1472	167	402	.415	41	119	.345	58	84	.690	26	75	101	215	114	0	46	97	4	433	1.2	2.6	5.3
REG. SEASON TOTALS	164	10	2975	338	777	.435	84	229	.367	97	152	.638	52	167	219	488	262	1	105	182	11	857	1.3	3.0	5.2

MAYES, CLYDE C. JR. b. March 17, 1953 Ht. 6-8 Wt. 230 College—Furman

SEASON—TEAM	G	GS	MIN	FGM	FGA	PCT	3FGM	3FGA	PCT	FTM	FTA	PCT	O-RB	D-RB	TOT	AST	PF	DQ	STL	TO	BLK	PTS	RPG	APG	PPG
75-76—Milwaukee	65	—	948	114	248	.460	—	—	—	56	97	.577	97	166	263	37	154	7	9	—	42	284	4.0	0.6	4.4
76-77—Indiana-Buffalo-Port.	9	—	52	5	19	.263	—	—	—	3	7	.429	10	6	16	3	12	0	0	—	4	13	1.8	0.3	1.4
REG. SEASON TOTALS	74	—	1000	119	267	.446	—	—	—	59	104	.567	107	172	279	40	166	7	9	—	46	297	3.8	0.5	4.0
PLAYOFF TOTALS	3	—	41	1	5	.200	—	—	—	3	4	.750	0	6	6	1	6	1	1	—	1	5	2.0	0.3	1.7

MAYES, THARON R. b. September 9, 1968 Ht. 6-3 Wt. 175 College—Florida State

SEASON—TEAM	G	GS	MIN	FGM	FGA	PCT	3FGM	3FGA	PCT	FTM	FTA	PCT	O-RB	D-RB	TOT	AST	PF	DQ	STL	TO	BLK	PTS	RPG	APG	PPG
91-92—Phil.-L.A. Clips	24	0	255	30	99	.303	15	41	.366	24	36	.667	3	13	16	35	41	0	16	31	2	99	0.7	1.5	4.1
REG. SEASON TOTALS	24	0	255	30	99	.303	15	41	.366	24	36	.667	3	13	16	35	41	0	16	31	2	99	0.7	1.5	4.1

MAYFIELD, KENDALL **(Ken)** b. May 11, 1948 Ht. 6-2 Wt. 185 College—Coffeyville CC/Tuskegee

SEASON—TEAM	G	GS	MIN	FGM	FGA	PCT	3FGM	3FGA	PCT	FTM	FTA	PCT	O-RB	D-RB	TOT	AST	PF	DQ	STL	TO	BLK	PTS	RPG	APG	PPG
75-76—New York	13	—	64	17	46	.370	—	—	—	3	3	1.000	1	7	8	4	18	0	0	—	0	37	0.6	0.3	2.8
REG. SEASON TOTALS	13	—	64	17	46	.370	—	—	—	3	3	1.000	1	7	8	4	18	0	0	—	0	37	0.6	0.3	2.8

MAYFIELD, WILLIAM HENRY **(Bill)** b. October 17, 1957 Ht. 6-7 Wt. 210 College—Iowa

SEASON—TEAM	G	GS	MIN	FGM	FGA	PCT	3FGM	3FGA	PCT	FTM	FTA	PCT	O-RB	D-RB	TOT	AST	PF	DQ	STL	TO	BLK	PTS	RPG	APG	PPG
80-81—Golden State	7	—	54	8	18	.444	0	0	—	1	2	.500	7	2	9	1	8	0	0	3	1	17	1.3	0.1	2.4
REG. SEASON TOTALS	7	—	54	8	18	.444	0	0	—	1	2	.500	7	2	9	1	8	0	0	3	1	17	1.3	0.1	2.4

MAYS, TRAVIS CORTEZ b. June 19, 1968 Ht. 6-2 Wt. 190 College—Texas

SEASON—TEAM	G	GS	MIN	FGM	FGA	PCT	3FGM	3FGA	PCT	FTM	FTA	PCT	O-RB	D-RB	TOT	AST	PF	DQ	STL	TO	BLK	PTS	RPG	APG	PPG
90-91—Sacramento	64	55	2145	294	724	.406	72	197	.365	255	331	.770	54	124	178	253	169	1	81	159	11	915	2.8	4.0	14.3
91-92—Atlanta	2	0	32	6	14	.429	3	6	.500	2	2	1.000	1	1	2	1	4	0	0	3	0	17	1.0	0.5	8.5
92-93—Atlanta	49	9	787	129	309	.417	29	84	.345	54	82	.659	20	33	53	72	59	0	21	51	3	341	1.1	1.5	7.0
REG. SEASON TOTALS	115	64	2964	429	1047	.410	104	287	.362	311	415	.749	75	158	233	326	232	1	102	213	14	1273	2.0	2.8	11.1
PLAYOFF TOTALS	1	0	20	2	4	.500	0	1	.000	0	0	—	0	1	1	—	3	0	0	1	0	4	1.0	0.0	4.0

MAZZA, MATTHEW ANTHONY (**Matt**) b. September 23, 1923 Ht. 6-3 Wt. 210 College—Canisius/Michigan State

SEASON—TEAM	G	GS	MIN	FGM	FGA	PCT	3FGM	3FGA	PCT	FTM	FTA	PCT	O-RB	D-RB	TOT	AST	PF	DQ	STL	TO	BLK	PTS	RPG	APG	PPG
49-50—Sheboygan	26	—	—	33	110	.300	—	—	—	32	45	.711	—	—	—	29	34	—	—	—	—	98	—	1.1	3.8
REG. SEASON TOTALS	26	—	—	33	110	.300	—	—	—	32	45	.711	—	—	—	29	34	—	—	—	—	98	—	1.1	3.8

McADOO, ROBERT ALLEN JR. (**Bob**) b. September 15, 1951 Ht. 6-9 Wt. 210 College—Vincennes/North Carolina

SEASON—TEAM	G	GS	MIN	FGM	FGA	PCT	3FGM	3FGA	PCT	FTM	FTA	PCT	O-RB	D-RB	TOT	AST	PF	DQ	STL	TO	BLK	PTS	RPG	APG	PPG
72-73—Buffalo	80	—	2562	585	1293	.452	—	—	—	271	350	.774	—	—	728	139	256	6	—	—	—	1441	9.1	1.7	18.0
73-74—Buffalo	74	—	3185	901	1647	.547	—	—	—	459	579	.793	281	836	1117	170	252	3	88	—	246	2261	15.1	2.3	30.6
74-75—Buffalo	82	—	3539	1095	2138	.512	—	—	—	641	796	.805	307	848	1155	179	278	3	92	—	174	2831	14.1	2.2	34.5
75-76—Buffalo	78	—	3328	934	1918	.487	—	—	—	559	734	.762	241	724	965	315	298	5	93	—	160	2427	12.4	4.0	31.1
76-77—Buffalo-N.Y.-K	72	—	2798	740	1445	.512	—	—	—	381	516	.738	199	727	926	205	262	3	77	—	99	1861	12.9	2.8	25.8
77-78—New York	79	—	3182	814	1564	.520	—	—	—	469	645	.727	236	774	1010	298	297	6	105	346	126	2097	12.8	3.8	26.5
78-79—N.Y.-Boston	60	—	2231	596	1127	.529	—	—	—	295	450	.656	130	390	520	168	189	3	74	217	67	1487	8.7	2.8	24.8
79-80—Detroit	58	—	2097	492	1025	.480	3	24	.125	235	322	.730	100	367	467	200	178	3	73	238	65	1222	8.1	3.4	21.1
80-81—Detroit-N.J.	16	—	321	68	157	.433	0	1	.000	29	41	.707	17	50	67	30	38	0	17	32	13	165	4.2	1.9	10.3
81-82—Los Angeles	41	0	746	151	330	.458	0	5	.000	90	126	.714	45	114	159	32	109	1	22	51	36	392	3.9	0.8	9.6
82-83—Los Angeles	47	1	1019	292	562	.520	0	1	.000	119	163	.730	76	171	247	39	153	2	40	68	40	703	5.3	0.8	15.0
83-84—Los Angeles	70	0	1456	352	748	.471	0	5	.000	212	264	.803	82	207	289	74	182	0	42	127	50	916	4.1	1.1	13.1
84-85—L.A. Lakers	66	0	1254	284	546	.520	0	1	.000	122	162	.753	79	216	295	67	170	0	18	95	53	690	4.5	1.0	10.5
85-86—Philadelphia	29	0	609	116	251	.462	0	0	—	62	81	.765	25	78	103	35	64	0	10	49	18	294	3.6	1.2	10.1
REG. SEASON TOTALS	852	1	28327	7420	14751	.503	3	37	.081	3944	5229	.754	1818	5502	8048	1951	2726	35	751	1223	1147	18787	9.4	2.3	22.1
PLAYOFF TOTALS	94	0	2714	698	1423	.491	2	8	.250	320	442	.724	180	531	711	127	318	9	72	145	151	1718	7.6	1.4	18.3
ALL-STAR TOTALS	4	2	88	24	41	.585	0	0	—	10	15	.667	10	10	20	4	15	0	1	3	1	58	5.0	1.0	14.5

McBRIDE, KENNETH S. (**Ken**) b. 1931 Ht. 6-3½ Wt. 195 College—Maryland State

SEASON—TEAM	G	GS	MIN	FGM	FGA	PCT	3FGM	3FGA	PCT	FTM	FTA	PCT	O-RB	D-RB	TOT	AST	PF	DQ	STL	TO	BLK	PTS	RPG	APG	PPG
54-55—Milwaukee	12	—	249	48	147	.327	—	—	—	21	29	.724	—	—	31	14	31	0	—	—	—	117	2.6	1.2	9.8
REG. SEASON TOTALS	12	—	249	48	147	.327	—	—	—	21	29	.724	—	—	31	14	31	0	—	—	—	117	2.6	1.2	9.8

McCANN, BRENDAN MICHAEL b. July 5, 1935 Ht. 6-2 Wt. 180 College—St. Bonaventure

SEASON—TEAM	G	GS	MIN	FGM	FGA	PCT	3FGM	3FGA	PCT	FTM	FTA	PCT	O-RB	D-RB	TOT	AST	PF	DQ	STL	TO	BLK	PTS	RPG	APG	PPG
57-58—New York	36	—	295	22	100	.220	—	—	—	25	37	.676	—	—	45	54	34	0	—	—	—	69	1.3	1.5	1.9
58-59—New York	1	—	7	0	3	.000	—	—	—	0	0	—	—	—	1	1	1	0	—	—	—	0	1.0	1.0	0.0
59-60—New York	4	—	29	1	10	.100	—	—	—	3	3	1.000	—	—	4	10	2	0	—	—	—	5	1.0	2.5	1.3
REG. SEASON TOTALS	41	—	331	23	113	.204	—	—	—	28	40	.700	—	—	50	65	37	0	—	—	—	74	1.2	1.6	1.8

McCANN, ROBERT GLEN (**Bob**) b. April 22, 1964 Ht. 6-7 Wt. 245 College—Upsala/Morehead State

SEASON—TEAM	G	GS	MIN	FGM	FGA	PCT	3FGM	3FGA	PCT	FTM	FTA	PCT	O-RB	D-RB	TOT	AST	PF	DQ	STL	TO	BLK	PTS	RPG	APG	PPG
89-90—Dallas	10	0	62	7	21	.333	0	0	—	12	14	.857	4	8	12	6	7	0	2	6	2	26	1.2	0.6	2.6
91-92—Detroit	26	0	129	13	33	.394	0	1	.000	4	13	.308	12	18	30	6	23	0	6	7	4	30	1.2	0.2	1.2
92-93—Minnesota	79	7	1536	200	410	.488	0	2	.000	95	152	.625	92	190	282	68	202	2	51	79	58	495	3.6	0.9	6.3
REG. SEASON TOTALS	115	7	1727	220	464	.474	0	3	.000	111	179	.620	108	216	324	80	232	2	59	92	64	551	2.8	0.7	4.8
PLAYOFF TOTALS	1	0	13	3	6	.500	0	0	—	0	0	—	1	1	2	—	2	0	0	2	1	6	2.0	0.0	6.0

McCANTS, MELVIN LAMONT (**Mel**) b. August 19, 1967 Ht. 6-8 Wt. 240 College—Purdue

SEASON—TEAM	G	GS	MIN	FGM	FGA	PCT	3FGM	3FGA	PCT	FTM	FTA	PCT	O-RB	D-RB	TOT	AST	PF	DQ	STL	TO	BLK	PTS	RPG	APG	PPG
89-90—L.A. Lakers	13	0	65	8	26	.308	0	0	—	6	8	.750	1	5	6	2	11	0	3	1	1	22	0.5	0.2	1.7
REG. SEASON TOTALS	13	0	65	8	26	.308	0	0	—	6	8	.750	1	5	6	2	11	0	3	1	1	22	0.5	0.2	1.7
PLAYOFF TOTALS	2	0	5	0	0	—	0	0	—	0	0	—	0	0	0	—	1	0	0	0	0	0	0.0	0.0	0.0

McCARRON, MICHAEL (**Mike**) b. March 2, 1922 d. October 2, 1991 Ht. 5-11 Wt. 180 College—Seton Hall

SEASON—TEAM	G	GS	MIN	FGM	FGA	PCT	3FGM	3FGA	PCT	FTM	FTA	PCT	O-RB	D-RB	TOT	AST	PF	DQ	STL	TO	BLK	PTS	RPG	APG	PPG
46-47—Toronto	60	—	—	236	838	.282	—	—	—	177	288	.615	—	—	—	59	184	—	—	—	—	649	—	1.0	10.8
49-50—Balt.-St. L.	8	—	—	3	15	.200	—	—	—	3	5	.600	—	—	—	3	5	—	—	—	—	9	—	0.4	1.1
REG. SEASON TOTALS	68	—	—	239	853	.280	—	—	—	180	293	.614	—	—	—	62	189	—	—	—	—	658	—	0.9	9.7

McCARTER, ANDRE EUGENE b. August 25, 1953　Ht. 6-3½　Wt. 190　College—UCLA

SEASON—TEAM	G	GS	MIN	FGM	FGA	PCT	3FGM	3FGA	PCT	FTM	FTA	PCT	O-RB	D-RB	TOT	AST	PF	DQ	STL	TO	BLK	PTS	RPG	APG	PPG
76-77—Kansas City	59	—	725	119	257	.463	—	—	—	32	45	.711	16	39	55	99	63	0	23	—	0	270	0.9	1.7	4.6
77-78—Kansas City	1	—	9	0	2	.000	—	—	—	0	0	—	0	1	1	0	1	0	0	0	0	0	1.0	0.0	0.0
80-81—Washington	43	—	448	51	135	.378	2	8	.250	18	24	.750	16	23	39	73	36	0	14	24	0	122	0.9	1.7	2.8
REG. SEASON TOTALS	103	—	1182	170	394	.431	2	8	.250	50	69	.725	32	63	95	172	100	0	37	24	0	392	0.9	1.7	3.8

McCARTER, WILLIE J. b. July 26, 1946　Ht. 6-3　Wt. 175　College—Drake

SEASON—TEAM	G	GS	MIN	FGM	FGA	PCT	3FGM	3FGA	PCT	FTM	FTA	PCT	O-RB	D-RB	TOT	AST	PF	DQ	STL	TO	BLK	PTS	RPG	APG	PPG
69-70—Los Angeles	40	—	861	132	349	.378	—	—	—	43	60	.717	—	—	83	93	71	0	—	—	—	307	2.1	2.3	7.7
70-71—Los Angeles	76	—	1369	247	592	.417	—	—	—	46	77	.597	—	—	122	126	152	0	—	—	—	540	1.6	1.7	7.1
71-72—Portland	39	—	612	103	257	.401	—	—	—	37	55	.673	—	—	43	85	58	0	—	—	—	243	1.1	2.2	6.2
REG. SEASON TOTALS	155	—	2842	482	1198	.402	—	—	—	126	192	.656	—	—	248	304	281	0	—	—	—	1090	1.6	2.0	7.0
PLAYOFF TOTALS	17	—	246	30	83	.361	—	—	—	2	7	.286	—	—	29	20	32	0	—	—	—	62	1.7	1.2	3.6

McCARTHY, JOHN JOSEPH (Johnny) b. April 25, 1934　Ht. 6-1　Wt. 185　College—Canisius

SEASON—TEAM	G	GS	MIN	FGM	FGA	PCT	3FGM	3FGA	PCT	FTM	FTA	PCT	O-RB	D-RB	TOT	AST	PF	DQ	STL	TO	BLK	PTS	RPG	APG	PPG
56-57—Rochester	72	—	1560	173	460	.376	—	—	—	130	193	.674	—	—	201	107	130	0	—	—	—	476	2.8	1.5	6.6
58-59—Cincinnati	47	—	1827	245	657	.373	—	—	—	116	174	.667	—	—	227	225	158	4	—	—	—	606	4.8	4.8	12.9
59-60—St. Louis	75	—	2383	240	730	.329	—	—	—	149	226	.659	—	—	301	328	233	3	—	—	—	629	4.0	4.4	8.4
60-61—St. Louis	79	—	2519	266	746	.357	—	—	—	122	226	.540	—	—	325	430	272	8	—	—	—	654	4.1	5.4	8.3
61-62—St. Louis	15	—	333	18	73	.247	—	—	—	12	27	.444	—	—	56	70	50	1	—	—	—	48	3.7	4.7	3.2
63-64—Boston	28	—	206	16	48	.333	—	—	—	5	13	.385	—	—	35	24	42	0	—	—	—	37	1.3	0.9	1.3
REG. SEASON TOTALS	316	—	8828	958	2714	.353	—	—	—	534	859	.622	—	—	1145	1184	885	16	—	—	—	2450	3.6	3.7	7.8
PLAYOFF TOTALS	27	—	808	63	162	.389	—	—	—	33	45	.733	—	—	96	132	78	0	—	—	—	159	3.6	4.9	5.9

McCARTY, HOWARD T. (Howie) b. 1919　d. 1973　Ht. 6-2　Wt. 190　College—Wayne State (Mich.)

SEASON—TEAM	G	GS	MIN	FGM	FGA	PCT	3FGM	3FGA	PCT	FTM	FTA	PCT	O-RB	D-RB	TOT	AST	PF	DQ	STL	TO	BLK	PTS	RPG	APG	PPG
45-46—Cleveland (N)	13	—	—	40	—	—	—	—	—	13	—	—	—	—	—	—	—	—	—	—	—	93	—	—	7.2
46-47—Detroit (N)	16	—	—	46	—	—	—	—	—	29	75	.387	—	—	—	—	—	—	—	—	—	121	—	—	7.6
46-47—Detroit	19	—	10	82	.122	—	—	—	—	1	10	.100	—	—	—	—	2	22	—	—	—	21	—	0.1	1.1
REG. NBA TOTALS	19	—	10	82	.122	—	—	—	—	1	10	.100	—	—	—	—	2	22	—	—	—	21	—	0.1	1.1
REG. NBL TOTALS	29	—	—	86	—	—	—	—	—	42	75	.387	—	—	—	—	—	—	—	—	—	214	—	—	7.4

McCLAIN, DWAYNE EDWARD b. February 7, 1963　Ht. 6-6　Wt. 185　College—Villanova

SEASON—TEAM	G	GS	MIN	FGM	FGA	PCT	3FGM	3FGA	PCT	FTM	FTA	PCT	O-RB	D-RB	TOT	AST	PF	DQ	STL	TO	BLK	PTS	RPG	APG	PPG
85-86—Indiana	45	4	461	69	180	.383	1	9	.111	18	35	.514	14	16	30	67	61	0	38	40	4	157	0.7	1.5	3.5
REG. SEASON TOTALS	45	4	461	69	180	.383	1	9	.111	18	35	.514	14	16	30	67	61	0	38	40	4	157	0.7	1.5	3.5

McCLAIN, THEODORE (Ted, Hound Dog) b. August 30, 1947　Ht. 6-2　Wt. 190　College—Tennessee State

SEASON—TEAM	G	GS	MIN	FGM	FGA	PCT	3FGM	3FGA	PCT	FTM	FTA	PCT	O-RB	D-RB	TOT	AST	PF	DQ	STL	TO	BLK	PTS	RPG	APG	PPG
71-72—Carolina (A)	64	—	900	148	415	.357	13	53	.245	110	142	.775	—	—	120	120	144	—	—	116	—	419	1.9	1.9	6.5
72-73—Carolina (A)	84	—	1816	325	652	.498	8	24	.333	145	204	.711	108	155	263	225	256	1	120	185	—	803	3.1	2.7	9.6
73-74—Carolina (A)	84	—	2582	423	872	.485	2	27	.074	251	325	.772	121	237	358	348	326	—	250	239	25	1099	4.3	4.1	13.1
74-75—Kentucky (A)	72	—	1971	256	582	.440	1	8	.125	104	138	.754	65	203	268	365	231	—	130	167	15	617	3.7	5.1	8.6
75-76—Ken.-N.Y. (A)	73	—	1927	267	631	.423	3	12	.250	136	170	.800	52	156	208	310	277	—	138	194	23	673	2.8	4.2	9.2
76-77—Denver	72	—	2002	245	551	.445	—	—	—	99	133	.744	52	177	229	324	255	9	106	—	13	589	3.2	4.5	8.2
77-78—Buffalo-Phil.	70	—	1020	123	280	.439	—	—	—	57	73	.781	20	92	112	157	124	2	58	90	6	303	1.6	2.2	4.3
78-79—Phoenix	36	—	465	62	132	.470	—	—	—	42	46	.913	25	44	69	60	51	0	19	54	—	166	1.9	1.7	4.6
REG. NBA TOTALS	178	—	3487	430	963	.447	—	—	—	198	252	.786	97	313	410	541	430	11	183	144	19	1058	2.3	3.0	5.9
REG. ABA TOTALS	377	—	9196	1419	3152	.450	27	124	.218	746	979	.762	346	751	1217	1368	1234	1	638	901	63	3611	3.2	3.6	9.6
NBA PLAYOFF TOTALS	25	—	304	37	90	.411	—	—	—	19	24	.792	12	24	36	50	36	0	21	21	2	93	1.4	2.0	3.7
ABA PLAYOFF TOTALS	39	—	1007	128	341	.375	1	13	.077	56	78	.718	29	84	156	127	130	0	41	78	6	313	4.0	3.3	8.0
ABA ALL-STAR TOTALS	1	—	25	6	8	.750	0	0	—	0	0	—	2	1	3	4	3	—	2	1	0	12	3.0	4.0	12.0

McCLOSKEY, JOHN WILLIAM (Jack) b. September 19, 1925　Ht. 6-2　Wt. 190　College—Pennsylvania

SEASON—TEAM	G	GS	MIN	FGM	FGA	PCT	3FGM	3FGA	PCT	FTM	FTA	PCT	O-RB	D-RB	TOT	AST	PF	DQ	STL	TO	BLK	PTS	RPG	APG	PPG
52-53—Philadelphia	1	—	16	3	9	.333	—	—	—	0	0	—	—	—	3	1	2	0	—	—	—	6	3.0	1.0	6.0
REG. SEASON TOTALS	1	—	16	3	9	.333	—	—	—	0	0	—	—	—	3	1	2	0	—	—	—	6	3.0	1.0	6.0

McCLOUD, GEORGE AARON b. May 27, 1967   Ht. 6-8 Wt. 215 College—Florida State

SEASON—TEAM	G	GS	MIN	FGM	FGA	PCT	3FGM	3FGA	PCT	FTM	FTA	PCT	O-RB	D-RB	TOT	AST	PF	DQ	STL	TO	BLK	PTS	RPG	APG	PPG
89-90—Indiana	44	0	413	45	144	.313	13	40	.325	15	19	.789	12	30	42	45	56	0	19	36	3	118	1.0	1.0	2.7
90-91—Indiana	74	0	1070	131	351	.373	43	124	.347	38	49	.776	35	83	118	150	141	1	40	91	11	343	1.6	2.0	4.6
91-92—Indiana	51	5	892	128	313	.409	32	94	.340	50	64	.781	45	87	132	116	95	1	26	62	11	338	2.6	2.3	6.6
92-93—Indiana	78	21	1500	216	525	.411	58	181	.320	75	102	.735	60	145	205	192	165	0	53	107	11	565	2.6	2.5	7.2
REG. SEASON TOTALS	247	26	3875	520	1333	.390	146	439	.333	178	234	.761	152	345	497	503	457	2	138	296	36	1364	2.0	2.0	5.5
PLAYOFF TOTALS	7	2	136	15	37	.405	5	18	.278	9	15	.600	4	10	14	20	21	0	6	9	2	44	2.0	2.9	6.3

McCONATHY, JOHN R. b. April 9, 1930   Ht. 6-5 Wt. 195 College—Northwestern State (La.)

SEASON—TEAM	G	GS	MIN	FGM	FGA	PCT	3FGM	3FGA	PCT	FTM	FTA	PCT	O-RB	D-RB	TOT	AST	PF	DQ	STL	TO	BLK	PTS	RPG	APG	PPG
51-52—Milwaukee	11	—	106	4	29	.138	—	—	—	6	14	.429	—	—	20	8	7	0	—	—	—	14	1.8	0.7	1.3
REG. SEASON TOTALS	11	—	106	4	29	.138	—	—	—	6	14	.429	—	—	20	8	7	0	—	—	—	14	1.8	0.7	1.3

McCONNELL, PAUL JOSEPH (Bucky) b. July 1, 1928   Ht. 5-10 Wt. 170 College—Marshall

SEASON—TEAM	G	GS	MIN	FGM	FGA	PCT	3FGM	3FGA	PCT	FTM	FTA	PCT	O-RB	D-RB	TOT	AST	PF	DQ	STL	TO	BLK	PTS	RPG	APG	PPG
52-53—Milwaukee	14	—	297	27	71	.380	—	—	—	14	29	.483	—	—	34	41	39	0	—	—	—	68	2.4	2.9	4.9
REG. SEASON TOTALS	14	—	297	27	71	.380	—	—	—	14	29	.483	—	—	34	41	39	0	—	—	—	68	2.4	2.9	4.9

McCORD, KEITH RENNAE b. June 22, 1957   Ht. 6-7 Wt. 210 College—Alabama-Birmingham/Alabama

SEASON—TEAM	G	GS	MIN	FGM	FGA	PCT	3FGM	3FGA	PCT	FTM	FTA	PCT	O-RB	D-RB	TOT	AST	PF	DQ	STL	TO	BLK	PTS	RPG	APG	PPG
80-81—Washington	2	—	9	2	4	.500	0	0	—	0	0	—	1	1	2	1	0	0	0	2	0	4	1.0	0.5	2.0
REG. SEASON TOTALS	2	—	9	2	4	.500	0	0	—	0	0	—	1	1	2	1	0	0	0	2	0	4	1.0	0.5	2.0

McCORMICK, TIMOTHY DANIEL (Tim) b. March 10, 1962   Ht. 6-11 Wt. 240 College—Michigan

SEASON—TEAM	G	GS	MIN	FGM	FGA	PCT	3FGM	3FGA	PCT	FTM	FTA	PCT	O-RB	D-RB	TOT	AST	PF	DQ	STL	TO	BLK	PTS	RPG	APG	PPG
84-85—Seattle	78	27	1584	269	483	.557	0	1	.000	188	263	.715	146	252	398	78	207	2	18	114	33	726	5.1	1.0	9.3
85-86—Seattle	77	42	1705	253	444	.570	1	2	.500	174	244	.713	140	263	403	83	219	4	19	110	28	681	5.2	1.1	8.8
86-87—Philadelphia	81	79	2817	391	718	.545	0	4	.000	251	349	.719	180	431	611	114	270	4	36	153	64	1033	7.5	1.4	12.8
87-88—Phil.-N.J.	70	55	2114	348	648	.537	0	2	.000	145	215	.674	146	321	467	118	234	3	32	111	23	841	6.7	1.7	12.0
88-89—Houston	81	0	1257	169	351	.481	0	4	.000	87	129	.674	87	174	261	54	193	0	18	68	24	425	3.2	0.7	5.2
89-90—Houston	18	0	116	10	29	.345	0	0	—	10	19	.526	8	19	27	3	24	0	3	10	1	30	1.5	0.2	1.7
90-91—Atlanta	56	7	689	93	187	.497	0	3	.000	66	90	.733	56	109	165	32	91	1	11	45	14	252	2.9	0.6	4.5
91-92—New York	22	0	108	14	33	.424	0	0	—	14	21	.667	14	20	34	9	18	0	2	8	0	42	1.5	0.4	1.9
REG. SEASON TOTALS	483	210	10390	1547	2893	.535	1	16	.063	935	1330	.703	777	1589	2366	491	1256	14	139	619	187	4030	4.9	1.0	8.3
PLAYOFF TOTALS	15	5	214	22	49	.449	0	1	.000	15	18	.833	11	46	57	6	35	0	4	7	4	59	3.8	0.4	3.9

McCRACKEN, PAUL GEORGE b. September 11, 1950   Ht. 6-4 Wt. 180 College—Cal State-Northridge

SEASON—TEAM	G	GS	MIN	FGM	FGA	PCT	3FGM	3FGA	PCT	FTM	FTA	PCT	O-RB	D-RB	TOT	AST	PF	DQ	STL	TO	BLK	PTS	RPG	APG	PPG
72-73—Houston	24	—	305	44	89	.494	—	—	—	23	39	.590	—	—	51	17	32	0	—	—	—	111	2.1	0.7	4.6
73-74—Houston	4	—	13	1	4	.250	—	—	—	0	0	—	1	5	6	2	3	0	—	0	0	2	1.5	0.5	0.5
76-77—Chicago	9	—	119	18	47	.383	—	—	—	11	18	.611	6	10	16	14	17	0	6	—	0	47	1.8	1.6	5.2
REG. SEASON TOTALS	37	—	437	63	140	.450	—	—	—	34	57	.596	7	15	73	33	52	0	6	—	0	160	2.0	0.9	4.3

McCRAY, CARLTON LAMONT (Scooter) b. February 8, 1960   Ht. 6-9 Wt. 215 College—Louisville

SEASON—TEAM	G	GS	MIN	FGM	FGA	PCT	3FGM	3FGA	PCT	FTM	FTA	PCT	O-RB	D-RB	TOT	AST	PF	DQ	STL	TO	BLK	PTS	RPG	APG	PPG
83-84—Seattle	47	6	520	47	121	.388	0	0	—	35	50	.700	45	70	115	44	73	1	11	34	19	129	2.4	0.9	2.7
84-85—Seattle	6	0	93	6	10	.600	0	0	—	3	4	.750	6	11	17	7	13	0	1	10	3	15	2.8	1.2	2.5
86-87—Cleveland	24	2	279	30	65	.462	0	0	—	20	41	.488	19	39	58	23	28	0	9	24	4	80	2.4	1.0	3.3
REG. SEASON TOTALS	77	8	892	83	196	.423	0	0	—	58	95	.611	70	120	190	74	114	1	21	68	26	224	2.5	1.0	2.9
PLAYOFF TOTALS	4	0	38	4	6	.667	0	1	.000	0	1	.000	3	3	6	3	8	0	1	0	0	8	1.5	0.8	2.0

McCRAY, RODNEY EARL b. August 29, 1961   Ht. 6-8 Wt. 235 College—Louisville

SEASON—TEAM	G	GS	MIN	FGM	FGA	PCT	3FGM	3FGA	PCT	FTM	FTA	PCT	O-RB	D-RB	TOT	AST	PF	DQ	STL	TO	BLK	PTS	RPG	APG	PPG
83-84—Houston	79	36	2081	335	672	.499	1	4	.250	182	249	.731	173	277	450	176	205	1	53	120	54	853	5.7	2.2	10.8
84-85—Houston	82	82	3001	476	890	.535	0	6	.000	231	313	.738	201	338	539	355	215	2	90	178	75	1183	6.6	4.3	14.4
85-86—Houston	82	82	2610	338	629	.537	0	3	.000	171	222	.770	159	361	520	292	197	2	50	130	58	847	6.3	3.6	10.3
86-87—Houston	81	81	3136	432	783	.552	0	9	.000	306	393	.779	190	388	578	434	172	2	88	208	53	1170	7.1	5.4	14.4
87-88—Houston	81	80	2689	359	746	.481	0	4	.000	288	367	.785	232	399	631	264	166	2	57	144	51	1006	7.8	3.3	12.4
88-89—Sacramento	68	65	2435	340	729	.466	5	22	.227	169	234	.722	143	371	514	293	121	0	57	168	36	854	7.6	4.3	12.6
89-90—Sacramento	82	82	3238	537	1043	.515	11	42	.262	273	348	.784	192	477	669	377	176	0	60	174	70	1358	8.2	4.6	16.6
90-91—Dallas	74	68	2561	336	679	.495	13	39	.333	159	198	.803	153	407	560	259	203	3	70	129	51	844	7.6	3.5	11.4
91-92—Dallas	75	48	2106	271	622	.436	25	85	.294	110	153	.719	149	319	468	219	180	2	48	115	30	677	6.2	2.9	9.0
92-93—Chicago	64	1	1019	92	204	.451	2	5	.400	36	52	.692	53	105	158	81	99	0	12	53	15	222	2.5	1.3	3.5
REG. SEASON TOTALS	768	629	24876	3516	6997	.503	57	219	.260	1925	2529	.761	1645	3442	5087	2750	1734	14	585	1419	493	9014	6.6	3.6	11.7
PLAYOFF TOTALS	46	39	1650	197	374	.527	0	6	.000	109	147	.741	81	190	271	206	99	0	33	87	33	503	5.9	4.5	10.9

McCULLOUGH, JOHN P. b. October 5, 1956 Ht. 6-4 Wt. 190 College—Oklahoma

SEASON—TEAM	G	GS	MIN	FGM	FGA	PCT	3FGM	3FGA	PCT	FTM	FTA	PCT	O-RB	D-RB	TOT	AST	PF	DQ	STL	TO	BLK	PTS	RPG	APG	PPG
81-82—Phoenix	8	0	23	9	13	.692	0	0	—	3	5	.600	1	3	4	3	3	0	2	3	0	21	0.5	0.4	2.6
REG. SEASON TOTALS	8	0	23	9	13	.692	0	0	—	3	5	.600	1	3	4	3	3	0	2	3	0	21	0.5	0.4	2.6

McDANIEL, XAVIER MAURICE (X-Man) b. June 4, 1963 Ht. 6-7 Wt. 205 College—Wichita State

SEASON—TEAM	G	GS	MIN	FGM	FGA	PCT	3FGM	3FGA	PCT	FTM	FTA	PCT	O-RB	D-RB	TOT	AST	PF	DQ	STL	TO	BLK	PTS	RPG	APG	PPG
85-86—Seattle	82	80	2706	576	1176	.490	2	10	.200	250	364	.687	307	348	655	193	305	8	101	248	37	1404	8.0	2.4	17.1
86-87—Seattle	82	82	3031	806	1583	.509	3	14	.214	275	395	.696	338	367	705	207	300	4	115	234	52	1890	8.6	2.5	23.0
87-88—Seattle	78	77	2703	687	1407	.488	14	50	.280	281	393	.715	206	312	518	263	230	2	96	223	52	1669	6.6	3.4	21.4
88-89—Seattle	82	10	2385	677	1385	.489	11	36	.306	312	426	.732	177	256	433	134	231	0	84	210	40	1677	5.3	1.6	20.5
89-90—Seattle	69	67	2432	611	1233	.496	5	17	.294	244	333	.733	165	282	447	171	231	2	73	187	36	1471	6.5	2.5	21.3
90-91—Seattle-Phoenix	81	79	2634	590	1186	.497	0	8	.000	193	267	.723	173	384	557	187	264	2	76	184	46	1373	6.9	2.3	17.0
91-92—New York	82	82	2344	488	1021	.478	12	39	.308	137	192	.714	176	284	460	149	241	3	57	147	24	1125	5.6	1.8	13.7
92-93—Boston	82	27	2215	457	924	.495	6	22	.273	191	241	.793	168	321	489	163	249	4	72	171	51	1111	6.0	2.0	13.5
93-94—Boston	82	5	1971	387	839	.461	10	41	.244	144	213	.676	142	258	400	126	193	0	48	116	39	928	4.9	1.5	11.3
REG. SEASON TOTALS	720	509	22421	5279	10754	.491	63	237	.266	2027	2824	.718	1852	2812	4664	1593	2244	25	722	1720	377	12648	6.5	2.2	17.6
PLAYOFF TOTALS	47	43	1674	360	770	.468	11	38	.289	123	185	.665	143	208	351	126	168	3	36	119	22	854	7.5	2.7	18.2
ALL-STAR TOTALS	1	0	13	1	9	.111	0	0	—	0	0	—	1	1	2	1	0	0	1	0	0	2	2.0	0.0	2.0

McDANIELS, JAMES RONALD (Jim) b. April 2, 1948 Ht. 6-11½ Wt. 230 College—Western Kentucky

SEASON—TEAM	G	GS	MIN	FGM	FGA	PCT	3FGM	3FGA	PCT	FTM	FTA	PCT	O-RB	D-RB	TOT	AST	PF	DQ	STL	TO	BLK	PTS	RPG	APG	PPG
71-72—Carolina (A)	58	—	2172	659	1276	.516	0	0	—	234	324	.722	249	565	814	97	251	—	—	167	—	1552	14.0	1.7	26.8
71-72—Seattle	12	—	235	51	123	.415	—	—	—	11	18	.611	—	—	82	9	26	0	—	—	—	113	6.8	0.8	9.4
72-73—Seattle	68	—	1095	154	386	.399	—	—	—	70	100	.700	—	—	345	78	140	4	—	—	—	378	5.1	1.1	5.6
73-74—Seattle	27	—	439	63	173	.364	—	—	—	23	43	.535	51	77	128	24	48	0	7	—	15	149	4.7	0.9	5.5
75-76—Kentucky (A)	29	—	365	78	165	.473	0	0	—	23	28	.821	40	84	124	21	64	—	8	37	17	179	4.3	0.7	6.2
75-76—Los Angeles	35	—	242	41	102	.402	—	—	—	9	9	1.000	26	48	74	15	40	1	4	—	10	91	2.1	0.4	2.6
77-78—Buffalo	42	—	694	100	234	.427	—	—	—	36	42	.857	46	135	181	44	112	3	4	50	37	236	4.3	1.0	5.6
REG. NBA TOTALS	184	—	2705	409	1018	.402	—	—	—	149	212	.703	123	260	810	170	366	8	15	50	62	967	4.4	0.9	5.3
REG. ABA TOTALS	87	—	2537	737	1441	.511	0	0	—	257	352	.730	289	649	938	118	315	0	8	204	17	1731	10.8	1.4	19.9
ABA PLAYOFF TOTALS	10	—	98	19	41	.463	0	0	—	4	7	.571	9	26	35	5	16	0	3	4	5	42	3.5	0.5	4.2
ABA ALL-STAR TOTALS	1	—	20	11	15	.733	0	0	—	2	3	.667	6	5	11	1	3	—	0	2	0	24	11.0	1.0	24.0

McDONALD, BENJAMIN (Ben) b. July 20, 1962 Ht. 6-8 Wt. 225 College—Cal State-Irvine

SEASON—TEAM	G	GS	MIN	FGM	FGA	PCT	3FGM	3FGA	PCT	FTM	FTA	PCT	O-RB	D-RB	TOT	AST	PF	DQ	STL	TO	BLK	PTS	RPG	APG	PPG
85-86—Cleveland	21	0	266	28	58	.483	0	1	.000	5	8	.625	15	23	38	9	30	0	7	10	1	61	1.8	0.4	2.9
86-87—Golden State	63	34	1284	164	360	.456	1	8	.125	24	38	.632	63	120	183	84	200	5	27	43	8	353	2.9	1.3	5.6
87-88—Golden State	81	41	2039	258	552	.467	9	35	.257	87	111	.784	133	202	335	138	246	4	39	93	8	612	4.1	1.7	7.6
88-89—Golden State	11	0	103	13	19	.684	0	0	—	9	15	.600	4	8	12	5	11	0	4	3	0	35	1.1	0.5	3.2
REG. SEASON TOTALS	176	75	3692	463	989	.468	10	44	.227	125	172	.727	215	353	568	236	487	9	77	149	17	1061	3.2	1.3	6.0
PLAYOFF TOTALS	10	0	85	3	21	.143	0	5	.000	2	4	.500	6	8	14	10	15	0	5	4	1	8	1.4	1.0	0.8

McDONALD, GLENN STUART b. March 18, 1952 Ht. 6-6 Wt. 190 College—Long Beach State

SEASON—TEAM	G	GS	MIN	FGM	FGA	PCT	3FGM	3FGA	PCT	FTM	FTA	PCT	O-RB	D-RB	TOT	AST	PF	DQ	STL	TO	BLK	PTS	RPG	APG	PPG
74-75—Boston	62	—	395	70	182	.385	—	—	—	28	37	.757	20	48	68	24	58	0	8	—	5	168	1.1	0.4	2.7
75-76—Boston	75	—	1019	191	456	.419	—	—	—	40	56	.714	56	79	135	68	123	0	39	—	20	422	1.8	0.9	5.6
76-77—Milwaukee	9	—	79	8	34	.235	—	—	—	3	4	.750	8	4	12	7	11	0	4	—	0	19	1.3	0.8	2.1
REG. SEASON TOTALS	146	—	1493	269	672	.400	—	—	—	71	97	.732	84	131	215	99	192	0	51	—	25	609	1.5	0.7	4.2
PLAYOFF TOTALS	19	—	98	10	38	.263	—	—	—	6	9	.667	2	12	14	6	16	0	2	—	0	26	0.7	0.3	1.4

McDONALD, RODERICK WILLIAM (Rod) b. April 9, 1945 Ht. 6-6 Wt. 205 College—Whitworth

SEASON—TEAM	G	GS	MIN	FGM	FGA	PCT	3FGM	3FGA	PCT	FTM	FTA	PCT	O-RB	D-RB	TOT	AST	PF	DQ	STL	TO	BLK	PTS	RPG	APG	PPG
70-71—Utah (A)	29	—	206	50	109	.459	2	2	1.000	15	25	.600	—	—	93	7	41	—	—	—	—	117	3.2	0.2	4.0
71-72—Utah (A)	33	—	231	34	76	.447	0	2	.000	27	37	.730	—	—	74	18	40	—	—	23	—	95	2.2	0.5	2.9
72-73—Utah (A)	25	—	142	27	63	.429	1	4	.250	15	19	.789	13	17	30	15	19	0	—	14	—	70	1.2	0.6	2.8
REG. ABA TOTALS	87	—	579	111	248	.448	3	8	.375	57	81	.704	13	17	197	40	100	0	—	37	—	282	2.3	0.5	3.2
ABA PLAYOFF TOTALS	9	—	36	12	18	.667	1	2	.500	1	3	.333	—	—	14	2	6	0	—	—	—	26	1.6	0.2	2.9

McDOWELL, HANK LEIGH b. November 13, 1959 Ht. 6-9 Wt. 215 College—Memphis State

SEASON—TEAM	G	GS	MIN	FGM	FGA	PCT	3FGM	3FGA	PCT	FTM	FTA	PCT	O-RB	D-RB	TOT	AST	PF	DQ	STL	TO	BLK	PTS	RPG	APG	PPG
81-82—Golden State	30	1	335	34	84	.405	0	0	—	27	41	.659	41	59	100	20	52	1	6	21	8	95	3.3	0.7	3.2
82-83—G.S.-Port.	56	0	505	58	126	.460	0	2	.000	47	61	.770	54	65	119	24	84	0	8	40	11	163	2.1	0.4	2.9
83-84—San Diego	57	0	611	85	197	.431	0	3	.000	38	56	.679	63	92	155	37	77	0	14	49	2	208	2.7	0.6	3.6
84-85—Houston	34	0	132	20	42	.476	0	1	.000	7	10	.700	7	15	22	9	22	0	3	8	5	47	0.6	0.3	1.4
85-86—Houston	22	0	204	42	42	.571	0	2	.000	17	25	.680	12	37	49	6	25	0	1	10	3	65	2.2	0.3	3.0
86-87—Milwaukee	7	0	70	8	17	.471	0	0	—	6	7	.857	9	10	19	2	14	0	2	3	0	22	2.7	0.3	3.1
REG. SEASON TOTALS	206	1	1857	229	508	.451	0	8	.000	142	200	.710	186	278	464	98	274	1	34	131	29	600	2.3	0.5	2.9
PLAYOFF TOTALS	15	0	37	2	8	.250	0	0	—	5	8	.625	4	6	10	4	8	0	0	2	0	9	0.7	0.3	0.6

McELROY, JAMES CHARLES JR. (Jim) b. October 4, 1953 Ht. 6-3 Wt. 190 College—Monroe County CC/Central Michigan

SEASON—TEAM	G	GS	MIN	FGM	FGA	PCT	3FGM	3FGA	PCT	FTM	FTA	PCT	O-RB	D-RB	TOT	AST	PF	DQ	STL	TO	BLK	PTS	RPG	APG	PPG
75-76—New Orleans	51	—	1134	151	296	.510	—	—	—	81	110	.736	34	76	110	107	70	0	44	—	4	383	2.2	2.1	7.5
76-77—New Orleans	73	—	2029	301	640	.470	—	—	—	169	217	.779	55	128	183	260	119	3	60	—	8	771	2.5	3.6	10.6
77-78—New Orleans	74	—	1760	287	607	.473	—	—	—	123	167	.737	44	104	148	292	110	0	58	141	34	697	2.0	3.9	9.4
78-79—New Orleans	79	—	2698	539	1097	.491	—	—	—	259	340	.762	61	154	215	453	183	1	148	237	49	1337	2.7	5.7	16.9
79-80—Detroit-Atlanta	67	—	1528	228	527	.433	5	21	.238	132	172	.767	32	67	99	227	123	2	46	131	19	593	1.5	3.4	8.9
80-81—Atlanta	54	—	680	78	202	.386	1	8	.125	48	59	.814	10	38	48	84	62	0	20	79	9	205	0.9	1.6	3.8
81-82—Atlanta	20	17	349	52	125	.416	1	5	.200	29	36	.806	6	11	17	39	44	0	8	22	4	134	0.9	2.0	6.7
REG. SEASON TOTALS	418	17	10178	1636	3494	.468	7	34	.206	841	1101	.764	242	578	820	1462	711	6	384	610	127	4120	2.0	3.5	9.9
PLAYOFF TOTALS	5	0	32	4	9	.444	0	1	.000	4	5	.800	1	1	2	4	1	0	0	2	0	12	0.4	0.8	2.4

McFARLAND, PATRICK ALOYSIUS (Pat) b. December 7, 1951 Ht. 6-5 Wt. 185 College—St. Joseph's (Pa.)

SEASON—TEAM	G	GS	MIN	FGM	FGA	PCT	3FGM	3FGA	PCT	FTM	FTA	PCT	O-RB	D-RB	TOT	AST	PF	DQ	STL	TO	BLK	PTS	RPG	APG	PPG
73-74—Denver (A)	67	—	757	159	359	.443	8	24	.333	35	52	.673	60	74	134	64	69	—	23	41	6	361	2.0	1.0	5.4
74-75—Denver (A)	70	—	945	200	424	.472	2	16	.125	52	66	.788	37	83	120	116	60	—	47	108	5	454	1.7	1.7	6.5
75-76—San Diego (A)	11	—	275	55	120	.458	1	2	.500	21	22	.955	17	27	44	39	20	—	6	29	1	132	4.0	3.5	12.0
REG. ABA TOTALS	148	—	1977	414	903	.458	11	42	.262	108	140	.771	114	184	298	219	149	0	76	178	12	947	2.0	1.5	6.4
ABA PLAYOFF TOTALS	5	—	30	2	8	.250	0	2	.000	2	2	1.000	1	2	3	2	3	0	0	6	0	6	0.6	0.4	1.2

McGAHA, FRED MELVIN (Mel) b. September 26, 1926 Ht. 6-1 Wt. 190 College—Arkansas

SEASON—TEAM	G	GS	MIN	FGM	FGA	PCT	3FGM	3FGA	PCT	FTM	FTA	PCT	O-RB	D-RB	TOT	AST	PF	DQ	STL	TO	BLK	PTS	RPG	APG	PPG
48-49—New York	51	—	—	62	195	.318	—	—	—	52	88	.591	—	—	—	51	104	—	—	—	—	176	—	1.0	3.5
REG. SEASON TOTALS	51	—	—	62	195	.318	—	—	—	52	88	.591	—	—	—	51	104	—	—	—	—	176	—	1.0	3.5
PLAYOFF TOTALS	2	—	—	0	3	.000	—	—	—	1	2	.500	—	—	—	2	6	—	—	—	—	1	—	1.0	0.5

McGEE, MICHAEL RAY (Mike) b. July 29, 1959 Ht. 6-5 Wt. 205 College—Michigan

SEASON—TEAM	G	GS	MIN	FGM	FGA	PCT	3FGM	3FGA	PCT	FTM	FTA	PCT	O-RB	D-RB	TOT	AST	PF	DQ	STL	TO	BLK	PTS	RPG	APG	PPG
81-82—Los Angeles	39	0	352	80	172	.465	0	4	.000	31	53	.585	34	15	49	16	59	0	18	34	3	191	1.3	0.4	4.9
82-83—Los Angeles	39	7	381	69	163	.423	1	7	.143	17	23	.739	33	20	53	26	50	1	11	27	5	156	1.4	0.7	4.0
83-84—Los Angeles	77	45	1425	347	584	.594	2	13	.154	61	113	.540	117	76	193	81	176	0	49	111	6	757	2.5	1.1	9.8
84-85—L.A. Lakers	76	3	1170	329	612	.538	22	61	.361	94	160	.588	97	68	165	71	147	1	39	81	7	774	2.2	0.9	10.2
85-86—L.A. Lakers	71	19	1213	252	544	.463	41	114	.360	42	64	.656	51	89	140	83	131	0	53	70	7	587	2.0	1.2	8.3
86-87—Atlanta	76	6	1420	311	677	.459	86	229	.376	80	137	.584	71	88	159	149	156	1	61	104	2	788	2.1	2.0	10.4
87-88—Atlanta-Sac.	48	0	1003	223	530	.421	53	160	.331	76	102	.745	55	73	128	71	81	0	52	65	6	575	2.7	1.5	12.0
88-89—New Jersey	80	49	2027	434	917	.473	93	255	.365	77	144	.535	73	116	189	116	184	1	80	124	12	1038	2.4	1.5	13.0
89-90—Phoenix	14	7	280	42	87	.483	8	23	.348	10	21	.476	11	25	36	16	28	0	8	14	1	102	2.6	1.1	7.3
REG. SEASON TOTALS	520	136	9271	2087	4286	.487	306	866	.353	488	817	.597	542	570	1112	629	1012	4	371	630	49	4968	2.1	1.2	9.6
PLAYOFF TOTALS	68	13	838	201	400	.503	21	61	.344	63	103	.612	63	46	109	55	100	0	23	54	3	486	1.6	0.8	7.1

McGILL, BILL (The Hill) b. September 16, 1939 Ht. 6-9½ Wt. 225 College—Utah

SEASON—TEAM	G	GS	MIN	FGM	FGA	PCT	3FGM	3FGA	PCT	FTM	FTA	PCT	O-RB	D-RB	TOT	AST	PF	DQ	STL	TO	BLK	PTS	RPG	APG	PPG
62-63—Chicago	60	—	590	181	353	.513	—	—	—	80	119	.672	—	—	161	38	118	1	—	—	—	442	2.7	0.6	7.4
63-64—Balt.-N.Y.	74	—	1784	456	937	.487	—	—	—	204	282	.723	—	—	414	121	217	7	—	—	—	1116	5.6	1.6	15.1
64-65—St. L.-L.A.	24	—	133	21	65	.323	—	—	—	13	17	.765	—	—	36	9	32	1	—	—	—	55	1.5	0.4	2.3
68-69—Denver (A)	78	—	1760	411	745	.552	0	0	—	180	264	.682	—	—	460	102	289	13	—	149	34	1002	5.9	1.3	12.8
69-70—Pitt.-L.A.-Dallas (A)	59	—	830	201	369	.545	0	0	—	77	108	.713	—	—	215	60	140	1	—	—	—	479	3.6	1.0	8.1
REG. NBA TOTALS	158	—	2507	658	1355	.486	—	—	—	297	418	.711	—	—	611	168	367	9	—	—	—	1613	3.9	1.1	10.2
REG. ABA TOTALS	137	—	2590	612	1114	.549	0	0	—	257	372	.691	—	—	675	162	429	14	—	149	—	1481	4.9	1.2	10.8
NBA PLAYOFF TOTALS	5	—	34	5	9	.556	—	—	—	1	1	1.000	—	—	9	2	9	1	—	—	—	11	1.8	0.4	2.2
ABA PLAYOFF TOTALS	7	—	96	19	39	.487	0	0	—	9	10	.900	—	—	23	6	26	2	—	4	—	47	3.3	0.9	6.7

McGINNIS, GEORGE F. b. August 12, 1950 Ht. 6-8 Wt. 235 College—Indiana

SEASON—TEAM	G	GS	MIN	FGM	FGA	PCT	3FGM	3FGA	PCT	FTM	FTA	PCT	O-RB	D-RB	TOT	AST	PF	DQ	STL	TO	BLK	PTS	RPG	APG	PPG
71-72—Indiana (A)	73	—	2179	465	999	.465	6	38	.158	298	462	.645	290	421	711	137	260	—	—	256	—	1234	9.7	1.9	16.9
72-73—Indiana (A)	82	—	3347	868	1755	.495	8	32	.250	517	778	.665	434	588	1022	205	348	0	160	401	—	2261	12.5	2.5	27.6
73-74—Indiana (A)	80	—	3266	789	1686	.468	5	34	.147	488	715	.683	422	775	1197	267	325	—	159	393	40	2071	15.0	3.3	25.9
74-75—Indiana (A)	79	—	3193	873	1934	.451	62	175	.354	545	753	.724	396	730	1126	495	303	—	206	422	56	2353	14.3	6.3	29.8
75-76—Philadelphia	77	—	2946	647	1552	.417	—	—	—	475	642	.740	260	707	967	359	334	13	198	—	41	1769	12.6	4.7	23.0
76-77—Philadelphia	79	—	2769	659	1439	.458	—	—	—	372	546	.681	324	587	911	302	299	4	163	—	37	1690	11.5	3.8	21.4
77-78—Philadelphia	78	—	2533	588	1270	.463	—	—	—	411	574	.716	282	528	810	294	287	6	137	312	27	1587	10.4	3.8	20.3
78-79—Denver	76	—	2552	603	1273	.474	—	—	—	509	765	.665	256	608	864	283	321	16	129	346	52	1715	11.4	3.7	22.6
79-80—Denver-Indiana	73	—	2208	400	886	.451	2	15	.133	270	488	.553	222	477	699	333	303	12	101	281	23	1072	9.6	4.6	14.7
80-81—Indiana	69	—	1845	348	768	.453	0	7	.000	207	385	.538	164	364	528	210	242	3	99	221	28	903	7.7	3.0	13.1
81-82—Indiana	76	4	1341	141	378	.373	0	3	.000	72	159	.453	93	305	398	204	198	4	96	131	28	354	5.2	2.7	4.7
REG. NBA TOTALS	528	4	16194	3386	7566	.448	2	25	.080	2316	3559	.651	1601	3576	5177	1985	1984	58	923	1291	236	9090	9.8	3.8	17.2
REG. ABA TOTALS	314	—	11985	2995	6374	.470	81	279	.290	1848	2708	.682	1542	2514	4056	1104	1236	0	525	1472	96	7919	12.9	3.5	25.2
NBA PLAYOFF TOTALS	34	0	1035	187	474	.395	0	0	—	121	189	.640	97	230	327	118	143	4	41	43	11	495	9.6	3.5	14.6
ABA PLAYOFF TOTALS	70	—	2680	599	1334	.449	29	100	.290	431	620	.695	345	556	901	286	301	0	74	281	27	1658	12.9	4.1	23.7
NBA ALL-STAR TOTALS	3	2	70	11	30	.367	0	0	—	8	17	.471	8	12	20	7	9	0	0	0	0	30	6.7	2.3	10.0
ABA ALL-STAR TOTALS	3	3	96	23	50	.460	0	2	.000	9	17	.529	15	23	38	8	13	—	5	14	2	55	12.7	2.7	18.3

McGLOCKLIN, JON P. b. June 10, 1943 Ht. 6-5 Wt. 205 College—Indiana

SEASON—TEAM	G	GS	MIN	FGM	FGA	PCT	3FGM	3FGA	PCT	FTM	FTA	PCT	O-RB	D-RB	TOT	AST	PF	DQ	STL	TO	BLK	PTS	RPG	APG	PPG
65-66—Cincinnati	72	—	852	153	363	.421	—	—	—	62	79	.785	—	—	133	88	77	0	—	—	—	368	1.8	1.2	5.1
66-67—Cincinnati	60	—	1194	217	493	.440	—	—	—	74	104	.712	—	—	164	93	84	0	—	—	—	508	2.7	1.6	8.5
67-68—San Diego	65	—	1876	316	757	.417	—	—	—	156	180	.867	—	—	199	178	117	0	—	—	—	788	3.1	2.7	12.1
68-69—Milwaukee	80	—	2888	662	1358	.487	—	—	—	246	292	.842	—	—	343	312	186	1	—	—	—	1570	4.3	3.9	19.6
69-70—Milwaukee	82	—	2966	639	1206	.530	—	—	—	169	198	.854	—	—	252	303	164	0	—	—	—	1447	3.1	3.7	17.6
70-71—Milwaukee	82	—	2891	574	1073	.535	—	—	—	144	167	.862	—	—	223	305	189	0	—	—	—	1292	2.7	3.7	15.8
71-72—Milwaukee	80	—	2213	374	733	.510	—	—	—	109	126	.865	—	—	181	231	146	0	—	—	—	857	2.3	2.9	10.7
72-73—Milwaukee	80	—	1951	351	699	.502	—	—	—	63	73	.863	—	—	158	236	119	0	—	—	—	765	2.0	3.0	9.6
73-74—Milwaukee	79	—	1910	329	693	.475	—	—	—	72	80	.900	33	106	139	241	128	1	43	—	7	730	1.8	3.1	9.2
74-75—Milwaukee	79	—	1853	323	651	.496	—	—	—	63	72	.875	25	94	119	255	142	2	51	—	6	709	1.5	3.2	9.0
75-76—Milwaukee	33	—	336	63	148	.426	—	—	—	9	10	.900	3	14	17	38	18	0	8	—	0	135	0.5	1.2	4.1
REG. SEASON TOTALS	792	—	20930	4001	8174	.489	—	—	—	1167	1381	.845	61	214	1928	2280	1370	4	102	—	13	9169	2.4	2.9	11.6
PLAYOFF TOTALS	55	—	1528	266	544	.489	—	—	—	75	91	.824	2	15	102	123	121	0	7	—	1	607	1.9	2.2	11.0
ALL-STAR TOTALS	1	—	7	1	2	.500	—	—	—	0	0	—	0	0	1	0	0	0	0	—	0	2	1.0	0.0	2.0

McGREGOR, GILBERT RAY (Gil) b. June 14, 1949 Ht. 6-8 Wt. 240 College—Wake Forest

SEASON—TEAM	G	GS	MIN	FGM	FGA	PCT	3FGM	3FGA	PCT	FTM	FTA	PCT	O-RB	D-RB	TOT	AST	PF	DQ	STL	TO	BLK	PTS	RPG	APG	PPG
71-72—Cincinnati	42	—	532	66	182	.363	—	—	—	39	56	.696	—	—	148	18	120	4	—	—	—	171	3.5	0.4	4.1
REG. SEASON TOTALS	42	—	532	66	182	.363	—	—	—	39	56	.696	—	—	148	18	120	4	—	—	—	171	3.5	0.4	4.1

McGRIFF, ELTON WAYNE (Mac) b. August 21, 1942 Ht. 6-9 Wt. 225 College—Creighton

SEASON—TEAM	G	GS	MIN	FGM	FGA	PCT	3FGM	3FGA	PCT	FTM	FTA	PCT	O-RB	D-RB	TOT	AST	PF	DQ	STL	TO	BLK	PTS	RPG	APG	PPG
67-68—Dallas (A)	20	—	369	49	89	.551	0	0	—	33	62	.532	—	—	114	2	65	3	—	21	—	131	5.7	0.1	6.6
68-69—Dallas-N.O.-Ken. (A)	36	—	495	75	171	.439	0	1	.000	57	90	.633	—	—	144	8	85	1	—	32	—	207	4.0	0.2	5.8
REG. ABA TOTALS	56	—	864	124	260	.477	0	1	.000	90	152	.592	—	—	258	10	150	4	—	53	—	338	4.6	0.2	6.0
ABA PLAYOFF TOTALS	13	—	267	38	91	.418	0	0	—	27	48	.563	—	—	99	8	49	3	—	26	—	103	7.6	0.6	7.9

McGUIRE, ALFRED (Allie) b. July 10, 1951 Ht. 6-3 Wt. 175 College—Marquette

SEASON—TEAM	G	GS	MIN	FGM	FGA	PCT	3FGM	3FGA	PCT	FTM	FTA	PCT	O-RB	D-RB	TOT	AST	PF	DQ	STL	TO	BLK	PTS	RPG	APG	PPG
73-74—New York	2	—	10	2	4	.500	—	—	—	0	0	—	0	2	2	1	2	0	0	—	0	4	1.0	0.5	2.0
REG. SEASON TOTALS	2	—	10	2	4	.500	—	—	—	0	0	—	0	2	2	1	2	0	0	—	0	4	1.0	0.5	2.0

McGUIRE, ALFRED JAMES (Al) b. September 7, 1928 Ht. 6-2 Wt. 180 College—St. John's

SEASON—TEAM	G	GS	MIN	FGM	FGA	PCT	3FGM	3FGA	PCT	FTM	FTA	PCT	O-RB	D-RB	TOT	AST	PF	DQ	STL	TO	BLK	PTS	RPG	APG	PPG
51-52—New York	59	—	788	72	167	.431	—	—	—	64	122	.525	—	—	121	107	136	8	—	—	—	208	2.1	1.8	3.5
52-53—New York	58	—	1231	112	287	.390	—	—	—	128	201	.637	—	—	167	145	206	8	—	—	—	352	2.9	2.5	6.1
53-54—New York	64	—	849	58	177	.328	—	—	—	58	133	.436	—	—	121	103	144	2	—	—	—	174	1.9	1.6	2.7
54-55—Baltimore	10	—	98	9	32	.281	—	—	—	5	7	.714	—	—	9	8	15	0	—	—	—	23	0.9	0.8	2.3
REG. SEASON TOTALS	191	—	2966	251	663	.379	—	—	—	255	463	.551	—	—	418	363	501	18	—	—	—	757	2.2	1.9	4.0
PLAYOFF TOTALS	24	—	339	31	83	.373	—	—	—	22	43	.512	—	—	28	30	60	3	—	—	—	84	1.2	1.3	3.5

McGUIRE, RICHARD JOSEPH (**Dick, Tricky Dick**) b. January 25, 1926   Ht. 6-0 Wt. 180 College—St. John's/Dartmouth

SEASON—TEAM	G	GS	MIN	FGM	FGA	PCT	3FGM	3FGA	PCT	FTM	FTA	PCT	O-RB	D-RB	TOT	AST	PF	DQ	STL	TO	BLK	PTS	RPG	APG	PPG
49-50—New York	68	—	—	190	563	.337	—	—	—	204	313	.652	—	—	—	386	160	—	—	—	—	584	—	5.7	8.6
50-51—New York	64	—	—	179	482	.371	—	—	—	179	276	.649	—	—	334	400	154	2	—	—	—	537	5.2	6.3	8.4
51-52—New York	64	—	2018	204	474	.430	—	—	—	183	290	.631	—	—	332	388	181	4	—	—	—	591	5.2	6.1	9.2
52-53—New York	61	—	1783	142	373	.381	—	—	—	153	269	.569	—	—	280	296	172	3	—	—	—	437	4.6	4.9	7.2
53-54—New York	68	—	2343	201	493	.408	—	—	—	220	345	.638	—	—	310	354	199	3	—	—	—	622	4.6	5.2	9.1
54-55—New York	71	—	2310	226	581	.389	—	—	—	195	303	.644	—	—	322	542	143	0	—	—	—	647	4.5	7.6	9.1
55-56—New York	62	—	1685	152	438	.347	—	—	—	121	193	.627	—	—	220	362	146	0	—	—	—	425	3.5	5.8	6.9
56-57—New York	72	—	1191	140	366	.383	—	—	—	105	163	.644	—	—	146	222	103	0	—	—	—	385	2.0	3.1	5.3
57-58—Detroit	69	—	2311	203	544	.373	—	—	—	150	225	.667	—	—	291	454	178	0	—	—	—	556	4.2	6.6	8.1
58-59—Detroit	71	—	2063	232	543	.427	—	—	—	191	258	.740	—	—	285	443	147	1	—	—	—	655	4.0	6.2	9.2
59-60—Detroit	68	—	1466	179	402	.445	—	—	—	124	201	.617	—	—	264	358	112	0	—	—	—	482	3.9	5.3	7.1
REG. SEASON TOTALS	738	—	17170	2048	5259	.389	—	—	—	1825	2836	.644	—	—	2784	4205	1695	13	—	—	—	5921	4.2	5.7	8.0
PLAYOFF TOTALS	63	—	1436	179	437	.410	—	—	—	163	275	.593	—	—	284	350	187	3	—	—	—	521	4.9	5.6	8.3
ALL-STAR TOTALS	7	—	151	12	31	.387	—	—	—	5	12	.417	—	—	23	38	11	0	—	—	—	29	3.3	5.4	4.1

McHALE, KEVIN EDWARD b. December 19, 1957   Ht. 6-10 Wt. 210 College—Minnesota

SEASON—TEAM	G	GS	MIN	FGM	FGA	PCT	3FGM	3FGA	PCT	FTM	FTA	PCT	O-RB	D-RB	TOT	AST	PF	DQ	STL	TO	BLK	PTS	RPG	APG	PPG
80-81—Boston	82	—	1645	355	666	.533	0	2	.000	108	159	.679	155	204	359	55	260	3	27	110	151	818	4.4	0.7	10.0
81-82—Boston	82	33	2332	465	875	.531	0	0	—	187	248	.754	191	365	556	91	264	1	30	137	185	1117	6.8	1.1	13.6
82-83—Boston	82	13	2345	483	893	.541	0	1	.000	193	269	.717	215	338	553	104	241	3	34	159	192	1159	6.7	1.3	14.1
83-84—Boston	82	10	2577	587	1055	.556	1	3	.333	336	439	.765	208	402	610	104	243	5	23	150	126	1511	7.4	1.3	18.4
84-85—Boston	79	31	2653	605	1062	.570	0	6	.000	355	467	.760	229	483	712	141	234	3	28	157	120	1565	9.0	1.8	19.8
85-86—Boston	68	62	2397	561	978	.574	0	0	—	326	420	.776	171	380	551	181	192	2	29	149	134	1448	8.1	2.7	21.3
86-87—Boston	77	77	3060	790	1307	.604	0	4	.000	428	512	.836	247	516	763	198	240	1	38	197	172	2008	9.9	2.6	26.1
87-88—Boston	64	63	2390	550	911	.604	0	0	—	346	434	.797	159	377	536	171	179	1	27	141	92	1446	8.4	2.7	22.6
88-89—Boston	78	74	2876	661	1211	.546	0	4	.000	436	533	.818	223	414	637	172	223	2	26	196	97	1758	8.2	2.2	22.5
89-90—Boston	82	25	2722	648	1181	.549	23	69	.333	393	440	.893	201	476	677	172	250	3	30	183	157	1712	8.3	2.1	20.9
90-91—Boston	68	10	2067	504	912	.553	15	37	.405	228	275	.829	145	335	480	126	194	2	25	140	146	1251	7.1	1.9	18.4
91-92—Boston	56	1	1398	323	634	.509	0	13	.000	134	163	.822	119	211	330	82	112	1	11	82	59	780	5.9	1.5	13.9
92-93—Boston	71	0	1656	298	649	.459	2	18	.111	164	195	.841	95	263	358	73	126	0	16	92	59	762	5.0	1.0	10.7
REG. SEASON TOTALS	971	399	30118	6830	12334	.554	41	157	.261	3634	4554	.798	2358	4764	7122	1670	2758	27	344	1893	1690	17335	7.3	1.7	17.9
PLAYOFF TOTALS	169	85	5716	1204	2145	.561	8	21	.381	766	972	.788	456	797	1253	274	571	8	65	326	281	3182	7.4	1.6	18.8
ALL-STAR TOTALS	7	0	125	24	48	.500	1	2	.500	12	14	.857	13	24	37	8	21	0	1	5	12	61	5.3	1.1	8.7

McHARTLEY, MAURICE FRANKLIN (**Mo**) b. August 1, 1942   Ht. 6-3 Wt. 200 College—North Carolina A&T

SEASON—TEAM	G	GS	MIN	FGM	FGA	PCT	3FGM	3FGA	PCT	FTM	FTA	PCT	O-RB	D-RB	TOT	AST	PF	DQ	STL	TO	BLK	PTS	RPG	APG	PPG
67-68—Dallas (A)	58	—	2175	330	825	.400	3	17	.176	225	324	.694	—	—	273	230	216	5	—	241	—	888	4.7	4.0	15.3
68-69—N.Y.-Miami (A)	76	—	2148	390	962	.405	6	27	.222	263	331	.795	—	—	211	269	251	5	—	269	—	1049	2.8	3.5	13.8
69-70—Miami-Pitt.-Dallas (A)	55	—	992	155	388	.399	6	36	.167	98	130	.754	—	—	115	142	158	3	—	—	—	414	2.1	2.6	7.5
REG. ABA TOTALS	189	—	5315	875	2175	.402	15	80	.188	586	785	.746	—	—	599	641	625	13	—	510	—	2351	3.2	3.4	12.4
ABA PLAYOFF TOTALS	25	—	699	127	337	.377	2	9	.222	90	114	.789	—	—	98	92	88	3	—	79	—	346	3.9	3.7	13.8

McINTOSH, KENNEDY (**Kenny**) b. January 21, 1949   Ht. 6-7 Wt. 225 College—Eastern Michigan

SEASON—TEAM	G	GS	MIN	FGM	FGA	PCT	3FGM	3FGA	PCT	FTM	FTA	PCT	O-RB	D-RB	TOT	AST	PF	DQ	STL	TO	BLK	PTS	RPG	APG	PPG
71-72—Chicago	43	—	405	57	168	.339	—	—	—	21	44	.477	—	—	89	18	41	0	—	—	—	135	2.1	0.4	3.1
72-73—Chicago-Seattle	59	—	1138	115	341	.337	—	—	—	40	67	.597	—	—	231	54	102	1	—	—	—	270	3.9	0.9	4.6
73-74—Seattle	69	—	2056	223	573	.389	—	—	—	65	107	.607	111	250	361	94	178	4	52	—	29	511	5.2	1.4	7.4
74-75—Seattle	6	—	101	6	29	.207	—	—	—	6	9	.667	6	9	15	7	12	0	4	—	3	18	2.5	1.2	3.0
REG. SEASON TOTALS	177	—	3700	401	1111	.361	—	—	—	132	227	.581	117	259	696	173	333	5	56	—	32	934	3.9	1.0	5.3

McINTYRE, ROBERT (**Bob**) b. January 23, 1944   Ht. 6-7 Wt. 215 College—St. John's

SEASON—TEAM	G	GS	MIN	FGM	FGA	PCT	3FGM	3FGA	PCT	FTM	FTA	PCT	O-RB	D-RB	TOT	AST	PF	DQ	STL	TO	BLK	PTS	RPG	APG	PPG
67-68—New Jersey (A)	21	—	451	70	187	.374	0	1	.000	34	58	.586	—	—	101	11	27	0	—	27	—	174	4.8	0.5	8.3
69-70—New York (A)	7	—	94	12	32	.375	1	3	.333	0	1	.000	—	—	20	5	8	0	—	—	—	25	2.9	0.7	3.6
REG. ABA TOTALS	28	—	545	82	219	.374	1	4	.250	34	59	.576	—	—	121	16	35	0	—	27	—	199	4.3	0.6	7.1

McKEE, GERALD (**Jerry**) b. August 4, 1946   Ht. 6-3 Wt. 190 College—Ohio

SEASON—TEAM	G	GS	MIN	FGM	FGA	PCT	3FGM	3FGA	PCT	FTM	FTA	PCT	O-RB	D-RB	TOT	AST	PF	DQ	STL	TO	BLK	PTS	RPG	APG	PPG
69-70—Indiana (A)	1	—	3	0	1	.000	0	0	—	0	0	—	—	—	0	0	0	0	—	—	—	0	0.0	0.0	0.0
REG. ABA TOTALS	1	—	3	0	1	.000	0	0	—	0	0	—	—	—	0	0	0	0	—	—	—	0	0.0	0.0	0.0

McKENNA, KEVIN ROBERT b. January 8, 1959 Ht. 6-5 Wt. 195 College—Creighton

SEASON—TEAM	G	GS	MIN	FGM	FGA	PCT	3FGM	3FGA	PCT	FTM	FTA	PCT	O-RB	D-RB	TOT	AST	PF	DQ	STL	TO	BLK	PTS	RPG	APG	PPG
81-82—Los Angeles	36	0	237	28	87	.322	0	2	.000	11	17	.647	18	11	29	14	45	0	10	20	2	67	0.8	0.4	1.9
83-84—Indiana	61	13	923	152	371	.410	3	17	.176	80	98	.816	30	65	95	114	133	3	46	62	5	387	1.6	1.9	6.3
84-85—New Jersey	29	7	535	61	134	.455	5	13	.385	38	43	.884	20	29	49	58	63	0	30	32	7	165	1.7	2.0	5.7
85-86—Washington	30	1	430	61	166	.367	27	77	.351	25	30	.833	9	27	36	23	54	1	29	18	2	174	1.2	0.8	5.8
86-87—New Jersey	56	3	942	153	337	.454	52	124	.419	43	57	.754	21	56	77	93	141	0	54	53	7	401	1.4	1.7	7.2
87-88—New Jersey	31	2	393	43	109	.394	16	50	.320	24	25	.960	4	27	31	40	55	1	15	19	2	126	1.0	1.3	4.1
REG. SEASON TOTALS	243	26	3460	498	1204	.414	103	283	.364	221	270	.819	102	215	317	342	491	5	184	204	25	1320	1.3	1.4	5.4
PLAYOFF TOTALS	1	0	2	0	0	—	0	0	—	0	0	—	0	0	0	—	0	0	0	0	0	0	0.0	0.0	0.0

McKENZIE, FORREST WALTON b. February 16, 1963 Ht. 6-7 Wt. 200 College—Loyola Marymount

SEASON—TEAM	G	GS	MIN	FGM	FGA	PCT	3FGM	3FGA	PCT	FTM	FTA	PCT	O-RB	D-RB	TOT	AST	PF	DQ	STL	TO	BLK	PTS	RPG	APG	PPG
86-87—San Antonio	6	0	42	7	28	.250	1	2	.500	2	2	1.000	2	5	7	1	9	0	1	3	0	17	1.2	0.2	2.8
REG. SEASON TOTALS	6	0	42	7	28	.250	1	2	.500	2	2	1.000	2	5	7	1	9	0	1	3	0	17	1.2	0.2	2.8

McKENZIE, STANLEY (Stan) b. October 6, 1944 Ht. 6-5 Wt. 210 College—New York University

SEASON—TEAM	G	GS	MIN	FGM	FGA	PCT	3FGM	3FGA	PCT	FTM	FTA	PCT	O-RB	D-RB	TOT	AST	PF	DQ	STL	TO	BLK	PTS	RPG	APG	PPG
67-68—Baltimore	50	—	653	73	182	.401	—	—	—	58	88	.659	—	—	121	24	98	1	—	—	—	204	2.4	0.5	4.1
68-69—Phoenix	80	—	1569	264	618	.427	—	—	—	219	287	.763	—	—	251	123	191	3	—	—	—	747	3.1	1.5	9.3
69-70—Phoenix	58	—	525	81	206	.393	—	—	—	58	73	.795	—	—	93	52	67	1	—	—	—	220	1.6	0.9	3.8
70-71—Portland	82	—	2290	398	902	.441	—	—	—	331	396	.836	—	—	309	235	238	2	—	—	—	1127	3.8	2.9	13.7
71-72—Portland	82	—	2036	410	834	.492	—	—	—	315	379	.831	—	—	272	148	240	2	—	—	—	1135	3.3	1.8	13.8
72-73—Port.-Houston	33	—	294	48	119	.403	—	—	—	30	37	.811	—	—	55	23	43	1	—	—	—	126	1.7	0.7	3.8
73-74—Houston	11	—	112	7	24	.292	—	—	—	6	8	.750	3	13	16	6	17	0	3	—	0	20	1.5	0.5	1.8
REG. SEASON TOTALS	396	—	7479	1281	2885	.444	—	—	—	1017	1268	.802	3	13	1117	611	894	10	3	—	0	3579	2.8	1.5	9.0
PLAYOFF TOTALS	7	—	71	8	29	.276	—	—	—	4	5	.800	0	0	9	3	14	0	0	—	0	20	1.3	0.4	2.9

McKEY, DERRICK WAYNE (Heavy D) b. October 10, 1966 Ht. 6-9 Wt. 225 College—Alabama-Birmingham

SEASON—TEAM	G	GS	MIN	FGM	FGA	PCT	3FGM	3FGA	PCT	FTM	FTA	PCT	O-RB	D-RB	TOT	AST	PF	DQ	STL	TO	BLK	PTS	RPG	APG	PPG
87-88—Seattle	82	4	1706	255	519	.491	11	30	.367	173	224	.772	115	213	328	107	237	3	70	108	63	694	4.0	1.3	8.5
88-89—Seattle	82	82	2804	487	970	.502	30	89	.337	301	375	.803	167	297	464	219	264	4	105	188	70	1305	5.7	2.7	15.9
89-90—Seattle	80	80	2748	468	949	.493	3	23	.130	315	403	.782	170	319	489	187	247	2	87	192	81	1254	6.1	2.3	15.7
90-91—Seattle	73	55	2503	438	847	.517	4	19	.211	235	278	.845	172	251	423	169	220	2	91	158	56	1115	5.8	2.3	15.3
91-92—Seattle	52	44	1757	285	604	.472	19	50	.380	188	222	.847	95	173	268	120	142	2	61	114	47	777	5.2	2.3	14.9
92-93—Seattle	77	68	2439	387	780	.496	40	112	.357	220	297	.741	121	206	327	197	208	5	105	152	58	1034	4.2	2.6	13.4
93-94—Indiana	76	76	2613	355	710	.500	9	31	.290	192	254	.756	129	273	402	327	248	1	111	228	49	911	5.3	4.3	12.0
REG. SEASON TOTALS	522	409	16570	2675	5379	.497	116	354	.328	1624	2053	.791	969	1732	2701	1326	1566	19	630	1140	424	7090	5.2	2.5	13.6
PLAYOFF TOTALS	61	50	2058	277	554	.500	18	61	.295	148	210	.705	135	200	335	196	205	3	57	132	58	720	5.5	3.2	11.8

McKINNEY, CARLTON B. b. October 21, 1964 Ht. 6-5 Wt. 210 College—Tulsa/Southern Methodist

SEASON—TEAM	G	GS	MIN	FGM	FGA	PCT	3FGM	3FGA	PCT	FTM	FTA	PCT	O-RB	D-RB	TOT	AST	PF	DQ	STL	TO	BLK	PTS	RPG	APG	PPG
89-90—L.A. Clippers	7	0	104	8	32	.250	0	1	.000	2	4	.500	4	8	12	7	15	1	6	7	1	18	1.7	1.0	2.6
91-92—New York	2	0	9	2	9	.222	0	0	—	0	0	—	0	1	1	0	1	0	0	0	0	4	0.5	0.0	2.0
REG. SEASON TOTALS	9	0	113	10	41	.244	0	1	.000	2	4	.500	4	9	13	7	16	1	6	7	1	22	1.4	0.8	2.4

McKINNEY, HORACE ALBERT (Bones) b. January 1, 1919 Ht. 6-6 Wt. 185 College—North Carolina/North Carolina St.

SEASON—TEAM	G	GS	MIN	FGM	FGA	PCT	3FGM	3FGA	PCT	FTM	FTA	PCT	O-RB	D-RB	TOT	AST	PF	DQ	STL	TO	BLK	PTS	RPG	APG	PPG
46-47—Washington	58	—	—	275	987	.279	—	—	—	145	210	.690	—	—	—	69	162	—	—	—	—	695	—	1.2	12.0
47-48—Washington	43	—	—	182	680	.268	—	—	—	121	188	.644	—	—	—	36	176	—	—	—	—	485	—	0.8	11.3
48-49—Washington	57	—	—	263	801	.328	—	—	—	197	279	.706	—	—	—	114	216	—	—	—	—	723	—	2.0	12.7
49-50—Washington	53	—	—	187	631	.296	—	—	—	118	152	.776	—	—	—	88	185	—	—	—	—	492	—	1.7	9.3
50-51—Wash.-Boston	44	—	—	102	327	.312	—	—	—	58	81	.716	—	—	198	85	136	6	—	—	—	262	4.5	1.9	6.0
51-52—Boston	63	—	1083	136	418	.325	—	—	—	65	80	.813	—	—	175	111	148	4	—	—	—	337	2.8	1.8	5.3
REG. SEASON TOTALS	318	—	1083	1145	3844	.298	—	—	—	704	990	.711	—	—	373	503	1023	10	—	—	—	2994	3.5	1.6	9.4
PLAYOFF TOTALS	23	—	20	82	268	.306	—	—	—	68	96	.708	—	—	16	25	82	4	—	—	—	232	3.2	1.1	10.1

McKINNEY, WILLIAM MERVIN (Billy) b. June 5, 1955 Ht. 6-0 Wt. 160 College—Northwestern

SEASON—TEAM	G	GS	MIN	FGM	FGA	PCT	3FGM	3FGA	PCT	FTM	FTA	PCT	O-RB	D-RB	TOT	AST	PF	DQ	STL	TO	BLK	PTS	RPG	APG	PPG
78-79—Kansas City	78	—	1242	240	477	.503	—	—	—	129	162	.796	20	65	85	253	121	0	58	124	3	609	1.1	3.2	7.8
79-80—Kansas City	76	—	1333	206	459	.449	1	10	.100	107	133	.805	20	66	86	248	87	0	58	89	5	520	1.1	3.3	6.8
80-81—Utah-Denver	84	—	2166	327	645	.507	2	12	.167	162	188	.862	36	148	184	360	231	3	99	158	11	818	2.2	4.3	9.7
81-82—Denver	81	27	1963	369	699	.528	0	17	.000	137	170	.806	29	113	142	338	186	0	69	115	16	875	1.8	4.2	10.8
82-83—Denver	68	38	1559	266	546	.487	0	7	.000	136	167	.814	21	100	121	288	142	0	39	101	5	668	1.8	4.2	9.8
83-84—San Diego	80	0	843	136	305	.446	0	3	.000	39	46	.848	7	47	54	161	84	0	27	48	0	311	0.7	2.0	3.9
85-86—Chicago	9	0	83	10	23	.435	0	0	—	2	2	1.000	1	4	5	13	9	0	3	2	0	22	0.6	1.4	2.4
REG. SEASON TOTALS	476	65	9189	1554	3154	.493	3	48	.063	712	868	.820	134	543	677	1661	860	3	353	637	40	3823	1.4	3.5	8.0
PLAYOFF TOTALS	19	3	334	59	118	.500	0	2	.000	26	37	.703	13	16	29	60	31	0	10	27	0	144	1.5	3.2	7.6

McLEMORE, McCOY JR. b. April 3, 1942 Ht. 6-7 Wt. 230 College—Moberly Area CC/Drake

SEASON—TEAM	G	GS	MIN	FGM	FGA	PCT	3FGM	3FGA	PCT	FTM	FTA	PCT	O-RB	D-RB	TOT	AST	PF	DQ	STL	TO	BLK	PTS	RPG	APG	PPG
64-65—San Francisco	78	—	1731	244	725	.337	—	—	—	157	220	.714	—	—	488	81	224	6	—	—	—	645	6.3	1.0	8.3
65-66—San Francisco	80	—	1467	225	528	.426	—	—	—	142	191	.743	—	—	488	55	197	4	—	—	—	592	6.1	0.7	7.4
66-67—Chicago	79	—	1382	258	670	.385	—	—	—	210	272	.772	—	—	374	62	189	2	—	—	—	726	4.7	0.8	9.2
67-68—Chicago	76	—	2100	374	940	.398	—	—	—	215	276	.779	—	—	430	130	219	4	—	—	—	963	5.7	1.7	12.7
68-69—Phoenix-Detroit	81	—	1620	282	722	.391	—	—	—	169	214	.790	—	—	404	94	186	4	—	—	—	733	5.0	1.2	9.0
69-70—Detroit	73	—	1421	233	500	.466	—	—	—	119	145	.821	—	—	336	83	159	3	—	—	—	585	4.6	1.1	8.0
70-71—Clev.-Milw.	86	—	2254	303	787	.385	—	—	—	204	261	.782	—	—	568	206	235	2	—	—	—	810	6.6	2.4	9.4
71-72—Milw.-Houston	27	—	246	28	71	.394	—	—	—	20	24	.833	—	—	73	22	33	1	—	—	—	76	2.7	0.8	2.8
REG. SEASON TOTALS	580	—	12221	1947	4943	.394	—	—	—	1236	1603	.771	—	—	3161	733	1442	26	—	—	—	5130	5.5	1.3	8.8
PLAYOFF TOTALS	18	—	239	34	91	.374	—	—	—	30	38	.789	—	—	49	17	31	1	—	—	—	98	2.7	0.9	5.4

McLEOD, GEORGE L. b. January 3, 1931 Ht. 6-5½ Wt. 200 College—Texas Christian

SEASON—TEAM	G	GS	MIN	FGM	FGA	PCT	3FGM	3FGA	PCT	FTM	FTA	PCT	O-RB	D-RB	TOT	AST	PF	DQ	STL	TO	BLK	PTS	RPG	APG	PPG
52-53—Baltimore	10	—	85	2	16	.125	—	—	—	8	15	.533	—	—	21	4	16	0	—	—	—	12	2.1	0.4	1.2
REG. SEASON TOTALS	10	—	85	2	16	.125	—	—	—	8	15	.533	—	—	21	4	16	0	—	—	—	12	2.1	0.4	1.2

McMAHON, JOHN JOSEPH (Jack) b. December 3, 1928 d. June 11, 1969 Ht. 6-1 Wt. 185 College—St. John's

SEASON—TEAM	G	GS	MIN	FGM	FGA	PCT	3FGM	3FGA	PCT	FTM	FTA	PCT	O-RB	D-RB	TOT	AST	PF	DQ	STL	TO	BLK	PTS	RPG	APG	PPG
52-53—Rochester	70	—	1665	176	534	.330	—	—	—	155	236	.657	—	—	183	186	253	16	—	—	—	507	2.6	2.7	7.2
53-54—Rochester	71	—	1891	250	691	.362	—	—	—	211	303	.696	—	—	211	238	221	6	—	—	—	711	3.0	3.4	10.0
54-55—Rochester	72	—	1807	251	721	.348	—	—	—	143	225	.636	—	—	211	246	179	1	—	—	—	645	2.9	3.4	9.0
55-56—Roch.-St. L.	70	—	1713	202	615	.328	—	—	—	110	185	.595	—	—	180	222	170	1	—	—	—	514	2.6	3.2	7.3
56-57—St. Louis	72	—	2344	239	725	.330	—	—	—	142	225	.631	—	—	222	367	213	2	—	—	—	620	3.1	5.1	8.6
57-58—St. Louis	72	—	2239	216	719	.300	—	—	—	134	221	.606	—	—	195	333	184	2	—	—	—	566	2.7	4.6	7.9
58-59—St. Louis	72	—	2235	248	692	.358	—	—	—	96	156	.615	—	—	164	298	221	2	—	—	—	592	2.3	4.1	8.2
59-60—St. Louis	25	—	334	33	93	.355	—	—	—	16	29	.552	—	—	24	49	42	1	—	—	—	82	1.0	2.0	3.3
REG. SEASON TOTALS	524	—	14228	1615	4790	.337	—	—	—	1007	1580	.637	—	—	1390	1939	1483	31	—	—	—	4237	2.7	3.7	8.1
PLAYOFF TOTALS	49	—	1518	191	505	.378	—	—	—	91	163	.558	—	—	149	203	163	7	—	—	—	473	3.0	4.1	9.7

McMILLAN, NATHANIEL (Nate, Mac) b. August 3, 1964 Ht. 6-5 Wt. 195 College—Chowan/North Carolina State

SEASON—TEAM	G	GS	MIN	FGM	FGA	PCT	3FGM	3FGA	PCT	FTM	FTA	PCT	O-RB	D-RB	TOT	AST	PF	DQ	STL	TO	BLK	PTS	RPG	APG	PPG
86-87—Seattle	71	50	1972	143	301	.475	0	7	.000	87	141	.617	101	230	331	583	238	4	125	155	45	373	4.7	8.2	5.3
87-88—Seattle	82	82	2453	235	496	.474	9	24	.375	145	205	.707	117	221	338	702	238	1	169	189	47	624	4.1	8.6	7.6
88-89—Seattle	75	74	2341	199	485	.410	15	70	.214	119	189	.630	143	245	388	696	236	3	156	211	42	532	5.2	9.3	7.1
89-90—Seattle	82	69	2338	207	438	.473	11	31	.355	98	153	.641	127	276	403	598	289	7	140	187	37	523	4.9	7.3	6.4
90-91—Seattle	78	0	1434	132	305	.433	17	48	.354	57	93	.613	71	180	251	371	211	6	104	122	20	338	3.2	4.8	4.3
91-92—Seattle	72	30	1652	177	405	.437	27	98	.276	54	84	.643	92	160	252	359	218	4	129	112	29	435	3.5	5.0	6.0
92-93—Seattle	73	25	1977	213	459	.464	25	65	.385	95	134	.709	84	222	306	384	240	6	173	139	33	546	4.2	5.3	7.5
93-94—Seattle	73	8	1887	177	396	.447	52	133	.391	31	55	.564	50	233	283	387	201	1	216	126	22	437	3.9	5.3	6.0
REG. SEASON TOTALS	606	338	16054	1483	3285	.451	156	476	.328	686	1054	.651	785	1767	2552	4080	1871	32	1212	1241	275	3808	4.2	6.7	6.3
PLAYOFF TOTALS	65	30	1548	142	371	.383	15	66	.227	71	115	.617	75	159	234	406	196	5	94	108	34	370	3.6	6.2	5.7

McMILLEN, CHARLES THOMAS (Tom) b. May 26, 1952 Ht. 6-11 Wt. 220 College—Maryland

SEASON—TEAM	G	GS	MIN	FGM	FGA	PCT	3FGM	3FGA	PCT	FTM	FTA	PCT	O-RB	D-RB	TOT	AST	PF	DQ	STL	TO	BLK	PTS	RPG	APG	PPG
75-76—Buffalo	50	—	708	96	222	.432	—	—	—	41	54	.759	64	122	186	69	87	1	7	—	6	233	3.7	1.4	4.7
76-77—Buffalo-N.Y.-K	76	—	1492	274	563	.487	—	—	—	96	123	.780	114	275	389	67	163	0	11	—	6	644	5.1	0.9	8.5
77-78—Atlanta	68	—	1683	280	568	.493	—	—	—	116	145	.800	151	265	416	84	233	8	33	109	16	676	6.1	1.2	9.9
78-79—Atlanta	82	—	1392	232	498	.466	—	—	—	106	119	.891	131	201	332	69	211	2	15	87	32	570	4.0	0.8	7.0
79-80—Atlanta	53	—	1071	191	382	.500	0	1	.000	81	107	.757	70	150	220	62	126	2	36	64	14	463	4.2	1.2	8.7
80-81—Atlanta	79	—	1564	253	519	.487	1	6	.167	80	108	.741	96	199	295	72	165	0	23	81	25	587	3.7	0.9	7.4
81-82—Atlanta	73	23	1792	291	572	.509	1	3	.333	140	170	.824	102	234	336	129	202	1	25	124	23	723	4.6	1.8	9.9
82-83—Atlanta	61	4	1364	198	424	.467	0	1	.000	108	133	.812	57	160	217	76	143	2	17	80	24	504	3.6	1.2	8.3
83-84—Washington	62	5	1294	222	447	.497	1	6	.167	127	156	.814	64	135	199	73	162	0	14	70	17	572	3.2	1.2	9.2
84-85—Washington	69	21	1547	252	534	.472	0	5	.000	112	135	.830	64	146	210	52	163	3	8	44	17	616	3.0	0.8	8.9
85-86—Washington	56	1	863	131	285	.460	0	1	.000	64	79	.810	44	69	113	35	85	0	9	34	10	326	2.0	0.6	5.8
REG. SEASON TOTALS	729	54	14770	2420	5014	.483	3	23	.130	1071	1329	.806	957	1956	2913	788	1740	19	198	693	190	5914	4.0	1.1	8.1
PLAYOFF TOTALS	26	0	430	58	132	.439	0	1	.000	23	29	.793	30	53	83	22	50	1	10	20	3	139	3.2	0.8	5.3

McMILLIAN, JAMES M. (Jim) b. March 11, 1948 Ht. 6-5 Wt. 225 College—Columbia

SEASON—TEAM	G	GS	MIN	FGM	FGA	PCT	3FGM	3FGA	PCT	FTM	FTA	PCT	O-RB	D-RB	TOT	AST	PF	DQ	STL	TO	BLK	PTS	RPG	APG	PPG
70-71—Los Angeles	81	—	1747	289	629	.459	—	—	—	100	130	.769	—	—	330	133	122	1	—	—	—	678	4.1	1.6	8.4
71-72—Los Angeles	80	—	3050	642	1331	.482	—	—	—	219	277	.791	—	—	522	209	209	0	—	—	—	1503	6.5	2.6	18.8
72-73—Los Angeles	81	—	2953	655	1431	.458	—	—	—	223	264	.845	—	—	447	221	176	0	—	—	—	1533	5.5	2.7	18.9
73-74—Buffalo	82	—	3322	600	1214	.494	—	—	—	325	379	.858	216	394	610	256	186	0	129	—	26	1525	7.4	3.1	18.6
74-75—Buffalo	62	—	2132	347	695	.499	—	—	—	194	231	.840	127	258	385	156	129	0	69	—	15	888	6.2	2.5	14.3
75-76—Buffalo	74	—	2610	492	918	.536	—	—	—	188	219	.858	134	256	390	205	141	0	88	—	14	1172	5.3	2.8	15.8
76-77—New York Knicks	67	—	2158	298	642	.464	—	—	—	67	86	.779	66	241	307	139	103	0	63	—	5	663	4.6	2.1	9.9
77-78—New York	81	—	1977	288	623	.462	—	—	—	115	134	.858	80	209	289	205	116	0	76	104	17	691	3.6	2.5	8.5
78-79—Portland	23	—	278	33	74	.446	—	—	—	17	21	.810	16	23	39	33	18	0	10	16	3	83	1.7	1.4	3.6
REG. SEASON TOTALS	631	—	20227	3644	7557	.482	—	—	—	1448	1741	.832	639	1381	3319	1557	1200	1	435	120	80	8736	5.3	2.5	13.8
PLAYOFF TOTALS	72	—	2722	497	1101	.451	—	—	—	200	253	.791	54	91	377	137	169	1	36	7	7	1194	5.2	1.9	16.6

McMILLON, SHELLIE JR. b. March 11, 1936 d. July 11, 1980 Ht. 6-5 Wt. 205 College—Bradley

SEASON—TEAM	G	GS	MIN	FGM	FGA	PCT	3FGM	3FGA	PCT	FTM	FTA	PCT	O-RB	D-RB	TOT	AST	PF	DQ	STL	TO	BLK	PTS	RPG	APG	PPG
58-59—Detroit	48	—	700	127	289	.439	—	—	—	55	104	.529	—	—	285	26	110	2	—	—	—	309	5.9	0.5	6.4
59-60—Detroit	75	—	1416	267	627	.426	—	—	—	132	199	.663	—	—	431	49	198	3	—	—	—	666	5.7	0.7	8.9
60-61—Detroit	78	—	1636	322	752	.428	—	—	—	140	201	.697	—	—	487	98	238	6	—	—	—	784	6.2	1.3	10.1
61-62—Detroit-St. L.	62	—	1225	265	591	.448	—	—	—	108	182	.593	—	—	368	59	202	10	—	—	—	638	5.9	1.0	10.3
REG. SEASON TOTALS	263	—	4977	981	2259	.434	—	—	—	435	686	.634	—	—	1571	232	748	21	—	—	—	2397	6.0	0.9	9.1
PLAYOFF TOTALS	9	—	168	28	71	.394	—	—	—	22	29	.759	—	—	39	9	37	3	—	—	—	78	4.3	1.0	8.7

McMULLAN, MALCOLM H. (Mal) b. August 23, 1927 Ht. 6-5 Wt. 210 College—Xavier (Ohio)/Kentucky

SEASON—TEAM	G	GS	MIN	FGM	FGA	PCT	3FGM	3FGA	PCT	FTM	FTA	PCT	O-RB	D-RB	TOT	AST	PF	DQ	STL	TO	BLK	PTS	RPG	APG	PPG
49-50—Indianapolis	58	—	—	123	380	.324	—	—	—	77	141	.546	—	—	—	87	212	—	—	—	—	323	—	1.5	5.6
50-51—Indianapolis	51	—	—	78	277	.282	—	—	—	48	82	.585	—	—	128	33	109	2	—	—	—	204	2.5	0.6	4.0
REG. SEASON TOTALS	109	—	—	201	657	.306	—	—	—	125	223	.561	—	—	128	120	321	2	—	—	—	527	2.5	1.1	4.8
PLAYOFF TOTALS	6	—	—	4	21	.190	—	—	—	6	9	.667	—	—	—	9	19	1	—	—	—	14	—	1.5	2.3

McNABB, CHESTER (Chet) b. 1921 Ht. 6-2 Wt. 200 College—Arizona State/West Texas State

SEASON—TEAM	G	GS	MIN	FGM	FGA	PCT	3FGM	3FGA	PCT	FTM	FTA	PCT	O-RB	D-RB	TOT	AST	PF	DQ	STL	TO	BLK	PTS	RPG	APG	PPG
47-48—Baltimore	2	—	—	0	1	.000	—	—	—	0	0	—	—	—	—	0	1	—	—	—	—	0	—	0.0	0.0
REG. SEASON TOTALS	2	—	—	0	1	.000	—	—	—	0	0	—	—	—	—	0	1	—	—	—	—	0	—	0.0	0.0

McNAMARA, MARK ROBERT b. June 8, 1959 Ht. 6-11 Wt. 235 College—Santa Clara/California

SEASON—TEAM	G	GS	MIN	FGM	FGA	PCT	3FGM	3FGA	PCT	FTM	FTA	PCT	O-RB	D-RB	TOT	AST	PF	DQ	STL	TO	BLK	PTS	RPG	APG	PPG
82-83—Philadelphia	36	2	182	29	64	.453	0	0	—	20	45	.444	34	42	76	7	42	1	3	36	3	78	2.1	0.2	2.2
83-84—San Antonio	70	3	1037	157	253	.621	0	0	—	74	157	.471	137	180	317	31	138	2	14	89	12	388	4.5	0.4	5.5
84-85—S.A.-K.C.	45	0	273	40	76	.526	0	0	—	32	62	.516	31	43	74	6	27	0	7	19	8	112	1.6	0.1	2.5
86-87—Philadelphia	11	1	113	14	30	.467	0	0	—	7	19	.368	17	19	36	2	17	0	1	8	0	35	3.3	0.2	3.2
87-88—Philadelphia	42	18	581	52	133	.391	0	0	—	48	66	.727	66	91	157	18	67	0	4	26	12	152	3.7	0.4	3.6
88-89—L.A. Lakers	39	0	318	32	64	.500	0	0	—	49	78	.628	38	62	100	10	51	0	4	24	3	113	2.6	0.3	2.9
89-90—L.A. Lakers	33	1	190	38	86	.442	0	0	—	26	40	.650	22	41	63	3	31	1	2	21	1	102	1.9	0.1	3.1
90-91—Orlando	2	0	13	0	1	.000	0	0	—	0	0	—	0	4	4	0	1	0	0	0	0	0	2.0	0.0	0.0
REG. SEASON TOTALS	278	25	2707	362	707	.512	0	0	—	256	467	.548	345	482	827	77	374	4	35	223	39	980	3.0	0.3	3.5
PLAYOFF TOTALS	8	0	16	5	9	.556	0	0	—	1	2	.500	0	4	4	—	1	0	0	0	0	11	0.5	0.0	1.4

McNAMEE, JOHN JOSEPH (Joe) b. September 24, 1926 Ht. 6-6 Wt. 210 College—San Francisco

SEASON—TEAM	G	GS	MIN	FGM	FGA	PCT	3FGM	3FGA	PCT	FTM	FTA	PCT	O-RB	D-RB	TOT	AST	PF	DQ	STL	TO	BLK	PTS	RPG	APG	PPG
50-51—Rochester	60	—	—	48	167	.287	—	—	—	27	42	.643	—	—	101	18	88	2	—	—	—	123	1.7	0.3	2.1
51-52—Roch.-Balt.	58	—	695	68	222	.306	—	—	—	30	50	.600	—	—	137	40	108	4	—	—	—	166	2.4	0.7	2.9
REG. SEASON TOTALS	118	—	695	116	389	.298	—	—	—	57	92	.620	—	—	238	58	196	6	—	—	—	289	2.0	0.5	2.4
PLAYOFF TOTALS	13	—	0	12	41	.293	—	—	—	9	12	.750	—	—	35	9	26	0	—	—	—	33	2.7	0.7	2.5

McNEALY, CHRISTOPHER (Chris) b. July 15, 1961 Ht. 6-7 Wt. 215 College—Santa Barbara CC/San Jose State

SEASON—TEAM	G	GS	MIN	FGM	FGA	PCT	3FGM	3FGA	PCT	FTM	FTA	PCT	O-RB	D-RB	TOT	AST	PF	DQ	STL	TO	BLK	PTS	RPG	APG	PPG
85-86—New York	30	6	627	70	144	.486	0	0	—	31	47	.660	62	141	203	41	88	2	38	35	12	171	6.8	1.4	5.7
86-87—New York	59	16	972	88	179	.492	0	0	—	52	80	.650	74	153	227	46	136	1	36	64	16	228	3.8	0.8	3.9
87-88—New York	19	0	265	23	74	.311	0	0	—	21	31	.677	24	40	64	23	50	1	16	17	2	67	3.4	1.2	3.5
REG. SEASON TOTALS	108	22	1864	181	397	.456	0	0	—	104	158	.658	160	334	494	110	274	4	90	116	30	466	4.6	1.0	4.3

McNEILL, LARRY (The Hawk) b. January 31, 1951 Ht. 6-9 Wt. 195 College—Marquette

SEASON—TEAM	G	GS	MIN	FGM	FGA	PCT	3FGM	3FGA	PCT	FTM	FTA	PCT	O-RB	D-RB	TOT	AST	PF	DQ	STL	TO	BLK	PTS	RPG	APG	PPG
73-74—Kansas City-Omaha	54	—	516	106	220	.482	—	—	—	99	140	.707	60	86	146	24	76	0	35	—	6	311	2.7	0.4	5.8
74-75—Kansas City-Omaha	80	—	1749	296	645	.459	—	—	—	189	241	.784	149	348	497	73	229	1	69	—	27	781	6.2	0.9	9.8
75-76—Kansas City	82	—	1613	295	610	.484	—	—	—	207	273	.758	157	353	510	72	244	2	51	—	32	797	6.2	0.9	9.7
76-77—N.Y.-G.S.	24	—	230	47	112	.420	—	—	—	52	61	.852	28	47	75	6	32	1	10	—	2	146	3.1	0.3	6.1
77-78—G.S.-Buffalo	46	—	940	162	356	.455	—	—	—	145	175	.829	80	122	202	47	114	1	18	67	11	469	4.4	1.0	10.2
78-79—Detroit	11	—	46	9	20	.450	—	—	—	11	12	.917	3	7	10	3	7	0	0	4	0	29	0.9	0.3	2.6
REG. SEASON TOTALS	297	—	5094	915	1963	.466	—	—	—	703	902	.779	477	963	1440	225	702	5	183	71	78	2533	4.8	0.8	8.5
PLAYOFF TOTALS	12	—	124	29	44	.659	—	—	—	19	24	.792	9	19	28	2	23	2	3	—	2	77	2.3	0.2	6.4

McNEILL, ROBERT J. (Bob) b. October 22, 1938 Ht. 6-1 Wt. 180 College—St. Joseph's (Pa.)

SEASON—TEAM	G	GS	MIN	FGM	FGA	PCT	3FGM	3FGA	PCT	FTM	FTA	PCT	O-RB	D-RB	TOT	AST	PF	DQ	STL	TO	BLK	PTS	RPG	APG	PPG
60-61—New York	75	—	1387	166	427	.389	—	—	—	105	126	.833	—	—	123	238	148	2	—	—	—	437	1.6	3.2	5.8
61-62—Phil.-L.A.	50	—	441	56	136	.412	—	—	—	26	34	.765	—	—	56	89	56	0	—	—	—	138	1.1	1.8	2.8
REG. SEASON TOTALS	125	—	1828	222	563	.394	—	—	—	131	160	.819	—	—	179	327	204	2	—	—	—	575	1.4	2.6	4.6
PLAYOFF TOTALS	5	—	30	4	7	.571	—	—	—	1	2	.500	—	—	6	5	6	0	—	—	—	9	1.2	1.0	1.8

McNULTY, CARL EDWIN b. February 14, 1930 Ht. 6-3 Wt. 185 College—Purdue

SEASON—TEAM	G	GS	MIN	FGM	FGA	PCT	3FGM	3FGA	PCT	FTM	FTA	PCT	O-RB	D-RB	TOT	AST	PF	DQ	STL	TO	BLK	PTS	RPG	APG	PPG
54-55—Milwaukee	1	—	14	1	6	.167	—	—	—	0	0	—	—	—	0	0	1	0	—	—	—	2	0.0	0.0	2.0
REG. SEASON TOTALS	1	—	14	1	6	.167	—	—	—	0	0	—	—	—	0	0	1	0	—	—	—	2	0.0	0.0	2.0

McPIPE, ROY b. May 5, 1950 Ht. 6-3 Wt. 205 College—Eastern Montana

SEASON—TEAM	G	GS	MIN	FGM	FGA	PCT	3FGM	3FGA	PCT	FTM	FTA	PCT	O-RB	D-RB	TOT	AST	PF	DQ	STL	TO	BLK	PTS	RPG	APG	PPG
74-75—Utah (A)	5	—	44	8	24	.333	2	4	.500	3	4	.750	2	3	5	1	5	—	1	10	0	21	1.0	0.2	4.2
REG. ABA TOTALS	5	—	44	8	24	.333	2	4	.500	3	4	.750	2	3	5	1	5	—	1	10	0	21	1.0	0.2	4.2

McQUEEN, COZELL b. January 18, 1962 Ht. 6-11 Wt. 235 College—North Carolina State

SEASON—TEAM	G	GS	MIN	FGM	FGA	PCT	3FGM	3FGA	PCT	FTM	FTA	PCT	O-RB	D-RB	TOT	AST	PF	DQ	STL	TO	BLK	PTS	RPG	APG	PPG
86-87—Detroit	3	0	7	3	3	1.000	0	0	—	0	0	—	3	5	8	0	1	0	0	0	1	6	2.7	0.0	2.0
REG. SEASON TOTALS	3	0	7	3	3	1.000	0	0	—	0	0	—	3	5	8	0	1	0	0	0	1	6	2.7	0.0	2.0

McREYNOLDS, THALES b. June 8, 1943 d. July 3, 1988 Ht. 6-3 Wt. 185 College—Miles

SEASON—TEAM	G	GS	MIN	FGM	FGA	PCT	3FGM	3FGA	PCT	FTM	FTA	PCT	O-RB	D-RB	TOT	AST	PF	DQ	STL	TO	BLK	PTS	RPG	APG	PPG
65-66—Baltimore	5	—	28	1	12	.083	—	—	—	1	2	.500	—	—	6	1	0	0	—	—	—	3	1.2	0.2	0.6
REG. SEASON TOTALS	5	—	28	1	12	.083	—	—	—	1	2	.500	—	—	6	1	0	0	—	—	—	3	1.2	0.2	0.6

McWILLIAMS, ERIC LEE b. April 18, 1950 Ht. 6-8 Wt. 200 College—Pasadena CC/Long Beach State

SEASON—TEAM	G	GS	MIN	FGM	FGA	PCT	3FGM	3FGA	PCT	FTM	FTA	PCT	O-RB	D-RB	TOT	AST	PF	DQ	STL	TO	BLK	PTS	RPG	APG	PPG
72-73—Houston	44	—	245	34	98	.347	—	—	—	18	37	.486	—	—	60	5	46	0	—	—	—	86	1.4	0.1	2.0
REG. SEASON TOTALS	44	—	245	34	98	.347	—	—	—	18	37	.486	—	—	60	5	46	0	—	—	—	86	1.4	0.1	2.0

MEARNS, GEORGE b. April 18, 1922 Ht. 6-3 Wt. 175 College—Rhode Island

SEASON—TEAM	G	GS	MIN	FGM	FGA	PCT	3FGM	3FGA	PCT	FTM	FTA	PCT	O-RB	D-RB	TOT	AST	PF	DQ	STL	TO	BLK	PTS	RPG	APG	PPG
46-47—Providence	57	—	—	128	478	.268	—	—	—	126	175	.720	—	—	—	35	137	—	—	—	—	382	—	0.6	6.7
47-48—Providence	24	—	—	23	115	.200	—	—	—	15	31	.484	—	—	—	10	65	—	—	—	—	61	—	0.4	2.5
REG. SEASON TOTALS	81	—	—	151	593	.255	—	—	—	141	206	.684	—	—	—	45	202	—	—	—	—	443	—	0.6	5.5

MEE, LaFARRELL DARNELL (Darnell) b. February 11, 1971 Ht. 6-5 Wt. 175 College—Western Kentucky

SEASON—TEAM	G	GS	MIN	FGM	FGA	PCT	3FGM	3FGA	PCT	FTM	FTA	PCT	O-RB	D-RB	TOT	AST	PF	DQ	STL	TO	BLK	PTS	RPG	APG	PPG
93-94—Denver	38	0	285	28	88	.318	5	24	.208	12	27	.444	17	18	35	16	34	0	15	18	13	73	0.9	0.4	1.9
REG. SEASON TOTALS	38	0	285	28	88	.318	5	24	.208	12	27	.444	17	18	35	16	34	0	15	18	13	73	0.9	0.4	1.9
PLAYOFF TOTALS	3	0	30	3	6	.500	1	4	.250	0	0	—	0	2	2	2	4	0	3	3	0	7	0.7	0.7	2.3

MEELY, CLIFF b. July 10, 1947 Ht. 6-8 Wt. 215 College—Northeastern JC/Colorado

SEASON—TEAM	G	GS	MIN	FGM	FGA	PCT	3FGM	3FGA	PCT	FTM	FTA	PCT	O-RB	D-RB	TOT	AST	PF	DQ	STL	TO	BLK	PTS	RPG	APG	PPG
71-72—Houston	77	—	1815	315	776	.406	—	—	—	133	197	.675	—	—	507	119	254	9	—	—	—	763	6.6	1.5	9.9
72-73—Houston	82	—	1694	268	657	.408	—	—	—	92	137	.672	—	—	496	91	263	6	—	—	—	628	6.0	1.1	7.7
73-74—Houston	77	—	1754	330	773	.427	—	—	—	90	140	.643	103	336	439	124	234	5	53	—	77	750	5.7	1.6	9.7
74-75—Houston	48	—	753	156	349	.447	—	—	—	68	94	.723	55	109	164	45	117	4	21	—	21	380	3.4	0.9	7.9
75-76—Houston-L.A.	34	—	313	52	132	.394	—	—	—	33	48	.688	22	75	97	19	61	1	14	—	8	137	2.9	0.6	4.0
REG. SEASON TOTALS	318	—	6329	1121	2687	.417	—	—	—	416	616	.675	180	520	1703	398	929	25	88	—	106	2658	5.4	1.3	8.4

MEENTS, SCOTT E. b. January 4, 1964 Ht. 6-10 Wt. 225 College—Illinois

SEASON—TEAM	G	GS	MIN	FGM	FGA	PCT	3FGM	3FGA	PCT	FTM	FTA	PCT	O-RB	D-RB	TOT	AST	PF	DQ	STL	TO	BLK	PTS	RPG	APG	PPG
89-90—Seattle	26	0	148	19	44	.432	0	0	—	17	23	.739	7	23	30	7	12	0	4	9	3	55	1.2	0.3	2.1
90-91—Seattle	13	0	53	7	28	.250	1	1	1.000	2	4	.500	3	7	10	8	5	0	7	6	4	17	0.8	0.6	1.3
REG. SEASON TOTALS	39	0	201	26	72	.361	1	1	1.000	19	27	.704	10	30	40	15	17	0	11	15	7	72	1.0	0.4	1.8
PLAYOFF TOTALS	2	0	8	2	4	.500	0	0	—	0	1	.000	0	1	1	—	1	0	1	0	0	4	0.5	0.0	2.0

MEHEN, RICHARD P. (**Dick**) b. May 20, 1922 d. December 14, 1986 Ht. 6-6 Wt. 195 College—Tennessee

SEASON—TEAM	G	GS	MIN	FGM	FGA	PCT	3FGM	3FGA	PCT	FTM	FTA	PCT	O-RB	D-RB	TOT	AST	PF	DQ	STL	TO	BLK	PTS	RPG	APG	PPG
47-48—Toledo (N)	57	—	—	151	—	—	—	—	—	85	125	.680	—	—	—	—	95	—	—	—	—	387	—	—	6.8
48-49—Waterloo (N)	62	—	—	315	—	—	—	—	—	211	304	.694	—	—	—	195	—	—	—	—	—	841	—	—	13.6
49-50—Waterloo	62	—	—	347	826	.420	—	—	—	198	281	.705	—	—	—	191	203	—	—	—	—	892	—	3.1	14.4
50-51—Balt.-Boston-Ft. Wayne	66	—	—	192	532	.361	—	—	—	90	123	.732	—	—	223	188	149	4	—	—	—	474	3.4	2.8	7.2
51-52—Milwaukee	65	—	2294	293	824	.356	—	—	—	117	167	.701	—	—	282	171	209	10	—	—	—	703	4.3	2.6	10.8
REG. NBA TOTALS	193	—	2294	832	2182	.381	—	—	—	405	571	.709	—	—	505	550	561	14	—	—	—	2069	3.9	2.8	10.7
REG. NBL TOTALS	119	—	—	466	—	—	—	—	—	296	429	.690	—	—	—	—	290	—	—	—	—	1228	—	—	10.3
NBA PLAYOFF TOTALS	3	—	0	12	29	.414	—	—	—	2	4	.500	—	—	14	3	9	0	—	—	—	26	4.7	1.0	8.7

MEINEKE, DONALD E. (**Don, Monk**) b. October 30, 1930 Ht. 6-7 Wt. 210 College—Dayton

SEASON—TEAM	G	GS	MIN	FGM	FGA	PCT	3FGM	3FGA	PCT	FTM	FTA	PCT	O-RB	D-RB	TOT	AST	PF	DQ	STL	TO	BLK	PTS	RPG	APG	PPG
52-53—Fort Wayne	68	—	2250	240	630	.381	—	—	—	245	313	.783	—	—	466	148	334	26	—	—	—	725	6.9	2.2	10.7
53-54—Fort Wayne	71	—	1466	135	393	.344	—	—	—	136	169	.805	—	—	372	81	214	6	—	—	—	406	5.2	1.1	5.7
54-55—Fort Wayne	68	—	1026	136	366	.372	—	—	—	119	170	.700	—	—	246	64	153	1	—	—	—	391	3.6	0.9	5.8
55-56—Rochester	69	—	1248	154	414	.372	—	—	—	181	232	.780	—	—	316	102	191	4	—	—	—	489	4.6	1.5	7.1
57-58—Cincinnati	67	—	792	125	351	.356	—	—	—	77	119	.647	—	—	226	38	155	3	—	—	—	327	3.4	0.6	4.9
REG. SEASON TOTALS	343	—	6782	790	2154	.367	—	—	—	758	1003	.756	—	—	1626	433	1047	40	—	—	—	2338	4.7	1.3	6.8
PLAYOFF TOTALS	25	—	508	40	114	.351	—	—	—	66	88	.750	—	—	100	26	73	5	—	—	—	146	4.0	1.0	5.8

MEINHOLD, CARL MARVIN (**Red**) b. March 29, 1926 Ht. 6-2 Wt. 185 College—Long Island University

SEASON—TEAM	G	GS	MIN	FGM	FGA	PCT	3FGM	3FGA	PCT	FTM	FTA	PCT	O-RB	D-RB	TOT	AST	PF	DQ	STL	TO	BLK	PTS	RPG	APG	PPG
47-48—Baltimore	48	—	—	108	356	.303	—	—	—	37	60	.617	—	—	—	16	64	—	—	—	—	253	—	0.3	5.3
48-49—Chicago-Prov.	50	—	—	101	306	.330	—	—	—	61	96	.635	—	—	—	47	60	—	—	—	—	263	—	0.9	5.3
REG. SEASON TOTALS	98	—	—	209	662	.316	—	—	—	98	156	.628	—	—	—	63	124	—	—	—	—	516	—	0.6	5.3
PLAYOFF TOTALS	11	—	—	17	67	.254	—	—	—	6	13	.462	—	—	—	6	—	—	—	—	—	40	—	0.0	3.6

MELCHIONNI, GARY DENNIS b. January 19, 1951 Ht. 6-2 Wt. 185 College—Duke

SEASON—TEAM	G	GS	MIN	FGM	FGA	PCT	3FGM	3FGA	PCT	FTM	FTA	PCT	O-RB	D-RB	TOT	AST	PF	DQ	STL	TO	BLK	PTS	RPG	APG	PPG
73-74—Phoenix	69	—	1251	202	439	.460	—	—	—	92	107	.860	46	96	142	142	85	1	41	—	9	496	2.1	2.1	7.2
74-75—Phoenix	68	—	1529	232	539	.430	—	—	—	114	141	.809	45	142	187	156	116	1	48	—	12	578	2.8	2.3	8.5
REG. SEASON TOTALS	137	—	2780	434	978	.444	—	—	—	206	248	.831	91	238	329	298	201	2	89	—	21	1074	2.4	2.2	7.8

MELCHIONNI, WILLIAM P. (**Bill**) b. October 19, 1944 Ht. 6-1 Wt. 165 College—Villanova

SEASON—TEAM	G	GS	MIN	FGM	FGA	PCT	3FGM	3FGA	PCT	FTM	FTA	PCT	O-RB	D-RB	TOT	AST	PF	DQ	STL	TO	BLK	PTS	RPG	APG	PPG
66-67—Philadelphia	73	—	692	138	353	.391	—	—	—	39	60	.650	—	—	98	98	73	0	—	—	—	315	1.3	1.3	4.3
67-68—Philadelphia	71	—	758	146	336	.435	—	—	—	33	47	.702	—	—	104	105	75	0	—	—	—	325	1.5	1.5	4.6
69-70—New York (A)	80	—	3157	479	1030	.465	5	28	.179	255	311	.820	—	—	230	457	282	7	—	—	—	1218	2.9	5.7	15.2
70-71—New York (A)	81	—	3284	561	1244	.451	2	22	.091	301	370	.814	—	—	237	672	273	—	—	—	—	1425	2.9	8.3	17.6
71-72—New York (A)	80	—	3326	672	1346	.499	2	19	.105	336	416	.808	—	—	248	669	275	—	—	314	—	1682	3.1	8.4	21.0
72-73—New York (A)	61	—	1849	291	646	.450	6	15	.400	163	194	.840	19	108	127	453	155	0	—	184	—	751	2.1	7.4	12.3
73-74—New York (A)	56	—	1146	116	276	.420	5	23	.217	59	71	.831	13	64	77	207	94	—	51	86	5	296	1.4	3.7	5.3
74-75—New York (A)	77	—	1384	201	413	.487	8	27	.296	62	78	.795	12	63	75	320	105	—	69	106	7	472	1.0	4.2	6.1
75-76—New York (A)	67	—	1191	149	358	.416	9	23	.391	79	93	.849	13	75	88	266	66	—	52	95	8	386	1.3	4.0	5.8
REG. NBA TOTALS	144	—	1450	284	689	.412	—	—	—	72	107	.673	—	—	202	203	148	0	—	—	—	640	1.4	1.4	4.4
REG. ABA TOTALS	502	—	15337	2469	5313	.465	37	157	.236	1255	1533	.819	57	310	1082	3044	1250	7	172	785	20	6230	2.2	6.1	12.4
NBA PLAYOFF TOTALS	10	—	55	8	26	.308	—	—	—	2	6	.333	—	—	7	11	4	0	—	—	—	18	0.7	1.1	1.8
ABA PLAYOFF TOTALS	45	—	1275	203	450	.451	3	18	.167	118	142	.831	6	20	91	227	139	5	4	65	1	527	2.0	5.0	11.7
ABA ALL-STAR TOTALS	3	—	66	8	20	.400	0	0	—	5	6	.833	3	8	11	8	4	0	1	6	0	21	3.7	2.7	7.0

MELVIN, EDWARD H. (**Ed**) b. February 13, 1916 Ht. 5-9 Wt. 170 College—Duquesne

SEASON—TEAM	G	GS	MIN	FGM	FGA	PCT	3FGM	3FGA	PCT	FTM	FTA	PCT	O-RB	D-RB	TOT	AST	PF	DQ	STL	TO	BLK	PTS	RPG	APG	PPG
46-47—Pittsburgh	57	—	—	99	376	.263	—	—	—	83	127	.654	—	—	—	37	150	—	—	—	—	281	—	0.6	4.9
REG. SEASON TOTALS	57	—	—	99	376	.263	—	—	—	83	127	.654	—	—	—	37	150	—	—	—	—	281	—	0.6	4.9

MEMINGER, DEAN P. (The Dream) b. May 13, 1948 Ht. 6-1 Wt. 175 College—Marquette

SEASON—TEAM	G	GS	MIN	FGM	FGA	PCT	3FGM	3FGA	PCT	FTM	FTA	PCT	O-RB	D-RB	TOT	AST	PF	DQ	STL	TO	BLK	PTS	RPG	APG	PPG
71-72—New York	78	—	1173	139	293	.474	—	—	—	79	140	.564	—	—	185	103	137	0	—	—	—	357	2.4	1.3	4.6
72-73—New York	80	—	1453	188	365	.515	—	—	—	81	129	.628	—	—	229	133	109	1	—	—	—	457	2.9	1.7	5.7
73-74—New York	78	—	2079	274	539	.508	—	—	—	103	160	.644	125	156	281	162	161	0	62	—	8	651	3.6	2.1	8.3
74-75—Atlanta	80	—	2177	233	500	.466	—	—	—	168	263	.639	84	130	214	397	160	0	118	—	11	634	2.7	5.0	7.9
75-76—Atlanta	68	—	1418	155	379	.409	—	—	—	100	152	.658	65	86	151	222	116	0	54	—	8	410	2.2	3.3	6.0
76-77—New York Knicks	32	—	254	15	36	.417	—	—	—	13	23	.565	12	14	26	29	17	0	8	—	1	43	0.8	0.9	1.3
REG. SEASON TOTALS	416	—	8554	1004	2112	.475	—	—	—	544	867	.627	286	386	1086	1046	700	1	242	—	28	2552	2.6	2.5	6.1
PLAYOFF TOTALS	45	—	779	66	145	.455	—	—	—	37	66	.561	9	15	104	82	85	1	4	—	0	169	2.3	1.8	3.8

MENCEL, CHARLES J. (Chuck) b. April 21, 1933 Ht. 6-0 Wt. 170 College—Minnesota

SEASON—TEAM	G	GS	MIN	FGM	FGA	PCT	3FGM	3FGA	PCT	FTM	FTA	PCT	O-RB	D-RB	TOT	AST	PF	DQ	STL	TO	BLK	PTS	RPG	APG	PPG
55-56—Minneapolis	69	—	973	120	375	.320	—	—	—	78	96	.813	—	—	110	132	74	1	—	—	—	318	1.6	1.9	4.6
56-57—Minneapolis	72	—	1848	243	688	.353	—	—	—	179	240	.746	—	—	237	201	95	0	—	—	—	665	3.3	2.8	9.2
REG. SEASON TOTALS	141	—	2821	363	1063	.341	—	—	—	257	336	.765	—	—	347	333	169	1	—	—	—	983	2.5	2.4	7.0
PLAYOFF TOTALS	8	—	150	19	55	.345	—	—	—	13	16	.813	—	—	18	14	11	0	—	—	—	51	2.3	1.8	6.4

MENGELT, JOHN P. (Crash) b. October 16, 1949 Ht. 6-2½ Wt. 195 College—Auburn

SEASON—TEAM	G	GS	MIN	FGM	FGA	PCT	3FGM	3FGA	PCT	FTM	FTA	PCT	O-RB	D-RB	TOT	AST	PF	DQ	STL	TO	BLK	PTS	RPG	APG	PPG
71-72—Cincinnati	78	—	1438	287	605	.474	—	—	—	208	252	.825	—	—	148	146	163	0	—	—	—	782	1.9	1.9	10.0
72-73—K.C.-Omaha-Detroit	79	—	1647	320	651	.492	—	—	—	127	160	.794	—	—	181	153	148	0	—	—	—	767	2.3	1.9	9.7
73-74—Detroit	77	—	1555	249	558	.446	—	—	—	182	229	.795	40	166	206	148	164	2	68	—	7	680	2.7	1.9	8.8
74-75—Detroit	80	—	1995	336	701	.479	—	—	—	211	248	.851	38	153	191	201	198	2	72	—	4	883	2.4	2.5	11.0
75-76—Detroit	67	—	1105	264	540	.489	—	—	—	192	237	.810	27	88	115	108	138	1	40	—	5	720	1.7	1.6	10.7
76-77—Chicago	61	—	1178	209	458	.456	—	—	—	89	113	.788	29	81	110	114	102	2	37	—	4	507	1.8	1.9	8.3
77-78—Chicago	81	—	1767	325	675	.481	—	—	—	184	238	.773	41	88	129	232	169	0	51	124	4	834	1.6	2.9	10.3
78-79—Chicago	75	—	1705	338	689	.491	—	—	—	150	182	.824	25	93	118	187	148	1	46	120	4	826	1.6	2.5	11.0
79-80—Chicago	36	—	387	90	166	.542	0	6	.000	39	49	.796	3	20	23	38	54	0	10	36	0	219	0.6	1.1	6.1
80-81—Golden State	2	—	11	0	4	.000	0	0	—	0	0	—	0	2	2	2	0	0	0	0	0	0	1.0	1.0	0.0
REG. SEASON TOTALS	636	—	12788	2418	5047	.479	0	6	.000	1382	1708	.809	203	689	1221	1329	1284	8	324	280	28	6218	1.9	2.1	9.8
PLAYOFF TOTALS	19	—	290	62	119	.521	0	0	—	43	55	.782	6	27	33	33	40	0	11	—	2	167	1.7	1.7	8.8

MENKE, KENNETH H. (Ken, Angles) b. October 2, 1922 Ht. 6-0 Wt. 170 College—Illinois

SEASON—TEAM	G	GS	MIN	FGM	FGA	PCT	3FGM	3FGA	PCT	FTM	FTA	PCT	O-RB	D-RB	TOT	AST	PF	DQ	STL	TO	BLK	PTS	RPG	APG	PPG
47-48—Fort Wayne (N)	44	—	—	39	—	—	—	—	—	45	57	.789	—	—	—	49	—	—	—	—	—	123	—	—	2.8
49-50—Waterloo	6	—	—	6	17	.353	—	—	—	3	8	.375	—	—	—	7	7	—	—	—	—	15	—	1.2	2.5
REG. NBA TOTALS	6	—	—	6	17	.353	—	—	—	3	8	.375	—	—	—	7	7	—	—	—	—	15	—	1.2	2.5
REG. NBL TOTALS	44	—	—	39	—	—	—	—	—	45	57	.789	—	—	—	49	—	—	—	—	—	123	—	—	2.8
NBL PLAYOFF TOTALS	1	—	—	1	—	—	—	—	—	0	—	—	—	—	—	1	—	—	—	—	—	2	—	—	2.0

MENYARD, DeWITT b. 1944 Ht. 6-10 Wt. 210 College—Allan Hancock/Utah

SEASON—TEAM	G	GS	MIN	FGM	FGA	PCT	3FGM	3FGA	PCT	FTM	FTA	PCT	O-RB	D-RB	TOT	AST	PF	DQ	STL	TO	BLK	PTS	RPG	APG	PPG
67-68—Houston (A)	71	—	1756	256	692	.370	0	0	—	131	197	.665	—	—	551	84	218	5	—	99	—	643	7.8	1.2	9.1
REG. ABA TOTALS	71	—	1756	256	692	.370	0	0	—	131	197	.665	—	—	551	84	218	5	—	99	—	643	7.8	1.2	9.1
ABA PLAYOFF TOTALS	3	—	64	7	18	.389	0	1	.000	1	3	.333	—	—	11	0	8	0	—	3	—	15	3.7	0.0	5.0
ABA ALL-STAR TOTALS	1	—	6	2	4	.500	0	0	—	0	1	.000	1	1	2	0	2	0	—	0	—	4	2.0	0.0	4.0

MERIWEATHER, JOE C. b. October 26, 1953 Ht. 6-10 Wt. 215 College—Southern Illinois

SEASON—TEAM	G	GS	MIN	FGM	FGA	PCT	3FGM	3FGA	PCT	FTM	FTA	PCT	O-RB	D-RB	TOT	AST	PF	DQ	STL	TO	BLK	PTS	RPG	APG	PPG
75-76—Houston	81	—	2042	338	684	.494	—	—	—	154	239	.644	163	353	516	82	219	4	36	—	120	830	6.4	1.0	10.2
76-77—Atlanta	73	—	2068	319	607	.526	—	—	—	182	255	.714	216	380	596	82	324	21	41	—	82	820	8.2	1.1	11.2
77-78—New Orleans	54	—	1277	194	411	.472	—	—	—	87	133	.654	135	237	372	58	188	8	18	94	118	475	6.9	1.1	8.8
78-79—N.O.N.Y.	77	—	1693	242	500	.484	—	—	—	126	187	.674	143	266	409	79	283	10	40	130	94	610	5.3	1.0	7.9
79-80—New York	65	—	1565	252	477	.528	0	1	.000	78	121	.645	122	228	350	66	239	8	37	112	120	582	5.4	1.0	9.0
80-81—Kansas City	74	—	1514	206	415	.496	0	0	—	148	213	.695	126	267	393	77	219	4	27	125	80	560	5.3	1.0	7.6
81-82—Kansas City	18	10	380	47	91	.516	0	0	—	31	40	.775	25	63	88	17	68	1	13	25	21	125	4.9	0.9	6.9
82-83—Kansas City	78	74	1706	258	453	.570	0	0	—	102	163	.626	150	274	424	64	285	4	47	118	86	618	5.4	0.8	7.9
83-84—Kansas City	73	31	1501	193	363	.532	0	0	—	94	123	.764	111	242	353	51	247	8	35	83	61	480	4.8	0.7	6.6
84-85—Kansas City	76	4	1061	121	243	.498	1	2	.500	96	124	.774	94	169	263	27	181	1	17	50	28	339	3.5	0.4	4.5
REG. SEASON TOTALS	669	119	14807	2170	4244	.511	1	3	.333	1098	1598	.687	1285	2479	3764	603	2253	69	311	737	810	5439	5.6	0.9	8.1
PLAYOFF TOTALS	10	0	199	24	49	.490	0	0	—	8	14	.571	12	19	31	5	31	1	5	9	7	56	3.1	0.5	5.6

MERIWETHER, PORTER L. b. March 16, 1940 Ht. 6-2 Wt. 180 College—Tennessee State

SEASON—TEAM	G	GS	MIN	FGM	FGA	PCT	3FGM	3FGA	PCT	FTM	FTA	PCT	O-RB	D-RB	TOT	AST	PF	DQ	STL	TO	BLK	PTS	RPG	APG	PPG
62-63—Syracuse	31	—	268	48	122	.393	—	—	—	23	33	.697	—	—	29	43	19	0	—	—	—	119	0.9	1.4	3.8
REG. SEASON TOTALS	31	—	268	48	122	.393	—	—	—	23	33	.697	—	—	29	43	19	0	—	—	—	119	0.9	1.4	3.8

MESCHERY, THOMAS N. (Tom) b. October 26, 1938 Ht. 6-6 Wt. 215 College—St. Mary's (Ca.)

SEASON—TEAM	G	GS	MIN	FGM	FGA	PCT	3FGM	3FGA	PCT	FTM	FTA	PCT	O-RB	D-RB	TOT	AST	PF	DQ	STL	TO	BLK	PTS	RPG	APG	PPG
61-62—Philadelphia	80	—	2509	375	929	.404	—	—	—	216	262	.824	—	—	729	145	330	15	—	—	—	966	9.1	1.8	12.1
62-63—San Francisco	64	—	2245	397	935	.425	—	—	—	228	313	.728	—	—	624	104	249	11	—	—	—	1022	9.8	1.6	16.0
63-64—San Francisco	80	—	2422	436	951	.458	—	—	—	207	295	.702	—	—	612	149	288	6	—	—	—	1079	7.7	1.9	13.5
64-65—San Francisco	79	—	2408	361	917	.394	—	—	—	278	370	.751	—	—	655	106	279	6	—	—	—	1000	8.3	1.3	12.7
65-66—San Francisco	80	—	2383	401	895	.448	—	—	—	224	293	.765	—	—	716	81	285	7	—	—	—	1026	9.0	1.0	12.8
66-67—San Francisco	72	—	1846	293	706	.415	—	—	—	175	244	.717	—	—	549	94	264	8	—	—	—	761	7.6	1.3	10.6
67-68—Seattle	82	—	2857	473	1008	.469	—	—	—	244	345	.707	—	—	840	193	323	14	—	—	—	1190	10.2	2.4	14.5
68-69—Seattle	82	—	2673	462	1019	.453	—	—	—	220	299	.736	—	—	822	194	304	7	—	—	—	1144	10.0	2.4	14.0
69-70—Seattle	80	—	2294	394	818	.482	—	—	—	196	248	.790	—	—	666	157	317	13	—	—	—	984	8.3	2.0	12.3
70-71—Seattle	79	—	1822	285	615	.463	—	—	—	162	216	.750	—	—	485	108	202	2	—	—	—	732	6.1	1.4	9.3
REG. SEASON TOTALS	778	—	23459	3877	8793	.441	—	—	—	2150	2885	.745	—	—	6698	1331	2841	89	—	—	—	9904	8.6	1.7	12.7
PLAYOFF TOTALS	39	—	1321	248	570	.435	—	—	—	140	173	.809	—	—	344	78	153	7	—	—	—	636	8.8	2.0	16.3
ALL-STAR TOTALS	1	—	8	1	3	.333	—	—	—	1	2	.500	—	—	1	1	1	0	—	—	—	3	1.0	1.0	3.0

MEYER, WILLIAM JOSEPH (Bill) b. August 30, 1943 Ht. 6-3 Wt. 195 College—Hiram Scott

SEASON—TEAM	G	GS	MIN	FGM	FGA	PCT	3FGM	3FGA	PCT	FTM	FTA	PCT	O-RB	D-RB	TOT	AST	PF	DQ	STL	TO	BLK	PTS	RPG	APG	PPG
67-68—Pittsburgh (A)	7	—	45	10	22	.455	0	0	—	2	2	1.000	—	—	5	1	7	0	—	2	—	22	0.7	0.1	3.1
REG. ABA TOTALS	7	—	45	10	22	.455	0	0	—	2	2	1.000	—	—	5	1	7	0	—	2	—	22	0.7	0.1	3.1

MEYERS, DAVID WILLIAM (Dave) b. April 21, 1953 Ht. 6-9 Wt. 215 College—UCLA

SEASON—TEAM	G	GS	MIN	FGM	FGA	PCT	3FGM	3FGA	PCT	FTM	FTA	PCT	O-RB	D-RB	TOT	AST	PF	DQ	STL	TO	BLK	PTS	RPG	APG	PPG
75-76—Milwaukee	72	—	1589	198	472	.419	—	—	—	135	210	.643	121	324	445	100	145	0	72	—	25	531	6.2	1.4	7.4
76-77—Milwaukee	50	—	1262	179	383	.467	—	—	—	127	192	.661	122	219	341	86	152	4	42	—	32	485	6.8	1.7	9.7
77-78—Milwaukee	80	—	2416	432	938	.461	—	—	—	314	435	.722	144	393	537	241	240	2	86	213	46	1178	6.7	3.0	14.7
79-80—Milwaukee	79	—	2204	399	830	.481	1	5	.200	156	246	.634	140	308	448	225	218	3	72	182	40	955	5.7	2.8	12.1
REG. SEASON TOTALS	281	—	7471	1208	2623	.461	1	5	.200	732	1083	.676	527	1244	1771	652	755	9	272	395	143	3149	6.3	2.3	11.2
PLAYOFF TOTALS	19	—	528	75	172	.436	0	3	.000	56	89	.629	45	78	123	51	65	1	17	40	17	206	6.5	2.7	10.8

MIASEK, STANLEY (Stan) b. August 8, 1924 d. October 18, 1989 Ht. 6-5 Wt. 210 College—None

SEASON—TEAM	G	GS	MIN	FGM	FGA	PCT	3FGM	3FGA	PCT	FTM	FTA	PCT	O-RB	D-RB	TOT	AST	PF	DQ	STL	TO	BLK	PTS	RPG	APG	PPG
46-47—Detroit	60	—	—	331	1154	.287	—	—	—	233	385	.605	—	—	—	93	208	—	—	—	—	895	—	1.6	14.9
47-48—Chicago	48	—	—	263	867	.303	—	—	—	190	310	.613	—	—	—	31	192	—	—	—	—	716	—	0.6	14.9
48-49—Chicago	58	—	—	169	488	.346	—	—	—	113	216	.523	—	—	—	57	208	—	—	—	—	451	—	1.0	7.8
49-50—Chicago	68	—	—	176	462	.381	—	—	—	146	221	.661	—	—	—	75	264	—	—	—	—	498	—	1.1	7.3
51-52—Baltimore	66	—	2174	258	707	.365	—	—	—	263	372	.707	—	—	639	140	257	12	—	—	—	779	9.7	2.1	11.8
52-53—Balt.-Milw.	65	—	1584	178	488	.365	—	—	—	156	248	.629	—	—	360	122	229	13	—	—	—	512	5.5	1.9	7.9
REG. SEASON TOTALS	365	—	3758	1375	4166	.330	—	—	—	1101	1752	.628	—	—	999	518	1358	25	—	—	—	3851	7.6	1.4	10.6
PLAYOFF TOTALS	8	—	0	36	96	.375	—	—	—	25	42	.595	—	—	—	4	38	1	—	—	—	97	—	0.5	12.1

MICHEAUX, LARRY WAYNE b. March 24, 1960 Ht. 6-9 Wt. 220 College—Houston

SEASON—TEAM	G	GS	MIN	FGM	FGA	PCT	3FGM	3FGA	PCT	FTM	FTA	PCT	O-RB	D-RB	TOT	AST	PF	DQ	STL	TO	BLK	PTS	RPG	APG	PPG
83-84—Kansas City	39	0	332	49	90	.544	0	0	—	21	39	.538	40	73	113	19	46	0	21	21	11	119	2.9	0.5	3.1
84-85—Milw.-Houston	57	0	565	91	157	.580	0	3	.000	29	43	.674	62	81	143	30	75	0	20	36	21	211	2.5	0.5	3.7
REG. SEASON TOTALS	96	0	897	140	247	.567	0	3	.000	50	82	.610	102	154	256	49	121	0	41	57	32	330	2.7	0.5	3.4
PLAYOFF TOTALS	8	0	122	18	37	.486	0	1	.000	10	20	.500	24	18	42	3	18	0	5	7	—	46	5.3	0.4	5.8

MIHALIK, ZIGMUND JOHN (Red) b. September 22, 1916 Ht. 6-0 Wt. 180 College—None

SEASON—TEAM	G	GS	MIN	FGM	FGA	PCT	3FGM	3FGA	PCT	FTM	FTA	PCT	O-RB	D-RB	TOT	AST	PF	DQ	STL	TO	BLK	PTS	RPG	APG	PPG
46-47—Pittsburgh	7	—	—	3	9	.333	—	—	—	0	0	—	—	—	—	0	10	—	—	—	—	6	—	0.0	0.9
46-47—Youngstown (N)	31	—	—	41	—	—	—	—	—	12	29	.414	—	—	—	—	—	—	—	—	—	94	—	—	3.0
REG. NBA TOTALS	7	—	—	3	9	.333	—	—	—	0	0	—	—	—	—	0	10	—	—	—	—	6	—	0.0	0.9
REG. NBL TOTALS	31	—	—	41	—	—	—	—	—	12	29	.414	—	—	—	—	—	—	—	—	—	94	—	—	3.0

MIKAN, EDWARD ANTON (Ed) b. October 20, 1925 Ht. 6-8 Wt. 230 College—DePaul

SEASON—TEAM	G	GS	MIN	FGM	FGA	PCT	3FGM	3FGA	PCT	FTM	FTA	PCT	O-RB	D-RB	TOT	AST	PF	DQ	STL	TO	BLK	PTS	RPG	APG	PPG
48-49—Chicago	60	—	—	229	729	.314	—	—	—	136	183	.743	—	—	—	62	191	—	—	—	—	594	—	1.0	9.9
49-50—Chicago-Roch.	65	—	—	89	321	.277	—	—	—	92	120	.767	—	—	—	42	143	—	—	—	—	270	—	0.6	4.2
50-51—Roch.-Wash.-Phil.	61	—	—	193	556	.347	—	—	—	137	189	.725	—	—	344	63	194	6	—	—	—	523	5.6	1.0	8.6
51-52—Philadelphia	66	—	1781	202	571	.354	—	—	—	116	148	.784	—	—	492	87	252	7	—	—	—	520	7.5	1.3	7.9
52-53—Phil.-Ind.	62	—	927	78	292	.267	—	—	—	79	98	.806	—	—	237	39	124	0	—	—	—	235	3.8	0.6	3.8
53-54—Boston	9	—	71	8	24	.333	—	—	—	5	9	.556	—	—	20	3	15	0	—	—	—	21	2.2	0.3	2.3
REG. SEASON TOTALS	323	—	2779	799	2493	.320	—	—	—	565	747	.756	—	—	1093	296	919	13	—	—	—	2163	5.5	0.9	6.7
PLAYOFF TOTALS	11	—	106	31	120	.258	—	—	—	29	35	.829	—	—	48	8	36	0	—	—	—	91	6.9	0.7	8.3

MIKAN, GEORGE LAWRENCE III (**Larry**) b. April 8, 1948 Ht. 6-7 Wt. 210 College—Minnesota

SEASON—TEAM	G	GS	MIN	FGM	FGA	PCT	3FGM	3FGA	PCT	FTM	FTA	PCT	O-RB	D-RB	TOT	AST	PF	DQ	STL	TO	BLK	PTS	RPG	APG	PPG
70-71—Cleveland	53	—	536	62	186	.333	—	—	—	34	55	.618	—	—	139	41	56	1	—	—	—	158	2.6	0.8	3.0
REG. SEASON TOTALS	53	—	536	62	186	.333	—	—	—	34	55	.618	—	—	139	41	56	1	—	—	—	158	2.6	0.8	3.0

MIKAN, GEORGE LAWRENCE JR. b. June 18, 1924 Ht. 6-10½ Wt. 245 College—DePaul

SEASON—TEAM	G	GS	MIN	FGM	FGA	PCT	3FGM	3FGA	PCT	FTM	FTA	PCT	O-RB	D-RB	TOT	AST	PF	DQ	STL	TO	BLK	PTS	RPG	APG	PPG
46-47—Chicago (N)	25	—	—	147	—	—	—	—	—	119	164	.726	—	—	—	—	96	—	—	—	—	413	—	—	16.5
47-48—Minneapolis (N)	56	—	—	406	—	—	—	—	—	383	509	.752	—	—	—	—	210	—	—	—	—	1195	—	—	21.3
48-49—Minneapolis	60	—	—	583	1403	.416	—	—	—	532	689	.772	—	—	—	218	260	—	—	—	—	1698	—	3.6	28.3
49-50—Minneapolis	68	—	—	649	1595	.407	—	—	—	567	728	.779	—	—	—	197	297	—	—	—	—	1865	—	2.9	27.4
50-51—Minneapolis	68	—	—	678	1584	.428	—	—	—	576	717	.803	—	—	958	208	308	14	—	—	—	1932	14.1	3.1	28.4
51-52—Minneapolis	64	—	2572	545	1414	.385	—	—	—	433	555	.780	—	—	866	194	286	14	—	—	—	1523	13.5	3.0	23.8
52-53—Minneapolis	70	—	2651	500	1252	.399	—	—	—	442	567	.780	—	—	1007	201	290	12	—	—	—	1442	14.4	2.9	20.6
53-54—Minneapolis	72	—	2362	441	1160	.380	—	—	—	424	546	.777	—	—	1028	174	268	4	—	—	—	1306	14.3	2.4	18.1
55-56—Minneapolis	37	—	765	148	375	.395	—	—	—	94	122	.770	—	—	308	53	153	6	—	—	—	390	8.3	1.4	10.5
REG. NBA TOTALS	439	—	8350	3544	8783	.404	—	—	—	3068	3924	.782	—	—	4167	1245	1862	50	—	—	—	10156	13.4	2.8	23.1
REG. NBL TOTALS	81	—	553	—	—	—	—	—	—	502	673	.746	—	—	—	—	306	—	—	—	—	1608	—	—	19.9
NBA PLAYOFF TOTALS	70	—	1500	563	1394	.404	—	—	—	554	705	.786	—	—	665	155	305	12	—	—	—	1680	13.9	2.2	24.0
NBL PLAYOFF TOTALS	21	—	160	—	—	—	—	—	—	141	196	.699	—	—	—	—	85	—	—	—	—	461	—	—	22.0
NBA ALL-STAR TOTALS	4	—	100	28	80	.350	—	—	—	22	27	.815	—	—	51	7	14	0	—	—	—	78	12.8	1.8	19.5

MIKKELSEN, ARILD VERNER (**Vern**) b. October 21, 1928 Ht. 6-7 Wt. 230 College—Hamline

SEASON—TEAM	G	GS	MIN	FGM	FGA	PCT	3FGM	3FGA	PCT	FTM	FTA	PCT	O-RB	D-RB	TOT	AST	PF	DQ	STL	TO	BLK	PTS	RPG	APG	PPG
49-50—Minneapolis	68	—	—	288	722	.399	—	—	—	215	286	.752	—	—	—	123	222	—	—	—	—	791	—	1.8	11.6
50-51—Minneapolis	64	—	—	359	893	.402	—	—	—	186	275	.676	—	—	655	181	260	13	—	—	—	904	10.2	2.8	14.1
51-52—Minneapolis	66	—	2345	363	866	.419	—	—	—	283	372	.761	—	—	681	180	282	16	—	—	—	1009	10.3	2.7	15.3
52-53—Minneapolis	70	—	2465	378	868	.435	—	—	—	291	387	.752	—	—	654	148	289	14	—	—	—	1047	9.3	2.1	15.0
53-54—Minneapolis	72	—	2247	288	771	.374	—	—	—	221	298	.742	—	—	615	119	264	7	—	—	—	797	8.5	1.7	11.1
54-55—Minneapolis	71	—	2559	440	1043	.422	—	—	—	447	598	.747	—	—	722	145	319	14	—	—	—	1327	10.2	2.0	18.7
55-56—Minneapolis	72	—	2100	317	821	.386	—	—	—	328	408	.804	—	—	608	173	319	17	—	—	—	962	8.4	2.4	13.4
56-57—Minneapolis	72	—	2198	322	854	.377	—	—	—	342	424	.807	—	—	630	121	312	18	—	—	—	986	8.8	1.7	13.7
57-58—Minneapolis	72	—	2390	439	1070	.410	—	—	—	370	471	.786	—	—	805	166	299	20	—	—	—	1248	11.2	2.3	17.3
58-59—Minneapolis	72	—	2139	353	904	.390	—	—	—	286	355	.806	—	—	570	159	246	8	—	—	—	992	7.9	2.2	13.8
REG. SEASON TOTALS	699	—	18443	3547	8812	.403	—	—	—	2969	3874	.766	—	—	5940	1515	2812	127	—	—	—	10063	9.4	2.2	14.4
PLAYOFF TOTALS	85	—	2103	396	999	.396	—	—	—	349	446	.783	—	—	585	152	397	27	—	—	—	1141	8.0	1.8	13.4
ALL-STAR TOTALS	6	—	110	27	70	.386	—	—	—	13	20	.650	—	—	52	8	20	0	—	—	—	67	8.7	1.3	11.2

MIKSIS, ALFONSE K. b. February 2, 1928 Ht. 6-7 Wt. 210 College—Western Illinois

SEASON—TEAM	G	GS	MIN	FGM	FGA	PCT	3FGM	3FGA	PCT	FTM	FTA	PCT	O-RB	D-RB	TOT	AST	PF	DQ	STL	TO	BLK	PTS	RPG	APG	PPG
49-50—Waterloo	8	—	—	5	21	.238	—	—	—	17	21	.810	—	—	—	4	22	—	—	—	—	27	—	0.5	3.4
REG. SEASON TOTALS	8	—	—	5	21	.238	—	—	—	17	21	.810	—	—	—	4	22	—	—	—	—	27	—	0.5	3.4

MILES, EDWARD JR. (**Eddie**) b. July 5, 1940 Ht. 6-4 Wt. 195 College—Seattle

SEASON—TEAM	G	GS	MIN	FGM	FGA	PCT	3FGM	3FGA	PCT	FTM	FTA	PCT	O-RB	D-RB	TOT	AST	PF	DQ	STL	TO	BLK	PTS	RPG	APG	PPG
63-64—Detroit	60	—	811	131	371	.353	—	—	—	62	87	.713	—	—	95	58	92	0	—	—	—	324	1.6	1.0	5.4
64-65—Detroit	76	—	2074	439	994	.442	—	—	—	166	223	.744	—	—	258	157	201	1	—	—	—	1044	3.4	2.1	13.7
65-66—Detroit	80	—	2788	634	1418	.447	—	—	—	298	402	.741	—	—	302	221	203	2	—	—	—	1566	3.8	2.8	19.6
66-67—Detroit	81	—	2419	582	1363	.427	—	—	—	261	338	.772	—	—	298	181	216	2	—	—	—	1425	3.7	2.2	17.6
67-68—Detroit	76	—	2303	561	1180	.475	—	—	—	282	369	.764	—	—	264	215	200	3	—	—	—	1404	3.5	2.8	18.5
68-69—Detroit	80	—	2252	441	983	.449	—	—	—	182	273	.667	—	—	283	180	201	0	—	—	—	1064	3.5	2.3	13.3
69-70—Detroit-Balt.	47	—	1295	238	541	.440	—	—	—	133	175	.760	—	—	177	86	107	0	—	—	—	609	3.8	1.8	13.0
70-71—Baltimore	63	—	1541	252	591	.426	—	—	—	118	147	.803	—	—	167	110	119	0	—	—	—	622	2.7	1.7	9.9
71-72—New York	42	—	198	23	64	.359	—	—	—	16	18	.889	—	—	16	17	46	0	—	—	—	62	0.4	0.4	1.5
REG. SEASON TOTALS	605	—	15681	3301	7505	.440	—	—	—	1518	2032	.747	—	—	1860	1225	1385	8	—	—	—	8120	3.1	2.0	13.4
PLAYOFF TOTALS	20	—	277	43	111	.387	—	—	—	13	17	.765	—	—	35	16	23	0	—	—	—	99	1.8	0.8	5.0
ALL-STAR TOTALS	1	—	28	8	16	.500	—	—	—	1	5	.200	—	—	1	0	1	0	—	—	—	17	1.0	0.0	17.0

MILITZOK, NATHAN (**Nat**) b. May 3, 1923 Ht. 6-3 Wt. 195 College—City College of New York/Hofstra/Cornell

SEASON—TEAM	G	GS	MIN	FGM	FGA	PCT	3FGM	3FGA	PCT	FTM	FTA	PCT	O-RB	D-RB	TOT	AST	PF	DQ	STL	TO	BLK	PTS	RPG	APG	PPG
46-47—N.Y.-Toronto	56	—	—	90	343	.262	—	—	—	64	112	.571	—	—	—	42	120	—	—	—	—	244	—	0.8	4.4
REG. SEASON TOTALS	56	—	—	90	343	.262	—	—	—	64	112	.571	—	—	—	42	120	—	—	—	—	244	—	0.8	4.4

MILLER, EDWIN B. (Eddie) b. June 18, 1931 Ht. 6-8 Wt. 225 College—Syracuse

SEASON—TEAM	G	GS	MIN	FGM	FGA	PCT	3FGM	3FGA	PCT	FTM	FTA	PCT	O-RB	D-RB	TOT	AST	PF	DQ	STL	TO	BLK	PTS	RPG	APG	PPG
52-53—Milw.-Balt.	70	—	2018	273	781	.350	—	—	—	187	287	.652	—	—	669	115	250	12	—	—	—	733	9.6	1.6	10.5
53-54—Baltimore	72	—	1657	244	600	.407	—	—	—	231	317	.729	—	—	537	95	194	0	—	—	—	719	7.5	1.3	10.0
REG. SEASON TOTALS	142	—	3675	517	1381	.374	—	—	—	418	604	.692	—	—	1206	210	444	12	—	—	—	1452	8.5	1.5	10.2
PLAYOFF TOTALS	2	—	93	13	34	.382	—	—	—	7	16	.438	—	—	36	5	9	0	—	—	—	33	18.0	2.5	16.5

MILLER, HARRY DAVID (Moose) b. July 28, 1923 Ht. 6-4 Wt. 230 College—Seton Hall/North Carolina

SEASON—TEAM	G	GS	MIN	FGM	FGA	PCT	3FGM	3FGA	PCT	FTM	FTA	PCT	O-RB	D-RB	TOT	AST	PF	DQ	STL	TO	BLK	PTS	RPG	APG	PPG
46-47—Toronto	53	—	—	58	260	.223	—	—	—	36	82	.439	—	—	—	42	119	—	—	—	—	152	—	0.8	2.9
REG. SEASON TOTALS	53	—	—	58	260	.223	—	—	—	36	82	.439	—	—	—	42	119	—	—	—	—	152	—	0.8	2.9

MILLER, JAY JULIAN (Jay Jay) b. July 19, 1943 Ht. 6-5 Wt. 210 College—Notre Dame

SEASON—TEAM	G	GS	MIN	FGM	FGA	PCT	3FGM	3FGA	PCT	FTM	FTA	PCT	O-RB	D-RB	TOT	AST	PF	DQ	STL	TO	BLK	PTS	RPG	APG	PPG
67-68—St. Louis	8	—	52	8	31	.258	—	—	—	4	7	.571	—	—	7	1	11	0	—	—	—	20	0.9	0.1	2.5
68-69—Milwaukee	3	—	27	2	10	.200	—	—	—	5	7	.714	—	—	2	0	4	0	—	—	—	9	0.7	0.0	3.0
68-69—L.A.-Indiana (A)	52	—	742	147	356	.413	0	0	—	127	176	.722	—	—	113	29	103	2	—	71	—	421	2.2	0.6	8.1
69-70—Indiana (A)	52	—	415	75	167	.449	0	1	.000	41	57	.719	—	—	80	16	72	2	—	—	—	191	1.5	0.3	3.7
70-71—Indiana (A)	2	—	9	4	5	.800	0	0	—	0	0	—	—	—	3	1	1	—	—	—	—	8	1.5	0.5	4.0
REG. NBA TOTALS	11	—	79	10	41	.244	—	—	—	9	14	.643	—	—	9	1	15	0	—	—	—	29	0.8	0.1	2.6
REG. ABA TOTALS	106	—	1166	226	528	.428	0	1	.000	168	233	.721	—	—	196	46	176	4	—	71	—	620	1.8	0.4	5.8
ABA PLAYOFF TOTALS	14	—	72	16	38	.421	—	—	—	4	10	.400	—	—	25	2	18	0	—	5	—	36	1.8	0.1	2.6

MILLER, LAWRENCE JAMES (Larry, Mills) b. April 4, 1946 Ht. 6-4½ Wt. 210 College—North Carolina

SEASON—TEAM	G	GS	MIN	FGM	FGA	PCT	3FGM	3FGA	PCT	FTM	FTA	PCT	O-RB	D-RB	TOT	AST	PF	DQ	STL	TO	BLK	PTS	RPG	APG	PPG
68-69—Los Angeles (A)	78	—	2871	473	1162	.407	42	139	.302	340	475	.716	—	—	599	177	193	0	—	182	—	1328	7.7	2.3	17.0
69-70—L.A.-Car. (A)	80	—	2037	317	758	.418	15	74	.203	223	331	.674	—	—	414	147	173	0	—	—	—	872	5.2	1.8	10.9
70-71—Carolina (A)	77	—	2140	364	795	.458	13	61	.213	197	272	.724	—	—	457	167	181	—	—	—	—	938	5.9	2.2	12.2
71-72—Carolina (A)	83	—	3199	562	1228	.458	12	47	.255	393	497	.791	—	—	399	235	232	—	—	191	—	1529	4.8	2.8	18.4
72-73—San Diego (A)	83	—	2700	450	1080	.417	0	7	.000	306	422	.725	171	184	355	281	174	0	—	168	—	1206	4.3	3.4	14.5
73-74—S.D.-Vir. (A)	80	—	1968	281	638	.440	0	3	.000	151	228	.662	87	122	209	144	138	—	56	120	6	713	2.6	1.8	8.9
74-75—Utah (A)	5	—	26	3	9	.333	0	0	—	3	3	1.000	1	0	1	4	0	—	1	2	0	9	0.2	0.8	1.8
REG. ABA TOTALS	486	—	14941	2450	5670	.432	82	331	.248	1613	2228	.724	259	306	2434	1155	1091	0	57	663	6	6595	5.0	2.4	13.6
ABA PLAYOFF TOTALS	9	—	153	20	61	.328	2	5	.400	19	23	.826	0	0	20	20	20	3	0	7	0	61	2.2	2.2	6.8

MILLER, OLIVER J. b. April 6, 1970 Ht. 6-9 Wt. 285 College—Arkansas

SEASON—TEAM	G	GS	MIN	FGM	FGA	PCT	3FGM	3FGA	PCT	FTM	FTA	PCT	O-RB	D-RB	TOT	AST	PF	DQ	STL	TO	BLK	PTS	RPG	APG	PPG
92-93—Phoenix	56	1	1069	121	255	.475	0	3	.000	71	100	.710	70	205	275	118	145	0	38	108	100	313	4.9	2.1	5.6
93-94—Phoenix	69	30	1786	277	455	.609	2	9	.222	80	137	.584	140	336	476	244	230	1	83	164	156	636	6.9	3.5	9.2
REG. SEASON TOTALS	125	31	2855	398	710	.561	2	12	.167	151	237	.637	210	541	751	362	375	1	121	272	256	949	6.0	2.9	7.6
PLAYOFF TOTALS	34	4	659	87	148	.588	0	2	.000	34	62	.548	47	121	168	64	98	0	27	55	71	208	4.9	1.9	6.1

MILLER, REGINALD WAYNE (Reggie) b. August 24, 1965 Ht. 6-7 Wt. 190 College—UCLA

SEASON—TEAM	G	GS	MIN	FGM	FGA	PCT	3FGM	3FGA	PCT	FTM	FTA	PCT	O-RB	D-RB	TOT	AST	PF	DQ	STL	TO	BLK	PTS	RPG	APG	PPG
87-88—Indiana	82	1	1840	306	627	.488	61	172	.355	149	186	.801	95	95	190	132	157	0	53	101	19	822	2.3	1.6	10.0
88-89—Indiana	74	70	2536	398	831	.479	98	244	.402	287	340	.844	73	219	292	227	170	2	93	143	29	1181	3.9	3.1	16.0
89-90—Indiana	82	82	3192	661	1287	.514	150	362	.414	544	627	.868	95	200	295	311	175	1	110	222	18	2016	3.6	3.8	24.6
90-91—Indiana	82	82	2972	596	1164	.512	112	322	.348	551	600	.918	81	200	281	331	165	1	109	163	13	1855	3.4	4.0	22.6
91-92—Indiana	82	82	3120	562	1121	.501	129	341	.378	442	515	.858	82	236	318	314	210	1	105	157	26	1695	3.9	3.8	20.7
92-93—Indiana	82	82	2954	571	1193	.479	167	419	.399	427	485	.880	67	191	258	262	182	0	120	145	26	1736	3.1	3.2	21.2
93-94—Indiana	79	79	2638	524	1042	.503	123	292	.421	403	444	.908	30	182	212	248	193	2	119	175	24	1574	2.7	3.1	19.9
REG. SEASON TOTALS	563	478	19252	3618	7265	.498	840	2152	.390	2803	3197	.877	523	1323	1846	1825	1252	7	709	1106	155	10879	3.3	3.2	19.3
PLAYOFF TOTALS	31	31	1199	240	493	.487	63	139	.453	205	238	.861	25	70	95	91	77	1	39	61	6	748	3.1	2.9	24.1
ALL-STAR TOTALS	1	0	14	2	3	.667	0	1	.000	0	0	—	0	1	1	3	1	0	1	0	0	4	1.0	3.0	4.0

MILLER, RICHARD MATHIAS (Dick) b. April 26, 1958 Ht. 6-6½ Wt. 220 College—Toledo

SEASON—TEAM	G	GS	MIN	FGM	FGA	PCT	3FGM	3FGA	PCT	FTM	FTA	PCT	O-RB	D-RB	TOT	AST	PF	DQ	STL	TO	BLK	PTS	RPG	APG	PPG
80-81—Indiana-Utah	8	—	53	4	9	.444	0	1	.000	0	0	—	2	5	7	5	5	0	4	8	0	8	0.9	0.6	1.0
REG. SEASON TOTALS	8	—	53	4	9	.444	0	1	.000	0	0	—	2	5	7	5	5	0	4	8	0	8	0.9	0.6	1.0

MILLER, ROBERT E. (Bob) b. July 9, 1956 Ht. 6-10 Wt. 230 College—Cincinnati

SEASON—TEAM	G	GS	MIN	FGM	FGA	PCT	3FGM	3FGA	PCT	FTM	FTA	PCT	O-RB	D-RB	TOT	AST	PF	DQ	STL	TO	BLK	PTS	RPG	APG	PPG
83-84—San Antonio	2	0	8	2	3	.667	0	0	—	0	0	—	2	3	5	1	5	0	0	1	1	4	2.5	0.5	2.0
REG. SEASON TOTALS	2	0	8	2	3	.667	0	0	—	0	0	—	2	3	5	1	5	0	0	1	1	4	2.5	0.5	2.0

MILLER, WALTER P. (**Walt**) b. July 30, 1915   Ht. 6-2 Wt. 190 College—Duquesne

SEASON—TEAM	G	GS	MIN	FGM	FGA	PCT	3FGM	3FGA	PCT	FTM	FTA	PCT	O-RB	D-RB	TOT	AST	PF	DQ	STL	TO	BLK	PTS	RPG	APG	PPG
37-38—Pittsburgh (N)	9	—	—	18	—	—	—	—	—	10	—	—	—	—	—	—	—	—	—	—	—	46	—	—	5.1
38-39—Pittsburgh (N)	19	—	—	52	—	—	—	—	—	44	—	—	—	—	—	—	—	—	—	—	—	148	—	—	7.8
45-46—Youngstown (N)	10	—	—	4	—	—	—	—	—	5	—	—	—	—	—	—	—	—	—	—	—	13	—	—	1.3
46-47—Pittsburgh	12	—	—	7	21	.333	—	—	—	9	18	.500	—	—	—	6	16	—	—	—	—	23	—	0.5	1.9
REG. NBA TOTALS	12	—	—	7	21	.333	—	—	—	9	18	.500	—	—	—	6	16	—	—	—	—	23	—	0.5	1.9
REG. NBL TOTALS	38	—	—	74	—	—	—	—	—	59	—	—	—	—	—	—	—	—	—	—	—	207	—	—	5.4

MILLER, WILLIAM RALPH (**Bill**) b. November 24, 1924   Ht. 6-3 Wt. 190 College—North Carolina

SEASON—TEAM	G	GS	MIN	FGM	FGA	PCT	3FGM	3FGA	PCT	FTM	FTA	PCT	O-RB	D-RB	TOT	AST	PF	DQ	STL	TO	BLK	PTS	RPG	APG	PPG
48-49—Chicago-St. L.	28	—	—	21	72	.292	—	—	—	11	20	.550	—	—	—	20	32	—	—	—	—	53	—	0.7	1.9
REG. SEASON TOTALS	28	—	—	21	72	.292	—	—	—	11	20	.550	—	—	—	20	32	—	—	—	—	53	—	0.7	1.9
PLAYOFF TOTALS	1	—	—	0	0	—	—	—	—	0	2	.000	—	—	—	0	—	—	—	—	—	0	—	—	0.0

MILLS, CHRISTOPHER LEMONTE (**Chris**) b. January 25, 1970   Ht. 6-6 Wt. 215 College—Kentucky/Arizona

SEASON—TEAM	G	GS	MIN	FGM	FGA	PCT	3FGM	3FGA	PCT	FTM	FTA	PCT	O-RB	D-RB	TOT	AST	PF	DQ	STL	TO	BLK	PTS	RPG	APG	PPG
93-94—Cleveland	79	18	2022	284	677	.419	38	122	.311	137	176	.778	134	267	401	128	232	3	54	89	50	743	5.1	1.6	9.4
REG. SEASON TOTALS	79	18	2022	284	677	.419	38	122	.311	137	176	.778	134	267	401	128	232	3	54	89	50	743	5.1	1.6	9.4
PLAYOFF TOTALS	3	1	112	19	38	.500	4	5	.800	9	11	.818	10	13	23	8	9	0	7	5	1	51	7.7	2.7	17.0

MILLS, JOHN (**Long John**) b. September 7, 1919   Ht. 6-8 Wt. 210 College—Western Kentucky

SEASON—TEAM	G	GS	MIN	FGM	FGA	PCT	3FGM	3FGA	PCT	FTM	FTA	PCT	O-RB	D-RB	TOT	AST	PF	DQ	STL	TO	BLK	PTS	RPG	APG	PPG
44-45—Cleveland (N)	29	—	—	29	—	—	—	—	—	42	—	—	—	—	—	—	—	—	—	—	—	100	—	—	3.4
45-46—Cleveland (N)	19	—	—	13	—	—	—	—	—	25	—	—	—	—	—	—	—	—	—	—	—	51	—	—	2.7
46-47—Pittsburgh	47	—	—	55	187	.294	—	—	—	71	129	.550	—	—	—	9	94	—	—	—	—	181	—	0.2	3.9
REG. NBA TOTALS	47	—	—	55	187	.294	—	—	—	71	129	.550	—	—	—	9	94	—	—	—	—	181	—	0.2	3.9
REG. NBL TOTALS	48	—	—	42	—	—	—	—	—	67	—	—	—	—	—	—	—	—	—	—	—	151	—	—	3.1
NBL PLAYOFF TOTALS	2	—	—	3	—	—	—	—	—	6	—	—	—	—	—	—	3	—	—	—	—	12	—	—	6.0

MILLS, TERRY RICHARD (**T**) b. December 21, 1967   Ht. 6-10 Wt. 250 College—Michigan

SEASON—TEAM	G	GS	MIN	FGM	FGA	PCT	3FGM	3FGA	PCT	FTM	FTA	PCT	O-RB	D-RB	TOT	AST	PF	DQ	STL	TO	BLK	PTS	RPG	APG	PPG
90-91—Denver-N.J.	55	2	819	134	288	.465	0	4	.000	47	66	.712	82	147	229	33	100	0	35	43	29	315	4.2	0.6	5.7
91-92—New Jersey	82	24	1714	310	670	.463	8	23	.348	114	152	.750	187	266	453	84	200	3	48	82	41	742	5.5	1.0	9.0
92-93—Detroit	81	46	2183	494	1072	.461	10	36	.278	201	254	.791	176	296	472	111	282	6	44	142	50	1199	5.8	1.4	14.8
93-94—Detroit	80	74	2773	588	1151	.511	24	73	.329	181	227	.797	193	479	672	177	309	6	64	153	62	1381	8.4	2.2	17.3
REG. SEASON TOTALS	298	146	7489	1526	3181	.480	42	136	.309	543	699	.777	638	1188	1826	405	891	15	191	420	182	3637	6.1	1.4	12.2
PLAYOFF TOTALS	4	0	77	10	27	.370	0	1	.000	7	11	.636	9	15	24	8	18	0	1	7	2	27	6.0	2.0	6.8

MINER, HAROLD DAVID (**Baby Jordan**) b. May 5, 1971   Ht. 6-5 Wt. 215 College—USC

SEASON—TEAM	G	GS	MIN	FGM	FGA	PCT	3FGM	3FGA	PCT	FTM	FTA	PCT	O-RB	D-RB	TOT	AST	PF	DQ	STL	TO	BLK	PTS	RPG	APG	PPG
92-93—Miami	73	0	1383	292	615	.475	3	9	.333	163	214	.762	74	73	147	73	130	2	34	92	8	750	2.0	1.0	10.3
93-94—Miami	63	31	1358	254	532	.477	4	6	.667	149	180	.828	75	81	156	95	132	0	31	95	13	661	2.5	1.5	10.5
REG. SEASON TOTALS	136	31	2741	546	1147	.476	7	15	.467	312	394	.792	149	154	303	168	262	2	65	187	21	1411	2.2	1.2	10.4
PLAYOFF TOTALS	4	0	57	12	26	.462	0	0	—	8	11	.727	3	5	8	2	4	0	1	2	0	32	2.0	0.5	8.0

MINNIEFIELD, DIRK DeWAYNE b. January 17, 1961   Ht. 6-3 Wt. 180 College—Kentucky

SEASON—TEAM	G	GS	MIN	FGM	FGA	PCT	3FGM	3FGA	PCT	FTM	FTA	PCT	O-RB	D-RB	TOT	AST	PF	DQ	STL	TO	BLK	PTS	RPG	APG	PPG
85-86—Cleveland	76	2	1131	167	347	.481	10	37	.270	73	93	.785	43	88	131	269	165	1	65	108	1	417	1.7	3.5	5.5
86-87—Clev.-Houston	74	52	1600	218	482	.452	11	39	.282	62	90	.689	29	111	140	348	174	2	72	157	7	509	1.9	4.7	6.9
87-88—G.S.-Boston	72	6	1070	108	221	.489	4	16	.250	41	55	.745	30	66	96	228	133	0	59	93	3	261	1.3	3.2	3.6
REG. SEASON TOTALS	222	60	3801	493	1050	.470	25	92	.272	176	238	.739	102	265	367	845	472	3	196	358	11	1187	1.7	3.8	5.3
PLAYOFF TOTALS	19	0	77	10	22	.455	2	5	.400	8	8	1.000	3	1	4	13	21	0	3	14	0	30	0.2	0.7	1.6

MINOR, DAVAGE (**Dave**) b. February 23, 1922   Ht. 6-2 Wt. 185 College—Toledo/UCLA

SEASON—TEAM	G	GS	MIN	FGM	FGA	PCT	3FGM	3FGA	PCT	FTM	FTA	PCT	O-RB	D-RB	TOT	AST	PF	DQ	STL	TO	BLK	PTS	RPG	APG	PPG
51-52—Baltimore	57	—	1558	185	522	.354	—	—	—	101	132	.765	—	—	275	160	161	2	—	—	—	471	4.8	2.8	8.3
52-53—Balt.-Milw.	59	—	1610	154	420	.367	—	—	—	98	132	.742	—	—	252	128	211	11	—	—	—	406	4.3	2.2	6.9
REG. SEASON TOTALS	116	—	3168	339	942	.360	—	—	—	199	264	.754	—	—	527	288	372	13	—	—	—	877	4.5	2.5	7.6

MINOR, MARK WILLIAM b. May 14, 1950   Ht. 6-6 Wt. 215 College—Ohio State

SEASON—TEAM	G	GS	MIN	FGM	FGA	PCT	3FGM	3FGA	PCT	FTM	FTA	PCT	O-RB	D-RB	TOT	AST	PF	DQ	STL	TO	BLK	PTS	RPG	APG	PPG
72-73—Boston	4	—	20	1	4	.250	—	—	—	3	4	.750	—	—	4	2	5	0	—	—	—	5	1.0	0.5	1.3
REG. SEASON TOTALS	4	—	20	1	4	.250	—	—	—	3	4	.750	—	—	4	2	5	0	—	—	—	5	1.0	0.5	1.3

MISAKA, WATARU (**Wat**) b. December 21, 1923   Ht. 5-7 Wt. 150 College—Utah

SEASON—TEAM	G	GS	MIN	FGM	FGA	PCT	3FGM	3FGA	PCT	FTM	FTA	PCT	O-RB	D-RB	TOT	AST	PF	DQ	STL	TO	BLK	PTS	RPG	APG	PPG
47-48—New York	3	—	—	3	13	.231	—	—	—	1	3	.333	—	—	—	0	7	—	—	—	—	7	—	0.0	2.3
REG. SEASON TOTALS	3	—	—	3	13	.231	—	—	—	1	3	.333	—	—	—	0	7	—	—	—	—	7	—	0.0	2.3

MITCHELL, ERNEST TODD (**Todd**) b. July 26, 1966   Ht. 6-7 Wt. 205 College—Purdue

SEASON—TEAM	G	GS	MIN	FGM	FGA	PCT	3FGM	3FGA	PCT	FTM	FTA	PCT	O-RB	D-RB	TOT	AST	PF	DQ	STL	TO	BLK	PTS	RPG	APG	PPG
88-89—Miami-S.A.	24	0	353	43	97	.443	0	0	—	37	64	.578	18	32	50	21	51	0	16	33	2	123	2.1	0.9	5.1
REG. SEASON TOTALS	24	0	353	43	97	.443	0	0	—	37	64	.578	18	32	50	21	51	0	16	33	2	123	2.1	0.9	5.1

MITCHELL, LELAND b. February 22, 1941   Ht. 6-4 Wt. 210 College—Pearl River CC/Mississippi State

SEASON—TEAM	G	GS	MIN	FGM	FGA	PCT	3FGM	3FGA	PCT	FTM	FTA	PCT	O-RB	D-RB	TOT	AST	PF	DQ	STL	TO	BLK	PTS	RPG	APG	PPG
67-68—New Orleans (A)	78	—	1091	122	350	.349	21	76	.276	56	85	.659	—	—	182	73	159	1	—	108	—	321	2.3	0.9	4.1
REG. ABA TOTALS	78	—	1091	122	350	.349	21	76	.276	56	85	.659	—	—	182	73	159	1	—	108	—	321	2.3	0.9	4.1
ABA PLAYOFF TOTALS	7	—	57	1	9	.111	0	4	.000	1	2	.500	—	—	3	3	8	0	—	5	—	3	0.4	0.4	0.4

MITCHELL, MICHAEL ANTHONY (**Mike**) b. January 1, 1956   Ht. 6-7½ Wt. 215 College—Auburn

SEASON—TEAM	G	GS	MIN	FGM	FGA	PCT	3FGM	3FGA	PCT	FTM	FTA	PCT	O-RB	D-RB	TOT	AST	PF	DQ	STL	TO	BLK	PTS	RPG	APG	PPG
78-79—Cleveland	80	—	1576	362	706	.513	—	—	—	131	178	.736	127	202	329	60	215	6	51	102	29	855	4.1	0.8	10.7
79-80—Cleveland	82	—	2802	775	1482	.523	0	6	.000	270	343	.787	206	385	591	93	259	4	70	172	77	1820	7.2	1.1	22.2
80-81—Cleveland	82	—	3194	853	1791	.476	4	9	.444	302	385	.784	215	287	502	139	199	0	63	175	52	2012	6.1	1.7	24.5
81-82—Clev.-S.A.	84	83	3063	753	1477	.510	0	7	.000	220	302	.728	244	346	590	82	277	4	60	153	43	1726	7.0	1.0	20.5
82-83—San Antonio	80	79	2803	686	1342	.511	0	3	.000	219	289	.758	188	349	537	98	248	6	57	126	52	1591	6.7	1.2	19.9
83-84—San Antonio	79	79	2853	779	1597	.488	6	14	.429	275	353	.779	188	382	570	93	251	6	62	141	73	1839	7.2	1.2	23.3
84-85—San Antonio	82	82	2853	775	1558	.497	5	23	.217	269	346	.777	145	272	417	151	219	1	61	144	27	1824	5.1	1.8	22.2
85-86—San Antonio	82	82	2970	802	1697	.473	0	12	.000	317	392	.809	134	275	409	188	175	0	56	184	25	1921	5.0	2.3	23.4
86-87—San Antonio	40	18	922	208	478	.435	1	2	.500	92	112	.821	38	65	103	38	68	0	19	51	9	509	2.6	1.0	12.7
87-88—San Antonio	68	20	1501	378	784	.482	3	12	.250	160	194	.825	54	144	198	68	101	0	31	52	13	919	2.9	1.0	13.5
REG. SEASON TOTALS	759	443	24537	6371	12912	.493	19	88	.216	2255	2894	.779	1539	2707	4246	1010	2012	27	530	1300	400	15016	5.6	1.3	19.8
PLAYOFF TOTALS	35	31	1163	273	544	.502	1	3	.333	99	130	.762	76	148	224	47	90	2	19	75	28	646	6.4	1.3	18.5
ALL-STAR TOTALS	1	0	15	6	12	.500	0	0	—	2	2	1.000	4	0	4	2	2	0	1	1	0	14	4.0	2.0	14.0

MITCHELL, MURRAY C. b. March 19, 1923   Ht. 6-6   College—Sam Houston State

SEASON—TEAM	G	GS	MIN	FGM	FGA	PCT	3FGM	3FGA	PCT	FTM	FTA	PCT	O-RB	D-RB	TOT	AST	PF	DQ	STL	TO	BLK	PTS	RPG	APG	PPG
49-50—Anderson	2	—	—	1	3	.333	—	—	—	0	0	—	—	—	—	2	1	—	—	—	—	2	—	1.0	1.0
REG. SEASON TOTALS	2	—	—	1	3	.333	—	—	—	0	0	—	—	—	—	2	1	—	—	—	—	2	—	1.0	1.0

MITCHELL, SAMUEL E. JR. (**Sam**) b. September 2, 1963   Ht. 6-7 Wt. 215 College—Mercer-Macon

SEASON—TEAM	G	GS	MIN	FGM	FGA	PCT	3FGM	3FGA	PCT	FTM	FTA	PCT	O-RB	D-RB	TOT	AST	PF	DQ	STL	TO	BLK	PTS	RPG	APG	PPG
89-90—Minnesota	80	30	2414	372	834	.446	0	9	.000	268	349	.768	180	282	462	89	301	7	66	96	54	1012	5.8	1.1	12.7
90-91—Minnesota	82	60	3121	445	1010	.441	0	9	.000	307	396	.775	188	332	520	133	338	13	66	104	57	1197	6.3	1.6	14.6
91-92—Minnesota	82	63	2151	307	725	.423	2	11	.182	209	266	.786	158	315	473	94	230	3	53	97	39	825	5.8	1.1	10.1
92-93—Indiana	81	1	1402	215	483	.445	4	23	.174	150	185	.811	93	155	248	76	207	1	23	51	10	584	3.1	0.9	7.2
93-94—Indiana	75	18	1084	140	306	.458	0	5	.000	82	110	.745	71	119	190	65	152	1	33	50	9	362	2.5	0.9	4.8
REG. SEASON TOTALS	400	172	10172	1479	3358	.440	6	57	.105	1016	1306	.778	690	1203	1893	457	1228	25	241	398	169	3980	4.7	1.1	10.0
PLAYOFF TOTALS	19	0	124	14	34	.412	0	1	.000	5	6	.833	5	13	18	5	26	0	2	6	2	33	0.9	0.3	1.7

MIX, STEVEN CHARLES (**Steve**) b. December 30, 1947   Ht. 6-7 Wt. 215 College—Toledo

SEASON—TEAM	G	GS	MIN	FGM	FGA	PCT	3FGM	3FGA	PCT	FTM	FTA	PCT	O-RB	D-RB	TOT	AST	PF	DQ	STL	TO	BLK	PTS	RPG	APG	PPG
69-70—Detroit	18	—	276	48	100	.480	—	—	—	23	39	.590	—	—	64	15	31	0	—	—	—	119	3.6	0.8	6.6
70-71—Detroit	35	—	731	111	249	.446	—	—	—	68	89	.764	—	—	164	34	72	0	—	—	—	290	4.7	1.0	8.3
71-72—Detroit	8	—	104	15	47	.319	—	—	—	7	12	.583	—	—	23	4	7	0	—	—	—	37	2.9	0.5	4.6
71-72—Denver (A)	1	—	4	1	1	1.000	0	0	—	0	0	—	—	—	1	0	1	—	—	0	—	2	1.0	0.0	2.0
73-74—Philadelphia	82	—	2969	495	1042	.475	—	—	—	228	288	.792	305	559	864	152	305	9	212	—	37	1218	10.5	1.9	14.9
74-75—Philadelphia	46	—	1748	280	582	.481	—	—	—	159	205	.776	155	345	500	99	175	6	79	—	21	719	10.9	2.2	15.6
75-76—Philadelphia	81	—	3039	421	844	.499	—	—	—	287	351	.818	215	447	662	216	288	6	158	—	29	1129	8.2	2.7	13.9
76-77—Philadelphia	75	—	1958	288	551	.523	—	—	—	215	263	.817	127	249	376	152	167	0	90	—	20	791	5.0	2.0	10.5
77-78—Philadelphia	82	—	1819	291	560	.520	—	—	—	175	220	.795	96	201	297	174	158	1	87	131	3	757	3.6	2.1	9.2
78-79—Philadelphia	74	—	1269	265	493	.538	—	—	—	161	201	.801	109	184	293	121	112	0	57	100	16	691	4.0	1.6	9.3
79-80—Philadelphia	81	—	1543	363	703	.516	4	10	.400	207	249	.831	114	176	290	149	114	0	67	132	9	937	3.6	1.8	11.6
80-81—Philadelphia	72	—	1327	288	575	.501	0	3	.000	200	240	.833	105	159	264	114	107	0	59	88	18	776	3.7	1.6	10.8
81-82—Philadelphia	75	0	1235	202	399	.506	1	4	.250	136	172	.791	92	133	225	93	86	0	42	67	17	541	3.0	1.2	7.2
82-83—Milw.-L.A.	58	20	809	137	283	.484	1	4	.250	75	88	.852	38	99	137	70	71	0	33	45	3	350	2.4	1.2	6.0
REG. NBA TOTALS	787	20	18827	3204	6428	.498	6	21	.286	1941	2417	.803	1356	2552	4159	1393	1693	22	884	563	173	8355	5.3	1.8	10.6
REG. ABA TOTALS	1	—	4	1	1	1.000	0	0	—	0	0	—	—	—	1	0	1	—	—	0	—	2	1.0	0.0	2.0
NBA PLAYOFF TOTALS	89	0	1442	244	494	.494	1	2	.500	153	177	.864	90	158	248	137	143	1	65	53	13	642	2.8	1.5	7.2
NBA ALL-STAR TOTALS	1	0	11	2	5	.400	0	0	—	0	0	—	—	—	0	0	2	0	0	—	0	4	2.0	0.0	4.0

MLKVY, WILLIAM P. **(Bill, Owl Without a Vowel)** b. January 19, 1931   Ht. 6-4   Wt. 190   College—Temple

SEASON—TEAM	G	GS	MIN	FGM	FGA	PCT	3FGM	3FGA	PCT	FTM	FTA	PCT	O-RB	D-RB	TOT	AST	PF	DQ	STL	TO	BLK	PTS	RPG	APG	PPG
52-53—Philadelphia	31	—	608	75	246	.305	—	—	—	31	48	.646	—	—	101	62	54	1	—	—	—	181	3.3	2.0	5.8
REG. SEASON TOTALS	31	—	608	75	246	.305	—	—	—	31	48	.646	—	—	101	62	54	1	—	—	—	181	3.3	2.0	5.8

MODZELEWSKI, STAN **(see Stanley J. Stutz)**

MOE, DOUGLAS EDWIN **(Doug)** b. September 21, 1938   Ht. 6-5½   Wt. 220   College—Elon/North Carolina

SEASON—TEAM	G	GS	MIN	FGM	FGA	PCT	3FGM	3FGA	PCT	FTM	FTA	PCT	O-RB	D-RB	TOT	AST	PF	DQ	STL	TO	BLK	PTS	RPG	APG	PPG
67-68—New Orleans (A)	78	—	3113	665	1610	.413	3	22	.136	551	693	.795	249	546	795	202	282	4	—	199	—	1884	10.2	2.6	24.2
68-69—Oakland (A)	75	—	2528	529	1227	.431	5	14	.357	360	444	.811	—	—	614	151	266	9	—	181	—	1423	8.2	2.0	19.0
69-70—Carolina (A)	80	—	2671	535	1254	.427	8	34	.235	304	399	.762	—	—	437	425	282	8	—	—	—	1382	5.5	5.3	17.3
70-71—Virginia (A)	78	—	2297	397	871	.456	2	10	.200	221	259	.853	—	—	473	270	284	—	—	—	—	1017	6.1	3.5	13.0
71-72—Virginia (A)	67	—	1472	175	415	.422	1	9	.111	104	129	.806	—	—	241	149	172	—	—	112	—	455	3.6	2.2	6.8
REG. ABA TOTALS	378	—	12081	2301	5377	.428	19	89	.213	1540	1924	.800	249	546	2560	1197	1286	21	—	492	—	6161	6.8	3.2	16.3
ABA PLAYOFF TOTALS	60	—	2142	411	968	.425	5	23	.217	259	342	.757	—	—	419	160	240	4	—	122	—	1086	7.0	2.7	18.1
ABA ALL-STAR TOTALS	3	—	91	13	31	.419	0	1	.000	10	16	.625	6	7	21	17	8	0	—	3	—	36	7.0	5.7	12.0

MOFFETT, LARRY b. November 5, 1954   Ht. 6-9   Wt. 210   College—Compton CC/Murray State (Ky.)/Nevada-Las Vegas

SEASON—TEAM	G	GS	MIN	FGM	FGA	PCT	3FGM	3FGA	PCT	FTM	FTA	PCT	O-RB	D-RB	TOT	AST	PF	DQ	STL	TO	BLK	PTS	RPG	APG	PPG
77-78—Houston	20	—	110	5	17	.294	—	—	—	6	10	.600	10	11	21	7	16	0	2	8	2	16	1.1	0.4	0.8
REG. SEASON TOTALS	20	—	110	5	17	.294	—	—	—	6	10	.600	10	11	21	7	16	0	2	8	2	16	1.1	0.4	0.8

MOGUS, LEO b. April 13, 1921   d. 1975   Ht. 6-4   Wt. 205   College—Youngstown

SEASON—TEAM	G	GS	MIN	FGM	FGA	PCT	3FGM	3FGA	PCT	FTM	FTA	PCT	O-RB	D-RB	TOT	AST	PF	DQ	STL	TO	BLK	PTS	RPG	APG	PPG
45-46—Youngstown (N)	16	—	—	61	—	—	—	—	—	66	98	.673	—	—	—	—	40	—	—	—	—	188	—	—	11.8
46-47—Clev.-Toronto	58	—	—	259	879	.295	—	—	—	235	325	.723	—	—	—	84	176	—	—	—	—	753	—	1.4	13.0
48-49—Balt.-Ft. Wayne-Ind.	52	—	—	172	509	.338	—	—	—	177	243	.728	—	—	—	104	170	—	—	—	—	521	—	2.0	10.0
49-50—Philadelphia	64	—	—	172	434	.396	—	—	—	218	300	.727	—	—	—	99	169	—	—	—	—	562	—	1.5	8.8
50-51—Philadelphia	57	—	—	43	122	.352	—	—	—	53	86	.616	—	—	102	32	60	0	—	—	—	139	1.8	0.6	2.4
REG. NBA TOTALS	231	—	—	646	1944	.332	—	—	—	683	954	.716	—	—	102	319	575	0	—	—	—	1975	1.8	1.4	8.5
REG. NBL TOTALS	16	—	—	61	—	—	—	—	—	66	98	.673	—	—	—	—	40	—	—	—	—	188	—	—	11.8
NBA PLAYOFF TOTALS	3	—	—	3	18	.167	—	—	—	4	7	.571	—	—	—	7	10	0	—	—	—	10	—	3.5	3.3

MOKESKI, PAUL KEEN **(Mo)** b. January 3, 1957   Ht. 7-0   Wt. 250   College—Kansas

SEASON—TEAM	G	GS	MIN	FGM	FGA	PCT	3FGM	3FGA	PCT	FTM	FTA	PCT	O-RB	D-RB	TOT	AST	PF	DQ	STL	TO	BLK	PTS	RPG	APG	PPG
79-80—Houston	12	—	113	11	33	.333	0	0	—	7	9	.778	14	15	29	2	24	0	1	10	6	29	2.4	0.2	2.4
80-81—Detroit	80	—	1815	224	458	.489	0	1	.000	120	200	.600	141	277	418	135	267	7	38	160	73	568	5.2	1.7	7.1
81-82—Clev.-Detroit	67	4	868	84	193	.435	0	3	.000	48	63	.762	59	149	208	35	171	2	33	55	40	216	3.1	0.5	3.2
82-83—Clev.-Milw.	73	19	1128	119	260	.458	0	1	.000	50	68	.735	76	184	260	49	223	9	21	67	44	288	3.6	0.7	3.9
83-84—Milwaukee	68	4	838	102	213	.479	1	3	.333	50	72	.694	51	115	166	44	168	1	11	44	29	255	2.4	0.6	3.8
84-85—Milwaukee	79	6	1586	205	429	.478	0	2	.000	81	116	.698	107	303	410	99	266	6	28	85	35	491	5.2	1.3	6.2
85-86—Milwaukee	45	0	521	59	139	.424	0	0	—	25	34	.735	36	103	139	30	92	1	6	25	25	143	3.1	0.7	2.4
86-87—Philadelphia	62	3	626	52	129	.403	0	1	.000	46	64	.719	45	93	138	22	126	0	18	22	13	150	2.2	0.4	2.4
87-88—Milwaukee	60	0	848	100	210	.476	0	4	.000	51	72	.708	70	151	221	62	194	5	27	49	29	251	3.7	0.4	4.2
88-89—Milwaukee	74	0	690	59	164	.360	7	26	.269	40	51	.784	63	124	187	36	153	0	29	35	21	165	2.5	0.5	2.2
89-90—Cleveland	38	1	449	63	150	.420	0	1	.000	25	36	.694	27	72	99	17	76	0	8	26	10	151	2.6	0.4	4.0
90-91—Golden State	36	1	257	21	59	.356	3	9	.333	12	15	.800	20	47	67	9	58	0	8	7	3	57	1.9	0.3	1.6
REG. SEASON TOTALS	694	38	9739	1099	2437	.451	11	51	.216	555	800	.694	709	1633	2342	500	1818	31	228	585	309	2764	3.4	0.7	4.0
PLAYOFF TOTALS	69	0	815	89	183	.486	1	4	.250	72	97	.742	59	148	207	33	166	3	26	39	23	251	3.0	0.5	3.6

MOLINAS, JACOB L. **(Jack)** b. October 1931   d. August 3, 1975   Ht. 6-6   Wt. 200   College—Columbia

SEASON—TEAM	G	GS	MIN	FGM	FGA	PCT	3FGM	3FGA	PCT	FTM	FTA	PCT	O-RB	D-RB	TOT	AST	PF	DQ	STL	TO	BLK	PTS	RPG	APG	PPG
53-54—Fort Wayne	29	—	993	108	278	.388	—	—	—	134	176	.761	—	—	209	47	74	2	—	—	—	350	7.2	1.6	12.1
REG. SEASON TOTALS	29	—	993	108	278	.388	—	—	—	134	176	.761	—	—	209	47	74	2	—	—	—	350	7.2	1.6	12.1

MOLIS, WAYNE J. b. April 17, 1943   Ht. 6-8   Wt. 230   College—Chicago Teachers/Lewis

SEASON—TEAM	G	GS	MIN	FGM	FGA	PCT	3FGM	3FGA	PCT	FTM	FTA	PCT	O-RB	D-RB	TOT	AST	PF	DQ	STL	TO	BLK	PTS	RPG	APG	PPG
66-67—New York	13	—	75	19	51	.373	—	—	—	7	13	.538	—	—	22	2	9	0	—	—	—	45	1.7	0.2	3.5
67-68—Oakland-Houston (A)	46	—	535	96	225	.427	2	3	.667	41	61	.672	—	—	170	39	49	1	—	26	—	235	3.7	0.8	5.1
REG. NBA TOTALS	13	—	75	19	51	.373	—	—	—	7	13	.538	—	—	22	2	9	0	—	—	—	45	1.7	0.2	3.5
REG. ABA TOTALS	46	—	535	96	225	.427	2	3	.667	41	61	.672	—	—	170	39	49	1	—	26	—	235	3.7	0.8	5.1
NBA PLAYOFF TOTALS	1	—	10	0	2	.000	—	—	—	0	0	—	—	—	1	1	1	0	—	—	—	0	1.0	1.0	0.0

MONCRIEF, SIDNEY A. b. September 21, 1957   Ht. 6-4 Wt. 190 College—Arkansas

SEASON—TEAM	G	GS	MIN	FGM	FGA	PCT	3FGM	3FGA	PCT	FTM	FTA	PCT	O-RB	D-RB	TOT	AST	PF	DQ	STL	TO	BLK	PTS	RPG	APG	PPG
79-80—Milwaukee	77	—	1557	211	451	.468	0	1	.000	232	292	.795	154	184	338	133	106	0	72	117	16	654	4.4	1.7	8.5
80-81—Milwaukee	80	—	2417	400	739	.541	2	9	.222	320	398	.804	186	220	406	264	156	1	90	145	37	1122	5.1	3.3	14.0
81-82—Milwaukee	80	80	2980	556	1063	.523	1	14	.071	468	573	.817	221	313	534	382	206	3	138	208	22	1581	6.7	4.8	19.8
82-83—Milwaukee	76	76	2710	606	1156	.524	1	10	.100	499	604	.826	192	245	437	300	180	1	113	197	23	1712	5.8	3.9	22.5
83-84—Milwaukee	79	79	3075	560	1125	.498	5	18	.278	529	624	.848	215	313	528	358	204	2	108	217	27	1654	6.7	4.5	20.9
84-85—Milwaukee	73	72	2734	561	1162	.483	9	33	.273	454	548	.828	149	242	391	382	197	1	117	184	39	1585	5.4	5.2	21.7
85-86—Milwaukee	73	72	2567	470	962	.489	33	103	.320	498	580	.859	115	219	334	357	178	1	103	174	18	1471	4.6	4.9	20.2
86-87—Milwaukee	39	30	992	158	324	.488	8	31	.258	136	162	.840	57	70	127	121	73	0	27	63	10	460	3.3	3.1	11.8
87-88—Milwaukee	56	51	1428	217	444	.489	5	31	.161	164	196	.837	58	122	180	204	109	0	41	86	12	603	3.2	3.6	10.8
88-89—Milwaukee	62	50	1594	261	532	.491	25	73	.342	205	237	.865	46	126	172	188	114	1	65	94	13	752	2.8	3.0	12.1
90-91—Atlanta	72	3	1096	117	240	.488	21	64	.328	82	105	.781	31	97	128	104	112	0	50	66	9	337	1.8	1.4	4.7
REG. SEASON TOTALS	767	513	23150	4117	8198	.502	110	387	.284	3587	4319	.831	1424	2151	3575	2793	1635	10	924	1551	226	11931	4.7	3.6	15.6
PLAYOFF TOTALS	93	71	3226	491	1033	.475	17	58	.293	488	602	.811	189	280	469	317	285	3	106	224	36	1487	5.0	3.4	16.0
ALL-STAR TOTALS	5	2	119	19	47	.404	1	1	1.000	19	22	.864	12	10	22	12	7	0	12	8	2	58	4.4	2.4	11.6

MONEY, ERIC V. b. February 6, 1955   Ht. 6-0 Wt. 170 College—Arizona

SEASON—TEAM	G	GS	MIN	FGM	FGA	PCT	3FGM	3FGA	PCT	FTM	FTA	PCT	O-RB	D-RB	TOT	AST	PF	DQ	STL	TO	BLK	PTS	RPG	APG	PPG
74-75—Detroit	66	—	889	144	319	.451	—	—	—	31	45	.689	27	61	88	101	121	3	33	—	2	319	1.3	1.5	4.8
75-76—Detroit	80	—	2267	449	947	.474	—	—	—	145	180	.806	77	130	207	338	243	4	137	—	11	1043	2.6	4.2	13.0
76-77—Detroit	73	—	1586	329	631	.521	—	—	—	90	114	.789	43	81	124	243	199	3	91	—	14	748	1.7	3.3	10.2
77-78—Detroit	76	—	2557	600	1200	.500	—	—	—	214	298	.718	90	119	209	356	237	5	123	322	12	1414	2.8	4.7	18.6
78-79—N.J.-Phil.	69	—	1979	444	893	.497	—	—	—	170	237	.717	70	92	162	331	202	2	87	235	12	1058	2.3	4.8	15.3
79-80—Phil.-Detroit	61	—	1549	273	546	.500	0	0	—	83	106	.783	31	73	104	254	146	3	53	155	11	629	1.7	4.2	10.3
REG. SEASON TOTALS	425	—	10827	2239	4536	.494	0	0	—	733	980	.748	338	556	894	1623	1148	20	524	712	62	5211	2.1	3.8	12.3
PLAYOFF TOTALS	20	—	505	96	210	.457	0	0	—	30	38	.789	18	24	42	93	62	1	23	22	1	222	2.1	4.7	11.1

MONROE, RODNEY EUGENE b. April 16, 1968   Ht. 6-3 Wt. 185 College—North Carolina State

SEASON—TEAM	G	GS	MIN	FGM	FGA	PCT	3FGM	3FGA	PCT	FTM	FTA	PCT	O-RB	D-RB	TOT	AST	PF	DQ	STL	TO	BLK	PTS	RPG	APG	PPG
91-92—Atlanta	38	0	313	53	144	.368	6	27	.222	19	23	.826	12	21	33	27	19	0	12	23	2	131	0.9	0.7	3.4
REG. SEASON TOTALS	38	0	313	53	144	.368	6	27	.222	19	23	.826	12	21	33	27	19	0	12	23	2	131	0.9	0.7	3.4

MONROE, VERNON EARL (Earl, Earl the Pearl) b. November 21, 1944   Ht. 6-3½ Wt. 185 College—Winston-Salem State

SEASON—TEAM	G	GS	MIN	FGM	FGA	PCT	3FGM	3FGA	PCT	FTM	FTA	PCT	O-RB	D-RB	TOT	AST	PF	DQ	STL	TO	BLK	PTS	RPG	APG	PPG
67-68—Baltimore	82	—	3012	742	1637	.453	—	—	—	507	649	.781	—	—	465	349	282	3	—	—	—	1991	5.7	4.3	24.3
68-69—Baltimore	80	—	3075	809	1837	.440	—	—	—	447	582	.768	—	—	280	392	261	1	—	—	—	2065	3.5	4.9	25.8
69-70—Baltimore	82	—	3051	695	1557	.446	—	—	—	532	641	.830	—	—	257	402	258	3	—	—	—	1922	3.1	4.9	23.4
70-71—Baltimore	81	—	2843	663	1501	.442	—	—	—	406	506	.802	—	—	213	354	220	3	—	—	—	1732	2.6	4.4	21.4
71-72—Balt.-N.Y.	63	—	1337	287	662	.434	—	—	—	175	224	.781	—	—	100	142	139	1	—	—	—	749	1.6	2.3	11.9
72-73—New York	75	—	2370	496	1016	.488	—	—	—	171	208	.822	—	—	245	288	195	1	—	—	—	1163	3.3	3.8	15.5
73-74—New York	41	—	1194	240	513	.468	—	—	—	93	113	.823	22	99	121	110	97	0	34	—	19	573	3.0	2.7	14.0
74-75—New York	78	—	2814	668	1462	.457	—	—	—	297	359	.827	56	271	327	270	200	0	108	—	29	1633	4.2	3.5	20.9
75-76—New York	76	—	2889	647	1354	.478	—	—	—	280	356	.787	48	225	273	304	209	1	111	—	22	1574	3.6	4.0	20.7
76-77—New York Knicks	77	—	2656	613	1185	.517	—	—	—	307	366	.839	45	178	223	366	197	0	91	—	23	1533	2.9	4.8	19.9
77-78—New York	76	—	2369	556	1123	.495	—	—	—	242	291	.832	47	135	182	361	189	0	60	179	19	1354	2.4	4.8	17.8
78-79—New York	64	—	1393	329	699	.471	—	—	—	129	154	.838	26	48	74	189	123	0	48	98	6	787	1.2	3.0	12.3
79-80—New York	51	—	633	161	352	.457	0	0	—	56	64	.875	16	20	36	67	46	0	21	28	3	378	0.7	1.3	7.4
REG. SEASON TOTALS	926	—	29636	6906	14898	.464	0	0	—	3642	4513	.807	260	976	2796	3594	2416	13	473	305	121	17454	3.0	3.9	18.8
PLAYOFF TOTALS	82	—	2715	567	1292	.439	0	0	—	337	426	.791	10	52	266	264	216	0	18	6	11	1471	3.2	3.2	17.9
ALL-STAR TOTALS	4	—	85	14	39	.359	0	0	—	12	17	.706	0	3	12	11	10	0	1	—	0	40	3.0	2.8	10.0

MONTGOMERY, HOWARD (Howie) b. August 22, 1940   Ht. 6-4½ Wt. 220 College—Texas-Pan American

SEASON—TEAM	G	GS	MIN	FGM	FGA	PCT	3FGM	3FGA	PCT	FTM	FTA	PCT	O-RB	D-RB	TOT	AST	PF	DQ	STL	TO	BLK	PTS	RPG	APG	PPG
62-63—San Francisco	20	—	364	65	153	.425	—	—	—	14	23	.609	—	—	69	21	35	1	—	—	—	144	3.5	1.1	7.2
REG. SEASON TOTALS	20	—	364	65	153	.425	—	—	—	14	23	.609	—	—	69	21	35	1	—	—	—	144	3.5	1.1	7.2

MOONEY, JAMES J. (Jim) b. July 8, 1930   Ht. 6-5 Wt. 215 College—Villanova

SEASON—TEAM	G	GS	MIN	FGM	FGA	PCT	3FGM	3FGA	PCT	FTM	FTA	PCT	O-RB	D-RB	TOT	AST	PF	DQ	STL	TO	BLK	PTS	RPG	APG	PPG
52-53—Philadelphia	18	—	529	54	148	.365	—	—	—	27	40	.675	—	—	70	35	50	1	—	—	—	135	3.9	1.9	7.5
REG. SEASON TOTALS	18	—	529	54	148	.365	—	—	—	27	40	.675	—	—	70	35	50	1	—	—	—	135	3.9	1.9	7.5

MOORE, ANDRE M. b. July 2, 1964   Ht. 6-9 Wt. 215 College—Illinois/Loyola (Ill.)

SEASON—TEAM	G	GS	MIN	FGM	FGA	PCT	3FGM	3FGA	PCT	FTM	FTA	PCT	O-RB	D-RB	TOT	AST	PF	DQ	STL	TO	BLK	PTS	RPG	APG	PPG
87-88—Denver-Milw.	10	0	50	9	27	.333	0	0	—	6	8	.750	6	8	14	6	6	0	2	4	1	24	1.4	0.6	2.4
REG. SEASON TOTALS	10	0	50	9	27	.333	0	0	—	6	8	.750	6	8	14	6	6	0	2	4	1	24	1.4	0.6	2.4

MOORE, EUGENE WILBERT (**Gene**) b. July 29, 1945 Ht. 6-9 Wt. 235 College—St. Louis

SEASON—TEAM	G	GS	MIN	FGM	FGA	PCT	3FGM	3FGA	PCT	FTM	FTA	PCT	O-RB	D-RB	TOT	AST	PF	DQ	STL	TO	BLK	PTS	RPG	APG	PPG
68-69—Kentucky (A)	76	—	2026	417	920	.453	0	2	.000	204	290	.703	318	499	817	90	311	18	—	160	—	1038	10.8	1.2	13.7
69-70—Kentucky (A)	83	—	2613	630	1390	.453	2	4	.500	209	311	.672	345	657	1002	188	382	25	—	—	—	1471	12.1	2.3	17.7
70-71—Texas (A)	84	—	2243	467	972	.480	2	6	.333	189	280	.675	285	565	850	101	303	—	—	—	—	1125	10.1	1.2	13.4
71-72—Dallas-N.Y. (A)	77	—	1412	253	545	.464	1	3	.333	89	120	.742	—	—	483	53	221	—	—	150	—	596	6.3	0.7	7.7
72-73—San Diego (A)	83	—	2481	400	804	.498	4	11	.364	180	260	.692	324	550	874	152	369	0	—	227	—	984	10.5	1.8	11.9
73-74—San Diego (A)	49	—	897	154	340	.453	1	7	.143	41	85	.482	96	196	292	59	133	—	26	74	51	350	6.0	1.2	7.1
74-75—St. Louis (A)	13	—	108	13	32	.406	0	0	—	4	4	1.000	15	27	42	5	11	—	4	12	7	30	3.2	0.4	2.3
REG. ABA TOTALS	465	—	11780	2334	5003	.467	10	33	.303	916	1350	.679	1383	2494	4360	648	1730	43	30	623	58	5594	9.4	1.4	12.0
ABA PLAYOFF TOTALS	47	—	933	196	440	.445	0	1	.000	87	120	.725	99	200	366	52	153	9	0	39	0	479	7.8	1.1	10.2
ABA ALL-STAR TOTALS	1	—	12	2	6	.333	0	1	.000	0	0	—	0	0	4	0	1	0	0	0	0	4	4.0	0.0	4.0

MOORE, JOHN BRIAN (**Johnny**) b. March 3, 1958 Ht. 6-1 Wt. 175 College—Texas

SEASON—TEAM	G	GS	MIN	FGM	FGA	PCT	3FGM	3FGA	PCT	FTM	FTA	PCT	O-RB	D-RB	TOT	AST	PF	DQ	STL	TO	BLK	PTS	RPG	APG	PPG
80-81—San Antonio	82	—	1578	249	520	.479	1	19	.053	105	172	.610	58	138	196	373	178	0	120	154	22	604	2.4	4.5	7.4
81-82—San Antonio	79	78	2294	309	667	.463	1	21	.048	122	182	.670	62	213	275	762	254	6	163	175	12	741	3.5	9.6	9.4
82-83—San Antonio	77	73	2552	394	841	.468	5	22	.227	148	199	.744	65	212	277	753	247	2	194	226	32	941	3.6	9.8	12.2
83-84—San Antonio	59	42	1650	231	518	.446	28	87	.322	105	139	.755	37	141	178	566	168	2	123	143	20	595	3.0	9.6	10.1
84-85—San Antonio	82	82	2689	416	910	.457	25	89	.281	189	248	.762	94	284	378	816	247	3	229	236	18	1046	4.6	10.0	12.8
85-86—San Antonio	28	23	856	150	303	.495	4	22	.182	59	86	.686	25	61	86	252	78	0	70	81	6	363	3.1	9.0	13.0
86-87—San Antonio	55	27	1234	198	448	.442	22	79	.278	56	70	.800	32	68	100	250	97	0	83	102	3	474	1.8	4.5	8.6
87-88—S.A.-N.J.	5	0	61	4	10	.400	0	1	.000	0	0	—	2	4	6	12	1	0	3	7	0	8	1.2	2.4	1.6
89-90—San Antonio	53	8	516	47	126	.373	8	34	.235	16	27	.593	16	36	52	82	55	0	32	39	3	118	1.0	1.5	2.2
REG. SEASON TOTALS	520	333	13430	1998	4343	.460	94	374	.251	800	1123	.712	391	1157	1548	3866	1325	13	1017	1163	116	4890	3.0	7.4	9.4
PLAYOFF TOTALS	41	25	1084	193	394	.490	10	32	.313	69	101	.683	41	91	132	344	121	0	70	74	13	465	3.2	8.4	11.3

MOORE, JOHN T. (**Jackie**) b. September 24, 1932 Ht. 6-5 Wt. 180 College—La Salle

SEASON—TEAM	G	GS	MIN	FGM	FGA	PCT	3FGM	3FGA	PCT	FTM	FTA	PCT	O-RB	D-RB	TOT	AST	PF	DQ	STL	TO	BLK	PTS	RPG	APG	PPG
54-55—Syr.-Milw.-Phil.	23	—	376	44	115	.383	—	—	—	22	47	.468	—	—	105	20	62	2	—	—	—	110	4.6	0.9	4.8
55-56—Philadelphia	54	—	402	50	129	.388	—	—	—	32	53	.604	—	—	117	26	80	1	—	—	—	132	2.2	0.5	2.4
56-57—Philadelphia	57	—	400	43	106	.406	—	—	—	37	46	.804	—	—	116	21	75	1	—	—	—	123	2.0	0.4	2.2
REG. SEASON TOTALS	134	—	1178	137	350	.391	—	—	—	91	146	.623	—	—	338	67	217	4	—	—	—	365	2.5	0.5	2.7
PLAYOFF TOTALS	9	—	53	8	20	.400	—	—	—	2	6	.333	—	—	17	2	14	0	—	—	—	18	1.9	0.2	2.0

MOORE, LAWRENCE (**Larry**) b. 1944 Ht. 6-7 Wt. 215 College—Nevada-Las Vegas

SEASON—TEAM	G	GS	MIN	FGM	FGA	PCT	3FGM	3FGA	PCT	FTM	FTA	PCT	O-RB	D-RB	TOT	AST	PF	DQ	STL	TO	BLK	PTS	RPG	APG	PPG
67-68—Anaheim (A)	12	—	78	8	33	.242	0	5	.000	11	13	.846	—	—	16	1	17	0	—	7	—	27	1.3	0.1	2.3
REG. ABA TOTALS	12	—	78	8	33	.242	0	5	.000	11	13	.846	—	—	16	1	17	0	—	7	—	27	1.3	0.1	2.3

MOORE, LOWES LEE b. May 5, 1957 Ht. 6-1 Wt. 170 College—West Virginia

SEASON—TEAM	G	GS	MIN	FGM	FGA	PCT	3FGM	3FGA	PCT	FTM	FTA	PCT	O-RB	D-RB	TOT	AST	PF	DQ	STL	TO	BLK	PTS	RPG	APG	PPG
80-81—New Jersey	71	—	1406	212	478	.444	4	27	.148	69	92	.750	43	125	168	228	179	1	61	108	17	497	2.4	3.2	7.0
81-82—Cleveland	4	0	70	19	38	.500	1	5	.200	6	8	.750	1	3	4	15	15	1	6	5	1	45	1.0	3.8	11.3
82-83—San Diego	37	3	642	81	190	.426	6	23	.261	42	56	.750	15	40	55	73	72	1	22	46	1	210	1.5	2.0	5.7
REG. SEASON TOTALS	112	3	2118	312	706	.442	11	55	.200	117	156	.750	59	168	227	316	266	3	89	159	19	752	2.0	2.8	6.7

MOORE, OTTO GEORGE (**Say No Moore**) b. August 27, 1946 Ht. 6-11 Wt. 205 College—Texas-Pan American

SEASON—TEAM	G	GS	MIN	FGM	FGA	PCT	3FGM	3FGA	PCT	FTM	FTA	PCT	O-RB	D-RB	TOT	AST	PF	DQ	STL	TO	BLK	PTS	RPG	APG	PPG
68-69—Detroit	74	—	1605	241	544	.443	—	—	—	88	168	.524	—	—	524	68	182	2	—	—	—	570	7.1	0.9	7.7
69-70—Detroit	81	—	2523	383	805	.476	—	—	—	194	305	.636	—	—	900	104	232	3	—	—	—	960	11.1	1.3	11.9
70-71—Detroit	82	—	1926	310	696	.445	—	—	—	121	219	.553	—	—	700	88	182	0	—	—	—	741	8.5	1.1	9.0
71-72—Phoenix	81	—	1624	260	597	.436	—	—	—	94	156	.603	—	—	540	88	212	2	—	—	—	614	6.7	1.1	7.6
72-73—Houston	82	—	2712	418	859	.487	—	—	—	127	211	.602	—	—	868	167	239	4	—	—	—	963	10.6	2.0	11.7
73-74—Houston-K.C.-Omaha	78	—	946	120	240	.500	—	—	—	39	62	.629	80	204	284	65	99	2	26	—	49	279	3.6	0.8	3.6
74-75—Detroit-N.O.	42	—	1066	118	262	.450	—	—	—	46	69	.667	92	238	330	83	148	3	21	—	40	282	7.9	2.0	6.7
75-76—New Orleans	81	—	2407	293	672	.436	—	—	—	144	226	.637	162	631	793	216	250	3	85	—	136	730	9.8	2.7	9.0
76-77—New Orleans	81	—	2084	193	477	.405	—	—	—	91	134	.679	170	466	636	181	231	3	54	—	117	477	7.9	2.2	5.9
REG. SEASON TOTALS	682	—	16893	2336	5152	.453	—	—	—	944	1550	.609	504	1539	5575	1060	1775	22	186	—	342	5616	8.2	1.6	8.2

MOORE, RICHARD L. b. 1945 Ht. 6-2 Wt. 190 College—Villanova/Hiram Scott

SEASON—TEAM	G	GS	MIN	FGM	FGA	PCT	3FGM	3FGA	PCT	FTM	FTA	PCT	O-RB	D-RB	TOT	AST	PF	DQ	STL	TO	BLK	PTS	RPG	APG	PPG
67-68—Denver (A)	18	—	211	24	71	.338	0	2	.000	21	28	.750	—	—	19	8	16	0	—	24	—	69	1.1	0.4	3.8
REG. ABA TOTALS	18	—	211	24	71	.338	0	2	.000	21	28	.750	—	—	19	8	16	0	—	24	—	69	1.1	0.4	3.8

MOORE, RONALD KEITH (Ron) b. January 16, 1962   Ht. 7-0 Wt. 260 College—Salem/West Virginia State

SEASON—TEAM	G	GS	MIN	FGM	FGA	PCT	3FGM	3FGA	PCT	FTM	FTA	PCT	O-RB	D-RB	TOT	AST	PF	DQ	STL	TO	BLK	PTS	RPG	APG	PPG
87-88—Detroit-Phoenix	14	0	59	9	29	.310	0	0	—	6	8	.750	2	6	8	1	21	0	5	4	0	24	0.6	0.1	1.7
REG. SEASON TOTALS	14	0	59	9	29	.310	0	0	—	6	8	.750	2	6	8	1	21	0	5	4	0	24	0.6	0.1	1.7

MOORE, TRACY LAMONT b. December 28, 1965   Ht. 6-4 Wt. 200 College—Tulsa

SEASON—TEAM	G	GS	MIN	FGM	FGA	PCT	3FGM	3FGA	PCT	FTM	FTA	PCT	O-RB	D-RB	TOT	AST	PF	DQ	STL	TO	BLK	PTS	RPG	APG	PPG
91-92—Dallas	42	2	782	130	325	.400	30	84	.357	65	78	.833	31	51	82	48	97	0	32	44	4	355	2.0	1.1	8.5
92-93—Dallas	39	1	510	103	249	.414	23	67	.343	53	61	.869	23	29	52	47	54	0	21	32	4	282	1.3	1.2	7.2
93-94—Detroit	3	0	10	2	3	.667	0	0	—	2	2	1.000	0	1	1	0	0	0	2	0	0	6	0.3	0.0	2.0
REG. SEASON TOTALS	84	3	1302	235	577	.407	53	151	.351	120	141	.851	54	81	135	95	151	0	55	76	8	643	1.6	1.1	7.7

MORELAND, JACK (Jackie) b. March 11, 1938 d. December 19, 1971   Ht. 6-7 Wt. 215 College—North Carolina State/Louisiana Tech

SEASON—TEAM	G	GS	MIN	FGM	FGA	PCT	3FGM	3FGA	PCT	FTM	FTA	PCT	O-RB	D-RB	TOT	AST	PF	DQ	STL	TO	BLK	PTS	RPG	APG	PPG
60-61—Detroit	64	—	1003	191	477	.400	—	—	—	86	132	.652	—	—	315	52	174	3	—	—	—	468	4.9	0.8	7.3
61-62—Detroit	74	—	1219	205	487	.421	—	—	—	139	186	.747	—	—	427	76	179	2	—	—	—	549	5.8	1.0	7.4
62-63—Detroit	78	—	1516	271	622	.436	—	—	—	145	214	.678	—	—	449	114	226	5	—	—	—	687	5.8	1.5	8.8
63-64—Detroit	78	—	1780	272	639	.426	—	—	—	164	210	.781	—	—	405	121	268	9	—	—	—	708	5.2	1.6	9.1
64-65—Detroit	54	—	732	103	296	.348	—	—	—	66	104	.635	—	—	183	69	151	4	—	—	—	272	3.4	1.3	5.0
67-68—New Orleans (A)	76	—	2332	459	1051	.437	2	4	.500	192	263	.730	—	—	619	138	289	13	—	124	—	1112	8.1	1.8	14.6
68-69—New Orleans (A)	78	—	2714	468	1109	.422	2	8	.250	221	313	.706	—	—	633	207	310	11	—	171	—	1159	8.1	2.7	14.9
69-70—New Orleans (A)	80	—	2321	317	765	.414	2	8	.250	139	176	.790	—	—	386	160	250	8	—	—	—	775	4.8	2.0	9.7
REG. NBA TOTALS	348	—	6250	1042	2521	.413	—	—	—	600	846	.709	—	—	1779	432	998	23	—	—	—	2684	5.1	1.2	7.7
REG. ABA TOTALS	234	—	7367	1244	2925	.425	6	20	.300	552	752	.734	—	—	1638	505	849	32	—	295	—	3046	7.0	2.2	13.0
NBA PLAYOFF TOTALS	14	—	223	44	90	.489	—	—	—	15	22	.682	—	—	62	16	50	1	—	—	—	103	4.4	1.1	7.4
ABA PLAYOFF TOTALS	28	—	829	143	342	.418	0	2	.000	61	92	.663	—	—	193	70	123	4	—	46	—	347	6.9	2.5	12.4

MORGAN, MUNDEN GUY (Guy) b. August 23, 1960   Ht. 6-8 Wt. 215 College—Wake Forest

SEASON—TEAM	G	GS	MIN	FGM	FGA	PCT	3FGM	3FGA	PCT	FTM	FTA	PCT	O-RB	D-RB	TOT	AST	PF	DQ	STL	TO	BLK	PTS	RPG	APG	PPG
82-83—Indiana	8	0	46	7	24	.292	0	0	—	1	4	.250	6	11	17	7	7	0	2	2	0	15	2.1	0.9	1.9
REG. SEASON TOTALS	8	0	46	7	24	.292	0	0	—	1	4	.250	6	11	17	7	7	0	2	2	0	15	2.1	0.9	1.9

MORGAN, REX b. October 27, 1948   Ht. 6-5 Wt. 190 College—Lakeland JC/Jacksonville

SEASON—TEAM	G	GS	MIN	FGM	FGA	PCT	3FGM	3FGA	PCT	FTM	FTA	PCT	O-RB	D-RB	TOT	AST	PF	DQ	STL	TO	BLK	PTS	RPG	APG	PPG
70-71—Boston	34	—	266	41	102	.402	—	—	—	35	54	.648	—	—	61	22	58	2	—	—	—	117	1.8	0.6	3.4
71-72—Boston	28	—	150	16	50	.320	—	—	—	23	31	.742	—	—	30	17	34	0	—	—	—	55	1.1	0.6	2.0
REG. SEASON TOTALS	62	—	416	57	152	.375	—	—	—	58	85	.682	—	—	91	39	92	2	—	—	—	172	1.5	0.6	2.8
PLAYOFF TOTALS	4	—	10	1	7	.143	—	—	—	1	3	.333	—	—	5	—	6	0	—	—	—	3	1.3	0.0	0.8

MORGENTHALER, ELMORE ROBERT (Elmo) b. August 3, 1922   Ht. 7-1 Wt. 230 College—Boston College/New Mexico School of Mines

SEASON—TEAM	G	GS	MIN	FGM	FGA	PCT	3FGM	3FGA	PCT	FTM	FTA	PCT	O-RB	D-RB	TOT	AST	PF	DQ	STL	TO	BLK	PTS	RPG	APG	PPG
46-47—Providence	11	—	—	4	13	.308	—	—	—	7	12	.583	—	—	—	3	3	—	—	—	—	15	—	0.3	1.4
48-49—Philadelphia	20	—	—	15	39	.385	—	—	—	12	18	.667	—	—	—	7	18	—	—	—	—	42	—	0.4	2.1
REG. SEASON TOTALS	31	—	—	19	52	.365	—	—	—	19	30	.633	—	—	—	10	21	—	—	—	—	57	—	0.3	1.8

MORNINGSTAR, DARREN b. April 22, 1969   Ht. 6-10 Wt. 235 College—Navy/Pittsburgh

SEASON—TEAM	G	GS	MIN	FGM	FGA	PCT	3FGM	3FGA	PCT	FTM	FTA	PCT	O-RB	D-RB	TOT	AST	PF	DQ	STL	TO	BLK	PTS	RPG	APG	PPG
93-94—Dallas-Utah	23	15	367	39	82	.476	0	0	—	18	30	.600	31	50	81	15	70	1	14	19	2	96	3.5	0.7	4.2
REG. SEASON TOTALS	23	15	367	39	82	.476	0	0	—	18	30	.600	31	50	81	15	70	1	14	19	2	96	3.5	0.7	4.2

MORRIS, CHRISTOPHER VERNARD (Chris) b. January 20, 1966   Ht. 6-8 Wt. 220 College—Auburn

SEASON—TEAM	G	GS	MIN	FGM	FGA	PCT	3FGM	3FGA	PCT	FTM	FTA	PCT	O-RB	D-RB	TOT	AST	PF	DQ	STL	TO	BLK	PTS	RPG	APG	PPG
88-89—New Jersey	76	48	2096	414	905	.457	64	175	.366	182	254	.717	188	209	397	119	250	4	102	190	60	1074	5.2	1.6	14.1
89-90—New Jersey	80	76	2449	449	1065	.422	61	193	.316	228	316	.722	194	228	422	143	219	1	130	185	79	1187	5.3	1.8	14.8
90-91—New Jersey	79	68	2553	409	962	.425	45	179	.251	179	244	.734	210	311	521	220	248	5	138	167	96	1042	6.6	2.8	13.2
91-92—New Jersey	77	74	2394	346	726	.477	22	110	.200	165	231	.714	199	295	494	197	211	2	129	171	81	879	6.4	2.6	11.4
92-93—New Jersey	77	57	2302	436	907	.481	17	76	.224	197	248	.794	227	227	454	106	171	2	144	119	52	1086	5.9	1.4	14.1
93-94—New Jersey	50	27	1349	203	454	.447	53	147	.361	85	118	.720	91	137	228	83	120	2	55	52	49	544	4.6	1.7	10.9
REG. SEASON TOTALS	439	350	13143	2257	5019	.450	262	880	.298	1036	1411	.734	1109	1407	2516	868	1219	16	698	884	417	5812	5.7	2.0	13.2
PLAYOFF TOTALS	13	11	396	78	162	.481	13	46	.283	28	31	.903	35	39	74	19	33	0	20	17	18	197	5.7	1.5	15.2

MORRIS, GLEN MAX (**Max**) b. March 14, 1925 Ht. 6-2 Wt. 195 College—Illinois/Northwestern

SEASON—TEAM	G	GS	MIN	FGM	FGA	PCT	3FGM	3FGA	PCT	FTM	FTA	PCT	O-RB	D-RB	TOT	AST	PF	DQ	STL	TO	BLK	PTS	RPG	APG	PPG
46-47—Chicago (N)	33	—	—	44	—	—	—	—	—	33	63	.524	—	—	—	—	59	—	—	—	—	121	—	—	3.7
47-48—Sheboygan (N)	39	—	—	132	—	—	—	—	—	132	215	.614	—	—	—	—	107	—	—	—	—	396	—	—	10.2
48-49—Sheboygan (N)	41	—	—	70	—	—	—	—	—	68	104	.654	—	—	—	—	83	—	—	—	—	208	—	—	5.1
49-50—Sheboygan	62	—	—	252	694	.363	—	—	—	277	415	.667	—	—	—	194	172	—	—	—	—	781	—	3.1	12.6
REG. NBA TOTALS	62	—	—	252	694	.363	—	—	—	277	415	.667	—	—	—	194	172	—	—	—	—	781	—	3.1	12.6
REG. NBL TOTALS	113	—	—	246	—	—	—	—	—	233	382	.610	—	—	—	—	249	—	—	—	—	725	—	—	6.4
NBA PLAYOFF TOTALS	3	—	—	14	40	.350	—	—	—	15	26	.577	—	—	—	14	8	—	—	—	—	43	—	4.7	14.3
NBL PLAYOFF TOTALS	12	—	—	12	—	—	—	—	—	4	10	.400	—	—	—	—	27	—	—	—	—	28	—	—	2.3

MORRIS, ISAIAH BUTCH b. April 2, 1969 Ht. 6-8 Wt. 230 College—San Jacinto/Arkansas

SEASON—TEAM	G	GS	MIN	FGM	FGA	PCT	3FGM	3FGA	PCT	FTM	FTA	PCT	O-RB	D-RB	TOT	AST	PF	DQ	STL	TO	BLK	PTS	RPG	APG	PPG
92-93—Detroit	25	0	102	26	57	.456	0	0	—	3	4	.750	6	6	12	4	14	0	3	8	1	55	0.5	0.2	2.2
REG. SEASON TOTALS	25	0	102	26	57	.456	0	0	—	3	4	.750	6	6	12	4	14	0	3	8	1	55	0.5	0.2	2.2

MORRISON, DWIGHT W. (**Red**) b. April 26, 1932 Ht. 6-8 Wt. 225 College—Idaho

SEASON—TEAM	G	GS	MIN	FGM	FGA	PCT	3FGM	3FGA	PCT	FTM	FTA	PCT	O-RB	D-RB	TOT	AST	PF	DQ	STL	TO	BLK	PTS	RPG	APG	PPG
54-55—Boston	71	—	1227	120	284	.423	—	—	—	72	115	.626	—	—	451	82	222	10	—	—	—	312	6.4	1.2	4.4
55-56—Boston	71	—	910	89	240	.371	—	—	—	44	89	.494	—	—	345	53	159	5	—	—	—	222	4.9	0.7	3.1
57-58—St. Louis	13	—	79	9	26	.346	—	—	—	3	4	.750	—	—	26	0	12	0	—	—	—	21	2.0	0.0	1.6
REG. SEASON TOTALS	155	—	2216	218	550	.396	—	—	—	119	208	.572	—	—	822	135	393	15	—	—	—	555	5.3	0.9	3.6
PLAYOFF TOTALS	10	—	65	5	15	.333	—	—	—	1	7	.143	—	—	25	1	27	1	—	—	—	11	2.5	0.1	1.1

MORRISON, JOHN RUSSELL b. May 2, 1945 Ht. 6-2 Wt. 190 College—Canisius

SEASON—TEAM	G	GS	MIN	FGM	FGA	PCT	3FGM	3FGA	PCT	FTM	FTA	PCT	O-RB	D-RB	TOT	AST	PF	DQ	STL	TO	BLK	PTS	RPG	APG	PPG
67-68—Denver (A)	9	—	76	10	34	.294	1	6	.167	6	9	.667	—	—	9	7	15	0	—	9	—	27	1.0	0.8	3.0
REG. ABA TOTALS	9	—	76	10	34	.294	1	6	.167	6	9	.667	—	—	9	7	15	0	—	9	—	27	1.0	0.8	3.0

MORRISON, MICHAEL FITZGERALD (**Mike**) b. August 16, 1967 Ht. 6-4 Wt. 195 College—Loyola (Maryland)

SEASON—TEAM	G	GS	MIN	FGM	FGA	PCT	3FGM	3FGA	PCT	FTM	FTA	PCT	O-RB	D-RB	TOT	AST	PF	DQ	STL	TO	BLK	PTS	RPG	APG	PPG
89-90—Phoenix	36	1	153	23	68	.338	2	7	.286	24	30	.800	7	13	20	11	20	0	2	23	0	72	0.6	0.3	2.0
REG. SEASON TOTALS	36	1	153	23	68	.338	2	7	.286	24	30	.800	7	13	20	11	20	0	2	23	0	72	0.6	0.3	2.0

MORTON, JOHN JR. (**Salt**) b. May 18, 1967 Ht. 6-3 Wt. 195 College—Seton Hall

SEASON—TEAM	G	GS	MIN	FGM	FGA	PCT	3FGM	3FGA	PCT	FTM	FTA	PCT	O-RB	D-RB	TOT	AST	PF	DQ	STL	TO	BLK	PTS	RPG	APG	PPG
89-90—Cleveland	37	3	402	48	161	.298	7	30	.233	43	62	.694	7	25	32	67	30	0	18	51	4	146	0.9	1.8	3.9
90-91—Cleveland	66	2	1207	120	274	.438	4	12	.333	113	139	.813	41	62	103	243	112	1	61	107	18	357	1.6	3.7	5.4
91-92—Clev.-Miami	25	0	270	36	93	.387	2	16	.125	32	38	.842	6	20	26	32	23	0	13	28	1	106	1.0	1.3	4.2
REG. SEASON TOTALS	128	5	1879	204	528	.386	13	58	.224	188	239	.787	54	107	161	342	165	1	92	186	23	609	1.3	2.7	4.8
PLAYOFF TOTALS	3	0	11	2	5	.400	0	0	—	4	4	1.000	0	0	0	—	1	0	0	2	0	8	0.0	0.0	2.7

MORTON, RICHARD b. February 2, 1966 Ht. 6-3 Wt. 190 College—Cal State-Fullerton

SEASON—TEAM	G	GS	MIN	FGM	FGA	PCT	3FGM	3FGA	PCT	FTM	FTA	PCT	O-RB	D-RB	TOT	AST	PF	DQ	STL	TO	BLK	PTS	RPG	APG	PPG
88-89—Indiana	2	0	11	3	4	.750	0	0	—	0	0	—	0	0	0	1	2	0	0	1	0	6	0.0	0.5	3.0
REG. SEASON TOTALS	2	0	11	3	4	.750	0	0	—	0	0	—	0	0	0	1	2	0	0	1	0	6	0.0	0.5	3.0

MOSLEY, GLENN E. b. December 26, 1955 Ht. 6-8 Wt. 195 College—Seton Hall

SEASON—TEAM	G	GS	MIN	FGM	FGA	PCT	3FGM	3FGA	PCT	FTM	FTA	PCT	O-RB	D-RB	TOT	AST	PF	DQ	STL	TO	BLK	PTS	RPG	APG	PPG
77-78—Philadelphia	6	—	21	5	13	.385	—	—	—	3	7	.429	0	5	5	2	5	0	0	5	0	13	0.8	0.3	2.2
78-79—San Antonio	26	—	221	31	75	.413	—	—	—	23	38	.605	27	37	64	19	35	0	8	20	10	85	2.5	0.7	3.3
REG. SEASON TOTALS	32	—	242	36	88	.409	—	—	—	26	45	.578	27	42	69	21	40	0	8	25	10	98	2.2	0.7	3.1
PLAYOFF TOTALS	3	—	6	2	3	.667	—	—	—	1	3	.333	0	1	1	1	0	0	0	1	5	0.3	0.3	1.7

MOSS, PERRY VICTOR b. November 11, 1958 Ht. 6-2 Wt. 185 College—Northeastern

SEASON—TEAM	G	GS	MIN	FGM	FGA	PCT	3FGM	3FGA	PCT	FTM	FTA	PCT	O-RB	D-RB	TOT	AST	PF	DQ	STL	TO	BLK	PTS	RPG	APG	PPG
85-86—Wash.-Phil.	72	0	1012	116	292	.397	7	32	.219	65	89	.730	34	81	115	108	132	1	56	79	15	304	1.6	1.5	4.2
86-87—Golden State	64	0	698	91	207	.440	1	14	.071	49	69	.710	29	66	95	90	96	0	42	57	3	232	1.5	1.4	3.6
REG. SEASON TOTALS	136	0	1710	207	499	.415	8	46	.174	114	158	.722	63	147	210	198	228	1	98	136	18	536	1.5	1.5	3.9
PLAYOFF TOTALS	15	0	73	10	22	.455	1	2	.500	9	10	.900	2	6	8	7	11	0	6	7	1	30	0.5	0.5	2.0

MOUNT, RICHARD CARL (Rick) b. January 5, 1947 Ht. 6-4 Wt. 185 College—Purdue

SEASON—TEAM	G	GS	MIN	FGM	FGA	PCT	3FGM	3FGA	PCT	FTM	FTA	PCT	O-RB	D-RB	TOT	AST	PF	DQ	STL	TO	BLK	PTS	RPG	APG	PPG
70-71—Indiana (A)	66	—	832	149	402	.371	23	79	.291	116	145	.800	—	—	71	107	127	—	—	—	—	437	1.1	1.6	6.6
71-72—Indiana (A)	78	—	2126	420	949	.443	57	180	.317	216	261	.828	—	—	155	230	233	—	—	142	—	1113	2.0	2.9	14.3
72-73—Kentucky (A)	61	—	1780	369	804	.459	9	30	.300	159	198	.803	50	88	138	194	172	0	—	119	—	906	2.3	3.2	14.9
73-74—Ken.-Utah (A)	52	—	753	179	410	.437	12	46	.261	59	71	.831	27	33	60	66	77	—	27	48	1	429	1.2	1.3	8.3
74-75—Memphis (A)	26	—	895	181	431	.420	20	47	.426	63	73	.863	14	37	51	79	44	—	28	41	7	445	2.0	3.0	17.1
REG. ABA TOTALS	283	—	6386	1298	2996	.433	121	382	.317	613	748	.820	91	158	475	676	653	0	55	350	8	3330	1.7	2.4	11.8
ABA PLAYOFF TOTALS	65	—	1498	290	714	.406	28	85	.329	120	143	.839	7	17	104	106	128	0	9	75	6	728	1.6	1.6	11.2

MOURNING, ALONZO b. February 8, 1970 Ht. 6-10 Wt. 240 College—Georgetown

SEASON—TEAM	G	GS	MIN	FGM	FGA	PCT	3FGM	3FGA	PCT	FTM	FTA	PCT	O-RB	D-RB	TOT	AST	PF	DQ	STL	TO	BLK	PTS	RPG	APG	PPG
92-93—Charlotte	78	78	2644	572	1119	.511	0	3	.000	495	634	.781	263	542	805	76	286	6	27	236	271	1639	10.3	1.0	21.0
93-94—Charlotte	60	59	2018	427	845	.505	0	2	.000	433	568	.762	177	433	610	86	207	3	27	199	188	1287	10.2	1.4	21.5
REG. SEASON TOTALS	138	137	4662	999	1964	.509	0	5	.000	928	1202	.772	440	975	1415	162	493	9	54	435	459	2926	10.3	1.2	21.2
PLAYOFF TOTALS	9	9	367	71	148	.480	0	2	.000	72	93	.774	28	61	89	13	37	1	6	37	31	214	9.9	1.4	23.8

MRAZOVICH, CHARLES (Chuck) b. February 26, 1924 Ht. 6-5 Wt. 185 College—Eastern Kentucky

SEASON—TEAM	G	GS	MIN	FGM	FGA	PCT	3FGM	3FGA	PCT	FTM	FTA	PCT	O-RB	D-RB	TOT	AST	PF	DQ	STL	TO	BLK	PTS	RPG	APG	PPG
50-51—Indianapolis	23	—	—	24	73	.329	—	—	—	28	46	.609	—	—	33	12	48	1	—	—	—	76	1.4	0.5	3.3
REG. SEASON TOTALS	23	—	—	24	73	.329	—	—	—	28	46	.609	—	—	33	12	48	1	—	—	—	76	1.4	0.5	3.3

MUELLER, ERWIN L. b. March 12, 1944 Ht. 6-8 Wt. 230 College—San Francisco

SEASON—TEAM	G	GS	MIN	FGM	FGA	PCT	3FGM	3FGA	PCT	FTM	FTA	PCT	O-RB	D-RB	TOT	AST	PF	DQ	STL	TO	BLK	PTS	RPG	APG	PPG
66-67—Chicago	80	—	2136	422	957	.441	—	—	—	171	260	.658	—	—	497	131	223	2	—	—	—	1015	6.2	1.6	12.7
67-68—Chicago-L.A.	74	—	1788	223	489	.456	—	—	—	107	185	.578	—	—	389	154	164	3	—	—	—	553	5.3	2.1	7.5
68-69—Chicago-Seattle	78	—	1355	144	384	.375	—	—	—	89	162	.549	—	—	297	186	143	1	—	—	—	377	3.8	2.4	4.8
69-70—Seattle-Detroit	78	—	2353	300	646	.464	—	—	—	189	263	.719	—	—	483	205	192	1	—	—	—	789	6.2	2.6	10.1
70-71—Detroit	52	—	1224	126	309	.408	—	—	—	60	108	.556	—	—	223	113	99	0	—	—	—	312	4.3	2.2	6.0
71-72—Detroit	42	—	605	68	197	.345	—	—	—	43	74	.581	—	—	147	57	64	0	—	—	—	179	3.5	1.4	4.3
72-73—Detroit	21	—	80	9	31	.290	—	—	—	5	7	.714	—	—	14	7	13	0	—	—	—	23	0.7	0.3	1.1
72-73—Virginia (A)	17	—	205	17	53	.321	0	0	—	3	10	.300	17	30	47	26	24	0	—	22	—	37	2.8	1.5	2.2
73-74—Memphis (A)	3	—	20	0	4	.000	0	0	—	2	5	.400	0	3	3	2	5	—	0	3	0	2	1.0	0.7	0.7
REG. NBA TOTALS	425	—	9541	1292	3013	.429	—	—	—	664	1059	.627	—	—	2050	853	898	7	—	—	—	3248	4.8	2.0	7.6
REG. ABA TOTALS	20	—	225	17	57	.298	0	0	—	5	15	.333	17	33	50	28	29	0	0	25	0	39	2.5	1.4	2.0
NBA PLAYOFF TOTALS	17	—	334	28	85	.329	—	—	—	15	28	.536	—	—	68	27	39	0	—	—	—	71	4.0	1.6	4.2
ABA PLAYOFF TOTALS	5	—	112	5	18	.278	1	1	1.000	6	7	.857	0	0	19	15	10	0	0	11	0	17	3.8	3.0	3.4

MULLANEY, JOSEPH A. (Joe) b. November 17, 1925 Ht. 6-0 Wt. 165 College—Holy Cross

SEASON—TEAM	G	GS	MIN	FGM	FGA	PCT	3FGM	3FGA	PCT	FTM	FTA	PCT	O-RB	D-RB	TOT	AST	PF	DQ	STL	TO	BLK	PTS	RPG	APG	PPG
49-50—Boston	37	—	—	9	70	.129	—	—	—	12	15	.800	—	—	—	52	30	—	—	—	—	30	—	1.4	0.8
REG. SEASON TOTALS	37	—	—	9	70	.129	—	—	—	12	15	.800	—	—	—	52	30	—	—	—	—	30	—	1.4	0.8

MULLENS, ROBERT J. (Bob) b. November 1, 1922 Ht. 6-1 Wt. 175 College—Fordham

SEASON—TEAM	G	GS	MIN	FGM	FGA	PCT	3FGM	3FGA	PCT	FTM	FTA	PCT	O-RB	D-RB	TOT	AST	PF	DQ	STL	TO	BLK	PTS	RPG	APG	PPG
46-47—N.Y.-Toronto	54	—	—	125	445	.281	—	—	—	64	102	.627	—	—	—	54	94	—	—	—	—	314	—	1.0	5.8
REG. SEASON TOTALS	54	—	—	125	445	.281	—	—	—	64	102	.627	—	—	—	54	94	—	—	—	—	314	—	1.0	5.8

MULLIN, CHRISTOPHER PAUL (Chris) b. July 30, 1963 Ht. 6-7 Wt. 220 College—St. John's

SEASON—TEAM	G	GS	MIN	FGM	FGA	PCT	3FGM	3FGA	PCT	FTM	FTA	PCT	O-RB	D-RB	TOT	AST	PF	DQ	STL	TO	BLK	PTS	RPG	APG	PPG
85-86—Golden State	55	30	1391	287	620	.463	5	27	.185	189	211	.896	42	73	115	105	130	1	70	75	23	768	2.1	1.9	14.0
86-87—Golden State	82	82	2377	477	928	.514	19	63	.302	269	326	.825	39	142	181	261	217	1	98	154	36	1242	2.2	3.2	15.1
87-88—Golden State	60	55	2033	470	926	.508	34	97	.351	239	270	.885	58	147	205	290	136	3	113	156	32	1213	3.4	4.8	20.2
88-89—Golden State	82	82	3093	830	1630	.509	23	100	.230	493	553	.892	152	331	483	415	178	1	176	296	39	2176	5.9	5.1	26.5
89-90—Golden State	78	78	2830	682	1272	.536	87	234	.372	505	568	.889	130	333	463	319	142	1	123	239	45	1956	5.9	4.1	25.1
90-91—Golden State	82	82	3315	777	1449	.536	40	133	.301	513	580	.884	141	302	443	329	176	2	173	245	63	2107	5.4	4.0	25.7
91-92—Golden State	81	81	3346	830	1584	.524	64	175	.366	350	420	.833	127	323	450	286	171	1	173	202	62	2074	5.6	3.5	25.6
92-93—Golden State	46	46	1902	474	930	.510	60	133	.451	183	226	.810	42	190	232	166	76	0	68	139	41	1191	5.0	3.6	25.9
93-94—Golden State	62	39	2324	410	869	.472	55	151	.364	165	219	.753	64	281	345	315	114	0	107	178	53	1040	5.6	5.1	16.8
REG. SEASON TOTALS	628	575	22611	5237	10208	.513	387	1113	.348	2906	3373	.862	795	2122	2917	2486	1340	10	1101	1684	394	13767	4.6	4.0	21.9
PLAYOFF TOTALS	33	33	1272	263	506	.520	23	49	.469	136	158	.861	29	117	146	105	85	0	43	88	32	685	4.4	3.2	20.8
ALL-STAR TOTALS	4	2	78	12	24	.500	2	2	1.000	7	8	.875	3	5	8	8	2	0	4	5	1	33	2.0	2.0	8.3

MULLINS, JEFFREY VINCENT JR. (Jeff, Pork Chop) b. March 18, 1942 Ht. 6-4 Wt. 190 College—Duke

SEASON—TEAM	G	GS	MIN	FGM	FGA	PCT	3FGM	3FGA	PCT	FTM	FTA	PCT	O-RB	D-RB	TOT	AST	PF	DQ	STL	TO	BLK	PTS	RPG	APG	PPG
64-65—St. Louis	44	—	492	87	209	.416	—	—	—	41	61	.672	—	—	102	44	60	0	—	—	—	215	2.3	1.0	4.9
65-66—St. Louis	44	—	587	113	296	.382	—	—	—	29	36	.806	—	—	69	66	68	1	—	—	—	255	1.6	1.5	5.8
66-67—San Francisco	75	—	1835	421	919	.458	—	—	—	150	214	.701	—	—	388	226	195	5	—	—	—	992	5.2	3.0	13.2
67-68—San Francisco	79	—	2805	610	1391	.439	—	—	—	273	344	.794	—	—	447	351	271	2	—	—	—	1493	5.7	4.4	18.9
68-69—San Francisco	78	—	2916	697	1517	.459	—	—	—	381	452	.843	—	—	460	339	251	4	—	—	—	1775	5.9	4.3	22.8
69-70—San Francisco	74	—	2861	656	1426	.460	—	—	—	320	378	.847	—	—	382	360	240	4	—	—	—	1632	5.2	4.9	22.1
70-71—San Francisco	75	—	2909	630	1308	.482	—	—	—	302	358	.844	—	—	341	332	246	5	—	—	—	1562	4.5	4.4	20.8
71-72—Golden State	80	—	3214	685	1466	.467	—	—	—	350	441	.794	—	—	444	471	260	5	—	—	—	1720	5.6	5.9	21.5
72-73—Golden State	81	—	3005	651	1321	.493	—	—	—	143	172	.831	—	—	363	337	201	2	—	—	—	1445	4.5	4.2	17.8
73-74—Golden State	77	—	2498	541	1144	.473	—	—	—	168	192	.875	86	190	276	305	214	2	69	—	22	1250	3.6	4.0	16.2
74-75—Golden State	66	—	1141	234	514	.455	—	—	—	71	87	.816	46	77	123	153	123	0	57	—	14	539	1.9	2.3	8.2
75-76—Golden State	29	—	311	58	120	.483	—	—	—	23	29	.793	12	20	32	39	36	0	14	—	1	139	1.1	1.3	4.8
REG. SEASON TOTALS	802	—	24574	5383	11631	.463	—	—	—	2251	2764	.814	144	287	3427	3023	2165	30	140	—	37	13017	4.3	3.8	16.2
PLAYOFF TOTALS	83	—	2255	462	1030	.449	—	—	—	160	213	.751	19	20	304	259	217	5	12	—	2	1084	3.7	3.1	13.1
ALL-STAR TOTALS	3	—	42	11	20	.550	—	—	—	0	0	—	0	0	5	6	6	0	0	—	0	22	1.7	2.0	7.3

MUNK, CHRISTIAN (Chris) b. August 5, 1967 Ht. 6-9 Wt. 225 College—USC

SEASON—TEAM	G	GS	MIN	FGM	FGA	PCT	3FGM	3FGA	PCT	FTM	FTA	PCT	O-RB	D-RB	TOT	AST	PF	DQ	STL	TO	BLK	PTS	RPG	APG	PPG
90-91—Utah	11	0	29	3	7	.429	0	0	—	7	12	.583	5	9	14	1	5	0	1	5	2	13	1.3	0.1	1.2
REG. SEASON TOTALS	11	0	29	3	7	.429	0	0	—	7	12	.583	5	9	14	1	5	0	1	5	2	13	1.3	0.1	1.2

MUNROE, GEORGE B. b. January 5, 1922 Ht. 5-11½ Wt. 170 College—Columbia/Dartmouth

SEASON—TEAM	G	GS	MIN	FGM	FGA	PCT	3FGM	3FGA	PCT	FTM	FTA	PCT	O-RB	D-RB	TOT	AST	PF	DQ	STL	TO	BLK	PTS	RPG	APG	PPG
46-47—St. Louis	59	—	—	164	623	.263	—	—	—	86	133	.647	—	—	—	17	91	—	—	—	—	414	—	0.3	7.0
47-48—Boston	21	—	—	27	91	.297	—	—	—	17	26	.654	—	—	—	3	20	—	—	—	—	71	—	0.1	3.4
REG. SEASON TOTALS	80	—	—	191	714	.268	—	—	—	103	159	.648	—	—	—	20	111	—	—	—	—	485	—	0.3	6.1
PLAYOFF TOTALS	6	—	—	16	36	.444	—	—	—	6	9	.667	—	—	—	1	10	—	—	—	—	38	—	0.2	6.3

MURDOCK, ERIC LLOYD b. June 14, 1968 Ht. 6-1 Wt. 190 College—Providence

SEASON—TEAM	G	GS	MIN	FGM	FGA	PCT	3FGM	3FGA	PCT	FTM	FTA	PCT	O-RB	D-RB	TOT	AST	PF	DQ	STL	TO	BLK	PTS	RPG	APG	PPG
91-92—Utah	50	0	478	76	183	.415	5	26	.192	46	61	.754	21	33	54	92	52	0	30	50	7	203	1.1	1.8	4.1
92-93—Milwaukee	79	78	2437	438	936	.468	31	119	.261	231	296	.780	95	189	284	603	177	2	174	207	7	1138	3.6	7.6	14.4
93-94—Milwaukee	82	76	2533	477	1019	.468	69	168	.411	234	288	.813	91	170	261	546	189	2	197	206	12	1257	3.2	6.7	15.3
REG. SEASON TOTALS	211	154	5448	991	2138	.464	105	313	.335	511	645	.792	207	392	599	1241	418	4	401	463	26	2598	2.8	5.9	12.3
PLAYOFF TOTALS	3	0	11	3	5	.600	0	1	.000	2	2	1.000	0	3	3	1	1	0	1	3	1	8	1.0	0.3	2.7

MURESAN, GHEORGHE b. February 14, 1971 Ht. 7-7 Wt. 320 College—Cluj (Romania)

SEASON—TEAM	G	GS	MIN	FGM	FGA	PCT	3FGM	3FGA	PCT	FTM	FTA	PCT	O-RB	D-RB	TOT	AST	PF	DQ	STL	TO	BLK	PTS	RPG	APG	PPG
93-94—Washington	54	2	650	128	235	.545	0	0	—	48	71	.676	66	126	192	18	120	1	28	54	48	304	3.6	0.3	5.6
REG. SEASON TOTALS	54	2	650	128	235	.545	0	0	—	48	71	.676	66	126	192	18	120	1	28	54	48	304	3.6	0.3	5.6

MURPHY, ALLEN b. July 15, 1952 Ht. 6-5 Wt. 190 College—Louisville

SEASON—TEAM	G	GS	MIN	FGM	FGA	PCT	3FGM	3FGA	PCT	FTM	FTA	PCT	O-RB	D-RB	TOT	AST	PF	DQ	STL	TO	BLK	PTS	RPG	APG	PPG
75-76—Kentucky (A)	29	—	248	43	114	.377	0	1	.000	27	37	.730	24	23	47	13	52	—	10	27	8	113	1.6	0.4	3.9
76-77—Los Angeles	2	—	18	1	5	.200	—	—	—	3	7	.429	3	1	4	0	5	0	0	—	0	5	2.0	0.0	2.5
REG. NBA TOTALS	2	—	18	1	5	.200	—	—	—	3	7	.429	3	1	4	0	5	0	0	—	0	5	2.0	0.0	2.5
REG. ABA TOTALS	29	—	248	43	114	.377	0	1	.000	27	37	.730	24	23	47	13	52	—	10	27	8	113	1.6	0.4	3.9

MURPHY, CALVIN JEROME (Cal) b. May 9, 1948 Ht. 5-9 Wt. 165 College—Niagara

SEASON—TEAM	G	GS	MIN	FGM	FGA	PCT	3FGM	3FGA	PCT	FTM	FTA	PCT	O-RB	D-RB	TOT	AST	PF	DQ	STL	TO	BLK	PTS	RPG	APG	PPG
70-71—San Diego	82	—	2020	471	1029	.458	—	—	—	356	434	.820	—	—	245	329	263	4	—	—	—	1298	3.0	4.0	15.8
71-72—Houston	82	—	2538	571	1255	.455	—	—	—	349	392	.890	—	—	258	393	298	6	—	—	—	1491	3.1	4.8	18.2
72-73—Houston	77	—	1697	381	820	.465	—	—	—	239	269	.888	—	—	149	262	211	3	—	—	—	1001	1.9	3.4	13.0
73-74—Houston	81	—	2922	671	1285	.522	—	—	—	310	357	.868	51	137	188	603	310	8	157	—	4	1652	2.3	7.4	20.4
74-75—Houston	78	—	2513	557	1152	.484	—	—	—	341	386	.883	52	121	173	381	281	8	128	—	4	1455	2.2	4.9	18.7
75-76—Houston	82	—	2995	675	1369	.493	—	—	—	372	410	.907	52	157	209	596	294	3	151	—	6	1722	2.5	7.3	21.0
76-77—Houston	82	—	2764	596	1216	.490	—	—	—	272	307	.886	54	118	172	386	281	6	144	—	8	1464	2.1	4.7	17.9
77-78—Houston	76	—	2900	852	1737	.491	—	—	—	245	267	.918	57	107	164	259	241	4	112	173	3	1949	2.2	3.4	25.6
78-79—Houston	82	—	2941	707	1424	.496	—	—	—	246	265	.928	78	95	173	351	288	5	117	187	6	1660	2.1	4.3	20.2
79-80—Houston	76	—	2676	624	1267	.493	1	25	.040	271	302	.897	68	82	150	299	269	3	143	162	9	1520	2.0	3.9	20.0
80-81—Houston	76	—	2014	528	1074	.492	4	17	.235	206	215	.958	33	54	87	222	209	0	111	129	6	1266	1.1	2.9	16.7
81-82—Houston	64	0	1204	277	648	.427	1	16	.063	100	110	.909	20	41	61	163	142	2	43	82	1	655	1.0	2.5	10.2
82-83—Houston	64	0	1423	337	754	.447	4	14	.286	138	150	.920	34	40	74	158	163	3	59	89	4	816	1.2	2.5	12.8
REG. SEASON TOTALS	1002	0	30607	7247	15030	.482	10	72	.139	3445	3864	.892	499	952	2103	4402	3250	53	1165	822	51	17949	2.1	4.4	17.9
PLAYOFF TOTALS	51	0	1660	388	817	.475	4	14	.286	165	177	.932	31	47	78	213	197	4	79	64	4	945	1.5	4.2	18.5
ALL-STAR TOTALS	1	0	15	3	5	.600	0	0	—	0	0	—	0	1	1	5	4	0	2	4	0	6	1.0	5.0	6.0

MURPHY, JAY DENNIS b. June 26, 1962 Ht. 6-9 Wt. 220 College—Boston College

SEASON—TEAM	G	GS	MIN	FGM	FGA	PCT	3FGM	3FGA	PCT	FTM	FTA	PCT	O-RB	D-RB	TOT	AST	PF	DQ	STL	TO	BLK	PTS	RPG	APG	PPG
84-85—L.A. Clippers	23	0	149	8	50	.160	0	1	.000	12	21	.571	6	35	41	4	21	0	1	8	2	28	1.8	0.2	1.2
85-86—L.A. Clippers	14	0	100	16	45	.356	0	2	.000	9	14	.643	7	8	15	3	12	0	4	5	3	41	1.1	0.2	2.9
86-87—Washington	21	0	141	31	72	.431	0	0	—	9	16	.563	17	22	39	5	21	0	3	6	2	71	1.9	0.2	3.4
87-88—Washington	9	0	46	8	23	.348	0	0	—	4	5	.800	4	12	16	1	5	0	0	5	0	20	1.8	0.1	2.2
REG. SEASON TOTALS	67	0	436	63	190	.332	0	3	.000	34	56	.607	34	77	111	13	59	0	8	24	7	160	1.7	0.2	2.4

MURPHY, JOHN FRANCIS (Moe) b. September 13, 1924 Ht. 6-2 Wt. 175 College—None

SEASON—TEAM	G	GS	MIN	FGM	FGA	PCT	3FGM	3FGA	PCT	FTM	FTA	PCT	O-RB	D-RB	TOT	AST	PF	DQ	STL	TO	BLK	PTS	RPG	APG	PPG
46-47—N.Y.-Phil.	20	—	—	11	40	.275	—	—	—	10	15	.667	—	—	—	0	8	—	—	—	—	32	—	0.0	1.6
REG. SEASON TOTALS	20	—	—	11	40	.275	—	—	—	10	15	.667	—	—	—	0	8	—	—	—	—	32	—	0.0	1.6

MURPHY, RICHARD D. (Dick) b. March 10, 1921 d. October 22, 1973 Ht. 6-1 Wt. 180 College—Manhattan/Marshall

SEASON—TEAM	G	GS	MIN	FGM	FGA	PCT	3FGM	3FGA	PCT	FTM	FTA	PCT	O-RB	D-RB	TOT	AST	PF	DQ	STL	TO	BLK	PTS	RPG	APG	PPG
46-47—N.Y.-Boston	31	—	—	15	75	.200	—	—	—	4	9	.444	—	—	—	8	15	—	—	—	—	34	—	0.3	1.1
REG. SEASON TOTALS	31	—	—	15	75	.200	—	—	—	4	9	.444	—	—	—	8	15	—	—	—	—	34	—	0.3	1.1

MURPHY, RONALD T. (Ronnie) b. July 29, 1964 Ht. 6-5 Wt. 225 College—Jacksonville

SEASON—TEAM	G	GS	MIN	FGM	FGA	PCT	3FGM	3FGA	PCT	FTM	FTA	PCT	O-RB	D-RB	TOT	AST	PF	DQ	STL	TO	BLK	PTS	RPG	APG	PPG
87-88—Portland	18	0	89	14	49	.286	1	4	.250	7	11	.636	5	6	11	6	14	0	5	8	1	36	0.6	0.3	2.0
REG. SEASON TOTALS	18	0	89	14	49	.286	1	4	.250	7	11	.636	5	6	11	6	14	0	5	8	1	36	0.6	0.3	2.0

MURPHY, TOD JAMES b. December 24, 1963 Ht. 6-9 Wt. 220 College—Cal State-Irvine

SEASON—TEAM	G	GS	MIN	FGM	FGA	PCT	3FGM	3FGA	PCT	FTM	FTA	PCT	O-RB	D-RB	TOT	AST	PF	DQ	STL	TO	BLK	PTS	RPG	APG	PPG
87-88—L.A. Clippers	1	0	19	1	1	1.000	0	0	—	3	4	.750	1	1	2	2	2	0	1	0	0	5	2.0	2.0	5.0
89-90—Minnesota	82	59	2493	260	552	.471	16	43	.372	144	203	.709	207	357	564	106	229	2	76	61	60	680	6.9	1.3	8.3
90-91—Minnesota	52	19	1063	90	227	.396	1	17	.059	70	105	.667	92	163	255	60	101	1	25	32	20	251	4.9	1.2	4.8
91-92—Minnesota	47	3	429	39	80	.488	1	2	.500	19	34	.559	36	74	110	11	40	0	9	18	8	98	2.3	0.2	2.1
93-94—Detroit-G.S.	9	0	67	6	12	.500	0	0	—	3	6	.500	4	6	10	4	10	0	2	1	0	15	1.1	0.4	1.7
REG. SEASON TOTALS	191	81	4071	396	872	.454	18	62	.290	239	352	.679	340	601	941	183	382	3	113	112	88	1049	4.9	1.0	5.5

MURRAY, KENNETH STANLEY JR. (Ken) b. April 20, 1928 Ht. 6-2 Wt. 195 College—St. Bonaventure

SEASON—TEAM	G	GS	MIN	FGM	FGA	PCT	3FGM	3FGA	PCT	FTM	FTA	PCT	O-RB	D-RB	TOT	AST	PF	DQ	STL	TO	BLK	PTS	RPG	APG	PPG
50-51—Balt.-Ft. Wayne	66	—	—	301	887	.339	—	—	—	248	332	.747	—	—	355	202	164	7	—	—	—	850	5.4	3.1	12.9
53-54—Fort Wayne	49	—	528	53	195	.272	—	—	—	43	60	.717	—	—	65	56	60	0	—	—	—	149	1.3	1.1	3.0
54-55—Balt.-Phil.	66	—	1590	187	535	.350	—	—	—	98	129	.760	—	—	179	224	126	1	—	—	—	472	2.7	3.4	7.2
REG. SEASON TOTALS	181	—	2118	541	1617	.335	—	—	—	389	521	.747	—	—	599	482	350	8	—	—	—	1471	3.3	2.7	8.1
PLAYOFF TOTALS	6	—	15	17	58	.293	—	—	—	6	7	.857	—	—	14	10	13	0	—	—	—	40	2.3	1.7	6.7

MURRAY, TRACY LAMONTE b. July 25, 1971 Ht. 6-7 Wt. 230 College—UCLA

SEASON—TEAM	G	GS	MIN	FGM	FGA	PCT	3FGM	3FGA	PCT	FTM	FTA	PCT	O-RB	D-RB	TOT	AST	PF	DQ	STL	TO	BLK	PTS	RPG	APG	PPG
92-93—Portland	48	14	495	108	260	.415	21	70	.300	35	40	.875	40	43	83	11	59	0	8	31	5	272	1.7	0.2	5.7
93-94—Portland	66	1	820	167	355	.470	50	109	.459	50	72	.694	43	68	111	31	76	0	21	37	20	434	1.7	0.5	6.6
REG. SEASON TOTALS	114	15	1315	275	615	.447	71	179	.397	85	112	.759	83	111	194	42	135	0	29	68	25	706	1.7	0.4	6.2
PLAYOFF TOTALS	2	0	11	3	6	.500	0	1	.000	0	0	—	3	0	3	1	3	0	1	0	0	6	1.5	0.5	3.0

MURRELL, WILLIE VERNON b. September 13, 1941 Ht. 6-6½ Wt. 225 College—Eastern Oklahoma State/Kansas State

SEASON—TEAM	G	GS	MIN	FGM	FGA	PCT	3FGM	3FGA	PCT	FTM	FTA	PCT	O-RB	D-RB	TOT	AST	PF	DQ	STL	TO	BLK	PTS	RPG	APG	PPG
67-68—Denver (A)	71	—	2495	498	1069	.466	3	11	.273	166	236	.703	—	—	637	64	200	1	—	116	—	1165	9.0	0.9	16.4
68-69—Miami (A)	75	—	2493	476	1019	.467	4	18	.222	191	269	.710	—	—	566	103	239	5	—	159	—	1147	7.5	1.4	15.3
69-70—Miami-Ken. (A)	82	—	1759	276	596	.463	7	17	.412	117	154	.760	—	—	452	66	201	2	—	—	—	676	5.5	0.8	8.2
REG. ABA TOTALS	228	—	6747	1250	2684	.466	14	46	.304	474	659	.719	—	—	1655	233	640	8	—	275	—	2988	7.3	1.0	13.1
ABA PLAYOFF TOTALS	24	—	689	130	278	.468	1	6	.167	56	69	.812	—	—	159	29	73	1	—	27	—	317	6.6	1.2	13.2

MURREY, DORIE S. b. September 7, 1943 Ht. 6-8 Wt. 215 College—Detroit

SEASON—TEAM	G	GS	MIN	FGM	FGA	PCT	3FGM	3FGA	PCT	FTM	FTA	PCT	O-RB	D-RB	TOT	AST	PF	DQ	STL	TO	BLK	PTS	RPG	APG	PPG
66-67—Detroit	35	—	311	33	82	.402	—	—	—	32	54	.593	—	—	102	12	57	2	—	—	—	98	2.9	0.3	2.8
67-68—Seattle	81	—	1494	211	484	.436	—	—	—	168	244	.689	—	—	600	68	273	7	—	—	—	590	7.4	0.8	7.3
68-69—Seattle	38	—	465	75	194	.387	—	—	—	62	97	.639	—	—	149	21	81	1	—	—	—	212	3.9	0.6	5.6
69-70—Seattle	81	—	1079	153	343	.446	—	—	—	136	186	.731	—	—	357	76	191	4	—	—	—	442	4.4	0.9	5.5
70-71—Port.-Balt.	71	—	716	78	178	.438	—	—	—	75	112	.670	—	—	221	32	149	4	—	—	—	231	3.1	0.5	3.3
71-72—Baltimore	51	—	421	43	113	.381	—	—	—	24	39	.615	—	—	126	17	76	2	—	—	—	110	2.5	0.3	2.2
REG. SEASON TOTALS	357	—	4486	593	1394	.425	—	—	—	497	732	.679	—	—	1555	226	827	20	—	—	—	1683	4.4	0.6	4.7
PLAYOFF TOTALS	17	—	93	13	27	.481	—	—	—	7	11	.636	—	—	33	1	6	0	—	—	—	33	1.9	0.1	1.9

MUSI, ANGELO JR. b. July 25, 1918 Ht. 5-9 Wt. 145 College—Temple

SEASON—TEAM	G	GS	MIN	FGM	FGA	PCT	3FGM	3FGA	PCT	FTM	FTA	PCT	O-RB	D-RB	TOT	AST	PF	DQ	STL	TO	BLK	PTS	RPG	APG	PPG
46-47—Philadelphia	60	—	—	230	818	.281	—	—	—	102	123	.829	—	—	—	26	120	—	—	—	—	562	—	0.4	9.4
47-48—Philadelphia	43	—	—	134	485	.276	—	—	—	51	73	.699	—	—	—	10	56	—	—	—	—	319	—	0.2	7.4
48-49—Philadelphia	58	—	—	194	618	.314	—	—	—	90	119	.756	—	—	—	81	108	—	—	—	—	478	—	1.4	8.2
REG. SEASON TOTALS	161	—	—	558	1921	.290	—	—	—	243	315	.771	—	—	—	117	284	—	—	—	—	1359	—	0.7	8.4
PLAYOFF TOTALS	25	—	—	77	306	.252	—	—	—	44	59	.746	—	—	—	16	58	—	—	—	—	198	—	0.6	7.9

MUSTAF, TERRAH JERROD (**Jerrod**) b. October 28, 1969 Ht. 6-10 Wt. 245 College—Maryland

SEASON—TEAM	G	GS	MIN	FGM	FGA	PCT	3FGM	3FGA	PCT	FTM	FTA	PCT	O-RB	D-RB	TOT	AST	PF	DQ	STL	TO	BLK	PTS	RPG	APG	PPG
90-91—New York	62	6	825	106	228	.465	0	1	.000	56	87	.644	51	118	169	36	109	0	15	61	14	268	2.7	0.6	4.3
91-92—Phoenix	52	3	545	92	193	.477	0	0	—	49	71	.690	45	100	145	45	59	0	21	51	16	233	2.8	0.9	4.5
92-93—Phoenix	32	9	336	57	130	.438	0	1	.000	33	53	.623	29	54	83	10	40	0	14	22	11	147	2.6	0.3	4.6
93-94—Phoenix	33	2	196	30	84	.357	0	0	—	13	22	.591	20	35	55	8	29	0	4	10	5	73	1.7	0.2	2.2
REG. SEASON TOTALS	179	19	1902	285	635	.449	0	2	.000	151	233	.648	145	307	452	99	237	0	54	144	46	721	2.5	0.6	4.0
PLAYOFF TOTALS	10	0	32	7	10	.700	0	0	—	4	5	.800	3	4	7	—	2	0	0	1	2	18	0.7	0.0	1.8

MUTOMBO, DIKEMBE MPOLONDO JEAN-JACQUE b. June 25, 1966 Ht. 7-2 Wt. 250 College—Georgetown

SEASON—TEAM	G	GS	MIN	FGM	FGA	PCT	3FGM	3FGA	PCT	FTM	FTA	PCT	O-RB	D-RB	TOT	AST	PF	DQ	STL	TO	BLK	PTS	RPG	APG	PPG
91-92—Denver	71	71	2716	428	869	.493	0	0	—	321	500	.642	316	554	870	156	273	1	43	252	210	1177	12.3	2.2	16.6
92-93—Denver	82	82	3029	398	781	.510	0	0	—	335	492	.681	344	726	1070	147	284	5	43	216	287	1131	13.0	1.8	13.8
93-94—Denver	82	82	2853	365	642	.569	0	1	.000	256	439	.583	286	685	971	127	262	2	59	206	336	986	11.8	1.5	12.0
REG. SEASON TOTALS	235	235	8598	1191	2292	.520	0	1	.000	912	1431	.637	946	1965	2911	430	819	8	145	674	833	3294	12.4	1.8	14.0
PLAYOFF TOTALS	12	12	511	50	108	.463	0	0	—	59	98	.602	40	104	144	21	42	0	8	30	69	159	12.0	1.8	13.3
ALL-STAR TOTALS	1	0	10	2	4	.500	0	0	—	0	0	—	1	1	2	1	0	0	1	2	0	4	2.0	1.0	4.0

MYERS, PETER E. (**Pete, Skeeter Hawk**) b. September 15, 1963 Ht. 6-6 Wt. 180 College—Faulkner State JC/Arkansas

SEASON—TEAM	G	GS	MIN	FGM	FGA	PCT	3FGM	3FGA	PCT	FTM	FTA	PCT	O-RB	D-RB	TOT	AST	PF	DQ	STL	TO	BLK	PTS	RPG	APG	PPG
86-87—Chicago	29	0	155	19	52	.365	0	6	.000	28	43	.651	8	9	17	21	25	0	14	10	2	66	0.6	0.7	2.3
87-88—San Antonio	22	0	328	43	95	.453	0	4	.000	26	39	.667	11	26	37	48	30	0	17	33	6	112	1.7	2.2	5.1
88-89—Phil.-N.Y.	33	0	270	31	73	.425	0	2	.000	33	48	.688	15	18	33	48	44	0	20	23	2	95	1.0	1.5	2.9
89-90—N.Y.-N.J.	52	2	751	89	225	.396	0	7	.000	66	100	.660	33	63	96	135	109	0	35	76	11	244	1.8	2.6	4.7
90-91—San Antonio	8	1	103	10	23	.435	0	1	.000	9	11	.818	2	16	18	14	14	0	3	14	3	29	2.3	1.8	3.6
93-94—Chicago	82	81	2030	253	556	.455	8	29	.276	136	194	.701	54	127	181	245	195	1	78	136	20	650	2.2	3.0	7.9
REG. SEASON TOTALS	226	84	3637	445	1024	.435	8	49	.163	298	435	.685	123	259	382	511	417	1	167	292	44	1196	1.7	2.3	5.3
PLAYOFF TOTALS	15	10	250	29	57	.509	0	4	.000	16	27	.593	11	11	22	29	23	0	8	17	5	74	1.5	1.9	4.9

NABER, ROBERT E. (**Bob**) b. September 3, 1929 Ht. 6-3 Wt. 185 College—Louisville

SEASON—TEAM	G	GS	MIN	FGM	FGA	PCT	3FGM	3FGA	PCT	FTM	FTA	PCT	O-RB	D-RB	TOT	AST	PF	DQ	STL	TO	BLK	PTS	RPG	APG	PPG
52-53—Indianapolis	4	—	11	0	4	.000	—	—	—	1	2	.500	—	—	5	1	6	0	—	—	—	1	1.3	0.3	0.3
REG. SEASON TOTALS	4	—	11	0	4	.000	—	—	—	1	2	.500	—	—	5	1	6	0	—	—	—	1	1.3	0.3	0.3

NACHAMKIN, BORIS ALEXANDER b. December 6, 1933 Ht. 6-6 Wt. 210 College—New York University

SEASON—TEAM	G	GS	MIN	FGM	FGA	PCT	3FGM	3FGA	PCT	FTM	FTA	PCT	O-RB	D-RB	TOT	AST	PF	DQ	STL	TO	BLK	PTS	RPG	APG	PPG
54-55—Rochester	6	—	59	6	20	.300	—	—	—	8	13	.615	—	—	19	3	6	0	—	—	—	20	3.2	0.5	3.3
REG. SEASON TOTALS	6	—	59	6	20	.300	—	—	—	8	13	.615	—	—	19	3	6	0	—	—	—	20	3.2	0.5	3.3

NAGEL, GERALD R. (**Jerry**) b. May 18, 1928 Ht. 6-1.5 Wt. 190 College—Loyola (Ill.)

SEASON—TEAM	G	GS	MIN	FGM	FGA	PCT	3FGM	3FGA	PCT	FTM	FTA	PCT	O-RB	D-RB	TOT	AST	PF	DQ	STL	TO	BLK	PTS	RPG	APG	PPG
49-50—Fort Wayne	14	—	—	6	28	.214	—	—	—	1	4	.250	—	—	—	18	11	—	—	—	—	13	—	1.3	0.9
REG. SEASON TOTALS	14	—	—	6	28	.214	—	—	—	1	4	.250	—	—	—	18	11	—	—	—	—	13	—	1.3	0.9

NAGY, FREDERICK KARL (**Fred, Fritz**) b. January 3, 1924 d. June 5, 1989 Ht. 6-1½ Wt. 185 College—North Carolina/Akron

SEASON—TEAM	G	GS	MIN	FGM	FGA	PCT	3FGM	3FGA	PCT	FTM	FTA	PCT	O-RB	D-RB	TOT	AST	PF	DQ	STL	TO	BLK	PTS	RPG	APG	PPG
47-48—Indianapolis (N)	39	—	—	42	—	—	—	—	—	42	63	.667	—	—	—	—	53	—	—	—	—	126	—	—	3.2
48-49—Indianapolis	50	—	—	94	271	.347	—	—	—	65	97	.670	—	—	—	68	84	—	—	—	—	253	—	1.4	5.1
REG. NBA TOTALS	50	—	—	94	271	.347	—	—	—	65	97	.670	—	—	—	68	84	—	—	—	—	253	—	1.4	5.1
REG. NBL TOTALS	39	—	—	42	—	—	—	—	—	42	63	.667	—	—	—	—	53	—	—	—	—	126	—	—	3.2
NBL PLAYOFF TOTALS	4	—	—	1	—	—	—	—	—	6	8	.750	—	—	—	—	2	—	—	—	—	8	—	—	2.0

NANCE, LARRY DONELL b. February 12, 1959 Ht. 6-10 Wt. 235 College—Clemson

SEASON—TEAM	G	GS	MIN	FGM	FGA	PCT	3FGM	3FGA	PCT	FTM	FTA	PCT	O-RB	D-RB	TOT	AST	PF	DQ	STL	TO	BLK	PTS	RPG	APG	PPG
81-82—Phoenix	80	0	1186	227	436	.521	0	1	.000	75	117	.641	95	161	256	82	169	2	42	104	71	529	3.2	1.0	6.6
82-83—Phoenix	82	82	2914	588	1069	.550	1	3	.333	193	287	.672	239	471	710	197	254	4	99	190	217	1370	8.7	2.4	16.7
83-84—Phoenix	82	82	2899	601	1044	.576	0	7	.000	249	352	.707	227	451	678	214	274	5	86	177	174	1451	8.3	2.6	17.7
84-85—Phoenix	61	55	2202	515	877	.587	1	2	.500	180	254	.709	195	341	536	159	185	2	88	136	104	1211	8.8	2.6	19.9
85-86—Phoenix	73	69	2484	582	1001	.581	0	8	.000	310	444	.698	169	449	618	240	247	6	70	210	130	1474	8.5	3.3	20.2
86-87—Phoenix	69	67	2569	585	1062	.551	1	5	.200	381	493	.773	188	411	599	233	223	4	86	149	148	1552	8.7	3.4	22.5
87-88—Phoenix-Clev.	67	60	2383	487	920	.529	2	6	.333	304	390	.779	193	414	607	207	242	10	63	155	159	1280	9.1	3.1	19.1
88-89—Cleveland	73	72	2526	496	920	.539	0	4	.000	267	334	.799	156	425	581	159	186	0	57	117	206	1259	8.0	2.2	17.2
89-90—Cleveland	62	53	2065	412	807	.511	1	1	1.000	186	239	.778	162	354	516	161	185	3	54	110	122	1011	8.3	2.6	16.3
90-91—Cleveland	80	78	2927	635	1211	.524	2	8	.250	265	330	.803	201	485	686	237	219	3	66	131	200	1537	8.6	3.0	19.2
91-92—Cleveland	81	81	2880	556	1032	.539	0	6	.000	263	320	.822	213	457	670	232	200	2	80	87	243	1375	8.3	2.9	17.0
92-93—Cleveland	77	77	2753	533	971	.549	0	4	.000	202	247	.818	184	484	668	223	223	3	54	107	198	1268	8.7	2.9	16.5
93-94—Cleveland	33	19	909	153	314	.487	0	0	—	64	85	.753	77	150	227	49	96	1	27	38	55	370	6.9	1.5	11.2
REG. SEASON TOTALS	920	795	30697	6370	11664	.546	8	55	.145	2939	3892	.755	2299	5053	7352	2393	2703	45	872	1711	2027	15687	8.0	2.6	17.1
PLAYOFF TOTALS	68	61	2428	440	813	.541	0	1	.000	190	256	.742	184	351	535	160	220	5	59	108	144	1070	7.9	2.4	15.7
ALL-STAR TOTALS	3	0	44	15	21	.714	0	0	—	3	4	.750	5	9	14	2	9	0	2	2	4	33	4.7	0.7	11.0

NAPOLITANO, PAUL WALLY b. February 3, 1923 Ht. 6-2 Wt. 185 College—San Francisco

SEASON—TEAM	G	GS	MIN	FGM	FGA	PCT	3FGM	3FGA	PCT	FTM	FTA	PCT	O-RB	D-RB	TOT	AST	PF	DQ	STL	TO	BLK	PTS	RPG	APG	PPG
47-48—Minneapolis (N)	52	—	—	72	—	—	—	—	—	11	21	.524	—	—	—	48	—	—	—	—	—	155	—	—	3.0
48-49—Indianapolis	1	—	—	0	0	—	—	—	—	0	0	—	—	—	—	0	0	—	—	—	—	0	—	0.0	0.0
REG. NBA TOTALS	1	—	—	0	0	—	—	—	—	0	0	—	—	—	—	0	0	—	—	—	—	0	—	0.0	0.0
REG. NBL TOTALS	52	—	—	72	—	—	—	—	—	11	21	.524	—	—	—	48	—	—	—	—	—	155	—	—	3.0
NBL PLAYOFF TOTALS	9	—	—	8	—	—	—	—	—	4	5	.800	—	—	—	3	—	—	—	—	—	20	—	—	2.2

NASH, CHARLES FRANCIS (Cotton) b. July 24, 1942 Ht. 6-6 Wt. 220 College—Kentucky

SEASON—TEAM	G	GS	MIN	FGM	FGA	PCT	3FGM	3FGA	PCT	FTM	FTA	PCT	O-RB	D-RB	TOT	AST	PF	DQ	STL	TO	BLK	PTS	RPG	APG	PPG
64-65—L.A.-S.F.	45	—	357	47	145	.324	—	—	—	43	52	.827	—	—	83	19	57	0	—	—	—	137	1.8	0.4	3.0
67-68—Kentucky (A)	39	—	786	106	305	.348	0	1	.000	121	162	.747	—	—	190	46	63	0	—	49	—	333	4.9	1.2	8.5
REG. NBA TOTALS	45	—	357	47	145	.324	—	—	—	43	52	.827	—	—	83	19	57	0	—	—	—	137	1.8	0.4	3.0
REG. ABA TOTALS	39	—	786	106	305	.348	0	1	.000	121	162	.747	—	—	190	46	63	0	—	49	—	333	4.9	1.2	8.5

NASH, ROBERT LEE JR. (Bob) b. August 24, 1950 Ht. 6-8 Wt. 195 College—San Jacinto/Hawaii

SEASON—TEAM	G	GS	MIN	FGM	FGA	PCT	3FGM	3FGA	PCT	FTM	FTA	PCT	O-RB	D-RB	TOT	AST	PF	DQ	STL	TO	BLK	PTS	RPG	APG	PPG
72-73—Detroit	36	—	169	16	72	.222	—	—	—	11	17	.647	—	—	34	16	30	0	—	—	—	43	0.9	0.4	1.2
73-74—Detroit	35	—	281	41	115	.357	—	—	—	24	39	.615	31	43	74	14	35	0	3	—	10	106	2.1	0.4	3.0
74-75—San Diego (A)	17	—	175	27	78	.346	0	2	.000	13	18	.722	20	35	55	12	30	—	4	16	2	67	3.2	0.7	3.9
77-78—Kansas City	66	—	800	157	304	.516	—	—	—	50	69	.725	75	94	169	46	75	0	27	47	18	364	2.6	0.7	5.5
78-79—Kansas City	82	—	1307	227	522	.435	—	—	—	69	86	.802	76	130	206	71	135	0	29	82	15	523	2.5	0.9	6.4
REG. NBA TOTALS	219	—	2557	441	1013	.435	—	—	—	154	211	.730	182	267	483	147	275	0	59	129	43	1036	2.2	0.7	4.7
REG. ABA TOTALS	17	—	175	27	78	.346	0	2	.000	13	18	.722	20	35	55	12	30	—	4	16	2	67	3.2	0.7	3.9
NBA PLAYOFF TOTALS	5	—	64	8	27	.296	—	—	—	8	10	.800	6	5	11	—	10	0	0	7	4	24	2.2	0.0	4.8

NATER, SWEN ERIC b. January 14, 1950 Ht. 6-11 Wt. 250 College—Cypress JC/UCLA

SEASON—TEAM	G	GS	MIN	FGM	FGA	PCT	3FGM	3FGA	PCT	FTM	FTA	PCT	O-RB	D-RB	TOT	AST	PF	DQ	STL	TO	BLK	PTS	RPG	APG	PPG
73-74—Vir.-S.A. (A)	79	—	2375	467	846	.552	0	1	.000	180	254	.709	286	712	998	129	214	—	32	200	63	1114	12.6	1.6	14.1
74-75—San Antonio (A)	78	—	2713	495	914	.542	0	1	.000	185	246	.752	369	910	1279	97	240	—	43	185	87	1175	16.4	1.2	15.1
75-76—N.Y.-Vir. (A)	76	—	1790	320	651	.492	0	4	.000	108	155	.697	229	537	766	55	238	—	31	170	51	748	10.1	0.7	9.8
76-77—Milwaukee	72	—	1960	383	725	.528	—	—	—	172	228	.754	266	599	865	108	214	6	54	—	51	938	12.0	1.5	13.0
77-78—Buffalo	78	—	2778	501	994	.504	—	—	—	208	272	.765	278	751	1029	216	274	3	40	225	47	1210	13.2	2.8	15.5
78-79—San Diego	79	—	2006	357	627	.569	—	—	—	132	165	.800	218	483	701	140	244	6	38	170	29	846	8.9	1.8	10.7
79-80—San Diego	81	—	2860	443	799	.554	0	2	.000	196	273	.718	352	864	1216	233	259	3	45	257	37	1082	15.0	2.9	13.4
80-81—San Diego	82	—	2809	517	935	.553	0	0	—	244	307	.795	295	722	1017	199	295	8	49	211	46	1278	12.4	2.4	15.6
81-82—San Diego	21	7	575	101	175	.577	1	1	1.000	59	79	.747	46	146	192	30	64	1	6	48	9	262	9.1	1.4	12.5
82-83—San Diego	7	0	51	6	20	.300	0	0	—	4	4	1.000	2	11	13	1	1	0	1	3	0	16	1.9	0.1	2.3
83-84—Los Angeles	69	0	829	124	253	.490	0	1	.000	63	91	.692	81	183	264	27	150	0	25	68	7	311	3.8	0.4	4.5
REG. NBA TOTALS	489	7	13868	2432	4528	.537	1	4	.250	1078	1419	.760	1538	3759	5297	954	1501	27	258	982	226	5943	10.8	2.0	12.2
REG. ABA TOTALS	233	—	6878	1282	2411	.532	0	6	.000	473	655	.722	884	2159	3043	281	692	0	106	555	201	3037	13.1	1.2	13.0
NBA PLAYOFF TOTALS	17	0	146	19	38	.500	0	0	—	20	26	.769	16	24	40	1	27	0	1	8	2	58	2.4	0.1	3.4
ABA PLAYOFF TOTALS	13	—	445	87	169	.515	0	0	—	19	35	.543	51	130	181	21	39	0	4	24	11	193	13.9	1.6	14.8
ABA ALL-STAR TOTALS	2	1	54	18	37	.486	0	0	—	5	6	.833	15	12	27	—	5	—	0	4	2	41	13.5	0.5	20.5

NATT, CALVIN LEON b. January 8, 1957   Ht. 6-6 Wt. 220 College—NE Louisiana

SEASON—TEAM	G	GS	MIN	FGM	FGA	PCT	3FGM	3FGA	PCT	FTM	FTA	PCT	O-RB	D-RB	TOT	AST	PF	DQ	STL	TO	BLK	PTS	RPG	APG	PPG
79-80—N.J.-Port.	78	—	2857	622	1298	.479	3	9	.333	306	419	.730	239	452	691	169	205	1	102	198	34	1553	8.9	2.2	19.9
80-81—Portland	74	—	2111	395	794	.497	4	8	.500	200	283	.707	149	282	431	159	188	2	73	163	18	994	5.8	2.1	13.4
81-82—Portland	75	71	2599	515	894	.576	2	8	.250	294	392	.750	193	420	613	150	175	1	62	140	36	1326	8.2	2.0	17.7
82-83—Portland	80	80	2879	644	1187	.543	3	20	.150	339	428	.792	214	385	599	171	184	2	63	203	29	1630	7.5	2.1	20.4
83-84—Portland	79	74	2638	500	857	.583	2	17	.118	275	345	.797	166	310	476	179	218	3	69	166	22	1277	6.0	2.3	16.2
84-85—Denver	78	76	2657	685	1255	.546	0	3	.000	447	564	.793	209	401	610	238	182	1	75	190	33	1817	7.8	3.1	23.3
85-86—Denver	69	62	2007	469	930	.504	2	6	.333	278	347	.801	125	311	436	164	143	0	58	130	13	1218	6.3	2.4	17.7
86-87—Denver	1	1	20	4	10	.400	0	0	—	2	2	1.000	2	3	5	2	2	0	1	1	0	10	5.0	2.0	10.0
87-88—Denver	27	7	533	102	208	.490	0	1	.000	54	73	.740	35	61	96	47	43	0	13	30	3	258	3.6	1.7	9.6
88-89—Denver-S.A.	24	0	353	47	116	.405	0	1	.000	57	79	.722	28	50	78	18	32	0	8	30	3	151	3.3	0.8	6.3
89-90—Indiana	14	0	164	20	31	.645	0	0	—	17	22	.773	10	25	35	9	14	0	1	5	0	57	2.5	0.6	4.1
REG. SEASON TOTALS	599	371	18818	4003	7580	.528	16	73	.219	2269	2954	.768	1370	2700	4070	1306	1386	10	525	1256	191	10291	6.8	2.2	17.2
PLAYOFF TOTALS	45	33	1504	320	636	.503	2	9	.222	184	250	.736	97	229	326	109	100	0	27	91	12	826	7.2	2.4	18.4
ALL-STAR TOTALS	1	0	11	1	3	.333	0	0	—	1	2	.500	0	3	3	1	1	0	0	1	0	3	3.0	1.0	3.0

NATT, KENNETH WAYNE (**Kenny**) b. October 5, 1958   Ht. 6-3 Wt. 185 College—NE Louisiana

SEASON—TEAM	G	GS	MIN	FGM	FGA	PCT	3FGM	3FGA	PCT	FTM	FTA	PCT	O-RB	D-RB	TOT	AST	PF	DQ	STL	TO	BLK	PTS	RPG	APG	PPG
80-81—Indiana	19	—	149	25	77	.325	2	8	.250	7	11	.636	9	6	15	10	18	0	5	10	1	59	0.8	0.5	3.1
82-83—Utah	22	0	210	38	73	.521	0	2	.000	9	14	.643	6	16	22	28	36	0	5	22	0	85	1.0	1.3	3.9
84-85—Utah-K.C.	8	0	29	2	6	.333	0	0	—	2	4	.500	2	1	3	3	3	0	2	3	0	6	0.4	0.4	0.8
REG. SEASON TOTALS	49	0	388	65	156	.417	2	10	.200	18	29	.621	17	23	40	41	57	0	12	35	1	150	0.8	0.8	3.1

NAULLS, WILLIAM DEAN (**Willie**) b. October 7, 1934   Ht. 6-6 Wt. 225 College—UCLA

SEASON—TEAM	G	GS	MIN	FGM	FGA	PCT	3FGM	3FGA	PCT	FTM	FTA	PCT	O-RB	D-RB	TOT	AST	PF	DQ	STL	TO	BLK	PTS	RPG	APG	PPG
56-57—St. L.-N.Y.	71	—	1778	293	820	.357	—	—		132	195	.677	—	—	617	84	186	1	—	—	—	718	8.7	1.2	10.1
57-58—New York	68	—	2369	472	1189	.397	—	—		284	344	.826	—	—	799	97	220	4	—	—	—	1228	11.8	1.4	18.1
58-59—New York	68	—	2061	405	1072	.378	—	—		258	311	.830	—	—	723	102	233	8	—	—	—	1068	10.6	1.5	15.7
59-60—New York	65	—	2250	551	1286	.428	—	—		286	342	.836	—	—	921	138	214	4	—	—	—	1388	14.2	2.1	21.4
60-61—New York	79	—	2976	737	1723	.428	—	—		372	456	.816	—	—	1055	191	268	5	—	—	—	1846	13.4	2.4	23.4
61-62—New York	75	—	2978	747	1798	.415	—	—		383	455	.842	—	—	867	192	260	6	—	—	—	1877	11.6	2.6	25.0
62-63—N.Y.-S.F.	70	—	1901	370	887	.417	—	—		166	207	.802	—	—	515	102	205	3	—	—	—	906	7.4	1.5	12.9
63-64—Boston	78	—	1409	321	769	.417	—	—		125	157	.796	—	—	356	64	208	0	—	—	—	767	4.6	0.8	9.8
64-65—Boston	71	—	1465	302	786	.384	—	—		143	176	.813	—	—	336	72	225	5	—	—	—	747	4.7	1.0	10.5
65-66—Boston	71	—	1433	328	815	.402	—	—		104	131	.794	—	—	319	72	197	4	—	—	—	760	4.5	1.0	10.7
REG. SEASON TOTALS	716	—	20620	4526	11145	.406	—	—		2253	2774	.812	—	—	6508	1114	2216	40	—	—	—	11305	9.1	1.6	15.8
PLAYOFF TOTALS	35	—	495	99	267	.371	—	—		50	67	.746	—	—	134	21	92	2	—	—	—	248	3.8	0.6	7.1
ALL-STAR TOTALS	4	—	77	17	50	.340	—	—		6	8	.750	—	—	26	2	8	0	—	—	—	40	6.5	0.5	10.0

NEAL, CRAIG DUANE b. February 16, 1964   Ht. 6-6 Wt. 170 College—Georgia Tech

SEASON—TEAM	G	GS	MIN	FGM	FGA	PCT	3FGM	3FGA	PCT	FTM	FTA	PCT	O-RB	D-RB	TOT	AST	PF	DQ	STL	TO	BLK	PTS	RPG	APG	PPG
88-89—Port.-Miami	53	0	500	45	123	.366	10	34	.294	14	23	.609	7	22	29	118	70	0	24	54	4	114	0.5	2.2	2.2
90-91—Denver	10	0	125	14	35	.400	3	9	.333	13	22	.591	2	14	16	37	26	1	4	19	0	44	1.6	3.7	4.4
REG. SEASON TOTALS	63	0	625	59	158	.373	13	43	.302	27	45	.600	9	36	45	155	96	1	28	73	4	158	0.7	2.5	2.5

NEAL, JAMES ELLERBE (**Jim**) b. May 21, 1930   Ht. 6-11 Wt. 235 College—Wofford

SEASON—TEAM	G	GS	MIN	FGM	FGA	PCT	3FGM	3FGA	PCT	FTM	FTA	PCT	O-RB	D-RB	TOT	AST	PF	DQ	STL	TO	BLK	PTS	RPG	APG	PPG
53-54—Syracuse	67	—	899	117	369	.317	—	—		78	132	.591	—	—	257	24	139	0	—	—	—	312	3.8	0.4	4.7
54-55—Baltimore	13	—	194	12	59	.203	—	—		15	22	.682	—	—	47	9	27	0	—	—	—	39	3.6	0.7	3.0
REG. SEASON TOTALS	80	—	1093	129	428	.301	—	—		93	154	.604	—	—	304	33	166	0	—	—	—	351	3.8	0.4	4.4
PLAYOFF TOTALS	11	—	100	13	35	.371	—	—		5	13	.385	—	—	27	2	14	0	—	—	—	31	2.5	0.2	2.8

NEAL, LLOYD b. December 10, 1950   Ht. 6-7 Wt. 225 College—Tennessee State

SEASON—TEAM	G	GS	MIN	FGM	FGA	PCT	3FGM	3FGA	PCT	FTM	FTA	PCT	O-RB	D-RB	TOT	AST	PF	DQ	STL	TO	BLK	PTS	RPG	APG	PPG
72-73—Portland	82	—	2723	455	921	.494	—	—		187	293	.638	—	—	967	146	305	6	—	—	—	1097	11.8	1.8	13.4
73-74—Portland	80	—	1517	246	502	.490	—	—		117	168	.696	150	344	494	89	190	0	45	—	73	609	6.2	1.1	7.6
74-75—Portland	82	—	2278	409	869	.471	—	—		189	295	.641	186	501	687	139	239	2	43	—	87	1007	8.4	1.7	12.3
75-76—Portland	68	—	2320	435	904	.481	—	—		186	268	.694	145	440	585	118	254	4	53	—	107	1056	8.6	1.7	15.5
76-77—Portland	58	—	955	160	340	.471	—	—		77	114	.675	87	168	255	58	148	0	8	—	35	397	4.4	1.0	6.8
77-78—Portland	61	—	1174	272	540	.504	—	—		127	177	.718	116	257	373	81	128	0	29	96	21	671	6.1	1.3	11.0
78-79—Portland	4	—	48	4	11	.364	—	—		1	1	1.000	2	7	9	1	7	0	0	6	1	9	2.3	0.3	2.3
REG. SEASON TOTALS	435	—	11015	1981	4087	.485	—	—		884	1316	.672	686	1717	3370	632	1271	12	178	102	324	4846	7.7	1.5	11.1
PLAYOFF TOTALS	22	—	253	37	84	.440	—	—		18	27	.667	23	58	81	19	39	0	2	6	12	92	3.7	0.9	4.2

NEALY, EDDIE CARL (**Ed**) b. February 19, 1960   Ht. 6-7 Wt. 240 College—Kansas State

SEASON—TEAM	G	GS	MIN	FGM	FGA	PCT	3FGM	3FGA	PCT	FTM	FTA	PCT	O-RB	D-RB	TOT	AST	PF	DQ	STL	TO	BLK	PTS	RPG	APG	PPG
82-83—Kansas City	82	61	1643	147	247	.595	0	0	—	70	114	.614	170	315	485	62	247	4	68	51	12	364	5.9	0.8	4.4
83-84—Kansas City	71	1	960	63	126	.500	0	0	—	48	60	.800	73	149	222	50	138	1	41	33	9	174	3.1	0.7	2.5
84-85—Kansas City	22	0	225	26	44	.591	0	0	—	10	19	.526	15	29	44	18	26	0	3	12	1	62	2.0	0.8	2.8
86-87—San Antonio	60	7	980	84	192	.438	4	31	.129	51	69	.739	96	188	284	83	144	1	40	36	11	223	4.7	1.4	3.7
87-88—San Antonio	68	1	837	50	109	.459	1	2	.500	41	63	.651	82	140	222	49	94	0	29	27	5	142	3.3	0.7	2.1
88-89—Chicago-Phoenix	43	0	258	13	36	.361	0	2	.000	4	9	.444	22	56	78	14	45	0	7	7	1	30	1.8	0.3	0.7
89-90—Chicago	46	0	503	37	70	.529	0	2	.000	30	41	.732	46	92	138	28	67	0	16	17	4	104	3.0	0.6	2.3
90-91—Phoenix	55	0	573	45	97	.464	5	16	.313	28	38	.737	44	107	151	36	46	0	24	19	4	123	2.7	0.7	2.2
91-92—Phoenix	52	4	505	62	121	.512	20	50	.400	16	24	.667	25	86	111	37	45	0	16	17	2	160	2.1	0.7	3.1
92-93—G.S.-Chicago	41	4	308	26	69	.377	8	27	.296	9	12	.750	12	52	64	15	41	0	12	7	2	69	1.6	0.4	1.7
REG. SEASON TOTALS	540	78	6792	553	1111	.498	38	130	.292	307	449	.684	585	1214	1799	392	893	6	256	226	51	1451	3.3	0.7	2.7
PLAYOFF TOTALS	33	0	376	30	68	.441	5	15	.333	19	27	.704	28	63	91	15	66	1	14	10	1	84	2.8	0.5	2.5

NEGRATTI, ALBERT EDWARD (**Al**) b. June 12, 1921   Ht. 6-3½ Wt. 200 College—Seton Hall

SEASON—TEAM	G	GS	MIN	FGM	FGA	PCT	3FGM	3FGA	PCT	FTM	FTA	PCT	O-RB	D-RB	TOT	AST	PF	DQ	STL	TO	BLK	PTS	RPG	APG	PPG
45-46—Rochester (N)	16	—	—	19	—	—	—	—	—	10	—	—	—	—	—	—	—	—	—	—	—	48	—	—	3.0
46-47—Rochester (N)	33	—	—	15	—	—	—	—	—	14	24	.583	—	—	—	—	—	—	—	—	—	44	—	—	1.3
46-47—Washington	11	—	—	13	69	.188	—	—	—	5	8	.625	—	5	20	—	—	—	—	—	—	31	—	0.5	2.8
REG. NBA TOTALS	11	—	—	13	69	.188	—	—	—	5	8	.625	—	5	20	—	—	—	—	—	—	31	—	0.5	2.8
REG. NBL TOTALS	49	—	—	34	—	—	—	—	—	24	24	.583	—	—	—	—	—	—	—	—	—	92	—	—	1.9
NBL PLAYOFF TOTALS	18	—	—	12	—	—	—	—	—	11	17	.647	—	—	32	—	—	—	—	—	—	35	—	—	1.9

NELSON, BARRY G. b. September 19, 1949   Ht. 6-10 Wt. 230 College—Duquesne

SEASON—TEAM	G	GS	MIN	FGM	FGA	PCT	3FGM	3FGA	PCT	FTM	FTA	PCT	O-RB	D-RB	TOT	AST	PF	DQ	STL	TO	BLK	PTS	RPG	APG	PPG
71-72—Milwaukee	28	—	102	15	36	.417	—	—	—	5	10	.500	—	—	20	7	21	0	—	—	—	35	0.7	0.3	1.3
REG. SEASON TOTALS	28	—	102	15	36	.417	—	—	—	5	10	.500	—	—	20	7	21	0	—	—	—	35	0.7	0.3	1.3
PLAYOFF TOTALS	2	—	5	0	0	—	—	—	—	0	0	—	—	—	1	1	1	0	—	—	—	0	0.5	0.5	0.0

NELSON, DONALD ARVID (**Don, Nellie**) b. May 15, 1940   Ht. 6-6 Wt. 210 College—Iowa

SEASON—TEAM	G	GS	MIN	FGM	FGA	PCT	3FGM	3FGA	PCT	FTM	FTA	PCT	O-RB	D-RB	TOT	AST	PF	DQ	STL	TO	BLK	PTS	RPG	APG	PPG
62-63—Chicago	62	—	1071	129	293	.440	—	—	—	161	221	.729	—	—	279	72	136	3	—	—	—	419	4.5	1.2	6.8
63-64—Los Angeles	80	—	1406	135	323	.418	—	—	—	149	201	.741	—	—	323	76	181	1	—	—	—	419	4.0	1.0	5.2
64-65—Los Angeles	39	—	238	36	85	.424	—	—	—	20	26	.769	—	—	73	24	40	1	—	—	—	92	1.9	0.6	2.4
65-66—Boston	75	—	1765	271	618	.439	—	—	—	223	326	.684	—	—	403	79	187	1	—	—	—	765	5.4	1.1	10.2
66-67—Boston	79	—	1202	227	509	.446	—	—	—	141	190	.742	—	—	295	65	143	0	—	—	—	595	3.7	0.8	7.5
67-68—Boston	82	—	1498	312	632	.494	—	—	—	195	268	.728	—	—	431	103	178	1	—	—	—	819	5.3	1.3	10.0
68-69—Boston	82	—	1773	374	771	.485	—	—	—	201	259	.776	—	—	458	92	198	2	—	—	—	949	5.6	1.1	11.6
69-70—Boston	82	—	2224	461	920	.501	—	—	—	337	435	.775	—	—	601	148	238	3	—	—	—	1259	7.3	1.8	15.4
70-71—Boston	82	—	2254	412	881	.468	—	—	—	317	426	.744	—	—	565	153	232	2	—	—	—	1141	6.9	1.9	13.9
71-72—Boston	82	—	2086	389	811	.480	—	—	—	356	452	.788	—	—	453	192	220	3	—	—	—	1134	5.5	2.3	13.8
72-73—Boston	72	—	1425	309	649	.476	—	—	—	159	188	.846	—	—	315	102	155	1	—	—	—	777	4.4	1.4	10.8
73-74—Boston	82	—	1748	364	717	.508	—	—	—	215	273	.788	90	255	345	162	189	1	19	—	13	943	4.2	2.0	11.5
74-75—Boston	79	—	2052	423	785	.539	—	—	—	263	318	.827	127	342	469	181	239	2	32	—	15	1109	5.9	2.3	14.0
75-76—Boston	75	—	943	175	379	.462	—	—	—	127	161	.789	56	126	182	77	115	0	14	—	7	477	2.4	1.0	6.4
REG. SEASON TOTALS	1053	—	21685	4017	8373	.480	—	—	—	2864	3744	.765	273	723	5192	1526	2451	21	65	—	35	10898	4.9	1.4	10.3
PLAYOFF TOTALS	150	—	3209	585	1175	.498	—	—	—	407	498	.817	60	135	719	210	399	5	13	—	7	1577	4.8	1.4	10.5

NELSON, LOUIS (**Louie, Sweets**) b. May 28, 1951   Ht. 6-3 Wt. 190 College—Washington

SEASON—TEAM	G	GS	MIN	FGM	FGA	PCT	3FGM	3FGA	PCT	FTM	FTA	PCT	O-RB	D-RB	TOT	AST	PF	DQ	STL	TO	BLK	PTS	RPG	APG	PPG
73-74—Capital	49	—	556	93	215	.433	—	—	—	53	73	.726	26	44	70	52	62	0	31	—	2	239	1.4	1.1	4.9
74-75—New Orleans	72	—	1898	307	679	.452	—	—	—	192	250	.768	75	121	196	178	186	1	65	—	6	806	2.7	2.5	11.2
75-76—New Orleans	66	—	2030	327	755	.433	—	—	—	169	230	.735	81	121	202	169	147	1	82	—	6	823	3.1	2.6	12.5
76-77—San Antonio	4	—	57	7	14	.500	—	—	—	4	7	.571	2	5	7	3	9	0	2	—	0	18	1.8	0.8	4.5
77-78—K.C.-N.J.	33	—	406	85	211	.403	—	—	—	57	84	.679	13	39	52	34	33	0	22	48	7	227	1.6	1.0	6.9
REG. SEASON TOTALS	224	—	4947	819	1874	.437	—	—	—	475	644	.738	197	330	527	436	437	2	202	48	21	2113	2.4	1.9	9.4

NELSON, RON b. October 7, 1946   Ht. 6-2 Wt. 175 College—New Mexico

SEASON—TEAM	G	GS	MIN	FGM	FGA	PCT	3FGM	3FGA	PCT	FTM	FTA	PCT	O-RB	D-RB	TOT	AST	PF	DQ	STL	TO	BLK	PTS	RPG	APG	PPG
70-71—Floridians (A)	59	—	490	72	172	.419	1	3	.333	41	54	.759	—	—	53	47	95	—	—	—	—	186	0.9	0.8	3.2
REG. ABA TOTALS	59	—	490	72	172	.419	1	3	.333	41	54	.759	—	—	53	47	95	—	—	—	—	186	0.9	0.8	3.2
ABA PLAYOFF TOTALS	1	—	2	0	1	.000	0	0	—	0	0	—	—	—	1	0	0	—	—	—	—	0	1.0	0.0	0.0

NEMELKA, RICHARD S. (Dick) b. October 1, 1943 Ht. 6-0 Wt. 175 College—Brigham Young

SEASON—TEAM	G	GS	MIN	FGM	FGA	PCT	3FGM	3FGA	PCT	FTM	FTA	PCT	O-RB	D-RB	TOT	AST	PF	DQ	STL	TO	BLK	PTS	RPG	APG	PPG
70-71—Utah (A)	39	—	504	82	213	.385	20	62	.323	32	49	.653	—	—	59	57	60	—	—	—	—	216	1.5	1.5	5.5
REG. ABA TOTALS	39	—	504	82	213	.385	20	62	.323	32	49	.653	—	—	59	57	60	—	—	—	—	216	1.5	1.5	5.5
ABA PLAYOFF TOTALS	9	—	51	7	21	.333	1	9	.111	4	5	.800	—	—	9	9	12	—	—	—	—	19	1.0	1.0	2.1

NESSLEY, MARTIN SCOTT b. February 16, 1965 Ht. 7-2 Wt. 260 College—Duke

SEASON—TEAM	G	GS	MIN	FGM	FGA	PCT	3FGM	3FGA	PCT	FTM	FTA	PCT	O-RB	D-RB	TOT	AST	PF	DQ	STL	TO	BLK	PTS	RPG	APG	PPG
87-88—L.A. Clips-Sac.	44	0	336	20	52	.385	0	0	—	8	18	.444	23	59	82	16	89	1	8	23	12	48	1.9	0.4	1.1
REG. SEASON TOTALS	44	0	336	20	52	.385	0	0	—	8	18	.444	23	59	82	16	89	1	8	23	12	48	1.9	0.4	1.1

NETOLICKY, ROBERT (Bob, Neto) b. August 2, 1942 Ht. 6-9 Wt. 225 College—Drake

SEASON—TEAM	G	GS	MIN	FGM	FGA	PCT	3FGM	3FGA	PCT	FTM	FTA	PCT	O-RB	D-RB	TOT	AST	PF	DQ	STL	TO	BLK	PTS	RPG	APG	PPG
67-68—Indiana (A)	71	—	2385	468	928	.504	0	1	.000	220	369	.596	313	506	819	69	162	0	—	143	—	1156	11.5	1.0	16.3
68-69—Indiana (A)	78	—	2721	583	1145	.509	0	5	.000	306	491	.623	313	485	798	87	231	4	—	178	—	1472	10.2	1.1	18.9
69-70—Indiana (A)	82	—	3222	673	1393	.483	2	7	.286	343	502	.683	337	539	876	123	206	2	—	—	—	1691	10.7	1.5	20.6
70-71—Indiana (A)	82	—	3137	651	1305	.499	2	8	.250	237	333	.712	—	—	774	104	192	—	—	—	—	1541	9.4	1.3	18.8
71-72—Indiana (A)	83	—	2905	522	1090	.479	4	19	.211	202	279	.724	—	—	764	83	185	—	—	166	—	1250	9.2	1.0	15.1
72-73—Dallas (A)	84	—	3409	650	1347	.483	0	4	.000	269	404	.666	338	513	851	239	166	0	—	214	—	1569	10.1	2.8	18.7
73-74—S.A.-Indiana (A)	75	—	1645	314	644	.488	2	6	.333	106	165	.642	173	220	393	94	113	—	28	98	33	736	5.2	1.3	9.8
74-75—Indiana (A)	59	—	1077	189	375	.504	2	12	.167	62	98	.633	98	133	231	49	108	—	9	55	18	442	3.9	0.8	7.5
75-76—Indiana (A)	4	—	53	8	21	.381	0	0	—	3	3	1.000	7	5	12	0	2	—	0	5	1	19	3.0	0.0	4.8
REG. ABA TOTALS	618	—	20554	4058	8248	.492	12	62	.194	1748	2644	.661	1579	2401	5518	848	1365	6	37	859	52	9876	8.9	1.4	16.0
ABA PLAYOFF TOTALS	73	—	2385	475	945	.503	0	4	.000	193	297	.650	158	255	645	61	177	2	0	52	1	1143	8.8	0.8	15.7
ABA ALL-STAR TOTALS	4	—	100	19	39	.487	0	0	—	8	15	.533	6	21	35	5	7	0	0	3	0	46	8.8	1.3	11.5

NEUMANN, JOHNNY b. September 11, 1951 Ht. 6-6 Wt. 200 College—Mississippi

SEASON—TEAM	G	GS	MIN	FGM	FGA	PCT	3FGM	3FGA	PCT	FTM	FTA	PCT	O-RB	D-RB	TOT	AST	PF	DQ	STL	TO	BLK	PTS	RPG	APG	PPG
71-72—Memphis (A)	77	—	1969	545	1328	.410	26	128	.203	293	385	.761	—	—	322	147	285	—	—	239	—	1409	4.2	1.9	18.3
72-73—Memphis (A)	79	—	2787	605	1283	.472	9	51	.176	329	423	.778	146	164	310	470	304	5	—	345	—	1548	3.9	5.9	19.6
73-74—Memphis-Utah (A)	87	—	2056	482	1070	.450	18	74	.243	166	215	.772	108	118	226	254	283	—	95	248	26	1148	2.6	2.9	13.2
74-75—Vir.-Indiana (A)	52	—	931	186	445	.418	21	78	.269	52	75	.693	42	47	89	135	131	—	26	82	11	445	1.7	2.6	8.6
75-76—Vir.-Ken. (A)	77	—	1589	393	949	.414	71	208	.341	151	189	.799	80	121	201	171	222	—	68	174	26	1008	2.6	2.2	13.1
76-77—Buffalo-L.A.	63	—	937	161	397	.406	—	—	—	59	87	.678	24	48	72	141	134	2	31	—	10	381	1.1	2.2	6.0
77-78—Indiana	20	—	216	35	86	.407	—	—	—	13	18	.722	5	9	14	27	24	0	6	22	1	83	0.7	1.4	4.2
REG. NBA TOTALS	83	—	1153	196	483	.406	—	—	—	72	105	.686	29	57	86	168	158	2	37	22	11	464	1.0	2.0	5.6
REG. ABA TOTALS	372	—	9332	2211	5075	.436	145	539	.269	991	1287	.770	376	450	1148	1177	1225	5	189	1088	63	5558	3.1	3.2	14.9
NBA PLAYOFF TOTALS	6	—	68	11	29	.379	—	—	—	2	4	.500	0	2	2	9	14	0	3	—	2	24	0.3	1.5	4.0
ABA PLAYOFF TOTALS	23	—	285	67	168	.399	6	22	.273	24	27	.889	18	18	36	22	41	0	10	26	3	164	1.6	1.0	7.1

NEUMANN, PAUL R. b. January 30, 1938 Ht. 6-1 Wt. 175 College—Stanford

SEASON—TEAM	G	GS	MIN	FGM	FGA	PCT	3FGM	3FGA	PCT	FTM	FTA	PCT	O-RB	D-RB	TOT	AST	PF	DQ	STL	TO	BLK	PTS	RPG	APG	PPG
61-62—Syracuse	77	—	1265	172	401	.429	—	—	—	133	172	.773	—	—	194	176	203	3	—	—	—	477	2.5	2.3	6.2
62-63—Syracuse	80	—	1581	237	503	.471	—	—	—	181	222	.815	—	—	200	227	221	5	—	—	—	655	2.5	2.8	8.2
63-64—Philadelphia	74	—	1973	324	732	.443	—	—	—	210	266	.789	—	—	246	291	211	1	—	—	—	858	3.3	3.9	11.6
64-65—Phil.-S.F.	76	—	2034	365	772	.473	—	—	—	234	303	.772	—	—	198	233	218	3	—	—	—	964	2.6	3.1	12.7
65-66—San Francisco	66	—	1729	343	817	.420	—	—	—	265	317	.836	—	—	208	184	174	0	—	—	—	951	3.2	2.8	14.4
66-67—San Francisco	78	—	2421	386	911	.424	—	—	—	312	390	.800	—	—	272	342	266	4	—	—	—	1084	3.5	4.4	13.9
REG. SEASON TOTALS	451	—	11003	1827	4136	.442	—	—	—	1335	1670	.799	—	—	1318	1453	1293	16	—	—	—	4989	2.9	3.2	11.1
PLAYOFF TOTALS	29	—	608	76	194	.392	—	—	—	65	85	.765	—	—	61	82	87	0	—	—	—	217	2.1	2.8	7.5

NEVITT, CHARLES GOODRICH (Chuck) b. June 13, 1959 Ht. 7-5 Wt. 250 College—North Carolina State

SEASON—TEAM	G	GS	MIN	FGM	FGA	PCT	3FGM	3FGA	PCT	FTM	FTA	PCT	O-RB	D-RB	TOT	AST	PF	DQ	STL	TO	BLK	PTS	RPG	APG	PPG
82-83—Houston	6	0	64	11	15	.733	0	0	—	1	4	.250	6	11	17	0	14	0	1	7	12	23	2.8	0.0	3.8
84-85—L.A. Lakers	11	0	59	5	17	.294	0	0	—	2	8	.250	5	15	20	3	20	0	0	10	15	12	1.8	0.3	1.1
85-86—Lakers-Detroit	29	0	126	15	43	.349	0	0	—	19	26	.731	13	19	32	7	35	0	4	12	19	49	1.1	0.2	1.7
86-87—Detroit	41	0	267	31	63	.492	0	0	—	14	24	.583	36	47	83	4	73	0	7	21	30	76	2.0	0.1	1.9
87-88—Detroit	17	0	63	7	21	.333	0	0	—	3	6	.500	4	14	18	0	12	0	1	2	5	17	1.1	0.0	1.0
88-89—Houston	43	0	228	27	62	.435	0	0	—	11	16	.688	17	47	64	3	51	1	5	22	29	65	1.5	0.1	1.5
89-90—Houston	3	0	9	2	2	1.000	0	0	—	0	0	—	0	3	3	1	3	0	0	2	1	4	1.0	0.3	1.3
91-92—Chicago	4	0	9	1	3	.333	0	0	—	0	0	—	0	1	1	1	2	0	0	3	0	2	0.3	0.3	0.5
93-94—San Antonio	1	0	1	0	0	—	0	0	—	3	6	.500	1	0	1	0	1	0	0	0	0	3	1.0	0.0	3.0
REG. SEASON TOTALS	155	0	826	99	226	.438	0	0	—	53	90	.589	82	157	239	19	211	1	18	80	111	251	1.5	0.1	1.6
PLAYOFF TOTALS	16	0	55	5	16	.313	0	0	—	6	10	.600	6	10	16	1	13	0	4	6	9	16	1.0	0.1	1.0

NEWBERN, MELVIN b. June 11, 1967 Ht. 6-4 Wt. 200 College—Minnesota

SEASON—TEAM	G	GS	MIN	FGM	FGA	PCT	3FGM	3FGA	PCT	FTM	FTA	PCT	O-RB	D-RB	TOT	AST	PF	DQ	STL	TO	BLK	PTS	RPG	APG	PPG
92-93—Detroit	33	1	311	42	113	.372	1	8	.125	34	60	.567	19	18	37	57	42	0	23	32	1	119	1.1	1.7	3.6
REG. SEASON TOTALS	33	1	311	42	113	.372	1	8	.125	34	60	.567	19	18	37	57	42	0	23	32	1	119	1.1	1.7	3.6

NEWLIN, MICHAEL F. (**Mike**) b. January 2, 1949 Ht. 6-4 Wt. 200 College—Utah

SEASON—TEAM	G	GS	MIN	FGM	FGA	PCT	3FGM	3FGA	PCT	FTM	FTA	PCT	O-RB	D-RB	TOT	AST	PF	DQ	STL	TO	BLK	PTS	RPG	APG	PPG
71-72—Houston	82	—	1495	256	618	.414	—	—	—	108	144	.750	—	—	228	135	233	6	—	—	—	620	2.8	1.6	7.6
72-73—Houston	82	—	2658	534	1206	.443	—	—	—	327	369	.886	—	—	340	409	301	5	—	—	—	1395	4.1	5.0	17.0
73-74—Houston	76	—	2591	510	1139	.448	—	—	—	380	444	.856	77	185	262	363	259	5	87	—	9	1400	3.4	4.8	18.4
74-75—Houston	79	—	2709	436	905	.482	—	—	—	265	305	.869	55	205	260	403	288	4	111	—	7	1137	3.3	5.1	14.4
75-76—Houston	82	—	3065	569	1123	.507	—	—	—	385	445	.865	72	264	336	457	263	5	106	—	5	1523	4.1	5.6	18.6
76-77—Houston	82	—	2119	387	850	.455	—	—	—	269	304	.885	53	151	204	320	226	2	60	—	3	1043	2.5	3.9	12.7
77-78—Houston	45	—	1181	216	495	.436	—	—	—	152	174	.874	36	84	120	203	128	1	52	120	4	584	2.7	4.5	13.0
78-79—Houston	76	—	1828	283	581	.487	—	—	—	212	243	.872	51	119	170	291	218	3	51	175	9	778	2.2	3.8	10.2
79-80—New Jersey	78	—	2510	611	1329	.460	45	152	.296	367	415	.884	101	163	264	314	195	1	115	231	4	1634	3.4	4.0	20.9
80-81—New Jersey	79	—	2911	632	1272	.497	10	30	.333	414	466	.888	78	141	219	299	237	2	87	248	9	1688	2.8	3.8	21.4
81-82—New York	76	32	1507	286	615	.465	7	23	.304	126	147	.857	36	55	91	170	194	2	33	104	3	705	1.2	2.2	9.3
REG. SEASON TOTALS	837	32	24574	4720	10133	.466	62	205	.302	3005	3456	.870	559	1367	2494	3364	2542	36	702	878	58	12507	3.0	4.0	14.9
PLAYOFF TOTALS	22	0	682	135	270	.500	0	0	—	55	65	.846	21	52	73	103	72	1	28	6	1	325	3.3	4.7	14.8

NEWMAN, JOHN SYLVESTER JR. (**Johnny**) b. November 28, 1963 Ht. 6-7 Wt. 195 College—Richmond

SEASON—TEAM	G	GS	MIN	FGM	FGA	PCT	3FGM	3FGA	PCT	FTM	FTA	PCT	O-RB	D-RB	TOT	AST	PF	DQ	STL	TO	BLK	PTS	RPG	APG	PPG
86-87—Cleveland	59	0	630	113	275	.411	1	22	.045	66	76	.868	36	34	70	27	67	0	20	46	7	293	1.2	0.5	5.0
87-88—New York	77	25	1589	270	620	.435	26	93	.280	207	246	.841	87	72	159	62	204	5	72	103	11	773	2.1	0.8	10.0
88-89—New York	81	80	2336	455	957	.475	97	287	.338	286	351	.815	93	113	206	162	259	4	111	153	23	1293	2.5	2.0	16.0
89-90—New York	80	69	2277	374	786	.476	45	142	.317	239	299	.799	60	131	191	180	254	3	95	143	22	1032	2.4	2.3	12.9
90-91—Charlotte	81	81	2477	478	1017	.470	30	84	.357	385	476	.809	94	160	254	188	278	7	100	189	17	1371	3.1	2.3	16.9
91-92—Charlotte	55	55	1651	295	618	.477	13	46	.283	236	308	.766	71	108	179	146	181	4	70	129	14	839	3.3	2.7	15.3
92-93—Charlotte	64	27	1471	279	534	.522	12	45	.267	194	240	.808	72	71	143	117	154	1	45	90	19	764	2.2	1.8	11.9
93-94—Cha.-N.J.	81	18	1697	313	664	.471	24	90	.267	182	225	.809	86	94	180	72	196	3	69	90	27	832	2.2	0.9	10.3
REG. SEASON TOTALS	578	355	14128	2577	5471	.471	248	809	.307	1795	2221	.808	599	783	1382	954	1593	27	582	943	140	7197	2.4	1.7	12.5
PLAYOFF TOTALS	36	20	829	150	328	.457	13	56	.232	105	137	.766	41	40	81	54	114	2	35	59	8	418	2.3	1.5	11.6

NEWMARK, DAVID L. (**Dave**) b. September 11, 1946 Ht. 7-0 Wt. 250 College—Columbia

SEASON—TEAM	G	GS	MIN	FGM	FGA	PCT	3FGM	3FGA	PCT	FTM	FTA	PCT	O-RB	D-RB	TOT	AST	PF	DQ	STL	TO	BLK	PTS	RPG	APG	PPG
68-69—Chicago	81	—	1159	185	475	.389	—	—	—	86	139	.619	—	—	347	58	205	7	—	—	—	456	4.3	0.7	5.6
69-70—Atlanta	64	—	612	127	296	.429	—	—	—	59	77	.766	—	—	174	42	128	3	—	—	—	313	2.7	0.7	4.9
70-71—Carolina (A)	31	—	457	100	209	.478	0	0	—	34	60	.567	—	—	157	28	84	—	—	—	—	234	5.1	0.9	7.5
REG. NBA TOTALS	145	—	1771	312	771	.405	—	—	—	145	216	.671	—	—	521	100	333	10	—	—	—	769	3.6	0.7	5.3
REG. ABA TOTALS	31	—	457	100	209	.478	0	0	—	34	60	.567	—	—	157	28	84	—	—	—	—	234	5.1	0.9	7.5
NBA PLAYOFF TOTALS	6	—	42	15	33	.455	—	—	—	4	4	1.000	—	—	12	2	8	0	—	—	—	34	2.0	0.3	5.7

NEWTON, BILL R. b. December 22, 1950 Ht. 6-9 Wt. 225 College—Louisiana State

SEASON—TEAM	G	GS	MIN	FGM	FGA	PCT	3FGM	3FGA	PCT	FTM	FTA	PCT	O-RB	D-RB	TOT	AST	PF	DQ	STL	TO	BLK	PTS	RPG	APG	PPG
72-73—Indiana (A)	24	—	117	24	56	.429	1	2	.500	9	18	.500	21	26	47	9	40	1	—	10	—	58	2.0	0.4	2.4
73-74—Indiana (A)	11	—	73	7	15	.467	0	0	—	1	2	.500	1	17	18	5	12	—	2	7	0	15	1.6	0.5	1.4
REG. ABA TOTALS	35	—	190	31	71	.437	1	2	.500	10	20	.500	22	43	65	14	52	1	2	17	0	73	1.9	0.4	2.1
ABA PLAYOFF TOTALS	4	—	7	2	5	.400	0	1	.000	0	0	—	0	0	5	0	3	0	0	1	0	4	1.3	0.0	1.0

NICHOLS, JACK EDWARD b. April 9, 1926 d. December 24, 1992 Ht. 6-7 Wt. 230 College—Washington/USC

SEASON—TEAM	G	GS	MIN	FGM	FGA	PCT	3FGM	3FGA	PCT	FTM	FTA	PCT	O-RB	D-RB	TOT	AST	PF	DQ	STL	TO	BLK	PTS	RPG	APG	PPG
48-49—Washington	34	—	—	153	392	.390	—	—	—	92	126	.730	—	—	—	56	118	—	—	—	—	398	—	1.6	11.7
49-50—Wash.-Tri-Cit	67	—	—	310	848	.366	—	—	—	259	344	.753	—	—	—	142	179	—	—	—	—	879	—	2.1	13.1
50-51—Tri-Cities	5	—	—	18	48	.375	—	—	—	10	13	.769	—	—	52	14	18	0	—	—	—	46	10.4	2.8	9.2
52-53—Milwaukee	69	—	2626	425	1170	.363	—	—	—	240	339	.708	—	—	533	196	237	9	—	—	—	1090	7.7	2.8	15.8
53-54—Milw.-Boston	75	—	1607	163	528	.309	—	—	—	113	152	.743	—	—	363	104	187	2	—	—	—	439	4.8	1.4	5.9
54-55—Boston	64	—	1910	249	656	.380	—	—	—	138	177	.780	—	—	533	144	238	10	—	—	—	636	8.3	2.3	9.9
55-56—Boston	60	—	1964	330	799	.413	—	—	—	200	253	.791	—	—	625	160	228	7	—	—	—	860	10.4	2.7	14.3
56-57—Boston	61	—	1372	195	537	.363	—	—	—	108	136	.794	—	—	374	85	185	4	—	—	—	498	6.1	1.4	8.2
57-58—Boston	69	—	1224	170	484	.351	—	—	—	59	80	.738	—	—	302	63	123	1	—	—	—	399	4.4	0.9	5.8
REG. SEASON TOTALS	504	—	10703	2013	5462	.369	—	—	—	1219	1620	.752	—	—	2782	964	1513	33	—	—	—	5245	6.9	1.9	10.4
PLAYOFF TOTALS	51	—	807	200	514	.389	—	—	—	119	161	.739	—	—	209	117	164	2	—	—	—	519	5.6	2.3	10.2

NICKS, ORLANDO CARL (Carl) b. October 6, 1958 Ht. 6-2 Wt. 180 College—Gulf Coast CC/Indiana State

SEASON—TEAM	G	GS	MIN	FGM	FGA	PCT	3FGM	3FGA	PCT	FTM	FTA	PCT	O-RB	D-RB	TOT	AST	PF	DQ	STL	TO	BLK	PTS	RPG	APG	PPG
80-81—Denver-Utah	67	—	1109	172	359	.479	0	4	.000	71	126	.563	37	73	110	149	141	0	60	116	3	415	1.6	2.2	6.2
81-82—Utah	80	1	1322	252	555	.454	0	5	.000	85	150	.567	67	94	161	89	184	0	66	101	4	589	2.0	1.1	7.4
82-83—Cleveland	9	2	148	26	59	.441	0	1	.000	11	17	.647	8	18	26	11	17	0	6	11	0	63	2.9	1.2	7.0
REG. SEASON TOTALS	156	3	2579	450	973	.462	0	10	.000	167	293	.570	112	185	297	249	342	0	132	228	7	1067	1.9	1.6	6.8

NIEMANN, RICHARD W. (Rich) b. July 2, 1946 Ht. 7-1½ Wt. 245 College—St. Louis

SEASON—TEAM	G	GS	MIN	FGM	FGA	PCT	3FGM	3FGA	PCT	FTM	FTA	PCT	O-RB	D-RB	TOT	AST	PF	DQ	STL	TO	BLK	PTS	RPG	APG	PPG
68-69—Detroit-Milw.	34	—	272	44	106	.415	—	—	—	19	25	.760	—	—	100	16	61	1	—	—	—	107	2.9	0.5	3.1
69-70—Boston	6	—	18	2	5	.400	—	—	—	2	2	1.000	—	—	6	2	10	0	—	—	—	6	1.0	0.3	1.0
69-70—Carolina (A)	63	—	1466	285	601	.474	0	0	—	141	192	.734	—	—	563	87	219	7	—	—	—	711	8.9	1.4	11.3
70-71—Floridians (A)	51	—	642	121	241	.502	0	0	—	43	60	.717	—	—	255	29	137	—	—	—	—	285	5.0	0.6	5.6
71-72—Dallas (A)	33	—	524	48	98	.490	0	0	—	25	34	.735	—	—	155	24	87	—	—	27	—	121	4.7	0.7	3.7
REG. NBA TOTALS	40	—	290	46	111	.414	—	—	—	21	27	.778	—	—	106	18	71	1	—	—	—	113	2.7	0.5	2.8
REG. ABA TOTALS	147	—	2632	454	940	.483	0	0	—	209	286	.731	—	—	973	140	443	7	—	27	—	1117	6.6	1.0	7.6
ABA PLAYOFF TOTALS	5	—	53	7	18	.389	0	0	—	3	3	1.000	—	—	12	2	11	0	—	—	—	17	2.4	0.4	3.4

NIEMIERA, JOHN RICHARD (Richie) b. May 26, 1921 Ht. 6-1 Wt. 165 College—Notre Dame

SEASON—TEAM	G	GS	MIN	FGM	FGA	PCT	3FGM	3FGA	PCT	FTM	FTA	PCT	O-RB	D-RB	TOT	AST	PF	DQ	STL	TO	BLK	PTS	RPG	APG	PPG
46-47—Fort Wayne (N)	13	—	—	28	—	—	—	—	—	17	23	.739	—	—	—	—	—	—	—	—	—	73	—	—	5.6
47-48—Fort Wayne (N)	59	—	—	118	—	—	—	—	—	97	135	.719	—	—	—	—	113	—	—	—	—	333	—	—	5.6
48-49—Fort Wayne	55	—	—	115	331	.347	—	—	—	132	165	.800	—	—	—	96	115	—	—	—	—	362	—	1.7	6.6
49-50—Ft. Wayne-And.	60	—	—	110	350	.314	—	—	—	104	139	.748	—	—	—	116	77	—	—	—	—	324	—	1.9	5.4
REG. NBA TOTALS	115	—	—	225	681	.330	—	—	—	236	304	.776	—	—	—	212	192	—	—	—	—	686	—	1.8	6.0
REG. NBL TOTALS	72	—	—	146	—	—	—	—	—	114	158	.722	—	—	—	—	113	—	—	—	—	406	—	—	5.6
NBA PLAYOFF TOTALS	8	—	—	11	27	.407	—	—	—	6	8	.750	—	—	—	8	10	—	—	—	—	28	—	1.0	3.5
NBL PLAYOFF TOTALS	10	—	—	21	—	—	—	—	—	12	16	.750	—	—	—	—	12	—	—	—	—	54	—	—	5.4

NILES, MICHAEL DONNELL (Mike) b. March 31, 1955 Ht. 6-6 Wt. 225 College—Cal State-Fullerton

SEASON—TEAM	G	GS	MIN	FGM	FGA	PCT	3FGM	3FGA	PCT	FTM	FTA	PCT	O-RB	D-RB	TOT	AST	PF	DQ	STL	TO	BLK	PTS	RPG	APG	PPG
80-81—Phoenix	44	—	231	48	138	.348	2	4	.500	17	37	.459	26	32	58	15	41	0	8	25	1	115	1.3	0.3	2.6
REG. SEASON TOTALS	44	—	231	48	138	.348	2	4	.500	17	37	.459	26	32	58	15	41	0	8	25	1	115	1.3	0.3	2.6
PLAYOFF TOTALS	2	—	4	0	5	.000	0	0	—	0	0	—	0	0	0	—	0	0	1	0	0	0	0.0	0.0	0.0

NIMPHIUS, KURT ALLEN b. March 13, 1958 Ht. 6-11 Wt. 225 College—Arizona State

SEASON—TEAM	G	GS	MIN	FGM	FGA	PCT	3FGM	3FGA	PCT	FTM	FTA	PCT	O-RB	D-RB	TOT	AST	PF	DQ	STL	TO	BLK	PTS	RPG	APG	PPG
81-82—Dallas	63	27	1085	137	297	.461	0	0	—	63	108	.583	92	203	295	61	190	5	17	56	82	337	4.7	1.0	5.3
82-83—Dallas	81	12	1515	174	355	.490	1	1	1.000	77	140	.550	157	247	404	115	287	11	24	66	111	426	5.0	1.4	5.3
83-84—Dallas	82	46	2284	272	523	.520	1	4	.250	101	162	.623	182	331	513	176	283	5	41	98	144	646	6.3	2.1	7.9
84-85—Dallas	82	40	2010	196	434	.452	0	6	.000	108	140	.771	136	272	408	183	262	4	30	95	126	500	5.0	2.2	6.1
85-86—Dallas-L.A. Clips	80	66	2226	351	694	.506	0	3	.000	194	262	.740	152	301	453	62	267	8	33	120	105	896	5.7	0.8	11.2
86-87—L.A. Clips-Detroit	66	11	1088	155	330	.470	0	4	.000	81	120	.675	80	107	187	25	156	1	20	63	54	391	2.8	0.4	5.9
87-88—San Antonio	72	7	919	128	257	.498	0	1	.000	60	83	.723	62	91	153	53	141	2	22	49	56	316	2.1	0.7	4.4
89-90—Philadelphia	38	1	314	38	91	.418	0	1	.000	14	30	.467	22	39	61	6	45	0	4	12	18	90	1.6	0.2	2.4
REG. SEASON TOTALS	564	210	11441	1451	2981	.487	2	20	.100	698	1045	.668	883	1591	2474	681	1631	36	191	559	696	3602	4.4	1.2	6.4
PLAYOFF TOTALS	25	0	306	26	65	.400	0	0	—	18	23	.783	34	47	81	18	52	0	2	14	19	70	3.2	0.7	2.8

NIX, DYRON PATRICK b. February 11, 1967 Ht. 6-7 Wt. 210 College—Tennessee

SEASON—TEAM	G	GS	MIN	FGM	FGA	PCT	3FGM	3FGA	PCT	FTM	FTA	PCT	O-RB	D-RB	TOT	AST	PF	DQ	STL	TO	BLK	PTS	RPG	APG	PPG
89-90—Indiana	20	0	109	14	39	.359	0	0	—	11	16	.688	8	18	26	5	15	0	3	7	1	39	1.3	0.3	2.0
REG. SEASON TOTALS	20	0	109	14	39	.359	0	0	—	11	16	.688	8	18	26	5	15	0	3	7	1	39	1.3	0.3	2.0

NIXON, NORMAN ELLARD (Norm) b. October 11, 1955 Ht. 6-2 Wt. 175 College—Duquesne

SEASON—TEAM	G	GS	MIN	FGM	FGA	PCT	3FGM	3FGA	PCT	FTM	FTA	PCT	O-RB	D-RB	TOT	AST	PF	DQ	STL	TO	BLK	PTS	RPG	APG	PPG
77-78—Los Angeles	81	—	2779	496	998	.497	—	—	—	115	161	.714	41	198	239	553	259	3	138	251	7	1107	3.0	6.8	13.7
78-79—Los Angeles	82	—	3145	623	1149	.542	—	—	—	158	204	.775	48	183	231	737	250	6	201	231	17	1404	2.8	9.0	17.1
79-80—Los Angeles	82	—	3226	624	1209	.516	1	8	.125	197	253	.779	52	177	229	642	241	1	147	288	14	1446	2.8	7.8	17.6
80-81—Los Angeles	79	—	2962	576	1210	.476	2	12	.167	196	252	.778	64	168	232	696	226	2	146	285	11	1350	2.9	8.8	17.1
81-82—Los Angeles	82	82	3024	628	1274	.493	3	12	.250	181	224	.808	38	138	176	652	264	3	132	238	7	1440	2.1	8.0	17.6
82-83—Los Angeles	79	79	2711	533	1123	.475	0	13	.000	125	168	.744	61	144	205	566	176	1	104	237	4	1191	2.6	7.2	15.1
83-84—San Diego	82	82	3053	587	1270	.462	11	46	.239	206	271	.760	56	147	203	914	180	1	94	257	4	1391	2.5	11.1	17.0
84-85—L.A. Clippers	81	81	2894	596	1281	.465	33	99	.333	170	218	.780	55	163	218	711	175	2	95	273	4	1395	2.7	8.8	17.2
85-86—L.A. Clippers	67	62	2138	403	921	.438	42	121	.347	131	162	.809	45	135	180	576	143	0	84	190	3	979	2.7	8.6	14.6
88-89—L.A. Clippers	53	30	1318	153	370	.414	8	29	.276	48	65	.738	13	65	78	339	69	0	46	118	0	362	1.5	6.4	6.8
REG. SEASON TOTALS	768	416	27250	5219	10805	.483	100	340	.294	1527	1978	.772	473	1518	1991	6386	1983	19	1187	2368	71	12065	2.6	8.3	15.7
PLAYOFF TOTALS	58	28	2287	440	921	.478	5	15	.333	142	186	.763	50	145	195	465	201	1	89	151	8	1027	3.4	8.0	17.7
ALL-STAR TOTALS	2	0	38	12	21	.571	0	0	—	1	2	.500	0	2	2	10	0	0	2	1	0	25	1.0	5.0	12.5

NOBLE, CHARLES E. (Chuck) b. July 24, 1931   Ht. 6-4 Wt. 195 College—Louisville

SEASON—TEAM	G	GS	MIN	FGM	FGA	PCT	3FGM	3FGA	PCT	FTM	FTA	PCT	O-RB	D-RB	TOT	AST	PF	DQ	STL	TO	BLK	PTS	RPG	APG	PPG
55-56—Fort Wayne	72	—	2013	270	767	.352	—	—	—	146	195	.749	—	—	261	282	253	3	—	—	—	686	3.6	3.9	9.5
56-57—Fort Wayne	54	—	1260	200	556	.360	—	—	—	76	102	.745	—	—	135	180	161	2	—	—	—	476	2.5	3.3	8.8
57-58—Detroit	61	—	1363	199	601	.331	—	—	—	56	77	.727	—	—	140	153	166	0	—	—	—	454	2.3	2.5	7.4
58-59—Detroit	65	—	939	189	560	.338	—	—	—	83	113	.735	—	—	115	114	126	0	—	—	—	461	1.8	1.8	7.1
59-60—Detroit	58	—	1621	276	774	.357	—	—	—	101	138	.732	—	—	201	265	172	2	—	—	—	653	3.5	4.6	11.3
60-61—Detroit	75	—	1655	196	566	.346	—	—	—	82	115	.713	—	—	180	287	195	4	—	—	—	474	2.4	3.8	6.3
61-62—Detroit	26	—	361	32	113	.283	—	—	—	8	15	.533	—	—	43	63	55	1	—	—	—	72	1.7	2.4	2.8
REG. SEASON TOTALS	411	—	9212	1362	3937	.346	—	—	—	552	755	.731	—	—	1075	1344	1128	12	—	—	—	3276	2.6	3.3	8.0
PLAYOFF TOTALS	29	—	591	79	244	.324	—	—	—	28	36	.778	—	—	63	86	71	2	—	—	—	186	2.2	3.0	6.4
ALL-STAR TOTALS	1	—	11	0	5	.000	—	—	—	0	0	—	—	—	1	3	1	0	—	—	—	0	1.0	3.0	0.0

NOEL, PAUL WENDEL b. August 4, 1924   Ht. 6-4 Wt. 185 College—Kentucky

SEASON—TEAM	G	GS	MIN	FGM	FGA	PCT	3FGM	3FGA	PCT	FTM	FTA	PCT	O-RB	D-RB	TOT	AST	PF	DQ	STL	TO	BLK	PTS	RPG	APG	PPG
47-48—New York	29	—	—	40	138	.290	—	—	—	19	30	.633	—	—	—	3	41	—	—	—	—	99	—	0.1	3.4
48-49—New York	47	—	—	70	277	.253	—	—	—	37	60	.617	—	—	—	33	84	—	—	—	—	177	—	0.7	3.8
49-50—New York	65	—	—	98	291	.337	—	—	—	53	87	.609	—	—	—	67	132	—	—	—	—	249	—	1.0	3.8
50-51—Rochester	52	—	—	49	174	.282	—	—	—	32	45	.711	—	—	81	34	61	1	—	—	—	130	1.6	0.7	2.5
51-52—Rochester	8	—	32	2	9	.222	—	—	—	2	3	.667	—	—	4	3	6	0	—	—	—	6	0.5	0.4	0.8
REG. SEASON TOTALS	201	—	32	259	889	.291	—	—	—	143	225	.636	—	—	85	140	324	1	—	—	—	661	1.4	0.7	3.3
PLAYOFF TOTALS	20	—	0	13	44	.295	—	—	—	10	16	.625	—	—	9	4	35	1	—	—	—	36	1.5	0.2	1.8

NOLAN, JAMES S. (Jim) b. June 9, 1927 d. April 19, 1983 Ht. 6-8 Wt. 210 College—Georgia Tech

SEASON—TEAM	G	GS	MIN	FGM	FGA	PCT	3FGM	3FGA	PCT	FTM	FTA	PCT	O-RB	D-RB	TOT	AST	PF	DQ	STL	TO	BLK	PTS	RPG	APG	PPG
49-50—Philadelphia	5	—	—	4	21	.190	—	—	—	0	0	—	—	—	—	4	14	—	—	—	—	8	—	0.8	1.6
REG. SEASON TOTALS	5	—	—	4	21	.190	—	—	—	0	0	—	—	—	—	4	14	—	—	—	—	8	—	0.8	1.6

NOLEN, PAUL E. b. September 3, 1929   Ht. 6-10 Wt. 215 College—Texas Tech

SEASON—TEAM	G	GS	MIN	FGM	FGA	PCT	3FGM	3FGA	PCT	FTM	FTA	PCT	O-RB	D-RB	TOT	AST	PF	DQ	STL	TO	BLK	PTS	RPG	APG	PPG
53-54—Baltimore	1	—	2	0	1	.000	—	—	—	0	0	—	—	—	1	0	1	0	—	—	—	0	1.0	0.0	0.0
REG. SEASON TOTALS	1	—	2	0	1	.000	—	—	—	0	0	—	—	—	1	0	1	0	—	—	—	0	1.0	0.0	0.0

NORDMANN, ROBERT (Bevo) b. December 11, 1939   Ht. 6-10 Wt. 225 College—St. Louis

SEASON—TEAM	G	GS	MIN	FGM	FGA	PCT	3FGM	3FGA	PCT	FTM	FTA	PCT	O-RB	D-RB	TOT	AST	PF	DQ	STL	TO	BLK	PTS	RPG	APG	PPG
61-62—Cincinnati	58	—	344	51	126	.405	—	—	—	29	57	.509	—	—	128	18	81	1	—	—	—	131	2.2	0.3	2.3
62-63—St. L.-N.Y.	53	—	1000	156	319	.489	—	—	—	59	122	.484	—	—	316	47	156	6	—	—	—	371	6.0	0.9	7.0
63-64—N.Y.-St. L.	19	—	259	27	66	.409	—	—	—	9	19	.474	—	—	65	5	51	1	—	—	—	63	3.4	0.3	3.3
64-65—Boston	3	—	25	3	5	.600	—	—	—	0	0	—	—	—	8	3	5	0	—	—	—	6	2.7	1.0	2.0
REG. SEASON TOTALS	133	—	1628	237	516	.459	—	—	—	97	198	.490	—	—	517	73	293	8	—	—	—	571	3.9	0.5	4.3
PLAYOFF TOTALS	2	—	5	0	1	.000	—	—	—	0	0	—	—	—	2	—	1	0	—	—	—	0	1.0	0.0	0.0

NORLANDER, JOHN A. (Johnny) b. March 5, 1921   Ht. 6-3 Wt. 180 College—Hamline

SEASON—TEAM	G	GS	MIN	FGM	FGA	PCT	3FGM	3FGA	PCT	FTM	FTA	PCT	O-RB	D-RB	TOT	AST	PF	DQ	STL	TO	BLK	PTS	RPG	APG	PPG
46-47—Washington	60	—	—	223	698	.319	—	—	—	180	276	.652	—	—	—	50	122	—	—	—	—	626	—	0.8	10.4
47-48—Washington	48	—	—	167	543	.308	—	—	—	135	182	.742	—	—	—	44	102	—	—	—	—	469	—	0.9	9.8
48-49—Washington	60	—	—	164	454	.361	—	—	—	116	171	.678	—	—	—	86	124	—	—	—	—	444	—	1.4	7.4
49-50—Washington	40	—	—	99	293	.338	—	—	—	53	85	.624	—	—	—	33	71	—	—	—	—	251	—	0.8	6.3
50-51—Washington	9	—	—	6	19	.316	—	—	—	9	14	.643	—	—	9	5	14	0	—	—	—	21	1.0	0.6	2.3
REG. SEASON TOTALS	217	—	—	659	2007	.328	—	—	—	493	728	.677	—	—	9	218	433	0	—	—	—	1811	1.0	1.0	8.3
PLAYOFF TOTALS	17	—	—	39	123	.317	—	—	—	33	43	.767	—	—	—	9	38	0	—	—	—	111	—	0.5	6.5

NORMAN, CONIEL (Connie) b. September 24, 1953   Ht. 6-3 Wt. 175 College—Arizona

SEASON—TEAM	G	GS	MIN	FGM	FGA	PCT	3FGM	3FGA	PCT	FTM	FTA	PCT	O-RB	D-RB	TOT	AST	PF	DQ	STL	TO	BLK	PTS	RPG	APG	PPG
74-75—Philadelphia	12	—	72	23	44	.523	—	—	—	2	3	.667	3	9	12	4	9	0	3	—	1	48	1.0	0.3	4.0
75-76—Philadelphia	65	—	818	183	422	.434	—	—	—	20	24	.833	51	50	101	66	87	1	28	—	7	386	1.6	1.0	5.9
78-79—San Diego	22	—	323	71	165	.430	—	—	—	19	23	.826	13	19	32	24	35	0	10	22	3	161	1.5	1.1	7.3
REG. SEASON TOTALS	99	—	1213	277	631	.439	—	—	—	41	50	.820	67	78	145	94	131	1	41	22	11	595	1.5	0.9	6.0
PLAYOFF TOTALS	1	—	1	1	1	1.000	—	—	—	0	0	—	0	1	1	0	0	0	0	—	0	2	1.0	0.0	2.0

NORMAN, KENNETH DARNEL (Ken, Snake) b. September 5, 1964 Ht. 6-8 Wt. 215 College—Wabash Valley/Illinois

SEASON—TEAM	G	GS	MIN	FGM	FGA	PCT	3FGM	3FGA	PCT	FTM	FTA	PCT	O-RB	D-RB	TOT	AST	PF	DQ	STL	TO	BLK	PTS	RPG	APG	PPG
87-88—L.A. Clippers	66	28	1435	241	500	.482	0	10	.000	87	170	.512	100	163	263	78	123	0	44	103	34	569	4.0	1.2	8.6
88-89—L.A. Clippers	80	79	3020	638	1271	.502	4	21	.190	170	270	.630	245	422	667	277	223	2	106	206	66	1450	8.3	3.5	18.1
89-90—L.A. Clippers	70	64	2334	484	949	.510	7	16	.438	153	242	.632	143	327	470	160	196	0	78	190	59	1128	6.7	2.3	16.1
90-91—L.A. Clippers	70	45	2309	520	1037	.501	6	32	.188	173	275	.629	177	320	497	159	192	0	63	139	63	1219	7.1	2.3	17.4
91-92—L.A. Clippers	77	24	2009	402	821	.490	4	28	.143	121	226	.535	158	290	448	125	145	0	53	100	66	929	5.8	1.6	12.1
92-93—L.A. Clippers	76	71	2477	498	975	.511	10	38	.263	131	220	.595	209	362	571	165	156	0	59	125	58	1137	7.5	2.2	15.0
93-94—Milwaukee	82	75	2539	412	919	.448	63	189	.333	92	183	.503	169	331	500	222	209	2	58	150	46	979	6.1	2.7	11.9
REG. SEASON TOTALS	521	386	16123	3195	6472	.494	94	334	.281	927	1586	.584	1201	2215	3416	1186	1244	4	461	1013	392	7411	6.6	2.3	14.2
PLAYOFF TOTALS	10	10	348	52	120	.433	3	10	.300	20	39	.513	33	57	90	27	26	0	8	7	3	127	9.0	2.7	12.7

NORRIS, AUDIE JAMES b. December 18, 1960 Ht. 6-9 Wt. 250 College—Jackson State

SEASON—TEAM	G	GS	MIN	FGM	FGA	PCT	3FGM	3FGA	PCT	FTM	FTA	PCT	O-RB	D-RB	TOT	AST	PF	DQ	STL	TO	BLK	PTS	RPG	APG	PPG
82-83—Portland	30	0	311	26	63	.413	0	0	—	14	30	.467	25	44	69	24	61	0	13	33	2	66	2.3	0.8	2.2
83-84—Portland	79	1	1157	124	246	.504	0	0	—	104	149	.698	82	175	257	76	231	2	30	114	34	352	3.3	1.0	4.5
84-85—Portland	78	13	1117	133	245	.543	0	3	.000	135	203	.665	90	160	250	47	221	7	42	100	33	401	3.2	0.6	5.1
REG. SEASON TOTALS	187	14	2585	283	554	.511	0	3	.000	253	382	.662	197	379	576	147	513	9	85	247	69	819	3.1	0.8	4.4
PLAYOFF TOTALS	20	0	214	32	55	.582	0	0	—	15	32	.469	31	40	71	12	43	1	7	18	8	79	3.6	0.6	4.0

NORRIS, SYLVESTER b. February 18, 1957 Ht. 6-11½ Wt. 225 College—Jackson State

SEASON—TEAM	G	GS	MIN	FGM	FGA	PCT	3FGM	3FGA	PCT	FTM	FTA	PCT	O-RB	D-RB	TOT	AST	PF	DQ	STL	TO	BLK	PTS	RPG	APG	PPG
79-80—San Antonio	17	—	189	18	43	.419	0	0	—	4	6	.667	10	33	43	6	41	1	3	19	12	40	2.5	0.4	2.4
REG. SEASON TOTALS	17	—	189	18	43	.419	0	0	—	4	6	.667	10	33	43	6	41	1	3	19	12	40	2.5	0.4	2.4

NORWOOD, WILLIE B. b. August 8, 1947 Ht. 6-7 Wt. 220 College—Alcorn State

SEASON—TEAM	G	GS	MIN	FGM	FGA	PCT	3FGM	3FGA	PCT	FTM	FTA	PCT	O-RB	D-RB	TOT	AST	PF	DQ	STL	TO	BLK	PTS	RPG	APG	PPG
71-72—Detroit	78	—	1272	222	440	.505	—	—	—	140	215	.651	—	—	316	43	229	4	—	—	—	584	4.1	0.6	7.5
72-73—Detroit	79	—	1282	249	504	.494	—	—	—	154	225	.684	—	—	324	56	182	0	—	—	—	652	4.1	0.7	8.3
73-74—Detroit	74	—	1178	247	484	.510	—	—	—	95	143	.664	95	134	229	58	156	2	60	—	9	589	3.1	0.8	8.0
74-75—Detroit	24	—	347	64	123	.520	—	—	—	31	42	.738	31	57	88	16	51	0	23	—	0	159	3.7	0.7	6.6
75-76—Seattle	64	—	1004	146	301	.485	—	—	—	152	203	.749	91	138	229	59	139	3	42	—	4	444	3.6	0.9	6.9
76-77—Seattle	76	—	1647	216	461	.469	—	—	—	151	206	.733	127	165	292	99	191	1	62	—	6	583	3.8	1.3	7.7
77-78—Detroit-Port.	35	—	611	74	181	.409	—	—	—	50	75	.667	49	70	119	33	101	1	31	56	3	198	3.4	0.9	5.7
REG. SEASON TOTALS	430	—	7341	1218	2494	.488	—	—	—	773	1109	.697	393	564	1597	364	1049	11	218	56	22	3209	3.7	0.8	7.5
PLAYOFF TOTALS	14	—	290	38	81	.469	—	—	—	16	23	.696	22	23	45	13	43	4	8	2	3	92	3.2	0.9	6.6

NOSTRAND, GEORGE THOMAS b. January 25, 1924 d. November 8, 1981 Ht. 6-8 Wt. 195 College—High Point/Wyoming

SEASON—TEAM	G	GS	MIN	FGM	FGA	PCT	3FGM	3FGA	PCT	FTM	FTA	PCT	O-RB	D-RB	TOT	AST	PF	DQ	STL	TO	BLK	PTS	RPG	APG	PPG
46-47—Toronto-Clev.	61	—	—	192	656	.293	—	—	—	98	210	.467	—	—	—	31	145	—	—	—	—	482	—	0.5	7.9
47-48—Providence	45	—	—	196	660	.297	—	—	—	129	239	.540	—	—	—	30	148	—	—	—	—	521	—	0.7	11.6
48-49—Prov.-Boston	60	—	—	212	651	.326	—	—	—	165	284	.581	—	—	—	94	164	—	—	—	—	589	—	1.6	9.8
49-50—Boston-Tri-Cit-Chicago	55	—	—	78	255	.306	—	—	—	56	99	.566	—	—	—	29	118	—	—	—	—	212	—	0.5	3.9
REG. SEASON TOTALS	221	—	—	678	2222	.305	—	—	—	448	832	.538	—	—	—	184	575	—	—	—	—	1804	—	0.8	8.2
PLAYOFF TOTALS	3	—	—	14	40	.350	—	—	—	5	7	.714	—	—	—	3	10	1	—	—	—	33	—	1.0	11.0

NOSZKA, STANLEY M. (Stan) b. September 19, 1920 Ht. 6-1 Wt. 185 College—Duquesne

SEASON—TEAM	G	GS	MIN	FGM	FGA	PCT	3FGM	3FGA	PCT	FTM	FTA	PCT	O-RB	D-RB	TOT	AST	PF	DQ	STL	TO	BLK	PTS	RPG	APG	PPG
45-46—Youngstown (N)	2	—	—	0	—	—	—	—	—	1	—	—	—	—	—	—	—	—	—	—	—	1	—	—	0.5
46-47—Pittsburgh	58	—	—	199	693	.287	—	—	—	109	157	.694	—	—	—	39	163	—	—	—	—	507	—	0.7	8.7
47-48—Boston	22	—	—	27	97	.278	—	—	—	24	35	.686	—	—	—	4	52	—	—	—	—	78	—	0.2	3.5
48-49—Boston	30	—	—	30	123	.244	—	—	—	15	30	.500	—	—	—	25	56	—	—	—	—	75	—	0.8	2.5
REG. NBA TOTALS	110	—	—	256	913	.280	—	—	—	148	222	.667	—	—	—	68	271	—	—	—	—	660	—	0.6	6.0
REG. NBL TOTALS	2	—	—	0	—	—	—	—	—	1	—	—	—	—	—	—	—	—	—	—	—	1	—	—	0.5
NBA PLAYOFF TOTALS	3	—	—	10	30	.333	—	—	—	5	8	.625	—	—	—	2	11	—	—	—	—	25	—	0.7	8.3

NOVAK, MICHAEL D. (Mike) b. April 23, 1915 d. August 15, 1978 Ht. 6-9 Wt. 220 College—Loyola (Ill.)

SEASON—TEAM	G	GS	MIN	FGM	FGA	PCT	3FGM	3FGA	PCT	FTM	FTA	PCT	O-RB	D-RB	TOT	AST	PF	DQ	STL	TO	BLK	PTS	RPG	APG	PPG
39-40—Chicago (N)	28	—	—	114	—	—	—	—	—	65	114	.570	—	—	—	—	62	—	—	—	—	293	—	—	10.5
40-41—Chicago (N)	23	—	—	56	—	—	—	—	—	34	74	.459	—	—	—	—	66	—	—	—	—	146	—	—	6.3
41-42—Chicago (N)	19	—	—	58	—	—	—	—	—	31	—	—	—	—	—	—	—	—	—	—	—	147	—	—	7.7
42-43—Chicago (N)	18	—	—	50	—	—	—	—	—	35	50	.700	—	—	—	—	51	—	—	—	—	135	—	—	7.5
43-44—Sheboygan (N)	22	—	—	39	—	—	—	—	—	14	—	—	—	—	—	—	—	—	—	—	—	92	—	—	4.2
44-45—Sheboygan (N)	27	—	—	88	—	—	—	—	—	57	—	—	—	—	—	—	—	—	—	—	—	233	—	—	8.6
45-46—Sheboygan (N)	34	—	—	111	—	—	—	—	—	88	144	.611	—	—	—	—	63	—	—	—	—	310	—	—	9.1
46-47—She.-Syr. (N)	36	—	—	153	—	—	—	—	—	73	136	.537	—	—	—	—	129	—	—	—	—	379	—	—	10.5
47-48—Syracuse (N)	60	—	—	211	—	—	—	—	—	124	201	.617	—	—	—	—	201	—	—	—	—	546	—	—	9.1
48-49—Rochester	60	—	—	124	363	.342	—	—	—	72	124	.581	—	—	—	112	188	—	—	—	—	320	—	1.9	5.3
49-50—Roch.-Phil.	60	—	—	37	149	.248	—	—	—	25	47	.532	—	—	—	61	139	—	—	—	—	99	—	1.0	1.7
53-54—Syracuse	5	—	24	0	7	.583	—	—	—	1	2	.500	—	—	2	2	9	0	—	—	—	1	0.4	0.4	0.2
REG. NBA TOTALS	125	—	24	161	519	.310	—	—	—	98	173	.566	—	—	2	175	336	0	—	—	—	420	0.4	1.4	3.4
REG. NBL TOTALS	267	—	—	880	—	—	—	—	—	521	719	.583	—	—	—	—	572	—	—	—	—	2281	—	—	8.5
NBA PLAYOFF TOTALS	4	—	0	6	22	.273	—	—	—	1	1	1.000	—	—	—	10	13	0	—	—	—	13	—	2.5	3.3
NBL PLAYOFF TOTALS	32	—	—	90	—	—	—	—	—	65	69	.565	—	—	—	—	77	—	—	—	—	245	—	—	7.7

NOWELL, MELVYN P. (Mel) b. December 27, 1939 Ht. 6-2 Wt. 170 College—Ohio State

SEASON—TEAM	G	GS	MIN	FGM	FGA	PCT	3FGM	3FGA	PCT	FTM	FTA	PCT	O-RB	D-RB	TOT	AST	PF	DQ	STL	TO	BLK	PTS	RPG	APG	PPG
62-63—Chicago	39	—	589	92	237	.388	—	—	—	48	66	.727	—	—	67	84	86	0	—	—	—	232	1.7	2.2	5.9
67-68—New Jersey (A)	76	—	1555	273	679	.402	9	32	.281	176	213	.826	—	—	193	155	188	1	—	142	—	731	2.5	2.0	9.6
REG. NBA TOTALS	39	—	589	92	237	.388	—	—	—	48	66	.727	—	—	67	84	86	0	—	—	—	232	1.7	2.2	5.9
REG. ABA TOTALS	76	—	1555	273	679	.402	9	32	.281	176	213	.826	—	—	193	155	188	1	—	142	—	731	2.5	2.0	9.6

NUTT, DENNIS CLAY b. March 25, 1963 Ht. 6-2 Wt. 170 College—Texas Christian

SEASON—TEAM	G	GS	MIN	FGM	FGA	PCT	3FGM	3FGA	PCT	FTM	FTA	PCT	O-RB	D-RB	TOT	AST	PF	DQ	STL	TO	BLK	PTS	RPG	APG	PPG
86-87—Dallas	25	0	91	16	40	.400	5	17	.294	20	22	.909	1	7	8	16	6	0	7	10	0	57	0.3	0.6	2.3
REG. SEASON TOTALS	25	0	91	16	40	.400	5	17	.294	20	22	.909	1	7	8	16	6	0	7	10	0	57	0.3	0.6	2.3
PLAYOFF TOTALS	1	0	10	1	5	.200	0	2	.000	0	0	—	1	1	2	1	0	0	0	1	0	2	2.0	1.0	2.0

OAKLEY, CHARLES b. December 18, 1963 Ht. 6-9 Wt. 245 College—Virginia Union

SEASON—TEAM	G	GS	MIN	FGM	FGA	PCT	3FGM	3FGA	PCT	FTM	FTA	PCT	O-RB	D-RB	TOT	AST	PF	DQ	STL	TO	BLK	PTS	RPG	APG	PPG
85-86—Chicago	77	30	1772	281	541	.519	0	3	.000	178	269	.662	255	409	664	133	250	9	68	175	30	740	8.6	1.7	9.6
86-87—Chicago	82	81	2980	468	1052	.445	11	30	.367	245	357	.686	299	775	1074	296	315	4	85	299	36	1192	13.1	3.6	14.5
87-88—Chicago	82	82	2816	375	776	.483	3	12	.250	261	359	.727	326	740	1066	248	272	2	68	241	28	1014	13.0	3.0	12.4
88-89—New York	82	82	2604	426	835	.510	12	48	.250	197	255	.773	343	518	861	187	270	1	104	248	14	1061	10.5	2.3	12.9
89-90—New York	61	61	2196	336	641	.524	0	3	.000	217	285	.761	258	469	727	146	220	3	64	165	16	889	11.9	2.4	14.6
90-91—New York	76	74	2739	307	595	.516	0	2	.000	239	305	.784	305	615	920	204	288	4	62	215	17	853	12.1	2.7	11.2
91-92—New York	82	82	2309	210	402	.522	0	3	.000	86	117	.735	256	444	700	133	258	2	67	123	15	506	8.5	1.6	6.2
92-93—New York	82	82	2230	219	431	.508	0	1	.000	127	176	.722	288	420	708	126	289	5	85	124	15	565	8.6	1.5	6.9
93-94—New York	82	82	2932	363	760	.478	0	3	.000	243	313	.776	349	616	965	218	293	4	110	193	18	969	11.8	2.7	11.8
REG. SEASON TOTALS	706	656	22578	2985	6033	.495	26	105	.248	1793	2436	.736	2679	5006	7685	1691	2455	34	713	1783	189	7789	10.9	2.4	11.0
PLAYOFF TOTALS	90	88	3178	368	791	.465	4	9	.444	241	327	.737	394	617	1011	166	310	4	100	198	23	981	11.2	1.8	10.9
ALL-STAR TOTALS	1	0	11	1	3	.333	0	0	—	0	0	—	1	2	3	3	3	0	0	0	0	2	3.0	3.0	2.0

O'BOYLE, JOHN W. b. March 7, 1928 Ht. 6-2 Wt. 185 College—Modesto JC/Colorado State

SEASON—TEAM	G	GS	MIN	FGM	FGA	PCT	3FGM	3FGA	PCT	FTM	FTA	PCT	O-RB	D-RB	TOT	AST	PF	DQ	STL	TO	BLK	PTS	RPG	APG	PPG
52-53—Milwaukee	5	—	97	8	26	.308	—	—	—	5	7	.714	—	—	10	5	20	1	—	—	—	21	2.0	1.0	4.2
REG. SEASON TOTALS	5	—	97	8	26	.308	—	—	—	5	7	.714	—	—	10	5	20	1	—	—	—	21	2.0	1.0	4.2

O'BRIEN, JAMES J. (Jimmy) b. April 9, 1949 Ht. 6-2 Wt. 170 College—Boston College

SEASON—TEAM	G	GS	MIN	FGM	FGA	PCT	3FGM	3FGA	PCT	FTM	FTA	PCT	O-RB	D-RB	TOT	AST	PF	DQ	STL	TO	BLK	PTS	RPG	APG	PPG
71-72—Pitt.-Ken. (A)	84	—	1778	173	436	.397	7	32	.219	65	80	.813	—	—	206	373	189	—	—	152	—	418	2.5	4.4	5.0
72-73—Kentucky (A)	68	—	1014	126	317	.397	0	9	.000	68	89	.764	27	65	92	174	103	0	—	77	—	320	1.4	2.6	4.7
73-74—Ken.-S.D. (A)	72	—	1320	211	513	.411	7	27	.259	79	95	.832	49	85	134	254	79	—	63	113	1	508	1.9	3.5	7.1
74-75—San Diego (A)	79	—	2036	210	525	.400	4	34	.118	125	142	.880	50	136	186	443	147	—	89	192	2	549	2.4	5.6	6.9
REG. ABA TOTALS	303	—	6148	720	1791	.402	18	102	.176	337	406	.830	126	286	618	1244	518	0	152	534	3	1795	2.0	4.1	5.9
ABA PLAYOFF TOTALS	30	—	610	57	148	.385	2	7	.286	46	55	.836	1	8	46	111	41	0	25	40	1	162	1.5	3.7	5.4

O'BRIEN, JAMES M. (Jim) b. November 7, 1951 Ht. 6-7 Wt. 200 College—Maryland

SEASON—TEAM	G	GS	MIN	FGM	FGA	PCT	3FGM	3FGA	PCT	FTM	FTA	PCT	O-RB	D-RB	TOT	AST	PF	DQ	STL	TO	BLK	PTS	RPG	APG	PPG
73-74—New York (A)	11	—	54	15	37	.405	0	4	.000	9	15	.600	13	4	17	6	5	—	3	8	3	39	1.5	0.5	3.5
74-75—Memphis (A)	47	—	611	88	203	.433	6	26	.231	47	60	.783	45	76	121	81	56	—	38	73	23	229	2.6	1.7	4.9
REG. ABA TOTALS	58	—	665	103	240	.429	6	30	.200	56	75	.747	58	80	138	87	61	0	41	81	26	268	2.4	1.5	4.6
ABA PLAYOFF TOTALS	7	—	42	6	19	.316	0	1	.000	2	2	1.000	2	6	8	8	3	0	3	1	0	14	1.1	1.1	2.0

O'BRIEN, RALPH E. (**Buckshot**) b. April 28, 1928 Ht. 5-9 Wt. 160 College—Butler

SEASON—TEAM	G	GS	MIN	FGM	FGA	PCT	3FGM	3FGA	PCT	FTM	FTA	PCT	O-RB	D-RB	TOT	AST	PF	DQ	STL	TO	BLK	PTS	RPG	APG	PPG
51-52—Indianapolis	64	—	1577	228	613	.372	—	—	—	122	149	.819	—	—	122	124	115	0	—	—	—	578	1.9	1.9	9.0
52-53—Ind.-Ft. Wayne-Balt.	55	—	758	96	286	.336	—	—	—	78	92	.848	—	—	70	56	74	0	—	—	—	270	1.3	1.0	4.9
REG. SEASON TOTALS	119	—	2335	324	899	.360	—	—	—	200	241	.830	—	—	192	180	189	0	—	—	—	848	1.6	1.5	7.1
PLAYOFF TOTALS	3	—	67	5	13	.385	—	—	—	7	7	1.000	—	—	4	3	3	0	—	—	—	17	1.3	1.0	5.7

O'BRIEN, ROBERT (**Bob**) b. January 26, 1927 Ht. 6-4½ Wt. 190 College—Kansas/Pepperdine

SEASON—TEAM	G	GS	MIN	FGM	FGA	PCT	3FGM	3FGA	PCT	FTM	FTA	PCT	O-RB	D-RB	TOT	AST	PF	DQ	STL	TO	BLK	PTS	RPG	APG	PPG
47-48—Philadelphia	22	—	—	17	81	.210	—	—	—	15	26	.577	—	—	—	1	40	—	—	—	—	49	—	0.0	2.2
48-49—Phil.-St. L.	24	—	—	10	50	.200	—	—	—	12	32	.375	—	—	—	9	32	—	—	—	—	32	—	0.4	1.3
REG. SEASON TOTALS	46	—	—	27	131	.206	—	—	—	27	58	.466	—	—	—	10	72	—	—	—	—	81	—	0.2	1.8
PLAYOFF TOTALS	9	—	—	9	38	.237	—	—	—	10	15	.667	—	—	—	3	13	—	—	—	—	28	—	0.3	3.1

O'CONNELL, DERMOTT F. (**Dermie**) b. April 13, 1928 d. October 5, 1988 Ht. 6-0 Wt. 175 College—Holy Cross

SEASON—TEAM	G	GS	MIN	FGM	FGA	PCT	3FGM	3FGA	PCT	FTM	FTA	PCT	O-RB	D-RB	TOT	AST	PF	DQ	STL	TO	BLK	PTS	RPG	APG	PPG
48-49—Boston	21	—	—	87	315	.276	—	—	—	30	56	.536	—	—	—	65	40	—	—	—	—	204	—	3.1	9.7
49-50—Boston-St. L.	61	—	—	111	425	.261	—	—	—	47	89	.528	—	—	—	91	91	—	—	—	—	269	—	1.5	4.4
REG. SEASON TOTALS	82	—	—	198	740	.268	—	—	—	77	145	.531	—	—	—	156	131	—	—	—	—	473	—	1.9	5.8

O'DONNELL, ANDREW J. (**Andy**) b. March 10, 1925 Ht. 6-1 Wt. 180 College—Loyola (Md.)

SEASON—TEAM	G	GS	MIN	FGM	FGA	PCT	3FGM	3FGA	PCT	FTM	FTA	PCT	O-RB	D-RB	TOT	AST	PF	DQ	STL	TO	BLK	PTS	RPG	APG	PPG
49-50—Baltimore	25	—	—	38	108	.352	—	—	—	14	18	.778	—	—	—	17	32	—	—	—	—	90	—	0.7	3.6
REG. SEASON TOTALS	25	—	—	38	108	.352	—	—	—	14	18	.778	—	—	—	17	32	—	—	—	—	90	—	0.7	3.6

OGDEN, CARLOS (**Bud**) b. December 29, 1946 Ht. 6-6 Wt. 215 College—Santa Clara

SEASON—TEAM	G	GS	MIN	FGM	FGA	PCT	3FGM	3FGA	PCT	FTM	FTA	PCT	O-RB	D-RB	TOT	AST	PF	DQ	STL	TO	BLK	PTS	RPG	APG	PPG
69-70—Philadelphia	47	—	357	82	172	.477	—	—	—	27	39	.692	—	—	86	31	62	2	—	—	—	191	1.8	0.7	4.1
70-71—Philadelphia	27	—	133	24	66	.364	—	—	—	18	26	.692	—	—	20	17	21	0	—	—	—	66	0.7	0.6	2.4
REG. SEASON TOTALS	74	—	490	106	238	.445	—	—	—	45	65	.692	—	—	106	48	83	2	—	—	—	257	1.4	0.6	3.5
PLAYOFF TOTALS	2	—	16	5	11	.455	—	—	—	2	4	.500	—	—	3	6	1	0	—	—	—	12	1.5	3.0	6.0

OGDEN, RALPH b. January 25, 1948 Ht. 6-5 Wt. 205 College—Santa Clara

SEASON—TEAM	G	GS	MIN	FGM	FGA	PCT	3FGM	3FGA	PCT	FTM	FTA	PCT	O-RB	D-RB	TOT	AST	PF	DQ	STL	TO	BLK	PTS	RPG	APG	PPG
70-71—San Francisco	32	—	162	17	71	.239	—	—	—	8	12	.667	—	—	32	9	17	0	—	—	—	42	1.0	0.3	1.3
REG. SEASON TOTALS	32	—	162	17	71	.239	—	—	—	8	12	.667	—	—	32	9	17	0	—	—	—	42	1.0	0.3	1.3
PLAYOFF TOTALS	2	—	15	1	5	.200	—	—	—	4	4	1.000	—	—	4	1	0	0	—	—	—	6	2.0	0.5	3.0

OGG, RAYMOND ALAN (**Alan**) b. July 5, 1967 Ht. 7-2 Wt. 245 College—Alabama-Birmingham

SEASON—TEAM	G	GS	MIN	FGM	FGA	PCT	3FGM	3FGA	PCT	FTM	FTA	PCT	O-RB	D-RB	TOT	AST	PF	DQ	STL	TO	BLK	PTS	RPG	APG	PPG
90-91—Miami	31	1	261	24	55	.436	0	2	.000	6	10	.600	15	34	49	2	53	1	6	8	27	54	1.6	0.1	1.7
91-92—Miami	43	0	367	46	84	.548	0	0	—	16	30	.533	30	44	74	7	73	0	5	19	28	108	1.7	0.2	2.5
92-93—Milw.-Wash.	6	0	29	5	13	.385	0	0	—	3	4	.750	3	7	10	4	6	0	1	3	3	13	1.7	0.7	2.2
REG. SEASON TOTALS	80	1	657	75	152	.493	0	2	.000	25	44	.568	48	85	133	13	132	1	12	30	58	175	1.7	0.2	2.2
PLAYOFF TOTALS	3	.0	15	1	3	.333	0	0	—	1	2	.500	0	1	1	—	3	0	1	0	3	3	0.3	0.0	1.0

O'GRADY, FRANCIS DAVID (**Buddy**) b. January 19, 1920 Ht. 5-11 Wt. 160 College—Georgetown

SEASON—TEAM	G	GS	MIN	FGM	FGA	PCT	3FGM	3FGA	PCT	FTM	FTA	PCT	O-RB	D-RB	TOT	AST	PF	DQ	STL	TO	BLK	PTS	RPG	APG	PPG
45-46—Rochester (N)	1	—	—	0	—	—	—	—	—	0	—	—	—	—	—	—	—	—	—	—	—	0	—	—	0.0
46-47—Washington	55	—	—	55	231	.238	—	—	—	38	53	.717	—	—	—	20	60	—	—	—	—	148	—	0.4	2.7
47-48—St. Louis	44	—	—	67	257	.261	—	—	—	36	54	.667	—	—	—	9	61	—	—	—	—	170	—	0.2	3.9
48-49—St. L.-Prov.	47	—	—	85	293	.290	—	—	—	49	71	.690	—	—	—	68	57	—	—	—	—	219	—	1.4	4.7
REG. NBA TOTALS	146	—	—	207	781	.265	—	—	—	123	178	.691	—	—	—	97	178	—	—	—	—	537	—	0.7	3.7
REG. NBL TOTALS	1	—	—	0	—	—	—	—	—	0	—	—	—	—	—	—	—	—	—	—	—	0	—	—	0.0
NBA PLAYOFF TOTALS	13	—	—	13	53	.245	—	—	—	8	8	1.000	—	—	—	10	—	—	—	—	—	34	0.0	0.0	2.6

O'HANLON, FRANCIS BRIAN (**Fran**) b. August 24, 1948 Ht. 6-1½ Wt. 175 College—Villanova

SEASON—TEAM	G	GS	MIN	FGM	FGA	PCT	3FGM	3FGA	PCT	FTM	FTA	PCT	O-RB	D-RB	TOT	AST	PF	DQ	STL	TO	BLK	PTS	RPG	APG	PPG
70-71—Floridians (A)	14	—	101	8	22	.364	0	1	.000	6	9	.667	—	—	4	13	18	—	—	—	—	22	0.3	0.9	1.6
REG. ABA TOTALS	14	—	101	8	22	.364	0	1	.000	6	9	.667	—	—	4	13	18	—	—	—	—	22	0.3	0.9	1.6

OHL, DONALD JAY (**Don**) b. April 18, 1936 Ht. 6-3 Wt. 190 College—Illinois

SEASON—TEAM	G	GS	MIN	FGM	FGA	PCT	3FGM	3FGA	PCT	FTM	FTA	PCT	O-RB	D-RB	TOT	AST	PF	DQ	STL	TO	BLK	PTS	RPG	APG	PPG
60-61—Detroit	79	—	2172	427	1085	.394	—	—	—	200	278	.719	—	—	256	265	224	3	—	—	—	1054	3.2	3.4	13.3
61-62—Detroit	77	—	2526	555	1250	.444	—	—	—	201	280	.718	—	—	267	244	173	2	—	—	—	1311	3.5	3.2	17.0
62-63—Detroit	80	—	2961	636	1450	.439	—	—	—	275	380	.724	—	—	239	325	234	3	—	—	—	1547	3.0	4.1	19.3
63-64—Detroit	71	—	2366	500	1224	.408	—	—	—	225	331	.680	—	—	180	225	219	3	—	—	—	1225	2.5	3.2	17.3
64-65—Baltimore	77	—	2821	568	1297	.438	—	—	—	284	388	.732	—	—	336	250	274	7	—	—	—	1420	4.4	3.2	18.4
65-66—Baltimore	73	—	2645	593	1334	.445	—	—	—	316	430	.735	—	—	280	290	208	1	—	—	—	1502	3.8	4.0	20.6
66-67—Baltimore	58	—	2024	452	1002	.451	—	—	—	276	354	.780	—	—	189	168	153	1	—	—	—	1180	3.3	2.9	20.3
67-68—Balt.-St. L.	70	—	1919	393	891	.441	—	—	—	197	254	.776	—	—	175	157	184	1	—	—	—	983	2.5	2.2	14.0
68-69—Atlanta	76	—	1995	385	901	.427	—	—	—	147	208	.707	—	—	170	221	232	5	—	—	—	917	2.2	2.9	12.1
69-70—Atlanta	66	—	984	176	372	.473	—	—	—	58	72	.806	—	—	71	98	113	1	—	—	—	410	1.1	1.5	6.2
REG. SEASON TOTALS	727	—	22413	4685	10806	.434	—	—	—	2179	2975	.732	—	—	2163	2243	2014	27	—	—	—	11549	3.0	3.1	15.9
PLAYOFF TOTALS	47	—	1482	320	749	.427	—	—	—	155	206	.752	—	—	161	130	154	3	—	—	—	795	3.4	2.8	16.9
ALL-STAR TOTALS	5	—	87	16	43	.372	—	—	—	14	15	.933	—	—	9	7	10	0	—	—	—	46	1.8	1.4	9.2

O'KEEFE, RICHARD T. (**Dick**) b. September 29, 1923 Ht. 6-2 Wt. 185 College—Santa Clara

SEASON—TEAM	G	GS	MIN	FGM	FGA	PCT	3FGM	3FGA	PCT	FTM	FTA	PCT	O-RB	D-RB	TOT	AST	PF	DQ	STL	TO	BLK	PTS	RPG	APG	PPG
47-48—Washington	37	—	—	63	257	.245	—	—	—	30	59	.508	—	—	—	18	85	—	—	—	—	156	—	0.5	4.2
48-49—Washington	50	—	—	70	274	.255	—	—	—	51	99	.515	—	—	—	43	119	—	—	—	—	191	—	0.9	3.8
49-50—Washington	68	—	—	162	529	.306	—	—	—	150	203	.739	—	—	—	74	247	—	—	—	—	474	—	1.1	7.0
50-51—Washington	17	—	—	21	102	.206	—	—	—	25	39	.641	—	—	37	25	48	0	—	—	—	67	2.2	1.5	3.9
REG. SEASON TOTALS	172	—	—	316	1162	.272	—	—	—	256	400	.640	—	—	37	160	499	0	—	—	—	888	2.2	0.9	5.2
PLAYOFF TOTALS	13	—	—	26	73	.356	—	—	—	20	28	.714	—	—	—	16	47	0	—	—	—	72	—	1.2	5.5

O'KEEFE, THOMAS V. (**Tommy**) b. July 16, 1926 Ht. 6-2 Wt. 185 College—Notre Dame/Georgetown

SEASON—TEAM	G	GS	MIN	FGM	FGA	PCT	3FGM	3FGA	PCT	FTM	FTA	PCT	O-RB	D-RB	TOT	AST	PF	DQ	STL	TO	BLK	PTS	RPG	APG	PPG
50-51—Balt.-Wash.	6	—	—	10	28	.357	—	—	—	3	4	.750	—	—	7	10	5	0	—	—	—	23	1.2	1.7	3.8
REG. SEASON TOTALS	6	—	—	10	28	.357	—	—	—	3	4	.750	—	—	7	10	5	0	—	—	—	23	1.2	1.7	3.8

O'KOREN, MICHAEL F. (**Mike**) b. February 7, 1958 Ht. 6-7 Wt. 205 College—North Carolina

SEASON—TEAM	G	GS	MIN	FGM	FGA	PCT	3FGM	3FGA	PCT	FTM	FTA	PCT	O-RB	D-RB	TOT	AST	PF	DQ	STL	TO	BLK	PTS	RPG	APG	PPG
80-81—New Jersey	79	—	2473	365	751	.486	5	18	.278	135	212	.637	179	299	478	252	243	8	86	146	27	870	6.1	3.2	11.0
81-82—New Jersey	80	32	2018	383	778	.492	8	23	.348	135	189	.714	111	194	305	192	175	0	83	147	13	909	3.8	2.4	11.4
82-83—New Jersey	46	14	803	136	259	.525	2	9	.222	34	48	.708	42	72	114	82	67	0	42	62	11	308	2.5	1.8	6.7
83-84—New Jersey	73	25	1191	186	385	.483	5	28	.179	53	87	.609	71	104	175	95	148	3	34	75	11	430	2.4	1.3	5.9
84-85—New Jersey	43	29	1119	194	393	.494	8	21	.381	42	67	.627	46	120	166	102	115	1	32	51	16	438	3.9	2.4	10.2
85-86—New Jersey	67	11	1031	160	336	.476	7	27	.259	23	39	.590	33	102	135	118	134	3	29	54	9	350	2.0	1.8	5.2
86-87—Washington	15	0	123	16	42	.381	0	2	.000	0	2	.000	6	8	14	13	10	0	2	6	0	32	0.9	0.9	2.1
87-88—New Jersey	4	0	52	9	16	.563	0	1	.000	0	4	.000	1	3	4	2	2	0	3	0	2	18	1.0	0.5	4.5
REG. SEASON TOTALS	407	111	8810	1449	2960	.490	35	129	.271	422	648	.651	489	902	1391	856	894	15	311	541	89	3355	3.4	2.1	8.2
PLAYOFF TOTALS	20	11	333	34	91	.374	0	3	.000	6	10	.600	21	40	61	33	59	2	6	20	5	74	3.1	1.7	3.7

OLAJUWON, HAKEEM ABDUL (**Hakeem the Dream**) b. January 21, 1963 Ht. 7-0 Wt. 250 College—Houston

SEASON—TEAM	G	GS	MIN	FGM	FGA	PCT	3FGM	3FGA	PCT	FTM	FTA	PCT	O-RB	D-RB	TOT	AST	PF	DQ	STL	TO	BLK	PTS	RPG	APG	PPG
84-85—Houston	82	82	2914	677	1258	.538	0	0	—	338	551	.613	440	534	974	111	344	10	99	234	220	1692	11.9	1.4	20.6
85-86—Houston	68	68	2467	625	1188	.526	0	0	—	347	538	.645	333	448	781	137	271	9	134	195	231	1597	11.5	2.0	23.5
86-87—Houston	75	75	2760	677	1332	.508	1	5	.200	400	570	.702	315	543	858	220	294	8	140	228	254	1755	11.4	2.9	23.4
87-88—Houston	79	79	2825	712	1385	.514	0	4	.000	381	548	.695	302	657	959	163	324	7	162	243	214	1805	12.1	2.1	22.8
88-89—Houston	82	82	3024	790	1556	.508	0	10	.000	454	652	.696	338	767	1105	149	329	10	213	275	282	2034	13.5	1.8	24.8
89-90—Houston	82	82	3124	806	1609	.501	1	6	.167	382	536	.713	299	850	1149	234	314	6	174	316	376	1995	14.0	2.9	24.3
90-91—Houston	56	50	2062	487	959	.508	0	4	.000	213	277	.769	219	551	770	131	221	5	121	174	221	1187	13.8	2.3	21.2
91-92—Houston	70	69	2636	591	1177	.502	0	1	.000	328	428	.766	246	599	845	157	263	7	127	187	304	1510	12.1	2.2	21.6
92-93—Houston	82	82	3242	848	1603	.529	0	8	.000	444	570	.779	283	785	1068	291	305	5	150	262	342	2140	13.0	3.5	26.1
93-94—Houston	80	80	3277	894	1694	.528	8	19	.421	388	542	.716	229	726	955	287	289	4	128	271	297	2184	11.9	3.6	27.3
REG. SEASON TOTALS	756	749	28331	7107	13761	.516	10	57	.175	3675	5212	.705	3004	6460	9464	1880	2954	71	1448	2385	2741	17899	12.5	2.5	23.7
PLAYOFF TOTALS	85	85	3463	902	1700	.531	2	9	.222	492	680	.724	341	704	1045	259	333	4	154	256	329	2298	12.3	3.0	27.0
ALL-STAR TOTALS	9	5	211	32	81	.395	0	0	—	25	46	.543	33	44	77	15	26	1	13	22	20	89	8.6	1.7	9.9

OLBERDING, MARK ALLEN b. April 21, 1956 Ht. 6-8 Wt. 230 College—Minnesota

SEASON—TEAM	G	GS	MIN	FGM	FGA	PCT	3FGM	3FGA	PCT	FTM	FTA	PCT	O-RB	D-RB	TOT	AST	PF	DQ	STL	TO	BLK	PTS	RPG	APG	PPG
75-76—S.D.-S.A. (A)	81	—	2055	302	607	.498	0	0	—	191	247	.773	184	346	530	142	249	—	50	141	37	795	6.5	1.8	9.8
76-77—San Antonio	82	—	1949	301	598	.503	—	—	—	251	316	.794	162	287	449	119	277	6	59	—	29	853	5.5	1.5	10.4
77-78—San Antonio	79	—	1773	231	480	.481	—	—	—	184	227	.811	104	269	373	131	235	1	45	118	26	646	4.7	1.7	8.2
78-79—San Antonio	80	—	1885	261	551	.474	—	—	—	233	290	.803	96	333	429	211	282	2	53	163	18	755	5.4	2.6	9.4
79-80—San Antonio	75	—	2111	291	609	.478	0	3	.000	210	264	.795	83	335	418	327	274	7	67	180	22	792	5.6	4.4	10.6
80-81—San Antonio	82	—	2408	348	685	.508	1	7	.143	315	380	.829	146	325	471	277	307	6	75	202	31	1012	5.7	3.4	12.3
81-82—San Antonio	68	63	2098	333	705	.472	2	12	.167	273	338	.808	118	321	439	202	253	5	57	139	29	941	6.5	3.0	13.8
82-83—Chicago	80	31	1817	251	522	.481	2	12	.167	194	248	.782	108	250	358	131	246	3	50	152	9	698	4.5	1.6	8.7
83-84—Kansas City	81	81	2160	249	504	.494	0	1	.000	261	318	.821	119	326	445	192	291	2	50	166	28	759	5.5	2.4	9.4
84-85—Kansas City	81	62	2277	265	528	.502	0	3	.000	293	352	.832	139	374	513	243	298	8	56	185	11	823	6.3	3.0	10.2
85-86—Sacramento	81	64	2157	225	403	.558	0	2	.000	162	210	.771	113	310	423	266	276	3	43	148	23	612	5.2	3.3	7.6
86-87—Sacramento	76	0	1002	69	165	.418	0	1	.000	116	131	.885	50	135	185	91	144	0	18	56	9	254	2.4	1.2	3.3
REG. NBA TOTALS	865	301	21637	2824	5750	.491	5	41	.122	2492	3074	.811	1238	3265	4503	2190	2883	43	573	1509	235	8145	5.2	2.5	9.4
REG. ABA TOTALS	81	—	2055	302	607	.498	0	0	—	191	247	.773	184	346	530	142	249	—	50	141	37	795	6.5	1.8	9.8
NBA PLAYOFF TOTALS	47	15	1366	204	435	.469	1	4	.250	112	144	.778	67	188	255	131	183	5	35	95	20	521	5.4	2.8	11.1
ABA PLAYOFF TOTALS	7	—	73	5	15	.333	0	0	—	3	6	.500	7	15	22	3	15	—	3	4	2	13	3.1	0.4	1.9

OLDHAM, JAWANN b. July 4, 1957 Ht. 7-0 Wt. 220 College—Seattle

SEASON—TEAM	G	GS	MIN	FGM	FGA	PCT	3FGM	3FGA	PCT	FTM	FTA	PCT	O-RB	D-RB	TOT	AST	PF	DQ	STL	TO	BLK	PTS	RPG	APG	PPG
80-81—Denver	4	—	21	2	6	.333	0	0	—	0	0	—	3	2	5	0	3	0	0	2	2	4	1.3	0.0	1.0
81-82—Houston	22	0	124	13	36	.361	0	0	—	8	14	.571	7	17	24	3	28	0	2	6	10	34	1.1	0.1	1.5
82-83—Chicago	16	0	171	31	58	.534	0	0	—	12	22	.545	18	29	47	5	30	1	5	13	13	74	2.9	0.3	4.6
83-84—Chicago	64	0	870	110	218	.505	0	0	—	39	66	.591	75	158	233	33	139	2	15	83	76	259	3.6	0.5	4.0
84-85—Chicago	63	0	993	89	192	.464	0	1	.000	34	50	.680	79	157	236	31	166	3	11	58	127	212	3.7	0.5	3.4
85-86—Chicago	52	47	1276	167	323	.517	0	1	.000	53	91	.582	112	194	306	37	206	6	28	86	134	387	5.9	0.7	7.4
86-87—New York	44	9	776	71	174	.408	0	1	.000	31	57	.544	51	128	179	19	95	1	22	48	71	173	4.1	0.4	3.9
87-88—Sacramento	54	13	946	119	250	.476	0	0	—	59	87	.678	82	222	304	33	143	2	12	62	110	297	5.6	0.6	5.5
89-90—Orlando-Lakers	6	0	45	3	6	.500	0	0	—	3	7	.429	4	12	16	1	9	0	2	4	3	9	2.7	0.2	1.5
90-91—Indiana	4	0	19	3	6	.500	0	0	—	0	0	—	0	3	3	0	1	0	0	0	0	6	0.8	0.0	1.5
REG. SEASON TOTALS	329	69	5241	608	1269	.479	0	3	.000	239	394	.607	431	922	1353	162	820	15	97	362	546	1455	4.1	0.5	4.4
PLAYOFF TOTALS	5	0	95	7	16	.438	0	0	—	0	0	—	9	15	24	3	19	1	6	12	7	14	4.8	0.6	2.8

OLDHAM, JOHN O. (Johnny) b. June 22, 1923 Ht. 6-3 Wt. 185 College—Western Kentucky

SEASON—TEAM	G	GS	MIN	FGM	FGA	PCT	3FGM	3FGA	PCT	FTM	FTA	PCT	O-RB	D-RB	TOT	AST	PF	DQ	STL	TO	BLK	PTS	RPG	APG	PPG
49-50—Fort Wayne	59	—	—	127	426	.298	—	—	—	103	145	.710	—	—	—	99	192	—	—	—	—	357	—	1.7	6.1
50-51—Fort Wayne	68	—	—	199	597	.333	—	—	—	171	292	.586	—	—	242	127	242	15	—	—	—	569	3.6	1.9	8.4
REG. SEASON TOTALS	127	—	—	326	1023	.319	—	—	—	274	437	.627	—	—	242	226	434	15	—	—	—	926	3.6	1.8	7.3
PLAYOFF TOTALS	7	—	—	18	43	.419	—	—	—	18	27	.667	—	—	5	9	28	1	—	—	—	54	1.7	1.3	7.7

OLEYNICK, FRANK b. February 20, 1955 Ht. 6-2½ Wt. 190 College—Seattle

SEASON—TEAM	G	GS	MIN	FGM	FGA	PCT	3FGM	3FGA	PCT	FTM	FTA	PCT	O-RB	D-RB	TOT	AST	PF	DQ	STL	TO	BLK	PTS	RPG	APG	PPG
75-76—Seattle	52	—	650	127	316	.402	—	—	—	53	77	.688	10	35	45	53	62	0	21	—	6	307	0.9	1.0	5.9
76-77—Seattle	50	—	516	81	223	.363	—	—	—	39	53	.736	13	32	45	60	48	0	13	—	4	201	0.9	1.2	4.0
REG. SEASON TOTALS	102	—	1166	208	539	.386	—	—	—	92	130	.708	23	67	90	113	110	0	34	—	10	508	0.9	1.1	5.0

OLIVE, JOHN b. March 1, 1955 Ht. 6-7 Wt. 215 College—Villanova

SEASON—TEAM	G	GS	MIN	FGM	FGA	PCT	3FGM	3FGA	PCT	FTM	FTA	PCT	O-RB	D-RB	TOT	AST	PF	DQ	STL	TO	BLK	PTS	RPG	APG	PPG
78-79—San Diego	34	—	189	13	40	.325	—	—	—	18	23	.783	3	16	19	3	32	0	4	13	0	44	0.6	0.1	1.3
79-80—San Diego	1	—	15	0	2	.000	0	0	—	0	0	—	0	1	1	0	2	0	0	2	0	0	1.0	0.0	0.0
REG. SEASON TOTALS	35	—	204	13	42	.310	0	0	—	18	23	.783	3	17	20	3	34	0	4	15	0	44	0.6	0.1	1.3

OLIVER, BRIAN DARNELL b. June 1, 1968 Ht. 6-4 Wt. 210 College—Georgia Tech

SEASON—TEAM	G	GS	MIN	FGM	FGA	PCT	3FGM	3FGA	PCT	FTM	FTA	PCT	O-RB	D-RB	TOT	AST	PF	DQ	STL	TO	BLK	PTS	RPG	APG	PPG
90-91—Philadelphia	73	4	800	111	272	.408	5	18	.278	52	71	.732	18	62	80	88	76	0	34	50	4	279	1.1	1.2	3.8
91-92—Philadelphia	34	0	279	33	100	.330	0	4	.000	15	22	.682	10	20	30	20	33	0	10	24	2	81	0.9	0.6	2.4
REG. SEASON TOTALS	107	4	1079	144	372	.387	5	22	.227	67	93	.720	28	82	110	108	109	0	44	74	6	360	1.0	1.0	3.4
PLAYOFF TOTALS	4	0	15	2	6	.333	0	0	—	2	2	1.000	0	0	0	1	4	0	1	0	0	6	0.0	0.3	1.5

OLIVER, JIMMY ALLEN b. July 12, 1969 Ht. 6-5 Wt. 205 College—Purdue

SEASON—TEAM	G	GS	MIN	FGM	FGA	PCT	3FGM	3FGA	PCT	FTM	FTA	PCT	O-RB	D-RB	TOT	AST	PF	DQ	STL	TO	BLK	PTS	RPG	APG	PPG
91-92—Cleveland	27	8	252	39	98	.398	1	9	.111	17	22	.773	9	18	27	20	22	0	9	9	2	96	1.0	0.7	3.6
93-94—Boston	44	6	540	89	214	.416	13	32	.406	25	33	.758	8	38	46	33	39	0	16	21	1	216	1.0	0.8	4.9
REG. SEASON TOTALS	71	14	792	128	312	.410	14	41	.341	42	55	.764	17	56	73	53	61	0	25	30	3	312	1.0	0.7	4.4

OLLRICH, GENE W. (**Moe**) b. June 30, 1922 Ht. 5-11 Wt. 160 College—Drake

SEASON—TEAM	G	GS	MIN	FGM	FGA	PCT	3FGM	3FGA	PCT	FTM	FTA	PCT	O-RB	D-RB	TOT	AST	PF	DQ	STL	TO	BLK	PTS	RPG	APG	PPG
49-50—Waterloo	14	—	—	17	72	.236	—	—	—	10	14	.714	—	—	—	24	34	—	—	—	—	44	—	1.7	3.1
REG. SEASON TOTALS	14	—	—	17	72	.236	—	—	—	10	14	.714	—	—	—	24	34	—	—	—	—	44	—	1.7	3.1

OLSEN, ENOCH ELI III (**Bud**) b. July 25, 1940 Ht. 6-8 Wt. 225 College—Louisville

SEASON—TEAM	G	GS	MIN	FGM	FGA	PCT	3FGM	3FGA	PCT	FTM	FTA	PCT	O-RB	D-RB	TOT	AST	PF	DQ	STL	TO	BLK	PTS	RPG	APG	PPG
62-63—Cincinnati	52	—	373	43	133	.323	—	—	—	27	39	.692	—	—	105	42	78	0	—	—	—	113	2.0	0.8	2.2
63-64—Cincinnati	49	—	513	85	210	.405	—	—	—	32	57	.561	—	—	149	29	78	0	—	—	—	202	3.0	0.6	4.1
64-65—Cincinnati	79	—	1372	224	512	.438	—	—	—	144	195	.738	—	—	333	84	203	5	—	—	—	592	4.2	1.1	7.5
65-66—Cin.-S.F.	59	—	602	81	193	.420	—	—	—	39	88	.443	—	—	192	20	81	1	—	—	—	201	3.3	0.3	3.4
66-67—San Francisco	40	—	348	75	167	.449	—	—	—	23	58	.397	—	—	103	32	51	1	—	—	—	173	2.6	0.8	4.3
67-68—Seattle	73	—	897	130	285	.456	—	—	—	17	62	.274	—	—	204	75	136	1	—	—	—	277	2.8	1.0	3.8
68-69—Boston-Detroit	17	—	113	15	42	.357	—	—	—	4	18	.222	—	—	25	11	14	0	—	—	—	34	1.5	0.6	2.0
69-70—Kentucky (A)	84	—	1375	158	330	.479	1	4	.250	26	73	.356	—	—	374	249	234	5	—	—	—	343	4.5	3.0	4.1
REG. NBA TOTALS	369	—	4218	653	1542	.423	—	—	—	286	517	.553	—	—	1111	293	641	8	—	—	—	1592	3.0	0.8	4.3
REG. ABA TOTALS	84	—	1375	158	330	.479	1	4	.250	26	73	.356	—	—	374	249	234	5	—	—	—	343	4.5	3.0	4.1
NBA PLAYOFF TOTALS	15	—	84	21	45	.467	—	—	—	4	12	.333	—	—	32	6	16	0	—	—	—	46	2.1	0.4	3.1
ABA PLAYOFF TOTALS	12	—	211	18	43	.419	0	1	.000	1	7	.143	—	—	61	39	45	2	—	—	—	37	5.1	3.3	3.1

O'MALLEY, V. GRADY (**Grady**) b. April 25, 1948 Ht. 6-5 Wt. 205 College—Manhattan

SEASON—TEAM	G	GS	MIN	FGM	FGA	PCT	3FGM	3FGA	PCT	FTM	FTA	PCT	O-RB	D-RB	TOT	AST	PF	DQ	STL	TO	BLK	PTS	RPG	APG	PPG
69-70—Atlanta	24	—	113	21	60	.350	—	—	—	8	19	.421	—	—	26	10	12	0	—	—	—	50	1.1	0.4	2.1
REG. SEASON TOTALS	24	—	113	21	60	.350	—	—	—	8	19	.421	—	—	26	10	12	0	—	—	—	50	1.1	0.4	2.1

O'NEAL, SHAQUILLE RASHAUN b. March 6, 1972 Ht. 7-1 Wt. 305 College—Louisiana State

SEASON—TEAM	G	GS	MIN	FGM	FGA	PCT	3FGM	3FGA	PCT	FTM	FTA	PCT	O-RB	D-RB	TOT	AST	PF	DQ	STL	TO	BLK	PTS	RPG	APG	PPG
92-93—Orlando	81	81	3071	733	1304	.562	0	2	.000	427	721	.592	342	780	1122	152	321	8	60	307	286	1893	13.9	1.9	23.4
93-94—Orlando	81	81	3224	953	1591	.599	0	2	.000	471	850	.554	384	688	1072	195	281	3	76	222	231	2377	13.2	2.4	29.3
REG. SEASON TOTALS	162	162	6295	1686	2895	.582	0	4	.000	898	1571	.572	726	1468	2194	347	602	11	136	529	517	4270	13.5	2.1	26.4
PLAYOFF TOTALS	3	3	126	23	45	.511	0	0	—	16	34	.471	17	23	40	7	13	0	2	10	9	62	13.3	2.3	20.7
ALL-STAR TOTALS	2	2	51	6	21	.286	0	0	—	10	20	.500	7	10	17	0	5	0	1	1	4	22	8.5	0.0	11.0

O'NEILL, MIKE b. 1927 Ht. 6-3 Wt. 210 College—California

SEASON—TEAM	G	GS	MIN	FGM	FGA	PCT	3FGM	3FGA	PCT	FTM	FTA	PCT	O-RB	D-RB	TOT	AST	PF	DQ	STL	TO	BLK	PTS	RPG	APG	PPG
52-53—Milwaukee	4	—	50	4	17	.235	—	—	—	4	4	1.000	—	—	9	3	10	1	—	—	—	12	2.3	0.8	3.0
REG. SEASON TOTALS	4	—	50	4	17	.235	—	—	—	4	4	1.000	—	—	9	3	10	1	—	—	—	12	2.3	0.8	3.0

ORMS, BARRY D. b. May 1, 1946 Ht. 6-3 Wt. 190 College—St. Louis

SEASON—TEAM	G	GS	MIN	FGM	FGA	PCT	3FGM	3FGA	PCT	FTM	FTA	PCT	O-RB	D-RB	TOT	AST	PF	DQ	STL	TO	BLK	PTS	RPG	APG	PPG
68-69—Baltimore	64	—	916	76	246	.309	—	—	—	29	60	.483	—	—	158	49	155	3	—	—	—	181	2.5	0.8	2.8
69-70—Indiana-Pitt. (A)	77	—	2091	272	695	.391	5	26	.192	152	276	.551	—	—	347	132	215	3	—	—	—	701	4.5	1.7	9.1
REG. NBA TOTALS	64	—	916	76	246	.309	—	—	—	29	60	.483	—	—	158	49	155	3	—	—	—	181	2.5	0.8	2.8
REG. ABA TOTALS	77	—	2091	272	695	.391	5	26	.192	152	276	.551	—	—	347	132	215	3	—	—	—	701	4.5	1.7	9.1
NBA PLAYOFF TOTALS	3	—	10	0	0	—	—	—	—	0	0	—	—	—	1	—	2	0	—	—	—	0	0.3	0.0	0.0

ORR, JOHN M. (**Johnny**) b. June 10, 1927 Ht. 6-3 Wt. 205 College—Beloit/Illinois

SEASON—TEAM	G	GS	MIN	FGM	FGA	PCT	3FGM	3FGA	PCT	FTM	FTA	PCT	O-RB	D-RB	TOT	AST	PF	DQ	STL	TO	BLK	PTS	RPG	APG	PPG
49-50—St. L.-Wat.	34	—	—	40	118	.339	—	—	—	12	14	.857	—	—	—	20	34	—	—	—	—	92	—	0.6	2.7
REG. SEASON TOTALS	34	—	—	40	118	.339	—	—	—	12	14	.857	—	—	—	20	34	—	—	—	—	92	—	0.6	2.7

ORR, LOUIS M. b. May 7, 1958 Ht. 6-8 Wt. 175 College—Syracuse

SEASON—TEAM	G	GS	MIN	FGM	FGA	PCT	3FGM	3FGA	PCT	FTM	FTA	PCT	O-RB	D-RB	TOT	AST	PF	DQ	STL	TO	BLK	PTS	RPG	APG	PPG
80-81—Indiana	82	—	1787	348	709	.491	0	6	.000	163	202	.807	172	189	361	132	153	0	55	123	25	859	4.4	1.6	10.5
81-82—Indiana	80	41	1951	357	719	.497	1	8	.125	203	254	.799	127	204	331	134	182	1	56	137	26	918	4.1	1.7	11.5
82-83—New York	82	14	1666	274	593	.462	0	2	.000	140	175	.800	94	134	228	94	134	0	64	93	24	688	2.8	1.1	8.4
83-84—New York	78	20	1640	262	572	.458	0	0	—	173	211	.820	101	127	228	61	142	0	66	95	17	697	2.9	0.8	8.9
84-85—New York	79	31	2452	372	766	.486	1	10	.100	262	334	.784	171	220	391	134	195	1	100	138	27	1007	4.9	1.7	12.7
85-86—New York	74	64	2237	330	741	.445	0	4	.000	218	278	.784	123	189	312	179	177	4	61	118	26	878	4.2	2.4	11.9
86-87—New York	65	8	1440	166	389	.427	1	5	.200	125	172	.727	102	130	232	110	123	0	47	70	18	458	3.6	1.7	7.0
87-88—New York	29	0	180	16	50	.320	0	1	.000	8	16	.500	13	21	34	9	27	0	6	14	0	40	1.2	0.3	1.4
REG. SEASON TOTALS	569	178	13353	2125	4539	.468	3	36	.083	1292	1642	.787	903	1214	2117	853	1133	6	455	788	163	5545	3.7	1.5	9.7
PLAYOFF TOTALS	22	0	393	56	143	.392	0	0	—	32	38	.842	37	46	83	13	46	1	14	24	6	144	3.8	0.6	6.5

ORTIZ, JOSE RAFAEL b. October 25, 1963 Ht. 6-10 Wt. 225 College—Oregon State

SEASON—TEAM	G	GS	MIN	FGM	FGA	PCT	3FGM	3FGA	PCT	FTM	FTA	PCT	O-RB	D-RB	TOT	AST	PF	DQ	STL	TO	BLK	PTS	RPG	APG	PPG
88-89—Utah	51	15	327	55	125	.440	0	1	.000	31	52	.596	30	28	58	11	40	0	8	36	7	141	1.1	0.2	2.8
89-90—Utah	13	0	64	19	42	.452	1	2	.500	3	5	.600	8	7	15	7	15	0	2	5	1	42	1.2	0.5	3.2
REG. SEASON TOTALS	64	15	391	74	167	.443	1	3	.333	34	57	.596	38	35	73	18	55	0	10	41	8	183	1.1	0.3	2.9

OSBORNE, CHARLES H. (**Chuck**) b. January 21, 1939 d. April 1979 Ht. 6-6 Wt. 210 College—Western Kentucky

SEASON—TEAM	G	GS	MIN	FGM	FGA	PCT	3FGM	3FGA	PCT	FTM	FTA	PCT	O-RB	D-RB	TOT	AST	PF	DQ	STL	TO	BLK	PTS	RPG	APG	PPG
61-62—Syracuse	4	—	21	1	8	.125	—	—	—	3	4	.750	—	—	9	1	3	0	—	—	—	5	2.3	0.3	1.3
REG. SEASON TOTALS	4	—	21	1	8	.125	—	—	—	3	4	.750	—	—	9	1	3	0	—	—	—	5	2.3	0.3	1.3

O'SHEA, KEVIN CHRISTOPHER b. July 10, 1925 Ht. 6-2 Wt. 175 College—Notre Dame

SEASON—TEAM	G	GS	MIN	FGM	FGA	PCT	3FGM	3FGA	PCT	FTM	FTA	PCT	O-RB	D-RB	TOT	AST	PF	DQ	STL	TO	BLK	PTS	RPG	APG	PPG
50-51—Minneapolis	63	—	87	267	.326		—	—	—	97	134	.724	—	—	125	100	99	1	—	—	—	271	2.0	1.6	4.3
51-52—Milw.-Balt.	65	—	1725	153	466	.328	—	—	—	144	210	.686	—	—	201	171	175	7	—	—	—	450	3.1	2.6	6.9
52-53—Baltimore	46	—	643	71	189	.376	—	—	—	48	81	.593	—	—	76	87	82	1	—	—	—	190	1.7	1.9	4.1
REG. SEASON TOTALS	174	—	2368	311	922	.337	—	—	—	289	425	.680	—	—	402	358	356	9	—	—	—	911	2.3	2.1	5.2
PLAYOFF TOTALS	5	—	0	1	7	.143	—	—	—	3	4	.750	—	—	5	1	8	0	—	—	—	5	1.3	0.3	1.0

O'SHIELDS, GARLAND L. (**Mule**) b. May 23, 1921 Ht. 6-1 Wt. 195 College—Spartanburg JC/Tennessee

SEASON—TEAM	G	GS	MIN	FGM	FGA	PCT	3FGM	3FGA	PCT	FTM	FTA	PCT	O-RB	D-RB	TOT	AST	PF	DQ	STL	TO	BLK	PTS	RPG	APG	PPG
46-47—Chicago	9	—	—	2	11	.182	—	—	—	0	2	.000	—	—	—	1	8	—	—	—	—	4	—	0.1	0.4
47-48—Syracuse (N)	5	—	—	3			—	—	—	3	4	.750	—	—	—	—	—	—	—	—	—	9	—	—	1.8
REG. NBA TOTALS	9	—	—	2	11	.182	—	—	—	0	2	.000	—	—	—	1	8	—	—	—	—	4	—	0.1	0.4
REG. NBL TOTALS	5	—	—	3			—	—	—	3	4	.750	—	—	—	—	—	—	—	—	—	9	—	—	1.8

OSTERKORN, WALTER RAYMOND (**Wally**) b. July 6, 1928 Ht. 6-5 Wt. 215 College—Illinois

SEASON—TEAM	G	GS	MIN	FGM	FGA	PCT	3FGM	3FGA	PCT	FTM	FTA	PCT	O-RB	D-RB	TOT	AST	PF	DQ	STL	TO	BLK	PTS	RPG	APG	PPG
51-52—Syracuse	66	—	1721	145	413	.351	—	—	—	199	335	.594	—	—	444	117	226	8	—	—	—	489	6.7	1.8	7.4
52-53—Syracuse	49	—	1016	85	262	.324	—	—	—	106	168	.631	—	—	217	61	129	2	—	—	—	276	4.4	1.2	5.6
53-54—Syracuse	70	—	2164	203	586	.346	—	—	—	209	361	.579	—	—	487	151	209	1	—	—	—	615	7.0	2.2	8.8
54-55—Syracuse	19	—	286	20	97	.206	—	—	—	16	32	.500	—	—	70	17	32	0	—	—	—	56	3.7	0.9	2.9
REG. SEASON TOTALS	204	—	5187	453	1358	.334	—	—	—	530	896	.592	—	—	1218	346	596	11	—	—	—	1436	6.0	1.7	7.0
PLAYOFF TOTALS	33	—	908	83	232	.358	—	—	—	92	157	.586	—	—	207	70	97	3	—	—	—	258	6.3	2.1	7.8

O'SULLIVAN, DANIEL JAMES (**Dan**) b. March 3, 1968 Ht. 6-10 Wt. 250 College—Fordham

SEASON—TEAM	G	GS	MIN	FGM	FGA	PCT	3FGM	3FGA	PCT	FTM	FTA	PCT	O-RB	D-RB	TOT	AST	PF	DQ	STL	TO	BLK	PTS	RPG	APG	PPG
90-91—Utah	21	0	85	7	16	.438	0	0	—	7	11	.636	5	12	17	4	18	0	1	4	1	21	0.8	0.2	1.0
92-93—N.J.-Milw.	6	0	17	3	5	.600	0	0	—	3	4	.750	2	4	6	1	4	0	1	0	0	9	1.0	0.2	1.5
93-94—Detroit	13	0	56	4	12	.333	0	0	—	9	12	.750	2	8	10	3	10	0	0	3	0	17	0.8	0.2	1.3
REG. SEASON TOTALS	40	0	158	14	33	.424	0	0	—	19	27	.704	9	24	33	8	32	0	2	7	1	47	0.8	0.2	1.2

OTHICK, MATTHEW BRIAN (**Matt**) b. March 16, 1969 Ht. 6-2 Wt. 165 College—Arizona

SEASON—TEAM	G	GS	MIN	FGM	FGA	PCT	3FGM	3FGA	PCT	FTM	FTA	PCT	O-RB	D-RB	TOT	AST	PF	DQ	STL	TO	BLK	PTS	RPG	APG	PPG
92-93—San Antonio	4	0	39	3	5	.600	2	4	.500	0	2	.000	1	1	2	7	7	0	1	4	0	8	0.5	1.8	2.0
REG. SEASON TOTALS	4	0	39	3	5	.600	2	4	.500	0	2	.000	1	1	2	7	7	0	1	4	0	8	0.5	1.8	2.0

OTTEN, DONALD F. (**Don**) b. April 18, 1921 d. September 18, 1985 Ht. 7-0 Wt. 250 College—Bowling Green

SEASON—TEAM	G	GS	MIN	FGM	FGA	PCT	3FGM	3FGA	PCT	FTM	FTA	PCT	O-RB	D-RB	TOT	AST	PF	DQ	STL	TO	BLK	PTS	RPG	APG	PPG
46-47—Tri-Cities (N)	44	—	—	200			—	—	—	169	261	.648	—	—	—	—	98	—	—	—	—	569	—	—	12.9
47-48—Tri-Cities (N)	60	—	—	282			—	—	—	260	392	.663	—	—	—	—	184	—	—	—	—	824	—	—	13.7
48-49—Tri-Cities (N)	64	—	—	301			—	—	—	297	424	.700	—	—	—	—	205	—	—	—	—	899	—	—	14.0
49-50—Tri-Cit-Wash.	64	—	—	242	648	.373	—	—	—	341	463	.737	—	—	—	91	246	—	—	—	—	825	—	1.4	12.9
50-51—Wash.-Balt.-Ft. Wayne	67	—	—	162	479	.338	—	—	—	246	308	.799	—	—	404	62	255	15	—	—	—	570	6.0	0.9	8.5
51-52—Ft. Wayne-Milw.	64	—	1789	222	636	.349	—	—	—	323	418	.773	—	—	435	123	218	11	—	—	—	767	6.8	1.9	12.0
52-53—Milwaukee	24	—	384	34	87	.391	—	—	—	64	91	.703	—	—	89	21	68	4	—	—	—	132	3.7	0.9	5.5
REG. NBA TOTALS	219	—	2173	660	1850	.357	—	—	—	974	1280	.761	—	—	928	297	787	30	—	—	—	2294	6.0	1.4	10.5
REG. NBL TOTALS	168	—	—	783			—	—	—	726	1077	.674	—	—	—	—	487	—	—	—	—	2292	—	—	13.6
NBA PLAYOFF TOTALS	5	—	0	18	51	.353	—	—	—	34	42	.810	—	—	19	14	22	1	—	—	—	70	6.3	2.8	14.0
NBL PLAYOFF TOTALS	12	—	—	58			—	—	—	73	93	.785	—	—	—	—	41	—	—	—	—	189	—	—	15.8

OTTEN, MAC WILLIAM b. December 16, 1925 Ht. 6-7 Wt. 220 College—Bowling Green

SEASON—TEAM	G	GS	MIN	FGM	FGA	PCT	3FGM	3FGA	PCT	FTM	FTA	PCT	O-RB	D-RB	TOT	AST	PF	DQ	STL	TO	BLK	PTS	RPG	APG	PPG
49-50—Tri-Cit-St. L.	59	—	—	51	155	.329	—	—	—	40	81	.494	—	—	—	36	119	—	—	—	—	142	—	0.6	2.4
REG. SEASON TOTALS	59	—	—	51	155	.329	—	—	—	40	81	.494	—	—	—	36	119	—	—	—	—	142	—	0.6	2.4

OUTLAW, CHARLES b. April 13, 1971 Ht. 6-8 Wt. 210 College—South Plains-Houston

SEASON—TEAM	G	GS	MIN	FGM	FGA	PCT	3FGM	3FGA	PCT	FTM	FTA	PCT	O-RB	D-RB	TOT	AST	PF	DQ	STL	TO	BLK	PTS	RPG	APG	PPG
93-94—L.A. Clippers	37	14	871	98	167	.587	0	2	.000	61	103	.592	81	131	212	36	94	1	36	31	37	257	5.7	1.0	6.9
REG. SEASON TOTALS	37	14	871	98	167	.587	0	2	.000	61	103	.592	81	131	212	36	94	1	36	31	37	257	5.7	1.0	6.9

OVERTON, CLAUDELL (Claude) b. December 16, 1927 Ht. 6-2 Wt. 195 College—East Central (Okla.)

SEASON—TEAM	G	GS	MIN	FGM	FGA	PCT	3FGM	3FGA	PCT	FTM	FTA	PCT	O-RB	D-RB	TOT	AST	PF	DQ	STL	TO	BLK	PTS	RPG	APG	PPG
52-53—Philadelphia	15	—	182	19	75	.253	—	—	—	20	30	.667	—	—	25	15	25	0	—	—	—	58	1.7	1.0	3.9
REG. SEASON TOTALS	15	—	182	19	75	.253	—	—	—	20	30	.667	—	—	25	15	25	0	—	—	—	58	1.7	1.0	3.9

OVERTON, DOUGLAS M. (Doug) b. August 3, 1969 Ht. 6-3 Wt. 190 College—La Salle

SEASON—TEAM	G	GS	MIN	FGM	FGA	PCT	3FGM	3FGA	PCT	FTM	FTA	PCT	O-RB	D-RB	TOT	AST	PF	DQ	STL	TO	BLK	PTS	RPG	APG	PPG
92-93—Washington	45	13	990	152	323	.471	3	13	.231	59	81	.728	25	81	106	157	81	0	31	72	6	366	2.4	3.5	8.1
93-94—Washington	61	1	749	87	216	.403	1	11	.091	43	52	.827	19	50	69	92	48	0	21	54	1	218	1.1	1.5	3.6
REG. SEASON TOTALS	106	14	1739	239	539	.443	4	24	.167	102	133	.767	44	131	175	249	129	0	52	126	7	584	1.7	2.3	5.5

OWENS, BILLY EUGENE b. May 1, 1969 Ht. 6-9 Wt. 220 College—Syracuse

SEASON—TEAM	G	GS	MIN	FGM	FGA	PCT	3FGM	3FGA	PCT	FTM	FTA	PCT	O-RB	D-RB	TOT	AST	PF	DQ	STL	TO	BLK	PTS	RPG	APG	PPG
91-92—Golden State	80	77	2510	468	891	.525	1	9	.111	204	312	.654	243	396	639	188	276	4	90	179	65	1141	8.0	2.4	14.3
92-93—Golden State	37	37	1201	247	493	.501	1	11	.091	117	183	.639	108	156	264	144	105	1	35	106	28	612	7.1	3.9	16.5
93-94—Golden State	79	72	2738	492	971	.507	3	15	.200	199	326	.610	230	410	640	326	269	5	83	214	60	1186	8.1	4.1	15.0
REG. SEASON TOTALS	196	186	6449	1207	2355	.513	5	35	.143	520	821	.633	581	962	1543	658	650	10	208	499	153	2939	7.9	3.4	15.0
PLAYOFF TOTALS	7	7	284	55	107	.514	0	1	.000	26	39	.667	25	38	63	26	25	0	12	13	4	136	9.0	3.7	19.4

OWENS, EDDIE b. December 26, 1953 Ht. 6-7 Wt. 210 College—Nevada-Las Vegas

SEASON—TEAM	G	GS	MIN	FGM	FGA	PCT	3FGM	3FGA	PCT	FTM	FTA	PCT	O-RB	D-RB	TOT	AST	PF	DQ	STL	TO	BLK	PTS	RPG	APG	PPG
77-78—Buffalo	8	—	63	9	21	.429	—	—	—	3	6	.500	5	5	10	5	9	0	1	3	0	21	1.3	0.6	2.6
REG. SEASON TOTALS	8	—	63	9	21	.429	—	—	—	3	6	.500	5	5	10	5	9	0	1	3	0	21	1.3	0.6	2.6

OWENS, JAMES L. (Red) b. September 2, 1925 d. October 11, 1988 Ht. 6-3 Wt. 185 College—Baylor

SEASON—TEAM	G	GS	MIN	FGM	FGA	PCT	3FGM	3FGA	PCT	FTM	FTA	PCT	O-RB	D-RB	TOT	AST	PF	DQ	STL	TO	BLK	PTS	RPG	APG	PPG
49-50—Tri-Cit-And.	61	—	—	86	288	.299	—	—	—	68	101	.673	—	—	—	73	152	—	—	—	—	240	—	1.2	3.9
51-52—Balt.-Milw.	29	—	626	83	252	.329	—	—	—	64	114	.561	—	—	102	64	92	5	—	—	—	230	3.5	2.2	7.9
REG. SEASON TOTALS	90	—	626	169	540	.313	—	—	—	132	215	.614	—	—	102	137	244	5	—	—	—	470	3.5	1.5	5.2
PLAYOFF TOTALS	8	—	0	26	89	.292	—	—	—	28	41	.683	—	—	—	19	37	2	—	—	—	80	—	2.4	10.0

OWENS, JIM b. May 1, 1950 Ht. 6-5 Wt. 200 College—Arizona State

SEASON—TEAM	G	GS	MIN	FGM	FGA	PCT	3FGM	3FGA	PCT	FTM	FTA	PCT	O-RB	D-RB	TOT	AST	PF	DQ	STL	TO	BLK	PTS	RPG	APG	PPG
73-74—Phoenix	17	—	101	21	39	.538	—	—	—	11	14	.786	1	8	9	15	6	0	5	—	0	53	0.5	0.9	3.1
74-75—Phoenix	41	—	432	56	145	.386	—	—	—	12	16	.750	7	36	43	49	27	0	16	—	2	124	1.0	1.2	3.0
REG. SEASON TOTALS	58	—	533	77	184	.418	—	—	—	23	30	.767	8	44	52	64	33	0	21	—	2	177	0.9	1.1	3.1

OWENS, KEITH KENSEL b. May 31, 1969 Ht. 6-7 Wt. 225 College—UCLA

SEASON—TEAM	G	GS	MIN	FGM	FGA	PCT	3FGM	3FGA	PCT	FTM	FTA	PCT	O-RB	D-RB	TOT	AST	PF	DQ	STL	TO	BLK	PTS	RPG	APG	PPG
91-92—L.A. Lakers	20	0	80	9	32	.281	0	0	—	8	10	.800	8	7	15	3	11	0	5	2	4	26	0.8	0.2	1.3
REG. SEASON TOTALS	20	0	80	9	32	.281	0	0	—	8	10	.800	8	7	15	3	11	0	5	2	4	26	0.8	0.2	1.3

OWENS, THOMAS WILLIAM (Tom) b. June 28, 1949 Ht. 6-10 Wt. 225 College—South Carolina

SEASON—TEAM	G	GS	MIN	FGM	FGA	PCT	3FGM	3FGA	PCT	FTM	FTA	PCT	O-RB	D-RB	TOT	AST	PF	DQ	STL	TO	BLK	PTS	RPG	APG	PPG
71-72—Memphis-Car. (A)	69	—	1118	197	402	.490	1	5	.200	109	175	.623	—	—	390	51	170	—	—	83	—	504	5.7	0.7	7.3
72-73—Carolina (A)	83	—	2209	393	727	.541	0	2	.000	193	284	.680	229	417	646	94	318	10	—	173	—	979	7.8	1.1	11.8
73-74—Carolina (A)	81	—	2284	444	843	.527	2	6	.333	226	294	.769	301	416	717	127	308	—	54	171	41	1116	8.9	1.6	13.8
74-75—St. L.-Memphis (A)	82	—	2647	511	969	.527	0	2	.000	217	289	.751	296	609	905	208	261	—	36	153	82	1239	11.0	2.5	15.1
75-76—Ken.-Indiana-S.A. (A)	74	—	1107	178	369	.482	0	0	—	92	129	.713	115	202	317	69	200	—	11	74	41	448	4.3	0.9	6.1
76-77—Houston	46	—	462	68	135	.504	—	—	—	52	76	.684	47	95	142	18	96	2	4	—	13	188	3.1	0.4	4.1
77-78—Portland	82	—	1714	313	639	.490	—	—	—	206	278	.741	195	346	541	160	263	7	33	152	37	832	6.6	2.0	10.1
78-79—Portland	82	—	2791	600	1095	.548	—	—	—	320	403	.794	263	477	740	301	329	15	59	247	58	1520	9.0	3.7	18.5
79-80—Portland	76	—	2337	518	1008	.514	1	2	.500	213	283	.753	189	384	573	194	270	5	45	174	53	1250	7.5	2.6	16.4
80-81—Portland	79	—	1843	322	630	.511	0	4	.000	191	250	.764	165	291	456	140	273	10	36	130	47	835	5.8	1.8	10.6
81-82—Indiana	74	40	1599	299	636	.470	1	2	.500	181	226	.801	142	230	372	127	259	7	41	137	37	780	5.0	1.7	10.5
82-83—Detroit	49	4	725	81	192	.422	0	0	—	45	66	.682	66	120	186	44	115	0	12	48	14	207	3.8	0.9	4.2
REG. NBA TOTALS	488	44	11471	2201	4335	.508	2	8	.250	1208	1582	.764	1067	1943	3010	984	1605	46	230	888	259	5612	6.2	2.0	11.5
REG. ABA TOTALS	389	—	9365	1723	3310	.521	3	15	.200	837	1171	.715	941	1644	2975	549	1257	10	101	654	164	4286	7.6	1.4	11.0
NBA PLAYOFF TOTALS	16	0	375	67	127	.528	0	0	—	25	37	.676	35	47	82	33	62	3	11	19	10	159	5.1	2.1	9.9
ABA PLAYOFF TOTALS	28	—	751	136	274	.496	0	1	.000	66	96	.688	90	148	238	36	102	0	6	33	15	338	8.5	1.3	12.1

PACE, JOSEPH (**Joe**) b. December 18, 1953   Ht. 6-10 Wt. 220 College—Coppin State/Maryland Eastern Shore

SEASON—TEAM	G	GS	MIN	FGM	FGA	PCT	3FGM	3FGA	PCT	FTM	FTA	PCT	O-RB	D-RB	TOT	AST	PF	DQ	STL	TO	BLK	PTS	RPG	APG	PPG
76-77—Washington	30	—	119	24	55	.436	—	—	—	16	29	.552	16	18	34	4	29	0	2	—	17	64	1.1	0.1	2.1
77-78—Washington	49	—	438	67	140	.479	—	—	—	57	93	.613	50	84	134	23	86	1	12	44	21	191	2.7	0.5	3.9
REG. SEASON TOTALS	79	—	557	91	195	.467	—	—	—	73	122	.598	66	102	168	27	115	1	14	44	38	255	2.1	0.3	3.2
PLAYOFF TOTALS	9	—	52	7	10	.700	—	—	—	11	15	.733	5	15	20	1	17	1	1	5	6	25	2.2	0.1	2.8

PACK, ROBERT JOHN JR. b. February 3, 1969   Ht. 6-2 Wt. 180 College—Tyler JC/USC

SEASON—TEAM	G	GS	MIN	FGM	FGA	PCT	3FGM	3FGA	PCT	FTM	FTA	PCT	O-RB	D-RB	TOT	AST	PF	DQ	STL	TO	BLK	PTS	RPG	APG	PPG
91-92—Portland	72	0	894	115	272	.423	0	10	.000	102	127	.803	32	65	97	140	101	0	40	92	4	332	1.3	1.9	4.6
92-93—Denver	77	1	1579	285	606	.470	1	8	.125	239	311	.768	52	108	160	335	182	1	81	185	10	810	2.1	4.4	10.5
93-94—Denver	66	4	1382	223	503	.443	6	29	.207	179	236	.758	25	98	123	356	147	1	81	204	9	631	1.9	5.4	9.6
REG. SEASON TOTALS	215	5	3855	623	1381	.451	7	47	.149	520	674	.772	109	271	380	831	430	2	202	481	23	1773	1.8	3.9	8.2
PLAYOFF TOTALS	26	0	384	52	136	.382	6	20	.300	42	59	.712	7	27	34	58	51	0	23	49	7	152	1.3	2.2	5.8

PACK, WAYNE (**Six-Pack**) b. July 5, 1950   Ht. 6-0 Wt. 165 College—Tennessee Tech

SEASON—TEAM	G	GS	MIN	FGM	FGA	PCT	3FGM	3FGA	PCT	FTM	FTA	PCT	O-RB	D-RB	TOT	AST	PF	DQ	STL	TO	BLK	PTS	RPG	APG	PPG
74-75—Indiana (A)	21	—	189	23	60	.383	5	17	.294	10	12	.833	7	13	20	13	21	—	6	13	0	61	1.0	0.6	2.9
REG. ABA TOTALS	21	—	189	23	60	.383	5	17	.294	10	12	.833	7	13	20	13	21	—	6	13	0	61	1.0	0.6	2.9

PADDIO, GERALD JAMES b. April 21, 1965   Ht. 6-7 Wt. 205 College—Seminole JC (Okla.)/Kilgore/Nevada-Las Vegas

SEASON—TEAM	G	GS	MIN	FGM	FGA	PCT	3FGM	3FGA	PCT	FTM	FTA	PCT	O-RB	D-RB	TOT	AST	PF	DQ	STL	TO	BLK	PTS	RPG	APG	PPG
90-91—Cleveland	70	22	1181	212	506	.419	6	24	.250	74	93	.796	38	80	118	90	71	0	20	71	6	504	1.7	1.3	7.2
92-93—Seattle	41	3	307	71	159	.447	2	8	.250	14	21	.667	17	33	50	33	24	0	14	16	6	158	1.2	0.8	3.9
93-94—Indiana-N.Y.-Wash.	18	1	137	22	60	.367	0	1	.000	9	16	.563	5	11	16	11	9	0	4	6	0	53	0.9	0.6	2.9
REG. SEASON TOTALS	129	26	1625	305	725	.421	8	33	.242	97	130	.746	60	124	184	134	104	0	38	93	12	715	1.4	1.0	5.5
PLAYOFF TOTALS	9	0	30	7	14	.500	0	1	.000	0	0	—	1	2	3	4	1	0	2	2	1	14	0.3	0.4	1.6

PAGETT, DANA P. b. March 29, 1949   Ht. 6-2 Wt. 180 College—USC

SEASON—TEAM	G	GS	MIN	FGM	FGA	PCT	3FGM	3FGA	PCT	FTM	FTA	PCT	O-RB	D-RB	TOT	AST	PF	DQ	STL	TO	BLK	PTS	RPG	APG	PPG
71-72—Virginia (A)	5	—	34	1	9	.111	1	3	.333	2	3	.667	—	—	3	6	8	—	—	3	—	5	0.6	1.2	1.0
REG. ABA TOTALS	5	—	34	1	9	.111	1	3	.333	2	3	.667	—	—	3	6	8	—	—	3	—	5	0.6	1.2	1.0

PAINE, FREDERICK VINCENT JR. (**Fred**) b. December 7, 1925   Ht. 6-5 Wt. 210 College—Westminster (Pa.)

SEASON—TEAM	G	GS	MIN	FGM	FGA	PCT	3FGM	3FGA	PCT	FTM	FTA	PCT	O-RB	D-RB	TOT	AST	PF	DQ	STL	TO	BLK	PTS	RPG	APG	PPG
48-49—Providence	3	—	—	3	19	.158	—	—	—	1	5	.200	—	—	—	1	3	—	—	—	—	7	—	0.3	2.3
REG. SEASON TOTALS	3	—	—	3	19	.158	—	—	—	1	5	.200	—	—	—	1	3	—	—	—	—	7	—	0.3	2.3

PALAZZI, TOGO ANTHONY b. August 8, 1932   Ht. 6-4 Wt. 205 College—Holy Cross

SEASON—TEAM	G	GS	MIN	FGM	FGA	PCT	3FGM	3FGA	PCT	FTM	FTA	PCT	O-RB	D-RB	TOT	AST	PF	DQ	STL	TO	BLK	PTS	RPG	APG	PPG
54-55—Boston	53	—	504	101	253	.399	—	—	—	45	60	.750	—	—	146	30	60	1	—	—	—	247	2.8	0.6	4.7
55-56—Boston	63	—	703	145	373	.389	—	—	—	85	124	.685	—	—	182	42	87	0	—	—	—	375	2.9	0.7	6.0
56-57—Boston-Syr.	63	—	1013	210	571	.368	—	—	—	136	175	.777	—	—	262	49	117	1	—	—	—	556	4.2	0.8	8.8
57-58—Syracuse	67	—	1001	228	579	.394	—	—	—	123	171	.719	—	—	243	42	125	0	—	—	—	579	3.6	0.6	8.6
58-59—Syracuse	71	—	1053	240	612	.392	—	—	—	115	158	.728	—	—	266	67	174	5	—	—	—	595	3.7	0.9	8.4
59-60—Syracuse	7	—	70	13	41	.317	—	—	—	4	8	.500	—	—	14	3	7	0	—	—	—	30	2.0	0.4	4.3
REG. SEASON TOTALS	324	—	4344	937	2429	.386	—	—	—	508	696	.730	—	—	1113	233	570	7	—	—	—	2382	3.4	0.7	7.4
PLAYOFF TOTALS	23	—	216	48	136	.353	—	—	—	25	39	.641	—	—	59	12	33	0	—	—	—	121	2.6	0.5	5.3

PALMER, ERROL b. 1945   Ht. 6-5 Wt. 195 College—DePaul

SEASON—TEAM	G	GS	MIN	FGM	FGA	PCT	3FGM	3FGA	PCT	FTM	FTA	PCT	O-RB	D-RB	TOT	AST	PF	DQ	STL	TO	BLK	PTS	RPG	APG	PPG
67-68—Minnesota (A)	63	—	1191	165	453	.364	0	0	—	170	253	.672	—	—	471	91	169	2	—	78	—	500	7.5	1.4	7.9
REG. ABA TOTALS	63	—	1191	165	453	.364	0	0	—	170	253	.672	—	—	471	91	169	2	—	78	—	500	7.5	1.4	7.9
ABA PLAYOFF TOTALS	6	—	75	10	25	.400	0	0	—	8	10	.800	—	—	27	7	17	0	—	7	—	28	4.5	1.2	4.7

PALMER, JAMES G. (**Jim**) b. June 8, 1933   Ht. 6-8 Wt. 225 College—Dayton

SEASON—TEAM	G	GS	MIN	FGM	FGA	PCT	3FGM	3FGA	PCT	FTM	FTA	PCT	O-RB	D-RB	TOT	AST	PF	DQ	STL	TO	BLK	PTS	RPG	APG	PPG
58-59—Cincinnati	67	—	1624	256	633	.404	—	—	—	178	246	.724	—	—	472	65	211	7	—	—	—	690	7.0	1.0	10.3
59-60—Cin.-N.Y.	74	—	1482	246	574	.429	—	—	—	119	174	.684	—	—	389	70	224	6	—	—	—	611	5.3	0.9	8.3
60-61—New York	55	—	688	125	310	.403	—	—	—	44	65	.677	—	—	179	30	128	0	—	—	—	294	3.3	0.5	5.3
REG. SEASON TOTALS	196	—	3794	627	1517	.413	—	—	—	341	485	.703	—	—	1040	165	563	13	—	—	—	1595	5.3	0.8	8.1

PALMER, JOHN S. (Bud) b. September 14, 1921 Ht. 6-4 Wt. 185 College—Princeton

SEASON—TEAM	G	GS	MIN	FGM	FGA	PCT	3FGM	3FGA	PCT	FTM	FTA	PCT	O-RB	D-RB	TOT	AST	PF	DQ	STL	TO	BLK	PTS	RPG	APG	PPG
46-47—New York	42	—	—	160	521	.307	—	—	—	81	121	.669	—	—	—	34	110	—	—	—	—	401	—	0.8	9.5
47-48—New York	48	—	—	224	710	.315	—	—	—	174	234	.744	—	—	—	45	149	—	—	—	—	622	—	0.9	13.0
48-49—New York	58	—	—	240	685	.350	—	—	—	234	307	.762	—	—	—	108	206	—	—	—	—	714	—	1.9	12.3
REG. SEASON TOTALS	148	—	—	624	1916	.326	—	—	—	489	662	.739	—	—	—	187	465	—	—	—	—	1737	—	1.3	11.7
PLAYOFF TOTALS	14	—	—	76	196	.388	—	—	—	49	68	.721	—	—	—	14	56	5	—	—	—	201	—	1.0	14.4

PALMER, WALTER SCOTT b. October 23, 1968 Ht. 7-2 Wt. 215 College—Dartmouth

SEASON—TEAM	G	GS	MIN	FGM	FGA	PCT	3FGM	3FGA	PCT	FTM	FTA	PCT	O-RB	D-RB	TOT	AST	PF	DQ	STL	TO	BLK	PTS	RPG	APG	PPG
90-91—Utah	28	0	85	15	45	.333	0	1	.000	10	15	.667	6	15	21	6	20	0	3	6	4	40	0.8	0.2	1.4
92-93—Dallas	20	0	124	27	57	.474	0	0	—	6	9	.667	12	32	44	5	29	0	1	10	5	60	2.2	0.3	3.0
REG. SEASON TOTALS	48	0	209	42	102	.412	0	1	.000	16	24	.667	18	47	65	11	49	0	4	16	9	100	1.4	0.2	2.1
PLAYOFF TOTALS	2	0	6	1	4	.250	0	0	—	0	0	—	0	1	1	—	3	0	0	1	0	2	0.5	0.0	1.0

PARHAM, ESTES FOSTER (Easy) b. December 27, 1921 d. October 1982 Ht. 6-3 Wt. 200 College—Texas Wesleyan

SEASON—TEAM	G	GS	MIN	FGM	FGA	PCT	3FGM	3FGA	PCT	FTM	FTA	PCT	O-RB	D-RB	TOT	AST	PF	DQ	STL	TO	BLK	PTS	RPG	APG	PPG
48-49—St. Louis	60	—	—	124	404	.307	—	—	—	96	172	.558	—	—	—	151	134	—	—	—	—	344	—	2.5	5.7
49-50—St. Louis	66	—	—	137	421	.325	—	—	—	88	178	.494	—	—	—	132	158	—	—	—	—	362	—	2.0	5.5
50-51—Philadelphia	7	—	—	3	7	.429	—	—	—	4	9	.444	—	—	12	3	5	0	—	—	—	10	1.7	0.4	1.4
REG. SEASON TOTALS	133	—	—	264	832	.317	—	—	—	188	359	.524	—	—	12	286	297	0	—	—	—	716	1.7	2.2	5.4
PLAYOFF TOTALS	2	—	—	5	13	.385	—	—	—	0	0	—	—	—	—	6	6	1	—	—	—	10	—	3.0	5.0

PARISH, ROBERT LEE (The Chief) b. August 30, 1953 Ht. 7-0 Wt. 235 College—Centenary

SEASON—TEAM	G	GS	MIN	FGM	FGA	PCT	3FGM	3FGA	PCT	FTM	FTA	PCT	O-RB	D-RB	TOT	AST	PF	DQ	STL	TO	BLK	PTS	RPG	APG	PPG
76-77—Golden State	77	—	1384	288	573	.503	—	—	—	121	171	.708	201	342	543	74	224	7	55	—	94	697	7.1	1.0	9.1
77-78—Golden State	82	—	1969	430	911	.472	—	—	—	165	264	.625	211	469	680	95	291	10	79	201	123	1025	8.3	1.2	12.5
78-79—Golden State	76	—	2411	554	1110	.499	—	—	—	196	281	.698	265	651	916	115	303	10	100	233	217	1304	12.1	1.5	17.2
79-80—Golden State	72	—	2119	510	1006	.507	0	1	.000	203	284	.715	247	536	783	122	248	6	58	225	115	1223	10.9	1.7	17.0
80-81—Boston	82	—	2298	635	1166	.545	0	1	.000	282	397	.710	245	532	777	144	310	9	81	191	214	1552	9.5	1.8	18.9
81-82—Boston	80	78	2534	669	1235	.542	0	0	—	252	355	.710	288	578	866	140	267	5	68	221	192	1590	10.8	1.8	19.9
82-83—Boston	78	76	2459	619	1125	.550	0	1	.000	271	388	.698	260	567	827	141	222	4	79	185	148	1509	10.6	1.8	19.3
83-84—Boston	80	79	2867	623	1140	.546	0	0	—	274	368	.745	243	614	857	139	266	7	55	184	116	1520	10.7	1.7	19.0
84-85—Boston	79	78	2850	551	1016	.542	0	0	—	292	393	.743	263	577	840	125	223	4	56	186	101	1394	10.6	1.6	17.6
85-86—Boston	81	80	2567	530	966	.549	0	0	—	245	335	.731	246	524	770	145	215	3	65	187	116	1305	9.5	1.8	16.1
86-87—Boston	80	80	2995	588	1057	.556	0	1	.000	227	309	.735	254	597	851	173	266	5	64	191	144	1403	10.6	2.2	17.5
87-88—Boston	74	73	2312	442	750	.589	0	1	.000	177	241	.734	173	455	628	115	198	5	55	154	84	1061	8.5	1.6	14.3
88-89—Boston	80	80	2840	596	1045	.570	0	0	—	294	409	.719	342	654	996	175	209	2	79	200	116	1486	12.5	2.2	18.6
89-90—Boston	79	78	2396	505	871	.580	0	0	—	233	312	.747	259	537	796	103	189	2	38	169	69	1243	10.1	1.3	15.7
90-91—Boston	81	81	2441	485	811	.598	0	1	.000	237	309	.767	271	585	856	66	197	1	66	153	103	1207	10.6	0.8	14.9
91-92—Boston	79	79	2285	468	874	.535	0	0	—	179	232	.772	219	486	705	70	172	2	68	131	97	1115	8.9	0.9	14.1
92-93—Boston	79	79	2146	416	777	.535	0	0	—	162	235	.689	246	494	740	61	201	3	57	120	107	994	9.4	0.8	12.6
93-94—Boston	74	74	1987	356	725	.491	0	0	—	154	208	.740	141	401	542	82	190	3	42	108	96	866	7.3	1.1	11.7
REG. SEASON TOTALS	1413	1015	42860	9265	17158	.540	0	6	.000	3964	5491	.722	4374	9599	13973	2085	4191	86	1165	3039	2252	22494	9.9	1.5	15.9
PLAYOFF TOTALS	178	151	6088	1125	2221	.507	0	1	.000	554	765	.724	565	1187	1752	233	613	16	145	364	303	2804	9.8	1.3	15.8
ALL-STAR TOTALS	9	1	142	36	68	.529	0	0	—	14	21	.667	16	37	53	8	15	0	4	10	8	86	5.9	0.9	9.6

PARK, MEDFORD R. (Med) b. April 11, 1933 Ht. 6-2 Wt. 205 College—Missouri

SEASON—TEAM	G	GS	MIN	FGM	FGA	PCT	3FGM	3FGA	PCT	FTM	FTA	PCT	O-RB	D-RB	TOT	AST	PF	DQ	STL	TO	BLK	PTS	RPG	APG	PPG
55-56—St. Louis	40	—	424	53	152	.349	—	—	—	44	70	.629	—	—	94	40	64	0	—	—	—	150	2.4	1.0	3.8
56-57—St. Louis	66	—	1130	118	324	.364	—	—	—	108	146	.740	—	—	200	94	137	2	—	—	—	344	3.0	1.4	5.2
57-58—St. Louis	71	—	1103	133	363	.366	—	—	—	118	162	.728	—	—	184	76	106	0	—	—	—	384	2.6	1.1	5.4
58-59—St. L.-Cin.	62	—	1126	145	361	.402	—	—	—	115	150	.767	—	—	188	108	93	0	—	—	—	405	3.0	1.7	6.5
59-60—Cincinnati	74	—	1849	226	582	.388	—	—	—	189	260	.727	—	—	301	214	180	2	—	—	—	641	4.1	2.9	8.7
REG. SEASON TOTALS	313	—	5632	675	1782	.379	—	—	—	574	788	.728	—	—	967	532	580	4	—	—	—	1924	3.1	1.7	6.1
PLAYOFF TOTALS	26	—	418	38	121	.314	—	—	—	53	77	.688	—	—	74	35	61	1	—	—	—	129	2.8	1.3	5.0

PARKER, ROBERT S. JR. (Sonny) b. March 22, 1955 Ht. 6-6½ Wt. 210 College—Mineral Area CC/Texas A&M

SEASON—TEAM	G	GS	MIN	FGM	FGA	PCT	3FGM	3FGA	PCT	FTM	FTA	PCT	O-RB	D-RB	TOT	AST	PF	DQ	STL	TO	BLK	PTS	RPG	APG	PPG
76-77—Golden State	65	—	889	154	292	.527	—	—	—	71	92	.772	85	88	173	59	77	0	53	—	26	379	2.7	0.9	5.8
77-78—Golden State	82	—	2069	406	783	.519	—	—	—	122	173	.705	167	222	389	155	186	0	135	128	36	934	4.7	1.9	11.4
78-79—Golden State	79	—	2893	512	1019	.502	—	—	—	175	222	.788	164	280	444	291	187	0	144	193	33	1199	5.6	3.7	15.2
79-80—Golden State	82	—	2849	483	988	.489	0	2	.000	237	302	.785	166	298	464	254	195	2	173	163	32	1203	5.7	3.1	14.7
80-81—Golden State	73	—	1317	191	388	.492	0	0	—	94	128	.734	101	93	194	106	112	0	67	84	15	476	2.7	1.5	6.5
81-82—Golden State	71	0	899	116	245	.473	0	0	—	48	72	.667	73	104	177	89	101	0	39	51	10	280	2.5	1.3	3.9
REG. SEASON TOTALS	452	0	10916	1862	3715	.501	0	2	.000	747	989	.755	756	1085	1841	954	858	2	611	619	150	4471	4.1	2.1	9.9
PLAYOFF TOTALS	10	0	120	19	36	.528	0	0	—	4	4	1.000	9	19	28	9	9	0	5	—	2	42	2.8	0.9	4.2

PARKHILL, BARRY b. May 10, 1951 Ht. 6-4 Wt. 185 College—Virginia

SEASON—TEAM	G	GS	MIN	FGM	FGA	PCT	3FGM	3FGA	PCT	FTM	FTA	PCT	O-RB	D-RB	TOT	AST	PF	DQ	STL	TO	BLK	PTS	RPG	APG	PPG
73-74—Virginia (A)	60	—	869	115	310	.371	3	16	.188	50	61	.820	13	52	65	96	151	—	28	80	12	283	1.1	1.6	4.7
74-75—Virginia (A)	78	—	1870	266	638	.417	0	8	.000	75	100	.750	27	106	133	226	228	—	50	170	11	607	1.7	2.9	7.8
75-76—St. Louis (A)	35	—	377	37	100	.370	1	11	.091	5	8	.625	2	24	26	64	46	—	9	29	7	80	0.7	1.8	2.3
REG. ABA TOTALS	173	—	3116	418	1048	.399	4	35	.114	130	169	.769	42	182	224	386	425	0	87	279	30	970	1.3	2.2	5.6
ABA PLAYOFF TOTALS	3	—	9	3	7	.429	0	0	—	0	0	—	0	1	1	2	0	0	1	0	0	6	0.3	0.7	2.0

PARKINSON, JACK GORDON b. March 4, 1924 Ht. 6-0 Wt. 175 College—Kentucky

SEASON—TEAM	G	GS	MIN	FGM	FGA	PCT	3FGM	3FGA	PCT	FTM	FTA	PCT	O-RB	D-RB	TOT	AST	PF	DQ	STL	TO	BLK	PTS	RPG	APG	PPG
49-50—Indianapolis	4	—	—	1	12	.083	—	—	—	1	1	1.000	—	—	—	2	3	—	—	—	—	3	—	0.5	0.8
REG. SEASON TOTALS	4	—	—	1	12	.083	—	—	—	1	1	1.000	—	—	—	2	3	—	—	—	—	3	—	0.5	0.8

PARKS, CHARLES (Charley) b. 1946 Ht. 6-5 Wt. 210 College—Idaho State

SEASON—TEAM	G	GS	MIN	FGM	FGA	PCT	3FGM	3FGA	PCT	FTM	FTA	PCT	O-RB	D-RB	TOT	AST	PF	DQ	STL	TO	BLK	PTS	RPG	APG	PPG
68-69—Denver (A)	2	—	5	0	1	.000	0	0	—	0	0	—	—	—	0	0	1	0	—	0	—	0	0.0	0.0	0.0
REG. ABA TOTALS	2	—	5	0	1	.000	0	0	—	0	0	—	—	—	0	0	1	0	—	—	—	0	0.0	0.0	0.0

PARKS, RICHARD E. (Rich) b. October 28, 1943 d. August 1978 Ht. 6-7 Wt. 235 College—Tulsa/St. Louis

SEASON—TEAM	G	GS	MIN	FGM	FGA	PCT	3FGM	3FGA	PCT	FTM	FTA	PCT	O-RB	D-RB	TOT	AST	PF	DQ	STL	TO	BLK	PTS	RPG	APG	PPG
67-68—Pittsburgh (A)	40	—	374	59	133	.444	1	3	.333	12	21	.571	—	—	116	14	68	3	—	19	—	131	2.9	0.4	3.3
REG. ABA TOTALS	40	—	374	59	133	.444	1	3	.333	12	21	.571	—	—	116	14	68	3	—	19	—	131	2.9	0.4	3.3
ABA PLAYOFF TOTALS	5	—	7	0	2	.000	0	1	.000	1	4	.250	—	—	2	0	3	0	—	—	—	1	0.4	0.0	0.2

PARR, JACK b. March 13, 1936 Ht. 6-9 Wt. 220 College—Kansas State

SEASON—TEAM	G	GS	MIN	FGM	FGA	PCT	3FGM	3FGA	PCT	FTM	FTA	PCT	O-RB	D-RB	TOT	AST	PF	DQ	STL	TO	BLK	PTS	RPG	APG	PPG
58-59—Cincinnati	66	—	1037	109	307	.355	—	—	—	44	73	.603	—	—	278	51	138	1	—	—	—	262	4.2	0.8	4.0
REG. SEASON TOTALS	66	—	1037	109	307	.355	—	—	—	44	73	.603	—	—	278	51	138	1	—	—	—	262	4.2	0.8	4.0

PARRACK, DOYLE KENNETH b. December 6, 1921 Ht. 6-0 Wt. 165 College—Oklahoma State

SEASON—TEAM	G	GS	MIN	FGM	FGA	PCT	3FGM	3FGA	PCT	FTM	FTA	PCT	O-RB	D-RB	TOT	AST	PF	DQ	STL	TO	BLK	PTS	RPG	APG	PPG
46-47—Chicago	58	—	—	110	413	.266	—	—	—	52	80	.650	—	—	—	20	77	—	—	—	—	272	—	0.3	4.7
REG. SEASON TOTALS	58	—	—	110	413	.266	—	—	—	52	80	.650	—	—	—	20	77	—	—	—	—	272	—	0.3	4.7
PLAYOFF TOTALS	7	—	—	0	9	.000	—	—	—	3	3	1.000	—	—	—	1	3	—	—	—	—	3	0.0	0.1	0.4

PARSLEY, CHARLES H. (Charlie) b. October 13, 1925 Ht. 6-2 Wt. 175 College—Western Kentucky

SEASON—TEAM	G	GS	MIN	FGM	FGA	PCT	3FGM	3FGA	PCT	FTM	FTA	PCT	O-RB	D-RB	TOT	AST	PF	DQ	STL	TO	BLK	PTS	RPG	APG	PPG
49-50—Philadelphia	9	—	—	8	31	.258	—	—	—	6	7	.857	—	—	—	8	7	—	—	—	—	22	—	0.9	2.4
REG. SEASON TOTALS	9	—	—	8	31	.258	—	—	—	6	7	.857	—	—	—	8	7	—	—	—	—	22	—	0.9	2.4

PASPALJ, ZARKO b. March 27, 1966 Ht. 6-9 Wt. 215 College—None

SEASON—TEAM	G	GS	MIN	FGM	FGA	PCT	3FGM	3FGA	PCT	FTM	FTA	PCT	O-RB	D-RB	TOT	AST	PF	DQ	STL	TO	BLK	PTS	RPG	APG	PPG
89-90—San Antonio	28	1	181	27	79	.342	0	1	.000	18	22	.818	15	15	30	10	37	0	3	21	7	72	1.1	0.4	2.6
REG. SEASON TOTALS	28	1	181	27	79	.342	0	1	.000	18	22	.818	15	15	30	10	37	0	3	21	7	72	1.1	0.4	2.6

PASSAGLIA, MARTIN HAROLD (Marty) b. April 22, 1919 Ht. 6-1½ Wt. 170 College—Santa Clara

SEASON—TEAM	G	GS	MIN	FGM	FGA	PCT	3FGM	3FGA	PCT	FTM	FTA	PCT	O-RB	D-RB	TOT	AST	PF	DQ	STL	TO	BLK	PTS	RPG	APG	PPG
46-47—Washington	43	—	—	51	221	.231	—	—	—	18	32	.563	—	—	—	9	44	—	—	—	—	120	—	0.2	2.8
48-49—Indianapolis	19	—	—	14	57	.246	—	—	—	3	4	.750	—	—	—	17	17	—	—	—	—	31	—	0.9	1.6
REG. SEASON TOTALS	62	—	—	65	278	.234	—	—	—	21	36	.583	—	—	—	26	61	—	—	—	—	151	—	0.4	2.4
PLAYOFF TOTALS	6	—	—	2	14	.143	—	—	—	1	3	.333	—	—	—	—	10	—	—	—	—	5	0.0	0.0	0.8

PASTUSHOK, GEORGE A. b. 1923 Ht. 6-1½ Wt. 195 College—Manhattan/St. John's

SEASON—TEAM	G	GS	MIN	FGM	FGA	PCT	3FGM	3FGA	PCT	FTM	FTA	PCT	O-RB	D-RB	TOT	AST	PF	DQ	STL	TO	BLK	PTS	RPG	APG	PPG
46-47—Providence	39	—	—	48	183	.262	—	—	—	25	46	.543	—	—	—	15	42	—	—	—	—	121	—	0.4	3.1
REG. SEASON TOTALS	39	—	—	48	183	.262	—	—	—	25	46	.543	—	—	—	15	42	—	—	—	—	121	—	0.4	3.1

PATRICK, MYLES b. November 16, 1954 Ht. 6-8 Wt. 220 College—Auburn

SEASON—TEAM	G	GS	MIN	FGM	FGA	PCT	3FGM	3FGA	PCT	FTM	FTA	PCT	O-RB	D-RB	TOT	AST	PF	DQ	STL	TO	BLK	PTS	RPG	APG	PPG
80-81—Los Angeles	3	—	9	2	5	.400	0	0	—	1	2	.500	1	1	2	1	3	0	0	1	0	5	0.7	0.3	1.7
REG. SEASON TOTALS	3	—	9	2	5	.400	0	0	—	1	2	.500	1	1	2	1	3	0	0	1	0	5	0.7	0.3	1.7

PATRICK, STANLEY A. (**Stan**) b. May 5, 1922 Ht. 6-3 Wt. 215 College—Santa Clara/Illinois

SEASON—TEAM	G	GS	MIN	FGM	FGA	PCT	3FGM	3FGA	PCT	FTM	FTA	PCT	O-RB	D-RB	TOT	AST	PF	DQ	STL	TO	BLK	PTS	RPG	APG	PPG
44-45—Chicago (N)	28	—	187	—	—	—	—	—	—	84	—	—	—	—	—	—	—	—	—	—	—	458	—	—	16.4
45-46—Chicago (N)	33	—	123	—	—	—	—	—	—	66	100	.660	—	—	—	—	42	—	—	—	—	312	—	—	9.5
46-47—Chicago (N)	42	—	72	—	—	—	—	—	—	36	67	.537	—	—	—	—	61	—	—	—	—	180	—	—	4.3
47-48—Flint (N)	48	—	149	—	—	—	—	—	—	90	144	.625	—	—	—	—	104	—	—	—	—	388	—	—	8.1
48-49—Hammond (N)	61	—	150	—	—	—	—	—	—	127	192	.661	—	—	—	—	97	—	—	—	—	427	—	—	7.0
49-50—Wat.-She.	53	—	116	294	.395		—	—	—	89	147	.605	—	—	—	74	76	—	—	—	—	321	—	1.4	6.1
REG. NBA TOTALS	53	—	116	294	.395		—	—	—	89	147	.605	—	—	—	74	76	—	—	—	—	321	—	1.4	6.1
REG. NBL TOTALS	212	—	681	—	—	—	—	—	—	403	503	.634	—	—	—	—	304	—	—	—	—	1765	—	—	8.3
NBA PLAYOFF TOTALS	3	—	4	7	.571		—	—	—	2	3	.667	—	—	—	—	1	2	—	—	—	—	10	0.0	0.3	3.3
NBL PLAYOFF TOTALS	16	—	39	—	—	—	—	—	—	16	26	.538	—	—	—	—	35	—	—	—	—	94	—	—	5.9

PATTERSON, GEORGE b. November 26, 1939 Ht. 6-7½ Wt. 230 College—Toledo

SEASON—TEAM	G	GS	MIN	FGM	FGA	PCT	3FGM	3FGA	PCT	FTM	FTA	PCT	O-RB	D-RB	TOT	AST	PF	DQ	STL	TO	BLK	PTS	RPG	APG	PPG
67-68—Detroit	59	—	559	44	133	.331	—	—	—	32	38	.842	—	—	159	51	85	0	—	—	—	120	2.7	0.9	2.0
REG. SEASON TOTALS	59	—	559	44	133	.331	—	—	—	32	38	.842	—	—	159	51	85	0	—	—	—	120	2.7	0.9	2.0
PLAYOFF TOTALS	1	—	4	0	0	—	—	—	—	0	0	—	—	—	1	1	0	0	—	—	—	0	1.0	1.0	0.0

PATTERSON, STEVEN J. (**Steve**) b. June 24, 1948 Ht. 6-9 Wt. 225 College—UCLA

SEASON—TEAM	G	GS	MIN	FGM	FGA	PCT	3FGM	3FGA	PCT	FTM	FTA	PCT	O-RB	D-RB	TOT	AST	PF	DQ	STL	TO	BLK	PTS	RPG	APG	PPG
71-72—Cleveland	65	—	775	94	263	.357	—	—	—	23	46	.500	—	—	228	54	80	0	—	—	—	211	3.5	0.8	3.2
72-73—Cleveland	62	—	710	71	198	.359	—	—	—	34	65	.523	—	—	228	51	79	1	—	—	—	176	3.7	0.8	2.8
73-74—Cleveland	76	—	1910	262	599	.437	—	—	—	69	112	.616	223	396	619	165	193	3	48	—	58	593	8.1	2.2	7.8
74-75—Cleveland	81	—	1269	161	387	.416	—	—	—	48	73	.658	112	217	329	93	128	1	21	—	20	370	4.1	1.1	4.6
75-76—Clev.-Chicago	66	—	918	84	220	.382	—	—	—	34	54	.630	80	148	228	80	93	1	16	—	16	202	3.5	1.2	3.1
REG. SEASON TOTALS	350	—	5582	672	1667	.403	—	—	—	208	350	.594	415	761	1632	443	573	6	85	—	94	1552	4.7	1.3	4.4

PATTERSON, TOMMIE J. (**Tommy**) b. October 15, 1948 Ht. 6-6 Wt. 220 College—Ouachita Baptist

SEASON—TEAM	G	GS	MIN	FGM	FGA	PCT	3FGM	3FGA	PCT	FTM	FTA	PCT	O-RB	D-RB	TOT	AST	PF	DQ	STL	TO	BLK	PTS	RPG	APG	PPG
72-73—Baltimore	23	—	92	21	49	.429	—	—	—	13	16	.813	—	—	22	3	18	0	—	—	—	55	1.0	0.1	2.4
73-74—Capital	2	—	8	0	1	.000	—	—	—	1	2	.500	1	1	2	2	0	0	0	—	0	1	1.0	1.0	0.5
REG. SEASON TOTALS	25	—	100	21	50	.420	—	—	—	14	18	.778	1	1	24	5	18	0	—	—	0	56	1.0	0.2	2.2
PLAYOFF TOTALS	1	—	1	0	0	—	—	—	—	0	0	—	0	0	0	—	0	0	0	—	0	0	0.0	0.0	0.0

PATTERSON, WORTHINGTON R. (**Worthy**) b. June 17, 1931 Ht. 6-2 Wt. 175 College—Connecticut

SEASON—TEAM	G	GS	MIN	FGM	FGA	PCT	3FGM	3FGA	PCT	FTM	FTA	PCT	O-RB	D-RB	TOT	AST	PF	DQ	STL	TO	BLK	PTS	RPG	APG	PPG
57-58—St. Louis	4	—	3	3	8	.375	—	—	—	1	2	.500	—	—	2	2	3	0	—	—	—	7	0.5	0.5	1.8
REG. SEASON TOTALS	4	—	3	3	8	.375	—	—	—	1	2	.500	—	—	2	2	3	0	—	—	—	7	0.5	0.5	1.8

PAULK, CHARLES (**Charlie**) b. 1946 Ht. 6-9 Wt. 220 College—Tulsa/Northeastern State

SEASON—TEAM	G	GS	MIN	FGM	FGA	PCT	3FGM	3FGA	PCT	FTM	FTA	PCT	O-RB	D-RB	TOT	AST	PF	DQ	STL	TO	BLK	PTS	RPG	APG	PPG
68-69—Milwaukee	17	—	217	19	84	.226	—	—	—	13	23	.565	—	—	78	3	26	0	—	—	—	51	4.6	0.2	3.0
70-71—Cincinnati	68	—	1213	274	637	.430	—	—	—	79	131	.603	—	—	320	27	186	6	—	—	—	627	4.7	0.4	9.2
71-72—Chicago-N.Y.	35	—	211	24	88	.273	—	—	—	15	21	.714	—	—	64	11	31	0	—	—	—	63	1.8	0.3	1.8
REG. SEASON TOTALS	120	—	1641	317	809	.392	—	—	—	107	175	.611	—	—	462	41	243	6	—	—	—	741	3.9	0.3	6.2
PLAYOFF TOTALS	7	—	13	3	10	.300	—	—	—	0	0	—	—	—	5	—	5	0	—	—	—	6	0.7	0.0	0.9

PAULSON, GERALD ARTHUR (**Jerry**) b. July 21, 1935 d. March 6, 1986 Ht. 6-2½ Wt. 185 College—Manhattan

SEASON—TEAM	G	GS	MIN	FGM	FGA	PCT	3FGM	3FGA	PCT	FTM	FTA	PCT	O-RB	D-RB	TOT	AST	PF	DQ	STL	TO	BLK	PTS	RPG	APG	PPG
57-58—Cincinnati	6	—	68	8	23	.348	—	—	—	4	6	.667	—	—	10	4	5	0	—	—	—	20	1.7	0.7	3.3
REG. SEASON TOTALS	6	—	68	8	23	.348	—	—	—	4	6	.667	—	—	10	4	5	0	—	—	—	20	1.7	0.7	3.3

PAULTZ, WILLIAM EDWARD (Billy, The Whopper) b. July 30, 1948 Ht. 6-11 Wt. 245 College—Cameron/St. John's

SEASON—TEAM	G	GS	MIN	FGM	FGA	PCT	3FGM	3FGA	PCT	FTM	FTA	PCT	O-RB	D-RB	TOT	AST	PF	DQ	STL	TO	BLK	PTS	RPG	APG	PPG
70-71—New York (A)	83	—	2758	510	973	.524	0	2	.000	201	269	.747	239	701	940	160	274	—	—	—	—	1221	11.3	1.9	14.7
71-72—New York (A)	83	—	2824	498	1021	.488	0	3	.000	207	299	.692	263	772	1035	128	298	—	—	214	—	1203	12.5	1.5	14.5
72-73—New York (A)	81	—	2800	532	1027	.518	0	2	.000	287	405	.709	279	736	1015	189	259	5	—	213	214	1351	12.5	2.3	16.7
73-74—New York (A)	77	—	2596	519	1051	.494	0	1	.000	222	308	.721	211	571	782	167	238	—	60	175	147	1260	10.2	2.2	16.4
74-75—New York (A)	80	—	2826	524	1080	.485	0	3	.000	214	286	.748	174	598	772	179	273	—	59	149	137	1262	9.7	2.2	15.8
75-76—San Antonio (A)	83	—	2958	566	1124	.504	0	2	.000	238	324	.735	210	652	862	340	232	—	61	231	253	1370	10.4	4.1	16.5
76-77—San Antonio	82	—	2694	521	1102	.473	—	—	—	238	320	.744	192	495	687	223	262	5	55	—	173	1280	8.4	2.7	15.6
77-78—San Antonio	80	—	2479	518	979	.529	—	—	—	230	306	.752	172	503	675	213	222	3	42	167	194	1266	8.4	2.7	15.8
78-79—San Antonio	79	—	2122	399	758	.526	—	—	—	114	194	.588	169	456	625	178	204	4	35	157	125	912	7.9	2.3	11.5
79-80—S.A.-Houston	84	—	2193	327	673	.486	0	0	—	109	182	.599	187	399	586	188	213	3	69	115	84	763	7.0	2.2	9.1
80-81—Houston	81	—	1659	262	517	.507	0	0	—	75	153	.490	111	280	391	105	182	1	28	89	72	599	4.8	1.3	7.4
81-82—Houston	65	3	807	89	226	.394	0	0	—	34	65	.523	54	126	180	41	99	0	15	45	22	212	2.8	0.6	3.3
82-83—Houston-S.A.	64	0	820	101	227	.445	0	0	—	27	59	.458	64	136	200	61	109	0	17	47	18	229	3.1	1.0	3.6
83-84—Atlanta	40	4	486	36	88	.409	0	0	—	17	33	.515	35	78	113	18	57	0	8	22	7	89	2.8	0.5	2.2
84-85—Utah	62	0	370	32	87	.368	0	0	—	18	28	.643	24	72	96	16	51	0	6	30	11	82	1.5	0.3	1.3
REG. NBA TOTALS	637	7	13630	2285	4657	.491	0	0	—	862	1340	.643	1008	2545	3553	1043	1399	16	275	672	706	5432	5.6	1.6	8.5
REG. ABA TOTALS	487	—	16762	3149	6276	.502	0	13	.000	1369	1891	.724	1376	4030	5406	1163	1574	5	180	982	751	7667	11.1	2.4	15.7
NBA PLAYOFF TOTALS	70	0	1616	215	505	.426	0	1	.000	85	129	.659	113	267	380	106	157	1	30	67	54	515	5.4	1.5	7.4
ABA PLAYOFF TOTALS	56	—	2172	372	733	.508	1	3	.333	206	285	.723	159	523	682	115	216	0	13	115	65	951	12.2	2.1	17.0
ABA ALL-STAR TOTALS	3	0	53	7	16	.438	0	0	—	3	3	1.000	3	6	11	8	5	—	1	2	3	17	3.7	2.7	5.7

PAXSON, JAMES EDWARD SR. (Jim) b. December 19, 1932 Ht. 6-6 Wt. 200 College—Dayton

SEASON—TEAM	G	GS	MIN	FGM	FGA	PCT	3FGM	3FGA	PCT	FTM	FTA	PCT	O-RB	D-RB	TOT	AST	PF	DQ	STL	TO	BLK	PTS	RPG	APG	PPG
56-57—Minneapolis	71	—	1274	138	485	.285	—	—	—	170	236	.720	—	—	266	86	163	—	—	—	—	446	3.7	1.2	6.3
57-58—Cincinnati	67	—	1795	225	639	.352	—	—	—	209	285	.733	—	—	350	139	183	2	—	—	—	659	5.2	2.1	9.8
REG. SEASON TOTALS	138	—	3069	363	1124	.323	—	—	—	379	521	.727	—	—	616	225	346	5	—	—	—	1105	4.5	1.6	8.0
PLAYOFF TOTALS	7	—	84	12	47	.255	—	—	—	13	22	.591	—	—	22	8	11	0	—	—	—	37	3.1	1.1	5.3

PAXSON, JAMES JOSEPH (Jim) b. July 9, 1957 Ht. 6-6 Wt. 200 College—Dayton

SEASON—TEAM	G	GS	MIN	FGM	FGA	PCT	3FGM	3FGA	PCT	FTM	FTA	PCT	O-RB	D-RB	TOT	AST	PF	DQ	STL	TO	BLK	PTS	RPG	APG	PPG
79-80—Portland	72	—	1270	189	460	.411	1	22	.045	64	90	.711	25	84	109	144	97	0	48	93	5	443	1.5	2.0	6.2
80-81—Portland	79	—	2701	585	1092	.536	2	30	.067	182	248	.734	74	137	211	299	172	1	140	131	9	1354	2.7	3.8	17.1
81-82—Portland	82	82	2756	662	1259	.526	8	35	.229	220	287	.767	75	146	221	276	159	0	129	144	12	1552	2.7	3.4	18.9
82-83—Portland	81	81	2740	682	1323	.515	4	25	.160	388	478	.812	68	106	174	231	160	0	140	156	17	1756	2.1	2.9	21.7
83-84—Portland	81	81	2686	680	1322	.514	17	59	.288	345	410	.841	68	105	173	251	165	0	122	142	10	1722	2.1	3.1	21.3
84-85—Portland	68	57	2253	508	988	.514	6	39	.154	196	248	.790	69	153	222	264	115	0	101	108	5	1218	3.3	3.9	17.9
85-86—Portland	75	31	1931	372	792	.470	20	62	.323	217	244	.889	42	106	148	278	156	3	94	112	5	981	2.0	3.7	13.1
86-87—Portland	72	1	1798	337	733	.460	26	98	.265	174	216	.806	41	98	139	237	134	0	76	108	12	874	1.9	3.3	12.1
87-88—Port.-Boston	45	3	801	137	298	.460	5	21	.238	68	79	.861	15	30	45	76	73	0	30	39	5	347	1.0	1.7	7.7
88-89—Boston	57	7	1138	202	445	.454	4	24	.167	84	103	.816	18	56	74	107	96	0	38	57	8	492	1.3	1.9	8.6
89-90—Boston	72	25	1283	191	422	.453	5	20	.250	73	90	.811	24	53	77	137	115	0	33	54	5	460	1.1	1.9	6.4
REG. SEASON TOTALS	784	368	21357	4545	9134	.498	98	435	.225	2011	2493	.807	519	1074	1593	2300	1442	4	951	1144	93	11199	2.0	2.9	14.3
PLAYOFF TOTALS	53	12	1107	212	458	.463	8	30	.267	122	151	.808	27	53	80	100	81	1	38	56	4	554	1.5	1.9	10.5
ALL-STAR TOTALS	2	0	31	10	16	.625	0	0	—	1	2	.500	1	2	3	3	0	0	2	4	0	21	1.5	1.5	10.5

PAXSON, JOHN MACBETH b. September 29, 1960 Ht. 6-2 Wt. 185 College—Notre Dame

SEASON—TEAM	G	GS	MIN	FGM	FGA	PCT	3FGM	3FGA	PCT	FTM	FTA	PCT	O-RB	D-RB	TOT	AST	PF	DQ	STL	TO	BLK	PTS	RPG	APG	PPG
83-84—San Antonio	49	0	458	61	137	.445	4	22	.182	16	26	.615	4	29	33	149	47	0	10	32	2	142	0.7	3.0	2.9
84-85—San Antonio	78	1	1259	196	385	.509	10	34	.294	84	100	.840	19	49	68	215	117	0	45	81	3	486	0.9	2.8	6.2
85-86—Chicago	75	3	1570	153	328	.466	15	51	.294	74	92	.804	18	76	94	274	172	2	55	63	2	395	1.3	3.7	5.3
86-87—Chicago	82	64	2689	386	793	.487	52	140	.371	106	131	.809	22	117	139	467	207	1	66	105	8	930	1.7	5.7	11.3
87-88—Chicago	81	30	1888	287	582	.493	33	95	.347	33	45	.733	16	88	104	303	154	2	49	64	1	640	1.3	3.7	7.9
88-89—Chicago	78	20	1738	246	513	.480	44	133	.331	31	36	.861	13	81	94	308	162	1	53	71	6	567	1.2	3.9	7.3
89-90—Chicago	82	82	2365	365	708	.516	33	92	.359	56	68	.824	27	92	119	335	176	1	83	85	6	819	1.5	4.1	10.0
90-91—Chicago	82	82	1971	317	578	.548	42	96	.438	34	41	.829	15	76	91	297	136	0	62	69	3	710	1.1	3.6	8.7
91-92—Chicago	79	79	1946	257	487	.528	12	44	.273	29	37	.784	21	75	96	241	142	0	49	44	5	555	1.2	3.1	7.0
92-93—Chicago	59	8	1030	105	233	.451	19	41	.463	17	20	.850	9	39	48	136	99	0	38	31	2	246	0.8	2.3	4.2
93-94—Chicago	27	0	343	30	68	.441	9	22	.409	1	2	.500	3	17	20	33	18	0	7	6	2	70	0.7	1.2	2.6
REG. SEASON TOTALS	772	369	17257	2403	4812	.499	273	770	.355	481	598	.804	167	739	906	2758	1430	7	517	651	44	5560	1.2	3.6	7.2
PLAYOFF TOTALS	119	57	2617	306	620	.494	45	122	.369	91	105	.867	11	98	109	306	249	6	65	71	3	748	0.9	2.6	6.3

PAYAK, JOHN JR. (Johnny) b. November 20, 1926 Ht. 6-4 Wt. 180 College—Bowling Green

SEASON—TEAM	G	GS	MIN	FGM	FGA	PCT	3FGM	3FGA	PCT	FTM	FTA	PCT	O-RB	D-RB	TOT	AST	PF	DQ	STL	TO	BLK	PTS	RPG	APG	PPG
49-50—Phil.-Wat.	52	—	—	98	331	.296	—	—	—	121	173	.699	—	—	86	113	—	—	—	—	—	317	—	1.7	6.1
52-53—Milwaukee	68	—	1470	128	373	.343	—	—	—	180	248	.726	—	—	114	140	194	7	—	—	—	436	1.7	2.1	6.4
REG. SEASON TOTALS	120	—	1470	226	704	.321	—	—	—	301	421	.715	—	—	114	226	307	7	—	—	—	753	1.7	1.9	6.3

PAYNE, KENNETH VICTOR (**Kenny**) b. November 25, 1966 Ht. 6-8 Wt. 220 College—Louisville

SEASON—TEAM	G	GS	MIN	FGM	FGA	PCT	3FGM	3FGA	PCT	FTM	FTA	PCT	O-RB	D-RB	TOT	AST	PF	DQ	STL	TO	BLK	PTS	RPG	APG	PPG
89-90—Philadelphia	35	4	216	47	108	.435	4	10	.400	16	18	.889	11	15	26	10	37	0	7	20	6	114	0.7	0.3	3.3
90-91—Philadelphia	47	6	444	68	189	.360	4	18	.222	26	29	.897	17	49	66	16	43	0	10	21	6	166	1.4	0.3	3.5
91-92—Philadelphia	49	3	353	65	145	.448	5	12	.417	9	13	.692	13	41	54	17	34	0	16	19	8	144	1.1	0.3	2.9
92-93—Philadelphia	13	0	154	38	90	.422	4	18	.222	4	4	1.000	4	20	24	18	15	0	5	7	2	84	1.8	1.4	6.5
REG. SEASON TOTALS	144	13	1167	218	532	.410	17	58	.293	55	64	.859	45	125	170	61	129	0	38	67	22	508	1.2	0.4	3.5
PLAYOFF TOTALS	3	0	10	2	5	.400	0	2	.000	2	2	1.000	1	1	2	—	3	0	0	1	0	6	0.7	0.0	2.0

PAYNE, TOM b. November 19, 1950 Ht. 7-2 Wt. 240 College—Kentucky

SEASON—TEAM	G	GS	MIN	FGM	FGA	PCT	3FGM	3FGA	PCT	FTM	FTA	PCT	O-RB	D-RB	TOT	AST	PF	DQ	STL	TO	BLK	PTS	RPG	APG	PPG
71-72—Atlanta	29	—	227	45	103	.437	—	—	—	29	46	.630	—	—	69	15	40	0	—	—	—	119	2.4	0.5	4.1
REG. SEASON TOTALS	29	—	227	45	103	.437	—	—	—	29	46	.630	—	—	69	15	40	0	—	—	—	119	2.4	0.5	4.1
PLAYOFF TOTALS	1	—	5	1	1	1.000	—	—	—	2	5	.400	—	—	4	—	1	0	—	—	—	4	4.0	0.0	4.0

PAYTON, GARY DWAYNE b. July 23, 1968 Ht. 6-4 Wt. 190 College—Oregon State

SEASON—TEAM	G	GS	MIN	FGM	FGA	PCT	3FGM	3FGA	PCT	FTM	FTA	PCT	O-RB	D-RB	TOT	AST	PF	DQ	STL	TO	BLK	PTS	RPG	APG	PPG
90-91—Seattle	82	82	2244	259	575	.450	1	13	.077	69	97	.711	108	135	243	528	249	3	165	180	15	588	3.0	6.4	7.2
91-92—Seattle	81	79	2549	331	734	.451	3	23	.130	99	148	.669	123	172	295	506	248	0	147	174	21	764	3.6	6.2	9.4
92-93—Seattle	82	78	2548	476	963	.494	7	34	.206	151	196	.770	95	186	281	399	250	1	177	148	21	1110	3.4	4.9	13.5
93-94—Seattle	82	82	2881	584	1159	.504	15	54	.278	166	279	.595	105	164	269	494	227	0	188	173	19	1349	3.3	6.0	16.5
REG. SEASON TOTALS	327	321	10222	1650	3431	.481	26	124	.210	485	720	.674	431	657	1088	1927	974	4	677	675	76	3811	3.3	5.9	11.7
PLAYOFF TOTALS	37	37	1142	176	389	.452	4	18	.222	42	70	.600	39	75	114	168	121	2	58	61	8	398	3.1	4.5	10.8
ALL-STAR TOTALS	1	0	17	3	4	.750	0	0	—	0	0	—	2	4	6	9	2	0	0	0	0	6	6.0	9.0	6.0

PAYTON, MELVIN E. (**Mel**) b. July 16, 1926 Ht. 6-4 Wt. 185 College—Tulane

SEASON—TEAM	G	GS	MIN	FGM	FGA	PCT	3FGM	3FGA	PCT	FTM	FTA	PCT	O-RB	D-RB	TOT	AST	PF	DQ	STL	TO	BLK	PTS	RPG	APG	PPG
51-52—Philadelphia	45	—	471	54	140	.386	—	—	—	21	28	.750	—	—	83	45	68	2	—	—	—	129	1.8	1.0	2.9
52-53—Indianapolis	66	—	1424	173	485	.357	—	—	—	120	161	.745	—	—	313	81	118	0	—	—	—	466	4.7	1.2	7.1
REG. SEASON TOTALS	111	—	1895	227	625	.363	—	—	—	141	189	.746	—	—	396	126	186	2	—	—	—	595	3.6	1.1	5.4
PLAYOFF TOTALS	5	—	54	8	19	.421	—	—	—	9	10	.900	—	—	9	1	13	0	—	—	—	25	1.8	0.2	5.0

PEARCY, GEORGE W. (**Wig**) b. July 2, 1919 Ht. 6-1 Wt. 165 College—Indiana State

SEASON—TEAM	G	GS	MIN	FGM	FGA	PCT	3FGM	3FGA	PCT	FTM	FTA	PCT	O-RB	D-RB	TOT	AST	PF	DQ	STL	TO	BLK	PTS	RPG	APG	PPG
46-47—Detroit	37	—	—	31	130	.238	—	—	—	32	44	.727	—	—	—	13	68	—	—	—	—	94	—	0.4	2.5
REG. SEASON TOTALS	37	—	—	31	130	.238	—	—	—	32	44	.727	—	—	—	13	68	—	—	—	—	94	—	0.4	2.5

PEARCY, HENRY EARL b. July 21, 1922 Ht. 6-1 Wt. 170 College—Indiana State

SEASON—TEAM	G	GS	MIN	FGM	FGA	PCT	3FGM	3FGA	PCT	FTM	FTA	PCT	O-RB	D-RB	TOT	AST	PF	DQ	STL	TO	BLK	PTS	RPG	APG	PPG
46-47—Detroit	29	—	—	24	108	.222	—	—	—	25	34	.735	—	—	—	7	20	—	—	—	—	73	—	0.2	2.5
REG. SEASON TOTALS	29	—	—	24	108	.222	—	—	—	25	34	.735	—	—	—	7	20	—	—	—	—	73	—	0.2	2.5

PECK, WILEY J. b. September 15, 1957 Ht. 6-7 Wt. 220 College—Mississippi State

SEASON—TEAM	G	GS	MIN	FGM	FGA	PCT	3FGM	3FGA	PCT	FTM	FTA	PCT	O-RB	D-RB	TOT	AST	PF	DQ	STL	TO	BLK	PTS	RPG	APG	PPG
79-80—San Antonio	52	—	628	73	169	.432	0	2	.000	34	55	.618	66	117	183	33	100	2	17	48	23	180	3.5	0.6	3.5
REG. SEASON TOTALS	52	—	628	73	169	.432	0	2	.000	34	55	.618	66	117	183	33	100	2	17	48	23	180	3.5	0.6	3.5
PLAYOFF TOTALS	2	—	9	0	3	.000	0	0	—	0	0	—	0	3	3	—	1	0	0	0	1	0	1.5	0.0	0.0

PEEK, RICHARD SHELBY (**Rich**) b. October 28, 1943 Ht. 6-11 Wt. 230 College—Louisiana Tech/Florida

SEASON—TEAM	G	GS	MIN	FGM	FGA	PCT	3FGM	3FGA	PCT	FTM	FTA	PCT	O-RB	D-RB	TOT	AST	PF	DQ	STL	TO	BLK	PTS	RPG	APG	PPG
67-68—Dallas (A)	51	—	759	101	209	.483	0	0	—	35	65	.538	—	—	197	22	94	1	—	49	—	237	3.9	0.4	4.6
REG. ABA TOTALS	51	—	759	101	209	.483	0	0	—	35	65	.538	—	—	197	22	94	1	—	49	—	237	3.9	0.4	4.6
ABA PLAYOFF TOTALS	8	—	137	18	37	.486	0	0	—	7	15	.467	—	—	42	3	17	1	—	10	—	43	5.3	0.4	5.4

PEELER, ANTHONY EUGENE b. November 25, 1969 Ht. 6-4 Wt. 215 College—Missouri

SEASON—TEAM	G	GS	MIN	FGM	FGA	PCT	3FGM	3FGA	PCT	FTM	FTA	PCT	O-RB	D-RB	TOT	AST	PF	DQ	STL	TO	BLK	PTS	RPG	APG	PPG
92-93—L.A. Lakers	77	11	1656	297	634	.468	46	118	.390	162	206	.786	64	115	179	166	193	0	60	123	14	802	2.3	2.2	10.4
93-94—L.A. Lakers	30	30	923	176	409	.430	14	63	.222	57	71	.803	48	61	109	94	93	0	43	59	8	423	3.6	3.1	14.1
REG. SEASON TOTALS	107	41	2579	473	1043	.453	60	181	.331	219	277	.791	112	176	288	260	286	0	103	182	22	1225	2.7	2.4	11.4

PEEPLES, GEORGE ALBERT b. October 30, 1943 Ht. 6-8 Wt. 205 College—Iowa

SEASON—TEAM	G	GS	MIN	FGM	FGA	PCT	3FGM	3FGA	PCT	FTM	FTA	PCT	O-RB	D-RB	TOT	AST	PF	DQ	STL	TO	BLK	PTS	RPG	APG	PPG
67-68—Indiana (A)	65	—	1203	138	339	.407	0	3	.000	115	188	.612	—	—	378	29	136	1	—	71	—	391	5.8	0.4	6.0
68-69—Indiana (A)	64	—	1111	122	278	.439	0	0	—	101	142	.711	—	—	358	33	137	2	—	73	—	345	5.6	0.5	5.4
69-70—Carolina (A)	83	—	2220	279	682	.409	0	7	.000	209	315	.663	—	—	685	123	232	0	—	—	—	767	8.3	1.5	9.2
70-71—Carolina (A)	82	—	2220	377	773	.488	0	1	.000	202	335	.603	—	—	771	110	279	—	—	—	—	956	9.4	1.3	11.7
71-72—Dallas (A)	6	—	125	11	25	.440	0	0	—	7	11	.636	—	—	35	5	10	2	—	9	—	29	5.8	0.8	4.8
72-73—Indiana (A)	9	—	56	4	14	.286	0	0	—	6	11	.545	3	12	15	4	14	0	—	6	—	14	1.7	0.4	1.6
REG. ABA TOTALS	309	—	6935	931	2111	.441	0	11	.000	640	1002	.639	3	12	2242	304	808	3	—	159	—	2502	7.3	1.0	8.1
ABA PLAYOFF TOTALS	24	—	607	59	144	.410	0	1	.000	49	73	.671	15	39	201	19	64	1	—	19	—	167	8.4	0.8	7.0

PELKINGTON, JOHN FRANCIS ROBERT JR. (Jake, Pelky) b. January 3, 1916 d. May 1, 1982 Ht. 6-6 Wt. 225 College—Manhattan

SEASON—TEAM	G	GS	MIN	FGM	FGA	PCT	3FGM	3FGA	PCT	FTM	FTA	PCT	O-RB	D-RB	TOT	AST	PF	DQ	STL	TO	BLK	PTS	RPG	APG	PPG
40-41—Akron Goodyear (N)	24	—	—	57	—	—	—	—	—	70	102	.686	—	—	—	—	87	—	—	—	—	184	—	—	7.7
42-43—Fort Wayne (N)	23	—	—	83	—	—	—	—	—	70	100	.700	—	—	—	—	65	—	—	—	—	236	—	—	10.3
43-44—Fort Wayne (N)	20	—	—	46	—	—	—	—	—	40	—	—	—	—	—	—	—	—	—	—	—	132	—	—	6.6
44-45—Fort Wayne (N)	30	—	—	85	—	—	—	—	—	76	—	—	—	—	—	—	—	—	—	—	—	246	—	—	8.2
45-46—Fort Wayne (N)	33	—	—	94	—	—	—	—	—	76	104	.731	—	—	—	—	89	—	—	—	—	264	—	—	8.0
46-47—Fort Wayne (N)	42	—	—	129	—	—	—	—	—	125	166	.753	—	—	—	—	117	—	—	—	—	383	—	—	9.1
47-48—Fort Wayne (N)	54	—	—	174	—	—	—	—	—	156	214	.729	—	—	—	—	156	—	—	—	—	504	—	—	9.3
48-49—Ft. Wayne-Balt.	54	—	—	193	469	.412	—	—	—	211	267	.790	—	—	—	131	216	—	—	—	—	597	—	2.4	11.1
REG. NBA TOTALS	54	—	—	193	469	.412	—	—	—	211	267	.790	—	—	—	131	216	—	—	—	—	597	—	2.4	11.1
REG. NBL TOTALS	226	—	—	668	—	—	—	—	—	613	686	.724	—	—	—	—	514	—	—	—	—	1949	—	—	8.6
NBA PLAYOFF TOTALS	3	—	—	13	33	.394	—	—	—	27	35	.771	—	—	—	3	13	1	—	—	—	53	—	1.0	17.7
NBL PLAYOFF TOTALS	34	—	—	82	—	—	—	—	—	73	66	.667	—	—	—	—	93	—	—	—	—	237	—	—	7.0

PELLOM, SAMUEL TROY (Sam) b. October 2, 1951 Ht. 6-9 Wt. 225 College—Buffalo (SUNY)

SEASON—TEAM	G	GS	MIN	FGM	FGA	PCT	3FGM	3FGA	PCT	FTM	FTA	PCT	O-RB	D-RB	TOT	AST	PF	DQ	STL	TO	BLK	PTS	RPG	APG	PPG
79-80—Atlanta	44	—	373	44	108	.407	0	0	—	21	30	.700	28	64	92	18	70	0	12	18	12	109	2.1	0.4	2.5
80-81—Atlanta	77	—	1472	186	380	.489	0	1	.000	81	116	.698	122	234	356	48	228	6	50	99	92	453	4.6	0.6	5.9
81-82—Atlanta	69	4	1037	114	251	.454	0	1	.000	61	79	.772	90	139	229	28	164	0	29	57	47	289	3.3	0.4	4.2
82-83—Atlanta-Milw.	6	0	29	6	16	.375	0	0	—	0	0	—	2	6	8	1	3	0	0	2	0	12	1.3	0.2	2.0
REG. SEASON TOTALS	196	4	2911	350	755	.464	0	2	.000	163	225	.724	242	443	685	95	465	6	91	176	151	863	3.5	0.5	4.4
PLAYOFF TOTALS	5	0	22	1	6	.167	0	0	—	1	3	.333	1	0	1	1	3	0	0	0	1	3	0.2	0.2	0.6

PENDER, JERRY LEE b. February 12, 1950 Ht. 6-2 Wt. 195 College—Merced/Fresno State

SEASON—TEAM	G	GS	MIN	FGM	FGA	PCT	3FGM	3FGA	PCT	FTM	FTA	PCT	O-RB	D-RB	TOT	AST	PF	DQ	STL	TO	BLK	PTS	RPG	APG	PPG
73-74—San Diego (A)	11	—	68	8	30	.267	1	3	.333	10	13	.769	3	2	5	4	11	—	6	9	0	27	0.5	0.4	2.5
REG. ABA TOTALS	11	—	68	8	30	.267	1	3	.333	10	13	.769	3	2	5	4	11	0	6	9	0	27	0.5	0.4	2.5

PEPLOWSKI, MICHAEL WALTER (Mike) b. October 15, 1970 Ht. 6-10 Wt. 270 College—Michigan State

SEASON—TEAM	G	GS	MIN	FGM	FGA	PCT	3FGM	3FGA	PCT	FTM	FTA	PCT	O-RB	D-RB	TOT	AST	PF	DQ	STL	TO	BLK	PTS	RPG	APG	PPG
93-94—Sacramento	55	19	667	76	141	.539	0	1	.000	24	44	.545	49	120	169	24	131	2	17	34	25	176	3.1	0.4	3.2
REG. SEASON TOTALS	55	19	667	76	141	.539	0	1	.000	24	44	.545	49	120	169	24	131	2	17	34	25	176	3.1	0.4	3.2

PERDUE, WILLIAM EDWARD III (Will) b. August 29, 1965 Ht. 7-0 Wt. 240 College—Vanderbilt

SEASON—TEAM	G	GS	MIN	FGM	FGA	PCT	3FGM	3FGA	PCT	FTM	FTA	PCT	O-RB	D-RB	TOT	AST	PF	DQ	STL	TO	BLK	PTS	RPG	APG	PPG
88-89—Chicago	30	0	190	29	72	.403	0	0	—	8	14	.571	18	27	45	11	38	0	4	15	6	66	1.5	0.4	2.2
89-90—Chicago	77	11	884	111	268	.414	0	5	.000	72	104	.692	88	126	214	46	150	0	19	65	26	294	2.8	0.6	3.8
90-91—Chicago	74	3	972	116	235	.494	0	3	.000	75	112	.670	122	214	336	47	147	1	23	75	57	307	4.5	0.6	4.1
91-92—Chicago	77	7	1007	152	278	.547	1	2	.500	45	91	.495	108	204	312	80	133	1	16	72	43	350	4.1	1.0	4.5
92-93—Chicago	72	16	998	137	246	.557	0	1	.000	67	111	.604	103	184	287	74	139	2	22	74	47	341	4.0	1.0	4.7
93-94—Chicago	43	6	397	47	112	.420	0	1	.000	23	32	.719	40	86	126	34	61	0	8	42	11	117	2.9	0.8	2.7
REG. SEASON TOTALS	373	43	4448	592	1211	.489	1	12	.083	290	464	.625	479	841	1320	292	668	4	92	343	190	1475	3.5	0.8	4.0
PLAYOFF TOTALS	64	0	556	76	147	.517	1	4	.250	41	73	.562	75	85	160	22	110	2	6	38	25	194	2.5	0.3	3.0

PERKINS, SAMUEL BRUCE (Sam) b. June 14, 1961 Ht. 6-9 Wt. 255 College—North Carolina

SEASON—TEAM	G	GS	MIN	FGM	FGA	PCT	3FGM	3FGA	PCT	FTM	FTA	PCT	O-RB	D-RB	TOT	AST	PF	DQ	STL	TO	BLK	PTS	RPG	APG	PPG
84-85—Dallas	82	42	2317	347	736	.471	9	36	.250	200	244	.820	189	416	605	135	236	1	63	102	63	903	7.4	1.6	11.0
85-86—Dallas	80	79	2626	458	910	.503	11	33	.333	307	377	.814	195	490	685	153	212	2	75	145	94	1234	8.6	1.9	15.4
86-87—Dallas	80	80	2687	461	957	.482	19	54	.352	245	296	.828	197	419	616	146	269	6	109	132	77	1186	7.7	1.8	14.8
87-88—Dallas	75	75	2499	394	876	.450	5	30	.167	273	332	.822	201	400	601	118	227	2	74	119	54	1066	8.0	1.6	14.2
88-89—Dallas	78	77	2860	445	959	.464	7	38	.184	274	329	.833	235	453	688	127	224	1	76	141	92	1171	8.8	1.6	15.0
89-90—Dallas	76	70	2668	435	883	.493	6	28	.214	330	424	.778	209	363	572	175	225	4	88	148	64	1206	7.5	2.3	15.9
90-91—L.A. Lakers	73	66	2504	368	744	.495	18	64	.281	229	279	.821	167	371	538	108	247	2	64	103	78	983	7.4	1.5	13.5
91-92—L.A. Lakers	63	63	2332	361	803	.450	15	69	.217	304	372	.817	192	364	556	141	192	1	64	83	62	1041	8.8	2.2	16.5
92-93—Lakers-Seattle	79	62	2351	381	799	.477	24	71	.338	250	305	.820	163	361	524	156	225	0	60	108	82	1036	6.6	2.0	13.1
93-94—Seattle	81	41	2170	341	779	.438	99	270	.367	218	272	.801	120	246	366	111	197	0	67	103	31	999	4.5	1.4	12.3
REG. SEASON TOTALS	767	655	25014	3991	8446	.473	213	693	.307	2630	3230	.814	1868	3883	5751	1370	2254	19	740	1184	697	10825	7.5	1.8	14.1
PLAYOFF TOTALS	81	74	2858	444	953	.466	51	147	.347	287	364	.788	187	441	628	153	268	4	81	129	89	1226	7.8	1.9	15.1

PERKINS, WARREN C. (Red) b. February 2, 1924 Ht. 6-3 Wt. 190 College—Tulane

SEASON—TEAM	G	GS	MIN	FGM	FGA	PCT	3FGM	3FGA	PCT	FTM	FTA	PCT	O-RB	D-RB	TOT	AST	PF	DQ	STL	TO	BLK	PTS	RPG	APG	PPG
49-50—Tri-Cities	60	—	—	128	422	.303	—	—	—	115	195	.590	—	—	—	114	260	—	—	—	—	371	—	1.9	6.2
50-51—Tri-Cities	66	—	—	135	428	.315	—	—	—	126	195	.646	—	—	319	143	232	13	—	—	—	396	4.8	2.2	6.0
REG. SEASON TOTALS	126	—	—	263	850	.309	—	—	—	241	390	.618	—	—	319	257	492	13	—	—	—	767	4.8	2.0	6.1
PLAYOFF TOTALS	2	—	—	1	1	1.000	—	—	—	0	0	—	—	—	—	1	4	0	—	—	—	2	—	0.5	1.0

PERRY, AULCIE b. July 3, 1950 Ht. 6-10 Wt. 210 College—Bethune-Cookman

SEASON—TEAM	G	GS	MIN	FGM	FGA	PCT	3FGM	3FGA	PCT	FTM	FTA	PCT	O-RB	D-RB	TOT	AST	PF	DQ	STL	TO	BLK	PTS	RPG	APG	PPG
74-75—Virginia (A)	21	—	415	81	186	.435	0	1	.000	19	30	.633	40	65	105	20	58	—	12	34	16	181	5.0	1.0	8.6
REG. ABA TOTALS	21	—	415	81	186	.435	0	1	.000	19	30	.633	40	65	105	20	58	—	12	34	16	181	5.0	1.0	8.6

PERRY, CURTIS R. b. September 13, 1948 Ht. 6-7 Wt. 220 College—SW Missouri State

SEASON—TEAM	G	GS	MIN	FGM	FGA	PCT	3FGM	3FGA	PCT	FTM	FTA	PCT	O-RB	D-RB	TOT	AST	PF	DQ	STL	TO	BLK	PTS	RPG	APG	PPG
70-71—San Diego	18	—	100	21	48	.438	—	—	—	11	20	.550	—	—	30	5	22	0	—	—	—	53	1.7	0.3	2.9
71-72—Houston-Milw.	75	—	1826	181	486	.372	—	—	—	76	119	.639	—	—	593	100	261	14	—	—	—	438	7.9	1.3	5.8
72-73—Milwaukee	67	—	2094	265	575	.461	—	—	—	83	126	.659	—	—	644	123	246	6	—	—	—	613	9.6	1.8	9.1
73-74—Milwaukee	81	—	2386	325	729	.446	—	—	—	78	134	.582	242	461	703	183	301	8	104	—	97	728	8.7	2.3	9.0
74-75—Phoenix	79	—	2688	437	917	.477	—	—	—	184	256	.719	347	593	940	186	288	10	108	—	78	1058	11.9	2.4	13.4
75-76—Phoenix	71	—	2353	386	776	.497	—	—	—	175	239	.732	197	487	684	182	269	5	84	—	66	947	9.6	2.6	13.3
76-77—Phoenix	44	—	1391	179	414	.432	—	—	—	112	142	.789	149	246	395	79	163	3	49	—	28	470	9.0	1.8	10.7
77-78—Phoenix	45	—	818	110	243	.453	—	—	—	51	65	.785	87	163	250	48	120	2	34	63	22	271	5.6	1.1	6.0
REG. SEASON TOTALS	480	—	13656	1904	4188	.455	—	—	—	770	1101	.699	1022	1950	4239	906	1670	48	379	63	291	4578	8.8	1.9	9.5
PLAYOFF TOTALS	52	—	1546	213	453	.470	—	—	—	72	109	.661	97	130	437	75	189	7	22	—	19	498	8.4	1.4	9.6

PERRY, ELLIOT LAMONTE b. March 28, 1969 Ht. 6-0 Wt. 155 College—Memphis State

SEASON—TEAM	G	GS	MIN	FGM	FGA	PCT	3FGM	3FGA	PCT	FTM	FTA	PCT	O-RB	D-RB	TOT	AST	PF	DQ	STL	TO	BLK	PTS	RPG	APG	PPG
91-92—L.A. Clips-Cha.	50	0	437	49	129	.380	1	7	.143	27	41	.659	14	25	39	78	36	0	34	50	3	126	0.8	1.6	2.5
93-94—Phoenix	27	9	432	42	113	.372	0	3	.000	21	28	.750	12	27	39	125	36	0	25	43	1	105	1.4	4.6	3.9
REG. SEASON TOTALS	77	9	869	91	242	.376	1	10	.100	48	69	.696	26	52	78	203	72	0	59	93	4	231	1.0	2.6	3.0
PLAYOFF TOTALS	4	0	13	1	7	.143	0	0	—	0	0	—	0	0	0	1	2	0	1	1	0	2	0.0	0.3	0.5

PERRY, RON b. December 29, 1943 Ht. 6-3 Wt. 190 College—Virginia Tech

SEASON—TEAM	G	GS	MIN	FGM	FGA	PCT	3FGM	3FGA	PCT	FTM	FTA	PCT	O-RB	D-RB	TOT	AST	PF	DQ	STL	TO	BLK	PTS	RPG	APG	PPG
67-68—Minnesota (A)	67	—	2125	339	878	.386	62	178	.348	118	179	.659	—	—	223	139	151	2	—	169	—	858	3.3	2.1	12.8
68-69—Miami-N.Y.-Indiana (A)	74	—	2385	402	1060	.379	67	192	.349	212	292	.726	—	—	241	244	255	8	—	201	—	1083	3.3	3.3	14.6
69-70—Car.-N.O. (A)	46	—	522	104	272	.382	10	35	.286	69	97	.711	—	—	53	37	78	1	—	—	—	287	1.2	0.8	6.2
REG. ABA TOTALS	187	—	5032	845	2210	.382	139	405	.343	399	568	.702	—	—	517	420	484	11	—	370	—	2228	2.8	2.2	11.9
ABA PLAYOFF TOTALS	17	—	202	34	114	.298	11	38	.289	18	27	.667	—	—	21	18	33	0	—	19	—	97	1.2	1.1	5.7

PERRY, TIMOTHY D. (Tim) b. June 4, 1965 Ht. 6-9 Wt. 220 College—Temple

SEASON—TEAM	G	GS	MIN	FGM	FGA	PCT	3FGM	3FGA	PCT	FTM	FTA	PCT	O-RB	D-RB	TOT	AST	PF	DQ	STL	TO	BLK	PTS	RPG	APG	PPG
88-89—Phoenix	62	15	614	108	201	.537	1	4	.250	40	65	.615	61	71	132	18	47	0	19	37	32	257	2.1	0.3	4.1
89-90—Phoenix	60	18	612	100	195	.513	1	1	1.000	53	90	.589	79	73	152	17	76	0	21	47	22	254	2.5	0.3	4.2
90-91—Phoenix	46	2	587	75	144	.521	0	5	.000	43	70	.614	53	73	126	27	60	1	23	32	43	193	2.7	0.6	4.2
91-92—Phoenix	80	69	2483	413	789	.523	3	8	.375	153	215	.712	204	347	551	134	237	2	44	141	116	982	6.9	1.7	12.3
92-93—Philadelphia	81	51	2104	287	613	.468	10	49	.204	147	207	.710	154	255	409	126	159	0	40	123	91	731	5.0	1.6	9.0
93-94—Philadelphia	80	68	2336	272	625	.435	73	200	.365	102	176	.580	117	287	404	94	154	1	60	80	82	719	5.1	1.2	9.0
REG. SEASON TOTALS	409	223	8736	1255	2567	.489	88	267	.330	538	823	.654	668	1106	1774	416	733	4	207	460	386	3136	4.3	1.0	7.7
PLAYOFF TOTALS	23	8	302	53	92	.576	0	0	—	31	52	.596	23	39	62	13	44	1	8	20	13	137	2.7	0.6	6.0

PERSON, CHUCK CONNORS (**Rifleman**) b. June 27, 1964 Ht. 6-8 Wt. 225 College—Auburn

SEASON—TEAM	G	GS	MIN	FGM	FGA	PCT	3FGM	3FGA	PCT	FTM	FTA	PCT	O-RB	D-RB	TOT	AST	PF	DQ	STL	TO	BLK	PTS	RPG	APG	PPG
86-87—Indiana	82	78	2956	635	1358	.468	49	138	.355	222	297	.747	168	509	677	295	310	4	90	211	16	1541	8.3	3.6	18.8
87-88—Indiana	79	71	2807	575	1252	.459	59	177	.333	132	197	.670	171	365	536	309	266	4	73	210	8	1341	6.8	3.9	17.0
88-89—Indiana	80	79	3012	711	1453	.489	63	205	.307	243	307	.792	144	372	516	289	280	12	83	308	18	1728	6.5	3.6	21.6
89-90—Indiana	77	73	2714	605	1242	.487	94	253	.372	211	270	.781	126	319	445	230	217	1	53	170	20	1515	5.8	3.0	19.7
90-91—Indiana	80	79	2566	620	1231	.504	69	203	.340	165	229	.721	121	296	417	238	221	1	56	184	17	1474	5.2	3.0	18.4
91-92—Indiana	81	81	2923	616	1284	.480	132	354	.373	133	197	.675	114	312	426	382	247	5	68	216	18	1497	5.3	4.7	18.5
92-93—Minnesota	78	75	2985	541	1248	.433	118	332	.355	109	168	.649	98	335	433	343	198	2	67	219	30	1309	5.6	4.4	16.8
93-94—Minnesota	77	37	2029	356	843	.422	100	272	.368	82	108	.759	55	198	253	185	164	0	45	121	12	894	3.3	2.4	11.6
REG. SEASON TOTALS	634	573	21992	4659	9911	.470	684	1934	.354	1297	1773	.732	997	2706	3703	2271	1903	29	535	1639	139	11299	5.8	3.6	17.8
PLAYOFF TOTALS	15	15	592	122	256	.477	25	64	.391	60	84	.714	16	74	90	55	51	1	13	37	2	329	6.0	3.7	21.9

PETERSEN, JAMES RICHARD (**Jim, Pete**) b. February 22, 1962 Ht. 6-10 Wt. 235 College—Minnesota

SEASON—TEAM	G	GS	MIN	FGM	FGA	PCT	3FGM	3FGA	PCT	FTM	FTA	PCT	O-RB	D-RB	TOT	AST	PF	DQ	STL	TO	BLK	PTS	RPG	APG	PPG
84-85—Houston	60	0	714	70	144	.486	0	0	—	50	66	.758	44	103	147	29	125	1	14	71	32	190	2.5	0.5	3.2
85-86—Houston	82	20	1664	196	411	.477	0	3	.000	113	160	.706	149	247	396	85	231	2	38	84	54	505	4.8	1.0	6.2
86-87—Houston	82	56	2403	386	755	.511	0	4	.000	152	209	.727	177	380	557	127	268	5	43	152	102	924	6.8	1.5	11.3
87-88—Houston	69	50	1793	249	488	.510	1	6	.167	114	153	.745	145	291	436	106	203	3	36	119	40	613	6.3	1.5	8.9
88-89—Sacramento	66	40	1633	278	606	.459	0	8	.000	115	154	.747	121	292	413	81	236	8	47	147	68	671	6.3	1.2	10.2
89-90—Golden State	43	19	592	60	141	.426	0	1	.000	52	73	.712	49	111	160	23	103	0	17	36	20	172	3.7	0.5	4.0
90-91—Golden State	62	21	834	114	236	.483	1	4	.250	50	76	.658	69	131	200	27	153	2	13	48	41	279	3.2	0.4	4.5
91-92—Golden State	27	2	169	18	40	.450	0	2	.000	7	10	.700	12	33	45	9	35	0	5	5	6	43	1.7	0.3	1.6
REG. SEASON TOTALS	491	208	9802	1371	2821	.486	2	28	.071	653	901	.725	766	1588	2354	487	1354	21	213	662	363	3397	4.8	1.0	6.9
PLAYOFF TOTALS	46	4	788	97	200	.485	0	0	—	47	71	.662	73	134	207	37	132	4	17	33	17	241	4.5	0.8	5.2

PETERSEN, LOY M. b. July 26, 1945 Ht. 6-5 Wt. 205 College—Oregon State

SEASON—TEAM	G	GS	MIN	FGM	FGA	PCT	3FGM	3FGA	PCT	FTM	FTA	PCT	O-RB	D-RB	TOT	AST	PF	DQ	STL	TO	BLK	PTS	RPG	APG	PPG
68-69—Chicago	38	—	299	44	109	.404	—	—	—	19	27	.704	—	—	41	25	39	0	—	—	—	107	1.1	0.7	2.8
69-70—Chicago	31	—	231	33	90	.367	—	—	—	26	39	.667	—	—	26	23	22	0	—	—	—	92	0.8	0.7	3.0
REG. SEASON TOTALS	69	—	530	77	199	.387	—	—	—	45	66	.682	—	—	67	48	61	0	—	—	—	199	1.0	0.7	2.9

PETERSON, EDWARD T. (**Ed**) b. June 27, 1924 d. March 20, 1984 Ht. 6-9 Wt. 230 College—Cornell

SEASON—TEAM	G	GS	MIN	FGM	FGA	PCT	3FGM	3FGA	PCT	FTM	FTA	PCT	O-RB	D-RB	TOT	AST	PF	DQ	STL	TO	BLK	PTS	RPG	APG	PPG
48-49—Syracuse (N)	63	—	165	—	—	—	—	—	—	104	177	.588	—	—	—	—	203	—	—	—	—	434	—	—	6.9
49-50—Syracuse	62	—	167	390	—	.428	—	—	—	111	185	.600	—	—	—	33	198	—	—	—	—	445	—	0.5	7.2
50-51—Syr.-Tri-Cit	53	—	130	384	—	.339	—	—	—	99	150	.660	—	288	66	188	9	—	—	—		359	5.4	1.2	6.8
REG. NBA TOTALS	115	—	297	774	—	.384	—	—	—	210	335	.627	—	—	288	99	386	9	—	—	—	804	5.4	0.9	7.0
REG. NBL TOTALS	63	—	165	—	—	—	—	—	—	104	177	.588	—	—	—	—	203	—	—	—	—	434	—	—	6.9
NBA PLAYOFF TOTALS	11	—	18	43	—	.419	—	—	—	8	14	.571	—	—	1	33	2	—	—	—		44	—	0.1	4.0
NBL PLAYOFF TOTALS	6	—	14	—	—	—	—	—	—	16	28	.571	—	—	—	—	21	—	—	—	—	44	—	—	7.3

PETERSON, MELVIN LOWELL (**Mel**) b. March 23, 1938 Ht. 6-4½ Wt. 185 College—Wheaton

SEASON—TEAM	G	GS	MIN	FGM	FGA	PCT	3FGM	3FGA	PCT	FTM	FTA	PCT	O-RB	D-RB	TOT	AST	PF	DQ	STL	TO	BLK	PTS	RPG	APG	PPG
63-64—Baltimore	2	—	3	1	1	1.000	—	—	—	0	0	—	—	—	1	0	2	0	—	—	—	2	0.5	0.0	1.0
67-68—Oakland (A)	77	—	1589	323	756	.427	9	34	.265	76	93	.817	—	—	451	104	161	1	—	114	—	731	5.9	1.4	9.5
68-69—Oakland (A)	51	—	709	132	263	.502	0	2	.000	12	15	.800	—	—	170	55	61	0	—	43	—	276	3.3	1.1	5.4
69-70—Los Angeles (A)	4	—	53	10	35	.286	0	4	.000	3	3	1.000	—	—	13	1	4	0	—	—	—	23	3.3	0.3	5.8
REG. NBA TOTALS	2	—	3	1	1	1.000	—	—	—	0	0	—	—	—	1	0	2	0	—	—	—	2	0.5	0.0	1.0
REG. ABA TOTALS	132	—	2351	465	1054	.441	9	40	.225	91	111	.820	—	—	634	160	226	1	—	157	—	1030	4.8	1.2	7.8
ABA PLAYOFF TOTALS	18	—	120	21	36	.583	1	2	.500	8	14	.571	—	—	34	6	13	0	—	6	—	51	1.9	0.3	2.8

PETERSON, ROBERT (**Bob**) b. January 25, 1932 Ht. 6-5 Wt. 210 College—Oregon

SEASON—TEAM	G	GS	MIN	FGM	FGA	PCT	3FGM	3FGA	PCT	FTM	FTA	PCT	O-RB	D-RB	TOT	AST	PF	DQ	STL	TO	BLK	PTS	RPG	APG	PPG
53-54—Balt.-Milw.	8	—	60	3	10	.300	—	—	—	9	11	.818	—	—	12	3	15	1	—	—	—	15	1.5	0.4	1.9
54-55—New York	37	—	503	62	169	.367	—	—	—	30	45	.667	—	—	154	31	80	2	—	—	—	154	4.2	0.8	4.2
55-56—New York	58	—	779	121	303	.399	—	—	—	68	104	.654	—	—	223	44	123	0	—	—	—	310	3.8	0.8	5.3
REG. SEASON TOTALS	103	—	1342	186	482	.386	—	—	—	107	160	.669	—	—	389	78	218	3	—	—	—	479	3.8	0.8	4.7
PLAYOFF TOTALS	3	—	71	7	15	.467	—	—	—	10	11	.909	—	—	16	5	3	0	—	—	—	24	5.3	1.7	8.0

PETRIE, GEOFFREY MICHAEL (**Geoff**) b. April 17, 1948　Ht. 6-4　Wt. 190　College—Princeton

SEASON—TEAM	G	GS	MIN	FGM	FGA	PCT	3FGM	3FGA	PCT	FTM	FTA	PCT	O-RB	D-RB	TOT	AST	PF	DQ	STL	TO	BLK	PTS	RPG	APG	PPG
70-71—Portland	82	—	3032	784	1770	.443	—	—	—	463	600	.772	—	—	280	390	196	1	—	—	—	2031	3.4	4.8	24.8
71-72—Portland	60	—	2155	465	1115	.417	—	—	—	202	256	.789	—	—	133	248	108	0	—	—	—	1132	2.2	4.1	18.9
72-73—Portland	79	—	3134	836	1801	.464	—	—	—	298	383	.778	—	—	273	350	163	2	—	—	—	1970	3.5	4.4	24.9
73-74—Portland	73	—	2800	740	1537	.481	—	—	—	291	341	.853	64	144	208	315	199	2	84	—	15	1771	2.8	4.3	24.3
74-75—Portland	80	—	3109	602	1319	.456	—	—	—	261	311	.839	38	171	209	424	215	1	81	—	13	1465	2.6	5.3	18.3
75-76—Portland	72	—	2557	543	1177	.461	—	—	—	277	334	.829	38	130	168	330	194	0	82	—	5	1363	2.3	4.6	18.9
REG. SEASON TOTALS	446	—	16787	3970	8719	.455	—	—	—	1792	2225	.805	140	445	1271	2057	1075	6	247	—	33	9732	2.8	4.6	21.8
ALL-STAR TOTALS	2	—	31	3	14	.214	—	—	—	2	2	1.000	1	1	2	5	1	0	1	—	0	8	1.0	2.5	4.0

PETROVIC, DRAZEN b. October 22, 1964　d. June 7, 1993　Ht. 6-5　Wt. 200　College—Zagreb (Yugoslavia)

SEASON—TEAM	G	GS	MIN	FGM	FGA	PCT	3FGM	3FGA	PCT	FTM	FTA	PCT	O-RB	D-RB	TOT	AST	PF	DQ	STL	TO	BLK	PTS	RPG	APG	PPG
89-90—Portland	77	0	967	207	427	.485	34	74	.459	135	160	.844	50	61	111	116	134	2	23	96	2	583	1.4	1.5	7.6
90-91—Port.-N.J.	61	0	1015	243	493	.493	23	65	.354	114	137	.832	51	59	110	86	132	0	43	81	1	623	1.8	1.4	10.2
91-92—New Jersey	82	82	3027	668	1315	.508	123	277	.444	232	287	.808	97	161	258	252	248	3	105	215	11	1691	3.1	3.1	20.6
92-93—New Jersey	70	67	2660	587	1134	.518	75	167	.449	315	362	.870	42	148	190	247	237	5	94	204	13	1564	2.7	3.5	22.3
REG. SEASON TOTALS	290	149	7669	1705	3369	.506	255	583	.437	796	946	.841	240	429	669	701	751	8	265	596	27	4461	2.3	2.4	15.4
PLAYOFF TOTALS	29	9	609	119	251	.474	11	34	.324	48	69	.696	16	35	51	42	68	0	12	50	1	297	1.8	1.4	10.2

PETRUSKA, RICHARD b. January 25, 1969　Ht. 6-10　Wt. 260　College—Loyola Marymount/UCLA

SEASON—TEAM	G	GS	MIN	FGM	FGA	PCT	3FGM	3FGA	PCT	FTM	FTA	PCT	O-RB	D-RB	TOT	AST	PF	DQ	STL	TO	BLK	PTS	RPG	APG	PPG
93-94—Houston	22	0	92	20	46	.435	7	15	.467	6	8	.750	9	22	31	1	15	0	2	15	3	53	1.4	0.0	2.4
REG. SEASON TOTALS	22	0	92	20	46	.435	7	15	.467	6	8	.750	9	22	31	1	15	0	2	15	3	53	1.4	0.0	2.4

PETTIT, ROBERT E. JR. (**Bob**) b. December 12, 1932　Ht. 6-9　Wt. 215　College—Louisiana State

SEASON—TEAM	G	GS	MIN	FGM	FGA	PCT	3FGM	3FGA	PCT	FTM	FTA	PCT	O-RB	D-RB	TOT	AST	PF	DQ	STL	TO	BLK	PTS	RPG	APG	PPG
54-55—Milwaukee	72	—	2659	520	1279	.407	—	—	—	426	567	.751	—	—	994	229	258	5	—	—	—	1466	13.8	3.2	20.4
55-56—St. Louis	72	—	2794	646	1507	.429	—	—	—	557	757	.736	—	—	1164	189	202	1	—	—	—	1849	16.2	2.6	25.7
56-57—St. Louis	71	—	2491	613	1477	.415	—	—	—	529	684	.773	—	—	1037	133	181	1	—	—	—	1755	14.6	1.9	24.7
57-58—St. Louis	70	—	2528	581	1418	.410	—	—	—	557	744	.749	—	—	1216	157	222	6	—	—	—	1719	17.4	2.2	24.6
58-59—St. Louis	72	—	2873	719	1640	.438	—	—	—	667	879	.759	—	—	1182	221	200	3	—	—	—	2105	16.4	3.1	29.2
59-60—St. Louis	72	—	2896	669	1526	.438	—	—	—	544	722	.753	—	—	1221	257	204	0	—	—	—	1882	17.0	3.6	26.1
60-61—St. Louis	76	—	3027	769	1720	.447	—	—	—	582	804	.724	—	—	1540	262	217	1	—	—	—	2120	20.3	3.4	27.9
61-62—St. Louis	78	—	3282	867	1928	.450	—	—	—	695	901	.771	—	—	1459	289	296	4	—	—	—	2429	18.7	3.7	31.1
62-63—St. Louis	79	—	3090	778	1746	.446	—	—	—	685	885	.774	—	—	1191	245	282	8	—	—	—	2241	15.1	3.1	28.4
63-64—St. Louis	80	—	3296	791	1708	.463	—	—	—	608	771	.789	—	—	1224	259	300	3	—	—	—	2190	15.3	3.2	27.4
64-65—St. Louis	50	—	1754	396	923	.429	—	—	—	332	405	.820	—	—	621	128	167	0	—	—	—	1124	12.4	2.6	22.5
REG. SEASON TOTALS	792	—	30690	7349	16872	.436	—	—	—	6182	8119	.761	—	—	12849	2369	2529	32	—	—	—	20880	16.2	3.0	26.4
PLAYOFF TOTALS	88	—	3545	766	1834	.418	—	—	—	708	915	.774	—	—	1304	241	277	1	—	—	—	2240	14.8	2.7	25.5
ALL-STAR TOTALS	11	—	360	81	193	.420	—	—	—	62	80	.775	—	—	178	23	25	0	—	—	—	224	16.2	2.1	20.4

PETTWAY, JERRY b. February 13, 1944　Ht. 6-3　Wt. 185　College—Northwood Institute

SEASON—TEAM	G	GS	MIN	FGM	FGA	PCT	3FGM	3FGA	PCT	FTM	FTA	PCT	O-RB	D-RB	TOT	AST	PF	DQ	STL	TO	BLK	PTS	RPG	APG	PPG
67-68—Houston (A)	76	—	1572	289	838	.345	16	57	.281	119	183	.650	—	—	274	103	132	2	—	82	—	713	3.6	1.4	9.4
68-69—Houston (A)	11	—	264	37	123	.301	0	5	.000	5	7	.714	—	—	29	17	19	0	—	16	—	79	2.6	1.5	7.2
REG. ABA TOTALS	87	—	1836	326	961	.339	16	62	.258	124	190	.653	—	—	303	120	151	2	—	98	—	792	3.5	1.4	9.1
ABA PLAYOFF TOTALS	3	—	62	12	29	.414	1	2	.500	4	5	.800	—	—	14	5	5	0	—	2	—	29	4.7	1.7	9.7

PHEGLEY, ROGER DALE b. October 16, 1956　Ht. 6-7　Wt. 205　College—Bradley

SEASON—TEAM	G	GS	MIN	FGM	FGA	PCT	3FGM	3FGA	PCT	FTM	FTA	PCT	O-RB	D-RB	TOT	AST	PF	DQ	STL	TO	BLK	PTS	RPG	APG	PPG
78-79—Washington	29	—	153	28	78	.359	—	—	—	24	29	.828	5	17	22	15	21	0	5	17	2	80	0.8	0.5	2.8
79-80—Wash.-N.J.	78	—	1512	350	733	.477	4	9	.444	177	203	.872	75	110	185	102	158	1	34	119	7	881	2.4	1.3	11.3
80-81—Cleveland	82	—	2269	474	965	.491	8	28	.286	224	267	.839	90	156	246	184	262	7	65	165	15	1180	3.0	2.2	14.4
81-82—Clev.-S.A.	81	9	1183	233	507	.460	5	31	.161	85	109	.780	61	93	154	114	152	0	36	66	8	556	1.9	1.4	6.9
82-83—San Antonio	62	4	599	120	267	.449	3	14	.214	43	56	.768	39	45	84	60	92	0	30	49	8	286	1.4	1.0	4.6
83-84—S.A.-Dallas	13	0	87	11	35	.314	2	5	.400	4	4	1.000	2	9	11	11	11	0	1	6	0	28	0.8	0.8	2.2
REG. SEASON TOTALS	345	13	5803	1216	2585	.470	22	87	.253	557	668	.834	272	430	702	486	696	8	171	422	40	3011	2.0	1.4	8.7
PLAYOFF TOTALS	14	0	49	9	23	.391	3	6	.500	5	6	.833	1	7	8	2	7	0	2	4	0	26	0.6	0.1	1.9

PHELAN, JAMES J. (**Jim**) b. March 19, 1929　Ht. 6-1　Wt. 175　College—La Salle

SEASON—TEAM	G	GS	MIN	FGM	FGA	PCT	3FGM	3FGA	PCT	FTM	FTA	PCT	O-RB	D-RB	TOT	AST	PF	DQ	STL	TO	BLK	PTS	RPG	APG	PPG
53-54—Philadelphia	4	—	33	0	6	.000	—	—	—	3	6	.500	—	—	5	2	9	0	—	—	—	3	1.3	0.5	0.8
REG. SEASON TOTALS	4	—	33	0	6	.000	—	—	—	3	6	.500	—	—	5	2	9	0	—	—	—	3	1.3	0.5	0.8

PHELAN, JOHN EDWARD (**Jack**) b. November 6, 1925 Ht. 6-5 Wt. 195 College—DePaul

SEASON—TEAM	G	GS	MIN	FGM	FGA	PCT	3FGM	3FGA	PCT	FTM	FTA	PCT	O-RB	D-RB	TOT	AST	PF	DQ	STL	TO	BLK	PTS	RPG	APG	PPG
49-50—Wat.-She.	55	—	—	87	268	.325	—	—	—	52	90	.578	—	—	—	57	151	—	—	—	—	226	—	1.0	4.1
REG. SEASON TOTALS	55	—	—	87	268	.325	—	—	—	52	90	.578	—	—	—	57	151	—	—	—	—	226	—	1.0	4.1
PLAYOFF TOTALS	3	—	—	4	10	.400	—	—	—	2	3	.667	—	—	—	3	10	—	—	—	—	10	—	1.0	3.3

PHELPS, MICHAEL (**Mike**) b. October 3, 1961 Ht. 6-4 Wt. 185 College—Alcorn State

SEASON—TEAM	G	GS	MIN	FGM	FGA	PCT	3FGM	3FGA	PCT	FTM	FTA	PCT	O-RB	D-RB	TOT	AST	PF	DQ	STL	TO	BLK	PTS	RPG	APG	PPG
85-86—Seattle	70	18	880	117	286	.409	1	12	.083	44	74	.595	29	60	89	71	86	0	45	62	1	279	1.3	1.0	4.0
86-87—Seattle	60	6	469	75	176	.426	1	10	.100	31	44	.705	16	34	50	64	60	0	21	32	2	182	0.8	1.1	3.0
87-88—L.A. Clippers	2	0	23	3	7	.429	0	0	—	3	4	.750	0	2	2	3	1	0	5	2	0	9	1.0	1.5	4.5
REG. SEASON TOTALS	132	24	1372	195	469	.416	2	22	.091	78	122	.639	45	96	141	138	147	0	71	96	3	470	1.1	1.0	3.6

PHILLIP, ANDREW MICHAEL (**Andy**) b. March 7, 1922 Ht. 6-2½ Wt. 195 College—Illinois

SEASON—TEAM	G	GS	MIN	FGM	FGA	PCT	3FGM	3FGA	PCT	FTM	FTA	PCT	O-RB	D-RB	TOT	AST	PF	DQ	STL	TO	BLK	PTS	RPG	APG	PPG
47-48—Chicago	32	—	—	143	425	.336	—	—	—	60	103	.583	—	—	—	74	75	—	—	—	—	346	—	2.3	10.8
48-49—Chicago	60	—	—	285	818	.348	—	—	—	148	219	.676	—	—	—	319	205	—	—	—	—	718	—	5.3	12.0
49-50—Chicago	65	—	—	284	814	.349	—	—	—	190	270	.704	—	—	—	377	210	—	—	—	—	758	—	5.8	11.7
50-51—Philadelphia	66	—	—	275	690	.399	—	—	—	190	253	.751	—	—	446	414	221	8	—	—	—	740	6.8	6.3	11.2
51-52—Philadelphia	66	—	2933	279	762	.366	—	—	—	232	308	.753	—	—	434	539	218	6	—	—	—	790	6.6	8.2	12.0
52-53—Phil.-Ft. Wayne	70	—	2690	250	629	.397	—	—	—	222	301	.738	—	—	364	397	229	9	—	—	—	722	5.2	5.7	10.3
53-54—Fort Wayne	71	—	2705	255	680	.375	—	—	—	241	330	.730	—	—	265	449	204	4	—	—	—	751	3.7	6.3	10.6
54-55—Fort Wayne	64	—	2332	202	545	.371	—	—	—	213	308	.692	—	—	290	491	166	1	—	—	—	617	4.5	7.7	9.6
55-56—Fort Wayne	70	—	2078	148	405	.365	—	—	—	112	199	.563	—	—	257	410	155	2	—	—	—	408	3.7	5.9	5.8
56-57—Boston	67	—	1476	105	277	.379	—	—	—	88	137	.642	—	—	181	168	121	1	—	—	—	298	2.7	2.5	4.4
57-58—Boston	70	—	1164	97	273	.355	—	—	—	42	71	.592	—	—	158	121	121	0	—	—	—	236	2.3	1.7	3.4
REG. SEASON TOTALS	701	—	15378	2323	6318	.368	—	—	—	1738	2499	.695	—	—	2395	3759	1925	31	—	—	—	6384	4.4	5.4	9.1
PLAYOFF TOTALS	67	—	1424	137	415	.330	—	—	—	154	220	.700	—	—	193	248	176	2	—	—	—	428	3.3	3.7	6.4
ALL-STAR TOTALS	5	—	113	15	31	.484	—	—	—	4	5	.800	—	—	25	31	8	0	—	—	—	34	5.0	6.2	6.8

PHILLIPS, DONALD EUGENE (**Gene**) b. October 25, 1948 Ht. 6-4 Wt. 175 College—Southern Methodist

SEASON—TEAM	G	GS	MIN	FGM	FGA	PCT	3FGM	3FGA	PCT	FTM	FTA	PCT	O-RB	D-RB	TOT	AST	PF	DQ	STL	TO	BLK	PTS	RPG	APG	PPG
71-72—Dallas (A)	28	—	174	30	76	.395	7	17	.412	11	14	.786	—	—	21	13	23	—	—	8	—	78	0.8	0.5	2.8
72-73—Dallas (A)	3	—	10	0	5	.000	0	3	.000	0	0	—	—	—	0	1	3	0	—	0	—	0	0.0	0.3	0.0
REG. ABA TOTALS	31	—	184	30	81	.370	7	20	.350	11	14	.786	—	—	21	14	26	0	—	8	—	78	0.7	0.5	2.5
ABA PLAYOFF TOTALS	1	—	2	0	0	—	0	0	—	0	0	—	—	—	—	0	0	0	—	—	—	0	0.0	0.0	0.0

PHILLIPS, EDDIE LEE b. September 29, 1961 Ht. 6-7 Wt. 225 College—Alabama

SEASON—TEAM	G	GS	MIN	FGM	FGA	PCT	3FGM	3FGA	PCT	FTM	FTA	PCT	O-RB	D-RB	TOT	AST	PF	DQ	STL	TO	BLK	PTS	RPG	APG	PPG
82-83—New Jersey	48	0	416	56	138	.406	0	2	.000	40	59	.678	27	50	77	29	58	0	14	50	8	152	1.6	0.6	3.2
REG. SEASON TOTALS	48	0	416	56	138	.406	0	2	.000	40	59	.678	27	50	77	29	58	0	14	50	8	152	1.6	0.6	3.2
PLAYOFF TOTALS	2	0	12	3	6	.500	0	2	.000	1	4	.250	3	2	5	3	2	0	0	1	0	7	2.5	1.5	3.5

PHILLIPS, GARY A. b. December 7, 1939 Ht. 6-3 Wt. 190 College—Houston

SEASON—TEAM	G	GS	MIN	FGM	FGA	PCT	3FGM	3FGA	PCT	FTM	FTA	PCT	O-RB	D-RB	TOT	AST	PF	DQ	STL	TO	BLK	PTS	RPG	APG	PPG
61-62—Boston	67	—	713	110	310	.355	—	—	—	50	86	.581	—	—	107	64	109	0	—	—	—	270	1.6	1.0	4.0
62-63—San Francisco	75	—	1801	256	643	.398	—	—	—	97	152	.638	—	—	225	137	185	7	—	—	—	609	3.0	1.8	8.1
63-64—San Francisco	66	—	2010	256	691	.370	—	—	—	146	218	.670	—	—	248	203	245	8	—	—	—	658	3.8	3.1	10.0
64-65—San Francisco	73	—	1541	198	553	.358	—	—	—	120	199	.603	—	—	189	148	184	3	—	—	—	516	2.6	2.0	7.1
65-66—San Francisco	67	—	867	106	303	.350	—	—	—	54	87	.621	—	—	134	113	97	0	—	—	—	266	2.0	1.7	4.0
REG. SEASON TOTALS	348	—	6932	926	2500	.370	—	—	—	467	742	.629	—	—	903	665	820	18	—	—	—	2319	2.6	1.9	6.7
PLAYOFF TOTALS	17	—	288	36	113	.319	—	—	—	34	51	.667	—	—	27	21	42	2	—	—	—	106	1.6	1.2	6.2

PHILLS, BOBBY RAY II b. December 20, 1969 Ht. 6-5 Wt. 215 College—Southern

SEASON—TEAM	G	GS	MIN	FGM	FGA	PCT	3FGM	3FGA	PCT	FTM	FTA	PCT	O-RB	D-RB	TOT	AST	PF	DQ	STL	TO	BLK	PTS	RPG	APG	PPG
91-92—Cleveland	10	0	65	12	28	.429	0	2	.000	7	11	.636	4	4	8	4	3	0	3	8	1	31	0.8	0.4	3.1
92-93—Cleveland	31	0	139	38	82	.463	2	5	.400	15	25	.600	6	11	17	10	19	0	10	18	2	93	0.5	0.3	3.0
93-94—Cleveland	72	53	1531	242	514	.471	1	12	.083	113	157	.720	71	141	212	133	135	1	67	63	12	598	2.9	1.8	8.3
REG. SEASON TOTALS	113	53	1735	292	624	.468	3	19	.158	135	193	.699	81	156	237	147	157	1	80	89	15	722	2.1	1.3	6.4
PLAYOFF TOTALS	10	2	89	14	36	.389	1	2	.500	6	8	.750	7	13	20	12	12	0	3	8	0	35	2.0	1.2	3.5

PIATKOWSKI, WALTER JR. (**Walt**) b. June 11, 1945   Ht. 6-8 Wt. 225 College—Bowling Green

SEASON—TEAM	G	GS	MIN	FGM	FGA	PCT	3FGM	3FGA	PCT	FTM	FTA	PCT	O-RB	D-RB	TOT	AST	PF	DQ	STL	TO	BLK	PTS	RPG	APG	PPG
68-69—Denver (A)	77	—	1819	399	956	.417	27	82	.329	117	151	.775	—	—	363	46	226	2	—	100	—	942	4.7	0.6	12.2
69-70—Denver (A)	74	—	1302	215	535	.402	11	50	.220	76	99	.768	—	—	252	41	180	1	—	—	—	517	3.4	0.6	7.0
71-72—Floridians (A)	6	—	28	3	16	.188	0	0	—	0	0	—	—	—	2	2	2	—	—	3	—	6	0.3	0.3	1.0
REG. ABA TOTALS	157	—	3149	617	1507	.409	38	132	.288	193	250	.772	—	—	617	89	408	3	—	103	—	1465	3.9	0.6	9.3
ABA PLAYOFF TOTALS	13	—	251	60	135	.444	2	13	.154	12	15	.800	—	—	40	10	41	1	—	13	—	134	3.1	0.8	10.3

PIERCE, RICKY CHARLES b. August 19, 1959   Ht. 6-4 Wt. 215 College—Walla Walla CC/Rice

SEASON—TEAM	G	GS	MIN	FGM	FGA	PCT	3FGM	3FGA	PCT	FTM	FTA	PCT	O-RB	D-RB	TOT	AST	PF	DQ	STL	TO	BLK	PTS	RPG	APG	PPG
82-83—Detroit	39	1	265	33	88	.375	1	7	.143	18	32	.563	15	20	35	14	42	0	8	18	4	85	0.9	0.4	2.2
83-84—San Diego	69	35	1280	268	570	.470	0	9	.000	149	173	.861	59	76	135	60	143	1	27	81	13	685	2.0	0.9	9.9
84-85—Milwaukee	44	3	882	165	307	.537	1	4	.250	102	124	.823	49	68	117	94	117	0	34	63	5	433	2.7	2.1	9.8
85-86—Milwaukee	81	8	2147	429	798	.538	3	23	.130	266	310	.858	94	137	231	177	252	6	83	107	6	1127	2.9	2.2	13.9
86-87—Milwaukee	79	31	2505	575	1077	.534	3	28	.107	387	440	.880	117	149	266	144	222	0	64	120	24	1540	3.4	1.8	19.5
87-88—Milwaukee	37	0	965	248	486	.510	3	14	.214	107	122	.877	30	53	83	73	94	0	21	57	7	606	2.2	2.0	16.4
88-89—Milwaukee	75	4	2078	527	1018	.518	8	36	.222	255	297	.859	82	115	197	156	193	1	77	112	19	1317	2.6	2.1	17.6
89-90—Milwaukee	59	0	1709	503	987	.510	46	133	.346	307	366	.839	64	103	167	133	158	2	50	129	7	1359	2.8	2.3	23.0
90-91—Milw.-Seattle	78	2	2167	561	1156	.485	46	116	.397	430	471	.913	67	124	191	168	170	1	60	147	13	1598	2.4	2.2	20.5
91-92—Seattle	78	78	2658	620	1306	.475	33	123	.268	417	455	.916	93	140	233	241	213	2	86	189	20	1690	3.0	3.1	21.7
92-93—Seattle	77	72	2218	524	1071	.489	42	113	.372	313	352	.889	58	134	192	220	167	0	100	160	7	1403	2.5	2.9	18.2
93-94—Seattle	51	0	1022	272	577	.471	6	32	.188	189	211	.896	29	54	83	91	84	0	42	64	5	739	1.6	1.8	14.5
REG. SEASON TOTALS	767	234	19896	4725	9441	.500	192	638	.301	2940	3353	.877	757	1173	1930	1571	1855	13	652	1247	130	12582	2.5	2.0	16.4
PLAYOFF TOTALS	89	31	2436	505	1071	.472	30	78	.385	333	384	.867	93	124	217	168	245	2	60	139	19	1373	2.4	1.9	15.4
ALL-STAR TOTALS	1	0	19	4	8	.500	0	0	—	1	1	1.000	0	2	2	2	2	0	0	2	0	9	2.0	2.0	9.0

PIETKIEWICZ, STANLEY THOMAS (**Stan**) b. July 14, 1956   Ht. 6-5 Wt. 200 College—Auburn

SEASON—TEAM	G	GS	MIN	FGM	FGA	PCT	3FGM	3FGA	PCT	FTM	FTA	PCT	O-RB	D-RB	TOT	AST	PF	DQ	STL	TO	BLK	PTS	RPG	APG	PPG
78-79—San Diego	4	—	32	1	8	.125	—	—	—	2	2	1.000	0	6	6	3	5	0	1	1	0	4	1.5	0.8	1.0
79-80—San Diego	50	—	577	91	179	.508	9	36	.250	37	46	.804	26	19	45	94	52	1	25	51	4	228	0.9	1.9	4.6
80-81—S.D.-Dallas	42	—	461	57	138	.413	19	48	.396	11	14	.786	13	29	42	77	28	0	15	22	2	144	1.0	1.8	3.4
REG. SEASON TOTALS	96	—	1070	149	325	.458	28	84	.333	50	62	.806	39	54	93	174	85	1	41	74	6	376	1.0	1.8	3.9

PILCH, JOHN A. b. July 11, 1925   Ht. 6-3 Wt. 185 College—Wyoming

SEASON—TEAM	G	GS	MIN	FGM	FGA	PCT	3FGM	3FGA	PCT	FTM	FTA	PCT	O-RB	D-RB	TOT	AST	PF	DQ	STL	TO	BLK	PTS	RPG	APG	PPG
51-52—Minneapolis	9	—	41	1	10	.100	—	—	—	3	6	.500	—	—	9	2	10	0	—	—	—	5	1.0	0.2	0.6
REG. SEASON TOTALS	9	—	41	1	10	.100	—	—	—	3	6	.500	—	—	9	2	10	0	—	—	—	5	1.0	0.2	0.6

PINCKNEY, EDWARD LEWIS (**Ed, E-Z Ed**) b. March 27, 1963   Ht. 6-9 Wt. 215 College—Villanova

SEASON—TEAM	G	GS	MIN	FGM	FGA	PCT	3FGM	3FGA	PCT	FTM	FTA	PCT	O-RB	D-RB	TOT	AST	PF	DQ	STL	TO	BLK	PTS	RPG	APG	PPG
85-86—Phoenix	80	24	1602	255	457	.558	0	2	.000	171	254	.673	95	213	308	90	190	3	71	148	37	681	3.9	1.1	8.5
86-87—Phoenix	80	65	2250	290	497	.584	0	2	.000	257	348	.739	179	401	580	116	196	1	86	135	54	837	7.3	1.5	10.5
87-88—Sacramento	79	7	1177	179	343	.522	0	2	.000	133	178	.747	94	136	230	66	118	0	39	77	32	491	2.9	0.8	6.2
88-89—Sac.-Boston	80	33	2012	319	622	.513	0	6	.000	280	350	.800	166	283	449	118	202	2	83	119	66	918	5.6	1.5	11.5
89-90—Boston	77	50	1082	135	249	.542	0	1	.000	92	119	.773	93	132	225	68	126	1	34	56	42	362	2.9	0.9	4.7
90-91—Boston	70	16	1165	131	243	.539	0	1	.000	104	116	.897	155	186	341	45	147	0	61	45	43	366	4.9	0.6	5.2
91-92—Boston	81	36	1917	203	378	.537	0	1	.000	207	255	.812	252	312	564	62	158	1	70	73	56	613	7.0	0.8	7.6
92-93—Boston	7	5	151	10	24	.417	0	—	—	12	13	.923	14	29	43	1	13	0	4	8	7	32	6.1	0.1	4.6
93-94—Boston	76	35	1524	151	289	.522	0	0	—	92	125	.736	160	318	478	62	131	0	58	62	44	394	6.3	0.8	5.2
REG. SEASON TOTALS	630	271	12880	1673	3102	.539	0	15	.000	1348	1758	.767	1208	2010	3218	628	1281	8	506	723	381	4694	5.1	1.0	7.5
PLAYOFF TOTALS	28	8	554	60	98	.612	0	1	.000	52	63	.825	63	72	135	10	57	0	19	21	12	172	4.8	0.4	6.1

PINONE, JOHN GABRIEL JR. b. February 19, 1961   Ht. 6-8 Wt. 230 College—Villanova

SEASON—TEAM	G	GS	MIN	FGM	FGA	PCT	3FGM	3FGA	PCT	FTM	FTA	PCT	O-RB	D-RB	TOT	AST	PF	DQ	STL	TO	BLK	PTS	RPG	APG	PPG
83-84—Atlanta	7	0	65	7	13	.538	0	0	—	6	10	.600	0	10	10	3	11	0	2	5	1	20	1.4	0.4	2.9
REG. SEASON TOTALS	7	0	65	7	13	.538	0	0	—	6	10	.600	0	10	10	3	11	0	2	5	1	20	1.4	0.4	2.9

PIONTEK, DAVID VINCENT (**Dave**) b. August 27, 1934   Ht. 6-5½ Wt. 230 College—Xavier (Ohio)

SEASON—TEAM	G	GS	MIN	FGM	FGA	PCT	3FGM	3FGA	PCT	FTM	FTA	PCT	O-RB	D-RB	TOT	AST	PF	DQ	STL	TO	BLK	PTS	RPG	APG	PPG
56-57—Rochester	71	—	1759	257	637	.403	—	—	—	122	183	.667	—	—	351	108	141	1	—	—	—	636	4.9	1.5	9.0
57-58—Cincinnati	71	—	1032	150	397	.378	—	—	—	95	151	.629	—	—	254	52	134	2	—	—	—	395	3.6	0.7	5.6
58-59—Cincinnati	72	—	1674	305	813	.375	—	—	—	156	227	.687	—	—	385	124	162	3	—	—	—	766	5.3	1.7	10.6
59-60—Cin.-St. L.	77	—	1833	292	728	.401	—	—	—	129	202	.639	—	—	461	118	211	5	—	—	—	713	6.0	1.5	9.3
60-61—St. Louis	29	—	254	47	96	.490	—	—	—	16	31	.516	—	—	68	19	31	0	—	—	—	110	2.3	0.7	3.8
61-62—Chicago	45	—	614	83	225	.369	—	—	—	39	59	.661	—	—	155	31	89	1	—	—	—	205	3.4	0.7	4.6
62-63—Cincinnati	48	—	457	60	158	.380	—	—	—	10	16	.625	—	—	96	26	67	0	—	—	—	130	2.0	0.5	2.7
REG. SEASON TOTALS	413	—	7623	1194	3054	.391	—	—	—	567	869	.652	—	—	1770	478	835	12	—	—	—	2955	4.3	1.2	7.2
PLAYOFF TOTALS	25	—	327	40	113	.354	—	—	—	24	37	.649	—	—	70	20	44	1	—	—	—	104	2.8	0.8	4.2

PIOTROWSKI, THOMAS TRACY (Tom) b. October 17, 1960 Ht. 7-1 Wt. 240 College—La Salle

SEASON—TEAM	G	GS	MIN	FGM	FGA	PCT	3FGM	3FGA	PCT	FTM	FTA	PCT	O-RB	D-RB	TOT	AST	PF	DQ	STL	TO	BLK	PTS	RPG	APG	PPG
83-84—Portland	18	0	78	12	26	.462	0	0	—	6	6	1.000	6	10	16	5	22	0	1	6	3	30	0.9	0.3	1.7
REG. SEASON TOTALS	18	0	78	12	26	.462	0	0	—	6	6	1.000	6	10	16	5	22	0	1	6	3	30	0.9	0.3	1.7

PIPPEN, SCOTTIE b. September 25, 1965 Ht. 6-7 Wt. 225 College—Central Arkansas

SEASON—TEAM	G	GS	MIN	FGM	FGA	PCT	3FGM	3FGA	PCT	FTM	FTA	PCT	O-RB	D-RB	TOT	AST	PF	DQ	STL	TO	BLK	PTS	RPG	APG	PPG
87-88—Chicago	79	0	1650	261	564	.463	4	23	.174	99	172	.576	115	183	298	169	214	3	91	131	52	625	3.8	2.1	7.9
88-89—Chicago	73	56	2413	413	867	.476	21	77	.273	201	301	.668	138	307	445	256	261	8	139	199	61	1048	6.1	3.5	14.4
89-90—Chicago	82	82	3148	562	1150	.489	28	112	.250	199	295	.675	150	397	547	444	298	6	211	278	101	1351	6.7	5.4	16.5
90-91—Chicago	82	82	3014	600	1153	.520	21	68	.309	240	340	.706	163	432	595	511	270	3	193	232	93	1461	7.3	6.2	17.8
91-92—Chicago	82	82	3164	687	1359	.506	16	80	.200	330	434	.760	185	445	630	572	242	2	155	253	93	1720	7.7	7.0	21.0
92-93—Chicago	81	81	3123	628	1327	.473	22	93	.237	232	350	.663	203	418	621	507	219	3	173	246	73	1510	7.7	6.3	18.6
93-94—Chicago	72	72	2759	627	1278	.491	63	197	.320	270	409	.660	173	456	629	403	227	1	211	232	58	1587	8.7	5.6	22.0
REG. SEASON TOTALS	551	455	19271	3778	7698	.491	175	650	.269	1571	2301	.683	1127	2638	3765	2862	1731	26	1173	1571	531	9302	6.8	5.2	16.9
PLAYOFF TOTALS	110	105	4301	765	1621	.472	60	196	.306	426	581	.733	241	607	848	573	383	6	210	349	107	2016	7.7	5.2	18.3
ALL-STAR TOTALS	4	3	93	21	46	.457	5	12	.417	10	16	.625	6	15	21	7	7	0	12	4	5	57	5.3	1.8	14.3

PITTMAN, CHARLES E. (Charlie) b. March 23, 1958 Ht. 6-8 Wt. 220 College—Merced/Maryland

SEASON—TEAM	G	GS	MIN	FGM	FGA	PCT	3FGM	3FGA	PCT	FTM	FTA	PCT	O-RB	D-RB	TOT	AST	PF	DQ	STL	TO	BLK	PTS	RPG	APG	PPG
82-83—Phoenix	28	0	170	19	40	.475	0	1	.000	25	37	.676	13	18	31	7	41	0	2	22	7	63	1.1	0.3	2.3
83-84—Phoenix	69	8	989	126	209	.603	0	2	.000	69	101	.683	76	138	214	70	129	1	16	81	22	321	3.1	1.0	4.7
84-85—Phoenix	68	3	1001	107	227	.471	0	2	.000	109	146	.747	90	137	227	69	144	1	20	100	21	323	3.3	1.0	4.8
85-86—Phoenix	69	17	1132	127	218	.583	0	0	—	99	141	.702	99	147	246	58	140	2	37	107	23	353	3.6	0.8	5.1
REG. SEASON TOTALS	234	28	3292	379	694	.546	0	5	.000	302	425	.711	278	440	718	204	454	4	75	310	73	1060	3.1	0.9	4.5
PLAYOFF TOTALS	21	4	336	42	74	.568	0	1	.000	30	46	.652	31	52	83	21	41	0	5	25	8	114	4.0	1.0	5.4

PLUMMER, GARY b. February 21, 1962 Ht. 6-9 Wt. 215 College—Boston

SEASON—TEAM	G	GS	MIN	FGM	FGA	PCT	3FGM	3FGA	PCT	FTM	FTA	PCT	O-RB	D-RB	TOT	AST	PF	DQ	STL	TO	BLK	PTS	RPG	APG	PPG
84-85—Golden State	66	0	702	92	232	.397	1	4	.250	65	92	.707	54	80	134	26	127	1	15	50	14	250	2.0	0.4	3.8
92-93—Denver	60	0	737	106	228	.465	0	3	.000	69	95	.726	53	120	173	40	141	1	14	78	11	281	2.9	0.7	4.7
REG. SEASON TOTALS	126	0	1439	198	460	.430	1	7	.143	134	187	.717	107	200	307	66	268	2	29	128	25	531	2.4	0.5	4.2

POLEE, DWAYNE L. b. March 2, 1963 Ht. 6-5 Wt. 180 College—Nevada-Las Vegas/Pepperdine

SEASON—TEAM	G	GS	MIN	FGM	FGA	PCT	3FGM	3FGA	PCT	FTM	FTA	PCT	O-RB	D-RB	TOT	AST	PF	DQ	STL	TO	BLK	PTS	RPG	APG	PPG
86-87—L.A. Clippers	1	0	6	1	4	.250	0	3	.000	0	0	—	0	0	0	0	3	0	1	1	0	2	0.0	0.0	2.0
REG. SEASON TOTALS	1	0	6	1	4	.250	0	3	.000	0	0	—	0	0	0	0	3	0	1	1	0	2	0.0	0.0	2.0

POLLARD, JAMES CLIFFORD (Jim, The Kangaroo Kid) b. July 9, 1922 d. January 22, 1993 Ht. 6-3½ Wt. 190 College—Stanford

SEASON—TEAM	G	GS	MIN	FGM	FGA	PCT	3FGM	3FGA	PCT	FTM	FTA	PCT	O-RB	D-RB	TOT	AST	PF	DQ	STL	TO	BLK	PTS	RPG	APG	PPG
47-48—Minneapolis (N)	59	—	—	310	—	—	—	—	—	140	207	.676	—	—	—	—	147	—	—	—	—	760	—	—	12.9
48-49—Minneapolis	53	—	—	314	792	.396	—	—	—	156	227	.687	—	—	—	142	144	—	—	—	—	784	—	2.7	14.8
49-50—Minneapolis	66	—	—	394	1140	.346	—	—	—	185	242	.764	—	—	—	252	143	—	—	—	—	973	—	3.8	14.7
50-51—Minneapolis	54	—	—	256	728	.352	—	—	—	117	156	.750	—	—	484	184	157	4	—	—	—	629	9.0	3.4	11.6
51-52—Minneapolis	65	—	2545	411	1155	.356	—	—	—	183	260	.704	—	—	593	234	199	4	—	—	—	1005	9.1	3.6	15.5
52-53—Minneapolis	66	—	2403	333	933	.357	—	—	—	193	251	.769	—	—	452	231	194	3	—	—	—	859	6.8	3.5	13.0
53-54—Minneapolis	71	—	2483	326	882	.370	—	—	—	179	230	.778	—	—	500	214	161	0	—	—	—	831	7.0	3.0	11.7
54-55—Minneapolis	63	—	1960	265	749	.354	—	—	—	151	186	.812	—	—	458	160	147	3	—	—	—	681	7.3	2.5	10.8
REG. NBA TOTALS	438	—	9391	2299	6379	.360	—	—	—	1164	1552	.750	—	—	2487	1417	1145	14	—	—	—	5762	7.8	3.2	13.2
REG. NBL TOTALS	59	—	—	310	—	—	—	—	—	140	207	.676	—	—	—	—	147	—	—	—	—	760	—	—	12.9
NBA PLAYOFF TOTALS	72	—	1724	349	1029	.339	—	—	—	279	372	.750	—	—	407	259	205	6	—	—	—	977	8.1	3.6	13.6
NBL PLAYOFF TOTALS	10	—	—	48	—	—	—	—	—	27	41	.659	—	—	—	—	29	—	—	—	—	123	—	—	12.3
NBA ALL-STAR TOTALS	4	—	97	21	69	.304	—	—	—	6	8	.750	—	—	22	13	8	0	—	—	—	48	5.5	3.3	12.0

POLSON, RALPH M. b. October 26, 1929 Ht. 6-7½ Wt. 205 College—Whitworth

SEASON—TEAM	G	GS	MIN	FGM	FGA	PCT	3FGM	3FGA	PCT	FTM	FTA	PCT	O-RB	D-RB	TOT	AST	PF	DQ	STL	TO	BLK	PTS	RPG	APG	PPG
52-53—N.Y.-Phil.	49	—	810	65	179	.363	—	—	—	61	96	.635	—	—	211	24	102	5	—	—	—	191	4.3	0.5	3.9
REG. SEASON TOTALS	49	—	810	65	179	.363	—	—	—	61	96	.635	—	—	211	24	102	5	—	—	—	191	4.3	0.5	3.9

POLYNICE, OLDEN (O.P.) b. November 21, 1964   Ht. 7-0 Wt. 250 College—Virginia

SEASON—TEAM	G	GS	MIN	FGM	FGA	PCT	3FGM	3FGA	PCT	FTM	FTA	PCT	O-RB	D-RB	TOT	AST	PF	DQ	STL	TO	BLK	PTS	RPG	APG	PPG
87-88—Seattle	82	0	1080	118	254	.465	0	2	.000	101	158	.639	122	208	330	33	215	1	32	81	26	337	4.0	0.4	4.1
88-89—Seattle	80	0	835	91	180	.506	0	2	.000	51	86	.593	98	108	206	21	164	0	37	46	30	233	2.6	0.3	2.9
89-90—Seattle	79	7	1085	156	289	.540	1	2	.500	47	99	.475	128	172	300	15	187	0	25	35	21	360	3.8	0.2	4.6
90-91—Seattle-L.A. Clips	79	30	2092	316	564	.560	0	1	.000	146	252	.579	220	333	553	42	192	1	43	88	32	778	7.0	0.5	9.8
91-92—L.A. Clippers	76	65	1834	244	470	.519	0	1	.000	125	201	.622	195	341	536	46	165	0	45	83	20	613	7.1	0.6	8.1
92-93—Detroit	67	18	1299	210	429	.490	0	1	.000	66	142	.465	181	237	418	29	126	0	31	54	21	486	6.2	0.4	7.3
93-94—Detroit-Sac.	68	65	2402	346	662	.523	0	2	.000	97	191	.508	299	510	809	41	189	2	42	78	67	789	11.9	0.6	11.6
REG. SEASON TOTALS	531	185	10627	1481	2848	.520	1	11	.091	633	1129	.561	1243	1909	3152	227	1238	4	255	465	217	3596	5.9	0.4	6.8
PLAYOFF TOTALS	18	0	269	37	64	.578	0	0	—	9	21	.429	31	57	88	3	49	1	10	7	5	83	4.9	0.2	4.6

PONDEXTER, CLIFTON (Cliff) b. September 15, 1954   Ht. 6-9 Wt. 235 College—Long Beach State

SEASON—TEAM	G	GS	MIN	FGM	FGA	PCT	3FGM	3FGA	PCT	FTM	FTA	PCT	O-RB	D-RB	TOT	AST	PF	DQ	STL	TO	BLK	PTS	RPG	APG	PPG
75-76—Chicago	75	—	1326	156	380	.411	—	—	—	122	182	.670	113	268	381	90	134	4	28	—	26	434	5.1	1.2	5.8
76-77—Chicago	78	—	996	107	257	.416	—	—	—	42	65	.646	77	159	236	41	82	0	34	—	11	256	3.0	0.5	3.3
77-78—Chicago	44	—	534	37	85	.435	—	—	—	14	20	.700	36	94	130	87	66	0	19	30	15	88	3.0	2.0	2.0
REG. SEASON TOTALS	197	—	2856	300	722	.416	—	—	—	178	267	.667	226	521	747	218	282	4	81	30	52	778	3.8	1.1	3.9
PLAYOFF TOTALS	3	—	12	0	1	.000	—	—	—	2	2	1.000	0	3	3	1	0	0	0	—	0	2	1.0	0.3	0.7

POPE, DAVID b. April 15, 1962   Ht. 6-7 Wt. 220 College—Norfolk State

SEASON—TEAM	G	GS	MIN	FGM	FGA	PCT	3FGM	3FGA	PCT	FTM	FTA	PCT	O-RB	D-RB	TOT	AST	PF	DQ	STL	TO	BLK	PTS	RPG	APG	PPG
84-85—Kansas City	22	0	129	17	53	.321	0	1	.000	7	13	.538	9	9	18	5	30	0	3	7	3	41	0.8	0.2	1.9
85-86—Seattle	11	0	74	9	20	.450	1	1	1.000	2	4	.500	6	5	11	4	11	0	2	2	1	21	1.0	0.4	1.9
REG. SEASON TOTALS	33	0	203	26	73	.356	1	2	.500	9	17	.529	15	14	29	9	41	0	5	9	4	62	0.9	0.3	1.9

POPSON, DAVID G. (Dave) b. May 17, 1964   Ht. 6-10 Wt. 220 College—North Carolina

SEASON—TEAM	G	GS	MIN	FGM	FGA	PCT	3FGM	3FGA	PCT	FTM	FTA	PCT	O-RB	D-RB	TOT	AST	PF	DQ	STL	TO	BLK	PTS	RPG	APG	PPG
88-89—L.A. Clips-Miami	17	0	106	16	40	.400	0	0	—	2	4	.500	12	15	27	8	17	0	1	10	3	34	1.6	0.5	2.0
90-91—Boston	19	0	64	13	32	.406	0	0	—	9	10	.900	7	7	14	2	12	0	1	6	2	35	0.7	0.1	1.8
91-92—Milwaukee	5	0	26	3	7	.429	0	1	.000	1	2	.500	2	3	5	3	5	0	2	4	1	7	1.0	0.6	1.4
REG. SEASON TOTALS	41	0	196	32	79	.405	0	1	.000	12	16	.750	21	25	46	13	34	0	4	20	6	76	1.1	0.3	1.9

POQUETTE, BENEDICT JAY (Ben, Gentle Ben) b. May 7, 1955   Ht. 6-9 Wt. 235 College—Central Michigan

SEASON—TEAM	G	GS	MIN	FGM	FGA	PCT	3FGM	3FGA	PCT	FTM	FTA	PCT	O-RB	D-RB	TOT	AST	PF	DQ	STL	TO	BLK	PTS	RPG	APG	PPG
77-78—Detroit	52	—	626	95	225	.422	—	—	—	42	60	.700	50	95	145	20	69	1	10	40	22	232	2.8	0.4	4.5
78-79—Detroit	76	—	1337	198	464	.427	—	—	—	111	142	.782	99	237	336	57	198	4	38	65	98	507	4.4	0.8	6.7
79-80—Utah	82	—	2349	296	566	.523	0	2	.000	139	167	.832	124	436	560	131	283	8	45	103	162	731	6.8	1.6	8.9
80-81—Utah	82	—	2808	324	614	.528	3	6	.500	126	162	.778	160	469	629	161	342	18	67	122	174	777	7.7	2.0	9.5
81-82—Utah	82	56	1698	220	428	.514	3	10	.300	97	120	.808	117	294	411	94	235	4	51	69	65	540	5.0	1.1	6.6
82-83—Utah	75	50	2331	329	697	.472	1	5	.200	166	221	.751	155	366	521	168	264	5	64	100	116	825	6.9	2.2	11.0
83-84—Cleveland	51	4	858	75	171	.439	1	5	.200	34	43	.791	57	125	182	49	114	1	20	28	33	185	3.6	1.0	3.6
84-85—Cleveland	79	6	1656	210	457	.460	3	17	.176	109	137	.796	148	325	473	79	220	3	47	70	58	532	6.0	1.0	6.7
85-86—Cleveland	81	3	1496	166	348	.477	2	10	.200	72	100	.720	121	252	373	78	187	2	33	68	32	406	4.6	1.0	5.0
86-87—Clev.-Chicago	58	2	604	62	122	.508	0	4	.000	40	50	.800	30	71	101	35	77	1	9	21	34	164	1.7	0.6	2.8
REG. SEASON TOTALS	718	121	15763	1975	4092	.483	13	59	.220	936	1202	.779	1061	2670	3731	872	1989	47	384	686	794	4899	5.2	1.2	6.8
PLAYOFF TOTALS	4	0	91	13	21	.619	0	0	—	4	5	.800	4	10	14	1	16	2	2	4	6	30	3.5	0.3	7.5

PORTER, HOWARD (Geezer) b. August 31, 1948   Ht. 6-8 Wt. 220 College—Villanova

SEASON—TEAM	G	GS	MIN	FGM	FGA	PCT	3FGM	3FGA	PCT	FTM	FTA	PCT	O-RB	D-RB	TOT	AST	PF	DQ	STL	TO	BLK	PTS	RPG	APG	PPG
71-72—Chicago	67	—	730	171	403	.424	—	—	—	59	77	.766	—	—	183	24	88	0	—	—	—	401	2.7	0.4	6.0
72-73—Chicago	43	—	407	98	217	.452	—	—	—	22	29	.759	—	—	118	16	52	1	—	—	—	218	2.7	0.4	5.1
73-74—Chicago	73	—	1229	296	658	.450	—	—	—	92	115	.800	86	199	285	32	116	0	23	—	39	684	3.9	0.4	9.4
74-75—N.Y.-Detroit	58	—	1163	201	412	.488	—	—	—	66	79	.835	79	175	254	19	93	0	23	—	26	468	4.4	0.3	8.1
75-76—Detroit	75	—	1482	298	635	.469	—	—	—	73	97	.753	81	214	295	25	133	0	31	—	36	669	3.9	0.3	8.9
76-77—Detroit	78	—	2200	465	962	.483	—	—	—	103	120	.858	155	303	458	53	202	0	50	—	73	1033	5.9	0.7	13.2
77-78—Detroit-N.J.	63	—	1323	309	635	.487	—	—	—	124	155	.800	100	179	279	42	134	0	29	55	38	742	4.4	0.7	11.8
REG. SEASON TOTALS	457	—	8534	1838	3922	.469	—	—	—	539	672	.802	501	1070	1872	211	818	1	156	55	212	4215	4.1	0.5	9.2
PLAYOFF TOTALS	36	—	663	151	329	.459	—	—	—	33	39	.846	51	72	152	18	59	0	18	—	15	335	4.2	0.5	9.3

PORTER, KEVIN b. April 17, 1950 Ht. 6-0 Wt. 175 College—St. Francis (Pa.)

SEASON—TEAM	G	GS	MIN	FGM	FGA	PCT	3FGM	3FGA	PCT	FTM	FTA	PCT	O-RB	D-RB	TOT	AST	PF	DQ	STL	TO	BLK	PTS	RPG	APG	PPG
72-73—Baltimore	71	—	1217	205	451	.455	—	—	—	62	101	.614	—	—	72	237	206	5	—	—	—	472	1.0	3.3	6.6
73-74—Capital	81	—	2339	477	997	.478	—	—	—	180	249	.723	79	100	179	469	319	14	95	—	9	1134	2.2	5.8	14.0
74-75—Washington	81	—	2589	406	827	.491	—	—	—	131	186	.704	55	97	152	650	320	12	152	—	11	943	1.9	8.0	11.6
75-76—Detroit	19	—	687	99	235	.421	—	—	—	42	56	.750	14	30	44	193	83	3	35	—	3	240	2.3	10.2	12.6
76-77—Detroit	81	—	2117	310	605	.512	—	—	—	97	133	.729	28	70	98	592	271	8	88	—	8	717	1.2	7.3	8.9
77-78—Detroit-N.J.	82	—	2813	495	1055	.469	—	—	—	244	320	.763	53	161	214	837	283	6	123	360	15	1234	2.6	10.2	15.0
78-79—Detroit	82	—	3064	534	1110	.481	—	—	—	192	266	.722	62	147	209	1099	302	5	158	337	5	1260	2.5	13.4	15.4
79-80—Washington	70	—	1494	201	438	.459	0	4	.000	110	137	.803	25	57	82	457	180	1	59	164	11	512	1.2	6.5	7.3
80-81—Washington	81	—	2577	446	859	.519	3	12	.250	191	247	.773	35	89	124	734	257	4	110	251	10	1086	1.5	9.1	13.4
82-83—Washington	11	0	210	21	40	.525	0	0	—	5	6	.833	2	3	5	46	30	0	10	21	0	47	0.5	4.2	4.3
REG. SEASON TOTALS	659	0	19107	3194	6617	.483	3	16	.188	1254	1701	.737	353	754	1179	5314	2251	58	830	1133	72	7645	1.8	8.1	11.6
PLAYOFF TOTALS	33	0	971	150	324	.463	0	1	.000	63	97	.649	26	40	68	191	128	5	33	4	0	363	2.1	5.8	11.0

PORTER, TERRY b. April 8, 1963 Ht. 6-3 Wt. 195 College—Wisconsin-Stevens Point

SEASON—TEAM	G	GS	MIN	FGM	FGA	PCT	3FGM	3FGA	PCT	FTM	FTA	PCT	O-RB	D-RB	TOT	AST	PF	DQ	STL	TO	BLK	PTS	RPG	APG	PPG
85-86—Portland	79	3	1214	212	447	.474	13	42	.310	125	155	.806	35	82	117	198	136	0	81	106	1	562	1.5	2.5	7.1
86-87—Portland	80	80	2714	376	770	.488	13	60	.217	280	334	.838	70	267	337	715	192	0	159	255	9	1045	4.2	8.9	13.1
87-88—Portland	82	82	2991	462	890	.519	24	69	.348	274	324	.846	65	313	378	831	204	1	150	244	16	1222	4.6	10.1	14.9
88-89—Portland	81	81	3102	540	1146	.471	79	219	.361	272	324	.840	85	282	367	770	187	1	146	248	8	1431	4.5	9.5	17.7
89-90—Portland	80	80	2781	448	969	.462	89	238	.374	421	472	.892	59	213	272	726	150	0	151	245	4	1406	3.4	9.1	17.6
90-91—Portland	81	81	2665	486	944	.515	130	313	.415	279	339	.823	52	230	282	649	151	2	158	189	12	1381	3.5	8.0	17.0
91-92—Portland	82	82	2784	521	1129	.461	128	324	.395	315	368	.856	51	204	255	477	155	1	127	188	12	1485	3.1	5.8	18.1
92-93—Portland	81	81	2883	503	1108	.454	143	345	.414	327	388	.843	58	258	316	419	122	0	101	199	10	1476	3.9	5.2	18.2
93-94—Portland	77	34	2074	348	836	.416	110	282	.390	204	234	.872	45	170	215	401	132	0	79	166	18	1010	2.8	5.2	13.1
REG. SEASON TOTALS	723	604	23208	3896	8239	.473	729	1892	.385	2497	2938	.850	520	2019	2539	5186	1429	5	1152	1840	90	11018	3.5	7.2	15.2
PLAYOFF TOTALS	81	73	2999	506	1047	.483	111	285	.389	385	461	.835	59	229	288	523	190	1	106	187	12	1508	3.6	6.5	18.6
ALL-STAR TOTALS	2	0	34	5	14	.357	1	7	.143	0	0	—	1	2	3	7	3	0	3	4	1	11	1.5	3.5	5.5

PORTER, WILLIE WILLIAM b. July 3, 1942 Ht. 6-7 Wt. 205 College—Tennessee State

SEASON—TEAM	G	GS	MIN	FGM	FGA	PCT	3FGM	3FGA	PCT	FTM	FTA	PCT	O-RB	D-RB	TOT	AST	PF	DQ	STL	TO	BLK	PTS	RPG	APG	PPG
67-68—Oakland-Pitt. (A)	56	—	1294	225	546	.412	0	0	—	199	294	.677	—	—	449	59	190	11	—	155	—	649	8.0	1.1	11.6
68-69—Minn.-Houston (A)	13	—	148	28	52	.538	0	0	—	17	31	.548	—	—	55	6	23	0	—	11	—	73	4.2	0.5	5.6
REG. ABA TOTALS	69	—	1442	253	598	.423	0	0	—	216	325	.665	—	—	504	65	213	11	—	166	—	722	7.3	0.9	10.5
ABA PLAYOFF TOTALS	14	—	167	19	43	.442	0	0	—	20	29	.690	—	—	69	6	43	0	—	18	—	58	4.9	0.4	4.1

PORTMAN, ROBERT M. (Bob) b. March 22, 1947 Ht. 6-5 Wt. 200 College—Creighton

SEASON—TEAM	G	GS	MIN	FGM	FGA	PCT	3FGM	3FGA	PCT	FTM	FTA	PCT	O-RB	D-RB	TOT	AST	PF	DQ	STL	TO	BLK	PTS	RPG	APG	PPG
69-70—San Francisco	60	—	813	177	398	.445	—	—	—	66	85	.776	—	—	224	28	77	0	—	—	—	420	3.7	0.5	7.0
70-71—San Francisco	68	—	1395	221	483	.458	—	—	—	77	106	.726	—	—	321	67	130	0	—	—	—	519	4.7	1.0	7.6
71-72—Golden State	61	—	553	89	221	.403	—	—	—	53	60	.883	—	—	133	26	69	0	—	—	—	231	2.2	0.4	3.8
72-73—Golden State	32	—	176	32	70	.457	—	—	—	20	26	.769	—	—	51	7	16	0	—	—	—	84	1.6	0.2	2.6
REG. SEASON TOTALS	221	—	2937	519	1172	.443	—	—	—	216	277	.780	—	—	729	128	292	0	—	—	—	1254	3.3	0.6	5.7
PLAYOFF TOTALS	11	—	149	24	61	.393	—	—	—	11	14	.786	—	—	30	3	14	0	—	—	—	59	2.7	0.3	5.4

POSTLEY, JOHN b. May 30, 1940 d. July 1970 Ht. 6-5 Wt. 220 College—Bethune-Cookman

SEASON—TEAM	G	GS	MIN	FGM	FGA	PCT	3FGM	3FGA	PCT	FTM	FTA	PCT	O-RB	D-RB	TOT	AST	PF	DQ	STL	TO	BLK	PTS	RPG	APG	PPG
67-68—Pittsburgh (A)	1	—	6	1	3	.333	0	0	—	0	0	—	—	—	6	1	1	0	—	1	—	2	6.0	1.0	2.0
REG. ABA TOTALS	1	—	6	1	3	.333	0	0	—	0	0	—	—	—	6	1	1	0	—	1	—	2	6.0	1.0	2.0

POWELL, CINCINNATUS (Cincy) b. February 25, 1942 Ht. 6-7 Wt. 225 College—Portland/Xavier (La.)

SEASON—TEAM	G	GS	MIN	FGM	FGA	PCT	3FGM	3FGA	PCT	FTM	FTA	PCT	O-RB	D-RB	TOT	AST	PF	DQ	STL	TO	BLK	PTS	RPG	APG	PPG
67-68—Dallas (A)	77	—	2524	533	1089	.489	1	4	.250	343	496	.692	—	—	694	106	254	7	—	190	—	1410	9.0	1.4	18.3
68-69—Dallas (A)	75	—	2573	555	1179	.471	2	7	.286	342	470	.728	—	—	671	173	275	5	—	212	—	1454	8.9	2.3	19.4
69-70—Dallas (A)	76	—	2624	562	1200	.468	2	12	.167	402	519	.775	—	—	682	192	250	6	—	—	—	1528	9.0	2.5	20.1
70-71—Kentucky (A)	81	—	2933	578	1173	.493	4	16	.250	302	398	.759	311	579	890	255	323	—	—	—	—	1462	11.0	3.1	18.0
71-72—Kentucky (A)	65	—	2288	430	907	.474	4	13	.308	185	256	.723	—	—	500	237	219	—	—	178	—	1049	7.7	3.6	16.1
72-73—Utah (A)	83	—	1985	423	853	.496	3	13	.231	167	240	.696	135	285	420	137	249	7	—	137	—	1016	5.1	1.7	12.2
73-74—Virginia (A)	82	—	2485	528	1167	.452	10	31	.323	209	296	.706	171	348	519	136	270	—	46	186	32	1275	6.3	1.7	15.5
74-75—Virginia (A)	60	—	1224	214	530	.404	5	17	.294	119	180	.661	74	132	206	94	138	—	27	91	8	552	3.4	1.6	9.2
REG. ABA TOTALS	599	—	18636	3823	8098	.472	31	113	.274	2069	2855	.725	691	1344	4582	1330	1978	25	73	994	40	9746	7.6	2.2	16.3
ABA PLAYOFF TOTALS	61	—	2020	412	989	.417	5	18	.278	242	321	.754	119	258	593	123	224	0	3	97	1	1071	9.7	2.0	17.6
ABA ALL-STAR TOTALS	2	—	47	9	15	.600	0	0	—	5	5	1.000	3	7	17	0	3	0	0	2	0	23	8.5	0.0	11.5

PRADD, MARLBERT (**Marl**) b. November 17, 1944 Ht. 6-3 Wt. 170 College—Dillard

SEASON—TEAM	G	GS	MIN	FGM	FGA	PCT	3FGM	3FGA	PCT	FTM	FTA	PCT	O-RB	D-RB	TOT	AST	PF	DQ	STL	TO	BLK	PTS	RPG	APG	PPG
67-68—New Orleans (A)	29	—	125	27	60	.450	0	0	—	20	27	.741	—	—	26	3	22	0	—	18	—	74	0.9	0.1	2.6
68-69—New Orleans (A)	50	—	323	81	186	.435	3	13	.231	93	119	.782	—	—	50	23	60	0	—	34	—	258	1.0	0.5	5.2
REG. ABA TOTALS	79	—	448	108	246	.439	3	13	.231	113	146	.774	—	—	76	26	82	0	—	52	—	332	1.0	0.3	4.2
ABA PLAYOFF TOTALS	13	—	57	13	31	.419	4	6	.667	10	18	.556	—	—	9	1	10	0	—	7	—	40	0.7	0.1	3.1

PRATT, MICHAEL P. (**Mike**) b. August 4, 1948 Ht. 6-4 Wt. 205 College—Kentucky

SEASON—TEAM	G	GS	MIN	FGM	FGA	PCT	3FGM	3FGA	PCT	FTM	FTA	PCT	O-RB	D-RB	TOT	AST	PF	DQ	STL	TO	BLK	PTS	RPG	APG	PPG
70-71—Kentucky (A)	78	—	1213	173	416	.416	3	11	.273	91	121	.752	—	—	225	188	135	—	—	—	—	440	2.9	2.4	5.6
71-72—Kentucky (A)	65	—	889	133	301	.442	16	40	.400	84	98	.857	—	—	158	98	151	—	—	81	—	366	2.4	1.5	5.6
REG. ABA TOTALS	143	—	2102	306	717	.427	19	51	.373	175	219	.799	—	—	383	286	286	—	—	81	—	806	2.7	2.0	5.6
ABA PLAYOFF TOTALS	25	—	488	80	187	.428	1	6	.167	42	52	.808	—	—	83	68	53	—	—	11	—	203	3.3	2.7	8.1

PRESSEY, PAUL MATTHEW b. December 24, 1958 Ht. 6-5 Wt. 205 College—Western Texas/Tulsa

SEASON—TEAM	G	GS	MIN	FGM	FGA	PCT	3FGM	3FGA	PCT	FTM	FTA	PCT	O-RB	D-RB	TOT	AST	PF	DQ	STL	TO	BLK	PTS	RPG	APG	PPG
82-83—Milwaukee	79	18	1528	213	466	.457	1	9	.111	105	176	.597	83	198	281	207	174	2	99	162	47	532	3.6	2.6	6.7
83-84—Milwaukee	81	18	1730	276	528	.523	2	9	.222	120	200	.600	102	180	282	252	241	6	86	157	50	674	3.5	3.1	8.3
84-85—Milwaukee	80	80	2876	480	928	.517	7	20	.350	317	418	.758	149	280	429	543	258	4	129	247	56	1284	5.4	6.8	16.1
85-86—Milwaukee	80	80	2704	411	843	.488	8	44	.182	316	392	.806	127	272	399	623	247	4	168	240	71	1146	5.0	7.8	14.3
86-87—Milwaukee	61	60	2057	294	616	.477	16	55	.291	242	328	.738	98	198	296	441	213	4	110	186	47	846	4.9	7.2	13.9
87-88—Milwaukee	75	75	2484	345	702	.491	8	39	.205	285	357	.798	130	245	375	523	233	6	112	198	34	983	5.0	7.0	13.1
88-89—Milwaukee	67	62	2170	307	648	.474	12	55	.218	187	241	.776	73	189	262	439	221	2	119	184	44	813	3.9	6.6	12.1
89-90—Milwaukee	57	2	1400	239	506	.472	6	43	.140	144	190	.758	59	113	172	244	149	3	71	109	23	628	3.0	4.3	11.0
90-91—San Antonio	70	18	1683	201	426	.472	16	57	.281	110	133	.827	50	126	176	271	174	1	63	130	32	528	2.5	3.9	7.5
91-92—San Antonio	56	7	759	60	161	.373	3	21	.143	28	41	.683	22	73	95	142	86	0	29	64	19	151	1.7	2.5	2.7
92-93—Golden State	18	0	268	29	66	.439	0	4	.000	21	27	.778	8	23	31	30	36	0	11	23	5	79	1.7	1.7	4.4
REG. SEASON TOTALS	724	420	19659	2855	5890	.485	79	356	.222	1875	2503	.749	901	1897	2798	3715	2032	32	997	1700	428	7664	3.9	5.1	10.6
PLAYOFF TOTALS	75	50	2269	321	682	.471	11	45	.244	228	313	.728	113	203	316	420	261	6	116	207	49	881	4.2	5.6	11.7

PRESSLEY, DOMINIC IVAN b. May 30, 1964 Ht. 6-2 Wt. 175 College—Boston College

SEASON—TEAM	G	GS	MIN	FGM	FGA	PCT	3FGM	3FGA	PCT	FTM	FTA	PCT	O-RB	D-RB	TOT	AST	PF	DQ	STL	TO	BLK	PTS	RPG	APG	PPG
88-89—Wash.-Chicago	13	0	124	9	31	.290	0	2	.000	5	9	.556	3	12	15	26	11	0	4	11	0	23	1.2	2.0	1.8
REG. SEASON TOTALS	13	0	124	9	31	.290	0	2	.000	5	9	.556	3	12	15	26	11	0	4	11	0	23	1.2	2.0	1.8

PRESSLEY, HAROLD b. July 14, 1963 Ht. 6-8 Wt. 210 College—Villanova

SEASON—TEAM	G	GS	MIN	FGM	FGA	PCT	3FGM	3FGA	PCT	FTM	FTA	PCT	O-RB	D-RB	TOT	AST	PF	DQ	STL	TO	BLK	PTS	RPG	APG	PPG
86-87—Sacramento	67	23	913	134	317	.423	7	28	.250	35	48	.729	68	108	176	120	96	1	40	63	21	310	2.6	1.8	4.6
87-88—Sacramento	80	49	2029	318	702	.453	36	110	.327	103	130	.792	139	230	369	185	211	4	84	135	55	775	4.6	2.3	9.7
88-89—Sacramento	80	36	2257	383	873	.439	119	295	.403	96	123	.780	216	269	485	174	215	1	93	124	76	981	6.1	2.2	12.3
89-90—Sacramento	72	10	1603	240	566	.424	46	148	.311	110	141	.780	94	215	309	149	148	0	58	88	36	636	4.3	2.1	8.8
REG. SEASON TOTALS	299	118	6802	1075	2458	.437	208	581	.358	344	442	.778	517	822	1339	628	670	6	275	410	188	2702	4.5	2.1	9.0

PREVIS, STEPHEN RICHARD (**Steve**) b. February 9, 1950 Ht. 6-2½ Wt. 185 College—North Carolina

SEASON—TEAM	G	GS	MIN	FGM	FGA	PCT	3FGM	3FGA	PCT	FTM	FTA	PCT	O-RB	D-RB	TOT	AST	PF	DQ	STL	TO	BLK	PTS	RPG	APG	PPG
72-73—Carolina (A)	30	—	147	23	60	.383	1	8	.125	8	15	.533	6	8	14	24	26	0	—	13	—	55	0.5	0.8	1.8
REG. ABA TOTALS	30	—	147	23	60	.383	1	8	.125	8	15	.533	6	8	14	24	26	0	—	13	—	55	0.5	0.8	1.8
ABA PLAYOFF TOTALS	2	—	11	1	7	.143	1	2	.500	0	0	—	—	—	—	3	3	2	0	—	4	—	3	1.5	1.5	1.5

PRICE, ANTHONY (**Tony**) b. January 5, 1957 Ht. 6-6½ Wt. 200 College—Pennsylvania

SEASON—TEAM	G	GS	MIN	FGM	FGA	PCT	3FGM	3FGA	PCT	FTM	FTA	PCT	O-RB	D-RB	TOT	AST	PF	DQ	STL	TO	BLK	PTS	RPG	APG	PPG
80-81—San Diego	5	—	29	2	7	.286	0	0	—	0	0	—	0	0	0	3	3	0	2	2	1	4	0.0	0.6	0.8
REG. SEASON TOTALS	5	—	29	2	7	.286	0	0	—	0	0	—	0	0	0	3	3	0	2	2	1	4	0.0	0.6	0.8

PRICE, HARTLEY BRENT (**Brent**) b. December 9, 1968 Ht. 6-1 Wt. 175 College—South Carolina/Oklahoma

SEASON—TEAM	G	GS	MIN	FGM	FGA	PCT	3FGM	3FGA	PCT	FTM	FTA	PCT	O-RB	D-RB	TOT	AST	PF	DQ	STL	TO	BLK	PTS	RPG	APG	PPG
92-93—Washington	68	9	859	100	279	.358	8	48	.167	54	68	.794	28	75	103	154	90	0	56	85	3	262	1.5	2.3	3.9
93-94—Washington	65	13	1035	141	326	.433	50	150	.333	68	87	.782	31	59	90	213	114	1	55	119	2	400	1.4	3.3	6.2
REG. SEASON TOTALS	133	22	1894	241	605	.398	58	198	.293	122	155	.787	59	134	193	367	204	1	111	204	5	662	1.5	2.8	5.0

PRICE, JAMES E. (Jim) b. November 27, 1949 Ht. 6-2½ Wt. 195 College—Louisville

SEASON—TEAM	G	GS	MIN	FGM	FGA	PCT	3FGM	3FGA	PCT	FTM	FTA	PCT	O-RB	D-RB	TOT	AST	PF	DQ	STL	TO	BLK	PTS	RPG	APG	PPG
72-73—Los Angeles	59	—	828	158	359	.440	—	—	—	60	73	.822	—	—	115	97	119	1	—	—	—	376	1.9	1.6	6.4
73-74—Los Angeles	82	—	2628	538	1197	.449	—	—	—	187	234	.799	120	258	378	369	229	2	157	—	29	1263	4.6	4.5	15.4
74-75—L.A.-Milw.	50	—	1870	317	717	.442	—	—	—	169	194	.871	62	136	198	286	182	1	111	—	24	803	4.0	5.7	16.1
75-76—Milwaukee	80	—	2525	398	958	.415	—	—	—	141	166	.849	74	187	261	395	264	3	148	—	32	937	3.3	4.9	11.7
76-77—Milw.-Buffalo-Denver	81	—	1828	253	567	.446	—	—	—	83	103	.806	50	181	231	261	247	3	128	—	20	589	2.9	3.2	7.3
77-78—Denver-Detroit	83	—	1929	294	656	.448	—	—	—	135	169	.799	57	203	260	260	200	0	114	175	9	723	3.1	3.1	8.7
78-79—Los Angeles	75	—	1207	171	344	.497	—	—	—	55	79	.696	26	97	123	218	128	0	66	100	12	397	1.6	2.9	5.3
REG. SEASON TOTALS	510	—	12815	2129	4798	.444	—	—	—	830	1018	.815	389	1062	1566	1886	1369	10	724	275	126	5088	3.1	3.7	10.0
PLAYOFF TOTALS	23	—	482	59	168	.351	—	—	—	20	32	.625	15	36	55	62	61	1	25	8	1	138	2.4	2.7	6.0
ALL-STAR TOTALS	1	—	17	3	9	.333	—	—	—	2	2	1.000	0	2	2	0	4	0	2	—	0	8	2.0	0.0	8.0

PRICE, MICHAEL (Mike) b. September 11, 1948 Ht. 6-3½ Wt. 200 College—Illinois

SEASON—TEAM	G	GS	MIN	FGM	FGA	PCT	3FGM	3FGA	PCT	FTM	FTA	PCT	O-RB	D-RB	TOT	AST	PF	DQ	STL	TO	BLK	PTS	RPG	APG	PPG
70-71—New York	56	—	251	30	81	.370	—	—	—	24	34	.706	—	—	29	12	57	0	—	—	—	84	0.5	0.2	1.5
71-72—New York	6	—	40	5	14	.357	—	—	—	9	11	.818	—	—	6	6	10	0	—	—	—	19	1.0	1.0	3.2
71-72—Indiana (A)	4	—	25	3	9	.333	0	0	—	0	0	—	—	—	5	1	4	—	4	—	—	6	1.3	0.3	1.5
72-73—Philadelphia	57	—	751	125	301	.415	—	—	—	38	47	.809	—	—	117	71	106	—	—	—	—	288	2.1	1.2	5.1
REG. NBA TOTALS	119	—	1042	160	396	.404	—	—	—	71	92	.772	—	—	152	89	173	0	—	—	—	391	1.3	0.7	3.3
REG. ABA TOTALS	4	—	25	3	9	.333	0	0	—	0	0	—	—	—	5	1	4	—	4	—	—	6	1.3	0.3	1.5
NBA PLAYOFF TOTALS	8	—	26	4	11	.364	—	—	—	4	6	.667	—	—	5	5	11	0	—	—	—	12	0.6	0.6	1.5

PRICE, WILLIAM MARK (Mark) b. February 15, 1964 Ht. 6-0 Wt. 175 College—Georgia Tech

SEASON—TEAM	G	GS	MIN	FGM	FGA	PCT	3FGM	3FGA	PCT	FTM	FTA	PCT	O-RB	D-RB	TOT	AST	PF	DQ	STL	TO	BLK	PTS	RPG	APG	PPG
86-87—Cleveland	67	0	1217	173	424	.408	23	70	.329	95	114	.833	33	84	117	202	75	1	43	105	4	464	1.7	3.0	6.9
87-88—Cleveland	80	79	2626	493	974	.506	72	148	.486	221	252	.877	54	126	180	480	119	1	99	184	12	1279	2.3	6.0	16.0
88-89—Cleveland	75	74	2728	529	1006	.526	93	211	.441	263	292	.901	48	178	226	631	98	0	115	212	7	1414	3.0	8.4	18.9
89-90—Cleveland	73	73	2706	489	1066	.459	152	374	.406	300	338	.888	66	185	251	666	89	0	114	214	5	1430	3.4	9.1	19.6
90-91—Cleveland	16	16	571	97	195	.497	18	53	.340	59	62	.952	8	37	45	166	23	0	42	56	2	271	2.8	10.4	16.9
91-92—Cleveland	72	72	2138	438	897	.488	101	261	.387	270	285	.947	38	135	173	535	113	0	94	159	12	1247	2.4	7.4	17.3
92-93—Cleveland	75	74	2380	477	986	.484	122	293	.416	289	305	.948	37	164	201	602	105	0	89	196	11	1365	2.7	8.0	18.2
93-94—Cleveland	76	73	2386	480	1005	.478	118	297	.397	238	268	.888	39	189	228	589	93	0	103	189	11	1316	3.0	7.8	17.3
REG. SEASON TOTALS	534	461	16752	3176	6553	.485	699	1707	.409	1735	1916	.906	323	1098	1421	3871	715	2	699	1315	64	8786	2.7	7.2	16.5
PLAYOFF TOTALS	43	43	1548	268	563	.476	52	149	.349	170	181	.939	19	93	112	301	76	1	58	140	5	758	2.6	7.0	17.6
ALL-STAR TOTALS	4	0	80	18	35	.514	9	19	.474	9	10	.900	1	5	6	13	9	0	5	8	1	54	1.5	3.3	13.5

PRIDDY, ROBERT B. (Bob) b. March 24, 1930 Ht. 6-3 Wt. 190 College—New Mexico State

SEASON—TEAM	G	GS	MIN	FGM	FGA	PCT	3FGM	3FGA	PCT	FTM	FTA	PCT	O-RB	D-RB	TOT	AST	PF	DQ	STL	TO	BLK	PTS	RPG	APG	PPG
52-53—Baltimore	16	—	149	14	38	.368	—	—	—	8	14	.571	—	—	36	7	36	3	—	—	—	36	2.3	0.4	2.3
REG. SEASON TOTALS	16	—	149	14	38	.368	—	—	—	8	14	.571	—	—	36	7	36	3	—	—	—	36	2.3	0.4	2.3
PLAYOFF TOTALS	1	—	1	0	0	—	—	—	—	0	0	—	—	—	0	—	1	0	—	—	—	0	0.0	0.0	0.0

PRITCHARD, JOHN D. b. January 23, 1927 Ht. 6-9 Wt. 220 College—Drake

SEASON—TEAM	G	GS	MIN	FGM	FGA	PCT	3FGM	3FGA	PCT	FTM	FTA	PCT	O-RB	D-RB	TOT	AST	PF	DQ	STL	TO	BLK	PTS	RPG	APG	PPG
49-50—Waterloo	7	—	—	9	29	.310	—	—	—	4	11	.364	—	—	8	14	—	—	—	—	—	22	—	1.1	3.1
REG. SEASON TOTALS	7	—	—	9	29	.310	—	—	—	4	11	.364	—	—	8	14	—	—	—	—	—	22	—	1.1	3.1

PRITCHARD, KEVIN LEE b. July 17, 1967 Ht. 6-3 Wt. 180 College—Kansas

SEASON—TEAM	G	GS	MIN	FGM	FGA	PCT	3FGM	3FGA	PCT	FTM	FTA	PCT	O-RB	D-RB	TOT	AST	PF	DQ	STL	TO	BLK	PTS	RPG	APG	PPG
90-91—Golden State	62	1	773	88	229	.384	5	31	.161	62	77	.805	16	49	65	81	104	1	30	59	8	243	1.0	1.3	3.9
91-92—Boston	11	0	136	16	34	.471	0	3	.000	14	18	.778	1	10	11	30	17	0	3	11	4	46	1.0	2.7	4.2
REG. SEASON TOTALS	73	1	909	104	263	.395	5	34	.147	76	95	.800	17	59	76	111	121	1	33	70	12	289	1.0	1.5	4.0

PUGH, LESLIE (Les) b. September 18, 1923 Ht. 6-7 Wt. 195 College—Ohio State

SEASON—TEAM	G	GS	MIN	FGM	FGA	PCT	3FGM	3FGA	PCT	FTM	FTA	PCT	O-RB	D-RB	TOT	AST	PF	DQ	STL	TO	BLK	PTS	RPG	APG	PPG
48-49—Providence	60	—	—	168	556	.302	—	—	—	125	167	.749	—	—	—	59	168	—	—	—	—	461	—	1.0	7.7
49-50—Baltimore	56	—	—	68	273	.249	—	—	—	115	136	.846	—	—	—	16	118	—	—	—	—	251	—	0.3	4.5
REG. SEASON TOTALS	116	—	—	236	829	.285	—	—	—	240	303	.792	—	—	—	75	286	—	—	—	—	712	—	0.6	6.1

PUGH, ROY b. 1923 Ht. 6-6 Wt. 210 College—Southern Methodist

SEASON—TEAM	G	GS	MIN	FGM	FGA	PCT	3FGM	3FGA	PCT	FTM	FTA	PCT	O-RB	D-RB	TOT	AST	PF	DQ	STL	TO	BLK	PTS	RPG	APG	PPG
47-48—Indianapolis (N)	4	—	—	1	—	—	—	—	—	2	4	.500	—	—	—	—	—	—	—	—	—	4	—	—	1.0
48-49—Ft. Wayne-Ind.-Phil.	23	—	—	13	51	.255	—	—	—	6	19	.316	—	—	—	9	17	—	—	—	—	32	—	0.4	1.4
REG. NBA TOTALS	23	—	—	13	51	.255	—	—	—	6	19	.316	—	—	—	9	17	—	—	—	—	32	—	0.4	1.4
REG. NBL TOTALS	4	—	—	1	—	—	—	—	—	2	4	.500	—	—	—	—	—	—	—	—	—	4	—	—	1.0

PULLARD, ANTHONY QUINN b. June 23, 1966 Ht. 6-10 Wt. 245 College—Oklahoma/McNeese State

SEASON—TEAM	G	GS	MIN	FGM	FGA	PCT	3FGM	3FGA	PCT	FTM	FTA	PCT	O-RB	D-RB	TOT	AST	PF	DQ	STL	TO	BLK	PTS	RPG	APG	PPG
92-93—Milwaukee	8	0	37	8	18	.444	0	0	—	1	3	.333	2	6	8	2	5	0	2	5	2	17	1.0	0.3	2.1
REG. SEASON TOTALS	8	0	37	8	18	.444	0	0	—	1	3	.333	2	6	8	2	5	0	2	5	2	17	1.0	0.3	2.1

PUTMAN, JAMES DONALD (**Don**) b. November 13, 1922 Ht. 6-1 Wt. 170 College—Colorado/Denver

SEASON—TEAM	G	GS	MIN	FGM	FGA	PCT	3FGM	3FGA	PCT	FTM	FTA	PCT	O-RB	D-RB	TOT	AST	PF	DQ	STL	TO	BLK	PTS	RPG	APG	PPG
46-47—St. Louis	58	—	—	156	635	.246	—	—	—	68	105	.648	—	—	—	30	106	—	—	—	—	380	—	0.5	6.6
47-48—St. Louis	42	—	—	105	399	.263	—	—	—	57	84	.679	—	—	—	25	95	—	—	—	—	267	—	0.6	6.4
48-49—St. Louis	59	—	—	98	330	.297	—	—	—	52	97	.536	—	—	—	140	132	—	—	—	—	248	—	2.4	4.2
49-50—St. Louis	57	—	—	51	200	.255	—	—	—	33	52	.635	—	—	—	90	116	—	—	—	—	135	—	1.6	2.4
REG. SEASON TOTALS	216	—	—	410	1564	.262	—	—	—	210	338	.621	—	—	—	285	449	—	—	—	—	1030	—	1.3	4.8
PLAYOFF TOTALS	12	—	—	17	79	.215	—	—	—	8	19	.421	—	—	—	10	28	1	—	—	—	42	—	0.8	3.5

QUICK, ROBERT L. (**Bob**) b. March 5, 1946 Ht. 6-5 Wt. 215 College—Xavier (Ohio)

SEASON—TEAM	G	GS	MIN	FGM	FGA	PCT	3FGM	3FGA	PCT	FTM	FTA	PCT	O-RB	D-RB	TOT	AST	PF	DQ	STL	TO	BLK	PTS	RPG	APG	PPG
68-69—Baltimore	28	—	154	30	73	.411	—	—	—	27	44	.614	—	—	25	12	14	0	—	—	—	87	0.9	0.4	3.1
69-70—Balt.-Detroit	34	—	364	63	139	.453	—	—	—	49	71	.690	—	—	75	14	50	0	—	—	—	175	2.2	0.4	5.1
70-71—Detroit	56	—	1146	155	341	.455	—	—	—	138	176	.784	—	—	230	56	142	1	—	—	—	448	4.1	1.0	8.0
71-72—Detroit	18	—	204	39	82	.476	—	—	—	34	45	.756	—	—	51	11	29	0	—	—	—	112	2.8	0.6	6.2
71-72—Dallas (A)	6	—	57	8	15	.533	0	0	—	10	10	1.000	—	—	14	1	9	—	—	4	—	26	2.3	0.2	4.3
REG. NBA TOTALS	136	—	1868	287	635	.452	—	—	—	248	336	.738	—	—	381	93	235	1	—	—	—	822	2.8	0.7	6.0
REG. ABA TOTALS	6	—	57	8	15	.533	0	0	—	10	10	1.000	—	—	14	1	9	—	—	4	—	26	2.3	0.2	4.3
NBA PLAYOFF TOTALS	2	—	9	2	3	.667	—	—	—	0	2	.000	—	—	1	—	1	0	—	—	—	4	0.5	0.0	2.0

QUINNETT, BRIAN RALPH b. May 30, 1966 Ht. 6-8 Wt. 235 College—Washington State

SEASON—TEAM	G	GS	MIN	FGM	FGA	PCT	3FGM	3FGA	PCT	FTM	FTA	PCT	O-RB	D-RB	TOT	AST	PF	DQ	STL	TO	BLK	PTS	RPG	APG	PPG
89-90—New York	31	0	193	19	58	.328	0	2	.000	2	3	.667	9	19	28	11	27	0	3	4	4	40	0.9	0.4	1.3
90-91—New York	68	5	1011	139	303	.459	15	43	.349	26	36	.722	65	80	145	53	100	0	22	52	13	319	2.1	0.8	4.7
91-92—N.Y.-Dallas	39	0	326	43	124	.347	13	41	.317	16	26	.615	16	35	51	12	32	0	16	16	8	115	1.3	0.3	2.9
REG. SEASON TOTALS	138	5	1530	201	485	.414	28	86	.326	44	65	.677	90	134	224	76	159	0	41	72	25	474	1.6	0.6	3.4
PLAYOFF TOTALS	6	0	52	6	12	.500	2	4	.500	0	0	—	5	4	9	5	4	0	1	3	0	14	1.5	0.8	2.3

RACKLEY, LUTHER JR. (**Luke**) b. June 11, 1946 Ht. 6-10 Wt. 220 College—Xavier (Ohio)

SEASON—TEAM	G	GS	MIN	FGM	FGA	PCT	3FGM	3FGA	PCT	FTM	FTA	PCT	O-RB	D-RB	TOT	AST	PF	DQ	STL	TO	BLK	PTS	RPG	APG	PPG
69-70—Cincinnati	66	—	1256	190	423	.449	—	—	—	124	195	.636	—	—	378	56	204	5	—	—	—	504	5.7	0.8	7.6
70-71—Cleveland	74	—	1434	219	470	.466	—	—	—	121	190	.637	—	—	394	66	186	3	—	—	—	559	5.3	0.9	7.6
71-72—Clev.-N.Y.	71	—	683	103	240	.429	—	—	—	50	88	.568	—	—	208	21	107	0	—	—	—	256	2.9	0.3	3.6
72-73—New York	1	—	2	0	0	—	—	—	—	0	0	—	—	—	1	0	2	0	—	—	—	0	1.0	0.0	0.0
72-73—Memphis (A)	57	—	893	170	344	.494	0	1	.000	78	120	.650	90	197	287	36	130	2	—	50	—	418	5.0	0.6	7.3
73-74—Philadelphia	9	—	68	5	13	.385	—	—	—	8	11	.727	5	17	22	0	11	0	3	—	4	18	2.4	0.0	2.0
REG. NBA TOTALS	221	—	3443	517	1146	.451	—	—	—	303	484	.626	5	17	1003	143	510	8	3	—	4	1337	4.5	0.6	6.0
REG. ABA TOTALS	57	—	893	170	344	.494	0	1	.000	78	120	.650	90	197	287	36	130	2	—	50	—	418	5.0	0.6	7.3
NBA PLAYOFF TOTALS	11	—	29	2	14	.143	—	—	—	4	4	1.000	—	—	7	1	7	0	—	—	0	8	0.6	0.1	0.7

RADER, HOWARD (**Howie**) b. March 29, 1921 d. February 2, 1991 Ht. 6-1 Wt. 190 College—Long Island University

SEASON—TEAM	G	GS	MIN	FGM	FGA	PCT	3FGM	3FGA	PCT	FTM	FTA	PCT	O-RB	D-RB	TOT	AST	PF	DQ	STL	TO	BLK	PTS	RPG	APG	PPG
46-47—Tri-Cities (N)	41	—	—	76	—	—	—	—	—	43	64	.672	—	—	—	—	93	—	—	—	—	195	—	—	4.8
47-48—Tri-Cities (N)	45	—	—	44	—	—	—	—	—	29	54	.537	—	—	—	—	90	—	—	—	—	117	—	—	2.6
48-49—Baltimore	13	—	—	7	45	.156	—	—	—	3	10	.300	—	—	14	25	—	—	—	—	—	17	—	1.1	1.3
REG. NBA TOTALS	13	—	—	7	45	.156	—	—	—	3	10	.300	—	—	14	25	—	—	—	—	—	17	—	1.1	1.3
REG. NBL TOTALS	86	—	—	120	—	—	—	—	—	72	118	.610	—	—	—	—	183	—	—	—	—	312	—	—	3.6
NBL PLAYOFF TOTALS	6	—	—	8	—	—	—	—	—	6	12	.500	—	—	—	—	11	—	—	—	—	22	—	—	3.7

RADFORD, MARK JEFFREY b. July 5, 1959 Ht. 6-4 Wt. 190 College—Oregon State

SEASON—TEAM	G	GS	MIN	FGM	FGA	PCT	3FGM	3FGA	PCT	FTM	FTA	PCT	O-RB	D-RB	TOT	AST	PF	DQ	STL	TO	BLK	PTS	RPG	APG	PPG
81-82—Seattle	43	0	369	54	100	.540	2	3	.667	35	69	.507	13	16	29	57	65	0	16	42	2	145	0.7	1.3	3.4
82-83—Seattle	54	2	439	84	172	.488	4	18	.222	30	73	.411	12	35	47	104	78	0	34	74	4	202	0.9	1.9	3.7
REG. SEASON TOTALS	97	2	808	138	272	.507	6	21	.286	65	142	.458	25	51	76	161	143	0	50	116	6	347	0.8	1.7	3.6

RADFORD, WAYNE b. May 29, 1956 Ht. 6-3 Wt. 205 College—Indiana

SEASON—TEAM	G	GS	MIN	FGM	FGA	PCT	3FGM	3FGA	PCT	FTM	FTA	PCT	O-RB	D-RB	TOT	AST	PF	DQ	STL	TO	BLK	PTS	RPG	APG	PPG
78-79—Indiana	52	—	649	83	175	.474	—	—	—	36	45	.800	25	43	68	57	61	0	30	45	1	202	1.3	1.1	3.9
REG. SEASON TOTALS	52	—	649	83	175	.474	—	—	—	36	45	.800	25	43	68	57	61	0	30	45	1	202	1.3	1.1	3.9

RADJA, DINO b. April 24, 1967   Ht. 6-11 Wt. 225 College—None

SEASON—TEAM	G	GS	MIN	FGM	FGA	PCT	3FGM	3FGA	PCT	FTM	FTA	PCT	O-RB	D-RB	TOT	AST	PF	DQ	STL	TO	BLK	PTS	RPG	APG	PPG
93-94—Boston	80	47	2303	491	942	.521	0	1	.000	226	301	.751	191	386	577	114	276	2	70	149	67	1208	7.2	1.4	15.1
REG. SEASON TOTALS	80	47	2303	491	942	.521	0	1	.000	226	301	.751	191	386	577	114	276	2	70	149	67	1208	7.2	1.4	15.1

RADOVICH, FRANK RAYMOND b. March 3, 1938   Ht. 6-8 Wt. 235 College—Indiana

SEASON—TEAM	G	GS	MIN	FGM	FGA	PCT	3FGM	3FGA	PCT	FTM	FTA	PCT	O-RB	D-RB	TOT	AST	PF	DQ	STL	TO	BLK	PTS	RPG	APG	PPG
61-62—Philadelphia	37	—	175	37	93	.398	—	—	—	13	26	.500	—	—	51	4	27	0	—	—	—	87	1.4	0.1	2.4
REG. SEASON TOTALS	37	—	175	37	93	.398	—	—	—	13	26	.500	—	—	51	4	27	0	—	—	—	87	1.4	0.1	2.4
PLAYOFF TOTALS	2	—	12	1	6	.167	—	—	—	2	4	.500	—	—	3	—	2	0	—	—	—	4	1.5	0.0	2.0

RADOVICH, GEORGE LEWIS (Moe) b. May 5, 1929   Ht. 6-0 Wt. 160 College—Wyoming

SEASON—TEAM	G	GS	MIN	FGM	FGA	PCT	3FGM	3FGA	PCT	FTM	FTA	PCT	O-RB	D-RB	TOT	AST	PF	DQ	STL	TO	BLK	PTS	RPG	APG	PPG
52-53—Philadelphia	4	—	33	5	13	.385	—	—	—	4	4	1.000	—	—	1	8	5	0	—	—	—	14	0.3	2.0	3.5
REG. SEASON TOTALS	4	—	33	5	13	.385	—	—	—	4	4	1.000	—	—	1	8	5	0	—	—	—	14	0.3	2.0	3.5

RADZISZEWSKI, RAYMOND A. (Ray) b. March 1, 1935   Ht. 6-5 Wt. 210 College—St. Joseph's (Pa.)

SEASON—TEAM	G	GS	MIN	FGM	FGA	PCT	3FGM	3FGA	PCT	FTM	FTA	PCT	O-RB	D-RB	TOT	AST	PF	DQ	STL	TO	BLK	PTS	RPG	APG	PPG
57-58—Philadelphia	1	—	6	0	3	.000	—	—	—	0	0	—	—	—	2	1	1	0	—	—	—	0	2.0	1.0	0.0
REG. SEASON TOTALS	1	—	6	0	3	.000	—	—	—	0	0	—	—	—	2	1	1	0	—	—	—	0	2.0	1.0	0.0

RAGELIS, RAYMOND ERNEST (Ray) b. December 10, 1928 d. September 19, 1983 Ht. 6-4 Wt. 205 College—Northwestern

SEASON—TEAM	G	GS	MIN	FGM	FGA	PCT	3FGM	3FGA	PCT	FTM	FTA	PCT	O-RB	D-RB	TOT	AST	PF	DQ	STL	TO	BLK	PTS	RPG	APG	PPG
51-52—Rochester	51	—	337	25	96	.260	—	—	—	18	29	.621	—	—	76	31	62	1	—	—	—	68	1.5	0.6	1.3
REG. SEASON TOTALS	51	—	337	25	96	.260	—	—	—	18	29	.621	—	—	76	31	62	1	—	—	—	68	1.5	0.6	1.3
PLAYOFF TOTALS	3	—	7	0	1	.000	—	—	—	0	0	—	—	—	1	1	0	0	—	—	—	0	0.3	0.3	0.0

RAIKEN, SHERWIN H. b. October 29, 1928   Ht. 6-2 Wt. 185 College—Villanova

SEASON—TEAM	G	GS	MIN	FGM	FGA	PCT	3FGM	3FGA	PCT	FTM	FTA	PCT	O-RB	D-RB	TOT	AST	PF	DQ	STL	TO	BLK	PTS	RPG	APG	PPG
52-53—New York	6	—	63	3	21	.143	—	—	—	3	8	.375	—	—	8	6	10	0	—	—	—	9	1.3	1.0	1.5
REG. SEASON TOTALS	6	—	63	3	21	.143	—	—	—	3	8	.375	—	—	8	6	10	0	—	—	—	9	1.3	1.0	1.5
PLAYOFF TOTALS	4	—	19	4	5	.800	—	—	—	0	1	.000	—	—	1	2	3	0	—	—	—	8	0.3	0.5	2.0

RAINS, EDWARD EUGENE (Ed) b. December 24, 1956   Ht. 6-7 Wt. 195 College—South Alabama

SEASON—TEAM	G	GS	MIN	FGM	FGA	PCT	3FGM	3FGA	PCT	FTM	FTA	PCT	O-RB	D-RB	TOT	AST	PF	DQ	STL	TO	BLK	PTS	RPG	APG	PPG
81-82—San Antonio	49	15	637	77	177	.435	0	2	.000	38	64	.594	37	43	80	40	74	0	18	25	2	192	1.6	0.8	3.9
82-83—San Antonio	34	1	292	33	83	.398	0	1	.000	29	43	.674	25	19	44	22	35	0	10	25	1	95	1.3	0.6	2.8
REG. SEASON TOTALS	83	16	929	110	260	.423	0	3	.000	67	107	.626	62	62	124	62	109	0	28	50	3	287	1.5	0.7	3.5
PLAYOFF TOTALS	8	0	41	5	11	.455	0	1	.000	4	9	.444	4	5	9	2	5	0	1	2	0	14	1.1	0.3	1.8

RAMBIS, DARRELL KURT (Kurt, Rambo) b. February 25, 1958   Ht. 6-8 Wt. 215 College—Santa Clara

SEASON—TEAM	G	GS	MIN	FGM	FGA	PCT	3FGM	3FGA	PCT	FTM	FTA	PCT	O-RB	D-RB	TOT	AST	PF	DQ	STL	TO	BLK	PTS	RPG	APG	PPG
81-82—Los Angeles	64	43	1131	118	228	.518	0	1	.000	59	117	.504	116	232	348	56	167	2	60	77	76	295	5.4	0.9	4.6
82-83—Los Angeles	78	77	1806	235	413	.569	0	2	.000	114	166	.687	164	367	531	90	233	2	105	145	63	584	6.8	1.2	7.5
83-84—Los Angeles	47	31	743	63	113	.558	0	0	—	42	66	.636	82	184	266	34	108	0	30	56	14	168	5.7	0.7	3.6
84-85—L.A. Lakers	82	46	1617	181	327	.554	0	0	—	68	103	.660	164	364	528	69	211	0	82	97	47	430	6.4	0.8	5.2
85-86—L.A. Lakers	74	74	1573	160	269	.595	0	0	—	88	122	.721	156	361	517	69	198	0	66	97	33	408	7.0	0.9	5.5
86-87—L.A. Lakers	78	10	1514	163	313	.521	0	0	—	120	157	.764	159	294	453	63	201	1	74	104	41	446	5.8	0.8	5.7
87-88—L.A. Lakers	70	20	845	102	186	.548	0	0	—	73	93	.785	103	165	268	54	103	0	39	59	13	277	3.8	0.8	4.0
88-89—Charlotte	75	75	2233	325	627	.518	0	3	.000	182	248	.734	269	434	703	159	208	4	100	148	57	832	9.4	2.1	11.1
89-90—Cha.-Phoenix	74	61	1904	190	373	.509	0	3	.000	82	127	.646	156	369	525	135	208	0	100	104	37	462	7.1	1.8	6.2
90-91—Phoenix	62	17	900	83	167	.497	0	2	.000	60	85	.706	77	189	266	64	107	1	25	45	11	226	4.3	1.0	3.6
91-92—Phoenix	28	5	381	38	82	.463	0	0	—	14	18	.778	23	83	106	37	46	0	12	25	14	90	3.8	1.3	3.2
92-93—Phoenix-Sac.	72	1	822	67	129	.519	0	2	.000	43	65	.662	77	150	227	53	122	0	43	42	18	177	3.2	0.7	2.5
93-94—L.A. Lakers	50	1	635	59	114	.518	0	1	.000	46	71	.648	84	105	189	32	89	0	22	26	23	164	3.8	0.6	3.3
REG. SEASON TOTALS	854	461	16104	1784	3341	.534	0	14	.000	991	1438	.689	1630	3297	4927	915	2001	10	758	1025	447	4559	5.8	1.1	5.3
PLAYOFF TOTALS	139	105	2565	284	495	.574	0	1	.000	151	215	.702	236	528	764	119	373	0	85	141	68	719	5.5	0.9	5.2

RAMSEY, CALVIN (Cal) b. July 13, 1937   Ht. 6-4 Wt. 200 College—New York University

SEASON—TEAM	G	GS	MIN	FGM	FGA	PCT	3FGM	3FGA	PCT	FTM	FTA	PCT	O-RB	D-RB	TOT	AST	PF	DQ	STL	TO	BLK	PTS	RPG	APG	PPG
59-60—St. L.-N.Y.	11	—	195	39	96	.406	—	—	—	19	33	.576	—	—	66	9	25	1	—	—	—	97	6.0	0.8	8.8
60-61—Syracuse	2	—	27	2	11	.182	—	—	—	2	4	.500	—	—	7	3	7	0	—	—	—	6	3.5	1.5	3.0
REG. SEASON TOTALS	13	—	222	41	107	.383	—	—	—	21	37	.568	—	—	73	12	32	1	—	—	—	103	5.6	0.9	7.9

RAMSEY, FRANK VERNON JR. b. July 13, 1931　Ht. 6-3　Wt. 190　College—Kentucky

SEASON—TEAM	G	GS	MIN	FGM	FGA	PCT	3FGM	3FGA	PCT	FTM	FTA	PCT	O-RB	D-RB	TOT	AST	PF	DQ	STL	TO	BLK	PTS	RPG	APG	PPG
54-55—Boston	64	—	1754	236	592	.399	—	—	—	243	322	.755	—	—	402	185	250	11	—	—	—	715	6.3	2.9	11.2
56-57—Boston	35	—	807	137	349	.393	—	—	—	144	182	.791	—	—	178	67	113	3	—	—	—	418	5.1	1.9	11.9
57-58—Boston	69	—	2047	377	900	.419	—	—	—	383	472	.811	—	—	504	167	245	8	—	—	—	1137	7.3	2.4	16.5
58-59—Boston	72	—	2013	383	1013	.378	—	—	—	341	436	.782	—	—	491	147	266	11	—	—	—	1107	6.8	2.0	15.4
59-60—Boston	73	—	2009	422	1062	.397	—	—	—	273	347	.787	—	—	506	137	251	10	—	—	—	1117	6.9	1.9	15.3
60-61—Boston	79	—	2019	448	1100	.407	—	—	—	295	354	.833	—	—	431	146	284	14	—	—	—	1191	5.5	1.8	15.1
61-62—Boston	79	—	1913	436	1019	.428	—	—	—	334	405	.825	—	—	387	109	245	10	—	—	—	1206	4.9	1.4	15.3
62-63—Boston	77	—	1541	284	743	.382	—	—	—	271	332	.816	—	—	288	95	259	13	—	—	—	839	3.7	1.2	10.9
63-64—Boston	75	—	1227	226	604	.374	—	—	—	196	233	.841	—	—	223	81	245	7	—	—	—	648	3.0	1.1	8.6
REG. SEASON TOTALS	623	—	15330	2949	7382	.399	—	—	—	2480	3083	.804	—	—	3410	1134	2158	87	—	—	—	8378	5.5	1.8	13.4
PLAYOFF TOTALS	98	—	2396	469	1105	.424	—	—	—	393	476	.826	—	—	494	151	362	14	—	—	—	1331	5.0	1.5	13.6

RAMSEY, RAYMOND L. (Ray) b. July 18, 1921　Ht. 6-2　Wt. 165　College—Bradley

SEASON—TEAM	G	GS	MIN	FGM	FGA	PCT	3FGM	3FGA	PCT	FTM	FTA	PCT	O-RB	D-RB	TOT	AST	PF	DQ	STL	TO	BLK	PTS	RPG	APG	PPG
47-48—Tri-Cities (N)	2	—	—	0	—	—	—	—	—	0	0	—	—	—	—	—	—	—	—	—	—	0	—	—	0.0
48-49—Baltimore	2	—	—	0	1	.000	—	—	—	2	2	1.000	—	—	0	0	—	—	—	—	—	2	—	0.0	1.0
REG. NBA TOTALS	2	—	—	0	1	.000	—	—	—	2	2	1.000	—	—	0	0	—	—	—	—	—	2	—	0.0	1.0
REG. NBL TOTALS	2	—	—	0	—	—	—	—	—	0	0	—	—	—	—	—	—	—	—	—	—	0	—	—	0.0

RANDALL, MARK CHRISTOPHER b. September 30, 1967　Ht. 6-9　Wt. 235　College—Kansas

SEASON—TEAM	G	GS	MIN	FGM	FGA	PCT	3FGM	3FGA	PCT	FTM	FTA	PCT	O-RB	D-RB	TOT	AST	PF	DQ	STL	TO	BLK	PTS	RPG	APG	PPG
91-92—Chicago-Minn.	54	0	441	68	149	.456	3	16	.188	32	43	.744	39	32	71	33	39	0	12	25	3	171	1.3	0.6	3.2
92-93—Minn.-Detroit	37	0	248	40	80	.500	1	8	.125	16	26	.615	27	28	55	11	33	0	4	17	2	97	1.5	0.3	2.6
93-94—Denver	28	0	155	17	50	.340	2	14	.143	22	28	.786	9	13	22	11	18	0	8	10	3	58	0.8	0.4	2.1
REG. SEASON TOTALS	119	0	844	125	279	.448	6	38	.158	70	97	.722	75	73	148	55	90	0	24	52	8	326	1.2	0.5	2.7
PLAYOFF TOTALS	2	0	6	0	1	.000	0	0	—	0	0	—	1	4	5	—	1	0	0	1	1	0	2.5	0.0	0.0

RANK, WALLACE ALIIFUA (Wally) b. March 1, 1958　Ht. 6-6½　Wt. 220　College—San Jose State

SEASON—TEAM	G	GS	MIN	FGM	FGA	PCT	3FGM	3FGA	PCT	FTM	FTA	PCT	O-RB	D-RB	TOT	AST	PF	DQ	STL	TO	BLK	PTS	RPG	APG	PPG
80-81—San Diego	25	—	153	21	57	.368	0	0	—	13	28	.464	17	13	30	17	33	1	7	26	1	55	1.2	0.7	2.2
REG. SEASON TOTALS	25	—	153	21	57	.368	0	0	—	13	28	.464	17	13	30	17	33	1	7	26	1	55	1.2	0.7	2.2

RANSEY, KELVIN b. May 3, 1958　Ht. 6-2　Wt. 170　College—Ohio State

SEASON—TEAM	G	GS	MIN	FGM	FGA	PCT	3FGM	3FGA	PCT	FTM	FTA	PCT	O-RB	D-RB	TOT	AST	PF	DQ	STL	TO	BLK	PTS	RPG	APG	PPG
80-81—Portland	80	—	2431	525	1162	.452	3	31	.097	164	219	.749	42	153	195	555	201	1	88	232	9	1217	2.4	6.9	15.2
81-82—Portland	78	68	2418	504	1094	.461	3	38	.079	242	318	.761	39	147	186	555	169	1	97	229	4	1253	2.4	7.1	16.1
82-83—Dallas	76	4	1607	343	746	.460	2	16	.125	152	199	.764	44	103	147	280	109	1	58	129	4	840	1.9	3.7	11.1
83-84—New Jersey	80	50	1937	300	700	.434	7	32	.219	145	183	.792	28	99	127	483	182	2	91	141	6	760	1.6	6.0	9.5
84-85—New Jersey	81	29	1689	300	654	.459	2	11	.182	122	142	.859	40	90	130	355	134	0	87	113	7	724	1.6	4.4	8.9
85-86—New Jersey	79	15	1504	231	505	.457	3	24	.125	121	148	.818	34	82	116	252	128	0	51	114	4	586	1.5	3.2	7.4
REG. SEASON TOTALS	474	166	11586	2207	4861	.454	20	152	.132	946	1209	.782	227	674	901	2480	923	5	472	958	34	5380	1.9	5.2	11.4
PLAYOFF TOTALS	14	6	306	45	117	.385	2	5	.400	14	19	.737	8	17	25	64	33	0	9	22	3	106	1.8	4.6	7.6

RANZINO, SAMUEL SALVADOR (Sam) b. June 21, 1927　Ht. 6-1　Wt. 185　College—North Carolina State

SEASON—TEAM	G	GS	MIN	FGM	FGA	PCT	3FGM	3FGA	PCT	FTM	FTA	PCT	O-RB	D-RB	TOT	AST	PF	DQ	STL	TO	BLK	PTS	RPG	APG	PPG
51-52—Rochester	39	—	234	30	90	.333	—	—	—	26	37	.703	—	—	39	25	63	2	—	—	—	86	1.0	0.6	2.2
REG. SEASON TOTALS	39	—	234	30	90	.333	—	—	—	26	37	.703	—	—	39	25	63	2	—	—	—	86	1.0	0.6	2.2

RASCOE, ROBERT B. (Bobby) b. July 22, 1940　Ht. 6-4　Wt. 205　College—Western Kentucky

SEASON—TEAM	G	GS	MIN	FGM	FGA	PCT	3FGM	3FGA	PCT	FTM	FTA	PCT	O-RB	D-RB	TOT	AST	PF	DQ	STL	TO	BLK	PTS	RPG	APG	PPG
67-68—Kentucky (A)	77	—	1606	245	563	.435	0	5	.000	190	249	.763	—	—	284	102	158	2	—	86	—	680	3.7	1.3	8.8
68-69—Kentucky (A)	78	—	1247	201	477	.421	3	15	.200	129	167	.772	—	—	150	105	131	1	—	93	—	534	1.9	1.3	6.8
69-70—Kentucky (A)	4	—	34	4	21	.190	0	1	.000	6	7	.857	—	—	4	1	3	0	—	—	—	14	1.0	0.3	3.5
REG. ABA TOTALS	159	—	2887	450	1061	.424	3	21	.143	325	423	.768	—	—	438	208	292	3	—	179	—	1228	2.8	1.3	7.7
ABA PLAYOFF TOTALS	12	—	251	42	90	.467	0	1	.000	34	36	.944	—	—	25	13	32	0	—	10	—	118	2.1	1.1	9.8

RASMUSSEN, BLAIR ALLEN b. November 13, 1962 Ht. 7-0 Wt. 250 College—Oregon

SEASON—TEAM	G	GS	MIN	FGM	FGA	PCT	3FGM	3FGA	PCT	FTM	FTA	PCT	O-RB	D-RB	TOT	AST	PF	DQ	STL	TO	BLK	PTS	RPG	APG	PPG
85-86—Denver	48	1	330	61	150	.407	0	0	—	31	39	.795	37	60	97	16	63	0	3	40	10	153	2.0	0.3	3.2
86-87—Denver	74	23	1421	268	570	.470	0	0	—	169	231	.732	183	282	465	60	224	6	24	79	58	705	6.3	0.8	9.5
87-88—Denver	79	45	1779	435	884	.492	0	0	—	132	170	.776	130	307	437	78	241	2	22	73	81	1002	5.5	1.0	12.7
88-89—Denver	77	22	1308	257	577	.445	0	0	—	69	81	.852	105	182	287	49	194	2	29	49	41	583	3.7	0.6	7.6
89-90—Denver	81	55	1995	445	895	.497	0	1	.000	111	134	.828	174	420	594	82	300	10	40	75	104	1001	7.3	1.0	12.4
90-91—Denver	70	69	2325	405	885	.458	2	5	.400	63	93	.677	170	508	678	70	307	15	52	81	132	875	9.7	1.0	12.5
91-92—Atlanta	81	61	1968	347	726	.478	5	23	.217	30	40	.750	94	299	393	107	233	1	35	51	48	729	4.9	1.3	9.0
92-93—Atlanta	22	6	283	30	80	.375	2	6	.333	9	13	.692	20	35	55	5	61	2	5	12	10	71	2.5	0.2	3.2
REG. SEASON TOTALS	532	282	11409	2248	4767	.472	9	35	.257	614	801	.767	913	2093	3006	467	1623	38	210	460	484	5119	5.7	0.9	9.6
PLAYOFF TOTALS	29	18	632	140	316	.443	0	0	—	65	81	.802	68	112	180	25	84	1	10	21	27	345	6.2	0.9	11.9

RATKOVICZ, GEORGE b. November 13, 1922 Ht. 6-7 Wt. 225 College—None

SEASON—TEAM	G	GS	MIN	FGM	FGA	PCT	3FGM	3FGA	PCT	FTM	FTA	PCT	O-RB	D-RB	TOT	AST	PF	DQ	STL	TO	BLK	PTS	RPG	APG	PPG
41-42—Chicago (N)	13	—	—	9	—	—	—	—	—	14	—	—	—	—	—	—	—	—	—	—	—	32	—	—	2.5
45-46—Chicago (N)	33	—	—	80	—	—	—	—	—	66	113	.584	—	—	—	—	91	—	—	—	—	226	—	—	6.8
46-47—Chicago (N)	37	—	—	43	—	—	—	—	—	26	58	.448	—	—	—	—	68	—	—	—	—	112	—	—	3.0
47-48—Rochester (N)	53	—	—	79	—	—	—	—	—	76	119	.639	—	—	—	—	135	—	—	—	—	234	—	—	4.4
48-49—Tri-Cities (N)	64	—	—	109	—	—	—	—	—	106	175	.606	—	—	—	—	207	—	—	—	—	324	—	—	5.1
49-50—Syracuse	62	—	—	162	439	.369	—	—	—	211	348	.606	—	—	124	201	—	—	—	—	535	—	2.0	8.6
50-51—Syracuse	66	—	—	264	636	.415	—	—	—	321	439	.731	—	—	547	193	256	11	—	—	—	849	8.3	2.9	12.9
51-52—Syracuse	66	—	1356	165	473	.349	—	—	—	163	242	.674	—	—	328	90	235	8	—	—	—	493	5.0	1.4	7.5
52-53—Balt.-Milw.	71	—	2235	208	619	.336	—	—	—	262	373	.702	—	—	522	217	287	16	—	—	—	678	7.4	3.1	9.5
53-54—Milwaukee	69	—	2170	197	501	.393	—	—	—	176	273	.645	—	—	523	154	255	11	—	—	—	570	7.6	2.2	8.3
54-55—Milwaukee	9	—	102	3	19	.158	—	—	—	10	23	.435	—	—	17	13	15	0	—	—	—	16	1.9	1.4	1.8
REG. NBA TOTALS	343	—	5863	999	2687	.372	—	—	—	1143	1698	.673	—	—	1937	791	1249	46	—	—	—	3141	6.9	2.3	9.2
REG. NBL TOTALS	200	—	—	320	—	—	—	—	—	288	465	.589	—	—	—	—	501	—	—	—	—	928	—	—	4.6
NBA PLAYOFF TOTALS	24	—	59	80	195	.410	—	—	—	99	148	.669	—	—	85	38	94	2	—	—	—	259	6.5	1.6	10.8
NBL PLAYOFF TOTALS	27	—	—	39	—	—	—	—	—	40	58	.672	—	—	—	—	74	—	—	—	—	118	—	—	4.4

RATLEFF, WILLIAM EDWARD (Ed) b. March 29, 1950 Ht. 6-6 Wt. 195 College—Long Beach State

SEASON—TEAM	G	GS	MIN	FGM	FGA	PCT	3FGM	3FGA	PCT	FTM	FTA	PCT	O-RB	D-RB	TOT	AST	PF	DQ	STL	TO	BLK	PTS	RPG	APG	PPG
73-74—Houston	81	—	1773	254	585	.434	—	—	—	103	129	.798	93	193	286	181	182	2	90	—	27	611	3.5	2.2	7.5
74-75—Houston	80	—	2563	392	851	.461	—	—	—	157	190	.826	185	274	459	259	231	5	146	—	51	941	5.7	3.2	11.8
75-76—Houston	72	—	2401	314	647	.485	—	—	—	168	206	.816	107	272	379	260	234	4	114	—	37	796	5.3	3.6	11.1
76-77—Houston	37	—	533	70	161	.435	—	—	—	26	42	.619	24	53	77	43	45	0	20	—	6	166	2.1	1.2	4.5
77-78—Houston	68	—	1163	130	310	.419	—	—	—	39	47	.830	56	106	162	153	109	0	60	67	22	299	2.4	2.3	4.4
REG. SEASON TOTALS	338	—	8433	1160	2554	.454	—	—	—	493	614	.803	465	898	1363	896	801	11	430	67	143	2813	4.0	2.7	8.3
PLAYOFF TOTALS	8	—	291	36	87	.414	—	—	—	17	20	.850	24	29	53	35	31	0	14	—	1	89	6.6	4.4	11.1

RATLIFF, MICHAEL D. (Mike) b. June 7, 1951 Ht. 6-10 Wt. 230 College—Wisconsin-Eau Claire

SEASON—TEAM	G	GS	MIN	FGM	FGA	PCT	3FGM	3FGA	PCT	FTM	FTA	PCT	O-RB	D-RB	TOT	AST	PF	DQ	STL	TO	BLK	PTS	RPG	APG	PPG
72-73—Kansas City-Omaha	58	—	681	98	235	.417	—	—	—	45	84	.536	—	—	194	38	111	1	—	—	—	241	3.3	0.7	4.2
73-74—Kansas City-Omaha	2	—	4	0	0	—	—	—	—	0	0	—	0	0	0	0	0	0	0	—	0	0	0.0	0.0	0.0
REG. SEASON TOTALS	60	—	685	98	235	.417	—	—	—	45	84	.536	0	0	194	38	111	1	0	—	0	241	3.2	0.6	4.0

RAUTINS, LEO R. b. March 20, 1960 Ht. 6-8 Wt. 215 College—Minnesota/Syracuse

SEASON—TEAM	G	GS	MIN	FGM	FGA	PCT	3FGM	3FGA	PCT	FTM	FTA	PCT	O-RB	D-RB	TOT	AST	PF	DQ	STL	TO	BLK	PTS	RPG	APG	PPG
83-84—Philadelphia	28	3	196	21	58	.362	0	0	—	6	10	.600	9	24	33	29	31	0	9	19	2	48	1.2	1.0	1.7
84-85—Atlanta	4	0	12	0	2	.000	0	0	—	0	0	—	1	1	2	3	3	0	0	1	0	0	0.5	0.8	0.0
REG. SEASON TOTALS	32	3	208	21	60	.350	0	0	—	6	10	.600	10	25	35	32	34	0	9	20	2	48	1.1	1.0	1.5
PLAYOFF TOTALS	3	0	5	1	3	.333	1	2	.500	0	0	—	2	0	2	1	2	0	1	0	0	3	0.7	0.3	1.0

RAY, CLIFFORD b. January 21, 1949 Ht. 6-9 Wt. 235 College—Oklahoma

SEASON—TEAM	G	GS	MIN	FGM	FGA	PCT	3FGM	3FGA	PCT	FTM	FTA	PCT	O-RB	D-RB	TOT	AST	PF	DQ	STL	TO	BLK	PTS	RPG	APG	PPG
71-72—Chicago	82	—	1872	222	445	.499	—	—	—	134	218	.615	—	—	869	254	296	5	—	—	—	578	10.6	3.1	7.0
72-73—Chicago	73	—	2009	254	516	.492	—	—	—	117	189	.619	—	—	797	271	232	5	—	—	—	625	10.9	3.7	8.6
73-74—Chicago	80	—	2632	313	612	.511	—	—	—	121	199	.608	285	692	977	246	281	5	58	—	173	747	12.2	3.1	9.3
74-75—Golden State	82	—	2519	299	573	.522	—	—	—	171	284	.602	259	611	870	178	305	9	95	—	116	769	10.6	2.2	9.4
75-76—Golden State	82	—	2184	212	404	.525	—	—	—	140	230	.609	270	506	776	149	247	2	78	—	83	564	9.5	1.8	6.9
76-77—Golden State	77	—	2018	263	450	.584	—	—	—	105	199	.528	199	416	615	112	242	5	74	—	81	631	8.0	1.5	8.2
77-78—Golden State	79	—	2268	272	476	.571	—	—	—	148	243	.609	236	522	758	147	291	4	74	150	90	692	9.6	1.9	8.8
78-79—Golden State	82	—	1917	231	439	.526	—	—	—	106	190	.558	213	395	608	136	264	4	47	153	50	568	7.4	1.7	6.9
79-80—Golden State	81	—	1683	203	383	.530	0	2	.000	84	149	.564	122	344	466	183	266	6	51	155	32	490	5.8	2.3	6.0
80-81—Golden State	66	—	838	64	152	.421	0	0	—	29	62	.468	73	144	217	52	194	2	24	74	13	157	3.3	0.8	2.4
REG. SEASON TOTALS	784	—	19940	2333	4450	.524	0	2	.000	1155	1963	.588	1657	3630	6953	1728	2618	52	501	532	638	5821	8.9	2.2	7.4
PLAYOFF TOTALS	60	—	1735	207	385	.538	0	0	—	82	139	.590	196	337	608	125	206	2	51	—	70	496	10.1	2.1	8.3

RAY, DONALD L. (Don, Duck) b. July 8, 1921   Ht. 6-6 Wt. 190 College—Western Kentucky

SEASON—TEAM	G	GS	MIN	FGM	FGA	PCT	3FGM	3FGA	PCT	FTM	FTA	PCT	O-RB	D-RB	TOT	AST	PF	DQ	STL	TO	BLK	PTS	RPG	APG	PPG
48-49—Tri-Cities (N)	46	—	—	123	—	—	—	—	—	80	117	.684	—	—	—	—	103	—	—	—	—	326	—	—	7.1
49-50—Tri-Cities	61	—	—	130	403	.323	—	—	—	104	149	.698	—	—	—	60	147	—	—	—	—	364	—	1.0	6.0
REG. NBA TOTALS	61	—	—	130	403	.323	—	—	—	104	149	.698	—	—	—	60	147	—	—	—	—	364	—	1.0	6.0
REG. NBL TOTALS	46	—	—	123	—	—	—	—	—	80	117	.684	—	—	—	—	103	—	—	—	—	326	—	—	7.1
NBA PLAYOFF TOTALS	3	—	—	4	13	.308	—	—	—	10	11	.909	—	—	—	—	7	1	—	—	—	18	—	0.0	6.0
NBL PLAYOFF TOTALS	6	—	—	16	—	—	—	—	—	17	21	.810	—	—	—	—	18	—	—	—	—	49	—	—	8.2

RAY, JAMES E. (Jim) b. January 12, 1934   Ht. 6-1½ Wt. 180 College—Toledo

SEASON—TEAM	G	GS	MIN	FGM	FGA	PCT	3FGM	3FGA	PCT	FTM	FTA	PCT	O-RB	D-RB	TOT	AST	PF	DQ	STL	TO	BLK	PTS	RPG	APG	PPG
56-57—Syracuse	4	—	43	2	11	.182	—	—	—	3	5	.600	—	—	5	3	4	0	—	—	—	7	1.3	0.8	1.8
59-60—Syracuse	4	—	21	1	6	.167	—	—	—	0	0	—	—	—	0	2	3	0	—	—	—	2	0.0	0.5	0.5
REG. SEASON TOTALS	8	—	64	3	17	.176	—	—	—	3	5	.600	—	—	5	5	7	0	—	—	—	9	0.6	0.6	1.1

RAY, JAMES EARL (James Earl) b. July 27, 1957   Ht. 6-8 Wt. 215 College—Jacksonville

SEASON—TEAM	G	GS	MIN	FGM	FGA	PCT	3FGM	3FGA	PCT	FTM	FTA	PCT	O-RB	D-RB	TOT	AST	PF	DQ	STL	TO	BLK	PTS	RPG	APG	PPG
80-81—Denver	18	—	148	15	49	.306	0	1	.000	7	10	.700	13	24	37	11	31	0	4	13	4	37	2.1	0.6	2.1
81-82—Denver	40	4	262	51	116	.440	1	1	1.000	21	36	.583	18	47	65	26	59	0	10	37	16	124	1.6	0.7	3.1
82-83—Denver	45	3	433	70	153	.458	0	1	.000	33	51	.647	37	89	126	39	83	2	24	50	19	173	2.8	0.9	3.8
REG. SEASON TOTALS	103	7	843	136	318	.428	1	3	.333	61	97	.629	68	160	228	76	173	2	38	100	39	334	2.2	0.7	3.2
PLAYOFF TOTALS	4	0	20	1	6	.167	0	0	—	1	4	.250	1	2	3	—	4	0	0	0	2	3	0.8	0.0	0.8

RAYL, JAMES R. (Jimmy, Splendid Splinter) b. June 21, 1941   Ht. 6-2 Wt. 175 College—Indiana

SEASON—TEAM	G	GS	MIN	FGM	FGA	PCT	3FGM	3FGA	PCT	FTM	FTA	PCT	O-RB	D-RB	TOT	AST	PF	DQ	STL	TO	BLK	PTS	RPG	APG	PPG
67-68—Indiana (A)	74	—	2193	317	819	.387	57	175	.326	195	243	.802	—	—	238	210	197	1	—	193	—	886	3.2	2.8	12.0
68-69—Indiana (A)	27	—	567	72	202	.356	34	92	.370	61	68	.897	—	—	67	63	80	2	—	50	—	239	2.5	2.3	8.9
REG. ABA TOTALS	101	—	2760	389	1021	.381	91	267	.341	256	311	.823	—	—	305	273	277	3	—	243	—	1125	3.0	2.7	11.1
ABA PLAYOFF TOTALS	3	—	118	15	42	.357	4	14	.286	5	7	.714	—	—	10	14	14	0	—	9	—	39	3.3	4.7	13.0

RAYMOND, CRAIG MILFORD b. April 5, 1945   Ht. 6-11 Wt. 240 College—Brigham Young

SEASON—TEAM	G	GS	MIN	FGM	FGA	PCT	3FGM	3FGA	PCT	FTM	FTA	PCT	O-RB	D-RB	TOT	AST	PF	DQ	STL	TO	BLK	PTS	RPG	APG	PPG
68-69—Philadelphia	27	—	177	22	64	.344	—	—	—	11	17	.647	—	—	68	8	46	2	—	—	—	55	2.5	0.3	2.0
69-70—Pitt.-L.A. (A)	80	—	2356	386	812	.475	0	1	.000	190	304	.625	—	—	796	154	274	8	—	—	—	962	10.0	1.9	12.0
70-71—Memphis (A)	56	—	1102	142	330	.430	0	1	.000	67	106	.632	—	—	289	91	124	—	—	—	—	351	5.2	1.6	6.3
71-72—Floridians (A)	64	—	889	104	227	.458	0	3	.000	48	76	.632	—	—	284	67	108	—	—	91	—	256	4.4	1.0	4.0
72-73—S.D.-Indiana (A)	14	—	168	12	39	.308	0	—	—	10	14	.714	23	50	73	7	24	0	—	15	—	34	5.2	0.5	2.4
REG. NBA TOTALS	27	—	177	22	64	.344	—	—	—	11	17	.647	—	—	68	8	46	2	—	—	—	55	2.5	0.3	2.0
REG. ABA TOTALS	214	—	4515	644	1408	.457	0	5	.000	315	500	.630	23	50	1442	319	530	8	—	106	—	1603	6.7	1.5	7.5
ABA PLAYOFF TOTALS	23	—	743	131	270	.485	0	0	—	74	96	.771	45	209	280	44	7	0	—	1	—	336	12.2	1.9	14.6

REA, CONNIE MACK b. January 27, 1935   Ht. 6-3 Wt. 175 College—Centenary/Vanderbilt

SEASON—TEAM	G	GS	MIN	FGM	FGA	PCT	3FGM	3FGA	PCT	FTM	FTA	PCT	O-RB	D-RB	TOT	AST	PF	DQ	STL	TO	BLK	PTS	RPG	APG	PPG
53-54—Baltimore	20	—	154	9	43	.209	—	—	—	5	16	.313	—	—	31	16	13	0	—	—	—	23	1.6	0.8	1.2
REG. SEASON TOTALS	20	—	154	9	43	.209	—	—	—	5	16	.313	—	—	31	16	13	0	—	—	—	23	1.6	0.8	1.2

REAVES, JOE L. b. May 27, 1950   Ht. 6-6 Wt. 220 College—Bethel College (Tenn.)

SEASON—TEAM	G	GS	MIN	FGM	FGA	PCT	3FGM	3FGA	PCT	FTM	FTA	PCT	O-RB	D-RB	TOT	AST	PF	DQ	STL	TO	BLK	PTS	RPG	APG	PPG
73-74—Phoenix	7	—	38	6	11	.545	—	—	—	4	11	.364	2	6	8	1	6	0	0	—	2	16	1.1	0.1	2.3
73-74—Memphis (A)	12	—	172	30	70	.429	0	0	—	4	6	.667	17	29	46	6	23	—	2	17	7	64	3.8	0.5	5.3
REG. NBA TOTALS	7	—	38	6	11	.545	—	—	—	4	11	.364	2	6	8	1	6	0	0	—	2	16	1.1	0.1	2.3
REG. ABA TOTALS	12	—	172	30	70	.429	0	0	—	4	6	.667	17	29	46	6	23	0	2	17	7	64	3.8	0.5	5.3

REDDOUT, FRANKLIN P. (Frank) b. 1931   Ht. 6-5 Wt. 195 College—Syracuse

SEASON—TEAM	G	GS	MIN	FGM	FGA	PCT	3FGM	3FGA	PCT	FTM	FTA	PCT	O-RB	D-RB	TOT	AST	PF	DQ	STL	TO	BLK	PTS	RPG	APG	PPG
53-54—Rochester	7	—	18	5	6	.833	—	—	—	3	4	.750	—	—	9	0	6	0	—	—	—	13	1.3	0.0	1.9
REG. SEASON TOTALS	7	—	18	5	6	.833	—	—	—	3	4	.750	—	—	9	0	6	0	—	—	—	13	1.3	0.0	1.9

REDMOND, MARLON BERNARD b. April 15, 1955   Ht. 6-6 Wt. 200 College—San Francisco

SEASON—TEAM	G	GS	MIN	FGM	FGA	PCT	3FGM	3FGA	PCT	FTM	FTA	PCT	O-RB	D-RB	TOT	AST	PF	DQ	STL	TO	BLK	PTS	RPG	APG	PPG
78-79—K.C.-Phil.	53	—	759	163	387	.421	—	—	—	31	50	.620	57	52	109	58	96	2	28	57	16	357	2.1	1.1	6.7
79-80—Kansas City	24	—	298	59	138	.428	0	9	.000	24	34	.706	18	34	52	19	27	0	4	19	9	142	2.2	0.8	5.9
REG. SEASON TOTALS	77	—	1057	222	525	.423	0	9	.000	55	84	.655	75	86	161	77	123	2	32	76	25	499	2.1	1.0	6.5
PLAYOFF TOTALS	1	—	2	0	2	.000	0	0	—	0	0	—	0	0	0	0	0	0	0	0	0	0	0.0	0.0	0.0

REED, HUBERT F. (Hub) b. October 4, 1936 Ht. 6-9 Wt. 220 College—Oklahoma City

SEASON—TEAM	G	GS	MIN	FGM	FGA	PCT	3FGM	3FGA	PCT	FTM	FTA	PCT	O-RB	D-RB	TOT	AST	PF	DQ	STL	TO	BLK	PTS	RPG	APG	PPG
58-59—St. Louis	65	—	950	136	317	.429	—	—	—	53	71	.746	—	—	317	32	171	2	—	—	—	325	4.9	0.5	5.0
59-60—St. L.-Cin.	71	—	1820	270	601	.449	—	—	—	134	184	.728	—	—	614	69	230	6	—	—	—	674	8.6	1.0	9.5
60-61—Cincinnati	75	—	1216	156	364	.429	—	—	—	85	122	.697	—	—	367	69	199	7	—	—	—	397	4.9	0.9	5.3
61-62—Cincinnati	80	—	1446	203	460	.441	—	—	—	60	82	.732	—	—	440	53	267	9	—	—	—	466	5.5	0.7	5.8
62-63—Cincinnati	80	—	1299	199	427	.466	—	—	—	74	98	.755	—	—	398	83	261	7	—	—	—	472	5.0	1.0	5.9
63-64—Los Angeles	46	—	386	33	91	.363	—	—	—	10	15	.667	—	—	107	23	73	0	—	—	—	76	2.3	0.5	1.7
64-65—Detroit	62	—	753	84	221	.380	—	—	—	40	58	.690	—	—	206	38	136	2	—	—	—	208	3.3	0.6	3.4
REG. SEASON TOTALS	479	—	7870	1081	2481	.436	—	—	—	456	630	.724	—	—	2449	367	1337	33	—	—	—	2618	5.1	0.8	5.5
PLAYOFF TOTALS	21	—	319	43	106	.406	—	—	—	21	30	.700	—	—	103	16	56	0	—	—	—	107	4.9	0.8	5.1

REED, RONALD LEE (Ron) b. November 2, 1942 Ht. 6-5 Wt. 205 College—Notre Dame

SEASON—TEAM	G	GS	MIN	FGM	FGA	PCT	3FGM	3FGA	PCT	FTM	FTA	PCT	O-RB	D-RB	TOT	AST	PF	DQ	STL	TO	BLK	PTS	RPG	APG	PPG
65-66—Detroit	57	—	997	186	524	.355	—	—	—	54	100	.540	—	—	339	92	133	1	—	—	—	426	5.9	1.6	7.5
66-67—Detroit	61	—	1248	223	600	.372	—	—	—	79	133	.594	—	—	423	81	145	2	—	—	—	525	6.9	1.3	8.6
REG. SEASON TOTALS	118	—	2245	409	1124	.364	—	—	—	133	233	.571	—	—	762	173	278	3	—	—	—	951	6.5	1.5	8.1

REED, WILLIS JR. b. June 25, 1942 Ht. 6-9½ Wt. 235 College—Grambling State

SEASON—TEAM	G	GS	MIN	FGM	FGA	PCT	3FGM	3FGA	PCT	FTM	FTA	PCT	O-RB	D-RB	TOT	AST	PF	DQ	STL	TO	BLK	PTS	RPG	APG	PPG
64-65—New York	80	—	3042	629	1457	.432	—	—	—	302	407	.742	—	—	1175	133	339	14	—	—	—	1560	14.7	1.7	19.5
65-66—New York	76	—	2537	438	1009	.434	—	—	—	302	399	.757	—	—	883	91	323	13	—	—	—	1178	11.6	1.2	15.5
66-67—New York	78	—	2824	635	1298	.489	—	—	—	358	487	.735	—	—	1136	126	293	9	—	—	—	1628	14.6	1.6	20.9
67-68—New York	81	—	2879	659	1346	.490	—	—	—	367	509	.721	—	—	1073	159	343	12	—	—	—	1685	13.2	2.0	20.8
68-69—New York	82	—	3108	704	1351	.521	—	—	—	325	435	.747	—	—	1191	190	314	7	—	—	—	1733	14.5	2.3	21.1
69-70—New York	81	—	3089	702	1385	.507	—	—	—	351	464	.756	—	—	1126	161	287	2	—	—	—	1755	13.9	2.0	21.7
70-71—New York	73	—	2855	614	1330	.462	—	—	—	299	381	.785	—	—	1003	148	228	1	—	—	—	1527	13.7	2.0	20.9
71-72—New York	11	—	363	60	137	.438	—	—	—	27	39	.692	—	—	96	22	30	0	—	—	—	147	8.7	2.0	13.4
72-73—New York	69	—	1876	334	705	.474	—	—	—	92	124	.742	—	—	590	126	205	0	—	—	—	760	8.6	1.8	11.0
73-74—New York	19	—	500	84	184	.457	—	—	—	42	53	.792	47	94	141	30	49	0	12	—	21	210	7.4	1.6	11.1
REG. SEASON TOTALS	650	—	23073	4859	10202	.476	—	—	—	2465	3298	.747	47	94	8414	1186	2411	58	12	—	21	12183	12.9	1.8	18.7
PLAYOFF TOTALS	78	—	2641	570	1203	.474	—	—	—	218	285	.765	4	18	801	149	275	4	2	—	0	1358	10.3	1.9	17.4
ALL-STAR TOTALS	7	—	161	38	84	.452	—	—	—	12	16	.750	0	0	58	7	20	1	0	—	0	88	8.3	1.0	12.6

REGAN, RICHARD JOSEPH (Richie) b. November 30, 1930 Ht. 6-2 Wt. 180 College—Seton Hall

SEASON—TEAM	G	GS	MIN	FGM	FGA	PCT	3FGM	3FGA	PCT	FTM	FTA	PCT	O-RB	D-RB	TOT	AST	PF	DQ	STL	TO	BLK	PTS	RPG	APG	PPG
55-56—Rochester	72	—	1746	240	681	.352	—	—	—	85	133	.639	—	—	174	222	179	4	—	—	—	565	2.4	3.1	7.8
56-57—Rochester	71	—	2100	257	780	.329	—	—	—	182	235	.774	—	—	205	222	179	1	—	—	—	696	2.9	3.1	9.8
57-58—Cincinnati	72	—	1648	202	569	.355	—	—	—	120	172	.698	—	—	175	185	174	0	—	—	—	524	2.4	2.6	7.3
REG. SEASON TOTALS	215	—	5494	699	2030	.344	—	—	—	387	540	.717	—	—	554	629	532	5	—	—	—	1785	2.6	2.9	8.3
PLAYOFF TOTALS	2	—	63	12	26	.462	—	—	—	0	1	.000	—	—	9	3	5	0	—	—	—	24	4.5	1.5	12.0
ALL-STAR TOTALS	1	—	21	2	7	.286	—	—	—	0	0		—	—	4	1	0	0	—	—	—	4	4.0	1.0	4.0

REHFELDT, DONALD (Don) b. January 7, 1927 d. October 17, 1980 Ht. 6-6 Wt. 210 College—Wisconsin

SEASON—TEAM	G	GS	MIN	FGM	FGA	PCT	3FGM	3FGA	PCT	FTM	FTA	PCT	O-RB	D-RB	TOT	AST	PF	DQ	STL	TO	BLK	PTS	RPG	APG	PPG
50-51—Baltimore	59	—	—	164	426	.385	—	—	—	103	139	.741	—	—	251	68	146	4	—	—	—	431	4.3	1.2	7.3
51-52—Balt.-Milw.	39	—	788	99	285	.347	—	—	—	63	80	.788	—	—	243	50	102	2	—	—	—	261	6.2	1.3	6.7
REG. SEASON TOTALS	98	—	788	263	711	.370	—	—	—	166	219	.758	—	—	494	118	248	6	—	—	—	692	5.0	1.2	7.1

REID, HERMAN JR. (J.R.) b. March 31, 1968 Ht. 6-9 Wt. 265 College—North Carolina

SEASON—TEAM	G	GS	MIN	FGM	FGA	PCT	3FGM	3FGA	PCT	FTM	FTA	PCT	O-RB	D-RB	TOT	AST	PF	DQ	STL	TO	BLK	PTS	RPG	APG	PPG
89-90—Charlotte	82	82	2757	358	814	.440	0	5	.000	192	289	.664	199	492	691	101	292	7	92	172	54	908	8.4	1.2	11.1
90-91—Charlotte	80	80	2467	360	773	.466	0	2	.000	182	259	.703	154	348	502	89	286	6	87	153	47	902	6.3	1.1	11.3
91-92—Charlotte	51	7	1257	213	435	.490	0	3	.000	134	190	.705	96	221	317	81	159	0	49	84	23	560	6.2	1.6	11.0
92-93—Cha.-S.A.	83	25	1887	283	595	.476	0	5	.000	214	280	.764	120	336	456	80	266	3	47	125	31	780	5.5	1.0	9.4
93-94—San Antonio	70	11	1344	260	530	.491	0	3	.000	107	153	.699	91	129	220	73	165	0	43	84	25	627	3.1	1.0	9.0
REG. SEASON TOTALS	366	205	9712	1474	3147	.468	0	18	.000	829	1171	.708	660	1526	2186	424	1168	16	318	618	180	3777	6.0	1.2	10.3
PLAYOFF TOTALS	14	2	276	35	81	.432	0	2	.000	30	40	.750	19	43	62	18	41	0	9	14	10	100	4.4	1.3	7.1

REID, JAMES (Jim) b. August 3, 1945 Ht. 6-6 Wt. 210 College—Winston-Salem State

SEASON—TEAM	G	GS	MIN	FGM	FGA	PCT	3FGM	3FGA	PCT	FTM	FTA	PCT	O-RB	D-RB	TOT	AST	PF	DQ	STL	TO	BLK	PTS	RPG	APG	PPG
67-68—Philadelphia	6	—	52	10	20	.500	—	—	—	1	5	.200	—	—	11	3	6	0	—	—	—	21	1.8	0.5	3.5
REG. SEASON TOTALS	6	—	52	10	20	.500	—	—	—	1	5	.200	—	—	11	3	6	0	—	—	—	21	1.8	0.5	3.5

REID, ROBERT KEITH b. August 30, 1955 Ht. 6-8 Wt. 210 College—St. Mary's (Texas)

SEASON—TEAM	G	GS	MIN	FGM	FGA	PCT	3FGM	3FGA	PCT	FTM	FTA	PCT	O-RB	D-RB	TOT	AST	PF	DQ	STL	TO	BLK	PTS	RPG	APG	PPG
77-78—Houston	80	—	1849	261	574	.455	—	—	—	63	96	.656	111	248	359	121	277	8	67	81	51	585	4.5	1.5	7.3
78-79—Houston	82	—	2259	382	777	.492	—	—	—	131	186	.704	129	354	483	230	302	7	75	131	48	895	5.9	2.8	10.9
79-80—Houston	76	—	2304	419	861	.487	0	3	.000	153	208	.736	140	301	441	244	281	2	132	164	57	991	5.8	3.2	13.0
80-81—Houston	82	—	2963	536	1113	.482	0	4	.000	229	303	.756	164	419	583	344	325	4	163	198	66	1301	7.1	4.2	15.9
81-82—Houston	77	75	2913	437	958	.456	1	10	.100	160	214	.748	175	336	511	314	297	2	115	157	48	1035	6.6	4.1	13.4
83-84—Houston	64	28	1936	406	857	.474	2	8	.250	81	123	.659	97	244	341	217	243	5	88	92	30	895	5.3	3.4	14.0
84-85—Houston	82	0	1763	312	648	.481	1	16	.063	88	126	.698	81	192	273	171	196	1	48	101	22	713	3.3	2.1	8.7
85-86—Houston	82	5	2157	409	881	.464	6	33	.182	162	214	.757	67	234	301	222	231	3	91	96	16	986	3.7	2.7	12.0
86-87—Houston	75	63	2594	420	1006	.417	53	162	.327	136	177	.768	47	242	289	323	232	2	75	104	21	1029	3.9	4.3	13.7
87-88—Houston	62	31	980	165	356	.463	13	34	.382	50	63	.794	38	87	125	67	118	0	27	41	5	393	2.0	1.1	6.3
88-89—Charlotte	82	54	2152	519	1214	.428	17	52	.327	152	196	.776	82	220	302	153	235	2	53	106	20	1207	3.7	1.9	14.7
89-90—Port.-Cha.	72	28	1202	175	447	.391	10	32	.313	54	86	.628	34	117	151	90	153	0	38	45	16	414	2.1	1.3	5.8
90-91—Philadelphia	3	0	37	2	14	.143	0	0	—	0	0	—	2	7	9	4	3	0	1	3	3	4	3.0	1.3	1.3
REG. SEASON TOTALS	919	284	25109	4443	9706	.458	103	354	.291	1459	1992	.732	1167	3001	4168	2500	2893	36	973	1319	403	10448	4.5	2.7	11.4
PLAYOFF TOTALS	79	37	2740	430	983	.437	8	53	.151	157	217	.724	110	281	391	335	277	3	106	148	41	1025	4.9	4.2	13.0

REID, WILLIAM JENNINGS JR. (**Billy**) b. September 10, 1957 Ht. 6-5 Wt. 190 College—Anderson JC/New Mexico/San Francisco

SEASON—TEAM	G	GS	MIN	FGM	FGA	PCT	3FGM	3FGA	PCT	FTM	FTA	PCT	O-RB	D-RB	TOT	AST	PF	DQ	STL	TO	BLK	PTS	RPG	APG	PPG
80-81—Golden State	59	—	597	84	185	.454	0	5	.000	22	39	.564	27	33	60	71	111	0	33	78	5	190	1.0	1.2	3.2
REG. SEASON TOTALS	59	—	597	84	185	.454	0	5	.000	22	39	.564	27	33	60	71	111	0	33	78	5	190	1.0	1.2	3.2

REISER, JOSEPH FRANCIS (**Chick**) b. December 17, 1914 Ht. 5-11 Wt. 165 College—Pratt Institute/New York University

SEASON—TEAM	G	GS	MIN	FGM	FGA	PCT	3FGM	3FGA	PCT	FTM	FTA	PCT	O-RB	D-RB	TOT	AST	PF	DQ	STL	TO	BLK	PTS	RPG	APG	PPG
43-44—Fort Wayne (N)	22	—	—	28	—	—	—	—	—	25	—	—	—	—	—	—	—	—	—	—	—	81	—	—	3.7
44-45—Fort Wayne (N)	30	—	—	82	—	—	—	—	—	53	—	—	—	—	—	—	—	—	—	—	—	217	—	—	7.2
45-46—Fort Wayne (N)	34	—	—	90	—	—	—	—	—	53	80	.663	—	—	—	—	93	—	—	—	—	233	—	—	6.9
46-47—Fort Wayne (N)	44	—	—	153	—	—	—	—	—	104	139	.748	—	—	—	—	153	—	—	—	—	410	—	—	9.3
47-48—Baltimore	47	—	202	628	322	—	—	—	—	137	185	.741	—	—	—	40	175	—	—	—	—	541	—	0.9	11.5
48-49—Baltimore	57	—	219	653	335	—	—	—	—	188	257	.732	—	—	—	132	202	—	—	—	—	626	—	2.3	11.0
49-50—Washington	67	—	197	646	305	—	—	—	—	212	254	.835	—	—	—	174	223	—	—	—	—	606	—	2.6	9.0
REG. NBA TOTALS	171	—	—	618	1927	.321	—	—	—	537	696	.772	—	—	—	346	600	—	—	—	—	1773	—	2.0	10.4
REG. NBL TOTALS	130	—	—	353	—	—	—	—	—	235	219	.717	—	—	—	—	246	—	—	—	—	941	—	—	7.2
NBA PLAYOFF TOTALS	16	—	—	49	191	.257	—	—	—	58	73	.795	—	—	—	20	72	3	—	—	—	156	—	1.3	9.8
NBL PLAYOFF TOTALS	24	—	—	77	—	—	—	—	—	45	47	.660	—	—	—	—	77	—	—	—	—	199	—	—	8.3

RELLFORD, RICHARD ALLEN b. February 16, 1964 Ht. 6-6 Wt. 230 College—Michigan

SEASON—TEAM	G	GS	MIN	FGM	FGA	PCT	3FGM	3FGA	PCT	FTM	FTA	PCT	O-RB	D-RB	TOT	AST	PF	DQ	STL	TO	BLK	PTS	RPG	APG	PPG
87-88—San Antonio	4	0	42	5	8	.625	0	0	—	6	8	.750	2	5	7	1	3	0	0	4	3	16	1.8	0.3	4.0
REG. SEASON TOTALS	4	0	42	5	8	.625	0	0	—	6	8	.750	2	5	7	1	3	0	0	4	3	16	1.8	0.3	4.0

RENNICKE, JOHN W. b. August 11, 1929 Ht. 6-2 Wt. 205 College—Drake

SEASON—TEAM	G	GS	MIN	FGM	FGA	PCT	3FGM	3FGA	PCT	FTM	FTA	PCT	O-RB	D-RB	TOT	AST	PF	DQ	STL	TO	BLK	PTS	RPG	APG	PPG
51-52—Milwaukee	6	—	54	4	18	.222	—	—	—	3	9	.333	—	—	9	1	7	0	—	—	—	11	1.5	0.2	1.8
REG. SEASON TOTALS	6	—	54	4	18	.222	—	—	—	3	9	.333	—	—	9	1	7	0	—	—	—	11	1.5	0.2	1.8

RENSBERGER, ROBERT LAMAR (**Rob**) b. March 7, 1921 Ht. 6-2 Wt. 170 College—Notre Dame

SEASON—TEAM	G	GS	MIN	FGM	FGA	PCT	3FGM	3FGA	PCT	FTM	FTA	PCT	O-RB	D-RB	TOT	AST	PF	DQ	STL	TO	BLK	PTS	RPG	APG	PPG
45-46—Chicago (N)	16	—	—	6	—	—	—	—	—	3	—	—	—	—	—	—	—	—	—	—	—	15	—	—	0.9
46-47—Chicago	3	—	—	0	7	.000	—	—	—	0	0	—	—	—	—	0	4	—	—	—	—	0	—	0.0	0.0
REG. NBA TOTALS	3	—	—	0	7	.000	—	—	—	0	0	—	—	—	—	0	4	—	—	—	—	0	—	0.0	0.0
REG. NBL TOTALS	16	—	—	6	—	—	—	—	—	3	—	—	—	—	—	—	—	—	—	—	—	15	—	—	0.9

RESTANI, KEVIN GILBERT (**Big Bird**) b. December 23, 1951 Ht. 6-9 Wt. 225 College—San Francisco

SEASON—TEAM	G	GS	MIN	FGM	FGA	PCT	3FGM	3FGA	PCT	FTM	FTA	PCT	O-RB	D-RB	TOT	AST	PF	DQ	STL	TO	BLK	PTS	RPG	APG	PPG
74-75—Milwaukee	76	—	1755	188	427	.440	—	—	—	35	49	.714	131	272	403	119	172	1	36	—	19	411	5.3	1.6	5.4
75-76—Milwaukee	82	—	1650	234	493	.475	—	—	—	24	42	.571	115	261	376	96	151	3	36	—	12	492	4.6	1.2	6.0
76-77—Milwaukee	64	—	1116	173	334	.518	—	—	—	12	24	.500	81	181	262	88	102	0	33	—	11	358	4.1	1.4	5.6
77-78—Milw.-K.C.	54	—	547	72	167	.431	—	—	—	9	13	.692	36	72	108	30	41	0	5	17	5	153	2.0	0.6	2.8
78-79—Milwaukee	81	—	1598	262	529	.495	—	—	—	51	73	.699	141	244	385	122	155	0	30	96	27	575	4.8	1.5	7.1
79-80—San Antonio	82	—	1966	369	727	.508	5	29	.172	131	161	.814	142	244	386	189	186	0	54	129	12	874	4.7	2.3	10.7
80-81—San Antonio	64	—	999	192	369	.520	3	8	.375	62	88	.705	71	103	174	81	103	0	16	68	14	449	2.7	1.3	7.0
81-82—S.A.-Clev.	47	0	483	32	88	.364	0	2	.000	10	16	.625	39	73	112	22	56	0	11	20	11	74	2.4	0.5	1.6
REG. SEASON TOTALS	550	0	10114	1522	3134	.486	8	39	.205	334	466	.717	756	1450	2206	747	966	4	221	330	111	3386	4.0	1.4	6.2
PLAYOFF TOTALS	9	0	118	19	36	.528	0	1	.000	4	9	.444	8	15	23	4	10	0	1	3	2	42	2.6	0.4	4.7

REYNOLDS, GEORGE b. November 23, 1947 Ht. 6-4 Wt. 195 College—Houston

SEASON—TEAM	G	GS	MIN	FGM	FGA	PCT	3FGM	3FGA	PCT	FTM	FTA	PCT	O-RB	D-RB	TOT	AST	PF	DQ	STL	TO	BLK	PTS	RPG	APG	PPG
69-70—Detroit	10	—	44	8	19	.421	—	—	—	5	7	.714	—	—	14	12	10	0	—	—	—	21	1.4	1.2	2.1
REG. SEASON TOTALS	10	—	44	8	19	.421	—	—	—	5	7	.714	—	—	14	12	10	0	—	—	—	21	1.4	1.2	2.1

REYNOLDS, JERRY (Ice) b. December 23, 1962 Ht. 6-8 Wt. 205 College—Madison Area Tech/Louisiana State

SEASON—TEAM	G	GS	MIN	FGM	FGA	PCT	3FGM	3FGA	PCT	FTM	FTA	PCT	O-RB	D-RB	TOT	AST	PF	DQ	STL	TO	BLK	PTS	RPG	APG	PPG
85-86—Milwaukee	55	8	508	72	162	.444	1	2	.500	58	104	.558	37	43	80	86	57	0	43	52	19	203	1.5	1.6	3.7
86-87—Milwaukee	58	24	963	140	356	.393	6	18	.333	118	184	.641	72	101	173	106	91	0	50	82	30	404	3.0	1.8	7.0
87-88—Milwaukee	62	21	1161	188	419	.449	3	7	.429	119	154	.773	70	90	160	104	97	0	74	104	32	498	2.6	1.7	8.0
88-89—Seattle	56	0	737	149	357	.417	3	15	.200	127	167	.760	49	51	100	62	58	0	53	57	26	428	1.8	1.1	7.6
89-90—Orlando	67	40	1817	309	741	.417	1	14	.071	239	322	.742	91	232	323	180	162	1	93	139	64	858	4.8	2.7	12.8
90-91—Orlando	80	9	1843	344	793	.434	10	34	.294	336	419	.802	88	211	299	203	123	0	95	172	56	1034	3.7	2.5	12.9
91-92—Orlando	46	16	1159	197	518	.380	3	24	.125	158	189	.836	47	102	149	151	69	0	63	96	17	555	3.2	3.3	12.1
REG. SEASON TOTALS	424	118	8188	1399	3346	.418	27	114	.237	1155	1539	.750	454	830	1284	892	657	1	471	702	244	3980	3.0	2.1	9.4
PLAYOFF TOTALS	18	0	97	19	48	.396	1	6	.167	14	23	.609	5	11	16	8	12	0	9	9	9	53	0.9	0.4	2.9

RHINE, KENDALL LEE b. February 13, 1943 Ht. 6-10 Wt. 240 College—Rice

SEASON—TEAM	G	GS	MIN	FGM	FGA	PCT	3FGM	3FGA	PCT	FTM	FTA	PCT	O-RB	D-RB	TOT	AST	PF	DQ	STL	TO	BLK	PTS	RPG	APG	PPG
67-68—Kentucky (A)	52	—	552	50	158	.316	0	1	.000	27	56	.482	—	—	235	31	120	2	—	36	—	127	4.5	0.6	2.4
68-69—Houston (A)	73	—	2116	255	629	.405	0	1	.000	149	265	.562	307	497	804	150	321	16	—	119	—	659	11.0	2.1	9.0
REG. ABA TOTALS	125	—	2668	305	787	.388	0	2	.000	176	321	.548	307	497	1039	181	441	18	—	155	—	786	8.3	1.4	6.3
ABA PLAYOFF TOTALS	5	—	62	5	17	.294	0	0	—	0	7	.000	—	—	15	4	16	—	—	4	—	10	3.0	0.8	2.0

RHODES, EUGENE STEPHEN (Gene) b. September 2, 1927 Ht. 6-1 Wt. 170 College—Western Kentucky

SEASON—TEAM	G	GS	MIN	FGM	FGA	PCT	3FGM	3FGA	PCT	FTM	FTA	PCT	O-RB	D-RB	TOT	AST	PF	DQ	STL	TO	BLK	PTS	RPG	APG	PPG
52-53—Indianapolis	65	—	1162	109	342	.319	—	—	—	119	169	.704	—	—	98	91	78	2	—	—	—	337	1.5	1.4	5.2
REG. SEASON TOTALS	65	—	1162	109	342	.319	—	—	—	119	169	.704	—	—	98	91	78	2	—	—	—	337	1.5	1.4	5.2
PLAYOFF TOTALS	2	—	51	4	14	.286	—	—	—	1	4	.250	—	—	7	5	5	0	—	—	—	9	3.5	2.5	4.5

RICE, GLEN ANTHONY b. May 28, 1967 Ht. 6-8 Wt. 220 College—Michigan

SEASON—TEAM	G	GS	MIN	FGM	FGA	PCT	3FGM	3FGA	PCT	FTM	FTA	PCT	O-RB	D-RB	TOT	AST	PF	DQ	STL	TO	BLK	PTS	RPG	APG	PPG
89-90—Miami	77	60	2311	470	1071	.439	17	69	.246	91	124	.734	100	252	352	138	198	1	67	113	27	1048	4.6	1.8	13.6
90-91—Miami	77	77	2646	550	1193	.461	71	184	.386	171	209	.818	85	296	381	189	216	0	101	166	26	1342	4.9	2.5	17.4
91-92—Miami	79	79	3007	672	1432	.469	155	396	.391	266	318	.836	84	310	394	184	170	0	90	145	35	1765	5.0	2.3	22.3
92-93—Miami	82	82	3082	582	1324	.440	148	386	.383	242	295	.820	92	332	424	180	201	0	92	157	25	1554	5.2	2.2	19.0
93-94—Miami	81	81	2999	663	1421	.467	132	346	.382	250	284	.880	76	358	434	184	186	0	110	130	32	1708	5.4	2.3	21.1
REG. SEASON TOTALS	396	379	14045	2937	6441	.456	523	1381	.379	1020	1230	.829	437	1548	1985	875	971	1	460	711	145	7417	5.0	2.2	18.7
PLAYOFF TOTALS	8	8	314	50	132	.379	10	35	.286	12	15	.800	9	37	46	15	21	0	13	20	2	122	5.8	1.9	15.3

RICHARDSON, CLINT DeWITT b. August 7, 1956 Ht. 6-3 Wt. 195 College—Seattle

SEASON—TEAM	G	GS	MIN	FGM	FGA	PCT	3FGM	3FGA	PCT	FTM	FTA	PCT	O-RB	D-RB	TOT	AST	PF	DQ	STL	TO	BLK	PTS	RPG	APG	PPG
79-80—Philadelphia	52	—	988	159	348	.457	1	3	.333	28	45	.622	55	68	123	107	97	0	24	64	15	347	2.4	2.1	6.7
80-81—Philadelphia	77	—	1313	227	464	.489	0	1	.000	84	108	.778	83	93	176	152	102	0	36	110	10	538	2.3	2.0	7.0
81-82—Philadelphia	77	0	1040	140	310	.452	2	2	1.000	69	88	.784	55	63	118	109	109	0	36	79	9	351	1.5	1.4	4.6
82-83—Philadelphia	77	1	1755	259	559	.463	0	6	.000	71	111	.640	98	149	247	168	164	0	71	99	18	589	3.2	2.2	7.6
83-84—Philadelphia	69	12	1571	221	473	.467	0	4	.000	79	103	.767	62	103	165	155	145	0	49	100	23	521	2.4	2.2	7.6
84-85—Philadelphia	74	20	1531	183	404	.453	1	3	.333	76	89	.854	60	95	155	157	143	0	37	78	15	443	2.1	2.1	6.0
85-86—Indiana	82	61	2224	335	736	.455	1	9	.111	123	147	.837	69	182	251	372	153	1	58	136	8	794	3.1	4.5	9.7
86-87—Indiana	78	14	1396	218	467	.467	6	17	.353	59	74	.797	51	92	143	241	106	0	49	85	7	501	1.8	3.1	6.4
REG. SEASON TOTALS	586	108	11818	1742	3761	.463	11	45	.244	589	765	.770	533	845	1378	1461	1019	1	360	751	105	4084	2.4	2.5	7.0
PLAYOFF TOTALS	72	1	1387	178	357	.499	0	3	.000	62	90	.689	73	120	193	120	152	0	48	70	14	418	2.7	1.7	5.8

RICHARDSON, JEROME JR. (Pooh) b. May 14, 1966 Ht. 6-1 Wt. 180 College—UCLA

SEASON—TEAM	G	GS	MIN	FGM	FGA	PCT	3FGM	3FGA	PCT	FTM	FTA	PCT	O-RB	D-RB	TOT	AST	PF	DQ	STL	TO	BLK	PTS	RPG	APG	PPG
89-90—Minnesota	82	48	2581	426	925	.461	23	83	.277	63	107	.589	55	162	217	554	143	0	133	141	25	938	2.6	6.8	11.4
90-91—Minnesota	82	82	3154	635	1350	.470	42	128	.328	89	165	.539	82	204	286	734	114	0	131	174	13	1401	3.5	9.0	17.1
91-92—Minnesota	82	82	2922	587	1261	.466	53	155	.342	123	178	.691	91	210	301	685	152	0	119	204	25	1350	3.7	8.4	16.5
92-93—Indiana	74	73	2396	337	703	.479	3	29	.103	92	124	.742	63	204	267	573	132	1	94	167	12	769	3.6	7.7	10.4
93-94—Indiana	37	25	1022	160	354	.452	3	12	.250	47	77	.610	28	82	110	237	78	0	32	88	3	370	3.0	6.4	10.0
REG. SEASON TOTALS	357	310	12075	2145	4593	.467	124	407	.305	414	651	.636	319	862	1181	2783	619	1	509	774	78	4828	3.3	7.8	13.5
PLAYOFF TOTALS	4	1	95	6	15	.400	1	1	1.000	4	6	.667	1	10	11	23	7	1	2	6	0	17	2.8	5.8	4.3

RICHARDSON, MICHEAL RAY (Micheal Ray, Sugar Ray) b. April 11, 1955 Ht. 6-5 Wt. 190 College—Montana

SEASON—TEAM	G	GS	MIN	FGM	FGA	PCT	3FGM	3FGA	PCT	FTM	FTA	PCT	O-RB	D-RB	TOT	AST	PF	DQ	STL	TO	BLK	PTS	RPG	APG	PPG
78-79—New York	72	—	1218	200	483	.414	—	—	—	69	128	.539	78	155	233	213	188	2	100	141	18	469	3.2	3.0	6.5
79-80—New York	82	—	3060	502	1063	.472	27	110	.245	223	338	.660	151	388	539	832	260	3	265	359	35	1254	6.6	10.1	15.3
80-81—New York	79	—	3175	523	1116	.469	23	102	.225	224	338	.663	173	372	545	627	258	2	232	302	35	1293	6.9	7.9	16.4
81-82—New York	82	79	3044	619	1343	.461	19	101	.188	212	303	.700	177	388	565	572	317	3	213	291	41	1469	6.9	7.0	17.9
82-83—G.S.-N.J.	64	51	2076	346	815	.425	8	51	.157	106	163	.650	113	182	295	432	240	4	182	244	24	806	4.6	6.8	12.6
83-84—New Jersey	48	25	1285	243	528	.460	14	58	.241	76	108	.704	56	116	172	214	156	4	103	118	20	576	3.6	4.5	12.0
84-85—New Jersey	82	82	3127	690	1470	.469	29	115	.252	240	313	.767	156	301	457	669	277	3	243	249	22	1649	5.6	8.2	20.1
85-86—New Jersey	47	39	1604	296	661	.448	4	27	.148	141	179	.788	77	173	250	340	163	2	125	150	11	737	5.3	7.2	15.7
REG. SEASON TOTALS	556	276	18589	3419	7479	.457	124	564	.220	1291	1870	.690	981	2075	3056	3899	1859	23	1463	1854	206	8253	5.5	7.0	14.8
PLAYOFF TOTALS	18	16	712	108	280	.386	6	29	.207	60	87	.690	32	67	99	129	63	1	50	50	4	282	5.5	7.2	15.7
ALL-STAR TOTALS	4	0	70	15	32	.469	0	3	.000	2	4	.500	5	5	10	10	9	0	9	7	0	32	2.5	2.5	8.0

RICHMOND, MITCHELL JAMES (Mitch, Rock) b. June 30, 1965 Ht. 6-5 Wt. 215 College—Moberly Area CC/Kansas State

SEASON—TEAM	G	GS	MIN	FGM	FGA	PCT	3FGM	3FGA	PCT	FTM	FTA	PCT	O-RB	D-RB	TOT	AST	PF	DQ	STL	TO	BLK	PTS	RPG	APG	PPG
88-89—Golden State	79	79	2717	649	1386	.468	33	90	.367	410	506	.810	158	310	468	334	223	5	82	269	13	1741	5.9	4.2	22.0
89-90—Golden State	78	78	2799	640	1287	.497	34	95	.358	406	469	.866	98	262	360	223	210	3	98	201	24	1720	4.6	2.9	22.1
90-91—Golden State	77	77	3027	703	1424	.494	40	115	.348	394	465	.847	147	305	452	238	207	0	126	230	34	1840	5.9	3.1	23.9
91-92—Sacramento	80	80	3095	685	1465	.468	103	268	.384	330	406	.813	62	257	319	411	231	1	92	247	34	1803	4.0	5.1	22.5
92-93—Sacramento	45	45	1728	371	782	.474	48	130	.369	197	233	.845	18	136	154	221	137	3	53	130	9	987	3.4	4.9	21.9
93-94—Sacramento	78	78	2897	635	1428	.445	127	312	.407	426	511	.834	70	216	286	313	211	3	103	216	17	1823	3.7	4.0	23.4
REG. SEASON TOTALS	437	437	16263	3683	7772	.474	385	1010	.381	2163	2590	.835	553	1486	2039	1740	1219	15	554	1293	131	9914	4.7	4.0	22.7
PLAYOFF TOTALS	17	17	686	147	304	.484	11	40	.275	57	62	.919	20	85	105	57	53	1	19	41	7	362	6.2	3.4	21.3
ALL-STAR TOTALS	1	1	24	5	16	.313	0	0	—	0	0	—	0	2	2	3	0	0	0	2	0	10	2.0	3.0	10.0

RICHTER, JOHN FRITZ b. March 12, 1937 Ht. 6-9 Wt. 225 College—Paul Smith's/North Carolina State

SEASON—TEAM	G	GS	MIN	FGM	FGA	PCT	3FGM	3FGA	PCT	FTM	FTA	PCT	O-RB	D-RB	TOT	AST	PF	DQ	STL	TO	BLK	PTS	RPG	APG	PPG
59-60—Boston	66	—	808	113	332	.340	—	—	—	59	117	.504	—	—	312	27	158	1	—	—	—	285	4.7	0.4	4.3
REG. SEASON TOTALS	66	—	808	113	332	.340	—	—	—	59	117	.504	—	—	312	27	158	1	—	—	—	285	4.7	0.4	4.3
PLAYOFF TOTALS	8	—	95	15	38	.395	—	—	—	5	14	.357	—	—	29	2	17	1	—	—	—	35	3.6	0.3	4.4

RICKETTS, RICHARD JAMES JR. (Dick) b. December 4, 1933 d. March 6, 1988 Ht. 6-7 Wt. 220 College—Duquesne

SEASON—TEAM	G	GS	MIN	FGM	FGA	PCT	3FGM	3FGA	PCT	FTM	FTA	PCT	O-RB	D-RB	TOT	AST	PF	DQ	STL	TO	BLK	PTS	RPG	APG	PPG
55-56—St. L.-Roch.	68	—	1943	235	752	.313	—	—	—	138	195	.708	—	—	490	206	287	14	—	—	—	608	7.2	3.0	8.9
56-57—Rochester	72	—	2114	299	869	.344	—	—	—	206	297	.694	—	—	437	127	307	12	—	—	—	804	6.1	1.8	11.2
57-58—Cincinnati	72	—	1620	215	664	.324	—	—	—	132	196	.673	—	—	410	114	277	8	—	—	—	562	5.7	1.6	7.8
REG. SEASON TOTALS	212	—	5677	749	2285	.328	—	—	—	476	688	.692	—	—	1337	447	871	34	—	—	—	1974	6.3	2.1	9.3
PLAYOFF TOTALS	2	—	31	5	15	.333	—	—	—	5	5	1.000	—	—	10	2	9	0	—	—	—	15	5.0	1.0	7.5

RIDER, ISAIAH JR. (J.R.) b. March 12, 1971 Ht. 6-5 Wt. 215 College—Allen County CC/Antelope Valley JC/Nevada-Las Vegas

SEASON—TEAM	G	GS	MIN	FGM	FGA	PCT	3FGM	3FGA	PCT	FTM	FTA	PCT	O-RB	D-RB	TOT	AST	PF	DQ	STL	TO	BLK	PTS	RPG	APG	PPG
93-94—Minnesota	79	60	2415	522	1115	.468	54	150	.360	215	265	.811	118	197	315	202	194	0	54	218	28	1313	4.0	2.6	16.6
REG. SEASON TOTALS	79	60	2415	522	1115	.468	54	150	.360	215	265	.811	118	197	315	202	194	0	54	218	28	1313	4.0	2.6	16.6

RIDGLE, JACKIE LENDELL b. February 13, 1948 Ht. 6-4½ Wt. 195 College—California

SEASON—TEAM	G	GS	MIN	FGM	FGA	PCT	3FGM	3FGA	PCT	FTM	FTA	PCT	O-RB	D-RB	TOT	AST	PF	DQ	STL	TO	BLK	PTS	RPG	APG	PPG
71-72—Cleveland	32	—	107	19	44	.432	—	—	—	19	26	.731	—	—	15	7	15	0	—	—	—	57	0.5	0.2	1.8
REG. SEASON TOTALS	32	—	107	19	44	.432	—	—	—	19	26	.731	—	—	15	7	15	0	—	—	—	57	0.5	0.2	1.8

RIEBE, MELVIN RUSSELL (Mel, Mouse) b. July 12, 1916 d. July 25, 1977 Ht. 5-11½ Wt. 180 College—Wooster

SEASON—TEAM	G	GS	MIN	FGM	FGA	PCT	3FGM	3FGA	PCT	FTM	FTA	PCT	O-RB	D-RB	TOT	AST	PF	DQ	STL	TO	BLK	PTS	RPG	APG	PPG
43-44—Cleveland (N)	18	—	—	113	—	—	—	—	—	97	134	.724	—	—	—	—	48	—	—	—	—	323	—	—	17.9
44-45—Cleveland (N)	30	—	—	223	—	—	—	—	—	161	—	—	—	—	—	—	86	—	—	—	—	607	—	—	20.2
45-46—Cleveland (N)	5	—	—	23	—	—	—	—	—	26	—	—	—	—	—	—	—	—	—	—	—	72	—	—	14.4
46-47—Cleveland	55	—	—	276	898	.307	—	—	—	111	173	.642	—	—	—	67	169	—	—	—	—	663	—	1.2	12.1
47-48—Boston	48	—	—	202	653	.309	—	—	—	85	137	.620	—	—	—	41	137	—	—	—	—	489	—	0.9	10.2
48-49—Boston-Prov.	43	—	—	172	589	.292	—	—	—	79	133	.594	—	—	—	104	110	—	—	—	—	423	—	2.4	9.8
REG. NBA TOTALS	146	—	—	650	2140	.304	—	—	—	275	443	.621	—	—	—	212	416	—	—	—	—	1575	—	1.5	10.8
REG. NBL TOTALS	53	—	—	359	—	—	—	—	—	284	134	.724	—	—	—	—	134	—	—	—	—	1002	—	—	18.9
NBA PLAYOFF TOTALS	6	—	—	23	80	.288	—	—	—	17	26	.654	—	—	—	5	13	—	—	—	—	63	—	0.8	10.5
NBL PLAYOFF TOTALS	4	—	—	23	—	—	—	—	—	20	—	—	—	—	—	—	8	—	—	—	—	66	—	—	16.5

RIEDY, ROBERT F. (Bob) b. August 26, 1945 Ht. 6-6 Wt. 215 College—Duke

SEASON—TEAM	G	GS	MIN	FGM	FGA	PCT	3FGM	3FGA	PCT	FTM	FTA	PCT	O-RB	D-RB	TOT	AST	PF	DQ	STL	TO	BLK	PTS	RPG	APG	PPG
67-68—Houston (A)	23	—	331	45	129	.349	0	0	—	41	67	.612	—	—	68	5	27	0	—	21	—	131	3.0	0.2	5.7
REG. ABA TOTALS	23	—	331	45	129	.349	0	0	—	41	67	.612	—	—	68	5	27	0	—	21	—	131	3.0	0.2	5.7

RIFFEY, JAMES R. **(Jim)** b. December 14, 1923   Ht. 6-4 Wt. 200 College—Tulane

SEASON—TEAM	G	GS	MIN	FGM	FGA	PCT	3FGM	3FGA	PCT	FTM	FTA	PCT	O-RB	D-RB	TOT	AST	PF	DQ	STL	TO	BLK	PTS	RPG	APG	PPG
50-51—Fort Wayne	35	—	—	65	185	.351	—	—	—	20	26	.769	—	—	61	16	54	0	—	—	—	150	1.7	0.5	4.3
REG. SEASON TOTALS	35	—	—	65	185	.351	—	—	—	20	26	.769	—	—	61	16	54	0	—	—	—	150	1.7	0.5	4.3

RIKER, THOMAS E. **(Tom)** b. February 28, 1950   Ht. 6-10 Wt. 225 College—South Carolina

SEASON—TEAM	G	GS	MIN	FGM	FGA	PCT	3FGM	3FGA	PCT	FTM	FTA	PCT	O-RB	D-RB	TOT	AST	PF	DQ	STL	TO	BLK	PTS	RPG	APG	PPG
72-73—New York	14	—	65	10	24	.417	—	—	—	15	24	.625	—	—	16	2	15	0	—	—	—	35	1.1	0.1	2.5
73-74—New York	17	—	57	13	29	.448	—	—	—	12	17	.706	9	6	15	3	6	0	0	—	0	38	0.9	0.2	2.2
74-75—New York	51	—	483	53	147	.361	—	—	—	46	82	.561	40	67	107	19	64	0	15	—	5	152	2.1	0.4	3.0
REG. SEASON TOTALS	82	—	605	76	200	.380	—	—	—	73	123	.593	49	73	138	24	85	0	15	—	5	225	1.7	0.3	2.7
PLAYOFF TOTALS	1	—	8	1	2	.500	—	—	—	0	0	—	1	1	2	1	1	0	0	—	0	2	2.0	1.0	2.0

RILEY, ERIC KENDALL b. June 2, 1970   Ht. 7-0 Wt. 245 College—Michigan

SEASON—TEAM	G	GS	MIN	FGM	FGA	PCT	3FGM	3FGA	PCT	FTM	FTA	PCT	O-RB	D-RB	TOT	AST	PF	DQ	STL	TO	BLK	PTS	RPG	APG	PPG
93-94—Houston	47	2	219	34	70	.486	0	1	.000	20	37	.541	24	35	59	9	30	0	5	15	9	88	1.3	0.2	1.9
REG. SEASON TOTALS	47	2	219	34	70	.486	0	1	.000	20	37	.541	24	35	59	9	30	0	5	15	9	88	1.3	0.2	1.9

RILEY, PATRICK JAMES **(Pat)** b. March 20, 1945   Ht. 6-4 Wt. 205 College—Kentucky

SEASON—TEAM	G	GS	MIN	FGM	FGA	PCT	3FGM	3FGA	PCT	FTM	FTA	PCT	O-RB	D-RB	TOT	AST	PF	DQ	STL	TO	BLK	PTS	RPG	APG	PPG
67-68—San Diego	80	—	1263	250	660	.379	—	—	—	128	202	.634	—	—	177	138	205	1	—	—	—	628	2.2	1.7	7.9
68-69—San Diego	56	—	1027	202	498	.406	—	—	—	90	134	.672	—	—	112	136	146	1	—	—	—	494	2.0	2.4	8.8
69-70—San Diego	36	—	474	75	180	.417	—	—	—	40	55	.727	—	—	57	85	68	0	—	—	—	190	1.6	2.4	5.3
70-71—Los Angeles	54	—	506	105	254	.413	—	—	—	56	87	.644	—	—	54	72	84	0	—	—	—	266	1.0	1.3	4.9
71-72—Los Angeles	67	—	926	197	441	.447	—	—	—	55	74	.743	—	—	127	75	110	0	—	—	—	449	1.9	1.1	6.7
72-73—Los Angeles	55	—	801	167	390	.428	—	—	—	65	82	.793	—	—	65	81	126	0	—	—	—	399	1.2	1.5	7.3
73-74—Los Angeles	72	—	1361	287	667	.430	—	—	—	110	144	.764	38	90	128	148	173	1	54	—	3	684	1.8	2.1	9.5
74-75—Los Angeles	46	—	1016	219	523	.419	—	—	—	69	93	.742	25	60	85	121	128	0	36	—	4	507	1.8	2.6	11.0
75-76—L.A.-Phoenix	62	—	813	117	301	.389	—	—	—	55	77	.714	16	34	50	57	112	0	22	—	6	289	0.8	0.9	4.7
REG. SEASON TOTALS	528	—	8187	1619	3914	.414	—	—	—	668	948	.705	79	184	855	913	1152	3	112	—	13	3906	1.6	1.7	7.4
PLAYOFF TOTALS	44	—	641	111	297	.374	—	—	—	29	38	.763	3	3	66	52	86	0	4	—	0	251	1.5	1.2	5.7

RILEY, ROBERT J. **(Bob)** b. July 6, 1948   Ht. 6-9 Wt. 235 College—Mount St. Mary's

SEASON—TEAM	G	GS	MIN	FGM	FGA	PCT	3FGM	3FGA	PCT	FTM	FTA	PCT	O-RB	D-RB	TOT	AST	PF	DQ	STL	TO	BLK	PTS	RPG	APG	PPG
70-71—Atlanta	7	—	39	4	9	.444	—	—	—	5	9	.556	—	—	12	1	5	0	—	—	—	13	1.7	0.1	1.9
REG. SEASON TOTALS	7	—	39	4	9	.444	—	—	—	5	9	.556	—	—	12	1	5	0	—	—	—	13	1.7	0.1	1.9

RILEY, RONALD JAY **(Ron)** b. November 11, 1950   Ht. 6-8 Wt. 200 College—USC

SEASON—TEAM	G	GS	MIN	FGM	FGA	PCT	3FGM	3FGA	PCT	FTM	FTA	PCT	O-RB	D-RB	TOT	AST	PF	DQ	STL	TO	BLK	PTS	RPG	APG	PPG
72-73—Kansas City-Omaha	74	—	1634	273	634	.431	—	—	—	79	116	.681	—	—	507	76	226	3	—	—	—	625	6.9	1.0	8.4
73-74—K.C.-Omaha-Houston	48	—	591	81	202	.401	—	—	—	24	38	.632	48	129	177	37	95	0	18	—	24	186	3.7	0.8	3.9
74-75—Houston	77	—	1578	196	470	.417	—	—	—	71	97	.732	137	243	380	130	197	3	56	—	22	463	4.9	1.7	6.0
75-76—Houston	65	—	1049	115	280	.411	—	—	—	38	56	.679	91	213	304	75	137	1	32	—	21	268	4.7	1.2	4.1
REG. SEASON TOTALS	264	—	4852	665	1586	.419	—	—	—	212	307	.691	276	585	1368	318	655	7	106	—	67	1542	5.2	1.2	5.8
PLAYOFF TOTALS	8	—	152	25	42	.595	—	—	—	6	16	.375	12	24	36	15	18	0	9	—	2	56	4.5	1.9	7.0

RINALDI, RICHARD P. **(Rich)** b. August 3, 1949   Ht. 6-3½ Wt. 195 College—St. Peter's

SEASON—TEAM	G	GS	MIN	FGM	FGA	PCT	3FGM	3FGA	PCT	FTM	FTA	PCT	O-RB	D-RB	TOT	AST	PF	DQ	STL	TO	BLK	PTS	RPG	APG	PPG
71-72—Baltimore	39	—	159	42	104	.404	—	—	—	20	30	.667	—	—	18	15	25	0	—	—	—	104	0.5	0.4	2.7
72-73—Baltimore	33	—	646	116	284	.408	—	—	—	48	64	.750	—	—	68	48	40	0	—	—	—	280	2.1	1.5	8.5
73-74—Capital	7	—	48	3	22	.136	—	—	—	3	4	.750	2	5	7	10	7	0	3	—	1	9	1.0	1.4	1.3
73-74—New York (A)	5	—	28	4	14	.286	0	1	.000	4	4	1.000	5	0	5	1	3	—	2	1	0	12	1.0	0.2	2.4
REG. NBA TOTALS	79	—	853	161	410	.393	—	—	—	71	98	.724	2	5	93	73	72	0	3	—	1	393	1.2	0.9	5.0
REG. ABA TOTALS	5	—	28	4	14	.286	0	1	.000	4	4	1.000	5	0	5	1	3	0	2	1	0	12	1.0	0.2	2.4
NBA PLAYOFF TOTALS	3	—	6	1	2	.500	—	—	—	0	0	—	0	0	0	1	3	0	0	—	0	2	0.0	0.3	0.7

RIORDAN, MICHAEL W. (Mike) b. July 9, 1945 Ht. 6-4 Wt. 200 College—Providence

SEASON—TEAM	G	GS	MIN	FGM	FGA	PCT	3FGM	3FGA	PCT	FTM	FTA	PCT	O-RB	D-RB	TOT	AST	PF	DQ	STL	TO	BLK	PTS	RPG	APG	PPG
68-69—New York	54	—	397	49	144	.340	—	—	—	28	42	.667	—	—	57	46	93	1	—	—	—	126	1.1	0.9	2.3
69-70—New York	81	—	1677	255	549	.464	—	—	—	114	165	.691	—	—	194	201	192	1	—	—	—	624	2.4	2.5	7.7
70-71—New York	82	—	1320	162	388	.418	—	—	—	67	108	.620	—	—	169	121	151	0	—	—	—	391	2.1	1.5	4.8
71-72—N.Y.-Balt.	58	—	1377	233	499	.467	—	—	—	84	124	.677	—	—	128	126	129	0	—	—	—	550	2.2	2.2	9.5
72-73—Baltimore	82	—	3466	652	1278	.510	—	—	—	179	218	.821	—	—	404	426	216	0	—	—	—	1483	4.9	5.2	18.1
73-74—Capital	81	—	3230	577	1223	.472	—	—	—	136	174	.782	120	260	380	264	237	2	102	—	14	1290	4.7	3.3	15.9
74-75—Washington	74	—	2191	520	1057	.492	—	—	—	98	117	.838	90	194	284	198	238	4	72	—	6	1138	3.8	2.7	15.4
75-76—Washington	78	—	1943	291	662	.440	—	—	—	71	96	.740	44	143	187	122	201	2	54	—	13	653	2.4	1.6	8.4
76-77—Washington	49	—	289	34	94	.362	—	—	—	11	15	.733	7	20	27	20	33	0	3	—	2	79	0.6	0.4	1.6
REG. SEASON TOTALS	639	—	15890	2773	5894	.470	—	—	—	788	1059	.744	261	617	1830	1524	1490	10	231	—	35	6334	2.9	2.4	9.9
PLAYOFF TOTALS	84	—	1648	253	567	.446	—	—	—	107	138	.775	20	53	199	111	203	1	20	—	4	613	2.4	1.3	7.3

RISEN, ARNOLD D. (Arnie, Stilts) b. October 9, 1924 Ht. 6-9 Wt. 200 College—Ohio State

SEASON—TEAM	G	GS	MIN	FGM	FGA	PCT	3FGM	3FGA	PCT	FTM	FTA	PCT	O-RB	D-RB	TOT	AST	PF	DQ	STL	TO	BLK	PTS	RPG	APG	PPG
45-46—Indianapolis (N)	18	—	—	77	—	—	—	—	—	65	110	.591	—	—	—	—	75	—	—	—	—	219	—	—	12.2
46-47—Indianapolis (N)	44	—	—	204	—	—	—	—	—	174	276	.630	—	—	—	—	150	—	—	—	—	582	—	—	13.2
47-48—Ind.-Roch. (N)	61	—	—	282	—	—	—	—	—	241	352	.685	—	—	—	—	198	—	—	—	—	805	—	—	13.2
48-49—Rochester	60	—	—	345	816	.423	—	—	—	305	462	.660	—	—	—	100	216	—	—	—	—	995	—	1.7	16.6
49-50—Rochester	62	—	—	206	598	.344	—	—	—	213	321	.664	—	—	—	92	228	—	—	—	—	625	—	1.5	10.1
50-51—Rochester	66	—	—	377	940	.401	—	—	—	323	440	.734	—	—	795	158	278	9	—	—	—	1077	12.0	2.4	16.3
51-52—Rochester	66	—	2396	365	926	.394	—	—	—	302	431	.701	—	—	841	150	258	3	—	—	—	1032	12.7	2.3	15.6
52-53—Rochester	68	—	2288	295	802	.368	—	—	—	294	429	.685	—	—	745	135	274	10	—	—	—	884	11.0	2.0	13.0
53-54—Rochester	72	—	2385	321	872	.368	—	—	—	307	430	.714	—	—	728	120	284	9	—	—	—	949	10.1	1.7	13.2
54-55—Rochester	69	—	1970	259	699	.371	—	—	—	279	375	.744	—	—	703	112	253	10	—	—	—	797	10.2	1.6	11.6
55-56—Boston	68	—	1597	189	493	.383	—	—	—	170	240	.708	—	—	553	88	300	17	—	—	—	548	8.1	1.3	8.1
56-57—Boston	43	—	935	119	307	.388	—	—	—	106	156	.679	—	—	286	53	163	4	—	—	—	344	6.7	1.2	8.0
57-58—Boston	63	—	1119	134	397	.338	—	—	—	114	167	.683	—	—	360	50	195	5	—	—	—	382	5.7	0.8	6.1
REG. NBA TOTALS	637	—	12690	2610	6850	.381	—	—	—	2413	3451	.699	—	—	5011	1058	2449	67	—	—	—	7633	9.7	1.7	12.0
REG. NBL TOTALS	123	—	—	563	—	—	—	—	—	480	738	.650	—	—	—	—	423	—	—	—	—	1606	—	—	13.1
NBA PLAYOFF TOTALS	61	—	1023	263	684	.385	—	—	—	264	390	.677	—	—	561	86	255	11	—	—	—	790	10.2	1.4	13.0
NBL PLAYOFF TOTALS	12	—	—	67	—	—	—	—	—	61	74	.730	—	—	—	—	44	—	—	—	—	195	—	—	16.3
NBA ALL-STAR TOTALS	3	—	58	9	24	.375	—	—	—	1	5	.200	—	—	21	3	11	0	—	—	—	19	7.0	1.0	6.3

RITTER, GOEBEL FRANKLIN (Tex) b. February 26, 1924 Ht. 6-2 Wt. 185 College—Eastern Kentucky

SEASON—TEAM	G	GS	MIN	FGM	FGA	PCT	3FGM	3FGA	PCT	FTM	FTA	PCT	O-RB	D-RB	TOT	AST	PF	DQ	STL	TO	BLK	PTS	RPG	APG	PPG
48-49—New York	55	—	—	123	353	.348	—	—	—	91	146	.623	—	—	—	57	71	—	—	—	—	337	—	1.0	6.1
49-50—New York	62	—	—	100	297	.337	—	—	—	125	176	.710	—	—	—	51	101	—	—	—	—	325	—	0.8	5.2
50-51—New York	34	—	—	39	103	.379	—	—	—	49	71	.690	—	—	65	37	52	1	—	—	—	127	1.9	1.1	3.7
REG. SEASON TOTALS	151	—	—	262	753	.348	—	—	—	265	393	.674	—	—	65	145	224	1	—	—	—	789	1.9	1.0	5.2
PLAYOFF TOTALS	13	—	—	21	71	.296	—	—	—	37	49	.755	—	—	2	10	42	2	—	—	—	79	0.7	0.8	6.1

RIVAS, RAMON b. June 3, 1966 Ht. 6-10 Wt. 260 College—Puerto Rico/Temple

SEASON—TEAM	G	GS	MIN	FGM	FGA	PCT	3FGM	3FGA	PCT	FTM	FTA	PCT	O-RB	D-RB	TOT	AST	PF	DQ	STL	TO	BLK	PTS	RPG	APG	PPG
88-89—Boston	28	0	91	12	31	.387	0	1	.000	16	25	.640	9	15	24	3	21	0	4	9	1	40	0.9	0.1	1.4
REG. SEASON TOTALS	28	0	91	12	31	.387	0	1	.000	16	25	.640	9	15	24	3	21	0	4	9	1	40	0.9	0.1	1.4

RIVERS, DAVID LEE b. January 20, 1965 Ht. 6-0 Wt. 175 College—Notre Dame

SEASON—TEAM	G	GS	MIN	FGM	FGA	PCT	3FGM	3FGA	PCT	FTM	FTA	PCT	O-RB	D-RB	TOT	AST	PF	DQ	STL	TO	BLK	PTS	RPG	APG	PPG
88-89—L.A. Lakers	47	0	440	49	122	.402	1	6	.167	35	42	.833	13	30	43	106	50	0	23	61	9	134	0.9	2.3	2.9
89-90—L.A. Clippers	52	11	724	80	197	.406	0	5	.000	59	78	.756	30	55	85	155	53	0	31	88	0	219	1.6	3.0	4.2
91-92—L.A. Clippers	15	0	122	10	30	.333	0	1	.000	10	11	.909	10	9	19	21	14	0	7	17	1	30	1.3	1.4	2.0
REG. SEASON TOTALS	114	11	1286	139	349	.398	1	12	.083	104	131	.794	53	94	147	282	117	0	61	166	10	383	1.3	2.5	3.4
PLAYOFF TOTALS	6	0	33	4	12	.333	0	2	.000	7	8	.875	1	3	4	6	6	0	0	4	0	15	0.7	1.0	2.5

RIVERS, GLENN ANTON (**Doc**) b. October 13, 1961 Ht. 6-4 Wt. 185 College—Marquette

SEASON—TEAM	G	GS	MIN	FGM	FGA	PCT	3FGM	3FGA	PCT	FTM	FTA	PCT	O-RB	D-RB	TOT	AST	PF	DQ	STL	TO	BLK	PTS	RPG	APG	PPG
83-84—Atlanta	81	47	1938	250	541	.462	2	12	.167	255	325	.785	72	148	220	314	286	8	127	174	30	757	2.7	3.9	9.3
84-85—Atlanta	69	58	2126	334	701	.476	15	36	.417	291	378	.770	66	148	214	410	250	7	163	176	53	974	3.1	5.9	14.1
85-86—Atlanta	53	50	1571	220	464	.474	0	16	.000	172	283	.608	49	113	162	443	185	2	120	141	13	612	3.1	8.4	11.5
86-87—Atlanta	82	82	2590	342	758	.451	4	21	.190	365	441	.828	83	216	299	823	287	5	171	217	30	1053	3.6	10.0	12.8
87-88—Atlanta	80	80	2502	403	890	.453	9	33	.273	319	421	.758	83	283	366	747	272	3	140	210	41	1134	4.6	9.3	14.2
88-89—Atlanta	76	76	2462	371	816	.455	43	124	.347	247	287	.861	89	197	286	525	263	6	181	158	40	1032	3.8	6.9	13.6
89-90—Atlanta	48	44	1526	218	480	.454	24	66	.364	138	170	.812	47	153	200	264	151	2	116	98	22	598	4.2	5.5	12.5
90-91—Atlanta	79	79	2586	444	1020	.435	88	262	.336	221	262	.844	47	206	253	340	216	2	148	125	47	1197	3.2	4.3	15.2
91-92—L.A. Clippers	59	25	1658	226	533	.424	26	92	.283	163	196	.832	23	124	147	233	166	2	111	92	19	641	2.5	3.9	10.9
92-93—New York	77	45	1886	216	494	.437	39	123	.317	133	162	.821	26	166	192	405	215	2	123	114	9	604	2.5	5.3	7.8
93-94—New York	19	19	499	55	127	.433	19	52	.365	14	22	.636	4	35	39	100	44	0	25	29	5	143	2.1	5.3	7.5
REG. SEASON TOTALS	723	605	21344	3079	6824	.451	269	837	.321	2318	2947	.787	589	1789	2378	4604	2335	39	1425	1534	309	8745	3.3	6.4	12.1
PLAYOFF TOTALS	64	62	2055	270	593	.455	32	100	.320	234	308	.760	51	189	240	455	222	5	111	134	14	806	3.8	7.1	12.6
ALL-STAR TOTALS	1	0	16	2	4	.500	0	0	—	5	11	.455	0	3	3	6	3	0	0	3	0	9	3.0	6.0	9.0

ROBBINS, AUSTIN (**Red**) b. September 30, 1944 Ht. 6-8 Wt. 200 College—Chipola JC/Tennessee

SEASON—TEAM	G	GS	MIN	FGM	FGA	PCT	3FGM	3FGA	PCT	FTM	FTA	PCT	O-RB	D-RB	TOT	AST	PF	DQ	STL	TO	BLK	PTS	RPG	APG	PPG
67-68—New Orleans (A)	73	—	2159	448	918	.488	2	6	.333	245	308	.795	366	528	894	73	157	0	—	115	—	1143	12.2	1.0	15.7
68-69—New Orleans (A)	76	—	2736	456	1035	.441	7	29	.241	291	361	.806	368	656	1024	142	200	1	—	121	—	1210	13.5	1.9	15.9
69-70—New Orleans (A)	82	—	3266	525	1091	.481	7	23	.304	285	366	.779	427	905	1332	182	251	1	—	—	—	1342	16.2	2.2	16.4
70-71—Utah (A)	82	—	2995	396	908	.436	11	44	.250	227	272	.835	303	673	976	178	203	—	—	—	—	1030	11.9	2.2	12.6
71-72—Utah (A)	78	—	2567	379	752	.504	29	71	.408	167	201	.831	—	—	711	124	171	—	—	86	—	954	9.1	1.6	12.2
72-73—San Diego (A)	58	—	1618	218	525	.415	9	30	.300	131	155	.845	159	258	417	99	134	2	—	85	—	576	7.2	1.7	9.9
73-74—S.D.-Ken. (A)	80	—	1627	276	577	.478	1	13	.077	116	136	.853	144	242	386	89	112	—	40	89	34	669	4.8	1.1	8.4
74-75—Ken.-Vir. (A)	57	—	1777	307	648	.474	3	10	.300	162	187	.866	153	262	415	114	106	—	31	97	31	779	7.3	2.0	13.7
REG. ABA TOTALS	586	—	18745	3005	6454	.466	69	226	.305	1624	1986	.818	1920	3524	6155	1001	1334	4	71	593	65	7703	10.5	1.7	13.1
ABA PLAYOFF TOTALS	67	—	2079	335	706	.475	9	32	.281	186	244	.762	138	296	729	109	155	0	4	84	5	865	10.9	1.6	12.9
ABA ALL-STAR TOTALS	3	—	53	12	25	.480	0	0	—	3	4	.750	6	5	11	2	5	0	0	3	0	27	3.7	0.7	9.0

ROBBINS, LEE ROY b. February 11, 1922 d. April 8, 1968 Ht. 6-3 Wt. 175 College—Colorado

SEASON—TEAM	G	GS	MIN	FGM	FGA	PCT	3FGM	3FGA	PCT	FTM	FTA	PCT	O-RB	D-RB	TOT	AST	PF	DQ	STL	TO	BLK	PTS	RPG	APG	PPG
47-48—Providence	31	—	—	72	260	.277	—	—	—	51	93	.548	—	—	—	7	93	—	—	—	—	195	—	0.2	6.3
48-49—Providence	16	—	—	9	25	.360	—	—	—	11	17	.647	—	—	—	12	24	—	—	—	—	29	—	0.8	1.8
REG. SEASON TOTALS	47	—	—	81	285	.284	—	—	—	62	110	.564	—	—	—	19	117	—	—	—	—	224	—	0.4	4.8

ROBERSON, RICK b. July 7, 1947 Ht. 6-9 Wt. 235 College—Cincinnati

SEASON—TEAM	G	GS	MIN	FGM	FGA	PCT	3FGM	3FGA	PCT	FTM	FTA	PCT	O-RB	D-RB	TOT	AST	PF	DQ	STL	TO	BLK	PTS	RPG	APG	PPG
69-70—Los Angeles	74	—	2005	262	586	.447	—	—	—	120	212	.566	—	—	672	92	256	7	—	—	—	644	9.1	1.2	8.7
70-71—Los Angeles	65	—	909	125	301	.415	—	—	—	88	143	.615	—	—	304	47	125	1	—	—	—	338	4.7	0.7	5.2
71-72—Cleveland	63	—	2207	304	688	.442	—	—	—	215	366	.587	—	—	801	109	251	7	—	—	—	823	12.7	1.7	13.1
72-73—Cleveland	62	—	2127	307	709	.433	—	—	—	167	290	.576	—	—	693	134	249	5	—	—	—	781	11.2	2.2	12.6
73-74—Portland	69	—	2060	364	797	.457	—	—	—	205	316	.649	251	450	701	133	252	4	65	—	55	933	10.2	1.9	13.5
74-75—New Orleans	16	—	339	48	108	.444	—	—	—	23	40	.575	39	79	118	23	49	0	7	—	8	119	7.4	1.4	7.4
75-76—Kansas City	74	—	709	73	180	.406	—	—	—	42	103	.408	74	159	233	53	126	1	18	—	17	188	3.1	0.7	2.5
REG. SEASON TOTALS	423	—	10356	1483	3369	.440	—	—	—	860	1470	.585	364	688	3522	591	1308	25	90	—	80	3826	8.3	1.4	9.0
PLAYOFF TOTALS	18	—	154	18	47	.383	—	—	—	10	17	.588	0	0	42	4	27	0	0	—	0	46	2.3	0.2	2.6

ROBERTS, ANTHONY JEROME b. April 15, 1955 Ht. 6-5½ Wt. 195 College—Oral Roberts

SEASON—TEAM	G	GS	MIN	FGM	FGA	PCT	3FGM	3FGA	PCT	FTM	FTA	PCT	O-RB	D-RB	TOT	AST	PF	DQ	STL	TO	BLK	PTS	RPG	APG	PPG
77-78—Denver	82	—	1598	311	736	.423	—	—	—	153	212	.722	135	216	351	105	212	1	40	118	7	775	4.3	1.3	9.5
78-79—Denver	63	—	1236	211	498	.424	—	—	—	76	110	.691	106	152	258	107	142	2	20	65	2	498	4.1	1.7	7.9
79-80—Denver	23	—	486	69	181	.381	0	1	.000	39	60	.650	54	55	109	20	52	1	13	28	3	177	4.7	0.9	7.7
80-81—Washington	26	—	350	54	144	.375	0	0	—	19	29	.655	18	50	68	20	52	0	11	28	0	127	2.6	0.8	4.9
83-84—Denver	19	0	197	34	91	.374	0	0	—	13	18	.722	20	31	51	13	43	1	5	17	1	81	2.7	0.7	4.3
REG. SEASON TOTALS	213	0	3867	679	1650	.412	0	1	.000	300	429	.699	333	504	837	265	501	5	89	256	13	1658	3.9	1.2	7.8
PLAYOFF TOTALS	16	0	480	99	232	.427	0	0	—	47	61	.770	50	71	121	36	66	3	13	30	7	245	7.6	2.3	15.3

ROBERTS, FREDERICK CLARK (**Fred**) b. August 14, 1960   Ht. 6-10 Wt. 220 College—Brigham Young

SEASON—TEAM	G	GS	MIN	FGM	FGA	PCT	3FGM	3FGA	PCT	FTM	FTA	PCT	O-RB	D-RB	TOT	AST	PF	DQ	STL	TO	BLK	PTS	RPG	APG	PPG
83-84—San Antonio	79	8	1531	214	399	.536	1	4	.250	144	172	.837	102	202	304	98	219	4	52	100	38	573	3.8	1.2	7.3
84-85—S.A.-Utah	74	0	1178	208	418	.498	1	1	1.000	150	182	.824	78	108	186	87	141	0	28	89	22	567	2.5	1.2	7.7
85-86—Utah	58	0	469	74	167	.443	1	2	.500	67	87	.770	31	49	80	27	72	0	8	53	6	216	1.4	0.5	3.7
86-87—Boston	73	11	1079	139	270	.515	0	3	.000	124	153	.810	54	136	190	62	129	1	22	89	20	402	2.6	0.8	5.5
87-88—Boston	74	14	1032	161	330	.488	0	6	.000	128	165	.776	60	102	162	81	118	0	16	68	15	450	2.2	1.1	6.1
88-89—Milwaukee	71	3	1251	155	319	.486	3	14	.214	104	129	.806	68	141	209	66	126	0	36	80	23	417	2.9	0.9	5.9
89-90—Milwaukee	82	66	2235	330	666	.495	2	11	.182	195	249	.783	107	204	311	147	210	5	56	130	25	857	3.8	1.8	10.5
90-91—Milwaukee	82	82	2114	357	670	.533	4	25	.160	170	209	.813	107	174	281	135	190	2	63	135	29	888	3.4	1.6	10.8
91-92—Milwaukee	80	63	1746	311	645	.482	19	37	.514	128	171	.749	103	154	257	122	177	0	52	122	40	769	3.2	1.5	9.6
92-93—Milwaukee	79	5	1488	226	428	.528	12	29	.414	135	169	.799	91	146	237	118	138	0	57	67	27	599	3.0	1.5	7.6
REG. SEASON TOTALS	752	252	14123	2175	4312	.504	43	132	.326	1345	1686	.798	801	1416	2217	943	1520	12	390	933	245	5738	2.9	1.3	7.6
PLAYOFF TOTALS	65	16	1053	145	293	.495	0	5	.000	111	142	.782	53	82	135	57	131	2	23	61	12	401	2.1	0.9	6.2

ROBERTS, JOSEPH (**Joe**) b. May 18, 1936   Ht. 6-6 Wt. 215 College—Ohio State

SEASON—TEAM	G	GS	MIN	FGM	FGA	PCT	3FGM	3FGA	PCT	FTM	FTA	PCT	O-RB	D-RB	TOT	AST	PF	DQ	STL	TO	BLK	PTS	RPG	APG	PPG
60-61—Syracuse	68	—	800	130	351	.370	—	—	—	62	104	.596	—	—	243	43	125	0	—	—	—	322	3.6	0.6	4.7
61-62—Syracuse	80	—	1642	243	619	.393	—	—	—	129	194	.665	—	—	538	50	230	4	—	—	—	615	6.7	0.6	7.7
62-63—Syracuse	33	—	466	73	196	.372	—	—	—	35	51	.686	—	—	155	16	66	1	—	—	—	181	4.7	0.5	5.5
67-68—Kentucky (A)	37	—	564	54	146	.370	1	3	.333	28	50	.560	—	—	139	14	64	1	—	30	—	137	3.8	0.4	3.7
REG. NBA TOTALS	181	—	2908	446	1166	.383	—	—	—	226	349	.648	—	—	936	109	421	5	—	—	—	1118	5.2	0.6	6.2
REG. ABA TOTALS	37	—	564	54	146	.370	1	3	.333	28	50	.560	—	—	139	14	64	1	—	30	—	137	3.8	0.4	3.7
NBA PLAYOFF TOTALS	9	—	84	11	32	.344	—	—	—	10	14	.714	—	—	32	—	12	0	—	—	—	32	3.6	0.0	3.6
ABA PLAYOFF TOTALS	5	—	63	5	15	.333	0	0	—	2	6	.333	—	—	15	1	13	0	—	3	—	12	3.0	0.2	2.4

ROBERTS, MARVIN JAMES (**Marv**) b. January 29, 1950   Ht. 6-8 Wt. 220 College—Utah State

SEASON—TEAM	G	GS	MIN	FGM	FGA	PCT	3FGM	3FGA	PCT	FTM	FTA	PCT	O-RB	D-RB	TOT	AST	PF	DQ	STL	TO	BLK	PTS	RPG	APG	PPG
71-72—Denver (A)	68	—	1047	217	533	.407	1	4	.250	86	120	.717	—	—	294	61	150	—	—	77	—	521	4.3	0.9	7.7
72-73—Denver (A)	77	—	1959	374	807	.463	1	3	.333	201	255	.788	180	218	398	95	194	3	—	110	—	950	5.2	1.2	12.3
73-74—Denver-Car. (A)	74	—	1599	266	598	.445	1	1	1.000	129	164	.787	161	210	371	119	153	—	47	100	7	662	5.0	1.6	8.9
74-75—Kentucky (A)	83	—	1370	201	467	.430	0	1	.000	127	164	.774	91	155	246	103	200	—	27	100	4	529	3.0	1.2	6.4
75-76—Ken.-Vir. (A)	72	—	1559	259	621	.417	0	0	—	107	137	.781	104	132	236	120	151	—	36	100	8	625	3.3	1.7	8.7
76-77—Los Angeles	28	—	209	27	76	.355	—	—	—	4	6	.667	9	16	25	19	34	0	4	—	2	58	0.9	0.7	2.1
REG. NBA TOTALS	28	—	209	27	76	.355	—	—	—	4	6	.667	9	16	25	19	34	0	4	—	2	58	0.9	0.7	2.1
REG. ABA TOTALS	374	—	7534	1317	3026	.435	3	9	.333	650	840	.774	536	715	1545	498	848	3	110	487	19	3287	4.1	1.3	8.8
ABA PLAYOFF TOTALS	24	—	422	86	178	.483	0	1	.000	45	57	.789	38	41	84	31	45	0	5	22	1	217	3.5	1.3	9.0

ROBERTS, STANLEY CORVET b. February 7, 1970   Ht. 7-0 Wt. 290 College—Louisiana State

SEASON—TEAM	G	GS	MIN	FGM	FGA	PCT	3FGM	3FGA	PCT	FTM	FTA	PCT	O-RB	D-RB	TOT	AST	PF	DQ	STL	TO	BLK	PTS	RPG	APG	PPG
91-92—Orlando	55	34	1118	236	446	.529	0	1	.000	101	196	.515	113	223	336	39	221	7	22	78	83	573	6.1	0.7	10.4
92-93—L.A. Clippers	77	76	1816	375	711	.527	0	0	—	120	246	.488	181	297	478	59	332	15	34	121	141	870	6.2	0.8	11.3
93-94—L.A. Clippers	14	14	350	43	100	.430	0	0	—	18	44	.409	27	66	93	11	54	2	6	24	25	104	6.6	0.8	7.4
REG. SEASON TOTALS	146	124	3284	654	1257	.520	0	1	.000	239	486	.492	321	586	907	109	607	24	62	223	249	1547	6.2	0.7	10.6
PLAYOFF TOTALS	5	5	149	26	50	.520	0	1	.000	5	18	.278	17	24	41	1	24	2	3	10	3	57	8.2	0.2	11.4

ROBERTS, WILLIAM (**Bill**) b. 1925   Ht. 6-9 Wt. 210 College—Wyoming

SEASON—TEAM	G	GS	MIN	FGM	FGA	PCT	3FGM	3FGA	PCT	FTM	FTA	PCT	O-RB	D-RB	TOT	AST	PF	DQ	STL	TO	BLK	PTS	RPG	APG	PPG
48-49—Chicago-Boston-St. L.	50	—	—	89	267	.333	—	—	—	44	63	.698	—	—	—	41	113	—	—	—	—	222	—	0.8	4.4
49-50—St. Louis	67	—	—	77	222	.347	—	—	—	28	39	.718	—	—	—	24	90	—	—	—	—	182	—	0.4	2.7
REG. SEASON TOTALS	117	—	—	166	489	.339	—	—	—	72	102	.706	—	—	—	65	203	—	—	—	—	404	—	0.6	3.5
PLAYOFF TOTALS	2	—	—	10	29	.345	—	—	—	2	5	.400	—	—	—	2	10	—	—	—	—	22	—	1.0	11.0

ROBERTSON, ALVIN CYRRALE b. July 22, 1962   Ht. 6-4 Wt. 190 College—Arkansas

SEASON—TEAM	G	GS	MIN	FGM	FGA	PCT	3FGM	3FGA	PCT	FTM	FTA	PCT	O-RB	D-RB	TOT	AST	PF	DQ	STL	TO	BLK	PTS	RPG	APG	PPG
84-85—San Antonio	79	9	1685	299	600	.498	4	11	.364	124	169	.734	116	149	265	275	217	1	127	167	24	726	3.4	3.5	9.2
85-86—San Antonio	82	82	2878	562	1093	.514	8	29	.276	260	327	.795	184	332	516	448	296	4	301	256	40	1392	6.3	5.5	17.0
86-87—San Antonio	81	78	2697	589	1264	.466	13	48	.271	244	324	.753	186	238	424	421	264	2	260	243	35	1435	5.2	5.2	17.7
87-88—San Antonio	82	82	2978	655	1408	.465	27	95	.284	273	365	.748	165	333	498	557	300	4	243	251	69	1610	6.1	6.8	19.6
88-89—San Antonio	65	65	2287	465	962	.483	9	45	.200	183	253	.723	157	227	384	393	259	6	197	231	36	1122	5.9	6.0	17.3
89-90—Milwaukee	81	81	2599	476	946	.503	4	26	.154	197	266	.741	230	329	559	445	280	2	207	217	17	1153	6.9	5.5	14.2
90-91—Milwaukee	81	81	2598	438	904	.485	23	63	.365	199	263	.757	191	268	459	444	273	5	246	212	16	1098	5.7	5.5	13.6
91-92—Milwaukee	82	79	2463	396	922	.430	67	210	.319	151	198	.763	175	175	350	360	263	5	210	223	32	1010	4.3	4.4	12.3
92-93—Milw.-Detroit	69	54	2006	247	539	.458	40	122	.328	84	128	.656	107	162	269	263	218	1	155	133	18	618	3.9	3.8	9.0
REG. SEASON TOTALS	702	611	22191	4127	8638	.478	195	649	.300	1715	2293	.748	1511	2213	3724	3606	2370	30	1946	1933	287	10164	5.3	5.1	14.5
PLAYOFF TOTALS	13	13	490	102	198	.515	6	17	.353	52	69	.754	27	42	69	81	53	1	36	39	2	262	5.3	6.2	20.2
ALL-STAR TOTALS	4	2	60	7	18	.389	0	0	—	4	4	1.000	3	10	13	7	3	0	2	10	0	18	3.3	1.8	4.5

ROBERTSON, OSCAR PALMER (The Big O) b. November 24, 1938   Ht. 6-5 Wt. 210 College—Cincinnati

SEASON—TEAM	G	GS	MIN	FGM	FGA	PCT	3FGM	3FGA	PCT	FTM	FTA	PCT	O-RB	D-RB	TOT	AST	PF	DQ	STL	TO	BLK	PTS	RPG	APG	PPG
60-61—Cincinnati	71	—	3032	756	1600	.473	—	—	—	653	794	.822	—	—	716	690	219	3	—	—	—	2165	10.1	9.7	30.5
61-62—Cincinnati	79	—	3503	866	1810	.478	—	—	—	700	872	.803	—	—	985	899	258	1	—	—	—	2432	12.5	11.4	30.8
62-63—Cincinnati	80	—	3521	825	1593	.518	—	—	—	614	758	.810	—	—	835	758	293	1	—	—	—	2264	10.4	9.5	28.3
63-64—Cincinnati	79	—	3559	840	1740	.483	—	—	—	800	938	.853	—	—	783	868	280	3	—	—	—	2480	9.9	11.0	31.4
64-65—Cincinnati	75	—	3421	807	1681	.480	—	—	—	665	793	.839	—	—	674	861	205	2	—	—	—	2279	9.0	11.5	30.4
65-66—Cincinnati	76	—	3493	818	1723	.475	—	—	—	742	881	.842	—	—	586	847	227	1	—	—	—	2378	7.7	11.1	31.3
66-67—Cincinnati	79	—	3468	838	1699	.493	—	—	—	736	843	.873	—	—	486	845	226	2	—	—	—	2412	6.2	10.7	30.5
67-68—Cincinnati	65	—	2765	660	1321	.500	—	—	—	576	660	.873	—	—	391	633	199	2	—	—	—	1896	6.0	9.7	29.2
68-69—Cincinnati	79	—	3461	656	1351	.486	—	—	—	643	767	.838	—	—	502	772	231	2	—	—	—	1955	6.4	9.8	24.7
69-70—Cincinnati	69	—	2865	647	1267	.511	—	—	—	454	561	.809	—	—	422	558	175	1	—	—	—	1748	6.1	8.1	25.3
70-71—Milwaukee	81	—	3194	592	1193	.496	—	—	—	385	453	.850	—	—	462	668	203	0	—	—	—	1569	5.7	8.2	19.4
71-72—Milwaukee	64	—	2390	419	887	.472	—	—	—	276	330	.836	—	—	323	491	116	0	—	—	—	1114	5.0	7.7	17.4
72-73—Milwaukee	73	—	2737	446	983	.454	—	—	—	238	281	.847	—	—	360	551	167	0	—	—	—	1130	4.9	7.5	15.5
73-74—Milwaukee	70	—	2477	338	772	.438	—	—	—	212	254	.835	71	208	279	446	132	0	77	—	4	888	4.0	6.4	12.7
REG. SEASON TOTALS	1040	—	43886	9508	19620	.485	—	—	—	7694	9185	.838	71	208	7804	9887	2931	18	77	—	4	26710	7.5	9.5	25.7
PLAYOFF TOTALS	86	—	3673	675	1466	.460	—	—	—	560	655	.855	15	39	578	769	267	3	15	—	4	1910	6.7	8.9	22.2
ALL-STAR TOTALS	12	—	380	88	172	.512	—	—	—	70	98	.714	0	0	69	81	41	0	0	—	0	246	5.8	6.8	20.5

ROBERTSON, TONY b. January 1, 1956   Ht. 6-4 Wt. 195 College—West Virginia

SEASON—TEAM	G	GS	MIN	FGM	FGA	PCT	3FGM	3FGA	PCT	FTM	FTA	PCT	O-RB	D-RB	TOT	AST	PF	DQ	STL	TO	BLK	PTS	RPG	APG	PPG
77-78—Atlanta	63	—	929	168	381	.441	—	—	—	37	53	.698	15	55	70	103	133	2	74	88	5	373	1.1	1.6	5.9
78-79—Golden State	12	—	74	15	40	.375	—	—	—	6	9	.667	6	4	10	4	10	0	8	8	0	36	0.8	0.3	3.0
REG. SEASON TOTALS	75	—	1003	183	421	.435	—	—	—	43	62	.694	21	59	80	107	143	2	82	96	5	409	1.1	1.4	5.5
PLAYOFF TOTALS	2	—	12	2	6	.333	—	—	—	1	2	.500	0	0	0	—	3	0	0	0	0	5	0.0	0.0	2.5

ROBEY, FREDERICK ROBERT (Rick) b. January 30, 1956   Ht. 6-11 Wt. 230 College—Kentucky

SEASON—TEAM	G	GS	MIN	FGM	FGA	PCT	3FGM	3FGA	PCT	FTM	FTA	PCT	O-RB	D-RB	TOT	AST	PF	DQ	STL	TO	BLK	PTS	RPG	APG	PPG
78-79—Indiana-Boston	79	—	1763	322	673	.478	—	—	—	174	224	.777	168	345	513	132	232	4	48	164	15	818	6.5	1.7	10.4
79-80—Boston	82	—	1918	379	727	.521	0	1	.000	184	269	.684	209	321	530	92	244	2	53	151	15	942	6.5	1.1	11.5
80-81—Boston	82	—	1569	298	547	.545	0	1	.000	144	251	.574	132	258	390	126	204	0	38	141	19	740	4.8	1.5	9.0
81-82—Boston	80	4	1186	185	375	.493	0	2	.000	84	157	.535	114	181	295	68	183	2	27	92	14	454	3.7	0.9	5.7
82-83—Boston	59	6	855	100	214	.467	0	0	—	45	78	.577	79	140	219	65	131	1	13	72	8	245	3.7	1.1	4.2
83-84—Phoenix	61	4	856	140	257	.545	1	1	1.000	61	88	.693	80	118	198	65	120	0	20	77	14	342	3.2	1.1	5.6
84-85—Phoenix	4	0	48	2	9	.222	0	0	—	1	2	.500	3	5	8	5	7	0	2	8	0	5	2.0	1.3	1.3
85-86—Phoenix	46	1	629	72	191	.377	0	3	.000	33	48	.688	40	108	148	58	92	1	19	66	5	177	3.2	1.3	3.8
REG. SEASON TOTALS	493	15	8824	1498	2993	.501	1	8	.125	726	1117	.650	825	1476	2301	611	1213	10	220	771	90	3723	4.7	1.2	7.6
PLAYOFF TOTALS	53	0	610	87	194	.448	0	3	.000	42	78	.538	55	84	139	29	107	0	13	44	11	216	2.6	0.5	4.1

ROBINSON, CLIFFORD RALPH (Cliff) b. December 16, 1966   Ht. 6-10 Wt. 225 College—Connecticut

SEASON—TEAM	G	GS	MIN	FGM	FGA	PCT	3FGM	3FGA	PCT	FTM	FTA	PCT	O-RB	D-RB	TOT	AST	PF	DQ	STL	TO	BLK	PTS	RPG	APG	PPG
89-90—Portland	82	0	1565	298	751	.397	12	44	.273	138	251	.550	110	198	308	72	226	4	53	129	53	746	3.8	0.9	9.1
90-91—Portland	82	11	1940	373	806	.463	6	19	.316	205	314	.653	123	226	349	151	263	2	78	133	76	957	4.3	1.8	11.7
91-92—Portland	82	7	2124	398	854	.466	1	11	.091	219	330	.664	140	276	416	137	274	11	85	154	107	1016	5.1	1.7	12.4
92-93—Portland	82	12	2575	632	1336	.473	19	77	.247	287	416	.690	165	377	542	182	287	8	98	173	163	1570	6.6	2.2	19.1
93-94—Portland	82	64	2853	641	1404	.457	13	53	.245	352	460	.765	164	386	550	159	263	0	118	169	111	1647	6.7	1.9	20.1
REG. SEASON TOTALS	410	94	11057	2342	5151	.455	51	204	.250	1201	1771	.678	702	1463	2165	701	1313	25	432	758	510	5936	5.3	1.7	14.5
PLAYOFF TOTALS	66	10	1547	252	594	.424	4	23	.174	127	228	.557	102	178	280	100	232	6	57	97	74	635	4.2	1.5	9.6
ALL-STAR TOTALS	1	0	18	5	8	.625	0	1	.000	0	0	—	1	1	2	5	0	0	1	0	0	10	2.0	5.0	10.0

ROBINSON, CLIFFORD TRENT (Cliff) b. March 13, 1960   Ht. 6-9½ Wt. 220 College—USC

SEASON—TEAM	G	GS	MIN	FGM	FGA	PCT	3FGM	3FGA	PCT	FTM	FTA	PCT	O-RB	D-RB	TOT	AST	PF	DQ	STL	TO	BLK	PTS	RPG	APG	PPG
79-80—New Jersey	70	—	1661	391	833	.469	1	4	.250	168	242	.694	174	332	506	98	178	1	61	137	34	951	7.2	1.4	13.6
80-81—New Jersey	63	—	1822	525	1070	.491	1	1	1.000	178	248	.718	120	361	481	105	216	6	58	182	52	1229	7.6	1.7	19.5
81-82—K.C.-Clev.	68	59	2175	518	1143	.453	0	4	.000	222	313	.709	174	435	609	120	222	4	88	149	103	1258	9.0	1.8	18.5
82-83—Cleveland	77	75	2601	587	1230	.477	0	5	.000	213	301	.708	190	666	856	145	272	7	61	224	58	1387	11.1	1.9	18.0
83-84—Cleveland	73	70	2402	533	1185	.450	1	2	.500	234	334	.701	156	597	753	185	195	2	51	187	32	1301	10.3	2.5	17.8
84-85—Washington	60	37	1870	422	896	.471	1	2	.500	158	213	.742	141	405	546	149	187	4	51	161	47	1003	9.1	2.5	16.7
85-86—Washington	78	78	2563	595	1255	.474	1	3	.333	269	353	.762	180	500	680	186	217	2	98	206	44	1460	8.7	2.4	18.7
86-87—Philadelphia	55	30	1586	338	729	.464	0	4	.000	139	184	.755	86	221	307	89	150	1	86	123	30	815	5.6	1.6	14.8
87-88—Philadelphia	62	51	2110	483	1041	.464	2	9	.222	210	293	.717	116	289	405	131	192	4	79	161	39	1178	6.5	2.1	19.0
88-89—Philadelphia	14	13	416	90	187	.481	0	1	.000	32	44	.727	19	56	75	32	37	0	17	34	2	212	5.4	2.3	15.1
91-92—L.A. Lakers	9	0	78	11	27	.407	0	1	.000	7	8	.875	7	12	19	9	4	0	5	7	0	29	2.1	1.0	3.2
REG. SEASON TOTALS	629	413	19284	4493	9596	.468	7	36	.194	1830	2533	.722	1363	3874	5237	1249	1870	31	655	1571	441	10823	8.3	2.0	17.2
PLAYOFF TOTALS	17	14	462	104	220	.473	0	0	—	42	66	.636	41	81	122	28	54	1	20	28	13	250	7.2	1.6	14.7

ROBINSON, DAVID MAURICE (The Admiral) b. August 6, 1965   Ht. 7-1   Wt. 235   College—Navy

SEASON—TEAM	G	GS	MIN	FGM	FGA	PCT	3FGM	3FGA	PCT	FTM	FTA	PCT	O-RB	D-RB	TOT	AST	PF	DQ	STL	TO	BLK	PTS	RPG	APG	PPG
89-90—San Antonio	82	81	3002	690	1300	.531	0	2	.000	613	837	.732	303	680	983	164	259	3	138	257	319	1993	12.0	2.0	24.3
90-91—San Antonio	82	81	3095	754	1366	.552	1	7	.143	592	777	.762	335	728	1063	208	264	5	127	270	320	2101	13.0	2.5	25.6
91-92—San Antonio	68	68	2564	592	1074	.551	1	8	.125	393	561	.701	261	568	829	181	219	2	158	182	305	1578	12.2	2.7	23.2
92-93—San Antonio	82	82	3211	676	1348	.501	3	17	.176	561	766	.732	229	727	956	301	239	5	127	241	264	1916	11.7	3.7	23.4
93-94—San Antonio	80	80	3241	840	1658	.507	10	29	.345	693	925	.749	241	614	855	381	228	3	139	253	265	2383	10.7	4.8	29.8
REG. SEASON TOTALS	394	392	15113	3552	6746	.527	15	63	.238	2852	3866	.738	1369	3317	4686	1235	1209	18	689	1203	1473	9971	11.9	3.1	25.3
PLAYOFF TOTALS	28	28	1108	233	461	.505	0	3	.000	191	271	.705	89	251	340	85	99	1	30	73	101	657	12.1	3.0	23.5
ALL-STAR TOTALS	5	3	108	33	57	.579	0	0	—	24	37	.649	11	25	36	4	15	0	7	5	8	90	7.2	0.8	18.0

ROBINSON, FLYNN JAMES b. April 28, 1941   Ht. 6-1   Wt. 190   College—Wyoming

SEASON—TEAM	G	GS	MIN	FGM	FGA	PCT	3FGM	3FGA	PCT	FTM	FTA	PCT	O-RB	D-RB	TOT	AST	PF	DQ	STL	TO	BLK	PTS	RPG	APG	PPG
66-67—Cincinnati	76	—	1140	274	599	.457	—	—	—	120	154	.779	—	—	133	110	197	3	—	—	—	668	1.8	1.4	8.8
67-68—Cin.-Chicago	75	—	2046	444	1010	.440	—	—	—	288	351	.821	—	—	272	219	184	1	—	—	—	1176	3.6	2.9	15.7
68-69—Chicago-Milw.	83	—	2616	625	1442	.433	—	—	—	412	491	.839	—	—	306	377	261	7	—	—	—	1662	3.7	4.5	20.0
69-70—Milwaukee	81	—	2762	663	1391	.477	—	—	—	439	489	.898	—	—	263	449	254	5	—	—	—	1765	3.2	5.5	21.8
70-71—Cincinnati	71	—	1368	374	817	.458	—	—	—	195	228	.855	—	—	143	138	161	0	—	—	—	943	2.0	1.9	13.3
71-72—Los Angeles	64	—	1007	262	535	.490	—	—	—	111	129	.860	—	—	115	138	139	2	—	—	—	635	1.8	2.2	9.9
72-73—L.A.-Balt.	44	—	630	133	288	.462	—	—	—	32	39	.821	—	—	62	85	71	0	—	—	—	298	1.4	1.9	6.8
73-74—San Diego (A)	49	—	779	185	405	.457	8	30	.267	52	68	.765	28	50	78	112	72	—	23	50	2	430	1.6	2.3	8.8
REG. NBA TOTALS	494	—	11569	2775	6082	.456	—	—	—	1597	1881	.849	—	—	1294	1516	1267	18	—	—	—	7147	2.6	3.1	14.5
REG. ABA TOTALS	49	—	779	185	405	.457	8	30	.267	52	68	.765	28	50	78	112	72	0	23	50	2	430	1.6	2.3	8.8
NBA PLAYOFF TOTALS	27	—	626	129	318	.406	—	—	—	70	88	.795	—	—	54	76	57	0	—	—	—	328	2.0	2.8	12.1
NBA ALL-STAR TOTALS	1	—	8	3	4	.750	—	—	—	0	0	—	—	—	1	2	2	0	—	—	—	6	1.0	2.0	6.0

ROBINSON, JACKIE b. May 20, 1955   Ht. 6-6   Wt. 210   College—Nevada-Las Vegas

SEASON—TEAM	G	GS	MIN	FGM	FGA	PCT	3FGM	3FGA	PCT	FTM	FTA	PCT	O-RB	D-RB	TOT	AST	PF	DQ	STL	TO	BLK	PTS	RPG	APG	PPG
78-79—Seattle	12	—	105	19	41	.463	—	—	—	8	15	.533	9	10	19	13	9	0	5	11	1	46	1.6	1.1	3.8
79-80—Detroit	7	—	51	9	17	.529	0	1	.000	9	11	.818	3	2	5	0	8	0	3	2	3	27	0.7	0.0	3.9
81-82—Chicago	3	0	29	3	9	.333	0	0	—	4	4	1.000	3	0	3	0	1	0	0	1	0	10	1.0	0.0	3.3
REG. SEASON TOTALS	22	0	185	31	67	.463	0	1	.000	21	30	.700	15	12	27	13	18	0	8	14	4	83	1.2	0.6	3.8

ROBINSON, JAMES b. August 31, 1970   Ht. 6-2   Wt. 180   College—Alabama

SEASON—TEAM	G	GS	MIN	FGM	FGA	PCT	3FGM	3FGA	PCT	FTM	FTA	PCT	O-RB	D-RB	TOT	AST	PF	DQ	STL	TO	BLK	PTS	RPG	APG	PPG
93-94—Portland	58	3	673	104	285	.365	23	73	.315	45	67	.672	34	44	78	68	69	0	30	52	15	276	1.3	1.2	4.8
REG. SEASON TOTALS	58	3	673	104	285	.365	23	73	.315	45	67	.672	34	44	78	68	69	0	30	52	15	276	1.3	1.2	4.8
PLAYOFF TOTALS	4	0	28	4	10	.400	1	2	.500	1	2	.500	2	1	3	6	2	0	1	0	1	10	0.8	1.5	2.5

ROBINSON, LARRY b. January 11, 1968   Ht. 6-5   Wt. 180   College—Eastern Oklahoma State/Centenary

SEASON—TEAM	G	GS	MIN	FGM	FGA	PCT	3FGM	3FGA	PCT	FTM	FTA	PCT	O-RB	D-RB	TOT	AST	PF	DQ	STL	TO	BLK	PTS	RPG	APG	PPG
90-91—G.S.-Wash.	36	10	425	62	150	.413	0	1	.000	15	27	.556	29	22	51	35	49	0	16	27	1	139	1.4	1.0	3.9
91-92—Boston	1	0	6	1	5	.200	0	0	—	0	0	—	2	0	2	1	3	0	0	1	0	2	2.0	1.0	2.0
92-93—Washington	4	0	33	6	16	.375	0	1	.000	3	5	.600	1	2	3	3	0	0	1	1	1	15	0.8	0.8	3.8
93-94—Houston	6	0	55	10	20	.500	2	8	.250	3	8	.375	4	6	10	6	8	0	7	10	0	25	1.7	1.0	4.2
REG. SEASON TOTALS	47	10	519	79	191	.414	2	10	.200	21	40	.525	36	30	66	45	60	0	24	39	2	181	1.4	1.0	3.9

ROBINSON, LEONARD EUGENE (Truck) b. October 4, 1951   Ht. 6-7   Wt. 225   College—Tennessee State

SEASON—TEAM	G	GS	MIN	FGM	FGA	PCT	3FGM	3FGA	PCT	FTM	FTA	PCT	O-RB	D-RB	TOT	AST	PF	DQ	STL	TO	BLK	PTS	RPG	APG	PPG
74-75—Washington	76	—	995	191	393	.486	—	—	—	60	115	.522	94	207	301	40	132	0	36	—	32	442	4.0	0.5	5.8
75-76—Washington	82	—	2055	354	779	.454	—	—	—	211	314	.672	139	418	557	113	239	3	42	—	107	919	6.8	1.4	11.2
76-77—Wash.-Atlanta	77	—	2777	574	1200	.478	—	—	—	314	430	.730	252	576	828	142	253	3	66	—	38	1462	10.8	1.8	19.0
77-78—New Orleans	82	—	3638	748	1683	.444	—	—	—	366	572	.640	298	990	1288	171	265	5	73	301	79	1862	15.7	2.1	22.7
78-79—N.O.-Phoenix	69	—	2537	566	1152	.491	—	—	—	324	462	.701	195	607	802	113	206	2	46	233	75	1456	11.6	1.6	21.1
79-80—Phoenix	82	—	2710	545	1064	.512	0	0	—	325	487	.667	213	557	770	142	262	2	58	251	59	1415	9.4	1.7	17.3
80-81—Phoenix	82	—	3088	647	1280	.505	0	0	—	249	396	.629	216	573	789	206	220	1	68	250	38	1543	9.6	2.5	18.8
81-82—Phoenix	74	72	2745	579	1128	.513	1	1	1.000	255	371	.687	202	519	721	179	215	2	42	202	28	1414	9.7	2.4	19.1
82-83—New York	81	76	2426	326	706	.462	0	0	—	118	201	.587	199	458	657	145	241	4	57	190	24	770	8.1	1.8	9.5
83-84—New York	65	63	2135	284	581	.489	0	0	—	133	206	.646	171	374	545	94	217	6	43	160	27	701	8.4	1.4	10.8
84-85—New York	2	1	35	2	5	.400	0	0	—	0	2	.000	6	3	9	3	3	0	2	5	3	4	4.5	1.5	2.0
REG. SEASON TOTALS	772	212	25141	4816	9971	.483	1	1	1.000	2355	3556	.662	1985	5282	7267	1348	2253	28	533	1592	510	11988	9.4	1.7	15.5
PLAYOFF TOTALS	74	25	1736	241	538	.448	0	0	—	122	198	.616	151	354	505	77	204	3	47	103	46	604	6.8	1.0	8.2
ALL-STAR TOTALS	2	0	45	6	13	.462	0	0	—	1	2	.500	4	7	11	3	6	0	0	7	0	13	5.5	1.5	6.5

ROBINSON, OLIVER LEON JR. b. March 13, 1960 Ht. 6-4 Wt. 185 College—Alabama-Birmingham

SEASON—TEAM	G	GS	MIN	FGM	FGA	PCT	3FGM	3FGA	PCT	FTM	FTA	PCT	O-RB	D-RB	TOT	AST	PF	DQ	STL	TO	BLK	PTS	RPG	APG	PPG
82-83—San Antonio	35	0	147	35	97	.361	1	11	.091	30	45	.667	6	11	17	21	18	0	4	13	2	101	0.5	0.6	2.9
REG. SEASON TOTALS	35	0	147	35	97	.361	1	11	.091	30	45	.667	6	11	17	21	18	0	4	13	2	101	0.5	0.6	2.9

ROBINSON, RONNIE b. March 9, 1951 Ht. 6-8½ Wt. 220 College—Memphis State

SEASON—TEAM	G	GS	MIN	FGM	FGA	PCT	3FGM	3FGA	PCT	FTM	FTA	PCT	O-RB	D-RB	TOT	AST	PF	DQ	STL	TO	BLK	PTS	RPG	APG	PPG
73-74—Utah-Memphis (A)	62	—	1170	174	394	.442	0	1	.000	49	73	.671	103	178	281	49	123	—	20	68	9	397	4.5	0.8	6.4
74-75—Memphis (A)	10	—	102	18	38	.474	0	0	—	4	6	.667	10	17	27	4	14	—	5	7	0	40	2.7	0.4	4.0
REG. ABA TOTALS	72	—	1272	192	432	.444	0	1	.000	53	79	.671	113	195	308	53	137	0	25	75	9	437	4.3	0.7	6.1

ROBINSON, RUMEAL JAMES (**Meal Time**) b. November 13, 1966 Ht. 6-2 Wt. 195 College—Michigan

SEASON—TEAM	G	GS	MIN	FGM	FGA	PCT	3FGM	3FGA	PCT	FTM	FTA	PCT	O-RB	D-RB	TOT	AST	PF	DQ	STL	TO	BLK	PTS	RPG	APG	PPG
90-91—Atlanta	47	16	674	108	242	.446	2	11	.182	47	80	.588	20	51	71	132	65	0	32	76	8	265	1.5	2.8	5.6
91-92—Atlanta	81	64	2220	423	928	.456	34	104	.327	175	275	.636	64	155	219	446	178	0	105	206	24	1055	2.7	5.5	13.0
92-93—New Jersey	80	28	1585	270	638	.423	20	56	.357	112	195	.574	49	110	159	323	169	2	96	140	12	672	2.0	4.0	8.4
93-94—N.J.-Cha.	31	0	396	55	152	.362	8	20	.400	13	29	.448	6	26	32	63	48	0	18	43	3	131	1.0	2.0	4.2
REG. SEASON TOTALS	239	108	4875	856	1960	.437	64	191	.335	347	579	.599	139	342	481	964	460	2	251	465	47	2123	2.0	4.0	8.9
PLAYOFF TOTALS	7	5	149	22	53	.415	2	7	.286	5	7	.714	4	9	13	36	19	0	6	24	0	51	1.9	5.1	7.3

ROBINSON, SAMUEL LEE (**Sam**) b. January 1, 1948 Ht. 6-7 Wt. 200 College—Long Beach State

SEASON—TEAM	G	GS	MIN	FGM	FGA	PCT	3FGM	3FGA	PCT	FTM	FTA	PCT	O-RB	D-RB	TOT	AST	PF	DQ	STL	TO	BLK	PTS	RPG	APG	PPG
70-71—Floridians (A)	83	—	2172	405	896	.452	4	19	.211	103	134	.769	—	—	410	112	182	—	—	—	—	917	4.9	1.3	11.0
71-72—Floridians (A)	51	—	686	126	300	.420	0	2	.000	54	68	.794	—	—	136	48	70	—	—	24	—	306	2.7	0.9	6.0
REG. ABA TOTALS	134	—	2858	531	1196	.444	4	21	.190	157	202	.777	—	—	546	160	252	—	—	24	—	1223	4.1	1.2	9.1
ABA PLAYOFF TOTALS	10	—	192	42	90	.467	0	0	—	21	23	.913	—	—	41	8	28	—	—	3	—	105	4.1	0.8	10.5

ROBINSON, WAYNE HOWARD b. April 19, 1958 Ht. 6-8 Wt. 217 College—Virginia Tech

SEASON—TEAM	G	GS	MIN	FGM	FGA	PCT	3FGM	3FGA	PCT	FTM	FTA	PCT	O-RB	D-RB	TOT	AST	PF	DQ	STL	TO	BLK	PTS	RPG	APG	PPG
80-81—Detroit	81	—	1592	234	509	.460	0	6	.000	175	240	.729	117	177	294	112	186	2	46	149	24	643	3.6	1.4	7.9
REG. SEASON TOTALS	81	—	1592	234	509	.460	0	6	.000	175	240	.729	117	177	294	112	186	2	46	149	24	643	3.6	1.4	7.9

ROBINSON, WILBERT JR. (**Wil**) b. December 25, 1949 Ht. 6-2 Wt. 175 College—West Virginia

SEASON—TEAM	G	GS	MIN	FGM	FGA	PCT	3FGM	3FGA	PCT	FTM	FTA	PCT	O-RB	D-RB	TOT	AST	PF	DQ	STL	TO	BLK	PTS	RPG	APG	PPG
73-74—Memphis (A)	45	—	956	166	402	.413	0	6	.000	57	67	.851	28	51	79	132	124	—	51	92	9	389	1.8	2.9	8.6
REG. ABA TOTALS	45	—	956	166	402	.413	0	6	.000	57	67	.851	28	51	79	132	124	0	51	92	9	389	1.8	2.9	8.6

ROBINZINE, WILLIAM CLINTARD (**Bill**) b. January 20, 1953 d. September 16, 1982 Ht. 6-7 Wt. 230 College—DePaul

SEASON—TEAM	G	GS	MIN	FGM	FGA	PCT	3FGM	3FGA	PCT	FTM	FTA	PCT	O-RB	D-RB	TOT	AST	PF	DQ	STL	TO	BLK	PTS	RPG	APG	PPG
75-76—Kansas City	75	—	1327	229	499	.459	—	—	—	145	198	.732	128	227	355	60	290	19	80	—	8	603	4.7	0.8	8.0
76-77—Kansas City	75	—	1594	307	677	.453	—	—	—	159	216	.736	164	310	474	95	283	7	86	—	13	773	6.3	1.3	10.3
77-78—Kansas City	82	—	1748	305	677	.451	—	—	—	206	271	.760	173	366	539	72	281	5	74	172	11	816	6.6	0.9	10.0
78-79—Kansas City	82	—	2179	459	837	.548	—	—	—	180	246	.732	218	420	638	104	367	16	105	179	15	1098	7.8	1.3	13.4
79-80—Kansas City	81	—	1917	362	723	.501	1	2	.500	200	274	.730	184	342	526	62	311	5	106	148	23	925	6.5	0.8	11.4
80-81—Clev.-Dallas	78	—	2016	392	826	.475	1	6	.167	218	281	.776	168	365	533	118	275	6	75	187	9	1003	6.8	1.5	12.9
81-82—Utah	56	9	651	131	294	.446	0	0	—	61	75	.813	56	88	144	49	156	5	37	83	5	323	2.6	0.9	5.8
REG. SEASON TOTALS	529	9	11432	2185	4533	.482	2	8	.250	1169	1561	.749	1091	2118	3209	560	1963	63	563	769	84	5541	6.1	1.1	10.5
PLAYOFF TOTALS	8	0	187	35	75	.467	0	0	—	13	18	.722	22	32	54	3	26	1	16	14	0	83	6.8	0.4	10.4

ROBISCH, DAVID GEORGE (**Dave, Robo**) b. December 22, 1949 Ht. 6-10 Wt. 235 College—Kansas

SEASON—TEAM	G	GS	MIN	FGM	FGA	PCT	3FGM	3FGA	PCT	FTM	FTA	PCT	O-RB	D-RB	TOT	AST	PF	DQ	STL	TO	BLK	PTS	RPG	APG	PPG
71-72—Denver (A)	84	—	2420	505	1138	.444	0	5	.000	294	419	.702	—	—	804	201	251	—	—	113	—	1304	9.6	2.4	15.5
72-73—Denver (A)	83	—	2647	521	1010	.516	0	1	.000	309	409	.756	248	496	744	170	271	8	—	134	—	1351	9.0	2.0	16.3
73-74—Denver (A)	84	—	2469	449	950	.473	0	0	—	318	411	.774	217	491	708	152	225	—	45	103	66	1216	8.4	1.8	14.5
74-75—Denver (A)	84	—	1899	392	779	.503	0	1	.000	304	346	.879	161	342	503	153	205	—	46	108	48	1088	6.0	1.8	13.0
75-76—S.D.-Indiana (A)	87	—	2789	436	1033	.422	0	3	.000	324	381	.850	281	513	794	166	200	—	71	113	59	1196	9.1	1.9	13.7
76-77—Indiana	80	—	1966	369	811	.455	—	—	—	213	256	.832	171	383	554	158	169	1	55	—	37	951	6.9	2.0	11.9
77-78—Indiana-L.A.	78	—	1277	177	430	.412	—	—	—	100	129	.775	100	252	352	88	130	1	39	71	29	454	4.5	1.1	5.8
78-79—Los Angeles	80	—	1219	150	336	.446	—	—	—	86	115	.748	82	203	285	97	108	0	20	53	25	386	3.6	1.2	4.8
79-80—Cleveland	82	—	2670	489	940	.520	0	3	.000	277	329	.842	225	433	658	192	211	2	53	138	53	1255	8.0	2.3	15.3
80-81—Clev.-Denver	84	—	2116	330	740	.446	0	0	—	200	247	.810	157	342	499	173	173	0	37	83	34	860	5.9	2.1	10.2
81-82—Denver	12	0	257	48	106	.453	0	0	—	48	55	.873	14	49	63	32	29	0	3	13	4	144	5.3	2.7	12.0
82-83—Denver	61	0	711	96	251	.382	0	1	.000	92	118	.780	34	117	151	53	61	0	10	45	9	284	2.5	0.9	4.7
83-84—Denver-S.A.-K.C.	31	0	340	35	96	.365	0	0	—	22	26	.846	15	43	58	20	36	1	3	12	2	92	1.9	0.6	3.0
REG. NBA TOTALS	508	0	10556	1694	3710	.457	0	4	.000	1038	1275	.814	798	1822	2620	813	917	5	220	415	193	4426	5.2	1.6	8.7
REG. ABA TOTALS	422	—	12224	2303	4910	.469	0	10	.000	1549	1966	.788	907	1842	3553	842	1152	8	162	571	173	6155	8.4	2.0	14.6
NBA PLAYOFF TOTALS	14	0	152	21	48	.438	0	0	—	7	11	.636	17	29	46	6	18	0	2	8	2	49	3.3	0.4	3.5
ABA PLAYOFF TOTALS	28	—	909	174	401	.434	0	0	—	116	152	.763	97	165	262	53	85	0	14	30	8	464	9.4	1.9	16.6

ROCHA, EPHRAIM J. (**Red**) b. September 18, 1923 Ht. 6-9 Wt. 185 College—Hawaii/Oregon State

SEASON—TEAM	G	GS	MIN	FGM	FGA	PCT	3FGM	3FGA	PCT	FTM	FTA	PCT	O-RB	D-RB	TOT	AST	PF	DQ	STL	TO	BLK	PTS	RPG	APG	PPG
47-48—St. Louis	48	—	—	232	740	.314	—	—	—	147	213	.690	—	—	—	39	209	—	—	—	—	611	—	0.8	12.7
48-49—St. Louis	58	—	—	223	574	.389	—	—	—	162	211	.768	—	—	—	157	251	—	—	—	—	608	—	2.7	10.5
49-50—St. Louis	65	—	—	275	679	.405	—	—	—	220	313	.703	—	—	—	155	257	—	—	—	—	770	—	2.4	11.8
50-51—Baltimore	64	—	—	297	843	.352	—	—	—	242	299	.809	—	—	511	147	242	9	—	—	—	836	8.0	2.3	13.1
51-52—Syracuse	66	—	2543	300	749	.401	—	—	—	254	330	.770	—	—	549	128	249	4	—	—	—	854	8.3	1.9	12.9
52-53—Syracuse	69	—	2454	268	690	.388	—	—	—	234	310	.755	—	—	510	137	257	5	—	—	—	770	7.4	2.0	11.2
54-55—Syracuse	72	—	2473	295	801	.368	—	—	—	222	284	.782	—	—	489	178	242	5	—	—	—	812	6.8	2.5	11.3
55-56—Syracuse	72	—	1883	250	692	.361	—	—	—	220	281	.783	—	—	416	131	244	6	—	—	—	720	5.8	1.8	10.0
56-57—Fort Wayne	72	—	1154	136	390	.349	—	—	—	109	144	.757	—	—	272	81	162	1	—	—	—	381	3.8	1.1	5.3
REG. SEASON TOTALS	586	—	10507	2276	6158	.370	—	—	—	1810	2385	.759	—	—	2747	1153	2113	30	—	—	—	6362	6.6	2.0	10.9
PLAYOFF TOTALS	39	—	961	165	458	.360	—	—	—	144	190	.758	—	—	197	58	169	9	—	—	—	474	6.6	1.5	12.2
ALL-STAR TOTALS	2	—	28	7	21	.333	—	—	—	6	6	1.000	—	—	7	5	6	0	—	—	—	20	3.5	2.5	10.0

ROCHE, JOHN MICHAEL (**Johnny**) b. September 26, 1949 Ht. 6-3 Wt. 170 College—South Carolina

SEASON—TEAM	G	GS	MIN	FGM	FGA	PCT	3FGM	3FGA	PCT	FTM	FTA	PCT	O-RB	D-RB	TOT	AST	PF	DQ	STL	TO	BLK	PTS	RPG	APG	PPG
71-72—New York (A)	82	—	2593	403	859	.469	12	35	.343	240	311	.772	—	—	172	259	211	—	—	188	—	1058	2.1	3.2	12.9
72-73—New York (A)	77	—	2615	404	909	.444	34	103	.330	265	347	.764	33	113	146	348	170	0	—	207	—	1107	1.9	4.5	14.4
73-74—N.Y.-Ken. (A)	84	—	2180	397	829	.479	36	105	.343	148	177	.836	34	88	122	363	157	—	57	184	15	978	1.5	4.3	11.6
74-75—Ken.-Utah (A)	58	—	1387	241	509	.473	13	44	.295	85	106	.802	21	72	93	191	103	—	49	105	7	580	1.6	3.3	10.0
75-76—Utah (A)	16	—	484	112	212	.528	9	26	.346	31	41	.756	5	20	25	79	47	—	14	51	1	264	1.6	4.9	16.5
75-76—Los Angeles	15	—	52	3	14	.214	—	—	—	2	4	.500	0	3	3	6	7	0	0	—	0	8	0.2	0.4	0.5
79-80—Denver	82	—	2286	354	741	.478	49	129	.380	175	202	.866	24	91	115	405	139	0	82	159	12	932	1.4	4.9	11.4
80-81—Denver	26	—	611	82	179	.458	9	27	.333	58	77	.753	5	32	37	140	44	0	17	52	8	231	1.4	5.4	8.9
81-82—Denver	39	2	501	68	150	.453	23	52	.442	28	38	.737	4	19	23	89	40	0	15	29	2	187	0.6	2.3	4.8
REG. NBA TOTALS	162	2	3450	507	1084	.468	81	208	.389	263	321	.819	33	145	178	640	230	0	114	240	22	1358	1.1	4.0	8.4
REG. ABA TOTALS	317	—	9259	1557	3318	.469	104	313	.332	769	982	.783	93	293	558	1240	688	0	120	735	23	3987	1.8	3.9	12.6
ABA PLAYOFF TOTALS	36	—	1239	259	543	.477	27	65	.415	115	156	.737	11	13	56	164	71	0	12	95	4	660	1.6	4.6	18.3

ROCK, EUGENE (**Gene**) b. November 4, 1921 Ht. 5-9½ Wt. 155 College—USC

SEASON—TEAM	G	GS	MIN	FGM	FGA	PCT	3FGM	3FGA	PCT	FTM	FTA	PCT	O-RB	D-RB	TOT	AST	PF	DQ	STL	TO	BLK	PTS	RPG	APG	PPG
47-48—Chicago	11	—	—	4	18	.222	—	—	—	2	4	.500	—	—	0	8	—	—	—	—	—	10	—	0.0	0.9
REG. SEASON TOTALS	11	—	—	4	18	.222	—	—	—	2	4	.500	—	—	0	8	—	—	—	—	—	10	—	0.0	0.9
PLAYOFF TOTALS	2	—	—	0	0	—	—	—	—	0	1	.000	—	—	—	0	—	—	—	—	—	0	—	—	0.0

ROCKER, JACK L. b. August 12, 1922 Ht. 6-5 Wt. 185 College—California Berkeley

SEASON—TEAM	G	GS	MIN	FGM	FGA	PCT	3FGM	3FGA	PCT	FTM	FTA	PCT	O-RB	D-RB	TOT	AST	PF	DQ	STL	TO	BLK	PTS	RPG	APG	PPG
47-48—Minneapolis (N)	5	—	—	2	—	—	—	—	—	0	0	—	—	—	—	—	—	—	—	—	—	4	—	—	0.8
47-48—Philadelphia	9	—	—	8	22	.364	—	—	—	1	1	1.000	—	—	—	3	2	—	—	—	—	17	—	0.3	1.9
REG. NBA TOTALS	9	—	—	8	22	.364	—	—	—	1	1	1.000	—	—	—	3	2	—	—	—	—	17	—	0.3	1.9
REG. NBL TOTALS	5	—	—	2	—	—	—	—	—	0	0	—	—	—	—	—	—	—	—	—	—	4	—	—	0.8

RODGERS, GUY WILLIAM JR. b. September 1, 1935 Ht. 6-0 Wt. 185 College—Temple

SEASON—TEAM	G	GS	MIN	FGM	FGA	PCT	3FGM	3FGA	PCT	FTM	FTA	PCT	O-RB	D-RB	TOT	AST	PF	DQ	STL	TO	BLK	PTS	RPG	APG	PPG
58-59—Philadelphia	45	—	1565	211	535	.394	—	—	—	61	112	.545	—	—	281	261	132	1	—	—	—	483	6.2	5.8	10.7
59-60—Philadelphia	68	—	2483	338	870	.389	—	—	—	111	181	.613	—	—	391	482	196	3	—	—	—	787	5.8	7.1	11.6
60-61—Philadelphia	78	—	2905	397	1029	.386	—	—	—	206	300	.687	—	—	509	677	262	3	—	—	—	1000	6.5	8.7	12.8
61-62—Philadelphia	80	—	2650	267	749	.356	—	—	—	121	182	.665	—	—	348	643	312	12	—	—	—	655	4.4	8.0	8.2
62-63—San Francisco	79	—	3249	445	1150	.387	—	—	—	208	286	.727	—	—	394	825	296	7	—	—	—	1098	5.0	10.4	13.9
63-64—San Francisco	79	—	2695	337	923	.365	—	—	—	198	280	.707	—	—	328	556	245	4	—	—	—	872	4.2	7.0	11.0
64-65—San Francisco	79	—	2699	465	1225	.380	—	—	—	223	325	.686	—	—	323	565	256	4	—	—	—	1153	4.1	7.2	14.6
65-66—San Francisco	79	—	2902	586	1571	.373	—	—	—	296	407	.727	—	—	421	846	241	6	—	—	—	1468	5.3	10.7	18.6
66-67—Chicago	81	—	3063	538	1377	.391	—	—	—	383	475	.806	—	—	346	908	243	1	—	—	—	1459	4.3	11.2	18.0
67-68—Chicago-Cin.	79	—	1546	148	426	.347	—	—	—	107	133	.805	—	—	150	380	167	1	—	—	—	403	1.9	4.8	5.1
68-69—Milwaukee	81	—	2157	325	862	.377	—	—	—	184	232	.793	—	—	226	561	207	2	—	—	—	834	2.8	6.9	10.3
69-70—Milwaukee	64	—	749	68	191	.356	—	—	—	67	90	.744	—	—	74	213	73	1	—	—	—	203	1.2	3.3	3.2
REG. SEASON TOTALS	892	—	28663	4125	10908	.378	—	—	—	2165	3003	.721	—	—	3791	6917	2630	45	—	—	—	10415	4.3	7.8	11.7
PLAYOFF TOTALS	46	—	1557	198	565	.350	—	—	—	112	175	.640	—	—	238	286	176	9	—	—	—	508	5.2	6.2	11.0
ALL-STAR TOTALS	4	—	101	10	27	.370	—	—	—	2	3	.667	—	—	13	25	13	0	—	—	—	22	3.3	6.3	5.5

RODGERS, WILLIAM DANIEL (Willie) b. September 11, 1945 Ht. 6-3 Wt. 195 College—Oklahoma

SEASON—TEAM	G	GS	MIN	FGM	FGA	PCT	3FGM	3FGA	PCT	FTM	FTA	PCT	O-RB	D-RB	TOT	AST	PF	DQ	STL	TO	BLK	PTS	RPG	APG	PPG
68-69—Denver (A)	40	—	294	27	80	.338	0	3	.000	31	52	.596	—	—	47	16	51	1	—	30	—	85	1.2	0.4	2.1
REG. ABA TOTALS	40	—	294	27	80	.338	0	3	.000	31	52	.596	—	—	47	16	51	1	—	30	—	85	1.2	0.4	2.1

RODMAN, DENNIS KEITH (Worm) b. May 13, 1961 Ht. 6-8 Wt. 210 College—Cooke County JC/SE Oklahoma State

SEASON—TEAM	G	GS	MIN	FGM	FGA	PCT	3FGM	3FGA	PCT	FTM	FTA	PCT	O-RB	D-RB	TOT	AST	PF	DQ	STL	TO	BLK	PTS	RPG	APG	PPG
86-87—Detroit	77	1	1155	213	391	.545	0	1	.000	74	126	.587	163	169	332	56	166	1	38	93	48	500	4.3	0.7	6.5
87-88—Detroit	82	32	2147	398	709	.561	5	17	.294	152	284	.535	318	397	715	110	273	5	75	156	45	953	8.7	1.3	11.6
88-89—Detroit	82	8	2208	316	531	.595	6	26	.231	97	155	.626	327	445	772	99	292	4	55	126	76	735	9.4	1.2	9.0
89-90—Detroit	82	43	2377	288	496	.581	1	9	.111	142	217	.654	336	456	792	72	276	2	52	90	60	719	9.7	0.9	8.8
90-91—Detroit	82	77	2747	276	560	.493	6	30	.200	111	176	.631	361	665	1026	85	281	7	65	94	55	669	12.5	1.0	8.2
91-92—Detroit	82	80	3301	342	635	.539	32	101	.317	84	140	.600	523	1007	1530	191	248	0	68	140	70	800	18.7	2.3	9.8
92-93—Detroit	62	55	2410	183	429	.427	15	73	.205	87	163	.534	367	765	1132	102	201	0	48	103	45	468	18.3	1.6	7.5
93-94—San Antonio	79	51	2989	156	292	.534	5	24	.208	53	102	.520	453	914	1367	184	229	0	52	138	32	370	17.3	2.3	4.7
REG. SEASON TOTALS	628	347	19334	2172	4043	.537	70	281	.249	800	1363	.587	2848	4818	7666	899	1966	19	453	940	431	5214	12.2	1.4	8.3
PLAYOFF TOTALS	97	39	2453	271	517	.524	2	22	.091	97	194	.500	301	513	814	82	341	3	56	129	72	641	8.4	0.8	6.6
ALL-STAR TOTALS	2	0	36	4	11	.364	0	0	—	0	0	—	10	7	17	1	2	0	1	4	1	8	8.5	0.5	4.0

ROGERS, HARRY J. (Tree) b. December 31, 1950 Ht. 6-7 Wt. 195 College—St. Louis

SEASON—TEAM	G	GS	MIN	FGM	FGA	PCT	3FGM	3FGA	PCT	FTM	FTA	PCT	O-RB	D-RB	TOT	AST	PF	DQ	STL	TO	BLK	PTS	RPG	APG	PPG
75-76—St. Louis (A)	18	—	298	60	124	.484	0	2	.000	17	24	.708	38	58	96	15	34	—	12	21	6	137	5.3	0.8	7.6
REG. ABA TOTALS	18	—	298	60	124	.484	0	2	.000	17	24	.708	38	58	96	15	34	—	12	21	6	137	5.3	0.8	7.6

ROGERS, JOHN BERNARD (Johnny) b. December 30, 1963 Ht. 6-10 Wt. 230 College—Stanford/Cal State-Irvine

SEASON—TEAM	G	GS	MIN	FGM	FGA	PCT	3FGM	3FGA	PCT	FTM	FTA	PCT	O-RB	D-RB	TOT	AST	PF	DQ	STL	TO	BLK	PTS	RPG	APG	PPG
86-87—Sacramento	45	15	468	90	185	.486	0	5	.000	9	15	.600	30	47	77	26	66	0	9	20	8	189	1.7	0.6	4.2
87-88—Cleveland	24	0	168	26	61	.426	0	2	.000	10	13	.769	8	19	27	3	23	0	4	10	3	62	1.1	0.1	2.6
REG. SEASON TOTALS	69	15	636	116	246	.472	0	7	.000	19	28	.679	38	66	104	29	89	0	13	30	11	251	1.5	0.4	3.6

ROGERS, MARSHALL LEE b. August 27, 1953 Ht. 6-1 Wt. 190 College—Texas-Pan American

SEASON—TEAM	G	GS	MIN	FGM	FGA	PCT	3FGM	3FGA	PCT	FTM	FTA	PCT	O-RB	D-RB	TOT	AST	PF	DQ	STL	TO	BLK	PTS	RPG	APG	PPG
76-77—Golden State	26	—	176	43	116	.371	—	—	—	14	15	.933	6	5	11	10	33	0	8	—	3	100	0.4	0.4	3.8
REG. SEASON TOTALS	26	—	176	43	116	.371	—	—	—	14	15	.933	6	5	11	10	33	0	8	—	3	100	0.4	0.4	3.8
PLAYOFF TOTALS	1	—	3	0	2	.000	—	—	—	2	2	1.000	0	1	1	—	0	0	0	—	0	2	1.0	0.0	2.0

ROGERS, RODNEY RAY JR. b. June 20, 1971 Ht. 6-7 Wt. 250 College—Wake Forest

SEASON—TEAM	G	GS	MIN	FGM	FGA	PCT	3FGM	3FGA	PCT	FTM	FTA	PCT	O-RB	D-RB	TOT	AST	PF	DQ	STL	TO	BLK	PTS	RPG	APG	PPG
93-94—Denver	79	14	1406	239	545	.439	35	92	.380	127	189	.672	90	136	226	101	195	3	63	131	48	640	2.9	1.3	8.1
REG. SEASON TOTALS	79	14	1406	239	545	.439	35	92	.380	127	189	.672	90	136	226	101	195	3	63	131	48	640	2.9	1.3	8.1
PLAYOFF TOTALS	12	0	190	19	49	.388	6	19	.316	17	27	.630	8	13	21	16	25	0	7	8	6	61	1.8	1.3	5.1

ROGES, ALBERT A. (Al) b. October 25, 1930 Ht. 6-4 Wt. 195 College—Los Angeles CC/Long Island University

SEASON—TEAM	G	GS	MIN	FGM	FGA	PCT	3FGM	3FGA	PCT	FTM	FTA	PCT	O-RB	D-RB	TOT	AST	PF	DQ	STL	TO	BLK	PTS	RPG	APG	PPG
53-54—Baltimore	67	—	1937	220	614	.358	—	—	—	130	179	.726	—	—	213	160	177	1	—	—	—	570	3.2	2.4	8.5
54-55—Balt.-Ft. Wayne	17	—	201	23	61	.377	—	—	—	15	24	.625	—	—	24	19	20	0	—	—	—	61	1.4	1.1	3.6
REG. SEASON TOTALS	84	—	2138	243	675	.360	—	—	—	145	203	.714	—	—	237	179	197	1	—	—	—	631	2.8	2.1	7.5

ROHLOFF, KENNETH LAWRANCE (Ken) b. April 18, 1939 Ht. 6-0 Wt. 195 College—North Carolina State

SEASON—TEAM	G	GS	MIN	FGM	FGA	PCT	3FGM	3FGA	PCT	FTM	FTA	PCT	O-RB	D-RB	TOT	AST	PF	DQ	STL	TO	BLK	PTS	RPG	APG	PPG
63-64—St. Louis	2	—	7	0	1	.000	—	—	—	0	0	—	—	—	0	1	4	0	—	—	—	0	0.0	0.5	0.0
REG. SEASON TOTALS	2	—	7	0	1	.000	—	—	—	0	0	—	—	—	0	1	4	0	—	—	—	0	0.0	0.5	0.0

ROLLINS, KENNETH H. (Kenny) b. September 14, 1923 Ht. 6-0 Wt. 170 College—Kentucky

SEASON—TEAM	G	GS	MIN	FGM	FGA	PCT	3FGM	3FGA	PCT	FTM	FTA	PCT	O-RB	D-RB	TOT	AST	PF	DQ	STL	TO	BLK	PTS	RPG	APG	PPG
48-49—Chicago	59	—	—	144	520	.277	—	—	—	77	104	.740	—	—	—	167	150	—	—	—	—	365	—	2.8	6.2
49-50—Chicago	66	—	—	144	421	.342	—	—	—	66	89	.742	—	—	—	131	129	—	—	—	—	354	—	2.0	5.4
52-53—Boston	43	—	426	38	115	.330	—	—	—	22	27	.815	—	—	45	46	63	1	—	—	—	98	1.0	1.1	2.3
REG. SEASON TOTALS	168	—	426	326	1056	.309	—	—	—	165	220	.750	—	—	45	344	342	1	—	—	—	817	1.0	2.0	4.9
PLAYOFF TOTALS	10	—	65	6	24	.250	—	—	—	8	8	1.000	—	—	8	9	20	0	—	—	—	20	1.3	0.9	2.0

ROLLINS, PHILIP LEE (Phil) b. January 19, 1934 Ht. 6-2 Wt. 190 College—Louisville

SEASON—TEAM	G	GS	MIN	FGM	FGA	PCT	3FGM	3FGA	PCT	FTM	FTA	PCT	O-RB	D-RB	TOT	AST	PF	DQ	STL	TO	BLK	PTS	RPG	APG	PPG
58-59—Phil.-Cin.	44	—	691	83	231	.359	—	—	—	63	90	.700	—	—	118	102	49	0	—	—	—	229	2.7	2.3	5.2
59-60—Cincinnati	72	—	1235	158	386	.409	—	—	—	77	127	.606	—	—	180	233	150	1	—	—	—	393	2.5	3.2	5.5
60-61—Cin.-St. L.-N.Y.	60	—	816	109	293	.372	—	—	—	58	88	.659	—	—	97	123	121	1	—	—	—	276	1.6	2.1	4.6
REG. SEASON TOTALS	176	—	2742	350	910	.385	—	—	—	198	305	.649	—	—	395	458	320	2	—	—	—	898	2.2	2.6	5.1

ROLLINS, WAYNE MONTE (Tree) b. June 16, 1955 Ht. 7-1 Wt. 255 College—Clemson

SEASON—TEAM	G	GS	MIN	FGM	FGA	PCT	3FGM	3FGA	PCT	FTM	FTA	PCT	O-RB	D-RB	TOT	AST	PF	DQ	STL	TO	BLK	PTS	RPG	APG	PPG
77-78—Atlanta	80	—	1795	253	520	.487	—	—	—	104	148	.703	179	373	552	79	326	16	57	121	218	610	6.9	1.0	7.6
78-79—Atlanta	81	—	1900	297	555	.535	—	—	—	89	141	.631	219	369	588	49	328	19	46	87	254	683	7.3	0.6	8.4
79-80—Atlanta	82	—	2123	287	514	.558	0	0	—	157	220	.714	283	491	774	76	322	12	54	99	244	731	9.4	0.9	8.9
80-81—Atlanta	40	—	1044	116	210	.552	0	1	.000	46	57	.807	102	184	286	35	151	7	29	57	117	278	7.2	0.9	7.0
81-82—Atlanta	79	39	2018	202	346	.584	0	0	—	79	129	.612	168	443	611	59	285	4	35	79	224	483	7.7	0.7	6.1
82-83—Atlanta	80	80	2472	261	512	.510	0	1	.000	98	135	.726	210	533	743	75	294	7	49	95	343	620	9.3	0.9	7.8
83-84—Atlanta	77	76	2351	274	529	.518	0	0	—	118	190	.621	200	393	593	62	297	9	35	101	277	666	7.7	0.8	8.6
84-85—Atlanta	70	60	1750	186	339	.549	0	0	—	67	93	.720	113	329	442	52	213	6	35	80	167	439	6.3	0.7	6.3
85-86—Atlanta	74	61	1781	173	347	.499	0	1	.000	69	90	.767	131	327	458	41	239	5	38	91	167	415	6.2	0.6	5.6
86-87—Atlanta	75	58	1764	171	313	.546	0	0	—	63	87	.724	155	333	488	22	240	1	43	61	140	405	6.5	0.3	5.4
87-88—Atlanta	76	59	1765	133	260	.512	0	0	—	70	80	.875	142	317	459	20	229	2	31	51	132	336	6.0	0.3	4.4
88-89—Cleveland	60	2	583	62	138	.449	0	1	.000	12	19	.632	38	101	139	19	89	0	11	22	38	136	2.3	0.3	2.3
89-90—Cleveland	48	19	674	57	125	.456	0	1	.000	11	16	.688	58	95	153	24	83	3	13	35	53	125	3.2	0.5	2.6
90-91—Detroit	37	0	202	14	33	.424	0	0	—	8	14	.571	13	29	42	4	35	0	2	15	20	36	1.1	0.1	1.0
91-92—Houston	59	5	697	46	86	.535	0	0	—	26	30	.867	61	110	171	15	85	0	14	18	62	118	2.9	0.3	2.0
92-93—Houston	42	0	247	11	41	.268	0	2	.000	9	12	.750	12	48	60	10	43	0	6	9	15	31	1.4	0.2	0.7
93-94—Orlando	45	1	384	29	53	.547	0	0	—	18	30	.600	33	63	96	9	55	1	7	13	35	76	2.1	0.2	1.7
REG. SEASON TOTALS	1105	460	23550	2572	4921	.523	0	7	.000	1044	1491	.700	2117	4538	6655	651	3314	92	505	1034	2506	6188	6.0	0.6	5.6
PLAYOFF TOTALS	79	40	1723	143	284	.504	0	1	.000	67	105	.638	135	291	426	29	250	10	33	75	128	353	5.4	0.4	4.5

ROMAR, LORENZO b. November 13, 1958 Ht. 6-1½ Wt. 175 College—Cerritos/Washington

SEASON—TEAM	G	GS	MIN	FGM	FGA	PCT	3FGM	3FGA	PCT	FTM	FTA	PCT	O-RB	D-RB	TOT	AST	PF	DQ	STL	TO	BLK	PTS	RPG	APG	PPG
80-81—Golden State	53	—	726	87	211	.412	2	6	.333	43	63	.683	10	46	56	136	64	0	27	52	3	219	1.1	2.6	4.1
81-82—Golden State	79	11	1259	203	403	.504	3	15	.200	79	96	.823	12	86	98	226	103	0	60	89	13	488	1.2	2.9	6.2
82-83—Golden State	82	64	2130	266	572	.465	10	33	.303	78	105	.743	23	115	138	455	142	0	98	141	5	620	1.7	5.5	7.6
83-84—G.S.-Milw.	68	9	1022	161	351	.459	4	33	.121	67	94	.713	21	72	93	193	77	0	55	63	8	393	1.4	2.8	5.8
84-85—Milw.-Detroit	9	0	51	3	16	.188	0	3	.000	5	5	1.000	0	0	0	12	7	0	4	5	0	11	0.0	1.3	1.2
REG. SEASON TOTALS	291	84	5188	720	1553	.464	19	90	.211	272	363	.749	66	319	385	1022	393	0	244	350	29	1731	1.3	3.5	5.9
PLAYOFF TOTALS	13	0	67	9	20	.450	0	3	.000	7	11	.636	0	3	3	15	9	0	0	5	0	25	0.2	1.2	1.9

ROOK, JERRY G. b. October 27, 1943 Ht. 6-5 Wt. 220 College—Arkansas State

SEASON—TEAM	G	GS	MIN	FGM	FGA	PCT	3FGM	3FGA	PCT	FTM	FTA	PCT	O-RB	D-RB	TOT	AST	PF	DQ	STL	TO	BLK	PTS	RPG	APG	PPG
69-70—New Orleans (A)	28	—	155	37	82	.451	0	2	.000	11	13	.846	—	—	31	10	21	0	—	—	—	85	1.1	0.4	3.0
REG. ABA TOTALS	28	—	155	37	82	.451	0	2	.000	11	13	.846	—	—	31	10	21	0	—	—	—	85	1.1	0.4	3.0

ROOKS, SEAN LESTER b. September 9, 1969 Ht. 6-10 Wt. 260 College—Arizona

SEASON—TEAM	G	GS	MIN	FGM	FGA	PCT	3FGM	3FGA	PCT	FTM	FTA	PCT	O-RB	D-RB	TOT	AST	PF	DQ	STL	TO	BLK	PTS	RPG	APG	PPG
92-93—Dallas	72	68	2087	368	747	.493	0	2	.000	234	389	.602	196	340	536	95	204	2	38	160	81	970	7.4	1.3	13.5
93-94—Dallas	47	28	1255	193	393	.491	0	1	.000	150	210	.714	84	175	259	49	109	0	21	80	44	536	5.5	1.0	11.4
REG. SEASON TOTALS	119	96	3342	561	1140	.492	0	3	.000	384	599	.641	280	515	795	144	313	2	59	240	125	1506	6.7	1.2	12.7

ROSE, ROBERT PAUL (**Bob**) b. December 27, 1964 Ht. 6-5 Wt. 185 College—George Mason

SEASON—TEAM	G	GS	MIN	FGM	FGA	PCT	3FGM	3FGA	PCT	FTM	FTA	PCT	O-RB	D-RB	TOT	AST	PF	DQ	STL	TO	BLK	PTS	RPG	APG	PPG
88-89—L.A. Clippers	2	0	3	0	1	.000	0	0	—	0	0	—	1	1	2	0	0	0	0	0	0	0	1.0	0.0	0.0
REG. SEASON TOTALS	2	0	3	0	1	.000	0	0	—	0	0	—	1	1	2	0	0	0	0	0	0	0	1.0	0.0	0.0

ROSENBERG, ALEXANDER (**Petey**) b. April 7, 1918 Ht. 5-10 Wt. 165 College—St. Joseph's (Pa.)

SEASON—TEAM	G	GS	MIN	FGM	FGA	PCT	3FGM	3FGA	PCT	FTM	FTA	PCT	O-RB	D-RB	TOT	AST	PF	DQ	STL	TO	BLK	PTS	RPG	APG	PPG
46-47—Philadelphia	51	—	—	60	287	.209	—	—	—	30	49	.612	—	—	—	27	64	—	—	—	—	150	—	0.5	2.9
REG. SEASON TOTALS	51	—	—	60	287	.209	—	—	—	30	49	.612	—	—	—	27	64	—	—	—	—	150	—	0.5	2.9
PLAYOFF TOTALS	9	—	—	1	12	.083	—	—	—	0	3	.000	—	—	—	3	4	—	—	—	—	2	0.0	0.3	0.2

ROSENBLUTH, LEONARD ROBERT (**Lennie**) b. January 22, 1933 Ht. 6-5 Wt. 200 College—North Carolina

SEASON—TEAM	G	GS	MIN	FGM	FGA	PCT	3FGM	3FGA	PCT	FTM	FTA	PCT	O-RB	D-RB	TOT	AST	PF	DQ	STL	TO	BLK	PTS	RPG	APG	PPG
57-58—Philadelphia	53	—	373	91	265	.343	—	—	—	53	84	.631	—	—	91	23	39	0	—	—	—	235	1.7	0.4	4.4
58-59—Philadelphia	29	—	205	43	145	.297	—	—	—	21	29	.724	—	—	54	6	20	0	—	—	—	107	1.9	0.2	3.7
REG. SEASON TOTALS	82	—	578	134	410	.327	—	—	—	74	113	.655	—	—	145	29	59	0	—	—	—	342	1.8	0.4	4.2
PLAYOFF TOTALS	4	—	11	3	9	.333	—	—	—	2	3	.667	—	—	3	—	0	0	—	—	—	8	0.8	0.0	2.0

ROSENSTEIN, HENRY (**Hank**) b. June 16, 1920 Ht. 6-4 Wt. 185 College—CCNY

SEASON—TEAM	G	GS	MIN	FGM	FGA	PCT	3FGM	3FGA	PCT	FTM	FTA	PCT	O-RB	D-RB	TOT	AST	PF	DQ	STL	TO	BLK	PTS	RPG	APG	PPG
46-47—N.Y.-Prov.	60	—	—	119	390	.305	—	—	—	144	225	.640	—	—	—	36	172	—	—	—	—	382	—	0.6	6.4
REG. SEASON TOTALS	60	—	—	119	390	.305	—	—	—	144	225	.640	—	—	—	36	172	—	—	—	—	382	—	0.6	6.4

ROSENTHAL, RICHARD ANTHONY (**Dick**) b. January 20, 1930 Ht. 6-5 Wt. 205 College—Notre Dame

SEASON—TEAM	G	GS	MIN	FGM	FGA	PCT	3FGM	3FGA	PCT	FTM	FTA	PCT	O-RB	D-RB	TOT	AST	PF	DQ	STL	TO	BLK	PTS	RPG	APG	PPG
54-55—Fort Wayne	67	—	1406	197	523	.377	—	—	—	130	181	.718	—	—	300	153	179	2	—	—	—	524	4.5	2.3	7.8
56-57—Fort Wayne	18	—	188	21	79	.266	—	—	—	9	17	.529	—	—	52	17	22	0	—	—	—	51	2.9	0.9	2.8
REG. SEASON TOTALS	85	—	1594	218	602	.362	—	—	—	139	198	.702	—	—	352	170	201	2	—	—	—	575	4.1	2.0	6.8
PLAYOFF TOTALS	11	—	209	27	84	.321	—	—	—	28	39	.718	—	—	48	26	39	1	—	—	—	82	4.4	2.4	7.5

ROTH, DOUGLAS KEITH (**Doug**) b. August 24, 1967 Ht. 6-11 Wt. 255 College—Tennessee

SEASON—TEAM	G	GS	MIN	FGM	FGA	PCT	3FGM	3FGA	PCT	FTM	FTA	PCT	O-RB	D-RB	TOT	AST	PF	DQ	STL	TO	BLK	PTS	RPG	APG	PPG
89-90—Washington	42	0	412	37	86	.430	0	1	.000	7	14	.500	44	76	120	20	70	1	8	16	13	81	2.9	0.5	1.9
REG. SEASON TOTALS	42	0	412	37	86	.430	0	1	.000	7	14	.500	44	76	120	20	70	1	8	16	13	81	2.9	0.5	1.9

ROTH, SCOTT EDWARD b. June 3, 1963 Ht. 6-8 Wt. 215 College—Wisconsin

SEASON—TEAM	G	GS	MIN	FGM	FGA	PCT	3FGM	3FGA	PCT	FTM	FTA	PCT	O-RB	D-RB	TOT	AST	PF	DQ	STL	TO	BLK	PTS	RPG	APG	PPG
87-88—Utah	26	0	201	30	74	.405	2	11	.182	22	30	.733	7	21	28	16	37	0	12	11	0	84	1.1	0.6	3.2
88-89—Utah-S.A.	63	3	536	59	167	.353	3	16	.188	60	87	.690	20	44	64	55	69	0	24	40	5	181	1.0	0.9	2.9
89-90—Minnesota	71	3	1061	159	420	.379	18	52	.346	150	201	.746	34	78	112	115	144	1	51	85	6	486	1.6	1.6	6.8
REG. SEASON TOTALS	160	6	1798	248	661	.375	23	79	.291	232	318	.730	61	143	204	186	250	1	87	136	11	751	1.3	1.2	4.7
PLAYOFF TOTALS	6	0	10	1	3	.333	0	0	—	0	0	—	0	0	—	0	0	0	2	0	0	2	0.0	0.0	0.3

ROTHENBERG, IRWIN P. (**Irv**) b. December 31, 1921 Ht. 6-7½ Wt. 215 College—Long Island University

SEASON—TEAM	G	GS	MIN	FGM	FGA	PCT	3FGM	3FGA	PCT	FTM	FTA	PCT	O-RB	D-RB	TOT	AST	PF	DQ	STL	TO	BLK	PTS	RPG	APG	PPG
46-47—Cleveland	29	—	—	36	167	.216	—	—	—	30	54	.556	—	—	—	15	62	—	—	—	—	102	—	0.5	3.5
47-48—Wash.-Balt.-St. L.	49	—	—	103	364	.283	—	—	—	87	150	.580	—	—	—	7	115	—	—	—	—	293	—	0.1	6.0
48-49—New York	53	—	—	101	367	.275	—	—	—	112	174	.644	—	—	—	68	174	—	—	—	—	314	—	1.3	5.9
REG. SEASON TOTALS	131	—	—	240	898	.267	—	—	—	229	378	.606	—	—	—	90	351	—	—	—	—	709	—	0.7	5.4
PLAYOFF TOTALS	11	—	—	9	53	.170	—	—	—	6	17	.353	—	—	—	2	21	—	—	—	—	24	—	0.2	2.2

ROTTNER, MARVIN (**Mickey**) b. March 23, 1919 Ht. 5-10.5 Wt. 180 College—Loyola (Ill.)

SEASON—TEAM	G	GS	MIN	FGM	FGA	PCT	3FGM	3FGA	PCT	FTM	FTA	PCT	O-RB	D-RB	TOT	AST	PF	DQ	STL	TO	BLK	PTS	RPG	APG	PPG
45-46—Sheboygan (N)	5	—	10	—	—	—	—	—	—	0	—	—	—	—	—	—	—	—	—	—	—	20	—	—	4.0
46-47—Chicago	56	—	—	190	655	.290	—	—	—	43	79	.544	—	—	—	93	109	—	—	—	—	423	—	1.7	7.6
47-48—Chicago	44	—	—	53	184	.288	—	—	—	11	34	.324	—	—	—	46	49	—	—	—	—	117	—	1.0	2.7
REG. NBA TOTALS	100	—	—	243	839	.290	—	—	—	54	113	.478	—	—	—	139	158	—	—	—	—	540	—	1.4	5.4
REG. NBL TOTALS	5	—	10	—	—	—	—	—	—	0	—	—	—	—	—	—	—	—	—	—	—	20	—	—	4.0
NBA PLAYOFF TOTALS	14	—	—	8	58	.138	—	—	—	2	7	.286	—	—	—	5	23	1	—	—	—	18	0.0	0.4	1.3
NBL PLAYOFF TOTALS	8	—	10	—	—	—	—	—	—	4	—	.000	—	—	—	—	5	—	—	—	—	24	—	—	3.0

ROUNDFIELD, DANNY THOMAS (Dan, Rounds) b. May 26, 1953 Ht. 6-8 Wt. 205 College—Central Michigan

SEASON—TEAM	G	GS	MIN	FGM	FGA	PCT	3FGM	3FGA	PCT	FTM	FTA	PCT	O-RB	D-RB	TOT	AST	PF	DQ	STL	TO	BLK	PTS	RPG	APG	PPG
75-76—Indiana (A)	67	—	767	131	309	.424	0	2	.000	77	122	.631	131	128	259	35	161	—	31	64	43	339	3.9	0.5	5.1
76-77—Indiana	61	—	1645	342	734	.466	—	—	—	164	239	.686	179	339	518	69	243	8	61	—	131	848	8.5	1.1	13.9
77-78—Indiana	79	—	2423	421	861	.489	—	—	—	218	300	.727	275	527	802	196	297	4	81	194	149	1060	10.2	2.5	13.4
78-79—Atlanta	80	—	2539	462	916	.504	—	—	—	300	420	.714	326	539	865	131	358	16	87	209	176	1224	10.8	1.6	15.3
79-80—Atlanta	81	—	2588	502	1007	.499	0	4	.000	330	465	.710	293	544	837	184	317	6	101	233	139	1334	10.3	2.3	16.5
80-81—Atlanta	63	—	2128	426	808	.527	0	1	.000	256	355	.721	231	403	634	161	258	8	76	178	119	1108	10.1	2.6	17.6
81-82—Atlanta	61	58	2217	424	910	.466	1	5	.200	285	375	.760	227	494	721	162	210	3	64	183	93	1134	11.8	2.7	18.6
82-83—Atlanta	77	76	2811	561	1193	.470	5	27	.185	337	450	.749	259	621	880	225	239	1	60	245	115	1464	11.4	2.9	19.0
83-84—Atlanta	73	72	2610	503	1038	.485	0	11	.000	374	486	.770	206	515	721	184	221	2	61	205	74	1380	9.9	2.5	18.9
84-85—Detroit	56	43	1492	236	505	.467	0	2	.000	139	178	.781	175	278	453	102	147	5	26	123	54	611	8.1	1.8	10.9
85-86—Washington	79	21	2321	322	660	.488	0	6	.000	273	362	.754	210	432	642	167	194	1	36	187	51	917	8.1	2.1	11.6
86-87—Washington	36	0	669	90	220	.409	1	5	.200	57	72	.792	64	106	170	39	77	0	11	49	16	238	4.7	1.1	6.6
REG. NBA TOTALS	746	270	23443	4289	8852	.485	7	61	.115	2733	3702	.738	2445	4798	7243	1620	2561	49	664	1806	1117	11318	9.7	2.2	15.2
REG. ABA TOTALS	67	—	767	131	309	.424	0	2	.000	77	122	.631	131	128	259	35	161	—	31	64	43	339	3.9	0.5	5.1
NBA PLAYOFF TOTALS	38	18	1304	225	478	.471	1	4	.250	126	174	.724	126	252	378	81	133	5	26	98	56	577	9.9	2.1	15.2
ABA PLAYOFF TOTALS	2	—	25	7	12	.583	0	0	—	8	9	.889	4	6	10	0	6	—	2	0	4	22	5.0	0.0	11.0
NBA ALL-STAR TOTALS	1	0	27	7	15	.467	0	0	—	4	9	.444	9	4	13	0	2	0	1	3	2	18	13.0	0.0	18.0

ROUX, GIFFORD H. (Giff) b. June 28, 1923 Ht. 6-5 Wt. 195 College—Kansas

SEASON—TEAM	G	GS	MIN	FGM	FGA	PCT	3FGM	3FGA	PCT	FTM	FTA	PCT	O-RB	D-RB	TOT	AST	PF	DQ	STL	TO	BLK	PTS	RPG	APG	PPG
46-47—St. Louis	60	—	—	142	478	.297	—	—	—	70	160	.438	—	—	—	17	95	—	—	—	—	354	—	0.3	5.9
47-48—St. Louis	46	—	—	68	258	.264	—	—	—	40	68	.588	—	—	—	12	60	—	—	—	—	176	—	0.3	3.8
48-49—St. L.-Prov.	45	—	—	29	118	.246	—	—	—	29	44	.659	—	—	—	20	30	—	—	—	—	87	—	0.4	1.9
REG. SEASON TOTALS	151	—	—	239	854	.280	—	—	—	139	272	.511	—	—	—	49	185	—	—	—	—	617	—	0.3	4.1
PLAYOFF TOTALS	8	—	—	13	53	.245	—	—	—	3	9	.333	—	—	—	9	—	—	—	—	—	29	—	0.0	3.6

ROWAN, RONALD LEWIS (Ron) b. April 23, 1962 Ht. 6-5 Wt. 200 College—Notre Dame/St. John's

SEASON—TEAM	G	GS	MIN	FGM	FGA	PCT	3FGM	3FGA	PCT	FTM	FTA	PCT	O-RB	D-RB	TOT	AST	PF	DQ	STL	TO	BLK	PTS	RPG	APG	PPG
86-87—Portland	7	0	16	4	9	.444	1	1	1.000	3	4	.750	1	0	1	1	1	0	4	3	0	12	0.1	0.1	1.7
REG. SEASON TOTALS	7	0	16	4	9	.444	1	1	1.000	3	4	.750	1	0	1	1	1	0	4	3	0	12	0.1	0.1	1.7

ROWE, CURTIS JR. b. July 2, 1949 Ht. 6-7 Wt. 225 College—UCLA

SEASON—TEAM	G	GS	MIN	FGM	FGA	PCT	3FGM	3FGA	PCT	FTM	FTA	PCT	O-RB	D-RB	TOT	AST	PF	DQ	STL	TO	BLK	PTS	RPG	APG	PPG
71-72—Detroit	82	—	2661	369	802	.460	—	—	—	192	287	.669	—	—	699	99	171	1	—	—	—	930	8.5	1.2	11.3
72-73—Detroit	81	—	3009	547	1053	.519	—	—	—	210	327	.642	—	—	760	172	191	0	—	—	—	1304	9.4	2.1	16.1
73-74—Detroit	82	—	2499	380	769	.494	—	—	—	118	169	.698	167	348	515	136	177	1	49	—	36	878	6.3	1.7	10.7
74-75—Detroit	82	—	2787	422	874	.483	—	—	—	171	227	.753	174	411	585	121	190	0	50	—	44	1015	7.1	1.5	12.4
75-76—Detroit	80	—	2998	514	1098	.468	—	—	—	252	342	.737	231	466	697	183	209	1	47	—	45	1280	8.7	2.3	16.0
76-77—Boston	79	—	2190	315	632	.498	—	—	—	170	240	.708	188	375	563	107	215	3	24	—	47	800	7.1	1.4	10.1
77-78—Boston	51	—	911	123	273	.451	—	—	—	66	89	.742	74	129	203	45	94	1	14	76	8	312	4.0	0.9	6.1
78-79—Boston	53	—	1222	151	346	.436	—	—	—	52	75	.693	79	163	242	69	105	2	15	88	13	354	4.6	1.3	6.7
REG. SEASON TOTALS	590	—	18277	2821	5847	.482	—	—	—	1231	1756	.701	913	1892	4264	932	1352	11	199	164	193	6873	7.2	1.6	11.6
PLAYOFF TOTALS	28	—	927	127	264	.481	—	—	—	69	95	.726	78	142	220	62	85	2	11	—	23	323	7.9	2.2	11.5
ALL-STAR TOTALS	1	—	8	0	2	.000	—	—	—	1	2	.500	0	2	2	0	2	0	—	0	—	1	2.0	0.0	1.0

ROWINSKI, JAMES (Jim) b. January 4, 1961 Ht. 6-8 Wt. 260 College—Purdue

SEASON—TEAM	G	GS	MIN	FGM	FGA	PCT	3FGM	3FGA	PCT	FTM	FTA	PCT	O-RB	D-RB	TOT	AST	PF	DQ	STL	TO	BLK	PTS	RPG	APG	PPG
88-89—Detroit-Phil.	9	0	15	1	4	.250	0	0	—	5	6	.833	1	4	5	0	0	0	0	0	0	7	0.6	0.0	0.8
89-90—Miami	14	0	112	14	32	.438	0	0	—	22	26	.846	17	12	29	5	19	0	1	10	2	50	2.1	0.4	3.6
REG. SEASON TOTALS	23	0	127	15	36	.417	0	0	—	27	32	.844	18	16	34	5	19	0	1	10	2	57	1.5	0.2	2.5

ROWLAND, DERRICK b. June 21, 1959 Ht. 6-5 Wt. 195 College—Potsdam (NY) State

SEASON—TEAM	G	GS	MIN	FGM	FGA	PCT	3FGM	3FGA	PCT	FTM	FTA	PCT	O-RB	D-RB	TOT	AST	PF	DQ	STL	TO	BLK	PTS	RPG	APG	PPG
85-86—Milwaukee	2	0	9	1	3	.333	0	0	—	1	2	.500	0	1	1	1	1	0	0	0	0	3	0.5	0.5	1.5
REG. SEASON TOTALS	2	0	9	1	3	.333	0	0	—	1	2	.500	0	1	1	1	1	0	0	0	0	3	0.5	0.5	1.5

ROWSOM, BRIAN MAURICE b. October 23, 1965 Ht. 6-9 Wt. 220 College—North Carolina-Wilmington

SEASON—TEAM	G	GS	MIN	FGM	FGA	PCT	3FGM	3FGA	PCT	FTM	FTA	PCT	O-RB	D-RB	TOT	AST	PF	DQ	STL	TO	BLK	PTS	RPG	APG	PPG
87-88—Indiana	4	0	16	0	6	.000	0	0	—	6	6	1.000	1	4	5	1	3	0	1	1	0	6	1.3	0.3	1.5
88-89—Charlotte	34	0	517	80	162	.494	1	1	1.000	65	81	.802	56	81	137	24	69	1	10	18	12	226	4.0	0.7	6.6
89-90—Charlotte	44	2	559	78	179	.436	1	2	.500	68	83	.819	44	87	131	22	58	0	18	25	11	225	3.0	0.5	5.1
REG. SEASON TOTALS	82	2	1092	158	347	.455	2	3	.667	139	170	.818	101	172	273	47	130	1	29	44	23	457	3.3	0.6	5.6

ROYAL, DONALD ADAM b. May 2, 1966 Ht. 6-8 Wt. 210 College—Notre Dame

SEASON—TEAM	G	GS	MIN	FGM	FGA	PCT	3FGM	3FGA	PCT	FTM	FTA	PCT	O-RB	D-RB	TOT	AST	PF	DQ	STL	TO	BLK	PTS	RPG	APG	PPG
89-90—Minnesota	66	0	746	117	255	.459	0	1	.000	153	197	.777	69	68	137	43	107	0	32	81	8	387	2.1	0.7	5.9
91-92—San Antonio	60	4	718	80	178	.449	0	0	—	92	133	.692	65	59	124	34	73	0	25	39	7	252	2.1	0.6	4.2
92-93—Orlando	77	0	1636	194	391	.496	0	3	.000	318	390	.815	116	179	295	80	179	4	36	113	25	706	3.8	1.0	9.2
93-94—Orlando	74	0	1357	174	347	.501	0	2	.000	199	269	.740	94	154	248	61	121	1	50	76	16	547	3.4	0.8	7.4
REG. SEASON TOTALS	277	4	4457	565	1171	.482	0	6	.000	762	989	.770	344	460	804	218	480	5	143	309	56	1892	2.9	0.8	6.8
PLAYOFF TOTALS	6	2	102	11	23	.478	0	0	—	14	21	.667	6	10	16	5	10	0	3	8	2	36	2.7	0.8	6.0

ROYALS, REGGIE b. September 18, 1954 Ht. 6-10½ Wt. 200 College—Florida State

SEASON—TEAM	G	GS	MIN	FGM	FGA	PCT	3FGM	3FGA	PCT	FTM	FTA	PCT	O-RB	D-RB	TOT	AST	PF	DQ	STL	TO	BLK	PTS	RPG	APG	PPG
74-75—San Diego (A)	2	—	11	2	4	.500	0	0	—	0	0	—	0	0	0	0	1	—	0	0	0	4	0.0	0.0	2.0
REG. ABA TOTALS	2	—	11	2	4	.500	0	0	—	0	0	—	0	0	—	0	1	—	0	0	0	4	0.0	0.0	2.0

ROYER, ROBERT D. **(Bob)** b. October 15, 1927 d. May 30, 1973 Ht. 5-10 Wt. 155 College—Kansas City JC/Indiana State

SEASON—TEAM	G	GS	MIN	FGM	FGA	PCT	3FGM	3FGA	PCT	FTM	FTA	PCT	O-RB	D-RB	TOT	AST	PF	DQ	STL	TO	BLK	PTS	RPG	APG	PPG
49-50—Denver	42	—	—	78	231	.338	—	—	—	41	58	.707	—	—	—	85	72	—	—	—	—	197	—	2.0	4.7
REG. SEASON TOTALS	42	—	—	78	231	.338	—	—	—	41	58	.707	—	—	—	85	72	—	—	—	—	197	—	2.0	4.7

RUDD, EDWARD DELANE **(Delaney)** b. November 8, 1962 Ht. 6-2 Wt. 195 College—Wake Forest

SEASON—TEAM	G	GS	MIN	FGM	FGA	PCT	3FGM	3FGA	PCT	FTM	FTA	PCT	O-RB	D-RB	TOT	AST	PF	DQ	STL	TO	BLK	PTS	RPG	APG	PPG
89-90—Utah	77	2	850	111	259	.429	16	56	.286	35	53	.660	12	43	55	177	81	0	22	88	1	273	0.7	2.3	3.5
90-91—Utah	82	0	874	124	285	.435	17	61	.279	59	71	.831	14	52	66	216	92	0	36	102	2	324	0.8	2.6	4.0
91-92—Utah	65	0	538	75	188	.399	11	47	.234	32	42	.762	15	39	54	109	64	0	15	49	1	193	0.8	1.7	3.0
92-93—Portland	15	1	95	7	36	.194	1	11	.091	11	14	.786	4	5	9	17	7	0	1	11	0	26	0.6	1.1	1.7
REG. SEASON TOTALS	239	3	2357	317	768	.413	45	175	.257	137	180	.761	45	139	184	519	244	0	74	250	4	816	0.8	2.2	3.4
PLAYOFF TOTALS	24	0	187	27	65	.415	7	26	.269	6	10	.600	3	6	9	49	27	0	7	10	0	67	0.4	2.0	2.8

RUDD, JOHN WILLIAM b. August 7, 1955 Ht. 6-7 Wt. 230 College—McNeese State

SEASON—TEAM	G	GS	MIN	FGM	FGA	PCT	3FGM	3FGA	PCT	FTM	FTA	PCT	O-RB	D-RB	TOT	AST	PF	DQ	STL	TO	BLK	PTS	RPG	APG	PPG
78-79—New York	58	—	723	59	133	.444	—	—	—	66	93	.710	69	98	167	35	95	1	17	59	8	184	2.9	0.6	3.2
REG. SEASON TOTALS	58	—	723	59	133	.444	—	—	—	66	93	.710	69	98	167	35	95	1	17	59	8	184	2.9	0.6	3.2

RUDOMETKIN, JOHN **(Rudo)** b. June 6, 1940 Ht. 6-6 Wt. 205 College—Allan Hancock/USC

SEASON—TEAM	G	GS	MIN	FGM	FGA	PCT	3FGM	3FGA	PCT	FTM	FTA	PCT	O-RB	D-RB	TOT	AST	PF	DQ	STL	TO	BLK	PTS	RPG	APG	PPG
62-63—New York	56	—	572	108	307	.352	—	—	—	73	95	.768	—	—	149	30	58	0	—	—	—	289	2.7	0.5	5.2
63-64—New York	52	—	696	154	326	.472	—	—	—	87	116	.750	—	—	164	26	86	0	—	—	—	395	3.2	0.5	7.6
64-65—N.Y.-S.F.	23	—	376	52	154	.338	—	—	—	34	50	.680	—	—	99	16	54	0	—	—	—	138	4.3	0.7	6.0
REG. SEASON TOTALS	131	—	1644	314	787	.399	—	—	—	194	261	.743	—	—	412	72	198	0	—	—	—	822	3.1	0.5	6.3

RUFFNER, PAUL b. October 15, 1948 Ht. 6-10 Wt. 225 College—Cerritos/Brigham Young

SEASON—TEAM	G	GS	MIN	FGM	FGA	PCT	3FGM	3FGA	PCT	FTM	FTA	PCT	O-RB	D-RB	TOT	AST	PF	DQ	STL	TO	BLK	PTS	RPG	APG	PPG
70-71—Chicago	10	—	60	15	35	.429	—	—	—	4	8	.500	—	—	16	2	10	0	—	—	—	34	1.6	0.2	3.4
71-72—Pittsburgh (A)	79	—	1059	182	381	.478	0	0	—	84	115	.730	—	—	341	52	178	—	—	69	—	448	4.3	0.7	5.7
73-74—Buffalo	20	—	51	11	27	.407	—	—	—	8	13	.615	4	7	11	0	10	0	1	—	1	30	0.6	0.0	1.5
74-75—Buffalo	22	—	103	22	47	.468	—	—	—	1	5	.200	12	10	22	7	22	0	3	—	3	45	1.0	0.3	2.0
75-76—St. Louis (A)	2	—	5	2	3	.667	0	0	—	0	0	—	1	2	3	0	0	—	0	0	0	4	1.5	0.0	2.0
REG. NBA TOTALS	52	—	214	48	109	.440	—	—	—	13	26	.500	16	17	49	9	42	0	4	—	4	109	0.9	0.2	2.1
REG. ABA TOTALS	81	—	1064	184	384	.479	0	0	—	84	115	.730	1	2	344	52	178	0	0	69	0	452	4.2	0.6	5.6
NBA PLAYOFF TOTALS	2	—	7	0	6	.000	—	—	—	0	0	—	0	2	4	—	0	0	0	—	0	0	2.0	0.0	0.0

RUKLICK, JOSEPH **(Joe)** b. August 3, 1938 Ht. 6-9 Wt. 220 College—Northwestern

SEASON—TEAM	G	GS	MIN	FGM	FGA	PCT	3FGM	3FGA	PCT	FTM	FTA	PCT	O-RB	D-RB	TOT	AST	PF	DQ	STL	TO	BLK	PTS	RPG	APG	PPG
59-60—Philadelphia	39	—	384	85	214	.397	—	—	—	26	36	.722	—	—	137	24	70	0	—	—	—	196	3.5	0.6	5.0
60-61—Philadelphia	29	—	223	43	120	.358	—	—	—	8	13	.615	—	—	62	10	38	0	—	—	—	94	2.1	0.3	3.2
61-62—Philadelphia	46	—	302	48	147	.327	—	—	—	12	26	.462	—	—	87	14	56	1	—	—	—	108	1.9	0.3	2.3
REG. SEASON TOTALS	114	—	909	176	481	.366	—	—	—	46	75	.613	—	—	286	48	164	1	—	—	—	398	2.5	0.4	3.5
PLAYOFF TOTALS	6	—	23	3	13	.231	—	—	—	1	2	.500	—	—	9	—	5	0	—	—	—	7	1.5	0.0	1.2

RULAND, JEFFREY ALAN (**Jeff**) b. December 16, 1958 Ht. 6-10 Wt. 275 College—Iona

SEASON—TEAM	G	GS	MIN	FGM	FGA	PCT	3FGM	3FGA	PCT	FTM	FTA	PCT	O-RB	D-RB	TOT	AST	PF	DQ	STL	TO	BLK	PTS	RPG	APG	PPG
81-82—Washington	82	0	2214	420	749	.561	1	3	.333	342	455	.752	253	509	762	134	319	7	44	237	58	1183	9.3	1.6	14.4
82-83—Washington	79	47	2862	580	1051	.552	1	3	.333	375	544	.689	293	578	871	234	312	12	74	297	77	1536	11.0	3.0	19.4
83-84—Washington	75	75	3082	599	1035	.579	1	7	.143	466	636	.733	265	657	922	296	285	8	68	342	72	1665	12.3	3.9	22.2
84-85—Washington	37	36	1436	250	439	.569	0	2	.000	200	292	.685	127	283	410	162	128	2	31	179	27	700	11.1	4.4	18.9
85-86—Washington	30	24	1114	212	383	.554	0	4	.000	145	200	.725	107	213	320	159	100	1	23	121	25	569	10.7	5.3	19.0
86-87—Philadelphia	5	2	116	19	28	.679	0	0	—	9	12	.750	12	16	28	10	13	0	0	10	4	47	5.6	2.0	9.4
91-92—Philadelphia	13	5	209	20	38	.526	0	0	—	11	16	.688	16	31	47	5	45	0	7	20	4	51	3.6	0.3	3.9
92-93—Detroit	11	0	55	5	11	.455	0	0	—	2	4	.500	9	9	18	2	16	0	2	6	0	12	1.6	0.2	1.1
REG. SEASON TOTALS	332	189	11088	2105	3734	.564	3	19	.158	1550	2159	.718	1082	2296	3378	1002	1218	30	249	1212	267	5763	10.2	3.0	17.4
PLAYOFF TOTALS	17	7	640	110	211	.521	0	4	.000	93	120	.775	62	101	163	67	60	1	14	71	13	313	9.6	3.9	18.4
ALL-STAR TOTALS	1	0	13	2	3	.667	0	0	—	2	2	1.000	1	3	4	2	2	0	1	2	0	6	4.0	2.0	6.0

RULE, BOBBY FRANK (**Bob, Golden**) b. June 29, 1944 Ht. 6-9 Wt. 220 College—Riverside CC/Colorado State

SEASON—TEAM	G	GS	MIN	FGM	FGA	PCT	3FGM	3FGA	PCT	FTM	FTA	PCT	O-RB	D-RB	TOT	AST	PF	DQ	STL	TO	BLK	PTS	RPG	APG	PPG
67-68—Seattle	82	—	2424	568	1162	.489	—	—	—	348	529	.658	—	—	776	99	316	10	—	—	—	1484	9.5	1.2	18.1
68-69—Seattle	82	—	3104	776	1655	.469	—	—	—	413	606	.682	—	—	941	141	322	8	—	—	—	1965	11.5	1.7	24.0
69-70—Seattle	80	—	2959	789	1705	.463	—	—	—	387	542	.714	—	—	825	144	278	6	—	—	—	1965	10.3	1.8	24.6
70-71—Seattle	4	—	142	47	98	.480	—	—	—	25	30	.833	—	—	46	7	14	0	—	—	—	119	11.5	1.8	29.8
71-72—Seattle-Phil.	76	—	2230	461	1058	.436	—	—	—	226	335	.675	—	—	534	116	189	4	—	—	—	1148	7.0	1.5	15.1
72-73—Phil.-Clev.	52	—	452	60	158	.380	—	—	—	20	31	.645	—	—	108	38	68	0	—	—	—	140	2.1	0.7	2.7
73-74—Cleveland	26	—	540	76	192	.396	—	—	—	34	46	.739	43	60	103	47	71	0	12	—	10	186	4.0	1.8	7.2
74-75—Milwaukee	1	—	11	0	1	.000	—	—	—	0	0	—	0	0	0	2	2	0	0	—	0	0	0.0	2.0	0.0
REG. SEASON TOTALS	403	—	11862	2777	6029	.461	—	—	—	1453	2119	.686	43	60	3333	594	1260	28	12	—	10	7007	8.3	1.5	17.4
ALL-STAR TOTALS	1	—	13	2	6	.333	—	—	—	1	1	1.000	0	0	4	0	2	0	0	—	0	5	4.0	0.0	5.0

RULLO, GENEROSO CHARLES (**Jerry**) b. June 23, 1923 Ht. 5-10 Wt. 165 College—Temple

SEASON—TEAM	G	GS	MIN	FGM	FGA	PCT	3FGM	3FGA	PCT	FTM	FTA	PCT	O-RB	D-RB	TOT	AST	PF	DQ	STL	TO	BLK	PTS	RPG	APG	PPG
46-47—Philadelphia	50	—	—	52	174	.299	—	—	—	23	47	.489	—	—	—	20	61	—	—	—	—	127	—	0.4	2.5
47-48—Baltimore	2	—	—	0	4	.000	—	—	—	0	0	—	—	—	—	0	1	—	—	—	—	0	—	0.0	0.0
48-49—Philadelphia	39	—	—	53	183	.290	—	—	—	31	45	.689	—	—	—	48	71	—	—	—	—	137	—	1.2	3.5
49-50—Philadelphia	4	—	—	3	9	.333	—	—	—	1	1	1.000	—	—	—	2	2	—	—	—	—	7	—	0.5	1.8
REG. SEASON TOTALS	95	—	—	108	370	.292	—	—	—	55	93	.591	—	—	—	70	135	—	—	—	—	271	—	0.7	2.9
PLAYOFF TOTALS	9	—	—	5	21	.238	—	—	—	3	3	1.000	—	—	—	1	10	1	—	—	—	13	0.0	0.1	1.4

RUSSELL, BRYON DEMETRISE b. December 31, 1970 Ht. 6-7 Wt. 225 College—Long Beach State

SEASON—TEAM	G	GS	MIN	FGM	FGA	PCT	3FGM	3FGA	PCT	FTM	FTA	PCT	O-RB	D-RB	TOT	AST	PF	DQ	STL	TO	BLK	PTS	RPG	APG	PPG
93-94—Utah	67	48	1121	135	279	.484	2	22	.091	62	101	.614	61	120	181	54	138	0	68	55	19	334	2.7	0.8	5.0
REG. SEASON TOTALS	67	48	1121	135	279	.484	2	22	.091	62	101	.614	61	120	181	54	138	0	68	55	19	334	2.7	0.8	5.0
PLAYOFF TOTALS	6	0	36	4	10	.400	2	3	.667	6	6	1.000	4	5	9	3	3	0	0	1	0	16	1.5	0.5	2.7

RUSSELL, CAZZIE LEE JR. b. June 7, 1944 Ht. 6-5½ Wt. 220 College—Michigan

SEASON—TEAM	G	GS	MIN	FGM	FGA	PCT	3FGM	3FGA	PCT	FTM	FTA	PCT	O-RB	D-RB	TOT	AST	PF	DQ	STL	TO	BLK	PTS	RPG	APG	PPG
66-67—New York	77	—	1696	344	789	.436	—	—	—	179	228	.785	—	—	251	187	174	1	—	—	—	867	3.3	2.4	11.3
67-68—New York	82	—	2296	551	1192	.462	—	—	—	282	349	.808	—	—	374	195	223	2	—	—	—	1384	4.6	2.4	16.9
68-69—New York	50	—	1645	362	804	.450	—	—	—	191	240	.796	—	—	209	115	140	1	—	—	—	915	4.2	2.3	18.3
69-70—New York	78	—	1563	385	773	.498	—	—	—	124	160	.775	—	—	236	135	137	0	—	—	—	894	3.0	1.7	11.5
70-71—New York	57	—	1056	216	504	.429	—	—	—	92	119	.773	—	—	192	77	74	0	—	—	—	524	3.4	1.4	9.2
71-72—Golden State	79	—	2902	689	1514	.455	—	—	—	315	378	.833	—	—	428	248	176	0	—	—	—	1693	5.4	3.1	21.4
72-73—Golden State	80	—	2429	541	1182	.458	—	—	—	172	199	.864	—	—	350	187	171	0	—	—	—	1254	4.4	2.3	15.7
73-74—Golden State	82	—	2574	738	1531	.482	—	—	—	208	249	.835	142	211	353	192	194	1	54	—	17	1684	4.3	2.3	20.5
74-75—Los Angeles	40	—	1055	264	580	.455	—	—	—	101	113	.894	34	81	115	109	56	0	27	—	2	629	2.9	2.7	15.7
75-76—Los Angeles	74	—	1625	371	802	.463	—	—	—	132	148	.892	50	133	183	122	122	0	53	—	3	874	2.5	1.6	11.8
76-77—Los Angeles	82	—	2583	578	1179	.490	—	—	—	188	219	.858	86	208	294	210	163	1	86	—	7	1344	3.6	2.6	16.4
77-78—Chicago	36	—	789	133	304	.438	—	—	—	49	57	.860	31	52	83	61	63	1	19	35	4	315	2.3	1.7	8.8
REG. SEASON TOTALS	817	—	22213	5172	11154	.464	—	—	—	2033	2459	.827	343	685	3068	1838	1693	7	239	35	33	12377	3.8	2.2	15.1
PLAYOFF TOTALS	72	—	1566	359	781	.460	—	—	—	134	154	.870	22	26	222	97	151	1	16	—	1	852	3.1	1.3	11.8
ALL-STAR TOTALS	1	—	20	4	13	.308	—	—	—	2	2	1.000	0	0	0	1	0	1	0	—	0	10	1.0	0.0	10.0

RUSSELL, FRANK b. April 17, 1949 Ht. 6-3 Wt. 180 College—Detroit

SEASON—TEAM	G	GS	MIN	FGM	FGA	PCT	3FGM	3FGA	PCT	FTM	FTA	PCT	O-RB	D-RB	TOT	AST	PF	DQ	STL	TO	BLK	PTS	RPG	APG	PPG
72-73—Chicago	23	—	131	29	77	.377	—	—	—	16	18	.889	—	—	17	15	12	0	—	—	—	74	0.7	0.7	3.2
REG. SEASON TOTALS	23	—	131	29	77	.377	—	—	—	16	18	.889	—	—	17	15	12	0	—	—	—	74	0.7	0.7	3.2

RUSSELL, MICHAEL CAMPANELLA (**Campy**) b. January 12, 1952 Ht. 6-8 Wt. 215 College—Michigan

SEASON—TEAM	G	GS	MIN	FGM	FGA	PCT	3FGM	3FGA	PCT	FTM	FTA	PCT	O-RB	D-RB	TOT	AST	PF	DQ	STL	TO	BLK	PTS	RPG	APG	PPG
74-75—Cleveland	68	—	754	150	365	.411	—	—	—	124	165	.752	43	109	152	45	100	0	21	—	3	424	2.2	0.7	6.2
75-76—Cleveland	82	—	1961	483	1003	.482	—	—	—	266	344	.773	134	211	345	107	231	5	69	—	10	1232	4.2	1.3	15.0
76-77—Cleveland	70	—	2109	435	1003	.434	—	—	—	288	370	.778	144	275	419	189	196	3	70	—	24	1158	6.0	2.7	16.5
77-78—Cleveland	72	—	2520	523	1168	.448	—	—	—	352	469	.751	154	304	458	278	193	3	88	206	12	1398	6.4	3.9	19.4
78-79—Cleveland	74	—	2859	603	1268	.476	—	—	—	417	523	.797	147	356	503	348	222	2	98	259	25	1623	6.8	4.7	21.9
79-80—Cleveland	41	—	1331	284	630	.451	1	9	.111	178	239	.745	76	149	225	173	113	1	72	148	20	747	5.5	4.2	18.2
80-81—New York	79	—	2865	508	1095	.464	8	26	.308	268	343	.781	109	244	353	257	248	2	99	212	8	1292	4.5	3.3	16.4
81-82—New York	77	63	2358	410	858	.478	25	57	.439	228	294	.776	86	150	236	284	221	1	77	195	12	1073	3.1	3.7	13.9
84-85—Cleveland	3	0	24	2	7	.286	0	1	.000	2	3	.667	0	5	5	3	3	0	0	5	0	6	1.7	1.0	2.0
REG. SEASON TOTALS	566	63	16781	3398	7397	.459	34	93	.366	2123	2750	.772	893	1803	2696	1684	1527	17	594	1025	114	8953	4.8	3.0	15.8
PLAYOFF TOTALS	20	0	605	120	288	.417	0	2	.000	91	108	.843	43	78	121	44	79	0	18	18	10	331	6.1	2.2	16.6
ALL-STAR TOTALS	1	0	13	2	8	.250	0	0	—	0	0	—	1	0	1	0	0	0	0	1	0	4	1.0	0.0	4.0

RUSSELL, PIERRE ANGELO b. December 13, 1949 Ht. 6-4½ Wt. 190 College—Kansas

SEASON—TEAM	G	GS	MIN	FGM	FGA	PCT	3FGM	3FGA	PCT	FTM	FTA	PCT	O-RB	D-RB	TOT	AST	PF	DQ	STL	TO	BLK	PTS	RPG	APG	PPG
71-72—Kentucky (A)	51	—	397	65	153	.425	0	3	.000	16	21	.762	—	—	93	51	56	—	—	33	—	146	1.8	1.0	2.9
72-73—Kentucky (A)	59	—	618	119	266	.447	2	17	.118	49	78	.628	54	75	129	61	80	0	—	33	—	289	2.2	1.0	4.9
REG. ABA TOTALS	110	—	1015	184	419	.439	2	20	.100	65	99	.657	54	75	222	112	136	0	—	66	—	435	2.0	1.0	4.0
ABA PLAYOFF TOTALS	12	—	37	7	12	.583	0	0	—	3	6	.500	—	—	12	2	5	0	—	1	—	17	1.0	0.2	1.4

RUSSELL, RUBIN B. JR. b. November 7, 1944 Ht. 6-3 Wt. 180 College—Parsons JC/North Texas

SEASON—TEAM	G	GS	MIN	FGM	FGA	PCT	3FGM	3FGA	PCT	FTM	FTA	PCT	O-RB	D-RB	TOT	AST	PF	DQ	STL	TO	BLK	PTS	RPG	APG	PPG
67-68—Dallas-Ken. (A)	26	—	269	56	158	.354	4	22	.182	25	41	.610	—	—	52	7	40	0	—	32	—	141	2.0	0.3	5.4
REG. ABA TOTALS	26	—	269	56	158	.354	4	22	.182	25	41	.610	—	—	52	7	40	0	—	32	—	141	2.0	0.3	5.4

RUSSELL, WALKER D. b. October 26, 1960 Ht. 6-5 Wt. 195 College—Oakland CC/Houston/Western Michigan

SEASON—TEAM	G	GS	MIN	FGM	FGA	PCT	3FGM	3FGA	PCT	FTM	FTA	PCT	O-RB	D-RB	TOT	AST	PF	DQ	STL	TO	BLK	PTS	RPG	APG	PPG
82-83—Detroit	68	1	757	67	184	.364	2	18	.111	47	58	.810	19	54	73	131	71	0	16	92	1	183	1.1	1.9	2.7
83-84—Detroit	16	0	119	14	42	.333	1	2	.500	12	13	.923	6	13	19	22	25	0	4	9	0	41	1.2	1.4	2.6
84-85—Atlanta	21	2	377	34	63	.540	1	1	1.000	14	17	.824	8	32	40	66	37	1	17	40	4	83	1.9	3.1	4.0
85-86—Detroit	1	0	2	0	1	.000	0	0	—	0	0	—	0	0	0	1	0	0	0	0	0	0	0.0	1.0	0.0
86-87—Indiana	48	0	511	64	165	.388	2	16	.125	27	37	.730	18	37	55	129	62	0	20	60	5	157	1.1	2.7	3.3
87-88—Detroit	1	0	1	0	1	.000	0	1	.000	0	0	—	0	0	0	1	0	0	0	0	0	0	0.0	1.0	0.0
REG. SEASON TOTALS	155	3	1767	179	456	.393	6	38	.158	100	125	.800	51	136	187	350	195	1	57	201	10	464	1.2	2.3	3.0
PLAYOFF TOTALS	7	0	10	2	5	.400	0	0	—	2	2	1.000	0	0	0	1	1	0	1	1	0	6	0.0	0.1	0.9

RUSSELL, WILLIAM FELTON (**Bill**) b. February 12, 1934 Ht. 6-9½ Wt. 220 College—San Francisco

SEASON—TEAM	G	GS	MIN	FGM	FGA	PCT	3FGM	3FGA	PCT	FTM	FTA	PCT	O-RB	D-RB	TOT	AST	PF	DQ	STL	TO	BLK	PTS	RPG	APG	PPG
56-57—Boston	48	—	1695	277	649	.427	—	—	—	152	309	.492	—	—	943	88	143	2	—	—	—	706	19.6	1.8	14.7
57-58—Boston	69	—	2640	456	1032	.442	—	—	—	230	443	.519	—	—	1564	202	181	2	—	—	—	1142	22.7	2.9	16.6
58-59—Boston	70	—	2979	456	997	.457	—	—	—	256	428	.598	—	—	1612	222	161	3	—	—	—	1168	23.0	3.2	16.7
59-60—Boston	74	—	3146	555	1189	.467	—	—	—	240	392	.612	—	—	1778	277	210	0	—	—	—	1350	24.0	3.7	18.2
60-61—Boston	78	—	3458	532	1250	.426	—	—	—	258	469	.550	—	—	1868	268	155	0	—	—	—	1322	23.9	3.4	16.9
61-62—Boston	76	—	3433	575	1258	.457	—	—	—	286	481	.595	—	—	1790	341	207	3	—	—	—	1436	23.6	4.5	18.9
62-63—Boston	78	—	3500	511	1182	.432	—	—	—	287	517	.555	—	—	1843	348	189	1	—	—	—	1309	23.6	4.5	16.8
63-64—Boston	78	—	3482	466	1077	.433	—	—	—	236	429	.550	—	—	1930	370	190	0	—	—	—	1168	24.7	4.7	15.0
64-65—Boston	78	—	3466	429	980	.438	—	—	—	244	426	.573	—	—	1878	410	204	1	—	—	—	1102	24.1	5.3	14.1
65-66—Boston	78	—	3386	391	943	.415	—	—	—	223	405	.551	—	—	1779	371	221	4	—	—	—	1005	22.8	4.8	12.9
66-67—Boston	81	—	3297	395	870	.454	—	—	—	285	467	.610	—	—	1700	472	258	4	—	—	—	1075	21.0	5.8	13.3
67-68—Boston	78	—	2953	365	858	.425	—	—	—	247	460	.537	—	—	1451	357	242	2	—	—	—	977	18.6	4.6	12.5
68-69—Boston	77	—	3291	279	645	.433	—	—	—	204	388	.526	—	—	1484	374	231	2	—	—	—	762	19.3	4.9	9.9
REG. SEASON TOTALS	963	—	40726	5687	12930	.440	—	—	—	3148	5614	.561	—	—	21620	4100	2592	24	—	—	—	14522	22.5	4.3	15.1
PLAYOFF TOTALS	165	—	7497	1003	2335	.430	—	—	—	667	1106	.603	—	—	4104	770	546	8	—	—	—	2673	24.9	4.7	16.2
ALL-STAR TOTALS	12	—	343	51	111	.459	—	—	—	18	34	.529	—	—	139	39	37	1	—	—	—	120	11.6	3.3	10.0

SADOWSKI, EDWARD FRANK (**Ed, Big Ed**) b. July 11, 1917 d. September 18, 1990 Ht. 6-5 Wt. 240 College—Seton Hall

SEASON—TEAM	G	GS	MIN	FGM	FGA	PCT	3FGM	3FGA	PCT	FTM	FTA	PCT	O-RB	D-RB	TOT	AST	PF	DQ	STL	TO	BLK	PTS	RPG	APG	PPG
40-41—Detroit (N)	24	—	—	95	—	—	—	—	—	66	101	.653	—	—	—	—	63	—	—	—	—	256	—	—	10.7
44-45—Fort Wayne (N)	1	—	—	4	—	—	—	—	—	2	—	—	—	—	—	—	—	—	—	—	—	10	—	—	10.0
45-46—Fort Wayne (N)	34	—	—	122	—	—	—	—	—	82	120	.683	—	—	—	—	94	—	—	—	—	326	—	—	9.6
46-47—Toronto-Clev.	53	—	329	891	—	.369	—	—	—	219	328	.668	—	—	—	46	194	—	—	—	—	877	—	0.9	16.5
47-48—Boston	47	—	308	953	—	.323	—	—	—	294	422	.697	—	—	—	74	182	—	—	—	—	910	—	1.6	19.4
48-49—Philadelphia	60	—	340	839	—	.405	—	—	—	240	350	.686	—	—	—	160	273	—	—	—	—	920	—	2.7	15.3
49-50—Phil.-Balt.	69	—	299	922	—	.324	—	—	—	274	373	.735	—	—	—	136	244	—	—	—	—	872	—	2.0	12.6
REG. NBA TOTALS	229	—	1276	3605	—	.354	—	—	—	1027	1473	.697	—	—	—	416	893	—	—	—	—	3579	—	1.8	15.6
REG. NBL TOTALS	59	—	221	—	—	—	—	—	—	150	221	.670	—	—	—	—	157	—	—	—	—	592	—	—	10.0
NBA PLAYOFF TOTALS	8	—	47	139	—	.338	—	—	—	58	85	.682	—	—	—	14	33	—	—	—	—	152	—	1.8	19.0
NBL PLAYOFF TOTALS	14	—	44	—	—	—	—	—	—	37	31	.710	—	—	—	—	38	—	—	—	—	125	—	—	8.9

SAILORS, KENNETH L. (Kenny) b. January 14, 1922 Ht. 5-10 Wt. 195 College—Wyoming

SEASON—TEAM	G	GS	MIN	FGM	FGA	PCT	3FGM	3FGA	PCT	FTM	FTA	PCT	O-RB	D-RB	TOT	AST	PF	DQ	STL	TO	BLK	PTS	RPG	APG	PPG
46-47—Cleveland	58	—	—	229	741	.309	—	—	—	119	200	.595	—	—	—	134	177	—	—	—	—	577	—	2.3	9.9
47-48—Chicago-Phil.-Prov.	44	—	—	207	689	.300	—	—	—	110	159	.692	—	—	—	59	162	—	—	—	—	524	—	1.3	11.9
48-49—Providence	57	—	—	309	906	.341	—	—	—	281	367	.766	—	—	—	209	239	—	—	—	—	899	—	3.7	15.8
49-50—Denver	57	—	—	329	944	.349	—	—	—	329	456	.721	—	—	—	229	242	—	—	—	—	987	—	4.0	17.3
50-51—Boston-Balt.	60	—	—	181	533	.340	—	—	—	131	180	.728	—	—	120	150	196	8	—	—	—	493	2.0	2.5	8.2
REG. SEASON TOTALS	276	—	—	1255	3813	.329	—	—	—	970	1362	.712	—	—	120	781	1016	8	—	—	—	3480	2.0	2.8	12.6
PLAYOFF TOTALS	2	—	—	6	16	.375	—	—	—	3	4	.750	—	—	—	4	8	1	—	—	—	15	—	2.0	7.5

SALLEY, JOHN THOMAS (Spider) b. May 16, 1964 Ht. 6-11 Wt. 250 College—Georgia Tech

SEASON—TEAM	G	GS	MIN	FGM	FGA	PCT	3FGM	3FGA	PCT	FTM	FTA	PCT	O-RB	D-RB	TOT	AST	PF	DQ	STL	TO	BLK	PTS	RPG	APG	PPG
86-87—Detroit	82	2	1463	163	290	.562	0	1	.000	105	171	.614	108	188	296	54	256	5	44	74	125	431	3.6	0.7	5.3
87-88—Detroit	82	16	2003	258	456	.566	0	0	—	185	261	.709	166	236	402	113	294	4	53	120	137	701	4.9	1.4	8.5
88-89—Detroit	67	21	1458	166	333	.498	0	2	.000	135	195	.692	134	201	335	75	197	3	40	100	72	467	5.0	1.1	7.0
89-90—Detroit	82	12	1914	209	408	.512	1	4	.250	174	244	.713	154	285	439	67	282	7	51	97	153	593	5.4	0.8	7.2
90-91—Detroit	74	1	1649	179	377	.475	0	1	.000	186	256	.727	137	190	327	70	240	7	52	91	112	544	4.4	0.9	7.4
91-92—Detroit	72	38	1774	249	486	.512	0	3	.000	186	260	.715	106	190	296	116	222	1	49	102	110	684	4.1	1.6	9.5
92-93—Miami	51	34	1422	154	307	.502	0	0	—	115	144	.799	113	200	313	83	192	7	32	101	70	423	6.1	1.6	8.3
93-94—Miami	76	45	1910	208	436	.477	2	3	.667	164	225	.729	132	275	407	135	260	4	56	94	78	582	5.4	1.8	7.7
REG. SEASON TOTALS	586	169	13593	1586	3093	.513	3	14	.214	1250	1756	.712	1050	1765	2815	713	1943	38	377	779	857	4425	4.8	1.2	7.6
PLAYOFF TOTALS	100	6	2531	285	562	.507	0	2	.000	256	367	.698	231	324	555	94	379	7	47	99	151	826	5.6	0.9	8.3

SALVADORI, ALBERT JULIAN (Al) b. May 6, 1945 Ht. 6-9½ Wt. 220 College—South Carolina

SEASON—TEAM	G	GS	MIN	FGM	FGA	PCT	3FGM	3FGA	PCT	FTM	FTA	PCT	O-RB	D-RB	TOT	AST	PF	DQ	STL	TO	BLK	PTS	RPG	APG	PPG
67-68—Oakland (A)	17	—	186	21	58	.362	1	1	1.000	11	16	.688	—	—	46	4	28	0	—	12	—	54	2.7	0.2	3.2
REG. ABA TOTALS	17	—	186	21	58	.362	1	1	1.000	11	16	.688	—	—	46	4	28	0	—	12	—	54	2.7	0.2	3.2

SAMPSON, RALPH LEE JR. b. July 7, 1960 Ht. 7-4 Wt. 235 College—Virginia

SEASON—TEAM	G	GS	MIN	FGM	FGA	PCT	3FGM	3FGA	PCT	FTM	FTA	PCT	O-RB	D-RB	TOT	AST	PF	DQ	STL	TO	BLK	PTS	RPG	APG	PPG
83-84—Houston	82	82	2693	716	1369	.523	1	4	.250	287	434	.661	293	620	913	163	339	16	70	294	197	1720	11.1	2.0	21.0
84-85—Houston	82	82	3086	753	1499	.502	0	6	.000	303	448	.676	227	626	853	224	306	10	81	326	168	1809	10.4	2.7	22.1
85-86—Houston	79	76	2864	624	1280	.488	2	15	.133	241	376	.641	258	621	879	283	308	12	99	285	129	1491	11.1	3.6	18.9
86-87—Houston	43	32	1326	277	566	.489	0	3	.000	118	189	.624	88	284	372	120	169	6	40	126	58	672	8.7	2.8	15.6
87-88—Houston-G.S.	48	44	1663	299	682	.438	2	11	.182	149	196	.760	140	322	462	122	164	3	41	171	88	749	9.6	2.5	15.6
88-89—Golden State	61	36	1086	164	365	.449	3	8	.375	62	95	.653	105	202	307	77	170	3	31	90	65	393	5.0	1.3	6.4
89-90—Sacramento	26	7	417	48	129	.372	1	4	.250	12	23	.522	11	73	84	28	66	1	14	34	22	109	3.2	1.1	4.2
90-91—Sacramento	25	4	348	34	93	.366	1	5	.200	5	19	.263	41	70	111	17	54	0	11	27	17	74	4.4	0.7	3.0
91-92—Washington	10	0	108	9	29	.310	0	2	.000	4	6	.667	11	19	30	4	11	2	3	22	8	22	3.0	0.4	2.2
REG. SEASON TOTALS	456	363	13591	2924	6012	.486	10	58	.172	1181	1786	.661	1174	2837	4011	1038	1590	52	390	1363	752	7039	8.8	2.3	15.4
PLAYOFF TOTALS	38	36	1307	283	569	.497	3	8	.375	142	202	.703	124	276	400	109	157	4	35	123	57	711	10.5	2.9	18.7
ALL-STAR TOTALS	3	2	66	21	33	.636	0	0	—	7	10	.700	5	14	19	2	13	0	0	6	1	49	6.3	0.7	16.3

SANDERS, ALBERT T. III (Al, Apple) b. January 1, 1950 d. May 4, 1994 Ht. 6-7 Wt. 240 College—Louisiana State

SEASON—TEAM	G	GS	MIN	FGM	FGA	PCT	3FGM	3FGA	PCT	FTM	FTA	PCT	O-RB	D-RB	TOT	AST	PF	DQ	STL	TO	BLK	PTS	RPG	APG	PPG
72-73—Virginia (A)	4	—	25	2	2	1.000	0	0	—	4	6	.667	—	5	5	0	4	0	—	3	—	8	1.3	0.0	2.0
REG. ABA TOTALS	4	—	25	2	2	1.000	0	0	—	4	6	.667	—	5	5	0	4	0	—	3	—	8	1.3	0.0	2.0

SANDERS, FRANKIE J. b. January 23, 1957 Ht. 6-6 Wt. 200 College—Southern

SEASON—TEAM	G	GS	MIN	FGM	FGA	PCT	3FGM	3FGA	PCT	FTM	FTA	PCT	O-RB	D-RB	TOT	AST	PF	DQ	STL	TO	BLK	PTS	RPG	APG	PPG
78-79—S.A.-Boston	46	—	479	105	246	.427	—	—	—	54	68	.794	35	75	110	52	69	1	21	55	6	264	2.4	1.1	5.7
80-81—Kansas City	23	—	186	34	77	.442	0	3	.000	20	22	.909	6	15	21	17	20	0	16	21	1	88	0.9	0.7	3.8
REG. SEASON TOTALS	69	—	665	139	323	.430	0	3	.000	74	90	.822	41	90	131	69	89	1	37	76	7	352	1.9	1.0	5.1
PLAYOFF TOTALS	9	—	50	9	18	.500	1	2	.500	4	4	1.000	4	1	5	2	8	0	3	8	0	23	0.6	0.2	2.6

SANDERS, JEFFERY RAYNARD (Jeff) b. January 14, 1966 Ht. 6-8 Wt. 240 College—Georgia Southern

SEASON—TEAM	G	GS	MIN	FGM	FGA	PCT	3FGM	3FGA	PCT	FTM	FTA	PCT	O-RB	D-RB	TOT	AST	PF	DQ	STL	TO	BLK	PTS	RPG	APG	PPG
89-90—Chicago	31	0	182	13	40	.325	0	0	—	2	4	.500	17	22	39	9	27	0	4	15	4	28	1.3	0.3	0.9
90-91—Charlotte	3	0	43	6	14	.429	0	0	—	1	2	.500	3	6	9	1	6	0	1	1	1	13	3.0	0.3	4.3
91-92—Atlanta	12	0	117	20	45	.444	0	0	—	7	9	.778	9	17	26	9	15	0	5	5	3	47	2.2	0.8	3.9
92-93—Atlanta	9	0	120	10	25	.400	0	0	—	4	8	.500	12	17	29	6	16	0	8	11	1	24	3.2	0.7	2.7
REG. SEASON TOTALS	55	0	462	49	124	.395	0	0	—	14	23	.609	41	62	103	25	64	0	18	32	9	112	1.9	0.5	2.0
PLAYOFF TOTALS	3	0	3	1	1	1.000	0	0	—	0	0	—	0	0	0	0	0	0	0	0	0	2	0.0	0.0	0.7

SANDERS, MICHAEL ANTHONY (Mike) b. May 7, 1960 Ht. 6-6 Wt. 210 College—UCLA

SEASON—TEAM	G	GS	MIN	FGM	FGA	PCT	3FGM	3FGA	PCT	FTM	FTA	PCT	O-RB	D-RB	TOT	AST	PF	DQ	STL	TO	BLK	PTS	RPG	APG	PPG
82-83—San Antonio	26	0	393	76	157	.484	0	2	.000	31	43	.721	31	63	94	19	57	0	18	28	6	183	3.6	0.7	7.0
83-84—Phoenix	50	0	586	97	203	.478	0	0	—	29	42	.690	40	63	103	44	101	0	23	44	12	223	2.1	0.9	4.5
84-85—Phoenix	21	11	418	85	175	.486	0	0	—	45	59	.763	38	51	89	29	59	0	23	34	4	215	4.2	1.4	10.2
85-86—Phoenix	82	5	1644	347	676	.513	3	15	.200	208	257	.809	104	169	273	150	236	3	76	143	31	905	3.3	1.8	11.0
86-87—Phoenix	82	4	1655	357	722	.494	2	17	.118	143	183	.781	101	170	271	126	210	1	61	105	23	859	3.3	1.5	10.5
87-88—Phoenix-Clev.	59	16	883	153	303	.505	0	1	.000	59	76	.776	38	71	109	56	131	1	31	50	9	365	1.8	0.9	6.2
88-89—Cleveland	82	82	2102	332	733	.453	3	10	.300	97	135	.719	98	209	307	133	230	2	89	104	32	764	3.7	1.6	9.3
89-90—Indiana	82	13	1531	225	479	.470	5	14	.357	55	75	.733	78	152	230	89	220	1	43	79	23	510	2.8	1.1	6.2
90-91—Indiana	80	7	1357	206	494	.417	4	20	.200	47	57	.825	73	112	185	106	198	1	37	65	26	463	2.3	1.3	5.8
91-92—Indiana-Clev.	31	20	633	92	161	.571	1	3	.333	36	47	.766	27	69	96	53	83	1	24	22	10	221	3.1	1.7	7.1
92-93—Cleveland	53	51	1189	197	396	.497	1	4	.250	59	78	.756	52	118	170	75	150	2	39	57	30	454	3.2	1.4	8.6
REG. SEASON TOTALS	648	209	12391	2167	4499	.482	19	86	.221	809	1052	.769	680	1247	1927	880	1675	12	464	731	206	5162	3.0	1.4	8.0
PLAYOFF TOTALS	67	35	1117	181	362	.500	3	9	.333	60	77	.779	70	98	168	85	166	0	43	73	22	425	2.5	1.3	6.3

SANDERS, THOMAS ERNEST (Satch) b. November 8, 1938 Ht. 6-6 Wt. 210 College—New York University

SEASON—TEAM	G	GS	MIN	FGM	FGA	PCT	3FGM	3FGA	PCT	FTM	FTA	PCT	O-RB	D-RB	TOT	AST	PF	DQ	STL	TO	BLK	PTS	RPG	APG	PPG
60-61—Boston	68	—	1084	148	352	.420	—	—	—	67	100	.670	—	—	385	44	131	1	—	—	—	363	5.7	0.6	5.3
61-62—Boston	80	—	2325	350	804	.435	—	—	—	197	263	.749	—	—	762	74	279	9	—	—	—	897	9.5	0.9	11.2
62-63—Boston	80	—	2148	339	744	.456	—	—	—	186	252	.738	—	—	576	95	262	6	—	—	—	864	7.2	1.2	10.8
63-64—Boston	80	—	2370	349	836	.417	—	—	—	213	280	.761	—	—	667	102	277	6	—	—	—	911	8.3	1.3	11.4
64-65—Boston	80	—	2459	374	871	.429	—	—	—	193	259	.745	—	—	661	92	318	15	—	—	—	941	8.3	1.2	11.8
65-66—Boston	72	—	1896	349	816	.428	—	—	—	211	276	.764	—	—	508	90	317	19	—	—	—	909	7.1	1.3	12.6
66-67—Boston	81	—	1926	323	755	.428	—	—	—	178	218	.817	—	—	439	91	304	6	—	—	—	824	5.4	1.1	10.2
67-68—Boston	78	—	1981	296	691	.428	—	—	—	200	255	.784	—	—	454	100	300	12	—	—	—	792	5.8	1.3	10.2
68-69—Boston	82	—	2184	364	847	.430	—	—	—	187	255	.733	—	—	574	110	293	9	—	—	—	915	7.0	1.3	11.2
69-70—Boston	57	—	1616	246	555	.443	—	—	—	161	183	.880	—	—	314	92	199	5	—	—	—	653	5.5	1.6	11.5
70-71—Boston	17	—	121	16	44	.364	—	—	—	7	8	.875	—	—	17	11	25	0	—	—	—	39	1.0	0.6	2.3
71-72—Boston	82	—	1631	215	524	.410	—	—	—	111	136	.816	—	—	353	98	257	7	—	—	—	541	4.3	1.2	6.6
72-73—Boston	59	—	423	47	149	.315	—	—	—	23	35	.657	—	—	88	27	82	0	—	—	—	117	1.5	0.5	2.0
REG. SEASON TOTALS	916	—	22164	3416	7988	.428	—	—	—	1934	2520	.767	—	—	5798	1026	3044	94	—	—	—	8766	6.3	1.1	9.6
PLAYOFF TOTALS	130	—	3039	465	1066	.436	—	—	—	212	296	.716	—	—	760	127	508	26	—	—	—	1142	5.8	1.0	8.8

SANFORD, RON b. June 11, 1946 Ht. 6-9 Wt. 215 College—New Mexico

SEASON—TEAM	G	GS	MIN	FGM	FGA	PCT	3FGM	3FGA	PCT	FTM	FTA	PCT	O-RB	D-RB	TOT	AST	PF	DQ	STL	TO	BLK	PTS	RPG	APG	PPG
71-72—Dallas (A)	1	—	2	0	0	—	0	0	—	0	0	—	—	—	0	0	1	—	—	0	—	0	0.0	0.0	0.0
REG. ABA TOTALS	1	—	2	0	0	—	0	0	—	0	0	—	—	—	0	1	—	—	—	—	—	0	0.0	0.0	0.0

SANTINI, ROBERT (Bob) b. February 17, 1935 Ht. 6-5 Wt. 190 College—Iona

SEASON—TEAM	G	GS	MIN	FGM	FGA	PCT	3FGM	3FGA	PCT	FTM	FTA	PCT	O-RB	D-RB	TOT	AST	PF	DQ	STL	TO	BLK	PTS	RPG	APG	PPG
55-56—New York	4	—	23	5	10	.500	—	—	—	1	2	.500	—	—	3	1	4	0	—	—	—	11	0.8	0.3	2.8
REG. SEASON TOTALS	4	—	23	5	10	.500	—	—	—	1	2	.500	—	—	3	1	4	0	—	—	—	11	0.8	0.3	2.8

SAPPLETON, WAYNE B. b. November 17, 1960 Ht. 6-9 Wt. 230 College—Loyola (Ill.)

SEASON—TEAM	G	GS	MIN	FGM	FGA	PCT	3FGM	3FGA	PCT	FTM	FTA	PCT	O-RB	D-RB	TOT	AST	PF	DQ	STL	TO	BLK	PTS	RPG	APG	PPG
84-85—New Jersey	33	0	298	41	87	.471	0	0	—	14	34	.412	28	47	75	7	50	0	7	21	4	96	2.3	0.2	2.9
REG. SEASON TOTALS	33	0	298	41	87	.471	0	0	—	14	34	.412	28	47	75	7	50	0	7	21	4	96	2.3	0.2	2.9

SAUL, FRANK BENJAMIN JR. (Pep) b. February 16, 1924 Ht. 6-2 Wt. 185 College—Seton Hall

SEASON—TEAM	G	GS	MIN	FGM	FGA	PCT	3FGM	3FGA	PCT	FTM	FTA	PCT	O-RB	D-RB	TOT	AST	PF	DQ	STL	TO	BLK	PTS	RPG	APG	PPG
49-50—Rochester	49	—	—	74	183	.404	—	—	—	34	47	.723	—	—	—	28	33	—	—	—	—	182	—	0.6	3.7
50-51—Rochester	65	—	—	105	310	.339	—	—	—	72	105	.686	—	—	84	68	85	0	—	—	—	282	1.3	1.0	4.3
51-52—Balt.-Minn.	64	—	1479	157	436	.360	—	—	—	119	153	.778	—	—	165	147	120	3	—	—	—	433	2.6	2.3	6.8
52-53—Minneapolis	70	—	1796	187	471	.397	—	—	—	142	200	.710	—	—	141	110	174	3	—	—	—	516	2.0	1.6	7.4
53-54—Minneapolis	71	—	1805	162	467	.347	—	—	—	128	170	.753	—	—	159	139	149	3	—	—	—	452	2.2	2.0	6.4
54-55—Milwaukee	65	—	1139	96	303	.317	—	—	—	95	123	.772	—	—	134	104	126	0	—	—	—	287	2.1	1.6	4.4
REG. SEASON TOTALS	384	—	6219	781	2170	.360	—	—	—	590	798	.739	—	—	683	596	687	9	—	—	—	2152	2.0	1.6	5.6
PLAYOFF TOTALS	49	—	1054	116	271	.428	—	—	—	89	122	.730	—	—	94	87	119	2	—	—	—	321	2.0	1.8	6.6

SAULDSBERRY, WOODROW JR. (Woody) b. July 11, 1934 Ht. 6-7 Wt. 220 College—Texas Southern

SEASON—TEAM	G	GS	MIN	FGM	FGA	PCT	3FGM	3FGA	PCT	FTM	FTA	PCT	O-RB	D-RB	TOT	AST	PF	DQ	STL	TO	BLK	PTS	RPG	APG	PPG
57-58—Philadelphia	71	—	2377	389	1082	.360	—	—	—	134	218	.615	—	—	729	58	245	3	—	—	—	912	10.3	0.8	12.8
58-59—Philadelphia	72	—	2743	501	1380	.363	—	—	—	110	176	.625	—	—	826	71	276	12	—	—	—	1112	11.5	1.0	15.4
59-60—Philadelphia	71	—	1848	325	974	.334	—	—	—	55	103	.534	—	—	447	112	203	2	—	—	—	705	6.3	1.6	9.9
60-61—St. Louis	69	—	1491	230	768	.299	—	—	—	56	100	.560	—	—	491	74	197	3	—	—	—	516	7.1	1.1	7.5
61-62—St. L.-Chicago	63	—	1765	298	869	.343	—	—	—	79	123	.642	—	—	536	90	179	5	—	—	—	675	8.5	1.4	10.7
62-63—Chicago-St. L.	77	—	2034	366	966	.379	—	—	—	107	163	.656	—	—	447	78	241	4	—	—	—	839	5.8	1.0	10.9
65-66—Boston	39	—	530	80	249	.321	—	—	—	11	22	.500	—	—	142	15	94	0	—	—	—	171	3.6	0.4	4.4
REG. SEASON TOTALS	462	—	12788	2189	6288	.348	—	—	—	552	905	.610	—	—	3618	498	1435	29	—	—	—	4930	7.8	1.1	10.7
PLAYOFF TOTALS	29	—	995	174	496	.351	—	—	—	35	62	.565	—	—	259	52	118	4	—	—	—	383	8.9	1.8	13.2
ALL-STAR TOTALS	1	—	18	5	11	.455	—	—	—	4	4	1.000	—	—	2	3	2	0	—	—	—	14	2.0	3.0	14.0

SAULTERS, GLYNN b. February 10, 1945 Ht. 6-2 Wt. 175 College—NE Louisiana

SEASON—TEAM	G	GS	MIN	FGM	FGA	PCT	3FGM	3FGA	PCT	FTM	FTA	PCT	O-RB	D-RB	TOT	AST	PF	DQ	STL	TO	BLK	PTS	RPG	APG	PPG
68-69—New Orleans (A)	22	—	120	22	70	.314	0	1	.000	15	22	.682	—	—	19	11	25	0	—	11	—	59	0.9	0.5	2.7
REG. ABA TOTALS	22	—	120	22	70	.314	0	1	.000	15	22	.682	—	—	19	11	25	0	—	11	—	59	0.9	0.5	2.7

SAUNDERS, JAMES FREDERICK (Fred) b. June 13, 1951 Ht. 6-7 Wt. 210 College—Syracuse

SEASON—TEAM	G	GS	MIN	FGM	FGA	PCT	3FGM	3FGA	PCT	FTM	FTA	PCT	O-RB	D-RB	TOT	AST	PF	DQ	STL	TO	BLK	PTS	RPG	APG	PPG
74-75—Phoenix	69	—	1059	176	406	.433	—	—	—	66	95	.695	82	171	253	80	151	3	41	—	15	418	3.7	1.2	6.1
75-76—Phoenix	17	—	146	28	64	.438	—	—	—	6	11	.545	11	26	37	13	23	0	5	—	1	62	2.2	0.8	3.6
76-77—Boston	68	—	1051	184	395	.466	—	—	—	35	53	.660	73	150	223	85	191	3	26	—	7	403	3.3	1.3	5.9
77-78—Boston-N.O.	56	—	643	99	234	.423	—	—	—	26	36	.722	38	73	111	46	106	3	21	42	14	224	2.0	0.8	4.0
REG. SEASON TOTALS	210	—	2899	487	1099	.443	—	—	—	133	195	.682	204	420	624	224	471	9	93	42	37	1107	3.0	1.1	5.3
PLAYOFF TOTALS	9	—	66	12	33	.364	—	—	—	5	6	.833	1	8	9	5	21	0	1	—	0	29	1.0	0.6	3.2

SAVAGE, DONALD JOSEPH (Don) b. April 9, 1928 Ht. 6-3 Wt. 205 College—Le Moyne

SEASON—TEAM	G	GS	MIN	FGM	FGA	PCT	3FGM	3FGA	PCT	FTM	FTA	PCT	O-RB	D-RB	TOT	AST	PF	DQ	STL	TO	BLK	PTS	RPG	APG	PPG
51-52—Syracuse	12	—	118	9	43	.209	—	—	—	18	28	.643	—	—	24	12	22	0	—	—	—	36	2.0	1.0	3.0
56-57—Syracuse	5	—	55	6	19	.316	—	—	—	6	7	.857	—	—	7	2	7	0	—	—	—	18	1.4	0.4	3.6
REG. SEASON TOTALS	17	—	173	15	62	.242	—	—	—	24	35	.686	—	—	31	14	29	0	—	—	—	54	1.8	0.8	3.2

SAWYER, ALAN LEIGH b. January 1, 1928 Ht. 6-5 Wt. 195 College—UCLA

SEASON—TEAM	G	GS	MIN	FGM	FGA	PCT	3FGM	3FGA	PCT	FTM	FTA	PCT	O-RB	D-RB	TOT	AST	PF	DQ	STL	TO	BLK	PTS	RPG	APG	PPG
50-51—Washington	33	—	—	87	215	.405	—	—	—	43	54	.796	—	—	125	25	75	1	—	—	—	217	3.8	0.8	6.6
REG. SEASON TOTALS	33	—	—	87	215	.405	—	—	—	43	54	.796	—	—	125	25	75	1	—	—	—	217	3.8	0.8	6.6

SCALES, DeWAYNE JAY (Hot Man) b. December 28, 1958 Ht. 6-8 Wt. 215 College—Louisiana State

SEASON—TEAM	G	GS	MIN	FGM	FGA	PCT	3FGM	3FGA	PCT	FTM	FTA	PCT	O-RB	D-RB	TOT	AST	PF	DQ	STL	TO	BLK	PTS	RPG	APG	PPG
80-81—New York	44	—	484	94	225	.418	1	6	.167	26	39	.667	47	85	132	10	54	0	12	30	4	215	3.0	0.2	4.9
81-82—New York	3	0	24	1	5	.200	0	0	—	1	2	.500	2	3	5	0	3	0	1	2	1	3	1.7	0.0	1.0
83-84—Washington	2	0	13	3	5	.600	0	0	—	0	2	.000	0	3	3	0	1	0	1	2	0	6	1.5	0.0	3.0
REG. SEASON TOTALS	49	0	521	98	235	.417	1	6	.167	27	43	.628	49	91	140	10	58	0	14	34	5	224	2.9	0.2	4.6

SCHADE, FRANK b. January 22, 1950 Ht. 6-1 Wt. 170 College—Wisconsin-Eau Claire/Texas-El Paso

SEASON—TEAM	G	GS	MIN	FGM	FGA	PCT	3FGM	3FGA	PCT	FTM	FTA	PCT	O-RB	D-RB	TOT	AST	PF	DQ	STL	TO	BLK	PTS	RPG	APG	PPG
72-73—Kansas City-Omaha	9	—	76	2	7	.286	—	—	—	6	6	1.000	—	—	6	10	12	0	—	—	—	10	0.7	1.1	1.1
REG. SEASON TOTALS	9	—	76	2	7	.286	—	—	—	6	6	1.000	—	—	6	10	12	0	—	—	—	10	0.7	1.1	1.1

SCHADLER, BERNARD R. (Ben) b. March 9, 1924 Ht. 6-2 Wt. 185 College—Northwestern

SEASON—TEAM	G	GS	MIN	FGM	FGA	PCT	3FGM	3FGA	PCT	FTM	FTA	PCT	O-RB	D-RB	TOT	AST	PF	DQ	STL	TO	BLK	PTS	RPG	APG	PPG
47-48—Chicago	37	—	—	23	116	.198	—	—	—	10	13	.769	—	—	6	40	—	—	—	—	—	56	—	0.2	1.5
48-49—Detroit-Wat. (N)	53	—	—	150	—	—	—	—	—	58	89	.652	—	—	—	104	—	—	—	—	—	358	—	—	6.8
REG. NBA TOTALS	37	—	—	23	116	.198	—	—	—	10	13	.769	—	—	6	40	—	—	—	—	—	56	—	0.2	1.5
REG. NBL TOTALS	53	—	—	150	—	—	—	—	—	58	89	.652	—	—	—	104	—	—	—	—	—	358	—	—	6.8
NBA PLAYOFF TOTALS	4	—	—	5	23	.217	—	—	—	0	2	.000	—	—	1	4	—	—	—	—	—	10	—	0.3	2.5

SCHAEFER, HERMAN H. (Herm) b. December 20, 1919 d. March 21, 1980 Ht. 6-0 Wt. 175 College—Indiana

SEASON—TEAM	G	GS	MIN	FGM	FGA	PCT	3FGM	3FGA	PCT	FTM	FTA	PCT	O-RB	D-RB	TOT	AST	PF	DQ	STL	TO	BLK	PTS	RPG	APG	PPG
41-42—Fort Wayne (N)	24	—	—	85	—	—	—	—	—	37	—	—	—	—	—	—	—	—	—	—	—	207	—	—	8.6
42-43—Fort Wayne (N)	21	—	—	36	—	—	—	—	—	12	—	—	—	—	—	—	—	—	—	—	—	84	—	—	4.0
45-46—Fort Wayne (N)	15	—	—	10	—	—	—	—	—	3	—	—	—	—	—	—	—	—	—	—	—	23	—	—	1.5
46-47—Indianapolis (N)	44	—	—	147	—	—	—	—	—	65	90	.722	—	—	—	45	—	—	—	—	—	359	—	—	8.2
47-48—Ind.-Minn. (N)	57	—	—	110	—	—	—	—	—	78	96	.813	—	—	—	74	—	—	—	—	—	298	—	—	5.2
48-49—Minneapolis	58	—	—	214	572	.374	—	—	—	174	213	.817	—	—	—	185	121	—	—	—	—	602	—	3.2	10.4
49-50—Minneapolis	65	—	—	122	314	.389	—	—	—	86	101	.851	—	—	—	203	104	—	—	—	—	330	—	3.1	5.1
REG. NBA TOTALS	123	—	—	336	886	.379	—	—	—	260	314	.828	—	—	—	388	225	—	—	—	—	932	—	3.2	7.6
REG. NBL TOTALS	161	—	—	388	—	—	—	—	—	195	186	.769	—	—	—	—	119	—	—	—	—	971	—	—	6.0
NBA PLAYOFF TOTALS	22	—	—	64	146	.438	—	—	—	47	54	.870	—	—	—	47	34	—	—	—	—	175	—	2.1	8.0
NBL PLAYOFF TOTALS	26	—	—	92	—	—	—	—	—	53	52	.808	—	—	—	—	31	—	—	—	—	237	—	—	9.1

SCHAEFFER, WILLIAM G. (Billy) b. December 11, 1951 Ht. 6-5 Wt. 200 College—St. John's

SEASON—TEAM	G	GS	MIN	FGM	FGA	PCT	3FGM	3FGA	PCT	FTM	FTA	PCT	O-RB	D-RB	TOT	AST	PF	DQ	STL	TO	BLK	PTS	RPG	APG	PPG
73-74—New York (A)	59	—	871	171	344	.497	2	9	.222	41	54	.759	49	92	141	37	140	—	24	53	9	385	2.4	0.6	6.5
74-75—New York (A)	27	—	280	61	131	.466	2	7	.286	15	25	.600	15	22	37	20	36	—	9	18	2	139	1.4	0.7	5.1
75-76—N.Y.-Vir. (A)	51	—	637	114	258	.442	2	10	.200	48	63	.762	39	72	111	37	72	—	19	35	9	278	2.2	0.7	5.5
REG. ABA TOTALS	137	—	1788	346	733	.472	6	26	.231	104	142	.732	103	186	289	94	248	0	52	106	20	802	2.1	0.7	5.9
ABA PLAYOFF TOTALS	5	—	23	8	16	.500	0	0	—	3	4	.750	6	3	9	3	3	0	0	1	0	19	1.8	0.6	3.8

SCHAFER, ROBERT THOMAS (Bob) b. 1933 Ht. 6-3 Wt. 195 College—Villanova

SEASON—TEAM	G	GS	MIN	FGM	FGA	PCT	3FGM	3FGA	PCT	FTM	FTA	PCT	O-RB	D-RB	TOT	AST	PF	DQ	STL	TO	BLK	PTS	RPG	APG	PPG
55-56—Phil.-St. L.	54	—	578	81	270	.300	—	—	—	62	81	.765	—	—	71	53	75	0	—	—	—	224	1.3	1.0	4.1
56-57—Syracuse	11	—	167	19	66	.288	—	—	—	11	13	.846	—	—	11	15	16	0	—	—	—	49	1.0	1.4	4.5
REG. SEASON TOTALS	65	—	745	100	336	.298	—	—	—	73	94	.777	—	—	82	68	91	0	—	—	—	273	1.3	1.0	4.2
PLAYOFF TOTALS	4	—	39	3	20	.150	—	—	—	5	6	.833	—	—	9	1	8	1	—	—	—	11	2.3	0.3	2.8

SCHARNUS, BENEDICT MICHAEL (Ben, Whitey) b. December 11, 1917 d. March 19, 1982 Ht. 6-2.5 Wt. 175 College—Seton Hall

SEASON—TEAM	G	GS	MIN	FGM	FGA	PCT	3FGM	3FGA	PCT	FTM	FTA	PCT	O-RB	D-RB	TOT	AST	PF	DQ	STL	TO	BLK	PTS	RPG	APG	PPG
46-47—Cleveland	51	—	—	33	165	.200	—	—	—	37	59	.627	—	—	—	19	83	—	—	—	—	103	—	0.4	2.0
48-49—Providence	1	—	—	0	1	.000	—	—	—	0	1	.000	—	—	—	0	0	—	—	—	—	0	—	0.0	0.0
REG. SEASON TOTALS	52	—	—	33	166	.199	—	—	—	37	60	.617	—	—	—	19	83	—	—	—	—	103	—	0.4	2.0
PLAYOFF TOTALS	3	—	—	6	21	.286	—	—	—	5	9	.556	—	—	—	2	10	1	—	—	—	17	—	0.7	5.7

SCHATZMAN, MARVIN J. (Marv) b. February 18, 1927 Ht. 6-5 Wt. 200 College—St. Louis

SEASON—TEAM	G	GS	MIN	FGM	FGA	PCT	3FGM	3FGA	PCT	FTM	FTA	PCT	O-RB	D-RB	TOT	AST	PF	DQ	STL	TO	BLK	PTS	RPG	APG	PPG
49-50—Baltimore	34	—	—	43	174	.247	—	—	—	29	50	.580	—	—	—	38	49	—	—	—	—	115	—	1.1	3.4
REG. SEASON TOTALS	34	—	—	43	174	.247	—	—	—	29	50	.580	—	—	—	38	49	—	—	—	—	115	—	1.1	3.4

SCHAUS, FREDERICK APPLETON (Fred) b. June 30, 1925 Ht. 6-5 Wt. 210 College—West Virginia

SEASON—TEAM	G	GS	MIN	FGM	FGA	PCT	3FGM	3FGA	PCT	FTM	FTA	PCT	O-RB	D-RB	TOT	AST	PF	DQ	STL	TO	BLK	PTS	RPG	APG	PPG
49-50—Fort Wayne	68	—	—	351	996	.352	—	—	—	270	330	.818	—	—	—	176	232	—	—	—	—	972	—	2.6	14.3
50-51—Fort Wayne	68	—	—	312	918	.340	—	—	—	404	484	.835	—	—	495	184	240	11	—	—	—	1028	7.3	2.7	15.1
51-52—Fort Wayne	62	—	2581	281	778	.361	—	—	—	310	372	.833	—	—	434	247	221	7	—	—	—	872	7.0	4.0	14.1
52-53—Fort Wayne	69	—	2541	240	719	.334	—	—	—	243	296	.821	—	—	413	245	261	11	—	—	—	723	6.0	3.6	10.5
53-54—Ft. Wayne-N.Y.	67	—	1515	161	415	.388	—	—	—	153	195	.785	—	—	267	109	176	3	—	—	—	475	4.0	1.6	7.1
REG. SEASON TOTALS	334	—	6637	1345	3826	.352	—	—	—	1380	1677	.823	—	—	1609	961	1130	32	—	—	—	4070	6.0	2.9	12.2
PLAYOFF TOTALS	21	—	453	78	230	.339	—	—	—	91	111	.820	—	—	85	55	86	4	—	—	—	247	5.0	2.6	11.8
ALL-STAR TOTALS	1	—	0	2	9	.222	—	—	—	4	4	1.000	—	—	4	2	3	0	—	—	—	8	4.0	2.0	8.0

SCHAYES, ADOLPH (**Dolph**) b. May 19, 1928 Ht. 6-8 Wt. 220 College—New York University

SEASON—TEAM	G	GS	MIN	FGM	FGA	PCT	3FGM	3FGA	PCT	FTM	FTA	PCT	O-RB	D-RB	TOT	AST	PF	DQ	STL	TO	BLK	PTS	RPG	APG	PPG
48-49—Syracuse (N)	63	—	—	271	—	—	—	—	—	267	370	.722	—	—	—	—	232	—	—	—	—	809	—	—	12.8
49-50—Syracuse	64	—	—	348	903	.385	—	—	—	376	486	.774	—	—	—	259	225	—	—	—	—	1072	—	4.0	16.8
50-51—Syracuse	66	—	—	332	930	.357	—	—	—	457	608	.752	—	—	1080	251	271	9	—	—	—	1121	16.4	3.8	17.0
51-52—Syracuse	63	—	2004	263	740	.355	—	—	—	342	424	.807	—	—	773	182	213	5	—	—	—	868	12.3	2.9	13.8
52-53—Syracuse	71	—	2668	375	1002	.374	—	—	—	512	619	.827	—	—	920	227	271	9	—	—	—	1262	13.0	3.2	17.8
53-54—Syracuse	72	—	2655	370	973	.380	—	—	—	488	590	.827	—	—	870	214	232	4	—	—	—	1228	12.1	3.0	17.1
54-55—Syracuse	72	—	2526	422	1103	.383	—	—	—	489	587	.833	—	—	887	213	247	6	—	—	—	1333	12.3	3.0	18.5
55-56—Syracuse	72	—	2517	465	1202	.387	—	—	—	542	632	.858	—	—	891	200	251	9	—	—	—	1472	12.4	2.8	20.4
56-57—Syracuse	72	—	2851	496	1308	.379	—	—	—	625	691	.904	—	—	1008	229	219	5	—	—	—	1617	14.0	3.2	22.5
57-58—Syracuse	72	—	2918	581	1458	.398	—	—	—	629	696	.904	—	—	1022	224	244	6	—	—	—	1791	14.2	3.1	24.9
58-59—Syracuse	72	—	2645	504	1304	.387	—	—	—	526	609	.864	—	—	962	178	280	9	—	—	—	1534	13.4	2.5	21.3
59-60—Syracuse	75	—	2741	578	1440	.401	—	—	—	533	597	.893	—	—	959	256	263	10	—	—	—	1689	12.8	3.4	22.5
60-61—Syracuse	79	—	3007	594	1595	.372	—	—	—	680	783	.868	—	—	960	296	296	9	—	—	—	1868	12.2	3.7	23.6
61-62—Syracuse	56	—	1480	268	751	.357	—	—	—	286	319	.897	—	—	439	120	167	4	—	—	—	822	7.8	2.1	14.7
62-63—Syracuse	66	—	1438	223	575	.388	—	—	—	181	206	.879	—	—	375	175	177	2	—	—	—	627	5.7	2.7	9.5
63-64—Philadelphia	24	—	350	44	143	.308	—	—	—	46	57	.807	—	—	110	48	76	3	—	—	—	134	4.6	2.0	5.6
REG. NBA TOTALS	996	—	29800	5863	15427	.380	—	—	—	6712	7904	.849	—	—	11256	3072	3432	90	—	—	—	18438	12.1	3.1	18.5
REG. NBL TOTALS	63	—	—	271	—	—	—	—	—	267	370	.722	—	—	—	—	232	—	—	—	—	809	—	—	12.8
NBA PLAYOFF TOTALS	97	—	2687	582	1491	.390	—	—	—	723	876	.825	—	—	1051	257	371	12	—	—	—	1887	12.2	2.6	19.5
NBL PLAYOFF TOTALS	6	—	—	27	—	—	—	—	—	32	42	.762	—	—	—	—	26	—	—	—	—	86	—	—	14.3
NBA ALL-STAR TOTALS	11	—	248	48	109	.440	—	—	—	42	50	.840	—	—	105	17	32	1	—	—	—	138	9.5	1.5	12.5

SCHAYES, DANIEL LESLIE (**Danny**) b. May 10, 1959 Ht. 6-11 Wt. 260 College—Syracuse

SEASON—TEAM	G	GS	MIN	FGM	FGA	PCT	3FGM	3FGA	PCT	FTM	FTA	PCT	O-RB	D-RB	TOT	AST	PF	DQ	STL	TO	BLK	PTS	RPG	APG	PPG
81-82—Utah	82	20	1623	252	524	.481	0	1	.000	140	185	.757	131	296	427	146	292	4	46	151	72	644	5.2	1.8	7.9
82-83—Utah-Denver	82	50	2284	342	749	.457	0	1	.000	228	295	.773	200	435	635	205	325	8	54	253	98	912	7.7	2.5	11.1
83-84—Denver	82	15	1420	183	371	.493	0	2	.000	215	272	.790	145	288	433	91	308	5	32	119	60	581	5.3	1.1	7.1
84-85—Denver	56	0	542	60	129	.465	0	0	—	79	97	.814	48	96	144	38	98	2	20	44	25	199	2.6	0.7	3.6
85-86—Denver	80	13	1654	221	440	.502	0	1	.000	216	278	.777	154	285	439	79	298	7	42	105	63	658	5.5	1.0	8.2
86-87—Denver	76	41	1556	210	405	.519	0	0	—	229	294	.779	120	260	380	85	266	5	20	95	74	649	5.0	1.1	8.5
87-88—Denver	81	74	2166	361	668	.540	0	2	.000	407	487	.836	200	462	662	106	323	9	62	155	92	1129	8.2	1.3	13.9
88-89—Denver	76	64	1918	317	607	.522	3	9	.333	332	402	.826	142	358	500	105	320	8	42	160	81	969	6.6	1.4	12.8
89-90—Denver	53	22	1194	163	330	.494	0	4	.000	225	264	.852	117	225	342	61	200	7	41	72	45	551	6.5	1.2	10.4
90-91—Milwaukee	82	38	2228	298	597	.499	0	5	.000	274	328	.835	174	361	535	98	264	4	55	106	61	870	6.5	1.2	10.6
91-92—Milwaukee	43	4	726	83	199	.417	0	0	—	74	96	.771	58	110	168	34	98	0	19	41	19	240	3.9	0.8	5.6
92-93—Milwaukee	70	7	1124	105	263	.399	0	3	.000	112	137	.818	72	177	249	78	148	1	36	65	36	322	3.6	1.1	4.6
93-94—Milw.-Lakers	36	6	363	28	84	.333	0	0	—	29	32	.906	31	48	79	13	45	0	10	23	10	85	2.2	0.4	2.4
REG. SEASON TOTALS	899	354	18798	2623	5366	.489	3	28	.107	2560	3167	.808	1592	3401	4993	1139	2985	60	479	1389	736	7809	5.6	1.3	8.7
PLAYOFF TOTALS	51	20	1153	166	308	.539	0	1	.000	151	184	.821	98	197	295	63	172	2	21	84	43	483	5.8	1.2	9.5

SCHECTMAN, OSCAR B. (**Ossie**) b. March 30, 1919 Ht. 6-1½ Wt. 175 College—Long Island University

SEASON—TEAM	G	GS	MIN	FGM	FGA	PCT	3FGM	3FGA	PCT	FTM	FTA	PCT	O-RB	D-RB	TOT	AST	PF	DQ	STL	TO	BLK	PTS	RPG	APG	PPG
46-47—New York	54	—	—	162	588	.276	—	—	—	111	179	.620	—	—	—	109	115	—	—	—	—	435	—	2.0	8.1
REG. SEASON TOTALS	54	—	—	162	588	.276	—	—	—	111	179	.620	—	—	—	109	115	—	—	—	—	435	—	2.0	8.1

SCHEFFLER, STEPHEN ROBERT (**Steve**) b. September 3, 1967 Ht. 6-9 Wt. 250 College—Purdue

SEASON—TEAM	G	GS	MIN	FGM	FGA	PCT	3FGM	3FGA	PCT	FTM	FTA	PCT	O-RB	D-RB	TOT	AST	PF	DQ	STL	TO	BLK	PTS	RPG	APG	PPG
90-91—Charlotte	39	0	227	20	39	.513	0	0	—	19	21	.905	21	24	45	9	20	0	6	4	2	59	1.2	0.2	1.5
91-92—Sac.-Denver	11	0	61	6	9	.667	0	0	—	9	12	.750	10	4	14	0	10	0	3	1	1	21	1.3	0.0	1.9
92-93—Seattle	29	5	166	25	48	.521	0	0	—	16	24	.667	15	21	36	5	37	0	6	5	1	66	1.2	0.2	2.3
93-94—Seattle	35	1	152	28	46	.609	0	0	—	19	20	.950	11	15	26	6	25	0	7	8	0	75	0.7	0.2	2.1
REG. SEASON TOTALS	114	6	606	79	142	.556	0	0	—	63	77	.818	57	64	121	20	92	0	22	18	4	221	1.1	0.2	1.9
PLAYOFF TOTALS	10	0	31	6	11	.545	0	0	—	4	6	.667	6	7	13	1	2	0	3	0	0	16	1.3	0.1	1.6

SCHEFFLER, THOMAS MARK (**Tom**) b. October 27, 1954 Ht. 6-11 Wt. 240 College—Purdue

SEASON—TEAM	G	GS	MIN	FGM	FGA	PCT	3FGM	3FGA	PCT	FTM	FTA	PCT	O-RB	D-RB	TOT	AST	PF	DQ	STL	TO	BLK	PTS	RPG	APG	PPG
84-85—Portland	39	0	268	21	51	.412	0	0	—	10	20	.500	18	58	76	11	48	0	8	15	11	52	1.9	0.3	1.3
REG. SEASON TOTALS	39	0	268	21	51	.412	0	0	—	10	20	.500	18	58	76	11	48	0	8	15	11	52	1.9	0.3	1.3
PLAYOFF TOTALS	3	0	10	2	3	.667	0	0	—	3	4	.750	3	2	5	—	0	0	1	1	0	7	1.7	0.0	2.3

SCHELLHASE, DAVID GENE JR. (**Dave**) b. October 14, 1944 Ht. 6-3½ Wt. 205 College—Purdue

SEASON—TEAM	G	GS	MIN	FGM	FGA	PCT	3FGM	3FGA	PCT	FTM	FTA	PCT	O-RB	D-RB	TOT	AST	PF	DQ	STL	TO	BLK	PTS	RPG	APG	PPG
66-67—Chicago	31	—	212	40	111	.360	—	—	—	14	22	.636	—	—	29	23	27	0	—	—	—	94	0.9	0.7	3.0
67-68—Chicago	42	—	301	47	138	.341	—	—	—	20	38	.526	—	—	47	37	43	0	—	—	—	114	1.1	0.9	2.7
REG. SEASON TOTALS	73	—	513	87	249	.349	—	—	—	34	60	.567	—	—	76	60	70	0	—	—	—	208	1.0	0.8	2.8
PLAYOFF TOTALS	3	—	8	1	5	.200	—	—	—	1	2	.500	—	—	1	—	0	0	—	—	—	3	0.3	0.0	1.0

SCHERER, HERBERT FREDERICK (Herb) b. December 21, 1929 Ht. 6-9½ Wt. 215 College—Long Island University

SEASON—TEAM	G	GS	MIN	FGM	FGA	PCT	3FGM	3FGA	PCT	FTM	FTA	PCT	O-RB	D-RB	TOT	AST	PF	DQ	STL	TO	BLK	PTS	RPG	APG	PPG
50-51—Tri-Cities	20	—	—	24	84	.286	—	—	—	20	35	.571	—	—	50	17	56	1	—	—	—	68	2.5	0.9	3.4
51-52—New York	12	—	167	19	65	.292	—	—	—	9	14	.643	—	—	26	6	25	0	—	—	—	47	2.2	0.5	3.9
REG. SEASON TOTALS	32	—	167	43	149	.289	—	—	—	29	49	.592	—	—	76	23	81	1	—	—	—	115	2.4	0.7	3.6

SCHINTZIUS, DWAYNE KENNETH b. October 14, 1968 Ht. 7-2 Wt. 280 College—Florida

SEASON—TEAM	G	GS	MIN	FGM	FGA	PCT	3FGM	3FGA	PCT	FTM	FTA	PCT	O-RB	D-RB	TOT	AST	PF	DQ	STL	TO	BLK	PTS	RPG	APG	PPG
90-91—San Antonio	42	7	398	68	155	.439	0	2	.000	22	40	.550	28	93	121	17	64	0	2	34	29	158	2.9	0.4	3.8
91-92—Sacramento	33	0	400	50	117	.427	0	4	.000	10	12	.833	43	75	118	20	67	1	6	19	28	110	3.6	0.6	3.3
92-93—New Jersey	5	0	35	2	7	.286	0	0	—	3	3	1.000	2	6	8	2	4	0	2	0	2	7	1.6	0.4	1.4
93-94—New Jersey	30	7	319	29	84	.345	0	0	—	10	17	.588	26	63	89	13	49	1	7	13	17	68	3.0	0.4	2.3
REG. SEASON TOTALS	110	14	1152	149	363	.410	0	6	.000	45	72	.625	99	237	336	52	184	2	17	66	76	343	3.1	0.5	3.1
PLAYOFF TOTALS	5	0	106	13	29	.448	0	0	—	3	6	.500	6	19	25	4	12	0	1	3	6	29	5.0	0.8	5.8

SCHLUETER, DALE WAYNE b. November 12, 1945 Ht. 6-10 Wt. 225 College—Colorado State

SEASON—TEAM	G	GS	MIN	FGM	FGA	PCT	3FGM	3FGA	PCT	FTM	FTA	PCT	O-RB	D-RB	TOT	AST	PF	DQ	STL	TO	BLK	PTS	RPG	APG	PPG
68-69—San Francisco	31	—	559	68	157	.433	—	—	—	45	82	.549	—	—	216	30	81	3	—	—	—	181	7.0	1.0	5.8
69-70—San Francisco	63	—	685	82	167	.491	—	—	—	60	97	.619	—	—	231	25	108	0	—	—	—	224	3.7	0.4	3.6
70-71—Portland	80	—	1823	257	527	.488	—	—	—	143	218	.656	—	—	629	192	265	4	—	—	—	657	7.9	2.4	8.2
71-72—Portland	81	—	2693	353	672	.525	—	—	—	241	326	.739	—	—	860	285	277	3	—	—	—	947	10.6	3.5	11.7
72-73—Philadelphia	78	—	1136	166	317	.524	—	—	—	86	123	.699	—	—	354	103	166	0	—	—	—	418	4.5	1.3	5.4
73-74—Atlanta	57	—	547	63	135	.467	—	—	—	38	50	.760	54	101	155	45	84	0	25	—	22	164	2.7	0.8	2.9
74-75—Buffalo	76	—	962	92	178	.517	—	—	—	84	121	.694	78	186	264	104	163	0	18	—	42	268	3.5	1.4	3.5
75-76—Buffalo	71	—	773	61	122	.500	—	—	—	54	81	.667	58	166	224	82	141	1	13	—	17	176	3.2	1.1	2.5
76-77—Phoenix	39	—	337	26	72	.361	—	—	—	18	31	.581	30	50	80	38	62	0	8	—	9	70	2.1	1.0	1.8
77-78—Portland	10	—	109	8	19	.421	—	—	—	9	18	.500	5	16	21	18	20	0	3	15	2	25	2.1	1.8	2.5
REG. SEASON TOTALS	586	—	9624	1176	2366	.497	—	—	—	778	1147	.678	225	519	3034	920	1367	11	67	15	91	3130	5.2	1.6	5.3
PLAYOFF TOTALS	17	—	109	14	26	.538	—	—	—	13	24	.542	7	14	43	4	21	0	2	—	3	41	2.5	0.2	2.4

SCHNELLBACHER, OTTO O. (The Claw) b. April 15, 1923 Ht. 6-5 Wt. 185 College—Kansas

SEASON—TEAM	G	GS	MIN	FGM	FGA	PCT	3FGM	3FGA	PCT	FTM	FTA	PCT	O-RB	D-RB	TOT	AST	PF	DQ	STL	TO	BLK	PTS	RPG	APG	PPG
48-49—Prov.-St. L.	43	—	—	93	280	.332	—	—	—	89	133	.669	—	—	—	64	109	—	—	—	—	275	—	1.5	6.4
REG. SEASON TOTALS	43	—	—	93	280	.332	—	—	—	89	133	.669	—	—	—	64	109	—	—	—	—	275	—	1.5	6.4
PLAYOFF TOTALS	2	—	—	6	20	.300	—	—	—	6	12	.500	—	—	—	6	9	1	—	—	—	18	—	3.0	9.0

SCHNITTKER, RICHARD D. (Dick) b. May 27, 1928 Ht. 6-5 Wt. 205 College—Ohio State

SEASON—TEAM	G	GS	MIN	FGM	FGA	PCT	3FGM	3FGA	PCT	FTM	FTA	PCT	O-RB	D-RB	TOT	AST	PF	DQ	STL	TO	BLK	PTS	RPG	APG	PPG
50-51—Washington	29	—	—	85	219	.388	—	—	—	123	139	.885	—	—	153	42	76	0	—	—	—	293	5.3	1.4	10.1
53-54—Minneapolis	71	—	1040	122	307	.397	—	—	—	86	132	.652	—	—	178	59	178	3	—	—	—	330	2.5	0.8	4.6
54-55—Minneapolis	72	—	1798	226	583	.388	—	—	—	298	362	.823	—	—	349	114	231	7	—	—	—	750	4.8	1.6	10.4
55-56—Minneapolis	72	—	1930	254	647	.393	—	—	—	304	355	.856	—	—	296	142	253	4	—	—	—	812	4.1	2.0	11.3
56-57—Minneapolis	70	—	997	113	351	.322	—	—	—	160	193	.829	—	—	185	52	144	3	—	—	—	386	2.6	0.7	5.5
57-58—Minneapolis	50	—	979	128	357	.359	—	—	—	201	237	.848	—	—	211	71	126	5	—	—	—	457	4.2	1.4	9.1
REG. SEASON TOTALS	364	—	6744	928	2464	.377	—	—	—	1172	1418	.827	—	—	1372	480	1008	22	—	—	—	3028	3.8	1.3	8.3
PLAYOFF TOTALS	35	—	502	45	135	.333	—	—	—	76	104	.731	—	—	83	25	83	3	—	—	—	166	2.4	0.7	4.7

SCHOENE, RUSSELL (Russ) b. April 16, 1960 Ht. 6-10 Wt. 210 College—Mineral Area CC/Tennessee Chattanooga

SEASON—TEAM	G	GS	MIN	FGM	FGA	PCT	3FGM	3FGA	PCT	FTM	FTA	PCT	O-RB	D-RB	TOT	AST	PF	DQ	STL	TO	BLK	PTS	RPG	APG	PPG
82-83—Phil.-Indiana	77	7	1222	207	435	.476	1	4	.250	61	83	.735	96	159	255	59	192	3	25	81	23	476	3.3	0.8	6.2
86-87—Seattle	63	0	579	71	190	.374	2	13	.154	29	46	.630	52	65	117	27	94	1	20	42	11	173	1.9	0.4	2.7
87-88—Seattle	81	2	973	208	454	.458	17	58	.293	51	63	.810	78	120	198	53	151	0	39	57	13	484	2.4	0.7	6.0
88-89—Seattle	69	1	774	135	349	.387	42	110	.382	46	57	.807	58	107	165	36	136	1	37	48	24	358	2.4	0.5	5.2
REG. SEASON TOTALS	290	10	3548	621	1428	.435	62	185	.335	187	249	.751	284	451	735	175	573	5	121	228	71	1491	2.5	0.6	5.1
PLAYOFF TOTALS	22	0	205	21	57	.368	4	17	.235	14	18	.778	10	28	38	7	31	1	4	4	4	60	1.7	0.3	2.7

SCHOLZ, DAVID A. (Dave) b. April 12, 1948 Ht. 6-8 Wt. 220 College—Illinois

SEASON—TEAM	G	GS	MIN	FGM	FGA	PCT	3FGM	3FGA	PCT	FTM	FTA	PCT	O-RB	D-RB	TOT	AST	PF	DQ	STL	TO	BLK	PTS	RPG	APG	PPG
69-70—Philadelphia	1	—	1	1	1	1.000	—	—	—	0	0	—	—	—	0	0	0	0	—	—	—	2	0.0	0.0	2.0
REG. SEASON TOTALS	1	—	1	1	1	1.000	—	—	—	0	0	—	—	—	0	0	0	0	—	—	—	2	0.0	0.0	2.0

SCHOON, MILTON W. (Milt) b. February 25, 1922 Ht. 6-8½ Wt. 230 College—Valparaiso

SEASON—TEAM	G	GS	MIN	FGM	FGA	PCT	3FGM	3FGA	PCT	FTM	FTA	PCT	O-RB	D-RB	TOT	AST	PF	DQ	STL	TO	BLK	PTS	RPG	APG	PPG
46-47—Detroit	41	—	—	43	199	.216	—	—	—	34	80	.425	—	—	—	12	75	—	—	—	—	120	—	0.3	2.9
47-48—Flint (N)	55	—	—	114	—	—	—	—	—	120	214	.561	—	—	—	—	194	—	—	—	—	348	—	—	6.3
48-49—Sheboygan (N)	57	—	—	81	—	—	—	—	—	109	184	.592	—	—	—	—	143	—	—	—	—	271	—	—	4.8
49-50—Sheboygan	62	—	—	150	366	.410	—	—	—	196	300	.653	—	—	—	84	190	—	—	—	—	496	—	1.4	8.0
REG. NBA TOTALS	103	—	—	193	565	.342	—	—	—	230	380	.605	—	—	—	96	265	—	—	—	—	616	—	0.9	6.0
REG. NBL TOTALS	112	—	—	195	—	—	—	—	—	229	398	.575	—	—	—	—	337	—	—	—	—	619	—	—	5.5
NBA PLAYOFF TOTALS	3	—	—	5	17	.294	—	—	—	7	10	.700	—	—	—	3	6	—	—	—	—	17	—	1.0	5.7
NBL PLAYOFF TOTALS	2	—	—	2	—	—	—	—	—	2	5	.400	—	—	—	—	10	—	—	—	—	6	—	—	3.0

SCHREMPF, DETLEF b. January 21, 1963 Ht. 6-9 Wt. 220 College—Washington

SEASON—TEAM	G	GS	MIN	FGM	FGA	PCT	3FGM	3FGA	PCT	FTM	FTA	PCT	O-RB	D-RB	TOT	AST	PF	DQ	STL	TO	BLK	PTS	RPG	APG	PPG
85-86—Dallas	64	12	969	142	315	.451	3	7	.429	110	152	.724	70	128	198	88	166	1	23	84	10	397	3.1	1.4	6.2
86-87—Dallas	81	5	1711	265	561	.472	33	69	.478	193	260	.742	87	216	303	161	224	2	50	110	16	756	3.7	2.0	9.3
87-88—Dallas	82	4	1587	246	539	.456	5	32	.156	201	266	.756	102	177	279	159	189	0	42	108	32	698	3.4	1.9	8.5
88-89—Dallas-Indiana	69	13	1850	274	578	.474	7	35	.200	273	350	.780	126	269	395	179	220	3	53	133	19	828	5.7	2.6	12.0
89-90—Indiana	78	18	2573	424	822	.516	17	48	.354	402	490	.820	149	471	620	247	271	6	59	180	16	1267	7.9	3.2	16.2
90-91—Indiana	82	3	2632	432	831	.520	15	40	.375	441	539	.818	178	482	660	301	262	3	58	175	22	1320	8.0	3.7	16.1
91-92—Indiana	80	4	2605	496	925	.536	23	71	.324	365	441	.828	202	568	770	312	286	4	62	191	37	1380	9.6	3.9	17.3
92-93—Indiana	82	60	3098	517	1085	.476	8	52	.154	525	653	.804	210	570	780	493	305	3	79	243	27	1567	9.5	6.0	19.1
93-94—Seattle	81	80	2728	445	903	.493	22	68	.324	300	390	.769	144	310	454	275	273	3	73	173	9	1212	5.6	3.4	15.0
REG. SEASON TOTALS	699	199	19753	3241	6559	.494	133	422	.315	2810	3541	.794	1268	3191	4459	2215	2196	25	499	1397	188	9425	6.4	3.2	13.5
PLAYOFF TOTALS	49	12	1254	185	404	.458	5	26	.192	184	234	.786	74	163	237	106	141	1	21	90	17	559	4.8	2.2	11.4
ALL-STAR TOTALS	1	0	13	1	3	.333	0	1	.000	1	2	.500	0	3	3	0	4	0	0	1	0	3	3.0	0.0	3.0

SCHULTZ, HOWARD HENRY (Howie, Stretch) b. July 3, 1922 Ht. 6-6 Wt. 220 College—Hamline

SEASON—TEAM	G	GS	MIN	FGM	FGA	PCT	3FGM	3FGA	PCT	FTM	FTA	PCT	O-RB	D-RB	TOT	AST	PF	DQ	STL	TO	BLK	PTS	RPG	APG	PPG
46-47—Anderson (N)	41	—	—	155	—	—	—	—	—	147	213	.690	—	—	—	—	124	—	—	—	—	457	—	—	11.1
47-48—Anderson (N)	60	—	—	213	—	—	—	—	—	179	258	.694	—	—	—	—	194	—	—	—	—	605	—	—	10.1
48-49—Anderson (N)	64	—	—	176	—	—	—	—	—	186	256	.727	—	—	—	—	204	—	—	—	—	538	—	—	8.4
49-50—And.-Ft. Wayne	67	—	—	179	671	.267	—	—	—	196	282	.695	—	—	—	169	244	—	—	—	—	554	—	2.5	8.3
51-52—Minneapolis	66	—	1301	89	315	.283	—	—	—	90	119	.756	—	—	246	102	197	13	—	—	—	268	3.7	1.5	4.1
52-53—Minneapolis	40	—	474	24	90	.267	—	—	—	43	62	.694	—	—	80	29	73	1	—	—	—	91	2.0	0.7	2.3
REG. NBA TOTALS	173	—	1775	292	1076	.271	—	—	—	329	463	.711	—	—	326	300	514	14	—	—	—	913	3.1	1.7	5.3
REG. NBL TOTALS	165	—	—	544	—	—	—	—	—	512	727	.704	—	—	—	—	522	—	—	—	—	1600	—	—	9.7
NBA PLAYOFF TOTALS	16	—	99	21	79	.266	—	—	—	19	27	.704	—	—	19	13	36	3	—	—	—	61	1.6	0.8	3.8
NBL PLAYOFF TOTALS	13	—	—	36	—	—	—	—	—	47	70	.671	—	—	—	—	46	—	—	—	—	119	—	—	9.2

SCHULZ, RICHARD A. (Dick) b. January 3, 1917 Ht. 6-2 Wt. 205 College—Wisconsin

SEASON—TEAM	G	GS	MIN	FGM	FGA	PCT	3FGM	3FGA	PCT	FTM	FTA	PCT	O-RB	D-RB	TOT	AST	PF	DQ	STL	TO	BLK	PTS	RPG	APG	PPG
42-43—Sheboygan (N)	1	—	—	0	—	—	—	—	—	0	—	—	—	—	—	—	—	—	—	—	—	0	—	—	0.0
43-44—Sheboygan (N)	20	—	—	18	—	—	—	—	—	10	—	—	—	—	—	—	—	—	—	—	—	46	—	—	2.3
44-45—Sheboygan (N)	29	—	—	86	—	—	—	—	—	71	—	—	—	—	—	—	—	—	—	—	—	243	—	—	8.4
45-46—Sheboygan (N)	29	—	—	56	—	—	—	—	—	66	94	.702	—	—	—	—	39	—	—	—	—	178	—	—	6.1
46-47—Clev.-Toronto	57	—	—	130	548	.237	—	—	—	94	138	.681	—	—	—	56	123	—	—	—	—	354	—	1.0	6.2
47-48—Baltimore	48	—	—	133	469	.284	—	—	—	117	160	.731	—	—	—	28	116	—	—	—	—	383	—	0.6	8.0
48-49—Washington	50	—	—	65	278	.234	—	—	—	65	91	.714	—	—	—	53	107	—	—	—	—	195	—	1.1	3.9
49-50—Wash.-Tri-Cit-She.	50	—	—	63	212	.297	—	—	—	83	110	.755	—	—	—	66	106	—	—	—	—	209	—	1.3	4.2
REG. NBA TOTALS	205	—	—	391	1507	.259	—	—	—	359	499	.719	—	—	—	203	452	—	—	—	—	1141	—	1.0	5.6
REG. NBL TOTALS	79	—	—	160	—	—	—	—	—	147	94	.702	—	—	—	—	39	—	—	—	—	467	—	—	5.9
NBA PLAYOFF TOTALS	25	—	—	40	197	.203	—	—	—	68	96	.708	—	—	—	36	78	—	—	—	—	148	—	1.4	5.9
NBL PLAYOFF TOTALS	21	—	—	52	—	—	—	—	—	67	61	.656	—	—	—	—	45	—	—	—	—	171	—	—	8.1

SCHURIG, ROGER PAUL b. April 3, 1942 Ht. 6-3 Wt. 185 College—Vanderbilt

SEASON—TEAM	G	GS	MIN	FGM	FGA	PCT	3FGM	3FGA	PCT	FTM	FTA	PCT	O-RB	D-RB	TOT	AST	PF	DQ	STL	TO	BLK	PTS	RPG	APG	PPG
67-68—Houston (A)	21	—	252	35	94	.372	3	8	.375	27	36	.750	—	—	29	18	38	0	—	23	—	100	1.4	0.9	4.8
REG. ABA TOTALS	21	—	252	35	94	.372	3	8	.375	27	36	.750	—	—	29	18	38	0	—	23	—	100	1.4	0.9	4.8

SCHWEITZ, JOHN ELWOOD b. April 19, 1960 Ht. 6-6 Wt. 210 College—Richmond

SEASON—TEAM	G	GS	MIN	FGM	FGA	PCT	3FGM	3FGA	PCT	FTM	FTA	PCT	O-RB	D-RB	TOT	AST	PF	DQ	STL	TO	BLK	PTS	RPG	APG	PPG
84-85—Seattle	19	0	110	25	74	.338	0	4	.000	7	10	.700	6	15	21	18	12	0	0	14	1	57	1.1	0.9	3.0
86-87—Detroit	3	0	7	0	1	.000	0	0	—	0	0	—	0	1	1	0	2	0	0	2	0	0	0.3	0.0	0.0
REG. SEASON TOTALS	22	0	117	25	75	.333	0	4	.000	7	10	.700	6	16	22	18	14	0	0	16	1	57	1.0	0.8	2.6

SCOLARI, FRED J. (**Freddie, Fat Freddie**) b. March 1, 1922 Ht. 5-10½ Wt. 180 College—San Francisco

SEASON—TEAM	G	GS	MIN	FGM	FGA	PCT	3FGM	3FGA	PCT	FTM	FTA	PCT	O-RB	D-RB	TOT	AST	PF	DQ	STL	TO	BLK	PTS	RPG	APG	PPG
46-47—Washington	58	—	—	291	989	.294	—	—	—	146	180	.811	—	—	—	58	159	—	—	—	—	728	—	1.0	12.6
47-48—Washington	47	—	—	229	780	.294	—	—	—	131	179	.732	—	—	—	58	153	—	—	—	—	589	—	1.2	12.5
48-49—Washington	48	—	—	196	633	.310	—	—	—	146	183	.798	—	—	—	100	150	—	—	—	—	538	—	2.1	11.2
49-50—Washington	66	—	—	312	910	.343	—	—	—	236	287	.822	—	—	—	175	181	—	—	—	—	860	—	2.7	13.0
50-51—Wash.-Syr.	66	—	—	302	923	.327	—	—	—	279	331	.843	—	—	218	255	183	1	—	—	—	883	3.3	3.9	13.4
51-52—Baltimore	64	—	2242	290	867	.334	—	—	—	353	423	.835	—	—	214	303	213	6	—	—	—	933	3.3	4.7	14.6
52-53—Balt.-Ft. Wayne	62	—	2123	277	809	.342	—	—	—	276	327	.844	—	—	209	233	212	4	—	—	—	830	3.4	3.8	13.4
53-54—Fort Wayne	64	—	1589	159	491	.324	—	—	—	144	180	.800	—	—	139	131	155	1	—	—	—	462	2.2	2.0	7.2
54-55—Boston	59	—	619	76	249	.305	—	—	—	39	49	.796	—	—	77	93	76	0	—	—	—	191	1.3	1.6	3.2
REG. SEASON TOTALS	534	—	6573	2132	6651	.321	—	—	—	1750	2139	.818	—	—	857	1406	1482	12	—	—	—	6014	2.7	2.6	11.3
PLAYOFF TOTALS	41	—	357	134	444	.302	—	—	—	141	178	.792	—	—	78	70	116	3	—	—	—	409	3.3	1.7	10.0
ALL-STAR TOTALS	1	—	15	5	9	.556	—	—	—	0	0	—	—	—	0	2	0	0	—	—	—	10	0.0	2.0	10.0

SCOTT, ALVIN LEROY b. September 14, 1955 Ht. 6-7 Wt. 185 College—Oral Roberts

SEASON—TEAM	G	GS	MIN	FGM	FGA	PCT	3FGM	3FGA	PCT	FTM	FTA	PCT	O-RB	D-RB	TOT	AST	PF	DQ	STL	TO	BLK	PTS	RPG	APG	PPG
77-78—Phoenix	81	—	1538	180	369	.488	—	—	—	132	191	.691	135	222	357	88	158	0	52	85	40	492	4.4	1.1	6.1
78-79—Phoenix	81	—	1737	212	396	.535	—	—	—	120	168	.714	104	256	360	126	139	2	80	99	62	544	4.4	1.6	6.7
79-80—Phoenix	79	—	1303	127	301	.422	1	3	.333	95	122	.779	89	139	228	98	101	0	47	92	53	350	2.9	1.2	4.4
80-81—Phoenix	82	—	1423	173	348	.497	1	6	.167	97	127	.764	101	167	268	114	124	0	60	77	70	444	3.3	1.4	5.4
81-82—Phoenix	81	38	1740	189	380	.497	0	2	.000	108	148	.730	97	197	294	149	169	0	59	98	70	486	3.6	1.8	6.0
82-83—Phoenix	81	9	1139	124	259	.479	0	2	.000	81	110	.736	60	164	224	97	133	0	48	64	31	329	2.8	1.2	4.1
83-84—Phoenix	65	5	735	55	124	.444	1	2	.500	56	72	.778	29	71	100	48	85	0	19	42	20	167	1.5	0.7	2.6
84-85—Phoenix	77	18	1238	111	259	.429	1	5	.200	53	74	.716	46	115	161	127	125	0	39	60	25	276	2.1	1.6	3.6
REG. SEASON TOTALS	627	70	10853	1171	2436	.481	4	20	.200	742	1012	.733	661	1331	1992	847	1034	2	404	617	371	3088	3.2	1.4	4.9
PLAYOFF TOTALS	61	1	878	88	206	.427	1	7	.143	47	72	.653	57	92	149	78	77	0	29	52	51	224	2.4	1.3	3.7

SCOTT, BYRON ANTOM b. March 28, 1961 Ht. 6-3 Wt. 195 College—Arizona State

SEASON—TEAM	G	GS	MIN	FGM	FGA	PCT	3FGM	3FGA	PCT	FTM	FTA	PCT	O-RB	D-RB	TOT	AST	PF	DQ	STL	TO	BLK	PTS	RPG	APG	PPG
83-84—Los Angeles	74	49	1637	334	690	.484	8	34	.235	112	139	.806	50	114	164	177	174	0	81	116	19	788	2.2	2.4	10.6
84-85—L.A. Lakers	81	65	2305	541	1003	.539	26	60	.433	187	228	.820	57	153	210	244	197	1	100	138	17	1295	2.6	3.0	16.0
85-86—L.A. Lakers	76	62	2190	507	989	.513	22	61	.361	138	176	.784	55	134	189	164	167	0	85	110	15	1174	2.5	2.2	15.4
86-87—L.A. Lakers	82	82	2729	554	1134	.489	65	149	.436	224	251	.892	63	223	286	281	163	0	125	144	18	1397	3.5	3.4	17.0
87-88—L.A. Lakers	81	81	3048	710	1348	.527	62	179	.346	272	317	.858	76	257	333	335	204	2	155	161	27	1754	4.1	4.1	21.7
88-89—L.A. Lakers	74	73	2605	588	1198	.491	77	193	.399	195	226	.863	72	230	302	231	181	1	114	157	27	1448	4.1	3.1	19.6
89-90—L.A. Lakers	77	77	2593	472	1005	.470	93	220	.423	160	209	.766	51	191	242	274	180	2	77	122	31	1197	3.1	3.6	15.5
90-91—L.A. Lakers	82	82	2630	501	1051	.477	71	219	.324	118	148	.797	54	192	246	177	146	0	95	85	21	1191	3.0	2.2	14.5
91-92—L.A. Lakers	82	82	2679	460	1005	.458	54	157	.344	244	291	.838	74	236	310	226	140	0	105	119	28	1218	3.8	2.8	14.9
92-93—L.A. Lakers	58	53	1677	296	659	.449	44	135	.326	156	184	.848	27	107	134	157	98	0	55	70	13	792	2.3	2.7	13.7
93-94—Indiana	67	2	1197	256	548	.467	27	74	.365	157	195	.805	19	91	110	133	80	0	62	103	9	696	1.6	2.0	10.4
REG. SEASON TOTALS	834	708	25290	5219	10630	.491	549	1481	.371	1963	2364	.830	598	1928	2526	2399	1730	6	1054	1325	225	12950	3.0	2.9	15.5
PLAYOFF TOTALS	158	122	4933	887	1810	.490	121	294	.412	402	495	.812	131	368	499	363	400	2	215	236	29	2297	3.2	2.3	14.5

SCOTT, CHARLES THOMAS (**Charlie**) b. December 15, 1948 Ht. 6-5½ Wt. 175 College—North Carolina

SEASON—TEAM	G	GS	MIN	FGM	FGA	PCT	3FGM	3FGA	PCT	FTM	FTA	PCT	O-RB	D-RB	TOT	AST	PF	DQ	STL	TO	BLK	PTS	RPG	APG	PPG
70-71—Virginia (A)	84	—	3185	902	1947	.463	16	65	.246	456	611	.746	—	—	438	472	298	—	—	—	—	2276	5.2	5.6	27.1
71-72—Virginia (A)	73	—	3061	985	2192	.449	29	110	.264	525	654	.803	—	—	374	347	261	—	—	340	—	2524	5.1	4.8	34.6
71-72—Phoenix	6	—	177	48	113	.425	—	—	—	17	21	.810	—	—	23	26	19	0	—	—	—	113	3.8	4.3	18.8
72-73—Phoenix	81	—	3062	806	1809	.446	—	—	—	436	556	.784	—	—	342	495	306	5	—	—	—	2048	4.2	6.1	25.3
73-74—Phoenix	52	—	2003	538	1171	.459	—	—	—	246	315	.781	64	158	222	271	194	6	99	—	22	1322	4.3	5.2	25.4
74-75—Phoenix	69	—	2592	703	1594	.441	—	—	—	274	351	.781	72	201	273	311	296	11	111	—	24	1680	4.0	4.5	24.3
75-76—Boston	82	—	2913	588	1309	.449	—	—	—	267	335	.797	106	252	358	341	356	17	103	—	24	1443	4.4	4.2	17.6
76-77—Boston	43	—	1581	326	734	.444	—	—	—	129	173	.746	52	139	191	196	155	3	60	—	12	781	4.4	4.6	18.2
77-78—Boston-L.A.	79	—	2473	435	994	.438	—	—	—	194	260	.746	62	187	249	378	252	6	110	238	17	1064	3.2	4.8	13.5
78-79—Denver	79	—	2617	393	854	.460	—	—	—	161	215	.749	54	156	210	428	284	12	78	255	30	947	2.7	5.4	12.0
79-80—Denver	69	—	1860	276	688	.401	2	11	.182	85	118	.720	51	115	166	250	197	3	47	163	23	639	2.4	3.6	9.3
REG. NBA TOTALS	560	—	19278	4113	9266	.444	2	11	.182	1809	2344	.772	461	1208	2034	2696	2059	63	608	656	152	10037	3.6	4.8	17.9
REG. ABA TOTALS	157	—	6246	1887	4139	.456	45	175	.257	981	1265	.775	—	—	812	819	559	—	—	340	—	4800	5.2	5.2	30.6
NBA PLAYOFF TOTALS	33	—	1177	195	494	.395	0	0	—	113	146	.774	46	95	141	133	158	14	40	21	12	503	4.3	4.0	15.2
ABA PLAYOFF TOTALS	12	—	504	115	281	.409	8	31	.258	83	110	.755	—	—	79	82	45	—	—	—	—	321	6.6	6.8	26.8
NBA ALL-STAR TOTALS	3	—	49	1	15	.067	0	0	—	2	2	1.000	1	2	5	7	6	0	0	—	1	4	1.7	2.3	1.3
ABA ALL-STAR TOTALS	2	—	44	11	27	.407	0	1	.000	5	9	.556	2	4	6	6	6	—	—	11	—	27	3.0	3.0	13.5

SCOTT, DENNIS EUGENE b. September 5, 1968 Ht. 6-8 Wt. 230 College—Georgia Tech

SEASON—TEAM	G	GS	MIN	FGM	FGA	PCT	3FGM	3FGA	PCT	FTM	FTA	PCT	O-RB	D-RB	TOT	AST	PF	DQ	STL	TO	BLK	PTS	RPG	APG	PPG
90-91—Orlando	82	73	2336	503	1183	.425	125	334	.374	153	204	.750	62	173	235	134	203	1	62	127	25	1284	2.9	1.6	15.7
91-92—Orlando	18	15	608	133	331	.402	29	89	.326	64	71	.901	14	52	66	35	49	1	20	31	9	359	3.7	1.9	19.9
92-93—Orlando	54	43	1759	329	763	.431	108	268	.403	92	117	.786	38	148	186	136	131	3	57	104	18	858	3.4	2.5	15.9
93-94—Orlando	82	37	2283	384	949	.405	155	388	.399	123	159	.774	54	164	218	216	161	0	81	93	32	1046	2.7	2.6	12.8
REG. SEASON TOTALS	236	168	6986	1349	3226	.418	417	1079	.386	432	551	.784	168	537	705	521	544	5	220	355	84	3547	3.0	2.2	15.0
PLAYOFF TOTALS	3	3	99	14	41	.341	7	22	.318	8	10	.800	1	5	6	3	7	0	2	8	3	43	2.0	1.0	14.3

SCOTT, JOHN RAYMOND (**Ray**) b. July 12, 1938 Ht. 6-9 Wt. 215 College—Portland

SEASON—TEAM	G	GS	MIN	FGM	FGA	PCT	3FGM	3FGA	PCT	FTM	FTA	PCT	O-RB	D-RB	TOT	AST	PF	DQ	STL	TO	BLK	PTS	RPG	APG	PPG
61-62—Detroit	75	—	2087	370	956	.387	—	—	—	255	388	.657	—	—	865	132	232	6	—	—	—	995	11.5	1.8	13.3
62-63—Detroit	76	—	2538	460	1110	.414	—	—	—	308	457	.674	—	—	772	191	263	9	—	—	—	1228	10.2	2.5	16.2
63-64—Detroit	80	—	2964	539	1307	.412	—	—	—	328	456	.719	—	—	1078	244	296	7	—	—	—	1406	13.5	3.1	17.6
64-65—Detroit	66	—	2167	402	1092	.368	—	—	—	220	314	.701	—	—	634	239	209	5	—	—	—	1024	9.6	3.6	15.5
65-66—Detroit	79	—	2652	544	1309	.416	—	—	—	323	435	.743	—	—	755	238	209	3	—	—	—	1411	9.6	3.0	17.9
66-67—Detroit-Balt.	72	—	2446	458	1144	.400	—	—	—	256	366	.699	—	—	760	160	215	2	—	—	—	1172	10.6	2.2	16.3
67-68—Baltimore	81	—	2924	490	1189	.412	—	—	—	348	447	.779	—	—	1111	167	252	2	—	—	—	1328	13.7	2.1	16.4
68-69—Baltimore	82	—	2168	386	929	.416	—	—	—	195	257	.759	—	—	722	133	212	1	—	—	—	967	8.8	1.6	11.8
69-70—Baltimore	73	—	1393	257	605	.425	—	—	—	139	173	.803	—	—	457	114	147	0	—	—	—	653	6.3	1.6	8.9
70-71—Virginia (A)	72	—	1552	420	933	.450	1	1	1.000	187	236	.792	—	—	573	123	180	—	—	—	—	1028	8.0	1.7	14.3
71-72—Virginia (A)	55	—	818	163	393	.415	2	4	.500	89	114	.781	—	—	252	40	90	—	—	55	—	417	4.6	0.7	7.6
REG. NBA TOTALS	684	—	21339	3906	9641	.405	—	—	—	2372	3293	.720	—	—	7154	1618	2035	33	—	—	—	10184	10.5	2.4	14.9
REG. ABA TOTALS	127	—	2370	583	1326	.440	3	5	.600	276	350	.789	—	—	825	163	270	—	—	55	—	1445	6.5	1.3	11.4
NBA PLAYOFF TOTALS	25	—	782	130	333	.390	—	—	—	61	102	.598	—	—	246	60	82	2	—	—	—	321	9.8	2.4	12.8
ABA PLAYOFF TOTALS	23	—	476	132	262	.504	0	0	—	75	94	.798	—	—	136	38	68	—	—	16	—	339	5.9	1.7	14.7

SCOTT, WILLIE b. 1947 Ht. 6-5 Wt. 210 College—Alabama State

SEASON—TEAM	G	GS	MIN	FGM	FGA	PCT	3FGM	3FGA	PCT	FTM	FTA	PCT	O-RB	D-RB	TOT	AST	PF	DQ	STL	TO	BLK	PTS	RPG	APG	PPG
69-70—Dallas (A)	8	—	51	6	15	.400	0	0	—	1	6	.167	—	—	4	2	16	0	—	—	—	—	13	0.5	0.3	1.6
REG. ABA TOTALS	8	—	51	6	15	.400	0	0	—	1	6	.167	—	—	4	2	16	0	—	—	—	—	13	0.5	0.3	1.6

SCRANTON, PAUL EARL JR. b. April 30, 1944 Ht. 6-5 Wt. 230 College—Pomona State

SEASON—TEAM	G	GS	MIN	FGM	FGA	PCT	3FGM	3FGA	PCT	FTM	FTA	PCT	O-RB	D-RB	TOT	AST	PF	DQ	STL	TO	BLK	PTS	RPG	APG	PPG
67-68—Anaheim (A)	5	—	41	4	9	.444	0	0	—	1	4	.250	—	—	16	1	5	0	—	1	—	9	3.2	0.2	1.8
REG. ABA TOTALS	5	—	41	4	9	.444	0	0	—	1	4	.250	—	—	16	1	5	0	—	1	—	9	3.2	0.2	1.8

SCURRY, CAREY b. December 4, 1962 Ht. 6-7 Wt. 190 College—NE Oklahoma A&M/Long Island University

SEASON—TEAM	G	GS	MIN	FGM	FGA	PCT	3FGM	3FGA	PCT	FTM	FTA	PCT	O-RB	D-RB	TOT	AST	PF	DQ	STL	TO	BLK	PTS	RPG	APG	PPG
85-86—Utah	78	0	1168	142	301	.472	1	11	.091	78	126	.619	97	145	242	85	171	2	78	96	66	363	3.1	1.1	4.7
86-87—Utah	69	5	753	123	247	.498	4	14	.286	94	134	.701	97	101	198	57	124	1	55	56	54	344	2.9	0.8	5.0
87-88—Utah-N.Y.	33	0	455	55	118	.466	3	8	.375	27	39	.692	30	54	84	50	81	0	49	43	23	140	2.5	1.5	4.2
REG. SEASON TOTALS	180	5	2376	320	666	.480	8	33	.242	199	299	.666	224	300	524	192	376	3	182	195	143	847	2.9	1.1	4.7
PLAYOFF TOTALS	8	0	111	18	42	.429	1	4	.250	4	9	.444	17	13	30	3	22	0	5	4	9	41	3.8	0.4	5.1

SEALS, BRUCE A. b. June 18, 1953 Ht. 6-8½ Wt. 210 College—Xavier (La.)

SEASON—TEAM	G	GS	MIN	FGM	FGA	PCT	3FGM	3FGA	PCT	FTM	FTA	PCT	O-RB	D-RB	TOT	AST	PF	DQ	STL	TO	BLK	PTS	RPG	APG	PPG
73-74—Utah (A)	78	—	1358	229	605	.379	19	90	.211	68	108	.630	100	179	279	54	199	—	57	81	57	545	3.6	0.7	7.0
74-75—Utah (A)	35	—	371	60	142	.423	0	3	.000	20	26	.769	43	54	97	13	67	—	15	24	16	140	2.8	0.4	4.0
75-76—Seattle	81	—	2435	388	889	.436	—	—	—	181	267	.678	157	350	507	119	314	11	64	—	44	957	6.3	1.5	11.8
76-77—Seattle	81	—	1977	378	851	.444	—	—	—	138	195	.708	118	236	354	93	262	6	49	—	58	894	4.4	1.1	11.0
77-78—Seattle	73	—	1322	230	551	.417	—	—	—	111	175	.634	62	164	226	81	210	4	41	103	33	571	3.1	1.1	7.8
REG. NBA TOTALS	235	—	5734	996	2291	.435	—	—	—	430	637	.675	337	750	1087	293	786	21	154	103	135	2422	4.6	1.2	10.3
REG. ABA TOTALS	113	—	1729	289	747	.387	19	93	.204	88	134	.657	143	233	376	67	266	0	72	105	73	685	3.3	0.6	6.1
NBA PLAYOFF TOTALS	15	—	273	42	105	.400	—	—	—	21	33	.636	22	34	56	11	36	0	7	6	8	105	3.7	0.7	7.0
ABA PLAYOFF TOTALS	18	—	301	50	112	.446	2	10	.200	13	23	.565	28	35	63	14	48	0	7	17	4	115	3.5	0.8	6.4

SEALY, MALIK b. February 1, 1970 Ht. 6-8 Wt. 190 College—St. John's

SEASON—TEAM	G	GS	MIN	FGM	FGA	PCT	3FGM	3FGA	PCT	FTM	FTA	PCT	O-RB	D-RB	TOT	AST	PF	DQ	STL	TO	BLK	PTS	RPG	APG	PPG
92-93—Indiana	58	2	672	136	319	.426	7	31	.226	51	74	.689	60	52	112	47	74	0	36	58	7	330	1.9	0.8	5.7
93-94—Indiana	43	5	623	111	274	.405	4	16	.250	59	87	.678	43	75	118	48	84	0	31	51	8	285	2.7	1.1	6.6
REG. SEASON TOTALS	101	7	1295	247	593	.417	11	47	.234	110	161	.683	103	127	230	95	158	0	67	109	15	615	2.3	0.9	6.1
PLAYOFF TOTALS	3	0	18	0	5	.000	0	1	.000	2	2	1.000	2	0	2	—	1	0	1	0	0	2	0.7	0.0	0.7

SEARCY, EDWIN (Ed) b. April 17, 1952 Ht. 6-6½ Wt. 210 College—St. John's

SEASON—TEAM	G	GS	MIN	FGM	FGA	PCT	3FGM	3FGA	PCT	FTM	FTA	PCT	O-RB	D-RB	TOT	AST	PF	DQ	STL	TO	BLK	PTS	RPG	APG	PPG
75-76—Boston	4	—	12	2	6	.333	—	—	—	2	2	1.000	0	0	0	1	4	0	0	—	0	6	0.0	0.3	1.5
REG. SEASON TOTALS	4	—	12	2	6	.333	—	—	—	2	2	1.000	0	0	0	1	4	0	0	—	0	6	0.0	0.3	1.5

SEARS, KENNETH ROBERT (Ken, Big Cat) b. August 17, 1933 Ht. 6-9 Wt. 200 College—Cal State-Santa Clara

SEASON—TEAM	G	GS	MIN	FGM	FGA	PCT	3FGM	3FGA	PCT	FTM	FTA	PCT	O-RB	D-RB	TOT	AST	PF	DQ	STL	TO	BLK	PTS	RPG	APG	PPG
55-56—New York	70	—	2069	319	728	.438	—	—	—	258	324	.796	—	—	616	114	201	4	—	—	—	896	8.8	1.6	12.8
56-57—New York	72	—	2516	343	821	.418	—	—	—	383	485	.790	—	—	614	101	226	2	—	—	—	1069	8.5	1.4	14.8
57-58—New York	72	—	2685	445	1014	.439	—	—	—	452	550	.822	—	—	785	126	251	7	—	—	—	1342	10.9	1.8	18.6
58-59—New York	71	—	2498	491	1002	.490	—	—	—	506	588	.861	—	—	658	136	237	6	—	—	—	1488	9.3	1.9	21.0
59-60—New York	64	—	2099	412	863	.477	—	—	—	363	418	.868	—	—	876	127	191	2	—	—	—	1187	13.7	2.0	18.5
60-61—New York	52	—	1396	241	568	.424	—	—	—	268	325	.825	—	—	293	102	165	6	—	—	—	750	5.6	2.0	14.4
62-63—N.Y.-S.F.	77	—	1141	161	304	.530	—	—	—	131	168	.780	—	—	206	95	128	0	—	—	—	453	2.7	1.2	5.9
63-64—San Francisco	51	—	519	53	120	.442	—	—	—	64	79	.810	—	—	94	42	71	0	—	—	—	170	1.8	0.8	3.3
REG. SEASON TOTALS	529	—	14923	2465	5420	.455	—	—	—	2425	2937	.826	—	—	4142	843	1470	27	—	—	—	7355	7.8	1.6	13.9
PLAYOFF TOTALS	9	—	88	16	37	.432	—	—	—	13	15	.867	—	—	29	9	10	0	—	—	—	45	3.2	1.0	5.0
ALL-STAR TOTALS	2	—	40	9	17	.529	—	—	—	9	10	.900	—	—	9	1	5	0	—	—	—	27	4.5	0.5	13.5

SEE, MARSHALL WAYNE (Wayne) b. November 3, 1923 Ht. 6-3 Wt. 190 College—Northern Arizona

SEASON—TEAM	G	GS	MIN	FGM	FGA	PCT	3FGM	3FGA	PCT	FTM	FTA	PCT	O-RB	D-RB	TOT	AST	PF	DQ	STL	TO	BLK	PTS	RPG	APG	PPG
49-50—Waterloo	61	—	—	113	303	.373	—	—	—	94	135	.696	—	—	—	143	147	—	—	—	—	320	—	2.3	5.2
REG. SEASON TOTALS	61	—	—	113	303	.373	—	—	—	94	135	.696	—	—	—	143	147	—	—	—	—	320	—	2.3	5.2

SEIKALY, RONY F. b. May 10, 1965 Ht. 6-11 Wt. 250 College—Syracuse

SEASON—TEAM	G	GS	MIN	FGM	FGA	PCT	3FGM	3FGA	PCT	FTM	FTA	PCT	O-RB	D-RB	TOT	AST	PF	DQ	STL	TO	BLK	PTS	RPG	APG	PPG
88-89—Miami	78	62	1962	333	744	.448	1	4	.250	181	354	.511	204	345	549	55	258	8	46	200	96	848	7.0	0.7	10.9
89-90—Miami	74	72	2409	486	968	.502	0	1	.000	256	431	.594	253	513	766	78	258	8	78	236	124	1228	10.4	1.1	16.6
90-91—Miami	64	59	2171	395	822	.481	2	6	.333	258	417	.619	207	502	709	95	213	2	51	205	86	1050	11.1	1.5	16.4
91-92—Miami	79	78	2800	463	947	.489	0	3	.000	370	505	.733	307	627	934	109	278	2	40	216	121	1296	11.8	1.4	16.4
92-93—Miami	72	64	2456	417	868	.480	1	8	.125	397	540	.735	259	587	846	100	260	3	38	203	83	1232	11.8	1.4	17.1
93-94—Miami	72	60	2410	392	803	.488	0	2	.000	304	422	.720	244	496	740	136	279	8	59	195	100	1088	10.3	1.9	15.1
REG. SEASON TOTALS	439	395	14208	2486	5152	.483	4	24	.167	1766	2669	.662	1474	3070	4544	573	1546	31	312	1255	610	6742	10.4	1.3	15.4
PLAYOFF TOTALS	8	6	282	33	67	.493	0	0	—	37	55	.673	30	47	77	12	37	1	5	20	12	103	9.6	1.5	12.9

SELBO, GLEN L. b. March 29, 1926 Ht. 6-3 Wt. 195 College—Western Michigan/Michigan/Wisconsin

SEASON—TEAM	G	GS	MIN	FGM	FGA	PCT	3FGM	3FGA	PCT	FTM	FTA	PCT	O-RB	D-RB	TOT	AST	PF	DQ	STL	TO	BLK	PTS	RPG	APG	PPG
47-48—Oshkosh (N)	59	—	—	157	—	—	—	—	—	62	100	.620	—	—	—	—	85	—	—	—	—	376	—	—	6.4
48-49—Oshkosh (N)	60	—	—	119	—	—	—	—	—	77	114	.675	—	—	—	—	94	—	—	—	—	315	—	—	5.3
49-50—Sheboygan	13	—	—	10	51	.196	—	—	—	22	29	.759	—	—	—	23	15	—	—	—	—	42	—	1.8	3.2
REG. NBA TOTALS	13	—	—	10	51	.196	—	—	—	22	29	.759	—	—	—	23	15	—	—	—	—	42	—	1.8	3.2
REG. NBL TOTALS	119	—	—	276	—	—	—	—	—	139	214	.650	—	—	—	—	179	—	—	—	—	691	—	—	5.8
NBL PLAYOFF TOTALS	4	—	—	5	—	—	—	—	—	5	6	.833	—	—	—	—	12	—	—	—	—	15	—	—	3.8

SELLERS, BRADLEY DONN (Brad) b. December 17, 1962 Ht. 7-0 Wt. 220 College—Wisconsin/Ohio State

SEASON—TEAM	G	GS	MIN	FGM	FGA	PCT	3FGM	3FGA	PCT	FTM	FTA	PCT	O-RB	D-RB	TOT	AST	PF	DQ	STL	TO	BLK	PTS	RPG	APG	PPG
86-87—Chicago	80	17	1751	276	606	.455	2	10	.200	126	173	.728	155	218	373	102	194	1	44	84	68	680	4.7	1.3	8.5
87-88—Chicago	82	76	2212	326	714	.457	1	7	.143	124	157	.790	107	143	250	141	174	0	34	91	66	777	3.0	1.7	9.5
88-89—Chicago	80	25	1732	231	476	.485	3	6	.500	86	101	.851	85	142	227	99	176	2	35	72	69	551	2.8	1.2	6.9
89-90—Seattle-Minn.	59	0	700	103	254	.406	0	5	.000	58	73	.795	39	50	89	33	74	1	17	46	22	264	1.5	0.6	4.5
91-92—Detroit	43	1	226	41	88	.466	0	1	.000	20	26	.769	15	27	42	14	20	0	1	15	10	102	1.0	0.3	2.4
92-93—Detroit-Minn.	54	4	533	49	130	.377	0	1	.000	37	39	.949	27	56	83	46	40	0	6	27	11	135	1.5	0.9	2.5
REG. SEASON TOTALS	398	123	7154	1026	2268	.452	6	30	.200	451	569	.793	428	636	1064	435	678	4	137	335	246	2509	2.7	1.1	6.3
PLAYOFF TOTALS	28	4	402	45	124	.363	0	0	—	30	34	.882	27	32	59	28	47	0	5	12	12	120	2.1	1.0	4.3

SELLERS, PHILLIP JR. (Phil) b. November 20, 1953 Ht. 6-4 Wt. 195 College—Rutgers

SEASON—TEAM	G	GS	MIN	FGM	FGA	PCT	3FGM	3FGA	PCT	FTM	FTA	PCT	O-RB	D-RB	TOT	AST	PF	DQ	STL	TO	BLK	PTS	RPG	APG	PPG
76-77—Detroit	44	—	329	73	190	.384	—	—	—	52	72	.722	19	22	41	25	56	0	22	—	0	198	0.9	0.6	4.5
REG. SEASON TOTALS	44	—	329	73	190	.384	—	—	—	52	72	.722	19	22	41	25	56	0	22	—	0	198	0.9	0.6	4.5
PLAYOFF TOTALS	1	—	6	1	4	.250	—	—	—	1	4	.250	1	1	2	—	2	0	0	—	0	3	2.0	0.0	3.0

SELTZ, ROLLAND A. (**Rollie**) b. January 25, 1924   Ht. 5-10½   Wt. 170   College—Hamline

SEASON—TEAM	G	GS	MIN	FGM	FGA	PCT	3FGM	3FGA	PCT	FTM	FTA	PCT	O-RB	D-RB	TOT	AST	PF	DQ	STL	TO	BLK	PTS	RPG	APG	PPG
46-47—Anderson (N)	41	—	—	123	—	—	—	—	—	104	143	.727	—	—	—	—	97	—	—	—	—	350	—	—	8.5
47-48—Anderson (N)	59	—	—	118	—	—	—	—	—	90	119	.756	—	—	—	—	110	—	—	—	—	326	—	—	5.5
48-49—Waterloo (N)	62	—	—	188	—	—	—	—	—	127	174	.730	—	—	—	—	139	—	—	—	—	503	—	—	8.1
49-50—Anderson	34	—	—	93	309	.301	—	—	—	80	104	.769	—	—	—	64	72	—	—	—	—	266	—	1.9	7.8
REG. NBA TOTALS	34	—	—	93	309	.301	—	—	—	80	104	.769	—	—	—	64	72	—	—	—	—	266	—	1.9	7.8
REG. NBL TOTALS	162	—	—	429	—	—	—	—	—	321	436	.736	—	—	—	—	346	—	—	—	—	1179	—	—	7.3
NBL PLAYOFF TOTALS	6	—	—	11	—	—	—	—	—	4	4	1.000	—	—	—	—	6	—	—	—	—	26	—	—	4.3

SELVAGE, LESTER REVELL (**Les**) b. March 7, 1943   Ht. 6-1   Wt. 175   College—NE Missouri State

SEASON—TEAM	G	GS	MIN	FGM	FGA	PCT	3FGM	3FGA	PCT	FTM	FTA	PCT	O-RB	D-RB	TOT	AST	PF	DQ	STL	TO	BLK	PTS	RPG	APG	PPG
67-68—Anaheim (A)	78	—	2432	371	1044	.355	147	461	.319	206	278	.741	—	—	217	247	239	3	—	195	—	1095	2.8	3.2	14.0
69-70—Los Angeles (A)	4	—	17	4	14	.286	0	4	.000	0	0	—	—	—	2	5	2	0	—	—	—	8	0.5	1.3	2.0
REG. ABA TOTALS	82	—	2449	375	1058	.354	147	465	.316	206	278	.741	—	—	219	252	241	3	—	195	—	1103	2.7	3.1	13.5
ABA PLAYOFF TOTALS	1	—	1	0	0	—	0	0	—	0	0	—	—	—	0	0	0	—	—	—	—	0	0.0	0.0	0.0

SELVY, FRANKLIN DELANO (**Frank**) b. November 9, 1932   Ht. 6-2½   Wt. 180   College—Furman

SEASON—TEAM	G	GS	MIN	FGM	FGA	PCT	3FGM	3FGA	PCT	FTM	FTA	PCT	O-RB	D-RB	TOT	AST	PF	DQ	STL	TO	BLK	PTS	RPG	APG	PPG
54-55—Balt.-Milw.	71	—	2668	452	1195	.378	—	—	—	444	610	.728	—	—	394	245	230	3	—	—	—	1348	5.5	3.5	19.0
55-56—St. Louis	17	—	444	67	183	.366	—	—	—	53	71	.746	—	—	54	35	38	1	—	—	—	187	3.2	2.1	11.0
57-58—St. L.-Minn.	38	—	426	44	167	.263	—	—	—	47	77	.610	—	—	88	35	44	0	—	—	—	135	2.3	0.9	3.6
58-59—New York	68	—	1448	233	605	.385	—	—	—	201	262	.767	—	—	248	96	113	1	—	—	—	667	3.6	1.4	9.8
59-60—Syr.-Minn.	62	—	1308	205	521	.393	—	—	—	153	208	.736	—	—	175	111	101	1	—	—	—	563	2.8	1.8	9.1
60-61—Los Angeles	77	—	2153	311	767	.405	—	—	—	210	279	.753	—	—	299	246	219	3	—	—	—	832	3.9	3.2	10.8
61-62—Los Angeles	79	—	2806	433	1032	.420	—	—	—	298	404	.738	—	—	412	381	232	0	—	—	—	1164	5.2	4.8	14.7
62-63—Los Angeles	80	—	2369	317	747	.424	—	—	—	192	269	.714	—	—	289	281	149	0	—	—	—	826	3.6	3.5	10.3
63-64—Los Angeles	73	—	1286	160	423	.378	—	—	—	78	122	.639	—	—	139	149	115	1	—	—	—	398	1.9	2.0	5.5
REG. SEASON TOTALS	565	—	14908	2222	5640	.394	—	—	—	1676	2302	.728	—	—	2098	1579	1241	10	—	—	—	6120	3.7	2.8	10.8
PLAYOFF TOTALS	52	—	1608	219	554	.395	—	—	—	151	192	.786	—	—	226	189	147	1	—	—	—	589	4.3	3.6	11.3
ALL-STAR TOTALS	2	—	30	2	10	.200	—	—	—	3	4	.750	—	—	7	2	5	0	—	—	—	7	3.5	1.0	3.5

SEMINOFF, JAMES (**Jim**) b. September 1, 1922   Ht. 6-2   Wt. 190   College—USC

SEASON—TEAM	G	GS	MIN	FGM	FGA	PCT	3FGM	3FGA	PCT	FTM	FTA	PCT	O-RB	D-RB	TOT	AST	PF	DQ	STL	TO	BLK	PTS	RPG	APG	PPG
46-47—Chicago	60	—	—	184	586	.314	—	—	—	71	130	.546	—	—	—	63	155	—	—	—	—	439	—	1.1	7.3
47-48—Chicago	48	—	—	113	381	.297	—	—	—	73	105	.695	—	—	—	89	105	—	—	—	—	299	—	1.9	6.2
48-49—Boston	58	—	—	153	487	.314	—	—	—	151	219	.689	—	—	—	229	195	—	—	—	—	457	—	3.9	7.9
49-50—Boston	65	—	—	85	283	.300	—	—	—	142	188	.755	—	—	—	249	154	—	—	—	—	312	—	3.8	4.8
REG. SEASON TOTALS	231	—	—	535	1737	.308	—	—	—	437	642	.681	—	—	—	630	609	—	—	—	—	1507	—	2.7	6.5
PLAYOFF TOTALS	16	—	—	47	194	.242	—	—	—	30	45	.667	—	—	—	16	48	1	—	—	—	124	0.0	1.0	7.8

SENESKY, GEORGE LAWRENCE b. April 4, 1922   Ht. 6-2   Wt. 180   College—St. Joseph's (Pa.)

SEASON—TEAM	G	GS	MIN	FGM	FGA	PCT	3FGM	3FGA	PCT	FTM	FTA	PCT	O-RB	D-RB	TOT	AST	PF	DQ	STL	TO	BLK	PTS	RPG	APG	PPG
46-47—Philadelphia	58	—	—	142	531	.267	—	—	—	82	124	.661	—	—	—	34	83	—	—	—	—	366	—	0.6	6.3
47-48—Philadelphia	47	—	—	158	570	.277	—	—	—	98	147	.667	—	—	—	52	90	—	—	—	—	414	—	1.1	8.8
48-49—Philadelphia	60	—	—	138	516	.267	—	—	—	111	152	.730	—	—	—	233	133	—	—	—	—	387	—	3.9	6.5
49-50—Philadelphia	68	—	—	227	709	.320	—	—	—	157	223	.704	—	—	—	264	164	—	—	—	—	611	—	3.9	9.0
50-51—Philadelphia	65	—	—	249	703	.354	—	—	—	181	238	.761	—	—	326	342	144	1	—	—	—	679	5.0	5.3	10.4
51-52—Philadelphia	57	—	1925	164	454	.361	—	—	—	146	194	.753	—	—	232	280	123	0	—	—	—	474	4.1	4.9	8.3
52-53—Philadelphia	69	—	2336	160	485	.330	—	—	—	93	146	.637	—	—	254	264	166	1	—	—	—	413	3.7	3.8	6.0
53-54—Philadelphia	58	—	771	41	119	.345	—	—	—	29	53	.547	—	—	66	84	79	—	—	—	—	111	1.1	1.4	1.9
REG. SEASON TOTALS	482	—	5032	1279	4087	.313	—	—	—	897	1277	.702	—	—	878	1553	982	2	—	—	—	3455	3.5	3.2	7.2
PLAYOFF TOTALS	32	—	120	125	391	.320	—	—	—	72	103	.699	—	—	19	51	71	0	—	—	—	322	3.8	1.6	10.1

SEWELL, TOM b. March 11, 1962   Ht. 6-5   Wt. 185   College—Amarillo/Lamar

SEASON—TEAM	G	GS	MIN	FGM	FGA	PCT	3FGM	3FGA	PCT	FTM	FTA	PCT	O-RB	D-RB	TOT	AST	PF	DQ	STL	TO	BLK	PTS	RPG	APG	PPG
84-85—Washington	21	0	87	9	36	.250	0	2	.000	2	4	.500	2	2	4	6	13	0	3	7	1	20	0.2	0.3	1.0
REG. SEASON TOTALS	21	0	87	9	36	.250	0	2	.000	2	4	.500	2	2	4	6	13	0	3	7	1	20	0.2	0.3	1.0

SEYMOUR, PAUL NORMAN b. January 30, 1928 Ht. 6-2 Wt. 180 College—Toledo

SEASON—TEAM	G	GS	MIN	FGM	FGA	PCT	3FGM	3FGA	PCT	FTM	FTA	PCT	O-RB	D-RB	TOT	AST	PF	DQ	STL	TO	BLK	PTS	RPG	APG	PPG
46-47—Toledo (N)	33	—	—	41	—	—	—	—	—	17	30	.567	—	—	—	—	—	—	—	—	—	99	—	—	3.0
47-48—Syracuse (N)	30	—	—	79	—	—	—	—	—	47	64	.734	—	—	—	—	54	—	—	—	—	205	—	—	6.8
47-48—Baltimore	22	—	—	27	101	.267	—	—	—	22	37	.595	—	—	—	6	34	—	—	—	—	76	—	0.3	3.5
48-49—Syracuse (N)	63	—	—	120	—	—	—	—	—	70	106	.660	—	—	—	—	150	—	—	—	—	310	—	—	4.9
49-50—Syracuse	62	—	—	175	524	.334	—	—	—	126	176	.716	—	—	—	189	157	—	—	—	—	476	—	3.0	7.7
50-51—Syracuse	51	—	—	125	385	.325	—	—	—	117	159	.736	—	—	194	187	138	0	—	—	—	367	3.8	3.7	7.2
51-52—Syracuse	66	—	2209	206	615	.335	—	—	—	186	245	.759	—	—	225	220	165	4	—	—	—	598	3.4	3.3	9.1
52-53—Syracuse	67	—	2684	306	798	.383	—	—	—	340	416	.817	—	—	246	294	210	3	—	—	—	952	3.7	4.4	14.2
53-54—Syracuse	71	—	2727	316	838	.377	—	—	—	299	368	.813	—	—	291	364	187	2	—	—	—	931	4.1	5.1	13.1
54-55—Syracuse	72	—	2950	375	1036	.362	—	—	—	300	370	.811	—	—	309	483	137	0	—	—	—	1050	4.3	6.7	14.6
55-56—Syracuse	57	—	1826	227	670	.339	—	—	—	188	233	.807	—	—	152	276	130	1	—	—	—	642	2.7	4.8	11.3
56-57—Syracuse	65	—	1235	143	442	.324	—	—	—	101	123	.821	—	—	130	193	91	0	—	—	—	387	2.0	3.0	6.0
57-58—Syracuse	64	—	763	107	315	.340	—	—	—	53	63	.841	—	—	107	93	88	0	—	—	—	267	1.7	1.5	4.2
58-59—Syracuse	21	—	266	32	98	.327	—	—	—	26	29	.897	—	—	39	36	25	0	—	—	—	90	1.9	1.7	4.3
59-60—Syracuse	4	—	7	0	4	.000	—	—	—	0	0	—	—	—	1	0	1	0	—	—	—	0	0.3	0.0	0.0
REG. NBA TOTALS	622	—	14667	2039	5826	.350	—	—	—	1758	2219	.792	—	—	1694	2341	1363	10	—	—	—	5836	3.1	3.8	9.4
REG. NBL TOTALS	126	—	—	240	—	—	—	—	—	134	200	.670	—	—	—	—	204	—	—	—	—	614	—	—	4.9
NBA PLAYOFF TOTALS	66	—	1652	208	632	.329	—	—	—	234	284	.824	—	—	164	257	185	5	—	—	—	650	3.0	3.9	9.8
NBL PLAYOFF TOTALS	14	—	—	36	—	—	—	—	—	19	26	.731	—	—	—	—	35	—	—	—	—	91	—	—	6.5
NBA ALL-STAR TOTALS	3	—	49	7	17	.412	—	—	—	7	8	.875	—	—	7	6	4	0	—	—	—	21	2.3	2.0	7.0

SHABACK, NICHOLAS (Nick) b. September 10, 1918 Ht. 5-11 Wt. 180 College—None

SEASON—TEAM	G	GS	MIN	FGM	FGA	PCT	3FGM	3FGA	PCT	FTM	FTA	PCT	O-RB	D-RB	TOT	AST	PF	DQ	STL	TO	BLK	PTS	RPG	APG	PPG
46-47—Cleveland	53	—	—	102	385	.265	—	—	—	38	53	.717	—	—	—	29	75	—	—	—	—	242	—	0.5	4.6
REG. SEASON TOTALS	53	—	—	102	385	.265	—	—	—	38	53	.717	—	—	—	29	75	—	—	—	—	242	—	0.5	4.6
PLAYOFF TOTALS	3	—	—	6	22	.273	—	—	—	3	5	.600	—	—	—	—	6	—	—	—	—	15	—	0.0	5.0

SHACKELFORD, RAY LYNN (Lynn) b. August 27, 1947 Ht. 6-5 Wt. 195 College—UCLA

SEASON—TEAM	G	GS	MIN	FGM	FGA	PCT	3FGM	3FGA	PCT	FTM	FTA	PCT	O-RB	D-RB	TOT	AST	PF	DQ	STL	TO	BLK	PTS	RPG	APG	PPG
69-70—Miami (A)	22	—	183	22	72	.306	4	13	.308	10	13	.769	—	—	27	11	34	0	—	—	—	58	1.2	0.5	2.6
REG. ABA TOTALS	22	—	183	22	72	.306	4	13	.308	10	13	.769	—	—	27	11	34	0	—	—	—	58	1.2	0.5	2.6

SHACKLEFORD, CHARLES EDWARD b. April 22, 1966 Ht. 6-10 Wt. 225 College—North Carolina State

SEASON—TEAM	G	GS	MIN	FGM	FGA	PCT	3FGM	3FGA	PCT	FTM	FTA	PCT	O-RB	D-RB	TOT	AST	PF	DQ	STL	TO	BLK	PTS	RPG	APG	PPG
88-89—New Jersey	60	0	484	83	168	.494	0	1	.000	21	42	.500	50	103	153	21	71	0	15	27	18	187	2.6	0.4	3.1
89-90—New Jersey	70	37	1557	247	535	.462	0	1	.000	79	115	.687	180	299	479	56	183	1	40	116	35	573	6.8	0.8	8.2
91-92—Philadelphia	72	62	1399	205	422	.486	0	1	.000	63	95	.663	145	270	415	46	205	3	38	62	51	473	5.8	0.6	6.6
92-93—Philadelphia	48	0	568	80	164	.488	0	2	.000	31	49	.633	65	140	205	26	92	1	13	36	25	191	4.3	0.5	4.0
REG. SEASON TOTALS	250	99	4008	615	1289	.477	0	5	.000	194	301	.645	440	812	1252	149	551	5	106	241	129	1424	5.0	0.6	5.7

SHAEFFER, CARL EDGEL b. October 25, 1924 d. October 25, 1974 Ht. 6-3½ Wt. 185 College—Alabama

SEASON—TEAM	G	GS	MIN	FGM	FGA	PCT	3FGM	3FGA	PCT	FTM	FTA	PCT	O-RB	D-RB	TOT	AST	PF	DQ	STL	TO	BLK	PTS	RPG	APG	PPG
49-50—Indianapolis	43	—	—	59	160	.369	—	—	—	32	57	.561	—	—	—	40	103	—	—	—	—	150	—	0.9	3.5
50-51—Indianapolis	10	—	—	6	22	.273	—	—	—	3	3	1.000	—	—	10	6	15	0	—	—	—	15	1.0	0.6	1.5
REG. SEASON TOTALS	53	—	—	65	182	.357	—	—	—	35	60	.583	—	—	10	46	118	0	—	—	—	165	1.0	0.9	3.1
PLAYOFF TOTALS	6	—	—	7	21	.333	—	—	—	7	14	.500	—	—	—	7	20	1	—	—	—	21	—	1.2	3.5

SHAFFER, LEE PHILIP II b. February 23, 1939 Ht. 6-7 Wt. 220 College—North Carolina

SEASON—TEAM	G	GS	MIN	FGM	FGA	PCT	3FGM	3FGA	PCT	FTM	FTA	PCT	O-RB	D-RB	TOT	AST	PF	DQ	STL	TO	BLK	PTS	RPG	APG	PPG
61-62—Syracuse	75	—	2083	514	1180	.436	—	—	—	239	310	.771	—	—	511	99	266	6	—	—	—	1267	6.8	1.3	16.9
62-63—Syracuse	80	—	2392	597	1393	.429	—	—	—	294	375	.784	—	—	524	97	249	5	—	—	—	1488	6.6	1.2	18.6
63-64—Philadelphia	41	—	1013	217	587	.370	—	—	—	102	133	.767	—	—	205	36	116	1	—	—	—	536	5.0	0.9	13.1
REG. SEASON TOTALS	196	—	5488	1328	3160	.420	—	—	—	635	818	.776	—	—	1240	232	631	12	—	—	—	3291	6.3	1.2	16.8
PLAYOFF TOTALS	13	—	387	99	238	.416	—	—	—	49	63	.778	—	—	82	15	41	0	—	—	—	247	6.3	1.2	19.0
ALL-STAR TOTALS	1	—	19	6	13	.462	—	—	—	0	0	—	—	—	1	1	3	0	—	—	—	12	1.0	1.0	12.0

SHANNON, EARL F. b. November 23, 1921 Ht. 5-11 Wt. 170 College—Rhode Island

SEASON—TEAM	G	GS	MIN	FGM	FGA	PCT	3FGM	3FGA	PCT	FTM	FTA	PCT	O-RB	D-RB	TOT	AST	PF	DQ	STL	TO	BLK	PTS	RPG	APG	PPG
46-47—Providence	57	—	—	245	722	.339	—	—	—	197	348	.566	—	—	—	84	169	—	—	—	—	687	—	1.5	12.1
47-48—Providence	45	—	—	123	469	.262	—	—	—	116	183	.634	—	—	—	49	106	—	—	—	—	362	—	1.1	8.0
48-49—Prov.-Boston	32	—	—	34	127	.268	—	—	—	39	58	.672	—	—	—	44	33	—	—	—	—	107	—	1.4	3.3
REG. SEASON TOTALS	134	—	—	402	1318	.305	—	—	—	352	589	.598	—	—	—	177	308	—	—	—	—	1156	—	1.3	8.6

SHANNON, HOWARD PAYNE (**Howie**) b. June 10, 1923 Ht. 6-2 Wt. 175 College—Kansas State/North Texas

SEASON—TEAM	G	GS	MIN	FGM	FGA	PCT	3FGM	3FGA	PCT	FTM	FTA	PCT	O-RB	D-RB	TOT	AST	PF	DQ	STL	TO	BLK	PTS	RPG	APG	PPG
48-49—Providence	55	—	—	292	802	.364	—	—	—	152	189	.804	—	—	—	125	154	—	—	—	—	736	—	2.3	13.4
49-50—Boston	67	—	—	222	646	.344	—	—	—	143	182	.786	—	—	—	174	148	—	—	—	—	587	—	2.6	8.8
REG. SEASON TOTALS	122	—	—	514	1448	.355	—	—	—	295	371	.795	—	—	—	299	302	—	—	—	—	1323	—	2.5	10.8

SHARE, CHARLES EDWARD (**Charlie**) b. March 14, 1927 Ht. 6-11½ Wt. 245 College—Bowling Green State

SEASON—TEAM	G	GS	MIN	FGM	FGA	PCT	3FGM	3FGA	PCT	FTM	FTA	PCT	O-RB	D-RB	TOT	AST	PF	DQ	STL	TO	BLK	PTS	RPG	APG	PPG
51-52—Fort Wayne	63	—	882	76	236	.322	—	—	—	96	155	.619	—	—	331	66	141	9	—	—	—	248	5.3	1.0	3.9
52-53—Fort Wayne	67	—	1044	91	254	.358	—	—	—	172	234	.735	—	—	373	74	213	13	—	—	—	354	5.6	1.1	5.3
53-54—Ft. Wayne-Milw.	68	—	1576	188	493	.381	—	—	—	188	275	.684	—	—	555	80	210	8	—	—	—	564	8.2	1.2	8.3
54-55—Milwaukee	69	—	1685	235	577	.407	—	—	—	351	492	.713	—	—	684	84	273	17	—	—	—	821	9.9	1.2	11.9
55-56—St. Louis	72	—	1975	315	733	.430	—	—	—	346	498	.695	—	—	774	131	318	13	—	—	—	976	10.8	1.8	13.6
56-57—St. Louis	72	—	1673	235	535	.439	—	—	—	269	393	.684	—	—	642	79	269	15	—	—	—	739	8.9	1.1	10.3
57-58—St. Louis	72	—	1824	216	545	.396	—	—	—	190	293	.648	—	—	749	130	279	15	—	—	—	622	10.4	1.8	8.6
58-59—St. Louis	72	—	1713	147	381	.386	—	—	—	139	184	.755	—	—	657	103	261	6	—	—	—	433	9.1	1.4	6.0
59-60—St. L.-Minn.	41	—	651	59	151	.391	—	—	—	53	80	.663	—	—	221	62	142	9	—	—	—	171	5.4	1.5	4.2
REG. SEASON TOTALS	596	—	13023	1562	3905	.400	—	—	—	1804	2604	.693	—	—	4986	809	2106	105	—	—	—	4928	8.4	1.4	8.3
PLAYOFF TOTALS	54	—	1076	124	285	.435	—	—	—	135	205	.659	—	—	352	59	224	17	—	—	—	383	6.5	1.1	7.1

SHARMAN, WILLIAM WALTON (**Bill**) b. May 25, 1926 Ht. 6-1 Wt. 190 College—USC

SEASON—TEAM	G	GS	MIN	FGM	FGA	PCT	3FGM	3FGA	PCT	FTM	FTA	PCT	O-RB	D-RB	TOT	AST	PF	DQ	STL	TO	BLK	PTS	RPG	APG	PPG
50-51—Washington	31	—	—	141	361	.391	—	—	—	96	108	.889	—	—	96	39	86	3	—	—	—	378	3.1	1.3	12.2
51-52—Boston	63	—	1389	244	628	.389	—	—	—	183	213	.859	—	—	221	151	181	3	—	—	—	671	3.5	2.4	10.7
52-53—Boston	71	—	2333	403	925	.436	—	—	—	341	401	.850	—	—	288	191	240	7	—	—	—	1147	4.1	2.7	16.2
53-54—Boston	72	—	2467	412	915	.450	—	—	—	331	392	.844	—	—	255	229	211	4	—	—	—	1155	3.5	3.2	16.0
54-55—Boston	68	—	2453	453	1062	.427	—	—	—	347	387	.897	—	—	302	280	212	2	—	—	—	1253	4.4	4.1	18.4
55-56—Boston	72	—	2698	538	1229	.438	—	—	—	358	413	.867	—	—	259	339	197	1	—	—	—	1434	3.6	4.7	19.9
56-57—Boston	67	—	2403	516	1241	.416	—	—	—	381	421	.905	—	—	286	236	188	1	—	—	—	1413	4.3	3.5	21.1
57-58—Boston	63	—	2214	550	1297	.424	—	—	—	302	338	.893	—	—	295	167	156	3	—	—	—	1402	4.7	2.7	22.3
58-59—Boston	72	—	2382	562	1377	.408	—	—	—	342	367	.932	—	—	292	179	173	1	—	—	—	1466	4.1	2.5	20.4
59-60—Boston	71	—	1916	559	1225	.456	—	—	—	252	291	.866	—	—	262	144	154	2	—	—	—	1370	3.7	2.0	19.3
60-61—Boston	61	—	1538	383	908	.422	—	—	—	210	228	.921	—	—	223	146	127	0	—	—	—	976	3.7	2.4	16.0
REG. SEASON TOTALS	711	—	21793	4761	11168	.426	—	—	—	3143	3559	.883	—	—	2779	2101	1925	27	—	—	—	12665	3.9	3.0	17.8
PLAYOFF TOTALS	78	—	2573	538	1262	.426	—	—	—	370	406	.911	—	—	285	201	220	6	—	—	—	1446	3.7	2.6	18.5
ALL-STAR TOTALS	8	—	194	40	104	.385	—	—	—	22	27	.815	—	—	31	16	16	0	—	—	—	102	3.9	2.0	12.8

SHASKY, JOHN PAUL b. July 31, 1964 Ht. 6-11½ Wt. 240 College—Minnesota

SEASON—TEAM	G	GS	MIN	FGM	FGA	PCT	3FGM	3FGA	PCT	FTM	FTA	PCT	O-RB	D-RB	TOT	AST	PF	DQ	STL	TO	BLK	PTS	RPG	APG	PPG
88-89—Miami	65	4	944	121	248	.488	0	2	.000	115	167	.689	96	136	232	22	94	0	14	46	13	357	3.6	0.3	5.5
89-90—Golden State	14	0	51	4	14	.286	0	0	—	2	6	.333	4	9	13	1	10	0	1	2	2	10	0.9	0.1	0.7
90-91—Dallas	57	0	510	51	116	.440	0	0	—	48	79	.608	58	76	134	11	75	0	14	27	20	150	2.4	0.2	2.6
REG. SEASON TOTALS	136	4	1505	176	378	.466	0	2	.000	165	252	.655	158	221	379	34	179	0	29	75	35	517	2.8	0.3	3.8

SHAVLIK, RONALD DEAN (**Ron**) b. December 4, 1933 d. June 27, 1983 Ht. 6-8 Wt. 200 College—North Carolina State

SEASON—TEAM	G	GS	MIN	FGM	FGA	PCT	3FGM	3FGA	PCT	FTM	FTA	PCT	O-RB	D-RB	TOT	AST	PF	DQ	STL	TO	BLK	PTS	RPG	APG	PPG
56-57—New York	7	—	72	4	22	.182	—	—	—	2	5	.400	—	—	22	0	12	0	—	—	—	10	3.1	0.0	1.4
57-58—New York	1	—	2	0	1	.000	—	—	—	0	0	—	—	—	1	0	0	0	—	—	—	0	1.0	0.0	0.0
REG. SEASON TOTALS	8	—	74	4	23	.174	—	—	—	2	5	.400	—	—	23	0	12	0	—	—	—	10	2.9	0.0	1.3

SHAW, BRIAN K. b. March 22, 1966 Ht. 6-6 Wt. 190 College—St. Mary's (Ca.)/Cal State-Santa Barbara

SEASON—TEAM	G	GS	MIN	FGM	FGA	PCT	3FGM	3FGA	PCT	FTM	FTA	PCT	O-RB	D-RB	TOT	AST	PF	DQ	STL	TO	BLK	PTS	RPG	APG	PPG
88-89—Boston	82	54	2301	297	686	.433	0	13	.000	109	132	.826	119	257	376	472	211	1	78	188	27	703	4.6	5.8	8.6
90-91—Boston	79	79	2772	442	942	.469	3	27	.111	204	249	.819	104	266	370	602	206	1	105	223	34	1091	4.7	7.6	13.8
91-92—Boston-Miami	63	26	1423	209	513	.407	5	23	.217	72	91	.791	50	154	204	250	115	0	57	99	22	495	3.2	4.0	7.9
92-93—Miami	68	45	1603	197	501	.393	43	130	.331	61	78	.782	70	187	257	235	163	2	48	96	19	498	3.8	3.5	7.3
93-94—Miami	77	52	2037	278	667	.417	73	216	.338	64	89	.719	104	246	350	385	195	1	71	173	21	693	4.5	5.0	9.0
REG. SEASON TOTALS	369	256	10136	1423	3309	.430	124	409	.303	510	639	.798	447	1110	1557	1944	890	5	359	779	123	3480	4.2	5.3	9.4
PLAYOFF TOTALS	22	22	637	99	214	.463	4	22	.182	45	59	.763	15	73	88	91	66	0	19	51	2	247	4.0	4.1	11.2

SHEA, ROBERT F. (**Bob**) b. September 11, 1924 Ht. 6-2 Wt. 195 College—Rhode Island

SEASON—TEAM	G	GS	MIN	FGM	FGA	PCT	3FGM	3FGA	PCT	FTM	FTA	PCT	O-RB	D-RB	TOT	AST	PF	DQ	STL	TO	BLK	PTS	RPG	APG	PPG
46-47—Providence	43	—	—	37	153	.242	—	—	—	19	33	.576	—	—	—	6	42	—	—	—	—	93	—	0.1	2.2
REG. SEASON TOTALS	43	—	—	37	153	.242	—	—	—	19	33	.576	—	—	—	6	42	—	—	—	—	93	—	0.1	2.2

SHEFFIELD, FREDERICK J. (Fred) b. November 5, 1923 Ht. 6-2 Wt. 165 College—Utah

SEASON—TEAM	G	GS	MIN	FGM	FGA	PCT	3FGM	3FGA	PCT	FTM	FTA	PCT	O-RB	D-RB	TOT	AST	PF	DQ	STL	TO	BLK	PTS	RPG	APG	PPG
46-47—Philadelphia	22	—		29	146	.199	—	—	—	16	26	.615	—	—		4	34	—	—	—	—	74	—	0.2	3.4
REG. SEASON TOTALS	22	—		29	146	.199	—	—	—	16	26	.615	—	—		4	34	—	—	—	—	74	—	0.2	3.4

SHELTON, CRAIG ANTHONY b. May 1, 1957 Ht. 6-7½ Wt. 210 College—Georgetown

SEASON—TEAM	G	GS	MIN	FGM	FGA	PCT	3FGM	3FGA	PCT	FTM	FTA	PCT	O-RB	D-RB	TOT	AST	PF	DQ	STL	TO	BLK	PTS	RPG	APG	PPG
80-81—Atlanta	55	—	586	100	219	.457	0	1	.000	35	58	.603	59	79	138	27	128	1	18	61	5	235	2.5	0.5	4.3
81-82—Atlanta	4	0	21	2	6	.333	0	0	—	1	2	.500	1	2	3	0	3	0	1	0	0	5	0.8	0.0	1.3
REG. SEASON TOTALS	59	0	607	102	225	.453	0	1	.000	36	60	.600	60	81	141	27	131	1	19	61	5	240	2.4	0.5	4.1

SHELTON, LONNIE JEWEL b. October 19, 1955 Ht. 6-8½ Wt. 240 College—Oregon State

SEASON—TEAM	G	GS	MIN	FGM	FGA	PCT	3FGM	3FGA	PCT	FTM	FTA	PCT	O-RB	D-RB	TOT	AST	PF	DQ	STL	TO	BLK	PTS	RPG	APG	PPG
76-77—New York Knicks	82	—	2104	398	836	.476	—	—	—	159	225	.707	220	413	633	149	363	10	125	—	98	955	7.7	1.8	11.6
77-78—New York	82	—	2319	508	988	.514	—	—	—	203	276	.736	204	376	580	195	350	11	109	228	112	1219	7.1	2.4	14.9
78-79—Seattle	76	—	2158	446	859	.519	—	—	—	131	189	.693	182	286	468	110	266	7	76	188	75	1023	6.2	1.4	13.5
79-80—Seattle	76	—	2243	425	802	.530	1	5	.200	184	241	.763	199	383	582	145	292	11	92	169	79	1035	7.7	1.9	13.6
80-81—Seattle	14	—	440	73	174	.420	0	0	—	36	55	.655	31	47	78	35	48	0	22	41	3	182	5.6	2.5	13.0
81-82—Seattle	81	81	2667	508	1046	.486	0	8	.000	188	240	.783	161	348	509	252	317	12	99	199	43	1204	6.3	3.1	14.9
82-83—Seattle	82	79	2572	437	915	.478	1	6	.167	141	187	.754	158	337	495	237	310	8	75	172	72	1016	6.0	2.9	12.4
83-84—Cleveland	79	78	2101	371	779	.476	1	5	.200	107	140	.764	140	241	381	179	279	9	76	165	55	850	4.8	2.3	10.8
84-85—Cleveland	57	14	1244	158	363	.435	0	5	.000	51	77	.662	82	185	267	96	187	3	44	74	18	367	4.7	1.7	6.4
85-86—Cleveland	44	1	682	92	188	.489	0	2	.000	14	16	.875	38	105	143	61	128	2	21	48	4	198	3.3	1.4	4.5
REG. SEASON TOTALS	673	253	18530	3416	6950	.492	3	31	.097	1214	1646	.738	1415	2721	4136	1459	2540	73	739	1284	559	8049	6.1	2.2	12.0
PLAYOFF TOTALS	52	10	1611	268	553	.485	0	4	.000	88	132	.667	157	256	413	101	228	10	52	110	43	624	7.9	1.9	12.0
ALL-STAR TOTALS	1	1	20	3	3	1.000	0	0	—	1	2	.500	4	5	9	1	4	0	1	2	0	7	9.0	1.0	7.0

SHEPHERD, BILLY L. b. November 18, 1949 Ht. 5-10 Wt. 165 College—Butler

SEASON—TEAM	G	GS	MIN	FGM	FGA	PCT	3FGM	3FGA	PCT	FTM	FTA	PCT	O-RB	D-RB	TOT	AST	PF	DQ	STL	TO	BLK	PTS	RPG	APG	PPG
72-73—Virginia (A)	16	—	68	7	35	.200	4	16	.250	9	10	.900	2	3	5	8	12	0	—	8	—	27	0.3	0.5	1.7
73-74—San Diego (A)	84	—	1738	200	530	.377	65	202	.322	42	66	.636	22	85	107	371	102	—	97	120	10	507	1.3	4.4	6.0
74-75—Memphis (A)	69	—	1315	161	386	.417	60	143	.420	52	72	.722	14	65	79	278	68	—	66	91	9	434	1.1	4.0	6.3
REG. ABA TOTALS	169	—	3121	368	951	.387	129	361	.357	103	148	.696	38	153	191	657	182	0	163	219	19	968	1.1	3.9	5.7
ABA PLAYOFF TOTALS	11	—	227	27	86	.314	11	39	.282	9	9	1.000	3	13	16	33	14	0	11	19	2	74	1.5	3.0	6.7

SHEPPARD, STEVE (Bear) b. March 21, 1954 Ht. 6-6 Wt. 215 College—Maryland

SEASON—TEAM	G	GS	MIN	FGM	FGA	PCT	3FGM	3FGA	PCT	FTM	FTA	PCT	O-RB	D-RB	TOT	AST	PF	DQ	STL	TO	BLK	PTS	RPG	APG	PPG
77-78—Chicago	64	—	698	119	262	.454	—	—	—	37	56	.661	67	64	131	43	72	0	14	46	3	275	2.0	0.7	4.3
78-79—Chicago-Detroit	42	—	279	36	76	.474	—	—	—	20	34	.588	25	22	47	19	26	0	8	25	1	92	1.1	0.5	2.2
REG. SEASON TOTALS	106	—	977	155	338	.459	—	—	—	57	90	.633	92	86	178	62	98	0	22	71	4	367	1.7	0.6	3.5

SHEROD, EDMUND b. September 13, 1959 Ht. 6-2 Wt. 170 College—Virginia Commonwealth

SEASON—TEAM	G	GS	MIN	FGM	FGA	PCT	3FGM	3FGA	PCT	FTM	FTA	PCT	O-RB	D-RB	TOT	AST	PF	DQ	STL	TO	BLK	PTS	RPG	APG	PPG
82-83—New York	64	37	1624	171	421	.406	1	13	.077	52	80	.650	43	106	149	311	112	2	96	104	14	395	2.3	4.9	6.2
REG. SEASON TOTALS	64	37	1624	171	421	.406	1	13	.077	52	80	.650	43	106	149	311	112	2	96	104	14	395	2.3	4.9	6.2
PLAYOFF TOTALS	6	0	23	1	5	.200	0	0	—	0	0	—	1	1	2	4	3	0	4	1	0	2	0.3	0.7	0.3

SHIPP, CHARLES WILLIAM (Charley, Jo-Jo) b. December 3, 1913 d. March 21, 1988 Ht. 6-1½ Wt. 200 College—Catholic

SEASON—TEAM	G	GS	MIN	FGM	FGA	PCT	3FGM	3FGA	PCT	FTM	FTA	PCT	O-RB	D-RB	TOT	AST	PF	DQ	STL	TO	BLK	PTS	RPG	APG	PPG
37-38—Akron Goodyear (N)	16	—	—	38	—	—	—	—	—	14	—	—	—	—	—		37	—	—	—	—	90	—	—	5.6
38-39—Akron Goodyear (N)	24	—	—	59	—	—	—	—	—	24	—	—	—	—	—		56	—	—	—	—	142	—	—	5.9
39-40—Oshkosh (N)	28	—	—	74	—	—	—	—	—	26	59	.441	—	—	—		64	—	—	—	—	174	—	—	6.2
40-41—Oshkosh (N)	22	—	—	46	—	—	—	—	—	21	38	.553	—	—	—		50	—	—	—	—	113	—	—	5.1
41-42—Oshkosh (N)	24	—	—	70	—	—	—	—	—	38	53	.717	—	—	—		54	—	—	—	—	178	—	—	7.4
42-43—Oshkosh (N)	23	—	—	52	—	—	—	—	—	36	67	.537	—	—	—		62	—	—	—	—	140	—	—	6.1
43-44—Oshkosh (N)	20	—	—	57	—	—	—	—	—	36	—	—	—	—	—		47	—	—	—	—	150	—	—	7.5
44-45—Fort Wayne (N)	30	—	—	31	—	—	—	—	—	16	—	—	—	—	—		57	—	—	—	—	78	—	—	2.6
45-46—Fort Wayne (N)	34	—	—	42	—	—	—	—	—	14	24	.583	—	—	—		49	—	—	—	—	98	—	—	2.9
46-47—Ft. Wayne-And. (N)	44	—	—	89	—	—	—	—	—	58	83	.699	—	—	—		98	—	—	—	—	236	—	—	5.4
47-48—Anderson (N)	55	—	—	103	—	—	—	—	—	63	95	.663	—	—	—		136	—	—	—	—	269	—	—	4.9
48-49—Waterloo (N)	56	—	—	104	—	—	—	—	—	59	90	.656	—	—	—		105	—	—	—	—	267	—	—	4.8
49-50—Waterloo	23	—	—	35	137	.255	—	—	—	37	51	.725	—	—	—	46	46	—	—	—	—	107	—	2.0	4.7
REG. NBA TOTALS	23	—	—	35	137	.255	—	—	—	37	51	.725	—	—	—	46	46	—	—	—	—	107	—	2.0	4.7
REG. NBL TOTALS	376	—	—	765	—	—	—	—	—	405	509	.619	—	—	—		815	—	—	—	—	1935	—	—	5.1
NBL PLAYOFF TOTALS	40	—	—	44	—	—	—	—	—	48	18	.611	—	—	—		65	—	—	—	—	136	—	—	3.4

SHORT, EUGENE (Gene) b. August 7, 1953   Ht. 6-7 Wt. 200 College—Jackson State

SEASON—TEAM	G	GS	MIN	FGM	FGA	PCT	3FGM	3FGA	PCT	FTM	FTA	PCT	O-RB	D-RB	TOT	AST	PF	DQ	STL	TO	BLK	PTS	RPG	APG	PPG
75-76—Seattle-N.Y.	34	—	222	32	91	.352	—	—	—	20	32	.625	19	29	48	10	36	0	8	—	3	84	1.4	0.3	2.5
REG. SEASON TOTALS	34	—	222	32	91	.352	—	—	—	20	32	.625	19	29	48	10	36	0	8	—	3	84	1.4	0.3	2.5

SHORT, PURVIS b. July 2, 1957   Ht. 6-7 Wt. 220 College—Jackson State

SEASON—TEAM	G	GS	MIN	FGM	FGA	PCT	3FGM	3FGA	PCT	FTM	FTA	PCT	O-RB	D-RB	TOT	AST	PF	DQ	STL	TO	BLK	PTS	RPG	APG	PPG
78-79—Golden State	75	—	1703	369	771	.479	—	—	—	57	85	.671	127	220	347	97	233	6	54	111	12	795	4.6	1.3	10.6
79-80—Golden State	62	—	1636	461	916	.503	0	6	.000	134	165	.812	119	197	316	123	186	4	63	122	9	1056	5.1	2.0	17.0
80-81—Golden State	79	—	2309	549	1157	.475	3	17	.176	168	205	.820	151	240	391	249	244	3	78	143	19	1269	4.9	3.2	16.1
81-82—Golden State	76	8	1782	456	935	.488	6	28	.214	177	221	.801	123	143	266	209	220	3	65	122	10	1095	3.5	2.8	14.4
82-83—Golden State	67	57	2397	589	1209	.487	4	15	.267	255	308	.828	145	209	354	228	242	3	94	194	14	1437	5.3	3.4	21.4
83-84—Golden State	79	76	2945	714	1509	.473	22	72	.306	353	445	.793	184	254	438	246	252	2	103	228	11	1803	5.5	3.1	22.8
84-85—Golden State	78	77	3081	819	1780	.460	47	150	.313	501	613	.817	157	241	398	234	255	4	116	241	27	2186	5.1	3.0	28.0
85-86—Golden State	64	63	2427	633	1313	.482	15	49	.306	351	406	.865	126	203	329	237	229	5	92	184	22	1632	5.1	3.7	25.5
86-87—Golden State	34	15	950	240	501	.479	4	17	.235	137	160	.856	55	82	137	86	103	1	45	68	7	621	4.0	2.5	18.3
87-88—Houston	81	11	1949	474	986	.481	5	21	.238	206	240	.858	71	151	222	162	197	0	58	118	14	1159	2.7	2.0	14.3
88-89—Houston	65	16	1157	198	480	.413	9	33	.273	77	89	.865	65	114	179	107	116	1	44	70	13	482	2.8	1.6	7.4
89-90—New Jersey	82	24	2213	432	950	.455	10	35	.286	198	237	.835	101	147	248	145	202	2	66	119	20	1072	3.0	1.8	13.1
REG. SEASON TOTALS	842	347	24549	5934	12507	.474	125	443	.282	2614	3174	.824	1424	2201	3625	2123	2479	34	878	1720	178	14607	4.3	2.5	17.3
PLAYOFF TOTALS	18	2	361	72	170	.424	0	5	.000	43	49	.878	23	29	52	30	49	0	13	26	2	187	2.9	1.7	10.4

SHOUSE, DEXTER WAYNE b. March 24, 1963   Ht. 6-2 Wt. 200 College—Panola JC/South Alabama

SEASON—TEAM	G	GS	MIN	FGM	FGA	PCT	3FGM	3FGA	PCT	FTM	FTA	PCT	O-RB	D-RB	TOT	AST	PF	DQ	STL	TO	BLK	PTS	RPG	APG	PPG
89-90—Philadelphia	3	0	18	0	4	.000	0	1	.000	0	0	—	0	0	0	2	2	0	1	2	1	0	0.0	0.7	0.0
REG. SEASON TOTALS	3	0	18	0	4	.000	0	1	.000	0	0	—	0	0	0	2	2	0	1	2	1	0	0.0	0.7	0.0

SHRIDER, RICHARD G. (Dick) b. February 7, 1923   Ht. 6-2 Wt. 190 College—Ohio

SEASON—TEAM	G	GS	MIN	FGM	FGA	PCT	3FGM	3FGA	PCT	FTM	FTA	PCT	O-RB	D-RB	TOT	AST	PF	DQ	STL	TO	BLK	PTS	RPG	APG	PPG
48-49—Detroit (N)	3	—	—	3	—	—	—	—	—	3	6	.500	—	—	—	—	—	—	—	—	—	9	—	—	3.0
48-49—New York	4	—	—	0	0	—	—	—	—	1	3	.333	—	—	—	2	2	—	—	—	—	1	—	0.5	0.3
REG. NBA TOTALS	4	—	—	0	0	—	—	—	—	1	3	.333	—	—	—	2	2	—	—	—	—	1	—	0.5	0.3
REG. NBL TOTALS	3	—	—	3	—	—	—	—	—	3	6	.500	—	—	—	—	—	—	—	—	—	9	—	—	3.0

SHUE, EUGENE WILLIAM (Gene) b. December 18, 1931   Ht. 6-2 Wt. 175 College—Maryland

SEASON—TEAM	G	GS	MIN	FGM	FGA	PCT	3FGM	3FGA	PCT	FTM	FTA	PCT	O-RB	D-RB	TOT	AST	PF	DQ	STL	TO	BLK	PTS	RPG	APG	PPG
54-55—Phil.-N.Y.	62	—	947	100	289	.346	—	—	—	59	78	.756	—	—	154	89	64	0	—	—	—	259	2.5	1.4	4.2
55-56—New York	72	—	1750	240	625	.384	—	—	—	181	237	.764	—	—	212	179	111	0	—	—	—	661	2.9	2.5	9.2
56-57—Fort Wayne	72	—	2470	273	710	.385	—	—	—	241	316	.763	—	—	421	238	137	0	—	—	—	787	5.8	3.3	10.9
57-58—Detroit	63	—	2333	353	919	.384	—	—	—	276	327	.844	—	—	333	172	150	1	—	—	—	982	5.3	2.7	15.6
58-59—Detroit	72	—	2745	464	1197	.388	—	—	—	338	421	.803	—	—	335	231	129	1	—	—	—	1266	4.7	3.2	17.6
59-60—Detroit	75	—	3338	620	1501	.413	—	—	—	472	541	.872	—	—	409	295	146	2	—	—	—	1712	5.5	3.9	22.8
60-61—Detroit	78	—	3361	650	1545	.421	—	—	—	465	543	.856	—	—	334	530	207	1	—	—	—	1765	4.3	6.8	22.6
61-62—Detroit	80	—	3143	580	1422	.408	—	—	—	362	447	.810	—	—	372	465	192	1	—	—	—	1522	4.7	5.8	19.0
62-63—New York	78	—	2288	354	894	.396	—	—	—	208	302	.689	—	—	191	259	171	0	—	—	—	916	2.4	3.3	11.7
63-64—Baltimore	47	—	963	81	276	.293	—	—	—	36	61	.590	—	—	94	150	98	2	—	—	—	198	2.0	3.2	4.2
REG. SEASON TOTALS	699	—	23338	3715	9378	.396	—	—	—	2638	3273	.806	—	—	2855	2608	1405	8	—	—	—	10068	4.1	3.7	14.4
PLAYOFF TOTALS	32	—	1171	207	488	.424	—	—	—	155	184	.842	—	—	133	132	75	0	—	—	—	569	4.2	4.1	17.8
ALL-STAR TOTALS	5	—	130	29	51	.569	—	—	—	8	12	.667	—	—	20	19	11	0	—	—	—	66	4.0	3.8	13.2

SHUMATE, JOHN H. b. April 6, 1952   Ht. 6-9 Wt. 235 College—Notre Dame

SEASON—TEAM	G	GS	MIN	FGM	FGA	PCT	3FGM	3FGA	PCT	FTM	FTA	PCT	O-RB	D-RB	TOT	AST	PF	DQ	STL	TO	BLK	PTS	RPG	APG	PPG
75-76—Phoenix-Buffalo	75	—	1976	332	592	.561	—	—	—	212	326	.650	143	411	554	127	159	2	82	—	34	876	7.4	1.7	11.7
76-77—Buffalo	74	—	2601	407	810	.502	—	—	—	302	450	.671	163	538	701	159	197	1	90	—	84	1116	9.5	2.1	15.1
77-78—Buffalo-Detroit	80	—	2760	391	773	.506	—	—	—	400	508	.787	157	525	682	180	200	2	90	232	52	1182	8.5	2.3	14.8
79-80—Detroit-Houston-S.A.	65	—	1337	207	392	.528	0	1	.000	165	216	.764	108	255	363	84	126	1	40	91	45	579	5.6	1.3	8.9
80-81—S.A.-Seattle	24	—	527	56	131	.427	0	0	—	55	76	.724	34	54	88	24	49	0	21	42	9	167	3.7	1.0	7.0
REG. SEASON TOTALS	318	—	9201	1393	2698	.516	0	1	.000	1134	1576	.720	605	1783	2388	574	731	6	323	365	224	3920	7.5	1.8	12.3
PLAYOFF TOTALS	12	—	440	63	112	.563	0	0	—	22	41	.537	32	58	90	30	38	0	13	5	17	148	7.5	2.5	12.3

SIBERT, SAM LEWIS b. February 11, 1949   Ht. 6-7 Wt. 215 College—Eastern Oklahoma State/Texas Tech/Kentucky State

SEASON—TEAM	G	GS	MIN	FGM	FGA	PCT	3FGM	3FGA	PCT	FTM	FTA	PCT	O-RB	D-RB	TOT	AST	PF	DQ	STL	TO	BLK	PTS	RPG	APG	PPG
72-73—Kansas City-Omaha	5	—	26	4	13	.308	—	—	—	4	5	.800	—	—	4	0	4	0	—	—	—	12	0.8	0.0	2.4
REG. SEASON TOTALS	5	—	26	4	13	.308	—	—	—	4	5	.800	—	—	4	0	4	0	—	—	—	12	0.8	0.0	2.4

SIBLEY, DONALD MARK b. November 13, 1950   Ht. 6-2 Wt. 175 College—Northwestern

SEASON—TEAM	G	GS	MIN	FGM	FGA	PCT	3FGM	3FGA	PCT	FTM	FTA	PCT	O-RB	D-RB	TOT	AST	PF	DQ	STL	TO	BLK	PTS	RPG	APG	PPG
73-74—Portland	28	—	124	20	56	.357	—	—	—	6	7	.857	9	16	25	13	23	0	4	—	1	46	0.9	0.5	1.6
REG. SEASON TOTALS	28	—	124	20	56	.357	—	—	—	6	7	.857	9	16	25	13	23	0	4	—	1	46	0.9	0.5	1.6

SICHTING, JERRY LEE b. November 29, 1956   Ht. 6-1½ Wt. 180 College—Purdue

SEASON—TEAM	G	GS	MIN	FGM	FGA	PCT	3FGM	3FGA	PCT	FTM	FTA	PCT	O-RB	D-RB	TOT	AST	PF	DQ	STL	TO	BLK	PTS	RPG	APG	PPG
80-81—Indiana	47	—	450	34	95	.358	0	5	.000	25	32	.781	11	32	43	70	38	0	23	28	1	93	0.9	1.5	2.0
81-82—Indiana	51	0	800	91	194	.469	1	9	.111	29	38	.763	14	41	55	117	63	0	33	42	1	212	1.1	2.3	4.2
82-83—Indiana	78	58	2435	316	661	.478	3	18	.167	92	107	.860	33	122	155	433	185	0	104	138	2	727	2.0	5.6	9.3
83-84—Indiana	80	80	2497	397	746	.532	6	20	.300	117	135	.867	44	127	171	457	179	0	90	144	8	917	2.1	5.7	11.5
84-85—Indiana	70	25	1808	325	624	.521	9	37	.243	112	128	.875	24	90	114	264	116	0	47	102	4	771	1.6	3.8	11.0
85-86—Boston	82	7	1596	235	412	.570	6	16	.375	61	66	.924	27	77	104	188	118	0	50	73	0	537	1.3	2.3	6.5
86-87—Boston	78	15	1566	202	398	.508	7	26	.269	37	42	.881	22	69	91	187	124	0	40	61	1	448	1.2	2.4	5.7
87-88—Boston-Port.	52	1	694	93	172	.541	10	22	.455	17	23	.739	9	27	36	93	60	0	21	22	0	213	0.7	1.8	4.1
88-89—Portland	25	1	390	46	104	.442	3	12	.250	7	8	.875	9	20	29	59	17	0	15	25	0	102	1.2	2.4	4.1
89-90—Cha.-Milw.	35	8	496	50	125	.400	3	12	.250	18	22	.818	3	16	19	94	40	0	16	22	2	121	0.5	2.7	3.5
REG. SEASON TOTALS	598	195	12732	1789	3531	.507	48	177	.271	515	601	.857	196	621	817	1962	940	0	439	657	19	4141	1.4	3.3	6.9
PLAYOFF TOTALS	47	4	655	64	153	.418	1	7	.143	11	17	.647	11	28	39	79	59	0	16	18	0	140	0.8	1.7	3.0

SIDLE, DONALD ROY (Don) b. June 21, 1946 d. May 1987 Ht. 6-8½ Wt. 215 College—Oklahoma

SEASON—TEAM	G	GS	MIN	FGM	FGA	PCT	3FGM	3FGA	PCT	FTM	FTA	PCT	O-RB	D-RB	TOT	AST	PF	DQ	STL	TO	BLK	PTS	RPG	APG	PPG
68-69—Miami (A)	77	—	1984	305	656	.465	0	4	.000	321	450	.713	—	—	551	73	212	3	—	142	—	931	7.2	0.9	12.1
69-70—Miami (A)	84	—	3493	639	1320	.484	1	6	.167	469	634	.740	432	650	1082	129	272	3	—	—	—	1748	12.9	1.5	20.8
70-71—Denver-Indiana (A)	84	—	2151	425	851	.499	2	9	.222	241	331	.728	—	—	635	97	233	—	—	—	—	1093	7.6	1.2	13.0
71-72—Indiana-Memphis (A)	69	—	960	175	384	.456	1	10	.100	124	195	.636	—	—	234	26	96	—	—	56	—	475	3.4	0.4	6.9
REG. ABA TOTALS	314	—	8588	1544	3211	.481	4	29	.138	1155	1610	.717	432	650	2502	325	813	6	—	198	—	4247	8.0	1.0	13.5
ABA PLAYOFF TOTALS	20	—	428	68	141	.482	0	1	.000	53	76	.697	—	—	122	21	43	1	—	23	—	189	6.1	1.1	9.5

SIEGFRIED, LARRY E. b. May 22, 1939   Ht. 6-4 Wt. 190 College—Ohio State

SEASON—TEAM	G	GS	MIN	FGM	FGA	PCT	3FGM	3FGA	PCT	FTM	FTA	PCT	O-RB	D-RB	TOT	AST	PF	DQ	STL	TO	BLK	PTS	RPG	APG	PPG
63-64—Boston	31	—	261	35	110	.318	—	—	—	31	39	.795	—	—	51	40	33	0	—	—	—	101	1.6	1.3	3.3
64-65—Boston	72	—	996	173	417	.415	—	—	—	109	140	.779	—	—	134	119	108	1	—	—	—	455	1.9	1.7	6.3
65-66—Boston	71	—	1675	349	825	.423	—	—	—	274	311	.881	—	—	196	165	157	1	—	—	—	972	2.8	2.3	13.7
66-67—Boston	73	—	1891	368	833	.442	—	—	—	294	347	.847	—	—	228	250	207	1	—	—	—	1030	3.1	3.4	14.1
67-68—Boston	62	—	1937	261	629	.415	—	—	—	236	272	.868	—	—	215	289	194	2	—	—	—	758	3.5	4.7	12.2
68-69—Boston	79	—	2560	392	1031	.380	—	—	—	336	389	.864	—	—	282	370	222	0	—	—	—	1120	3.6	4.7	14.2
69-70—Boston	78	—	2081	382	902	.424	—	—	—	220	257	.856	—	—	212	299	187	2	—	—	—	984	2.7	3.8	12.6
70-71—San Diego	53	—	1673	146	378	.386	—	—	—	130	153	.850	—	—	207	346	146	0	—	—	—	422	3.9	6.5	8.0
71-72—Houston-Atlanta	31	—	558	43	123	.350	—	—	—	32	37	.865	—	—	42	72	53	0	—	—	—	118	1.4	2.3	3.8
REG. SEASON TOTALS	550	—	13632	2149	5248	.409	—	—	—	1662	1945	.854	—	—	1567	1950	1307	7	—	—	—	5960	2.8	3.5	10.8
PLAYOFF TOTALS	79	—	1826	301	753	.400	—	—	—	256	307	.834	—	—	199	209	249	5	—	—	—	858	2.5	2.6	10.9

SIEWERT, RALPH PAUL (Sky) b. December 31, 1923 d. June 1991 Ht. 7-1 Wt. 235 College—Dakota Wesleyan

SEASON—TEAM	G	GS	MIN	FGM	FGA	PCT	3FGM	3FGA	PCT	FTM	FTA	PCT	O-RB	D-RB	TOT	AST	PF	DQ	STL	TO	BLK	PTS	RPG	APG	PPG
46-47—St. L.-Toronto	21	—	—	6	44	.136	—	—	—	8	15	.533	—	—	—	4	18	—	—	—	—	20	—	0.2	1.0
REG. SEASON TOTALS	21	—	—	6	44	.136	—	—	—	8	15	.533	—	—	—	4	18	—	—	—	—	20	—	0.2	1.0

SIKMA, JACK WAYNE b. November 14, 1955   Ht. 6-11 Wt. 250 College—Illinois Wesleyan

SEASON—TEAM	G	GS	MIN	FGM	FGA	PCT	3FGM	3FGA	PCT	FTM	FTA	PCT	O-RB	D-RB	TOT	AST	PF	DQ	STL	TO	BLK	PTS	RPG	APG	PPG
77-78—Seattle	82	—	2238	342	752	.455	—	—	—	192	247	.777	196	482	678	134	300	6	68	186	40	876	8.3	1.6	10.7
78-79—Seattle	82	—	2958	476	1034	.460	—	—	—	329	404	.814	232	781	1013	261	295	4	82	253	67	1281	12.4	3.2	15.6
79-80—Seattle	82	—	2793	470	989	.475	0	1	.000	235	292	.805	198	710	908	279	232	5	68	202	77	1175	11.1	3.4	14.3
80-81—Seattle	82	—	2920	595	1311	.454	0	5	.000	340	413	.823	184	668	852	248	282	5	78	201	93	1530	10.4	3.0	18.7
81-82—Seattle	82	82	3049	581	1212	.479	2	13	.154	447	523	.855	223	815	1038	277	268	5	102	213	107	1611	12.7	3.4	19.6
82-83—Seattle	75	71	2564	484	1043	.464	0	8	.000	400	478	.837	213	645	858	233	263	4	87	190	65	1368	11.4	3.1	18.2
83-84—Seattle	82	82	2993	576	1155	.499	0	2	.000	411	480	.856	225	686	911	327	301	6	95	236	92	1563	11.1	4.0	19.1
84-85—Seattle	68	68	2402	461	943	.489	2	10	.200	335	393	.852	164	559	723	285	239	1	83	160	91	1259	10.6	4.2	18.5
85-86—Seattle	80	78	2790	508	1100	.462	0	13	.000	355	411	.864	146	602	748	301	293	4	92	214	73	1371	9.4	3.8	17.1
86-87—Milwaukee	82	82	2536	390	842	.463	0	2	.000	265	313	.847	208	614	822	203	328	14	88	160	90	1045	10.0	2.5	12.7
87-88—Milwaukee	82	82	2923	514	1058	.486	3	14	.214	321	348	.922	195	514	709	279	316	11	93	157	80	1352	8.6	3.4	16.5
88-89—Milwaukee	80	80	2587	360	835	.431	82	216	.380	266	294	.905	141	482	623	289	300	6	85	145	61	1068	7.8	3.6	13.4
89-90—Milwaukee	71	70	2250	344	827	.416	68	199	.342	230	260	.885	109	383	492	229	244	5	76	139	48	986	6.9	3.2	13.9
90-91—Milwaukee	77	44	1940	295	691	.427	46	135	.341	166	197	.843	108	333	441	143	218	4	65	130	64	802	5.7	1.9	10.4
REG. SEASON TOTALS	1107	739	36943	6396	13792	.464	203	618	.328	4292	5053	.849	2542	8274	10816	3488	3879	80	1162	2586	1048	17287	9.8	3.2	15.6
PLAYOFF TOTALS	102	45	3558	556	1249	.445	11	45	.244	338	407	.830	226	719	945	244	432	17	97	209	80	1461	9.3	2.4	14.3
ALL-STAR TOTALS	7	0	147	24	51	.471	0	2	.000	7	8	.875	12	30	42	11	20	0	9	6	7	55	6.0	1.6	7.9

SILAS, JAMES EDWARD (Snake, Captain Late) b. February 11, 1949 Ht. 6-2 Wt. 190 College—Stephen F. Austin

SEASON—TEAM	G	GS	MIN	FGM	FGA	PCT	3FGM	3FGA	PCT	FTM	FTA	PCT	O-RB	D-RB	TOT	AST	PF	DQ	STL	TO	BLK	PTS	RPG	APG	PPG
72-73—Dallas (A)	78	—	2417	341	679	.502	0	0	—	389	467	.833	109	227	336	244	262	2	—	192	—	1071	4.3	3.1	13.7
73-74—San Antonio (A)	84	—	3096	486	1017	.478	0	1	.000	349	420	.831	83	260	343	319	256	—	90	220	8	1321	4.1	3.8	15.7
74-75—San Antonio (A)	82	—	3105	578	1136	.509	0	2	.000	430	486	.885	73	237	310	398	232	—	111	230	17	1586	3.8	4.9	19.3
75-76—San Antonio (A)	84	—	3112	718	1384	.519	0	2	.000	564	647	.872	111	224	335	452	263	—	155	254	24	2000	4.0	5.4	23.8
76-77—San Antonio	22	—	356	61	142	.430	—	—	—	87	107	.813	7	25	32	50	36	0	13	—	3	209	1.5	2.3	9.5
77-78—San Antonio	37	—	311	43	97	.443	—	—	—	60	73	.822	4	19	23	38	29	0	11	30	1	146	0.6	1.0	3.9
78-79—San Antonio	79	—	2171	466	922	.505	—	—	—	334	402	.831	35	148	183	273	215	1	76	199	20	1266	2.3	3.5	16.0
79-80—San Antonio	77	—	2293	513	999	.514	0	4	.000	339	382	.887	45	122	167	347	206	2	61	192	14	1365	2.2	4.5	17.7
80-81—San Antonio	75	—	2055	476	997	.477	0	2	.000	374	440	.850	44	187	231	285	129	0	51	159	12	1326	3.1	3.8	17.7
81-82—Cleveland	67	34	1447	251	573	.438	0	0	—	246	286	.860	26	83	109	222	109	0	40	107	6	748	1.6	3.3	11.2
REG. NBA TOTALS	357	34	8633	1810	3730	.485	0	11	.000	1440	1690	.852	161	584	745	1215	724	3	252	687	56	5060	2.1	3.4	14.2
REG. ABA TOTALS	328	—	11730	2123	4216	.504	0	5	.000	1732	2020	.857	376	948	1324	1413	1013	2	356	896	49	5978	4.0	4.3	18.2
NBA PLAYOFF TOTALS	27	0	745	148	330	.448	0	0	—	101	125	.808	18	46	64	95	57	1	32	60	2	397	2.4	3.5	14.7
ABA PLAYOFF TOTALS	14	—	591	93	202	.460	0	1	.000	61	82	.744	16	44	60	92	45	0	24	39	2	247	4.3	6.6	17.6
ABA ALL-STAR TOTALS	2	1	46	11	17	.647	0	0	—	19	19	1.000	1	2	3	10	9	—	2	2	0	41	1.5	5.0	20.5

SILAS, PAUL THERON b. July 12, 1943 Ht. 6-7 Wt. 230 College—Creighton

SEASON—TEAM	G	GS	MIN	FGM	FGA	PCT	3FGM	3FGA	PCT	FTM	FTA	PCT	O-RB	D-RB	TOT	AST	PF	DQ	STL	TO	BLK	PTS	RPG	APG	PPG
64-65—St. Louis	79	—	1243	140	375	.373	—	—	—	83	164	.506	—	—	576	48	161	1	—	—	—	363	7.3	0.6	4.6
65-66—St. Louis	46	—	586	70	173	.405	—	—	—	35	61	.574	—	—	236	22	72	0	—	—	—	175	5.1	0.5	3.8
66-67—St. Louis	77	—	1570	207	482	.429	—	—	—	113	213	.531	—	—	669	74	208	4	—	—	—	527	8.7	1.0	6.8
67-68—St. Louis	82	—	2652	399	871	.458	—	—	—	299	424	.705	—	—	958	162	243	4	—	—	—	1097	11.7	2.0	13.4
68-69—Atlanta	79	—	1853	241	575	.419	—	—	—	204	333	.613	—	—	745	140	166	0	—	—	—	686	9.4	1.8	8.7
69-70—Phoenix	78	—	2836	373	804	.464	—	—	—	250	412	.607	—	—	916	214	266	5	—	—	—	996	11.7	2.7	12.8
70-71—Phoenix	81	—	2944	338	789	.428	—	—	—	285	416	.685	—	—	1015	247	227	3	—	—	—	961	12.5	3.0	11.9
71-72—Phoenix	80	—	3082	485	1031	.470	—	—	—	433	560	.773	—	—	955	343	201	2	—	—	—	1403	11.9	4.3	17.5
72-73—Boston	80	—	2618	400	851	.470	—	—	—	266	380	.700	—	—	1039	251	197	1	—	—	—	1066	13.0	3.1	13.3
73-74—Boston	82	—	2599	340	772	.440	—	—	—	264	337	.783	334	581	915	186	246	3	63	—	20	944	11.2	2.3	11.5
74-75—Boston	82	—	2661	312	749	.417	—	—	—	244	344	.709	348	677	1025	224	229	3	60	—	22	868	12.5	2.7	10.6
75-76—Boston	81	—	2662	315	740	.426	—	—	—	236	333	.709	365	660	1025	203	227	3	56	—	33	866	12.7	2.5	10.7
76-77—Denver	81	—	1959	206	572	.360	—	—	—	170	255	.667	236	370	606	132	183	0	58	—	23	582	7.5	1.6	7.2
77-78—Seattle	82	—	2172	184	464	.397	—	—	—	109	186	.586	289	377	666	145	182	0	65	152	16	477	8.1	1.8	5.8
78-79—Seattle	82	—	1957	170	402	.423	—	—	—	116	194	.598	259	316	575	115	177	3	31	98	19	456	7.0	1.4	5.6
79-80—Seattle	82	—	1595	113	299	.378	0	0	—	89	136	.654	204	232	436	66	120	0	25	83	5	315	5.3	0.8	3.8
REG. SEASON TOTALS	1254	—	34989	4293	9949	.432	0	0	—	3196	4748	.673	2035	3213	12357	2572	3105	32	358	333	138	11782	9.9	2.1	9.4
PLAYOFF TOTALS	163	—	4619	396	998	.397	0	0	—	332	480	.692	339	628	1527	335	469	7	81	73	34	1124	9.4	2.1	6.9
ALL-STAR TOTALS	2	—	30	2	10	.200	0	0	—	4	5	.800	0	2	11	3	3	0	4	—	0	8	5.5	1.5	4.0

SILLIMAN, MICHAEL BARNWELL (Mike) b. May 4, 1944 Ht. 6-6½ Wt. 225 College—Army

SEASON—TEAM	G	GS	MIN	FGM	FGA	PCT	3FGM	3FGA	PCT	FTM	FTA	PCT	O-RB	D-RB	TOT	AST	PF	DQ	STL	TO	BLK	PTS	RPG	APG	PPG
70-71—Buffalo	36	—	366	36	79	.456	—	—	—	19	39	.487	—	—	62	23	37	0	—	—	—	91	1.7	0.6	2.5
REG. SEASON TOTALS	36	—	366	36	79	.456	—	—	—	19	39	.487	—	—	62	23	37	0	—	—	—	91	1.7	0.6	2.5

SIMMONS, CORNELIUS LEO (Connie) b. March 15, 1925 d. April 15, 1989 Ht. 6-8 Wt. 225 College—None

SEASON—TEAM	G	GS	MIN	FGM	FGA	PCT	3FGM	3FGA	PCT	FTM	FTA	PCT	O-RB	D-RB	TOT	AST	PF	DQ	STL	TO	BLK	PTS	RPG	APG	PPG
46-47—Boston	60	—	—	246	768	.320	—	—	—	128	189	.677	—	—	—	62	130	—	—	—	—	620	—	1.0	10.3
47-48—Boston-Balt.	45	—	—	162	545	.297	—	—	—	62	108	.574	—	—	—	24	122	—	—	—	—	386	—	0.5	8.6
48-49—Baltimore	60	—	—	299	794	.377	—	—	—	181	265	.683	—	—	—	116	215	—	—	—	—	779	—	1.9	13.0
49-50—New York	60	—	—	241	729	.331	—	—	—	198	299	.662	—	—	—	102	203	—	—	—	—	680	—	1.7	11.3
50-51—New York	66	—	—	229	613	.374	—	—	—	146	208	.702	—	—	426	117	222	8	—	—	—	604	6.5	1.8	9.2
51-52—New York	66	—	1558	227	600	.378	—	—	—	175	254	.689	—	—	471	121	214	8	—	—	—	629	7.1	1.8	9.5
52-53—New York	65	—	1707	240	637	.377	—	—	—	249	340	.732	—	—	458	127	252	9	—	—	—	729	7.0	2.0	11.2
53-54—New York	72	—	2006	255	713	.358	—	—	—	210	305	.689	—	—	484	128	234	1	—	—	—	720	6.7	1.8	10.0
54-55—Balt.-Syr.	36	—	862	137	384	.357	—	—	—	72	114	.632	—	—	220	61	109	2	—	—	—	346	6.1	1.7	9.6
55-56—Rochester	68	—	903	144	428	.336	—	—	—	78	129	.605	—	—	235	82	142	2	—	—	—	366	3.5	1.2	5.4
REG. SEASON TOTALS	598	—	7036	2180	6211	.351	—	—	—	1499	2211	.678	—	—	2294	940	1843	30	—	—	—	5859	6.2	1.6	9.8
PLAYOFF TOTALS	62	—	879	278	728	.382	—	—	—	286	391	.731	—	—	317	96	256	8	—	—	—	842	7.4	1.5	13.6

SIMMONS, GRANT M. b. March 7, 1943 Ht. 6-3 Wt. 190 College—Nebraska

SEASON—TEAM	G	GS	MIN	FGM	FGA	PCT	3FGM	3FGA	PCT	FTM	FTA	PCT	O-RB	D-RB	TOT	AST	PF	DQ	STL	TO	BLK	PTS	RPG	APG	PPG
67-68—Denver (A)	78	—	2264	292	688	.424	1	22	.045	208	295	.705	—	—	240	182	236	3	—	153	—	793	3.1	2.3	10.2
68-69—Denver (A)	17	—	252	22	59	.373	1	2	.500	20	29	.690	—	—	26	15	42	2	—	17	—	65	1.5	0.9	3.8
REG. ABA TOTALS	95	—	2516	314	747	.420	2	24	.083	228	324	.704	—	—	266	197	278	5	—	170	—	858	2.8	2.1	9.0
ABA PLAYOFF TOTALS	7	—	154	13	37	.351	0	1	.000	12	16	.750	—	—	22	15	21	1	—	10	—	38	3.1	2.1	5.4

SIMMONS, JOHN EARL (Johnny) b. July 7, 1924 Ht. 6-1 Wt. 185 College—New York University

SEASON—TEAM	G	GS	MIN	FGM	FGA	PCT	3FGM	3FGA	PCT	FTM	FTA	PCT	O-RB	D-RB	TOT	AST	PF	DQ	STL	TO	BLK	PTS	RPG	APG	PPG
46-47—Boston	60	—	—	120	429	.280	—	—	—	78	127	.614	—	—	—	29	78	—	—	—	—	318	—	0.5	5.3
REG. SEASON TOTALS	60	—	—	120	429	.280	—	—	—	78	127	.614	—	—	—	29	78	—	—	—	—	318	—	0.5	5.3

SIMMONS, LIONEL JAMES (L-Train) b. November 14, 1968 Ht. 6-7 Wt. 210 College—La Salle

SEASON—TEAM	G	GS	MIN	FGM	FGA	PCT	3FGM	3FGA	PCT	FTM	FTA	PCT	O-RB	D-RB	TOT	AST	PF	DQ	STL	TO	BLK	PTS	RPG	APG	PPG
90-91—Sacramento	79	79	2978	549	1301	.422	3	11	.273	320	435	.736	193	504	697	315	249	0	113	230	85	1421	8.8	4.0	18.0
91-92—Sacramento	78	78	2895	527	1162	.454	1	5	.200	281	365	.770	149	485	634	337	205	0	135	218	132	1336	8.1	4.3	17.1
92-93—Sacramento	69	68	2502	468	1055	.444	1	11	.091	298	364	.819	156	339	495	312	197	4	95	196	38	1235	7.2	4.5	17.9
93-94—Sacramento	75	74	2702	436	996	.438	6	17	.353	251	323	.777	168	394	562	305	189	2	104	183	50	1129	7.5	4.1	15.1
REG. SEASON TOTALS	301	299	11077	1980	4514	.439	11	44	.250	1150	1487	.773	666	1722	2388	1269	840	6	447	827	305	5121	7.9	4.2	17.0

SIMON, WALTER J. (Walt) b. December 1, 1939 Ht. 6-6 Wt. 200 College—Benedict

SEASON—TEAM	G	GS	MIN	FGM	FGA	PCT	3FGM	3FGA	PCT	FTM	FTA	PCT	O-RB	D-RB	TOT	AST	PF	DQ	STL	TO	BLK	PTS	RPG	APG	PPG
67-68—New Jersey (A)	78	—	2518	433	955	.453	1	15	.067	169	266	.635	—	—	524	212	272	8	—	173	—	1036	6.7	2.7	13.3
68-69—New York (A)	68	—	2750	570	1296	.440	6	27	.222	290	417	.695	—	—	554	234	289	5	—	183	—	1436	8.1	3.4	21.1
69-70—New York (A)	81	—	2696	454	1030	.441	1	20	.050	253	338	.749	—	—	474	294	296	5	—	—	—	1162	5.9	3.6	14.3
70-71—Kentucky (A)	84	—	1411	274	578	.474	1	11	.091	100	156	.641	—	—	315	156	253	—	—	—	—	649	3.8	1.9	7.7
71-72—Kentucky (A)	67	—	1111	243	464	.524	1	10	.100	109	156	.699	—	—	233	137	157	—	—	72	—	596	3.5	2.0	8.9
72-73—Kentucky (A)	83	—	2403	432	897	.482	3	17	.176	143	191	.749	122	273	395	336	271	6	—	156	—	1010	4.8	4.0	12.2
73-74—Kentucky (A)	80	—	1164	233	492	.474	2	13	.154	57	68	.838	62	147	209	117	133	—	38	77	10	525	2.6	1.5	6.6
REG. ABA TOTALS	541	—	14053	2639	5712	.462	15	113	.133	1121	1592	.704	184	420	2704	1486	1671	24	38	661	10	6414	5.0	2.7	11.9
ABA PLAYOFF TOTALS	59	—	1435	231	514	.449	0	18	.000	93	118	.788	3	6	264	162	204	1	24	45	14	555	4.5	2.7	9.4
ABA ALL-STAR TOTALS	1	—	21	8	11	.727	0	0	—	2	3	.667	3	1	4	1	3	0	0	2	0	18	4.0	1.0	18.0

SIMPSON, RALPH DEREK b. August 10, 1949 Ht. 6-5 Wt. 200 College—Michigan State

SEASON—TEAM	G	GS	MIN	FGM	FGA	PCT	3FGM	3FGA	PCT	FTM	FTA	PCT	O-RB	D-RB	TOT	AST	PF	DQ	STL	TO	BLK	PTS	RPG	APG	PPG
70-71—Denver (A)	81	—	1820	460	1108	.415	17	60	.283	215	285	.754	—	—	231	168	152	—	—	—	—	1152	2.9	2.1	14.2
71-72—Denver (A)	84	—	3006	920	2000	.460	3	22	.136	457	568	.805	—	—	398	258	244	—	—	266	—	2300	4.7	3.1	27.4
72-73—Denver (A)	81	—	2589	732	1670	.438	5	24	.208	421	556	.757	140	231	371	222	241	2	127	283	—	1890	4.6	2.7	23.3
73-74—Denver (A)	75	—	2244	597	1395	.428	2	24	.083	208	276	.754	113	213	326	191	190	—	103	196	12	1404	4.3	2.5	18.7
74-75—Denver (A)	82	—	2863	694	1374	.505	1	12	.083	303	402	.754	108	283	391	442	214	—	166	314	19	1692	4.8	5.4	20.6
75-76—Denver (A)	84	—	3121	619	1211	.511	4	24	.167	273	350	.780	121	333	454	597	183	—	153	360	23	1515	5.4	7.1	18.0
76-77—Detroit	77	—	1597	356	834	.427	—	—	—	138	195	.708	48	133	181	180	100	0	68	—	5	850	2.4	2.3	11.0
77-78—Detroit-Denver	64	—	1323	216	576	.375	—	—	—	85	104	.817	53	104	157	159	90	1	75	126	7	517	2.5	2.5	8.1
78-79—Phil.-N.J.	68	—	979	174	433	.402	—	—	—	76	111	.685	35	61	96	126	57	0	37	100	5	424	1.4	1.9	6.2
79-80—New Jersey	8	—	81	18	47	.383	0	2	.000	5	10	.500	6	5	11	14	3	0	9	12	0	41	1.4	1.8	5.1
REG. NBA TOTALS	217	—	3980	764	1890	.404	0	2	.000	304	420	.724	142	303	445	479	250	1	189	238	17	1832	2.1	2.2	8.4
REG. ABA TOTALS	487	—	15643	4022	8758	.459	32	166	.193	1877	2437	.770	482	1060	2171	1878	1224	2	549	1419	54	9953	4.5	3.9	20.4
NBA PLAYOFF TOTALS	17	—	252	45	109	.413	0	0	—	16	23	.696	6	18	24	41	21	0	4	22	2	106	1.4	2.4	6.2
ABA PLAYOFF TOTALS	38	—	1501	322	731	.440	4	16	.250	186	226	.823	35	91	181	185	104	0	43	146	7	834	4.8	4.9	21.9
ABA ALL-STAR TOTALS	5	—	118	25	62	.403	0	1	.000	5	7	.714	4	4	15	7	3	—	3	11	0	55	3.0	1.4	11.0

SIMS, H. DOUGLAS (Doug) b. June 29, 1943 Ht. 6-7 Wt. 195 College—Kent State

SEASON—TEAM	G	GS	MIN	FGM	FGA	PCT	3FGM	3FGA	PCT	FTM	FTA	PCT	O-RB	D-RB	TOT	AST	PF	DQ	STL	TO	BLK	PTS	RPG	APG	PPG
68-69—Cincinnati	4	—	12	2	5	.400	—	—	—	0	0	—	—	—	4	0	4	0	—	—	—	4	1.0	0.0	1.0
REG. SEASON TOTALS	4	—	12	2	5	.400	—	—	—	0	0	—	—	—	4	0	4	0	—	—	—	4	1.0	0.0	1.0

SIMS, ROBERT ANTELL JR. (Bob) b. October 9, 1938 Ht. 6-5 Wt. 220 College—Pepperdine

SEASON—TEAM	G	GS	MIN	FGM	FGA	PCT	3FGM	3FGA	PCT	FTM	FTA	PCT	O-RB	D-RB	TOT	AST	PF	DQ	STL	TO	BLK	PTS	RPG	APG	PPG
61-62—L.A.-St. L.	65	—	1345	193	491	.393	—	—	—	123	216	.569	—	—	183	154	187	4	—	—	—	509	2.8	2.4	7.8
67-68—Anaheim (A)	2	—	19	2	7	.286	0	0	—	4	6	.667	—	—	1	2	6	1	—	0	—	8	0.5	1.0	4.0
REG. NBA TOTALS	65	—	1345	193	491	.393	—	—	—	123	216	.569	—	—	183	154	187	4	—	—	—	509	2.8	2.4	7.8
REG. ABA TOTALS	2	—	19	2	7	.286	0	0	—	4	6	.667	—	—	1	2	6	1	—	0	—	8	0.5	1.0	4.0

SIMS, SCOTT ALAN b. April 18, 1955 Ht. 6-1 Wt. 170 College—Missouri

SEASON—TEAM	G	GS	MIN	FGM	FGA	PCT	3FGM	3FGA	PCT	FTM	FTA	PCT	O-RB	D-RB	TOT	AST	PF	DQ	STL	TO	BLK	PTS	RPG	APG	PPG
77-78—San Antonio	12	—	95	10	26	.385	—	—	—	10	15	.667	5	8	13	20	16	0	3	19	0	30	1.1	1.7	2.5
REG. SEASON TOTALS	12	—	95	10	26	.385	—	—	—	10	15	.667	5	8	13	20	16	0	3	19	0	30	1.1	1.7	2.5

SINGLETON, MCKINLEY b. October 29, 1961 Ht. 6-5 Wt. 175 College—Shelby State CC/Alabama-Birmingham

SEASON—TEAM	G	GS	MIN	FGM	FGA	PCT	3FGM	3FGA	PCT	FTM	FTA	PCT	O-RB	D-RB	TOT	AST	PF	DQ	STL	TO	BLK	PTS	RPG	APG	PPG
86-87—New York	2	0	10	2	3	.667	0	1	.000	0	0	—	0	0	0	1	1	0	0	0	0	4	0.0	0.5	2.0
REG. SEASON TOTALS	2	0	10	2	3	.667	0	1	.000	0	0	—	0	0	0	1	1	0	0	0	0	4	0.0	0.5	2.0

SINICOLA, EMILIO J. (**Zeke**) b. January 25, 1929   Ht. 5-10 Wt. 165 College—Niagara

SEASON—TEAM	G	GS	MIN	FGM	FGA	PCT	3FGM	3FGA	PCT	FTM	FTA	PCT	O-RB	D-RB	TOT	AST	PF	DQ	STL	TO	BLK	PTS	RPG	APG	PPG
51-52—Fort Wayne	3	—	15	1	4	.250	—	—	—	0	2	.000	—	—	1	0	2	0	—	—	—	2	0.3	0.0	0.7
53-54—Fort Wayne	9	—	53	4	16	.250	—	—	—	3	6	.500	—	—	1	3	8	0	—	—	—	11	0.1	0.3	1.2
REG. SEASON TOTALS	12	—	68	5	20	.250	—	—	—	3	8	.375	—	—	2	3	10	0	—	—	—	13	0.2	0.3	1.1

SITTON, CHARLES E. (**Charlie**) b. July 3, 1962   Ht. 6-8 Wt. 210 College—Oregon State

SEASON—TEAM	G	GS	MIN	FGM	FGA	PCT	3FGM	3FGA	PCT	FTM	FTA	PCT	O-RB	D-RB	TOT	AST	PF	DQ	STL	TO	BLK	PTS	RPG	APG	PPG
84-85—Dallas	43	0	304	39	94	.415	0	2	.000	13	25	.520	24	36	60	26	50	0	7	19	6	91	1.4	0.6	2.1
REG. SEASON TOTALS	43	0	304	39	94	.415	0	2	.000	13	25	.520	24	36	60	26	50	0	7	19	6	91	1.4	0.6	2.1

SKILES, SCOTT ALLEN b. March 5, 1964   Ht. 6-1 Wt. 190 College—Michigan State

SEASON—TEAM	G	GS	MIN	FGM	FGA	PCT	3FGM	3FGA	PCT	FTM	FTA	PCT	O-RB	D-RB	TOT	AST	PF	DQ	STL	TO	BLK	PTS	RPG	APG	PPG
86-87—Milwaukee	13	0	205	18	62	.290	3	14	.214	10	12	.833	6	20	26	45	18	0	5	21	1	49	2.0	3.5	3.8
87-88—Indiana	51	2	760	86	209	.411	6	20	.300	45	54	.833	11	55	66	180	97	0	22	76	3	223	1.3	3.5	4.4
88-89—Indiana	80	13	1571	198	442	.448	20	75	.267	130	144	.903	21	128	149	390	151	1	64	177	2	546	1.9	4.9	6.8
89-90—Orlando	70	32	1460	190	464	.409	52	132	.394	104	119	.874	23	136	159	334	126	0	36	90	4	536	2.3	4.8	7.7
90-91—Orlando	79	66	2714	462	1039	.445	93	228	.408	340	377	.902	57	213	270	660	192	2	89	252	4	1357	3.4	8.4	17.2
91-92—Orlando	75	63	2377	359	868	.414	91	250	.364	248	277	.895	36	166	202	544	188	0	74	233	5	1057	2.7	7.3	14.1
92-93—Orlando	78	78	3086	416	891	.467	80	235	.340	289	324	.892	52	238	290	735	244	4	86	267	2	1201	3.7	9.4	15.4
93-94—Orlando	82	46	2303	276	644	.429	68	165	.412	195	222	.878	42	147	189	503	171	1	47	193	2	815	2.3	6.1	9.9
REG. SEASON TOTALS	528	300	14476	2005	4619	.434	413	1119	.369	1361	1529	.890	248	1103	1351	3391	1187	8	423	1309	23	5784	2.6	6.4	11.0
PLAYOFF TOTALS	2	0	23	4	8	.500	0	2	.000	1	1	1.000	1	0	1	3	2	0	0	5	0	9	0.5	1.5	4.5

SKINNER, ALBERT L. JR. (**Al**) b. June 16, 1952   Ht. 6-3 Wt. 195 College—Massachusetts

SEASON—TEAM	G	GS	MIN	FGM	FGA	PCT	3FGM	3FGA	PCT	FTM	FTA	PCT	O-RB	D-RB	TOT	AST	PF	DQ	STL	TO	BLK	PTS	RPG	APG	PPG
74-75—New York (A)	51	—	773	130	266	.489	1	3	.333	72	94	.766	42	78	120	121	111	—	29	68	13	333	2.4	2.4	6.5
75-76—New York (A)	83	—	2082	330	702	.470	2	8	.250	203	241	.842	96	211	307	280	252	—	91	169	50	865	3.7	3.4	10.4
76-77—New York Nets	79	—	2256	382	887	.431	—	—	—	231	292	.791	112	251	363	289	279	7	103	—	53	995	4.6	3.7	12.6
77-78—N.J.-Detroit	77	—	1551	222	488	.455	—	—	—	162	203	.798	67	157	224	146	242	6	65	161	20	606	2.9	1.9	7.9
78-79—N.J.-Phil.	45	—	643	91	214	.425	—	—	—	99	114	.868	27	59	86	89	114	2	40	72	3	281	1.9	2.0	6.2
79-80—Philadelphia	2	—	10	1	2	.500	0	0	—	0	0	—	0	0	0	2	1	0	0	2	0	2	0.0	1.0	1.0
REG. NBA TOTALS	203	—	4460	696	1591	.437	0	0	—	492	609	.808	206	467	673	526	636	15	208	235	76	1884	3.3	2.6	9.3
REG. ABA TOTALS	134	—	2855	460	968	.475	3	11	.273	275	335	.821	138	289	427	401	363	—	120	237	63	1198	3.2	3.0	8.9
NBA PLAYOFF TOTALS	5	—	47	6	17	.353	0	0	—	6	8	.750	5	5	10	11	6	0	3	6	1	18	2.0	2.2	3.6
ABA PLAYOFF TOTALS	14	—	296	45	103	.437	1	1	1.000	42	54	.778	25	25	50	28	46	—	21	26	2	133	3.6	2.0	9.5

SKINNER, TALVIN (**Tab**) b. September 10, 1952   Ht. 6-5 Wt. 210 College—Maryland-Eastern Shore

SEASON—TEAM	G	GS	MIN	FGM	FGA	PCT	3FGM	3FGA	PCT	FTM	FTA	PCT	O-RB	D-RB	TOT	AST	PF	DQ	STL	TO	BLK	PTS	RPG	APG	PPG
74-75—Seattle	73	—	1574	142	347	.409	—	—	—	63	97	.649	135	209	344	85	161	0	49	—	17	347	4.7	1.2	4.8
75-76—Seattle	72	—	1224	132	285	.463	—	—	—	49	80	.613	89	175	264	67	116	1	50	—	7	313	3.7	0.9	4.3
REG. SEASON TOTALS	145	—	2798	274	632	.434	—	—	—	112	177	.633	224	384	608	152	277	1	99	—	24	660	4.2	1.0	4.6
PLAYOFF TOTALS	15	—	297	25	59	.424	—	—	—	25	34	.735	17	36	53	19	35	0	14	—	4	75	3.5	1.3	5.0

SKOOG, MYER UPTON (**Whitey**) b. November 2, 1926   Ht. 5-11 Wt. 180 College—Minnesota

SEASON—TEAM	G	GS	MIN	FGM	FGA	PCT	3FGM	3FGA	PCT	FTM	FTA	PCT	O-RB	D-RB	TOT	AST	PF	DQ	STL	TO	BLK	PTS	RPG	APG	PPG
51-52—Minneapolis	35	—	988	102	296	.345	—	—	—	30	38	.789	—	—	122	60	94	4	—	—	—	234	3.5	1.7	6.7
52-53—Minneapolis	68	—	996	102	264	.386	—	—	—	46	61	.754	—	—	121	82	137	2	—	—	—	250	1.8	1.2	3.7
53-54—Minneapolis	71	—	1877	212	530	.400	—	—	—	72	97	.742	—	—	224	179	234	5	—	—	—	496	3.2	2.5	7.0
54-55—Minneapolis	72	—	2365	330	836	.395	—	—	—	125	155	.806	—	—	303	251	265	10	—	—	—	785	4.2	3.5	10.9
55-56—Minneapolis	72	—	2311	340	854	.398	—	—	—	155	193	.803	—	—	291	255	232	5	—	—	—	835	4.0	3.5	11.6
56-57—Minneapolis	23	—	656	78	220	.355	—	—	—	44	47	.936	—	—	72	76	65	1	—	—	—	200	3.1	3.3	8.7
REG. SEASON TOTALS	341	—	9193	1164	3000	.388	—	—	—	472	591	.799	—	—	1133	903	1027	27	—	—	—	2800	3.3	2.6	8.2
PLAYOFF TOTALS	34	—	929	115	286	.402	—	—	—	50	73	.685	—	—	125	70	130	5	—	—	—	280	3.7	2.1	8.2

SLADE, JEFFREY ALAN (**Jeff**) b. March 1, 1941   Ht. 6-6 Wt. 220 College—Kenyon

SEASON—TEAM	G	GS	MIN	FGM	FGA	PCT	3FGM	3FGA	PCT	FTM	FTA	PCT	O-RB	D-RB	TOT	AST	PF	DQ	STL	TO	BLK	PTS	RPG	APG	PPG
62-63—Chicago	3	—	20	2	5	.400	—	—	—	0	1	.000	—	—	7	0	3	0	—	—	—	4	2.3	0.0	1.3
REG. SEASON TOTALS	3	—	20	2	5	.400	—	—	—	0	1	.000	—	—	7	0	3	0	—	—	—	4	2.3	0.0	1.3

SLAUGHTER, JAMES W. (Jim) b. May 13, 1928 Ht. 6-11 Wt. 215 College—South Carolina

SEASON—TEAM	G	GS	MIN	FGM	FGA	PCT	3FGM	3FGA	PCT	FTM	FTA	PCT	O-RB	D-RB	TOT	AST	PF	DQ	STL	TO	BLK	PTS	RPG	APG	PPG
51-52—Baltimore	28	—	525	53	165	.321	—	—	—	41	68	.603	—	—	148	25	81	0	—	—	—	147	5.3	0.9	5.3
REG. SEASON TOTALS	28	—	525	53	165	.321	—	—	—	41	68	.603	—	—	148	25	81	0	—	—	—	147	5.3	0.9	5.3

SLAUGHTER, JOSE DAN b. September 9, 1960 Ht. 6-5 Wt. 215 College—Portland

SEASON—TEAM	G	GS	MIN	FGM	FGA	PCT	3FGM	3FGA	PCT	FTM	FTA	PCT	O-RB	D-RB	TOT	AST	PF	DQ	STL	TO	BLK	PTS	RPG	APG	PPG
82-83—Indiana	63	1	515	89	238	.374	9	41	.220	38	59	.644	34	34	68	52	93	0	36	42	7	225	1.1	0.8	3.6
REG. SEASON TOTALS	63	1	515	89	238	.374	9	41	.220	38	59	.644	34	34	68	52	93	0	36	42	7	225	1.1	0.8	3.6

SLOAN, GERALD EUGENE (Jerry, Spider) b. March 28, 1942 Ht. 6-5½ Wt. 195 College—Evansville Tech

SEASON—TEAM	G	GS	MIN	FGM	FGA	PCT	3FGM	3FGA	PCT	FTM	FTA	PCT	O-RB	D-RB	TOT	AST	PF	DQ	STL	TO	BLK	PTS	RPG	APG	PPG
65-66—Baltimore	59	—	952	120	289	.415	—	—	—	98	139	.705	—	—	230	110	176	7	—	—	—	338	3.9	1.9	5.7
66-67—Chicago	80	—	2942	525	1214	.432	—	—	—	340	427	.796	—	—	726	170	293	7	—	—	—	1390	9.1	2.1	17.4
67-68—Chicago	77	—	2454	369	959	.385	—	—	—	289	386	.749	—	—	591	229	291	11	—	—	—	1027	7.7	3.0	13.3
68-69—Chicago	78	—	2939	488	1170	.417	—	—	—	333	447	.745	—	—	619	276	313	6	—	—	—	1309	7.9	3.5	16.8
69-70—Chicago	53	—	1822	310	737	.421	—	—	—	207	318	.651	—	—	372	165	179	3	—	—	—	827	7.0	3.1	15.6
70-71—Chicago	80	—	3140	592	1342	.441	—	—	—	278	389	.715	—	—	701	281	289	5	—	—	—	1462	8.8	3.5	18.3
71-72—Chicago	82	—	3035	535	1206	.444	—	—	—	258	391	.660	—	—	691	211	309	8	—	—	—	1328	8.4	2.6	16.2
72-73—Chicago	69	—	2412	301	733	.411	—	—	—	94	133	.707	—	—	475	151	235	5	—	—	—	696	6.9	2.2	10.1
73-74—Chicago	77	—	2860	412	921	.447	—	—	—	194	273	.711	150	406	556	149	273	3	183	—	10	1018	7.2	1.9	13.2
74-75—Chicago	78	—	2577	380	865	.439	—	—	—	193	258	.748	177	361	538	161	265	5	171	—	17	953	6.9	2.1	12.2
75-76—Chicago	22	—	617	84	210	.400	—	—	—	55	78	.705	40	76	116	22	77	1	27	—	5	223	5.3	1.0	10.1
REG. SEASON TOTALS	755	—	25750	4116	9646	.427	—	—	—	2339	3239	.722	367	843	5615	1925	2700	61	381	—	32	10571	7.4	2.5	14.0
PLAYOFF TOTALS	51	—	1888	294	689	.427	—	—	—	128	189	.677	42	116	412	109	187	4	27	—	1	716	8.1	2.1	14.0
ALL-STAR TOTALS	2	—	40	6	17	.353	—	—	—	0	1	.000	0	0	7	4	10	0	0	—	0	12	3.5	2.0	6.0

SLUBY, TOM GRIFFIN b. February 18, 1962 Ht. 6-4 Wt. 200 College—Notre Dame

SEASON—TEAM	G	GS	MIN	FGM	FGA	PCT	3FGM	3FGA	PCT	FTM	FTA	PCT	O-RB	D-RB	TOT	AST	PF	DQ	STL	TO	BLK	PTS	RPG	APG	PPG
84-85—Dallas	31	0	151	30	58	.517	0	2	.000	13	21	.619	5	7	12	16	18	0	3	11	0	73	0.4	0.5	2.4
REG. SEASON TOTALS	31	0	151	30	58	.517	0	2	.000	13	21	.619	5	7	12	16	18	0	3	11	0	73	0.4	0.5	2.4

SMART, JONATHAN KEITH (Keith) b. September 21, 1964 Ht. 6-1 Wt. 175 College—Garden City CC/Indiana

SEASON—TEAM	G	GS	MIN	FGM	FGA	PCT	3FGM	3FGA	PCT	FTM	FTA	PCT	O-RB	D-RB	TOT	AST	PF	DQ	STL	TO	BLK	PTS	RPG	APG	PPG
88-89—San Antonio	2	0	12	0	2	.000	0	1	.000	2	2	1.000	0	1	1	2	0	0	0	2	0	2	0.5	1.0	1.0
REG. SEASON TOTALS	2	0	12	0	2	.000	0	1	.000	2	2	1.000	0	1	1	2	0	0	0	2	0	2	0.5	1.0	1.0

SMAWLEY, BELUS VAN b. March 20, 1918 Ht. 6-1½ Wt. 195 College—Appalachian State

SEASON—TEAM	G	GS	MIN	FGM	FGA	PCT	3FGM	3FGA	PCT	FTM	FTA	PCT	O-RB	D-RB	TOT	AST	PF	DQ	STL	TO	BLK	PTS	RPG	APG	PPG
46-47—St. Louis	22	—	—	113	352	.321	—	—	—	36	47	.766	—	—	—	10	37	—	—	—	—	262	—	0.5	11.9
47-48—St. Louis	48	—	—	212	688	.308	—	—	—	111	150	.740	—	—	—	18	88	—	—	—	—	535	—	0.4	11.1
48-49—St. Louis	59	—	—	352	946	.372	—	—	—	210	281	.747	—	—	—	183	145	—	—	—	—	914	—	3.1	15.5
49-50—St. Louis	61	—	—	287	832	.345	—	—	—	260	314	.828	—	—	—	215	160	—	—	—	—	834	—	3.5	13.7
50-51—Syr.-Balt.	60	—	—	252	663	.380	—	—	—	227	267	.850	—	—	178	161	145	4	—	—	—	731	3.0	2.7	12.2
51-52—Baltimore	11	—	0	13	63	.206	—	—	—	14	17	.824	—	—	—	18	8	9	0	—	—	—	40	1.6	0.7	3.6
REG. SEASON TOTALS	261	—	0	1229	3544	.347	—	—	—	858	1076	.797	—	—	196	595	584	4	—	—	—	3316	2.8	2.3	12.7
PLAYOFF TOTALS	11	—	0	54	169	.320	—	—	—	20	29	.690	—	—	—	3	31	1	—	—	—	128	—	0.3	11.6

SMILEY, A. JOHN (Jack, Smiles) b. December 22, 1922 Ht. 6-3 Wt. 190 College—Illinois

SEASON—TEAM	G	GS	MIN	FGM	FGA	PCT	3FGM	3FGA	PCT	FTM	FTA	PCT	O-RB	D-RB	TOT	AST	PF	DQ	STL	TO	BLK	PTS	RPG	APG	PPG
47-48—Fort Wayne (N)	60	—	—	105	—	—	—	—	—	90	135	.667	—	—	—	—	168	—	—	—	—	300	—	—	5.0
48-49—Fort Wayne	59	—	—	141	571	.247	—	—	—	112	164	.683	—	—	—	138	202	—	—	—	—	394	—	2.3	6.7
49-50—And.-Wat.	59	—	—	98	364	.269	—	—	—	136	201	.677	—	—	—	161	193	—	—	—	—	332	—	2.7	5.6
REG. NBA TOTALS	118	—	—	239	935	.256	—	—	—	248	365	.679	—	—	—	299	395	—	—	—	—	726	—	2.5	6.2
REG. NBL TOTALS	60	—	—	105	—	—	—	—	—	90	135	.667	—	—	—	—	168	—	—	—	—	300	—	—	5.0
NBL PLAYOFF TOTALS	4	—	—	7	—	—	—	—	—	6	8	.750	—	—	—	—	11	—	—	—	—	20	—	—	5.0

SMITH, ADRIAN HOWARD (Odie) b. October 5, 1936 Ht. 6-1½ Wt. 180 College—Booneville JC/Northeast Miss. CC/Kentucky

SEASON—TEAM	G	GS	MIN	FGM	FGA	PCT	3FGM	3FGA	PCT	FTM	FTA	PCT	O-RB	D-RB	TOT	AST	PF	DQ	STL	TO	BLK	PTS	RPG	APG	PPG
61-62—Cincinnati	80	—	1462	202	499	.405	—	—	—	172	222	.775	—	—	151	167	101	0	—	—	—	576	1.9	2.1	7.2
62-63—Cincinnati	79	—	1522	241	544	.443	—	—	—	223	275	.811	—	—	174	141	157	1	—	—	—	705	2.2	1.8	8.9
63-64—Cincinnati	66	—	1524	234	576	.406	—	—	—	154	197	.782	—	—	147	145	164	1	—	—	—	622	2.2	2.2	9.4
64-65—Cincinnati	80	—	2745	463	1016	.456	—	—	—	284	342	.830	—	—	220	240	199	2	—	—	—	1210	2.8	3.0	15.1
65-66—Cincinnati	80	—	2982	531	1310	.405	—	—	—	408	480	.850	—	—	287	256	276	1	—	—	—	1470	3.6	3.2	18.4
66-67—Cincinnati	81	—	2636	502	1147	.438	—	—	—	343	380	.903	—	—	205	187	272	0	—	—	—	1347	2.5	2.3	16.6
67-68—Cincinnati	82	—	2783	480	1035	.464	—	—	—	320	386	.829	—	—	185	272	259	6	—	—	—	1280	2.3	3.3	15.6
68-69—Cincinnati	73	—	1336	243	562	.432	—	—	—	217	269	.807	—	—	105	127	166	1	—	—	—	703	1.4	1.7	9.6
69-70—Cin.-S.F.	77	—	1087	153	416	.368	—	—	—	152	170	.894	—	—	82	133	122	0	—	—	—	458	1.1	1.7	5.9
70-71—San Francisco	21	—	247	38	89	.427	—	—	—	35	41	.854	—	—	24	30	24	0	—	—	—	111	1.1	1.4	5.3
71-72—Virginia (A)	53	—	686	87	195	.446	2	11	.182	92	103	.893	—	—	46	42	89	—	—	34	—	268	0.9	0.8	5.1
REG. NBA TOTALS	719	—	18324	3087	7194	.429	—	—	—	2308	2762	.836	—	—	1580	1698	1740	12	—	—	—	8482	2.2	2.4	11.8
REG. ABA TOTALS	53	—	686	87	195	.446	2	11	.182	92	103	.893	—	—	46	42	89	—	—	34	—	268	0.9	0.8	5.1
NBA PLAYOFF TOTALS	36	—	746	107	282	.379	—	—	—	92	112	.821	—	—	61	80	60	0	—	—	—	306	1.7	2.2	8.5
ABA PLAYOFF TOTALS	11	—	297	46	99	.465	1	5	.200	32	37	.865	—	—	19	17	28	—	—	11	—	125	1.7	1.5	11.4
NBA ALL-STAR TOTALS	1	—	26	9	18	.500	—	—	—	6	6	1.000	—	—	8	3	5	0	—	—	—	24	8.0	3.0	24.0

SMITH, ALAN RICHARD (Al) b. January 15, 1947 Ht. 6-1 Wt. 185 College—Bradley

SEASON—TEAM	G	GS	MIN	FGM	FGA	PCT	3FGM	3FGA	PCT	FTM	FTA	PCT	O-RB	D-RB	TOT	AST	PF	DQ	STL	TO	BLK	PTS	RPG	APG	PPG
71-72—Denver (A)	83	—	1764	292	675	.433	32	107	.299	153	211	.725	—	—	226	249	244	—	—	163	—	769	2.7	3.0	9.3
72-73—Denver (A)	83	—	2343	315	767	.411	17	90	.189	272	352	.773	68	146	214	477	295	7	—	261	—	919	2.6	5.7	11.1
73-74—Denver (A)	76	—	2435	311	779	.399	22	72	.306	187	242	.773	56	185	241	619	257	—	100	273	7	831	3.2	8.1	10.9
74-75—Utah (A)	80	—	2037	225	582	.387	34	94	.362	157	193	.813	39	108	147	375	230	—	59	201	3	641	1.8	4.7	8.0
75-76—Utah (A)	15	—	392	42	105	.400	6	17	.353	48	59	.814	13	24	37	73	45	—	10	29	2	138	2.5	4.9	9.2
REG. ABA TOTALS	337	—	8971	1185	2908	.407	111	380	.292	817	1057	.773	176	463	865	1793	1071	7	169	927	12	3298	2.6	5.3	9.8
ABA PLAYOFF TOTALS	18	—	449	59	154	.383	5	16	.313	39	45	.867	2	10	55	68	55	0	2	47	0	162	3.1	3.8	9.0

SMITH, CHARLES ANTON (Tony) b. June 14, 1968 Ht. 6-4 Wt. 205 College—Marquette

SEASON—TEAM	G	GS	MIN	FGM	FGA	PCT	3FGM	3FGA	PCT	FTM	FTA	PCT	O-RB	D-RB	TOT	AST	PF	DQ	STL	TO	BLK	PTS	RPG	APG	PPG
90-91—L.A. Lakers	64	1	695	97	220	.441	0	7	.000	40	57	.702	24	47	71	135	80	0	28	69	12	234	1.1	2.1	3.7
91-92—L.A. Lakers	63	0	820	113	283	.399	0	11	.000	49	75	.653	31	45	76	109	91	0	39	50	8	275	1.2	1.7	4.4
92-93—L.A. Lakers	55	9	752	133	275	.484	2	11	.182	62	82	.756	46	41	87	63	72	1	50	40	7	330	1.6	1.1	6.0
93-94—L.A. Lakers	73	31	1617	272	617	.441	16	50	.320	85	119	.714	106	89	195	148	128	1	59	76	14	645	2.7	2.0	8.8
REG. SEASON TOTALS	255	41	3884	615	1395	.441	18	79	.228	236	333	.709	207	222	429	455	371	2	176	235	41	1484	1.7	1.8	5.8
PLAYOFF TOTALS	16	0	153	22	48	.458	2	6	.333	9	14	.643	9	4	13	9	25	1	6	12	1	55	0.8	0.6	3.4

SMITH, CHARLES DANIEL b. July 16, 1965 Ht. 6-10 Wt. 240 College—Pittsburgh

SEASON—TEAM	G	GS	MIN	FGM	FGA	PCT	3FGM	3FGA	PCT	FTM	FTA	PCT	O-RB	D-RB	TOT	AST	PF	DQ	STL	TO	BLK	PTS	RPG	APG	PPG
88-89—L.A. Clippers	71	56	2161	435	878	.495	0	3	.000	285	393	.725	173	292	465	103	273	6	68	146	89	1155	6.5	1.5	16.3
89-90—L.A. Clippers	78	76	2732	595	1145	.520	1	12	.083	454	572	.794	177	347	524	114	294	6	86	162	119	1645	6.7	1.5	21.1
90-91—L.A. Clippers	74	74	2703	548	1168	.469	0	7	.000	384	484	.793	216	392	608	134	267	4	81	165	145	1480	8.2	1.8	20.0
91-92—L.A. Clippers	49	25	1310	251	539	.466	0	6	.000	212	270	.785	95	206	301	56	159	2	41	69	98	714	6.1	1.1	14.6
92-93—New York	81	68	2172	358	764	.469	0	2	.000	287	367	.782	170	262	432	142	254	4	48	155	96	1003	5.3	1.8	12.4
93-94—New York	43	21	1105	176	397	.443	8	16	.500	87	121	.719	66	99	165	50	144	4	26	64	45	447	3.8	1.2	10.4
REG. SEASON TOTALS	396	320	12183	2363	4891	.483	9	46	.196	1709	2207	.774	897	1598	2495	599	1391	26	350	761	592	6444	6.3	1.5	16.3
PLAYOFF TOTALS	45	38	1148	172	371	.464	0	3	.000	102	135	.756	71	112	183	54	168	3	25	71	50	446	4.1	1.2	9.9

SMITH, CHARLES EDWARD IV b. November 29, 1967 Ht. 6-1 Wt. 160 College—Georgetown

SEASON—TEAM	G	GS	MIN	FGM	FGA	PCT	3FGM	3FGA	PCT	FTM	FTA	PCT	O-RB	D-RB	TOT	AST	PF	DQ	STL	TO	BLK	PTS	RPG	APG	PPG
89-90—Boston	60	0	519	59	133	.444	0	7	.000	53	76	.697	14	55	69	103	75	0	35	36	3	171	1.2	1.7	2.9
90-91—Boston	5	0	30	3	7	.429	0	0	—	3	5	.600	0	2	2	6	7	0	1	3	0	9	0.4	1.2	1.8
REG. SEASON TOTALS	65	0	549	62	140	.443	0	7	.000	56	81	.691	14	57	71	109	82	0	36	39	3	180	1.1	1.7	2.8
PLAYOFF TOTALS	3	0	9	1	2	.500	0	0	—	0	0	—	1	0	1	3	0	0	1	0	0	2	0.3	1.0	0.7

SMITH, CHRIS G. b. May 17, 1970 Ht. 6-3 Wt. 190 College—Connecticut

SEASON—TEAM	G	GS	MIN	FGM	FGA	PCT	3FGM	3FGA	PCT	FTM	FTA	PCT	O-RB	D-RB	TOT	AST	PF	DQ	STL	TO	BLK	PTS	RPG	APG	PPG
92-93—Minnesota	80	6	1266	125	289	.433	2	14	.143	95	120	.792	32	64	96	196	96	1	48	68	16	347	1.2	2.5	4.3
93-94—Minnesota	80	16	1617	184	423	.435	10	39	.256	95	141	.674	15	107	122	285	131	1	38	101	18	473	1.5	3.6	5.9
REG. SEASON TOTALS	160	22	2883	309	712	.434	12	53	.226	190	261	.728	47	171	218	481	227	2	86	169	34	820	1.4	3.0	5.1

SMITH, CLINTON b. January 19, 1964 Ht. 6-6 Wt. 210 College—Central Arizona/Ohio State/Cleveland State

SEASON—TEAM	G	GS	MIN	FGM	FGA	PCT	3FGM	3FGA	PCT	FTM	FTA	PCT	O-RB	D-RB	TOT	AST	PF	DQ	STL	TO	BLK	PTS	RPG	APG	PPG
86-87—Golden State	41	0	341	50	117	.427	0	2	.000	27	36	.750	26	30	56	45	36	0	13	26	1	127	1.4	1.1	3.1
90-91—Washington	5	0	45	2	4	.500	0	0	—	3	6	.500	2	2	4	4	3	0	1	1	0	7	0.8	0.8	1.4
REG. SEASON TOTALS	46	0	386	52	121	.430	0	2	.000	30	42	.714	28	32	60	49	39	0	14	27	1	134	1.3	1.1	2.9

SMITH, DELBERT BOWER (Deb) b. January 7, 1920 Ht. 6-3 Wt. 180 College—Utah

SEASON—TEAM	G	GS	MIN	FGM	FGA	PCT	3FGM	3FGA	PCT	FTM	FTA	PCT	O-RB	D-RB	TOT	AST	PF	DQ	STL	TO	BLK	PTS	RPG	APG	PPG
46-47—St. Louis	48	—	—	32	119	.269	—	—	—	9	21	.429	—	—	—	6	47	—	—	—	—	73	—	0.1	1.5
REG. SEASON TOTALS	48	—	—	32	119	.269	—	—	—	9	21	.429	—	—	—	6	47	—	—	—	—	73	—	0.1	1.5
PLAYOFF TOTALS	1	—	—	0	0	—	—	—	—	0	1	.000	—	—	—	—	1	—	—	—	—	0	—	—	0.0

SMITH, DEREK ERVIN b. November 1, 1961 Ht. 6-7 Wt. 220 College—Louisville

SEASON—TEAM	G	GS	MIN	FGM	FGA	PCT	3FGM	3FGA	PCT	FTM	FTA	PCT	O-RB	D-RB	TOT	AST	PF	DQ	STL	TO	BLK	PTS	RPG	APG	PPG
82-83—Golden State	27	0	154	21	51	.412	0	2	.000	17	25	.680	10	28	38	2	40	0	0	11	4	59	1.4	0.1	2.2
83-84—San Diego	61	20	1297	238	436	.546	1	6	.167	123	163	.755	54	116	170	82	165	2	33	78	22	600	2.8	1.3	9.8
84-85—L.A. Clippers	80	80	2762	682	1271	.537	3	19	.158	400	504	.794	174	253	427	216	317	8	77	230	52	1767	5.3	2.7	22.1
85-86—L.A. Clippers	11	9	339	100	181	.552	1	2	.500	58	84	.690	20	21	41	31	35	2	9	33	13	259	3.7	2.8	23.5
86-87—Sacramento	52	42	1658	338	757	.446	9	33	.273	178	228	.781	60	122	182	204	184	3	46	126	23	863	3.5	3.9	16.6
87-88—Sacramento	35	18	899	174	364	.478	8	23	.348	87	113	.770	35	68	103	89	108	2	21	48	17	443	2.9	2.5	12.7
88-89—Sac.-Phil.	65	38	1295	216	496	.435	7	31	.226	129	188	.686	61	106	167	128	164	4	43	88	23	568	2.6	2.0	8.7
89-90—Philadelphia	75	7	1405	261	514	.508	16	36	.444	130	186	.699	62	110	172	109	198	2	35	85	20	668	2.3	1.5	8.9
90-91—Boston	2	0	16	1	4	.250	0	1	.000	3	4	.750	0	0	0	5	3	0	1	1	1	5	0.0	2.5	2.5
REG. SEASON TOTALS	408	214	9825	2031	4074	.499	45	153	.294	1125	1495	.753	476	824	1300	866	1214	23	265	700	175	5232	3.2	2.1	12.8
PLAYOFF TOTALS	14	3	149	23	43	.535	0	2	.000	13	18	.722	4	12	16	9	32	0	5	15	1	59	1.1	0.6	4.2

SMITH, DONALD (Don) b. October 10, 1951 Ht. 6½ Wt. 165 College—Dayton

SEASON—TEAM	G	GS	MIN	FGM	FGA	PCT	3FGM	3FGA	PCT	FTM	FTA	PCT	O-RB	D-RB	TOT	AST	PF	DQ	STL	TO	BLK	PTS	RPG	APG	PPG
74-75—Philadelphia	54	—	538	131	321	.408	—	—	—	21	21	1.000	14	16	30	47	45	0	20	—	3	283	0.6	0.9	5.2
REG. SEASON TOTALS	54	—	538	131	321	.408	—	—	—	21	21	1.000	14	16	30	47	45	0	20	—	3	283	0.6	0.9	5.2

SMITH, DONALD A. (see Zaid Abdul-Aziz)

SMITH, DONALD E. b. July 27, 1920 Ht. 6-2 Wt. 190 College—Minnesota

SEASON—TEAM	G	GS	MIN	FGM	FGA	PCT	3FGM	3FGA	PCT	FTM	FTA	PCT	O-RB	D-RB	TOT	AST	PF	DQ	STL	TO	BLK	PTS	RPG	APG	PPG
42-43—Oshkosh (N)	13	—	—	22	—	—	—	—	—	15	—	—	—	—	—	—	—	—	—	—	—	59	—	—	4.5
46-47—Ind. (N)	2	—	—	1	—	—	—	—	—	1	2	.500	—	—	—	—	—	—	—	—	—	3	—	—	1.5
47-48—Minneapolis (N)	57	—	—	69	—	—	—	—	—	62	94	.660	—	—	—	—	98	—	—	—	—	200	—	—	3.5
48-49—Minneapolis	8	—	—	2	13	.154	—	—	—	2	3	.667	—	—	—	2	6	—	—	—	—	6	—	0.3	0.8
REG. NBA TOTALS	8	—	—	2	13	.154	—	—	—	2	3	.667	—	—	—	2	6	—	—	—	—	6	—	0.3	0.8
REG. NBL TOTALS	72	—	—	92	—	—	—	—	—	78	102	.657	—	—	—	—	98	—	—	—	—	262	—	—	3.6
NBL PLAYOFF TOTALS	12	—	—	14	—	—	—	—	—	11	12	.750	—	—	—	—	23	—	—	—	—	39	—	—	3.3

SMITH, DOUGLAS (Doug) b. September 17, 1969 Ht. 6-10 Wt. 230 College—Missouri

SEASON—TEAM	G	GS	MIN	FGM	FGA	PCT	3FGM	3FGA	PCT	FTM	FTA	PCT	O-RB	D-RB	TOT	AST	PF	DQ	STL	TO	BLK	PTS	RPG	APG	PPG
91-92—Dallas	76	32	1707	291	702	.415	0	11	.000	89	121	.736	129	262	391	129	259	5	62	97	34	671	5.1	1.7	8.8
92-93—Dallas	61	42	1524	289	666	.434	0	4	.000	56	74	.757	96	232	328	104	280	12	48	115	52	634	5.4	1.7	10.4
93-94—Dallas	79	42	1684	295	678	.435	2	9	.222	106	127	.835	114	235	349	119	287	3	82	93	38	698	4.4	1.5	8.8
REG. SEASON TOTALS	216	116	4915	875	2046	.428	2	24	.083	251	322	.780	339	729	1068	352	826	20	192	305	124	2003	4.9	1.6	9.3

SMITH, EDWARD BERNARD (Ed) b. July 5, 1929 Ht. 6-6 Wt. 195 College—Harvard

SEASON—TEAM	G	GS	MIN	FGM	FGA	PCT	3FGM	3FGA	PCT	FTM	FTA	PCT	O-RB	D-RB	TOT	AST	PF	DQ	STL	TO	BLK	PTS	RPG	APG	PPG
53-54—New York	11	—	104	11	45	.244	—	—	—	6	10	.600	—	—	26	9	15	0	—	—	—	28	2.4	0.8	2.5
REG. SEASON TOTALS	11	—	104	11	45	.244	—	—	—	6	10	.600	—	—	26	9	15	0	—	—	—	28	2.4	0.8	2.5

SMITH, ELMORE b. May 9, 1949 Ht. 7-1 Wt. 250 College—Wiley/Kentucky State

SEASON—TEAM	G	GS	MIN	FGM	FGA	PCT	3FGM	3FGA	PCT	FTM	FTA	PCT	O-RB	D-RB	TOT	AST	PF	DQ	STL	TO	BLK	PTS	RPG	APG	PPG
71-72—Buffalo	78	—	3186	579	1275	.454	—	—	—	194	363	.534	—	—	1184	111	306	10	—	—	—	1352	15.2	1.4	17.3
72-73—Buffalo	76	—	2829	600	1244	.482	—	—	—	188	337	.558	—	—	946	192	295	16	—	—	—	1388	12.4	2.5	18.3
73-74—Los Angeles	81	—	2922	434	949	.457	—	—	—	147	249	.590	204	702	906	150	309	8	71	—	393	1015	11.2	1.9	12.5
74-75—Los Angeles	74	—	2341	346	702	.493	—	—	—	112	231	.485	210	600	810	145	255	6	84	—	216	804	10.9	2.0	10.9
75-76—Milwaukee	78	—	2809	498	962	.518	—	—	—	222	351	.632	201	692	893	97	268	7	78	—	238	1218	11.4	1.2	15.6
76-77—Milw.-Clev.	70	—	1464	241	507	.475	—	—	—	117	213	.549	114	325	439	43	207	4	35	—	144	599	6.3	0.6	8.6
77-78—Cleveland	81	—	1996	402	809	.497	—	—	—	205	309	.663	178	500	678	57	241	4	50	141	176	1009	8.4	0.7	12.5
78-79—Cleveland	24	—	332	69	130	.531	—	—	—	18	26	.692	45	61	106	13	60	0	7	42	16	156	4.4	0.5	6.5
REG. SEASON TOTALS	562	—	17879	3169	6578	.482	—	—	—	1203	2079	.579	952	2880	5962	808	1941	55	325	183	1183	7541	10.6	1.4	13.4
PLAYOFF TOTALS	13	—	387	86	172	.500	—	—	—	34	52	.654	36	82	118	8	53	0	17	5	25	206	9.1	0.6	15.8

SMITH, GARFIELD b. November 18, 1945   Ht. 6-9 Wt. 235 College—Eastern Kentucky

SEASON—TEAM	G	GS	MIN	FGM	FGA	PCT	3FGM	3FGA	PCT	FTM	FTA	PCT	O-RB	D-RB	TOT	AST	PF	DQ	STL	TO	BLK	PTS	RPG	APG	PPG
70-71—Boston	37	—	281	42	116	.362	—	—	—	22	56	.393	—	—	95	9	53	0	—	—	—	106	2.6	0.2	2.9
71-72—Boston	26	—	134	28	66	.424	—	—	—	6	31	.194	—	—	37	8	22	0	—	—	—	62	1.4	0.3	2.4
72-73—San Diego (A)	71	—	1055	116	244	.475	0	0	—	28	93	.301	140	166	306	39	197	4	—	33	—	260	4.3	0.5	3.7
REG. NBA TOTALS	63	—	415	70	182	.385	—	—	—	28	87	.322	—	—	132	17	75	0	—	—	—	168	2.1	0.3	2.7
REG. ABA TOTALS	71	—	1055	116	244	.475	0	0	—	28	93	.301	140	166	306	39	197	4	—	33	—	260	4.3	0.5	3.7
NBA PLAYOFF TOTALS	4	—	6	1	5	.200	—	—	—	0	3	.000	—	—	1	—	1	0	—	—	—	2	0.3	0.0	0.5
ABA PLAYOFF TOTALS	4	—	63	5	17	.294	0	0	—	2	7	.286	—	—	21	1	9	0	—	1	—	12	5.3	0.3	3.0

SMITH, GREGORY DARNELL (**Greg**) b. January 28, 1947   Ht. 6-5 Wt. 195 College—Western Kentucky

SEASON—TEAM	G	GS	MIN	FGM	FGA	PCT	3FGM	3FGA	PCT	FTM	FTA	PCT	O-RB	D-RB	TOT	AST	PF	DQ	STL	TO	BLK	PTS	RPG	APG	PPG
68-69—Milwaukee	79	—	2207	276	613	.450	—	—	—	91	155	.587	—	—	804	137	264	12	—	—	—	643	10.2	1.7	8.1
69-70—Milwaukee	82	—	2368	339	664	.511	—	—	—	125	174	.718	—	—	712	156	304	8	—	—	—	803	8.7	1.9	9.8
70-71—Milwaukee	82	—	2428	409	799	.512	—	—	—	141	213	.662	—	—	589	227	284	5	—	—	—	959	7.2	2.8	11.7
71-72—Milw.-Houston	82	—	2256	309	671	.461	—	—	—	111	168	.661	—	—	483	222	259	4	—	—	—	729	5.9	2.7	8.9
72-73—Houston-Port.	76	—	1610	234	485	.482	—	—	—	75	128	.586	—	—	383	122	218	8	—	—	—	543	5.0	1.6	7.1
73-74—Portland	67	—	878	99	228	.434	—	—	—	48	79	.608	65	124	189	78	126	1	41	—	6	246	2.8	1.2	3.7
74-75—Portland	55	—	519	71	146	.486	—	—	—	32	48	.667	29	60	89	27	96	1	22	—	6	174	1.6	0.5	3.2
75-76—Portland	1	—	3	0	1	.000	—	—	—	0	0	—	0	0	0	0	2	0	0	—	0	0	0.0	0.0	0.0
REG. SEASON TOTALS	524	—	12269	1737	3607	.482	—	—	—	623	965	.646	94	184	3249	969	1553	39	63	—	12	4097	6.2	1.8	7.8
PLAYOFF TOTALS	24	—	783	117	222	.527	—	—	—	35	62	.565	0	0	205	58	79	1	0	—	0	269	8.5	2.4	11.2

SMITH, JAMES OLIVER (**Jim**) b. April 12, 1958   Ht. 6-9 Wt. 225 College—Ohio State

SEASON—TEAM	G	GS	MIN	FGM	FGA	PCT	3FGM	3FGA	PCT	FTM	FTA	PCT	O-RB	D-RB	TOT	AST	PF	DQ	STL	TO	BLK	PTS	RPG	APG	PPG
81-82—San Diego	72	3	858	86	169	.509	0	0	—	39	85	.459	72	110	182	46	185	5	22	47	51	211	2.5	0.6	2.9
82-83—Detroit	4	0	18	3	4	.750	0	0	—	2	4	.500	0	5	5	0	4	0	0	0	0	8	1.3	0.0	2.0
REG. SEASON TOTALS	76	3	876	89	173	.514	0	0	—	41	89	.461	72	115	187	46	189	5	22	47	51	219	2.5	0.6	2.9

SMITH, JOHN JR. b. May 24, 1944   Ht. 7-0 Wt. 235 College—Southern Colorado

SEASON—TEAM	G	GS	MIN	FGM	FGA	PCT	3FGM	3FGA	PCT	FTM	FTA	PCT	O-RB	D-RB	TOT	AST	PF	DQ	STL	TO	BLK	PTS	RPG	APG	PPG
68-69—Dallas (A)	77	—	2172	246	623	.395	0	0	—	116	214	.542	271	538	809	58	328	19	—	117	—	608	10.5	0.8	7.9
69-70—Dallas-Pitt.-N.Y. (A)	70	—	1190	105	284	.370	0	2	.000	56	94	.596	—	—	404	58	185	5	—	—	—	266	5.8	0.8	3.8
REG. ABA TOTALS	147	—	3362	351	907	.387	0	2	.000	172	308	.558	271	538	1213	116	513	24	—	117	—	874	8.3	0.8	5.9
ABA PLAYOFF TOTALS	9	—	141	16	34	.471	0	1	.000	7	13	.538	—	—	44	8	21	0	—	4	—	39	4.9	0.9	4.3

SMITH, KEITH LEWAYNE b. March 9, 1964   Ht. 6-3 Wt. 195 College—Loyola Marymount

SEASON—TEAM	G	GS	MIN	FGM	FGA	PCT	3FGM	3FGA	PCT	FTM	FTA	PCT	O-RB	D-RB	TOT	AST	PF	DQ	STL	TO	BLK	PTS	RPG	APG	PPG
86-87—Milwaukee	42	4	461	57	150	.380	3	9	.333	21	28	.750	13	19	32	43	74	0	25	30	3	138	0.8	1.0	3.3
REG. SEASON TOTALS	42	4	461	57	150	.380	3	9	.333	21	28	.750	13	19	32	43	74	0	25	30	3	138	0.8	1.0	3.3

SMITH, KENNETH (**Kenny**) b. March 8, 1965   Ht. 6-3 Wt. 170 College—North Carolina

SEASON—TEAM	G	GS	MIN	FGM	FGA	PCT	3FGM	3FGA	PCT	FTM	FTA	PCT	O-RB	D-RB	TOT	AST	PF	DQ	STL	TO	BLK	PTS	RPG	APG	PPG
87-88—Sacramento	61	60	2170	331	694	.477	12	39	.308	167	204	.819	40	98	138	434	140	1	92	184	8	841	2.3	7.1	13.8
88-89—Sacramento	81	81	3145	547	1183	.462	46	128	.359	263	357	.737	49	177	226	621	173	0	102	249	7	1403	2.8	7.7	17.3
89-90—Sac.-Atlanta	79	51	2421	378	811	.466	26	83	.313	161	196	.821	18	139	157	445	143	0	79	169	8	943	2.0	5.6	11.9
90-91—Houston	78	78	2699	522	1003	.520	49	135	.363	287	340	.844	36	127	163	554	131	0	106	237	11	1380	2.1	7.1	17.7
91-92—Houston	81	80	2735	432	910	.475	54	137	.394	219	253	.866	34	143	177	562	112	0	104	227	7	1137	2.2	6.9	14.0
92-93—Houston	82	82	2422	387	744	.520	96	219	.438	195	222	.878	28	132	160	446	110	0	80	163	7	1065	2.0	5.4	13.0
93-94—Houston	78	78	2209	341	711	.480	89	220	.405	135	155	.871	24	114	138	327	121	0	59	126	4	906	1.8	4.2	11.6
REG. SEASON TOTALS	540	510	17801	2938	6056	.485	372	961	.387	1427	1727	.826	229	930	1159	3389	930	1	622	1355	52	7675	2.1	6.3	14.2
PLAYOFF TOTALS	38	38	1200	167	355	.470	59	126	.468	78	97	.804	11	75	86	168	63	0	35	65	6	471	2.3	4.4	12.4

SMITH, KENNETH WAYNE (**Ken**) b. July 12, 1953   Ht. 6-7 Wt. 185 College—Lon Morris/Tulsa

SEASON—TEAM	G	GS	MIN	FGM	FGA	PCT	3FGM	3FGA	PCT	FTM	FTA	PCT	O-RB	D-RB	TOT	AST	PF	DQ	STL	TO	BLK	PTS	RPG	APG	PPG
75-76—San Antonio (A)	19	—	164	34	83	.410	1	5	.200	13	16	.813	9	15	24	7	22	—	4	8	0	82	1.3	0.4	4.3
REG. ABA TOTALS	19	—	164	34	83	.410	1	5	.200	13	16	.813	9	15	24	7	22	—	4	8	0	82	1.3	0.4	4.3

SMITH, LaBRADFORD CORVEY b. April 3, 1969 Ht. 6-3 Wt. 200 College—Louisville

SEASON—TEAM	G	GS	MIN	FGM	FGA	PCT	3FGM	3FGA	PCT	FTM	FTA	PCT	O-RB	D-RB	TOT	AST	PF	DQ	STL	TO	BLK	PTS	RPG	APG	PPG
91-92—Washington	48	5	708	100	246	.407	2	21	.095	45	56	.804	30	51	81	99	98	0	44	63	1	247	1.7	2.1	5.1
92-93—Washington	69	33	1546	261	570	.458	8	23	.348	109	127	.858	26	80	106	186	178	2	58	103	9	639	1.5	2.7	9.3
93-94—Wash.-Sac.	66	2	877	124	306	.405	21	60	.350	63	84	.750	34	50	84	109	96	2	40	50	5	332	1.3	1.7	5.0
REG. SEASON TOTALS	183	40	3131	485	1122	.432	31	104	.298	217	267	.813	90	181	271	394	372	4	142	216	15	1218	1.5	2.2	6.7

SMITH, LARRY (Mr. Mean) b. January 18, 1958 Ht. 6-8 Wt. 225 College—Alcorn State

SEASON—TEAM	G	GS	MIN	FGM	FGA	PCT	3FGM	3FGA	PCT	FTM	FTA	PCT	O-RB	D-RB	TOT	AST	PF	DQ	STL	TO	BLK	PTS	RPG	APG	PPG
80-81—Golden State	82	—	2578	304	594	.512	0	0	—	177	301	.588	433	561	994	93	316	10	70	146	63	785	12.1	1.1	9.6
81-82—Golden State	74	55	2213	220	412	.534	0	1	.000	88	159	.553	279	534	813	83	291	7	65	105	54	528	11.0	1.1	7.1
82-83—Golden State	49	41	1433	180	306	.588	0	0	—	53	99	.535	209	276	485	46	186	5	36	83	20	413	9.9	0.9	8.4
83-84—Golden State	75	63	2091	244	436	.560	0	0	—	94	168	.560	282	390	672	72	274	6	61	124	22	582	9.0	1.0	7.8
84-85—Golden State	80	78	2497	366	690	.530	0	0	—	155	256	.605	405	464	869	96	285	5	78	160	54	887	10.9	1.2	11.1
85-86—Golden State	77	74	2441	314	586	.536	0	1	.000	112	227	.493	384	472	856	95	286	7	62	135	50	740	11.1	1.2	9.6
86-87—Golden State	80	78	2374	297	544	.546	0	1	.000	113	197	.574	366	551	917	95	295	7	71	135	56	707	11.5	1.2	8.8
87-88—Golden State	20	10	499	58	123	.472	0	1	.000	11	27	.407	79	103	182	25	63	1	12	36	11	127	9.1	1.3	6.4
88-89—Golden State	80	78	1897	219	397	.552	0	0	—	18	58	.310	272	380	652	118	248	2	61	110	54	456	8.2	1.5	5.7
89-90—Houston	74	0	1300	101	213	.474	0	2	.000	20	55	.364	180	272	452	69	203	3	56	70	28	222	6.1	0.9	3.0
90-91—Houston	81	28	1923	128	263	.487	0	0	—	12	50	.240	302	407	709	88	265	6	83	93	22	268	8.8	1.1	3.3
91-92—Houston	45	7	800	50	92	.543	0	1	.000	4	11	.364	107	149	256	33	121	3	21	44	7	104	5.7	0.7	2.3
92-93—San Antonio	66	13	833	38	87	.437	0	0	—	9	22	.409	103	165	268	28	133	2	23	39	16	85	4.1	0.4	1.3
REG. SEASON TOTALS	883	525	22879	2519	4743	.531	0	7	.000	866	1630	.531	3401	4724	8125	941	2966	64	699	1280	457	5904	9.2	1.1	6.7
PLAYOFF TOTALS	31	18	657	56	112	.500	0	1	.000	20	29	.690	99	120	219	43	101	0	27	28	20	132	7.1	1.4	4.3

SMITH, MICHAEL JOHN b. May 19, 1965 Ht. 6-10 Wt. 225 College—Brigham Young

SEASON—TEAM	G	GS	MIN	FGM	FGA	PCT	3FGM	3FGA	PCT	FTM	FTA	PCT	O-RB	D-RB	TOT	AST	PF	DQ	STL	TO	BLK	PTS	RPG	APG	PPG
89-90—Boston	65	7	620	136	286	.476	2	28	.071	53	64	.828	40	60	100	79	51	0	9	54	1	327	1.5	1.2	5.0
90-91—Boston	47	3	389	95	200	.475	6	24	.250	22	27	.815	21	35	56	43	27	0	6	37	2	218	1.2	0.9	4.6
REG. SEASON TOTALS	112	10	1009	231	486	.475	8	52	.154	75	91	.824	61	95	156	122	78	0	15	91	3	545	1.4	1.1	4.9
PLAYOFF TOTALS	6	0	22	6	10	.600	0	3	.000	7	7	1.000	0	0	0	1	3	0	1	1	0	19	0.0	0.2	3.2

SMITH, OTIS FITZGERALD b. January 30, 1964 Ht. 6-5 Wt. 210 College—Jacksonville

SEASON—TEAM	G	GS	MIN	FGM	FGA	PCT	3FGM	3FGA	PCT	FTM	FTA	PCT	O-RB	D-RB	TOT	AST	PF	DQ	STL	TO	BLK	PTS	RPG	APG	PPG
86-87—Denver	28	0	168	33	79	.418	0	2	.000	12	21	.571	17	17	34	22	30	0	1	19	1	78	1.2	0.8	2.8
87-88—Denver-G.S.	72	18	1549	325	662	.491	13	41	.317	178	229	.777	126	121	247	155	160	0	91	107	42	841	3.4	2.2	11.7
88-89—Golden State	80	5	1597	311	715	.435	7	37	.189	174	218	.798	128	202	330	140	165	1	88	129	40	803	4.1	1.8	10.0
89-90—Orlando	65	35	1644	348	708	.492	10	40	.250	169	222	.761	117	183	300	147	174	0	76	102	57	875	4.6	2.3	13.5
90-91—Orlando	75	39	1885	407	902	.451	9	46	.196	221	301	.734	176	213	389	169	190	1	85	140	35	1044	5.2	2.3	13.9
91-92—Orlando	55	5	877	116	318	.365	8	21	.381	70	91	.769	40	76	116	57	85	1	36	62	13	310	2.1	1.0	5.6
REG. SEASON TOTALS	375	102	7720	1540	3384	.455	47	187	.251	824	1082	.762	604	812	1416	690	804	3	377	559	188	3951	3.8	1.8	10.5
PLAYOFF TOTALS	7	0	68	11	30	.367	0	0	—	7	11	.636	7	11	18	10	6	0	2	6	3	29	2.6	1.4	4.1

SMITH, PETE b. 1947 Ht. 6-6 Wt. 205 College—Cincinnati/Valdosta State/Pepperdine

SEASON—TEAM	G	GS	MIN	FGM	FGA	PCT	3FGM	3FGA	PCT	FTM	FTA	PCT	O-RB	D-RB	TOT	AST	PF	DQ	STL	TO	BLK	PTS	RPG	APG	PPG
72-73—San Diego (A)	5	—	32	2	12	.167	0	2	.000	0	0	—	3	5	8	1	5	0	—	5	—	4	1.6	0.2	0.8
REG. ABA TOTALS	5	—	32	2	12	.167	0	2	.000	0	0	—	3	5	8	1	5	0	—	5	—	4	1.6	0.2	0.8

SMITH, PHILIP ARNOLD (Phil) b. April 22, 1952 Ht. 6-4 Wt. 185 College—San Francisco

SEASON—TEAM	G	GS	MIN	FGM	FGA	PCT	3FGM	3FGA	PCT	FTM	FTA	PCT	O-RB	D-RB	TOT	AST	PF	DQ	STL	TO	BLK	PTS	RPG	APG	PPG
74-75—Golden State	74	—	1055	221	464	.476	—	—	—	127	158	.804	51	89	140	135	141	0	62	—	0	569	1.9	1.8	7.7
75-76—Golden State	82	—	2793	659	1383	.477	—	—	—	323	410	.788	133	243	376	362	223	0	108	—	18	1641	4.6	4.4	20.0
76-77—Golden State	82	—	2880	631	1318	.479	—	—	—	295	376	.785	101	231	332	328	227	0	98	—	29	1557	4.0	4.0	19.0
77-78—Golden State	82	—	2940	648	1373	.472	—	—	—	316	389	.812	100	200	300	393	219	2	108	266	27	1612	3.7	4.8	19.7
78-79—Golden State	59	—	2288	489	977	.501	—	—	—	194	255	.761	48	164	212	261	159	3	101	170	23	1172	3.6	4.4	19.9
79-80—Golden State	51	—	1552	325	685	.474	7	22	.318	135	171	.789	28	118	146	187	154	1	62	121	15	792	2.9	3.7	15.5
80-81—San Diego	76	—	2378	519	1057	.491	4	18	.222	237	313	.757	49	107	156	372	231	1	84	176	18	1279	2.1	4.9	16.8
81-82—S.D.-Seattle	74	41	2042	340	761	.447	5	27	.185	163	223	.731	51	135	186	307	213	0	67	155	27	848	2.5	4.1	11.5
82-83—Seattle	79	17	1238	175	400	.438	3	8	.375	101	133	.759	27	103	130	216	113	0	44	102	8	454	1.6	2.7	5.7
REG. SEASON TOTALS	659	58	19166	4007	8418	.476	19	75	.253	1891	2428	.779	588	1390	1978	2561	1680	7	734	990	165	9924	3.0	3.9	15.1
PLAYOFF TOTALS	49	0	1210	234	517	.453	0	1	.000	120	167	.719	43	107	150	143	99	1	49	6	18	588	3.1	2.9	12.0
ALL-STAR TOTALS	2	0	40	9	20	.450	0	—	—	2	6	.333	1	6	7	8	4	0	1	—	0	20	3.5	4.0	10.0

SMITH, RANDOLPH (**Randy**) b. December 12, 1948 Ht. 6-3 Wt. 180 College—Buffalo State

SEASON—TEAM	G	GS	MIN	FGM	FGA	PCT	3FGM	3FGA	PCT	FTM	FTA	PCT	O-RB	D-RB	TOT	AST	PF	DQ	STL	TO	BLK	PTS	RPG	APG	PPG
71-72—Buffalo	76	—	2094	432	896	.482	—	—	—	158	254	.622	—	—	368	189	202	2	—	—	—	1022	4.8	2.5	13.4
72-73—Buffalo	82	—	2603	511	1154	.443	—	—	—	192	264	.727	—	—	391	422	247	1	—	—	—	1214	4.8	5.1	14.8
73-74—Buffalo	82	—	2745	531	1079	.492	—	—	—	205	288	.712	87	228	315	383	261	6	203	—	4	1267	3.8	4.7	15.5
74-75—Buffalo	82	—	3001	610	1261	.484	—	—	—	236	295	.800	95	249	344	534	247	2	137	—	3	1456	4.2	6.5	17.8
75-76—Buffalo	82	—	3167	702	1422	.494	—	—	—	383	469	.817	104	313	417	484	274	5	153	—	4	1787	5.1	5.9	21.8
76-77—Buffalo	82	—	3094	702	1504	.467	—	—	—	294	386	.762	134	323	457	441	264	2	176	—	8	1698	5.6	5.4	20.7
77-78—Buffalo	82	—	3314	789	1697	.465	—	—	—	443	554	.800	110	200	310	458	224	2	172	286	11	2021	3.8	5.6	24.6
78-79—San Diego	82	—	3111	693	1523	.455	—	—	—	292	359	.813	102	193	295	395	177	1	177	255	5	1678	3.6	4.8	20.5
79-80—Cleveland	82	—	2677	599	1326	.452	10	53	.189	233	283	.823	93	163	256	363	190	1	125	200	7	1441	3.1	4.4	17.6
80-81—Cleveland	82	—	2199	486	1043	.466	1	28	.036	221	271	.815	46	147	193	357	132	0	113	195	14	1194	2.4	4.4	14.6
81-82—New York	82	40	2033	348	748	.465	3	11	.273	122	151	.808	53	102	155	255	199	1	91	124	1	821	1.9	3.1	10.0
82-83—S.D.-Atlanta	80	16	1406	273	565	.483	3	18	.167	114	131	.870	37	59	96	206	139	1	56	98	0	663	1.2	2.6	8.3
REG. SEASON TOTALS	976	56	31444	6676	14218	.470	17	110	.155	2893	3705	.781	861	1977	3597	4487	2556	22	1403	1158	57	16262	3.7	4.6	16.7
PLAYOFF TOTALS	24	0	914	168	361	.465	0	0	—	84	103	.816	18	91	109	157	80	1	43	0	2	420	4.5	6.5	17.5
ALL-STAR TOTALS	2	0	44	15	21	.714	0	0	—	5	6	.833	4	4	8	9	5	0	3	3	1	35	4.0	4.5	17.5

SMITH, REGINALD D. (**Reggie**) b. August 21, 1970 Ht. 6-10 Wt. 250 College—Texas Christian

SEASON—TEAM	G	GS	MIN	FGM	FGA	PCT	3FGM	3FGA	PCT	FTM	FTA	PCT	O-RB	D-RB	TOT	AST	PF	DQ	STL	TO	BLK	PTS	RPG	APG	PPG
92-93—Portland	23	0	68	10	27	.370	0	1	.000	3	14	.214	15	6	21	1	16	0	4	4	1	23	0.9	0.0	1.0
93-94—Portland	43	9	316	29	72	.403	0	0	—	18	38	.474	40	59	99	4	47	0	12	12	6	76	2.3	0.1	1.8
REG. SEASON TOTALS	66	9	384	39	99	.394	0	1	.000	21	52	.404	55	65	120	5	63	0	16	16	7	99	1.8	0.1	1.5

SMITH, ROBERT (**Bobby, Bingo**) b. February 26, 1946 Ht. 6-5 Wt. 210 College—Tulsa

SEASON—TEAM	G	GS	MIN	FGM	FGA	PCT	3FGM	3FGA	PCT	FTM	FTA	PCT	O-RB	D-RB	TOT	AST	PF	DQ	STL	TO	BLK	PTS	RPG	APG	PPG
69-70—San Diego	75	—	1198	242	567	.427	—	—	—	66	96	.688	—	—	328	75	119	0	—	—	—	550	4.4	1.0	7.3
70-71—Cleveland	77	—	2332	495	1106	.448	—	—	—	178	234	.761	—	—	429	258	175	4	—	—	—	1168	5.6	3.4	15.2
71-72—Cleveland	82	—	2734	527	1190	.443	—	—	—	178	224	.795	—	—	502	247	222	3	—	—	—	1232	6.1	3.0	15.0
72-73—Cleveland	73	—	1068	268	603	.444	—	—	—	64	81	.790	—	—	199	108	80	0	—	—	—	600	2.7	1.5	8.2
73-74—Cleveland	82	—	2612	536	1179	.455	—	—	—	139	169	.822	134	301	435	198	242	4	89	—	30	1211	5.3	2.4	14.8
74-75—Cleveland	82	—	2636	585	1212	.483	—	—	—	132	160	.825	108	299	407	229	227	1	80	—	26	1302	5.0	2.8	15.9
75-76—Cleveland	81	—	2338	495	1121	.442	—	—	—	111	136	.816	83	258	341	155	231	0	58	—	36	1101	4.2	1.9	13.6
76-77—Cleveland	81	—	2135	513	1149	.446	—	—	—	148	181	.818	92	225	317	152	211	3	61	—	30	1174	3.9	1.9	14.5
77-78—Cleveland	82	—	1581	369	840	.439	—	—	—	108	135	.800	65	142	207	91	155	1	38	81	21	846	2.5	1.1	10.3
78-79—Cleveland	72	—	1650	361	784	.460	—	—	—	83	106	.783	77	129	206	121	188	2	43	75	7	805	2.9	1.7	11.2
79-80—Clev.-S.D.	78	—	2123	385	891	.432	23	81	.284	100	115	.870	94	165	259	100	209	4	62	81	17	893	3.3	1.3	11.4
REG. SEASON TOTALS	865	—	22407	4776	10642	.449	23	81	.284	1307	1637	.798	653	1519	3630	1734	2059	22	431	237	167	10882	4.2	2.0	12.6
PLAYOFF TOTALS	18	—	470	88	216	.407	0	0	—	25	28	.893	16	38	54	35	48	1	14	1	4	201	3.0	1.9	11.2

SMITH, ROBERT JOSEPH (**Bobby**) b. August 20, 1937 Ht. 6-4 Wt. 190 College—West Virginia

SEASON—TEAM	G	GS	MIN	FGM	FGA	PCT	3FGM	3FGA	PCT	FTM	FTA	PCT	O-RB	D-RB	TOT	AST	PF	DQ	STL	TO	BLK	PTS	RPG	APG	PPG
59-60—Minneapolis	10	—	130	13	54	.241	—	—	—	11	16	.688	—	—	33	14	10	0	—	—	—	37	3.3	1.4	3.7
61-62—Los Angeles	3	—	7	0	1	.000	—	—	—	0	0	—	—	—	0	0	1	0	—	—	—	0	0.0	0.0	0.0
REG. SEASON TOTALS	13	—	137	13	55	.236	—	—	—	11	16	.688	—	—	33	14	11	0	—	—	—	37	2.5	1.1	2.8

SMITH, ROBERT LEROY b. March 10, 1955 Ht. 5-11½ Wt. 165 College—Arizona Western/Nevada-Las Vegas

SEASON—TEAM	G	GS	MIN	FGM	FGA	PCT	3FGM	3FGA	PCT	FTM	FTA	PCT	O-RB	D-RB	TOT	AST	PF	DQ	STL	TO	BLK	PTS	RPG	APG	PPG
77-78—Denver	45	—	378	50	97	.515	—	—	—	21	24	.875	6	30	36	39	52	0	18	20	3	121	0.8	0.9	2.7
78-79—Denver	82	—	1479	184	436	.422	—	—	—	159	180	.883	41	105	146	208	165	1	58	95	13	527	1.8	2.5	6.4
79-80—Utah-N.J.	65	—	809	118	269	.439	8	26	.308	80	92	.870	20	59	79	92	105	1	26	53	4	324	1.2	1.4	5.0
80-81—Cleveland	1	—	20	2	5	.400	0	0	—	4	4	1.000	1	2	3	3	6	1	0	3	0	8	3.0	3.0	8.0
81-82—Milwaukee	17	1	316	52	110	.473	2	10	.200	10	12	.833	1	13	14	44	35	0	10	14	1	116	0.8	2.6	6.8
82-83—S.D.-S.A.	12	0	68	7	24	.292	0	2	.000	9	10	.900	1	5	6	8	13	0	5	6	0	23	0.5	0.7	1.9
84-85—Cleveland	7	0	48	4	17	.235	0	4	.000	8	10	.800	0	4	4	7	6	0	2	3	0	16	0.6	1.0	2.3
REG. SEASON TOTALS	229	1	3118	417	958	.435	10	42	.238	291	332	.877	70	218	288	401	382	3	119	194	21	1135	1.3	1.8	5.0
PLAYOFF TOTALS	26	0	208	31	68	.456	2	8	.250	16	19	.842	10	13	23	39	25	0	10	12	0	80	0.9	1.5	3.1

SMITH, SAM b. January 27, 1944 Ht. 6-7 Wt. 230 College—Louisville/Kentucky Wesleyan

SEASON—TEAM	G	GS	MIN	FGM	FGA	PCT	3FGM	3FGA	PCT	FTM	FTA	PCT	O-RB	D-RB	TOT	AST	PF	DQ	STL	TO	BLK	PTS	RPG	APG	PPG
67-68—Minnesota (A)	77	—	2175	284	750	.379	2	6	.333	185	280	.661	—	—	586	81	171	1	—	94	—	755	7.6	1.1	9.8
68-69—Kentucky (A)	62	—	1421	173	437	.396	1	10	.100	114	172	.663	—	—	390	64	143	0	—	70	—	461	6.3	1.0	7.4
69-70—Kentucky (A)	81	—	2405	307	724	.424	1	4	.250	163	249	.655	—	—	719	109	202	4	—	—	—	778	8.9	1.3	9.6
70-71—Ken.-Utah (A)	35	—	302	39	93	.419	1	5	.200	24	39	.615	—	—	81	20	42	—	—	—	—	103	2.3	0.6	2.9
REG. ABA TOTALS	255	—	6303	803	2004	.401	5	25	.200	486	740	.657	—	—	1776	274	558	5	—	164	—	2097	7.0	1.1	8.2
ABA PLAYOFF TOTALS	32	—	895	131	304	.431	0	4	.000	70	105	.667	—	—	222	34	64	0	—	23	—	332	6.9	1.1	10.4

SMITH, SAM b. January 8, 1955   Ht. 6-4 Wt. 200 College—Seminole JC/Nevada-Las Vegas

SEASON—TEAM	G	GS	MIN	FGM	FGA	PCT	3FGM	3FGA	PCT	FTM	FTA	PCT	O-RB	D-RB	TOT	AST	PF	DQ	STL	TO	BLK	PTS	RPG	APG	PPG
78-79—Milwaukee	16	—	125	19	47	.404	—	—	—	18	24	.750	0	9	9	16	12	0	8	8	7	56	0.6	1.0	3.5
79-80—Chicago	30	—	496	97	230	.422	8	35	.229	57	63	.905	22	32	54	42	54	0	25	33	7	259	1.8	1.4	8.6
REG. SEASON TOTALS	46	—	621	116	277	.419	8	35	.229	75	87	.862	22	41	63	58	66	0	33	41	14	315	1.4	1.3	6.8

SMITH, STEVEN DELANO (**Steve**) b. March 31, 1969   Ht. 6-8 Wt. 205 College—Michigan State

SEASON—TEAM	G	GS	MIN	FGM	FGA	PCT	3FGM	3FGA	PCT	FTM	FTA	PCT	O-RB	D-RB	TOT	AST	PF	DQ	STL	TO	BLK	PTS	RPG	APG	PPG
91-92—Miami	61	59	1806	297	654	.454	40	125	.320	95	127	.748	81	107	188	278	162	1	59	152	19	729	3.1	4.6	12.0
92-93—Miami	48	43	1610	279	619	.451	53	132	.402	155	197	.787	56	141	197	267	148	3	50	129	16	766	4.1	5.6	16.0
93-94—Miami	78	77	2776	491	1076	.456	91	262	.347	273	327	.835	156	196	352	394	217	6	84	202	35	1346	4.5	5.1	17.3
REG. SEASON TOTALS	187	179	6192	1067	2349	.454	184	519	.355	523	651	.803	293	444	737	939	527	10	193	483	70	2841	3.9	5.0	15.2
PLAYOFF TOTALS	8	8	292	51	114	.447	16	33	.485	26	31	.839	20	16	36	26	14	0	8	13	3	144	4.5	3.3	18.0

SMITH, THOMAS F.X. (**Tom**) b. July 5, 1927   Ht. 6-1 Wt. 165 College—St. Peter's

SEASON—TEAM	G	GS	MIN	FGM	FGA	PCT	3FGM	3FGA	PCT	FTM	FTA	PCT	O-RB	D-RB	TOT	AST	PF	DQ	STL	TO	BLK	PTS	RPG	APG	PPG
51-52—New York	1	—	3	0	6	.000	—	—	—	4	6	.667	—	—	0	2	2	0	—	—	—	4	0.0	2.0	4.0
REG. SEASON TOTALS	1	—	3	0	6	.000	—	—	—	4	6	.667	—	—	0	2	2	0	—	—	—	4	0.0	2.0	4.0

SMITH, WILLIAM A. (**Bill**) b. February 14, 1949   Ht. 7-½ Wt. 220 College—Syracuse

SEASON—TEAM	G	GS	MIN	FGM	FGA	PCT	3FGM	3FGA	PCT	FTM	FTA	PCT	O-RB	D-RB	TOT	AST	PF	DQ	STL	TO	BLK	PTS	RPG	APG	PPG
71-72—Portland	22	—	448	72	173	.416	—	—	—	38	64	.594	—	—	135	19	73	3	—	—	—	182	6.1	0.9	8.3
72-73—Portland	8	—	43	9	15	.600	—	—	—	5	8	.625	—	—	8	1	8	0	—	—	—	23	1.0	0.1	2.9
REG. SEASON TOTALS	30	—	491	81	188	.431	—	—	—	43	72	.597	—	—	143	20	81	3	—	—	—	205	4.8	0.7	6.8

SMITH, WILLIAM C. (**Willie**) b. October 26, 1953   Ht. 6-2½ Wt. 180 College—Seminole JC/Missouri

SEASON—TEAM	G	GS	MIN	FGM	FGA	PCT	3FGM	3FGA	PCT	FTM	FTA	PCT	O-RB	D-RB	TOT	AST	PF	DQ	STL	TO	BLK	PTS	RPG	APG	PPG
76-77—Chicago	2	—	11	0	1	.000	—	—	—	0	0	—	0	0	0	0	1	0	0	—	0	0	0.0	0.0	0.0
77-78—Indiana	1	—	7	0	0	—	—	—	—	0	0	—	0	0	0	1	1	0	0	0	0	0	0.0	1.0	0.0
78-79—Portland	13	—	131	23	44	.523	—	—	—	12	17	.706	7	6	13	17	19	0	10	14	1	58	1.0	1.3	4.5
79-80—Cleveland	62	—	1051	121	315	.384	17	71	.239	40	52	.769	56	65	121	259	110	1	75	95	1	299	2.0	4.2	4.8
REG. SEASON TOTALS	78	—	1200	144	360	.400	17	71	.239	52	69	.754	63	71	134	277	131	1	85	109	2	357	1.7	3.6	4.6

SMITH, WILLIAM F. (**Bill**) b. April 26, 1939   Ht. 6-5 Wt. 190 College—St. Peter's

SEASON—TEAM	G	GS	MIN	FGM	FGA	PCT	3FGM	3FGA	PCT	FTM	FTA	PCT	O-RB	D-RB	TOT	AST	PF	DQ	STL	TO	BLK	PTS	RPG	APG	PPG
61-62—New York	9	—	83	8	33	.242	—	—	—	7	8	.875	—	—	16	7	6	0	—	—	—	23	1.8	0.8	2.6
REG. SEASON TOTALS	9	—	83	8	33	.242	—	—	—	7	8	.875	—	—	16	7	6	0	—	—	—	23	1.8	0.8	2.6

SMITS, RIK (**The Dunking Dutchman**) b. August 23, 1966   Ht. 7-4 Wt. 265 College—Marist

SEASON—TEAM	G	GS	MIN	FGM	FGA	PCT	3FGM	3FGA	PCT	FTM	FTA	PCT	O-RB	D-RB	TOT	AST	PF	DQ	STL	TO	BLK	PTS	RPG	APG	PPG
88-89—Indiana	82	71	2041	386	746	.517	0	1	.000	184	255	.722	185	315	500	70	310	14	37	130	151	956	6.1	0.9	11.7
89-90—Indiana	82	82	2404	515	967	.533	0	1	.000	241	297	.811	135	377	512	142	328	11	45	143	169	1271	6.2	1.7	15.5
90-91—Indiana	76	38	1690	342	705	.485	0	0	—	144	189	.762	116	241	357	84	246	3	24	86	111	828	4.7	1.1	10.9
91-92—Indiana	74	55	1772	436	855	.510	0	2	.000	152	193	.788	124	293	417	116	231	4	29	130	100	1024	5.6	1.6	13.8
92-93—Indiana	81	81	2072	494	1017	.486	0	0	—	167	228	.732	126	306	432	121	285	5	27	147	75	1155	5.3	1.5	14.3
93-94—Indiana	78	75	2113	493	923	.534	0	1	.000	238	300	.793	135	348	483	156	281	11	49	151	82	1224	6.2	2.0	15.7
REG. SEASON TOTALS	473	402	12092	2666	5213	.511	0	5	.000	1126	1462	.770	821	1880	2701	689	1681	48	211	787	688	6458	5.7	1.5	13.7
PLAYOFF TOTALS	31	24	805	179	358	.500	0	1	.000	84	105	.800	47	109	156	43	124	3	20	64	25	442	5.0	1.4	14.3

SMREK, MICHAEL FRANK (**Mike**) b. August 31, 1962   Ht. 7-0 Wt. 250 College—Canisius

SEASON—TEAM	G	GS	MIN	FGM	FGA	PCT	3FGM	3FGA	PCT	FTM	FTA	PCT	O-RB	D-RB	TOT	AST	PF	DQ	STL	TO	BLK	PTS	RPG	APG	PPG
85-86—Chicago	38	5	408	46	122	.377	0	2	.000	16	29	.552	46	64	110	19	95	0	6	29	23	108	2.9	0.5	2.8
86-87—L.A. Lakers	35	3	233	30	60	.500	0	0	—	16	25	.640	13	24	37	5	70	1	4	19	13	76	1.1	0.1	2.2
87-88—L.A. Lakers	48	2	421	44	103	.427	0	0	—	44	66	.667	27	58	85	8	105	3	7	30	42	132	1.8	0.2	2.8
88-89—San Antonio	43	18	623	72	153	.471	0	0	—	49	76	.645	42	87	129	12	102	2	13	48	58	193	3.0	0.3	4.5
89-90—Golden State	13	3	107	10	24	.417	0	0	—	1	6	.167	11	23	34	1	18	0	4	9	11	21	2.6	0.1	1.6
90-91—G.S.-L.A. Clips	15	0	95	9	27	.333	0	0	—	6	12	.500	7	19	26	4	27	1	3	3	3	24	1.7	0.3	1.6
91-92—Golden State	2	0	3	0	0	—	0	0	—	0	0	—	0	1	1	0	0	0	0	0	0	0	0.5	0.0	0.0
REG. SEASON TOTALS	194	31	1890	211	489	.431	0	2	.000	132	214	.617	146	276	422	49	417	7	37	138	150	554	2.2	0.3	2.9
PLAYOFF TOTALS	21	0	72	3	16	.188	0	0	—	5	9	.556	4	9	13	—	21	0	1	3	10	11	0.6	0.0	0.5

SMYTH, JOSEPH GEORGE (**Joe**) b. May 22, 1929   Ht. 6-3½ Wt. 215 College—Niagara

SEASON—TEAM	G	GS	MIN	FGM	FGA	PCT	3FGM	3FGA	PCT	FTM	FTA	PCT	O-RB	D-RB	TOT	AST	PF	DQ	STL	TO	BLK	PTS	RPG	APG	PPG
53-54—N.Y.-Balt.	40	—	495	48	138	.348	—	—	—	35	65	.538	—	—	98	49	53	0	—	—	—	131	2.5	1.2	3.3
REG. SEASON TOTALS	40	—	495	48	138	.348	—	—	—	35	65	.538	—	—	98	49	53	0	—	—	—	131	2.5	1.2	3.3

SNYDER, RICHARD J. JR. (**Dick**) b. February 1, 1944 Ht. 6-5 Wt. 210 College—Davidson

SEASON—TEAM	G	GS	MIN	FGM	FGA	PCT	3FGM	3FGA	PCT	FTM	FTA	PCT	O-RB	D-RB	TOT	AST	PF	DQ	STL	TO	BLK	PTS	RPG	APG	PPG
66-67—St. Louis	55	—	676	144	333	.432	—	—	—	46	61	.754	—	—	91	59	82	1	—	—	—	334	1.7	1.1	6.1
67-68—St. Louis	75	—	1622	257	613	.419	—	—	—	129	167	.772	—	—	194	164	215	5	—	—	—	643	2.6	2.2	8.6
68-69—Phoenix	81	—	2108	399	846	.472	—	—	—	185	255	.725	—	—	328	211	213	2	—	—	—	983	4.0	2.6	12.1
69-70—Phoenix-Seattle	82	—	2437	456	863	.528	—	—	—	169	208	.813	—	—	323	342	277	8	—	—	—	1081	3.9	4.2	13.2
70-71—Seattle	82	—	2824	645	1215	.531	—	—	—	302	361	.837	—	—	257	352	249	6	—	—	—	1592	3.1	4.3	19.4
71-72—Seattle	73	—	2534	496	937	.529	—	—	—	218	259	.842	—	—	228	283	200	3	—	—	—	1210	3.1	3.9	16.6
72-73—Seattle	82	—	3060	473	1022	.463	—	—	—	186	216	.861	—	—	323	311	216	2	—	—	—	1132	3.9	3.8	13.8
73-74—Seattle	74	—	2670	572	1189	.481	—	—	—	194	224	.866	90	216	306	265	257	4	90	—	26	1338	4.1	3.6	18.1
74-75—Cleveland	82	—	2590	498	988	.504	—	—	—	165	195	.846	37	201	238	281	226	3	69	—	43	1161	2.9	3.4	14.2
75-76—Cleveland	82	—	2274	441	881	.501	—	—	—	155	188	.824	50	148	198	220	215	0	59	—	33	1037	2.4	2.7	12.6
76-77—Cleveland	82	—	1685	316	693	.456	—	—	—	127	149	.852	47	102	149	160	177	2	45	—	30	759	1.8	2.0	9.3
77-78—Cleveland	58	—	660	112	252	.444	—	—	—	56	64	.875	9	40	49	56	74	0	23	48	19	280	0.8	1.0	4.8
78-79—Seattle	56	—	536	81	187	.433	—	—	—	43	51	.843	15	33	48	63	52	0	14	36	6	205	0.9	1.1	3.7
REG. SEASON TOTALS	964	—	25676	4890	10019	.488	—	—	—	1975	2398	.824	248	740	2732	2767	2453	36	300	84	157	11755	2.8	2.9	12.2
PLAYOFF TOTALS	31	—	572	97	233	.416	—	—	—	30	41	.732	14	31	50	49	55	1	16	8	11	224	1.6	1.6	7.2

SOBEK, GEORGE EDWARD (**Chips**) b. February 10, 1920 d. April 9, 1990 Ht. 6-1½ Wt. 180 College—Notre Dame

SEASON—TEAM	G	GS	MIN	FGM	FGA	PCT	3FGM	3FGA	PCT	FTM	FTA	PCT	O-RB	D-RB	TOT	AST	PF	DQ	STL	TO	BLK	PTS	RPG	APG	PPG
45-46—Indianapolis (N)	1	—	—	2	—	—	—	—	—	1	—	—	—	—	—	—	—	—	—	—	—	5	—	—	5.0
46-47—Toledo (N)	42	—	—	186	—	—	—	—	—	179	248	.722	—	—	—	106	—	—	—	—	—	551	—	—	13.1
47-48—Toledo (N)	48	—	—	118	—	—	—	—	—	124	170	.729	—	—	—	110	—	—	—	—	—	360	—	—	7.5
48-49—Hammond (N)	57	—	—	143	—	—	—	—	—	232	322	.720	—	—	—	167	—	—	—	—	—	518	—	—	9.1
49-50—Sheboygan	60	—	—	95	251	.378	—	—	—	156	205	.761	—	—	—	95	158	—	—	—	—	346	—	1.6	5.8
REG. NBA TOTALS	60	—	—	95	251	.378	—	—	—	156	205	.761	—	—	—	95	158	—	—	—	—	346	—	1.6	5.8
REG. NBL TOTALS	148	—	—	449	—	—	—	—	—	536	740	.723	—	—	—	383	—	—	—	—	—	1434	—	—	9.7
NBA PLAYOFF TOTALS	3	—	—	10	20	.500	—	—	—	12	16	.750	—	—	—	3	15	2	—	—	—	32	—	1.0	10.7
NBL PLAYOFF TOTALS	7	—	—	18	—	—	—	—	—	20	27	.741	—	—	—	25	—	—	—	—	—	56	—	—	8.0

SOBERS, RICKY BRAD b. January 15, 1953 Ht. 6-3 Wt. 200 College—Southern Idaho/Nevada-Las Vegas

SEASON—TEAM	G	GS	MIN	FGM	FGA	PCT	3FGM	3FGA	PCT	FTM	FTA	PCT	O-RB	D-RB	TOT	AST	PF	DQ	STL	TO	BLK	PTS	RPG	APG	PPG
75-76—Phoenix	78	—	1898	280	623	.449	—	—	—	158	192	.823	80	179	259	215	253	6	106	—	7	718	3.3	2.8	9.2
76-77—Phoenix	79	—	2005	414	834	.496	—	—	—	243	289	.841	82	152	234	238	258	3	93	—	14	1071	3.0	3.0	13.6
77-78—Indiana	79	—	3019	553	1221	.453	—	—	—	330	400	.825	92	235	327	584	308	10	170	352	23	1436	4.1	7.4	18.2
78-79—Indiana	81	—	2825	553	1194	.463	—	—	—	298	338	.882	118	183	301	450	315	8	138	304	23	1404	3.7	5.6	17.3
79-80—Chicago	82	—	2673	470	1002	.469	21	68	.309	200	239	.837	75	167	242	426	294	4	136	282	17	1161	3.0	5.2	14.2
80-81—Chicago	71	—	1803	355	769	.462	17	66	.258	231	247	.935	46	98	144	284	225	3	98	206	17	958	2.0	4.0	13.5
81-82—Chicago	80	6	1938	363	801	.453	19	76	.250	195	254	.768	37	105	142	301	238	6	73	217	18	940	1.8	3.8	11.8
82-83—Washington	41	39	1438	234	534	.438	23	55	.418	154	185	.832	35	67	102	218	158	3	61	147	14	645	2.5	5.3	15.7
83-84—Washington	81	81	2624	508	1115	.456	29	111	.261	221	264	.837	51	128	179	377	278	10	117	222	17	1266	2.2	4.7	15.6
84-85—Seattle	71	12	1490	280	628	.446	8	28	.286	132	162	.815	27	76	103	252	156	0	49	158	9	700	1.5	3.5	9.9
85-86—Seattle	78	0	1279	240	541	.444	13	43	.302	110	125	.880	29	70	99	180	139	1	44	85	2	603	1.3	2.3	7.7
REG. SEASON TOTALS	821	138	22992	4250	9262	.459	130	447	.291	2272	2695	.843	672	1460	2132	3525	2622	54	1085	1973	161	10902	2.6	4.3	13.3
PLAYOFF TOTALS	29	4	875	156	343	.455	4	16	.250	71	85	.835	25	54	79	117	122	5	27	24	8	387	2.7	4.0	13.3

SOBIE, RONALD CHARLES (**Ron, formerly Ronald Charles Sobieszczyk**) b. September 21, 1934 Ht. 6-3 Wt. 195 College—DePaul

SEASON—TEAM	G	GS	MIN	FGM	FGA	PCT	3FGM	3FGA	PCT	FTM	FTA	PCT	O-RB	D-RB	TOT	AST	PF	DQ	STL	TO	BLK	PTS	RPG	APG	PPG
56-57—New York	71	—	1378	166	442	.376	—	—	—	152	199	.764	—	—	326	129	158	0	—	—	—	484	4.6	1.8	6.8
57-58—New York	55	—	1399	217	539	.403	—	—	—	196	239	.820	—	—	263	125	147	3	—	—	—	630	4.8	2.3	11.5
58-59—New York	50	—	857	144	400	.360	—	—	—	112	133	.842	—	—	154	78	84	0	—	—	—	400	3.1	1.6	8.0
59-60—N.Y.-Minn.	16	—	234	37	108	.343	—	—	—	31	37	.838	—	—	48	21	32	0	—	—	—	105	3.0	1.3	6.6
REG. SEASON TOTALS	192	—	3868	564	1489	.379	—	—	—	491	608	.808	—	—	791	353	421	3	—	—	—	1619	4.1	1.8	8.4

SOBIESZCZYK, RONALD CHARLES (**see Ronald Charles Sobie**)

SOJOURNER, MIKE b. October 16, 1953 Ht. 6-9 Wt. 225 College—Utah

SEASON—TEAM	G	GS	MIN	FGM	FGA	PCT	3FGM	3FGA	PCT	FTM	FTA	PCT	O-RB	D-RB	TOT	AST	PF	DQ	STL	TO	BLK	PTS	RPG	APG	PPG
74-75—Atlanta	73	—	2129	378	775	.488	—	—	—	95	146	.651	196	446	642	93	217	10	35	—	57	851	8.8	1.3	11.7
75-76—Atlanta	67	—	1602	248	524	.473	—	—	—	80	119	.672	126	323	449	58	174	2	38	—	40	576	6.7	0.9	8.6
76-77—Atlanta	51	—	551	95	203	.468	—	—	—	41	57	.719	49	97	146	21	66	0	15	—	9	231	2.9	0.4	4.5
REG. SEASON TOTALS	191	—	4282	721	1502	.480	—	—	—	216	322	.671	371	866	1237	172	457	12	88	—	106	1658	6.5	0.9	8.7

SOJOURNER, WILLARD (Willie, Rainbow) b. September 10, 1948 Ht. 6-8 Wt. 225 College—Weber State

SEASON—TEAM	G	GS	MIN	FGM	FGA	PCT	3FGM	3FGA	PCT	FTM	FTA	PCT	O-RB	D-RB	TOT	AST	PF	DQ	STL	TO	BLK	PTS	RPG	APG	PPG
71-72—Virginia (A)	84	—	1313	222	448	.496	0	0	—	124	193	.642	—	—	514	56	222	—	—	86	—	568	6.1	0.7	6.8
72-73—Virginia (A)	64	—	1065	199	410	.485	0	0	—	84	128	.656	121	243	364	75	187	4	—	80	—	482	5.7	1.2	7.5
73-74—New York (A)	82	—	1316	202	419	.482	0	3	.000	54	64	.844	110	225	335	54	205	—	24	85	88	458	4.1	0.7	5.6
74-75—New York (A)	79	—	1020	155	324	.478	1	3	.333	49	70	.700	94	181	275	42	190	—	16	63	64	360	3.5	0.5	4.6
REG. ABA TOTALS	309	—	4714	778	1601	.486	1	6	.167	311	455	.684	325	649	1488	227	804	4	40	314	152	1868	4.8	0.7	6.0
ABA PLAYOFF TOTALS	32	—	297	44	91	.484	0	0	—	14	20	.700	24	23	76	18	52	0	2	30	21	102	2.4	0.6	3.2

SOMERSET, WILLARD F. (Willie) b. March 17, 1942 Ht. 5-10 Wt. 170 College—Duquesne

SEASON—TEAM	G	GS	MIN	FGM	FGA	PCT	3FGM	3FGA	PCT	FTM	FTA	PCT	O-RB	D-RB	TOT	AST	PF	DQ	STL	TO	BLK	PTS	RPG	APG	PPG
65-66—Baltimore	8	—	98	18	43	.419	—	—	—	9	11	.818	—	—	15	9	21	0	—	—	—	45	1.9	1.1	5.6
67-68—Houston (A)	61	—	2334	467	1042	.448	33	107	.308	359	460	.780	—	—	305	225	211	5	—	164	—	1326	5.0	3.7	21.7
68-69—Houston-N.Y. (A)	74	—	3118	619	1510	.410	36	139	.259	484	583	.830	—	—	332	280	261	4	—	215	—	1758	4.5	3.8	23.8
REG. NBA TOTALS	8	—	98	18	43	.419	—	—	—	9	11	.818	—	—	15	9	21	0	—	—	—	45	1.9	1.1	5.6
REG. ABA TOTALS	135	—	5452	1086	2552	.426	69	246	.280	843	1043	.808	—	—	637	505	472	9	—	379	—	3084	4.7	3.7	22.8
ABA PLAYOFF TOTALS	3	—	131	30	73	.411	4	14	.286	27	34	.794	—	—	25	9	11	0	—	16	—	91	8.3	3.0	30.3
ABA ALL-STAR TOTALS	1	—	17	2	7	.286	0	0	—	2	2	1.000	—	3	3	3	3	0	—	1	—	6	3.0	3.0	6.0

SORENSON, DAVID LOWELL (Dave) b. July 8, 1948 Ht. 6-8 Wt. 225 College—Ohio State

SEASON—TEAM	G	GS	MIN	FGM	FGA	PCT	3FGM	3FGA	PCT	FTM	FTA	PCT	O-RB	D-RB	TOT	AST	PF	DQ	STL	TO	BLK	PTS	RPG	APG	PPG
70-71—Cleveland	79	—	1940	353	794	.445	—	—	—	184	229	.803	—	—	486	163	181	3	—	—	—	890	6.2	2.1	11.3
71-72—Cleveland	76	—	1162	213	475	.448	—	—	—	106	136	.779	—	—	301	81	120	1	—	—	—	532	4.0	1.1	7.0
72-73—Clev.-Phil.	58	—	755	124	293	.423	—	—	—	64	90	.711	—	—	210	36	107	0	—	—	—	312	3.6	0.6	5.4
REG. SEASON TOTALS	213	—	3857	690	1562	.442	—	—	—	354	455	.778	—	—	997	280	408	4	—	—	—	1734	4.7	1.3	8.1

SOVRAN, GINO b. December 17, 1924 Ht. 6-2 Wt. 175 College—Assumption (Ont.)/Detroit

SEASON—TEAM	G	GS	MIN	FGM	FGA	PCT	3FGM	3FGA	PCT	FTM	FTA	PCT	O-RB	D-RB	TOT	AST	PF	DQ	STL	TO	BLK	PTS	RPG	APG	PPG
46-47—Toronto	6	—	—	5	15	.333	—	—	—	1	2	.500	—	—	—	1	5	—	—	—	—	11	—	0.2	1.8
REG. SEASON TOTALS	6	—	—	5	15	.333	—	—	—	1	2	.500	—	—	—	1	5	—	—	—	—	11	—	0.2	1.8

SPAIN, JOHN KENNETH (Ken) b. October 6, 1946 d. October 1990 Ht. 6-9 Wt. 235 College—Houston

SEASON—TEAM	G	GS	MIN	FGM	FGA	PCT	3FGM	3FGA	PCT	FTM	FTA	PCT	O-RB	D-RB	TOT	AST	PF	DQ	STL	TO	BLK	PTS	RPG	APG	PPG
70-71—Pittsburgh (A)	11	—	112	8	22	.364	0	0	—	8	17	.471	—	—	40	2	17	—	—	—	—	24	3.6	0.2	2.2
REG. ABA TOTALS	11	—	112	8	22	.364	0	0	—	8	17	.471	—	—	40	2	17	—	—	—	—	24	3.6	0.2	2.2

SPANARKEL, JAMES GERARD (Jim) b. June 28, 1957 Ht. 6-5 Wt. 190 College—Duke

SEASON—TEAM	G	GS	MIN	FGM	FGA	PCT	3FGM	3FGA	PCT	FTM	FTA	PCT	O-RB	D-RB	TOT	AST	PF	DQ	STL	TO	BLK	PTS	RPG	APG	PPG
79-80—Philadelphia	40	—	442	72	153	.471	0	2	.000	54	65	.831	27	27	54	51	58	0	12	57	6	198	1.4	1.3	5.0
80-81—Dallas	82	—	2317	404	866	.467	1	10	.100	375	423	.887	142	155	297	232	230	3	117	172	20	1184	3.6	2.8	14.4
81-82—Dallas	82	1	1755	270	564	.479	8	24	.333	279	327	.853	99	111	210	206	140	0	86	111	9	827	2.6	2.5	10.1
82-83—Dallas	48	4	722	91	197	.462	2	10	.200	88	113	.779	27	57	84	78	59	0	27	55	3	272	1.8	1.6	5.7
83-84—Dallas	7	0	54	7	16	.438	1	2	.500	9	13	.692	5	2	7	5	8	0	6	4	0	24	1.0	0.7	3.4
REG. SEASON TOTALS	259	5	5290	844	1796	.470	12	48	.250	805	941	.855	300	352	652	572	495	3	248	399	38	2505	2.5	2.2	9.7
PLAYOFF TOTALS	5	0	8	0	2	.000	0	0	—	2	2	1.000	0	1	1	1	1	0	0	0	0	2	0.2	0.2	0.4

SPARKS, DANIEL E. (Dan) b. April 17, 1945 Ht. 6-7½ Wt. 200 College—Vincennes/Weber State

SEASON—TEAM	G	GS	MIN	FGM	FGA	PCT	3FGM	3FGA	PCT	FTM	FTA	PCT	O-RB	D-RB	TOT	AST	PF	DQ	STL	TO	BLK	PTS	RPG	APG	PPG
68-69—Miami (A)	64	—	1138	153	396	.386	0	0	—	113	165	.685	—	—	287	43	171	5	—	70	—	419	4.5	0.7	6.5
69-70—Miami (A)	3	—	52	7	18	.389	0	0	—	5	6	.833	—	—	16	2	7	0	—	—	—	19	5.3	0.7	6.3
REG. ABA TOTALS	67	—	1190	160	414	.386	0	0	—	118	171	.690	—	—	303	45	178	5	—	70	—	438	4.5	0.7	6.5
ABA PLAYOFF TOTALS	12	—	251	29	65	.446	0	0	—	19	30	.633	—	—	57	8	35	0	—	14	—	77	4.8	0.7	6.4

SPARROW, GUY P. b. November 2, 1932 Ht. 6-6 Wt. 220 College—Detroit

SEASON—TEAM	G	GS	MIN	FGM	FGA	PCT	3FGM	3FGA	PCT	FTM	FTA	PCT	O-RB	D-RB	TOT	AST	PF	DQ	STL	TO	BLK	PTS	RPG	APG	PPG
57-58—New York	72	—	1661	318	838	.379	—	—	—	165	257	.642	—	—	461	69	232	6	—	—	—	801	6.4	1.0	11.1
58-59—N.Y.-Phil.	67	—	842	129	406	.318	—	—	—	78	138	.565	—	—	244	67	158	3	—	—	—	336	3.6	1.0	5.0
59-60—Philadelphia	11	—	80	14	45	.311	—	—	—	2	8	.250	—	—	23	6	20	0	—	—	—	30	2.1	0.5	2.7
REG. SEASON TOTALS	150	—	2583	461	1289	.358	—	—	—	245	403	.608	—	—	728	142	410	9	—	—	—	1167	4.9	0.9	7.8

SPARROW, RORY DARNELL b. June 12, 1958 Ht. 6-2 Wt. 175 College—Villanova

SEASON—TEAM	G	GS	MIN	FGM	FGA	PCT	3FGM	3FGA	PCT	FTM	FTA	PCT	O-RB	D-RB	TOT	AST	PF	DQ	STL	TO	BLK	PTS	RPG	APG	PPG
80-81—New Jersey	15	—	212	22	63	.349	0	0	—	12	16	.750	7	11	18	32	15	0	13	18	3	56	1.2	2.1	3.7
81-82—Atlanta	82	82	2610	366	730	.501	1	15	.067	124	148	.838	53	171	224	424	240	2	87	145	13	857	2.7	5.2	10.5
82-83—Atlanta-N.Y.	81	58	2428	392	810	.484	5	22	.227	147	199	.739	61	169	230	397	255	4	107	197	5	936	2.8	4.9	11.6
83-84—New York	79	74	2436	350	738	.474	10	39	.256	108	131	.824	48	141	189	539	230	4	100	210	8	818	2.4	6.8	10.4
84-85—New York	79	41	2292	326	662	.492	7	31	.226	122	141	.865	38	131	169	557	200	2	81	150	9	781	2.1	7.1	9.9
85-86—New York	74	74	2344	345	723	.477	5	20	.250	101	127	.795	50	120	170	472	182	1	85	154	14	796	2.3	6.4	10.8
86-87—New York	80	30	1951	263	590	.446	11	42	.262	71	89	.798	29	86	115	432	160	0	67	140	6	608	1.4	5.4	7.6
87-88—N.Y.-Chicago	58	25	1044	117	293	.399	2	13	.154	24	33	.727	15	57	72	167	79	1	41	58	3	260	1.2	2.9	4.5
88-89—Miami	80	79	2613	444	982	.452	18	74	.243	94	107	.879	55	161	216	429	168	0	103	204	17	1000	2.7	5.4	12.5
89-90—Miami	82	25	1756	210	510	.412	8	40	.200	59	77	.766	37	101	138	298	140	0	49	99	4	487	1.7	3.6	5.9
90-91—Sacramento	80	74	2375	371	756	.491	31	78	.397	58	83	.699	45	141	186	362	189	1	83	126	16	831	2.3	4.5	10.4
91-92—Chicago-Lakers	46	0	489	58	151	.384	3	15	.200	8	13	.615	3	25	28	83	57	0	12	33	5	127	0.6	1.8	2.8
REG. SEASON TOTALS	836	562	22550	3264	7008	.466	101	389	.260	928	1164	.797	441	1314	1755	4192	1915	15	828	1534	103	7557	2.1	5.0	9.0
PLAYOFF TOTALS	30	20	782	100	240	.417	5	16	.313	52	65	.800	16	35	51	161	82	3	26	54	1	257	1.7	5.4	8.6

SPEARS, MARION ODICCA (**Odie**) b. June 26, 1925 d. March 28, 1985 Ht. 6-4½ Wt. 205 College—Western Kentucky

SEASON—TEAM	G	GS	MIN	FGM	FGA	PCT	3FGM	3FGA	PCT	FTM	FTA	PCT	O-RB	D-RB	TOT	AST	PF	DQ	STL	TO	BLK	PTS	RPG	APG	PPG
48-49—Chicago	57	—	—	200	631	.317	—	—	—	131	197	.665	—	—	—	97	200	—	—	—	—	531	—	1.7	9.3
49-50—Chicago	68	—	—	277	775	.357	—	—	—	158	230	.687	—	—	—	159	250	—	—	—	—	712	—	2.3	10.5
51-52—Rochester	66	—	1673	225	570	.395	—	—	—	116	152	.763	—	—	303	163	225	8	—	—	—	566	4.6	2.5	8.6
52-53—Rochester	62	—	1414	198	494	.401	—	—	—	199	243	.819	—	—	251	113	227	15	—	—	—	595	4.0	1.8	9.6
53-54—Rochester	72	—	1633	184	505	.364	—	—	—	183	238	.769	—	—	310	109	211	5	—	—	—	551	4.3	1.5	7.7
54-55—Rochester	71	—	1888	226	585	.386	—	—	—	220	271	.812	—	—	299	148	252	6	—	—	—	672	4.2	2.1	9.5
55-56—Fort Wayne	72	—	1378	166	468	.355	—	—	—	159	201	.791	—	—	231	121	191	2	—	—	—	491	3.2	1.7	6.8
56-57—Ft. Wayne-St. L.	11	—	118	12	38	.316	—	—	—	19	22	.864	—	—	15	7	24	0	—	—	—	43	1.4	0.6	3.9
REG. SEASON TOTALS	479	—	8104	1488	4066	.366	—	—	—	1185	1554	.763	—	—	1409	917	1580	36	—	—	—	4161	4.0	1.9	8.7
PLAYOFF TOTALS	32	—	573	74	215	.344	—	—	—	58	91	.637	—	—	89	44	114	5	—	—	—	206	3.2	1.4	6.4

SPECTOR, ARTHUR EDWARD (**Art, Speed**) b. October 17, 1920 d. June 18, 1987 Ht. 6-4 Wt. 200 College—Villanova

SEASON—TEAM	G	GS	MIN	FGM	FGA	PCT	3FGM	3FGA	PCT	FTM	FTA	PCT	O-RB	D-RB	TOT	AST	PF	DQ	STL	TO	BLK	PTS	RPG	APG	PPG
46-47—Boston	55	—	—	123	460	.267	—	—	—	83	150	.553	—	—	—	46	130	—	—	—	—	329	—	0.8	6.0
47-48—Boston	48	—	—	67	243	.276	—	—	—	60	92	.652	—	—	—	17	106	—	—	—	—	194	—	0.4	4.0
48-49—Boston	59	—	—	130	434	.300	—	—	—	64	116	.552	—	—	—	77	111	—	—	—	—	324	—	1.3	5.5
49-50—Boston	7	—	—	2	12	.167	—	—	—	1	4	.250	—	—	—	3	4	—	—	—	—	5	—	0.4	0.7
REG. SEASON TOTALS	169	—	—	322	1149	.280	—	—	—	208	362	.575	—	—	—	143	351	—	—	—	—	852	—	0.8	5.0
PLAYOFF TOTALS	3	—	—	2	9	.222	—	—	—	2	4	.500	—	—	—	—	9	—	—	—	—	6	—	0.0	2.0

SPENCER, ANDRE b. July 20, 1964 Ht. 6-6 Wt. 210 College—Bakersfield/Northern Arizona

SEASON—TEAM	G	GS	MIN	FGM	FGA	PCT	3FGM	3FGA	PCT	FTM	FTA	PCT	O-RB	D-RB	TOT	AST	PF	DQ	STL	TO	BLK	PTS	RPG	APG	PPG
92-93—Atlanta-G.S.	20	1	422	73	163	.448	0	2	.000	41	54	.759	38	43	81	24	64	0	17	26	7	187	4.1	1.2	9.4
93-94—G.S.-Sac.	28	1	349	52	118	.441	0	0	—	55	77	.714	30	43	73	22	43	0	19	21	7	159	2.6	0.8	5.7
REG. SEASON TOTALS	48	2	771	125	281	.445	0	2	.000	96	131	.733	68	86	154	46	107	0	36	47	14	346	3.2	1.0	7.2

SPENCER, ELMORE b. December 6, 1969 Ht. 7-0 Wt. 270 College—Georgia/Connors St. JC/Clark County CC/Nevada-Las Vegas

SEASON—TEAM	G	GS	MIN	FGM	FGA	PCT	3FGM	3FGA	PCT	FTM	FTA	PCT	O-RB	D-RB	TOT	AST	PF	DQ	STL	TO	BLK	PTS	RPG	APG	PPG
92-93—L.A. Clippers	44	4	280	44	82	.537	0	0	—	16	32	.500	17	45	62	8	54	0	8	26	18	104	1.4	0.2	2.4
93-94—L.A. Clippers	76	63	1930	288	540	.533	0	2	.000	97	162	.599	96	319	415	75	208	3	30	168	127	673	5.5	1.0	8.9
REG. SEASON TOTALS	120	67	2210	332	622	.534	0	2	.000	113	194	.582	113	364	477	83	262	3	38	194	145	777	4.0	0.7	6.5
PLAYOFF TOTALS	2	0	4	0	2	.000	0	0	—	0	0	—	1	0	1	—	1	0	0	0	0	0	0.5	0.0	0.0

SPENCER, FELTON LaFRANCE b. January 5, 1968 Ht. 7-0 Wt. 265 College—Louisville

SEASON—TEAM	G	GS	MIN	FGM	FGA	PCT	3FGM	3FGA	PCT	FTM	FTA	PCT	O-RB	D-RB	TOT	AST	PF	DQ	STL	TO	BLK	PTS	RPG	APG	PPG
90-91—Minnesota	81	46	2099	195	381	.512	0	1	.000	182	252	.722	272	369	641	25	337	14	48	77	121	572	7.9	0.3	7.1
91-92—Minnesota	61	54	1481	141	331	.426	0	0	—	123	178	.691	167	268	435	53	241	7	27	70	79	405	7.1	0.9	6.6
92-93—Minnesota	71	48	1296	105	226	.465	0	0	—	83	127	.654	134	190	324	17	243	10	23	70	66	293	4.6	0.2	4.1
93-94—Utah	79	79	2210	256	507	.505	0	0	—	165	272	.607	235	423	658	43	304	5	41	127	67	677	8.3	0.5	8.6
REG. SEASON TOTALS	292	227	7086	697	1445	.482	0	1	.000	553	829	.667	808	1250	2058	138	1125	36	139	344	333	1947	7.0	0.5	6.7
PLAYOFF TOTALS	16	16	492	47	105	.448	0	0	—	33	50	.660	61	74	135	7	73	3	3	24	20	127	8.4	0.4	7.9

SPICER, LEWIS G. (**Lou**) b. November 12, 1922 d. June 23, 1981 Ht. 6-2 Wt. 195 College—Syracuse

SEASON—TEAM	G	GS	MIN	FGM	FGA	PCT	3FGM	3FGA	PCT	FTM	FTA	PCT	O-RB	D-RB	TOT	AST	PF	DQ	STL	TO	BLK	PTS	RPG	APG	PPG
46-47—Providence	4	—	—	0	7	.000	—	—	—	1	2	.500	—	—	—	0	3	—	—	—	—	1	—	0.0	0.3
REG. SEASON TOTALS	4	—	—	0	7	.000	—	—	—	1	2	.500	—	—	—	0	3	—	—	—	—	1	—	0.0	0.3

SPITZER, CRAIG W. b. December 18, 1945 Ht. 7-0 Wt. 225 College—Tulane

SEASON—TEAM	G	GS	MIN	FGM	FGA	PCT	3FGM	3FGA	PCT	FTM	FTA	PCT	O-RB	D-RB	TOT	AST	PF	DQ	STL	TO	BLK	PTS	RPG	APG	PPG
67-68—Chicago	10	—	44	8	21	.381	—	—	—	2	3	.667	—	—	24	0	4	0	—	—	—	18	2.4	0.0	1.8
REG. SEASON TOTALS	10	—	44	8	21	.381	—	—	—	2	3	.667	—	—	24	0	4	0	—	—	—	18	2.4	0.0	1.8
PLAYOFF TOTALS	1	—	3	0	3	.000	—	—	—	0	0	—	—	—	3	1	0	0	—	—	—	0	3.0	1.0	0.0

SPOELSTRA, ARTHUR CORNELIUS (**Art**) b. September 11, 1932 Ht. 6-9 Wt. 220 College—Western Kentucky

SEASON—TEAM	G	GS	MIN	FGM	FGA	PCT	3FGM	3FGA	PCT	FTM	FTA	PCT	O-RB	D-RB	TOT	AST	PF	DQ	STL	TO	BLK	PTS	RPG	APG	PPG
54-55—Rochester	70	—	1127	159	399	.398	—	—	—	108	156	.692	—	—	285	58	170	2	—	—	—	426	4.1	0.8	6.1
55-56—Rochester	72	—	1640	226	576	.392	—	—	—	163	238	.685	—	—	436	95	248	11	—	—	—	615	6.1	1.3	8.5
56-57—Rochester	69	—	1176	217	559	.388	—	—	—	88	120	.733	—	—	220	56	168	5	—	—	—	522	3.2	0.8	7.6
57-58—Minn.-N.Y.	67	—	1305	161	419	.384	—	—	—	127	187	.679	—	—	332	57	225	11	—	—	—	449	5.0	0.9	6.7
REG. SEASON TOTALS	278	—	5248	763	1953	.391	—	—	—	486	701	.693	—	—	1273	266	811	29	—	—	—	2012	4.6	1.0	7.2
PLAYOFF TOTALS	3	—	28	7	14	.500	—	—	—	1	1	1.000	—	—	9	—	11	0	—	—	—	15	3.0	0.0	5.0

SPRAGGINS, WARREN BRUCE (**Bruce**) b. 1940 Ht. 6-5½ Wt. 190 College—Virginia Union

SEASON—TEAM	G	GS	MIN	FGM	FGA	PCT	3FGM	3FGA	PCT	FTM	FTA	PCT	O-RB	D-RB	TOT	AST	PF	DQ	STL	TO	BLK	PTS	RPG	APG	PPG
67-68—New Jersey (A)	70	—	1590	306	686	.446	2	5	.400	238	336	.708	—	—	329	66	173	2	—	81	—	852	4.7	0.9	12.2
REG. ABA TOTALS	70	—	1590	306	686	.446	2	5	.400	238	336	.708	—	—	329	66	173	2	—	81	—	852	4.7	0.9	12.2

SPREWELL, LATRELL FONTAINE b. September 8, 1970 Ht. 6-5 Wt. 190 College—Three Rivers CC/Alabama

SEASON—TEAM	G	GS	MIN	FGM	FGA	PCT	3FGM	3FGA	PCT	FTM	FTA	PCT	O-RB	D-RB	TOT	AST	PF	DQ	STL	TO	BLK	PTS	RPG	APG	PPG
92-93—Golden State	77	69	2741	449	968	.464	73	198	.369	211	283	.746	79	192	271	295	166	2	126	203	52	1182	3.5	3.8	15.4
93-94—Golden State	82	82	3533	613	1417	.433	141	391	.361	353	456	.774	80	321	401	385	158	0	180	226	76	1720	4.9	4.7	21.0
REG. SEASON TOTALS	159	151	6274	1062	2385	.445	214	589	.363	564	739	.763	159	513	672	680	324	2	306	429	128	2902	4.2	4.3	18.3
PLAYOFF TOTALS	3	3	122	26	60	.433	8	23	.348	8	12	.667	1	8	9	21	15	0	2	9	3	68	3.0	7.0	22.7
ALL-STAR TOTALS	1	0	15	3	8	.375	0	2	.000	3	7	.429	4	3	7	1	1	0	0	2	0	9	7.0	1.0	9.0

SPRIGGS, LARRY MICHAEL b. September 8, 1959 Ht. 6-7 Wt. 230 College—San Jacinto/Howard

SEASON—TEAM	G	GS	MIN	FGM	FGA	PCT	3FGM	3FGA	PCT	FTM	FTA	PCT	O-RB	D-RB	TOT	AST	PF	DQ	STL	TO	BLK	PTS	RPG	APG	PPG
81-82—Houston	4	0	37	7	11	.636	0	0	—	0	2	.000	2	4	6	4	7	0	2	4	0	14	1.5	1.0	3.5
82-83—Chicago	9	0	39	8	20	.400	0	0	—	5	7	.714	2	7	9	3	3	0	1	2	2	21	1.0	0.3	2.3
83-84—Los Angeles	38	0	363	44	82	.537	0	2	.000	36	50	.720	16	45	61	30	55	0	12	34	4	124	1.6	0.8	3.3
84-85—L.A. Lakers	75	32	1292	194	354	.548	0	3	.000	112	146	.767	77	150	227	132	195	2	47	115	13	500	3.0	1.8	6.7
85-86—L.A. Lakers	43	7	471	88	192	.458	0	1	.000	38	49	.776	28	53	81	49	78	0	18	54	9	214	1.9	1.1	5.0
REG. SEASON TOTALS	169	39	2202	341	659	.517	0	6	.000	191	254	.752	125	259	384	218	338	2	80	209	28	873	2.3	1.3	5.2
PLAYOFF TOTALS	30	0	297	55	106	.519	0	2	.000	39	51	.765	21	47	68	40	50	0	5	33	6	149	2.3	1.3	5.0

SPRINGER, JAMES E. (**Jim**) b. June 17, 1926 Ht. 6-9 Wt. 235 College—Canterbury

SEASON—TEAM	G	GS	MIN	FGM	FGA	PCT	3FGM	3FGA	PCT	FTM	FTA	PCT	O-RB	D-RB	TOT	AST	PF	DQ	STL	TO	BLK	PTS	RPG	APG	PPG
47-48—And.-Ind. (N)	25	—	—	12	—	—	—	—	—	25	40	.625	—	—	—	29	—	—	—	—	—	49	—	—	2.0
48-49—Indianapolis	2	—	—	0	0	—	—	—	—	1	1	1.000	—	—	—	0	0	—	—	—	—	1	—	0.0	0.5
REG. NBA TOTALS	2	—	—	0	0	—	—	—	—	1	1	1.000	—	—	—	0	0	—	—	—	—	1	—	0.0	0.5
REG. NBL TOTALS	25	—	—	12	—	—	—	—	—	25	40	.625	—	—	—	29	—	—	—	—	—	49	—	—	2.0
NBL PLAYOFF TOTALS	3	—	—	0	—	—	—	—	—	0	2	.000	—	—	—	3	—	—	—	—	—	0	—	—	0.0

SPRUILL, JAMES WINFRED (**Jim**) b. February 26, 1923 Ht. 6-2½ Wt. 225 College—Rice

SEASON—TEAM	G	GS	MIN	FGM	FGA	PCT	3FGM	3FGA	PCT	FTM	FTA	PCT	O-RB	D-RB	TOT	AST	PF	DQ	STL	TO	BLK	PTS	RPG	APG	PPG
48-49—Indianapolis	1	—	—	1	3	.333	—	—	—	0	0	—	—	—	—	0	3	—	—	—	—	2	—	0.0	2.0
REG. SEASON TOTALS	1	—	—	1	3	.333	—	—	—	0	0	—	—	—	—	0	3	—	—	—	—	2	—	0.0	2.0

STACEY, ROBERT L. (**see Stacey Arceneaux**)

STACOM, KEVIN M. b. September 4, 1951 Ht. 6-3 Wt. 185 College—Holy Cross/Providence

SEASON—TEAM	G	GS	MIN	FGM	FGA	PCT	3FGM	3FGA	PCT	FTM	FTA	PCT	O-RB	D-RB	TOT	AST	PF	DQ	STL	TO	BLK	PTS	RPG	APG	PPG
74-75—Boston	61	—	447	72	159	.453	—	—	—	29	33	.879	30	25	55	49	65	0	11	—	3	173	0.9	0.8	2.8
75-76—Boston	77	—	1114	170	387	.439	—	—	—	68	91	.747	62	99	161	128	117	0	23	—	5	408	2.1	1.7	5.3
76-77—Boston	79	—	1051	179	438	.409	—	—	—	46	58	.793	40	57	97	117	65	0	19	—	3	404	1.2	1.5	5.1
77-78—Boston	55	—	1006	206	484	.426	—	—	—	54	71	.761	26	80	106	111	60	0	28	69	3	466	1.9	2.0	8.5
78-79—Indiana-Boston	68	—	831	128	342	.374	—	—	—	44	60	.733	30	55	85	112	47	0	29	80	1	300	1.3	1.6	4.4
81-82—Milwaukee	7	0	90	14	34	.412	1	2	.500	1	2	.500	2	5	7	7	6	0	1	9	0	30	1.0	1.0	4.3
REG. SEASON TOTALS	347	0	4539	769	1844	.417	1	2	.500	242	315	.768	190	321	511	524	360	0	111	158	15	1781	1.5	1.5	5.1
PLAYOFF TOTALS	26	0	227	16	53	.302	—	—	—	9	12	.750	9	10	19	21	24	0	5	—	0	41	0.7	0.8	1.6

STAGGS, JAMES ERVIN (Erv) b. 1948 Ht. 6-6 Wt. 195 College—Cheyney State

SEASON—TEAM	G	GS	MIN	FGM	FGA	PCT	3FGM	3FGA	PCT	FTM	FTA	PCT	O-RB	D-RB	TOT	AST	PF	DQ	STL	TO	BLK	PTS	RPG	APG	PPG
69-70—Miami (A)	53	—	1058	189	474	.399	2	7	.286	73	114	.640	—	—	122	76	155	7	—	—	—	453	2.3	1.4	8.5
REG. ABA TOTALS	53	—	1058	189	474	.399	2	7	.286	73	114	.640	—	—	122	76	155	7	—	—	—	453	2.3	1.4	8.5

STALLWORTH, DAVID A. (Dave, The Rave) b. December 20, 1941 Ht. 6-7 Wt. 200 College—Wichita State

SEASON—TEAM	G	GS	MIN	FGM	FGA	PCT	3FGM	3FGA	PCT	FTM	FTA	PCT	O-RB	D-RB	TOT	AST	PF	DQ	STL	TO	BLK	PTS	RPG	APG	PPG
65-66—New York	80	—	1893	373	820	.455	—	—	—	258	376	.686	—	—	492	186	237	4	—	—	—	1004	6.2	2.3	12.6
66-67—New York	76	—	1889	380	816	.466	—	—	—	229	320	.716	—	—	472	144	226	4	—	—	—	989	6.2	1.9	13.0
69-70—New York	82	—	1375	239	557	.429	—	—	—	161	225	.716	—	—	323	139	194	2	—	—	—	639	3.9	1.7	7.8
70-71—New York	81	—	1565	295	685	.431	—	—	—	169	230	.735	—	—	352	106	175	1	—	—	—	759	4.3	1.3	9.4
71-72—N.Y.-Balt.	78	—	2040	336	778	.432	—	—	—	152	188	.809	—	—	433	158	217	3	—	—	—	824	5.6	2.0	10.6
72-73—Baltimore	73	—	1217	180	435	.414	—	—	—	78	101	.772	—	—	236	112	139	1	—	—	—	438	3.2	1.5	6.0
73-74—Capital	45	—	458	75	187	.401	—	—	—	47	55	.855	52	73	125	25	61	0	28	—	4	197	2.8	0.6	4.4
74-75—New York	7	—	57	5	18	.278	—	—	—	0	0	—	6	14	20	2	10	0	3	—	3	10	2.9	0.3	1.4
REG. SEASON TOTALS	522	—	10494	1883	4296	.438	—	—	—	1094	1495	.732	58	87	2453	872	1259	15	31	—	7	4860	4.7	1.7	9.3
PLAYOFF TOTALS	40	—	579	92	230	.400	—	—	—	52	68	.765	0	0	137	36	79	0	0	—	0	236	3.4	0.9	5.9

STALLWORTH, ISAAC (Bud) b. January 18, 1950 Ht. 6-5 Wt. 190 College—Kansas

SEASON—TEAM	G	GS	MIN	FGM	FGA	PCT	3FGM	3FGA	PCT	FTM	FTA	PCT	O-RB	D-RB	TOT	AST	PF	DQ	STL	TO	BLK	PTS	RPG	APG	PPG
72-73—Seattle	77	—	1225	198	522	.379	—	—	—	86	114	.754	—	—	225	58	138	0	—	—	—	482	2.9	0.8	6.3
73-74—Seattle	67	—	1019	188	479	.392	—	—	—	48	77	.623	51	123	174	33	129	0	21	—	12	424	2.6	0.5	6.3
74-75—New Orleans	73	—	1668	298	710	.420	—	—	—	125	182	.687	78	168	246	46	208	4	59	—	11	721	3.4	0.6	9.9
75-76—New Orleans	56	—	1051	211	483	.437	—	—	—	85	124	.685	42	103	145	53	135	1	30	—	17	507	2.6	0.9	9.1
76-77—New Orleans	40	—	526	126	272	.463	—	—	—	17	29	.586	19	52	71	23	76	1	19	—	11	269	1.8	0.6	6.7
REG. SEASON TOTALS	313	—	5489	1021	2466	.414	—	—	—	361	526	.686	190	446	861	213	686	6	129	—	51	2403	2.8	0.7	7.7

STANCZAK, EDMUND A. (Ed, Moose) b. August 15, 1921 Ht. 6-3 Wt. 205 College—None

SEASON—TEAM	G	GS	MIN	FGM	FGA	PCT	3FGM	3FGA	PCT	FTM	FTA	PCT	O-RB	D-RB	TOT	AST	PF	DQ	STL	TO	BLK	PTS	RPG	APG	PPG
46-47—Anderson (N)	44	—	—	142	—	—	—	—	—	118	201	.587	—	—	—	—	109	—	—	—	—	402	—	—	9.1
47-48—Anderson (N)	55	—	—	73	—	—	—	—	—	61	102	.598	—	—	—	—	95	—	—	—	—	207	—	—	3.8
48-49—Anderson (N)	64	—	—	191	—	—	—	—	—	202	275	.735	—	—	—	—	209	—	—	—	—	584	—	—	9.1
49-50—Anderson	57	—	—	159	456	.349	—	—	—	203	270	.752	—	—	—	67	166	—	—	—	—	521	—	1.2	9.1
50-51—Boston	17	—	—	11	48	.229	—	—	—	35	43	.814	—	—	—	34	6	6	0	—	—	57	2.0	0.4	3.4
REG. NBA TOTALS	74	—	—	170	504	.337	—	—	—	238	313	.760	—	—	—	34	73	172	0	—	—	578	2.0	1.0	7.8
REG. NBL TOTALS	163	—	—	406	—	—	—	—	—	381	578	.659	—	—	—	—	413	—	—	—	—	1193	—	—	7.3
NBA PLAYOFF TOTALS	8	—	—	14	48	.292	—	—	—	23	30	.767	—	—	—	10	26	1	—	—	—	51	—	1.3	6.4
NBL PLAYOFF TOTALS	13	—	—	17	—	—	—	—	—	27	46	.587	—	—	—	—	41	—	—	—	—	61	—	—	4.7

STANSBURY, TERENCE R. b. February 27, 1961 Ht. 6-5 Wt. 175 College—Temple

SEASON—TEAM	G	GS	MIN	FGM	FGA	PCT	3FGM	3FGA	PCT	FTM	FTA	PCT	O-RB	D-RB	TOT	AST	PF	DQ	STL	TO	BLK	PTS	RPG	APG	PPG
84-85—Indiana	74	14	1278	210	458	.459	4	25	.160	102	126	.810	39	75	114	127	205	2	47	80	12	526	1.5	1.7	7.1
85-86—Indiana	74	17	1331	191	441	.433	9	53	.170	107	132	.811	29	110	139	206	200	2	59	139	8	498	1.9	2.8	6.7
86-87—Seattle	44	0	375	67	156	.429	11	29	.379	31	50	.620	8	16	24	57	78	0	13	29	0	176	0.5	1.3	4.0
REG. SEASON TOTALS	192	31	2984	468	1055	.444	24	107	.224	240	308	.779	76	201	277	390	483	4	119	248	20	1200	1.4	2.0	6.3

STARKS, JOHN LEVELL b. August 10, 1965 Ht. 6-5 Wt. 185 College—Northern Oklahoma/Rogers St./Oklahoma JC/Oklahoma St.

SEASON—TEAM	G	GS	MIN	FGM	FGA	PCT	3FGM	3FGA	PCT	FTM	FTA	PCT	O-RB	D-RB	TOT	AST	PF	DQ	STL	TO	BLK	PTS	RPG	APG	PPG
88-89—Golden State	36	0	316	51	125	.408	10	26	.385	34	52	.654	15	26	41	27	36	0	23	39	3	146	1.1	0.8	4.1
90-91—New York	61	10	1173	180	410	.439	27	93	.290	79	105	.752	30	101	131	204	137	1	59	74	17	466	2.1	3.3	7.6
91-92—New York	82	0	2118	405	902	.449	94	270	.348	235	302	.778	45	146	191	276	231	4	103	150	18	1139	2.3	3.4	13.9
92-93—New York	80	51	2477	513	1199	.428	108	336	.321	263	331	.795	54	150	204	404	234	3	91	173	12	1397	2.6	5.1	17.5
93-94—New York	59	54	2057	410	977	.420	113	337	.335	187	248	.754	37	148	185	348	191	4	95	184	6	1120	3.1	5.9	19.0
REG. SEASON TOTALS	318	115	8141	1559	3613	.431	352	1062	.331	798	1038	.769	181	571	752	1259	829	12	371	620	56	4268	2.4	4.0	13.4
PLAYOFF TOTALS	55	33	1738	246	617	.399	86	253	.340	184	240	.767	21	122	143	254	192	2	67	140	5	762	2.6	4.6	13.9
ALL-STAR TOTALS	1	0	20	4	9	.444	1	3	.333	0	0	—	1	2	3	3	1	0	1	2	0	9	3.0	3.0	9.0

STARR, KEITH EDWARD b. March 14, 1954 Ht. 6-6½ Wt. 195 College—Pittsburgh

SEASON—TEAM	G	GS	MIN	FGM	FGA	PCT	3FGM	3FGA	PCT	FTM	FTA	PCT	O-RB	D-RB	TOT	AST	PF	DQ	STL	TO	BLK	PTS	RPG	APG	PPG
76-77—Chicago	17	—	65	6	24	.250	—	—	—	2	2	1.000	6	4	10	6	11	0	1	—	0	14	0.6	0.4	0.8
REG. SEASON TOTALS	17	—	65	6	24	.250	—	—	—	2	2	1.000	6	4	10	6	11	0	1	—	0	14	0.6	0.4	0.8

STAVERMAN, LARRY JOSEPH b. October 11, 1936 Ht. 6-7 Wt. 205 College—Thomas More

SEASON—TEAM	G	GS	MIN	FGM	FGA	PCT	3FGM	3FGA	PCT	FTM	FTA	PCT	O-RB	D-RB	TOT	AST	PF	DQ	STL	TO	BLK	PTS	RPG	APG	PPG
58-59—Cincinnati	57	—	681	101	215	.470	—	—	—	45	59	.763	—	—	218	54	103	0	—	—	—	247	3.8	0.9	4.3
59-60—Cincinnati	49	—	479	70	149	.470	—	—	—	47	64	.734	—	—	180	36	98	0	—	—	—	187	3.7	0.7	3.8
60-61—Cincinnati	66	—	944	111	249	.446	—	—	—	79	93	.849	—	—	287	86	164	4	—	—	—	301	4.3	1.3	4.6
62-63—Chicago	33	—	602	94	194	.485	—	—	—	49	62	.790	—	—	158	43	94	3	—	—	—	237	4.8	1.3	7.2
63-64—Balt.-Detroit-Cin.	60	—	674	98	212	.462	—	—	—	69	90	.767	—	—	176	32	118	3	—	—	—	265	2.9	0.5	4.4
REG. SEASON TOTALS	265	—	3380	474	1019	.465	—	—	—	289	368	.785	—	—	1019	251	577	10	—	—	—	1237	3.8	0.9	4.7
PLAYOFF TOTALS	7	—	70	11	23	.478	—	—	—	15	19	.789	—	—	26	5	16	0	—	—	—	37	3.7	0.7	5.3

STEELE, LARRY NELSON b. May 5, 1949 Ht. 6-5 Wt. 180 College—Kentucky

SEASON—TEAM	G	GS	MIN	FGM	FGA	PCT	3FGM	3FGA	PCT	FTM	FTA	PCT	O-RB	D-RB	TOT	AST	PF	DQ	STL	TO	BLK	PTS	RPG	APG	PPG
71-72—Portland	72	—	1311	148	308	.481	—	—	—	70	97	.722	—	—	282	161	198	8	—	—	—	366	3.9	2.2	5.1
72-73—Portland	66	—	1301	159	329	.483	—	—	—	71	89	.798	—	—	154	156	181	4	—	—	—	389	2.3	2.4	5.9
73-74—Portland	81	—	2648	325	680	.478	—	—	—	135	171	.789	89	221	310	323	295	10	217	—	32	785	3.8	4.0	9.7
74-75—Portland	76	—	2389	265	484	.548	—	—	—	122	146	.836	86	140	226	287	254	6	183	—	16	652	3.0	3.8	8.6
75-76—Portland	81	—	2382	322	651	.495	—	—	—	154	203	.759	77	215	292	324	289	8	170	—	19	798	3.6	4.0	9.9
76-77—Portland	81	—	1680	326	652	.500	—	—	—	183	227	.806	71	117	188	172	216	3	118	—	13	835	2.3	2.1	10.3
77-78—Portland	65	—	1132	210	447	.470	—	—	—	100	122	.820	34	79	113	87	138	2	59	66	5	520	1.7	1.3	8.0
78-79—Portland	72	—	1488	203	483	.420	—	—	—	112	136	.824	58	113	171	142	208	4	74	96	10	518	2.4	2.0	7.2
79-80—Portland	16	—	446	62	146	.425	0	4	.000	22	27	.815	13	32	45	67	53	0	25	33	1	146	2.8	4.2	9.1
REG. SEASON TOTALS	610	—	14777	2020	4180	.483	0	4	.000	969	1218	.796	428	917	1781	1719	1832	45	846	195	96	5009	2.9	2.8	8.2
PLAYOFF TOTALS	27	—	525	67	158	.424	0	0	—	51	62	.823	26	38	64	39	60	0	26	15	2	185	2.4	1.4	6.9

STEPHENS, EVERETTE LOUIS b. October 21, 1966 Ht. 6-2 Wt. 175 College—Purdue

SEASON—TEAM	G	GS	MIN	FGM	FGA	PCT	3FGM	3FGA	PCT	FTM	FTA	PCT	O-RB	D-RB	TOT	AST	PF	DQ	STL	TO	BLK	PTS	RPG	APG	PPG
88-89—Indiana	35	0	209	23	72	.319	2	10	.200	17	22	.773	11	12	23	37	22	0	9	29	4	65	0.7	1.1	1.9
90-91—Milwaukee	3	0	6	2	3	.667	0	0	—	2	2	1.000	0	0	0	2	0	0	0	0	0	6	0.0	0.7	2.0
REG. SEASON TOTALS	38	0	215	25	75	.333	2	10	.200	19	24	.792	11	12	23	39	22	0	9	29	4	71	0.6	1.0	1.9

STEPHENS, JOHN FRANCIS (Jack) b. May 18, 1933 Ht. 6-3 Wt. 185 College—Notre Dame

SEASON—TEAM	G	GS	MIN	FGM	FGA	PCT	3FGM	3FGA	PCT	FTM	FTA	PCT	O-RB	D-RB	TOT	AST	PF	DQ	STL	TO	BLK	PTS	RPG	APG	PPG
55-56—St. Louis	72	—	2219	248	643	.386	—	—	—	247	357	.692	—	—	377	207	144	6	—	—	—	743	5.2	2.9	10.3
REG. SEASON TOTALS	72	—	2219	248	643	.386	—	—	—	247	357	.692	—	—	377	207	144	6	—	—	—	743	5.2	2.9	10.3
PLAYOFF TOTALS	7	—	116	12	41	.293	—	—	—	15	25	.600	—	—	23	9	9	0	—	—	—	39	3.3	1.3	5.6

STEPPE, MICHAEL HOLBROOK (Brook) b. November 7, 1959 Ht. 6-5 Wt. 195 College—DeKalb/Georgia Tech

SEASON—TEAM	G	GS	MIN	FGM	FGA	PCT	3FGM	3FGA	PCT	FTM	FTA	PCT	O-RB	D-RB	TOT	AST	PF	DQ	STL	TO	BLK	PTS	RPG	APG	PPG
82-83—Kansas City	62	6	606	84	176	.477	1	7	.143	76	100	.760	25	48	73	68	92	0	26	55	3	245	1.2	1.1	4.0
83-84—Indiana	61	13	857	148	314	.471	0	3	.000	134	161	.832	43	79	122	79	93	0	34	83	6	430	2.0	1.3	7.0
84-85—Detroit	54	0	486	83	178	.466	0	1	.000	87	104	.837	25	32	57	36	61	0	16	43	4	253	1.1	0.7	4.7
86-87—Sacramento	34	7	665	95	199	.477	3	9	.333	73	88	.830	21	40	61	81	56	0	18	54	3	266	1.8	2.4	7.8
88-89—Portland	27	2	244	33	78	.423	5	9	.556	32	37	.865	13	19	32	16	32	0	11	13	1	103	1.2	0.6	3.8
REG. SEASON TOTALS	238	28	2858	443	945	.469	9	29	.310	402	490	.820	127	218	345	280	334	0	105	248	17	1297	1.4	1.2	5.4
PLAYOFF TOTALS	4	0	20	2	7	.286	0	1	.000	4	6	.667	1	2	3	2	3	0	0	2	0	8	0.8	0.5	2.0

STEVENS, BARRY WAYNE b. January 17, 1963 Ht. 6-5 Wt. 195 College—Iowa State

SEASON—TEAM	G	GS	MIN	FGM	FGA	PCT	3FGM	3FGA	PCT	FTM	FTA	PCT	O-RB	D-RB	TOT	AST	PF	DQ	STL	TO	BLK	PTS	RPG	APG	PPG
92-93—Golden State	2	0	6	1	2	.500	0	0	—	0	0	—	2	0	2	0	1	0	0	0	0	2	1.0	0.0	1.0
REG. SEASON TOTALS	2	0	6	1	2	.500	0	0	—	0	0	—	2	0	2	0	1	0	0	0	0	2	1.0	0.0	1.0

STEVENS, WAYNE b. June 19, 1936 Ht. 6-3½ Wt. 185 College—Cincinnati

SEASON—TEAM	G	GS	MIN	FGM	FGA	PCT	3FGM	3FGA	PCT	FTM	FTA	PCT	O-RB	D-RB	TOT	AST	PF	DQ	STL	TO	BLK	PTS	RPG	APG	PPG
59-60—Cincinnati	8	—	49	3	19	.158	—	—	—	7	10	.700	—	—	16	4	4	0	—	—	—	13	2.0	0.5	1.6
REG. SEASON TOTALS	8	—	49	3	19	.158	—	—	—	7	10	.700	—	—	16	4	4	0	—	—	—	13	2.0	0.5	1.6

STEWART, DENNIS EDWARD b. April 11, 1947 Ht. 6-6 Wt. 220 College—Michigan

SEASON—TEAM	G	GS	MIN	FGM	FGA	PCT	3FGM	3FGA	PCT	FTM	FTA	PCT	O-RB	D-RB	TOT	AST	PF	DQ	STL	TO	BLK	PTS	RPG	APG	PPG
70-71—Baltimore	2	—	6	1	4	.250	—	—	—	2	2	1.000	—	—	3	1	0	0	—	—	—	4	1.5	0.5	2.0
70-71—Floridians (A)	10	—	66	15	44	.341	1	3	.333	5	7	.714	—	—	14	1	12	—	—	—	—	36	1.4	0.1	3.6
REG. NBA TOTALS	2	—	6	1	4	.250	—	—	—	2	2	1.000	—	—	3	1	0	0	—	—	—	4	1.5	0.5	2.0
REG. ABA TOTALS	10	—	66	15	44	.341	1	3	.333	5	7	.714	—	—	14	1	12	—	—	—	—	36	1.4	0.1	3.6

STEWART, LARRY b. September 21, 1968   Ht. 6-8 Wt. 220 College—Coppin State

SEASON—TEAM	G	GS	MIN	FGM	FGA	PCT	3FGM	3FGA	PCT	FTM	FTA	PCT	O-RB	D-RB	TOT	AST	PF	DQ	STL	TO	BLK	PTS	RPG	APG	PPG
91-92—Washington	76	43	2229	303	590	.514	0	3	.000	188	233	.807	186	263	449	120	225	3	51	112	44	794	5.9	1.6	10.4
92-93—Washington	81	8	1823	306	564	.543	0	2	.000	184	253	.727	154	229	383	146	191	1	47	153	29	796	4.7	1.8	9.8
93-94—Washington	3	0	35	3	8	.375	0	0	—	7	10	.700	1	6	7	2	4	0	2	2	1	13	2.3	0.7	4.3
REG. SEASON TOTALS	160	51	4087	612	1162	.527	0	5	.000	379	496	.764	341	498	839	268	420	4	100	267	74	1603	5.2	1.7	10.0

STEWART, NORMAN E. (**Norm**) b. January 20, 1935   Ht. 6-5 Wt. 205 College—Missouri

SEASON—TEAM	G	GS	MIN	FGM	FGA	PCT	3FGM	3FGA	PCT	FTM	FTA	PCT	O-RB	D-RB	TOT	AST	PF	DQ	STL	TO	BLK	PTS	RPG	APG	PPG
56-57—St. Louis	5	—	37	4	15	.267	—	—	—	2	6	.333	—	—	5	2	9	0	—	—	—	10	1.0	0.4	2.0
REG. SEASON TOTALS	5	—	37	4	15	.267	—	—	—	2	6	.333	—	—	5	2	9	0	—	—	—	10	1.0	0.4	2.0

STIPANOVICH, STEPHEN SAMUEL (**Steve**) b. November 17, 1960   Ht. 7-0 Wt. 250 College—Missouri

SEASON—TEAM	G	GS	MIN	FGM	FGA	PCT	3FGM	3FGA	PCT	FTM	FTA	PCT	O-RB	D-RB	TOT	AST	PF	DQ	STL	TO	BLK	PTS	RPG	APG	PPG
83-84—Indiana	81	73	2426	392	816	.480	3	16	.188	183	243	.753	116	446	562	170	303	4	73	161	67	970	6.9	2.1	12.0
84-85—Indiana	82	66	2315	414	871	.475	1	11	.091	297	372	.798	141	473	614	199	265	4	71	184	78	1126	7.5	2.4	13.7
85-86—Indiana	79	65	2397	416	885	.470	2	10	.200	242	315	.768	173	450	623	206	261	1	75	146	69	1076	7.9	2.6	13.6
86-87—Indiana	81	81	2761	382	760	.503	1	4	.250	307	367	.837	184	486	670	180	304	9	106	130	97	1072	8.3	2.2	13.2
87-88—Indiana	80	80	2692	411	828	.496	3	15	.200	254	314	.809	157	505	662	183	302	8	90	156	69	1079	8.3	2.3	13.5
REG. SEASON TOTALS	403	365	12591	2015	4160	.484	10	56	.179	1283	1611	.796	771	2360	3131	938	1435	26	415	777	380	5323	7.8	2.3	13.2
PLAYOFF TOTALS	4	4	149	21	38	.553	0	1	.000	13	19	.684	7	23	30	3	14	0	3	4	2	55	7.5	0.8	13.8

STITH, BRYANT LAMONICA b. December 10, 1970   Ht. 6-5 Wt. 208 College—Virginia

SEASON—TEAM	G	GS	MIN	FGM	FGA	PCT	3FGM	3FGA	PCT	FTM	FTA	PCT	O-RB	D-RB	TOT	AST	PF	DQ	STL	TO	BLK	PTS	RPG	APG	PPG
92-93—Denver	39	12	865	124	278	.446	0	4	.000	99	119	.832	39	85	124	49	82	0	24	44	5	347	3.2	1.3	8.9
93-94—Denver	82	82	2853	365	811	.450	2	9	.222	291	351	.829	119	230	349	199	165	0	116	131	16	1023	4.3	2.4	12.5
REG. SEASON TOTALS	121	94	3718	489	1089	.449	2	13	.154	390	470	.830	158	315	473	248	247	0	140	175	21	1370	3.9	2.0	11.3
PLAYOFF TOTALS	12	12	413	43	102	.422	0	1	.000	50	60	.833	23	33	56	26	23	0	11	14	2	136	4.7	2.2	11.3

STITH, SAMUEL ELWOOD (**Sam**) b. July 22, 1937   Ht. 6-2 Wt. 185 College—St. Bonaventure

SEASON—TEAM	G	GS	MIN	FGM	FGA	PCT	3FGM	3FGA	PCT	FTM	FTA	PCT	O-RB	D-RB	TOT	AST	PF	DQ	STL	TO	BLK	PTS	RPG	APG	PPG
61-62—New York	32	—	440	59	162	.364	—	—	—	23	38	.605	—	—	51	60	55	0	—	—	—	141	1.6	1.9	4.4
REG. SEASON TOTALS	32	—	440	59	162	.364	—	—	—	23	38	.605	—	—	51	60	55	0	—	—	—	141	1.6	1.9	4.4

STITH, THOMAS ALVIN (**Tom**) b. January 21, 1939   Ht. 6-5 Wt. 210 College—St. Bonaventure

SEASON—TEAM	G	GS	MIN	FGM	FGA	PCT	3FGM	3FGA	PCT	FTM	FTA	PCT	O-RB	D-RB	TOT	AST	PF	DQ	STL	TO	BLK	PTS	RPG	APG	PPG
62-63—New York	25	—	209	37	110	.336	—	—	—	3	10	.300	—	—	39	18	23	0	—	—	—	77	1.6	0.7	3.1
REG. SEASON TOTALS	25	—	209	37	110	.336	—	—	—	3	10	.300	—	—	39	18	23	0	—	—	—	77	1.6	0.7	3.1

STIVRINS, ALEX FRANK b. November 29, 1962   Ht. 6-8 Wt. 220 College—Creighton/Colorado

SEASON—TEAM	G	GS	MIN	FGM	FGA	PCT	3FGM	3FGA	PCT	FTM	FTA	PCT	O-RB	D-RB	TOT	AST	PF	DQ	STL	TO	BLK	PTS	RPG	APG	PPG
85-86—Seattle	3	0	14	1	4	.250	0	0	—	1	4	.250	3	0	3	1	2	0	0	3	0	3	1.0	0.3	1.0
92-93—Atl.-L.A. Clips-Milw.-Phoe.	19	0	76	19	39	.487	0	2	.000	3	4	.750	7	12	19	3	11	0	2	7	2	41	1.0	0.2	2.2
REG. SEASON TOTALS	22	0	90	20	43	.465	0	2	.000	4	8	.500	10	12	22	4	13	0	2	10	2	44	1.0	0.2	2.0

STOCKTON, JOHN HOUSTON (**Stock**) b. March 26, 1962   Ht. 6-1 Wt. 175 College—Gonzaga

SEASON—TEAM	G	GS	MIN	FGM	FGA	PCT	3FGM	3FGA	PCT	FTM	FTA	PCT	O-RB	D-RB	TOT	AST	PF	DQ	STL	TO	BLK	PTS	RPG	APG	PPG
84-85—Utah	82	5	1490	157	333	.471	2	11	.182	142	193	.736	26	79	105	415	203	3	109	150	11	458	1.3	5.1	5.6
85-86—Utah	82	38	1935	228	466	.489	2	15	.133	172	205	.839	33	146	179	610	227	2	157	168	10	630	2.2	7.4	7.7
86-87—Utah	82	2	1858	231	463	.499	7	38	.184	179	229	.782	32	119	151	670	224	1	177	164	14	648	1.8	8.2	7.9
87-88—Utah	82	79	2842	454	791	.574	24	67	.358	272	324	.840	54	183	237	1128	247	5	242	262	16	1204	2.9	13.8	14.7
88-89—Utah	82	82	3171	497	923	.538	16	66	.242	390	452	.863	83	165	248	1118	241	3	263	308	14	1400	3.0	13.6	17.1
89-90—Utah	78	78	2915	472	918	.514	47	113	.416	354	432	.819	57	149	206	1134	233	3	207	272	18	1345	2.6	14.5	17.2
90-91—Utah	82	82	3103	496	978	.507	58	168	.345	363	434	.836	46	191	237	1164	233	1	234	298	16	1413	2.9	14.2	17.2
91-92—Utah	82	82	3002	453	939	.482	83	204	.407	308	366	.842	68	202	270	1126	234	3	244	286	22	1297	3.3	13.7	15.8
92-93—Utah	82	82	2863	437	899	.486	72	187	.385	293	367	.798	64	173	237	987	224	2	199	266	21	1239	2.9	12.0	15.1
93-94—Utah	82	82	2969	458	868	.528	48	149	.322	272	338	.805	72	186	258	1031	236	3	199	266	22	1236	3.1	12.6	15.1
REG. SEASON TOTALS	816	612	26148	3883	7578	.512	359	1018	.353	2745	3340	.822	535	1593	2128	9383	2302	26	2031	2440	164	10870	2.6	11.5	13.3
PLAYOFF TOTALS	84	67	3013	421	887	.475	51	161	.317	322	392	.821	71	198	269	929	260	0	178	249	26	1215	3.2	11.1	14.5
ALL-STAR TOTALS	6	3	134	21	40	.525	5	9	.556	4	6	.667	1	14	15	55	14	0	12	27	1	51	2.5	9.2	8.5

STOKES, GREGORY LEWIS (Greg) b. August 5, 1963   Ht. 6-10 Wt. 220 College—Iowa

SEASON—TEAM	G	GS	MIN	FGM	FGA	PCT	3FGM	3FGA	PCT	FTM	FTA	PCT	O-RB	D-RB	TOT	AST	PF	DQ	STL	TO	BLK	PTS	RPG	APG	PPG
85-86—Philadelphia	31	13	350	56	119	.471	0	1	.000	14	21	.667	27	30	57	17	56	0	14	19	11	126	1.8	0.5	4.1
89-90—Sacramento	11	0	34	1	9	.111	0	0	—	2	2	1.000	2	3	5	0	8	0	0	3	0	4	0.5	0.0	0.4
REG. SEASON TOTALS	42	13	384	57	128	.445	0	1	.000	16	23	.696	29	33	62	17	64	0	14	22	11	130	1.5	0.4	3.1
PLAYOFF TOTALS	7	7	90	8	28	.286	0	0	—	11	13	.846	6	7	13	4	12	0	2	4	6	27	1.9	0.6	3.9

STOKES, MAURICE (Mo) b. June 17, 1933 d. April 6, 1970 Ht. 6-7 Wt. 240 College—St. Francis (Pa.)

SEASON—TEAM	G	GS	MIN	FGM	FGA	PCT	3FGM	3FGA	PCT	FTM	FTA	PCT	O-RB	D-RB	TOT	AST	PF	DQ	STL	TO	BLK	PTS	RPG	APG	PPG
55-56—Rochester	67	—	2323	403	1137	.354	—	—	—	319	447	.714	—	—	1094	328	276	11	—	—	—	1125	16.3	4.9	16.8
56-57—Rochester	72	—	2761	434	1249	.347	—	—	—	256	385	.665	—	—	1256	331	287	12	—	—	—	1124	17.4	4.6	15.6
57-58—Cincinnati	63	—	2460	414	1181	.351	—	—	—	238	333	.715	—	—	1142	403	226	9	—	—	—	1066	18.1	6.4	16.9
REG. SEASON TOTALS	202	—	7544	1251	3567	.351	—	—	—	813	1165	.698	—	—	3492	1062	789	32	—	—	—	3315	17.3	5.3	16.4
PLAYOFF TOTALS	1	—	39	3	12	.250	—	—	—	6	7	.857	—	—	15	2	3	0	—	—	—	12	15.0	2.0	12.0
ALL-STAR TOTALS	3	—	87	15	43	.349	—	—	—	9	15	.600	—	—	42	12	8	0	—	—	—	39	14.0	4.0	13.0

STOLKEY, ARTHUR F. (Art) b. October 23, 1920   Ht. 6-1 Wt. 180 College—Detroit

SEASON—TEAM	G	GS	MIN	FGM	FGA	PCT	3FGM	3FGA	PCT	FTM	FTA	PCT	O-RB	D-RB	TOT	AST	PF	DQ	STL	TO	BLK	PTS	RPG	APG	PPG
46-47—Detroit	23	—	—	36	164	.220	—	—	—	30	44	.682	—	—	—	38	72	—	—	—	—	102	—	1.7	4.4
REG. SEASON TOTALS	23	—	—	36	164	.220	—	—	—	30	44	.682	—	—	—	38	72	—	—	—	—	102	—	1.7	4.4

STOLL, RANDY C. b. 1945   Ht. 6-7 Wt. 235 College—Washington State

SEASON—TEAM	G	GS	MIN	FGM	FGA	PCT	3FGM	3FGA	PCT	FTM	FTA	PCT	O-RB	D-RB	TOT	AST	PF	DQ	STL	TO	BLK	PTS	RPG	APG	PPG
67-68—Anaheim (A)	25	—	403	66	138	.478	0	0	—	10	25	.400	—	—	91	12	42	0	—	28	—	142	3.6	0.5	5.7
REG. ABA TOTALS	25	—	403	66	138	.478	0	0	—	10	25	.400	—	—	91	12	42	0	—	28	—	142	3.6	0.5	5.7

STONE, GEORGE (Radar) b. February 9, 1946   Ht. 6-7½ Wt. 215 College—John Marshall

SEASON—TEAM	G	GS	MIN	FGM	FGA	PCT	3FGM	3FGA	PCT	FTM	FTA	PCT	O-RB	D-RB	TOT	AST	PF	DQ	STL	TO	BLK	PTS	RPG	APG	PPG
68-69—Los Angeles (A)	74	—	2199	437	964	.453	28	74	.378	261	337	.774	—	—	504	57	254	8	—	124	—	1163	6.8	0.8	15.7
69-70—Los Angeles (A)	83	—	2639	512	1194	.429	65	206	.316	239	306	.781	—	—	551	145	280	4	—	—	—	1328	6.6	1.7	16.0
70-71—Utah (A)	78	—	1734	372	808	.460	50	157	.318	121	156	.776	—	—	363	106	173	—	—	—	—	915	4.7	1.4	11.7
71-72—Utah-Car. (A)	24	—	381	49	123	.398	1	9	.111	25	28	.893	—	—	62	25	40	—	—	22	—	124	2.6	1.0	5.2
REG. ABA TOTALS	259	—	6953	1370	3089	.444	144	446	.323	646	827	.781	—	—	1480	333	747	12	—	146	—	3530	5.7	1.3	13.6
ABA PLAYOFF TOTALS	35	—	1148	249	597	.417	18	83	.217	93	118	.788	—	—	262	71	97	0	—	—	—	609	7.5	2.0	17.4

STOVALL, PAUL L. b. August 16, 1948 d. January 9, 1978 Ht. 6-5 Wt. 225 College—Pratt CC/Arizona State

SEASON—TEAM	G	GS	MIN	FGM	FGA	PCT	3FGM	3FGA	PCT	FTM	FTA	PCT	O-RB	D-RB	TOT	AST	PF	DQ	STL	TO	BLK	PTS	RPG	APG	PPG
72-73—Phoenix	25	—	211	26	76	.342	—	—	—	24	38	.632	—	—	61	13	37	0	—	—	—	76	2.4	0.5	3.0
73-74—San Diego (A)	13	—	194	36	73	.493	0	0	—	28	44	.636	21	37	58	12	32	—	4	21	6	100	4.5	0.9	7.7
REG. NBA TOTALS	25	—	211	26	76	.342	—	—	—	24	38	.632	—	—	61	13	37	0	—	—	—	76	2.4	0.5	3.0
REG. ABA TOTALS	13	—	194	36	73	.493	0	0	—	28	44	.636	21	37	58	12	32	0	4	21	6	100	4.5	0.9	7.7

STRAWDER, JOE TOM b. September 21, 1940   Ht. 6-10 Wt. 235 College—Bradley

SEASON—TEAM	G	GS	MIN	FGM	FGA	PCT	3FGM	3FGA	PCT	FTM	FTA	PCT	O-RB	D-RB	TOT	AST	PF	DQ	STL	TO	BLK	PTS	RPG	APG	PPG
65-66—Detroit	79	—	2180	250	613	.408	—	—	—	176	256	.688	—	—	820	78	305	10	—	—	—	676	10.4	1.0	8.6
66-67—Detroit	79	—	2156	281	660	.426	—	—	—	188	262	.718	—	—	791	82	344	19	—	—	—	750	10.0	1.0	9.5
67-68—Detroit	73	—	2029	206	456	.452	—	—	—	139	215	.647	—	—	685	85	312	18	—	—	—	551	9.4	1.2	7.5
REG. SEASON TOTALS	231	—	6365	737	1729	.426	—	—	—	503	733	.686	—	—	2296	245	961	47	—	—	—	1977	9.9	1.1	8.6
PLAYOFF TOTALS	6	—	177	14	42	.333	—	—	—	14	22	.636	—	—	65	9	27	1	—	—	—	42	10.8	1.5	7.0

STRICKER, WILLIAM LOUIS (Bill) b. January 22, 1948   Ht. 6-8½ Wt. 220 College—Pacific

SEASON—TEAM	G	GS	MIN	FGM	FGA	PCT	3FGM	3FGA	PCT	FTM	FTA	PCT	O-RB	D-RB	TOT	AST	PF	DQ	STL	TO	BLK	PTS	RPG	APG	PPG
70-71—Portland	1	—	2	2	3	.667	—	—	—	0	0	—	—	—	0	0	1	0	—	—	—	4	0.0	0.0	4.0
REG. SEASON TOTALS	1	—	2	2	3	.667	—	—	—	0	0	—	—	—	0	0	1	0	—	—	—	4	0.0	0.0	4.0

STRICKLAND, RODNEY (Rod) b. July 11, 1966   Ht. 6-3 Wt. 185 College—DePaul

SEASON—TEAM	G	GS	MIN	FGM	FGA	PCT	3FGM	3FGA	PCT	FTM	FTA	PCT	O-RB	D-RB	TOT	AST	PF	DQ	STL	TO	BLK	PTS	RPG	APG	PPG
88-89—New York	81	10	1358	265	567	.467	19	59	.322	172	231	.745	51	109	160	319	142	2	98	148	3	721	2.0	3.9	8.9
89-90—N.Y.-S.A.	82	24	2140	343	756	.454	8	30	.267	174	278	.626	90	169	259	468	160	3	127	170	14	868	3.2	5.7	10.6
90-91—San Antonio	58	56	2076	314	651	.482	11	33	.333	161	211	.763	57	162	219	463	125	0	117	156	11	800	3.8	8.0	13.8
91-92—San Antonio	57	54	2053	300	659	.455	5	15	.333	182	265	.687	92	173	265	491	122	0	118	160	17	787	4.6	8.6	13.8
92-93—Portland	78	35	2474	396	816	.485	4	30	.133	273	381	.717	120	217	337	559	153	1	131	199	24	1069	4.3	7.2	13.7
93-94—Portland	82	58	2889	528	1093	.483	2	10	.200	353	471	.749	122	248	370	740	171	0	147	257	24	1411	4.5	9.0	17.2
REG. SEASON TOTALS	438	237	12990	2146	4542	.472	49	177	.277	1315	1837	.716	532	1078	1610	3040	873	6	738	1090	93	5656	3.7	6.9	12.9
PLAYOFF TOTALS	33	24	1053	176	389	.452	1	16	.063	78	112	.696	45	91	136	267	96	2	39	83	7	431	4.1	8.1	13.1

STRICKLAND, ROGER (The Rifle) b. September 4, 1940　Ht. 6-5　Wt. 200　College—Jacksonville

SEASON—TEAM	G	GS	MIN	FGM	FGA	PCT	3FGM	3FGA	PCT	FTM	FTA	PCT	O-RB	D-RB	TOT	AST	PF	DQ	STL	TO	BLK	PTS	RPG	APG	PPG
63-64—Baltimore	1	—	4	1	3	.333	—	—	—	0	0	—	—	—	0	0	1	0	—	—	—	2	0.0	0.0	2.0
REG. SEASON TOTALS	1	—	4	1	3	.333	—	—	—	0	0	—	—	—	0	0	1	0	—	—	—	2	0.0	0.0	2.0

STROEDER, JOHN b. July 24, 1958　Ht. 6-10　Wt. 260　College—Montana

SEASON—TEAM	G	GS	MIN	FGM	FGA	PCT	3FGM	3FGA	PCT	FTM	FTA	PCT	O-RB	D-RB	TOT	AST	PF	DQ	STL	TO	BLK	PTS	RPG	APG	PPG
87-88—Milwaukee	41	0	271	29	79	.367	0	2	.000	20	30	.667	24	47	71	20	48	0	3	24	12	78	1.7	0.5	1.9
88-89—S.A.-G.S.	5	0	22	2	5	.400	0	0	—	0	0	—	5	9	14	3	3	0	0	3	2	4	2.8	0.6	0.8
REG. SEASON TOTALS	46	0	293	31	84	.369	0	2	.000	20	30	.667	29	56	85	23	51	0	3	27	14	82	1.8	0.5	1.8
PLAYOFF TOTALS	1	0	1	1	1	1.000	1	1	1.000	0	0	—	0	0	0	—	0	0	0	0	0	3	0.0	0.0	3.0

STRONG, DEREK LAMAR b. February 9, 1968　Ht. 6-8　Wt. 225　College—Xavier (Ohio)

SEASON—TEAM	G	GS	MIN	FGM	FGA	PCT	3FGM	3FGA	PCT	FTM	FTA	PCT	O-RB	D-RB	TOT	AST	PF	DQ	STL	TO	BLK	PTS	RPG	APG	PPG
91-92—Washington	1	0	12	0	4	.000	0	0	—	3	4	.750	1	4	5	1	1	0	0	1	0	3	5.0	1.0	3.0
92-93—Milwaukee	23	0	339	42	92	.457	4	8	.500	68	85	.800	40	75	115	14	20	0	11	13	1	156	5.0	0.6	6.8
93-94—Milwaukee	67	11	1131	141	341	.413	3	13	.231	159	206	.772	109	172	281	48	69	1	38	61	14	444	4.2	0.7	6.6
REG. SEASON TOTALS	91	11	1482	183	437	.419	7	21	.333	230	295	.780	150	251	401	63	90	1	49	75	15	603	4.4	0.7	6.6

STROTHERS, WILLIAM LAMONT (Lamont) b. May 10, 1968　Ht. 6-4　Wt. 190　College—Christopher Newport

SEASON—TEAM	G	GS	MIN	FGM	FGA	PCT	3FGM	3FGA	PCT	FTM	FTA	PCT	O-RB	D-RB	TOT	AST	PF	DQ	STL	TO	BLK	PTS	RPG	APG	PPG
91-92—Portland	4	0	17	4	12	.333	0	2	.000	2	4	.500	1	0	1	1	2	0	1	2	1	10	0.3	0.3	2.5
92-93—Dallas	9	0	138	20	61	.328	2	13	.154	8	10	.800	8	6	14	13	13	0	8	15	0	50	1.6	1.4	5.6
REG. SEASON TOTALS	13	0	155	24	73	.329	2	15	.133	10	14	.714	9	6	15	14	15	0	9	17	1	60	1.2	1.1	4.6

STROUD, JOHN BUSBY b. October 29, 1957　Ht. 6-7　Wt. 215　College—Mississippi

SEASON—TEAM	G	GS	MIN	FGM	FGA	PCT	3FGM	3FGA	PCT	FTM	FTA	PCT	O-RB	D-RB	TOT	AST	PF	DQ	STL	TO	BLK	PTS	RPG	APG	PPG
80-81—Houston	9	—	88	11	34	.324	0	0	—	3	4	.750	7	6	13	9	7	0	1	4	0	25	1.4	1.0	2.8
REG. SEASON TOTALS	9	—	88	11	34	.324	0	0	—	3	4	.750	7	6	13	9	7	0	1	4	0	25	1.4	1.0	2.8

STROUD, WILLIAM D. (Red) b. May 2, 1941　Ht. 6-0　Wt. 160　College—Mississippi State

SEASON—TEAM	G	GS	MIN	FGM	FGA	PCT	3FGM	3FGA	PCT	FTM	FTA	PCT	O-RB	D-RB	TOT	AST	PF	DQ	STL	TO	BLK	PTS	RPG	APG	PPG
67-68—New Orleans (A)	7	—	33	5	11	.455	1	1	1.000	9	10	.900	—	—	2	1	7	0	—	9	—	20	0.3	0.1	2.9
REG. ABA TOTALS	7	—	33	5	11	.455	1	1	1.000	9	10	.900	—	—	2	1	7	0	—	9	—	20	0.3	0.1	2.9

STUMP, EUGENE ANDREW (Gene) b. November 13, 1923　Ht. 6-2½　Wt. 185　College—DePaul

SEASON—TEAM	G	GS	MIN	FGM	FGA	PCT	3FGM	3FGA	PCT	FTM	FTA	PCT	O-RB	D-RB	TOT	AST	PF	DQ	STL	TO	BLK	PTS	RPG	APG	PPG
47-48—Boston	43	—	—	59	247	.239	—	—	—	24	38	.632	—	—	—	18	66	—	—	—	—	142	—	0.4	3.3
48-49—Boston	56	—	193	580	.333	—	—	—	92	129	.713	—	—	—	56	102	—	—	—	—	478	—	1.0	8.5	
49-50—Minn.-Wat.	49	—	—	63	213	.296	—	—	—	37	54	.685	—	—	—	44	59	—	—	—	—	163	—	0.9	3.3
REG. SEASON TOTALS	148	—	—	315	1040	.303	—	—	—	153	221	.692	—	—	—	118	227	—	—	—	—	783	—	0.8	5.3
PLAYOFF TOTALS	3	—	—	1	3	.333	—	—	—	0	0	—	—	—	—	2	—	—	—	—	—	2	0.0	0.0	0.7

STUTZ, STANLEY J. (Stan, formerly Stan Modzelewski) b. April 14, 1920　d. October 28, 1975　Ht. 5-10　Wt. 170　College—Rhode Island

SEASON—TEAM	G	GS	MIN	FGM	FGA	PCT	3FGM	3FGA	PCT	FTM	FTA	PCT	O-RB	D-RB	TOT	AST	PF	DQ	STL	TO	BLK	PTS	RPG	APG	PPG
46-47—New York	60	—	—	172	641	.268	—	—	—	133	170	.782	—	—	—	49	127	—	—	—	—	477	—	0.8	8.0
47-48—New York	47	—	—	109	501	.218	—	—	—	113	135	.837	—	—	—	57	121	—	—	—	—	331	—	1.2	7.0
48-49—Baltimore	59	—	—	121	431	.281	—	—	—	131	159	.824	—	—	—	82	149	—	—	—	—	373	—	1.4	6.3
REG. SEASON TOTALS	166	—	—	402	1573	.256	—	—	—	377	464	.813	—	—	—	188	397	—	—	—	—	1181	—	1.1	7.1
PLAYOFF TOTALS	11	—	—	32	117	.274	—	—	—	40	49	.816	—	—	—	8	31	—	—	—	—	104	—	0.7	9.5

SUITER, GARY G. b. January 18, 1945　Ht. 6-9　Wt. 235　College—Midwestern State

SEASON—TEAM	G	GS	MIN	FGM	FGA	PCT	3FGM	3FGA	PCT	FTM	FTA	PCT	O-RB	D-RB	TOT	AST	PF	DQ	STL	TO	BLK	PTS	RPG	APG	PPG
70-71—Cleveland	30	—	140	19	54	.352	—	—	—	4	9	.444	—	—	41	2	20	0	—	—	—	42	1.4	0.1	1.4
REG. SEASON TOTALS	30	—	140	19	54	.352	—	—	—	4	9	.444	—	—	41	2	20	0	—	—	—	42	1.4	0.1	1.4

SUMPTER, BARRY b. November 11, 1965　Ht. 6-11　Wt. 245　College—Louisville/Austin Peay

SEASON—TEAM	G	GS	MIN	FGM	FGA	PCT	3FGM	3FGA	PCT	FTM	FTA	PCT	O-RB	D-RB	TOT	AST	PF	DQ	STL	TO	BLK	PTS	RPG	APG	PPG
88-89—L.A. Clippers	1	0	1	0	1	.000	0	0	—	0	0	—	0	0	0	0	0	0	0	0	0	0	0.0	0.0	0.0
REG. SEASON TOTALS	1	0	1	0	1	.000	0	0	—	0	0	—	0	0	0	0	0	0	0	0	0	0	0.0	0.0	0.0

SUNDERLAGE, DON J. b. December 20, 1929 d. July 15, 1961 Ht. 6-1 Wt. 180 College—Illinois

SEASON—TEAM	G	GS	MIN	FGM	FGA	PCT	3FGM	3FGA	PCT	FTM	FTA	PCT	O-RB	D-RB	TOT	AST	PF	DQ	STL	TO	BLK	PTS	RPG	APG	PPG
53-54—Milwaukee	68	—	2232	254	748	.340	—	—	—	252	337	.748	—	—	225	187	263	8	—	—	—	760	3.3	2.8	11.2
54-55—Minneapolis	45	—	404	33	133	.248	—	—	—	48	73	.658	—	—	56	37	57	0	—	—	—	114	1.2	0.8	2.5
REG. SEASON TOTALS	113	—	2636	287	881	.326	—	—	—	300	410	.732	—	—	281	224	320	8	—	—	—	874	2.5	2.0	7.7
ALL-STAR TOTALS	1	—	6	1	2	.500	—	—	—	2	2	1.000	—	—	0	1	1	0	—	—	—	4	0.0	1.0	4.0

SUNDVOLD, JON THOMAS (Sunny) b. July 2, 1961 Ht. 6-2 Wt. 170 College—Missouri

SEASON—TEAM	G	GS	MIN	FGM	FGA	PCT	3FGM	3FGA	PCT	FTM	FTA	PCT	O-RB	D-RB	TOT	AST	PF	DQ	STL	TO	BLK	PTS	RPG	APG	PPG
83-84—Seattle	73	2	1284	217	488	.445	9	37	.243	64	72	.889	23	68	91	239	81	0	29	81	1	507	1.2	3.3	6.9
84-85—Seattle	73	1	1150	170	400	.425	12	38	.316	48	59	.814	17	53	70	206	87	0	36	85	1	400	1.0	2.8	5.5
85-86—San Antonio	70	4	1150	220	476	.462	21	60	.350	39	48	.813	22	58	80	261	110	0	34	85	0	500	1.1	3.7	7.1
86-87—San Antonio	76	42	1765	365	751	.486	50	149	.336	70	84	.833	20	78	98	315	109	1	35	97	0	850	1.3	4.1	11.2
87-88—San Antonio	52	12	1024	176	379	.464	26	64	.406	43	48	.896	14	34	48	183	54	0	27	57	2	421	0.9	3.5	8.1
88-89—Miami	68	8	1338	307	675	.455	48	92	.522	47	57	.825	18	69	87	137	78	0	27	87	1	709	1.3	2.0	10.4
89-90—Miami	63	2	867	148	363	.408	44	100	.440	44	52	.846	15	56	71	102	69	0	25	52	0	384	1.1	1.6	6.1
90-91—Miami	24	0	225	43	107	.402	15	35	.429	11	11	1.000	3	6	9	24	11	0	7	16	0	112	0.4	1.0	4.7
91-92—Miami	3	0	8	1	3	.333	1	1	1.000	0	0	—	0	0	0	2	2	0	0	0	0	3	0.0	0.7	1.0
REG. SEASON TOTALS	502	71	8811	1647	3642	.452	226	576	.392	366	431	.849	132	422	554	1469	601	1	220	560	5	3886	1.1	2.9	7.7
PLAYOFF TOTALS	10	3	157	25	57	.439	4	18	.222	5	6	.833	2	5	7	25	6	0	4	9	0	59	0.7	2.5	5.9

SURHOFF, RICHARD C. JR. (Dick) b. November 16, 1929 d. May 1, 1987 Ht. 6-4 Wt. 210 College—Long Island University/Marshall

SEASON—TEAM	G	GS	MIN	FGM	FGA	PCT	3FGM	3FGA	PCT	FTM	FTA	PCT	O-RB	D-RB	TOT	AST	PF	DQ	STL	TO	BLK	PTS	RPG	APG	PPG
52-53—New York	26	—	187	13	61	.213	—	—	—	19	30	.633	—	—	25	9	36	1	—	—	—	45	1.0	0.3	1.7
53-54—Milwaukee	32	—	358	43	129	.333	—	—	—	47	62	.758	—	—	69	23	53	0	—	—	—	133	2.2	0.7	4.2
REG. SEASON TOTALS	58	—	545	56	190	.295	—	—	—	66	92	.717	—	—	94	32	89	1	—	—	—	178	1.6	0.6	3.1
PLAYOFF TOTALS	4	—	13	2	4	.500	—	—	—	0	0	—	—	—	2	2	2	0	—	—	—	4	0.5	0.5	1.0

SUTOR, GEORGE J. b. September 14, 1943 Ht. 6-8 Wt. 240 College—La Salle

SEASON—TEAM	G	GS	MIN	FGM	FGA	PCT	3FGM	3FGA	PCT	FTM	FTA	PCT	O-RB	D-RB	TOT	AST	PF	DQ	STL	TO	BLK	PTS	RPG	APG	PPG
67-68—Kentucky (A)	1	—	5	0	0	—	0	0	—	0	0	—	—	—	1	0	2	0	—	0	—	0	1.0	0.0	0.0
68-69—Minnesota (A)	64	—	886	139	397	.350	0	2	.000	71	114	.623	—	—	348	27	170	8	—	60	—	349	5.4	0.4	5.5
69-70—Car.-Miami (A)	14	—	147	12	46	.261	0	1	.000	7	17	.412	—	—	55	3	31	0	—	—	—	31	3.9	0.2	2.2
REG. ABA TOTALS	79	—	1038	151	443	.341	0	3	.000	78	131	.595	—	—	404	30	203	8	—	60	—	380	5.1	0.4	4.8
ABA PLAYOFF TOTALS	1	—	3	0	1	.000	0	0	—	0	1	.000	—	—	—	0	2	0	—	1	—	0	0.0	0.0	0.0

SUTTLE, DANE LEE b. August 9, 1961 Ht. 6-3 Wt. 190 College—Pepperdine

SEASON—TEAM	G	GS	MIN	FGM	FGA	PCT	3FGM	3FGA	PCT	FTM	FTA	PCT	O-RB	D-RB	TOT	AST	PF	DQ	STL	TO	BLK	PTS	RPG	APG	PPG
83-84—Kansas City	40	1	469	109	214	.509	0	3	.000	40	47	.851	21	25	46	46	46	0	20	32	0	258	1.2	1.2	6.5
84-85—Kansas City	6	0	24	6	13	.462	0	1	.000	2	2	1.000	0	3	3	2	3	0	1	1	0	14	0.5	0.3	2.3
REG. SEASON TOTALS	46	1	493	115	227	.507	0	4	.000	42	49	.857	21	28	49	48	49	0	21	33	0	272	1.1	1.0	5.9

SUTTON, GREGORY RAY (Greg) b. December 3, 1967 Ht. 6-2 Wt. 170 College—Langston/Oral Roberts

SEASON—TEAM	G	GS	MIN	FGM	FGA	PCT	3FGM	3FGA	PCT	FTM	FTA	PCT	O-RB	D-RB	TOT	AST	PF	DQ	STL	TO	BLK	PTS	RPG	APG	PPG
91-92—San Antonio	67	2	601	93	240	.388	26	89	.292	34	45	.756	6	41	47	91	111	0	26	70	9	246	0.7	1.4	3.7
REG. SEASON TOTALS	67	2	601	93	240	.388	26	89	.292	34	45	.756	6	41	47	91	111	0	26	70	9	246	0.7	1.4	3.7
PLAYOFF TOTALS	2	0	15	2	6	.333	0	2	.000	3	3	1.000	0	0	0	2	3	0	1	0	1	7	0.0	1.0	3.5

SWAGERTY, KEITH M. b. October 30, 1945 Ht. 6-7 Wt. 235 College—Pacific

SEASON—TEAM	G	GS	MIN	FGM	FGA	PCT	3FGM	3FGA	PCT	FTM	FTA	PCT	O-RB	D-RB	TOT	AST	PF	DQ	STL	TO	BLK	PTS	RPG	APG	PPG
68-69—Houston (A)	77	—	2447	362	883	.410	0	5	.000	256	421	.608	326	496	822	92	238	5	—	112	—	980	10.7	1.2	12.7
69-70—Kentucky (A)	3	—	30	2	9	.222	0	1	.000	3	3	1.000	—	—	6	3	4	0	—	—	—	7	2.0	1.0	2.3
REG. ABA TOTALS	80	—	2477	364	892	.408	0	6	.000	259	424	.611	326	496	828	95	242	5	—	112	—	987	10.4	1.2	12.3

SWAIN, BENNIE S. b. December 16, 1933 Ht. 6-8 Wt. 220 College—Texas Southern

SEASON—TEAM	G	GS	MIN	FGM	FGA	PCT	3FGM	3FGA	PCT	FTM	FTA	PCT	O-RB	D-RB	TOT	AST	PF	DQ	STL	TO	BLK	PTS	RPG	APG	PPG
58-59—Boston	58	—	708	99	244	.406	—	—	—	67	110	.609	—	—	262	29	127	3	—	—	—	265	4.5	0.5	4.6
REG. SEASON TOTALS	58	—	708	99	244	.406	—	—	—	67	110	.609	—	—	262	29	127	3	—	—	—	265	4.5	0.5	4.6
PLAYOFF TOTALS	5	—	27	2	6	.333	—	—	—	1	2	.500	—	—	14	1	4	0	—	—	—	5	2.8	0.2	1.0

SWANSON, NORMAN P. (Norm) b. October 4, 1930 Ht. 6-6 Wt. 210 College—Detroit

SEASON—TEAM	G	GS	MIN	FGM	FGA	PCT	3FGM	3FGA	PCT	FTM	FTA	PCT	O-RB	D-RB	TOT	AST	PF	DQ	STL	TO	BLK	PTS	RPG	APG	PPG
53-54—Rochester	63	—	611	31	137	.226	—	—	—	38	64	.594	—	—	110	33	91	3	—	—	—	100	1.7	0.5	1.6
REG. SEASON TOTALS	63	—	611	31	137	.226	—	—	—	38	64	.594	—	—	110	33	91	3	—	—	—	100	1.7	0.5	1.6
PLAYOFF TOTALS	6	—	23	3	7	.429	—	—	—	2	3	.667	—	—	5	—	5	0	—	—	—	8	0.8	0.0	1.3

SWARTZ, DANIEL S. **(Dan, Dogpatch)** b. December 23, 1934　Ht. 6-4　Wt. 215　College—Kentucky/Morehead State

SEASON—TEAM	G	GS	MIN	FGM	FGA	PCT	3FGM	3FGA	PCT	FTM	FTA	PCT	O-RB	D-RB	TOT	AST	PF	DQ	STL	TO	BLK	PTS	RPG	APG	PPG
62-63—Boston	39	—	335	57	150	.380	—	—	—	61	72	.847	—	—	88	21	92	0	—	—	—	175	2.3	0.5	4.5
REG. SEASON TOTALS	39	—	335	57	150	.380	—	—	—	61	72	.847	—	—	88	21	92	0	—	—	—	175	2.3	0.5	4.5
PLAYOFF TOTALS	1	—	4	0	0	—	—	—	—	0	0	—	—	—	0	—	0	0	—	—	—	0	0.0	0.0	0.0

SWIFT, HARLEY E. JR. **(Skeeter)** b. June 19, 1946　Ht. 6-3½　Wt. 210　College—East Tennessee State

SEASON—TEAM	G	GS	MIN	FGM	FGA	PCT	3FGM	3FGA	PCT	FTM	FTA	PCT	O-RB	D-RB	TOT	AST	PF	DQ	STL	TO	BLK	PTS	RPG	APG	PPG
69-70—New Orleans (A)	66	—	1089	215	546	.394	38	125	.304	139	168	.827	—	—	100	77	208	4	—	—	—	607	1.5	1.2	9.2
70-71—Memphis-Pitt. (A)	80	—	2134	402	895	.449	39	150	.260	206	246	.837	—	—	233	269	264	—	—	—	—	1049	2.9	3.4	13.1
71-72—Pittsburgh (A)	79	—	2340	401	856	.468	33	100	.330	224	265	.845	—	—	200	309	277	—	—	252	—	1059	2.5	3.9	13.4
72-73—Dallas (A)	42	—	1123	177	374	.473	19	49	.388	128	149	.859	20	62	82	150	140	1	—	136	—	501	2.0	3.6	11.9
73-74—San Antonio (A)	16	—	153	23	67	.343	1	12	.083	16	20	.800	5	11	16	15	26	—	3	13	0	63	1.0	0.9	3.9
REG. ABA TOTALS	283	—	6839	1218	2738	.445	130	436	.298	713	848	.841	25	73	631	820	915	5	3	401	0	3279	2.2	2.9	11.6

SYDNOR, WALLACE B. **(Buck)** b. September 19, 1921　Ht. 5-10　Wt. 175　College—Western Kentucky

SEASON—TEAM	G	GS	MIN	FGM	FGA	PCT	3FGM	3FGA	PCT	FTM	FTA	PCT	O-RB	D-RB	TOT	AST	PF	DQ	STL	TO	BLK	PTS	RPG	APG	PPG
46-47—Chicago	15	—	—	5	26	.192	—	—	—	5	10	.500	—	—	—	0	6	—	—	—	—	15	—	0.0	1.0
REG. SEASON TOTALS	15	—	—	5	26	.192	—	—	—	5	10	.500	—	—	—	0	6	—	—	—	—	15	—	0.0	1.0

SZCZERBIAK, WALTER **(Walt)** b. August 21, 1949　Ht. 6-6　Wt. 210　College—George Washington

SEASON—TEAM	G	GS	MIN	FGM	FGA	PCT	3FGM	3FGA	PCT	FTM	FTA	PCT	O-RB	D-RB	TOT	AST	PF	DQ	STL	TO	BLK	PTS	RPG	APG	PPG
71-72—Pittsburgh (A)	53	—	598	149	237	.629	0	2	.000	35	53	.660	—	—	150	41	100	—	—	50	—	333	2.8	0.8	6.3
REG. ABA TOTALS	53	—	598	149	237	.629	0	2	.000	35	53	.660	—	—	150	41	100	—	—	50	—	333	2.8	0.8	6.3

TANNENBAUM, SIDNEY **(Sid)** b. October 8, 1925　d. September 4, 1986　Ht. 6-0　Wt. 160　College—New York University

SEASON—TEAM	G	GS	MIN	FGM	FGA	PCT	3FGM	3FGA	PCT	FTM	FTA	PCT	O-RB	D-RB	TOT	AST	PF	DQ	STL	TO	BLK	PTS	RPG	APG	PPG
47-48—New York	24	—	—	90	360	.250	—	—	—	62	74	.838	—	—	—	37	33	—	—	—	—	242	—	1.5	10.1
48-49—N.Y.-Balt.	46	—	—	146	501	.291	—	—	—	99	120	.825	—	—	—	125	74	—	—	—	—	391	—	2.7	8.5
REG. SEASON TOTALS	70	—	—	236	861	.274	—	—	—	161	194	.830	—	—	—	162	107	—	—	—	—	633	—	2.3	9.0
PLAYOFF TOTALS	6	—	—	17	62	.274	—	—	—	13	16	.813	—	—	—	14	13	—	—	—	—	47	—	2.3	7.8

TARPLEY, ROY JAMES JR. b. November 28, 1964　Ht. 6-11　Wt. 245　College—Michigan

SEASON—TEAM	G	GS	MIN	FGM	FGA	PCT	3FGM	3FGA	PCT	FTM	FTA	PCT	O-RB	D-RB	TOT	AST	PF	DQ	STL	TO	BLK	PTS	RPG	APG	PPG
86-87—Dallas	75	1	1405	233	499	.467	1	3	.333	94	139	.676	180	353	533	52	232	3	56	101	79	561	7.1	0.7	7.5
87-88—Dallas	81	9	2307	444	888	.500	0	5	.000	205	277	.740	360	599	959	86	313	8	103	172	86	1093	11.8	1.1	13.5
88-89—Dallas	19	6	591	131	242	.541	0	1	.000	66	96	.688	77	141	218	17	70	2	28	45	30	328	11.5	0.9	17.3
89-90—Dallas	45	35	1648	314	696	.451	0	6	.000	130	172	.756	189	400	589	67	160	0	79	117	70	758	13.1	1.5	16.8
90-91—Dallas	5	5	171	43	79	.544	0	1	.000	16	18	.889	16	39	55	12	20	0	6	13	9	102	11.0	2.4	20.4
REG. SEASON TOTALS	225	56	6122	1165	2404	.485	1	16	.063	511	702	.728	822	1532	2354	234	795	13	272	448	274	2842	10.5	1.0	12.6
PLAYOFF TOTALS	24	4	806	171	335	.510	0	4	.000	65	92	.707	115	192	307	32	99	4	29	48	43	407	12.8	1.3	17.0

TART, LEVERN DONIHUE **(Doc)** b. June 1, 1942　Ht. 6-3　Wt. 195　College—Bradley

SEASON—TEAM	G	GS	MIN	FGM	FGA	PCT	3FGM	3FGA	PCT	FTM	FTA	PCT	O-RB	D-RB	TOT	AST	PF	DQ	STL	TO	BLK	PTS	RPG	APG	PPG
67-68—Oakland-N.J. (A)	73	—	2853	633	1500	.422	1	15	.067	451	566	.797	—	—	394	249	212	0	—	277	—	1718	5.4	3.4	23.5
68-69—N.Y.-Hous.-Den. (A)	61	—	1403	274	649	.422	0	3	.000	193	255	.757	—	—	195	143	141	2	—	149	—	741	3.2	2.3	12.1
69-70—New York (A)	80	—	3210	756	1528	.495	11	35	.314	412	526	.783	—	—	546	264	268	4	—	—	—	1935	6.8	3.3	24.2
70-71—N.Y.-Texas (A)	60	—	1806	357	862	.414	10	34	.294	198	253	.783	—	—	239	174	171	—	—	—	—	922	4.0	2.9	15.4
REG. ABA TOTALS	274	—	9272	2020	4539	.445	22	87	.253	1254	1600	.784	—	—	1374	830	792	6	—	426	—	5316	5.0	3.0	19.4
ABA PLAYOFF TOTALS	11	—	414	102	230	.443	4	18	.222	59	72	.819	—	—	53	69	35	—	—	—	—	267	4.8	6.3	24.3
ABA ALL-STAR TOTALS	2	—	40	5	20	.250	1	2	.500	5	5	1.000	2	1	6	4	2	0	—	4	—	16	3.0	2.0	8.0

TATUM, WILLIAM EARL **(Earl)** b. July 26, 1953　Ht. 6-4½　Wt. 185　College—Marquette

SEASON—TEAM	G	GS	MIN	FGM	FGA	PCT	3FGM	3FGA	PCT	FTM	FTA	PCT	O-RB	D-RB	TOT	AST	PF	DQ	STL	TO	BLK	PTS	RPG	APG	PPG
76-77—Los Angeles	68	—	1249	283	607	.466	—	—	—	72	100	.720	83	153	236	118	168	1	85	—	22	638	3.5	1.7	9.4
77-78—L.A.-Indiana	82	—	2522	510	1087	.469	—	—	—	153	196	.781	79	216	295	296	257	5	140	184	40	1173	3.6	3.6	14.3
78-79—Boston-Detroit	79	—	1233	280	627	.447	—	—	—	52	71	.732	41	84	125	73	165	3	78	88	34	612	1.6	0.9	7.7
79-80—Cleveland	33	—	225	36	94	.383	2	6	.333	11	19	.579	11	15	26	20	29	0	16	17	5	85	0.8	0.6	2.6
REG. SEASON TOTALS	262	—	5229	1109	2415	.459	2	6	.333	288	386	.746	214	468	682	507	619	9	319	289	101	2508	2.6	1.9	9.6
PLAYOFF TOTALS	11	—	356	67	134	.500	0	0	—	16	24	.667	16	38	54	27	34	2	15	—	9	150	4.9	2.5	13.6

TAYLOR, ANTHONY PAUL b. November 30, 1965　Ht. 6-4　Wt. 175　College—Oregon

SEASON—TEAM	G	GS	MIN	FGM	FGA	PCT	3FGM	3FGA	PCT	FTM	FTA	PCT	O-RB	D-RB	TOT	AST	PF	DQ	STL	TO	BLK	PTS	RPG	APG	PPG
88-89—Miami	21	7	368	60	151	.397	0	2	.000	24	32	.750	11	23	34	43	37	0	22	20	5	144	1.6	2.0	6.9
REG. SEASON TOTALS	21	7	368	60	151	.397	0	2	.000	24	32	.750	11	23	34	43	37	0	22	20	5	144	1.6	2.0	6.9

TAYLOR, BRIAN DWIGHT b. June 9, 1951 Ht. 6-2 Wt. 185 College—Princeton

SEASON—TEAM	G	GS	MIN	FGM	FGA	PCT	3FGM	3FGA	PCT	FTM	FTA	PCT	O-RB	D-RB	TOT	AST	PF	DQ	STL	TO	BLK	PTS	RPG	APG	PPG
72-73—New York (A)	63	—	2038	395	767	.515	4	25	.160	168	226	.743	77	126	203	175	219	5	—	137	—	962	3.2	2.8	15.3
73-74—New York (A)	75	—	2505	363	762	.476	8	29	.276	100	143	.699	92	122	214	341	192	—	154	164	22	834	2.9	4.5	11.1
74-75—New York (A)	79	—	2611	472	920	.513	10	46	.217	150	196	.765	86	146	232	282	216	—	221	152	26	1104	2.9	3.6	14.0
75-76—New York (A)	54	—	1733	354	724	.489	32	76	.421	164	207	.792	70	92	162	204	138	—	125	153	22	904	3.0	3.8	16.7
76-77—Kansas City	72	—	2488	501	995	.504	—	—	—	225	275	.818	88	150	238	320	206	1	199	—	16	1227	3.3	4.4	17.0
77-78—Denver	39	—	1222	182	403	.452	—	—	—	88	115	.765	30	68	98	132	120	1	71	77	6	452	2.5	3.4	11.6
78-79—San Diego	20	—	212	30	83	.361	—	—	—	16	18	.889	13	13	26	20	34	0	24	17	0	76	1.3	1.0	3.8
79-80—San Diego	78	—	2754	418	895	.467	90	239	.377	130	162	.802	76	112	188	335	246	6	147	141	25	1056	2.4	4.3	13.5
80-81—San Diego	80	—	2312	310	591	.525	44	115	.383	146	185	.789	58	93	151	440	212	0	118	111	23	810	1.9	5.5	10.1
81-82—San Diego	41	40	1274	165	328	.503	23	63	.365	90	110	.818	26	70	96	229	113	1	47	82	9	443	2.3	5.6	10.8
REG. NBA TOTALS	330	40	10262	1606	3295	.487	157	417	.376	695	865	.803	291	506	797	1476	931	9	606	428	82	4064	2.4	4.5	12.3
REG. ABA TOTALS	271	—	8887	1584	3173	.499	54	176	.307	582	772	.754	325	486	811	1002	765	5	500	606	70	3804	3.0	3.7	14.0
ABA PLAYOFF TOTALS	37	—	1334	208	473	.440	12	37	.324	73	95	.768	51	56	123	133	117	0	66	81	8	501	3.3	3.6	13.5
ABA ALL-STAR TOTALS	2	1	50	12	22	.545	0	1	.000	3	5	.600	0	1	5	11	7	—	4	1	0	27	2.5	5.5	13.5

TAYLOR, CORNELIUS F. (**Jay**) b. October 3, 1967 Ht. 6-3 Wt. 190 College—Eastern Illinois

SEASON—TEAM	G	GS	MIN	FGM	FGA	PCT	3FGM	3FGA	PCT	FTM	FTA	PCT	O-RB	D-RB	TOT	AST	PF	DQ	STL	TO	BLK	PTS	RPG	APG	PPG
89-90—New Jersey	17	0	114	21	52	.404	3	13	.231	6	9	.667	5	6	11	5	9	0	5	10	3	51	0.6	0.3	3.0
REG. SEASON TOTALS	17	0	114	21	52	.404	3	13	.231	6	9	.667	5	6	11	5	9	0	5	10	3	51	0.6	0.3	3.0

TAYLOR, FREDRICK OLLIE (**Fred**) b. February 5, 1948 Ht. 6-5½ Wt. 180 College—Texas-Pan American

SEASON—TEAM	G	GS	MIN	FGM	FGA	PCT	3FGM	3FGA	PCT	FTM	FTA	PCT	O-RB	D-RB	TOT	AST	PF	DQ	STL	TO	BLK	PTS	RPG	APG	PPG
70-71—Phoenix	54	—	552	110	284	.387	—	—	—	78	125	.624	—	—	86	51	113	0	—	—	—	298	1.6	0.9	5.5
71-72—Phoenix-Cin.	34	—	283	36	117	.308	—	—	—	15	32	.469	—	—	54	18	40	0	—	—	—	87	1.6	0.5	2.6
REG. SEASON TOTALS	88	—	835	146	401	.364	—	—	—	93	157	.592	—	—	140	69	153	0	—	—	—	385	1.6	0.8	4.4

TAYLOR, JEFFREY (**Jeff**) b. January 1, 1960 Ht. 6-4 Wt. 175 College—Texas Tech

SEASON—TEAM	G	GS	MIN	FGM	FGA	PCT	3FGM	3FGA	PCT	FTM	FTA	PCT	O-RB	D-RB	TOT	AST	PF	DQ	STL	TO	BLK	PTS	RPG	APG	PPG
82-83—Houston	44	5	774	64	160	.400	0	1	.000	30	46	.652	25	53	78	110	82	1	40	60	15	158	1.8	2.5	3.6
86-87—Detroit	12	0	44	6	10	.600	0	0	—	9	10	.900	1	3	4	3	4	0	2	8	1	21	0.3	0.3	1.8
REG. SEASON TOTALS	56	5	818	70	170	.412	0	1	.000	39	56	.696	26	56	82	113	86	1	42	68	16	179	1.5	2.0	3.2

TAYLOR, LEONARD CHESTER JR. b. May 2, 1966 Ht. 6-8 Wt. 220 College—California

SEASON—TEAM	G	GS	MIN	FGM	FGA	PCT	3FGM	3FGA	PCT	FTM	FTA	PCT	O-RB	D-RB	TOT	AST	PF	DQ	STL	TO	BLK	PTS	RPG	APG	PPG
89-90—Golden State	10	0	37	0	6	.000	0	1	.000	11	16	.688	4	8	12	1	4	0	0	5	0	11	1.2	0.1	1.1
REG. SEASON TOTALS	10	0	37	0	6	.000	0	1	.000	11	16	.688	4	8	12	1	4	0	0	5	0	11	1.2	0.1	1.1

TAYLOR, OLIVER HAROLD (**Ollie**) b. March 7, 1947 Ht. 6-2 Wt. 195 College—Houston

SEASON—TEAM	G	GS	MIN	FGM	FGA	PCT	3FGM	3FGA	PCT	FTM	FTA	PCT	O-RB	D-RB	TOT	AST	PF	DQ	STL	TO	BLK	PTS	RPG	APG	PPG
70-71—New York (A)	80	—	1617	251	496	.506	5	12	.417	187	277	.675	—	—	307	146	231	—	—	—	—	694	3.8	1.8	8.7
71-72—New York (A)	82	—	1891	245	542	.452	0	6	.000	218	308	.708	—	—	330	153	213	—	—	153	—	708	4.0	1.9	8.6
72-73—San Diego (A)	69	—	2121	325	757	.429	11	55	.200	286	425	.673	156	209	365	275	191	1	—	207	—	947	5.3	4.0	13.7
73-74—N.Y.-Car. (A)	31	—	519	65	150	.433	2	4	.500	58	86	.674	34	54	88	54	63	—	20	58	6	190	2.8	1.7	6.1
REG. ABA TOTALS	262	—	6148	886	1945	.456	18	77	.234	749	1096	.683	190	263	1090	628	698	1	20	418	6	2539	4.2	2.4	9.7
ABA PLAYOFF TOTALS	31	—	994	118	270	.437	3	9	.333	83	116	.716	3	0	148	73	92	0	2	87	0	322	4.8	2.4	10.4

TAYLOR, ROLAND MORRIS (**Fatty**) b. March 13, 1946 Ht. 6-0 Wt. 180 College—Dodge City CC/LaSalle

SEASON—TEAM	G	GS	MIN	FGM	FGA	PCT	3FGM	3FGA	PCT	FTM	FTA	PCT	O-RB	D-RB	TOT	AST	PF	DQ	STL	TO	BLK	PTS	RPG	APG	PPG
69-70—Washington (A)	83	—	1994	243	520	.467	1	6	.167	178	264	.674	—	—	377	201	285	4	—	—	—	665	4.5	2.4	8.0
70-71—Virginia (A)	84	—	1629	180	393	.458	4	22	.182	175	256	.684	—	—	263	225	228	—	—	—	—	539	3.1	2.7	6.4
71-72—Virginia (A)	84	—	2669	306	680	.450	1	15	.067	164	258	.636	—	—	416	321	302	—	—	206	—	777	5.0	3.8	9.3
72-73—Virginia (A)	78	—	2553	316	679	.465	3	7	.429	150	248	.605	137	181	318	374	266	3	210	237	—	785	4.1	4.8	10.1
73-74—Virginia (A)	80	—	2812	292	709	.412	3	19	.158	185	256	.723	124	253	377	416	270	—	215	279	15	772	4.7	5.2	9.7
74-75—Denver (A)	76	—	2018	251	586	.428	6	21	.286	129	172	.750	85	136	221	337	238	—	172	248	16	637	2.9	4.4	8.4
75-76—Virginia (A)	76	—	2483	243	600	.405	11	51	.216	125	173	.723	117	224	341	401	212	—	206	247	16	622	4.5	5.3	8.2
76-77—Denver	79	—	1548	132	314	.420	—	—	—	37	65	.569	90	121	211	288	202	0	132	—	9	301	2.7	3.6	3.8
REG. NBA TOTALS	79	—	1548	132	314	.420	—	—	—	37	65	.569	90	121	211	288	202	0	132	—	9	301	2.7	3.6	3.8
REG. ABA TOTALS	561	—	16158	1831	4167	.439	29	141	.206	1106	1627	.680	463	794	2313	2275	1801	7	803	1217	47	4797	4.1	4.1	8.6
NBA PLAYOFF TOTALS	1	—	1	0	0	—	—	—	—	0	0	—	0	0	0	0	0	0	0	—	0	0	0.0	0.0	0.0
ABA PLAYOFF TOTALS	53	—	1336	127	313	.406	3	14	.214	74	104	.712	28	35	200	167	163	0	35	89	5	331	3.8	3.2	6.2

TAYLOR, RONALD (Ron) b. November 21, 1947 Ht. 7-1 Wt. 265 College—USC

SEASON—TEAM	G	GS	MIN	FGM	FGA	PCT	3FGM	3FGA	PCT	FTM	FTA	PCT	O-RB	D-RB	TOT	AST	PF	DQ	STL	TO	BLK	PTS	RPG	APG	PPG
69-70—Wash.-N.Y. (A)	75	—	910	156	327	.477	0	0	—	57	102	.559	—	—	293	64	218	11	—	—	—	369	3.9	0.9	4.9
70-71—Virginia (A)	1	—	25	1	9	.111	0	0	—	0	1	.000	—	—	0	4	2	—	—	—	—	2	0.0	4.0	2.0
71-72—Pittsburgh (A)	1	—	4	0	1	.000	0	0	—	0	0	—	—	—	1	0	5	—	—	1	—	0	1.0	0.0	0.0
REG. ABA TOTALS	77	—	939	157	337	.466	0	0	—	57	103	.553	—	—	294	68	225	11	—	1	—	371	3.8	0.9	4.8
ABA PLAYOFF TOTALS	2	—	5	0	4	.000	0	0	—	0	1	.000	—	—	2	0	0	0	—	—	—	0	1.0	0.0	0.0

TAYLOR, VINCENT CALDWELL (Vince) b. September 11, 1960 Ht. 6-5 Wt. 180 College—Duke

SEASON—TEAM	G	GS	MIN	FGM	FGA	PCT	3FGM	3FGA	PCT	FTM	FTA	PCT	O-RB	D-RB	TOT	AST	PF	DQ	STL	TO	BLK	PTS	RPG	APG	PPG
82-83—New York	31	0	321	37	102	.363	0	0	—	21	32	.656	19	17	36	41	54	1	20	30	2	95	1.2	1.3	3.1
REG. SEASON TOTALS	31	0	321	37	102	.363	0	0	—	21	32	.656	19	17	36	41	54	1	20	30	2	95	1.2	1.3	3.1

TEAGLE, TERRY MICHAEL b. April 10, 1960 Ht. 6-5 Wt. 195 College—Baylor

SEASON—TEAM	G	GS	MIN	FGM	FGA	PCT	3FGM	3FGA	PCT	FTM	FTA	PCT	O-RB	D-RB	TOT	AST	PF	DQ	STL	TO	BLK	PTS	RPG	APG	PPG
82-83—Houston	73	44	1708	332	776	.428	10	29	.345	87	125	.696	74	120	194	150	171	0	53	137	18	761	2.7	2.1	10.4
83-84—Houston	68	0	616	148	315	.470	7	27	.259	37	44	.841	28	50	78	63	81	1	13	62	4	340	1.1	0.9	5.0
84-85—Detroit-G.S.	21	3	349	74	137	.540	2	4	.500	25	35	.714	22	21	43	14	36	0	13	15	5	175	2.0	0.7	8.3
85-86—Golden State	82	52	2158	475	958	.496	4	25	.160	211	265	.796	96	139	235	115	241	2	71	136	34	1165	2.9	1.4	14.2
86-87—Golden State	82	0	1650	370	808	.458	0	10	.000	182	234	.778	68	107	175	105	190	0	68	117	13	922	2.1	1.3	11.2
87-88—Golden State	47	4	958	248	546	.454	1	9	.111	97	121	.802	41	40	81	61	95	0	32	80	4	594	1.7	1.3	12.6
88-89—Golden State	66	41	1569	409	859	.476	2	12	.167	182	225	.809	110	153	263	96	173	2	79	116	17	1002	4.0	1.5	15.2
89-90—Golden State	82	49	2376	538	1122	.480	3	14	.214	244	294	.830	114	253	367	155	231	3	91	144	15	1323	4.5	1.9	16.1
90-91—L.A. Lakers	82	0	1498	335	757	.443	0	9	.000	145	177	.819	82	99	181	82	165	1	31	83	8	815	2.2	1.0	9.9
91-92—L.A. Lakers	82	0	1602	364	805	.452	1	4	.250	151	197	.766	91	92	183	113	148	0	66	114	9	880	2.2	1.4	10.7
92-93—Houston	2	0	25	2	7	.286	0	0	—	1	2	.500	0	3	3	2	1	0	0	1	0	5	1.5	1.0	2.5
REG. SEASON TOTALS	687	193	14509	3295	7090	.465	30	143	.210	1362	1719	.792	726	1077	1803	956	1532	9	517	1005	127	7982	2.6	1.4	11.6
PLAYOFF TOTALS	45	3	885	203	450	.451	0	4	.000	89	114	.781	39	59	98	42	104	1	29	54	10	495	2.2	0.9	11.0

TEMPLE, COLLIS JR. b. November 8, 1952 Ht. 6-8 Wt. 220 College—Louisiana State

SEASON—TEAM	G	GS	MIN	FGM	FGA	PCT	3FGM	3FGA	PCT	FTM	FTA	PCT	O-RB	D-RB	TOT	AST	PF	DQ	STL	TO	BLK	PTS	RPG	APG	PPG
74-75—San Antonio (A)	24	—	102	17	41	.415	0	1	.000	8	10	.800	14	17	31	15	29	—	4	12	4	42	1.3	0.6	1.8
REG. ABA TOTALS	24	—	102	17	41	.415	0	1	.000	8	10	.800	14	17	31	15	29	—	4	12	4	42	1.3	0.6	1.8

TERRELL, IRA EDMONDSON b. June 19, 1954 Ht. 6-8 Wt. 205 College—Southern Methodist

SEASON—TEAM	G	GS	MIN	FGM	FGA	PCT	3FGM	3FGA	PCT	FTM	FTA	PCT	O-RB	D-RB	TOT	AST	PF	DQ	STL	TO	BLK	PTS	RPG	APG	PPG
76-77—Phoenix	78	—	1751	277	545	.508	—	—	—	111	176	.631	99	288	387	103	165	0	41	—	47	665	5.0	1.3	8.5
78-79—N.O.-Port.	49	—	732	93	198	.470	—	—	—	35	53	.660	44	102	146	41	100	0	22	53	28	221	3.0	0.8	4.5
REG. SEASON TOTALS	127	—	2483	370	743	.498	—	—	—	146	229	.638	143	390	533	144	265	0	63	53	75	886	4.2	1.1	7.0
PLAYOFF TOTALS	1	—	6	0	4	.000	—	—	—	0	0	—	0	2	2	—	0	0	0	0	0	0	2.0	0.0	0.0

TERRY, ALLEN CHARLES (Chuck) b. September 27, 1950 Ht. 6-6 Wt. 215 College—Long Beach State

SEASON—TEAM	G	GS	MIN	FGM	FGA	PCT	3FGM	3FGA	PCT	FTM	FTA	PCT	O-RB	D-RB	TOT	AST	PF	DQ	STL	TO	BLK	PTS	RPG	APG	PPG
72-73—Milwaukee	67	—	693	55	162	.340	—	—	—	17	24	.708	—	—	145	40	116	1	—	—	—	127	2.2	0.6	1.9
73-74—Milwaukee	7	—	32	4	12	.333	—	—	—	0	0	—	1	2	3	4	4	0	2	—	0	8	0.4	0.6	1.1
73-74—San Antonio (A)	61	—	1093	132	294	.449	1	2	.500	36	41	.878	67	99	166	72	139	—	18	33	5	301	2.7	1.2	4.9
74-75—San Antonio (A)	79	—	1186	148	313	.473	3	8	.375	39	53	.736	77	140	217	69	146	—	37	37	3	338	2.7	0.9	4.3
75-76—New York (A)	66	—	970	96	246	.390	6	21	.286	22	29	.759	45	99	144	38	116	—	36	21	6	220	2.2	0.6	3.3
76-77—New York Nets	61	—	1075	128	318	.403	—	—	—	48	62	.774	43	100	143	39	120	0	58	—	10	304	2.3	0.6	5.0
REG. NBA TOTALS	135	—	1800	187	492	.380	—	—	—	65	86	.756	44	102	291	83	240	1	60	—	10	439	2.2	0.6	3.3
REG. ABA TOTALS	206	—	3249	376	853	.441	10	31	.323	97	123	.789	189	338	527	179	401	0	91	91	14	859	2.6	0.9	4.2
NBA PLAYOFF TOTALS	5	—	18	4	5	.800	—	—	—	0	0	—	0	3	3	1	2	0	0	—	0	8	0.6	0.2	1.6
ABA PLAYOFF TOTALS	16	—	261	23	56	.411	0	2	.000	7	10	.700	13	32	45	10	30	0	3	9	1	53	2.8	0.6	3.3

TERRY, CARLOS FERNANDO b. June 22, 1956 d. March 12, 1989 Ht. 6-4½ Wt. 215 College—Winston-Salem State

SEASON—TEAM	G	GS	MIN	FGM	FGA	PCT	3FGM	3FGA	PCT	FTM	FTA	PCT	O-RB	D-RB	TOT	AST	PF	DQ	STL	TO	BLK	PTS	RPG	APG	PPG
80-81—Washington	26	—	504	80	160	.500	0	6	.000	28	42	.667	43	73	116	70	68	1	27	57	13	188	4.5	2.7	7.2
81-82—Washington	13	0	60	3	15	.200	0	3	.000	3	4	.750	5	7	12	8	15	0	3	5	1	9	0.9	0.6	0.7
82-83—Washington	55	3	514	39	106	.368	0	2	.000	10	15	.667	27	72	99	46	79	1	24	20	13	88	1.8	0.8	1.6
REG. SEASON TOTALS	94	3	1078	122	281	.434	0	11	.000	41	61	.672	75	152	227	124	162	2	54	82	27	285	2.4	1.3	3.0
PLAYOFF TOTALS	3	0	5	0	0	—	0	0	—	0	0	—	0	1	1	—	0	0	0	0	0	0	0.3	0.0	0.0

TERRY, CLAUDE LEWIS b. January 12, 1950 Ht. 6-5 Wt. 195 College—Stanford

SEASON—TEAM	G	GS	MIN	FGM	FGA	PCT	3FGM	3FGA	PCT	FTM	FTA	PCT	O-RB	D-RB	TOT	AST	PF	DQ	STL	TO	BLK	PTS	RPG	APG	PPG
72-73—Denver (A)	68	—	667	120	285	.421	10	24	.417	74	114	.649	—	—	75	62	111	0	—	69	—	324	1.1	0.9	4.8
73-74—Denver (A)	60	—	587	113	255	.443	14	35	.400	60	69	.870	26	45	71	73	64	—	12	57	3	300	1.2	1.2	5.0
74-75—Denver (A)	70	—	989	193	364	.530	10	25	.400	70	92	.761	57	83	140	111	82	—	33	80	2	466	2.0	1.6	6.7
75-76—Denver (A)	79	—	1349	232	500	.464	13	55	.236	80	89	.899	42	110	152	146	116	—	40	96	5	557	1.9	1.8	7.1
76-77—Buffalo-Atlanta	45	—	545	96	191	.503	—	—	—	36	44	.818	12	34	46	58	48	0	20	—	1	228	1.0	1.3	5.1
77-78—Atlanta	27	—	166	25	68	.368	—	—	—	9	11	.818	3	12	15	7	14	0	6	8	0	59	0.6	0.3	2.2
REG. NBA TOTALS	72	—	711	121	259	.467	—	—	—	45	55	.818	15	46	61	65	62	0	26	8	1	287	0.8	0.9	4.0
REG. ABA TOTALS	277	—	3592	658	1404	.469	47	139	.338	284	364	.780	125	238	438	392	373	0	85	302	10	1647	1.6	1.4	5.9
ABA PLAYOFF TOTALS	28	—	330	43	117	.368	1	19	.053	17	23	.739	9	25	37	32	38	0	8	23	2	104	1.3	1.1	3.7
ABA ALL-STAR TOTALS	1	—	25	5	12	.417	1	3	.333	3	5	.600	0	0	3	3	2	—	0	0	0	14	3.0	3.0	14.0

THACKER, THOMAS PORTER (**Tom, Tack**) b. November 2, 1939 Ht. 6-2 Wt. 170 College—Cincinnati

SEASON—TEAM	G	GS	MIN	FGM	FGA	PCT	3FGM	3FGA	PCT	FTM	FTA	PCT	O-RB	D-RB	TOT	AST	PF	DQ	STL	TO	BLK	PTS	RPG	APG	PPG
63-64—Cincinnati	48	—	457	53	181	.293	—	—	—	26	53	.491	—	—	115	51	51	0	—	—	—	132	2.4	1.1	2.8
64-65—Cincinnati	55	—	470	56	168	.333	—	—	—	23	47	.489	—	—	127	41	64	0	—	—	—	135	2.3	0.7	2.5
65-66—Cincinnati	50	—	478	84	207	.406	—	—	—	15	38	.395	—	—	119	61	85	0	—	—	—	183	2.4	1.2	3.7
67-68—Boston	65	—	782	114	272	.419	—	—	—	43	84	.512	—	—	161	69	165	2	—	—	—	271	2.5	1.1	4.2
68-69—Indiana (A)	18	—	346	40	117	.342	0	2	.000	18	31	.581	—	—	67	52	51	0	—	26	—	98	3.7	2.9	5.4
69-70—Indiana (A)	70	—	1016	70	212	.330	10	39	.256	38	69	.551	—	—	211	185	177	2	—	—	—	188	3.0	2.6	2.7
70-71—Indiana (A)	8	—	92	6	17	.353	0	3	.000	1	1	1.000	—	—	22	7	18	—	—	—	—	13	2.8	0.9	1.6
REG. NBA TOTALS	218	—	2187	307	828	.371	—	—	—	107	222	.482	—	—	522	222	365	2	—	—	—	721	2.4	1.0	3.3
REG. ABA TOTALS	96	—	1454	116	346	.335	10	44	.227	57	101	.564	—	—	300	244	246	2	—	26	—	299	3.1	2.5	3.1
NBA PLAYOFF TOTALS	31	—	217	25	82	.305	—	—	—	9	19	.474	—	—	51	19	46	0	—	—	—	59	1.6	0.6	1.9
ABA PLAYOFF TOTALS	30	—	578	48	155	.310	3	16	.188	34	58	.586	—	—	125	105	90	1	—	33	—	133	4.2	3.5	4.4

THEARD, FLOYD b. September 5, 1944 d. April 11, 1985 Ht. 6-1½ Wt. 170 College—Kentucky State

SEASON—TEAM	G	GS	MIN	FGM	FGA	PCT	3FGM	3FGA	PCT	FTM	FTA	PCT	O-RB	D-RB	TOT	AST	PF	DQ	STL	TO	BLK	PTS	RPG	APG	PPG
69-70—Denver (A)	25	—	406	39	113	.345	0	1	.000	18	28	.643	—	—	51	44	49	1	—	—	—	96	2.0	1.8	3.8
REG. ABA TOTALS	25	—	406	39	113	.345	0	1	.000	18	28	.643	—	—	51	44	49	1	—	—	—	96	2.0	1.8	3.8

THEUS, REGGIE WAYNE b. October 13, 1957 Ht. 6-6.5 Wt. 205 College—Nevada Las Vegas

SEASON—TEAM	G	GS	MIN	FGM	FGA	PCT	3FGM	3FGA	PCT	FTM	FTA	PCT	O-RB	D-RB	TOT	AST	PF	DQ	STL	TO	BLK	PTS	RPG	APG	PPG
78-79—Chicago	82	—	2753	537	1119	.480	—	—	—	264	347	.761	92	136	228	429	270	2	93	303	18	1338	2.8	5.2	16.3
79-80—Chicago	82	—	3029	566	1172	.483	28	105	.267	500	597	.838	143	186	329	515	262	4	114	348	20	1660	4.0	6.3	20.2
80-81—Chicago	82	—	2820	543	1097	.495	18	90	.200	445	550	.809	124	163	287	426	258	1	122	259	20	1549	3.5	5.2	18.9
81-82—Chicago	82	82	2838	560	1194	.469	25	100	.250	363	449	.808	115	197	312	476	243	1	87	277	16	1508	3.8	5.8	18.4
82-83—Chicago	82	81	2856	749	1567	.478	21	91	.231	434	542	.801	91	209	300	484	281	6	143	321	17	1953	3.7	5.9	23.8
83-84—Chicago-K.C.	61	35	1498	262	625	.419	7	42	.167	214	281	.762	50	79	129	352	171	3	50	156	12	745	2.1	5.8	12.2
84-85—Kansas City	82	80	2543	501	1029	.487	5	38	.132	334	387	.863	106	164	270	656	250	0	95	307	18	1341	3.3	8.0	16.4
85-86—Sacramento	82	82	2919	546	1137	.480	6	35	.171	405	490	.827	73	231	304	788	231	3	112	327	20	1503	3.7	9.6	18.3
86-87—Sacramento	79	76	2872	577	1223	.472	17	78	.218	429	495	.867	86	180	266	692	208	3	78	289	16	1600	3.4	8.8	20.3
87-88—Sacramento	73	73	2653	619	1318	.470	16	59	.271	320	385	.831	72	160	232	463	173	0	59	234	16	1574	3.2	6.3	21.6
88-89—Atlanta	82	82	2517	497	1067	.466	17	58	.293	285	335	.851	86	156	242	387	236	0	108	194	16	1296	3.0	4.7	15.8
89-90—Orlando	76	71	2350	517	1178	.439	26	105	.248	378	443	.853	75	146	221	407	194	1	60	226	12	1438	2.9	5.4	18.9
90-91—New Jersey	81	81	2955	583	1247	.468	52	144	.361	292	343	.851	69	160	229	378	231	0	85	252	35	1510	2.8	4.7	18.6
REG. SEASON TOTALS	1026	743	34603	7057	14973	.471	238	945	.252	4663	5644	.826	1182	2167	3349	6453	3008	24	1206	3493	236	19015	3.3	6.3	18.5
PLAYOFF TOTALS	17	11	542	89	218	.408	2	15	.133	64	77	.831	17	30	47	97	58	1	18	48	2	244	2.8	5.7	14.4
ALL-STAR TOTALS	2	1	27	4	12	.333	0	0	—	0	0	—	1	1	2	4	1	0	2	6	0	8	1.0	2.0	4.0

THIBEAUX, PETER C. b. October 3, 1961 Ht. 6-7 Wt. 210 College—St. Mary's (Ca.)

SEASON—TEAM	G	GS	MIN	FGM	FGA	PCT	3FGM	3FGA	PCT	FTM	FTA	PCT	O-RB	D-RB	TOT	AST	PF	DQ	STL	TO	BLK	PTS	RPG	APG	PPG
84-85—Golden State	51	1	461	94	195	.482	0	2	.000	43	67	.642	29	40	69	17	85	1	11	34	17	231	1.4	0.3	4.5
85-86—Golden State	42	8	531	100	233	.429	2	5	.400	29	48	.604	28	47	75	28	82	1	23	39	15	231	1.8	0.7	5.5
REG. SEASON TOTALS	93	9	992	194	428	.453	2	7	.286	72	115	.626	57	87	144	45	167	2	34	73	32	462	1.5	0.5	5.0

THIEBEN, WILLIAM BERNHARD (**Bill**) b. March 28, 1935 Ht. 6-6½ Wt. 215 College—Hofstra

SEASON—TEAM	G	GS	MIN	FGM	FGA	PCT	3FGM	3FGA	PCT	FTM	FTA	PCT	O-RB	D-RB	TOT	AST	PF	DQ	STL	TO	BLK	PTS	RPG	APG	PPG
56-57—Fort Wayne	58	—	633	90	256	.352	—	—	—	57	87	.655	—	—	207	17	78	0	—	—	—	237	3.6	0.3	4.1
57-58—Detroit	27	—	243	42	143	.294	—	—	—	16	27	.593	—	—	65	7	44	0	—	—	—	100	2.4	0.3	3.7
REG. SEASON TOTALS	85	—	876	132	399	.331	—	—	—	73	114	.640	—	—	272	24	122	0	—	—	—	337	3.2	0.3	4.0
PLAYOFF TOTALS	2	—	28	6	7	.857	—	—	—	2	6	.333	—	—	6	3	5	0	—	—	—	14	3.0	1.5	7.0

THIGPEN, JUSTUS b. August 13, 1947   Ht. 6-1 Wt. 170 College—Flint JC/Weber State

SEASON—TEAM	G	GS	MIN	FGM	FGA	PCT	3FGM	3FGA	PCT	FTM	FTA	PCT	O-RB	D-RB	TOT	AST	PF	DQ	STL	TO	BLK	PTS	RPG	APG	PPG
69-70—Pittsburgh (A)	3	—	58	5	19	.263	0	0	—	1	3	.333	—	—	8	4	14	1	—	—	—	11	2.7	1.3	3.7
72-73—Detroit	18	—	99	23	57	.404	—	—	—	0	0	—	—	—	9	8	18	0	—	—	—	46	0.5	0.4	2.6
73-74—Kansas City-Omaha	1	—	2	1	3	.333	—	—	—	0	0	—	1	0	1	0	0	0	0	—	0	2	1.0	0.0	2.0
REG. NBA TOTALS	19	—	101	24	60	.400	—	—	—	0	0	—	1	0	10	8	18	0	—	—	0	48	0.5	0.4	2.5
REG. ABA TOTALS	3	—	58	5	19	.263	0	0	—	1	3	.333	—	—	8	4	14	1	—	—	—	11	2.7	1.3	3.7

THIRDKILL, DAVID b. April 12, 1960   Ht. 6-7 Wt. 215 College—Southern Idaho/Bradley

SEASON—TEAM	G	GS	MIN	FGM	FGA	PCT	3FGM	3FGA	PCT	FTM	FTA	PCT	O-RB	D-RB	TOT	AST	PF	DQ	STL	TO	BLK	PTS	RPG	APG	PPG
82-83—Phoenix	49	2	521	74	170	.435	1	7	.143	45	78	.577	28	44	72	36	93	1	19	48	4	194	1.5	0.7	4.0
83-84—Detroit	46	0	291	31	72	.431	0	1	.000	15	31	.484	9	22	31	27	44	0	10	19	3	77	0.7	0.6	1.7
84-85—Detroit-Milw.-S.A.	18	3	183	20	38	.526	0	1	.000	11	19	.579	10	7	17	4	22	0	5	14	3	51	0.9	0.2	2.8
85-86—Boston	49	0	385	54	110	.491	0	1	.000	55	88	.625	27	43	70	15	55	0	11	19	3	163	1.4	0.3	3.3
86-87—Boston	17	0	89	10	24	.417	0	1	.000	5	16	.313	5	14	19	2	12	0	2	5	0	25	1.1	0.1	1.5
REG. SEASON TOTALS	179	5	1469	189	414	.457	1	11	.091	131	232	.565	79	130	209	84	226	1	47	105	13	510	1.2	0.5	2.8
PLAYOFF TOTALS	18	0	69	7	22	.318	0	3	.000	7	15	.467	1	9	10	5	9	0	2	7	0	21	0.6	0.3	1.2

THOMAS, CARL b. October 3, 1969   Ht. 6-4 Wt. 175 College—Eastern Michigan

SEASON—TEAM	G	GS	MIN	FGM	FGA	PCT	3FGM	3FGA	PCT	FTM	FTA	PCT	O-RB	D-RB	TOT	AST	PF	DQ	STL	TO	BLK	PTS	RPG	APG	PPG
91-92—Sacramento	1	0	31	5	12	.417	1	2	.500	1	2	.500	0	0	0	1	3	0	1	1	0	12	0.0	1.0	12.0
REG. SEASON TOTALS	1	0	31	5	12	.417	1	2	.500	1	2	.500	0	0	0	1	3	0	1	1	0	12	0.0	1.0	12.0

THOMAS, CHARLES b. October 3, 1969   Ht. 6-3 Wt. 175 College—Eastern Michigan

SEASON—TEAM	G	GS	MIN	FGM	FGA	PCT	3FGM	3FGA	PCT	FTM	FTA	PCT	O-RB	D-RB	TOT	AST	PF	DQ	STL	TO	BLK	PTS	RPG	APG	PPG
91-92—Detroit	36	0	156	18	51	.353	2	17	.118	10	15	.667	6	16	22	22	20	0	4	17	1	48	0.6	0.6	1.3
REG. SEASON TOTALS	36	0	156	18	51	.353	2	17	.118	10	15	.667	6	16	22	22	20	0	4	17	1	48	0.6	0.6	1.3

THOMAS, IRVING b. January 2, 1966   Ht. 6-9 Wt. 230 College—Kentucky/Florida State

SEASON—TEAM	G	GS	MIN	FGM	FGA	PCT	3FGM	3FGA	PCT	FTM	FTA	PCT	O-RB	D-RB	TOT	AST	PF	DQ	STL	TO	BLK	PTS	RPG	APG	PPG
90-91—L.A. Lakers	26	0	108	17	50	.340	0	0	—	12	21	.571	14	17	31	10	24	0	4	13	1	46	1.2	0.4	1.8
REG. SEASON TOTALS	26	0	108	17	50	.340	0	0	—	12	21	.571	14	17	31	10	24	0	4	13	1	46	1.2	0.4	1.8
PLAYOFF TOTALS	3	0	5	1	1	1.000	0	0	—	0	0	—	0	0	0	—	0	0	0	0	0	2	0.0	0.0	0.7

THOMAS, ISIAH LORD III b. April 30, 1961   Ht. 6-1 Wt. 185 College—Indiana

SEASON—TEAM	G	GS	MIN	FGM	FGA	PCT	3FGM	3FGA	PCT	FTM	FTA	PCT	O-RB	D-RB	TOT	AST	PF	DQ	STL	TO	BLK	PTS	RPG	APG	PPG
81-82—Detroit	72	72	2433	453	1068	.424	17	59	.288	302	429	.704	57	152	209	565	253	2	150	299	17	1225	2.9	7.8	17.0
82-83—Detroit	81	81	3093	725	1537	.472	36	125	.288	368	518	.710	105	223	328	634	318	8	199	326	29	1854	4.0	7.8	22.9
83-84—Detroit	82	82	3007	669	1448	.462	22	65	.338	388	529	.733	103	224	327	914	324	8	204	307	33	1748	4.0	11.1	21.3
84-85—Detroit	81	81	3089	646	1410	.458	29	113	.257	399	493	.809	114	247	361	1123	288	8	187	302	25	1720	4.5	13.9	21.2
85-86—Detroit	77	77	2790	609	1248	.488	26	84	.310	365	462	.790	83	194	277	830	245	9	171	289	20	1609	3.6	10.8	20.9
86-87—Detroit	81	81	3013	626	1353	.463	19	98	.194	400	521	.768	82	237	319	813	251	5	153	343	20	1671	3.9	10.0	20.6
87-88—Detroit	81	81	2927	621	1341	.463	30	97	.309	305	394	.774	64	214	278	678	217	0	141	273	17	1577	3.4	8.4	19.5
88-89—Detroit	80	76	2924	569	1227	.464	33	121	.273	287	351	.818	49	224	273	663	209	0	133	298	20	1458	3.4	8.3	18.2
89-90—Detroit	81	81	2993	579	1322	.438	42	136	.309	292	377	.775	74	234	308	765	206	0	139	322	19	1492	3.8	9.4	18.4
90-91—Pittsburgh	48	46	1657	289	665	.435	19	65	.292	179	229	.782	35	125	160	446	118	4	75	185	10	776	3.3	9.3	16.2
91-92—Detroit	78	78	2918	564	1264	.446	25	86	.291	292	378	.772	68	179	247	560	194	2	118	252	15	1445	3.2	7.2	18.5
92-93—Detroit	79	79	2922	526	1258	.418	61	198	.308	278	377	.737	71	161	232	671	222	2	123	284	18	1391	2.9	8.5	17.6
93-94—Detroit	58	56	1750	318	763	.417	39	126	.310	181	258	.702	46	113	159	399	126	0	68	202	6	856	2.7	6.9	14.8
REG. SEASON TOTALS	979	971	35516	7194	15904	.452	398	1373	.290	4036	5316	.759	951	2527	3478	9061	2971	48	1861	3682	249	18822	3.6	9.3	19.2
PLAYOFF TOTALS	111	109	4216	825	1869	.441	81	234	.346	530	689	.769	134	390	524	987	363	8	234	369	38	2261	4.7	8.9	20.4
ALL-STAR TOTALS	11	10	318	76	133	.571	6	15	.400	27	35	.771	12	15	27	97	17	0	31	41	0	185	2.5	8.8	16.8

THOMAS, JAMES EDWARD (**Jim**) b. October 19, 1960   Ht. 6-3 Wt. 190 College—Indiana

SEASON—TEAM	G	GS	MIN	FGM	FGA	PCT	3FGM	3FGA	PCT	FTM	FTA	PCT	O-RB	D-RB	TOT	AST	PF	DQ	STL	TO	BLK	PTS	RPG	APG	PPG
83-84—Indiana	72	15	1219	187	403	.464	1	11	.091	80	110	.727	59	90	149	130	115	1	60	69	6	455	2.1	1.8	6.3
84-85—Indiana	80	52	2059	347	726	.478	8	42	.190	183	234	.782	74	187	261	234	195	2	76	131	5	885	3.3	2.9	11.1
85-86—L.A. Clippers	6	0	69	6	15	.400	0	0	—	1	2	.500	3	5	8	12	12	0	5	9	1	13	1.3	2.0	2.2
90-91—Minnesota	3	0	14	1	4	.250	0	0	—	0	0	—	0	0	0	1	0	0	1	1	0	2	0.0	0.3	0.7
REG. SEASON TOTALS	161	67	3361	541	1148	.471	9	53	.170	264	346	.763	136	282	418	377	322	3	142	210	12	1355	2.6	2.3	8.4

THOMAS, JOSEPH RANDLE (**Joe**) b. March 9, 1948   Ht. 6-5½ Wt. 205 College—Marquette

SEASON—TEAM	G	GS	MIN	FGM	FGA	PCT	3FGM	3FGA	PCT	FTM	FTA	PCT	O-RB	D-RB	TOT	AST	PF	DQ	STL	TO	BLK	PTS	RPG	APG	PPG
70-71—Phoenix	39	—	204	23	86	.267	—	—	—	9	20	.450	—	—	43	17	19	0	—	—	—	55	1.1	0.4	1.4
REG. SEASON TOTALS	39	—	204	23	86	.267	—	—	—	9	20	.450	—	—	43	17	19	0	—	—	—	55	1.1	0.4	1.4

THOMAS, RONALD MORTON **(Ron)** b. November 19, 1950 Ht. 6-6 Wt. 215 College—Trinity Valley CC/Louisville

SEASON—TEAM	G	GS	MIN	FGM	FGA	PCT	3FGM	3FGA	PCT	FTM	FTA	PCT	O-RB	D-RB	TOT	AST	PF	DQ	STL	TO	BLK	PTS	RPG	APG	PPG
72-73—Kentucky (A)	31	—	369	62	132	.470	0	2	.000	21	41	.512	53	62	115	23	73	2	—	21	—	145	3.7	0.7	4.7
73-74—Kentucky (A)	71	—	976	128	273	.469	1	7	.143	37	63	.587	112	177	289	62	156	—	48	71	7	294	4.1	0.9	4.1
74-75—Kentucky (A)	79	—	830	115	256	.449	1	3	.333	57	119	.479	124	176	300	46	133	—	51	71	14	288	3.8	0.6	3.6
75-76—Kentucky (A)	83	—	1117	134	277	.484	1	2	.500	55	94	.585	148	223	371	67	168	—	61	71	18	324	4.5	0.8	3.9
REG. ABA TOTALS	264	—	3292	439	938	.468	3	14	.214	170	317	.536	437	638	1075	198	530	2	160	234	39	1051	4.1	0.8	4.0
ABA PLAYOFF TOTALS	50	—	665	98	188	.521	0	1	.000	32	62	.516	57	90	222	37	106	0	18	45	6	228	4.4	0.7	4.6

THOMAS, TERRY C. b. August 20, 1953 Ht. 6-8 Wt. 220 College—Detroit

SEASON—TEAM	G	GS	MIN	FGM	FGA	PCT	3FGM	3FGA	PCT	FTM	FTA	PCT	O-RB	D-RB	TOT	AST	PF	DQ	STL	TO	BLK	PTS	RPG	APG	PPG
75-76—Detroit	28	—	136	28	65	.431	—	—	—	21	29	.724	15	21	36	3	21	1	4	—	2	77	1.3	0.1	2.8
REG. SEASON TOTALS	28	—	136	28	65	.431	—	—	—	21	29	.724	15	21	36	3	21	1	4	—	2	77	1.3	0.1	2.8
PLAYOFF TOTALS	4	—	6	0	5	.000	—	—	—	0	0	—	1	0	1	—	1	0	0	—	0	0	0.3	0.0	0.0

THOMAS, WILLIS **(Lefty)** b. 1937 Ht. 6-2 Wt. 185 College—Harbor JC/Tennessee State

SEASON—TEAM	G	GS	MIN	FGM	FGA	PCT	3FGM	3FGA	PCT	FTM	FTA	PCT	O-RB	D-RB	TOT	AST	PF	DQ	STL	TO	BLK	PTS	RPG	APG	PPG
67-68—Denver-Anaheim (A)	62	—	1068	243	550	.442	0	3	.000	69	93	.742	—	—	114	55	107	1	—	94	—	555	1.8	0.9	9.0
REG. ABA TOTALS	62	—	1068	243	550	.442	0	3	.000	69	93	.742	—	—	114	55	107	1	—	94	—	555	1.8	0.9	9.0

THOMPSON, BERNARD b. August 30, 1962 Ht. 6-6 Wt. 210 College—Fresno State

SEASON—TEAM	G	GS	MIN	FGM	FGA	PCT	3FGM	3FGA	PCT	FTM	FTA	PCT	O-RB	D-RB	TOT	AST	PF	DQ	STL	TO	BLK	PTS	RPG	APG	PPG
84-85—Portland	59	0	535	79	212	.373	0	8	.000	39	51	.765	37	39	76	52	79	0	31	35	10	197	1.3	0.9	3.3
85-86—Phoenix	61	20	1281	195	399	.489	0	2	.000	127	157	.809	58	83	141	132	151	0	51	90	10	517	2.3	2.2	8.5
86-87—Phoenix	24	2	331	42	105	.400	0	3	.000	27	33	.818	20	11	31	18	53	0	11	16	5	111	1.3	0.8	4.6
87-88—Phoenix	37	7	566	74	159	.465	0	2	.000	43	60	.717	40	36	76	51	75	1	21	21	1	191	2.1	1.4	5.2
88-89—Houston	23	0	222	20	59	.339	0	2	.000	22	26	.846	9	19	28	13	33	0	13	19	1	62	1.2	0.6	2.7
REG. SEASON TOTALS	204	29	2935	410	934	.439	0	17	.000	258	327	.789	164	188	352	266	391	1	127	181	27	1078	1.7	1.3	5.3
PLAYOFF TOTALS	2	0	10	0	5	.000	0	0	—	2	2	1.000	1	2	3	2	1	0	0	0	1	2	1.5	1.0	1.0

THOMPSON, CORNELIUS ALLEN **(Corny)** b. February 5, 1960 Ht. 6-8 Wt. 225 College—Connecticut

SEASON—TEAM	G	GS	MIN	FGM	FGA	PCT	3FGM	3FGA	PCT	FTM	FTA	PCT	O-RB	D-RB	TOT	AST	PF	DQ	STL	TO	BLK	PTS	RPG	APG	PPG
82-83—Dallas	44	2	520	43	137	.314	0	0	—	36	46	.783	41	79	120	34	92	0	12	31	7	122	2.7	0.8	2.8
REG. SEASON TOTALS	44	2	520	43	137	.314	0	0	—	36	46	.783	41	79	120	34	92	0	12	31	7	122	2.7	0.8	2.8

THOMPSON, DAVID O'NEIL b. July 13, 1954 Ht. 6-4½ Wt. 195 College—North Carolina State

SEASON—TEAM	G	GS	MIN	FGM	FGA	PCT	3FGM	3FGA	PCT	FTM	FTA	PCT	O-RB	D-RB	TOT	AST	PF	DQ	STL	TO	BLK	PTS	RPG	APG	PPG
75-76—Denver (A)	83	—	3101	807	1567	.515	3	19	.158	541	681	.794	228	297	525	308	282	—	136	250	102	2158	6.3	3.7	26.0
76-77—Denver	82	—	3001	824	1626	.507	—	—	—	477	623	.766	138	196	334	337	236	1	114	—	53	2125	4.1	4.1	25.9
77-78—Denver	80	—	3025	826	1584	.521	—	—	—	520	668	.778	156	234	390	362	213	1	92	245	99	2172	4.9	4.5	27.2
78-79—Denver	76	—	2670	693	1353	.512	—	—	—	439	583	.753	109	165	274	225	180	2	70	186	82	1825	3.6	3.0	24.0
79-80—Denver	39	—	1239	289	617	.468	7	19	.368	254	335	.758	56	118	174	124	106	0	39	116	38	839	4.5	3.2	21.5
80-81—Denver	77	—	2620	734	1451	.506	10	39	.256	489	615	.795	107	180	287	231	231	3	53	250	60	1967	3.7	3.0	25.5
81-82—Denver	61	5	1246	313	644	.486	4	14	.286	276	339	.814	57	91	148	117	149	1	34	142	29	906	2.4	1.9	14.9
82-83—Seattle	75	64	2155	445	925	.481	2	10	.200	298	380	.784	96	174	270	222	142	0	47	163	33	1190	3.6	3.0	15.9
83-84—Seattle	19	0	349	89	165	.539	0	1	.000	62	73	.849	18	26	44	13	30	0	10	27	13	240	2.3	0.7	12.6
REG. NBA TOTALS	509	69	16305	4213	8365	.504	23	83	.277	2815	3616	.778	737	1184	1921	1631	1287	8	459	1129	407	11264	3.8	3.2	22.1
REG. ABA TOTALS	83	—	3101	807	1567	.515	3	19	.158	541	681	.794	228	297	525	308	282	—	136	250	102	2158	6.3	3.7	26.0
NBA PLAYOFF TOTALS	27	2	971	249	539	.462	1	3	.333	120	161	.745	42	73	115	101	83	1	24	63	27	619	4.3	3.7	22.9
ABA PLAYOFF TOTALS	13	—	508	127	237	.536	1	4	.250	88	105	.838	32	51	83	39	54	—	16	50	5	343	6.4	3.0	26.4
NBA ALL-STAR TOTALS	4	4	115	33	49	.673	0	0	—	9	17	.529	3	13	16	10	13	0	6	8	1	75	4.0	2.5	18.8
ABA ALL-STAR TOTALS	1	1	34	9	18	.500	0	0	—	11	13	.846	0	8	8	2	4	—	0	0	0	29	8.0	2.0	29.0

THOMPSON, GEORGE b. November 29, 1947 Ht. 6-2 Wt. 215 College—Marquette

SEASON—TEAM	G	GS	MIN	FGM	FGA	PCT	3FGM	3FGA	PCT	FTM	FTA	PCT	O-RB	D-RB	TOT	AST	PF	DQ	STL	TO	BLK	PTS	RPG	APG	PPG
69-70—Pittsburgh (A)	54	—	1017	259	587	.441	7	32	.219	176	260	.677	—	—	94	73	109	0	—	—	—	701	1.7	1.4	13.0
70-71—Pittsburgh (A)	82	—	2470	575	1220	.471	23	90	.256	347	485	.715	—	—	291	207	217	—	—	—	—	1520	3.5	2.5	18.5
71-72—Pittsburgh (A)	70	—	2904	696	1448	.481	41	132	.311	455	584	.779	—	—	353	257	201	—	—	217	—	1888	5.0	3.7	27.0
72-73—Memphis (A)	80	—	2925	579	1269	.456	20	73	.274	549	700	.784	95	170	265	403	246	1	—	245	—	1727	3.3	5.0	21.6
73-74—Memphis (A)	78	—	2732	539	1134	.475	10	54	.185	410	519	.790	93	180	273	396	234	—	117	210	24	1498	3.5	5.1	19.2
74-75—Milwaukee	73	—	1983	306	691	.443	—	—	—	168	214	.785	50	131	181	225	203	5	66	—	6	780	2.5	3.1	10.7
REG. NBA TOTALS	73	—	1983	306	691	.443	—	—	—	168	214	.785	50	131	181	225	203	5	66	—	6	780	2.5	3.1	10.7
REG. ABA TOTALS	364	—	12048	2648	5658	.468	101	381	.265	1937	2548	.760	188	350	1276	1336	1007	1	117	672	24	7334	3.5	3.7	20.1
ABA ALL-STAR TOTALS	3	—	60	14	27	.519	0	2	.000	2	2	1.000	0	3	3	5	3	0	0	5	0	30	1.0	1.7	10.0

THOMPSON, JOHN R. JR. b. September 2, 1941 Ht. 6-10 Wt. 230 College—Providence

SEASON—TEAM	G	GS	MIN	FGM	FGA	PCT	3FGM	3FGA	PCT	FTM	FTA	PCT	O-RB	D-RB	TOT	AST	PF	DQ	STL	TO	BLK	PTS	RPG	APG	PPG
64-65—Boston	64	—	699	84	209	.402	—	—	—	62	105	.590	—	—	230	16	141	1	—	—	—	230	3.6	0.3	3.6
65-66—Boston	10	—	72	14	30	.467	—	—	—	4	6	.667	—	—	30	3	15	0	—	—	—	32	3.0	0.3	3.2
REG. SEASON TOTALS	74	—	771	98	239	.410	—	—	—	66	111	.595	—	—	260	19	156	1	—	—	—	262	3.5	0.3	3.5
PLAYOFF TOTALS	6	—	32	3	14	.214	—	—	—	7	7	1.000	—	—	16	1	4	0	—	—	—	13	2.7	0.2	2.2

THOMPSON, JOHN SIGRED (Jack) b. March 26, 1946 Ht. 6-1 Wt. 185 College—South Carolina

SEASON—TEAM	G	GS	MIN	FGM	FGA	PCT	3FGM	3FGA	PCT	FTM	FTA	PCT	O-RB	D-RB	TOT	AST	PF	DQ	STL	TO	BLK	PTS	RPG	APG	PPG
68-69—Indiana (A)	2	—	4	1	3	.333	0	1	.000	0	0	—	—	—	1	2	0	0	—	2	—	2	0.5	1.0	1.0
REG. ABA TOTALS	2	—	4	1	3	.333	0	1	.000	0	0	—	—	—	1	2	0	0	—	2	—	2	0.5	1.0	1.0

THOMPSON, KEVIN LAMONT b. February 7, 1971 Ht. 6-11 Wt. 260 College—North Carolina State

SEASON—TEAM	G	GS	MIN	FGM	FGA	PCT	3FGM	3FGA	PCT	FTM	FTA	PCT	O-RB	D-RB	TOT	AST	PF	DQ	STL	TO	BLK	PTS	RPG	APG	PPG
93-94—Portland	14	0	58	6	14	.429	0	1	.000	1	2	.500	7	6	13	3	11	0	0	5	2	13	0.9	0.2	0.9
REG. SEASON TOTALS	14	0	58	6	14	.429	0	1	.000	1	2	.500	7	6	13	3	11	0	0	5	2	13	0.9	0.2	0.9

THOMPSON, LaSALLE III (Tank) b. June 23, 1961 Ht. 6-10 Wt. 255 College—Texas

SEASON—TEAM	G	GS	MIN	FGM	FGA	PCT	3FGM	3FGA	PCT	FTM	FTA	PCT	O-RB	D-RB	TOT	AST	PF	DQ	STL	TO	BLK	PTS	RPG	APG	PPG
82-83—Kansas City	71	3	987	147	287	.512	0	1	.000	89	137	.650	133	242	375	33	186	1	40	96	61	383	5.3	0.5	5.4
83-84—Kansas City	80	38	1915	333	637	.523	0	0	—	160	223	.717	260	449	709	86	327	8	71	168	145	826	8.9	1.1	10.3
84-85—Kansas City	82	77	2458	369	695	.531	0	0	—	227	315	.721	274	580	854	130	328	4	98	202	128	965	10.4	1.6	11.8
85-86—Sacramento	80	64	2377	411	794	.518	0	1	.000	202	276	.732	252	518	770	168	295	8	71	184	109	1024	9.6	2.1	12.8
86-87—Sacramento	82	53	2166	362	752	.481	0	5	.000	188	255	.737	237	450	687	122	290	6	69	143	126	912	8.4	1.5	11.1
87-88—Sacramento	69	9	1257	215	456	.471	2	5	.400	118	164	.720	138	289	427	68	217	1	54	109	73	550	6.2	1.0	8.0
88-89—Sac.-Indiana	76	71	2329	416	850	.489	0	1	.000	227	281	.808	224	494	718	81	285	12	79	179	94	1059	9.4	1.1	13.9
89-90—Indiana	82	60	2126	223	471	.473	1	5	.200	107	134	.799	175	455	630	106	313	11	65	150	71	554	7.7	1.3	6.8
90-91—Indiana	82	77	1946	276	565	.488	1	5	.200	72	104	.692	154	409	563	147	265	4	63	168	63	625	6.9	1.8	7.6
91-92—Indiana	80	49	1299	168	359	.468	0	2	.000	58	71	.817	98	283	381	102	207	0	52	98	34	394	4.8	1.3	4.9
92-93—Indiana	63	0	730	104	213	.488	0	1	.000	29	39	.744	55	123	178	34	137	0	29	47	24	237	2.8	0.5	3.8
93-94—Indiana	30	1	282	27	77	.351	0	0	—	16	30	.533	26	49	75	16	59	1	10	23	8	70	2.5	0.5	2.3
REG. SEASON TOTALS	877	502	19872	3051	6156	.496	4	26	.154	1493	2029	.736	2026	4341	6367	1093	2909	56	701	1567	936	7599	7.3	1.2	8.7
PLAYOFF TOTALS	28	14	547	71	163	.436	0	0	—	36	45	.800	49	99	148	28	79	0	16	37	25	178	5.3	1.0	6.4

THOMPSON, MYCHAL GEORGE b. January 30, 1955 Ht. 6-10 Wt. 235 College—Minnesota

SEASON—TEAM	G	GS	MIN	FGM	FGA	PCT	3FGM	3FGA	PCT	FTM	FTA	PCT	O-RB	D-RB	TOT	AST	PF	DQ	STL	TO	BLK	PTS	RPG	APG	PPG
78-79—Portland	73	—	2144	460	938	.490	—	—	—	154	269	.572	198	406	604	176	270	10	67	205	134	1074	8.3	2.4	14.7
80-81—Portland	79	—	2790	569	1151	.494	0	1	.000	207	323	.641	223	463	686	284	260	5	62	241	170	1345	8.7	3.6	17.0
81-82—Portland	79	78	3129	681	1303	.523	0	0	—	280	446	.628	258	663	921	319	233	2	69	245	107	1642	11.7	4.0	20.8
82-83—Portland	80	80	3017	505	1033	.489	0	1	.000	249	401	.621	183	570	753	380	213	1	68	281	110	1259	9.4	4.8	15.7
83-84—Portland	79	74	2648	487	929	.524	0	2	.000	266	399	.667	235	453	688	308	237	2	84	235	108	1240	8.7	3.9	15.7
84-85—Portland	79	55	2616	572	1111	.515	0	0	—	307	449	.684	211	407	618	205	216	0	78	231	104	1451	7.8	2.6	18.4
85-86—Portland	82	78	2569	503	1011	.498	0	0	—	198	309	.641	181	427	608	176	267	5	76	196	35	1204	7.4	2.1	14.7
86-87—S.A.-Lakers	82	7	1890	359	797	.450	1	2	.500	219	297	.737	138	274	412	115	202	1	45	134	71	938	5.0	1.4	11.4
87-88—L.A. Lakers	80	0	2007	370	722	.512	0	3	.000	185	292	.634	198	291	489	66	251	1	38	113	79	925	6.1	0.8	11.6
88-89—L.A. Lakers	80	8	1994	291	521	.559	0	1	.000	156	230	.678	157	310	467	48	224	0	58	97	59	738	5.8	0.6	9.2
89-90—L.A. Lakers	70	70	1883	281	562	.500	0	0	—	144	204	.706	173	304	477	43	207	0	33	79	73	706	6.8	0.6	10.1
90-91—L.A. Lakers	72	4	1077	113	228	.496	0	2	.000	62	88	.705	74	154	228	21	112	0	23	47	23	288	3.2	0.3	4.0
REG. SEASON TOTALS	935	454	27764	5191	10306	.504	1	12	.083	2427	3707	.655	2229	4722	6951	2141	2692	27	701	2104	1073	12810	7.4	2.3	13.7
PLAYOFF TOTALS	104	23	2708	449	897	.501	0	0	—	234	361	.648	224	403	627	126	309	4	56	156	106	1132	6.0	1.2	10.9

THOMPSON, PAUL STANFORD b. May 25, 1961 Ht. 6-6 Wt. 210 College—Tulane

SEASON—TEAM	G	GS	MIN	FGM	FGA	PCT	3FGM	3FGA	PCT	FTM	FTA	PCT	O-RB	D-RB	TOT	AST	PF	DQ	STL	TO	BLK	PTS	RPG	APG	PPG
83-84—Cleveland	82	10	1731	309	662	.467	9	39	.231	115	149	.772	120	192	312	122	192	2	70	73	37	742	3.8	1.5	9.0
84-85—Clev.-Milw.	49	27	942	189	459	.412	6	30	.200	69	87	.793	57	101	158	78	119	1	56	57	25	453	3.2	1.6	9.2
85-86—Philadelphia	23	8	432	70	194	.361	2	12	.167	37	43	.860	27	36	63	24	49	1	15	30	17	179	2.7	1.0	7.8
REG. SEASON TOTALS	154	45	3105	568	1315	.432	17	81	.210	221	279	.792	204	329	533	224	360	4	141	160	79	1374	3.5	1.5	8.9
PLAYOFF TOTALS	3	0	34	5	12	.417	0	2	.000	3	5	.600	1	4	5	2	3	0	4	4	1	13	1.7	0.7	4.3

THOMPSON, STEPHEN M. b. December 2, 1968 Ht. 6-4 Wt. 185 College—Syracuse

SEASON—TEAM	G	GS	MIN	FGM	FGA	PCT	3FGM	3FGA	PCT	FTM	FTA	PCT	O-RB	D-RB	TOT	AST	PF	DQ	STL	TO	BLK	PTS	RPG	APG	PPG
91-92—Orlando-Sac.	19	0	91	14	37	.378	0	1	.000	3	8	.375	11	8	19	8	9	0	6	5	3	31	1.0	0.4	1.6
REG. SEASON TOTALS	19	0	91	14	37	.378	0	1	.000	3	8	.375	11	8	19	8	9	0	6	5	3	31	1.0	0.4	1.6

THOMPSON, WILLIAM STANSBURY (**Billy, B.T. Express**) b. December 1, 1963   Ht. 6-7 Wt. 220 College—Louisville

SEASON—TEAM	G	GS	MIN	FGM	FGA	PCT	3FGM	3FGA	PCT	FTM	FTA	PCT	O-RB	D-RB	TOT	AST	PF	DQ	STL	TO	BLK	PTS	RPG	APG	PPG
86-87—L.A. Lakers	59	0	762	142	261	.544	0	1	.000	48	74	.649	69	102	171	60	148	1	15	61	30	332	2.9	1.0	5.6
87-88—L.A. Lakers	9	0	38	3	13	.231	0	0	—	8	10	.800	2	7	9	1	11	0	1	6	0	14	1.0	0.1	1.6
88-89—Miami	79	58	2273	349	716	.487	0	4	.000	156	224	.696	241	331	572	176	260	8	56	189	105	854	7.2	2.2	10.8
89-90—Miami	79	45	2142	375	727	.516	2	4	.500	115	185	.622	238	313	551	166	237	1	54	156	89	867	7.0	2.1	11.0
90-91—Miami	73	46	1481	205	411	.499	0	4	.000	89	124	.718	120	192	312	111	161	3	32	117	48	499	4.3	1.5	6.8
91-92—Golden State	1	0	1	0	0	—	0	0	—	0	0	—	0	0	0	0	0	0	0	0	0	0	0.0	0.0	0.0
REG. SEASON TOTALS	300	149	6697	1074	2128	.505	2	13	.154	416	617	.674	670	945	1615	514	817	13	158	529	272	2566	5.4	1.7	8.6
PLAYOFF TOTALS	3	0	27	6	11	.545	0	0	—	2	2	1.000	3	3	6	2	2	0	4	0	0	14	2.0	0.7	4.7

THOREN, DUANE W. (**Skip**) b. April 5, 1943   Ht. 6-10 Wt. 230 College—Illinois

SEASON—TEAM	G	GS	MIN	FGM	FGA	PCT	3FGM	3FGA	PCT	FTM	FTA	PCT	O-RB	D-RB	TOT	AST	PF	DQ	STL	TO	BLK	PTS	RPG	APG	PPG
67-68—Minnesota (A)	63	—	1203	206	475	.434	0	1	.000	102	164	.622	—	—	436	59	124	3	—	77	—	514	6.9	0.9	8.2
68-69—Miami (A)	78	—	2645	532	1100	.484	0	2	.000	241	392	.615	391	655	1046	195	324	11	—	180	—	1305	13.4	2.5	16.7
69-70—Miami (A)	29	—	1020	164	364	.451	0	2	.000	92	155	.594	—	—	393	75	112	2	—	—	—	420	13.6	2.6	14.5
REG. ABA TOTALS	170	—	4868	902	1939	.465	0	5	.000	435	711	.612	391	655	1875	329	560	16	—	257	—	2239	11.0	1.9	13.2
ABA PLAYOFF TOTALS	14	—	454	75	157	.478	0	0	—	42	73	.575	42	113	182	21	53	3	—	32	—	192	13.0	1.5	13.7
ABA ALL-STAR TOTALS	1	—	17	1	4	.250	0	0	—	0	0	—	—	5	5	2	3	0	—	1	—	2	5.0	2.0	2.0

THORN, RODNEY KING (**Rod**) b. May 23, 1941   Ht. 6-4 Wt. 195 College—West Virginia

SEASON—TEAM	G	GS	MIN	FGM	FGA	PCT	3FGM	3FGA	PCT	FTM	FTA	PCT	O-RB	D-RB	TOT	AST	PF	DQ	STL	TO	BLK	PTS	RPG	APG	PPG
63-64—Baltimore	75	—	2594	411	1015	.405	—	—		258	353	.731	—	—	360	281	187	3	—	—	—	1080	4.8	3.7	14.4
64-65—Detroit	74	—	1770	320	750	.427	—	—		176	243	.724	—	—	266	161	122	0	—	—	—	816	3.6	2.2	11.0
65-66—Detroit-St. L.	73	—	1739	306	728	.420	—	—		168	236	.712	—	—	210	145	144	0	—	—	—	780	2.9	2.0	10.7
66-67—St. Louis	67	—	1166	233	524	.445	—	—		125	172	.727	—	—	160	118	88	0	—	—	—	591	2.4	1.8	8.8
67-68—Seattle	66	—	1668	377	835	.451	—	—		252	342	.737	—	—	265	230	117	1	—	—	—	1006	4.0	3.5	15.2
68-69—Seattle	29	—	567	131	283	.463	—	—		71	97	.732	—	—	83	80	58	0	—	—	—	333	2.9	2.8	11.5
69-70—Seattle	19	—	105	20	45	.444	—	—		15	24	.625	—	—	16	17	8	0	—	—	—	55	0.8	0.9	2.9
70-71—Seattle	63	—	767	141	299	.472	—	—		69	102	.676	—	—	103	182	60	0	—	—	—	351	1.6	2.9	5.6
REG. SEASON TOTALS	466	—	10376	1939	4479	.433	—	—		1134	1569	.723	—	—	1463	1214	784	4	—	—	—	5012	3.1	2.6	10.8
PLAYOFF TOTALS	19	—	275	45	116	.388	—	—		39	45	.867	—	—	45	21	22	0	—	—	—	129	2.4	1.1	6.8

THORNTON, DALLAS (**Big D**) b. September 1, 1946   Ht. 6-4 Wt. 190 College—Kentucky Wesleyan

SEASON—TEAM	G	GS	MIN	FGM	FGA	PCT	3FGM	3FGA	PCT	FTM	FTA	PCT	O-RB	D-RB	TOT	AST	PF	DQ	STL	TO	BLK	PTS	RPG	APG	PPG
68-69—Miami (A)	45	—	756	108	249	.434	2	9	.222	79	125	.632	—	—	119	63	92	1	—	80	—	297	2.6	1.4	6.6
69-70—Miami (A)	5	—	114	15	35	.429	0	2	.000	14	17	.824	—	—	22	11	14	0	—	—	—	44	4.4	2.2	8.8
REG. ABA TOTALS	50	—	870	123	284	.433	2	11	.182	93	142	.655	—	—	141	74	106	1	—	80	—	341	2.8	1.5	6.8
ABA PLAYOFF TOTALS	7	—	118	23	59	.390	0	7	.000	21	34	.618	—	—	23	6	9	0	—	8	—	67	3.3	0.9	9.6

THORNTON, ROBERT GEORGE (**Bob**) b. July 10, 1962   Ht. 6-10 Wt. 225 College—Saddleback CC/Cal State-Irvine

SEASON—TEAM	G	GS	MIN	FGM	FGA	PCT	3FGM	3FGA	PCT	FTM	FTA	PCT	O-RB	D-RB	TOT	AST	PF	DQ	STL	TO	BLK	PTS	RPG	APG	PPG
85-86—New York	71	23	1323	125	274	.456	0	0	—	86	162	.531	113	177	290	43	209	5	30	83	7	336	4.1	0.6	4.7
86-87—New York	33	4	282	29	67	.433	0	1	.000	13	20	.650	18	38	56	8	48	0	4	24	3	71	1.7	0.2	2.2
87-88—N.Y.-Phil.	48	2	593	65	130	.500	0	2	.000	34	55	.618	46	66	112	15	103	1	11	35	3	164	2.3	0.3	3.4
88-89—Philadelphia	54	0	449	47	111	.423	1	3	.333	32	60	.533	36	56	92	15	87	0	8	23	7	127	1.7	0.3	2.4
89-90—Philadelphia	56	0	592	48	112	.429	1	3	.333	26	51	.510	45	88	133	17	105	1	20	35	12	123	2.4	0.3	2.2
90-91—Minnesota	12	1	110	4	13	.308	0	0	—	8	10	.800	1	14	15	1	18	0	0	9	3	16	1.3	0.1	1.3
91-92—Utah	2	0	6	1	7	.143	0	0	—	2	2	1.000	2	0	2	0	1	0	0	0	0	4	1.0	0.0	2.0
REG. SEASON TOTALS	276	30	3355	319	714	.447	2	9	.222	201	360	.558	261	439	700	99	571	7	73	209	35	841	2.5	0.4	3.0
PLAYOFF TOTALS	16	—	121	9	23	.391	0	0	—	8	14	.571	15	9	24	5	25	0	2	3	1	26	1.5	0.3	1.6

THORPE, OTIS HENRY b. August 5, 1962   Ht. 6-10 Wt. 245 College—Providence

SEASON—TEAM	G	GS	MIN	FGM	FGA	PCT	3FGM	3FGA	PCT	FTM	FTA	PCT	O-RB	D-RB	TOT	AST	PF	DQ	STL	TO	BLK	PTS	RPG	APG	PPG
84-85—Kansas City	82	23	1918	411	685	.600	0	2	.000	230	371	.620	187	369	556	111	256	2	34	187	37	1052	6.8	1.4	12.8
85-86—Sacramento	75	18	1675	289	492	.587	0	0	—	164	248	.661	137	283	420	84	233	3	35	123	34	742	5.6	1.1	9.9
86-87—Sacramento	82	82	2956	567	1050	.540	0	3	.000	413	543	.761	259	560	819	201	292	11	46	189	60	1547	10.0	2.5	18.9
87-88—Sacramento	82	82	3072	622	1226	.507	0	6	.000	460	609	.755	279	558	837	266	264	3	62	228	56	1704	10.2	3.2	20.8
88-89—Houston	82	82	3135	521	961	.542	0	2	.000	328	450	.729	272	515	787	202	259	6	82	225	37	1370	9.6	2.5	16.7
89-90—Houston	82	82	2947	547	998	.548	0	10	.000	307	446	.688	258	476	734	261	270	5	66	229	24	1401	9.0	3.2	17.1
90-91—Houston	82	82	3039	549	988	.556	3	7	.429	334	480	.696	287	559	846	197	278	10	73	217	20	1435	10.3	2.4	17.5
91-92—Houston	82	82	3056	558	943	.592	0	7	.000	304	463	.657	285	577	862	250	307	7	52	237	37	1420	10.5	3.0	17.3
92-93—Houston	72	69	2357	385	690	.558	0	2	.000	153	256	.598	219	370	589	181	234	3	43	151	19	923	8.2	2.5	12.8
93-94—Houston	82	82	2909	449	801	.561	0	2	.000	251	382	.657	271	599	870	189	253	1	66	185	28	1149	10.6	2.3	14.0
REG. SEASON TOTALS	803	684	27064	4898	8834	.554	3	41	.073	2944	4248	.693	2454	4866	7320	1942	2646	51	559	1971	352	12743	9.1	2.4	15.9
PLAYOFF TOTALS	49	46	1740	260	442	.588	1	2	.500	117	188	.622	139	282	421	112	162	3	31	85	13	638	8.6	2.3	13.0
ALL-STAR TOTALS	1	0	4	1	1	1.000	0	0	—	0	0	—	0	0	0	0	0	0	0	0	0	2	0.0	0.0	2.0

THREATT, SEDALE EUGENE b. September 10, 1961 Ht. 6-2 Wt. 185 College—West Virginia Tech

SEASON—TEAM	G	GS	MIN	FGM	FGA	PCT	3FGM	3FGA	PCT	FTM	FTA	PCT	O-RB	D-RB	TOT	AST	PF	DQ	STL	TO	BLK	PTS	RPG	APG	PPG
83-84—Philadelphia	45	0	464	62	148	.419	1	8	.125	23	28	.821	17	23	40	41	65	1	13	33	2	148	0.9	0.9	3.3
84-85—Philadelphia	82	0	1304	188	416	.452	4	22	.182	66	90	.733	21	78	99	175	171	2	80	99	16	446	1.2	2.1	5.4
85-86—Philadelphia	70	27	1754	310	684	.453	1	24	.042	75	90	.833	21	100	121	193	157	1	93	102	5	696	1.7	2.8	9.9
86-87—Phil.-Chicago	68	8	1446	239	534	.448	7	32	.219	95	119	.798	26	82	108	259	164	0	74	89	13	580	1.6	3.8	8.5
87-88—Chicago-Seattle	71	0	1055	216	425	.508	3	27	.111	57	71	.803	23	65	88	160	100	0	60	63	8	492	1.2	2.3	6.9
88-89—Seattle	63	0	1220	235	476	.494	11	30	.367	63	77	.818	31	86	117	238	155	0	83	77	4	544	1.9	3.8	8.6
89-90—Seattle	65	18	1481	303	599	.506	8	32	.250	130	157	.828	43	72	115	216	164	0	65	77	8	744	1.8	3.3	11.4
90-91—Seattle	80	57	2066	433	835	.519	10	35	.286	137	173	.792	25	74	99	273	191	0	113	138	8	1013	1.2	3.4	12.7
91-92—L.A. Lakers	82	82	3070	509	1041	.489	20	62	.323	202	243	.831	43	210	253	593	231	1	168	182	16	1240	3.1	7.2	15.1
92-93—L.A. Lakers	82	82	2893	522	1028	.508	14	53	.264	177	215	.823	47	226	273	564	248	1	142	173	11	1235	3.3	6.9	15.1
93-94—L.A. Lakers	81	20	2278	411	852	.482	5	33	.152	138	155	.890	28	125	153	344	186	1	110	106	19	965	1.9	4.2	11.9
REG. SEASON TOTALS	789	294	19031	3428	7038	.487	84	358	.235	1163	1418	.820	325	1141	1466	3056	1832	7	1001	1139	110	8103	1.9	3.9	10.3
PLAYOFF TOTALS	49	15	1200	224	477	.470	10	36	.278	78	95	.821	19	71	90	198	121	1	64	69	3	536	1.8	4.0	10.9

THURMOND, NATHANIEL (Nate) b. July 25, 1941 Ht. 6-11 Wt. 230 College—Bowling Green

SEASON—TEAM	G	GS	MIN	FGM	FGA	PCT	3FGM	3FGA	PCT	FTM	FTA	PCT	O-RB	D-RB	TOT	AST	PF	DQ	STL	TO	BLK	PTS	RPG	APG	PPG
63-64—San Francisco	76	—	1966	219	554	.395	—	—	—	95	173	.549	—	—	790	86	184	2	—	—	—	533	10.4	1.1	7.0
64-65—San Francisco	77	—	3173	519	1240	.419	—	—	—	235	357	.658	—	—	1395	157	232	3	—	—	—	1273	18.1	2.0	16.5
65-66—San Francisco	73	—	2891	454	1119	.406	—	—	—	280	428	.654	—	—	1312	111	223	7	—	—	—	1188	18.0	1.5	16.3
66-67—San Francisco	65	—	2755	467	1068	.437	—	—	—	280	445	.629	—	—	1382	166	183	3	—	—	—	1214	21.3	2.6	18.7
67-68—San Francisco	51	—	2222	382	929	.411	—	—	—	282	438	.644	—	—	1121	215	137	1	—	—	—	1046	22.0	4.2	20.5
68-69—San Francisco	71	—	3208	571	1394	.410	—	—	—	382	621	.615	—	—	1402	253	171	0	—	—	—	1524	19.7	3.6	21.5
69-70—San Francisco	43	—	1919	341	824	.414	—	—	—	261	346	.754	—	—	762	150	110	1	—	—	—	943	17.7	3.5	21.9
70-71—San Francisco	82	—	3351	623	1401	.445	—	—	—	395	541	.730	—	—	1128	257	192	1	—	—	—	1641	13.8	3.1	20.0
71-72—Golden State	78	—	3362	628	1454	.432	—	—	—	417	561	.743	—	—	1252	230	214	1	—	—	—	1673	16.1	2.9	21.4
72-73—Golden State	79	—	3419	517	1159	.446	—	—	—	315	439	.718	—	—	1349	280	240	2	—	—	—	1349	17.1	3.5	17.1
73-74—Golden State	62	—	2463	308	694	.444	—	—	—	191	287	.666	249	629	878	165	179	4	41	—	179	807	14.2	2.7	13.0
74-75—Chicago	80	—	2756	250	686	.364	—	—	—	132	224	.589	259	645	904	328	271	6	46	—	195	632	11.3	4.1	7.9
75-76—Chicago-Clev.	78	—	1393	142	337	.421	—	—	—	62	123	.504	115	300	415	94	160	1	22	—	98	346	5.3	1.2	4.4
76-77—Cleveland	49	—	997	100	246	.407	—	—	—	68	106	.642	121	253	374	83	128	2	16	—	81	268	7.6	1.7	5.5
REG. SEASON TOTALS	964	—	35875	5521	13105	.421	—	—	—	3395	5089	.667	744	1827	14464	2575	2624	34	125	—	553	14437	15.0	2.7	15.0
PLAYOFF TOTALS	81	—	2875	379	912	.416	—	—	—	208	335	.621	62	143	1101	227	266	4	11	—	51	966	13.6	2.8	11.9
ALL-STAR TOTALS	5	—	104	14	43	.326	—	—	—	3	8	.375	1	2	44	2	5	0	0	—	0	31	8.8	0.4	6.2

THURSTON, JOHN MELVIN (Mel) b. January 16, 1919 Ht. 6-0 Wt. 175 College—Canisius

SEASON—TEAM	G	GS	MIN	FGM	FGA	PCT	3FGM	3FGA	PCT	FTM	FTA	PCT	O-RB	D-RB	TOT	AST	PF	DQ	STL	TO	BLK	PTS	RPG	APG	PPG
46-47—Tri-Cities (N)	39	—	—	39	—	—	—	—	—	36	59	.610	—	—	—	—	62	—	—	—	—	114	—	—	2.9
47-48—Tri-Cities (N)	34	—	—	36	—	—	—	—	—	38	61	.623	—	—	—	—	—	—	—	—	—	110	—	—	3.2
47-48—Providence	14	—	—	32	113	.283	—	—	—	14	28	.500	—	—	—	4	42	—	—	—	—	78	—	0.3	5.6
REG. NBA TOTALS	14	—	—	32	113	.283	—	—	—	14	28	.500	—	—	—	4	42	—	—	—	—	78	—	0.3	5.6
REG. NBL TOTALS	73	—	—	75	—	—	—	—	—	74	120	.617	—	—	—	—	62	—	—	—	—	224	—	—	3.1

TIDRICK, HOWARD BENJAMIN (Hal) b. August 4, 1915 d. April 2, 1974 Ht. 6-1 Wt. 190 College—Washington & Jefferson

SEASON—TEAM	G	GS	MIN	FGM	FGA	PCT	3FGM	3FGA	PCT	FTM	FTA	PCT	O-RB	D-RB	TOT	AST	PF	DQ	STL	TO	BLK	PTS	RPG	APG	PPG
44-45—Sheboygan (N)	1	—	—	0	—	—	—	—	—	0	—	—	—	—	—	—	—	—	—	—	—	0	—	—	0.0
46-47—Toledo (N)	44	—	—	232	—	—	—	—	—	115	165	.697	—	—	—	—	105	—	—	—	—	579	—	—	13.2
47-48—Toledo (N)	59	—	—	267	—	—	—	—	—	189	243	.778	—	—	—	—	149	—	—	—	—	723	—	—	12.3
48-49—Ind.-Balt.	61	—	—	194	616	.315	—	—	—	164	205	.800	—	—	—	101	191	—	—	—	—	552	—	1.7	9.0
REG. NBA TOTALS	61	—	—	194	616	.315	—	—	—	164	205	.800	—	—	—	101	191	—	—	—	—	552	—	1.7	9.0
REG. NBL TOTALS	104	—	—	499	—	—	—	—	—	304	408	.745	—	—	—	—	254	—	—	—	—	1302	—	—	12.5
NBA PLAYOFF TOTALS	3	—	—	5	19	.263	—	—	—	3	5	.600	—	—	—	1	16	2	—	—	—	13	—	0.3	4.3
NBL PLAYOFF TOTALS	5	—	—	19	—	—	—	—	—	14	23	.609	—	—	—	—	15	—	—	—	—	52	—	—	10.4

TIEMAN, DANIEL THEODORE (Dan) b. November 30, 1940 Ht. 6-0 Wt. 185 College—Thomas More

SEASON—TEAM	G	GS	MIN	FGM	FGA	PCT	3FGM	3FGA	PCT	FTM	FTA	PCT	O-RB	D-RB	TOT	AST	PF	DQ	STL	TO	BLK	PTS	RPG	APG	PPG
62-63—Cincinnati	29	—	176	15	57	.263	—	—	—	4	10	.400	—	—	22	27	18	0	—	—	—	34	0.8	0.9	1.2
REG. SEASON TOTALS	29	—	176	15	57	.263	—	—	—	4	10	.400	—	—	22	27	18	0	—	—	—	34	0.8	0.9	1.2

TILLIS, DARREN b. February 23, 1960 Ht. 6-11 Wt. 215 College—Cleveland State

SEASON—TEAM	G	GS	MIN	FGM	FGA	PCT	3FGM	3FGA	PCT	FTM	FTA	PCT	O-RB	D-RB	TOT	AST	PF	DQ	STL	TO	BLK	PTS	RPG	APG	PPG
82-83—Boston-Clev.	52	4	526	76	181	.420	0	1	.000	16	28	.571	41	89	130	18	76	3	8	22	30	168	2.5	0.3	3.2
83-84—Golden State	72	1	730	108	254	.425	0	2	.000	41	63	.651	75	109	184	24	176	1	12	51	60	257	2.6	0.3	3.6
REG. SEASON TOTALS	124	5	1256	184	435	.423	0	3	.000	57	91	.626	116	198	314	42	252	4	20	73	90	425	2.5	0.3	3.4

TINGLE, ROBERT JACKSON (**Jack**) b. December 30, 1924 d. September 22, 1958 Ht. 6-4 Wt. 205 College—Kentucky

SEASON—TEAM	G	GS	MIN	FGM	FGA	PCT	3FGM	3FGA	PCT	FTM	FTA	PCT	O-RB	D-RB	TOT	AST	PF	DQ	STL	TO	BLK	PTS	RPG	APG	PPG
47-48—Washington	37	—	—	36	137	.263	—	—	—	17	33	.515	—	—	—	7	45	—	—	—	—	89	—	0.2	2.4
48-49—Minneapolis	2	—	—	1	6	.167	—	—	—	0	0	—	—	—	—	1	2	—	—	—	—	2	—	0.5	1.0
REG. SEASON TOTALS	39	—	—	37	143	.259	—	—	—	17	33	.515	—	—	—	8	47	—	—	—	—	91	—	0.2	2.3

TINSLEY, GEORGE T. b. September 19, 1946 Ht. 6-5 Wt. 205 College—Kentucky Wesleyan

SEASON—TEAM	G	GS	MIN	FGM	FGA	PCT	3FGM	3FGA	PCT	FTM	FTA	PCT	O-RB	D-RB	TOT	AST	PF	DQ	STL	TO	BLK	PTS	RPG	APG	PPG
69-70—Wash.-Ken. (A)	82	—	1446	175	407	.430	1	8	.125	162	218	.743	—	—	325	76	192	3	—	—	—	513	4.0	0.9	6.3
71-72—Floridians (A)	51	—	418	70	174	.402	5	22	.227	46	62	.742	—	—	60	38	79	—	—	26	—	191	1.2	0.7	3.7
REG. ABA TOTALS	133	—	1864	245	581	.422	6	30	.200	208	280	.743	—	—	385	114	271	3	—	26	—	704	2.9	0.9	5.3
ABA PLAYOFF TOTALS	15	—	284	44	96	.458	2	7	.286	32	44	.727	—	—	65	19	35	0	—	2	—	122	4.3	1.3	8.1

TISDALE, WAYMAN LAWRENCE b. June 9, 1964 Ht. 6-9 Wt. 260 College—Oklahoma

SEASON—TEAM	G	GS	MIN	FGM	FGA	PCT	3FGM	3FGA	PCT	FTM	FTA	PCT	O-RB	D-RB	TOT	AST	PF	DQ	STL	TO	BLK	PTS	RPG	APG	PPG
85-86—Indiana	81	60	2277	516	1002	.515	0	2	.000	160	234	.684	191	393	584	79	290	3	32	188	44	1192	7.2	1.0	14.7
86-87—Indiana	81	15	2159	458	892	.513	0	2	.000	258	364	.709	217	258	475	117	293	9	50	139	26	1174	5.9	1.4	14.5
87-88—Indiana	79	57	2378	511	998	.512	0	2	.000	246	314	.783	168	323	491	103	274	5	54	145	34	1268	6.2	1.3	16.1
88-89—Indiana-Sac.	79	35	2434	532	1036	.514	0	4	.000	317	410	.773	187	422	609	128	290	7	55	172	52	1381	7.7	1.6	17.5
89-90—Sacramento	79	79	2937	726	1383	.525	0	6	.000	306	391	.783	185	410	595	108	251	3	54	153	54	1758	7.5	1.4	22.3
90-91—Sacramento	33	31	1116	262	542	.483	0	1	.000	136	170	.800	75	178	253	66	99	2	23	82	28	660	7.7	2.0	20.0
91-92—Sacramento	72	71	2521	522	1043	.500	0	2	.000	151	198	.763	135	334	469	106	248	3	55	124	79	1195	6.5	1.5	16.6
92-93—Sacramento	76	75	2283	544	1069	.509	0	2	.000	175	231	.758	127	373	500	108	277	8	52	117	47	1263	6.6	1.4	16.6
93-94—Sacramento	79	77	2557	552	1102	.501	0	0	—	215	266	.808	159	401	560	139	290	4	37	124	52	1319	7.1	1.8	16.7
REG. SEASON TOTALS	659	500	20662	4623	9066	.510	0	21	.000	1964	2578	.762	1444	3092	4536	954	2312	42	412	1244	416	11210	6.9	1.4	17.0
PLAYOFF TOTALS	4	0	108	19	31	.613	0	0	—	13	23	.565	5	11	16	9	17	1	1	5	0	51	4.0	2.3	12.8

TODOROVICH, MARKO JOHN (**Mike**) b. June 11, 1923 Ht. 6-5 Wt. 220 College—Washington (Mo.)/Notre Dame/Wyoming

SEASON—TEAM	G	GS	MIN	FGM	FGA	PCT	3FGM	3FGA	PCT	FTM	FTA	PCT	O-RB	D-RB	TOT	AST	PF	DQ	STL	TO	BLK	PTS	RPG	APG	PPG
47-48—Sheboygan (N)	60	—	—	277	—	—	—	—	—	223	343	.650	—	—	—	—	182	—	—	—	—	777	—	—	13.0
48-49—Sheboygan (N)	60	—	—	239	—	—	—	—	—	170	281	.605	—	—	—	—	183	—	—	—	—	648	—	—	10.8
49-50—St. L.-Tri-Cit	65	—	—	263	852	.309	—	—	—	266	370	.719	—	—	—	207	230	—	—	—	—	792	—	3.2	12.2
50-51—Tri-Cities	66	—	—	221	715	.309	—	—	—	211	301	.701	—	—	455	179	197	5	—	—	—	653	6.9	2.7	9.9
REG. NBA TOTALS	131	—	—	484	1567	.309	—	—	—	477	671	.711	—	—	455	386	427	5	—	—	—	1445	6.9	2.9	11.0
REG. NBL TOTALS	120	—	—	516	—	—	—	—	—	393	624	.630	—	—	—	—	365	—	—	—	—	1425	—	—	11.9
NBA PLAYOFF TOTALS	3	—	—	6	31	.194	—	—	—	19	24	.792	—	—	—	8	14	1	—	—	—	31	—	2.7	10.3

TOLBERT, BYRON THOMAS (**Tom, Fabian**) b. October 16, 1965 Ht. 6-7 Wt. 240 College—Cal State-Irvine/Cerritos College/Arizona

SEASON—TEAM	G	GS	MIN	FGM	FGA	PCT	3FGM	3FGA	PCT	FTM	FTA	PCT	O-RB	D-RB	TOT	AST	PF	DQ	STL	TO	BLK	PTS	RPG	APG	PPG
88-89—Charlotte	14	0	117	17	37	.459	0	3	.000	6	12	.500	7	14	21	7	20	0	2	2	4	40	1.5	0.5	2.9
89-90—Golden State	70	21	1347	218	442	.493	5	18	.278	175	241	.726	122	241	363	58	191	0	23	79	25	616	5.2	0.8	8.8
90-91—Golden State	62	32	1371	183	433	.423	7	21	.333	127	172	.738	87	188	275	76	195	4	35	80	38	500	4.4	1.2	8.1
91-92—Golden State	35	0	310	33	86	.384	2	8	.250	22	40	.550	14	41	55	21	73	0	10	20	6	90	1.6	0.6	2.6
92-93—Orlando	72	61	1838	226	454	.498	9	28	.321	122	168	.726	133	279	412	91	192	4	33	124	21	583	5.7	1.3	8.1
93-94—L.A. Clippers	49	6	640	74	177	.418	6	16	.375	33	45	.733	36	72	108	30	61	0	13	39	15	187	2.2	0.6	3.8
REG. SEASON TOTALS	302	120	5623	751	1629	.461	29	94	.309	485	678	.715	399	835	1234	283	732	8	116	344	109	2016	4.1	0.9	6.7
PLAYOFF TOTALS	9	0	116	14	33	.424	1	3	.333	3	11	.273	0	18	18	8	29	0	3	4	4	32	2.0	0.9	3.6

TOLBERT, RAYMOND LEE (**Ray**) b. September 10, 1958 Ht. 6-9 Wt. 225 College—Indiana

SEASON—TEAM	G	GS	MIN	FGM	FGA	PCT	3FGM	3FGA	PCT	FTM	FTA	PCT	O-RB	D-RB	TOT	AST	PF	DQ	STL	TO	BLK	PTS	RPG	APG	PPG
81-82—N.J.-Seattle	64	0	607	100	202	.495	0	2	.000	19	35	.543	50	76	126	33	83	0	12	45	15	219	2.0	0.5	3.4
82-83—Seattle-Detroit	73	2	1107	157	314	.500	0	3	.000	52	103	.505	72	170	242	50	153	1	26	83	47	366	3.3	0.7	5.0
83-84—Detroit	49	0	475	64	121	.529	0	1	.000	23	45	.511	45	53	98	26	88	1	12	26	20	151	2.0	0.5	3.1
87-88—N.Y.-Lakers	25	0	259	35	69	.507	0	0	—	19	30	.633	23	32	55	10	39	0	8	21	5	89	2.2	0.4	3.6
88-89—Atlanta	50	0	341	40	94	.426	0	0	—	23	37	.622	31	57	88	16	55	0	13	35	13	103	1.8	0.3	2.1
REG. SEASON TOTALS	261	2	2789	396	800	.495	0	6	.000	136	250	.544	221	388	609	135	418	2	71	210	100	928	2.3	0.5	3.6
PLAYOFF TOTALS	5	0	33	3	5	.600	0	0	—	4	8	.500	1	4	5	1	7	0	4	0	0	10	1.0	0.2	2.0

TOLSON, BYRON DEAN (**Dean**) b. November 25, 1951 Ht. 6-8 Wt. 195 College—Arkansas

SEASON—TEAM	G	GS	MIN	FGM	FGA	PCT	3FGM	3FGA	PCT	FTM	FTA	PCT	O-RB	D-RB	TOT	AST	PF	DQ	STL	TO	BLK	PTS	RPG	APG	PPG
74-75—Seattle	19	—	87	16	37	.432	—	—	—	11	17	.647	12	10	22	5	12	0	4	—	6	43	1.2	0.3	2.3
76-77—Seattle	60	—	587	137	242	.566	—	—	—	85	159	.535	73	84	157	27	83	0	32	—	21	359	2.6	0.5	6.0
77-78—Seattle	1	—	7	0	1	.000	—	—	—	0	0	—	0	0	0	2	2	0	0	—	0	0	0.0	2.0	0.0
REG. SEASON TOTALS	80	—	681	153	280	.546	—	—	—	96	176	.545	85	94	179	34	97	0	36	1	27	402	2.2	0.4	5.0
PLAYOFF TOTALS	4	—	22	1	8	.125	—	—	—	2	2	1.000	4	3	7	1	3	0	0	—	0	4	1.8	0.3	1.0

TOMJANOVICH, RUDOLPH (Rudy T.) b. November 24, 1948　Ht. 6-8　Wt. 220　College—Michigan

SEASON—TEAM	G	GS	MIN	FGM	FGA	PCT	3FGM	3FGA	PCT	FTM	FTA	PCT	O-RB	D-RB	TOT	AST	PF	DQ	STL	TO	BLK	PTS	RPG	APG	PPG
70-71—San Diego	77	—	1062	168	439	.383	—	—	—	73	112	.652	—	—	381	73	124	0	—	—	—	409	4.9	0.9	5.3
71-72—Houston	78	—	2689	500	1010	.495	—	—	—	172	238	.723	—	—	923	117	193	2	—	—	—	1172	11.8	1.5	15.0
72-73—Houston	81	—	2972	655	1371	.478	—	—	—	250	335	.746	—	—	938	178	225	1	—	—	—	1560	11.6	2.2	19.3
73-74—Houston	80	—	3227	788	1470	.536	—	—	—	385	454	.848	230	487	717	250	230	0	89	—	66	1961	9.0	3.1	24.5
74-75—Houston	81	—	3134	694	1323	.525	—	—	—	289	366	.790	184	429	613	236	230	1	76	—	24	1677	7.6	2.9	20.7
75-76—Houston	79	—	2912	622	1202	.517	—	—	—	221	288	.767	167	499	666	188	206	1	42	—	19	1465	8.4	2.4	18.5
76-77—Houston	81	—	3130	733	1437	.510	—	—	—	287	342	.839	172	512	684	172	198	1	57	—	27	1753	8.4	2.1	21.6
77-78—Houston	23	—	849	217	447	.485	—	—	—	61	81	.753	40	98	138	32	63	0	15	38	5	495	6.0	1.4	21.5
78-79—Houston	74	—	2641	620	1200	.517	—	—	—	168	221	.760	170	402	572	137	186	0	44	138	18	1408	7.7	1.9	19.0
79-80—Houston	62	—	1834	370	778	.476	22	79	.278	118	147	.803	132	226	358	109	161	2	32	98	10	880	5.8	1.8	14.2
80-81—Houston	52	—	1264	263	563	.467	12	51	.235	65	82	.793	78	130	208	81	121	0	19	58	6	603	4.0	1.6	11.6
REG. SEASON TOTALS	768	—	25714	5630	11240	.501	34	130	.262	2089	2666	.784	1173	2783	6198	1573	1937	8	374	332	175	13383	8.1	2.0	17.4
PLAYOFF TOTALS	37	—	1041	213	436	.489	1	10	.100	84	109	.771	67	122	189	59	78	1	11	17	8	511	5.1	1.6	13.8
ALL-STAR TOTALS	5	—	89	12	32	.375	0	0	—	0	0	—	10	17	27	2	9	0	1	0	1	24	5.4	0.4	4.8

TONEY, ANDREW b. November 23, 1957　Ht. 6-3　Wt. 185　College—Southwestern Louisiana

SEASON—TEAM	G	GS	MIN	FGM	FGA	PCT	3FGM	3FGA	PCT	FTM	FTA	PCT	O-RB	D-RB	TOT	AST	PF	DQ	STL	TO	BLK	PTS	RPG	APG	PPG
80-81—Philadelphia	75	—	1768	399	806	.495	9	29	.310	161	226	.712	32	111	143	273	234	5	59	219	10	968	1.9	3.6	12.9
81-82—Philadelphia	77	1	1909	511	979	.522	25	59	.424	227	306	.742	43	91	134	283	269	5	64	214	17	1274	1.7	3.7	16.5
82-83—Philadelphia	81	81	2474	626	1250	.501	22	76	.289	324	411	.788	42	183	225	365	255	0	80	271	17	1598	2.8	4.5	19.7
83-84—Philadelphia	78	72	2556	593	1125	.527	12	38	.316	390	465	.839	57	136	193	373	251	1	70	297	23	1588	2.5	4.8	20.4
84-85—Philadelphia	70	65	2237	450	914	.492	39	105	.371	306	355	.862	35	142	177	363	211	1	65	224	24	1245	2.5	5.2	17.8
85-86—Philadelphia	6	0	84	11	36	.306	0	2	.000	3	8	.375	2	3	5	12	8	0	2	7	0	25	0.8	2.0	4.2
86-87—Philadelphia	52	12	1058	197	437	.451	22	67	.328	133	167	.796	16	69	85	188	78	0	18	112	8	549	1.6	3.6	10.6
87-88—Philadelphia	29	15	522	72	171	.421	9	27	.333	58	72	.806	8	39	47	108	35	0	11	50	6	211	1.6	3.7	7.3
REG. SEASON TOTALS	468	246	12608	2859	5718	.500	138	403	.342	1602	2010	.797	235	774	1009	1965	1341	12	369	1394	105	7458	2.2	4.2	15.9
PLAYOFF TOTALS	72	49	2146	485	1015	.478	12	51	.235	272	346	.786	56	112	168	323	265	3	58	257	18	1254	2.3	4.5	17.4
ALL-STAR TOTALS	2	0	40	10	16	.625	0	1	.000	1	1	1.000	0	1	1	10	3	0	4	4	0	21	0.5	5.0	10.5

TONEY, SEDRIC ANDRE b. April 13, 1962　Ht. 6-2　Wt. 180　College—Phillips Business/Western Nebraska CC/Dayton

SEASON—TEAM	G	GS	MIN	FGM	FGA	PCT	3FGM	3FGA	PCT	FTM	FTA	PCT	O-RB	D-RB	TOT	AST	PF	DQ	STL	TO	BLK	PTS	RPG	APG	PPG
85-86—Atlanta-Phoenix	13	0	230	28	66	.424	3	10	.300	21	31	.677	3	22	25	26	24	0	6	22	0	80	1.9	2.0	6.2
87-88—New York	21	0	139	21	48	.438	5	14	.357	10	11	.909	3	5	8	24	20	0	9	12	1	57	0.4	1.1	2.7
88-89—Indiana	2	0	9	1	5	.200	0	3	.000	0	1	.000	1	1	2	0	1	0	0	2	0	2	1.0	0.0	1.0
89-90—Atlanta-Sac.	64	9	968	87	250	.348	23	63	.365	67	83	.807	14	46	60	174	106	1	33	73	0	264	0.9	2.7	4.1
93-94—Cleveland	12	0	64	2	12	.167	0	1	.000	2	2	1.000	1	2	3	11	8	0	0	5	0	6	0.3	0.9	0.5
REG. SEASON TOTALS	112	9	1410	139	381	.365	31	91	.341	100	128	.781	22	76	98	235	159	1	48	114	1	409	0.9	2.1	3.7
PLAYOFF TOTALS	3	0	15	3	6	.500	3	6	.500	2	2	1.000	0	0	0	2	4	0	1	2	0	11	0.0	0.7	3.7

TONKOVICH, ANDREW EDWARD (Andy) b. November 1, 1922　Ht. 6-1　Wt. 185　College—Marshall

SEASON—TEAM	G	GS	MIN	FGM	FGA	PCT	3FGM	3FGA	PCT	FTM	FTA	PCT	O-RB	D-RB	TOT	AST	PF	DQ	STL	TO	BLK	PTS	RPG	APG	PPG
48-49—Providence	17	—	—	19	71	.268	—	—	—	6	9	.667	—	—	—	10	12	—	—	—	—	44	—	0.6	2.6
REG. SEASON TOTALS	17	—	—	19	71	.268	—	—	—	6	9	.667	—	—	—	10	12	—	—	—	—	44	—	0.6	2.6

TOOLSON, ANDREW K. (Andy) b. January 19, 1966　Ht. 6-6　Wt. 210　College—Brigham Young

SEASON—TEAM	G	GS	MIN	FGM	FGA	PCT	3FGM	3FGA	PCT	FTM	FTA	PCT	O-RB	D-RB	TOT	AST	PF	DQ	STL	TO	BLK	PTS	RPG	APG	PPG
90-91—Utah	47	15	470	50	124	.403	12	32	.375	25	33	.758	32	35	67	31	58	0	14	24	2	137	1.4	0.7	2.9
REG. SEASON TOTALS	47	15	470	50	124	.403	12	32	.375	25	33	.758	32	35	67	31	58	0	14	24	2	137	1.4	0.7	2.9
PLAYOFF TOTALS	2	0	4	0	2	.000	0	1	.000	0	0	—	0	0	0	1	0	0	1	0	0	0	0.0	0.5	0.0

TOOMAY, JOHN C. (Jack) b. August 9, 1922　Ht. 6-6½　Wt. 215　College—Pacific

SEASON—TEAM	G	GS	MIN	FGM	FGA	PCT	3FGM	3FGA	PCT	FTM	FTA	PCT	O-RB	D-RB	TOT	AST	PF	DQ	STL	TO	BLK	PTS	RPG	APG	PPG
47-48—Chicago-Prov.	23	—	—	61	191	.319	—	—	—	60	91	.659	—	—	—	7	71	—	—	—	—	182	—	0.3	7.9
48-49—Balt.-Wash.	36	—	—	32	84	.381	—	—	—	36	53	.679	—	—	—	12	65	—	—	—	—	100	—	0.3	2.8
49-50—Denver	62	—	—	204	514	.397	—	—	—	186	264	.705	—	—	—	94	213	—	—	—	—	594	—	1.5	9.6
REG. SEASON TOTALS	121	—	—	297	789	.376	—	—	—	282	408	.691	—	—	—	113	349	—	—	—	—	876	—	0.9	7.2
PLAYOFF TOTALS	1	—	—	1	5	.200	—	—	—	5	7	.714	—	—	—	6	1	—	—	—	—	7	—	0.0	7.0

TOONE, BERNARD b. July 14, 1956　Ht. 6-9　Wt. 210　College—Marquette

SEASON—TEAM	G	GS	MIN	FGM	FGA	PCT	3FGM	3FGA	PCT	FTM	FTA	PCT	O-RB	D-RB	TOT	AST	PF	DQ	STL	TO	BLK	PTS	RPG	APG	PPG
79-80—Philadelphia	23	—	124	23	64	.359	1	7	.143	8	10	.800	12	22	34	12	20	0	4	16	5	55	1.5	0.5	2.4
REG. SEASON TOTALS	23	—	124	23	64	.359	1	7	.143	8	10	.800	12	22	34	12	20	0	4	16	5	55	1.5	0.5	2.4
PLAYOFF TOTALS	4	—	6	0	4	.000	0	1	.000	0	0	—	0	1	1	1	1	0	0	0	0	0	0.3	0.3	0.0

TORGOFF, IRVING **(Irv)** b. March 6, 1917 d. October 21, 1993 Ht. 6-1.5 Wt. 195 College—Long Island University

SEASON—TEAM	G	GS	MIN	FGM	FGA	PCT	3FGM	3FGA	PCT	FTM	FTA	PCT	O-RB	D-RB	TOT	AST	PF	DQ	STL	TO	BLK	PTS	RPG	APG	PPG
39-40—Detroit (N)	26	—	—	64	—	—	—	—	—	43	67	.642	—	—	—	—	58	—	—	—	—	171	—	—	6.6
46-47—Washington	58	—	—	187	684	.273	—	—	—	116	159	.730	—	—	—	30	173	—	—	—	—	490	—	0.5	8.4
47-48—Washington	47	—	—	111	541	.205	—	—	—	117	144	.813	—	—	—	32	153	—	—	—	—	339	—	0.7	7.2
48-49—Balt.-Phil.	42	—	—	59	226	.261	—	—	—	50	64	.781	—	—	—	44	110	—	—	—	—	168	—	1.0	4.0
REG. NBA TOTALS	147	—	—	357	1451	.246	—	—	—	283	367	.771	—	—	—	106	436	—	—	—	—	997	—	0.7	6.8
REG. NBL TOTALS	26	—	—	64	—	—	—	—	—	43	67	.642	—	—	—	—	58	—	—	—	—	171	—	—	6.6
NBA PLAYOFF TOTALS	8	—	—	13	84	.155	—	—	—	13	19	.684	—	—	—	7	25	3	—	—	—	39	—	0.9	4.9
NBL PLAYOFF TOTALS	3	—	—	10	—	—	—	—	—	7	—	—	—	—	—	—	7	—	—	—	—	27	—	—	9.0

TORMOHLEN, EUGENE R. **(Gene, Bumper)** b. May 12, 1937 Ht. 6-9 Wt. 250 College—Tennessee

SEASON—TEAM	G	GS	MIN	FGM	FGA	PCT	3FGM	3FGA	PCT	FTM	FTA	PCT	O-RB	D-RB	TOT	AST	PF	DQ	STL	TO	BLK	PTS	RPG	APG	PPG
62-63—St. Louis	7	—	47	5	10	.500	—	—	—	2	10	.200	—	—	15	5	11	0	—	—	—	12	2.1	0.7	1.7
63-64—St. Louis	51	—	640	94	250	.376	—	—	—	22	46	.478	—	—	216	50	128	3	—	—	—	210	4.2	1.0	4.1
65-66—St. Louis	71	—	775	144	324	.444	—	—	—	54	82	.659	—	—	314	60	138	3	—	—	—	342	4.4	0.8	4.8
66-67—St. Louis	63	—	1036	172	403	.427	—	—	—	50	84	.595	—	—	347	73	177	4	—	—	—	394	5.5	1.2	6.3
67-68—St. Louis	77	—	714	98	262	.374	—	—	—	33	56	.589	—	—	226	68	94	0	—	—	—	229	2.9	0.9	3.0
69-70—Atlanta	2	—	11	2	4	.500	—	—	—	0	0	—	—	—	4	1	3	0	—	—	—	4	2.0	0.5	2.0
REG. SEASON TOTALS	271	—	3223	515	1253	.411	—	—	—	161	278	.579	—	—	1122	257	551	10	—	—	—	1191	4.1	0.9	4.4
PLAYOFF TOTALS	26	—	169	24	60	.400	—	—	—	11	18	.611	—	—	62	21	38	0	—	—	—	59	2.4	0.8	2.3

TOSHEFF, WILLIAM MARK **(Bill)** b. June 2, 1926 Ht. 6-1 Wt. 175 College—Indiana

SEASON—TEAM	G	GS	MIN	FGM	FGA	PCT	3FGM	3FGA	PCT	FTM	FTA	PCT	O-RB	D-RB	TOT	AST	PF	DQ	STL	TO	BLK	PTS	RPG	APG	PPG
51-52—Indianapolis	65	—	2055	213	651	.327	—	—	—	182	221	.824	—	—	216	222	204	7	—	—	—	608	3.3	3.4	9.4
52-53—Indianapolis	67	—	2459	253	783	.323	—	—	—	253	314	.806	—	—	229	243	243	5	—	—	—	759	3.4	3.6	11.3
53-54—Milwaukee	71	—	1825	168	578	.291	—	—	—	156	210	.743	—	—	163	196	207	3	—	—	—	492	2.3	2.8	6.9
REG. SEASON TOTALS	203	—	6339	634	2012	.315	—	—	—	591	745	.793	—	—	608	661	654	15	—	—	—	1859	3.0	3.3	9.2
PLAYOFF TOTALS	4	—	134	3	34	.088	—	—	—	10	10	1.000	—	—	11	11	14	0	—	—	—	16	2.8	2.8	4.0

TOUGH, ROBERT **(Bob, Red)** b. August 28, 1920 Ht. 6-0 Wt. 185 College—St. John's

SEASON—TEAM	G	GS	MIN	FGM	FGA	PCT	3FGM	3FGA	PCT	FTM	FTA	PCT	O-RB	D-RB	TOT	AST	PF	DQ	STL	TO	BLK	PTS	RPG	APG	PPG
45-46—Fort Wayne (N)	5	—	—	12	—	—	—	—	—	5	—	—	—	—	—	—	—	—	—	—	—	29	—	—	5.8
46-47—Fort Wayne (N)	44	—	—	124	—	—	—	—	—	55	81	.679	—	—	—	—	73	—	—	—	—	303	—	—	6.9
47-48—Fort Wayne (N)	60	—	—	129	—	—	—	—	—	48	71	.676	—	—	—	—	98	—	—	—	—	306	—	—	5.1
48-49—Fort Wayne	53	—	—	183	661	.277	—	—	—	100	138	.725	—	—	—	99	101	—	—	—	—	466	—	1.9	8.8
49-50—Balt.-Wat.	29	—	—	43	153	.281	—	—	—	37	40	.925	—	—	—	38	40	—	—	—	—	123	—	1.3	4.2
REG. NBA TOTALS	82	—	—	226	814	.278	—	—	—	137	178	.770	—	—	—	137	141	—	—	—	—	589	—	1.7	7.2
REG. NBL TOTALS	109	—	—	265	—	—	—	—	—	108	152	.678	—	—	—	—	171	—	—	—	—	638	—	—	5.9
NBL PLAYOFF TOTALS	16	—	—	35	—	—	—	—	—	23	31	.742	—	—	—	—	27	—	—	—	—	93	—	—	5.8

TOWE, MONTE CORWIN b. September 27, 1953 Ht. 5-7 Wt. 150 College—North Carolina State

SEASON—TEAM	G	GS	MIN	FGM	FGA	PCT	3FGM	3FGA	PCT	FTM	FTA	PCT	O-RB	D-RB	TOT	AST	PF	DQ	STL	TO	BLK	PTS	RPG	APG	PPG
75-76—Denver (A)	64	—	576	72	179	.402	9	42	.214	36	44	.818	6	49	55	136	84	—	37	81	5	189	0.9	2.1	3.0
76-77—Denver	51	—	409	56	138	.406	—	—	—	18	25	.720	8	26	34	87	61	0	16	—	0	130	0.7	1.7	2.5
REG. NBA TOTALS	51	—	409	56	138	.406	—	—	—	18	25	.720	8	26	34	87	61	0	16	—	0	130	0.7	1.7	2.5
REG. ABA TOTALS	64	—	576	72	179	.402	9	42	.214	36	44	.818	6	49	55	136	84	—	37	81	5	189	0.9	2.1	3.0
NBA PLAYOFF TOTALS	1	—	6	2	3	.667	—	—	—	0	0	—	0	0	0	1	0	0	0	—	0	4	0.0	1.0	4.0
ABA PLAYOFF TOTALS	4	—	30	3	8	.375	0	0	—	4	5	.800	0	0	0	6	6	—	1	5	0	10	0.0	1.5	2.5
ABA ALL-STAR TOTALS	1	—	11	1	3	.333	0	0	—	0	0	—	0	0	0	2	0	0	0	0	0	2	0.0	2.0	2.0

TOWER, KEITH RAYMOND b. May 15, 1970 Ht. 6-11 Wt. 250 College—Notre Dame

SEASON—TEAM	G	GS	MIN	FGM	FGA	PCT	3FGM	3FGA	PCT	FTM	FTA	PCT	O-RB	D-RB	TOT	AST	PF	DQ	STL	TO	BLK	PTS	RPG	APG	PPG
93-94—Orlando	11	0	32	4	9	.444	0	0	—	0	0	—	0	6	6	1	6	0	0	0	0	8	0.5	0.1	0.7
REG. SEASON TOTALS	11	0	32	4	9	.444	0	0	—	0	0	—	0	6	6	1	6	0	0	0	0	8	0.5	0.1	0.7

TOWERY, WILLIAM CARLISLE **(Blackie)** b. June 20, 1920 Ht. 6-4½ Wt. 210 College—Western Kentucky

SEASON—TEAM	G	GS	MIN	FGM	FGA	PCT	3FGM	3FGA	PCT	FTM	FTA	PCT	O-RB	D-RB	TOT	AST	PF	DQ	STL	TO	BLK	PTS	RPG	APG	PPG
41-42—Fort Wayne (N)	24	—	—	64	—	—	—	—	—	35	—	—	—	—	—	—	92	—	—	—	—	163	—	—	6.8
42-43—Fort Wayne (N)	23	—	—	53	—	—	—	—	—	33	53	.623	—	—	—	—	71	—	—	—	—	139	—	—	6.0
43-44—Fort Wayne (N)	22	—	—	48	—	—	—	—	—	33	—	—	—	—	—	—	74	—	—	—	—	129	—	—	5.9
44-45—Fort Wayne (N)	1	—	—	0	—	—	—	—	—	1	—	—	—	—	—	—	—	—	—	—	—	1	—	—	1.0
46-47—Fort Wayne (N)	41	—	—	100	—	—	—	—	—	80	134	.597	—	—	—	—	123	—	—	—	—	280	—	—	6.8
47-48—Fort Wayne (N)	59	—	—	139	—	—	—	—	—	129	187	.690	—	—	—	—	194	—	—	—	—	407	—	—	6.9
48-49—Ft. Wayne-Ind.	60	—	—	203	771	.263	—	—	—	195	263	.741	—	—	—	171	243	—	—	—	—	601	—	2.9	10.0
49-50—Baltimore	68	—	—	222	678	.327	—	—	—	153	202	.757	—	—	—	142	244	—	—	—	—	597	—	2.1	8.8
REG. NBA TOTALS	128	—	—	425	1449	.293	—	—	—	348	465	.748	—	—	—	313	487	—	—	—	—	1198	—	2.4	9.4
REG. NBL TOTALS	170	—	—	404	—	—	—	—	—	311	374	.647	—	—	—	—	554	—	—	—	—	1119	—	—	6.6
NBL PLAYOFF TOTALS	29	—	—	63	—	—	—	—	—	36	26	.500	—	—	—	—	90	—	—	—	—	162	—	—	5.6

TOWNES, LINTON RODNEY b. November 30, 1959 Ht. 6-7 Wt. 195 College—James Madison

SEASON—TEAM	G	GS	MIN	FGM	FGA	PCT	3FGM	3FGA	PCT	FTM	FTA	PCT	O-RB	D-RB	TOT	AST	PF	DQ	STL	TO	BLK	PTS	RPG	APG	PPG
82-83—Portland	55	0	516	105	234	.449	9	25	.360	28	38	.737	30	35	65	31	81	0	19	33	5	247	1.2	0.6	4.5
83-84—Milw.-S.D.	4	0	19	4	8	.500	0	0	—	0	0	—	0	1	1	1	4	0	1	1	2	8	0.3	0.3	2.0
84-85—San Antonio	1	0	8	0	6	.000	0	0	—	2	2	1.000	1	0	1	0	1	0	0	0	0	2	1.0	0.0	2.0
REG. SEASON TOTALS	60	0	543	109	248	.440	9	25	.360	30	40	.750	31	36	67	32	86	0	20	34	7	257	1.1	0.5	4.3
PLAYOFF TOTALS	8	0	66	17	35	.486	1	4	.250	6	7	.857	4	2	6	5	12	0	0	3	0	41	0.8	0.6	5.1

TOWNSEND, RAYMOND ANTHONY b. December 20, 1955 Ht. 6-3½ Wt. 185 College—UCLA

SEASON—TEAM	G	GS	MIN	FGM	FGA	PCT	3FGM	3FGA	PCT	FTM	FTA	PCT	O-RB	D-RB	TOT	AST	PF	DQ	STL	TO	BLK	PTS	RPG	APG	PPG
78-79—Golden State	65	—	771	127	289	.439	—	—	—	50	68	.735	11	44	55	91	70	0	27	51	6	304	0.8	1.4	4.7
79-80—Golden State	75	—	1159	171	421	.406	4	26	.154	60	84	.714	33	56	89	116	113	0	60	65	4	406	1.2	1.5	5.4
81-82—Indiana	14	0	95	11	41	.268	2	9	.222	11	20	.550	2	11	13	10	18	0	3	6	0	35	0.9	0.7	2.5
REG. SEASON TOTALS	154	0	2025	309	751	.411	6	35	.171	121	172	.703	46	111	157	217	201	0	90	122	10	745	1.0	1.4	4.8

TRAPP, GEORGE b. July 11, 1948 Ht. 6-8.5 Wt. 205 College—Pasadena CC/Long Beach State

SEASON—TEAM	G	GS	MIN	FGM	FGA	PCT	3FGM	3FGA	PCT	FTM	FTA	PCT	O-RB	D-RB	TOT	AST	PF	DQ	STL	TO	BLK	PTS	RPG	APG	PPG
71-72—Atlanta	60	—	890	144	388	.371	—	—	—	105	139	.755	—	—	183	51	144	2	—	—	—	393	3.1	0.9	6.6
72-73—Atlanta	77	—	1853	359	824	.436	—	—	—	150	194	.773	—	—	455	127	274	11	—	—	—	868	5.9	1.6	11.3
73-74—Detroit	82	—	1489	333	693	.481	—	—	—	99	134	.739	97	216	313	81	226	2	47	—	33	765	3.8	1.0	9.3
74-75—Detroit	78	—	1472	288	652	.442	—	—	—	99	131	.756	71	205	276	63	210	1	37	—	14	675	3.5	0.8	8.7
75-76—Detroit	76	—	1091	278	602	.462	—	—	—	63	88	.716	79	150	229	50	167	3	33	—	23	619	3.0	0.7	8.1
76-77—Detroit	6	—	68	15	29	.517	—	—	—	3	4	.750	4	6	10	3	13	0	0	—	1	33	1.7	0.5	5.5
REG. SEASON TOTALS	379	—	6863	1417	3188	.444	—	—	—	519	690	.752	251	577	1466	375	1034	19	117	—	71	3353	3.9	1.0	8.8
PLAYOFF TOTALS	31	—	518	115	249	.462	—	—	—	28	40	.700	21	58	118	23	89	1	4	—	9	258	3.8	0.7	8.3

TRAPP, JOHN QUINCY b. October 2, 1945 Ht. 6-7 Wt. 215 College—Pasadena CC/Nevada-Las Vegas

SEASON—TEAM	G	GS	MIN	FGM	FGA	PCT	3FGM	3FGA	PCT	FTM	FTA	PCT	O-RB	D-RB	TOT	AST	PF	DQ	STL	TO	BLK	PTS	RPG	APG	PPG
68-69—San Diego	25	—	142	29	80	.363	—	—	—	19	29	.655	—	—	49	5	38	0	—	—	—	77	2.0	0.2	3.1
69-70—San Diego	70	—	1025	185	434	.426	—	—	—	72	104	.692	—	—	309	49	200	3	—	—	—	442	4.4	0.7	6.3
70-71—San Diego	82	—	2080	322	766	.420	—	—	—	142	188	.755	—	—	510	138	337	16	—	—	—	786	6.2	1.7	9.6
71-72—Los Angeles	58	—	759	139	314	.443	—	—	—	51	73	.699	—	—	180	42	130	3	—	—	—	329	3.1	0.7	5.7
72-73—L.A.-Phil.	44	—	889	171	420	.407	—	—	—	90	122	.738	—	—	200	49	150	4	—	—	—	432	4.5	1.1	9.8
72-73—Denver (A)	25	—	342	54	128	.422	0	2	.000	19	32	.594	27	45	72	20	76	0	—	25	—	127	2.9	0.8	5.1
REG. NBA TOTALS	279	—	4895	846	2014	.420	—	—	—	374	516	.725	—	—	1248	283	855	26	—	—	—	2066	4.5	1.0	7.4
REG. ABA TOTALS	25	—	342	54	128	.422	0	2	.000	19	32	.594	27	45	72	20	76	0	—	25	—	127	2.9	0.8	5.1
NBA PLAYOFF TOTALS	10	—	71	8	33	.242	—	—	—	4	7	.571	—	—	16	5	9	0	—	—	—	20	1.6	0.5	2.0
ABA PLAYOFF TOTALS	5	—	51	7	16	.438	0	0	—	8	12	.667	—	—	7	2	13	—	—	1	—	22	1.4	0.4	4.4

TRESVANT, JOHN B. b. November 6, 1939 Ht. 6-7 Wt. 215 College—Seattle

SEASON—TEAM	G	GS	MIN	FGM	FGA	PCT	3FGM	3FGA	PCT	FTM	FTA	PCT	O-RB	D-RB	TOT	AST	PF	DQ	STL	TO	BLK	PTS	RPG	APG	PPG
64-65—St. Louis	4	—	35	4	11	.364	—	—	—	6	9	.667	—	—	18	6	9	0	—	—	—	14	4.5	1.5	3.5
65-66—St. L.-Detroit	61	—	969	171	400	.428	—	—	—	142	190	.747	—	—	364	72	179	2	—	—	—	484	6.0	1.2	7.9
66-67—Detroit	68	—	1553	256	585	.438	—	—	—	164	234	.701	—	—	483	88	246	8	—	—	—	676	7.1	1.3	9.9
67-68—Detroit-Cin.	85	—	2473	396	867	.457	—	—	—	250	384	.651	—	—	709	160	344	18	—	—	—	1042	8.3	1.9	12.3
68-69—Cin.-Seattle	77	—	2482	380	820	.463	—	—	—	202	330	.612	—	—	686	166	300	9	—	—	—	962	8.9	2.2	12.5
69-70—Seattle-L.A.	69	—	1499	264	595	.444	—	—	—	206	284	.725	—	—	425	112	204	4	—	—	—	734	6.2	1.6	10.6
70-71—L.A.-Balt.	75	—	1517	202	436	.463	—	—	—	146	205	.712	—	—	382	86	196	1	—	—	—	550	5.1	1.1	7.3
71-72—Baltimore	65	—	1227	162	360	.450	—	—	—	121	148	.818	—	—	323	83	175	6	—	—	—	445	5.0	1.3	6.8
72-73—Baltimore	55	—	541	85	182	.467	—	—	—	41	59	.695	—	—	156	33	101	0	—	—	—	211	2.8	0.6	3.8
REG. SEASON TOTALS	559	—	12296	1920	4256	.451	—	—	—	1278	1843	.693	—	—	3546	806	1754	48	—	—	—	5118	6.3	1.4	9.2
PLAYOFF TOTALS	40	—	862	104	251	.414	—	—	—	66	95	.695	—	—	246	44	115	3	—	—	—	274	6.2	1.1	6.9

TRIPTOW, RICHARD FLOYD (Dick, Tiptoe) b. November 3, 1922 Ht. 6-0 Wt. 170 College—DePaul

SEASON—TEAM	G	GS	MIN	FGM	FGA	PCT	3FGM	3FGA	PCT	FTM	FTA	PCT	O-RB	D-RB	TOT	AST	PF	DQ	STL	TO	BLK	PTS	RPG	APG	PPG
44-45—Chicago (N)	30	—	—	113	—	—	—	—	—	73	—	—	—	—	—	—	—	—	—	—	—	299	—	—	10.0
45-46—Chicago (N)	34	—	—	68	—	—	—	—	—	85	127	.669	—	—	—	77	—	—	—	—	—	221	—	—	6.5
46-47—Chicago (N)	44	—	—	59	—	—	—	—	—	60	90	.667	—	—	—	71	—	—	—	—	—	178	—	—	4.0
47-48—Tri-Cit-Ft. Wayne (N)	57	—	—	92	—	—	—	—	—	87	138	.630	—	—	—	109	—	—	—	—	—	271	—	—	4.8
48-49—Fort Wayne	55	—	—	116	417	.278	—	—	—	102	141	.723	—	96	—	107	—	—	—	—	—	334	—	1.7	6.1
49-50—Baltimore	4	—	—	0	5	.000	—	—	—	2	2	1.000	—	1	—	5	—	—	—	—	—	2	—	0.3	0.5
REG. NBA TOTALS	59	—	—	116	422	.275	—	—	—	104	143	.727	—	97	—	112	—	—	—	—	—	336	—	1.6	5.7
REG. NBL TOTALS	165	—	—	332	—	—	—	—	—	305	355	.654	—	—	—	257	—	—	—	—	—	969	—	—	5.9
NBL PLAYOFF TOTALS	18	—	—	39	—	—	—	—	—	22	33	.576	—	—	—	38	—	—	—	—	—	100	—	—	5.6

TRIPUCKA, PETER KELLY (**Kelly**) b. February 16, 1959 Ht. 6-6 Wt. 225 College—Notre Dame

SEASON—TEAM	G	GS	MIN	FGM	FGA	PCT	3FGM	3FGA	PCT	FTM	FTA	PCT	O-RB	D-RB	TOT	AST	PF	DQ	STL	TO	BLK	PTS	RPG	APG	PPG
81-82—Detroit	82	82	3077	636	1281	.496	5	22	.227	495	621	.797	219	224	443	270	241	0	89	280	16	1772	5.4	3.3	21.6
82-83—Detroit	58	58	2252	565	1156	.489	14	37	.378	392	464	.845	126	138	264	237	157	0	67	187	20	1536	4.6	4.1	26.5
83-84—Detroit	76	75	2493	595	1296	.459	2	17	.118	426	523	.815	119	187	306	228	190	0	65	190	17	1618	4.0	3.0	21.3
84-85—Detroit	55	43	1675	396	831	.477	2	5	.400	255	288	.885	66	152	218	135	118	1	49	118	14	1049	4.0	2.5	19.1
85-86—Detroit	81	81	2626	615	1236	.498	12	25	.480	380	444	.856	116	232	348	265	167	0	93	183	10	1622	4.3	3.3	20.0
86-87—Utah	79	76	1865	291	621	.469	19	52	.365	197	226	.872	54	188	242	243	147	0	85	167	11	798	3.1	3.1	10.1
87-88—Utah	49	21	976	139	303	.459	31	74	.419	59	68	.868	30	87	117	105	68	1	34	68	4	368	2.4	2.1	7.5
88-89—Charlotte	71	65	2302	568	1215	.467	30	84	.357	440	508	.866	79	188	267	224	196	0	88	236	16	1606	3.8	3.2	22.6
89-90—Charlotte	79	73	2404	442	1029	.430	38	104	.365	310	351	.883	82	240	322	224	220	1	75	176	16	1232	4.1	2.8	15.6
90-91—Charlotte	77	1	1289	187	412	.454	15	45	.333	152	167	.910	46	130	176	159	130	0	33	92	13	541	2.3	2.1	7.0
REG. SEASON TOTALS	707	575	20959	4434	9380	.473	168	465	.361	3106	3660	.849	937	1766	2703	2090	1634	3	678	1697	137	12142	3.8	3.0	17.2
PLAYOFF TOTALS	25	23	750	145	314	.462	0	5	.000	101	118	.856	41	52	93	57	65	2	22	61	5	391	3.7	2.3	15.6
ALL-STAR TOTALS	2	0	21	3	7	.429	0	0	—	1	2	.500	0	1	1	4	1	0	1	3	0	7	0.5	2.0	3.5

TRUITT, ANSLEY HOOVER b. August 24, 1950 Ht. 6-9 Wt. 215 College—California Berkeley

SEASON—TEAM	G	GS	MIN	FGM	FGA	PCT	3FGM	3FGA	PCT	FTM	FTA	PCT	O-RB	D-RB	TOT	AST	PF	DQ	STL	TO	BLK	PTS	RPG	APG	PPG
72-73—Dallas (A)	16	—	86	18	42	.429	0	0	—	3	9	.333	10	28	38	2	9	0	—	7	—	39	2.4	0.1	2.4
REG. ABA TOTALS	16	—	86	18	42	.429	0	0	—	3	9	.333	10	28	38	2	9	0	—	7	—	39	2.4	0.1	2.4

TSCHOGL, JOHN MARK b. April 25, 1950 Ht. 6-6 Wt. 210 College—Cal-Santa Barbara

SEASON—TEAM	G	GS	MIN	FGM	FGA	PCT	3FGM	3FGA	PCT	FTM	FTA	PCT	O-RB	D-RB	TOT	AST	PF	DQ	STL	TO	BLK	PTS	RPG	APG	PPG
72-73—Atlanta	10	—	94	14	40	.350	—	—	—	2	4	.500	—	—	21	6	25	0	—	—	—	30	2.1	0.6	3.0
73-74—Atlanta	64	—	499	59	166	.355	—	—	—	10	17	.588	33	43	76	33	69	0	17	—	20	128	1.2	0.5	2.0
74-75—Philadelphia	39	—	623	53	148	.358	—	—	—	13	22	.591	52	59	111	30	80	2	25	—	25	119	2.8	0.8	3.1
REG. SEASON TOTALS	113	—	1216	126	354	.356	—	—	—	25	43	.581	85	102	208	69	174	2	42	—	45	277	1.8	0.6	2.5
PLAYOFF TOTALS	3	—	11	5	8	.625	—	—	—	0	0	—	0	0	4	1	0	0	0	—	0	10	1.3	0.3	3.3

TSIOROPOULOS, LOUIS C. (**Lou**) b. August 31, 1930 Ht. 6-5 Wt. 195 College—Kentucky

SEASON—TEAM	G	GS	MIN	FGM	FGA	PCT	3FGM	3FGA	PCT	FTM	FTA	PCT	O-RB	D-RB	TOT	AST	PF	DQ	STL	TO	BLK	PTS	RPG	APG	PPG
56-57—Boston	52	—	670	79	256	.309	—	—	—	69	89	.775	—	—	207	33	135	6	—	—	—	227	4.0	0.6	4.4
57-58—Boston	70	—	1819	198	624	.317	—	—	—	142	207	.686	—	—	434	112	242	8	—	—	—	538	6.2	1.6	7.7
58-59—Boston	35	—	488	60	190	.316	—	—	—	25	33	.758	—	—	110	20	74	0	—	—	—	145	3.1	0.6	4.1
REG. SEASON TOTALS	157	—	2977	337	1070	.315	—	—	—	236	329	.717	—	—	751	165	451	14	—	—	—	910	4.8	1.1	5.8
PLAYOFF TOTALS	11	—	239	25	85	.294	—	—	—	19	29	.655	—	—	64	14	40	4	—	—	—	69	5.8	1.3	6.3

TUCKER, ALBERT AMES (**Al, Tuck**) b. February 24, 1943 Ht. 6-8 Wt. 190 College—Oklahoma Baptist

SEASON—TEAM	G	GS	MIN	FGM	FGA	PCT	3FGM	3FGA	PCT	FTM	FTA	PCT	O-RB	D-RB	TOT	AST	PF	DQ	STL	TO	BLK	PTS	RPG	APG	PPG
67-68—Seattle	81	—	2368	437	989	.442	—	—	—	186	263	.707	—	—	605	111	262	6	—	—	—	1060	7.5	1.4	13.1
68-69—Seattle-Cin.	84	—	1885	361	809	.446	—	—	—	158	244	.648	—	—	439	74	186	2	—	—	—	880	5.2	0.9	10.5
69-70—Chicago-Balt.	61	—	819	146	285	.512	—	—	—	70	87	.805	—	—	166	38	86	0	—	—	—	362	2.7	0.6	5.9
70-71—Baltimore	31	—	276	52	115	.452	—	—	—	25	31	.806	—	—	73	7	33	0	—	—	—	129	2.4	0.2	4.2
70-71—Floridians (A)	14	—	331	66	149	.443	3	7	.429	34	42	.810	—	—	65	12	40	—	—	—	—	169	4.6	0.9	12.1
71-72—Floridians (A)	81	—	1799	377	810	.465	30	82	.366	157	199	.789	—	—	392	100	205	—	—	129	—	941	4.8	1.2	11.6
REG. NBA TOTALS	257	—	5348	996	2198	.453	—	—	—	439	625	.702	—	—	1283	230	567	8	—	—	—	2431	5.0	0.9	9.5
REG. ABA TOTALS	95	—	2130	443	959	.462	33	89	.371	191	241	.793	—	—	457	112	245	—	—	129	—	1110	4.8	1.2	11.7
NBA PLAYOFF TOTALS	4	—	5	2	2	1.000	—	—	—	0	0	—	—	—	0	0	0	0	—	—	—	4	0.0	0.0	1.0
ABA PLAYOFF TOTALS	9	—	216	33	85	.388	1	7	.143	19	24	.792	—	—	46	16	28	—	—	3	—	86	5.1	1.8	9.6

TUCKER, JAMES D. (**Jim**) b. December 11, 1932 Ht. 6-7½ Wt. 185 College—Duquesne

SEASON—TEAM	G	GS	MIN	FGM	FGA	PCT	3FGM	3FGA	PCT	FTM	FTA	PCT	O-RB	D-RB	TOT	AST	PF	DQ	STL	TO	BLK	PTS	RPG	APG	PPG
54-55—Syracuse	20	—	287	39	116	.336	—	—	—	27	38	.711	—	—	97	12	50	0	—	—	—	105	4.9	0.6	5.3
55-56—Syracuse	70	—	895	101	290	.348	—	—	—	66	83	.795	—	—	232	38	166	2	—	—	—	268	3.3	0.5	3.8
56-57—Syracuse	9	—	119	17	44	.386	—	—	—	0	1	.000	—	—	20	2	26	0	—	—	—	34	2.2	0.2	3.8
REG. SEASON TOTALS	99	—	1301	157	450	.349	—	—	—	93	122	.762	—	—	349	52	242	2	—	—	—	407	3.5	0.5	4.1
PLAYOFF TOTALS	15	—	131	21	61	.344	—	—	—	14	17	.824	—	—	40	3	28	0	—	—	—	56	2.7	0.2	3.7

TUCKER, KELVIN TRENT (Trent) b. December 20, 1959 Ht. 6-5 Wt. 195 College—Minnesota

SEASON—TEAM	G	GS	MIN	FGM	FGA	PCT	3FGM	3FGA	PCT	FTM	FTA	PCT	O-RB	D-RB	TOT	AST	PF	DQ	STL	TO	BLK	PTS	RPG	APG	PPG
82-83—New York	78	59	1830	299	647	.462	14	30	.467	43	64	.672	75	141	216	195	235	1	56	70	6	655	2.8	2.5	8.4
83-84—New York	63	21	1228	225	450	.500	6	16	.375	25	33	.758	43	87	130	138	124	0	63	54	8	481	2.1	2.2	7.6
84-85—New York	77	46	1819	293	606	.483	29	72	.403	38	48	.792	74	114	188	199	195	0	75	64	15	653	2.4	2.6	8.5
85-86—New York	77	23	1788	349	740	.472	41	91	.451	79	100	.790	70	99	169	192	167	0	65	70	8	818	2.2	2.5	10.6
86-87—New York	70	15	1691	325	691	.470	68	161	.422	77	101	.762	49	86	135	166	169	1	116	78	13	795	1.9	2.4	11.4
87-88—New York	71	4	1248	193	455	.424	69	167	.413	51	71	.718	32	87	119	117	158	3	53	47	6	506	1.7	1.6	7.1
88-89—New York	81	24	1824	263	579	.454	118	296	.399	43	55	.782	55	121	176	132	163	0	88	59	6	687	2.2	1.6	8.5
89-90—New York	81	2	1725	253	606	.417	95	245	.388	66	86	.767	57	117	174	173	159	0	74	73	8	667	2.1	2.1	8.2
90-91—New York	65	13	1194	191	434	.440	64	153	.418	17	27	.630	33	72	105	111	120	0	44	46	9	463	1.6	1.7	7.1
91-92—Phoenix-S.A.	24	0	415	60	129	.465	19	48	.396	16	20	.800	8	29	37	27	39	0	21	14	3	155	1.5	1.1	6.5
92-93—Chicago	69	0	909	143	295	.485	52	131	.397	18	22	.818	16	55	71	82	65	0	24	18	6	356	1.0	1.2	5.2
REG. SEASON TOTALS	756	207	15671	2594	5632	.461	575	1410	.408	473	627	.754	512	1008	1520	1532	1594	5	679	593	88	6236	2.0	2.0	8.2
PLAYOFF TOTALS	66	8	1059	142	316	.449	50	120	.417	30	43	.698	30	64	94	100	107	0	44	38	5	364	1.4	1.5	5.5

TURNER, ANDRE D. b. December 13, 1964 Ht. 5-11 Wt. 160 College—Memphis State

SEASON—TEAM	G	GS	MIN	FGM	FGA	PCT	3FGM	3FGA	PCT	FTM	FTA	PCT	O-RB	D-RB	TOT	AST	PF	DQ	STL	TO	BLK	PTS	RPG	APG	PPG
86-87—Boston	3	0	18	2	5	.400	0	1	.000	0	0	—	1	1	2	1	1	0	0	5	0	4	0.7	0.3	1.3
87-88—Houston	12	0	99	12	34	.353	1	7	.143	10	14	.714	4	4	8	23	13	0	7	12	1	35	0.7	1.9	2.9
88-89—Milwaukee	4	0	13	3	6	.500	0	0	—	0	0	—	0	3	3	0	2	0	2	4	0	6	0.8	0.0	1.5
89-90—L.A. Clips-Cha.	11	0	115	11	38	.289	0	2	.000	4	4	1.000	4	4	8	23	6	0	8	12	0	26	0.7	2.1	2.4
90-91—Philadelphia	70	1	1407	168	383	.439	12	33	.364	64	87	.736	36	116	152	311	124	0	63	95	0	412	2.2	4.4	5.9
91-92—Washington	70	3	871	111	261	.425	1	16	.063	61	77	.792	17	73	90	177	59	0	57	84	2	284	1.3	2.5	4.1
REG. SEASON TOTALS	170	4	2523	307	727	.422	14	59	.237	139	182	.764	62	201	263	535	205	0	137	212	3	767	1.5	3.1	4.5
PLAYOFF TOTALS	8	0	189	21	48	.438	3	9	.333	13	16	.813	2	11	13	35	12	0	11	8	0	58	1.6	4.4	7.3

TURNER, ELSTON HOWARD b. June 10, 1959 Ht. 6-5 Wt. 200 College—Mississippi

SEASON—TEAM	G	GS	MIN	FGM	FGA	PCT	3FGM	3FGA	PCT	FTM	FTA	PCT	O-RB	D-RB	TOT	AST	PF	DQ	STL	TO	BLK	PTS	RPG	APG	PPG
81-82—Dallas	80	62	1996	282	639	.441	0	4	.000	97	138	.703	143	158	301	189	182	1	75	116	3	661	3.8	2.4	8.3
82-83—Dallas	59	16	879	96	238	.403	2	3	.667	20	30	.667	68	84	152	88	75	0	47	59	0	214	2.6	1.5	3.6
83-84—Dallas	47	1	536	54	150	.360	1	9	.111	28	34	.824	42	51	93	59	40	0	26	29	0	137	2.0	1.3	2.9
84-85—Denver	81	2	1491	181	388	.466	1	6	.167	51	65	.785	88	128	216	158	152	0	96	70	7	414	2.7	2.0	5.1
85-86—Denver	73	0	1324	165	379	.435	0	9	.000	39	53	.736	64	137	201	165	150	1	70	80	6	369	2.8	2.3	5.1
86-87—Chicago	70	4	936	112	252	.444	1	8	.125	23	31	.742	34	81	115	102	97	1	30	31	4	248	1.6	1.5	3.5
87-88—Chicago	17	0	98	8	30	.267	0	0	—	1	2	.500	8	2	10	9	5	0	8	10	0	17	0.6	0.5	1.0
88-89—Denver	78	12	1746	151	353	.428	2	7	.286	33	56	.589	109	178	287	144	209	2	90	60	8	337	3.7	1.8	4.3
REG. SEASON TOTALS	505	97	9006	1049	2429	.432	7	46	.152	292	409	.714	556	819	1375	914	910	5	442	455	28	2397	2.7	1.8	4.7
PLAYOFF TOTALS	43	4	735	97	200	.485	3	4	.750	21	33	.636	51	79	130	86	79	1	33	35	2	218	3.0	2.0	5.1

TURNER, GARY D. b. 1945 Ht. 6-7 Wt. 200 College—Texas Christian

SEASON—TEAM	G	GS	MIN	FGM	FGA	PCT	3FGM	3FGA	PCT	FTM	FTA	PCT	O-RB	D-RB	TOT	AST	PF	DQ	STL	TO	BLK	PTS	RPG	APG	PPG
67-68—Houston (A)	2	—	21	2	2	1.000	0	0	—	2	3	.667	—	—	3	0	2	0	—	2	—	6	1.5	0.0	3.0
REG. ABA TOTALS	2	—	21	2	2	1.000	0	0	—	2	3	.667	—	—	3	0	2	0	—	2	—	6	1.5	0.0	3.0

TURNER, HENRY b. August 18, 1966 Ht. 6-7 Wt. 205 College—Cal State-Fullerton

SEASON—TEAM	G	GS	MIN	FGM	FGA	PCT	3FGM	3FGA	PCT	FTM	FTA	PCT	O-RB	D-RB	TOT	AST	PF	DQ	STL	TO	BLK	PTS	RPG	APG	PPG
89-90—Sacramento	36	1	315	58	122	.475	0	3	.000	40	65	.615	22	28	50	22	40	0	17	26	7	156	1.4	0.6	4.3
REG. SEASON TOTALS	36	1	315	58	122	.475	0	3	.000	40	65	.615	22	28	50	22	40	0	17	26	7	156	1.4	0.6	4.3

TURNER, HERSCHELL C. b. March 29, 1938 Ht. 6-2 Wt. 195 College—Nebraska

SEASON—TEAM	G	GS	MIN	FGM	FGA	PCT	3FGM	3FGA	PCT	FTM	FTA	PCT	O-RB	D-RB	TOT	AST	PF	DQ	STL	TO	BLK	PTS	RPG	APG	PPG
67-68—Pitt.-Anaheim (A)	41	—	500	51	159	.321	6	26	.231	23	47	.489	—	—	74	45	72	1	—	45	—	131	1.8	1.1	3.2
REG. ABA TOTALS	41	—	500	51	159	.321	6	26	.231	23	47	.489	—	—	74	45	72	1	—	45	—	131	1.8	1.1	3.2

TURNER, JACKIE LEE (Jack) b. June 29, 1930 Ht. 6-4 Wt. 170 College—Western Kentucky

SEASON—TEAM	G	GS	MIN	FGM	FGA	PCT	3FGM	3FGA	PCT	FTM	FTA	PCT	O-RB	D-RB	TOT	AST	PF	DQ	STL	TO	BLK	PTS	RPG	APG	PPG
54-55—New York	65	—	922	111	308	.360	—	—	—	60	76	.789	—	—	154	77	76	0	—	—	—	282	2.4	1.2	4.3
REG. SEASON TOTALS	65	—	922	111	308	.360	—	—	—	60	76	.789	—	—	154	77	76	0	—	—	—	282	2.4	1.2	4.3
PLAYOFF TOTALS	2	—	16	2	6	.333	—	—	—	1	3	.333	—	—	4	2	1	0	—	—	—	5	2.0	1.0	2.5

TURNER, JEFFREY STEVEN (**Jeff**) b. April 9, 1962 Ht. 6-9 Wt. 240 College—Vanderbilt

SEASON—TEAM	G	GS	MIN	FGM	FGA	PCT	3FGM	3FGA	PCT	FTM	FTA	PCT	O-RB	D-RB	TOT	AST	PF	DQ	STL	TO	BLK	PTS	RPG	APG	PPG
84-85—New Jersey	72	36	1429	171	377	.454	0	3	.000	79	92	.859	88	130	218	108	243	8	29	90	7	421	3.0	1.5	5.8
85-86—New Jersey	53	1	650	84	171	.491	0	1	.000	58	78	.744	45	92	137	14	125	4	21	49	3	226	2.6	0.3	4.3
86-87—New Jersey	76	22	1003	151	325	.465	0	1	.000	76	104	.731	80	117	197	60	200	6	33	81	13	378	2.6	0.8	5.0
89-90—Orlando	60	15	1105	132	308	.429	2	10	.200	42	54	.778	52	175	227	53	161	4	23	61	12	308	3.8	0.9	5.1
90-91—Orlando	71	43	1683	259	532	.487	6	15	.400	85	112	.759	108	255	363	97	234	5	29	126	10	609	5.1	1.4	8.6
91-92—Orlando	75	42	1591	225	499	.451	1	8	.125	79	114	.693	62	184	246	92	229	6	24	106	16	530	3.3	1.2	7.1
92-93—Orlando	75	20	1479	231	437	.529	10	17	.588	56	70	.800	74	178	252	107	192	2	19	66	9	528	3.4	1.4	7.0
93-94—Orlando	68	51	1536	199	426	.467	18	55	.327	35	45	.778	79	192	271	60	239	1	23	75	11	451	4.0	0.9	6.6
REG. SEASON TOTALS	550	230	10476	1452	3075	.472	37	110	.336	510	669	.762	588	1323	1911	591	1623	36	201	654	81	3451	3.5	1.1	6.3
PLAYOFF TOTALS	6	0	39	3	8	.375	0	0	—	1	1	1.000	2	5	7	5	13	0	0	4	0	7	1.2	0.8	1.2

TURNER, JOHN F. (**Jack**) b. June 5, 1939 Ht. 6-5 Wt. 200 College—Louisville

SEASON—TEAM	G	GS	MIN	FGM	FGA	PCT	3FGM	3FGA	PCT	FTM	FTA	PCT	O-RB	D-RB	TOT	AST	PF	DQ	STL	TO	BLK	PTS	RPG	APG	PPG
61-62—Chicago	42	—	567	84	221	.380	—	—	—	32	42	.762	—	—	85	44	51	0	—	—	—	200	2.0	1.0	4.8
REG. SEASON TOTALS	42	—	567	84	221	.380	—	—	—	32	42	.762	—	—	85	44	51	0	—	—	—	200	2.0	1.0	4.8

TURNER, JOHN L. b. November 30, 1967 Ht. 6-8 Wt. 245 College—Allegany CC/Georgetown/Phillips

SEASON—TEAM	G	GS	MIN	FGM	FGA	PCT	3FGM	3FGA	PCT	FTM	FTA	PCT	O-RB	D-RB	TOT	AST	PF	DQ	STL	TO	BLK	PTS	RPG	APG	PPG
91-92—Houston	42	0	345	43	98	.439	0	0	—	31	59	.525	38	40	78	12	40	0	6	32	4	117	1.9	0.3	2.8
REG. SEASON TOTALS	42	0	345	43	98	.439	0	0	—	31	59	.525	38	40	78	12	40	0	6	32	4	117	1.9	0.3	2.8

TURNER, WILLIAM R. III (**Bill**) b. February 18, 1944 Ht. 6-7 Wt. 220 College—Akron

SEASON—TEAM	G	GS	MIN	FGM	FGA	PCT	3FGM	3FGA	PCT	FTM	FTA	PCT	O-RB	D-RB	TOT	AST	PF	DQ	STL	TO	BLK	PTS	RPG	APG	PPG
67-68—San Francisco	42	—	482	68	157	.433	—	—	—	36	60	.600	—	—	155	16	74	1	—	—	—	172	3.7	0.4	4.1
68-69—San Francisco	79	—	1486	222	535	.415	—	—	—	175	230	.761	—	—	380	67	231	6	—	—	—	619	4.8	0.8	7.8
69-70—S.F.-Cin.	72	—	1170	197	468	.421	—	—	—	123	167	.737	—	—	304	43	193	3	—	—	—	517	4.2	0.6	7.2
70-71—San Francisco	18	—	200	26	82	.317	—	—	—	13	20	.650	—	—	42	8	24	0	—	—	—	65	2.3	0.4	3.6
71-72—Golden State	62	—	597	71	181	.392	—	—	—	40	53	.755	—	—	131	22	67	1	—	—	—	182	2.1	0.4	2.9
72-73—Port.-L.A.	21	—	125	19	58	.328	—	—	—	4	7	.571	—	—	27	11	16	0	—	—	—	42	1.3	0.5	2.0
REG. SEASON TOTALS	294	—	4060	603	1481	.407	—	—	—	391	537	.728	—	—	1039	167	605	11	—	—	—	1597	3.5	0.6	5.4
PLAYOFF TOTALS	22	—	284	37	87	.425	—	—	—	22	31	.710	—	—	62	16	47	2	—	—	—	96	2.8	0.7	4.4

TURPIN, MELVIN HARRISON (**Mel**) b. December 28, 1960 Ht. 6-11 Wt. 250 College—Kentucky

SEASON—TEAM	G	GS	MIN	FGM	FGA	PCT	3FGM	3FGA	PCT	FTM	FTA	PCT	O-RB	D-RB	TOT	AST	PF	DQ	STL	TO	BLK	PTS	RPG	APG	PPG
84-85—Cleveland	79	45	1949	363	711	.511	0	0	—	109	139	.784	155	297	452	36	211	3	38	118	87	835	5.7	0.5	10.6
85-86—Cleveland	80	69	2292	456	838	.544	0	4	.000	185	228	.811	182	374	556	55	260	6	65	134	106	1097	7.0	0.7	13.7
86-87—Cleveland	64	1	801	169	366	.462	0	0	—	55	77	.714	62	128	190	33	90	1	11	63	40	393	3.0	0.5	6.1
87-88—Utah	79	0	1011	199	389	.512	1	3	.333	71	98	.724	88	148	236	32	157	2	26	71	68	470	3.0	0.4	5.9
89-90—Washington	59	12	818	110	209	.526	0	2	.000	56	71	.789	88	133	221	27	135	0	15	45	47	276	3.7	0.5	4.7
REG. SEASON TOTALS	361	127	6871	1297	2513	.516	1	9	.111	476	613	.777	575	1080	1655	183	853	12	155	431	348	3071	4.6	0.5	8.5
PLAYOFF TOTALS	11	0	76	15	28	.536	0	0	—	3	4	.750	6	8	14	2	8	0	5	7	5	33	1.3	0.2	3.0

TWARDZIK, DAVE JOHN (**Pinball**) b. September 20, 1950 Ht. 6-1 Wt. 180 College—Old Dominion

SEASON—TEAM	G	GS	MIN	FGM	FGA	PCT	3FGM	3FGA	PCT	FTM	FTA	PCT	O-RB	D-RB	TOT	AST	PF	DQ	STL	TO	BLK	PTS	RPG	APG	PPG
72-73—Virginia (A)	80	—	1357	141	306	.461	2	9	.222	178	212	.840	45	113	158	184	202	1	—	122	—	462	2.0	2.3	5.8
73-74—Virginia (A)	57	—	1413	163	343	.475	3	15	.200	168	214	.785	52	129	181	170	173	—	60	118	8	497	3.2	3.0	8.7
74-75—Virginia (A)	76	—	2679	359	657	.546	1	6	.167	317	384	.826	94	153	247	404	238	—	132	266	11	1036	3.3	5.3	13.6
75-76—Virginia (A)	43	—	871	100	216	.463	3	16	.188	113	139	.813	28	61	89	125	107	—	62	93	3	316	2.1	2.9	7.3
76-77—Portland	74	—	1937	263	430	.612	—	—	—	239	284	.842	75	127	202	247	228	6	128	—	15	765	2.7	3.3	10.3
77-78—Portland	75	—	1820	242	409	.592	—	—	—	183	234	.782	36	98	134	244	186	2	107	158	4	667	1.8	3.3	8.9
78-79—Portland	64	—	1570	203	381	.533	—	—	—	261	299	.873	39	80	119	176	185	5	84	127	4	667	1.9	2.8	10.4
79-80—Portland	67	—	1594	183	394	.464	4	7	.571	197	252	.782	52	104	156	273	149	2	77	131	1	567	2.3	4.1	8.5
REG. NBA TOTALS	280	—	6921	891	1614	.552	4	7	.571	880	1069	.823	202	409	611	940	748	15	396	416	24	2666	2.2	3.4	9.5
REG. ABA TOTALS	256	—	6320	763	1522	.501	9	46	.196	776	949	.818	219	456	675	883	720	1	254	599	22	2311	2.6	3.4	9.0
NBA PLAYOFF TOTALS	25	—	559	74	134	.552	0	0	—	68	85	.800	10	29	39	62	79	3	30	22	2	216	1.6	2.5	8.6
ABA PLAYOFF TOTALS	7	—	112	10	24	.417	0	1	.000	17	21	.810	7	7	15	8	15	0	3	7	0	37	2.1	1.1	5.3
ABA ALL-STAR TOTALS	1	—	15	4	4	1.000	0	0	—	6	7	.857	1	0	1	3	6	—	4	0	0	14	1.0	3.0	14.0

TWYMAN, JOHN KENNEDY (**Jack**) b. May 11, 1934   Ht. 6-6 Wt. 210 College—Cincinnati

SEASON—TEAM	G	GS	MIN	FGM	FGA	PCT	3FGM	3FGA	PCT	FTM	FTA	PCT	O-RB	D-RB	TOT	AST	PF	DQ	STL	TO	BLK	PTS	RPG	APG	PPG
55-56—Rochester	72	—	2186	417	987	.422	—	—	—	204	298	.685	—	—	466	171	239	4	—	—	—	1038	6.5	2.4	14.4
56-57—Rochester	72	—	2338	449	1023	.439	—	—	—	276	363	.760	—	—	354	123	251	4	—	—	—	1174	4.9	1.7	16.3
57-58—Cincinnati	72	—	2178	465	1028	.452	—	—	—	307	396	.775	—	—	464	110	224	3	—	—	—	1237	6.4	1.5	17.2
58-59—Cincinnati	72	—	2713	710	1691	.420	—	—	—	437	558	.783	—	—	653	209	277	6	—	—	—	1857	9.1	2.9	25.8
59-60—Cincinnati	75	—	3023	870	2063	.422	—	—	—	598	762	.785	—	—	664	260	275	10	—	—	—	2338	8.9	3.5	31.2
60-61—Cincinnati	79	—	2920	796	1632	.488	—	—	—	405	554	.731	—	—	672	225	279	5	—	—	—	1997	8.5	2.8	25.3
61-62—Cincinnati	80	—	2991	739	1542	.479	—	—	—	353	435	.811	—	—	638	215	323	5	—	—	—	1831	8.0	2.7	22.9
62-63—Cincinnati	80	—	2623	641	1335	.480	—	—	—	304	375	.811	—	—	598	214	286	7	—	—	—	1586	7.5	2.7	19.8
63-64—Cincinnati	68	—	1996	447	993	.450	—	—	—	189	228	.829	—	—	364	137	267	7	—	—	—	1083	5.4	2.0	15.9
64-65—Cincinnati	80	—	2236	479	1081	.443	—	—	—	198	239	.828	—	—	383	137	239	4	—	—	—	1156	4.8	1.7	14.5
65-66—Cincinnati	73	—	943	224	498	.450	—	—	—	95	117	.812	—	—	168	60	122	1	—	—	—	543	2.3	0.8	7.4
REG. SEASON TOTALS	823	—	26147	6237	13873	.450	—	—	—	3366	4325	.778	—	—	5424	1861	2782	56	—	—	—	15840	6.6	2.3	19.2
PLAYOFF TOTALS	34	—	1095	245	556	.441	—	—	—	131	159	.824	—	—	255	62	131	2	—	—	—	621	7.5	1.8	18.3
ALL-STAR TOTALS	6	—	117	38	68	.559	—	—	—	13	20	.650	—	—	21	8	14	0	—	—	—	89	3.5	1.3	14.8

TYLER, TERRY CHRISTOPHER b. October 30, 1956   Ht. 6-7 Wt. 215 College—Detroit

SEASON—TEAM	G	GS	MIN	FGM	FGA	PCT	3FGM	3FGA	PCT	FTM	FTA	PCT	O-RB	D-RB	TOT	AST	PF	DQ	STL	TO	BLK	PTS	RPG	APG	PPG
78-79—Detroit	82	—	2560	456	946	.482	—	—	—	144	219	.658	211	437	648	89	254	3	104	141	201	1056	7.9	1.1	12.9
79-80—Detroit	82	—	2672	430	925	.465	2	12	.167	143	187	.765	228	399	627	129	237	3	107	175	220	1005	7.6	1.6	12.3
80-81—Detroit	82	—	2549	476	895	.532	0	8	.000	148	250	.592	198	369	567	136	215	2	112	163	180	1100	6.9	1.7	13.4
81-82—Detroit	82	0	1989	336	643	.523	1	4	.250	142	192	.740	154	339	493	126	182	1	77	121	160	815	6.0	1.5	9.9
82-83—Detroit	82	56	2543	421	880	.478	2	15	.133	146	196	.745	180	360	540	157	221	3	103	120	160	990	6.6	1.9	12.1
83-84—Detroit	82	7	1602	313	691	.453	2	13	.154	94	132	.712	104	181	285	76	151	1	63	78	59	722	3.5	0.9	8.8
84-85—Detroit	82	53	2004	422	855	.494	0	8	.000	106	148	.716	148	275	423	63	192	0	49	76	90	950	5.2	0.8	11.6
85-86—Sacramento	71	52	1651	295	649	.455	0	3	.000	84	112	.750	109	204	313	94	159	0	64	94	108	674	4.4	1.3	9.5
86-87—Sacramento	82	48	1930	329	664	.495	1	3	.333	101	140	.721	116	212	328	73	151	1	55	78	78	760	4.0	0.9	9.3
87-88—Sacramento	74	28	1185	184	407	.452	1	7	.143	41	64	.641	87	155	242	56	85	0	43	43	47	410	3.3	0.8	5.5
88-89—Dallas	70	11	1057	169	360	.469	1	9	.111	47	62	.758	74	135	209	40	90	0	24	51	39	386	3.0	0.6	5.5
REG. SEASON TOTALS	871	255	21742	3831	7915	.484	10	82	.122	1196	1702	.703	1609	3066	4675	1039	1937	14	801	1140	1342	8868	5.4	1.2	10.2
PLAYOFF TOTALS	17	2	272	61	134	.455	0	1	.000	31	40	.775	23	32	55	8	26	0	8	11	10	153	3.2	0.5	9.0

TYRA, CHARLES E. (**Charlie**) b. August 16, 1935   Ht. 6-8 Wt. 235 College—Louisville

SEASON—TEAM	G	GS	MIN	FGM	FGA	PCT	3FGM	3FGA	PCT	FTM	FTA	PCT	O-RB	D-RB	TOT	AST	PF	DQ	STL	TO	BLK	PTS	RPG	APG	PPG
57-58—New York	68	—	1182	175	490	.357	—	—	—	150	224	.670	—	—	480	34	175	3	—	—	—	500	7.1	0.5	7.4
58-59—New York	69	—	1586	240	606	.396	—	—	—	129	190	.679	—	—	485	33	180	2	—	—	—	609	7.0	0.5	8.8
59-60—New York	74	—	2033	406	952	.426	—	—	—	133	189	.704	—	—	598	80	258	8	—	—	—	945	8.1	1.1	12.8
60-61—New York	59	—	1404	199	549	.362	—	—	—	120	173	.694	—	—	394	82	164	7	—	—	—	518	6.7	1.4	8.8
61-62—Chicago	78	—	1606	193	534	.361	—	—	—	133	214	.621	—	—	610	86	210	7	—	—	—	519	7.8	1.1	6.7
REG. SEASON TOTALS	348	—	7811	1213	3131	.387	—	—	—	665	990	.672	—	—	2567	315	987	27	—	—	—	3091	7.4	0.9	8.9
PLAYOFF TOTALS	2	—	55	12	28	.429	—	—	—	6	9	.667	—	—	31	1	5	0	—	—	—	30	15.5	0.5	15.0

UNSELD, WESTLEY SISSEL (**Wes**) b. March 14, 1946   Ht. 6-7½ Wt. 245 College—Louisville

SEASON—TEAM	G	GS	MIN	FGM	FGA	PCT	3FGM	3FGA	PCT	FTM	FTA	PCT	O-RB	D-RB	TOT	AST	PF	DQ	STL	TO	BLK	PTS	RPG	APG	PPG
68-69—Baltimore	82	—	2970	427	897	.476	—	—	—	277	458	.605	—	—	1491	213	276	4	—	—	—	1131	18.2	2.6	13.8
69-70—Baltimore	82	—	3234	526	1015	.518	—	—	—	273	428	.638	—	—	1370	291	250	2	—	—	—	1325	16.7	3.5	16.2
70-71—Baltimore	74	—	2904	424	846	.501	—	—	—	199	303	.657	—	—	1253	293	235	2	—	—	—	1047	16.9	4.0	14.1
71-72—Baltimore	76	—	3171	409	822	.498	—	—	—	171	272	.629	—	—	1336	278	218	1	—	—	—	989	17.6	3.7	13.0
72-73—Baltimore	79	—	3085	421	854	.493	—	—	—	149	212	.703	—	—	1260	347	168	0	—	—	—	991	15.9	4.4	12.5
73-74—Capital	56	—	1727	146	333	.438	—	—	—	36	55	.655	152	365	517	159	121	1	56	—	16	328	9.2	2.8	5.9
74-75—Washington	73	—	2904	273	544	.502	—	—	—	126	184	.685	318	759	1077	297	180	1	115	—	68	672	14.8	4.1	9.2
75-76—Washington	78	—	2922	318	567	.561	—	—	—	114	195	.585	271	765	1036	404	203	3	84	—	59	750	13.3	5.2	9.6
76-77—Washington	82	—	2860	270	551	.490	—	—	—	100	166	.602	243	634	877	363	253	5	87	—	45	640	10.7	4.4	7.8
77-78—Washington	80	—	2644	257	491	.523	—	—	—	93	173	.538	286	669	955	326	234	2	98	173	45	607	11.9	4.1	7.6
78-79—Washington	77	—	2406	346	600	.577	—	—	—	151	235	.643	274	556	830	315	204	2	71	156	37	843	10.8	4.1	10.9
79-80—Washington	82	—	2973	327	637	.513	1	2	.500	139	209	.665	334	760	1094	366	249	5	65	153	61	794	13.3	4.5	9.7
80-81—Washington	63	—	2032	225	429	.524	2	4	.500	55	86	.640	207	466	673	170	171	1	52	97	36	507	10.7	2.7	8.0
REG. SEASON TOTALS	984	—	35832	4369	8586	.509	3	6	.500	1883	2976	.633	2085	4974	13769	3822	2762	29	628	579	367	10624	14.0	3.9	10.8
PLAYOFF TOTALS	119	—	4889	513	1040	.493	0	1	.000	234	385	.608	306	742	1777	453	371	5	67	69	55	1260	14.9	3.8	10.6
ALL-STAR TOTALS	5	—	77	14	28	.500	0	0	—	3	5	.600	2	4	36	6	10	0	2	—	0	31	7.2	1.2	6.2

UPLINGER, HAROLD F. (**Hal**) b. September 30, 1929   Ht. 6-4 Wt. 185 College—Long Island University

SEASON—TEAM	G	GS	MIN	FGM	FGA	PCT	3FGM	3FGA	PCT	FTM	FTA	PCT	O-RB	D-RB	TOT	AST	PF	DQ	STL	TO	BLK	PTS	RPG	APG	PPG
53-54—Baltimore	23	—	268	33	94	.351	—	—	—	20	22	.909	—	—	31	26	42	0	—	—	—	86	1.3	1.1	3.7
REG. SEASON TOTALS	23	—	268	33	94	.351	—	—	—	20	22	.909	—	—	31	26	42	0	—	—	—	86	1.3	1.1	3.7

UPSHAW, KELVIN PARNELL b. January 24, 1963   Ht. 6-2   Wt. 180   College—Northeastern Oklahoma A & M/Utah

SEASON—TEAM	G	GS	MIN	FGM	FGA	PCT	3FGM	3FGA	PCT	FTM	FTA	PCT	O-RB	D-RB	TOT	AST	PF	DQ	STL	TO	BLK	PTS	RPG	APG	PPG
88-89—Miami-Boston	32	0	617	99	212	.467	3	15	.200	18	26	.692	10	39	49	117	80	1	26	55	3	219	1.5	3.7	6.8
89-90—Boston-Dallas-G.S.	40	0	387	64	146	.438	4	15	.267	28	37	.757	9	32	41	54	53	0	27	27	1	160	1.0	1.4	4.0
90-91—Dallas	48	1	514	104	231	.450	7	29	.241	55	64	.859	20	35	55	86	77	0	28	39	5	270	1.1	1.8	5.6
REG. SEASON TOTALS	120	1	1518	267	589	.453	14	59	.237	101	127	.795	39	106	145	257	210	1	81	121	9	649	1.2	2.1	5.4
PLAYOFF TOTALS	3	0	24	5	12	.417	0	0	—	0	0	—	0	2	2	5	4	0	1	1	0	10	0.7	1.7	3.3

VACENDAK, STEPHEN T. (Steve) b. August 15, 1944   Ht. 6-1½   Wt. 185   College—Duke

SEASON—TEAM	G	GS	MIN	FGM	FGA	PCT	3FGM	3FGA	PCT	FTM	FTA	PCT	O-RB	D-RB	TOT	AST	PF	DQ	STL	TO	BLK	PTS	RPG	APG	PPG
67-68—Pittsburgh (A)	9	—	73	13	35	.371	0	0	—	10	15	.667	—	—	15	8	14	0	—	9	—	36	1.7	0.9	4.0
68-69—Minnesota (A)	60	—	1589	288	716	.402	2	8	.250	167	215	.777	—	—	210	166	158	1	—	139	—	745	3.5	2.8	12.4
69-70—Pitt.-Miami (A)	14	—	173	15	59	.254	0	2	.000	13	22	.591	—	—	13	20	22	0	—	—	—	43	0.9	1.4	3.1
REG. ABA TOTALS	83	—	1835	316	810	.390	2	10	.200	190	252	.754	—	—	238	194	194	1	—	148	—	824	2.9	2.3	9.9
ABA PLAYOFF TOTALS	14	—	230	41	92	.446	0	0	—	37	41	.902	—	—	20	14	26	0	—	17	—	119	1.4	1.0	8.5

VALENTINE, DARNELL TERRELL b. February 3, 1959   Ht. 6-2   Wt. 185   College—Kansas

SEASON—TEAM	G	GS	MIN	FGM	FGA	PCT	3FGM	3FGA	PCT	FTM	FTA	PCT	O-RB	D-RB	TOT	AST	PF	DQ	STL	TO	BLK	PTS	RPG	APG	PPG
81-82—Portland	82	14	1387	187	453	.413	0	9	.000	152	200	.760	48	101	149	270	187	1	94	127	3	526	1.8	3.3	6.4
82-83—Portland	47	36	1298	209	460	.454	0	1	.000	169	213	.793	34	83	117	293	139	1	101	131	5	587	2.5	6.2	12.5
83-84—Portland	68	60	1893	251	561	.447	0	3	.000	194	246	.789	49	78	127	395	179	1	107	149	6	696	1.9	5.8	10.2
84-85—Portland	75	59	2278	321	679	.473	0	2	.000	230	290	.793	54	165	219	522	189	1	143	194	5	872	2.9	7.0	11.6
85-86—Port.-L.A. Clips	62	29	1217	161	388	.415	4	14	.286	130	175	.743	32	93	125	246	123	0	72	115	2	456	2.0	4.0	7.4
86-87—L.A. Clippers	65	52	1759	275	671	.410	13	56	.232	163	200	.815	38	112	150	447	148	3	116	167	10	726	2.3	6.9	11.2
87-88—L.A. Clippers	79	31	1636	223	533	.418	15	33	.455	101	136	.743	37	119	156	382	135	0	122	148	8	562	2.0	4.8	7.1
88-89—Cleveland	77	4	1086	136	319	.426	3	14	.214	91	112	.813	22	81	103	174	88	0	57	83	7	366	1.3	2.3	4.8
90-91—Cleveland	65	60	1841	230	496	.464	6	25	.240	143	172	.831	37	135	172	351	170	2	98	126	12	609	2.6	5.4	9.4
REG. SEASON TOTALS	620	345	14395	1993	4560	.437	41	157	.261	1373	1744	.787	351	967	1318	3080	1358	9	910	1240	58	5400	2.1	5.0	8.7
PLAYOFF TOTALS	26	21	707	114	248	.460	1	2	.500	84	95	.884	17	33	50	177	79	3	40	56	4	313	1.9	6.8	12.0

VALENTINE, RONNIE L. (Ron) b. November 27, 1957   Ht. 6-7   Wt. 210   College—Old Dominion

SEASON—TEAM	G	GS	MIN	FGM	FGA	PCT	3FGM	3FGA	PCT	FTM	FTA	PCT	O-RB	D-RB	TOT	AST	PF	DQ	STL	TO	BLK	PTS	RPG	APG	PPG
80-81—Denver	24	—	123	37	98	.378	1	2	.500	9	19	.474	10	20	30	7	23	0	7	16	4	84	1.3	0.3	3.5
REG. SEASON TOTALS	24	—	123	37	98	.378	1	2	.500	9	19	.474	10	20	30	7	23	0	7	16	4	84	1.3	0.3	3.5

VALLELY, JOHN STEPHEN b. October 3, 1948   Ht. 6-3   Wt. 185   College—Orange Coast/UCLA

SEASON—TEAM	G	GS	MIN	FGM	FGA	PCT	3FGM	3FGA	PCT	FTM	FTA	PCT	O-RB	D-RB	TOT	AST	PF	DQ	STL	TO	BLK	PTS	RPG	APG	PPG
70-71—Atlanta	51	—	430	73	204	.358	—	—	—	45	59	.763	—	—	34	47	50	0	—	—	—	191	0.7	0.9	3.7
71-72—Atlanta-Houston	49	—	366	69	171	.404	—	—	—	30	45	.667	—	—	32	37	50	0	—	—	—	168	0.7	0.8	3.4
REG. SEASON TOTALS	100	—	796	142	375	.379	—	—	—	75	104	.721	—	—	66	84	100	0	—	—	—	359	0.7	0.8	3.6

VAN ARSDALE, RICHARD ALBERT (Dick) b. February 22, 1943   Ht. 6-4½   Wt. 210   College—Indiana

SEASON—TEAM	G	GS	MIN	FGM	FGA	PCT	3FGM	3FGA	PCT	FTM	FTA	PCT	O-RB	D-RB	TOT	AST	PF	DQ	STL	TO	BLK	PTS	RPG	APG	PPG
65-66—New York	79	—	2289	359	838	.428	—	—	—	251	351	.715	—	—	376	184	235	5	—	—	—	969	4.8	2.3	12.3
66-67—New York	79	—	2892	410	913	.449	—	—	—	371	509	.729	—	—	555	247	264	3	—	—	—	1191	7.0	3.1	15.1
67-68—New York	78	—	2348	316	725	.436	—	—	—	227	339	.670	—	—	424	230	225	0	—	—	—	859	5.4	2.9	11.0
68-69—Phoenix	80	—	3388	612	1386	.442	—	—	—	454	644	.705	—	—	548	388	245	2	—	—	—	1678	6.9	4.9	21.0
69-70—Phoenix	77	—	2966	592	1166	.508	—	—	—	459	575	.798	—	—	264	338	282	5	—	—	—	1643	3.4	4.4	21.3
70-71—Phoenix	81	—	3157	609	1346	.452	—	—	—	553	682	.811	—	—	316	329	246	1	—	—	—	1771	3.9	4.1	21.9
71-72—Phoenix	82	—	3096	545	1178	.463	—	—	—	529	626	.845	—	—	334	297	232	1	—	—	—	1619	4.1	3.6	19.7
72-73—Phoenix	81	—	2979	532	1118	.476	—	—	—	426	496	.859	—	—	326	268	221	2	—	—	—	1490	4.0	3.3	18.4
73-74—Phoenix	78	—	2832	514	1028	.500	—	—	—	361	423	.853	66	155	221	324	241	2	96	—	17	1389	2.8	4.2	17.8
74-75—Phoenix	70	—	2419	421	895	.470	—	—	—	282	339	.832	52	137	189	195	177	2	81	—	11	1124	2.7	2.8	16.1
75-76—Phoenix	58	—	1870	276	570	.484	—	—	—	195	235	.830	39	98	137	140	113	2	52	—	11	747	2.4	2.4	12.9
76-77—Phoenix	78	—	1535	227	498	.456	—	—	—	145	166	.873	31	86	117	120	94	0	35	—	5	599	1.5	1.5	7.7
REG. SEASON TOTALS	921	—	31771	5413	11661	.464	—	—	—	4253	5385	.790	188	476	3807	3060	2575	25	264	—	44	15079	4.1	3.3	16.4
PLAYOFF TOTALS	34	—	968	124	294	.422	—	—	—	88	105	.838	10	13	82	94	89	1	13	—	2	336	2.4	2.8	9.9
ALL-STAR TOTALS	3	—	38	8	16	.500	—	—	—	0	1	.000	0	0	8	5	1	0	0	—	0	16	2.7	1.7	5.3

VAN ARSDALE, THOMAS ARTHUR (Tom) b. February 22, 1943 Ht. 6-5 Wt. 215 College—Indiana

SEASON—TEAM	G	GS	MIN	FGM	FGA	PCT	3FGM	3FGA	PCT	FTM	FTA	PCT	O-RB	D-RB	TOT	AST	PF	DQ	STL	TO	BLK	PTS	RPG	APG	PPG
65-66—Detroit	79	—	2041	312	834	.374	—	—	—	209	290	.721	—	—	309	205	251	1	—	—	—	833	3.9	2.6	10.5
66-67—Detroit	79	—	2134	347	887	.391	—	—	—	272	347	.784	—	—	341	193	241	3	—	—	—	966	4.3	2.4	12.2
67-68—Detroit-Cin.	77	—	1514	211	545	.387	—	—	—	188	252	.746	—	—	225	155	202	5	—	—	—	610	2.9	2.0	7.9
68-69—Cincinnati	77	—	3059	547	1233	.444	—	—	—	398	533	.747	—	—	356	208	300	6	—	—	—	1492	4.6	2.7	19.4
69-70—Cincinnati	71	—	2544	620	1376	.451	—	—	—	381	492	.774	—	—	463	155	247	3	—	—	—	1621	6.5	2.2	22.8
70-71—Cincinnati	82	—	3146	749	1642	.456	—	—	—	377	523	.721	—	—	499	181	294	3	—	—	—	1875	6.1	2.2	22.9
71-72—Cincinnati	73	—	2598	550	1205	.456	—	—	—	299	396	.755	—	—	350	198	241	1	—	—	—	1399	4.8	2.7	19.2
72-73—K.C. Omaha-Phil.	79	—	2311	445	1043	.427	—	—	—	250	308	.812	—	—	358	152	224	2	—	—	—	1140	4.5	1.9	14.4
73-74—Philadelphia	78	—	3041	614	1433	.428	—	—	—	298	350	.851	88	305	393	202	300	6	62	—	3	1526	5.0	2.6	19.6
74-75—Phil.-Atlanta	82	—	2843	593	1385	.428	—	—	—	322	424	.759	77	201	278	223	257	5	91	—	3	1508	3.4	2.7	18.4
75-76—Atlanta	75	—	2026	346	785	.441	—	—	—	126	166	.759	35	151	186	146	202	5	57	—	7	818	2.5	1.9	10.9
76-77—Phoenix	77	—	1425	171	395	.433	—	—	—	102	145	.703	47	137	184	67	163	0	20	—	3	444	2.4	0.9	5.8
REG. SEASON TOTALS	929	—	28682	5505	12763	.431	—	—	—	3222	4226	.762	247	794	3942	2085	2922	40	230	—	16	14232	4.2	2.2	15.3
ALL-STAR TOTALS	3	—	23	6	16	.375	—	—	—	1	3	.333	0	0	3	2	3	0	0	—	0	13	1.0	0.7	4.3

VAN BREDA KOLFF, JAN MICHAEL (V.B.K.) b. December 16, 1951 Ht. 6-7 Wt. 200 College—Vanderbilt

SEASON—TEAM	G	GS	MIN	FGM	FGA	PCT	3FGM	3FGA	PCT	FTM	FTA	PCT	O-RB	D-RB	TOT	AST	PF	DQ	STL	TO	BLK	PTS	RPG	APG	PPG
74-75—Denver (A)	84	—	1639	155	342	.453	0	3	.000	177	211	.839	121	237	358	181	164	—	48	122	43	487	4.3	2.2	5.8
75-76—Vir.-Ken. (A)	80	—	1978	223	488	.457	2	6	.333	165	198	.833	144	292	436	182	164	—	65	144	96	613	5.5	2.3	7.7
76-77—New York Nets	72	—	2398	271	609	.445	—	—	—	195	228	.855	156	304	460	117	205	2	74	—	68	737	6.4	1.6	10.2
77-78—New Jersey	68	—	1419	107	292	.366	—	—	—	87	123	.707	66	178	244	105	192	7	52	73	46	301	3.6	1.5	4.4
78-79—New Jersey	80	—	1998	196	423	.463	—	—	—	146	183	.798	108	274	382	180	235	4	85	135	74	538	4.8	2.3	6.7
79-80—New Jersey	82	—	2399	212	458	.463	7	20	.350	130	155	.839	103	326	429	247	307	11	100	158	76	561	5.2	3.0	6.8
80-81—New Jersey	78	—	1426	100	245	.408	2	8	.250	98	117	.838	48	154	202	129	214	3	38	108	50	300	2.6	1.7	3.8
81-82—New Jersey	41	0	452	41	82	.500	0	2	.000	62	76	.816	17	31	48	32	63	1	12	29	13	144	1.2	0.8	3.5
82-83—New Jersey	13	0	63	5	14	.357	0	0	—	5	6	.833	2	11	13	5	9	0	2	3	2	15	1.0	0.4	1.2
REG. NBA TOTALS	434	0	10155	932	2123	.439	9	30	.300	723	888	.814	500	1278	1778	815	1225	28	363	506	329	2596	4.1	1.9	6.0
REG. ABA TOTALS	164	—	3617	378	830	.455	2	9	.222	342	409	.836	265	529	794	363	328	—	113	266	139	1100	4.8	2.2	6.7
NBA PLAYOFF TOTALS	4	0	97	8	21	.381	0	0	—	5	6	.833	11	12	23	7	9	0	2	6	4	21	5.8	1.8	5.3
ABA PLAYOFF TOTALS	22	—	378	38	80	.475	0	0	—	40	45	.889	35	41	76	31	39	—	10	25	11	116	3.5	1.4	5.3

VAN BREDA KOLFF, WILLEM H. (Butch) b. October 28, 1922 Ht. 6-3 Wt. 185 College—Princeton/New York University

SEASON—TEAM	G	GS	MIN	FGM	FGA	PCT	3FGM	3FGA	PCT	FTM	FTA	PCT	O-RB	D-RB	TOT	AST	PF	DQ	STL	TO	BLK	PTS	RPG	APG	PPG
46-47—New York	16	—	—	7	34	.206	—	—	—	11	17	.647	—	—	—	6	10	—	—	—	—	25	—	0.4	1.6
47-48—New York	44	—	—	53	192	.276	—	—	—	74	120	.617	—	—	—	29	81	—	—	—	—	180	—	0.7	4.1
48-49—New York	59	—	—	127	401	.317	—	—	—	161	240	.671	—	—	—	143	148	—	—	—	—	415	—	2.4	7.0
49-50—New York	56	—	—	55	167	.329	—	—	—	96	134	.716	—	—	—	78	111	—	—	—	—	206	—	1.4	3.7
REG. SEASON TOTALS	175	—	—	242	794	.305	—	—	—	342	511	.669	—	—	—	256	350	—	—	—	—	826	—	1.5	4.7
PLAYOFF TOTALS	15	—	—	28	88	.318	—	—	—	36	50	.720	—	—	—	13	29	—	—	—	—	92	—	0.9	6.1

VANCE, ELLIS EUGENE (Gene) b. February 25, 1923 Ht. 6-3 Wt. 195 College—Illinois

SEASON—TEAM	G	GS	MIN	FGM	FGA	PCT	3FGM	3FGA	PCT	FTM	FTA	PCT	O-RB	D-RB	TOT	AST	PF	DQ	STL	TO	BLK	PTS	RPG	APG	PPG
47-48—Chicago	48	—	—	163	617	.264	—	—	—	76	126	.603	—	—	—	49	193	—	—	—	—	402	—	1.0	8.4
48-49—Chicago	56	—	—	222	657	.338	—	—	—	131	181	.724	—	—	—	167	217	—	—	—	—	575	—	3.0	10.3
49-50—Tri-Cities	35	—	—	110	325	.338	—	—	—	86	120	.717	—	—	—	121	145	—	—	—	—	306	—	3.5	8.7
50-51—Tri-Cities	28	—	—	44	110	.400	—	—	—	43	61	.705	—	—	88	53	91	0	—	—	—	131	3.1	1.9	4.7
51-52—Milwaukee	7	—	118	7	26	.269	—	—	—	9	14	.643	—	—	15	9	18	0	—	—	—	23	2.1	1.3	3.3
REG. SEASON TOTALS	174	—	118	546	1735	.315	—	—	—	345	502	.687	—	—	103	399	664	0	—	—	—	1437	2.9	2.3	8.3
PLAYOFF TOTALS	10	—	0	32	132	.242	—	—	—	23	33	.697	—	—	—	17	43	3	—	—	—	87	—	1.7	8.7

VANDEWEGHE, ERNEST MAURICE III (Kiki) b. August 1, 1958 Ht. 6-8 Wt. 220 College—UCLA

SEASON—TEAM	G	GS	MIN	FGM	FGA	PCT	3FGM	3FGA	PCT	FTM	FTA	PCT	O-RB	D-RB	TOT	AST	PF	DQ	STL	TO	BLK	PTS	RPG	APG	PPG
80-81—Denver	51	—	1376	229	537	.426	0	7	.000	130	159	.818	86	184	270	94	116	0	29	86	24	588	5.3	1.8	11.5
81-82—Denver	82	78	2775	706	1260	.560	1	13	.077	347	405	.857	149	312	461	247	217	1	52	189	29	1760	5.6	3.0	21.5
82-83—Denver	82	79	2909	841	1537	.547	15	51	.294	489	559	.875	124	313	437	203	198	0	66	177	38	2186	5.3	2.5	26.7
83-84—Denver	78	71	2734	895	1603	.558	11	30	.367	494	580	.852	84	289	373	238	187	1	53	156	50	2295	4.8	3.1	29.4
84-85—Portland	72	69	2502	618	1158	.534	11	33	.333	369	412	.896	74	154	228	106	116	0	37	116	22	1616	3.2	1.5	22.4
85-86—Portland	79	76	2791	719	1332	.540	1	8	.125	523	602	.869	92	124	216	187	161	0	54	177	17	1962	2.7	2.4	24.8
86-87—Portland	79	79	3029	808	1545	.523	39	81	.481	467	527	.886	86	165	251	220	137	0	52	139	17	2122	3.2	2.8	26.9
87-88—Portland	37	7	1038	283	557	.508	22	58	.379	159	181	.878	36	73	109	71	68	0	21	48	7	747	2.9	1.9	20.2
88-89—Port.-N.Y.	45	1	934	200	426	.469	19	48	.396	80	89	.899	26	45	71	69	78	0	19	41	11	499	1.6	1.5	11.1
89-90—New York	22	15	563	102	231	.442	10	19	.526	44	48	.917	15	38	53	41	28	0	15	26	3	258	2.4	1.9	11.7
90-91—New York	75	72	2420	458	927	.494	51	141	.362	259	288	.899	78	102	180	110	122	0	42	108	10	1226	2.4	1.5	16.3
91-92—New York	67	0	956	188	383	.491	26	66	.394	65	81	.802	31	57	88	57	87	0	15	27	8	467	1.3	0.9	7.0
92-93—L.A. Clippers	41	3	494	92	203	.453	12	37	.324	58	66	.879	12	36	48	25	45	0	13	20	7	254	1.2	0.6	6.2
REG. SEASON TOTALS	810	548	24521	6139	11699	.525	218	592	.368	3484	3997	.872	893	1892	2785	1668	1560	2	468	1310	243	15980	3.4	2.1	19.7
PLAYOFF TOTALS	68	46	1890	419	822	.510	20	58	.345	235	259	.907	53	135	188	134	132	1	39	89	27	1093	2.8	2.0	16.1
ALL-STAR TOTALS	2	0	40	10	17	.588	0	0	—	1	2	.500	1	5	6	2	2	0	1	0	0	21	3.0	1.0	10.5

VANDEWEGHE, ERNEST MAURICE JR. (**Ernie, Doc**) b. September 12, 1928   Ht. 6-3 Wt. 195 College—Colgate

SEASON—TEAM	G	GS	MIN	FGM	FGA	PCT	3FGM	3FGA	PCT	FTM	FTA	PCT	O-RB	D-RB	TOT	AST	PF	DQ	STL	TO	BLK	PTS	RPG	APG	PPG
49-50—New York	42	—	—	164	390	.421	—	—	—	93	140	.664	—	—	—	78	126	—	—	—	—	421	—	1.9	10.0
50-51—New York	44	—	—	135	336	.402	—	—	—	68	97	.701	—	—	195	121	144	6	—	—	—	338	4.4	2.8	7.7
51-52—New York	57	—	1507	200	457	.438	—	—	—	124	160	.775	—	—	264	164	188	3	—	—	—	524	4.6	2.9	9.2
52-53—New York	61	—	1745	272	625	.435	—	—	—	187	244	.766	—	—	342	144	242	11	—	—	—	731	5.6	2.4	12.0
53-54—New York	15	—	271	37	103	.359	—	—	—	25	31	.806	—	—	39	29	38	1	—	—	—	99	2.6	1.9	6.6
55-56—New York	5	—	77	10	31	.323	—	—	—	2	2	1.000	—	—	13	12	15	0	—	—	—	22	2.6	2.4	4.4
REG. SEASON TOTALS	224	—	3600	818	1942	.421	—	—	—	499	674	.740	—	—	853	548	753	21			—	2135	4.7	2.4	9.5
PLAYOFF TOTALS	43	—	754	146	347	.421	—	—	—	136	174	.782	—	—	199	91	179	5	—	—	—	428	5.1	2.1	10.0

VAN EXEL, NICKEY MAXWELL (**Nick**) b. November 27, 1971   Ht. 6-1 Wt. 170 College—Trinity Valley CC/Cincinnati

SEASON—TEAM	G	GS	MIN	FGM	FGA	PCT	3FGM	3FGA	PCT	FTM	FTA	PCT	O-RB	D-RB	TOT	AST	PF	DQ	STL	TO	BLK	PTS	RPG	APG	PPG
93-94—L.A. Lakers	81	80	2700	413	1049	.394	123	364	.338	150	192	.781	47	191	238	466	154	1	85	145	8	1099	2.9	5.8	13.6
REG. SEASON TOTALS	81	80	2700	413	1049	.394	123	364	.338	150	192	.781	47	191	238	466	154	1	85	145	8	1099	2.9	5.8	13.6

VAN LIER, NORMAN ALLEN III (**Norm**) b. April 1, 1947   Ht. 6-2 Wt. 175 College—St. Francis (Pa.)

SEASON—TEAM	G	GS	MIN	FGM	FGA	PCT	3FGM	3FGA	PCT	FTM	FTA	PCT	O-RB	D-RB	TOT	AST	PF	DQ	STL	TO	BLK	PTS	RPG	APG	PPG
69-70—Cincinnati	81	—	2895	302	749	.403	—	—	—	166	224	.741	—	—	409	500	329	18	—	—	—	770	5.0	6.2	9.5
70-71—Cincinnati	82	—	3324	478	1138	.420	—	—	—	359	440	.816	—	—	583	832	343	12	—	—	—	1315	7.1	10.1	16.0
71-72—Cin.-Chicago	79	—	2415	334	761	.439	—	—	—	237	300	.790	—	—	357	542	239	5	—	—	—	905	4.5	6.9	11.5
72-73—Chicago	80	—	2882	474	1064	.445	—	—	—	166	211	.787	—	—	438	567	269	5	—	—	—	1114	5.5	7.1	13.9
73-74—Chicago	80	—	2863	427	1051	.406	—	—	—	288	370	.778	114	263	377	548	282	4	162	—	7	1142	4.7	6.9	14.3
74-75—Chicago	70	—	2590	407	970	.420	—	—	—	236	298	.792	86	242	328	403	246	5	139	—	14	1050	4.7	5.8	15.0
75-76—Chicago	76	—	3026	361	987	.366	—	—	—	235	319	.737	138	272	410	500	298	9	150	—	26	957	5.4	6.6	12.6
76-77—Chicago	82	—	3097	300	729	.412	—	—	—	238	306	.778	108	262	370	636	268	3	129	—	16	838	4.5	7.8	10.2
77-78—Chicago	78	—	2524	200	477	.419	—	—	—	172	229	.751	86	198	284	531	279	9	144	200	5	572	3.6	6.8	7.3
78-79—Milwaukee	38	—	555	30	77	.390	—	—	—	47	52	.904	8	32	40	158	108	4	43	49	3	107	1.1	4.2	2.8
REG. SEASON TOTALS	746	—	26171	3313	8003	.414	—	—	—	2144	2749	.780	540	1269	3596	5217	2661	74	767	249	71	8770	4.8	7.0	11.8
PLAYOFF TOTALS	38	—	1549	198	509	.389	—	—	—	134	171	.784	34	95	191	234	154	5	47	—	9	530	5.0	6.2	13.9
ALL-STAR TOTALS	3	—	37	2	7	.286	—	—	—	1	2	.500	2	1	3	3	5	0	2	—	1	5	1.0	1.0	1.7

VANOS, NICHOLAS (**Nick**) b. April 13, 1963 d. August 16, 1987 Ht. 7-2 Wt. 260 College—Cal State-Santa Clara

SEASON—TEAM	G	GS	MIN	FGM	FGA	PCT	3FGM	3FGA	PCT	FTM	FTA	PCT	O-RB	D-RB	TOT	AST	PF	DQ	STL	TO	BLK	PTS	RPG	APG	PPG
85-86—Phoenix	11	0	202	23	72	.319	0	0	—	8	23	.348	21	39	60	16	34	0	2	20	5	54	5.5	1.5	4.9
86-87—Phoenix	57	14	640	65	158	.411	0	2	.000	38	59	.644	67	113	180	43	94	0	19	48	23	168	3.2	0.8	2.9
REG. SEASON TOTALS	68	14	842	88	230	.383	0	2	.000	46	82	.561	88	152	240	59	128	0	21	68	28	222	3.5	0.9	3.3

VAN ZANT, DENNIS b. June 1, 1952   Ht. 6-9 Wt. 210 College—Azusa Pacific

SEASON—TEAM	G	GS	MIN	FGM	FGA	PCT	3FGM	3FGA	PCT	FTM	FTA	PCT	O-RB	D-RB	TOT	AST	PF	DQ	STL	TO	BLK	PTS	RPG	APG	PPG
75-76—San Antonio (A)	1	—	2	0	0	—	0	0	—	2	2	1.000	0	1	1	0	1	—	0	0	0	2	1.0	0.0	2.0
REG. ABA TOTALS	1	—	2	0	0	—	0	0	—	2	2	1.000	0	1	1	0	1	—	0	0	0	2	1.0	0.0	2.0

VAUGHN, CHARLES (**Chico**) b. February 19, 1940   Ht. 6-3 Wt. 215 College—Southern Illinois

SEASON—TEAM	G	GS	MIN	FGM	FGA	PCT	3FGM	3FGA	PCT	FTM	FTA	PCT	O-RB	D-RB	TOT	AST	PF	DQ	STL	TO	BLK	PTS	RPG	APG	PPG
62-63—St. Louis	77	—	1845	295	708	.417	—	—	—	188	261	.720	—	—	258	252	201	3	—	—	—	778	3.4	3.3	10.1
63-64—St. Louis	68	—	1340	238	538	.442	—	—	—	107	148	.723	—	—	126	129	166	0	—	—	—	583	1.9	1.9	8.6
64-65—St. Louis	75	—	1965	344	811	.424	—	—	—	182	242	.752	—	—	173	157	192	2	—	—	—	870	2.3	2.1	11.6
65-66—St. L.-Detroit	56	—	1219	182	474	.384	—	—	—	106	144	.736	—	—	109	140	99	1	—	—	—	470	1.9	2.5	8.4
66-67—Detroit	50	—	680	85	226	.376	—	—	—	50	74	.676	—	—	67	75	54	0	—	—	—	220	1.3	1.5	4.4
67-68—Pittsburgh (A)	74	—	2858	512	1350	.379	137	410	.334	308	416	.740	—	—	298	142	203	0	—	171	—	1469	4.0	1.9	19.9
68-69—Minnesota (A)	69	—	2301	415	1170	.355	145	523	.277	253	329	.769	—	—	165	107	178	1	—	150	—	1228	2.4	1.6	17.8
69-70—Pittsburgh (A)	21	—	401	66	180	.367	24	82	.293	48	70	.686	—	—	28	22	53	1	—	—	—	204	1.3	1.0	9.7
REG. NBA TOTALS	326	—	7049	1144	2757	.415	—	—	—	633	869	.728	—	—	733	753	712	6	—	—	—	2921	2.2	2.3	9.0
REG. ABA TOTALS	164	—	5560	993	2700	.368	306	1015	.301	609	815	.747	—	—	491	271	434	2	—	321	—	2901	3.0	1.7	17.7
NBA PLAYOFF TOTALS	27	—	631	98	226	.434	—	—	—	44	61	.721	—	—	62	62	91	2	—	—	—	240	2.3	2.3	8.9
ABA PLAYOFF TOTALS	20	—	633	101	293	.345	30	114	.263	68	85	.800	—	—	59	45	58	1	—	35	—	300	3.0	2.3	15.0
ABA ALL-STAR TOTALS	1	—	4	2	2	1.000	2	2	1.000	0	0	—	—	—	0	0	0	0	—	1	—	6	0.0	0.0	6.0

VAUGHN, DAVID b. June 4, 1952   Ht. 7-0 Wt. 220 College—Nevada-Las Vegas/Oral Roberts

SEASON—TEAM	G	GS	MIN	FGM	FGA	PCT	3FGM	3FGA	PCT	FTM	FTA	PCT	O-RB	D-RB	TOT	AST	PF	DQ	STL	TO	BLK	PTS	RPG	APG	PPG
74-75—Virginia (A)	83	—	2507	422	998	.423	0	2	.000	125	229	.546	276	618	894	132	274	—	79	195	126	969	10.8	1.6	11.7
75-76—Virginia (A)	10	—	86	12	33	.364	0	0	—	5	8	.625	8	11	19	3	15	—	0	5	2	29	1.9	0.3	2.9
REG. ABA TOTALS	93	—	2593	434	1031	.421	0	2	.000	130	237	.549	284	629	913	135	289	—	79	200	128	998	9.8	1.5	10.7

VAUGHN, VIRGIL V. b. May 15, 1918 Ht. 6-4 Wt. 205 College—Kentucky Wesleyan

SEASON—TEAM	G	GS	MIN	FGM	FGA	PCT	3FGM	3FGA	PCT	FTM	FTA	PCT	O-RB	D-RB	TOT	AST	PF	DQ	STL	TO	BLK	PTS	RPG	APG	PPG
46-47—Boston	17	—	—	15	78	.192	—	—	—	15	28	.536	—	—	—	10	18	—	—	—	—	45	—	0.6	2.6
47-48—Syracuse (N)	11	—	—	29	—	—	—	—	—	5	9	.556	—	—	—	—	—	—	—	—	—	63	—	—	5.7
REG. NBA TOTALS	17	—	—	15	78	.192	—	—	—	15	28	.536	—	—	—	10	18	—	—	—	—	45	—	0.6	2.6
REG. NBL TOTALS	11	—	—	29	—	—	—	—	—	5	9	.556	—	—	—	—	—	—	—	—	—	63	—	—	5.7
NBL PLAYOFF TOTALS	3	—	—	2	—	—	—	—	—	6	11	.545	—	—	—	3	—	—	—	—	—	10	—	—	3.3

VAUGHT, LOY STEPHEN b. February 27, 1967 Ht. 6-9 Wt. 240 College—Michigan

SEASON—TEAM	G	GS	MIN	FGM	FGA	PCT	3FGM	3FGA	PCT	FTM	FTA	PCT	O-RB	D-RB	TOT	AST	PF	DQ	STL	TO	BLK	PTS	RPG	APG	PPG
90-91—L.A. Clippers	73	0	1178	175	359	.487	0	2	.000	49	74	.662	124	225	349	40	135	2	20	49	23	399	4.8	0.5	5.5
91-92—L.A. Clippers	79	38	1687	271	551	.492	4	5	.800	55	69	.797	160	352	512	71	165	1	37	66	31	601	6.5	0.9	7.6
92-93—L.A. Clippers	79	4	1653	313	616	.508	1	4	.250	116	155	.748	164	328	492	54	172	2	55	83	39	743	6.2	0.7	9.4
93-94—L.A. Clippers	75	56	2118	373	695	.537	0	5	.000	131	182	.720	218	438	656	74	221	5	76	96	22	877	8.7	1.0	11.7
REG. SEASON TOTALS	306	98	6636	1132	2221	.510	5	16	.313	351	480	.731	666	1343	2009	239	693	10	188	294	115	2620	6.6	0.8	8.6
PLAYOFF TOTALS	8	0	86	13	26	.500	1	1	1.000	6	7	.857	6	24	30	4	10	0	5	4	2	33	3.8	0.5	4.1

VERGA, ROBERT BRUCE (Bob) b. September 7, 1945 Ht. 6-1 Wt. 190 College—Duke

SEASON—TEAM	G	GS	MIN	FGM	FGA	PCT	3FGM	3FGA	PCT	FTM	FTA	PCT	O-RB	D-RB	TOT	AST	PF	DQ	STL	TO	BLK	PTS	RPG	APG	PPG
67-68—Dallas (A)	31	—	1285	280	633	.442	13	50	.260	162	218	.743	—	—	138	74	93	1	—	95	—	735	4.5	2.4	23.7
68-69—Denver-N.Y.-Houston (A)	63	—	1804	416	1006	.414	19	68	.279	336	454	.740	—	—	233	188	200	1	—	195	—	1187	3.7	3.0	18.8
69-70—Carolina (A)	82	—	3411	867	1984	.437	66	215	.307	458	565	.811	—	—	430	290	268	3	—	—	—	2258	5.2	3.5	27.5
70-71—Carolina (A)	75	—	2009	550	1202	.458	10	44	.227	302	419	.721	—	—	280	182	223	—	—	—	—	1412	3.7	2.4	18.8
71-72—Car.-Pitt. (A)	70	—	2029	459	1046	.439	19	52	.365	285	398	.716	—	—	237	253	198	—	—	224	—	1222	3.4	3.6	17.5
73-74—Portland	21	—	216	42	93	.452	—	—	—	20	32	.625	11	7	18	17	22	0	12	—	0	104	0.9	0.8	5.0
REG. NBA TOTALS	21	—	216	42	93	.452	—	—	—	20	32	.625	11	7	18	17	22	0	12	—	0	104	0.9	0.8	5.0
REG. ABA TOTALS	321	—	10538	2572	5871	.438	127	429	.296	1543	2054	.751	—	—	1318	987	982	5	—	514	—	6814	4.1	3.1	21.2
ABA PLAYOFF TOTALS	4	—	156	48	102	.471	4	16	.250	8	11	.727	—	—	11	10	14	0	—	—	—	108	2.8	2.5	27.0
ABA ALL-STAR TOTALS	1	—	16	6	14	.429	1	3	.333	1	2	.500	—	—	5	2	1	0	—	0	—	14	5.0	2.0	14.0

VERHOEVEN, PETER GERARD b. February 15, 1959 Ht. 6-9 Wt. 220 College—Fresno State

SEASON—TEAM	G	GS	MIN	FGM	FGA	PCT	3FGM	3FGA	PCT	FTM	FTA	PCT	O-RB	D-RB	TOT	AST	PF	DQ	STL	TO	BLK	PTS	RPG	APG	PPG
81-82—Portland	71	22	1207	149	296	.503	0	0	—	51	72	.708	106	148	254	52	215	4	42	55	22	349	3.6	0.7	4.9
82-83—Portland	48	0	527	87	171	.509	0	1	.000	21	31	.677	44	52	96	32	95	2	18	40	9	195	2.0	0.7	4.1
83-84—Portland	43	0	327	50	100	.500	0	1	.000	17	25	.680	27	34	61	20	75	0	22	21	11	117	1.4	0.5	2.7
84-85—Kansas City	54	0	366	51	108	.472	0	0	—	21	25	.840	28	35	63	17	85	1	15	20	7	123	1.2	0.3	2.3
85-86—Golden State	61	5	749	90	167	.539	1	2	.500	25	43	.581	65	95	160	29	141	3	29	30	17	206	2.6	0.5	3.4
86-87—Indiana	5	0	44	5	14	.357	0	0	—	0	0	—	2	5	7	2	11	1	2	0	1	10	1.4	0.4	2.0
REG. SEASON TOTALS	282	27	3220	432	856	.505	1	4	.250	135	196	.689	272	369	641	152	622	11	128	166	67	1000	2.3	0.5	3.5
PLAYOFF TOTALS	3	0	19	0	0	—	0	0	—	2	2	1.000	0	0	0	—	10	0	1	1	0	2	0.0	0.0	0.7

VETRA, GUNDARS b. May 22, 1967 Ht. 6-6 Wt. 195 College—None

SEASON—TEAM	G	GS	MIN	FGM	FGA	PCT	3FGM	3FGA	PCT	FTM	FTA	PCT	O-RB	D-RB	TOT	AST	PF	DQ	STL	TO	BLK	PTS	RPG	APG	PPG
92-93—Minnesota	13	0	89	19	40	.475	3	3	1.000	4	6	.667	4	4	8	6	12	0	2	2	0	45	0.6	0.5	3.5
REG. SEASON TOTALS	13	0	89	19	40	.475	3	3	1.000	4	6	.667	4	4	8	6	12	0	2	2	0	45	0.6	0.5	3.5

VIANNA, JOAO b. November 15, 1966 Ht. 6-9 Wt. 215 College—None

SEASON—TEAM	G	GS	MIN	FGM	FGA	PCT	3FGM	3FGA	PCT	FTM	FTA	PCT	O-RB	D-RB	TOT	AST	PF	DQ	STL	TO	BLK	PTS	RPG	APG	PPG
91-92—Dallas	1	0	9	1	2	.500	0	0	—	0	0	—	0	0	0	2	3	0	0	1	0	2	0.0	2.0	2.0
REG. SEASON TOTALS	1	0	9	1	2	.500	0	0	—	0	0	—	0	0	0	2	3	0	0	1	0	2	0.0	2.0	2.0

VINCENT, JAMES SAMUEL (Sam) b. May 18, 1963 Ht. 6-2 Wt. 185 College—Michigan State

SEASON—TEAM	G	GS	MIN	FGM	FGA	PCT	3FGM	3FGA	PCT	FTM	FTA	PCT	O-RB	D-RB	TOT	AST	PF	DQ	STL	TO	BLK	PTS	RPG	APG	PPG
85-86—Boston	57	0	432	59	162	.364	1	4	.250	65	70	.929	11	37	48	69	59	0	17	49	4	184	0.8	1.2	3.2
86-87—Boston	46	5	374	60	136	.441	0	0	—	51	55	.927	5	22	27	59	33	0	13	33	1	171	0.6	1.3	3.7
87-88—Seattle-Chicago	72	27	1501	210	461	.456	8	21	.381	145	167	.868	35	117	152	381	145	0	55	136	16	573	2.1	5.3	8.0
88-89—Chicago	70	56	1703	274	566	.484	2	17	.118	106	129	.822	34	156	190	335	124	0	53	142	10	656	2.7	4.8	9.4
89-90—Orlando	63	45	1657	258	564	.457	1	14	.071	188	214	.879	37	157	194	354	108	1	65	132	20	705	3.1	5.6	11.2
90-91—Orlando	49	17	975	152	353	.431	3	19	.158	99	120	.825	17	90	107	197	74	0	30	91	5	406	2.2	4.0	8.3
91-92—Orlando	39	18	885	150	349	.430	1	13	.077	110	130	.846	19	82	101	148	55	1	35	72	4	411	2.6	3.8	10.5
REG. SEASON TOTALS	396	168	7527	1163	2591	.449	16	88	.182	764	885	.863	158	661	819	1543	598	2	268	655	60	3106	2.1	3.9	7.8
PLAYOFF TOTALS	52	10	546	82	227	.361	1	8	.125	62	78	.795	14	32	46	87	54	0	16	47	4	227	0.9	1.7	4.4

VINCENT, JAY FLETCHER b. June 10, 1959 Ht. 6-8 Wt. 220 College—Michigan State

SEASON—TEAM	G	GS	MIN	FGM	FGA	PCT	3FGM	3FGA	PCT	FTM	FTA	PCT	O-RB	D-RB	TOT	AST	PF	DQ	STL	TO	BLK	PTS	RPG	APG	PPG
81-82—Dallas	81	62	2626	719	1448	.497	1	4	.250	293	409	.716	182	383	565	176	308	8	89	194	21	1732	7.0	2.2	21.4
82-83—Dallas	81	73	2726	622	1272	.489	0	3	.000	269	343	.784	217	375	592	212	295	4	70	188	45	1513	7.3	2.6	18.7
83-84—Dallas	61	5	1421	252	579	.435	0	1	.000	168	215	.781	81	166	247	114	159	1	30	113	10	672	4.0	1.9	11.0
84-85—Dallas	79	47	2543	545	1138	.479	0	4	.000	351	420	.836	185	519	704	169	226	0	48	170	22	1441	8.9	2.1	18.2
85-86—Dallas	80	3	1994	442	919	.481	0	3	.000	222	274	.810	107	261	368	180	193	2	66	145	21	1106	4.6	2.3	13.8
86-87—Washington	51	17	1386	274	613	.447	0	3	.000	130	169	.769	69	141	210	85	127	0	40	77	17	678	4.1	1.7	13.3
87-88—Denver	73	8	1755	446	958	.466	1	4	.250	231	287	.805	80	229	309	143	198	1	46	137	26	1124	4.2	2.0	15.4
88-89—Denver-S.A.	29	4	646	104	257	.405	1	3	.333	40	60	.667	38	72	110	27	63	0	6	42	4	249	3.8	0.9	8.6
89-90—Phil.-Lakers	41	6	459	86	183	.470	1	2	.500	41	49	.837	20	42	62	18	52	0	18	33	5	214	1.5	0.4	5.2
REG. SEASON TOTALS	576	225	15556	3490	7367	.474	4	27	.148	1745	2226	.784	979	2188	3167	1124	1621	16	413	1099	171	8729	5.5	2.0	15.2
PLAYOFF TOTALS	38	12	971	170	415	.410	0	2	.000	150	174	.862	65	112	177	46	107	1	24	73	9	490	4.7	1.2	12.9

VIRDEN, CLAUDE FELTON b. November 25, 1947 Ht. 6-5½ Wt. 200 College—Murray State (Ky.)

SEASON—TEAM	G	GS	MIN	FGM	FGA	PCT	3FGM	3FGA	PCT	FTM	FTA	PCT	O-RB	D-RB	TOT	AST	PF	DQ	STL	TO	BLK	PTS	RPG	APG	PPG
72-73—Kentucky (A)	31	—	825	130	327	.398	0	2	.000	46	59	.780	49	105	154	74	84	0	—	49	—	306	5.0	2.4	9.9
REG. ABA TOTALS	31	—	825	130	327	.398	0	2	.000	46	59	.780	49	105	154	74	84	0	—	49	—	306	5.0	2.4	9.9

VOCE, GARY ANTHONY b. November 24, 1965 Ht. 6-9 Wt. 245 College—Notre Dame

SEASON—TEAM	G	GS	MIN	FGM	FGA	PCT	3FGM	3FGA	PCT	FTM	FTA	PCT	O-RB	D-RB	TOT	AST	PF	DQ	STL	TO	BLK	PTS	RPG	APG	PPG
89-90—Cleveland	1	0	4	1	3	.333	0	0	—	0	0	—	2	0	2	0	0	0	0	0	0	2	2.0	0.0	2.0
REG. SEASON TOTALS	1	0	4	1	3	.333	0	0	—	0	0	—	2	0	2	0	0	0	0	0	0	2	2.0	0.0	2.0

VOLKER, FLOYD W. b. June 21, 1921 Ht. 6-4 Wt. 205 College—Wyoming

SEASON—TEAM	G	GS	MIN	FGM	FGA	PCT	3FGM	3FGA	PCT	FTM	FTA	PCT	O-RB	D-RB	TOT	AST	PF	DQ	STL	TO	BLK	PTS	RPG	APG	PPG
47-48—Oshkosh (N)	57	—	—	102	—	—	—	—	—	31	66	.470	—	—	—	133	—	—	—	—	—	235	—	—	4.1
48-49—Oshkosh (N)	64	—	—	166	—	—	—	—	—	78	134	.582	—	—	—	190	—	—	—	—	—	410	—	—	6.4
49-50—Ind.-Denver	54	—	163	527	.309		—	—	—	71	129	.550	—	—	112	169	—	—	—	—	—	397	—	2.1	7.4
REG. NBA TOTALS	54	—	—	163	527	.309	—	—	—	71	129	.550	—	—	112	169	—	—	—	—	—	397	—	2.1	7.4
REG. NBL TOTALS	121	—	—	268	—	—	—	—	—	109	200	.545	—	—	—	323	—	—	—	—	—	645	—	—	5.3
NBL PLAYOFF TOTALS	11	—	—	34	—	—	—	—	—	13	21	.619	—	—	—	37	—	—	—	—	—	81	—	—	7.4

VOLKOV, ALEXANDER (Sasha) b. March 29, 1964 Ht. 6-10 Wt. 235 College—Kiev Institute (Russia)

SEASON—TEAM	G	GS	MIN	FGM	FGA	PCT	3FGM	3FGA	PCT	FTM	FTA	PCT	O-RB	D-RB	TOT	AST	PF	DQ	STL	TO	BLK	PTS	RPG	APG	PPG
89-90—Atlanta	72	4	937	137	284	.482	13	34	.382	70	120	.583	52	67	119	83	166	3	36	52	22	357	1.7	1.2	5.0
91-92—Atlanta	77	27	1516	251	569	.441	35	110	.318	125	198	.631	103	162	265	250	178	2	66	102	30	662	3.4	3.2	8.6
REG. SEASON TOTALS	149	31	2453	388	853	.455	48	144	.333	195	318	.613	155	229	384	333	344	5	102	154	52	1019	2.6	2.2	6.8

VON NIEDA, STANLEY L. JR. (Whitey) b. June 19, 1922 Ht. 6-1 Wt. 175 College—Penn State

SEASON—TEAM	G	GS	MIN	FGM	FGA	PCT	3FGM	3FGA	PCT	FTM	FTA	PCT	O-RB	D-RB	TOT	AST	PF	DQ	STL	TO	BLK	PTS	RPG	APG	PPG
47-48—Tri-Cities (N)	60	—	—	276	—	—	—	—	—	174	287	.606	—	—	—	144	—	—	—	—	—	726	—	—	12.1
48-49—Tri-Cities (N)	64	—	—	247	—	—	—	—	—	147	226	.650	—	—	—	141	—	—	—	—	—	641	—	—	10.0
49-50—Tri-Cit.-Balt.	59	—	—	120	336	.357	—	—	—	73	115	.635	—	—	143	127	—	—	—	—	—	313	—	2.4	5.3
REG. NBA TOTALS	59	—	—	120	336	.357	—	—	—	73	115	.635	—	—	143	127	—	—	—	—	—	313	—	2.4	5.3
REG. NBL TOTALS	124	—	—	523	—	—	—	—	—	321	513	.626	—	—	—	285	—	—	—	—	—	1367	—	—	11.0
NBL PLAYOFF TOTALS	12	—	—	61	—	—	—	—	—	28	51	.549	—	—	—	29	—	—	—	—	—	150	—	—	12.5

VRANES, DANIEL LaDREW (Danny) b. October 29, 1958 Ht. 6-8 Wt. 220 College—Utah

SEASON—TEAM	G	GS	MIN	FGM	FGA	PCT	3FGM	3FGA	PCT	FTM	FTA	PCT	O-RB	D-RB	TOT	AST	PF	DQ	STL	TO	BLK	PTS	RPG	APG	PPG
81-82—Seattle	77	1	1075	143	262	.546	0	1	.000	89	148	.601	71	127	198	56	150	0	28	68	22	375	2.6	0.7	4.9
82-83—Seattle	82	73	2054	226	429	.527	0	1	.000	115	209	.550	177	248	425	120	254	2	53	102	49	567	5.2	1.5	6.9
83-84—Seattle	80	72	2174	258	495	.521	0	1	.000	153	236	.648	150	245	395	132	263	4	51	121	54	669	4.9	1.7	8.4
84-85—Seattle	76	70	2163	186	402	.463	1	4	.250	67	127	.528	154	282	436	152	256	4	76	119	57	440	5.7	2.0	5.8
85-86—Seattle	80	19	1569	131	284	.461	0	4	.000	39	75	.520	115	166	281	68	218	3	63	58	31	301	3.5	0.9	3.8
86-87—Philadelphia	58	6	817	59	138	.428	1	5	.200	21	45	.467	51	95	146	30	127	0	35	26	25	140	2.5	0.5	2.4
87-88—Philadelphia	57	5	772	53	121	.438	0	3	.000	15	35	.429	45	72	117	36	100	0	27	25	33	121	2.1	0.6	2.1
REG. SEASON TOTALS	510	246	10624	1056	2131	.496	2	19	.105	499	875	.570	763	1235	1998	594	1368	13	333	519	271	2613	3.9	1.2	5.1
PLAYOFF TOTALS	15	7	235	23	61	.377	0	1	.000	5	9	.556	26	36	62	12	34	1	4	8	7	51	4.1	0.8	3.4

VRANKOVIC, STOJAN b. January 22, 1964 Ht. 7-2 Wt. 260 College—None

SEASON—TEAM	G	GS	MIN	FGM	FGA	PCT	3FGM	3FGA	PCT	FTM	FTA	PCT	O-RB	D-RB	TOT	AST	PF	DQ	STL	TO	BLK	PTS	RPG	APG	PPG
90-91—Boston	31	0	166	24	52	.462	0	0	—	10	18	.556	15	36	51	4	43	1	1	24	29	58	1.6	0.1	1.9
91-92—Boston	19	0	110	15	32	.469	0	0	—	7	12	.583	8	20	28	5	22	0	0	10	17	37	1.5	0.3	1.9
REG. SEASON TOTALS	50	0	276	39	84	.464	0	0	—	17	30	.567	23	56	79	9	65	1	1	34	46	95	1.6	0.2	1.9
PLAYOFF TOTALS	2	0	7	2	2	1.000	0	0	—	0	1	.000	0	2	2	1	2	0	0	1	0	4	1.0	0.5	2.0

VROMAN, BRETT GRANT b. December 25, 1955 Ht. 7-0 Wt. 230 College—UCLA/Nevada-Las Vegas

SEASON—TEAM	G	GS	MIN	FGM	FGA	PCT	3FGM	3FGA	PCT	FTM	FTA	PCT	O-RB	D-RB	TOT	AST	PF	DQ	STL	TO	BLK	PTS	RPG	APG	PPG
80-81—Utah	11	—	93	10	27	.370	0	1	.000	14	19	.737	7	18	25	9	26	1	5	9	5	34	2.3	0.8	3.1
REG. SEASON TOTALS	11	—	93	10	27	.370	0	1	.000	14	19	.737	7	18	25	9	26	1	5	9	5	34	2.3	0.8	3.1

WADE, MARK A. b. October 15, 1965 Ht. 6-1 Wt. 160 College—El Camino CC/Oklahoma/Nevada-Las Vegas

SEASON—TEAM	G	GS	MIN	FGM	FGA	PCT	3FGM	3FGA	PCT	FTM	FTA	PCT	O-RB	D-RB	TOT	AST	PF	DQ	STL	TO	BLK	PTS	RPG	APG	PPG
87-88—Golden State	11	0	123	3	20	.150	0	2	.000	2	4	.500	3	12	15	34	13	0	7	13	1	8	1.4	3.1	0.7
89-90—Dallas	1	0	3	0	0	—	0	0	—	0	0	—	0	0	0	2	0	0	0	0	0	0	0.0	2.0	0.0
REG. SEASON TOTALS	12	0	126	3	20	.150	0	2	.000	2	4	.500	3	12	15	36	13	0	7	13	1	8	1.3	3.0	0.7

WAGER, CLINTON B. (Clint) b. January 20, 1920 Ht. 6-6 Wt. 230 College—St. Mary's (Minn.)

SEASON—TEAM	G	GS	MIN	FGM	FGA	PCT	3FGM	3FGA	PCT	FTM	FTA	PCT	O-RB	D-RB	TOT	AST	PF	DQ	STL	TO	BLK	PTS	RPG	APG	PPG
43-44—Oshkosh (N)	22	—	—	79	—	—	—	—	—	72	—	—	—	—	—	—	—	—	—	—	—	230	—	—	10.5
44-45—Oshkosh (N)	27	—	—	70	—	—	—	—	—	28	—	—	—	—	—	—	—	—	—	—	—	168	—	—	6.2
45-46—Oshkosh (N)	34	—	—	68	—	—	—	—	—	31	48	.646	—	—	—	—	83	—	—	—	—	167	—	—	4.9
46-47—Oshkosh (N)	44	—	—	68	—	—	—	—	—	50	69	.725	—	—	—	—	142	—	—	—	—	186	—	—	4.2
47-48—Oshkosh (N)	59	—	—	90	—	—	—	—	—	56	93	.602	—	—	—	—	169	—	—	—	—	236	—	—	4.0
48-49—Hammond (N)	61	—	—	125	—	—	—	—	—	82	146	.562	—	—	—	—	236	—	—	—	—	332	—	—	5.4
49-50—Fort Wayne	63	—	—	57	203	.281	—	—	—	29	47	.617	—	—	—	90	175	—	—	—	—	143	—	1.4	2.3
REG. NBA TOTALS	63	—	—	57	203	.281	—	—	—	29	47	.617	—	—	—	90	175	—	—	—	—	143	—	1.4	2.3
REG. NBL TOTALS	247	—	—	500	—	—	—	—	—	319	356	.615	—	—	—	—	630	—	—	—	—	1319	—	—	5.3
NBA PLAYOFF TOTALS	4	—	—	11	25	.440	—	—	—	8	10	.800	—	—	—	8	22	3	—	—	—	30	—	2.0	7.5
NBL PLAYOFF TOTALS	20	—	—	41	—	—	—	—	—	24	21	.619	—	—	—	—	68	—	—	—	—	106	—	—	5.3

WAGNER, DANIEL EARNEST (Danny) b. August 1, 1922 Ht. 6-0 Wt. 170 College—Schreiner JC/Texas

SEASON—TEAM	G	GS	MIN	FGM	FGA	PCT	3FGM	3FGA	PCT	FTM	FTA	PCT	O-RB	D-RB	TOT	AST	PF	DQ	STL	TO	BLK	PTS	RPG	APG	PPG
47-48—Flint (N)	50	—	—	96	—	—	—	—	—	59	92	.641	—	—	—	—	82	—	—	—	—	251	—	—	5.0
48-49—Sheboygan (N)	62	—	—	111	—	—	—	—	—	109	146	.747	—	—	—	—	120	—	—	—	—	331	—	—	5.3
49-50—Sheboygan	11	—	—	19	54	.352	—	—	—	31	35	.886	—	—	—	18	22	—	—	—	—	69	—	1.6	6.3
REG. NBA TOTALS	11	—	—	19	54	.352	—	—	—	31	35	.886	—	—	—	18	22	—	—	—	—	69	—	1.6	6.3
REG. NBL TOTALS	112	—	—	207	—	—	—	—	—	168	238	.706	—	—	—	—	202	—	—	—	—	582	—	—	5.2
NBL PLAYOFF TOTALS	2	—	—	3	—	—	—	—	—	1	1	1.000	—	—	—	—	9	—	—	—	—	7	—	—	3.5

WAGNER, MILTON JR. (Milt) b. February 20, 1963 Ht. 6-5 Wt. 185 College—Louisville

SEASON—TEAM	G	GS	MIN	FGM	FGA	PCT	3FGM	3FGA	PCT	FTM	FTA	PCT	O-RB	D-RB	TOT	AST	PF	DQ	STL	TO	BLK	PTS	RPG	APG	PPG
87-88—L.A. Lakers	40	4	380	62	147	.422	2	10	.200	26	29	.897	4	24	28	61	42	0	6	22	4	152	0.7	1.5	3.8
90-91—Miami	13	1	116	24	57	.421	6	17	.353	9	11	.818	0	7	7	15	14	0	2	12	3	63	0.5	1.2	4.8
REG. SEASON TOTALS	53	5	496	86	204	.422	8	27	.296	35	40	.875	4	31	35	76	56	0	8	34	7	215	0.7	1.4	4.1
PLAYOFF TOTALS	5	0	14	2	5	.400	0	1	.000	2	2	1.000	0	2	2	3	3	0	0	1	0	6	0.4	0.6	1.2

WAGNER, PHILLIP C. (Phil) b. December 18, 1945 Ht. 6-2 Wt. 190 College—Georgia Tech

SEASON—TEAM	G	GS	MIN	FGM	FGA	PCT	3FGM	3FGA	PCT	FTM	FTA	PCT	O-RB	D-RB	TOT	AST	PF	DQ	STL	TO	BLK	PTS	RPG	APG	PPG
68-69—Indiana (A)	12	—	180	11	41	.268	1	4	.250	13	17	.765	—	—	23	14	28	0	—	18	—	36	1.9	1.2	3.0
REG. ABA TOTALS	12	—	180	11	41	.268	1	4	.250	13	17	.765	—	—	23	14	28	0	—	18	—	36	1.9	1.2	3.0

WAITERS, GRANVILLE S. b. January 8, 1961 Ht. 6-11 Wt. 225 College—Ohio State

SEASON—TEAM	G	GS	MIN	FGM	FGA	PCT	3FGM	3FGA	PCT	FTM	FTA	PCT	O-RB	D-RB	TOT	AST	PF	DQ	STL	TO	BLK	PTS	RPG	APG	PPG
83-84—Indiana	78	8	1040	123	238	.517	0	1	.000	31	51	.608	64	163	227	60	164	2	24	65	85	277	2.9	0.8	3.6
84-85—Indiana	62	2	703	85	190	.447	0	1	.000	29	50	.580	57	113	170	30	107	2	16	55	44	199	2.7	0.5	3.2
85-86—Houston	43	0	156	13	39	.333	0	1	.000	1	6	.167	15	13	28	8	30	0	4	11	10	27	0.7	0.2	0.6
86-87—Chicago	44	26	534	40	93	.430	0	1	.000	5	9	.556	38	49	87	22	83	1	10	16	31	85	2.0	0.5	1.9
87-88—Chicago	22	0	114	9	29	.310	0	1	.000	0	2	.000	9	19	28	1	26	0	2	6	15	18	1.3	0.0	0.8
REG. SEASON TOTALS	249	39	2547	270	589	.458	0	5	.000	66	118	.559	183	357	540	121	410	5	56	153	185	606	2.2	0.5	2.4
PLAYOFF TOTALS	13	0	34	4	7	.571	0	0	—	0	0	—	2	4	6	—	4	0	1	1	4	8	0.5	0.0	0.6

WAKEFIELD, ANDRE b. January 11, 1955 Ht. 6-2½ Wt. 175 College—Southern Idaho/Loyola (Ill.)

SEASON—TEAM	G	GS	MIN	FGM	FGA	PCT	3FGM	3FGA	PCT	FTM	FTA	PCT	O-RB	D-RB	TOT	AST	PF	DQ	STL	TO	BLK	PTS	RPG	APG	PPG
78-79—Chicago-Detroit	73	—	586	62	177	.350	—	—	—	48	69	.696	25	51	76	70	70	0	19	73	2	172	1.0	1.0	2.4
79-80—Utah	8	—	47	6	15	.400	0	0	—	3	3	1.000	0	4	4	3	13	0	1	8	0	15	0.5	0.4	1.9
REG. SEASON TOTALS	81	—	633	68	192	.354	0	0	—	51	72	.708	25	55	80	73	83	0	20	81	2	187	1.0	0.9	2.3

WALK, NEAL EUGENE b. July 29, 1948 Ht. 6-10 Wt. 250 College—Florida

SEASON—TEAM	G	GS	MIN	FGM	FGA	PCT	3FGM	3FGA	PCT	FTM	FTA	PCT	O-RB	D-RB	TOT	AST	PF	DQ	STL	TO	BLK	PTS	RPG	APG	PPG
69-70—Phoenix	82	—	1394	257	547	.470	—	—	—	155	242	.640	—	—	455	80	225	2	—	—	—	669	5.5	1.0	8.2
70-71—Phoenix	82	—	2033	426	945	.451	—	—	—	205	268	.765	—	—	674	117	282	8	—	—	—	1057	8.2	1.4	12.9
71-72—Phoenix	81	—	2142	506	1057	.479	—	—	—	256	344	.744	—	—	665	151	295	9	—	—	—	1268	8.2	1.9	15.7
72-73—Phoenix	81	—	3114	678	1455	.466	—	—	—	279	355	.786	—	—	1006	287	323	11	—	—	—	1635	12.4	3.5	20.2
73-74—Phoenix	82	—	2549	573	1245	.460	—	—	—	235	297	.791	235	602	837	331	255	8	73	—	57	1381	10.2	4.0	16.8
74-75—N.O.-N.Y.	67	—	1125	198	473	.419	—	—	—	86	105	.819	91	248	339	123	177	3	37	—	23	482	5.1	1.8	7.2
75-76—New York	82	—	1340	262	607	.432	—	—	—	79	99	.798	98	291	389	119	209	3	26	—	22	603	4.7	1.5	7.4
76-77—New York Knicks	11	—	135	28	57	.491	—	—	—	6	7	.857	5	22	27	6	22	0	4	—	3	62	2.5	0.5	5.6
REG. SEASON TOTALS	568	—	13832	2928	6386	.459	—	—	—	1301	1717	.758	429	1163	4392	1214	1788	44	140	—	105	7157	7.7	2.1	12.6
PLAYOFF TOTALS	8	—	102	22	53	.415	—	—	—	6	8	.750	0	5	40	4	17	0	1	—	2	50	5.0	0.5	6.3

WALKER, ANDREW MARTIN (**Andy**) b. March 25, 1955 Ht. 6-4 Wt. 190 College—Niagara

SEASON—TEAM	G	GS	MIN	FGM	FGA	PCT	3FGM	3FGA	PCT	FTM	FTA	PCT	O-RB	D-RB	TOT	AST	PF	DQ	STL	TO	BLK	PTS	RPG	APG	PPG
76-77—New Orleans	40	—	438	72	156	.462	—	—	—	36	47	.766	23	52	75	32	59	0	20	—	7	180	1.9	0.8	4.5
REG. SEASON TOTALS	40	—	438	72	156	.462	—	—	—	36	47	.766	23	52	75	32	59	0	20	—	7	180	1.9	0.8	4.5

WALKER, BRADY W. b. March 15, 1921 Ht. 6-6 Wt. 205 College—Brigham Young

SEASON—TEAM	G	GS	MIN	FGM	FGA	PCT	3FGM	3FGA	PCT	FTM	FTA	PCT	O-RB	D-RB	TOT	AST	PF	DQ	STL	TO	BLK	PTS	RPG	APG	PPG
48-49—Providence	59	—	—	202	556	.363	—	—	—	87	155	.561	—	—	68	100	—	—	—	—	—	491	—	1.2	8.3
49-50—Boston	68	—	—	218	583	.374	—	—	—	72	114	.632	—	—	109	100	—	—	—	—	—	508	—	1.6	7.5
50-51—Boston-Balt.	66	—		164	416	.394	—	—	—	72	103	.699	—	—	354	111	82	2	—	—	—	400	5.4	1.7	6.1
51-52—Baltimore	35	—	699	89	217	.410	—	—	—	26	34	.765	—	—	195	40	38	0	—	—	—	204	5.6	1.1	5.8
REG. SEASON TOTALS	228	—	699	673	1772	.380	—	—	—	257	406	.633	—	—	549	328	320	2	—	—	—	1603	5.4	1.4	7.0

WALKER, CHESTER (**Chet, Chet the Jet**) b. February 22, 1940 Ht. 6-6½ Wt. 215 College—Bradley

SEASON—TEAM	G	GS	MIN	FGM	FGA	PCT	3FGM	3FGA	PCT	FTM	FTA	PCT	O-RB	D-RB	TOT	AST	PF	DQ	STL	TO	BLK	PTS	RPG	APG	PPG
62-63—Syracuse	78	—	1992	352	751	.469	—	—	—	253	362	.699	—	—	561	83	220	3	—	—	—	957	7.2	1.1	12.3
63-64—Philadelphia	76	—	2775	492	1118	.440	—	—	—	330	464	.711	—	—	784	124	232	3	—	—	—	1314	10.3	1.6	17.3
64-65—Philadelphia	79	—	2187	377	936	.403	—	—	—	288	388	.742	—	—	528	132	200	2	—	—	—	1042	6.7	1.7	13.2
65-66—Philadelphia	80	—	2603	443	982	.451	—	—	—	335	468	.716	—	—	636	201	238	3	—	—	—	1221	8.0	2.5	15.3
66-67—Philadelphia	81	—	2691	561	1150	.488	—	—	—	445	581	.766	—	—	660	188	232	4	—	—	—	1567	8.1	2.3	19.3
67-68—Philadelphia	82	—	2623	539	1172	.460	—	—	—	387	533	.726	—	—	607	157	252	3	—	—	—	1465	7.4	1.9	17.9
68-69—Philadelphia	82	—	2753	554	1145	.484	—	—	—	369	459	.804	—	—	640	144	244	0	—	—	—	1477	7.8	1.8	18.0
69-70—Chicago	78	—	2726	596	1249	.477	—	—	—	483	568	.850	—	—	604	192	203	1	—	—	—	1675	7.7	2.5	21.5
70-71—Chicago	81	—	2927	650	1398	.465	—	—	—	480	559	.859	—	—	588	179	187	2	—	—	—	1780	7.3	2.2	22.0
71-72—Chicago	78	—	2588	619	1225	.505	—	—	—	481	568	.847	—	—	473	178	171	0	—	—	—	1719	6.1	2.3	22.0
72-73—Chicago	79	—	2455	597	1248	.478	—	—	—	376	452	.832	—	—	395	179	166	1	—	—	—	1570	5.0	2.3	19.9
73-74—Chicago	82	—	2661	572	1178	.486	—	—	—	439	502	.875	131	275	406	200	201	1	68	—	4	1583	5.0	2.4	19.3
74-75—Chicago	76	—	2452	524	1076	.487	—	—	—	413	480	.860	114	318	432	169	181	0	49	—	6	1461	5.7	2.2	19.2
REG. SEASON TOTALS	1032	—	33433	6876	14628	.470	—	—	—	5079	6384	.796	245	593	7314	2126	2727	23	117	—	10	18831	7.1	2.1	18.2
PLAYOFF TOTALS	105	—	3688	687	1531	.449	—	—	—	542	689	.787	36	85	737	212	286	3	23	—	2	1916	7.0	2.0	18.2
ALL-STAR TOTALS	7	—	125	20	46	.435	—	—	—	17	20	.850	0	2	18	9	11	0	0	—	0	57	2.6	1.3	8.1

WALKER, CLARENCE (**Foots**) b. May 21, 1951 Ht. 6-1 Wt. 170 College—Vincennes/West Georgia

SEASON—TEAM	G	GS	MIN	FGM	FGA	PCT	3FGM	3FGA	PCT	FTM	FTA	PCT	O-RB	D-RB	TOT	AST	PF	DQ	STL	TO	BLK	PTS	RPG	APG	PPG
74-75—Cleveland	72	—	1070	111	275	.404	—	—	—	80	117	.684	47	99	146	192	126	0	80	—	7	302	2.0	2.7	4.2
75-76—Cleveland	81	—	1280	143	369	.388	—	—	—	84	108	.778	53	129	182	288	136	0	98	—	5	370	2.2	3.6	4.6
76-77—Cleveland	62	—	1216	157	349	.450	—	—	—	89	115	.774	55	105	160	254	124	1	83	—	4	403	2.6	4.1	6.5
77-78—Cleveland	81	—	2496	287	641	.448	—	—	—	159	221	.719	76	218	294	453	218	0	176	181	24	733	3.6	5.6	9.0
78-79—Cleveland	55	—	1753	208	448	.464	—	—	—	137	175	.783	59	139	198	321	153	0	130	127	18	553	3.6	5.8	10.1
79-80—Cleveland	76	—	2422	258	568	.454	1	9	.111	195	243	.802	78	209	287	607	202	2	155	157	12	712	3.8	8.0	9.4
80-81—New Jersey	41	—	1172	72	169	.426	2	9	.222	88	111	.793	22	80	102	253	105	0	52	85	1	234	2.5	6.2	5.7
81-82—New Jersey	77	54	1861	156	378	.413	3	9	.333	141	194	.727	31	119	150	398	179	1	120	107	6	456	1.9	5.2	5.9
82-83—New Jersey	79	10	1388	114	250	.456	2	12	.167	116	149	.779	30	106	136	264	134	1	78	104	3	346	1.7	3.3	4.4
83-84—New Jersey	34	0	378	32	90	.356	2	5	.400	24	27	.889	8	23	31	81	37	0	20	31	3	90	0.9	2.4	2.6
REG. SEASON TOTALS	658	64	15036	1538	3537	.435	10	44	.227	1113	1460	.762	459	1227	1686	3111	1414	5	992	792	83	4199	2.6	4.7	6.4
PLAYOFF TOTALS	22	0	330	41	97	.423	0	0	—	27	33	.818	14	21	35	64	37	0	14	8	4	109	1.6	2.9	5.0

WALKER, DARRELL b. March 9, 1961   Ht. 6-4 Wt. 180 College—Westark CC/Arkansas

SEASON—TEAM	G	GS	MIN	FGM	FGA	PCT	3FGM	3FGA	PCT	FTM	FTA	PCT	O-RB	D-RB	TOT	AST	PF	DQ	STL	TO	BLK	PTS	RPG	APG	PPG
83-84—New York	82	0	1324	216	518	.417	4	15	.267	208	263	.791	74	93	167	284	202	1	127	194	15	644	2.0	3.5	7.9
84-85—New York	82	66	2489	430	989	.435	0	17	.000	243	347	.700	128	150	278	408	244	2	167	204	21	1103	3.4	5.0	13.5
85-86—New York	81	35	2023	324	753	.430	0	10	.000	190	277	.686	100	120	220	337	216	1	146	192	36	838	2.7	4.2	10.3
86-87—Denver	81	25	2020	358	742	.482	0	4	.000	272	365	.745	157	170	327	282	229	0	120	187	37	988	4.0	3.5	12.2
87-88—Washington	52	0	940	114	291	.392	0	6	.000	82	105	.781	43	84	127	100	105	2	62	69	10	310	2.4	1.9	6.0
88-89—Washington	79	78	2565	286	681	.420	0	9	.000	142	184	.772	135	372	507	496	215	2	155	184	23	714	6.4	6.3	9.0
89-90—Washington	81	81	2883	316	696	.454	2	21	.095	138	201	.687	173	541	714	652	220	1	139	173	30	772	8.8	8.0	9.5
90-91—Washington	71	65	2305	230	535	.430	0	9	.000	93	154	.604	140	358	498	459	199	2	78	154	33	553	7.0	6.5	7.8
91-92—Detroit	74	4	1541	161	381	.423	0	10	.000	65	105	.619	85	153	238	205	134	0	63	79	18	387	3.2	2.8	5.2
92-93—Detroit-Chicago	37	2	511	34	96	.354	0	1	.000	12	26	.462	22	36	58	53	63	0	33	25	2	80	1.6	1.4	2.2
REG. SEASON TOTALS	720	356	18601	2469	5682	.435	6	102	.059	1445	2027	.713	1057	2077	3134	3276	1827	11	1090	1461	225	6389	4.4	4.6	8.9
PLAYOFF TOTALS	34	3	508	64	174	.368	0	1	.000	49	76	.645	37	45	82	48	58	0	34	51	6	177	2.4	1.4	5.2

WALKER, HORACE b. April 17, 1938   Ht. 6-3½ Wt. 210 College—Michigan State

SEASON—TEAM	G	GS	MIN	FGM	FGA	PCT	3FGM	3FGA	PCT	FTM	FTA	PCT	O-RB	D-RB	TOT	AST	PF	DQ	STL	TO	BLK	PTS	RPG	APG	PPG
61-62—Chicago	65	—	1331	149	439	.339	—	—	—	140	193	.725	—	—	466	69	194	2	—	—	—	438	7.2	1.1	6.7
REG. SEASON TOTALS	65	—	1331	149	439	.339	—	—	—	140	193	.725	—	—	466	69	194	2	—	—	—	438	7.2	1.1	6.7

WALKER, JAMES (Jimmy) b. April 8, 1944   Ht. 6-3 Wt. 205 College—Providence

SEASON—TEAM	G	GS	MIN	FGM	FGA	PCT	3FGM	3FGA	PCT	FTM	FTA	PCT	O-RB	D-RB	TOT	AST	PF	DQ	STL	TO	BLK	PTS	RPG	APG	PPG
67-68—Detroit	81	—	1585	289	733	.394	—	—	—	134	175	.766	—	—	135	226	204	1	—	—	—	712	1.7	2.8	8.8
68-69—Detroit	69	—	1639	312	670	.466	—	—	—	182	229	.795	—	—	157	221	172	1	—	—	—	806	2.3	3.2	11.7
69-70—Detroit	81	—	2869	666	1394	.478	—	—	—	355	440	.807	—	—	242	248	203	4	—	—	—	1687	3.0	3.1	20.8
70-71—Detroit	79	—	2765	524	1201	.436	—	—	—	344	414	.831	—	—	207	268	173	0	—	—	—	1392	2.6	3.4	17.6
71-72—Detroit	78	—	3083	634	1386	.457	—	—	—	397	480	.827	—	—	231	315	198	2	—	—	—	1665	3.0	4.0	21.3
72-73—Houston	81	—	3079	605	1301	.465	—	—	—	244	276	.884	—	—	268	442	207	0	—	—	—	1454	3.3	5.5	18.0
73-74—Houston-K.C. Omaha	75	—	2958	582	1240	.469	—	—	—	273	333	.820	39	165	204	307	170	0	81	—	9	1437	2.7	4.1	19.2
74-75—Kansas City-Omaha	81	—	3122	553	1164	.475	—	—	—	247	289	.855	51	188	239	226	222	2	85	—	13	1353	3.0	2.8	16.7
75-76—Kansas City	73	—	2490	459	950	.483	—	—	—	231	267	.865	49	128	177	176	186	2	87	—	14	1149	2.4	2.4	15.7
REG. SEASON TOTALS	698	—	23590	4624	10039	.461	—	—	—	2407	2903	.829	139	481	1860	2429	1735	12	253	—	36	11655	2.7	3.5	16.7
PLAYOFF TOTALS	12	—	346	70	151	.464	—	—	—	28	35	.800	1	9	19	26	29	1	5	—	1	168	1.6	2.2	14.0
ALL-STAR TOTALS	2	—	30	4	12	.333	—	—	—	3	6	.500	0	0	3	1	3	0	0	—	0	11	1.5	0.5	5.5

WALKER, KENNETH (Kenny, Sky) b. August 18, 1964   Ht. 6-8 Wt. 220 College—Kentucky

SEASON—TEAM	G	GS	MIN	FGM	FGA	PCT	3FGM	3FGA	PCT	FTM	FTA	PCT	O-RB	D-RB	TOT	AST	PF	DQ	STL	TO	BLK	PTS	RPG	APG	PPG
86-87—New York	68	64	1719	285	581	.491	0	4	.000	140	185	.757	118	220	338	75	236	7	49	75	49	710	5.0	1.1	10.4
87-88—New York	82	61	2139	344	728	.473	0	1	.000	138	178	.775	192	197	389	86	290	5	63	83	59	826	4.7	1.0	10.1
88-89—New York	79	2	1163	174	356	.489	5	20	.250	66	85	.776	101	129	230	36	190	1	41	44	45	419	2.9	0.5	5.3
89-90—New York	68	21	1595	204	384	.531	2	5	.400	125	173	.723	131	212	343	49	178	1	33	60	52	535	5.0	0.7	7.9
90-91—New York	54	8	771	83	191	.435	0	1	.000	64	82	.780	63	94	157	13	92	0	18	30	30	230	2.9	0.2	4.3
93-94—Washington	73	4	1397	132	274	.482	0	3	.000	87	125	.696	118	171	289	33	156	1	26	44	59	351	4.0	0.5	4.8
REG. SEASON TOTALS	424	160	8784	1222	2514	.486	7	34	.206	620	828	.749	723	1023	1746	292	1142	15	230	336	294	3071	4.1	0.7	7.2
PLAYOFF TOTALS	26	4	355	31	74	.419	0	1	.000	27	37	.730	17	40	57	15	63	0	4	9	11	89	2.2	0.6	3.4

WALKER, PHILLIP B. (Phil) b. March 20, 1956   Ht. 6-3 Wt. 190 College—Millersville State

SEASON—TEAM	G	GS	MIN	FGM	FGA	PCT	3FGM	3FGA	PCT	FTM	FTA	PCT	O-RB	D-RB	TOT	AST	PF	DQ	STL	TO	BLK	PTS	RPG	APG	PPG
77-78—Washington	40	—	384	57	161	.354	—	—	—	64	96	.667	21	31	52	54	39	0	14	62	5	178	1.3	1.4	4.5
REG. SEASON TOTALS	40	—	384	57	161	.354	—	—	—	64	96	.667	21	31	52	54	39	0	14	62	5	178	1.3	1.4	4.5
PLAYOFF TOTALS	4	—	17	1	8	.125	—	—	—	4	5	.800	1	1	2	2	5	0	0	3	0	6	0.5	0.5	1.5

WALKER, WALTER FREDERICK (Wally) b. July 18, 1954   Ht. 6-6½ Wt. 195 College—Virginia

SEASON—TEAM	G	GS	MIN	FGM	FGA	PCT	3FGM	3FGA	PCT	FTM	FTA	PCT	O-RB	D-RB	TOT	AST	PF	DQ	STL	TO	BLK	PTS	RPG	APG	PPG
76-77—Portland	66	—	627	137	305	.449	—	—	—	67	100	.670	45	63	108	51	92	0	14	—	2	341	1.6	0.8	5.2
77-78—Port.-Seattle	77	—	1104	204	461	.443	—	—	—	75	120	.625	87	132	219	77	138	1	26	77	10	483	2.8	1.0	6.3
78-79—Seattle	60	—	969	168	343	.490	—	—	—	58	96	.604	66	111	177	69	127	0	12	68	26	394	3.0	1.2	6.6
79-80—Seattle	70	—	844	139	274	.507	0	0	—	48	64	.750	64	106	170	53	102	0	21	50	4	326	2.4	0.8	4.7
80-81—Seattle	82	—	1796	290	626	.463	0	3	.000	109	169	.645	105	210	315	122	168	1	53	115	15	689	3.8	1.5	8.4
81-82—Seattle	70	70	1965	302	629	.480	0	2	.000	90	134	.672	108	197	305	218	215	2	36	111	28	694	4.4	3.1	9.9
82-83—Houston	82	59	2251	362	806	.449	1	4	.250	72	116	.621	137	236	373	199	202	3	37	144	22	797	4.5	2.4	9.7
83-84—Houston	58	18	612	118	241	.490	2	6	.333	6	18	.333	26	66	92	55	65	0	17	33	4	244	1.6	0.9	4.2
REG. SEASON TOTALS	565	147	10168	1720	3685	.467	3	15	.200	525	817	.643	638	1121	1759	844	1109	7	216	598	111	3968	3.1	1.5	7.0
PLAYOFF TOTALS	64	8	743	99	217	.456	0	0	—	45	65	.692	56	67	123	44	136	1	16	34	11	243	1.9	0.7	3.8

WALLACE, MICHAEL JOHN (**Red**) b. July 12, 1918 d. July 7, 1977 Ht. 6-1 Wt. 185 College—Scranton

SEASON—TEAM	G	GS	MIN	FGM	FGA	PCT	3FGM	3FGA	PCT	FTM	FTA	PCT	O-RB	D-RB	TOT	AST	PF	DQ	STL	TO	BLK	PTS	RPG	APG	PPG
46-47—Boston-Toronto	61	—	—	225	809	.278	—	—	—	106	196	.541	—	—	—	58	167	—	—	—	—	556	—	1.0	9.1
REG. SEASON TOTALS	61	—	—	225	809	.278	—	—	—	106	196	.541	—	—	—	58	167	—	—	—	—	556	—	1.0	9.1

WALLER, DWIGHT b. October 5, 1945 Ht. 6-7 Wt. 225 College—Tennessee State

SEASON—TEAM	G	GS	MIN	FGM	FGA	PCT	3FGM	3FGA	PCT	FTM	FTA	PCT	O-RB	D-RB	TOT	AST	PF	DQ	STL	TO	BLK	PTS	RPG	APG	PPG
68-69—Atlanta	11	—	29	2	9	.222	—	—	—	3	7	.429	—	—	10	1	8	0	—	—	—	7	0.9	0.1	0.6
69-70—Denver (A)	7	—	87	10	24	.417	0	1	.000	9	19	.474	—	—	38	4	12	0	—	—	—	29	5.4	0.6	4.1
71-72—Denver (A)	2	—	10	2	4	.500	0	0	—	0	0	—	—	—	5	1	3	—	—	1	—	4	2.5	0.5	2.0
REG. NBA TOTALS	11	—	29	2	9	.222	—	—	—	3	7	.429	—	—	10	1	8	0	—	—	—	7	0.9	0.1	0.6
REG. ABA TOTALS	9	—	97	12	28	.429	0	1	.000	9	19	.474	—	—	43	5	15	0	—	1	—	33	4.8	0.6	3.7

WALLER, JAMIE ANTONIO b. November 20, 1964 Ht. 6-4 Wt. 215 College—Virginia Union

SEASON—TEAM	G	GS	MIN	FGM	FGA	PCT	3FGM	3FGA	PCT	FTM	FTA	PCT	O-RB	D-RB	TOT	AST	PF	DQ	STL	TO	BLK	PTS	RPG	APG	PPG
87-88—New Jersey	9	0	91	16	40	.400	0	2	.000	10	18	.556	9	4	13	3	13	0	4	11	1	42	1.4	0.3	4.7
REG. SEASON TOTALS	9	0	91	16	40	.400	0	2	.000	10	18	.556	9	4	13	3	13	0	4	11	1	42	1.4	0.3	4.7

WALSH, JAMES PATRICK (**Jim**) b. August 29, 1930 d. March 4, 1976 Ht. 6-4 Wt. 195 College—Stanford

SEASON—TEAM	G	GS	MIN	FGM	FGA	PCT	3FGM	3FGA	PCT	FTM	FTA	PCT	O-RB	D-RB	TOT	AST	PF	DQ	STL	TO	BLK	PTS	RPG	APG	PPG
57-58—Philadelphia	10	—	72	5	27	.185	—	—	—	10	17	.588	—	—	15	8	9	0	—	—	—	20	1.5	0.8	2.0
REG. SEASON TOTALS	10	—	72	5	27	.185	—	—	—	10	17	.588	—	—	15	8	9	0	—	—	—	20	1.5	0.8	2.0

WALTERS, REX ANDREW b. March 12, 1970 Ht. 6-4 Wt. 190 College—DeAnza CC/Northwestern/Kansas

SEASON—TEAM	G	GS	MIN	FGM	FGA	PCT	3FGM	3FGA	PCT	FTM	FTA	PCT	O-RB	D-RB	TOT	AST	PF	DQ	STL	TO	BLK	PTS	RPG	APG	PPG
93-94—New Jersey	48	0	386	60	115	.522	14	28	.500	28	34	.824	6	32	38	71	41	0	15	30	3	162	0.8	1.5	3.4
REG. SEASON TOTALS	48	0	386	60	115	.522	14	28	.500	28	34	.824	6	32	38	71	41	0	15	30	3	162	0.8	1.5	3.4
PLAYOFF TOTALS	1	0	1	1	1	1.000	0	0	—	0	0	—	0	0	0	—	0	0	0	0	0	2	0.0	0.0	2.0

WALTHER, PAUL G. (**Lefty**) b. March 23, 1927 Ht. 6-3 Wt. 165 College—Tennessee

SEASON—TEAM	G	GS	MIN	FGM	FGA	PCT	3FGM	3FGA	PCT	FTM	FTA	PCT	O-RB	D-RB	TOT	AST	PF	DQ	STL	TO	BLK	PTS	RPG	APG	PPG
49-50—Minn.-Ind.	53	—	—	114	290	.393	—	—	—	63	109	.578	—	—	—	56	123	—	—	—	—	291	—	1.1	5.5
50-51—Indianapolis	63	—	213	634	.336	—	—	—	145	209	.694	—	—	226	221	201	8	—	—	—	571	3.6	3.6	9.1
51-52—Indianapolis	55	—	1903	220	549	.401	—	—	—	231	308	.750	—	—	246	137	171	6	—	—	—	671	4.5	2.5	12.2
52-53—Indianapolis	67	—	2468	227	645	.352	—	—	—	264	354	.746	—	—	284	205	260	7	—	—	—	718	4.2	3.1	10.7
53-54—Philadelphia	64	—	2067	138	392	.352	—	—	—	145	206	.704	—	—	257	220	199	5	—	—	—	421	4.0	3.4	6.6
54-55—Fort Wayne	68	—	820	56	161	.348	—	—	—	54	88	.614	—	—	155	131	115	1	—	—	—	166	2.3	1.9	2.4
REG. SEASON TOTALS	370	—	7258	968	2671	.362	—	—	—	902	1274	.708	—	—	1168	974	1069	27	—	—	—	2838	3.7	2.6	7.7
PLAYOFF TOTALS	23	—	255	40	106	.377	—	—	—	63	87	.724	—	—	40	35	59	1	—	—	—	143	2.5	1.6	6.2
ALL-STAR TOTALS	1	—	17	1	4	.250	—	—	—	0	0	—	—	—	2	2	1	0	—	—	—	2	2.0	2.0	2.0

WALTHOUR, ISAAC (**Rabbit**) b. 1928 Ht. 5-11 Wt. 175 College—None

SEASON—TEAM	G	GS	MIN	FGM	FGA	PCT	3FGM	3FGA	PCT	FTM	FTA	PCT	O-RB	D-RB	TOT	AST	PF	DQ	STL	TO	BLK	PTS	RPG	APG	PPG
53-54—Milwaukee	4	—	30	1	6	.167	—	—	—	0	0	—	—	—	1	2	6	0	—	—	—	2	0.3	0.5	0.5
REG. SEASON TOTALS	4	—	30	1	6	.167	—	—	—	0	0	—	—	—	1	2	6	0	—	—	—	2	0.3	0.5	0.5

WALTON, LLOYD b. November 23, 1953 Ht. 6½ Wt. 160 College—Moberly Area CC/Marquette

SEASON—TEAM	G	GS	MIN	FGM	FGA	PCT	3FGM	3FGA	PCT	FTM	FTA	PCT	O-RB	D-RB	TOT	AST	PF	DQ	STL	TO	BLK	PTS	RPG	APG	PPG
76-77—Milwaukee	53	—	678	88	188	.468	—	—	—	53	65	.815	15	36	51	141	52	0	40	—	2	229	1.0	2.7	4.3
77-78—Milwaukee	76	—	1264	154	344	.448	—	—	—	54	83	.651	26	50	76	253	94	0	77	107	13	362	1.0	3.3	4.8
78-79—Milwaukee	75	—	1381	157	327	.480	—	—	—	61	90	.678	34	70	104	356	103	0	72	123	9	375	1.4	4.7	5.0
79-80—Milwaukee	76	—	1243	110	242	.455	1	3	.333	49	71	.690	33	58	91	285	68	0	43	112	2	270	1.2	3.8	3.6
80-81—Kansas City	61	—	821	90	218	.413	0	1	.000	26	33	.788	13	35	48	208	45	0	32	80	2	206	0.8	3.4	3.4
REG. SEASON TOTALS	341	—	5387	599	1319	.454	1	4	.250	243	342	.711	121	249	370	1243	362	0	264	422	28	1442	1.1	3.6	4.2
PLAYOFF TOTALS	18	—	201	21	51	.412	0	1	.000	11	17	.647	4	8	12	57	14	0	12	24	4	53	0.7	3.2	2.9

WALTON, WILLIAM THEODORE III (**Bill**) b. November 5, 1952   Ht. 7-0 Wt. 240 College—UCLA

SEASON—TEAM	G	GS	MIN	FGM	FGA	PCT	3FGM	3FGA	PCT	FTM	FTA	PCT	O-RB	D-RB	TOT	AST	PF	DQ	STL	TO	BLK	PTS	RPG	APG	PPG
74-75—Portland	35	—	1153	177	345	.513	—	—	—	94	137	.686	92	349	441	167	115	4	29	—	94	448	12.6	4.8	12.8
75-76—Portland	51	—	1687	345	732	.471	—	—	—	133	228	.583	132	549	681	220	144	3	49	—	82	823	13.4	4.3	16.1
76-77—Portland	65	—	2264	491	930	.528	—	—	—	228	327	.697	211	723	934	245	174	5	66	—	211	1210	14.4	3.8	18.6
77-78—Portland	58	—	1929	460	882	.522	—	—	—	177	246	.720	118	648	766	291	145	3	60	206	146	1097	13.2	5.0	18.9
79-80—San Diego	14	—	337	81	161	.503	0	0	—	32	54	.593	28	98	126	34	37	0	8	37	38	194	9.0	2.4	13.9
82-83—San Diego	33	32	1099	200	379	.528	0	0	—	65	117	.556	75	248	323	120	113	0	34	105	119	465	9.8	3.6	14.1
83-84—San Diego	55	46	1476	288	518	.556	0	2	.000	92	154	.597	132	345	477	183	153	1	45	177	88	668	8.7	3.3	12.1
84-85—L.A. Clippers	67	37	1647	269	516	.521	0	2	.000	138	203	.680	168	432	600	156	184	0	50	174	140	676	9.0	2.3	10.1
85-86—Boston	80	2	1546	231	411	.562	0	0	—	144	202	.713	136	408	544	165	210	1	38	151	106	606	6.8	2.1	7.6
86-87—Boston	10	0	112	10	26	.385	0	0	—	8	15	.533	11	20	31	9	23	0	1	15	10	28	3.1	0.9	2.8
REG. SEASON TOTALS	468	117	13250	2552	4900	.521	0	4	.000	1111	1683	.660	1103	3820	4923	1590	1298	17	380	865	1034	6215	10.5	3.4	13.3
PLAYOFF TOTALS	49	0	1197	230	438	.525	0	1	.000	68	101	.673	95	349	444	145	149	4	32	36	83	528	9.1	3.0	10.8
ALL-STAR TOTALS	1	1	31	6	14	.429	0	0	—	3	3	1.000	2	8	10	2	3	0	3	4	2	15	10.0	2.0	15.0

WANZER, ROBERT FRANCIS (**Bobby**) b. June 4, 1921   Ht. 6-0 Wt. 170 College—Colgate/Seton Hall

SEASON—TEAM	G	GS	MIN	FGM	FGA	PCT	3FGM	3FGA	PCT	FTM	FTA	PCT	O-RB	D-RB	TOT	AST	PF	DQ	STL	TO	BLK	PTS	RPG	APG	PPG
47-48—Rochester (N)	40	—	—	55			—	—	—	57	69	.826	—	—	—	—	38	—	—	—	—	167	—	—	4.2
48-49—Rochester	60	—	—	202	533	.379	—	—	—	209	254	.823	—	—	—	186	132	—	—	—	—	613	—	3.1	10.2
49-50—Rochester	67	—	—	254	614	.414	—	—	—	283	351	.806	—	—	—	214	102	—	—	—	—	791	—	3.2	11.8
50-51—Rochester	68	—	—	252	628	.401	—	—	—	232	273	.850	—	—	232	181	129	0	—	—	—	736	3.4	2.7	10.8
51-52—Rochester	66	—	2498	328	772	.425	—	—	—	377	417	.904	—	—	333	262	201	5	—	—	—	1033	5.0	4.0	15.7
52-53—Rochester	70	—	2577	318	866	.367	—	—	—	384	473	.812	—	—	351	252	206	7	—	—	—	1020	5.0	3.6	14.6
53-54—Rochester	72	—	2538	322	835	.386	—	—	—	314	428	.734	—	—	392	254	171	2	—	—	—	958	5.4	3.5	13.3
54-55—Rochester	72	—	2376	324	820	.395	—	—	—	294	374	.786	—	—	374	247	163	2	—	—	—	942	5.2	3.4	13.1
55-56—Rochester	72	—	1980	245	651	.376	—	—	—	259	360	.719	—	—	272	225	151	0	—	—	—	749	3.8	3.1	10.4
56-57—Rochester	21	—	159	23	49	.469	—	—	—	36	46	.783	—	—	25	9	20	0	—	—	—	82	1.2	0.4	3.9
REG. NBA TOTALS	568	—	12128	2268	5768	.393	—	—	—	2388	2976	.802	—	—	1979	1830	1275	16	—	—	—	6924	4.5	3.2	12.2
REG. NBL TOTALS	40	—	—	55	—	—	—	—	—	57	69	.826	—	—	—	—	38	—	—	—	—	167	—	—	4.2
NBA PLAYOFF TOTALS	38	—	710	171	402	.425	—	—	—	212	241	.880	—	—	186	134	123	3	—	—	—	554	5.8	3.5	14.6
NBL PLAYOFF TOTALS	11	—	—	21	—	—	—	—	—	24	28	.857	—	—	—	—	5	—	—	—	—	66	—	—	6.0
NBA ALL-STAR TOTALS	5	—	131	17	43	.395	—	—	—	12	14	.857	—	—	17	17	17	1	—	—	—	46	3.4	3.4	9.2

WARBINGTON, PERRY b. September 7, 1952   Ht. 6-2 Wt. 165 College—Lake City CC/Georgia Southern College

SEASON—TEAM	G	GS	MIN	FGM	FGA	PCT	3FGM	3FGA	PCT	FTM	FTA	PCT	O-RB	D-RB	TOT	AST	PF	DQ	STL	TO	BLK	PTS	RPG	APG	PPG
74-75—Philadelphia	5	—	70	4	21	.190	—	—	—	2	2	1.000	2	6	8	16	16	0	0	—	0	10	1.6	3.2	2.0
REG. SEASON TOTALS	5	—	70	4	21	.190	—	—	—	2	2	1.000	2	6	8	16	16	0	0	—	0	10	1.6	3.2	2.0

WARD, GERALD W. (**Gerry**) b. September 6, 1941   Ht. 6-4 Wt. 200 College—Boston College

SEASON—TEAM	G	GS	MIN	FGM	FGA	PCT	3FGM	3FGA	PCT	FTM	FTA	PCT	O-RB	D-RB	TOT	AST	PF	DQ	STL	TO	BLK	PTS	RPG	APG	PPG
63-64—St. Louis	24	—	139	16	53	.302	—	—	—	11	17	.647	—	—	21	21	26	0	—	—	—	43	0.9	0.9	1.8
64-65—Boston	3	—	30	2	18	.111	—	—	—	1	1	1.000	—	—	5	6	6	0	—	—	—	5	1.7	2.0	1.7
65-66—Philadelphia	66	—	838	67	189	.354	—	—	—	39	60	.650	—	—	89	80	163	3	—	—	—	173	1.3	1.2	2.6
66-67—Chicago	76	—	1042	117	307	.381	—	—	—	87	138	.630	—	—	179	130	169	2	—	—	—	321	2.4	1.7	4.2
REG. SEASON TOTALS	169	—	2049	202	567	.356	—	—	—	138	216	.639	—	—	294	237	364	5	—	—	—	542	1.7	1.4	3.2
PLAYOFF TOTALS	14	—	118	13	34	.382	—	—	—	3	6	.500	—	—	10	11	27	0	—	—	—	29	0.7	0.8	2.1

WARD, HENRY LORETTE b. January 30, 1952   Ht. 6-4 Wt. 195 College—Jackson State

SEASON—TEAM	G	GS	MIN	FGM	FGA	PCT	3FGM	3FGA	PCT	FTM	FTA	PCT	O-RB	D-RB	TOT	AST	PF	DQ	STL	TO	BLK	PTS	RPG	APG	PPG
75-76—San Antonio (A)	61	—	688	154	333	.462	6	23	.261	16	27	.593	45	95	140	35	99	—	16	45	10	330	2.3	0.6	5.4
76-77—San Antonio	27	—	171	34	90	.378	—	—	—	15	17	.882	10	23	33	6	30	0	6	—	5	83	1.2	0.2	3.1
REG. NBA TOTALS	27	—	171	34	90	.378	—	—	—	15	17	.882	10	23	33	6	30	0	6	—	5	83	1.2	0.2	3.1
REG. ABA TOTALS	61	—	688	154	333	.462	6	23	.261	16	27	.593	45	95	140	35	99	—	16	45	10	330	2.3	0.6	5.4
NBA PLAYOFF TOTALS	1	—	1	2	3	.667	—	—	—	0	0	—	0	0	0	0	0	0	0	—	0	4	0.0	0.0	4.0
ABA PLAYOFF TOTALS	5	—	18	4	12	.333	2	2	1.000	0	0	—	1	1	2	0	6	—	1	1	1	10	0.4	0.0	2.0

WARE, JAMES EDWARD (**Jim**) b. May 2, 1944   Ht. 6-7½ Wt. 210 College—Oklahoma City

SEASON—TEAM	G	GS	MIN	FGM	FGA	PCT	3FGM	3FGA	PCT	FTM	FTA	PCT	O-RB	D-RB	TOT	AST	PF	DQ	STL	TO	BLK	PTS	RPG	APG	PPG
66-67—Cincinnati	33	—	201	30	97	.309	—	—	—	10	17	.588	—	—	69	6	35	0	—	—	—	70	2.1	0.2	2.1
67-68—San Diego	30	—	228	25	97	.258	—	—	—	23	34	.676	—	—	77	7	28	1	—	—	—	73	2.6	0.2	2.4
68-69—Dallas (A)	1	—	15	3	4	.750	0	0	—	1	2	.500	—	—	7	1	4	0	—	1	—	7	7.0	1.0	7.0
REG. NBA TOTALS	63	—	429	55	194	.284	—	—	—	33	51	.647	—	—	146	13	63	1	—	—	—	143	2.3	0.2	2.3
REG. ABA TOTALS	1	—	15	3	4	.750	0	0	—	1	2	.500	—	—	7	1	4	0	—	1	—	7	7.0	1.0	7.0
NBA PLAYOFF TOTALS	3	—	13	5	13	.385	—	—	—	0	0	—	—	—	2	1	0	—	—	—	—	10	0.7	0.0	3.3

WARLEY, BENJAMIN VALLENTINA (Ben) b. September 4, 1936 Ht. 6-6 Wt. 205 College—Tennessee State

SEASON—TEAM	G	GS	MIN	FGM	FGA	PCT	3FGM	3FGA	PCT	FTM	FTA	PCT	O-RB	D-RB	TOT	AST	PF	DQ	STL	TO	BLK	PTS	RPG	APG	PPG
62-63—Syracuse	26	—	206	50	111	.450	—	—	—	25	35	.714	—	—	86	4	42	1	—	—	—	125	3.3	0.2	4.8
63-64—Philadelphia	79	—	1740	215	494	.435	—	—	—	220	305	.721	—	—	619	71	274	5	—	—	—	650	7.8	0.9	8.2
64-65—Philadelphia	64	—	900	94	253	.372	—	—	—	124	176	.705	—	—	277	53	170	6	—	—	—	312	4.3	0.8	4.9
65-66—Phil.-Balt.	57	—	773	116	284	.408	—	—	—	64	97	.660	—	—	217	25	129	2	—	—	—	296	3.8	0.4	5.2
66-67—Baltimore	62	—	1037	125	312	.401	—	—	—	134	170	.788	—	—	325	51	176	6	—	—	—	384	5.2	0.8	6.2
67-68—Anaheim (A)	71	—	2297	435	985	.442	52	166	.313	313	389	.805	—	—	608	96	276	12	—	161	—	1235	8.6	1.4	17.4
60-69—Los Angeles (A)	35	—	876	172	423	.407	31	121	.256	116	155	.748	—	—	194	26	127	6	—	53	—	491	5.5	0.7	14.0
69-70—Denver (A)	42	—	475	60	170	.353	15	58	.259	58	76	.763	—	—	110	30	98	0	—	—	—	193	2.6	0.7	4.6
REG. NBA TOTALS	288	—	4656	600	1454	.413	—	—	—	567	783	.724	—	—	1524	204	791	20	—	—	—	1767	5.3	0.7	6.1
REG. ABA TOTALS	148	—	3648	667	1578	.423	98	345	.284	487	620	.785	—	—	912	152	501	18	—	214	—	1919	6.2	1.0	13.0
NBA PLAYOFF TOTALS	10	—	109	9	32	.281	—	—	—	13	20	.650	—	—	39	3	16	0	—	—	—	31	3.9	0.3	3.1
ABA PLAYOFF TOTALS	10	—	129	16	38	.421	7	16	.438	6	10	.600	—	—	29	11	27	1	—	—	—	45	2.9	1.1	4.5
ABA ALL-STAR TOTALS	1	—	17	2	7	.286	0	3	.000	4	4	1.000	—	1	1	3	2	0	—	2	—	8	1.0	3.0	8.0

WARLICK, ROBERT LEE (Bob) b. March 20, 1941 Ht. 6-5 Wt. 205 College—Pueblo JC/Pepperdine/Denver

SEASON—TEAM	G	GS	MIN	FGM	FGA	PCT	3FGM	3FGA	PCT	FTM	FTA	PCT	O-RB	D-RB	TOT	AST	PF	DQ	STL	TO	BLK	PTS	RPG	APG	PPG
65-66—Detroit	10	—	78	11	38	.289	—	—	—	2	6	.333	—	—	16	10	8	0	—	—	—	24	1.6	1.0	2.4
66-67—San Francisco	12	—	65	15	52	.288	—	—	—	6	11	.545	—	—	20	10	4	0	—	—	—	36	1.7	0.8	3.0
67-68—San Francisco	69	—	1320	257	610	.421	—	—	—	97	171	.567	—	—	264	159	164	1	—	—	—	611	3.8	2.3	8.9
68-69—Milw.-Phoenix	66	—	997	213	509	.418	—	—	—	87	142	.613	—	—	152	132	122	0	—	—	—	513	2.3	2.0	7.8
69-70—Los Angeles (A)	29	—	711	112	309	.362	0	1	.000	65	96	.677	—	—	114	76	70	0	—	—	—	289	3.9	2.6	10.0
REG. NBA TOTALS	157	—	2460	496	1209	.410	—	—	—	192	330	.582	—	—	452	311	298	1	—	—	—	1184	2.9	2.0	7.5
REG. ABA TOTALS	29	—	711	112	309	.362	0	1	.000	65	96	.677	—	—	114	76	70	0	—	—	—	289	3.9	2.6	10.0
NBA PLAYOFF TOTALS	12	—	234	55	120	.458	—	—	—	28	37	.757	—	—	53	25	26	2	—	—	—	138	4.4	2.1	11.5

WARNER, CARNELL b. August 12, 1948 Ht. 6-9 Wt. 225 College—Jackson State

SEASON—TEAM	G	GS	MIN	FGM	FGA	PCT	3FGM	3FGA	PCT	FTM	FTA	PCT	O-RB	D-RB	TOT	AST	PF	DQ	STL	TO	BLK	PTS	RPG	APG	PPG
70-71—Buffalo	65	—	1293	156	376	.415	—	—	—	79	143	.552	—	—	452	53	140	2	—	—	—	391	7.0	0.8	6.0
71-72—Buffalo	62	—	1239	162	366	.443	—	—	—	58	78	.744	—	—	379	54	125	2	—	—	—	382	6.1	0.9	6.2
72-73—Buffalo-Clev.	72	—	1370	174	421	.413	—	—	—	59	90	.656	—	—	522	72	178	3	—	—	—	407	7.3	1.0	5.7
73-74—Clev.-Milw.	72	—	1405	174	349	.499	—	—	—	85	114	.746	106	291	397	71	204	8	27	—	42	433	5.5	1.0	6.0
74-75—Milwaukee	79	—	2519	248	541	.458	—	—	—	106	155	.684	238	574	812	127	267	8	49	—	54	602	10.3	1.6	7.6
75-76—Los Angeles	81	—	2512	251	524	.479	—	—	—	89	128	.695	223	499	722	106	283	5	55	—	46	591	8.9	1.3	7.3
76-77—Los Angeles	14	—	170	25	53	.472	—	—	—	4	6	.667	21	48	69	11	28	0	.1	—	2	54	4.9	0.8	3.9
REG. SEASON TOTALS	445	—	10508	1190	2630	.452	—	—	—	480	714	.672	588	1412	3353	494	1225	26	132	—	144	2860	7.5	1.1	6.4
PLAYOFF TOTALS	21	—	561	54	123	.439	—	—	—	13	19	.684	37	135	172	26	81	3	8	—	14	121	8.2	1.2	5.8

WARREN, JOHN II (Johnny) b. July 7, 1947 Ht. 6-3 Wt. 180 College—St. John's

SEASON—TEAM	G	GS	MIN	FGM	FGA	PCT	3FGM	3FGA	PCT	FTM	FTA	PCT	O-RB	D-RB	TOT	AST	PF	DQ	STL	TO	BLK	PTS	RPG	APG	PPG
69-70—New York	44	—	272	44	108	.407	—	—	—	24	35	.686	—	—	40	30	53	0	—	—	—	112	0.9	0.7	2.5
70-71—Cleveland	82	—	2610	380	899	.423	—	—	—	180	217	.829	—	—	344	347	299	13	—	—	—	940	4.2	4.2	11.5
71-72—Cleveland	68	—	969	144	345	.417	—	—	—	49	58	.845	—	—	133	91	92	0	—	—	—	337	2.0	1.3	5.0
72-73—Cleveland	40	—	290	54	111	.486	—	—	—	18	19	.947	—	—	42	34	45	0	—	—	—	126	1.1	0.9	3.2
73-74—Cleveland	69	—	790	132	291	.454	—	—	—	35	41	.854	42	86	128	62	117	1	27	—	6	299	1.9	0.9	4.3
REG. SEASON TOTALS	303	—	4931	754	1754	.430	—	—	—	306	370	.827	42	86	687	564	606	14	27	—	6	1814	2.3	1.9	6.0
PLAYOFF TOTALS	10	—	22	2	5	.400	—	—	—	0	0	—	0	0	3	2	6	0	0	—	0	4	0.3	0.2	0.4

WARREN, ROBERT G. (Bobby, Colonel) b. July 17, 1946 Ht. 6-5 Wt. 190 College—Vanderbilt

SEASON—TEAM	G	GS	MIN	FGM	FGA	PCT	3FGM	3FGA	PCT	FTM	FTA	PCT	O-RB	D-RB	TOT	AST	PF	DQ	STL	TO	BLK	PTS	RPG	APG	PPG
68-69—Los Angeles (A)	76	—	2045	285	645	.442	31	89	.348	297	385	.771	—	—	349	155	252	6	—	175	—	898	4.6	2.0	11.8
69-70—Los Angeles (A)	72	—	1672	266	647	.411	25	107	.234	176	238	.739	—	—	277	141	190	1	—	—	—	733	3.8	2.0	10.2
70-71—Memphis (A)	46	—	763	146	367	.398	21	81	.259	107	133	.805	—	—	144	85	87	—	—	—	—	420	3.1	1.8	9.1
71-72—Memphis-Car. (A)	75	—	1801	313	707	.443	11	55	.200	213	268	.795	—	—	259	182	165	—	—	140	—	850	3.5	2.4	11.3
72-73—Car.-Dallas-Utah (A)	77	—	1571	244	504	.484	5	19	.263	236	274	.861	92	150	242	147	212	2	—	143	—	729	3.1	1.9	9.5
73-74—Utah-S.A. (A)	59	—	799	110	255	.431	0	6	.000	63	73	.863	53	51	104	74	73	—	21	62	13	283	1.8	1.3	4.8
74-75—San Antonio (A)	71	—	992	127	265	.479	2	7	.286	77	91	.846	42	70	112	91	109	—	35	68	9	333	1.6	1.3	4.7
75-76—San Diego (A)	10	—	265	36	81	.444	1	3	.333	28	32	.875	27	32	59	23	35	—	9	23	6	101	5.9	2.3	10.1
REG. ABA TOTALS	486	—	9908	1527	3471	.440	96	367	.262	1197	1494	.801	214	303	1546	898	1123	9	65	611	28	4347	3.2	1.8	8.9
ABA PLAYOFF TOTALS	35	—	935	142	321	.442	17	58	.293	86	104	.827	9	12	187	92	108	—	2	30	2	387	5.3	2.6	11.1

WARRICK, BRYAN ANTHONY b. July 22, 1959 Ht. 6-5 Wt. 195 College—St. Joseph's (Pa.)

SEASON—TEAM	G	GS	MIN	FGM	FGA	PCT	3FGM	3FGA	PCT	FTM	FTA	PCT	O-RB	D-RB	TOT	AST	PF	DQ	STL	TO	BLK	PTS	RPG	APG	PPG
82-83—Washington	43	20	727	65	171	.380	0	5	.000	42	57	.737	15	54	69	126	103	5	21	71	8	172	1.6	2.9	4.0
83-84—Washington	32	0	254	27	66	.409	1	3	.333	8	16	.500	5	17	22	43	37	0	9	20	3	63	0.7	1.3	2.0
84-85—L.A. Clippers	58	1	713	85	173	.491	1	4	.250	44	57	.772	10	48	58	153	85	0	23	70	6	215	1.0	2.6	3.7
85-86—Milw.-Indiana	36	5	685	85	182	.467	3	12	.250	54	68	.794	10	59	69	115	79	0	27	53	2	227	1.9	3.2	6.3
REG. SEASON TOTALS	169	26	2379	262	592	.443	5	24	.208	148	198	.747	40	178	218	437	304	5	80	214	19	677	1.3	2.6	4.0

WASHBURN, CHRISTOPHER SCOTT (**Chris**) b. May 13, 1965 Ht. 6-11 Wt. 255 College—North Carolina State

SEASON—TEAM	G	GS	MIN	FGM	FGA	PCT	3FGM	3FGA	PCT	FTM	FTA	PCT	O-RB	D-RB	TOT	AST	PF	DQ	STL	TO	BLK	PTS	RPG	APG	PPG
86-87—Golden State	35	2	385	57	145	.393	0	1	.000	18	51	.353	36	65	101	16	51	0	6	39	8	132	2.9	0.5	3.8
87-88—G.S.-Atlanta	37	0	260	36	81	.444	0	0	—	18	31	.581	28	47	75	6	29	0	5	17	8	90	2.0	0.2	2.4
REG. SEASON TOTALS	72	2	645	93	226	.412	0	1	.000	36	82	.439	64	112	176	22	80	0	11	56	16	222	2.4	0.3	3.1
PLAYOFF TOTALS	6	0	31	3	7	.429	0	0	—	5	6	.833	0	1	1	2	2	0	0	4	0	11	0.2	0.3	1.8

WASHINGTON, DONALD MAURICE JR. (**Don**) b. April 22, 1952 Ht. 6-8 Wt. 210 College—North Carolina

SEASON—TEAM	G	GS	MIN	FGM	FGA	PCT	3FGM	3FGA	PCT	FTM	FTA	PCT	O-RB	D-RB	TOT	AST	PF	DQ	STL	TO	BLK	PTS	RPG	APG	PPG
74-75—Denver (A)	50	—	438	79	183	.432	0	2	.000	38	56	.679	41	48	89	30	92	—	12	49	19	196	1.8	0.6	3.9
75-76—Utah (A)	6	—	58	12	18	.667	0	0	—	0	0	—	4	9	13	3	19	—	1	3	1	24	2.2	0.5	4.0
REG. ABA TOTALS	56	—	496	91	201	.453	0	2	.000	38	56	.679	45	57	102	33	111	—	13	52	20	220	1.8	0.6	3.9
ABA PLAYOFF TOTALS	4	—	26	5	10	.500	0	0	—	1	1	1.000	2	4	6	2	9	—	1	4	2	11	1.5	0.5	2.8

WASHINGTON, DUANE E. b. August 31, 1964 Ht. 6-4 Wt. 195 College—Laredo JC/Middle Tennessee State

SEASON—TEAM	G	GS	MIN	FGM	FGA	PCT	3FGM	3FGA	PCT	FTM	FTA	PCT	O-RB	D-RB	TOT	AST	PF	DQ	STL	TO	BLK	PTS	RPG	APG	PPG
87-88—New Jersey	15	0	156	18	42	.429	2	4	.500	16	20	.800	5	17	22	34	23	0	12	9	0	54	1.5	2.3	3.6
92-93—L.A. Clippers	4	0	28	0	5	.000	0	0	—	0	0	—	0	2	2	5	2	0	1	2	0	0	0.5	1.3	0.0
REG. SEASON TOTALS	19	0	184	18	47	.383	2	4	.500	16	20	.800	5	19	24	39	25	0	13	11	0	54	1.3	2.1	2.8

WASHINGTON, DWAYNE ALONZO (**Pearl**) b. January 6, 1964 Ht. 6-2 Wt. 195 College—Syracuse

SEASON—TEAM	G	GS	MIN	FGM	FGA	PCT	3FGM	3FGA	PCT	FTM	FTA	PCT	O-RB	D-RB	TOT	AST	PF	DQ	STL	TO	BLK	PTS	RPG	APG	PPG
86-87—New Jersey	72	61	1600	257	538	.478	4	24	.167	98	125	.784	37	92	129	301	184	5	92	175	7	616	1.8	4.2	8.6
87-88—New Jersey	68	10	1379	245	547	.448	11	49	.224	132	189	.698	54	64	118	206	163	2	91	141	4	633	1.7	3.0	9.3
88-89—Miami	54	8	1065	164	387	.424	1	14	.071	82	104	.788	49	74	123	226	101	0	73	122	4	411	2.3	4.2	7.6
REG. SEASON TOTALS	194	79	4044	666	1472	.452	16	87	.184	312	418	.746	140	230	370	733	448	7	256	438	15	1660	1.9	3.8	8.6

WASHINGTON, JAMES H. (**Jim**) b. July 1, 1943 Ht. 6-7 Wt. 215 College—Villanova

SEASON—TEAM	G	GS	MIN	FGM	FGA	PCT	3FGM	3FGA	PCT	FTM	FTA	PCT	O-RB	D-RB	TOT	AST	PF	DQ	STL	TO	BLK	PTS	RPG	APG	PPG
65-66—St. Louis	65	—	1104	158	393	.402	—	—	—	68	120	.567	—	—	353	43	176	4	—	—	—	384	5.4	0.7	5.9
66-67—Chicago	77	—	1475	252	604	.417	—	—	—	88	159	.553	—	—	468	56	181	1	—	—	—	592	6.1	0.7	7.7
67-68—Chicago	82	—	2525	418	915	.457	—	—	—	187	274	.682	—	—	825	113	233	1	—	—	—	1023	10.1	1.4	12.5
68-69—Chicago	80	—	2705	440	1023	.430	—	—	—	241	356	.677	—	—	847	104	226	0	—	—	—	1121	10.6	1.3	14.0
69-70—Philadelphia	79	—	2459	401	842	.476	—	—	—	204	273	.747	—	—	734	104	262	5	—	—	—	1006	9.3	1.3	12.7
70-71—Philadelphia	78	—	2501	395	829	.476	—	—	—	259	340	.762	—	—	747	97	258	6	—	—	—	1049	9.6	1.2	13.4
71-72—Phil.-Atlanta	84	—	2961	393	885	.444	—	—	—	256	323	.793	—	—	736	146	276	3	—	—	—	1042	8.8	1.7	12.4
72-73—Atlanta	75	—	2833	308	713	.432	—	—	—	163	224	.728	—	—	801	174	252	5	—	—	—	779	10.7	2.3	10.4
73-74—Atlanta	73	—	2519	297	612	.485	—	—	—	134	196	.684	207	528	735	156	249	5	49	—	74	728	10.1	2.1	10.0
74-75—Atlanta-Buffalo	80	—	1579	191	421	.454	—	—	—	62	93	.667	110	280	390	111	167	5	34	—	26	444	4.9	1.4	5.6
75-76—Buffalo	1	—	7	0	1	.000	—	—	—	0	0	—	1	0	1	1	0	0	0	—	0	0	1.0	1.0	0.0
REG. SEASON TOTALS	774	—	22668	3253	7238	.449	—	—	—	1662	2358	.705	318	808	6637	1105	2280	35	83	—	100	8168	8.6	1.4	10.6
PLAYOFF TOTALS	42	—	1106	151	340	.444	—	—	—	67	112	.598	3	4	300	58	111	2	0	—	0	369	7.1	1.4	8.8

WASHINGTON, KERMIT ALAN (**Special K**) b. September 17, 1951 Ht. 6-8 Wt. 230 College—American International

SEASON—TEAM	G	GS	MIN	FGM	FGA	PCT	3FGM	3FGA	PCT	FTM	FTA	PCT	O-RB	D-RB	TOT	AST	PF	DQ	STL	TO	BLK	PTS	RPG	APG	PPG
73-74—Los Angeles	45	—	400	73	151	.483	—	—	—	26	49	.531	62	85	147	19	77	0	21	—	18	172	3.3	0.4	3.8
74-75—Los Angeles	55	—	949	87	207	.420	—	—	—	72	122	.590	106	244	350	66	155	2	25	—	32	246	6.4	1.2	4.5
75-76—Los Angeles	36	—	492	39	90	.433	—	—	—	45	66	.682	51	114	165	20	76	0	11	—	26	123	4.6	0.6	3.4
76-77—Los Angeles	53	—	1342	191	380	.503	—	—	—	132	187	.706	182	310	492	48	183	1	43	—	52	514	9.3	0.9	9.7
77-78—L.A.-Boston	57	—	1617	247	507	.487	—	—	—	170	246	.691	215	399	614	72	188	3	47	107	64	664	10.8	1.3	11.6
78-79—San Diego	82	—	2764	350	623	.562	—	—	—	227	330	.688	296	504	800	125	317	11	85	185	121	927	9.8	1.5	11.3
79-80—Portland	80	—	2657	421	761	.553	0	3	.000	231	360	.642	325	517	842	167	307	8	73	170	131	1073	10.5	2.1	13.4
80-81—Portland	73	—	2120	325	571	.569	0	1	.000	181	288	.628	236	450	686	149	258	5	85	144	86	831	9.4	2.0	11.4
81-82—Portland	20	4	418	38	78	.487	0	0	—	24	41	.585	40	77	117	29	56	0	9	19	16	100	5.9	1.5	5.0
87-88—Golden State	6	1	56	7	14	.500	0	0	—	2	2	1.000	9	10	19	0	13	0	4	4	4	16	3.2	0.0	2.7
REG. SEASON TOTALS	507	5	12815	1778	3382	.526	0	4	.000	1110	1691	.656	1522	2710	4232	695	1630	30	403	629	550	4666	8.3	1.4	9.2
PLAYOFF TOTALS	9	0	263	30	60	.500	0	2	.000	12	17	.706	35	58	93	14	18	0	10	11	6	72	10.3	1.6	8.0
ALL-STAR TOTALS	1	0	14	1	6	.167	0	0	—	2	4	.500	4	4	8	1	4	0	0	1	1	4	8.0	1.0	4.0

WASHINGTON, RICHARD LEE b. July 15, 1955 Ht. 6-10½ Wt. 220 College—UCLA

SEASON—TEAM	G	GS	MIN	FGM	FGA	PCT	3FGM	3FGA	PCT	FTM	FTA	PCT	O-RB	D-RB	TOT	AST	PF	DQ	STL	TO	BLK	PTS	RPG	APG	PPG
76-77—Kansas City	82	—	2265	446	1034	.431	—	—		177	254	.697	201	497	698	85	324	13	63	—	90	1069	8.5	1.0	13.0
77-78—Kansas City	78	—	2231	425	891	.477	—	—		150	199	.754	188	466	654	118	324	12	74	191	73	1000	8.4	1.5	12.8
78-79—Kansas City	18	—	161	14	41	.341	—	—		10	16	.625	11	37	48	7	31	0	7	15	3	38	2.7	0.4	2.1
79-80—Milwaukee	75	—	1092	197	421	.468	0	0	—	46	76	.605	95	181	276	55	166	2	26	63	48	440	3.7	0.7	5.9
80-81—Dallas-Clev.	80	—	1812	340	747	.455	1	2	.500	119	159	.748	158	295	453	129	273	3	46	129	61	800	5.7	1.6	10.0
81-82—Cleveland	18	2	313	50	115	.435	0	2	.000	9	15	.600	32	43	75	15	51	0	8	35	2	109	4.2	0.8	6.1
REG. SEASON TOTALS	351	2	78/4	1472	3249	.453	1	4	.250	511	719	.711	685	1519	2204	409	1169	30	224	433	277	3456	6.3	1.2	9.8
PLAYOFF TOTALS	11	0	164	36	67	.537	0	0	—	3	6	.500	10	23	33	3	39	1	5	9	9	/5	3.0	0.3	6.8

WASHINGTON, ROBERT (**Bobby**) b. July 11, 1947 Ht. 5-11½ Wt. 175 College—Eastern Kentucky

SEASON—TEAM	G	GS	MIN	FGM	FGA	PCT	3FGM	3FGA	PCT	FTM	FTA	PCT	O-RB	D-RB	TOT	AST	PF	DQ	STL	TO	BLK	PTS	RPG	APG	PPG
69-70—Kentucky (A)	2	—	5	0	1	.000	0	0	—	0	0	—	—	—	0	0	0	0	—	—	—	0	0.0	0.0	0.0
70-71—Cleveland	47	—	823	123	310	.397	—	—		104	140	.743	—	—	105	190	105	0	—	—	—	350	2.2	4.0	7.4
71-72—Cleveland	69	—	967	123	309	.398	—	—		104	128	.813	—	—	129	223	135	1	—	—	—	350	1.9	3.2	5.1
REG. NBA TOTALS	116	—	1790	246	619	.397	—	—		208	268	.776	—	—	234	413	240	1	—	—	—	700	2.0	3.6	6.0
REG. ABA TOTALS	2	—	5	0	1	.000	0	0	—	0	0	—	—	—	0	0	0	0	—	—	—	0	0.0	0.0	0.0

WASHINGTON, STANLEY (**Stan**) b. January 23, 1952 Ht. 6-4 Wt. 190 College—San Diego

SEASON—TEAM	G	GS	MIN	FGM	FGA	PCT	3FGM	3FGA	PCT	FTM	FTA	PCT	O-RB	D-RB	TOT	AST	PF	DQ	STL	TO	BLK	PTS	RPG	APG	PPG
74-75—Washington	1	—	4	0	1	.000	—	—	—	0	0	—	0	0	0	0	1	0	0	—	0	0	0.0	0.0	0.0
REG. SEASON TOTALS	1	—	4	0	1	.000	—	—	—	0	0	—	0	0	0	0	1	0	0	—	0	0	0.0	0.0	0.0

WASHINGTON, THOMAS (**Trooper**) b. April 21, 1944 Ht. 6-7 Wt. 225 College—Cheyney

SEASON—TEAM	G	GS	MIN	FGM	FGA	PCT	3FGM	3FGA	PCT	FTM	FTA	PCT	O-RB	D-RB	TOT	AST	PF	DQ	STL	TO	BLK	PTS	RPG	APG	PPG
67-68—Pittsburgh (A)	63	—	1844	312	596	.523	2	2	1.000	106	186	.570	303	369	672	102	189	4	—	110	—	732	10.7	1.6	11.6
68-69—Minnesota (A)	69	—	2625	421	839	.502	0	6	.000	190	316	.601	367	501	868	178	239	2	—	190	—	1032	12.6	2.6	15.0
69-70—Pitt.-L.A. (A)	81	—	2353	320	582	.550	4	8	.500	155	240	.646	—	—	822	196	285	8	—	—	—	799	10.1	2.4	9.9
70-71—Floridians (A)	57	—	1876	216	426	.507	0	2	.000	102	167	.611	—	—	606	187	184	—	—	—	—	534	10.6	3.3	9.4
71-72—New York (A)	80	—	2510	387	678	.571	0	0	—	107	166	.645	—	—	750	161	291	—	—	188	—	881	9.4	2.0	11.0
72-73—New York (A)	76	—	2027	229	425	.539	0	0	—	63	101	.624	174	379	553	203	242	5	—	183	—	521	7.3	2.7	6.9
REG. ABA TOTALS	426	—	13235	1885	3546	.532	6	18	.333	723	1176	.615	844	1249	4271	1027	1430	19	—	671	—	4499	10.0	2.4	10.6
ABA PLAYOFF TOTALS	66	—	2015	256	472	.542	0	2	.000	73	139	.525	169	271	748	161	218	5	—	82	—	585	11.3	2.4	8.9
ABA ALL-STAR TOTALS	1	—	15	2	5	.400	0	0	—	2	2	1.000	4	1	5	1	3	0	—	0	—	6	5.0	1.0	6.0

WASHINGTON, WILSON JR. b. August 3, 1955 Ht. 6-10 Wt. 235 College—Old Dominion

SEASON—TEAM	G	GS	MIN	FGM	FGA	PCT	3FGM	3FGA	PCT	FTM	FTA	PCT	O-RB	D-RB	TOT	AST	PF	DQ	STL	TO	BLK	PTS	RPG	APG	PPG
77-78—Phil.-N.J.	38	—	561	100	206	.485	—	—		29	53	.547	50	106	156	10	75	2	18	63	37	229	4.1	0.3	6.0
78-79—New Jersey	62	—	1139	218	434	.502	—	—		66	104	.635	88	206	294	47	186	5	31	98	67	502	4.7	0.8	8.1
REG. SEASON TOTALS	100	—	1700	318	640	.497	—	—		95	157	.605	138	312	450	57	261	7	49	161	104	731	4.5	0.6	7.3

WATSON, ROBERT E. (**Bobby**) b. March 22, 1930 Ht. 6-0 Wt. 160 College—Kentucky

SEASON—TEAM	G	GS	MIN	FGM	FGA	PCT	3FGM	3FGA	PCT	FTM	FTA	PCT	O-RB	D-RB	TOT	AST	PF	DQ	STL	TO	BLK	PTS	RPG	APG	PPG
54-55—Milwaukee	63	—	702	72	223	.323	—	—	—	31	45	.689	—	—	87	79	67	0	—	—	—	175	1.4	1.3	2.8
REG. SEASON TOTALS	63	—	702	72	223	.323	—	—	—	31	45	.689	—	—	87	79	67	0	—	—	—	175	1.4	1.3	2.8

WATTS, DONALD EARL (**Slick**) b. July 22, 1951 Ht. 6-1 Wt. 175 College—Xavier (La.)

SEASON—TEAM	G	GS	MIN	FGM	FGA	PCT	3FGM	3FGA	PCT	FTM	FTA	PCT	O-RB	D-RB	TOT	AST	PF	DQ	STL	TO	BLK	PTS	RPG	APG	PPG
73-74—Seattle	62	—	1424	198	510	.388	—	—	—	100	155	.645	72	110	182	351	207	8	115	—	13	496	2.9	5.7	8.0
74-75—Seattle	82	—	2056	232	551	.421	—	—	—	93	153	.608	95	167	262	499	254	7	190	—	12	557	3.2	6.1	6.8
75-76—Seattle	82	—	2776	433	1015	.427	—	—	—	199	344	.578	112	253	365	661	270	3	261	—	16	1065	4.5	8.1	13.0
76-77—Seattle	79	—	2627	428	1015	.422	—	—	—	172	293	.587	81	226	307	630	256	5	214	—	25	1028	3.9	8.0	13.0
77-78—Seattle-N.O.	71	—	1584	219	558	.392	—	—	—	92	156	.590	60	119	179	294	184	1	108	168	31	530	2.5	4.1	7.5
78-79—Houston	61	—	1046	92	227	.405	—	—	—	41	67	.612	35	68	103	243	143	1	73	71	14	225	1.7	4.0	3.7
REG. SEASON TOTALS	437	—	11513	1602	3876	.413	—	—	—	697	1168	.597	455	943	1398	2678	1314	25	961	239	111	3901	3.2	6.1	8.9
PLAYOFF TOTALS	17	—	522	79	177	.446	—	—	—	27	52	.519	19	39	58	120	66	1	43	7	7	185	3.4	7.1	10.9

WATTS, RONALD MICHAEL (**Ron**) b. May 21, 1943 Ht. 6-6 Wt. 210 College—Wake Forest

SEASON—TEAM	G	GS	MIN	FGM	FGA	PCT	3FGM	3FGA	PCT	FTM	FTA	PCT	O-RB	D-RB	TOT	AST	PF	DQ	STL	TO	BLK	PTS	RPG	APG	PPG
65-66—Boston	1	—	3	1	2	.500	—	—	—	0	0	—	—	—	1	1	1	0	—	—	—	2	1.0	1.0	2.0
66-67—Boston	27	—	89	11	44	.250	—	—	—	16	23	.696	—	—	38	1	16	0	—	—	—	38	1.4	0.0	1.4
REG. SEASON TOTALS	28	—	92	12	46	.261	—	—	—	16	23	.696	—	—	39	2	17	0	—	—	—	40	1.4	0.1	1.4
PLAYOFF TOTALS	1	—	5	1	6	.167	—	—	—	1	2	.500	—	—	2	—	3	0	—	—	—	3	2.0	0.0	3.0

WATTS, SAMUEL D. (Sam) b. March 14, 1948　Ht. 6-3　Wt. 185　College—Northwest CC/Great Falls/Florida A&M

SEASON—TEAM	G	GS	MIN	FGM	FGA	PCT	3FGM	3FGA	PCT	FTM	FTA	PCT	O-RB	D-RB	TOT	AST	PF	DQ	STL	TO	BLK	PTS	RPG	APG	PPG
70-71—Pittsburgh (A)	54	—	650	109	287	.380	14	41	.341	49	67	.731	—	—	99	45	106	—	—	—	—	281	1.8	0.8	5.2
REG. ABA TOTALS	54	—	650	109	287	.380	14	41	.341	49	67	.731	—	—	99	45	106	—	—	—	—	281	1.8	0.8	5.2

WEATHERSPOON, CLARENCE (Baby Barkley) b. September 8, 1970　Ht. 6-7　Wt. 240　College—Southern Mississippi

SEASON—TEAM	G	GS	MIN	FGM	FGA	PCT	3FGM	3FGA	PCT	FTM	FTA	PCT	O-RB	D-RB	TOT	AST	PF	DQ	STL	TO	BLK	PTS	RPG	APG	PPG
92-93—Philadelphia	82	82	2654	494	1053	.469	1	4	.250	291	408	.713	179	410	589	147	188	1	85	176	67	1280	7.2	1.8	15.6
93-94—Philadelphia	82	82	3147	602	1246	.483	4	17	.235	298	430	.693	254	578	832	192	152	0	100	195	116	1506	10.1	2.3	18.4
REG. SEASON TOTALS	164	164	5801	1096	2299	.477	5	21	.238	589	838	.703	433	988	1421	339	340	1	185	371	183	2786	8.7	2.1	17.0

WEATHERSPOON, NICK LEVOTER (Spoon) b. July 20, 1950　Ht. 6-7　Wt. 195　College—Illinois

SEASON—TEAM	G	GS	MIN	FGM	FGA	PCT	3FGM	3FGA	PCT	FTM	FTA	PCT	O-RB	D-RB	TOT	AST	PF	DQ	STL	TO	BLK	PTS	RPG	APG	PPG
73-74—Capital	65	—	1216	199	483	.412	—	—	—	96	139	.691	133	264	397	38	179	1	48	—	16	494	6.1	0.6	7.6
74-75—Washington	82	—	1347	256	562	.456	—	—	—	103	138	.746	132	214	346	51	212	2	65	—	21	615	4.2	0.6	7.5
75-76—Washington	64	—	1083	218	458	.476	—	—	—	96	137	.701	85	189	274	55	172	2	46	—	16	532	4.3	0.9	8.3
76-77—Wash.-Seattle	62	—	1657	310	690	.449	—	—	—	91	144	.632	120	308	428	53	168	1	52	—	28	711	6.9	0.9	11.5
77-78—Chicago	41	—	611	86	194	.443	—	—	—	37	42	.881	57	68	125	32	74	0	19	49	10	209	3.0	0.8	5.1
78-79—San Diego	82	—	2642	479	998	.480	—	—	—	176	238	.739	179	275	454	135	287	6	80	184	37	1134	5.5	1.6	13.8
79-80—San Diego	57	—	1124	164	378	.434	0	0	—	63	91	.692	83	125	208	54	136	1	34	86	17	391	3.6	0.9	6.9
REG. SEASON TOTALS	453	—	9680	1712	3763	.455	0	0	—	662	929	.713	789	1443	2232	418	1228	13	344	319	145	4086	4.9	0.9	9.0
PLAYOFF TOTALS	31	—	715	115	235	.489	0	0	—	51	73	.699	46	104	150	26	95	1	18	—	8	281	4.8	0.8	9.1

WEBB, ANTHONY JEROME (Spud) b. July 13, 1963　Ht. 5-7　Wt. 135　College—Midland/North Carolina State

SEASON—TEAM	G	GS	MIN	FGM	FGA	PCT	3FGM	3FGA	PCT	FTM	FTA	PCT	O-RB	D-RB	TOT	AST	PF	DQ	STL	TO	BLK	PTS	RPG	APG	PPG
85-86—Atlanta	79	8	1229	199	412	.483	2	11	.182	216	275	.785	27	96	123	337	164	1	82	159	5	616	1.6	4.3	7.8
86-87—Atlanta	33	0	532	71	162	.438	1	6	.167	80	105	.762	6	54	60	167	65	1	34	70	2	223	1.8	5.1	6.8
87-88—Atlanta	82	1	1347	191	402	.475	1	19	.053	107	131	.817	16	130	146	337	125	0	63	131	11	490	1.8	4.1	6.0
88-89—Atlanta	81	6	1219	133	290	.459	1	22	.045	52	60	.867	21	102	123	284	104	0	70	83	6	319	1.5	3.5	3.9
89-90—Atlanta	82	46	2184	294	616	.477	1	19	.053	162	186	.871	38	163	201	477	185	0	105	141	12	751	2.5	5.8	9.2
90-91—Atlanta	75	64	2197	359	803	.447	54	168	.321	231	266	.868	41	133	174	417	180	0	118	146	6	1003	2.3	5.6	13.4
91-92—Sacramento	77	77	2724	448	1006	.445	73	199	.367	262	305	.859	30	193	223	547	193	1	125	229	24	1231	2.9	7.1	16.0
92-93—Sacramento	69	68	2335	342	789	.433	37	135	.274	279	328	.851	44	149	193	481	177	0	104	194	6	1000	2.8	7.0	14.5
93-94—Sacramento	79	62	2567	373	810	.460	55	164	.335	204	251	.813	44	178	222	528	182	1	93	168	23	1005	2.8	6.7	12.7
REG. SEASON TOTALS	657	332	16334	2410	5290	.456	225	743	.303	1593	1907	.835	267	1198	1465	3575	1375	4	794	1321	95	6638	2.2	5.4	10.1
PLAYOFF TOTALS	39	6	725	114	249	.458	7	23	.304	86	105	.819	19	66	85	198	64	0	30	51	2	321	2.2	5.1	8.2

WEBB, JEFFREY WILLIAM (Jeff) b. July 6, 1948　Ht. 6-4　Wt. 170　College—Kansas State

SEASON—TEAM	G	GS	MIN	FGM	FGA	PCT	3FGM	3FGA	PCT	FTM	FTA	PCT	O-RB	D-RB	TOT	AST	PF	DQ	STL	TO	BLK	PTS	RPG	APG	PPG
70-71—Milwaukee	29	—	300	27	78	.346	—	—	—	11	15	.733	—	—	24	19	33	0	—	—	—	65	0.8	0.7	2.2
71-72—Milw.-Phoenix	46	—	238	40	100	.400	—	—	—	16	23	.696	—	—	35	23	29	0	—	—	—	96	0.8	0.5	2.1
REG. SEASON TOTALS	75	—	538	67	178	.376	—	—	—	27	38	.711	—	—	59	42	62	0	—	—	—	161	0.8	0.6	2.1
PLAYOFF TOTALS	9	—	23	4	7	.571	—	—	—	3	3	1.000	—	—	1	2	2	0	—	—	—	11	0.1	0.2	1.2

WEBB, MARCUS L. b. May 9, 1970　Ht. 6-9　Wt. 255　College—Alabama

SEASON—TEAM	G	GS	MIN	FGM	FGA	PCT	3FGM	3FGA	PCT	FTM	FTA	PCT	O-RB	D-RB	TOT	AST	PF	DQ	STL	TO	BLK	PTS	RPG	APG	PPG
92-93—Boston	9	0	51	13	25	.520	0	1	.000	13	21	.619	5	5	10	2	11	0	1	5	2	39	1.1	0.2	4.3
REG. SEASON TOTALS	9	0	51	13	25	.520	0	1	.000	13	21	.619	5	5	10	2	11	0	1	5	2	39	1.1	0.2	4.3

WEBBER, MAYCE EDWARD CHRISTOPHER III (Chris) b. March 1, 1973　Ht. 6-10　Wt. 260　College—Michigan

SEASON—TEAM	G	GS	MIN	FGM	FGA	PCT	3FGM	3FGA	PCT	FTM	FTA	PCT	O-RB	D-RB	TOT	AST	PF	DQ	STL	TO	BLK	PTS	RPG	APG	PPG
93-94—Golden State	76	76	2438	572	1037	.552	0	14	.000	189	355	.532	305	389	694	272	247	4	93	206	164	1333	9.1	3.6	17.5
REG. SEASON TOTALS	76	76	2438	572	1037	.552	0	14	.000	189	355	.532	305	389	694	272	247	4	93	206	164	1333	9.1	3.6	17.5
PLAYOFF TOTALS	3	3	109	22	40	.550	0	2	.000	3	10	.300	13	13	26	27	11	0	3	9	9	47	8.7	9.0	15.7

WEBER, FOREST JOHN (Jake) b. March 18, 1918　Ht. 6-6　Wt. 225　College—Purdue

SEASON—TEAM	G	GS	MIN	FGM	FGA	PCT	3FGM	3FGA	PCT	FTM	FTA	PCT	O-RB	D-RB	TOT	AST	PF	DQ	STL	TO	BLK	PTS	RPG	APG	PPG
45-46—Indianapolis (N)	5	—	—	7	—	—	—	—	—	4	—	—	—	—	—	—	—	—	—	—	—	18	—	—	3.6
46-47—N.Y.-Prov.	50	—	—	59	202	.292	—	—	—	55	79	.696	—	—	—	4	111	—	—	—	—	173	—	0.1	3.5
REG. NBA TOTALS	50	—	—	59	202	.292	—	—	—	55	79	.696	—	—	—	4	111	—	—	—	—	173	—	0.1	3.5
REG. NBL TOTALS	5	—	—	7	—	—	—	—	—	4	—	—	—	—	—	—	—	—	—	—	—	18	—	—	3.6

WEBSTER, ELNARDO b. March 6, 1948 Ht. 6-5 Wt. 200 College—Wharton County JC/St. Peter's

SEASON—TEAM	G	GS	MIN	FGM	FGA	PCT	3FGM	3FGA	PCT	FTM	FTA	PCT	O-RB	D-RB	TOT	AST	PF	DQ	STL	TO	BLK	PTS	RPG	APG	PPG
71-72—N.Y.-Memphis (A)	19	—	237	50	109	.459	1	4	.250	21	29	.724	—	—	44	16	39	—	—	35	—	122	2.3	0.8	6.4
REG. ABA TOTALS	19	—	237	50	109	.459	1	4	.250	21	29	.724	—	—	44	16	39	—	—	35	—	122	2.3	0.8	6.4

WEBSTER, MARVIN NATHANIEL **(The Human Eraser)** b. April 13, 1952 Ht. 7-1 Wt. 235 College—Morgan State

SEASON—TEAM	G	GS	MIN	FGM	FGA	PCT	3FGM	3FGA	PCT	FTM	FTA	PCT	O-RB	D-RB	TOT	AST	PF	DQ	STL	TO	BLK	PTS	RPG	APG	PPG
75-76—Denver (A)	38	—	398	55	120	.458	0	1	.000	55	78	.705	63	111	174	30	60	—	9	38	52	165	4.6	0.8	4.3
76-77—Denver	80	—	1276	198	400	.495	—	—	—	143	220	.650	152	332	484	62	149	2	23	—	118	539	6.1	0.8	6.7
77-78—Seattle	82	—	2910	427	851	.502	—	—	—	290	461	.629	361	674	1035	203	262	8	48	257	162	1144	12.6	2.5	14.0
78-79—New York	60	—	2027	264	558	.473	—	—	—	150	262	.573	198	457	655	172	183	6	24	170	112	678	10.9	2.9	11.3
79-80—New York	20	—	298	38	79	.481	0	0	—	12	16	.750	28	52	80	9	39	1	3	20	11	88	4.0	0.5	4.4
80-81—New York	82	—	1708	159	341	.466	1	4	.250	104	163	.638	162	303	465	72	187	2	27	103	97	423	5.7	0.9	5.2
81-82—New York	82	32	1883	199	405	.491	0	0	—	108	170	.635	184	306	490	99	211	2	22	90	90	506	6.0	1.2	6.2
82-83—New York	82	0	1472	168	331	.508	0	1	.000	106	180	.589	176	267	443	49	210	3	35	102	131	442	5.4	0.6	5.4
83-84—New York	76	5	1290	112	239	.469	0	0	—	66	117	.564	146	220	366	53	187	2	34	85	100	290	4.8	0.7	3.8
86-87—Milwaukee	15	0	102	10	19	.526	1	1	1.000	6	8	.750	12	14	26	3	17	0	3	8	7	27	1.7	0.2	1.8
REG. NBA TOTALS	579	37	12966	1575	3223	.489	2	6	.333	985	1597	.617	1419	2625	4044	722	1445	26	219	835	828	4137	7.0	1.2	7.1
REG. ABA TOTALS	38	—	398	55	120	.458	0	1	.000	55	78	.705	63	111	174	30	60	—	9	38	52	165	4.6	0.8	4.3
NBA PLAYOFF TOTALS	48	0	1382	177	365	.485	0	0	—	108	167	.647	150	273	423	68	144	2	12	83	94	462	8.8	1.4	9.6
ABA PLAYOFF TOTALS	13	—	155	21	50	.420	0	0	—	15	28	.536	24	47	71	9	28	—	1	15	14	57	5.5	0.7	4.4

WEDMAN, SCOTT DEAN b. July 29, 1952 Ht. 6-7 Wt. 215 College—Colorado

SEASON—TEAM	G	GS	MIN	FGM	FGA	PCT	3FGM	3FGA	PCT	FTM	FTA	PCT	O-RB	D-RB	TOT	AST	PF	DQ	STL	TO	BLK	PTS	RPG	APG	PPG
74-75—Kansas City-Omaha	80	—	2554	375	806	.465	—	—	—	139	170	.818	202	288	490	129	270	2	81	—	27	889	6.1	1.6	11.1
75-76—Kansas City	82	—	2968	538	1181	.456	—	—	—	191	245	.780	199	407	606	199	280	8	103	—	36	1267	7.4	2.4	15.5
76-77—Kansas City	81	—	2743	521	1133	.460	—	—	—	206	241	.855	187	319	506	227	226	3	100	—	23	1248	6.2	2.8	15.4
77-78—Kansas City	81	—	2961	607	1192	.509	—	—	—	221	254	.870	144	319	463	201	242	2	99	158	22	1435	5.7	2.5	17.7
78-79—Kansas City	73	—	2498	561	1050	.534	—	—	—	216	271	.797	135	251	386	144	239	4	76	106	30	1338	5.3	2.0	18.3
79-80—Kansas City	68	—	2347	569	1112	.512	7	22	.318	145	181	.801	114	272	386	145	230	1	84	112	45	1290	5.7	2.1	19.0
80-81—Kansas City	81	—	2902	685	1437	.477	25	77	.325	140	204	.686	128	305	433	226	294	4	97	161	46	1535	5.3	2.8	19.0
81-82—Cleveland	54	39	1638	260	589	.441	5	23	.217	66	90	.733	128	176	304	133	189	4	73	73	14	591	5.6	2.5	10.9
82-83—Clev.-Boston	75	35	1793	374	788	.475	10	32	.313	85	107	.794	98	184	282	117	228	6	43	126	17	843	3.8	1.6	11.2
83-84—Boston	68	5	916	148	333	.444	2	13	.154	29	35	.829	41	98	139	67	107	0	27	43	7	327	2.0	1.0	4.8
84-85—Boston	78	5	1127	220	460	.478	17	34	.500	42	55	.764	57	102	159	94	111	0	23	47	10	499	2.0	1.2	6.4
85-86—Boston	79	19	1402	286	605	.473	17	48	.354	45	68	.662	66	126	192	83	127	0	38	54	22	634	2.4	1.1	8.0
86-87—Boston	6	2	78	9	27	.333	1	2	.500	1	2	.500	3	6	9	6	6	0	2	3	2	20	1.5	1.0	3.3
REG. SEASON TOTALS	906	105	25927	5153	10713	.481	84	251	.335	1526	1923	.794	1502	2853	4355	1771	2549	34	846	883	301	11916	4.8	2.0	13.2
PLAYOFF TOTALS	85	2	1961	368	812	.453	27	70	.386	119	171	.696	105	217	322	150	189	1	63	90	20	882	3.8	1.8	10.4
ALL-STAR TOTALS	1	0	20	4	5	.800	0	0	—	0	0	—	0	6	6	2	2	0	1	—	0	8	6.0	2.0	8.0

WEHR, RICHARD WADE **(Dick)** b. December 9, 1925 Ht. 6-4 Wt. 180 College—Rice/Indiana

SEASON—TEAM	G	GS	MIN	FGM	FGA	PCT	3FGM	3FGA	PCT	FTM	FTA	PCT	O-RB	D-RB	TOT	AST	PF	DQ	STL	TO	BLK	PTS	RPG	APG	PPG
48-49—Indianapolis	9	—	—	5	21	.238	—	—	—	2	6	.333	—	—	—	3	12	—	—	—	—	12	—	0.3	1.3
REG. SEASON TOTALS	9	—	—	5	21	.238	—	—	—	2	6	.333	—	—	—	3	12	—	—	—	—	12	—	0.3	1.3

WEIDNER, BRANT CLIFFORD b. October 28, 1960 Ht. 6-10 Wt. 230 College—William & Mary

SEASON—TEAM	G	GS	MIN	FGM	FGA	PCT	3FGM	3FGA	PCT	FTM	FTA	PCT	O-RB	D-RB	TOT	AST	PF	DQ	STL	TO	BLK	PTS	RPG	APG	PPG
83-84—San Antonio	8	0	38	2	9	.222	0	0	—	4	4	1.000	4	7	11	0	5	0	0	2	2	8	1.4	0.0	1.0
REG. SEASON TOTALS	8	0	38	2	9	.222	0	0	—	4	4	1.000	4	7	11	0	5	0	0	2	2	8	1.4	0.0	1.0

WEISS, ROBERT WILLIAM **(Bob)** b. May 7, 1942 Ht. 6-3 Wt. 180 College—Penn State

SEASON—TEAM	G	GS	MIN	FGM	FGA	PCT	3FGM	3FGA	PCT	FTM	FTA	PCT	O-RB	D-RB	TOT	AST	PF	DQ	STL	TO	BLK	PTS	RPG	APG	PPG
65-66—Philadelphia	7	—	30	3	9	.333	—	—	—	0	0	—	—	—	7	4	10	0	—	—	—	6	1.0	0.6	0.9
66-67—Philadelphia	6	—	29	5	10	.500	—	—	—	2	5	.400	—	—	3	10	8	0	—	—	—	12	0.5	1.7	2.0
67-68—Seattle	82	—	1614	295	686	.430	—	—	—	213	254	.839	—	—	150	342	137	0	—	—	—	803	1.8	4.2	9.8
68-69—Milw.-Chicago	77	—	1478	189	499	.379	—	—	—	128	160	.800	—	—	162	199	174	1	—	—	—	506	2.1	2.6	6.6
69-70—Chicago	82	—	2544	365	855	.427	—	—	—	213	253	.842	—	—	227	474	206	0	—	—	—	943	2.8	5.8	11.5
70-71—Chicago	82	—	2237	278	659	.422	—	—	—	226	269	.840	—	—	189	387	216	1	—	—	—	782	2.3	4.7	9.5
71-72—Chicago	82	—	2450	358	832	.430	—	—	—	212	254	.835	—	—	170	377	212	1	—	—	—	928	2.1	4.6	11.3
72-73—Chicago	82	—	2086	279	655	.426	—	—	—	159	189	.841	—	—	148	295	151	1	—	—	—	717	1.8	3.6	8.7
73-74—Chicago	79	—	1708	263	564	.466	—	—	—	142	170	.835	32	71	103	303	156	0	104	—	12	668	1.3	3.8	8.5
74-75—Buffalo	76	—	1338	102	261	.391	—	—	—	54	67	.806	21	83	104	260	146	0	82	—	19	258	1.4	3.4	3.4
75-76—Buffalo	66	—	995	89	183	.486	—	—	—	35	48	.729	13	53	66	150	94	0	48	—	14	213	1.0	2.3	3.2
76-77—Washington	62	—	768	62	133	.466	—	—	—	29	37	.784	15	54	69	130	66	0	53	—	7	153	1.1	2.1	2.5
REG. SEASON TOTALS	783	—	17277	2288	5346	.428	—	—	—	1413	1706	.828	81	261	1398	2931	1576	4	287	—	52	5989	1.8	3.7	7.6
PLAYOFF TOTALS	53	—	1103	167	392	.426	—	—	—	73	91	.802	8	26	89	164	111	1	14	—	2	407	1.7	3.1	7.7

WEITZMAN, RICHARD L. (Rick) b. April 30, 1946 Ht. 6-2 Wt. 185 College—Northeastern

SEASON—TEAM	G	GS	MIN	FGM	FGA	PCT	3FGM	3FGA	PCT	FTM	FTA	PCT	O-RB	D-RB	TOT	AST	PF	DQ	STL	TO	BLK	PTS	RPG	APG	PPG
67-68—Boston	25	—	75	12	46	.261	—	—	—	9	13	.692	—	—	10	8	8	0	—	—	—	33	0.4	0.3	1.3
REG. SEASON TOTALS	25	—	75	12	46	.261	—	—	—	9	13	.692	—	—	10	8	8	0	—	—	—	33	0.4	0.3	1.3
PLAYOFF TOTALS	3	—	5	2	3	.667	—	—	—	0	0	—	—	—	1	1	0	0	—	—	—	4	0.3	0.3	1.3

WELLS, OWEN b. December 9, 1950 Ht. 6-7 Wt. 200 College—Detroit

SEASON—TEAM	G	GS	MIN	FGM	FGA	PCT	3FGM	3FGA	PCT	FTM	FTA	PCT	O-RB	D-RB	TOT	AST	PF	DQ	STL	TO	BLK	PTS	RPG	APG	PPG
74-75—Houston	33	—	214	42	100	.420	—	—	—	15	22	.682	12	23	35	22	38	0	9	—	3	99	1.1	0.7	3.0
REG. SEASON TOTALS	33	—	214	42	100	.420	—	—	—	15	22	.682	12	23	35	22	38	0	9	—	3	99	1.1	0.7	3.0
PLAYOFF TOTALS	4	—	5	3	5	.600	—	—	—	0	0	—	0	1	1	1	1	0	—	0	6	0.3	0.3	1.5

WELLS, RALPH E. b. September 3, 1940 d. August 2, 1968 Ht. 6-1 Wt. 180 College—Northwestern

SEASON—TEAM	G	GS	MIN	FGM	FGA	PCT	3FGM	3FGA	PCT	FTM	FTA	PCT	O-RB	D-RB	TOT	AST	PF	DQ	STL	TO	BLK	PTS	RPG	APG	PPG
62-63—Chicago	3	—	48	1	7	.143	—	—	—	0	7	.000	—	—	6	7	6	0	—	—	—	2	2.0	2.3	0.7
REG. SEASON TOTALS	3	—	48	1	7	.143	—	—	—	0	7	.000	—	—	6	7	6	0	—	—	—	2	2.0	2.3	0.7

WELP, CHRISTIAN ANSGAR (Chris) b. January 2, 1964 Ht. 7-0 Wt. 245 College—Washington

SEASON—TEAM	G	GS	MIN	FGM	FGA	PCT	3FGM	3FGA	PCT	FTM	FTA	PCT	O-RB	D-RB	TOT	AST	PF	DQ	STL	TO	BLK	PTS	RPG	APG	PPG
87-88—Philadelphia	10	0	132	18	31	.581	0	0	—	12	18	.667	11	13	24	5	25	0	5	9	5	48	2.4	0.5	4.8
88-89—Philadelphia	72	0	843	99	222	.446	0	1	.000	48	73	.658	59	134	193	29	176	0	23	42	41	246	2.7	0.4	3.4
89-90—S.A.-G.S.	27	3	198	23	61	.377	0	0	—	19	25	.760	18	30	48	9	58	0	6	15	8	65	1.8	0.3	2.4
REG. SEASON TOTALS	109	3	1173	140	314	.446	0	1	.000	79	116	.681	88	177	265	43	259	0	34	66	54	359	2.4	0.4	3.3
PLAYOFF TOTALS	3	0	22	1	3	.333	0	0	—	0	2	.000	0	7	7	—	7	0	0	1	0	2	2.3	0.0	0.7

WENNINGTON, WILLIAM PERCEY (Bill) b. December 26, 1964 Ht. 7-0 Wt. 245 College—St. John's

SEASON—TEAM	G	GS	MIN	FGM	FGA	PCT	3FGM	3FGA	PCT	FTM	FTA	PCT	O-RB	D-RB	TOT	AST	PF	DQ	STL	TO	BLK	PTS	RPG	APG	PPG
85-86—Dallas	56	3	562	72	153	.471	0	4	.000	45	62	.726	32	100	132	21	83	0	11	21	22	189	2.4	0.4	3.4
86-87—Dallas	58	0	560	56	132	.424	0	2	.000	45	60	.750	53	76	129	24	95	0	13	39	10	157	2.2	0.4	2.7
87-88—Dallas	30	0	125	25	49	.510	1	2	.500	12	19	.632	14	25	39	4	33	0	5	9	9	63	1.3	0.1	2.1
88-89—Dallas	65	9	1074	119	275	.433	1	9	.111	61	82	.744	82	204	286	46	211	3	16	54	35	300	4.4	0.7	4.6
89-90—Dallas	60	2	814	105	234	.449	0	4	.000	60	75	.800	64	134	198	41	144	2	20	50	21	270	3.3	0.7	4.5
90-91—Sacramento	77	23	1455	181	415	.436	1	5	.200	74	94	.787	101	239	340	69	230	4	46	51	59	437	4.4	0.9	5.7
93-94—Chicago	76	0	1371	235	482	.488	0	2	.000	72	88	.818	117	236	353	70	214	4	43	75	29	542	4.6	0.9	7.1
REG. SEASON TOTALS	422	37	5961	793	1740	.456	3	28	.107	369	480	.769	463	1014	1477	275	1010	13	154	299	185	1958	3.5	0.7	4.6
PLAYOFF TOTALS	26	0	151	12	33	.364	1	1	1.000	7	10	.700	15	14	29	10	37	0	1	7	5	32	1.1	0.4	1.2

WENSTROM, MATTHEW WILLIAM (Matt) b. November 4, 1970 Ht. 7-1 Wt. 250 College—North Carolina

SEASON—TEAM	G	GS	MIN	FGM	FGA	PCT	3FGM	3FGA	PCT	FTM	FTA	PCT	O-RB	D-RB	TOT	AST	PF	DQ	STL	TO	BLK	PTS	RPG	APG	PPG
93-94—Boston	11	0	37	6	10	.600	0	0	—	6	10	.600	6	6	12	0	7	0	0	4	2	18	1.1	0.0	1.6
REG. SEASON TOTALS	11	0	37	6	10	.600	0	0	—	6	10	.600	6	6	12	0	7	0	0	4	2	18	1.1	0.0	1.6

WERDANN, ROBERT b. September 12, 1970 Ht. 6-11 Wt. 250 College—St. John's

SEASON—TEAM	G	GS	MIN	FGM	FGA	PCT	3FGM	3FGA	PCT	FTM	FTA	PCT	O-RB	D-RB	TOT	AST	PF	DQ	STL	TO	BLK	PTS	RPG	APG	PPG
92-93—Denver	28	0	149	18	59	.305	0	1	.000	17	31	.548	23	29	52	7	38	1	6	12	4	53	1.9	0.3	1.9
REG. SEASON TOTALS	28	0	149	18	59	.305	0	1	.000	17	31	.548	23	29	52	7	38	1	6	12	4	53	1.9	0.3	1.9

WERTIS, RAYMOND A. (Ray) b. January 1, 1922 Ht. 5-11 Wt. 175 College—St. John's

SEASON—TEAM	G	GS	MIN	FGM	FGA	PCT	3FGM	3FGA	PCT	FTM	FTA	PCT	O-RB	D-RB	TOT	AST	PF	DQ	STL	TO	BLK	PTS	RPG	APG	PPG
46-47—Toronto-Clev.	61	—	—	79	366	.216	—	—	—	56	91	.615	—	—	—	39	82	—	—	—	—	214	—	0.6	3.5
47-48—Providence	7	—	—	13	72	.181	—	—	—	6	14	.429	—	—	—	6	13	—	—	—	—	32	—	0.9	4.6
REG. SEASON TOTALS	68	—	—	92	438	.210	—	—	—	62	105	.590	—	—	—	45	95	—	—	—	—	246	—	0.7	3.6
PLAYOFF TOTALS	3	—	—	6	26	.231	—	—	—	4	5	.800	—	—	—	6	6	—	—	—	—	16	—	2.0	5.3

WESLEY, DAVID b. November 14, 1970 Ht. 6-0 Wt. 190 College—Temple JC/Baylor

SEASON—TEAM	G	GS	MIN	FGM	FGA	PCT	3FGM	3FGA	PCT	FTM	FTA	PCT	O-RB	D-RB	TOT	AST	PF	DQ	STL	TO	BLK	PTS	RPG	APG	PPG
93-94—New Jersey	60	0	542	64	174	.368	11	47	.234	44	53	.830	10	34	44	123	47	0	38	52	4	183	0.7	2.1	3.1
REG. SEASON TOTALS	60	0	542	64	174	.368	11	47	.234	44	53	.830	10	34	44	123	47	0	38	52	4	183	0.7	2.1	3.1
PLAYOFF TOTALS	3	0	18	3	7	.429	1	4	.250	2	2	1.000	0	0	0	3	0	0	2	4	0	9	0.0	1.0	3.0

WESLEY, WALTER (Walt) b. January 25, 1945 Ht. 6-11 Wt. 230 College—Kansas

SEASON—TEAM	G	GS	MIN	FGM	FGA	PCT	3FGM	3FGA	PCT	FTM	FTA	PCT	O-RB	D-RB	TOT	AST	PF	DQ	STL	TO	BLK	PTS	RPG	APG	PPG
66-67—Cincinnati	64	—	909	131	333	.393	—	—	—	52	123	.423	—	—	329	19	161	2	—	—	—	314	5.1	0.3	4.9
67-68—Cincinnati	66	—	918	188	404	.465	—	—	—	76	152	.500	—	—	281	34	168	2	—	—	—	452	4.3	0.5	6.8
68-69—Cincinnati	82	—	1334	245	534	.459	—	—	—	134	207	.647	—	—	403	47	191	0	—	—	—	624	4.9	0.6	7.6
69-70—Chicago	72	—	1407	270	648	.417	—	—	—	145	219	.662	—	—	455	68	184	1	—	—	—	685	6.3	0.9	9.5
70-71—Cleveland	82	—	2425	565	1241	.455	—	—	—	325	473	.687	—	—	713	83	295	5	—	—	—	1455	8.7	1.0	17.7
71-72—Cleveland	82	—	2185	412	1006	.410	—	—	—	196	291	.674	—	—	711	76	245	4	—	—	—	1020	8.7	0.9	12.4
72-73—Clev.-Phoenix	57	—	474	77	202	.381	—	—	—	26	46	.565	—	—	151	31	77	1	—	—	—	180	2.6	0.5	3.2
73-74—Capital	39	—	400	71	151	.470	—	—	—	26	43	.605	63	73	136	14	74	1	9	—	20	168	3.5	0.4	4.3
74-75—Phil.-Milw.	45	—	247	42	93	.452	—	—	—	16	27	.593	18	45	63	12	51	0	7	—	5	100	1.4	0.3	2.2
75-76—Los Angeles	1	—	7	1	2	.500	—	—	—	2	4	.500	0	1	1	1	2	0	0	—	0	4	1.0	1.0	4.0
REG. SEASON TOTALS	590	—	10306	2002	4614	.434	—	—	—	998	1585	.630	81	119	3243	385	1448	16	16	—	25	5002	5.5	0.7	8.5
PLAYOFF TOTALS	8	—	83	18	41	.439	—	—	—	6	12	.500	0	0	28	2	16	0	0	—	0	42	3.5	0.3	5.3

WEST, JEFFERY DOUGLAS (Doug, Fresh) b. May 27, 1967 Ht. 6-6 Wt. 200 College—Villanova

SEASON—TEAM	G	GS	MIN	FGM	FGA	PCT	3FGM	3FGA	PCT	FTM	FTA	PCT	O-RB	D-RB	TOT	AST	PF	DQ	STL	TO	BLK	PTS	RPG	APG	PPG
89-90—Minnesota	52	0	378	53	135	.393	3	11	.273	26	32	.813	24	46	70	18	61	0	10	31	6	135	1.3	0.3	2.6
90-91—Minnesota	75	1	824	118	246	.480	0	1	.000	58	84	.690	56	80	136	48	115	0	35	41	23	294	1.8	0.6	3.9
91-92—Minnesota	80	72	2540	463	894	.518	4	23	.174	186	231	.805	107	150	257	281	239	1	66	120	26	1116	3.2	3.5	14.0
92-93—Minnesota	80	80	3104	646	1249	.517	2	23	.087	249	296	.841	89	158	247	235	279	1	85	165	21	1543	3.1	2.9	19.3
93-94—Minnesota	72	61	2182	434	891	.487	1	8	.125	187	231	.810	61	170	231	172	236	3	65	137	24	1056	3.2	2.4	14.7
REG. SEASON TOTALS	359	214	9028	1714	3415	.502	10	66	.152	706	874	.808	337	604	941	754	930	5	261	494	100	4144	2.6	2.1	11.5

WEST, JERRY ALAN b. May 28, 1938 Ht. 6-2½ Wt. 180 College—West Virginia

SEASON—TEAM	G	GS	MIN	FGM	FGA	PCT	3FGM	3FGA	PCT	FTM	FTA	PCT	O-RB	D-RB	TOT	AST	PF	DQ	STL	TO	BLK	PTS	RPG	APG	PPG
60-61—Los Angeles	79	—	2797	529	1264	.419	—	—	—	331	497	.666	—	—	611	333	213	1	—	—	—	1389	7.7	4.2	17.6
61-62—Los Angeles	75	—	3087	799	1795	.445	—	—	—	712	926	.769	—	—	591	402	173	4	—	—	—	2310	7.9	5.4	30.8
62-63—Los Angeles	55	—	2163	559	1213	.461	—	—	—	371	477	.778	—	—	384	307	150	1	—	—	—	1489	7.0	5.6	27.1
63-64—Los Angeles	72	—	2906	740	1529	.484	—	—	—	584	702	.832	—	—	443	403	200	2	—	—	—	2064	6.2	5.6	28.7
64-65—Los Angeles	74	—	3066	822	1655	.497	—	—	—	648	789	.821	—	—	447	364	221	2	—	—	—	2292	6.0	4.9	31.0
65-66—Los Angeles	79	—	3218	818	1731	.473	—	—	—	840	977	.860	—	—	562	480	243	1	—	—	—	2476	7.1	6.1	31.3
66-67—Los Angeles	66	—	2670	645	1389	.464	—	—	—	602	686	.878	—	—	392	447	160	1	—	—	—	1892	5.9	6.8	28.7
67-68—Los Angeles	51	—	1919	476	926	.514	—	—	—	391	482	.811	—	—	294	310	152	1	—	—	—	1343	5.8	6.1	26.3
68-69—Los Angeles	61	—	2394	545	1156	.471	—	—	—	490	597	.821	—	—	262	423	156	1	—	—	—	1580	4.3	6.9	25.9
69-70—Los Angeles	74	—	3106	831	1673	.497	—	—	—	647	785	.824	—	—	338	554	160	3	—	—	—	2309	4.6	7.5	31.2
70-71—Los Angeles	69	—	2845	667	1351	.494	—	—	—	525	631	.832	—	—	320	655	180	1	—	—	—	1859	4.6	9.5	26.9
71-72—Los Angeles	77	—	2973	735	1540	.477	—	—	—	515	633	.814	—	—	327	747	209	0	—	—	—	1985	4.2	9.7	25.8
72-73—Los Angeles	69	—	2460	618	1291	.479	—	—	—	339	421	.805	—	—	289	607	138	0	—	—	—	1575	4.2	8.8	22.8
73-74—Los Angeles	31	—	967	232	519	.447	—	—	—	165	198	.833	30	86	116	206	80	0	81	—	23	629	3.7	6.6	20.3
REG. SEASON TOTALS	932	—	36571	9016	19032	.474	—	—	—	7160	8801	.814	30	86	5376	6238	2435	17	81	—	23	25192	5.8	6.7	27.0
PLAYOFF TOTALS	153	—	6321	1622	3460	.469	—	—	—	1213	1506	.805	0	2	855	970	451	3	0	—	0	4457	5.6	6.3	29.1
ALL-STAR TOTALS	12	—	341	62	137	.453	—	—	—	36	50	.720	0	0	47	55	28	0	0	—	0	160	3.9	4.6	13.3

WEST, MARK ANDRE b. November 5, 1960 Ht. 6-10 Wt. 245 College—Old Dominion

SEASON—TEAM	G	GS	MIN	FGM	FGA	PCT	3FGM	3FGA	PCT	FTM	FTA	PCT	O-RB	D-RB	TOT	AST	PF	DQ	STL	TO	BLK	PTS	RPG	APG	PPG
83-84—Dallas	34	0	202	15	42	.357	0	0	—	7	22	.318	19	27	46	13	55	0	1	12	15	37	1.4	0.4	1.1
84-85—Milw.-Clev.	66	25	888	106	194	.546	0	1	.000	43	87	.494	90	161	251	15	197	7	13	59	49	255	3.8	0.2	3.9
85-86—Cleveland	67	26	1172	113	209	.541	0	0	—	54	103	.524	97	225	322	20	235	6	27	91	62	280	4.8	0.3	4.2
86-87—Cleveland	78	13	1333	209	385	.543	0	2	.000	89	173	.514	126	213	339	41	229	5	22	106	81	507	4.3	0.5	6.5
87-88—Clev.-Phoenix	83	41	2098	316	573	.551	0	1	.000	170	285	.596	165	358	523	74	265	4	47	173	147	802	6.3	0.9	9.7
88-89—Phoenix	82	32	2019	243	372	.653	0	0	—	108	202	.535	167	384	551	39	273	4	35	103	187	594	6.7	0.5	10.5
89-90—Phoenix	82	79	2399	331	530	.625	0	0	—	199	288	.691	212	516	728	45	277	5	36	126	184	861	8.9	0.5	10.5
90-91—Phoenix	82	64	1957	247	382	.647	0	0	—	135	206	.655	171	393	564	37	266	2	32	86	161	629	6.9	0.5	7.7
91-92—Phoenix	82	11	1436	196	310	.632	0	0	—	109	171	.637	134	238	372	22	239	2	14	82	81	501	4.5	0.3	6.1
92-93—Phoenix	82	82	1558	175	285	.614	0	0	—	86	166	.518	153	305	458	29	243	3	16	93	103	436	5.6	0.4	5.3
93-94—Phoenix	82	50	1236	162	286	.566	0	0	—	58	116	.500	112	183	295	33	214	4	31	74	109	382	3.6	0.4	4.7
REG. SEASON TOTALS	820	423	16298	2113	3568	.592	0	4	.000	1058	1819	.582	1446	3003	4449	368	2493	42	274	1005	1179	5284	5.4	0.4	6.4
PLAYOFF TOTALS	79	66	1598	186	322	.578	0	0	—	85	143	.594	142	254	396	33	263	8	21	73	117	457	5.0	0.4	5.8

WEST, ROLAND D. b. June 6, 1944 Ht. 6-4 Wt. 180 College—Cincinnati

SEASON—TEAM	G	GS	MIN	FGM	FGA	PCT	3FGM	3FGA	PCT	FTM	FTA	PCT	O-RB	D-RB	TOT	AST	PF	DQ	STL	TO	BLK	PTS	RPG	APG	PPG
67-68—Baltimore	4	—	14	2	5	.400	—	—	—	0	0	—	—	—	5	0	3	0	—	—	—	4	1.3	0.0	1.0
REG. SEASON TOTALS	4	—	14	2	5	.400	—	—	—	0	0	—	—	—	5	0	3	0	—	—	—	4	1.3	0.0	1.0

WESTBROOK, DEXTER b. 1943 Ht. 6-8 Wt. 200 College—Providence

SEASON—TEAM	G	GS	MIN	FGM	FGA	PCT	3FGM	3FGA	PCT	FTM	FTA	PCT	O-RB	D-RB	TOT	AST	PF	DQ	STL	TO	BLK	PTS	RPG	APG	PPG
67-68—N.J.-Pitt. (A)	12	—	127	19	39	.487	0	0	—	10	14	.714	—	—	23	5	30	0	—	—	13	—	48	1.9	0.4	4.0
REG. ABA TOTALS	12	—	127	19	39	.487	0	0	—	10	14	.714	—	—	23	5	30	0	—	—	13	—	48	1.9	0.4	4.0

WESTPHAL, PAUL DOUGLAS b. November 30, 1950 Ht. 6-4 Wt. 195 College—USC

SEASON—TEAM	G	GS	MIN	FGM	FGA	PCT	3FGM	3FGA	PCT	FTM	FTA	PCT	O-RB	D-RB	TOT	AST	PF	DQ	STL	TO	BLK	PTS	RPG	APG	PPG
72-73—Boston	60	—	482	89	212	.420	—	—	—	67	86	.779	—	—	67	69	88	0	—	—	—	245	1.1	1.2	4.1
73-74—Boston	82	—	1165	238	475	.501	—	—	—	112	153	.732	49	94	143	171	173	1	39	—	34	588	1.7	2.1	7.2
74-75—Boston	82	—	1581	342	670	.510	—	—	—	119	156	.763	44	119	163	235	192	0	78	—	33	803	2.0	2.9	9.8
75-76—Phoenix	82	—	2960	657	1329	.494	—	—	—	365	440	.830	74	185	259	440	218	3	210	—	38	1679	3.2	5.4	20.5
76-77—Phoenix	81	—	2600	682	1317	.518	—	—	—	362	439	.825	57	133	190	459	171	1	134	—	21	1726	2.3	5.7	21.3
77-78—Phoenix	80	—	2481	809	1568	.516	—	—	—	396	487	.813	41	123	164	437	162	0	138	280	31	2014	2.1	5.5	25.2
78-79—Phoenix	81	—	2641	801	1496	.535	—	—	—	339	405	.837	35	124	159	529	159	1	111	232	26	1941	2.0	6.5	24.0
79-80—Phoenix	82	—	2665	692	1317	.525	26	93	.280	382	443	.862	46	141	187	416	162	0	119	207	35	1792	2.3	5.1	21.9
80-81—Seattle	36	—	1078	221	500	.442	6	25	.240	153	184	.832	11	57	68	148	70	0	46	78	14	601	1.9	4.1	16.7
81-82—New York	18	12	451	86	194	.443	2	8	.250	36	47	.766	9	13	22	100	61	1	19	47	8	210	1.2	5.6	11.7
82-83—New York	80	59	1978	318	693	.459	14	48	.292	148	184	.804	19	96	115	439	180	1	87	196	16	798	1.4	5.5	10.0
83-84—Phoenix	59	2	865	144	313	.460	7	26	.269	117	142	.824	8	35	43	148	69	0	41	77	6	412	0.7	2.5	7.0
REG. SEASON TOTALS	823	73	20947	5079	10084	.504	55	200	.275	2596	3166	.820	393	1120	1580	3591	1705	8	1022	1117	262	12809	1.9	4.4	15.6
PLAYOFF TOTALS	107	8	2449	553	1149	.481	6	29	.207	225	285	.789	40	106	153	353	241	2	89	89	23	1337	1.4	3.3	12.5
ALL-STAR TOTALS	5	4	128	43	68	.632	0	2	.000	11	16	.688	3	4	7	24	14	0	6	11	5	97	1.4	4.8	19.4

WETZEL, JOHN FRANCIS b. October 22, 1944 Ht. 6-5 Wt. 190 College—Virginia Tech

SEASON—TEAM	G	GS	MIN	FGM	FGA	PCT	3FGM	3FGA	PCT	FTM	FTA	PCT	O-RB	D-RB	TOT	AST	PF	DQ	STL	TO	BLK	PTS	RPG	APG	PPG
67-68—Los Angeles	38	—	434	52	119	.437	—	—	—	35	46	.761	—	—	84	51	55	0	—	—	—	139	2.2	1.3	3.7
70-71—Phoenix	70	—	1091	124	288	.431	—	—	—	83	101	.822	—	—	153	114	156	1	—	—	—	331	2.2	1.6	4.7
71-72—Phoenix	51	—	419	31	82	.378	—	—	—	24	30	.800	—	—	65	56	71	0	—	—	—	86	1.3	1.1	1.7
72-73—Atlanta	28	—	504	42	94	.447	—	—	—	14	17	.824	—	—	58	39	41	1	—	—	—	98	2.1	1.4	3.5
73-74—Atlanta	70	—	1232	107	252	.425	—	—	—	41	57	.719	39	131	170	138	147	1	73	—	19	255	2.4	2.0	3.6
74-75—Atlanta	63	—	785	87	204	.426	—	—	—	68	77	.883	34	80	114	77	108	1	51	—	8	242	1.8	1.2	3.8
75-76—Phoenix	37	—	249	22	46	.478	—	—	—	20	24	.833	8	30	38	19	30	0	9	—	3	64	1.0	0.5	1.7
REG. SEASON TOTALS	357	—	4714	465	1085	.429	—	—	—	285	352	.810	81	241	682	494	608	4	133	—	30	1215	1.9	1.4	3.4
PLAYOFF TOTALS	5	—	38	3	7	.429	—	—	—	2	2	1.000	0	2	4	4	8	0	0	—	0	8	0.8	0.8	1.6

WHATLEY, ENNIS b. August 11, 1962 Ht. 6-3 Wt. 180 College—Alabama-Birmingham

SEASON—TEAM	G	GS	MIN	FGM	FGA	PCT	3FGM	3FGA	PCT	FTM	FTA	PCT	O-RB	D-RB	TOT	AST	PF	DQ	STL	TO	BLK	PTS	RPG	APG	PPG
83-84—Chicago	80	73	2159	261	556	.469	0	2	.000	146	200	.730	63	134	197	662	223	4	119	268	17	668	2.5	8.3	8.4
84-85—Chicago	70	44	1385	140	313	.447	1	9	.111	68	86	.791	34	67	101	381	141	1	66	144	10	349	1.4	5.4	5.0
85-86—Clev.-Wash.-S.A.	14	1	107	15	35	.429	0	0	—	5	10	.500	4	10	14	23	10	0	5	10	1	35	1.0	1.6	2.5
86-87—Washington	73	72	1816	246	515	.478	0	2	.000	126	165	.764	58	136	194	392	172	0	92	138	10	618	2.7	5.4	8.5
87-88—Atlanta	5	0	24	4	9	.444	0	0	—	3	4	.750	0	4	4	2	3	0	2	4	0	11	0.8	0.4	2.2
88-89—L.A. Clippers	8	0	90	12	33	.364	0	0	—	10	11	.909	2	14	16	22	15	0	7	11	1	34	2.0	2.8	4.3
91-92—Portland	23	0	209	21	51	.412	0	4	.000	27	31	.871	6	15	21	34	12	0	14	14	3	69	0.9	1.5	3.0
93-94—Atlanta	82	1	1004	120	236	.508	0	6	.000	52	66	.788	22	77	99	181	93	0	59	78	2	292	1.2	2.2	3.6
REG. SEASON TOTALS	355	191	6794	819	1748	.469	1	23	.043	437	573	.763	189	457	646	1697	669	5	364	667	44	2076	1.8	4.8	5.8
PLAYOFF TOTALS	28	2	241	18	60	.300	0	1	.000	10	12	.833	4	23	27	31	31	0	16	21	0	46	1.0	1.1	1.6

WHEELER, CLINTON b. October 27, 1959 Ht. 6-1 Wt. 185 College—William Paterson

SEASON—TEAM	G	GS	MIN	FGM	FGA	PCT	3FGM	3FGA	PCT	FTM	FTA	PCT	O-RB	D-RB	TOT	AST	PF	DQ	STL	TO	BLK	PTS	RPG	APG	PPG
87-88—Indiana	59	0	513	62	132	.470	0	0	—	25	34	.735	19	21	40	103	37	0	36	52	2	149	0.7	1.7	2.5
88-89—Miami-Port.	28	0	354	45	87	.517	0	1	.000	15	20	.750	17	14	31	54	26	0	27	24	0	105	1.1	1.9	3.8
REG. SEASON TOTALS	87	0	867	107	219	.489	0	1	.000	40	54	.741	36	35	71	157	63	0	63	76	2	254	0.8	1.8	2.9

WHITAKER, LUCIAN CARY (**Skippy**) b. August 29, 1930 Ht. 6-1 Wt. 185 College—Kentucky

SEASON—TEAM	G	GS	MIN	FGM	FGA	PCT	3FGM	3FGA	PCT	FTM	FTA	PCT	O-RB	D-RB	TOT	AST	PF	DQ	STL	TO	BLK	PTS	RPG	APG	PPG
54-55—Boston	3	—	15	1	6	.167	—	—	—	0	0	—	—	—	1	1	4	0	—	—	—	2	0.3	0.3	0.7
REG. SEASON TOTALS	3	—	15	1	6	.167	—	—	—	0	0	—	—	—	1	1	4	0	—	—	—	2	0.3	0.3	0.7

WHITE, ERIC LANCE b. December 30, 1965 Ht. 6-8 Wt. 200 College—Pepperdine

SEASON—TEAM	G	GS	MIN	FGM	FGA	PCT	3FGM	3FGA	PCT	FTM	FTA	PCT	O-RB	D-RB	TOT	AST	PF	DQ	STL	TO	BLK	PTS	RPG	APG	PPG
87-88—L.A. Clippers	17	4	352	66	124	.532	1	1	1.000	45	57	.789	31	31	62	9	32	0	7	21	3	178	3.6	0.5	10.5
88-89—Utah-L.A. Clips	38	0	436	62	120	.517	0	0	—	34	42	.810	34	36	70	17	40	0	10	26	1	158	1.8	0.4	4.2
REG. SEASON TOTALS	55	4	788	128	244	.525	1	1	1.000	79	99	.798	65	67	132	26	72	0	17	47	4	336	2.4	0.5	6.1

WHITE, HERBERT THOMAS (**Herb**) b. June 15, 1948 Ht. 6-2 Wt. 195 College—Georgia

SEASON—TEAM	G	GS	MIN	FGM	FGA	PCT	3FGM	3FGA	PCT	FTM	FTA	PCT	O-RB	D-RB	TOT	AST	PF	DQ	STL	TO	BLK	PTS	RPG	APG	PPG
70-71—Atlanta	38	—	315	34	84	.405	—	—	—	22	39	.564	—	—	48	47	62	2	—	—	—	90	1.3	1.2	2.4
REG. SEASON TOTALS	38	—	315	34	84	.405	—	—	—	22	39	.564	—	—	48	47	62	2	—	—	—	90	1.3	1.2	2.4

WHITE, HUBERT JR. (Hubie) b. January 26, 1940 Ht. 6-4 Wt. 205 College—Villanova

SEASON—TEAM	G	GS	MIN	FGM	FGA	PCT	3FGM	3FGA	PCT	FTM	FTA	PCT	O-RB	D-RB	TOT	AST	PF	DQ	STL	TO	BLK	PTS	RPG	APG	PPG
62-63—San Francisco	29	—	271	40	111	.360	—	—	—	12	18	.667	—	—	35	28	47	0	—	—	—	92	1.2	1.0	3.2
63-64—Philadelphia	23	—	196	31	105	.295	—	—	—	17	28	.607	—	—	42	12	28	0	—	—	—	79	1.8	0.5	3.4
69-70—Miami (A)	54	—	824	146	363	.402	7	43	.163	62	84	.738	—	—	155	56	147	2	—	—	—	361	2.9	1.0	6.7
70-71—Pittsburgh (A)	14	—	166	17	61	.279	2	7	.286	10	13	.769	—	—	32	14	28	—	—	—	—	46	2.3	1.0	3.3
REG. NBA TOTALS	52	—	467	71	216	.329	—	—	—	29	46	.630	—	—	77	40	75	0	—	—	—	171	1.5	0.8	3.3
REG. ABA TOTALS	68	—	990	163	424	.384	9	50	.180	72	97	.742	—	—	187	70	175	2	—	—	—	407	2.8	1.0	6.0

WHITE, JOSEPH HENRY (Jo Jo) b. November 16, 1946 Ht. 6-3 Wt. 190 College—Kansas

SEASON—TEAM	G	GS	MIN	FGM	FGA	PCT	3FGM	3FGA	PCT	FTM	FTA	PCT	O-RB	D-RB	TOT	AST	PF	DQ	STL	TO	BLK	PTS	RPG	APG	PPG
69-70—Boston	60	—	1328	309	684	.452	—	—	—	111	135	.822	—	—	169	145	132	1	—	—	—	729	2.8	2.4	12.2
70-71—Boston	75	—	2787	693	1494	.464	—	—	—	215	269	.799	—	—	376	361	255	5	—	—	—	1601	5.0	4.8	21.3
71-72—Boston	79	29	3261	770	1788	.431	—	—	—	285	343	.831	—	—	446	416	227	1	—	—	—	1825	5.6	5.3	23.1
72-73—Boston	82	—	3250	717	1665	.431	—	—	—	178	228	.781	—	—	414	498	185	2	—	—	—	1612	5.0	6.1	19.7
73-74—Boston	82	—	3238	649	1445	.449	—	—	—	190	227	.837	100	251	351	448	185	1	105	—	25	1488	4.3	5.5	18.1
74-75—Boston	82	—	3220	658	1440	.457	—	—	—	186	223	.834	84	227	311	458	207	1	128	—	17	1502	3.8	5.6	18.3
75-76—Boston	82	—	3257	670	1492	.449	—	—	—	212	253	.838	61	252	313	445	183	2	107	—	20	1552	3.8	5.4	18.9
76-77—Boston	82	—	3333	638	1488	.429	—	—	—	333	383	.869	87	296	383	492	193	5	118	—	22	1609	4.7	6.0	19.6
77-78—Boston	46	—	1641	289	690	.419	—	—	—	103	120	.858	53	127	180	209	109	2	49	117	7	681	3.9	4.5	14.8
78-79—Boston-G.S.	76	—	2338	404	910	.444	—	—	—	139	158	.880	42	158	200	347	173	1	80	212	7	947	2.6	4.6	12.5
79-80—Golden State	78	—	2052	336	706	.476	1	6	.167	97	114	.851	42	139	181	239	186	0	88	157	13	770	2.3	3.1	9.9
80-81—Kansas City	13	—	236	36	82	.439	0	0	—	11	18	.611	3	18	21	37	21	0	11	18	1	83	1.6	2.8	6.4
REG. SEASON TOTALS	837	—	29941	6169	13884	.444	1	6	.167	2060	2471	.834	472	1468	3345	4095	2056	21	686	504	112	14399	4.0	4.9	17.2
PLAYOFF TOTALS	80	—	3428	732	1629	.449	0	0	—	256	309	.828	57	178	358	452	241	3	63	—	7	1720	4.5	5.7	21.5
ALL-STAR TOTALS	7	—	124	29	60	.483	0	0	—	6	11	.545	2	7	27	21	6	0	4	—	1	64	3.9	3.0	9.1

WHITE, RANDY (Bird) b. November 4, 1967 Ht. 6-8 Wt. 240 College—Louisiana Tech

SEASON—TEAM	G	GS	MIN	FGM	FGA	PCT	3FGM	3FGA	PCT	FTM	FTA	PCT	O-RB	D-RB	TOT	AST	PF	DQ	STL	TO	BLK	PTS	RPG	APG	PPG
89-90—Dallas	55	2	707	93	252	.369	1	14	.071	50	89	.562	78	95	173	21	124	0	24	47	6	237	3.1	0.4	4.3
90-91—Dallas	79	29	1901	265	665	.398	6	37	.162	159	225	.707	173	331	504	63	308	6	81	131	44	695	6.4	0.8	8.8
91-92—Dallas	65	12	1021	145	382	.380	4	27	.148	124	162	.765	96	140	236	31	157	1	31	68	22	418	3.6	0.5	6.4
92-93—Dallas	64	20	1433	235	540	.435	10	42	.238	138	184	.750	154	216	370	49	226	4	63	108	45	618	5.8	0.8	9.7
93-94—Dallas	18	3	320	45	112	.402	6	20	.300	19	33	.576	30	53	83	11	46	0	10	18	10	115	4.6	0.6	6.4
REG. SEASON TOTALS	281	66	5382	783	1951	.401	27	140	.193	490	693	.707	531	835	1366	175	861	11	209	372	127	2083	4.9	0.6	7.4
PLAYOFF TOTALS	1	0	2	0	0	—	0	0	—	0	0	—	0	0	0	0	0	0	0	0	0	0	0.0	0.0	0.0

WHITE, RORY WILBUR b. August 16, 1959 Ht. 6-8 Wt. 215 College—South Alabama

SEASON—TEAM	G	GS	MIN	FGM	FGA	PCT	3FGM	3FGA	PCT	FTM	FTA	PCT	O-RB	D-RB	TOT	AST	PF	DQ	STL	TO	BLK	PTS	RPG	APG	PPG
82-83—Phoenix	65	0	626	127	234	.543	0	1	.000	70	109	.642	47	58	105	30	54	0	16	51	2	324	1.6	0.5	5.0
83-84—Phoenix-Milw.-S.D.	36	2	372	80	170	.471	0	0	—	26	47	.553	37	37	74	15	31	0	15	24	3	186	2.1	0.4	5.2
84-85—L.A. Clippers	80	14	1106	144	279	.516	0	0	—	90	130	.692	94	101	195	34	115	0	35	87	20	378	2.4	0.4	4.7
85-86—L.A. Clippers	75	30	1761	355	684	.519	1	9	.111	164	222	.739	82	99	181	74	161	2	74	95	8	875	2.4	1.0	11.7
86-87—L.A. Clippers	68	35	1545	265	552	.480	0	3	.000	94	144	.653	90	104	194	79	159	1	47	73	19	624	2.9	1.2	9.2
REG. SEASON TOTALS	324	81	5410	971	1919	.506	1	13	.077	444	652	.681	350	399	749	232	520	3	187	330	52	2387	2.3	0.7	7.4
PLAYOFF TOTALS	3	0	40	7	14	.500	0	1	.000	2	4	.500	1	9	10	—	4	0	0	1	0	16	3.3	0.0	5.3

WHITE, RUDOLPH (Rudy) b. June 23, 1953 Ht. 6-2 Wt. 195 College—Arizona State

SEASON—TEAM	G	GS	MIN	FGM	FGA	PCT	3FGM	3FGA	PCT	FTM	FTA	PCT	O-RB	D-RB	TOT	AST	PF	DQ	STL	TO	BLK	PTS	RPG	APG	PPG
75-76—Houston	32	—	284	42	102	.412	—	—	—	18	25	.720	13	25	38	30	32	0	19	—	5	102	1.2	0.9	3.2
76-77—Houston	46	—	368	47	106	.443	—	—	—	15	25	.600	13	28	41	35	39	0	11	—	1	109	0.9	0.8	2.4
77-78—Houston	21	—	219	31	85	.365	—	—	—	14	18	.778	8	13	21	22	24	0	8	22	0	76	1.0	1.0	3.6
79-80—Houston	9	—	106	13	24	.542	0	0	—	10	13	.769	0	9	9	5	8	0	5	8	0	36	1.0	0.6	4.0
80-81—G.S.-Seattle	16	—	208	23	65	.354	0	1	.000	15	16	.938	1	10	11	20	23	0	9	12	1	61	0.7	1.3	3.8
REG. SEASON TOTALS	124	—	1185	156	382	.408	0	1	.000	72	97	.742	35	85	120	112	126	0	52	42	7	384	1.0	0.9	3.1
PLAYOFF TOTALS	1	—	2	1	3	.333	0	0	—	0	0	—	1	0	1	—	0	0	1	—	0	2	1.0	0.0	2.0

WHITE, TONY F. b. February 15, 1965 Ht. 6-2 Wt. 170 College—Tennessee

SEASON—TEAM	G	GS	MIN	FGM	FGA	PCT	3FGM	3FGA	PCT	FTM	FTA	PCT	O-RB	D-RB	TOT	AST	PF	DQ	STL	TO	BLK	PTS	RPG	APG	PPG
87-88—Chicago-N.Y.-G.S.	49	0	581	111	249	.446	0	6	.000	39	54	.722	12	19	31	59	57	0	20	47	2	261	0.6	1.2	5.3
REG. SEASON TOTALS	49	0	581	111	249	.446	0	6	.000	39	54	.722	12	19	31	59	57	0	20	47	2	261	0.6	1.2	5.3

WHITE, WILLIE b. August 20, 1962 Ht. 6-3 Wt. 195 College—Tennessee Chattanooga

SEASON—TEAM	G	GS	MIN	FGM	FGA	PCT	3FGM	3FGA	PCT	FTM	FTA	PCT	O-RB	D-RB	TOT	AST	PF	DQ	STL	TO	BLK	PTS	RPG	APG	PPG
84-85—Denver	39	0	234	52	124	.419	4	11	.364	21	31	.677	15	21	36	29	24	0	5	30	2	129	0.9	0.7	3.3
85-86—Denver	43	4	343	74	168	.440	6	21	.286	19	23	.826	17	27	44	53	24	0	18	25	2	173	1.0	1.2	4.0
REG. SEASON TOTALS	82	4	577	126	292	.432	10	32	.313	40	54	.741	32	48	80	82	48	0	23	55	4	302	1.0	1.0	3.7
PLAYOFF TOTALS	14	3	144	29	64	.453	3	7	.429	7	12	.583	10	10	20	23	10	0	6	18	0	68	1.4	1.6	4.9

WHITEHEAD, JEROME CLAY b. September 30, 1956 Ht. 6-10 Wt. 220 College—Riverside CC/Marquette

SEASON—TEAM	G	GS	MIN	FGM	FGA	PCT	3FGM	3FGA	PCT	FTM	FTA	PCT	O-RB	D-RB	TOT	AST	PF	DQ	STL	TO	BLK	PTS	RPG	APG	PPG
78-79—San Diego	31	—	152	15	34	.441	—	—	—	8	18	.444	16	34	50	7	29	0	3	11	4	38	1.6	0.2	1.2
79-80—S.D.-Utah	50	—	553	58	114	.509	0	0	—	10	35	.286	56	111	167	24	97	3	8	36	17	126	3.3	0.5	2.5
80-81—Dallas-Clev.-S.D.	48	—	688	83	180	.461	0	1	.000	28	56	.500	58	156	214	26	122	2	20	56	9	194	4.5	0.5	4.0
81-82—San Diego	72	63	2214	406	726	.559	0	0	—	184	241	.763	231	433	664	102	290	16	48	141	44	996	9.2	1.4	13.8
82-83—San Diego	46	23	905	164	306	.536	0	0	—	72	87	.828	105	156	261	42	139	2	21	65	15	400	5.7	0.9	8.7
83-84—San Diego	70	1	921	144	294	.490	0	0	—	88	107	.822	94	151	245	19	159	2	17	59	12	376	3.5	0.3	5.4
84-85—Golden State	79	78	2536	421	825	.510	0	0	—	184	235	.783	219	403	622	53	322	8	45	141	43	1026	7.9	0.7	13.0
85-86—Golden State	81	3	1079	126	294	.429	0	0	—	60	97	.619	94	234	328	19	176	2	18	64	19	312	4.0	0.2	3.9
86-87—Golden State	73	1	937	147	327	.450	0	1	.000	79	113	.699	110	152	262	24	175	1	16	50	12	373	3.6	0.3	5.1
87-88—Golden State	72	27	1221	174	360	.483	0	0	—	59	82	.720	109	212	321	39	209	3	32	49	21	407	4.5	0.5	5.7
88-89—G.S.-S.A.	57	4	622	72	182	.396	0	0	—	31	47	.660	49	85	134	19	115	1	23	24	4	175	2.4	0.3	3.1
REG. SEASON TOTALS	679	200	11828	1810	3642	.497	0	2	.000	803	1118	.718	1141	2127	3268	374	1833	40	251	696	200	4423	4.8	0.6	6.5
PLAYOFF TOTALS	10	0	100	9	27	.333	0	0	—	4	10	.400	5	9	14	3	22	1	2	1	2	22	1.4	0.3	2.2

WHITNEY, CHARLES VINCENT (**Hawkeye**) b. June 22, 1957 Ht. 6-5 Wt. 235 College—North Carolina State

SEASON—TEAM	G	GS	MIN	FGM	FGA	PCT	3FGM	3FGA	PCT	FTM	FTA	PCT	O-RB	D-RB	TOT	AST	PF	DQ	STL	TO	BLK	PTS	RPG	APG	PPG
80-81—Kansas City	47	—	782	149	306	.487	2	6	.333	50	65	.769	29	77	106	68	98	0	47	48	6	350	2.3	1.4	7.4
81-82—Kansas City	23	4	266	25	71	.352	0	1	.000	4	7	.571	13	27	40	19	31	0	12	14	1	54	1.7	0.8	2.3
REG. SEASON TOTALS	70	4	1048	174	377	.462	2	7	.286	54	72	.750	42	104	146	87	129	0	59	62	7	404	2.1	1.2	5.8

WHITNEY, CHRISTOPHER ANTOINE (**Chris**) b. October 5, 1971 Ht. 6-0 Wt. 170 College—Lincoln Trail/Clemson

SEASON—TEAM	G	GS	MIN	FGM	FGA	PCT	3FGM	3FGA	PCT	FTM	FTA	PCT	O-RB	D-RB	TOT	AST	PF	DQ	STL	TO	BLK	PTS	RPG	APG	PPG
93-94—San Antonio	40	4	339	25	82	.305	10	30	.333	12	15	.800	5	24	29	53	53	0	11	37	1	72	0.7	1.3	1.8
REG. SEASON TOTALS	40	4	339	25	82	.305	10	30	.333	12	15	.800	5	24	29	53	53	0	11	37	1	72	0.7	1.3	1.8

WHITNEY, HENRY LEE (**Hank**) b. April 28, 1939 Ht. 6-7 Wt. 235 College—Iowa State

SEASON—TEAM	G	GS	MIN	FGM	FGA	PCT	3FGM	3FGA	PCT	FTM	FTA	PCT	O-RB	D-RB	TOT	AST	PF	DQ	STL	TO	BLK	PTS	RPG	APG	PPG
67-68—New Jersey (A)	37	—	1159	217	552	.393	0	0	—	157	220	.714	—	—	477	56	158	3	—	54	—	591	12.9	1.5	16.0
68-69—N.Y.-Houston (A)	49	—	892	131	329	.398	0	1	.000	89	130	.685	—	—	254	56	144	1	—	72	—	351	5.2	1.1	7.2
69-70—Carolina (A)	59	—	981	170	403	.422	0	0	—	57	88	.648	—	—	371	56	200	4	—	—	—	397	6.3	0.9	6.7
REG. ABA TOTALS	145	—	3032	518	1284	.403	0	1	.000	303	438	.692	—	—	1102	168	502	8	—	126	—	1339	7.6	1.2	9.2
ABA PLAYOFF TOTALS	4	—	60	17	33	.515	0	0	—	4	9	.444	—	—	21	2	12	0	—	—	—	38	5.3	0.5	9.5

WICKS, SIDNEY b. September 19, 1949 Ht. 6-9 Wt. 225 College—Santa Monica/UCLA

SEASON—TEAM	G	GS	MIN	FGM	FGA	PCT	3FGM	3FGA	PCT	FTM	FTA	PCT	O-RB	D-RB	TOT	AST	PF	DQ	STL	TO	BLK	PTS	RPG	APG	PPG
71-72—Portland	82	—	3245	784	1837	.427	—	—	—	441	621	.710	—	—	943	350	186	1	—	—	—	2009	11.5	4.3	24.5
72-73—Portland	80	—	3152	761	1684	.452	—	—	—	384	531	.723	—	—	870	440	253	3	—	—	—	1906	10.9	5.5	23.8
73-74—Portland	75	—	2853	685	1492	.459	—	—	—	314	412	.762	196	488	684	326	214	2	90	—	63	1684	9.1	4.3	22.5
74-75—Portland	82	—	3162	692	1391	.497	—	—	—	394	558	.706	231	646	877	287	289	5	108	—	80	1778	10.7	3.5	21.7
75-76—Portland	79	—	3044	580	1201	.483	—	—	—	345	512	.674	245	467	712	244	250	5	77	—	53	1505	9.0	3.1	19.1
76-77—Boston	82	—	2642	464	1012	.458	—	—	—	310	464	.668	268	556	824	169	331	14	64	—	61	1238	10.0	2.1	15.1
77-78—Boston	81	—	2413	433	927	.467	—	—	—	217	329	.660	223	450	673	171	318	9	67	226	46	1083	8.3	2.1	13.4
78-79—San Diego	79	—	2022	312	676	.462	—	—	—	147	226	.650	159	246	405	126	274	4	70	180	36	771	5.1	1.6	9.8
79-80—San Diego	71	—	2146	210	496	.423	0	1	.000	83	152	.546	138	271	409	213	241	5	76	167	52	503	5.8	3.0	7.1
80-81—San Diego	49	—	1083	125	286	.437	0	1	.000	76	150	.507	79	144	223	111	168	3	40	94	40	326	4.6	2.3	6.7
REG. SEASON TOTALS	760	—	25762	5046	11002	.459	0	2	.000	2711	3955	.685	1539	3268	6620	2437	2524	51	592	667	431	12803	8.7	3.2	16.8
PLAYOFF TOTALS	9	—	261	42	81	.519	0	0	—	34	47	.723	26	57	83	16	37	2	13	—	3	118	9.2	1.8	13.1
ALL-STAR TOTALS	4	—	81	18	40	.450	0	0	—	13	18	.722	5	5	17	3	10	0	2	—	1	49	4.3	0.8	12.3

WIDBY, GEORGE RONALD (**Ron**) b. March 9, 1945 Ht. 6-4 Wt. 210 College—Tennessee

SEASON—TEAM	G	GS	MIN	FGM	FGA	PCT	3FGM	3FGA	PCT	FTM	FTA	PCT	O-RB	D-RB	TOT	AST	PF	DQ	STL	TO	BLK	PTS	RPG	APG	PPG
67-68—New Orleans (A)	20	—	137	27	70	.386	0	3	.000	4	7	.571	—	—	45	4	18	0	—	7	—	58	2.3	0.2	2.9
REG. ABA TOTALS	20	—	137	27	70	.386	0	3	.000	4	7	.571	—	—	45	4	18	0	—	7	—	58	2.3	0.2	2.9
ABA PLAYOFF TOTALS	6	—	31	8	19	.421	2	3	.667	0	2	.000	—	—	17	1	5	0	—	2	—	18	2.8	0.2	3.0

WIER, MURRAY NEAL b. December 12, 1926 Ht. 5-9 Wt. 155 College—Iowa

SEASON—TEAM	G	GS	MIN	FGM	FGA	PCT	3FGM	3FGA	PCT	FTM	FTA	PCT	O-RB	D-RB	TOT	AST	PF	DQ	STL	TO	BLK	PTS	RPG	APG	PPG
48-49—Tri-Cities (N)	60	—	—	80	—	—	—	—	—	79	113	.699	—	—	—	91	—	—	—	—	—	239	—	—	4.0
49-50—Tri-Cities	56	—	—	157	480	.327	—	—	—	115	166	.693	—	—	—	107	141	—	—	—	—	429	—	1.9	7.7
REG. NBA TOTALS	56	—	—	157	480	.327	—	—	—	115	166	.693	—	—	—	107	141	—	—	—	—	429	—	1.9	7.7
REG. NBL TOTALS	60	—	—	80	—	—	—	—	—	79	113	.699	—	—	—	91	—	—	—	—	—	239	—	—	4.0
NBA PLAYOFF TOTALS	3	—	—	3	9	.333	—	—	—	4	8	.500	—	—	—	4	—	—	—	—	—	10	—	0.0	3.3
NBL PLAYOFF TOTALS	6	—	—	13	—	—	—	—	—	9	13	.692	—	—	—	15	—	—	—	—	—	35	—	—	5.8

WIESENHAHN, ROBERT B. JR. (Bob) b. December 22, 1938 Ht. 6-4 Wt. 215 College—Cincinnati

SEASON—TEAM	G	GS	MIN	FGM	FGA	PCT	3FGM	3FGA	PCT	FTM	FTA	PCT	O-RB	D-RB	TOT	AST	PF	DQ	STL	TO	BLK	PTS	RPG	APG	PPG
61-62—Cincinnati	60	—	326	51	161	.317	—	—	—	17	30	.567	—	—	112	23	50	0	—	—	—	119	1.9	0.4	2.0
REG. SEASON TOTALS	60	—	326	51	161	.317	—	—	—	17	30	.567	—	—	112	23	50	0	—	—	—	119	1.9	0.4	2.0
PLAYOFF TOTALS	2	—	6	1	4	.250	—	—	—	1	1	1.000	—	—	2	—	0	0	—	—	—	3	1.0	0.0	1.5

WIGGINS, MITCHELL LEE b. September 28, 1959 Ht. 6-4 Wt. 185 College—Truett-McConnell/Clemson/Florida State

SEASON—TEAM	G	GS	MIN	FGM	FGA	PCT	3FGM	3FGA	PCT	FTM	FTA	PCT	O-RB	D-RB	TOT	AST	PF	DQ	STL	TO	BLK	PTS	RPG	APG	PPG
83-84—Chicago	82	40	2123	399	890	.448	7	29	.241	213	287	.742	138	190	328	187	278	8	106	139	11	1018	4.0	2.3	12.4
84-85—Houston	82	24	1575	318	657	.484	6	23	.261	96	131	.733	110	125	235	119	195	1	83	90	13	738	2.9	1.5	9.0
85-86—Houston	78	0	1198	222	489	.454	1	12	.083	86	118	.729	87	72	159	101	155	1	59	62	5	531	2.0	1.3	6.8
86-87—Houston	32	19	788	153	350	.437	0	5	.000	49	65	.754	74	59	133	76	82	1	44	50	3	355	4.2	2.4	11.1
89-90—Houston	66	52	1852	416	853	.488	0	3	.000	192	237	.810	133	153	286	104	165	0	85	87	1	1024	4.3	1.6	15.5
91-92—Philadelphia	49	0	569	88	229	.384	0	1	.000	35	51	.686	43	51	94	22	67	0	20	25	1	211	1.9	0.4	4.3
REG. SEASON TOTALS	389	135	8105	1596	3468	.460	14	73	.192	671	889	.755	585	650	1235	609	942	11	397	453	34	3877	3.2	1.6	10.0
PLAYOFF TOTALS	29	0	539	105	212	.495	0	3	.000	23	31	.742	45	48	93	34	55	0	19	34	3	233	3.2	1.2	8.0

WILBURN, KENNETH (Ken) b. June 8, 1944 Ht. 6-6 Wt. 195 College—Central State (Ohio)

SEASON—TEAM	G	GS	MIN	FGM	FGA	PCT	3FGM	3FGA	PCT	FTM	FTA	PCT	O-RB	D-RB	TOT	AST	PF	DQ	STL	TO	BLK	PTS	RPG	APG	PPG
67-68—Chicago	3	—	26	5	9	.556	—	—	—	1	4	.250	—	—	10	2	4	0	—	—	—	11	3.3	0.7	3.7
68-69—Chicago	4	—	14	3	8	.375	—	—	—	1	4	.250	—	—	3	1	1	0	—	—	—	7	0.8	0.3	1.8
68-69—Minn.-N.Y.-Denver (A)	47	—	465	76	198	.384	0	0	—	38	71	.535	—	—	199	26	68	1	—	—	47	190	4.2	0.6	4.0
REG. NBA TOTALS	7	—	40	8	17	.471	—	—	—	2	8	.250	—	—	13	3	5	0	—	—	—	18	1.9	0.4	2.6
REG. ABA TOTALS	47	—	465	76	198	.384	0	0	—	38	71	.535	—	—	199	26	68	1	—	—	47	190	4.2	0.6	4.0
ABA PLAYOFF TOTALS	7	—	93	16	33	.485	0	0	—	4	16	.250	—	—	32	5	21	0	—	—	11	36	4.6	0.7	5.1

WILCUTT, D.C. b. March 25, 1923 Ht. 6-2 Wt. 165 College—St. Louis

SEASON—TEAM	G	GS	MIN	FGM	FGA	PCT	3FGM	3FGA	PCT	FTM	FTA	PCT	O-RB	D-RB	TOT	AST	PF	DQ	STL	TO	BLK	PTS	RPG	APG	PPG
48-49—St. Louis	22	—	—	18	51	.353	—	—	—	15	18	.833	—	—	—	31	9	—	—	—	—	51	—	1.4	2.3
49-50—St. Louis	37	—	—	24	73	.329	—	—	—	29	42	.690	—	—	—	49	27	—	—	—	—	77	—	1.3	2.1
REG. SEASON TOTALS	59	—	—	42	124	.339	—	—	—	44	60	.733	—	—	—	80	36	—	—	—	—	128	—	1.4	2.2
PLAYOFF TOTALS	2	—	—	3	7	.429	—	—	—	0	0	—	—	—	—	4	2	—	—	—	—	6	—	2.0	3.0

WILEY, EUGENE (Gene) b. November 12, 1937 Ht. 6-10 Wt. 220 College—Wichita State

SEASON—TEAM	G	GS	MIN	FGM	FGA	PCT	3FGM	3FGA	PCT	FTM	FTA	PCT	O-RB	D-RB	TOT	AST	PF	DQ	STL	TO	BLK	PTS	RPG	APG	PPG
62-63—Los Angeles	75	—	1488	109	236	.462	—	—	—	23	68	.338	—	—	504	40	180	4	—	—	—	241	6.7	0.5	3.2
63-64—Los Angeles	78	—	1510	146	273	.535	—	—	—	45	75	.600	—	—	510	44	225	4	—	—	—	337	6.5	0.6	4.3
64-65—Los Angeles	80	—	2002	175	376	.465	—	—	—	56	111	.505	—	—	690	105	235	11	—	—	—	406	8.6	1.3	5.1
65-66—Los Angeles	67	—	1386	123	289	.426	—	—	—	43	76	.566	—	—	490	63	171	3	—	—	—	289	7.3	0.9	4.3
67-68—Oakland-Dallas (A)	9	—	85	7	20	.350	0	0	—	4	8	.500	—	—	20	2	10	0	—	2	—	18	2.2	0.2	2.0
REG. NBA TOTALS	300	—	6386	553	1174	.471	—	—	—	167	330	.506	—	—	2194	252	811	22	—	—	—	1273	7.3	0.8	4.2
REG. ABA TOTALS	9	—	85	7	20	.350	0	0	—	4	8	.500	—	—	20	2	10	0	—	2	—	18	2.2	0.2	2.0
NBA PLAYOFF TOTALS	27	—	710	52	103	.505	—	—	—	16	37	.432	—	—	272	34	80	2	—	—	—	120	10.1	1.3	4.4

WILEY, MICHAEL ANTHONY b. October 16, 1957 Ht. 6-9 Wt. 200 College—Long Beach State

SEASON—TEAM	G	GS	MIN	FGM	FGA	PCT	3FGM	3FGA	PCT	FTM	FTA	PCT	O-RB	D-RB	TOT	AST	PF	DQ	STL	TO	BLK	PTS	RPG	APG	PPG
80-81—San Antonio	33	—	271	76	138	.551	0	2	.000	36	48	.750	22	42	64	11	38	1	8	28	6	188	1.9	0.3	5.7
81-82—San Diego	61	1	1013	203	359	.565	0	5	.000	98	141	.695	67	115	182	52	127	1	40	71	16	504	3.0	0.9	8.3
REG. SEASON TOTALS	94	1	1284	279	497	.561	0	7	.000	134	189	.709	89	157	246	63	165	2	48	99	22	692	2.6	0.7	7.4
PLAYOFF TOTALS	3	0	5	0	1	.000	0	0	—	2	2	1.000	0	0	0	—	2	0	0	0	0	2	0.0	0.0	0.7

WILEY, MORLON DAVID b. September 24, 1966 Ht. 6-4 Wt. 190 College—Long Beach State

SEASON—TEAM	G	GS	MIN	FGM	FGA	PCT	3FGM	3FGA	PCT	FTM	FTA	PCT	O-RB	D-RB	TOT	AST	PF	DQ	STL	TO	BLK	PTS	RPG	APG	PPG
88-89—Dallas	51	1	408	46	114	.404	6	24	.250	13	16	.813	13	34	47	76	61	0	25	34	6	111	0.9	1.5	2.2
89-90—Orlando	40	2	638	92	208	.442	17	46	.370	28	38	.737	13	39	52	114	65	0	45	63	3	229	1.3	2.9	5.7
90-91—Orlando	34	0	350	45	108	.417	6	12	.500	17	25	.680	4	13	17	73	37	1	24	34	0	113	0.5	2.1	3.3
91-92—Orlando-S.A.-Atlanta	53	19	870	83	193	.430	14	42	.333	24	35	.686	24	57	81	180	89	0	47	60	3	204	1.5	3.4	3.8
92-93—Atlanta-Dallas	58	15	995	96	254	.378	54	154	.351	17	26	.654	29	62	91	181	127	2	65	80	3	263	1.6	3.1	4.5
93-94—Miami-Dallas	16	0	158	9	29	.310	3	10	.300	0	0	—	0	10	10	23	21	0	15	17	0	21	0.6	1.4	1.3
REG. SEASON TOTALS	252	37	3419	371	906	.409	100	288	.347	99	140	.707	83	215	298	647	400	3	221	288	15	941	1.2	2.6	3.7

WILFONG, ALVA WINFRED (Win) b. March 18, 1933 d. May 18, 1985 Ht. 6-2 Wt. 185 College—Memphis State/Missouri

SEASON—TEAM	G	GS	MIN	FGM	FGA	PCT	3FGM	3FGA	PCT	FTM	FTA	PCT	O-RB	D-RB	TOT	AST	PF	DQ	STL	TO	BLK	PTS	RPG	APG	PPG
57-58—St. Louis	71	—	1360	196	543	.361	—	—	—	163	238	.685	—	—	290	163	199	3	—	—	—	555	4.1	2.3	7.8
58-59—St. Louis	63	—	741	99	285	.347	—	—	—	62	82	.756	—	—	121	50	102	0	—	—	—	260	1.9	0.8	4.1
59-60—Cincinnati	72	—	1992	283	764	.370	—	—	—	161	207	.778	—	—	352	265	229	1	—	—	—	727	4.9	3.7	10.1
60-61—Cincinnati	62	—	717	106	305	.348	—	—	—	72	89	.809	—	—	147	87	119	1	—	—	—	284	2.4	1.4	4.6
REG. SEASON TOTALS	268	—	4810	684	1897	.361	—	—	—	458	616	.744	—	—	910	565	649	5	—	—	—	1826	3.4	2.1	6.8
PLAYOFF TOTALS	16	—	208	26	88	.295	—	—	—	28	39	.718	—	—	47	28	31	0	—	—	—	80	2.9	1.8	5.0

WILKENS, LEONARD RANDOLPH (Lenny) b. October 28, 1937 Ht. 6-1 Wt. 185 College—Providence

SEASON—TEAM	G	GS	MIN	FGM	FGA	PCT	3FGM	3FGA	PCT	FTM	FTA	PCT	O-RB	D-RB	TOT	AST	PF	DQ	STL	TO	BLK	PTS	RPG	APG	PPG
60-61—St. Louis	75	—	1898	333	783	.425	—	—	—	214	300	.713	—	—	335	212	215	5	—	—	—	880	4.5	2.8	11.7
61-62—St. Louis	20	—	870	140	364	.385	—	—	—	84	110	.764	—	—	131	116	63	0	—	—	—	364	6.6	5.8	18.2
62-63—St. Louis	75	—	2569	333	834	.399	—	—	—	222	319	.696	—	—	403	381	256	6	—	—	—	888	5.4	5.1	11.8
63-64—St. Louis	78	—	2526	334	808	.413	—	—	—	270	365	.740	—	—	335	359	287	7	—	—	—	938	4.3	4.6	12.0
64-65—St. Louis	78	—	2854	434	1048	.414	—	—	—	416	558	.746	—	—	365	431	283	7	—	—	—	1284	4.7	5.5	16.5
65-66—St. Louis	69	—	2692	411	954	.431	—	—	—	422	532	.793	—	—	322	429	248	4	—	—	—	1244	4.7	6.2	18.0
66-67—St. Louis	78	—	2974	448	1036	.432	—	—	—	459	583	.787	—	—	412	442	280	6	—	—	—	1355	5.3	5.7	17.4
67-68—St. Louis	82	—	3169	546	1246	.438	—	—	—	546	711	.768	—	—	438	679	255	3	—	—	—	1638	5.3	8.3	20.0
68-69—Seattle	82	—	3463	644	1462	.440	—	—	—	547	710	.770	—	—	511	674	294	8	—	—	—	1835	6.2	8.2	22.4
69-70—Seattle	75	—	2802	448	1066	.420	—	—	—	438	556	.788	—	—	378	683	212	6	—	—	—	1334	5.0	9.1	17.8
70-71—Seattle	71	—	2641	471	1125	.419	—	—	—	461	574	.803	—	—	319	654	201	3	—	—	—	1403	4.5	9.2	19.8
71-72—Seattle	80	—	2989	479	1027	.466	—	—	—	480	620	.774	—	—	338	766	209	4	—	—	—	1438	4.2	9.6	18.0
72-73—Cleveland	75	—	2973	572	1275	.449	—	—	—	394	476	.828	—	—	346	628	221	2	—	—	—	1538	4.6	8.4	20.5
73-74—Cleveland	74	—	2483	462	994	.465	—	—	—	289	361	.801	80	197	277	522	165	2	97	—	17	1213	3.7	7.1	16.4
74-75—Portland	65	—	1161	134	305	.439	—	—	—	152	198	.768	38	82	120	235	96	1	77	—	9	420	1.8	3.6	6.5
REG. SEASON TOTALS	1077	—	38064	6189	14327	.432	—	—	—	5394	6973	.774	118	279	5030	7211	3285	63	174	—	26	17772	4.7	6.7	16.5
PLAYOFF TOTALS	64	—	2403	359	899	.399	—	—	—	313	407	.769	0	0	373	372	258	7	0	—	0	1031	5.8	5.8	16.1
ALL-STAR TOTALS	9	—	182	30	75	.400	—	—	—	25	32	.781	0	0	22	26	15	0	—	—	0	85	2.4	2.9	9.4

WILKERSON, ROBERT LEE (Bob) b. August 15, 1954 Ht. 6-6½ Wt. 195 College—Indiana

SEASON—TEAM	G	GS	MIN	FGM	FGA	PCT	3FGM	3FGA	PCT	FTM	FTA	PCT	O-RB	D-RB	TOT	AST	PF	DQ	STL	TO	BLK	PTS	RPG	APG	PPG
76-77—Seattle	78	—	1552	221	573	.386	—	—	—	84	122	.689	96	162	258	171	136	0	72	—	8	526	3.3	2.2	6.7
77-78—Denver	81	—	2780	382	936	.408	—	—	—	157	210	.748	98	376	474	439	275	3	126	294	21	921	5.9	5.4	11.4
78-79—Denver	80	—	2425	396	869	.456	—	—	—	119	173	.688	100	314	414	284	190	0	118	196	21	911	5.2	3.6	11.4
79-80—Denver	75	—	2381	430	1030	.417	7	34	.206	166	222	.748	85	231	316	243	194	1	93	193	27	1033	4.2	3.2	13.8
80-81—Chicago	80	—	2238	330	715	.462	1	10	.100	137	163	.840	86	196	282	272	170	0	102	175	23	798	3.5	3.4	10.0
81-82—Cleveland	65	38	1805	284	679	.418	3	18	.167	145	185	.784	60	190	250	237	188	3	92	138	25	716	3.8	3.6	11.0
82-83—Cleveland	77	11	1702	213	511	.417	0	4	.000	93	124	.750	62	180	242	189	157	0	68	160	16	519	3.1	2.5	6.7
REG. SEASON TOTALS	536	49	14883	2256	5313	.425	11	66	.167	901	1199	.751	587	1649	2236	1835	1310	7	671	1156	141	5424	4.2	3.4	10.1
PLAYOFF TOTALS	22	0	679	86	220	.391	0	1	.000	32	50	.640	33	80	113	107	75	2	27	42	6	204	5.1	4.9	9.3

WILKES, JACKSON KEITH (Keith, see Jamaal Abdul-Lateef Wilkes)

WILKES, JAMAAL ABDUL-LATEEF (Silk, formerly Jackson Keith Wilkes) b. May 2, 1953 Ht. 6-6.5 Wt. 190 College—UCLA

SEASON—TEAM	G	GS	MIN	FGM	FGA	PCT	3FGM	3FGA	PCT	FTM	FTA	PCT	O-RB	D-RB	TOT	AST	PF	DQ	STL	TO	BLK	PTS	RPG	APG	PPG
74-75—Golden State	82	—	2515	502	1135	.442	—	—	—	160	218	.734	203	468	671	183	222	0	107	—	22	1164	8.2	2.2	14.2
75-76—Golden State	82	—	2716	617	1334	.463	—	—	—	227	294	.772	193	527	720	167	222	0	102	—	31	1461	8.8	2.0	17.8
76-77—Golden State	76	—	2579	548	1147	.478	—	—	—	247	310	.797	155	423	578	211	222	1	127	—	16	1343	7.6	2.8	17.7
77-78—Los Angeles	51	—	1490	277	630	.440	—	—	—	106	148	.716	113	267	380	182	162	1	77	107	22	660	7.5	3.6	12.9
78-79—Los Angeles	82	—	2915	626	1242	.504	—	—	—	272	362	.751	164	445	609	227	275	2	134	224	27	1524	7.4	2.8	18.6
79-80—Los Angeles	82	—	3111	726	1358	.535	3	17	.176	189	234	.808	176	349	525	250	220	1	129	157	28	1644	6.4	3.0	20.0
80-81—Los Angeles	81	—	3028	786	1495	.526	1	13	.077	254	335	.758	146	289	435	235	223	1	121	207	29	1827	5.4	2.9	22.6
81-82—Los Angeles	82	82	2906	744	1417	.525	0	4	.000	246	336	.732	153	240	393	143	240	1	89	164	24	1734	4.8	1.7	21.1
82-83—Los Angeles	80	80	2552	684	1290	.530	0	6	.000	203	268	.757	146	197	343	182	221	0	65	150	17	1571	4.3	2.3	19.6
83-84—Los Angeles	75	74	2507	542	1055	.514	2	8	.250	208	280	.743	130	210	340	214	205	0	72	137	41	1294	4.5	2.9	17.3
84-85—L.A. Lakers	42	8	761	148	303	.488	0	1	.000	51	66	.773	35	59	94	41	65	0	19	49	3	347	2.2	1.0	8.3
85-86—L.A. Clippers	13	1	195	26	65	.400	1	3	.333	22	27	.815	13	16	29	15	19	0	7	16	2	75	2.2	1.2	5.8
REG. SEASON TOTALS	828	245	27275	6226	12471	.499	7	52	.135	2185	2878	.759	1627	3490	5117	2050	2296	7	1049	1211	262	14644	6.2	2.5	17.7
PLAYOFF TOTALS	113	29	3799	785	1689	.465	0	6	.000	250	344	.727	251	467	718	246	326	3	137	145	53	1820	6.4	2.2	16.1
ALL-STAR TOTALS	3	0	54	13	27	.481	0	0	—	7	7	1.000	6	8	14	7	3	0	4	4	0	33	4.7	2.3	11.0

WILKES, JAMES ROBERT b. March 12, 1958 Ht. 6-7 Wt. 200 College—UCLA

SEASON—TEAM	G	GS	MIN	FGM	FGA	PCT	3FGM	3FGA	PCT	FTM	FTA	PCT	O-RB	D-RB	TOT	AST	PF	DQ	STL	TO	BLK	PTS	RPG	APG	PPG
80-81—Chicago	48	—	540	85	184	.462	0	1	.000	29	42	.690	36	60	96	30	86	0	25	34	12	199	2.0	0.6	4.1
81-82—Chicago	57	22	862	128	266	.481	0	1	.000	58	80	.725	62	97	159	64	112	0	30	62	18	314	2.8	1.1	5.5
82-83—Detroit	9	0	129	11	34	.324	0	1	.000	12	15	.800	9	10	19	10	22	0	3	5	1	34	2.1	1.1	3.8
REG. SEASON TOTALS	114	22	1531	224	484	.463	0	3	.000	99	137	.723	107	167	274	104	220	0	58	101	31	547	2.4	0.9	4.8
PLAYOFF TOTALS	2	0	5	0	1	.000	0	0	—	0	0	—	1	1	1	1	0	0	1	2	0	0	0.5	0.5	0.0

WILKINS, EDDIE LEE (**Eddie Lee**) b. May 7, 1962   Ht. 6-10 Wt. 220 College—Gardner-Webb

SEASON—TEAM	G	GS	MIN	FGM	FGA	PCT	3FGM	3FGA	PCT	FTM	FTA	PCT	O-RB	D-RB	TOT	AST	PF	DQ	STL	TO	BLK	PTS	RPG	APG	PPG
84-85—New York	54	16	917	116	233	.498	0	2	.000	66	122	.541	86	176	262	16	155	3	21	64	16	298	4.9	0.3	5.5
86-87—New York	24	10	454	56	127	.441	0	1	.000	27	58	.466	45	62	107	6	67	1	9	28	2	139	4.5	0.3	5.8
88-89—New York	71	2	584	114	245	.465	0	1	.000	61	111	.550	72	76	148	7	110	1	10	56	16	289	2.1	0.1	4.1
89-90—New York	79	0	972	141	310	.455	0	2	.000	89	147	.605	114	151	265	16	152	1	18	73	18	371	3.4	0.2	4.7
90-91—New York	68	1	668	114	255	.447	0	1	.000	51	90	.567	69	111	180	15	91	0	17	50	7	279	2.6	0.2	4.1
92-93—Philadelphia	26	0	192	55	97	.567	0	2	.000	48	78	.615	14	26	40	2	34	1	7	17	1	158	1.5	0.1	6.1
REG. SEASON TOTALS	322	29	3787	596	1267	.470	0	9	.000	342	606	.564	400	602	1002	62	609	7	82	288	60	1534	3.1	0.2	4.8
PLAYOFF TOTALS	15	0	93	18	35	.514	0	0	—	12	23	.522	12	12	24	—	14	0	2	8	0	48	1.6	0.0	3.2

WILKINS, GERALD BERNARD (**Doug E. Fresh**) b. September 11, 1963   Ht. 6-6 Wt. 210 College—Moberly Area CC/Tennessee Chattanooga

SEASON—TEAM	G	GS	MIN	FGM	FGA	PCT	3FGM	3FGA	PCT	FTM	FTA	PCT	O-RB	D-RB	TOT	AST	PF	DQ	STL	TO	BLK	PTS	RPG	APG	PPG
85-86—New York	81	53	2025	437	934	.468	7	25	.280	132	237	.557	92	116	208	161	155	0	68	157	9	1013	2.6	2.0	12.5
86-87—New York	80	73	2758	633	1302	.486	26	74	.351	235	335	.701	120	174	294	354	165	0	88	214	18	1527	3.7	4.4	19.1
87-88—New York	81	78	2703	591	1324	.446	39	129	.302	191	243	.786	106	164	270	326	183	1	90	212	22	1412	3.3	4.0	17.4
88-89—New York	81	58	2414	462	1025	.451	51	172	.297	186	246	.756	95	149	244	274	166	1	115	169	22	1161	3.0	3.4	14.3
89-90—New York	82	80	2609	472	1032	.457	39	125	.312	208	259	.803	133	238	371	330	188	0	95	194	21	1191	4.5	4.0	14.5
90-91—New York	68	56	2164	380	804	.473	9	43	.209	169	206	.820	78	129	207	275	181	0	82	161	23	938	3.0	4.0	13.8
91-92—New York	82	82	2344	431	964	.447	38	108	.352	116	159	.730	74	132	206	219	195	4	76	113	17	1016	2.5	2.7	12.4
92-93—Cleveland	80	35	2079	361	797	.453	16	58	.276	152	181	.840	74	140	214	183	154	1	78	94	18	890	2.7	2.3	11.1
93-94—Cleveland	82	82	2768	446	975	.457	84	212	.396	194	250	.776	106	197	303	255	186	0	105	131	38	1170	3.7	3.1	14.3
REG. SEASON TOTALS	717	597	21864	4213	9157	.460	309	946	.327	1583	2116	.748	878	1439	2317	2377	1573	7	797	1445	188	10318	3.2	3.3	14.4
PLAYOFF TOTALS	50	41	1542	276	616	.448	19	70	.271	93	117	.795	47	97	144	186	130	1	52	88	8	664	2.9	3.7	13.3

WILKINS, JACQUES DOMINIQUE (**Dominique, Human Highlight Film**) b. January 12, 1960   Ht. 6-8 Wt. 215 College—Georgia

SEASON—TEAM	G	GS	MIN	FGM	FGA	PCT	3FGM	3FGA	PCT	FTM	FTA	PCT	O-RB	D-RB	TOT	AST	PF	DQ	STL	TO	BLK	PTS	RPG	APG	PPG
82-83—Atlanta	82	82	2697	601	1220	.493	2	11	.182	230	337	.682	226	252	478	129	210	1	84	180	63	1434	5.8	1.6	17.5
83-84—Atlanta	81	81	2961	684	1429	.479	0	11	.000	382	496	.770	254	328	582	126	197	1	117	215	87	1750	7.2	1.6	21.6
84-85—Atlanta	81	81	3023	853	1891	.451	25	81	.309	486	603	.806	226	331	557	200	170	0	135	225	54	2217	6.9	2.5	27.4
85-86—Atlanta	78	78	3049	888	1897	.468	13	70	.186	577	705	.818	261	357	618	206	170	0	138	251	49	2366	7.9	2.6	30.3
86-87—Atlanta	79	79	2969	828	1787	.463	31	106	.292	607	742	.818	210	284	494	261	149	0	117	215	51	2294	6.3	3.3	29.0
87-88—Atlanta	78	76	2948	909	1957	.464	38	129	.295	541	655	.826	211	291	502	224	162	0	103	218	47	2397	6.4	2.9	30.7
88-89—Atlanta	80	80	2997	814	1756	.464	29	105	.276	442	524	.844	256	297	553	211	138	0	117	181	52	2099	6.9	2.6	26.2
89-90—Atlanta	80	79	2888	810	1672	.484	59	183	.322	459	569	.807	217	304	521	200	141	0	126	174	47	2138	6.5	2.5	26.7
90-91—Atlanta	81	81	3078	770	1640	.470	85	249	.341	476	574	.829	261	471	732	265	156	0	123	201	65	2101	9.0	3.3	25.9
91-92—Atlanta	42	42	1601	424	914	.464	37	128	.289	294	352	.835	103	192	295	158	77	0	52	122	24	1179	7.0	3.8	28.1
92-93—Atlanta	71	70	2647	741	1584	.468	120	316	.380	519	627	.828	187	295	482	227	116	0	70	184	27	2121	6.8	3.2	29.9
93-94—Atlanta-L.A. Clips	74	74	2635	698	1588	.440	85	295	.288	442	522	.847	182	299	481	169	126	0	92	172	30	1923	6.5	2.3	26.0
REG. SEASON TOTALS	907	903	33493	9020	19335	.467	524	1684	.311	5455	6706	.813	2594	3701	6295	2376	1812	2	1274	2338	596	24019	6.9	2.6	26.5
PLAYOFF TOTALS	51	51	2019	488	1138	.429	19	79	.241	350	426	.822	141	191	332	135	116	0	71	144	32	1345	6.5	2.6	26.4
ALL-STAR TOTALS	8	3	159	38	95	.400	2	8	.250	28	38	.737	16	11	27	15	13	0	6	8	4	106	3.4	1.9	13.3

WILKINS, JEFFREY (**Jeff**) b. March 9, 1955   Ht. 6-11.5 Wt. 230 College—Black Hawk/Illinois State

SEASON—TEAM	G	GS	MIN	FGM	FGA	PCT	3FGM	3FGA	PCT	FTM	FTA	PCT	O-RB	D-RB	TOT	AST	PF	DQ	STL	TO	BLK	PTS	RPG	APG	PPG
80-81—Utah	56	—	1058	117	260	.450	0	0	—	27	40	.675	62	212	274	40	169	3	32	59	46	261	4.9	0.7	4.7
81-82—Utah	82	62	2274	314	718	.437	0	3	.000	137	176	.778	120	491	611	90	248	4	32	134	77	765	7.5	1.1	9.3
82-83—Utah	81	34	2307	389	816	.477	0	3	.000	156	200	.780	154	442	596	132	251	4	41	186	42	934	7.4	1.6	11.5
83-84—Utah	81	1	1734	249	520	.479	0	3	.000	134	182	.736	109	346	455	73	205	1	27	109	42	632	5.6	0.9	7.8
84-85—Utah	79	0	1505	285	582	.490	0	1	.000	61	80	.763	78	288	366	81	173	0	35	91	18	631	4.6	1.0	8.0
85-86—Utah-S.A.	75	4	1126	147	374	.393	0	0	—	58	93	.624	74	198	272	46	157	1	11	52	21	352	3.6	0.6	4.7
REG. SEASON TOTALS	454	101	10004	1501	3270	.459	0	10	.000	573	771	.743	597	1977	2574	462	1203	13	178	631	246	3575	5.7	1.0	7.9
PLAYOFF TOTALS	24	1	478	81	176	.460	0	1	.000	44	57	.772	23	92	115	18	65	0	4	26	12	206	4.8	0.8	8.6

WILKINSON, DALE WAYNE b. March 18, 1960   Ht. 6-10 Wt. 220 College—Idaho State

SEASON—TEAM	G	GS	MIN	FGM	FGA	PCT	3FGM	3FGA	PCT	FTM	FTA	PCT	O-RB	D-RB	TOT	AST	PF	DQ	STL	TO	BLK	PTS	RPG	APG	PPG
84-85—Detroit-L.A. Clips	12	0	45	4	16	.250	0	1	.000	6	7	.857	1	3	4	2	10	0	0	4	0	14	0.3	0.2	1.2
REG. SEASON TOTALS	12	0	45	4	16	.250	0	1	.000	6	7	.857	1	3	4	2	10	0	0	4	0	14	0.3	0.2	1.2

WILLIAMS, AARON b. October 2, 1971   Ht. 6-9 Wt. 220 College—Xavier (Ohio)

SEASON—TEAM	G	GS	MIN	FGM	FGA	PCT	3FGM	3FGA	PCT	FTM	FTA	PCT	O-RB	D-RB	TOT	AST	PF	DQ	STL	TO	BLK	PTS	RPG	APG	PPG
93-94—Utah	6	0	12	2	8	.250	0	0	—	0	1	.000	1	2	3	1	4	0	0	1	0	4	0.5	0.2	0.7
REG. SEASON TOTALS	6	0	12	2	8	.250	0	0	—	0	1	.000	1	2	3	1	4	0	0	1	0	4	0.5	0.2	0.7

WILLIAMS, ALFRED (**Al**) b. January 3, 1948   Ht. 6-6 Wt. 210 College—Drake

SEASON—TEAM	G	GS	MIN	FGM	FGA	PCT	3FGM	3FGA	PCT	FTM	FTA	PCT	O-RB	D-RB	TOT	AST	PF	DQ	STL	TO	BLK	PTS	RPG	APG	PPG
70-71—Kentucky (A)	11	—	70	19	43	.442	0	0	—	5	10	.500	—	—	26	5	13	—	—	—	—	43	2.4	0.5	3.9
REG. ABA TOTALS	11	—	70	19	43	.442	0	0	—	5	10	.500	—	—	26	5	13	—	—	—	—	43	2.4	0.5	3.9

WILLIAMS, ARTHUR T. (**Hambone**) b. September 29, 1939　Ht. 6-2　Wt. 180　College—San Diego CC/Cal Poly-Pomona

SEASON—TEAM	G	GS	MIN	FGM	FGA	PCT	3FGM	3FGA	PCT	FTM	FTA	PCT	O-RB	D-RB	TOT	AST	PF	DQ	STL	TO	BLK	PTS	RPG	APG	PPG
67-68—San Diego	79	—	1739	265	718	.369	—	—	—	113	165	.685	—	—	286	391	204	0	—	—	—	643	3.6	4.9	8.1
68-69—San Diego	79	—	1987	227	592	.383	—	—	—	105	149	.705	—	—	364	524	238	0	—	—	—	559	4.6	6.6	7.1
69-70—San Diego	80	—	1545	189	464	.407	—	—	—	88	118	.746	—	—	292	503	168	0	—	—	—	466	3.7	6.3	5.8
70-71—Boston	74	—	1141	150	330	.455	—	—	—	60	83	.723	—	—	205	233	182	1	—	—	—	360	2.8	3.1	4.9
71-72—Boston	81	—	1326	161	339	.475	—	—	—	90	119	.756	—	—	256	327	204	2	—	—	—	412	3.2	4.0	5.1
72-73—Boston	81	—	974	110	261	.421	—	—	—	43	56	.768	—	—	182	236	136	1	—	—	—	263	2.2	2.9	3.2
73-74—Boston	67	—	617	73	168	.435	—	—	—	27	32	.844	20	95	115	163	100	0	44	—	3	173	1.7	2.4	2.6
74-75—San Diego (A)	7	—	89	8	12	.667	0	0	—	0	0	—	3	9	12	20	15	—	7	10	0	16	1.7	2.9	2.3
REG. NBA TOTALS	541	—	9329	1175	2872	.409	—	—	—	526	722	.729	20	95	1700	2377	1232	4	44	—	3	2876	3.1	4.4	5.3
REG. ABA TOTALS	7	—	89	8	12	.667	0	0	—	0	0	—	3	9	12	20	15	—	7	10	0	16	1.7	2.9	2.3
NBA PLAYOFF TOTALS	39	—	527	68	163	.417	—	—	—	31	43	.721	4	19	95	135	90	1	7	—	0	167	2.4	3.5	4.3

WILLIAMS, BERNARD (**Bernie**) b. December 30, 1945　Ht. 6-3　Wt. 175　College—La Salle

SEASON—TEAM	G	GS	MIN	FGM	FGA	PCT	3FGM	3FGA	PCT	FTM	FTA	PCT	O-RB	D-RB	TOT	AST	PF	DQ	STL	TO	BLK	PTS	RPG	APG	PPG
69-70—San Diego	72	—	1228	251	641	.392	—	—	—	96	122	.787	—	—	155	165	124	0	—	—	—	598	2.2	2.3	8.3
70-71—San Diego	56	—	708	112	338	.331	—	—	—	68	81	.840	—	—	85	113	76	1	—	—	—	292	1.5	2.0	5.2
71-72—Virginia (A)	78	—	1667	349	816	.428	18	65	.277	113	142	.796	—	—	154	134	178	—	—	123	—	829	2.0	1.7	10.6
72-73—Virginia (A)	71	—	1513	356	831	.428	10	58	.172	166	193	.860	60	65	125	137	150	0	—	136	—	888	1.8	1.9	12.5
73-74—Virginia (A)	6	—	51	6	19	.316	1	2	.500	2	2	1.000	0	4	4	7	3	—	1	5	0	15	0.7	1.2	2.5
REG. NBA TOTALS	128	—	1936	363	979	.371	—	—	—	164	203	.808	—	—	240	278	200	1	—	—	—	890	1.9	2.2	7.0
REG. ABA TOTALS	155	—	3231	711	1666	.427	29	125	.232	281	337	.834	60	69	283	278	331	0	1	264	0	1732	1.8	1.8	11.2
ABA PLAYOFF TOTALS	14	—	380	87	198	.439	2	5	.400	20	28	.714	0	0	47	24	42	0	0	35	0	196	3.4	1.7	14.0

WILLIAMS, BRIAN CARSON b. April 6, 1969　Ht. 6-11　Wt. 240　College—Maryland/Arizona

SEASON—TEAM	G	GS	MIN	FGM	FGA	PCT	3FGM	3FGA	PCT	FTM	FTA	PCT	O-RB	D-RB	TOT	AST	PF	DQ	STL	TO	BLK	PTS	RPG	APG	PPG
91-92—Orlando	48	2	905	171	324	.528	0	0	—	95	142	.669	115	157	272	33	139	2	41	86	53	437	5.7	0.7	9.1
92-93—Orlando	21	0	240	40	78	.513	0	1	.000	16	20	.800	24	32	56	5	48	2	14	25	17	96	2.7	0.2	4.6
93-94—Denver	80	1	1507	251	464	.541	0	3	.000	137	211	.649	138	308	446	50	221	3	49	104	87	639	5.6	0.6	8.0
REG. SEASON TOTALS	149	3	2652	462	866	.533	0	4	.000	248	373	.665	277	497	774	88	408	7	104	215	157	1172	5.2	0.6	7.9
PLAYOFF TOTALS	12	0	289	42	76	.553	0	0	—	27	41	.659	33	56	89	11	36	0	4	17	11	111	7.4	0.9	9.3

WILLIAMS, CHARLES E. (**Charlie, Toothpick**) b. September 5, 1943　Ht. 6-0　Wt. 175　College—Seattle

SEASON—TEAM	G	GS	MIN	FGM	FGA	PCT	3FGM	3FGA	PCT	FTM	FTA	PCT	O-RB	D-RB	TOT	AST	PF	DQ	STL	TO	BLK	PTS	RPG	APG	PPG
67-68—Pittsburgh (A)	78	—	3042	642	1573	.408	51	178	.287	290	429	.676	—	—	377	173	295	6	—	270	—	1625	4.8	2.2	20.8
68-69—Minnesota (A)	66	—	2282	484	1298	.373	66	212	.311	203	286	.710	—	—	246	163	222	6	—	204	—	1237	3.7	2.5	18.7
69-70—Pittsburgh (A)	26	—	925	193	537	.359	16	75	.213	104	135	.770	—	—	78	94	80	1	—	—	—	506	3.0	3.6	19.5
70-71—Pitt.-Memphis (A)	88	—	2242	501	1217	.412	33	136	.243	204	291	.701	—	—	210	250	243	—	—	—	—	1239	2.4	2.8	14.1
71-72—Memphis (A)	82	—	2583	480	1258	.382	41	174	.236	294	395	.744	—	—	228	253	250	—	—	233	—	1295	2.8	3.1	15.8
72-73—Memphis-Utah (A)	32	—	370	37	115	.322	3	20	.150	41	57	.719	4	14	18	59	54	1	—	34	—	118	0.6	1.8	3.7
REG. ABA TOTALS	372	—	11444	2337	5998	.390	210	795	.264	1136	1593	.713	4	14	1157	992	1144	14	—	741	—	6020	3.1	2.7	16.2
ABA PLAYOFF TOTALS	30	—	1022	218	527	.414	19	79	.241	100	139	.719	—	—	103	60	107	4	—	76	—	555	3.4	2.0	18.5
ABA ALL-STAR TOTALS	2	—	12	1	7	.143	0	2	.000	2	2	1.000	—	—	0	2	2	0	—	3	—	4	0.0	1.0	2.0

WILLIAMS, CHARLES LEON (**Chuckie**) b. December 31, 1953　Ht. 6-3　Wt. 180　College—Kansas State

SEASON—TEAM	G	GS	MIN	FGM	FGA	PCT	3FGM	3FGA	PCT	FTM	FTA	PCT	O-RB	D-RB	TOT	AST	PF	DQ	STL	TO	BLK	PTS	RPG	APG	PPG
76-77—Cleveland	22	—	65	14	47	.298	—	—	—	9	12	.750	3	1	4	7	7	0	1	—	0	37	0.2	0.3	1.7
REG. SEASON TOTALS	22	—	65	14	47	.298	—	—	—	9	12	.750	3	1	4	7	7	0	1	—	0	37	0.2	0.3	1.7

WILLIAMS, CHARLES LINWOOD (**Buck**) b. March 8, 1960　Ht. 6-8　Wt. 225　College—Maryland

SEASON—TEAM	G	GS	MIN	FGM	FGA	PCT	3FGM	3FGA	PCT	FTM	FTA	PCT	O-RB	D-RB	TOT	AST	PF	DQ	STL	TO	BLK	PTS	RPG	APG	PPG
81-82—New Jersey	82	82	2825	513	881	.582	0	1	.000	242	388	.624	347	658	1005	107	285	5	84	235	84	1268	12.3	1.3	15.5
82-83—New Jersey	82	82	2961	536	912	.588	0	4	.000	324	523	.620	365	662	1027	125	270	4	91	246	110	1396	12.5	1.5	17.0
83-84—New Jersey	81	81	3003	495	926	.535	0	4	.000	284	498	.570	355	645	1000	130	298	3	81	237	125	1274	12.3	1.6	15.7
84-85—New Jersey	82	82	3182	577	1089	.530	1	4	.250	336	538	.625	323	682	1005	167	293	7	63	238	110	1491	12.3	2.0	18.2
85-86—New Jersey	82	82	3070	500	956	.523	0	2	.000	301	445	.676	329	657	986	131	294	9	73	244	96	1301	12.0	1.6	15.9
86-87—New Jersey	82	82	2976	521	936	.557	0	1	.000	430	588	.731	322	701	1023	129	315	8	78	280	91	1472	12.5	1.6	18.0
87-88—New Jersey	70	70	2637	466	832	.560	1	1	1.000	346	518	.668	298	536	834	109	266	5	68	189	44	1279	11.9	1.6	18.3
88-89—New Jersey	74	72	2446	373	702	.531	0	3	.000	213	320	.666	249	447	696	78	223	0	61	142	36	959	9.4	1.1	13.0
89-90—Portland	82	82	2801	413	754	.548	0	1	.000	288	408	.706	250	550	800	116	285	4	69	168	39	1114	9.8	1.4	13.6
90-91—Portland	80	80	2582	358	595	.602	0	0	—	217	308	.705	227	524	751	97	247	2	47	137	47	933	9.4	1.2	11.7
91-92—Portland	80	80	2519	340	563	.604	0	1	.000	221	293	.754	260	444	704	108	244	4	62	130	41	901	8.8	1.4	11.3
92-93—Portland	82	82	2498	270	528	.511	0	1	.000	138	214	.645	232	458	690	75	270	0	81	101	61	678	8.4	0.9	8.3
93-94—Portland	81	81	2636	291	524	.555	0	1	.000	201	296	.679	315	528	843	80	239	1	58	111	47	783	10.4	1.0	9.7
REG. SEASON TOTALS	1040	1038	36136	5653	10198	.554	2	24	.083	3541	5337	.663	3872	7492	11364	1452	3529	52	916	2458	931	14849	10.9	1.4	14.3
PLAYOFF TOTALS	87	87	3236	397	757	.524	0	0	—	311	460	.676	310	531	841	104	315	9	82	174	59	1105	9.7	1.2	12.7
ALL-STAR TOTALS	3	0	61	10	19	.526	0	0	—	5	11	.455	7	17	24	6	3	0	1	4	2	25	8.0	2.0	8.3

WILLIAMS, CLIFFORD L. (**Cliff**) b. April 15, 1945 Ht. 6-3 Wt. 180 College—Bowling Green

SEASON—TEAM	G	GS	MIN	FGM	FGA	PCT	3FGM	3FGA	PCT	FTM	FTA	PCT	O-RB	D-RB	TOT	AST	PF	DQ	STL	TO	BLK	PTS	RPG	APG	PPG
68-69—Detroit	3	—	18	2	9	.222	—	—	—	0	0	—	—	—	3	2	7	0	—	—	—	4	1.0	0.7	1.3
REG. SEASON TOTALS	3	—	18	2	9	.222	—	—	—	0	0	—	—	—	3	2	7	0	—	—	—	4	1.0	0.7	1.3

WILLIAMS, COREY b. April 24, 1970 Ht. 6-2 Wt. 190 College—Oklahoma State

SEASON—TEAM	G	GS	MIN	FGM	FGA	PCT	3FGM	3FGA	PCT	FTM	FTA	PCT	O-RB	D-RB	TOT	AST	PF	DQ	STL	TO	BLK	PTS	RPG	APG	PPG
92-93—Chicago	35	0	242	31	85	.365	1	3	.333	18	22	.818	19	12	31	23	24	0	4	11	2	81	0.9	0.7	2.3
93-94—Minnesota	4	0	46	5	13	.385	0	1	.000	1	1	1.000	1	5	6	6	6	0	2	2	0	11	1.5	1.5	2.8
REG. SEASON TOTALS	39	0	288	36	98	.367	1	4	.250	19	23	.826	20	17	37	29	30	0	6	13	2	92	0.9	0.7	2.4

WILLIAMS, DONALD EDGAR (**Don, Duck**) b. August 2, 1956 Ht. 6-2 Wt. 180 College—Notre Dame

SEASON—TEAM	G	GS	MIN	FGM	FGA	PCT	3FGM	3FGA	PCT	FTM	FTA	PCT	O-RB	D-RB	TOT	AST	PF	DQ	STL	TO	BLK	PTS	RPG	APG	PPG
79-80—Utah	77	—	1794	232	519	.447	0	12	.000	42	60	.700	21	85	106	183	166	0	100	107	11	506	1.4	2.4	6.6
REG. SEASON TOTALS	77	—	1794	232	519	.447	0	12	.000	42	60	.700	21	85	106	183	166	0	100	107	11	506	1.4	2.4	6.6

WILLIAMS, EARL (**Earl the Twirl**) b. March 24, 1951 Ht. 6-7½ Wt. 230 College—Winston-Salem State

SEASON—TEAM	G	GS	MIN	FGM	FGA	PCT	3FGM	3FGA	PCT	FTM	FTA	PCT	O-RB	D-RB	TOT	AST	PF	DQ	STL	TO	BLK	PTS	RPG	APG	PPG
74-75—Phoenix	79	—	1040	163	394	.414	—	—	—	45	103	.437	156	300	456	95	146	0	28	—	32	371	5.8	1.2	4.7
75-76—Detroit	46	—	562	73	152	.480	—	—	—	22	44	.500	103	148	251	18	81	0	22	—	20	168	5.5	0.4	3.7
76-77—New York Nets	1	—	7	0	2	.000	—	—	—	3	6	.500	1	1	2	1	2	0	0	—	1	3	2.0	1.0	3.0
78-79—Boston	20	—	273	54	123	.439	—	—	—	14	24	.583	41	64	105	12	41	0	12	20	9	122	5.3	0.6	6.1
REG. SEASON TOTALS	146	—	1882	290	671	.432	—	—	—	84	177	.475	301	513	814	126	270	0	62	20	62	664	5.6	0.9	4.5

WILLIAMS, EDWARD (**Chuck**) b. June 6, 1946 Ht. 6-2 Wt. 175 College—Colorado

SEASON—TEAM	G	GS	MIN	FGM	FGA	PCT	3FGM	3FGA	PCT	FTM	FTA	PCT	O-RB	D-RB	TOT	AST	PF	DQ	STL	TO	BLK	PTS	RPG	APG	PPG
70-71—Pittsburgh (A)	83	—	1795	268	613	.437	1	4	.250	249	317	.785	—	—	185	170	161	—	—	—	—	786	2.2	2.0	9.5
71-72—Denver (A)	84	—	1580	263	583	.451	0	4	.000	205	275	.745	—	—	157	160	144	—	—	98	—	731	1.9	1.9	8.7
72-73—San Diego (A)	83	—	3074	488	1020	.478	1	7	.143	493	623	.791	71	158	229	582	275	8	—	231	—	1470	2.8	7.0	17.7
73-74—S.D.-Ken. (A)	90	—	2876	405	918	.441	4	12	.333	299	382	.783	80	170	250	557	198	—	89	256	11	1113	2.8	6.2	12.4
74-75—Memphis (A)	81	—	3171	476	963	.494	10	24	.417	212	260	.815	60	160	220	576	165	—	115	171	18	1174	2.7	7.1	14.5
75-76—Denver (A)	79	—	2529	339	660	.514	0	4	.000	188	231	.814	41	169	210	375	215	—	115	180	7	866	2.7	4.7	11.0
76-77—Denver-Buffalo	65	—	867	78	210	.371	—	—	—	68	87	.782	26	75	101	132	60	0	32	—	3	224	1.6	2.0	3.4
77-78—Buffalo	73	—	2002	208	436	.477	—	—	—	114	138	.826	29	108	137	317	137	0	48	156	4	530	1.9	4.3	7.3
REG. NBA TOTALS	138	—	2869	286	646	.443	—	—	—	182	225	.809	55	183	238	449	197	0	80	156	7	754	1.7	3.3	5.5
REG. ABA TOTALS	500	—	15025	2239	4757	.471	16	55	.291	1646	2088	.788	252	657	1251	2420	1158	8	319	936	36	6140	2.5	4.8	12.3
ABA PLAYOFF TOTALS	37	—	1133	162	348	.466	1	3	.333	116	133	.872	19	57	105	152	82	0	21	88	9	441	2.8	4.1	11.9
ABA ALL-STAR TOTALS	2	—	38	4	9	.444	0	0	—	4	8	.500	—	—	0	1	6	4	—	0	1	12	0.5	3.0	6.0

WILLIAMS, EUGENE (**Gene**) b. April 1, 1947 Ht. 6-7 Wt. 235 College—Kansas State

SEASON—TEAM	G	GS	MIN	FGM	FGA	PCT	3FGM	3FGA	PCT	FTM	FTA	PCT	O-RB	D-RB	TOT	AST	PF	DQ	STL	TO	BLK	PTS	RPG	APG	PPG
69-70—Kentucky (A)	1	—	8	0	1	.000	0	0	—	0	0	—	—	—	0	0	2	0	—	—	—	0	0.0	0.0	0.0
REG. ABA TOTALS	1	—	8	0	1	.000	0	0	—	0	0	—	—	—	0	2	0	—	—	—	0	0.0	0.0	0.0

WILLIAMS, FREEMAN JR. b. May 15, 1956 Ht. 6-4 Wt. 190 College—Portland State

SEASON—TEAM	G	GS	MIN	FGM	FGA	PCT	3FGM	3FGA	PCT	FTM	FTA	PCT	O-RB	D-RB	TOT	AST	PF	DQ	STL	TO	BLK	PTS	RPG	APG	PPG
78-79—San Diego	72	—	1195	335	683	.490	—	—	—	76	98	.776	48	50	98	83	88	0	42	99	2	746	1.4	1.2	10.4
79-80—San Diego	82	—	2118	645	1343	.480	42	128	.328	194	238	.815	103	89	192	166	145	0	72	171	9	1526	2.3	2.0	18.6
80-81—San Diego	82	—	1976	642	1381	.465	48	141	.340	253	297	.852	75	54	129	164	157	0	91	166	5	1585	1.6	2.0	19.3
81-82—S.D.-Atlanta	60	10	997	276	623	.443	28	94	.298	140	166	.843	23	39	62	86	103	1	29	107	0	720	1.0	1.4	12.0
82-83—Utah	18	3	210	36	101	.356	2	7	.286	18	25	.720	3	14	17	10	30	0	6	12	1	92	0.9	0.6	5.1
85-86—Washington	9	0	110	25	67	.373	7	14	.500	12	17	.706	4	8	12	7	10	0	7	13	1	69	1.3	0.8	7.7
REG. SEASON TOTALS	323	13	6606	1959	4198	.467	127	384	.331	693	841	.824	256	254	510	516	533	1	247	568	18	4738	1.6	1.6	14.7
PLAYOFF TOTALS	1	0	4	0	2	.000	0	1	.000	0	0	—	0	0	0	0	0	0	0	0	0	0	0.0	0.0	0.0

WILLIAMS, GUS (The Wizard) b. October 10, 1953 Ht. 6-2 Wt. 175 College—USC

SEASON—TEAM	G	GS	MIN	FGM	FGA	PCT	3FGM	3FGA	PCT	FTM	FTA	PCT	O-RB	D-RB	TOT	AST	PF	DQ	STL	TO	BLK	PTS	RPG	APG	PPG
75-76—Golden State	77	—	1728	365	853	.428	—	—	—	173	233	.742	62	97	159	240	143	2	140	—	26	903	2.1	3.1	11.7
76-77—Golden State	82	—	1930	325	701	.464	—	—	—	112	150	.747	72	161	233	292	218	4	121	—	19	762	2.8	3.6	9.3
77-78—Seattle	79	—	2572	602	1335	.451	—	—	—	227	278	.817	83	173	256	294	198	2	185	189	41	1431	3.2	3.7	18.1
78-79—Seattle	76	—	2266	606	1224	.495	—	—	—	245	316	.775	111	134	245	307	162	3	158	190	29	1457	3.2	4.0	19.2
79-80—Seattle	82	—	2969	739	1533	.482	7	36	.194	331	420	.788	127	148	275	397	160	1	200	181	37	1816	3.4	4.8	22.1
81-82—Seattle	80	80	2876	773	1592	.486	9	40	.225	320	436	.734	92	152	244	549	163	0	172	197	36	1875	3.1	6.9	23.4
82-83—Seattle	80	80	2761	660	1384	.477	2	43	.047	278	370	.751	72	133	205	643	117	0	182	230	26	1600	2.6	8.0	20.0
83-84—Seattle	80	80	2818	598	1306	.458	4	25	.160	297	396	.750	67	137	204	675	151	0	189	232	25	1497	2.6	8.4	18.7
84-85—Washington	79	78	2960	638	1483	.430	51	176	.290	251	346	.725	72	123	195	608	159	1	178	213	32	1578	2.5	7.7	20.0
85-86—Washington	77	67	2284	434	1013	.428	30	116	.259	138	188	.734	52	114	166	453	113	0	96	160	15	1036	2.2	5.9	13.5
86-87—Atlanta	33	0	481	53	146	.363	5	18	.278	27	40	.675	8	32	40	139	53	0	17	54	5	138	1.2	4.2	4.2
REG. SEASON TOTALS	825	385	25645	5793	12570	.461	108	454	.238	2399	3173	.756	818	1404	2222	4597	1637	13	1638	1646	291	14093	2.7	5.6	17.1
PLAYOFF TOTALS	99	24	3215	782	1644	.476	9	39	.231	356	483	.737	136	172	308	469	243	4	174	201	40	1929	3.1	4.7	19.5
ALL-STAR TOTALS	2	1	41	12	28	.429	0	1	.000	4	4	1.000	3	0	3	13	2	0	2	5	0	28	1.5	6.5	14.0

WILLIAMS, GUY BERNARD b. July 1, 1960 Ht. 6-9 Wt. 200 College—San Francisco/Washington State

SEASON—TEAM	G	GS	MIN	FGM	FGA	PCT	3FGM	3FGA	PCT	FTM	FTA	PCT	O-RB	D-RB	TOT	AST	PF	DQ	STL	TO	BLK	PTS	RPG	APG	PPG
84-85—Washington	21	0	119	29	63	.460	1	4	.250	2	5	.400	15	12	27	9	17	0	5	8	2	61	1.3	0.4	2.9
85-86—Golden State	5	0	25	2	5	.400	0	0	—	3	6	.500	0	6	6	0	7	1	1	0	2	7	1.2	0.0	1.4
REG. SEASON TOTALS	26	0	144	31	68	.456	1	4	.250	5	11	.455	15	18	33	9	24	1	6	8	4	68	1.3	0.3	2.6

WILLIAMS, HENRY (Hank) b. April 28, 1952 Ht. 6-5½ Wt. 215 College—Jacksonville

SEASON—TEAM	G	GS	MIN	FGM	FGA	PCT	3FGM	3FGA	PCT	FTM	FTA	PCT	O-RB	D-RB	TOT	AST	PF	DQ	STL	TO	BLK	PTS	RPG	APG	PPG
74-75—Utah (A)	40	—	468	76	173	.439	3	22	.136	18	23	.783	31	65	96	26	74	—	14	32	4	173	2.4	0.7	4.3
REG. ABA TOTALS	40	—	468	76	173	.439	3	22	.136	18	23	.783	31	65	96	26	74	—	14	32	4	173	2.4	0.7	4.3
ABA PLAYOFF TOTALS	2	—	7	2	6	.333	0	0	—	0	0	—	1	1	2	0	2	—	0	0	0	4	1.0	0.0	2.0

WILLIAMS, HERBERT L. (Herb) b. February 16, 1958 Ht. 6-11 Wt. 255 College—Ohio State

SEASON—TEAM	G	GS	MIN	FGM	FGA	PCT	3FGM	3FGA	PCT	FTM	FTA	PCT	O-RB	D-RB	TOT	AST	PF	DQ	STL	TO	BLK	PTS	RPG	APG	PPG
81-82—Indiana	82	75	2277	407	854	.477	2	7	.286	126	188	.670	175	430	605	139	200	0	53	137	178	942	7.4	1.7	11.5
82-83—Indiana	78	74	2513	580	1163	.499	0	7	.000	155	220	.705	151	432	583	262	230	4	54	229	171	1315	7.5	3.4	16.9
83-84—Indiana	69	53	2279	411	860	.478	0	4	.000	207	295	.702	154	400	554	215	193	4	60	207	108	1029	8.0	3.1	14.9
84-85—Indiana	75	70	2557	575	1211	.475	1	9	.111	224	341	.657	154	480	634	252	218	1	54	265	134	1375	8.5	3.4	18.3
85-86—Indiana	78	74	2770	627	1275	.492	1	12	.083	294	403	.730	172	538	710	174	244	2	50	210	184	1549	9.1	2.2	19.9
86-87—Indiana	74	67	2526	451	939	.480	0	9	.000	199	269	.740	143	400	543	174	255	9	59	145	93	1101	7.3	2.4	14.9
87-88—Indiana	75	37	1966	311	732	.425	0	6	.000	126	171	.737	116	353	469	98	244	1	37	119	146	748	6.3	1.3	10.0
88-89—Indiana-Dallas	76	66	2470	322	739	.436	0	5	.000	133	194	.686	135	458	593	124	236	5	46	149	134	777	7.8	1.6	10.2
89-90—Dallas	81	19	2199	295	665	.444	2	9	.222	108	159	.679	76	315	391	119	243	4	51	106	106	700	4.8	1.5	8.6
90-91—Dallas	60	36	1832	332	655	.507	0	4	.000	83	130	.638	86	271	357	95	197	3	30	113	88	747	6.0	1.6	12.5
91-92—Dallas	75	26	2040	367	851	.431	1	6	.167	124	171	.725	106	348	454	94	189	2	35	114	98	859	6.1	1.3	11.5
92-93—New York	55	0	571	72	175	.411	0	0	—	14	21	.667	44	102	146	19	78	0	21	22	28	158	2.7	0.3	2.9
93-94—New York	70	3	774	103	233	.442	0	1	.000	27	42	.643	56	126	182	28	108	1	18	39	43	233	2.6	0.4	3.3
REG. SEASON TOTALS	948	600	26774	4853	10352	.469	7	79	.089	1820	2604	.699	1568	4653	6221	1793	2635	36	568	1855	1511	11533	6.6	1.9	12.2
PLAYOFF TOTALS	33	4	411	52	102	.510	0	0	—	26	36	.722	22	45	67	17	60	1	5	23	18	130	2.0	0.5	3.9

WILLIAMS, JAMES (Fly) b. February 18, 1953 Ht. 6-5 Wt. 200 College—Austin Peay

SEASON—TEAM	G	GS	MIN	FGM	FGA	PCT	3FGM	3FGA	PCT	FTM	FTA	PCT	O-RB	D-RB	TOT	AST	PF	DQ	STL	TO	BLK	PTS	RPG	APG	PPG
74-75—St. Louis (A)	71	—	1239	297	643	.462	2	14	.143	69	101	.683	72	109	181	142	156	—	64	177	10	665	2.5	2.0	9.4
REG. ABA TOTALS	71	—	1239	297	643	.462	2	14	.143	69	101	.683	72	109	181	142	156	—	64	177	10	665	2.5	2.0	9.4
ABA PLAYOFF TOTALS	2	—	8	1	5	.200	0	1	.000	0	0	—	0	1	1	0	2	—	0	1	0	2	0.5	0.0	1.0

WILLIAMS, JAYSON b. February 22, 1968 Ht. 6-10 Wt. 240 College—St. John's

SEASON—TEAM	G	GS	MIN	FGM	FGA	PCT	3FGM	3FGA	PCT	FTM	FTA	PCT	O-RB	D-RB	TOT	AST	PF	DQ	STL	TO	BLK	PTS	RPG	APG	PPG
90-91—Philadelphia	52	1	508	72	161	.447	1	2	.500	37	56	.661	41	70	111	16	92	1	9	40	6	182	2.1	0.3	3.5
91-92—Philadelphia	50	8	646	75	206	.364	0	0	—	56	88	.636	62	83	145	12	110	1	20	44	20	206	2.9	0.2	4.1
92-93—New Jersey	12	2	139	21	46	.457	0	0	—	7	18	.389	22	19	41	0	24	0	4	8	4	49	3.4	0.0	4.1
93-94—New Jersey	70	0	877	125	293	.427	0	0	—	72	119	.605	109	154	263	26	140	1	17	35	36	322	3.8	0.4	4.6
REG. SEASON TOTALS	184	11	2170	293	706	.415	1	2	.500	172	281	.612	234	326	560	54	366	3	50	127	66	759	3.0	0.3	4.1
PLAYOFF TOTALS	6	0	27	4	8	.500	0	0	—	1	2	.500	5	2	7	—	6	0	0	3	0	9	1.2	0.0	1.5

WILLIAMS, JOHN (Hot Rod) b. August 9, 1962 Ht. 6-11 Wt. 245 College—Tulane

SEASON—TEAM	G	GS	MIN	FGM	FGA	PCT	3FGM	3FGA	PCT	FTM	FTA	PCT	O-RB	D-RB	TOT	AST	PF	DQ	STL	TO	BLK	PTS	RPG	APG	PPG
86-87—Cleveland	80	80	2714	435	897	.485	0	1	.000	298	400	.745	222	407	629	154	197	0	58	139	167	1168	7.9	1.9	14.6
87-88—Cleveland	77	50	2106	316	663	.477	0	1	.000	211	279	.756	159	347	506	103	203	2	61	104	145	843	6.6	1.3	10.9
88-89—Cleveland	82	10	2125	356	700	.509	1	4	.250	235	314	.748	173	304	477	108	188	1	77	102	134	948	5.8	1.3	11.6
89-90—Cleveland	82	29	2776	528	1070	.493	0	0	—	325	440	.739	220	443	663	168	214	2	86	143	167	1381	8.1	2.0	16.8
90-91—Cleveland	43	14	1293	199	430	.463	0	1	.000	107	164	.652	111	179	290	100	126	2	36	63	69	505	6.7	2.3	11.7
91-92—Cleveland	80	12	2432	341	678	.503	0	4	.000	270	359	.752	228	379	607	196	191	2	60	83	182	952	7.6	2.5	11.9
92-93—Cleveland	67	13	2055	263	560	.470	0	0	—	212	296	.716	127	288	415	152	171	2	48	116	105	738	6.2	2.3	11.0
93-94—Cleveland	76	72	2660	394	825	.478	0	0	—	252	346	.728	207	368	575	193	219	3	78	139	130	1040	7.6	2.5	13.7
REG. SEASON TOTALS	587	280	18161	2832	5823	.486	1	11	.091	1910	2598	.735	1447	2715	4162	1174	1509	14	504	889	1099	7575	7.1	2.0	12.9
PLAYOFF TOTALS	41	2	1272	194	384	.505	0	0	—	144	190	.758	96	184	280	84	132	4	36	64	50	532	6.8	2.0	13.0

WILLIAMS, JOHN SAM (Rock) b. October 26, 1966 Ht. 6-9 Wt. 280 College—Louisiana State

SEASON—TEAM	G	GS	MIN	FGM	FGA	PCT	3FGM	3FGA	PCT	FTM	FTA	PCT	O-RB	D-RB	TOT	AST	PF	DQ	STL	TO	BLK	PTS	RPG	APG	PPG
86-87—Washington	78	6	1773	283	624	.454	8	36	.222	144	223	.646	130	236	366	191	173	1	129	122	30	718	4.7	2.4	9.2
87-88—Washington	82	37	2428	427	910	.469	5	38	.132	188	256	.734	127	317	444	232	217	3	117	145	34	1047	5.4	2.8	12.8
88-89—Washington	82	1	2413	438	940	.466	19	71	.268	225	290	.776	158	415	573	356	213	1	142	157	70	1120	7.0	4.3	13.7
89-90—Washington	18	18	632	130	274	.474	2	18	.111	65	84	.774	27	109	136	84	33	0	21	43	9	327	7.6	4.7	18.2
90-91—Washington	33	11	941	164	393	.417	10	41	.244	73	97	.753	42	135	177	133	63	0	39	68	6	411	5.4	4.0	12.5
92-93—L.A. Clippers	74	8	1638	205	477	.430	12	53	.226	70	129	.543	88	228	316	142	188	1	83	79	23	492	4.3	1.9	6.6
93-94—L.A. Clippers	34	6	725	81	188	.431	5	20	.250	24	36	.667	37	90	127	97	85	1	25	35	10	191	3.7	2.9	5.6
REG. SEASON TOTALS	401	87	10550	1728	3806	.454	61	277	.220	789	1115	.708	609	1530	2139	1235	972	7	556	649	182	4306	5.3	3.1	10.7
PLAYOFF TOTALS	13	5	332	35	80	.438	2	5	.400	24	41	.585	20	34	54	30	38	2	15	20	4	96	4.2	2.3	7.4

WILLIAMS, KENNETH RAY (Kenny) b. June 9, 1969 Ht. 6-9 Wt. 205 College—Barton County CC/Elizabeth City State

SEASON—TEAM	G	GS	MIN	FGM	FGA	PCT	3FGM	3FGA	PCT	FTM	FTA	PCT	O-RB	D-RB	TOT	AST	PF	DQ	STL	TO	BLK	PTS	RPG	APG	PPG
90-91—Indiana	75	0	527	93	179	.520	0	3	.000	34	50	.680	56	75	131	31	81	0	11	41	31	220	1.7	0.4	2.9
91-92—Indiana	60	6	565	113	218	.518	0	4	.000	26	43	.605	64	65	129	40	99	0	20	22	41	252	2.2	0.7	4.2
92-93—Indiana	57	0	844	150	282	.532	0	3	.000	48	68	.706	102	126	228	38	87	1	21	28	45	348	4.0	0.7	6.1
93-94—Indiana	68	1	982	191	391	.488	0	4	.000	45	64	.703	93	112	205	52	99	0	24	45	49	427	3.0	0.8	6.3
REG. SEASON TOTALS	260	7	2918	547	1070	.511	0	14	.000	153	225	.680	315	378	693	161	366	1	76	136	166	1247	2.7	0.6	4.8
PLAYOFF TOTALS	17	0	105	10	26	.385	0	0	—	2	6	.333	6	11	17	7	20	0	6	6	5	22	1.0	0.4	1.3

WILLIAMS, KEVIN EUGENE b. September 11, 1961 Ht. 6-2 Wt. 180 College—St. John's

SEASON—TEAM	G	GS	MIN	FGM	FGA	PCT	3FGM	3FGA	PCT	FTM	FTA	PCT	O-RB	D-RB	TOT	AST	PF	DQ	STL	TO	BLK	PTS	RPG	APG	PPG
83-84—San Antonio	19	0	200	25	58	.431	0	1	.000	25	32	.781	4	9	13	43	42	1	8	22	4	75	0.7	2.3	3.9
84-85—Cleveland	46	4	413	58	134	.433	0	5	.000	47	64	.734	19	44	63	61	86	1	22	49	4	163	1.4	1.3	3.5
86-87—Seattle	65	0	703	132	296	.446	0	7	.000	55	66	.833	47	36	83	66	154	1	45	63	8	319	1.3	1.0	4.9
87-88—Seattle	80	9	1084	199	450	.442	1	7	.143	103	122	.844	61	66	127	96	207	1	62	68	7	502	1.6	1.2	6.3
88-89—N.J.-L.A. Clips	50	0	547	81	200	.405	1	6	.167	46	59	.780	28	42	70	53	91	0	30	52	11	209	1.4	1.1	4.2
REG. SEASON TOTALS	260	13	2947	495	1138	.435	2	26	.077	276	343	.805	159	197	356	319	580	4	167	254	34	1268	1.4	1.2	4.9
PLAYOFF TOTALS	21	0	332	53	112	.473	0	4	.000	30	40	.750	25	17	42	40	60	0	19	14	1	136	2.0	1.9	6.5

WILLIAMS, LORENZO b. July 15, 1969 Ht. 6-9 Wt. 200 College—Polk CC/Stetson

SEASON—TEAM	G	GS	MIN	FGM	FGA	PCT	3FGM	3FGA	PCT	FTM	FTA	PCT	O-RB	D-RB	TOT	AST	PF	DQ	STL	TO	BLK	PTS	RPG	APG	PPG
92-93—Cha.-Orlando-Boston	27	7	179	17	36	.472	0	0	—	2	7	.286	17	38	55	5	29	0	5	8	17	36	2.0	0.2	1.3
93-94—Orlando-Cha.-Dallas	38	11	716	49	110	.445	0	1	.000	12	28	.429	95	122	217	25	92	0	18	22	46	110	5.7	0.7	2.9
REG. SEASON TOTALS	65	18	895	66	146	.452	0	1	.000	14	35	.400	112	160	272	30	121	0	23	30	63	146	4.2	0.5	2.2
PLAYOFF TOTALS	1	0	3	1	1	1.000	0	0	—	0	0	—	1	0	1	—	0	0	0	0	0	2	1.0	0.0	2.0

WILLIAMS, MICHAEL GEORGE (Mike) b. August 14, 1963 Ht. 6-8 Wt. 255 College—Cincinnati/Bradley

SEASON—TEAM	G	GS	MIN	FGM	FGA	PCT	3FGM	3FGA	PCT	FTM	FTA	PCT	O-RB	D-RB	TOT	AST	PF	DQ	STL	TO	BLK	PTS	RPG	APG	PPG
89-90—Sac.-Atlanta	21	0	102	6	18	.333	0	1	.000	3	6	.500	5	18	23	2	30	0	3	3	7	15	1.1	0.1	0.7
REG. SEASON TOTALS	21	0	102	6	18	.333	0	1	.000	3	6	.500	5	18	23	2	30	0	3	3	7	15	1.1	0.1	0.7

WILLIAMS, MICHEAL DOUGLAS b. July 23, 1966 Ht. 6-2 Wt. 175 College—Baylor

SEASON—TEAM	G	GS	MIN	FGM	FGA	PCT	3FGM	3FGA	PCT	FTM	FTA	PCT	O-RB	D-RB	TOT	AST	PF	DQ	STL	TO	BLK	PTS	RPG	APG	PPG
88-89—Detroit	49	0	358	47	129	.364	2	9	.222	31	47	.660	9	18	27	70	44	0	13	42	3	127	0.6	1.4	2.6
89-90—Phoenix-Cha.	28	1	329	60	119	.504	0	3	.000	36	46	.783	12	20	32	81	39	0	22	33	1	156	1.1	2.9	5.6
90-91—Indiana	73	37	1706	261	523	.499	1	7	.143	290	330	.879	49	127	176	348	202	1	150	150	17	813	2.4	4.8	11.1
91-92—Indiana	79	76	2750	404	824	.490	8	33	.242	372	427	.871	73	209	282	647	262	7	233	240	22	1188	3.6	8.2	15.0
92-93—Minnesota	76	76	2661	353	791	.446	26	107	.243	419	462	.907	84	189	273	661	268	7	165	227	23	1151	3.6	8.7	15.1
93-94—Minnesota	71	66	2206	314	687	.457	10	45	.222	333	397	.839	67	154	221	512	193	3	118	203	24	971	3.1	7.2	13.7
REG. SEASON TOTALS	376	256	10010	1439	3073	.468	47	204	.230	1481	1709	.867	294	717	1011	2319	1008	18	701	895	90	4406	2.7	6.2	11.7
PLAYOFF TOTALS	12	8	295	48	108	.444	3	10	.300	56	65	.862	9	17	26	68	36	2	24	19	0	155	2.2	5.7	12.9

WILLIAMS, MILTON (**Milt**) b. November 22, 1945   Ht. 6-2½ Wt. 185 College—Lincoln (Mo.)/Campbell

SEASON—TEAM	G	GS	MIN	FGM	FGA	PCT	3FGM	3FGA	PCT	FTM	FTA	PCT	O-RB	D-RB	TOT	AST	PF	DQ	STL	TO	BLK	PTS	RPG	APG	PPG
70-71—New York	5	—	13	1	1	1.000	—	—	—	2	3	.667	—	—	0	2	3	0	—	—	—	4	0.0	0.4	0.8
71-72—Atlanta	10	—	127	23	53	.434	—	—	—	21	29	.724	—	—	4	20	18	0	—	—	—	67	0.4	2.0	6.7
73-74—Seattle	53	—	505	62	149	.416	—	—	—	41	63	.651	19	28	47	103	82	1	25	—	0	165	0.9	1.9	3.1
74-75—St. Louis (A)	4	—	95	11	19	.579	0	0	—	0	0	—	4	9	13	12	10	—	10	10	0	22	3.3	3.0	5.5
REG. NBA TOTALS	68	—	645	86	203	.424	—	—	—	64	95	.674	19	28	51	125	103	1	25	—	0	236	0.8	1.8	3.5
REG. ABA TOTALS	4	—	95	11	19	.579	0	0	—	0	0	—	4	9	13	12	10	—	10	10	0	22	3.3	3.0	5.5

WILLIAMS, NATHANIEL RUSSELL (**Nate**) b. May 2, 1950   Ht. 6-4½ Wt. 220 College—Utah State

SEASON—TEAM	G	GS	MIN	FGM	FGA	PCT	3FGM	3FGA	PCT	FTM	FTA	PCT	O-RB	D-RB	TOT	AST	PF	DQ	STL	TO	BLK	PTS	RPG	APG	PPG
71-72—Cincinnati	81	—	2173	418	968	.432	—	—	—	127	172	.738	—	—	372	174	300	11	—	—	—	963	4.6	2.1	11.9
72-73—Kansas City-Omaha	80	—	1979	417	874	.477	—	—	—	106	133	.797	—	—	339	128	272	9	—	—	—	940	4.2	1.6	11.8
73-74—Kansas City-Omaha	82	—	2513	538	1165	.462	—	—	—	193	236	.818	118	226	344	182	290	5	149	—	34	1269	4.2	2.2	15.5
74-75—K.C. Omaha-N.O.	85	—	1945	474	988	.480	—	—	—	181	220	.823	102	235	337	145	251	3	97	—	30	1129	4.0	1.7	13.3
75-76—New Orleans	81	—	1935	421	948	.444	—	—	—	197	239	.824	135	225	360	107	253	6	109	—	17	1039	4.4	1.3	12.8
76-77—New Orleans	79	—	1776	414	917	.451	—	—	—	146	194	.753	107	199	306	92	200	0	76	—	16	974	3.9	1.2	12.3
77-78—N.O.-G.S.	73	—	1249	312	724	.431	—	—	—	101	121	.835	65	139	204	74	181	3	57	83	34	725	2.8	1.0	9.9
78-79—Golden State	81	—	1299	284	567	.501	—	—	—	102	117	.872	68	139	207	61	169	0	55	93	5	670	2.6	0.8	8.3
REG. SEASON TOTALS	642	—	14869	3278	7151	.458	—	—	—	1153	1432	.805	595	1163	2469	963	1916	37	543	176	136	7709	3.8	1.5	12.0

WILLIAMS, REGGIE (**Silk**) b. March 5, 1964   Ht. 6-7 Wt. 195 College—Georgetown

SEASON—TEAM	G	GS	MIN	FGM	FGA	PCT	3FGM	3FGA	PCT	FTM	FTA	PCT	O-RB	D-RB	TOT	AST	PF	DQ	STL	TO	BLK	PTS	RPG	APG	PPG
87-88—L.A. Clippers	35	14	857	152	427	.356	13	58	.224	48	66	.727	55	63	118	58	108	1	29	63	21	365	3.4	1.7	10.4
88-89—L.A. Clippers	63	17	1303	260	594	.438	30	104	.288	92	122	.754	70	109	179	103	181	1	81	114	29	642	2.8	1.6	10.2
89-90—L.A. Clips-Clev.-S.A.	47	17	743	131	338	.388	6	37	.162	52	68	.765	28	55	83	53	102	2	32	45	14	320	1.8	1.1	6.8
90-91—S.A.-Denver	73	46	1896	384	855	.449	57	157	.363	166	197	.843	133	173	306	133	253	9	113	112	41	991	4.2	1.8	13.6
91-92—Denver	81	80	2623	601	1277	.471	56	156	.359	216	269	.803	145	260	405	235	270	4	148	173	68	1474	5.0	2.9	18.2
92-93—Denver	79	79	2722	535	1167	.458	33	122	.270	238	296	.804	132	296	428	295	284	6	126	194	76	1341	5.4	3.7	17.0
93-94—Denver	82	68	2654	418	1014	.412	64	230	.278	165	225	.733	98	294	392	300	288	3	117	163	66	1065	4.8	3.7	13.0
REG. SEASON TOTALS	460	321	12798	2481	5672	.437	259	864	.300	977	1243	.786	661	1250	1911	1177	1486	26	646	864	315	6198	4.2	2.6	13.5
PLAYOFF TOTALS	21	12	454	71	176	.403	20	52	.385	29	37	.784	23	49	72	45	61	1	11	33	12	191	3.4	2.1	9.1

WILLIAMS, RICHARD C. (**Rickey**) b. March 12, 1957   Ht. 6-1 Wt. 175 College—New Mexico/Long Beach State

SEASON—TEAM	G	GS	MIN	FGM	FGA	PCT	3FGM	3FGA	PCT	FTM	FTA	PCT	O-RB	D-RB	TOT	AST	PF	DQ	STL	TO	BLK	PTS	RPG	APG	PPG
82-83—Utah	44	0	346	56	135	.415	0	3	.000	35	53	.660	15	23	38	37	42	0	20	38	4	147	0.9	0.8	3.3
REG. SEASON TOTALS	44	0	346	56	135	.415	0	3	.000	35	53	.660	15	23	38	37	42	0	20	38	4	147	0.9	0.8	3.3

WILLIAMS, ROBERT (**Bob**) b. May 12, 1931   Ht. 6-6 Wt. 230 College—Florida A&M

SEASON—TEAM	G	GS	MIN	FGM	FGA	PCT	3FGM	3FGA	PCT	FTM	FTA	PCT	O-RB	D-RB	TOT	AST	PF	DQ	STL	TO	BLK	PTS	RPG	APG	PPG
55-56—Minneapolis	20	—	173	21	46	.457	—	—	—	24	45	.533	—	—	54	7	36	1	—	—	—	66	2.7	0.4	3.3
56-57—Minneapolis	4	—	30	1	4	.250	—	—	—	2	3	.667	—	—	5	0	2	0	—	—	—	4	1.3	0.0	1.0
REG. SEASON TOTALS	24	—	203	22	50	.440	—	—	—	26	48	.542	—	—	59	7	38	1	—	—	—	70	2.5	0.3	2.9

WILLIAMS, ROBERT AARON (**Rob**) b. May 5, 1961   Ht. 6-2 Wt. 175 College—Houston

SEASON—TEAM	G	GS	MIN	FGM	FGA	PCT	3FGM	3FGA	PCT	FTM	FTA	PCT	O-RB	D-RB	TOT	AST	PF	DQ	STL	TO	BLK	PTS	RPG	APG	PPG
82-83—Denver	74	33	1443	191	468	.408	2	15	.133	131	174	.753	37	99	136	361	221	4	89	185	12	515	1.8	4.9	7.0
83-84—Denver	79	66	1924	309	671	.461	15	47	.319	171	209	.818	54	140	194	464	268	4	84	169	5	804	2.5	5.9	10.2
REG. SEASON TOTALS	153	99	3367	500	1139	.439	17	62	.274	302	383	.789	91	239	330	825	489	8	173	354	17	1319	2.2	5.4	8.6
PLAYOFF TOTALS	12	11	283	45	101	.446	7	16	.438	17	19	.895	7	25	32	61	46	2	11	27	2	114	2.7	5.1	9.5

WILLIAMS, ROBERT ERIC (**Pete**) b. March 10, 1965   Ht. 6-7 Wt. 190 College—Mount San Antonio/Arizona

SEASON—TEAM	G	GS	MIN	FGM	FGA	PCT	3FGM	3FGA	PCT	FTM	FTA	PCT	O-RB	D-RB	TOT	AST	PF	DQ	STL	TO	BLK	PTS	RPG	APG	PPG
85-86—Denver	53	11	573	67	111	.604	0	0	—	17	40	.425	47	99	146	14	68	1	19	19	23	151	2.8	0.3	2.8
86-87—Denver	5	0	10	1	2	.500	0	0	—	0	0	—	0	1	1	1	1	0	0	1	0	2	0.2	0.2	0.4
REG. SEASON TOTALS	58	11	583	68	113	.602	0	0	—	17	40	.425	47	100	147	15	69	1	19	20	23	153	2.5	0.3	2.6
PLAYOFF TOTALS	4	0	18	2	4	.500	0	1	.000	0	0	—	1	3	4	3	2	0	0	0	0	4	1.0	0.8	1.0

WILLIAMS, RONALD ROBERT (**Ron, Fritz**) b. September 24, 1944 Ht. 6-3 Wt. 190 College—West Virginia

SEASON—TEAM	G	GS	MIN	FGM	FGA	PCT	3FGM	3FGA	PCT	FTM	FTA	PCT	O-RB	D-RB	TOT	AST	PF	DQ	STL	TO	BLK	PTS	RPG	APG	PPG
68-69—San Francisco	75	—	1472	238	567	.420	—	—	—	109	142	.768	—	—	178	247	176	3	—	—	—	585	2.4	3.3	7.8
69-70—San Francisco	80	—	2435	452	1046	.432	—	—	—	277	337	.822	—	—	190	424	287	7	—	—	—	1181	2.4	5.3	14.8
70-71—San Francisco	82	—	2809	426	977	.436	—	—	—	331	392	.844	—	—	244	480	301	9	—	—	—	1183	3.0	5.9	14.4
71-72—Golden State	80	—	1932	291	614	.474	—	—	—	195	234	.833	—	—	147	308	232	1	—	—	—	777	1.8	3.9	9.7
72-73—Golden State	73	—	1016	180	409	.440	—	—	—	75	83	.904	—	—	81	114	108	0	—	—	—	435	1.1	1.6	6.0
73-74—Milwaukee	71	—	1130	192	393	.489	—	—	—	60	68	.882	19	50	69	153	114	1	49	—	2	444	1.0	2.2	6.3
74-75—Milwaukee	46	—	526	62	165	.376	—	—	—	24	29	.828	10	33	43	71	70	2	23	—	2	148	0.9	1.5	3.2
75-76—Los Angeles	9	—	158	17	43	.395	—	—	—	10	13	.769	2	17	19	21	15	0	3	—	0	44	2.1	2.3	4.9
REG. SEASON TOTALS	516	—	11478	1858	4214	.441	—	—	—	1081	1298	.833	31	100	971	1818	1303	23	75	—	4	4797	1.9	3.5	9.3
PLAYOFF TOTALS	32	—	671	104	248	.419	—	—	—	52	59	.881	6	21	57	94	76	2	9	—	3	260	1.8	2.9	8.1

WILLIAMS, SAMUEL H. (**Sam**) b. January 22, 1945 Ht. 6-3 Wt. 180 College—Burlington CC/Iowa

SEASON—TEAM	G	GS	MIN	FGM	FGA	PCT	3FGM	3FGA	PCT	FTM	FTA	PCT	O-RB	D-RB	TOT	AST	PF	DQ	STL	TO	BLK	PTS	RPG	APG	PPG
68-69—Milwaukee	55	—	628	78	228	.342	—	—	—	72	134	.537	—	—	109	61	106	1	—	—	—	228	2.0	1.1	4.1
69-70—Milwaukee	11	—	44	11	24	.458	—	—	—	5	11	.455	—	—	7	3	5	0	—	—	—	27	0.6	0.3	2.5
REG. SEASON TOTALS	66	—	672	89	252	.353	—	—	—	77	145	.531	—	—	116	64	111	1	—	—	—	255	1.8	1.0	3.9
PLAYOFF TOTALS	2	—	16	4	7	.571	—	—	—	0	2	.000	—	—	4	1	5	0	—	—	—	8	2.0	0.5	4.0

WILLIAMS, SAMUEL KEITH b. March 7, 1959 Ht. 6-8 Wt. 215 College—Pasadena CC/Arizona State

SEASON—TEAM	G	GS	MIN	FGM	FGA	PCT	3FGM	3FGA	PCT	FTM	FTA	PCT	O-RB	D-RB	TOT	AST	PF	DQ	STL	TO	BLK	PTS	RPG	APG	PPG
81-82—Golden State	59	22	1073	154	277	.556	0	0	—	49	89	.551	91	217	308	38	156	0	45	64	76	357	5.2	0.6	6.1
82-83—Golden State	75	28	1533	252	479	.526	0	1	.000	123	171	.719	153	240	393	45	244	4	71	101	89	627	5.2	0.6	8.4
83-84—G.S.-Phil.	77	12	1434	204	431	.473	0	1	.000	92	140	.657	121	218	339	62	209	3	68	99	106	500	4.4	0.8	6.5
84-85—Philadelphia	46	8	488	58	148	.392	0	1	.000	28	47	.596	38	68	106	11	92	1	26	44	26	144	2.3	0.2	3.1
REG. SEASON TOTALS	257	70	4528	668	1335	.500	0	3	.000	292	447	.653	403	743	1146	156	701	8	210	308	297	1628	4.5	0.6	6.3
PLAYOFF TOTALS	9	0	81	3	14	.214	0	0	—	4	12	.333	5	13	18	3	9	0	2	9	6	10	2.0	0.3	1.1

WILLIAMS, SCOTT CHRISTOPHER b. March 21, 1968 Ht. 6-10 Wt. 230 College—North Carolina

SEASON—TEAM	G	GS	MIN	FGM	FGA	PCT	3FGM	3FGA	PCT	FTM	FTA	PCT	O-RB	D-RB	TOT	AST	PF	DQ	STL	TO	BLK	PTS	RPG	APG	PPG
90-91—Chicago	51	0	337	53	104	.510	1	2	.500	20	28	.714	42	56	98	16	51	0	12	23	13	127	1.9	0.3	2.5
91-92—Chicago	63	0	690	83	172	.483	0	3	.000	48	74	.649	90	157	247	50	122	0	13	35	36	214	3.9	0.8	3.4
92-93—Chicago	71	5	1369	166	356	.466	0	7	.000	90	126	.714	168	283	451	68	230	3	55	73	66	422	6.4	1.0	5.9
93-94—Chicago	38	11	638	114	236	.483	1	5	.200	60	98	.612	69	112	181	39	112	1	16	44	21	289	4.8	1.0	7.6
REG. SEASON TOTALS	223	16	3034	416	868	.479	2	17	.118	218	326	.669	369	608	977	173	515	4	96	175	136	1052	4.4	0.8	4.7
PLAYOFF TOTALS	63	0	939	108	227	.476	0	4	.000	62	98	.633	92	173	265	43	161	2	21	52	41	278	4.2	0.7	4.4

WILLIAMS, SYLVESTER (**Sly, The Garbage Man**) b. January 26, 1958 Ht. 6-7 Wt. 210 College—Rhode Island

SEASON—TEAM	G	GS	MIN	FGM	FGA	PCT	3FGM	3FGA	PCT	FTM	FTA	PCT	O-RB	D-RB	TOT	AST	PF	DQ	STL	TO	BLK	PTS	RPG	APG	PPG
79-80—New York	57	—	556	104	267	.390	0	4	.000	58	90	.644	65	56	121	36	73	0	19	49	8	266	2.1	0.6	4.7
80-81—New York	67	—	1976	349	708	.493	2	8	.250	185	268	.690	159	257	416	180	199	0	116	141	18	885	6.2	2.7	13.2
81-82—New York	60	27	1521	349	628	.556	2	9	.222	131	173	.757	100	127	227	142	153	0	77	114	16	831	3.8	2.4	13.9
82-83—New York	68	6	1385	314	647	.485	2	19	.105	176	259	.680	94	196	290	133	166	3	73	133	3	806	4.3	2.0	11.9
83-84—Atlanta	13	1	258	34	114	.298	1	9	.111	36	46	.783	19	31	50	16	33	0	14	18	1	105	3.8	1.2	8.1
84-85—Atlanta	34	20	867	167	380	.439	4	15	.267	79	123	.642	45	123	168	94	83	1	28	78	8	417	4.9	2.8	12.3
85-86—Boston	6	0	54	5	21	.238	0	4	.000	7	12	.583	7	8	15	2	15	0	1	7	1	17	2.5	0.3	2.8
REG. SEASON TOTALS	305	54	6617	1322	2765	.478	11	68	.162	672	971	.692	489	798	1287	603	722	4	328	540	55	3327	4.2	2.0	10.9
PLAYOFF TOTALS	7	0	138	29	59	.492	1	1	1.000	3	3	1.000	14	16	30	11	11	0	6	15	1	62	4.3	1.6	8.9

WILLIAMS, THOMAS RAY (**Ray**) b. October 14, 1954 Ht. 6-2½ Wt. 190 College—San Jacinto/Minnesota

SEASON—TEAM	G	GS	MIN	FGM	FGA	PCT	3FGM	3FGA	PCT	FTM	FTA	PCT	O-RB	D-RB	TOT	AST	PF	DQ	STL	TO	BLK	PTS	RPG	APG	PPG
77-78—New York	81	—	1550	305	689	.443	—	—	—	146	207	.705	85	124	209	363	211	4	108	242	15	756	2.6	4.5	9.3
78-79—New York	81	—	2370	575	1257	.457	—	—	—	251	313	.802	104	187	291	504	274	4	128	285	19	1401	3.6	6.2	17.3
79-80—New York	82	—	2582	687	1384	.496	7	37	.189	333	423	.787	149	263	412	512	295	5	167	256	24	1714	5.0	6.2	20.9
80-81—New York	79	—	2742	616	1335	.461	16	68	.235	312	382	.817	122	199	321	432	270	4	185	235	37	1560	4.1	5.5	19.7
81-82—New Jersey	82	69	2732	639	1383	.462	9	54	.167	387	465	.832	117	208	325	488	302	9	199	290	43	1674	4.0	6.0	20.4
82-83—Kansas City	72	68	2170	419	1068	.392	15	74	.203	256	333	.769	93	234	327	569	248	3	120	335	26	1109	4.5	7.9	15.4
83-84—New York	76	63	2230	418	939	.445	25	81	.309	263	318	.827	67	200	267	449	274	5	162	219	26	1124	3.5	5.9	14.8
84-85—Boston	23	5	459	55	143	.385	6	23	.261	31	46	.674	16	41	57	90	56	1	30	42	5	147	2.5	3.9	6.4
85-86—Atlanta-S.A.-N.J.	47	21	827	117	306	.382	6	19	.316	115	126	.913	35	51	86	187	124	2	61	101	4	355	1.8	4.0	7.6
86-87—New Jersey	32	14	800	131	290	.452	7	28	.250	49	60	.817	26	49	75	185	111	4	38	94	9	318	2.3	5.8	9.9
REG. SEASON TOTALS	655	240	18462	3962	8794	.451	91	384	.237	2143	2673	.802	814	1556	2370	3779	2165	41	1198	2099	208	10158	3.6	5.8	15.5
PLAYOFF TOTALS	40	8	889	166	412	.403	7	35	.200	86	106	.811	39	71	110	202	128	2	43	109	2	425	2.8	5.1	10.6

WILLIAMS, WALTER ANDER JR. (Walt) b. April 16, 1970 Ht. 6-8 Wt. 230 College—Maryland

SEASON—TEAM	G	GS	MIN	FGM	FGA	PCT	3FGM	3FGA	PCT	FTM	FTA	PCT	O-RB	D-RB	TOT	AST	PF	DQ	STL	TO	BLK	PTS	RPG	APG	PPG
92-93—Sacramento	59	26	1673	358	823	.435	61	191	.319	224	302	.742	115	150	265	178	209	6	66	179	29	1001	4.5	3.0	17.0
93-94—Sacramento	57	4	1356	226	580	.390	38	132	.288	148	233	.635	71	164	235	132	200	6	52	145	23	638	4.1	2.3	11.2
REG. SEASON TOTALS	116	30	3029	584	1403	.416	99	323	.307	372	535	.695	186	314	500	310	409	12	118	324	52	1639	4.3	2.7	14.1

WILLIAMS, WARD M. b. June 26, 1923 Ht. 6-4 Wt. 195 College—Indiana

SEASON—TEAM	G	GS	MIN	FGM	FGA	PCT	3FGM	3FGA	PCT	FTM	FTA	PCT	O-RB	D-RB	TOT	AST	PF	DQ	STL	TO	BLK	PTS	RPG	APG	PPG
48-49—Fort Wayne	53	—	—	61	257	.237	—	—	—	93	124	.750	—	—	—	82	158	—	—	—	—	215	—	1.5	4.1
REG. SEASON TOTALS	53	—	—	61	257	.237	—	—	—	93	124	.750	—	—	—	82	158	—	—	—	—	215	—	1.5	4.1

WILLIAMS, WILLIE EARL b. July 28, 1946 Ht. 6-7 Wt. 200 College—Florida State

SEASON—TEAM	G	GS	MIN	FGM	FGA	PCT	3FGM	3FGA	PCT	FTM	FTA	PCT	O-RB	D-RB	TOT	AST	PF	DQ	STL	TO	BLK	PTS	RPG	APG	PPG
70-71—Boston-Cin.	25	—	105	10	42	.238	—	—	—	3	5	.600	—	—	23	8	14	0	—	—	—	23	0.9	0.3	0.9
REG. SEASON TOTALS	25	—	105	10	42	.238	—	—	—	3	5	.600	—	—	23	8	14	0	—	—	—	23	0.9	0.3	0.9

WILLIAMSON, JOHN LEE (Super John) b. November 10, 1952 Ht. 6-2 Wt. 190 College—New Mexico State

SEASON—TEAM	G	GS	MIN	FGM	FGA	PCT	3FGM	3FGA	PCT	FTM	FTA	PCT	O-RB	D-RB	TOT	AST	PF	DQ	STL	TO	BLK	PTS	RPG	APG	PPG
73-74—New York (A)	77	—	2264	482	982	.491	2	11	.182	150	190	.789	68	145	213	243	254	—	86	208	27	1116	2.8	3.2	14.5
74-75—New York (A)	75	—	1872	370	768	.482	3	13	.231	123	147	.837	51	98	149	197	188	—	61	148	23	866	2.0	2.6	11.5
75-76—New York (A)	76	—	2255	519	1153	.450	8	42	.190	187	232	.806	70	120	190	188	224	—	76	185	33	1233	2.5	2.5	16.2
76-77—N.Y.-Indiana	72	—	2481	618	1347	.459	—	—	—	259	329	.787	42	151	193	201	246	4	107	—	13	1495	2.7	2.8	20.8
77-78—Indiana-N.J.	75	—	2731	723	1649	.438	—	—	—	331	391	.847	66	161	227	214	236	6	94	228	10	1777	3.0	2.9	23.7
78-79—New Jersey	74	—	2451	635	1367	.465	—	—	—	373	437	.854	53	143	196	255	215	3	89	233	12	1643	2.6	3.4	22.2
79-80—N.J.-Wash.	58	—	1374	359	817	.439	11	35	.314	116	138	.841	38	61	99	126	137	1	36	92	19	845	1.7	2.2	14.6
80-81—Washington	9	—	112	18	56	.321	1	6	.167	5	6	.833	0	7	7	17	13	0	4	12	1	42	0.8	1.9	4.7
REG. NBA TOTALS	288	—	9149	2353	5236	.449	12	41	.293	1084	1301	.833	199	523	722	813	847	14	330	565	55	5802	2.5	2.8	20.1
REG. ABA TOTALS	228	—	6391	1371	2903	.472	13	66	.197	460	569	.808	189	363	552	628	666	0	223	541	83	3215	2.4	2.8	14.1
NBA PLAYOFF TOTALS	4	—	123	34	81	.420	2	6	.333	16	19	.842	4	4	8	9	15	0	4	18	0	86	2.0	2.3	21.5
ABA PLAYOFF TOTALS	29	—	903	192	392	.490	2	10	.200	62	86	.721	31	49	80	76	101	0	21	72	12	448	2.8	2.6	15.4

WILLIFORD, DUNCAN VANN (Vann) b. January 26, 1948 Ht. 6-6 Wt. 195 College—North Carolina State

SEASON—TEAM	G	GS	MIN	FGM	FGA	PCT	3FGM	3FGA	PCT	FTM	FTA	PCT	O-RB	D-RB	TOT	AST	PF	DQ	STL	TO	BLK	PTS	RPG	APG	PPG
70-71—Carolina (A)	38	—	295	62	141	.440	3	9	.333	21	37	.568	—	—	68	15	34	—	—	—	—	148	1.8	0.4	3.9
REG. ABA TOTALS	38	—	295	62	141	.440	3	9	.333	21	37	.568	—	—	68	15	34	—	—	—	—	148	1.8	0.4	3.9

WILLIS, KEVIN ALVIN (Devo, Fresh) b. September 6, 1962 Ht. 7-0 Wt. 240 College—Michigan State

SEASON—TEAM	G	GS	MIN	FGM	FGA	PCT	3FGM	3FGA	PCT	FTM	FTA	PCT	O-RB	D-RB	TOT	AST	PF	DQ	STL	TO	BLK	PTS	RPG	APG	PPG
84-85—Atlanta	82	19	1785	322	690	.467	2	9	.222	119	181	.657	177	345	522	36	226	4	31	104	49	765	6.4	0.4	9.3
85-86—Atlanta	82	59	2300	419	811	.517	0	6	.000	172	263	.654	243	461	704	45	294	6	66	177	44	1010	8.6	0.5	12.3
86-87—Atlanta	81	81	2626	538	1003	.536	1	4	.250	227	320	.709	321	528	849	62	313	4	65	173	61	1304	10.5	0.8	16.1
87-88—Atlanta	75	55	2091	356	687	.518	0	2	.000	159	245	.649	235	312	547	28	240	2	68	138	42	871	7.3	0.4	11.6
89-90—Atlanta	81	51	2273	418	805	.519	2	7	.286	168	246	.683	253	392	645	57	259	4	63	144	47	1006	8.0	0.7	12.4
90-91—Atlanta	80	80	2373	444	881	.504	4	10	.400	159	238	.668	259	445	704	99	235	2	60	153	40	1051	8.8	1.2	13.1
91-92—Atlanta	81	80	2962	591	1224	.483	6	37	.162	292	363	.804	418	840	1258	173	223	0	72	197	54	1480	15.5	2.1	18.3
92-93—Atlanta	80	80	2878	616	1218	.506	7	29	.241	196	300	.653	335	693	1028	165	264	1	68	213	41	1435	12.9	2.1	17.9
93-94—Atlanta	80	80	2867	627	1257	.499	9	24	.375	268	376	.713	335	628	963	150	250	2	79	188	38	1531	12.0	1.9	19.1
REG. SEASON TOTALS	722	585	22155	4331	8576	.505	31	128	.242	1760	2532	.695	2576	4644	7220	815	2304	25	572	1487	416	10453	10.0	1.1	14.5
PLAYOFF TOTALS	49	49	1722	302	592	.510	2	10	.200	115	169	.680	169	277	446	41	194	3	39	85	31	721	9.1	0.8	14.7
ALL-STAR TOTALS	1	0	14	4	10	.400	0	0	—	0	0	—	4	0	4	0	1	0	0	0	0	8	4.0	0.0	8.0

WILLOUGHBY, WILLIAM WESLEY (Bill) b. May 20, 1957 Ht. 6-8 Wt. 205 College—None

SEASON—TEAM	G	GS	MIN	FGM	FGA	PCT	3FGM	3FGA	PCT	FTM	FTA	PCT	O-RB	D-RB	TOT	AST	PF	DQ	STL	TO	BLK	PTS	RPG	APG	PPG
75-76—Atlanta	62	—	870	113	284	.398	—	—	—	66	100	.660	103	185	288	31	87	0	37	—	29	292	4.6	0.5	4.7
76-77—Atlanta	39	—	549	75	169	.444	—	—	—	43	63	.683	65	105	170	13	64	1	19	—	23	193	4.4	0.3	4.9
77-78—Buffalo	56	—	1079	156	363	.430	—	—	—	64	80	.800	76	143	219	38	131	2	24	56	47	376	3.9	0.7	6.7
79-80—Cleveland	78	—	1447	219	457	.479	1	9	.111	96	127	.756	122	207	329	72	189	0	32	68	62	535	4.2	0.9	6.9
80-81—Houston	55	—	1145	150	287	.523	0	3	.000	49	64	.766	74	153	227	64	102	0	18	74	31	349	4.1	1.2	6.3
81-82—Houston	69	42	1475	240	464	.517	3	7	.429	56	77	.727	107	157	264	75	146	1	31	78	60	539	3.8	1.1	7.8
82-83—S.A.-N.J.	62	0	1146	147	324	.454	6	14	.429	43	55	.782	63	138	201	64	139	0	25	61	17	343	3.2	1.0	5.5
83-84—New Jersey	67	2	936	124	258	.481	0	7	.000	55	63	.873	75	118	193	56	106	2	23	53	24	303	2.9	0.8	4.5
REG. SEASON TOTALS	488	44	8647	1224	2606	.470	10	40	.250	472	629	.750	685	1206	1891	413	964	4	209	390	293	2930	3.9	0.8	6.0
PLAYOFF TOTALS	24	0	447	44	121	.364	0	1	.000	32	42	.762	33	61	94	23	45	0	14	24	19	120	3.9	1.0	5.0

WILSON, COATLEN OTHELL (Othell) b. October 26, 1961   Ht. 6-0   Wt. 190   College—Virginia

SEASON—TEAM	G	GS	MIN	FGM	FGA	PCT	3FGM	3FGA	PCT	FTM	FTA	PCT	O-RB	D-RB	TOT	AST	PF	DQ	STL	TO	BLK	PTS	RPG	APG	PPG
84-85—Golden State	74	23	1260	134	291	.460	3	16	.188	54	76	.711	35	96	131	217	122	0	77	95	12	325	1.8	2.9	4.4
86-87—Sacramento	53	2	789	82	185	.443	3	18	.167	43	54	.796	28	53	81	207	67	0	42	77	4	210	1.5	3.9	4.0
REG. SEASON TOTALS	127	25	2049	216	476	.454	6	34	.176	97	130	.746	63	149	212	424	189	0	119	172	16	535	1.7	3.3	4.2

WILSON, GEORGE (Jiff) b. May 9, 1942   Ht. 6-8   Wt. 230   College—Cincinnati

SEASON—TEAM	G	GS	MIN	FGM	FGA	PCT	3FGM	3FGA	PCT	FTM	FTA	PCT	O-RB	D-RB	TOT	AST	PF	DQ	STL	TO	BLK	PTS	RPG	APG	PPG
64-65—Cincinnati	39	—	288	41	155	.265	—	—	—	9	30	.300	—	—	102	11	59	0	—	—	—	91	2.6	0.3	2.3
65-66—Cincinnati	47	—	276	54	138	.391	—	—	—	27	42	.643	—	—	98	17	56	0	—	—	—	135	2.1	0.4	2.9
66-67—Cin.-Chicago	55	—	573	85	234	.363	—	—	—	58	86	.674	—	—	206	15	92	0	—	—	—	228	3.7	0.3	4.1
67-68—Seattle	77	—	1236	179	498	.359	—	—	—	109	155	.703	—	—	470	56	218	1	—	—	—	467	6.1	0.7	6.1
68-69—Phoenix-Phil.	79	—	1846	272	663	.410	—	—	—	153	235	.651	—	—	721	108	232	5	—	—	—	697	9.1	1.4	8.8
69-70—Philadelphia	67	—	836	118	304	.388	—	—	—	122	172	.709	—	—	317	52	145	3	—	—	—	358	4.7	0.8	5.3
70-71—Buffalo	46	—	713	92	269	.342	—	—	—	56	69	.812	—	—	230	48	99	1	—	—	—	240	5.0	1.0	5.2
REG. SEASON TOTALS	410	—	5768	841	2261	.372	—	—	—	534	789	.677	—	—	2144	307	901	10	—	—	—	2216	5.2	0.7	5.4
PLAYOFF TOTALS	12	—	101	8	31	.258	—	—	—	7	11	.636	—	—	42	10	20	0	—	—	—	23	3.5	0.8	1.9

WILSON, ISAIAH (Bunny) b. May 31, 1948   Ht. 6-2½   Wt. 175   College—Baltimore

SEASON—TEAM	G	GS	MIN	FGM	FGA	PCT	3FGM	3FGA	PCT	FTM	FTA	PCT	O-RB	D-RB	TOT	AST	PF	DQ	STL	TO	BLK	PTS	RPG	APG	PPG
71-72—Detroit	48	—	322	63	177	.356	—	—	—	41	56	.732	—	—	47	41	32	0	—	—	—	167	1.0	0.9	3.5
72-73—Memphis (A)	30	—	386	68	159	.428	3	8	.375	51	64	.797	18	—	21	39	72	46	0	—	41	—	190	1.3	2.4	6.3
REG. NBA TOTALS	48	—	322	63	177	.356	—	—	—	41	56	.732	—	—	47	41	32	0	—	—	—	167	1.0	0.9	3.5
REG. ABA TOTALS	30	—	386	68	159	.428	3	8	.375	51	64	.797	18	21	39	72	46	0	—	41	—	190	1.3	2.4	6.3

WILSON, JAMES (Jim) b. 1948   Ht. 5-10½   Wt. 175   College—Cheyney

SEASON—TEAM	G	GS	MIN	FGM	FGA	PCT	3FGM	3FGA	PCT	FTM	FTA	PCT	O-RB	D-RB	TOT	AST	PF	DQ	STL	TO	BLK	PTS	RPG	APG	PPG
70-71—Pittsburgh (A)	6	—	44	1	8	.125	0	0	—	4	6	.667	—	—	6	8	3	—	—	—	—	6	1.0	1.3	1.0
REG. ABA TOTALS	6	—	44	1	8	.125	0	0	—	4	6	.667	—	—	6	8	3	—	—	—	—	6	1.0	1.3	1.0

WILSON, JASPER b. July 12, 1947   Ht. 6-6   Wt. 200   College—Southern

SEASON—TEAM	G	GS	MIN	FGM	FGA	PCT	3FGM	3FGA	PCT	FTM	FTA	PCT	O-RB	D-RB	TOT	AST	PF	DQ	STL	TO	BLK	PTS	RPG	APG	PPG
68-69—New Orleans (A)	66	—	756	128	339	.378	5	12	.417	82	127	.646	—	—	173	43	127	1	—	63	—	343	2.6	0.7	5.2
69-70—New Orleans (A)	4	—	59	8	21	.381	1	2	.500	6	8	.750	—	—	14	2	6	0	—	—	—	23	3.5	0.5	5.8
REG. ABA TOTALS	70	—	815	136	360	.378	6	14	.429	88	135	.652	—	—	187	45	133	1	—	63	—	366	2.7	0.6	5.2
ABA PLAYOFF TOTALS	10	—	92	11	42	.262	0	5	.000	17	23	.739	—	—	26	2	20	0	—	4	—	39	2.6	0.2	3.9

WILSON, MICHAEL (Mike) b. September 15, 1959   Ht. 6-3   Wt. 180   College—Marquette

SEASON—TEAM	G	GS	MIN	FGM	FGA	PCT	3FGM	3FGA	PCT	FTM	FTA	PCT	O-RB	D-RB	TOT	AST	PF	DQ	STL	TO	BLK	PTS	RPG	APG	PPG
83-84—Washington	6	0	26	0	2	.000	0	1	.000	1	2	.500	1	0	1	3	5	0	0	3	0	1	0.2	0.5	0.2
84-85—Clev.-N.J.	19	0	267	36	77	.468	0	0	—	27	36	.750	14	17	31	35	21	0	14	20	5	99	1.6	1.8	5.2
86-87—N.J.-Atlanta	7	0	45	3	10	.300	0	0	—	2	2	1.000	1	3	4	7	10	0	1	5	0	8	0.6	1.0	1.1
REG. SEASON TOTALS	32	0	338	39	89	.438	0	1	.000	30	40	.750	16	20	36	45	36	0	15	28	5	108	1.1	1.4	3.4

WILSON, NIKITA FRANCISCUS b. February 25, 1964   Ht. 6-8   Wt. 200   College—Louisiana State

SEASON—TEAM	G	GS	MIN	FGM	FGA	PCT	3FGM	3FGA	PCT	FTM	FTA	PCT	O-RB	D-RB	TOT	AST	PF	DQ	STL	TO	BLK	PTS	RPG	APG	PPG
87-88—Portland	15	0	54	7	23	.304	0	0	—	5	6	.833	2	9	11	3	7	0	0	5	0	19	0.7	0.2	1.3
REG. SEASON TOTALS	15	0	54	7	23	.304	0	0	—	5	6	.833	2	9	11	3	7	0	0	5	0	19	0.7	0.2	1.3

WILSON, RICHARD (Rick) b. February 7, 1956   Ht. 6-4½   Wt. 200   College—Louisville

SEASON—TEAM	G	GS	MIN	FGM	FGA	PCT	3FGM	3FGA	PCT	FTM	FTA	PCT	O-RB	D-RB	TOT	AST	PF	DQ	STL	TO	BLK	PTS	RPG	APG	PPG
78-79—Atlanta	61	—	589	81	197	.411	—	—	—	24	44	.545	20	56	76	72	66	1	30	41	8	186	1.2	1.2	3.0
79-80—Atlanta	5	—	59	2	14	.143	0	0	—	4	6	.667	2	1	3	11	3	0	4	8	1	8	0.6	2.2	1.6
REG. SEASON TOTALS	66	—	648	83	211	.393	0	0	—	28	50	.560	22	57	79	83	69	1	34	49	9	194	1.2	1.3	2.9
PLAYOFF TOTALS	1	—	1	0	0	—	0	0	—	0	0	—	0	0	0	0	0	0	0	0	0	0	0.0	0.0	0.0

WILSON, RICKY b. July 16, 1964   Ht. 6-3   Wt. 195   College—George Mason

SEASON—TEAM	G	GS	MIN	FGM	FGA	PCT	3FGM	3FGA	PCT	FTM	FTA	PCT	O-RB	D-RB	TOT	AST	PF	DQ	STL	TO	BLK	PTS	RPG	APG	PPG
87-88—N.J.-S.A.	24	1	420	43	110	.391	10	26	.385	29	40	.725	2	25	27	69	40	0	23	25	3	125	1.1	2.9	5.2
REG. SEASON TOTALS	24	1	420	43	110	.391	10	26	.385	29	40	.725	2	25	27	69	40	0	23	25	3	125	1.1	2.9	5.2
PLAYOFF TOTALS	2	0	9	0	2	.000	0	0	—	0	0	—	0	0	0	1	2	0	0	1	0	0	0.0	0.5	0.0

WILSON, ROBERT E. (**Bobby**) b. January 15, 1951   Ht. 6-2½ Wt. 175 College—Pasadena CC/Northeastern JC/Wichita State

SEASON—TEAM	G	GS	MIN	FGM	FGA	PCT	3FGM	3FGA	PCT	FTM	FTA	PCT	O-RB	D-RB	TOT	AST	PF	DQ	STL	TO	BLK	PTS	RPG	APG	PPG
74-75—Chicago	48	—	425	115	225	.511	—	—	—	46	58	.793	18	34	52	36	54	1	22	—	1	276	1.1	0.8	5.8
75-76—Chicago	58	—	856	197	489	.403	—	—	—	43	58	.741	32	62	94	52	96	1	25	—	2	437	1.6	0.9	7.5
76-77—Boston	25	—	131	19	59	.322	—	—	—	11	13	.846	3	6	9	14	19	0	3	—	0	49	0.4	0.6	2.0
77-78—Indiana	12	—	86	14	36	.389	—	—	—	2	3	.667	6	6	12	8	16	0	2	6	1	30	1.0	0.7	2.5
REG. SEASON TOTALS	143	—	1498	345	809	.426	—	—	—	102	132	.773	59	108	167	110	185	2	52	6	4	792	1.2	0.8	5.5
PLAYOFF TOTALS	10	—	93	17	41	.415	—	—	—	10	12	.833	2	9	11	4	10	0	4	—	0	44	1.1	0.4	4.4

WILSON, ROBERT F. (**Bobby**) b. 1944   Ht. 6-7½ Wt. 215 College—Kansas

SEASON—TEAM	G	GS	MIN	FGM	FGA	PCT	3FGM	3FGA	PCT	FTM	FTA	PCT	O-RB	D-RB	TOT	AST	PF	DQ	STL	TO	BLK	PTS	RPG	APG	PPG
67-68—Dallas (A)	69	—	1562	226	581	.389	1	2	.500	163	265	.615	—	—	450	55	209	8	—	127	—	616	6.5	0.8	8.9
REG. ABA TOTALS	69	—	1562	226	581	.389	1	2	.500	163	265	.615	—	—	450	55	209	8	—	127	—	616	6.5	0.8	8.9
ABA PLAYOFF TOTALS	6	—	50	7	25	.280	1	1	1.000	6	13	.462	—	—	26	2	12	1	—	7	—	21	4.3	0.3	3.5

WILSON, ROBERT JR. (**Bob**) b. March 8, 1926   Ht. 6-4 Wt. 185 College—West Virginia State

SEASON—TEAM	G	GS	MIN	FGM	FGA	PCT	3FGM	3FGA	PCT	FTM	FTA	PCT	O-RB	D-RB	TOT	AST	PF	DQ	STL	TO	BLK	PTS	RPG	APG	PPG
51-52—Milwaukee	63	—	1308	79	264	.299	—	—	—	78	135	.578	—	—	210	108	172	8	—	—	—	236	3.3	1.7	3.7
REG. SEASON TOTALS	63	—	1308	79	264	.299	—	—	—	78	135	.578	—	—	210	108	172	8	—	—	—	236	3.3	1.7	3.7

WILSON, STEPHEN EARL (**Steve**) b. October 16, 1948   Ht. 6-5 Wt. 185 College—Hanover

SEASON—TEAM	G	GS	MIN	FGM	FGA	PCT	3FGM	3FGA	PCT	FTM	FTA	PCT	O-RB	D-RB	TOT	AST	PF	DQ	STL	TO	BLK	PTS	RPG	APG	PPG
70-71—Denver (A)	39	—	261	52	132	.394	8	33	.242	22	41	.537	—	—	48	29	43	—	—	—	—	134	1.2	0.7	3.4
71-72—Denver (A)	9	—	36	5	23	.217	0	2	.000	4	7	.571	—	—	4	6	9	—	—	3	—	14	0.4	0.7	1.6
REG. ABA TOTALS	48	—	297	57	155	.368	8	35	.229	26	48	.542	—	—	52	35	52	—	—	3	—	148	1.1	0.7	3.1

WILSON, THOMAS E. (**Bubba**) b. August 7, 1955   Ht. 6-3 Wt. 175 College—Western Carolina

SEASON—TEAM	G	GS	MIN	FGM	FGA	PCT	3FGM	3FGA	PCT	FTM	FTA	PCT	O-RB	D-RB	TOT	AST	PF	DQ	STL	TO	BLK	PTS	RPG	APG	PPG
79-80—Golden State	16	—	143	7	25	.280	0	0	—	3	6	.500	6	10	16	12	11	0	2	8	0	17	1.0	0.8	1.1
REG. SEASON TOTALS	16	—	143	7	25	.280	0	0	—	3	6	.500	6	10	16	12	11	0	2	8	0	17	1.0	0.8	1.1

WILSON, TREVOR b. March 16, 1968   Ht. 6-8 Wt. 210 College—UCLA

SEASON—TEAM	G	GS	MIN	FGM	FGA	PCT	3FGM	3FGA	PCT	FTM	FTA	PCT	O-RB	D-RB	TOT	AST	PF	DQ	STL	TO	BLK	PTS	RPG	APG	PPG
90-91—Atlanta	25	0	162	21	70	.300	0	2	.000	13	26	.500	16	24	40	11	13	0	5	17	1	55	1.6	0.4	2.2
93-94—Lakers-Sac.	57	13	1221	187	388	.482	0	2	.000	92	166	.554	120	153	273	72	123	0	38	93	11	466	4.8	1.3	8.2
REG. SEASON TOTALS	82	13	1383	208	458	.454	0	4	.000	105	192	.547	136	177	313	83	136	0	43	110	12	521	3.8	1.0	6.4

WINCHESTER, KENNARD NORMAN JR. b. September 3, 1966   Ht. 6-5 Wt. 210 College—James Madison/Averett

SEASON—TEAM	G	GS	MIN	FGM	FGA	PCT	3FGM	3FGA	PCT	FTM	FTA	PCT	O-RB	D-RB	TOT	AST	PF	DQ	STL	TO	BLK	PTS	RPG	APG	PPG
90-91—Houston	64	1	607	98	245	.400	8	20	.400	35	45	.778	34	33	67	25	70	0	16	30	13	239	1.0	0.4	3.7
91-92—Houston-N.Y.	19	0	81	13	30	.433	1	2	.500	8	10	.800	6	9	15	8	5	0	2	2	2	35	0.8	0.4	1.8
92-93—Houston	39	0	340	61	139	.439	4	19	.211	17	22	.773	17	32	49	13	40	0	10	15	10	143	1.3	0.3	3.7
REG. SEASON TOTALS	122	1	1028	172	414	.415	13	41	.317	60	77	.779	57	74	131	46	115	0	28	47	25	417	1.1	0.4	3.4
PLAYOFF TOTALS	3	0	11	3	5	.600	0	0	—	0	1	.000	0	0	0	2	0	0	0	1	0	6	0.0	0.7	2.0

WINDIS, TONY JOHN b. January 27, 1933   Ht. 6-1 Wt. 160 College—Wyoming

SEASON—TEAM	G	GS	MIN	FGM	FGA	PCT	3FGM	3FGA	PCT	FTM	FTA	PCT	O-RB	D-RB	TOT	AST	PF	DQ	STL	TO	BLK	PTS	RPG	APG	PPG
59-60—Detroit	9	—	193	16	60	.267	—	—	—	4	6	.667	—	—	47	32	20	0	—	—	—	36	5.2	3.6	4.0
REG. SEASON TOTALS	9	—	193	16	60	.267	—	—	—	4	6	.667	—	—	47	32	20	0	—	—	—	36	5.2	3.6	4.0

WINDSOR, JOHN T. b. April 3, 1940   Ht. 6-8 Wt. 220 College—Stanford

SEASON—TEAM	G	GS	MIN	FGM	FGA	PCT	3FGM	3FGA	PCT	FTM	FTA	PCT	O-RB	D-RB	TOT	AST	PF	DQ	STL	TO	BLK	PTS	RPG	APG	PPG
63-64—San Francisco	11	—	68	10	27	.370	—	—	—	7	8	.875	—	—	26	2	13	0	—	—	—	27	2.4	0.2	2.5
REG. SEASON TOTALS	11	—	68	10	27	.370	—	—	—	7	8	.875	—	—	26	2	13	0	—	—	—	27	2.4	0.2	2.5

WINFIELD, LEROY (Lee) b. February 4, 1947   Ht. 6-2½ Wt. 175 College—North Texas

SEASON—TEAM	G	GS	MIN	FGM	FGA	PCT	3FGM	3FGA	PCT	FTM	FTA	PCT	O-RB	D-RB	TOT	AST	PF	DQ	STL	TO	BLK	PTS	RPG	APG	PPG
69-70—Seattle	64	—	771	138	288	.479	—	—	—	87	116	.750	—	—	98	102	95	0	—	—	—	363	1.5	1.6	5.7
70-71—Seattle	79	—	1605	334	716	.466	—	—	—	162	244	.664	—	—	193	225	135	1	—	—	—	830	2.4	2.8	10.5
71-72—Seattle	81	—	2040	343	692	.496	—	—	—	175	262	.668	—	—	218	290	198	1	—	—	—	861	2.7	3.6	10.6
72-73—Seattle	53	—	1061	143	332	.431	—	—	—	62	108	.574	—	—	126	186	92	3	—	—	—	348	2.4	3.5	6.6
73-74—Buffalo	36	—	433	37	105	.352	—	—	—	33	52	.635	19	24	43	47	42	0	15	—	5	107	1.2	1.3	3.0
74-75—Buffalo	68	—	1259	164	312	.526	—	—	—	49	68	.721	45	81	126	134	106	1	43	—	30	377	1.9	2.0	5.5
75-76—Kansas City	22	—	214	32	66	.485	—	—	—	9	14	.643	8	16	24	19	14	0	10	—	6	73	1.1	0.9	3.3
REG. SEASON TOTALS	403	—	7383	1191	2511	.474	—	—	—	577	864	.668	72	121	828	1003	682	6	68	—	41	2959	2.1	2.5	7.3
PLAYOFF TOTALS	7	—	77	7	18	.389	—	—	—	4	7	.571	5	6	11	11	10	1	3	—	1	18	1.6	1.6	2.6

WINGATE, DAVID GROVER STACEY JR. b. December 15, 1963   Ht. 6-5 Wt. 185 College—Georgetown

SEASON—TEAM	G	GS	MIN	FGM	FGA	PCT	3FGM	3FGA	PCT	FTM	FTA	PCT	O-RB	D-RB	TOT	AST	PF	DQ	STL	TO	BLK	PTS	RPG	APG	PPG
86-87—Philadelphia	77	9	1612	259	602	.430	13	52	.250	149	201	.741	70	86	156	155	169	1	93	128	19	680	2.0	2.0	8.8
87-88—Philadelphia	61	22	1419	218	545	.400	10	40	.250	99	132	.750	44	57	101	119	125	0	47	104	22	545	1.7	2.0	8.9
88-89—Philadelphia	33	6	372	54	115	.470	2	6	.333	27	34	.794	12	25	37	73	43	0	9	35	2	137	1.1	2.2	4.2
89-90—San Antonio	78	2	1856	220	491	.448	0	13	.000	87	112	.777	62	133	195	208	154	2	89	127	18	527	2.5	2.7	6.8
90-91—San Antonio	25	0	563	53	138	.384	1	9	.111	29	41	.707	24	51	75	46	66	0	19	42	5	136	3.0	1.8	5.4
91-92—Washington	81	72	2127	266	572	.465	1	18	.056	105	146	.719	80	189	269	247	162	1	123	124	21	638	3.3	3.0	7.9
92-93—Charlotte	72	55	1471	180	336	.536	1	6	.167	79	107	.738	49	125	174	183	135	1	66	89	9	440	2.4	2.5	6.1
93-94—Charlotte	50	36	1005	136	283	.481	4	12	.333	34	51	.667	30	104	134	104	85	0	42	53	6	310	2.7	2.1	6.2
REG. SEASON TOTALS	477	202	10425	1386	3082	.450	32	156	.205	609	824	.739	371	770	1141	1135	939	5	488	702	102	3413	2.4	2.4	7.2
PLAYOFF TOTALS	27	0	538	69	148	.466	4	5	.800	23	37	.622	19	45	64	63	62	3	28	25	5	165	2.4	2.3	6.1

WINGO, HARTHORNE NATHANIEL (Wingy) b. September 9, 1947   Ht. 6-8 Wt. 210 College—Friendship JC

SEASON—TEAM	G	GS	MIN	FGM	FGA	PCT	3FGM	3FGA	PCT	FTM	FTA	PCT	O-RB	D-RB	TOT	AST	PF	DQ	STL	TO	BLK	PTS	RPG	APG	PPG
72-73—New York	13	—	59	9	22	.409	—	—	—	2	6	.333	—	—	16	1	9	0	—	—	—	20	1.2	0.1	1.5
73-74—New York	60	—	536	82	172	.477	—	—	—	48	76	.632	72	94	166	25	85	0	7	—	14	212	2.8	0.4	3.5
74-75—New York	82	—	1686	233	506	.460	—	—	—	141	187	.754	163	293	456	84	215	2	48	—	35	607	5.6	1.0	7.4
75-76—New York	57	—	533	72	163	.442	—	—	—	40	60	.667	46	61	107	18	59	0	19	—	8	184	1.9	0.3	3.2
REG. SEASON TOTALS	212	—	2814	396	863	.459	—	—	—	231	329	.702	281	448	745	128	368	2	74	—	57	1023	3.5	0.6	4.8
PLAYOFF TOTALS	11	—	104	21	47	.447	—	—	—	8	12	.667	11	14	32	8	10	0	5	—	0	50	2.9	0.7	4.5

WINKLER, MARVIN (Marv) b. February 18, 1948   Ht. 6-1½ Wt. 170 College—Southwestern Louisiana

SEASON—TEAM	G	GS	MIN	FGM	FGA	PCT	3FGM	3FGA	PCT	FTM	FTA	PCT	O-RB	D-RB	TOT	AST	PF	DQ	STL	TO	BLK	PTS	RPG	APG	PPG
70-71—Milwaukee	3	—	14	3	10	.300	—	—	—	2	2	1.000	—	—	4	2	3	0	—	—	—	8	1.3	0.7	2.7
71-72—Indiana (A)	20	—	155	15	54	.278	2	4	.500	8	14	.571	—	—	16	12	16	—	12	—	—	40	0.8	0.6	2.0
REG. NBA TOTALS	3	—	14	3	10	.300	—	—	—	2	2	1.000	—	—	4	2	3	0	—	—	—	8	1.3	0.7	2.7
REG. ABA TOTALS	20	—	155	15	54	.278	2	4	.500	8	14	.571	—	—	16	12	16	—	12	—	—	40	0.8	0.6	2.0
NBA PLAYOFF TOTALS	5	—	8	0	4	.000	—	—	—	0	0	—	—	—	0	1	3	0	—	—	—	0	0.0	0.2	0.0

WINSLOW, RICKIE O'NEAL b. July 26, 1964   Ht. 6-8 Wt. 225 College—Houston

SEASON—TEAM	G	GS	MIN	FGM	FGA	PCT	3FGM	3FGA	PCT	FTM	FTA	PCT	O-RB	D-RB	TOT	AST	PF	DQ	STL	TO	BLK	PTS	RPG	APG	PPG
87-88—Milwaukee	7	0	45	3	13	.231	0	1	.000	1	2	.500	3	4	7	2	9	0	1	4	0	7	1.0	0.3	1.0
REG. SEASON TOTALS	7	0	45	3	13	.231	0	1	.000	1	2	.500	3	4	7	2	9	0	1	4	0	7	1.0	0.3	1.0

WINTERS, BRIAN JOSEPH b. March 1, 1952   Ht. 6-4 Wt. 185 College—South Carolina

SEASON—TEAM	G	GS	MIN	FGM	FGA	PCT	3FGM	3FGA	PCT	FTM	FTA	PCT	O-RB	D-RB	TOT	AST	PF	DQ	STL	TO	BLK	PTS	RPG	APG	PPG
74-75—Los Angeles	68	—	1516	359	810	.443	—	—	—	76	92	.826	39	99	138	195	168	1	74	—	18	794	2.0	2.9	11.7
75-76—Milwaukee	78	—	2795	618	1333	.464	—	—	—	180	217	.829	66	183	249	366	240	0	124	—	25	1416	3.2	4.7	18.2
76-77—Milwaukee	78	—	2717	652	1308	.498	—	—	—	205	242	.847	64	167	231	337	228	1	114	—	29	1509	3.0	4.3	19.3
77-78—Milwaukee	80	—	2751	674	1457	.463	—	—	—	246	293	.840	87	163	250	393	239	4	124	236	27	1594	3.1	4.9	19.9
78-79—Milwaukee	79	—	2575	662	1343	.493	—	—	—	237	277	.856	48	129	177	383	243	1	83	257	40	1561	2.2	4.8	19.8
79-80—Milwaukee	80	—	2623	535	1116	.479	38	102	.373	184	214	.860	48	175	223	362	208	0	101	186	28	1292	2.8	4.5	16.2
80-81—Milwaukee	69	—	1771	331	697	.475	18	51	.353	119	137	.869	32	108	140	229	185	2	70	136	10	799	2.0	3.3	11.6
81-82—Milwaukee	61	13	1289	404	806	.501	36	93	.387	123	156	.788	51	119	170	253	187	1	57	118	9	967	2.8	4.1	15.9
82-83—Milwaukee	57	12	1361	255	587	.434	22	68	.324	73	85	.859	35	75	110	156	132	2	45	81	4	605	1.9	2.7	10.6
REG. SEASON TOTALS	650	25	19938	4490	9457	.475	114	314	.363	1443	1713	.842	470	1218	1688	2674	1830	12	792	1014	190	10537	2.6	4.1	16.2
PLAYOFF TOTALS	41	9	1352	269	549	.490	19	48	.396	80	99	.808	26	92	118	192	123	3	52	96	16	637	2.9	4.7	15.5
ALL-STAR TOTALS	2	1	30	5	12	.417	0	0	—	0	0	—	2	4	6	2	4	0	1	3	0	10	3.0	1.0	5.0

WINTERS, VOISE LEE b. October 12, 1962   Ht. 6-8 Wt. 200 College—Bradley

SEASON—TEAM	G	GS	MIN	FGM	FGA	PCT	3FGM	3FGA	PCT	FTM	FTA	PCT	O-RB	D-RB	TOT	AST	PF	DQ	STL	TO	BLK	PTS	RPG	APG	PPG
85-86—Philadelphia	4	0	17	3	13	.231	0	1	.000	0	0	—	1	2	3	0	1	0	1	2	0	6	0.8	0.0	1.5
REG. SEASON TOTALS	4	0	17	3	13	.231	0	1	.000	0	0	—	1	2	3	0	1	0	1	2	0	6	0.8	0.0	1.5

WISE, ALLEN HARPER (**Skip**) b. July 25, 1955 Ht. 6-3 Wt. 180 College—Clemson

SEASON—TEAM	G	GS	MIN	FGM	FGA	PCT	3FGM	3FGA	PCT	FTM	FTA	PCT	O-RB	D-RB	TOT	AST	PF	DQ	STL	TO	BLK	PTS	RPG	APG	PPG
75-76—San Antonio (A)	2	—	10	2	4	.500	0	0	—	0	0	—	1	2	3	1	4	—	0	2	0	4	1.5	0.5	2.0
REG. ABA TOTALS	2	—	10	2	4	.500	0	0	—	0	0	—	1	2	3	1	4	—	0	2	0	4	1.5	0.5	2.0

WISE, WILLIE M. b. March 3, 1947 Ht. 6-6 Wt. 220 College—San Francisco CC/Drake

SEASON—TEAM	G	GS	MIN	FGM	FGA	PCT	3FGM	3FGA	PCT	FTM	FTA	PCT	O-RB	D-RB	TOT	AST	PF	DQ	STL	TO	BLK	PTS	RPG	APG	PPG
69-70—Los Angeles (A)	82	—	2709	483	1014	.476	4	17	.235	278	427	.651	283	669	952	204	301	8	—	—	—	1248	11.6	2.5	15.2
70-71—Utah (A)	82	—	2676	491	1059	.464	5	17	.294	312	467	.668	—	—	807	204	297	—	—	—	—	1299	9.8	2.5	15.8
71-72—Utah (A)	84	—	3300	743	1471	.505	6	18	.333	459	633	.725	282	612	894	286	299	—	—	282	—	1951	10.6	3.4	23.2
72-73—Utah (A)	83	—	3131	672	1404	.479	3	18	.167	476	607	.784	217	465	682	277	278	5	—	236	—	1823	8.2	3.3	22.0
73-74—Utah (A)	82	—	3292	714	1458	.490	2	16	.125	396	501	.790	170	453	623	302	246	—	118	202	43	1826	7.6	3.7	22.3
74-75—Virginia (A)	16	—	574	128	296	.432	1	4	.250	77	111	.694	32	70	102	54	50	—	26	45	3	334	6.4	3.4	20.9
75-76—Virginia (A)	46	—	1343	247	595	.415	0	6	.000	135	175	.771	89	173	262	125	135	—	53	125	13	629	5.7	2.7	13.7
76-77—Denver	75	—	1403	237	513	.462	—	—	—	142	218	.651	76	177	253	142	180	2	60	—	18	616	3.4	1.9	8.2
77-78—Seattle	2	—	10	0	3	.000	—	—	—	1	4	.250	2	1	3	0	2	0	0	0	0	1	1.5	0.0	0.5
REG. NBA TOTALS	77	—	1413	237	516	.459	—	—	—	143	222	.644	78	178	256	142	182	2	60	0	18	617	3.3	1.8	8.0
REG. ABA TOTALS	475	—	17025	3478	7297	.477	21	96	.219	2133	2921	.730	1073	2442	4322	1452	1606	13	197	890	59	9110	9.1	3.1	19.2
NBA PLAYOFF TOTALS	6	—	106	14	41	.341	—	—	—	17	25	.680	6	22	28	3	16	0	0	—	1	45	4.7	0.5	7.5
ABA PLAYOFF TOTALS	68	—	2592	564	1120	.504	2	10	.200	292	411	.710	124	373	644	224	223	1	25	124	10	1422	9.5	3.3	20.9
ABA ALL-STAR TOTALS	3	—	95	20	40	.500	0	0	—	9	11	.818	10	12	22	7	6	0	1	4	1	49	7.3	2.3	16.3

WITTE, LUKE b. October 19, 1950 Ht. 7-0 Wt. 235 College—Ohio State

SEASON—TEAM	G	GS	MIN	FGM	FGA	PCT	3FGM	3FGA	PCT	FTM	FTA	PCT	O-RB	D-RB	TOT	AST	PF	DQ	STL	TO	BLK	PTS	RPG	APG	PPG
73-74—Cleveland	57	—	728	105	243	.432	—	—	—	46	62	.742	80	147	227	41	91	0	8	—	22	256	4.0	0.7	4.5
74-75—Cleveland	39	—	271	33	96	.344	—	—	—	19	31	.613	38	54	92	15	42	0	4	—	22	85	2.4	0.4	2.2
75-76—Cleveland	22	—	99	11	32	.344	—	—	—	9	15	.600	9	29	38	4	14	0	1	—	1	31	1.7	0.2	1.4
REG. SEASON TOTALS	118	—	1098	149	371	.402	—	—	—	74	108	.685	127	230	357	60	147	0	13	—	45	372	3.0	0.5	3.2
PLAYOFF TOTALS	7	—	28	6	11	.545	—	—	—	4	4	1.000	4	5	9	4	4	0	0	—	0	16	1.3	0.6	2.3

WITTMAN, H. GREGORY (**Greg**) b. May 10, 1947 Ht. 6-8 Wt. 210 College—Western Carolina

SEASON—TEAM	G	GS	MIN	FGM	FGA	PCT	3FGM	3FGA	PCT	FTM	FTA	PCT	O-RB	D-RB	TOT	AST	PF	DQ	STL	TO	BLK	PTS	RPG	APG	PPG
69-70—Denver (A)	50	—	453	80	204	.392	4	17	.235	32	59	.542	—	—	98	15	87	2	—	—	—	196	2.0	0.3	3.9
70-71—Texas-Fla. (A)	10	—	70	6	25	.240	0	1	.000	4	9	.444	—	—	19	0	21	—	—	—	—	16	1.9	0.0	1.6
REG. ABA TOTALS	60	—	523	86	229	.376	4	18	.222	36	68	.529	—	—	117	15	108	2	—	—	—	212	2.0	0.3	3.5
ABA PLAYOFF TOTALS	2	—	4	1	2	.500	1	1	1.000	1	3	.333	—	—	0	2	0	—	—	—	—	4	0.0	0.0	2.0

WITTMAN, RANDY SCOTT b. October 28, 1959 Ht. 6-6 Wt. 210 College—Indiana

SEASON—TEAM	G	GS	MIN	FGM	FGA	PCT	3FGM	3FGA	PCT	FTM	FTA	PCT	O-RB	D-RB	TOT	AST	PF	DQ	STL	TO	BLK	PTS	RPG	APG	PPG
83-84—Atlanta	78	1	1071	160	318	.503	2	5	.400	28	46	.609	14	57	71	71	82	0	17	32	0	350	0.9	0.9	4.5
84-85—Atlanta	41	22	1168	187	352	.531	2	7	.286	30	41	.732	16	57	73	125	58	0	28	57	7	406	1.8	3.0	9.9
85-86—Atlanta	81	79	2760	467	881	.530	5	16	.313	104	135	.770	51	119	170	306	118	0	81	114	14	1043	2.1	3.8	12.9
86-87—Atlanta	71	65	2049	398	792	.503	4	12	.333	100	127	.787	30	94	124	211	107	0	39	88	16	900	1.7	3.0	12.7
87-88—Atlanta	82	82	2412	376	787	.478	0	0	—	71	89	.798	39	131	170	302	117	0	50	82	18	823	2.1	3.7	10.0
88-89—Sac.-Indiana	64	13	1120	130	286	.455	3	6	.500	28	41	.683	26	54	80	111	43	0	23	32	2	291	1.3	1.7	4.5
89-90—Indiana	61	0	544	62	122	.508	1	2	.500	5	6	.833	4	26	30	39	21	0	7	23	4	130	0.5	0.6	2.1
90-91—Indiana	41	0	355	35	79	.443	0	5	.000	4	6	.667	6	27	33	25	9	0	10	10	4	74	0.8	0.6	1.8
91-92—Indiana	24	0	115	8	19	.421	0	0	—	1	2	.500	1	8	9	11	4	0	2	3	0	17	0.4	0.5	0.7
REG. SEASON TOTALS	543	262	11594	1823	3636	.501	17	53	.321	371	493	.753	187	573	760	1201	559	0	257	441	65	4034	1.4	2.2	7.4
PLAYOFF TOTALS	38	30	1105	225	417	.540	0	2	.000	37	50	.740	21	57	78	115	68	0	22	42	6	487	2.1	3.0	12.8

WITTS, GARRETT DAVID (**Garry**) b. July 3, 1959 Ht. 6-7 Wt. 190 College—Holy Cross

SEASON—TEAM	G	GS	MIN	FGM	FGA	PCT	3FGM	3FGA	PCT	FTM	FTA	PCT	O-RB	D-RB	TOT	AST	PF	DQ	STL	TO	BLK	PTS	RPG	APG	PPG
81-82—Washington	46	0	493	49	84	.583	1	2	.500	33	40	.825	29	33	62	38	74	1	17	35	4	132	1.3	0.8	2.9
REG. SEASON TOTALS	46	0	493	49	84	.583	1	2	.500	33	40	.825	29	33	62	38	74	1	17	35	4	132	1.3	0.8	2.9
PLAYOFF TOTALS	4	0	28	2	2	1.000	0	0	—	1	2	.500	2	1	3	2	6	0	1	0	0	5	0.8	0.5	1.3

WOHL, DAVID BRUCE (**Dave**) b. November 2, 1949 Ht. 6-2 Wt. 185 College—Pennsylvania

SEASON—TEAM	G	GS	MIN	FGM	FGA	PCT	3FGM	3FGA	PCT	FTM	FTA	PCT	O-RB	D-RB	TOT	AST	PF	DQ	STL	TO	BLK	PTS	RPG	APG	PPG
71-72—Philadelphia	79	—	1628	243	567	.429	—	—	—	156	206	.757	—	—	150	228	229	2	—	—	—	642	1.9	2.9	8.1
72-73—Port.-Buffalo	78	—	1933	254	568	.447	—	—	—	103	133	.774	—	—	109	326	227	3	—	—	—	611	1.4	4.2	7.8
73-74—Buffalo-Houston	67	—	1055	121	277	.437	—	—	—	75	102	.735	11	35	46	236	136	3	76	—	2	317	0.7	3.5	4.7
74-75—Houston	75	—	1722	203	462	.439	—	—	—	79	106	.745	26	86	112	340	184	1	75	—	9	485	1.5	4.5	6.5
75-76—Houston	50	—	700	66	163	.405	—	—	—	38	49	.776	9	47	56	112	112	2	26	—	1	170	1.1	2.2	3.4
76-77—Houston-N.Y.	51	—	986	116	290	.400	—	—	—	61	89	.685	16	65	81	142	115	2	39	—	6	293	1.6	2.8	5.7
77-78—New Jersey	10	—	118	12	34	.353	—	—	—	11	12	.917	1	3	4	13	24	0	3	16	0	35	0.4	1.3	3.5
REG. SEASON TOTALS	410	—	8142	1015	2361	.430	—	—	—	523	697	.750	63	236	558	1397	1027	13	219	16	18	2553	1.4	3.4	6.2
PLAYOFF TOTALS	4	—	8	3	3	1.000	—	—	—	0	0	—	0	1	1	2	0	1	—	0	6	0.3	0.5	1.5	

WOLF, JOSEPH JAMES (**Joe**) b. December 17, 1964 Ht. 6-11 Wt. 230 College—North Carolina

SEASON—TEAM	G	GS	MIN	FGM	FGA	PCT	3FGM	3FGA	PCT	FTM	FTA	PCT	O-RB	D-RB	TOT	AST	PF	DQ	STL	TO	BLK	PTS	RPG	APG	PPG
87-88—L.A. Clippers	42	26	1137	136	334	.407	3	15	.200	45	54	.833	51	136	187	98	139	8	38	76	16	320	4.5	2.3	7.6
88-89—L.A. Clippers	66	15	1450	170	402	.423	2	14	.143	44	64	.688	83	188	271	113	152	1	32	94	16	386	4.1	1.7	5.8
89-90—L.A. Clippers	77	19	1325	155	392	.395	5	25	.200	55	71	.775	63	169	232	62	129	0	30	77	24	370	3.0	0.8	4.8
90-91—Denver	74	38	1593	234	519	.451	2	15	.133	69	83	.831	136	264	400	107	244	8	60	95	31	539	5.4	1.4	7.3
91-92—Denver	67	0	1160	100	277	.361	1	11	.091	53	66	.803	97	143	240	61	124	1	32	60	14	254	3.6	0.9	3.8
92-93—Boston-Port.	23	0	165	20	44	.455	0	1	.000	13	16	.813	14	34	48	5	24	0	7	7	1	53	2.1	0.2	2.3
REG. SEASON TOTALS	340	98	6830	815	1968	.414	13	01	.160	279	354	.788	444	934	1378	446	812	18	199	409	102	1922	3.9	1.3	5.5
PLAYOFF TOTALS	2	0	20	1	2	.500	0	0	—	0	0	—	2	2	4	—	1	0	0	0	1	2	2.0	0.0	1.0

WOOD, DAVID b. November 30, 1964 Ht. 6-9 Wt. 230 College—Skagit Valley/Nevada-Reno

SEASON—TEAM	G	GS	MIN	FGM	FGA	PCT	3FGM	3FGA	PCT	FTM	FTA	PCT	O-RB	D-RB	TOT	AST	PF	DQ	STL	TO	BLK	PTS	RPG	APG	PPG
88-89—Chicago	2	0	2	0	0	—	0	0	—	0	0	—	0	0	0	0	0	0	0	0	0	0	0.0	0.0	0.0
90-91—Houston	82	13	1421	148	349	.424	28	90	.311	108	133	.812	107	139	246	94	236	4	58	89	16	432	3.0	1.1	5.3
92-93—San Antonio	64	2	598	52	117	.444	5	21	.238	46	55	.836	38	59	97	34	93	1	13	29	12	155	1.5	0.5	2.4
93-94—Detroit	78	3	1182	119	259	.459	22	49	.449	62	82	.756	104	135	239	51	201	3	39	35	19	322	3.1	0.7	4.1
REG. SEASON TOTALS	226	18	3203	319	725	.440	55	160	.344	216	270	.800	249	333	582	179	530	8	110	153	47	909	2.6	0.8	4.0
PLAYOFF TOTALS	8	0	64	4	7	.571	2	2	1.000	2	4	.500	2	6	8	4	15	0	3	1	0	12	1.0	0.5	1.5

WOOD, JAMES HOWARD (**Howard**) b. May 20, 1959 Ht. 6-7 Wt. 235 College—Tennessee

SEASON—TEAM	G	GS	MIN	FGM	FGA	PCT	3FGM	3FGA	PCT	FTM	FTA	PCT	O-RB	D-RB	TOT	AST	PF	DQ	STL	TO	BLK	PTS	RPG	APG	PPG
81-82—Utah	42	3	342	55	120	.458	0	1	.000	34	52	.654	22	43	65	9	37	0	8	15	6	144	1.5	0.2	3.4
REG. SEASON TOTALS	42	3	342	55	120	.458	0	1	.000	34	52	.654	22	43	65	9	37	0	8	15	6	144	1.5	0.2	3.4

WOOD, MARTIN ALPHONZO (**Al**) b. June 2, 1958 Ht. 6-6 Wt. 210 College—North Carolina

SEASON—TEAM	G	GS	MIN	FGM	FGA	PCT	3FGM	3FGA	PCT	FTM	FTA	PCT	O-RB	D-RB	TOT	AST	PF	DQ	STL	TO	BLK	PTS	RPG	APG	PPG
81-82—Atlanta-S.D.	48	5	930	179	381	.470	3	24	.125	93	119	.782	51	83	134	58	108	4	31	71	9	454	2.8	1.2	9.5
82-83—San Diego	76	47	1822	343	740	.464	15	50	.300	124	161	.770	96	140	236	134	188	5	55	111	36	825	3.1	1.8	10.9
83-84—Seattle	81	81	2236	467	945	.494	3	21	.143	223	271	.823	94	181	275	166	207	1	64	126	32	1160	3.4	2.0	14.3
84-85—Seattle	80	79	2545	515	1061	.485	7	33	.212	166	214	.776	99	180	279	236	187	3	84	120	52	1203	3.5	3.0	15.0
85-86—Seattle	78	34	1749	355	817	.435	5	37	.135	187	239	.782	80	164	244	114	171	2	57	107	19	902	3.1	1.5	11.6
86-87—Dallas	54	0	657	121	310	.390	7	25	.280	109	139	.784	39	55	94	34	83	0	19	34	11	358	1.7	0.6	6.6
REG. SEASON TOTALS	417	246	9939	1980	4254	.465	40	190	.211	902	1143	.789	459	803	1262	742	944	15	310	569	159	4902	3.0	1.8	11.8
PLAYOFF TOTALS	5	5	157	26	56	.464	0	1	.000	8	12	.667	7	27	34	10	16	0	1	7	1	60	6.8	2.0	12.0

WOOD, OSIE LEON III (**Leon**) b. March 25, 1962 Ht. 6-3 Wt. 185 College—Arizona/Cal State-Fullerton

SEASON—TEAM	G	GS	MIN	FGM	FGA	PCT	3FGM	3FGA	PCT	FTM	FTA	PCT	O-RB	D-RB	TOT	AST	PF	DQ	STL	TO	BLK	PTS	RPG	APG	PPG
84-85—Philadelphia	38	1	269	50	134	.373	4	30	.133	18	26	.692	3	15	18	45	17	0	8	25	0	122	0.5	1.2	3.2
85-86—Phil.-Wash.	68	1	1198	184	466	.395	41	114	.360	123	155	.794	25	65	90	182	70	0	34	87	0	532	1.3	2.7	7.8
86-87—New Jersey	76	7	1733	187	501	.373	60	200	.300	123	154	.799	23	97	120	370	126	0	48	108	3	557	1.6	4.9	7.3
87-88—S.A.-Atlanta	52	8	909	136	312	.436	52	127	.409	76	99	.768	17	40	57	174	50	0	26	39	1	400	1.1	3.3	7.7
89-90—New Jersey	28	2	200	16	49	.327	4	21	.190	14	16	.875	1	11	12	47	16	0	6	8	0	50	0.4	1.7	1.8
90-91—Sacramento	12	0	222	25	63	.397	12	38	.316	19	21	.905	5	14	19	49	10	0	5	12	0	81	1.6	4.1	6.8
REG. SEASON TOTALS	274	19	4531	598	1525	.392	173	530	.326	373	471	.792	74	242	316	867	289	0	127	279	4	1742	1.2	3.2	6.4
PLAYOFF TOTALS	10	0	21	6	15	.400	2	3	.667	8	10	.800	0	1	1	3	0	0	0	3	0	22	0.1	0.3	2.2

WOOD, ROBERT A. (**Bob**) b. October 7, 1921 Ht. 5-10½ College—Northern Illinois

SEASON—TEAM	G	GS	MIN	FGM	FGA	PCT	3FGM	3FGA	PCT	FTM	FTA	PCT	O-RB	D-RB	TOT	AST	PF	DQ	STL	TO	BLK	PTS	RPG	APG	PPG
49-50—Sheboygan	6	—	—	3	14	.214	—	—	—	1	1	1.000	—	—	—	1	6	—	—	—	—	7	—	0.2	1.2
REG. SEASON TOTALS	6	—	—	3	14	.214	—	—	—	1	1	1.000	—	—	—	1	6	—	—	—	—	7	—	0.2	1.2

WOODS, JAMES THOMAS JR. (**Tommy**) b. June 10, 1943 Ht. 6-6½ Wt. 225 College—East Tennessee State

SEASON—TEAM	G	GS	MIN	FGM	FGA	PCT	3FGM	3FGA	PCT	FTM	FTA	PCT	O-RB	D-RB	TOT	AST	PF	DQ	STL	TO	BLK	PTS	RPG	APG	PPG
67-68—Kentucky (A)	18	—	184	14	43	.326	0	1	.000	14	16	.875	—	—	55	4	25	0	—	9	—	42	3.1	0.2	2.3
REG. ABA TOTALS	18	—	184	14	43	.326	0	1	.000	14	16	.875	—	—	55	4	25	0	—	9	—	42	3.1	0.2	2.3

WOODS, RANDOLPH (**Randy**) b. September 23, 1970 Ht. 6-0 Wt. 185 College—La Salle

SEASON—TEAM	G	GS	MIN	FGM	FGA	PCT	3FGM	3FGA	PCT	FTM	FTA	PCT	O-RB	D-RB	TOT	AST	PF	DQ	STL	TO	BLK	PTS	RPG	APG	PPG
92-93—L.A. Clippers	41	1	174	23	66	.348	3	14	.214	19	26	.731	6	8	14	40	26	0	14	16	1	68	0.3	1.0	1.7
93-94—L.A. Clippers	40	0	352	49	133	.368	27	78	.346	20	35	.571	13	16	29	71	40	0	24	34	2	145	0.7	1.8	3.6
REG. SEASON TOTALS	81	1	526	72	199	.362	30	92	.326	39	61	.639	19	24	43	111	66	0	38	50	3	213	0.5	1.4	2.6

WOODSON, MICHAEL DEAN (**Mike**) b. March 24, 1958 Ht. 6-5 Wt. 200 College—Indiana

SEASON—TEAM	G	GS	MIN	FGM	FGA	PCT	3FGM	3FGA	PCT	FTM	FTA	PCT	O-RB	D-RB	TOT	AST	PF	DQ	STL	TO	BLK	PTS	RPG	APG	PPG
80-81—New York	81	—	949	165	373	.442	1	5	.200	49	64	.766	33	64	97	75	95	0	36	54	12	380	1.2	0.9	4.7
81-82—N.J.-K.C.	83	74	2331	538	1069	.503	7	25	.280	221	286	.773	102	145	247	222	220	3	142	153	35	1304	3.0	2.7	15.7
82-83—Kansas City	81	3	2426	584	1154	.506	7	33	.212	298	377	.790	84	164	248	254	203	0	137	174	59	1473	3.1	3.1	18.2
83-84—Kansas City	71	12	1838	389	816	.477	2	8	.250	247	302	.818	62	113	175	175	174	2	83	115	28	1027	2.5	2.5	14.5
84-85—Kansas City	78	3	1998	530	1068	.496	5	21	.238	264	330	.800	69	129	198	143	216	1	117	139	28	1329	2.5	1.8	17.0
85-86—Sacramento	81	51	2417	510	1073	.475	2	13	.154	242	289	.837	94	132	226	197	215	1	92	145	37	1264	2.8	2.4	15.6
86-87—L.A. Clippers	74	66	2126	494	1130	.437	34	123	.276	240	290	.828	68	94	162	196	201	1	100	168	16	1262	2.2	2.6	17.1
87-88—L.A. Clippers	80	77	2534	562	1263	.445	18	78	.231	296	341	.868	64	126	190	273	210	1	109	186	26	1438	2.4	3.4	18.0
88-89—Houston	81	79	2259	410	936	.438	31	89	.348	195	237	.823	51	143	194	206	195	1	89	136	18	1046	2.4	2.5	12.9
89-90—Houston	61	11	972	160	405	.395	12	41	.293	62	86	.721	25	63	88	66	100	1	42	49	11	394	1.4	1.1	6.5
90-91—Houston-Clev.	15	3	171	26	77	.338	1	7	.143	11	13	.846	3	10	13	15	18	0	5	12	5	64	0.9	1.0	4.3
REG. SEASON TOTALS	786	379	20021	4368	9364	.466	120	443	.271	2125	2615	.813	655	1183	1838	1822	1847	11	952	1331	275	10981	2.3	2.3	14.0
PLAYOFF TOTALS	13	7	348	59	148	.399	3	13	.231	37	41	.902	17	13	30	34	35	0	10	23	4	158	2.3	2.6	12.2

WOOLLARD, ROBERT GEORGE (**Bob**) b. July 27, 1940 Ht. 6-10 Wt. 225 College—Wake Forest

SEASON—TEAM	G	GS	MIN	FGM	FGA	PCT	3FGM	3FGA	PCT	FTM	FTA	PCT	O-RB	D-RB	TOT	AST	PF	DQ	STL	TO	BLK	PTS	RPG	APG	PPG
69-70—Miami (A)	19	—	234	32	82	.390	0	1	.000	20	25	.800	—	—	69	6	42	1	—	—	—	84	3.6	0.3	4.4
REG. ABA TOTALS	19	—	234	32	82	.390	0	1	.000	20	25	.800	—	—	69	6	42	1	—	—	—	84	3.6	0.3	4.4

WOOLRIDGE, ORLANDO VERNADA b. December 16, 1959 Ht. 6-9 Wt. 215 College—Notre Dame

SEASON—TEAM	G	GS	MIN	FGM	FGA	PCT	3FGM	3FGA	PCT	FTM	FTA	PCT	O-RB	D-RB	TOT	AST	PF	DQ	STL	TO	BLK	PTS	RPG	APG	PPG
81-82—Chicago	75	12	1188	202	394	.513	0	3	.000	144	206	.699	82	145	227	81	152	1	23	107	24	548	3.0	1.1	7.3
82-83—Chicago	57	38	1627	361	622	.580	0	3	.000	217	340	.638	122	176	298	97	177	1	38	157	44	939	5.2	1.7	16.5
83-84—Chicago	75	74	2544	570	1086	.525	1	2	.500	303	424	.715	130	239	369	136	253	6	71	188	60	1444	4.9	1.8	19.3
84-85—Chicago	77	76	2816	679	1225	.554	0	5	.000	409	521	.785	158	277	435	135	185	0	58	178	38	1767	5.6	1.8	22.9
85-86—Chicago	70	59	2248	540	1090	.495	4	23	.174	364	462	.788	150	200	350	213	186	2	49	174	47	1448	5.0	3.0	20.7
86-87—New Jersey	75	53	2638	556	1067	.521	1	8	.125	438	564	.777	118	249	367	261	243	4	54	213	86	1551	4.9	3.5	20.7
87-88—New Jersey	19	12	622	110	247	.445	0	2	.000	92	130	.708	31	60	91	71	73	2	13	48	20	312	4.8	3.7	16.4
88-89—L.A. Lakers	74	0	1491	231	494	.468	0	1	.000	253	343	.738	81	189	270	58	130	0	30	103	65	715	3.6	0.8	9.7
89-90—L.A. Lakers	62	2	1421	306	550	.556	0	5	.000	176	240	.733	49	136	185	96	160	2	39	73	46	788	3.0	1.5	12.7
90-91—Denver	53	50	1823	490	983	.498	0	4	.000	350	439	.797	141	220	361	119	145	2	69	152	23	1330	6.8	2.2	25.1
91-92—Detroit	82	61	2113	452	907	.498	1	9	.111	241	353	.683	109	151	260	88	154	0	41	133	33	1146	3.2	1.1	14.0
92-93—Detroit-Milw.	58	47	1555	289	599	.482	0	9	.000	120	177	.678	87	98	185	115	122	1	27	79	27	698	3.2	2.0	12.0
93-94—Philadelphia	74	1	1955	364	773	.471	1	14	.071	208	302	.689	103	195	298	139	186	1	41	142	56	937	4.0	1.9	12.7
REG. SEASON TOTALS	851	485	24041	5150	10037	.513	8	88	.091	3315	4501	.737	1361	2335	3696	1609	2166	22	553	1747	569	13623	4.3	1.9	16.0
PLAYOFF TOTALS	36	12	905	161	327	.492	0	2	.000	106	148	.716	43	87	130	42	105	2	20	55	26	428	3.6	1.2	11.9

WORKMAN, HAYWOODE WILVON b. January 23, 1966 Ht. 6-3 Wt. 180 College—Winston Salem State/Oral Roberts

SEASON—TEAM	G	GS	MIN	FGM	FGA	PCT	3FGM	3FGA	PCT	FTM	FTA	PCT	O-RB	D-RB	TOT	AST	PF	DQ	STL	TO	BLK	PTS	RPG	APG	PPG
89-90—Atlanta	6	0	16	2	3	.667	0	0	—	2	2	1.000	0	3	3	2	3	0	3	0	0	6	0.5	0.3	1.0
90-91—Washington	73	56	2034	234	515	.454	12	50	.240	101	133	.759	51	191	242	353	162	1	87	135	7	581	3.3	4.8	8.0
93-94—Indiana	65	52	1714	195	460	.424	18	56	.321	93	116	.802	32	172	204	404	152	0	85	151	4	501	3.1	6.2	7.7
REG. SEASON TOTALS	144	108	3764	431	978	.441	30	106	.283	196	251	.781	83	366	449	759	317	1	175	286	11	1088	3.1	5.3	7.6
PLAYOFF TOTALS	16	15	511	45	131	.344	6	21	.286	32	38	.842	11	40	51	112	40	0	28	38	1	128	3.2	7.0	8.0

WORKMAN, MARK CECIL b. March 10, 1930 d. December 21, 1983 Ht. 6-9 Wt. 215 College—West Virginia

SEASON—TEAM	G	GS	MIN	FGM	FGA	PCT	3FGM	3FGA	PCT	FTM	FTA	PCT	O-RB	D-RB	TOT	AST	PF	DQ	STL	TO	BLK	PTS	RPG	APG	PPG
52-53—Milw.-Phil.	65	—	1030	130	408	.319	—	—	—	70	113	.619	—	—	193	37	166	5	—	—	—	330	3.0	0.6	5.1
53-54—Baltimore	14	—	151	25	60	.417	—	—	—	6	10	.600	—	—	37	7	31	0	—	—	—	56	2.6	0.5	4.0
REG. SEASON TOTALS	79	—	1181	155	468	.331	—	—	—	76	123	.618	—	—	230	44	197	5	—	—	—	386	2.9	0.6	4.9

WORKMAN, THOMAS EDWIN (**Tom, Hawk**) b. November 14, 1944 Ht. 6-7 Wt. 225 College—Seattle

SEASON—TEAM	G	GS	MIN	FGM	FGA	PCT	3FGM	3FGA	PCT	FTM	FTA	PCT	O-RB	D-RB	TOT	AST	PF	DQ	STL	TO	BLK	PTS	RPG	APG	PPG
67-68—St. L.-Balt.	20	—	95	19	40	.475	—	—	—	18	23	.783	—	—	25	3	17	0	—	—	—	56	1.3	0.2	2.8
68-69—Baltimore	21	—	86	22	54	.407	—	—	—	9	15	.600	—	—	27	2	16	0	—	—	—	53	1.3	0.1	2.5
69-70—Detroit	2	—	6	0	1	.000	—	—	—	0	0	—	—	—	0	0	1	0	—	—	—	0	0.0	0.0	0.0
69-70—Los Angeles (A)	26	—	445	116	251	.462	1	4	.250	77	98	.786	—	—	94	22	69	0	—	—	—	310	3.6	0.8	11.9
70-71—Utah-Denver (A)	56	—	679	133	303	.439	3	19	.158	86	105	.819	—	—	179	48	113	—	—	—	—	355	3.2	0.9	6.3
REG. NBA TOTALS	43	—	187	41	95	.432	—	—	—	27	38	.711	—	—	52	5	34	0	—	—	—	109	1.2	0.1	2.5
REG. ABA TOTALS	82	—	1124	249	554	.449	4	23	.174	163	203	.803	—	—	273	70	182	0	—	—	—	665	3.3	0.9	8.1
NBA PLAYOFF TOTALS	1	—	2	0	1	.000	—	—	—	0	0	—	—	—	1	0	0	0	—	—	—	0	1.0	0.0	0.0
ABA PLAYOFF TOTALS	3	—	9	3	7	.429	0	0	—	0	0	—	—	—	3	0	0	0	—	—	—	6	1.0	0.0	2.0

WORSLEY, WILLIE JAMES b. November 13, 1945 Ht. 5-10 Wt. 175 College—Texas-El Paso

SEASON—TEAM	G	GS	MIN	FGM	FGA	PCT	3FGM	3FGA	PCT	FTM	FTA	PCT	O-RB	D-RB	TOT	AST	PF	DQ	STL	TO	BLK	PTS	RPG	APG	PPG
68-69—New York (A)	24	—	460	36	123	.293	10	30	.333	63	84	.750	—	—	35	39	48	0	—	32	—	145	1.5	1.6	6.0
REG. ABA TOTALS	24	—	460	36	123	.293	10	30	.333	63	84	.750	—	—	35	39	48	0	—	32	—	145	1.5	1.6	6.0

WORTHEN, SAMUEL LEE (**Sam**) b. January 17, 1958 Ht. 6-5½ Wt. 195 College—McLennan CC/Marquette

SEASON—TEAM	G	GS	MIN	FGM	FGA	PCT	3FGM	3FGA	PCT	FTM	FTA	PCT	O-RB	D-RB	TOT	AST	PF	DQ	STL	TO	BLK	PTS	RPG	APG	PPG
80-81—Chicago	64	—	945	95	192	.495	0	4	.000	45	60	.750	22	93	115	115	115	0	57	91	6	235	1.8	1.8	3.7
81-82—Utah	5	0	22	2	5	.400	0	0	—	0	0	—	1	0	1	3	3	0	0	2	0	4	0.2	0.6	0.8
REG. SEASON TOTALS	69	0	967	97	197	.492	0	4	.000	45	60	.750	23	93	116	118	118	0	57	93	6	239	1.7	1.7	3.5
PLAYOFF TOTALS	1	0	1	0	0	—	0	0	—	0	0	—	0	0	0	0	0	0	0	0	0	0	0.0	0.0	0.0

WORTHY, JAMES AGER b. February 27, 1961 Ht. 6-9 Wt. 225 College—North Carolina

SEASON—TEAM	G	GS	MIN	FGM	FGA	PCT	3FGM	3FGA	PCT	FTM	FTA	PCT	O-RB	D-RB	TOT	AST	PF	DQ	STL	TO	BLK	PTS	RPG	APG	PPG
82-83—Los Angeles	77	1	1970	447	772	.579	1	4	.250	138	221	.624	157	242	399	132	221	2	91	178	64	1033	5.2	1.7	13.4
83-84—Los Angeles	82	53	2415	495	890	.556	0	6	.000	195	257	.759	157	358	515	207	244	5	77	181	70	1185	6.3	2.5	14.5
84-85—L.A. Lakers	80	76	2696	610	1066	.572	0	7	.000	190	245	.776	169	342	511	201	196	0	87	198	67	1410	6.4	2.5	17.6
85-86—L.A. Lakers	75	73	2454	629	1086	.579	0	13	.000	242	314	.771	136	251	387	201	195	0	82	149	77	1500	5.2	2.7	20.0
86-87—L.A. Lakers	82	82	2819	651	1207	.539	0	13	.000	292	389	.751	158	308	466	226	206	0	108	168	83	1594	5.7	2.8	19.4
87-88—L.A. Lakers	75	72	2655	617	1161	.531	2	16	.125	242	304	.796	129	245	374	289	175	1	72	155	55	1478	5.0	3.9	19.7
88-89—L.A. Lakers	81	81	2960	702	1282	.548	2	23	.087	251	321	.782	169	320	489	288	175	0	108	182	56	1657	6.0	3.6	20.5
89-90—L.A. Lakers	80	80	2960	711	1298	.548	15	49	.306	248	317	.782	160	318	478	288	190	0	99	160	49	1685	6.0	3.6	21.1
90-91—L.A. Lakers	78	74	3008	716	1455	.492	26	90	.289	212	266	.797	107	249	356	275	117	0	104	127	35	1670	4.6	3.5	21.4
91-92—L.A. Lakers	54	54	2108	450	1007	.447	9	43	.209	166	204	.814	98	207	305	252	89	0	76	127	23	1075	5.6	4.7	19.9
92-93—L.A. Lakers	82	69	2359	510	1142	.447	30	111	.270	171	211	.810	73	174	247	278	87	0	92	137	27	1221	3.0	3.4	14.9
93-94—L.A. Lakers	80	2	1597	340	838	.406	32	111	.288	100	135	.741	48	133	181	154	80	0	45	97	18	812	2.3	1.9	10.2
REG. SEASON TOTALS	926	717	30001	6878	13204	.521	117	486	.241	2447	3184	.769	1561	3147	4708	2791	1975	8	1041	1859	624	16320	5.1	3.0	17.6
PLAYOFF TOTALS	143	125	5297	1267	2329	.544	14	67	.209	474	652	.727	257	490	747	463	352	2	177	298	96	3022	5.2	3.2	21.1
ALL-STAR TOTALS	7	3	142	34	77	.442	0	3	.000	6	9	.667	12	14	26	9	10	0	7	4	4	74	3.7	1.3	10.6

WRIGHT, BRADFORD WILLIAM (**Brad**) b. March 26, 1962 Ht. 6-11 Wt. 225 College—UCLA

SEASON—TEAM	G	GS	MIN	FGM	FGA	PCT	3FGM	3FGA	PCT	FTM	FTA	PCT	O-RB	D-RB	TOT	AST	PF	DQ	STL	TO	BLK	PTS	RPG	APG	PPG
86-87—New York	14	0	138	20	46	.435	0	1	.000	12	28	.429	25	28	53	1	20	0	3	13	6	52	3.8	0.1	3.7
87-88—Denver	2	0	7	1	5	.200	0	0	—	0	0	—	0	1	1	0	3	0	0	2	0	2	0.5	0.0	1.0
REG. SEASON TOTALS	16	0	145	21	51	.412	0	1	.000	12	28	.429	25	29	54	1	23	0	3	15	6	54	3.4	0.1	3.4

WRIGHT, HOWARD GREGORY b. December 20, 1967 Ht. 6-8 Wt. 220 College—Stanford

SEASON—TEAM	G	GS	MIN	FGM	FGA	PCT	3FGM	3FGA	PCT	FTM	FTA	PCT	O-RB	D-RB	TOT	AST	PF	DQ	STL	TO	BLK	PTS	RPG	APG	PPG
90-91—Atlanta-Orlando-Dallas	15	0	164	19	47	.404	0	1	.000	16	24	.667	12	33	45	3	28	0	4	11	5	54	3.0	0.2	3.6
92-93—Orlando	4	0	10	4	5	.800	0	0	—	0	2	.000	1	1	2	0	0	0	0	0	0	8	0.5	0.0	2.0
REG. SEASON TOTALS	19	0	174	23	52	.442	0	1	.000	16	26	.615	13	34	47	3	28	0	4	11	5	62	2.5	0.2	3.3

WRIGHT, HOWARD L. (**Howie**) b. February 22, 1947 Ht. 6-3 Wt. 185 College—Austin Peay

SEASON—TEAM	G	GS	MIN	FGM	FGA	PCT	3FGM	3FGA	PCT	FTM	FTA	PCT	O-RB	D-RB	TOT	AST	PF	DQ	STL	TO	BLK	PTS	RPG	APG	PPG
70-71—Kentucky (A)	52	—	612	94	245	.384	9	42	.214	40	49	.816	—	—	80	63	89	—	—	—	—	237	1.5	1.2	4.6
71-72—Kentucky (A)	1	—	4	0	0	—	0	0	—	0	1	.000	—	—	0	0	0	—	—	1	—	0	0.0	0.0	0.0
REG. ABA TOTALS	53	—	616	94	245	.384	9	42	.214	40	50	.800	—	—	80	63	89	—	—	1	—	237	1.5	1.2	4.5
ABA PLAYOFF TOTALS	5	—	36	7	20	.350	2	8	.250	4	9	.444	—	—	2	4	6	—	—	4	—	20	0.4	0.8	4.0

WRIGHT, JOSEPH A. (**Joby**) b. September 5, 1950 Ht. 6-8 Wt. 220 College—Indiana

SEASON—TEAM	G	GS	MIN	FGM	FGA	PCT	3FGM	3FGA	PCT	FTM	FTA	PCT	O-RB	D-RB	TOT	AST	PF	DQ	STL	TO	BLK	PTS	RPG	APG	PPG
72-73—Seattle	77	—	931	133	278	.478	—	—	—	37	89	.416	—	—	218	36	164	0	—	—	—	303	2.8	0.5	3.9
73-74—Memphis (A)	3	—	31	5	16	.313	0	0	—	2	2	1.000	9	5	14	0	7	—	0	4	1	12	4.7	0.0	4.0
75-76—S.D.-Vir. (A)	23	—	305	50	109	.459	0	0	—	21	38	.553	29	30	59	2	54	—	5	24	4	121	2.6	0.1	5.3
REG. NBA TOTALS	77	—	931	133	278	.478	—	—	—	37	89	.416	—	—	218	36	164	0	—	—	—	303	2.8	0.5	3.9
REG. ABA TOTALS	26	—	336	55	125	.440	0	0	—	23	40	.575	38	35	73	2	61	0	5	28	5	133	2.8	0.1	5.1

WRIGHT, LARRY GLENN b. November 23, 1954 Ht. 6½ Wt. 170 College—Grambling State

SEASON—TEAM	G	GS	MIN	FGM	FGA	PCT	3FGM	3FGA	PCT	FTM	FTA	PCT	O-RB	D-RB	TOT	AST	PF	DQ	STL	TO	BLK	PTS	RPG	APG	PPG
76-77—Washington	78	—	1421	262	595	.440	—	—	—	88	115	.765	32	66	98	232	170	0	55	—	5	612	1.3	3.0	7.8
77-78—Washington	70	—	1466	283	570	.496	—	—	—	76	107	.710	31	71	102	260	195	3	68	134	15	642	1.5	3.7	9.2
78-79—Washington	73	—	1658	276	589	.469	—	—	—	125	168	.744	48	92	140	298	166	3	69	119	13	677	1.9	4.1	9.3
79-80—Washington	76	—	1286	229	500	.458	4	16	.250	96	108	.889	40	82	122	222	144	3	49	108	18	558	1.6	2.9	7.3
80-81—Detroit	45	—	997	140	303	.462	2	7	.286	53	66	.803	26	62	88	153	114	1	42	74	7	335	2.0	3.4	7.4
81-82—Detroit	1	0	6	0	1	.000	0	0	—	0	0	—	0	0	0	0	2	0	1	0	0	0	0.0	0.0	0.0
REG. SEASON TOTALS	343	0	6834	1190	2558	.465	6	23	.261	438	564	.777	177	373	550	1165	791	10	283	436	58	2824	1.6	3.4	8.2
PLAYOFF TOTALS	49	0	870	166	348	.477	0	1	.000	65	81	.802	21	44	65	133	131	2	37	55	7	397	1.3	2.7	8.1

WRIGHT, LAWRENCE (**Lonnie**) b. January 23, 1944   Ht. 6-2 Wt. 205 College—Colorado State

SEASON—TEAM	G	GS	MIN	FGM	FGA	PCT	3FGM	3FGA	PCT	FTM	FTA	PCT	O-RB	D-RB	TOT	AST	PF	DQ	STL	TO	BLK	PTS	RPG	APG	PPG
67-68—Denver (A)	38	—	896	146	346	.422	2	9	.222	79	121	.653	—	—	96	68	96	0	—	43	—	373	2.5	1.8	9.8
68-69—Denver (A)	69	—	2538	453	1089	.416	19	86	.221	205	276	.743	—	—	290	175	250	2	—	160	—	1130	4.2	2.5	16.4
69-70—Denver (A)	79	—	2237	393	952	.413	54	193	.280	121	175	.691	—	—	216	149	278	7	—	—	—	961	2.7	1.9	12.2
70-71—Denver-Fla. (A)	72	—	1398	199	558	.357	17	74	.230	93	133	.699	—	—	153	116	162	—	—	—	—	508	2.1	1.6	7.1
71-72—Floridians (A)	77	—	1638	252	599	.421	19	73	.260	95	117	.812	—	—	158	133	197	—	—	89	—	618	2.1	1.7	8.0
REG. ABA TOTALS	335	—	8707	1443	3544	.407	111	435	.255	593	822	.721	—	—	913	641	983	9	—	292	—	3590	2.7	1.9	10.7
ABA PLAYOFF TOTALS	33	—	905	110	335	.328	6	34	.176	57	76	.750	—	—	100	78	88	0	—	26	—	283	3.0	2.4	8.6

WRIGHT, LEROY b. May 6, 1938   Ht. 6-9 Wt. 220 College—Pacific

SEASON—TEAM	G	GS	MIN	FGM	FGA	PCT	3FGM	3FGA	PCT	FTM	FTA	PCT	O-RB	D-RB	TOT	AST	PF	DQ	STL	TO	BLK	PTS	RPG	APG	PPG
67-68—Pittsburgh (A)	17	—	331	24	60	.400	0	0	—	9	22	.409	—	—	108	14	49	1	—	20	—	57	6.4	0.8	3.4
68-69—Minnesota (A)	10	—	95	4	13	.308	0	0	—	0	5	.000	—	—	30	1	15	0	—	2	—	8	3.0	0.1	0.8
REG. ABA TOTALS	27	—	426	28	73	.384	0	0	—	9	27	.333	—	—	138	15	64	1	—	22	—	65	5.1	0.6	2.4
ABA PLAYOFF TOTALS	14	—	195	9	31	.290	0	1	.000	8	22	.364	—	—	73	8	32	2	—	8	—	26	5.2	0.6	1.9

WRIGHT, LUTHER A. JR. b. September 22, 1971   Ht. 7-2 Wt. 270 College—Seton Hall

SEASON—TEAM	G	GS	MIN	FGM	FGA	PCT	3FGM	3FGA	PCT	FTM	FTA	PCT	O-RB	D-RB	TOT	AST	PF	DQ	STL	TO	BLK	PTS	RPG	APG	PPG
93-94—Utah	15	2	92	8	23	.348	0	1	.000	3	4	.750	6	4	10	0	21	0	1	6	2	19	0.7	0.0	1.3
REG. SEASON TOTALS	15	2	92	8	23	.348	0	1	.000	3	4	.750	6	4	10	0	21	0	1	6	2	19	0.7	0.0	1.3

WUYCIK, DENNIS MARK b. March 29, 1950   Ht. 6-6 Wt. 215 College—North Carolina

SEASON—TEAM	G	GS	MIN	FGM	FGA	PCT	3FGM	3FGA	PCT	FTM	FTA	PCT	O-RB	D-RB	TOT	AST	PF	DQ	STL	TO	BLK	PTS	RPG	APG	PPG
72-73—Carolina (A)	83	—	973	151	329	.459	0	4	.000	75	108	.694	69	110	179	79	165	3	—	116	—	377	2.2	1.0	4.5
73-74—Carolina (A)	49	—	492	88	190	.463	1	2	.500	51	77	.662	51	55	106	31	88	—	16	40	4	228	2.2	0.6	4.7
74-75—St. Louis (A)	25	—	219	34	74	.459	0	1	.000	11	19	.579	17	21	38	18	40	—	6	25	1	79	1.5	0.7	3.2
REG. ABA TOTALS	157	—	1684	273	593	.460	1	7	.143	137	204	.672	137	186	323	128	293	3	22	181	5	684	2.1	0.8	4.4
ABA PLAYOFF TOTALS	15	—	94	8	24	.333	0	1	.000	8	12	.667	1	2	19	3	14	0	0	9	0	24	1.3	0.2	1.6

WYDNER, A.J. b. September 11, 1964   Ht. 6-2 Wt. 180 College—Massachusetts/Fairfield

SEASON—TEAM	G	GS	MIN	FGM	FGA	PCT	3FGM	3FGA	PCT	FTM	FTA	PCT	O-RB	D-RB	TOT	AST	PF	DQ	STL	TO	BLK	PTS	RPG	APG	PPG
90-91—Boston	6	0	39	3	12	.250	0	1	.000	6	8	.750	1	2	3	8	1	0	1	4	0	12	0.5	1.3	2.0
REG. SEASON TOTALS	6	0	39	3	12	.250	0	1	.000	6	8	.750	1	2	3	8	1	0	1	4	0	12	0.5	1.3	2.0

YARDLEY, GEORGE HARRY III b. November 3, 1928   Ht. 6-5 Wt. 195 College—Stanford

SEASON—TEAM	G	GS	MIN	FGM	FGA	PCT	3FGM	3FGA	PCT	FTM	FTA	PCT	O-RB	D-RB	TOT	AST	PF	DQ	STL	TO	BLK	PTS	RPG	APG	PPG
53-54—Fort Wayne	63	—	1489	209	492	.425	—	—	—	146	205	.712	—	—	407	99	166	3	—	—	—	564	6.5	1.6	9.0
54-55—Fort Wayne	60	—	2150	363	869	.418	—	—	—	310	416	.745	—	—	594	126	205	7	—	—	—	1036	9.9	2.1	17.3
55-56—Fort Wayne	71	—	2353	434	1067	.407	—	—	—	365	492	.742	—	—	686	159	212	2	—	—	—	1233	9.7	2.2	17.4
56-57—Fort Wayne	72	—	2691	522	1273	.410	—	—	—	503	639	.787	—	—	755	147	231	2	—	—	—	1547	10.5	2.0	21.5
57-58—Detroit	72	—	2843	673	1624	.414	—	—	—	655	808	.811	—	—	768	97	226	3	—	—	—	2001	10.7	1.3	27.8
58-59—Detroit-Syr.	61	—	1839	446	1042	.428	—	—	—	317	407	.779	—	—	431	65	159	2	—	—	—	1209	7.1	1.1	19.8
59-60—Syracuse	73	—	2402	546	1205	.453	—	—	—	381	467	.816	—	—	579	122	227	3	—	—	—	1473	7.9	1.7	20.2
REG. SEASON TOTALS	472	—	15767	3193	7572	.422	—	—	—	2677	3434	.780	—	—	4220	815	1426	22	—	—	—	9063	8.9	1.7	19.2
PLAYOFF TOTALS	46	—	1693	324	767	.422	—	—	—	285	349	.817	—	—	457	112	143	2	—	—	—	933	9.9	2.4	20.3
ALL-STAR TOTALS	6	—	131	26	60	.433	—	—	—	12	17	.706	—	—	35	4	13	0	—	—	—	64	5.8	0.7	10.7

YATES, BARRY b. January 30, 1946   Ht. 6-7 Wt. 215 College—Nebraska/Maryland

SEASON—TEAM	G	GS	MIN	FGM	FGA	PCT	3FGM	3FGA	PCT	FTM	FTA	PCT	O-RB	D-RB	TOT	AST	PF	DQ	STL	TO	BLK	PTS	RPG	APG	PPG
71-72—Philadelphia	24	—	144	31	83	.373	—	—	—	7	11	.636	—	—	40	7	14	0	—	—	—	69	1.7	0.3	2.9
REG. SEASON TOTALS	24	—	144	31	83	.373	—	—	—	7	11	.636	—	—	40	7	14	0	—	—	—	69	1.7	0.3	2.9

YATES, WAYNE E. b. November 7, 1937   Ht. 6-8 Wt. 235 College—Memphis State

SEASON—TEAM	G	GS	MIN	FGM	FGA	PCT	3FGM	3FGA	PCT	FTM	FTA	PCT	O-RB	D-RB	TOT	AST	PF	DQ	STL	TO	BLK	PTS	RPG	APG	PPG
61-62—Los Angeles	37	—	263	31	105	.295	—	—	—	10	22	.455	—	—	94	16	72	1	—	—	—	72	2.5	0.4	1.9
REG. SEASON TOTALS	37	—	263	31	105	.295	—	—	—	10	22	.455	—	—	94	16	72	1	—	—	—	72	2.5	0.4	1.9
PLAYOFF TOTALS	4	—	12	3	8	.375	—	—	—	1	2	.500	—	—	5	1	2	0	—	—	—	7	1.3	0.3	1.8

YELVERTON, CHARLES W. (**Charlie**) b. December 5, 1948   Ht. 6-2 Wt. 190 College—Fordham

SEASON—TEAM	G	GS	MIN	FGM	FGA	PCT	3FGM	3FGA	PCT	FTM	FTA	PCT	O-RB	D-RB	TOT	AST	PF	DQ	STL	TO	BLK	PTS	RPG	APG	PPG
71-72—Portland	69	—	1227	206	530	.389	—	—	—	133	188	.707	—	—	201	81	145	2	—	—	—	545	2.9	1.2	7.9
REG. SEASON TOTALS	69	—	1227	206	530	.389	—	—	—	133	188	.707	—	—	201	81	145	2	—	—	—	545	2.9	1.2	7.9

YONAKOR, RICHARD ROBERT (**Rich**) b. October 3, 1958 Ht. 6-9 Wt. 220 College—North Carolina

SEASON—TEAM	G	GS	MIN	FGM	FGA	PCT	3FGM	3FGA	PCT	FTM	FTA	PCT	O-RB	D-RB	TOT	AST	PF	DQ	STL	TO	BLK	PTS	RPG	APG	PPG
81-82—San Antonio	10	0	70	14	26	.538	0	0	—	5	7	.714	13	14	27	3	7	0	1	2	2	33	2.7	0.3	3.3
REG. SEASON TOTALS	10	0	70	14	26	.538	0	0	—	5	7	.714	13	14	27	3	7	0	1	2	2	33	2.7	0.3	3.3
PLAYOFF TOTALS	2	0	4	1	2	.500	0	0	—	0	0	—	0	1	1	1	1	0	1	0	0	2	0.5	0.5	1.0

YOUNG, DANNY RICHARDSON b. July 26, 1962 Ht. 6-4 Wt. 175 College—Wake Forest

SEASON—TEAM	G	GS	MIN	FGM	FGA	PCT	3FGM	3FGA	PCT	FTM	FTA	PCT	O-RB	D-RB	TOT	AST	PF	DQ	STL	TO	BLK	PTS	RPG	APG	PPG
84-85—Seattle	3	0	26	2	10	.200	0	1	.000	0	0	—	0	3	3	2	2	0	3	2	0	4	1.0	0.7	1.3
85-86—Seattle	82	29	1901	227	449	.506	24	74	.324	90	106	.849	29	91	120	303	113	0	110	92	9	568	1.5	3.7	6.9
86-87—Seattle	73	26	1482	132	288	.458	29	79	.367	59	71	.831	23	90	113	353	72	0	74	85	3	352	1.5	4.8	4.8
87-88—Seattle	77	0	949	89	218	.408	22	77	.286	43	53	.811	18	57	75	218	69	0	52	37	2	243	1.0	2.8	3.2
88-89—Portland	48	2	952	115	250	.460	17	50	.340	50	64	.781	17	57	74	123	50	0	55	45	3	297	1.5	2.6	6.2
89-90—Portland	82	8	1393	138	328	.421	16	59	.271	91	112	.813	29	93	122	231	84	0	82	80	4	383	1.5	2.8	4.7
90-91—Portland	75	1	897	103	271	.380	36	104	.346	41	45	.911	22	53	75	141	49	0	50	50	7	283	1.0	1.9	3.8
91-92—Port.-L.A. Clips	62	5	1023	100	255	.392	23	70	.329	57	67	.851	16	59	75	172	53	0	46	47	4	280	1.2	2.8	4.5
92-93—Detroit	65	2	836	69	167	.413	22	68	.324	28	32	.875	13	34	47	119	36	0	31	30	5	188	0.7	1.8	2.9
REG. SEASON TOTALS	567	73	9459	975	2236	.436	189	582	.325	459	550	.835	167	537	704	1662	528	0	503	468	37	2598	1.2	2.9	4.6
PLAYOFF TOTALS	53	1	710	80	186	.430	19	59	.322	40	49	.816	20	44	64	119	59		32	37	4	219	1.2	2.2	4.1

YOUNG, MICHAEL WAYNE b. January 2, 1961 Ht. 6-7 Wt. 220 College—Houston

SEASON—TEAM	G	GS	MIN	FGM	FGA	PCT	3FGM	3FGA	PCT	FTM	FTA	PCT	O-RB	D-RB	TOT	AST	PF	DQ	STL	TO	BLK	PTS	RPG	APG	PPG
84-85—Phoenix	2	0	11	2	6	.333	0	1	.000	0	0	—	1	1	2	0	0	0	0	0	0	4	1.0	0.0	2.0
85-86—Philadelphia	2	0	2	0	2	.000	0	0	—	0	0	—	0	0	0	0	0	0	0	0	0	0	0.0	0.0	0.0
89-90—L.A. Clippers	45	2	459	92	194	.474	8	26	.308	27	38	.711	36	50	86	24	47	0	25	15	3	219	1.9	0.5	4.9
REG. SEASON TOTALS	49	2	472	94	202	.465	8	27	.296	27	38	.711	37	51	88	24	47	0	25	15	3	223	1.8	0.5	4.6
PLAYOFF TOTALS	3	0	3	1	4	.250	0	0	—	0	0	—	1	0	1	—	0	0	0	0	0	2	0.3	0.0	0.7

YOUNG, PERRY b. August 4, 1963 Ht. 6-5 Wt. 210 College—Virginia Tech

SEASON—TEAM	G	GS	MIN	FGM	FGA	PCT	3FGM	3FGA	PCT	FTM	FTA	PCT	O-RB	D-RB	TOT	AST	PF	DQ	STL	TO	BLK	PTS	RPG	APG	PPG
86-87—Chicago-Port.	9	0	72	6	21	.286	0	0	—	1	2	.500	3	5	8	7	14	0	5	4	1	13	0.9	0.8	1.4
REG. SEASON TOTALS	9	0	72	6	21	.286	0	0	—	1	2	.500	3	5	8	7	14	0	5	4	1	13	0.9	0.8	1.4

ZASLOFSKY, MAX (**Slats**) b. December 7, 1925 d. October 15, 1985 Ht. 6-2 Wt. 170 College—Chicago/St. John's

SEASON—TEAM	G	GS	MIN	FGM	FGA	PCT	3FGM	3FGA	PCT	FTM	FTA	PCT	O-RB	D-RB	TOT	AST	PF	DQ	STL	TO	BLK	PTS	RPG	APG	PPG
46-47—Chicago	61	—	—	336	1020	.329	—	—	—	205	278	.737	—	—	—	40	121	—	—	—	—	877	—	0.7	14.4
47-48—Chicago	48	—	—	373	1156	.323	—	—	—	261	333	.784	—	—	—	29	125	—	—	—	—	1007	—	0.6	21.0
48-49—Chicago	58	—	—	425	1216	.350	—	—	—	347	413	.840	—	—	—	149	156	—	—	—	—	1197	—	2.6	20.6
49-50—Chicago	68	—	—	397	1132	.351	—	—	—	321	381	.843	—	—	—	155	185	—	—	—	—	1115	—	2.3	16.4
50-51—New York	66	—	—	302	853	.354	—	—	—	231	298	.775	—	228	136	150	3	—	—	—	—	835	3.5	2.1	12.7
51-52—New York	66	—	2113	322	958	.336	—	—	—	287	380	.755	—	194	156	183	5	—	—	—	—	931	2.9	2.4	14.1
52-53—New York	29	—	722	123	320	.384	—	—	—	98	142	.690	—	75	55	81	1	—	—	—	—	344	2.6	1.9	11.9
53-54—Balt.-Milw.-Ft. Wayne	65	—	1881	278	756	.368	—	—	—	255	357	.714	—	160	154	142	1	—	—	—	—	811	2.5	2.4	12.5
54-55—Fort Wayne	70	—	1862	269	821	.328	—	—	—	247	352	.702	—	191	203	130	0	—	—	—	—	785	2.7	2.9	11.2
55-56—Fort Wayne	9	—	182	29	81	.358	—	—	—	30	35	.857	—	16	16	18	1	—	—	—	—	88	1.8	1.8	9.8
REG. SEASON TOTALS	540	—	6760	2854	8313	.343	—	—	—	2282	2969	.769	—	864	1093	1291	11	—	—	—	—	7990	2.8	2.0	14.8
PLAYOFF TOTALS	63	—	732	306	850	.360	—	—	—	287	372	.772	—	121	101	174	4	—	—	—	—	899	2.8	1.6	14.3
ALL-STAR TOTALS	1	—	25	3	7	.429	—	—	—	5	5	1.000	—	4	2	0	0	—	—	—	—	11	4.0	2.0	11.0

ZAWOLUK, ROBERT MICHAEL (**Zeke**) b. October 13, 1930 Ht. 6-7 Wt. 215 College—St. John's

SEASON—TEAM	G	GS	MIN	FGM	FGA	PCT	3FGM	3FGA	PCT	FTM	FTA	PCT	O-RB	D-RB	TOT	AST	PF	DQ	STL	TO	BLK	PTS	RPG	APG	PPG
52-53—Indianapolis	41	—	622	55	150	.367	—	—	—	77	116	.664	—	—	146	31	83	1	—	—	—	187	3.6	0.8	4.6
53-54—Philadelphia	71	—	1795	203	540	.376	—	—	—	186	230	.809	—	—	330	99	220	6	—	—	—	592	4.6	1.4	8.3
54-55—Philadelphia	67	—	1117	138	375	.368	—	—	—	155	199	.779	—	—	256	87	147	3	—	—	—	431	3.8	1.3	6.4
REG. SEASON TOTALS	179	—	3534	396	1065	.372	—	—	—	418	545	.767	—	—	732	217	450	10	—	—	—	1210	4.1	1.2	6.8
PLAYOFF TOTALS	2	—	18	1	6	.167	—	—	—	0	2	.000	—	—	2	—	5	0	—	—	—	2	1.0	0.0	1.0

ZELLER, DAVID A. (**Dave**) b. June 8, 1939 Ht. 6-1½ Wt. 175 College—Miami (Ohio)

SEASON—TEAM	G	GS	MIN	FGM	FGA	PCT	3FGM	3FGA	PCT	FTM	FTA	PCT	O-RB	D-RB	TOT	AST	PF	DQ	STL	TO	BLK	PTS	RPG	APG	PPG
61-62—Cincinnati	61	—	278	36	102	.353	—	—	—	18	24	.750	—	—	27	58	37	0	—	—	—	90	0.4	1.0	1.5
REG. SEASON TOTALS	61	—	278	36	102	.353	—	—	—	18	24	.750	—	—	27	58	37	0	—	—	—	90	0.4	1.0	1.5
PLAYOFF TOTALS	2	—	5	1	2	.500	—	—	—	0	0	—	—	—	1	1	0	0	—	—	—	2	0.5	0.5	1.0

ZELLER, GARY LYNN b. November 20, 1947   Ht. 6-3 Wt. 205 College—Drake

SEASON—TEAM	G	GS	MIN	FGM	FGA	PCT	3FGM	3FGA	PCT	FTM	FTA	PCT	O-RB	D-RB	TOT	AST	PF	DQ	STL	TO	BLK	PTS	RPG	APG	PPG
70-71—Baltimore	50	—	226	34	115	.296	—	—	—	15	28	.536	—	—	27	7	43	0	—	—	—	83	0.5	0.1	1.7
71-72—Baltimore	28	—	471	83	229	.362	—	—	—	22	35	.629	—	—	65	30	62	0	—	—	—	188	2.3	1.1	6.7
71-72—New York (A)	12	—	82	7	30	.233	0	1	.000	4	6	.667	—	—	10	2	16	—	—	9	—	18	0.8	0.2	1.5
REG. NBA TOTALS	78	—	697	117	344	.340	—	—	—	37	63	.587	—	—	92	37	105	0	—	—	—	271	1.2	0.5	3.5
REG. ABA TOTALS	12	—	82	7	30	.233	0	1	.000	4	6	.667	—	—	10	2	16	—	—	9	—	18	0.8	0.2	1.5
NBA PLAYOFF TOTALS	15	—	67	12	35	.343	—	—	—	2	7	.286	—	—	13	4	15	0	—	—	—	26	0.9	0.3	1.7
ABA PLAYOFF TOTALS	3	—	9	1	1	1.000	0	0	—	0	1	.000	—	—	1	0	7	—	—	3	—	2	0.3	0.0	0.7

ZELLER, HARRY RAYMOND (**Hank**) b. July 10, 1918   Ht. 6-4 Wt. 210 College—Pittsburgh/Washington & Jefferson

SEASON—TEAM	G	GS	MIN	FGM	FGA	PCT	3FGM	3FGA	PCT	FTM	FTA	PCT	O-RB	D-RB	TOT	AST	PF	DQ	STL	TO	BLK	PTS	RPG	APG	PPG
46-47—Pittsburgh	48	—	—	120	382	.314	—	—	—	122	177	.689	—	—	—	31	177	—	—	—	—	362	—	0.6	7.5
REG. SEASON TOTALS	48	—	—	120	382	.314	—	—	—	122	177	.689	—	—	—	31	177	—	—	—	—	362	—	0.6	7.5

ZENO, ANTHONY MICHAEL (**Tony**) b. October 1, 1957   Ht. 6-8 Wt. 210 College—Arizona State

SEASON—TEAM	G	GS	MIN	FGM	FGA	PCT	3FGM	3FGA	PCT	FTM	FTA	PCT	O-RB	D-RB	TOT	AST	PF	DQ	STL	TO	BLK	PTS	RPG	APG	PPG
79-80—Indiana	8	—	59	6	21	.286	0	0	—	2	2	1.000	3	11	14	1	13	0	4	9	3	14	1.8	0.1	1.8
REG. SEASON TOTALS	8	—	59	6	21	.286	0	0	—	2	2	1.000	3	11	14	1	13	0	4	9	3	14	1.8	0.1	1.8

ZEVENBERGEN, PHIL b. April 13, 1964   Ht. 6-10 Wt. 230 College—Seattle Pacific/Edmonds CC/Washington

SEASON—TEAM	G	GS	MIN	FGM	FGA	PCT	3FGM	3FGA	PCT	FTM	FTA	PCT	O-RB	D-RB	TOT	AST	PF	DQ	STL	TO	BLK	PTS	RPG	APG	PPG
87-88—San Antonio	8	0	58	15	27	.556	0	0	—	0	2	.000	4	9	13	3	12	0	3	4	1	30	1.6	0.4	3.8
REG. SEASON TOTALS	8	0	58	15	27	.556	0	0	—	0	2	.000	4	9	13	3	12	0	3	4	1	30	1.6	0.4	3.8
PLAYOFF TOTALS	1	0	1	0	0	—	0	0	—	0	0	—	0	0	0	—	0	0	0	0	0	0	0.0	0.0	0.0

ZOET, JIM b. December 30, 1953   Ht. 7-1 Wt. 240 College—Kent State

SEASON—TEAM	G	GS	MIN	FGM	FGA	PCT	3FGM	3FGA	PCT	FTM	FTA	PCT	O-RB	D-RB	TOT	AST	PF	DQ	STL	TO	BLK	PTS	RPG	APG	PPG
82-83—Detroit	7	0	30	1	5	.200	0	0	—	0	0	—	3	5	8	1	9	0	1	4	3	2	1.1	0.1	0.3
REG. SEASON TOTALS	7	0	30	1	5	.200	0	0	—	0	0	—	3	5	8	1	9	0	1	4	3	2	1.1	0.1	0.3

ZOPF, WILLIAM CHARLES JR. (**Bill, Zip**) b. June 7, 1948   Ht. 6-1½ Wt. 170 College—Duquesne

SEASON—TEAM	G	GS	MIN	FGM	FGA	PCT	3FGM	3FGA	PCT	FTM	FTA	PCT	O-RB	D-RB	TOT	AST	PF	DQ	STL	TO	BLK	PTS	RPG	APG	PPG
70-71—Milwaukee	53	—	398	49	135	.363	—	—	—	20	36	.556	—	—	46	73	34	0	—	—	—	118	0.9	1.4	2.2
REG. SEASON TOTALS	53	—	398	49	135	.363	—	—	—	20	36	.556	—	—	46	73	34	0	—	—	—	118	0.9	1.4	2.2

ZUNIC, MATTHEW (**Matt, Mad Matt**) b. December 19, 1919   Ht. 6-7 Wt. 195 College—George Washington

SEASON—TEAM	G	GS	MIN	FGM	FGA	PCT	3FGM	3FGA	PCT	FTM	FTA	PCT	O-RB	D-RB	TOT	AST	PF	DQ	STL	TO	BLK	PTS	RPG	APG	PPG
47-48—Flint (N)	57	—	—	123	—	—	—	—	—	85	128	.664	—	—	—	—	209	—	—	—	—	331	—	—	5.8
48-49—Washington	56	—	—	98	323	.303	—	—	—	77	109	.706	—	—	—	50	182	—	—	—	—	273	—	0.9	4.9
REG. NBA TOTALS	56	—	—	98	323	.303	—	—	—	77	109	.706	—	—	—	50	182	—	—	—	—	273	—	0.9	4.9
REG. NBL TOTALS	57	—	—	123	—	—	—	—	—	85	128	.664	—	—	—	—	209	—	—	—	—	331	—	—	5.8
NBA PLAYOFF TOTALS	9	—	—	7	39	.179	—	—	—	12	19	.632	—	—	—	6	26	1	—	—	—	26	—	0.7	2.9

INDEX

All persons who appear in the encyclopedia are indexed with the exception of those whose names appear only in the All-Time Player Directory or only in draft lists, boxscores, other statistical listings, or acknowledgments. Boldface numerals denote references to photos.